Contents

KT-440-018

OPPOSITE FISHERMEN, KOVALAM PREVIOUS PAGE TRADITIONAL DANCERS, BHUBANESWAR

Introduction to
India

India, it is often said, is not a country, but a continent. Stretching from the frozen summits of the Himalayas to the tropical greenery of Kerala, its expansive borders encompass an incomparable range of landscapes, cultures and people. Walk the streets of any Indian city and you'll rub shoulders with representatives of several of the world's great faiths, a multitude of castes and outcastes, fair-skinned, turbanned Punjabis and dark-skinned Tamils. You'll also encounter temple rituals that have been performed since the time of the Egyptian Pharaohs, onion-domed mosques erected centuries before the Taj Mahal was ever dreamt of, and quirky echoes of the British Raj on virtually every corner.

That so much of India's past remains discernible today is all the more astonishing given the pace of change since Independence in 1947. Spurred by the free-market reforms of the early 1990s, the **economic revolution** started by Rajiv Gandhi has transformed the country with new consumer goods, technologies and ways of life. Today the land where the Buddha lived and taught, and whose religious festivals are as old as the rivers that sustain them, is the second largest producer of computer software in the world, with its own satellites and nuclear weapons.

However, the presence in even the most far-flung market towns of internet cafés, smart phones and Tata Nano cars has thrown into sharp relief the **problems** that have bedevilled India since long before it became the world's largest secular democracy. Poverty remains a harsh fact of life for around forty percent of India's inhabitants; no other nation on earth has slum settlements on the scale of those in Delhi, Mumbai and Kolkata (Calcutta), nor so many malnourished children, uneducated women and homes without access to clean water and waste disposal.

Many first-time visitors find themselves unable to see past such glaring disparities. Others come expecting a timeless ascetic wonderland and are surprised to encounter one

ABOVE FROM LEFT ELEPHANT SANCTUARY, KERALA (P.1076); MAKING OPIUM TEA NEAR JODHPUR (P.174); ANJUNA FLEA MARKET (P.696)

of the most materialistic societies on the planet. Still more find themselves intimidated by what may seem, initially, an incomprehensible and bewildering continent. But for all its jarring juxtapositions, intractable paradoxes and frustrations, India remains an utterly compelling destination. Intricate and worn, its distinctive patina – the stream of life in its crowded bazaars, the ubiquitous *filmi* music, the pungent melange of diesel fumes, cooking spices, dust and dung smoke – casts a spell that few forget from the moment they step off a plane. Love it or hate it – and most travellers oscillate between the two – India will shift the way you see the world.

Where to go

The best Indian itineraries are the simplest. It just isn't possible to see everything in a single expedition, even if you spent a year trying. Far better, then, to concentrate on one or two specific regions and, above all, to be flexible. Although it requires a deliberate change of pace to venture away from the urban centres, rural India has its own very distinct pleasures. In fact, while Indian cities are undoubtedly adrenalin-fuelled, upbeat places, it is possible – and certainly less stressful – to travel for months around the Subcontinent and rarely have to set foot in one.

The most-travelled circuit in the country, combining spectacular monuments with the flat, fertile landscape that for many people is archetypally Indian, is the so-called **Golden Triangle** in the north: Delhi itself, the colonial capital; Agra, home of the Taj Mahal; and the Pink City of Jaipur in **Rajasthan**. Rajasthan is probably the single most popular state with travellers, who are drawn by its desert scenery, the imposing medieval forts and palaces of Jaisalmer, Jodhpur, Udaipur and Bundi, and by the colourful traditional dress.

East of Delhi, the River Ganges meanders through some of India's most densely populated regions to reach the extraordinary holy Hindu city of **Varanasi** (also known as Benares), where to witness the daily rituals of life and death focused around the

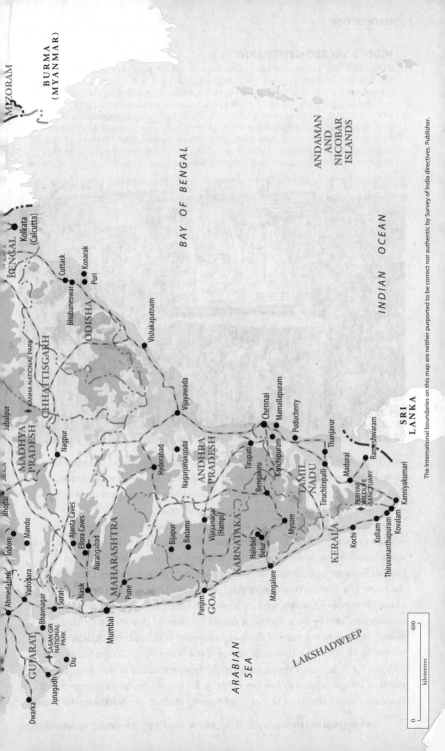

The International boundaries on this map are neither purported to be correct nor authentic by Survey of India directives. Publisher.

INDIA'S SACRED GEOGRAPHY

It's hard to think of a more visibly religious country than India. The very landscape of the Subcontinent – its rivers, waterfalls, trees, hilltops, mountains and rocks – comprises a vast sacred geography for adherents of the dozen or more faiths rooted here. Connecting the country's countless holy places is a network of pilgrimage routes along which tens of thousands of worshippers may be moving at any one time – on regular trains, specially decorated buses, tinsel-covered bicycles, barefoot, alone or in noisy family groups. For the visitor, joining devotees in the teeming temple precincts of the south, on the *ghats* at Varanasi, at the Sufi shrines of Ajmer and Delhi, before the naked Jain colossi of Sravanabelagola, or at any one of the innumerable religious festivals that punctuate the astrological calendar is to experience India at its most intense.

waterfront *ghats* (bathing places) is to glimpse the continuing practice of India's most ancient religious traditions. Further east still is the great city of **Kolkata (Calcutta)**, the capital until early last century of the British Raj and now a teeming metropolis that epitomizes contemporary India's most pressing problems.

The majority of travellers follow the well-trodden Ganges route to reach Nepal, perhaps unaware that the **Indian Himalayas** offer superlative trekking and mountain scenery to rival any in the range. With travel in Kashmir still largely limited to its capital, Srinagar, and central valley area, **Himachal Pradesh** – where Dharamsala is the home of a Tibetan community that includes the Dalai Lama himself – and the remote province of **Ladakh**, with its mysterious lunar landscape and cloud-swept monasteries, have become the major targets for journeys into the mountains. Less visited, but possessing some of Asia's highest peaks, is the niche of **Uttarakhand** bordering Nepal, where the glacial source of the sacred River Ganges has attracted pilgrims for more than a thousand years. At the opposite end of the chain, **Sikkim**, north of Bengal, is another low-key trekking destination, harbouring scenery and a Buddhist culture similar to that of neighbouring Bhutan. The **Northeast Hill States**,

CLOCKWISE FROM TOP LEFT PALOLEM BEACH (P.720); LAMAYURU GOMPA (P.501); FISHING VILLAGE NEAR KOVALAM (P.1033)

INDIAN RAILWAYS

India's **railways**, which daily transport millions of commuters, pilgrims, animals and hessian-wrapped packages between the four corners of the Subcontinent, are often cited as the best thing the British Raj bequeathed to its former colony. And yet, with its hierarchical legion of clerks, cooks, coolies, bearers, ticket inspectors, station managers and ministers, the network has become a quintessentially Indian institution.

Travelling across India by rail – whether you rough it in dirt-cheap second-class, or pamper yourself with starched cotton sheets and hot meals in an a/c carriage – is likely to yield some of the most memorable moments of your trip. Open around the clock, the stations in themselves are often great places to watch the world go by, with hundreds of people from all walks of life eating, sleeping, buying and selling, regardless of the hour. This is also where you'll grow familiar with one of the unforgettable sounds of the Subcontinent: the robotic drone of the chai-wallah, dispensing cups of hot, sweet tea.

connected to eastern India by a slender neck of land, boast remarkably diverse landscapes and an incredible fifty percent of India's biodiversity.

Heading south from Kolkata (Calcutta) along the coast, your first likely stop is Konarak in **Orissa**, site of the famous Sun Temple, a giant carved pyramid of stone that lay submerged under sand until its rediscovery at the start of the twentieth century. **Tamil Nadu**, further south, has also retained its own tradition of magnificent architecture, with towering *gopura* gateways dominating towns whose vast temple complexes are still the focus of everyday life. Of them all, Madurai, in the far south, is the most stunning, but you could spend months wandering between the sacred sites of the Kaveri Delta and the fragrant Nilgiri Hills, draped in the tea terraces that have become the hallmark of south Indian landscapes. **Kerala**, near the southernmost tip of the Subcontinent on the western coast, is India at its most tropical and relaxed, its lush backwaters teeming with simple wooden craft of all shapes and sizes, and red-roofed towns and villages all but invisible beneath a canopy of palm trees. Further up the coast is **Goa**, the former Portuguese colony whose 100km coastline is fringed with beaches to suit all tastes and budgets, from upmarket package tourists to long-staying backpackers, and whose towns hold whitewashed Christian churches that could almost have been transplanted from Europe.

North of here sits **Mumbai**, an ungainly beast that has been the major focus of the nationwide drift to the big cities. Centre of the country's formidable popular movie industry, it reels along on an undeniable energy that, after a few days of acclimatization, can prove addictive. Beyond Mumbai is the state of **Gujarat**, renowned for the unique culture and crafts of the barren Kutch region.

On a long trip, it makes sense to pause and rest every few weeks. Certain places have fulfilled that function for generations, such as the Himalayan resort of **Manali**, epicentre of India's hashish-producing area, and the many former colonial hill stations that dot the country, from **Ootacamund (Ooty)**, in the far south, to that archetypal British retreat, **Shimla**, immortalized in the writing of Rudyard Kipling. Elsewhere, the combination of sand and the sea, and a picturesque rural or religious backdrop – such as at **Varkala** in Kerala, **Gokarna** in Karnataka, and the remoter beaches of Goa – are usually enough to loosen even the tightest itineraries.

When to go

India's weather is extremely varied, something you must take into account when planning your trip. The most influential feature of the Subcontinent's climate is the wet season, or **monsoon**. This breaks on the Keralan coast at the end of May, working its way northeast across the country over the following month and a half. While it lasts, regular and prolonged downpours are interspersed with bursts of hot sunshine, and the pervasive humidity can be intense. At the height of the monsoon – especially in the jungle regions of the northwest and the low-lying delta lands of Bengal – flooding can severely disrupt communications, causing widespread destruction. In the Himalayan foothills, landslides are common, and entire valley systems can be cut off for weeks.

By September, the monsoon has largely receded from the north, but it takes another couple of months before the clouds disappear altogether from the far south. The east

INDIAN FOOD

Indian cooking is as varied as the country itself, with dozens of distinctive regional **culinary traditions** ranging from the classic Mughlai cuisine of the north to the feisty coconut- and chilli-infused flavours of the south; these are often a revelation to first-time visitors, whose only contact with Indian food will probably have been through the stereotypical Anglo-Indian dishes served up in the majority of restaurants overseas. Best known is the cuisine of north India, with its signature biryanis, tandooris and rich cream- and yogurt-based sauces accompanied with thick naan breads, evidence of the region's long contact with Central Asia. The food of south India is light years away, exemplified by the ubiquitous vegetarian "meal" – a huge mound of rice served on a banana leaf and accompanied with fiery pickles – or by the classic masala dosa, a crisp rice pancake wrapped around a spicy potato filling. There's also a host of regional cuisines to explore – Punjabi, Bengali, Gujarati, Goan, Keralan and Kashmiri, to name just a few of the most distinctive – each of which has its own special dishes, spices and cooking techniques.

coast of Andhra Pradesh and Tamil Nadu, and the south of Kerala, get a second drenching between October and December, when the "northwest" or "retreating" monsoon sweeps in from the Bay of Bengal. By December, however, most of the Subcontinent enjoys clear skies and relatively cool temperatures.

Mid-winter sees the most marked contrasts between the climates of north and south India. While Delhi, for example, may be ravaged by chill winds blowing off the snowfields of the Himalayas, the Tamil plains and coastal Kerala, more than 1000km south, still stew under fierce post-monsoon sunshine. As spring gathers pace, the centre of the Subcontinent starts to heat up again, and by late March thermometers nudge 33°C across most of the Gangetic Plains and Deccan plateau. Temperatures peak in May and early June, when anyone who can retreats to the hill stations. Above the baking Subcontinental land mass, hot air builds up and sucks in humidity from the southwest, causing the onset of the monsoon in late June, and bringing relief to millions of overheated Indians.

The best time to visit most of the country, therefore, is during the **cool, dry season**, between November and March. Delhi, Agra, Varanasi, Rajasthan and Madhya Pradesh are ideal at this time, and temperatures in Goa and central India remain comfortable. The heat of the south is never less than intense but it becomes stifling in May and June, so aim to be in Tamil Nadu and Kerala between January and March. From this time onwards, the Himalayas grow more accessible, and the trekking season reaches its peak in August and September while the rest of the Subcontinent is being soaked by the rains.

AVERAGE TEMPERATURES AND RAINFALL

	Jan	Feb	Mar	Apr	May	Jun	Jul	Aug	Sep	Oct	Nov	Dec
CHENNAI (TN)												
Max/min °C	28/20	31/21	33/23	36/26	38/27	37/27	35/26	34/26	34/25	32/24	29/22	28/21
Max/min °F	83/68	87/70	91/74	96/79	100/81	99/81	95/78	94/78	93/77	89/75	85/72	83/70
Rainfall (mm)	28	33	5	13	38	71	122	137	160	157	152	152
DELHI												
Max/min °C	21/7	24/9	31/14	36/20	41/26	39/28	36/27	34/26	34/24	34/18	29/11	23/8
Max/min °F	70/63	75/48	88/57	97/68	106/79	102/82	97/81	93/79	93/75	93/64	84/52	73/46
Rainfall (mm)	23	18	13	8	13	74	180	173	117	10	3	10
KOLKATA (CALCUTTA) (WB)												
Max/min °C	27/13	29/15	34/21	36/24	36/25	33/26	32/26	32/26	32/26	32/24	29/18	26/13
Max/min °F	81/55	84/59	93/70	97/75	97/77	91/79	90/79	90/79	90/79	90/75	84/64	79/55
Rainfall (mm)	10	31	36	43	140	297	325	328	252	114	20	5
MUMBAI (M)												
Max/min °C	28/19	28/19	30/22	32/24	33/27	32/26	29/25	29/24	29/24	32/24	32/23	31/21
Max/min °F	82/66	82/66	86/72	90/75	91/81	90/79	84/77	84/75	84/75	90/75	90/73	88/70
Rainfall (mm)	3	3	3	0	18	485	617	340	264	64	13	3
PANJIM (GOA)												
Max/min °C	32/19	32/21	32/23	33/25	33/26	30/24	29/24	28/24	29/24	32/24	33/22	32/21
Max/min °F	90/66	90/70	90/73	91/77	91/79	86/75	84/75	82/75	84/75	90/75	91/72	90/70
Rainfall (mm)	0	0	0	0	50	580	650	400	150	90	10	0

Author picks

Our authors have crossed the length and breadth of India in search of the most impressive monuments, sumptuous food and memorable journeys. Here's a list of their personal highlights.

Naga knees up The spectacular Hornbill Festival, held in a village near the town of Kohima in early December, brings together the tribes of Nagaland dressed in astonishingly beautiful traditional finery for shows of martial arts, dance, wrestling, archery and a rock concert. **See p.860**

Swimming with Rajan Retired timber elephant Rajan's dips in the translucent turquoise water of Havelock Beach, in the Andaman Islands, offer a unique sub-aqua photo opportunity. **See p.939**

Dancing monks On the banks of the Brahmaputra River, the Hindu monasteries (*sattras*) of Majuli host chimeric dance plays performed by white-turbaned monks. **See p.847**

Masked trance Nothing encapsulates the otherworldly feel of the deep south like the masked spirit possession *theyyem* rituals enacted in villages around the town of Kannur, Kerala. See p.1081

Cave treasure Shown in a languid hipshot pose holding a blue lotus bloom, the figure of Padmapani in Ajanta's Cave 1 is the great masterpiece of ancient Indian art. **See p.645**

Gilded vision Hypnotic *kirtans* (hymns) mingle to magical effect with the reflections of the Sikhs' holiest shrine in the shimmering Amrit Samovar tank – an intoxicating image of spirituality. See p.520

To the source Follow a winding dirt trail through the high Himalayas to the source of the sacred River Ganges, where yogis and sadhus bathe in icy water emanating from the snout of a glacier. **See p.311**

Slow cooking *Dum Pukt*, in Mumbai's *ITC Maratha*, ranks among just a handful of kitchens in India capable of recreating the recipes of the Muslim courts of Hyderabad and Awadh, slow-cooked in terracotta pots sealed with dough. **See p.611**

> Our author recommendations don't end here. We've flagged up our favourite places – a perfectly sited hotel, an atmospheric café, a special restaurant – throughout the guide, highlighted with the ★ symbol.

FROM TOP NAGA MEN PERFORMING TRADITIONAL WAR DANCE; THE SOURCE OF THE GANGES; THEYYEM PERFORMANCE

32

things not to miss

It's not possible to see everything India has to offer in one trip, and we don't suggest you try. What follows is a selective taste of the country's highlights: outstanding buildings, natural wonders, spectacular festivals and unforgettable journeys. All highlights have a page reference to take you straight to the Guide, where you can find out more. Coloured numbers refer to chapters in the Guide section.

1 JAISALMER
Page 183
Honey-coloured citadel, emerging from the sands of the Thar Desert.

2 BANDHAVGARH NATIONAL PARK
Page 381
Deep in the eastern tracts of Madhya Pradesh, this park is rich in animal and birdlife, including tigers and leopards.

3 KONARK
Page 896
A colossal thirteenth-century temple, buried under sand until its rediscovery by the British.

4 GOKARNA
Page 1125
The beautiful beaches on the edge of this temple town are popular with budget travellers fleeing the commercialism of nearby Goa.

5 TAJ MAHAL
Page 233
Simply the world's greatest building: Shah Jahan's monument to love fully lives up to all expectations.

6 THRISSUR PURAM
Page 1074

More than one hundred sumptuously caparisoned elephants march in Kerala's biggest temple festival, accompanied by ear-shattering south Indian drum orchestras.

7 KHAJURAHO
Page 365

Immaculately preserved temples renowned for their uncompromisingly erotic carvings.

8 KOCHI
Page 1059

This atmospheric harbourside is strung with elegant Chinese fishing nets.

9 KEOLADEO NATIONAL PARK, BHARATPUR
Page 159

Asia's most famous bird reserve, where millions of migrants nest each winter. The perfect antidote to the frenzy and pollution of nearby Agra and Jaipur.

10 TIKSE
Page 489

The most architecturally impressive of the many dramatic monasteries within striking distance of Leh.

11 ORCHHA
Page 360

This semi-ruined former capital of the Bundela rajas is an architectural gem, rising up through the surrounding forest.

10

12 VARANASI
Page 269

City of Light, founded by Shiva, where the bathing *ghats* beside the Ganges teem with pilgrims.

13 MEHERANGARH FORT, JODHPUR
Page 176

The epitome of Rajput power and extravagance, its ramparts towering above a labyrinthine, blue-painted old city.

14 AMRITSAR
Page 519

The largest city in Punjab, and site of the fabled Golden Temple, the Sikhs' holiest shrine.

15 MAMALLAPURAM
Page 963

A fishing and stone-carving village, with magnificent boulder friezes, shrines and the sea-battered Shore Temple.

16 RAJASTHANI HANDICRAFTS
Page 138

The teeming bazaars of the Pink City in Jaipur burst with vibrant cloth, jewellery, Persian-style pottery and semiprecious stones. Simply the best place to shop in the Subcontinent.

17 KATHAKALI
Page 1026

Kerala is the place to experience *kathakali* and other esoteric ritual theatre forms.

18 ELLORA CAVES
Page 637

Buddhist, Hindu and Jain caves, and the colossal Hindu Kailash temple, carved from a spectacular volcanic ridge at the heart of the Deccan plateau.

12

13

14

23

24

19 RATH YATRA, PURI
Page 891

Three colossal chariots with brightly coloured canopies are pulled by crowds of devotees through the streets of eastern India's holiest town.

20 GANGOTRI
Page 311

An atmospheric village on the Ganges that serves as a base for the trek into the heart of the Hindu faith – Gomukh, the source of the Ganges.

21 HAMPI/VIJAYANAGAR
Page 1131

Deserted capital of the last great Hindu empire, scattered over a bizarre landscape of giant golden-brown boulders.

22 UDAIPUR
Page 202

Arguably the most romantic city in India, with ornate Rajput palaces floating in the middle of two shimmering lakes.

23 PALOLEM
Page 720

Exquisite crescent-shaped beach in Goa's relaxed south, famous for its dolphins and local alcoholic spirit, *feni*.

24 DURGA PUJA
Page 733

An exuberant festival held in September or October, when every street and village erects a shrine to the goddess Durga. Kolkata (Calcutta) has the most lavish festivities.

25 MANALI–LEH HIGHWAY
Page 455

India's epic Himalayan road trip, along the second highest highway in the world, is the most popular approach to Ladakh, and revered by motorbikers, cyclists and drivers alike.

25

26 PUSHKAR CAMEL MELA
Page 172

November sees the largest livestock market on earth, where 200,000 Rajasthani herders in traditional costume converge on the desert oasis of Pushkar to trade and bathe in the sacred lake.

27 DHARAMSALA
Page 418

Perched on the edge of the Himalayas, this is the home of the Dalai Lama and Tibetan Buddhism in exile.

28 VARKALA
Page 1037

This pleasantly low-key Keralan resort boasts sheer red cliffs, amazing sea views and a legion of Ayurvedic masseurs.

29 MADURAI
Page 997

Definitive south Indian city, centred on a spectacular medieval temple.

30 ZANSKAR
Page 504

A barren moonscape with extraordinary scenery and challenging trails over the high passes.

31 BOATING ON THE BACKWATERS OF KERALA
Page 1046

Lazy boat trips wind through the lush tropical waterways of India's deep south.

32 FATEHPUR SIKRI
Page 247

The Mughal emperor Akbar's elegant palace complex now lies deserted on a ridge near Agra, but remains one of India's architectural masterpieces.

Itineraries

India's simply too vast and too complex to explore in a single trip. It makes more sense to focus on one, two or perhaps three regions, depending on your time frame. The following itineraries showcase both the classic attractions and less well known gems of six distinct areas, from the icy heights of the Himalayas to the sweltering tropical backwaters of Kerala.

THE GOLDEN TRIANGLE

No other region of India packs in as many awe-inspiring monuments as the so-called "Golden Triangle" connecting Delhi, Agra and Jaipur. Allow at least a week to complete the circuit, with a diversion south to the tiger reserve at Ranthambore if you've time to spare.

❶ Delhi Start out at Shah Jahan's mighty Red Fort in the Mughal Old City, then work your way south through the medieval monuments of the southern suburbs. **See p.76**

❷ Agra Cross the Yamuna River by boat in the early morning for an unforgettable view of the Taj just after sunrise, then spend the rest of the day ticking off the city's other Mughal splendours. **See p.230**

❸ Fatehpur Sikri Overnight at a guesthouse below the deserted capital of emperor Akbar to see its deep red sandstone architecture at its most ethereal, in the diffuse light of dusk and dawn. **See p.247**

❹ Keoladeo National Park Bicycle safaris along the dirt tracks and banks that crisscross this teeming bird reserve offer a perfect antidote to the noise and traffic of India's northern cities. **See p.159**

❺ Jaipur Approach the ochre-walled palace of Amber Fort on elephant back, before spending

a day in the textile and gemstone bazaars of the Rajasthani capital – a riot of quintessentially Indian colour. **See p.127**

❻ Shekhawati Set on the fringes of the Thar Desert, the painted havelis (walled mansions) in the market towns of this once rich area make the ideal stopover on the journey back to Delhi. **See p.142**

AROUND THE "LAND OF KINGS"

India's dazzling desert state, Rajasthan, tends to be the destination of choice for most first-time travellers to India, and with good reason. You'll need at least a month to really do it justice, or three weeks at a pinch.

❶ Jaipur The Pink City, with its hectic streets and flamboyant Rajput architecture, is a real baptism of fire. Hilltop viewpoints such as the Tiger Fort and Monkey Temple offer welcome respite from the mayhem. **See p.127**

❷ Ranthambore If sighting a tiger is a priority, aim to spend at least a couple of nights at a camp near this world-famous reserve, where big cats prowl the shores of a ruin-studded lake. **See p.159**

❸ Pushkar Ringed by the white domes and sacred ghats of Hindu shrines, Pushkar makes a perfect base for leisurely desert walks and souvenir hunts. **See p.168**

ABOVE BACKWATERS NEAR ALLEPPEY, KERALA; JODHPUR, RAJASTHAN

THE GOLDEN TRIANGLE
AROUND THE "LAND OF KINGS"
THE DEEP SOUTH

❹ Udaipur Dine by candlelight on a haveli rooftop for the ultimate view of the Sisodia Maharanas' fairytale palaces, rising from the banks of glassy Fateh Sagar lake. **See p.202**

❺ Jodhpur Perched on the rim of sheer sandstone cliffs, Rajasthan's most spectacular medieval fortress, Meherangarh, towers above a warrenous old city painted a hundred shades of sky blue. **See p.174**

❻ Jaislamer A long trip across the Thar is rewarded by the sublime vision of Jai Sigh's yellow-stone citadel floating above the sandflats. Camel treks can take you deep into the surrounding desert. **See p.183**

❼ Bikaner Some quirky early twentieth-century architecture and a temple where thousands of rats run free are two vestiges of this city's former prominence on the trans-Thar caravan route. **See p.195**

❽ Nawalgarh After a succession of big cities, this small town on the fringes of the desert, famed for its elaborately painted merchants'

houses, makes an enjoyable base for trips to nearby adobe villages. **See p.142**

THE DEEP SOUTH

From the boulder-strewn plains of Tamil Nadu to the lush, intensely tropical coastal strip of Kerala, the Deep South offers a succession of dramatic landscapes and world-class historic monuments. You'll need at least three weeks to cover this route comfortably, or two at a rushed pace travelling with your own transport.

❶ Chennai The old colonial hub of Fort St George is the standout sight of the Tamil capital, but there's also a wealth of succulent southern cuisine on offer. **See p.952**

❷ Mammalapuram Sculpted a dozen or more centuries ago by the Pallava kings, Mammalapuram holds a tempting combination of ancient stonework and breezy tropical beaches. **See p.963**

❸ Puducherry Soak up the lingering Gallic ambience of France's former colony on the

Coromandel coast, ideally from the confines of a heritage hotel. **See p.975**

❹ **Thanjavur** The mighty Brihadishwara temple and famous collection of Chola bronzes in the town museum make Thanjavur the perfect springboard for explorations of the Kaveri Delta region. **See p.988**

❺ **Tiruchirapalli (Trichy)** Gaze from the summit of Trichy's exotic rock fort across the Kaveri River to the largest temple complex in India, on the island of Srirangam. **See p.993**

❻ **Madurai** The shrine of the Fish-Eyed Goddess is Tamil Nadu's greatest living monument, renowned for its soaring, multicoloured, deity-encrusted gateway towers. **See p.997**

❼ **Periyar** Scale the Western Ghat range to enter the jungles of Kerala's Cardamom Hills, where the Periyar Wildlife Sanctuary offers the chance to sight elephants from a punted raft. **See p.1050**

❽ **Alleppey** This former colonial trading port provides the entry point for trips into the surrounding backwater region of Kuttanad – a watery world like no other in Asia. **See p.1043**

❾ **Fort Cochin** The heritage hotels, arty cafés and funky boutiques of Kerala's historic harbour town are the ideal end point for a tour of India's far south. **See p.1061**

HIMALAYAN ODYSSEY

Experience the contrasting landscapes of the world's greatest mountain range with this two- to three-week journey from the northern plains to the fringes of the Tibetan Plateau and idyllic Vale of Kashmir.

❶ **Shimla** Trundle on the toy train from Kalka through the foothills to this quintessentially Raj-era hill station, from where a magnificent spread of distant snow peaks is visible. **See p.403**

❷ **Manali** Lush forests of deodar cedars, apple orchards and giant, ice-dusted summits flank the hill resort of Manali, in the Kullu Valley – starting point of the trans-Himalayan Highway. **See p.441**

❸ **Leh** A breathless, two-day journey across a vast desert of scree and dizzying passes brings you to the capital of Ladakh, marooned in the high Indus Valley. **See p.479**

❹ **The Ladakhi lakes** Charter a jeep for the trip southeast to the hypnotically beautiful altitude lakes of Pangong Tso and Tso Moriri. **See p.492**

❺ **Kargil** Fairytale Buddhist monasteries and stupendous mountain scenery characterize the long haul to the mid-point on the journey to Kashmir, marked by this Shia Muslim market town. **See p.502**

❻ **Srinagar** Laze on the deck of a houseboat sipping spiced tea while the shadows lengthen on the surrounding mountainsides and shikhara canoes filled with fruit and flowers paddle past. **See p.470**

RHODODENDRONS AND RED PANDAS

Kolkata, the capital of West Bengal, is the launch pad for this classic trip through the tea estates around Darjeeling to Sikkim, a beautiful, predominantly Buddhist region in the lap of the Himalayas. You could cover the route in a fortnight; with an additional week, consider a multistage trek into the high country further north.

❶ **Kolkata** Join the flood of commuters crossing the Howrah Bridge, admire the spectacular monuments of the British Empire and discover one of India's tastiest regional cuisines. **See p.732**

❷ **Darjeeling** Amazing views of distant Kanchenjunga (the world's second highest mountain), a quaint Raj-era vibe and the famous Toy Train ride up from the plains account for the perennial appeal of India's principal tea hub. **See p.769**

❸ **Rumtek** A quiet alternative to nearby Gangtok (the Sikkimese capital), Rumtek is also the site of a spectacular Buddhist monastery. **See p.817**

❹ **Maenam Sanctuary** Tackle the lung-stretching, 1000m ascent of Maenam mountain from Ravangla town for a tantalizing panoramic view of the snow peaks to the north. **See p.823**

❺ **Pemayangtse** The poster boy for northeast Himalayan monasteries, Pemayangtse offers the added bonus of spectacular vistas of Kanchenjunga. **See p.825**

❻ **Varshey Rhododendron Sanctuary** Travellers with a botanical bent shouldn't miss the chance to trek through this tract of pristine rhododendron forest near the Nepali border, home to red pandas and black bears. **See p.825**

THROUGH THE HEART OF INDIA

Despite its extraordinary wealth of historic monuments, the Deccan region of central India sees comparatively few visitors. The rewards for those who do make it are

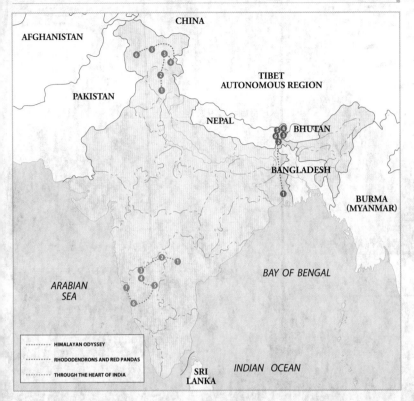

considerable: a succession of astonishing temple sites, crumbling tombs, mosques and deserted capitals spanning sixteen centuries of civilization. Allow at least three weeks for this unforgettable trip.

❶ Hyderabad The convoluted ruins of medieval Golconda, on the outskirts of the city, followed by a climb of the Charminar ("Four Minarets") mosque and a slap-up Hyderabdi feast are the perfect preamble for what lies ahead. **See p.909**

❷ Bidar Resembling a town on the central Asia Silk Route, Bidar's rambling fort-palace, madrasa, tombs and metal workshops recall this region's medieval Persian roots. **See p.1147**

❸ Bijapur For three centuries, Bijapur served as the capital of the Deccan. An unparalleled crop of monuments survive from the sixteenth and seventeenth centuries, including India's largest domed tomb, the mighty Golgumbaz. **See p.1142**

❹ Badami, Aihole and Pattadakal The Deccan's ancient Hindu heyday is represented by this trio of wonderful sites – a feast of enigmatic rock-cut caves, monkey-infested temples and tumbledown forts – in the middle of nowhere. **See p.1139**

❺ Hampi Rent a bicycle to explore the expansive, beautifully carved remains of medieval India's most splendid city, set amid a dreamy landscape of banana groves and boulder hills. **See p.1131**

❻ Gokarna This compact pilgrimage town on the Konkan coast holds plenty of traditional atmosphere, and a crop of gorgeous beaches around the headland to the south. **See p.1125**

❼ Goa For a self-indulgent spell soaking up the rays and surf of the Konkan, Goa's hard to beat. Aim for one of the less-developed resorts such as Agonda or Patnem in the south of the state. **See p.670**

COMMUTERS, CHURCHGATE STATION, MUMBAI

Basics

Getting there

With most overland routes into India (except from Nepal) effectively blocked by closed or trouble-prone borders, the only practicable way of getting to India is by plane. There are numerous nonstop services from the UK, plus a few from North America and one from Australia. Most of these arrive at either Delhi or Mumbai, although there are also nonstop flights from the UK into Kolkata, Chennai and Bengaluru.

Fares worldwide always depend on the season, with the highest being roughly from November to March, when the weather in India is best; fares drop during the shoulder seasons – April to May and August to early October – and you'll get the best prices during the low season, June and July. The most expensive fares of all are those coinciding with **Diwali** in October/November, when demand peaks as Indian emigrants travel home for holidays with their families.

For Goa or Kerala, you may find it cheaper to pick up a bargain **package deal** from a tour operator (see p.30). Indian law prohibits the sale of flight-only tickets by charter companies, but operators sometimes get around this by tacking budget "bunk-house" accommodation to their tickets, which (if it exists at all) travellers ditch on arrival. Note also that the Indian government places a restriction of 28 days on the period of time a charter ticket can cover. If you wish to stay in the country for longer than that, you technically have to take a scheduled flight. Nor is it possible to fly in on a charter and out on a scheduled flight, or vice versa.

Packages

Lots of operators run **package holidays** to India, covering activities ranging from trekking and wildlife-watching through to general sightseeing or just lying on the beach, not to mention more specialist-interest tours focusing on anything from steam locomotives to food. In addition, many companies can also arrange **tailor-made tours** where you plan your own itinerary. Specialist trips such as trekking and tailor-made tours do not necessarily work out a lot more expensive than organizing everything independently, especially if you want a degree of comfort. Tour operators pay a lot less for better-class hotels and flights than you would, plus they save you time and hassle by knowing the best hotels, routes and sights to feature. On the other hand, a typical package tour can rather isolate you from the country, shutting you off in air-conditioned hotels and cars.

Flights from the UK and Ireland

It takes between eight and eleven hours to fly from the UK direct to India. A number of carriers fly nonstop from London Heathrow to Delhi and Mumbai; these currently include Air India (Wairindia.com), Jet Airways (Wjetairways.com), Virgin Atlantic (Wvirgin-atlantic.com) and British Airways (Wba.com), who also fly nonstop to Kolkata, Chennai and Bengaluru. Numerous other European and Middle Eastern carriers offer one-stop services via their home city in Europe or the Gulf. From elsewhere in the UK and Ireland you'll have to take an indirect flight, changing planes at either Heathrow or somewhere else in Europe, the Middle East or Asia. Both scheduled fares and flight-only charters usually start from around £500.

Flights from the US and Canada

India is on the other side of the planet from the US and Canada. If you live on the east coast it's quicker to travel via Europe, while from the west coast it's roughly the same distance (and price) whether you travel via Europe or the Pacific. There are currently nonstop flights from **New York** to Delhi and Mumbai on Air India and Continental (Wcontinental.com), to Mumbai on Delta (Wdelta.com) and from **Chicago** to Delhi on American Airlines (Waa.com). Otherwise, you'll probably stop over somewhere in Europe (most often London), the Gulf, or both. Nonstop

A BETTER KIND OF TRAVEL

At Rough Guides we are passionately committed to travel. We believe it helps us understand the world we live in and the people we share it with – and of course tourism is vital to many developing economies. But the scale of modern tourism has also damaged some places irreparably, and climate change is accelerated by most forms of transport, especially flying. All Rough Guides' flights are carbon-offset, and every year we donate money to a variety of environmental charities.

flights take around 15–16 hours, with fares from New York to Mumbai/Delhi starting at around US$1250. There are currently no nonstop flights from the **west coast**; count on a minimum 22 hours' travel time. Fares start at around US$1500.

There are also no nonstop flights from **Canada** to India – you'll have to travel via a connecting city in the US, Europe or Asia with a minimum travel time of around 20 hours. Fares start at around Can$1100 from Toronto and Can$1200 from Vancouver.

Flights from Australia and New Zealand

The only nonstop flight to India from either **Australia** or **New Zealand** at present is Qantas's (Wqantas.com.au) service from Sydney to Mumbai (with a flying time of around 13hr); otherwise, you'll have to make at least one change of plane in a southeast Asian hub city (usually Kuala Lumpur, Singapore or Bangkok). Fares start from around Aus$1700. Flying from New Zealand, the cheapest fares to India start at around NZ$2000 from Auckland; add on approximately NZ$200 for flights from Wellington or Christchurch.

Round-the-world tickets

If India is only one stop on a longer journey, you might want to consider buying a **Round-the-World (RTW) ticket**. Some travel agents can sell you an "off-the-shelf" RTW ticket that will have you touching down in about half a dozen cities (Delhi and Mumbai feature on many itineraries); others will have to assemble one for you, which can be tailored to your needs but is apt to be more expensive. Prices start around £1700/US$2700 for a RTW ticket including India, valid for one year.

Agents and operators

TRAVEL AGENTS

North South Travel UK ☎ 01245 608 291, Wnorthsouthtravel .co.uk. Friendly, competitive travel agency, offering discounted fares worldwide. Profits are used to support projects in the developing world, especially the promotion of sustainable tourism.

STA Travel UK ☎ 0871 2300 040, US ☎ 1 800 781 4040, Australia ☎ 134 782, New Zealand ☎ 0800 474 400, South Africa ☎ 0861 781 781; W statravel.co.uk. Worldwide specialists in independent travel; also student IDs, travel insurance, car rental, rail passes, and more. Good discounts for students and under-26s.

Trailfinders UK ☎ 0845 058 5858, Ireland ☎ 01 677 7888, Australia ☎ 1300 780 212; W trailfinders.com. One of the best-informed and most efficient agents for independent travellers.

Travel CUTS Canada ☎ 1 866 246 9762, US ☎ 1 800 592 2887; W travelcuts.com. Canadian youth and student travel firm.

USIT Ireland ☎ 01 602 1906, Northern Ireland ☎ 028 9032 7111; W usit.ie. Ireland's main student and youth travel specialists.

PACKAGE-HOLIDAY COMPANIES

Audley Travel UK ☎ 01993 838300, W audleytravel.com. Tailor-made and small-group tours that use interesting accommodation (homestays, tented camps and heritage properties); they're also strong on wildlife.

Bales UK ☎ 0845 057 1819, W balesworldwide.com. Wide range of group and tailor-made tours covering most of India. They won four awards in 2012.

Cox & Kings UK ☎ 020 7873 5000, W coxandkings.co.uk, US ☎ 1 800 999 1758, W coxandkings.com. Established in India in 1758, with upmarket group and private tours, many featuring Rajasthan and Agra, plus the Palace on Wheels.

Exodus UK ☎ 0845 287 7606, Ireland ☎ 01 804 7153, US ☎ 1 800 843 4277, Canada ☎ 1 866 338 8735, Australia ☎ 1300 655 433, New Zealand ☎ 0800 838 747; W exodus.co.uk. Experienced specialists in small-group itineraries, treks and overland tours.

Explore Worldwide UK ☎ 0845 291 4541, US ☎ 1 800 486 9096, Australia ☎ 02 8913 0700, New Zealand ☎ 09 524 5118; W explore.co.uk. Wide range of small-group adventure holidays.

GeoEx US ☎ 1 800 777 8183, W geoex.com. Unusual tours, ranging from Tamil Nadu temple trips to Sikkim village walks.

High Places UK ☎ 0114 275 7500, W highplaces.co.uk. Sheffield-based trekking and mountaineering specialists; they also run an interesting sixteen-day tour through Kerala.

Insider Tours UK ☎ 01233 811771, W insider-tours.com. Some of the most original, "hands-on" and ethical itineraries on the market, taking visitors to wonderful off-track corners of Kerala, Goa, the Northeast and elsewhere.

Kerala Connections UK ☎ 01892 722440, W keralaconnect .co.uk. Itineraries in Kerala, as well as Tamil Nadu, Karnataka, Goa and the Andamans, for a wide range of budgets.

Lakshmi Tours UK ☎ 01985 844183, W lakshmitoursindia.com. Special-interest tours (drawing, textiles, Ayurveda) for small groups, mostly focusing on Rajasthan and Kerala.

Mountain Kingdoms UK ☎ 01453 844400, W mountainkingdoms.co.uk. Quality treks in Sikkim, Garhwal, Himachal Pradesh, Ladakh and Arunachal Pradesh, plus a Kerala spice trail.

Myths and Mountains US ☎ 1 800 670 6984 or ☎ 775 832 5454, W mythsandmountains.com. Special-interest trips (tailor-made or group) to some very unusual places, ranging from tribal Chhattisgarh to deepest Gujarat, with the emphasis on culture, crafts and religion.

Peregrine UK ☎ 0845 863 9667, Australia ☎ 03 8601 4444; W peregrineadventures.com. Small-group wildlife and culture tours in Rajasthan and south India, plus trekking in Ladakh.

SD Enterprises ☎ 020 8903 3411, W indiarail.co.uk. Run by Indian rail experts, SD Enterprises put together itineraries for independent travellers wanting to explore India by train, plus a range of non-choo choo choices.

Steppes Discovery UK ☎ 01285 643333, US ☎ 1 800 352 7606; Ⓦ steppesdiscovery.co.uk. Nature-tour specialist offering small groups or tailor-made trips with an accent on conservation and ecology.
Voyages Jules Verne UK ☎ 0845 166 7003, Ⓦ vjv.co.uk. Classic heritage tours, including some by rail.
Western & Oriental Travel UK ☎ 020 7666 1234, Ⓦ wandotravel.com. Award-winning, upmarket agency with tailor-made itineraries ranging from Himalayan treks to southern temple tours, with the emphasis on culture, history and wildlife.

Entry requirements

Almost everyone needs a visa before travelling to India. If you're going to study or work, you'll need to apply for a special student or business visa; otherwise, a standard tourist visa will suffice.

Tourist visas

Tourist visas are valid for six months from the date of issue (not of departure from your home country or entry into India), and vary in price according to your nationality. Fees were hiked to £82 for UK citizens in early 2013 but cost around £32/US$48 for most other applicants. You're asked to specify whether you need a single-entry or a multiple-entry visa; as the same rates apply to both, it makes sense to ask for the latter just in case you decide to go back within six months.

Visas in the UK, US, Canada and Australia are no longer issued by Indian embassies themselves, but by various third-party companies or sub-contractors (see below). The firms' websites give all the details you need to make your application. Read the small print carefully and always **make sure you've allowed plenty of time**. Processing time is usually two to three working days but it's wiser to leave at least a week. **Postal applications** take a minimum of ten working days plus time in transit, and often longer.

Elsewhere in the world, visas are still issued by the relevant local embassy or consulate, though the same caveats apply. Bear in mind too that Indian High Commissions, embassies and consulates observe Indian public holidays as well as local ones, so always check opening hours in advance.

Visa agencies

In many countries it's possible to pay a **visa agency** or "visa expediter" (see below) to process the visa on your behalf, which typically costs £60–70/US$100–120, plus the price of the visa. This is worth considering if you're not able to get to your nearest Indian High Commission, embassy or consulate yourself. Prices vary from company to company, as do turnaround times. Two weeks is about standard, but you can get a visa in as little as 24 hours if you're prepared to pay premium rates. For a full rundown of services, check the company websites, from where you can usually download visa application forms.

Visa extensions

It is no longer possible to **extend a tourist visa** in India, though exceptions may be made in special circumstances such as serious illness. Many travellers who want to spend more time in India go to a neighbouring country such as Nepal for a new visa when their old one expires, but there is no guarantee a new one will be issued right away, as you are not officially allowed to spend more than six months in the country within one year.

INDIAN EMBASSIES, HIGH COMMISSIONS, CONSULATES AND VISA-PROCESSING CENTRES ABROAD

Australia c/o VFS Global (Ⓦ vfs-in-au.net). Offices in all states except Tasmania and NT – see website for contact details.
Canada c/o VFS Global (Ⓦ in.vfsglobal.ca). Nine offices countrywide – see website for contact details.
Ireland Embassy: 6 Leeson Park, Dublin 6 ☎ 01 497 0843, Ⓦ indianembassy.ie.
Nepal c/o Indian Visa Service Centre (IVSC), House no.296, Kapurdhara Marg, Kathmandu ☎ 01 400 1516, Ⓦ indianembassy.org.np.
New Zealand High Commission: 180 Molesworth St, PO Box 4045, Wellington ☎ 04 473 6390, Ⓦ hicomind.org.nz.
South Africa 852 Schoeman St, PO Box 40216, Arcadia 0007, Pretoria ☎ 012 342 2593, Ⓦ indiainsouthafrica.com; 1 Eton Rd, Parktown, PO Box 6805, Johannesburg 2000 ☎ 011 482 8484 to 9; The Old Station Building (4th floor), 160 Pine St, PO Box 3276, Durban 4001 ☎ 031 307 7020, Ⓦ indcondurban.co.za.
Sri Lanka High Commission: 36–38 Galle Rd, Colombo 3 ☎ 011 232 7587, Ⓦ hcicolombo.org. Consulate: 31 Rajapihilla Mawatha, PO Box 47, Kandy ☎ 081 222 4563.
UK c/o VFS Global (Ⓦ in.vfsglobal.co.uk). Offices in London, Birmingham, Manchester, Cardiff, Edinburgh and Glasgow – see website for contact details.
US c/o Travisa (Ⓦ indiavisa.travisaoutsourcing.com). Offices in Washington, New York, San Francisco, Chicago and Houston – see website for contact details.

VISA AGENCIES

CIBT UK ☎ 0844 736 0211, Ⓦ uk.cibtvisas.co.uk, US ☎ 1 800 929 2428, Ⓦ www.cibt.com.
India Visa 24 UK ☎ 0800 084 5037, Ⓦ indiavisa24.co.uk.

India Visa Company UK ☎ 020 8582 1117,
ⓦ indiavisacompany.com.
India Visa Office UK ☎ 0844 800 4018, ⓦ indiavisaheadoffice
.co.uk.
Travel Document Systems US: Washington ☎ 1 800 874 5100,
New York ☎ 1 877 874 5104, San Francisco ☎ 1 888 874 5100;
ⓦ traveldocs.com.
Visa Connection US & Canada ☎ 1 866 566 8472,
ⓦ visaconnection.biz.
Visa Link Australia ☎ 03 9673 1500, ⓦ visalink.com.au.

Getting around

Inter-city transport in India may not be the fastest or the most comfortable in the world, but it's cheap and goes more or less everywhere. You generally have the option of train or bus, sometimes plane, and occasionally even boat. Transport around town comes in even more permutations, ranging in Kolkata, for example, from human-pulled rickshaws to a state-of-the-art metro system.

Whether you're on road or rail, public transport or your own vehicle, India offers the chance to try out some classics: narrow-gauge railways, steam locomotives, the Ambassador car and the Enfield Bullet motorbike – indeed some people come to India for these alone.

By train

Travelling by train is one of India's classic experiences. The national rail network covers almost the entire country; only a few places (such as the mountainous regions of Sikkim, Ladakh, Uttarakhand and most of Himachal Pradesh) are inaccessible by train. Although the railway system might look like chaos, it does work, and generally better than you might expect. Trains are often late, of course, sometimes by hours rather than minutes, but they do run, and when the train you've been waiting for rolls into the station, the reservation you made halfway across the country several weeks ago will be on a list pasted to the side of your carriage.

It's worth bearing in mind, with journeys frequently lasting twelve hours or more, that an **overnight train** can save you a day's travelling and a night's hotel bill, assuming you sleep well on trains. When travelling overnight, always padlock your bag to your bunk; an attached chain is usually provided beneath the seat of the lower bunk.

Types of train

There are three basic types of passenger train in India. You're most likely to use long-distance **inter-city trains** (called "express" or "mail") along with the speedier "**super-fast**" air-conditioned trains – these include the various "Rajdhani" expresses, which link Delhi with cities nationwide, and "Shatabdi" expresses, daytime trains that connect major cities, mostly within an eight-hour travelling distance. There are also painfully slow local "**passenger**" trains, which stop everywhere, and which you'll only use if you want to get right off the beaten track. In addition to these three basic types of train, there are also a few dedicated **tourist trains** and other special services, such as the famous Palace on Wheels (see p.34) and the toy train to Darjeeling (see p.779).

Classes of train travel

Indian Railways distinguishes between no fewer than seven **classes** of travel. Different types of train carry different classes of carriage, though you'll seldom have more than four to choose from any one service. The simplest and cheapest class, used by the majority of Indians, is **second-class unreserved** (or "second seating"). These basic carriages have hard wooden seats and often become incredibly packed during the day – bearable for shortish daytime journeys, but best avoided for longer trips and (especially) overnight travel, unless you're exceptionally hardy or unusually poor. On the plus side, fares in second-class unreserved are so cheap as to be virtually free. It also represents a way of getting on a train at the last minute if you haven't been able to secure a reserved seat.

Far more civilized, and only around fifty percent more expensive, is **second-class sleeper** ("sleeper class"), consisting of carriages of three-tiered padded bunks that convert to seats during the day. All seats in these carriages must be booked in advance even for daytime journeys, meaning that they don't get horrendously overcrowded like second-class unreserved, although there's usually still plenty going on, with itinerant chai- and coffee-sellers, travelling musicians, beggars and sweepers passing through the carriages. Overnight trips in second-class sleeper compartments are reasonably comfy. **First class** consists of non-a/c seating in comfortable if ageing compartments of two to four berths, though this class is being phased out and is now found on relatively few trains.

The other four classes are all air-conditioned (available only on inter-city and super-fast trains). **A/c chair car** (often denoted as "CC") is found almost exclusively on superfast services and consists of comfortable reclining seats; they're really designed for daytime travel, since they don't convert to bunks, and aren't generally found on overnight services. Shatabdi expresses are made up entirely of chair-car carriages (ordinary a/c chair car and, for double the price, an executive a/c chair car).

There are three classes of air-conditioned sleepers. The cheapest, **third-class a/c**, has open carriages with three-tier bunks – basically the same as second-class sleeper, except with a/c. Less crowded (and found on more services) is **second-class a/c**, which has two-tier berths. Most comfortable of all is **first-class a/c**, which consists of two-tier bunks in two- or four-person private compartments, complete with carpeting and relatively presentable bathrooms – although fares can work out only slightly cheaper than taking a plane.

Note that bed linen is provided free on most a/c services, while bottled water, snacks and simple meals are included in the ticket price of Rajdhani and Shatabdi services.

Ladies' compartments exist on all overnight trains for women travelling on their own or with other women; they are usually small and can be full of noisy kids, but can give untold relief to women travellers who otherwise might have to endure incessant staring in the open section of the carriage. They can be a good place to meet Indian women, particularly if you like (or are with) children. Some stations also have ladies-only waiting rooms.

Timetables and fares

Fares, **timetables** and availability of berths can be checked online at Indian Railway's cumbersome website (Ⓦindianrail.gov.in), or via the more streamlined, privately run Ⓦcleartrip.com. Indian Railways' *Trains at a Glance* (₹45; updated twice a year) contains timetables of all inter-city and superfast trains and is available from information counters and newsstands at all main stations.

All rail fares are calculated according to the exact **distance** travelled. *Trains at a Glance* prints a chart of fares by kilometres, and also gives the distance in kilometres of stations along each route in the timetables, making it possible to calculate what the basic fare will be for any given journey.

Indrail passes

Indrail passes, sold to foreigners and Indians resident abroad, cover all fares and reservation fees for periods ranging from half a day to ninety days, but are considerably more expensive than buying tickets individually. The pass is designed for nation-wide travel, so if you only use it, say, between Delhi, Agra and the cities of Rajasthan, you won't be getting your money's worth. The pass does, however, save you queuing for tickets and it allows you to make and cancel reservations with impunity (and without charge), and generally smooths your way in. For example, if you need to find a seat or berth on a "full" train, pass-holders get priority for tourist quota places. Indrail passes are available, in sterling or US dollars, at main station tourist counters in India and outside the country at IR agents and sometimes at Air India offices. A seven-day pass costs US$80 in second class, US$135 in first, and US$270 in a/c class. There's a full list of prices and overseas IR agents at Ⓦindianrail.gov.in /international_Tourist.html.

Reserving tickets

It's important to plan your train journeys in advance, as demand often makes it impossible to buy a long-distance ticket on the same day that you want to travel – although the Tatkal quota system (see p.34) has made life a little easier. Travellers following tight itineraries tend to buy their departure tickets from particular towns the moment they arrive to avoid having to trek out to the station again. At most large stations, it's possible to reserve tickets for journeys starting elsewhere in the country.

RAIL RECORDS

Comprising 108,706km (67,547 miles) of track and 7500 locomotives, which transport an average of 13 million passengers every day, India's **rail network** is the second largest in the world, with a workforce of around 1.4 million.

One record the country's transport ministers are somewhat less proud of, however, is the Indian Railways' **accident rate**. Four to five hundred crashes occur annually in India, causing between seven and eight hundred fatalities, which makes this the most dangerous rail network in the world, by a long chalk. Having said that, travelling by rail is considerably safer than using the buses. According to the most recent statistics, nearly 135,000 people died on the roads in 2010.

Online booking can be done through Indian Railways' official reservation site, ⓦ irctc.co.in, although the site only works during Indian opening hours and can be frustratingly difficult to use. A more dependable option is the privately run ⓦ cleartrip .com, which charges ₹100 per ticket to process purchases; major foreign credit cards are accepted but you will first have to register with them and Indian Railways – check out ⓦ seat61.com/India .htm#book-fromoutside for a clear explanation of this convoluted procedure. Bookings may be made from ninety days in advance right up to four hours before the scheduled departure time of the train. Cleartrip. com also handles **Tatkal tickets** (see below). Having booked your travel, you can then print out your own e-tickets, taking this along with some photo ID, such as a passport, when you board the train.

When **reserving a ticket in person** at a railway station, the first thing you'll have to do is fill in a little form at the booking office stating your name, age and sex, your proposed date of travel, and the train you wish to catch (giving the train's **name and number**). Most stations have computerized booking counters and you'll be told immediately whether or not seats are available. **Reservation offices** in the main stations are generally open from Monday to Saturday from 8am to 8pm, and on Sunday to 2pm. In larger cities, major stations have special tourist sections to cut queues for foreigners, with helpful English-speaking staff. Elsewhere, buying a ticket can often involve a longish wait, though women can often bypass this by simply walking to the head of the queue and forming their own "ladies' queue". A few stations also operate a number system of queueing, allowing you to repair to the chai stall until your number is called. A good alternative to queueing yourself is to get someone else to buy your ticket for you. Many **travel agents** will do this for a small fee (typically around ₹50–100); alternatively, ask at your guesthouse if they can sort it out.

Quotas and late-availability tickets

If there are no places available on the train you want, you have a number of choices. First, some seats and berths are set aside as a "**tourist quota**" – ask at the tourist counter of the reservations hall if you can get in on this, or else try the stationmaster. This quota is available in advance but usually only at major or originating stations. Failing that, other special quotas, such as one for "emergencies", only released on the day of travel, may remain unused – however, if you get a booking on the emergency quota and a pukka emergency or VIP turns up, you lose the reservation. Alternatively, you can stump up extra cash for a **Tatkal** ticket, which guarantees you access to a special ten percent quota on most trains, though certain catches and conditions apply. Bookable online and at any computerized office, these are released from 8am two days before the train departs, and there's a surcharge of ₹75–150, depending on the class of travel.

RAC – or "Reservation Against Cancellation" – tickets are another option, giving you priority if sleepers do become available. The ticket clerk should be able to tell you your chances. With an RAC ticket you are allowed onto the train and can sit until the conductor can find you a berth. The worst sort of ticket to have is a **wait-listed** one – identifiable by the letter "W" prefixing your passenger number – which will allow you onto the train but not in a reserved compartment; in this case go and see the ticket inspector as soon as possible to persuade him to find you a place if one is free. Wait-listed ticket holders are not allowed onto Shatabdi and Rajdhani trains. For short journeys or on minor routes you won't need to reserve tickets in advance.

Luxury tourist trains

Inspired by the Orient Express, Indian Railways offers high-end holiday packages aboard luxury **tourist trains**. The flagship of the scheme is the **Palace on Wheels** (ⓦ palaceonwheels.net), with sumptuous ex-maharajas' carriages updated into modern air-conditioned coaches, still decorated with the original designs. An all-inclusive, eight-day whistle-stop tour (Sept–April weekly) starts at US$2920 per person for the full trip, with discounts off-season (Sept and April). Note that the train is often booked up for months ahead, so early reservations are advised.

The Palace on Wheels has proved so popular that it has spawned a number of similar heritage trains, including Royal Rajasthan on Wheels, Maharajas' Express and The Deccan Odyssey. Details of all these tours, including fares and toll-free numbers in major Western countries, can be found on the Palace on Wheels website.

By plane

Considering the huge distances involved in getting around the country, and the time it takes to get from A to B, **flying** is an attractive option, despite the cost – the journey from Delhi to Chennai, for example, takes a mere 2 hours 30 minutes by plane compared to 36 hours on the train. Delays and cancellations can whittle away the time advantage, especially over small distances, but if you're short of time and plan to cover a lot of ground, flying can be a godsend. There was a proliferation of private airlines in the early years of the millennium but competition has seen some fold or get bought out by more established companies. At the time of writing, Kingfisher Airlines' fleet was grounded and it's uncertain whether the company will survive.

As with train tickets, **booking flights** is most easily done online via the airline's website. Larger carriers also have offices in major cities, as well as at the airports they fly to; these are listed in the relevant Guide chapters. Children under twelve pay half fare and under-twos (one per adult) pay ten percent.

DOMESTIC AIRLINES

Air India W airindia.com.
Air India Express W airindiaexpress.in.
Go Air W goair.in.
IndiGo Airlines W book.goindigo.in.
Jet Airways/JetKonnect W jetairways.com.
Kingfisher Airlines W flykingfisher.com.
SpiceJet W spicejet.com.

By bus

Although trains are generally the most characterful and comfortable way to travel in India, there are some places, particularly in the Himalayas, not covered by the rail network, or where trains are inconvenient. By contrast, **buses** go almost everywhere, usually more frequently than trains (though mostly in daylight hours), and are also sometimes faster (including in parts of Rajasthan and other places without broadgauge track). Going by bus also usually saves you the bother of reserving a ticket in advance.

Services vary enormously in terms of price and standard. Ramshackle **government-run buses**, packed with people, livestock and luggage, cover most routes, both short- and long-distance. In addition, popular routes between larger cities, towns and resorts are usually covered by **private buses**. These tend to be more comfortable, with extra legroom, tinted windows and padded reclining seats. Note, however, that smaller private bus companies may be only semilegal and have little backup in case of breakdown.

The description of the service usually gives some clue about the level of comfort. "Ordinary" buses usually have minimally padded, bench-like seats with upright backs. "Deluxe" or "Luxury" are more or less interchangeable terms but sometimes the term deluxe signifies a luxury bus past its sell-by date;

occasionally a bus will be described as a "2 by 2" which means a deluxe bus with just two seats on either side of the aisle. When applied to government services, these may hardly differ from "ordinary" buses, but with private companies, they should guarantee a softer, individual seat. It's worth asking when booking if your bus will have a video or music system (a "video bus"), as their deafening noise ruins any chances of sleep. Always try to avoid the back seats – they accentuate bumpy roads.

Luggage travels in the hatch of private buses – for which you may have to part with about ₹10–20 for the safekeeping of your bags. On state-run buses, you can usually squeeze it into an unobtrusive corner, although you may sometimes be requested to have it travel on the roof (you may be able to travel up there yourself if the bus is too crowded, though it's dangerous and illegal); check that it's well secured (ideally, lock it there) and not liable to get squashed. Baksheesh is in order for whoever puts it up there for you.

Buying a bus ticket is usually less of an ordeal than buying a train ticket, although at large city bus stations there may be twenty or so counters, assigned to different routes. When you buy your ticket you'll be given the registration number of the bus and, sometimes, a seat number. As at railway stations, women can form a separate, quicker, "ladies' queue". You can usually only pay on board on most ordinary state buses, and at bus stands outside major cities. Prior booking is usually available and preferable for express and private services, and it's a good idea to check with the agent exactly where the bus will depart from. You can usually pay on board private buses too, though doing so reduces your chances of a seat.

By boat

Apart from river ferries, few **boat services** run in India. The Andaman Islands are connected to Kolkata and Chennai by boat – as well as to each other. Kerala has a regular passenger service with a number of services operating out of Alappuzha and Kollam, including the popular "backwater trip" between the two. The Sunderbans in the delta region to the south of Kolkata is only accessible by boat.

By car

It is much more usual for tourists to be driven in India than it is for them to drive themselves; **car rental** firms operate on the basis of supplying **vehicles with drivers**. You can arrange them through any tourist office or taxi firm, and local taxi drivers hanging around hotels and city ranks are also available for day hire. Cars will cost around ₹1500 (£17/US$27) per day, which should include a maximum of 200km, with additional kilometres charged at around ₹6–7 per kilometre. On longer trips, the driver sleeps in the car, for which his firm may charge an additional ₹150–200. You should generally tip the driver around ₹150 per day, too.

Most tourists succumb to the romance of that quintessentially Indian automobile, the **Hindustan Ambassador** Mark IV, based on the design of the old British Morris Oxford. Sadly, however, the car's appalling suspension and back-breaking seats make it among the most uncomfortable rides in the world. Older models, in particular, can make for some gruelling journeys, with dashboards that become burning-hot and suffocating fumes plaguing the front seats. All in all, you'll be much better off in a modern two- or four-door hatchback – ask your rental company for the options. Air-conditioning adds considerably to the rate, and with larger cars such as SUVs, the daily rate of ₹1500 tends only to cover the first 80km, after which stiff additional per-kilometre charges apply.

A handful of big international chains offer **self-drive** car rental in India, but unless you've had plenty of experience on the country's notoriously dangerous roads, we strongly recommend you leave the driving to an expert. If you do drive yourself, expect the unexpected, and expect other drivers to take whatever liberties they can get away with. **Traffic** in the cities is particularly undisciplined; vehicles cut in and out without warning, and pedestrians, cyclists and cows wander nonchalantly down the middle of the road. In the country the roads are narrow, often in terrible repair, and hogged by overloaded Tata trucks that move aside for nobody, while something slow-moving like a bullock cart or a herd of goats can take up the whole road. It is particularly dangerous to drive at night – cyclists and cart drivers hardly ever have lights. If you are involved in an **accident**, it might be an idea to leave the scene quickly and go straight to the police to report it; mobs can assemble fast, especially if pedestrians or cows are involved.

To **import a car or motorbike** into India, you'll have to show a *carnet de passage*, a document intended to ensure that you don't sell the vehicle illegally. These are available from motoring organizations such as the AA. It's also worth bringing a few basic spares, as parts for foreign makes can be hard to find in India, although low-quality imitations are more widely available. All in all, this option is arduous, and bringing a vehicle to India is something of a commitment.

By motorbike

Riding a **motorbike** in India is not for the faint-hearted. Besides the challenging road and traffic conditions (see above) with the resultant stress and fatigue, simply running an unfamiliar bike can become a nightmare.

Buying a motorbike in India is only for the brave. If it's an old classic you're after, the 350- or 500cc Enfield Bullet, sold cheapest in Puducherry, on the Tamil Nadu coast, leads the field, with models becoming less idiosyncratic the more recent they are. If low price and practicality are your priorities, a smaller model from the likes of Bajaj, built in India but based on dependable old Japanese designs, may fit the bill if not the image. Delhi's Karol Bagh area is renowned for its motorcycle shops and rental agencies (see opposite). Obviously, you'll have to haggle over the price, but you can expect to pay half to twothirds of the original price for a bike in reasonable condition. Given the right bargaining skills, you can sell it again later for a similar price – perhaps to another foreign traveller – by advertising it in hotels and restaurants. A certain amount of bureaucracy is involved in transferring vehicle ownership to a new owner but a garage should be able to put you on to a broker ("auto consultant") who, for a modest commission (around ₹1000–2000), will help you find a seller or a buyer, and do the necessary paperwork.

Motorbike **rental** is available in many tourist towns and can be fun for local journeys, but the condition of the bike can be hit and miss. However, unless you know your stuff, this is a better strategy than diving in and buying a machine. Unlike with sales, it's in a rental outfit's interest to rent you a bike that works. Mechanically, the important thing to establish is the condition of the chain and sprockets, whether the machine starts and runs smoothly and, not least, whether both brakes and lights work (even so, riding at night is inadvisable). An in-depth knowledge of mechanics is not so necessary as every town has a bike mender who will be no stranger to Enfields.

A recommended firm in Delhi, both for purchasing bikes and for rental, is **Bulletwallas** (ⓦbulletwallas.com), at 7 Arakashan Rd, Multani Dhanda in the Paharganj district. An Aussie-run outfit, they specialize in Enfields, selling new, used and customized machines with only quality parts.

Without doubt the least stressful way of enjoying India on a motorbike, especially a temperamental but characterful Enfield, is joining one of several **motorbike tours**. They focus on the best locales with minimal traffic and amazing landscapes – the Himalayas, Rajasthan and Kerala – and remove much of the stress from what is still an adventure.

MOTORBIKE TOUR AGENCIES

Blazing Trails UK ☎ 01902 894009, ⓦ blazingtrailstours.com.
Classic Bike Adventure India Goa ☎ 0832 226 8467,
ⓦ classic-bike-india.com.
Ferris Wheels Motorcycle Safaris Australia ☎ 02 9970 6370,
ⓦ ferriswheels.com.au.
Himalayan Roadrunners US ☎ 802 738 6500, ⓦ ridehigh.com.
Live India UK ☎ 0845 224 1917, ⓦ liveindia.co.uk.

By bicycle

In many ways a **bicycle** is the ideal form of transport in India, offering total independence without loss of contact with local people. You can camp out, though there are cheap lodgings in almost every village – take the bike into your room with you – and, if you get tired of pedalling, you can put it on top of a bus as luggage, or transport it by train.

Bringing a bike from abroad requires no *carnet* or special paperwork but spare parts and accessories may be of different sizes and standards in India, so you may have to improvise. Bring basic spares and tools, and a pump. **Buying a bike** in India couldn't be easier, since most towns have cycle shops and even entire markets devoted to bikes. The advantages of a local bike are that spare parts are easy to get, locally produced tools and parts will fit, and your bike will not draw a crowd every time you park it. Disadvantages are that Indian bikes tend to be heavier and less state-of-the-art than ones from abroad; mountain bikes are beginning to appear in cities and bigger towns, but with insufficient gears and a low level of equipment, they're not worth buying. Selling should be quite easy: you won't get a tremendously good deal at a cycle market but you may well be able to sell privately, or even to a rental shop.

Bicycles can be **rented** in most towns, usually for local use only: this is a good way to find out if your legs and bum can survive an Indian bike before buying one. Rates can be anything from ₹25 to ₹150 per day and you may have to leave a deposit or your passport as security. Several adventure-tour operators offer bicycle tours of the country (see p.30), with most customers bringing their own cycles.

As for **contacts**, International Bicycle Fund in the US (☎ 206 767 0848, ⓦ ibike.org) publishes information and offers advice on bicycle travel around the world and maintains a useful website. In India, the Cycling Federation of India, C-5A/262, DDA Flats, Janak Puri, New Delhi 110058 (☎ 011 2375 3528, ⓦ cyclingfederationofindia.org), is the main cycle-sports organization.

City transport

Transport around towns takes various forms. City **buses** can get unbelievably crowded, so beware of pickpockets, razor-carrying, pocket-slitters and "Eve-teasers" (see p.72); the same applies to **suburban trains** in Mumbai (Chennai is about the only other place where you might want to use trains for local city transport). Any visitor to Delhi or Kolkata will be amazed by the clean efficiency of India's two **metro** systems.

You can also take **taxis**, usually rather battered Ambassadors (painted black and yellow in the large cities) and Maruti omnivans. With luck, the driver will agree to use the meter; in theory you're within your rights to call the police if he doesn't, but the usual compromise is to agree a fare for the journey before you get in. Naturally, it helps to have an idea in advance what the fare should be, though any figures quoted in this or any other guide should be treated as being the broadest of guidelines only. From places such as main stations, you may be able to find other passengers to share a taxi to the town centre. Many stations, and certainly most airports, operate **pre-paid taxi schemes** with set fares that you pay before departure; more expensive pre-paid limousines are also available.

That most Indian of vehicles, the **auto-rickshaw** – commonly referred to as just an "auto" – is the front half of a motor scooter with a couple of seats mounted on the back. Cheaper than taxis, better at nipping in and out of traffic, and usually metered (although, again, very few drivers are willing to use theirs and you should agree a fare before setting off), auto-rickshaws are a little unstable and their drivers often rather reckless but that's all part of the fun. In major tourist centres rickshaw-wallahs can, however, hassle you endlessly on the street, often shoving themselves right in your path to prevent you from ignoring them, and once you're inside they may try to take you to several shops before reaching your destination. In general it is better to hail a rickshaw than to take one that's been following you, and to avoid those that hang around outside posh hotels.

Some towns also have larger versions of auto-rickshaws known as **tempos** (or Vikrams), with six or eight seats behind, which usually ply fixed routes at flat fares. Here and there, you'll also come across horse-drawn carriages, or **tongas**. Tugged by underfed and often lame horses, these are the least popular with tourists.

Slower and cheaper still is the **cycle rickshaw** – basically a glorified tricycle. Foreign visitors often feel uncomfortable about travelling this way; except in the major tourist cities, cycle rickshaw-wallahs are invariably emaciated pavement-dwellers who earn only a pittance for their pains. In the end, though, to deny them your custom on those grounds is spurious logic; they will earn even less if you don't use them. As a foreigner you'll probably be quoted grossly inflated fares, but ask yourself if it's really worth haggling over tiny sums, which they could probably do with more than you.

Only in Kolkata do rickshaw-wallahs continue to haul the city's pukka rickshaws on foot.

If you want to see a variety of places around town, consider renting a taxi, rickshaw or auto-rickshaw for the day. Find a driver who speaks English reasonably well and agree a price beforehand. You will probably find it a lot cheaper than you imagine: the driver will invariably act as a guide and source of local knowledge, so tipping is usually in order.

Accommodation

There are far more Indians travelling around their own country at any one time – whether for holidays, on pilgrimages or for business – than there are foreign tourists, and a vast infrastructure of hotels and guesthouses caters for their needs. On the whole, accommodation, like so many other things in India, provides good value for money, though in the major cities, especially, there are luxury establishments that charge international prices for providing Western-style comforts and service.

Budget accommodation

While accommodation prices in India are generally on the up, there's still an abundance of inexpensive **hotels** and **hostels**, catering for foreign backpackers, tourists and less well-off Indians. Most charge ₹300–500 for a double room, although rates outside big cities and tourist centres may fall below ₹200 (roughly £2.30/US$3.60). The rock-bottom option is usually in a dormitory of a hostel or hotel, where you may still pay less than ₹100. Even cheaper still are **dharamshalas**, hostels run by religious establishments and used by pilgrims (see p.40).

Budget accommodation varies from filthy fleapits to homely guesthouses and, naturally, tends to be cheaper the further you get off the beaten track. It's most expensive in Delhi, Mumbai, Goa and resorts of Kerala, where prices are at least double those for equivalent accommodation in most other parts of the country.

The cheapest rooms usually have flimsy beds and thin, lumpy mattresses. Shared showers and toilets with only cold water are also the norm at the bottom of the range, although increasing numbers of places are offering en-suite bathrooms (or "attached" rooms, as they're known locally) and hot water, either on tap or in a bucket. Even so, it's always wise to check out the state of the bathrooms and toilets before taking a room. Bed bugs and mosquitoes are other things to check for – splotches of blood around the bed and on the walls where people have squashed them are telltale signs.

ACCOMMODATION PRICING

Accommodation prices quoted throughout this guide are for the cheapest double room during the main tourist season, where one exists, but not for short spikes during peak periods, such as those that occur in the hill stations from April to July or in Rajasthan, Goa and Kerala over Christmas and New Year. Notable regional price fluctuations, including slack periods when great discounts can be had, are mentioned in the accommodation listings throughout the guide chapters.

Where two prices are given, it denotes the cost of a double with shared bathroom first ("non attached"), followed by the en-suite ("attached") option. Dorm prices per person are also quoted separately where applicable. If the review states that a hotel has some air-conditioned rooms, you can usually reckon on them costing 50–100 percent more than the non-a/c ones.

Note that all hotels and guesthouses are required by law to have an official list of approved room prices. Some establishments, especially the cheaper ones, ignore this rule, while others do not display the rates. It is always worth asking for the "tariff list", if you cannot see it, as a starting point for any bargaining.

If a **taxi driver** or **rickshaw-wallah** tells you that the place you ask for is full, closed or has moved, it's more than likely that it's because he wants to take you to a hotel that pays him commission – added, in some cases, to your bill. Hotel touts operate in many popular tourist spots, working for commission from the hotels they take you to; this can become annoying and they should be given a wide berth unless you are desperate.

Mid-range hotels

Even if you value your creature comforts, you don't need to pay through the nose for them. A large clean room, freshly made bed, your own spotless bathroom and hot and cold running water can still cost as little as ₹500 (£5.70/US$9) in cheaper areas. Extras that bump up the price include local taxes, a TV, mosquito nets, a balcony and, above all, **air-conditioning**. Abbreviated in this book (and in India itself) as a/c, air-conditioning is not necessarily the advantage you might expect – in some hotels you can find yourself paying double for a system that is so dust-choked and noisy as to be more of a drawback than an advantage. Some offer **air-coolers** instead of a/c – these can be noisy and are less effective than full-blown a/c, but much better than just a fan. They're only found in drier climes as they don't work in areas of extreme humidity such as along the coasts of south India and the Bay of Bengal. Many medium-priced hotels also have attached restaurants, and also offer room service.

Most state governments run their own chain of hotels. They are usually good value but far less well run than comparable places in the private sector. We've reviewed such chain hotels throughout this guide. Bookings for state-run hotels can be made in advance through the state tourist offices throughout the country.

Upmarket hotels

The boom of the past decade has seen a proliferation in the number of luxury hotels throughout India. Roughly speaking they fall into two categories.

Pitched primarily at visiting businessmen, smart, Western-style hotels with air-conditioning and swanky interiors are to be found predominantly in towns and city centres. Because competition among them is rife, tariffs tend to represent good value for money, especially in the upper-mid-range bracket. Formal five-star chains such as *Taj*, India's premier hotel group, charge international rates – as most of their guests are on expense accounts or staying as part of discounted tour packages. Note that many top-end hotels offer significant **reductions to their rack rates** if you **book online**.

Holding more appeal for foreign visitors are the **heritage properties** that have mushroomed all across the country in recent years. Rajasthan started the trend, with old forts, palaces, hunting lodges, havelis and former hunting camps converted into accommodation for high-spending tourists. Brimming with old-world atmosphere, they deliver a quintessentially Indian "experience", often in the most exotic locations, with turbaned bellboys and antique automobiles adding to the colonial-era ambience. Other states were quick to get in on the act, and these days you can stay in fabulous Tamil mansions, colonial tea bungalows in the Nilgiris, wooden, gabled-roofed *tharavadaku* in the Keralan backwaters and Portuguese *palacios* in Goa. Quite a few wildlife sanctuaries also offer atmospheric, high-end accommodation in former hunting lodges, tented camps or treehouses, while down in Kerala, you can experience the lakes and lagoons of the backwaters on a converted rice barge. Reviews of the best heritage accommodation options appear in the relevant accounts in the Guide.

Other options

Many railway stations have "**retiring rooms**": basic private rooms with a bed and bathroom (some stations have dorms, too). They can be handy if you're catching an early morning train and are usually amongst the cheapest accommodation available anywhere, but can be noisy. Retiring rooms cannot be booked in advance and are allocated on a first-come-first-served basis; just turn up and ask if there's a vacancy.

TOP FIVE SPECIAL PLACES TO STAY

Elsewhere, Aswem Quality Goan beach huts under swaying palms. See p.703
Imperial, Delhi The capital's classiest hotel occupies an Art Deco building. See p.107
Lake Palace, Udaipur Lavishly converted palace in the middle of the lake. See p.208

Oriental Guest House, Leh Superfriendly family guesthouse with sweeping mountain views. See p.485
Shergarh, Kanha National Park Eco-friendly and relaxing jungle hideaway. See p.381

ACCOMMODATION PRACTICALITIES

Check-out time is often noon, but confirm this when you arrive: some expect you out by 9am, but many others operate a 24hr system, under which you are simply obliged to leave by the same time as you arrived. Some places let you use their facilities after the official check-out time, sometimes for a small charge, while a few won't even let you leave your baggage after check-out unless you pay for another night.

Not all hotels offer **single rooms**, so it can often work out more expensive to travel alone; in hotels that don't, you may be able to negotiate a slight discount. It's not unusual to find rooms with three or four beds, however – great value for families and small groups.

In cheap hotels and hostels, you needn't expect any additions to your basic bill, but as you go up the scale, you'll find **taxes** and **service charges** creeping in, sometimes adding as much as a third on top of the original tariff. Service is generally ten percent but taxes are a matter for local governments and vary from state to state.

Like most other things in India, the price of a room may well be open to **negotiation**. If you think the price is too high, or if all the hotels in town are empty, try haggling. You may get nowhere – but nothing ventured, nothing gained.

In one or two places, it's possible to rent rooms in people's homes. In Rajasthan, Mumbai and Kerala the local tourist offices run "**paying guest**" or "homestay" schemes to place tourists with families offering lodging. Servas (Ⓦservas.org), established in 1949 as a peace organization, is now devoted to providing homestays, representing more than six hundred hosts in India; you have to join before travelling by applying to the local Servas secretary (located via the website) – you then get a list of hosts to contact in the place you are visiting. Some people provide free accommodation, others are just day-hosts. There is no guarantee a bed will be provided – it's up to the individual. More recent web-based hosting options include Ⓦcouchsurfing.org and Ⓦairbnb.com.

Camping is generally restricted to wildlife reserves, where the Forest Department lay on low-impact accommodation under canvas for visitors, and to beach resorts in which building is restricted by local coastal protection laws. Except on mountain treks, it's not usual simply to pitch a tent in the countryside.

YMCAs and **YWCAs**, confined to big cities, are plusher and pricier than mid-range hotels. They are usually good value but are often full and some are exclusively single-sex. Official and non-official **youth hostels**, some run by state governments, are spread haphazardly across the country. They give HI cardholders a discount but rarely exclude non-members, nor do they usually impose daytime closing. Prices match the cheapest hotels; where there is a youth hostel, it usually has a dormitory and may well be the best budget accommodation available – which goes especially for the Salvation Army ones.

Finally, **religious institutions**, particularly Sikh *gurudwaras*, offer accommodation for pilgrims and visitors, which may include tourists; a donation is often expected, and certainly appreciated, but some of the bigger ones charge a fixed, nominal fee. Pilgrimage sites, especially those far from other accommodation, also have **dharamshalas** where visitors can stay – very cheap and very simple, usually with basic, communal washing facilities; some charitable institutions even have rooms with simple attached bathrooms. *Dharamshalas*, like *gurudwaras*, offer accommodation either on a donations system or charge a nominal fee, which can be as low as ₹25.

Food and drink

Indian food has a richly deserved reputation as one of the world's great cuisines. Stereotyped abroad as the ubiquitous "curry", the cooking of the Subcontinent covers a wealth of different culinary styles, with myriad regional variations and specialities, from the classic creamy meat and fruit Mughlai dishes of the north through to the banana-leaf vegetarian thalis of the south.

The basic distinction in Indian food is between the cuisines of the north and south. **North Indian food** (which is the style generally found in Indian restaurants abroad) is characterized by its rich meat and vegetable dishes in thick tomato, onion and yogurt-based sauces, accompanied by thick breads. **South Indian food**, by contrast, is almost exclusively vegetarian, with spicy chilli and coconut flavours and lots of rice, either served in its natural state or made into one of the south's distinctive range of pancakes, such as the dosa, *iddli* and *uttapam*.

For **vegetarians**, in particular, Indian food is a complete delight. Some of the Subcontinent's best food is meat-free, and even confirmed carnivores will find themselves tucking into delicious dhals and vegetable curries with relish. Most religious Hindus, and the majority of people in the south, don't eat meat or fish, while some orthodox Brahmins and Jains also avoid onions and garlic, which are thought to inflame the baser instincts. **Veganism** is not common, however; if you're vegan, you'll have to keep your eyes open for eggs and dairy products. Many eating places state whether they are vegetarian or non-vegetarian either on signs outside or at the top of the menu. The terms used in India (and throughout our eating listings) are "veg" and "non-veg". You'll also see "pure veg", which means that no eggs or alcohol are served. As a rule, **meat-eaters** should exercise caution in India: even when meat is available, especially in the larger towns, its quality can be poor, except in the best restaurants, and you won't get much in a dish anyway – especially in cheaper canteens where it's mainly there for flavouring. Hindus, of course, do not eat beef and Muslims shun pork, so you'll only find those in a few Christian enclaves such as the beach areas of Goa, and Tibetan areas. Note that what is called "mutton" on menus is in fact goat.

Where to eat

Broadly speaking, eating establishments divide into three main types: cheap and unpretentious local cafés (known variously as *dhabas*, *bhojanalayas* and *udipis*); Indian restaurants aimed at more affluent locals; and tourist restaurants. **Dhabas** and **bhojanalayas** are cheap cafés, where food is basic but often good, consisting of vegetable curry, dhal (a kind of lentil broth), rice or Indian bread (the latter more standard in the north) and sometimes meat. Often found along the sides of highways, *dhabas* traditionally cater to truck drivers – one way of telling a good *dhaba* is to judge from the number of trucks parked outside. *Bhojanalayas* are basic eating places, usually found in towns (especially around bus stands and train stations) in the north and centre of the country; they tend to be vegetarian, especially those signed as "Vaishno". Both *dhabas* and *bhojanalayas* can be grubby – look them over before you commit

> We give more **advice** on drinking water in the Health section (see box, p.47). There's a glossary of food terms in the Language section (see p.1193).

yourself. The same is rarely true of their southern equivalent, **udipi** canteens, which offer cheap, delicious snacks such as masala dosa, *iddli*, *vada* and rice-based dishes, all freshly cooked to order and served by uniformed waiters.

There are all sorts of **Indian restaurants**, veg and non-veg and typically catering to Indian businessmen and middle-class families. These are the places to go for reliably good Indian food at bargain prices. The more expensive Indian restaurants, such as those in five-star hotels, can be very expensive by local standards, but offer a rare chance to try top-notch classic Indian cooking, and still at significantly cheaper prices than you'd pay back home – assuming you could find Indian food that good.

Tourist restaurants, found across India wherever there are significant numbers of Western visitors, cater specifically for foreign travellers with unadventurous tastebuds, serving up a stereotypical array of pancakes, omelettes, chips, muesli and fruit salad, along with a basic range of curries. The downside is that they tend to be relatively pricey, while the food can be very hit and miss – Indian spaghetti bolognaise, enchiladas and chicken chowmein can be every bit as weird as you might expect. International-style **fast food**, including burgers (without beef – usually chicken or mutton) and pizzas, is also available in major cities.

Indian food

What Westerners call a "curry" covers a huge variety of dishes, each made with a different masala, or mix of **spices**. Curry powder does not exist in India, the nearest equivalent being garam masala ("hot mix"), a combination of spices added to a dish at the last stage of cooking to spice it up. Commonly used spices include chilli, turmeric, garlic, ginger, cinnamon, cardamom, cloves, coriander – both leaf and seed – cumin and saffron. These are not all added at the same time, and some (particularly cardamom and cloves) are used whole, so beware of chewing on them.

Chilli is another key element in the Indian spice cabinet but the idea that all Indian food is fiery hot is a complete myth. North Indian food, in particular, tends to be quite mildly spiced, often more so than Indian food in restaurants abroad. South Indian food can be hotter but not invariably so. If you don't like hot food, there are mild dishes such as korma and biriyani where meat or vegetables are cooked with rice. Indians tend to assuage the effects of chilli with chutney, *dahi* (curd) or *raita* (curd with mint and cucumber, or other herbs and vegetables). Otherwise,

Somewhat confusingly, places serving traditional meals in India frequently call themselves "**hotels**", even though they do not offer accommodation. This is particularly common in the south, where you'll often come across men waving signs on roadsides advertising a "hotel", when it's no more than a lunch stop.

beer is one of the best things for washing chilli out of your mouth; the essential oils that cause the burning sensation dissolve in alcohol, but not in water.

Vegetarian curries are usually identified (even on menus in English) by the Hindi names of their main ingredients, such as *paneer* (cheese), *alu* (potatoes), *chana* (chickpeas) or *mutter* (peas). **Meat curries** are more often given specific names such as *korma* or *dopiaza*, to indicate the kind of masala used or the method of cooking.

North Indian food

North Indian cooking has been heavily influenced by the various Muslim invaders who arrived in the Subcontinent from Central Asia and Persia and who gave Indian cooking many of its most popular dishes and accompaniments, such as the biriyani and the naan bread, as well as its relatively greater emphasis on meat compared to the south. The classic north Indian fusion of native and Central Asian influences (although it can be found as far south as Hyderabad) is so-called **Mughlai cooking**, the creation of the Mughal dynasty. Mostly non-veg, the food is mildly spiced but extremely rich, using ingredients such as cream, almonds, sultanas and saffron – the classic korma sauce is the best-known example.

The other big northern style is **tandoori**. The name refers to the deep clay oven (*tandoor*) in which the food is cooked. Tandoori chicken is marinated in yogurt, herbs and spices before cooking. Boneless pieces of meat, marinated and cooked in the same way are known as tikka; they may be served in a medium-strength masala (tikka masala), one thickened with almonds (*pasanda*), or in a rich butter sauce (*murg makhani* or butter chicken). Breads such as naan and *roti* are also baked in the *tandoor*.

A main dish – which may be a curry, but could also be a dry dish such as a kebab, or a tandoori dish without a masala – is usually served with a dhal (lentils) and bread such as chapattis or naan. Rice is usually an optional extra in north India and has to be ordered separately. Many restaurants also offer set meals, or **thalis**. A thali is a stainless-steel tray

with a number of little dishes in it, containing a selection of curries, a chutney and a sweet. In the middle you'll get bread and usually rice. In many places, waiters will keep coming round with refills until you've had enough.

In north India, food is usually served with **bread**, which comes in a number of varieties, all of them flatbreads rather than loaves. **Chapatti** is a generic term for breads, but tends to refer to the simplest, unleavened type. It's usually made from wheat flour. The term **roti** is likewise generic, and a roti can be exactly the same as a chapatti, but the term tends to refer more to a thicker bread baked in a *tandoor*. **Naan** is a leavened bread, thick and chewy, and invariably baked in a *tandoor*; it's a favourite in non-veg restaurants as it best accompanies rich meaty dishes. You may also come across fried breads, of which **paratha** (or *parantha*) is rolled out, basted with ghee, folded over and rolled out again several times before cooking, and often stuffed with ingredients such as potato (*alu paratha*); it's popular for breakfast. **Puris** are little fried puffballs. **Poppadum** (*papad*) is a crisp wafer made from lentil flour and is typically served as an appetizer.

There's an enormous variety of regional cuisines across the north. **Bengalis** love fish and cook a mean *mangsho* (meat) curry as well as exotic vegetable dishes such as *mo-cha* – cooked banana flower. They also like to include fish bones for added flavour in their vegetable curries – a nasty surprise for vegetarians. **Tibetans** and **Bhotias** from the Himalayas have a simple diet of *thukpa* (meat soup) and *momo* (meat dumplings), as well as a salty tea made with either rancid yak butter (where available) or with ordinary butter. In **Punjab** and much of northern India, home cooking consists of dhal and vegetables along with *roti* and less rice than the Bengalis. Food in **Gujarat**, predominantly veg, is often cooked with a bit of sugar. Certain combinations are traditional and seasonally repeated, such as *makki ki roti* (fried corn bread) with *sarson ka sag* (mustard-leaf greens) around Punjab and other parts of north India. *Baingan bharta* (pured roast aubergine) is commonly eaten with plain yogurt and *roti*. In good Muslim cooking from the north, delicately made *rumali roti* ("handkerchief" bread) often accompanies rich meat and chicken dishes.

South Indian food

The food of south India is a world away from that of the north. Southern cooking also tends to use a significantly different repertoire of spices, with sharper, simpler flavours featuring coconut, tamarind, curry leaves and plenty of dried red and

FIVE TOP PLACES TO EAT

Apoorva, Mumbai Top-quality Mangalorean coconut-based delights. See p.613
Blackbeard's Bistro, Havelock Island Chilled-out traveller haunt with superb seafood. See p.941
Le Club, Puducherry A stylish touch of French *je ne sais quoi*. See p.979

Karim's, Old Delhi Atmospheric spot for tasty kebabs and mouth-watering Mughlai dishes. See p.114
Sarovaram, Ernakulam Quintessential pure-veg Keralan food in simple surroundings. See p.1068

fresh green chillies. **Rice** is king, not only eaten in its natural form, but also made into regional staples such as *iddlis* (steamed rice cakes) and dosas (fermented rice-batter pancakes), such as the ubiquitous masala dosa, a potato curry wrapped in a crispy lentil-flour pancake. The lavish naans, *parathas*, *rotis* and other breads that are such a feature of north Indian cooking aren't usually available, apart from the fluffy little *puri*. Meat is comparatively uncommon in the Brahmin-dominated temple towns of Tamil Nadu, but available throughout Kerala, where there are sizeable Christian and Muslim minorities.

Set meals are another common feature in the south, where they are generally referred to simply as "meals". They generally consist of a mound of rice surrounded by various vegetable curries, *sambar* dhal, chutney and curd, and usually accompanied by *puris* and *rasam*, a thin, hot, peppery soup. Traditionally served on a round metal tray or thali (also found in north India), with each side dish in a separate metal bowl, set meals are sometimes served up on a section of banana leaf instead. In most traditional restaurants, you can eat as much as you want, and staff circulate with refills of everything. In the south even more than elsewhere, eating with your fingers is *de rigueur* and cutlery may be unavailable in cheap restaurants.

Wherever you eat, remember to use only your **right hand**, and wash your hands before you start. Try and avoid getting food on the palm of your hand by eating with the tips of your fingers.

Snacks and street food

India abounds in **snacks** and **street food**. *Chana puri*, a chickpea curry with a *puri* (or sometimes another type of bread, a *kulcha*) to dunk, is a great favourite in the north; *iddli sambar* – lentil and vegetable sauce with rice cakes to dunk – is the southern equivalent. Street finger-food includes *bhel puris* (a Mumbai speciality consisting of a mix of puffed rice, deep fried vermicelli, potato and crunchy *puri* with tamarind sauce), *pani puris* (the

same *puris* dunked in peppery and spicy water – only for the seasoned), *bhajis* (deep-fried cakes of vegetables in chickpea flour), samosas (vegetables or occasionally meat in a pastry triangle, fried), and pakoras (vegetables or potato dipped in chickpea flour batter and deep-fried). In the south, you'll also come across the ever-popular *vada*, a spicy deep-fried lentil cake which looks rather like a doughnut.

Kebabs are common in the north, most frequently **seekh** kebab, minced lamb grilled on a skewer, but also **shami** kebab, small minced-lamb cutlets. Kebabs rolled into griddle-fried bread, known as *kathi* rolls, originated in Kolkata but are now available in other cities as well. With all street snacks, though, remember that food left lying around attracts germs – make sure it's freshly cooked. Be especially careful with snacks involving water, such as *pani puris*, and cooking oil, which is often recycled. Generally, it's a good idea to acclimatize to Indian conditions before you start eating street snacks.

You won't find anything called "**Bombay mix**" in India, but there's no shortage of dry spicy snack mixes, often referred to as *channa chur*. Jackfruit chips are sometimes sold as a savoury snack – though they are rather bland – and cashew nuts are a real bargain. Peanuts, also known as "monkey nuts" or *mumfuli*, usually come roasted and unshelled.

Non-Indian food

Chinese food is widely available in any urban area. It's generally cooked by Indian chefs and isn't exactly authentic, except in the few Indian cities, most notably Kolkata, that have large Chinese communities, where you can get very good Chinese cuisine.

Tourist restaurants and backpacker cafés nationwide offer a fair choice of **Western food**, from unpretentious little bakeries serving cakes and sandwiches to smart tourist restaurants dishing up fine Italian cooking on candlelit terraces. However, quality is variable. Delhi and Mumbai are also home to a range of specialist non-Indian restaurants

PAAN

You may be relieved to know that the red stuff people spit all over the streets isn't blood, but juice produced by chewing **paan** – a digestive, commonly taken after meals, and also a mild stimulant, found especially in the northeast, where it is fresh and much stronger.

Paan consists of chopped or shredded nut (always referred to as betel nut, though in fact it comes from the areca palm), wrapped in a leaf (which *does* come from the betel vine) that is first prepared with ingredients such as *katha* (a red paste), *chuna* (slaked white lime), *mitha masala* (a mix of sweet spices, which can be ingested) and *zarda* (chewing tobacco, not to be swallowed on any account, especially if made with *chuna*). The triangular package thus formed is wedged inside your cheek and chewed slowly. In the case of *chuna* and *zarda* paans, you should spit out the juice as you go.

Paan, and paan masala, a mix of betel nut, fennel seeds, sweets and flavourings, are sold by paan-wallahs, often from tiny stalls squeezed between shops. Paan-wallahs develop big reputations; those in the tiny roads of Varanasi are the most renowned, asking astronomical prices for paan made to elaborate specifications including silver and even gold foil. Paan is an acquired taste; novices should start off, and preferably stick with, the sweet and harmless *mitha* variety, which is perfectly all right to ingest.

featuring Tex-Mex, Thai, Japanese, Italian and French cuisines – these are usually found in luxury hotels.

In addition to these places, international **fast-food** chains such as Pizza Hut, Domino's, KFC and McDonald's serve the same standard fare as elsewhere in the world at much cheaper prices.

Sweets

Most Indians have rather a sweet tooth and **Indian sweets**, usually made of milk, can be very sweet indeed. Of the more solid type, *barfi*, a kind of fudge made from milk which has been boiled down and condensed, varies from moist and delicious to dry and powdery. It comes in various flavours from plain creamy white to *pista* (pistachio) in livid green and is often sold covered with silver leaf (which you eat). Smoother-textured, round *penda* and thin diamonds of *kaju katli*, plus moist *sandesh* and the harder *paira*, both popular in Bengal, are among many other sweets made from *chhana* or boiled-down milk. Crunchier *mesur* is made with chickpeas; numerous types of gelatinous halwa, not the Middle Eastern variety, include the rich *gajar ka halwa* made from carrots and cream.

Jalebis, circular orange tubes made of deep-fried treacle and dripping with syrup, are as sickly as they look. *Gulab jamuns*, deep-fried spongy dough balls soaked in syrup, are just as unhealthy. Another popular sweet is the round ladoo, essentially made from sugar, ghee and flour, though the ingredients may vary from region to region. Among Bengali sweets, widely considered to be the best are *rasgullas*, rosewater-flavoured cream-cheese balls

floating in syrup. *Ras malai*, found throughout north India, is similar, but soaked in cream instead of syrup. Down south, *payasam* – a rice or vermicelli pudding flavoured with cardamom, saffron and nuts – is a popular dessert, with special versions served during major festivals.

Chocolate is improving rapidly in India and you'll find various Cadbury's and Amul bars. None of the various indigenous brands of imitation Swiss and Belgian chocolates are worth eating.

Among the large **icecream** vendors, Kwality (now owned and branded as Wall's), Vadilal's, Gaylord and Dollops stand out. Uniformed men push carts of ice cream around and the bigger companies have many imitators, usually quite obvious. Some have no scruples – stay away from water ices unless you have a seasoned constitution. Icecream parlours selling elaborate concoctions including sundaes have really taken off; Connaught Circus in Delhi has several. Be sure to try **kulfi**, a pistachio- and cardamom-flavoured frozen sweet which is India's answer to ice cream; bhang kulfi (popular during the festival of Holi) is laced with cannabis and has an interesting kick to it, but should be approached with caution.

Fruit

What **fruit** is available varies with region and season, but there's always a fine choice. Ideally, you should peel all fruit, including apples, or soak them in strong iodine or potassium permanganate solution for half an hour. Roadside vendors sell fruit which they often cut up and serve sprinkled with salt and even masala – don't buy anything that looks like it's been hanging around for a while.

Mangoes of various kinds are usually on offer but not all are sweet enough to eat fresh – some are used for pickles or curries. Indians are very picky about their mangoes, which they feel and smell before buying; if you don't know the art of choosing the fruit, you could be sold the leftovers. Among the species appearing at different times in the season, which lasts from spring to summer, look out for Alphonso and Langra. Bananas of one sort or another are also on sale all year round, and oranges and tangerines are generally easy to come by, as are sweet melons and thirst-quenching watermelons.

Tropical fruits such as coconuts, papayas (pawpaws) and pineapples are more common in the south, while things such as lychees and pomegranates are very seasonal. In the north, temperate fruit from the mountains can be much like that in Europe and North America, with strawberries, apricots and even rather soft apples available in season.

Among less familiar fruit, the *chiku*, which looks like a kiwi and tastes a bit like a pear, is worth a mention, as is the watermelon-sized jackfruit, whose spiny green exterior encloses sweet, slightly rubbery yellow segments, each containing a seed. Individual segments are sold at roadside stalls.

Non-alcoholic drinks

India sometimes seems to run on **tea**, or chai, grown in Darjeeling, Assam and the Nilgiri Hills, and sold by chai-wallahs on just about every street corner. Tea is usually made by putting tea leaves, milk and water in a pan, boiling it all up, straining it into a cup or glass with lots of sugar and pouring back and forth from one cup to another to stir. Ginger and/or cardamom are often added. If you're quick off the mark, you can get them to hold the sugar. English tea it isn't, but most travellers get used to it. Sometimes, especially in tourist spots, you might get a pot of European-style "tray" tea, generally consisting of a tea bag in lukewarm water – you'd do better to stick to the pukka Indian variety, unless, that is, you are in a traditional tea-growing area.

Instant **coffee** is becoming increasingly common, and in some cases is more popular than tea, especially in the south. In the north, most coffee is instant, although increasing numbers of cafés and restaurants are now investing in proper coffee machines, especially in tourist centres. Café society has finally arrived in the major cities, and Delhi and Mumbai now have a fair share of trendy coffee shops serving real cappuccino and espresso. In the south, coffee is just as common as tea, and far better than it is in the north. One of the best places to get it is in

outlets of the *India Coffee House* chain, found in every southern town and occasionally in the north. A whole ritual is attached to the drinking of milky Keralan coffee in particular, poured in flamboyant sweeping motions between tall glasses to cool it down.

Soft drinks are ubiquitous. Coca-Cola and Pepsi returned to India in the early 1990s after being banned from the country for seventeen years and have now largely replaced their old Indian equivalents such as Campa Cola and Thums Up, although you'll still find the pleasantly lemony Limca (rumoured to have dubious connections to Italian companies, and to contain additives banned there). All contain a lot of sugar but little else: adverts for Indian soft drinks have been known to boast "Absolutely no natural ingredients!" None will quench your thirst for long.

More recommendable is **water**, either treated or boiled tap water (see box, p.47) or bottled water (though quality may be suspect). You'll also find cartons of Frooti, Jumpin, Réal and similar brands of **fruit juice** drinks, which come in mango, guava, apple and lemon varieties. If the carton looks at all mangled, it is best not to touch it as it may have been recycled. At larger stations, there will be a stall on the platform selling Himachali apple juice. Better still, green **coconuts**, common around coastal areas especially in the south, are cheaper than any of these and sold on the street by vendors who will hack off the top for you with a machete and give you a straw to suck up the coconut water (you then scoop out the flesh and eat it). You will also find street stalls selling freshly made sugar-cane juice: delicious, and not in fact too sweet, but not always as safe healthwise as you might like.

India's greatest cold drink, **lassi**, is made with beaten curd and drunk either sweetened with sugar, salted, or mixed with fruit. Varying widely from smooth and delicious to insipid and watery, it is sold at virtually every café, restaurant and canteen in the country. Freshly made milk shakes are also commonly available at establishments with blenders. They'll also sell you what they call a fruit juice, but which is usually fruit, water and sugar (or salt) liquidized and strained; also, street vendors selling fresh fruit juice in less than hygienic conditions are apt to add salt and garam masala. With all such drinks, however appetizing they may seem, you should exercise great caution in deciding where to drink them.

Alcohol

Prohibition, once widespread in India, is now only fully enforced in Gujarat and some of the northeastern hill states, although Tamil Nadu, Andhra Pradesh and some other states retain partial prohibition in the form of "dry" days, high taxes, restrictive licences, and health warnings on labels.

Alcoholic enclaves in prohibition states can become major drinking centres: Daman and Diu in Gujarat, and Puducherry and Karaikal in Tamil Nadu are the main ones. Goa, Sikkim and Mahé (Kerala) join them as places where the booze flows especially freely and cheaply. Interestingly, all were outside the British Raj. Liquor permits – free, and available from Indian embassies, high commissions and tourist offices abroad, from tourist offices in Delhi, Mumbai, Kolkata and Chennai, and even at airports on arrival – allow those travellers who bother to apply for one to evade certain restrictions in Gujarat.

Beer is widely available, if rather expensive by local standards. Price varies from state to state, but you can usually expect to pay around ₹80–150 for a 650ml bottle. A pub culture, not dissimilar to that of the West, has taken root amongst the wealthier classes in cities like Bengaluru and Mumbai and also in Delhi. Kingfisher, King's Black Label and Foster's are the leading brands, but there are plenty of others. All lagers, which tend to contain chemical additives including glycerine, are usually pretty palatable if you can get them cold. In certain places, notably unlicensed restaurants in Tamil Nadu and Kerala, beer comes in the form of "special tea" – a teapot of beer, which you pour into and drink from a teacup to disguise what it really is.

A cheaper, and often delicious, alternative to beer in Goa and Kerala and other southern states is **toddy** (palm wine). In Bengal it is made from the date palm, and is known as *taddy*. Sweet and non-alcoholic when first tapped, it ferments within twelve hours. In the Himalayas, the Bhotia people, of Tibetan stock, drink *chang*, a beer made from millet, and one of the nicest drinks of all – *tumba*, where fermented millet is placed in a bamboo flask and topped with hot water, then sipped through a bamboo pipe.

Spirits usually take the form of "Indian Made Foreign Liquor" (IMFL), although the recently legitimized foreign liquor industry is expanding rapidly. Some Scotch, such as Seagram's Hundred Pipers, is now being bottled in India and sold at a premium, as is Smirnoff vodka, among other known brands. Some of the brands of Indian whisky are not too bad and are affordable in comparison; gin and brandy can be pretty rough, while Indian rum is sweet and distinctive. In Goa, *feni* is a spirit distilled from coconut or cashew fruit. Steer well clear of illegally distilled *arak* (*araq*) however, which often contains methanol (wood alcohol) and other poisons. A look through the press, especially at festival times, will soon reveal numerous cases of blindness and death as a result of drinking bad hooch (or "spurious liquor" as it's called). Licensed country liquor, sold in several states under such names as *bangla*, is an acquired taste. Unfortunately, Indian **wine** – despite the efforts of a few pioneering vineyards such as Grovers (near Bengaluru) – is still generally of a poor quality, and also expensive, while foreign wine available in upmarket restaurants and luxury hotels comes with an exorbitant price-tag.

Health

There are plenty of scare stories about the health risks of travelling in India, but in fact cases of serious illness are very much the exception rather than the rule. Standards of hygiene and sanitation have increased greatly over the past couple of decades and there's no reason you can't stay healthy throughout your trip – indeed many travellers now visit the Subcontinent without even experiencing the traditional dose of "Delhi belly". Having said that, it's still important to be careful, keep your resistance high and to be aware of the dangers of untreated water, mosquito bites and undressed open cuts.

It's worth knowing, if you are ill and can't get to a doctor, that almost any medicine can be bought over the counter without a prescription.

Precautions

When it comes to **food**, be wary of dishes that appear to have been reheated. Anything boiled, fried or grilled (and thus sterilized) in your presence is usually all right, though seafood and meat can pose real risks if they're not fresh; anything that has been left out for any length of time, or stored in a fridge during a power cut, is best avoided. Raw unpeeled fruit and vegetables should always be viewed with suspicion, and you should steer clear of salads unless you know they have been washed in purified water.

Be vigilant about **personal hygiene**: wash your hands often, especially before eating. Keep all cuts clean, treat them with iodine or antiseptic (a liquid or dry spray is better in the heat) and cover them to prevent infection.

Advice on avoiding **mosquitoes** is offered under "Malaria" (see p.48). If you do get bites or itches, try not to scratch them: it's difficult, but infection and tropical ulcers can result if you do. Tiger balm and even dried soap may relieve the itching.

Finally, especially if you are going on a long trip, have a **dental check-up** before you leave home.

Vaccinations

No **inoculations** are legally required for entry into India, but diphtheria, typhoid and hepatitis A jabs are recommended for travellers to many parts of the country, and it's worth ensuring that you are up to date with tetanus, polio and other boosters. Vaccinations for hepatitis B, rabies, meningitis, Japanese encephalitis and TB are only advised if you're travelling to remote areas or working in environments with an increased exposure to infectious diseases.

Transmitted through contaminated food and water or through saliva, **hepatitis A** can lay a victim low for several months with exhaustion, fever and diarrhoea. Symptoms include yellowing of the whites of the eyes, general malaise, orange urine (though dehydration could also cause that) and light-coloured stools. If you think you have it, get a diagnosis as soon as possible, steer clear of alcohol, get lots of rest – and try to avoid passing it on. More serious is **hepatitis B**, transmitted like AIDS through blood or sexual contact.

Typhoid fever is also spread through contaminated food or water, but is rare in most parts of India. It produces a persistent high temperature with malaise, headaches and abdominal pains, followed by diarrhoea.

Cholera, spread the same way as hepatitis A and typhoid, causes sudden attacks of watery diarrhoea with cramps and debilitation. Again, this disease rarely occurs in India, breaking out in isolated epidemics; there is a vaccination but it offers very little protection. Most medical authorities now recommend immunization against meningococcal **meningitis (ACWY)** too. Spread by airborne bacteria (through coughs and sneezes for example), it is a very unpleasant disease that attacks the lining of the brain and can be fatal.

Rabies is widespread throughout the country, and the best advice is to give dogs and monkeys a wide berth – do not play with animals at all, no matter how cute they might look. If you're bitten or scratched and it breaks the skin, immediately wash the wound gently with soap or detergent, apply alcohol or iodine if possible, and go straight away, to the nearest hospital for an anti-rabies jab.

For up-to-the-minute information, make an appointment at a travel clinic. These clinics also sell travel accessories, including mosquito nets and first-aid kits.

MEDICAL RESOURCES FOR TRAVELLERS

International Society for Travel Medicine W istm.org. A full list of clinics worldwide specializing in travel health.

IN THE UK AND IRELAND
Hospital for Tropical Diseases Travel Clinic UK T 020 7387 4411, W thehtd.org.
MASTA (Medical Advisory Service for Travellers Abroad) UK T 0870 606 2782, W masta-travel-health.com. Forty clinics across the UK.
Tropical Medical Bureau Republic of Ireland T 1850 487674, W tmb.ie.

IN THE US AND CANADA
Canadian Society for International Health Canada W csih.org. Extensive list of travel health centres in Canada.

WHAT ABOUT THE WATER?
One of the chief concerns of many prospective visitors to India is whether the water is safe to drink. Tap water is best avoided, even though locals happily gulp it down, but many hotels and restaurants have modern filtration systems that remove most of the risks. **Bottled water**, available in all but the most remote places, is an even safer bet, though it has a major drawback – namely the **plastic pollution** it causes. Visualize the size of the pile you'd leave behind you after getting through a couple of bottles per day, imagine that multiplied by millions and you have something along the lines of the amount of non-biodegradable landfill waste generated each year by tourists alone.

The best solution as regards your health and the environment is to purify your own water. **Chemical sterilization** using **chlorine** is completely effective, fast and inexpensive, and you can remove the nasty taste it leaves with neutralizing tablets or lemon juice.

Alternatively, invest in some kind of **purifying filter** incorporating chemical sterilization to kill even the smallest viruses. An ever-increasing range of compact, lightweight products are available these days through outdoor shops and large pharmacies, but pregnant women or anyone with thyroid problems should check that iodine isn't used as the chemical sterilizer.

IN AUSTRALIA, NEW ZEALAND AND SOUTH AFRICA

Heat trouble

The sun and the heat can cause a few unexpected problems. Before they've acclimatized, many people get a bout of **prickly heat rash**, an infection of the sweat ducts caused by excessive perspiration that doesn't dry off. A cool shower, zinc oxide powder (sold in India) and loose cotton clothes should help. **Dehydration** is another possible problem, so make sure you're drinking enough liquid, and drink rehydration salts frequently, especially when hot and/or tired. The main danger sign is irregular urination (only once a day for instance); dark urine definitely means you should drink more (although it could also indicate hepatitis).

The **sun** can burn, or even cause sunstroke; a high-factor sun block is vital on exposed skin, especially when you first arrive. A light hat is also a very good idea, especially if you're doing a lot of walking around in the sun.

Finally, be aware that overheating can cause **heatstroke**, which is potentially fatal. Signs are a very high body temperature, without a feeling of fever but accompanied by headaches and disorientation. Lowering body temperature (taking a tepid shower for example) and resting in an air-conditioned room is the first step in treatment; also take in plenty of fluids and seek medical advice if the condition doesn't improve after 24 hours.

Malaria

Malaria is one of the Subcontinent's big killers and it's essential that you check with your doctor whether you'll need to take anti-malarial medication for your visit. The disease, caused by a parasite carried in the saliva of female Anopheles mosquitoes, can be found in many parts of India, and is especially prevalent in the northeast, although non-existent in the high Himalayan regions (there's a useful malaria map of the country at ⓦ fitfortravel .nhs.uk, showing varying levels of risk across the country). Malaria has a variable incubation period of a few days to several weeks, so you can become ill long after being bitten – which is why it's important to carry on taking the tablets even after you've returned home.

Ideas about appropriate **antimalarial medication** tend to vary from country to country and prophylaxis remains a controversial subject; it's important that you get expert medical advice on which treatment is right for you. In addition, resistance to established antimalarial drugs is growing alarmingly – none of the following provides complete protection, so avoiding being bitten in the first place remains important. Chloroquine- and proguanil-resistant strains of malaria are particularly prevalent in **Assam and the northeast**; travellers to this region might consider taking a course of malarone, doxycycline or mefloquine instead.

The most established regime – widely prescribed in Europe, but not in North America – is a combination of **chloroquine** (trade names Nivaquin or Avloclor) taken weekly either on its own or in conjunction with a daily dose of **proguanil** (Paludrine). You need to start this regime a week before arriving in a malarial area and continue it for four weeks after leaving. In India chloroquine is easy to come by but proguanil isn't, so stock up before you arrive. **Mefloquine** (Lariam) is a newer and stronger treatment. As a prophylactic, you need take just one tablet weekly, starting two weeks before entering a risk area and continuing for four weeks after leaving. Mefloquine is a very powerful and effective antimalarial, though there have been widely reported concerns about its side effects, including psychological problems.

Doxycycline is often prescribed in Australasia. One tablet is taken daily, starting a day or two before entering a malarial zone and continuing for four weeks after leaving. It's not suitable for children under ten and it can cause thrush in women, while three percent of users develop a sensitivity to light, causing a rash, so it's not ideal for beach holidays. It also interferes with the effectiveness of the contraceptive pill. **Malarone** (a combination of atovaquone and proguanil) is the most recent drug to come on the market. The bonus is that you only have to start taking it two days before you enter a malarial zone and continue for just a week after leaving, meaning that, although it's expensive, it can prove economical for short trips.

Malarial symptoms

The first signs of malaria are remarkably similar to a severe **flu**, and may take months to appear: if you suspect anything go to a hospital or clinic for a blood test immediately. The shivering, burning

A TRAVELLERS' FIRST-AID KIT

Below are items you might want to take, especially if you're planning to go trekking – all are available in India itself, at a fraction of what you might pay at home:

- Antiseptic cream
- Insect repellent and cream such as Anthisan for soothing bites
- Plasters/Band-Aids
- A course of Flagyl antibiotics
- Water sterilization tablets or water purifier
- Lint and sealed bandages
- Knee supports
- Imodium (Lomotil) for emergency diarrhoea treatment
- A mild oral anesthetic such as Bonjela for soothing ulcers or mild toothache
- Paracetamol/aspirin
- Multivitamin and mineral tablets
- Rehydration sachets
- Hypodermic needles and sterilized skin wipes

fever and headaches come in waves, usually in the early evening. Malaria is not infectious, but some strains are dangerous and occasionally even fatal when not treated promptly, in particular, the chloroquine-resistant cerebral malaria. This virulent and lethal strain of the disease, which affects the brain, is treatable, but has to be diagnosed early. Erratic body temperature, lack of energy and aches are the first key signs.

Preventing mosquito bites

The best way of combating malaria is, of course, to avoid getting bitten: malarial mosquitoes are active from dusk until dawn and during this time you should use mosquito **repellent** and take all necessary precautions. Sleep under a mosquito net if possible, burn mosquito coils (widely available in India, but easy to break in transit) or electrically heated repellents such as All Out. An Indian brand of repellent called Odomos is widely available and very effective, though most travellers bring their own from home, usually one containing the noxious but effective compound DEET. DEET can cause rashes and a strength of more than thirty percent is not advised for those with sensitive skin. A natural alternative is citronella or, in the UK, Mosi-guard Natural, made from a blend of eucalyptus oils; those with sensitive skin should still use DEET on clothes and nets. Mosquito "buzzers" – plug-in contraptions that smoulder tablets of DEET compounds slowly overnight – are pretty useless, but wrist and ankle bands are as effective as spray and a good alternative for sensitive skin. Though active all night, female Anopheles mosquitoes

prefer to bite in the evening, so be especially careful at that time. Wear long sleeves, skirts and trousers, avoid dark colours, which attract mosquitoes, and put repellent on all exposed skin.

Dengue fever and Japanese encephalitis

Another illness spread by mosquito bites is **dengue fever**, whose symptoms are similar to those of malaria, plus aching bones. There is no vaccine available and the only treatment is complete rest, with drugs to assuage the fever. Japanese encephalitis, a mosquito-borne viral infection causing fever, muscle pains and headaches, is most prevalent in wet, rural rice-growing areas. However, it only rarely affects travellers, and the vaccine isn't usually recommended unless you plan to spend much time around paddy fields during and immediately after the monsoons.

Intestinal troubles

Diarrhoea is the most common bane of travellers. When mild and not accompanied by other major symptoms, it may just be your stomach reacting to unfamiliar food. Accompanied by cramps and vomiting, it could well be food poisoning. In either case, it will probably pass of its own accord in 24–48 hours without treatment. In the meantime, it is essential to replace the fluids and salts you're losing, so take lots of water with oral rehydration salts (commonly referred to as ORS, or called Electrolyte in India). If you can't get ORS, use half a teaspoon of salt and eight of sugar in a litre of water, and if you are too ill to drink, seek medical help immediately. Travel clinics and pharmacies sell double-ended moulded plastic spoons with the exact ratio of sugar to salt.

While you are suffering, it's a good idea to avoid greasy food, heavy spices, caffeine and most fruit and dairy products. Some say bananas and pawpaws are good, as are *kitchri* (a simple dhal and rice preparation) and rice soup and coconut water, while curd or a soup made from Marmite or Vegemite (if you happen to have some with you) are forms of protein that can be easily absorbed by your body when you have the runs. **Drugs** like Lomotil or Imodium simply plug you up – undermining the body's efforts to rid itself of infection – though they can be useful if you have to travel. If symptoms persist for more than a few days, a course of antibiotics may be necessary; this should be seen as a last resort, following medical advice.

Sordid though it may seem, it's a good idea to look at what comes out when you go to the toilet. If your diarrhoea contains blood or mucus and if you are suffering other symptoms including rotten-egg belches and farts, the cause may be dysentery or giardia. With a fever, it could well be caused by **bacillic dysentery**, and may clear up without treatment. If you're sure you need it, a course of antibiotics such as tetracycline should sort you out, but they also destroy gut flora in your intestines (which help protect you – curd can replenish them to some extent). If you start a course, be sure to finish it, even after the symptoms have gone. Similar symptoms, without fever, indicate **amoebic dysentery**, which is much more serious, and can damage your gut if untreated. The usual cure is a course of Metronidazole (Flagyl) or Fasigyn, both antibiotics which may themselves make you feel ill, and must not be taken with alcohol. Symptoms of **giardia** are similar – including frothy stools, nausea and constant fatigue – for which the treatment is again Metronidazole. If you suspect that you have either of these, seek medical help, and only start on the Metronidazole (750mg three times daily for a week for adults) if there is definitely blood in your diarrhoea and it is impossible to see a doctor.

Finally, bear in mind that oral drugs, such as malaria pills and the Pill, are likely to be largely ineffective if taken while suffering from diarrhoea.

Bites and creepy crawlies

Worms may enter your body through skin (especially the soles of your feet) or food. An itchy anus is a common symptom, and you may even see them in your stools. They are easy to treat: if you suspect you have them, get some worming tablets such as Mebendazole (Vermox) from any pharmacy.

Biting insects and similar animals other than mosquitoes may also aggravate you. The obvious suspects are **bed bugs** – look for signs of squashed ones around beds in cheap hotels. An infested mattress can be left in the hot sun all day to get rid of them, but they often live in the frame or even in walls or floors. **Head** and **body lice** can also be a nuisance, but medicated soap and shampoo (preferably brought with you from home) usually see them off. Avoid **scratching bites**, which can lead to infection. Bites from ticks and lice can spread **typhus**, characterized by fever, muscle aches, headaches and, later, red eyes and a measles-like rash. If you think you have it, seek treatment (tetracycline is usually prescribed).

Snakes are unlikely to bite unless accidentally disturbed, and most are harmless in any case. To see one at all, you need to search stealthily – walk heavily and they usually oblige by disappearing. If you do get bitten, remember what the snake looked like (kill it if you can), try not to move the affected part, and seek medical help: antivenins are available in most hospitals. A few **spiders** have poisonous bites too. Remove **leeches**, which may attach themselves to you in jungle areas, with salt or a lit cigarette: never just pull them off.

Altitude sickness

At high altitudes, you may develop symptoms of **acute mountain sickness** (AMS). Just about everyone who ascends to around 4000m or higher experiences mild symptoms, but serious cases are rare. The simple cure – descent – almost always brings immediate recovery.

AMS is caused by the fact that at high elevations there is not only less oxygen, but also lower atmospheric pressure. This can have all sorts of weird effects on the body: it can cause the brain to swell and the lungs to fill with fluid, and even bring on uncontrollable farting. The syndrome varies from one person to the next but symptoms include breathlessness, headaches and dizziness, nausea, difficulty sleeping and appetite loss. More extreme cases may involve disorientation and loss of balance, and the coughing up of pink frothy phlegm.

AMS strikes without regard for fitness – in fact, young people seem to be more susceptible, possibly because they're more reluctant to admit they feel sick and they dart about more energetically. Most people are capable of acclimatizing to very high altitudes but the process takes time and must be done in stages. The golden rule is not to go too high, too fast; or if you do, spend the night at a lower height ("Climb High, Sleep Low"). Above 3000m, you should not ascend more than 500m per day; take mandatory acclimatization days at 3500m and 4000m – more if you feel unwell – and try to spend these days day-hiking to higher altitudes .

The general symptoms of AMS can be treated with the drug acetazolamide (Diamox) but this is not advised as it will block the early signs of severe AMS, which can be fatal. It is better to stay put for a day or two, eat a high-carbohydrate diet, drink plenty of water (three litres a day is recommended), take paracetamol or aspirin for the headaches, and descend if the AMS persists or worsens. If you fly direct to a high-altitude destination such as Leh, be especially careful to acclimatize (plan for three days of initial rest); you'll certainly want to avoid doing anything strenuous at first.

Other precautions to take at high altitudes include avoiding alcohol and sleeping pills, drinking more liquid, and protecting your skin against UV solar glare.

HIV and AIDS

HIV/AIDS is as much of a risk in India as anywhere else, despite the government's reluctance to admit it. As yet only NGOs and foreign agencies such as the WHO have embarked on awareness and prevention campaigns. As elsewhere in the world, high-risk groups include prostitutes and intravenous drug users. It is extremely unwise to contemplate casual sex without a condom – carry some with you (preferably brought from home as Indian ones may be less reliable) and insist upon using them.

Should you need an **injection** or a **transfusion** in India, make sure that new, sterile equipment is used; any blood you receive should be from voluntary rather than commercial donor banks. If you have a shave from a barber, make sure he uses a clean blade and don't undergo processes such as ear-piercing, acupuncture or tattooing unless you can be sure that the equipment is sterile.

Getting medical help

Pharmacies can usually advise on minor medical problems, and most doctors in India speak English. Also, many hotels keep a **doctor** on call; if you do get ill and need medical assistance, take advice as to the best facilities around. Basic medications are made to Indian Pharmacopoea (IP) standards, and most medicines are available without prescription, but always check the sell-by date. **Hospitals** have variable standards: private clinics and mission hospitals are often better than state-run ones but may not have the same facilities. Hospitals in big cities, including university or medical-school

---

AYURVEDIC MEDICINE

Ayurveda, a Sanskrit word meaning the "knowledge for prolonging life", is a five-thousand-year-old holistic medical system that is widely practised in India. Ayurvedic doctors and clinics in large towns deal with foreigners as well as their usual patients, and some **pharmacies** specialize in Ayurvedic preparations, including toiletries such as soaps, shampoos and toothpastes.

Ayurveda assumes the fundamental sameness of self and nature. Unlike the allopathic medicines of the West, which depend on finding out what's ailing you and then killing it, Ayurveda looks at the whole patient: disease is regarded as a symptom of **imbalance**, so it's the imbalance that's treated, not the disease. Ayurvedic theory holds that the body is controlled by three forces, which reflect the forces within the self: *pitta*, the force of the sun, is hot, and rules the digestive processes and metabolism; *kapha*, likened to the moon, the creator of tides and rhythms, has a cooling effect and governs the body's organs; and *vata*, wind, relates to movement and the nervous system. The healthy body is one that has the three forces in balance. To diagnose an imbalance, the Ayurvedic **vaid** (doctor) responds not only to the physical complaint but also to family background, daily habits and emotional traits.

Imbalances are typically treated with herbal remedies designed to alter whichever of the three forces is out of whack. Made according to traditional formulae, using indigenous plants, Ayurvedic medicines are cheaper than branded or imported drugs. In addition, the doctor may prescribe various forms of yogic cleansing to rid the body of waste substances. To the uninitiated, these techniques will sound rather off-putting – for instance, swallowing a long strip of cloth, a short section at a time, and then pulling it back up again to remove mucus from the stomach. Ayurvedic **massage** with herbal oils is especially popular in Kerala where courses of treatments are available to combat a wide array of ailments.

hospitals, are generally pretty good, and cities such as Delhi, Mumbai and Bengaluru boast state-of-the-art medical facilities but at a price. Many hospitals require patients (even emergency cases) to buy necessities such as medicines, plaster casts and vaccines, and to pay for X-rays, before procedures are carried out. Remember to keep receipts for insurance reimbursements.

However, **government hospitals** provide all surgical and after-care services free of charge and in most other state medical institutions charges are usually so low that for minor treatment the expense may well be lower than the initial "excess" on your insurance. You will, however, need a companion to stay, or you'll have to come to an arrangement with one of the hospital cleaners, to help you out in hospital – relatives are expected to wash, feed and generally take care of the patient. Beware of scams by private clinics in tourist towns such as Agra where there have been reports of overcharging and misdiagnosis by doctors to claim insurance money. Addresses of foreign consulates (who will advise in an emergency), as well as clinics and hospitals, can be found in the Directory sections in the accounts of major towns in this book.

The media

With well over a billion people and a literacy rate approaching seventy percent, India produces a staggering 4700 daily papers in more than three hundred languages, plus another 39,000 journals and weeklies. There are a large number of English-language daily newspapers, both national and regional.

The most prominent of the nationals are the *Times of India*, *The Hindu*, *The Deccan Chronicle*, *The Hindustan Times*, *The Telegraph*, *The Economic Times* and the *New Indian Express* (usually the most critical of the government). All are pretty dry and sober, concentrating on Indian news; *The Independent* and Kolkata's *Telegraph* tend to have better coverage of world news than the rest. *Asian Age*, published simultaneously in India, London and New York, is a conservative tabloid that sports a motley collection of the world's more colourful stories. All the major Indian newspapers have websites (see opposite), with the *Times of India*, *The Hindu* and the *Hindustan Times* providing the most up-to-date and detailed news services.

India's press is the freest in Asia and attacks on the government are often quite outspoken. However,

as in the West, most papers can be seen as part of the political establishment, and are unlikely to print anything that might upset the "national consensus".

There are also a number of *Time/Newsweek*-style **news magazines**, with a strong emphasis on politics. The best of these are *India Today* and *Frontline*, published by *The Hindu*. Others include *Outlook*, which presents the most readable, broadly themed analysis, *Sunday* and *The Week*. As they give more of an overview of stories and issues than the daily papers, you will probably get a better insight into Indian politics, and most tend to have a higher proportion of international news, too. *Business India* is more financially oriented and *The India Magazine* more cultural. Film **fanzines** and gossip mags are very popular (*Screen* and *Filmfare* are the best, though you'd have to be reasonably *au fait* with Indian movies to follow a lot of it), but magazines and periodicals in English cover all sorts of popular and minority interests, so it's worth having a look through what's available.

Foreign publications such as the *International Herald Tribune*, *Time* and *The Economist* are all available in the main cities, though it's easier (and cheaper) to read the day's edition for free online. For a read through the British press, try the British Council in Delhi, Mumbai, Kolkata and Chennai; the USIS is the American equivalent. Expat-oriented bookstalls, such as those in New Delhi's Khan Market, stock slightly out-of-date and expensive copies of magazines like *Vogue* and *NME*.

BBC World Service radio (@bbc.co.uk/world service) can be picked up at 94.3FM in most major cities, on short wave on frequencies ranging from 5790–15310kHz, and on medium wave (AM) at 1413KHz (212m) between about 8.30am and 10.30pm (Indian time). It also broadcasts online. The Voice of America (@voa.gov) can be found on 15.75MHz (19) and (75.75MHz (39.5m), among other frequencies. Radio Canada (@rcinet.ca) broadcasts in English on 6165 and 7255KHz (48.6 and 41.3m) at 6.30–7.30am and on 9635 and 11,975 KHz (31 and 25m) at 8.30–9.30pm.

The government-run **TV company**, Doordarshan, which broadcasts a sober diet of edifying programmes, has tried to compete with the onslaught of mass access to **satellite TV**. The main broadcaster in English is Rupert Murdoch's Star TV network, which incorporates the BBC World Service and Zee TV (with Z News), a progressive blend of Hindi-oriented chat, film, news and music programmes. Star Sports, ESPN and Ten Sports churn out a mind-boggling amount of cricket, extensive coverage of English Premier League football, plenty of tennis and a few other sports. Other channels include CNN, the Discovery Channel, the immensely popular Channel V, hosted by scantily clad Mumbai models and DJs, and a couple of American soap and chat stations. There are now numerous local-language channels as well.

NEWS AND MEDIA ONLINE

Ⓦ **guardian.co.uk/world/india** High-quality news features are the meat of this "Special Report" section of the *Guardian's* award-winning website, which also has links to its archived India articles and an excellent dossier on Kashmir. Access is free.

Ⓦ **indiatoday.digitaltoday.in** Homepage of India's best-selling news magazine.

Ⓦ **samachar.com** One of the best news gateway sites, featuring headlines and links to leading Indian newspapers.

Ⓦ **tehelka.com** Alternative news webzine, famous for exposing corruption scandals in government.

Ⓦ **timesofindia.indiatimes.com,** Ⓦ **thehindu.com,** Ⓦ **hindustantimes.com,** Ⓦ **deccanherald.com** Websites of some of India's leading daily papers, with detailed national coverage.

Festivals and holidays

Virtually every temple in every town or village across the country has its own festival. The biggest and most spectacular include Puri's Rath Yatra festival in June or July, the Hemis festival in Ladakh, also held in June or July, Pushkar's camel fair in November, Kullu's Dussehra, Madurai's three annual festivals and, of course, the Kumbh Mela, held at Allahabad, Haridwar, Nasik and Ujjain. While mostly religious in nature, merry-making rather than solemnity are generally the order of the day, and onlookers are usually welcome. Indeed, if you're lucky enough to coincide with a local festival, it may well prove to be the highlight of your trip.

There isn't space to list every festival in every village across India here, but local festivals are listed throughout the body of the Guide. The calendar below includes details of the main national and regional celebrations. Hindu, Sikh, Buddhist and Jain festivals follow the Indian **lunar calendar** and their dates therefore vary from year to year – we've given the lunar month (Magha, Phalguna, Chaitra, and so on), where relevant, in the listings below. The lunar calendar adds a leap month every two or

three years to keep it in line with the seasons. Muslim festivals follow the **Islamic calendar**, whose year is shorter and which thus loses about eleven days per annum against the Gregorian.

You may, while in India, be lucky enough to be invited to a **wedding**. These are jubilant affairs, always scheduled on auspicious days. A Hindu bride dresses in red for the ceremony, and marks the parting of her hair with red *sindur* and her forehead with a *bindi*. She wears gold or bone bangles, which she keeps on for the rest of her married life. Although the practice is officially illegal, large dowries often change hands. These are usually paid by the bride's family to the groom, and can be contentious; poor families feel obliged to save for years to get their daughters married.

PRINCIPAL INDIAN HOLIDAYS

India has only four **national public holidays** as such: Jan 26 (Republic Day); Aug 15 (Independence Day); Oct 2 (Gandhi's birthday); and Dec 25 (Christmas Day). Each state, however, has its own calendar of public holidays; you can expect most businesses to close on the major holidays of their own religion. The Hindu lunar calendar months are given in brackets below.

Key: B=Buddhist; C=Christian; H=Hindu; J=Jain; M=Muslim; N=non-religious; P=Parsi; S=Sikh.

Jan–Feb (Magha–Phalguna)

H Pongal (1 Magha): Tamil harvest festival celebrated with decorated cows, processions and *rangolis* (chalk designs on the doorsteps of houses). *Pongal* is a sweet porridge made from newly harvested rice and eaten by all, including the cows. The festival is also known as Makar Sankranti, and celebrated in Karnataka, Andhra Pradesh and the east of India.

H Ganga Sagar: Pilgrims come from all over the country to Sagar Dwip, on the mouth of the Hooghly 150km south of Kolkata, to bathe during Makar Sankranti.

H Vasant Panchami (5 Magha): One-day spring festival in honour of Saraswati, the goddess of learning, celebrated with kite-flying, the wearing of yellow saris and the blessing of schoolchildren's books and pens by the goddess.

N Republic Day (Jan 26): A military parade in Delhi typifies this state celebration of India's republic-hood, followed on Jan 29 by the "Beating the Retreat" ceremony outside the presidential palace in Delhi.

N Goa Carnival: Goa's own Mardi Gras features float processions and *feni*-induced mayhem in the state capital, Panjim.

N International Kite Festival at Aurangabad (Maharashtra).

H Teppa Floating Festival (16 Magha) at Madurai (Tamil Nadu). Meenakshi and Shiva are towed around the temple tank in boats lit with fairy lights – a prelude to the Tamil marriage season.

N Elephanta Music and Dance Festival (Mumbai).

Feb–March (Phalguna). Classical Indian dance performed with the famous rock-cut caves in Mumbai harbour as a backdrop.

B Losar (1 Phalguna): Tibetan New Year celebrations among Tibetan and Himalayan Buddhist communities, especially at Dharamsala (HP).

H Shivratri (10 Phalguna): Anniversary of Shiva's *tandav* (creation) dance, and his wedding anniversary. Popular family festival but also a sadhu festival of pilgrimage and fasting, especially at important Shiva temples.

H Holi (15 Phalguna): Water festival held during Dol Purnima (full moon) to celebrate the beginning of spring, most popular in the north. Expect to be bombarded with water, paint, coloured powder and other mixtures; they can permanently stain clothing, so don't go out in your Sunday best.

N Khajuraho Dance Festival: The country's finest dancers perform in front of Madhya Pradesh's famous erotic sculpture-carved shrines.

C Carnival (Mardi Gras): The last day before Lent, forty days before Easter, is celebrated in Goa, as in the rest of the Catholic world.

March–April (Chaitra)

H Gangaur (3 Chaitra): Rajasthani festival (also celebrated in Bengal and Odisha) in honour of Parvati, marked with singing and dancing.

H Ramanavami (9 Chaitra): Birthday of Rama, the hero of the Ramayana, celebrated with readings of the epic and discourses on Rama's life and teachings.

C Easter (movable feast): Celebration of the resurrection of Christ. Good Friday in particular is a day of festivity.

P Pateti: Parsi new year, also known as Nav Roz, celebrating the creation of fire. Feasting, services and present-giving.

P Khorvad Sal (a week after Pateti): Birthday of Zarathustra (aka Zoroaster). Celebrated in the Parsis' fire temples, and with feasting at home.

H Chittirai, Madurai (Tamil Nadu): Elephant-led procession.

April–May (Vaisakha)

HS Baisakhi (1 Vaisakha): To the Hindus, it's the solar new year, celebrated with music and dancing; to the Sikhs, it's the anniversary of the foundation of the Khalsa (Sikh brotherhood) by Guru Gobind Singh. Processions and feasting follow readings of the Granth Sahib scriptures.

J Mahavir Jayanti (13 Vaisakha): Birthday of Mahavira, the founder of Jainism. The main Jain festival of the year, observed by visits to sacred Jain sites, especially in Rajasthan and Gujarat, and with present-giving.

H Puram Thrissur (Kerala): Frenzied drumming and elephant parades.

B Buddha Jayanti (16 Vaisakha): Buddha's birthday. He achieved enlightenment and nirvana on the same date. Sarnath (UP) and Bodh Gaya (Bihar) are the main centres of celebration.

May–June (Jyaishtha)

H Ganga Dussehra (10 Jyaishtha): Bathing festival to celebrate the descent to earth of the goddess of the Ganges.

June–July (Ashadha)

H Rath Yatra (2 Ashadha): Festival held in Puri (and other places, especially in the south) to commemorate Krishna's (Lord Jagannath's) journey to Mathura.

H Teej (3 Ashadha): Festival in honour of Parvati to welcome the monsoon. Particularly celebrated in Rajasthan.

B Hemis Leh (Ladakh): Held sometime between late June and mid-July, this spectacular festival features *chaam* (lama dances) to signify the victory of Buddhism over evil.

July–Aug (Shravana)

H Naag Panchami (3 Shravana): Snake festival in honour of the *naga* snake deities. Mainly celebrated in Rajasthan and Maharashtra.

H Raksha Bandhan/Narial Purnima (16 Shravana): Festival to honour the sea god Varuna. Brothers and sisters exchange gifts, the sister tying a thread known as a *rakhi* to her brother's wrist. Brahmins, after a day's fasting, change the sacred thread they wear.

N Independence Day (Aug 15): India's biggest secular celebration, on the anniversary of Independence from Britain.

Aug–Sept (Bhadraparda)

H Ganesh Chaturthi (4 Bhadraparda): Festival dedicated to Ganesh, especially celebrated in Maharashtra. In Mumbai, huge processions carry images of the god to immerse in the sea.

H Onam: Keralan harvest festival, celebrated with snake-boat races. The Nehru Trophy snake-boat race at Alappuzha (held on the 2nd Sat of Aug) is the most spectacular, with long boats crewed by 150 rowers.

H Janmashtami (23 Bhadraparda): Krishna's birthday, an occasion for fasting and celebration, especially in Agra, Mumbai, Mathura (UP) and Vrindaban (UP).

H Avani Mula Madurai (Tamil Nadu): Celebration of the coronation of Shiva.

Sept–Oct (Ashvina)

H Dussehra (1–10 Ashvina): Ten-day festival (usually two days' public holiday) associated with vanquishing demons, in particular Rama's victory over Ravana in the Ramayana, and Durga's over the buffalo-headed Mahishasura (particularly in West Bengal, where it is called Durga Puja). Dussehra celebrations include performances of the Ram Lila (life of Rama). Best in Mysore (Karnataka), Ahmedabad (Gujarat) and Kullu (Himachal Pradesh). Durga Puja is best seen in Kolkata where it is an occasion for exchanging gifts, and every locality has its own competing street-side image.

N Mahatma Gandhi's Birthday (Oct 2): Solemn commemoration of independent India's founding father.

Oct–Nov (Kartika)

H Diwali (Deepavali) (15 Kartika): Festival of lights, and India's biggest, to celebrate Rama's and Sita's homecoming in the Ramayana. Festivities include the lighting of oil lamps and firecrackers, and the giving and receiving of sweets and gifts. Diwali coincides with Kali Puja, celebrated in temples dedicated to the wrathful goddess, especially in Bengal, and often accompanied by the ritual sacrifice of goats.

J Jain New Year (15 Kartika): Coincides with Diwali, so Jains celebrate alongside Hindus.

S Nanak Jayanti (16 Kartika): Guru Nanak's birthday marked by prayer readings and processions, especially in Amritsar and in the rest of the Punjab, and at Patna (Bihar).

Nov–Dec (Margashirsha or Agrahayana)

H Sonepur Mela: World's largest cattle fair at Sonepur (Bihar).
N Pushkar Camel Fair. Camel herders don their finest attire for this massive livestock market on the fringes of the Thar Desert in Rajasthan.
N Hampi Festival (Karnataka): Government-sponsored music and dance festival.

Dec–Jan (Pausa)

CN Christmas (Dec 25): Popular in Christian areas of Goa and Kerala, and in big cities.
N Posh Mela (Dec 27): Held in Shantiniketan near Kolkata (Calcutta), a festival renowned for *baul* music.

Moveable

H Kumbh Mela: Major three-yearly festival held at one of four holy cities: Nasik (Maharashtra), Ujjain (MP), Haridwar (UP) or Prayag (Maharashtra) as well as at Allahabad (UP). The Maha Kumbh Mela or "Great" Kumbh Mela, the largest religious fair in India, is held every twelve years in Allahabad (UP); the next festival is due to take place in 2016 (April 22 to May 21) in Ujjain.
M Ramadan: The month during which Muslims may not eat, drink or smoke from sunrise to sunset, and should abstain from sex. Future estimated dates are: June 28–July 27, 2014, June 17 to July 16, 2015 and June 6 to July 5, 2016.
M Id ul-Fitr: Feast to celebrate the end of Ramadan. The precise date of the festival depends on exactly when the new moon is sighted, and so cannot be predicted with complete accuracy. Estimated dates (though these may vary by a day or two) are: July 28, 2014, July 17, 2015 and July 6, 2016.

Sports

India is not perhaps a place that most people associate with sports, but cricket, hockey and football (soccer) all have their place.

Cricket is by far the most popular of these, and a fine example of how something quintessentially British (well, English) has become something quintessentially Indian. Travellers to India will find it hard to get away from the game – it's everywhere, especially on television. Cricketing heroes such as the legendary batting maestro Sachin Tendulkar and superstar Indian captain Mahendra Dhoni live under the constant scrutiny of the media and public; expectations are high and disappointments acute. India versus Pakistan matches are especially emotive – the entire country received a fillip when India beat

their arch-rivals in the final of the inaugural Twenty20 World Cup in 2007 by a nail-biting five runs. Besides spectator cricket, you'll see games being played on open spaces all around the country.

Test matches are rare, but inter-state cricket is easy to catch – the most prestigious competition is the Ranji Trophy. Occasionally, in cities like Kolkata, you may even come across a match blocking a road, and will have to be patient as the players begrudgingly let your vehicle continue.

Horseracing can be a good day out, especially if you enjoy a flutter. The racecourse at Kolkata is the most popular, often attracting crowds of more than fifty thousand, especially on New Year's Day. There are several other racecourses around the country, mostly in larger cities such as Mumbai, Delhi, Pune, Hyderabad, Mysore, Bengaluru and Ooty. Other (mainly) spectator sports include **polo**, originally from upper Kashmir, but taken up by the British to become one of the symbols of the Raj. Certain Rajasthani princes, such as the late Hanut Singh of Jodhpur, were considered to be the best polo players in the world between the 1930s and 1950s, but since the 1960s, when the privy purses were abolished, they have been unable to maintain their stables, and the tradition of polo has declined. Today, it's mainly the army who plays the game; the best place to catch a match is at the Delhi Gymkhana during the winter season. Polo, in more or less its original form, is still played on tiny mountain ponies in Ladakh; a good place to see a game played in traditional style is in Leh during the Ladakh Festival in early September.

After years in the doldrums, **Indian hockey**, which used to regularly furnish the country with Olympic medals, is making a strong comeback. The haul of medals dried up in the 1960s when international hockey introduced astro-turf – which was, and still is, a rare surface in India. However, hockey remains very popular, especially in schools and colleges and, interestingly, amongst the tribal girls of Odisha, who supply the Indian national team with a regular clutch of players.

Football (soccer) is similarly popular with a keenly contested national championship. The best teams are based in Kolkata and include three legendary clubs – Mohan Bagan, East Bengal and Mohamadan Sporting – who all command fanatical support. Unlike most of the league, these teams employ professional players and even include some minor internationals, mostly from Africa. International soccer tournaments are becoming increasingly common.

Tennis in India has always been a sport for the middle and upper classes. The country has produced a number of world-class players, such as the men's duo of Mahesh Bhupati and Leander Paes, who briefly achieved a world number-one ranking in the men's doubles in 1999, while the glamorous young Sania Mirza, the first ever Indian to break into the WTA's Top 50 ranked players, rivals the nation's cricketers in popularity.

Volleyball is very popular throughout India, especially in the resorts of Goa. Standards aren't particularly high and joining a game is quite easy. Since the arrival on the Formula 1 scene of Kingfisher tycoon Vijay Malia's Force India team, **motor racing** has also grown in popularity and since 2011 the country has hosted a Grand Prix at the spanking new track at Noida outside Delhi. Golf is widely followed, too, again among the middle classes; the second oldest golf course in the world is in Kolkata, and one of the highest in the world is at Shimla.

One indigenous sport you're likely to see in north India is **kabadi**, played on a small (badminton-sized) court, and informally on any suitable open area. The game, with seven players in each team, consists of a player from each team alternately attempting to "tag" as many members of the opposing team as possible in the space of a single breath (cheating is impossible; the player has to maintain a continuous chant of "kabadikabadikabadikabadi" etc), and getting back to his/her own side of the court without being caught. The game can get quite rough, with slaps and kicks in tagging allowed, and the defending team must try to tackle and pin the attacker so as not to allow him or her to even touch the dividing line. Tagged victims are required to leave the court. Although still an amateur sport, kabadi is taken very seriously with state and national championships, and now features in the Asian Games.

Popular with devotees of the monkey god, Hanuman, **Indian wrestling**, or *kushti*, has a small but dedicated following. Wrestlers are known as *pahalwaans* or "strong men" and can be seen exercising early in the morning with clubs and weights along river *ghats* such as those in Varanasi or Kolkata.

Trekking and outdoor activities

India offers plenty of opportunities for adventure sports, including trekking, mountaineering, whitewater rafting, caving and diving – just make sure you've got comprehensive insurance (see p.67) before getting stuck in.

Trekking

Though **trekking** in India is not nearly as commercialized as in neighbouring Nepal, the country can claim some of the world's most spectacular routes, especially in the Ladakh and Zanskar Himalayas, where the mountain passes frequently top 5000m. Himalayan routes are not all extreme, with relatively gentle short trails exploring the Singalila Range around Darjeeling, low-level forest walks through the rhododendron-clad hillsides of Sikkim and the well-beaten pilgrim trails of Garhwal. Trekking is also becoming more popular in the Western Ghats and Nilgiris of the south.

Hiring a **guide-cum-cook** is recommended whenever possible, especially on more difficult and less frequented routes, where the consequences of getting lost or running out of supplies could be serious. Porters (with or without ponies) can also make your trip a lot less arduous, and on longer routes where a week or more's worth of provisions have to be carried, they may be essential. You'll usually be approached in towns and villages leading to the trailhead by men touting for work. Finding out what the going day rate is can be difficult, and you should expect to have to haggle.

If the prospect of organizing a trek yourself seems too daunting, consider employing a **trekking company** to do it for you. Agencies at places like Manali, Leh, Darjeeling and Gangtok are detailed in the Guide, while specialist tour operators also offer trips based around trekking (see p.30).

Himachal Pradesh is the easiest state in which to plan a trek. Uttarkhand sees fewer trekkers, and there are plenty of opportunities to wander off the beaten track and either escape the hordes of pilgrims or, alternatively, to join them on their way to the sacred sites of Badrinath, Gangotri, Joshimath and Kedarnath. There are also exciting and exotic high-mountain trekking opportunities in the ancient Buddhist kingdoms of Ladakh and Zanskar, where trails can vary in length from relatively short four-day excursions to epics of ten days or more. At the eastern end of the Himalayas, Darjeeling makes a good base from which to explore the surrounding mountains. Neighbouring Sikkim has the greatest variations in altitude, from steamy river valleys to the third highest massif in the world. Shorter and less strenuous treks are available in the Ghats and the Nilgiri hills of southern India, with Munnar and Wayanad in Kerala, the Kodagu region of Karnataka and Ooty in Tamil Nadu proving the main springboards.

Having the right **equipment** for a trek is important, but hi-tech gear isn't essential – bring what you need to be comfortable but keep weight to a minimum. You can rent equipment in places such as Leh and Darjeeling, but otherwise, you'll have to buy what you need or bring it with you. Make sure everything (zips, for example) is in working order before you set off. Clothes should be lightweight and versatile, especially considering the range of temperatures you might encounter: dress in layers for maximum flexibility.

Mountaineering

Mountaineering is a more serious venture, requiring planning and organization; if you've never climbed, don't start in the Himalayas. Mountaineering institutes at Darjeeling, Uttarkashi and Dharamsala run training courses. The one at Uttarkashi in Uttarakhand (W nimindia.net) is popular with foreigners: you can learn rock- and ice-climbing skills and expedition techniques for a fraction of what you'd pay in the West, but the 28-day basic mountaineering course run by Siachen Glacier veterans of the Indian army is extremely gruelling. Permission for mountaineering expeditions should be sought at least six months in advance from the Indian Mountaineering Federation, Anand Niketan, Benito Juarez Road, New Delhi 110021 (T 011 2411 1211, W indmount.org). Peak fees range from US$1500 to US$4000, according to

height, and expeditions must be accompanied by an IMF liaison officer equipped to the same standard as the rest of the party. The IMF can also supply lists of local mountaineering clubs; climbing with such clubs enables you to get to know local climbers, and obtain permits for otherwise restricted peaks.

Skiing

Despite the mammoth spread of the Himalayas, **skiing** in India remains relatively undeveloped. The only options for organized skiing are the western Himalayas, in particular Uttarakhand, Himachal Pradesh and Kashmir; the eastern Himalayas have unreliable snowfall at skiing altitudes.

The ski area at **Auli** (see p.316), near Joshimath in Uttarakhand, has had money poured into it but suffers from a short season, limited (though cheap) skiing and non-existent après-ski activity. In **Himachal Pradesh**, the skiing in the vicinity of Shimla is far too underdeveloped to warrant a detour, but the possibilities around Manali are more enticing because of the prospect of virgin powder: two or three surface tows operate in the Solang Nala for three months every winter. By far the most promising prospect at present, however, is **Gulmarg** (see p.474) in Kashmir. On a plateau at 2600m, the former British hill station boasts the highest ski lift in the world – and some of the most dependably fine powder snow to be had anywhere. Skiers are dropped at nearly 4000m by a French-built gondola, from where the off-piste possibilities are truly world class. A New Zealand company is threatening to start heli-skiing in this area, but for the time being Gulmarg offers a refreshingly wild experience that's a world away from the lift queues and crowded après-ski bars of the Alps. Guided trips are organized by British, IMFGA-qualified team, Mountain Tracks (W ski-gulmarg.co.uk).

Whitewater rafting

Though not as well known as some of the mighty rivers of Nepal, the **rivers** Chenab and Beas in Himachal Pradesh, the Rangit and Teesta in Sikkim, the Zanskar and Indus in Ladakh, and the Ganges in Uttarakhand all combine exciting waters with magnificent scenery. Kullu, Manali, Leh, Gangtok and Rishikesh are among the main rafting centres. Prices start at around ₹800 per day including food, but it's worth sounding out a few agents to find the best deals. For more details see the relevant accounts in the Guide.

Caving

Meghalaya has the best **caving** potential of all the Indian states. The three main areas are the East Khasi hills, the South Garo hills and the Jainta hills (home to the 21.4km-long Krem Kotsati–Umlawan cave, the longest system in mainland Asia). **Potholing** contacts can be found in the Meghalaya account (see p.851).

Diving and snorkelling

Because of the number of rivers draining into the sea around the Subcontinent, India's **coastal waters** are generally silt-laden and too murky for decent diving or snorkelling. However, in many areas abundant hard coral and colourful fish make up for the relatively poor visibility. India also counts two beautiful tropical-island archipelagos in its territory, both surrounded by exceptionally clear seas. Served by well-equipped and reputable diving centres, the Andaman Islands and Lakshadweep offer world-class diving on a par with just about anything in Asia. Don't come here expecting rock-bottom prices though. Compared to Thailand, India's dive schools are pricey, typically charging around US$60–70 for a one-tank outing, to US$400–450 for an open-water course.

For independent travellers, the most promising destination for both scuba diving and snorkelling is the **Andaman Islands** in the Bay of Bengal, around 1000km east of the mainland. Part of a chain of submerged mountains that stretch north from Sumatra to the coast of Myanmar (Burma), this isolated archipelago is ringed by gigantic coral reefs whose crystal-clear waters are teeming with tropical fish and other marine life. Given the high cost of diving courses, most visitors stick to snorkelling, but if you already have your PADI permit, you might want to do a couple of dives on Havelock island or around Cinque Island or the Mahatma Gandhi Marine Reserve, accessed from Port Blair. If you want to do an open-water course, book ahead as places tend to be in short supply especially during the peak season, between December and February.

Lakshadweep is a classic coconut palm-covered atoll, some 400km west of Kerala in the Arabian Sea. The shallow lagoons, extensive coral reefs and exceptionally good visibility make this a perfect option for both first-timers and more experienced divers – though the one and only hotel is an extremely pricey five-star.

PADI-approved dive schools also work out of a handful of resorts in Goa, including Palolem (see p.721). Although the waters off the Goan coast have poor visibility, these schools take clients further south to an island off the shores of neighbouring Karnataka where conditions are much better.

As with other countries, qualified divers should take their current certification card and/or logbook; if you haven't used it for one year or more, it is unlikely you will be asked to take the supposedly mandatory refresher test.

Camel trekking

The way to experience the desert in style is from the top of a camel. The one-humped Arabian camel, or dromedary, common in desert regions of Rajasthan, is well adapted to the terrain, with long double eyelashes to keep sand out of its eyes, nostrils that it can close, and broad, soft, padded feet that are ideal for walking on sand. Riding on a camel is smoother than riding on a horse because the camel moves its left and then right legs together, rather than front and then back legs, giving it a more rolling gait. They are usually docile, good-tempered animals, but the male goes into rut in spring, when it becomes rather grumpy and can kick and bite, and spit its regurgitated stomach contents in anger.

Camel treks can be arranged at Jaisalmer (see p.185) and Bikaner (see p.200). Some treks stick to the beaten track, and take you to the popular tourist sights. Others specialize in heading off deep into the desert for a feeling of isolation and remoteness. Typically, camel treks include two days in the saddle and a night spent camping in the desert, but you can opt for longer or shorter trips.

Yoga, meditation and ashrams

The birthplace of yoga and the spiritual home of the world's most famous meditation traditions, India offers unrivalled opportunities for spiritual nourishment, ranging from basic yoga and pranayama classes to extended residential meditation retreats.

Yoga is taught virtually everywhere in India and there are several internationally known centres where you can train to become a teacher. **Meditation** is similarly practised all over the country and specific courses are available in temples, meditation centres, monasteries and ashrams. **Ashrams** are communities where people work, live and study together, drawn by a common, usually spiritual, goal.

Details of yoga and meditation courses and ashrams are provided throughout the Guide. Most centres offer courses that you can enrol on at short notice, but many of the more popular ones (see p.60) need to be booked well in advance.

Yoga

Yoga (Sanskrit for "to unite" and root of the word "yoke") aims to help the practitioner unite his or her individual consciousness with the divine. This is achieved by raising awareness of one's self through spiritual, mental and physical exercises and discipline. **Hatha yoga**, the most popular form of yoga in the West, is based on physical postures called *asanas*, which stretch, relax and tone the muscular system of the body and also massage the internal organs. Each *asana* has a beneficial effect on a particular muscle group or organ, and although they vary widely in difficulty, consistent practice will lead to improved suppleness and health benefits. For serious practitioners, however, Hatha yoga is seen simply as the first step leading to more subtle stages of meditation which commence when the energies of the body have been awakened and sensitized by stretching and relaxing. Other forms of yoga include *raja* yoga, which includes moral discipline, and *bhakti* yoga, the yoga of devotion, which entails a commitment to one's guru or teacher. *Jnana* yoga (the yoga of knowledge) is centred around the deep philosophies that underlie Hindu spiritual thinking.

Rishikesh, in Uttarakhand, is India's yoga capital, with a bumper crop of ashrams offering all kinds of courses (see p.308). The country's most famous teachers, however, work from institutes further south. **Iyengar** yoga is one of the most famous approaches studied today, named after its founder, B.K.S. Iyengar (a student of the great yoga teacher Sri Tirumalai Krishnamacharya), with its main centre, the Ramamani Iyengar Memorial Yoga Institute, in Pune, Maharashtra (🅦bksiyengar.com). Iyengar's style is based upon precise physical alignment during each posture. With much practise, and the aid of props such as blocks, straps and chairs, the student can attain perfect physical balance and, the theory goes, perfect balance of mind will follow. Iyengar yoga has a strong therapeutic element and has been used successfully for treating a wide variety of structural and internal problems.

Ashtanga yoga is an approach developed by K Pattabhi Jois of Mysore (🅦kpjayi.org), who also studied under Krishnamacharya. Unlike Iyengar yoga, which centres around a collection of separate *asanas*, Ashtanga links various postures into a series of flowing moves called *vinyasa*, with the aim of developing strength and agility. The perfect synchronization of movement with breath is a key objective throughout these sequences. Although a powerful form, it can be frustrating for beginners as each move has to be perfected before moving on to the next one.

The son of Krishnamacharya, T.K.V. Desikachar, established a third major branch in modern yoga, emphasizing a more versatile and adaptive approach to teaching, focused on the situation of the individual practitioner. This style became known as Viniyoga, although Desikachar has long tried to distance himself from the term. In the mid-1970s, he co-founded the Krishnamacharya Yoga Mandiram (🅦kym.org), now a flagship institute in Chennai, in neighbouring Tamil Nadu and, in 2006, an offshoot now steered by his son Kausthub, called the Krishnamacharya Healing and Yoga Foundation (🅦khyf.net).

The other most influential Indian yoga teacher of the modern era has been Swami Vishnu Devananda, an acolyte of the famous sage Swami Sivanda, who established the International Sivananda Yoga Vedanta Center (🅦sivananda.org), with more than twenty branches in India and abroad. **Sivananda**-style yoga tends to introduce elements in a different order from its counterparts – teaching practices regarded by others as advanced to relative beginners. This fast-forward approach has proved particularly popular with Westerners, who flock in their thousands to intensive introductory courses staged at centres all over India – the most renowned of them at Neyyar Dam, in the hills east of the Keralan capital, Thiruvananthapuram.

Meditation

Meditation is often practised after a session of yoga, when the energy of the body has been awakened, and is an essential part of both Hindu and Buddhist practice. In both religions, meditation is considered the most powerful tool for understanding the true nature of mind and self, an essential step on the path to **enlightenment**. In Vedanta, meditation's aim is to realize the true self as non-dual Brahman or godhead – the foundation of all consciousness and life. *Moksha* (or liberation – the nirvana of the Buddhists), achieved through disciplines of yoga and meditation, eventually helps believers release the soul from endless cycles of birth and rebirth.

Vipassana meditation is a technique, originally taught by the Buddha, whereby practitioners learn to become more aware of physical sensations and mental processes. Courses last for a minimum of ten days and are austere – involving 4am starts, around ten hours of meditation a day, no solid food after noon, segregation of the sexes, and no talking for the duration (except with the leaders of the course). Courses are free for all first-time students, to allow everyone an opportunity to learn and benefit from the technique. Vipassana is taught in more than 25 centres throughout India including in Bodhgaya, Bengaluru, Chennai, Hyderabad and Jaipur.

Tibetan Buddhist meditation is attracting more and more followers around the world. With its four distinct schools, Tibetan Buddhism incorporates a huge variety of meditation practices, including Vipassana, known as *shiné* in Tibetan, and various visualization techniques involving the numerous deities that make up the complex and colourful Tibetan pantheon. India, with its large Tibetan diaspora, has become a major centre for people wanting to study Tibetan Buddhism and medicine. Dharamsala in Himachal Pradesh, home to the Dalai Lama and Tibetan government-in-exile, is the main centre for Tibetan studies, offering numerous opportunities for one-on-one study with the Tibetan monks and nuns who live there. Other major Tibetan diaspora centres in India include Darjeeling in West Bengal and Bylakuppe near Mysore in Karnataka. For further details of courses available locally, see the relevant Guide chapters.

Ashrams and centres

Ashrams can range in size from just a handful of people to several thousand, and their rules, regulations and restrictions vary enormously. Some offer on-site accommodation, others will require you to stay in the nearest town or village. Some charge Western prices, others local prices, and some operate on a donation basis. Many ashrams have set programmes each day, while others are less structured, teaching as and when requested. In addition to these traditional Indian places to learn yoga and meditation techniques, dozens of smaller centres open in the coastal resorts of Goa and Kerala during the winter, several of them staffed by internationally famous teachers. The more prominent of these are listed below.

COURSES AND ASHRAMS

Ashiyana Tropical Retreat Centre Junasa Waddo, Mandrem, Goa
W ashiyana-yoga-goa.com. If you like your yoga retreats to be

drop-dead gorgeous, look no further than here. Perched on the banks of a river facing the sea, the centre offers world-class yoga, massage, meditation and *satsang* tuition – from resident and visiting teachers – with accommodation in beautifully designed Indonesian-style treehouses. Daily and weekly rates include workshops.

Astanga Yoga Nilayam 235 8th Cross, 3rd stage, Gokulam, Mysore 570002, Karnataka ☎ 98801 85500, W kpjayi.org. Run by students of Pattabhi Jois, one of the great innovators of yoga in India, and offering tuition in dynamic yoga, affiliated with martial arts. Courses last between one and six months and need to be booked in advance.

Brahmani Centre Tito's White House, Anjuna, Goa ☎ 95456 20578, W brahmaniyoga.com. Offers drop-in yoga classes – mainly Ashtanga, with a few taster sessions in other styles, plus Pranayama and *bhajan* devotional singing – by top-notch teachers. All levels of ability are catered for.

Divine Life Society PO Shivanandanagar, Muni ki Reti, Rishikesh, District Tehri Garhwal, Uttarakhand ☎ 0135 430040, W sivanandadlshq.org. The original Sivananda ashram – well organized if institutional, with several retreats and courses on all aspects and forms of yoga.

Harmonic Healing & Eco Retreat Centre Patnem, Goa ☎ 80071 98029, W harmonicingoa.com. Yoga, pilates, reiki initiations, energy balancing and Thai massages from internationally acclaimed teachers, along with lessons in Bollywood dance and classical Indian singing, all with one of the loveliest beach panoramas in Goa.

International Society for Krishna Consciousness (ISKCON) 3c Albert Rd, Kolkata ☎ 033 247 3757; Bhaktivedanta Swami Marg, Raman Reti, Vrindavan ☎ 0565 442478, W iskcon.com. Large and well-run international organization with major ashrams and temples in Mayapur, north of Kolkata in West Bengal, Vrindavan in west UP and centres in numerous other locations, both in India and abroad. Promotes *bhakti* yoga (the yoga of devotion) through good deeds, right living and chanting – a way of life rather than a short course.

Mata Amritanandamayi Math Amritapuri, Vallikkavu, Kerala ☎ 0476 289 7578, W amritapuri.org. The ashram of the famous "Hugging Saint", Amma, visited annually by hundreds of thousands, who pass through for *darshan* and a hug from the smiley guru, whose charitable works have earned her near-divine status in the south.

Osho Commune International 17 Koregaon Park, Pune, Maharashtra 411001 ☎ 020 6601 9999, W osho.com. Established by the enigmatic Osho, who generated a huge following of both Western and Indian devotees, this "Meditation Resort" (see p.662) is set in 31 acres of beautifully landscaped gardens and offers a variety of courses in personal therapy, healing and meditation.

Prasanthi Nilayam Puttaparthi, Andhra Pradesh ☎ 08555 87236, W sathyasai.org. The ashram of Satya Sai Baba, one of India's most revered and popular gurus who died in 2011. There is still a worldwide following of millions, despite the deaths of four followers in mysterious circumstances in 2000, with international btranches. The ashram is four or five hours by bus from Bangalore. Visitors sometimes comment on the strict security staffing and rigid rules and regulations. Cheap accommodation is available in dormitories or "flats" for four people. There is no need to book in advance, though you should phone to check availability (see p.923).

Purple Valley Centre Assagao, Goa ☎ 08 32 226 8364, ⓦ yogagoa.com. Purple Valley has accommodation for up to forty guests and what must be one of the most beautiful yoga *shalas* (practice areas) in India. Their teachers include Nancy Gilgoff and Sharath Rangaswamy, grandson of the illustrious Ashtanga Guru, Shri K. Pattabhi Jois.

Root Institute for Wisdom Culture Bodhgaya, Bihar ☎ 0631 220 0714, ⓦ rootinstitute.com. Regular seven- to ten-day courses on Tibetan Buddhism and meditation are held here from Oct to March, and there are facilities for individual retreats. Accommodation for longer stays should be booked well in advance (see p.799).

Saccidananda Ashram Thanneepalli, Kullithalai, near Tiruchirapelli, Tamil Nadu ☎ 04323 22260, ⓦ bedegriffiths.com. Also known as Shantivanam (meaning Peace Forest in Sanskrit), it is situated on the banks of the sacred River Cauvery. Founded by Father Bede Griffiths, a visionary Benedictine monk, it presents a curious but sympathetic fusion of Christianity and Hinduism. Visitors can join in the services and rituals or just relax here. Accommodation is in simple huts dotted around the grounds and meals are communal. Very busy during the major Christian festivals.

Sivananda Yoga Vedanta Dhanwantari Ashram Thiruvananthapuram, Kerala ☎ 0471 227 3093, ⓦ sivananda.org. An offshoot of the original Divine Life Society, this yoga-based ashram focuses on *asanas*, breathing techniques (*pranayama*) and meditation. They also run month-long yoga teacher-training programmes, but book well in advance. There are branches in Madurai, Chennai, Delhi, Uttarkashi and worldwide – see the website for details.

Tushita Meditation Centre McLeod Ganj, Dharamsala 176219, Himachal Pradesh ☎ 01892 221866, ⓦ tushita.info. Offers a range of Tibetan meditation courses. A ten-day course costs in the region of ₹4000; book well in advance.

Vipassana International Academy Runs a wide variety of 3- to 45-day courses in Vipassana meditation at eighteen centres across India and more worldwide. See ⓦ dhamma.org for details.

Culture and etiquette

Cultural differences extend to all sorts of little things. While allowances will usually be made for foreigners, visitors unacquainted with Indian customs may need a little preparation to avoid causing offence or making fools of themselves. The list of do's and don'ts here is hardly exhaustive: when in doubt, watch what the Indian people around you are doing.

Eating and the right-hand rule

The biggest minefield of potential faux pas has to do with **eating**. This is usually done with the fingers, and requires practice to get absolutely right. Rule one is: **eat with your right hand only**. In India, as right across Asia, the left hand is for wiping your bottom, cleaning your feet and other unsavoury functions (you also put on and take off your shoes with your left hand), while the right hand is for eating, shaking hands and so on.

Quite how rigid individuals are about this tends to vary, with brahmins (who, at the top of the hierarchical ladder, are one of the two "right-handed castes") and southerners likely to be the strictest. While you can hold a cup or utensil in your left hand, and you can get away with using it to help tear your chapatti, you should not eat, pass food or wipe your mouth with your left hand.

This rule extends beyond food. In general, do not pass anything to anyone with your left hand, or point at anyone with it either; and Indians won't be impressed if you put it in your mouth. In general, you should accept things given to you with your right hand – though using both hands is a sign of respect.

The other rule to beware of when eating or drinking is that your lips should not touch other people's food – *jhutha*, or sullied food, is strictly taboo. Don't, for example, take a bite out of a chapatti and pass it on. When drinking out of a cup or bottle to be shared with others, don't let it touch your lips, but rather pour it directly into your mouth. This custom also protects you from things like hepatitis. It is customary to wash your hands before and after eating.

Temples and religion

Religion is taken very seriously in India; it's important always to show due respect to religious buildings, shrines, images, and people at prayer. When entering a **temple or mosque**, remove your shoes and leave them at the door (socks are acceptable and protect your feet from burning-hot stone ground). Some temples – Jain ones in particular – do not allow you to enter wearing or carrying leather articles, and forbid entry to menstruating women. In the southern state of Kerala, most Hindu temples are closed to non-Hindus, but those that aren't require men to remove their shirts before entering (women must wear long dresses or skirts).

In a mosque, non-Muslims would not normally be allowed in at prayer time and women are sometimes not let in at all. In a Hindu temple, you are not often allowed into the inner sanctum; and at a Buddhist *stupa* or monument, you should always walk round clockwise (ie, with the *stupa* on your right). Hindus are very superstitious about taking photographs of images of deities and inside temples; if in doubt, desist. Do not take photos of funerals or cremations.

Funeral processions are private affairs, and should be left in peace. In Hindu funerals, the body is normally carried to the cremation site within hours of death by white-shrouded relatives (white is the colour of mourning). The eldest son is expected to shave his head and wear white following the death of a parent. At Varanasi and other places, you may see cremations; such occasions should be treated with respect and photographs should not be taken.

Dress

Indian people are very conservative about dress. **Women** are expected to dress modestly, with legs and shoulders covered. Trousers are acceptable, but shorts and short skirts are offensive to many. **Men** should always wear a shirt in public, and avoid skimpy shorts away from beach areas. These rules are particularly important in temples and mosques. Cover your head with a cap or cloth when entering a *dargah* (Sufi shrine) or Sikh *gurudwara*; women in particular are also required to cover their limbs. Men are similarly expected to dress appropriately with their legs and head covered. Caps are usually available on loan, often free, for visitors, and sometimes cloth is available to cover up your arms and legs.

Never mind sky-clad Jains (see p.1177) or *naga sadhus*, **nudity** is not acceptable in India. Topless bathing is not uncommon in Goa (though it is in theory prohibited), but you can be sure the locals don't like it.

In general, Indians find it hard to understand why rich Westerners should wander round in ragged clothes or imitate the lowest ranks of Indian society, who would love to have something more decent to wear. Staying well groomed and dressing "respectably" vastly improves the impression you make on local people and reduces sexual harassment for women, too.

Other possible gaffes

Kissing and **embracing** are regarded in India as part of sex: do not do them in public. In more conservative areas (ie outside Westernized parts of big cities or tourist enclaves), it is not even a good idea for couples to hold hands, though Indian men can sometimes be seen holding hands as a sign of "brotherliness". Be aware of your **feet**. When entering a private home, you should normally remove your shoes (follow your host's example);

when sitting, avoid pointing the soles of your feet at anyone. Accidental contact with one's foot is always followed by an apology.

Indian English can be very formal and even ceremonious. Indian people may well call you "sir" or "madam", even "good lady" or "kind sir". At the same time, you should be aware that your English may seem rude to them. In particular, swearing is taken rather seriously, and casual use of the F-word is likely to shock.

Meeting people

Westerners have an ambiguous status in Indian eyes. In one way, you represent the rich sahib, whose culture dominates the world, and the old colonial mentality has not completely disappeared. On the other hand, as a non-Hindu, you are an outcaste, your presence in theory polluting to an orthodox or high-caste Hindu, while to members of all religions, your morals and your standards of spiritual and physical cleanliness are suspect.

As a traveller, you will constantly come across people who want to strike up a **conversation**. English not being their first language, they may not be familiar with the conventional ways of doing this, and thus their opening line may seem abrupt if at the same time very formal. "Excuse me good gentleman, what is your native place?" is a typical one. It is also the first in a series of questions that Indian men seem sometimes to have learnt from a single book in order to ask Western tourists. Some of the questions may baffle at first ("What is your qualification?" "Are you in service?"), some may be queries about the ways of the West or the purpose of your trip, but mostly they will be about your family and your job.

You may find it odd or even intrusive that complete strangers should want to know that sort of thing, but these subjects are considered polite conversation between strangers in India, and help people place one another in terms of social position. Your family, job, even income, are not considered "personal" subjects, and it is completely normal to ask people about them. Asking the same questions back will not be taken amiss – far from it. Being curious does not have the "nosey" stigma in India that it has in the West.

Things that Indian people are likely to find strange about you are lack of religion (you could adopt one), travelling alone, leaving your family to come to India, being an unmarried couple (letting people think you are married can make life easier), and travelling second class or staying in cheap hotels when, as a tourist, you are relatively rich. You will probably end up having to explain the same things many times to many different people; on the other hand, you can ask questions too, so you could take it as an opportunity to ask things you want to know about India. English-speaking Indians and members of the large and growing middle class in particular are usually extremely well informed and well educated.

Shopping

So many beautiful and exotic souvenirs are on sale in India, at such low prices, that it's sometimes hard to know what to buy first. On top of that, all sorts of things (such as made-to-measure clothes) that would be vastly expensive at home are much more reasonably priced in India. Even if you lose weight during your trip, your baggage might well put on quite a bit – unless of course you post some of it home.

Where to shop

Quite a few items sold in tourist areas are made elsewhere and, needless to say, it's more fun (and cheaper) to pick them up at source. Best buys are noted in the relevant sections of the Guide, along with a few specialities that can't be found outside their regions. India is awash with **street hawkers**, often very young kids. Although they can be annoying and should be dealt with firmly if you are not interested, do not write them off completely as they sometimes have decent souvenirs at lower than shop prices and are open to hard bargaining.

Virtually all the state governments in India run handicraft "**emporia**", most with branches in the major cities such as Delhi, Mumbai, Chennai and Kolkata. These four cities also have **Central Cottage Industries Emporiums**. Goods in these emporiums are generally of a high quality, even if their fixed prices are a little expensive, and they are worth a visit to get an idea of what crafts are available and how much they should cost.

Bargaining

Whatever you **buy** (except food and cigarettes), you will almost always be expected to **haggle** over the price. Bargaining is very much a matter of personal style, but should always be lighthearted, never acrimonious. There are no hard and fast rules – it's really a question of how much something is worth to you. It's a good plan, therefore, to have an idea of how much you want to pay. Bid low and let the shopkeeper argue you up. If they'll settle for your price or less, you have a deal. If not, you don't, but you've had a pleasant conversation and no harm is done.

Don't worry too much about the first quoted prices. Some people suggest paying a third of the opening price, but it really depends on the shop, the goods and the shopkeeper's impression of you. You may not be able to get the seller much below the first quote; on the other hand, you may end up paying as little as a tenth of it. If you bid too low, you may be hustled out of the shop for offering an "insulting" price, but this is all part of the game, and you'll no doubt be welcomed as an old friend if you return the next day. More often, however, if you start to walk away, the price will magically come down, so that's a useful tactic.

"Green" tourists are easily spotted, so try and look like you know what you are up to, even on your first day, or leave it till later; you could wait and see what the going rate is first.

Haggling is a little bit like bidding in an auction, and similar rules apply. Don't start haggling for something if you know you don't want it, and never let any figure pass your lips that you are not prepared to pay – having mentioned a price, you are obliged to pay it. If the seller asks you how much you would pay for something and you don't want it, say so.

Sometimes rickshaw-wallahs and taxi drivers stop unasked at shops where they get a small **commission** simply for bringing customers. In places like Jaipur and Agra where this is common practice,

---

CRAFTS GALORE

No country in the world produces such a tempting array of arts and crafts as India. Intensely colourful, delicately worked, exquisitely ornate and immensely varied, India's crafts have the added advantage of being amazingly inexpensive. Every part of the country has its **specialities** – textiles in Rajasthan, metalwork in Karnataka, carpets in Kashmir, *thangkas* in Ladakh, leatherware in Maharashtra and batik in Orissa – but everywhere you'll see beautiful things that you'll find hard to resist buying. Whether it's sumptuous fabrics, intricate carvings or garish knick-knacks, India offers a feast of artistic creations that you'll want to gorge on.

tourists sometimes even strike a deal with their drivers – agreeing to stop at five shops and splitting the commission for the time wasted. If you're taken to a shop by a tout or driver and you buy something, you pay around fifty percent extra. Stand firm about not entering shops and getting to your destination if you have no appetite for such shenanigans. If you want a bargain, shop alone, and never let anybody on the street take you to a shop – if you do, they'll be getting a commission and you'll be paying it.

Travelling with children

Travelling with kids can be both challenging and rewarding. Indians are very tolerant of **children** so you can take them almost anywhere without restriction, and they always help break the ice with strangers.

However the main problem with children, especially small children, is their extra vulnerability. Even more than their parents, they need protection from the sun, unsafe drinking water, heat and unfamiliar food. All that chilli in particular may be a problem, even with older kids, if they're not used to it. Remember too, that diarrhoea, perhaps just a nuisance to you, could be dangerous for a child: rehydration salts (see p.48) are vital if your child goes down with it. Make sure too, if possible, that your child is aware of the dangers of rabies; keep children away from animals and consider a rabies jab.

For babies, nappies (diapers) are available in most large towns at similar prices to the West, but it's worth taking an additional pack in case of emergencies, and bringing sachets of Calpol or similar, which aren't readily available in India. And if your baby is on powdered milk, it might be an idea to bring some of that: you can certainly get it in India, but it may not taste the same. Dried baby food could also be worth taking – any café or chai-wallah should be able to supply you with boiled water.

For touring, hiking or walking, child-carrier backpacks are ideal; some even come with mosquito nets these days. As for luggage, bring as little as possible so you can manage the kids more easily. If your child is small enough, a fold-up buggy is also well worth packing, even if you no longer use a buggy at home, as kids tire so easily in the heat. If you want to cut down on long train or bus journeys by flying, remember that children under 2 travel for ten percent of the adult fare, and under-12s for half price.

Travel essentials

Costs

For Western visitors, India is still one of the world's less expensive countries. A little foreign currency can go a long way, and you can be confident of getting good value for your money, whether you're setting out to keep your budget to a minimum or to enjoy the opportunities that spending a bit more will make possible.

What you spend obviously depends on where you go, where you stay, how you get around, what you eat and what you buy. Outside the tourist resorts of Kerala and Goa, you could just about survive on a **budget** of as little as ₹800 (£9/US$15) per day, if you eat in local *dhabas*, stay in the cheapest hotels and don't travel too much. In reality, most backpackers nowadays tend to spend at least double that. On ₹2000 (£23/US$36) per day you'll be able to afford comfortable mid-range hotels, and meals in smarter restaurants, regular rickshaw or taxi rides and entrance fees to monuments. Spend around ₹5000 (£57/US$90) per day and you can stay in smart hotels, eat in the top restaurants, travel first class on trains and afford chauffeur-driven cars. Although it is possible to travel very comfortably in India, it's also possible to spend a great deal of money, if you want to experience the very best the country has to offer, and there are plenty of hotels now charging US$500 per night, sometimes even more.

Budget **accommodation** is still very good value, however. Cheap double rooms start from around ₹400 (£4.50/US$7) per night, while a no-frills vegetarian **meal** in an ordinary restaurant will typically cost no more than ₹100. Long-distance **transport** can work out to be phenomenally good value if you stick to state buses and standard second-class non-a/c trains, but soon starts to add up if you opt for air-conditioned carriages on the superfast inter-city services. The 200km trip from Delhi to Agra, for example, can cost anywhere from ₹88 (£1/US$1.60) in second class unreserved up to ₹820 (£9/US$15) in first-class a/c.

Where you are also makes a difference: Mumbai is notoriously pricey, especially for accommodation, and Delhi is also substantially more expensive than most parts of the country. Upscale visitor accommodation in Kerala costs almost as much as it does in Europe, although fierce competition tends to keep prices at the lower end of the budget spectrum down in the tourist towns of Rajasthan.

ASI ENTRANCE FEES

The Archeological Survey of India (ASI), who manage many of India's most popular monuments, such as the Taj Mahal, currently operates a **two-tier entry system** at all its sites, whereby foreign visitors, including non-resident Indians, pay a lot more than Indian residents; we've listed entrance fees for both foreigners and Indian residents throughout the Guide.

Out in the sticks, on the other hand, and particularly away from your fellow tourists, you will often find things incredibly cheap, though your choice will obviously be more limited.

Don't make any rigid assumptions at the outset of a long trip that your money will last for a certain number of weeks or months. On any one day it may be possible to spend very little, but cumulatively you won't be doing yourself any favours if you don't make sure you keep yourself well rested and properly fed. As a foreigner in India, you will find yourself penalized by double-tier entry prices to museums and historic sites (see box above) as well as in upmarket hotels and airfares, both of which are levied at a higher rate and in dollars.

Some independent travellers tend to indulge in wild and highly competitive **penny-pinching**, which Indian people find rather pathetic – they have a fair idea of what you can earn at home. Bargain where appropriate, but don't begrudge a few rupees to someone who's worked hard for them: consider what their services would cost in your own country, and how much more valuable the money is to them than it is to you. Even if you get a bad deal on every rickshaw journey you make, it will only add a minuscule fraction to the cost of your trip. Remember too, that every pound or dollar you spend in India goes that much further and luxuries you can't afford at home become possible here: sometimes it's worth spending more simply because you get more for it. At the same time, don't pay well over the odds for something if you know what the going rate is. Thoughtless extravagance can, particularly in remote areas that see a dispro-portionate number of tourists, contribute to inflation, putting even basic goods and services beyond the reach of local people.

Crime and personal safety

In spite of the crushing poverty and the yawning gulf between rich and poor, India is, on the whole, a **safe** country in which to travel. As a tourist, however, you are an obvious target for the tiny number of thieves (who may include some of your fellow travellers), and stand to face serious problems if you do lose

your passport and money or bank cards. Common sense, therefore, suggests a few precautions.

Beware of crowded locations, such as packed buses or trains, in which it is easy for pickpockets to operate – slashing pockets or bags with razor blades is not unheard of in certain locations, and itching powder is sometimes used to distract the unwary. Don't leave valuables unattended on the beach when you go for a swim; backpacks in dormitory accommodation are also obvious targets, as is luggage on the roof of buses. Even monkeys rate a mention here, since it's not unknown for them to steal things from hotel rooms with open windows, or even to snatch bags from unsuspecting shoulders.

Budget travellers would do well to carry a **padlock**, as these are usually used to secure the doors of cheap hotel rooms and it's reassuring to know you have the only key. You can also use them to lock your bag to seats or racks in trains, for which a length of chain also comes in handy. Don't put valuables in your luggage for bus or plane journeys: keep them with you at all times. If your baggage is on the roof of a bus, make sure it is well secured. On trains and buses, the prime time for theft is just before you leave, so keep a particular eye on your gear then, beware of deliberate diversions, and don't put your belongings next to open windows. Remember that routes popular with tourists tend to be popular with thieves too. Druggings leading to theft and worse are rare but not unheard of, so you are best advised to politely refuse food and drink from fellow passengers or passing strangers, unless you are completely confident it's the family picnic you are sharing or have seen the food purchased from a vendor.

However, **don't get paranoid**; the best way of enjoying the country is to stay relaxed but with your wits about you. Crime levels in India are a long way below those of Western countries and violent crime against tourists is almost unheard of. Virtually none of the people who approach you on the street intend any harm: most want to sell you something (though this is not always made apparent immedi-ately), some want to practise their English, others (if you're a woman) to chat you up, while more than a few just want to add your address to their book or

DRUGS

India is a centre for the production of **cannabis** and to a lesser extent **opium**, and derivatives of these drugs are widely available. **Charas** (hashish) is produced all along the Himalayas, while **ganja** (marijuana) is the more common form in the south. The use of cannabis is frowned upon by respectable Indians – if you see anyone in a movie smoking a chillum, you can be sure it's the baddie. Sadhus, on the other hand, are allowed to smoke it legally as part of their religious devotion to Shiva, who is said to have originally discovered its narcotic properties.

Bhang (a preparation made from marijuana leaves, which it is claimed sometimes contains added hallucinogenic ingredients such as *datura*) is legal and widely available in bhang shops: it is used to make sweets and drinks such as the notoriously potent bhang lassis which have waylaid many an unwary traveller. Bhang shops also frequently sell ganja, low-quality *charas* and opium (*chandu*), mainly from Rajasthan and Madhya Pradesh. Opium derivatives morphine and heroin are widespread too, with addiction an increasing problem among the urban poor. "Brown sugar" that you may be offered on the street is number-three heroin; Varanasi is becoming notorious for its heroin problem. Use of other illegal drugs such as LSD, ecstasy and cocaine is largely confined to tourists in party locations such as Goa.

All of these drugs except bhang are strictly controlled under Indian **law**. Anyone arrested with less than five grams of cannabis, which they are able to prove is for their own use, is liable to a six-month maximum, but cases can take years to come to trial (two is normal, and eight not unheard of). Police raids and searches are particularly common in Manali, the Kullu Valley (and on buses from those places to Delhi, especially at harvest time) and the beach areas of Goa. "Paying a fine now" may be possible on arrest (though it will probably mean all the money you have), but once you are booked in at the station, your chances are slim; a minority of the population languishing in Indian jails are foreigners on drugs charges.

have a snap taken with you. Anyone offering wonderful-sounding moneymaking schemes, however, is almost certain to be a con artist.

If you do feel threatened, it's worth looking for help. **Tourism police** are found sitting in clearly marked booths in the main railway stations, especially in big tourist centres, where they will also have a booth in the main bus station. In addition, they may have a marked booth outside major tourist sites.

Be wary of **credit card fraud**; a credit card can be used to make duplicate forms by which your account is then billed for fictitious transactions, so don't let shops or restaurants take your card away to process – insist they do it in front of you or follow them to the point of transaction.

It's not a bad idea to keep US$200 or so separately from the rest of your money, along with your travellers' cheque receipts, insurance policy number and phone number for claims, and a photocopy of the pages in your passport containing personal data and your Indian visa. This will cover you in case you do lose all your valuables.

If the worst happens and you get **robbed**, the first thing to do is report the theft as soon as possible to the local police. They are very unlikely to recover your belongings but you need a report from them in order to claim on your travel insurance. Dress smartly and expect an uphill battle

– city cops in particular tend to be jaded from too many insurance and travellers' cheque scams.

Losing your passport is a real hassle, but does not necessarily mean the end of your trip. First, report the loss immediately to the police, who will issue you with the all-important "complaint form" that you need to be able to travel around and check into hotels, as well as claim back any expenses incurred in replacing your passport from your insurer. A complaint form, however, will not allow you to change money or travellers' cheques. If you've run out of cash, your best bet is to ask your hotel manager to help you out (staff will have seen your passport when you checked in, and the number will be in the register). The next thing to do is telephone your nearest embassy or consulate in India. Normally, passports have to be applied for and collected in person, but if you are stranded, it is usually possible to arrange to receive the necessary forms in the post. However, you still have to go to the embassy or consulate to pick up your new passport. Emergency passports are the cheapest form of replacement, but are normally only valid for the few days of your return flight. If you're not sure when you're leaving India, you'll have to obtain a more costly full passport; these can only be issued by high commissions, embassies and larger consulates in Delhi or Mumbai, although they can be arranged through consulates in Chennai, Kolkata or Panjim (Goa).

Duty free allowance

Anyone over 17 can bring in one US quart (0.95 litre – but nobody's going to quibble about the other 5ml) of spirits, or a bottle of wine and 250ml spirits; plus 200 cigarettes, or 50 cigars, or 250g tobacco. You may be required to register anything valuable on a tourist baggage re-export form to make sure you can take it home with you, and to fill in a currency declaration form if carrying more than US$10,000 or the equivalent.

Electricity

Generally 220V 50Hz AC, though direct current supplies also exist, so check before plugging in. Most sockets are triple round-pin (accepting European-size double round-pin plugs). British, Irish and Australasian plugs will need an adaptor, preferably universal; American and Canadian appliances will need a transformer too, unless multivoltage. Power cuts and voltage variations are very common; voltage stabilizers should be used to run sensitive appliances such as laptops.

Gay and lesbian travellers

Homosexuality is not generally open or accepted in India, but in a landmark decision in July 2009, the High Court declared unconstitutional the Victorian ban on gay sex between consenting adults, as a result of which it is now legal. Prejudice is still ingrained however, especially in conservative areas such as Rajasthan.

For **lesbians**, making contacts is difficult; even the Indian women's movement does not readily promote lesbianism as an issue that needs confronting. The only public faces of a hidden scene are the organizations in Delhi (see below). For **gay men**, homosexuality is no longer solely the preserve of the alternative scene of actors and artists, and is increasingly accepted by the upper classes, but Mumbai remains much more a centre for gay life than Delhi, let alone traditionalist Rajasthan. Following the High Court ruling however, there are now gay nights in several Delhi clubs, and *Time Out Delhi* has a section on gay and lesbian events.

One group of people you may come across are **hijras**, who look like transvestites and are accepted as a transitional "third sex" between male and female. Pukka *hijras* are born with genitals that are neither fully male nor female, but some are eunuchs, who undergo castration to become *hijras* because they are transsexuals (physically male but psychologically female). They live in their own "families" and have a niche in Indian society, but not an easy one. At weddings, their presence is supposed to bring good luck, and they are usually given baksheesh for putting in a brief appearance. Generally, however, they have a low social status, face widespread discrimination, and many make a living by begging or prostitution.

GAY AND LESBIAN CONTACTS AND RESOURCES

Campaign for Lesbian Rights (CALERI)/Shakhi PO Box 3526, Lajpat Nagar, New Delhi 110065 ✉ caleri@hotmail.com. Collective working for lesbian rights.

Gay Delhi ⓦ gaydelhi.tripod.com. Weekly social meetings and other events for gay men in Delhi.

Humsafar Trust ⓦ humsafar.org. Set up to promote safe sex among gay men, the website also has lots of links and up-to-date information.

Indian Dost ⓦ indiandost.com/delhigay.php. The Delhi page of a website for gay men in India.

International Gay and Lesbian Human Rights Commission ⓦ glhrc.org. Latest news on the human rights situation for gay people worldwide, including regular bulletins on India.

Purple Dragon Lobby of the Tarntawan Place Hotel, 119/5-10 Suriwong Rd, Bangkok 10500, Thailand ☎ +662 238 3227, ⓦ purpledrag.com. Thai-based tour operator offering various gay-friendly tours of India.

Sangini PO Box 7532, Vasant Kunj, New Delhi 110070, ⓦ sanginii .org. Lesbian information, support and contacts. Helpline (Tues noon–3pm & Fri 6–8pm) on ☎ 011 5567 6450.

Insurance

It's imperative that you take out proper **travel insurance** before setting off for India. In addition to covering medical expenses and emergency flights, travel insurance also insures your money and belongings against loss or theft. Before paying for a new policy, however, it's worth checking whether you are already covered: some all-risks home insurance policies may cover your possessions when overseas, and many private medical schemes include cover when abroad. In Canada, provincial health plans usually provide partial medical cover for mishaps overseas, while holders of official student/teacher/youth cards in Canada and the US are entitled to meagre accident coverage and hospital in-patient benefits. Students will often find that their student health coverage extends during the vacations and for one term beyond the date of last enrolment.

ROUGH GUIDES TRAVEL INSURANCE

Rough Guides has teamed up with WorldNomads.com to offer great travel insurance deals. Policies are available to residents of more than 150 countries, with cover for a wide range of adventure sports, 24hr emergency assistance, high levels of medical and evacuation cover and a stream of travel safety information. Roughguides.com users can take advantage of their policies online 24/7, from anywhere in the world – even if you're already travelling. And since plans often change when you're on the road, you can extend your policy and even claim online. Roughguides.com users who buy travel insurance with WorldNomads.com can also leave a positive footprint and donate to a community development project. For more information, go to ⓦ roughguides.com/travel-insurance.

After exhausting the possibilities above, you might want to contact a specialist travel insurance company, or consider the travel insurance deal offered by Rough Guides (see box above). A typical travel insurance policy usually provides cover for the loss of baggage, tickets and – up to a certain limit – cash or cheques, as well as cancellation or curtailment of your journey. Most of them exclude so-called dangerous sports unless an extra premium is paid: in India this can mean scuba diving, whitewater rafting, windsurfing and trekking with ropes, though probably not jeep safaris. Many policies can be chopped and changed to exclude coverage you don't need – for example, sickness and accident benefits can often be excluded or included at will. If you do take medical coverage, ascertain whether benefits will be paid as treatment proceeds or only after return home, and whether there is a 24-hour medical emergency number. When securing baggage cover, make sure that the per-article limit – typically under £500 – will cover your most valuable possession. If you need to make a claim, you should keep receipts for medicines and medical treatment, and in the event you have anything stolen, you must obtain an official statement from the police.

Internet

All large cities and tourist towns now have at least a few (usually dozens) of places where you can get online, either at cyber cafés or your hotel or guesthouse. Prices typically range from around ₹20/hr in big cities to ₹90/hr in more remote places. Broadband has now reached more or less everywhere though speeds can still be painfully slow and computers rather antiquated, making it difficult to load complex websites or to perform online transactions (like booking a train ticket). Recent years have seen a proliferation of wi-fi connections, so getting your own device online is far easier than in the past.

Laundry

In India, no one goes to the laundry: if they don't do their own, they send it out to a *dhobi*. Wherever you are staying, there will either be an in-house *dhobi*, or one very close by to call on. The *dhobi* will take your dirty washing to a *dhobi ghat*, a public clothes-washing area (the bank of a river for example), where it is shown some old-fashioned discipline: separated, soaped and given a damn good thrashing to beat the dirt out of it. Then it is hung out to dry in the sun and, once dried, taken to the ironing sheds where every garment is endowed with razor-sharp creases and then matched to its rightful owner by hidden cryptic markings. Your clothes will come back from the *dhobi* absolutely spotless, though this kind of violent treatment does take it out of them: buttons get lost and eventually the cloth starts to fray. If you'd rather not entrust your Savile Row made-to-measure to their tender mercies, head instead for the dry-cleaners in large towns.

Living in India

It is illegal for a foreign tourist to work in India, and there's no shortage of English teachers, but you may consider doing some voluntary charitable work. Several charities welcome volunteers on a medium-term commitment, say over two months. People visiting India on business or with employment arranged in advance may apply for a business visa, and non-resident Indians are entitled to stay for up to five years.

If you want to spend your time working as a volunteer for an **NGO (Non-Governmental Organization)**, you should make arrangements well before you arrive by contacting the body in question, rather than on spec. Special visas are generally not required unless you intend to work for longer than six months. For information about which NGOs are operating across the country, log on to ⓦ indianngos.com and select options from a drop-down list.

VOLUNTEERING RESOURCES

Animal Aid 6900 37th Ave SW, Seattle, WA 98126, US; Badi Village, across from T.B. Hospital, Main Rd, Udaipur 313004, Rajasthan ☎ 0294 251 3359; ⊕ animalaidunlimited.com. Animal welfare group working to alleviate animal suffering in Udaipur, Rajasthan (see p.211). No special skills are required, though volunteers with veterinary knowledge are especially welcome.

Children Walking Tall "The Mango House", House 148/3, near Vrundavan Hospital, Karaswada, Mapusa, Bardez, Goa 403526 ☎ 98221 24 802, ⊕ childrenwalkingtall.com. A British-run operation that works with slum children in north Goa. Volunteers are needed to distribute clothes and fruit, sort through donations, teach or organize fundraising events.

Concern India Foundation A-52, 1st Floor, Amar Colony, Lajpat Nagar-IV, New Delhi 110024 ☎ 011 2622 4482 or ☎ 011 2622 4483, ⊕ concernindia.org. Charitable trust supporting grassroots NGOs working with disadvantaged people.

Darjeeling Children's Trust Rewang House, Dr. Zakir Hussein Rd, Darjeeling ☎ 09474 030016, ⊕ darjeelingchildrenstrust.com. Retired Major Pasang Wangdi helps run the UK-based charity, supporting eight primary schools, all within walking distance of the Chowrasta. Volunteers who are willing to give a week or more of their time are welcome.

DISHA Foundation Disha Path, near JDA Park, Nirman Nagar-C, Jaipur 302019, Rajasthan ☎ 0141 239 3319, ⊕ dishafoundation .org. Resource centre for children with cerebral palsy and other disabilities. Needs donations, sponsors, and volunteers with time or specific skills.

Friends of Shekhewati C/o Apani Dhani, Nawalgarh 333042, Rajasthan ☎ 01594 222 239, ⊕ apanidhani.com/friend. Conservation group aiming to save Shekhawati's art heritage; needs writers, photographers, architects and architecture students to volunteer their services.

Goa Animal Welfare Trust (GAWT) Old Police Station, Bansai, Cacora-Curchorem, Salcete, Goa 403706 ☎ 0832 265 3677, ⊕ gawt.org. GAWT does sterling work with stray and mistreated animals, and welcome volunteers in centres around Goa.

Mandore Medical and Relief Society 10-D Near Government Bus Stand, Paota, Jodhpur 342006, Rajasthan ☎ 0291 254 5210, ⊕ mandore.com. Guesthouse which takes on volunteers for periods as short as a week to work in health awareness and education projects in rural areas around Jodhpur.

Salaam Baalak Trust 2nd Floor, DDA Community Centre, Gali Chandiwali, Paharganj, Delhi 110055 ☎ 011 2358 4164, ⊕ salaambaalaktrust.com. Charity working to help street children in Delhi's Paharganj (see p.85).

Sambhali Trust Durg Niwas Guesthouse, 1 Old Public Park, Raika Bagh, Jodhpur 342001, Rajasthan ☎ 0291 251 2385, ⊕ sambhali-trust.org. Locally based NGO dedicated to providing education, training and empowerment to girls and women from underprivileged backgrounds in rural Rajasthan.

Seva Mandir Old Fatehpura, Udaipur 313004, Rajasthan ☎ 0294 245 1041, ⊕ sevamandir.org. NGO working in tribal villages in the Udaipur district; takes interns to help with development projects.

SOS Children's Villages of India A-7 Nizamuddin (West), New Delhi 110013 ☎ 011 2435 7299, ⊕ soscvindia.org. SOS has projects in different parts of India, including Delhi and Rajasthan, giving shelter to distressed children by providing a healthy environment and education including vocational training.

Left luggage

Most stations in India have "cloakrooms" (sometimes called parcel offices) for passengers to leave their baggage. These can be extremely handy if you want to go sightseeing in a town and move on the same day. In theory, you need a train ticket or Indrail pass to deposit luggage, but staff don't always ask; they may, however, refuse to take your bag if you can't lock it. Losing your reclaim ticket causes problems; the clerk will be assumed to have stolen the bag if he can't produce it, so there'll be untold running around to obtain clearance before you can get your bag without it. Make sure, when checking baggage in, that the cloakroom will be open when you need to pick it up. The standard charge is currently ₹10 for the first 24 hours, plus ₹15 per day afterwards.

Mail

Mail can take anything from six days to three weeks to get to or from India, depending on where you are and the country you are mailing to; ten days is about the norm. Most **post offices** are open Monday to Friday from 10am to 5pm and Saturday from 10am to noon, but town GPOs keep longer hours (usually Mon–Sat 9.30am–1pm & 2–5.30pm). **Stamps** are not expensive, but you'll have to stick them on yourself as they tend not to be self-adhesive (every post office keeps a pot of evil-smelling glue for this purpose). Aerogrammes and postcards cost the same to anywhere in the world. Ideally, you should also have mail franked in front of you

Sending a parcel from India can be a performance. First take it to a tailor to have it wrapped in cheap cotton cloth, stitched up and sealed with wax. Next, take it to the post office, fill in and attach the relevant customs forms, buy your stamps, see them franked and dispatch it. Surface mail is incredibly cheap, and takes an average of six months to arrive – it may take half, or four times that, however. It's a good way to dump excess baggage and souvenirs, but don't send anything fragile this way.

Maps

Getting good maps of India, in India, can be difficult. The government – in an archaic suspicion of cartography, and in spite of clear coverage of the country on Google – forbids the sale of detailed maps of border areas, which includes the entire coastline.

It therefore makes sense to bring a **full country map** of India with you. Freytag & Berndt produce the best country map, while Nelles covers parts of the country with 1:1,500,000 regional maps. These are generally excellent, but cost a fortune if you buy the complete set. Their double-sided map of the Himalayas is useful for roads and planning and has some detail but is not sufficient as a trekking map. Ttk, a Chennai-based company, publishes basic state maps which are widely available in India, and in some specialized travel and map shops in the UK such as Stanfords; these are poorly drawn but useful for road distances. The Indian Railways map at the back of the publication *Trains at a Glance* (see p.33) is useful for planning railway journeys.

If you need larger-scale **city maps** than the ones we provide in this guide – which are keyed to show recommended hotels and restaurants – you can sometimes get them from tourist offices, though the plans published free online at Google Maps are vastly superior (simply print them off at an internet café or before you leave home). Eicher has a series of glossy, *A–Z*-style books (Delhi, Mumbai, Kolkata, Chennai and Bengaluru (Bangalore) only), produced in India and available at all good bookstores.

As for **trekking maps**, the US Army Map Service produced maps in the 1960s which, with a scale of 1:250,000, remain sufficiently accurate on topography, but are of course outdated on the latest road developments. Most other maps you can buy are based on these, and they're still the best available for most of the Himalayan regions. Leomann Maps (1:200,000) also cover the northwest Himalayan regions. These are not contour maps and are therefore better for planning and basic reference than for trekking. The Survey of India publishes a rather poor 1:250,000 series for trekkers in the Uttarakhand Himalayas – simplified versions of their own infinitely more reliable maps, produced for the military, which are absolutely impossible for an outsider to get hold of.

Money

India's unit of currency is the **rupee**, usually abbreviated "₹" and divided into a hundred paise. Almost all money is paper, with notes of 5, 10, 20, 50, 100, 500 and 1000 rupees. Coins in circulation are 1, 2, 5 and 10 rupees, the latter two gradually replacing the paper versions. Note that it's technically illegal to take rupees in or out of India (although they are widely available at overseas forexes), so you might want to wait until you arrive before changing money.

Banknotes, especially lower denominations, can get into a terrible state. Don't accept torn banknotes, since no one else will be prepared to take them and you'll be left saddled with the things, though you can change them at the Reserve Bank of India and large branches of other big banks. Don't pass them on to beggars; they can't use them either, so it amounts to an insult.

Large denominations can also be a problem, as change is usually in short supply. Many Indian people cannot afford to keep much lying around, and you shouldn't necessarily expect shopkeepers or rickshaw-wallahs to have it (and they may – as may you – try to hold onto it if they do). Larger notes – like the ₹500 note – are good for travelling with and can be changed for smaller denominations at hotels and other suitable establishments. A word of warning – the ₹500 note looks remarkably similar to the ₹100 note.

At the time of writing, the **exchange rate** was approximately ₹88 to £1, or ₹55 to US$1, and ₹72 to £1. You can check latest exchange rates online at ⓦ xe.com.

ATMs, cards and travellers' cheques

The easiest way to access your money in India is with **plastic**, though it's a good idea to also have some backup in the form of cash or travellers' cheques. You will find **ATMs** at main banks in all major towns, cities and tourist areas, though your card issuer may well add a foreign transaction fee, and the Indian bank will also levy a small charge, generally around ₹25.

Your card issuer, and sometimes the ATM itself, imposes limits on the amount you may withdraw in a day – typically ₹10,000–20,000. Note, too, that the first time you try to take money out after arriving in India your request may be refused – a standard security procedure aimed at preventing fraud. Telephone your bank or credit card's 24 hour line for the block to be removed – or better still telephone your bank before you leave home to warn them.

Credit cards are accepted for payment at major hotels, top restaurants, some shops and airline offices, but virtually nowhere else. American Express, MasterCard and Visa are the likeliest to be accepted. Beware of people making extra copies of the receipt, in order to fraudulently bill you later; always insist that the transaction is made before your eyes.

One big downside of relying on plastic as your

main access to cash, of course, is that cards can easily get lost or stolen, so take along a couple of alternatives if you can, keep an emergency stash of cash just in case, and make a note of your home bank's telephone number and website addresses for emergencies.

US dollars are the easiest **currency** to convert, with euros and pounds sterling not far behind. Major hard currencies can be changed easily in tourist areas and big cities, less so elsewhere. If you enter the country with more than US$10,000 or the equivalent, you are supposed to fill in a currency declaration form.

In addition to cash and plastic (or as a generally less convenient alternative to the latter), consider carrying some **travellers' cheques**. You pay a small commission (usually one percent) to buy these with cash in the same currency, a little more to convert from a different currency, but they have the advantage over cash that, if lost or stolen, they can be replaced. Not all banks, however, accept them. Well-known brands such as Thomas Cook and American Express are your best bet, but in some places even American Express is only accepted in US dollars and not as pounds sterling. Visa and American Express offer **pre-paid cards** that you can load up with credit before you leave home and use in ATMs like a debit card – effectively travellers' cheques in plastic form.

Changing money

Changing money in regular **banks**, especially government-run banks such as the State Bank of India (SBI), can be a time-consuming business, involving lots of form-filling and queueing at different counters, so it's best to change substantial amounts at any one time. You'll have no such problems, however, with **private companies** such as Thomas Cook, American Express or forex agents. Major cities and main tourist centres usually have several **licensed currency exchange bureaux**; rates usually aren't as good as at a bank but transactions are generally a lot quicker and there's less paperwork to complete.

Outside **banking hours** (Mon–Fri 10am– 2/4pm, Sat 10am–noon), large hotels may change money, probably at a lower rate, and exchange bureaux have longer opening hours. Banks in the arrivals halls at Delhi, Mumbai and Chennai airports stay open 24 hours.

Wherever you change money, hold on to **exchange receipts** ("encashment certificates"); they will be required if you want to change back any excess rupees when you leave the country and to buy air tickets and reserve train berths with rupees at special counters for foreigners. The State Bank of India now charges for tax clearance forms.

Opening hours

Standard shop opening hours in India are Monday to Saturday 9.30am to 6pm. Most big stores, at any rate, keep those hours, while smaller shops vary from town to town, region to region, and one to another, but usually keep longer hours. Government tourist offices are open Monday to Friday 9.30am to 5pm, Saturday 9.30am to 1pm, closed on the second Saturday of the month; state-run tourist offices are likely to be open Monday to Friday 10am to 5pm.

Phones

Since the mobile (cellphone) revolution, privately run phone **international direct-dialling** facilities – **STD/ISD** (Standard Trunk Dialling/International Subscriber Dialling) places – have become far less common so you can't always rely on finding one. In addition, calling from them will cost more than dialling from a mobile if you have an Indian SIM card. Visitors therefore nearly all bring their own phones these days, and buy an Indian SIM to cover their trip.

SIM cards are sold through most cellphone shops and network outlets. Unfortunately, in the wake of the 2008 Mumbai terror attacks, the process of obtaining one has become more complicated for foreigners. You have to provide a photocopy of your passport (photo and visa pages), fill in a form and be registered at an Indian address, though the hotel you are staying in usually suffices. There is an initial connection fee ranging from

---

CALLING HOME FROM ABROAD

Note that the initial zero is omitted from the area code when dialing the UK, Ireland, Australia and New Zealand from abroad.

Australia international access code + 61
Ireland international access code + 353
New Zealand international access code + 64
South Africa international access code + 27
UK international access code + 44
US and Canada international access code + 1

₹50–250, depending on the dealer and network.

Coverage varies from state to state, but the largest national network providers are best – Vodaphone, Airtel and Tata DoCoMo. Once your retailer has unlocked your phone and you have paid for the initial card, it can be topped up ("re-charged" as it's known) by amounts ranging from ₹10–1000, though only by paying certain figures (check with the retailer) will you get the full amount in credits. Call charges to the UK and US from most Indian networks cost ₹2–3 per minute. Also, get your card supplier to turn on the "do not disturb" option, or you'll be plagued with spam calls and spam texts from the phone company.

Indian **mobile** numbers are ten-digit, starting with an 8 or (more common) a 9. However, if you are calling from outside the state where the mobile is based (but not from abroad), you need to add a zero in front of that.

Calling an Indian mobile or landline from a UK landline, you can save a lot of money by dialling via a company such as Ratebuster (Ⓦ ratebuster.co.uk), which requires no sign-up but uses an 0845 number, or better still by signing up cost-free with a VoIP provider such as 18185 (Ⓦ 18185.com). In the US you can make cheap calls via reasonable monthly deals on Phone.com (Ⓦ phone.com).

Photography

Beware of pointing your camera at anything that might be considered "strategic", including airports and anything military. Remember too that some people prefer not to be photographed, so it's a good idea to ask before you take a snapshot of them. More likely, you'll get people, especially kids, volunteering to pose and it's quite common for Indians to ask you to be in their snaps.

Most photo shops can now transfer **digital** images onto a CD – useful in order to free up memory space. **Camera film**, sold at average Western prices, is still available in India (but check the date on the box, and note that false boxes containing outdated film are often sold). It's becoming harder to get film developed, however, and dubious quality makes it better done back at home anyway. If you're after **slide film**, buy it in the big cities and don't expect to find specialist brands.

Sexism and women's issues

India is not a country that provides huge obstacles to women travellers. In the days of the Raj, many upper-class women travelled through India alone,

as did the female flower children of the hippie era. Plenty of women travel solo today, but few get through their trip without any hassle, so it's good to prepare yourself to be a little bit thick-skinned.

Indian streets are almost without exception male-dominated – something that may take a bit of getting used to, particularly if you find yourself subjected to incessant staring, whistling and name calling. This can usually be stopped by ignoring the gaze and quickly moving on, or by firmly telling the offender to stop looking at you. Most of your fellow travellers on trains and buses will be men, who may start up most unwelcome conversations about sex, divorce and the freedom of relationships in the West. These cannot often be avoided, but demonstrating too much enthusiasm to discuss such topics can lure men into thinking that you are easy about sex, and the situation could become threatening. At its worst in larger cities, all this can become very tiring. You can get round it to a certain extent by joining women in public places, and you'll notice an immense difference if you join up with a male travelling companion. In this case, expect Indian men to approach him (assumed, of course, to be your husband – an assumption it is sometimes advantageous to go along with) and talk to him about you quite happily as if you were not there. Beware, however, if you are (or look) of Indian origin with a non-Indian male companion: this may well cause you harassment, as you might be seen to have brought shame on your family by adopting the loose morals of the West.

In addition to staring and suggestive comments and looks, **sexual harassment**, or "Eve teasing" as it is bizarrely known, is likely to be a nuisance, but not generally a threat. Expect to get groped in crowds and to have men "accidentally" squeeze past you at any opportunity. It tends to be worse in cities than in small towns and villages but being followed can be a real problem wherever you are.

In time you'll learn to gauge a situation – sometimes wandering around on your own may attract so much unwanted attention that you may prefer to stay in one place until you've recharged your batteries or your male fan club has moved on. It's always best to dress modestly – a *salwar kameez* is perfect, as is any baggy clothing – and refrain from smoking or drinking in public, which only reinforces prejudices that Western women are "loose" and "easy".

Returning an unwanted touch with a punch or slap is perfectly in order (Indian women often become aggressive when offended), and does serve to vent a little frustration. It should also attract

RAPE, MURDER AND AN "EVERYDAY EXPERIENCE"

On December 16, 2012 , a 23-year-old physiotherapy student and her boyfriend boarded a bus at Munirka in South Delhi. Unknown to her, the driver was on a joyride and the five other male passengers were his friends. Beating her boyfriend unconscious, they gang-raped and brutally abused her in the back of the bus. They then dumped the unfortunate couple naked on a road near the airport. The rape victim was rushed to hospital with serious internal injuries, and was even flown for emergency treatment to Singapore, but ten days after the attack she died. The incident suddenly brought to public attention the high frequency of rape and sexual assault in Delhi, and sparked off violent protests that lasted for several days. The perpetrators were arrested and the government hurriedly brought in the death penalty for rape, but real change will need a shift in public attitudes. As another female medical student told the press, sexual harassment in Delhi is an "everyday experience" for women in the city.

In the aftermath, more rape cases gained publicity, perhaps because the victims were emboldened to report the crimes and the press eager to continue focusing on the now hot issue. In mid-March 2013, a Swiss woman, camping in a remote part of Madhya Pradesh, was also raped and her husband assaulted. Again, the attackers were swiftly arrested. Despite these horrific cases, India remains a generally safe destination, especially if the common-sense precautions recommended here are followed.

attention and urge someone to help you, or at least deal with the offending man – a man transgressing social norms is always out of line and any passer-by will want to let him know it. If you feel someone getting too close in a crowd or on a bus, brandishing your left shoe in his face can be very effective.

Going to watch a Bollywood movie at the cinema is a fun and essential part of your trip to India but, at cheap cinemas especially, such an occasion is rarely without hassle. If you do go to the cinema, it's best to go to an upmarket theatre, or at least to go with a group of people and sit in the balcony area, where it's a bit more expensive but the crowd is much more sedate.

Violent sexual assaults on tourists are extremely rare but the number of reported cases of rape is slowly rising (see box above), and you should always take precautions: avoid quiet, dimly lit streets and alleys at night, as well as remote rural locations; if you find a trustworthy rickshaw/taxi driver in the day keep him for the night journey; and try to get someone to accompany you to your hotel whenever possible. While Indian women are still quite timid about reporting rape – it is considered as much a disgrace to the victim as to the perpetrator – Western victims should always report it to the police, and before leaving the area try to let other tourists, or locals, know, in the hope that pressure from the community may uncover the offender and see him brought to justice.

The **practicalities of travel** take on a new dimension for lone women travellers. Often you can turn your gender to your advantage. For example, on inter-city buses the driver and conductor will often take you under their wing, and there will be countless other instances of kindness wherever you travel. You'll be more welcome in some private houses than a group of Western males, and may find yourself learning the finer points of Indian cooking around the family's clay stove. Women frequently get preference at bus and railway stations where they can join a separate "ladies' queue", and use ladies' waiting rooms. On overnight trains the enclosed ladies' compartments are peaceful havens (unless filled with noisy children); you could also try to share a berth section with a family where you are usually drawn into the security of the group and are less exposed to lustful gazes. In hotels watch out for "peep-holes" in your door (and in the common bathrooms), and be sure to cover your window when changing and when sleeping.

Lastly, bring your own supply of **tampons**, which are not widely available outside main cities.

Time

India is all in one time zone and remains the same year round: GMT+5hr 30min. This makes it 5hr 30min ahead of London, 10hr 30min ahead of New York, 13hr 30min ahead of LA, 4hr 30min behind Sydney and 6hr 30min behind NZ; however, summertime in those places will change the difference by an hour. Indian time is referred to as IST (Indian Standard Time, which cynics refer to as "Indian stretchable time").

Tipping and baksheesh

As a well-off visitor you'll be expected to be liberal with your **tips**. Low-paid workers in hotels and restaurants often accept lower pay than they should in the expectation of generous tips during the tourist season. **Ten percent** should be regarded as acceptable if you've received good service – more if the staff have really gone out of their way to be helpful. A tip of ₹10–20 suffices at most restaurants other than the really posh ones in top-end hotels. Taxi and auto-rickshaw wallahs will not expect tips unless you've made unplanned diversions or stops. What to **tip your driver** at the end of long tours, however, is a trickier issue, especially if you've been forking out ₹150–200 for their daily allowance, as well as paying for meals. The simple answer is to give what you think they deserve, and what you can afford. Drivers working for tour operators, even more than hotel staff and waiters, depend on tips to get through the off-season (many are paid only ₹200–300 per day because their bosses know that foreign customers tend to tip well).

Alms giving (baksheesh) is common throughout India; people with disabilities and mutilations often congregate in city centres and popular resorts, where they survive from begging. In such cases a few coins up to ₹5–10 should be sufficient. Kids demanding money, pens, sweets or the like are a different case: yielding to any request only encourages them to pester others.

Toilets

Western-style toilets are becoming much more common in India now, especially in hotels and lodges in touristy areas, though you'll probably still come across a few traditional "squat" toilets – basically a hole in the ground. Paper, if used, often goes in a bucket next to the loo rather than down it. Instead, Indians use a jug of water and their left hand, a method you may also come to prefer, but if you do use paper, keep some handy. Some guesthouses and hotels do supply it, but don't count on; it's a good idea to stock up before going too far off the beaten track as it's not available everywhere. Travelling is especially difficult for women as facilities are limited or non-existent, especially when travelling by road rather than by rail. However, toilets in the a/c carriages of trains are usually kept clean, as are those in mid-range and air-conditioned restaurants. The latest development is tourist toilets at every major historical site. For ₹5 you get water, mirrors, toilet paper and a clean sit-down loo.

Tourist information

The main tourist website for India is ⓦincredibleindia.org. The Indian government also maintains a number of **tourist offices abroad**, whose staff are usually helpful and knowledgeable. Other sources of information include the websites of Indian embassies and tourist offices, travel agents (who are in business for themselves, so their advice may not always be totally unbiased), and Indian Railways representatives abroad (see p.33).

Inside India, both national and local governments run tourist information offices, providing general travel advice and handing out an array of printed material, from city maps to glossy leaflets on specific destinations. The Indian government's tourist department, whose main offices are on Janpath in New Delhi (see p.106) and opposite Churchgate railway station in Mumbai (see p.608), has branches in most regional capitals. These, however, operate independently of the state government information counters and their commercial bureaux run by the state tourism development corporations, usually referred to by their initials (e.g. MPTDC in Madhya Pradesh, RTDC in Rajasthan, and so on), which offer a wide range of travel facilities, including guided tours, car rental and their own hotels. A list of state tourist office websites is given in the Delhi chapter (see p.33).

Just to confuse things further, the Indian government's tourist office has a corporate wing, too. The Indian Tourism Development Corporation (ITDC) is responsible for the *Ashok* chain of hotels and operates tour and travel services, frequently competing with its state counterparts.

There's all sorts of information available about India **online** – we've listed the best websites in relevant places throughout the Guide. One particularly good general site is ⓦindiamike.com, which features lively chat rooms, bulletin boards, photo archives and banks of members' travel articles.

INDIA TOURISM OFFICES OVERSEAS

Australia Glasshouse Shopping Complex, 135 King St, Sydney NSW 2000 ☎ 02 9555, ⊕ info@indiatourism.com.au.
Canada 60 Bloor St (West), Suite 1003, Toronto, ON M4W 3B8 ☎ 1 416 962 3787 or ☎ 1 416 962 3788, ⊕ info@indiatourismcanada.ca.
South Africa PO Box 412542, Craighall 2024, Hyde Lane, Lancaster Gate, Johannesburg 2000 ☎ 011 325 0880, ⊕ goito@global.co.za.
UK 7 Cork St, London W1S 3LH ☎ 020 7437 3677, ⊕ london5 @indiatouristoffice.org.
US 1270 Ave of Americas, Suite 1808 (18th floor), New York, NY 10020 ☎ 1 212 586 4901, ⊕ ny@itonyc.com; 3550 Wilshire Blvd, Suite 204, Los Angeles, CA 90010-2485 ☎ 1 213 380 8855, ⊕ indiatourismla@aol.com.

TRAVEL ADVICE

Australian Department of Foreign Affairs Ⓦ smartraveller
.gov.au.
British Foreign & Commonwealth Office Ⓦ fco.gov.uk.
Canadian Department of Foreign Affairs Ⓦ voyage.gc.ca.
Irish Department of Foreign Affairs Ⓦ foreignaffairs.gov.ie.
New Zealand Ministry of Foreign Affairs Ⓦ safetravel.govt.nz.
South African Department of Foreign Affairs Ⓦ dfa.gov.za.
US State Department Ⓦ travel.state.gov.

Travellers with disabilities

Disability is common in India; many conditions that
would be curable in the West, such as cataracts, are
permanent disabilities here because people can't
afford the treatment. Those with disabilities are
unlikely to receive the best treatment available, and
the choice is usually between staying at home to
be looked after by your family and going out on the
street to beg for alms.

For **travellers with a disability**, this has its
advantages and disadvantages: disability doesn't
get the same embarrassed reaction from Indian
people that it does from some able-bodied
Westerners. On the other hand, you'll be lucky to
see a state-of-the-art wheelchair or a disabled loo,
and the streets are full of all sorts of obstacles that
would be hard for a blind or wheelchair-bound
tourist to negotiate independently. Kerbs are often
high, pavements uneven and littered, and ramps
non-existent. There are potholes all over the place
and open sewers. Some of the more expensive
hotels have ramps for the movement of luggage
and equipment, but if that makes them accessible
to wheelchairs, it is by accident rather than design.
Nonetheless, the 1995 Persons with Disabilities Act
specifies access for all to public buildings, and is

sometimes enforced. A visit to Delhi by the wheelchair-bound astro-physicist Stephen Hawking
resulted in the appearance of ramps at several Delhi
tourist sights including the Red Fort, Qutub Minar
and Jantar Mantar. Following a 1997 court case,
most major Indian airports have also been made a
lot more accessible for chair users.

If you walk with difficulty, you will find India's
many street obstacles and steep stairs hard going.
Another factor that can be a problem is the
constant barrage of people proffering things (hard
to wave aside if you are, for instance, on crutches),
and all that queueing, not to mention heat, will take
it out of you if you have a condition that makes you
tire quickly. A light, folding camp-stool is one thing
that could be invaluable if you have limited walking
or standing power.

Then again, Indian people are likely to be very
helpful if, for example, you need their help getting
on and off buses or up stairs. Taxis and rickshaws are
easily affordable and very adaptable; if you rent one
for a day, the driver is certain to help you on and off,
and perhaps even around the sites you visit. If you
employ a guide, they may also be prepared to help
you with steps and obstacles.

If complete independence is out of the question,
going with an able-bodied companion might be
on the cards. Some package tour operators try to
cater for travellers with disabilities – Bales and
Somak among them – but you should always
contact any operator and discuss your exact needs
with them before making a booking. You should
also make sure you are covered by any insurance
policy you take out.

For more information about disability issues in
India, check the Disability India Network website at
Ⓦ disabilityindia.org.

Delhi

HUMAYUN'S TOMB

1

Delhi

Delhi is the symbol of old India and new…even the stones here whisper to our ears of the ages of long ago and the air we breathe is full of the dust and fragrances of the past, as also of the fresh and piercing winds of the present.

Jawaharlal Nehru

India's capital, Delhi is the hub of the country: a buzzing international metropolis which draws people from across India and the globe. Home to fifteen million people, it's big, sprawling and still growing. Yet tucked away inside Delhi's modern suburbs and developments are tombs, temples and ruins dating back centuries; in some places, the remains of whole cities from the dim and distant past nestle among homes and highways built in just the last decade or two. The result is a city full of fascinating nooks and crannies that you could happily spend weeks, or even months, exploring.

From a tourist's perspective, Delhi is divided into two main parts. **Old Delhi** is the city of the Mughals and dates back to the seventeenth century. It's the capital's most frenetic quarter, and its most Islamic, a reminder that for more than seven hundred years Delhi was a Muslim-ruled city. While many of the buildings enclosing Old Delhi's teeming bazaars have a tale to tell, its greatest monuments are undoubtedly the magnificent constructions of the Mughals, most notably the mighty **Red Fort**, and the **Jama Masjid**, India's largest and most impressive mosque.

To the south, encompassing the modern city centre, is **New Delhi**, built by the British to be the capital of their empire's key possession. A spacious city of tree lined boulevards, New Delhi is also impressive in its own way. The **Rajpath**, stretching from **India Gate** to the Presidential Palace, is at least as mighty a statement of imperial power as the Red Fort, and it's among the broad avenues of New Delhi that you'll find most of the city's museums, not to mention its prime shopping area, centred around the colonnaded facades of **Connaught Place**, the heart of downtown Delhi.

As the city expands, however – which it is doing at quite a pace – the centre of New Delhi is becoming too small to house the shops, clubs, bars and restaurants needed to cater to the affluent and growing middle class. Many businesses are moving into **South Delhi**, the vast area beyond the colonial city. Here, among the modern developments, and new business and shopping areas, is where you'll find some of Delhi's most ancient and fascinating attractions. Facing each other at either end of Lodi Road, for example, lie the constructions marking two ends of the great tradition of Mughal garden tombs: **Humayun's Tomb**, its genesis, and **Safdarjang's Tomb**, its last gasp. Here too, you'll find the remains of the six cities that preceded Old Delhi, most notably the **Qutb Minar** and the rambling ruins of **Tughluqabad**.

As a place to hit India for the first time, Delhi isn't a bad choice. The city is used to foreigners: hotels in all price ranges cater specifically for foreign tourists, and you'll meet plenty of experienced fellow travellers who can give you tips and pointers. And there's certainly no shortage of things to see and do while you acclimatize yourself to the Subcontinent. Quite apart from its historical treasures, Delhi has a host of **museums** and art treasures, cultural performances and crafts that showcase the country's diverse heritage. The city's growing **nightlife** scene boasts designer bars, chic

Delhi history p.82	**Recommended trains from Delhi** p.103
Sound-and-light shows p.92	**Delhi scams** p.104
Travel agents and tour operators p.102	**City and regional tours** p.105

QAWWALI CONCERT, HAZRAT NIZAMUDDIN DARGAH

Highlights

❶ **Rajpath** The centrepiece of Lutyens' imperial New Delhi, this wide boulevard epitomizes the spirit of the British Raj. **See p.83**

❷ **Paharganj** Frenetic market and hotel district opposite the New Delhi railway station. **See p.85**

❸ **National Museum** The country's finest museum, with exhibits from more than five thousand years of Indian culture. **See p.87**

❹ **Humayun's Tomb** An elegant red-brick forerunner of the Taj Mahal, whose lovely gardens offer an escape from the heat. **See p.89**

❺ **Hazrat Nizamuddin** A Sufi shrine in a deeply traditional Muslim quarter, where hypnotic *qawwali* music is performed every Thursday. **See p.90**

❻ **Red Fort** Delhi's most famous monument, this imposing sandstone fort is a ghostly vestige of Mughal splendour. **See p.92**

❼ **Jama Masjid** Shah Jahan's great mosque, with huge minarets offering bird's-eye views over the old city. **See p.96**

❽ **Qutb Minar Complex** The ruins of Delhi's first incarnation, a thirteenth-century city dominated by an impressive Victory Tower. **See p.100**

HIGHLIGHTS ARE MARKED ON THE MAP ON PP.80–81

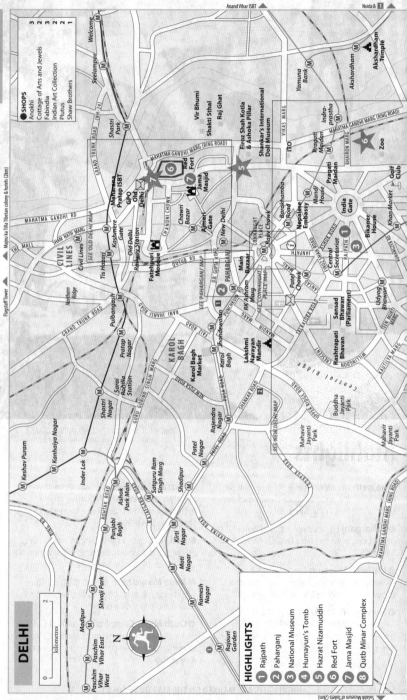

DELHI

0 ————— 2
kilometres

N

SHOPS
Anokhi 3
Cottage of Arts and Jewels 2
Fabindia 3
Indian Art Collection 2
Plutus 2
Shaw Brothers 1

HIGHLIGHTS
1 Rajpath
2 Paharganj
3 National Museum
4 Humayun's Tomb
5 Hazrat Nizamuddin
6 Red Fort
7 Jama Masjid
8 Qutb Minar Complex

1

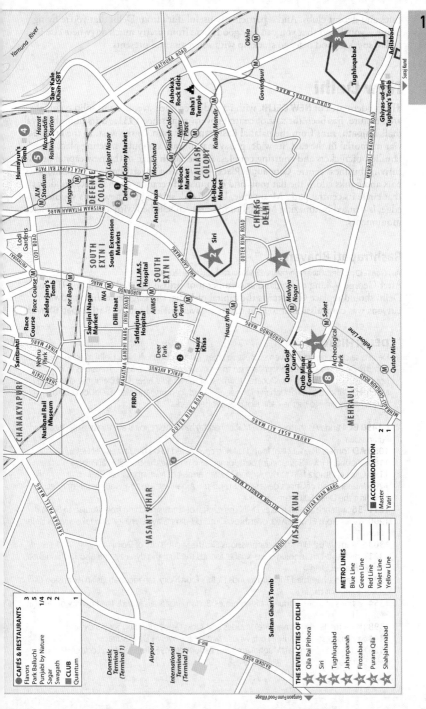

● CAFÉS & RESTAURANTS
Flavors 3
Park Balluchi 5
Punjabi by Nature 1/4
Sagar 2
Swagath 2
■ CLUB
Quantum 1

THE SEVEN CITIES OF DELHI
Qila Rai Pithora
Siri
Tughluqabad
Jahanpanah
Firozabad
Purana Qila
Shahjahanabad

METRO LINES
Blue Line
Green Line
Red Line
Violet Line
Yellow Line

■ ACCOMMODATION
Master 2
Yatri 1

1

cafés and decent clubs. And – particularly useful if it's from Delhi that you're flying home – you'll find that you can buy goods here from pretty much anywhere else in India, so it's a good place to stock up with souvenirs and presents.

New Delhi

The modern area of **NEW DELHI**, with its wide tree lined avenues and solid colonial architecture, has been the seat of central government since 1931. At its hub, the royal mall, **Rajpath**, runs from the palatial **Rashtrapati Bhavan**, in the west, to the **India Gate** war memorial in the east. Its wide, grassy margins are a popular meeting place for families, picnickers and courting couples. At the north edge of the new capital lies the thriving business centre, **Connaught Place**, where neon advertisements for restaurants, bars and banks adorn the flat roofs and colonnaded verandas of the white buildings that circle its central park. Meanwhile, Lodi Road, skirting the new city's southern edge, is flanked by amazing Mughal tombs and embellished with a park full of ancient monuments.

Rashtrapati Bhavan

Vijay Chowk • ⓦ presidentofindia.nic.in/rashtrapati_bhavan.html • ⓜ Central Secretariat

After George V, king of England and emperor of British India, decreed in 1911 that Delhi should replace Calcutta as the capital of India, the English architect **Edwin Lutyens** was commissioned to plan the new governmental centre. **Rashtrapati Bhavan**,

---

DELHI HISTORY

Delhi is said to consist of seven successive cities, with British-built New Delhi making an eighth. In truth, Delhi has centred historically on three main areas: Lal Kot and extensions to its northeast, where the city was located for most of the Middle Ages; Old Delhi, the city of the Mughals, founded by Shah Jahan in the seventeenth century; and New Delhi, built by the British just in time to be the capital of independent India.

c.1450 BC Pandavas (heroes of the Mahabharata) have their capital at Indraprastha, near Purana Qila
1060 AD Tomars (Rajput clan) found Lal Kot, considered to be the first city of Delhi
1180 Chauhans (rival Rajput clan) oust Tomars and rename the city Qila Lal Pithora
1191 Qila Lal Pithora falls to the Afghan Muslim armies of Muhammad of Ghor
1206 Muhammad of Ghor's general, Qutb-ud-din Aibak, sets up as an independent ruler, founding the Delhi Sultanate
1211–36 Sultan Iltutmish makes Delhi the capital of lands stretching from Punjab to Bengal
1290 Khaljis, from Central Asia, overthrow Qutb-ud-din's "Slave Dynasty" and take over as Delhi sultans
1303 Sultan Ala-ud-Din Khalji commissions Siri, the second city of Delhi
1321 Ghiyas-ud-Din Tughluq ousts Khaljis, founds the Tughluq dynasty, and also Tughluqabad, the third city of Delhi
1326 Sultan Muhammad Tughluq founds Delhi's fourth city, Jahanpanah, as an extension of Lal Kot, joining it to Siri
1354 As the sultanate gradually disintegrates, Sultan Firoz Shah founds the fifth city of Delhi at Firozabad
1398 Timur the Lame (Tamerlaine) invades and sacks Delhi, founding Sayyid dynasty
1444 Sayyids ousted by Buhul Lodi, whose family take over as Delhi sultans
1526 First Battle of Panipat: Mughal emperor Babur defeats Sultan Ibrahim Lodi, ending the Delhi Sultanate

the official residence of the president of India, is one of the largest and most grandiose of the Raj constructions, built by Lutyens and Herbert Baker between 1921 and 1929. Despite its classical columns, Mughal-style domes and chhatris and Indian filigree work, the whole building is unmistakeably British in character. Its majestic proportions are best appreciated from India Gate to the east – though with increasing pollution, the view is often clouded by a smoggy haze. The apartments inside are strictly private, but the **gardens** at the west side are open to the public for two weeks in February or March (exact date changes annually; entrance via gate 35, accessed from Church Road; free). Modelled on Mughal pleasure parks, with a typically ordered square pattern of quadrants dissected by waterways and refreshed by fountains, Lutyens' gardens extend beyond the normal confines to include tennis courts, butterfly enclosures, vegetable and fruit patches and a swimming pool.

Rajpath

Ⓜ Central Secretariat

Vijay Chowk, immediately in front of Rashtrapati Bhavan, leads into the wide, straight **Rajpath**, flanked with gardens and fountains that are floodlit at night, and the scene of annual **Republic Day** celebrations (Jan 26). Rajpath runs east to **India Gate**. Designed by Lutyens in 1921, the high arch, reminiscent of the Arc de Triomphe in Paris, commemorates ninety thousand Indian soldiers killed fighting for the British in World War I, and bears the names of more than three thousand British and Indian soldiers who died on the Northwest frontier and in the Afghan War of 1919. The extra memorial beneath the arch honours the lives lost in the Indo-Pakistan War of 1971.

1540 Sher Shah Suri ousts Babur's son Humayun and founds the sixth city of Delhi at Purana Qila

1556 Humayun retakes Delhi but dies the following year

1565 Humayun's son Akbar shifts the Mughal capital from Delhi to Agra

1638 Akbar's grandson Shah Jahan shifts the capital back to Delhi, creating its seventh city at Shahjahanabad (Old Delhi)

1739 Persian emperor Nadir Shah sacks Delhi, slaughtering 15,000 of its inhabitants as Mughal power crumbles

1784 The Marathas (see p.1159) subdue Delhi, making the emperor their vassal

1803 In the Battle of Delhi, Britain's East India Company defeat the Marathas and take over as effective rulers

1857 In the great uprising (First War of Independence), Delhi supports the insurgents, but the British retake the city with bloody reprisals, deposing the Mughals and expelling Muslim Delhiites for two years

1911 The British decide on a new Indian capital at Delhi as opposition to colonial rule mounts in Calcutta

1931 New Delhi officially inaugurated as capital of the Raj

1947 British hand over power in Delhi to India's first elected government, but Hindu mobs drive many Muslims from the city, while Hindu and Sikh refugees flood in from Punjab and Bengal

1957 Delhi Development Authority (DDA) founded to plan the city's development

1975–77 Indira Gandhi's Emergency: forced evictions of Muslim slum-dwellers in Old Delhi

1984 Indira Gandhi's assassination, followed by sectarian riots targetting Delhi's Sikh population

1992 Delhi gains status of Capital Territory (CT), with its own government, but not full statehood; BJP take power in CT elections

1998 Congress Party wrests the CT from the BJP, and holds power to this day

2002 First metro line opens

2013 Gang rape and murder of a student paramedic sparks worldwide protests

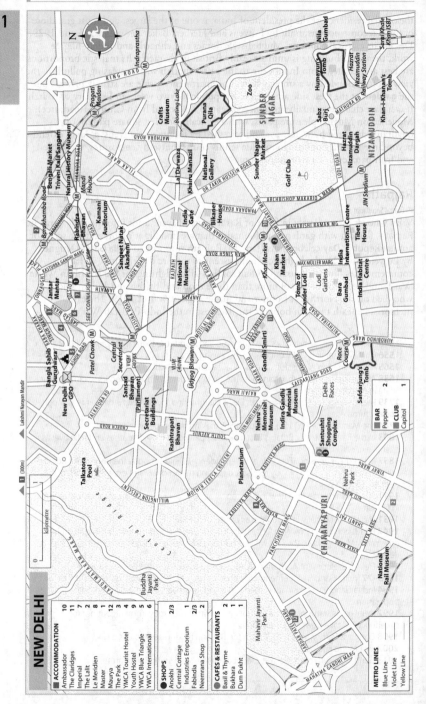

NEW DELHI

■ ACCOMMODATION

Ambassador	10
The Claridges	11
Imperial	7
The Lalit	2
Le Meridien	8
Master	12
Maurya	3
The Park	4
YMCA Tourist Hostel	9
Youth Hostel	5
YWCA Blue Triangle	6
YWCA International	

● SHOPS

Anokhi	2/3
Central Cottage	
Industries Emporium	1
Fabindia	2/3
Neemrana Shop	2

■ CAFÉS & RESTAURANTS

Basil & Thyme	2
Bukhara	1
Dum Pukht	1

METRO LINES

Blue Line	
Violet Line	
Yellow Line	

■ BAR

Pepper	2

■ CLUB

Capitol	1

1

Connaught Place and around

Ⓦ connaughtplacemall.com • Ⓜ Rajiv Chowk

New Delhi's commercial hub, **Connaught Place** (known as "CP"), with its classical colonnades, is radically different from the bazaars of Old Delhi, which it superseded. Named after a minor British royal of the day, it takes the form of a circle, divided by eight radial roads and three ring roads into blocks lettered A–N. The term Connaught Place originally referred to the inner circle (now renamed Rajiv Chowk after Rajiv Gandhi), the outer one being Connaught Circus (now Indira Chowk, after Rajiv's mum). CP is crammed with restaurants, bars, shops, cinemas, banks and airline offices.

Jantar Mantar

Sansad Marg • Daily sunrise–sunset • ₹100 (₹5) • Ⓦ jantarmantar.org • Ⓜ Rajiv Chowk or Shivaji Stadium

South of Connaught Place on Sansad Marg, the **Jantar Mantar** was built in 1725, the first of five open-air observatories designed by the ruler of Jaipur, Jai Singh II, and precursor to his larger one in Jaipur (see p.130). Huge red- and white- slanting stone structures looming over palm trees and neat flowerbeds were used to calculate time, solar and lunar calendars and astrological movements with an admirable degree of accuracy.

Bangla Sahib Gurudwara

Ashok Rd by New Delhi GPO • Ⓦ banglasahib.org • Ⓜ Shivaji Stadium

Southwest of Connaught Place, by the New Delhi General Post Office, the vast white marble structure of **Bangla Sahib Gurudwara** is Delhi's biggest Sikh temple, topped by a huge, golden, onion-shaped dome that is visible from some distance. The temple commemorates a 1664 visit to Delhi by the eighth Sikh guru, Hare Krishan, and welcomes visitors; deposit shoes at the information centre, where you can also enlist the services of a free guide. Remember to cover your head and dress conservatively. Live devotional music (vocals, harmonium and tabla) is relayed throughout the complex, and everybody is invited to share a simple meal of dhal and chapattis, served three times daily.

Lakshmi Narayan Mandir

Mandir Marg • Daily 4.30am–1.30pm & 2.30–9pm • Ⓜ Ramakrishna Ashram Marg or Shivaji Stadium

Lakshmi Narayan Mandir, northwest of New Delhi GPO and directly west of Connaught Place, is a modern Hindu temple that also welcomes tourists (deposit cameras, shoes and mobile phones at the entrance). With its white, cream and red brick domes, it was commissioned by a wealthy merchant family, the Birlas (hence its alternative name, Birla Mandir). The main shrine is dedicated to Lakshmi, goddess of wealth (on the right), and her consort Narayana, aka Vishnu, the preserver of life (on the left, holding a conch). At the back is a tiny ornate chamber decorated with coloured stones and mirrors and dedicated to Krishna, one of Vishnu's earthly incarnations. Devotional music is played throughout, and quotes from Hindu scriptures, many translated into English, adorn the walls.

Paharganj

Ⓜ Ramakrishna Ashram Marg or New Delhi

North of Connaught Place and directly west of New Delhi railway station, **Paharganj**, centred around Main Bazaar, provides the first experience of the Subcontinent for many budget travellers. Packed with cheap hotels, restaurants, cafés and *dhabas*, and with a busy fruit and vegetable market halfway along, it's also a paradise for shoestring shoppers seeking psychedelic clothing, joss sticks, bags and oils of patchouli or sandalwood.

There is also a less-visible underside to life in Paharganj, in the shape of the **street children**. Most are runaways who've left difficult homes, often hundreds of kilometres away, and the majority sleep on the streets and inhale solvents to numb their pain. The Salaam Baalak Trust (Ⓦ salaambaalaktrust.com), a local NGO working to help them,

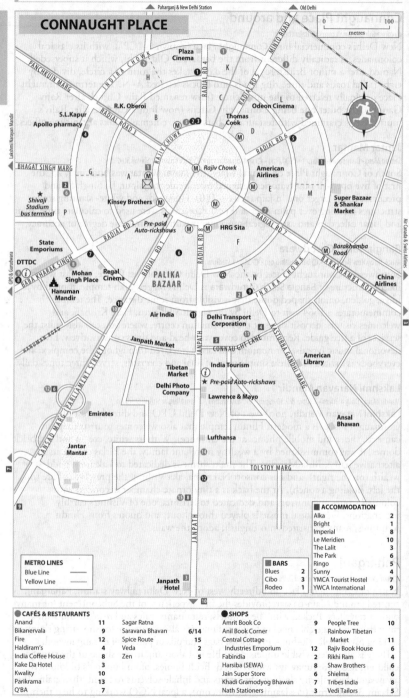

Paharganj & New Delhi Station

Old Delhi

CONNAUGHT PLACE

0   100
metres

N

Plaza Cinema

PANCHKUIN MARG

INDIRA CHOWK

MINTO ROAD

RADIAL RD 4

RADIAL RD 5

K

R.K. Oberoi

RADIAL ROAD 3

H

B

Thomas Cook

Odeon Cinema

L

S.L.Kapur

Apollo pharmacy

Lakshmi Narayan Mandir

C

RAJIV CHOWK

D

RADIAL RD 6

BHAGAT SINGH MARG

G

A

Rajiv Chowk

American Airlines

E

Super Bazaar & Shankar Market

M

Shivaji Stadium bus terminal

Kinsey Brothers

P

RADIAL RD 2

Pre-paid Auto-rickshaws

HRG Sita

RADIAL RD 1

RADIAL RD 8

RADIAL RD 7

BARAKHAMBA ROAD

Barakhamba Road

China Airlines

Air Canada & Swiss Airlines

State Emporiums

DTTCC

GPO & Gurudwara

BABA KHARAK SINGH

Mohan Singh Place

Regal Cinema

Hanuman Mandir

HANUMAN ROAD

PALIKA BAZAAR

INDIRA CHOWK

F

N

Air India

Janpath Market

JANPATH

Delhi Transport Corporation

CONNAUGHT LANE

KASTURBA GANDHI MARG

American Library

SANSAD MARG (PARLIAMENT STREET)

Emirates

Tibetan Market

Delhi Photo Company

India Tourism

Pre-paid Auto-rickshaws

Lawrence & Mayo

Ansal Bhawan

Jantar Mantar

Lufthansa

TOLSTOY MARG

JANPATH

METRO LINES
Blue Line
Yellow Line

Janpath Hotel

■ **BARS**
Blues	2
Cibo	3
Rodeo	1

■ **ACCOMMODATION**
Alka	2
Bright	1
Imperial	8
Le Meridien	10
The Lalit	3
The Park	6
Ringo	5
Sunny	4
YMCA Tourist Hostel	7
YWCA International	9

● **CAFÉS & RESTAURANTS**
Anand	11
Bikanervala	9
Fire	12
Haldiram's	4
India Coffee House	8
Kake Da Hotel	3
Kwality	10
Parikrama	13
Q'BA	7

Sagar Ratna	1
Saravana Bhavan	6/14
Spice Route	15
Veda	2
Zen	5

● **SHOPS**
Amrit Book Co	9
Anil Book Corner	1
Central Cottage Industries Emporium	12
Fabindia	2
Harsiba (SEWA)	6
Jain Super Store	6
Khadi Gramodyog Bhawan	7
Nath Stationers	3

People Tree	10
Rainbow Tibetan Market	11
Rajiv Book House	4
Rikhi Ram	6
Shaw Brothers	6
Shielma	8
Tribes India	8
Vedi Tailors	5

organizes **walking tours** of Paharganj conducted by former street children. Tours last two hours, usually start at 10am and cost ₹200. For bookings, contact ☎98731 30383 or ✉salaamwalk@yahoo.com. Proceeds go towards providing shelter, education and healthcare for the children themselves.

National Museum

11 Janpath • Tues–Sun 10am–5pm • ₹300 (₹10), camera ₹300 (₹20) • ⓦ nationalmuseumindia.gov.in • Ⓜ Udyog Bhawan

The **National Museum**, just south of Rajpath, provides a good overview of Indian culture and history. The foreigners' entry fee includes a free audio tour (₹150 in English for Indian citizens), but you need to leave a passport, driving licence, credit card or ₹2000 (or US$40/£40/€40) as a deposit, and the exhibits the tour covers are rather random. At a trot, you can see the museum in a couple of hours, but to get the best out of your visit you should set aside at least half a day.

The most important exhibits are on the ground floor, kicking off in **room 4** with the Harappan civilization. The Gandhara sculptures in **room 6** betray a very obvious Greco-Roman influence. **Room 9** has some very fine bronzes, most especially those of the Chola period (from south India between the ninth and the thirteenth centuries), and a fifteenth-century statue of Devi from Vijanaraya in south India, by the left-hand wall. Among the late medieval sculptures in **room 10** is a fearsome, vampire-like, late Chola *dvarapala* (a guardian figure built to flank the doorway to a shrine), also from south India, and a couple of performing musicians from Mysore. **Room 12** is devoted to the Mughals, and in particular their miniature paintings. Look out also for two paintings depicting a subject you wouldn't expect – the nativity of Jesus. It's worth popping upstairs to the **textiles**, and the **musical instruments** collection on the second floor is outstanding. The **Central Asian antiquities** collection includes a large number of paintings, documents, ceramics and textiles from Eastern Turkestan (Xinjiang) and the Silk Route, dating from between the third and twelfth centuries. On your way out, take a look at the massive twelve-tiered temple chariot from Tamil Nadu, an extremely impressive piece of woodwork in a glass shelter just by the southern entrance gate.

Nehru Memorial Museum

Museum Tues–Sun 9am–5pm • Free • ⓦ nehrumemorial.com **Planetarium** 40min astronomy shows in English Tues–Sun 11.30am & 3pm • ₹50 • ⓦ nehruplanetarium.org

The **Nehru Memorial Museum** was home to India's first prime minister, Jawaharlal Nehru, and is now preserved in his memory. One of Nehru's passions was astronomy, and there's a **planetarium** in the grounds of the house.

Indira Gandhi Memorial Museum

1 Safdarjang Rd • Tues–Sun 9.30am–5pm • Free • Ⓜ Race Course

Nehru's daughter, Indira Gandhi, despite her excesses during the 1975–77 Emergency (see p.1165), is still remembered by many with respect and affection. The **Indira Gandhi Memorial Museum** occupies the house where she was assassinated by her Sikh bodyguards in 1984; her bloodstained sari, chemically preserved, is on display, and there's a section devoted to her son Rajiv, including the clothes he was wearing when Sri Lankan Tamil separatists assassinated him in 1991.

Gandhi Smriti

5 Tees January Marg • Tues–Sun (& closed 2nd Sat of each month) 10am–5pm • Free • ⓦ gandhismriti.gov.in • Ⓜ Race Course

Still more tragic than the deaths of Rajiv and Indira Gandhi was the 1948 assassination of the nation's founder, Mahatma Gandhi, who shared their surname but was not

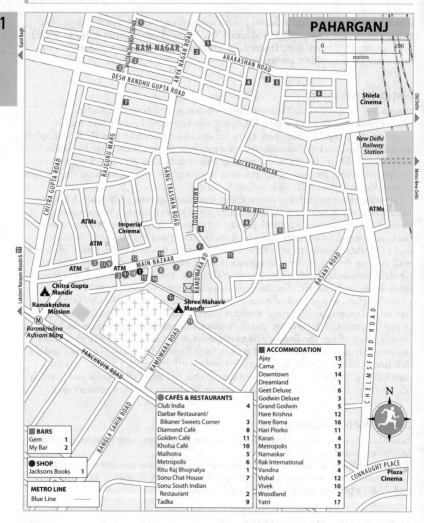

PAHARGANJ

CAFÉS & RESTAURANTS

Club India	4
Darbar Restaurant/	
Bikaner Sweets Corner	3
Diamond Café	8
Golden Café	11
Kholsa Café	10
Malhotra	5
Metropolis	6
Ritu Raj Bhojnalya	1
Sonu Chat House	7
Sonu South Indian	
Restaurant	2
Tadka	9

ACCOMMODATION

Ajay	15
Cama	7
Downtown	14
Dreamland	1
Geet Deluxe	6
Godwin Deluxe	3
Grand Godwin	5
Hare Krishna	12
Hare Rama	16
Hari Piorko	11
Karan	4
Metropolis	13
Namaskar	8
Rak International	9
Vandna	4
Vishal	12
Vivek	10
Woodland	2
Yatri	17

BARS

Gem	1
My Bar	2

SHOP

Jacksons Books	1

METRO LINE

Blue Line

related. The **Gandhi Smriti** is the house where the Mahatma lived his last days. He had come to Delhi to quell the sectarian rioting that accompanied Partition, but Hindu sectarian extremists hated him for protecting Muslims, and on 30 January 1948, one of them shot him dead. Visitors can view an exhibition about his life, and follow in his last footsteps to the spot where he died.

National Gallery of Modern Art

Jaipur House, India Gate (by Shershah Rd) • Tues–Sun 10am–5pm • ₹150 (₹10) • ⓦ ngmaindia.gov.in • Ⓜ Khan Market

Once the residence of the Maharaja of Jaipur, the extensive **National Gallery of Modern Art** is a rich showcase of Indian contemporary art. The permanent displays, focusing on post-1930s work, exhibit many of India's most important pieces of modern art, including work by the "Bengali Renaissance" artists Abanendranath Tagore and

Nandalal Bose, the great poet and artist Rabindranath Tagore, and Jamini Roy, whose work, reminiscent of Modigliani's, reflects the influence of Indian folk art. Also on show are the romantic paintings and etchings of Thomas Daniell and his nephew William, British artists of the Bombay or Company School, which combined Indian delicacy with Western realism. The ground-floor galleries are used for temporary exhibitions.

National Handicrafts and Handlooms Museum

Pragati Maidan, Bhairon Marg • Daily 9.30am–5pm • Free • ⓦ nationalcraftsmuseum.nic.in • ⓜ Indraprastha

Immediately north of Purana Qila (see below), the **National Handicrafts and Handlooms Museum** (NHHM, or **Crafts Museum**) is a dynamic exhibition of the rural arts and crafts of India, divided into three sections. The **exhibition galleries** show a range of textiles, carvings, ceramics, painting and metalwork from across India, while the **village complex** displays an assortment of traditional homes from different parts of the country. The **craft demonstrations** do feature a few artisans actually at work, but mostly they are more like shops selling crafts typical of different Indian regions. There's also a library and a fixed-price museum **shop**.

Purana Qila

Daily sunrise–sunset • ₹100 (₹5) • Bus #453, #454, #457 or #458 from New Delhi railway station gate 2 (Ajmeri Gate side) – ask for the zoo, which is the same stop

The majestic fortress of **Purana Qila**, whose crumbling ramparts dominate busy Mathura Road, east of India Gate, is thought to stand on the site of Indraprastha, the Pandava city of Mahabharata fame. Considered to be the sixth city of Delhi, it was begun by Humayun, the second Mughal emperor, as Din-Panah, and renamed Shergarh by Sher Shah Suri, who displaced him in 1540 and oversaw most of the construction.

Most of the inside of the fortress is taken up by pleasant lawns and gardens, but two important buildings survive. Of them, the **Qila-i-Kuhna Masjid** is one of Sher Shah's finest monuments. Constructed in 1541 in the Afghan style, it has five elegant arches, embellished with white and black marble to complement the red sandstone. The geometric patterns and carved Arabic calligraphy around the main doorway all represent a more sophisticated degree of decorative artwork than anything seen before in Delhi. Previous decorative carving on buildings had been in plaster, but here it's in stone, a more serious affair as it's obviously much harder to work.

The Purana Qila's other main building, the **Sher Mandal**, is a red-sandstone octagonal observatory and library built for Sher Shah. It was here in 1556 that the emperor Humayun died. He stumbled down its treacherously steep steps while hurrying to answer the muezzin's call to prayer, just a year after he had defeated Sher Shah's son Sikander Suri and regained power.

Humayun's Tomb

Hazrat Nizamuddin • Daily sunrise–sunset • ₹250 (₹10) • The tomb is 500m from Hazrat Nizamuddin railway station (one stop from New Delhi Station on the suburban line), and easily accessible by bus (#181 or #894 from Chelmsford Rd by New Delhi station; #893, #894 or #966 from Kasturba Gandhi Marg by Connaught Place), or by pre-paid auto from Connaught Place (₹60)

Close to the medieval Muslim centre of Nizamuddin, **Humayun's Tomb** stands at the crossroads of the Lodi and Mathura roads. Late afternoon is the best time to photograph it. Delhi's first Mughal mausoleum, it was constructed to house the remains of the second Mughal emperor, Humayun, and was built under the watchful eye of Haji Begum, his senior widow and mother of Akbar, who camped here for the duration, and is now buried alongside her husband. The grounds were later used to

1

inter several prominent Mughals, and served as a refuge for the last emperor, Bahadur Shah II, before his capture by the British in 1857.

The tomb's sombre, Persian-style elegance marks this as one of Delhi's finest historic sites. Constructed of red sandstone, inlaid with black and white marble, on a commanding podium looking towards the Yamuna River, it stands in the centre of the formal *charbagh*, or quartered garden. The octagonal structure is crowned with a double dome that soars to a height of 38m. Though it was the very first Mughal garden tomb – to be followed by Akbar's at Sikandra (see p.241) and, of course, the Taj Mahal at Agra (see p.233), for which it can be seen as a prototype – Humayun's mausoleum has antecedents in Delhi in the form of Ghiyas-ud-Din Tughluq's tomb at Tughluqabad (see p.99), and that of Sikandar Lodi in Lodi Gardens (see opposite). From the second of those it adopted its octagonal shape and the high central arch that was to be such a typical feature of Mughal architecture – you'll see it at the Taj, and in Delhi's Jama Masjid (see p.96), for example.

Within the grounds southeast of the main mausoleum, another impressive square mausoleum, with a double dome and two graves bearing Koranic inscriptions, is that of Humayun's barber, a man considered to be important because he was trusted with holding a razor to the emperor's throat.

Nila Gumbad

Nearby but outside the compound (so you'll have to walk right round for a closer look) stands the **Nila Gumbad** ("blue dome"), an octagonal tomb with a dome of blue tiles, supposedly built by one of Akbar's nobles to honour a faithful servant, and which may possibly predate Humayun's Tomb.

Tomb of Khan-i-Khanan

Daily sunrise–sunset • ₹100 (₹5)

On your way round to the Nila Gumbad (depending on your route), you pass the **tomb of Khan-i-Khanan**, a Mughal general who died in 1626; unfortunately, the tomb looks rather ragged as the facing was all stripped for use in Safdarjang's tomb, and the garden that surrounded it has mostly gone. Nearby, the blue-domed structure in the middle of the road junction in front of the entrance to Humayun's tomb is a seventeenth-century tomb called **Sabz Burj** – the tiles on its dome are not original, but the result of a recent restoration.

Nizamuddin

Just across the busy Mathura Road from Humayun's Tomb, and now engulfed by a busy road network and plush suburbs, the self-contained *mahalla* (village) of **Nizamuddin**, with its lack of traffic, ancient mosques and tombs and slow pace of life, is so different from the surrounding city that to enter it is like passing through a time warp. At its heart, surrounded by a tangle of narrow alleyways lined with shops and market stalls, lies one of Sufism's greatest shrines, the **Hazrat Nizamuddin Dargah**, which draws a constant stream of devotees from far and wide.

Hazrat Nizamuddin Dargah

The marble *dargah* is the tomb of Sheikh Nizam-ud-Din Aulia (1236–1325), fourth saint of the Chishtiya Sufi order founded by Khwaja Muin-ud-din Chishti of Ajmer (see box, p.164), and was built the year the sheikh died, but has been through several renovations, and the present mausoleum dates from 1562. Lattice screens and arches in the inner sanctum surround the actual tomb (closed to women), which is surrounded by a marble rail and a canopy of mother-of-pearl. Sheikh Nizam-ud-Din's disciple, the poet and chronicler **Amir Khusrau** – considered to be the first Urdu poet and the founder of *khyal*, the most common form of north Indian classical music – lies in a contrasting red-sandstone tomb in front of his master's mausoleum.

Religious song and music play an important role among the Chishtiyas, as among several Sufi orders, and *qawwals* (bards) gather to sing in the evenings (especially on Thursdays and feast days). Comprising a chorus led by solo singing accompanied by clapping and usually a harmonium combined with a *dholak* (double-membraned barrel drum) and tabla (paired hand-drums), the hypnotic rhythm of their **qawwali music** is designed to lull its audience into a state of *mast* (spiritual intoxication), which is believed to bring the devotee closer to God.

Jamat Khana Masjid

The oldest building in the area, the red-sandstone mosque of **Jamat Khana Masjid**, looms over the main *dargah* on its western side. It was commissioned in 1325 by Khizr Khan, the son of the Khalji sultan Ala-ud-Din. Enclosed by marble lattice screens next to Amir Khusrau's mausoleum, the tomb of **Princess Jahanara**, Shah Jahan's favourite daughter, is topped by a hollow filled with grass in compliance with her wish to have nothing but grass covering her grave. Just east of the *dargah* compound, the elegant 64-pillared white marble **Chausath Khamba** was built as a mausoleum for the family of a Mughal politician who had been governor of Gujarat, and the building, with its low, wide form and elegant marble screens, bears the unmistakeable evidence of Gujarati influence. The compound containing the Chausath is usually locked, but the caretaker should be on hand somewhere nearby to open it up should you want to take a closer look.

Lodi Gardens

Lodi Rd • Daily: April–Sept 5am–8pm, Oct–March 6am–8pm • Free • Ⓜ Khan Market or Jor Bagh

The leafy, pleasant **Lodi Gardens**, 2km west of Nizamuddin along Lodi Road, form part of a belt of fifteenth- and sixteenth-century monuments that now stand incongruously amid golf greens, large bungalows and elite estates. The park is especially full in the early mornings and early evenings, when fitness enthusiasts come for brisk walks or to jog through the manicured gardens against a backdrop of much-graffitied medieval monuments; it's also a popular lovers' hangout. The gardens, a ₹40 auto-ride from Connaught Place, also contain the **National Bonsai Park**, which has a fine selection of diminutive trees. The best time to come is at sunset, when the light is soft and the tombs are all lit up.

Near the centre of the gardens, the imposing **Bara Gumbad** ("large dome") is a square, late fifteenth-century tomb capped by the eponymous dome, its monotonous exterior relieved by grey and black stones and its interior adorned with painted stuccowork. **Shish Gumbad** ("glazed dome"), a similar tomb 50m north, still bears a few traces of the blue tiles liberally used to form friezes below the cornice and above the entrance. Inside, plasterwork is inscribed with ornate Koranic inscriptions.

The octagonal **tomb of Muhammad Shah** (ruled 1434–45) of the Sayyid dynasty stands 300m southwest of Bara Gumbad, surrounded by verandas and pierced by arches and sloping buttresses. Enclosed within high walls and a square garden, 300m north of Bara Gumbad, the **tomb of Sikandar Lodi** (ruled 1489–1517) repeats the octagonal theme, with a central chamber encircled by a veranda. **Athpula** ("eight piers"), a sixteenth-century ornamental bridge, lies east, in the northwest corner of the park.

Safdarjang's Tomb

Aurobindo Marg (opposite Lodi Rd) • Daily dawn–dusk • ₹100 (₹5) • Ⓜ Jor Bagh

The two-storeyed tomb of **Safdarjang** was the very last of India's great Mughal garden tombs. Built between 1753 and 1774, it dates from the period after Nadir Shah's sacking of the city, by which time the empire was reduced to a fraction of its former size and most of the capital's grander buildings lay in ruins. Safdarjang was the Mughal nawab (governor) of Avadh who briefly became vizier before being overthrown for his

1

Shi'ite beliefs. Emblematic of the decadence and degeneracy that characterized the twilight of the Mughal era, the mausoleum sports an elongated, tapered dome and absurdly ornate interior filled with swirling plasterwork. In *City of Djinns*, William Dalrymple aptly describes its quirky design as "blowzy Mughal rococo" typifying an age "not so much decaying into impoverished anonymity as one whoring and drinking itself into extinction". Facing east, it's at its most photogenic in the morning.

National Rail Museum

Service Rd, Chanakyapuri •Tues–Sun 9am–5.30pm • ₹20, video ₹100 • Bus #620 from Shivaji Stadium terminal by Connaught Place, or a pre-paid auto from Connaught Place (₹60)

The cream of India's royal coaches and oldest engines are on permanent display at the **National Rail Museum** in the embassy enclave of Chanakyapuri, southwest of Connaught Place. Some 27 locomotives and seventeen carriages – including the teak carriage of the maharaja of Mysore, trimmed in gold and ivory, and the cabin used by the Prince of Wales in 1876 – are kept in the grounds. A steam-hauled miniature "Joy Train" does a circuit of the grounds (₹20) whenever it has enough passengers.

The covered section of the museum houses models of famous engines and coaches, displays of old tickets, and even the skull of an elephant hit by a train near Bombay in 1894. The pride of the collection, however, is a model of India's very first train, a steam engine that made its inaugural journey of 21 miles from Bombay to Thane in 1853.

Old Delhi (Shahjahanabad)

Though it's not in fact the oldest part of Delhi, the seventeenth-century city of **Shahjahanabad**, built for the Mughal emperor Shah Jahan, is known as **OLD DELHI**. Construction began on the city in 1638, and within eleven years it was substantially complete, surrounded by more than 8km of ramparts pierced by fourteen main gates. It boasted a beautiful main thoroughfare, **Chandni Chowk**, an imposing citadel, the **Red Fort** (Lal Qila), and an impressive congregational mosque, the **Jama Masjid**. Today much of the wall has crumbled, and of the fourteen gates only four remain, but it's still a fascinating area, crammed with interesting nooks and crannies, though you'll need stamina, patience, time and probably a fair few chai stops along the way to endure the crowds and traffic. Old Delhi is served by metro stations at Chandni Chowk (actually nearer Old Delhi train station), Chawri Bazaar, and the Ajmeri Gate side of New Delhi Railway Station (the metro stop's name of "New Delhi" is, in this instance, misleading).

The Red Fort (Lal Qila)

Netaji Subhash Marg • **Fort** Tues–Sun sunrise–sunset • ₹250 (₹10) **Museums** 10am–5pm • ₹5 • Ⓜ Chandni Chowk

The largest of Old Delhi's monuments is **Lal Qila**, known in English as the **Red Fort** because of the red sandstone from which it was built. It was commissioned by Shah Jahan to be his residence and modelled on the fort at Agra. Work started in 1638, and the emperor moved in ten years later. The fort contains all the trappings you'd expect at the centre of Mughal government: halls of public and private audience,

---

SOUND-AND-LIGHT SHOWS

Each night except Monday, a **sound-and-light show** takes place in the **Red Fort**: the palaces are dramatically lit, and a historical commentary blares from crackly loudspeakers. The show starts after sunset and lasts an hour (in English Feb–April, Sept & Oct 8.30pm, May–Aug 9pm, Nov–Jan 7.30pm; weekdays ₹60, weekends and public holidays ₹80; ☎011 2327 4580). The mosquitoes are ferocious, so bring repellent. Heavy monsoon rains may affect summer shows.

domed and arched marble palaces, plush private apartments, a mosque and elaborately designed gardens. The ramparts, which stretch for more than 2km, are interrupted by two gates – **Lahori Gate** to the west, through which you enter, and Delhi Gate to the south. Shah Jahan's son, Aurangzeb, added barbicans to both gates. In those days, the Yamuna River ran along the eastern wall, feeding both the moat and a "stream of paradise" which ran through every pavilion. As the Mughal Empire declined, the fort fell into disrepair. It was attacked and plundered by the Persian emperor Nadir Shah in 1739, and by the British in 1857. Nevertheless, it remains an

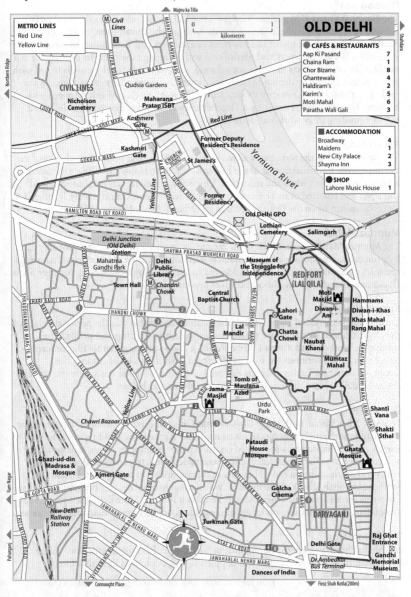

OLD DELHI

METRO LINES
Red Line
Yellow Line

0 ———— 1
kilometre

CAFÉS & RESTAURANTS
Aap Ki Pasand — 7
Chaina Ram — 1
Chor Bizarre — 8
Ghantewala — 4
Haldiram's — 2
Karim's — 5
Moti Mahal — 6
Paratha Wali Gali — 3

ACCOMMODATION
Broadway — 4
Maidens — 1
New City Palace — 2
Shayma Inn — 3

SHOP
Lahore Music House — 1

1

impressive testimony to Mughal grandeur. Keep your ticket stub as you will have to show it several times (for example, to enter the museums).

The main entrance to the fort from Lahori Gate opens onto **Chatta Chowk**, a covered street flanked with arched cells that used to house Delhi's most talented jewellers, carpet-makers, goldsmiths and silk-weavers, but is now given over to souvenir-sellers. At the end, a path to the left leads to the **Museum of the Struggle for Independence**, depicting resistance to British rule.

Diwan-i-Am

The **Naubhat Khana** ("Musicians' Gallery") marked the entrance into the royal quarters. Beyond it, a path leads ahead through wide lawns to the **Diwan-i-Am**, or Hall of Public Audience, where the emperor used to meet commoners and hold court. In those days it was strewn with silk carpets and partitioned with hanging tapestries. Its centrepiece is a marble dais on which sat the emperor's throne, surrounded by twelve panels inlaid with precious stones, mostly depicting birds and flowers. The most famous of them, in the middle at the top (and not easy to see), shows the mythological Greek Orpheus with his lute. The panels were made by a Florentine jeweller and imported from Italy, but the surrounding inlay work was done locally.

Rang Mahal

The pavilions along the fort's east wall face spacious gardens and overlook the banks of the Yamuna River. Immediately east of the Diwan-i-Am, **Rang Mahal**, the "Palace of Colour", housed the emperor's wives and mistresses. Originally, its ceiling was overlaid with gold and silver and reflected onto a central pool in the marble floor. Unfortunately, it suffered a lot of vandalism when the British used it as an Officers' Mess after the 1857 uprising.

Mumtaz Mahal

The **Mumtaz Mahal**, south of the main *zenana*, or women's quarters, and probably used by princesses, now houses an **Archeological Museum**, displaying manuscripts, paintings, ceramics and textiles, with a section devoted to the last Mughal emperor, Bahadur Shah II; exhibits include his silk robes and silver hookah pipe.

Khas Mahal

On the northern side of Rang Mahal, the marble **Khas Mahal** was the personal palace of the emperor, split into separate apartments for worship, sleeping and sitting. The southern chamber, **Tosh Khana** ("Robe Room"), has a stunning marble filigree screen on its north wall, surmounted by a panel carved with the scales of justice. The octagonal tower projecting over the east wall of the Khas Mahal was where the emperor appeared daily before throngs gathered on the riverbanks below.

Diwan-i-Khas

North of Khas Mahal, in the large **Diwan-i-Khas** ("Hall of Private Audience"), the emperor would address the highest nobles of his court. Today it's the finest building in the fort, a marble pavilion shaded by a roof raised on stolid pillars meeting in ornate scalloped arches and embellished with delicate inlays of flowers made from semiprecious stones. On the north and south walls you can still make out the inscription of a couplet in Persian attributed to Shah Jahan's prime minister, which roughly translates as: "If there be paradise upon this earthly sphere/It is here, oh it is here, oh it is here". More than just a paean, the verse refers to the deliberate modelling of the gardens on the Koranic description of heaven.

The hammams

A little further north are the **hammams**, or baths, sunk into the marble floor inlaid with patterns of precious stones, and dappled in jewel-coloured light that filters

FROM TOP JAMA MASJID (P.96); QUTB MINAR COMPLEX (P.100); CHANDNI CHOWK (P.96) >

1

through stained-glass windows. The western chamber contained hot baths while the eastern apartment, with fountains of rosewater, was used as a dressing room.

Moti Masjid

Next to the hammams, the sweetly fashioned **Moti Masjid**, or Pearl Mosque, triple-domed in white marble, was added by Aurangzeb in 1659, but unfortunately it's currently closed to the public.

Jama Masjid

Urdu Bazaar Rd • 8am till 30min before sunset; closed for 30min in the afternoon for afternoon prayers (in summer opens 7am) • ₹300 (in principle this is a camera charge, but in practise all foreigners have to pay it) • No shorts, short skirts or sleeveless tops • ⓜ Chawri Bazaar

A wonderful piece of Mughal pomp, the red-and-white **Jama Masjid** is India's largest mosque. Its courtyard is large enough to accommodate the prostrated bodies of 25,000 worshippers. It was designed by Shah Jahan and built by a workforce of five thousand people between 1644 and 1656. Originally called Masjid-i-Jahanuma ("mosque commanding a view of the world"), this grand structure stands on Bho Jhala, one of Shahjahanabad's two hills, and looks east to the sprawling Red Fort, and down on the seething streets of Old Delhi. Broad, red-sandstone staircases lead to gateways on the east, north and southern sides, where worshippers and visitors alike must remove their shoes (the custodian will guard them for you for a small tip).

Once inside the courtyard, your eyes will be drawn to the three bulbous marble domes crowning the **main prayer hall** on the west side (facing Mecca), fronted by a series of high cusped arches, and sheltering the *mihrab*, the central niche in the west wall indicating the direction of prayer. The pool in the centre is used for ritual ablutions. At each corner of the square yard a slender minaret crowned with a marble dome rises to the sky, and it's worth climbing the **tower** (₹100; women must be accompanied by a man) south of the main sanctuary for a view over Delhi. In the northeast corner a white shrine protects a collection of Muhammad's relics, including his sandals, a hair from his beard and his "footprint" miraculously embedded in a marble slab.

Chandni Chowk

Old Delhi's main thoroughfare, **Chandni Chowk** was once a sublime canal lined with trees and some of the most opulent bazaars in the whole of Asia. The British paved over the canal after 1857. Rickshaws are now allowed to operate along Chandni Chowk after the abolition of a 2007 ban, but traffic is extremely congested, and the best way to take it in is on foot. Along the way, look out for numbered "heritage buildings" signposted at intervals, with placards outside explaining their historical importance, especially during the 1857 uprising.

Lal Mandir

Daily 6am–noon & 6–9pm • Free but donations appreciated, especially for the bird hospital • ⓜ Chandni Chowk

At Chandni Chowk's eastern end, opposite the Red Fort, the **Lal Mandir** Jain temple is not as ornate as the Jain temples in Rajasthan (see p.212 & p.216), but it does boast detailed carvings, and gilded paintwork in the antechambers surrounding the main shrine. Remove your shoes and leave any leather articles at the kiosk before entering. The attached **bird hospital** puts into practice the Jain principle that all life is sacred by rescuing injured birds, with each species having its own ward; the sparrow ward is largely occupied by victims of ceiling fans, with which these poor critters frequently collide.

Raj Ghat

Mahatma Gandhi Marg • Daily 10am–8pm • Free

When Shah Jahan established his city in 1638, its eastern edges bordered the Yamuna River, and a line of *ghats*, or steps leading to the water, was installed along the riverbanks. *Ghats* have been used in India for centuries, for mundane things like washing clothes and bathing, but also for worship and funeral cremation. **Raj Ghat**, east of Delhi Gate – really more a park than a *ghat* – is the place where Mahatma Gandhi was cremated, on the day after his assassination in 1948. The Mahatma's *samadhi* (cremation memorial), a low black plinth inscribed with his reputed last words, "Hai Ram" ("Oh God"), receives a steady stream of visitors, and he is remembered through prayers here every Friday evening at 5pm, and on the anniversaries of his birth and death (Oct 2 & Jan 30).

North of Raj Ghat, memorials also mark the places where Jawaharlal Nehru (at Shanti Vana), his daughter Indira Gandhi (at Shakti Sthal), and his grandson Rajiv Gandhi (at Vir Bhumi) were cremated.

Gandhi Memorial Museum

Jawaharlal Nehru Marg • Tues–Sun 9.30am–5.30pm • Free

Opposite Raj Ghat's southwest corner, the small **Gandhi Memorial Museum** houses some of Gandhi's photographs and writings, and at weekends you can watch a film on his political and personal life (English Sat 4pm; Hindi Sun 4pm; 1hr).

Firoz Shah Kotla

Mahatma Gandhi Marg • Tues–Sun sunrise–sunset • ₹100 (₹5)

Supposedly, Firoz Shah, sultan of Delhi from 1351 to 1358, had a whole fifth city of Delhi built – Firozabad, founded in 1354. Today few traces survive of what was in any case probably never more than a suburb of the main city, but what does remain is the fortified palace of **Firoz Shah Kotla**, now a crumbling ruin with ornamental gardens 1500m south of Delhi Gate. Its most incongruous and yet distinctive element is the third-century BC polished sandstone **Ashokan pillar**, carried down the Yamuna River by raft from Ambala. For a reasonable view of the column, you'll need to climb to the top of the building, entering the compound through a gate on the west side, then mounting a stairway in the northeast corner. From the top you also get a view of the neighbouring mosque and *baoli* (step-well), as well as the lawns that make the site such a pleasant place to visit.

Old Delhi GPO and around

Netaji Subhash Marg leads north from the Red Fort and under a railway bridge to Old Delhi GPO. Just before the post office, on the east side of the road, **Lothian Cemetery**, the burial ground for officers of the East India Company from 1808 until just after the 1857 uprising, had become very run-down, but was being renovated at last check. In the middle of the road in front of the post office, the remains of the East India Company's **Magazine** or arsenal is now used mainly as an unofficial public toilet, so watch your step if you cross the street to explore it. Another part of the magazine, with a memorial plaque, stands on a second traffic island just to the north. Continuing north along Lothian Road, you'll pass another remnant of Company days on your right in the form of the old **Residency**, now the Archeology Department of Guru Gobind Singh Indraprastha University.

St James's Church

Lothian Rd • Daily 8.30am–1pm & 2.30–5pm

A couple of hundred metres north of the Residency is the rather fine cream-and-white baroque facade of **St James's Church**, commissioned in 1836 by **James Skinner**, the son

1

of a Scottish Company-wallah and a Rajput princess. Because of his mixed ancestry, and the increasing racism of the British regime, Skinner was refused a commission in the Company's army, but set up his own irregular cavalry unit (Skinner's Horse, also called the Yellow Boys after their uniform) and made himself pretty much indispensable to the Company in northern India. Though he was continually snubbed over pay and rank, his astounding victories over the forces of the maharajah of Jaipur and the great Sikh leader Maharajah Ranjit Singh eventually forced the Company to begrudgingly grant him the rank of Lieutenant Colonel and absorb his cavalrymen into its ranks. Skinner died in 1842 and is buried just in front of the altar.

Qudsia Gardens

Yamuna Marg

The double-arched **Kashmiri Gate**, on the west side of Lothian Road just 300m north of St James's Church, was where the Mughal court would leave Delhi every summer bound for the cool valley of Kashmir. To its north is Maharana Pratap ISBT, beyond which, across the busy Lala Hardev Sahai Marg, the peaceful **Qudsia Gardens** are a fading remnant of the magnificent pleasure parks commissioned in the mid-eighteenth century by Queen Qudsia, favourite mistress of Muhammad Shah, and mother of Ahmed Shah.

Nicholson Cemetery

Lala Hardev Sahai Marg • Daily: summer 8am–6pm; winter 9am–5pm

Just west of the Qudsia Gardens is Delhi's oldest burial ground, **Nicholson Cemetery**, named after Brigadier General John Nicholson, who was shot down while leading the British attack to regain Delhi from the 1857 insurgents.

South Delhi

Most of the early settlements of Delhi, including its first city at Qila Rai Pithora (around the Qutb Minar), are to be found not in "Old Delhi" but in **South Delhi**, the area south of Lutyens' carefully planned boulevards, where the rapid expansion of suburban Delhi has swallowed up what was previously countryside. Whole villages have been embedded within it, and the area is littered with monuments from the past. Meanwhile, as the centre becomes more and more congested, South Delhi's housing enclaves and colonies are increasingly home to the newest shopping centres and the most happening locales.

Hauz Khas

Ⓜ Green Park

Set amid parks and woodland 4km south of Safdarjang's Tomb, the wealthy suburban development of **Hauz Khas** is typical of South Delhi in being a thoroughly modern area dotted with remnants of antiquity. The modern part takes the form of Hauz Khas village, a shopping area packed with chic boutiques and smart restaurants. There's also a very pleasant deer park and a rose garden, but of most interest to visitors, apart from the upmarket **shopping** possibilities (see pp.116–118), are the ruins of a fourteenth-century reservoir at the western end of the village.

Sultan Ala-ud-Din Khalji had the reservoir (or "tank") built in 1304 to supply water to his citadel at Siri, Delhi's "second city", and it was known after him as **Hauz-i-Alai**. Half a century later, it was expanded by Firoz Shah, who added a two-storey seminary and a mosque at its northern end. Among the anonymous tombs scattered throughout the area is that of Firoz Shah himself, directly overlooking the southern corner of the tank. Its high walls, lofty dome, and doorway spanned by a lintel with a stone railing outside are fine examples of Hindu Indian traditions effectively blended with Islamic architecture.

Siri itself was located a couple of kilometres east of Hauz Khas, and the remains of its ramparts can be seen from Khel Gaon Marg. Much of the site has been given over to parkland, which makes it pleasant enough to visit, but part of it has been subsumed by a village built to house athletes competing in the 1982 Asian Games.

The Baha'i Temple

Bahapur, Kalkaji • Tues–Sun: April–Sept 9am–7pm; Oct–March 9am–6pm (you may be asked to wait briefly outside during services, which are on the hour 9am–noon & 3–5pm) • ⓦ bahaihouseofworship.in • Ⓜ Kalkaji Mandir

Often compared visually to the Sydney Opera House, Delhi's **Baha'i Temple** is an iconic piece of modern architecture that dominates the surrounding suburban sprawl. Twenty-seven spectacular giant white petals of marble in the shape of an unfolding lotus spring from nine pools and walkways, to symbolize the nine unifying spiritual paths of the Baha'i faith; each petal alcove contains an extract from the Baha'i holy scriptures. Set amid well-maintained gardens, the temple is at its most impressive at sunset.

Ashoka's Rock Edict

Off Raja Dhirsain Marg, northwest of the Baha'i Temple • Ⓜ Nehru Place

Ashoka's Rock Edict is a ten-line epigraph inscribed in ancient Brahmi script on a smooth, sloping rock. The rock, now protected by a shelter in its own little park, was used as a slide by neighbourhood kids until 1966, when local residents noticed the ancient inscription, which was promulgated by the Mauryan emperor Ashoka the Great in the third century BC, and shows there must have been an important settlement nearby. It states that the emperor's exertions in the cause of dharma (righteousness) had brought the people closer to the gods, and that through their efforts this attainment could be increased even further.

Tughluqabad

Daily sunrise–sunset • ₹100 (₹5) • Ⓜ Tughluqabad

Some 15km southeast of Connaught Place on the Mehrauli–Badarpur Road (the entrance is 1km east of the junction with Guru Ravidas Marg), a rocky escarpment holds the crumbling 6.5km-long battlements of the third city of Delhi, **Tughluqabad**, built during the short reign of Ghiyas-ud-din Tughluq (1320–24). After the king's death the city was deserted, probably due to the lack of a clean water source nearby. The most interesting area is the high-walled **citadel** in the southwestern part of the site, though only a long underground passage, the ruins of several halls and a tower now remain. The grid pattern of some of the city streets to the north is still traceable. The palace area is to the west of the entrance, and the former bazaar to the east.

The southernmost of Tughlaqabad's thirteen gates still looks down on a causeway, breached by the modern road, which rises above the flood plain, to link the fortress with **Ghiyas-ud-Din Tughluq's tomb** (same hours and ticket as Tughlaqabad). The tomb is entered through a massive red-sandstone gateway leading into a courtyard surrounded by cloisters in the defensive walls. In the middle, surrounded by a well-kept lawn, stands the distinctive mausoleum, its sloping sandstone walls topped by a marble dome, and in its small way a precursor to the fine series of garden tombs built by the Mughals, which began here in Delhi with that of Humayun (see p.89). Inside the mausoleum are the graves of Ghiyas-ud-Din, his wife and their son Muhammad Shah

1

II. Ghiyas-ud-Din's chief minister, Jafar Khan, is buried in the eastern bastion, and interred in the cloister nearby is the sultan's favourite dog.

The later fortress of **Adilabad** (free entry), built by Muhammad Shah II in much the same style as his father's citadel, and now in ruins, stands on a hillock to the southeast.

Qutb Minar Complex

Ladha Sarai, Mehrauli · Daily sunrise–sunset · ₹250 (₹10) · Ⓜ Saket

Above the foundations of Lal Kot, the "first city of Delhi" founded in the eleventh century by the Tomar Rajputs, stand the first monuments of Muslim India, known as the **Qutb Minar Complex**. You'll find it 13km south of Connaught Place off Aurobindo Marg. One of Delhi's most famous landmarks, the fluted red-sandstone tower of the **Qutb Minar** tapers upwards from the ruins, covered with intricate carvings and deeply inscribed verses from the Koran, to a height of just over 72m. In times past it was considered one of the "Wonders of the East", second only to the Taj Mahal; but historian John Keay was perhaps more representative of the modern eye when he claimed that the tower had "an unfortunate hint of the factory chimney and the brick kiln; a wisp of white smoke trailing from its summit would not seem out of place".

Work on the Qutb Minar started in 1202; it was Qutb-ud-Din Aibak's victory tower, celebrating the advent of the Muslim dominance of Delhi (and much of the Subcontinent) that was to endure until 1857. For Qutb-ud-Din, who died four years after gaining power, it marked the eastern extremity of the Islamic faith, casting the shadow of God over east and west. It was also a minaret, from which the muezzin called the faithful to prayer. Only the first storey has been ascribed to Qutb-ud-din's own short reign; the other four were built under his successor Iltutmish, and the top was restored in 1369 under Firoz Shah, using marble to face the red sandstone.

The Quwwat-ul-Islam mosque

Adjacent to the tower lie the ruins of India's first mosque, **Quwwat-ul-Islam** ("the Might of Islam"), commissioned by Qutb-ud-Din and built using the remains of 27 Hindu and Jain temples with the help of Hindu artisans whose influence can be seen in the detail of the masonry and the indigenous corbelled arches. Steps lead to an impressive courtyard flanked by cloisters and supported by pillars unmistakeably taken from a Hindu temple and adapted to accord with strict Islamic law forbidding iconic worship – all the faces of the decorative figures carved into the columns have been removed. Especially fine ornamental arches, rising as high as 16m, remain of what was once the prayer hall. Beautifully carved sandstone screens, combining Koranic calligraphy with the Indian lotus, form a facade immediately to the west of the mosque, facing Mecca. The thirteenth-century Delhi sultan Iltutmish and his successors had the building extended, enlarging the prayer hall and the cloisters and introducing geometric designs, calligraphy, glazed tiles set in brick, and squinches (arches set diagonally to a square to support a dome).

Alai Minar

The Khalji sultan Ala-ud-Din had the mosque extended to the north, and aimed to build a tower even taller than the Qutb Minar, but his **Alai Minar** never made it beyond the first storey, which still stands, and is regarded as a monument to the folly of vain ambition. Ala-ud-Din also commissioned the **Alai Darwaza**, an elegant mausoleum-like gateway with stone lattice screens, to the south of the Qutb Minar.

The Iron Pillar

In complete contrast to the mainly Islamic surroundings, an **Iron Pillar** (7.2m) stands in the precincts of Qutb-ud-Din's original mosque, bearing fourth-century Sanskrit inscriptions of the Gupta period attributing it to the memory of King Chandragupta II (375–415 AD). Once topped with an image of the Hindu bird god, Garuda, the extraordinarily pure but rust-free pillar has puzzled metallurgists. Its rust resistance is apparently due to its containing as much as one percent phosphorous, which has acted as a chemical catalyst to create a protective layer of an unusual compound called misawite around the metal. The pillar was evidently transplanted here by the Tomars, but it's not known from where.

Archeological Park

Anuvrat Marg, Mehrauli • Daily sunrise–sunset • Free • Ⓜ Saket or Qutab Minar

The area south of the Qutb Minar Complex, rich with remains from all sorts of historical periods, has been turned into an **Archeological Park**. Here, within a very pleasant stroll of each other, and of Qutab Minar metro station, you'll find: the tomb of Ghiyas-ud-Din Balban, one of the Slave Dynasty sultans (reigned 1265–87), believed to be the first building in India constructed with true arches; the beautiful 1528 mosque and tomb of the poet Jamali Kamali (you may need to find the caretaker to open up the tomb for you); and the octagonal Mughal tomb of Muhammad Quli Khan, one of Akbar's courtiers, which was occupied in the early nineteenth century by Sir Thomas Metcalfe, the East India Company's resident at the Mughal court, who rather bizarrely converted it into a country house. Metcalfe made his mark on the area in other ways too, restoring a Lodi-period dovecote and constructing "follies" – mock-ancient pavilions, a typical feature of English country estates of the time, except that Metcalfe's were Indian in style. The park extends over more than a hundred hectares and contains more than eighty monuments, including tombs, mosques, gateways and *baolis*, dating from every century between the thirteenth and the twentieth.

Akshardham Temple

Noida Link Rd, Akshardham • Tues–Sun 9.30am–6.30pm • Free • Ⓦ akshardham.com • Ⓜ Akshardham

Across Nizamuddin Bridge on the east side of the Yamuna River, the opulent **Akshardham Temple** was erected in 2005 by the Gujarat-based Shri Swaminarayan sect. The temple is a stunning piece of art, embellished with wonderful carvings made using the same tools and techniques as in ancient times. Cameras, mobile phones, mirrors and any electronic equipment, including USB keys, are prohibited and should be deposited at the cloakroom outside. Visitors may not enter wearing shorts or skirts above the knee. The **main shrine** is surrounded by a pink sandstone relief (you must walk round it clockwise) whose theme is elephants; wild, domesticated or in legend. Inside, the centrepiece and main object of devotion is a 3m-high gold statue of the sect's founder, Bhagwan Shri Swaminarayan, attended by four disciples. Behind it are paintings depicting scenes from his life, and also personal objects such as his sandals and even some of his hair and nail clippings. The four subsidiary shrines are devoted to conventional Hindu gods.

ARRIVAL AND DEPARTURE DELHI

Delhi is India's main point of arrival for overseas visitors, and the major transport hub for north India, containing the country's main international **airport** as well as four **long-distance railway** stations and three **intercity bus** terminals. It seldom takes more than a day to arrange an onward journey. Scores of travel agents (see box, p.102) sell bus and air tickets, while many hotels (budget or otherwise) will book private buses for you. There's an ever-expanding network of internal flights, but it's still best to book as far ahead as possible; at peak times such as Diwali, demand is very high. While you can buy tickets directly from the airlines (see p.102), it can save time and legwork to book through an agency (see box, p.102). Some airlines still require you to reconfirm your flight between a week and 72 hours before leaving.

BY PLANE

Indira Gandhi International (IGI) Airport (Ⓣ 0124 337 6000, Ⓦ newdelhiairport.in), 20km southwest of the centre, has two separate terminals: international and some

domestic flights use Terminal 3, while other domestic services are at Terminal 1. Note if flying out on an e-ticket that you will not be allowed into the terminal without a printout of it. There are ATMs in the arrivals hall, plus Punjab

1

National Bank and Thomas Cook to change money. For those seeking accommodation, 24hr desks, including Indian Tourism (ITDC) and Delhi Tourism and Transport Development Corporation (DTTDC), have a list of approved hotels and can secure you reservations. The two terminals are adjacent but 6km apart by road; a free AAI shuttle bus, running every twenty minutes, connects them.

Airport Express Link The quickest and easiest option for getting to or from the city is the Airport Express Link metro line (ⓦdelhiairportexpress.com), which takes travellers between the airport and New Delhi rail station in forty minutes for ₹120; when the line is fully operational, the journey time should be less than twenty minutes.

Buses There is a 24hr city bus service (every 10–20min; 40min; ₹75, plus ₹25 for baggage) between the airport (both terminals) and Maharana Pratap Inter-state Bus Terminal (ISBT) in Old Delhi via Connaught Place, New Delhi Station (Ajmeri Gate side) and the Red Fort.

Taxis A taxi is particularly advisable if you leave or arrive late at night. There are several official pre-paid taxi kiosks in the arrival area; the fare will be around ₹350 to the city centre, with a 25 percent surcharge between 11pm and 5am; kiosk prices vary, so check a few first. Note that even these pre-paid taxi drivers may try to take you to hotels not of your choice (see box, p.104). Many hotels, including some of the Paharganj budget options, offer pick-up services from the airport, where you will be met with a driver bearing your name on a placard. This presents the smoothest and most reliable method of getting to your hotel from the airport,

though prices vary considerably, starting from around ₹300, but often twice as much or more. Most tourists leaving on night-flights book a taxi to the airport in advance (around ₹300; 30–60min) through their hotel.

Auto-rickshaws The auto-rickshaws that wait in line at the departure gate constitute the most precarious and least reliable form of transport from the airport, especially at night, though they're cheaper than a taxi; fares are around ₹180–200. A pre-paid auto from CP costs ₹160.

Airlines Air India, Safdarjung Airport, Aurobindo Marg ⓣ011 2462 2220; Go Air, Terminal 1-D, IGI Airport ⓣ011 2567 4480 or ⓣ1800 222111; IndiGo, Level 1, Tower C, Global Business Park, MG Rd, Gurgaon ⓣ99103 83838; Jet and JetKonnect, Jetair House, 13 Community Centre, Yusuf Sarai ⓣ011 3984 1111; Kingfisher, C-12 SDA Commercial Complex, opposite IIT Main Gate, Gamal Abdel Nasser Marg ⓣ1800 200 9000; PIA, 23 Narain Manzil (5th floor), 23 Barakhamba Rd ⓣ011 2373 7791; Royal Nepal Airlines, 44 Janpath ⓣ011 2332 0817; SpiceJet, 319 Udyog Vihar, Phase IV, Gurgaon ⓣ1800 180 3333; Sri Lankan Airlines, 312 World Trade Centre, Barakhamba Rd ⓣ011 4152 8630; Thai, *Hotel Intercontinental Eros*, American Plaza, Nehru Place ⓣ011 4149 7777.

BY TRAIN

Delhi has four major railway stations. All are notorious for theft: don't take your eyes off your luggage for a moment. Old Delhi and New Delhi stations are served by stops on the metro, but travelling on it with heavy baggage is

---

TRAVEL AGENTS AND TOUR OPERATORS

Don't book flights or excursions through any agency that you're directed to by a street tout, and that goes double for any agency spuriously trying to pass itself off as a tourist information office.

The Rajasthan Tourism Development Corporation Bikaner House, Pandara Rd ⓣ011 2338 3837 or ⓣ011 2338 6069, ⓦrtdc.in. Organizes package tours including wildlife tours and trips on the *Palace on Wheels* and *Royal Rajasthan on Wheels* trains.

The Delhi Tourism and Transport Development Corporation Coffee Home (opposite Hanuman Temple), Baba Kharak Singh Marg ⓣ011 2336 3607 or ⓣ011 2336 5358, ⓦdelhitourism.gov.in. Offers day-trips to Agra (₹1100) and three-day "Golden Triangle" excursions to Agra, Fatehpur Sikri, Jaipur and

Amber (₹4600).

Hotel Namaskar 917 Chandiwalan (off Main Bazaar), Paharganj ⓣ011 2358 2233, ⓦnamaskarhotel.com. Offers competitively priced car tours around Rajasthan and UP.

Ashok Travels and Tours Janpath Hotel, Janpath ⓣ011 2334 9067, ⓔtours@attindiatourism.com. The India Tourism Development Corporation's commercial arm, Ashok Travels, sells excursions and air tickets.

TICKETING

For **ticketing**, recommended operators specializing in international and domestic flights include:

Aa Bee Travel In the lobby of Hare Rama Guest House at T-298 off Main Bazaar, Paharganj ⓣ011 2356 2171 or ⓣ011 2356 2117, ⓔaabee@mail.com. A reliable firm for competitively priced air and private bus tickets.

Student Travel Information Centre G-55 Connaught Place ⓣ011 4620 6600, ⓦstatravel.co.in. Represents STA Travel in India, sells tickets and issues or renews ISIC cards.

RECOMMENDED TRAINS FROM DELHI

The trains below are recommended as the fastest and/or most convenient for specific cities. Daily unless marked.

Destination	Name	No.	From	Departs	Duration
Agra	Bhopal Shatabdi*	#12002	ND	6am	2hr 6min
	Taj Express	#12180	HN	7.10am	2hr 55min
	Mangala Express	#12618	HN	9.20am	3hr
	Kerala Express	#12626	ND	11.30am	2hr 55min
Ahmedabad	Ashram Express	#12916	OD	3.20pm	16hr 20min
	Rajdhani Express*	#12958	ND	7.55pm	13hr 40min
Ajmer	Shatabdi Express*	#12015	ND	6.05am	6hr 40min
	Ahmedabad Mail	#19106	OD	10.20pm	8hr 20min
Chandigarh	Shatabdi Express*	#12011	ND	7.40am	3hr 25min
	Paschim Express	#12925	ND	11.05am	4hr 52min
	Shatabdi Express*	#12005	ND	5.25pm	3hr 25min
Chennai	Tamil Nadu Express	#12622	ND	10.30pm	32hr 45min
	GT Express	#12616	HN	6.40pm	35hr 35min
Haridwar	Shatabdi Express*	#12017	ND	6.50am	4hr 35min
	Janshatabdi Express*	#12055	ND	5.50am	4hr 07min
Jaipur	Shatabdi Express*	#12015	ND	6.05am	4hr 25min
	Ashram Express	#12916	OD	3.20pm	5hr 05min
Jhansi	Shatabdi Express*	#12002	ND	6am	4hr 45min
Kolkata	Kolkata Rajdhani* (exc Fri)	#12302	ND	5pm	16hr 55min
	Sealdah Rajdhani*	#12314	ND	4.30pm	17hr 45min
	Poorva Express (Tu, W, Sa, Su)	#2304	ND	4.20pm	24hr 25min
	Kalka Mail	#12312	OD	5.48am	26hr 07min
Mumbai	Rajdhani Express*	#12952	ND	4.30pm	16hr 05min
Udaipur	Mewar Express	#12963	HN	7.05pm	12hr 15min
Varanasi	Shiv Ganga Express	#12560	ND	6.55pm	12hr 35min
	Swatantras Express	#12562	ND	8.40pm	11hr 50min
Vasco da Gama	Goa Express	#12780	HN	3.05pm	39hr 25min

OD Old Delhi, ND New Delhi, HN Hazrat Nizamuddin
*a/c only

prohibited, though you may possibly get away with it out of peak hours. Many southbound trains leave from New Delhi, but all trains to Rajasthan, except those to Bharatpur, Kota and Sawai Madhopur, leave from either Old Delhi or Sarai Rohilla stations. Quite a few trains to south and central India leave from Hazrat Nizamuddin station, so check carefully when you buy your ticket. Bookings for all trains can be made at New Delhi station.

New Delhi station New Delhi station is at the eastern end of Paharganj Main Bazaar, within easy walking distance of many of the area's budget hotels. The station has two exits: take the Paharganj exit for Connaught Place and most points south, and the Ajmeri Gate exit for Old Delhi. Cycle rickshaws from both sides can take you to Connaught Place – just 500m down the road – but cannot enter Connaught Place itself. Both exits have pre-paid auto-rickshaw booths (₹40 to CP, ₹60 to Chandni Chowk, plus ₹10 for baggage). New Delhi railway station has a very efficient booking office (Mon–Sat 8am–8pm, Sun 8am–2pm) for foreign tourists, on the first floor (above ground) of the main departure building. Staff will give you advice on the fastest trains, and you should have little difficulty finding a seat or berth; foreigners must show passports, and may possibly be asked to pay in foreign currency or show exchange certificates. Ignore roadside advice to book train tickets elsewhere, and don't try buying one at the reservations building down the road – you'll be faced with a confusion of queues and crowds. Ignore claims that the tourist booking office has moved or is closed, and ignore touts who claim to be directing you to it (see box, p.104).

Old Delhi station Old Delhi station (officially called Delhi Junction), west of the Red Fort, is well connected to the city by taxis, auto-rickshaws and cycle-rickshaws; for autos

1

DELHI SCAMS

Delhi can be a headache for the first-time visitor because of **scams** to entrap the unwary – even down to dumping dung onto visitors' shoes and, then charging them to clean it off. The most common wheeze, though, is for taxi drivers or touts to convince you that the hotel you've chosen is full, closed or has just burned to the ground so as to take you to one that pays them commission. They may even pretend to phone your hotel to check, or will take you to a travel agent (often claiming to be a "tourist office") who will do it, dialling for you (a different number); the "receptionist" on the line will corroborate the story, or deny all knowledge of your reservation. The driver or tout will then take you to a "very good hotel" – usually in Karol Bagh – where you'll be charged well over the odds for a night's accommodation. To **reduce the risk of being caught out**, write down your taxi's registration number (make sure the driver sees you doing it), and insist on going to your hotel with no stops en route. Heading for Paharganj, your driver may try to take you to a hotel of his choice rather than yours. To avoid this, you could ask to be dropped at New Delhi railway station and walk from there. You may even encounter fake "doormen" outside hotels who'll tell you the place is full; check at reception first, and even if the claim is true, never follow the tout to anywhere he recommends. These problems can be avoided by **reserving in advance**; many hotels will arrange for a car and driver to meet you at your point of arrival.

New Delhi railway station is the worst place for touts; assume that anyone who approaches you here – even in uniform – with offers of help, or to direct you to the foreigners' booking hall, is up to no good. Most are trying to lure travellers to the fake "official" tourist offices opposite the Paharganj entrance, where you'll end up paying way over the odds, often for unconfirmed tickets. And don't believe stories that the foreigners' booking hall has closed.

On **Connaught Place** and along **Janpath**, steer clear of phoney "tourist information offices" (which touts may try to divert you to – a typical CP tout chat-up line is to inform you which block you are on, so be suspicious of anyone who comes up and tells you that unasked), and never do business with any travel agency that tries to disguise itself as a tourist information office. For the record, India Tourism is at 88 Janpath and the DTTDC is at *Coffee Home* on Baba Kharak Singh Marg (and note that DTTDC's old office at N-36 Connaught Place has closed, and all the "tourist offices" surrounding it are phoney).

Finally, be aware that taxi, auto and rental-car drivers get a hefty commission for taking you to certain shops, which will be added to your bill should you buy anything. You can assume that auto-wallahs who accost you on the street do so with the intention of overcharging you, or of taking you to shops which pay them commission rather than straight to where you want to go. Always hail a taxi or auto-rickshaw yourself, rather than taking one whose driver approaches you, and don't let them take you to places where you haven't asked to go.

there's a booth selling fixed-price pre-paid tickets – Connaught Place is ₹85, plus ₹8 per piece of baggage. The country's only international train service, the Samjhauta Express, departs from Old Delhi – political situation allowing – every Tuesday and Thursday for Lahore in Pakistan, but always check in advance that the train is running and that foreigners may use it, as these things are liable to change.

Hazrat Nizamuddin and Sarai Rohilla The other long-distance stations are Hazrat Nizamuddin station, southeast of the centre, for trains from Agra (except the Shatabdi Express); and Sarai Rohilla station, west of Old Delhi station, for some services from Rajasthan. Hazrat Nizamuddin has a pre-paid auto booth; Connaught Place is ₹90 (plus ₹5/piece of baggage), slightly less from Sarai Rohilla, but you may sometimes find it hard to get any autos to accept the slip from the pre-paid booth at Hazrat Nizamuddin unless you pay extra. You may be lucky and

find a local train to New Delhi, but they tend to be sardine-can packed, and buying a ticket can be a real scrum.

BY BUS

Buses are of most use for travelling to mountainous areas of neighbouring states that aren't served by trains, but they may also be faster than trains on shorter routes. On longer routes there's usually a choice between the ramshackle state-run buses and more comfortable private buses, which some see as potentially more dangerous, as they travel faster and often overnight.

State buses Most state-run intercity buses use Maharana Pratap ISBT, north of Old Delhi railway station (☎011 2386 0290; ⓜ Kashmere Gate), 20min and ₹85 (plus ₹10 for baggage) from Connaught Place by pre-paid auto. Try to arrive an hour or so before departure to allow time to find the correct counter (there are thirty or so) and book your ticket. Ask for the numbers of both platform and licence plate to ensure you board the right bus. Services for Uttarakhand hill stations like Nainital (6 daily; 9hr), Almora (2 daily; 12hr) and Ramnagar (for Corbett National Park; hourly; 7–8hr) leave from Anand Vihar ISBT in East Delhi (☎011 2214 8097; Ⓜ Anand Vihar; bus #85 from Shivaji Stadium off Connaught Place; ₹100 plus ₹10 for baggage by pre-paid auto from CP). Buses to Agra (every 30min; 5–6hr), and some to Ajmer (10 daily; 9hr) and Jaipur (hourly; 6hr) leave from the Sarai Kale Khan ISBT east of Hazrat Nizamuddin Station (☎011 2435 8343; ₹80 plus ₹10 for baggage by pre-paid auto from CP). For Jaipur (28 daily; 6hr), Udaipur (1 daily; 20hr), Jodhpur (1 daily; 12hr) and Ajmer (3 daily; 9hr), the Rajasthan Roadways terminal at Bikaner House, India Gate (☎011 2338 3469; ₹50 plus ₹10 for baggage by pre-paid auto from CP), has

by far the best service, including some deluxe buses.

Private buses Private deluxe buses usually depart from near the Ramakrishna Mission at the end of Main Bazaar, Paharganj, but some pick up passengers at hotels. Popular destinations include Kullu, Manali and Dharamsala, which are not accessible by train, as well as Pushkar and the Uttarakhand (Uttaranchal) hill stations. You can book tickets a day or two in advance at the agencies in Paharganj or Connaught Place.

International buses The only international service is to Lahore in Pakistan, leaving from Dr Ambedkar Terminal on Jawaharlal Nehru Marg (near Delhi Gate) daily except Sunday at 6am (☎011 2331 8180, Ⓦdtc .nic.in/lahorebus.htm).

GETTING AROUND

Even with the addition of a metro system, **public transport** in Delhi is still inadequate for the city's population and size, and increased car ownership is adding to the general chaos. **Cows** have been banned from much of central Delhi, but not the more traditional districts. In an effort to reduce pollution, buses, taxis and auto-rickshaws have all now been converted from petrol and diesel to run on **Compressed Natural Gas** (CNG), but most inner-city thoroughfares are still choked with exhaust fumes and congested.

The metro Delhi's metro system is being built in several phases, with work projected to continue until at least 2021. There are so far six lines: red, yellow, blue, green, violet and an airport express line. In the next phase of construction (phase 3), the Violet Line is to be extended northwards, and new outer ring lines are to be built. For progress updates, see Ⓦdelhimetrorail.com. The minimum fare is currently ₹8, while the highest fare from the centre is ₹25. The metro is wheelchair accessible, and each station should have an ATM. Women have reserved seats and the whole first carriage to themselves, and it's wise to use it, especially during peak hours, when trains can be very full indeed.

Children under 90cm (3ft) tall travel free if accompanied by an adult. Photography is prohibited, as in principle is baggage weighing more than 15kg, or measuring more than 60cm x 45cm x 25cm.

Buses With auto- and cycle rickshaws so cheap and plentiful, few tourists use Delhi's often overcrowded buses, but they do prove useful from time to time, and some are even a/c. Fares range from ₹15–25.

By auto-rickshaw Auto-rickshaws are often the most effective form of transport around Delhi. In Connaught Place, and in front of the tourist office on Janpath, as well as at stations and bus terminals, there are pre-paid

---

CITY AND REGIONAL TOURS

The **DTTDC tourist office** (see p.106), daily except Monday, organizes a/c bus tours of New Delhi (9am–1.30pm; ₹200) and Old Delhi (2.15–5.45pm; ₹200), or a full-day tour which covers both (9am–5.45pm; ₹300). All start outside the DTTDC office at *Coffee Home*, opposite the Hanuman Temple on Baba Kharak Singh Marg. From the same place, depending on demand, they sometimes run a "Delhi by Evening" tour (₹200), which includes sound-and-light shows at the Red Fort, and an Agra day-trip (Wed, Sat & Sun; depart 7am, return 10pm; ₹1100).

DTTDC also run HoHo, a hop-on, hop-off tour (daily except Mon 8.30am–6.30pm) on two routes, a half-hourly red route covering Old and central New Delhi, and an hourly green route covering South Delhi. Tickets cost ₹600 (₹300) on either route for one day, or ₹1000 (₹500) on both routes for two days, and can be bought on the bus or from the DTTDC kiosk opposite Hanuman Temple on Baba Kharak Singh Marg (☎011 4094 0000, Ⓦhohodelhi.com).

Delhi Transport Corporation (☎011 2375 2774 or ☎011 2375 2244, Ⓦdtc.nic.in) runs one-day tours for ₹200, starting from Scindia House in Connaught Place (corner of Janpath) at 9.30am, or the Red Fort at 9.45am. All the five-star **hotels** offer their own, door-to-door packages, and many hotels in and around Paharganj, such as *Namaskar* and *Metropolis*, can arrange city tours by taxi for around ₹1000, which is good value when shared between three or four people.

1

auto-rickshaw kiosks, charging certified official fares. Otherwise you'll need to negotiate a price before getting in; prices for foreigners vary according to your haggling skills, but as a sample fare, it should cost about ₹70–80 from Connaught Place to Old Delhi.

By cycle rickshaw Cycle rickshaws are not allowed in Connaught Place and parts of New Delhi, but are handy for short journeys to outlying areas and around Paharganj. They're also nippier than motorized traffic in Old Delhi. Rates should be roughly half that demanded by autos, but remember that your rickshaw-wallah will be among Delhi's poorest citizens, see how hard he works, and unless he gives you reason not to, be prepared to tip generously.

By taxis Delhi's taxis (white, or black and yellow) cost around fifty percent more than auto-rickshaws. Drivers belong to local taxi stands, where you can make bookings and fix prices; if you flag a taxi on the street you're letting yourself in for some hectic haggling. A surcharge of around 25 percent operates between 11pm and 5am. Alternatively, radiocab firms such as Mega Cabs (☎011 4141 4141, ⓦ megacabs.com) and Quick Cabs (☎011 4533 3333, ⓦ quickcabs.in) offer a 24hr call-a-cab service with meters, though expect to pay a bit more than usual.

By bicycle Cycling in the large avenues of New Delhi takes some getting used to and can be hazardous for those not used to chaotic traffic. Bicycle rental is hard to come by, but

you can buy bikes pretty cheaply at Jhandewalan market, (by Jhandewalan metro station).

Chauffeur-driven cars For local sightseeing and journeys beyond the city confines, chauffeur-driven cars are very good value, especially for groups of three or four. Many budget hotels offer cars and drivers, as does the DTTDC (see below), and the booths at the southern end of the Tibetan Market on Janpath. DTTDC rates are ₹1365 for a 10hr day within Delhi (more in an a/c vehicle), which includes 100km mileage. Alternatively, there's Kumar Tourist Taxi Service, K-14 Connaught Place (☎011 2341 5930, ⓦ kumarindiatours.com). Driving yourself in Delhi can be dangerous, and is not advisable.

Car rental Avis, *Oberoi Hotel*, Dr Zakir Hussain Marg ☎011 2430 4452 or ☎1800 103 2847; Hertz, Plot 11a, Shivaji Marg, Moti Nagar (near IGI Airport) ☎0124 301 4724, ⓔ ocr.rangapuri@orixindia.com.

Motorcbike dealers The Karol Bagh area has many good bike shops selling new or secondhand Enfields. Reliable dealers include Inder Motors, 1744-A/55 basement, Hardhyan Singh Nalwala St, Abdul Aziz Rd (closed Mon; ☎011 2875 0869, ⓦ lallisingh.com), two blocks east of Ajmal Khan Rd, turning right at the *chowki*, then the third alley on the left. Also worth trying is Ess Aar Motors, 1-E/13 Jhandewalan Extension, between Karol Bagh and Paharganj (☎011 2367 8836, ⓦ essaarmotors.in).

INFORMATION

Tourist information There are reasonably helpful tourist offices at the international and domestic airports, railway stations and bus terminals, and India Tourism at 88 Janpath, just south of Connaught Place (Mon–Fri 9am–6pm, Sat 9am–2pm; ☎011 2332 0005 or 011 2332 0008), is a good place to pick up information on historical sites, city tours, shopping and cultural events, as well as free city maps. DTTDC have an office at *Coffee Home*, 1 Annexe, Emporium Complex, Baba Kharak Singh Marg, opposite the Hanuman Temple (daily 7am–9pm; ☎011 2336 5358, ⓦ delhitourism.nic.in), plus a kiosk just outside this, and others in the two airport terminals. Beware of any other firms that look like or claim to be tourist offices (see box, p.104).

State tourist offices Andaman and Nicobar Islands, 12 Chanakyapuri (near Chanakya Theatre) ☎011 2687 1443, ⓦ go2andaman.com; Andhra Pradesh, Andhra Bhawan, 1 Ashoka Rd ☎011 2338 1293, ⓦ aptourism.in; Arunachal Pradesh, Arunachal Bhawan, Kautilya Marg, Chanakyapuri ☎011 2301 3915, ⓦ arunachaltourism.in; Assam, State Emporia Complex, B-1 Baba Kharak Singh Marg ☎011 2334 5897, ⓦ assamtourism.org; Bihar, Room 6, *Hotel Janpath*, Janpath ☎011 2336 8371, ⓦ bstdc.bih.nic.in; Chandigarh, 21-B Telegraph Lane, Harish Chandra Mathur Lane, off Kasturba Gandhi Marg behind Max Muller Bhawan ☎011 2335 3359, ⓦ citcochandigarh.com;

Chhattisgarh, 3rd floor, Chanakya Bhawan (opposite Chanakya Cinema), Malcha Marg, Chanakyapuri ☎011 2611 6823, ⓦ chhattisgarhtourism.net; Daman and Diu (no Delhi office) ☎0260 225 5104, ⓦ diutourism.co.in; Goa, Goa Sadan, 18 Amrita Shergil Marg, near Khan Market ☎011 2462 9968, ⓦ goa-tourism.com; Gujarat, A-6 State Emporia Building, Baba Kharak Singh Marg ☎011 2374 4015, ⓦ gujarattourism.com; Haryana, Chanderlok Building, 36 Janpath ☎011 2332 4910 or ☎011 2332 4911, ⓦ haryanatourism.gov.in; Himachal Pradesh, Chanderlok Building, 36 Janpath ☎011 2332 5320, ⓦ hptdc.nic.in; Jammu & Kashmir, Rooms 14 & 15, *Hotel Janpath*, Janpath ☎011 2374 4938 or ☎011 2374 4948, ⓦ jktourism.org; Jharkhand, Room 2, *Hotel Janpath*, Janpath ☎011 2336 5545, ⓦ jharkhandtourism.in; Karnataka, C-4 State Emporia Building, Baba Kharak Singh Marg ☎011 2336 3863, ⓦ travel2karnataka.com; Kerala, Travancore House, Kasturba Gandhi Marg, near Bharatiya Vidya Bhawan ☎011 2338 2067, ⓦ keralatourism.org; Lakshadweep, Lakshadweep House, 16 State Guest House Area, Chanakyapuri ☎011 2410 1170, ⓦ lakshadweeptourism.nic.in; Madhya Pradesh, Room 12, *Hotel Janpath*, Janpath ☎011 2336 6528, ⓦ mptourism .com; Maharashtra, Room 10, *Hotel Janpath*, Janpath ☎011 2336 6940, ⓦ maharashtratourism.gov.in; Manipur, C-7 State Emporia Building, Baba Kharak Singh Marg

☎011 2374 6359, ⊛manipur.nic.in/tourism.htm; Meghalaya, Meghalaya House, 9 Aurangzeb Rd ☎011 2301 4417, ⊛megtourism.gov.in; Mizoram (no Delhi office) ☎0389 233 3475, ⊛mizotourism.nic.in; Nagaland (no Delhi office) ☎0370 224 3124, ⊛tourismnagaland. com; Odisha (Orissa), B-4 State Emporia Building, Baba Kharak Singh Marg ☎011 2336 4580, ⊛orissa-tourism. com; Puducherry, 3 Sardar Patel Marg, Chanakyapuri ☎011 2611 1302, ⊛tourism.puducherry.gov.in; Punjab, Room 11, *Hotel Janpath*, Janpath ☎011 2334 3055, ⊛punjabtourism.gov.in; Rajasthan, Bikaner House, Pandara Rd, near India Gate ☎011 2338 3837, ⊛rajasthantourismindia.com; Sikkim, Sikkim House, 14 Panchsheel Marg, Chanakyapuri ☎011 2611 5346, ⊛sikkimtourism.travel; Tamil Nadu, C-1 State Emporia Building, Baba Kharak Singh Marg ☎011 2374 5427, ⊛tamilnadutourism.org; Tripura, Tripura Bhavan, Kautilya Marg, Chanakyapuri ☎011 2301 5157, ⊛tripuratourism. nic.in; Uttarakhand (Garhwal), GMVN, 102 Inder Prakash

Building, Barakhamba Rd ☎011 2335 0481, ⊛gmvnl.com; Uttarakhand (Kumaon) KMVN, 103 Inder Prakash Building, Barakhamba Rd ☎011 2371 2246, ⊛kmvn.gov.in; Uttar Pradesh, Chandralok Building, 36 Janpath ☎011 2332 2251, ⊛up-tourism.com; West Bengal, A-2 State Emporia Building, Baba Kharak Singh Marg ☎011 2374 2840, ⊛westbengaltourism.gov.in.

Listings Exhibitions and cultural events are listed in *Delhi Diary* and *Delhi City*, which are usually available for free at big hotels or at the GOI tourist office. Entertainment listings can be found in fortnightly *Time Out Delhi* and monthly *First City*, available from bookshops and street stalls. Online, apart from the DTTDC's website, it's worth checking the Delhi pages of *India for You* at ⊛indfy.com/delhi/tourism.html for sightseeing information (click on "Tourist Places to Visit"), the Delhi city government's tourism pages at ⊛delhigovt.nic.in/page.asp for general information, and for current listings ⊛delhilive.com.

ACCOMMODATION

Delhi has a vast range of **accommodation**, from dirt-cheap lodges to extravagant international hotels. Bookings for upmarket hotels can be made at airport and railway station tourist desks; budget travellers will have to hunt around independently. Don't believe touts, taxi drivers or auto-wallahs telling you there are no rooms at your hotel, and avoid the places they recommend in Karol Bagh (see box, p.104).

CONNAUGHT PLACE AND CENTRAL NEW DELHI

You pay a premium to stay on Connaught Place, so if you want value for money, stay elsewhere. To its south, grander hotels on and around Janpath and along Sansad Marg cater mainly for business travellers and tourist groups, but there are some very good ones among them. Only a couple of the budget travellers' lodges that once dotted the lanes off the northern end of Janpath remain, and they're often full, so book ahead.

Alka P-16, Connaught Place ☎011 2334 4000, ⊛hotelalka.com; map p.86. "The best alternative to luxury", they reckon, but the rooms, though a/c and carpeted, are pretty poky – the cheaper ones don't even have a window, though they do try to make up for it with mirrors to create an illusion of more space. On the plus side, there's a reasonable vegetarian restaurant, and an annexe on M-block for when the main hotel is full. Breakfast included. ₹6458

Bright M-85, Connaught Place ☎011 4330 2222, ⊛hotelbrightdelhi.in; map p.86. A former budget hotel now reborn as quite an impressive mid-range option. The rooms are on the small side, but done out in tasteful silverish decor with marble and mosaic-tile bathrooms, and there's also free wi-fi. Breakfast included. ₹7250

★ **Imperial** Janpath, Connaught Place end ☎011 2334 1234, ⊛theimperialindia.com; map p.86. Delhi's classiest hotel, in a beautiful 1933 Art Deco building set amid large, palm-shaded gardens. The rooms are stylish, as

is the cool lobby done out in cream and gold, while corridors double up as galleries exhibiting fascinating eighteenth- and nineteenth-century prints of India. Staff maintain just the right degree of courteousness, and there are a number of excellent restaurants including the renowned *Spice Route* (see p.112). ₹**20,650**

The Lalit Off Barakhamba Rd and Tolstoy Marg, southeast of Connaught Place ☎011 4444 7777, ⊛thelalit.com; map p.84. A stylish, modern hotel, with cool, elegant rooms and a spacious lobby decorated with some impressive works of art. Prices depend on demand, so they're lower when business is slack, and this is the maximum rack rate for a standard double, including breakfast: ₹**17,117**

★ **Master** R-500 New Rajendra Nagar ☎011 2874 1089, ⊛master-guesthouse.com; map pp.80–81 A lovely little *pension*-style guesthouse, comfortable, secure and family-run, with four a/c double rooms of different sizes (a bathroom between each pair), free wi-fi and a secluded roof terrace. Located on the edge of the green belt just 10min by auto-rickshaw from Connaught Place (or bus #910 from Shivaji Terminal behind Block P) and not far from Karol Bagh metro. Vegetarian meals are available and rates include breakfast. Book ahead. ₹**3250**

Le Meridien Windsor Place, Janpath ☎011 2371 0101, ⊛lemeridien.com/newdelhi; map p.84. Busy five-star with glass-walled elevators that take you up to bedrooms set around a massive atrium. The whole ensemble looks

1

like a housing scheme in a sci-fi movie, though the rooms are spacious and comfortable within, and service is excellent. Facilities include a swimming pool, health club, choice of restaurants and bars, wheelchair access throughout, including a room adapted for wheelchair users. Price varies with demand; this is the top rack rate for a standard double: ₹18,307

★ **The Park** 15 Sansad Marg ☎011 2374 3000 or ☎1800 117 275, ⓦtheparkhotels.com; map p.86. They don't come much snazzier than this place, with its super-cool lobby, ultra-modern rooms, and en-suite bathrooms screened off by frosted glass walls. Service is snappy, the atmosphere is relaxed, and all the facilities you'd expect are here, including a bar, a good restaurant (see p.112) and a pool. A cut above your run-of-the-mill five-star. ₹15,350

Ringo 17 Scindia House, Connaught Lane ☎011 2331 0605, ⓔringo_guest_house@yahoo.co.in; map p.86. An old backpacker favourite that's traded in its dorms for single and double rooms, which are plain but decent, some attached, and arranged around a central terrace that makes a pretty congenial little hangout. ₹500/₹700

Sunny 152 Scindia House, Connaught Lane ☎011 2331 2909, ⓔsunnyguesthouse1234@hotmail.com; map .86. Another former backpacker dorm hotel now offering cheap but rather box-like single and double rooms, some attached, with hot water at 30min notice. ₹400/₹800

YMCA Tourist Hostel Jai Singh Marg, southwest of Connaught Place ☎011 2336 1915, ⓦnewdelhiymca .org; map p.84. A rather staid establishment popular with American budget travellers, with institutional corridors that belie the spacious if simple rooms, and good restaurants, a large swimming pool (April–Sept only) and attractive gardens. Wheelchair friendly. Rates include breakfast and supper. ₹2525

YWCA Blue Triangle Ashok Rd, southwest of Connaught Place ☎011 2336 0133, ⓦywcaofdelhi.org (but book via ⓦbtfhonline.com); map p.84. Open to men and women, rooms here are nice and big, with large attached bathrooms. The whole place is clean, quiet and respectable, with lawns outside to relax on, but you'll need to book ahead to secure a room. Rates include breakfast. ₹2752

YWCA International 10 Sansad Marg, southwest of Connaught Place ☎011 2336 1561, ⓦywcaindia.org; map p.86. Clean and airy a/c rooms with private bathrooms, though not as nice as at the *Blue Triangle* (but cheaper); set meals are available in the restaurant. Women are given priority but men can also stay, and there's wheelchair access. Rates include breakfast and a free copy of *The Times of India* every morning. ₹2570

PAHARGANJ

Running west from New Delhi railway station, the Paharganj area is backpacker territory, with innumerable lodges offering inexpensive and mid-range accommodation. Some are good value; others offer very little for very little, and many suffer from slamming-door syndrome and people shouting till dawn (especially if windows face inwards onto the communal stairwell), so choose carefully if you value peace and quiet. Some hotels here run a 24hr checkout system, which means you check out at the same time you checked in – good if you arrived late, bad if you arrived early.

Ajay 5084-A Main Bazaar ☎011 2358 3125, ⓦajayguesthouse.com; map p.88. Tucked away down an alley off the Main Bazaar, this well-run place with marble decor has clean rooms, some a/c, with bathroom and TV, but not all with windows. There's a pool table, internet access and a 24hr bakery downstairs, next to a big café area for breakfast or snacks. 24hr checkout. Wi-fi costs ₹65/day. ₹800

Downtown 4583 Main Bazaar ☎011 4154 1529, ⓔltctravel@rediffmail.com; map p.88. This friendly lodging, just off the Main Bazaar, is bright and breezy, and not bad value, but it's worth asking for a room with an outside window. Noon checkout. Dorm ₹150; double ₹500

Hare Krishna 1572–3 Main Bazaar ☎011 4154 1340 or ☎011 4154 1341, ⓦharekrishnaguesthouse.com; map p.88. Rooms at this very popular backpacker guesthouse are clean, the best are spacious, and all are attached. There's hot running water and a pleasant rooftop café-restaurant, but the lower floors can be pretty noisy. Wi-fi is ₹100/day. 24hr checkout. ₹600

Hare Rama T-298 off Main Bazaar ☎011 4734 3333, ⓦhareramaguesthouse.com; map p.88. Attached rooms, reasonable cleanliness and low prices, but hard beds and iffy hot water at this busy hotel down an alley off the Main Bazaar. Bonus points include the Aa Bee travel agency and a 24hr cheap internet café in the lobby, and a 24hr restaurant on the roof. 24hr checkout. ₹500

Hari Piorko 4775 Main Bazaar, by Tooti Chowk ☎011 2358 7888 or ☎011 2358 7999, ⓦhotelharipiorkodelhi. com; map p.88. This bright hotel, slap-bang in the middle of the Paharganj action, with a balcony restaurant overlooking it all, is the new kid on the block and generally gets a thumbs-up from tourists who don't want to slum it too much. The rooms are nice and fresh, and there's lots of marble and mock stone cladding about the place, but it can be very busy-busy at times. 24hr checkout. ₹1390

Metropolis 1634–5 Main Bazaar ☎011 2356 1782, ⓦmetropolistouristhome.com; map p.88. Main Bazaar's most upmarket and comfortable hotel, recently refurbished. A few double rooms have large windows and bathtubs, but others are windowless. All are a/c with a TV, fridge and balcony, and there's a good restaurant and bar, with seating downstairs or on the roof terrace. ₹2000

Namaskar 917 Chandiwalan, off Main Bazaar ☎011 2358 2233, ⓦnamaskarhotel.com; map p.88. Popular family-run budget hotel off the Main Bazaar with a variety of attached rooms, some large with a/c (₹650), but not all the cheaper ones have hot showers or outside windows. The staff are very attentive and helpful, but they also run tours which they can sometimes be pushy about selling. ₹400

Rak International Tooti Chowk, 820 Main Bazaar ☎011 2356 2478, ⓦhotelrakinternational.com; map p.88. One of the most consistently popular Paharganj choices, in a small square off the Main Bazaar, with good value and large, cool rooms, a/c (₹250 extra), TV, fridge and hot water. There's also wi-fi and a pleasant rooftop restaurant. ₹1100

Vishal 1575–80 Main Bazaar ☎011 2356 2123, ⓔvishalhotel@hotmail.com; map p.88. Most of the rooms here are arranged around a grubby atrium, and they're all attached, but it's worth stumping up ₹100 more for a newer, cleaner room. ₹600

Vivek 1534–50 Main Bazaar ☎011 4154 1436, ⓦvivekhotel.com; map p.88. A longstanding travellers' favourite, with a 24hr rooftop restaurant, and decent if unremarkable rooms, with attached baths and hot water, some a/c; the best have windows facing the street, and there's even room service. ₹750

Yatri 3/4 Jhansi Rd, off Punchkuin Rd, by Delhi Heart and Lung Institute ☎011 2362 5563, ⓦyatrihouse .com; map pp.80–81. This guesthouse, tucked away up a small residential street a 10min walk from Paharganj, is like staying in a private home, with clean and quiet attached rooms, hot water, TV, wi-fi and a small enclosed garden for breakfast or just for relaxing, though it's a little pricey for what you get. Book well in advance. Breakfast included. ₹5000

RAM NAGAR

Directly north of Paharganj, a 5min walk from New Delhi railway station and just beyond the flyover section of Desh Bandhu Gupta Rd, Ram Nagar is lined with hotels and a few restaurants. Accommodation tends to be slightly more expensive than in Paharganj, but the rooms are generally better.

Cama 3037 Chowk Chuna Mandi, Rajguru Marg ☎011 2358 0245, ⓔhotelcama@yahoo.com; map p.88. The best-value hotel on this street between Paharganj and Ram Nagar, though it looks grander from the outside than on the inside. Amid the warren of small rooms, all attached with hot water, some have balconies, and some even have a/c. ₹550

★ **Geet Deluxe** 8570 Arakashan Rd ☎011 2361 6140 to 43, ⓔhotelgeetdx@gmail.com; map p.88. A cut above the other mid-range options in this area, well kept with nice touches and a certain charm, offering clean,

decent-sized rooms, all with TV, and either a/c or air-cooled. ₹1175

Grand Godwin 8502/41 Arakashan Rd ☎011 2354 6891 to 8, ⓦgodwinhotels.com; map p.88. A good choice for a bit of comfort: rooms here are all well appointed and well kept, with central a/c, and there are super deluxe rooms and even suites, as well as a multi-cuisine restaurant. Rates include a buffet breakfast. The *Godwin Deluxe*, next door, is run by the same people and has similar rooms and prices. ₹3253

Karan and **Vandna** 47 Arakashan Rd ☎011 2362 8821 and ☎011 2362 8823; map p.88. Two hotels next to each other and jointly run. The *Karan* has smaller and simpler rooms, while the *Vandna* – with mosaics of Krishna and the Qutb Minar flanking the doorway – has slightly larger rooms, costing just ₹100 more. All the rooms in both hotels are attached with hot water and TVs, but mattresses are rather hard. ₹500

Woodland 8235/6 Multani Danda, Arakashan Rd ☎011 4154 1304 to 7, ⓦhotelwoodland.com; map p.88. Popular hotel with a choice of big a/c (₹850), or less expensive smaller, non-a/c rooms. If you want a cheaper room still (₹100 less), they'll send you to their sister establishment, the *Dreamland*, just across the street. ₹600

OLD DELHI

Few tourists stay in Old Delhi: it's less central than Connaught Place and Paharganj, and it's dirtier, noisier and more crowded, with hotels geared mostly to Indian visitors rather than foreigners. The hotels around Old Delhi station in particular are bad value. Still, there are a couple of good upmarket options on the area's fringes and some reasonable budget hotels around the Jama Masjid, and of all the areas in town to stay in, this is by far the most colourful.

Broadway 4/15A Asaf Ali Rd ☎011 4366 3600, ⓦhotelbroadwaydelhi.com; map p.93. On the southern edge of Old Delhi, close to Delhi Gate, this mid-range hotel has a lot of old-fashioned charm and an excellent restaurant specializing in Kashmiri feasts (see p.113), and a bar. Rooms are a little sombre, but they're clean and well equipped, and some look out to the Jama Masjid. Breakfast included. ₹5502

★ **Maidens** 7 Sham Nath Marg, Civil Lines; ☎011 2397 5464, ⓦmaidenshotel.com; map p.93. A nice bit of understated luxury in a lovely old colonial mansion dating back to Company days; quiet and relaxing with comfortable period rooms, big bathrooms and leafy gardens as well as a swimming pool and a good restaurant. ₹9980

New City Palace 726 Jama Masjid Motor Market ☎011 2327 9548, ⓔnewcitypalace@hotmail.com; map p.93. Though it doesn't quite live up to its billing of "a home for

1

palatial comfort", this budget hotel is clean and well situated, directly behind the Jama Masjid (reserve ahead if you want a room with a view). Showers are hot and the best rooms have a/c, though not all the cheaper ones have outside windows, and you may need to ask for a change of sheets. 24hr checkout. ₹600

Shayma Inn 5050/12 Netaji Subhash Marg ☎ 011 2327 0712, ✉ shaymainn@yahoo.in; map p.93. A range of reasonably cosy rooms above the hubbub of Netaji Subhash Marg on the east side of Old Delhi, and handy for the Red Fort and Jama Masjid. ₹1650

SOUTH DELHI

Most of the accommodation south of Connaught Place lies firmly in the luxury category, although there are a few guesthouses in Sunder Nagar, the odd mid-range hotel tucked away in a residential area and a modern youth hostel near the exclusive diplomatic enclave in Chanakyapuri.

Ambassador Sujan Singh Park, off Subramaniam Bharti Marg ☎ 011 2463 2600, ✪ tajhotels.com; map p.84. Low-key but well-run and classy, this is a friendly place with comfortably-sized rooms and huge bathrooms, plus a couple of good restaurants and free use of the pool and health club at the other Taj Group hotel, *Taj Mahal*. Breakfast included. ₹18,206

The Claridges 12 Aurangzeb Rd ☎ 011 3955 5000, ✪ claridges.com; map p.84. One of Delhi's oldest and finest establishments, oozing elegant 1930s style from its facade to its rooms and even its bathrooms. Facilities include four restaurants, a vodka bar and a swimming pool. ₹3338

Maurya Sardar Patel Marg, Chanakyapuri ☎ 011 2611 2233, ✪ itchotels.in/itcmaurya; map p.84. An extremely plush hotel on the edge of Chanakyapuri, opposite the Ridge forest, with an imposing range of luxury rooms and two of the best restaurants in Delhi (see p.114). It regularly hosts visiting heads of state, with Bill Clinton among those who have stayed here. Promotional rates are often available. ₹22,000

Youth Hostel 5 Nyaya Marg, off Kautilya Marg, Chanakyapuri ☎ 011 2611 6285, ✪ yhaindia.org; map p.84. Away from the bustling city centre, this modern and eco-friendly blue concrete building, with dorms (a/c ₹500) and a/c or non-a/c singles and doubles, is the showpiece-cum-administration centre of the Indian YHA. You need to be an HI member to stay here (maximum stay seven days) but you can join on the spot (₹30). All rates include breakfast. Dorm ₹275, double ₹800

MAJNU KA TILLA

If you want to avoid Delhi's hustle and bustle, or have a change from Indian culture and cuisine, the Tibetan colony at Majnu Ka Tilla, a couple of kilometres north of Old Delhi, offers excellent-value budget hotels with immaculately kept rooms, much nicer than what you'd get for the same price in Paharganj. It's a relatively quiet district with Tibetan food, internet facilities and money changers close by, but it isn't very convenient for central Delhi (Connaught Place is ₹100 away by auto; Vidhan Sabha metro is a 15min walk, or ₹20 by rickshaw). Book ahead, as hotels are often full here. There's only one main drag in Majnu ka Tilla, so everything's pretty easy to find.

Lhasa House 16 New Camp, just east of the main street ☎ 011 2393 9777 or ☎ 011 2393 9888, ✉ lhasahouse@ rediffmail.com. The rooms are a bit smaller and simpler than at *Wongdhen House* next door, but all are attached, with TV and fan. The cheapest rooms are on the top floor, but otherwise no different from the pricier ones. ₹325

White House 44 New Camp ☎ 011 2381 3644, ✉ whitehouse02@yahoo.com. On the Tibetan colony's main street (such as it is), 100m north of the other two hotels mentioned here; the rooms are quite large, attached, with TV, and certainly well kept, but the mattresses are a bit on the hard side. Again, you pay more to stay on the lower floors. ₹300

★ **Wongdhen House** 15-A New Camp, just east of the main drag, next to Lhasa House ☎ 011 2381 6689, ✉ 2wongdhenhouse@gmail.com. Friendly guesthouse with a choice of rooms, all attached and some overlooking the Yamuna River. There's free wi-fi and a good restaurant (Tibetan food, or breakfast items), plus a terrace with a great river view. ₹700

EATING

Most restaurants close around 11pm, but those with bars usually stay open until midnight. If you're looking for a **late-night** meal, you have a number of choices: eat in one of the restaurants in a top hotel, or the 24hr coffee shop or bar at the *Lalit*; try a snack in Paharganj's round-the-clock rooftop cafés; or head to Pandara Rd market (open till 1.30am).

CONNAUGHT PLACE

Connaught Place ("CP") is dominated by upmarket restaurants and Western-style fast-food places, with a few cheap and cheerful restaurants hidden away if you know where to look. The Bengali Market, on Tansen Marg, off Barakhamba Rd, is a good place for sweets and snacks.

Anand 15/96 Scinidia House, Connaught Lane, three doors from Sunny Guest House ☎ 011 2331 3349; map p.86. Good, cheap eats including great spicy biriyanis (mutton biryani ₹127.50), non-veg dishes (butter chicken ₹127.50) and thalis (₹134 veg, ₹154 non-veg). Daily 11am–11pm.

1

Bikanervala 1st floor, Rajiv Gandhi Bhawan, between the two state emporium buildings, Baba Kharak Singh Marg ☎97177 44098, ⍟bikanervala.com; map p.86. Sparkling canteen-style restaurant serving snacks, meals (thalis ₹160–185), ice creams, sweets and *namkeens*. They also do takeaways and deliveries. Daily 11am–11pm.

Fire Park Hotel, 15 Sansad Marg ☎011 2374 3000 ext 1827; map p.86. Scintillating if expensive modern restaurant whose contemporary Indian cuisine bears a strong hint of European influence. The menu is seasonal, with lighter dishes in summer, fierier ones in winter. Typical dishes include *daab chingri* (prawns in mustard and coconut sauce; ₹1150) or *mathan murg* (curried chicken cooked in a clay pot; ₹795). Booking is advisable for the evening sitting, but shouldn't be necessary at lunchtime. Daily 12.30–2.45pm & 7.30–11.45pm.

Haldiram's 6-L Connaught Place ☎011 4768 5300, ⍟haldiram.com; map p.86. A branch of the Old Delhi sweet and snack house (see p.114) and a great place to stop for a thick sweet lassi (₹60), a *pao bhaji* (₹82) or even a cheeky banana split (₹113). They even have low-sugar and sugar-free sweets. Daily 10am–10.30pm.

India Coffee House 2nd floor, Mohan Singh Place Shopping Complex, Baba Kharak Singh Marg ☎011 2334 2994; map p.86. When the Indian Coffee Board closed its coffee house, a group of ex-workers formed a co-op to take them over, calling them "India Coffee House", and this branch, opened in 1957, was the first. A real relic of Nehruvian India, with a large open-air roof terrace, it serves coffee, snacks and basic meals (masala dosa ₹30) to an eclectic cross-section of downtown New Delhi's daytime population. If you prefer Italian-style concoctions with frothy steamed milk, chains such as *Barista* and *Café Coffee Day* have branches on almost every CP block, but the coffee here is more refreshing, more Indian, and, at just ₹15 a cup, a lot cheaper. Daily 9am–9pm.

★ **Kake Da Hotel** 67 Municipal Market, Outer Ring, Connaught Place; map p.86. A perenially popular diner (the term "hotel" does not imply accommodation) that's been here so long it's become a Delhi institution, known for unpretentious but reliably good Punjabi curries, mostly non-veg, such as butter chicken (₹140) or sag meat (*palak* mutton; ₹140). Takeaway available. Daily noon–11.30pm.

Kwality 7 Regal Building, Sansad Marg ☎011 2374 2310; map p.86. Originally set up to serve American GIs during World War II, this is one of CP's better mid-market choices, quite elegantly decorated with lots of mirrors and chandeliers (though the odd mouse has been spotted). Good choices include chicken tikka with green peas (₹355), and spicy fish jalfrezi (₹395). Meals served daily noon–3.30pm & 7–11pm, with snacks served in between times.

Parikrama Kasturba Gandhi Marg ☎011 2372 1616; map p.86. Novel and expensive Indian (mainly tandoori)

and Chinese cuisine in a revolving restaurant affording superb views over Delhi; a single rotation takes ninety minutes. Specialities include *murg pasandey parikrama* (chicken breast stuffed with minced chicken and nuts in a cashew-nut sauce; ₹450) and *murg tikka parikrama* (chicken tikka in a spicy cashew-nut marinade; ₹650). Booking advisable. Daily 12.30–11pm.

Q'BA E-42/43 Connaught Place ☎011 4517 3333, ⍟qba.co.in; map p.86. Cool and stylish upmarket bar-restaurant on two floors and two terraces, with views over CP. Its "world cuisine" largely boils down to Indian, Italian and Thai, but the choice is still impressive, with a Goan fish curry for ₹550, or old favourites such as chicken tikka masala (₹525), and there's a buffet lunch for ₹651. Daily 12.30–3pm & 7–11.30pm.

Sagar Ratna K-15 Connaught Place ☎011 2341 2470; map p.86. The CP branch of the renowned *Defence Colony* restaurant (see p.115), great for *vadas*, dosas or a south Indian veg thali (₹155). Takeaways and delivery available. Daily 8am–11pm.

Saravana Bhavan P-15 Connaught Place and 46 Janpath ☎011 2331 7755; map p.86. Excellent low-priced south Indian snacks and meals, including thalis (noon–4pm & 7–10.30pm only; ₹165) and quick lunches (10am–3pm only; ₹105), as well as the usual dosas, *iddlis* and *uttapams*. The mini tiffin (₹105) has a taste of everything. Daily 8am–11pm.

Spice Route Hotel Imperial, Janpath ☎011 2334 1234; map p.86. This beautifully decorated restaurant, rarified and expensive – if perhaps a little overpriced – specializes in spicy Southeast Asian and Keralan cuisine. A sumptuous Thai tiger prawn curry will set you back ₹1500, a *kochi masala* (Keralan chicken curry) ₹700, or there's an evenings-only tasting menu for ₹4500. If you want to eat really well in the CP vicinity, this is one of your best bets. Daily 12.30–2.45pm & 7–11.45pm.

Veda H-27 Connaught Place ☎011 4151 3535; map p.86. CP's swankiest restaurant, heavy on the "ambience" (all smoochy red and black decor with low lights), which is what you pay for here, though the food isn't at all bad, with main dishes such as Peshawari kebabs (₹1075) and *malai fish tikka* (₹1475). Daily noon–10pm.

Zen B-25 Connaught Place; map p.86. Excellent Chinese meals, plus a few Thai and Japanese dishes, served in a relaxed and traditional style, as well as Western snacks (3–7pm), and a broad selection of wines, spirits and beers. Try the shredded lamb in spring onion and coriander (₹325) or the crabmeat and asparagus in garlic sauce (₹595). Daily 11am–11pm.

PAHARGANJ AND RAM NAGAR

With so much good food on offer in Delhi, it's a shame to dine in Paharganj, even if that's where your hotel is. Most of the restaurants on the Main Bazaar are geared to unadventurous foreign tastebuds, offering poor imitations of Western, Israeli, Japanese, and even Thai dishes, or sloppy, insipid versions of Indian curries for foreigners who can't handle chilli. Most serve breakfasts of toast, porridge, muesli and omelettes, though they'll do you a *paratha* as well. Eating options in Ram Nagar are more indigenous. If you decide to eat in any of the *dhabas* opposite New Delhi Station, especially those with waiters outside trying to hustle you in, and unless you can read the price list in Hindi, always ask the price of a dish before ordering, or you're likely to be overcharged.

Club India 4797 Main Bazaar ☎ 011 2358 9392; map p.88. First-floor and rooftop restaurant with the best views over central Paharganj, lively music and the usual travellers' breakfast options (set breakfasts ₹75–135), plus Israeli, Japanese, Tibetan and even tandoori dishes. Thalis go for ₹150 (veg) and ₹200 (non-veg). Daily 8am–11pm.

Darbar Restaurant and Bikaner Sweets Corner 9002 Multani Dhanda Chowk, just off Desh Bandhu Gupta Rd ☎ 011 2351 6666; map p.88. Upstairs, it's a no-nonsense, moderately priced, veg restaurant, serving tasty thalis (₹120–150) and north Indian veg dishes such as *malai kofta* (₹150); it also has a takeaway service and delivers orders over ₹300 within 1km radius. Downstairs, it's a wonderful sweets emporium, with all sorts of multicoloured Bengali and Rajasthani confections, plus *namkeens* and savouries. Daily 8.30am–11pm.

Diamond Café 5069 Main Bazaar ☎ 011 2358 8176; map p.88. Backpacker restaurant with a good if typical traveller menu (spag bol ₹150, hummus with tahina ₹80), including a choice of set breakfasts (Continental, Indian, American, Israeli; ₹120–140), fruit salads, pancakes and also some Indian dishes. Daily 8am–11pm.

Golden Café 1 Nehru Bazaar, Ramdwara Rd, opposite Sri Mahavir Mandir ☎ 98108 19367 or ☎ 98108 19377; map p.88. Cheap and cheerful café popular with Korean and Japanese travellers, serving mainly Chinese dishes. You can start with a wonton soup (₹60 veg, ₹70 non-veg), followed by Szechwan-style pork (₹140) or tofu with mushrooms and bamboo shoots (₹115). Daily 11am–11pm.

Kholsa Café 5024 Main Bazaar; map p.88. Tiny, long-established backpacker restaurant, similar to the *Diamond Café*, but slightly cheaper – a relic of the overland trail. Breakfasts here go for ₹90–130, and they still do hippie-traveller favourites such as banana pancakes (₹50). Daily 7.30am–midnight.

Malhotra 1833–4 Laksmi Narain Rd ☎ 011 2358 1849; map p.88. A tourist favourite, offering passable Indian, Chinese and Continental dishes at reasonable prices (chicken tikka masala ₹150). They also do thalis (₹155 veg, ₹255 non-veg) and various breakfast options. Daily 7am–11pm.

Metropolis 1634 Main Bazaar ☎ 011 2356 1782; map p.88. Cosy a/c ground-floor restaurant in the hotel of same

name (downstairs or on the roof terrace). Paharganj's priciest venue serves full breakfasts, reasonable curries and tandoori specials, plus Western dishes, beer, spirits, cocktails and non-alcoholic "mocktails". Try their mutton *kurma* (₹375). Daily 8am–11pm.

Ritu Raj Bhojnalya Arakashan Rd, below Delhi Continental Hotel ☎ 99903 82854; map p.88. Cheap, popular *dhaba* serving excellent Indian breakfasts, simple veg curries, and south Indian snacks. A great place for *chana* rice (₹70) or a thali (₹70–110). Daily 8.30am–11.30pm.

Sonu Chat House 5046 Main Bazaar ☎ 81301 57379; map p.88. Popular cheap diner serving noodles, soup, samosas, curries, veg biriyanis (₹80) and even masala dosa (₹55) to the backpacker crowd. Daily 8.30am–12.30am.

Sonu South Indian Restaurant 8849/2 Multani Dhanda Chowk, off Desh Bandhu Gupta Rd, Ram Nagar ☎ 011 6800 6800; map p.88. Basic south Indian grub (masala dosa, *iddlis*, *vadas* and the like) at low prices. A masala dosa goes for ₹60, a thali for ₹100–135. Daily 8am–11pm.

Tadka 4986 Ramdwara Rd (Nehru Bazaar) ☎ 011 3291 5216; map p.88. The best dining in Paharganj: a clean, bright, modern little restaurant serving low-priced Indian veg dishes such as *palak paneer* or *shahi* (tomato) *paneer* (both ₹130). They'll deliver to any address within 2km. Daily 9am–10.30pm.

OLD DELHI

Old Delhi's crowded streets contain numerous simple food-halls that serve surprisingly good, and invariably fiery, Indian dishes for as little as ₹50. Upmarket eating is thin on the ground, but some of the mid-range places serve food every bit as good as the posh restaurants of South Delhi, and the sweets and snacks in Old Delhi are the best in town.

Aap ki Pasand 15 Netaji Subhash Marg ☎ 011 2326 0373, ⊕ aapkipasandtea.com; map p.93. You can get a chai on any street corner, but for a superior cuppa, head to this refined tea room, where ₹100 will buy you a bone china cup of first- or second-flush Darjeeling, Assam or Nilgiri; you can buy it all by the packet as well (in which case the taster is free). Mon–Sat 10am–7pm.

Chaina Ram 6499 Fatehpuri Chowk, next to Fatehpuri Mosque ☎ 011 2395 0747; map p.93. Established in Karachi in 1901, and forced to relocate in 1947, this little shop is well known for its Sindhi-style sweets; the delicately aromatic Karachi halwa with almonds and pistachios (₹400–800/kg), is the best in town. Daily 8am–8.30pm.

Chor Bizarre Hotel Broadway, 4/15 Asaf Ali Rd ☎ 011 4366 3600; map p.93. A wide selection of excellent Indian cuisine including specialities from around the country, but above all from Kashmir. Eccentric, delightful decor featuring a four-poster bed, sewing table and a servery

1

made from a 1927 vintage Fiat. The speciality is a Kashmiri *tarami* (sampler of various dishes; ₹675). Daily noon–3.30pm & 7.30–11pm.

Ghantewala 1862-A Chandni Chowk ☎011 2328 0490; map p.93. Established in 1790, this famous confectioner supplied sweets to the last Mughal emperors; its *ladoo* (₹390/kg) was already renowned in the nineteenth century, but their speciality is a nutty, butterscotch-like sweet called *sohan halwa* (₹510/kg). Mon–Sat 8am–9pm.

★ **Haldiram's** 1454 Chandni Chowk ☎011 4768 5114, ⊛haldiram.com; map p.93. Very clean, low-priced snack-bar and takeaway with sweets and samosas downstairs, drinks and snacks upstairs, including excellent *puris*, lassis (₹60), lime sodas, kulfis and thalis (₹130–185). If you've never tried one, check the *raj kachori* (₹68), a crunchy pastry shell enclosing a tangy chickpea curry with yogurt. Daily 10am–10.30pm.

★ **Karim's** Gali Kababian (20m from the junction with Kasturba Hospital Rd, then left under Jawahar Hotel) ☎011 2326 4981, ⊛karimhoteldelhi.com; map p.93. A perennial Delhi favourite, located in a passage down a side street, opposite the south gate of the Jama Masjid, consisting of four eating halls (same kitchen) offering the best meat dishes in the old city, at moderate prices, with delicious fresh kebabs, hot breads and great Mughlai curries. A full dish of mutton korma will set you back ₹210, but half-dishes are also available. Daily 9am–11pm.

Moti Mahal 3704 Netaji Subhash Marg ☎011 2327 3011, ⊛motimahal1947.com; map p.93. Renowned for its tandoori chicken, this medium-priced restaurant is a local favourite – one of the first Punjabi restaurants in town – with both indoor seating and a large open-air courtyard. Their speciality is *murg musallam* (chicken with kidney, egg and mincemeat; ₹330). Every day except Tues at 8.30pm, they have live *qawwali* and *ghazali* music. Daily noon–12.30am.

Paranthe Wali Gali Off Chandni Chowk, opposite the Central Bank; map p.93. Head down this alleyway by Kanwarji Raj Kumar Sweet Shop (itself pretty good), and you'll be rewarded with *parathas* filled with anything from *paneer* and *gobi* to *mutter* and *mooli*, all cooked to order and served with a small selection of curries for ₹30–50. There are three *paratha*-wallahs in the alley, all good, but the most renowned is the first one, *Pandit Babu Ram*. Daily 9am–11pm.

SOUTH DELHI

The enclaves and villages spread across the vast area of South Delhi offer countless eating options, and most of its upmarket shopping zones (Hauz Khas, Defence Colony, Ansal Plaza and the like) contain several good restaurants. Dilli Haat, the tourist market in Safdarjang, has 25 food stalls offering dishes from nearly every state in India.

Pandara Rd Market's restaurants and snack bars, just south of India Gate, stay open until 1.30am.

Basil & Thyme Santushti Shopping Complex ☎011 2467 3322; map p.84. Bistro-style Mediterranean eating with dishes like moussaka (₹465), and desserts including tiramisú (₹285); the menu changes every six months and there are daily specials. The early closing time however, means it's lunch not supper, unless you want to make that tea. Book ahead for peak times (1–2pm) in particular. Mon–Sat 10.30am–6pm.

Bukhara Maurya Hotel, Sardar Patel Marg, Chanakyapuri ☎011 2611 2233; map p.84. Delhi's top restaurant, specializing in succulently tender tandoori kebabs (₹1750 for a Peshwari lamb kebab, ₹1800 for tandoori pomfret), with a menu that's short but very sweet, and a kitchen separated from the eating area by a glass partition, so you can watch the chefs at work. Bill Clinton is among the celebs who flock here. At lunchtime there's a set meal for ₹2500. Daily 12.30–2.40pm & 7–11.40pm.

Dum Pukht Maurya Hotel, Sardar Patel Marg, Chanakyapuri ☎011 2611 2233; map p.84. *Bukhara* isn't the only super-top destination in the *Maurya Hotel*: this place, which specializes in the *dum* (slow-cooked casserole) cuisine of Avadh (eastern Uttar Pradesh), is also among the city's best restaurants, offering very elegant surroundings and absolutely punctillious service. The house speciality is *raan-e-dum-pukht* (₹2350), a *dum*-cooked leg of lamb so tender it falls off the bone and melts on the tongue. Daily 7–11.30pm.

Flavors C-52 Defence Colony ☎011 2464 5644, ⊛flavorsofitaly.in; ⊛Mool Chand or Lajpat Nagar; map pp.80–81. Run by an Indian/Italian couple, this is one of Delhi's very best Italian restaurants, where you'll find excellent risotto (₹400–500), great pasta (₹450–500) and pizzas (₹350–500), plus wonderful tiramisú. Daily 11am–11.30pm.

Park Balluchi Deer Park, Hauz Khas ☎011 2685 9369, ⊛parkballuchi.com; ⊛Green Park; map pp.80–81. Kebabs and Baluchi dishes (from Baluchistan, now split between Pakistan and Iran) amid pleasant sylvan surroundings. The speciality is a *murg potli* kebab, served on a flaming sword (₹525). Daily noon–midnight.

★ **Punjabi by Nature** Priya Cinema Complex, Basant Lok, Vasant Vihar ☎011 4151 6666, ⊛punjabibynature .in; map pp.80–81. It's quite a haul from the centre (₹120 by pre-paid auto from CP), but this restaurant has made a big name for itself among Delhi foodies with its fabulous Punjabi and north Indian cuisine. The Amritsari fish tikka (₹795) is succulent, but for something really special, try the *raan-e-Punjab* (leg of lamb, ₹1025). There's a more easily accessible branch on the third floor of City Square Mall, Raja Garden (☎011 4222 5656 or ☎011 4222 5757), by Rajaouri Garden metro (exit gate 4). Daily 12.30–11.30pm.

Sagar 18 Defence Colony Market; ⓜLajpat Nagar; map pp.80–81. Delicious, inexpensive south Indian vegetarian food, with *vadas*, *iddlis*, *ravas* and dosas (₹65–100), plus great thalis (₹155). They've also opened a north Indian restaurant a few doors down at no. 24, and they have branches all over town, but the original is still the best. Daily 8am–11pm.

Swagath 14 Defence Colony Market; ⓜLajpat Nagar; map pp.80–81. A non-veg offshoot of *Sagar*, a few doors away. There are Indian and Chinese meat dishes on the menu, but ignore those and go for the Mangalore-style seafood – the Swagath special (chilli and tamarind), *gassi* (coconut sauce) and *hariyali* (green masala) dishes are all great (all ₹435 with pomfret or ₹585 with prawns). Daily 11am–11.45pm.

NIGHTLIFE AND ENTERTAINMENT

With an ever-increasing number of pubs and clubs, Delhi's **nightlife** scene is in full swing. During the week, lounge and dance bars are your best bet, but come the weekend the **clubs** really take off. Most, if not all, of the ones popular with Delhi's young jet-set are in the luxury hotels, and many don't allow "stag entry" (men unaccompanied by women), which makes them a whole lot more comfortable for women, but is tough luck if you're male and alone. India Gate and Rajpath attract nightly **people's parties** where large crowds mill about, snacking and eating ice cream; these are not advisable for women on their own, as you're likely to get hassled. For **drinking**, the five-star hotels all have plush and expensive bars, and many of the better ones have dance floors. Quite a few bars have happy hours with BOGOF offers ("buy one get one free") on beer and Indian liquors. Lounge bars with laidback music have become very popular, and there are some good ones scattered about the southern suburbs. The drinking age in Delhi is 25.

BARS

Blues N-17 Connaught Place ☎011 4707 8866; map p.86. Snazzy bar and restaurant, offering an eclectic range of live music (6.30–9.30pm nightly; Thurs is rock night). The bar staff are all pros at mixing extravagant cocktails. Happy hour is 4–8pm, after which there's a ₹300 minimum charge, and lone males may not be allowed in. Daily noon–12.30am.

Cibo Janpath Hotel, Janpath ☎011 4302 9291; map p.86. An Indianized version of Mediterranean ambience, including an outside dining area decorated with gilded statues and Italian food, and through the tiled doorway, a bar surrounded by gilt fireplaces. It all just about manages to be chic rather than kitsch, though it works pretty well as either. Daily 10am–midnight.

Gem 1050 Main Bazar, Paharganj ☎011 6462 8999; map p.88. Not a place to seek out over other options in town, but the beer's cheap (₹120 for a 650ml bottle), and it's handy if you're in Paharganj and don't want to venture too far afield for a beer, though women won't be comfortable drinking here without a male companion. For a classier drink in the area, try the *Metropolis Hotel* (see p.108). Daily 9am–midnight.

My Bar 5136 Main Bazar, Paharganj ☎98104 10411; map, p.88. A large and lively bar that also serves food, and quite a fun hangout, although it's the cheap beer (₹70 for a 650ml bottle) that you really come for. Daily 11am–midnight.

Pepper Forte Grand Complex, Chanakya Lane (behind Akbar Bhawan), Chanakyapuri ☎011 2687 8320; map, p.84. Cool, twin-level bar with a small dancefloor, DJs spinning sounds (mainly hip-hop) from 10.30pm, and a BOGOF happy hour 3–9pm, but it's mostly of note for its Tuesday gay nights. Men pay ₹1000 to get in after 10.30pm Sun–Thurs, ₹1500 Fri & Sat; women get in free. Daily 3pm–2am.

Rodeo A-12 Connaught Place ☎011 2371 3781; map p.86. Saloon-style bar with Wild West waiters, swinging-saddle bar stools, pitchers of beer, michelada (beer with lime, salt and chilli), tequila slammers, and Mexican-style bar snacks (tacos, enchiladas, fajitas, quesadillas). Happy hour is 3.30–7.30pm. Daily noon–12.30am.

CLUBS

Capitol Ashok Hotel, 50-B Diplomatic Enclave, Chanakyapuri ☎011 2687 9802; map p.84. An upmarket disco playing unashamedly commercial filmi and pop music to a crowd of the city's gilded youth, with a bar specializing in cocktails. Prices vary according to the night, but there's typically a ₹1000 per couple entry fee, with no "stag entry" allowed. Daily 9pm–2am or later.

Quantum L-1 Center Stage Mall (5th floor), Sector 18, Noida ☎0120 457 1091; ⓦquantumlive.com; map pp.80–81. Across the river, and indeed just across the state line in UP, this is the biggest and most kicking club in town, modelled on London's *Fabric*, with three floors (dancefloor, chill-out and VIP), a roof terrace and Indian and international DJs playing international dance music, usually trance, techno or house. Entry is typically ₹2000 per couple ("stag entry" is not usually allowed). Fri & Sat 10pm–4am.

DANCE AND DRAMA

Dances of India Parsi Anjuman Hall, Bahadur Shah Zafar Marg, near Delhi Gate ☎011 2623 4689. Excellent classical, folk and tribal dance featuring six to seven items every night from different parts of India,

1

usually including Bharatnatyam, Kathakali, Bhawai and the graceful dance of the northeastern state of Manipur. These were formerly held daily at 6.45pm, but have been suspended during construction of Delhi Gate metro station, though they should resume when work on that is completed.

Kamani Auditorium 1 Copernicus Marg ☎011 4350 3351 or ☎011 4350 3352, ⓦkamaniauditorium.org. Bharatnatyam and other dance performances.

Sangeet Natak Akademi Rabindra Bhavan, 35 Firoz Shah Rd ☎011 2338 7246 to 8, ⓦsangeetnatak.com. Delhi's premier performing arts institution, putting on performances of classical dance and music from across India.

Triveni Kala Sangam 205 Tansen Marg, just south of the Bengali Market ☎011 2371 8833. A cultural complex incorporating two theatres and four art galleries, which puts on assorted dance shows and art exhibitions as well as running art, dance and music classes.

CINEMAS

Bollywood movies without subtitles are shown at cinemas such as the Regal (☎011 2336 2245) in Connaught Place, the Imperial in Rajguru Marg, Paharganj, or the Shiela (☎011 2367 2100) on Desh Bandhu Gupta Rd, north of New Delhi railway station. Tickets cost ₹25–100. CP's Odeon (☎011 3989 4040) and Plaza (☎011 4760 4200) cinemas are plusher and nowadays more popular. In addition, some of the cultural centres (see p.115) occasionally run international film festivals. If you want to see Hindi films with English subtitles, your best bet is to buy them on DVD.

SPORTS AND OUTDOOR ACTIVITIES

The recreational activity most likely to appeal to visitors in the pre-monsoon months has to be a dip in one of Delhi's **swimming pools**. Unfortunately most public pools require you to take out membership; aside from Siri Fort Sports Complex, try Talkatora Pool, Park Rd (☎011 2301 8178). Luxury hotels usually restrict their pools to residents, but may allow outsiders to join their health clubs.

Children's Riding Club Safdarjang Rd, behind Safdarjang's Tomb ☎011 2301 1891. Horserides for adults at 7.30am and for children at 3.30pm; you'll need to take out membership (₹5000/month) and pay ₹4000/session plus a ₹4000 deposit.

Delhi Races Kamal Ataturk Rd ☎011 2379 2869. Regular horse racing Tues from 1.30pm, sometimes other days too. Men usually ₹65, women ₹35. Mobile phones not allowed inside (you can deposit them at the entrance).

Indian Mountaineering Foundation 6 Benito Juárez Marg ☎011 2411 1211, ⓦindmount.org.

Official organization governing mountaineering and permits throughout India, with a library and an outdoor climbing wall. Some equipment can be rented here, and you can get information on local crags and climbing groups.

Siri Fort Sports Complex Siri Fort ☎011 2649 7482, ⓦdda.org.in. An Olympic-sized swimming pool, a toddlers' pool, plus tennis, squash and badminton courts are among the facilities here, the most central of the city's fourteen sports complexes. Out-of-towners can use it for ₹100 (₹40) a day.

SHOPPING

Although the traditional places to **shop** in Delhi are around **Connaught Place** (particularly the underground Palika Bazaar) and **Chandni Chowk**, a number of suburbs created by the rapid growth of the city are emerging as fashionable shopping districts. To check prices and quality for crafts, you can't do better than the **state emporiums** on Baba Kharak Singh Marg. Unlike the markets of Old Delhi, most shops in New Delhi take credit cards; beware of touts trying to sweet-talk you into visiting supposed "government shops" which pay them a commission. In all bazaars and street markets, the rule is to **haggle**.

ART, ANTIQUES, CRAFTS AND JEWELLERY

For crafts and jewellery, the government emporiums on Baba Kharak Singh Marg should be your first stop, especially if you want to check prices. Paharganj and Janpath's Tibetan market are good for trinkets such as cheap jewellery, decorated boxes and sandalwood carvings. For upmarket art, antiques (remember that to export anything more than a hundred years old you will need a permit) and jewellery, there's Sunder Nagar Market (map p.84).

Central Cottage Industries Emporium Jawahar Vyapar Bhawan, Janpath, opposite Imperial Hotel

☎011 2336 5611, ⓦcottageemporium.in; map p.86. Popular and convenient multistorey government-run complex, with handicrafts, carpets, leather and reproduction miniatures at fixed (if fractionally high) rates. Jewellery ranges from tribal silver anklets to costume pieces and precious stones. Mon–Sat 10am–7pm.

Cottage of Arts and Jewels 50 Hauz Khas Village ☎011 2696 7418; map pp.80–81. Interesting, eccentric mix of jewellery, curios and papier-mâché crafts, plus film posters and old photographs. The best of the collection, including miniatures and precious stones, is not on display: ask to see it. Daily except Tues noon–6pm.

Neemrana Shop 22-B Khan Market ☎011 4358 7183, ⓦ neemranahotels.com/neemrana-shop; map p.84. Run by the renowned hotel group of the same name, the shop has a chic clientele and offers a range of clothes and a small collection of antiques and *objets d'art*. Mon–Sat 10am–8pm, Sun 11am–7pm.

Plutus 10 Hauz Khas Village ☎011 2651 4210, ⓦ plutusexports.com; map pp.80–81. An attractively presented, upmarket shop selling replica antiques, bronze statues and an assorted collection of silver and gold jewellery. Daily 11am–7pm.

BOOKS

Given that some of the best English literature nowadays is coming out of India, and that many English-language titles are published here at prices far lower than you'll find them in North America, the British Isles or Australasia, Delhi can be a very good place to stock up on books, both new and used. On Sundays there's also Daryaganj Market by Delhi Gate in Old Delhi – an excellent place to search for book bargains.

Amrit Book Co N-21 Connaught Place ☎011 2331 7331; map p.86. A good all-round bookshop selling a wide selection of fiction and non-fiction from India and elsewhere. Mon–Sat 11am–8pm, Sun noon–7pm.

Anil Book Corner By the Plaza Cinema, H-Block, Connaught Place ☎011 2371 3223; map p.86. Huge, dusty piles of used books at relatively low prices – you never know what you might find here, but you may need to search hard. Daily 10am–7.30pm.

Jacksons Books 5106 Main Bazaar, Paharganj ☎98990 89274; map p.88. Paharganj's best address for secondhand books in English – expect to find the sort of novels that backpackers like to read, plus travel guidebooks to India and neighbouring countries. Daily 10am–10pm.

Rajiv Book House 30 Palika Bazar, Connaught Place ☎011 2332 3692; map p.86. A compact but well-stocked little bookshop and an excellent place to buy the latest Indian novels as well as books on Indian art, religion, cookery and current affairs. If you buy a few, they may even offer a discount. Daily 10.30am–7pm.

FABRICS AND CLOTHES

Delhi's fabric and clothes shops sell anything from high-quality silks, homespun cottons, saris, Kashmiri shawls and traditional *kurta* pyjamas to multicoloured tie-dyed T-shirts and other hippie gear. For T-shirts and tie-dyed clothing, try Paharganj or the Tibetan Market. For bargain Western-style trousers, skirts and shirts, the export-surplus market at Sarojini Nagar (pp.80–81) is very good. Roadside stalls behind the Tibetan Market off Janpath sell lavishly embroidered and mirrored spreads from Rajasthan and

Gujarat, but silks and fine cotton are best bought in government emporiums on Baba Kharak Singh Marg.

Anokhi 5 & 6 Santushti Shopping Complex ☎011 2688 3076, ⓦ anokhi.com; map p.84. Soft cotton and raw silk clothes and soft furnishings; particularly renowned for hand-block printed cottons combining traditional and contemporary designs. Also at 32 Khan Market and 16 N-Block Market. Mon–Sat 10am–7pm (Khan Market and N-Block market branches open daily 10am–8pm).

Fabindia 5, 7 & 14, N-Block Market, Greater Kailash ☎011 4669 3724, ⓦ fabindia.com; map pp.80–81. Spread over several shops in the market, with everything from furnishings and interiors to chic cotton clothing for men, women and children and wearable block-printed cottons, sourced from villages across India; also sells organic spices, jams and pickles, and has branches around town including Khan Market (central hall, above nos. 20 & 21), 38 Santushti Shopping Complex, and B-28 Connaught Place. Daily 10am–8pm (Khan Market daily 10am–8pm; Santushti Shopping Complex Mon–Sat 10am–7pm; Connaught Place daily 11am–8pm).

Harsiba (SEWA) 5 Rajiv Gandhi Bhawan, between the two state emporium buildings, Baba Kharak Singh Marg ☎011 3948 9374, ⓦ sewa.org; map p.86. Lovely clothes, accessories and furnishings made by self-employed women, mostly working at home, and sold through their own co-operatively run outlet. Daily 10am–7pm.

Khadi Gramodyog Bhawan 24 Regal Building, corner of Sansad Marg and Connaught Place ☎011 2336 0902, ⓦ kvic.org.in; map p.86. Government-run and a great place to pick up hardy, lightweight travelling clothes. Reasonably priced, ready-made traditional Indian garments include *salwar kameez*, woollen waistcoats, pyjamas, shawls and caps, plus rugs, cloth by the metre, tea, incense, cards and tablecloths. Mon–Sat 10am–7.45pm.

People Tree 8 Regal Building, Sansad Marg, Connaught Place ☎011 2374 4877, ⓦ peopletreeonline .com; map p.86. An interesting selection of alternative designs, with an emphasis on T-shirts, ethnic chic and jewellery. Mon–Sat 10.30am–7pm.

Rainbow Tibetan Market 1 Janpath ☎011 2332 8582; map p.86. A wide range of T-shirts with witty Indian designs and slogans – not designed for tourists particularly, but great as souvenirs. Daily 11am–8pm.

Shaw Brothers D-47 Ground Floor, Defence Colony ☎011 2469 0364, ⓦ shawbrothersonline.com; map pp.80–81. Upmarket purveyors of shawls, rugs, pashminas and silks. They also have a smaller but more conveniently located branch at 8 Palika Bazar, Connaught Place (☎011 2332 9080). Daily 10am–9pm (both branches).

1

Vedi Tailors M-60 Connaught Place ☎011 2341 6901, ⓦ veditailors.com; map p.86. Originally established in Rangoon in 1926, this gents' tailor can run you up a made-to-measure suit for anything from ₹8000 to ₹30,000, depending on fabric and cut. They usually take a week, but for a little extra they can do it in 24hr. S.L. Kapur at G-7 (☎011 2332 5917; similar hours) is an equally reputable firm offering a similar service. Mon–Sat 11.30am–8pm.

MUSIC AND MUSICAL INSTRUMENTS

Lahore Music House Netaji Subhash Marg, Old Delhi (nextdoor to Moti Mahal restaurant) ☎011 2327 1305, ⓦ lmhindia.com; map p.93. Long-established north Indian musical instrument makers with a reputation for quality. Mon–Sat 10am–7pm.

Rikhi Ram G-8, Outer Circle, Connaught Place ☎011 2332 7685, ⓦ rikhiram.com; map p.86. Once sitar makers to the likes of renowned musician Ravi Shankar, and still maintaining an exclusive air, with prices to match. Check out the display of their own unique instrumental inventions. Mon–Sat 12.30–8pm.

Shielma 11 Palika Bazar, Connaught Place ☎011 2332 2900; map p.86. CDs of classical, folk and film music, plus DVDs of Hindi (and English) movies – a good place to find Bollywood classics with English subtitles. Daily 10.30am–8pm.

MISCELLANEOUS

Indian Art Collection 1 Hauz Khas Village ☎98187 16702; map pp.80–81. Old Bollywood film posters are the speciality here, mostly in the ₹1000–5000 range. You can buy them framed, but it's generally easier to have them rolled up and slipped into in a protective tube. They also sell a variety of superior bric-a-brac including old metal trays, maps and advertising placards – well worth a browse. Mon–Sat 10.30am–7.30pm, Sun 11am–5pm.

Jain Super Store 172 Palika Bazaar, Connaught Place ☎011 2332 1031, ⓦ jainperfumers.com; map p.86. Essential oils (including gift packs), natural perfumes and their own in-house fragrances, as well as joss sticks, scented candles and aroma diffusers. Mon–Sat 11am–8pm, Sun noon–6pm.

Nath Stationers (The Card Shop) B-38 Connaught Place ☎011 2371 3218; map p.86. A small shop with a big selection of greeting cards featuring Indian artwork and designs. Mon–Sat 12.30–6pm.

Tribes India 2 Rajiv Gandhi Bhawan, between the two state emporium buildings, Baba Kharak Singh Marg ☎011 2334 1282, ⓦ tribesindia.com; map p.86. Crafts by indigenous "tribal" peoples from across India, often very different from other traditional Indian products. it's a fair trade outlet, guaranteeing a decent rate to the artisans who make the items on sale. Daily 10.30am–7pm.

DIRECTORY

Banks and exchange Almost every block on Connaught Place has an ATM, as do metro stations, and there are several along Chandni Chowk and Asaf Ali Rd in Old Delhi. You can also change money at numerous exchange offices in Connaught Place and Paharganj, including Lucky Forex (see opposite), and all major hotels have exchange facilities. Thomas Cook is upstairs at C-33 Connaught Place (☎011 6627 1971 or ☎1800 209 9100).

Embassies, consulates and high commissions Australia, 1/50-G Shanti Path, Chanakyapuri ☎011 4139 9900; Bangladesh, EP-39, D Radha Krishan Marg, Chanakyapuri ☎011 2412 1389; Bhutan, Chandragupta Marg, Chanakyapuri ☎011 2688 9230; Burma (Myanmar), 3/50-F Nyaya Marg, Chanakyapuri ☎011 2467 8822; Canada, 7/8 Shanti Path, Chanakyapuri ☎011 4178 2000; China, 50-D Shanti Path, Chanakyapuri (entrance for visa applications in Nyaya Marg) ☎011 2611 2345; Ireland, 230 Jor Bagh (near Safdarjang's Tomb) ☎011 2462 6733; Malaysia, 50-M Satya Marg, Chanakyapuri ☎011 2611 1291 to 3; Maldives, B-2 Anand Niketan ☎011 4143 5709; Nepal, Barakhamba Rd by Mandi House Chowk, southeast of Connaught Place ☎011 2332 9969; New Zealand, Sir Edmund Hillary Marg, Chanakyapuri ☎011 4688 3170; Pakistan, 2/50-G Shanti Path, Chanakyapuri ☎011 2611 0601; Singapore, E-6 Chandragupta Marg, Chanakyapuri ☎011 4600 0800; South Africa, B-18 Vasant Marg, Vasant Vihar ☎011 2614 9411; Sri Lanka, 27 Kautilya Marg, Chanakyapuri ☎011 2301 0201 to 3; Thailand, 56-N Nyaya Marg, Chanakyapuri ☎011 2611 8103 or 4; UK, Shanti Path, Chanakyapuri ☎011 2687 2161; US, Shanti Path, Chanakyapuri ☎011 2419 8000.

Hospitals All India Institute of Medical Sciences (AIIMS), Ansari Nagar, Aurobindo Marg (☎011 2658 8500, ⓦ aiims .edu), has a 24hr emergency service, as does Dr Ram Manohar Lohia Hospital, Baba Kharak Singh Marg (☎011 2334 8200, ⓦ rmlh.nic.in). Private clinics include East West Medical Centre, B-28 Greater Kailash Part I (☎011 2469 9229, ⓦ eastwestrescue.com) and Indraprastha Apollo Hospital, Sarita Vihar, Delhi–Mathura Rd (☎011 2692 5801, ⓦ apollohospdelhi.com). The US embassy maintains a list of hospitals and doctors on its website at ⓦ newdelhi .usembassy.gov/service/other-citizen-services/medical-information.html.

Internet Sunrise N-9/II Connaught Place (daily 10am–7.30pm or later; ₹40/hr); Shivam, 651 Tooti Chowk, just off Main Bazaar, Paharganj (9.30am–8.30pm; ₹30/hr); Kesri, 5111 Main Bazaar, Paharganj (near Kholsa Café; daily 10am–10.30pm; ₹50/hr); Shiva Parcels, T-138 General Market (off Ramiwara Rd), Paharganj (daily 10am–midnight; ₹25/hr).

Left luggage ₹10–37/day at the railway stations. Most hotels in Paharganj offer a left-luggage service.

Money transfers Western Union and MoneyGram transfers can be picked up at post offices including the Old and New Delhi GPOs and also the branch post office in Connaught Place (but Mon–Fri 10am–4pm only). Be sure to specify the correct post office, as with poste restante (see below).

Opticians Lawrence & Mayo, 76 Janpath; R.K. Oberoi, H-14 Connaught Place.

Pharmacies Apollo, G-8 Connaught Place (☎011 2371 1838) and at New Delhi Station (*Ginger Hotel*; ☎011 2323 2878) is open 24hr.

Photographic services Kinsey Brothers, 2-A Connaught Place (under *India Today)*; Delhi Photo Company, 78 Janpath.

Police ☎100 (national number). Delhi has a dedicated squad of tourist police based at the airport, main stations and major tourist sights and hotel areas, whose aim is specifically to help tourists in trouble. If you need to involve the police, your hotel reception or the Government of India tourist office will direct you to the appropriate station.

Postal services Poste restante (Mon–Sat 9am–5pm) is available at the GPO (Gole PO) on the roundabout at the intersection of Baba Kharak Singh Marg and Ashoka Rd (sale of stamps Mon–Sat 9am–8pm). You must show your passport to claim mail or check the register for parcels. Have mail for this post office addressed to "Poste Restante, New Delhi GPO, Gole Dakhana, Delhi 110001",

as letters sent to "Poste Restante, Delhi" will go to Old Delhi GPO, north of the railway line on Lothian Rd (but if you want mail to be held there, specify "Old Delhi GPO, Lothian Rd, Delhi 110006" just to be sure). There is a branch office at A-6 Connaught Place (Mon–Sat 10am–5.45pm).

Telephones Lucky Forex, 1126 Main Bazaar, Paharganj (daily 10am–9pm) has low-cost international calls (₹7/min to the UK, North America, Australia and New Zealand), and – in case you get an answering machine – the first ten seconds are free.

Visa extensions and exit formalities Tourist visas cannot normally be extended, but in exceptional cases you may be able to get an exemption from the Ministry of Home Affairs, Foreigners' Division, Jaisalmer House, 26 Man Singh Rd (Mon–Fri 10am–noon). If your total stay will exceed six months, you will need to register at the Foreigner's Regional Registration Office (FRRO), East Block 8, Level 2, Sector 1, Ramakrishna Puram (Mon–Fri 9.30am–1.30pm & 2–4pm; ☎011 2671 1443). Further information can be found at ⊚immigrationindia.nic.in and ⊚indianfrro.gov.in/frro. Should you need a tax clearance certificate, the Foreign Section of the Income Tax Office (ITO) is at Central Revenue Building, Indraprastha Estate (Mon–Fri 10am–1pm & 2–5pm; ☎011 2337 9161 ext 1650); have foreign exchange certificates and ATM receipts to hand.

Rajasthan

UDAIPUR

Rajasthan

The state of Rajasthan emerged after Partition from a mosaic of twenty-two feudal kingdoms, known in the British era as Rajputana, "Land of Kings". Running northeast from Mount Abu, near the border with Gujarat, to within a stone's throw of the ruins of ancient Delhi, its backbone is formed by the bare brown hills of the Aravalli Range, which divide the fertile Dhundar basin from the shifting sands of the mighty Thar Desert, one of the driest places on earth.

2

Rajasthan's extravagant **palaces**, **forts** and finely carved **temples** comprise one of the country's richest crops of architectural monuments. But these exotic buildings are not the only legacy of the region's prosperous and militaristic history. Rajasthan's strong adherence to tradition is precisely what makes it a compelling place to travel around. Swaggering moustaches, heavy silver anklets, bulky red, yellow or orange turbans, pleated veils and mirror-inlaid saris may be part of the complex language of **caste**, but to most outsiders they epitomize India at its most exotic.

Colour also distinguishes Rajasthan's most important tourist cities. **Jaipur**, the vibrant state capital, is known as the "Pink City" thanks to the reddish paint applied to its ornate facades and palaces. **Jodhpur**, the "Blue City", is centred on a labyrinthine old walled town, whose sky-blue mass of cubic houses is overlooked by India's most imposing hilltop fort. Further west, the magical desert city of **Jaisalmer**, built from local sandstone, is termed the "Golden City". In the far south of the state, **Udaipur** hasn't gained a colour tag yet, but it could be called the "White City": coated in decaying limewash, its waterside palaces and havelis are framed by a distant vista of sawtooth hills.

The route stringing together these four cities has become one of the most heavily trodden tourist trails in India. But it's easy to escape into more remote areas. Northwest of Jaipur, the desert region of **Shekhawati** is dotted with atmospheric market towns and innumerable richly painted havelis, while the desert city of **Bikaner** is also well worth a stopover for its fine fort, havelis and the unique "rat temple" at nearby Deshnok. The same is true of **Bundi**, in the far south of the state, with its magnificent, muralled fort and blue-washed old town, as well as the superbly prominent fort at **Chittaurgarh** nearby, not to mention the engaging hill station and remarkable Jain temples of **Mount Abu**.

Another attraction is Rajasthan's wonderful **wildlife sanctuaries**. Of these, the tiger sanctuary at **Ranthambore** is deservedly the most popular, while the **Keoladeo National Park** at **Bharatpur**, on the eastern border of Rajasthan near Agra, is unmatched in South Asia for its incredible avian population, offering a welcome respite from the frenetic cities that inevitably dominate most visitors' itineraries.

PAINTED STORKS, KEOLADEO NATIONAL PARK, BHARATPUR

Highlights

❶ **Keoladeo National Park, Bharatpur** Flocks of rare birds – and birdwatchers – travel from across Asia and Europe each winter to visit this remarkable wetland sanctuary. **See p.159**

❷ **Ranthambore National Park** One of the easiest places in the world to see tigers in the wild, thanks to its large and exhibitionist population of big cats. **See p.159**

❸ **Savitri Temple, Pushkar** For optimum views of the famous lake and whitewashed holy town, climb to the hilltop Savitri Temple at sunset. **See p.169**

❹ **Mehrangarh Fort, Jodhpur** Spectacular hilltop citadel, with maximum-impact views of

the Blue City below. **See p.176**

❺ **Jaisalmer Fort** One of India's most beautiful forts, its massive, honey-coloured bastions enclosing a labyrinth of narrow streets dotted with sandstone havelis and temples. **See p.183**

❻ **Camel trekking** There's no better way to experience the Thar Desert than by riding a camel through it. **See p.185 & p.200**

❼ **Udaipur** Rajasthan's – if not India's – most romantic city: a fairy-tale ensemble of lakes, floating palaces and sumptuous Rajput architecture ringed by dramatic green hills. **See p.202**

HIGHLIGHTS ARE MARKED ON THE MAP ON PP.124–125

HIGHLIGHTS

1. Keoladeo National Park, Bharatpur
2. Ranthambore National Park
3. Savitri Temple, Pushkar
4. Mehrangarh Fort, Jodhpur
5. Jaisalmer Fort
6. Camel trekking
7. Udaipur

PAKISTAN

Thar Desert (Great Indian Desert)

Indira Gandhi Canal

RAJASTH

GUJARAT

Ganganagar

Suratgarh

Kali Bangan

Bikaner

Gajner

Kolayat   Deshnok

Nokha

NH-15

Kishangarh

Bhuttewala

Ramgarh

Bada Bagh

Lodurva

Amar Sagar   **6**

Sam   **5** Jaisalmer

Khuhri

Phalodi

Keechen

Pokaran

Dechhu   Osian

Merta Rd

Mandor

4 Jodhpur

Shiv

NH-15

Balotra   Luni

Barmer   Pali   Marw

Sinoari

NH-15   NH-8

Jalor   Sanderao   Mundwara

Falna   Sadri Rajs

Ranakpur

KUMBALGARH SANCTUARY

Sanchor   Sirohi   Nathdwara

Pindwara   Nagda

Gogunda   Ek

Mt Abu   Abu Rd   Udaipur   **7**

Jaisamar

Rishdeo   Sal

Palanpur

Dungarpur

Himatnagar

Rann of Kutch

Little Rann of Kutch

Ahmedabad

Bhuj

Mumbai

Mahi

N

Na

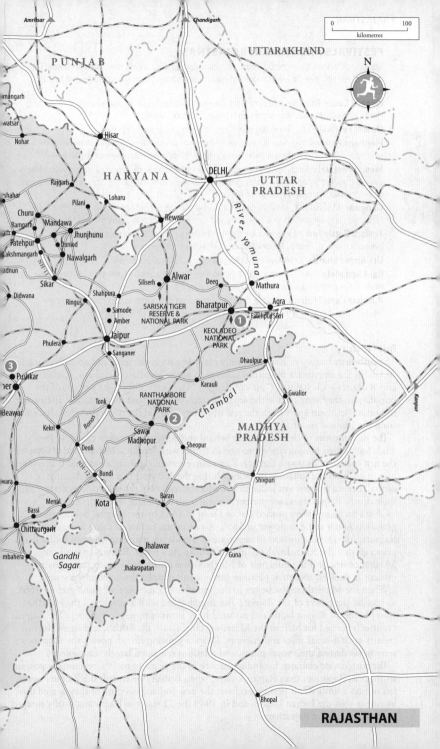

RAJASTHAN

2

FESTIVALS AND FAIRS IN RAJASTHAN

Rajasthan's vibrant local costumes are at their most dazzling during the state's **festivals**. For dates of specific events, ask at tourist offices; most festivals fall on days determined by the lunar calendar.

Nagaur Cattle Fair (late Jan/early Feb). Thousands of farmers and around seventy thousand steers, cows and bullocks descend on Nagaur, south of Bikaner.

Desert Festival (Feb). Three-day event in Sam, near Jaisalmer. See p.192

Elephant Festival (Feb/March). Parades of brightly painted elephants march through the streets of Jaipur, concluding with an extraordinary elephant-versus-*mahout* tug of war.

Mewar Festival (March/April). The ranas of Udaipur welcome the onset of spring with three days of traditional dances, the lighting of a sacred fire, and music by the city's famous bagpipe orchestra. Women play a prominent role.

Gangaur (March/April). In homage to Gauri, the consort of Lord Shiva, wives pray for their husbands, and unmarried girls wish for good suitors. At its best in Jaisalmer and Mount Abu.

Tilwara Cattle Fair (held over a fortnight in March or April). One of Rajasthan's biggest livestock markets, held at Tilwara, 93km southwest of Jodhpur.

Urs Ajmer Sharif (April/May). India's largest Islamic festival. See p.164.

Rani Sati Mela (Aug). Vast crowds gather in Jhunjhunu for a day of prayers and dances in memory of a merchant's widow who committed *sati* in 1595.

Pushkar Camel Fair (Nov). More than three hundred thousand visitors converge on the world's largest livestock market and Rajasthan's most colourful festival. See p.172.

Brief history

The turbulent history of Rajasthan only really begins in the sixth and seventh centuries AD, with the emergence of warrior clans such as the Sisodias, Chauhans, Kachchwahas and Rathores – the **Rajputs** ("sons of Kings") Never exceeding eight percent of the population, they were to rule the separate states of **Rajputana** for centuries. Their code of honour set them apart from the rest of society – as did the myth that they descended from the sun and moon.

The Rajput codes of chivalry that lay behind endless clashes between clans and family feuds found their most savage expression in battles with Muslims. **Muhammad of Ghor** was the first to march his troops through Rajasthan, eventually gaining a foothold that enabled him to establish the **Sultanate** in Delhi. During the 350 years that followed, much of central, eastern and western India came under the control of the sultans, but, despite all their efforts, Rajput resistance prevented them from ever taking over Rajputana.

Ghor's successors were pushed out of Delhi in 1483 by the Mughal Babur, whose grandson **Akbar** came to power in 1556. Aware of the futility of using force against the Rajputs, Akbar chose instead to negotiate in friendship, and married Rani Jodha Bai, a princess from the Kachchwaha family of Amber. As a result, Rajputs entered the Mughal courts, and the influence of Mughal ideas on art and architecture remains evident in palaces, mosques, pleasure gardens and temples throughout the state.

When the Mughal empire began to decline after the accession of Aurangzeb in 1658, so too did the power of the Rajputs. Aurangzeb sided with a new force, the **Marathas**, who plundered Rajput lands and extorted huge sums of protection money. The Rajputs eventually turned for help to the Marathas' chief rivals, the **British**, and signed formal treaties as to mutual allies and enemies. Despite growing British power, the Rajputs were never denied their royal status, and relations remained largely amicable.

The nationwide clamour for Independence in the years up to 1947 eventually proved stronger in Rajasthan than Rajput loyalty; when British rule ended, the Rajputs were left out on a limb. With persuasion from the new Indian government they agreed one by one to join the Indian Union, and in 1949 the 22 states of Rajputana finally merged to form the state of **Rajasthan**.

Modern Rajasthan remains among the poorest and most staunchly traditional regions of India, although attempts to raise educational and living standards are gradually bearing fruit. Since 1991, Rajasthan has tripled its literacy rate, a feat unmatched by any other state, while several universities have been established and new industries have benefited from an electricity supply that now reaches most villages. Irrigation schemes have also improved crop production in this arid region, although the severe threat of **drought** remains an acute problem, and the greatest single threat to Rajasthan's future prosperity.

GETTING AROUND AND INFORMATION   RAJASTHAN

By public transport Trains connect all major cities and many smaller towns, while the reliable state-run bus company, RSTDC, and various private operators have regular services between cities. Be aware that although private companies tend to operate the most comfortable modern coaches, they may also cram too many passengers on board and make unscheduled stops during the journey to tout for custom.

Climate Rajasthan's climate reaches the extremes common to desert regions, with temperatures topping 45°C during the hottest months of May and June. The monsoon breaks over central and eastern Rajasthan in July, continuing, in theory at least, through until September, although in recent years rainfall has become increasingly unpredictable and sporadic. The fierce summer heat lingers until mid-September or October, when night temperatures drop considerably. The best time to visit is between November and February, when daytime temperatures rarely exceed 30°C; in midwinter, you'll need a shawl or thick jumper if you're outdoors at night.

Jaipur and around

A flamboyant showcase of Rajasthani architecture, **JAIPUR** has long been established on tourist itineraries as the third corner of India's "Golden Triangle". At the heart of Jaipur lies the **Pink City**, the old walled quarter, whose **bazaars** rank among the most vibrant in Asia, renowned for their textiles and jewellery. For all its colour, however, Jaipur's heavy traffic, dense crowds and pushy traders make it a taxing place to explore, and many visitors stay just long enough to catch a train to more laidback destinations further west or south. If you can put up with the urban stress, however, the city's modern outlook and commercial hustle and bustle offer a stimulating contrast to many other places in the state.

Jaipur's attractions fall into three distinct areas. At the heart of the urban sprawl, the historic **Pink City** is where you'll find the fine City Palace and the Hawa Mahal along with myriad bazaars stuffed with enticing Rajasthani handicrafts. The much leafier and less hectic area **south of the Pink City** is home to the Ram Niwas Gardens and Central Museum, while the city's **outskirts** are dotted with a string of intriguing relics of royal rule, most notably Nahargarh Fort, the cenotaphs at Royal Gaitor, and the temples (and monkeys) of Galta.

Brief history

Established in 1727, Jaipur is one of Rajasthan's youngest cities, founded by (and named after) **Jai Singh II** of the **Kachchwaha** family, who ruled a sizeable portion of northern Rajasthan from their fort at nearby Amber. The Kachchwaha Rajputs had been the first to ally themselves with the Mughals, in 1561, and, by the time of Jai Singh's accession, the free flow of trade, art and ideas had won them great prosperity. Jai Singh's fruitful 43-year reign was followed by an inevitable battle for succession, and the state was thrown into turmoil. Much of its territory was lost to Marathas and Jats, and the British quickly moved in to take advantage of Rajput infighting. Following Independence, Jaipur became **state capital** of Rajasthan in 1956.

Today, with a population of more than three million, Jaipur is the state's most advanced commercial and business centre and its most prosperous city – some estimates put it among the world's 25 fastest growing cities, with an annual population growth of around 4 percent, and gleaming new high-rises springing up on an almost weekly basis. Evidence of Jaipur's severe growing pains can be seen in older parts of the city, however, with creaking infrastructure and traffic-choked roads frequently approaching gridlock during the morning and evening rush hours.

The Pink City

At the heart of Jaipur lies Jai Singh's original city, popularly known as the **Pink City**, enclosed by walls and imposing gateways. One of the Pink City's most striking features is its regular **grid-plan**, with wide, straight streets, broadening to spacious squares

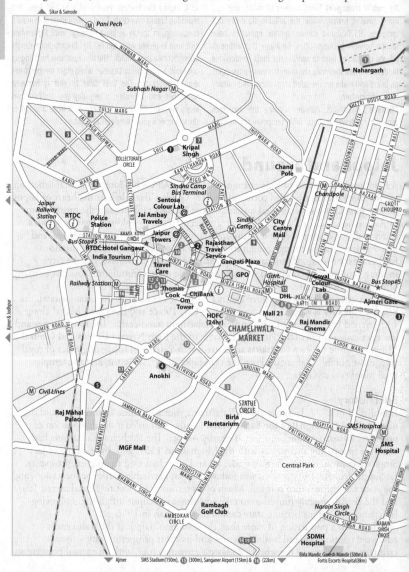

(*choupads*) at major intersections – a design created in accordance with the *Vastu Shastra*, a series of ancient Hindu architectural treatises. Another eye-catching city characteristic is its uniform **pink colour**, intended to camouflage the poor-quality materials from which its buildings were originally constructed.

City Palace

Daily 9am–5pm, last entry 4.30pm • ₹300 including audioguide (₹75), video ₹200; same ticket also valid for Jaigarh Fort at Amber if used within 24hr • To reach the palace entrance, go through the small archway on the north side of Tripolia Bazaar just west of the junction with Chaura Rasta and follow the road as it veers round to the right, past the Jantar Mantar (see p.130); the entrance is past here, on your left

2

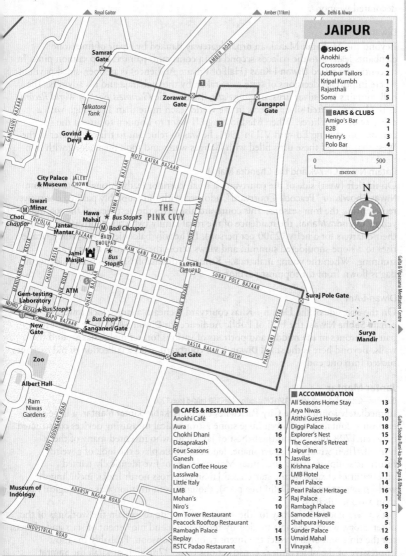

JAIPUR

● SHOPS	
Anokhi	4
Crossroads	4
Jodhpur Tailors	2
Kripal Kumbh	1
Rajasthali	3
Soma	5

■ BARS & CLUBS	
Amigo's Bar	2
B2B	1
Henry's	3
Polo Bar	4

● CAFÉS & RESTAURANTS	
Anokhi Café	13
Aura	4
Chokhi Dhani	16
Dasaprakash	9
Four Seasons	12
Ganesh	11
Indian Coffee House	8
Lassiwala	7
Little Italy	13
LMB	5
Mohan's	2
Niro's	10
Om Tower Restaurant	6
Peacock Rooftop Restaurant	6
Rambagh Palace	14
Replay	15
RSTC Padao Restaurant	1

■ ACCOMMODATION	
All Seasons Home Stay	13
Arya Niwas	9
Atithi Guest House	10
Diggi Palace	18
Explorer's Nest	15
The General's Retreat	17
Jaipur Inn	7
Jasvilas	2
Krishna Palace	4
LMB Hotel	11
Pearl Palace	14
Pearl Palace Heritage	16
Raj Palace	1
Rambagh Palace	19
Samode Haveli	3
Shahpura House	5
Sunder Palace	12
Umaid Mahal	6
Vinayak	8

At the heart of the Pink City stands the magnificent **City Palace**, having originally built by Jai Singh in the 1720s and has lost none of its original pomp and splendour. The royal family still occupies part of the palace, advancing in procession on formal occasions through the grand **Tripolia Gate** on its southern side. Less exalted visitors enter through a modest gate on the eastern side of the palace that leads into the first of the two main courtyards, centred on the elegant **Mubarak Mahal**. Built as a reception hall in 1899, the building now holds the museum's **textile collection**, housing some of the elaborately woven and brocaded fabrics that formerly graced the royal wardrobe. On the north side of the courtyard, the **Armoury** is probably the finest such collection in Rajasthan, a vast array of blood-curdling but often beautifully decorated weapons.

Diwan-i-Khas

Beyond the Mubarak Mahal, an ornate gateway flanked by a pair of fine stone elephants leads into the palace's second main courtyard, painted deep salmon pink. In its centre the raised **Diwan-i-Khas** (Hall of Private Audience) is an open-sided pavilion where important decisions of state were taken by the maharaja and his advisers. The hall contains two silver urns, or *gangajalis*, listed in the *Guinness Book of World Records* as the largest crafted silver objects in the world, each more than 1.5m high with a capacity of 8182 litres. When Madho Singh II went to London to attend the coronation of King Edward VII in 1901, he was so reluctant to trust the water in the West that he had these urns filled with Ganges water and took them along with him.

Pritam Niwas Chowk and the Chandra Mahal

On the left (west) side of the courtyard, a small corridor leads through to the **Pritam Niwas Chowk**, or "Peacock Courtyard", adorned with four superbly painted doorways representing the four seasons. This courtyard also gives the best view of the soaring yellow **Chandra Mahal**, the residence of the royal family (who allow private tours of their quarters for a hefty ₹2500 per person). Its heavily balconied seven-storey facade rises to a slope-shouldered summit, and views across the city from its peak are stunning. When the young maharaja – Kumar Padmanabh Singh – is in residence his flag is flown from the topmost pavilion.

Diwan-i-Am

On the east side of the Diwan-i-Khas courtyard, beneath a large clock tower, sits the ornate **Sabha Niwas**, the Hall of Public Audience (or **Diwan-i-Am**), bare except for a pair of thrones in the middle and portraits of various former maharajas around the walls. Beyond here is the small **Diwan-i-Am courtyard**, with a collection of old carriages tucked into one end.

Jantar Mantar
Daily 9am–4.30pm, last entry 4pm • ₹150 (₹40); audioguide ₹150; guided tours ₹200

Immediately south of the City Palace lies the remarkable **Jantar Mantar**, a large grassy enclosure containing eighteen huge stone astronomical measuring devices constructed between 1728 and 1734 at the behest of Jai Singh, who invented many of them himself. Their strange, abstract shapes lend the whole place the look of a weird futuristic sculpture park. The Jantar Mantar is one of five identically named observatories created by the star-crazed Jai Singh across north India, including the well-known example in Delhi (see p.85), though his motivation was astrological rather than astronomical.

It's a very good idea to pay for the services of a **guide** to explain the workings of the observatory, which was able to identify the position and movement of stars and planets, tell the time and even predict the intensity of the monsoon. Probably the most impressive of the observatory's constructions is the 27m-high sundial, the **Samrat**

Yantra, which can calculate the time to within two seconds. A more original device, the **Jaiprakash Yantra**, consists of two hemispheres laid in the ground, each composed of six curving marble slabs with a suspended ring in the centre, whose shadow marks the day, time and zodiac symbol – vital for calculating auspicious days for marriage.

Hawa Mahal

Daily 9am–4.30pm, last entry 4pm • ₹50 (₹10); audioguide ₹124 (₹90); guided tours ₹200

Jaipur's most instantly recognizable landmark, the **Hawa Mahal**, or "Palace of Winds", stands to the east of the City Palace – it's best appreciated from the outside during the early morning, when it glows orange-pink in the rays of the rising sun. Built in 1799 to enable the women of the court to watch street processions while remaining in purdah, its five-storey facade, decked out with hundreds of finely screened windows and balconies, makes the building seem far larger than it really is; in fact, it's little more than a facade. To get inside the palace itself you need to walk for five minutes around the rear of the building, following the lane that runs north from Tripolia Bazaar. Once inside, you can climb up the back of the facade to the screened niches from where the ladies of the court would once have looked down, and which still offer superb views over the mayhem of Jaipur below.

Govind Devji

Kanwar Nagar, near the Pradeep Rawat Memorial Hospital • Closed noon–4pm • Free • ⓦ govinddevji.net

North of the City Palace is the **Govind Devji**, the family temple of the maharajas of Jaipur. The temple is dedicated to Krishna in his character of Govinda, who is considered to be the guardian deity of the rulers of Jaipur. The principal shrine houses a sacred image of Govinda thought to be five thousand years old, which was brought from Vrindavan (near Agra) in 1735.

Iswari Minar Swarg Suli

Daily 9.30am–4.30pm • ₹20 (₹10) • To reach the minaret, go through the archway off Tripolia Bazaar which leads to the City Palace, but then head round to the left, away from the palace, and you'll see the minaret ahead of you

Just west of the City Palace, the slender **Iswari Minar Swarg Suli**, or **Ishwar Lat** (Heaven-piercing Minaret), was built by Jai Singh II's son and successor, Iswari Singh, to celebrate a minor victory over a combined Maratha-Rajput force in 1747. Its summit offers the definitive view of the Pink City.

Albert Hall

Central Museum Tues–Sun 10am–4.30pm (last entry 4pm) • ₹150 (₹30); audioguide ₹124 (₹90)

Immediately south of the Pink City, the wide road leading out from New Gate is flanked by the surprisingly lush **Ram Niwas Gardens**, named after their creator, Maharaja Ram Singh (1835–80). Standing sentinel in amongst these gardens is the city's florid **Albert Hall**, a prominent city landmark. Built in 1867, it exhibits a whimsical mix of Venetian and Mughal styles (Italian below, Indian on top) and today houses the city's **Central Museum**. The bulk of the collection focuses on regional and Indian themes, including fine displays of Jaipur pottery, Hindu statuary and Mughal and Rajasthani miniature paintings, supported by an eclectic array of artefacts from around the globe – everything from Egyptian antiquities to decorative tiles from Stoke-on-Trent, with forays into Japan, Myanmar and Persia.

Museum of Indology

24 Gangawal Park • Daily 8am–4pm • ₹100 (₹20) including guided tour, plus tip

South of the Albert Hall off Jawaharlal Nehru Road, the **Museum of Indology** is home to assorted curiosities collected by the late Acharya Vyakul, stuffed into a rambling suburban house. Exhibits include oddities such as a map of India painted on a grain of rice, letters written on a hair and a glass bed, along with enormous quantities of junk, all heaped up together in great mouldering piles.

Nahargarh

Fort Daily 24hr • Free **Palace apartments** Daily 10am–5.30pm • ₹30 (₹10)

Teetering on the edge of the hills north of Jaipur is the dramatic **Nahargarh**, or "Tiger Fort", built by Jai Singh II in 1734 and offering superb views of Jaipur, best enjoyed towards dusk. The fort's imposing walls sprawl for nearly 1km along the ridgetop, although the only significant surviving structures within are the **palace apartments**, built inside the old fort by Madho Singh II between 1883 and 1892 as a love nest in which he kept his most treasured concubines away from the disapproving eyes of his courtiers and four official wives.

Vehicles can only get to the fort along a road that branches off Amber Road, a 15km journey from Jaipur. It's simpler to **walk** to the fort along the steep path that climbs up from the north side of the city centre, a stiff fifteen to twenty-minute walk, although the path is a bit tricky to find, so you might want to take a rickshaw to the bottom. Try to avoid going up too late in the day or returning after dark – the fort is popular with delinquent teenagers and other unsavoury types, and the atmosphere can be a tad seedy at the best of times. There are a couple of **cafés** in the palace complex; the RSTC *Padao Restaurant* (see p.137) has the best views.

Royal Gaitor

Daily 9am–4.30pm • Free, camera ₹10, video ₹20

On the northern edge of the city centre, the walled funerary complex of **Royal Gaitor** contains the stately marble mausoleums (chhatris) of Jaipur's ruling family. The compound consists of two main courtyards, each crammed full of imposing memorials. The first (and more modern) courtyard is dominated by the grandiose twentieth-century cenotaph of **Madho Singh II** (d. 1922), a ruler of famously gargantuan appetites, whose four wives and fifty-odd concubines bore him "around 125" children. The second, older, courtyard is home to the elaborate tomb of **Jai Singh II** (d. 1743), the founder of Jaipur and the first ruler to be interred at Gaitor.

On the ridgetop above Gaitor (reachable via a steep path) lies the **Ganesh Mandir**, the second of the city's two major Ganesh temples – a huge building instantly recognizable from the huge swastika painted on its side.

Galta "Monkey Palace"

Daily sunrise–sunset • Free; camera ₹50, video ₹150 • To reach Galta by vehicle you'll need to drive 10km around the hills behind Jaipur or it's a stiff 20min walk following the path beyond Suraj Pole gate on the eastern edge of the Pink City and climbing steeply up to the Surya Mandir on the crest of the hill above the main temple complex

Nestling in a steep-sided valley 3km east of Jaipur, **Galta** comprises a picturesque collection of 250-year-old temples squeezed into a narrow rocky ravine. Galta owes its sacred status in large part to a freshwater spring that seeps constantly through the rocks in the otherwise dry valley, keeping two **tanks** full. These putrid-smelling ponds are now the domain of more than five thousand macaque monkeys, which have earned Galta its nickname of the "Monkey Palace". For many tourists the sight of the splashing monkeys outstrips the attraction of the temples themselves, though the assorted shrines, dedicated variously to Krishna, Rama and Hanuman, are attractively atmospheric. It's also worth walking up to the spectacularly situated **Surya Mandir**, perched above the tanks on the ridgetop, which boasts dramatic views of the city below.

Sisodia Rani-ka-Bagh

Daily 8am–5pm • ₹10 or ₹20 between 5–8pm

On your way to Galta it's worth stopping off at the small royal pleasure palace and lush gardens of **Sisodia Rani-ka-Bagh**, built by Maharaja Sawai Jai Singh in 1728 as a gift to his second queen, Sisodia, a princess from Udaipur. The walls of the garden are adorned with Radha-Krishna murals and its design exhibits both Mughal and Indian influences.

ARRIVAL AND DEPARTURE   **JAIPUR**   **2**

Jaipur is Rajasthan's main **transport hub**, with frequent bus and train services to all major destinations around the state, as well as nationwide (and some international) air connections. Short journeys to destinations like Bharatpur, Ajmer (for Pushkar) and towns in Shekhawati are usually best made by bus; one exception is Sawai Madhopur, which is most easily reached by train.

By plane Jaipur's modern Sanganer airport (📞0141 225 0623) is 15km south of the city centre and is used by Air India Express (IX), Air India Regional (CD), GoAir (G8), Indian Airlines (IC), IndiGo (6E), Jet Airways & JetKonnect (9W) and SpiceJet (SG). There are airport buses into town; alternatively, a rickshaw will cost around ₹300, a taxi ₹400–450.

Destinations Ahmedabad (6E, SG); Bengaluru (Bangalore; G8, 6E, SG); Chennai (6E, SG); Delhi (IX, CD, IC, 9W, SG); Goa (G8, SG); Guwahati (6E, SG); Hyderabad (6E, SG); Indore (9W); Jammu (SG); Kolkata (Calcutta; 6E); Mumbai (IC, G8, 6E, 9W, SG,); Pune (SG); Srinagar (SG)and Udaipur (9W). Air India Express flies to Dubai 3–4 times a week, and Air Arabia once a week.

By train The city's railway station (📞0141 220 4531) lies 1.5km west of the Pink City. Bookings for trains should be made at least a day in advance at the computerized reservations hall just outside the main station (Mon–Sat 8am–8pm, Sun 8am–2pm; 📞135); go to the special "Foreign Tourist and Freedom Fighter" counter, number 769.

By bus State buses from all over Rajasthan and further afield pull in at the Inter-state Bus Terminal (also known as "Sindhu Camp") on Station Rd. For longer journeys, faster but less frequent deluxe Gold Line ("Volvo") and Silver Line government services guarantee seats (enquiries on 📞0141 220 4445, bookings up to 24hr in advance on

RECOMMENDED TRAINS FROM JAIPUR

Destination	Name	No.	Departs	Arrives
Abu Road	Aravali Express	9708	(daily) 9am	5.10pm
Agra	UDZ Kurj Express	9666	(daily) 6.15am	11am
	Sealdah Express	2988	(daily) 3pm	7.25pm
	Shatabdi Express	2035	(exc Thurs) 7.05am	10.35pm
Ajmer	Shatabdi Express	2015	(daily) 10.35am	12.45pm
	Aravali Express	9708	(daily) 9am	11.15am
Alwar	Jammu Tawi Express	2413	(daily) 4.30pm	6.37pm
	Shatabdi Express	2016	(daily) 5.50pm	7.32pm
Bikaner	Bikaner Intercity	2468	(daily) 3pm	9.40pm
	Hanumangarh Special	9734	(daily) 9.15pm	4.40am
Chittaurgarh	Udaipur Express	2992	(daily) 2pm	7.05pm
Delhi	Jaisalmer Express	4060	(daily) 5am	11.10am
	Shatabdi Express	2016	(exc Wed) 4.30pm	10.40pm
Jaisalmer	Jaisalmer Express	4659	(daily) 11.45pm	11.15am
Jodhpur	Marudhar Express	4853/4863/4865	(daily) 11.35am	5pm
	Ranthambore Express	2465	(daily) 5pm	10pm
	Jaisalmer Express	4659	(daily) 11.45pm	4.45am
Kota	Ranthambhore Express	2466	(daily) 11.05am	2.45pm
	Mumbai Superfast	2956	(daily) 2.10pm	5.25pm
Sawai Madhopur				
(for Ranthambore	Ranthambhore Express	2466	(daily) 11.05am	1.15pm
National Park)	Mumbai Superfast	2956	(daily) 2.10pm	4pm
Udaipur	Udaipur Special	9721	(daily) 6.45am	1.45pm
Varanasi	Marudhar Express	4866	(Wed) 3.45pm	9.30am

2

0141 220 5790). For other services it's easier to just turn up at the bus stand and head for the relevant booking office – destinations are listed outside each cabin. The deluxe services have their own separate booking hatch on platform 3 (open 24hr). You can book tickets for private buses at the string of agents on Station Rd. A reliable company is Jai Ambay Travels (daily 7.30am–9am; 0141 220 5177), on Station Rd near the junction with MI Rd; you can buy tickets just prior to departure, but it's a good idea to get them in advance (you can also book by phone).

Destinations There are frequent services to pretty much every major town in Rajasthan and beyond. There's an RTDC bus for Pushkar daily at 3.15pm; otherwise catch one of the regular buses for Ajmer and change there, or take a private

bus – Jai Ambay Travels' comfortable non-a/c and a/c coaches leave at 9.15am and 10am respectively. Jai Ambay Travels also sell tickets for direct private buses to Agra (4 daily; 5hr 30min), Ajmer (hourly; 2hr 30min), Bharatpur (hourly; 4hr 30min), Bikaner (5 daily; 6hr), Bundi (2 daily; 4hr), Chittaurgarh (1 daily; 6hr), Delhi (4 daily; 5hr 30min), Jaisalmer (2 nightly, including 8pm sleeper; 12hr), Jodhpur (4 daily, including 10pm sleeper; 6–7hr), Kota (2 daily; 5hr), Nawalgarh (hourly; 3hr) and Udaipur (4 nightly including a 10pm a/c sleeper; 9hr). While state bus services run more frequently (except to Jaisalmer) than private buses, their routes often take them via rural villages resulting in longer travel times and sometimes, overcrowding.

GETTING AROUND

Jaipur is very spread out, and although it's possible to explore the Pink City on foot (despite the crowds), you may need some form of transport to get you there from your hotel. It's best to avoid the morning and evening rush hours.

By rickshaw Auto-rickshaws are available all over the city, as are cycle rickshaws, though these can take forever to get anywhere in the heavy traffic. Prepaid auto-rickshaws can be booked at the kiosks (open 24hr) in front of the railway station and in front of the bus station. Rates for these are much cheaper than you're likely to get on the street (₹483/₹260 for a full/half-day's rental, for example, or just ₹350 for a roundtrip to Amber, including waiting time).

By taxi Cars with driver can be rented through most hotels or through any RTDC office, usually costing ₹700 for a half-day, or ₹1200/day.

By bus Bus route #5 is very useful; it starts at Collectorate Circle, passes through Khasa Kothi then proceeds east

down MI Rd before entering the Pink City via the Sanganeri Gate (Johari Bazaar). The route then passes by the Hawa Mahal before continuing on to Amber, its final destination. The bus costs ₹10/₹12 between Bani Park/Khasa Kothi and the Pink City or ₹20/₹22 if you are travelling all the way to Amber.

By metro At the time of writing, work was nearing completion on one of two new city metro rail lines; the 12km East–West Corridor linking Mansarovar to Badi Chaupar via the railway station and Chand Pol is expected to begin operating by the end of 2013. Phase two, the North–South Corridor, will eventually link the city with the airport.

INFORMATION AND TOURS

Tourist information The RTDC has tourist information offices on Platform 1 of the railway station (daily 7am–10pm; 0141 220 0778); on MI Rd opposite the GPO (daily 10am–5pm; 0141 237 5466); and on platform 3 at the state bus terminal (daily 7am–10pm; 0141 220 6720). RTDC tours (see below) can be booked through any of these offices. There's an India Tourism office at the Khasa Kothi hotel (Mon–Fri 9.30am–6pm, Sat 9am–2pm; 0141 237 2200), with a good range of leaflets and countrywide information.

Events The monthly Jaipur City Guide (₹45), available at some hotels, bookshops and newspaper stalls, has listings of all the latest events in the city. The Jaipur Literature

Festival (jaipurliteraturefestival.org) is one of Asia's biggest bookfests, held over five days in late January at the Diggi Palace hotel. Jaipur's SMS Stadium (smsstadium .com) hosts annual Indian Premier League (IPL) cricket fixtures. For tickets, see ipltickets.net.

Attraction tickets A great-value way to see five of Jaipur's biggest attractions (Amber Fort, Jantar Mantar, Hawa Mahal, Nahargarh Fort and Albert Hall) is to buy a composite ticket for ₹300 (₹50). You can buy these passes at the ticket offices of each named attraction, and they are valid for two consecutive days.

Guided city tours One very inexpensive, albeit very rushed, way to see Jaipur's main attractions is on one of the

JAIPUR BUS SCAM

Buses arriving from Delhi or Agra skirt the southern side of the city, stopping briefly at Narain Singh Circle, where rickshaw-wallahs frequently board the bus and, with the connivance of the bus driver, announce that it's the end of the line ("bus going to yard") – a ploy to get you aboard their rickshaws and into a hotel that pays them commission.

two guided tours run by the RTDC (5hr half-day tour ₹250; 9hr full-day tour ₹300; entrance, camera and transport fees not included), which cram in most of the major city sights. They also run a "Pink City by Night" tour (6.30–10.30pm; ₹375), which includes (vegetarian) dinner at Nahargarh Fort. Tours depart from (and can be booked through) any of the RTDC offices listed above or through the RTDC *Hotel Gangaur* on MI Rd.

ACCOMMODATION

Jaipur has a wide range of accommodation, mostly found west of the city centre, along (or close to) MI Rd and in the upmarket suburb of Bani Park. It's a good idea to book ahead, particularly around the Elephant Festival (first half of March). Note that almost all the places listed below offer free pick up from the bus or train station, and all have internet access (and most have wi-fi as well). Be aware that commission-seeking auto-rickshaw wallahs can be a problem.

All Seasons Home Stay 63 Hathroi Fort, behind Vidhayakpuri Police Station ☏0141 236 9443, ⓦallseasonshomestayjaipur.com. The rooms in this family house each come with a/c, TVs, private bathrooms and garden-view terraces or balconies. Some also have attached kitchens (fridge and cooking gas costs an extra ₹200/day). There's free wi-fi and tasty home-cooked meals. ₹1250

Arya Niwas Sansar Chandra Rd (behind Amber Tower) ☏0141 237 2456, ⓦaryaniwas.com. Dependable old hotel with free wi-fi, arranged around a couple of intimate courtyards, with a lovely expanse of lawn and spacious veranda out front. Rooms are nicely furnished; all come with TVs and a/c, apart from a few air-cooled singles. They also offer city tours, including a 3hr guided stroll of the Pink City. Popular with groups. ₹1720

Atithi Guest House 1 Park House Scheme, just off MI Rd ☏0141 237 8679, ⓔatithijaipur@hotmail .com. Long-established red-brick guesthouse and still one of the nicer budget places in town, with pleasant, modern tiled rooms (air-cooled and a/c) and an attractive rooftop terrace. There's a smart café and the popular *Mohan's* restaurant is a 2min stroll away. Wi-fi ₹75/day. ₹1100

★ **Diggi Palace** SMS Hospital Rd ☏0141 237 3091, ⓦhoteldiggipalace.com. One of the city's most appealing heritage hotels, occupying a characterful old haveli set amid huge gardens in a conveniently central location. Recent renovations have brought the hotel a little more upmarket. ₹5000

Explorer's Nest 3 Purohit Ji Ka Bagh, nr. Jalupura Crossing ☏0141 400 2580, ⓦjaipurbedbreakfast.com. Home to five clean and cosy bedrooms (fan or a/c), this basic hostel-cum-homestay is tucked into a quiet residential neighbourhood just off MI Rd. There's wi-fi, book swapping facilities and a kitchen you can use, plus home-cooked meals. It can be tricky to find, so call for a free pick up. ₹650

The General's Retreat 9 Sardar Patel Marg, nr Chomu Circle ☏0141 237 7134, ⓦgeneralsretreat.com. Dating back to the 1960s, this quaint ex-general's mansion with lush garden is home to eleven clean, bright and cosy en-suite a/c rooms, adorned with old photographs, period furnishings and gorgeous Rajasthani fabrics, plus a convivial rooftop dining room. ₹2800

Jaipur Inn Shiv Marg, Bani Park ☏0141 220 1121, ⓦjaipurinn.com. Reliable, pleasantly old-fashioned budget option, with comfortable and well-equipped rooms with TV and a/c (the rear garden rooms are nicest), plus breezy rooftop terrace and café. Free wi-fi. ₹1500

Jasvilas C-9, Sawai Jai Singh Highway, Bani Park ☏0141 220 4638, ⓦjasvilas.com. Welcoming family-run guesthouse in a gracious old suburban mansion, with spacious and comfortable a/c rooms, a neat little pool and attractive enclosed gardens. ₹4700

Krishna Palace E-26 Durga Marg, Bani Park ☏0141 220 1395, ⓦkrishnapalace.com. Set in a rather grand, haveli-style building, this friendly, family-run budget option offers a range of bright and comfortable air-cooled and a/c rooms with TVs, decorated with traditional Rajasthani touches. Free wi-fi. ₹750

LMB Hotel Johari Bazaar ☏0141 256 5844, ⓦhotellmb.com. This mid-range hotel next door to the well-known *Laxmi Mishthan Bhandar (LMB)* restaurant is one of few places to stay within the Pink City. The cheaper "Executive" rooms are neat and comfortable; the more expensive *Madhu Yamini* or "Royal Deluxe" rooms aren't worth the extra splurge. Avoid the noisy rooms overlooking Johari Bazaar. ₹2925

★ **Pearl Palace** Hari Kishan Somani Marg, Hathroi Fort ☏0141 237 3700, ⓦhotelpearlpalace.com. One of the best guesthouses in Rajasthan, with a selection of spotless and excellent-value modern air-cooled and a/c rooms (a few with shared bathroom) attractively decorated with local arts and crafts, plus a mixed dorm. The well-drilled staff can take care of all your needs, and facilities include 24hr money exchange, internet access, a silver shop, wi-fi and travel ticketing, plus an excellent rooftop restaurant (see p.137). Advance bookings recommended. Dorm ₹150, double ₹450/₹800

★ **Pearl Palace Heritage** 54 Gopal Bari, Lane no.2, Ajmer Rd ☏0141 237 5242, ⓦpearlpalaceheritage .com. Striking sister hotel to the excellent *Pearl Palace*, with a much more upmarket heritage theme – each of the

2

spacious, painstakingly designed a/c rooms is highly unique and features traditional wooden doors, assorted artworks and artefacts. There's a superb sequence of stone carvings adorning the first-floor corridors – a miniature museum in itself. Rooms have TVs, free wi-fi and spotless en-suite bathrooms, some of which feature jacuzzi tubs. For this quality, room rates are a steal. ₹2360

Raj Palace Jorawar Singh Gate, Amer Rd ☎0141 263 4077, ⓦrajpalace.com. One of the smartest addresses in Jaipur, regularly patronized by Bollywood film stars and Arab sheikhs alike. Its location on the edge of the Pink City can't be beaten, while the setting – in a wonderful old haveli built in 1727 – is pure romance. Facilities include a beautiful little pool and sumptuous spa. US$450

Rambagh Palace Bhawani Singh Marg ☎0141 221 1919, ⓦtajhotels.com. This opulent palace complex, set amid 47 acres of beautiful gardens, is indisputably the grandest hotel in Jaipur, and one of the most romantic places to stay in India. Rooms are superbly equipped, with Rajasthani artworks, reproduction antique furniture and all mod-cons. Facilities include a clutch of fine restaurants and bars (see opposite), indoor and outdoor pools (guests only) and a Jiva spa. Even if you can't afford to stay, call in for afternoon tea (₹1500/person). Check the website for discounts, especially in summer. US$850

★ **Samode Haveli** Gangapole ☎0141 263 2370, ⓦsamode.com. In an unbeatably central location on the northeastern edge of the Pink City, this superb old haveli is brimming with atmosphere, centred on an idyllic courtyard and with the prettiest pool in town. Rooms are a mishmash: it's worth paying a little more for a suite. In summer (May–Sept), rates can fall by forty percent. US$300

Shahpura House Devi Marg, Bani Park ☎0141 220 2293, ⓦshahpurahouse.com. Charismatic but affordable 200-year-old heritage hotel, superbly decorated throughout with lavish murals and Rajasthani architectural touches. Rooms all come with a/c, mini-bar and bathtub, and are attractively furnished with old wooden furniture; there's also a small pool. ₹4700

★ **Sunder Palace** 46 Sanjay Marg, Hathroi Fort, Ajmer Rd ☎0141 236 0878, ⓦsunderpalace.com. One of the city's standout budget options, with spotless, attractively decorated modern rooms (fan, air-cooled or a/c), all with sparkling attached bathrooms at very competitive prices. There's a choice of garden café or tranquil rooftop restaurant (see below), while the two friendly brothers who run the place can also take care of money exchange, travel arrangements and anything else you're likely to think of. There's also internet, wi-fi, a souvenir shop, a book-swap library and a cushy day room with games, TV and common shower for early/late arrivals. Advance bookings recommended. ₹500

Umaid Mahal C-20/B-2 Bihari Marg, Bani Park ☎0141 220 1952, ⓦumaidmahal.com. Extravagantly decorated heritage-style modern hotel, with virtually every surface covered in colourful traditional murals. The spacious a/c rooms are attractively furnished with antique-style wooden furniture, and there's also a nice basement pool and bar. Check website for discounts. ₹2500

Vinayak 4 Kabir Marg, Bani Park ☎0141 220 5260, ⓔvinayakguesthouse.yahoo.co.in. Another reliable family-run budget option in Bani Park with a mix of spartan single and double rooms (some with shared bathrooms, and a few with a/c), a nice rooftop, cosy communal lounge and wi-fi. ₹250/₹400

EATING

★ **Anokhi Café** 2nd Floor, KK Square Mall, Prithviraj Rd ☎0141 400 7244. If you've overloaded on curries and need a respite, this veggie-friendly café attached to the Anokhi boutique is the perfect tonic. There's real coffee, fresh juices, terrific cakes and cookies, plus sandwiches, falafels, bean burgers, pizzas and amazing salads (mains ₹175–420). Most ingredients are sourced from their own organic farm. Daily 9.30am–7.30pm.

★ **Aura** Sunder Palace Hotel, Sanjay Marg, Hathroi Fort ☎0141 236 0878. Breezy, tranquil, flower-filled rooftop restaurant at a popular guesthouse, specializing in tasty, pure-veg Indian cooking, including lunch and dinner thalis, at bargain prices, plus wicked Nutella pancakes and home-cooked daily specials. Mains ₹70–95. Daily 7am–10.30pm.

Chokhi Dhani 22km south of Jaipur on the Tonk Rd ☎0141277 0554, ⓦchokhanidhani.com. This Rajasthani theme-park-cum-restaurant attracts droves of well-heeled Jaipuris, especially at weekends, when the whole place gets wildly busy. The ₹450/₹650 entrance fee includes an evening meal plus access to a wide range of attractions (though tips are expected at many) – elephant, camel and bullock-cart rides, folk dances, puppet shows, magicians and chapatti-making demonstrations, to name just a few. When you've done with the entertainment, make for the mud-walled dining hall where you'll be sat on the floor and served an authentically original Rajasthani village thali quite unlike anything you'll find in the restaurants of Jaipur, with lots of rustic rural delicacies like cornflour chapattis, *gatta* and unusual curried vegetables. It's all a bit hokey, but fun. The higher entrance fee includes a meal in the posher a/c food hall. An auto-rickshaw charges ₹300–350 for the roundtrip. Mon–Sat 6–11pm, Sun 11am–11pm.

Dasaprakash 5 Kamal Mansion, MI Rd ☎0141 237 1313. This unpretentious a/c restaurant serves up a tasty range of classic south Indian veg dishes – *iddlis*, *vadas*, *uttapams*, *upuma*, thalis (₹225), and no less than seventeen types of dosa – plus a selection of ice cream sundaes in various colour combinations. Mains ₹85–160. Daily 9am–11pm.

Four Seasons Subhash Marg ☎0141 237 4600. Generally reckoned to be the best Indian veg restaurant in town, with top-notch dosas and *uttapams* along with a big choice of delicious north Indian curries. You may have to queue, especially later on in the evening when the place fills with locals. No alcohol. Mains ₹110–250. Daily 11am–11pm (no tandoor items 5–7pm).

Ganesh Restaurant Nehru Bazaar ☎0141 231 2380. An unprepossessing stairway leads up between two shops, about 20m west of the New Gate, to this tiny basic food joint sitting atop the old city wall. The "kitchen" is an open fire pit above the street, and, despite appearances, the Indian veg food (mains ₹65–110) is delicious – try the buttery garlic naan with the cashew nut masala. Daily 9.30am–11pm.

Indian Coffee House Panch Batti, MI Rd ☎0141 231 2380. Tucked down an alleyway off MI Rd this hard-to-find hangout's been serving coffee and dirt cheap has snacks such as pakoras and samosas for more than fifty years The interiors are shabby, but for ₹27 a brew, you'd expect nothing less. Daily 8.30am–9.30pm.

Lassiwala 312 MI Rd. A Jaipur institution for its sublime lassis (₹34), served in old-style terracotta mugs. Its popularity has sparked a small lassi-wallah-war, with two impostors setting up shop to the right (as you face it) of the original – check for the correct street number (clearly displayed). Daily 7.30am until the lassis are sold out (usually by early afternoon).

Little Italy KK Square Mall, Prithviraj Rd ☎0141 402 2444. Svelte modern restaurant serving passable – if not particularly authentic – pizza, pasta, salads, risotto and a few Italian-style meat dishes, plus assorted Mexican snacks. Also has a decent selection of Indian wines. Mains around ₹300. Daily noon–11pm.

LMB Johari Bazaar ☎0141 265 5844. The veg food at this Pink City institution (mains from ₹130, thali ₹405) is disappointingly pedestrian, so stick to the sweet counter outside, which dishes up a famous *paneer ghewar* (honeycomb cake soaked in treacle) and piping hot *tikkis* in spicy mango sauce. Daily 8am–11.30pm.

Mohan's 14 Motilal Atal Rd, opposite Hotel Neelam ☎0141 510 4299. Cosy and unpretentious little veg restaurant, popular with locals thanks to its well-prepared and excellent-value Indian food, with virtually everything under ₹75. There's not much room, so you might end up sharing a table. There's another branch on Nehru Bazaar, near to *Atithi Guest House*. Daily 8am–10pm.

Niro's MI Rd ☎0141 237 4493, ⓦnirosindia.com. Some of the best non-veg food in Jaipur, with Rajasthani specialities such as *sula* (lamb), *lal maans* (mutton) and *gatta* along with a big choice of tandoori dishes and other meat and veg curries, plus Western and Chinese. Try a (goat) brain masala, if you dare! Mains ₹155–300. Licensed. Daily 10am–4pm & 6–11pm.

Om Tower Restaurant Om Tower, Church Rd, off MI Rd ☎0141 236 6683, ⓦhotelomtower.com. Rajasthan's first revolving restaurant, on the fourteenth floor of the landmark Om Tower. The head-spinning views are the main attraction; the north Indian food (veg only) is acceptable but rather expensive (mains ₹170–385). No alcohol. Daily noon–4pm & 7–11pm.

★ **Peacock Rooftop Restaurant** Pearl Palace hotel, Hari Kishan Somani Marg ☎0141 237 3700. The city's most appealing rooftop restaurant (licensed), with quirky original decor featuring cute metal chairs and a striking peacock canopy – particularly pretty after dark. There's a big menu of veg and non-veg Indian options, all well prepared, with flavoursome sauces, crisp breads and cold beers, plus Chinese, pizzas and the usual Western snacks. It gets busy, so it's a good idea to book ahead. Mains ₹80–350.

Rambagh Palace Bhawani Singh Marg ☎0141 221 1919, ⓦtajhotels.com. Jaipur's most opulent hotel serves up a handful of memorable dining options. Choose between *Suarna Mahal*, offering Indian fine-dining in a superbly over-the-top Neoclassical-style dining room, or tuck into Italian food at the more laidback *Steam* restaurant built inside the carriages of an old steam train in the hotel's grounds. Mains at both start at around ₹850, but for *Suvarna Mahal*, non-guests must cough up ₹2500 for entry (plus tax) into the hotel (redeemable against food and drink). Reservations strongly recommended. Steam daily 7pm–midnight; Suvarna Mahal daily noon–3pm & 7pm–midnight.

★ **Replay** Ridhi Tower, Tonk Rd ☎0141 271 2782. The Italian and Mexican dishes served at this hip restaurant-lounge opposite the SMS Stadium are much better than average, and the breezy rooftop setting lends further appeal. There's a decent wine list too. Mains from ₹300. Daily 11am–midnight.

RSTC Padao Restaurant Palace Complex, Nahargarh Fort ☎0141 514 8044. This is a particularly iconic spot to dine as the sun sets over Jaipur. Entrance costs ₹50 including tea/coffee or a soft drink. Daily 5–11pm.

DRINKING AND ENTERTAINMENT

Amigo's Bar Ninth floor of the Om Tower, Church Rd, off MI Rd ☎0141 236 6683, ⓦhotelomtower.com. Popular for its fine city views, reasonable drinks list (including a few cocktails) and passable Tex-Mex snacks. Daily 11am–11pm.

B2B Country Inn, Kasa Kothi Circle, MI Rd ☎0141 403 3300. This is Jaipur's best stab at a Western-style club, attracting a mix of locals and foreigners alike with its impressive drinks list and "couples only" dance floor. Wed, Fri & Sat 8.30pm–2am.

2

Henry's Ground floor of the Hotel Park Prime, Prithviraj Rd ☎0141 236 0202. The city's most appealing English-style pub, complete with oak bar and sporting memorabilia; alternatively, the same hotel also has a breezy rooftop bar (*The Terrace Grill*) with a small pool and city views – particularly attractive after dark. Henry's daily noon–11.30pm; Terrace Grill daily 7.30–11.30pm.

Polo Bar Rambagh Palace Bhawani Singh Marg ☎0141 221 1919, ⊛tajhotels.com. For a truly enchanting evening, sink old-fashioned tipples in this memorable hotel's swanky, colonial-style *Polo* bar. A cover charge of ₹2500 applies. Daily noon–midnight.

Raj Mandir Cinema Bhagwan Das Rd. If you visit one cinema while you're in India, it should be the Raj Mandir, just off MI Rd. Boasting a stunning Art Deco lobby and 1500-seat auditorium, Mandir shows four movies a day (usually at 12.30pm, 3.30pm, 6.30pm and 9.30pm). There's always a long queue for tickets though (₹60/₹80 or ₹150 for a box), so get yours an hour or so before the show starts. New (Hollywood) movies are often shown in English during the first week of their release.

SHOPPING

If you come across an Indian handicraft object or garment abroad, chances are it will have been bought in Jaipur. As a regular tourist, you'll find it harder to hunt out the best merchandise here, but as a source of souvenirs, perhaps only Delhi can surpass it. In keeping with Maharaja Jai Singh's original city divisions, different streets are reserved for purveyors of different goods. **Bapu Bazaar**, on the south side of the Pink City, is the best place for clothes and textiles, including Jaipur's famous **block-print** work and *bandhani* **tie-dye**. On the opposite side of town, along Amber Rd just beyond Zorawar Gate, rows of emporiums are stacked with gorgeous patchwork wall-hangings and **embroidery**; these places do a steady trade with bus parties of wealthy tourists, so be prepared to be hassled; haggle hard. For old-style Persian-influenced vases, along with tiles, plates and candleholders, visit the outlets of the city's renowned **blue potteries** along Amber Rd or the workshop of the late Kripal Singh (see below).

Anokhi 2nd Floor, KK Square Mall, Prithviraj Rd ⊛anokhi.com. This is the place to buy high-quality "ethnic" Indian evening wear, *salwar kameez* and shirts. They also do lovely bedspreads, quilts, tablecloths and cushion covers. Daily 9.30am–8pm.

Crossroads 1st Floor, KK Square Mall, Prithviraj Rd ☎0141 237 9400. This big bookshop has a superb selection of English-language fiction and India-related titles. Daily 10.30am–9pm.

Jodhpur Tailors Moti Lal Atal Rd (behind Hotel Neelam) ☎93515 84026. One of the best tailors in town.

Hand-stitched suits run from around ₹8000, or you could just pick up a shirt (from ₹800), trousers (₹2000) or jodhpurs (₹2800). Mon–Sat 11.30am–8pm.

Kripal Kumbh Shiv Marg, near the Jaipur Inn ⊛kripalkumbh.com. The former workshop-cum-home of Jaipur's most famous ceramist, the late Kripal Singh, full of attractive and affordable examples of the city's traditional blue-and-white pottery. They also claim to be the only workshop in Jaipur producing entirely lead-free pottery that can safely be used with hot food (as well as featuring colours such as red and orange, which

---

JEWELLERY AND GEMSTONES IN JAIPUR

The two best places for silver jewellery are **Johari Bazaar**, the broad street running north of Sanganeri Gate in the Pink City, and **Chameliwala Market**, just off MI Road in the tangle of alleyways behind the *Copper Chimney* restaurant. The latter also has the city's best selection of gems, though it's also a hard place to shop in peace, thanks to a particularly slippery breed of scam merchant, known locally as *lapkars*. These young men – usually smartly dressed and speaking excellent English – will regale you with beguiling tales about how you can buy gems in Jaipur and sell them back home for a massive profit. This is nonsense, of course, but by the time you realize this you'll be thousands of kilometres away with a handful of worthless cut-glass "gems" wondering where all the mysterious entries on your credit-card bill came from. If you're paying for gemstones or jewellery with a credit card in Jaipur, don't let it out of your sight, and never agree to leave a docket as security.

There's a government-sponsored **gem-testing laboratory** (Mon–Fri & every first and third Sat of month 10am–5pm; ☎0141 256 8221) at the Gem and Jewellery Export Promotion Council, 2nd floor, Rajasthan Chamber Bhavan, MI Rd near Ajmeri Gate, where you can have gemstones tested for authenticity. The cost is ₹1000 per stone, with reports delivered the following working day (or ₹1600 per stone for a same-day report if you deliver the stone before 1pm).

are impossible with lead glazes). Mon–Sat 10am–6pm.

Rajasthali MI Rd, opposite Ajmeri Gate ⓦrajasthali.gov .in. This large, government-run emporium gives you an idea of the range of handicrafts available and approximate costs – although you'll probably find similar items at cheaper prices in the Pink City bazaars. Mon–Sat 11am–7.30pm.

Soma A-5 Jamnalal Bajaj Marg ⓦsomashop.com. Similar range of block-printed clothes (ladieswear only) and fabrics to Anokhi, though at slightly cheaper prices. Daily 10am–8pm.

DIRECTORY

Banks and exchange There are many ATMs around town, especially along MI Rd, and many private exchange places in Jaipur (try Thomas Cook on MI Rd, Mon–Sat 9.30am–5.30pm) offering more or less the same rates as the banks. Many of the guesthouses and hotels can change money (though rates can be poor); both *Sunder Palace Hotel* and the *Pearl Palace Hotel* have 24hr money-changing facilities.

Hospitals For emergencies, the government-run SMS Hospital (☎0141 256 0291), on Sawai Ram Singh Rd, is best; treatment is usually free for foreigners. Private hospitals include the Santokba Durlabhji Memorial Hospital or SDMH (Bhawani Singh Marg, ☎0141 256 6251) and the well-equipped Fortis Escorts Hospital on JLN Rd in Malviya Nagar, 8km south of town (☎0141 254 7000).

Left luggage The left luggage counter at the main bus station costs ₹10/bag/24 hours.

Meditation The Dhamma Thali Vipassana Centre (☎0141 268 0220, ⓦthali.dhamma.org), located in beautiful countryside on the road to Galta, is one of fifty centres across the world set up to promote the practice of Vipassana meditation. Courses generally run for ten days (see website for schedule and details) and are free, but a donation is expected.

Photography Sentosa Colour Lab (Mon–Sat 10am–8pm), Ganpati Plaza (on the side facing MI Rd), and Goyal Colour Lab (Mon–Sat 10.30am–8pm), next to *Lassiwalla* on MI Rd, both offer good digital and print services.

Police station The main police post is on Station Rd opposite the railway station (☎0141 220 2677).

Post and couriers For poste restante, go to the GPO on MI Rd (Mon–Sat 10am–6pm). Parcels and registered mail are kept at the sorting office behind the main desks; packages

are cotton-wrapped and sewn at the concession (Mon–Sat 10am–4pm) by the main entrance. It's preferable to bring your own box. If you're sending a parcel, take it to the customs office on the first floor to have it checked before wrapping and posting; this will speed up delivery by about ten days. The city's DHL office is at G-8, C Scheme, Vinobha Marg, behind Standard Chartered Bank (Mon–Sat 9.30am–7.30pm; ☎0141 236 1159).

Swimming pools The nicest hotel pool currently open to non-guests is at the *Alsisar Haveli* (a pricey ₹250/hr); cheaper options include the pools at the following hotels: *Shahpura House* (₹200/3hr), *Madhuban* (₹150 for a day), *Raj Mahal* (₹270/3hr) and *Narain Niwas* (₹250/hr).

Travel agents It's usually easiest to arrange something through your hotel or guesthouse. Alternatively, try the reputable Rajasthan Travel Service, on the ground floor of Ganpati Plaza on MI Rd (☎0141 408 0808, ⓦrajasthantravelservice.com) or Travel Care, on the ground floor of Jaipur Towers (Mon–Sat 9.30am–6.30pm; ☎0141 237 1832, ⓦtravelcareindia.com), agents for virtually every domestic airline and most major international operators, including Air India, BA, Air France, KLM, Lufthansa, Thai Airways, Singapore Airlines and Gulf Air.

Volunteering Local NGO TAABAR (ⓦtaabar.org), opposite the railway station, provides street children and runaways with shelter, food and education, and also operates a mobile health clinic. Volunteers are welcome.

Yoga Rajasthan Swasthya Yoga Parishad, New Police Academy Rd (☎0141 230 1698) and Madhavanand Ashram (☎0141 220 0317), in Bani Park. There are also free daily yoga classes from 6–7am at the Madhavanand Girls College, along Behari Marg (also in Bani Park), and 6.30–7.30am near the temple (use Gate 3) in Central Park.

Around Jaipur

Forts, palaces, temples and assorted ruins from a thousand years of Kachchhaha history adorn the hills and valleys near Jaipur. The superb palace at **Amber** provides the most obvious destination for a day-trip, easily combined with a visit to the impressive fort of **Jaigarh**.

HOT AIR BALLOONING

For bird's-eye views of the Pink City, Sky Waltz (☎97172 95801, ⓦskywaltz.com) proffers hot air balloon safaris (1hr; US$240 including transfers) between April and February. They have a number of launch sites in and around the city including Amber, one of the prettiest, and Samode, an hour north of Jaipur.

2

Amber

On the crest of a rocky hill 11km north of Jaipur, **AMBER** (or Amer) was the capital of the leading **Kachchwaha** Rajput clan from 1037 until 1727, when Jai Singh established his new city at Jaipur. Amber's palace buildings are less impressive than those at Jaipur, but the natural setting – perched high on a narrow rocky ridge above the surrounding countryside and fortified by natural hills and high ramparts – is unforgettably dramatic.

Visit Amber early in the day if you want to avoid the big coach parties and if you're there in the afternoon, stay on to watch the atmospheric Amber Sound-and-Light Show from the lakeside Kesar Kiyari complex below the fort.

The palace complex

Palace Daily 8am–6pm, last entry 5.30pm; Shri Sila Devi temple closed noon–4pm • ₹200 (₹25), audioguide ₹150 (100) • Sound-and-light Show Daily English 6.30pm, Hindi 7.30pm. ₹200 (₹100)

The path from the village climbs to Suraj Pole (Sun Gate) and the large **Jaleb Chowk** courtyard at the entrance to the main **palace complex**, where you'll find the ticket office and assorted official guides (₹200). On the left-hand side of the courtyard is the **Shri Sila Devi temple**, dedicated to Sila, an aspect of Kali. The statue within is one of the most revered in Jaipur, framed by an unusual arch formed from stylized carvings of banana leaves.

Next to the Shri Sila Devi temple, a steep flight of steps ascends to **Singh Pole** (Lion Gate), the entrance to the main palace. The architectural style is distinctly Rajput, though it's clear from the mirrored mosaics covering the walls that Mughal ideas also crept in.

Singh Pole leads into the first of the palace's three main courtyards, on the far side of which stands the **Diwan-i-Am** (Hall of Public Audience), constructed in 1639. This open-sided pavilion is notably similar in its overall conception to contemporary Mughal audience halls in Delhi and Agra, even if the architectural details are essentially Rajput.

Diagonally opposite, the exquisitely painted **Ganesh Pole** marks the entrance to a second courtyard, its right-hand side filled with a miniature fountain-studded garden, behind which lie the rooms of the **Sukh Mahal**, set into the side of the courtyard. The marble rooms here were cooled by water channelled through small conduits carved into the walls, an early and ingenious system of air-conditioning – the central room has a particularly finely carved example.

On the opposite side of the courtyard, the dazzling **Sheesh Mahal** houses what were the private chambers of the maharaja and his queen, its walls and ceilings decorated with intricate mosaics fashioned out of shards of mirror and coloured glass. On the far side of the courtyard beyond the Sheesh Mahal, a narrow stairwell winds up to the small **Jas Mandir**, decorated with similar mosaics and guarded from the sun by delicate marble screens.

From the rear of the Sheesh Mahal courtyard, a narrow corridor transports you into a further expansive courtyard at the heart of the **Palace of Man Singh I**, the oldest part of the palace complex. The buildings here are plain and austere compared to later structures, though they would originally have been richly decorated and furnished. The pillared *baradari* in the centre of the courtyard was once a meeting area for the maharanis, shrouded from men's eyes by flowing curtains.

Amber town

Below the palace, the atmospheric but little-visited **Amber town** is full of remnants of Kachchwaha rule. One of the most striking local landmarks is the unusual **Jagat Shiromani Temple**. Built by Man Singh after the death in battle of his son and would-have-been successor, the temple is a large and florid structure located to the south of Amer Road. Its shrine is topped by an enormous *shikhara* and fronted by an unusually large, two-storey *mandapa* with a curved roof inspired by those on Mughal pavilions.

The town is also home to the excellent **Anokhi Museum of Hand Printing** (Kheri Gate; Tues–Sat 10.30am–5pm, Sun 11am–4.30pm mid-July to April ₹30, camera ₹50, video ₹150; ⓦanokhi.com/museum), a ten-minute walk north west from the temple towards Sagar Lake (look out for the blue-and-white signs). Housed in an attractive old haveli, the museum has an interesting collection of hand block-printed textiles and garments, along with live demonstrations of printing and carving by resident craftsmen. There's a bijou shop and café here too.

ARRIVAL AND INFORMATION   AMBER

It's a pleasant 15min uphill walk from the tourist office to the palace. Alternatively, you could rent a jeep (they hang out along the main road and around the tourist office and charge ₹300 for the return trip, including 1hr 30min waiting time) or waddle up on an elephant (daily 7.30am–11.30am & 3.30pm–5pm; ₹900).

By bus Bus #5 to Amber starts from Collectorate Circle in Jaipur, travels down the Sawaj Jai Singh Highway, along MI Rd (with a stop outside the GPO) and into the Pink City via the Ajmeri Gate where you'll find a stop on the main road in front of the Hawa Mahal (every 5–10min; 20–30min, ₹22).

By auto-rickshaw An auto will cost around ₹300 return, including a couple of hours' waiting time.
Tourist information There's a small tourist office (daily 8am–4pm) opposite the elephant stables.

Jaigarh
Daily 9am–4.30pm • ₹85 (₹35)

Perched high on the hills behind Amber Palace, the rugged **Jaigarh** fort offers incredible vistas over the hills and plains below. The fort was built in 1600, though as the Kachchwahas were on friendly terms with the Mughals, it saw few battles. At the centre of the fort, a small **museum** has the usual old maps and photographs, plus a selection of cannons dating back to 1588. None of them, however, can hold a candle to the immense **Jaivana** cannon, the largest in Asia, which sits in solitary splendour at the highest point of the fort, five minutes' walk beyond the museum. Needing one hundred kilos of gunpowder for a single shot, the Jaivana could supposedly hurl a cannonball 35km – though its true military value was never gauged since it was never fired in battle.

ARRIVAL AND DEPARTURE   JAIGARH

On foot Most people walk to Jaigarh from Amber Palace, a steep 15–20min climb. The path to the fort goes from just below the entrance to the palace, branching off from near the top of the zigzagging road (the one used by elephants; not the pedestrian path).

By car By car or jeep, you'll need to follow the much longer road that leads to both Jaigarh and Nahargarh; jeeps can be rented in Amber town for the return trip to the fort (₹500, including 2hr waiting time).

Samode

Hidden among the Aravalli Hills 42km northwest of Jaipur, **SAMODE** is notable for its impeccably restored eighteenth-century **palace**, now an award-winning heritage hotel, the *Samode Palace* (non-guests have to shell out a hefty ₹1000, redeemable against food and drink inside, to visit). Some three hundred steps lead up from the palace to a hilltop **fort**, with panoramic views.

ARRIVAL AND DEPARTURE   SAMODE

By bus Local buses to Samode depart Platform 4 of the main Bus Station (Sindhu Camp) between 5am and 10pm
(every 30min) and take 2hr. Taxis cost from ₹1500.

ACCOMMODATION

★ **Samode Palace** ☏ 01423 240014, ⓦ samode.com. The hotel offers uncompromisingly romantic rooms covered with murals and filled with antiques. It's popular
with groups, but the lovely rooftop pool and Indian fusion restaurant is for independent travellers only. Rates drop by 30 percent May–Sept. <u>US$375</u>

Sanganer

SANGANER, 16km south of Jaipur, is the busiest centre for handmade **textiles** in the region, and the best place to watch traditional block printers in action. There are a couple of large factories here, but most of the printing is done as a cottage industry in family homes. The town itself has ruined palaces and a handful of elegant Jain **temples**, including the Shri Digamber temple near Tripolia Gate.

2

ARRIVAL AND DEPARTURE	SANGANER

By bus Government buses and minibuses to Sanganer from Jaipur run from Chand Pol via Ajmer Rd (every 15min; 1hr), or you can catch government bus #3A from Ajmeri Gate.

Shekhawati

Northwest of Jaipur, the land becomes increasingly arid and inhospitable, with farms and fields gradually giving way to wind-blown expanses of undulating semidesert dotted with endless *khejri* trees and isolated houses enclosed in stockades of thorn. Although now something of a backwater, this region, known as **Shekhawati**, once lay on an important caravan route connecting Delhi and Sind (now in Pakistan) with the Gujarati coast, before the rise of Bombay and Calcutta diverted the trans-Thar trade south and eastwards. Having grown rich on trade and taxes, Shekhawati's Marwari merchants and landowning *thakurs* spent their fortunes competing with one another to build the grand, ostentatiously decorated **havelis** that still line the streets of the region's dusty little towns – an incredible concentration of mansions, palaces and cenotaphs plastered inside and out with elaborate and colourful **murals**. Considering the wealth of traditional art here, and the region's proximity to Jaipur, however, most of Shekhawati still feels surprisingly far off the tourist trail.

GETTING AROUND	SHEKHAWATI

By bus and jeep Getting around is best done by road. Regular local buses, always overcrowded, connect Shekhawati's main towns, while jeeps also shuttle between towns and villages, picking up as many passengers as they can cram in.

By train The recently upgraded metre-to broad-gauge line links main towns in the Shekhawati region with Sikar and Delhi. Services between Jaipur and Bikaner (still metre-gauge) tend to be slow and unreliable.

Nawalgarh

At the centre of Shekhawati, surrounded by desert and *khejri* scrub, the lively little market town of **NAWALGARH** makes – along with nearby Mandawa – the most

VISITING SHEKHAWATI'S HAVELIS

A number of Shekhawati's havelis, particularly in Nawalgarh, have now been restored and opened as museums. Most, however, remain in a state of picturesque dilapidation and are still occupied by local families, while others have been abandoned, and are now empty apart from a solitary **chowkidar** (caretaker-cum-guard). Visitors are welcome to look around inside some havelis in return for a small tip (₹30 is sufficient), while others remain closed to outsiders. If in doubt just stick your head in the front door and ask, but remember that you're effectively entering someone's private home, so never go inside without permission. Visiting times are usually between sunrise and sunset. Be aware of "guide touts", who accost you on the street with offers of haveli tours. They might take you to a haveli or two, but they are not licensed guides, and their sole objective is to get you to a shop that pays them commission.

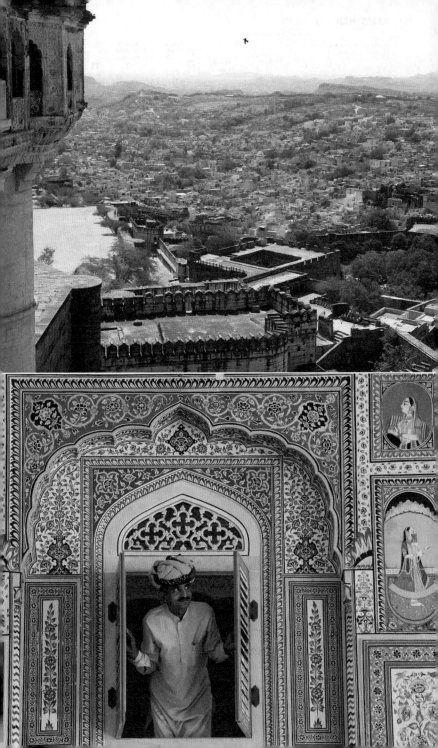

2

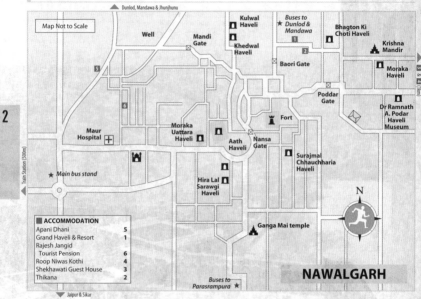

NAWALGARH

convenient and congenial base for exploring the region, with a bumper crop of painted havelis and a picturesque bazaar, along with a decent range of accommodation.

Dr Ramnath A. Podar Haveli Museum

Rambilas Podar Rd • Daily: summer 8am–7pm; winter 8.30am–6.30pm • ₹100 (₹80), camera ₹30, video ₹50 • ⓦ podarhavelimuseum.org

The logical place to start a tour of Nawalgarh is on the east side of town at the magnificent Anandi Lal Podar Haveli, which now houses the **Dr Ramnath A. Podar Haveli Museum**. Built in 1920, this is one of the few havelis in Shekhawati to have been restored to its original glory, and boasts the most vivid murals in town, including steam trains, soldiers drilling with rifles, and a clever 3D-like panel of a bull's head that transmogrifies into that of an elephant as you move from left to right. There's also a mildly diverting series of **exhibits** showcasing aspects of Rajasthani life, including musical instruments and traditional costumes.

Morarka Haveli

Naya Bazaar • Daily 8am–6pm • ₹50 (Free)

A short walk to the north of the Dr Ramnath A. Podar Haveli Museum lies the fine **Morarka Haveli**, decorated with murals of Shiva, Parvati, Krishna and Jesus, plus a *baithak* complete with a fine old hand-pulled fan (*punkah*). Directly opposite the Morarka Haveli lies the eye-catching **Krishna (Gher Ka) Mandir**, dating from the mid-eighteenth century, a florid mass of delicate chhatris.

Bhagton ki Choti Haveli

Near Podar Gate • Daily 8am–6pm • ₹40

About 200m east of the Morarka Haveli, the unrestored, 150-year-old **Bhagton ki Choti Haveli** has an unusually varied selection of murals including a European-style angel and Queen Victoria (over the arches by the right of the main door). On the left, a *trompe-l'oeil* picture shows seven women in the shape of an elephant, while other pictures show Europeans riding bicycles, along with a steamboat and a train.

The fort

At the heart of town, the **fort** (Bala Qila) has more or less vanished under a clutch of modern buildings huddled around a central courtyard that now hosts the town's colourful vegetable market. The dilapidated building on the far left-hand side of the courtyard (by the Bank of Baroda) boasts a magnificent, eerily echoing **Sheesh Mahal**, covered in mirrorwork, which once served as the dressing room of the maharani of Nawalgarh, its ceiling decorated with pictorial maps of Nawalgarh and Jaipur. You'll have to pay ₹20–30 to see the room; if no one's around, ask at the sweet factory on the opposite side of the courtyard.

2

Aath Haveli

Near Nansa Gate

Heading west from the fort through the Nansa Gate (signed, confusingly, as the "Rambilas Podar Memorial Gate") and following the road around brings you to the so-called **Aath Haveli** ("Eight Havelis", built by eight brothers, although only six were actually completed), a complex of heavily decorated mansions featuring murals – some of which are in a poor condition – in a range of styles depicting the usual mishmash of subjects both ancient and modern.

Moraka Uattara Haveli

Near Nansa Gate • Daily 8am–6pm • ₹50

The newly restored **Moraka Uattara Haveli**, opposite the Aath Haveli, also has a richly painted exterior and *mardana* (men's) courtyard, with elephants and horses framed in a mass of florid decoration.

Surajmal Chhauchharia Haveli

Near Jangid Hospital

Havelis dot the streets south and southeast of the Nansa Gate, one of the quietest and most atmospheric parts of town. These include the **Surajmal Chhauchharia Haveli**, whose murals feature two small pictures of Europeans floating past in a hot-air balloon. The painter took some playful licence as to the mechanics involved, with the passengers keeping their balloons aloft by blowing into them through small pipes.

ARRIVAL AND DEPARTURE
NAWALGARH

By train The railway station is 1km west of the bus station. Trains link Nawalgarh with Jhuhujunu, Sikar and Delhi, and there are erratic services to Bikaner and Jaipur. For timetable information, check out ⊚ indianrail.gov.in.

By bus Nawalgarh's bus and jeep stand is 1.5km west of town, around ₹60–100 by auto-rickshaw to the town's various hotels and guesthouses. RSRTC buses leave the main bus stand for Jaipur every 15min between 6am and 7.30pm (3hr 30min), and less frequently during the night; there's also a deluxe service at 8am. Some private buses also serve Jaipur, though these drop passengers 5km

outside the centre so are best avoided. Other services include Jhunjhunu (every 15–30min; 1hr) and Bikaner (hourly; 3hr 30min). There are also buses to Ajmer (6 daily; 3hr 30min), Delhi (8 daily; 8hr), Jodhpur (4 daily; 6hr 30min) and two evening departures to Jaipur Airport (8.15pm & 9.15pm; 4hr 30min). Buses to Fatehpur (1–2 hourly; 1hr 15min), Dundlod and Mandawa (every 30min; 20min & 45min respectively) leave from the bus stand just past Baori Gate on the north edge of town. Local destinations are also served by shared jeep, which leave when full.

GETTING AROUND AND INFORMATION

Getting around For trips around the region, you can either jump on and off cheap, cramped village-to-village jeeps or rent a vehicle through *Apani Dhani* (see p.146) or the *Rajesh Jangid Tourist Pension* (see p.146). Cycles can also be rented at both of these places for ₹50/day.

Tours The owners of the *Apani Dhani* and the *Rajesh Jangid Tourist Pension* also run socially responsible tours of

Shekhawati including jeep tours of nearby towns and other places of interest (₹1900–2500); walking tours of Nawalgarh (₹350/person); and tours by camel cart (₹1500/3hr). Alternatively, Babloo Sharma at the Moraka Haveli (☏ 98281 91232; beware of imitators in the streets outside) can also arrange car and walking tours at similar prices, plus horseriding excursions (₹1500/hr). The *Roop Niwas Kothi*

2

hotel also offers horseriding jaunts on its stable of pure-bred Marwari steeds (₹1000/hr), as well as short camel rides (₹800/hr) and more extended horse and camel safaris – see ⓦroyalridingholidays.com for full details.

ACCOMMODATION

★ **Apani Dhani** Northwest edge of town ☎0159 422 2239, ⓦapanidhani.com. Occupying a fetching cluster of mud-walled Rajasthani village-style huts (with clean attached bathrooms) dripping with bougainvillea, this eight-room eco-resort offers a perfect example of sustainable local tourism – a proportion of room rates (5 percent) goes to support environmental and educational projects and local artisans earn some income through involvement in the resort's stimulating programme of craft and cultural activities. Guests share the premises with the owner's extended family, giving it the feel of a homestay, and rooms (especially those in the slightly more expensive superior category) have plenty of rustic charm. There's also excellent organic pure veg food (nearly all of the fresh produce is plucked from the resort's extensive home garden), as well as wi-fi and activities including tie-dye and cookery classes, plus tours (see p.145). No alcohol. Book ahead. ₹995

Grand Haveli and Resort Baori Gate ☎0159 422 5301, ⓦgrandhaveli.com. Occupying the beautifully restored, century-old Patnawalo ki Haveli, the individual rooms and suites here are a mixed bag; some feature *jharokas* and coloured frescos, others are plain and poky – ask to see a couple first. There are also two restaurants (one on the rooftop) and a bar. ₹4500

Rajesh Jangid Tourist Pension On the western edge of town, just north of Maur Hospital ☎0159 422 4060, ⓦtouristpension.com. Homely guesthouse offering simple but spotless and good-value rooms in a sociable Brahmin family home; most have solar-heated water and the most expensive boast beautiful murals. There's also excellent pure veg food and free wi-fi, while activities include jeep tours (see p.145), Hindi classes and workshops in tie-dying, cooking and bangle-making. ₹550

Roop Niwas Kothi 1km east of the town centre ☎0159 422 2008, ⓦroopniwaskothi.com. Popular with passing coach parties, this rambling Raj-era mansion has a certain faded elegance, old-fashioned rooms, a nice swimming pool (non-guests pay ₹150/hr) and plenty of period charm at a fairly modest price. ₹3500

Shekhawati Guest House 1km east of the town centre, 200m south of the Roop Niwas Kothi ☎0159 422 4658, ⓦshekhawatiguesthouse.com. Run by charming owner Kalpana Singh, this friendly family guesthouse offers accommodation either in neat and clean, if rather dark, air-cooled rooms in the main house or in slightly more expensive garden cottages (with fan). Fresh produce is used in meals (veg and non-veg) and served in the breezy garden restaurant. There are also free cookery lessons, and tours can be arranged. ₹600

Thikana (also known locally as Vishnu Basotia's) 100m west of the Bhagton ki Choti Haveli ☎0159 422 2152, ⓦheritagethikana.com. Friendly family-run hotel in an unbeatably central location, with nicely furnished rooms and lovely views from the upstairs terrace – though the slightly chintzy pink modern building doesn't really live up to its billing as a "heritage" hotel. ₹1600

Dundlod

The most obvious target for a day-trip from Nawalgarh is **DUNDLOD**, 7km north and the site of an old fort and some large havelis. The musty **fort** (sunrise–sunset; ₹20) is worth a quick visit for its fine old Diwan-i-Khana, filled with antique European furniture. Dundlod's most interesting haveli is the meticulously restored **Seth Arjun Das Goenka Haveli** (daily 8am–7pm; ₹40; ⓦgoenkahaveli.com) of 1870, its interior covered in a profusion of finely detailed frescoes on assorted religious themes. Close by lies the delicate chhatri of Ram Dutt Goenka of 1888, with vibrant friezes lining its dome.

ARRIVAL AND DEPARTURE DUNDLOD

By bus Although buses to Dundlod leave every 30min from Nawalgarh's bus stand north of Baori Gate, you could also walk across the fields – a leisurely 2hr ramble.

ACCOMMODATION

Dundlod Fort ☎0159 425 2519, ⓦdundlod.com. The fort houses a heritage hotel; rooms are a bit shabby and overpriced for what you get, though the public areas are atmospheric and it's a good place to organize horseriding tours (3–12 days) on one of the castle's thoroughbred mounts. ₹3500

Parasrampura

Buses run every 30min or so between Parasrampura and Nawalgarh and take around 1hr

The serene hamlet of **PARASRAMPURA**, 20km southeast of Nawalgarh, is prettified by some of Shekhawati's oldest painted buildings. Monuments include the **Gopinath temple**, built in 1742, whose murals depict the torments of hell alongside images of the famous local Rajput ruler, Sardul Singh, with his five sons. Some of the paintings are unfinished, as the artists were diverted to decorate the chhatri of **Rajul Singh**, who died that same year. The large dome of this exquisite memorial contains a flourish of lively murals, once again including images of hell, and of Sardul Singh with his sons. Parasrampura's modest **fort** is on the west bank of the dry riverbed.

Jhunjhunu

Spreading in a mass of brick and concrete from the base of a rocky hill, **JHUNJHUNU** is a busy and fairly unprepossessing town, though it preserves an interesting old central bazaar and a fine collection of painted havelis. Jhunjhunu is usually visited as a day-trip from nearby Nawalgarh or Mandawa, though it has a couple of decent accommodation options if you want to stay.

Khetri Mahal

West of Nehru Bazaar • ₹20

Hidden away in the alleyways west of Nehru Bazaar is Jhunjhunu's most striking building, the magnificent **Khetri Mahal** of 1770, a superb, open-sided sandstone palace with cusped Islamic-style arches that wouldn't look out of place amid the great Indo-Islamic monuments of Fatehpur Sikri. The whole edifice seems incongruously grand amid the modest streets of central Jhunjhunu and is largely abandoned, save for the upper terraces that serve as impromptu open-air classrooms for local schoolchildren. A covered ramp, wide enough for horses, winds up to the roof, from where there are sweeping views over the town and across to the massive ramparts of the sturdy **Badalgarh Fort** (currently closed to the public) on a nearby hilltop.

Futala Market

Stretching east of the Khetri Mahal is Jhunjhunu's main bazaar, centred around **Futala Market**, a fascinating and hopelessly confusing tangle of narrow streets crammed with dozens of tiny, charmingly old-fashioned shops. On the northern edge of the bazaar, facing each other across the small square of Chabutra Chowk, lie the two so-called **Modi havelis**, boasting the usual range of murals – the one on the eastern side of the chowk is the most impressive, entered via a grand, 3m-high ramp.

Nehru Bazaar

Jhunjhunu's finest havelis are spread out along **Nehru Bazaar**, immediately east of the main bazaar. Heading east, you'll first reach the striking **Kaniram Narsinghdas Tibrewala Haveli** of 1883, perched on a platform above the surrounding vegetable stalls and sporting a fine selection of paintings inside (the entrance is around the back).

Further east down Nehru Bazaar, entered via an impressive ramp up from street level, the **Mohanlal Ishwardas Modi Haveli** has a good selection of entertainingly naïve portraits. Unusual oval miniatures of various Indian bigwigs frame the entrance to the zenana (women's) courtyard, while in the zenana itself a long frieze of miniature portraits runs around the top of the arches showing assorted European and Indian personages sporting a range of flouncy costumes, silly hats and magnificent moustaches.

Bihari Ji Temple
South of Cloth Market Rd

To the northeast of Nehru Bazaar, the striking little **Bihari Ji Temple** features some of the oldest murals in Shekhawati, painted in 1776 in black and brown vegetable pigments, including a dramatic depiction inside the central dome of Hanuman's monkey army taking on the forces of the many-headed demon king Ravana.

Dargah of Kamaruddin Shah

West of the Khetri Mahal at the foot of the craggy Nehara Pahar lies the **Dargah of Kamaruddin Shah**, an atmospheric complex comprising a mosque and madrasa arranged around a pretty courtyard (still retaining some of its original murals), with the ornate *dargah* (tomb) of the Sufi saint Kamaruddin Shah in the centre. Women must wear headscarves.

Mertani Baori
Near Pipli Circle

North of the town centre lies the **Mertani Baori**, one of the region's most impressive step-wells. Constructed in 1783 by Mertani, the widow of Sardul Singh, this step-well is thought to be a staggering 30m deep.

Rani Sati Mandir
Off Rani Sati Rd

To the northeast of town is the extraordinary **Rani Sati Mandir**, dedicated to a merchant's wife who commited sati in 1595. The shrine is reputedly the richest temple in the country after Tirupati in Andhra Pradesh – although similar claims are made for the Nathdwara temple (see p.212) – receiving hundreds of thousands of pilgrims each year and millions of rupees in donations. It's immense popularity bears witness to the enduring awe with which satis are regarded in the state.

ARRIVAL AND DEPARTURE — JHUNJHUNU

By train The train station is around 1.5km southwest of the main bazaar. Services link Jhunjhunu with Nawalgarh, Sikar and Delhi, and there are slow and often unreliable services to Jaipur and Bikaner too. For up-to-date timetable information, check out ⊚ indianrail.gov.in.

By bus The government bus stand (☎ 0159 223 2664) is just south of the town centre. There are frequent services to Nawalgarh (every 30min; 1hr) and towns throughout Shekhawati, as well as to Bikaner (4 daily; 5hr 30min), Jaipur (ever 30min; 4hr), Jodhpur (6 daily; 7hr), Ajmer (2 daily; 4hr) and Delhi (hourly, including a 9pm sleeper bus; 7hr). Buses to Mandawa (every 45min; 45min–1hr) also stop by Mandawa Circle near the *RTDC Tourist Bungalow*.

GETTING AROUND AND INFORMATION

By rickshaw Jhunjhunu is quite spread out, and walking around can be tiring, but many of the streets of the old town are too narrow for cars; rickshaws operate as taxis, picking up as many passengers as they can.

Tourist information There's a tourist office within the *RTDC Tourist Bungalow* (Mon–Sat 10am–5pm), near the Mandawa Circle, but it's rarely manned.

Tours Laxmi Jangid, the owner of *Jamuna Resort*, offers full-day tours around Shekhawati by car or jeep for ₹2200, as well as shorter camel tours (2hr; ₹800/person) and 3–5 day cycling trips to local towns.

ACCOMMODATION

There are no good restaurants in town, and you'll almost certainly end up eating where you're staying.

Fresco Palace Paramveer Path, off Station Rd ☎ 0159 239 5233. Pleasant modern hotel (although there aren't many frescoes in evidence), with comfortable, slightly chintzy rooms (all a/c) and a relaxing garden restaurant. ₹2000

Jamuna Resort Delhi–Sikar Rd ☎ 0159 223 2871, ⊚ shivshekhawati.com. This attractive village-style resort on the eastern edge of town comprises a cluster of thatch-roofed cottages (all a/c) set amid extensive grounds complete with pool (non-guests ₹100) and garden restaurant. The more expensive rooms are exquisitely decorated with mirrorwork and traditional murals. They also run courses in Indian cooking and art, plus free yoga classes. Also a good place to arrange tours (see opposite). ₹1500

Sangam Paramveer Path, opposite the government bus stand ☎0159 223 2544. Basic cheapie with large,

bare and shabby rooms – many of which are past their best. Request one away from the noisy main road. ₹500

Shiv Shekhawati Khemi Shakti Rd, near Muni Ashram ☎0159 223 2651 or ☎0159 512 695, ⓦshivshekhawati .com. Decent hotel with large, clean rooms (all a/c), but no restaurant. ₹1000

Mandawa

Rising from a flat, featureless landscape roughly midway between Jhunjhunu and Fatehpur, **MANDAWA** was founded by the Shekhawats in 1755 and is now the most tourist-oriented place in Shekhawati, although the handicraft shops, touts and guides detract very little from the town's profusion of beautifully dilapidated mansions.

The havelis

Tours usually begin with the **Naveti Haveli** (now the State Bank of Bikaner & Jaipur), on the main bazaar. Duck through the metal gate to the right of the bank (no charge) for a look at Mandawa's most entertaining murals, including well-preserved images of a bird-man attempting to take flight, the Wright Brothers' aeroplane, a man using a telephone and a strongman pulling a car.

A ten-minute walk west from here brings you to an interesting cluster of buildings centred around the **Nand Lal Murmuria Haveli**. The murals here are relatively modern, dating from the 1930s and executed in a decidedly flowery and sentimental style, perhaps influenced by contemporary European magazines, with images of various Venetian scenes, George V, Nehru riding a horse and the legendary Maratha warrior Shivaji. Next door, the sun-faded **Goenka Double Haveli** (not to be confused with either of the other Goenka havelis nearby) is one of the largest and grandest in Mandawa, with two separate entrances and striking elephants and horses on the facade.

South of the main bazaar, the **Gulab Rai Wadia Haveli** is one of the finest in town. The south-facing exterior wall is particularly interesting, with unusually racy (albeit modestly small) murals depicting, amongst other things, a Kama Sutra-like scene in a railway carriage. The interior of the haveli is entered via a grand ramp, with

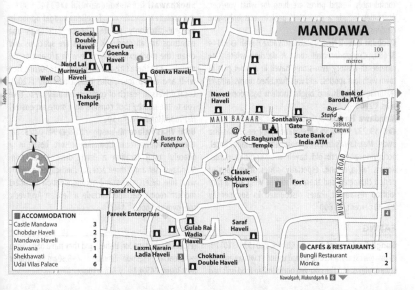

2

Belgian-glass mirrorwork over the finely carved door leading into the zenana (women's) courtyard.

Immediately south of here lies the almost equally fine **Laxmi Narain Ladia Haveli**. The zenana courtyard boasts naïve paintings of a plane and a steamship, along with a cannon being pulled by horses and a tiger attacking a centaur. Some 100m further south, the unusually large **Chokhani Double Haveli** (₹40) consists of two separate wings built for two brothers; look for the miserable British soldiers and chillum-smoking sadhu facing one another in the recess at the centre of the facade.

ARRIVAL AND INFORMATION   MANDAWA

By bus Buses from Jhunjhunu, Nawalgarh, Jaipur and Bikaner arrive at Subash Chowk, near Sonthaliya Gate in the east of town, except for the fast services that drop you at the highway junction (an auto into town should cost ₹40). From Fatehpur, most buses pull in at a stand in the centre, just off the main bazaar, and since the town is so small, both bus stands are within walking distance of most hotels. Jeeps ply the same routes. There are frequent services to Jhunjhunu (every 30min; 1hr), Nawalgarh (every 30min; 45min) and Fatehpur (every 30min; 1hr), plus a handful of buses (mostly in the morning) to Jaipur (4hr), Bikaner (3hr 30min) and Delhi (7hr).

Tours Walking tours of Mandawa's havelis can be arranged through your hotel, from ₹150/person.

Most guesthouses and hotels can also arrange trips out into the surrounding desert either by jeep or on horseback, on camel or in camel-drawn carts. Prices for all these activities vary wildly, but are usually cheapest if booked through *Shekhawati* Hotel (see below), who also rent bicycles for ₹50/hr. Classic Shekhawati Tours (☎01592 223144, ✉classicshekhamnd@yahoo .co.in), by the fort entrance, arranges more upmarket day and overnight tented camel safaris (₹5500), though you'll need to book a few days in advance.

Services The State Bank of Bikaner & Jaipur (Mon–Fri 10am–2pm, Sat 10am–noon) changes travellers' cheques and cash. Internet access is available at most hotels from ₹40/hr.

ACCOMMODATION

Castle Mandawa Fort ☎0159 222 3124 or ☎0141 510 6081, ⊛castlemandawa.com. Mandawa's fanciest accommodation, set in the old town fort, with an atmospheric mishmash of buildings around a sand-filled courtyard. All rooms are different, so look at several before you decide, since standards of comfort and decor vary considerably – and prices are high for what you get. Amenities include a spa, gym, pool (guests only) and gardens. ₹6930

Chobdar Haveli Near Gulab Rai Wadia Haveli ☎93144 32690, ⊛chobdarhaveli.com. A dazzling white, late nineteenth-century, two-storey haveli in a quiet part of town with four spotless and well-furnished rooms (all a/c) featuring big beds and bright modern bathrooms with tubs. ₹2200

Mandawa Haveli Nr Sonthaliya Gate, Main Bazaar ☎0159 222 3088, ⊛hotelmandawa.free.fr. Far and away Mandawa's most atmospheric heritage hotel, occupying a superb old haveli with original murals. Rooms (all a/c) and, especially, suites, have bags of period character, and there's also free wi-fi and a nice rooftop restaurant. Rates discounted in summer by 20–40 percent. ₹1800

Paawana Main Bazaar ☎0159 222 3663, ⊛hotelpaawana.com. Recently opened hotel in a neat modern building (done up with the obligatory murals) and offering attractively furnished a/c rooms at surprisingly affordable prices. There's a great street-view restaurant. ₹1500

Shekhawati Off Mukundgarh Rd ☎93146 98079, ⊛hotelshekhawati.com. Excellent budget option in an eye-catchingly painted house (although the paintings are all modern). Rooms are spacious and clean (the more expensive come with a/c and pretty murals), and there's also food, internet (₹50/hr), free wi-fi and cheap tours, plus henna painting (₹200). Local drivers in search of commission may try to take you to the nearby (but considerably more expensive) *Heritage Mandawa*. ₹350

Udai Vilas Palace Mukundgarh Rd ☎94140 23378, ⊛uvpmandawa.com. Upmarket resort hotel in a peaceful rural location a 5min drive south from Mandawa, set amid three acres of landscaped grounds with fine desert views and accommodation in smart modern rooms. Facilities include a Keralan Ayurvedic spa, gym and pool. ₹4400

EATING

Bungli Restaurant Goenka Chowk ☎01571 310129, ⊛bunglirestaurant.com. *Bungli* wouldn't win awards for style or views, but the non-veg north Indian food isn't bad

(especially the tandoori dishes) and they run a daily "yoga + breakfast" session (summer 7–8.30am & winter 8–9.30am; ₹450). Daily 7am–10pm.

Monica West of the fort. This rooftop restaurant (follow the signs from the entrance road to the fort), dishes up probably the best food in town, with well-prepared veg and non-veg north Indian standards (mains ₹100–380) along with cold beer. Friendly but discreet service. Daily 8am–10pm.

Fatehpur

Lying just off NH-11, **FATEHPUR** is the closest town in Shekhawati to Bikaner, 116km west, and a convenient place to stop if you're taking the northern route across the Thar. The town itself is fairly run-down, but it does have several elaborately painted mansions.

Fatehpur's most celebrated muralled abode is the **Nadine Le Prince Haveli** near Chauhan Well (daily 9am–12.30pm & 2.30–6pm; ₹250; ⓦcultural-centre.com), an 1802 mansion restored to its original splendour by its current owner Nadine Le Prince, a French artist who purchased the haveli in 1998. Some local aficionados complain about the manner in which the haveli has been restored – with large-scale repainting of murals, rather than the simple cleaning and preservation of existing art – but the overall effect is undeniably impressive, and the haveli as a whole is one of the few in Shekhawati where you get a real sense of how these lavish mansions would originally have looked.

Close to the Nadine Le Prince Haveli on Churu-Sikar Road, the imposing **Jagannath Singania Haveli** (closed to visitors) towers over the main road north. Most of the exterior paintings have faded; the best are on the western facade of the small building around the back, including Krishna and Radha framed by elephants and some heavily bewhiskered Europeans toting guns.

South from the Jagannath Singania Haveli, the **Geori Shankar Haveli** (next to an unusually fine bangle stall) is the polar opposite of the Nadine Le Prince Haveli, dilapidated but hugely atmospheric, and still inhabited by a number of impoverished local families.

ARRIVAL AND DEPARTURE   FATEHPUR

By bus Fatehpur has two bus stands, near each other in the centre of town on the main Sikar–Churu (north–south) road. Buses from the government Roadways stand, furthest south, serve Jaipur (every 30min; 3hr 30min), Bikaner (every 30min; 3hr 30min–4hr) and Delhi (2 daily; 6hr). Private buses run from the stand further north along the bazaar to Mandawa (every 30min; 45min), Jhunjhunu (every 30min; 1hr), Mahansar (every 30min; 45min) and Ramgarh (every 30min; 30min). Arriving in Fatehpur, note that many buses drop passengers off at the NH-11 intersection, about 1km south of town.

ACCOMMODATION

RTDC Hotel Haveli Just off NH-11 ☏0157 123 0293, ⓦtdc.in/haveli.htm. Set in spacious grounds, this is the town's only plausible hotel, though its large and light rooms (some with a/c) don't quite compensate for the dodgy plumbing and general air of neglect. Licensed. ₹1180

Mahansar

The relative inaccessibility of **MAHANSAR**, marooned amid a sea of scrub and drifting sand north of Mandawa, has ensured that its monuments remain among the least visited in the region, making the village a peaceful place to hole up for a day or two.

Otherwise known as the "Gold Shop Haveli", the **Sona ki Dukan Haveli** (daily, no set hours; ₹100; ask around the shops for the key), right in the middle of the village, is home to Shekhawati's finest paintings. The murals in the entrance hall are the most striking, and depict the exploits of Rama, the incarnations of Vishnu and the life of Krishna, all painted in superb detail and picked out in lavish gold leaf (hence the haveli's name).

While you're here, it's also worth having a look at the nearby **Raghunath Mandir**, covered in colourful floral murals and offering good views over town from its chhatri-fringed rooftop.

By bus Mahansar bus station is to the west of town. Services run to Nawalgarh (2hr 30min), Mandawa (1hr 30min) and Fatehpur (45min).

ACCOMMODATION

Narayan Niwas Castle Mahansar ☎0159 526 4322, ⓦmehansarcastle.com. This quirky hotel, managed by Mahansar's royal family, is in a crumbling 1768 abode that's home to fourteen rooms of varying standards, including two memorably appointed heritage rooms (#1 and #5) and some cheaper but still deeply atmospheric standard doubles (albeit stronger on period charm than creature comforts). ₹1720

Ramgarh

RAMGARH, 20km north of Fatehpur, was founded in 1791 and developed as something of a status symbol by disaffected members of the wealthy Poddar merchant family, who made every effort for the town to outshine nearby Churu, which they left following a dispute with the local *thakur* over taxes. They succeeded in their aim: Ramgarh is one of the most beautiful – but also still one of the least-visited – towns in Shekhawati, with the usual fine havelis along with an exceptional array of religious architecture as well.

Starting from the bus stand on the west side of town, follow either of the two roads east into the town centre. After about five minutes' walk you'll reach the **Poddar family havelis** (daily 8am–7pm; free), a superb cluster of ornate mansions decorated with scenes from local folk stories and a frequently repeated motif, comprising three fishes joined at the mouth, which is unique to Ramgarh. Just beyond here lies the town's main square, surrounded by the disintegrating remains of further lavishly painted havelis.

Turn left here and head through the Churu Gate, beyond which the road is lined with a dense cluster of extraordinarily ornate temples and memorial chhatris erected by various members of the Poddar clan, their rooftops capped with a fantastical array of domes and arcades.

By jeep and bus Inter-village jeeps and buses run to Fatehpur (45min), Mandawa (1hr 30min) and Nawalgarh (2hr 30min).

By car You can reach Ramgarh on day-trips from Fatehpur, Mandawa and Nawalgarh with your own vehicle, which is by far the quickest option.

Lakshmangarh

The small town of **LAKSHMANGARH**, 20km south of Fatehpur, is another archetypal, but seldom visited, Shekhawati destination, its neat grid of streets (a layout inspired by that of Jaipur's Pink City) dotted with dozens of ornate havelis in various stages of picturesque decay. Lakshmangarh is dominated by its dramatic nineteenth-century **fort**, which crowns a rocky outcrop on the west side of town; it's now closed to the public, though you can walk up the steep track to the entrance to enjoy the fine views. Looking down from here you can see the extensive **Char Chowk Haveli** (Four-Courtyard Haveli), off to the left, the finest in town and one of the largest in Shekhawati.

By bus or car Numerous buses run to Fatehpur (45min), Sikar (1hr), where there's a train station, and Nawalgarh (2hr); you can also reach Lakshmangarh on day-trips from these destinations with your own vehicle.

East of Jaipur

The area **east of Jaipur**, interspersed with the forested slopes of the Aravalli Hills, holds an inviting mixture of historic towns and wildlife sanctuaries. To the northeast is the fortified town of **Alwar**, convenient for the **Sariska Tiger Reserve and National Park**. Further east are the former princely capitals of **Deeg** and **Bharatpur**, and India's finest bird sanctuary, **Keoladeo National Park**. The wildlife sanctuary at **Ranthambore**, in idyllic scenery southeast of Jaipur, offers the best chance in India of spotting wild tigers.

Alwar

Roughly 140km northeast from Jaipur towards Delhi, the large, bustling town of **ALWAR** sprawls across a valley beneath one of eastern Rajasthan's larger and more impressive **forts**, whose massive ramparts straggle impressively along craggy ridges above. The town is mostly visited as a jumping-off point for Sariska National Park, though it has a number of interesting attractions in its own right, including a fine palace and a string of colourful bazaars.

City Palace

Museum Tues–Sun 10am–5pm • ₹10 (₹5)

Alwar's principal attraction is its rambling and atmospheric **City Palace**, or Vinai Vilas Mahal, a sprawling complex of ornate but slightly dilapidated buildings, covered in crumbling ochre plaster and studded with endless canopied balconies. Most of the palace's innumerable rooms are now put to more mundane use as government offices, while the courtyard in front provides open-air office space for dozens of typists, lined up behind clanking old antique metal machines, and lawyers, who prosecute their business under the trees.

The palace's time-warped **museum**, on the top floor, has extensive collections of weapons and miniature paintings, alongside a medley of objects belonging to former maharajas ranging from musical instruments to stuffed animals.

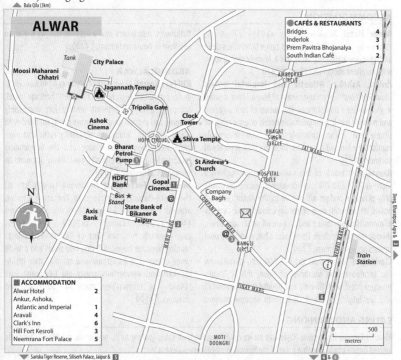

Steps at the left-hand end of the main facade lead up to a large **tank**, flanked by symmetrical *ghats*, pavilions and a terrace on which stands the delicate **Moosi Maharani Chhatri**, built in memory of Bhaktawar Singh's mistress, who immolated herself on his funeral pyre.

Bala Qila

Perched high above Alwar is **Bala Qila** fort, whose well-preserved walls climb dramatically up and down the thickly wooded hillsides that rise above the town. There's not much actually to see inside the fort – besides a temple and a few old cannons – but it's a pleasant walk up from town, with fine views and fresh hill breezes. It takes about two hours to make the return trip on foot up to the fort's outermost gate, or about twice that to reach the topmost point of the fortifications. If you don't want to walk, you'll have to arrange for a taxi through your hotel or the tourist office – the road up is too steep for cycle rickshaws.

ARRIVAL AND INFORMATION
ALWAR

By train The railway station is around 1.5km east of the centre. Trains run to and from Delhi, Jaipur, Jodhpur, Ajmer and Ahmedabad (but not Bharatpur). For Jaipur, the best service is the *Ajmer Shatabdi* #2015 (daily; dep. 8.40am, arr. 10.30am); for Delhi, the *Ashram Express* #2915 (daily; dep. 6.40am, arr. 10.10am) is one of the faster services.

By bus Alwar's bus stand is right in the middle of town. Buses depart for Bharatpur via Deeg (every 15min; 4hr), Sariska (every 30min; 1hr–1hr 30min), Delhi (every 30min; 5hr) and Jaipur (hourly; 4hr).

Getting around There are plenty of cycle rickshaws, but surprisingly few autos (try the railway station).

Tourist information The RTDC office is south of the station (Mon–Fri 10am–5pm; ☎ 0144 234 7348).

Services You can change currency and travellers' cheques at the State Bank of Bikaner & Jaipur, in the centre of town, which also has an ATM that accepts foreign Visa and MasterCards; if this isn't working, try the HDFC ATM nearby. Internet cafés are plentiful, and generally charge around ₹20/hr.

ACCOMMODATION

Alwar Hotel 26 Manu Marg ☎ 0144 270 0012, ⓦ alwarhotel.com. This bijou mid-range hotel offers clean and spacious a/c rooms, wi-fi and a homely dining room with excellent north Indian food. ₹2630

Ankur, Ashoka, Atlantic and Imperial hotels Clustered together on the corner of Manu Marg, a 5min walk from the bus station. This group of four adjacent and more or less indistinguishable hotels offers a range of simple but cheap, tolerably clean and reasonably comfortable fan and a/c rooms. There are always plenty of vacancies. ₹650

Aravali Just south of the railway station on Nehru Marg ☎ 0144 233 2883, ⓦ hotelaraveli.co.in. The town's only plausible budget alternative to the *Ankur* group of hotels. It's definitely seen better days, and the wide variety of rooms (fan, air-cooled and a/c) are all rather run-down, though reasonably clean. There's also a bar, wi-fi and a pool (guests only) in summer. ₹700

Clark's Inn Shanti Kuni ☎ 0144 700 600, ⓦ clarksinn .in. Located to the southeast of town, this is Alwar's smartest hotel, with friendly and helpful staff. Rooms (all a/c) are bright, cosy and clean, with spotless modern

bathrooms, and there's also a licensed bar, wi-fi and an excellent in-house restaurant. ₹4200

AROUND ALWAR

Hill Fort Kesroli 12km east of Alwar ☎ 0146 828 9352, ⓦ neemranahotels.com. India's oldest heritage hotel, occupying a rugged fifteenth-century fort impeccably restored and centred on a lush inner courtyard filled with plants and birds. Rooms are pleasantly rustic and have great views over Kesroli village and the surrounding countryside, as does the pretty pool. Wi-fi. Discounts in summer of 20 percent. ₹3000

Neemrana Fort-Palace Neemrana (just north of the Delhi–Jaipur NH-8 close to the state border, around 75km from Alwar, 120km from Delhi and 140km from Jaipur) ☎ 0149 424 6006, ⓦ neemranahotels.com. One of Rajasthan's longest-running heritage hotels, offering two pools and a wide range of rooms in Rajasthani and colonial style inside the vast and wonderfully crusty old Neemrana Fort (1464) – a labyrinthine maze of courtyards and corridors. ₹4500

EATING AND DRINKING

Alwar is famous throughout Rajasthan for its cavity-causing milk cakes (*palang torh*), which you can buy at the stalls around Hope Circus. Note that none of the following places serves alcohol.

Bridges Clark's Inn, Shanti Kuni ☏0144 700 600. Smart a/c street-facing non-veg multicuisine restaurant featuring hearty north and south Indian, Chinese and Continental standards, plus sandwiches and pizza. Afterwards, drop into the adjacent *Cloud* 9, also at the hotel, for a nightcap. Mains ₹125–250. Daily 7am–11pm.

Inderlok Company Bagh Rd, near Nangli Circle ☏0144 270 0398. Popular a/c veg restaurant serving good pan-India dishes, including unusual *paneer* varieties, along with a few Oriental mains. Mains ₹90–140. Daily noon–3pm & 7–11pm.

Prem Pavitra Bhojanalya Old Bus Stand ☏0144 233 5284. This cosy little restaurant dishes up the best food in town, with a very short, very cheap menu of simple north Indian staples (mains ₹30–75) such as *palek paneer* and *aloo paratha*. The entrance is easily missed: go up the road roughly opposite the State Bank of Jaipur & Bikaner, past the Bharat Petroleum petrol station. It's on the left about 50m up. Daily 10am–10pm.

South Indian Café Opposite the Gopal Cinema ☏0144 270 1217. Simple little a/c café serving reasonably priced thalis and a short menu of specialities from southern Indian, including masala dosas with mango chutney. Mains ₹40–70. Daily 9am–9pm.

Siliserh Palace

Daily, no set hours • ₹50

Fifteen kilometres south of Alwar, **Siliserh Palace** is easily visited en route to or from Sariska if you've got your own vehicle (there's no public transport here). Maharaja Vijay Singh had the palace built in 1845 to win over a beautiful commoner, a certain Sheela, who agreed to marriage on the condition that she live within sight of her family's modest home. The whitewashed palace itself is fairly humdrum, but the Shangri-La setting, on the edge of a ten-square-kilometre lake ringed by jungle-clad hills, is idyllic. It's a nice spot to while away an afternoon, and you can rent paddle-boats (₹200/30min) and motorboats (₹600 for 15min).

Sariska Tiger Reserve and National Park

Alwar is the access point for **Sariska Tiger Reserve and National Park**, a former maharaja's hunting ground managed since 1979 by Project Tiger. Accustomed to being overshadowed by the more famous Ranthambore, Sariska was suddenly thrust into the headlines in 2005 when it was discovered that its tiger population, estimated at around 28 in 2003, had all but vanished due to poaching – one of India's biggest-ever conservation scandals. As a result, tigers were reintroduced to Sariska in 2008, with the arrival of one male and two females airlifted from Ranthambore, followed by a further two tigers in 2009 and 2010. Fortunately, these desperate measures reaped rewards with the birth of two cubs in 2012, increasing Sariska's current tiger tally to seven.

One silver lining from the whole affair is that the number of visitors to the sanctuary has dwindled significantly, and for birders and wildlife enthusiasts put off by the crowds and hassle of Ranthambore, Sariska's relative serenity comes as a welcome relief. The 881-square-kilometre sanctuary is home to abundant **wildlife** including *sambar*, *chital*, wild boar, nilgai and other antelopes, jackals, mongooses, monkeys, peacocks, porcupines, and numerous birds. The park is also dotted with a number of evocative ruins and other man-made structures, including the old **Kankwari Fort**, and a **Hanuman temple** deep within the park that gets surprisingly lively on Saturdays and Tuesdays, when visitors to the temple are allowed into the park for free.

ESSENTIALS   **SARISKA TIGER RESERVE**

Opening times Sariska is open daily from October to June (summer 6–9.30am & 2–5.30pm; winter 7–10am & 3.30–7pm).

Tickets Entrance to the park costs ₹475/person (₹75) in a Canter or ₹505 (₹105) in a Gypsy (jeep). You rent vehicles from the entrance and pay an additional ₹150 (Canter) or ₹200 (Gypsy) for the privilege plus ₹13/₹42 for a compulsory guide and ₹400 for a video camera. Buy your tickets online (☒rajasthanwildlife.in) or from the park's ticket office on the day. Private vehicles are allowed into the park on Saturdays and Tuesdays (to visit the temple), but are restricted to metalled roads.

ARRIVAL AND DEPARTURE

By bus The park lies 35km southwest of Alwar on the main Alwar–Jaipur road; buses between the two (every 30min; 1hr) will stop, on request, at the *Sariska Palace* hotel, a 5min walk from the park.

By taxi Alternatively, you may be able to arrange a taxi through a hotel in Alwar (around ₹1100 for the roundtrip), which also gives you time to visit Siliserh (see p.155) on the way back.

ACCOMMODATION

Alwar Bagh 20km from Sariska (and 14km from Alwar) on the Sariska–Alwar highway ☎0294 515 1412, ⊛alwarbagh.com. Large and comfortable a/c rooms in a sequence of attractive lemon-yellow and salmon-pink buildings arranged around spacious gardens, plus a fine pool. Very tranquil, and much better value than the various places closer to the park. **₹3500**

RTDC Hotel Tiger Den ☎0144 284 1342, ⊛rtdc.cin /tigerden.htm. Attractive, if rather overpriced, option conveniently situated right next to the park entrance, with spacious, old-fashioned fan-cooled and a/c rooms, plus a

nice garden, though service can be lackadaisical. Rates are half board. Licensed. **₹2420**

Sariska Palace A couple of minutes' drive down the main road from the park entrance ☎011 2841 325, ⊛thesariskapalace.in. This former maharaja's residence has plenty of atmosphere, though rooms in the main building are surprisingly shabby given the hefty price, while those in the various modern annexes scattered around the grounds are poky and boring. There's also a pool (₹500 for non-guests), clay tennis court and large swathes of manicured lawns to loll around on. **₹9800**

Deeg

Some 30km northwest of Bharatpur, the dusty little market town of **DEEG** is the unlikely home of one of eastern Rajasthan's most lavish **palaces** (daily except Fri 9.30am–5.30pm; ₹100 (₹5)), a fascinating blend of Mughal and Hindu architectural styles constructed by the local Jat overlords in the mid-eighteenth century. The extensive complex comprises a large number of finely carved buildings scattered around extensive *charbagh*-style gardens dotted with thirty-odd water jets – though sadly the water channels are dry and the fountains are only switched on during local festivals.

As you enter the palace, the first and largest of the various *bhawans*, the **Gopal Bhawan**, lies immediately ahead, a spacious and plushly furnished hall that originally served as Surajmal's summer residence. Behind it lies the first of the palace's two large tanks, the **Gopal Sagar**. On the opposite side of the gardens lies the ornate **Kesav Bhawan**, or "Monsoon Palace", a richly carved open-sided pavilion surrounded by a deep water channel dotted with hundreds of tiny fountains. This unusual structure was designed to recreate the cool ambience of the rainy season, with water released from rooftop pipes to imitate a shower of monsoon rain, while metal balls were agitated by further streams of pressurized water to simulate the sound of thunder. Immediately behind here is the second of the palace's **tanks**, its stepped *ghats* usually covered in washing laid out by local housewives, while beyond rise the enormous walls of the town's huge fort.

ARRIVAL AND INFORMATION · DEEG

By bus Deeg is served by bus from Alwar (every 15min; 3hr) and Bharatpur (every 15min; 1hr).

Information The town is easily visited as a day-trip from

Bharatpur, or en route between Bharatpur and Alwar. There's nowhere to stay.

Bharatpur

The walled town of **BHARATPUR** is just a stone's throw from the border with Uttar Pradesh and a mere 18km from the magnificent abandoned city of Fatehpur Sikri (see p.247). The town itself has an interesting mix of bazaars, palaces and temples, but the real reason to come here is to visit India's most famous bird sanctuary, the **Keoladeo National Park** (see p.159), on the town's southern edge, one of India's, if not the world's, top ornithological destinations.

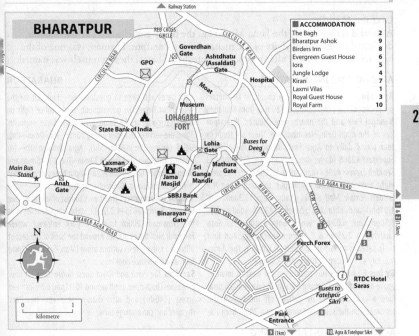

BHARATPUR

■ ACCOMMODATION	
The Bagh	2
Bharatpur Ashok	9
Birders Inn	8
Evergreen Guest House	6
Iora	5
Jungle Lodge	4
Kiran	7
Laxmi Vilas	1
Royal Guest House	3
Royal Farm	10

Lohagarh

Museum Tues–Sun 9.30am–5pm • ₹50 (₹5), camera ₹10, video ₹20

Bharatpur was founded by the Jat king Surajmal, who constructed the virtually impregnable **Lohagarh** (Iron Fort) at the heart of town in 1732; time and modern development have had little effect on its magnificent 11km-long bastions and immense moat. You're most likely to enter the fort from the south, though it's worth having a look at the impressive **Ashtdhatu** (or Eight-Metal) **Gate**, named on account of the number of different metals that apparently went into the making of its extremely solid-looking doors.

The fort is home to no less than three large royal palaces in various stages of dereliction, all built by the Jats between 1730 and 1850. The best preserved is the large orange **Kamra Khas Mahal**, on the west side of the fort, which now serves as the town's recently upgraded **museum**, home to a large collection of finely carved sculptures, weapons and a superb little marble hammam (baths), plus the usual ragtag collection of miniature paintings and other regal memorabilia.

Ganga Mandir

Near Lohia Gate

Immediately south of the fort lies the unusual **Ganga Mandir**, a large Hindu temple dedicated to the proprietary goddess of India's most sacred river, though the elaborately carved sandstone building itself looks more like a Neoclassical French chateau than a Subcontinental temple.

Jama Masjid

Jama Masjid Market

Beyond the Ganga Mandir, narrow roads snake southwest through Bharatpur's characteristic bazaar district to reach the imposing **Jama Masjid**, set high on a raised platform above the busy surrounding streets.

Laxman Mandir

A short distance east of the Jama Masjid lies the finely embellished **Laxman Mandir**, dedicated to the family deity of the maharajas of Bharatpur. Laxman, was one of the brothers of Lord Rama, after whose other brother, Bharat, the town itself was named.

ARRIVAL AND INFORMATION   BHARATPUR

By train The railway station is a couple of kilometres northwest of the town centre, a ₹60 ride from Keoladeo National Park and the nearby guesthouses. Bharatpur lies on the main Delhi–Mumbai line. There are three or four trains daily to Agra Fort, including the *Howrah Superfast* #2308 (daily; dep. 4.52am, arr. 6.15am) and *Sealdah Express* #2988 (daily; dep. 5.32pm, arr. 7.25pm); eight services to Sawai Madhopur, the best being the Golden *Temple Mail* #2904 (daily; dep. 10.30am, arr. 1.01pm) and *Kota Jan Shatabdi* #2060 (daily; dep. 3.50pm, arr. 6.02pm), which both continue to Kota (arriving at 2.25pm & 7.40pm respectively), and four daily services to Jaipur, the best of which is the *Ajmer Intercity* #2195 (dep. 6.10am, arr. 9.30am).

By bus Bharatpur's bus stand is in the west of town. If you're arriving from Fatehpur Sikri you'll save yourself time (and a rickshaw fare) by getting off the bus at the crossroads on the southeast side of town 200m from the

park gates and close to guesthouses – look out for the prominent Rajasthan government tourist office right on the crossroads, or the large *RTDC Hotel Saras* opposite. There are services to Jaipur (every 30min; 3hr 30min–4hr), Delhi (every 30min–1hr; 5hr), Agra (hourly; 1hr–1hr 30min), Fatehpur Sikri (every 30min–1hr; 30–45min) and Deeg (hourly; 1hr). Deluxe Agra–Jaipur buses stop in front of *Hotel Saras* (every 30min after 2pm).

Tourist information The town's tourist office (Mon–Sat 9.30am–6pm; ☎ 05644 222542, ⬥ bharatpur.nic.in) is at the crossroads 200m from the park entrance where Fatehpur Sikri buses pull in. Around the back of the tourist office is a railway reservations office (Mon–Sat 8am–2pm) for making advance bookings.

Services *The Perch* and *Royal Guest House* forex on New Civil Lines (both open untill around 10/11pm) offer internet access (₹40/hr) and also change cash and travellers' cheques and can arrange taxis.

ACCOMMODATION AND EATING

All the town's best hotels and guesthouses are located near the entrance to Keoladeo National Park, some 3km south of the town centre itself. Bharatpur's reputation as a tourist-friendly oasis has made it an attractive base for day-trippers to Agra and the Taj Mahal – a day-trip by taxi to Agra and back should cost about ₹1400, including parking and taxes. There are no independent restaurants in Bharatpur – most people eat where they're staying.

The Bagh Agra–Achnera Rd, 1km past Laxmi Vilas Palace ☎ 0564 422 8333, ⬥ thebagh.com. This idyllic upmarket hotel occupies a cluster of pink, low-rise buildings scattered around *charbagh*-style gardens that are home to more than fifty species of bird. Rooms are cool, spacious and attractively furnished, and there's also a spa and large pool. ₹**6000**

Bharatpur Ashok (formerly the Bharatpur Forest Lodge) 1km inside park ☎ 0564 422 2722, ⬥ forestlodgebharatpur.com. In a pleasantly sylvan setting inside the park (note that you'll have to pay one day's park entrance fee for every night you stay here), this very sleepy hotel has spacious and comfortable old-fashioned rooms with balconies overlooking the sanctuary, a pleasant garden out the back and a passable restaurant. Relatively expensive, but the setting is pretty much unbeatable. ₹**4700**

★ **Birders' Inn** Near the park entrance ☎ 0564 422 7346, ⬥ birdersinn.com. The most inviting place in town, usually full of serious birdwatchers who gather nightly to compare checklists in the pleasant courtyard garden and superb a/c multicuisine restaurant. Rooms (all a/c) are large, smart and excellent value. Free wi-fi and free pick up. Licensed. ₹**2400**

Evergreen Guest House Gauri-Shankar Colony ☎ 0564 422 5917 or ☎ 09602 83286. One of the cheapest options in Bharatpur, with simple but clean rooms in a family home with fan and private bathroom (though hot water comes in a bucket in some rooms), and a pretty garden restaurant. ₹**300**

Iora 54 Gauri-Shankar Colony ☎ 98280 41294, ⬥ ioraguesthouse.com. Owned by an amateur photographer, the six rooms here (air-cooled or a/c) are comfortable, and there's good veg food. ₹**700**

Jungle Lodge Gauri-Shankar Colony ☎ 0564 422 5622, ⬥ junglelodge.dk. This friendly place is run by a knowledgeable naturalist and has clean and spacious rooms (fan, air-cooled and a/c) overlooking a tranquil garden. The cute little restaurant and evening fires (in winter) give the place a pleasantly sociable feel, and there are bikes and binoculars for rent, plus internet access (₹30/hr) and wi-fi (₹15/hr). ₹**600**

★ **Kiran** 364 Rajendra Nagar ☎ 0564 422 3845, ⬥ kiranguesthouse.com. Run by an extremely friendly and helpful pair of brothers (one of whom is a certified naturalist), this place offers eight clean and comfortable fan-cooled, air-cooled and a/c rooms at rock-bottom prices. There's free collection (and drop-off) from the bus and train stations, plus wi-fi and binoculars for rent (₹50). **₹300**

Laxmi Vilas Palace Agra Rd ☎ 0564 422 3523, ⓦ laxmivilas.com. Former royal palace, set amid extensive grounds east of town with heated pool. It's all a trifle kitsch, but undeniably romantic, with reasonably priced a/c rooms complete with four-poster beds and other regal decorative touches. **₹7700**

Royal Guest House Civil Line, nr. Tourist Reception Centre ☎ 05644 23 0283, ⓦ royalguesthousebharatpur .com. Functional fan-cooled and a/c rooms in a family-run guesthouse with free wi-fi, money exchange and a travel counter. They also own the more tranquil *Royal Farm*, a pricier option 3km out of town (₹1300); make sure you know which place you're getting when you book. **₹400**

2

Keoladeo National Park

Keoladeo National Park is India's premier birdwatching sanctuary – an avian wonderland that attracts vast numbers of feathered creatures thanks to its strategic location, protected status and extensive wetlands. Some 385 species have been recorded here, including around two hundred year-round residents along with 190-odd migratory species from as far afield as Tibet, China, Siberia and even Europe, who fly south to escape the northern winter. Keoladeo is probably best known for its stupendous array of **aquatic birds**, which descend en masse on the park's wetlands following the dramatic arrival of the monsoon in July. These include the majestic saras crane and a staggering two thousand painted storks, as well as snake-necked darters, spoonbills, white ibis and grey pelicans. There are also various **mammals** in the park, including wild boar, mongoose, antelope, jackal, jungle cat, *chital*, nilgai and *sambar*.

The **best time to visit** is following the monsoon (roughly Oct–March), when the weather is dry but the lakes are still full and the migratory birds in residence (although mists in December and January can hinder serious birdwatching). Rajasthan's decade of **drought** finally came to an end in 2012 with an unusually long monsoon. Consistent rainfall combined with a series of three new permanent irrigation channels – designed to keep the water level in the lakes consistent – replenished Keoladeo's waterways which had all but dried up during the drought.

INFORMATION **KEOLADEO NATIONAL PARK**

Opening times Daily: April–Sept 6am–6pm; Oct–March 6.30am–5.30pm.

Entry fee ₹400 (₹200), video ₹200.

Getting around The park entrance is around 4km south of Bharatpur railway station; free maps are available here. A single road passes through the park, while numerous small paths cut around lakes and across marshes and provide excellent cover for birdwatching. You can hire a guide at the gate (₹100/hr for up to five people), who will probably have binoculars for you to borrow. Although you can stroll through the park on foot, the best way to get around and cover more ground is by bicycle, available at the main entrance (₹25; note that bikes from outside aren't currently allowed into the park), or by cycle rickshaw (₹70/hr) – drivers are trained by the park authorities and very clued up. During the winter, gondola-style boats (₹25/person, minimum four people) offer short rides across the wetlands, assuming there's enough water.

Eating and drinking The *Bharatpur Ashok Hotel* (see opposite) at the north end of the park is a reliable place to get a drink or something to eat.

Ranthambore National Park

No Indian nature reserve can guarantee a tiger sighting, but at **RANTHAMBORE NATIONAL PARK** the odds are probably better than anywhere else: the park is relatively small and the resident tigers are famously unperturbed by humans, hunting in broad daylight and rarely shying away from cameras or jeep-loads of tourists. Combine the big cats' bravado with the park's proximity to the Delhi–Agra–Jaipur "Golden Triangle", and you'll understand why Ranthambore attracts the number of visitors it does.

With more than eighty thousand visitors a year, Ranthambore is one of India's most popular national parks and can get ridiculously busy throughout the cool winter months, especially around Diwali and New Year. The summer months from April to

2

June are a lot quieter, but obviously very hot. There are currently around forty adult tigers in the park, plus healthy populations of *chital*, nilgai, jackals, leopards, jungle cats and a wide array of birds. The original core section of the national park is flanked by three **buffer zones**, designed to provide space for the park's ever-expanding number of young territory-seeking tigers.

Ranthambore Fort

Daily 6am–6pm • Free, note that you don't have to pay the park entry fee if you're just going to the fort • The easiest way to visit the fort is to go on a tour; these can be arranged through the *Tiger Safari* hotel (₹1000/jeep), or just ask at your hotel to see if they can arrange a jeep.

It's well worth setting aside some time from the tigers to visit the dramatic **Ranthambore Fort**, set atop a rocky crag near the entrance to the national park, although actually, since it's officially within the core zone, there's still the chance of spotting a tiger en route. The fort was founded in 944 by the Chauhan Rajputs and, following the decisive defeat of Prithviraj III by Muhammad of Ghor in 1192, became a key strategic focus in Rajput resistance to the expanding power of the Delhi Sultanate.

A few kilometres along the road into the park, a twisting flight of two hundred eroded stone steps leads up through gateways and crumbling fortifications to reach the fort, enclosed by some 7km of walls and bastions that snake around the ridgetop, offering fine views over the surrounding countryside. The numerous remains within the fort include a mosque, a large tank, assorted chhatris and several temples – the one dedicated to Ganesh is particularly revered, and people from all over the country write to the elephant-headed god's shrine here to invite him to their weddings.

ESSENTIALS   RANTHAMBORE NATIONAL PARK

Rules about visiting Ranthambore change frequently, so don't be surprised if the following information has become obsolete by the time you arrive. At present, the number of vehicles allowed into the park is strictly controlled, with a maximum of around fifteen six-seater jeeps (also known as "Gypsys") and 25 Canters (open-top buses seating twenty people) being allowed in during each morning and afternoon session.

Tour times Tours run daily every morning and afternoon, and last around 3hr. Departure times vary slightly depending on sunrise, leaving between 6.30am and 7am and between 2.30pm and 3pm. Dress in layers: early mornings can be surprisingly cold.

Prices Seats officially cost ₹795 in a Canter and ₹927 in a jeep (or ₹395/528 for Indian residents); all prices include the park entrance fee, vehicle rental and guide fees; video cameras ₹400.

Booking If you want to book your own seat, the best option is to reserve online at ⊕ rajasthanwildlife.in, but you will still have to go to the ticket office on the day of your safari around 45min before departure to show your booking confirmation and ID before your boarding pass is issued. The alternative is to

make for the Tiger Reserve Tourist Centre (daily 5.30–6.30am & 12.30–1.30pm) near *Tiger Safari* hotel, about 7km along Ranthambore Rd, where you can buy tickets for tours on the day. A much easier option is to book a seat in a jeep or Canter through your hotel – in fact it's a good idea to book your safari at the same time you book your room (or even before). You'll pay a surcharge for this, which can be anything from ₹100 for a seat in a Canter/jeep booked through a cheaper hotel up to ₹2000 for a place in a jeep booked through a top-end establishment. Stricter ticketing rules have now discouraged the practice of touting – hotels must supply names and passport details of their guests to make a booking, and tickets are not transferable, nor refundable. In practice, seats in a Canter average at around ₹1200, and jeeps, ₹1600.

CANTER OR GYPSY

Obviously, most visitors prefer the much smaller and quieter jeeps (Gypsys), but demand usually outstrips supply. It's worth emphasizing that your chances of seeing a tiger are the same whether you're in a Canter or a jeep, even though travelling by jeep may feel more like a "real" safari. You shouldn't have any problems getting a seat in a Canter if you book the day before (except possibly on Fri and Sun between Oct 1 and April, 15 when five to eight Canters are block-booked by the *Palace on Wheels* and *Royal Rajasthan on Wheels*). If you want to go in a jeep it's best to book ahead, although you might get lucky, especially from around April through to June, when visitor numbers fall significantly. Your chances drop considerably around public holidays.

Zones The park is split into nine zones – five core zones (thought to be best for tiger spotting) and four recently added buffer zones. Zones are randomly allocated upon booking. If you are given the same zone twice, you may be able to request an alternate zone, but the final decision lies with the park authorities.

When to visit The core section of Ranthambore is closed annually from July 1 to September 30 with the exception of the four buffer zones, which remain open year round. The best time to visit is during the dry season (Oct–March), when the lack of water entices the larger animals out to the lakeside. During and immediately after the monsoons they're more likely to remain in the forest. More information can be gleaned from Project Tiger's excellent booklet, *The Ultimate Ranthambore Guide* (₹250), on sale in local souvenir shops.

ARRIVAL AND INFORMATION

Ranthambore is reached via the small town of Sawai Madhopur. An auto-rickshaw from the bus stops or train station to guesthouses along Ranthambore Rd should cost from ₹50.

By train Sawai Madhopur is served by trains on the main Mumbai–Delhi line, and is thus easily accessible from Bharatpur, Agra, Jaipur, Delhi and Kota. The station is right in the middle of the newer, commercial part of town, otherwise known as Bajaria, close to the Bundi and Jaipur bus stands. Daily services run to Jaipur (9.45am, 10.40am, 2.35pm & 6.35pm; 2hr 5min–2hr 25min), Bharatpur (7.05am & 12.30pm; 2hr 20min–2hr 30min), Jodhpur (2.35pm; 7hr 30min), Kota (8.10am, 1.05pm, 1.35pm, 4.10pm, 6.07pm & 7.30pm; 1hr 15min–1hr 35min), Delhi (6.28am, 7.05am, 12.30pm & 1.08am; 4hr 30min–6hr), Mumbai (1.05pm, 4.10pm, 8.38pm & 10.05pm; 13–16hr) and Udaipur (11.50pm; 7hr 30min).

By bus Ongoing improvements to the previously awful roads around Ranthambore are gradually making bus travel a quicker and more comfortable option, although taking the train is still preferable for most destinations. Note that for Bundi, it's easiest to take a train to Kota and then catch a bus, or catch a direct bus all the way. Buses to Kota, Bundi and Jaipur depart from the Bundi stand, east of the Main Bazaar (near the overpass) with additional Jaipur services departing from the Jaipur stand, close to the post office circle. Services depart for Jaipur (3 daily; 5hr), Bundi (2 daily; 4–5hr), and Ajmer (1 daily; 8hr).

Tourist information The friendly staff in the tourist office (Mon–Sat 10am–5pm; ☏ 07462 220808), located in the train station, hand out free maps of the town.

Services There are exchange facilities at many hotels and in the State Bank of India in Sawai Madhopur. ATMs are plentiful and the internet cafés scattered around town charge around ₹50/hr.

ACCOMMODATION AND EATING

Most of the area's numerous hotels and guesthouses are strung out along the 14km road between Sawai Madhopur's new town and the national park; some of the better places are featured on ⊛ hotelsranthambhore.com. Accommodation prices in Ranthambore are significantly above average, and genuine budget accommodation is almost non-existent (hoteliers claim that they only really see six months' business every year – and therefore have to charge double prices). Ranthambore has few options for dining, most people eat where they're staying.

Aman-i-Khás Ranthambore Rd ☏ 0746 225 2052, ⊛ amanresorts.com. Situated in a very quiet rural setting, this place rivals *Vanyavilas* (see p.162) for tasteful opulence (and even outdoes it for wallet-crunching expense). Accommodation is in ten superb, cavernous luxury tents, and there's also a traditional step-well for swimming and a spa tent. Closed May–Sept. **US$1100**

★ **Khem Villas** On the far side of the park entrance ☏ 0746 225 2347, ⊛ khemvillas.com. Delightful little eco-resort set amid ten acres of carefully nurtured wilderness that is home to abundant birdlife and other fauna. Accommodation is in a mix of rooms, luxury tents or stylish little cottages with private verandas and open-to-the-sky showers, and there's also home-grown organic vegetarian food and an interesting range of excursions. Full board. **₹11,000**

Nahargarh Khilchipur Village, Ranthambore Rd, 2km south of park entrance ☏ 0746 225 2281, ⊛ nahargarh.com. Superbly theatrical-looking hotel, built in the style of an old-fashioned Rajput palace and looking every bit the regal retreat. Rooms are sumptuously decorated in traditional style and there's also a large pool, free wi-fi and licensed bar. **₹9590**

Raj Palace Resort Ranthambore Rd, 2km from town ☏ 0746 222 4793, ⊛ rajpalaceranthambhore.com. One of the best-value places in Ranthambore, with spacious and clean modern a/c rooms in the main building and some slightly more homely a/c "cottages" around the gardens at the back, plus a pool (non-guests ₹200/hr). **₹3500**

Rajputana Resort Ranthambore Rd, 3km from town ☏ 0941 201 428, ⊛ hotelrajputanaranthambhore.com. One of the cheapest options in town. Rooms (a few with a/c) are bright and adorned with colourful flowery bed linen. Some rooms are poky so ask to see a few first. **₹600**

2

2

Ranthambhore Bagh Ranthambore Rd, 3km from town ☎0746 222 1748, ☻ranthambhore.com. The upper-floor a/c rooms in this rambling hotel are average but the twelve fabric-lined fully furnished en-suite tents (all with air-coolers and attached bathrooms) feel wonderfully authentic, and are scattered in a pretty garden (make sure you get one away from the road). ₹3880

Ranthambhore Palace Ranthambore Rd, 2.5km from town ☎0746 222 0383, ☻hotelranthambhorepalace.com. This brand-new high rise is home to a selection of smart, well-furnished and good value rooms with a/c, TVs and private modern bathrooms, plus wi-fi and a pleasant roof restaurant. Great value at current rates. ₹800

RTDC Castle Jhoomar Baori On a hillside 7km out of town ☎0746 222 0495, ☻rtdc.in/jhoomarbaori.htm. Coral pink former royal hunting lodge on a lofty hilltop site close to the park, with superb views from the roof terrace and large, atmospheric – albeit disappointingly shabby – a/c rooms. ₹5750

★ **Sawai Madhopur Lodge** Ranthambore Rd, 1.5km from town ☎0746 222 0541, ☻tajhotels.com. Occupying an atmospheric 1930s hunting lodge, this luxury heritage hotel has bags of charm, with pleasantly leafy grounds and accommodation in beautifully appointed colonial-style rooms (the stylish luxury rooms are the best), plus a pool (non-guests ₹400) and attractive restaurant home to extravagant daily lunch and dinner buffets (₹750). Rates are full board. US$350

★ **Tiger Safari** Ranthambore Rd, 2.5 km from town ☎0746 222 1137, ☻tigersafariresort.com. The best of Ranthambore's cheaper hotels, well-geared to travellers, with helpful service and comfortably furnished rooms (almost all with a/c) plus spacious cottages around the rear garden. There's also internet access (free for the first two hours), wi-fi, a pool (free to non-guests), free station pick up/drop-off station, and a pleasant garden restaurant. ₹1290

Vanyavilas Ranthambore Rd, about 7km from town ☎0746 222 3999, ☻oberoihotels.com. Superbly stylish (and expensive) jungle resort centred around a lavishly decorated building home to an excellent restaurant specializing in royal Rajasthani cuisine. Scattered around the rustic grounds are beautifully equipped wooden-floored, hand-embroidered a/c tents, walled gardens, an outdoor pool, lakeside spa and lookout tower. US$1200

Ajmer and around

The Nag Pahar ("Snake Mountain"), a steeply shelving spur of the Aravallis west of Jaipur, forms an appropriately epic backdrop for **AJMER**, home of the great Sufi saint **Khwaja Muin-ud-Din Chishti**, who founded the Chishtiya Sufi order. His tomb, the **Dargah Khwaja Sahib**, remains one of the most important Islamic shrines in the world. The streams of pilgrims and dervishes (it is believed that seven visits here are the equivalent of one to Mecca) especially pick up during Muharram (Muslim New Year) and Eid, and for the saint's anniversary day, or **Urs Mela** (see box, p.164).

Although Ajmer's dusty modern roads are choked with traffic, the narrow lanes of the bazaars around the **Dargah Khwaja Sahib** retain an almost medieval character, with lines of rose-petal stalls and shops selling prayer mats, beads and lengths of gold-edged green silk offerings. Finely arched Mughal gateways still stand at the main entrances to the **old city**, whose skyscape of mosque minarets and domes is overlooked from on high by the crumbling **Taragarh** – for centuries India's most strategically important fortress.

While most of Rajasthan consisted of princely states, Ajmer was under British rule, and colonial-era relics can be found scattered across the city, among them the **Jubilee clock tower** opposite the railway station and the **King Edward Memorial Hall** a little to the west. The famous **Mayo College**, originally built as a school for princes and now a leading educational institution, is known in society circles as the "Eton of the East".

For Hindu pilgrims and foreign travellers, Ajmer is important primarily as a jumping-off place for **Pushkar**, a twenty-minute bus ride away, and most stay only for as long as it takes to catch a bus out. As a day-trip from Pushkar, however it's a highly worthwhile excursion, and as a stronghold of Islam, Ajmer is unique in Hindu-dominated Rajasthan.

Brief history

A fort was first established at Ajmer in the tenth century by local Rajput chieftain Ajay Pal Chauhan, whose clan, the Chauhans, went on to become the dominant power in eastern Rajasthan until they were beaten in 1193 by Muhammad of Ghor (see p.1157). The Delhi sultans allowed the Chauhans to carry on ruling as their tributaries, but in 1365, with Delhi on the wane as a regional power, Ajmer fell to the kingdom of Mewar (Udaipur).

During the sixteenth century, the city became the object of rivalry between Mewar and the neighbouring kingdom of Marwar (Jodhpur). The Marwaris took it in 1532, but the presence of Khwaja Muin-ud-Din Chishti's *dargah* made Ajmer an important prize for the Muslim Mughals, and Akbar's forces marched in just 27 years later.

The Mughals held onto Ajmer for more than two centuries, but as their empire began to fragment, the neighbouring Rajput kingdoms once again started giving the city covetous looks. It was eventually taken in 1770 by the Marathas, who subsequently sold the city to the East India Company for ₹50,000 in 1818. Thus, while most of Hindu-dominated Rajasthan retained internal independence during the Raj, Ajmer was a little Muslim enclave of directly ruled British territory, only reunited with Jodhpur and Udaipur, its former overlords, when it became part of Rajasthan in 1956.

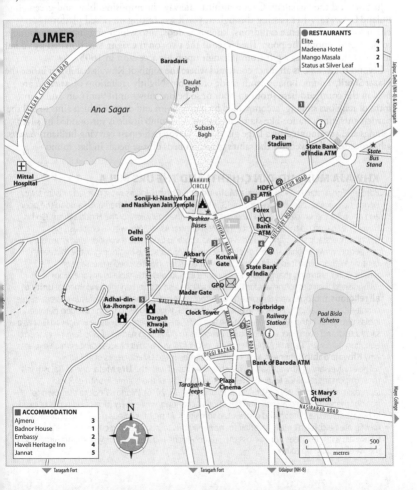

Dargah Khwaja Sahib

Dargah Bazaar • Daily 5am to midnight; tomb closed daily 3–4pm, except Thurs when it's shut 2.30–3.30pm • ⑩ dargahajmer.com

Housing the tomb of the revered Sufi saint, Khwaja Muin-ud-Din Chishti, the **Dargah Khwaja Sahib**, or Dargah Sharif, is the most important Muslim shrine in India, attracting thousands of pilgrims daily. Founded in the thirteenth century, the *dargah* contains structures financed by many Muslim rulers, particularly the three great Mughals – Shah Jahan, Jahangir and, especially, Akbar, who came to the *dargah* to pray for a male heir and rewarded it with a new mosque when his wish was granted.

You enter the complex through the lofty **Nizam Gate**, donated by the nizam of Hyderabad in 1911. Once inside, you may be accosted by stern-looking young men claiming they are "official guides". In fact, they are *khadims*, hereditary priests who lead pilgrims through rituals in the *dargah* in exchange for donations. Their services are not compulsory, whatever they may say.

Beyond the Nizam Gate lies the smaller **Shajahani Gate**, commissioned by Shah Jahan. Carry on through this to reach a courtyard, from where steps lead up on the right to the **Akbari Masjid (Akbar's Mosque)**, built by a grateful Akbar following the birth of his son Salim, the future emperor Jahangir.

Just beyond the Shajahani Gate is a third gateway, the imposing, blue-and-green **Buland Darwaza**. After passing through it, you'll see, resting on raised platforms on either side, two immense cauldrons, known as **degs**, into which pilgrims throw money to be shared among the poor. The larger of the two, on the right, was donated by Akbar in 1567; the other was a gift from Jahangir upon his accession in 1605.

Beyond the *khanas* is an inner courtyard where the tomb of Khwaja Sahib lies inside the **Mazar Sharif**, a domed mausoleum made of marble. Nightly recitations of *qawwali* are held in the courtyard here (from an hour or so before sunset until 9pm), an exuberant form of religious singing, accompanied by harmonium and drums, which aims to lull the participants into a trance-like state called *mast*. The **tomb** inside is surrounded by silver railings and surmounted by a large gilt dome. Devotees file past carrying brilliant *chadars*, gilt-brocaded silk covers for the saint's grave, on beds of rose petals in flat, round

KHWAJA MUIN-UD-DIN CHISHTI AND THE URS MELA

Born in Afghanistan in 1156, **Khwaja Muin-ud-Din Chishti**, India's most revered Muslim saint, began his religious career at the age of 13, when he distributed his inheritance among the poor and adopted the simple life of an itinerant Sufi *fakir* (the equivalent of the Hindu sadhu). On his travels, he soaked up the teachings of the great Central Asian Sufis, whose emphasis on mysticism, ecstatic states and pure devotion as a path to God were revolutionizing Islam during this period. Khwaja Sahib and his disciples settled in Ajmer at the beginning of the thirteenth century. Withdrawing into a life of meditation and fasting, he preached a message of renunciation, affirming that personal experience of God was attainable to anyone who relinquished their ties to the world. More radically, he also insisted on the fundamental **unity of all religions**: mosques and temples, he asserted, were merely material manifestations of a single divinity. Khwaja Sahib thus became one of the first religious figures to bridge the gap between India's two great faiths. After he died at the age of 97, his followers lauded the Bhagavad Gita as a sacred text, and even encouraged Hindu devotees to pray using names of God familiar to them, equating Ram with "Rahman", the Merciful Aspect of Allah – a spirit of acceptance which explains why **Khwaja Sahib's** shrine in Ajmer continues to be loved by adherents of all faiths.

The anniversary of Khwaja Sahib's death is celebrated with the **Urs Mela**, one of Rajasthan's most important religious festivals, held on the sixth day of the Islamic month of Rajab (approximately May 5, 2014, April 26, 2015 and April 13, 2016). Pilgrims flock to the town to honour the saint with *qawwali* (Sufi devotional) chanting, while *kheer* (rice pudding) is cooked in huge vats at the *dargah* and distributed to visitors. At night religious gatherings called *mehfils* are held. It isn't really an affair for non-religious tourists, but the city does take on a festive air, with devotees from across the Subcontinent and beyond converging on Ajmer for the week leading up to it.

head-baskets. Visitors are blessed, lightly brushed with peacock feathers and given the chance to touch the cloth covering the tomb in return for an offering.

Subsidiary shrines in the inner courtyard include one belonging to a daughter of Shah Jahan, plus a handful of generals and governors, and some Afghani companions of the saint. The delicately carved marble mosque behind the saint's tomb, the **Jama Masjid** or Shahjahani Masjid, was commissioned by Shah Jahan in 1628 and took nine years to build. Despite its grand scale, the emperor deliberately had it built without a dome so as not to upstage the saint's mausoleum next door.

2

Adhai-din-ka-Jhonpra

Andar Kot Rd

Often overlooked by visitors, the **Adhai-din-ka-Jhonpra**, or "two-and-a-half-day hut", to the south of town is the oldest surviving monument in the city, and one of the finest examples of medieval architecture in Rajasthan. Originally built in 660 AD as a Jain temple, and converted in 1153 into a Hindu college, it was destroyed forty years later by the invading Afghan chieftain Muhammad of Ghor, who later had it renovated as a mosque. Tradition holds that its name derives from the speed with which it was constructed, but in fact the reconstruction took fifteen years, using materials plundered from Hindu and Jain temples; the name actually refers to a *fakirs'* festival that used to be held here in the eighteenth century, a *jhonpra* (hut) being the abode of a *fakir* (Sufi mendicant). Defaced Hindu motifs are still clearly discernible on the pillars and ceilings, but the mosque's most beautiful features are the bands of Koranic calligraphy that decorate its seven-arched facade.

Akbar's Fort

Museum Rd • **Museum** Tues–Sun 9.45am–5.15pm • ₹50 (₹5)

The small but attractive **Akbar's Fort** encloses a rectangular pavilion made of golden sandstone that was used by Akbar and his son Jahangir; it was here in 1616 that Jahangir received Sir Thomas Roe, the first British ambassador to be granted an official audience, after four years of trailing between the emperor's encampments. Today, the old palace houses a small **museum**, displaying mainly Hindu and Jain statues.

Nasiyan Jain Temple

Prithivi Raj Marg • Daily 8.30am–5.30pm • ₹10

Perhaps the most bizarre sight in Ajmer is the mirrored **Soniji-ki-Nasiya** hall adjoining the **Nasiyan Jain Temple**, or "Red Temple", in the heart of town. Commissioned in the 1820s by an Ajmeri diamond magnate, the hall contains a huge diorama-style display commemorating the life of Rishabha (or Adinath), the first Jain *tirthankara*. The glowing tableau (containing a tonne of gold) features a huge procession of soldiers and elephants carrying the infant *tirthankara* from Ayodhya to Mount Sumeru to be blessed, while musicians and deities fly overhead. Admission to the main temple alongside is restricted to Jains.

Ana Sagar

Laid out in the twelfth century, the artificial lake northwest of Ajmer known as **Ana Sagar** is worth a visit to see the line of exquisite white-marble pavilions called **baradaris**, or summer shelters, erected by Shah Jahan on the lake's eastern shore. Modelled on the Diwan-i-Am in Delhi's Red Fort, four of the five pavilions remain beautifully preserved, standing in the shade of trees and ornamental gardens laid out by Jahangir – particularly beautiful an hour or so before sunset.

By train Ajmer's railway station (☏ 0145 243 2535) is on the main Delhi–Ahmedabad railway line and slap-bang in the centre of town. The computerized reservations hall (daily 8am–2pm & 2.15–10pm) is on the first floor of the south wing; get there early in the morning to avoid queues or shell out a little extra for a travel agent.

By bus The State Bus Stand (☏ 0145 242 9398) lies some 2km to the northeast of the train station on the Jaipur Rd – an auto-rickshaw from here into town costs around ₹60. The majority of travellers visit Ajmer on a day-trip from Pushkar, but note that buses to and from Pushkar don't travel through the centre of Ajmer en route to the bus stand, so you'll have to traipse into town from the bus stand and then back out again at the end of your visit. State buses – including services to Pushkar (roughly every 15min until about 8.30pm, and afterwards hourly until dawn) – depart from bays 23 & 24 of the State Bus Stand. Deluxe buses operate to Jaipur (3 daily; 4-5hrs)

and to Delhi via Jaipur (2 daily; 10hr). Seats on private buses – many of which have connecting services from Pushkar – can be reserved at travel agents along Kutchery Rd towards Prithviraj Marg.

Tourist information The RTDC runs tourist offices near the state bus stand next to the *RTDC Hotel Khadim* (Mon–Sat 10am–5pm; ☏ 0145 262 7426) and at the railway station (daily 9am–5pm; no phone – it's just inside the station's smaller, southern entrance).

Services There are State Bank of India ATMs opposite the GPO on Prithviraj Marg and near the tourist office, a Bank of Baroda ATM between the *Elite* and *Honey Dew* restaurants, and ICICI and HDFC ATMs at either end of Sardar Patel Marg (the road that *Mango Masala* restaurant is on). You can exchange cash and travellers' cheques in the State Bank of India. Internet cafés charge ₹30/hr. There's a left luggage office (open 24hr) directly opposite the tourist information office in the railway station.

ACCOMMODATION

Ajmer's hotels aren't great value; you're better off staying in Pushkar and visiting from there. Accommodation also tends to get chock-full during the Urs Mela (see box, p.164). Note that many cheaper hotels tend to operate a 24hr check-out system.

Ajmeru Off Prithviraj Marg, just inside Kotwali Gate ☏ 0145 243 1103, ⊛ hotelajmeru.com. This comfortable modern hotel is one of the best value places to stay in town, with bright, clean and well-kept fan, air-cooled and a/c rooms with attached bathrooms and cable TV. 24hr checkout. ₹800

Badnor House New Civil Lines, near RTDC Hotel Khadim ☏ 0145 262 7579, ⊛ badnorhouse.com. Tucked into a residential area, this friendly homestay offers clean modern rooms in a newly built block away from the owner's house, all

with a/c, attached bathrooms and TVs. ₹2500

Embassy Jaipur Rd, opposite City Powerhouse ☏ 0145 242 5519, ⊛ hotelembassyajmer.com. Comfortable modern three-star. All rooms come with a/c, TV and mini-bar, and there's also the good in-house *Silver Leaf* restaurant (see below). No wi-fi. ₹1900

★ **Haveli Heritage Inn** Kutchery Rd, Phul Nawas ☏ 0145 262 1607, ⊛ haveliheritageinn.com. In an old house from the 1870s that was once used as the state HQ of the Indian Congress Party – Nehru and Gandhi both

RECOMMENDED TRAINS FROM AJMER

Destination	Name	No.	Departs	Arrives
Abu Road	*Ahmedabad Mail*	9106	6.50am (daily)	11.47pm
	Aravali Express	9708	11.25am (daily)	5pm
Agra	*Sealdah Express*	2988	12.50pm (daily)	7.25pm
	Ajmer–Agra Intercity	2196	3pm (daily)	9.50pm
Alwar	*Ajmer Shatabdi*	2016	3.45pm (daily)	7.32pm
	Jammu Tawi Express	2413	2.15pm (daily)	6.37pm
Chittaurgarh	*Udaipur Express*	2992	4.10pm (daily)	9.05pm
	Ratlam Express	9654	1.25pm (daily)	5.05pm
Jaipur	*Ajmer Express*	2991	11.30am (daily)	1.25pm
	Bhopal–Jaipur Express	9712	6.55am (daily)	9.25am
	Aravali Express	9707	4.35pm (daily)	6.55pm
Jodhpur	Fast passenger train	54802	2.30pm (daily)	7.40pm
New Delhi	*Ajmer Shatabdi*	2016	3.45pm (daily)	10.40pm
	Rajdhani Express	2957	12.55am (daily)	7.30am
Udaipur	*Udaipur Daily Special*	9721	8.55am (daily)	1.45pm
	Udaipur Express	2992	4.10pm (daily)	9.30pm

stayed here (in Room 2). It actually sounds grander than it is, but if you think of this as a *pension* rather than a haveli, you'll get the right idea – the big attractions are the peaceful atmosphere and the delightful family that runs it. Rooms (air-cooled and a/c) are bright, spacious and attractively furnished, and there's free wi-fi and great home cooking too. ₹**1275**

Jannat Dargah Bazaar, near Nizam Gate ☎0145 243 2494, ⊛ajmerhoteljannat.com. A stone's throw from the Dargah Khwaja Sahib, and the best hotel in the area, *Jannat* fills up quickly on Thurs and Fri, but usually has space the rest of the week. There's a range of rooms, all modern and clean, some with a/c and TVs, plus a good restaurant and friendly service. 24hr check-out. ₹**2500**

EATING

Note that none of the following serves alcohol; if you want a **drink**, find a local bottle shop or try room service in your hotel.

Elite Station Rd ☎0145 242 9544. Reliable veg restaurant serving moderately priced curries and thalis (₹60–120), plus a sprinkling of vegetarian Chinese, Continental and south Indian options. You can eat either inside in the white-tablecloth dining room or outside in the garden. Daily 10.30am–11pm.

★ **Madeena Hotel** Station Rd (directly opposite the train station). Muslim establishment serving very tasty non-veg Mughlai curries, mostly involving "mutton" (ie goat), in the form of korma, mughlai, *keema*, masala or biriyani, in full or half portions (₹50–90) with freshly baked tandoori breads. There are also

chicken, egg and veg options. Daily 9am–11pm.
Mango Masala Sardar Patel Marg ☎0145 242 2100, ⊛mangomasala.com. Popular, studenty place serving pizzas, snacks, veg burgers, salads, shakes, mocktails and ice-cream sodas, as well as veg set-meals and thalis, and lots of *paneer* curries. Mains ₹79–189. Daily 11am–11pm.
Status at Silver Leaf Embassy Hotel, Jaipur Rd. Sedate veg restaurant featuring plush white loungers, with a big selection of curries (most around ₹110–195), plus Chinese and passable Italian dishes, snacks and breakfasts. Daily 8am–11pm.

Taragarh Fort

Daily sunrise–sunset • Free

Three kilometres to the southwest of Ajmer, and just visible on the ridge high above the city, **Taragarh** (the Star Fort) was for two thousand years the most important strategic objective for invading armies in northwest India. Any ruler who successfully breached its walls, rising from a ring of forbidding escarpments, effectively controlled the region's trade. The fort is now badly ruined but is still visited in large numbers by pilgrims, who come to pay their respects at what must be one of the few shrines in the world devoted to a tax inspector. The **Dargah of Miran Sayeed Hussein Khangsawar** honours Muhammad of Ghor's chief revenue collector, slain in the Rajput attack of 1202 when, following one of the fort's rare defeats, the entire Muslim population of the fort was put to the sword.

ARRIVAL AND DEPARTURE   TARAGARH FORT

On foot The best way of getting to Taragarh is to take a 90min hike along the ancient paved pathway from Ajmer, with superb views across the plains and neighbouring hills; to pick up the trailhead, follow the lane behind the Dargah Khwaja Sahib, past the Adhai-din-ka-Jhonpra and on towards the saddle in the ridge visible to the south

By auto or jeep Autos (around ₹350 return) and jeeps (₹60) leave from behind the Plaza Cinema on Diggi Chowk, west of the train station; ask for the "Ta-ra-garh jeeps", pronouncing all the syllables clearly, or you may end up at the main Dargah Khwaja Sahib. To return to Ajmer, catch a jeep from the lot on the northeast side of the village, near the Dargah.

Pushkar

According to legend, **PUSHKAR**, 15km northwest of Ajmer, came into existence when Lord Brahma, the Creator, dropped a lotus flower (*pushpa*) to earth from his hand (*kar*). At the three spots where the petals landed, water magically appeared in the midst of the desert to form three small blue lakes, and it was on the banks of the largest of these that Brahma subsequently convened a gathering of some 900,000 celestial beings – the entire Hindu pantheon. Surrounded by whitewashed temples and bathing *ghats*, the lake is today revered as one of India's most sacred sites: Pushkaraj Maharaj, literally "Pushkar King of Kings". During the auspicious full-moon phase of October/ November (the anniversary of the gods' mass meeting, or *yagya*), its waters are believed to cleanse the soul of all impurities, drawing pilgrims from all over the country. Alongside this annual religious festival, Rajasthani villagers also buy and sell livestock at what has become the largest **camel market** (*unt mela*) in the world, when more than 150,000 dealers, tourists and traders fill the dunes west of the lake.

The temples

There are more than five hundred **temples** in and around Pushkar, although some, like the splendid **Vishnu Temple**, are out of bounds to non-Hindus. Pushkar's most important shrine, the **Brahma Temple** (closed 1.30–3pm daily), houses a four-headed image of Brahma in its main sanctuary, and is one of the few temples in India devoted to him. Raised on a stepped platform in the centre of a courtyard, the inevitably crowded chamber is surrounded on three sides by smaller subsidiary shrines topped with flat roofs providing views across the desert to **Savitri Temple** on the summit of a nearby hill. The one-hour climb to the top of that hill is rewarded by matchless vistas over the town, surrounded on all sides by desert, and is best done before dawn, to reach the summit for sunrise, though it's also a great spot to watch the sun set. The temple itself is modern, but the image of Savitri is thought to date back to the seventh century.

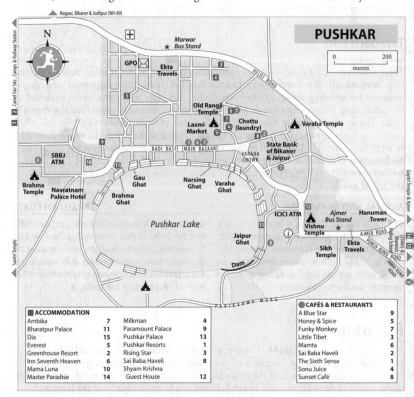

■ ACCOMMODATION			
Ambika	7	Milkman	4
Bharatpur Palace	11	Paramount Palace	9
Dia	15	Pushkar Palace	13
Everest	5	Pushkar Resorts	1
Greenhouse Resort	2	Rising Star	3
Inn Seventh Heaven	6	Sai Baba Haveli	8
Mama Luna	10	Shyam Krishna	
Master Paradise	14	Guest House	12

● CAFÉS & RESTAURANTS	
A Blue Star	9
Honey & Spice	5
Funky Monkey	7
Little Tibet	3
Mamta	6
Sai Baba Haveli	2
The Sixth Sense	1
Sonu Juice	4
Sunset Café	8

The lake and ghats

Everything in Pushkar revolves around the **lake**. Five hundred beautiful whitewashed temples encircle the lake, connected to the water by 52 *ghats* – one for each of Rajasthan's maharajas, who built separate guesthouses in which to stay during their visits here. Primary among the *ghats* is **Gau Ghat**, sometimes called Main Ghat, from which ashes of Mahatma Gandhi, Jawaharlal Nehru and Shri Lal Bahadur Shastri were sprinkled into the lake. **Brahma Ghat** marks the spot where Brahma himself is said to have worshipped, while at the large **Varaha Ghat**, just off the market square, Vishnu is believed to have appeared in the form of Varaha (a boar), the third of his nine earthly incarnations. At all the *ghats* visitors should remove their shoes at a reverential distance from the lake and refrain from smoking and taking photos.

Indian and Western tourists alike are urged by local Brahmin priests to worship at the lake; that is, to make **Pushkar Puja**. This traditional ritual involves the repetition of prayers while scattering rose petals into the lake, and then being asked for a donation. On completion of the puja, a red thread taken from a temple is tied around your wrist. Labelled the "Pushkar passport" by locals, this simple token means that you'll no longer attract pushy Pushkar priests and can wander unhindered onto the *ghats*. Indians usually give a sum of ₹21 or ₹31; ₹51 or, at most, ₹101 should suffice for a foreign tourist. (Hindus never give monetary gifts ending in "0"; the number "1" is considered auspicious and believed to symbolize new beginnings.) A favourite trick of (usually phoney) priests is to ask how much you want to pay, then say a blessing for assorted members of your family, and demand the amount you stated times the number of family members blessed; don't be bullied by such cheap tricks into giving any more than you agreed.

ARRIVAL AND INFORMATION

By train Pushkar's railway station is to the northeast of town. The daily service between Pushkar and Ajmer #59608 (dep. 3.30pm, arr. 4.50pm) is more of a tourist train. For all other destinations, you need to take a train from Ajmer (see box, p.166).

By bus There are two bus stands; buses to Ajmer leave from

the Ajmer Bus Stand in the east of town while government and private inter-city buses for destinations further afield (such as Bundi, Delhi, Jaipur, Jaisalmer, Jodhpur and Bikaner – most of which also stop en route at Ajmer) leave from the Marwar Bus Stand (☎0145 242 9398), located to the north of town. There are services to Ajmer (every 15min; 30min),

BRAHMA, SAVITRI AND GAYITRI

Although **Brahma**, the Creator, is one of the trinity of top Hindu gods, along with Vishnu (the Preserver) and Shiva (the Destroyer), his importance has dwindled since Vedic times and he has nothing like the following of the other two. The story behind his temple here in Pushkar serves to explain why this is so, and also reveals the significance of the temples here named after Brahma's wives, **Savitri** and **Gayitri**.

The story goes that Lord Brahma was to marry Savitri, a river goddess, at a sacrificial ritual called a *yagna*, which had to be performed at a specific, astrologically auspicious moment. But Savitri, busy dressing for the ceremony, failed to show up on time. Without a wife, the Creator could not perform the *yagna* at the right moment, so he had to find another consort quickly. The only unmarried woman available was a shepherdess of the untouchable Gujar caste named Gayitri, whom the gods hastily purified by passing her through the mouth of a cow (*gaya* means "cow", and *tri*, "passed through"). When Savitri finally arrived, she was furious that Brahma had married someone else and cursed him, saying that henceforth he would be worshipped only at Pushkar. She also proclaimed that the Gujar caste would gain liberation after death only if their ashes were scattered on Pushkar lake – a belief that has persisted to this day. After casting her curses, disgruntled Savitri flew off to the highest hill above the town. To placate her, it was agreed that she should have her temple on that hilltop, while Gayitri occupied the lower hill on the opposite, eastern side of the lake, and that Savitri would always be worshipped before Gayitri, which is exactly how pilgrims do it, visiting Savitri's temple first, and Gayitri's temple afterwards.

Bikaner (9 daily; 6hr 30min), Bundi (2 daily; 5hr), Delhi (hourly, including overnight sleeper services; 10hr), Jaipur (hourly; 3hr 30min), Jodhpur (1 daily plus 1 nightly; 6hr) and Jaisalmer (2 nightly; 10hr). For Udaipur, change at Ajmer. Further destinations are served from Ajmer (see p.166), and connecting services are available, but it's not unknown for people who have bought tickets at agencies in Pushkar to find their seats double-booked when they try boarding in Ajmer. If possible, make bookings for bus journeys from Ajmer in Ajmer itself. Services to Delhi are often reserved days ahead.

Getting around There are very few cycle rickshaws and autos in Pushkar, so you'll probably have to walk to your hotel. There are a number of places just east of the Ajmer Bus Stand renting out scooters and motorbikes for around ₹200/day. Malakar Bicycle Shop, by the Ajmer Bus Stand (the unsigned pink shop next to EKTA TRAVELS), has basic bicycles for ₹40/24hr.

Tourist information Pushkar's tourist office (daily 10am–5pm; 24hr during camel fair; ☎0145 277 2040) is located inside the main gate of the *RTDC Hotel Sarovar*.

ACCOMMODATION

Prices rise dramatically during the camel fair, with increases of anything from two to five times the normal rate.

Ambika Opposite Old Rangji Temple ☎0145 277 3154. Right in the thick of the action, with simple but cheap and clean whitewashed rooms, all attached, some with views over the street below – colourful, if a bit noisy. Good value during the camel fair. ₹300

Bharatpur Palace Main Bazaar ☎0145 277 2320, ✉bharatpurpalace_pushkar@yahoo.co.in. A bit basic and overpriced for what you get, but the location's wonderful, right on the lake, with views across the *ghats* from some rooms and delicious home-cooked meals. A couple of rooms have a/c; cheaper ones have shared bathrooms. ₹250/₹400

★ Día Next to Masters Paradise Resort, Panch Kund Rd ☎0145 277 2585, ⓦinn-seventh-heaven.com/Dia. Gorgeous low-key sister-property to *Inn Seventh Heaven*; situated above the owner's home, the four attractively furnished rooms here feature breezy private balconies and terraces in a very peaceful location on the edge of town, around 500m from the Ajmer Bus Stand. ₹2800

Everest Near Main Gau (Ghandi Ghat) ☎0145 277 3417, ⓦpushkarhoteleverest.com. Nice, friendly and family-run guesthouse in a peaceful residential location

above town. Rooms (all attached, some with a/c) are spotlessly clean, with modern bathrooms and a lovely rooftop restaurant. Book swap and wi-fi available. ₹300

★ Greenhouse Resort Kishanpura Rd, Tilore, about 8km from Pushkar ☎0145 230 0079, ⓦthegreenhouseresort.com. A gorgeous eco-resort set in ten acres featuring twenty chic tents with attached bathrooms, pretty gardens, a huge pool, spa, licensed bar and an eco-styled air-cooled restaurant. The resort's greenhouses supply the hotel with fresh veg, seasonal strawberries and roses. ₹8800

★ Inn Seventh Heaven Chhoti Basti ☎0145 510 5455, ⓦinn-seventh-heaven.com. Beautiful hotel in a fine old haveli, mixing traditional and contemporary styles to memorable effect, with vine-draped balconies around a spacious interior courtyard and a range of beautifully furnished rooms. Excellent value. ₹1000

★ Mama Luna Bari Mohalia, Badi Basti ☎098283 97281, ⓦhotelmamaluna.com. The spacious rooms (all attached, with fan or a/c) in this popular guesthouse are painted in bright Rajasthani hues. There's a leafy rooftop

---

RAJASTHAN'S ETHNIC MINORITIES

Like most Indian states, Rajasthan has a number of "tribal" peoples who live outside the social mainstream. Many are nomadic, and often called "Gypsies" – indeed the Romanies of Europe are thought to have originated among these Rajasthani Gypsy tribes. The most prominent are the **Kalbeliyas**, found largely in Pushkar. The Kalbeliyas discovered how to charm snakes, and they used to sing and dance for royalty, as they now do for tourists, but living on the margins of society, they suffer similar discriminations as their brethren in Europe.

The **Bhopas** are a green-eyed tribe of nomads who used to work as entertainers to the maharajas, and to this day they make a living as itinerant poets and storytellers. They are asked to perform particularly where someone is sick, as their songs are believed to aid recovery.

In the Jodhpur region, many tourists take an excursion into the countryside to visit the **Bishnoi** (see p.181), a religious rather than strictly ethnic group, whose tree-hugging beliefs chime with those of hippies in the West. Living in close proximity to them, though with a very different lifestyle, are the **Bhils**, great hunters who used to hire themselves out as soldiers in the armies of the Rajput kingdoms. They have their own language and religion, and their dances have become very popular, especially at Holi.

restaurant, free daily yoga classes (5.30–6.30pm) for in-house guests and good wi-fi on upper floors. Excellent value at current rates. ₹250

Master Paradise Panch Kund Rd ☎ 0145 277 3933, ⓦ masterparadise.com. Spotless, well-kept three-star in a peaceful setting just outside town, with lovely gardens, a pool (non-guests ₹100), steam bath and jacuzzi. ₹2550

Milkman Maili Mohalla ☎ 0145 277 3452. Intimate and sociable little family-run place hidden away in the backstreets with a range of cosy, well-kept rooms (fan, air-cooled or a/c; some with shared bath) and a nice rooftop café, garden and terrace, plus a six-bedroom dorm. Good value. Dorm ₹100, double ₹250/₹400

Paramount Palace Bari Basti ☎ 0145 277 2428, ⓦ pushkar-paramount.com. Relaxed guesthouse near the Brahma Temple with a mixed bag of rooms, all with fans and attached bathrooms. The cheaper ground-floor rooms are dark and poky, but the upstairs rooms to the front with dusky pink balconies and stunning town views are lovely. There's also free wi-fi and a nice rooftop restaurant. ₹250

Pushkar Palace Choti Basti ☎ 0145 277 3001, ⓦ hotelpushkarpalace.com. Attractive hotel occupying an old maharaja's palace in a plum position overlooking the lake. The whole place has lots of charm, with period-style rooms (most with lake views) and a pretty courtyard garden, though rates are a bit steep – and exorbitant during the camel fair. ₹8220

Pushkar Resorts Motisar Rd, Ganehra ☎ 0112 649 4531, ⓦ sewara.com. Tranquil resort, inconveniently situated 5km out of town in the desert, with forty a/c cottages in pristine gardens and a kidney-shaped pool. Their restaurant has a non-veg menu and an alcohol licence. Booking recommended. ₹3223

Rising Star Near Marwar Bus Stand, Mali Mohalla, Choti Basti ☎ 0145 277 2328, ⓔ risingstarpushkar @hotmail.com. The friendly family running this cute homestay keep their handful of rooms (all attached, some with a/c) lovely and tidy – the nicest have balconies. Free wi-fi. ₹400

Sai Baba Haveli Off Varaha Chowk ☎ 0145 510 5161, ⓔ lola_singh_modiano@hotmail.com. Run by a French-Indian couple, this place offers a range of fan and air-cooled rooms with attached bathrooms in an attractive old house set around a pleasant garden patio. There's also a good restaurant (see p.172). ₹250

Shyam Krishna Guest House Main Bazaar near Vishnu temple ☎ 0145 277 2461. Attractively tranquil guesthouse with a variety of rooms (some with shared bathroom) set around a garden in a lovely old blue-washed former temple compound. Excellent value, especially during the camel fair. ₹300/₹500

EATING

As Pushkar is sacred to Lord Brahma, all food within city limits is strictly veg: meat, eggs and alcohol are banned. Pushkar's sweet speciality is **malpua**, which is basically a chapatti fried in syrup, sold at sweetshops around town, and on Halwai Gali, the street directly opposite Gau Ghat.

A Blue Star Jammi Kund Rd ☎ 98283 55263. Peaceful painted restaurant on the outskirts of town serving good Israeli dishes such as falafel, hummus and eggplant pita wraps, plus toasted sandwiches and excellent wood-fired pizzas (₹80). Daily 9am–10pm.

Funky Monkey Near SBBJ Bank, Mahadev Chowk ☎ 98298 73439, ⓦ funkymonkeycafe.in. Tiny café with just a handful of orange tables, and a good menu featuring pasta, pizza, sandwiches, pancakes, juices, real coffee and lassis. There's also free wi-fi and a TV showing sport and movies. Daily 6am–1am.

★ **Honey & Spice** Laxmi Market, Main Bazaar ☎ 0145 510 55505. Much more imaginative than your average Pushkar backpacker café, with a short but sweet menu of tasty and nutritious vegetarian wholefood dishes (₹55–90) and cakes, plus juices, lassis and speciality teas. Daily 7am–7pm.

Little Tibet Payal Guest House, Main Bazaar. Attractive garden restaurant set beneath the overhanging boughs of an enormous tree, serving decent Tibetan and Indian food alongside the usual medley of faux Italian, Israeli and Mexican tourist fodder accompanied by the inevitable chillout soundtrack – and even sleepier service. Mains ₹65–170. Daily 8am–10.30pm.

Mamta Near Brahma Temple ☎ 0145 227 2114. This is where a lot of Pushkar's Indian visitors come to eat, not surprisingly as it serves the best thalis and veg curries (from ₹60) in town. What's available depends on what vegetables are in season, but there's always a good selection. Daily 8am–10pm.

Sai Baba Haveli Off Varaha Chowk. The usual Indian veg curries (₹60–95) plus great pasta and the best pizza (₹75–130) in Pushkar (the *tandoor* doubles as a pizza oven). You can sit out front or, more atmospherically, in the garden. There's Gypsy dancing on Saturdays at 8pm, usually accompanied by a buffet. Daily 8am–11pm.

★ **The Sixth Sense** On the top floor of the Inn Seventh Heaven. This stylish café-restaurant offers a welcome alternative to Pushkar's grungy backpacker cafés, with a small but carefully chosen range of Indian and Italian food using fresh seasonal ingredients, plus snacks, fresh juices, fruit tarts and awesome eggless pancake breakfasts. Mains ₹45–120. Daily 8.30am–11pm.

2

KARTIKA PURNIMA AND PUSHKAR CAMEL FAIR

Hindus visit Pushkar year-round to take a dip in the redemptory waters of the lake, but there's one particular day when bathing here is believed to relieve devotees of all their sins. That day is the full moon (*purnima*) of the **Kartika** month (usually Nov). During the five days leading up to and including the full moon, Pushkar hosts thousands of celebrating devotees, following prescribed rituals on the lakeside and in the Brahma Temple.

At the same time, a huge, week-long **camel fair** is held west of the town, with hordes of herders from all over Rajasthan gathering to parade, race and trade more than forty thousand animals. With the harvest safely in the bag and the surplus livestock sold, the villagers, for this brief week or so, have a little money to spend enjoying themselves, which creates a lighthearted atmosphere that's generally absent from most other Rajasthani livestock fairs, backed up with entertainments including camel races, moustache competitions and a popular funfair, complete with an eye-catching sequence of enormous big wheels.

The popularity of Pushkar's fair has – inevitably – had an effect on the event, with camera-toting package tourists now bumping elbows with the event's traditional pilgrims and camel traders. But while the commercialism can be off-putting, the festive environment and coming together of cultures does produce some spontaneous mirth: in 2004, the second prize in the moustache contest was won by a Mancunian.

INFORMATION

Dates The dates of the next camel fairs are: 9–17, Nov 2013, Oct 30–Nov 6 2014, 18–25 Nov, 2015.

When to go It's best to get here for the first two or three days to see the *mela* in full swing; by the final few days of the festival most of the buying and selling has been done and the bulk of the herders have packed up and gone home. The day before the festival officially starts is also good – pretty much all the traders and livestock have arrived, but there are relatively few tourists around.

Booking accommodation It's best to book a room as far ahead as possible, though if you arrive early in the day – and with a bit of hunting – securing accommodation shouldn't be a problem. If you get stuck, you could try the RTDC runs a Tourist Village close to the fairgrounds, offering dormitory beds (₹350), tents and huts (some a/c), complete with private bathrooms, it offers from ₹2750 – ask at the tourist office or check ⊚ rtdc.in. Additional luxury temporary campsites are offered by *Royal Camp* (reservations c/o WelcomHeritage, ☏ 0291 257 2321, ⊚ welcomheritagehotels.com; ₹19500) and *Royal Desert Camp* (reservations c/o *Pushkar Palace* or *Jagat Palace* hotels or ⊚ rajasthanroyaldesertcamp.com; ₹11000).

Sonu Juice Main Bazaar. Almost every juice combination you can think of is sold here (from ₹20) along with muesli, so it makes a great spot for breakfast. Daily 7am–9pm.

Sunset Café East side of the lake ☏ 0145 277 2382. The perfect place to enjoy Pushkar's legendary lakeside sunsets, with great views (though the outside seats fill up quickly towards dusk) and an impressive selection of juices, lassis and shakes, along with the usual range of Italian, Mexican, Tibetan and Chinese food. Mains ₹50–120. Daily 7.30am–midnight.

SHOPPING

Though it isn't a craft centre as such, Pushkar is a good place to pick up touristy souvenirs, with its shops conveniently strung out along the Main Bazaar. As well as lots of hippie-type clothes, T-shirts, silver jewellery and Hindi music, not to mention ceramic chillums (Pushkar's rival those of Hampi and Pondicherry in the south), you'll find lac bangles, Rajasthani textiles, incense, essential oils and – always handy for a paint fight – Holi dyes. For new and used books, there's a slew of shops on the Main Bazaar just south of Varaha Chowk.

DIRECTORY

Banks and exchange There's a useful State Bank of Bikaner & Jaipur ATM near the Brahma Temple. Alternatively, you can change cash or travellers' cheques quickly at the many forex offices in the Main Bazaar.

Camel safaris A number of places arrange short camel rides and safaris (including overnight trips) in the desert around Pushkar – try EKTA Travels (see p.170), who run trips for around ₹170/hr.

Dance The Colleena Shakhti Dance Center (⊚ colleenashakti.com) in the old Rangji Temple runs intensive courses in Odissi dance, plus drop-in sessions covering a range of styles.

Horseriding Shannu's Riding School on Panch Kund Rd, near the Roadways Bus Stand (☎0145 277 2043) offers 1–2hr rides in the morning and evening on hardy Marwari steeds from ₹350/hr.

Hospital Government Hospital, opposite the GPO near Marwar Bus Stand (☎0145 277 2029).

Laundry Chhotu, just off Varaha Chowk (daily 7am–8.30pm). Bring clothes early for same-day service.

Police Next to the GPO (☎0145 277 2046).

Post office In the north of town near the Marwar Bus Stand (Mon–Sat 9am–5pm).

Swimming pools The *Navratan Palace Hotel* charges non-guests ₹100 to use theirs between noon and 5pm, or you can use the smaller pool at the *Om* hotel (Ajmer Rd) if you take a meal or drink.

Travel agents EKTA Travels acts as Indian Railways' agent in Pushkar and can arrange tickets for train journeys out of any station in India for a ₹50 charge, and also handles bus and plane tickets. They have offices at both the Marwar (☎0145 277 2931) and Ajmer bus stands (☎0145 277 2888).

Yoga and meditation Experienced teacher Yogesh Yogi runs intensive yoga and meditation courses (3–30 days) in the tranquil Pushkar Yoga Garden (☎9828 279835, ⓦpushkaryoga.org), on Vamdev road opposite the Ajmer Bus Stand, behind the Sikh *gurudwara*.

Jodhpur and around

On the eastern fringe of the Thar Desert, **JODHPUR**, dubbed "the Blue City" after the colour-wash of its old town houses, huddles below the mighty **Mehrangarh Fort**, the most spectacular citadel in Rajasthan, which dominates the cityscape from atop its huge sandstone plinth.

Blue originally denoted a high-caste Brahmin residence, resulting from the addition of indigo to lime-based whitewash, which was thought to protect buildings from insects, and to keep them cool in summer. Over time the colour caught on – there's now even a blue-wash mosque on the road from the Jalori Gate, west of the fort.

The bazaars of the old city, with different areas assigned to different trades, radiate out from the 1910 **Sardar Market** with its tall **clock tower**, a distinctive local landmark marking the centre of town. Most of the ramparts on the south side of the old city have been dismantled, leaving **Jalori Gate** and **Sojati Gate** looking rather forlorn as gates without a wall.

Jodhpur was once the most important town of Marwar, the largest princely state in Rajputana, and now has a population of around a million. Most people stay just long enough to visit the fort, though there's plenty to justify a longer visit. Getting lost in the blue maze of the old city you'll stumble across Muslim tie-dyers, puppet-makers and traditional spice markets, while Jodhpur's famed cubic roofscape, best viewed at sunset, is a photographer's dream.

Brief history

The **kingdom of Marwar** came into existence in 1381 when Rao Chanda, chief of the **Rathore** Rajput clan, seized the fort of Mandor (see p.181) from its former rulers, the Parihars. In 1459, the Rathore chief **Rao Jodha** moved from the exposed site at Mandor to a massive steep-sided escarpment, naming his new capital Jodhpur, after himself. His high barricaded fort proved virtually impregnable, and the city soon amassed great wealth from trade. The Mughals were keen to take over Jodhpur, and **Akbar** got his hands on the city in 1561, but he eventuallly allowed Marwar to keep its internal independence so long as the Rathore maharajas allied themselves to him.

In the eighteenth century, Marwar, Mewar (Udaipur) and Jaipur sealed a triple alliance to retain their independence against the Mughals, though the three states were as often at each other's throats as they were allied together. At the end of the century, maharaja **Man Singh** found himself under pressure from the expanding Maratha empire to his south, so in 1818 he turned for help to a new power, the **British**. Under the terms of his deal with them – not unlike Marwar's old arrangement with the Mughals – the kingdom retained its internal independence, but had to pay the East India Company an annual tribute equivalent to the one previously enforced by the Marathas.

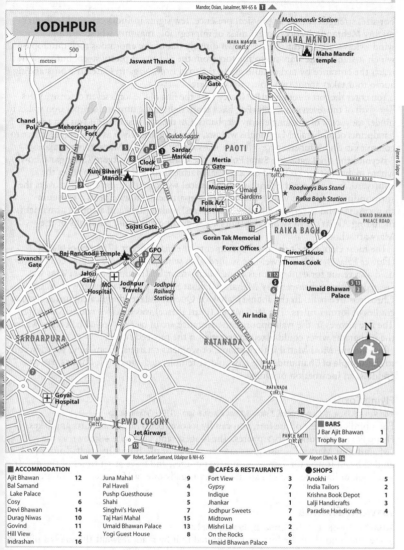

■ ACCOMMODATION				● CAFÉS & RESTAURANTS		● SHOPS	
Ajit Bhawan	12	Juna Mahal	9	Fort View	3	Anokhi	5
Bal Samand		Pal Haveli	4	Gypsy	7	India Tailors	2
Lake Palace	1	Pushp Guesthouse	3	Indique	1	Krishna Book Depot	1
Cosy	6	Shahi	5	Jhankar	1	Lalji Handicrafts	3
Devi Bhawan	14	Singhvi's Haveli	7	Jodhpur Sweets	7	Paradise Handicrafts	4
Durag Niwas	10	Taj Hari Mahal	15	Midtown	4		
Govind	11	Umaid Bhawan Palace	13	Mishri Lal	2		
Hill View	2	Yogi Guest House	8	On the Rocks	6		
Indrashan	16			Umaid Bhawan Palace	5		

■ BARS

J Bar Ajit Bhawan	1
Trophy Bar	2

The last but one maharaja before Independence, **Umaid Singh**, is commemorated by the immense Umaid Bhawan Palace. In 1930 he agreed in principle with the British to incorporate Marwar into an independent India. Despite the loss of official status, his descendants retain much of their wealth, alongside a great deal of influence and genuine respect in Jodhpur.

Mehrangarh Fort

Daily 9am–5pm • ₹300 (₹50) entry includes audio tour if you leave ID, credit card or deposit; audio tour for Indian visitors costs ₹150; camera ₹100, video ₹200; elevator ₹20; guide ₹200 • Ⓦ mehrangarh.org

For size, strength and sheer physical presence, few sights in India can rival Jodhpur's mighty **Mehrangarh Fort**, a great mass of impregnable masonry whose soaring, windowless walls appear to have grown directly out of the enormous rock outcrop on which it stands. The walk up to the fort from the old city is pretty steep, but you can reach the entrance by taxi or auto along the road from Nagauri Gate. The outstanding audio tour takes about two hours to complete.

You enter the fort through **Jai Pol** (or Jey Pol), the first of the fort's seven defensive gates. The sixth of the seven gates, **Loha Pol**, has a sharp right-angle turn and sharper iron spikes to hinder the ascent of charging enemy elephants. On the wall just inside it you can see the handprints of Maharaja Man Singh's widows, placed there in 1843 as they left the palace to commit sati on his funeral pyre – the last mass sati by wives of a Marwari maharaja.

Beyond the final gate, the **Suraj Pol**, lies the **Coronation Courtyard** (Shangar Chowk), where maharajas are crowned on a special marble throne. Looking up from the courtyard, you can see the fantastic *jali* (lattice) work that almost entirely covers the surrounding sandstone walls. The adjoining apartments now serve as a **museum** showcasing solid silver *howdahs* (elephant seats), palanquins and assorted armaments including Akbar's own sword. Upstairs are some fine **miniature paintings** of the Marwari school.

The most elaborate of the royal apartments, the magnificent 1724 **Phool Mahal** (Flower Palace), with its jewel-like stained-glass windows and gold filigree ceiling, was used as a venue for dancing, music and poetry recitals. The nearby **Takhat Vilas** was created by nineteenth-century Maharaja Takhat Singh, its ceiling hung with huge Christmas tree balls. In the **Jhanki Mahal**, or Queen's Palace, there's a colourful array of cradles of former rulers. The **Moti Mahal** (Pearl Palace) was used for councils of state. The five alcoves in the wall opposite the entrance are in fact concealed balconies where the maharaja's wives could listen in secretly on the proceedings.

Beyond the Moti Mahal is the **Zenana**, or women's quarters. From here, you descend to the **Temple of Chamunda**, the city's oldest temple, dedicated to Jodhpur's patron goddess, an incarnation of Durga.

Flying Fox
Tours start at 9.30am, 10.30am, 11.30am, 2.30pm, 3.30pm, 4.30pm & 5pm • ₹1199 • Ⓦ flyingfox.asia

For a bird's-eye view of the fort, you can fly its over courtyards, ramparts and lakes via **Flying Fox**; a network of six zipwires. The longest (and last) wire – known as the "Magnificent Marwar" – also gives amazing views of the Blue City itself. Tours are guided by an instructor, last about ninety minutes, and leave at set times of the day. If you book online three days in advance, they usually offer a 15 percent discount.

Jaswant Thanda
Fort Rd • Daily 9am–5pm • ₹30 (₹15); camera ₹25, video ₹50; guide ₹80

Some 500m north of the fort, and connected to it by road, **Jaswant Thanda** is a pillared marble memorial to the popular ruler Jaswant Singh II (1878–95), who purged Jodhpur of bandits, initiated irrigation systems and boosted the economy. The cenotaphs of members of the royal family who have died since Jaswant are close to his memorial; those who preceded him are commemorated by chhatris at Mandor (see p.181). In the morning, this southwest-facing spot is an excellent place from which to photograph the fort.

Umaid Bhawan Palace
Circuit House Rd • **Museum** Daily 9am–5pm • ₹50 (₹25), camera ₹50, video ₹100

Dominating the city's southeast horizon is the **Umaid Bhawan Palace**, a colossal Indo-Saracenic heap commissioned by Maharaja Umaid Singh in 1929 as a famine relief project, keeping three thousand labourers gainfully employed for sixteen years at a total cost of more than ₹9 million. The furniture and fittings for its 374 rooms were originally ordered from Maples in London during World War II, but were sunk by a U-boat en route to India. The maharaja was thus forced to turn to Stephen Norblin, a wartime Polish refugee, who gave the palace its fabulous Art Deco interiors.

The present incumbent, Maharaja Gaj Singh, occupies only one-third of the palace; the rest is given over to a luxury **hotel** (see p.179) and a rather dull **museum**, containing assorted European crockery and glassware, plus a mildly entertaining gallery of clocks and barometers, some in the form of railway locomotives, lighthouses and windmills. Far more interesting (and expensive) is the palace itself, its Art Deco furniture and fittings nearly all original, enlivened with lashings of typically Rajasthani gilt and sweeping staircases. To see them, non-guests will need to spend a minimum of ₹2000 per person at the hotel's bar or one of its restaurants (see p.180). If you're coming to eat here, it's a good idea to reserve in advance.

Umaid Gardens

High Court Rd · **Gardens and Zoo** Daily except Tues 9.45am–5.15pm · ₹75, camera ₹15, video ₹40 **Sardar Government Museum** Tues–Sun 9.45am–5.15pm · ₹50 (₹10)

The **Umaid Gardens** are home to the city's depressing **zoo**, whose animals are housed in enclosures scattered around the park, and the **Sardar Government Museum**, exhibiting the usual collection of skinned, stuffed, decapitated and pickled animals, along with a few other Rajasthani artefacts.

ARRIVAL AND DEPARTURE   JODHPUR

Jodhpur stands at the nexus of Rajasthan's main tourist routes, with connections northeast to Jaipur, Pushkar and Delhi, south to Udaipur and Ahmedabad, and west to Jaisalmer. Buses for most destinations are faster than the train.

By plane Jodhpur's Civil Airport (📞 2912512934) is 4km south of the city and currently served by Air India (airport & 2 West Patel Nagar, Circuit House Rd; 📞 0291 251 0758) and Jet Airways (Residency Rd & airport; 📞 0291 251 5551) who operate flights to Delhi and Mumbai. A pre-paid auto-rickshaw into town from the airport costs ₹150–200; taxis ₹400.

By train The railway station is on Station Rd, 300m south of Sojati Gate. There's a computerized reservations office (Mon–Sat 8am–8pm, Sun 8am–2pm), just north of the station behind the GPO. *Govind* hotel allows customers at its *Fort View* restaurant (see p.180) to leave baggage free of charge and use toilet facilities while waiting for a train. Note that there are no direct trains to Udaipur or Chittaurgarh – it's much easier to catch the bus.

By bus Government buses leave from the Roadways (Raika Bagh) Bus Stand just east of town – turn up an hour or so before departure to buy a ticket. For timetable information, it's best to ask your hotel or guesthouse to ring on your behalf (📞 0291 254 4686 or 📞 0291 254 4989). Most private buses leave from the stand on Pal Rd, 4km west of the centre (about ₹80 by auto); a few private buses leave from Kalpataru Cinema, 4km southwest of town (₹60 by auto). Private buses for Jaisalmer leave from Bombay Motors Circle, nearby, where they also drop you off. You can book tickets on private buses at most travel agents and a lot of hotels (for a ₹50 fee). Currently, there are services to Agra (daily; 15hr), Ajmer (2 daily; 5hr), Delhi (2 daily; 12hr), Jaipur (daily; 7hr), Jaisalmer (13 daily; 5hr), Mount Abu (daily; 7hr) and Udaipur (3 daily; 7hr).

GETTING AROUND AND INFORMATION

Motorcycle rental Jodhpur Travels, Station Rd (a few doors south of the *Govind* hotel; daily 6am–11pm; 📞 94606 87264) has motorbikes and mopeds for rent from ₹350/day.

Tourist information The tourist office (Mon–Fri 9.30am–6pm; 📞 0291 254 5083) is next to the *RTDC Goomar Hotel* on High Court Rd. Online, 🖥 jodhpur.nic.in and 🖥 maharajajodhpur.com both have lots of interesting background information on the city.

ACCOMMODATION

Jodhpur has plenty of good accommodation in all price brackets, although commission rackets are a real problem. Most guesthouses offer wi-fi and free pick ups; if not, take an auto to a point nearby and then walk.

2

RECOMMENDED TRAINS FROM JODHPUR

All the following trains run daily. There's also the once-weekly *Thar Express* to Karachi in Pakistan (Sat at 1am; 24hr), which departs from Bagat Ki Kothi station, 4km south of the city.

Destination	Name	No.	Departs	Arrives
Abu Road	*Ahmedabad Express*	9224	6am	10.37am
	Ranakpur Express	4707	3pm	7.57pm
Agra	*Howrah Superfast*	2308	8.30pm	6.15am
Ajmer	Fast passenger train	54801	7am	12.40pm
Alwar	*Jaisalmer–Delhi Express*	4060	11pm	7.12am
Bikaner	*Ranakpur Express*	4708	10am	3.35pm
	Barmer-Kalka Express	4888	10.45am	4.25pm
Jaipur	*Jaipur Intercity Express*	2466	6.10am	10.50am
	Mandor Express	2462	8pm	12.50am
Jaisalmer	*Delhi–Jaisalmer Express*	4659	5.10am	11pm
	Jaisalmer Express	4810	11.45pm	5.30am
New Delhi	*Mandor Express*	2462	8pm	6.25am
	Jaisalmer–Delhi Express	4660	11pm	11.10am
Sawai Madhopur	*Intercity Express*	2466	6.10am	1.15pm
	Bhopal passenger train	54812	8.05am	12.25pm

Ajit Bhawan Airport Rd ☎0291 251 0410, ⊚ajitbhawan.com. Despite the Flintstones-like theme-park design, this self-contained resort – built to resemble a *dhani* village – gets rave reviews for its try-hard attitude and relaxing environment. Accommodation is in cute little round chalets, tents or more conventional rooms, and there's a quaint waterfall-fed pool (₹565/day non-guests), thatch-roofed outdoor restaurant, a bar and spa. ₹18,000

Bal Samand Lake Palace 8km north of Jodhpur along Mandore Rd ☎0291 257 2321, ⊚welcomheritagehotels.com. Among the most attractive heritage hotels in the state, converted from the maharaja's lakeside summer palace, with ten beautiful "Palace Suites" in the main building – all huge, airy and exquisitely furnished–plus cheaper standard rooms in the palace's former stables, near reception. US$143

Cosy Bhram Puri, Chuna ki Choki, Navchokiya ☎0291 261 2066, ⊚cosyguesthouse.com. Friendly little guesthouse in a pretty blue-washed building buried deep in the maze of lanes in the west of the old city (call for free pickup; it's tricky to find otherwise). Rooms (fan, air-cooled and a/c; a few with shared bathroom) are simple but neat and cosy, and there are killer views of the fort from the rooftop terrace. ₹200/₹300

★**Devi Bhawan** Ratanada Circle, Defence Laboratory Rd ☎0291 251 2215, ⊚devibhawan.com. Set in surprisingly lush gardens, this eighty-year-old refuge is home to spotless a/c rooms furnished with period fittings and colourful Rajasthani fabrics. The gorgeous pool is one of the nicest in town and there's a breezy restaurant that spills onto a terrace shaded by neem trees. Book ahead. ₹2470

Durag Niwas 1st Old Public Park Lane, Raika Bagh ☎0291 251 2385, ⊚durag-niwas.com. Very friendly and well-run little place with cosy air-cooled and a/c rooms, all with private bathrooms, set around a peaceful courtyard. Also runs various programmes helping disadvantaged local women (half the guests are usually long-stay volunteers). Gay-and-lesbian-friendly. ₹400

★**Govind** Station Rd ☎0291 262 2758, ⊚govindhotel.com. A longstanding travellers' favourite, with bright, spotless rooms (some with a/c; all air-cooled in summer), a clean dorm, excellent rooftop restaurant (see opposite) with wi-fi and friendly, professional management who also arrange tours. There's also an in-house internet café and travel agents (see p.180), and it's conveniently close to the station. Dorm ₹200, double ₹700

Hill View Old City, on the road up to the fort about 200m beyond Krishna Prakash hotel ☎0291 244 1763. Sociable guesthouse run by hotelier turned local Congress politician Zafran and family. Rooms (all attached) are basic but very cheap, and there are fine views over town. ₹250

Indrashan 593 High Court Colony, 3km south of town ☎0291 244 0665, ⊚indrashan.com. Five cosy rooms in an authentic homestay in a quiet residential area, with sumptuous cooking classes (₹1500) that draw amateur chefs from around the world. Non-guests are welcome for dinner if they call ahead. ₹4125

★**Juna Mahal** Ada Bazaar, off Daga St ☎0291 279 0366, ⊚junamahal.com. This 370-year-old haveli has just five great-value boutique suites (all a/c) adorned with eye-catching artefacts, plus nice bathrooms and balconies. There's veg food, free wi-fi and free pick up from the railway station. ₹1600

Pal Haveli Near Gulab Sagar Lake ☎0291 329 3328, ⊚palhaveli.com. Atmospheric heritage hotel in the heart of the old city with attractively furnished rooms and plenty of period character. Standard ("Royal Heritage") rooms are reasonably affordable, though the "Historical" rooms are only slightly nicer, and almost twice the price. There's also a fabulous rooftop restaurant (see below) and bar. ₹4300

Pushp Guesthouse Nr Manak Chowk ☎0291 264 8494, ⓦpushpguesthouse.com. Tucked up a side alley in the heart of the Old City, *Pushp* is run by a friendly family and has five clean jewel-coloured rooms (fan, a/c or air-cooled), a nice fabric-adorned rooftop café and city views. ₹400

★ **Shahi** Gandhi St, City Police district, off Katla Bazaar opposite Narsingh Temple ☎0291 262 3802, ⓦshahiguesthouse.net. Welcoming family guesthouse occupying a quirky 350-year-old haveli buried deep in the warren of lanes beneath the fort's southwest wall – and with superb views of it from the roof. The six rooms (all a/c) are brimming with character, decorated with a medley of quaint murals and assorted curios. Call for free pickup (it's difficult to find otherwise). ₹2800

Singhvi's Haveli Ramdevji-ka Chowk ☎0291 262 4293, ⓦsinghvihaveli.com. This family-run guesthouse in a 500-year-old haveli rears up from the old town under the quieter western end of Mehrangarh Fort. The mishmash of rooms (all attached, some with a/c) range from cheap 'n'

cheerful doubles to a fabulous mirrorwork-adorned Maharani Suite. There's a veg restaurant and the wi-fi works all over the property. ₹400

Taj Hari Mahal 5 Residency Rd, 1km south of town ☎0291 243 9700, ⓦtajhotels.com. All the luxury you'd expect from a five-star *Taj* hotel, with swanky traditional-style decor, two good restaurants including *Marwar*), a spa and good-sized pool, and spacious and attractively furnished rooms (US$280).

Umaid Bhawan Palace Circuit House Rd ☎0291 251 0101, ⓦtajhotels.com. The maharaja of Jodhpur's princely pile (see p.177) ranks among the world's grandest hotels, with celebrity guests and lashings of trendy Art Deco. But being king or queen for a day can be a solitary experience – some find the oversized suites, stately salons and dark, marbled passageways a bit foreboding. US$1030

Yogi Guest House Manak Chowk, Old City (about 50m down the road in front of the Krishna Prakash hotel) ☎0291 264 3436, ⓦyogiguesthouse.com. One of the better guesthouses located just north of Sardar Bazaar, with lovely blue decor and clean, comfy rooms (most with a/c) with wobbly old walls. There are excellent fort views from the rooftop restaurant. Free wi-fi. ₹450

EATING AND DRINKING

Local specialities include *mirchi bada*, a big chilli covered in wheatgerm and potato and then deep-fried like a pakora. Cheap drinks can be found in the grungy, male-dominated bars around the *Midtown* restaurant on Station Rd.

CAFÉS AND RESTAURANTS

Fort View Govind Hotel, Station Rd ☎0291 262 2758. A cut above the usual tourist places, with good, reasonably priced veg curries and thalis (₹70–120), local specialities such as *makhania* lassi (₹50) and excellent *gulab jamun* (not the Bengali sweet, but a savoury Rajasthani dish made with *mawa*), plus good breakfast options, including real coffee. Also has wi-fi coverage, and you can hang out here while waiting for a bus or train (baggage storage facilities are available). Licensed. Daily 7am–midnight.

Gypsy C Rd, Sardarpura ☎0291 510 3882. Downstairs it's a run-of-the-mill diner selling Indian snacks and ice cream. Upstairs it's a comfortable restaurant serving one thing only: an unlimited and delicious veg thali (₹136), which they keep refilling for as long as you carry on eating. There's another branch 50m away on A Rd. Daily 11am-3.30pm & 7pm-11pm

★ **Indique,** Pal Haveli, Near Gulab Sagar Lake ☎0291 329 3328 ☎0291 329 3328. Far and away the most atmospheric dining spot in town. Tables sit on two levels of the hotel's significant rooftop, with stunning views of the fort, the Blue City and the Umaid Bhawan Palace. The veg and non-veg food (₹250–480) isn't quite as good as the

view, but the restaurant is licensed, and a great spot for sundowners. Bookings are recommended. Daily noon–3pm & 6pm-10.30pm.

Jhankar Choti Haveli, Makarana Mohalla ☎98280 31291. The veg restaurant in this 500-year-old building spans three floors, with obligatory rooftop seating, but it's the enchanting courtyard garden restaurant that steals the show; sit under the shade of neem trees and dine on home-style Rajasthani specialities (₹95–150) such as *raboi* and *ker sangri*. Services include free internet and wi-fi. Daily 7am–11pm.

Jodhpur Sweets C Rd, Sardarpura, next to Gypsy. The best sweet shop in town, and an excellent place to try *makhan wada*, *mawa kachori* or any other Rajasthani or Bengali sweets. Daily 7am–10pm

★ **Midtown** On a side road off Station Rd opposite the station ☎0291 263 7001. Bright, clean and friendly pure-veg restaurant with a delicious range of curries, south Indian dishes, Gujarati and Rajasthani thalis and other Rajasthani specialities, as well as some pizza and Chinese. Mains ₹90–180. Licensed. Daily 7am–11pm.

Mishri Lal In the eastern arch of the south gate to Sardar Market. The most famous purveyor of *makhania* lassi (₹25 a cup), made with cream, yogurt, saffron and cardamom, deliciously rich and thick. Daily 8.30am–9pm.

On the Rocks Next to Ajit Bhawan hotel, Airport Rd ☏ 0291 230 2701. Upmarket garden restaurant specializing in kebabs and tandoori cuisine. Though the service is slow, it's fun and festive at night. The lunch crowd is mostly tour groups. Mains ₹135–195 veg, ₹235–265 non-veg. Daily 8am–11pm.

Umaid Bhawan Palace Circuit House Rd ☏ 0291 251 0101, ⊛ tajhotels.com. The opulent *Umaid Bhawan Palace* boasts various eating and drinking possibilities, though whatever you do you'll have to stump up a ₹2000 minimum charge, payable on entry and redeemable against anything you eat or drink (advance reservations for the restaurants are also strongly recommended) – although this at least gives you the chance to wander around the hotel's opulent Art Deco interior. *The Pillars* veranda café has sweeping views over the palace

gardens and offers light snacks during the day. Full meals are available at the *Risala* multicuisine restaurant, set in a lavish, old-world European-style dining room, and at *The Pillars* at night. The Pillars 6.30am–11pm; Risala 1–3pm & 7.30–11pm.

BARS

J Bar Ajit Bhawan Airport Rd ☏ 0291 251 0410. Comfy chairs, cool decor and a long beverage list make this smart hotel bar a good spot for evening drinks, and there's a great menu too. Daily 11am–11pm.

Trophy Bar Umaid Bhawan Palace, Circuit House Rd ☏ 0291 251 0101. Adorned with hunting trophies of former maharajahs, including stuffed animals and a 2m-long elephant tusk, this is easily the most memorable place for a drink in the city, if you can afford the ₹2000 minimum charge. Daily 11am–3 & 6pm–11pm.

SHOPPING

Jodhpur's first-rate antique reproductions – everything from chests of drawers to sculptures of Jain *tirthankaras* – attract dealers from around the world. There's a line of shops selling them along Umaid Bhawan Palace Rd east of the Circuit House. Other good buys in town include textiles, patchwork bedcovers, bandhani (tye-dye) fabric and Jodhpur riding britches.

Anokhi Rani Bagh. Close to *Ajit Bhawan* hotel, this small branch of the famous Jaipur store displays a selection of their famed block-printed products - quilts, clothing, bags and saris. Daily 10.30am–8pm.

Lalji Handicrafts Umaid Bhawan Palace Rd. Huge warehouse-like shop stuffed with all sorts of unusual bric-a-brac including old enamel signs and colonial-era prints. Daily 9am–7pm.

India Tailors High Court Rd, 75m east of the junction with Nai Sarak. Despite its small and

unprepossessing appearance, this little shop can't be beaten for custom-made suits or Jodhpur riding britches, and counts the maharaja among its customers. Daily 10am–8pm.

Krishna Book Depot Upstairs at Krishna Art and Export in Sardar Market. The first floor of this handily located bookshop, just east of the north gate, is stuffed with a selection of new and used English language books and Indian travel titles. Daily 10.30am–7.30pm.

DIRECTORY

Banks and exchange There are plenty of ATMs on MG Rd 100m east of Sojati Gate, plus one on Station Rd near *Govind* hotel, and plenty east of the tourist office. Forex offices can be found north of the clock tower in Sardar Market and on Hanwant Vihar just north of Circuit House.

Cooking class Lavi at the *Govind* hotel runs Indian cooking classes on demand for ₹600/person.

Festival Jodhpur's annual two-day Marwar Festival, held at the full moon of the Hindu month of Ashvina (Oct 7–8, 2014; Oct 26–27, 2015; Oct 14–15, 2016) is a showcase of performing arts, mainly music and dance.

Hospital The best private hospital is the Goyal on Residency Rd in the Sindhi Colony, 2km south of town (☏ 0291 243 2144).

Police ☏ 0291 265 0777. There's a police tourist assistance booth by the clock tower in Sardar Market.

Post office The GPO is opposite the *Govind* hotel on Station Rd. Stamps can be bought in the section through the right-hand entrance (Mon–Sat 9am–3pm, Sun 9am–1pm).

Swimming pool Non-guests can use the lovely pool at the *Ajit Bhawan* hotel (see p.178) for ₹565/day, or the smaller pools at *Ratan Vilas* (₹400/day) and *Devi Bhawan* (₹300/3hr).

Travel agents Staff at the *Govind* hotel (see p.178) can book train, bus and plane tickets for a modest service charge (₹50), and can also arrange car rental from ₹1500/day, camel safaris to Osian and tours to local Bisnoi villages.

Mandor

Some 9km north of Jodhpur lies the sleepy village of **MANDOR**, home to a superb sequence of **royal cenotaphs** erected in memory of the kingdom's former rulers.

Mandor served as the capital of the Parihar Rajputs from the sixth century until 1381, when they were ousted by Rathore Rao Chauhan, and although the capital was moved to Jodhpur in 1459, the Marwari rulers continued to have their memorial cenotaphs (*dewals*) erected here. Temple-like in their sombre dark red sandstone, the cenotaphs grew in size and grandeur as the Rathore kingdom prospered (the canopy-like chhatris next to them are for lesser royals). The largest is Ajit Singh's, built in 1724. His six queens, along with assorted mistresses, concubines, maids and entertainers – 84 women in all – committed sati on his funeral pyre.

At the end of the gardens, on the far side of the chhatris, you'll find the octagonal **Ek Thamba Mahal** (Single Pillared Palace), a three-storey pagoda-like affair built at the beginning of the eighteenth century for royal ladies to watch public events without breaking their purdah. Behind it is a small **museum** (Tues–Sun 9.45am–5.15pm; ₹60 (₹5)), home to a few dull sculptures and paintings. Much more interesting are the extensive remains of **Mandor Fort**, citadel of the Parihar and Rathore Rajputs when Mandor was their capital, reached via a flight of steps behind the mildly diverting museum.

ARRIVAL AND DEPARTURE   MANDOR

By bus Mandor can be reached on minibuses #1, #5 and #7 from Jodhpur's Sojati Gate. Services operate between 7.30am and 8.30pm daily.

ACCOMMODATION

Mandore Guest House Close to the gardens on Dadawari Lane ☏ 0291 254 5210, ⊛ mandore.com. It's actually more of a miniature resort than a guesthouse, with accommodation in a mix of air-cooled and a/c rooms and (rather dark) round huts set in a tree-studded garden. ₹2140

The Bishnoi villages

Good and inexpensive tours of the Bishnoi villages are run by several guesthouses in Jodhpur including *Govind* hotel, *Durag Niwas* and *Yogi's Guest House*; rates start at around ₹800/person in a couple (cheaper in larger groups)

Jodhpur's surroundings can be explored on organized "**village safaris**", which take small groups of tourists out into rural Rajasthan, usually stopping at four or five **Bishnoi villages** where you can taste traditional food, drink opium tea and watch crafts such as spinning and carpet-making. You might also spot nilgai (bluebull) antelopes and gazelles.

The Bishnois – a religious sect rather than an ethnic group in the usual sense – are among the world's earliest tree-huggers. Their origins go back to a drought in the year 1485. Observing that this was caused largely by deforestation, a guru by the name of Jambeshwar Bhagavan formulated 29 rules for living in harmony with nature and the environment – his followers are called Bishnoi after the Marwari word for 29. As well as enforcing strict vegetarianism, Jambeshwar's rules forbid the killing of animals or felling of live trees. In particular, Bishnoi hold the **khejri** tree sacred. In 1730, at the village of **Khejadali**, workers sent by the maharaja of Marwar to make lime for the construction of a palace started felling *khejri* trees to burn the local limestone. A woman by the name of Amrita Devi put her arms around a tree and declared that if they wanted to cut it down, they would have to cut her head off first. The leader of the working party ordered her decapitation, upon which her three daughters followed her example, and were similarly beheaded. Bishnoi people from the whole of the surrounding region then converged on the site to defend the trees – 363 of them gave their lives doing so. When news reached the maharaja, he ordered the felling to cease and banned cutting down trees and hunting animals in Bishnoi territory. Today, a small temple marks the place where all this happened, while in its grounds, 363 *khejri* trees commemorate the martyrs.

Although it is possible to go to Khejadali by bus, you'll be hard put to find a villager who speaks English, and it's a lot better to go with a tour group, which will also visit other villages. Most tours stop at Khejadali for lunch. This is usually followed by an **opium ceremony** in which opium is dissolved in water in a specially designed wooden vessel, and poured through a strainer into a second receptacle. The process is repeated twice more, and the resulting tea is drunk from the palm of a hand. Strictly speaking, it's illegal, but blind eyes are turned to this kind of traditional opium use, though in fact opium addiction is something of a social problem in rural Rajasthan.

Osian

Rajasthan's largest group of early Jain and Hindu temples lies on the outskirts of the small town of **OSIAN** (or **Osiyan**), 64km north of Jodhpur. The temples date from the eighth to the twelfth centuries when Osian was a regional trading centre. The town's ruler and population apparently converted to Jainism in the eleventh century, and the town is still an important Jain pilgrimage centre.

The town centre is dominated by the imposing twelfth-century **Sachiya Mata Temple**, overlooking the whole of Osian from its elevated hilltop position. At the very top of the complex, the main shrine to Sachiya (an incarnation of Durga) is unusually decorated with multicoloured mirrorwork and topped by a cluster of finely carved *shikharas*.

A five-minute walk from the Sachiya Mata Temple lies Osian's most beautiful monument, the **Mahavira Jain Temple** (daily 5am–10pm; ₹10, ₹100 camera & video; no leather items permitted, and women should not enter while menstruating). Built in the eighth century, renovated in the tenth, and restored quite recently, the temple's beautifully carved central shrine is fronted by twenty elegant pillars and surrounded by shrines to further *tirthankaras*. A trio of smaller temples lies nearby, including a pair of Surya temples and the unusual **Peeplaj Temple**, surrounded by gargoyle-like projecting elephants, along with a massive Pratihara-period (eighth and ninth centuries) step-well.

Just south of the bus stop lies Osian's oldest collection of temples, centred on the **Vishnu and Harihara temples**, also built in the Pratihara period. The nine temples in this group retain a considerable amount of decorative carving, particularly in the surrounding friezes.

LEGEND OF THE THAR

Legend ascribes the **creation of the Thar** to Rama, hero of the Ramayana. In it, Rama, an earthly incarnation of the god Vishnu, has to rescue his wife Sita from the clutches of the demon Ravana, who is holding her on the island of Sri Lanka. To cross to the island, Rama loads his bow with a magical arrow that will dry up the ocean, but the sea god Sagara begs him not to shoot, offering him free passage instead. Well, says Rama, my bow is now drawn and must be shot, where shall I aim it? There is a sea to the north, replies Sagara, where evil-doers drink my water and hurt me; shoot your arrow there, and you'll be doing me a favour. So Rama takes aim and shoots, drying up the sea that Sagara has described, and creating the desert of Marwar ("Land of the Dead"). By Rama's special boon, this new land, though desert, is blessed, full of sweet herbs and fit for grazing cattle.

In fact, the legend would seem to be based on some degree of truth, for the fossil record shows that back in the Jurassic period (206–144 million years ago), the Thar was indeed covered by sea. Indeed, you may notice that slabs of sandstone often bear tell-tale ripple marks showing that they once formed part of the seabed.

ARRIVAL AND INFORMATION

By bus Government buses from Jodhpur (every 30min–1hr; 1hr 30min) drop you at the stand on the main road just south of town.

Tours Camel treks around Osian can also be arranged through the *Govind* and *Cosy* guesthouses in Jodhpur; rates start at around ₹850/person/day (minimum two people) plus transport costs (roundtrip by taxi from ₹1500).

ACCOMMODATION

Priest Bhanu Sarma Guesthouse Opposite the Mahavira temple ☎0292 227 4331. Run by the knowledgeable (Hindu) priest of the same name who looks after the (Jain) temple, rooms are basic but clean with shared bathrooms and buckets for hot water. Priest Bhanu can act as a guide for the local temples and you can also arrange camel safaris and tours of local Bishnoi villages from here. ₹400

Reggie's Camel Camp Reservations c/o the India Safari Club in Jodhpur on ☎0291 243 7023, ⓦ camelcamposian.com. A comfortable and welcoming luxury hotel amid the desert on the outskirts of town, with carpeted a/c tents and a stunning pool. Full board. US$260

Jaisalmer and around

In the remote westernmost corner of Rajasthan, **JAISALMER** is the quintessential desert town, its golden, sand-coloured ramparts rising out of the arid Thar like a scene from the *Arabian Nights*. Rampant commercialism may have dampened the romantic vision somewhat, but even with all the touts and tour buses, the town deservedly remains one of India's most popular destinations. Villagers dressed in voluminous red and orange turbans still outnumber foreigners in the bazaar, while the exquisite sandstone architecture of the "Golden City" is quite unlike anything else in India.

The streets of Jaisalmer are flanked with numerous pale honey-coloured facades, covered with latticework and floral designs, but the city's real showpieces are its **havelis**, commissioned by wealthy merchants during the eighteenth and nineteenth centuries.

Brief history

Rawal Jaisal of the Bhati clan founded Jaisalmer in 1156 as a replacement for his less easily defensible capital at Lodurva. Constant wars with Jodhpur and Bikaner followed, as did conflict with the sultans of Delhi. In 1298, a seven-year siege of the fort by the forces of Ala-ud-Din Khalji (see p.1157) ended when the men of the city rode out to their deaths while the women committed *johar* – although the Bhatis soon resumed their rule. The city was again besieged by Sultanate forces in 1326, resulting in another desperate act of *johar*, but Gharsi Bhati managed to negotiate the return of his kingdom as a vassal state of Delhi, after which it remained in Bhati hands.

In 1570 the ruler of Jaisalmer married one of his daughters to Akbar's son, cementing an alliance between Jaisalmer and the Mughal Empire. Its position on the overland route between Delhi and Central Asia made it an important entrepôt for goods such as silk, opium and spices, and the city grew rich on the proceeds, as the magnificent havelis of its merchants bear witness. However, the emergence of Bombay and Surat as major ports meant that overland trade diminished, and with it Jaisalmer's wealth. The death-blow came with Partition, when Jaisalmer's life-line trade route was severed by the new, highly sensitive Pakistani border. The city took on renewed strategic importance during the Indo-Pakistani wars of 1965 and 1971, and it is now a major **military outpost**, with jet aircraft regularly roaring past the ramparts.

Jaisalmer Fort

Palace of the Maharawal Daily 9am–6pm; last tour 5pm • ₹300 (₹200) including camera fee and audioguide (although you'll need to leave either a ₹2000 cash deposit or your passport for the equipment); students ₹150 (₹100); video ₹150, camera (for Indians) ₹100 **Jain temples** Daily 8am–noon • ₹150 including camera/video/mobile phone fees

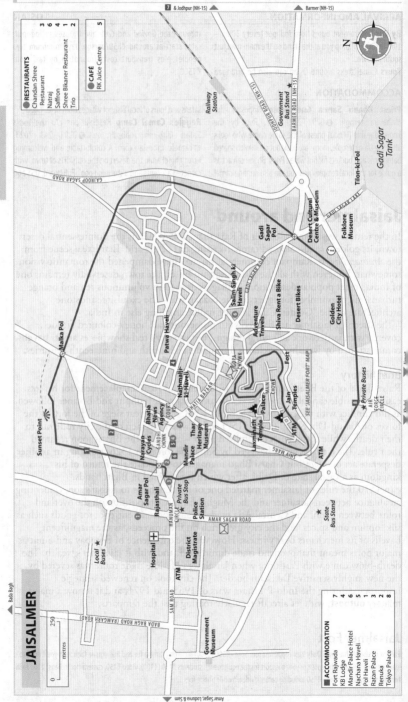

SEE JAISALMER FORT MAP

JAISALMER

0   250
     metres

RESTAURANTS

Chandan Shree	3
Restaurant	4
Natraj	6
Saffron	1
Shree Bikaner Restaurant	1
Trio	2

CAFÉ

RK Juice Centre	5

ACCOMMODATION

Fort Rajwada	7
KB Lodge	4
Mandir Palace Hotel	6
Nachana Haveli	5
Pol Haveli	1
Ratan Palace	3
Renuka	2
Tokyo Palace	8

& Jodhpur (NH-15)

Barmer (NH-15)

Railway Station

Government Bus Stand

Barmer Road (NH-15)

Jodhpur Road (NH-15)

Gadi Sagar Tank

Tilon-ki-Pol

Gadi Sagar Pol

Desert Cultural Centre & Museum

Folklore Museum

Gadi Sagar Road

Gadisar Road

(Ramgarh Road) Bada Bagh Road

Ghadroop Sagar Road

Malka Pol

Sunset Point

Patwa Haveli

Salim Singh ki Haveli

Shiva Rent a Bike

Adventure Travels

Desert Bikes

Golden City Hotel

Nathmalji ki-Haveli

Gopa Chowk

Bhatia Bazaar

Fort

Main Chowk

Laxminath Temple

Palace

Jain Temples

Shiv Marg

ATM

Private Buses

Air Force Circle

Bhatia News Agency

Court Rd

Sandhi Chowk

Thar Heritage Museum

Narayan Cycles

Mandir Palace

Amar Sagar Pol

Rajasthali

Private Bus Stop

Hanuman Circle

Police Station

Amar Sagar Road

State Bus Stand

Hospital

District Magistrate

Sam Road

Government Museum

Local Buses

ATM

Amar Sagar, Lodurva & Sam

Bada Bagh

CAMEL SAFARIS FROM JAISALMER

Few visitors who make it as far as Jaisalmer pass up the opportunity to go on a **camel trek**, which provides an irresistibly romantic chance to cross the barren sands and sleep under one of the starriest skies in the world. Sandstorms, sore backsides and camel farts aside, the safaris are usually great fun. Treks normally last from one to four days, with **prices** varying from ₹750 to ₹2000 per night. The highlight is spending a night under the desert stars, and most travellers find that an overnight trip, departing around 3pm one day and returning the next at noon, is sufficient. Unfortunately, the price you pay is not an adequate gauge of the quality of services you get, and it pays to shop around and ask other travellers for recommendations. We've listed a few dependable operators below, though the list is far from exhaustive. Make sure you'll be provided with your own camel, an adequate supply of blankets (it can get very cold at night), food cooked with mineral water and a campfire. You should also make sure that your operator is committed to either burning or removing all rubbish (including plastic bottles).

The traditional Jaisalmer camel safari used to head west out of town to Amar Sagar, Lodurva, Sam and Kuldera (see p.193). Some operators still cover these areas, although encroaching development and crowds of other tourists (around Sam especially) mean that there is very little sense of the real desert hereabouts. The better operators are constantly seeking out new and unspoilt areas to trek through – this usually means an initial drive out of Jaisalmer of around 50–60km, though it's worth it to avoid the crowds. Longer seven- to ten-day treks to Pokaran, Barmer and Bikaner can also be arranged, though these shouldn't be attempted lightly.

Finally, don't book anything until you get to Jaisalmer. Touts trawl trains and buses from Jodhpur, but they usually represent dodgy outfits, or pretend to represent one of the well-established operators. Some offer absurdly cheap rooms (typically ₹100) if you agree to book a camel trek with them, and then rescind their offer (of a room) if you change your mind. Guesthouse notice-boards are filled with sorry stories of tourists who accepted. As a rule of thumb, any firm that has to tout for business – and that includes hotels – is worth avoiding.

SPECIALIST AGENCIES

Specialist agencies allow you to book direct through their offices in Jaisalmer. Reliable outfits include:

Adventure Travels Just south of the First Fort Gate ☎94141 49176, ⓦadventurecamels.com. With more than 25 years of experience, this operator gets rave reviews for seeking out remote locations and providing fringe amenities, like real mattresses and sheets, plus hearty food.

Sahara Travels Gopa Chowk ☎0299 225 2609, ⓦsaharatravelsjaisalmer.com. Dependable operator established in 1989 by the late "Mr Desert" offering well-priced safaris with comfy cot beds, adequate blankets and a decent supply of food and drink.

HOTEL-ORGANIZED SAFARIS

Nearly all hotels offer camel safaris. The following two get good reviews:

Renuka Near Gandhi Chowk ☎912992 252757. Friendly, reliable camel safaris at some of the lowest rates in town – guides speak decent English and facilities aren't bad, given the price.

Shahi Palace Off Shiv Marg ☎0299 225 5920. Safaris organized through *Shahi Palace* aren't the cheapest, but feedback on comfort and location is good. Rough Guides readers get 10 percent off if they show this guide.

Every part of Jaisalmer Fort is made of soft yellow Jurassic sandstone. Outside, the thick **walls**, punctuated with barrel-sided bastions, drop almost 100m to the town below, while inside narrow winding streets are flanked with carved golden facades. Two thousand people still live within its walls; seventy percent of them are Brahmins and the rest, living primarily on the east side, are predominantly Rajput. A paved road punctuated by four huge gateways winds up to the fort's **main chowk** (square) – large round stones lie atop the ramparts above the entrance, waiting to be pushed down on the heads of any approaching enemy. The main chowk was the scene of the three terrible acts of *johar* during the fourteenth and fifteenth centuries, when the women

2

of the royal palace, which overlooks the chowk, had a huge fire built, and jumped from the palace walls into it.

The chowk is dominated by the **Palace of the Maharawal**, open to the public as the **Fort Palace Museum**. The palace's balconied, five-storey facade displays some of the finest masonry in Jaisalmer, while the ornate marble throne to the left of the palace entrance is where the monarch (known in Jaisalmer as the maharawal rather than the maharaja) would have addressed his troops. Inside, the museum offers an intriguing snapshot of the life of Jaisalmer's potentates through the ages, with artefacts ranging from a fancy silver coronation throne to more homely items, such as the bed and thali dish of a nineteenth-century ruler. There's also an interesting array of other exhibits – from fifteenth-century sculptures (including an unusual bearded Rama) through to local stamps and banknotes, while the rooftop terrace gives unrivalled views over the city and the surrounding countryside.

The fort has a number of Hindu temples, including the venerable **Laxminath Temple** of 1494, however none is as impressive as the complex of seven **Jain temples**. The temples, connected by small corridors and stairways, were built between the twelfth and fifteenth centuries with yellow and white marble shrines and exquisite sculpted motifs covering the walls, ceilings and pillars. Two of the seven temples are open

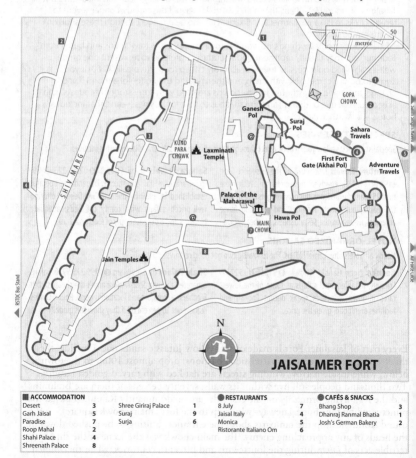

JAISALMER FORT

■ ACCOMMODATION				● RESTAURANTS		● CAFÉS & SNACKS	
Desert	3	Shree Giriraj Palace	1	8 July	7	Bhang Shop	3
Garh Jaisal	5	Suraj	9	Jaisal Italy	4	Dhanraj Ranmal Bhatia	1
Paradise	7	Surja	6	Monica	5	Josh's German Bakery	2
Roop Mahal	2			Ristorante Italiano Om	6		
Shahi Palace	4						
Shreenath Palace	8						

between 8am and noon; the other five only open from 11am to noon, when the whole place gets overrun with coach parties, so it's best to visit before 11am to see the first two temples, then come back later to see the rest.

Nathmalji-ki-Haveli

Court Rd • Daily 8am–8pm • Free

Just north of Bhatia Bazaar (take the small road between the Ajanta Photo Studio and Dev Handicrafts), the **Nathmalji-ki-Haveli** was built in 1885 for Jaisalmer's prime minister by two brother stonemasons, one of whom built the left half, the other the right, as a result of which the two sides are subtly different. It's guarded by two elephants, and the first-floor bay window above the main doorway is surmounted by a frieze of little figures including elephants, horses, a steam train and a horse-drawn carriage.

Patwa Haveli

Kumhar Para • Daily 8am–8pm • ₹20 **Government museums** Daily 10am–5pm • ₹50 combined ticket (₹20) **Kothari Patwa Haveli Museum** Daily 9am–6pm • ₹150 (₹50), video ₹70, camera ₹50

The finely decorated **Patwa Haveli**, or Patwon-ki-Haveli, lies a couple of blocks north of the Nathmalji-ki-Haveli down a street to the right, its exterior a positive riot of exuberantly carved *jharokhas* (protruding balconies). The haveli was constructed in the first half of the nineteenth century by the Patwa merchants – five brothers from a Jain family who were bankers and traders in brocade and opium. There are actually five separate suites within the haveli. Two are closed to visitors. Two, preserved in their original condition, are open as **government museums**. One, the **Kothari Patwa Haveli Museum** has various traditional artefacts on display and replica mirrorwork on the walls, giving you some idea of how the haveli would originally have looked. As well as visiting the interior of the Patwa Haveli, it's worth taking a little stroll down the street whose entrance it bridges, to check out the stonework on four impressive neighbouring havelis.

Salim Singh ki Haveli

Asani Rd • Daily: summer 8am–7pm, winter 8am–6pm • ₹20, camera ₹50, video ₹50

The third of Jaisalmer's famous trio of havelis, the **Salim Singh ki Haveli**, lies on the east side of town and is immediately recognizable by the lavishly carved overhanging rooftop balcony that gives the whole building a strangely top-heavy appearance. Its upper floor, enclosed by an overhanging balcony, is best seen from the roof of *Natraj* restaurant.

Mandir Palace

Gandhi Chowk • Daily 8am–6pm • ₹50, joint entry into palace (₹40) and museum (₹20), video camera ₹30, camera ₹30

Portions of the **Mandir Palace**, now partly converted into a heritage hotel (see p.190), can be visited, though its most striking feature, the elegant **Badal Vilas tower**, is best seen from the west, just outside Amar Sagar Pol.

Gadi Sagar Tank

South of town through an imposing triple gateway lies **Gadi Sagar Tank**, once Jaisalmer's sole water supply, flanked with sandstone *ghats* and temples – a peaceful spot, staring out into the desert; you can rent boats here for a spin on the water (₹50 for 30min).

Folklore Museum

Gadi Sagar Rd • Daily 8am–6pm • ₹50 (₹10)

The **Folklore Museum**, near the main gate of the Gadi Sagar Tank, has displays of folk art and textiles, along with opium and betel nut paraphernalia from the personal collection of the museum's proprietor, N.K. Sharma.

Desert Cultural Centre & Museum

Gadi Sagar Rd • Daily 10am–6pm • ₹50, camera & video ₹50 (₹20)

Local curiosities including musical instruments, fossils, tools, utensils and rare manuscripts are on display at the **Desert Cultural Centre & Museum**, next to the tourist office on the main road. The main exhibit is a cloth painting depicting the life of the local folk hero Pabuji, a legendary figure credited with introducing the camel to Rajasthan.

Thar Heritage Museum

Off Court Rd • Daily 9am–9pm • ₹40, ₹20 camera & video camera

In the centre of town, the modest little **Thar Heritage Museum** is one of Jaisalmer's more interesting museums. Showcasing the personal collection of local historian L.N. Khatri, who may be on hand to explain some of the stories and customs behind the quirky array of local artefacts on display, exhibits range from bits of fossilized tree and old chillums through to camel regalia and antique musical instruments.

ARRIVAL AND DEPARTURE | JAISALMER

By plane Jaisalmer's airport lies 14km west of town on Khuri Rd. There are no flights at present. A new passenger terminal was finished in 2012, but at the time of writing was still waiting for its official opening. When it does open, it's expected that flights will resume – probably to Delhi via Jaipur, and possibly also to Mumbai via Udaipur, though exact details remain vague.

By train Jaisalmer's railway station (☎0299 225 2354) is 2km east of the city on the Jodhpur Rd; reservationless travellers can calmly enquire among the sandwich-board-toting hoteliers lined up in the parking lot. The majority offer free rides; otherwise an auto-rickshaw into town will cost around ₹80. The following trains run daily. For all other destinations, you're best off taking a bus. Note that night trains can get very cold – close to freezing in winter.

Destiantions The #4660 *Jaisalmer–Delhi Express*, which departs at 5.15pm, stops at, among other places, Pokaran (6.40pm), Phalodi (7.56pm), Osian (8.58pm), Jodhpur (10.25pm), Jaipur (4.50am), Alwar (7.12am) and New Delhi (11.10am). The overnight #4809 *Jaisalmer–Jodhpur Express* departs at 11.30pm, arriving in Jodhpur at 5.15am. There are two daily services to Bikaner: the #4703 departs at 11.10am and arrives at Bikaner's Lalgarh Station at

4.40pm, while the #4701 departs at 10.30pm and arrives at 4.35am into Bikaner Junction. You can also travel straight to Kolkata by train on the weekly *Jaisalmer–Howrah SF Express* #12372 departing Jaisalmer on Thurs at 12.20am, arriving in Kolkata at 4.30pm the next day.

By bus Most government buses (☎0299 225 1541) depart from the Government Bus Stand east of town on Barmer Rd, although earlymorning departures leave from the more conveniently located State Bus Stand at the southern end of Amar Sagar Rd; check when you buy your ticket. Private buses operate from Hanuman Circle (until 6.30am) and Air Force Circle south of the fort. Tickets for private buses can be purchased from any of the numerous travel agents around town – try Swagat Travels or Hanuman Travels, just north of Hanuman Circle, or from Adventure Travels (see box, 185). Local buses to places such as Lodurva, Khuhri and Sam leave from the stand north of Hanuman Circle.

Destinations Abu Rd (daily; 7hr), Bikaner (3 daily; 7hr), Delhi via Jodhpur, Jaipur (2 daily; 13hr), Jodhpur (more or less hourly from 5am–6.30pm; 5–6hr), Pushkar (daily; 9hr), Udaipur (2 daily; 8–9hr), Ajmer and Jaipur (5pm daily; 18hr) and.

GETTING AROUND AND INFORMATION

Bicycle rental Narayan Cycles, in the street directly opposite *Nachana Haveli* hotel (100m up on the left, just where the street starts to bend); ₹10/hr.

Motorbike rental There are a couple of places south of

Gopa Chowk including Desert Bikes (☎94141 50033) and Shiva Rent a Bike (☎94620 94620), with bikes and scooters for ₹400–500/day or from ₹100/hr.

Tourist information RTDC's tourist office (Mon–Sat 10am–5pm; ☎0299 225 2406), southeast of town near Gadi Sagar Pol, is of little use, and its "recommended" operators pay for the privilege. Online, it's worth having a look at ⊕ jaisalmer.org.uk and ⊕ jaisalmer.nic.in.

ACCOMMODATION

Jaisalmer has plenty of accommodation, and fierce competition keeps prices low. The basic choice is between in one of the old places within the wonderfully atmospheric fort – but read "Jaisalmer in Jeopardy" first (see box below) – or in one of the newer places outside (many of which are built in traditional sandstone and come with superb fort views). Most places offer free pick-up from the bus or railway stations, and the majority have internet access. Almost all offer camel treks, which vary in standard and price, and some managers, even at reputable hotels, can be uncomfortably pushy if you don't arrange a safari through them.

IN THE FORT

Desert ☎0299 225 0602, ⓦdeserthotel.com; map p.186. Friendly little budget place with cheaper rooms downstairs (including a couple of bargain singles with shared bathroom), and brighter rooms upstairs, some with fort views. ₹250/₹300

Garh Jaisal ☎0299 225 3836, ⓦhotelgarhjaisal.com; map p.186. Charming and efficien tly run haveli with seven smart colour-themed rooms with balconies, a/c and superb views across town. Rates include breakfast and their awesome roof terrace has arguably the best panoramas in the fort. US$125

Paradise ☎0299 225 2674, ⓦparadiseonfort.com; map p.186. Atmospheric old haveli with a leafy courtyard and a wide selection of rooms, ranging from cheap downstairs rooms with common baths to prettily decorated upstairs rooms with a/c, some of which come with balconies and views. ₹250

★ **Shreenath Palace** Nr. Jain temples ☎0299 225 2907, ⓦhotelinjaisalmer.com; map p.186. Atmospheric 450-year-old haveli – a former prime minister's abode – run by a charming family. Rooms (all a/c) feature intricate archways, balconies and private bathrooms; the Rajasthani rooms are a bit poky, so it's worth splashing out on one of the charming suites. ₹2500

Suraj ☎0299 225 1623, ⓦhotelsurajjaisalmer .webs.com; map p.186. This superbly atmospheric haveli of 1526 is one of the nicest places to stay in the fort with simple but charactertful and hugely spacious heritage rooms (all with fan) and a privileged rooftop view of the Jain temples. ₹1850

Surja East Fort Wall ☎94147 61394, ⓦhotelsurja.com; map p.186. A range of basic attached fan and a/c rooms (the more expensive ones with fine views) and a relaxing rooftop terrace with one of the best panoramas in town. Free wi-fi. ₹500

JAISALMER IN JEOPARDY

Erected on a base of soft bantonite clay, sand and sandstone, the foundations of **Jaisalmer Fort** are rapidly eroding due to huge increases in water consumption, mainly related to tourism. At the height of the season, around 120 litres per head are pumped into the area – and due to problems with the drainage system, a large proportion of this water seeps back into the soil beneath the fort, weakening its foundations. The results have been disastrous. In 1998 six people died when an exterior wall gave way, and five more bastions fell in 2000 and 2001. Jaisalmer is now listed among the World Monument Fund's 100 Most Endangered Sites.

An international campaign, **Jaisalmer in Jeopardy** (JiJ; ⓦjaisalmer-in-jeopardy.org), has been set up to facilitate repairs throughout the fort, including assistance with upgrading underground sewerage. The scheme relies largely on donations; see the website for details if you'd like to help. Despite the work so far carried out, however, some authorities think the best way to save the fort would be to evacuate its two thousand inhabitants and start repairs to the drainage system from scratch, an expensive and time-consuming venture much opposed by the guesthouse owners inside whose earnings depend on tourism.

Given all this, some people (and guidebooks) suggest that travellers **should avoid staying in the fort** in order to relieve pressure on its crumbling foundations. Unfortunately, this also has a serious side effect in that it deprives many local hoteliers – some of whom have been in the fort for decades, and who are in no way responsible for Jaisalmer's current plight – of a living. We have therefore continued to list certain guesthouses within the fort. All are long-established, low-impact, and occupy original and largely unmodified buildings. On the other hand, we haven't listed any of the fort's modern, custom-built hotels. Remember, too, that if you do stay in the fort, you can do your bit by minimizing your water usage as much as possible.

2

IN TOWN

KB Lodge Opposite Patwa Haveli ☎0299 223 5833, ⓦkillabhawan.com; map p.184. An efficiently run modern hotel a stone's throw from the havelis with just a handful of tastefully furnished yellow-walled rooms (some with a/c). Discounts in summer. ₹**1930**

Mandir Palace Hotel Gandhi Chowk ☎0299 225 2788, ⓦmandirpalace.com; map p.184. Occupying part of the exquisite Mandir Palace (see p.187), with pleasantly spacious rooms sporting discreet heritage touches, attractive public areas (including the fine old Durbar Hall, now housing a miniature museum) and a pool (non-guests ₹400/hr). ₹**7000**

Nachana Haveli Gandhi Chowk ☎0299 225 1910, ⓦnachanahaveli.com; map p.184. This venerable old haveli is one of the best choices in its class. The atmospheric ground-floor rooms (all a/c) are virtually windowless but have stone walls and are attractively decorated with antique fittings; the suites upstairs are brighter, and have fort views. There's also the good *Saffron* rooftop restaurant (see p.192). ₹**3800**

Pol Haveli Near Geeta Ashram, Dedansar Rd ☎0299 225 0131, ⓦhotelpolhaveli.com; map p.184. Attractive guesthouse in a stylish little sandstone building. Rooms (fan or a/c) are neat and comfortable (although larger ones are slightly lacking in furniture), and there's a lovely rooftop terrace for idle lounging and fort-gazing. Wi-fi and free pick up from train station. ₹**500**

Ratan Palace Off Gandhi Chowk ☎0299 225 2757, ⓔhotelrenuka@rediffmail.com; map p.184. One of the best cheapies in this part of town, with a friendly owner and hassle-free accommodation in old-fashioned but spotless rooms (the cheapest with shared bathrooms; the more expensive with a/c). They run good camel treks (see box, p.185) and have, slightly larger and more expensive rooms (from ₹500) in the

Renuka guesthouse just down the street. ₹**450**

Roop Mahal Off Shiv Marg ☎0299 225 1700, ⓦhotelroopmahal.com; map p.186. Comfortable guesthouse in a good central location, with bright, inexpensive modern rooms (some with fort views and cheap a/c), helpful staff and a pleasant rooftop restaurant. There's also wi-fi and plenty of parking space. ₹**350**

★ **Shahi Palace** Off Shiv Marg ☎0299 225 5920, ⓦshahipalacehotel.com; map p.186. Outstanding little hotel tucked just south of the fort in a stylish modern sandstone building with stunning fort views from the rooftop terrace restaurant and immaculate rooms. The only caveat is that the cheaper rooms are a bit small – it's well worth coughing up for one of the superb larger a/c rooms. The same family also run the slightly cheaper *Oasis Haveli* (☎0299 225 0871) and Star Haveli (☎0299 2250 941) next door. ₹**350**

Shree Giriraj Palace Near Gopa Chowk ☎0299 225 2268; map p.186. Simple, friendly local hotel with some of the cheapest rooms in town, including ultra-cheap shared-bath doubles, plus budget attached and a/c rooms – great value at current prices. ₹**350**

Tokyo Palace Nr Air Force Circle ☎0299 225 5483, ⓦtokyopalace.net; map p.184. Newly built hotel with a nice selection of comfy, cosily furnished rooms (all attached, with fan or a/c), plus six-bed dorms, 50m from the private bus stop. There's free wi-fi and a small pool, plus 20 percent discounts between April and July. Dorm ₹**150**, double ₹**500**

OUT OF TOWN

Fort Rajwada Off Jodhpur Rd, 3.5km east of town ☎0299 225 3233, ⓦfortrajwada.com; map p.184. A reliable resort hotel on the outskirts of town, with five-star facilities (pool, bar, good restaurant and grand coffee shop), and 25 percent discounts April–Sept. ₹**5500**

EATING AND DRINKING

RESTAURANTS

8 July Main Chowk, in the fort ☎0299 225 2814; map p.186. Recommended for its privileged terrace view of the fort's bustling main chowk and palace rather than for its food, though it has a good selection of smoothies, lassis, juices and snacks, along with Indian, Italian, Chinese and Mexican mains (₹95–160). Homesick Brits/Aussies will love the Marmite/Vegemite and toast breakfast option. Daily 7.30am–10pm.

Chandan Shree Restaurant Just west of Amar Sagar Pol; map p.184. Popular local diner for inexpensive veg curries (₹65–110) and thalis (₹70–150), as well as Rajasthani specialities such as *govind gatta* and *ker sangri*. Daily 11am–3pm & 7–10pm.

Jaisal Italy Inside first fort gate ☎92147 16005; map p.186. Italian restaurant with great pasta dishes

(₹130–200), served in heaped portions at reasonable prices, plus thin-crust pizzas and salads, and a superb terrace directly opposite the main ramparts – beautiful at night. Daily 8.30am–10pm.

★ **Monica** Near the first fort gate; map p.186. Moderately priced Rajasthani and tandoori dishes, along with delicious veg and non-veg thalis (₹145/210). Mains ₹65–145. Daily 8am–11pm.

Natraj Opposite the Salim Singh ki Haveli ☎0299 225 2667; map p.184. Friendly rooftop non-veg restaurant, popular for its excellent, gently spiced Mughlai chicken, *malai kofta* and other Indian dishes (mains ₹125–300). Licensed. Daily 8.30am–10pm.

★ **Ristorante Italiano Om** In the fort, nr Cannon Point ☎86960 04251; map p.186. A great breakfast spot with a handful of atmospheric dining options –

intimate rooftop, private balcony or cute café-esque dining room. Service is slow (it's a bit of a one-man show) but their pizzas are good, there's real coffee and their Indian cuisine shines – try the cashew nut curry or go for the in-house thali (₹200). Mains ₹80–150. Daily 7am–10pm.

Saffron Nachana Haveli, Gandhi Chowk ☎0299 225 2110; map p.184. Slightly upmarket restaurant with fine tandoori and Mughlai food, plus Indian veg, Italian and Chinese options (mains ₹75–190), plus live music every other night. Daily 8.30am–10pm.

Shree Bikaner Restaurant North of Hanuman Circle; map p.184. No-frills pure veg restaurant serving up Punjabi veg curries (₹45–100), a choice of Rajasthani, Gujarati and Bengali thalis (₹80–125), and a wonderful *dal bati churma* (a traditional Rajasthani dish consisting of baked wheatflour balls served with dhal and sweet *churma* sauce; ₹135), which they'll keep refilling till you've had enough. Daily noon–3.30pm & 7.30–11pm.

Trio Gandhi Chowk, next to Mandir Palace ☎0299 225 2733; map p.184. Slightly upscale choice known for its sumptuous tandoori and Mughlai meat dishes (non veg mains ₹210–280), alongside some Rajasthani specialities and a reasonable veg selection. Book early for the best tables overlooking the Mandir Palace

and the fort. Daily 6.30–11am, noon–3.30pm & 6.30–10.30pm.

CAFÉS AND SNACKS

Bhang shop Gopa Chowk; map p.186. If you like bhang – and be warned that it doesn't agree with everybody – this is one of the best places in the country to get it, with a whole menu of bhang-laced drinks and sweets, and a choice of different strengths. Unlicensed.

Dhanraj Ranmal Bhatia Court Rd; map p.186. Wonderful, moist milk-based sweets (*ladoo*, *barfi* and the like), plus great samosas and *mirchi badas*; you can even watch them being made, as they do it all out front. Daily 9am–9pm.

Joshi's German Bakery Gopa Chowk ☎99298 04517; map p.186. Bakery-cum-internet café serving up a scrumptious range of fresh cakes, croissants and cookies, especially in the morning during winter (Nov–April), plus sandwiches and snacks (₹55–250). Too bad the coffee's instant. Daily 8am–8pm.

RK Juice Center Bhatia Bazaar; map p.184. Wonderful freshly pressed juices using whatever fruits are available on the day (usually including some or all of orange, pomegranate, pineapple, banana, carrot and ginger). They promise not to add ice or tap water (though they do use it to rinse out the juice extractor). Daily 7am–late.

SHOPPING

Jaisalmer is one of the best places in India to shop for souvenirs. Prices are comparatively high and the salesmen push hard, but the choice of goods is excellent – virtually the whole **fort** has now been turned into an enormous souvenir bazaar, while there are dozens of further places along **Bhatia Bazaar**. Jaisalmer is a particularly good place to pick up textiles, fabrics and leatherwork (including camel leather bags and shoes), as well as cheap hippie-style clothes. If you want to check prices, drop into Rajasthali (Mon–Sat 10.30am–7pm), the official Rajasthan state crafts emporium outside Amar Sagar Pol, whose uninspiring offerings are fixed and marked. There are also numerous shops in the fort selling new and used English books.

DIRECTORY

Banks and exchange There are ATMs just inside Amar Sagar Pol, one directly opposite the gate on the outside, one by the District Magistrate's office on Sam Rd, and a couple just outside the southern edge of the fort. There's a cluster of exchange bureaux in Gandhi Chowk, while the reliable Adventure Travels (see box, p.185) also change cash and travellers' cheques.

Doctor Dr S.K. Dube (☎02992 251560) speaks good English; he charges ₹500 per consultation or ₹800 for a call out to your hotel.

Festival Jaisalmer's Desert Festival is held over three days at the full moon in the lunar month of Magha (Feb 12–14, 2014; Feb 1–3, 2015; Feb 19–21, 2016). Unlike many of the region's other festivals, this is not a livestock fair, but a festival of performing arts, and generally a fun occasion, with folk dancing, turban-tying competitions, camel racing and craft bazaars. Main events are held at Dedansar Polo

Ground. Room prices rise and hotels tend to get full at this time.

Hospital The government T.B. Hospital is on Sam Rd, west of Hanuman Circle (☎0299 225 5627), but a better bet is the small, private Maheshwari Hospital off Sam Rd opposite the court and District Magistrate's office (☎0299 225 0024).

Police Just south of Hanuman Circle on Amar Sagar Rd (☎0299 225 2233).

Post office The main post office, with poste restante, is on Amar Sagar Rd 200m south of Hanuman Circle; there's a smaller office opposite the fort wall behind Gopa Chowk (both Mon–Sat 10.30am–1pm & 2–5pm).

Swimming pool Non-guests can use the pools at the *Mandir Palace Hotel* (₹400/hr) and the small pool at the *Golden City* hotel (₹100) on the south side of town. Alternatively, try the pools at *Fort Rajwada, Gorbandh*

Palace and *Jawahar Niwas Palace* hotels, out of town; these usually cost around ₹250–300.

Travel agents The excellent Adventure Travels (see box, p.185) can arrange bus, train and plane tickets for a modest commission, plus currency exchange, and can also sort out hotel bookings.

Amar Sagar

Get there by rickshaw (₹350 return) or cycle from town

Seven kilometres northwest of Jaisalmer is **AMAR SAGAR**, a small and peaceful town set around a large artificial lake (empty during the dry season) where you'll find the eighteenth-century Amar Singh Palace and three Jain temples, including the **Adeshwar Nath Temple**, commissioned in 1928 by a member of the same family who put up the Patwa Haveli in Jaisalmer (daily dawn–dusk; ₹100, ₹100 camera, R150 video (free)).

2

Lodurva

There is just one bus a day to Lodurva (3.30pm), so taking a rickshaw or taxi is a more convenient and leisurely option (₹450/₹500 respectively for the roundtrip including stops at Amar Sagar and Bada Bagh) – or, if feeling energetic, you could cycle there

A further 10km northwest of Amar Sagar, **LODURVA** was the capital of the Bhati Rajputs from the eighth century until the twelfth, when it was sacked by Muhammad of Ghor, after which the Bhatis moved their capital to Jaisalmer. Only a few **Jain temples**, rebuilt in the seventeenth century, remain. The main temple (daily 8am–5pm; ₹100 including camera/video fee (free)), dedicated to Parshvanath, features an ornately carved 8m *toran* (arch), just inside the entrance to the main temple compound, perhaps the most exquisite in Rajasthan, plus a finely carved exterior.

Kuldara

Daily sunrise–sunset • ₹10, vehicles ₹150 • No public transport; a jeep to Kuldara costs ₹600 for the roundtrip

South of the Sam road, around 25km west of Jaisalmer, the ghost village of **KULDARA** was one of 84 villages abandoned, for unknown reasons, simultaneously one night in 1825 by the Paliwal Brahmin community, which had settled here in the thirteenth century. The Paliwals' sense of industry and order is attested by their homes, each with its living quarters, guest room, kitchen and stables, and parking space for a camel. You can take an atmospheric stroll through them to the temple at the heart of the village.

Sam

The daily bus to Sam (4pm) departs from the local bus stand in Jaisalmer; jeeps and taxis to Sam cost about ₹1000/₹1500 for the roundtrip

The huge, rolling sand dunes 40km west of Jaisalmer are known as **SAM**, though strictly this is the name of a small village further west. Unfortunately, the once pristine desert here has now vanished beneath endless tented camps, as around five thousand tourists descend daily to watch sunset and make merry in the desert. If you've come to the Thar in search of vast crowds, psychotic camel touts and endless piles of windblown plastic, then you'll be in seventh heaven. If not, the entire area is best given a wide berth. You can overnight here in one of the numerous tented camps, but we wouldn't recommend it.

Khuhri

A rather nicer place to watch the sun set over the dunes than Sam is the village of **KHUHRI**, 42km south of Jaisalmer. Many camel safaris either start here or pass through – most time their arrival so that tourists can see flamboyantly dressed local women arriving with large jugs on their heads to fill up with water at caste-specific wells. The village also has a certain charm – many of its homes are still made of mud and thatch rather than concrete, their exterior surfaces beautifully decorated with ornate white murals. Unfortunately, tourist development has already eroded much of Khuhri's traditional character. Virtually every building has been converted into a guesthouse, while ugly new concrete buildings and endless signboards are beginning to mushroom on every available space, accompanied by the usual tide of discarded plastic and other rubbish.

ARRIVAL AND DEPARTURE KHUHRI

By bus Five daily buses (9.30am, 2pm, 3pm, 4pm & 5pm; 90min) depart from the local bus stand in Jaisalmer. Return services depart Khuhri at 8am, 9am, 11am and 3pm.

By jeep/taxi A jeep/taxi will set you back ₹1000/₹1500 for the roundtrip.

ACCOMMODATION

Badal House Call ahead for a pick up at the bus stop ☎081073 39097. Despite the profusion of guesthouses in Khuhri (and upmarket tented camps around it), prices tend to be steep. If you do want to stay in the desert, you probably can't do better than the very simple but extremely peaceful *Badal House*. Owned by the charming Badul Singh this welcoming homestay is a good place to chill out for a few days and get a feel of village life. You stay in huts or rooms and they can also arrange well-priced, authentic camel safaris (₹600/person). Full board. ₹**600**

Pokaran

Some 110km east of Jaisalmer at the road and rail junctions between Jodhpur, Bikaner and the west is the quiet and little-visited town of **POKARAN**. Pokaran became the centre of international attention in May 1998 when three massive **nuclear explosions** were detonated 200m beneath the sands of the Thar Desert, 20km northwest of the town, announcing India's arrival as one of the world's fully fledged atomic powers. Despite its unwelcome moment of international fame, Pokaran remains something of an outpost, but there are a couple of places to stay should you need.

ARRIVAL AND DEPARTURE POKARAN

By train For Jaisalmer (2hr 30min), trains depart at 3.30am and 8.33am; and to Jodhpur (4hr) at 1.20am and 7.05pm.

By bus All Jaisalmer buses bound for Jodhpur and Bikaner go via Pokaran – services depart approximately every hour between 5am and 6.30pm.

ACCOMMODATION

Fort Pokaran ☎0299 422 2274, ⊛fortpokaran.com. You can find excellent accommodation at Pokaran's sixteenth-century fort, a wonderful old sandstone building that feels more authentic for having only been partly restored. ₹**4600**

Phalodi

The main highway and railway line wind in tandem east from Jaisalmer across the desert, separating at the small junction settlement of **PHALODI**, almost exactly midway between Jaisalmer and Bikaner. This scruffy salt-extraction colony is the jumping-off place for one of Rajasthan's most beautiful natural sights at keechen.

ARRIVAL AND DEPARTURE PHALODI

By train For Jaisalmer (3hr 45min), trains depart at 1.51am and 7.17am; to Jodhpur (2hr 30min) at 2.27am and 8.01pm; and to Bikaner (Lalgarh Junction) (2hr 25min) at 1.55pm.

By bus There are hourly RSRTC departures to Jaisalmer, Jodhpur and Bikaner. If you are only stopping for a few hours to visit Keechen's cranes, ensure you know when the last bus leaves to your final destination.

On a tour If your next destination is Bikaner, naturalist Jitu Solanki, owner of Bikaner's *Vinayak Guesthouse* (see p.201), can collect you in Phalodi or Pokaran in his jeep and take you on to Bikaner, visiting Keechen and Gajner Wildlife Sanctuary en route.

ACCOMMODATION

Chetnya Palace Next to the old Jaisalmer Bus Stand ⓣ0292 522 3945. Its shabby rooms are uninspiring, but this is the best budget option in town. ₹400

Lal Niwas Dadhas Mohalla ⓣ0292 522 3813, ⓦlalniwas.com. This three hundred-year-old red-sandstone haveli has been converted into a low-key heritage hotel, with slightly dog-eared a/c rooms, and a tiny pool. ₹3520

Keechen

From Phalodi, the best way to get to Keechen is to rent a bicycle from one of the stalls in town – a pleasant, mostly flat ride on well-surfaced roads; alternatively, jump in an auto-rickshaw (₹250) or taxi (₹500) for a tour

Around 6km east of Phalodi, the village of **KEECHEN** hosts four thousand **demoiselle cranes** that migrate here each winter from their breeding grounds in Central Asia. Known locally as *kurja*, the birds are encouraged to return by the villagers, who scatter grain for them twice a day – a custom that has persisted for 150 years or more. At feeding times (6–7am & 5–6pm), the flock descends en masse on a fenced-off area just outside the village, where you can watch them at close quarters.

Bikaner and around

The bustling city of **BIKANER** has little of the aesthetic magic of neighbouring Jaisalmer, Jodhpur or Jaipur, but is worth a visit thanks to the impressive **Junagarh Fort**, as well as for the chance to explore its atmospheric old city, dotted with a rich array of quirky, early twentieth-century havelis. Near to town are a government **camel-breeding farm** and the remarkable world-famous **rat temple** at Deshnok.

Junagarh Fort

Daily 10am–5.30pm (last entry 4.30pm) • ₹200 (including camera), ₹20, plus ₹30 camera fee), video ₹100; combined ticket including entrance, camera and audioguide ₹250

Built at ground level and defended only by high walls and a wide moat, **Junagarh Fort** isn't as immediately imposing as the mighty hill forts elsewhere in Rajasthan, though its richly decorated interiors are as magnificent as any in the state. The fort was built between 1587 and 1593, and progressively enlarged and embellished by later rulers. The entrance price includes a **guided tour**, but if you wish to explore the fort on your own and at your own pace, opt for the audioguide.

Entering the fort, look out for handprints set in stone near the second gate, **Daulat Pol**, which bear witness to the satis of various royal women. From here a passageway climbs up to the small Vikram Vilas courtyard, beyond which you'll find the main courtyard. Opening onto the main courtyard is the **Karan Mahal**, built in the seventeenth century to commemorate a victory over the Mughal emperor Aurangzeb and adorned with gold-leaf painting and an old *punkah* (fan). Next to here in the **Rai Niwas** are Maharaja Gai Singh's ivory slippers, one of Akbar's swords, and a representation of the Pisces zodiac sign which looks remarkably like a dinosaur in a headscarf.

Beyond here is the **Anup Mahal** (Diwan-i-Khas), the grandest room in the palace, with stunning red and gold filigree decorative painting and a red satin throne framed by an arc of glass and mirrors. The carpet was made by inmates of Bikaner jail – a manufacturing tradition that has only recently ceased. After such a hectic display of opulence, the **Badal Mahal** ("cloud palace"), built in the mid-nineteenth century for Maharaja Sardar Singh (1851–72) is pleasantly understated. Upstairs, a room exhibits beds of nails, sword blades and spear heads used by sadhus to demonstrate their immunity to pain, while across the terrace in the finely painted **Gaj Mandar** is the maharaja's chaste single bed and the maharani's more accommodating double.

2

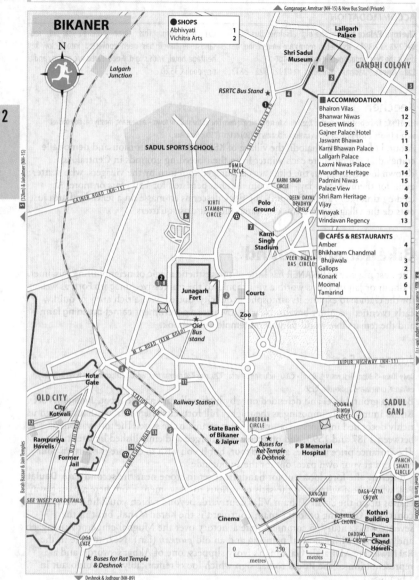

BIKANER

N

Ganganagar, Amritsar (NH-15) & New Bus Stand (Private)

● **SHOPS**
Abhivyati	1
Vichitra Arts	2

Lalgarh Junction

Lalgarh Palace

Shri Sadul Museum

GANDHI COLONY

RSRTC Bus Stand

SADUL SPORTS SCHOOL

GAINER ROAD (NH-15)

UMUL CIRCLE

KARNI SINGH CIRCLE

KIRTI STAMBH CIRCLE

Polo Ground

DEEN DAYAL UPADHYA CIRCLE

Karni Singh Stadium

KARNI SINGH CIRCLE

VEER DURGA DAS CIRCLE

■ **ACCOMMODATION**
Bhairon Vilas	8
Bhanwar Niwas	12
Desert Winds	7
Gajner Palace Hotel	5
Jaswant Bhawan	11
Karni Bhawan Palace	3
Lallgarh Palace	1
Laxmi Niwas Palace	2
Marudhar Heritage	14
Padmini Niwas	15
Palace View	4
Shri Ram Heritage	9
Vijay	10
Vinayak	6
Vrindavan Regency	13

■ **CAFÉS & RESTAURANTS**
Amber	4
Bhikharam Chandmal Bhujiwala	3
Gallops	2
Konark	5
Moomal	6
Tamarind	1

Junagarh Fort

Courts

Zoo

Old Bus stand

M G ROAD (IKEM ROAD)

JAIPUR HIGHWAY (NH-11)

Kote Gate

STATION ROAD

Railway Station

POONAN SINGH CIRCLE

SADUL GANJ

OLD CITY

City Kotwali

Rampuriya Havelis

Former Jail

Barah Bazaar & Jain Temples

SEE 'INSET' FOR DETAILS

AMBEDKAR CIRCLE

State Bank of Bikaner & Jaipur

Buses for Rat Temple & Deshnok

P B Memorial Hospital

PANCH SHATI CIRCLE

Camel Farm & 157,000m

Cinema

RANGARI CHOWK

DAGA-SITYA CHOWK

KOTHRIAN KA CHOWK

Kothari Building

DADDHO KA CHOWK

Punan Chand Haweli

0   250
metres

0   25
metres

GOGA GATE

★ Buses for Rat Temple & Deshnok

Deshnok & Jodhpur (NH-89)

The next part of the palace, the twentieth-century **Ganga Niwas**, created by Maharaja Ganga Singh (1887–1943), can be reached either via a long and labyrinthine passageway from the Gaj Mandar or, more directly, from the Vikram Vilas courtyard (see above). This section of the palace is centred on the cavernous **Diwan-i-Am**, dominated by a World War I de Havil and biplane, a present from the British to Bikaner's state forces. Next door is the early twentieth-century office of Ganga Singh, followed by several further rooms stuffed full of guns and swords.

Prachina Museum

Juagarh Fort • Daily 9am–6pm • ₹100 (₹20), camera ₹20, video ₹100 • ⓦ prachinamuseum.org

Within the fort complex, the **Prachina Museum** houses a pretty collection of objects (glassware, crockery, cutlery and walking sticks) demonstrating the growing influence of Europe on Rajasthani style in the early twentieth century. A whole circa-1900 salon has been recreated, and there's also an interesting collection of Rajasthani textiles and clothing.

The old city

Bikaner's labyrinthine **old city** is notable for its profusion of unusual **havelis** whose idiosyncratic architecture demonstrates an unlikely fusion of indigenous sandstone carving with Art Nouveau and red-brick British municipal style. The city is confusing to navigate, so accept getting lost as part of the experience.

The Rampuriya havelis

Entering the old city through Kote Gate, bear left (south) down Old Jail Road. After 300m, turn right just past the florid pink gateway to a Hindu temple to reach the City Kotwali (the old city's central police station). Follow the road past here to reach the three striking **Rampuriya havelis**, commissioned in the 1920s by three brothers from a Jain trading family and faced with reliefs of a mixture of personages, including Maharaja Ganga Singh, Britain's George V and Queen Mary, and Krishna and Radha.

Rangari Chowk, Kothrion ka Chowk and Daga Sita Chowk

Turn left just before the third Rampuriya Haveli, walking past the boarded-up 1918 **Golchha Haveli**, and continue roughly straight ahead, following the road as it makes two dog-legs to the right, to emerge after 100m onto a street full of ironmongers. Turn right here and continue for 300m to reach the small square called **Rangari Chowk**, centred on a neat white Hindu temple. Walk along the right-hand side of the temple and straight ahead you will see the small, triangular square called **Kothrion ka Chowk**, lined by handsome havelis. Follow the road as it swings round to the left, past the **Kothari Building** (on your right), with five wonderfully extravagant Art Nouveau balconies, to reach the small **Daga Sitya Chowk**. A house on the left still has fading murals of steam trains, while Diamond House, on the right, gets wider as it goes up, each storey overhanging the one below it. Retrace your steps back to just before Kothrion ka Chowk, then turn left to reach the **Punan Chand Haveli** boasting an amazingly carved floral facade. Turn round again and head back towards Kothrion ka Chowk, then take the first left to reach the large **Daddho ka Chowk**, surrounded by fine havelis.

Bhandreshwar (Bhandasar) Temple

Cross the Daddho ka Chowk to where the street ends at a T-junction, then turn right and continue for around 400m to reach **Barah Bazaar**, centred on a large pillar painted in the colours of the Indian flag. Follow the street round to the left and you'll eventually reach the **Bhandreshwar (Bhandasar) Temple**, unusual among Jain temples in being covered in a rich, almost gaudy, array of paintings. Porcelain tiles imported from Victorian England decorate the main altar, and steps lead up the unusually large tower, where you get a great view over the old city.

Lallgarh Palace

Dr Karni Singhji Rd

The sturdy red-sandstone **Lallgarh Palace** in the north of the town is home to the royal family of Bikaner, although parts have now been converted into a pair of hotels, and there's also the Shri Sadul Museum. It was built during the reign of Ganga Singh, who lived here from 1902, and the sheer scale and profusion of the exterior decoration is impressive, even if it lacks the romantic allure of older Rajasthani palaces.

Shri Sadul Museum

Mon–Sat 10am–5.30pm • ₹50 (₹25), video ₹150

The **Shri Sadul Museum** houses an enormous and surprisingly engrossing collection of old photographs showing various viceregal visits, pictures of Ganga Singh at the signing of the Versailles Treaty and plenty of royal processions including an evocative 1940s railway carriage.

National Research Centre on Camels

Daily noon–6pm • ₹50 (₹20), camera ₹30; camel ride ₹50; guided tour ₹100 • Around ₹150–200 roundtrip by auto including waiting time

What claims to be Asia's largest camel-breeding farm, the **National Research Centre on Camels** lies out in the desert 10km south of Bikaner. Bikaner is renowned for its famously sturdy beasts – the camel corps was a much-feared component of the imperial battle formation – but the growing proliferation of motor vehicles has severely reduced the camel's traditional role as the staple means of rural transport. It's best to take a guided tour of the farm; aim to be here at 3.30–4pm, when you'll be wowed by the sight of four hundred stampeding dromedaries arriving from the desert for their daily chow. A small **museum** showcases each species through a series of photographs. There's also a kiosk selling camel milk and milk-based products such as ice cream (₹30); many visitors make the journey here for a taste of the *kesar* (saffron) kulfi alone. There's also a small leather shop and paintings.

The temple of rats

Daily 5am–8/10pm • Free, ₹20 camera, ₹50 video • There are trains from Bikaner (1hr–1hr 30min) at 9.30am and 11.05am, with return services from Deshnok at 2.38pm and 3.03pm; buses for Deshnok from Bikaner leave roughly every 15min (45min) from the main bus stand, stopping on the east side of Ambedkar Circle near PB Memorial Hospital, and just south of Goga Gate Circle, near the southeast corner of the old city

The **Karni Mata Temple** in DESHNOK, 30km south of Bikaner, is one of India's more bizarre attractions. Step inside the Italian-marble arched doorway and everywhere you'll see free-roaming rats, known as *kabas*, which devotees believe are reincarnated souls saved from the wrath of Yama, the god of death. The innermost shrine, made of rough stone and logs cut from sacred *jal* trees, houses the yellow-marble image of Karniji (see box below). This in turn is encased by a much grander marble building. Pilgrims bring offerings for the rats to eat inside the main shrine, and it's considered auspicious to eat the leftovers after they've been nibbled by the *kabas*. Some pilgrims spend hours searching for a glimpse of the temple's venerated white rat, while it's also considered fortunate for a rat to run over your feet (stand still for a while – preferably next to some

---

THE DESHNOK DEVI

Members of the Charan caste of musicians believe that incarnations of the goddess Durga periodically appear among them, one of whom was **Karni Mata**, born at a village near Phalodi in 1387, who went on to perform miracles such as water divination and bringing the dead back to life, eventually becoming the region's most powerful cult leader. According to legend, one of Karni Mata's followers came to her because her son was grievously ill, but by the time they got to him, he had died. Karni Mata went to Yama, the god of the underworld, to ask for him back, but Yama refused. Knowing that of all the creatures upon the earth, only rats were outside Yama's dominion, Karni Mata decreed that all Charans would henceforth be reincarnated as rats, thus escaping Yama's power. It is these sacred rats (*kabas*) that inhabit the Deshnok temple.

RECOMMENDED TRAINS FROM BIKANER

Destination	Name	No.	Departs	Arrives
Abu Road	Ranakpur Express	4707	9.30am (daily)	7.57pm
	Ahmedabad Express	9224	12.35am (daily)	10.37am
Agra	Howrah Superfast	2308	6.45pm (daily)	6.15am
Delhi	Rohilla Intercity	2471	9.15pm (daily)	5.25am
	Assam Express*	5610	6.45pm (daily)	7.20am
Jaipur	Jaipur Intercity	2467	6am (daily)	12.35am
	Kota Special	9733	11pm (daily)	5.30am
Jaisalmer	Lalgarh–Jaisalmer Express*	4704	7.15am (daily)	1.15pm
	Bikaner–Jaisalmer Express	4702	10.55pm (daily)	4.30am
Jodhpur	Ranakpur Express	4707	9.30am (daily)	2.45pm
	Barmer Express	4887	11.05am (daily)	3.45pm
	Ahmedabad Express	9224	12.35am (daily)	5.35am

*From Lalgarh Junction

food), but whatever you do don't step on one, or you'll have to donate a gold model of a rat to placate the deity. Shoes have to be removed at the gate, leaving you to wander among the rat droppings barefoot or in your socks.

ARRIVAL AND DEPARTURE

BIKANER AND AROUND

Bikaner is very spread out, with widely scattered accommodation. The RSRTC Bus Stand (☎ 0151 2523800) is 1.5km north of town, near Lallgarh Palace; the old bus stand (used by some private buses) and railway station are both centrally located, although a few trains arrive at Lalgarh Junction, on the northwestern edge of town. An auto ride across town from the state bus stand to the railway station should cost around ₹40.

By train The railway station is on Station Rd (☎ 0151 220 0131), just east of the old city. There are no direct trains to Ajmer – it's much easier to take the bus.

By bus Private buses are run by a handful of firms, most of which have offices at the Old Bus Stand on the south side of Junagarh Fort – shop around until you find a service that suits. Most private services depart from outside these offices, though check when you book your ticket (there's also a newer private bus stand inconveniently located 5km north of town along the Ganganagar road, though few operators ever use it). The most comfortable long-distance buses are run by

Chandra Travels and Milan Travels (☎ 092142 01220), and Neelam has a daily service to Agra (12hr). Alternatively, most guesthouses should be able to book tickets for you, for a small fee (₹50). Services run to destinations including Ajmer (7 daily; 6hr), Amritsar (daily; 13hr), Delhi (6 daily; 10hr) via Mandawa (5hr), Jaipur (hourly; 7hr), Jaisalmer (3 daily; 7hr), Jhunjhunu (3 daily; 5hr), Jodhpur (every 30min; 6hr), Nawalgarh (5 daily; 5hr 30min), Phalodi (hourly; 3hr 30min), Pokaran (5 daily; 5hr) and Udaipur (daily; 13hr). Buses to Shekhawati leave from the Khatri Bus Stand, about 3.5km east of town along the Jaipur highway.

GETTING AROUND AND INFORMATION

Bicycle rental Available for ₹30/hr from a couple of shacks just south of the main post office, opposite the southwest corner of the fort.

Tourist information The helpful tourist office (Mon–Fri 10am–5pm; ☎ 0151 222 6701) is in the *RTDC Dholamaru Hotel* at Pooran Singh Circle. Online, check out the excellent ⓦ realbikaner.com.

Tours Jitu Solanki (see box, p.200) is a government-approved guide and can arrange Bikaner city tours (₹200) and jeep tours to Keechen and Gajner Wildlife Sanctuary, while Vijay Singh Rathore at the *Vijay guesthouse* runs an enjoyable one-day tour combining Gajner, Kolayat, Deshnok and the camel farm for ₹1500. Both can organize cars/jeeps and offer day and overnight trips to Shekhawati's towns and havelis.

ACCOMMODATION

Bikaner has a surprisingly large selection of hotels, though the cheap flophouses along Station Rd are insalubrious and best avoided.

★ **Bhairon Vilas** Next to Junagarh Fort ☎ 0151 254 4751, ⓦ hotelbhaironvilas.tripod.com. Charming heritage

hotel in an old royal haveli, surrounded by an attractive garden and kitted out with quirky antiques and family curios.

2

CAMEL SAFARIS FROM BIKANER

Bikaner offers a good alternative to Jaisalmer as a starting point for **camel treks** into the Thar Desert. This eastern part of the desert, while just as scenic as the western Thar, is not nearly as congested with fellow trekkers, with the result that local people in the villages along the route don't wait around all day for the chance to sell Pepsi to tourists. Wildlife is also abundant, with plentiful blackbuck, nilgai and desert foxes.

Your choices of **operator** are somewhat limited. The city's leading and longest-established operator is the personable Vijay Singh Rathore (aka "Camel Man"), based at *Vijay guesthouse* (see below). Full details of his various treks are posted at ⓦ camelman.com; rates start from ₹1000 per person per day. Slightly cheaper safaris are also offered by *Vino Guesthouse*, 3km south of the train station, and by Thar Camel Safari, c/o the *Meghsar Castle* hotel or direct on ☏ 93512 06093. Another possibility is the *Vinayak guesthouse*'s (see opposite) jeep safaris, led by Jitu Solanki, a trained zoologist. These offer fascinating insights into the desert's wildlife and enivronment, and include visits to remote Bishnoi villages. Safaris can be customized to focus on particular areas of interest, including specialized wildlife, birdwatching, snake-spotting and photographic tours.

Rooms (all a/c and with TVs) are a mixed bag; it's worth spending a little extra to get one of the more spacious and atmospheric heritage rooms. There's also a good restaurant, bijou bar and boutique, plus a pool planned for 2013. Free wi-fi. ₹1600

Bhanwar Niwas Old City ☏ 0151 220 1043, ⓦ bhanwarniwas.com. Bikaner's most ostentatious haveli, built for a textile tycoon in the late 1920s and crammed with kitsch fittings and furniture, complete with a 1927 Buick in the lobby, an atmospheric *fin de siècle* dining room and an array of memorably chintzy rooms. ₹5870

Desert Winds North of Kirti Stambh Circle ☏ 0151 254 2202, ⓦ hoteldesertwinds.in. Welcoming, medium-sized hotel with spotlessly clean and comfy rooms (all a/c) and a decent veg restaurant. A much friendlier, if low-key, alternative to the *Harasar Haveli* next door, minus the tour groups. Free wi-fi, plus sunrise and sunset desert tours for ₹1000/person. ₹1720

Gajner Palace Hotel 32km southwest of Bikaner ☏ 0153 427 5061 to 9, ⓦ hrhindia.com. This grand affair in red sandstone was built in the early twentieth century as a hunting lodge for the maharajas of Bikaner. The hotel overlooks a lake, and staff can arrange jaunts through the surrounding Gajner Wildlife Sanctuary. ₹8450

Jaswant Bhawan Alakhsagar Rd (go out of the rear exit of the train station) ☏ 0151 254 8848, ⓦ hoteljaswantbhawan.com. Relaxing hotel in a nice old house very close to the station. Surprisingly quiet given the location, with very well priced, comfortable fan, air-cooled and a/c rooms. ₹1000

Karni Bhawan Palace Gandhi Colony, 1km east of Lallgarh Palace ☏ 0151 252 4701 to 5, or ☏ 1800 180 2933 or ☏ 1800 180 2944, ⓦ hrhindia.com. On the outside it looks like an oversized English suburban house, but the interior is period and wonderful, with superb (if overpriced) Art Deco suites (₹7050) in the main building,

complete with original 1930s furniture (but don't bother with the standard rooms in the annexe). Big discounts in summer. ₹4230

Laxmi Niwas Palace Lallgarh Palace ☏ 0151 220 2777, ⓦ laxminiwaspalace.com. The better of two palatial hotels in the Lallgarh Palace complex, offering large rooms with period English furniture. Rooms at the neighbouring *Lallgarh Palace Hotel* are slightly cheaper and less impressive, though still boast plenty of colonial character. ₹10,900

Marudhar Heritage Gangashahar Rd ☏ 0151 252 2524, ⓔ hmheritage2000@yahoo.co.in. Friendly, tranquil hotel near the station with a variety of neat and clean air-cooled and a/c rooms, all attached. Free pick up. ₹550

Padmini Niwas 148 Sadulganj, off Jaipur Rd 1.5 km east of the city centre ☏ 0151 252 2794, ⓦ hotelpadmininiwas.com. A pleasant, welcoming guesthouse with a lovely garden and spacious, clean rooms (air-cooled or a/c), and a neat, if tiny, pool (non-guests ₹100). No wi-fi. ₹700

Palace View Lallgarh Palace Campus ☏ 0151 254 3625, ⓔ hotelpalaceview@gmail.com. In a quiet location to the north of town, *Palace View* has comfortable, clean and pleasantly old-fashioned rooms (most a/c), a homely little dining room and views of Lallgarh Palace. ₹1000

Shri Ram Heritage Sadulganj, 1.5 km east of the city centre ☏ 0151 252 2651 or ☏ 92144 04100, ⓔ shriramhotel@yahoo.com. Friendly suburban hotel affiliated with YHA India. The more expensive rooms are spacious and very comfortably furnished, though the cheaper ones are a bit cramped. There are also five-bed dorms. Dorm ₹200, double ₹500

Vijay Opposite Sophia School, 5km east of centre along the Jaipur Highway ☏ 0151 223 1244, ⓦ camelman .com. Sociable family guesthouse with spacious and comfortable air-cooled rooms (some with optional a/c) at bargain prices. There's also camping space, plus a nice garden with alfresco dining area, free bicycles and a Royal Enfield motorbike for rent. The owner also has a house in Thelasar, a little-visited village in Shekhawati, where you can also go and stay as part of an overnight tour. ₹400

Vinayak Old Ginani ☎94144 30948, ⓦvinayakdesertsafari.com. Friendly and family run, *Vinayak* offers simple but clean and cheap singles and doubles (all attached, some with hot water bucket showers), plus

mattresses on the rooftop for early or late winter arrivals (₹100). Wi-fi and bicycles are complimentary, free cooking lessons are available and there are motorbikes for rent (₹300/ day). Good for camel safaris (see box opposite). ₹350

Vrindavan Regency Shiv Shakti Mall ☎0151 220 0446, ⓦhotelvrindavanregency.com. The best of the cluster of hotels near the railway station with clean, if slightly gloomy, a/c rooms and suites, plus a decent restaurant open until late. ₹1200

EATING AND DRINKING

Bikaner is famous for sweets such as *kaju katli*, made with cashew nuts, and *tirangi*, a three-coloured confection made with cashews, almonds and pistachios.

Amber Station Rd ☎0151 222 0333. Simple yet clean local restaurant popular with Westerners, with a long menu of Indian veg standards along with a few snacks. Mains ₹115–195, thali ₹128–168. Daily 10am–10pm.

Bhikharam Chandmal Bhujiawala Just off Station Rd on the road to Kote Gate (the English sign is very small and easy to miss). Top *mithai* shop, known for its excellent Bengali and Rajasthani sweets, although the staff speak little English and aren't particularly helpful. Daily 8am–8pm.

Gallops Court Rd ☎0151 320 0833. Pleasant but seriously overpriced a/c restaurant opposite the fort that has grown fat on the easy pickings of passing coach parties. The food's not bad, however, with a range of north Indian veg and non-veg standards, plus a few local specialities, served in big portions. Usually full of tour groups at lunchtime, though quieter and nicer in the evenings. Most non-veg mains ₹200–325. Licensed. Daily noon–3pm & 7.30–10.30pm.

Konark Rani Bazaar, near the railway station. Bright basement joint popular with families, featuring a cake shop on one side and a smarter north Indian veg restaurant on the other, with pizza, burgers and Chinese dishes also on the menu. Friendly management. Mains ₹80–140, thali ₹110. Daily 10am–11pm.

Moomal Panch Shati Circle ☎0151 254 9575. Popular with well-heeled locals, this white-linen restaurant serves sumptuous south Indian veg food – the cashew and cherry Moomal Special alone is worth the trip. Mains around ₹120–200. Daily 11am–4pm & 6–10.30pm.

Tamarind Bhairon Vilas ☎0151 254 4751. Spilling onto a tamarind tree-shaded lawn, this decor-orientated licensed restaurant is highly atmospheric, with dusky pink walls, black leather chairs and white tablecloths. There's a small menu of veg mains (₹80–250) and it's a good place for a lazy breakfast. It's licensed and the bijou boutique bar is great for a drink afterwards. Daily 8am–10.30pm.

SHOPPING

Bikaner is famous for its skilled lacquerwork and handicrafts, and for its handwoven woollen *pattu* (a kind of shawl-cum-blanket).

Abhivyakti Ganganar Rd, near the bus stand ☎0151 252 2139. This is the best place to buy *pattu* and the manager can arrange visits to villages to see how the textiles are woven by local women's co-ops. They don't pay commission to auto drivers, so don't believe anyone if they

tell you that the shop's closed. Mon–Sat 9am–5pm, Sun 9am–noon.

Vichitra Arts Bhairon Vilas ☎98292 91431. Sells boutique womenswear, accessories and miniature paintings by local artist Shiv Swami. Daily 9am–11pm.

DIRECTORY

Banks and exchange There are ATMs directly opposite the station, and another one 100m south; on Station Rd almost opposite the road from Kote Gate; and between *RTDC Hotel Dhola Maru* and Panch Shati Circle. Thomas Cook (Mon–Sat 9am–6pm), inside the entrance to the fort, changes cash and travellers' cheques.

Festival Bikaner's colourful camel fair (Jan 15–17, 2014; Jan 4–6, 2015; Jan 23–24, 2016) has the usual camel races and camel hairstyle competitions, plus dancing and firework displays. Most of the action takes

place at the polo ground north of town near *Harasar Haveli* hotel. Advance accommodation booking recommended.

Hospital PBM Memorial Hospital by Ambedkar Circle (☎0151 222 6334).

Police Station Rd (☎0151 252 2225).

Post office Just west of the fort (Mon–Fri 10am–5pm; closed 1.30–2pm).

Swimming pool The *Padmini Niwas* hotel allows non-guests to use their bijou pool for ₹100.

Udaipur

Spreading around the shores of the idyllic Lake Pichola and backdropped by a majestic ring of craggy green hills, **UDAIPUR** seems to encapsulate India at its most quintessentially romantic, with its intricate sequence of ornately turreted and balconied palaces, whitewashed havelis and bathing *ghats* clustered around the waters of the lake – or, in the case of the *Lake Palace* hotel and Jag Mandir, floating magically upon them. Not that the city is quite perfect. Insensitive lakeside development, appalling traffic along the **old city**'s maze of tightly winding streets and vast hordes of tourists mean that Udaipur is far from unspoilt or undiscovered. Even so, it remains a richly rewarding place to visit, and although it's possible to take in most of the sights in a few days, many people spend at least a week exploring the city and the various attractions scattered about the surrounding countryside.

Brief history

Udaipur is a relatively young city by Indian standards, having been established in the mid-sixteenth century by Udai Singh II of the **Sisodia** family, rulers of the state of **Mewar**, which covered much of present-day southern Rajasthan. The Sisodias are traditionally considered to be the foremost of all the Rajput royal dynasties. The present Sisodia maharana is the seventy-sixth in the unbroken line of Mewar suzerains, which makes the Mewar household the longest lasting of all royal families of Rajasthan, and perhaps the oldest surviving dynasty in the world.

The state of Mewar was established by Guhil in 568 AD. His successors set up their capital first at Nagda and then, in 734, at the mighty fort of Chittaurgarh, from where they established control over much of present-day southern Rajasthan (see p.219). By the time **Udai Singh II** inherited the throne of Mewar in 1537, however, it was clear that Chittaurgarh's days were numbered. Udai began looking for a location for a new city, to be named Udaipur, eventually choosing a swampy site beside Lake Pichola, protected on all sides by outcrops of the Aravalli Range. The Mughal emperor Akbar duly captured Chittaurgarh after a protracted seige in 1568, but by then Udai was firmly established in his new capital, where he remained unmolested until his death in 1572. His son, the heroic **Pratap Singh**, continued to defy Akbar and spent much of his reign doggedly defending his kingdom's freedom against the overwhelming military muscle of the Mughal army.

Following Akbar's death, peace finally ensued, and the city – gradually emerging up around the city's grand **City Palace**, on the east shore of the lake – prospered until 1736, when Mewar suffered the first of repeated attacks by the **Marathas**, who gradually reduced the city to poverty until being finally driven off by the British in the early eighteenth century. The Sisodias thenceforth allied themselves to the British, while preserving their independence until 1947, when the famous old state of Mewar was finally merged into the newly created nation of India.

Lake Pichola

Udaipur's idyllic **Lake Pichola** provides the city's most memorable views, a beautiful frame for the City Palace buildings, havelis, *ghats*, temple towers and other structures which crowd its eastern side – best seen from a boat trip around the lake (see box, p.204). The lake's two **island palaces** are among Udaipur's most famous features. **Jag Niwas**, now the *Lake Palace* hotel, was built in amalgamated Rajput-Mughal style as a summer palace during the reign of Jagat Singh (1628–52), after whom it was named. Unfortunately, as a security measure following the 2008 gun attacks in Mumbai, non-guests can no longer visit the hotel. The **Jag Mandir** palace, on the island to the south, is arranged around a large garden guarded by stone elephants. The main building here is the **Gol Mahal**, which has detailed stone inlay work within its domed

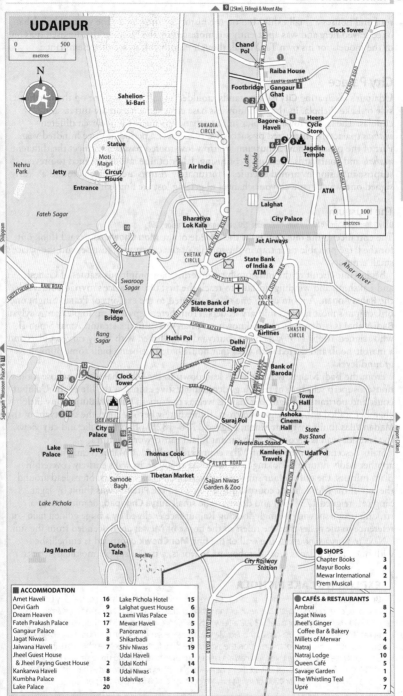

UDAIPUR

0   500

metres

N

Shilpgram ◄

Sajjangarh 'Monsoon Palace' & ▶ ◄

Airport (20km) ▶

▲ 9 (25km), Eklingji & Mount Abu

Clock Tower

Chand Pol

Raiba House

Footbridge

Gangaur Ghat

Bagore-ki Haveli

Heera Cycle Store

Lake Pichola

Jagdish Temple

ATM

Lalghat

City Palace

0   100

metres

Sahelion-ki-Bari

SUKADIA CIRCLE

Statue

Moti Magri

Nehru Park

Jetty

Circut House

Entrance

Fateh Sagar

Air India

Bharatiya Lok Kala

Jet Airways

CHETAK CIRCLE

GPO

State Bank of India & ATM

FATEH SAGAR ROAD

CHHOTA CHETAK RD   **RANI ROAD**

Swaroop Sagar

New Bridge

Rang Sagar

Hathi Pol

HOSPITAL ROAD

State Bank of Bikaner and Jaipur

COURT CIRCLE

ASHWINI BAZAAR

Delhi Gate

Indian Airlines

SHASTRI CIRCLE

Ahar River

MOCHIWADA ROAD

Clock Tower

BARA BAZAAR

Bank of Baroda

SEE INSET

City Palace

Jetty

Lake Palace

Thomas Cook

Tibetan Market

Samode Bagh

Town Hall

Ashoka Cinema Hall

Suraj Pol

BHATTIYANI CHOHTTA

State Bus Stand

Private Bus Stand

Kamlesh Travels

Udai Pol

LAKE PALACE ROAD

Sajjan Niwas Garden & Zoo

Lake Pichola

Jag Mandir

Dutch Tala

Rope Way

City Railway Station

STATION ROAD

AHMEDABAD ROAD

▼ 21 (5km) & Ahmedabad

■ ACCOMMODATION

Amet Haveli	16	Lake Pichola Hotel	15
Devi Garh	9	Lalghat guest House	6
Dream Heaven	12	Laxmi Vilas Palace	10
Fateh Prakash Palace	17	Mewar Haveli	5
Gangaur Palace	3	Panorama	13
Jagat Niwas	8	Shikarbadi	21
Jaiwana Haveli	7	Shiv Niwas	19
Jheel Guest House		Udai Haveli	1
& Jheel Paying Guest House	2	Udai Kothi	14
Kankarwa Haveli	8	Udai Niwas	4
Kumbha Palace	18	Udaivilas	11
Lake Palace	20		

● SHOPS

Chapter Books	3
Mayur Books	4
Mewar International	2
Prem Musical	1

● CAFÉS & RESTAURANTS

Ambrai	8
Jagat Niwas	3
Jheel's Ginger	
Coffee Bar & Bakery	2
Millets of Merwar	4
Natraj	6
Natraj Lodge	10
Queen Café	5
Savage Garden	1
The Whistling Teal	9
Upré	7

roof and houses a small exhibition on the history of the island. The young Shah Jahan once stayed here and was apparently so impressed by the building that he used it as one of the models for his own Taj Mahal, though it's difficult to see the resemblance.

City Palace

Udaipur's fascinating **City Palace** stands moulded in soft yellow stone on the northeast side of Lake Pichola, its thick windowless base crowned with ornate turrets and cupolas. The largest royal complex in Rajasthan, it is made up of eleven different *mahals* (palaces) constructed by successive rulers over a period of three hundred years. Part of the palace is now a **museum**. Narrow low-roofed passages connect the different *mahals* and courtyards, creating a confusing, labyrinthine layout designed to prevent surprise intrusion by armed enemies – fortunately visitors are directed around a clearly signed one-way circuit, so your chances of getting lost are limited.

The museum

Daily 9.30am–4.30pm • ₹100, camera ₹200, video ₹200; audioguide ₹250; guide ₹250

The entrance to the **museum** is on the far side of the **Moti Chowk** courtyard (look out for the large portable tiger trap in the middle of the courtyard), just beyond the palace's small **armoury**.

Begin your circuit of the museum by wandering past propitious statues of Ganesh and Lakshmi, and winding upstairs to reach the first of the palace's myriad courtyards, the **Rajya Angan**. A room off to one side is devoted to the exploits of Pratap Singh, one of Udaipur's most famous military leaders. From here, steps lead up to pleasantly sylvan **Badi Mahal** (Garden Palace; also known as Amar Vilas after its creator, Amar Singh II, who reigned 1695–1755), its main courtyard embellished with finely carved pillars and a marble pool, and dotted with trees that flourish despite being built some 30m above ground level.

From the Badi Mahal, twisting steps lead down to the **Dilkushal Mahal**, whose rooms house a superb selection of paintings depicting festive events in the life of the Udaipur court and portraits of the maharanas, as well as the superb **Kanch ki Burj**, a tiny little chamber walled with red zigzag mirrors. Immediately beyond here, the courtyard of the **Madan Vilas** (built by Bhim Singh, reigned 1778–1828) offers fine lake and city views; the lakeside wall is decorated with quaint inlaid mirrorwork pictures.

Stairs descend from the Madan Vilas courtyard to the **Moti Mahal** (Pearl Palace), another oddly futuristic-looking little mirrored chamber, its walls entirely covered in plain mirrors, the only colour supplied by its stained-glass windows. Steps lead around the top of the Mor Chowk courtyard (see below) to the **Pitam Niwas** (built by Jagat Singh II, reigned 1734–90) and down to the small **Surya Choupad**, dominated by a striking image showing a kingly-looking Rajput face enclosed by a huge golden halo – a reference to the belief that the rulers of the house of Mewar are descended from the sun.

Next to Surya Choupad, the wall of the fine **Mor Chowk** courtyard is embellished with one of the palace's most flamboyant artworks, a trio of superb mosaic peacocks

---

EXPLORING LAKE PICHOLA

Boat rides around Lake Pichola depart from the jetty towards the south end of the City Palace complex, offering unforgettable views of the various palaces. Circuits of the lake take 45min and cost ₹300 before 3pm, or a hefty ₹500 afterwards, plus an additional ₹25 for the City Palace entry ticket (see above). All trips stop at the Jag Mandir. Tours depart hourly on the hour from 10am to 6pm. To make the most of them, sit on the side of the boat facing the palace (they usually run anticlockwise around the lake). You can also rent your own boat (seating up to seven people) here for ₹4000. Alternatively, on the waterfront between the *Jaiwana* and *Kankarwa* havelis, you can take a 30min boat ride for ₹200 or rent a private boat for ₹2000 for up to ten people.

> ## CITY PALACE ACCESS
> Note that to reach certain parts of the City Palace, including the *Fateh Prakash Palace* and *Shiv Niwas* hotels, the Durbar Hall, Crystal Gallery and the jetty for boats around Lake Pichola and over to the *Lake Palace* hotel, you'll have to fork out ₹25 for a **general entrance ticket** to the City Palace complex. You don't have to buy this ticket if you're just visiting the City Palace Museum or the courtyard outside, or if you're actually staying at any of the three hotels.

(*mor*), commissioned by Sajjan Singh in 1874, each made from around five thousand pieces of glass and coloured stone. On the other side of the courtyard is the opulent little **Manek Mahal** (Ruby Palace), its walls mirrored in rich reds and greens.

From the Manek Mahal, a long corridor winds past the kitsch apartments of queen mother Shri Gulabkunwar (1928–73) and through the **Zenana Mahal** (Women's Palace), whose long sequence of rooms now houses a huge array of paintings depicting royal fun and frolics in Mewar. Continue onwards to emerge, finally, into the last and largest of the palace's courtyards, **Lakshmi Chowk**, the centrepiece of the Zenana Mahal. The museum exit is at the far end of the chowk.

Government Museum
Daily 10am–4.30pm • ₹50

The small **Government Museum**, opposite the entrance to the City Palace Museum, is of interest for its impressive sculpture gallery of pieces from Kumbalgarh, including some outstanding works in black marble.

Durbar Hall
Crystal Gallery Daily 9am–6.30pm • ₹550 including audioguide

More interesting than the Government Museum in many ways – and certainly far more atmospheric – is the vast **Durbar Hall** in the Fateh Prakash Palace (the building immediately behind the main City Palace building, which now houses the *Fateh Prakash Palace* hotel). This huge, wonderfully time-warped Edwardian-era ballroom was built to host state banquets, royal functions and the like, and remains full of period character, complete with huge chandeliers, creaky old furniture and fusty portraits. In a gallery overlooking the hall is the eccentric **Crystal Gallery**, housing an array of fine British crystal ordered by Sajjan Singh in the 1880s and featuring outlandishly kitsch items including crystal chairs, tables and lamps – there's even a crystal hookah and a crystal bed. The extortionate entrance charge is a bit of a turn-off, though it does include an audioguide and non-alcoholic refreshments at the hotel's *Surya Dharshan Bar*.

Mewar Sound-and-Light show
Daily: Sept–Feb 7pm; March and April 7.30pm; May–Aug 8pm • From ₹150 (English), ₹100 (Hindi)

Every evening, fifteen years of history is revived at the palace, as special effects and commentary recount stories from the Kingdom of Mewar. The Mewar Sound-and-Light show is held in Manek Chowk, and commentary is in English between September and April, and in Hindi for the rest of the year.

Jagdish Temple
City Palace Rd

Just north of the City Palace, **Jagdish Temple** is one of Udaipur's most popular and vibrant shrines. Built in 1652 and dedicated to Lord Jagannath, an aspect of Vishnu, its outer walls and towering *shikhara* are heavily carved with figures of Vishnu, scenes from the life of Krishna and dancing *apsaras* (nymphs). The circular *mandapa* leads to the sanctuary where a black stone image of Jagannath sits shrouded in flowers, while a small raised shrine in front of the temple protects a bronze Garuda. Subsidiary shrines to Shiva, Ganesh, Surya and Durga stand at each corner of the main temple.

Bagore-ki-Haveli

Gangaur Ghat Marg • **Museum** Daily 10am–5pm • ₹30 (₹20), camera ₹30, video ₹100

North of Jagdish Temple, a lane leads to Gangaur Ghat and the **Bagore-ki-Haveli**, a 138-room lakeside haveli of 1751. A section of the building has been converted into a worthwhile **museum**, arranged on two floors around one of the rambling haveli's several courtyards. The upper floor has several immaculately restored rooms with original furnishings and artworks, plus some fine murals. The lower floor has rooms full of women's clothes, musical instruments, kitchen equipment and – the undisputed highlight – what is claimed to be the world's largest turban. Traditional **music and dance** shows (₹100 (₹60), camera ₹50, video ₹50) are staged here nightly at 7pm.

Bharatiya Lok Kala

Saheli Marg • Daily 9am–5.30pm • ₹40 (₹25), camera ₹10, video ₹50

Just north of Chetak Circle in the new city, the hoary old **Bharatiya Lok Kala** museum is home to a mildly interesting collection of exhibits covering the folk traditions of Rajasthan and India, with dusty displays of colourful masks, puppets and musical instruments. Short, amusing **puppet shows** (tip expected) are staged throughout the day on demand (the performers will probably hunt you down and drag you into the theatre shortly after your arrival), while there's an hour-long show, with music, dancing and more puppets, daily at 6pm (₹60 (₹40), camera ₹10, video ₹50).

Sahelion-ki-Bari

Saheli Marg • Daily 8am–8pm • ₹5

Northeast of Moti Magri, **Sahelion-ki-Bari**, the "garden of the maids of honour", was laid out by Sangram Singh (1710–34) as a summer retreat for the diversion and entertainment of the ladies of the royal household – though the fountains weren't installed until the reign of Fateh Singh (1884–1930). The gardens are centred on a peaceful courtyard enclosing a large pool and surrounded by attractive formal walled gardens, at the back of which four elephant statues surround Udaipur's most striking fountain – a fanciful tiered creation that looks a bit like a huge, multicoloured cake stand.

Ropeway

Daily 9am–9pm • ₹300 (₹72) return • ⓦ udaipurropeway.com

Just south of the old city, opposite Deen Dayal Park, pairs of ruby-red cable cars float up to the summit of Machlan Magra hill on the Ropeway. The panoramic views, taking in sights such as Lake Pichola, Jag Mandir and the Monsoon Palace, from its summit are stunning, especially at sunset. East of the Dutch Tala (lake) a winding pathway provides an alternative ascent route used by pilgrims visiting the small hilltop Karni Mata temple.

Shilpgram

Daily 11am–7pm • ₹50 (₹30), camera/video ₹50

Some 4km west of town, the popular rural arts and crafts centre of **Shilpgram** was set up to promote the traditional architecture, music and crafts of the tribal people of western India, with displays dedicated to the diverse lifestyles and customs of the region's rural population. Around thirty replica houses and huts in traditional style are arranged in a village-like compound, with examples of buildings from various states.

Musicians, puppeteers and dancers – *hijras* (eunuchs) among them – hang out around the houses and strike up on the approach of visitors (tip expected), while you may also see people weaving, potting and embroidering as they would in their original homes – though most of the actual handicrafts on sale are fifth-rate, if that. Despite its honourable intentions, many tourists find the atmosphere contrived and resent the hustling by musicians and their ilk. Even so, it's well worth a visit if only for the scenic journey out along the road around Fateh Sagar Lake. It's best done by bicycle but you can also get there by auto-rickshaw; this costs around ₹250 including waiting time.

Sajjangarh (Monsoon Palace)

Daily 9am–sunset, last entry 5pm • ₹160 (₹20), plus ₹79 for car shuttle up the hill or ₹130 if you come in your own taxi

High on a hill 5km west of the city and inside the **Sajjangarh Wildlife Sanctuary**, the so-called "Monsoon Palace", **Sajjangarh**, was begun in 1883 by Maharana Sajjan Singh to serve as a summer retreat, complete with a nine-storey observatory from which the royal family proposed to watch the monsoon clouds travelling across the countryside below. Unfortunately, the maharana's untimely death the following year put paid to the planned observatory, and although the palace itself was finished by Singh's successor, Maharana Fateh Singh, it was found to be impossible to pump water up to it, and the whole place was abandoned shortly afterwards. The large though rather plain building is now a somewhat melancholy sight, but the views over Udaipur, more than 300m below, are unrivalled. The journey up to the palace takes a good fifteen minutes by taxi (around ₹300 for the roundtrip); the climb is too steep to tackle by bicycle (₹5), although some people try.

ARRIVAL AND DEPARTURE

UDAIPUR

By plane Flights from Dabok Airport (☎0294 265 5453), 20km east of Udaipur, serve Delhi, Jaipur, Jodhpur and Mumbai. Pre-paid taxis from the airport cost ₹550 or ₹450 from the city. Airline offices in Udaipur include Air India in Mumal Towers on Sacheli Marg Rd in Madhuban (☎0294 241 0999) and Jet Airways, near the Blue Circle Bus Centre and GPO, also on Sacheli Marg (☎0294 656 191).

By train Trains pull in at Udaipur City Station, southeast of the city centre. Services from Udaipur are surprisingly limited; those we've listed (see box below) are the best of a bad bunch. Note that there are no direct services to Jodhpur (change at Kota). You can save a trip to the station by

booking tickets through travel agents in town (see p.211) for a surcharge of around ₹50–75, or your guesthouse, which will change you about what you'd pay for a rickshaw to the station and back.

By bus Government buses leave from the main RSTRC bus stand at Udai Pol; from here pre-paid auto cost ₹45 to the City Palace area. Private buses depart from across City Station Rd, and are a better option for longer and (especially) overnight journeys. It's easiest to book tickets for private buses through one of the many travel agents in town (usually for a modest surcharge of around ₹20) or, for ease, through your hotel/guesthouse. If you want to book your own ticket you'll need to make

RECOMMENDED TRAINS FROM UDAIPUR

Destination	Name	No.	Departs	Arrives
Ahmedabad	*Ahmedabad Fast Passenger*	52927	8.10am (daily)	9.05pm
	Ahmedabad Express	9943	5.45pm (daily)	4.25am
Ajmer	*Ajmer Express*	2991	6.15am (daily)	11.25am
	Udaipur Jaipur Daily Special	9722	2.15am (daily)	7.10am
Bundi	*Mewar Express*	2964	6.15pm (daily)	10.40pm
Chittaurgarh	*Mewar Express*	2964	6.15pm (daily)	8.30pm
Jaipur	*Ajmer Express*	2991	1.25pm (daily)	6.30am
Kota	*Mewar Express*	2964	6.15pm (daily)	11.40pm
Mumbai (Bandra)	*Bandra Express*	2996	9.35pm (Tues, Thurs, Sat)	2.20pm
New Delhi	*Mewar Express*	2964	6.15pm (daily)	6.30am
Sawai Madhopur	*Mewar Express*	2964	6.15pm (daily)	1.06am

a reservation with one of the bus company offices around Udai Pol – try the reliable Kamlesh Travels (☎0294 248 5823) who operate the best a/c sleeper coaches to Mumbai, Delhi and Jaipur. Other destinations include Agra (2 daily; 14hr), Ajmer (hourly; 7hr), Chittaurgarh (every 30min; 2hr 30min), Delhi (4 daily; 14hr), Mumbai (daily; 15hr) via Ahmedabad (5hr), Jaipur (hourly; 9hr), Jaisalmer (daily; 12hr), Jodhpur (6 daily; 7hr) and Mount Abu (2 daily; 4hr). Local buses to destinations such as Nagda, Eklingji, Nathdwara and Kankroli leave regularly from the RSTRC bus stand.

GETTING AROUND AND INFORMATION

By auto-rickshaw Auto-rickshaws are the usual means of transport; there are no cycle rickshaws in town. Rickshaw sightseeing tours cost around ₹500 for 5–6hr.

Bicycle and motorbike rental Renting a bicycle is another possibility, although traffic around the city is bad. Heera Cycle Store at 86 Gangaur Ghat Marg near Jagdish Temple (daily 7.30am–9pm; ☎0294 513 0625), rents out basic bicycles for ₹80/day. They also have Vespas (from ₹300/day) and Enfields (₹500/day); you'll need to bring your passport and leave a hard-currency deposit.

Tourist information The main tourist office (Mon–Sat 10am–5pm; ☎0294 241 1535) is in Fateh Memorial on Airport Rd at Suraj Pol, on the east side of the city, with desks at the airport and railway station.

Tours Tours to Ranakpur, Kumbalgarh, Nathdwara and Eklingji are offered by some of the innumerable travel agents dotted around the city centre (see p.224), as well as car rental with driver (usually around ₹1800/day for up to 300km).

ACCOMMODATION

Most accommodation is on the east side of Lake Pichola, although there are a growing number of excellent places on the far more peaceful northwestern side of the lake, just across the bridge by Chand Pol.

EAST OF LAKE PICHOLA

Fateh Prakash Palace City Palace ☎0294 252 8016, ⓦhrhindia.com. The best location in the city, right in the heart of the City Palace complex, with prices to match. Most of the rooms have superb lake views, although some are rather small and characterless for the price. U̲S̲$̲4̲2̲0̲

Gangaur Palace 339 "Ashoka Haveli" Gangaur Ghat Marg ☎0294 242 2303, ⓦashokahaveli.com. Popular and reliable budget hotel in an atmospheric traditional haveli. There's a wide range of rooms of varying standards (fan and a/c), including some with lake views, though prices for the smarter rooms can be a bit steep – try bargaining. Facilities include a miniature arts shop, in-house painting lessons (₹100/hr) and a breakfast-worthy French bakery. ₹̲5̲0̲0̲

★ **Jagat Niwas** 23–25 Lalghat ☎0294 242 2860, ⓦjagatniwaspalace.com. Beautifully restored seventeenth-century haveli right on the lakeside, with 29 pleasant a/c rooms (some with lake views) and a good restaurant (see p.210). The Raj rooms have lovely lakeside jharokhas, and are worth the splurge. ₹̲1̲9̲9̲0̲

★ **Jaiwana Haveli** 14 Lalghat ☎0294 241 1103, ⓦjaiwanahaveli.com. Good-value lakeside haveli accommodation with a range of spotless modern rooms; some have a/c, and the more expensive ones have fine lake views, as does the good rooftop restaurant. Best to book ahead. ₹̲2̲4̲1̲5̲

Jheel Guesthouse & Jheel Paying Guesthouse 52–56 Gangor Ghat ☎0294 242 1352, ⓦjheelguesthouse.com. These neighbouring sister-guesthouses offer seven good-value rooms apiece (all with attached bathrooms); the older wing is home to more basic fan-cooled doubles (₹400) while those in the newer building come with a/c and superb lake views (some even have balconies). ₹̲1̲2̲0̲0̲

Kankarwa Haveli 26 Lalghat ☎0294 241 1457, ⓦindianheritagehotels.com. Romantically restored haveli right on the waterfront. Not quite as pristine as the nearby Jagat Niwas, but equally as atmospheric, with colourful, antiquey rooms (all a/c; some with superb lake views) and an excellent rooftop veg restaurant (for guests only). ₹̲4̲1̲5̲0̲

Kumbha Palace 104 Bhatiyani Chohatta ☎98280 59506, ⓦhotelkumbhapalace.com. Friendly, Dutch-owned guesthouse hidden under the east walls of City Palace and backed by a bougainvillea-filled garden. Their single and double rooms (a few with a/c) are simple but bright and clean, there's free wi-fi and the whole place is refreshingly peaceful. ₹̲5̲5̲0̲

★ **Lake Palace** Lake Pichola ☎0294 252 8800, ⓦtajhotels.com. One of India's most famous and romantic hotels, sailing in magnificent isolation on its own island amid the serene waters of Lake Pichola. Accommodation is in a selection of luxurious rooms and suites while facilities include a spa, pool, butler service and limousine rental. U̲S̲$̲8̲5̲0̲

Lalghat Guest House 33 Lalghat ☎0294 252 5301, ⓦlalghat.com. One of the oldest guesthouses in Udaipur, and still going strong thanks to its superb lakeside position and cheapish rates. There's a mix of no-frills single and double rooms (some with shared bathrooms, some a/c, and a few with lakeside views), plus a nicer-than-average ten-person dorm. Dorm ₹̲1̲0̲0̲, double ₹̲3̲5̲0̲/₹̲5̲0̲0̲

Mewar Haveli 34–35 Lalghat ☎0294 252 1140, ⓦmewarhaveli.com. Spotless and well-run modern mid-range hotel in a very central location. The twelve rooms (some with a/c and lake views) are chintzy but comfortable, and there are further lake views from the attractive rooftop restaurant. ₹**1340**

Shiv Niwas City Palace ☏ 0294 252 8016, ⊛ hrhindia .com. This upmarket heritage hotel trades on its superb location inside the City Palace complex, with grand public areas, a dreamy pool (non-guests ₹350) and a lavish spa. The viewless standard ("palace") rooms are disappointingly small and ordinary given the price tag; suites (₹35,800) are far more memorable, with genuine old-world atmosphere and marvellous lake views. 20 percent discounts in summer. ₹**17,330**

★ **Udai Haveli** 40 Ganesh Ghati, Gadiya Devra ☏ 93525 06701, ✉ jituvishawat@hotmail.com. This excellent family-run guesthouse located up a quiet side street near *Savage Garden* restaurant is one of the best-value cheapies in town. The nine rooms (a couple with shared bathrooms) are neat and clean with bright, modern bathrooms. Delicious home-cooked food is served on the breezy rooftop. ₹**200**/₹**250**

Udai Niwas Gangaur Marg ☏ 0294 241 4303, ⊛ hoteludainiwas.com. Bright modern high-rise hotel with a range of smart rooms in various price categories (the more expensive ones have a/c and nice bathrooms), travel office and restaurant showing evening movies (7pm), although road noise and the periodic outbursts of massively amplified music from the nearby Jagdish Temple mean that it's not particularly peaceful. ₹**500**

NORTHWESTERN SIDE OF LAKE PICHOLA

★ **Amet Haveli** Chand Pol ☏ 0294 243 4009, ⊛ amethaveliudaipur.com. This fine old white haveli is one of the best lakefront properties in town. Rooms are beautifully decorated with traditional touches and come with a/c, TV and lake views, though you might want to spend a little more to get one of the superb suites, with big windows right over the water. Also home to the excellent *Ambrai* restaurant (see p.210). ₹**6700**

Dream Heaven Hanuman Ghat, Chand Pol ☏ 0294 243 1038, ⊛ dreamheaven.co.in. Deservedly popular (book ahead) guesthouse with a good range of clean and reasonably priced rooms; some have superb lake views (₹1500), as does the convivial wi-fi-enabled rooftop restaurant. ₹**800**

Lake Pichola Hotel Piplia Haveli, Chand Pol ☏ 0294 243 1197, ⊛ lakepicholahotel.com. This long-established hotel won't win any design awards but the lakeside location and City Palace views are just about perfect, and prices quite reasonable. Don't bother with the

viewless standard rooms, though. All rooms have a/c and TV. Also home to the excellent *Upre* rooftop restaurant (see p.210) and bar. ₹**5500**

★ **Panorama** Hanuman Ghat, Chand Pol ☏ 0294 243 1027 or ☏ 94143 52523, ⊛ panoramaguesthouse.in. Excellent budget hotel, efficiently run by friendly management and with cheap, cosy and excellent-value rooms (some with superb lake views and balconies; a few with a/c). There's internet and wi-fi, and also a nice rooftop restaurant with lovely lake views and good-value food. Book ahead. ₹**400**

Udai Kothi Chand Pol ☏ 0294 243 2810, ⊛ udaikothi .com. Smart and spotless modern hotel in traditional style, with lots of flowery murals and chintzy architectural touches. Rooms all come with TV, a/c and plenty of slightly twee furnishings; there's also a pool (non-guests ₹500) and a lovely garden. ₹**4700**

OUTSIDE THE CITY CENTRE

Laxmi Vilas Palace Off Fateh Sagar Rd ☏ 0294 252 9711, ⊛ thelalit.com. Luxury hotel occupying a nineteenth-century hilltop guesthouse above Fateh Sagar Lake. It's strong on creature comforts, with well-equipped rooms and a huge pool, although less atmospheric than the similarly priced hotels in the City Palace. US$**650**

★ **Udaivilas** Haridasji Ki Magri ☏ 0294 243 3300, ⊛ oberoihotels.com. Udaipur's most opulent hotel, occupying a sprawling palace, embellished with acres of marble and a novel "moated pool" that flows around the outside of the main building. Suites come with infinity swimming pools and private butlers, and the spa is pure indulgence. US$**1060**

AROUND UDAIPUR

★ **Devi Garh** Delwara Village, 25km north of Udaipur ☏ 0295 328 9211, ⊛ deviresorts.in. Hidden away in the Aravalli Hills a 40min drive north of Udaipur, this luxury hotel occupies the magnificent seventeenth-century Devi Garh palace, mixing traditional Rajasthani palace opulence with contemporary style to memorable effect. Facilities include a superb spa and a spectacular pool. Suites only. US$**350**

Shikarbadi Goverdhan Vilas, 5km south of Udaipur on the NH-8 ☏ 0294 258 3201, ⊛ hrhindia.com. Former royal hunting lodge with its own pool, lake, deer park and stud farm – less ostentatious (and significantly cheaper) than the palaces in town. Suites (₹9870) in the old 1930s block have more character than the newer a/c rooms. ₹**8450**

EATING, DRINKING AND ENTERTAINMENT

Bagore-ki-Haveli (see p.206) has nightly dance performances, while Shilpgram (see p.206) often hosts out-of-town performers. Many of Udaipur's tourist cafés screen the James Bond movie *Octopussy*, with its manic boat and auto-rickshaw chases round the city's landmarks, every evening at 7pm.

2

★ **Ambrai** Amet Haveli, Chand Pol ☎0294 243 1085. In a superlative setting facing the City Palace, this is one of the few lakeside restaurants where the cooking lives up to its location, although prices are creeping up. The menu features an extensive selection of north Indian veg and non-veg dishes (including top-notch tandooris), plus a few Chinese and European offerings. Even if you're not hungry, come for a sundowner and watch the sun set over the lake. Non-veg mains ₹185–515. Licensed. Daily 7.30am–10.30pm.

Jagat Niwas 23–25 Lalghat. Popular restaurant in the hotel of the same name, serving up well-prepared north Indian standards (non-veg mains ₹225–335), with nice views over the lake from its comfy window seats. Daily 8am–10pm.

Jheels Ginger Coffee Bar and Bakery Jheel Paying Guest House, 56 Gangaur Ghat ☎94610 16511. Grab one of the idyllic lakeside tables at this charming ground-floor café, which serves up all sorts of coffees and yummy treats including chocolate tart (₹30), muffins (₹50), sandwiches, sundaes and ice creams. They offer free wi-fi too. For something a bit more substantial, their rooftop restaurant is pretty good. Daily 8am–9pm.

★ **Millets of Merwar** Nr. Hanuman Ghat Hotel, Chand Pol ☎87693 48440, ⊛milletsofmerwar.com. Indulge in healthy cuisine in this rustic lakeview café with vegan, organic and gluten-free options, including pasta (from ₹120), soups, thali (₹150), Indian and Thai curries (₹60–120), salads and corn/millet flour pizzas, plus shakes and juices. They also organize walks to crafts villages (₹500) and offer water bottle refills for ₹5. Daily 8am–10.30pm.

Natraj New Bapu Bazaar (behind Town Hall Road's Ashok Cinema). Udaipur's top thali joint for more than twenty years, but well off the tourist trail and fiendishly hard to find (from Suraj Pol gate, head north up Bapu Bazaar, turn right after 30m, then left, and it's 20m up on your right). Easily the best cheap meal in town – just ₹80 for unlimited portions of veg curries, soups, dhal, curd and chapattis. A newer, posher tourist-orientated outlet (*Natraj Lodge*) on Station Rd, offers a similar experience for a slightly more expensive ₹130. Daily 10.30am–3.30pm & 6.30–10.30pm.

Queen Café Chand Pol. This homely and unpretentious little café offers a refreshing alternative to Udaipur's mainstream tourist restaurants, with an authentic taste of home-style vegetarian Indian cooking including mild banana, mango and pumpkin curries (most mains ₹60–80). Daily 8.30am–9pm.

Savage Garden 22 Chand Pol ☎0294 242 5440. Stylish restaurant set in an old haveli given a funky modern makeover, with loads of blue and white paint and minimalist decor. Food is Middle Eastern and European, with slight gourmet pretensions, and the menu is short but well chosen. Mains ₹190–550. Daily 11am–11pm.

Upré Lake Pichola Hotel, Chand Pol ☎0294 243 1197. Chic, smart and surprisingly lush rooftop restaurant serving good veg and non veg dishes (mains ₹220–530) with licensed bar, plunge pool, open kitchen and cushy loungers. Grab one of the lamplit balcony tables for the best views over the city and lake. Daily 11am–11pm.

The Whistling Teal Raj Palace hotel, 103 Bhattiyani Chohatta ☎0294 242 2067. Attractive, tented garden restaurant serving well-prepared north Indian and Rajasthani veg and non-veg dishes (mains ₹100–350) – pricier than average, but worth it. There are also hookah pipes with fruit-flavoured tobacco (₹250), plus good coffee, and you can sip drinks from the bar astride horse saddle stools. Daily 8.30am–10.30pm.

SHOPPING

Udaipur is one of Rajasthan's top shopping destinations, with an eclectic array of local artisanal specialities along with other crafts from across the state. The city's particular speciality is **miniature painting**, with numerous shops selling traditional Mewari-style works on paper and silk. Many places also do a good line in leather and cloth-bound **stationery** using handmade paper. Udaipur is well known for its **silver jewellery** – Jagdish St, Bara Bazaar and Moti Chohatta, around the clock tower, are home to lots of shops. Lalghat and the branches leading off it are home to **bookshops** selling new and secondhand titles, some of which let you exchange used books.

DIRECTORY

Banks and exchange There are ATMs all over the new city, plus a particularly handy 24hr machine on the street leading to the City Palace. Lots of places around Jagdish Temple offer forex. Mewar International (daily 9am–10pm), on Lalghat, changes cash and travellers' cheques, and gives cash advances on Visa and MasterCard.

Cooking lessons Available at numerous places around town. Try the *Panorama guesthouse* (see p.209), who charge (from ₹500 for 3hr classes) or the homely little

Queen Café (see above), who charge (₹900 for 3hr).

Doctor Dr. Virendra Bhandari (☎98290 91084) will visit hotels/guesthouses.

Horseriding Various places around town offer horseriding expeditions into the surrounding countryside. The reputable *Kumbha Palace* hotel (see p.208) runs half- and full-day excursions (₹1500/₹2500), plus longer trips from their tranquil *Krishna Ranch*, 7km out of the city, where they also have nice rooms (₹1250). Princess Trails (☎98290 42012, princesstrails.com) specializes in extended, four- to eight-day safaris on thoroughbred Mewari mounts.

Hospital Aravalli Hospital (private), 332 Ambamata Rd (ⓣ 0294 243 0222).

Music The enthusiastic Rajesh Prajapat at the Prem Musical Instrument shop (ⓣ 94143 43583), adjacent to the *Gangaur Palace* hotel, offers sitar and tabla lessons (₹400 for 90min) and can also arrange flute lessons with his brother, or musical appreciation classes if you just want to learn more about Indian music.

Painting lessons Lessons in traditional Indian painting are offered by many places around town; the *Gangaur Palace* hotel is a reliable option (₹100/hr).

Photography Mewar International (see above), on Lalghat behind the Jagdish Temple, burn CDs and DVDs, sell memory cards and have equipment to download photos from most types of digital cameras; they also offer backup and photo recovery from defective memory cards.

Post office Parcels are best sent from the GPO at Chetak Circle (Mon–Fri 10am–5pm).

Swimming pool The lovely rooftop pool at *Udai Kothi* costs ₹500/day for non-guests. Otherwise, try the *Mahendra Prakash Palace* hotel (₹300).

Travel agents Virtually every shop and guesthouse around the Jagdish Temple seems to offer bus and rail ticketing. Reliable agents include Mewar International on Lalghat behind the Jagdish Temple, which also stocks books; Gangaur Tour 'n' Travels, close by at 28 Gangaur Ghat (ⓣ 94141 60476); and the travel agency inside the *Udai Niwas* hotel.

Volunteer work The Animal Aid Society, Badi Village, opposite T.B. Hospital, 8km northeast of the city (ⓣ 99505 31639, ⓦ animalaidunlimited.com) run by a friendly American expat couple, maintains a pet hospital where volunteers and visitors are encouraged and no special skills are required – just a willingness to work with animals, usually including street dogs, cows, donkeys, cats and monkeys.

Yoga Ashtanga Yoga Ashram (aka "Raiba House"), Chand Pol (ⓣ 0294 252 4872). Daily 90min Hatha yoga classes for all standards at 8.30am and 6pm (let them know you're coming a day in advance). Free, but donations appreciated – proceeds go to a local animal charity. Individual lessons also available.

Around Udaipur

North of the city are the historic temples of **Nagda**, **Eklingji**, **Nathdwara** and **Kankroli**, while to the northwest, en route to Jodhpur, lie the superb Jain temples of **Ranakpur** and the rambling fort at **Kumbalgarh**. Renting a car or motorcycle saves time, though local buses serve both routes.

Nagda

Regular buses leave for Kailashpuri (the Nagda turn-off) every 30min from Udaipur's main bus stand; Nagda is a further 3km away down this side road – rent a bicycle from the shop at the junction to get there, take an auto-rickshaw or walk

Dating back to 626 AD, the ragged remnants of the ancient capital of Mewar, **NAGDA**, stand next to a lake 20km northeast of Udaipur. Most of the buildings here were either destroyed by the Mughals or submerged by the lake, which has expanded naturally over the centuries. All that survives is a fine pair of tenth-century Vaishnavite temples known as **Saas-Bahu** – literally "mother-in-law" and "daughter-in-law". The more impressive mother-in-law temple has lost its *shikhara* (tower) but preserves a wealth of carving inside, while within the *mandapa*, a marriage area is marked by four ornate pillars, bearing images of the gods Brahma, Vishnu, Shiva and Surya to which couples are supposed to pay homage.

Eklingji

Main temple daily 10.30am–1.30pm & 5.30–8.30pm • Free • Frequent buses leave for Eklingji from Udaipur's main bus stand, dropping passengers off close to the temple

Returning to the main road, you can continue to **EKLINGJI** via the road or along a path that leads behind the old protective walls and downhill. Ask for directions at the bike shop. The god **Eklingji**, a manifestation of Shiva, has been the protective deity of the rulers of Mewar ever since the eighth century, when Bappa Rawal was bestowed with the title *darwan* (servant) of Eklingji by his guru. To this day, the maharana of Udaipur still visits the 108-temple complex every Monday evening (the day traditionally celebrated all over India as being sacred to Shiva) and the whole place is usually lively with local pilgrims seeking his blessings. The milky-white marble **main temple** is crowned by an elaborate two-storey *mandapa* guarded by stone elephants; inside, a four-faced black marble lingam marks the precise spot where Bappa Rawal received his accolade.

2 Nathdwara

Nathdwara is on NH-8, and sees a constant flow of buses en route north and south

The temple dedicated to Krishna – known also as **Nath**, the favourite avatar (incarnation) of Vishnu – at **NATHDWARA**, "Gateway to God", is one of the richest temples in India, and gets incredibly crowded during major religious festivals. It dates from the seventeenth century when a chariot laden with an image of Krishna – being carried from Mathura to Udaipur to save it from destruction by Aurangzeb – became stuck in the mud here. Its bearers interpreted the event as a divine sign, establishing the new **Shri Nathji Temple** where it had stopped.

The temple lies about 1km south of the town's bus stop, surrounded by a fascinating tangle of narrow streets where stalls display incense, perfumes and small Krishna statues. The temple opens for worship eight times daily, when the image is woken, dressed, washed, fed and put to bed. Don't miss the radiant *pichwai* paintings in the main sanctuary, made of hand-spun cloth and coloured with strong vegetable pigments. You could also ask a guide to show you the "footsteps of Krishna", a process that requires rubbing rose petals on the marble floor.

Ranakpur

Some 90km north of Udaipur, the spectacular **Jain temples** at **RANAKPUR** boast marblework on a par with that of the more famous Dilwara shrines at Mount Abu (see p.216). The temples are hidden away in a beautiful wooded valley, deep in the Aravalli Hills, which was originally gifted to the Jain community in the fifteenth century by Rana Kumbha, the Hindu ruler of Mewar.

The **main temple** (noon–5pm; free, camera or mobile with camera ₹100, video ₹100) was built in 1439 according to a strict system of measurement based on the number 72 (the age at which the founder of Jainism, Mahavira, achieved nirvana). The entire temple sits on a pedestal measuring 72 yards square and is held up by 1440 (72 x 20) individually carved pillars. Inside, there are 72 elaborately carved shrines, some octagonal in shape, along with the main deity (a 72-inch-tall image of the four-faced Adinath, the first *tirthankara*) encased in the central sanctum. The carving on the walls, columns and the domed ceilings is superb. Friezes depicting the life of the *tirthankara* are etched into the walls, while musicians and dancers have been modelled out of brackets between the pillars and the ceiling.

Three smaller temples nestle among the trees in the enclosure in front of the main temple. The most impressive is the **Parshwanath Temple**, around 100m from the main temple, with a small but finely carved shrine, while a further 100m walk brings you to the simpler **Neminath Temple**. Close by (a short walk across the car park) is a contemporary Hindu temple dedicated to **Surya**.

ARRIVAL AND DEPARTURE   RANAKPUR

By bus Ranakpur is a bumpy bus ride from Udaipur (hourly; 2hr 30min), or from Jodhpur (8 daily; 4–5hr) via the market town of Falna (the nearest railway station) on the NH-14, from where there are four daily buses to Abu Rd (5–6hr). Buses stop right outside the Jain temples, which are 2–4km from the hotels; if you're lucky, you might find an auto or jeep at the bus stop – if not you'll have to ring your hotel and ask to be picked up, or (worst-case scenario) walk.

By taxi Ranakpur can also be visited as a day-trip from

Udaipur, either on its own or in combination with nearby return Kumbalgarh; count on around ₹1800 for the return trip by car.

Trekking If you wish to visit Kumbalgarh too, think about trekking between the two sites, a beautiful hike through an unspoilt section of the Aravalli Hills. As Kumbalgarh is on the top of the range, it's easier to hike down from there to Ranakpur (see below); guides and rangers may be arranged at the hotels listed below for the 6hr uphill climb in the other direction.

ACCOMMODATION AND EATING

Accommodation in Ranakpur is relatively expensive. There are no restaurants outside the hotels and guesthouses, although you can enjoy a delicious pure veg thali lunch at the temple (noon–1.30pm) for a bargain ₹40.

Fateh Bagh 4km south of the temples ☎0293 428 6186, ⊚hrhindia.com. Ranakpur's most authentic accommodation, a 200-year-old palace transported piece by piece for 50km, and rebuilt here. Rooms are comfy and characterful, and facilities include a pool, spa and Ayurveda centre. ₹8455

King's Abode 3km south of the temples ☎90019 99491, ⊚kingsabode.in. Grey stone walls and a lush inner courtyard give this hotel plenty of character. It's 28 a/c double rooms are spacious and equipped with plenty of mod cons, while the higher-category rooms have private pools. There's a big swimming pool, plus jacuzzi, spa and restaurant, and treks and nature walks can be arranged. ₹6460

Mana 5km south of the temples ☎90019 99568, ⊚manahotels.in. Angular Scandinavian-styled *Mana* is unashamedly modern and unlike anything else in Ranakpur, exhibiting plenty of timber, glass and steel. Chic rooms and cottages within the 3.5-acre garden all feature a/c, TVs and phones, plus bright modern bathrooms with tubs, whilst the slender infinity pool flows right into the restaurant/bar. ₹6000

Ranakpur Hill Resort 3km south of the temples ☎02934 286411, ⊚ranakpurhillresort.com. Chintzy little resort with a range of great-value rooms (air-cooled and a/c) of varying standards, and some less appealing tents (available Oct–March only). It also has a decent-sized pool and a small Ayurveda centre, and can arrange half-day horse safaris. Rooms & tents ₹2500

Shivika Lake Hotel 2km south of the temples ☎02934 285078 or ☎99299 18419, ⊚shivikalakehotel.com. One of the few budget options in Ranakpur, although the rooms (some with a/c) are disappointingly shabby given the price; don't be fooled by the website pics. Local treks (₹400/person) and jeep safaris (₹750/person) can be arranged here and there's a gorgeously positioned swimming pool with forested lake backdrop. ₹800

Kumbalgarh

Fort Daily 8am–5.30pm • ₹100 (₹5) Sound-and-light show 7pm • ₹200 (₹100)

The remote hilltop fort of **KUMBALGARH**, 80km north of Udaipur, is the most formidable of the 32 constructed or restored by Rana Kumbha of Chittaurgarh in the fifteenth century. Protected by a series of monumental walls and bastions, it was only successfully besieged once, when a confederacy led by Akbar poisoned the water supply. Aside from the fort itself, Kumbalgarh is worth a visit to experience the idyllic Aravalli countryside, dotted with tribal villages and offreing striking views.

The most memorable panorama of all is from the pinnacle of the rather plain **palace** building, crowning the summit of the fort, with striking bird's-eye views over the numerous Jain and Hindu **temples** clustered around the main gate and scattered over the hills below. The oldest are thought to date from the second century; the **tombs** of the great Rana Kumbha himself (murdered by his eldest son) and his grandson Prithviraj (poisoned by his brother-in-law) stand to the east. Some 36km of crenellated ramparts wind around the rim of the hilltop, and it's possible to walk around them in two comfortable days, sleeping rough or in tents; a guide is compulsory (from ₹800/day). Be sure to take sufficient food and water.

Kumbalgarh Wildlife Sanctuary

₹160 (₹10), camera ₹400

Lining the deep valley that plunges west from the fort down to the plains, the **Kumbalgarh Wildlife Sanctuary** comprises a dense area of woodland that offers a refuge for wolves and leopards. With a local guide, you can trek through it to Ranakpur, a

2

rewarding and easy hike of between four and five hours (the alternative is a long journey on an infrequent country bus). Entry **permits** are obtainable from the District Forest Officer at **Kelwara**, 7km down the road, though local guides – contactable through the hotels listed below, or at local shops, or at the café just inside the fort gates – can obtain permits for you, and will charge from ₹800 to do the walk with you, or ₹2000 including entry fees to go round in a jeep.

ARRIVAL AND DEPARTURE   KUMBALGARH

By taxi Kumbalgarh and Ranakpur can easily be visited as a (longish) day-trip from Udaipur (around ₹1800 for the roundtrip by taxi for up to four people).

By shared jeep Otherwise, take a shared jeep from Chetak Circle to Kelwara, 7km down the road, from where you should be able to pick up a jeep or rickshaw to Kumbalgarh.

ACCOMMODATION

The Aodhi 1km below the fort ☏ 0295 424 2341, ⓦ hrhhotels.com. A peaceful and welcoming heritage hotel with stylishly furnished rooms (some with nice views), a big pool and jeep safaris to local villages (2hr, ₹1550). ₹8450

Club Mahindra Fort Kumbalgarh, 5km down the Kelwara road ☏ 0295 424 2171, ⓦ clubmahindra.com. A modern upmarket hotel with spa, recently renovated, with superb views from its pool and garden terrace. ₹2400

Silent Valley 7km from the fort on the Udawad Rd ☏ 94154 07259, ⓦ hotelsilentvalleykumbhalgarh .com. The eight basic rooms (all attached, with a/c) are nothing special, but the tranquil nature-filled location is idyllic, there's good food and the staff are welcoming. Horseriding, treks and jeep safaris can be arranged. It's hard to find, so call for pick up. ₹2500

Mount Abu

Rajasthan's only bona fide hill station, **MOUNT ABU** (1220m) is a major Indian resort, popular above all with honeymooners who flock here during the winter wedding season (Nov to March) and with visiting holiday-makers from nearby Gujarat. Mount Abu's hokey commercialism is aimed squarely at these local vacationers rather than foreign tourists, but the sight of lovestruck honeymooners shyly holding hands and jolly parties of Gujarati tourists on the loose lends the whole place a charmingly idiosyncratic holiday atmosphere quite unlike anywhere else in Rajasthan – and the fresh air is exhilarating after the heat of the desert plains. The town also occupies an important place in Rajput history, being the site of the famous *yagna agnikund* fire ceremony, conducted in the eighth century AD, from which all Rajputs claim mythological descent.

Note that during the peak months of April to June and at almost any major festival time (especially Diwali in Nov), and even during weekends, the town's population of thirty thousand mushrooms, room rates skyrocket, and peace and quiet are at a premium.

At the centre of town, **Nakki Lake** is popular in the late afternoon for pony and pedalo rides (₹50/30min). Of several panoramic viewpoints on the fringes of town above the plains, **Sunset Point** is the favourite – though the hordes of holiday-makers and hawkers also make it one of the noisiest and least romantic. **Honeymoon Point**, also known as Ganesh Point (after the adjacent temple), and **Anadhra Point** offer breathtaking views over the plain at any time of day, and tend to be more peaceful. 4pm is a good time to visit, but don't try to take clifftop paths between Sunset and Honeymoon points, as tourists have been mugged here.

Brahma Kumaris Museum

Off Nakki Lake Rd • Daily 8am–8pm • Free

The **Brahma Kumaris Museum**, between the polo ground and the lake, is devoted to the spiritual ideals of the Brahma Kumaris ("children of Brahma"), whose

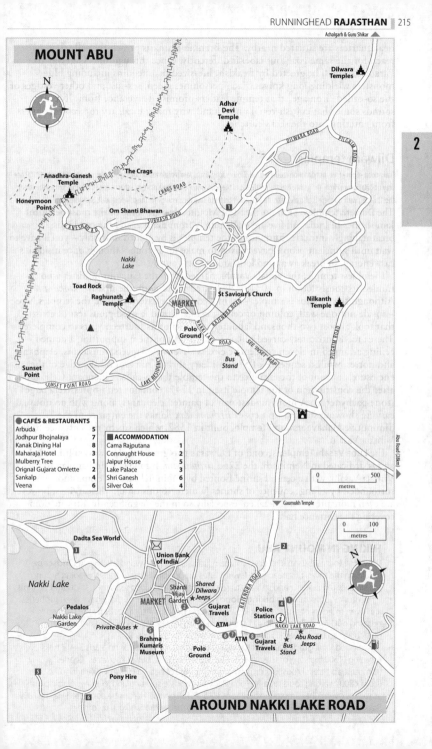

MOUNT ABU

Achalgarh & Guru Shikar

Dilwara Temples

N

DILWARA ROAD
PILGRIM ROAD

Adhar Devi Temple

Anadhra-Ganesh Temple

The Crags

CRAGS ROAD

Honeymoon Point

Om Shanti Bhawan

SURBASH ROAD

G. ANESH RD

Nakki Lake

Toad Rock

Raghunath Temple

St Saviour's Church

MARKET

Nilkanth Temple

Polo Ground

RAJENDRA ROAD

PILGRIM ROAD

SEE INSET MAP

Bus Stand

NAKKI LAKE ROAD

Sunset Point

SUNSET POINT ROAD

LAKE RESIDENCE

Abu Road (28km)

Gaumukh Temple

● CAFÉS & RESTAURANTS	
Arbuda	5
Jodhpur Bhojnalaya	7
Kanak Dining Hal	8
Maharaja Hotel	3
Mulberry Tree	1
Orignal Gujarat Omlette	2
Sankalp	4
Veena	6

■ ACCOMMODATION	
Cama Rajputana	1
Connaught House	2
Jaipur House	5
Lake Palace	3
Shri Ganesh	6
Silver Oak	4

0 — 500 metres

---

0 — 100 metres

Dadta Sea World

Union Bank of India

Nakki Lake

Shanti Vijay Garden

Shared Dilwara Jeeps

MARKET

RAJENDRA ROAD

Pedalos

Nakki Lake Garden

Gujarat Travels

Police Station

Private Buses

ATM

NAKKI LAKE ROAD

Brahma Kumaris Museum

ATM

Gujarat Travels

Abu Road Jeeps

Bus Stand

Polo Ground

Pony Hire

N

AROUND NAKKI LAKE ROAD

headquarters are situated nearby. The Brahma Kumaris preach that all religions reach for the same goal, but label it differently. Once through the "Gateway to Paradise," you'll be greeted by freakish, life-sized mannequins including blue monsters wielding long knives. Each personifies greed, sex-lust and other vestiges of the so-called "iron age" that temple leaders promise deliverance from. If it all sounds somewhat cultish you'll understand why many locals try to keep foreigners from entering into the sect's clutches.

Dilwara temples

Daily noon–6pm • Free, but donation requested, no photography, usual Jain temple restrictions apply • You can charter a jeep (₹100 one way or ₹200 return) from the junction at the north end of the polo ground, or take a place in a shared one (₹10) from just up the street; the 1hr-long walk up there is also pleasant, though many prefer to save their energy for the downhill walk back into town

The **Dilwara temples**, 3km northeast of Mount Abu, are some of the most beautiful Jain shrines in India. All five are made purely from marble, and the carving is breathtakingly intricate. Entrance to the temples is by guided tour only – you'll have to wait until sufficient people have arrived to make up a group – though once inside it's easy enough to break away and look around on your own.

The oldest temple, the **Vimala Vasahi**, named after the Gujarati minister who funded its construction in 1031, is dedicated to Adinath, the first *tirthankara*. Although the exterior is simple – as, indeed, are the exteriors of all the temples here – inside not one wall, column or ceiling is unadorned, a prodigious feat of artistry that took almost two thousand labourers and sculptors fourteen years to complete. There are 48 intricately carved pillars inside, eight of them supporting a domed ceiling arranged in eleven concentric circles alive with dancers, musicians, elephants and horses, while a sequence of 57 subsidiary shrines run around the edge of the enclosure. In front of the entrance to the temple the so-called "Elephant Cell" (added after the construction of the temple itself in 1147) contains ten impressively large stone pachyderms. A more modest pair of painted elephants, along with an unusual carving showing stacked-up tiers of *tirthankaras*, flanks the entrance to the diminutive **Mahaveerswami Temple**, built in 1582, which sits by the entrance to the Vimala Vasahi.

The **Luna Vasahi Temple**, second of Dilwara's two great temples, was built in 1231, and is dedicated to Neminath, the 22nd *tirthankara*. It follows a similar plan to the Vimala Vasahi, with a central shrine fronted by a minutely carved dome and surrounded by a long sequence of shrines (a mere 48 this time). The carvings, however, are even more precise and detailed, especially so in the magnificently intricate dome covering the entrance hall.

HIKING IN MOUNT ABU

Down in Mount Abu's market area, you gain little sense of the wonderfully wild **landscape** enfolding the town, but head for a few minutes up one of the many trails threading around the sides of the plateau, and it's easy to see why the area has inspired sages, saints and pilgrims for centuries. Unfortunately **hiking alone** is not recommended, as there have been robberies and even murders of unaccompanied visitors, and police will turn back anyone spotted heading out alone. There's also a chance of running into bears and leopards – bears, in particular, can be dangerous if surprised, or when with their young.

Two good local **guides** are Lalit Kanojia at the *Shri Ganesh* hotel, who leads 3–4hr treks every morning (₹600/person); or the experienced Mahendra Dan, better known as "Charles" (🔟 mount-abu-treks.blogspot.com), who runs a range of half-day (from ₹400) and full-day (from ₹800) walking tours focusing on village life, wildlife spotting and local Ayurvedic plants, as well as overnight camping expeditions (₹1500, full board). He can be contacted via the *Lake Palace* hotel or on ☎ 94141 54854, or emailed on ✉ mahendradan@gmail.com.

The remaining two temples, both fifteenth-century, are less spectacular. The **Bhimasah Pittalhar Temple** houses a huge gilded image of the first *tirthankara*, Adinath, installed in 1468, which measures more than 2.5m high and weighs in at around 4.5 tons. The large three-storey **Khartar Vasahi Temple** (near the entrance to the temples) was built in 1458 and is consecrated to Parshvanath. The temple is topped by a high grey stone tower and boasts some intricate carving in places, though overall it's only a pale shadow of the earlier temples.

Hindu temples

On the north side of town, en route to the Dilwara temples, a flight of more than four hundred steps climbs up to the **Adhar Devi Temple** (dedicated to Durga). The small main shrine is cut into the rocky hilltop and entered by clambering under a very low overhang. There are fine views from the terrace above, where there's another tiny shrine cut out of solid rock. The milk-coloured water of the **Doodh Baori** well at the foot of the steps is considered to be a source of pure milk (*doodh*) for gods and sages.

A further 8km northeast (not served by public transport, so you'd need to hire a jeep or a taxi), the temple complex at **ACHALGARH** is dominated by the **Achaleshwar Mahadeo Temple**, believed to have been created when Lord Shiva placed his toe on the spot to still an earthquake. Its sanctuary holds a yoni with a hole in it that is said to reach into the netherworld. Nearby, the **Jamadagni Ashram** is site of the *yagna agnikund*, where the sage Vashishtha presided over the fire ritual that produced the four Rajput clans (the Parmars, Parihars, Solankis and Chauhans).

The lesser visited, but more dramatically situated, **Gaumukh Temple** lies 7km south of the market area and is also not served by public transport, so you'll have to hire a jeep or taxi. Standing at the head of a steep flight of 750 steps, the small pool inside the shrine – which continues to flow even during times of drought – is believed to hold water from the sacred Sarawati Ganga River. Pilgrims come here to perform puja, to invoke the blessings of India's two greatest *rishis* (sages), Vashishtha and Vishwamitra, who are thought to have meditated and debated here.

The last important Hindu pilgrimage site on Mount Abu is the Atri Rishi Temple at **Guru Shikar**, 15km northeast of town, which at 1772m above sea level marks the highest point in Rajasthan. You can enjoy superb panoramic vistas either from the temple itself, or from the drinks stall at the bottom of the steps leading up to it. There's no public transport there, however, so you'll have to rent a jeep – going rates are ₹800, so make the most of it by visiting the other temples en route.

ARRIVAL AND INFORMATION   **MOUNT ABU**

Mount Abu is accessible only by road. The nearest railhead is at Abu Rd, from where buses make the 45min ascent up to Mount Abu itself. Entering Mount Abu, you have to pay a ₹10 entry fee (plus an additional ₹10 for a car or jeep).

By train There's a computerized train booking office (daily 8am–2pm) upstairs at the tourist office. Buses to Abu Rd leave Mount Abu every hour between 6am and 9pm (₹30); jeeps leave when full (from next to the bus stand), and taxis can be hired at the corner by the *Jodhpur Bhojnalaya* restaurant for ₹400.

By bus Government buses run from the State Bus Stand on Nakki Lake Rd. Private buses are run by a string of operators along Nakki Lake Rd west of the State Bus Stand (Gujarat Travels is a reliable option). There are currently private services to Ajmer (1 nightly; 7hr), Ahmedabad (3 daily; 6hr), Jaipur (1 nightly; 11hr), Jodhpur (1 daily; 6hr) and Udaipur (3 daily; 4hr).

Tourist information The RSTC Tourist Office (Mon–Sat 10am–1.30pm & 2–5pm; ☏02974 235151) is opposite the main bus stand; there's also information online at ⊚ mountabu.com.

Services To change travellers' cheques the best bet is the Union Bank of India (Mon–Fri 10am–3pm, Sat 10am–12.30pm), hidden away in the bazaar near the post office. The State Bank of India has an ATM in front of the tourist office, and there are two more between there and the polo ground. Internet cafés in the bazaar generally charge ₹30/hr.

Tours *Shri Ganesh* guesthouse runs forest treks and jeep tours (₹600 for the vehicle for 3–4hr) out to places like Achalgarh and Guru Shikar.

2

RECOMMENDED TRAINS FROM ABU ROAD

Destination	Name	No.	Departs	Arrives
Ahmedabad	*Ahmedabad Express*	9224	10.57am (daily)	3pm
	Ahmedabad Mail	9106	12.55pm (daily)	4.55pm
Ajmer	*Aravali Express*	9707	10.02am (daily)	4.25pm
	Haridwar Mail	9105	2.51pm (daily)	8.25pm
Jaipur	*Aravali Express*	9707	10.02am (daily)	6.55pm
	Haridwar Mail	9105	2.51pm (daily)	11pm
Jodhpur	*Jammu Tawi Express*	9223	3.22pm (daily)	8pm
Mumbai (Bandra)	*Aravali Express*	9708	5.10pm (daily)	6.35am
	Surya Nagri Express	2479	11.38pm (daily)	11.35am
New Delhi	*Rajdhani Express*	2957	8.54pm (daily)	7.30am
	Ashram Express	2915	10.05pm (daily)	10.10am

ACCOMMODATION

The steady stream of pilgrims and honeymoon couples ensures that Mount Abu has plenty of hotels, lots of them offering luxuries for newlyweds in special "couple rooms". Check-out time in most places is a chippy 9am. Prices rocket in high season (April–June & Nov–Dec), especially at weekends, reaching their peak during Diwali.

Cama Rajputana Adhar Devi Rd ☎0297 423 8205, ⓦcamahotelsindia.com. Attractive resort-style place occupying a neatly refurbished colonial building in sprawling grounds. Rooms (all a/c) are cool and spacious, while the extensive facilities include a bar, billiard room and a big pool (guests only). Popular with tour groups. ₹6550

★ **Connaught House** Rajendra Rd ☎0297 423 8560, ⓦjodhanaheritage.com. Easily Mount Abu's most memorable accommodation option, occupying a time-warped colonial-era retreat set in a flower-filled garden with sweeping views. Rooms (all a/c) in the old house are beautifully preserved, with period furniture and decor; those in the modern block on the hill above are much less atmospheric. ₹7045

Jaipur House South of the lake ☎0297 423 5176. A fine old summer palace perched on a hilltop above town, with some of the town's best and most spacious accommodation (and superb town views) in tastefully decorated suites with wooden furnishings – although the "deluxe" rooms, in an ugly modern block halfway down the drive, are dull and overpriced. ₹5285

Lake Palace Nakki Lake Rd ☎0297 423 7154, ⓦsavshantihotels.com. One of the town's best mid-range options, in a scenic position facing Nakki Lake, with good service and a range of well-maintained modern rooms (all a/c, the more expensive ones with lake view and balcony). ₹3600

★ **Shri Ganesh** Southwest of the polo ground, near Sophia High School ☎0297 423 7292, ⓔlalit_ganesh@yahoo.co.in. Easily the best budget hotel in town, and the only one geared towards foreign backpackers. Rooms are simple, if shabby (some attached, some with very hard beds), and there are dorm beds (₹100–150/person), plus Indian cooking lessons (₹250), guided walks, jeep tours (see p.217), internet access, and free pick up from the bus stand. ₹300/₹400

Silver Oak 100m north of the main bus stand ☎0297 423 8301, ⓦhotelsilveroak.com. A warm welcome and spacious rooms (some with a/c and modern bathrooms) make this one of the best-value guesthouses in town; request one of the nicer front rooms, which open onto sunny garden terraces. ₹2250

EATING AND DRINKING

Mount Abu's predominantly middle-class Gujarati visitors are typically hard to please when it comes to food, so standards are exceptionally high and prices low. Meat is rare; if you get carniverous cravings, you could try a couple of non-veg Punjabi restaurants in the bazaar.

Arbuda Nakki Lake Rd ☎94144 49794. Perennially popular spot with a huge veggie menu ranging from pizza, burgers and sandwiches through to Chinese, south Indian, Gujarati and Punjabi (mains ₹60–120), as well as good fresh juices. Lightning-fast, friendly service and a popular, airy terrace. Daily 8am–11pm.

Jodhpur Bhojnalaya Nakki Lake Rd, opposite Bank of

Baroda ☎0297 423 5382. The best place in town for authentic Rajasthani veg food, heavy on ghee and spices. It's famous for its definitive *dhal bati churma* (a traditional Rajasthani dish consisting of baked wheatflour balls served with dhal and sweet *churma*, ₹90), and also has the usual big list of Indian veg dishes and thali (₹150). Daily 11am–3pm & 7–11pm.

★ **Kanak Dining Hall** Nakki Lake Rd ☎ 0297 423 8305. Friendly place offering the best Gujarati all-you-can-eat thalis in town – a superb array of subtly spiced veg delicacies for a very modest ₹100/head. Come hungry – portions are limitless. They also have a Punjabi thali (₹120) and a range of veg dishes. Daily 11.30am–3pm & 7–10.30pm.

Mulberry Tree Nakki Lake Rd ☎ 0297 423 8392. The multicuisine non-veg restaurant at *Hotel Hilltone* is Mount Abu's smartest dining option, with tables neatly laid indoors or on the front lawn. From the open kitchen come Indian and continental dishes (₹160-300) including sizzlers, pasta and steak. Licensed. Daily 8–10.30am, noon–3pm & 7.30–10.30pm.

Orignal Gujarat Omlette Nakki Lake Rd. The place to go if you need an eggy snack, omelette sandwiches are ₹40 a go at this little shack – one of a few omelette sellers opposite the northern tip of the Polo Ground.

Sankalp Opposite Hotel Samrat on Nakki Lake Rd ☎ 0297 423 5161. Branch of a south Indian chain offering the usual dishes (*iddlis*, dosas, *uttapams* and the like) in comfortable, modern a/c surrounds, with specialities such as veg pulao (₹85) or tomato *masala uthappa* (₹155), or if you really want to go to town, a 1m-long dosa (₹500). Daily 8am–10pm.

Veena Nakki Lake Rd ☎ 0297 423 8033. Open-air seating next to the main road. Brightly lit and kind of tacky when it's got the latest *filmi* hits blaring out, but the fast food is second to none and they have a welcome open fire on the terrace most evenings. Try a tangy *pao bhaji* (₹50–90) or melt-in-the-mouth dosas (₹60–100). Daily 11am–11pm.

Chittaurgarh

The belt of hilly land east of Udaipur is the most fertile in Rajasthan, watered by several perennial rivers and guarded by a sequence of imposing forts perched atop the craggy ridges that crisscross the region.

The first major settlement you'll come across is the historic town of **CHITTAURGARH** (or **Chittor**), 115km northeast of Udaipur. Of all the former Rajput capitals, Chittaurgarh – former capital of the kingdom or Merwar before Udaipur – was the strongest bastion of Hindu resistance against the Muslim invaders and it is home to one of Rajasthan's most spectacular and historic forts, rising majestically above a verdant tapestry of plains. No less than three mass suicides (*johars*) were committed over the centuries by the female inhabitants of this honey-coloured **fort**. As a symbol of Rajput chivalry and militarism only Jodhpur's Meherangarh Fort compares.

Some visitors squeeze a tour of Chittaurgarh into a day-trip, or en route between Bundi and Udaipur, but it's well worth stopping overnight to give yourself plenty of time to explore the fort properly.

Brief history

The origins of Chittor Fort are obscure, but probably date back to the seventh century. It was seized by **Bappa Rawal**, founder of the Mewar dynasty, in 734, and remained the Mewar capital for the next 834 years, bar a couple of brief interruptions. Despite its commanding position and formidable appearance, however, Chittor was far from invincible, and was sacked three times over the centuries, by **Ala-ud-Din-Khalji** (1303), **Sultan Bahadur Shah** (1535) and **Akbar** (1568). It was this last attack which convinced the then ruler of Mewar, Udai Singh, to decamp to a more remote and easily defensible site at Udaipur. Chittaurgarh was eventually ceded back to the Rajputs in 1616 on condition that it not be refortified, but the royal family of Mewar, by now firmly ensconced in Udaipur, never resettled here, and the entire fort, which once boasted a population of more than 50,000 still houses a couple of thousand people.

The fort

Fort Daily 7am–6pm • ₹100 (₹5), video camera ₹25; plus ₹5/rickshaw; guides ₹250 **Archeological museum** Daily except Fri 10am–5pm • ₹50 • Sound-and-light show; daily 7pm; Fri & Tues in English • ₹200 (₹75) • The fort lies approximately 2km east of town: autos from the bus and train stations should cost ₹150

The entire **fort** is 5km long and 1km wide, and you could easily spend a whole day up here nosing around the myriad remains, although most visitors content themselves

2

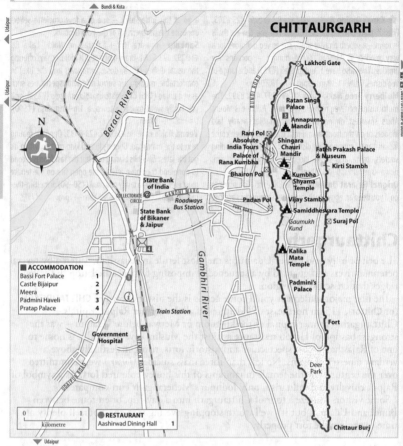

with a few hours. **Tours** of the fort are most easily made by auto-rickshaw (₹300–400 for around 3hr); alternatively, take a rickshaw to the entrance and explore on foot, or (perhaps best) rent a **bike** from the shop on the road leading west from the crossroads outside the station or from Padmini Haveli in the fort (₹150/hr). It's a long, steep climb up to the fort, but most of the roads on the plateau itself are flat.

The ascent to the fort, protected by massive bastions, begins at **Padan Pol** in the east of town and winds upwards through a further six gateways. The houses of those who still inhabit the fort are clustered to the north of the final gate, Rama Pol, where you buy your ticket.

Entering the fort, you first reach the slowly deteriorating fifteenth-century **Palace of Rana Kumbha** (reigned 1433–68), built by the ruler who presided over the period of Mewar's greatest prosperity. The main palace building still stands five storeys high, though it's difficult now to make much sense of the confusing tangle of partially ruined walls and towers. Every evening, hourly sound-and-light shows bring the palace to life, and recount the harrowing history – battles and stories – of the fort.

Opposite the palace stands the intricately carved fifteenth-century **Shingara Chauri Mandir**, a small but lavishly adorned Jain temple dedicated to Shantinath, the sixteenth *tirthankara*. Nearby, the modern **Fateh Prakash Palace**, a large, plain edifice built for the maharana of Udaipur in the 1920s, is home to a small

archeological museum, containing a fine array of Jain and Hindu carvings recovered from various places around the fort.

A couple of hundred metres further on lies the imposing **Kumbha Shyama Temple**, constructed by (and named after) Rana Kumbha. A black statue of Garuda stands in its own pavilion in front of the shrine, while an image of Varaha, the boar incarnation of Vishnu, occupies a niche at the rear. A second shrine stands close by within the small walled enclosure, dedicated to **Meerabai**, a Jodhpur princess and poet famed for her devotion to Krishna.

The Vijay Stambh and beyond

The main road within the fort continues south to its focal point, **Vijay Stambh**, the soaring "tower of victory" erected by Rana Kumbha to commemorate his 1440 victory over the Muslim sultan Mehmud Khilji of Malwa. This magnificent sand-coloured tower, whose nine storeys rise 36m, took a decade to build; its walls are lavishly carved with mythological scenes and images from all Indian religions, including Arabic inscriptions in praise of Allah. You can climb the dark narrow stairs to the very summit for free by showing your fort entry ticket.

The area around the Vijay Stambh is littered with an impressive number of further remains, including a pair of monumental gateways and a number of florid temples, including the superbly decorated **Samiddhesvara Temple**, whose shrine houses an image of the *trimurti*, a composite, three-headed image of Shiva, Brahma and Vishnu. A path leads from here down to the **Gaumukh Kund**, a large reservoir fed by an underground stream that trickles through carved mouths (*mukh*) of cows (*gau*) and commands superb views across the plains.

Buildings further south include the **Kalika Mata Temple**, and **Padmini's Palace**, its rather plain buildings enclosing a series of attractive little walled gardens leading to a tower overlooking the small lake. The road continues south to the point once used for hurling traitors to their deaths, then returns north along the eastern ridge to **Suraj Pol** gate, with spectacular vistas across a patchwork of farmland. Several temples line the route, but the most impressive monument is **Kirti Stambh**. The inspiration for the tower of victory, this smaller "tower of fame" was built by Digambaras as a monument to the first *tirthankara* Adinath, whose unclad image appears throughout its six storeys.

ARRIVAL AND INFORMATION   CHITTAURGARH

By train Chittaurgarh's railway station is to the south of the city.

By bus The Roadways (aka "Kothwali") Bus Stand is on the west bank of the Ghambiri, 2km north of the train station. There are buses to Ajmer (7 daily; 5hr), Bundi (3 daily; 4hr 30min), Udaipur (roughly hourly; 2hr 30min) and Kota (2 daily; 4hr 30min).

Tourist information The RTDC tourist office (Mon–Sat 10am–1.30pm & 2–5pm; ☎01472 241089) stands just north of the railway station on Station Rd and has details

RECOMMENDED TRAINS FROM CHITTAURGARH

Destination	Name	No.	Departs	Arrives
Ajmer	*Udaipur–Ajmer Express*	2991	8.42am (daily)	11.25pm
	Ratlam–Ajmer Express	9653	10.10am (daily)	1.55pm
Bundi	*City Link Express*	9019	2.55pm (daily)	5.33pm
	Mewar Express	2964	8.50pm (daily)	10.40pm
Jaipur	*Gwalior Superfast*	9666	12.35am (daily)	6am
	Udaipur Jaipur Express	2991	8.42am (daily)	1.25am
Kota	*Nimach–Kota Express*	9019	2.55pm (daily)	6.50pm
New Delhi	*Mewar Express*	2964	8.50pm (daily)	6.30am
Udaipur	*Mewar Express*	2963	5.05am (daily)	7.20am
	Ajmer–Udaipur Express	2992	7.25pm (daily)	9.30pm

of registered guides (from ₹250 for up to 4hr).

Services None of the banks exchange money. There are many internet cafés (typically ₹30/hr) and ATMs around Collectorate Circle. You can purchase train tickets and arrange taxis through the *Padmini Haveli* (see below) in the fort – the owners are both registered national guides and can arrange day–trips to Bassi villages and Bijaipur through their travel agency, Absolute India Tours. They also rent good mountain bicycles for ₹150/hr.

ACCOMMODATION AND EATING

Accommodation in Chittor is relatively pricey; the only really cheap places are the slightly grim hotels around the railway station and in the middle of town. You'll probably end up eating where you're staying, unless you fancy trying one of the rough-and-ready *dhabas* in the town centre or around the railway station. If you're just coming to the fort for the day, arrange a delicious veg lunch (₹400) at the *Padmini Haveli*; book a day in advance.

Aashirwad Dining Hall Next to Shree Ji Hotel ☎94141 10110. Popular little veg thali joint (₹70) open for lunch only. Daily noon–3pm.

Bassi Fort Palace Bassi, 24km east of Chittaurgarh ☎0147 222 5321, ⓦbassifortpalace.com. Attractive heritage hotel, occupying the town's florid palace, with sixteen comfortable rooms and spacious grounds where a sacred tree is believed to grant all one's wishes. **₹2250**

Castle Bijaipur ☎0147 227 6351, ⓦcastlebijaipur .com. This lovely hotel occupies a superb 350-year-old castle set in a tranquil and unspoilt rural location a 45min (32km) drive east of Chittor. Rooms are decorated with traditional Rajasthani wooden furniture and artefacts, and there's a pool, Ayurvedic massages, daily group yoga and meditation sessions (individual tuition on request), plus cycle, jeep and horse safaris to nearby villages. They also have tented accommodation (₹4800) a few kilometres away in an even more remote rural location at Pangarh Lake. Breakfast included. **₹4800**

Meera Neemuch Rd ☎0147 224 0266, ⓦhotelmeerachittaurgarh.com. The best cheapie in town, with a wide selection of fan and a/c rooms, and some very quirkily decorated suites; facilities include an inexpensive restaurant and a good bar. **₹860**

★ **Padmini Haveli** Anna Poorna Temple Rd, Fort ☎0147 224 1251, ⓦthepadminihaveli.com. Easily the best place to stay in town, right in the heart of Chittor Fort. Run by a charming husband-and-wife team – both national guides – and their family, this is authentic Rajasthani hospitality at its best, and the pure veg food is excellent. Rooms (all a/c) are characterful and adorned with beautiful fabrics and (unusually) Hermès sculptures; bathrooms feature solid granite sinks. Views from the rooftop sunset terrace are spectacular. **₹3200**

Pratap Palace Opposite the GPO on Shri Gurukul Rd ☎0147 224 0099, ⓦhotelpratappalacechittaurgarh .com. Functional mid-range hotel, a bit shabby in places, but with an attractive garden and good food. The smarter deluxe rooms are best (though rather expensive); the cheaper rooms are relatively unappealing and overpriced. They have a decent non-veg restaurant (mains ₹150–400; daily 8am–10pm) and can also arrange countryside tours from *Castle Bijaipur* (see above). **₹2500**

Bundi

The walled town of **BUNDI**, 37km north of Kota, lies in the north of the former Hadoti state, shielded by jagged outcrops of the Vindhya Range. The site was the capital of the Hadachauhans, but although settled in 1241, 25 years before neighbouring Kota, Bundi never amounted to more than a modest market centre, and remains relatively untouched by modern development. The palace alone justifies a visit thanks to its superb collection of **murals**, while the well-preserved **old town**, crammed with crumbling havelis, picturesque old bazaars and a surprising number of flamboyant *baoris* or "step-wells" (giant water tanks designed to collect the precious monsoon rains), makes this one of southern Rajasthan's most appealing destinations – a fact recognized by the ever-increasing numbers of foreign tourists who are now visiting the place.

The palace

Daily 8am–7pm • ₹100 (₹25), camera ₹50, video ₹100 • If you want a guide, try the extremely informative Keshav Bhati (☎94143 94241, @bharat_bhati@yahoo.com) who charges around ₹600 (plus palace entry fees) for a tour of the entire palace, and also offers city tours and visits to regional sights, including his hometown of Kota

Bundi's **palace** was one of the few royal abodes in Rajasthan untouched by Mughal influence, and its appearance is surprisingly homogenous considering the number of times it was added to over the years.

A short steep path winds up to the main gateway, **Hathi Pol**, surmounted by elephant carvings, beyond which lies the palace's principal courtyard. On the right-hand side, steps lead up to the **Ratan Doulat**, the early seventeenth-century Diwan-i-Am, or Hall of Public Audience, an open terrace with a simple marble throne overlooking the courtyard below.

At the far end of the Ratan Daulat, further steps lead up to the **Chhatra Mahal**. Go through the open-sided turquoise-painted pavilion on the southern side of the courtyard and the room beyond to reach a superb little **antechamber** (or "dressing room"), every surface covered in finely detailed murals from the 1780s embellished with gold and silver leaf. The opposite side of the courtyard is flanked by a pavilion with columns supported on the backs of quaint black trumpeting elephants, at the back of which you'll find a well-preserved old squat toilet, offering the best view from any public convenience in Rajasthan.

From the Chhatra Mahal courtyard, a narrow flight of steps leads up to an even smaller courtyard flanked by the superbly decorated **Phool Mahal** (built in 1607,

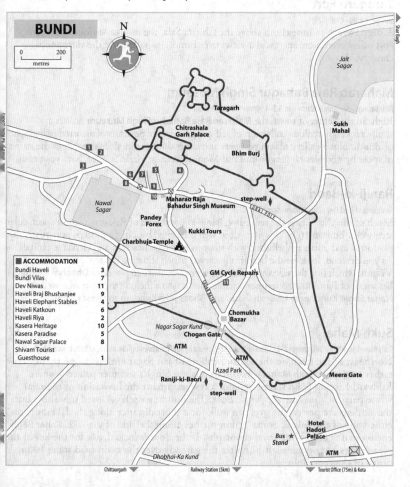

BUNDI

N

0   200
metres

Jait Sagar

Taragarh

Chitrashala Garh Palace

Sukh Mahal

Bhim Burj

Nawal Sagar

step-well

Maharao Raja Bahadur Singh Museum

Pandey Forex

Kukki Tours

Charbhuja Temple

ACCOMMODATION

Bundi Haveli	3
Bundi Vilas	7
Dev Niwas	11
Haveli Braj Bhushanjee	9
Haveli Elephant Stables	4
Haveli Katkoun	6
Haveli Riya	2
Kasera Heritage	10
Kasera Paradise	5
Nawal Sagar Palace	8
Shivam Tourist Guesthouse	1

GM Cycle Repairs

Chomukha Bazar

Nagar Sagar Kund

Chogan Gate

ATM

ATM

Azad Park

Meera Gate

Raniji-ki-Baori

step-well

Hotel Hadoti Palace

Bus Stand

ATM

Dhabhai-Ka Kund

Chittaurgarh   Railway Station (5km)   Tourist Office (75m) & Kota

though the murals date from the 1860s), whose murals include a vast procession featuring regiments of soldiers in European dress and a complete camel corps.

From here, further narrow steps ascend to the **Badal Mahal** (Cloud Palace), home to what are often regarded as the finest paintings in the whole of southern Rajasthan. A vividly coloured ring of Krishnas and Radhas dance around the highest part of the vaulted dome, flanked by murals showing Krishna being driven to his wedding by Ganesh, and Rama returning from Sri Lanka to Ayodhya.

Chittra Sala

Sunrise–sunset • Free

There are further outstanding murals in the **Chittra Sala**, just above the palace. At the rear left-hand corner of the garden inside, steps lead up to a small courtyard embellished with an outstanding sequence of murals painted in an unusual muted palette of turquoises, blues and blacks, the majority devoted to magical depictions of scenes from the life of Krishna.

Taragarh Fort

Sunrise–sunset • ₹100 (₹25)

A steep twenty-minute climb above the Chittra Sala, the monkey-infested **Taragarh Fort** offers even more spectacular views over Bundi, its palace and the surrounding countryside.

Maharao Raja Bahadur Singh Museum

Near Surang Gate • Daily 9.30am–1pm & 2–4.30pm • ₹50, camera ₹50

Right in the centre of town, the **Maharao Raja Bahadur Singh Museum** houses a skull-crackingly tedious collection of self-congratulatory portraits of assorted maharajas of Bundi, plus a gallery of stuffed tigers and other dumb animals massacred in the name of sport by notables ranging from Lord Mountbatten to Haile Selassie. Save your cash.

Raniji-ki-Baori

Southwest of Azad Park • Daily 9.30am–5pm • ₹70 (₹15)

South of the Old City is the rewarding **Raniji-ki-Baori**, one of Rajasthan's most spectacular step-wells. Built in 1699, this 46m-deep well is reached by a flight of steps punctuated by platforms and pillars embellished with sinuous S-shaped brackets and elephant capitals. As you descend, look for the beautifully carved panels showing the ten avatars of Lord Vishnu, which line the side walls. The nineteenth-century step-well of **Dhabhai-ka Kund** lies south of Ranji-ki-Baori; other notable Bundi *baoris* include the twin step-wells of **Nagar Sagar Kund**, near Chogan Gate, and **Bhora-ji-ka Kund**, to the west of town.

Sukh Mahal

Daily 9am–5pm • ₹50 (₹20), camera ₹50 • Count on around ₹80 return by auto from town to Sukh Mahal, or ₹120 to Kshar Bagh

Northeast of the town on the southern shore of Jait Sagar tank is the pretty but now rather neglected **Sukh Mahal** – Rao Raja Vishnu Singh's summer palace – where Rudyard Kipling (who stayed here for a few months at the invitation of the raja) wrote parts of *Kim* and *The Jungle Book*. The building itself is closed to visitors but the gardens are pretty, and you can walk for a short distance along the lakeshore on either side of the palace. Some 1.5km further along the side of the lake, **Kshar Bagh** encloses sixty crumbling royal cenotaphs. If the door is locked, ask for the key at the *chowkidar*'s hut on your left just after the gateway over the main road some 100m north of the cenotaphs.

ARRIVAL AND INFORMATION

By train The railway station is around 5km south of town (₹100 or so by auto-rickshaw). Two evening trains run to Kota: *Kota Express* #29019 (dep. 5.35pm, arr. 6.50pm) and *Merwar Express* #2964 (dep. 22.42pm, arr. 23.40pm). To Chittaurgarh there are morning trains at 7.20am (*Haldighati Passenger* #59812, arr. 10.50am) and 9.38am (*Dehra Dun Express* #29020, arr. 12.05pm). The *Mewar Express* #2963, which currently passes through Bundi at 2.04am nightly, arrives in Udaipur at 7.20am.

By bus Buses arrive in the southeast part of town near the post office, from where it's around ₹40 by auto-rickshaw to the palace and guesthouses. Heading south, there are regular buses to Kota (every 30min; 45min–1hr), and services to Chittaurgarh (2 daily; 4hr) and Udaipur (3 daily; 6hr 30min). Heading north, there are buses to Sawai Madhopur (for Ranthambore National Park; 4 daily; 4hr 30min); alternatively, take a bus to Kota and a train from there (see p.227). Buses are the best way of reaching Ajmer (every 30min; 4hr), Jaipur (every 30min; 5hr) and Jodhpur (4 daily; 10hr).

BUNDI

Tourist information The town's tourist office (Mon–Fri 9.30am–6pm; ☎0747 244 3697) is south of town near the Circuit House.

Services You can change money at Pandey Forex, about 100m south of the palace, and at the *Kasera Heritage* guesthouse; there are also several ATMs in the southern end of town. Dozens of places offer internet access from ₹40/hr. Lots of places rent out motorbikes (from ₹250/day), and a few also have bicycles (around ₹50/day; try GM Cycle Repairs in the bazaar). The *Hadoti Palace Hotel*'s big pool costs ₹400/hr.

Events The annual Bundi Festival takes place around mid-November, and is a celebration of Hadoti heritage with a very local, country-fair feel.

Tours Jovial archaeology enthusiast "Kukki" (☎98284 04527) runs engaging half-day and full-day tours (from ₹600) to prehistoric rock painting sites in Bundi's rural hinterland, plus visits to villages and vulture colonies.

ACCOMMODATION AND EATING

★ **Bundi Haveli** 107 Balchand Para ☎0747 244 6716, ⊕hotelbundihaveli.com. Traditional old haveli given a stylish contemporary makeover, with beautifully furnished a/c rooms (many with *jharokhas*), a pretty rooftop restaurant (non-veg mains ₹175–260) and facilities including wi-fi, internet access and money exchange. Excellent value at current rates. ₹1235

★ **Bundi Vilas** Balchand Para ☎0747 512 0694, ⊕bundivilas.com. Tucked up against the palace's lower rampart walls, the seven charming rooms and suites (all a/c) of this 300-year-old family-run haveli are tastefully decorated and high on creature comforts. There's a pretty rooftop restaurant, and the rooftop suites are the most romantic in town. ₹4100

Dev Niwas Opposite Purani Kothwali ☎98290 42128, ⊕devniwas.com. Otherwise known as the *Maaji Sahib ki Haveli*, this sociable guesthouse dates back three centuries and is home to 21 clean rooms and suites (all with attached bathrooms and a/c), plus a nice rooftop restaurant. ₹1200

Haveli Braj Bhushanjee Near Surang Gate ☎0747 244 2322, ⊕kiplingsbundi.com. Wonderfully atmospheric 150-year-old haveli, with original murals, antiques and assorted artworks adorning virtually every surface. Rooms (all a/c and TV) are similarly engaging, and immaculately maintained. ₹1285

Haveli Elephant Stables Palace Approach Rd ☎99281 54064, ✉elephantstable_guesthouse@hotmail.com. Accommodation in the palace's former elephant stables, a pretty and very peaceful spot underneath the fort's huge walls. Rooms (fan and air-cooled, the cheapest with squat toilet) are basic, but at this price and in this location you

can't really complain. ₹250

Haveli Katkoun Balchand Para ☎0747 244 4311, ⊕havelikatkoun.free.fr. Budget guesthouse with gleaming marble floors and a range of spacious and smart single/double rooms, the best of which have a/c and palace views. ₹500

Haveli Riya Balchand Para ☎0747 244 4211. Friendly family guesthouse with a selection of rooms at bargain prices, some a little basic, but all neat and clean. There's a nice little rooftop café. ₹250

Kasera Paradise Near Surang Gate ☎0747 244 4679, ⊕kaseraparadise.com. Tucked away in a peaceful little lane just behind the *Braj Bhushanjee*, this attractive guesthouse occupies a meticulously restored sixteenth-century haveli with a range of variously priced a/c rooms, all nicely furnished and decorated with traditional murals. Their *Out of the Blue* rooftop restaurant serves decent pasta and pizzas (₹130–190) and sibling *Kasera Heritage* (₹1000) has more rooms just over the road. ₹1200

Nawal Sagar Palace Balchand Para ☎0747 230 0644, ⊕nawalsagarpalace.com. Situated right beside the lake, this recently renovated hotel has spacious and clean heritage rooms (the more expensive with a/c and lake views), plus an emerald lawn and decent rooftop restaurant. ₹400

Shivam Tourist Guesthouse Balchand Para ☎0747 244 7892, ⊕shivam-bundi.co.in. Extremely sociable little family guesthouse with friendly management, eight clean and pleasantly decorated attached rooms (the best on the upper floors), good home cooking (plus cooking classes) and free wi-fi. ₹300

Kota

KOTA, 230km south of Jaipur on a fertile plain fed by Rajasthan's largest river, the Chambal, is one of the state's dirtier and less appealing cities. With a population nudging 700,000, it is one of Rajasthan's major commercial and industrial hubs, with hydro, atomic and thermal power stations lining the banks of the Chambal, alongside Asia's largest fertilizer plant, whose enormous chimneys provide a not-very-scenic backdrop to many views of the town. Kota is worth a visit if only for its fine city palace, which houses one of the better museums in Rajasthan, while the old town has a commercial hustle and bustle, which makes a nice contrast to somnolent Bundi, a 45-minute drive away.

City Palace

Maharao Madho Singh Museum Daily except official holidays 10am–4.30pm; it's possible to visit the museum out of hours for an extra ₹30 • Combined entrance to museum and palace ₹150 (₹25) including camera, video ₹100

On the southern side of the town centre, around 2km from the bus station, lies the **City Palace**, a well-preserved cluster of blue and pink royal residences; construction on them began in 1625 and continued sporadically until the early years of the twentieth century. The palace now houses the excellent **Maharao Madho Singh Museum**. The first room is filled with a selection of luxury items belonging to the maharaja, while diagonally across the courtyard lies the dazzling **Raj Mahal**, built by Rao Madho Singh (ruled 1625–49), richly decorated with paintings and mirrorwork, which served as the ruler's public audience hall. From the Raj Mahal, a corridor leads into a further sequence of rooms housing a well-stocked armoury and a small art gallery, and a depressing wildlife gallery, filled with the moth-eaten remains of various leopards and tigers.

Exit the museum then follow the steps up past the Raj Mahal to reach a series of finely painted palace buildings. Three storeys up is the **Barah Mahal**, one of whose rooms is richly decorated with dozens of square miniatures placed together on the wall like tiles and depicting a range of religious and contemporary scenes, from Krishna lifting Mount Goverdhan to exotic-looking European ladies and gentlemen.

Kishore Sagar and around

Government Museum Daily except official holidays 10am–5pm • ₹50 (₹5); no cameras

Kishore Sagar, an artificial lake built in 1346, gives some visual relief from the city's grim industrial backdrop, if its water levels are buoyant; the red-and-white palace in its centre, **Jag Mandir**, was commissioned by Prince Dher Deh of Bundi in 1346. On the northern edge of the lake the dusty **Government Museum** serves as the dispiriting home for an excellent collection of local stone carvings, extracted from local temples in the Hadoti (Bundi-Kota) region (signs in Hindi only, if at all).

On the edge of the river a few kilometres south of the fort, crocodiles and gharial sometimes sun themselves in a shallow pond in the **Chambal Gardens** (₹5); boats from here offer leisurely jaunts (₹500 for up to five people for 1hr) on the crocodile-infested River Chambal.

RECOMMENDED TRAINS FROM KOTA

Destination	Name	No.	Departs	Arrives
Agra	*Avadh Express* (Agra Fort)	9037	2.50pm (Mon, Wed, Thurs & Sat)	9.55pm
	Haldighati Passenger	59811	9pm (daily)	6am
Bundi	*Dehra Dun Express*	9020A	9am (daily)	9.36am
Chittaurgarh	*Dehra Dun Express*	9020A	9am (daily)	12.05pm
Jaipur	*Dayodaya Express*	2181	8am (daily)	11.50pm
	Jaipur Express	2955	8.50am (daily)	12.50pm
	Ranthambore Express	2465	12.34pm (daily)	4.45pm
Mumbai (Central)	*Jaipur–Mumbai SF*	2956	5.35pm (daily)	7.40am
New Delhi (Nizamuddin)	*Kota Jan Shatabdi*	2059	5.55am (daily)	12.30pm
	Golden Temple Mail	2903	11.15am (daily)	6.35pm
	Mewar Express	2964	11.55pm (daily)	6.30am
Sawai Madhopur (for Ranthambore National Park)	*Dayodaya Express*	2181	8am (daily)	9.30am
	Golden Temple Mail	2903	11.15am (daily)	12.25
	Ranthambore Express	2465	12.40pm (daily)	2.25pm
	Dehra Dun Express	9019	7.30pm (daily)	9.10pm

ARRIVAL AND INFORMATION   KOTA

By train Kota is a surprisingly large and sprawling city, and you'll need a rickshaw to cover the sights, especially if arriving at the railway station, 2km to the north of town.

By bus Arriving at the central bus stand just north of Kishore Sagar, on Bundi Rd, it's a long but feasible walk through the bustling main bazaar to the City Palace. Buses leave regularly to Bundi (every 7min 7am–8.30pm; 45min–1hr), Ajmer (every 30min; 6hr), Chittor (5 daily; 4hr), Jaipur (every 30min; 6hr) and Udaipur (7 daily; 6hr). Services to Ajmer and Udaipur usually stop in Bundi en route.

Tourist information Kota's Tourist Office (Mon–Fri 9am–5pm; ☎0744 232 7695) is in the *RTDC Chambal Hotel*, just north of the Kishor Sagar.

Services The best place for changing travellers' cheques is the inconveniently located State Bank of Bikaner & Jaipur (Mon–Fri 9.30am–5pm & Sat 9.30am–2pm) in the south of town. There are several ATMs scattered around the road intersection by the *Navrang* hotel.

ACCOMMODATION AND EATING

Brijraj Bhawan Civil Lines ☎0744 245 0529, ⓦindianheritagehotels.com. An idyllic retreat in the heart of noisy Kota, occupying a fine old colonial mansion set in a peaceful spot overlooking the river. Rooms are pure Victorian period pieces, all scrupulously maintained and very comfortable. ₹6710

Navrang Station Rd ☎0744 232 3294. The nicest cheap hotel in town, with a mix of simple air-cooled and more attractively furnished a/c rooms, all with TV. There's also a modern pure veg restaurant (*Venue*), which has a good selection of north Indian veg mains (mains (₹60–95) plus dosas, pizzas and Chinese dishes. The adjacent *Phul Plaza* is reasonable too, but not quite so appealing. ₹600

Sukhdham Kothi Civil Lines ☎0744 232 0081, ⓦsukhdhamkothi.com. Marvellously atmospheric guesthouse located in a hundred-year-old stone mansion set amid extensive gardens. Comfy and atmospheric rooms with old wooden furniture and assorted nineteenth-century bric-a-brac. ₹1900

Umed Bhawan Palace Palace/Station Rd, Khelri Phatak ☎0744 232 5262, ⓦwelcomheritagehotels .com. Occupying a huge and rather ugly former royal residence, this fancy hotel offers upmarket comforts (and a fair bit of chintz) at a reasonable price. ₹6560

Uttar Pradesh

THE TAJ MAHAL

Uttar Pradesh

Uttar Pradesh, "the Northern State" – formerly the United Provinces, but always UP – is the heartland of Hinduism and Hindi, dominating the nation in culture, religion, language and politics. A vast, steamy plain of the Ganges, it boasts a history that's very much the history of India, and its temples and monuments – Buddhist, Hindu and Muslim – are among the most impressive in the country.

Western UP, which adjoins Delhi, has always been close to India's centre of power. Its main city, **Agra**, once the Mughal capital, is home to the Taj Mahal, and a short hop from the abandoned Mughal city of Fatehpur Sikri. **Central UP** constituted the **Kingdom of Avadh**, the last centre of independent Muslim rule in northern India until the British unceremoniously took it over, fuelling the resentment that led to the 1857 uprising, in which its capital **Lucknow** (now UP's state capital), played such a celebrated role.

In **eastern UP** lies Hinduism's holiest city, the *tirtha* (crossing-place) of **Varanasi**, where it's believed death transports the soul to final liberation. Sacred since antiquity, it was frequented by Mahavira, the founder of Jainism, and also by Buddha, who preached his first sermon in nearby **Sarnath**.

Although UP was once a thriving centre of Islamic jurisprudence and culture, many Muslims departed during the years after Independence, and the Muslim population now comprises just eighteen percent. As the heart of what is known as the "cow belt" (equivalent to America's "bible belt"), UP has been plagued by caste politics and was for some years dominated by the Hindu sectarian BJP. It acquired an unfortunate reputation as the focus of bitter communal tensions, most notoriously in the wake of the 1992 destruction of the Babri Masjid mosque in **Ayodhya** (east of Lucknow, near Faizabad), which sparked off sectarian riots across India. In recent years, state politics have been dominated by two largely local left-wing parties, the socialist Samajwadi party (SP) and the mainly low-caste Bahujan Samaj party (BSP).

Agra

The splendour of **AGRA** – India's capital under the Mughals – remains undiminished, from the massive fort to the magnificent **Taj Mahal**. Along with Delhi, 204km northwest, and Jaipur in Rajasthan, Agra is the third apex of the "Golden Triangle", India's most popular tourist itinerary. Although it's possible to see Agra on a day-trip from Delhi, the Taj alone deserves so much more – a fleeting visit would miss the subtleties of its many moods, as the light changes from sunrise to sunset – while the city's other sights and Fatehpur Sikri can easily fill several days.

Most of the city's major Mughal monuments, including the Taj Mahal, are lined up along the banks of the **Yamuna River**, which bounds the city's eastern edge. They date

VARANASI

Highlights

❶ Taj Mahal The world's most beautiful building, and India's top tourist sight, marking the zenith and prefection of Mughal architecture, never fails to impress. **See p.233**

❷ Akbar's mausoleum, Sikandra The great Mughal's tomb looks just as it does in old miniatures, with tame monkeys and deer wandering in its ornamental gardens. **See p.241**

❸ Fatehpur Sikri An awesomely grand, deserted palace complex in what was once the imperial capital of Mughal India, straddling an arid ridge near the Rajasthani border. **See p.247**

❹ Kalinjar Fort In the dusty badlands on the southern edge of the state, and well off the usual tourist trail, this remote fort well repays the effort of getting to it. **See p.268**

❺ Varanasi Take a boat on the Ganges before dawn to watch the sun rise over India's most ancient and sacred city. **See p.269**

❻ Sarnath Evocative ruins on the site where the Buddha gave his first sermon. **See p.282**

HIGHLIGHTS ARE MARKED ON THE MAP ON P.232

from the later phase of Mughal rule and the reigns of Akbar, Jahangir and Shah Jahan – exemplifying the ever-increasing extravagance which, by Shah Jahan's time, had already begun to strain the imperial coffers and sow the seeds of political and military decline.

Brief history

Agra remained a minor administrative centre until 1504, when the Delhi sultan, **Sikandar Lodi**, moved his capital here to keep a check on the warring factions of his empire. The ruins of his city can still be seen on the Yamuna River's east bank. After defeating the last Lodi sultan, Ibrahim Lodi, at Panipat in 1526, **Babur**, the founder of the Mughal empire, sent ahead his son **Humayun** to capture Agra. In gratitude for their benevolent treatment at his hands, the family of the raja of Gwalior rewarded the

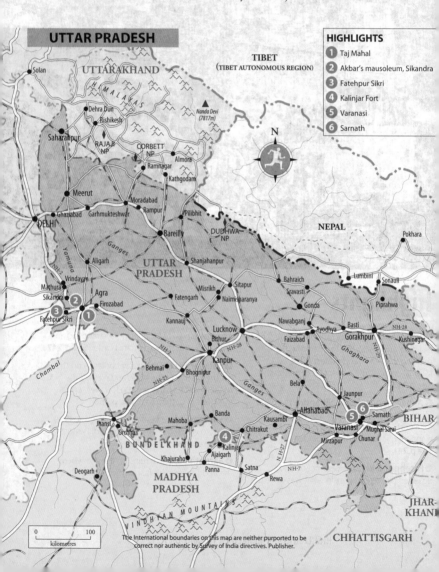

UTTAR PRADESH

HIGHLIGHTS

1. Taj Mahal
2. Akbar's mausoleum, Sikandra
3. Fatehpur Sikri
4. Kalinjar Fort
5. Varanasi
6. Sarnath

The international boundaries on this map are neither purported to be correct nor authentic by Survey of India directives. Publisher.

Mughal with jewellery and precious stones – among them the legendary **Koh-i-noor Diamond**, now among Britain's crown jewels.

Agra saw its heyday under Humayun's son, **Akbar the Great** (1556–1605), when Agra Fort was built, and it remained the empire's capital for more than a century. Even when **Shah Jahan**, Jahangir's son and successor, built a new city in Delhi – Shahjahanabad, now known as Old Delhi – his heart remained in Agra. He pulled down many of the earlier red-sandstone structures in the fort, replacing them with his trademark – exquisite marble buildings. The empire flourished under his successor Aurangzeb (1658–1707), although his intolerance towards non-Muslims stirred up a hornets' nest. Agra was occupied successively by the Jats, the Marathas and eventually the British.

The Taj Mahal

Described by Bengali poet Rabindranath Tagore as "a teardrop on the face of eternity", the **Taj Mahal** is undoubtedly the zenith of Mughal architecture. Volumes have been written on its perfection, and its image adorns countless glossy brochures and guidebooks; nonetheless, the reality never fails to overwhelm all who see it, and few words can do it justice.

The magic of the monument is strangely undiminished by the crowds of tourists who visit, as small and insignificant as ants in the face of the immense mausoleum. That said, the Taj is at its most alluring in the relative quiet of early morning, shrouded in mist and bathed with a soft red glow. As its vast marble surfaces fall into shadow or reflect the sun, its colour changes from soft grey and yellow to pearly cream and dazzling white. This play of light is an important decorative device, symbolically implying the presence of Allah, who is never represented in physical form. To really appreciate it fully however, you'd have to stick around from dawn until dusk.

Overlooking the Yamuna River, the Taj Mahal stands at the northern end of a vast walled garden. Though its layout follows a distinctly Islamic theme, representing Paradise, it is above all a monument to romantic love. **Shah Jahan** built the Taj to enshrine the body of his favourite wife, Arjumand Bann Begum, better known by her official palace title, **Mumtaz Mahal** ("Chosen One of the Palace"), who died shortly after giving birth to her fourteenth child in 1631 – the number of children she bore the emperor is itself a tribute to her hold on him, given the number of other wives and concubines that the emperor would have been able to call on. The emperor was devastated by her death, and set out to create an unsurpassed monument to her memory – its name, "Taj Mahal", is simply a shortened, informal version of Mumtaz Mahal's palace title. Construction by a workforce of some twenty thousand men from all over Asia commenced in 1632 and took more than twenty years, not being completed until 1653. Marble was brought from Makrana, near Ajmer in Rajasthan, and semi-precious stones for decoration – onyx, amethyst, lapis lazuli, turquoise, jade, crystal, coral and mother-of-pearl – were carried to Agra from Persia, Russia, Afghanistan, Tibet, China and the Indian Ocean. Eventually, Shah Jahan's pious and intolerant son Aurangzeb seized power, and the former emperor was interned in Agra Fort, where as legend would have it he lived out his final years gazing wistfully at the Taj Mahal. When he died in January 1666, his body was carried across the river to lie alongside his beloved wife in his peerless tomb.

The Chowk-i-Jilo Khana

The south, east and west **entrances** all lead into the **Chowk-i-Jilo Khana** forecourt. The main entrance into the complex, an arched gateway topped with delicate domes and adorned with Koranic verses and inlaid floral designs, stands at the northern edge of Chowk-i-Jilo Khana, directly aligned with the Taj, but shielding it from the view of those who wait outside.

The charbagh

Once through the gateway from the Chowk-i-Jilo Khana, you'll see the Taj itself at the end of the huge **charbagh** (literally "four gardens"), a garden dissected into four quadrants by waterways (usually dry), evoking the Koranic description of Paradise, where rivers flow with water, milk, wine and honey. Introduced by Babur from Central Asia, *charbaghs* remained fashionable throughout the Mughal era. Unlike other Mughal mausoleums such as Akbar's (see p.241) and Humayun's (see p.89), the Taj isn't at the centre of the *charbagh*, but at the northern end, presumably to exploit its riverside setting.

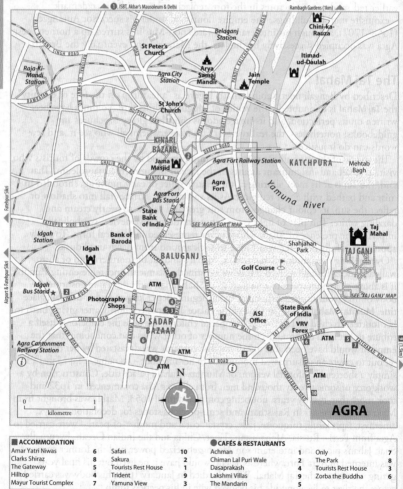

THE TAJ MAHAL: A MONUMENT UNDER THREAT

Despite the seemingly impregnable sense of serenity and other-worldliness which clings to the Taj, in reality, India's most famous building faces **serious threats** from traffic and industrial pollution, and from the millions of tourists who visit it each year. Marble is all but impervious to the onslaught of wind and rain that erodes softer sandstone, but it has no natural defence against the sulphur dioxide that lingers in a dusty haze and shrouds the monument; sometimes the smog is so dense that the tomb cannot be seen from the fort. Sulphur dioxide mixes with atmospheric moisture and settles as sulphuric acid on the surface of the tomb, making the smooth white marble yellow and flaky, and forming a subtle fungus that experts have named "marble cancer".

The main sources of pollution are the continuous flow of **vehicles** along the national highways that skirt the city, and the seventeen hundred **factories** in and around Agra – chemical effluents belched out from their chimneys are well beyond recommended safety limits. Despite laws demanding the installation of pollution-control devices, the imposition of a ban on all petrol- and diesel-fuelled traffic within 500m of the Taj Mahal, and an exclusion zone banning new industrial plants from an area of 10,400 square kilometres around the complex, pollutants in the atmosphere have continued to rise.

Cleaning work on the Taj Mahal rectifies the problem to some extent, but the chemicals used will themselves eventually affect the marble – attendants already shine their torches on "repaired" sections of marble to demonstrate how they've lost their translucency. The government has responded by setting up a pollution monitoring station to check on levels of N_2O and SO_2 in the atmosphere, but in 2007 a parliamentary committee reported that, aside from the threat from these acidic gases, particulate matter in the air was slowly turning the Taj yellow; the report recommended treatment with a non-corrosive clay pack – something like a building-sized face-pack – to remove particle deposits from the marble.

From time to time scare reports surface to the effect that the Taj's four minarets are listing and in danger of keeling over. Luckily, this proves to be a false alarm: the minarets were deliberately constructed leaning slightly outwards in order to counteract an optical illusion which would have made them appear to lean inwards when seen from ground level if they were actually exactly vertical. Despite their lean, they are quite stable.

The Taj

At the far end of the *charbagh*, steps up to the high square marble platform on which the **mausoleum** itself sits, each corner marked by a tall, tapering minaret. To the west of the tomb is a domed red-sandstone **mosque** and to the east a replica **jawab**, put there to complete the architectural symmetry of the complex – it cannot be used as a mosque as it faces away from Mecca.

The Taj is essentially square in shape, with pointed arches cut into its sides and topped with a huge central dome that rises for over 55m, its height accentuated by a crowning brass spire almost 17m high. On approach, the tomb looms ever larger and grander, but not until you are close do you appreciate both its sheer size and the extraordinarily fine detail of relief carving, highlighted by floral patterns of precious stones. Arabic verses praising the glory of Paradise fringe the archways, proportioned exactly so that each letter appears to be the same size when viewed from the ground.

The south face of the tomb is the main entrance to the **interior:** a high octagonal chamber whose weirdly echoing interior is flushed with pale light. A marble screen, decorated with precious stones and cut so finely that it seems almost translucent, protects the cenotaph of Mumtaz Mahal in the centre, perfectly aligned with the doorway and the distant gateway into the Chowk-i-Jilo Khana, and that of Shah Jahan crammed in next to it – the only object which breaks the perfect symmetry of the entire complex. The inlay work on the marble tombs is the finest in Agra, and no pains were spared in perfecting it – some of the petals and leaves are made of up to sixty separate stone fragments. Ninety-nine names of Allah adorn the top of Mumtaz's tomb, and set into Shah Jahan's is a pen box, the hallmark of a male ruler. These cenotaphs, in accordance with Mughal tradition, are only representations of the real coffins, which lie in the same positions in a crypt below.

The museum

In theory daily except Fri 9am–5pm (but sometimes closed for no apparent reason) • ₹5

The Taj's **museum**, in the enclosure's western wall, features exquisite miniature paintings, two marble pillars believed to have come from the fort and portraits of Mughal rulers including Shah Jahan and Mumtaz Mahal, as well as architectural drawings of the Taj and examples of *pietra dura* stone inlay work.

INFORMATION

TAJ MAHAL

Opening hours Daily except Fri, sunrise–sunset.

Tickets ₹750 (₹20); ticket valid all day, but only for one entrance; also gives tax-free entry to other sites if used on the same day, giving ₹50 off the admission fee at Agra Fort, and ₹10 off at Sikandra, Itimad-ud-daulah and Fatehpur Sikri. Ticket queues are longest at the west gate; shortest at the south gate; the east gate ticket office is 500m down the road, by the Shilpgram crafts village. You are not allowed to enter with food (and none is available inside), nor with a mobile phone or a travel guidebook – these can be deposited at lockers near the entrances. Foreigners are given a free bottle of water and a pair of shoe covers on entry.

Night visits It's possible to see the Taj by moonlight on the night of the full moon itself and on the two days before and after. Four hundred visitors are admitted per night (in batches of fifty between 8pm and midnight, but not on Fridays or during Ramadan). Tickets (₹750 (₹510)) have to be purchased a day in advance from the ASI office, 22 The Mall (Mon–Sat 10am–6pm; ☎0562 222 7261). If a

viewing is cancelled, you get a refund.

Viewing the Taj for free You can see the Taj for free from a Taj Ganj hotel rooftop (many have restaurants with a Taj view), or by heading down the eastern side of the compound to a small Krishna temple by the river, where you can see the Taj, and also take a little boat ride (₹200–1000, depending on the size of your camera) to see it from the river. From Mehtab Bagh on the opposite bank of the river (daily sunrise–sunset; ₹100 (₹5)), the view is breathtaking, especially at dawn. You cross the river on the road bridge north of Agra Fort, and turn right when you reach the far bank, following the metalled road until it enters the village of Katchpura and becomes a rough track that eventually emerges at a small Dalit shrine on the riverside, directly opposite the Taj and next to the entrance of Mehtab Bagh. You can see the Taj from the garden's floodlit walkways, and from outside the gardens on the riverbank, but unfortunately you can no longer access the gardens by boat from across the river by the Taj itself.

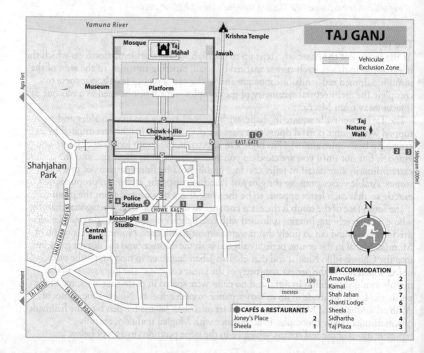

Agra Fort

Daily sunrise–sunset • ₹300 (₹20), ₹50 discount for foreigners on production of a Taj ticket for the same day

The high red-sandstone ramparts of **Agra Fort** dominate a bend in the Yamuna River 2km northwest of the Taj Mahal. Akbar laid the foundations of this majestic citadel, built between 1565 and 1573 in the form of a half moon, on the remains of earlier Rajput fortifications. The structure developed as the seat and stronghold of the Mughal Empire for successive generations: Akbar commissioned the walls and gates, his grandson, Shah Jahan, had most of the principal buildings erected, and Aurangzeb, the last great emperor, was responsible for the ramparts.

The curved sandstone bastions reach a height of over 20m and stretch for around two and a half kilometres, punctuated by a sequence of massive gates, (although only the **Amar Singh Pol** is currently open to visitors). The original and grandest entrance was through the western side, via the **Delhi Gate** and **Hathi Pol** or "Elephant Gate" (closed to the public), now flanked by two red-sandstone towers faced in marble, but once guarded by colossal stone elephants with riders which were destroyed by Aurangzeb in 1668. Access to this and to much of the fort is restricted, and only those parts open to the public are described below.

There's nowhere to buy drinks inside the fort, and exploring the complex can be thirsty work, so unless you're happy to take your chances at the public drinking taps, it's a good idea to take water in with you.

Diwan-i-Am and the great courtyard

Entrance to the fort is through the **Amar Singh Pol**, actually three separate gates placed close together and at right angles to each other to disorientate any potential attackers and to deprive them of the space in which to use battering weapons against the fortifications. From here a ramp climbs gently uphill flanked by high walls (another defensive measure), through a second gate to the spacious courtyard, with tree-studded lawns, which surrounds the graceful **Diwan-i-Am** ("Hall of Public Audience"). Open on three sides, the pillared hall, which replaced an earlier wooden structure, was commissioned by Shah Jahan in 1628. The elegance of the setting would have been enhanced by the addition of brocade, carpets and satin canopies for audiences with the emperor.

The ornate throne alcove – built to house a gem-encrusted Peacock Throne, which was eventually moved to Delhi, only to be looted from there by Nadir Shah and finishing up in Tehran – is inlaid in marble decorated with flowers and foliage in bas-relief, and connects to the royal chambers within. In front of the alcove, the **Baithak**, a small marble table, is where ministers would have sat to deliver petitions and receive commands. This is also where trials would have been conducted, and justice speedily implemented.

The area to the north of the Diwan-i-Am courtyard is, sadly, closed to visitors, though you can make out the delicate white marble domes and chhatris of the striking, if rather clumsily proportioned, **Moti Masjid** ("Pearl Mosque") rising beyond the courtyard walls, best seen from the Diwan-i-Am itself. Directly in front of the Diwan-i-Am an incongruously Gothic Christian tomb marks the **grave of John Russell Colvin**, lieutenant governor of the Northwestern Provinces, who died here during the 1857 uprising, when Agra's British population barricaded themselves inside the fort.

> ## SOUND-AND-LIGHT SHOW
>
> Every night after sunset (exact times vary from day to day), a **sound-and-light show** takes place at Agra Fort in front of the Diwan-i-Am. The show lasts an hour, during which time lights play on various parts of the fort as a commentary takes you through the history of the great Mughals. It's fun, but nothing spectacular. Tickets for the English performance cost ₹150 (₹40), and can be bought at the gate.

3

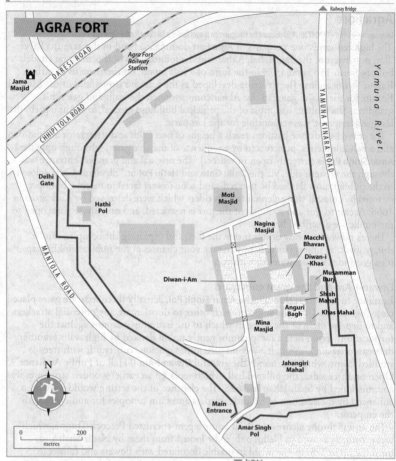

The royal pavilions

Heading through the small door to the left of the throne alcove in the Diwan-i-Am and climbing the stairs beyond brings you out onto the upper level of the **Macchi Bhavan** (Fish Palace), a large but relatively plain two-storey structure overlooking a spacious, grassy courtyard. This was once strewn with fountains and flowerbeds, interspersed with tanks and water channels stocked with fish on which the emperor and his courtiers would practise their angling skills, though the maharaja of Bharatpur subsequently removed some of its marble fixtures to his palace in Deeg, and William Bentinck (governor general from 1828 to 1835) auctioned off much of the palace's original mosaics and fretwork.

Nagina Masjid

On the north side of the courtyard (to the left as you enter) a small door leads to the exquisite little **Nagina Masjid** (Gem Mosque), made entirely of marble. Capped with three domes and approached from a marble-paved courtyard, it was commissioned by Shah Jahan for the ladies of the *zenana* (harem). At the rear on the right, a small balcony with beautifully carved lattice screens offers a discreet viewpoint from where members of the harem were able to inspect luxury goods – silks, jewellery and brocade – laid out for sale by merchants in the courtyard below, without themselves being seen.

The raised terrace on the far side of the Macchi Bhavan is adorned by two **thrones**, one black slate, the other white marble. The white one was used by Shah Jahan, the black one by the future emperor Jahangir to watch elephant fights in the eastern enclosure. It now serves, somewhat less gloriously, as a favoured perch for couples posing for photos against the backdrop of the distant Taj.

Diwan-i-Khas

To your right (as you face the river), a high terrace overlooking the Yamuna is topped with a sequence of lavish royal apartments designed to catch the cool breezes blowing across the waters below. The first is the delicate **Diwan-i-Khas** (Hall of Private Audience), erected in 1635, where the emperor would have received kings, dignitaries and ambassadors, and is one of the most finely decorated buildings in the fort, with paired marble pillars and peacock arches inlaid with lapis lazuli and jasper.

Mina Masjid

A passageway behind the Diwan-i-Khas leads to the tiny **Mina Masjid**, a plain white marble mosque built for Shah Jahan and traditionally said to have been used by him during his imprisonment here.

Musamman Burj

Beyond, the passageway leads to a two-storey pavilion known as the **Musamman Burj**, famous as the spot where he is said to have caught his last glimpse of the Taj Mahal before he died, and the most elaborately decorated structure in the fort. Its lattice-screen balustrade is dotted with ornamental niches and with exquisite *pietra dura* inlay covering almost every surface. In front of the tower a courtyard, paved with marble octagons, centres on a **pachisi board** where the emperor, following his father's example at Fatehpur Sikri (see p.247), played *pachisi* (a form of ludo) using dancing girls as pieces.

Anguri Bagh

Beyond the Musamman Burj, another large courtyard, the **Anguri Bagh** (Grape Garden), is a miniature *charbagh*, its east side flanked by the marble building known as **Khas Mahal** (Private Palace), possibly a drawing room or the emperor's sleeping chamber. The palace is flanked by two so-called **Golden Pavilions**, their curved roofs covered with gilded copper tiles in a style inspired by the thatched roofs of Bengali village huts.

In front of the Khas Mahal, steps descend into the northeast corner of the Anguri Bagh and the **Shish Mahal** (Glass Palace), where royal women bathed in the soft lamplight reflected from the mirror-work mosaics that covered the walls and ceiling; the building is currently locked, so you can only peek in through the windows.

The Jahangiri Mahal

South of the Khas Mahal lies the huge **Jahangiri Mahal** (Jahangir's Palace), although the name is misleading since it was actually built for Jahangir's father, Akbar, and probably served not as a royal palace, but as a harem. Compared to the classic Mughal designs of the surrounding buildings, this robust sandstone structure has quite a few Hindu elements mixed up with traditional Mughal and Islamic motifs.

From the central courtyard, a gateway leads out through the main gateway into the palace, whose impressive facade shows a characteristic mix of Mughal and Indian motifs, with Islamic pointed arches and inlaid mosaics combined with Hindu-style overhanging eaves supported by heavily carved brackets. Immediately in front of the palace sits **Jahangir's Hauz** (Jahangir's Cistern), a giant bowl with steps inside and out, made in 1611 from a single block of porphyry and inscribed in Persian. Filled with rosewater, it would have been used by the emperor as a bathtub, and it's also believed that the emperor took it with him on his travels around the empire – though it seems difficult to credit this, given the bath's size and weight.

Jama Masjid

Jama Masjid Rd

Opposite Agra Fort, and overlooking Agra Fort railway station, is the city's principal mosque, the soaring red-sandstone **Jama Masjid** (Friday Mosque). Built in 1648, it was originally connected directly to the fort's principal entrance, the Delhi Gate, by a large courtyard, but the British ran a railway line between the two, leaving the mosque stranded in no-man's land on the far side of the tracks.

Standing on a high plinth above the chaotic streets of the surrounding bazaar (of which it affords fine views), the mosque is crowned by three large sandstone domes covered in distinctive zigzagging bands of marble. Five huge arches lead into the main prayer hall, topped by a prettily inlaid band of sandstone decorated in abstract floral patterns; inside, the mihrab is surrounded by delicate flourishes of Koranic script, inlaid in black, a design mirrored in the principal archway.

Kinari Bazaar

The space around the base of the mosque is now filled with the crowded – but refreshingly hassle-free – streets of **Kinari Bazaar**, a fascinating warren crammed full with shops and stalls, though the numbers of people, scooters, cycle rickshaws and cows pushing their way through the streets make exploring it a slow and tiring business. Opposite the northeast corner of the complex, look out for the **petha-wallahs**, purveyors of Agra's most famous sweet (see p.245).

Itimad-ud-daulah

Moti Bagh • Daily sunrise–sunset • ₹110 (₹10)

On the east bank of the Yamuna River some 3km north of Agra Fort, the beautiful **Itimad-ud-daulah** (pronounced "Atma Dolla"), is the tomb of Mirza Ghiyas Beg, *wazir* (chief minister) and father-in-law of Emperor Jahangir, who gave him the title of Itimad-ud-daulah, or "Pillar of the State". The tomb is popularly known among Agra's rickshaw-wallahs as the "**Baby Taj**", and though it's much smaller and less successfully proportioned than its more famous relative, it does foreshadow the Taj in being the first building in Mughal Agra to be faced entirely in marble, with lavish use of *pietra dura* inlay to decorate its translucent exterior walls.

The tomb sits at the centre of a *charbagh* garden, though here entered from the eastern (rather than the usual southern) side, presumably to highlight its setting against the backdrop of the Yamuna River – another element of its design which anticipates that of the Taj. The building's undersized rooftop pavilion replaces the usual dome, and has four stocky minarets stuck onto each corner. However, these imperfections seem unimportant given the superbly intricate **inlay work** that covers virtually the entire tomb – an incredible profusion of floral and geometrical patterning in muted reds, oranges, browns and greys that give it the appearance of an enormous, slightly hallucinogenic experiment in medieval op-art. Elegant inlaid designs showing characteristic Persian motifs including wine vases, trees and honeysuckles adorn the arches of the four entrances, and the walls inside are covered in rather eroded and clumsily restored paintings of more vases, flowers and cypresses.

Chini-ka-Rauza

Around 1km north of Itimad-ud-daulah is the **Chini-ka-Rauza**, built between 1628 and 1639 as the mausoleum of Afzal Khan, a Persian poet from Shiraz who was one of Shah Jahan's ministers. As befits his origins, Afzal Khan's tomb is of purely Persian design, the only such building in Agra.

Rambagh

Mahatma Gandi Marg • Daily sunrise–sunset • ₹110 (₹10)

A kilometre or so north of the Chini-ka-Rauza, amid the dusty sprawl of northern Agra, the **Rambagh** gardens are one of the very few surviving remains in India from the reign of the Mughal dynasty's founder Babur, though there's little left to see here now. The gardens were originally laid out in 1526 following the Persian *charbagh* plan, which would subsequently prove the prototype for all later Mughal gardens in the Subcontinent.

Akbar's mausoleum

Mathura Rd • Daily 6am–5pm • ₹110 (₹10) • Autos ₹100 each way, or take a Mathura-bound bus from Agra Fort Bus Stand

Given the Mughal tradition of magnificent tombs, it is no surprise that the mausoleum of the most distinguished Mughal ruler was one of the most ambitious structures of its time. **Akbar's mausoleum** borders the side of the main highway to Mathura at **SIKANDRA**, 10km northwest of Agra.

The complex is entered via its huge **Buland Darwaza** (Great Gate), surmounted by four marble minarets, and overlaid with marble and coloured tiles in repetitive geometrical patterns, bearing the Koranic inscription "These are the gardens of Eden, enter them and live forever". Through the gateway, extensive, park-like **gardens** are divided by fine raised sandstone walkways into the four equal quadrants of the typical Mughal *charbagh* design. Langur monkeys may be seen along the path, while deer roam through the tall grasses, just as they do in the Mughal miniature paintings dating from the era when the tomb was constructed, lending the whole place a magically peaceful and rural atmosphere.

The mausoleum

The **mausoleum** itself sits in the middle of the gardens, at the centre of the *charbagh* and directly in front of Buland Darwaza. The entire structure is one of the strangest in Mughal Agra, its huge square base topped not by the usual dome but by a three-storey open-sided sandstone construction crowned with a solid-looking marble pavilion. The mishmash design may be attributable to Jahangir, who ordered changes in the mausoleum's design halfway through its construction, Akbar himself having neglected to leave finished plans for his mausoleum. By the standards of India's other Mughal buildings, it's architecturally a failure, but not without a certain whimsical charm, and much of the inlay work around the lower storey is exquisite.

A high marble gateway in the mausoleum's southern facade frames an elaborate lattice screen shielding a small vestibule painted with rich sea-blue frescoes and Koranic verses. From here a ramp leads down into a large, echoing and absolutely plain subterranean **crypt**, lit by a single skylight, in the centre of which stands Akbar's grave, decorated with the pen-box motif, the symbol of a male ruler, which can also be seen on Shah Jahan's tomb in the Taj Mahal.

Mariam's Tomb

Daily 6am–5pm • ₹100 (₹5)

Off the road on the opposite side, 1km north of Sikandra, lies the altogether more modest **Mariam's tomb**, the mausoleum of Akbar's wife and Jahangir's mother Mariam Zamani.

ARRIVAL AND DEPARTURE   AGRA

BY PLANE

Kheria airport The airport, 7km southwest of town (☎0562 240 0569), is currently served only by three weekly flights to Varanasi and Khajuraho with Air India. Further services are expected in the future.

Airlines Air India, c/o Tourism Guild of Agra, Shilpgram

(☎0562 654 3736); Jet, *Clarks Shiraz* hotel (☎0562 222 6527).

BY TRAIN

Railway Stations Agra has six stations, but visitors generally use only two of them. The busiest is Agra

Cantonment ("Cantt"), in the southwest, which serves Delhi, Gwalior, Jhansi and most points south. Trains from Rajasthan pull in close to the Jama Masjid at Agra Fort station (a few also stop at Agra Cantt). Agra Cantt is more convenient for the hotels around Sadar Bazaar, while Agra Fort Station is slightly closer to the Taj Ganj area; both are a fair way from the hotels along Fatehabad Rd. There's a pre-paid auto-rickshaw/taxi booth at Agra Cantonment Station (₹100/150 to Taj Ganj); drivers may try to intercept you before you reach the pre-paid booth so as to overcharge you and work some commission scam. Cycle rickshaws wait in the forecourt outside, but are slow if you're going to Fatehabad Rd or Taj Ganj. Cycle rickshaw and auto drivers may try to earn commission by taking you to a hotel of their choosing, and may therefore claim (falsely, of course) that the hotel of your choice is closed.

Tickets Train tickets, especially to the capital, should be booked several days in advance if possible at either Agra Cantonment or Agra Fort stations; both have computerized booking offices and separate tourist counters.

BY BUS

Travelling by bus along the main highways, especially to the capital on the Grand Trunk road and to Jaipur on NH-11, is considerably more hair-raising than doing the same journeys by train; accidents, most of them head-on collisions with other buses or trucks, are disconcertingly frequent. Agra has three bus stands, but Agra Fort Bus Stand is now used for local services only.

Idgah Bus Stand, near Cantonment station in the southwest of town, has services to Fatehpur Sikri (every 30min; 1hr–1hr 30min), Delhi (every 30min; 5–6hr), Madhya Pradesh and Rajasthan. For Rajasthani destinations beyond Jaipur, take a bus to Jaipur (hourly; 5–6hr) and pick up a connecting service (an exception is Ajmer, which has three daily direct services, taking 9hr). One scam to be aware of on buses to Idgah, especially from Jaipur, is that they may make a stop in the suburbs, about 6km out, where auto-wallahs (often in collusion with the bus drivers) may claim that your vehicle has reached the end of the line, and that you need to disembark; if there are still Indian passengers on the bus, sit tight till you get to Idgah.

Transport Nagar ISBT, 12km north of town at Transport Nagar, just off the Delhi–Agra highway. Buses from here serve UP destinations such as Lucknow (2 daily; 9hr 30min) and Varanasi (1 daily; 14hr), as well as to Haridwar (3 daily; 10hr), Rishikesh (3 daily; 12hr) and Dehra Dun (4 daily; 13hr). An auto into town will cost some ₹100, but if you're really determined to get into Agra on the cheap, you can

RECOMMENDED TRAINS FROM AGRA

The trains below are recommended as the fastest and/or most convenient for specific cities. All those listed here run daily.

Destination	Name	No.	From	Departs	Duration
Chennai	GT Express	#12616	AC	9.50pm	32hr 25min
	Tamil Nadu Express	#12622	AC	1.10am	30hr 05min
Delhi (New Delhi)	Karnataka Express	#12627	AC	6.45am	3hr 45min
	Kerala Express	#12625	AC	10.28am	3hr 12min
	Jhelum Express	#11077	AC	5.10pm	3hr 35min
	Shatabdi Express*	#12001	AC	8.35pm	2hr 10min
Gwalior	Shatabdi Express*	#12002	AC	8.11am	1hr 19min
	Punjab Mail	#12138	AC	8.55pm	1hr 40min
Jaipur	Ajmer Intercity Express	#12195	AF	5.10am	4hr 20min
	Udaipur Express	#19665	AC	5.40pm	4hr 40min
Jhansi	Shatabdi Express*	#12002	AC	8.11am	2hr 34min
	Punjab Mail	#12138	AC	8.55pm	3hr 30min
Jodhpur	Howrah–Jodhpur Exp	#12307	AC	8.10pm	9hr 50min
Khajuraho	Khajuraho Express	#19666	AC	11.05am	8hr 25min
	Sampark Kranti Exp	#12488/ 02448	AC	11.20pm	7hr 15min
Kolkata (Howrah)	Ajmer–Sealdah Express	#12988	AF	7.50pm	20hr 05min
Udaipur	Udaipur Express	#19665	AC	5.40pm	12hr 30min
Varanasi	Marudhar Express	#14854/ 64/66	AF	9.20pm	13hr 10min
Vasco da Gama	Goa Express	#12780	AC	5.50pm	36hr 40min

AC Agra Cantonment, AF Agra Fort
*a/c only

walk down to the highway and pick up a shared auto (₹10) to Baghwan Talkies, and another one from there to Gwalior Rd or Agra Fort bus station (₹25).

RSRTC buses Deluxe and a/c Rajasthan Roadways (RSRTC, bookable on ⓦrsrtc.com) non-stop services to Jaipur (9 daily; 4hr) leave from the forecourt of *Hotel Shakpura*, next to the Idgah bus stand.

Private buses Hotels and travel agents can book seats on private buses to Delhi, Gwalior, Khajuraho, Lucknow and Nainital. The 12hr ride to Khajuraho (leaving at 5am) is a bit gruelling – it's better to take the train, or failing that, take a train to Jhansi (3hr) and pick up a bus there (5hr).

GETTING AROUND

Agra is very spread out and its sights too widely separated for you to get between them easily on foot, so you'll probably spend a fair amount of time in rickshaws or taxis. Getting from one part of the city to another can prove surprisingly time-consuming, and crossing from one side of the Yamuna River to the other is particularly tedious, with only two over-used and under-maintained bridges. Motorized vehicles are excluded from a small area around the Taj, supposedly to protect it from pollution. On rickshaws and taxis, haggle hard: Agra sees so many "fresh" tourists that drivers almost always quote significantly inflated prices to start with (the best policy, if a rickshaw driver names a silly price, is simply to walk away – they'll usually chase after you and offer a more realistic fare). Also, note that the main agenda for many rickshaw and taxi drivers is to get you into shops that pay them **commission**, added to your bill of course; if they offer you a ride for an absurdly low price, this is what their aim is.

By cycle rickshaw Cycle rickshaws are good for short trips and provide a livelihood for some of the city's poorest inhabitants, as well as being cleaner and greener than autos, but are slow for long journeys, and rickshaw drivers are the biggest source of hassle in Agra – attempt to walk anywhere, and they will be constantly on your case. Walking on the right-hand side of the street makes it harder for them to follow you. It's always wiser to hail a rickshaw of your own choice rather than go with a driver who pesters you (almost always with the intention of overcharging or working a commission scam).

By auto-rickshaw Auto-rickshaws are faster than cycle rickshaws, though the same caveats apply. Fares, including waiting time, are very reasonable if you haggle. Sample fares from Taj Ganj are ₹40–50 to Sadar Bazaar or Agra Fort, ₹120 to Agra Cantt Station.

By taxi Taxis are handy for longer trips to Sikandra or Fatehpur Sikri; agree a fare before you set off. There are taxi ranks at the stations, or your hotel should be able to arrange a vehicle.

INFORMATION AND TOURS

Tourist information Agra has two tourist offices, India Tourism at 191 The Mall (Mon–Fri 9am–5pm, Sat 9am–2pm; ☎0562 222 6368), and UP Tourism at 64 Taj Rd (Mon–Sat 10am–5pm; ☎0562 222 6378); there is also an information booth (24hr; ☎0562 242 1204) at Cantonment Station.

Tours UP Tourism runs a whistlestop tour (daily except Fri) of Agra, aimed mainly at day-trippers from Delhi. The tour leaves the Cantonment Station at 10.30am (coinciding with the *Taj Express* from Delhi), but depends on demand – call UP Tourism at the station (☎0562 242 1204) to check whether it's running on any particular day. The full-day tour (₹1700 (₹300)) including all entrance and guide fees) whisks you at breakneck speed around the Taj, Agra Fort and Fatehpur Sikri, ending at around 6pm in time for the *Taj Express* back to Delhi; you can also join the tour just for the afternoon visit to Fatehpur Sikri (₹550 (₹300)). Tours can be booked either through the UP Tourism or India Tourism offices.

ACCOMMODATION

Most budget travellers end up in **Taj Ganj**, the jumble of narrow lanes immediately south of the Taj. With their unrivalled rooftop views and laidback cafés, the little guesthouses here can be great places to stay. There are more modern and upmarket lodgings along **Fatehabad Rd**, southwest of Taj Ganj, while the leafier **Cantonment** area and the adjacent **Sadar Bazaar** have places to suit every budget.

TAJ GANJ

★ **Amarvilas** East Gate ☎0562 223 1515, ⓦoberoi hotels.com; map p.236. Easily the loveliest (and most expensive) hotel in Agra, virtually a work of art in its own right, constructed in a serene blend of Mughal and Moorish styles around a gorgeous *charbagh*-style courtyard water garden. Most rooms have Taj views. Facilities include a large pool, idyllic terraced gardens, two smart restaurants

and a very chichi bar. ₹48,902

Kamal Chowk Kagzi ☎0562 233 0126, ⓔhotelkamal @hotmail.com; map p.236. Right in the thick of the Taj Ganj action, with well-maintained rooms (all attached, with hot running water), free wi-fi and a great view from the rooftop restaurant. ₹650

Shah Jahan Chowk Kagzi ☎0562 320 0240, ⓔshahjahan.hotel@gmail.com; map p.236. There's a wide range of rooms here (a/c double ₹700), but all are good value, and even the cheapest doubles are attached with hot showers, although there are a few non-attached singles (₹200). There's also a rooftop restaurant with good Taj views, and wi-fi downstairs. **₹350**

Shanti Lodge Chowk Kagzi ☎0562 233 1973, ⓦhotel shantilodge.com; map p.236. Deservedly popular backpacker lodge with superb Taj views from the rooftop restaurant, a mixed bag of rooms – those in the annexe are newer and larger, with Taj views – and a rooftop restaurant. There are also good deals for single occupancy, although the cheapest single rooms (₹250) don't have hot running water. **₹400**

Sheela East Gate ☎0562 329 3437, ⓦhotelsheelaagra .com; map p.236. Clean and spacious ground-floor rooms ranged around a lovely little garden, with fan, air-cooled and a/c options, friendly staff and a good restaurant. All rooms are attached, but the cheapest have hot water in buckets only, so it's worth paying ₹200 more for an upgrade. **₹600**

Sidhartha West Gate ☎0562 233 0901, ⓦhotel sidhartha.com; map p.236. Bigger and better rooms than the other Taj Ganj budget joints, set around a restaurant in a leafy courtyard that includes fragments of Mughal-era walls, but they've raised their prices way above the competition, so they're no longer great value, especially as non-a/c rooms supply hot water in a bucket only. **₹800**

Taj Plaza East Gate ☎0562 223 2515; map p.236. A slightly more upmarket alternative to the nearby Taj Ganj guesthouses, this small, modern hotel has a range of clean, bright air-cooled and a/c rooms with cable TV; the most expensive a/c ones (₹2500) have good Taj views. Despite the relatively high prices, hot water is only available at 20min notice, and wi-fi costs ₹100 extra/day. **₹1500**

CANTONMENT AND SADAR BAZAAR

Clarks Shiraz 54 Taj Rd ☎0562 222 6121, ⓦhotelclarksshiraz.com; map p.234. Sprawling five-star in a pleasant Cantonment setting with small but cosy rooms, the more expensive of which have distant Taj views. Facilities include two restaurants, two bars, a swimming pool, an Ayurvedic massage centre and a health club. **₹7869**

Hilltop 21 The Mall ☎0562 222 6836, ⓔhotel hilltopagra@yahoo.com; map p.234. Set in pleasant grounds with peacocks and parrots, this place is a little bit ramshackle, and the cheaper rooms are on the small side, but they're all good value. If you're utterly strapped for cash, you could go for the ultra-basic cell-like rooms with shared bath, and you can camp for ₹50/person. *Rough Guide* readers are promised a discount. **₹150/₹350**

Sakura Near Idgah Bus Station ☎0562 242 0169, ⓔashu_sakura@yahoo.com; map p.234. Well-run and good-value guesthouse on the west side of town. It doesn't look too inviting from the outside, but the rooms (of which there's quite a variety, including a/c rooms from ₹900) are

large, bright, spacious and nicely furnished, and the manager is extremely helpful and a mine of local information. The only drawback is the location: handy for Idgah bus and Cantonment train stations, but a bit of a hike from everywhere else. **₹600**

★ **Tourists Rest House** Kutchery Rd, Baluganj ☎0562 246 3961, ⓦdontworrychickencurry.com; map p.234. One of Agra's top budget options, with a range of bright, competitively priced rooms around a tranquil leafy courtyard; all super-clean, and all attached with hot running water, some a/c (₹750). There's also free wi-fi, free bus and train reservations, and free pick-up from bus or train stations with a day's notice. **₹350**

Yamuna View 6-B The Mall ☎0562 246 2990, ⓦhotelyamunaviewagra.com; map p.234. Conveniently central, low-key five-star. Rooms are stylish in an understated kind of way, and facilities include a pool, a bar and a couple of smart restaurants, including the *Mandarin* (see opposite). **₹6745**

FATEHABAD ROAD AND AROUND

Amar Yatri Niwas Fatehabad Rd ☎0562 223 3030, ⓦamaryatriniwas.com; map p.234. Good-value mid-range hotel with well-maintained rooms (the cheaper ones small but still very comfortable) and a multicuisine restaurant. **₹2137**

The Gateway Fatehabad Rd ☎0562 660 2000, ⓦthegatewayhotels.com; map p.234. Rooms at this stylish hotel (some with distant Taj views) are among the most attractive in Agra, cheerfully decorated in orange and white, while public areas are pleasantly plush and there's the usual range of five-star amenities including a pool. Discounts are usually available on the official (rack) rate. **₹11,804**

Mayur Tourist Complex Fatehabad Rd ☎0562 233 2302, ⓦmayurcomplex.com; map p.234. Dinky pagoda-like cottages with attached bathrooms around a large garden (generally peaceful, but often used for weddings Nov–Jan). Facilities include a multicuisine restaurant-cum-beer bar, and a swimming pool and health centre. **₹3400**

Safari Shaheed Nagar, Shamsabad Rd ☎0562 248 0106, ⓔhotelsafari@hotmail.com; map p.234. Friendly and relaxed hotel. Rooms (fan, air-cooled and a/c) are rather old, but clean, attached and well looked-after, and there are distant views of the Taj from the rooftop café. Good value, though the location is a bit out of the way. **₹450**

Trident Tajnagri, Fatehabad Rd ☎0562 233 5000, ⓦtridenthotels.com; map p.234. A peaceful five-star, whose cheerful rooms (including two adapted for wheelchair users) are in low-lying buildings around a spacious garden with a large pool and multicuisine restaurant. Despite being located a couple of kilometres out of town, it's actually quite handy for the Taj's eastern entrance, with a direct road round the back of the hotel. **₹12,928**

EATING

Agra is the home of **Mughlai cooking**, renowned for its rich cream- and curd-based sauces, accompanied by naan and tandoori breads roasted in earthen ovens, pulao rice dishes and milky sweets such as *kheer*. **Taj Ganj** has innumerable scruffy little travellers' cafés, though standards of hygiene are often suspect and the food is generally uninspiring, with slow service the norm. Taj Ganj's saving grace is the **rooftop cafés**, many with fine Taj views, which cap most of its buildings. Local **specialities** of Agra include *petha* (crystallized pumpkin) – the best is the Panchi brand, available at various outlets all over town, particularly in the row of *petha* shops in Kinari Bazaar along the northeast side of the Jama Masjid (past *Chimman Lal Puri Wale*). Look out too for *ghazak*, a rock-hard candy with nuts, and *dalmoth*, a crunchy mix made with black lentils. Agra's restaurants – including even apparently reputable places – are not immune to the epidemic of **credit-card fraud** (see p.66). It's best not to pay by credit card except in the city's five-star establishments, or, if you do, to supervise the operation carefully.

Achman Agra–Delhi Highway (NH-2), Dayal Bagh, 5km out of town near Baghwan Talkies ☎0562 406 4401; map p.234. Veg restaurant highly rated among Agra-wallahs in the know, famous for its *navratan* korma (a mildly spiced mix of nuts, dried fruit and *paneer*; ₹185) and *malai* kofta (₹155), as well as wonderful stuffed naans (₹48). Well off the tourist trail in the north of the city, but ideally placed for dinner on your way home from Sikandra (to which it's about halfway), and reachable by shared auto from Agra Fort bus station or Gwalior Rd. Daily noon–11pm.

★ **Chimman Lal Puri Wale** Opposite northeast wall of Jama Masjid ☎0562 246 1430; map p.234. An Agra institution for five generations, this much-loved little café-restaurant looks a touch grubby from the outside, but serves delicious *puri* thalis, with two veg dishes and a sweet – all for ₹50. Ideal pit-stop after visiting the Jama Masjid. Daily 7am–10pm.

Dasaprakash Meher Theatre Complex, 1 Gwalior Rd, close to the Tourists Rest House ☎0562 246 3535, ⓦdasaprakash.in; map p.234. Offshoot of a famous Chennai restaurant, serving a limited menu of top-notch south Indian food, with special Mysore or spicy coriander versions of masala dosa (₹140), thalis (₹125–300) and an extensive ice cream menu – the "hot fudge bonanza split" (₹120) wins by a nose. Daily noon–11pm.

Joney's Place Chowk Kazgi, Taj Ganj; map p.236. Oldest of the Taj Ganj travellers' cafés, going since 1978, and open early in case you need breakfast ahead of a dawn visit to the Taj. The breakfasts are pretty good, or there's spaghetti, macaroni, veg or non-veg curries (such as *alu gobi* at ₹50), thalis (₹80) and even (on occasion) hummus (₹20) and a version of falafel (₹40). Daily 5am–10pm.

Lakshmi Villas 50-A Taj Rd, Sadar Bazaar ☎0562 222 5616; map p.234. A good, and much cheaper, alternative to *Dasaprakash*, this unpretentious and deservedly popular south Indian café in the middle of Sadar Bazaar offers the usual menu of *iddlis*, dosas and *uttapams* (masala dosa ₹70), plus thalis (served noon–3.30pm & 7–10.30pm only; ₹120). Daily 8am–10.30pm.

The Mandarin Yamuna View hotel ☎0562 246 2990; map p.234. One of the best non-Indian restaurants in town, this stylish Chinese offers a possibly welcome change

from Mughlai curries and masala dosas. The menu features a good selection of delicately prepared dishes like stir-fried vegetables in almond sauce (₹305) and chicken in honey chilli (₹415), with the emphasis on light ingredients and subtle flavours. Daily noon–11pm.

Only 45 Taj Rd (at Mall Rd) ☎0562 222 6834; map p.234. One of Agra's most popular north Indian restaurants, usually packed with local families and tourist groups and known for its well-prepared tandoori and Mughlai creations, though there's also a wide selection of more mainstream north Indian meat and veg standards including a sumptuous chicken Mughlai (₹210) or *malai* kofta (₹145), plus a few Chinese and Continental offerings. There's seating in an indoor a/c dining room or in the pleasant courtyard. Daily 7am–10pm.

The Park 183-A Taj Rd, Sadar Bazaar ☎94566 75101; map p.234. A long-established favourite with both locals and tourists, this simple a/c restaurant dishes up an excellent range of classic Mughlai chicken dishes, along with more mainstream tandooris and meat and veg curries accompanied by superb naan breads, plus a modest selection of Continental and Chinese favourites. Specialities include *rogan josh* (₹155) and chicken *badami* (with almonds; ₹250). Daily 10am–11pm.

Sheela East Gate, Taj Ganj; map p.236. The most dependable and pleasant place to eat near the Taj, with seating outside in the shady garden or inside the narrow café. The menu features a good choice of simple Indian dishes, including chicken curry (₹110) and veg biriyani (₹80), as well as drinks and snacks, and the fruit lassis are more of a yogurty dessert than a drink. Daily 6am–11pm.

Tourists Rest House Kutchery Rd, Baluganj; map p.234. Atmospheric, candlelit garden restaurant serving a modest selection of breakfasts and Indian veg dishes to a clientele of foreign backpackers. The veg curries are surprisingly good, but they often omit the chilli for the benefit of European tourists, so tell them if you want it spicy. Try the tasty vegetable kofta (₹85), rounded off with banana custard (₹65). Daily 7am–10pm.

Zorba the Buddha E-19 Shopping Arcade, Sadar Bazaar ☎0562 222 6091, ⓦzorbarestaurantagra .com; map p.234. Aimed unashamedly at foreign tourists, though you'll find Indian people eating here too, this prettily decorated little place promises no chilli unless you ask for it, and offers, along with Indian veg dishes, odd specialities such as a Hawaiian spree (vegetables and pineapple in pineapple sauce; ₹250) or a fiesta (vegetables in tomato and cashew sauce; ₹250), all generally tasty and well presented. Daily noon–10pm. Closed in June.

SHOPPING

Agra is renowned for its **marble** tabletops, vases and trays, inlaid with semi-precious stones in ornate floral designs, in imitation of those found in the Taj Mahal. It is also an excellent place to buy **leather**: Agra's shoe industry supplies all India, and its tanneries export bags, briefcases and jackets. **Carpets** and **dhurries** are manufactured here too, and traditional embroidery continues to thrive. *Zari* and *zardozi* are brightly coloured, the latter building up three-dimensional patterns with fantastic motifs; *chikan* uses more delicate overlay techniques. **Shilpgram** is an extensive crafts village close to the Taj Mahal's East Gate, with arts and handicrafts from all over India, and occasional live music and dance performances. Shopping or browsing around The Mall, MG Rd, Munro Rd, Kinari Bazaar, Sadar Bazaar and the Taj Complex is fun, but you need to know what you're buying and be prepared to haggle. A lot of private shops try to **disguise themselves** to look like state-run "cottage" or "handlooms" outlets – an indication of their level of integrity. The official-sounding (but private) Cottage Industries Exposition on the Fatehabad Rd is well presented but outrageously expensive (it's one of the places you're likely to be taken to by commission-seeking rickshaw-wallahs). Shops in the big hotels may be pricey, but their quality and service are usually more reliable.

Scams Agra sees a large amount of credit-card fraud; be wary of ordering anything to be sent overseas, never let your credit card out of your sight, even for the transaction to be authorized, and make sure that all documentation is filled in correctly and fully so as not to allow unauthorized later additions. A list of stores against whom complaints have been lodged is maintained by the local police department. Remember that if you arrive at any shop in a rickshaw or taxi, the prices of anything you buy will be inflated to cover the driver's commission. If you're planning on buying, ask to be dropped off nearby, and then walk to the shop (not allowing your driver to see where you are going).

DIRECTORY

Banks and exchange There are ATMs at Cantonment railway station and dotted around the city. The State Bank of India on MG Rd north of Baluganj, with a branch just north of Fatehabad Rd in the Cantonment, does not always accept travellers' cheques, but Allahabad Bank at *Clarks Shiraz* hotel does. For longer hours, less messing about, and usually better rates and lower commission charges, there are private exchange offices in Taj Ganj, and in the Tourist Complex Area around *Amar Yatri Niwas* hotel (VRV forex, opposite *Amar Yatri Niwas* on Fatehabad Rd, for example).

Hospitals Clean and dependable private hospitals with English-speaking doctors: SR Hospital, Namenar Rd (☎0562 226 9411); GG Nursing Home, 106/2 Sanjay Place (☎0562 285 3952); Pushpanjali, Delhi Gate (☎0562 402 4000). The District Hospital, MG Rd, Chipitola (☎0562 246 6099) gives free treatment, and may be preferable for minor injuries. Avoid backstreet clinics, even if recommended by your hotel manager, and in particular, if you fall ill with what appears to be food poisoning, do not go to a clinic or doctor suggested by someone in the restaurant concerned.

Internet There's plenty of internet access available around town, particularly in Taj Ganj; rates are typically ₹30/hr. Many hotels and guesthouses have their own internet connections.

Photography Numerous places on MG Rd, a block north of The Mall, can download and burn digital images to disc or make prints, as can Moonlight Studio (corner of West Gate and Chowk Kagzi) in Taj Ganj.

Police There are police stations on Chowk Kagzi in Taj Ganj (☎0562 233 1015) and on Mahatma Gandhi Rd in Sadar Bazaar, slightly south of the intersection with Fatehpur Sikri Rd (☎0562 222 6561). Agra has a dedicated tourist police force to protect tourists; they can be contacted through UP Tourism or on ☎94544 02764, or in an emergency on ☎1073.

Post The Head Post Office is on The Mall, near India Tourism.

Swimming The pools at most of Agra's hotels are usually reserved for the use of hotel guests only, though a few places admit outsiders for a fee. These currently include the *Yamuna View* (₹400), Mayur Tourist Complex (₹300), and (both near *Amar Yatri Niwas*) the *Amar* (₹500) and *Mansingh Palace* (₹400).

Travel agenices The *Tourists Rest House* has a travel agency called Bag Packers (☎0562 225 0246, ⊛bagpackertravels.com), which can organize car rental with driver and tailor-made tours of Agra and/or Rajasthan, starting from Agra or Delhi; they can also book train tickets and accept payment from foreign credit or debit cards.

Fatehpur Sikri

The ghost city of **FATEHPUR SIKRI**, former imperial capital of the great Mughal emperor **Akbar**, straddles the crest of a rocky ridge on the Agra–Jaipur highway, 45km southwest of Agra and 21km east of Bharatpur. The city was built here between 1569 and 1585 as a result of the emperor's enthusiasm for the local Muslim divine **Sheikh Salim Chishti** (see p.250), though the move away from Agra may also have had something to do with Akbar's weariness of the crowds and his desire to create a new capital that was an appropriate symbol of imperial power. The fusion of Hindu and Muslim traditions in its architecture says a lot about the religious and cultural tolerance of Akbar's reign.

Fatehpur Sikri's period of pre-eminence was brief, however, and after 1585 it would never again serve as the seat of the Mughal emperor. The reasons for the **city's abandonment** remain enigmatic. The theory that the city's water supply proved incapable of sustaining its population is no longer widely accepted – even after the city had been deserted, the nearby lake to its northwest still yielded good water. A more likely explanation is that the city was simply the victim of the vagaries of the empire's day-to-day military contingencies. Shortly after the new capital was established, the empire was threatened by troubles in the Punjab, and Akbar moved to the more strategically situated Lahore to deal with them. These military preoccupations kept Akbar at Lahore for over a decade, and at the end of this period he decided, apparently for no particular reason, to return to Agra rather than Fatehpur Sikri.

The Royal Palace

Daily sunrise–sunset • ₹260 (₹20), video ₹25

Shunning the Hindu tradition of aligning towns with the cardinal compass points, Akbar chose to construct his new capital following the natural features of the terrain, which is why the principal thoroughfare, town walls, and many of the most important buildings face southwest or northeast. The mosque and most private apartments do not follow the main axis, but face west towards Mecca, according to Muslim tradition, with the palace crowning the highest point on the ridge.

There are two **entrances** to the **Royal Palace** and court complex. Independent travellers mostly use the one on the west side, by Jodhbai's Palace; organized tours tend to use that on the east, by the Diwan-i-Am. Official **guides** offer their services at the booking office (₹250 for 2hr in a group of up to five people). There's nowhere to buy drinks in the palace, so take water in with you; you're not allowed to eat inside.

Diwan-i-Am

A logical place to begin a tour of the palace complex is the **Diwan-i-Am**, where important festivals were held, and where citizens could exercise their right to petition the emperor. Unlike the ornate pillared Diwan-i-Am buildings at the forts in Agra and Delhi, it is basically just a large courtyard, surrounded by a continuous colonnaded walkway with Hindu-style square columns and capitals, and broken only by the small pavilion, flanked by elaborately carved *jali* screens, in which the emperor himself would have sat – the position of the royal platform forced the emperor's subjects to approach him from the side in an attitude of humility.

The Diwan-i-Khas courtyard

A doorway in the northwest corner of the Diwan-i-Am leads to the centre of the *mardana* (men's quarters), a large, irregularly shaped enclosure dotted with a strikingly eclectic range of buildings. At the far (northern) end of the enclosure stands the tall **Diwan-i-Khas** ("Hall of Private Audience"), topped with four chhatris and embellished with the heavily carved Hindu-style brackets, large overhanging eaves and corbelled arches which are typical of the architecture of Fatehpur Sikri.

3

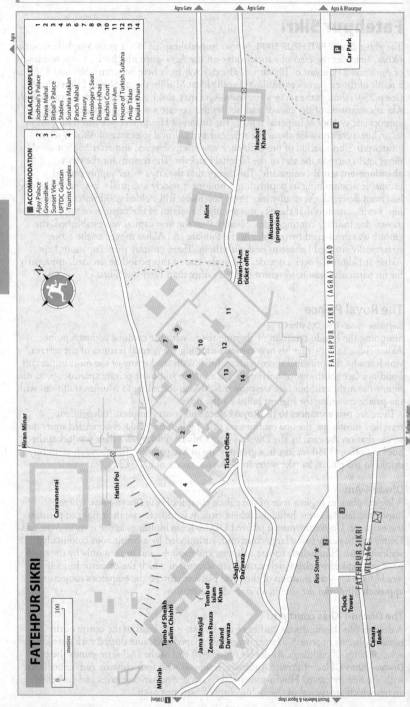

FATEHPUR SIKRI

	PALACE COMPLEX
1	Jodhbai's Palace
2	Hawa Mahal
3	Birbal's Palace
4	Stables
5	Sunahra Makan
6	Panch Mahal
7	Treasury
8	Astrologer's Seat
9	Diwan-i-Khas
10	Pachisi Court
11	Diwan-i-Am
12	House of Turkish Sultana
13	Anup Talao
14	Daulat Khana

	ACCOMMODATION
2	Ajay Palace
3	Goverdhan
1	Sunset View
	UPTDC Gulistan
4	Tourist Complex

Agra Gate

Agra Gate

Agra & Bharatpur

Car Park

Agra

Naubat Khana

Mint

Museum (proposed)

Diwan-i-Am ticket office

FATEHPUR SIKRI (AGRA) ROAD

Hiran Minar

Hathi Pol

Caravanserai

Ticket Office

Shahi Darwaza

Tomb of Sheikh Salim Chishti

Tomb of Islam Khan

Jama Masjid

Zenana Rauza

Buland Darwaza

Mihrab

0   100
metres

N

Railway station

Bus Stand

FATEHPUR SIKRI VILLAGE

Clock Tower

Canara Bank

Biscuit bakeries & liquor shop (100m)

The interior of the building consists of a single high hall (despite the impression, from the outside that this is a two-storey building) centred on an elaborately corbelled column known as the **Throne Pillar**, supporting a large circular platform from which four balustraded bridges radiate outwards. Seated upon this throne, the emperor held discussions with representatives of diverse religions, aiming to synthesize India's religions into one. The pillar symbolizes this project by incorporating motifs drawn from Hinduism, Buddhism, Islam and Christianity.

Next to the Diwan-i-Khas lies the three-roomed **Treasury**, its brackets embellished by mythical sea creatures, guardians of the treasures of the deep; it's also known as Ankh Michauli, meaning hide and seek, which it's said was played here. In fact, both names are probably just fanciful inventions, and the building most likely served as a multipurpose pavilion which could be used for a variety of functions, as could most buildings in Mughal palaces. Attached to it is the so-called **Astrologer's Seat**, a small pavilion embellished with elaborate Jain carvings.

In the middle of the courtyard, separating the Diwan-i-Khas from the buildings on the opposite (south) side of the complex is the **Pachisi Court**, a giant board used to play *pachisi* (similar to ludo). Akbar is said to have been a fanatical player, using slave girls dressed in colourful costumes as live pieces. Abu'l Fazl, the court chronicler, related that at "times more than two hundred persons participated, and no one was allowed to go home until he had played sixteen rounds. This could take up to three months. If one of the players lost his patience and became restless, he was made to drink a cupful of wine. Seen superficially, this appears to be just a game. But His Majesty pursues higher objectives. He weighs up the talents of his people and teaches them to be affable."

House of the Turkish Sultana

Diagonally opposite the *pachisi* board, the **House of the Turkish Sultana** (or Anup Talao Pavilion) gained its name from the popular belief that it was the residence of one of Akbar's favourite wives, the Sultana Ruqayya Begum – though this seems unlikely given its location in the centre of the men's quarters. The name was probably made up by nineteenth-century guides to titillate early tourists, and the building is more likely to have served as a simple pleasure pavilion. Its superbly carved stone walls are covered with a profusion of floral and geometrical designs, plus some partially vandalized animal carvings.

South of here is the **Anup Talao** (Peerless Pool), a pretty little ornamental pond divided by four walkways connected to a small "island" in the middle – a layout reminiscent of the raised walkways inside the Diwan-i-Khas.

The Daulat Khana

Facing the Turkish Sultana's house from the other side of the Anup Talao are Akbar's former private sleeping and living quarters, the **Daulat Khana** ("Abode of Fortune"). The room on the ground floor with alcoves in its walls was the emperor's library, where he would be read to (he himself was illiterate) from a collection of fifty thousand manuscripts he allegedly took everywhere with him. Behind the library is the imperial sleeping chamber, the **Khwabgah** ("House of Dreams"), with an enormous raised bed in its centre.

Panch Mahal

One of Fatehpur Sikri's most famous structures, the **Panch Mahal** or "Five-Storeyed Palace", looms northwest of here, marking the beginning of the **zenana** (women's quarters) which make up the entire western side of the palace complex. The palace tapers to a final single kiosk and is supported by 176 columns of varying designs; the ground floor contains 84 pillars – an auspicious number in Hindu astrology. The open spaces between the pillars were originally covered with latticed screens, so that ladies of the *zenana* could observe goings-on in the courtyard of the *mardana* below without themselves being seen.

The women's quarters

Directly behind the Panch Mahal, a courtyard garden was reserved for the *zenana* (harem). The adjoining **Sunahra Makan** (Golden House), also known as Mariam's House, is variously thought to have been the home of the emperor's mother or of Akbar's wife Mariam. It is enlivened by the faded remains of paintings on its walls (whose now vanished golden paint gave the pavilion its name), by the lines of verse penned by Abu'l Fazl, inscribed around the ceiling in blue bands, and by the quaint little carvings tucked into the brackets supporting the roof, including several elephants and a tiny carving of Rama attended by Hanuman (on the north side of the building, facing the *zenana* courtyard garden).

Solemnly presiding over the whole complex is the main harem, known as **Jodhbai's Palace**. The residence of several of the emperor's senior wives, this striking building is the grandest and largest in the entire city, and looks decidedly Hindu even in the eclectic context of Fatehpur Sikri, having been modelled after Rajput palaces such as those at Gwalior and Orchha.

On the north side of the palace, the **Hawa Mahal** ("Palace of the Winds"), a small screened tower with a delicately carved chamber, was designed to catch the evening breeze, while a raised covered walkway, lined with five large chhatris, leads from here to a (now vanished) lake.

Northwest of Jodhbai's Palace lies a third women's palace, known as **Birbal's Palace** – though this is another misnomer, as Birbal, Akbar's favourite courtier, was a man and would have been most unwelcome in the middle of the *zenana*. It's more likely to have been the residence of two of Akbar's senior wives.

Jama Masjid

Daily dawn–dusk • Free

Southwest of the palace complex, with the village of Fatehpur Sikri nestling at its base, stands the **Jama Masjid** or Dargah Mosque, one of the finest in the whole of India. Unfortunately, pestilential self-appointed "guides" make it all but impossible to enjoy the place in peace. The mosque was apparently completed in 1571, before work on the palace commenced, showing the religious significance which Akbar accorded the entire site. This was due to its connections with the Sufi saint **Sheikh Salim Chishti**, who is buried here, and who played a crucial role in the founding of Fatehpur Sikri by prophesying the birth of a son to the emperor: when one of Akbar's wives, Rani Jodhabai, a Hindu Rajput princess from Amber, became pregnant she was sent here until the birth of her son Salim, who later became the emperor Jahangir. Fatehpur Sikri was constructed in the saint's honour.

Buland Darwaza

The neck-cricking **Buland Darwaza** (Great Gate), a spectacular entrance scaled by an impressive flight of steps, was added around 1576 to commemorate Akbar's military campaign in Gujarat. Flanked by domed kiosks, the archway of the simple sandstone memorial is inscribed with a message from the Koran: "Said Jesus Son of Mary (peace be on him): The world is but a bridge – pass over without building houses on it. He who hopes for an hour hopes for eternity; the world is an hour – spend it in prayer for the rest is unseen." The numerous horseshoes nailed to the doors here date from the beginning of the twentieth century – an odd instance of British folk superstition in this very Islamic place.

Tomb of Sheikh Salim

The gate leads into a vast cloistered courtyard, far larger than in any mosque previously built in India. The **prayer hall**, on the west (left) side, is the focus of the mosque,

punctuated by an enormous gateway. More eye-catching is the exquisite **Tomb of Sheikh Salim Chishti**, directly ahead as you enter the courtyard. Much of this was originally crafted in red sandstone and only later faced in marble: the beautiful lattice screens – another design feature probably imported from Gujarat, though it would later become a staple of Mughal architecture – are unusually intricate, with striking serpentine exterior brackets supporting the eaves.

AKBAR'S HAREM

Although remembered primarily for his liberal approach to religion, Akbar was typically Mughal in his attitudes to women, whom he collected in much the same way as a philatelist amasses stamps. At its height of splendour, the **royal harem** at Fatehpur Sikri held around five thousand women, guarded by a legion of eunuchs. Its doors were closed to outsiders, but rumours permeated the sandstone walls and several notable travellers were smuggled inside the Great Mughals' seraglios, leaving for posterity often lurid accounts of the emperors' private lives.

The size of Akbar's harem grew in direct proportion to his empire. With each new conquest, he would be gifted by the defeated rulers and nobles their most beautiful daughters, who, together with their maidservants, would be installed in the luxurious royal **zenana**. In all, the emperor is thought to have kept three hundred wives; their ranks were swollen by a constant flow of concubines (*kaniz*), dancing girls (*kanchni*) and female slaves (*bandis*), or "silver bodied damsels with musky tresses" as one chronicler described them, purchased from markets across Asia. Screened from public view by ornately pierced stone *jali* windows were women from the four corners of the Mughal empire, as well as Afghans, Turks, Iranians, Arabs, Tibetans, Russians and Abyssinians, and even one Portuguese, sent as presents or tribute.

The **eunuchs** who presided over them came from similarly diverse backgrounds. While some were hermaphrodites, others had been forcibly castrated, either as punishment following defeat on the battlefield, or after having been donated by their fathers as payment of backdated revenue – an all too common custom at the time.

Akbar is said to have consumed prodigious quantities of Persian wine, *araq* (a spirit distilled from sugar cane), bhang and opium. The lavish dance recitals held in the harem, as well as sexual liaisons conducted on the top pavilion of the Panch Mahal and in the *zenana* itself, would have been fuelled by these substances. Over time, Akbar's hedonistic ways incurred the disapproval of his highest clerics – the *Ulema*. The Koran expressly limits the number of wives a man may take to four, but one verse also admits a lower form of marriage, known as *muta*, more like an informal pact, which could be entered into with non-Muslims. Akbar's abuse of this long-lapsed law was heavily criticized by his Sunni head priest during their religious disquisitions.

What life must actually have been like for the women who lived in Akbar's harem one can only imagine, but it is known that alcoholism and drug addiction were widespread, and that some also risked their lives to conduct illicit affairs with male lovers, smuggled in disguised as physicians or under heavy Muslim veils.

In fact, the notion that the harem was a gilded prison whose inmates whiled their lifetimes away in idle vanity and dalliance is something of a myth. Many women in the *zenana* were immensely rich in their own right, and wielded enormous influence on the court. Jahangir's wife, Nur Jahan, virtually ran the empire from behind the screen of purdah during the last five years of her husband's ailing reign, while her mother-in-law owned a ship that traded between Surat and the Red Sea, a tradition continued by Shah Jahan's daughter, who grew immensely wealthy through her business enterprises.

Partly as a result of the money and power at the women's disposal, jealousies in the harem were also rife, and the work of maintaining order and calm among the thousands of foster mothers, aunties, the emperor's relatives and all his wives, minor wives, paramours, musicians, dancers, amazons and slaves, was a major preoccupation. As Akbar's court chronicler wryly observed, "The government of the kingdom is but an amusement compared with such a task, for it is within the (harem) that intrigue is enthroned."

ARRIVAL AND INFORMATION

By train There are five daily trains from Fatehpur Sikri to Agra (1hr–1hr 15min), overnight services to Lucknow and to Kota, Bundi and Chittaurgarh, and even a direct (though not conveniently timed) train to Mumbai; the station also has a computer reservation office, and is a good place to make bookings as there isn't usually any queue.

By bus Buses leave either from the crowded bus stand in the centre of the village or from the bus stop on the bypass near Agra Gate, about 1.5km from town (about ₹20 by auto-rickshaw from the village, also connected by a ₹5 CNG bus to the palace entrance) – it's usually quickest to pick up a bus from Agra Gate, especially if you're heading to Jaipur (hourly; 4hr). Services from the bus stand itself go to Agra's Idgah Bus Stand (every 30min; 1hr–1hr 30min) and to Bharatpur (hourly; 30–45min). There are shared jeeps from the village to Agra (₹30), but they depart very full, the driving isn't marvellous and they frequently have accidents. Note that buses back to Agra dry up around 4.30pm, so it's best to get to the bus stand by 4pm to be sure of transport back – failing that, you should be able to pick up transport on the main road by Agra Gate.

Getting around Transport around the village takes the form of tongas and auto-rickshaws, but for most people it's just as easy to walk.

Services Canara Bank has an ATM. The *Hotel Goverdhan* will change cash dollars, pounds or euros, offers free tourist information and can arrange tours of Rajasthan.

ACCOMMODATION AND EATING

You'll probably **eat** where you stay. If you want to go out, try the *Goverdhan* or the *Ajay Palace* hotel. Fatehpur Sikri's delicious biscuits are not to be missed – you can savour them hot out of the oven each evening at the bakeries on the lane leading up from the bazaar to the Jama Masjid.

Ajay Palace Agra Rd ☎ 05613 282950. Simple hotel in the village, with small, plain rooms, all clean with attached bathrooms (though hot water comes in buckets). There's also a nice little rooftop terrace and good food. **₹300**

★ **Goverdhan** Buland Gate Rd, just east of the bus stand ☎ 94125 26585, ⊕ hotelfatehpursikriviews.com. A wide range of well-kept rooms (all attached with hot running water) arranged around a neat lawn, as well as good food (made with filtered water), wi-fi and a friendly and helpful proprietor. **₹400**

Sunset View 100m west of the Jama Masjid ☎ 94123 84416. Backpacker guesthouse offering neat, clean, if basic rooms and superb views over the Jama Masjid and the countryside beyond. Most rooms are attached, but hot water comes in buckets. **₹100/₹250**

UPTDC Gulistan Tourist Complex Agra Rd, 1km east of the village ☎ 05613 282490, ⊕ rahigulistan @up-tourism.com. A low-rise, modern building in red sandstone, which looks rather like an academic institution, and has decent if functional rooms, plus a restaurant, a pool room and a beer bar. **₹600**

Jhansi

Despite its seventeenth-century fort, the rail- and road-junction town of **JHANSI**, in an anomalous promontory of UP that thrusts south into Madhya Pradesh, is not very exciting. Most visitors stop only long enough to catch a connecting bus to **Khajuraho**, 175km southeast in Madhya Pradesh. Like Avadh (see p.256), Jhansi was an independent state until the British summarily annexed it in 1854, and was consequently a major centre of support for the 1857 uprising, under the leadership of **Rani Lakshmibai**, its last ruler's widow, and the uprising's great heroine.

Jhansi Fort

Daily sunrise–sunset • ₹100 (₹5), video camera ₹25 • **Sound-and-light show** (English version) daily: April–Sept 8.45pm; Oct–March 7.45pm • ₹250 (₹20)

Dominating it all from a bare brown craggy hill, **Jhansi Fort**, built in 1613 by Bir Singh Joo Deo, raja of Orchha, is worth visiting primarily for the **views** from its ramparts. Rani Lakshmibai is supposed to have leapt over the west wall on horseback to escape the British, though she must have had a very athletic horse to do so. Inside the fort are a couple of unremarkable temples, plus an old cistern and the ruins of a palace.

Rani Lakshmi Mahal

Nehru Marg • Daily sunrise–sunset • ₹100 (₹5) • No photography allowed

Two minutes' walk from the roundabout below the fort, the **Rani Lakshmi Mahal** is a small stately home in "Bundela style" (lots of ornate balconies and domed roofs), built as a palace for the rani. The home was the scene of a brutal massacre in 1858, when British troops bayoneted all its occupants (they murdered some five thousand people in all after recapturing Jhansi from the insurgents).

St Jude's Shrine

Jail Rd

The grounds of a Cantonment seminary between the station and the GPO hold one of the most important Catholic pilgrimage sites in India, **St Jude's Shrine**. A bone belonging to Jude the Apostle, patron saint of hopeless causes, is said to be buried in the foundations of the sombre grey-and-white cathedral. On his feast day, October 28, thousands come to plead their causes.

ARRIVAL AND INFORMATION

By train Jhansi is the most convenient main railway station for Orchha. The station is on the west side of town, 1.5km from the centre, near the Civil Lines area. To Khajuraho, there is a day train, the #19666 *Udaipur–Khajuraho Express*, which leaves at 2.35pm daily to arrive at 7.30pm, and there's also a night train, the #12448/02448 *Sampark Kranti Express*, which departs Jhansi at 2.25am to arrive at Khajuraho at a bright and early 6.35am. Numerous trains serve Agra, mostly taking around 3hr, although the #12001 *Shatabdi Express* at 5.59pm takes only 2hr 30min. To Lucknow (5–8 daily; 5hr 10min–7hr 20min), the #11109 *Intercity Express* at 6.10am, arriving at noon, is the most convenient.

By bus The bus stand on the eastern edge of town – 1.5km from the centre, 3km from the station – has only one daily departure for Khajuraho (₹125) – you're usually better off taking a shared tempo to Orchha and an onward bus from there, or better still, go by train.

By tempo Shared tempos for Orchha (45min; ₹20) wait alongside the bus stand, but they tend to dry up around 5pm. There are also shared tempos from the bus stand to the train station. An auto from Jhansi to Orchha will cost around ₹200.

Tourist information The UP Tourist Office at the *Hotel Veerangana* on Shivpuri Rd (Mon–Sat 10am–5pm; ☎0510 244 1267) provides town plans and information on Bundelkhand and the route to Khajuraho, but they often close up before time. At the station, UP Tourism have a kiosk on platform 1 (Mon–Sat 10am–5pm, but closed on the second Sat of the month, and often closed for breaks as it has a staff of only one), and MP Tourism have one next door (daily 10am–5pm; ☎0510 244 2622), with information about getting to Khajuraho.

Banks There are ATMs all over town, including one in the station forecourt. The State Bank of India is on Jhokan Bagh Rd near Elite Cross.

ACCOMMODATION AND EATING

With Orchha just down the road, few people **stay** in Jhansi. Most Jhansi hotels operate 24hr checkout.

Jhansi Shastri Marg, Cantonment (opposite the GPO) ☎0510 247 0360, ✉jhansihotel@sancharnet.in. A former haunt of British burra sahibs, with a well-stocked and atmospheric colonial bar and restaurant, some a/c rooms (₹1500) and a small garden. ₹**1200**

Let's Eat 6 Shastri Marg, Cantonment (opposite *Raj Palace* hotel) ☎99350 85029. A bright, a/c restaurant serving snacks and meals, largely chicken (butter, *handi* or *do pyaza*, all ₹200), as well as various breakfast options. Daily 9.30am–11pm.

Nav Bharat Shastri Marg, Sadar Bazaar (300m up the street from *Let's Eat*) ☎0510 247 0025. Veg or non-veg thalis, dosas, curries, burgers and sizzlers, served up fast-food-style. Thalis cost ₹115 veg, ₹150 non-veg. Daily except Tues 10am–10pm.

Railway Refreshment Rooms In the station. A cheap and handy alternative to the restaurants in town, serving breakfast (omelettes and such like) 6–11am, lunch 11am–3pm, supper 7–10pm (with surprisingly good freshly cooked thalis; ₹22 veg, ₹27 non-veg), and tea and snacks the rest of the time. Daily 24hr.

Raj Palace Shastri Marg, Cantonment (near the GPO) ☎0510 274 0554, ✉hotelrajpalacejhansi@rediffmail.com. A friendly hotel in a quiet location. The rooms are quite spacious and presentable, and are all attached, but they don't all have widows, and there's hot running water

6am–1pm only (though they'll do you a bucket of hot water any time outside those hours). ₹800

Sharma Sweets Shastri Marg, Sadar Bazaar (next door to Nav Bharat) ☎ 0510 247 1666. A good spot for a bit of *mithai* confectionery – the nutty dry fruit *ladoo* (₹30/ piece) is wonderful. Daily 8am–10pm.

Lucknow

UP's state capital, **LUCKNOW**, is best remembered for the ordeal of its British residents during a five-month **siege** of the Residency in 1857. Less remembered are the atrocities perpetrated by the British when they recaptured the city. Lucknow saw the last days of Muslim rule in India, and the summary British deposition in 1856 of Wajid Ali Shah, the last nawab of **Avadh**, was one of the main causes of the 1857 uprising.

Extraordinary sandstone **monuments**, now engulfed by modern Lucknow, still testify to the euphoric atmosphere of the Islamic Avadh's unique culture. European-inspired edifices, too, are prominent on the skyline, often embellished with flying buttresses, turrets, cupolas and floral patterns, but the brick and mortar with which they were constructed means that they are not ageing as well as the earlier stone buildings, and colonial Lucknow is literally crumbling away.

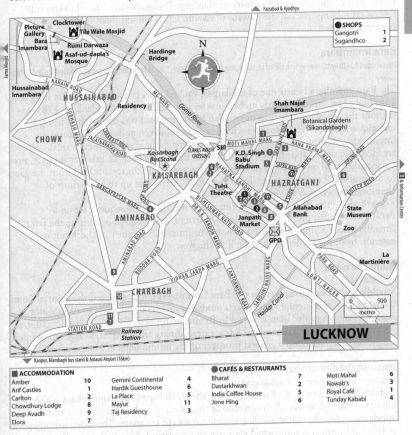

● SHOPS	
Gangotri	1
Sugandhco	2

■ ACCOMMODATION					
Amber	10	Gemini Continental	4	Moti Mahal	6
Arif Castles	1	Hardik Guesthouse	6	Nawab's	3
Carlton	2	La Place	5	Royal Café	1
Chowdhury Lodge	8	Mayur	11	Tunday Kababi	4
Deep Avadh	9	Taj Residency	3		
Elora	7				

● CAFÉS & RESTAURANTS			
Bharat	7		
Dastarkhwan	2		
India Coffee House	5		
Jone Hing	6		

Brief history

Avadh (Oudh, as the British spelt it) broke away from the Mughal Empire in the mid-eighteenth century after its nawab, Safdarjang, was thrown out of office in Delhi for being a Shi'ite, but as the Mughal Empire declined, Avadh became the centre of Muslim power. Under the decadent later nawabs, the arts flourished. Lucknow, the Avadhi capital, became a magnet for artisans. Courtesans became poets, singers and dancers, and under the last nawab the amorous musical form called *thumri* emerged here (see p.1185). The city was also an important repository of Shi'a culture and Islamic jurisprudence, its Farangi Mahal law school attracting students from China and Central Asia.

The patronage of the Shi'a nawabs also produced new expressions of the faith, notably in the annual **Muharram** processions. Held in memory of the martyrdom of Muhammad's grandson Hussain (the second Shi'ite Imam) at Karbala in Iraq, these developed into elaborate affairs with **tazia**, ornate paper reproductions of Hussein's Karbala shrine, being carried through the streets. During the rest of the year the *tazia* images are kept in Imambara (houses of the Imam); these range from humble rooms in poor Shi'a households to the **Great Imambara** built by Asaf-ud-daula in 1784.

Hussainabad

In the west of the city, in the vicinity of Hardinge Bridge around "old" Lucknow, lie several crumbling relics of the nawabs of Avadh. Chief among them is the Great or **Bara Imambara**.

Bara Imambara

Hussainabad Rd • Daily sunrise–sunset, closed on Sun during Muharram • ₹350 (₹35), ticket includes Hussainabad Imambara and Picture Gallery

The **Bara Imambara** boasts one of the largest vaulted halls in the world – 50m long and 15m high. Flat on top, slightly arched inside, and built by Asaf-ud-daula in 1784 without the aid of a single iron or wooden beam, the roof was constructed using a technique known as *kara dena*, in which bricks are broken and angled to form an interlocking section and then covered with concrete – here several metres thick. The arcaded structure is approached through what must have been an extravagant gate, now pockmarked and on the verge of collapse. Two successive courtyards lead from the gates to the unusually festive-looking Imambara itself. Steps lead up to a labyrinth of chambers known as *bhulbhulaiya* – the "maze".

Overlooking the Bara Imambara from the south, the **Asfi Mosque** is set on a two-tiered arcaded plinth with two lofty minarets. Even though it is inside the Bara Imambara compound, it is closed to non-Muslims, but anyone can check out its exterior, from the gardens adjoining it to the west.

Rumi Darwaza

Hussainabad Rd

Straddling the main road west of the Bara Imambara's entrance gates, the colossal **Rumi Darwaza** is an ornamental victory arch modelled on one of the gates to Asia Minor in Istanbul (known to the Islamic world in Byzantine times as "Rum"). Now decaying, it sports elaborate floral patterns and a few extraordinary trumpets; steps lead up to open chambers that command a general prospect of the monuments of Hussainabad.

Hussainabad Imambara and around

Hussainabad Rd • Same hours and ticket as Bara Imambara

A short distance west of the Rumi Darwaza, the lavish **Hussainabad Imambara** is also known as the Chhota (small) Imambara, or the Palace of Lights, thanks to its fairy-tale appearance when decorated and illuminated for special occasions. The raised bathing pool in front of it, which is approached via a spacious courtyard, adds to the overall atmosphere.

A central gilded dome dominates the whole ensemble, busy with minarets, small domes and arches and even a crude miniature Taj Mahal. Built in 1837 by Muhammad Ali Shah, partly to provide famine relief through employment, the Imambara houses a silver-faced throne, plus the tombs of important Avadhi personalities. The dummy gate opposite the main entrance was used by ceremonial musicians, while the unfinished watchtower is known as the Satkhanda or "Seven Storeys", even though only four were ever constructed.

Beyond the Hussainabad Tank is the isolated 67-metre-high **Hussainabad Clocktower**, an ambitious Gothic affair completed in 1887 which carries the largest clock in India. Southwest of the Hussainabad Imambara, and surrounded by ruins, are the two soaring minarets and three domes of the **Jama Masjid**. Commissioned by Muhammad Ali Shah, who ruled Avadh 1837–42, the mosque was only completed after his death.

Muhammad Ali Shah Art Gallery

Hussainabad Rd • Same hours and ticket as Bara Imambara

Close to the clocktower monolith lies **Taluqdar's Hall**, built by Muhammad Ali Shah to house the offices of the Hussainabad Trust and the dusty **Picture Gallery**, also known as the **Muhammad Ali Shah Art Gallery**. Arranged chronologically, the portraits of nawabs graphically demonstrate the decline of their civilization, as the figures become progressively portlier. In a famous image, the androgynous-looking last nawab, Wajid Ali Shah (1847–56), is shown in a daringly low-cut top that reveals his left nipple.

The Residency

Daily sunrise–sunset; museum daily 8am–4.30pm • ₹100 (₹5), video cameras ₹25

The blasted **Residency** rests in peace amid landscaped gardens southeast of Hardinge Bridge – a battle-scarred ruin left exactly as it stood when the siege was finally relieved by Sir Colin Campbell on November 17, 1857 (see box, p.258). Its cannonball-shattered tower became a shrine to the tenacity of the British in India, and continued to be maintained as such even after Independence.

During the siege, every building in the complex was utilized for the hard-fought defence of the compound. The **Treasury**, on the right through the **Baillie Guard Gate**, served as an arsenal, while the sumptuous **Banqueting Hall**, immediately west, was a makeshift hospital, and the extensive single-storey **Dr Fayrer's House**, just south, housed women and children. Most of the original structures, such as **Begum Kothi**, were left standing to impede direct fire from the enemy. On the lawn outside Begum Kothi, a large cross honours the astute Sir Henry Lawrence, responsible for building its defences, who died shortly after hostilities began.

The pockmarked Residency itself holds a small **museum**. On the ground floor, the **Model Room**, the only one with its roof intact, houses a large model of the defences and of the Residency and a small but excellent collection of images, including etchings showing wall breaches blocked up with billiard tables and a soldier blacking up in preparation for a dash across enemy lines.

Hazratganj

With its shops and upmarket restaurants and hotels, and a concentration of banks and other services, **Hazratganj** is the modern centre of Lucknow. Though not as bustling as the older Kaiserbagh and Aminabad neighbourhoods to its west, Hazratganj still has quite a buzz, plus a handful of interesting sights.

Shah Najaf Imambara

Rana Pratap Marg (opposite *Carlton Hotel*) • Daily except Fri sunrise–sunset • Free

With its huge dome, the **Shah Najaf Imambara**, named after the tomb of Ali in Iraq, is at its best when adorned with lights during the holy month of Muharram. Its musty

THE LUCKNOW RESIDENCY SIEGE

The insurgent sepoys who entered Lucknow on June 30, 1857, found the city rife with resentment against the recent British takeover of the kingdom of Avadh. The tiny and isolated **British garrison**, under the command of Sir Henry Lawrence, took refuge in the **Residency**, which became the focus of a fierce struggle.

Less than a third of the three thousand British residents and loyal Indians who crammed into the Residency survived the four-and-a-half-month siege. So unhygienic were their living conditions that those who failed to succumb to gangrenous and tetanus-infected wounds often fell victim to cholera and scurvy. While a barrage of heavy artillery was maintained by both sides, the insurgents attempted to tunnel under the defences and lay mines, but among the British were former tin-miners in the 32nd (Cornish) Regiment, who were far more adept at such things, and were able to follow the sounds of enemy chipping, defuse mines, and even blow up several sepoy-controlled buildings.

Morale remained high among the 1400 **noncombatants**, who included fifty schoolboys from La Martinière (see below), and class distinctions were upheld throughout. While the wives of European soldiers and non-commissioned officers, children and servants took refuge in the *tikhana* (cellar), the "ladies" of the Residency occupied the higher and airier chambers, until the unfortunate loss of one Miss Palmer's leg on July 1 persuaded them of the gravity of their predicament. Sir Henry Lawrence was fatally wounded the next day. The wealthier officers managed to maintain their own private hoard of supplies, living in much their usual style. Matters improved when, after three months, Brigadier-General Sir Henry Havelock arrived with reinforcements, and the normal round of visits and invitations to supper was resumed despite the inconvenient shortage of good food and wine. Not until November 17 was the siege finally broken by a force of Sikhs and Highlanders under Sir Colin Campbell. Their offers of tea, however, were turned down by the Residency women; they were used to taking it with milk, which the soldiers could not supply.

interior holds some incredibly garish chandeliers used in processions, several *tazia*, and the silver-faced tomb of the decadent and profligate Ghazi-ud-Din-Haidar (ruled 1814–27), buried with three of his queens.

Sikandrabagh

Rana Pratap Marg • **Botanical Gardens** Mon–Fri: April–Sept 5–9.15am; Oct–March 6–9.15am (last entry ticket sold 8.30am) • ₹1

The Imambara was commandeered as an insurgent stronghold in 1857, and the crucial battle that enabled the British to relieve the Residency was fought in the adjacent pleasure gardens of **Sikandrabagh** on November 16. It took one and a half hours of bombardment by Sir Colin Campbell's soldiers to breach the defences of the two thousand sepoys; then the Sikhs and 93rd Highlanders poured through. There was no escape for the terrified sepoys, some of whom are said to have believed the bloodstained, red-faced, kilted Scots to be the ghosts of a group of European women slaughtered at Kanpur earlier in the uprising. Driven against the north wall, the sepoys were either bayoneted or shot, and the dead and dying piled shoulder-high. Tranquil once again, Sikandrabagh is now home to the National Botanical Research Institute and the beautiful **Botanical Gardens**, with manicured lawns, conservatories, nurseries and herb, rose and bougainvillea gardens.

La Martinière

La Martinière Rd

Towards the east of Lucknow, an extraordinary chateau-like building has become almost a symbol of the city – **La Martinière** remains to this day an exclusive boys' school in the finest colonial tradition. It was built as a country retreat by Major-General Claude Martin, a French soldier-adventurer taken prisoner by the British in Puducherry. The enigmatic Martin later joined the East India Company, made his fortune in indigo, and served both the British and the nawabs of Avadh. The building is an outrageous but intriguing amalgam, crowned by flying walkways; Greco-Roman figures on the parapets give it a busy silhouette, gigantic heraldic lions gaze across the grounds, and a large bronze cannon graces the front. Martin himself is buried in the basement. During the uprising, La Martinière was occupied by insurgent forces, its boys having been evacuated to the Residency.

The zoo

Rana Pratap Marg • Tues–Sun 8am–5pm • ₹100 (₹20–25)

Close to the centre of Hazratganj, its grounds dotted with derelict Avadhi monuments, Lucknow's small **zoo** also serves as an amusement park with a miniature train to view the animals.

The State Museum

Tues–Sun 10am–4pm • ₹50 (₹5), camera ₹20

Inside the zoo, the **State Museum** exhibits delicate, speckled-red-sandstone sculpture from the Mathura school of the Kushana and Gupta periods (first to sixth centuries AD). Besides sculpture from Gandhara, Mahoba, Nalanda and Sravasti, it has a gallery of terracotta artefacts and even an Egyptian mummy. Musical instruments, paintings and costumes provide atmosphere in the Avadh gallery, while the natural history section is a taxidermist's dream.

ARRIVAL AND DEPARTURE

LUCKNOW

By plane Amausi airport is 16km south of town on the Kanpur Rd (around ₹400 by taxi from the city centre, or ₹150 by auto). Destinations include Delhi (12 daily with Jet, Go and IndiGo; 1hr), Mumbai (5 daily with Air India, Jet, Go and IndiGo; 2hr 5min–2hr 15min), Patna (2 daily with Jet and IndiGo; 1hr–1hr 15min) and Bangalore (1 daily with IndiGo; 2hr 30min). Air India's office is at 9 Rani Laxmi Bai Marg (by *Gemini Continental* hotel; ☎0522 262 0927); Jet are based at the airport (☎0522 243 4009).

By train Lucknow's busy railway station (with a computerized reservations office at the eastern end of its forecourt) is in Charbagh, 4km southwest of Hazratganj (₹65 by auto). It's quite a remarkable building, its roof studded with prominent chhatris of different sizes. Note that Lucknow Junction is actually a separate station from Lucknow, adjoining it to the west (off the same forecourt); make sure you go to the correct station to get your train.

Destinations Trains to Delhi include the #12003 *Shatabdi Express*, which leaves at 3.35pm to arrive in New Delhi at 10.05pm. Overnight services include the #12553 *Vaishali Express* at 10.25pm, which reaches New Delhi at 6.30am, and the #12229 *Lucknow Mail* at 10.10pm, arriving in New Delhi at 6.50am. To Agra, the #14863/14865/14853 *Marudhar Express* leaves daily at half past midnight, arriving in Agra Fort at 5.55am, while the *Intercity Express* #12179 departs Lucknow at 3.45pm to reach Agra Cantonment at 9.35pm. The *Pushpak Express* #12533 is the most convenient service to Mumbai (daily 7.45pm, arriving 8.05pm). The fastest daily service to Kolkata is

the #13006 *Amritsar–Howrah Mail* (dep. 10.50am, arr. 7.20am next day). The #14236 *Bareilly–Varanasi Express* leaves at 11.15pm for Varanasi, arriving at 6.50am; daytime services include the #13006 *Amritsar–Howrah Mail* (dep. 10.50am, arr. 4.40pm). The #13009 *Doon Express* at 6.30pm is the best service for Dehra Dun (arr. 7.10am). Ramnagar is served by the 4.45pm *Dheradun Express* #14265/55321 (arr. 6.15am). Both stop at Haridwar, but inconveniently, in the wee hours. Also to Uttarakhand, the #13019 *Bagh Express* leaves at 12.25am to reach Kathgodam, the railhead for Nainital, at 9.30am. For Khajuraho, the #12533 *Pushpak Express* at 7.45pm reaches Jhansi at 1.30am, which ought to give you enough time to pick up the #12448/02448 *Sampark Kranti Express* at 2.25am, arriving in Khajuraho at 6.35am; if you want to play it safe, you can take the earlier #11110 *Intercity Express* at 4.2pm to reach Jhansi at 10.35pm. For Nepal, daily overnight trains to Gorakhpur – where you can get a bus to the Sonauli border, and then buses to Kathmandu and Pokhara on the other side – include the #15708 *Amritsar–Katihar Express* (12.50am, arr. 5.50am), and the #11015 *Kushinagar Express* (1.55am, arr. 7.15am).

By bus Most intercity buses operate from Alambagh Bus Stand, 3km southwest of the station (₹120 from Hazratganj by auto, or ₹7–10 on shared Vikrams from Charbagh or Ashoka Marg). A few buses use the more central Kaiserbagh Bus Stand (₹50 by cycle rickshaw from Hazratganj), which has departures to Dehra Dun (2 daily; 10hr 30min), Haridwar (1 daily; 10hr), Gorakhpur (hourly; 8hr) and Sonauli (5 daily; 12hr).

GETTING AROUND

By tempo Multiseater tempos (Vikrams) have more or less taken over from city buses, plying regular routes such as from Charbagh to the GPO.

Car rental Cars (with driver) can be hired from Great Value

Travels at *Hotel Clarks Avadh*, 8 MG Marg by Clarks Avadh Crossing (☎0522 262 7228), or UP Tours (see p.262) at the *Hotel Gomti* (☎0522 261 2659).

INFORMATION AND TOURS

Tourist information The UP Tourism office is inconveniently located at C-13 Vipin Khand in Gomti Nagar, 3km east of town (Mon–Fri 10am–5pm; ☎0522 230 4870). If all you need is a town plan, you can pick one up from their tour agency, UP Tours at *Hotel Gomti*, 6 Sapru Marg (Mon–Sat 9.30am–6.30pm; ☎0522 261 2659). Lucknow also has offices of both GMVN (for Garhwal, western Uttarakhand), at 4-7-RF Khushnuma Complex, Bahadur Marg (☎0522 220 7844), and KMVN (for Kumaon, eastern Uttarakhand), A-4, Sarang Manor Flats, Shah Najaf Rd, behind *Hotel Gomti* (☎0522 261 5866).

Tours Comprehensive daily city tours (₹650), which must be booked in advance through UP Tours (see p.262), and only run if they have three or more takers, leave the *Hotel Gomti* at 9.30am and return at 2.30pm. You can also be picked up from the station (at 9am) and from various other hotels. The price includes guide and entrance fees. A 2hr Heritage Walk starts bright and early at 7.30am daily (₹150) from Tile Wale Masjid north of Shah Najaf Imambara; for details contact Naved Zia on ☎94150 13047.

ACCOMMODATION

There's a concentration of budget hotels around Subhaj Marg, north of the station, with more upmarket places mainly within easy each of Hazratganj in the centre of town.

Amber Subhash Marg, Naka Hindola ☎0522 268 3201, ✉amberhotel@yahoo.com. Good value near the station: a range of spacious rooms at different prices, all attached, most with a/c but a few just air-cooled. The cheapest rooms go quickly. 24hr checkout. ₹**500**

Arif Castles 4 Rana Pratap Marg ☎0522 409 8777, ⊛arifcastles.com. Quite well-appointed in marble, brass and light blue, this "business class hotel", as it calls itself, has cool rooms, a/c, cable TV and an Avadhi cuisine restaurant. Rates include breakfast. ₹**5085**

Carlton Shah Najaf Rd ☎0522 222 4021. Fabled Lucknow address, a *fin-de-siècle* Euro-Avadhi edifice with big rooms, ancient plumbing and musty hunting trophies. Currently closed for total refurbishment, and should eventually emerge spanking new.

Chowdhury Lodge 3 Vidhan Sabha Marg ☎0522 393 2397. Grimy, *paan*-stained city-centre cheapie down an alley by a filling station. The attached and non-attached rooms are certainly nowhere near luxury, although there are some a/c rooms (₹800), and hot water comes in a bucket, but especially for singles (₹150/₹250), it's very cheap indeed. ₹**200**/₹**350**

Deep Avadh Aminabad Rd, Naka Hindola ☎0522 268 4381 to 7, ✉deepavadh@sify.com. Good a/c rooms in various sizes with 24hr room service, as well as two restaurants, bar and travel desk, in an interesting part of town close to the station and on the edge of bustling Aminabad. 24hr checkout. ₹**1644**

Elora 3 Lalbagh ☎0522 221 1307. Friendly, popular place with a good range of clean rooms, including some with a/c (₹1000). Facilities include cable TV in all rooms,

24hr room service and a multicuisine restaurant. ₹**800**

Gemini Continental 10 Rani Laximbai Marg ☎0522 401 1111, ⊛geminicontinental.com. Snazzy, upscale hotel in the centre of town. Spacious, modern rooms with great views, mini-bar, cable TV, a/c and 24hr room service. Buffet breakfast is included, but wi-fi is ₹550 extra. ₹**8437**

Hardik Guest House 16 Rana Pratap Marg, by the junction with Jopling Rd ☎0522 220 9497. Clean, comfortable and justifiably popular family-run guesthouse with friendly, helpful staff, a/c rooms and good home-cooking, although it's getting slightly worn around the edges, and it's a bit pricey for what you get. ₹**2500**

La Place 6 Shah Najaf Rd, Hazratganj ☎0522 405 5000, ⊛sarovarhotels.com. Small but smart modern business hotel crackling with brisk efficiency. Facilities include wi-fi, a business centre and executive offices, but no pool. Breakfast included. Discounts usually available. ₹**8213**

Mayur Subhash Marg, at Station Rd, Charbagh (above Bharat restaurant) ☎0522 245 1824. The cheapest rooms are pretty poky, and those at the other end of the range are better value. The attached rooms all have hot running water, but only the a/c rooms (₹950) have a shower as such (in the others, it's taps and a bucket). Located opposite the train station, and handy for early morning get-aways and late-night arrivals. 24hr checkout. ₹**300**/₹**500**

Taj Residency Vipin Khand, Gomti Nagar ☎0522 239 3939, ⊛tajhotels.com. Built in Avadhi style, this is easily Lucknow's most elegant and comfortable hotel, with a swimming pool and a range of restaurants, but inconveniently situated 3km east of town. Breakfast included. ₹**12,366**

EATING

The rich traditional **Lucknavi cuisine** – featuring Mughlai dishes as well as the local *dum pukht* (steam casserole) style, sometimes known as *handi* after the pot it's cooked in – is available from food stalls throughout the city, in places such as Shami Avadh Bazaar, near the K.D. Singh Babu Stadium, the Chowk, Aminabad and behind the Tulsi Theatre in Hazratganj. Luknavi "kebabs" – extremely delicious – are in fact fried patties of very finely minced meat. The bazaars are the place to get Lucknow's popular breakfast speciality *paya-khulcha*, a spicy mutton soup served with hot breads.

Bharat Subhash Marg, at Station Rd, Charbagh ☎0522 326 8053. Cheap *dhaba* opposite the station serving good dosas (₹40), curries and thalis (veg ₹120, non-veg ₹155). Daily 6am–11pm.

Dastarkhwan China Gate ☎0522 262 5297. One of a number of open-air diners in this little street by UP Press Club, with non-veg Mughlai dishes (such as *rogan josh*, ₹65), kebabs (₹35–65) and biriyanis (₹65). Daily 1.30–10.30pm.

Indian Coffee House 1 Ashok Marg ☎0522 322 9556. Once a hotbed of Lucknow's political intelligentsia, nicknamed the "maternity ward" for the ideas it gave birth to, now reborn as a bright, new café serving excellent filter coffee (at ₹45, rather pricier than in most *ICH* branches) plus cakes, shakes, snacks and Avadhi, south Indian or Chinese food (*shahi* kebabs ₹80, masala dosa ₹45). Daily 8am–10pm.

Jone Hing MG Marg, Hazratganj ☎93357 11772. Chinese restaurant serving the usual sweet-and-sour, chop suey and chowmein, plus specialities such as Manchurian chicken lollipop (drumsticks in sauce, ₹180) or chilli fish (₹195). Daily 11am–11pm.

Moti Mahal 75 MG Marg, Hazratganj ☎0522 404 8101. The sweet shop at the front has some great milky confections, including sugar-free ones; the family restaurant upstairs serves excellent veg curries, including three types of *dum aloo* (Lucknavi, Banarsi or Kashmiri, all ₹100). Daily 11am–11pm.

Nawab's In Capoor's hotel, 52 MG Marg, Hazratganj ☎0522 405 4300. A refined restaurant, with live *qawwali* music in the evening (except Tues). Top dishes include *murg nawabi*, a mild, creamy dish of chicken in cashew butter (₹325), or there's a great mushroom tikka masala (₹195). Daily noon–11pm.

Royal Café 9–7 Shah Najaf Rd ☎0522 402 3535. A lively place that's popular among Lucknavi families. They have plenty of veg dishes, of course, but they tend to specialize in chicken, with half a Royal Café special chicken (with hard-boiled egg and dried fruit) or chicken *handi* for ₹270, and there are also Chinese and Continental dishes. Daily 10am–11.30pm.

★ Tunday Kababi Naaz Cinema Rd, just off Aminabad main chowk. For an authentic Avadhi gastronomic experience, head to this popular and inexpensive place (the best in a street of them), where tandoori chicken and kebabs are prepared out front and served up within. A plate of four kebabs will set you back ₹25 for beef, ₹55 for mutton. Daily 11.30am–11.30pm.

DIRECTORY

Banks and exchange There are plenty of ATMs around town (at the station and the bus stand, and on MG Rd and Shah Najaf Rd); otherwise, there's Allahabad Bank on Park Rd in Hazratganj and the State Bank of India (SBI) on MG Marg.

LUCKNAVI CRAFTS

Chikan is a long-standing Lucknavi tradition of embroidery, in which designs are built up to form delicate floral patterns along edges on saris and on necklines and collars of *kurtas*. Workshops can be found around the Chowk, the market area of old Lucknow, and shops and showrooms in Hazratganj (especially Janpath Market), Nazirabad and Aminabad.

Lucknow is also renowned for its *ittar* (or *attar*), concentrated perfume sold in small vials – an acquired (and expensive) taste. Small balls of cotton wool are daubed with the scent and placed neatly within the top folds of the ear; musicians believe that the aroma heightens their senses. Popular *ittar* include *ambar* from amber, *khus* from a flowering plant and rose-derived *ghulab*.

Gangotri MG Marg, Hazratganj (half a block west of Lalbagh) ☎0522 262 4377. The UP state crafts emporium has a variety of carvings, carpets, enamel ware, brass figurines, clothes and textiles. The fixed prices here are higher than those in the markets, but the quality is assured and you don't have to haggle. Mon–Sat 10.30am–7.30pm.

Sugandhco D-4 Janpath Market (on the south side of the market) ☎0522 262 1748. The smell of sweet perfume greets you as you enter this well-established dealer of top-whack own-brand ittar and incense, which is also sold in other shops around town. Mon–Sat noon–7.30pm.

Festivals November's Lucknow Festival (details from UP Tourism) is an opportunity to sample the city's vibrant traditions of music and dance.

Internet Meeting Point, Sapru Marg near the junction with Ashok Marg (daily 8.30am–8pm; ₹20/hr); United Cyber Café, 1st floor, Rani Sultanat Plaza, MG Marg, opposite Janpath

Market (daily 10am–10pm; ₹20/hr). In Charbagh, in the back alleys opposite *Hotel Mayur*, a few small places, with just a couple of terminals each, charge the same price.

Travel agents Thomas Cook, 68 Hazratganj, 1st Floor (☎ 0522 645 9454); UP Tours, *Hotel Gomti*, 6 Sapru Marg (☎ 0522 261 2659).

Allahabad and around

The administrative and industrial city of **ALLAHABAD**, 135km west of Varanasi and 227km southeast of Lucknow, is also known as **Prayag** ("confluence"): the point where the Yamuna and Ganges rivers meet the mythical Saraswati River (see box, p.264). Sacred to Hindus, the **sangam** (which also means "confluence"), east of the city, is one of the great pilgrimage destinations of India. Allahabad comes alive during its *melas* (fairs) – the annual **Magh Mela** (Jan/Feb), and the colossal **Maha Kumbh Mela**, held every twelve years (2025 and 2037 are the next ones).

Allahabad is a pleasant city to visit, with vast open riverside scenery and good amenities, but is without major temples or monuments. At the junction of the fertile Doab, the "two-river" valley between the Yamuna and the Ganges, it did however possess a crucial strategic significance; its massive **fort**, built by the emperor Akbar in 1583, is still used by the military. Another Mughal, Jahangir's son Khusrau, was murdered here by his brother Shah Jahan, who went on to become emperor. Allahabad was briefly the centre of power after the 1857 uprising, when the British moved the headquarters of their Northwestern Provinces here from Agra; the formal transfer of power from the East India Company to the Crown took place here the following year.

Central Allahabad is split in two by the railway line, with the chaotic and congested **Old City** or **Chowk** south of Allahabad Junction station, and the grid of the **Civil Lines** (the residential quarter of the Raj military town) to the north.

Allahabad also makes a good base from which to venture into the remoter parts of **Bundelkhand** (see p.268) to the south.

All Saints' Cathedral

Mahatma Gandhi Marg

A kilometre north of Allahabad Junction railway station, the yellow-and-red sandstone bulk of the Gothic **All Saints' Cathedral** dominates the surrounding avenues. Designed by Sir William Emerson, architect of Kolkata's Victoria Memorial, the cathedral retains much of its stained glass, and an impressive altar of inlaid marble. Plaques provide interesting glimpses of Allahabad in the days of the Raj, while flying buttresses and snarling gargoyles on the exterior resemble something you might see in an English county town – an impression subverted by the palm trees in the garden. Sunday services continue to attract large congregations, as do Masses at the flamboyant **St Joseph's Roman Catholic Cathedral**, a short distance northeast.

Allahabad Museum

Kamla Nehru Marg • Tues–Sun 10.30am–4.45pm, closed the Sun following the 2nd Sat of the month • ₹100 (₹5)

On the edge of the pleasant **Chandra Shekhar Azad Park**, the grounds of the **Allahabad Museum** are dotted with pieces of ancient sculpture. Inside, you'll find early terracotta artefacts, eighth-century sculptures from the Buddhist site of Kausambi, and a striking twelfth-century image from Khajuraho of Shiva and Parvati. A copious collection of modern Indian art includes work by Haldar, Sajit Khastgir and Rathin Mitra, as well as Jamini Roy, who was inspired by folk art. European paintings concentrate on spiritual

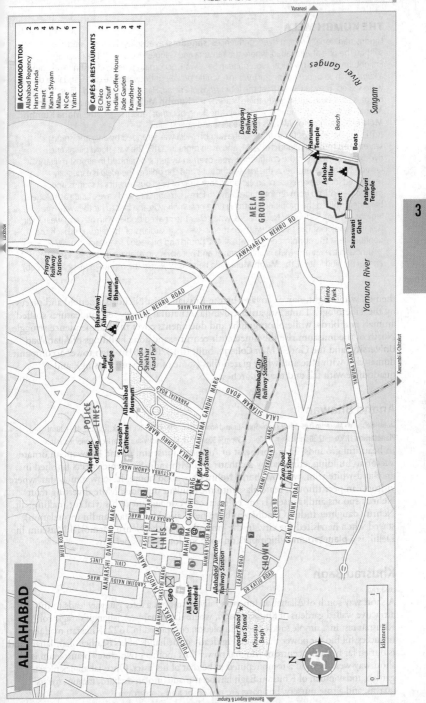

ALLAHABAD

ACCOMMODATION
Allahabad Regency	2
Harsh Ananda	3
Ilawart	4
Kanha Shyam	5
Milan	7
N Cee	6
Yatrik	1

CAFÉS & RESTAURANTS
El Chico	2
Hot Stuff	1
Indian Coffee House	3
Jade Garden	4
Kamdhenu	3
Tandoor	4

Varanasi

River Ganges

Sangam

Beach

Daraganj Railway Station

Hanuman Temple

Boats

Ashoka Pillar

Fort

Patalpuri Temple

Saraswati Ghat

MELA GROUND

JAWAHARLAL NEHRU RD

Yamuna River

Minto Park

Kaushambi & Chitrakut

YAMUNA BANK RD

MALVIYA MARG

MOTILAL NEHRU ROAD

Anand Bhawan

Bharadwaj Ashram

Muir College

Chandra Shekhar Azad Park

Allahabad Museum

PANNALAL ROAD

KAMLA NEHRU MARG

LALA SITARAM ROAD

Allahabad City Railway Station

Prayag Railway Station

Lucknow

POLICE LINES

State Bank of India

St Joseph's Cathedral

MAHATMA GANDHI MARG

MARG

SWAMI VIVEKANAND MARG

ZERO RD

Zero Road Bus Stand

KASTURBA GANDHI MARG

MG Marg Bus Stand

MUIR ROAD

MAHARSHI DAYANAND MARG

SARDAR PATEL MARG

TASHKENT MARG

CIVIL LINES

MAHATMA GANDHI MARG

SMITH RD

SWAMI VIVEKANAND MARG

GRAND TRUNK ROAD

CHOWK

CIVIL LINES

SAROJINI NAIDU MARG

NAWAB YUSUF ROAD

Allahabad Junction Railway Station

LEADER ROAD

DR KATJU ROAD

LAL BAHADUR SHASTRI MARG

PURSHOTTAMDAS TANDON MARG

GPO

All Saints' Cathedral

Leader Road Bus Stand

Khusrau Bagh

N

0   1   kilometre

Samaami Airport & Kanpur

3

THE KUMBH MELA

Hindus traditionally regard river confluences (**sangams**) as auspicious places, and none more so than the one at Allahabad, where the Yamuna and Ganges rivers meet the River of Enlightenment, the mythical subterranean Saraswati. According to legend, Vishnu was carrying a *kumbha* (pot) of *amrita* (nectar), when a scuffle broke out between the gods, and four drops were spilled. They fell to earth at the four *tirthas* of Prayag, Haridwar, Nasik and Ujjain. The event is commemorated every three years by the **Kumbh Mela**, held at each *tirtha* in turn; the Allahabad sangam is known as Tirtharaja, the "King of *tirthas*", and its *mela*, the **Maha Kumbh Mela** or "Great" Kumbh Mela, is the greatest and holiest of all.

The largest religious fair in India, Maha Kumbh Mela was attended by an astonishing **seventeen million** pilgrims in 2001, and even more in 2013. The vast flood plains and riverbanks adjacent to the confluence were overrun by tents, organized in almost military fashion by the government, the local authorities and the police. The *mela* is especially renowned for the presence of an extraordinary array of religious ascetics – sadhus and *mahants* – enticed from remote hideaways in forests, mountains and caves. Once astrologers have determined the propitious bathing time or *kumbhayog*, the first to hit the water are legions of Naga Sadhus or Naga Babas, who cover their naked bodies with ash and wear their hair in dreadlocks. The sadhus, who see themselves as guardians of the faith, approach the confluence at the appointed time with all the pomp and bravado of a charging army.

Although the Kumbh Mela is only triennial, and not always in Allahabad, there is a smaller annual bathing festival, the **Magh Mela**, held here every year in the month of Magha (Jan–Feb).

themes, with bright, naive canvases by the Russian artist Nicholas Roerich, and pieces by the Tibetologist Lama Angarika Govinda. A natural history section features stuffed animals and birds, while photographs and documents cover the Independence struggle. North of the museum rise the nineteenth-century sandstone buildings of **Allahabad University**, and the Gothic **Muir College**, built in 1870. A 61m-high tower accompanies domes clad with blue and white glazed tiles (some of which are missing), and a quadrangle with tall and elegant arches.

Anand Bhawan

Motilal Nehru Rd • **Museum** Tues–Sun 9.30am–5pm • Ground floor free, first floor ₹50 (₹10); no tickets sold 12.45–1.30pm
Planetarium 11.30am, 12.30pm, 1.30pm, 2.30pm, 3.30pm, 4.30pm • ₹40, all in Hindi with a 30min lecture prior to the show

In beautiful grounds, 1km northeast of Allhabad museum, **Anand Bhawan**, an ornate Victorian building, crowned by a chhatri and with Indo-Saracenic effects finished in grey-and-white trim, was **Jawaharlal Nehru's** boyhood home. It's now a museum, where visitors can peer through plate glass into the opulent interiors. More diverting than Nehru's spoons and trousers is the colonial court document of his trial for making salt. Nehru's daughter Indira Gandhi was born here, and Mahatma Gandhi (no relation) stayed when he visited the city. In the grounds, as at the Nehru Memorial Museum in Delhi, is a **planetarium**, which puts on six hour-long shows per day.

Khusrau Bagh

Leader Rd

A short way south of Allahabad Junction railway station, a lofty gateway leads to the attractive walled gardens of **Khusrau Bagh**, where the remains of Jahangir's tragic son Khusrau rest in a simple sandstone mausoleum, completed in 1622. Khusrau made an unsuccessful bid for power that ended in death at the hands of his brother Shah Jahan, and is buried far from the centre of Mughal power. His mother's two-storey mausoleum is a short way west, beyond a tomb reputed to be that of his sister. Once Jahangir's pleasure garden, today much of Khusrau Bagh has been made into an orchard, famous for its guavas, and a rose nursery, but parts are unkempt and overgrown.

The river frontage

Most of Allahabad's river frontage is along the Yamuna, where women perform *arati* or evening worship at **Saraswati Ghat** by floating *diya* downstream. Immediately to the west, in **Minto Park**, a memorial marks the spot where, in 1858, the British Raj was born, as India officially passed from the East India Company to the Crown.

The fort

East of Saraswati Ghat, Akbar's **fort** is best appreciated from boats on the river (see box below). Much of it is still occupied by the military, and public access is restricted to the leafy corner around the **Patalpuri Temple**, approached through any of the three massive gates. Much of the superstructure is neglected; the **zenana** with its columned hall does survive, but can only be viewed with prior permission. At the main gate, a poorly restored polished stone **Ashoka Pillar** is inscribed with the emperor's edicts and dated to 242 BC.

Hanuman Temple

Where the fort's eastern battlements meet the river, a muddy *ghat* is busy with boatmen jostling for custom from pilgrims heading to the sangam. Inland along the base of the fort, with the flood plain of the sangam to the right, a road leads past rows of stalls catering to pilgrims visiting the brightly painted **Hanuman Temple**. Unusually, the large sunken image of the monkey god inside is reclining rather than standing erect; during the annual floods the waters rise to touch his feet before once again receding.

ARRIVAL AND DEPARTURE ALLAHABAD AND AROUND

By plane Bamrauli airport, 18km west on the Kanpur Rd, has daily flights to Delhi with Air India, whose office is at the airport (☎0532 258 1370).

By train Allahabad has four railway stations, but all express trains use Allahabad Junction. Most hotels are nearby; be sure to use the right exit for the area where you plan to stay. Destinations include Delhi (25–29 daily; 7hr 5min–17hr 25min), Agra (23–26 daily; 5hr 33min–10hr 17min), Luicknow (11–12 daily; 4hr 20min–8hr 55min), Varanasi (11–16 daily; 2hr 25min–4hr 5min) and Satna (for Khajuraho; 19–23 daily; 2hr 35min–3hr 50min).

By bus Leader Road Bus Stand, used by buses from western destinations such as Agra, Lucknow, Kausambi and Delhi, is opposite Allahabad Junction station's south gates on the city side. Zero Road Bus Stand, serving Mahoba, Satna and Chitrakut to the south (with connections for Khajuraho) is 1km southeast. Buses from all over and especially points east, including Varanasi (every 15min; 3hr 30min), use the larger MG Marg Bus Stand, next to the *Hotel Ilawart*; because of their frequency, buses are more convenient than trains for the journey to Varanasi.

GETTING AROUND AND INFORMATION

By rickshaw Cycle- and auto-rickshaws are the most common modes of transport; a trip to the sangam from the Civil Lines crossing costs around ₹50 (hang on to your vehicle for the return journey).

THE SANGAM

Around 7km from the centre of the Civil Lines, overlooked by the eastern ramparts of the fort, wide flood plains and muddy banks protrude towards the sacred **sangam**. At the point at which the brown Ganges meets the greenish Yamuna, *pandas* (priests) perch on small platforms to perform puja and assist the devout in their ritual ablutions in the shallow waters. Beaches and *ghats* here are littered with the shorn hair of pilgrims who come to offer *pind* for their deceased parents, and women sit around selling cone-shaped pyramids of bright red and orange *tilak* powder.

Boats to the sangam, used by pilgrims and tourists alike, can be rented at the *ghat* immediately east of the fort, for the recommended government rate of ₹30/head. However, most pilgrims pay around ₹60 and you can be charged as much as ₹200. Official prices for a sixteen-seat boat are ₹300 but can soar to more than ₹2000 during the *melas*. On the way to the sangam, high-pressure aquatic salesmen loom up on the placid waters selling offerings such as coconuts for pilgrims to discard at the confluence. Once abandoned, the offerings are fished up and sold on to other pilgrims.

Car rental Car rental through general travel agencies such as Varuna in Tulsiani Plaza, next to *Harsh* a hotel on MG Marg (☎ 0532 242 7287, ✉ varunatravels@hotmail.com), costs in the region of ₹1400/day, plus mileage. UP Tours, next to *Ilawart* hotel on MG Marg, can also supply a car and driver.

Tourist information At *Ilawart* hotel, 35 MG Marg, Civil Lines (Mon–Sat 10am–5pm, but closed on the second Sat of the month; ☎ 0532 240 8873).

ACCOMMODATION

Allahabad Regency 16 Tashkent Marg ☎ 0532 240 7835, ⊛ hotelallahabadregency.com. Nineteenth-century colonial bungalow with a good garden restaurant, a sauna, jacuzzi, swimming pool and gym. The rooms are very well done out, but a bit on the small side – it's worth paying ₹675 more for a suite-like split-level "duplex" room. ₹**4047**

Harsh Ananda 118/116 MG Marg ☎ 0532 242 7897, ⊛ hotelharshananda.com. An old colonial bungalow refurbished to make a very stylish hotel, with a lawn out front and fireplaces in some of the rooms, all of which are tastefully decorated in relaxing cream and brown tones. ₹**3597**

Ilawart 35 MG Marg Civil Lines ☎ 0532 260 7440, ✉ rahiilawart@up-tourism.com. The new block, where the standard rooms are located, overlooks the bus stand, so choose your room carefully to avoid noise. The older block is quieter, and has been completely refurbished, but the rooms are pricier. As well as rooms, there's a dorm, a restaurant with haphazard service but good food, and a bar. Run by UP Tourism. Dorm ₹**200**, double ₹**1686**

Kanha Shyam Strachey Rd, Civil Lines ☎ 0532 256 0123 to 32, ⊛ hotelkanhashyam.com. Classy four-star with quite stately rooms done out in burgundy and dark wood. There's a lounge bar, a 24hr coffee shop and a rooftop restaurant. ₹**7307**

Milan 46 Leader Rd ☎ 0532 240 3776 or 7, ⊛ hotelmilan.in. A cut above the other hotels in the area south of the station, and not a bad mid-range choice; following renovation, it should emerge gleaming bright and spanking new some time in 2013. ₹**550**

N Cee 108 Leader Rd ☎ 0532 240 1166. Popular budget hotel south of the railway line in the busy bazaar area. Rooms are small, but it's cheap and friendly (and often full), with 24hr checkout. ₹**450**

Yatrik 33 Sardar Patel Marg ☎ 0532 226 0921 to 6, ⊛ www.hotelyatrik.com. Good upmarket choice, with more character than its rival the *Kanha Shyam*. Popular, well run and with a beautiful garden graced with elegant palms, and a pool (April–Sept). 24hr check-out. ₹**3927**

EATING

Most of the better **cafés** and **restaurants** are in the Civil Lines area. In the early evening, the snack stalls along MG Marg ply their specialities.

El Chico 24 MG Marg ☎ 0532 242 0075. One of the city's best, a smart place with good Indian, Chinese and Western cuisine, including grills, sizzlers, Szechwan-style chicken (₹250) or baked fish in cheese sauce (₹290). Daily 9am–11pm.

Hot Stuff 21 Sardar Patel Marg ☎ 0532 226 1168. Popular hangout for Allahabad's young and trendy, offering burgers (₹50, or ₹65 with Coke and fries), shakes (₹75), Chinese food and ice cream. Daily 10.30am–10.30pm.

Indian Coffee House MG Marg, set back from the road ☎ 0532 262 4827. Allahabad branch of the coffee co-op, serving great filter coffee and basic cheap snacks (masala dosa ₹35; nothing over ₹40) with no frills or pretensions. Daily 8am–9pm.

Jade Garden 123–127 MG Marg ☎ 0532 256 1408.

Small garden restaurant offering Chinese food of the chop suey, chowmein and sweet-and-sour variety, plus veg and non-veg Indian dishes. Lemon chicken, ginger chicken or chicken Manchurian are all ₹250. Daily 11am–11pm.

Kamdhenu 37 MG Marg, in the beautiful nineteenth-century Palace Theatre building ☎ 0532 329 7244. Famous Allahabad sweetshop whose specialities include milk cake with almonds (₹17/piece), and less cloyingly sweet fig and nut confections. Daily 8.30am–10.30pm.

Tandoor 33 MG Marg ☎ 0532 242 7291. Reliable non-veg restaurant, and one of the best places in the city for Indian food, serving all the tandoori classics including chicken tikka (₹140), kebabs and Mughlai curries (*rogan josh* ₹115). Daily 10.30am–10.30pm.

DIRECTORY

Banks There are several ATMs along MG Marg, and there's a State Bank of India inconveniently located at Kutchery Rd, Police Lines.

Internet Businet and Vishal Internet in Maya Bazaar, next to *Tandoor* restaurant (both daily 10am–9pm; ₹15/hr);

Angelica's Cyber Point opposite *Hotel Samrat* down an alley off MG Marg (daily 9am–10pm; ₹20/hr).

Post office Allahabad's main post office (known as the GPO or HPO) is at Sarojini Naidu Marg, near All Saints' Cathedral in the Civil Lines.

CLOCKWISE FROM TOP THE RESIDENCY, LUCKNOW (P.257); SARNATH (P.282); SADHU, KUMBH MELA (P.264) >

Kausambi

Just 63km south of Allahabad, on the banks of the Yamuna, are the extensive ruins of **Kausambi**, a major Buddhist centre where Buddha himself once preached. The city flourished between the eighth century BC and the sixth century AD; archeological evidence suggests even earlier habitation. According to legend, it was founded by descendants of the Pandavas, after floods destroyed their city of Hastinapur. Mud ramparts (originally faced with brick) tower over the fields, running along an irregular 6km perimeter, and sections remain of a defensive moat. Within the complex, excavations have revealed a paved road, brick houses, wells, tanks and drains, a monastery with cloisters, a large *stupa* and the ruins of a palace. The only standing feature is a damaged sandstone column ascribed to **Ashoka** – a second column, moved by the Mughals, now graces the gates of the fort at Allahabad. If you have your own vehicle or hire a taxi (around ₹1400 from Varuna Travels or UP Tours), Kausambi is a straightforward day-trip from Allahabad. Otherwise, there are buses from Leader Road stand (₹31).

Chitrakut

The sprawling pilgrimage town of **CHITRAKUT (also called Sitapur)** is 128km southwest of Alllahabad, and easily accessible by both train and bus. It's also a good place to catch onward transport to Kalinjar and Khajuraho. Together with its twin town of **Karbi**, 8km east (where there are train connections to Allahabad, Kolkata and Delhi), Chitrakut is a major Vaishnavite pilgrimage centre, like a smaller version of Varanasi, without the hustle. Most of its religious and leisure activity revolves around the charming central **Ramghat**, where boats with electric-blue mattresses and pillows create a pretty picture against a backdrop of ashrams and *ghats* to either side of the narrow, slow-moving river.

Kalinjar

About 88km southwest of Chitrakut, the abandoned star-shaped fortress of **KALINJAR** looks down on the Gangetic valley from the final escarpments of the craggy Vindhya hills, above the town of the same name. Much of the fort has been reclaimed by dry shrubby forest, populated by monkeys; once-grand avenues are now rocky footpaths that wind through the few crumbling yet ornately carved buildings that remain. Kalinjar has no tourist facilities to speak of – most of those who do come are either on day-trips from Chitrakut or Allahabad, or stay in Banda, which is on major train and bus routes and is connected to Kalinjar by local buses.

Steep steps lead straight up for 3km from Kalinjar village to the fort's main gate, **Alam Darwaza**, but the southern **Panna Gate** has rock carvings depicting seven deer (like the fort's seven gates, these represent the then-known planets). Beneath **Bara Darwaza**, the "Large Gate", in the artificial cave of Sita Sej, a stone couch dating from the fourth century holds some of Kalinjar's earliest inscriptions. The fort's colossal rambling **battlements** provide sweeping views of the Gangetic plain and the Vindhya hills.

> **BUNDELKHAND**
>
> The harshness of the terrain in the **Bundelkhand** region, south of Lucknow along the Madhya Pradesh border, and the all but unbearable heat in the summer, make it the most difficult, if intriguing, part of the state to control, and even today, its labyrinthine hills and valleys are home to infamous bands of outlaw **dacoits**. Many of these have become folk-heroes among local villagers, who shelter them from the almost equally brutal police force. The most celebrated in recent years was **Phoolan Devi**, the "Bandit Queen", from a village near Behmai who was kidnapped by a dacoit gang, became the leader's lover, and took over from him after he was killed. She eventually surrendered to the police, was released in 1994, and even became an MP for the socialist Samajwadi Party before being assassinated in 2001.

Varanasi

Older than history, older than tradition, older even than legend, and looks twice as old as all of them put together.

Mark Twain

The great Hindu city of **VARANASI**, also known as **Banaras** or **Benares**, stretches along the River Ganges, its waterfront dominated by long flights of stone *ghats* where thousands of pilgrims and residents come for their daily ritual ablutions. Known to the devout as **Kashi**, the Luminous – the City of Light, founded by Shiva – Varanasi is one of the oldest living cities in the world. It has maintained its religious life since the sixth century BC in one continuous tradition, in part by remaining outside the mainstream of political activity and historical development of the Subcontinent, and stands at the centre of the Hindu universe, the focus of a religious geography that reaches from the Himalayan cave of Amarnath in Kashmir to India's southern tip at Kanniyakumari, Puri to the east, and Dwarka to the west. Located next to a ford on an ancient trade route, Varanasi is among the holiest of all *tirthas* – "crossing places", that allow the devotee access to the divine and enable gods and goddesses to come down to earth. It has attracted pilgrims, seekers, *sannyasins* and students of the *Vedas* throughout its history, including sages such as Buddha, Mahavira (founder of the Jain faith) and the great Hindu reformer Shankara.

Anyone who dies in Varanasi attains instant *moksha*, or enlightenment. Widows and the elderly come here to live out their final days, finding shelter in temples, assisted by alms from the faithful. Western visitors since the Middle Ages have marvelled at the strangeness of this most alien of Indian cities: the tight mesh of alleys, the religious accoutrements, the host of deities – and the proximity of death.

The ghats

The great riverbanks at Varanasi, built high with eighteenth- and nineteenth-century pavilions and palaces, temples and terraces, are lined by stone steps – the **ghats** – which stretch along the whole waterfront, changing dramatically in appearance with the seasonal fluctuations of the river level. Each of the hundred *ghats*, big and small, is marked by a lingam, and occupies its own special place in the religious geography of the city. Some have crumbled over the years while others continue to thrive, visited by early-morning bathers, brahmin priests offering puja, and people practising meditation and yoga. Hindus regard the Ganges as *amrita*, the elixir of life, which brings purity to the living and salvation to the dead, but in reality the river is scummy with effluent, so don't be tempted to join the bathers; never mind the chemicals and human body parts, it's the level of heavy metals, dumped by factories upstream, that are the real cause for concern. Whether Ganga water still has the power to absolve sin if sterilized is a contentious point among the faithful; current thinking has it that boiling is acceptable but chemical treatment ruins it.

For centuries, pilgrims have traced the perimeter of the city by a ritual circumambulation, paying homage to shrines on the way. Among the most popular routes is the **Panchatirthi Yatra**, which takes in the *pancha* (five) *tirthi* (crossings) of Asi, Dash, Manikarnaka, Panchganga, and finally Adi Kesh. To gain merit or appease the gods, the devotee, accompanied by a *panda* (priest), recites a *sankalpa* (statement of intent) and performs a ritual at each stage of the journey. For the casual visitor, however, the easiest way to see the *ghats* is to follow a south–north sequence either by boat or on foot.

Asi Ghat

At the clay-banked **Asi Ghat**, where the River Asi runs into the Ganges, pilgrims bathe prior to worshipping at a huge lingam under a peepal tree. A small marble temple just off the *ghat* houses another lingam called **Asisangameshvara**, the "Lord of the Confluence of the Asi". Traditionally, pilgrims continued from these to **Lolarka Kund**, the "Trembling Sun", a rectangular tank 15m below ground level, approached by steep steps, but it's now almost abandoned – except during the Lolarka Mela fair (Aug/Sept),

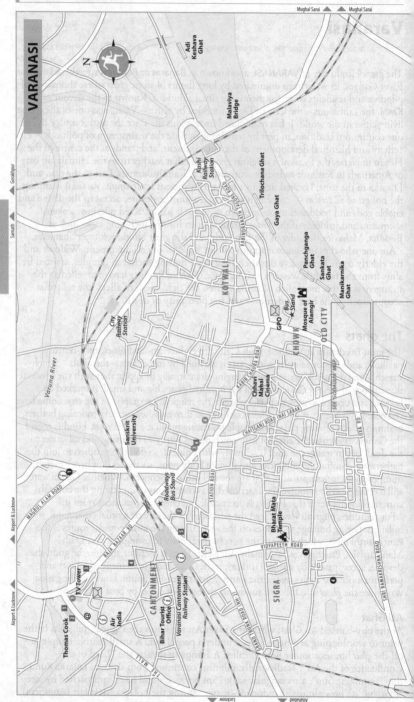

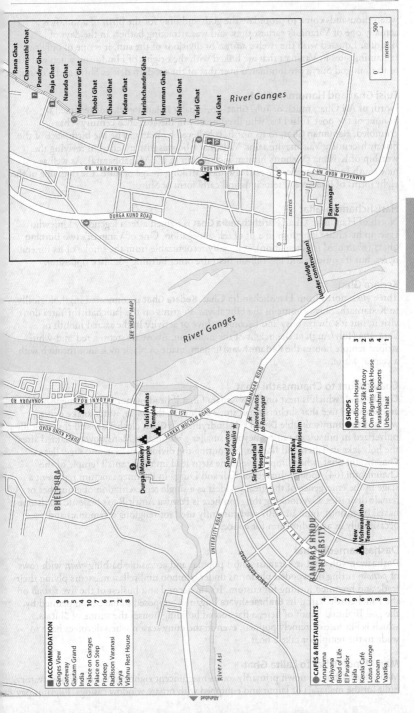

3

■ ACCOMMODATION
Ganges View	9
Gateway	3
Gautam Grand	5
India	4
Palace on Ganges	10
Palace on Step	7
Pradeep	6
Radisson Varanasi	1
Surya	2
Vishnu Rest House	8

● SHOPS
Handloom House	3
Mehrotra Silk Factory	2
Om Pilgrims Book House	5
Paraslakshmi Exports	4
Urban Haat	1

● CAFÉS & RESTAURANTS
Annapurna	4
Ashiyana	1
Bread of Life	7
El Parador	2
Haifa	9
Kerala Café	6
Lotus Lounge	5
Poonam	3
Vaatika	8

when thousands come to propitiate the gods and pray for the birth of a son. It is actually one of Varanasi's earliest sites, and was attracting bathers in the days of Buddha. Equated with the twelve *adityas* or divisions of the sun, it is one of only two remaining sites in Varanasi that are linked with the origins of Hinduism, when worship of the sun god Surya predominated over that of the modern deities Shiva and Vishnu.

Tulsi Ghat and Hanuman Ghat

North of Asi Ghat, much of **Tulsi Ghat** – originally Lolarka *ghat*, but renamed in honour of the poet Tulsi Das, who lived nearby in the sixteenth century – has crumbled. **Hanuman Ghat**, to its north, is believed by many to be the birthplace of the fifteenth-century Vaishnavite saint, Vallabha, who was instrumental in reviving the worship of Krishna (Vishnu's human incarnation in the Mahabharata). As well as a new south Indian temple, the *ghat* also has a striking image of **Ruru**, the dog, one of the eight forms of **Bhairava**, a ferocious and early form of Shiva.

Harishchandra Ghat

North of Hanuman Ghat, **Harishchandra Ghat** is named after a legendary king who gave up his entire kingdom in a fit of self-abnegation. One of Varanasi's two **burning ghats** (*ghats* used for cremation), it is easily recognizable from the smoke of its funeral pyres, but it's quieter and less full-on than the other burning *ghat* (see opposite).

Kedara Ghat

Three *ghats* north from Harishchandra Ghat, **Kedara Ghat** is connected mythologically to Kedarnath, Shiva's home in the Himalayas. Pilgrims on the Panchatirthi Yatra don't visit it, but it's always busy and becomes a hive of activity in the sacred month of Shravana (July/Aug), at the height of the monsoon. Above its steps, a red-and-white-striped temple houses the **Kedareshvara lingam**, made of black rock shot through with a vein of white.

Chauki Ghat to Chaumsathi Ghat

Chauki Ghat, which is next on from Kedara Ghat if heading north, is distinguished by an enormous tree that shelters small stone shrines to the *nagas*, water-snake deities, while at the unmistakeable **Dhobi** ("Laundrymen's") **Ghat**, clothes are still rhythmically pulverized in pursuit of purity. Beyond smaller *ghats* such as **Mansarowar**, named after the holy lake in Tibet, and **Narada**, honouring the divine musician and sage, lies **Chaumsathi Ghat**, where impressive stone steps lead up to the small temple of the **Chaumsathi (64) Yoginis**. Images of Kali and Durga in its inner sanctum represent a stage in the emergence of the great goddess as a single representation of a number of female divinities. Overlooking the *ghats* here is Peshwa Amrit Rao's majestic sandstone haveli (mansion), built in 1807 and currently used for religious ceremonies and occasionally as an auditorium for concerts.

Dashaswamedh Ghat

Dashaswamedh Ghat is Varanasi's most popular and accessible bathing *ghat*, with rows of *pandas* sitting on wooden platforms under bamboo umbrellas, masseurs plying their trade and boatmen jostling for custom. It's the second and busiest of the five *tirthas* on the Panchatirthi Yatra. Its **Brahmeshvara** lingam is supposed to have been planted by the god Brahma. South of here, a flat-roofed building houses the shrine of **Shitala**, which is likewise extremely popular, even in the rainy season when devotees have to wade to the temple or take a boat.

Man Mandir Ghat to Lalita Ghat

Man Mandir Ghat is known primarily for its magnificent eighteenth-century observatory, built for the maharaja of Jaipur and equipped with ornate window casings. Pilgrims pay homage to the important lingam of Someshvara, the lord of the moon, alongside, before crossing **Tripurabhairavi Ghat** to **Mir Ghat** and the **New Vishwanatha Temple**, built by conservative brahmins who claimed that the main Vishwanatha lingam was rendered impure when Harijans (Untouchables) entered the sanctum in 1956. At Mir Ghat, the **Dharma Kupa**, the Well of Dharma, is surrounded by subsidiary shrines and the lingam of **Dharmesha**, where it is said that Yama, the Lord of Death, obtained his jurisdiction over all the dead of the world – except here in Varanasi.

To the north is **Lalita Ghat**, renowned for its **Ganga Keshava** shrine to Vishnu and the **Nepali Temple** (daily 5am–8pm; ₹15), a Kathmandu-style wooden structure which houses an image of **Pashupateshvara** – Shiva's manifestation at Pashupatinath, in the Kathmandu Valley – and sporting a small selection of erotic carvings.

Manikarnika Ghat

North of Lalita lies Varanasi's pre-eminent cremation ground, **Manikarnika Ghat**. Such grounds are usually held to be inauspicious, and located on the fringes of cities, but the entire city of Shiva is regarded as **Mahashamshana**, the "Great Cremation Ground", for the corpse of the entire universe. The *ghat* is perpetually crowded with funeral parties, as well as the **Doms**, its Untouchable guardians, busy and preoccupied with facilitating final release for those lucky enough to pass away here. Seeing bodies being cremated so publicly has always exerted a great fascination for visitors to the city, but photography is strictly taboo; even having a camera visible may be construed as intent, and provoke hostility. Wood touts descend on tourists at the *ghat* explaining the finer metaphysical points of transmutation ("cremation is education") before subtly shifting to the practicalities of how much wood is needed to burn one body, the neverending cycle of inflation and would you like to give a donation. The amounts written down in their "ledgers" are unbelievable.

Lying at the centre of the five *tirthas*, Manikarnika Ghat symbolizes both creation and destruction, epitomized by the juxtaposition of the sacred well of **Manikarnika Kund**, said to have been dug by Vishnu at the time of creation, and the hot, sandy ash-infused soil of cremation grounds where time comes to an end. In Hindu mythology, Manikarnika Kund predates the arrival of the Ganga and has its source deep in the Himalayas. Vishnu carved the *kund* (water tank) with his discus, and filled it with perspiration from his exertions in creating the world at the behest of Shiva. When Shiva quivered with delight, his earring fell into this pool, which as Manikarnika – "Jewelled Earring" – became the first *tirtha* in the world. Every year, after the floodwaters of the river have receded to leave the pool caked in alluvial deposits, the *kund* is re-dug. Its surroundings are cleaned and painted with bright folk art depicting the presiding goddess, **Manikarni Devi**.

Scindia Ghat

Bordering Manikarnika to the north is the picturesque **Scindia Ghat**, its tilted Shiva temple lying partially submerged in the river, after falling in as a result of the sheer weight of the *ghat*'s construction in the mid-nineteenth century. Above the *ghat*, several of Varanasi's most influential shrines are hidden within the tight maze of alleyways of the area known as **Siddha Kshetra** (the "Field of Fulfilment").

BOAT TRIPS ON THE GANGES

All along the *ghats*, and especially at the main ones such as Dashaswamedh, the prices of **boat** (*bajra*) **rental** are highly inflated, with local boatmen under pressure from touts to fleece tourists and pilgrims. Renting a boat to catch the dawn in particular can be a bit of a free-for-all, and haggling is essential. There used to be an official rate, which everyone ignored, but it's now down to your bargaining skills – expect to pay around ₹200 for an hour in a small (one- to four-person) boat, or ₹300 in a larger (five- to ten-person) one.

Panchganga Ghat to Adi Keshava Ghat

North of Lakshmanbala Ghat, with its commanding views of the river, lies one of the most dramatic – and contentious – *ghats*, **Panchganga**, dominated by Varanasi's largest riverside building, the great **Mosque of Alamgir**, known locally as Beni Madhav-ka-Darera. With its minarets now much shortened, the mosque stands on the ruins of the **Bindu Madhava**, a Vishnu temple that extended from Panchganga to Rama Ghat before it was destroyed by Aurangzeb and replaced with the mosque. Panchganga also bears testimony to more favourable Hindu-Muslim relations, being the site of the initiation of the medieval saint of the Sufi tradition, Kabir, the son of a humble Muslim weaver who is venerated by Hindus and Muslims alike. Along the riverfront lies a curious array of three-sided cells, submerged during the rainy season, some with lingams, others with images of Vishnu, and some empty and used for meditation or yoga. Above **Trilochana Ghat**, further north, is the holy ancient lingam of the three (*tri*)-eyed (*lochana*) Shiva. Beyond it, the river bypasses some of Varanasi's oldest precincts, now predominantly Muslim in character; the *ghats* themselves gradually become less impressive and are usually of the *kaccha* (clay-banked) variety. At **Adi Keshava Ghat** (the "Original Vishnu"), on the outskirts of the city, the Varuna River flows into the Ganga. Unapproachable during the rainy season, when it is completely submerged, the *ghat* marks the place where Vishnu supposedly landed as an emissary of Shiva, and stands on the original site of the city before it spread southwards. Around Adi Keshava are a number of Ganesha shrines.

The Old City

At the heart of Varanasi, between Dashaswamedh Ghat and Godaulia to the south and west and Manikarnika Ghat on the river to the north, lies the maze of ramshackle alleys that comprise the **Old City**, or Vishwanatha Khanda. The whole area buzzes with the activity of pilgrims, *pandas* and stalls selling offerings to the faithful, and there are lingams and shrines tucked into every corner. If you get lost just head for the river.

The Golden Temple and around

Accessed from Vishwanatha Mandir Lane to the north of Vishwanatha Gali, but closed to non-Hindus, the **Vishwanatha Mandir** temple complex, also called Visheshwara (the "Lord of All"), is popularly known as the **Golden Temple**, due to the gold plating on its massive spire. Because it is largely hidden behind walls, non-Hindus have to make do with glimpses of it from adjacent buildings. Vishwanatha's history has been fraught. Sacked by successive Muslim rulers, it was repeatedly rebuilt and destroyed; in 1785, Queen Ahilyabai Holkar of Indore built the temple that stands today. Its simple white domes tower over the **Jnana Vapi** ("Wisdom Well"), immediately north, housed in an open-arcaded hall built in 1828, where Shiva cooled his lingam after the construction of Vishwanatha.

Adjacent to the temple, guarded by armed police to protect it from Hindu fanatics, stands the **Jnana Vapi Mosque**, also known as the Great Mosque of Aurangzeb. Close by, the temple of **Annapurna Bhavani** is dedicated to Shakti, the divine female energy. Manifest in many forms, including the awesome Kali and Durga with their weapons and gruesome garlands of skulls, she's seen here as the provider of sustenance and carries a cooking pot. Nearby is a stunning image, faced in silver against a black surround, of **Shani** or Saturn. Slightly north, across the main road, the thirteenth-century **Razia's Mosque** stands atop the ruins of a still earlier Vishwanatha temple that was destroyed under the Sultanate.

Bharat Mata

Vidyapeeth Rd

About 3km northwest of Godaulia, outside the Old City, the modern temple of **Bharat Mata** ("Mother India"), inaugurated by Mahatma Gandhi, is unusual in that it has a

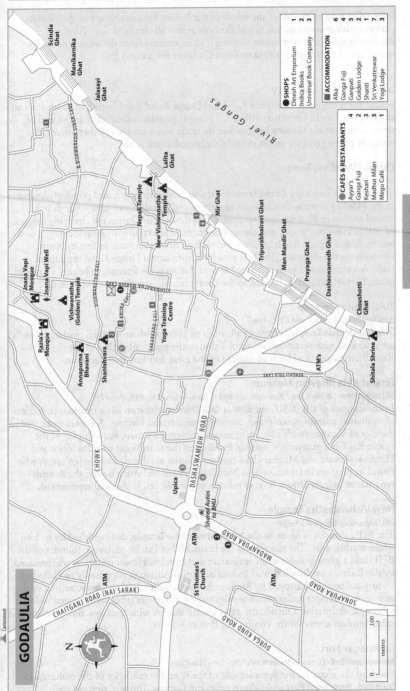

GODAULIA

N

Cantonment

CHAITGANJ ROAD (NAI SARAK)

ATM

St Thomas's
Church

DURGA KUND ROAD

SONAPURA ROAD

MADANPURA ROAD

ATM

ATM

Shared Autos
to BHU

DASHASWAMEDH ROAD

Upica

CHOWK

BENGALI TOLA LANE

ATM's

Razia's
Mosque

Annapurna
Bhavani

Shanishtvara

Vishwanatha
(Golden) Temple

Jnana Vapi
Mosque

Jnana Vapi Well

Yoga Training
Centre

VISHWANATHA MANDIR LANE

SARAKI GALI

SAHARKARD GALI

New Vishwanatha
Temple

Nepali Temple

Mir Ghat

Lalita
Ghat

Tripurabhairavi Ghat

Man Mandir Ghat

Prayaga Ghat

Dashaswamedh Ghat

Choushotti
Ghat

Shitala Shrine

River Ganges

Jalasayi
Ghat

Manikarnika
Ghat

Scindia
Ghat

VISHWANATHA GALI

0   100
metres

● **SHOPS**
Dinesh Art Emporium 1
Indica Books 2
Universal Book Company ... 3

■ **ACCOMMODATION**
Alka 6
Ganga Fuji 4
Ganpati 5
Golden Lodge 1
Shanti 7
Sri Venkateswar 3
Yogi Lodge 3

● **CAFÉS & RESTAURANTS**
Ayyar's 4
Ganga Fuji 2
Keshari 3
Madhur Milan 5
Megu Café 1

3

huge relief map in marble of the whole of the Indian Subcontinent and the Tibetan plateau, with mountains, rivers and the holy *tirthas* all clearly visible. Pilgrims circumambulate the map before viewing it in its entirety from the second floor. The temple can be reached by rickshaw from Godaulia for around ₹50.

South of the Old City

Inland from the ghats, Sonapura Road and Durga Kund Road both lead south towards the Banaras Hindu University (BHU). The most popular tourist sight at this end of town is the famous **Monkey Temple**, but there are also a couple of other interesting temples, plus a good art museum and a maharajah's fort to see.

Durga (Monkey) Temple
Durga Kund Rd

The nineteenth-century **Durga Temple** – stained red with ochre, and popularly known as the **Monkey Temple**, thanks to its aggressive and irritable monkeys – stands in a walled enclosure 4km south of Godaulia. It is devoted to Durga, the terrifying aspect of Shiva's consort, Parvati, and the embodiment of **Shakti** (divine female energy), and was built in a typical north Indian style, with an ornate *shikhara* in five segments, symbolizing the elements. The best views are from across Durga *kund*, the adjoining tank. A forked stake in the courtyard is used during some festivals to behead sacrificial goats. Non-Hindus are admitted to the courtyard, but not the inner sanctum.

Tulsi Manas Temple
Durga Kund Rd • Daily 5.30am–noon & 3.30–9pm

The **Tulsi Manas Temple** is open to all. Built in 1964 of white-streaked marble, its walls are inscribed with verses by Goswami Tulsidas, the poet and author of the Ramcharitmanas, the Hindi equivalent of the great Sanskrit epic Ramayana.

Bharat Kala Bhawan Museum
BHU campus • Mon–Sat: May & June 7.30am–1pm; July–April 10.30am–4.30pm • ₹100 (₹10), camera ₹50

In the campus of the BHU, the **Bharat Kala Bhawan Museum** has a fabulous collection of miniature paintings, sculpture, contemporary art and bronzes. A gallery dedicated to the city of Varanasi, with a stunning nineteenth-century map, has a display of the recent Raj Ghat excavations and old etchings of the city. Along with Buddhist and Hindu sculpture and Mughal glass, further galleries are devoted to foreign artists who found inspiration in India, such as Nicholas Roerich and Alice Boner; the Bengali renaissance painter Jamini Roy, so influenced by folk art, is also well represented.

New Vishwanatha Temple
BHU campus • Daily 4am–noon & 1–9pm

The BHU campus is home to the **New Vishwanatha Temple**, distinguished by its lofty white-marble spire. The temple was the brainchild of Pandit Malaviya, founder of the BHU and a great believer in an egalitarian and casteless Hindu revival. It was financed by the Birlas, a wealthy Marwari industrial family. Although supposedly modelled on an original temple destroyed by Aurangzeb, the building displays characteristics of the new wave of temple architecture, amalgamating influences from various parts of India with a garish interior. Outside the gates a small market with teashops, flower-sellers and other vendors caters for the continuous flow of visitors.

Ramnagar Fort
Ramnagar (south bank of the river) • **Museum** Daily 10am–5pm • ₹150 (₹20)

South of the *ghats*, on the opposite side of the river, the residence of the maharaja of Varanasi, **Ramnagar Fort** looks down upon the Ganges. The best views of the

> ## RAM LILA
> Varanasi is renowned for its **Ram Lila**, held during Dussehra (Oct), during which episodes from the Ramayana are re-enacted throughout the city and the maharaja sponsors three weeks of elaborate celebrations. Across the courtyard, a section is devoted to the Ram Lila procession and festivities.

fortifications – especially impressive in late afternoon – are to be had from the bridge to the fort, which is reached by a road heading south from the BHU area. This was previously a seasonal pontoon bridge, but that is now being replaced with a new permanent bridge – while that is under construction, shared autos to the fort from the BHU are taking a detour via the next crossing south. The fort can also be reached by chartering a boat from Dashaswamedh Ghat.

Inside, the fort bears testimony to the wealth of the maharaja and his continuing influence. A dusty and poorly kept **museum** provides glimpses of a decadent past: horse-drawn carriages, old motor cars, palanquins, ornate gilded and silver *howdahs* (elephant seats), hookahs, costumes and old silk in a sorry state are all part of the collection, along with an armoury, some minute ivory carvings, an astronomical clock and hunting trophies. Some visitors have reported having tea with the affable maharaja after chance encounters.

ARRIVAL AND DEPARTURE VARANASI

By plane Babatpur airport is 22km northwest of the city. From Cantonment station, a pre-paid taxi costs ₹540; a pre-paid auto is ₹275 (or around ₹350 from town if you don't pre-pay). Allow at least 90min from the Old City. Destinations include: Delhi (6 daily with Air India, Jet and SpiceJet; 1hr 20min); Kolkata (1 daily with JetKonnect; 1hr 20min); Mumbai (1 daily with Air India; 2hr). Airline offices include Air India, 52 Yadunath Marg, Cantonment ☎ 0542 250 2547 and Jet Airways, at the airport ☎ 0542 262 2577.

By train Varanasi Cantonment (officially, Varanasi Junction) is the most conveniently located station, with pre-paid auto and taxi booths (if they are not staffed, the tourist office in the station can sort you out), and a foreign tourists' reservations office (Mon–Sat 8am–8pm, Sun 8am–2pm). Many trains on the main east–west Delhi–Kolkata line bypass Varanasi but stop at Mughal Sarai, 17km east of town and around 45min away by road or rail. There are retiring rooms at Mughal Sarai station and local buses to Varanasi (in Varanasi, pick them up at Roadways Bus Stand, or directly across GT Rd). Trains from the north and east may stop at Varanasi City station before they reach Cantonment, but transport into town from there is sparser.

Destinations The fastest train to Agra and Jaipur is the daily #12307 *Howrah–Jodhpur Express*, which leaves Mughal Sarai at 9.50am, arriving at Agra Fort at 7.45pm, Jaipur just after midnight, and Jodhpur at 6am, but there's also an overnight service from Varanasi itself, the #14853/14863/14865 *Marudhar Express* (dep. 5.20–6.15pm, depending on the day, arr. Agra Fort 5.55am, Jaipur 11.20am, Jodhpur 5pm). For Delhi, though a couple of *Rajdhani* express trains pass through Mughal Sarai around 1am, the most convenient trains leave from

Varanasi, including the #12559 *Shiv Ganga Express* (dep. 7.15pm, arr. New Delhi 7.40am). The best daytime service, the #12875 *Neelachal Express* (dep. 7.38am, arr. New Delhi 9.40pm) runs Tues, Fri and Sun only. To Kolkata, convenient overnight services include the #12344 *Vibhuti Express*, leaving Varanasi at 6.10pm, for a chirpy 7.30am arrival at Howrah; you can get a faster service from Mughal Sarai (the 1.38am #12314 *Sealdah Rajdhani* takes only 8hr 30min), but it's hardly worth the extra effort. The *Mahanagri Express* #11094 is the fastest train to Mumbai (dep. 11.25am, arr. Mumbai CST 2.15pm next day). The most convenient train to Patna is the 2.35pm *Secunderabad–Patna Express* #12791, which reaches Patna at 7.10pm. For an earlier arrival, the 7.55am #12402 *Magadh Express* from Mughal Sarai gets in at 11.30am. To Gaya the #13010 *Doon Express* leaves Varanasi at 4.15pm and arrives at 9.17pm. To Uttarakhand, the #13009 *Doon Express* (dep. 10.30am, arr. Dehra Dun 7.10am next day) is the best option for Dehra Dun, but a section of the #14265 *Dehra Dun Express* (dep. 8.30am) also serves Ramnagar (arr. 6.15am next day). For Khajuraho, there's the three-times weekly #21108 *Khajuraho Link Express* (Mon, Wed & Sat 6.05pm, arr. 5.15am); otherwise take a train to Satna (the four-weekly #11062/11066 *Lokmanyatilak Express* does it overnight, dep. 11.20pm, arr. at 6.55am), where you can pick up a bus for the 3hr journey.

By bus Most buses terminate a couple of hundred metres east of the railway station along the main Grand Trunk Rd and at the Roadways Bus Stand (☎ 0542 220 3476). Buses from Nepal are met by the rickshaw mafia (see p.278).

3

Destinations From the Roadways Bus Stand on GT Rd, UPSRTC run hourly buses 5.30am–8.30pm to the Nepal border at Sonauli (10hr) via Gorakhpur (7hr), and there are good and regular buses for Allahabad (every 15min; 3hr 30min), making road a better option than rail. For Bihar, buses are few and far between (with none at all to Patna), and road conditions not great, so rail is your best bet.

GETTING AROUND AND INFORMATION

By rickshaw Cycle rickshaws are the easiest way to get around Varanasi, and often defy death and traffic jams by cycling up the wrong side of the road; a ride from Godaulia to Cantonment railway station costs around ₹50. Auto-rickshaws should be faster, but due to the volume of traffic they rarely are for short rides across town. Godaulia to the railway station should cost ₹70.

Car rental The tourist office can arrange car rental at around ₹1400/day for a car with driver within a 200km radius of Varanasi.

Motorcycles Mechanics and workshops specializing in Enfields are clustered in the Jagatganj area, near the Sanskrit University.

Tourist information The main UP Tourism office is at Urban Haat, Sanskritik Sankul (Mon–Sat, closed 2nd Sat of the month, 10am–5pm; ☎ 0542 250 5033, ✉ up_tourism _varanasi@yahoo.co.in), though their tourist information counter (daily 7am–7pm; ☎ 0542 250 6670) inside the Cantonment railway station is their main office for giving out information – the boss, Uma Shankar, is extremely helpful and is backed up by a force of tourist police (same

phone number) to defend tourists from crime. The India Tourism office is in the Cantonment district, away from the Old City and *ghats*, just off The Mall on Stranger Rd (Mon–Fri 9am–5.30pm, Sat 9am–2pm; ☎ 0542 250 1784). It gives out information on the whole of India, but staff can assist with booking accommodation in Varanasi. They also maintain a booth at the airport (in principle open the same hours). The shabby Bihar Government tourist office at 3rd Floor, Hans Sarowar, Englishia Lane, Jawaharlal Nehru Market, Cantonment (☎ 0542 222 3821), is useful if you're heading east into that state. The local branch of the National Informatics Centre has some interesting information about Varanasi on their website at ⊕ varanasi.nic.in.

Tours To experience the *ghats* at sunrise, or the peace of Sarnath, you're best off eschewing guided tours and making your own arrangements. If your time is very limited, official guides, organized through the India Tourism office, can be useful (₹950/day for up to five people, slightly more for bigger groups), but never go shopping with a guide, official or not, nor ask them to take you to any shop.

ACCOMMODATION

Most of Varanasi's better and more expensive hotels lie on its peripheries, though to experience the full ambience of the city, stay close to the *ghats* and the lanes of the **Old City**, where top-floor rooms, with views and more light, are generally the best. If you want to stay with a local family, ask at UP Tourism's station office about their **paying guesthouse** scheme

GODAULIA

Alka D-3/23 Mir Ghat ☎ 0542 239 8445, ⊕ hotelalkavns .com; map p.275. You'll need to book well ahead in high season (Oct–March), but this is a good mid-range riverside

choice, with a variety of well-maintained quality rooms, plus a terrace and a pleasant little lawn overlooking the river. ₹500/₹600

Ganga Fuji D-7/21 Sakarkand Gali ☎ 0542 232 7333,

TOUT DODGING

Like Agra and Delhi, Varanasi is rife with **touts**, and you'll have to be careful of scams, especially on arrival. Many hotels pay a **commission** of up to eighty percent of the room rate (for every day you stay) to whoever takes you to the door – a cost that is passed on to you.

All English-speaking rickshaw drivers are part of this racket, and avoiding it takes persistence. At Cantonment railway station, you can phone your hotel of choice, who will send someone to pick you up (the tourist office will even do this for you). If you want to make your own way to the hotels of the old town, walk away from the bus or railway station to the main road, find a non-English-speaking cycle rickshaw driver, and ask to be taken to Godaulia, 3km southeast – a ₹50 ride. Rickshaws are unable to penetrate the maze of lanes around Vishwanatha Temple and are banned from the central part of Godaulia. Again, you can call a hotel from here to come and find you – if you attempt to get to a hotel yourself, touts may try to attach themselves and claim a commission on arrival. When trying to find hotels in the old town that don't pay commission to touts, it's common to hear that they have "burned down" or "flooded"; touts may also try to remove signs directing people to them.

Ⓦgangafujihomevaranasi.com; map p.275. Well-run family guesthouse near the Golden Temple, with a range of tastefully decorated rooms, some with a/c (₹990). Scrupulously clean (though it's down a rather dirty alley) and the bathrooms are immaculate. ₹330/₹550

Ganpati D-3/24 Mir Ghat ☏0542 239 0057 or 9, Ⓦganpatiguesthouse.com; map p.275. Rooms here – ideally booked in advance – overlook the Ganges or are arranged around a courtyard, and there's free wi-fi, a restaurant and a sociable balcony overlooking the river. The 10am checkout time is a bit inconvenient. ₹500/₹1200

Golden Lodge D-8/35 Kalika Gali, near Shanishvara ☏0542 239 8788, Ⓔgoldenvaranasi@gmail.com; map p.275. Friendly staff, a range of attached and non-attached double rooms (plus some non-attached singles), and a decent restaurant, but make sure the price they quote includes tax and service or they may try to add those to your bill when you leave. ₹300/₹450

Shanti Guest House CK-8/129 Garwasi Tola, near Manikarnika Ghat ☏0542 239 2568, Ⓔvaranasishanti @yahoo.com; map p.275. An old favourite – though in need of a lick of paint – tucked away near the burning *ghats*. Large building with loads of (generally) clean double rooms with attached bathrooms, as well as dorm beds and non-attached singles (₹100). Excellent views from the lively rooftop restaurant, and free boat rides at sunrise and sunset. Dorm ₹70, double ₹200

Sri Venkateswar D-5/64 Dashaswamedh Rd ☏0542 239 2357, Ⓔvenlodge@yahoo.com; map p.275. Simple but clean and close to the *ghats* and to Vishwanatha Temple, capturing the ambience of the Old City. Large rooms, nice courtyard, friendly staff, 24hr checkout and no intoxicants allowed. ₹650

Yogi Lodge D-8/29 Kalika Gali ☏0542 239 2588, Ⓦyogilodge.com; map p.275. An old budget-traveller favourite in the heart of the Old City that's been going for years; very well run, with a safe for valuables. Spotless restaurant, clean rooms and dorms, but the bathrooms are shared. Dorm ₹100, double ₹200

SOUTH OF GODAULIA, NEAR THE RIVER

★ **Ganges View** Asi Ghat ☏0542 231 3218, Ⓦhotelgangesview.com; map pp.270–271. In a lovely old house deocrated with paintings, the rooms are small but tastefully and stylishly decorated (those on the upper storey have the best views), and there's a wonderful big veranda looking out onto the river. Wi-fi is free and breakfast is included. ₹5500

Palace on Ganges B-1/158 Asi Ghat ☏0542 231 5050, Ⓦpalaceonganges.com; map pp.270–271. The only luxury hotel on the Ganges, with 42 individually decorated rooms representing the states of India – the Gujarati room is particularly colourful. Facilities include central a/c, TV,

mini-bar, tour desk and rooftop restaurant with live music nightly. ₹5500

Palace on Step D-21/11 Rana Ghat ☏0542 245 0970, Ⓦpalaceonstep.com; map pp.270–271. Originally two hotels (separated by a big banyan tree), now combined to make one, with rooms ranging from budget to a/c, but all immaculate, though you pay a premium (₹2000) if you want views over the *ghats* (which you get from the hotel's terrace anyway). ₹1000

Vishnu Rest House D-24/17 Pandey Ghat ☏0542 245 0206; map pp.270–271. Ramshackle riverside lodge, with rooms, dorms and a patio and café overlooking the Ganges; popular and often booked up, but an offshoot, the adjoining *Lord Vishnu Guest House*, has better-value rooms and a great roof terrace too. Best approached via the *ghats*, south of Dashaswamedh. Dorm ₹90, double ₹300

CANTONMENT AND AROUND

Gateway Nadesar Palace Grounds, Raja Bazaar Rd, ☏0542 666 0001 or ☏1800 111825, Ⓦthegateway hotels.com; map pp.270–271. The poshest gaff in town, set in vast grounds (explore them by buggy, or on a birdwatching walk), with stately rooms, fine dining, a pool and fitness centre. ₹16,148

Gautam Grand Parade Kothi ☏0542 220 8288, Ⓔhotelgautamgrand@.yahoo.co.in; map pp.270–271. Good-value modern hotel near the station; the rooms (some a/c) are not huge, but they're reasonably well-kept, each with a balcony. There's also 24hr room service and the staff are eager to please. ₹850

India 59 Patel Nagar ☏0542 250 7593, Ⓦtheindia hotel.com; map pp.270–271. A three-star hotel that makes a pretty good attempt at being stylish. The rooms are quite smart and modern (cool white with pinewood – even the laminated floor doesn't look too naff) with attached bathrooms and a/c; and a health and fitness centre, a rooftop bar, basement lounge bar, and three restaurants, including the excellent *Palm Springs*. ₹6866

Pradeep Kabir Chaura Rd, Jagatganj ☏0542 220 4963, Ⓦhotelpradeep.com; map pp.270–271. Comfortable, quite smart and popular with tour groups; away from, but within striking distance of, the *ghats*. Has the *Poonam* restaurant (see p.281), plus another restaurant on the roof, and 24hr room service. ₹2922

Radisson Varanasi The Mall ☏0542 250 1515 or ☏1800 1800 333, Ⓦradisson.com/varanasiin; map pp.270–271. One of Varanasi's best-value luxury places, with classy and well-appointed rooms, stylish but not huge, plus a swimming pool, free wi-fi, two restaurants, a bar and a coffee lounge. Large buffet breakfast included. ₹10,117

Surya S-20/51, A5 The Mall ☏0542 250 8465 or 6, Ⓦhotelsuryavns.com; map pp.270–271. Well-run, comfortable and relaxing hotel arranged around a small

WHAT'S IN A NAME?

The **Yogi Lodge** (near Vishwanatha Temple), **Vishnu Rest House** (overlooking the river) and **Shanti Guest House** (near Manikarnika Ghat), three of the Old City's most popular guesthouses, face dubious competition from lookalike hotels copying their names and paying rickshaw-wallahs to divert customers. Bogus Vishnu lodges have sprung up with names like *Old Vishnu Lodge*, *Vishnu Guest House*, *Real Vishnu Guest House* and *New Vishnu Guest House*, and several more "Shanti" lodges and "Yogi" lodges are playing the same name game. Legally, the con merchants are safe, as no one owns the copyright to such universal Indian words as "Yogi", "Vishnu" and "Shanti", but tourists should beware: no hotel that pays commission to touts or tries to trick you like this is going to be honest in other ways either.

lawn that doubles up as an alfresco restaurant. Rooms are small but well kept, with modern bathrooms, and many have balconies. Facilities include a tour desk, foreign exchange, a pool (₹200 for non-guests) and a decent restaurant. You can also camp (₹300/person). **₹3035**

EATING AND DRINKING

Most of the Old City **cafés** are vegetarian, and alcohol is not tolerated, but the Cantonment is less constrained, and some hotels have bars. After an early morning boat trip, try the traditional snack of *kachori*, savoury deep-fried pastry bread sold in the Old City next to the *ghats* – but avoid the chai stalls here as the cups are washed in the river.

Stomach disorders are common in Varanasi, so stick to bottled or treated water and be careful when choosing where you eat. Among hotel restaurants, *Vishnu Rest House* on Pandey Ghat does excellent thalis and the *Yogi Lodge* must have the cleanest kitchen in the Old City, dishing out non-spicy curries and travellers' favourites.

GODAULIA

Ayyar's Dashaswamedh Rd (below Banaras Lodge) ☏ 93364 62618; map p.275. Small, inexpensive café at the back of a shopping arcade, serving south Indian food, including great masala dosas (₹35), excellent filter coffee (₹20) and delicious milk drinks. Daily 7am–10pm.

Ganga Fuji D-5/8 Kalika Gali, Dashaswamedh ☏ 98396 14340; map p.275. Pleasant little restaurant near Vishwanatha, with live classical music from 7.30pm and a friendly host who guides diners through the multicuisine menu, with Chinese, Japanese and Continental options. North Indian dishes are particularly good, but light on spices for the benefit of European tourists; a biriyani goes for ₹120 veg, ₹180 with chicken. Daily 7.30am–10pm.

Keshari D-14/8, Teri Neem, off Dashaswamedh Rd ☏ 0542 240 1472; map p.275. The menu lists a huge variety of veg curries, "all items available". The *paneer* tomato (₹80) and the mushroom masala (₹120) are particular favourites, but every dish is delicious. Daily 9am–10.30pm.

Madhur Milan Dashaswamedh Rd, just past Vishwanatha Lane ☏ 95650 63977; map p.275. Cheap and very popular café, great for dosas, sweets, *kachoris* and samosas (₹10; watch them being fried out front, and grab them while they're piping hot). Thalis ₹60–150. Daily 6am–11pm.

Megu Café D-8/1 Kalika Gali ☏ 92365 19262; map p.275. Down the alley leading to the *Golden Lodge* and *Yogi Lodge*, this small place run by a Japanese-Indian couple (shoes off at the door), serves a short menu of Japanese treats including veg sushi rolls (₹120), veg tempura (₹120) and ginger chicken (₹130). Mon–Sat 10am–4pm.

THE REST OF THE TOWN

Annapurna J-12/16A Ramkatora ☏ 0542 220 0151, ⊛ sriannapurna.com; map pp.270–271. Gleaming multicuisine restaurant serving Continental, Subcontinental and Chinese veg food (thali ₹160); also does home delivery, and even delivers thalis at two hours' notice to any train passing through Varanasi (give train name and number, plus coach and seat number). Daily 9am–10pm.

Ashiyana Major Singh Place, Lt Rohan Marg, Cantonment ☏ 0542 250 3764; map pp.270–271. Chinese and Indian meals, snacks and drinks served in an a/c lounge or on a rather noisy lawn. Try the chicken *dopiaza* (₹110), or chicken tikka masala (₹190). Daily 10.30am–10.30pm.

Bread of Life B-3/322 Sonapura Rd ☏ 0542 227 5012; map pp.270–271. Bakery providing brown bread, cinnamon rolls (₹35) and confectionery, with a small, clean restaurant serving Western food such as minestrone (₹80) and veg moussaka (₹100), plus a few Chinese options. Profits go to charity, but service is slow. Daily 7am–10pm.

El Parador Maldahia Rd (off Parade Kothi) ☏ 98394 33861; map pp.270–271. Remarkable restaurant serving outstanding Mexican, Italian, Greek and French cuisine in a bistro atmosphere. You can start with spinach and mushroom enchiladas (₹300), and follow them up with a filet mignon (₹550). All their pasta is homemade, and they have a bakery for bread and cakes too. Daily 11am–10pm.

Haifa B-1/107 Asi Rd ☎0542 231 2960; map pp.270–271. Laidback place serving approximations of Middle Eastern dishes – including hummus, fresh-baked pittas and falafel – as well as the more usual Indian fare. The "Middle Eastern thali" (a selection of *mezze* with pitta) is a great deal at ₹150. Daily 7.30am–10pm.

Kerala Café Durga Kund Rd, Bhelpura Thana ☎0542 227 5105; map pp.270–271. A very popular south Indian restaurant with good snacks (dosas, *vadas*, *uttapams* and the like – a masala dosa will set you back ₹35) and lemon rice, coconut rice, sambar rice or curd rice (₹40). Daily 8am–10pm.

Lotus Lounge B-14/27 Mansarowar Ghat ☎98385 67717; map pp.270–271. Not a lounge at all, but a bright and breezy terrace restaurant overlooking the *ghats*, and

serving an eclectic mix of international cuisine from chicken satay (₹220) to Thai red chicken curry (₹200) and veg moussaka (₹180), plus pastas and salads. Daily 8am–10pm.

Poonam Hotel Pradeep, Kabir Chaura Rd, Jagatganj ☎0542 220 4963; map pp.270–271. Good, moderately priced Mughlai food served in a comfortable a/c environment. A Mughlai biriyani will set you back ₹300, or you can try a *murg methi malai* (chicken with cashewnut and green fenugreek) for ₹260. Daily 6.30am–11pm.

Vaatika Asi Ghat ☎0542 801 9477; map pp.270–271. A leafy terrace right on the *ghat*, serving good pizza (₹150–200) and pasta (₹120–170), plus freshly made juices and salads (all vegetables sterilized in permanganate, all water boiled and filtered). Daily 7.30am–10pm.

3

SHOPPING

Hustlers and rickshaw drivers are always keen to drag tourists into commission-paying stores, but avoiding those, **shopping in Varanasi** can be great, and it's worth seeking out the city's rich silk-weaving and brasswork. The best **areas to browse** are the Thatheri Bazaar (for brass), or Jnana Vapi and the Vishwanatha Gali in Godaulia with its Temple Bazaar (for silk brocade and jewellery).

CRAFTS

Dinesh Art Emporium D-5/5 Saraswati Phatak (a few doors from Golden Temple post office) ☎93361 50159; map p.275. Batik T-shirts, wall hangings and cushion covers, which they make themselves upstairs (if you're interested, they'll take you up for a look). Daily 10am–8pm.

Handloom House D-64/132K Sigra (off Vidyapeeth Rd) ☎0542 222 1742, ⓦhandloomhouse.in; map pp.270–271. This government-run emporium offers fixed prices and assured quality on silk, cotton, saris, shirts, sheets and cushion covers. Mon–Sat 10am–8pm, Sun 11am–6pm.

Open Hand Café and Shop B-1/128-3 Dumraun Bagh Colony, Asi ☎0542 236 9751, ⓦopenhand.in. Near *Haifa* restaurant, this community-run project sells bed linen, clothes, bags and cards and it doubles up as a café, so you can enjoy filter coffee and chocolate cake while you shop. Mon–Sat 8am–8pm.

Urban Haat Sanskritik Sankul, Chowka Ghat ☎0542 250 5033; pp.270–271. You pay ₹2 to enter UP Tourism's crafts fair, where you can see artisans working on crafts from UP and elsewhere in India. There are also food stalls, and an open-air theatre with dance and music shows. Daily 10am–9pm.

SILK

Sales pitches tend to become most aggressive when it comes to silk. You need to be wary of the hard sell, and also to be aware that well-known reputable firms spawn crooked imitators using the same names to fool tourists. Qazi Sadullahpura, near the Chhavi Mahal Cinema, lies at the heart of a fascinating Muslim neighbourhood devoted to the production of silk.

★ **Mehrotra Silk Factory** SC-21/72 Englishia Lane, off Station Rd near the railway station ☎0542 220 0189, ⓦmehrotrasilk.in; map pp.270–271. Highly recommended, and will happily run you up a shirt and deliver it to your hotel, as well as selling ready-made scarves, shawls and bedsheets at very good prices; they also have a branch at K-4/8A Lalghat, and offer free hotel or station pick-ups for customers (this shop is particularly plagued by spurious imitators: on no account ask a rickshaw-wallah or guide to bring you here, as they will almost certainly take you to a commission-paying imitator instead). Daily 10am–8pm.

Paraslakshmi Exports D-61/16, Sidhgiribagh ☎0542 241 1496; map pp.270–271. A wide range of silk fabrics as well as scarves, shawls and bedspreads at fixed prices; offers free pick-ups for customers, and it is wise to take them up on this. Daily 10am–7pm.

BOOKS

Indica Books D-40/18 Madanpura Rd, Godaulia ☎0542 245 0818, ⓦindicabooks.com; map p.275. A large selection of books on Hinduism, religious philosophy and what they call "Indology", including their own publications. There's also a good selection of Indian and foreign fiction and non-fiction in English at the front. Mon–Sat 10am–8pm.

Om Pilgrims Book House B-27/98 A-8, Nawabganj Rd, Durga Kund ☎0542 231 4060, ⓦpilgrimsonlineshop.com; map pp.270–271. A funny old place, a bit like a Victorian books emporium, in an old house, specializing in books on religion, particularly Buddhism, but also books on Varanasi and the Ganges, and even a few antiquarian books. Mon–Sat 10am–6pm.

Universal Book Company D40/60 Madanpura Rd, Godaulia ☎0542 245 0042; map p.275. A modern

bookshop with lots of Indian literature, as well as books on Indian history, culture and religion. Mon–Sat 10am–8.30pm.

DIRECTORY

Banks and exchange There are plenty of ATMs in town, including on Godaulia roundabout. Several cheap hotels, as well as the upmarket ones, will change money. Thomas Cook by *Radisson* hotel (Mon–Sat 9.30am–6.30pm) changes cash and travellers' cheques with a minimum of fuss.

Hospitals Sir Sunderlal Hospital, Benares Hindu University (☎0542 236 9169); Shiv Prasad Gupta Hospital (government-run), Kabir Chaura (☎0542 221 4723); Ram Krishna Mission Hospital, Luxa (☎0542 245 1727).

Internet Cyber Point, Bengali Tola Lane (daily 11am–11pm; ₹20/hr), with others nearby; Cyber Café, Parade Kothi (50m towards the station from *Gautam Grand* hotel; daily 9am–9pm; ₹15/hr).

Music The International Music Ashram, D33/81 Kalishpura, near Dasashwamedh Ghat in the Old City (☎0542 245 2302, ✉keshvaraonayak@hotmail.com), is an excellent place to get a few lessons in tabla, sitar and theory.

Pharmacies Every hospital has a neighbouring 24hr pharmacy.

Post The main post office in the Old City is on Kabir Chaura Rd near Kotwali police station at the top end of the Chowk district. The one in the Cantonment is off Raja Bazaar Rd near the big TV mast at its top end. Branch offices are located in *Clarks* hotel, on the Mall in the Cantonment, on Dashaswamedh Rd near the river, and on Vishwanatha Mandir Lane north of *Ganga Fuji* restaurant.

Travel agencies General travel agencies include the friendly Nova Travels, S-21/119C Shubhash Nagar, near Parade Kothi (☎0542 220 8361), and Thomas Cook, S-20/51-5 Varunapul, The Mall (☎0542 250 9946).

Yoga There is a yoga institute at the Benares Hindu University, but the Yoga Training Cente (D-5/15 Shakarkand Lane, near Mir Ghat; ☎99198 57895) in Godaulia is more central; alternatively try Yogi Rakesh Pandeep, B-4/35 Hanuman Ghat (☎94158 17882).

Sarnath

Ten kilometres north of Varanasi, the ruins and temples at **SARNATH** are a Buddhist pilgrimage centre, and also popular with day-trippers from Varanasi. It was here, around 530 BC, just five weeks after he had found enlightenment, that Buddha gave his first ever sermon. According to Buddhist belief, this set in motion the Dharmachakra ("Wheel of Law"), a new cycle of rebirths and reincarnations leading eventually to ultimate enlightenment for everybody. During the rainy season, when Buddha and his followers sought respite from their round of itinerant teaching, they would retire to Sarnath. Also known as **Rishipatana**, the place of the *rishis*, or **Mrigadaya**, the deer park, Sarnath's name derives from Saranganatha, the Lord of the Deer.

Over the centuries, the settlement flourished as a centre of Buddhist (particularly Hinayana) art and teaching. Seventh-century Chinese pilgrim Xuan Zhang recounted seeing thirty monasteries, supporting some three thousand monks, and a life-sized brass statue of the Buddha turning the Wheel of Law, but Indian Buddhism floundered under the impact of Muslim invasions and the rise of Hinduism. Sarnath's expanding Buddhist settlement eventually dissolved in the wake of this religious and political metamorphosis. Except for the **Dhamekh Stupa**, much of the site lay in ruins for almost a millennium, prey to vandalism and pilfering, until 1834, when Alexander Cunningham, head of the Archaeological Survey, excavated the site. Today it is once more an important Buddhist centre, and its avenues house missions from all over the Buddhist world.

The main site

Daily sunrise–sunset • ₹100 (₹5), video camera ₹25

Dominated by the huge bulk of the Dhamekh Stupa, the extensive archeological excavations of the main site of Sarnath are maintained within an immaculate park. As you enter from the southwest, the pillaged remains of the **Dharmarajika Stupa** lie immediately to the north: within its core the *stupa* holds a green marble casket containing relics of Buddha (Ashoka gathered these up from seven original locations and redistributed them among numerous *stupas* nationwide including this one) and precious objects, including decayed pearls and gold leaf. Commemorating the spot where the Buddha delivered his first sermon, Dharmarajika is attributed to the reign of Ashoka in the third century BC, but was extended a further six times.

Adjacent to Dharmarajika Stupa are the ruins of the **main shrine**, where Ashoka is said to have meditated. To the west stands the lower portion of an **Ashoka Pillar** – minus its famous capital, which is now housed in the museum. The ruins of four monasteries, dating from the third to the twelfth centuries, are also contained within the compound; all bear the same hallmark of a central courtyard surrounded by monastic cells.

Dhamekh Stupa

The most impressive of the site's remains is the **Dhamekh Stupa**, also known as the **Dharma Chakra Stupa**, which stakes a competing claim to be the exact spot of Buddha's first sermon. The *stupa* is composed of a cylindrical tower rising 33.5m from a stone drum, ornamented with bas-relief foliage and geometric patterns; the eight-arched niches halfway up may once have held statues of the Buddha.

3

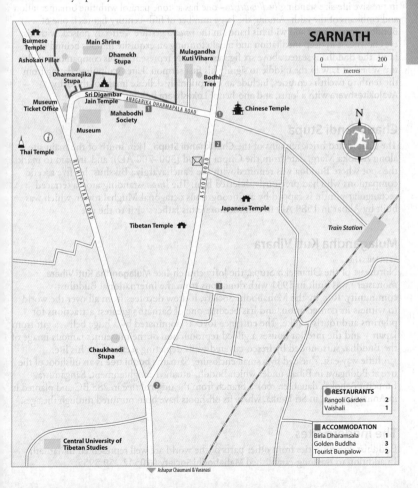

SARNATH

Burmese Temple

Main Shrine

Ashokan Pillar

Dhamekh Stupa

Dharmarajika Stupa

Mulagandha Kuti Vihara

Bodhi Tree

0   200
metres

Museum Ticket Office

Sri Digambar Jain Temple

ANAGARIKA DHARMAPALA ROAD

Museum

Mahabodhi Society

Chinese Temple

N

Thai Temple

BHISHPATTAN ROAD

ASHOK ROAD

Japanese Temple

Tibetan Temple

Train Station

Chaukhandi Stupa

Central University of Tibetan Studies

Ashapur Chaumani & Varanasi

RESTAURANTS
Rangoli Garden   2
Vaishali   1

ACCOMMODATION
Birla Dharamsala   1
Golden Buddha   3
Tourist Bungalow   2

Sri Digamber Jain Temple

In its own enclosure outside the main site, so accessible for free, the **Sri Digamber Jain Temple**, or Shreyanshnath Temple, is believed to mark the birthplace of Shreyanshnath, the eleventh Jain *tirthankara*. Built in 1824, the interior houses a large image of the saint, as well as attractive frescoes depicting the life of Mahavira, the contemporary of Buddha who founded the Jain religion.

The museum

Daily 8am–4.45pm • ₹5 (ticket office across the street); leave cameras and mobiles in lockers at the entrance

Opposite the gates to the main site, the **museum** is designed to look like a *vihara*. Its small but renowned collection of Buddhist and brahmanist antiquities consists mostly of sculpture made from Chunar sandstone. The most famous exhibit is the **lion capital**, removed here from the Ashoka column on the main site. Commissioned by Ashoka (273–232 BC), the great Mauryan king and convert to the *dharma*, it has become the emblem of modern India: four alert and beautifully sculpted lions guard the four cardinal points, atop a circular platform. Belonging to the first and second centuries AD are two impressive life-size standing *bodhisattvas* – one has a stone parasol with fine ornamentation and emblems of the faith. Among the large number of fifth-century figures is one of **Buddha**, cross-legged and with his hands in the *mudra* gesture. Perfectly poised, with his eyes downcast in deep meditation and a halo forming an exquisite nimbus behind his head, the Buddha is seated above six figures, possibly representing his companions, with the Wheel of Law in the middle to signify his first sermon. Later sculptures, dating from the tenth to twelfth centuries, include an exceptionally delicate image of the deity **Avalokiteshvara** with a lotus, and another of **Lokeshvara** holding a bowl.

Chaukhandi Stupa

The dilapidated brick remains of the **Chaukhandi Stupa**, 1km south of the main site along Ashoka Marg, date from the Gupta period (300–700 AD), and are said to mark the spot where Buddha was reunited with the Panchavargiya Bikshus, his five ascetic companions who had previously deserted him. The *stupa*, standing atop a terraced rectangular plinth, is capped by an incongruous octagonal Mughal tower, which was built by Akbar in 1589 AD to commemorate his father's visit to the site.

Mulagandha Kuti Vihara

No set hours • Free

Northeast of the Dhamekh Stupa, the lofty church-like **Mulagandha Kuti Vihara** monastery was built in 1931 with donations from the international Buddhist community. Run by the Mahabodhi Society, it drew devotees from all over the world to witness its consecration, and has become one of Sarnath's greatest attractions for pilgrims and tourists alike. The entrance foyer is dominated by a huge bell – a gift from Japan – and the interior houses a gilded reproduction of the museum's famous image of the Buddha, surrounded by fresco-covered walls depicting scenes from his life.

A little way east, shielded by a small enclosure, Sarnath's **bodhi tree** is an offshoot of the tree at Bodhgaya in Bihar, under which Buddha attained enlightenment. Sangamitra, Emperor Ashoka's daughter, took a branch from the original tree in 288 BC and planted it in Anuradhapura, in Sri Lanka, where its offshoots have been nurtured through the ages.

The modern sites

Buddhist communities from other parts of the world are well represented in Sarnath. In addition to the long-established **Mahabodhi Society** (☎0542 259 5955,

@mahabodhisocietyofindia.wordpress.com), the **Central University of Tibetan Studies** (☎0542 258 5242, @cuts.ac.in), just out of Sarnath toward Varanasi, offers degree courses in Tibetan philosophy and the ancient language of Pali. Close to the post office is the traditional-style **Tibetan Temple** with frescoes and a good collection of *thangkas* (Tibetan Buddhist paintings): its central image is a colossal Shakyamuni, or "Buddha Calling the Earth to Witness" (his enlightenment). Two hundred metres to the east of the main gates is the **Chinese Temple**, while to the northwest, the **Burmese Temple** houses a white marble image of the Buddha flanked by two disciples. Behind the *Tourist Bungalow* is the **Japanese Temple**, run by the Mrigdayavana Mahavihara Society.

ARRIVAL AND INFORMATION   SARNATH

By bus Sarnath-bound blue buses from Varanasi (₹10) run along GT Rd past Cantonment station and eastward, but are sporadic and can get crowded. A lot more buses run to Ashapur Chaumani, 2km south of Sarnath, from where you can walk or take a local rickshaw.

By auto-rickshaw A pre-paid auto from Varanasi Cantonment station costs ₹110; shared autos (₹20/person) also sometimes run.

Tourist office UP Modern Recreation Centre (Mon–Sat 10am–5pm).

ACCOMMODATION AND EATING

Birla Dharamsala Anagarika Dharmapala Rd (next to the Mahabodhi Society gates). One of a number of guesthouses run by religious institutions for pilgrims, this one is very central, spartan but clean, and subject to religious rules (no alcohol and no sex, for example), with both attached and non-attached rooms. ₹200/₹600

Golden Buddha Near Tibetan Temple ☎0542 258 7933, @goldenbuddha@rediffmail.com. Sarnath's most comfortable option, with a lush garden, good restaurant, and lovely old-fashioned rooms (and well worth the ₹150 extra for a deluxe upstairs room). ₹950

Rangoli Garden Restaurant SA-14/97 Ashok Rd (opposite the radio station) ☎0542 259 5325. Just past Chukhandi Stupa, at the crossroad on the way from Varanasi, this is a very popular spot for good north and south Indian food and has an outdoor sitting area. Non-veg mains around ₹120–200. Mon–Sat 10am–10pm.

Tourist Bungalow Ashok Rd (opposite the post office) ☎0542 259 5965, @rahimrigdav@up-tourism.com. The UP state-run hotel is institutional and functional, but it's got large rooms, all attached, some a/c (₹1237), and a dorm. Dorm ₹150, double ₹900

Vaishali At the junction of Anagarika Dharmapala Rd and Ashok Rd ☎93361 33640, @vaishalirestaurant .com. Upstairs restaurant with a choice of North Indian, South Indian or Chinese. You can get a masala dosa for ₹50, or *paneer* mushroom masala for ₹120. Daily 8.30am–9pm.

Gorakhpur

Some 230km north of Varanasi, **GORAKHPUR** rose to prominence as a waystation on a pilgrims' route linking Kushinagar (the place of Buddha's enlightenment) and **Lumbini** (his birthplace, across the border in Nepal), and is now known primarily as a gateway to Nepal. It was named after the Shaivite yogi **Gorakhnath**, and holds a large ashram and temple dedicated to him. Tourists and pilgrims tend to hurry through, their departure hastened by the town's infamous flies and mosquitoes. It does however, have a bustling bazaar, adequate amenities and a few passable hotels.

ARRIVAL AND INFORMATION   GORAKHPUR

By plane The airport (currently served only five times weekly by Jet to Delhi) is 7km east of Gorakhpur towards Kushinagar. Taxis charge ₹200 into town.

By train Daily trains from Gorakhpur include the #12555 *Gorakdam Express* at 4.35pm for Lucknow (arr. 9.40pm) and New Delhi (arr. 5.50am), and the #15018 *Gorakhpur–Lokmanyatilak Express* at 5.30am for Mumbai (arr. at *Kurla* 6.40pm next day) via Varanasi (arr. 11.05am); other trains to Varanasi (6hr) include the overnight #55149

Gorakhpur–Manduadih passenger train (it has sleepers), which leaves at 11.15pm, arriving 6.15am.

By bus Gorakhpur has three bus stands: the Railway Bus Stand, near the station (200m up Station Rd, which is opposite the station, marked by a statue of Maharana Pratap Singh on horseback), for services from the Nepalese border at Sonauli and Kushinagar; the Kacheri Bus Stand, 1km southwest of the station, for buses from Allahabad, Lucknow and Varanasi; and Pedleyganj, 2km southeast of

3

the station, used by some Varanasi services.

By rickshaw Cycle rickshaws are the main means of transport around town, with few hotels more than 2km from the station.

Services There are ATMs around town including several in Golghar (1km southwest of the station) and directly outside the station; the State Bank of India on Bank Rd will change travellers' cheques. The GPO is on Park Rd at Golghar.

ACCOMMODATION AND EATING

Gorakhpur **hotels** range from dingy flophouses near the station to mid-range places in Golghar (1km southwest) and Niyamachak (1.5km west). For **eating**, there's a row of cheap *dhabas* opposite the station. All the following hotels have 24hr checkout.

Bobina Nepal Rd, Niyamachak ☎0551 233 6663 or 4, ⓦhotelbobina.com. The public areas look a bit windswept, but this is a very good-value mid-range choice, with spacious a/c (₹1349) and non-a/c rooms, a decent restaurant and bar, and even a pool. Often full, so it's worth booking ahead. ₹843

Bobis Golghar ☎0551 233 2233. A multicuisine restaurant where lunch is served noon–3pm, supper 7–10.30pm, with snacks and cakes from the adjoining bakery served in between times. A mutton curry here will set you back ₹140, a chicken curry ₹135, and there are also Chinese and Continental options.

Clarks Inn Grand Park Rd, near Golghar ☎0551 220 5015, ⓦclarksinngrand.in. Gorakhpur's most upmarket

option, an unexciting but reliable business hotel with large rooms, a fitness centre and a pool. Breakfast included. ₹6745

Railway retiring rooms If you're taking a train out, you can use the retiring rooms at the station, which are excellent value, all with big bathrooms, come with or without a/c, and can be hired for 12hr or 24hr. There are also single rooms (₹150) and dorms (₹75). Very handy if you need to catch an early train. ₹275

Standard Station Rd, by the statue of Maharana Pratap Singh ☎0551 220 1439. Cleanest of the cheap hotels opposite the station. Rooms are attached, but hot water comes in a bucket (₹10). ₹450

Kushinagar

Set against a pastoral landscape 53km east of Gorakhpur, the small village of **KUSHINAGAR** is revered as the site of Buddha's death and cremation, and final liberation (**Mahaparinirvana**) from the cycles of death and rebirth. During his lifetime, **Kushinara**, as it was then called, was a small kingdom of the Mallas, surrounded by forest. It remained forgotten until the late nineteenth century, when archeologists began excavations based on the writings of the seventh-century Chinese pilgrims.

Set in a leafy park in the heart of Kushinagar, the **Mahaparinirvana Temple** (or **Nirvana Stupa**), dated to the reign of Kumaragupta I (413–455 AD), was extensively rebuilt by Burmese Buddhists in 1927. The large gilded **reclining Buddha** inside the shrine was reconstructed from the remains of an earlier Malla image. At the road crossing immediately southwest, the **Matha Kuwar** shrine holds a tenth-century Buddha made of blue schist rock, also covered in gilt. It's usually locked up (you can look in through the windows), but the caretaker may offer to open it up for you if he's around. Just round the corner, there's a **Bauddha Museum** (Tues–Fri and most Sats 10.30am–4.30pm; ₹10 (₹3), camera ₹20), housing a so-so collection of ancient Buddhist sculpture, not all original; the most interesting exhibits are the small pieces in a case of antiquities unearthed locally. The crumbling bricks of the **Ramabhar Stupa**, about 1.5km southeast of the main site (around ₹50 for the roundtrip by rickshaw), are thought to be the original **Mukutabandhana Stupa**, erected to mark the spot where Buddha was cremated.

Today Kushinagar is rediscovering its roots as a centre of international Buddhism, and is home to several monasteries sponsored by Buddhists from Tibet, Burma, Thailand, Sri Lanka and Japan. The strikingly simple **Japanese Temple** consists of a single circular chamber housing a great golden image of Buddha, softly lit through small, stained-glass windows. In stark contrast, the recently constructed **Thai Monastery** is a large complex of lavish, traditionally styled temples and shrines.

GETTING TO NEPAL

Gorakhpur is a convenient jumping-off point for western **Nepal**, offering access to Pokhara and even Kathmandu. Direct buses to or from Kathmandu and Pokhara are not a good deal – it's much better to get a bus to Sonauli, cross over, and pick up onward transport connections on the other side.

  Buses for Sonauli (3hr) depart from Gorakhpur's Railway Bus Stand between 4.30am and 9pm: deluxe buses leave from in front of the railway station. For onward destinations in Nepal, you'll need to get to Bhairawa, 5km north of the border post (around ₹20 by local bus, ₹50 by rickshaw). There are buses and minibuses from Bhairawa every half-hour or so to Kathmandu (8–9hr) and Pokhara (7–9hr), but set off early from Gorakhpur to get your connecting bus in daylight and enjoy the views.

  Coming the other way, private buses for Gorakhpur leave Sonauli almost hourly in the mornings (5–11am).

ACCOMMODATION

Rahi Tourist Bungalow Maharaj Ganj, Sonauli (1km short of the border) ☎05522 238201, ✉rahinrajana @up-tourism.com. This UP state government-run hotel has a range of rooms, including a/c (₹700), and a dorm

(₹100). There's more choice over the border in Nepal; and in Bhairawa, 4km up the road from the border, where the budget *Mt Everest* and more upmarket *Yeti* are popular options. ₹350

VISAS AND MONEY

Nepalese visas (valid for one month) are available at the border for US$30. There is a State Bank of India on the Indian side of the border; moneychangers across the border will also cash travellers' cheques. Indian ₹500 and ₹1000 notes are **illegal** in Nepal; yours may be confiscated, and you can even be arrested for having them on you.

3

ARRIVAL AND INFORMATION

KUSHINAGAR

By bus Regular buses link Kushinagar with Gorakhpur (1hr 30min). Buses drop you on the NH-28 highway at the junction with the road into town.
Tourist information UP Tourism maintains an office (Mon–Sat 10am–5pm; ☎05564 273045) at *Pathik Niwas*.
Tours India Tourism and UP Tourism run comprehensive tours of the whole "Buddhist Circuit" of Uttar Pradesh,

which can be booked in Kushinagar, or at UP Tourism in Delhi (see p.106). *Yama Café* organize a 13km hike to surrounding villages and holy sites (8am–4pm; ₹750 /person including breakfast and lunch; minimum five people).
Services There's a moneychanger next to *Yama Café*, and you can also change money at the *Lotus Nikko* hotel.

ACCOMMODATION AND EATING

Most of the temples offer **accommodation** for visiting pilgrims in return for a donation.

Linh Son 300m from the NH-28 highway, on the left ☎99368 37270, ⊕linhsonnepalindiatemple.org. The bright, modern guesthouse attached to this Chinese-Vietnamese temple is one of the best in town, with clean, spacious doubles with attached baths and hot water. The adjoining temple is also pretty resplendent. ₹500
Lotus Nikko next to the Japanese Temple ☎05564 273026, ⊕lotusnikkohotels.com. Very large rooms, more like suites, each with a sitting and eating area, make this Kushinagar's top hotel, but it's sometimes booked up by tour groups. ₹7182
Pathik Niwas 500m from the NH-28 highway, on the right ☎05564 273046, ✉rahipathikniwas@ up-tourism.com. The UP state-run hotel has ground-floor rooms around a garden (sometimes used for

weddings), all attached, and ranging from plain and institutional to luxury cottage suites called "American Huts" (₹1573). ₹700
Shree Birla 300m from the NH-28 highway, on the right ☎05564 273090. A very simple Indian guesthouse adjoining an Indian Buddhist shrine, and matching its cream-and-russet paintwork. A few rooms are attached (the price for these is no different), but all are pretty basic. ₹250
★ **Yama Café** 300m from the NH-28 highway, next to Linh Son Temple ☎99561 12749. Small, but clean and pleasant, restaurant with a short menu of home-cooked Indian, Tibetan and Chinese food – the vegetable- or chicken-noodle soup (₹50 and ₹70, respectively) is particularly recommended. They also sell postcards and devotional items. Daily 8am–8pm.

Uttarakhand

AARTI CEREMONY IN HARIDWAR

Uttarakhand

Northeast of Delhi, bordering Nepal and Tibet, the mountains of the Garhwal and Kumaon regions rise from the fertile sub-Himalayan plains. Together they form the state of Uttarakhand, which was shorn free from lowland Uttar Pradesh in 2000 after years of agitation, and changed its name from Uttaranchal in 2007. The region has its own distinct languages and cultures, and successive deep river valleys shelter fascinating micro-civilizations, where Hinduism meets animism and Buddhist influence is never too far away. Although not as high as the giants of Nepal, further east, or as the Karakoram, the snow peaks here rank among the most beautiful mountains of the inner Himalayas, forming an almost continuous chain that culminates in Nanda Devi, the highest mountain in India at 7816m.

Garhwal is the more visited region, busy with pilgrims who flock to its holy spots. At **Haridwar**, the Ganges thunders out from the foothills on its long journey to the sea. The nearby ashram town of **Rishikesh** is familiar from one of the classic East-meets-West images of the 1960s; it was where the Beatles came to stay with the Maharishi. From here pilgrims set off for the high temples known as the Char Dham – **Badrinath**, **Kedarnath**, **Yamunotri** and **Gangotri**, the source of the Ganges. Earthier pursuits are on offer at **Mussoorie**, a British hill station that's now a popular Indian resort. The less-visited **Kumaon** region remains largely unspoilt, and boasts pleasant small towns with panoramic mountain views, among them **Kausani**, **Ranikhet**, and the tiny hamlet of **Kasar Devi**, as well as the Victorian hill station of **Nainital**, where a lakeside promenade throngs with visitors escaping the heat of the plains. Further down, the forests at **Corbett Tiger Reserve** offer the chance to go tiger-spotting from the back of an elephant. Both districts abound in classic treks, many leading through the *bugyals* – summer pastures, where rivers are born and paths meet.

Brief history

The first known inhabitants of Garhwal and Kumaon were the **Kuninda** in the second century BC. A Himalayan tribal people practising an early form of Shaivism, they traded salt with Tibet and shared connections with contemporaneous Indo-Greek civilization. As evidenced by a second-century Ashokan edict at Kalsi in western Garhwal, Buddhism made some inroads in the region, but Garhwal and Kumaon remained Brahmanical. The Kuninda eventually succumbed to the **Guptas** around the fourth century AD, who, despite controlling much of the north Indian plains, failed to make a lasting impact in the hills. Between the seventh and the fourteenth

Highlights

❶ **Char Dham** The pilgrim circuit to the four sacred sites of Garhwal reveals a cross-section of the Indian Himalayas' most superb scenery. **See p.295**

❷ **Haridwar** The spectacular nightly *aarti* ceremony in one of Hinduism's holiest cities sees thousands of the devout sending candles down the Ganges. **See p.300**

❸ **Rishikesh** This busy pilgrimage place on the banks of the turquoise Ganges is a renowned yoga and meditation centre. **See p.304**

❹ **Gangotri** Trek beyond the tree line to the Gaumukh Glacier, source of the Ganges, where

sadhus offer accommodation for spiritual retreats. **See p.312**

❺ **Valley of the Flowers** The lush meadows of this remote, hidden valley are a botanist's dream: come in monsoon season to see the flowers in full bloom. **See p.318**

❻ **Kuari Pass trek** A five-day trail through the upper reaches of Garhwal, offering stunning views of the Great Himalayan Watershed. **See p.319**

❼ **Corbett Tiger Reserve** Established in the 1930s, India's most famous nature reserve is renowned for its population of tigers. **See p.322**

HIGHLIGHTS ARE MARKED ON THE MAP ON PP.292–293

UTTARAKHAND

0 ——— 50
kilometres

HIGHLIGHTS

1. Char Dam
2. Haridwar
3. Rishikesh
4. Gangotri
5. Valley of the Flowers
6. Kuari Pass trek
7. Corbett Tiger Reserve

TIBET
(TIBET AUTONOMOUS REGION)

Mana Pass

Kamet
(7756m)

Vasudhara
Waterfall

Satopanth
(7075m)

Badrinath

Sudarshan
(6507m)

Nandanvan

Nilkanth
(6596m)

Lanka

Bhojbasa

Gomukh

Tapovan

Bhaironghati

Bhagirathi
(6856m)

Chaukhamba
(7138m)

Harsil

Bhagirathi

Gangotri

Shivling
(6543m)

Gangotri
Glacier

Jogin
(6465m)

Kedarnath (6940m)

Madhmaheshwar

Har-ki-Dun

Swargarohini
(6252m)

Khatling
Glacier

Rudranath

Osla

Bandarpunch
(6316m)

Khatling

Kedarnath

Chandrashila
(3930m)

Taluka

Yamunotri

Janki Chatti

Rambara

Gaurikund

Tungnath

Sankri

Kharsali

Dodi Tal

Guptkashi

Netwar

Hanuman Chatti

Agoda

Kalyani

Sonprayag

Okhimath

Purola

Yamuna

Uttarkashi

Gangi

Mandakini

GARHWAL

Barkot

BudhaKedar

Ghuttu

Bhilangna

Rudra

Nowgaon

Bhagirathi

Ghamsali

Alakananda

Deoban

Nag Tiba
(3027m)

Sarkhanda Devi
(3030m)

Srinagar

Chakrata

Dhanolti

New
Tehri

Pauri

Tons

Kempty Falls

Dhanaulti

Chamba

Devaprayag

HIMACHAL
PRADESH

Mussoorie

Kunjapuri
(2240m)

Kalsi

Dehra Dun

Narendranagar

Nilkanth Mahadev

Lansdowne

Rishikesh

Kunnao

RAJAJI
NATIONAL
PARK

Chilla

Haridwar

Bijnor

Roorkee

Yamunanagar

Saharanpur

Ganges

UTTAR PRADESH

Delhi

The International boundaries on this map are neither purported to be correct nor authentic by Survey of India directives. Publisher.

centuries, the Shaivite **Katyuri** dominated lands of varying extent from the modern-day **Baijnath** valley in Kumaon, where their stone temples still stand, and Brahmanical culture flourished, highlighted by the rise of **Jageshwar** as a major pilgrimage centre. In following centuries, Kumaon prospered further under the **Chandras**, who took learning and art to new levels, while Garhwal fell under the Panwar rajas. In 1803, the westward expansion of the Nepali Gurkhas engulfed both regions, but their brief rule ended with the Sugauli Treaty of 1816, resulting in annexation of both regions by the British.

The Birth of Uttaranchal

Following Independence, Garhwal and Kumaon became part of Uttar Pradesh, but failure by the administration in Lucknow to develop the region led to increasingly violent calls for a **separate state**. Things came to a head in October 1994 when a peaceful protest march to Delhi was violently disrupted in Mussoorie by the UP police. The sympathetic high-caste BJP took up the separatist cause after coming to power in March 1998, leading to the creation of India's 27th state, originally called Uttaranchal, on November 9, 2000.

The process of creating the new state was somewhat acrimonious. Deep cultural **differences** characterize Garhwal and Kumaon, and both regions hoped to host the new capital. Dehra Dun, in lowland Garhwal, was eventually chosen, upsetting the Kumaonis considerably. Meanwhile, in Haridwar – culturally a part of the plains – farmers took to the streets to demand things remain as they were. In January 2007, the state reverted to its historical name, Uttarakhand, meaning "northern country". More than a dozen years after it was created, scores of old and new problems continue to face the young state.

On the environmental front, deforestation in the hills has led to a rapid loss of arable land, while global warming continues to shrink glaciers at an alarming rate. As both water and power shortages continue to impact much of the state, many of Uttarakhand's controversial hydro-electric projects have been scrapped or stalled over a scrum of political, religious and environmental concerns. Yet while officialdom founders, groups such as the **Himalayan Environmental Studies and Conservation Organization** (HESCO), inspired by self-reliance crusader Dr. Anil Joshi, are taking sustainable development into their own hands, working to meld local resources and modern technology.

GETTING AROUND   **UTTARAKHAND**

Most roads are well maintained by the army to support its large presence in the border areas, but getting around isn't always comfortable or easy: the monsoon season (Aug & Sept) brings frequent landslides that cause long delays, while during winter (Dec–Feb), many roads are blocked with snow. Buses ply many of the high mountain roads, but for these most locals prefer tightly crammed jeeps.

Dehra Dun

Capital of Uttarakhand since 2000, **DEHRA DUN**, 255km north of Delhi, is pleasantly located at just below 700m, as the Himalayan foothills begin their dramatic rise, so it never gets too hot in summer, and snows rarely appear in winter. It stands at the centre of the 120km-long **Doon Valley** (*dun* or *doon* literally means "valley"), hemmed in by the Yamuna to the west and the Ganges at Rishikesh to the east. A popular retirement spot, and renowned for its elite public schools, Dehra Dun has been occupied in turn by Sikhs, Mughals and Gurkhas, but it is the British influence that is most apparent. Driven by its status as state capital, increasing local and government investment led to a commercial and IT boom in the city, though this has stagnated somewhat in recent years. The accompanying noise and traffic problems are at their most intense around the markets near the tall Victoria **Clock Tower**, and along Gandhi and Rajpur roads.

GARHWAL

As the sacred land that holds the sources of the mighty Ganges and Yamuna rivers, **Garhwal** has been the heartland of Hindu identity since the ninth century when, in the wake of the decline of Buddhism in northern India, the reformer Shankara incorporated many of the mountains' ancient shrines into the fold of Hinduism. He founded the four main **yatra** (pilgrimage) temples, deep within the Himalayas, known as the **Char Dham** – **Badrinath**, **Kedarnath**, and the less-visited pair of **Gangotri** and **Yamunotri**. Each year, between May and November, once the snows have melted, streams of pilgrims penetrate high into the mountains, passing by way of **Rishikesh**, the land of yogis and ashrams.

For more than a millennium, the *yatris* (pilgrims) came on foot. However, the annual event has been transformed in the last few years; roads blasted by the military through the mountains during the war against China in the early 1960s are now the lifelines for a new form of motorized *yatra*. Eastern Garhwal in particular is getting rich, and the fabric of hill society is changing rapidly – visitors hoping to experience the old Garhwal should spend at least part of their time well away from the principal *yatra* routes. In addition to their spiritual significance, the hills are now becoming established as a centre for **adventure sports**, offering all levels of trekking, whitewater rafting, paragliding, skiing and climbing.

Forest Research Institute

3km northwest of Clock Tower on Kaulagarh Rd • Mon–Fri 9.30am–5.30pm • ₹10 • ☏ 0135 2759382, ⊛ fri.icfre.gov.in • Vikram #6 from Connaught Place

The chateau-like **Forest Research Institute**, an impressive red-brick, Raj-era structure completed in the 1920s, sits in sprawling grounds. The institute is devoted to the preservation of India's much-threatened woodlands, and is responsible for training most of India's forest officers. There's a large and interesting **museum** holding wood samples, insects, furniture, pickled animal embryos and the like.

ARRIVAL AND DEPARTURE

DEHRA DUN

By bus The Inter-state Bus Terminal (ISBT) is located in the far southwest of town, linked to the central railway station and budget hotels on Gandhi Rd by auto-rickshaw (₹120) or Vikram #5 (₹10). Buses to Mussoorie run from just north of the train station entrance.

Destinations Delhi (hourly; 7hr); Dharamsala (2 daily; 14hr); Haridwar (every 30min; 2hr); Joshimath (daily; 12hr); Manali (3pm; 14hr); Mussoorie (hourly; 1hr); Nainital (8 daily; 7hr); Rishikesh (every 30min; 1hr 30min); Shimla (4 daily; 10hr); Uttarkashi (2 daily; 8hr).

By train The station is off Gandhi Rd, about 2km southwest of the Clock Tower. The best daily trains to Delhi are the overnight #14042 *Mussoorie Express* (dep. 9.20pm; arr. Delhi Sarai Rohilla 8.50am), the a/c #12018 *Shatabdi Express* (dep. 5pm; arr. New Delhi 10.45pm) and the #12056 *Janshatabdi Express* (dep. 5.10am; arr. New Delhi 11.15am). The *Doon Express* #13010 is the most convenient options for Lucknow (dep. 8.25pm; arr. 8.20am) as well as Varanasi (arr. 4pm) and Kolkata (arr. 6.55am the second morning). For Agra, the #14310 *Ujjaiyani Express* (Tues & Wed; dep. 6am; arr. 4.55pm) is the fastest.

GETTING AROUND AND INFORMATION

By Vikram These blue, eight-seater auto-rickshaws are Dehra Dun's cheapest mode of transport; they are numbered by their routes and cost ₹4–10.
Car rental GMVN's head office, 74/1 Rajpur Rd (Mon–Sat 10am–5pm; ☏ 0135 2746817); Drona Travels, *Hotel*

Drona, 45 Gandhi Rd (Mon–Sat 10am–5pm; ☏ 0135 2653309).
Tourist information GMVN Tourist Office, *Hotel Drona*, 45 Gandhi Rd (Mon–Sat 10am–5pm; ☏ 0135 2653217, ⊛ gmvnl.com).

ACCOMMODATION

Dehra Dun has a good selection of mid-range **hotels**, many of them strung along Rajpur Rd as it heads north to Mussoorie. What little budget accommodation there is can be found between the railway station and the Clock Tower – or in the old-fashioned railway retiring rooms.

Ashrey 10 Tyagi Rd ☏ 0135 2623388. In a quiet, but central, spot, just a 3min walk south of Princes Chowk; the

private lawn in front complements the spotless, spacious and well-furnished new rooms with flatscreen TVs, some with a/c (₹2000). Good value. **₹1000**

Great Value 74-C Rajpur Rd, 2.5km north of the Clock Tower ☎ 0135 2744086, ⊚ greatvaluehotel.com. Large, well-run chain hotel with good facilities including a nice garden, a bar and bright, spotless rooms equipped with wi-fi (₹120/hr). **₹3200**

Moti Mahal 7 Rajpur Rd ☎ 0135 2651277, ⊚ hotelmotimahal.net. A bright, modern hotel with a fancy restaurant; double-glazing keeps the noise and fumes out of the immaculate a/c rooms (₹1800), all of which have posh fittings such as flatscreen TVs. **₹1000**

Saurab 1 Raja Rd ☎ 0135 2728041, ⊚ hotelsaurab .com. The best budget option within easy walking distance of the train station. It's good value: clean, spacious attached rooms with TVs, hot water, a multicuisine restaurant, friendly staff and a travel desk. **₹850.**

★ **White House** 15/7 Subhash Rd (aka Lytton Rd) ☎ 0135 2656594. Atmospheric old Art Deco Raj residence near Astley Hall, with huge verandas, lofty ceilings, sturdy furniture (rather hard beds) and a friendly owner. All rooms are attached and some have a/c (₹990). A peaceful retreat from the centre of Dehra Dun, yet only a few minutes' walk away. **₹825**

EATING AND DRINKING

Black Pepper 3 Astley Hall, Rajpur Rd ☎ 0135 2657781. This cool, grotto-style restaurant appeals to families and bright young things, with a wide range of Indian, Chinese and Continental meals, from chicken sizzler (₹395) to Goan fish curry (₹425). The upstairs bar is equally inviting (Carlsberg ₹280). Daily 9am–2.30am.

★ **Kumar Foods** 15B Rajpur Rd. Excellent veg and non-veg cooking, with a lengthy menu of north and south Indian, Chinese and Continental dishes, from chicken stroganoff (₹260) to *paneer* tikka masala (₹180), served in comfortable surroundings at reasonable prices. Save for room for fantastic *mithai* (sweets). There's a pure veg branch 40m further north. Daily 11am–10pm.

Moti Mahal 7 Rajpur Rd ☎ 0135 2651277. In the hotel of the same name, this sleek, a/c restaurant is the place for a spot of posh nosh, especially chicken and *paneer*, although there are also Chinese options. Non-veg favorites include chicken *karahi* (₹220) and that great Anglo-Bangladeshi contribution to Indian cuisine, chicken tikka masala (₹280). Daily 11am–10pm.

Tirupati 27-B Rajpur Rd ☎ 93581 10244. This clean and friendly multicuisine restaurant serves everything from chowmein (₹95) to cheese pizza (₹125), but particularly strong on south Indian dishes. While a north Indian thali will set you back ₹140, for ₹145 you can try a south Indian combination featuring dosa, *iddli*, *vada* and *kheer* (rice pudding). Daily 10am–10pm.

DIRECTORY

ATMs and banks A number of ATMs surround the Clock Tower; the State Bank of India on Convent Rd changes travellers' cheques, as do many of the banks along Rajpur Rd.

Bookshop Natraj Bookshop (17 Rajpur Rd; Mon-Sat 10am–1.30pm & 3–8pm), known locally as The Green Bookshop, is one of the oldest and best independent bookstores in the country.

Internet access There are numerous cyber cafés on the main streets, including Webex on Lytton Rd just south of White House (₹40/hr) and Harsh Computers on Neshvilla Rd (₹20/hr).

Post office The GPO is on Rajpur Rd (Mon–Sat 10am–6pm).

Treks and tours The GMVN's head office (74/1 Rajpur Rd; Mon–Sat 10am–5pm; ☎ 0135 2746817, ✉ gmvn @sacharnett.in) books GMVN accommodation and tours throughout Garhwal; similar services are also available at Drona Travels (Hotel Drona complex, 45 Gandhi Rd; Mon–Sat 10am–5pm; ☎ 0135 2653309). For treks, good options include Garhwal Adventure Tours (151 Araghar; ☎ 0135 2677769, ✉ garhwaltrekking@rediffmail.com), an experienced organization used to working with tour groups such as Exodus, and Cliff Climbers (51–61 Bazaar; ☎ 0135 2651235), the best trekking and mountaineering equipment dealers in the region.

Mussoorie

Spreading for 15km along a high serrated ridge, **MUSSOORIE** is the closest hill station to Delhi, just 278km north of the capital and 34km north of Dehra Dun, from where it is visible on a clear day. At an altitude of 2000m, it gives travellers from the plains their first glimpse of the snow-covered Himalayan **peaks** of western Garhwal, as well as dramatic views of the Dehra Dun valley below.

These days, Mussoorie is a highly popular weekend retreat for middle-class Indians up from the plains. Most foreign visitors come to Mussoorie to **study** Hindi at the excellent Landour Language School, but the town also makes a handy base for **treks** into the western interior of Garhwal. Dominated by the long Bandarpunch Massif (6316m), with Swargarohini (6252m) in the west and the Gangotri group in the east, Mussoorie's mountain panorama may not be as dramatic as at some other hill stations, but it forms a pleasant backdrop to the busy holiday town.

Mussoorie centres on the 2km pedestrian-only **Mall**, bookended by the town's two most lively hubs: Library Bazaar (also called Gandhi Chowk) to the west and Kulri Bazaar to the east.

Happy Valley

3km west of the Library near Convent Hill

Home to more than five thousand Tibetans, **Happy Valley** was the first Tibetan settlement in India following the Dalai Lama's 1959 escape from Tibet. Although the headquarters for the Tibetan government-in-exile moved to Dharamsala in 1960, Happy Valley remains a bastion of Tibetan culture, with a large school, a lively bazaar and numerous *gompas*, including the small but beautiful **Shedup Choephelling**, the first of its kind to be built in India, surrounded by gardens and fluttering prayer flags overlooking the Doon Valley.

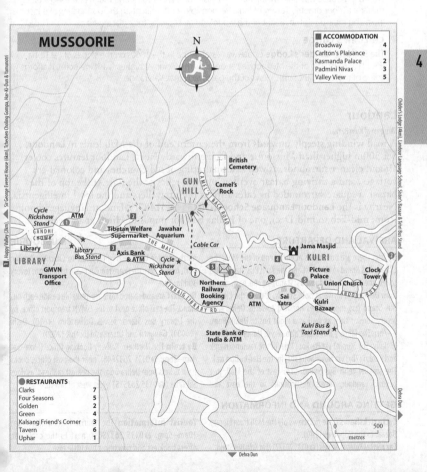

MUSSOORIE

N

■ **ACCOMMODATION**
Broadway	4
Carlton's Plaisance	1
Kasmanda Palace	2
Padmini Nivas	3
Valley View	5

British Cemetery

GUN HILL
Camel's Rock

CAMEL'S BACK ROAD

Cycle Rickshaw Stand
ATM
GANDHI CHOWK
Library
LIBRARY
GMVN Transport Office
Library Bus Stand
Tibetan Welfare Supermarket
Jawahar Aquarium
THE MALL
Cable Car
Axis Bank & ATM
Cycle Rickshaw Stand
KINRAIG LIBRARY RD
Northern Railway Booking Agency
ATM
State Bank of India & ATM

Jama Masjid
KULRI
Picture Palace
Clock Tower
Union Church
LANDOUR BAZAR
Sai Yatra
Kulri Bazaar
Kulri Bus & Taxi Stand

Happy Valley (2km)
Sir George Everest House (6km), Tibetan Choling Gompa, Har-Ki-Dun & Yamunotri
Childer's Lodge (4km), Landour Language School, Sister's Bazaar & Tehri Bus Stand
Dehra Dun

● **RESTAURANTS**
Clarks	7
Four Seasons	5
Golden	2
Green	4
Kalsang Friend's Corner	3
Tavern	6
Uphar	1

0   500
metres

Dehra Dun

4

MUSSOORIE'S MOUNTAIN VIEWPOINTS

While Mussoorie's busy Mall faces away from the snows and towards Dehra Dun, a number of vantage points are within a short walk of the centre, offering glimpses of Himalyan giants such as Bandar Punch I (6316m) and II (6102m) and Kalanag Peak (6387m).

GUN HILL

The most popular of Mussoorie's viewpoints, **Gun Hill** (2024m) rises like a volcano over central Mussoorie, offering superb Himalayan views when the weather is right. It can be ascended by a footpath forking up from the Mall, or by a 400m cable-car ride starting from the Ropeway station (10am–7pm; ₹75 return) about halfway down the Mall.

CAMEL'S BACK ROAD

Rounding the northern base of Gun Hill is the pleasant 4km promenade of **Camel's Back Road**, a scenic northerly arch connecting Library and Kulri bazaars. Along the way are several worthy viewpoints, as well as the distinctive Camel's Rock and an old British cemetery (closed to visitors).

SIR GEORGE EVEREST'S HOUSE

The 6km hike from Library Bazaar to the former home and laboratory of **Sir George Everest** is rewarded with fantastic views of both the Himalayas and the Doon Valley. The abandoned, crumbling house was built by the famous Welsh surveyor in 1833, and much of the work of the Great Trigonometric Survey of India, responsible for demarcating the boundaries of British India and measuring the height of the world's greatest peaks, took place here.

CHILDER'S LODGE

The 300-acre **Childer's Lodge** estate was established in the 1860s on the slopes of Lal Tibba (Red Hill), 5km east of the Mall above Landour. As the vicinity's highest vantage point, it affords some of the best panoramic views of the Garhwal Himalayan range.

Landour

5km east of Kulri Bazaar

A road winding steeply upwards from the eastern end of the Mall leads to **Landour**. Set 300m higher than Mussoorie and facing towards Tibet, Landour features cooler air and cleaner surrounds, as well as a smattering of old churches and colonial-era cottages, and a thriving bazaar overflowing with relics of the Raj. At the top of the bazaar, a square surrounded by cafés attracts both travellers and the local intelligentsia. Nearby is the **Landour Language School** (☎0135 2631487, ⊕landourlanguageschool .com; mid-Feb to mid-Dec), one of India's best for pupils of Hindi at all levels.

ARRIVAL AND DEPARTURE
MUSSOORIE

By bus There are bus stands at either end of the Mall; the Library Bus Stand to the west and the Kulri Bus Stand (also called the Masonic Lodge Bus Stand) to the east. Buses from Dehra Dun arrive at both stands, though the Library Bus Stand has more buses heading towards Dehra Dun (every 30min; 1hr), as well as a night bus to Delhi (8pm; 6–7hr). The Library Bus Stand also serves Hanuman Chatti (3 daily; 5hr 30min) via Barkot (3hr) for the Yamunotri trek and Sankri (7hr) via Nowgaon (3hr) for the Har-ki-Dun trek. The smaller Tehri Bus Stand, 5km east of the Mall, just beyond Landour, serves destinations to the east and

northeast: for Uttarkashi, first head to Chamba (hourly; 4hr), from where there are regular buses to Gangotri (every 30min; 5hr).

By taxi Cars and shared taxis are available beside each bus stand. The taxi office next to the GMVN transport office, by the Library Bus Stand, serves Dehra Dun (₹610), Delhi (₹6000), Gangotri and Uttarkashi (both ₹12000).

By train The Northern Railway Booking Office (Mon–Sat 8am–2pm; ☎0135 2632846), near the post office, books train tickets from Dehra Dun, the nearest railhead, as does Sai Yatra (☎0135 2635151), just west of Tavern.

GETTING AROUND AND INFORMATION

Cycle rickshaws Cycle rickshaws ply the Mall from Library Bazaar to the Ropeway (₹40).

Car rental Kulwant Travels (☎0135 2632717) at Kulri Bus Stand.

Tourist information The tourist bureau (Mon–Sat 10am–5pm; ☎0135 2632863), next to the cable car, offers booklets and brochures but little else.

Tours GMVN transport office (Mon–Sat 8am–5pm; ☎0135 2631281), next to the Library Bus Stand, runs tours of the town and further afield. Trek Himalaya, on the steep street opposite the cable car (Daily 9.30am–8pm; ☎0135 2630491, ⓦtrekhimalaya.com), can put together trekking packages.

Services There are several ATMs along the Mall, including at State Bank of India and Axis Bank, both of which change money; there are two further ATMs along the Mall. Internet access is available at Banares Cyber Café near *Green* restaurant (₹15/hr). There's a post office towards the Kulri end of the Mall (Mon–Fri 9am–5pm, Sat 9am–4pm).

ACCOMMODATION

Mussoorie's high season runs from mid-May to mid-July, with June being the busiest (and costliest) month of the year. Prices are reduced during the shoulder season which includes Christmas and New Year's, April and May, and the "Bengali season" of Oct and Nov; rates are slashed by as much as fifty percent the rest of the year.

Broadway Camel's Back Rd ☎0135 2632243. Set in a rambling old nineteenth-century wooden building, this guesthouse is perched on the edge of Kulri Bazaar with charming, bright window boxes, lovely views and a friendly atmosphere. A good bet for budget travellers. ₹1250

Carlton's Plaisance Happy Valley Rd, 1.5km west of town ☎0135 2632800, ⓦcarltonplaisance.com. Atmospheric Raj-era house with a more modern annexe, both stuffed full of period memorabilia. Edmund Hillary stayed here and loved it, and George Everest's house is just up the road. Lovely gardens and an ideal base for gentle rambles away from the town. Book two weeks ahead in season. ₹3000

Kasmanda Palace The Mall ☎0135 2632424, ⓦkasmandapalace.com. A short, stiff climb up from the Mall leads to this beautiful, whitewashed, ex-maharaja's summer palace, bought from a British officer in 1915 and now a heritage hotel. Comfortable and quiet with lavish rooms, beautiful gardens, historical charm and wall-mounted rhino heads. Book far ahead in season. ₹6000

★ **Padmini Nivas** The Mall ☎0135 2631093, ⓦhotelpadmininivas.com. Just below the Mall, with a beautiful rose garden and fruit trees, plus excellent views and lovely, fresh rooms, most of them with a veranda. It was founded by a British colonel in the 1840s, and was later home to Padmini, a Gujarati queen. ₹3000

Valley View The Mall ☎0135 2632324. Friendly, clean place towering over the centre of the Mall and close to all its amenities, with a good restaurant and sunny terraces overlooking the Doon Valley – views that are even better from the hotel's pricier, wood-panelled super-deluxe rooms (₹3000). Off-season discounts of up to seventy percent. ₹2700

EATING

Clarks The Mall, Kulri ☎0135 2632393. This multicuisine restaurant manages to maintain a period atmosphere of sorts. Housed in a nineteenth-century hotel with lofty ceilings and plush furnishings, it offers separate menus for non-veg Indian and Chinese cuisine, a favourite being the chicken *rara* Punjabi (₹200). A bar and bakery are also attached. Daily 10am–10pm.

Four Seasons The Mall, Kulri. Not as much fun as the *Tavern* across the street, but locals claim the mostly Indian menu here is the best in town. The *murgh makhani* (butter chicken; ₹190/375 for half/full) may have you convinced, as well. Free delivery to your hotel (for orders over ₹350). Daily 11am–11pm.

Golden Landour Bazaar. A popular, if unremarkable, local place next to the old Clock Tower, serving Tibetan, Chinese and Indian dishes, and breakfasts. Mains ₹40–100. Daily 11am–10pm.

Green The Mall, Kulri. Justifiably popular and friendly restaurant in the heart of Kulri, serving Indian, Chinese and snack food. Foreigners tend to love the Kashmiri *kufta* (₹150), while locals swear by the *dal makhani*

(₹120). In season, you may have to queue. Daily 8.30am–11pm.

★ **Kalsang Friend's Corner** The Mall, by the post office. This cosy diner, decked with Chinese lanterns, Tibetan prayer flags and "Free Tibet" stickers-serves tasty Chinese, Indian and Thai dishes alongside hearty Tibetan food, including lengthy lists of *momos* (dumplings; ₹69–144), *thukpas* (noodle soups; ₹84–129) and pork dishes. Daily 11.30am–10.30pm.

Tavern The Mall, Kulri. Hip place near the Picture Palace, offering pricey Western, Thai, Chinese and Indian dishes, including chilli prawns (₹520). There's a small bar with beers from ₹200 and live music most nights, as well as a billiards hall upstairs with pool (₹80/hr) and snooker tables (₹120). Daily 11am–11pm.

Uphar Gandhi Chowk. Clean and ultra-friendly north and south Indian veg food joint with an ice-cream bar (₹35/scoop). Easily one of the best eating spots in the Library area. The specialty is Punjabi food; try the *sarson ka saag* (mustard curry) and *makki ki roti* (spicy, boiled mustard leaves with Indian corn bread; ₹145). Daily 12.30–4.30pm & 6.30–10.30pm.

4

4

HAR-KI-DUN VALLEY TREK

Tucked away in the northwest corner of Garhwal is the stunning "Valley of the Gods", reached by a relatively undemanding three-day (38km) trek from Sankri. A lush, forested valley striped with glacial streams from the snow-clad peaks of **Swargarohini** ("Ascent to Heaven"; 6252m) and **Bandarpunch** ("Monkey's Tail"; 6316m), Har-ki-Dun is home to the Himalayan black bear and the elusive snow leopard, and falls within the Govind Wildlife Sanctuary and National Park (April–Nov; ₹350 (₹50) for up to three days; nominal camping fees extra).

The sparse local population traces its lineage back to the Mahabharata, and like the Pandavas of the epic, they practise a form of polyandry and follow intriguing religious customs, including witchcraft. Worship at Taluka's Duryodhana temple, for example, consists of throwing shoes at the idol; at Pakola, the image has its back to the congregation. Their distinctive alpine buildings have beautifully carved wooden doors and windows, with the mortar construction punctuated by wooden slats.

To reach the **trailhead** at Sankri, board a Yamunotri-bound bus from Mussoorie's Library Bus Stand and change at Nowgaon, 9km before Barkot, for a jeep to Sankri. On the way you'll pass the forest checkpoint at Neitwar, 13km before Sankri. The official trail begins here, although jeeps can continue to Taluka (1900m), 14km further along through deodar and sycamore woods. The second day's hike is 13km to Seema, just below the village of Osla (2559m), while the third day's hike is 14km to Har-ki-Dun campsite (3566m), an excellent base from which to explore the *bugyals* (high alpine meadows) below the Swargarohini to the east, and the Jaundhar Glacier, a day-trip to the northwest. Note that you'll need to take your own food to Har-ki-Dun as there are no *dhabas* after Seema; forest bungalows can be found at each campsite (Sankri, Taluka, Seema and Har-ki-Dun).

Haridwar

At **HARIDWAR** – the Gates (*dwar*) of God (*Hari*) – 214km northeast of Delhi, the **River Ganges** emerges from its final rapids past the Shivalik Hills to begin its long slow journey across northern India to the Bay of Bengal. Stretching for roughly 3km along a narrow strip of land between the craggy wooded hills to the west and the river to the east, Haridwar is especially revered by Hindus, for whom the **Har-ki-Pairi** *ghat* (literally the "Footstep of God") marks the exact spot where the river leaves the mountains. As a road and rail junction, Haridwar links the Gangetic plains with the mountains of Uttarakhand and their holy pilgrimage (*yatra*) network. Along with Nasik, Ujjain and Allahabad, Haridwar is one of the four holy *tirthas* or "crossings" that serve as the focus of the massive **Kumbh Mela** festival (see box, p.264). Every twelve years (next due in 2022), millions of pilgrims come to bathe at a preordained moment in the turbulent waters of the channelled river around Har-ki-Pairi.

Har-ki-Pairi

Split by a barrage north of Haridwar, the **Ganges** flows through the town in two principal channels, divided by a long sliver of land. The natural stream lies to the east, while the embankment of the fast-flowing canal to the west holds the *ghats* and ashrams around **Har-ki-Pairi temple**. Bridges and walkways connect the various islands, and metal chains are placed in the river to protect bathers from being swept away.

The clock tower opposite Har-ki-Pairi *ghat* is an excellent vantage point, especially during evening worship. At both dawn and dusk, the spectacular ceremony of **Ganga Aarti** – devotion to the life-bestowing goddess Ganga – draws crowds of thousands. Lights float down the river and priests perform elaborate choreographed movements while swinging torches to the accompaniment of gongs and music. As soon as they've finished the river shallows fill up with people looking for coins thrown in by the devout. The *ghat* area is free to visit, although a donation is required to visit the section at the bottom of the first staircase.

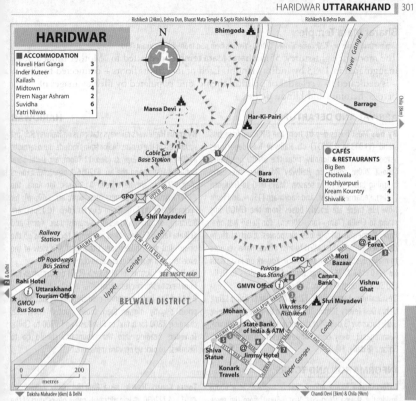

HARIDWAR

■ ACCOMMODATION	
Haveli Hari Ganga	3
Inder Kuteer	7
Kailash	5
Midtown	4
Prem Nagar Ashram	2
Suvidha	6
Yatri Niwas	1

● CAFÉS & RESTAURANTS	
Big Ben	5
Chotiwala	2
Hoshiyarpuri	1
Kream Kountry	4
Shivalik	3

Haridwar's markets

Haridwar's teeming network of **markets** is the other main focus of interest. **Bara Bazaar**, at the top of town, is a good place to buy a *danda* (bamboo staff) for treks in the mountains. Stalls in the colourful **Moti Bazaar** in the centre of town, on the Jawalapur road, sell everything from clothes to spices.

Hilltop temples

Cable car daily: April–Oct 7.30am–7pm; Nov–March 8.30am–5pm • Mansa Devi ₹48 return; Chandi Devi ₹117 return

High above Haridwar, on the crest of a ridge, the gleaming white *shikhara* of the **Mansa Devi** temple dominates both town and valley. Believing the revered goddess to be a granter of wishes, devotees tie pieces of thread to the branches of holy tree that stands nearby. The temple is easily reached by **cable car** (known as "Udan Khatola") from a base station off Upper Road in the heart of town, while the steep 1.5km walk is pleasant enough early in the morning; pedestrian traffic along the trail can become intense later in the day during *yatra* season. None of the shrines and temples up top holds any great architectural interest, but you do get excellent views along the river.

Rising above the opposite bank of the Ganges, about 4km to the south of Mansa Devi, is another hill, Neel Parvat, crowned with another hilltop temple, **Chandi Devi**. While its earliest roots trace back to the eighth century, the temple was built in 1929 by the king of Kashmir. This temple is also reachable by cable car or a 3km hike from Chandi *ghat*, which passes the impressive Kamraj ki-Kali temple on the way.

Bharat Mata Temple

5km north of Haridwar • ₹20; camera/video ₹20/40 • Vikrams from next to *Shivalik* restaurant (₹10)

The modern, eight-storey, 55m **Bharat Mata temple**, dedicated to "Mother India", was inaugurated in 1983 by Indira Gandhi. Each of its various floors – connected by lifts – is dedicated to a celestial or political theme, and populated by lifelike images of heroes, heroines and Hindu deities.

ARRIVAL AND DEPARTURE   HARIDWAR

By bus Most buses depart from the UP Roadways bus stand (☎01334 227037) on Railway Rd (departures listed below). Additionally, from the GMOU bus stand (about 200m south on Railway Rd) there are early morning buses in *yatra* season (May–Oct) to Gangotri (12hr), Kedarnath (10hr) and Badrinath (15hr), and from Nov–Jun there are hourly buses from the GMOU bus stand to Chilla (7am–1pm; 30min), for Rajaji National Park. Numerous private bus companies, most of them clustered behind the GMVN tourist office, have services to major destinations in the south. Konark on Jassa Ram Rd (☎01334 222630) has three daily services to Delhi (10.30am, 10pm & 11pm; 5–6hr).

Destinations Agra (hourly; 12hr); Amritsar (3 daily; 12hr); Dehra Dun (every 30min; 1hr 30min); Delhi (every 30min; 6hr); Lucknow (3 daily; 12hr); Nainital (9 daily; 9hr 30min); Ramnagar (13 daily; 6hr); Rishikesh (every 30min; 45min); Shimla (8 daily; 14hr).

By train Haridwar's railways station is on Railway Rd, just southwest of the centre. Major trains include the overnight #14042 *Mussoorie Express* (dep. 11.10pm; arr. Delhi Sarai Rohilla 8.50am) and the a/c #12056 *Janshatabdi Express* (dep 6.22am; arr. New Delhi 11.10am); for Agra, the #18478 *Kalingautkal Express* (dep. 6am; arr. 3.50pm); for Lucknow, the #13010 *Doon Express* (dep 10.15pm; arr. 8.20am), which continues to Varanasi (arr. 4pm) and Kolkata (arr. 6.55am second morning). Local trains on the branch line to Rishikesh aren't that useful in view of the excellent and more frequent road connections.

By Vikram Vikrams for Rishikesh (₹30) depart when full from next to *Shivalik* restaurant.

By taxi The Taxi Association near the railway station sets prices slightly higher than those quoted elsewhere, charging ₹800 for a taxi to Rishikesh and ₹700 to Chilla. Travellers heading into the mountains should go to Rishikesh to pick up onward transport.

INFORMATION AND TOURS

Information Tourist information is available at a booth inside the station (Mon–Sat 10am–5pm), from the more helpful GMVN tourist office (Mon–Sat 10am–5pm; ☎01334 224240) near Lalita Rao Bridge on Upper Rd, or from the state tourism office at *Rahi Motel* on Railway Rd, southwest of the bus stand (Mon–Sat 10am–5pm; ☎01334 265304).

Tours Konark Travels, Jassa Ram Rd (daily 7am–9pm; ☎01334 222630, ⊚konarktravels.com), offers tours of the state by bus or car; Mohan's (Mon–Sat 8am–10.30pm; ☎01334 220910, ⊚mohansadventure.in), across from *Big Ben* restaurant, runs more adventure-based tours such as rafting, mountain biking and rock climbing.

ACCOMMODATION

Haveli Hari Ganga 21 Ramghat, Bara Baaar ☎01334 265207, ⊚havelihariganga.com. A lovely haveli set up by two merchant brothers in 1917, now converted into a beautiful heritage hotel with massage and spa rooms, a vegetarian restaurant and a private *ghat* for *aarti*. Superior rooms come with Ganges views (₹7000) while all rooms have wi-fi available for a fee. **₹5500**

Inder Kuteer Sharwan Nath Nagar ☎01334 226336. This friendly hotel near the river has small attached rooms with hard beds and hot water, as well as a terrace with great rooftop views. Best value in this price range. **₹500**

Kailash Shivmurti Chowk, Railway Rd ☎01334 227789, ⊚hotelkailash.com. Handy mostly for the nearby railway station, the rooms here are all either air-cooled or a/c (₹750). Most are beginning to show their age, though some have little balconies overlooking the busy street. Up to fifty percent discount off-season. **₹450**

Midtown In an alley off Upper Rd, opposite Chotiwallah restaurant ☎01334 227507, ⊚midtownhotel.in. The name fits at this centrally located hotel, set about midway between the transport hubs and Har-ki-Pairi *ghat*. It's Haridwar's best-value mid-range hotel, with clean rooms and friendly staff. Rooms at the front have balconies, while some have a/c (₹1600). There's wi-fi access, and thirty percent discounts from Nov–Feb. **₹950**

Prem Nagar Ashram Jawalapur Rd, 2km west of the station ☎01334 226345, ⊚manavdharam.org. Very calm and peaceful, if rather removed from town (₹5 by shared Vikram), this ashram has been around since 1944. The staff are charming and the rooms clean and cheap. **₹400**

Suvidha Sharwan Nath Nagar, behind Chitra Talkies cinema ☎01334 227023, ⊚hotelsuvidhadeluxe.com. Comfortable, plush place with air-cooled and a/c (₹1950) rooms in a pleasant location near the river, away from the bustle of the bazaars and main roads. The rooftop has a

16-inch telescope to look at the hilltop temples (₹50/10min). **₹1250**

Yatri Niwas Upper Rd, 250m from Har-ki-Pairi ☎ 97191 02222. Built in 1904 and recently renovated, this family-run hotel is popular among travellers for its handy location near the *ghats*, as well as for its pleasant marble courtyard, useful travel desk and all-a/c rooms complete with flatscreen TVs and wi-fi. **₹2000**

EATING

As a holy city, Haridwar is strictly vegetarian and booze-free.

Big Ben Hotel Ganga, Railway Rd. Sleek a/c restaurant with big windows overlooking a busy corner, with a good range of veg curries, set meals, decent breakfasts (₹140–180) and a few Chinese and Continental dishes including cheese steak (₹145) and veg steak (₹125); they mean "cutlets". Daily 8.30am–10.30pm.

Chotiwala Upper Rd. Established in 1937, this comfortable, dimlylit restaurant is still one of the best around, offering good Indian food as well as breakfast (tea, coffee, toast and the like), some Chinese dishes and, of course, killer thalis (₹110–130). Daily 10am–11pm.

Hoshiyarpuri Upper Rd. Also established in 1937, this busy, friendly, *dhaba*-like restaurant close to Har-ki-Pairi serves delicious Indian (especially Punjabi) dishes such as

dal makhani (₹70), a host of Chinese mains (₹60–150) and great desserts like *kheer* (creamed rice pudding; ₹30). Daily 11am–4pm & 7pm–4am.

Kream Kountry Railway Rd. Bright new canteen serving Indian snacks and fast food, from kulfi (₹25) to cheese pizza (₹95), as well as softy ice cream cones for just ₹10. Daily 11am–11pm.

Shivalik Railway Rd ☎ 01334 226868. Housed in the hotel of the same name, *Shivalik's* chef prides himself on his small selection of Chinese dishes and tasty south Indian snacks. There are a few worthy combo deals to choose from (₹125–180), and the Continental breakfast (₹150) and deluxe thali (₹170) are both good value. Daily 8am–11pm.

DIRECTORY

Banks and ATMs Several banks with ATMs are found along Railway Rd, including the State Bank of India and Canara Bank, both of which also change cash; there are more ATMs on Upper St, as well as Sai Forex for foreign exchange (☎ 01134 228483).

Internet There are several internet cafés scattered along

the streets behind Railway Rd, such as at Jimmy Hotel (₹20/hr). On Upper St, the Sai Forex office has an attached a/c internet café (₹40/hr).

Post office The GPO is on Upper Rd (Mon–Sat 10am–5pm).

Rajaji National Park

15 Nov–15 June daily 6–9am & 3–6pm • ₹600 (₹150) plus ₹500 (₹250) per vehicle; camera ₹50 (free), video camera ₹5000 (₹2500); mandatory local guide ₹200 • ⓦ rajajinationalpark.in

RAJAJI NATIONAL PARK, part of the same forest belt as Corbett Tiger Reserve, 180km east, spans around 830 square kilometres of the Himalayan foothills immediately east and west of Haridwar. Of the park's eight **entry points**, the most useful are the main gates at **Chilla**, near Haridwar, and the gates at **Kunnao**, close to Rishikesh.

Although largely surrounded by development and dotted with settlements of the **Van Gujjars**, a nomadic tribe whose summer homes have traditionally fallen within the park, for the time being Rajaji remains pristine and its wildlife resilient. Less developed than Corbett, it contains a similar range of fauna, most notably elephants, but also antelope, anteater, leopard and tigers, the last numbering at least thirteen at last count.

Chilla

9km east of Haridwar

Neither attractive nor interesting, **Chilla**, set beside the Ganges barrage and its massive electricity pylons, marks the main entrance to Rajaji National Park. It makes a good and relatively quiet base for explorations of the park. Meanwhile, **Chilla Beach** – occasionally used by large river turtles – lies within walking distance through the woods, 1km north along the Ganges.

ARRIVAL AND GETTING AROUND

By bus and taxi Hourly buses (7am–1pm) run to Chilla from Haridwar's GMOU bus stand. Taxis charge ₹700 one way.

Jeep hire Jeeps can be hired by the gate in Chilla (3hr drive ₹1100)

ACCOMMODATION

Chilla Tourist Bungalow 5min walk from park gates, Chilla ☎01382 266678, ⍉gmvnl.com. This GMVN bungalow, bookable through the GMVN tourist office in Haridwar (see p.302), offers clean and cosy deluxe and a/c rooms (₹1900), all attached with TVs and hot water, while there are also huts, grassy camping facilities and dorms as well as a restaurant and gardens overlooking the dam. Staff can arrange jeep tours

through the park. Dorm ₹200, double ₹1500
Forest Rest Houses Rajaji National Park. Scattered throughout the park itself are ten simple forest resthouses, bookable through the Rajaji National Park Office in Dehra Dun (5/1 Ansari Marg; ☎0135 2621669) or with help from Mohan's in Haridwar (see p.302). The one at Chilla is the largest, and the only one with meals available. ₹1500

Rishikesh

RISHIKESH, 238km northeast of Delhi and just 24km north of Haridwar, huddles along the steep wooded banks of the fast-flowing Ganges as it exits the mountains of Garwhal to crash onto the plains to the south. The centre for all manner of New Age and Hindu activity, its many ashrams – some ascetic, some opulent – continue to draw devotees and followers of all sorts of weird and wonderful gurus, with the large **Shivananda Ashram** in particular renowned as a yoga centre. Rishikesh is also emerging as an **adventure-sports** hub, with rafting, trekking and mountaineering all on offer.

Rishikesh has one or two ancient shrines, but its main role has always been as a way-station for *sannyasin*, yogis and travellers heading for the high Himalayas. The arrival of the Beatles, who came here to meet the Maharishi in 1968, was one of the first manifestations of the lucrative expansion of the *yatra* pilgrimage circuit; these days it's easy to see why Ringo thought it was "just like Butlin's". By far the best times to visit are in winter and spring, when the mountain temples are shut by the snows – without the *yatra* razzmatazz, you get a sense of the tranquillity that was the original appeal of the place. At other times, a walk upriver leads easily away from the bustle to secluded spots among giant rocks ideally suited for yoga, meditation or an invigorating dip in the cold water (but not a swim: fast currents make that too dangerous).

Confusingly, the name Rishikesh applies to a loose association of distinct areas, encompassing several scattered hamlets on both sides of the river. The town of **Rishikesh** itself sprawls to the south of the Chandrabagha riverbed, home to Triveni Ghat, the train station, bus stand and the commercial and communications hubs. A short ride north of town is the footbridge (*jhula*) of Ram Jhula, linking **Swarg Ashram** on the east bank, while 2km further upstream is a second footbridge, **Lakshman Jhula**. The settlements in both areas are largely traffic-free, spiritual hubs dotted with ashrams, temples, hotels and restaurants.

Triveni Ghat

Southern end of Ghat Rd

Most pilgrims passing through Rishikesh en route to the Himalayan shrines of the Char Dham pause for a dip and puja at **Triveni Ghat**, near the centre of town. The river here looks especially spectacular during evening *arati*, when *diya* lights (₹5–10) float on the water.

Bharat Mandir

Rishikesh's oldest temple, **Bharat Mandir** features a black stone image of Vishnu, believed

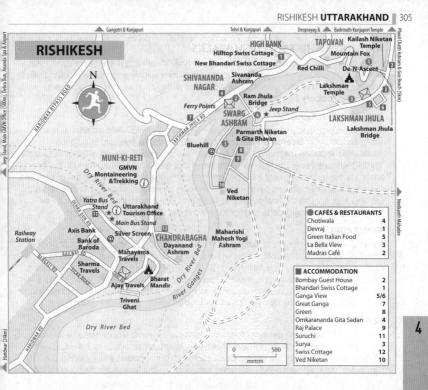

to have been consecrated by the great ninth-century Hindu revivalist Shankara; the event is commemorated during Basant Panchami, to mark the first day of spring. A sacred trio of entangled trees stands near the entrance, taken to represent the Hindu Tri Dev (Trinity).

Swarg Ashram

The dense-knit complex of cafés, shops and ashrams collectively known as **Swarg Ashram**, opposite Shivananda Ashram, backs on to forest-covered hills where caves are still inhabited by sadhus. The most conspicuous of the area's many ashram-temples is **Parmarth Niketan**, whose large courtyard is crammed with brightly clad gods and goddesses. Next door is **Gita Bhavan**, which runs a free Ayurvedic dispensary up the street (daily 8am–noon & 2–8pm); they also sell books, saris and *khadi* handloom cloth. The river can be crossed at this point either by the Ram Jhula footbridge or the nearby ferry (₹10).

Lakshman Jhula

Most travellers find **Lakshman Jhula**, a pair of lively settlements straddling the footbridge of the same name, to be the most appealing part of Rishikesh. The east bank is also linked by a 2km path from Swarg Ashram that skirts the river, passing beautiful sandy beaches sheltered by large boulders. Most striking on the east bank is the enormous, gaudy, thirteen-storey **Kailash Niketan Temple**, just north of the bridge. The dramatic landscape and turquoise river (brown during the monsoon) are best appreciated from the *Devraj Coffee Corner* on the west side (see p.308), where travellers spend days watching daredevil monkeys cavorting on the bridge and pouncing on unsuspecting passers-by.

AROUND RISHIKESH: LOCAL WALKS

Plenty of paths wind through the forests around Rishikesh, offering walkers a welcome escape from the bustle of town. There's a chance you'll encounter wildlife along the way; keep a safe distance from wild elephants. Also, bring a guide or walking partner as there have been incidents of **robbery** along the trails.

NEELKANTH MAHADEV

Winding steeply through the forests from Swarg Ashram is an old, 10km pilgrim trail to the small Shiva shrine of **Neelkanth Mahadev**. It marks the spot where Lord Shiva once swallowed the poison that turned his throat blue, earning himself the nickname of Neelkanth, "the blue-throated one". The recently blasted road that takes a long detour through the forest has made the small settlement a less peaceful retreat during *yatra* season. The trail offers some stunning vantage points and passes by Mahesh Yogi's overgrown ashram (of Beatles fame), crossing a spur before the final descent to Neelkanth. One or both legs are often done by shared jeep (₹70/person), departing from the stand just south of Ram Jhula Bridge.

KUNJAPURI

The small white Shakti temple of **Kunjapuri**, 10km west of town, stands at the sharp point of an almost perfectly conical hill 1645m high, with panoramic views into the high Himalayas to the north as well as back towards Rishikesh and Haridwar to the south. A popular sunrise and sunset spot, it gets most traffic during the Navratri (April and Oct) and Dussehra (Oct) festivals. It's a 3–4hr hike from Lakshman Jhula, passing through pleasant countryside, or a short bus ride to Hindola Khal (every 15min from the Yatra Bus Stand), followed by a 3km (45min) walk up the hill.

BEACHES

The motorable track running north of Lakshman Jhula passes several secluded beaches before arriving at the beautiful ashram of **Phool Chatti** (5km upstream), set at a bend in the river with sandy beaches that include the famous **Goa Beach**, with giant boulders and appealing, but sometimes hazardous swimming – swimmers are regularly swept away when the current is strong.

ARRIVAL AND DEPARTURE   RISHIKESH AND AROUND

By train Rishikesh lies at the end of a small branch railway line from Haridwar, linked by six daily trains (1hr). The daily #54472 train connects Delhi, but is painfully slow (7am; 10hr 15min); there are plenty of faster services from Haridwar.

By bus There are two important bus stands in Rishikesh: the Main Bus Stand (for lowland destinations throughout the region) and the Yatra Bus Stand (also known as the Tehri Bus Stand; April–Oct for mountain destinations to the north), both of which have recently been combined off Dehra Dun Rd to the north of Rishikesh town. During *yatra* season it's recommended to book at least the day before your journey. Mountain roads are treacherous and tedious, landslides are not uncommon during the monsoon period, and only early departures reach the Char Dham in a day. Plenty of private bus companies have offices around

Lakshman Jhula and Swarg Ashram.

Destinations Agra (6pm; 12hr); Badrinath (6 daily; 12hr); Dehra Dun (hourly; 1hr 30min); Delhi (12 daily; 7hr); Gangotri (5.30am; 11–12hr); Haridwar (every 30min; 30min); Kedarnath (4.30am; 10hr); Nainital (9am; 8–9hr); Uttarkashi (6 daily; 7–8hr); Yamunotri (7am; 12hr).

By jeep Jeeps depart when full from the jeep stand (daily 4–8am) by the main GMVN office on Haridwar Bypass Rd, to the west of town. Although slightly more expensive than buses, they are much faster. When booked in advance through agencies, such as Sharma Travels (86 Haridwar Rd; ☎ 0135 2430364), you may be able to arrange to be picked up from west-bank hotels.

By Vikram Vikrams to Haridwar depart from Dehra Dun Rd (₹30/person).

GETTING AROUND AND INFORMATION

By Vikram and jeep Vikrams to Lakshman Jhula can be hired from near Rishikesh's railway station for about ₹50 (₹15/person). On the east bank of the river, jeeps from the northern edge of Swarg Ashram connect to the centre of Lakshman Jhula (₹10).

By ferry Ferries cross the Ganges near Ram Jhula outside monsoon season (daily 7.30am–7pm; ₹10

oneway, ₹15 return).

Car rental Reliable agencies include Ajay Travels (☎ 0135 2430644) at *Hotel Neelkanth*, Haridwar Rd, and Mahayama Travels (☎ 0135 2432968) at the Urvasi Complex on Dehra Dun Rd. The GMVN office also rents cars.

Information The Uttarakhand Tourist Office (Mon–Sat 10am–5pm; ☎ 0135 2430209) is just north of the bus stands in the newly built TFC Building. The GMVN (Mon–Sat 10am–5pm; ☎ 0135 2430799) has two offices: the larger Yatra Office is behind the jeep stand on Haridwar Bypass Rd, Natraj Chowk, while a smaller Mountaineering and Trekking branch is on Lakshman Jhula Rd in Muni-ki-Reti. Each can provide plenty of local information, though in practice they restrict themselves to selling their own tours and booking accommodation in their tourist lodges.

ACCOMMODATION

Rishikesh town has plenty of hotels but an excess of noise and pollution; the only reason to stay here is to be near the bus station. New Agers tend to prefer Swarg Ashram and the east bank of the river, away from the noise and near the ashrams, while backpackers head for the cheap little guesthouses of Lakshman Jhula or the more disconnected huddle of hotels on the High Bank.

Bhandari Swiss Cottage High Bank ☎ 0135 2432939; ⓦ bhandariswisscottagerishikesh.com. This popular backpacker retreat has a range of good-value fan and a/c (₹1000) attached rooms spanning its three storeys; the priciest ones are on top. There's a cosy café and restaurant area with wi-fi (₹30/hr), and yoga classes are on offer. If it's full, the similarly-priced *New Bhandari Swiss Cottage* (☎ 0135 2435322) and the *Hill Top Swiss Cottage* (☎ 0135 2442896) are handy neighbours. ₹200

Bombay Guest House Lakshman Jhula ☎ 0135 3250038. Basic accommodation with shared baths off a leafy courtyard; handy for exploring the unspoilt upper reaches of this stretch of the river and popular with long-term and hippyie travellers. The owner rents bikes and arranges rafting. ₹260

Ganga View Lakshman Jhula ☎ 0135 2440320. A good-value choice among the many, generally similar, small budget hotels in the area – this one has nice fresh rooms, all with attached bathrooms and hot water, and it's set off the main drag, making it reasonably quiet. More expensive rooms are up the stairs to the back (₹300–350), while the best face the river (₹500–600). A second location is 50m downstream. ₹200

Great Ganga Lakshman Jhula Rd, near Ram Jhula Bridge ☎ 0135 2442243, ⓦ thegreatganga.com. It's worth braving the steep and very grotty pathway to reach this comfortable upmarket hotel. The spotless rooms have river-facing balconies, big windows and lovely views. If you really want to push the boat out, go for a suite (₹9050). There's also a spa, travel desk and multicuisine restaurant. ₹3350

Green Swarg Ashram ☎ 0135 2431242, ⓦ hotelgreen .com. Popular little travellers' hotel tucked behind Gita Bhavan Ashram. All rooms have attached bathrooms, most with running hot water and a/c (₹1300), plus there's a roof terrace, wi-fi, travel desk, yoga classes (₹150–200), and a restaurant that serves under-spiced Indian and Italian food. ₹750

Omkarananda Gita Sadan Lakshman Jhula Rd, near Ram Jhula Bridge ☎ 0135 243 6346, ⓔ omkara@vsnl .com. Run by the ashram of the same name, this lovely all-a/c guesthouse has a relaxed atmosphere, plain but spacious and immaculately clean rooms, great views over the river towards Swarg Ashram, and even a four-person family suite (₹2500), but you'll need to book ahead. ₹1500

Raj Palace Swarg Ashram, behind Parmarth Niketan ☎ 0135 2440079, ⓦ rajhotels.in. Well-managed hotel popular with yoga students due to its location near the ashrams as well as its large, sunny yoga room and rooftop café. The rooms are basic but clean, all either air-cooled or a/c (₹1250), and there's a good travel desk and off-season discounts of up to fifty percent. ₹600

Suruchi Opposite Yatra Bus Stand ☎ 0135 2432602. Friendly but rather bland hotel offering decent, carpeted a/c (₹800) and non-a/c rooms with attached bathrooms and hot water. There's also a basic restaurant and café

4

ADVENTURE ACTIVITIES IN RISHIKESH

Adventure activities have become one of Rishikesh's top draws, most notably **rafting**. There are numerous established river camps on the Ganges above Rishikesh, operating from late September to as late as June, with excursions ranging from half-day runs to extended camping-rafting expeditions. The GMVN's **Mountaineering and Trekking** division on Lakshman Jhula Road in Muni-ki-Reti (☎ 0135 2430799, ⓦ gmvnl.com) rents equipment, arranges guides, and organizes ski trips to Auli, treks across Garhwal, and, along with their Yatra Office, run numerous tours, such as a four-day, all-inclusive package to Badrinath for ₹6560.

With the town's seasonal tourism boom has come a dramatic rise of unregulated tour and travel operators with no insurance cover for their drivers, cars or tourists. Ask for recommended **travel agents** at your hotel or at the tourist office, or try one of the reliable local firms in Tapovan (on the west bank of Lakshman Jhula): Red Chilli (☎ 0135 2434021, ⓦ redchilliadventure.com), De-N-Ascent (☎ 0135 2442354, ⓦ kayakhimalaya.com) and Mountain Fox (☎ 0135 2442909, ⓦ mountainfoxadventure.com).

downstairs, but the main attraction here is that it's convenient for early Char Dham buses. ₹**450**

★ **Surya** Lakshman Jhula ☎0135 2440211, ⓦ hotellaxmanjhula.com. Just above *Café Coffee Day*, *Surya* is a backpacker favourite for its laid-back vibe, its location in the heart of Lakshman Jhula, and its fantastic Ganges views. The best of its clean, marble-floored rooms are those facing the river (₹600–950) in front, though the darker back rooms are quieter. There's also a cosy rooftop restaurant. ₹**500**

Swiss Cottage Chandrabhaga ☎0135 2435012, ⓔ shivgangamylove@rediff.mail.com. Rishikesh's first guesthouse, founded in 1961 by Swami Brahmananda, disciple of Swami Shivanandaa. It's a small but peaceful haven with a friendly owner and a motley assortment of attached rooms; popular with long-term visitors and good value (single ₹300), so often booked up. ₹**600**

Ved Niketan Swarg Ashram ☎0135 2430279. Enormous orange ashram with manicured garden grounds on the east bank of the river, with cheap accommodation (single ₹150) that is very popular with budget travellers. There are evening and morning Hatha yoga classes (Mon–Sat 8–9.30am & 4–5.30pm). ₹**300**

EATING

Chotiwala Swarg Ashram ☎0135 2430070, ⓦ chotiwalarestaurant.com. Two neighbouring establishments with the same name vie for custom and constantly attempt to outdo each other. The one closest to the river has slightly better service and a congenial roof terrace, but both places are large, busy and open early for breakfast; the extensive menus include express thalis (₹99–150) as well as ice cream, sweets and cold drinks. Daily 8.30am–9.30pm.

Devraj Coffee Corner Lakshman Jhula, just west of the bridge. A great spot for a break: enjoy cinnamon rolls, muesli, fruit curd, apple strudel and superb cakes (₹20–40), or dine on pizzas, veg sizzlers, curries, veggie burgers (₹130), or even the odd attempt at a Mexican dish, while watching the Ganges and the pilgrims flow past. Daily 8am–9pm.

Green Italian Food Swarg Ashram. Pizzas and pastas head the list of treats at this slick, spotless offshoot of the *Green hotel*'s in-house Italian restaurant. There's a choice of spaghetti or penne with a range of veg sauces, or veg cannelloni with a choice of three veg fillings (₹150), good pizzas (margherita ₹135), plus a range of set breakfasts (₹50–110). Daily 8am–10pm.

La Bella View Lakshman Jhula, east bank. The Ganges view from the upstairs tables in this low-key, thatched-roof restaurant is only slightly better than from the cosier, cushion-clad Both share downstairs area a menu spanning Indian to Israeli, with emphasis on Italian dishes like pasta al pesto (₹120) and pizza margherita (₹110). Daily 9am–11pm.

Madras Café Opposite ferry quay, by Ram Jhula Bridge. Busy, welcoming restaurant, with great filter coffee and reasonably priced south Indian food. The "Himalayan Health Pullao" (₹100) is worth a try, made with vegetable sprouts and Ayurvedic herbs, but there's also the "Himalayan Health Pancake" (₹130), a wholewheat pancake toped with mixed fruit, curd and honey. Daily 8am–10pm.

ASHRAMS, YOGA AND MEDITATION

Maharishi Mahesh Yogi's beautifully situated ashram, home to the Beatles in 1968, stands empty on a high forested bluff above the river, claimed by the Forest Department since its lease expired more than fifteen years ago. While there are no longer classes here, Rishikesh has plenty of other reputable ashrams welcoming students of yoga with courses of varying cost and duration – from one day to several months. Guests must be respectful of ashrams' strict rules governing conduct. Be warned that complaints of theft and harassment in ashrams are surprisingly common.

Parmarth Niketan Ashram Swarg Ashram ☎0135 2440077, ⓦ parmarth.com. This giant ashram right next to the river houses more than a thousand simple rooms with daily yoga classes, a range of yoga courses, nightly *aarti* ceremonies and a common dining hall. They also sponsor a yoga week in early March (ⓦ internationalyogafestival.com).

Phool Chatti Ashram 5km north of Lakshman Jhula ☎0135 6981303, ⓦ phoolchattiyoga.com. Peaceful ashram with lush gardens in a pristine setting far away from the noise of town. They specialize in seven-day, all-inclusive yoga and meditation retreats (from ₹8000/person), mostly aimed towards beginners and intermediate-level.

Sivananda Ashram ☎0135 2430040, ⓦ sivananda online.org. Large institution, with branches all over the world, run by the Divine Life Society and founded by Swami Sivananda (who passed into *maha samadhi* – final liberation – in 1963). It has a well-stocked library, a forest retreat and a charitable hospital. The most rigid schedule begins at 4am, with nearly constant lessons in meditation and yoga on offer. For long-term stays, contact the secretary two months in advance through their website. Stays are donation-based.

DIRECTORY

Banks and ATMs Banks in town include the Bank of Baroda and the nearby Axis Bank, both on Dehra Dun Rd, with ATMs. There are also several banks with ATMs further north: on Lakshman Jhula Rd by the GMVN trekking office, on the east

bank near Ram Jhula Bridge and in Swarg Ashram. Numerous travel agents in Lakshman Jhula will change cash.
Internet Blue Hill Travel and Cyber Café (₹20/hr) in Swarg Ashram near Parmarth Niketan.

Post office The main post office is on Ghat Rd near Triveni Ghat (Mon–Fri 10am–4pm, Sat 10am–1pm), with branch offices in Lakshman Jhula and near both sides of Ram Jhula Bridge.

Uttarkashi

The largest town in the interior of Garhwal, **UTTARKASHI** makes a convenient stopover to break up the road from Rishikesh (148km south) to Gangotri (100km northeast). Discerning travellers, however, are beginning to linger longer in this picturesque town to hike the unspoiled trails of Garhwal's interior or to gear up for longer treks such as to Dodi Tal (see box below).

Occupying the flat and fertile valley floor of the Bhagirathi, Uttarkashi is no stranger to natural disasters; the town made the news when it was hit by severe floods in 1978, an earthquake in 1991, and a massive landslide in 2003 that wiped out several hotels along the main road as well as the bus stand and tourist office. No one was hurt in the last, but the large gap in the centre of town remains today. Efforts have since been made to secure the hillside against landslides, but in 2012 another flood wiped out the bridge to Gangotri.

ARRIVAL AND DEPARTURE
UTTARKASHI

By bus All buses to and from Uttarkashi park on Gangotri Rd in the centre of town.
Destinations Chamba (every 30min; 5hr); Hanuman Chatti (2 daily; 7hr); Mussoorie (2 daily; 9hr); Rishikesh (9 daily; 7hr); Sangam Chatti (3 daily; 45min).

By jeep Shared jeeps depart from a jeep stand 500m north of the town centre, leaving when full for Gangotri (5am–2pm; 5hr). For Rishikesh (6hr), Haridwar (7hr) and other destinations south, another cluster of jeeps waits by the petrol station opposite the *Old Bandhari Hotel*.

4

THE DODI TAL TREK

One of Garhwal's all-time classic treks, the **Dodi Tal trek** links the Gangotri and Yamunotri regions without straying into high glacial terrain. It's a relatively short and easy hike, but local villagers are keen to offer their services as porters or guides, taking hikers off the beaten track to visit the villages. Carry as much of your own food as possible and bring a tent.

From **Uttarkashi**, catch a morning bus (45min) or jeep heading to Sangam Chatti (1350m), from where it's a 7km climb through fields and woodland to **Agoda** (2286m), where you can set up camp or head to the *Tourist Bungalow* at the far end of the village. On the second day, follow the trail from Agoda as it climbs west of the Asi Ganga and zigzags steadily upwards through lush pine and spruce forests, with a smattering of chai shops en route. After 14km and a final undulation, you will reach the lake of **Dodi Tal** (3024m), set against a backdrop of thickly forested hills and said to be the spot where Lord Ganesha was both born and beheaded. Near the basic forest bungalow in the clearing are chai shops and areas for camping.

On the third day you'll make the 4km hike to Dharwa Top, following the well-marked path along (and often across) the stream that feeds Dodi Tal, which can get steep and entail scrambling, until you emerge above the tree line. A further 2km along, the trail heads left to a small pass, then zigzags up scree to **Dharwa Top** (4130m), the highest point of the trek, offering superb panoramas of the Srikanta Range. A leftward path beyond the top leads to camping and water, but if you've still got sufficient energy and daylight, you can continue along the main route, which takes about four more hours and 13km to rejoin the tree line at **Sima**, where there's basic hut accommodation.

The following day's beautiful 12km trail from Sima kicks off with a steep 1.5km scramble alongside a stream before easing past forest and *bugyal* (alpine meadow). A well-defined rocky path drops steadily through two villages and zigzags down to the Hanuman Ganga, finally emerging at **Hanuman Chatti** (see p.310), from where buses and jeeps connect with Barkot, Uttarkashi, Mussoorie and other points in Garhwal. The Dodi Tal trek can easily be tied in with hikes in the **Har-ki-Dun** (see box, p.300) and **Yamunotri** areas (see p.311).

INFORMATION

Guides and trekking companies The town has an abundance of experienced mountain guides – most of them graduates of its highly esteemed Nehru Institute of Mountaineering (☏01374 222123; �🌐nimindia.org; one-month mountaineering courses $650 (₹5000)). Specialist operators include Mount Support, BD Nautial Bhawan, Bhatwari Rd (☏01374 222419, ✉mountsupport@rediffmail.com), on the main road, who also have equipment for rent and porters for hire.

Supplies Uttarkashi's busy and well-stocked market is ideal for picking up supplies before high-altitude treks.

ACCOMMODATION AND EATING

Amba Main market ☏96392 31472. Basic, friendly and well-kept hotel in the middle of town, offering green-painted rooms with balconies over the busy lanes of the market. Discounts of fifty percent are available outside of the summer *yatra* season. ₹**600**

GMVN Tourist Bungalow Main market ☏01374 222271. A comfortable three-storey complex set around an attractive lawn dotted with plastic chairs. Rooms are clean and spacious with TVs and marble floors, and there's an attached dorm. Prices come down slightly July–Oct and are slashed during low season (Nov & April). Dorm ₹**280**, double ₹**1760**

Hillview Gangotri Rd, 300m up from the bus stand. Set in the hotel of the same name, this is one of the best restaurants in town, offering an assortment of Chinese and Indian dishes as well as snacks and breakfasts. The veg thali is a good deal (₹50), but the special thali is even better (₹120). Daily 8.30am–10pm.

★ **Monal Tourist Home** 2km north of town ☏01374 222270, �🌐monaluttarkashi.com. The best deal around, this welcoming guesthouse is run by the ever-friendly Deependar Panwar, a graduate of the Nehru Institute of Mountaineering and a great source of local information. He's enlisted local experts to open up a wide range of activities in the area, from hiking, mountain biking and angling to classes for cooking, yoga and Hindi. Both the A and B Wings are clean and well kept, but the A wing is more attractive with more spacious rooms and a cosy veranda. Within Wing B is a bright, big-windowed restaurant and sitting area, combined with a small library and a computer with internet access (₹40/hr). ₹**600**

DIRECTORY

ATMs There are three ATMs in town: Bank of Baroda near Hillview on Gangotri Rd, and State Bank and PNB in the main market area.

Internet Ravi Cyberworld, near the market (₹40/hr).
Post office The post office (Mon–Sat 9.30am–5pm) is west of the main market, near the river.

The trek to Yamunotri

Cradled in a deep cleft in the lap of Bandarpunch, and thus denied mountain vistas, the temple of **Yamunotri** (3291m), 223km northeast of Rishikesh, marks the source of the Yamuna, India's second holiest river after the Ganges. The least dramatic but most beautiful of the four *dhams* (temples) of Garhwal, it's also the least spoiled and commercial. **Access** (mid-April to early Nov; exact dates vary annually) has become easier following road improvements; from the roadhead at Janki Chatti it's a mere 5km along a trail that follows the turbulent ice-blue river as it runs below rocky crags, with snowy peaks in the distance. The walk can also be combined with the **Dodi Tal trek** linking nearby Hanuman Chatti to Uttarkashi (see box, p.309).

Janki Chatti and around

The riverside hamlet of **HANUMAN CHATTI** (2400m) is the western terminus of the famous trek to Dodi Tal (see box, p.309); 6km beyond this is the enchanting little village of **JANKI CHATTI** (2475m), which marks the end of the motorable road from Rishikesh and the start of the trail to Yamunotri. While in Janki Chatti, it's worth making the 1km detour across the river to the traditional Garhwali village of **KHARSALI**, home to the *pandas* (pilgrim priests) of Yamunotri. Among the dry-stone buildings with their beautifully carved wooden beams stands a unique three-storey Shiva temple – dedicated to Someshwar, lord of the mythical intoxicant Soma.

Yamunotri

5km hike north of Janki Chatti • Mid-April to early Nov

The trail from Janki Chatti becomes steeper as well as more dramatic and beautiful as it passes through rocky forested crags to reach **YAMUNOTRI** (3291m), cradled in a deep cleft in the lap of Bandarpunch. Built around three piping-hot sulphur springs by the river, Yamunotri's temple is new and architecturally uninteresting; it has to be completely rebuilt every few years due to the impact of heavy winter snows and monsoon rains. Its main shrine – actually part of the top spring, worshipped as the source of the river – holds a small silver image of the goddess Yamuna, bedecked with garlands. The daughter of Surya, the sun, and Sangya, consciousness, Yamuna is the twin sister of Yama, the lord of death; all who bathe in her waters are spared a painful end, while food cooked in the water is considered to be *prasad* (divine offering). Most pilgrims also bathe in the **hot spring** (free); both male and female pools have been built.

Technically, the source of the Yamuna is the glacial lake of **Saptarishi Kund**, a hard, steep 12km trek up the mountain alongside the river that eases towards its end near the base of Kalinda Parbat. Both this trek and the route over the challenging Yamunotri Pass to Har-ki-Dun (see box, p.300) necessitate at least one day's acclimatization, adequate clothing and a guide, available from the GMVN tourist lodge.

ARRIVAL AND DEPARTURE   THE TREK TO YAMUNOTRI

HANUMAN CHATTI

During *yatra* season, Hanuman Chatti is connected by direct buses to Dehra Dun (8hr), Mussoorie (5hr 30min), Rishikesh (12hr), Gangotri (11hr) and Uttarkashi (7hr), although most services are for Barkot (2hr 30min), from where there are more frequent connections available to all these destinations.

Regular shared jeeps link to Janki Chatti (20min).

JANKI CHATTI

Shared jeeps connect Janki Chatti with Hanuman Chatti (20min) and Barkot (2hr), from where there are regular rides to Uttarkashi (6–7hr).

ACCOMMODATION AND EATING

HANUMAN CHATTI

GMVN Tourist Bungalow ☎01375 224236. This excellent and well-kept tourist bungalow has attached river-facing rooms and a decent dorm. A simple restaurant is attached. Dorm ₹**160**, double ₹**680**

JANKI CHATTI

Atithi Niwas ☎94121 49931, ⊛hotelatithiniwas .com. One of the better hotels in town, with twelve double rooms that come with attached bathrooms, hot water, TVs, a basic restaurant and mountain views all around. ₹**1700**

Mandakini Near jeep stand ☎94129 33148. This pink and white three-storey hotel has 25 clean rooms, 24hr hot water (brought on request), a small restaurant and internet service. ₹**600**

YAMUNOTRI

In addition to the GMVN bungalow, several ashrams offer beds starting around ₹300/person. Among the best of the ashrams are Ramananda, overlooking the temple, and Hanuman Mandir, run by the famous Rambharose Das, aka Nepali Baba. Otherwise, there's the Yamuna Ashram and the much smaller Kali Kamli Dharamshala.

Gangotri and the Gaumukh Glacier trek

Set amid tall deodar and pine forests at the head of the Bhagirathi gorge, 248km north of Rishikesh at 3140m, **Gangotri** is the most remote of Garhwal's Char Dham (see box, p.295). The jeep drive from Uttarkashi is breathtaking – in more ways than one – as it winds high above the Bhagirathi and crosses one of the world's highest bridges, over the gorge near **Lanka**. Although the wide Alaknanda, which flows past Badrinath, may have a better technical claim to be the main channel of the Ganges, Gangotri is for Hindus the spiritual source of the great river, while its physical source is the ice cave of **Gaumukh** on the Gangotri Glacier, 14km further up the valley. From here, the **River Bhagirathi** begins its tempestuous descent through a series of mighty gorges, carving great channels and cauldrons in the rock and foaming in whitewater pools.

Gangotri

Road accessible mid-April to early Nov

Although most of the nearby snow peaks are obscured by the desolate craggy mountains looming immediately above **GANGOTRI**, the town itself is redolent of the atmosphere of the high Himalayas, populated by a mixed cast of Hindu pilgrims and foreign trekkers. Across the river from the temple, a loose development of ashrams and guesthouses dwarfed by great rocky outcrops and huge trees leads down to **Dev Ghat**, overlooking the confluence with the Kedar Ganga. Near the centre of the town, webbed together by stone pathways and metal footbridges, is the impressive waterfall-fed pool of **Gaurikund**.

Gangotri's unassuming **temple**, overlooking the river just beyond a small market on the left bank, is one of India's holiest sites. Built early in the eighteenth century by the Gurkha general Amar Singh Thapa, the simple structure consists of a squat *shikhara* surrounded by four smaller replicas; it commemorates the legend of the goddess Ganga, enticed to earth by King Bhagirath's acts of penance in order to revitalize the ashes of his ancestors. Inside the temple is a silver image of the goddess, while a slab of stone adjacent to the temple is venerated as **Bhagirath Shila**, the spot where the legendary king performed his meditation. Steps lead down to the main riverside *ghat*, where the devout bathe in the freezing waters of the river to cleanse their bodies and souls of sin.

ARRIVAL AND DEPARTURE
GANGOTRI

By bus and jeep The bus and jeep stands both lie just beyond the west entrance to town. Jeeps connect Gangotri to Uttarkashi (departing when full, 5.30am–2pm; 5hr), from where there are connections further south. During *yatra* season (May–Oct), early morning buses link Rishikesh (11hr) and Haridwar (12hr).

ACCOMMODATION AND EATING

A number of *dhabas* and cafés on both sides of Gangotri's river serve thalis, good breakfasts and much-needed, warming chai. For pilgrims heading toward Gaumukh, the market area also marks the last chance to buy gloves and woolly hats. All hotels provide buckets of hot water for bathing (₹30).

Bhagirathi Sadan Across the river from the temple ☎ 013772 22244. A well-kept riverside option on the quieter side of the bridge, with small green rooms with attached bathrooms and a shared patio overlooking the river. ₹300

Gangaputra Guesthouse 200m east of jeep stand ☎ 994589 31025. Small hotel with three clean, green-carpeted double rooms sharing a cosy balcony over the main drag. The downstairs restaurant, serving north and south Indian food and equipped with a generator, is one of the town's best (thalis ₹120): it gets crowded during the frequent power outages. ₹400

Krishna Restaurant 100m east of jeep stand ☎ 94101 99108. The cleanest and best restaurant in town, serving a good range of meals from cheesy spaghetti (₹130) to classic thalis (₹80–120). Daily 8.30am–9.30pm.

Gaumukh Glacier Trek

Mid-April to early Nov • ₹600 (₹150) for two days; ₹250 (₹50) per extra day; video camera ₹1500

A flight of steps beside the Gangotri Temple begins the 20km trek to **Gaumukh Glacier**, one of the most beautiful and accessible glaciers in the inner Himalayas.

Leaving Gangotri, the trail rises gently above the north bank of the river, offering increasingly spectacular mountain vistas. Just 2km along is the **forest checkpoint**, where permits are inspected. About 9km further is the oasis of **Chirbasa**, where the skyline becomes dominated by magnificent buttresses and glass-like walls, culminating in the sharp pinnacles of Bhagirathi 3 (6454m) and Bhagirathi 1 (6856m). The path then climbs above the tree line, passing across a steep rocky area prone to landslides. Just around the bend, beyond a stream crossing, 5km from Chirbasa, is the cold grey hamlet of **Bhojbasa**, cowering in the shadows of the surrounding peaks. Most visitors spend a night here before the final push to the glacier.

From Bhojbasa, it's a further 4km up the giant boulder-strewn path to reach **Gaumukh** ("the cow's mouth"), bringing into view the beautiful **Shivling Peak** (6543m), the "Indian

Matterhorn", and providing a closer look at the Bhagirathi peaks and the huge expanse of the Gangotri Glacier – 23km long, and up to 4km wide – sweeping like a gigantic highway through the heart of the mountains. At the source, the river emerges with great force from a cavern in the glacier. The steadily retreating ice is in a constant state of flux, so the huge greyish-blue snout of the glacier continually changes appearance as chunks of ice tumble into the gushing water. Visitors are advised to keep 500m back from the glacier's mouth: many pilgrims have been crushed to death by falling ice while attempting to collect holy water. It's well worth braving the cold to reach Gaumukh for **sunrise**, though it's also rewarding in the afternoon, when the source is lit by the sun. From the glacier, most hikers return to Gangotri via Bhojbasa, while others may continue beyond the glacier to the meadow of Tapovan (6km) or further afield.

ACCOMMODATION AND EATING   GAUMUKH GLACIER TREK

There's a good place to camp (free) down by the river in Bhojbasa, but you'll need your own tent.

GMVN Tourist Bungalow Bhojbasa. Beds are available within the row of large, six-person canvas tents here, but there are no private rooms. Guests huddle in the small, friendly restaurant (thali ₹195), the warmest spot in Bhojbasa, which is also the place to arrange a mountain guide if you plan to cross the glaciers. **₹320**

Kedarnath and around

It's hard to imagine a more dramatic setting for a temple than **Kedarnath** (3583m). Reached by a 14km trek from the town of **Gaurikund**, Kedarnath sits 223km northeast of Rishikesh, close to the source of the Mandakini, and overlooked by tumbling glaciers and giant buttresses of ice, snow and rock. The third of the sacred Char Dham sites, Kedarnath is among the most important shrines in the Himalayas and as one of India's twelve *jyotrilinga* – lingams of light – attracts hordes of Hindu pilgrims (*yatri*) in the summer months. The area makes a refreshing change from the rocky and desolate valleys of west Garhwal, with lush hanging gorges, immaculately terraced hillsides and abundant apple orchards. Kedarnath is also a good base for short treks to the beautiful lakes of Vasuki Tal and Gandhi Sarovar.

Gaurikund

Accessible early April to early Nov

The small but bustling town of **GAURIKUND**, at the end of the motorable road from the south, is revered as the place where Gauri, also called Parvati, paid her penance and eventually won the heart of Shiva. In town are a set of hot springs and a temple enshrining an image of Parvati, although the latter's religious significance far exceeds its visual appeal. For the vast majority, Gaurikund is most important as the starting point of the trek up to the **temple of Kedarnath** (see opposite).

ARRIVAL AND DEPARTURE   GAURIKUND

By bus and jeep There are early morning departures from the bus stand in town for Rishikesh and Haridwar (10–12hr) as well as Rudraprayag (4–5hr), useful for Joshimath, Badrinath and Kumaon; in *yatra* season there's also a 7am direct bus to Badrinath (12hr). The nearby jeep stand serves the same destinations, although most jeeps head first to Rudraprayag (4hr).

ACCOMMODATION AND EATING

Annapurna Bazaar Road ☎ 01364 269209. One of the better-run private hotels in town, *Annapurna* has large, clean, carpeted doubles with sunny balconies, plus dorms. Dorm ₹**200**, double ₹**500**

GMVN Tourist Bungalow Near Kedarnath trailhead

☎ 01364 269202. Gaurikund's most welcoming option, offering clean and cosy doubles with hot water on demand, and a mixture of squat and Western-style toilets. There's also a restaurant offering breakfasts, soups, salads and veg thalis (₹120). Dorm ₹**220**, double ₹**940**

The trek to Kedarnath

14km north of Gaurikund • April to early Nov • Horses for the upward trek ₹700 (₹1000 in high season); four-man *dholis* ₹3500

So popular is the six-hour **Kedarnath trek** on the *yatra* trail that the path up from Gaurikund is being slowly stripped of its vegetation, used for fuel and to feed the ponies that carry wealthier pilgrims. The large pony track that climbs from Gaurikund is dotted with chai shops, traversing the hillside through the disappearing forests to the village of **Rambara**, 7km up and halfway to Kedarnath. An untidy heap of cafés and resthouses, Rambara also signals the end of the tree line. Several conspicuous short cuts scar the hillside as the track rises steeply to **Garur Chatti** before levelling off just 1km short of Kedarnath. Suddenly, rounding a corner, you come face to face with the incredible south face of the peak of Kedarnath (6940m) at the end of the valley, with the temple town dwarfed beneath it in the distance.

4

Kedarnath

KEDARNATH itself is not a very attractive town – in fact it's almost unbearable at the height of the pilgrimage season (May, June & Sept). It's a grey place, whose central thoroughfare stretches 500m between the temple and the bridge, lined with resthouses and *dharamshalas*, pilgrim shops and administrative offices. However, the sheer power of its location tends to sweep away any negative impressions, and it's always possible to escape to explore the incredible high-altitude scenery.

Kedarnath Temple

The imposing **Kedarnath Temple** was originally constructed by Guru Shankara in the ninth century. Built of stone with a large *mandapa* (fore-chamber), it houses an

---

TREKS AROUND KEDARNATH

Beginning near the main bridge just before town, a paved pathway crosses the Mandakini to the left of the valley and ends 4km north at the Chorabari **Glacier** (1–2hr) At its edge lies **Chorabari Tal**, a lake also known as **Gandhi Sarovar** as some of the Mahatma's ashes were scattered here. The source of the Mandakini lies around 800m before the lake, emerging from a hole in the moraine on extremely suspect ground. An alternative route to the lake begins from the small bridge just behind the temple, across which the main track may be reached after a scramble up the rough boulder-strewn moraine.

Another walk is to the ancient shrine of **Bhairava**, visible from Kedarnath's main temple and just under 1km to the east of town. It is connected by another well-marked path running diagonally along the hillside, and surrounded with fluttering prayer flags. A cliff known as **Bhairava Jhamp** rises nearby, said to be where fanatical pilgrims used to leap to their deaths in hopes of instant liberation – until the British banned the practice in the nineteenth century.

A longer, more difficult path (consider hiring a guide in Kedarnath) leads from near the GMVN Tourist Bungalow to **Vakuki Tal** (4135m), 9km away (4–5hr). Set in a desolate high mountain valley surrounded by the snow-clad Chaukhamba peaks, the little lake is crystal clear.

impressive stone image of Shiva's bull, Nandi. Within the inner sanctum, open to all, *pandas* (pilgrim priests) sit around a rock considered to be Shiva's upraised bottom, left here as he plunged head-first into the ground when fleeing Bhim, one of the Pandavas. Mendicant sadhus congregate in the elevated courtyard in front of the temple.

ACCOMMODATION AND EATING   KEDARNATH

Bharat Seva Ashram Beyond the temple, to the left ☎ 01364 27213. Housed in a large red building with more than one hundred beds in relatively clean and comfortable rooms, some with private bathrooms. ₹500/₹650
GMVN Tourist Bungalow Centre of town ☎ 01364 263228. Large, clean and anonymous double rooms with sitting areas and attached bathrooms. Hot water is

available on demand in the early mornings. There's also a small restaurant with decent breakfasts and thalis (₹120) and great mountain views. Dorm ₹160, double ₹960
Shri Badrinath Kedarnath Mandi Samiti Just behind the temple. This canteen, run by the temple committee, serves curries and *aloo paratha*. Daily 5am–1am.

Joshimath

The scattered administrative town of **JOSHIMATH** clings to the side of a deep valley 250km northeast of Rishikesh, with tantalizing glimpses of the snow-capped peaks high above and the prospect, far below, of the road disappearing into a sunless canyon at Vishnu Prayag, the confluence with the Dhauli Ganga. Few of the thousands of pilgrims who pass through en route to Badrinath linger, but Joshimath has close links with **Shankara**, the ninth-century reformer who attained enlightenment here beneath a mulberry tree before going on to establish **Jyotirmath**, one of the four centres of Hinduism (*dhams*) at the four cardinal points. The town itself consists of a long drawn-out **Upper Bazaar**, and, around 1km from the main market, a **Lower Bazaar** that holds the colourful Narsingh, Navadurga, Vasudev and Gauri Shankar **temples**. A 4km **cable car** (mid-April to mid-Nov 9.20am–4.30pm; mid-Nov to mid-April 8.10am–5.50pm; ₹500 return) links the town to the slopes of **Auli**, one of India's better ski resorts, attracting visitors throughout the year for its views of the High Himalayas.

ARRIVAL AND DEPARTURE   JOSHIMATH

Despite considerable effort on the part of the military, the roads around Joshimath are notoriously prone to landslides during the monsoon season, making for routine delays.

By bus Buses depart from near the GMOU office in the centre of the main market, Upper Bazaar to Rishikesh (10hr) and Haridwar (11hr), stopping off in Karnaprayag (3hr 30min), from where there are frequent connections to Kumaon via Gwaldam. During *yatra* season, there are also regular buses from the Joshimath bus stand, just above the

main market, to Govind Ghat (1hr) and Badrinath (2hr), as well as a daily service to Gaurikund (11hr).
By jeep The jeep stand is located beside the Joshimath bus stand, with jeeps departing when full for Govind Ghat (45min) and Badrinath (2hr), as well as down to Karnaprayag (3hr) and Rishikesh (9–10hr).

INFORMATION AND TOURS

Tourist information The tourist office (Mon–Fri & usually Sat 10am–5pm, ☎ 01389 222181) is by the new GMVN block above Upper Bazaar.
Trekking and skiing Eskimo Adventure Company (☎ 97568 35647 or ☎ 01389 222864, ✉ aeskimoadventures@rediffmail .com), opposite *Hotel Sriram* in the main market; Himalayan Snow Runner (☎ 94120 82247 or ☎ 01389 222687,

🌐 himalayansnowrunner.com), near the cable car in the west of Upper Bazaar.
Services There are two ATMs (PNB and SBI) in the main market. For internet access, try KCE Uniyal Infotech by the jeep stand in Upper Bazaar (₹50/hr); there's another cyber cafe near *Marwari* restaurant, to the west along Upper Bazaar.

ACCOMMODATION AND EATING

Dronagiri 1km west of main market ☎ 01389 222254, 🌐 dronagirihotel.com. Although not the most centrally

located, this is the most comfortable hotel in town, offering attached rooms with good views, running hot water, a clean multicuisine restaurant, internet access and satellite TV. ₹1500

GMVN Tourist Rest House Up a short lane 400m from the Upper Bazaar ☎01389 222118. Centrally located, with basic but decent attached rooms as well as a dorm, and a café serving simple meals and veg thalis (₹80). The new block, up above the old and accessed by the lane opposite the GMOU office, is better

(☎01389 222226; ₹800), especially the rooms with front-facing views. ₹600

Marwari 500m west of main market. One of the brightest, biggest and best of the *dhabas* along Bazaar Rd, with the standard variety of north and south Indian and Chinese dishes, an attached sweets shop and cosy, numbered booths. A "super thali" costs ₹75. Daily 6am–midnight.

Badrinath

Accessible May–Oct

BADRINATH, "Lord of the Berries", just 40km from the Tibetan border, is the most popular of Garhwal's four main pilgrimage temples, and one of Hinduism's holiest sites. Founded by Shankara in the ninth century, it lies near the source of the Alaknanda, the main tributary of the holy Ganges. Badrinath's setting is dazzling, deep in a valley beneath the sharp, snowy pyramid of Nilkantha (6596m), but the town itself, sprawled to the south and east beyond the temple, is largely grubby and unattractive. Immediately south of the temple, on the west bank of the Alaknanda, is the old **village** of Badrinath, its traditional stone buildings and small market seeming like relics from a bygone age.

4

Badri Narayan

Badrinath's **temple** is known as **Badri Narayan**, and is dedicated to Vishnu, said to have done penance in the mythical Badrivan ("Forest of Berries") that once covered the mountains of Uttarakhand. Unusually, it is made of wood, and the entire facade is repainted each May after the snow has receded and the temple has reopened for the season. From a distance, its bright colours, which contrast strikingly with the concrete buildings, snowy peaks and deep blue skies, resemble a Tibetan *gompa*; there's some debate as to whether the temple was formerly a Buddhist shrine. Inside, where photography is strictly taboo, the black stone image of **Badri Vishal** is seated like a *bodhisattva* in the lotus position (some Hindus regard Buddha as an incarnation of Vishnu). *Pandas* (pilgrim priests) sit around the cloisters carrying on the business of worship and a booth enables visitors to pay in advance for *darshan* (devotional rituals) chosen from a long menu.

This site, on the west bank of the turbulent Alaknanda, may well have been selected because of the sulphurous **Tapt Kund** hot springs on the embankment right beneath the temple, used for ritual bathing.

Mana

The main road north of Badrinath heads into increasingly border-sensitive territory, but visitors can normally take local buses and taxis 4km on to the end of the road where the intriguing Bhotia village of **MANA** nestles – check the current situation before setting out. It's also possible to walk to Mana along a clear footpath by the road. The village itself consists of a warren of small lanes and buildings piled virtually on top of each other; the local Bhotia people, Buddhists of Tibetan origin who formerly traded across the high Mana Pass, now tend livestock and ponies and sell yak meat and brightly coloured, handmade carpets. Past the village and over a natural rock bridge, a path leads up the true left bank of the river towards the mountain of Satopanth (7075m), to the base of the impressive 145m **waterfall** of **Vasudhara**, considered to be the source of the Alaknanda. Walking time is just an hour and a half and, unusually, there are no chai stalls en route.

ARRIVAL AND INFORMATION   BADRINATH

By bus Badrinath's bus station is near the southern edge of town; buses depart from here every 2hr from 5.30am until 1.30pm to Joshimath (2hr), Rishikesh (12hr) and Haridwar (13hr), the later departures making an overnight halt en route to lowland destinations. During *yatra* season, one daily bus runs to Gaurikund (7am; 12–13hr).

By jeeps Shared jeeps depart from 5am until early afternoon from just outside the bus stand, connecting the same destinations as the buses.

Services SBI has an ATM just across the bridge by the temple steps, though service is occasionally interrupted. Internet access is available from Naithani's Internet (daily 8am–8pm; ₹50/hr).

ACCOMMODATION AND EATING

Badrinath is awash with rough, flea-bitten budget hotels strung along the main road. The most atmospheric area for cafés and chai shops is the old section around the temple, but the more commercial east bank holds a few more upmarket restaurants, along with numerous bog-standard *dhabas*.

GMVN Devlok Bazar 50m east of post office ☏01381 222212. Set closer to the action than most other hotels, *Devlok* has a somewhat institutional feel but spacious, pleasant rooms, a restaurant serving Marwari and Gujarati thalis (₹100), great views of Neelkanth and excellent local advice. **₹1650**

Panchali Tourist Guest House Across from the south entrance to the bus station ☏94107 43596, ✉ rameshnaithani.05@gmail.com. This small family-run guesthouse, convenient for catching early buses heading south, has eight well-kept rooms with clean bathrooms, hot water buckets for ₹30 and a welcoming owner. **₹400**

Sarovar Portico 200m south of the bus station ☏93103 33317, ⓦ sarovarhotels.com. Marking the southern entrance into town, this remains Badrinath's poshest hotel, with plentiful amenities including a luxurious café-lounge. Rates include breakfast. **₹5500**

Hemkund and the Valley of the Flowers

Trail to Ghangaria open mid-April to early Nov • Hemkund pilgrim season June–Oct • **Valley of Flowers National Park** Late May–Oct daily 6am–6pm (last entry 3pm) • Three-day permit ₹600 (₹150)

Starting from the mountain hamlet of **Govind Ghat**, 28km south of Badrinath, an important pilgrim trail winds 14km up a steep stone path to the overgrown village of Gangharia (3048m), also known as Ghovind Dham. This one-street town is a stopover point for hundreds of Sikh pilgrims en route to Hemkund, as well as for a small trickle of visitors to the Valley of Flowers. Overnight stays are prohibited at both sites.

From Ghangaria, it is a further 6km trek along a steep path to reach the snow-melt lake of **Hemkund** (4329m). In the Sikh holy book, the Guru Granth Sahib, Govind Singh recalled meditating at a lake surrounded by seven high mountains; only in the twentieth century was Hemkund discovered to be that lake. A large *gurudwara* and a small shrine to Lakshmana, the brother of Rama of Ramayana fame, now stand alongside.

An alternative trail forks left from just above Ghangaria, climbing 5km to the mountain *bugyals* of the Bhyundar Valley – the **Valley of the Flowers**. Starting at an altitude of 3352m, the valley was discovered in 1931 by the visionary mountaineer Frank Smythe, who named it for its multitude of rare and beautiful flora. The meadows are at their best during the monsoon, from mid-July until mid-August. Due to the no-camping rule, it is unfortunately impossible to explore the 10km valley in its entirety in the space of a day's hike from Ghangaria.

ARRIVAL AND INFORMATION   HEMKUND AND THE VALLEY OF THE FLOWERS

By bus and jeep Buses and shared jeeps run frequently from early morning until mid-afternoon between Joshimath (45min) and Badrinath (1hr), stopping along Badrinath Rd in Govind Ghat, just above the trailhead. From there, it's possible to travel by horse to Ghangaria (₹720 up, ₹400 down). Helicopters depart from Govind Ghat's helipad to Ghangaria (₹3500).

Information The tourist information office in the centre of Ghangaria (daily 6pm–8pm) exists only to screen a nightly documentary on the Valley of Flowers (6pm; 20min; ₹20), provided the town's power is up and running.

Permits Three-day permits for the Valley of the Flowers can be bought from the ticket office, about 300m up the trail from Ghangaria towards Hemkund, to the left.

KUARI PASS TREK

The old route over the **KUARI PASS** (4268m) in northeastern Garhwal, also called the Curzon Trail after the British Viceroy who traversed parts of it in 1905, provides some stunning mountain views. Officially renamed the **Nehru Trail** after Independence, the popular five-day trail crosses the high ranges without entering the permanent snowline. An ideal expedition for those not equipped to tackle glacial terrain, the trail over Kuari Pass follows alpine meadows and crosses several major streams, skirting the outer western edge of the Nanda Devi National Park. The trail affords excellent views of Trisul (7120m), the trident, Nanda Ghunti (6309m), and the elusive tooth-like Changabang (6864m), while to the far north on the border with Tibet rises the unmistakeable pyramid of Kamet (7756m). Camping equipment is needed, especially on the pass, and guides can be negotiated in Joshimath or Ghat.

Though the original trailhead lies much further south at Gwaldam, most people begin the trek at Ghat, which is connected by shared jeeps to Nandaprayag (1hr 15min). From Ghat, it's a 62km trek to Auli, near Joshimath, crossing the Kuari Pass (3640m) on the sixth day, while an alternative ending takes you to the hot springs of Tapovan in the Dhauli Ganga Valley. The best time for the trek is from May to June and mid-September to November.

Using the Kuari Pass as a base, a climb to the peak of **Pangerchuli** (5183m), 12km up and down, is thoroughly recommended – the views from the summit reveal almost the entire route, including breathtaking mountain vistas. Although snow may be encountered on the climb, it is not a technical peak and no special equipment (save a good stick) is necessary. One descent from Kuari Pass is the picturesque and less abrupt 24km route through forest to the ski centre of **Auli** via Chitrakantha, while a worthy alternative is the gruelling, knee-grinding 22km descent down to the small village of **Tapovan**, overlooking the Dhauli Ganga and its hot-spring-fed tank, and connected by local transport to Joshimath, just 11km away.

4

ACCOMMODATION

GMVN Tourist Guest House Ghangaria. This airy pink complex offers good value, with clean, spacious rooms set off the busy pathway towards the forested banks of the Pushpavati. Open June 1 to October 5. Dorm ₹280, double ₹1100

Priya Ghangaria ☏ 01389 222595. This basic hotel is a notch above many of those that surround it, with a spacious shared balcony and decent, if not quite spotless, rooms, reasonably clean bedding and white-tile bathrooms. The downstairs restaurant serves the usual blend of Punjabi, Chinese and Garhwali dishes:

try the *jholi* (₹40) or the *jhangora ki kheer* (sweet millet porridge; ₹90). ₹400

Shri Nanda Lokpal Palace Ghangaria ☏ 94101 04010, ⊛ hotelnandalokpal.com. This purple and orange three-storey block, just to the right of the trail as it reaches Ghangaria, houses clean, cosy rooms that are among the town's best. There's also a friendly owner, a handy generator and a restaurant serving pricey *jholi* (curry sauce flavoured with curd; ₹100). Prices are slashed up to eighty percent outside the peak season. ₹2850

Nainital

The small, peanut-shaped crater lake of Nainital, set in a mountain hollow at an altitude of 1938m, 277km north of Delhi, gives its name to the largest town in Kumaon. Discovered for Europeans in 1841 by Mr Barron, a wealthy sugar merchant, **NAINITAL** swiftly became a popular escape from the summer heat of the lowlands, and remains one of India's top hill stations. Throughout the year, and especially between March and July, hordes of tourists and honeymooners pack the **Mall**, a 1.5km promenade of restaurants, hotels and souvenir shops that links **Mallital** (head of the lake), the older, colonial part of Nainital at the north end, with **Tallital** (foot of the lake).

Nainital's position within striking range of the inner Himalayas – the peaks are visible from vantage points above town – makes it a good base for exploring Kumaon. When the town's commercialism gets a bit much, it's always possible to escape into the beautiful surrounding country, to lakes such as **Sat Tal** (23km away), where the foothills begin their sudden drop towards the plains to the south, or to the forested ridges around **Kilbury** (12km) and the old Shiva temple at **Mukteshwar** (51km), both of which offer up stunning Himalayan vistas.

The Flats

The popular **Nainital Boat Club** stands at the edge of the large plain known as the **Flats**, the result of a huge landslide in 1880 that buried the *Victoria Hotel*, along with 150 people. Surrounded by the cheap and lively **Tibetan Market**, a **gurdwara**, the gleaming **Jama Masjid** and the rebuilt **Naina Devi Temple**, the Flats now hosts a large field for sporting events. A favourite pastime for day-trippers is to **rent a boat** (₹160) on the lake from next to the boat club, on the northwest corner.

High Altitude Zoo

A steep 1.5km climb from the southern end of the Mall • Tues–Sun 10am–4.30pm • ₹25, camera ₹25, video ₹200 • ☎ 05942 237927

Overlooking the town is Nainital's excellent **High Altitude Zoo**, home to all sorts of exotic creatures such as Siberian tigers, Tibetan wolves, leopards and Himalayan black bears. It's well managed, with detailed explanations in English and a tiny Shiva temple tucked away at the top.

Snow View and around

Cable car The Mall, near *Mayur Restaurant* • Daily: May & June 8am–8pm; July–April 10am–5pm • ₹150 return

A cable car climbs from the Mall to **Snow View** (2270m), from where good views of the snow-clad peaks are most likely early in the morning, especially from October to March. Otherwise it's a 2km hike along a choice of steep trails. The top gets overcrowded in season, with a carnival atmosphere of rides, stalls, go-karting, cafés, a promenade and the viewpoint itself.

About halfway up to Snow View, conspicuous thanks to its abundant prayer flags, lies the small Tibetan *gompa* (temple) of **Gadhan Kunkyop Ling**, which has recently been rebuilt in traditional *gompa* style. Beyond Snow View, trails lead on for 4km to **Naina Peak** (2611m), also called **China Peak** (*Naina* means China), the highest point around Nainital, with good views in all directions.

ARRIVAL AND DEPARTURE — NAINITAL

By bus Buses for most destinations run from Tallital Bus Stand in the south of town. Most buses to Ramnagar, however, depart from Sukhatal Bus Stand, west of Mallital, although two morning services also depart from Tallital. More connections throughout Kumaon are available from the nearby transport hubs of Bhowali (20min) and Haldwani (1hr 30min).

By jeep Shared jeeps congregate near the Tallital Bus Stand, linking Bhowali (20min) and Haldwani (1hr 30min),

as well as destinations further north in Kumaon such as Almora (3hr) and Ranikhet (2hr 30min).

Destinations Almora (daily; 3hr); Bowhali (every 30min; 20min); Delhi (9.30am & 8.30pm; 9hr); Haridwar (8 daily; 7–8hr); Kathgodam (every 30min; 30min); Pithorogarh (daily; 8–9hr); Ramnagar (4 daily; 3hr); Ranikhet (daily; 3hr 30min); Rishikesh (8 daily; 8–9hr).

By train The Railway Reservation Office (Mon–Sat

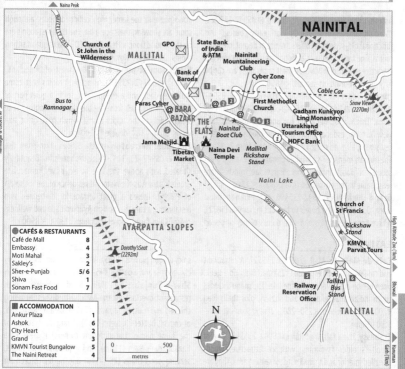

NAINITAL

Naina Peak ▲

Church of St John in the Wilderness

MALLITAL

GPO

State Bank of India & ATM

Nainital Mountaineering Club

Bank of Baroda

Cyber Zone

Cable Car

Bus to Ramnagar

Paras Cyber

BARA BAZAAR

First Methodist Church

Snow View (2270m)

Gadham Kunkyop Ling Monastery

THE FLATS

Nainital Boat Club

Uttarakhand Tourism Office

HDFC Bank

Jama Masjid

Tibetan Market

Naina Devi Temple

Mallital Rickshaw Stand

Naini Lake

Church of St Francis

AYARPATTA SLOPES

Dorothy's Seat (2292m)

Rickshaw Stand

KMVN Parvat Tours

SOUTH MALL

THE MALL

High Altitude Zoo (1km)

Bhowali

Hanuman Garh (3km)

● CAFÉS & RESTAURANTS	
Café de Mall	8
Embassy	4
Moti Mahal	3
Sakley's	2
Sher-e-Punjab	5/6
Shiva	1
Sonam Fast Food	7

■ ACCOMMODATION	
Ankur Plaza	1
Ashok	6
City Heart	2
Grand	3
KMVN Tourist Bungalow	5
The Naini Retreat	4

Railway Reservation Office

Tallital Bus Stand

TALLITAL

N

0   500
metres

4

Rahimangar & Corbett NP

9am–noon & 2–5pm, Sun 9am–2pm; ☎05942 231010) is by the Tallital Bus Stand. The nearest railway station is at Kathgodam (35km south; linked by regular buses), from where the #15014 *Raniket Express* connects Old Delhi (dep. 8.40pm; arr. 3.55am), the #14119 *Dehra Dun Express* connects Haridwar (dep. 7.45pm; arr. 2.30am) and Dehra Dun (arr 4.20am), the #13020 *Kathgodam–Howrah Express* connects Lucknow (dep. 9.55pm; arr. 5.55am), Gorakhpur (arr. 12.20pm), for crossings into Nepal, and Kolkata (arr. Howrah Station 12.40pm) on the second afternoon.

GETTING AROUND AND INFORMATION

Cycle rickshaw The cycle rickshaw stand is in Tallital; the journey from the Mall to Mallital costs ₹10.

Vehicle rental Bikes and motorbikes can be rented from *City Heart* hotel, while agencies along the Mall, among them KMVN Parvat Tours (☎05942 235656) and Hina Tours (☎05942 235860), rent cars.

Tourist information There's an Uttarakhand Tourism office on the Mall near Mallital (Mon–Sat 10am–5pm; ☎05942 235337), but you'll find better information online (ⓦnainitaltourism.com).

Tours, trekking and mountaineering The KMVN representative, Parvat Tours (Mon–Sat 10am–5pm; ☎05942 235656), on the Mall in Tallital, organizes tours and books accommodation at KMVN lodges. For more advice on trekking and mountaineering, call in at Nainital Mountaineering Club, CRST Inter College Building (☎05942 235051), opposite *City Heart* hotel in Mallital, which offers mountain courses and climbing trips (starting at ₹600 (₹300)).

ACCOMMODATION

As a holiday town, Nainital is full of hotels, but budget accommodation is hard to come by in season. Rates are highest between March and July, peaking from May to June. On the whole, rooms are cheaper in Tallital than in Mallital.

Ankur Plaza Opposite cable car station, Mallital ☎05942 235448, ⓦhotelankurplaza.com. High prices in season, but friendly management and good bargains off-season (double from ₹1250), when this is among the best budget options. Rooms are cosy, showing attention to detail if not great taste, and come with breakfast for two. ₹2500

Ashok 100m from Tallital Bus Stand ☎05942 235721, ⓦashoknainital.com. Handy for early buses, this functional old-style hotel offers a range of decent, compact rooms, fine for a short stay, although its surrounds aren't as attractive as those in Mallital. Most room rates are cut by fifty percent during off-season. ₹1800

★ **City Heart** Above Mallital rickshaw stand ☎05942 235228 or ☎94112 68115, ⓦcityhearthotelnainital .com. This welcoming hotel has some of the best lake views in town, especially from the upper rooms and rooftop restaurant, all with cable TV and hot water from 7–11am. The friendly manager is a wildlife photographer and a great source of local information. Rates are much more reasonable in the off-season (from ₹800). ₹2500

Grand The Mall ☎05942 235406, ⓦthegrandnainital .com. One of the first hotels to be built in Nainital (1872), where time seems to stand still: there's plenty of period atmosphere in the large, high-ceilinged rooms, although some are showing their age a bit. The cheapest rooms are on the ground floor, all featuring LCD TVs and quaint sitting rooms. Open April–Nov. ₹2600

KMVN Tourist Bungalow 200m west of bus stand, Tallital ☎05942 235570. Functional rooms that come with breakfast, and a cheap dorm, set in a quiet part of Tallital, a short walk from the bus stand. A lengthy set of stairs connects the upper rooms, which have great lake views. Dorm ₹300, double ₹2200

The Naini Retreat Ayarpatta Slopes, 1km from the Mall ☎05942 235105, ⓦleisurehotels.in. Beautifully situated high above the lake in extensive, immaculate grounds, this was the historical residence of the maharaja of Pilibhit. There's a great terrace for barbecues, two restaurants, a café, bar and an Ayurvedic spa and wellness centre. Lake-facing rooms start from ₹13000. ₹8500

EATING

Café de Mall The Mall ☎05942 235527. A restaurant and café with a small espresso (₹25) machine, and a sleek, open eating area overlooking the lake. The menu includes south Indian snacks, pizzas and sizzlers, plus thalis (veg ₹200–230, non-veg ₹250–280). Daily 9am–4pm & 5.30–10pm.

Embassy The Mall, Mallital ☎05942 235597. One of Nainital's older favourites, with an attractive, wood-panelled interior and a small outdoor seating area. They are strongest on tandoori, Chinese and Tibetan dishes, but also offer pizzas (₹95–150) and sizzlers (₹195–295). Daily 10.30am–11pm.

Moti Mahal The Mall, Mallital ☎05946 221713. Among the favourites in town for Punjabi cuisine, Moti Mahal has a cosy set of booths and serves Chinese and Indian dishes (chicken curry ₹150) as well as snack foods, sandwiches and pizzas (margherita ₹120). Daily 9.30am–10.30pm.

Sakley's The Mall, Mallital. Since 1944 Sakley's has been serving posh if pricey international cuisine including seafood dishes such as steamed fish delight (₹325) and spicy dragon prawns (₹495). Alternatively, pop in for a very civilized tea and a pastry (₹45–70). Daily 10am–10pm.

Sher-e-Punjab The Mall. Good non-veg Indian restaurant overlooking the Mall, with dishes including chicken and mutton sagwala (₹150), karahi, handi and, of course, butter chicken (₹350). A larger restaurant of the same name (but different owners) is near Bara Bazaar (daily 9am–11pm), and is popular with locals, serving good thalis (₹90–140) and butter chicken for the same price as at the Mall restaurant. Daily 10.30am–10pm.

Shiva Bara Bazaar, Mallital. Cheap, good and popular dhaba with tasty mutter paneer (₹90) and mushroom dishes, among other veg options. Thalis ₹125–150. The next-door clone (to the right) is equally good. Daily 11am–11pm.

Sonam Fast Food Tibetan Market, Mallital. Tiny but popular café up an alley in the market, serving up hot plates of veg momos (steamed dumplings; ₹50), chowmein (from ₹40) and thukpa (soup; ₹50), though there's not much in the way of seating. Daily 11am–9pm.

DIRECTORY

Banks and ATMs There are a handful of ATMs along the Mall and in Mallital. The State Bank of India (Mon–Fri 10am–4pm, Sat 10am–1pm) and the Bank of Baroda, both near the Post Office in Mallital, change cash, as does the HDFC Bank further south along the Mall. It's a good idea to change cash here if you are moving on into the mountains, as there are few banks further north that will do so.

Internet access Cyberia, by the path to the cable car (₹35/hr); Paras Cyber, Bara Bazaar (₹30/hr).

Corbett Tiger Reserve

Based at Ramnagar 63km southwest of Nainital, **Corbett Tiger Reserve** is one of India's premier wildlife reserves. Established in 1936 by Jim Corbett (among others) as the Hailey National Park, India's first, and later renamed in his honour, it is one of Himalayan India's last expanses of wilderness. Almost the entire 1288-square-kilometre park, spread over the foothills of Kumaon, is sheltered by a buffer zone of mixed deciduous and giant *sal* forests, which provide impenetrable cover for wildlife. The core area of 520 square kilometres at its heart remains out of bounds, and safaris on foot are only permissible in the fringe forests.

Corbett is famous for its big cats, in particular, the **tiger** – it was the first designated Project Tiger Reserve in 1973 – but its 180 or so tigers are elusive, and sightings are far from guaranteed. Nonetheless, the project has proven more successful in Uttarakhand (both in Corbett and the nearby Rajaji National Park) than in any of its other twenty-odd reserves. While the very survival of the tiger in India remains in serious jeopardy (see p.1182), Corbett does seem to be prioritizing the needs of tigers over those of other wildlife and of tourists. **Poaching**, however, is not unheard of, though it's Corbett's **elephants** that face the most serious threat.

The reservoir within the park also shelters populations of **gharial**, a long-snouted, fish-eating crocodile, and **maggar**, a large marsh crocodile, as well as other reptiles. Jackal are common, and wild boar often run through the camps in the evenings. The grasslands around Dhikala are home to deer species such as the spotted **chital**, hog and barking **deer** and the larger **sambar**, while rhesus and common langur, the two main classes of Indian **monkey**, are both abundant, and happy to provide in-camp entertainment. Bird life ranges from water birds such as the pied kingfisher to **birds of prey**, including the crested serpent eagle and the Himalayan grey-headed fishing eagle. Late spring (April–June) is the best time to see wildlife, when low water levels force animals into the open. Of the camp's five zones, by far the best one for sighting big game is the picturesque **Dhikala** camp, deep into the park near the reservoir.

Ramnagar

Situated in the rich farm-belt of the terai, on the southeastern fringes of the great forests, the busy market town of **RAMNAGAR** is the administrative hub for Corbett Tiger Reserve. Permits and accommodation reservations are issued at the **reception**

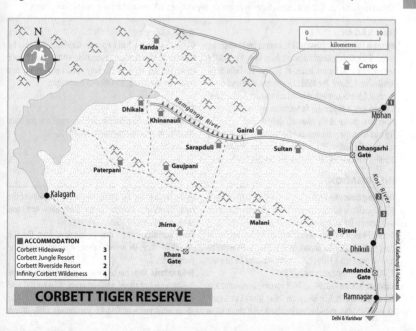

■ ACCOMMODATION	
Corbett Hideaway	3
Corbett Jungle Resort	1
Corbett Riverside Resort	2
Infinity Corbett Wilderness	4

CORBETT TIGER RESERVE

office. There's little to do around Ramnagar itself except go **fishing**. At Lohachaur, 15km north along the River Kosi, good anglers are in with a chance of landing the legendary mahseer, a redoubtable battling river carp.

Dhikala

Beautifully situated overlooking the Ramganga reservoir and the forested hills beyond, Corbett's main camp, **DHIKALA**, lies 49km northwest of Ramnagar and 31km west of Dhangarhi Gate. As you can only stray beyond the confines of the camp on elephant-back or in a car or jeep, the whole place has something of the air of a military encampment. It's normally possible to see plenty of animals and birds from the Dhikala **watchtower**, a 1km wander down the path near the restaurant (turn left where the path meets a junction); bring binoculars, remain quiet and don't wear bright colours or perfume. Chital, sambar and various other deer species find refuge in the savannah grasslands known as the *chaur*, behind the camp to the south, and tigers are occasionally drawn in looking for prey. Two-hour **elephant rides from the camp** (see opposite) explore this sea of grass, rarely penetrating far into the deep jungles beyond; try to convince your *mahout* (elephant driver) to venture in, as they can be quite magical.

Dikhuli resorts

A number of self-contained **resorts** have sprung up on the fringes of Corbett, close to the town of **Dikhuli** (about 9km north of Ramnagar). These provide a higher standard of accommodation than in Dhikala or Ramnagar as well as guides for expeditions in the neighbouring forests, which can be as rich in wildlife as the park, minus all the restrictions and bureaucracy.

ARRIVAL AND DEPARTURE   CORBETT TIGER RESERVE

The nearest town to Corbett Tiger Reserve is Ramnagar, which is the best place to arrange tours and accommodation. Visitors may enter the CTR in private vehicles or on tours easily arranged in Ramnagar or any of the outlying resorts.

RAMNAGAR

By train The railway station is 1km south of the town centre (beyond the *Corbett Kingdom* hotel); from here, the #25014 *Corbett Park Link Express* leaves at 9.55pm for Delhi Sarai Rohilla (arr. 3.55am). The #55322 *Ramnagar-Varanasi Express* leaves at 8.50pm, connecting with Lucknow (arr. 7.30am) and Varanasi (arr. 3.45pm). For faster trains and connections to other parts change at Moradabad (7 daily; 1–2hr).

By bus From the main bus stand in the town centre, buses run to Delhi (every 30min; 8hr), Dehra Dun (9 daily; 6hr 30min), Haridwar (9 daily; 5hr) and Nainital (4 daily; 3hr).

DHIKALA

Dhikala can be reached by private transport, but only by those with an overnight reservation within the Dhikala camp. For day-trippers, the only option is the daily bus tour from the Reception Office in Ramnagar.

DHIKULI

Dhikuli resorts offer pick up from Ramnagar's bus and train stations, while auto-rickshaws charge ₹100–150.

INFORMATION

Opening hours Mid-June to mid-Nov daily 6.30–9.30am & 1.30–5.30pm (check at reception for seasonal changes in park hours); Jhirna zone open year-round

Entry Fees Three-day permit ₹1000 (₹200); additional days ₹450 (₹100); 4hr permit ₹450 (₹100); vehicle charge for overnight trip ₹1500 (₹500); vehicle charge for day-trip ₹500 (₹250); mandatory guide ₹200

Contact Details ☎05947 251489, ⊛corbettnationalpark.in

Information The CTR Reception Office (daily 6am–4pm; ☎05947 251489, ⊛ corbettnationalpark.in) is about 100m to the north of the bus stand, on the opposite side of the road. There's also a visitors' centre (daily 6am–4pm) and museum at Dhangarhi Gate.

Park permits Permits may be obtained from the CTR Reception Office; 4hr permits can be picked up at any of the park's gates.

Jeep safaris Jeeps can be arranged at the reception centre in Ramnagar (see above), while other operators can be found outside Ramnagar's bus stand – shop around and be clear about what you're getting for your money (fuel, driver's accommodation and a specific number of 3hr safaris should all be included). A petrol 4WD, such as a Maruti Gypsy, is best as it is quiet and built for the terrain. Girish at *Govind* restaurant in Ramnagar (☎ 05947 251615) can help arrange tours.

Guides All jeep safaris must be accompanied by a guide (₹200/day) – who may or may not be able to identify wildlife or speak English – allotted to your jeep by a rota system. If you require a guide with specific knowledge, contact the Field Director one month in advance with your request (☎ 05947 253977). Alternatively, you may choose your own guide by opting to visit wildlife areas outside of the park; again, Girish can help (see opposite).

Gates The closest of the various park gates from Ramnagar is at Amdanda (1km north) on the road to Bijrani (11km). Another useful gate is Dhangarhi (18km

north of Ramnagar), which provides access to the park's northern and northwestern portions, including the main camp of Dhikala. Khara gate (20km west of Ramnagar) links Jhirna in the south of the park, the only area to remain open year-round.

Bus tours The park runs daily bus tours (5.30am & noon; ₹2000 (₹1000)) to Dhikala from Ramnagar, providing the only means of reaching the camp without staying the night.

Elephant rides Two-hour rides are offered in each of the five camps, both mornings and evenings, for ₹1000 (₹300).

Services There are a several ATMs in Ramnagar, including Bank of Baroda on Ranikhet Rd and SBI at the train station. There are several internet cafés (₹30–40/hr) on the main road south of the bus stand.

ACCOMMODATION

RAMNAGAR

Anand 100m south of the main bus stand ☎ 05947 254385. This modest option in the town's noisy centre offers clean, simple rooms, all with an attached bathroom and TV. There's a spotless little restaurant attached. ₹500

Corbett Kingdom 400m south of the bus stand ☎ 05947 251601, ⓦ corbettkingdom.com. Next to a none-too-clean irrigation ditch near the town centre, this flashy three-storey hotel is Ramnagar's best, offering a/c rooms with flatscreen TVs and big windows. The hotel's ample amenities include a multicuisine restaurant, travel desk and a small pool. ₹2500

Corbett Motel Less than 1km south of the train station ☎ 05947 253033 or ☎ 98374 68933, ⓦ corbettmotel.com. Spartan but clean rooms, tents and a good restaurant in a leafy mango orchard just beyond the bustle of town. Friendly owner Karan arranges safaris and tours, and can arrange pick up from the town centre when the driver isn't on safari (otherwise it's a ₹50 auto-rickshaw ride). Tent ₹800, double ₹1000

KMVN Tourist Lodge Next to CTR Reception Office, about 100m north of bus stand ☎ 05947 251225. As institutional as any KMVN lodge, in a central but relatively quiet location with a dorm and basic restaurant as well as spacious but spartan doubles, some with a/c (₹1750). Dorm ₹200, double ₹1300

JIM CORBETT (1875–1955)

Hunter of man-eating tigers, photographer, conservationist and author, **Jim Corbett** was born in Nainital of English and Irish parentage. A childhood spent around the Corbett winter home just outside Kaladhungi (29km southeast of Ramnagar) instilled in young Jim a love for close communion with nature and an instinctive understanding of jungle ways.

Known locally as "Carpet Sahib", a mispronunciation of his name, Jim Corbett was called upon time and time again to rid the hills of Kumaon of **man-eating tigers** and leopards. Normally shy of human contact, such animals become man-eaters when infirmity brought upon by old age or wounds renders them unable to hunt their usual prey. Many of those killed by Corbett were found to have suppurating wounds caused by porcupine quills embedded deep in their paws.

One of Corbett's most memorable exploits was the killing of the **Champawat tiger**, which was responsible for a documented 436 human deaths, and was bold enough to steal its victims from the midst of human habitation. By the mid-1930s, though, Corbett had become dismayed with the increasing number of hunters in the Himalayas and the resultant decline in wildlife, and diverted his energies into conservation, swapping his gun for a movie camera and spending months capturing tigers on film. His adventures are described in books such as *My India*, *Jungle Lore* and *Man-Eaters of Kumaon*; Martin Booth's *Carpet Sahib* is an excellent biography of a remarkable man. Unhappy in post-Independence India, Jim Corbett retired to East Africa, where he continued his conservation efforts until his death at the age of eighty.

For a further glimpse into Corbett's life, head to his family's former winter retreat near Kaladhungi, which has been turned into the **Jim Corbett Museum** (Mon–Sat: summer 8am–6pm; winter 8am–5pm; ₹50 (₹10)).

DHIKALA

All accommodation within the park is bookable via the CTR reception office in Ramnagar (see p.324); however, bookings (online or by telephone) for Dhikala should be made at least thirty days in advance (twenty for Indian nationals) during peak season. KMVN run a canteen for guests, *Parvat*, with both Indian and Western food available, while on the other side of the camp is a *dhaba* serving similar food.

Dhikala Forest Lodges ⊕05947 251489, ⓦdhikalaforestlodge.in. Surrounded by a small fence, the *Dhikala Forest Lodge* complex has just over one hundred beds, spread between rooms in various wings and a pair of twelve bed dormitories with rather uncomfortable bunk beds (no bedding supplied) and common bathrooms. Dorm ₹400, double ₹2000

DHIKULI RESORTS

Corbett Hideaway 10km north of Ramnagar ⊕05947 284132, ⓦcorbetthideaway.com. Luxurious terracotta-coloured huts with all mod cons as well as an exhaustive slew of extra amenities, from a thatched-roof grillhouse to a poolside bar, all dotted around a pleasant orchard on a bluff overlooking the Kosi River and pretending, without great success, to be rustic. Safaris and the usual tours arranged. ₹8000

Corbett Jungle Resort 29km north of Ramnagar (9km beyond Dhangarhi Gate), Mohan ⊕05947 287820, ⓦcorbettjungleresort.com. Wood-panelled stone cottages in a leafy mango orchard above the Kosi, complete with a curvacious pool. Food, trekking and jeep safaris are included in the package deals (from ₹9555), and there are good off-season discounts. ₹3800

Corbett Riverside Resort 11km north of Ramnagar ⊕05947 284125, ⓦcorbettriverside.com. A picturesque setting, 10km north of Ramnagar looking across the river to forest-covered cliffs. Amenities include a pool, volleyball court, billiards hall and a travel desk where you can arrange various safaris and horseback rides. The super-ritzy Presidential Suites along the river's edge (₹15080) have verandas directly above the river beach. ₹4420

Infinity Corbett Wilderness 9km north of Ramnagar ⊕05947 251279, ⓦinfinityresorts.com. Corbett's most ostentatious resort overlooks the Kosi River and the forested hills beyond, with large comfortable rooms, a library, well-stocked bar, swimming pool, gym and spa. Safaris cost (a lot) extra. Activities include nature trails with the resort's own naturalists, jungle rides, fishing, trekking and films. ₹10000

Ranikhet

The small and deliberately undeveloped hill station of **RANIKHET** (1824m), 50km west of Almora, is essentially an army cantonment, home to the Kumaon Rifles. New construction is confined to the **Sadar Bazaar** area, while the rest of the town above it, climbing towards the crest of the hill, retains its peacefully pleasant atmosphere in the shade of tall pine woods. Forest trails abound, including a shortcut from the bazaar to the Mall (something of a misnomer, as it's a quiet road with few buildings apart from officers' messes), which starts just above the town and continues south for 3km along the wooded crest of the ridge.

KRC Shawl and Tweed Factory

Above the Narsingh Stadium Parade Ground, at the very start of the Mall • Summer Mon–Sat 9am–7pm, Sun 10am–5pm; winter Mon–Sat 10am–6pm, Sun 10am–5pm

The **KRC Shawl and Tweed Factory**, in an old church equipped with looms and wheels, allows visitors to watch the weavers in action, a fascinating display of concentration, dexterity and counting. The herringbone and houndstooth tweeds are sold in the shop next door (all woollen items range from ₹575 to about ₹1000).

ARRIVAL AND DEPARTURE | RANIKHET

By train There's a railway reservation office (Mon–Fri 9am–1pm & 2–4pm, Sat 9.30–1pm & 2–3pm) next to the post office, handy for booking trains from the nearest station in Kathgodam.

By bus Buses from all over Kumaon, including the railway station at Kathgodam, 84km away, arrive at one of two stands on either end of the bazaar: the KMOU stand to the west at Gandhi Chowk, and the UP Roadways stand (⊕84760 07549) east of the bazaar. Long-haul buses to

Delhi, Lucknow, Dehra Dun and Haridwar depart from the UP Roadways stand, while all other regional destinations are served by the KMOU stand.

Destinations Almora (hourly; 2hr 30min); Bageshwar (4 daily; 5hr); Bhowali (6 daily; 2hr); Delhi (4 daily; 11–12hr); Dehra Dun (2 daily; 10–11hr); Haldwani (6 daily; 3hr 30min); Haridwar (2 daily; 9–10hr); Kathgodam (6 daily; 3hr); Lucknow (daily; 11–12hr); Nainital (daily; 2hr 30min); Ramnagar (hourly; 4hr 30min).

By jeep Shared jeeps depart when full from beside both bus stands for many of the same destinations, including Almora (2hr) and Haldwani (3hr).

GETTING AROUND

Jeeps Shared jeeps leave when full for the Mall (₹10; 10min) from the small stand above Gandhi Chowk.

Taxis The taxi rank is just above the KMOU Bus Stand.

ACCOMMODATION AND EATING

If you're just passing through Ranikhet, the hotels in the busy bazaar are sufficient, but the Mall is better for an extended stay. Eating choices are pretty limited; the best of them are within the better hotels, but there are a few good cafés and *dhabas* in the bazaar.

★ **Chevron Rosemount** 500m east of the Mall from the turn-off just south of Hotel Meghdoot ☎ 05966 221391, ⓦ chevronhotels.com. A beautifully restored 1897 colonial mansion, deep in the woods, all pine and teak with lovely rooms, a restaurant and gardens complete with tennis, croquet, badminton and snow views from the deckchairs on the lawn. There's also a four-person cottage (₹11,100). ₹**4100**

Meghdoot The Mall, 3km south of town centre ☎ 05966 220475, ⓦ hotelmeghdootranikhet.com. Comfortable suites set back from balconies full of potted plants and flowers, with running hot water, parking and room service, plus a good mid-range restaurant that serves up a range of tasty biriyani (from ₹95 veg), pulao and other non-veg dishes. ₹**900**

★ **Ranikhet Club** The Mall, 2km south of town centre ☎ 05966 220611. For a taste of Indian military life and a good dose of colonial nostalgia, men and women can join the Ranikhet Club (₹50/day). In addition to the classy old restaurant (veg sizzler ₹150), there's a rustic bar (Kingfisher ₹120), cards room and billiards room, each featuring men with grand moustaches calling each other chaps. Acceptable dress for evening visits includes shirts, ties, leather shoes, lounge suits and "national dress". There are also a few exorbitantly priced rooms available (from ₹4500). Daily 7am–10.30pm.

DIRECTORY

Banks and ATMs There are several ATMs in town, including one at the State Bank of India (Mon–Fri 10am–4pm).
Post office The main post office is on the Mall (Mon–Sat 9am–5pm), not far beyond the Ranikhet Club.

Internet Ranikhet Cyber Cafe (daily 7.30am–7.30pm; ₹25/hr) is attached to *Ranikhet Inn*, above Gandhi Chowk.

Almora and around

Spread out over a hilltop overlooking terraced fields, 67km north of Nainital, **ALMORA** (1646m) is Kumaon's official and cultural capital. Founded by the Chand dynasty in 1560, and occupied successively by the Gurkhas and the British, it remains a major market town, and has attracted an eclectic assortment of visitors over the years, including Swami Vivekananda, Timothy Leary and the Tibetologist author of *The Way of the White Clouds*, Lama Angarika Govinda. While many foreign visitors prefer the nearby traveller colony of **Kasar Devi**, around 8km north, Almora has a few of its own attractions and makes a practical base for regional excursions.

Almora bazaars

Although most of Almora's official business is conducted along the hectic **Mall**, the **bazaars**, immediately above and parallel to it along the crest of the saddle, hold much more of interest. These pedestrian-only flagstone lanes teem with local crowds in the evenings, while its faded, carved facades evoke a distant past. The most impressive example of the old architectural style is found at the Khazanchi Mohalla, which once belonged to the state treasurers. Stretching about 1.5km from Lal Bazaar to Thana Bazaar, the various markets offer everything from *khadi* (home-spun) cotton textiles to *tamta* (local copperware).

The temples

Towards the top of town, just north of the market area, a compound holds a group of Chand-period stone **temples**. The main one, a squat single-storey structure, is dedicated to **Nanda Devi**, the goddess embodied in the region's highest mountain. More typical of Kumaoni temple architecture are two larger Shaivite painted stone temples, capped with umbrella-like wooden roofs covering their stone *amalaka* (circular crowns). During September a large fair is held here in honour of Nanda Devi.

ARRIVAL AND DEPARTURE ALMORA

By train There's a computerized railway reservation centre (Mon–Sat 9am–noon & 2–5pm) at the KMVN *Holiday Home* hotel, on the Mall 1km west of the centre, useful for booking trains from the nearest railway station at Kathgodam.

By bus Buses arrive and depart from a pair of nearby adjacent bus stands located the middle of the Mall. Tickets for Kumaoni destinations can be bought from the KMOU office (☎94105 01878), while tickets for Dehra Dun, Haridwar and Delhi should be purchased from the UTC office (☎84760 07548),

50m east and down some steps by Deewan's Sweets.

Destinations Bageshwar (every 30min; 4hr); Baijnath (every 30min; 3hr); Bowhali (hourly; 2hr 30min); Dehra Dun (4 daily; 12hr); Delhi (4 daily; 12hr); Haldwani (hourly; 4hr); Haridwar (2 daily; 11hr); Kausani (every 30min; 2hr); Ranikhet (hourly; 2hr).

By jeep The jeep stand is by the Bharat filling station on the Mall, just west of the *Shikhar* hotel. Jeeps depart when full for Kasar Devi (15min), Binsar (1hr), Bageshwar (2hr), Ranikhet (2hr) and Kausani (2hr 30min).

INFORMATION AND TOURS

Tourist information The tourist office is next to the *Savoy Hotel* (Mon–Sat 10am–5pm; ☎05962 230180).

Tours and treks The best places to find out about taxi excursions, treks and other activities, or to hire equipment

and guides, are Discover Himalaya (☎05962 231470, ✉discoverhimalaya@indiatimes.com) and High Adventure (☎05962 232277), both on the Mall by *Hotel Kailas*.

ACCOMMODATION

Bansal Lal Bazaar, at the top of the steep lane opposite Hotel Shikhar ☎05962 230864. Spotless, simple rooms with en suites (free hot bucket water), fantastic rooftop views and very friendly management, who'll deliver their renowned lassis (₹25–40) and *tikkis* (₹35) to your room. The top room is the largest and most attractive. Fixed price year round. **₹300**

Kailas The Mall, above the GPO ☎05962 230624, ✉jawaharlalshah@india.com. They aren't kidding when they call this ramshackle heap "a hotel like no other". People either view it as (almost literally) a dump or as a charming old place inspired by Nek Chand's rock garden in Chandigarh (see p.515). It's run by the aged and charming Mr Shah, who'll happily regale guests with fascinating tales of times gone by. **₹300**

Khim's Guest House Off Kasar Devi Rd, 3.5km north of Almora ☎94120 44865, ✉khims_guest_house@yahoo. com. Extremely laid-back guesthouse favoured by ageing, old-school hippies, and a lovely place to chill out for a week or two. It offers simple unattached rooms, or cottages with attached bathrooms, and there's an excellent library on the Himalayan region, one of the best in the entire country. **₹800/₹350**

Shikhar The Mall, 150m northeast of the bus stand ☎05962 230253, ✇hotelshikhar.in. Marking the centre of town, *Shikhar* has a wide range of rooms, some at very reasonable prices and most with balconies, while the grounds feature giant verandas overlooking the valley. The gloomy but cavernous restaurant serves good breakfasts, and there's a tiny internet café outside. Fixed prices year round. **₹700/₹400**

EATING

Cafés and restaurants are strung along the Mall, especially around the bazaar area; locally grown and prepared Kumaon rice and black dhal are particularly delicious. Hotels such as the *Savoy* can produce a feast of Kumaoni dishes, if given plenty of advance notice.

Chatpat Chicken Corner The Mall, 300m west of the bus stand. Plain and simple, brightly lit place serving tasty roast chicken for under ₹100. Daily 11am–10.30pm.

Glory The Mall, near Shikhar Hotel ☎05962 230279. Multicuisine café/restaurant, strong on north Indian cooking, with dishes from masala dosa (₹50) to butter chicken (half

₹160, full ₹270) as well as a smattering of Chinese food. Also good for breakfast. Daily 8.30am–1pm.

New Soni The Mall, near the bus stand. Excellent, Sikh-run *dhaba* famed for its chicken (half ₹100, full ₹200) and mutton dishes (₹140); it can get crowded. Daily 10am–1pm.

DIRECTORY

Banks and ATMs There are many ATMs along the Mall.

The State Bank of India (Mon–Fri 10am–1pm) will change

travellers' cheques (preferably Amex), but not cash – Nainital is the nearest town for that.

Kasar Devi

8km north of Almora

Spread among the cedar and rhododendron forest below the unassuming hilltop temple of Kasar Devi (of Swami Vivekanda fame), 8km north of Almora, is the pleasant hamlet of **KASAR DEVI**. Nicknamed "hippieland" by some of the locals, it plays host to a thriving long-term travellers' scene.

ARRIVAL AND DEPARTURE   KASAR DEVI

By jeep Shared jeeps run when full between Almora's jeep stand and Kasar Devi (15min; ₹30), dropping off passengers along Binsar Rd.

ACCOMMODATION AND EATING

Mohan's Binsar Retreat Binsar Rd ⊕05926 251118, ⓦmohansbinsarretreat.com. The pick of Kasar Devi accommodation, attracting guests and non-guests alike to its breezy terrace café with lazy chairs overlooking the valley. Rooms all come with fireplaces and kettles, plus there's wi-fi and a good restaurant, housed in a gazebo. Full and half-board options available. ₹2200

New Dolma Binsar Rd ⊕05926 251118. Run by Tibetans, *New Dolma* is perched above the road with a view of the Himalayas; you can enjoy your *momos* (₹40–60), special *thukpa* (₹60) and chowmein (₹30–60) on the broad

outdoor terrace or inside the chequered-floor diner. There are also some luridly painted rooms upstairs (₹600). Daily 8am–10pm.

Rainbow Guest House Off Binsar Rd, near Mohan's ⊕05962 251105 or ⊕97203 20664, ⓦrainbow-cafe .eu5.org. Reached by a small path off the main road, this good-value guesthouse has well-kept rooms with hot water, kettles and wi-fi connection. There are also terraces with mountain views, a small library, a spacious restaurant with thalis (from ₹120), and a friendly owner who can arrange treks to the surrounding villages. ₹800

Binsar

BINSAR, known locally as Jhandi Dhar ("hill top"), 33km north of Almora, rises in isolation to a commanding 2412m. Though it was once the summer capital of the Chandras, Kumaon's kings, little of that era remains aside from the bulbous stone Shiva temple of **Bineshwar** (₹650 (₹250)), 3km below the summit. Most visitors come to see the 300km panorama of Himalayan peaks along the northern horizon, including, from west to east, Kedarnath, Chaukhamba, Trisul, Nandaghunti, Nanda Devi, Nandakot and Panchuli. Closer at hand, you can enjoy quiet forest walks through oak and rhododendron woods. Recently designated a nature sanctuary, Binsar is rich in alpine flora, ferns, hanging moss and wild flowers.

ARRIVAL AND DEPARTURE   BINSAR

By taxi Binsar is easily visited as a day-trip from Almora. There's no bus, but a return taxi from Almora's jeep stand costs around ₹1000.

ACCOMMODATION

KMVN Tourist Rest House 2km before Zero Point, Binsar Wildlife Sanctuary ⊕05962 80176. At the end of the road near the top of a steep hill, this KMVN place offers bland but comfortable wood-panelled rooms that

run on solar power and often go dark in the evening: bring a torch. There's basic veg and non-veg food available. The mountain views from the broad garden terrace are wonderful. ₹2400

Jageshwar

JAGESHWAR, 25km northeast of Almora, is the very heart of Kumaon, a place where language and customs seem to have resisted change. An idyllic small river meanders through dark pines for 3km off the main road from **Artola**, stumbling onto a complex of 124 ancient shrines and temples that cluster at the base of venerable deodar trees. Jageshwar village retains much of its traditional charm, with stone-paved lanes and beautifully carved wooden doors and windows painted in green, turquoise and other striking colours. Good local **walks** include the steep 3km ascent through beautiful pine forests to the hamlet and stone temples of **Vriddha** or **Briddh Jageshwar** (Old Jageshwar), with an extensive panorama from the mountains of Garhwal to the massifs of western Nepal. A trail from here leads 12km along an undulating ridge to Binsar; the trail finally emerges from the woods near the stone temple of **Bineshwar**.

ARRIVAL AND DEPARTURE — JAGESHWAR

By bus A daily bus runs from Almora at noon (1hr 30min), returning from Jageshwar's main temple gate around 8am.

By taxi A return taxi from Almora costs about ₹1000.

ACCOMMODATION AND EATING

Tara Guest House Up the hill from Jageshwar Temple ☎ 05962 263068, ⊛ jageshwar.co.uk. This tiny, family-run block has five basic rooms with twin beds, Western-style toilets and small patios overlooking the temple, in a quiet setting a few minutes off the road. Hot water, good breakfasts and thalis are available on request, prepared by the friendly owner, who offers advice and guidance on local excursions. ₹550

Kausani

Spread out east to west along a narrow pine-covered ridge 52km northwest of Almora, the village of **KAUSANI** has become a popular resort thanks to its spectacular Himalayan panorama. It's a simple day-trip from Almora, though as the peaks – Nanda Choti, Trisul, Nanda Devi and Panchol – are at their best at dawn and dusk, it's well worth an overnight stay. The tourist scene is growing, and a number of new hotels and restaurants have sprung up in recent years to cater for the very seasonal demand. Up the hill from the town centre are several **ashrams**, including one that once housed Mahatma Gandhi, who walked here in 1929, thirty years before the road came through.

There are numerous possibilities for short **day-hikes** in the woods and terraced valleys around Kausani, among them the scenic hike to the Kausani Tea Estate (4km north), and the pleasant trail down the valley to the temples of **Baijnath** (10km). Further afield is the important pilgrimage site of **Bageshwar** and the trailhead for the Pindari Glacier, a few hours away in Song.

ARRIVAL AND INFORMATION — KAUSANI

By bus and shared jeep Kausani is connected by regular buses and shared jeeps to Almora (every 30min; 2hr 30min) and Baijnath (hourly; 30min), from where buses continue to Bageshwar (1hr 30min) to the east and Gwaldam (1hr 30min) and Karnaprayag (3–4hr) to the northwest, for destinations in Garhwal.

Services The State Bank of India has an ATM. There's internet at *Hill Queen Restaurant*, near Snow View Point above town (₹30/hr), which has telescopes for admiring the peaks and stars. Power outages are frequent across town.

ACCOMMODATION AND EATING

Outside high season (April 15–June 15 & Oct 1–Nov 15), room rates are slashed roughly in half.

Anashakti Ashram Snow View Rd, looking down on the Mall ☎ 05962 258028. Guests prepared to observe house rules, such as attending compulsory prayers and not smoking, are welcome to stay at Gandhi's pleasant but spartan former ashram, run completely on solar power, for a donation. Either way, it's worth visiting the main prayer hall, which doubles as a Gandhi museum (daily 7am–noon & 4–7pm; free; no photos).

★ **Uttarakhand** Up the steps north from the bus stand ☎ 05962 258012, ⊛ uttarakhandkausani.com. This foreigner-friendly place run by 25-year-old owner Vipin, a nature enthusiast and great source of information on hikes, has clean doubles and a broad terrace with fantastic Himalayan views; the second-storey rooms with satellite TV and flush bidet toilets are the best value. A good hangout spot is in the thatched-roof viewing tower, equipped with a telescope and rising above the hotel's *Garden Restaurant*, which hosts Kausani's only tandoor oven (full chicken ₹350). Wi-fi around the lobby. ₹1050

PINDARI GLACIER TREK

One of Uttarakhand's lesser-traversed trails connects the most accessible glacier in the Kumaon region, the **Pindari Glacier**, which stretches more than 3km in length and almost 0.5km in width. Passing through pristine high mountain country and a host of tiny Himalayan villages, the trail follows the Pindar River to its source, offering views along the way of the region's giants, among them Nanda Kot (6861m), Panwali Dwar (6663m) and Maiktoli (6m).

Beginning and ending in **Song** (1600m), the trail covers about 90km roundtrip and takes six days to complete, crossing over the Dhakuri Pass (2680m) and beyond the final settlement of Khati to reach Zero Point at the edge of the Pindari Glacier (3660m).

The whole trek can be done tea-house style, as basic government lodges dot the trail; near the glacier itself, you can opt to stay with a locally famous Sadhu who goes by the name Baba Ji. However, camping equipment and sleeping bags are highly recommended. Guides and porters are easily arranged in Song, connected to Bageshwar by jeeps (1hr 30min) and buses (2hr). The Pindari Glacier has also caught the attention of mountain bikers: two-wheel tours are run by Mike McLean (❿ mountainbikekerala.com) in April and October.

Baijnath

At the bottom of the broad Garur Valley lies the quiet town of **BAIJNATH** (1126m), 16km north of Kausani and sprawled along the banks of the Gomti River. This was once the capital city of the Katyur dynasty, which ruled much of Garhwal and Kumaon from the seventh to the fourteenth centuries; their stone temples, built between the ninth and twelfth centuries, still stand at a bend in the river. Eighteen towering shrines rise from the temple grounds, each a beautiful example of the medieval *nagara* style, the tallest of them devoted to Lord Shiva. The main temple, however, is devoted to Shiva's consort, Parvati, its 1.5m schist image of the goddess being one of the few in the complex to have withstood the ravages of time.

ARRIVAL AND DEPARTURE
BAIJNATH

By bus and jeep Regular buses and jeeps link Baijnath with Bageshwar (1hr), Kausani (30min) and Gwaldam (1hr 30min); jeeps and buses congregate 500m south of the temples, across the river.

ACCOMMODATION AND EATING

KMVN Tourist Rest House 200m north of the temples, off the main road to the left ☏ 05963 250101. A modern hotel in a quiet setting with large en-suite rooms with hot water, some with a/c (₹1300). There's also a dorm, restaurant and garden area with good views of the Trisul. Dorm ₹**180**, double ₹**800**

Bageshwar

Nestled 74km north of Almora, **BAGESHWAR** is one of Kumaon's most important pilgrimage towns, spread along the lush and lovely Gomti River valley. Pilgrims still flock to its huddle of ancient temples, highlighted by the fifteenth-century Bagnath Temple, built by the Chandras, in the centre of town. Most foreign travellers use the town as a base for the Pindari Glacier trek (see box above); Bageshwar's market is a great place to stock up on supplies.

ARRIVAL AND DEPARTURE
BAGESHWAR

By bus and jeep The bus and jeep stands are in the west of town, within a short walk of the town centre; regular buses connect Baijnath (1hr), Kausani (1hr 30min), Almora (3hr), Bowhali (6hr), Haldwani (7hr 30min) and Song (2hr) for the Pindari Glacier trek.

ACCOMMODATION AND EATING

KMVN Tourist Resthouse 2km south of the bus station across a bridge ☏ 05963 220034. The basic rooms are passable, with large bathrooms with geysers, but it's worth paying the extra for the deluxe rooms (₹700). The attached restaurant serves standard hot meals. Staff can get you sorted for the Pindari trek, as well as other regional excursions. ₹**600**

Madhya Pradesh and Chhattisgarh

SCULPTURES ON THE FACADE OF
PARSVANATH TEMPLE, KHAJURAHO

5

Madhya Pradesh and Chhattisgarh

Hot, dusty Madhya Pradesh is a vast landlocked expanse of scrub-covered hills, sun-parched plains and one third of India's forests. Stretching from beyond the headwaters of the mighty Narmada River to the fringes of the Western Ghats, it's a transitional zone between the Gangetic lowlands in the north and the high, dry Deccan plateau to the south. Despite its diverse array of exceptional attractions, ranging from ancient temples and hilltop forts to some of India's best tiger reserves, Madhya Pradesh receives only a fraction of the tourist traffic that pours between Delhi, Agra, Varanasi and the south. For those who make the effort, this gem of a state is both culturally rewarding and largely hassle-free.

In the centre of Madhya Pradesh, the state capital **Bhopal**, though synonymous with industrial disaster (see box, p.341), has a vibrant Muslim heritage and some interesting museums. Nearby is **Sanchi**, one of India's most significant Buddhist sites. The hill station of **Pachmarhi**, meanwhile, has echoes of the Raj, numerous hiking routes and the little-visited Satpura National Park.

In the north of the state, the city of **Gwalior** has a stunning hilltop fort and is within striking distance of **Datia's** Rajput palace, the Scindia family's mausoleums at **Shivpuri**, and **Orchha**, the atmospheric ruined capital of the Bundella rajas. Further east is the state's biggest attraction, the cluster of magnificent sandstone temples at **Khajuraho**, renowned for their intricate erotic carvings.

Nondescript **Jabalpur** is the biggest city in eastern Madhya Pradesh, a region that has few historic sites but does boast the **Kanha**, **Bandhavgarh** and **Pench** reserves, among the last strongholds for many endangered species, most notably the **tiger**. Alongside **Orchha** and **Khajuraho**, these parks are the only places in Madhya Pradesh you're likely to meet more than a handful of foreign tourists.

Western Madhya Pradesh is home to **Indore**, a modern city of industry. Though of little interest in itself, Indore is a good base for exploring **Mandu**, the romantic former capital of the Malwa sultans, the Hindu pilgrimage centres of **Omkareshwar** and **Maheshwar**, and the holy city of **Ujjain**, one of the sites of the Kumbh Mela.

The best time to visit Madhya Pradesh is during the relatively cool winter months (Nov–Feb). In April, May and June, daytime temperatures frequently exceed 40°C, but if you can stand the heat, this is the best time to catch glimpses of tigers in the national parks. The increasingly meagre rains finally sweep in from the southeast in late June or early July.

JAMA MASJID, MANDU

Highlights

① Sanchi India's finest Buddhist monument, Sanchi is a carefully restored *stupa* complex with intricately carved gateways. **See p.344**

② Pachmarhi Central India's only hill station, where you can trek to the top of a sacred Shiva peak, hunt out prehistoric rock art or simply relax in the refreshingly cool air. **See p.350**

③ Orchha Madhya Pradesh at its most exotic, Orchha boasts crumbling riverside tombs and ornate Rajput palaces amid lush, tranquil countryside. **See p.360**

④ Khajuraho These renowned temples are swathed in thought-provoking erotic sculpture. Lost for centuries in thick jungle, they have since been beautifully restored. **See p.365**

⑤ Kanha National Park The most famous of Madhya Pradesh's national parks, Kanha is archetypal Kipling country and teems with wildlife, most notably majestic tigers. **See p.378**

⑥ Mandu A medieval fort on a plateau where the emperor got down to serious pleasure-seeking in his vast harem, theatre, steam baths and pavilions. **See p.386**

HIGHLIGHTS ARE MARKED ON THE MAP ON P.336

5

Brief history

Any exploration of central India will be illuminated if you have a grasp of its long and turbulent history. Most of the marauding armies that have swept across the Subcontinent over the last two millennia passed through this corridor, leaving in their wake a bumper crop of monuments. The very first traces of settlement in Madhya Pradesh are the 10,000-year-old paintings on the lonely hilltop of Bhimbetka, near Bhopal. Aboriginal rock art was still being created here during the Mauryan emperor Ashoka's evangelical dissemination of Buddhism, in the second century BC. Nearby **Sanchi** is this era's most impressive relic. By the end of the first millennium AD, central India was divided into several kingdoms. The Paramaras, whose ruler Raja Bhoj founded Bhopal, controlled the southern and central area, known as Malwa, while the Chandellas, responsible for some of the Subcontinent's most exquisite temples – most notably at Khajuraho – held sway in the north.

Muslim influence started to grow in the thirteenth century, and by the mid-sixteenth century the whole region was under Mughal rule, which left its mark on the architecture

MADHYA PRADESH & CHHATTISGARH

N

HIGHLIGHTS

1. Sanchi
2. Pachmarhi
3. Orchha
4. Khajuraho
5. Kanha National Park
6. Mandu

5

CHHATTISGARH

In November 2000, sixteen districts seceded from Madhya Pradesh to form the state of **Chhattisgarh**, which has rich mineral resources but is badly affected by violent **Naxalite** (Maoist rebel groups) activities. As such, it receives a mere trickle of foreign visitors. While there are few notable attractions, the state has fascinating tribal groups, particularly in the **Bastar** region, which also boasts beautiful landscapes. However, before travelling anywhere south of the capital, **Raipur**, you must obtain up-to-date information about the **state of security** around your intended destination. **Violent conflict** between Naxalite guerrillas and state-sponsored militias continues to blight parts of southern Chhattisgarh, with some remote areas more or less permanently controlled by the rebels.

VISITING CHHATTISGARH

Parts of the state, however, are safe to visit, and two excellent operators run trips that explore the state's rich indigenous culture in areas virtually untouched by tourism. The Chhattisgarh Tourism Board's website (🌐chhattisgarhtourism.net) is a useful resource.

Shergarh Mukki, just outside Kanha National Park ☏ 90981 87246, 🌐shergarh.com. This exceptional camp (see p.381) runs two- to three-day cycle tours from Kanha National Park in Madhya Pradesh and through the pristine countryside of eastern Chhattisgarh to the Bhoromdeo Wildlife Reserve, which is home to tigers, leopards and more than 180 species of birds. Along the way you visit fascinating Gond and Baiga tribal villages and markets. Prices start at ₹4800/person/day.

Bhoromdeo Jungle Camp Bhoromdeo, a 2hr 30min drive from Raipur ☏94255 58230, 🌐bhoromdeojungleretreat.com. *Shergarh*'s tours finish at this tranquil lodge at the edge of the Bhoromdeo Wildlife Reserve. Accommodation is provided in attractive en-suite rooms thoughtfully decorated with local crafts. The owner offers sensitively run cycle and trekking tours to Kanha that involve homestays in local villages and camping. Visits to tribal markets, cookery classes and pottery sessions can all be organized. Close to the lodge is a beautiful eleventh-century Shiva temple known as the "Khajuraho of Chhattisgarh" for its erotic carvings. Prices start at ₹2500 per person per day.

and culture of Mandu, Gwalior and Bhopal, in particular. The Marathas briefly took control before the arrival of the British in the seventeenth century. Under the **British**, the middle of India was known as the "Central Provinces", and administered jointly from Nagpur (now in Maharashtra), and the summer capital Pachmarhi.

Madhya Pradesh, or **MP**, only came into being after Independence, when the Central Provinces were amalgamated with a number of smaller princedoms. Since then, the state, more than ninety percent Hindu and with a substantial rural and tribal population, has remained far more stable than neighbouring Uttar Pradesh and Bihar. Major civil unrest between Hindus and Muslims was virtually unheard of until the Bhopal riots of 1992–93, sparked off by events in Ayodhya (see p.1165). Now Hindu-Muslim relations in MP are relatively cordial again, the state has turned to focus on the latest enemy – recurring **drought** across the poverty-stricken plains and the social and environmental consequences of the damming of the Narmada River. The state remains one of India's poorest, despite flourishing automotive, cement and soybean industries, and the state government see tourism as one way of boosting Madhya Pradesh's economic prospects.

GETTING AROUND   MADHYA PRADESH

By bus Getting around Madhya Pradesh without your own vehicle normally involves a lot of bone-shaking bus journeys, usually under the auspices of MPSRTC, the state road transport authority.

By train For longer distances, trains are the best bet. The Central Railway, the main line between Mumbai and Kolkata, scythes straight through the middle of the state, forking at Itarsi junction. One branch veers north towards Bhopal, Jhansi, Gwalior and Agra, while the other continues northeast to Varanasi and eastern India via Jabalpur. In the far west, at Indore and the holy city of Ujjain, you can pick up the Western Railway, which heads up through eastern Rajasthan to Bharatpur and Delhi.

5

ACCOMMODATION

MP Tourism accommodation Madhya Pradesh Tourism (commonly known as MP Tourism) has hotels, lodges and the odd hostel scattered throughout the state, of variable standards but often in excellent locations; book them at any MP Tourism office or online at ⓦ mptourism.com.

Hotel taxes Most mid-range and top-end hotels in Madhya Pradesh charge "luxury" taxes and service charges on their rooms that can total more than 20 percent (although annoyingly few include them in their published rates). All the hotel prices given in this chapter include all taxes and other additional charges.

Bhopal

With around 1.8 million inhabitants, **BHOPAL**, Madhya Pradesh's capital, sprawls out from the eastern shores of a huge artificial lake, its packed old city surrounded by modern concrete suburbs and green hills. The nineteenth-century **mosques** emphasize its enduring Muslim legacy, while the hectic **bazaars** of the walled old city are worth a visit. Elsewhere, a couple of good archeological **museums** house hoards of ancient sculpture and the lakeside **Bharat Bhavan** ranks among India's premier centres for performing and visual arts. The **Museum of Man** on the city's outskirts is the country's most comprehensive exhibition of *adivasi* houses, culture and technology. Despite all this, Bhopal will always be known for the 1984 **gas disaster**, which continues to cast a long shadow over the city and its people.

Bhopal has two separate centres. Spread over the hills to the south of the lakes, the partially pedestrianized **New Market** area is a mix of shopping arcades, internet cafés, ice cream parlours, cinemas and office blocks. Once you've squeezed through the strip of

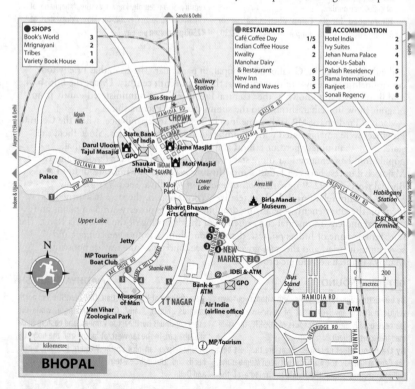

● SHOPS	
Book's World	3
Mrignayani	2
Tribes	1
Variety Book House	4

● RESTAURANTS	
Café Coffee Day	1/5
Indian Coffee House	4
Kwality	2
Manohar Dairy & Restaurant	6
New Inn	3
Wind and Waves	5

■ ACCOMMODATION	
Hotel India	2
Ivy Suites	3
Jehan Numa Palace	4
Noor-Us-Sabah	1
Palash Reseidency	5
Rama International	7
Ranjeet	6
Sonali Regency	8

BHOPAL

land that divides the Upper and (smaller) Lower lakes, sweeping avenues, civic buildings and gardens give way to the more heavily congested **old city**. This area includes the **Jama Masjid** and the bazaar, centred on **Chowk**, a dense grid of streets between the **Moti Masjid** and Hamidia Road. The art **galleries** and **museums** are on side roads off New Market, or along the hilly southern edge of the Upper Lake.

Brief history

Bhopal's name is said to derive from the eleventh-century **Raja Bhoj**, who was instructed by his court gurus to atone for the murder of his mother by linking up the nine rivers flowing through his kingdom. A dam, or *pal*, was built across one of them, and the ruler established a new capital around the two resultant lakes – **Bhojapal**. By the end of the seventeenth century, **Dost Mohammed Khan**, an erstwhile general of Aurangzeb, had occupied the now deserted site to carve out his own kingdom from the chaos left in the wake of the Mughal Empire. The Muslim dynasty he established became one of central India's leading royal families. Under the Raj, its members were among the select few to merit the accolade of a nineteen-gun salute from the British. In the nineteenth century, Bhopal was presided over largely by female rulers, who revamped the city with noble civic works, including the three sandstone **mosques** that still dominate the skyline.

Today, Bhopal carries the burden of the appalling Union Carbide factory gas disaster of 1984 (see box, p.341), with residents quick to remind you of their continuing legal and medical plight. In 1992, Hindu-Muslim rioting broke out following the destruction of the Babri Masjid in Ayodhya. However, the many tales of Hindus sheltering their Muslim friends from the mobs at this time and vice versa demonstrate the long tradition of religious tolerance in the city. In recent years, Bhopal – and Madhya Pradesh in general – has remained true to its lenient nature, with little of the political and religious intolerance that afflicts many other north Indian states.

The bazaar

Chowk • Daily except Mon • Dawn–dusk

Bhopal's lively **bazaar** provides a welcome splash of colour after the dismal, traffic-filled streets around the railway station. Famous for *zarda*, purdah, *garda* and *namarda* (tobacco, veils, dust and eunuchs), it retains a strong Muslim ambience, with overhanging balconies intricately carved with Islamic geometric designs. Each of the narrow streets radiating from the central square specializes in a different type of merchandise, including Chanderi silk saris, bass drums and clarinets, tussar silk, silver jewellery and Bhopal's famous beaded purses. At the heart of the market loom the rich red-sandstone walls and stumpy minarets of the **Jama Masjid**, built in 1837 by Kudsia Begum.

Imam Square

Southwest of Chowk

Imam Square was once the epicentre of royal Bhopal. Nowadays, it's little more than a glorified traffic island, only worth stopping at to admire the **Moti Masjid** on its eastern edge. The "Pearl Mosque", erected in 1860 by Sikander Begum, Kudsia's daughter, is a diminutive and much less imposing version of Shah Jahan's Jama Masjid in Old Delhi, notable more for its slender, gold-topped minarets and sandstone cupolas than its size.

Lining the opposite, northern side of the square near the ceremonial archway is a more eccentric nineteenth-century pile. A fusion of Italian, Gothic and Islamic influences, the **Shaukat Mahal** was originally designed by a French architect. Unfortunately, both it and the elegant **Sadar Manzil** ("Hall of Public Audience") are now government offices and closed to visitors.

5

Darul Uloom Tajul Masajid

A 5min walk west of Imam Square • Daily except Fri dawn–dusk ; closed during Id-ul-Fitr • Free

With its matching pair of colossal pink minarets soaring high above the city skyline, the **Darul Uloom Tajul Masajid** lives up to the epithet of "mother of all mosques", as denoted by the extra "a" in its name. Whether Bhopal's most impressive monument also deserves to be dubbed the biggest in India, as locals claim, is less certain. Work on the building commenced under Sultan Jehan Begum (1868–1901), the eighth ruler of Bhopal. After the death of her domineering husband, the widow queen embarked on a spending spree that left the city with a postal system, new schools and a railway, but which all but impoverished the state – and the Tajul Masajid was never actually completed.

Birla Mandir museum

East of the Lower Lake • Tues–Sun 10.30am–5.30pm • ₹100 (₹10)

The **Birla Mandir museum** collection includes some of the finest stone sculpture in Madhya Pradesh, informatively displayed with explanatory panels in English in the main galleries. The museum is in a detached mansion beside Birla Mandir, the garish modern Hindu Lakshmi Narayan temple that stands high on Arera Hill overlooking the Lower Lake. Aside from the museum itself, the **temple gardens**, which overlook the city, are a fine place to watch the sunset.

The exhibition is divided between Vishnu, the mother goddesses and Shiva. The **Vishnu** section contains some interesting representations of the god's diverse and frequently bizarre reincarnations, while in the **Devi** gallery next door, a cadaverous Chamunda (the goddess Du rga in her most terrifying aspect) stands incongruously amid a row of voluptuous maidens and fertility figures. The **Shiva** room, by contrast, is altogether more subdued. Finally, have a look at the replicas of the 3500-year-old **Harappan** artefacts encased under the stairs.

Bharat Bhavan Arts Centre

Lake Drive Road, on the eastern tip of the Upper Lake • Tues–Sun: Feb–Oct 2–8pm; Nov–Jan 1–7pm • ₹10, free on Fri

The **Bharat Bhavan Arts Centre** was set up in 1982 as part of a wider government project to promote visual and performing arts in Indian state capitals. The initiative fizzled out after prime minister Indira Gandhi's death, but Bharat Bhavan has since become provincial India's pre-eminent arts centre.

Inside Goan architect Charles Correa's campus of concrete domes and dour brickwork are temporary exhibitions as well as a large split-level **permanent collection** of modern Indian painting and sculpture. Rather incongruously placed amid the latter, look out for an eighteenth-century gilt-framed landscape by the Daniells – the uncle-nephew duo employed as a part of the Company School of Painting during the Raj.

Bharat Bhavan has a gallery devoted exclusively to **adivasi art**, in search of which talent scouts spent months roaming remote regions. Among their more famous discoveries was the Gond painter **Jangarh Singh Shyam**. Many of his works are on display here, along with a colourful assemblage of masks, terracottas, woodcarvings and ritual paraphernalia.

Museum of Man

Just off Shamla Hills Rd, south of the Upper Lake • Tues–Sun: March–Aug 11am–6.30pm; Sept–Feb 10am–5.30pm • ₹10, vehicle ₹10 video ₹50 • A roundtrip by auto-rickshaw from the city centre costs around ₹200–300 including waiting time

The story of India's indigenous minorities – the *adivasi*, literally "original inhabitants" – is all too familiar. Dispossessed of their land by large-scale development projects or exploitative moneylenders, the "tribals" have seen a gradual erosion of their traditional

5

THE BHOPAL GAS TRAGEDY

At 12.05am on December 3, 1984, a lethal cloud of methyl isocyanate (MIC), a toxic chemical used in the manufacture of pesticides, exploded at the huge, US-owned Union Carbide plant on the northern edge of Bhopal.

Highly reactive, MIC must be kept under constant pressure at a temperature of 0°C – yet cost-conscious officials had reduced the pressure to save some $70 a day. When water entered tank E-610 through badly maintained and leaking valves to contaminate the MIC, a massive reaction was triggered. Wind dispersed the gas throughout the densely populated residential districts and slums. There was neither a warning siren nor adequate emergency procedures in place, leaving the thick cloud of gas to blind and suffocate its victims. The leak killed 1600 instantly (according to official figures) and between 7000 and 10,000 in the aftermath, but the figure now totals well over 23,000 in the years since the incident. More than 500,000 people were exposed to the gas, of whom about one fifth have been left with chronic and incurable health problems, often passed on to children born in years following the tragedy. The water in the community pumps of the affected residential areas remains contaminated with dangerous toxic chemicals that seeped out from the now-deserted factory. Campaigners say the factory still contains thousands of tonnes of toxic waste.

EVADING RESPONSIBILITY

Though the incidence of TB, cancers, infertility and cataracts in the affected area remains way above the national average, the factory officials initially said the effect of MIC was akin to that of tear gas, causing only temporary health problems. They accepted moral responsibility for the accident, but blamed the Indian government for inadequate safety standards when it came to the issue of compensation. Only in 1989 did Union Carbide agree to pay an average of ₹25,000 to each adult victim – a paltry sum that didn't even cover loans for the medical bills in the first five years, let alone compensate for the loss of life and livelihoods and other consequences of the disaster. In 2001, the Bhopal Memorial Hospital and Research Centre opened to treat patients.

Despite both US and Indian former bosses being charged with serious offences – including manslaughter – the government and factory authorities had been keen to sweep the whole episode under the carpet. It took until June 2010 for some measure of justice to be dispensed, when a Bhopal court gave seven former factory employees two-year prison sentences for causing "death by negligence". The court also fined the former Indian unit of Union Carbide ₹500,000. NGOs and local campaigners dismissed the ruling as completely inadequate. Warren Anderson, the former CEO of Union Carbide in the US, has yet to face justice; in 2002, a Bhopal court directed India's Central Bureau of Investigation to pursue his extradition, but the US authorities have so far refused to extradite him. (Anderson fled India after the court there granted him bail.)

After much lobbying, the government in 2005 launched a legal case to recoup money from Dow Chemical, which bought Union Carbide in 2001 but denies ongoing liability. To date, little progress has been made but people in Bhopal continue to stage regular protests and rallies.

FIND OUT MORE

If you're interested in learning more about the disaster or volunteering your services, contact the Sambhavna Trust at Bafna Colony, Berasia Road, Bhopal (☎0755 273 0914, ⌨bhopal.org). *Five Past Midnight in Bhopal* by Dominique Lapierre and Javier Moro, and the Booker Prize-nominated *Animal's People* by Indra Sinha are both highly recommended further reading.

culture. The **Museum of Man**, or the Rashtriya Manav Sangrahalaya, is an enlightened attempt to redress the balance.

Overlooking New Market on one side and the majestic sweep of Upper Lake on the other, the 200-acre hilltop site includes a reconstructed Keralan coastal village and a winding trail where each tribal group from the state has contributed an interpretation own creation myth. A large exhibition hall draws on all the daily and ritual elements in the *adivasi* lifestyle, and dotted among the forest scrub are botanical trails, a research centre and a permanent open-air display of traditional *adivasi* buildings.

5

Van Vihar Zoological Park

Lake Drive Rd, south of the Upper Lake • Sat–Thurs Fri 7–11am & 2–6pm • ₹200 (₹20) • For transport around the park, an auto-rickshaw is ₹200 plus the ₹20 entrance fee for the driver

A trip to the **Van Vihar Zoological Park** ties in nicely with a visit to the Museum of Man next door – keep the same auto-rickshaw for the whole trip. The stars of the park are a couple of regal white tigers, but there are also gharial, leopards, Himalayan bears and tigers. You can get a longer look at the 207 species of birds by taking a boat from the jetty 0.5km northeast of the park gate.

ARRIVAL AND DEPARTURE

BHOPAL

BY PLANE

Bhopal's airport is 12km north of the city: a taxi to/from the city centre costs around ₹400, an auto-rickshaw roughly half that. Air India (☎0755 277 0480) has an office in Airlines House on Bhadbhada Rd, TT Nagar, while Jet Airways (☎0755 276 0371) is based in Ranjit Towers on MP Nagar Rd, a 15min auto-rickshaw ride south of New Market. Ventura AirConnect (☎1860 500 4455, ⓦventuraairconnect.in), which has an office in Palash Residency, has flights to various cities and towns within Madhya Pradesh.

Destinations Ahmedabad (1 daily; 1hr 30min); Delhi (2 daily; 1hr 15min–40min); Gwalior (3 weekly; 1hr 20min); Hyderabad (1 daily; 2hr 5min); Indore (1–2 daily; 45min); Jabalpur (6 weekly; 1hr 10min); Khajuraho (3 weekly; 1hr 10min); Lucknow (1 daily; 1hr 30min); Mumbai (2 daily; 1hr 35min); Raipur (1 daily; 1hr 35min).

BY TRAIN

The main railway station, Bhopal Junction, is close to the centre: to reach the hotel district, leave by the exit on platforms 4 or 5 and head to the busy corner of Hamidia Rd. Approaching Bhopal from the south, most trains also stop briefly at Habibganj Station, a long way out. There's a pre-paid taxi and auto-rickshaw booth outside the railway station on Hamidia Rd. The quickest and most convenient train to Delhi is the *Shatabdi Express* #12001, which travels via Jhansi (for Orchha/Khajuraho; 3hr

6min), Gwalior and Agra. One of the most convenient trains to Mumbai is the *Punjab Mail* #12138 (daily 4.55pm; 14hr 40min).

Destinations Agra (every 30min–1hr; 5hr 45min–9hr 10min); Delhi (every 30min–1hr; 8–13hr 10min); Gwalior (every 30min–1hr; 4hr 16min–8hr 25min); Indore (6–7 daily; 3hr 50min–6hr 15min); Jabalpur (7–8 daily; 5hr 15min–12hr 50min); Jhansi (every 30min–1hr; 3hr 6min–5hr); Mumbai (7–8 daily; 13hr 40min–16hr 30min); Varanasi (1 daily; 16hr 15min).

BY BUS

The main state bus stand, used by services to/from Indore, Pachmarhi, and Sanchi, is a 10min walk southwest of the railway station on Hamidia Rd. MP Tourism runs quick and comfortable a/c buses between Bhopal and Indore; for Ujjain, get off at Dewas and pick up a local bus for the remaining 37km. Bus services to destinations beyond Madhya Pradesh generally arrive at and depart from the Inter-State Bus Terminal (ISBT), located close to the Habibganj railway station (though the train is almost always a better bet for these journeys).

Tickets Tickets should be booked in advance, either online (ⓦmptourism.com) or at *Palash Residency* (see opposite), where the buses arrive and depart.

Destinations Indore (every 30min; 4–5hr); Pachmarhi (6–7 daily; 6hr 30min–7hr 30min); Sanchi (every 30min; 1hr 30min).

GETTING AROUND

By auto-rickshaw Most of Bhopal's principal places of interest are so far apart that the best way of getting around is by auto-rickshaw.

By taxi Taxis can be organized through your hotel or one of the MP Tourism offices.

INFORMATION

Tourist information The MP Tourism head office (☎0755 277 8383, ⓦmptourism.com; Mon–Sat 10am–5.30pm) is inconveniently located in Paryatan Bhawan on Bhadbhada Rd, 2km south of New Market. There are also smaller branches at the railway station

(platform 1 exit; daily 8am–8pm; ☎0755 274 6827) and at the airport (opens to meet incoming flights). You can book an MP Tourism tour, hotel or a/c bus to Indore at the booth (daily 8am–8pm; ☎0755 329 5040) at *Palash Residency* (see opposite).

TOURS

Tours MP Tourism runs a city bus tour (Tues–Sun 11am–3.30pm; ₹60), which leaves from *Palash Residency*.

MP Tourism's Boat Club operates speedboat trips (₹40/5min) on the Upper Lake.

ACCOMMODATION

If you're not bothered by traffic noise and fumes, **Hamidia Rd**, Bhopal's busy main thoroughfare, is the most convenient **place to stay**. Shoestring options are thin on the ground and even the dingiest dives will slap a ten percent **"luxury" tax** onto your bill (and often a service charge too). Most of Bhopal's top hotels are close to **Upper Lake** in the Shamla Hills area, a 15min ride from the railway station.

Hotel India New Market ☎0755 255 4594. Smoothly run by the *Indian Coffee House* co-operative, this hotel has clean and comfortable mid-range rooms with attached bathrooms, TVs and phones. A/c costs extra. It's very popular, so book in advance. ₹1300

★ **Ivy Suites** A. Nadir Colony, Shamla Hills ☎0755 423 5508, ⒲ivysuites.com. Tucked away in a smart housing estate, this wonderfully relaxed guesthouse has ten spacious rooms, each thoughtfully furnished with paintings, books and plants; those upstairs have ivy-filled balconies overlooking the Upper Lake. ₹4200

Jehan Numa Palace 157 Shamla Hills Rd ☎0755 266 1100, ⒲hoteljehanumapalace.com. Bhopal's top hotel is a palazzo-style building set around a central courtyard covered by bougainvillea-clad walkways. The luxurious rooms are all of a high standard, though the cheaper ones are a bit tight, and there are three fabulous restaurants. ₹8500

Noor-Us-Sabah Palace Grounds, VIP Rd ☎0755 522 3333, ⒲noorussabahpalace.com. The "Light of Dawn" is an impeccably renovated 1920s nawab's palace, perched on a hill overlooking the Upper Lake. Opulent rooms come with elegant mirrors, regal red furniture and private balconies, and there's a pool and a fine restaurant. ₹7950

Palash Residency T T Nagar Rd, near New Market ☎0755 255 3006, ⒲mptourism.com. One of the better MP Tourism-run hotels, albeit overpriced. Each of the rooms has plenty of space, flatscreen TVs, kettles and small baskets of toiletries. There's a restaurant and bar, and rates include breakfast. Booking is advised. ₹3550

Rama International Hamidia Rd ☎0755 274 0542. Set back from the main road, and very popular with Indian tourists, *Rama International* is a rambling, relatively peaceful hotel with clean and simple rooms (all have private bathrooms and either fans or a/c). ₹650

Ranjeet Hamidia Rd ☎0755 274 0500. The green marble lobby gives off a subterranean feel, but the rooms here are bright enough and come with complimentary breakfast. Those at the front can be very noisy, so ask for one at the back. 24hr checkout. ₹650

Sonali Regency Just off Hamidia Rd ☎0755 274 0880, Ⓔsonali@mantrafreenet.com. Quieter than the other hotels in the area, and although the cheapest rooms are boxy and the beds a bit hard, they all boast TVs and clean private bathrooms. Nice touches like free newspapers, internet access, 24hr checkout and good service give *Sonali Regency* the edge over its similarly-priced competitors nearby. ₹650

EATING

Decent restaurants are relatively thin on the ground. The larger hotels serve uniform multicuisine menus, while the canteens opposite the bus stand do thalis and *subzi*, rice and dhal for next to nothing. For breakfast, try the local favourites, *poha* (a steamed rice cake) and *katchori* (a fried, lentil-stuffed snack).

Café Coffee Day Lake View Drive ☎0755 266 8822, ⒲cafecoffeeday.com. This outpost of the Indian chain has a great location overlooking the Upper Lake, and the coffee (from around ₹50) is as reliable as ever. There's another branch on Bhadbada Rd, near New Market. Daily 9am–10.30pm.

Indian Coffee House Hotel India ☎0755 255 4594. Aside from a couple of vintage coffee posters, the dining hall is nondescript, but the filter coffee (₹12), south Indian breakfast options (₹40–90), main meals (₹60–260) and service from the white-suited waiters are all excellent. Daily 8am–10.30pm.

Kwality New Market ☎0755 255 4744. Popular branch of the national chain, with outdoor seating, a busy self-service canteen area and a more sedate a/c dining room. There is a vast array of veg snacks (₹30–150) like *pani puri* and economical "mini meals", as well as so-so pizzas and better Chinese and Indian mains. Daily 8am–10.30pm.

Manohar Dairy & Restaurant Hamidia Rd ☎0755 274 0454. Bustling fast-food-style joint where yellow-shirted waiters dish up a steady stream of *katchoris*, veg burgers, pizzas and ice cream sundaes. There's also an attached sweet shop. Snacks ₹30–100. Daily 8am–11pm.

New Inn Bhadbhada Rd, New Market ☎0755 422 3777. Behind the glass frontage, incongruously decorated with a dragon motif, is a garish mix of yellow and orange walls and brown leather seats. Thankfully the keenly priced food – particularly the kebabs (₹80–155) and the south Indian breakfast options (₹30–60) – is far better judged. Daily 8am–10pm.

Wind and Waves Lake Drive Rd ☎0755 266 1523. While the standard MP Tourism menu (Indian, Chinese and some Continental dishes) holds few surprises, the setting – conveniently close to the museums and boat club, and overlooking the Upper Lake – is appealing, and there's a bar (beer from around ₹220) upstairs. Daily noon–3pm & 7–10.30pm.

SHOPPING

THE BAZAARS

Chowk (bazaar Mon–Sat) is the best place for silk and silver. The New Market area has some bigger stores.

Mrignayani New Market ☎0755 255 4162. The state-run, fixed-price Mrignayani has everything from batiks to bedspreads; there's also a branch on Hamidia Rd. Tues–Sun 11am–8pm.

Tribes New Market ☎0755 257 9644. Close to the New Market branch of Mrignayani, this national government-run store sells a selection of *adivasi* goods at fixed prices. Tues–Sun 11am–8pm.

BOOKSTORES

Book's World Bhadbada Rd, New Market, opposite Variety Book House. Worth a look – although most of its secondhand books are trashy fiction, you can sometimes dig out the odd gem. Daily 10am–6pm.

Variety Book House Bhadbada Rd, New Market ☎0755 255 6022. Bhopal's best collection of English-language, fiction, non-fiction and magazines. Daily 10am–9pm.

DIRECTORY

Banks and exchange Only the main banks in New Market and the top hotels offer foreign exchange. ATMs are common: the State Bank of India is by the GPO; IDBI bank is opposite.

Hospital The public Hamidia Hospital (☎0755 254 0222) is on Sultania Rd, between Imam Square and the Darul Uloom Tajul Masajid. The small, private Hajela Hospital (☎0755 277

3392), on Sultania Rd in Geetanjali, also has a good reputation.

Internet Try the unnamed internet café near *Ranjeet* hotel or Hub, opposite the State Bank of India in New Market. (20/hr).

Post office The Head Post Office is just off Bhadbhada Rd, in New Market; there's also a GPO on Sultania Rd near the Darul Uloom Tajul Masajid.

Around Bhopal

A wealth of impressive ancient monuments lie within a couple of hours' journey from Bhopal. To the northeast, the third-century BC *stupas* at **Sanchi** are an easy day-trip. Its peaceful setting also makes an ideal base for visits to more *stupas* at **Satdhara** or **Udaigiri**'s rock-cut caves and the nearby Column of Heliodorus at **Besnagar**. South towards Hoshangabad and the Narmada Valley, the prehistoric cave paintings at **Bhimbetka** can be visited in a day by bus.

Sanchi

From a distance, the smooth-sided hemispherical object that appears on a hillock overlooking the main train line at **Sanchi**, 46km northeast of Bhopal, has the surreal air of an upturned satellite dish. In fact, the giant stone mound stands as testimony to a much older means of communing with the cosmos. Quite apart from being India's finest Buddhist monument, the **Great Stupa** is one of the earliest religious structures in the Subcontinent. It presides over a complex of ruined temples and monasteries that collectively provide a rich and unbroken record of the development of Buddhist art and architecture from the faith's first emergence in central India during the third century BC, until it was eventually squeezed out by the resurgence of Brahmanism during the medieval era.

Brief history

Unlike other famous Buddhist centres in eastern India and Nepal, Sanchi has no known connection with Buddha himself. It first became a place of pilgrimage when the Mauryan emperor **Ashoka**, who married a woman from nearby Besnagar (see p.349), erected a polished stone pillar and brick-and-mortar *stupa* here midway through the third century BC. The complex was enlarged by successive dynasties, but after the eclipse of Buddhism, Sanchi lay deserted and overgrown until its rediscovery in 1818 by General Taylor of the Bengal Cavalry. In the following years a swarm of heavy-handed treasure hunters invaded the site, yet the explorer Sir Alexander Cunningham was the only one to find anything more than rubble; in 1851, he unearthed two soapstone relic boxes, containing bone fragments and bearing the names of two of Buddha's most noted followers, Sariputra and Maha-Mogalanasa. Historians equated the discovery with "finding the graves of Saints Peter and Paul". The find transformed Sanchi, for centuries neglected, into a Buddhist place of pilgrimage once again.

By the 1880s, amateur archeologists had left the ruins in a sorry state. Deep gouges gaped from the sides of *stupas* 1 and 2, a couple of ceremonial gateways had completely collapsed and much of the masonry was plundered by local villagers. **Restoration work** made little impact until 1912, when the jungle was hacked away, the main *stupas* and temples rebuilt, lawns and trees planted and a museum erected to house what sculpture had not been shipped off to Delhi or London.

The Great Stupa
Daily 8am–6pm · ₹250 (₹10), video ₹25, car ₹10

Floating serenely above a vast expanse of open plains, Sanchi's ruins have preserved the tranquillity that attracted the original occupants. Most visitors find a couple of hours sufficient to explore the site, though you could easily spend several days poring over the four exquisite gateways, or **toranas**, surrounding the Great Stupa. Paved walkways and steps lead around the hilltop enclosure, dotted with interpretative panels and shady trees.

Stupa 1, the **Great Stupa**, stands at the western edge of the plateau and is surrounded by some of the richest and best-preserved ancient sculpture you're likely to see in situ. Fragments of the original construction, a much smaller version built in the third century BC by Ashoka, lie entombed beneath the thick outer shell of lime plaster added a century later. The **Shungas** were responsible for the raised processional balcony, and the two graceful staircases that curve gently around the sides of the drum from the paved walkway at ground level, as well as the aerial-like *chhattra* and its square enclosure which crown the top of the mound. Four elaborate gateways were added by the **Satavahanas** in the first century BC, followed by the four serene meditating **Buddhas** that greet you as you pass through the main entrances. Carved out of local sandstone, these were installed during the Gupta era, around 450 AD, by which time figurative depictions of Buddha had become acceptable (elsewhere in Sanchi, Buddha is represented by an empty throne, a wheel, a pair of footprints and even a parasol).

As you move gradually closer to the *stupa*, the extraordinary wealth of sculpture adorning the **toranas** slips slowly into focus. Every conceivable space on the 8m upright posts and three curving cross-bars teems with delicate figures of humans, demigods

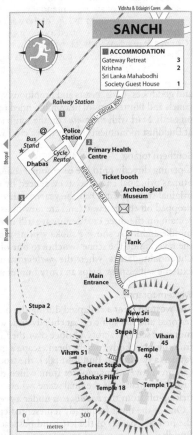

Vidisha & Udaigiri Caves

SANCHI

N

■ ACCOMMODATION	
Gateway Retreat	3
Krishna	2
Sri Lanka Mahabodhi Society Guest House	1

Railway Station

BHOPAL - VIDISHA ROAD

Bus Stand

Police Station

Cycle Rental

Dhabas

Primary Health Centre

MONUMENTS ROAD

Ticket booth

Archeological Museum

Tank

Main Entrance

Stupa 2

New Sri Lankan Temple

Stupa 3

Vihara 45

Vihara 51

Temple 40

The Great Stupa

Ashoka's Pillar

Temple 18

Temple 17

0   300
metres

5

STUPAS

The hemispherical mounds known as *stupas* have been central to Buddhist worship since the sixth century BC, when Buddha himself modelled the first prototype. Asked by one of his disciples for a symbol to help disseminate his teachings after his death, Buddha took his begging bowl, teaching staff and a length of cloth – his only worldly possessions – and arranged them into the form of a *stupa*, using the cloth as a base, the upturned bowl as the dome and the stick as the projecting finial, or spire.

Originally, *stupas* were simple burial mounds, but as the religion spread, the basic components multiplied and became imbued with **symbolic significance**. The main dome, or **anda** – representing the "divine axis" linking heaven and earth – grew larger, while the wooden railings, or **vedikas**, surrounding it were replaced by massive stone ones. A raised ambulatory terrace, or **medhi**, was added to the vertical sides of the drum, along with two flights of stairs and four ceremonial entrances, carefully aligned with the cardinal points. Finally, crowning the tip of the *stupa*, the single spike evolved into a three-tiered umbrella, or **chhattra**, standing for the Three Jewels of Buddhism: the Buddha, the Law and the community of monks.

The *chhattra*, usually enclosed within a low square stone railing, or **harmika**, formed the topmost point of the axis, directly above the reliquary in the heart of the *stupa*. Ranging from bits of bone wrapped in cloth to fine caskets of precious metals, crystal and carved stone, the reliquaries were the "seeds" and their protective mounds the "egg". Excavations of the 84,000 *stupas* scattered around the Subcontinent have shown that the solid interiors were also sometimes built as elaborate **mandalas** – symbolic patterns that exerted a beneficial influence over the *stupa* and those who walked around it. The ritual of circumambulation, or **pradhakshina**, which enabled the worshipper to tap into cosmic energy and be transported from the mundane to the divine realms, was always carried out in a clockwise direction from the east, imitating the sun's passage across the heavens.

and goddesses, birds, beasts and propitious symbols. In between are purely decorative panels and illustrations of heaven intended to inspire worshippers to lead meritorious lives on earth. Start with the *torana* on the south side, which is the oldest, and, as is the custom at Buddhist monuments, proceed in a clockwise direction around the *stupa*.

Southern torana

Opening directly onto the ceremonial staircase, the **southern torana** was the Great Stupa's principal entrance, as evidenced by the proximity of the stump of Ashoka's original stone pillar. Over the years, some of the panels with the best sculpture have dropped off the gateway (and are now housed in the site museum), but those that remain on the three crossbeams are still in reasonable condition. A carved frieze on the middle architrave shows Ashoka visiting a *stupa* in a traditional show of veneration. On the reverse side the scene switches to one of the Buddha's previous incarnations, the **Chhaddanta Jataka**, where the *bodhisattva* adopts the guise of an elephant who, in extreme selflessness, helps an ivory hunter saw off his own (six) tusks.

Western torana

The **western torana** collapsed during the nineteenth century, but has been skilfully restored and has some of Sanchi's liveliest sculpture. In the top right panel, a troupe of monkeys scurries across a bridge over the Ganges, made by the *bodhisattva*, their leader, from his own body to help them escape a gang of soldiers. According to the **Mahakapi Jataka** (a traditional Buddhist tale), the troops were dispatched by the local king to capture a coveted mango tree from which the monkeys had been feeding. You can also just about make out the final scene, where the repentant monarch gets a stern ticking-off from the *bodhisattva* under a *peepal* tree.

One of the most frequently represented episodes from the life of Buddha features on the first two panels of the left-hand post facing the *stupa*. In the **Temptation of Mara**, Buddha, who has vowed to remain under the *bodhi* tree until he attains enlightenment, heroically ignores the attempts of the evil demon Mara to distract him with violent threats and her seductive daughters.

Northern torana

Crowned with a fragmented Wheel of Law and two tridents symbolizing the Buddhist trinity, the **northern torana** is the most elaborate and best preserved of the four gateways. Scenes crammed onto its two vertical posts include Buddha performing an aerial promenade and a monkey presenting him with a bowl of honey. Straddling the two pillars, a bas-relief on both faces of the lowest crossbeam depicts the **Vessantara Jataka** (another traditional Buddhist tale), telling of a *bodhisattva*-prince banished by his father for giving away a magical rain-making elephant. A better view of the inner, south-facing side of the plaque can be had from the balcony of the *stupa*'s raised terrace. Note the little tableau on the far right showing the royal family trudging through the jungle.

Eastern torana

Leaning languorously into space from the right capital of the **eastern torana** is Sanchi's most celebrated piece of sculpture, the sensuous **salabhanjika**, or wood-nymph. The full-breasted fertility goddess is one of several such figures that once blessed worshippers as they entered the Great Stupa. Most of the others are now in museums in Los Angeles and London.

Panels on the inner face of the pillar below the *salabhanjika* depict scenes from the life of the Buddha, including his conception when the *bodhisattva* entered the body of his mother, Maya, in the form of a white elephant. The front face of the middle architrave picks up the tale some years later, when the young Buddha, represented by a riderless horse, makes his **great departure** from the palace where he grew up to begin the life of a wandering ascetic. The reverse side shows the fully enlightened Buddha, symbolized by an empty throne.

Elsewhere around the enclosure

Of the dozens of other numbered ruins around the 400m enclosure, only a handful are of more than passing interest. The smaller, plainer but immaculately restored **Stupa 3**, immediately northeast of Stupa 1, is upstaged by its slightly older cousin in every way but one. In 1851, a pair of priceless reliquaries was discovered deep in the middle of the mound. The caskets were found to contain relics belonging to two of Buddha's closest disciples. In one, fragments of bone were encased with beads made from pearls, crystal, amethyst, lapis lazuli and gypsum, while on the lid, the initial of the saint they are thought to have belonged to, Sariputra, was painted in ink. Previously kept in London's British Museum, both are now in the new Buddhist temple outside the *stupa* enclosure and are brought out for public view for one day in late November.

The eastern edge

From Stupa 3, pick your way through the clutter of pillars, small *stupa*s and exposed temple floors nearby to the large complex of interconnecting raised terraces at the far **eastern edge** of the site. The most intact monastery of the bunch, **Vihara 45**, dates from the ninth and tenth centuries and has the usual layout of cells ranged around a central courtyard. Originally, a colossal, richly decorated sanctuary tower soared high above the complex, but this collapsed, leaving the inner sanctum exposed. The river goddesses Ganga and Yamuna number among the skilfully sculpted figures flanking the entrance to the shrine itself. Inside, Buddha still reigns supreme.

The enclosure's tenth-century eastern **boundary wall** is the best place from which to enjoy Sanchi's serene **views**. To the northeast, a huge, sheer-sided rock rises from the midst of Vidisha, near the site of the ancient city that sponsored the monasteries here (traces of the **pilgrimage** trail between Besnagar and Sanchi can still be seen crossing the hillside below). South from the hill, a wide expanse of well-watered wheat-fields

5

stretches off towards the angular sandstone ridges of the Raisen escarpment.

The southern area

The **southern area** of the enclosure harbours some of Sanchi's most interesting temples. Pieces of burnt wood dug from the foundations of **Temple 40** prove that the present apsidal-ended *chaitya* was built on top of an earlier structure contemporaneous with the Mauryan Stupa 1. **Temple 17** is a fine example of early Gupta architecture and the precursor of the classical Hindu design developed later in Orissa and Khajuraho.

Before leaving the enclosure, hunt out the stump of **Ashoka's Pillar** on the right of Stupa 1's southern *torana*. The Mauryan emperor erected columns like this all over the empire to mark sacred sites and pilgrims' trails. Its finely polished shaft was originally crowned with the magnificent lion capital now housed in the site museum. The inscription etched around its base is in the Brahmi script, recording Ashoka's edicts in Pali, the early Buddhist language and forerunner of Sanskrit.

The western slope

A flight of steps beside Stupa 1 leads down the **western slope** of Sanchi hill to the village, passing two notable monuments. The bottom portions of the thick stone walls of **Vihara 51** have been carefully restored to show its floorplan of 22 cells around a paved central courtyard. Further down, the second-century BC **Stupa 2** stands on an artificial ledge, well below the main enclosure – probably because its relics were less important than those of *stupas* 1 and 3. The ornamental railings and gateways around it are certainly no match for those up the hill, although the carvings of lotus medallions and mythical beasts that decorate them are worth close scrutiny. The straps dangling from some of the horseriders' saddles are believed to mark the first appearance in India of stirrups.

The archeological museum

Daily except Fri 10am–5pm • ₹5

Sanchi's small **archeological museum**, to the left of the road up to the hilltop, houses a modest collection of artefacts, mostly fragments of sculpture, jewellery, pottery, weapons and tools. Its **main hall** contains the most impressive pieces, including the famous Ashokan lion-capital (see above) and two damaged *salabhanjikas* from the gateways of *Stupa* 1. Also of note are the distinctive Mathuran red-sandstone Buddhas.

ARRIVAL AND INFORMATION   SANCHI

By train There are four daily trains (28min–1hr 45min) between Bhopal and Sanchi; those travelling to Sanchi are much quicker than those travelling from Sanchi. The nearest mainline station is Vidisha, 10km northeast and connected by plenty of local buses; there are daily trains to/ from Mumbai and Delhi.

By bus Buses from Bhopal to Sanchi (1hr 30min) depart every 30mins from the Hamidia Rd bus stand. To catch a bus back to Bhopal, wait opposite the *Gateway Retreat* (see below) and flag one down.

Information A handful of wooden stalls surround the bus stand, constituting Sanchi's tiny bazaar, where there's also an internet café. Staff at the *Gateway Retreat* can provide local information. You can rent bicycles for around ₹50/day from the bazaar. Power cuts occur frequently, so bring a torch. The *dhabas* and stalls by the bus stand serve inexpensive thalis. Try the local speciality, sweet coconut *nariyal* samosas.

ACCOMMODATION AND EATING

Gateway Retreat On the Bhopal–Vidisha Rd ☏ 07482 266723. MP Tourism's accommodation option is Sanchi's smartest, with slightly overpriced whitewashed a/c rooms set in neatly tended grounds. It's often busy, so book ahead. There also a reliable, if unexciting, restaurant here, as well as Sanchi's only bar. **₹2140**

Krishna Above the chemist shop on the Bhopal–Vidisha Rd ☏ 07482 266610. This friendly, family-run place has the best set-up for backpackers, with clean tiled rooms (the best are at the back), squat or sit-down toilets and a roof terrace facing the *stupas*. Inexpensive pancakes, sandwiches, noodles and Indian main meals are also available. **₹500**

Sri Lanka Mahabodhi Society Guest House Near the railway station ☏ 07482 266699. Low-cost accommodation – primarily aimed at visiting Buddhists, though other tourists are very welcome – offering spartan rooms with shared facilities facing a shady garden, and more comfortable (and expensive) attached rooms. ₹300

Satdhara

Perched on the edge of a dramatic ravine amid rolling hills 30km north of Bhopal, the rarely visited **Satdhara** ("seven streams") is well worth the detour for *stupa* enthusiasts, though you'll need your own vehicle to get here. There are 34 **stupas** dating from the Mauryan period in the third century BC, and fourteen monasteries, three of which have substantial foundations still visible. Several *stupas* and two of the **monasteries** have been reconstructed using original methods and materials, and others are under renovation.

Stupa 1, standing 13m high and with a *medhi* (broad circumambulatory path) around the base, is the most impressive of the *stupas*. Immediately behind it is the imposing 3m-tall foundation platform of **Monastery 1**, while to the right are two circular **mills**, where oxen still push a great stone around a rut to crush the lime, sand and stone rubble for cement – the technique used by the original architects.

Vidisha and around

The main reason to call in at the bustling market town of **Vidisha**, a 56km train or bus ride from Bhopal, and also served by buses from nearby Sanchi, is to hop on a tonga to the archeological sites at **Udaigiri** and **Besnagar**.

The museum

Behind the railway station in the east of town • Tues–Sun 10am–5pm • ₹50 (₹5)

If you're not pushed for time, it's worth popping into Vidisha's small **museum** for a quick look. The majority of its pieces, such as Kubera Yaksha, the 3m, pot-bellied male fertility figure in the hallway, are second-century Hindu artefacts unearthed at Besnagar.

Udaigiri

6km west of Vidisha • Daily sunrise–sunset • Free • Take a tonga or auto-rickshaw from Vidisha (around ₹100), hire a bike from one of the shops in Vidisha's bazaar or cycle from Sanchi, though this is more strenuous (1–2hr)

A modest collection of ruined temples and fifth-century rock-cut caves stand just 6km west of Vidisha at **Udaigiri**. The caves, many decorated by Hindu and Jain mendicants, lie scattered around a long, thin outcrop of sandstone surrounded by wheat fields.

Once you've left Vidisha, a left turn just after crossing the Betwa River leads along a gently undulating tree lined avenue for 2–3km. As it approaches the hillside, the road takes a sharp left turn towards the village. Stop here, at the base of the near-vertical rock face, to climb a steep flight of steps to **Cave 19**, which has worn reliefs of gods and demons around the doorways, and a **Jain cave temple** on the northern edge of the ridge. Ask the *chowkidar* to unlock the doors for you.

The site's *pièce de résistance*, a 4m-high image of the boar-headed hero Varaha, stands carved into **Cave 5**. Vishnu adopted this guise to rescue the earth-goddess, Prithvi, from the churning primordial ocean. Varaha's left foot rests on a naga king wearing a hood of thirteen cobra heads, while the river goddesses Ganga and Yamuna hold water vessels on either side. In the background you can see Brahma and Agni, the Vedic fire-god. The scene is seen as an allegory of the emperor Chandra Gupta II's conquest of northern India.

Besnagar

5km west of the Udaigiri turn-off • Daily sunrise–sunset • Free • Take a tonga or auto-rickshaw (around ₹150-300) from Vidisha or Sanchi

The ruins of ancient **Besnagar**, known locally as **Khambaba**, are in a tiny village down the main road from Vidisha. During the Mauryan and Shunga empires, between the third and first centuries BC, a thriving provincial capital overlooked the confluence of the Beas

5

and Betwa rivers. The emperor Ashoka himself was once governor here and even married a local banker's daughter. Now, a few mounds and some scattered pieces of masonry are all that remain. Yet one small monument makes the short detour worthwhile. The sixteen-sided stone pillar in an enclosed courtyard, known as the **Column of Heliodorus**, was erected in 113 BC by a Bactrian-Greek envoy from Taxila, the capital city of Gandhara (now the northwest frontier region of Pakistan), who converted to the local Vaishnavite cult during his long diplomatic posting here. The shaft, dedicated to Krishna's father Vasudeva, was originally crowned with a statue of Vishnu's vehicle Garuda.

Bhimbetka

45km southeast of Bhopal • Daily sunrise–sunset • ₹10 (₹2) • Regular buses (every 30min–1hr; 1hr) run from Bhopal's Hamidia Rd bus stand to the town of Obaidullaganj, 7km away from Bhimbetka, from where you can take an auto-rickshaw (around ₹100) to the site

Shortly after NH-12 peels away from the main Bhopal–Hoshangabad road, 45km southeast of Bhopal, a long line of boulders appears high on a scrub-covered ridge to the west. The hollows, overhangs and crevices eroded over the millennia from the crags of this malleable sandstone outcrop harbour one of the world's largest collections of **prehistoric rock art**. Discovered in 1957, **Bhimbetka** makes a fascinating day-trip.

Around half the thousand **shelters** so far catalogued along the 10km-long hilltop contain rock paintings, dating from three different periods. The oldest (around ten thousand years old) are green outline drawings of human figures and large red images of animals. The second, more prolific phase accounts for the bulk of Bhimbetka's rock art, and were created in the "Stone Age" – between 8000 and 5000 BC. These friezes depict dynamic hunting scenes full of rampaging animals, initiation ceremonies, burials, masked dances, sports, wars, pregnant women and a drinking party. Bhimbetka's third and final spate of cave painting took place during the early historic period; the stylized, geometric figures bear a strong resemblance to the art still produced by the region's *adivasi* groups.

From the car park at the top of the hill, a paved pathway winds through the jumble of rocks containing the most striking and accessible of Bhimbetka's art. The *chowkidars* will show you around for a bit of baksheesh. Look out for the Paleolithic images in green, the wonderful "X-ray" animals filled in with cross-hatching and complex geometric designs, and the recurrent image of a bull chasing a human figure and a crab – believed to represent a struggle between the totemic heroes of three different tribes.

Pachmarhi

Among the last tracts of central India mapped by the British, the **Mahadeo Hills** weren't explored until 1857, when Captain J. Forsyth and his party of Bengal Lancers stumbled upon an idyllic saucer-shaped plateau at the heart of the range, strewn with huge boulders and crisscrossed by streams. Five years later a road was cut from the railhead at **Piparia**, and by the end of the century **Pachmarhi** had become the summer capital of the entire Central Provinces, complete with a military sanatorium, churches, clubhouses, racecourse and polo pitch.

Aside from the faded Raj atmosphere and myriad walks and **hikes**, the main incentive to travel up here is in order to scramble around the surrounding forest in search of **prehistoric rock art** or to visit **Satpura National Park**, home to a handful of (elusive) tigers and leopards.

Pachmarhi town, more than 1000m above sea level, is clean, green and relaxed, despite the presence of a large military cantonment in its midst. It has retained a distinctly colonial ambience, enhanced by the elegant British bungalows and church spires that nose incongruously above the tropical tree line. In the evenings families stroll and picnic in the parklands, while army bands and scout troops march around the maidans.

5

Satpura National Park

Satpura National Park Daily sunrise–sunset • ₹500 plus vehicle seating up to seven ₹1550 **Ticket office** Daily: April–Oct 8am– noon & 4–8pm; Nov–March 9am–1pm & 3–7pm **Bison Lodge** Tues–Sun: April–Oct 8am–noon & 4–7pm; Nov–March 9am–1pm & 3–7pm • Free

The 524-square-kilometre **Satpura National Park**, around 3km southwest of town and dominated by the rugged Mahadeo Hills, is worth a visit to see the Indian bison, barking deer, sambar, jackals and wild dogs, although you'll be very lucky to see any of the handful of tigers and leopards. Entry permits are available from the Forestry Commission **ticket office** at Bison Lodge, a five-minute walk south of *Hotel Amaltas* (see opposite). **Bison Lodge** also has a small museum with displays on the park's flora and fauna.

Pachmarhi Hill

There is a fine panoramic view over the town on one side and the thickly forested valley of Jambu Dwip on the other from the top of **Pachmarhi Hill**. The craggy cliffs lining the north side of the uninhabited gorge below are riddled with hidden rock-shelters and caves. To get to the hill simply head to the whitewashed Muslim shrine in the Babu Lines area of town (1km southwest of the bus stand); from here it is a fifteen-minute climb to the summit.

The Jata Shankar cave

The **Jata Shankar cave** is a thirty minute walk along a well-beaten track from the bus stand, twisting north from the main bazaar into the hillside through a narrow steep-sided canyon to this sacred cave, a prominent point in the Shivratri *yatra*. En route, in a small cluster of prehistoric rock-shelters just off the path, look out for **Harper's cave**, named for its naturally formed seated figure of a man playing a harp. Beyond it, at the head of a dark chasm, the Jata Shankar cave itself lurks at the foot of a long flight of stone steps. The grotto's name, which literally means "Shiva's hairstyle", derives from the rock formation around a natural lingam on the cave floor, which supposedly resembles the god's matted dreadlocks.

THE PANDAV CAVES, FAIRY POOL AND BIG FALLS WALK

A two- to three-hour walk around the eastern fringes of the plateau strings together a small cluster of interesting sights. First head up to the **Pandav Caves** (40min), which occupy a knobbly sandstone hillock just east of the road between the ATC cantonment (an army training centre) and the petrol pump. Hindu mythology tells these five (*panch*) simple cells (*marhi*) sheltered the Pandava brothers of Mahabharata fame during their thirteen-year exile. Yet archeologists maintain a group of Buddhist monks excavated the bare stone chambers and pillared verandas around the first century BC. Rejoin the road in front of the caves and head around the back of the hill to the melancholy **British cemetery**. Beyond that, the road becomes a dirt track leading to a small car park. If you plan to head on to Fairy Pool or Big Falls, you will need to buy an entry permit first (see above). From the car park, take the footpath down the hill through the woods for about twenty minutes till the trail flattens out, and turn right at a fork to descend to **Apsara Vihar**, or "Fairy Pool" – a popular bathing and picnic spot at the foot of a small waterfall.

A five-minute scramble over the boulders downstream takes you to the 150m-high **Rajat Prapat**, or "Big Falls". If you walk back to the fork and continue along the trail, a five-minute walk brings you to a railing facing the 105m-high falls. Beyond this point you will need a guide to find the 2km trail down to the deep, cold pool at the bottom.

SHIVRATRI MELA

Popular during the summer with Indian tourists, especially on long holiday weekends, Pachmarhi remains sleepy for much of the rest of the year. The big exception to this is during the annual **Shivratri Mela** (Feb/March), when thousands of pilgrims pour through en route to the top of nearby Chauragarh Mountain. The festival marks the anniversary of Shiva's *tandav* dance and his wedding anniversary.

Chauragarh

The 23km climb to the sacred summit of **Chauragarh Mountain,** on the south rim of the plateau, follows the main *yatra* trail used by pilgrims during the Shivratri *mela*. The first 8km can be covered by bike. From the bazaar, head south across the lake towards the crossroads in front of the *Amaltas Hotel*, then take the road to **Mahadeo cave**, passing a vantage point above the narrow **Handi Kho** ravine, just before the road makes its first sharp descent at the turn-off for **Priyadarshini**, or "Forsyth's Point".

The **footpath** proper begins at the very bottom of the valley, after the road has plunged down a sequence of hairpin bends. Before setting off, make a brief diversion up the *khud* behind the modern **temple** to the Mahadeo cave, where pilgrims take a purifying dip in the cool spring water. From here, a strenuous two-hour climb follows an ancient trail to the top of the mountain, which is crammed with tens of thousands of worshippers and sadhus during the Shivratri festival. At the summit, where a temple houses the all-powerful Chauragarh lingam, a thicket of orange tridents surrounds a bright blue statue of Shiva. The views are suitably sublime.

ARRIVAL AND DEPARTURE   PACHMARHI

By train The nearest railway station is Piparia (or Pipariya), 52km northeast of Pachmarhi and on the Mumbai–Howrah line. If you're coming from Bhopal, you'll need to catch a connecting train from Itarsi Junction.
Destinations Itarsi Junction (13–18 daily; 1hr 26min–2hr); Jabalpur (13–16 daily; 2hr–3hr 19min); Nagpur (1 daily; 7hr); Satna (for Khajuraho; 5–8 daily; 5– 6hr).

By bus or shared jeep Regular buses travel between Bhopal's main bus station and Pachmarhi. Frequent buses and shared jeeps (every 30min or so; 1hr) shuttle between Piparia and Pachmarhi.
Destinations Indore (2 daily; 12–13hr); Nagpur (2–3 daily; 8–9hr); Pachmarhi (6–7 daily; 6hr 30min–7hr 30min).

GETTING AROUND AND INFORMATION

By jeep Any of the MP Tourism hotels can organize jeep rental (₹1500/day). Shared jeeps also do the rounds of Pachmarhi's main sights; a seat costs ₹150–200/day.
Bike rental Shops in the bazaar have a few bikes for rent (around ₹50/day); take a chain and padlock (bring your own) and hide the bike in the bushes while you are trekking to stop it being pinched.
Tourist information The main MP Tourism information

office (Mon–Fri 10am–5pm; ☎07578 252100) is next to *Amaltas Hotel* near the military training area, Tehsil, on the far side of a lotus-filled lake, a 5min jeep or auto-rickshaw ride south of the bus station. There's also a small information booth at the bus station (Mon–Fri 10am–5pm; ☎07578 252029). If you are considering any walks more ambitious than those mentioned in this account, it is worth investing in a local guide.

TOURS

Bison Lodge Near the roundabout, around 1km southwest of town centre. Guides are available from *Bison Lodge*. Most of the longer hikes go through Satpura National Park, and so require a permit that you will need to obtain from the Forestry Commission office at the same address (see opposite).
Satpura Adventure Club ☎94243 77866,

✉ shailendra.sahu84@yahoo.com. Based at *Saket Hotel* (see p.354), the Satpura Adventure Club can organize guides from ₹300/day. The guides are young tribal men with expert local knowledge of the area, though they may not speak English, and the fees go directly to them and their villages. The agency also offers parasailing, and can arrange rock climbing and homestays.

5

ACCOMMODATION

Accommodation in Pachmarhi is in short supply during the *melas*, over Christmas and New Year, and May–June, when you should book well in advance. Outside of these times, it should be possible to negotiate a good discount almost everywhere. Budget accommodation centres on the bazaar, but most of the MP Tourism hotels are near Tehsil.

Amaltas Near Tehsil, around 1km southwest of the town centre ☎07578 252098, ⓦmptourism.com. MP Tourism hotel in an old British-built building with a collection of a/c "deluxe" (₹2460) rooms with the odd flash of character such as a curved wall or marble fireplace (room no. 5 is particularly good). The standard rooms, in a separate annexe, are less appealing. **₹2140**

★ **Evelyn's Own** Tehsil, near Golf View, around 2.5km southwest of the town centre ☎07578 252056, ⓔevelynsown@gmail.com. A colonial-era bungalow with homely rooms (they vary in quality, so ask to see a few), lush garden, small pool and tennis court. But the real draw is the owner, former army colonel Bunny Rao and his wife Pramila. Both are a mine of information. **₹1500**

Forsyth Lodge Near the village of Sarangpur, opposite the Madai entrance to the park ☎07575 21306, ⓦforsythlodge.com. Named after a pioneering British captain (see p.378), this wonderful lodge is set amid 44 acres of jungle. It has twelve beautiful cottages, a pool and well-trained staff and guides. Rates (listed for two people) include full board, jeep and elephant safaris. **₹24,000**

Golf View Tehsil, overlooking the golf course, around 2.5km southwest of the town centre ☎07578 252115, ⓦgolfviewpachmarhi.com. One of Pachmarhi's smarter hotels, *Golf View* has classy attached rooms with 1920s-style furniture, fireplaces, high ceilings and modern features like tea/coffee-makers and whirlpool baths. Outside you find manicured lawns, mango trees and, rather unexpectedly, a running track. **₹8600**

Hotel Highlands Main Rd, about 600m before the bus stand ☎07578 252099, ⓦmptourism.com. MP Tourism's most affordable option has attached rooms with TV and either fans or a/c in whitewashed cottages with green corrugated iron roofs. Although comfortable, they could do with a fresh lick of paint. **₹2030**

Reni Pani Jungle Lodge On the northern edge of the park, near Reni Pani village ☎07578 252079, ⓦrenipanijunglelodge.com. Under the same management as Bhopal's *Jehan Numa Palace* (see p.343), this secluded top-end lodge has a collection of spacious, tastefully designed cottages set beside a stream or surrounded by jungle. There's a pool, and a range of gu ided trips inside the park are on offer. Rates include full board. **₹17,200**

Rock-End Manor Near Tehsil, around 2km southwest of the town centre ☎07578 252079, ⓦmptourism .com. MP Tourism's well-restored British bungalow is a long-established favourite of visiting VIPs for its Raj-style rooms (they feel more like suites) and stately atmosphere. Easy chairs on the veranda offer views over the hills and the flower garden. Rates include full board. **₹4990**

Saket Patel Marg, in the heart of the bazaar, a 5min walk from the bus stand ☎07578 252165, ⓔhotelsaket2003@yahoo.com. Friendly hotel offering clean rooms with TV, attached bathroom (some with squat toilets) and luminous stars on the ceilings. The more expensive ones are bigger and have tubs, a/c and small balconies. **₹720**

EATING

Khalsa *Hotel Khalsa*, bottom end of bazaar, off the main road ☎07578 252298. A Sikh-run place with predictably good veg and non-veg Punjabi food (including a tasty Peshwari naan), plus a decent attempt at a Gujarati thali. The bizarre dining room features fake tree-trunk roof supports and fairy lights. Mains from ₹50. Daily noon–3pm & 7–10.30pm.

Rock-End Manor Rock-End Manor hotel ☎07578 252079. All the MP Tourism properties have restaurants serving the solid but hardly earth-shattering north Indian and Chinese menu (mains ₹90–310), but the Raj-era charm here elevates it above the others – given the surroundings, fish and chips seems the most appropriate choice. Book a table in advance during the peak season. Daily noon–3pm & 7–10.30pm.

Gwalior

Straddling the main Delhi-Mumbai train line, **GWALIOR** is northern Madhya Pradesh's largest city and boasts one of India's most magnificent hilltop forts. The sandstone **citadel**, with its temples and palaces, peers down from the edge of a sheer-sided plateau above a haze of exhaust fumes and busy streets. The city's other unmissable attraction is the extraordinarily flamboyant **Jai Vilas Palace**, owned by the local ruling family, the **Scindias**. Their personalities and influence are everywhere, from the **chhatris** (cenotaphs) north of Jayaji Chowk to the excellent **Sarod Ghar** classical music museum.

Despite its proximity to Agra, 119km north, Gwalior sees few foreign tourists and its drab modern centre lacks the charm of its nearby Rajasthani counterparts. That said, it is a worthwhile place to pause for a day, particularly around late November or early December, when the old **Mughal tombs** host one of India's premier classical music events, the **Tansen Festival**.

Brief history

An inscription unearthed in a now-defunct sun temple suggests that Gwalior was first occupied in the sixth century BC by Hun invaders from the north. Local legend, however, attributes the founding of the fort to the Kuchwaha prince **Suraj Sen**, said to have been cured of leprosy during the tenth century by the hermit **Gwalipa** after whom the city is named. The Kuchwahas' successors, the Parihars, were brutally overthrown in 1232 by **Iltutmish**.

A third Rajput dynasty, the **Tomars**, retook Gwalior in 1398, ushering in the city's golden age. Under **Man Singh**, who ascended to the Tomar *gadi* (throne) in 1486, the hilltop gained the magnificent palaces and fortifications that were to earn it the epithet "the pearl in the necklace of the castles of Hind". Skirmishes with neighbouring powers dogged the Rajputs' rule until 1517, when the **Lodis** from Delhi besieged the fort for a

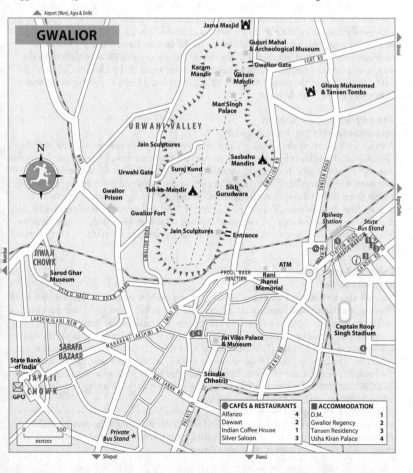

second time and Man Singh was slain. Thereafter, Gwalior was ruled by a succession of Muslim overlords before falling to Akbar.

With the decline of the Mughals, Gwalior became the base of the most powerful of the four Maratha clans, the **Scindias**, in 1754. Twenty-six years later, British troops conquered the fort and Gwalior became a British feudatory state ruled by a succession of puppet rajas. The most famous of these, Jayaji Rao Scindia, remained loyal to the British during the 1857 uprising, although 6500 of his troops joined the opposing forces led by Tantia Tope and **Rani Lakshmi Bai** of Jhansi. Both rebel leaders were killed in the ensuing battle, and the maharaja quickly resumed his role as host of some of the grandest viceregal dinners, royal visits and tiger hunts ever witnessed by the Raj. The Scindias remained influential after Independence, and still live in Gwalior.

The fort

North of the modern city • **Fort** Daily sunrise–sunset • ₹100 (₹5), video ₹25 • Guides around ₹250/3hr • **English-language sound-and-light show** Daily: March–Oct 8.30pm; Nov–Feb 7.30pm • ₹250 (₹75); tickets available from the fort or the MP Tourism office at *Tansen Residency* hotel

Gwalior's imposing **fort** sprawls over a 3km-long outcrop of sandstone. Its mighty turreted battlements encompass six palaces, three temples and several water tanks and cisterns, as well as a prestigious public school and a Sikh *gurudwara*.

Two routes wind up the hill. In the west, a driveable track just off Gwalior Road climbs the steep gorge of the **Urwahi valley** to the **Urwahi Gate**, passing a line of rock-cut Jain statues along the way. The other, more accessible **Gwalior Gate** is on the northeast corner of the cliff. Official **guides** tout for trade at the Urwahi Gate and the cold drinks shop at the entrance to the palace complex. There's a nightly **sound-and-light** show in the Man Mandir.

The archeological museum

Tues–Sun 10am–5pm • ₹100 (₹10), camera ₹30, video ₹200

A short walk north of the Gwalior Gate, just outside the fort compound, the modest Gujuri Mahal was built by Man Singh to woo his favourite rani, Mrignayani, when she was still a peasant girl. The elegant sandstone palace now houses the **archeological museum**, whose large collection of sculptures, inscriptions and paintings is well worth a look, even if the labels are woefully uninformative. Highlights include the twin Ashoka lion capitals from Vidisha in gallery two, and gallery nine's erotic bas-relief, but the most famous exhibit is the exquisitely carved **salabhanjika**, a small female figurine. Noted for her sensuous curves and sublime facial expression, the statue is often dubbed "India's Mona Lisa".

The Man Singh Palace

South of the Gwalior Gate

Entered via the **Hathiya** ("elephant") **Paur** gateway, with its twin turrets and ornate blue tilework, the **Man Singh Palace** was declared "the noblest specimen of Hindu domestic architecture in northern India" by nineteenth-century explorer Sir Alexander Cunningham. Built between 1486 and 1517 by the Tomar ruler Man Singh, it's also known as the Chit Mandir ("Painted Palace") for the rich ceramic **mosaics** encrusting its facade. The best-preserved fragments of tilework, on its south side, can be seen from the bank left of the main Hathiya Paur gateway. Spread in luxurious bands of turquoise, emerald green and yellow across the ornate stonework are tigers, elephants, peacocks and crocodiles brandishing flowers.

By contrast, the **interior** of the four-storey palace is very plain. However, there are some fine pierced-stone *jali* screens, behind which the women of the palace would assemble to receive instruction from Gwalior's great music gurus. The circular chambers in the lower storeys were once dungeons.

The Teli-ka-Mandir and Suraj Kund

On the south side of the plateau, the 30m-tall **Teli-ka-Mandir** is the fort's oldest surviving monument. Dating from the mid-eighth century, it consists of a huge rectangular sanctuary tower capped with an unusual vaulted-arch roof, whose *peepal*-leaf shape derives from the *chaitya* windows of much earlier rock-cut Buddhist caves. In the aftermath of the 1857 Indian uprising, the Vishnu temple was used by the British as a soda factory, and restoration work continues. At the head of the Urwahi ravine, just north of the Teli-ka-Mandir, the **Suraj Kund** is the 100m-long tank whose waters are reputed to have cured the tenth-century ruler Suraj Sen, later Suraj Pal, of leprosy.

The Sasbahu mandirs

At the eastern edge of the fort, the **Sasbahu**, or "mother-and-daughter-in-law", temples overlook the city near an unsightly TV mast. The larger one has a three-storey *mandapa* (assembly hall), supported by four intricate pillars, while the smaller one consists of an open-sided porch with a pyramidal roof. Both were erected late in the eleventh century and are dedicated to Vishnu.

The Sikh gurudwara

South of the Sasbahu *mandirs*, the huge, gold-tipped, white-domed marble building to the south is a modern **Sikh gurudwara**, built to commemorate a Sikh hero who was imprisoned in the fort. Before entering, cover your arms, legs and head, remove your socks and shoes and wash your feet in the tank at the bottom of the steps.

The Jain sculptures

Near the Urwahi Gate at the southern entrance to the fort, the sheer sandstone cliffs around the fort harbour some imposing rock-cut **Jain sculptures**. Carved between the seventh and fifteenth centuries, most of the large honey-coloured figures depict the 24 Jain teacher-saviours – the *tirthankaras*, or "Crossing Makers" – standing with their arms held stiffly at their sides, or sitting cross-legged, the palms of their hands upturned. Many lost their faces and genitalia when Mughal emperor Babur's iconoclastic army descended on the city in 1527.

The larger of the two main groups lines the southwestern approach to the fort, along the sides of the **Urwahi** ravine. The largest image, to the side of the road near Urwahi Gate, portrays Adinath, 19m tall, with decorative nipples, a head of tightly curled hair and drooping ears, standing on a lotus bloom beside several smaller statues. A little further from the fort, on the other side of the road, another company of *tirthankaras* enjoys a more dramatic situation, looking over a natural gorge. All have lost their faces, save a proud trio sheltered by a delicate canopy.

The third collection stands on the southeast corner of the plateau, overlooking the city from a narrow ledge. To get here, follow Gwalior Road north along the foot of the cliff from Phool Bagh junction, near the **Rani Jhansi memorial**, until you see a paved path winding up the hill from behind a row of houses on the left. Once again, the *tirthankaras*, which are numbered, occupy deep recesses hewn from the rock wall. One of the few not defaced by the Muslim invaders, number 10, is still revered by Gwalior's small Jain community as a shrine.

The old town and south of the fort

A number of interesting Islamic monuments are tucked away down the narrow backstreets of Gwalior's predominantly Muslim **old town**, clustered around the north and northeast corners of the hill. One of the main landmarks in this area is the **Jama Masjid**, erected in 1661, which stands close to the Gujuri Mahal near the main entrance to the fort.

5

The tombs of Ghaus Mohammed and Tansen
Off Tansen Rd, 1km east of the Jama Masjid

The city's most famous Muslim building is the sixteenth-century **Tomb of Ghaus Mohammed**, an Afghan prince who helped Babur take Gwalior fort. It's a fine specimen of early Mughal architecture, and a popular local shrine. Elegant hexagonal pavilions stand at each of its four corners; in the centre, the large central dome retains a few remnants of its blue-glazed tiles. The tomb's walls are inlaid with exquisite pierced-stone *jali* screens.

The second and smaller of the tombs in the gardens is that of the famous Mughal singer-musician **Tansen**, one of the "Nine Jewels" of Emperor Akbar's court. Every year, performers and aficionados from all over India flock here for Gwalior's annual **music festival** (Nov/Dec). Local superstition holds that the leaves of the **tamarind tree** growing on the plinth nearby have a salutary effect on the singing voice, which is why its bottom branches have been stripped bare.

The Jai Vilas Palace
Palace Rd, south of the fort • Daily except Wed 10am–5pm • ₹350 (₹60), camera ₹70, video ₹120

The **Jai Vilas Palace** is one of India's most grandiose and eccentric nineteenth-century relics, although the lack of labelling and information make it an unsatisfactory experience.

The palace was built in 1875 during the reign of Maharaja Jayaji Rao Scindia. He dispatched his friend Colonel Michael Filose on a grand tour of Europe to seek inspiration; Filose returned with a vast shipment of furniture, fabric, paintings, tapestries and cut glass, together with the blueprints for a building that borrowed heavily from Buckingham Palace, Versailles, Greek ruins and Italian-Baroque stately homes. The result is a shamelessly over-the-top blend of Doric, Tuscan and Corinthian architecture.

The Scindias, who still occupy part of the palace, have opened two wings to the public. The first wing, a **museum**, includes countless Mughal paintings, Persian rugs, gold and silver ornaments and antique furniture that belonged to the estate of Louis XVI before the French Revolution.

A still more extravagant wing lies across the courtyard from the museum. The **durbar hall** was where the maharaja entertained important visitors. A sweeping Belgian glass staircase leads from the lobby upstairs to the gargantuan assembly hall, which has the world's biggest chandeliers. At over three and a half tonnes apiece, they could not be installed until the strength of the roof had been tested with eight elephants. The rug lining the floor of the hall, woven by inmates of Gwalior jail, took twelve years to complete and, at over 40m in length, is the largest handmade carpet in Asia.

Sarod Ghar museum
Ustad Hafiz Ali Khan Marg, Jiwaji Ganj, southwest of the fort • Tues–Sun 10am–1pm & 2–4pm • Free • ⓦ sarod.com

The **Sarod Ghar** music museum occupies the beautiful ancestral home of the Bangash family, whose ancestors, originally Afghan horse-traders who settled in India, produced a dynasty of musical virtuosos, including **Ustad Hafiz Ali Khan** and his son **Ustad Amjad Ali Khan**. The museum traces Gwalior's rich musical legacy, from Tansen, who performed in Mughal emperor Akbar's court, to the invention by Gulam Ali Khan Bangash of the **sarod**, whose ethereal tones accompany you as you progress through the galleries.

The Scindia chhatris
Palace Rd, just south of the Jai Vilas Palace

Two characteristically ostentatious Scindia family tombs are found in the south of Gwalior. Inside a walled courtyard, the **chhatris** feature intricate stonework and ornately painted scenes of life inside the nineteenth-century Maratha royal court. Built in 1817 to commemorate Maharaja Jiyaji Rao Scindia, the larger of the pair is most remarkable for the intricate outside panelling of interwoven flowers. The second chhatri is a more compact and finely detailed version of the former. Constructed in

1843 for the recently departed Maharaja Janakaji Scindia, sculptures and carvings depict the hectic lifestyle of a king.

ARRIVAL AND INFORMATION
GWALIOR

By plane The airport is 9km north of the city; a taxi to the centre costs around ₹500–600. Air India (Tansen Marg; ☎0751 237 6820) has flights between both Delhi and Mumbai.
Destinations Delhi (1 daily; 50min) and Mumbai (1 daily; 1hr 40min).

By train Gwalior's railway station lies in the east of the city, just off Station Rd and a short walk from numerous hotels. The quickest train to Delhi is the *Shatabdi Express* #12001 (daily 7.05pm; 3hr 35min), which travels via Agra (1hr 25min). Travelling in the opposite direction, the *Shatabdi Express* #12002 (daily 9.30am) is the quickest train to both Jhansi and Bhopal.
Destinations Agra (every 30min–1hr; 1hr 20min–2hr 25min); Bhopal (every 30min–1hr; 4hr 30min–8hr 17min); Delhi (every 30min–1hr; 3hr 35min–6hr 55min); Indore (1–3 daily; 10hr 15min–12hr 15min); Jhansi (every 30min–1hr; 1hr 10min–3hr 20min); Khajuraho (1 daily; 6hr 40min).

By bus The state bus stand is just around the corner from the railway station, just off Station Rd, and has services to Agra, Datia, Jhansi and Shivpuri. The private bus stand is inconveniently situated on the southwestern edge of Gwalior. It is only really worth considering if you are travelling long distances.
Destinations Agra (every 30min–1hr; 3hr–3hr 30min); Datia (every 30min–1hr; 1hr 30min–2hr); Jhansi (every 30min–1hr; 3hr 30min–4hr); Shivpuri (every 30min–1hr; 2hr 30min).

Tourist information MP Tourism has an office at *Tansen Residency* on Gandhi Rd (daily 10am–6pm; ☎0751 223 4557); it runs a daily bus tour of the city (8hr 30min; ₹105). There is also an MP Tourism booth in the railway station on platform 1 (daily 9am–7pm; ☎0751 404 0777).

Internet There are several internet cafés on Padav Rd, including Gwala's Cyber Zone. ₹20/hr.

Money The State Bank of India, at the heart of the bazaar district near the GPO on Jayaji Chowk, changes foreign currency. There are numerous ATMs, including one next to the tourist office booth in the station and another on MLB Rd.

ACCOMMODATION

Standards at Gwalior's hotels are low, especially at the budget end of the market. In addition, many shoestring hotels, particularly those near the railway station, refuse to take foreigners.

D.M. Link Rd, near the state bus stand ☎0751 234 2083. Probably the best low-cost choice in Gwalior, with minuscule but clean and quiet rooms; the cheaper ones have squat toilets. The ancient TVs are locked inside cabinets, lest you were thinking of pinching one. Mosquitoes can be a problem here, so put up a net. **₹600**

Gwalior Regency Link Rd, near the state bus stand ☎0751 234 0670, ⓦhotelregencygroup.com. Efficient, if not particularly friendly, mid-range hotel aimed primarily at business travellers. As well as smart, modern a/c en suites, there is a small pool, gym, coffee shop, a good restaurant and a bar-disco. **₹4700**

Tansen Residency 6-A Gandhi Rd ☎0751 234 0370, ⓦmptourism.com. This MP Tourism-run hotel is a reasonable choice for a night. Set in its own gardens, it has has well-furnished but cramped a/c rooms, plus a pool, restaurant and bar. It's popular, so book in advance. **₹2700**

Usha Kiran Palace Jayendraganj, Lakshar ☎0751 244 4000, ⓦtajhotels.com. Romantic 120-year-old palace set in nine acres of landscaped gardens. Charming rooms have Indian-style divans, 1930s-era furniture and silk cushions. There's a pool and spa, and cookery and yoga classes are available. **₹10,000**

EATING

Alfanzo Mahdav Rao Scindia Marg ☎0751 655 5501. A modern a/c restaurant with subdued lighting and a large fish tank. The food – north Indian and Chinese veg standards – is well prepared, though service is over-attentive. Mains ₹140–220. Daily 12.30–4pm & 7–10.30pm.

Dawaat *Gwalior Regency* ☎0751 234 0670. The tandoori kebabs – fish, chicken and *paneer* – are the highlights of this hotel restaurant, which also serves south Indian options, biriyanis and decent Indian-style Chinese food. Mains ₹150–325. Daily 8am–11pm.

Indian Coffee House Station Rd. Low-key place with white-turbaned waiters, it consistently produces the goods, from toast and filter coffee (from ₹12) and south Indian breakfast options (₹40–90) to more substantial meals (₹60–260). Daily 8am–10.30pm.

★ **Silver Saloon** Usha Kiran Palace ☎0751 244 4000. If you can't afford to stay at the hotel, a visit to its exemplary restaurant is the next best thing. Gourmet Mughal, Marathi, Nepalese and international dishes are served impeccably in evocative surroundings; expect to pay upwards of ₹500 for dinner. Afterwards, head to the hotel's *Bada Bar* for a drink and a game of billiards. Daily 8am–11pm.

5

Datia

Constructed by Bir Singh Deo at the height of the Bundela's "golden age", the little-visited majestic palace at **DATIA**, 30km northwest of Jhansi and 71km southeast of Gwalior, is one of India's finest Rajput buildings.

Presiding over a mass of white- and blue-washed brick houses from its seat atop a rock outcrop, the **Nrsing Dev Palace** stands in the north of town. Half the fun of visiting the labyrinthine palace is trying to find a path from its pitch-black subterranean chambers, hewn out of the solid base of the hill for use during the hot season, to the rani's airy apartment on the top floor. In between, a maze of cross-cutting corridors, flying walkways, walls encrusted with fragments of ceramic tiles, latticed screens and archways, hidden passages, pavilions and suites of apartments lead you in ever-decreasing circles until you eventually run out of staircases. The views from the upper storeys are breathtaking.

ARRIVAL AND DEPARTURE DATIA

By train Datia railway station, 2km southwest of the bus station, sits on the main Delhi–Mumbai train line, though services are fairly limited.

By bus The bus station is just south of the centre. Regular buses connect Datia with both Jhansi (every 30min–1hr; 1hr–1hr 30min) and Gwalior (every 30min–1hr; 1hr 30min–2hr). If you're coming from Shivpuri, 97km west, you'll need to change buses at Karera.

ACCOMODATION

Datia Tourist Motel 5km from the railway station ☎ 07522 238125, ⊛ mptourism.com. Most people visit Datia on a day-trip, but if you want to stay the night, try this MP Tourism hotel, which has four plain a/c rooms, a restaurant and not much else. ₹**1710**

Shivpuri

SHIVPURI, 112km south of Gwalior and the former summer capital of the Scindias, is worth a stop-off to see the **Madhav Rao Scindia Chhatri** (daily 8am–noon & 3–8pm; ₹40, camera ₹10, video ₹40), a white marble synthesis of Hindu and Islamic architectural styles with spires and pavilions. There are also several other lesser chhatris, and tranquil gardens, complete with Victorian lamps and ornamental balustrades. Nearby, the **Madhav National Park** (daily sunrise–4.30pm; vehicle ₹1500 (₹400), guide ₹150, camera ₹40, video ₹300) has deer, leopards, sloth bears, crocodiles and blackbucks, as well as a Scindia-era hunting lodge and castle.

ARRIVAL AND INFORMATION SHIVPURI

By bus or train Shivpuri is linked to Gwalior by train (1–4 daily; 2hr 27min–3hr 45min), but state buses (every 30min–1hr; 3hr) are more convenient.

ACCOMMODATION

Shivpuri Tourist Village ☎ 07492 223760, ⊛ mptourism.com. This MP Tourism-run hotel has a pleasant, if rather bland and overpriced, collection of a/c rooms, as well as a restaurant-bar (mains ₹70–310) and a swimming pool. Staff can organize jeep hire and trips to Madhav National Park. ₹**2700**

Orchha

An essential stop en route to or from Khajuraho, **ORCHHA** ("hidden place") certainly lives up to its name, residing amid a tangle of scrubby *dhak* forest eighteen kilometres southeast of Jhansi. In spite of its tumbledown state, the fortified and now deserted medieval town remains an architectural gem, its guano-splashed temple *shikharas*, derelict palaces, havelis and weed-choked sandstone cenotaphs floating serenely above the banks of the River Betwa. Clustered around the foot of the exotic ruins, the sleepy village makes an excellent spot to unwind after the hassle of northern cities. However, it's now firmly established on the tour-group circuit, so try to spend a night or two here after the coach parties have moved off.

Brief history

After being chased by several generations of Delhi sultans from various capitals around central India, the Bundela dynasty finally settled at the former Malwan fort of **Orchha** in the fifteenth century. Work on Orchha's magnificent fortifications, palaces and temples was started by Raja **Rudra Pratap**, and continued after he was killed in 1531 trying to wrestle a cow from the clutches of a tiger. Thereafter, the dynasty's fortunes depended on the goodwill of their mighty neighbours, the **Mughals**. After being defeated in battle by Akbar, the proud and pious **Madhukar Shah** nearly signed his clan's death warrant by showing up at the imperial court with a red *tilak* smeared on his forehead – a mark at that time banned by the emperor. Madhukar's bold gesture, however, earned Akbar's respect, and the two became friends – an alliance fostered in the following years by Orchha's most illustrious raja.

   During his 22-year rule, **Bir Singh Deo** erected 52 forts and palaces, including the citadel at Jhansi, the rambling Nrsing Dev at Datia and many of Orchha's finest buildings. In 1627, he was killed by bandits while returning from the Deccan with a camel train full of booty. Afterwards, relations with the Mughals rapidly deteriorated, and the Bundelas eventually fled Orchha for the comparative safety of **Tikamgarh**. Apart from the *Sheesh Mahal*, now a hotel (see p.364), the magnificent monuments have lain virtually deserted ever since.

The monuments

Across the bridge, just east of the market • Daily 8am–6pm • "Day passport" for all the monuments ₹250 (₹10), camera ₹25, video ₹200
English-language sound-and-light show Daily: Nov–Feb 6.30pm; March–Oct 7.30pm • ₹250 (₹75), children ₹150 (₹40)

The best-preserved of Orchha's scattered **palaces**, **temples**, **tombs** and **gardens** lie within comfortable walking distance of the village and can be seen – at breakneck speed – in a day; yet to get the most out of a trip you should plan on staying the night. A sound-and-light show is held every night throughout the year.

Raj Mahal

Just beyond the bridge, the first building you come to across Orchha's medieval granite bridge is the well-preserved ruin of the royal palace, or **Raj Mahal**. Of the two rectangular courtyards inside, the second, formerly used by the Bundela ranis, is the most dramatic. Opulent royal quarters, raised balconies and interlocking walkways rise in symmetrical tiers on all four sides, crowned by domed pavilions and turrets; the apartments projecting into the quadrangle on the ground floor belonged to the most-favoured queens. As you wander around, look out for the fragments of mirror inlay and vibrant **painting** plastered over their walls and ceilings. Some of the friezes are in remarkable condition, depicting Vishnu's various outlandish incarnations, court and hunting scenes, and lively festivals.

Rai Praveen Mahal

Reached via a path that leads from the Raj Mahal around the northern side of the hill, the **Rai Praveen Mahal** is a small, double-storeyed brick apartment built by Raja Indramani for his concubine in the mid-1670s. The gifted poetess, musician and dancer Rai Praveen beguiled the Mughal emperor Akbar when she was sent to him as a gift, but was eventually returned to Orchha to live out her remaining days. Set amid the well-watered lawns of the **Anand Mahal gardens**, the building has a main assembly

5

hall on the ground floor (used to host music and dance performances), a boudoir upstairs and cool underground apartments.

Jahangir Mahal

South of the Rai Praveen Mahal, Orchha's most admired palace, the **Jahangir Mahal** was built by Bir Singh Deo as a monumental welcome present for the Mughal emperor when he paid a state visit here in the seventeenth century. Jahangir had come to invest his old ally with the sword of Abdul Fazal – the emperor's erstwhile enemy whom Bir Singh had murdered some years earlier. Entered through an ornate ceremonial gateway, the main, east-facing facade is still encrusted with turquoise tiles. Two stone elephants flank the stairway, holding bells in their trunks to announce the arrival of the raja, and there are three storeys of elegant hanging balconies, terraces, apartments and onion domes piled around a central courtyard. This palace, however, has a much lighter feel, with countless windows and pierced stone screens looking out over the exotic Orchha skyline to the west, and a sea of treetops and ruined temples in the other direction.

Sheesh Mahal

Just west of the Jahangir Mahal and built during the early eighteenth century, long after Orchha's demise, the **Sheesh Mahal** ("Palace of Mirrors") was originally intended to be an exclusive country retreat for the local raja, Udait Singh. Following Independence, the property was inherited by the state government, who converted it into a hotel. The rather squat palace stands between the Raj Mahal and the Jahangir Mahal, at the far end of an open-sided courtyard. Covered in a coat of whitewash and stripped of most of its Persian rugs and antiques, the building retains only traces of its former splendour, though there are stunning views from its upper terraces and turrets. If they're not occupied, check out the palatial suites (rooms 1 and 2), which contain original bathroom fittings.

Saket Museum of Ramayana Correlogram

Tues–Sun 10am–5pm • Free

A short walk south of the Raj Mahal, the small **Saket Museum of Ramayana Correlogram** has an intriguing collection of Hindu folk art from across India. Highlights include Mithila paintings (produced using paint made from cow's milk) from Bihar and colourful masks from Odisha and Uttar Pradesh.

Ram Raja Mandir

Daily 8am–noon & 8–10pm • Free

The **Ram Raja Mandir** stands at the end of the small bazaar, in a cool marble-tiled courtyard. Local legend has it that Madhukar Shah constructed the building as a palace for his wife, Rani Ganesha, and it only became a temple after a Rama icon, which the queen had dutifully carried all the way from her home town of Ayodhya, could not be lifted from the spot where she first set it down; it remains there to this day, and the temple is a popular pilgrimage site.

Hardaul ka Baithak

Opposite the Ram Raja Mandir • No fixed opening times • Free

A path leads through the Mughal-style Phool Bagh ornamental garden to **Hardaul ka Baithak**, a grand pavilion where Bir Singh Deo's second son, Hardaul, ally of Jahangir and romantic paragon, once held court. Newlyweds come here to seek blessing from Hardaul, who, despite being poisoned by his jealous brother who accused him of intimacy with his sister-in-law, is thought to confer good luck. The tall towers rising above the gardens like disregarded bridge supports are *dastgirs* ("wind-catchers"), Persian-style cooling towers that provided air-conditioning for the neighbouring palace, Palkhi Mahal; they're thought to be the only ones of their kind surviving in India.

Chatturbuj Mandir
No fixed opening times • Free

With its huge pointed *shikharas* soaring high above the village just south of the market, **Chatturbuj Mandir** is the temple originally built to house Rani Ganesha's icon. In cruciform shape, representing the four-armed Vishnu, with seven storeys and spacious courtyards ringed by arched balconies, it epitomizes the regal Bundelkhand style, inspired by the Mughals, with Rajput, Persian and European touches. It's unusual for a Hindu temple, with few carvings and a wealth of space – perhaps to accommodate followers of the **bhakti** cult (a form of worship involving large congregations of people rather than a small elite of priests). You can climb up the narrow staircases between storeys to the temple's roof, pierced by an ornate *shikhara* whose niches shelter nesting vultures.

Lakshmi Narayan Mandir
Around 1km west of the village • No fixed opening times • Free

The solitary **Lakshmi Narayan temple** crowns a rocky hillock just under 1km west of Orchha village, at the end of a long, paved pathway. It takes around fifteen minutes to walk here from the market, for which you are rewarded with fine views and excellent seventeenth-and nineteenth-century paintings. For a small tip, the *chowkidar* will lead you through the galleries inside the temple. Look out for the frieze depicting the battle of Jhansi, in which the rani appears in an upper room of the fort next to her horse, while musket-bearing British troops scuttle about below. Elsewhere, episodes from the much-loved Krishna story crop up alongside portraits of the Bundela rajas and their military and architectural achievements, while a side pillar bears a sketch of two very inebriated English soldiers.

Orchha Nature Reserve
On the east side of the bridge, around 700m south of the market • Daily 8am–6pm • ₹150 (₹20)

The **Orchha Nature Reserve** is a good place to spend a spare morning or afternoon. Here you can take an idle wander or cycle along a peaceful nature trail (around 12km in length) in the company of monkeys and peacocks.

Chhatris
Around 1km south of the market • No fixed opening times • Free

A solemn row of pale brown weed-choked domes and spires, the fourteen riverside **chhatris**, the cenotaphs of Bundelkhand's former rulers (including that of Bir Sing Deo), are Orchha's most melancholy ruins and best admired at sunrise or sunset.

ARRIVAL AND INFORMATION	**ORCHHA**

By tempo and bus Packed tempos and buses (departing when full; 20–40min) shuttle between Jhansi bus station and Orchha's main crossroads, 18km away. If you're on a bus from Khajuraho/Bamitha to Jhansi you can ask to be dropped off at the turning on the main road, and pick up a tempo for the remaining 7km. If you're heading in the opposite direction, don't bank on being able to flag down a bus on the highway, as they're often full. Instead, get to Jhansi bus station, from where they depart. There is one daily bus direct from Jhansi to Khajuraho (the departure time fluctuates, so ask locally; 5hr), as well as numerous ones between Jhansi and Bamitha, a 15min auto-rickshaw ride from Khajuraho.

By auto-rickshaw An auto-rickshaw between Jhansi and Orchha costs about ₹200–250 (more at night).

By taxi A taxi between Jhansi and Orchha costs around ₹450–500 (more at night); one between Orchha and Khajuraho costs around ₹2200–2600. The MP Tourism office (see p.364) and the better hotels can organize them for you.

By train Orchha's small railway station is 3.5km from the centre of the village (around ₹50 by auto-rickshaw). A local train (1 daily; 5–6hr) trundles between Orchha and Khajuraho. It generally departs from Orchha in the morning, and returns from Khajuraho in the early afternoon – exact times fluctuate, so check locally. You can't book tickets in advance, but there's usually no shortage of seats.

5

Jhansi station (see p.254) has a far wider range of train services, including those running to and from Khajuraho (1–2 daily; 4hr 10min–4hr 55min).

Tourist information The MP Tourism offices (daily 7am–10pm) at the *Sheesh Mahal* (☎07680 252624) and *Betwa Retreat* (☎07680 252618) can provide information and organize river-rafting trips (₹1200/1hr 30min, ₹2000/2hr 30min).

ACCOMMODATION

Most of the smarter hotels will allow non-guests to use their pools for around ₹150–300.

Amar Mahal Bypass Rd, 200m south of the market ☎07680 252102, ⊛amarmahal.com. A Mughal-themed hotel whose attached rooms, each with elegantly carved wooden beds and elaborately painted ceilings, are set around a series of peaceful, interlinked courtyards. As well as a restaurant, there's a pool, yoga sessions and a mini spa (all open to non-guests). ₹**4700**

Betwa Retreat Off Tikamgarh Rd, a 10min walk south of the market ☎07680 252618, ⊛mptourism.com. An MP Tourism lodge with faded but tastefully decorated salmon-coloured cottages and comfy a/c "Swiss" tents, each with a TV, fridge and marble bathroom set in a peaceful garden close to the river. There's a restaurant, bar and small pool. ₹**2460**

Bundelkhand Riverside Off Jhansi Rd, around 600m north of the market ☎07680 252612, ⊛bundelkhand riverside.com. The former hunting lodge of Orchha's last maharaja, dating back to 1895, *Bundelkhand Riverside* has a blend of traditional Indian and British colonial architecture, spacious art-filled attached rooms (most with river views), a good restaurant and a pool. ₹**4230**

Friends of Orchha ☎99933 85405, ⊛orchha.org. This NGO offers homestays with local families; accommodation (price listed for the room) is basic, but the families provide food (₹40–130/meal) and the experience offers a wonderful insight into traditional Orchha life. ₹**550**

Ganpati Jhansi Rd ☎07680 252765. Welcoming, family-run hotel with a range of rooms set around a small garden, from where there are spectacular views of the old fortifications. All the rooms are clean and have attached bathrooms; the more expensive have a/c and some (notably no.21) boast vistas of their own. ₹**800**

★ **Sheesh Mahal** Jehangir Mahal Rd, next to the Raj Mahal ☎07680 252624, ⊛mptourism.com. The local raja's former country bolthole in the heart of the fort is now an atmospheric hotel with eight charming (and very good value) a/c rooms and a personalized approach. If you can afford it, treat yourself to a romantic night in the Maharaja suite (₹5360) – perks include a vast marble bathtub and the ultimate loo with a view. Advance booking recommended. ₹**2460**

Shri Mahant Guesthouse Overlooking the market ☎07680 252715. Backpacker stalwart in the heart of the action: the rooms are a little claustrophobic and gloomy, and the most basic have squat toilets, but for a few more rupees you get air-coolers, TV and Western-style toilets. ₹**300**

Shri Mahant Hotel Lakshmi Narayan Temple Rd, 200m northwest of the market ☎07680 252341, ✉shri.mahant.hotel@yahoo.com. Run by the same people as *Shri Mahant Guesthouse*, this relaxed place is well away from the tourist scrum; there are scruffy, fairly clean a/c rooms in the older part of hotel and smarter, modern a/c en suites (costing around ₹400 more) in the newer annexe. ₹**800**

EATING

Most of the restaurants in the centre of Orchha boast interchangeable, traveller-orientated menus and views across to the fort. If you want a bit more variety and some non-veg options, try the restaurants in the smarter hotels such as *Bundhelkhand Riverside*. The delicious local delicacy, *kalakand* (milk cake), can be bought from the small stalls in the market.

Betwa Tarang On the approach to the Fort Bridge. A first-floor, veg restaurant with reasonable (though rather pricey for Orchha) pizzas and pasta, as well as better (and less expensive) Indian and Chinese dishes. Mains ₹80–240. Daily 8am–10pm.

Bhola On the approach to the Fort Bridge. Established, if rather scruffy little restaurant with an eclectic menu that jumps from Korean, Dutch and Israeli dishes to veg Indian staples. Traveller favourites also feature, such as banana pancakes and the "Hail to the queen" (a sweet concotion of ice cream, chocolates and crushed biscuits). Mains ₹40–140. Daily 8am–10pm.

Jharokha Hotel Sheesh Mahal ☎07680 252624.

If you're not staying here, soak up the palace's evocative surroundings in the colonnaded dining hall, which has tasty veg and non-veg food (standouts include the fish, chicken and mutton curries), and live music and dancing in the evenings. Mains ₹70–310. Daily 8–10am, noon–3pm & 7–10.30pm.

Ram Raja On the approach to the Fort Bridge ☎07680 252697. Cheerful little place with an extensive breakfast menu (served all day) that features hash browns, peanut butter or Nutella on toast and as many kinds of eggs as you can possibly think of. They also serve simple veg Indian meals and *momos* (Tibetan dumplings). Mains ₹45–200. Daily 8am–10pm.

DIRECTORY

Bike rental A bike can be a useful way to get around Orchha; several companies in town rent them out for around ₹50/day.

Internet The cyber café next to *Bhola* restaurant offers internet and Skype access for around ₹20/hr.

Money You can change travellers' cheques at Canara Bank on Jhansi Rd, just off the main square, and there is a State Bank of India ATM on Tikamgarh Rd, close to the bus stand.

Khajuraho

The resplendent Hindu temples of **KHAJURAHO**, immaculately restored after almost a millennium of abandonment and neglect, and now a UNESCO World Heritage site, are an essential stop on any itinerary of India's historic monuments. Famed for the delicate sensuality – and forthright **eroticism** – of their sculpture, they were built between the tenth and twelfth centuries AD and remain the greatest architectural achievement of the **Chandella** dynasty.

Waves of Afghan invaders soon hastened the decline of the Chandellas, however, who abandoned the temples shortly after they were built for more secure ground. The temples gradually fell out of use and by the sixteenth century had been swallowed by the surrounding jungle. It took "rediscovery" by the British in 1838 before these masterpieces were fully appreciated in India, let alone internationally. It is still not known exactly why the temples were built and there are a number of competing theories (see box, p.369); some say they are a "how to" guide for Brahmin boys while others claim they symbolize the wedding party of Shiva and Parvati.

Some 400km southeast of Agra and the same distance west of Varanasi, Khajuraho might look central on maps of the Subcontinent, but remains almost as **remote** from the Indian mainstream as it was when the temples were built – which is presumably what spared them the depredations of the marauders, invaders and zealots who devastated so many early Hindu sites. However, a train route now crosses this extended flood plain, making Khajuraho much easier to visit today.

Khajuraho village

The sheer splendour of the temples rather overshadows **Khajuraho village**. Still, if you stay a night or two, you'll discover a relaxed pace of life, especially in the evening when the local market and open-air restaurants create a very sociable atmosphere. Facilities for visitors are concentrated in the uncluttered avenues of the village; the gates of the western group of temples open immediately onto its main square, which is surrounded by hotels, cafés and curio shops where you should brace yourself for some hard selling.

THE TEMPLES OF KHAJURAHO

The exquisite intricacy of the **temples** themselves – of which the most spectacular are **Kandariya Mahadeva**, **Vishvanatha** and **Lakshmana**, all in the conglomeration known as the **Western Group** – was made possible by the soft fawn-coloured sandstone used in their construction. Considering the propensity of such stone to crumble, they have withstood the ravages of time remarkably well. Much of the **ornate sculpture** adorning their walls is in such high relief as to be virtually three-dimensional, with strains of pink in the stone helping to imbue the figures with flesh-like tones. The incredible skill of the artisans is evident throughout, with friezes as little as 10cm wide crammed with naturalistic details of ornaments, jewellery, hairstyles and even manicured nails. To add to the beauty of the whole ensemble, the temples subtly change hue as the day progresses, passing from a warm pink at sunrise to white at midday and back to pink at sunset. Dramatic **floodlights** pick them out in the evening, and they glow white when the moon is out.

5

The Archeological Museum

South side of the main square • Daily except Fri 9am–5pm • Free entry with a ticket for the western group of temples

The small **Archeological Museum** is principally noteworthy for a remarkable sculpture of a pot-bellied dancing Ganesh; among the other exhibits is a range of carvings and statues from the temples. There are long-standing (though rather vague) plans to move the museum to a new site close to the Tourist Facilitation Centre.

The Adivart State Museum of Tribal and Folk Art

Chandella Cultural Centre, just east of the Tourist Facilitation Centre • Tues–Sun 10am–5pm • ₹50

The **Adivart State Museum of Tribal and Folk Art** has a small but interesting collection of paintings, sculptures and artwork by Madhya Pradesh's many tribal groups. It also has a range of original paintings and prints for sale.

The western group of temples

Entrance opposite the main village square • Daily sunrise–sunset • ₹250 (₹10), camera ₹25; self-guided audio tour ₹100 **English-language sound-and-light show** Daily: March–Aug 7.30pm; Sept–Feb 6.30pm • ₹350 (₹120)

Stranded like a fleet of stone ships amid pristine lawns and flowerbeds fringed with bougainvillea, the **western group** of temples is Khajuraho's prime attraction. With the exception of Matangesvara, just outside the main complex, all are now virtually devoid of religious significance, and only spring back to life during Shivratri (see box, p.353). Visitors must remove their shoes before entering individual temples. An informative self-guided **audio tour** is available from the temple booking office, and there's a nightly **sound-and-light** show (50min).

Varaha

Just inside the complex a small open *mandapa* pavilion, built between the tenth and eleventh centuries, houses a huge, highly polished sandstone image of **Vishnu** as the boar – **Varaha**. Carved in low relief on its body, 674 figures in neat rows represent the major gods and goddesses of the Hindu pantheon. Lord of the earth, water and heaven, the alert boar straddles Shesha the serpent, accompanied by what T.S. Burt (see box, p.369) conjectured must have been the most beautiful form of **Prithvi**, the earth goddess – all that remains are her feet, and a hand on the neck of the boar. Above the image the lotus ceiling stands out in relief.

Lakshmana

Beyond Varaha, adjacent to the Matangesvara temple across the boundary wall, the richly carved **Lakshmana** temple, dating from around 950 AD, is the oldest of the western group. It stands on a high plinth covered with processional friezes of horses, elephants and camels, as well as soldiers, domestic scenes, musicians and dancers. Among explicit sexual images is a man sodomizing a horse, flanked by shocked female onlookers. The sheer energy of the work gives the whole temple an astounding sense of movement and vitality.

While the plinth depicts the human world, the temple itself, the *adhisthana*, brings one into contact with the celestial realm. Two tiers of carved panels decorate its exterior, with gods and goddesses attended by *apsaras*, "celestial nymphs", and figures in complicated sexual acts on the lower tier and in the recesses. Fine detail includes a magnificent dancing Ganesh on the south face, a master architect with his students on the east, and heavenly musicians and dancers.

The mandapa and inner sanctum

Successive pyramidal roofs over the *mandapa* and the porch rise to a clustered tower made of identical superimposed elements. Small porches with sloping eaves project from the *mandapa* and passageway, with exquisite columns, each with eight figures, at each corner of the platform supported by superb brackets in the form of

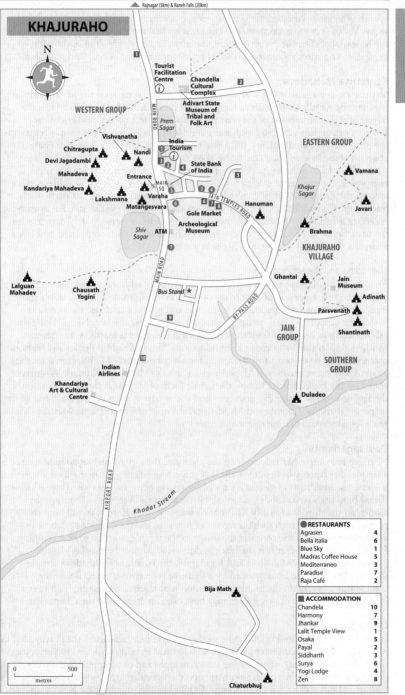

KHAJURAHO

Rajnagar (5km) & Raneh Falls (20km)

Tourist Facilitation Centre
Chandella Cultural Complex
Adivart State Museum of Tribal and Folk Art

WESTERN GROUP

Prem Sagar

EASTERN GROUP

Vishvanatha
Chitragupta
Nandi
Devi Jagadambi
Mahadeva
Entrance
Kandariya Mahadeva
Lakshmana
Varaha
Matangesvara
Gole Market
Archeological Museum
Shiv Sagar
ATM

India Tourism
State Bank of India
Jain Temples Road
Hanuman
Vamana
Khajur Sagar
Javari
Brahma

KHAJURAHO VILLAGE

Lalguan Mahadev
Chausath Yogini
Bus Stand
By-Pass Road

Ghantai
Jain Museum
Adinath
Parsvanath
Shantinath

JAIN GROUP

SOUTHERN GROUP

Indian Airlines
Khandariya Art & Cultural Centre

Airport Road

Duladeo

Khodar Stream

RESTAURANTS

Agrasen	4
Bella Italia	6
Blue Sky	1
Madras Coffee House	5
Mediterraneo	3
Paradise	7
Raja Café	2

ACCOMMODATION

Chandela	10
Harmony	7
Jhankar	9
Lalit Temple View	1
Osaka	5
Payal	2
Siddharth	3
Surya	6
Yogi Lodge	4
Zen	8

Bija Math

0   500
metres

Chaturbhuj

Airport (1km), Jhansi, Panna National Park & Railway Station (3km)

apsaras. The inner sanctum, the *garbha griha*, is reached through a door whose lintel shows Vishnu's consort **Lakshmi**, accompanied by **Brahma** and **Shiva**; a frieze depicts the **Navagraha**, the nine planets. Inside, the main image is of Vishnu as the triple-headed, four-armed Vaikuntha, attended by his incarnations as boar and man-lion.

Kandariya Mahadeva

Sharing a common platform with other temples in the western corner of the enclosure, the majestic **Kandariya Mahadeva** temple, built between 1025 and 1050 AD, is the largest and most imposing of the western group. A perfect consummation of the five-part design instigated in Lakshmana and Vishvanatha, this Shiva temple represents the pinnacle of Chandellan art, its ornate roofs soaring dramatically to culminate 31m above the base in a *shikhara* consisting of 84 smaller replicas.

Kandariya Mahadeva is especially popular with visitors for the extraordinarily energetic and provocative erotica that ornaments its three tiers, covering almost every facet of the exterior. Admiring crowds can always be found in front of a particularly fine image of a couple locked in **mithuna** (sexual intercourse) with a maiden assisting on either side. One of Khajuraho's most familiar motifs, it seems to defy nature, with the male figure suspended upside down on his head; only when considered as if from above do the sinuous intertwined limbs begin to make sense.

The torana and the seven mothers

An elaborate garland at the entrance to the temple, carved from a single stone, acts as a *torana*, the ritual gateway of a marriage procession. Both inside and out, lavish and intricate images of gods, goddesses, musicians and nymphs celebrate the occasion; within the sanctuary a dark passage leads to its central *shivalingam*. Niches along the exterior contain images of **Ganesh**, **Virabhadra** and the **Sapta Matrikas**, the Seven Mothers responsible for dressing the bridegroom, Shiva. Wrathful deities and fearsome protectors, the seven consist of Brahmi, a female counterpart of Shiva, seated on the swan of Brahma; a three-eyed Maheshvari on Shiva's bull Nandi; Kumari; Vaishnavi, seated on the bird Garuda; Varahi, the female form of Vishnu as the boar; Narasimhi, the female form of Vishnu as man-lion; and the terrifying Chamunda, the slayer of the *asuras* or "demons" Chanda and Munda, and the only one of the Sapta Matrikas who is not a female representation of a major male god.

Devi Jagadambi

North of Kandariya Mahadeva along the platform, the earlier **Devi Jagadambi** temple is a simpler structure, whose outer walls lack projecting balconies. Originally dedicated to Vishnu, its prominent *mandapa* is capped by a massive pyramidal roof. Three *bhandas* (belts) bind the *jangha* (body), adorned with exquisite and sensuous carvings; the erotica on the third is arguably Khajuraho's finest. Vishnu appears throughout the panels, all decorated with sinuous figures of nymphs, gods and goddesses, some in amorous embrace. Some consider the image in the temple sanctum to be a standing Parvati, others argue that it is the black goddess Kali, known here as Jagadambi.

Between Kandariya Mahadeva and Jagadambi, the remains of **Mahadeva** temple shelter a 1m high lion accompanied by a figure of indeterminate sex. Recurring throughout Khajuraho, the highly stylized lion motif, seen here rearing itself over a kneeling warrior with drawn sword, may have been an emblem of the Chandellas.

Chitragupta

Beyond the platform, and similar to its southern neighbour, Jagadambi, the heavily (and in places clumsily) restored **Chitragupta** temple is unusual in being dedicated to **Surya**, the sun god. Ornate depictions of hunting scenes, nymphs and dancing girls accompany processional friezes, while on the southern aspect a particularly vigorous ten-headed Vishnu embodies all his ten incarnations. Within the inner chamber, the fiery Surya rides a chariot driven by seven horses. The small and relatively insignificant temple in front of Chitragupta, also heavily restored and now known as **Parvati**, may originally have been a Vishnu temple, but holds an interesting image of the goddess Ganga riding on a crocodile.

Vishvanatha

Laid out along the same lines as Lakshmana, **Vishvanatha**, in the northeast corner of the enclosure – the third of the three main western group shrines – can be precisely

---

THE EROTIC ART OF KHAJURAHO

Prurient eyes have been hypnotized by the unabashed **erotica** of Khajuraho ever since its "rediscovery" in February 1838. A young British officer of the Bengal Engineers, **T.S. Burt**, had deviated from his official itinerary when he came upon the ancient temples all but engulfed by jungle.

Frank representations of oral sex, masturbation and copulation with animals may have fitted into the mores of the tenth-century Chandellas, but, as Burt relates, were hardly calculated to meet with the approval of the upstanding officers of Queen Victoria:

"I found…seven Hindoo temples, most beautifully and exquisitely carved as to workmanship, but the sculptor had at times allowed his subject to grow a little warmer than there was any absolute necessity for his doing; indeed some of the sculptures here were extremely indecent and offensive…The palki (palanquin) bearers, however, appeared to take great delight at those, to them, very agreeable novelties, which they took care to point out to all present."

Burt found the inscription on the steps of the Vishvanatha temple that enabled historians to attribute the site to the Chandellas, and to piece together their genealogy, but it was several years before Major-General Sir Alexander Cunningham produced detailed plans of Khajuraho, drawing the distinction between "western" and "eastern" groups. Cunningham thought all the sculptures "highly indecent, and most of them disgustingly obscene."

TANTRIC CULTS TO CELESTIAL ENTERTAINMENT

The erotic images remain the subject of a disproportionate amount of controversy and debate among academics and curious tourists alike. The task of explanation is made more difficult by the fact that even the Chandellas themselves barely mentioned the temples in their literature, and the very name "Khajuraho" may be misleading, simply taken from that of the nearby village. Among attempts to account for the sexual content of the carvings have been suggestions of links with **Tantric** cults, which use sex as a pivotal part of worship. Some claim they were inspired by the **Kama Sutra**, and similarly intended to serve as a manual on love, while others argue the sculptures were designed to entertain the gods, diverting their wrath and thus protecting the temples against natural calamities. Alternatively, the geometric qualities of certain images have been put forward as evidence that each represents a **yantra**, a pictorial form of a mantra, for use in meditation.

The sixteen large panels depicting sexual union that appear along the northern and southern aspects of the three principal temples – Kandariya Mahadeva, Lakshmana and Vishvanatha – are mostly concerned with the junction of the male and the female elements of the temples, the **mandapa** and the **garbha griha** (the "womb"). They might therefore have been intended as a visual pun, elaborated by artistic licence.

A MARRIAGE PARTY

A radical approach that ties history and architecture with living traditions has been proposed by Shobita Punja in her book *Divine Ecstasy*. Citing historic references to Khajuraho under the name of Shivpuri – the "City of Shiva" – she uses ancient Sanskrit texts to suggest that the dramatic temples and their celestial hordes represent the **marriage party of Shiva and Parvati**, taking place in a mythical landscape that stretches along the Vindhya hills to Kalinjar in the east. Thus Punja argues the lower panel on Vishvanatha's southern walls shows Shiva as a bridegroom accompanied by his faithful bull, Nandi, while the intertwined limbs of the panel above – the couple locked in *mithuna*, assisted by a maiden to either side – show the consummation, with the lustful Brahma a pot-bellied voyeur at their feet.

5

dated to 1002 AD as the work of the ruler Dhangadeva. Unlike some other temples at Khajuraho, which may have changed their presiding deities, Vishvanatha is most definitely a Shiva temple, as confirmed by the open *mandapa* pavilion in front of the main temple, where a monolithic seated **Nandi** waits obediently. Large panels between the balconies once more show *mithuna*, with amorous couples embracing among the sensuous nymphs. Idealized representations of the female form include women in such poses as writing letters, playing music and cuddling babies. Decorative elephant motifs appear to the south of Vishvanatha, and lions guard its northern aspect.

Matangesvara

The simplicity of the **Matangesvara** temple, outside the complex gates, shows it to be one of Khajuraho's oldest structures, but although built early in the tenth century it remains in everyday use. Deep balconies project from the walls of its circular sanctuary, inside which a pillar-like *shivalingam* emerges from the pedestal yoni, the vulva – the recurring symbol of the union of Shiva. During the annual festival of Shivratri, the great wedding of Shiva and Parvati, the shrine becomes a hive of activity, drawing pilgrims for ceremonies that hark back to Khajuraho's distant past.

Chausath Yogini

Southwest of Shiv Sagar are the remains of the curious temple of **Chausath Yogini** – the "Sixty-Four Yoginis". Dating from the ninth century, it consists of 35 small granite shrines clustered around a quadrangle; there were originally 64 shrines, with the presiding goddess's temple at the centre. Only fourteen other temples, all in northern India, are known to have been dedicated to these wrathful and bloodthirsty female attendants of the goddess Kali. Around 1km further west lie the ruins of **Lalguan Mahadev**, a small temple dedicated to Shiva.

The eastern group

East of the village • Daily sunrise–sunset • Free

The two separate networks of temples that make up Cunningham's **eastern group** are reached via the two forks of the road east of the village. One is the tightly clustered **Jain group**, while slightly north are a number of shrines and two larger temples, **Vamana** and **Javari**, both dating from the late eleventh century.

The temples to the north

On the north side of Jain Temples Road a more modern temple is home to a 2m-high image of monkey god **Hanuman** that may predate all of Khajuraho's temples and shrines. As the road forks left along the eastern shore of the murky Khajur Sagar lake, at the edge of Khajuraho village, it passes the remains of a single-room temple erroneously referred to as the **Brahma** temple. It is in fact a shrine to Shiva, as demonstrated by its *chaturmukha* – "four-faced" – lingam. While the eastern and western faces carry benign expressions, and the north face bears the gentler aspect of Uma, the female manifestation of Shiva, the ferocious southern face is surrounded by images of death and destruction. Crowning the lingam is the rounded form of **Sadashiva**, Shiva the Infinite at the centre of the cosmos.

KAHAJURAHO HASSLE

Touts in Kahjuraho can be a pain, but the most common hassle for tourists is being approached by children who offer to take you to visit their school, hospital or village – a visit that ends with demands for money. There's a Tourist Police booth on Main Road; go here if you have any serious problems.

5

Vamana Temple

The largest of the Khajuraho village temples, **Vamana**, stands alone in a field 200m further north. Erected slightly earlier than Javari, in a fully evolved Chandella style, Vamana has a simple uncluttered *shikhara* that rises in bands covered with arch-like motifs. Figures including seductive celestial nymphs form two bands around the *jangha*, the body of the temple, while a superb doorway leads to the inner sanctum, which is dedicated to Vamana, an incarnation of Vishnu. On the way to the Jain group, the road runs near what survives of a late tenth-century temple, known as **Ghantai** for its fine columns sporting bells (*ghantai*), garlands and other motifs.

The Jain group temples

1.5km southeast of Jain Temples Rd **Jain Museum** Mon–Sat dawn–6pm • ₹5

The temple of **Parsvanath**, dominating the walled enclosure of the **Jain group**, is probably older than the main temples of Khajuraho, judging by its relatively simple ground plan. Its origins are a mystery; although officially classified as a Jain monument, it may have been a Hindu temple that was donated to the Jains who settled here at a later date. Certainly, the animated sculpture of Khajuraho's other Hindu temples is well represented on the two horizontal bands around the walls, and the upper one is crowded with Hindu gods in intimate entanglements. Among Khajuraho's finest work, they include Brahma and his consort; a beautiful Vishnu; a rare image of the god of love, **Kama**, shown with his quiver of flower arrows embracing his consort **Rati**; and two graceful female figures. A narrow strip above the two main bands depicts celestial musicians playing cymbals, drums, stringed instruments and flutes. Inside, beyond an ornate hall, a black monolithic stone is dedicated to the Jain lord Parsvanath, inaugurated as recently as 1860 to replace an image of another *tirthankara*, Adinath.

Immediately north of Parsvanath, **Adinath**'s own temple, similar but smaller, has undergone drastic renovation. Three tiers of sculpture surround its original structure, of which only the sanctum, *shikhara* and vestibule survive; the incongruous *mandapa* is a much later addition. Inside the *garbha griha* stands the black image of the *tirthankara* Adinath himself. The huge 4.5m-high statue of the sixteenth *tirthankara*, **Shantinath**, in his newer temple, is the most important image in this working Jain complex. With its slender beehive *shikharas*, the temple attracts pilgrims from all over India, including naked sadhus.

Sculpture in the small circular **Jain Museum**, at the entrance to the Jain temples, includes stone carvings of all 24 *tirthankaras*.

The southern group

South of Khajuraho village • No fixed opening times • Free

Khajuraho's **southern group** consists of three widely separated temples. The nearest to town, **Duladeo**, is down a dirt track south of the Jain group, 1.5km from the main square. Built early in the twelfth century, Duladeo bears witness to the decline of temple architecture in the late Chandellan period, noticeable particularly in its sculpture. Nonetheless, its main hall contains some exquisite carving, and the angular rippled exterior of the main temple is unique to Khajuraho.

Across the Khodar stream and south along Airport Road, a small road leads left to the disproportionately tall, tapering **Chaturbhuj**. A forerunner to Duladeo, built around 1100 AD and bearing some resemblance to the Javari temple of the Eastern group, Chaturbhuj is plainer than Duladeo and devoid of erotica. A remarkable image of Vishnu, however, graces its inner sanctum.

To reach the third temple, **Bija Math**, return to the cluster of houses before Chaturbhuj and take a right along the dirt track through the small village. The structure lay below a suspiciously large mound of mud until 1998, when an excavation discovered the delicately carved platform. Unfortunately, the temple itself has disintegrated into the debris of ornate sculpture lying strewn around the site.

Raneh Falls

Around 20km northwest of Khajuraho Daily dawn–dusk • ₹150 (₹80) • An auto-rickshaw from Khajuraho costs around ₹300, including waiting time; a taxi costs around ₹1000

The **Raneh Falls** crash through a valley of black and pink basalt. Despite what you might be told, gharials (reptiles similar to crocodiles) are rarely seen here outside of the monsoon months, which is also when the falls are at their most spectacular (at other times they can be little more than a trickle). You can avoid the additional entry fees for auto-rickshaws and taxis by walking the 3.5km from the ticket office (around 45min).

5

ARRIVAL AND DEPARTURE

KHAJURAHO

By plane The airport is 5km south of the main square of Khajuraho village; a taxi into town costs around ₹150–250. A new, larger airport capable of handling international flights is being built nearby.

Destinations Bhopal (3 weekly, via Rewa; 4hr 5min); Delhi (1–2 daily, some via Varanasi; 2hr 35min–2hr 50min); Varanasi (1–2 daily; 50min).

By train The railway station is 2km south of the airport; a taxi into the village costs around ₹200–300. Tickets for all but the slow train to/from Orchha get booked up quickly, so plan your journey well in advance. The only exception to this is the slow train to/from Orchha; tickets aren't available in advance, but you can almost always find a seat (note that you can also travel between Khajuraho and Orchha via Jhansi). For trains to a wider range of destinations, head to Satna, 125km east.

Destinations Agra (1–2 daily; 8hr–8hr 25min); Delhi (1

daily; 11hr 10min); Gwalior (1 daily; 6hr 40min); Jaipur (1 daily; 13hr 10min); Jhansi (1–2 daily; 4hr 10min–4hr 55min); Orchha (1 daily; 5–6hr); Udaipur (1 daily; 21hr).

By bus The bus stand, less than 1km southeast of the main square, is within walking distance of most of the hotels; alternatively an auto-rickshaw costs around ₹50–60. There's a daily bus to Jhansi (generally 9am; about 4hr 30min), 174km to the west, that continues on to Gwalior (around 8–9hr) and then Agra (around 11hr 30min–12hr). Three daily buses connect Khajuraho and Satna (3hr 30min), and there are frequent buses to Bamitha (every 10–15min; 30min), 11km away, which has a far greater range of services, including to Jhansi.

By taxi A taxi to Orchha costs ₹2200–2600; to Satna fares are generally a bit lower. Ignore requests from drivers for extortionate "road tolls" and firmly agree a price first.

GETTING AROUND

By taxi Taxis and rental cars are available through most hotels and the *Raja Café* (see p.375). A day's sightseeing around Khajuraho costs in the region of ₹1200.

By rickshaw Auto-rickshaws charge around ₹650–700

for a full-day of temple-spotting; cycle rickshaws cost about half this.

By bike Many places rent out bikes (around ₹50/day), including Mohammad Bilal on Jain Temples Rd.

INFORMATION AND TOURS

Tourist information The MP Tourism office, in the Tourist Facilitation Centre (☎07686 274051; daily except Sun and 2nd and 3rd Sat of the month 10am–5pm), provides local information and can book accommodation and car rental. There's also a small India Tourism office just off the main square (Mon–Fri 9.30am–6pm; ☎07686 272347).

Guides Guide rates are set by the government: ₹750 for one to five people for half a-day, ₹950 for a full day;

there's a surcharge (₹300 for a half day, ₹400 for a full day) for tours in languages other than Hindi and English. There are several recommended, highly experienced guides including Ganga, owner of the *Harmony* hotel (see p.374) and a Tantra expert, Mr D.S. Rajput, Mr Mama and Mr Chandel, all three of whom can be contacted through the *Raja Café*, and Anurag Sukla (☎9425 143963).

FESTIVALS AND DANCE IN KHAJURAHO

Khajuraho is a bustling epicentre during **Phalguna** (Feb/March), when the festival of **Maha Shivratri** draws pilgrims from all over the region to commemorate the marriage of Shiva and Parvati. It also hosts one of India's premier dance events, the **Khajuraho Festival of Dance** in February; the precise date for the festival tends to be confirmed late, so confirm with the India Tourism or MP Tourism offices (see above), and book as soon as you can. The Khandariya Art and Cultural Centre (☎07686 274031), 1km south of the village centre, hosts performances of dances (₹350) from across India most evenings, and has a good selection of fixed-price arts and crafts for sale. There are also shows of traditional dances (₹350) from the local area at the Tourist Facilitation Centre (see above) every evening.

5

ACCOMMODATION

For travellers coming from elsewhere in Madhya Pradesh, Khajuraho's **touts** and commission system can be a shock. Avoid going into **hotels** with taxi, or auto-rickshaw drivers and be firm about where you want to stay. The sheer number of hotels means competition is fierce, so standards are high in all price ranges and substantial **discounts** can be negotiated. The India Tourism office (see p.373) can organize **homestays** in nearby villages.

Chandela Airport Rd ☏07686 272355, ⓦtajhotels .com. This smart, if not quite luxurious, resort has attractive attached cottages in eleven acres of neatly tended gardens, with all the hallmarks of the *Taj Group*: mini-golf, tennis and croquet, fitness centre, pool, coffee shop, bar and two restaurants. Good deals are available via the website. ₹8800

Harmony Jain Temples Rd ☏07686 274135, ⓦhotel harmonyonline.com. The Mediterranean influence in the design lends an air of spaciousness to this long-established hotel, which has a range of budget and mid-range attached rooms – each airy, clean and complete with a flatscreen TV – and a bird-filled courtyard. The food's pretty good too. If you're interested in finding out about the future, ask the hotel can put you in touch with face- and palm readers. ₹600

Jhankar By-Pass Rd ☏07686 274063, ⓦmptourism .com. Away from the tourist and tout scrum near the Western group, this well-kept though dated MP Tourism hotel is a big hit with Indian tourists. The clean a/c doubles are brightened up with paintings of the temples. ₹2140

★ **Lalit Temple View** Main Rd ☏07686 272111, ⓦthelalit.com. If money is no object, this is the place to stay. Sumptuous rooms look out either towards the temples or the enticing pool and shaded groves of *mahua* trees. The spa treatments, however, are the real selling point and include Ayurvedic and Thai massage and reflexology. ₹12,300

Osaka Off Jain Temples Rd ☏07686 272839, ⓔosaka4guest@ymail.com. A decent choice for anyone on a budget, *Osaka* has a handful of large but faded rooms with tiled floors and private bathrooms. Rooms vary, so look at a few; some come with ancient a/c units. Mosquitoes can be a problem. ₹300

Payal Across the fields northeast of the centre ☏07686 274064, ⓦmptourism.com. Run by MP Tourism, this sleepy hotel has pleasant gardens and an inviting pool in which to cool off. While the rooms, all with mini verandas and either fans or a/c, could do with a spruce up, they're certainly comfortable. ₹1385

Siddharth Opposite the Western group temples ☏07686 274627, ⓔhotelsiddharth@rediffmail.com. The staff at this mid-range hotel are amiable, but the en-suite rooms are a bit tired and frayed around the edges. Still, the a/c deluxe double (₹2500) at the front has wonderful temple views and the rooftop restaurant produces some of the town's best Indian food. ₹1000

Surya Jain Temples Rd ☏07686 274144, ⓦhotel suryakhajuraho.com. This popular and efficiently run hotel has clean and comfortable rooms (though annoyingly hot water isn't available all day), a lush garden, 24hr internet/wi-fi access, a book exchange, yoga and massage sessions and an alfresco eating area. ₹650

Yogi Lodge On a cul-de-sac between the row of shops behind Raja Café ☏07686 274158, ⓔyogi_sharm @yahoo.com. The shoestring rooms here are pretty clean and have attached bathrooms, though are still somewhat austere (and not all had hot running water at the time of writing, though this is apparently on the horizon). But you can't argue with the price, particularly as it includes free yoga and meditation sessions. ₹300

Zen Jain Temples Rd ☏07686 274228, ⓦhotelzen khajuraho.co.in. The Zen-influenced garden complete with lotus ponds and pet rabbit is the focal point of this place, which has reasonably priced rooms with TVs and attached or shared bathrooms. The on-site Italian restaurant serves great chocolate cake, and yoga and meditation classes are on offer. ₹500

EATING

Many rooftop restaurants erroneously claim you can see the evening sound-and-light shows from their establishments – what you actually get are occasional flashes of light and muffled voices.

Agrasen Jain Temples Rd. The potplant-filled, lantern-lit restaurant produces the typical traveller-orientated menu with a little more flair than the norm; there's a lot of choice for breakfast, plus economical thalis and tasty lassis (try the coconut flavour). Mains ₹70–350. Daily 6.30am–10.30pm.

Bella Italia Jain Temples Rd ☏98934 54795. *Bella Italia* is a more economical alternative to *Mediterraneo* for thin-crust pizzas (₹175–260), pastas and crêpes. In the early evening, hundreds of parrots congregate in the

neighbouring trees to make an almighty racket, before settling down for the night around 8pm. Daily 7am–10.30pm.

Blue Sky Main Rd. While it's a bit of a tourist trap, this rooftop restaurant offers a unique experience: a table in a (slightly precarious) treehouse – just ring the bell for service. Even if you don't have a head for heights, the thalis, Indian mains and Chinese dishes aren't bad (mains ₹80–250). The refreshing *jeevan rakshak ghol* (mineral water, lime juice, sugar and salt) is hard to beat on a hot day. Daily 8am–10pm.

Madras Coffee House Jain Temples Rd ☎94253 42194. This modest, rather scruffy canteen is popular with locals and frugal travellers for an inexpensive south Indian breakfast of dosas, *vadas* and *uttapams* or a lunchtime or evening thali. Dishes ₹40–150. Daily 8am–9pm.

★ **Mediterraneo** Jain Temples Rd ☎07686 272246. Authentic thin-crust pizzas (₹290–375) from a wood-fired oven, handmade pasta, home-baked bread, sweet and savoury crêpes, a superb Dutch-style apple pie and unparalleled espressos and cappuccinos make this the top joint in town, though the prices do reflect this. Daily 8am–10pm.

Paradise Airport Rd. This rooftop terrace and restaurant overlooking Shiv Sagar lake is ideal for a sundowner with cocktails, Kingfishers or even some Indian wine and "champagne" on offer; there's also a menu of traveller classics such as banana pancakes. Beer around ₹200. 9am–11pm.

Raja Café Main Square ☎07686 272307. A buzzing one-stop shop: as well as offering official guides, internet access and a bookstore, *Raja* also does a good line in Continental dishes like rösti, goulash and Southern fried chicken, as well as excellent Indian and Chinese options (mains ₹120–280). Try the banana flambée for dessert, or settle for a cold beer. Daily 8am–10pm.

DIRECTORY

Banks and Exchange Foreign currency can be changed at the State Bank of India on the main square (Mon–Fri 10.30am–2.30pm & 3–4.30pm, Sat 10.30am–1.30pm); it has an ATM opposite Shiv Sagar lake, and there's a Union Bank ATM next to *Raja Café* (see above).

Internet Most hotels and several cyber cafés along Jain Temples Rd provide low-cost wi-fi/internet acces.
Post office The post office is in the Tourist Facilitation Centre.

Panna National Park

According to official figures in 2006, **Panna National Park**, 37km south of Khajuraho, was home to 24 tigers. Just three years later, however, the state government admitted that there were no longer any tigers left, blaming the shocking drop on poachers. Since then tigers have been relocated here from other parks and numbers are slowly increasing (though you'll need a healthy dose of luck to actually spot one). Panna also boasts two hundred species of birds (it's a wonderful place for birders), as well as sloth bears, wolves and pythons.

ARRIVAL AND DEPARTURE
PANNA NATIONAL PARK

By taxi or bus A taxi from Khajuraho should cost around ₹1800. Khajuraho–Satna buses (3 daily; around 45min–1hr 30min) pass by the park, though taking a taxi is undoubtedly easier.

INFORMATION AND TOURS

Opening times Panna National Park is open mid-Oct to June (daily except Wed: winter 6.30am–noon & 3–5.45pm; summer 5–11am & 4–7pm).
Entry fees ₹2000 (₹1000) for a jeep seating up to six tourists, plus ₹200 per safari for a compulsory guide.

Tours Several hotels and travel agences, including *Raja Café* (see above), offer safaris (around ₹1800/vehicle, excluding entry and guide fees) in Panna, though for wildlife spotting it's far better to stay a night at one of the lodges close to the park.

ACCOMMODATION

Sarai at Toria Near Toria village ☎96852 93130, ⓦsaraiattoria.com. Run by a wildlife photographer and a renowned conservation biologist, this eco-friendly lodge on the west bank of the River Ken is easily the best place to stay in the area, with a collection of delightful cottages. Rates include full board and safaris. ₹**13,750**

Jabalpur

After running in tandem across an endless expanse of wheat fields and tribal villages, the main Kolkata to Mumbai road and train lines converge on eastern Madhya Pradesh's largest city. However, **JABALPUR**, 330km east of Bhopal, is only really worth visiting en route to the **Marble Rocks**, gouged by the Narmada River nearby, or to the national parks and tiger reserves, **Kanha**, **Bandhavgarh** and **Pench**, all half a day's journey away.

5

Rani Durgawati Museum

2km west of the railway station, near Russel Chowk • Tues–Sun 10am–5pm • ₹30 (₹5), camera ₹20, video ₹50

If you have some time to kill in Jabalpur, visit the **Rani Durgawati Museum**, which houses a predictable assortment of ancient temple sculpture, bronze plates and seals recording regional dynastic histories, plus a better than you might except display on the state's *adivasi* minorities.

Madan Mahal and Tilwara Ghat

Five kilometres west of the railway station in the direction of the Marble Rocks (see opposite), the main highway skirts a large moraine of enormous granite boulders, on the top of which stand the ruins of the **Madan Mahal** – a fortress-cum-pleasure-palace built by the Gond ruler Madan Shah in 1116. Another kilometre west, you reach an impressive bridge spanning the Narmada River. Known locally as **Tilwara Ghat**, the handful of shrines near the water's edge below marks one of the sacred places where Mahatma Gandhi's ashes were scattered.

ARRIVAL AND INFORMATION	JABALPUR

By plane The airport is 21km northwest of the city centre; taxis to Jabalpur cost ₹700–800, an auto-rickshaw around half that.

Destinations Bhopal (2 daily except Sun; 1hr 10min); Delhi (4 weekly; 1hr 55min).

By bus The shambolic city bus stand is a short way south of the bazaar, west of Naudra Bridge.

Destinations Kanha National Park (3 daily; 5hr); Mandla (every 30min–1hr; 3hr).

By train The railway station is 2km east of the centre; an auto-rickshaw costs ₹20–30. For Khajuraho, you need to catch one of the early trains to Satna, from where you can take an onward bus to Khajuraho. To reach Bandhavgarh National Park, take a train to Umaria, from where regular shared jeeps and taxis head to the park gate.

Destinations Bhopal (5–6 daily; 6hr–12hr 25min); Delhi (3–4 daily; 13hr 55min–17hr 55min); Indore (2 daily; 11hr 25min–13hr 50min); Mumbai (6–11 daily; 16hr 20min–20hr); Nagpur (3–4 daily; 8hr 50min–19hr); Patna (5–6 daily; 13hr 5min–17hr 20min); Satna (every 1–2hr; 2hr 40min–3hr 40min); Umaria (2 daily; 2hr 49min–4hr); Varanasi (5–9 daily; 9hr 50min–12hr 10min).

Car hire A car for a one-way trip to Kanha National Park costs around ₹3500. Most hotels can organize one, or try

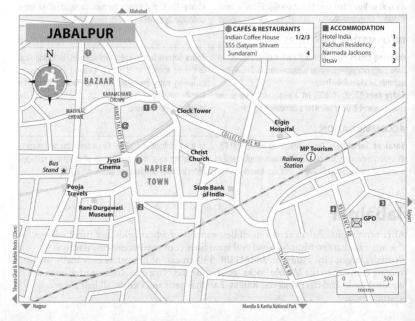

JABALPUR

N

Allahabad

BAZAAR

KARAMCHAND CHOWK

MALVNAC CHOWK

VINOD TALKIES ROAD

Clock Tower

Elgin Hospital

COLLECTORATE RD

MP Tourism

Bus Stand ★

Jyoti Cinema

NAPIER TOWN

Christ Church

Railway Station (i)

Pooja Travels

State Bank of India

Rani Durgawati Museum

RESIDENCE RD

GPO

STATION RD

Tilwara Ghat & Marble Rocks (22km)

Nagpur

Mandla & Kanha National Park ▼

Airport

0   500
metres

● CAFÉS & RESTAURANTS		■ ACCOMMODATION	
Indian Coffee House	1/2/3	Hotel India	1
SSS (Satyam Shivam		Kalchuri Residency	4
Sundaram)	4	Narmada Jacksons	3
		Utsav	2

Pooja Travels (☎0761 261 0118), which has an office close to the bus stand.

Tourist information The MP Tourism office is inside the main arrivals hall at the railway station (☎0761 267 7690, ⓦmptourism.com; daily except Sun and second and third Sat of month 11am–5pm). It runs boat cruises (₹1300–1500) on the Narmada River.

ACCOMMODATION AND EATING

Hotel India Near Karamchand Chowk ☎0761 248 0093, ⓔicwcsltdjbp@rediffmail.com. Owned by the co-operative society behind the *Indian Coffee House* chain – and run with the same quiet professionalism – this hotel has well-appointed, very clean attached rooms with TVs and phones. 24hr checkout. ₹1600

Indian Coffee House inside Hotel India ☎0761 248 0093. The *Hotel India* branch has black and red seats, glass walls, and a (normally dry) water feature, as well as top Chinese and south and north Indian meals and snacks (₹40–260) and filter coffee. Daily 8am–10.30pm.

Kalchuri Residency Residency Rd ☎0761 267 8491, ⓦmptourism.com. MP Tourism's welcoming hotel, close to the railway station in the Civil Lines area of town, has care-worn but ample a/c rooms, plus a decent restaurant and bar. ₹3210

Narmada Jacksons Civil Lines ☎0761 400 1122, ⓦjacksons-hotel.net. The smartest place to stay in Jabalpur has a stately entrance and lobby, and bland business-traveller-orientated en suites (the bathrooms could do with some modernization). There's also a pool, Ayurvedic spa, sauna, steam room and restaurant. ₹4600

★ **SSS (Satyam Shivam Sundaram)** Near Jyoti Cinema, Naudra Bridge ☎0761 240 1130. This understated local pure-veg canteen is popular for its superior bottomless thalis, wide range of dhals and unbeatable prices (₹30–90). The mushroom curry is particularly good. Daily 10am–10pm.

Utsav Russel Chowk ☎0761 401 7269, ⓦhotelutsav.com. While *Utsav's* keenly priced rooms are pretty grungy, their attached bathrooms, TVs and phones help to make them acceptable for a night. It's on the corner of a busy junction, so bring earplugs. 24hr checkout. ₹550

DIRECTORY

Banks and Exchange Change cash and travellers' cheques at the State Bank of India, around 1km west of the railway station, or at the *Rishi Regency* hotel opposite, which has a 24hr exchange counter. Note that there are no exchange facilities at the tiger reserves.

Internet There are several internet cafés, including Cyber Junction on Vined Talkies Rd.

The Marble Rocks

West of Jabalpur, the Narmada River suddenly narrows, plunges over a series of dramatic waterfalls, then squeezes through a seam of milky white marble before continuing on its westward course across the Deccan. The 30m cliffs and globulous shapes worn by the water out of the rock may not be so spectacular, but the **Marble Rocks**, known locally as **Bheraghat**, are a good place to while away an idle afternoon.

Bheraghat

Bheraghat village itself, overlooking the gorge, is a sleepy little place, with few signs of activity beyond the ringing of chisels in the workshops of its many **marble-carvers**. Most pieces on display in the shop fronts are heavy-duty Hanumans, *shivalingams* and various deities, destined for sites around India.

Mandapur Temple and the Dhuandhar

Bheraghat is also something of a **religious site**. At the southern end of town, from the fork in the river, 107 stone steps lead up to the tenth-century **Mandapur temple**, a circular building known for the 64 beautifully carved Tantric goddesses, or Chausath Yogini, which stand in its enclosure. Beyond the temple, at the far end of the gorge, the Dhuandhar, or "Smoke Cascade", waterfall is particularly dramatic after the monsoons.

ARRIVAL AND DEPARTURE

THE MARBLE ROCKS

By tempo, auto-rickshaw or taxi Excruciately slow tempos (around 45min) connect Jabalpur and Bheraghat, or you can take a much quicker auto-rickshaw (around ₹400) or taxi (around ₹700).

5

BOAT TRIPS

From Bheraghat's main street, a flight of steps leads down to the river and the **ghats**, from where **rowing boats** (₹21–31/head on a shared basis; ₹250–450 for the whole boat) ferry visitors up the gorge, although these don't run during the monsoon (July to mid-Oct). Avoid the boatmen who try and squeeze in 25 passengers. Once underway, the boatman begins his spiel, in Hindi, pointing out the more interesting **rock formations**. The most appreciative noises from the other passengers are not reserved for the "monkey's leap" (jumped over by Hanuman on his way to Lanka), but for the places used as Bollywood film locations. Look out for the enormous **bees' nests** dangling from the crevices in the rock. The formations are floodlit after dark.

ACCOMMODATION AND EATING

Hotel River View Close to Motel Marble Rocks ☎ 0761 290 5937, ⓦ marblerock-hotelriverview.com. A cheaper alternative to *Motel Marble Rocks* is this nearby place whose smarter rooms and garden have good views of the gorge; sheets could be cleaner, however. There's also a decent veg restaurant. **₹1000**

Motel Marble Rocks Just off the road out to the falls ☎ 0761 283 0424, ⓦ mptourism.com. If you want to stay the night, head to MP Tourism's pleasant motel, a converted colonial bungalow, complete with veranda, garden and easy chairs from which to enjoy the vistas. There's a small restaurant; service is friendly but glacially slow. **₹2780**

From Jabalpur to Kanha

From Jabalpur, the bone-shaking journey to Kanha takes you into some of eastern Madhya Pradesh's most isolated rural districts. When Captain J. Forsyth and his Bengal Lancers pushed through en route to the uncharted interior at the end of the nineteenth century, this landscape was a virtually unbroken tract of *sal* forest teeming with Indian bison, deer and tigers. Since then, the local Baiga tribals have taken up the plough, and all but a few patches of forest clinging to the ridges of nearby hillsides have been logged, cleared for farmland or simply burned as firewood by the burgeoning populations of sharecroppers.

Kanha National Park

Widely considered the greatest of India's wildlife reserves, **Kanha National Park** encompasses some 940 square kilometres of deciduous forest, savanna grassland, hills and gently meandering rivers – home to hundreds of species of birds and animals, including **tigers**. Despite the arduous overland haul to the park, few travellers are disappointed by its beauty, which is particularly striking at dawn. Tiger sightings are not guaranteed, but even a fleeting glimpse of one should be considered a great privilege. Moreover, the wealth of other creatures and some of central India's most quintessentially Kiplingesque countryside make it a wonderful place to spend a few days.

From the main gates, at **Kisli** in the west, and **Mukki**, 35km away in the south, a complex network of driveable dirt tracks fans out across the park, taking in a good cross-section of its diverse terrain. Which animals you see from your open-top jeep largely depends on where your guide decides to take you. Kanha is perhaps best known for the broad sweeps of grassy rolling meadows, or **maidans**, along its river valleys, which support large concentrations of deer. The park has several different species, including the endangered "twelve-horned" **barasingha** (swamp deer), plucked from the verge of extinction in the 1960s. The ubiquitous **chital** (spotted deer – the staple diet of Kanha's tigers) congregates in especially large numbers during the rutting season in early July, when it's not uncommon to see several thousand at one time.

The **woodlands** carpeting the spurs of the Maikal Ridge that taper into the core zone from the south consist of *sal*, teak and moist deciduous forest oddly reminiscent of northern Europe. Troupes of langur monkeys crash through the canopy, while **gaur**, the world's largest wild cattle, forage through the fallen leaves; years of exposure to snap-happy humans seem to have left the awesome, hump-backed bulls impervious to camera flashes, but it's still wise to keep a safe distance. Higher up, you may catch sight of a **dhol** (wild dog) as well as porcupines, pythons, sloth bears, wild boar, mouse deer or the magnificent **sambar**. You might even spot a **leopard**, although these shy animals tend to steer well clear of vehicles. Kanha also supports an exotic and colourful array of **birds**, including Indian rollers, bee-eaters, golden orioles, paradise flycatchers, egrets, some outlandish **hornbills** and numerous kingfishers and birds of prey.

Kanha's tigers

Kanha's **tigers**, are its biggest draw, and the jeep drivers and guides, who are well aware of this, scan the sandy tracks for pug marks and respond to the agitated alarm calls of nearby animals. Although the Kanha zone has been a prime site for spotting tigers in the past, at the time of research sightings here were less common here than in Kisli, Sarhi and Mukki. "Elephant shows" – in which visitors disembark from their jeeps to take a short elephant ride in pursuit of a tiger that has been spotted – were banned at the time of writing, but may well be reintroduced in the future; currently "elephant joyrides" (see p.380) are on offer, which although not geared towards wildlife-spotting, are fun experiences. If you're intent on **seeing a tiger**, plan on spending three nights at the park and taking around five excursions; the cats are most often spotted lounging among camouflaging brakes of bamboo or in the tall elephant grass lining streams and waterholes.

ARRIVAL AND DEPARTURE   KANHA NATIONAL PARK

The easiest way to get to Kanha is via Jabalpur, which is well connected by air and rail to most other parts of the country. It is also possible to travel via Nagpur, 226km away, which has a busy railway station and airport.

By bus Daily buses leave Jabalpur for Kisli (via Mandla) at 7am, 11am and noon (around 5hr). All stop briefly at the barrier in Khatia, 4km down the road from Kisli. Buses back to Jabalpur leave Khatia at 6am, 8am and 1.30pm. There are more frequent departures in both directions from Mandla (2hr from Kanha, 3hr from Jabalpur). There are also daily buses to/from Nagpur (6hr 30min) from nearby Balaghat.

By taxi A taxi to/from Jabalpur costs around ₹3500 one way.

FROM HUNTERS TO POACHERS

Central portions of the Kanha Valley were designated a wildlife sanctuary in 1933. Previously, the whole area was one enormous viceregal hunting ground, its game the exclusive preserve of high-ranking British army officers and civil servants seeking trophies for their colonial bungalows. Not until the 1950s though, after a particularly voracious hunter bagged thirty tigers in a single shoot, did the government declare Kanha a bona fide national park. Kanha was one of the original participants in Indira Gandhi's **Project Tiger** (see p.1182), which helped numbers recover. The forest department claims there are around 78 tigers, but guides and naturalists say 40–45 is a more accurate estimate (for most of India's tiger reserves, halving the official figures will generally give you a more realistic idea). As part of a long-term project, the park has expanded to encompass a large protective buffer zone – a move not without its opponents among the local tribal community, who depend on the forest for food and firewood. Over the years, the authorities have had a hard time reconciling the needs of the villagers with the demands of conservation and tourism; but for the time being at least, an equitable balance seems to have been struck.

Yet serious challenges remain: although poaching is now largely under control here, it still remains a threat; illegal timber-felling continues; the buffer zone is increasingly being encroached upon; and there is little effort to check the growth of new hotels. There have also been problems when tigers have strayed outside the park's boundaries and killed cattle and some local villagers have responded by leaving out poison. Visit the website of campaign organization Travel Operators for Tigers (w toftigers.org) to find out what role travellers can play in protecting India's tigers.

5

INFORMATION

Opening hours Kanha is open from Oct 16 until the monsoon arrives at the end of June (daily except Wed: winter 6.30am–noon & 3–5.45pm; summer 5–11am & 4–7pm).

Entry fees ₹2030 (₹1030) for the Kisli, Sarhi and Mukki zones of the park or ₹3030 (₹1530) for the "premium" Kanha zone per safari for a jeep seating up to six tourists, plus ₹200 per safari for a compulsory guide. Note that prices are likely to be hiked in the future. Entry tickets should be booked as far in advance as possible (see box below). For the shorter afternoon safaris, it is best to book a ticket for a zone that is close to your hotel – the Kisli, Sari and Kahna zones are close to the Khatia gate, while the Mukki zone, predictably enough, is close to the Mukki gate.

Jeep hire If you're not staying on a "Jungle Plan" package (see below) you will have to hire an open-top jeep – or "gypsy" (around ₹2200 for a morning safari and ₹1600 for an afternoon safari) to get around the park. These are available through most hotels, private operators in Khatia

or at the main gates: try and get a group together and book at least a day in advance. Jeeps can comfortably sit four people (excluding the guide and driver), although you can squeeze in six at a push. At the time of research a maximum of 140 vehicles were allowed into the park per day; this number is likely to be reduced in the future. Note that walking inside the park is strictly forbidden.

Elephant rides At the time of writing, "elephant joyrides" (7am & 8.30am; 1hr; ₹1500 (₹500)/person; minimum two people) had been introduced for a trial period in the park. Lodges can book them for you.

Money There is now an ATM close to the Khatia gate, but it is still worth bringing some money with you.

When to visit During peak season (Nov–Feb), the nights and early mornings can get very cold, and there are frequent frosts, so bring warm clothing. The heat between March and June keeps visitor numbers down, but tiger sightings are more common then, when the cats are forced to come out to the waterholes and streams.

ACCOMMODATION

MP Tourism has two lodges in **Kisli**, atmospherically situated inside the park proper, and one close to the **Mukki** gate. Private hotels outside the west gate, in and around the village of **Khatia**, range from walk-in budget lodges to five-star resorts, while those close to Mukki are generally high-end places; all should be booked several days in advance (and up to three months in the high season). However, at any hotel it's worth asking about discounts. The Khatia hotels are scattered along a 6km stretch of road that sees very little traffic during the day, so make sure you are dropped off at the right place. To reach the Mukki hotels from Khatia, you will require your own transport. Avoid visiting during **Indian holidays** like Diwali and Holi, when hotels are packed. Many hotels offer **"Jungle Plan"** packages; these include accommodation, food and safaris.

Baghira Log Huts Kisli ☎07649 277227 or ☎07649 277310, ⓦmptourism.com. MP Tourism's *Baghira Log Huts*, in the core zone, has spacious a/c chalets with private bath; nos. 1–8 overlook a meadow where animals come to graze. There's also a decent restaurant and bar; rates

include full board. ₹**4690**

Chitvan Mukki ☎07636 290644, ⓦchitvan.com. In a peaceful location surrounded by fields, the attractive *Chitvan* is accessed via a small bridge over a lily pond. As well as spacious, tasteful rooms, it has a curvy swimming

---

ONLINE BOOKING FOR THE TIGER RESERVES

Top-end, mid-range and even some budget lodges at Kanha, Bandhavgarh, Pench and Panna will take care of your **park entry ticket** if you have booked with them in advance – this is by far the easiest option and is strongly recommended. However, if you're planning to look for a place to stay on arrival (or are staying at a budget lodge that can't or won't book a ticket for you), you'll need to book an entry ticket yourself via the (often temperamental, particularly with regards to accepting foreign payments via its netbanking facility) MP Online website (ⓦmponline.gov.in). Tickets are limited, so do this as far **in advance** as possible, especially during the high season.

Booking – inevitably – is more confusing than it needs to be. On the **website**, click on "Citizen services", then "Reservations", then "National parks", then "Book now". After selecting the relevant park, you can choose which area of that park you want to book a safari slot for and whether you want a morning or afternoon safari. On the form itself, in the "Vehicle" category, select "light motorised vehicle (LMV)", though note that this doesn't mean that your vehicle is booked; you will still need to organize one via your lodge (something, again, that is worth doing in advance).

pool, a mini spa, vegetable and herb gardens, and 14 acres of grounds ideal for an idle wander or a birdwatching session. Rates include full board, nature walk and visit to the village of a local tribe. ₹6500

Kanha Safari Lodge Mukki ☏07636 290715, ⓦmptourism.com. MP Tourism's tree-filled lodge on the quieter side of the park overlooks the river and has pristine fan-cooled and a/c rooms with blue-tiled bathrooms, kettles and (rather redundant) TVs in villa-style buildings, plus a restaurant and bar. Rates include full board. ₹3290

Kipling Camp 4km south of Khatia ☏07649 277218, ⓦkiplingcamp.com. A British-run camp in a secluded forest location offering five-star comfort, plus the company of Tara, the elephant made famous by Mark Shand's book (see p.1188). Beautiful cottages have exposed wooden beams, cane chairs and private verandas, and there's a great photo-filled bar with a well-stocked library. Rates include full board, trips to nearby villages and markets, and birdwatching walks. ₹9990

Pugmark Resort Khatia ☏07649 277291, ⓦpugmark resort.com. Cheerful turquoise and green rooms, with either fans or a/c, are set in overgrown gardens with a campfire at the centre. There's also an attractive restaurant, open to non-guests. It's a winding 15min walk from the main road; follow the signs. Rates are on a Jungle Plan basis, and include accommodation, food and safaris for two people. ₹10,000

★ **Shergarh** Mukki ☏9098 187346, ⓦshergarh.com. Katie and Jehan Bhujwala run an intimate, environmentally friendly and socially responsible camp of luxury tents, each with a smart attached bathroom and private veranda. Outstanding service and thoughtful touches (such as personal hot water bottles for chilly early morning safaris) create a wonderfully serene environment. The excellent chef makes use of organic produce from the camp's butterfly-filled gardens, while the small lake in the centre is home to kingfishers and cormorants. Rates are on a Jungle Plan basis, and include accommodation, food and safaris for two people. ₹20,000

Singinawa Mukki ☏07636 200031, ⓦsinginawa.in. Top-end lodge that combines an eco-friendly "plastic-free" ethos with luxury: accommodation is in tasteful cottages (some with wheelchair access), 55 acres of wildlife-filled grounds, a lovely pool and the fascinating company of Nanda SJB Rana, a wildlife photographer and filmmaker, and his wife Latika, a leading wildlife biologist. Rates include full board. ₹20,500

Tourist Hotel Kisli ☏07649 277227 or ☏07649 277310, ⓦmptourism.com. Located close to *Baghira Log Huts* in the core zone, and also run by MP Tourism, *Tourist Hostel* has 24 dorm beds and is an excellent budget choice. Rates include full board. ₹1090

Van Vihar Khatia, 500m off the main road from Khatia Gate ☏94258 55779, ✉vanvihar99@yahoo .com. This stalwart shoestring choice has a salmon-pink colour scheme and variable rooms that could be cleaner: the cheapest have squat toilets and are pretty shabby, but the more expensive a/c ones are acceptable for the price. Staff can help organize park entry tickets and jeep hire. ₹700

Bandhavgarh National Park

Madhya Pradesh's second national park, **Bandhavgarh**, tucked away in the hilly northeast of the state, has one of the highest relative densities of **tigers** of any of India's reserves and shelters some fascinating ruins. Although it's a long haul to Bandhavgarh from either Jabalpur (195km) or Khajuraho (237km), it's worth it – not only to track tigers but also, as all the accommodation is close to the park gates, to watch the array of birdlife from the comfort of your lodge.

Though there are flat grassy maidans in the south of the park, Bandhavgarh is predominantly rugged and hilly, with *sal* trees in the valleys, and mixed forest in the upper reaches, which shelter a diverse avian population. Bandhavgarh's headquarters and main gate are in the village of **Tala**, connected to Umaria, 32km southwest, by a road slicing through the park's narrow midriff.

On the whole, jeep safaris tend to stick to the core area where the chances of spotting a **tiger** (there are estimated to be around 35–45) are high. Deer species include gazelle, barking deer, nilgai (blueball) and *chital* (spotted deer). Sloth bears, porcupines, *sambar* and muntjac also hide away in the forest, while hyenas, foxes and jackals appear occasionally in the open country. If you're very fortunate, you may catch sight of an elusive leopard. Look out too for some very **exotic birds**, including red jungle fowl, white-naped woodpecker, painted spurfowl and long-billed vultures. Perhaps the most enjoyable way of viewing game is to take an **elephant ride** in the misty dawn.

5

CALL OF THE WILD

For serious wildlife enthusiasts, there are a few very experienced naturalists in Tala, who can be contacted through your hotel. S.K. Tiwari of **Skay's Camp** (☎07627 265309, ⓦskayscamp.in) specializes in nature photography, and has an impressive knowledge of Indian flora and fauna.

The crumbling ramparts of the **fort** crown a hill in the centre of the park, 300m above the surrounding terrain. Its ramparts offer spectacular views and the best birdwatching in the park. Beneath the fort are a few modest temples, the rock-cut cells of monks and soldiers, and a massive stone Vishnu reclining on his cobra near a pool that dates from the tenth century. Tigers may be found in the area; they're more likely to stick to the lower levels, and there are no instances of people actually being harmed by tigers here or even suddenly coming across them – but the risks are real nonetheless.

Brief history

Bandhavgarh, one of India's newer national parks, has a long history. Legend dates the construction of its hilltop **fort** to the time of the epic Ramayana (around 800 BC). Excavations of caves tunnelled into the rock below the fort have revealed inscriptions scratched into the sandstone in the first century BC, from which time Bandhavgarh served as a base for a string of dynasties, including the **Chandellas**, responsible for the Khajuraho temples. They ruled here until the **Bhagels** took over in the twelfth century, staking a claim to the region that is still held by their direct descendant, the maharaja of Rewa. The dynasty shifted to Rewa in 1617, allowing Bandhavgarh to be slowly consumed by forest, bamboo and grasslands that provided prime hunting ground for the Rewa kings. The present maharaja ended his hunting days in 1968 when he donated the area to the state as parkland. In 1986, two more chunks of forest were added to the original core zone, giving the park a total area of 448 square kilometres.

ARRIVAL AND DEPARTURE   **BANDHAVGARH NATIONAL PARK**

By train The closest station to Bandhavgarh is Umaria, which is linked to the park by shared jeeps and taxis (around ₹600–800), as well as a couple of morning buses (1hr). Destinations Agra (1 daily; 13hr 24min); Bhopal (3 daily; 8hr 34min–12hr 5min); Delhi (1 daily; 17hr 19min); Gwalior (1 daily; 11hr 39min); Indore (1 daily; 17hr 50min); Jabalpur (2 daily; 2hr 49min–4hr); Jhansi (1 daily; 9hr 56min); Satna (for connections to Khajuraho; 1 daily; 3hr 9min); Varanasi (1–2 daily; 9hr 44min–10hr 54min).

By taxi Travelling by taxi to and from Khajuraho or Jabalpur takes roughly 5hr and costs upwards of ₹3500.

INFORMATION

Opening times Bandhavgarh is open from mid-Oct until the end of June (daily except Wed dawn–dusk). The best time to visit is during the hotter months between March and June, when thirsty tigers and their prey are forced out to the waterholes and the park's three perennial streams; the heat can be trying at this time, however. Visiting in the cooler months, when wildlife viewing is still good, is more comfortable.

Entry fees ₹4030 (₹2030) for the "premium" Tala zone (where you generally have a better chance of spotting tigers), ₹2030 (₹1030) for the rest of the park, for a jeep seating up to six tourists, plus ₹200 per safari for a compulsory guide. It's possible to book online (see box, p.380).

Jeeps Jeeps (₹1600–2200/safari) can be booked at the park headquarters or through your hotel.

ACCOMMODATION AND EATING

Most of Bandhavgarh's hotels, all of which are in and around **Tala**, cater for travellers on a higher budget, and offer **"Jungle Plan"** packages, which include accommodation, meals and two jeep safaris. The only places to eat outside the hotels are the inexpensive *dhabas* on Tala's main road.

Bandhavgarh Jungle Lodge Close to the river ☎07627 265317, ⓦbandhavgarhjunglelodge.com. Rustic (but eminently comfortable) mud-walled huts with thatched roofs and brown and beige interiors, lush gardens and enthusiastic staff give this lodge plenty of character. Deer can often be seen at the nearby meadow. Rates are on a Jungle Plan basis, and include accommodation, food and safaris for two people. US$450

Tiger's Den Resort Umaria Rd ☎011 2704 9446, ⓦtigerdenbandhavgarh.com. This efficient and friendly lodge has a cluster of large cottages with soothing decor and bathtubs in flower-filled gardens, plus an atmospheric wooden dining room. Rates include full board. ₹5000

Tiger Trails 2.5km beyond Tala; book through Indian Adventures ☎022 2640 8742, ⓦindianadventures.com. One of the better-value deals in Tala: cosy cottages have tiled roofs and exposed brickwork, while the alfresco dining room overlooks a little lake, which is great for birdwatching. Rates are on a Jungle Plan basis, and include accommodation, food and safaris for two people. ₹14,600

★ **Treehouse Hideaway** Ketkiya Village ☎011 2588 9516, ⓦtreehousehideaway.com. Blending seamlessly into the surrounding jungle, these stunning treehouses, made from local materials, are far removed from anything you may have played in as a child, combining top-end comforts with a sense of adventure. The camp has 21 acres of forest and even its own watering hole, which is sometimes visited by tigers. Rates are on a Jungle Plan basis, and include accommodation, food and safaris for two people. ₹25,000

White Tiger Forest Lodge Umaria Rd, next to the barrier over the main road ☎07627 265366, ⓦmptourism.com. MP Tourism's large complex has snug a/c and fan rooms with attached bathrooms, linked by raised walkways, and a restaurant and bar. Rooms 17–21 are in bungalows with verandas overlooking the river, which attracts myriad birds and – very occasionally – tigers. Rates include full board. ₹4690

Pench Tiger Reserve

Far quieter than its more famous counterparts, **Pench Tiger Reserve** has an estimated 20–25 tigers and sightings are relatively common. The 758-square-kilometre park, made up largely of tropical deciduous forest, is also home to leopards, jackals, deer and 250 species of birds.

ARRIVAL AND DEPARTURE

PENCH TIGER RESERVE

By bus or shared jeep Daily buses link Jabalpur (192km; every 2–3hr; 4–5hr) and Nagpur (92km; every 2–3hr; 2hr 30min) with Khawasa, from where you can catch a shared jeep the 12km to Turia, which is 2km away from the main gates and most of the hotels.

By taxi Hiring a taxi from Jabalpur will cost around ₹3500. From Nagpur it will cost in the region of ₹2500.

INFORMATION

Opening times The park is open mid-October to July (daily except Wed dawn to dusk).

Entry fees ₹2030 (₹1030) for a jeep seating up to six tourists, plus ₹200 per safari for a compulsary guide. It is possible to book in advance online (see box, p.380).

Jeeps Jeeps (₹1600–2200/safari) can be booked at the park headquarters or through your hotel; it's worth doing this in advance.

ACCOMMODATION

Kipling's Court Turia ☎07695 232830, ⓦmptourism.com. This MP Tourism-run lodge offers no-nonsense lodgings in fan-cooled and a/c rooms, as well as twelve great-value dorm beds (₹1090), plus pleasant grounds and a small pool. Rates include full board. ₹3690

Pench Jungle Camp ☎07695 232817, ⓦwildlife-camp-india.com. Luxury tents with wicker furniture and attached bathrooms, a handful of appealing cottages and some more traditional hotel rooms, plus a pool. ₹16,500

Indore

The state's economic powerhouse and the biggest city in western Madhya Pradesh, **INDORE** is huge, modern and pretty dull. If you find yourself with time to kill en route to or from **Mandu**, 98km southwest, however, you could stop and check out a couple of worthwhile sights. For centuries a stopover on the pilgrimage trails to Omkareshwar and Ujjain, Indore became the capital of Malhar Rao's **Holkar** dynasty

5

in the eighteenth century. Later, Rao's daughter-in-law, **Ahilya Bai**, took over control of the state, which then stretched as far as the Ganges and the Punjab, and founded modern Indore. When she died in 1795, the state plunged into a series of bloody conflicts, which only ended in 1818 when the dynasty secured a small but rich dominion with Indore as the capital. The city expanded in the nineteenth century, fuelled by trade in cotton and opium, and the maverick Holkar maharajas remained in power until Independence. Since then it's become a major and affluent industrial hub.

Indore's sights lie west of the railway line, in and around the **bazaar**. Two broad thoroughfares, MG Road and Jawahar Marg, form the north and south boundaries of this cluttered and chaotic district, which is interrupted in the east by the confluence of the Saraswati and Khan rivers. The city's principal landmark is the eighteenth-century former Holkar palace of **Raj Wada**, which presides over a palm-fringed square in the heart of the city and boasts a seven-storey gateway. Most of the palace collapsed after a fire in 1984, and only the facade and a temple survive.

Jain Kanch Mandir

Off Jawahar Marg, in the bazaar • Daily 10am–5pm • Free; no photography

The **Jain Kanch Mandir** or "Mirror Temple", deep in the bazaar district, is one of the city's more eccentric religious monuments; surprisingly, for a faith renowned for its austerity, the interior is decked with multicoloured glass **mosaics**.

Central Museum of Indore

AB Rd • Tues–Sun 10am–5pm • ₹100 (₹10)

The **Central Museum of Indore** houses Holkar-era swords, shields and armour, as well as terracotta, coins, paintings and fossils from throughout Madhya Pradesh. There is also a smaller selection of modern art and religious sculptures.

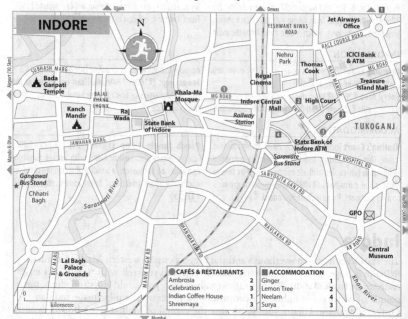

● CAFÉS & RESTAURANTS		■ ACCOMMODATION	
Ambrosia	2	Ginger	1
Celebration	3	Lemon Tree	2
Indian Coffee House	1	Neelam	4
Shreemaya	3	Surya	3

Lal Bagh Palace

5

Just off BLC Marg • Tues–Sun 10am–5pm • ₹100 (₹5)

The **Lal Bagh Palace** is an extravagant Neoclassical creation. Given a limitless budget, its British designers produced a vast stately home dripping with Doric columns, gilt stucco, crystal chandeliers and replica Rococo furniture. The Lal Bagh's main entrance is via a pair of grandiose wrought-iron gates, modelled on those at Buckingham Palace. Inside, a vast array of family heirlooms is housed in the former durbar hall, banquet rooms and the ballroom. Check out the jewel-encrusted portrait of Tukoji Rao (1902–25) – the ruler responsible for completing the palace – in the billiards room.

ARRIVAL AND DEPARTURE | INDORE

By plane The airport is 11.5km west of the city centre; a taxi into town costs around ₹300.

Destinations Ahmedabad (1 daily; 1hr 15min); Bhopal (1–2 daily; 40min); Delhi (3 daily; 1hr 25min); Jaipur (1 daily; 1hr 40min); Lucknow (1 daily; 1hr 55min); Mumbai (3 daily; 1hr 15min); Nagpur (1 daily; 1hr); Pune (1 daily; 1hr 5min); Raipur (1 daily; 1hr 50min).

By train The railway station is right in the city centre; two branches of the Western Railway connect Indore to cities in northern India.

Destinations Agra (1 daily; 12hr 55min); Ahmedabad (1 daily; 10hr); Bhopal (5 daily; 4hr 50min–6hr 35min); Delhi (2 daily; 13hr 20min–16hr 45min); Gwalior (1–2 daily; 11hr 2min–12hr 10min); Jabalpur (2 daily; 12hr–13hr 40min); Jaipur (2 daily; 10hr 35min–15hr 25min); Jhansi (1 daily; 9hr 22min); Mumbai (1 daily; 14hr 5min).

By bus The main bus stand, Sarawate, is a short walk south from platform 1 of the railway station beyond the overpass;

regular buses to Bhopal and Omkareshwar depart from here. Other buses – including those to Ujjain, Dhamnod (for connections to Maheshwar), Mandu and Dhar (connected to Mandu by half-hourly buses) – depart from the Gangawal bus stand, 3km west.

By MP Tourism bus MP Tourism runs fast a/c buses between Bhopal and Indore (7 daily; 4hr–4hr 30min); it also sometimes has buses to Ujjain and Omkareshwar. Tickets should be booked in advance, either online (ⓦmptourism.com) or at the MP Tourism office, where the buses arrive and depart.

Destinations Bhopal (every 30min; 4–5hr); Dhamnod (every 30min–1hr; 2–3hr); Dhar (every 30min–1hr; 2hr); Mandu (2 daily; 3hr 30min–4hr); Omkareshwar (every 30min–1hr; 3–4hr); Ujjain (every 30min–1hr; 1hr 30min–2hr).

By taxi A taxi to Ujjain, Maheshwar or Omkareshwar costs ₹1750–2500; one to Mandu costs ₹2100–3000.

ACCOMMODATION

Most of Indore's **hotels** cater for business visitors and are scattered around the prosperous suburb of **Tukoganj**. Budget travellers should ignore the dire lodges opposite the bus stand, and head for the better-value hotels along **Chhoti Gwaltoli**, just east of the railway station beneath the big Patel flyover (though note that not all are willing to accept foreign guests).

Ginger AB Rd, near Shanivar Darpan ⓣ 1860 266 3333, ⓦgingerhotels.com. The Indore outpost of this chain of mid-range hotels is a reliable choice: service is efficient, the en suites are equipped with wi-fi and flatscreen TVs, and there is a *Café Coffee Day* on site. The only downside is the location, a 10–15min auto-rickshaw ride north of the railway station. Book online in advance to knock around 50 percent off the rack rates. ₹3999

★ **Lemon Tree** RNT Rd ⓣ0731 442 3232, ⓦlemon treehotels.com. With a bright yellow exterior, smart service and sleek attached rooms set around a vast atrium decorated with modern art, this is the pick of Indore's top-end hotels. There's a restaurant, café, sports bar and fitness centre, and the rooms have nice touches like kettles, ergonomic chairs and orthopaedic mattresses. The rate

quoted here is for an advance online booking; rack rates are significantly higher. ₹5200

Neelam 33/2 Patel Bridge Corner ⓣ0731 246 6001, ⓣ251 8774. Despite its location on a dingy alley, this friendly establishment is the best of the budget options. Lining a central courtyard, the compact rooms with tiny attached bathrooms (some have squat toilets) are pretty clean and have TVs and phones. 24hr checkout. ₹500

Surya 5/5 Nath Mandir Rd ⓣ0731 407 9111, ⓦsuryaindore.com. While the rooms at this established mid-range hotel are showing their age, they're still comfortable, particularly those in the "executive" class (well worth the extra ₹250 or so). Service is good, and there's an excellent multicuisine restaurant and bar. ₹2350

EATING

Ambrosia Hotel Fortune Landmark, Vijaynagar, 3km northeast of the city centre ⓣ0731 398 84444. The

grand dining room has the air of a stately home, and the extensive Indian, Chinese and international menu (try the

5

mutton *rogan josh*) is suitably lofty. Not quite the food of the gods, but still pretty good. Mains ₹150–350. Daily noon–3pm & 7–11pm.

Celebration RNT Rd, in the annexe to the right of Hotel Shreemaya ☎ 0731 252 6666. A hygienic bakery and café renowned for its sweet goodies, including cavity-inducing black forest, pineapple and chocolate truffle cakes (around ₹50 a slice), as well as savoury snacks like *katchoris*. Daily 7.30am–10.30pm.

Indian Coffee House Next to Rampura Building, off MG Rd ☎ 0731 243 2226. Waiters in turbans and cummerbunds

serve quality south Indian veg breakfast items, north Indian meals and filter coffee (from ₹12). There's another branch in the Commissioner's Office compound off MG Rd. Mains ₹50–150. Daily 8am–10.30pm.

★ **Shreemaya** *Hotel Shreemaya*, RNT Rd ☎ 0731 423 4888. Adjoining veg and non-veg restaurants with curvy Art Deco-style ceilings, frosted glasswork and mouthwatering food: the vast chicken biriyani, *missi roti* and – if you have any space left – chocolate brownie and ice cream are not to be missed. Mains ₹140–270. Daily noon–3pm & 7–10.30pm.

DIRECTORY

Banks The State Bank of Indore has a foreign exchange office opposite their main branch on Raj Wada, and has an ATM on RNT Rd. ICICI Bank, 576 MG Rd, and Thomas Cook (☎ 0731 254 2525, ⊛ thomascook.in), Yeshwant Niwas Rd, are efficient alternatives. There are countless

other ATMs through the city.

Internet Internet access is available at Rimzim in the Silver Mall, off RNT Rd.

Travel agents President Travels at Hotel President, 163 RNT Rd (☎ 0731 253 3472) is a reliable agency.

Mandu

Set against the rugged Vindhya hills, the medieval ghost-town of **MANDU**, 98km southwest of Indore, is one of central India's most atmospheric monuments. Visit at the height of the monsoons, when the rocky plateau and its steeply shelving sides are carpeted with green vegetation, and you'll understand why the Malwa sultans christened their capital **Shadiabad** – "City of Joy".

Even during the relentless heat of the dry season, the ruins are an exotic spectacle. Elegant Islamic palaces, mosques and mausoleums crumble beside large medieval reservoirs and precipitous ravines, while below, an endless vista of scorched plains and tiny villages stretches off to the horizon. Mandu can be visited as a day-trip from Indore, but you'll enjoy it more if you spend a night or two, giving you time not only to explore the ruins, but also to witness the memorable sunsets over the Narmada Valley.

Mandu's monuments derive from a unique school of Islamic architecture that flourished here, and at Dhar, between 1400 and 1516. The elegantly simple buildings are believed to have exerted a considerable influence on the Mughal architects responsible for the Taj Mahal. Mandu's platform, a 23-square-kilometre plateau, is separated from the body of hills to the north by the **Kakra Khoh** ("deep ravine"). A narrow causeway forms a natural bridge across the gorge, carrying the present road across and up via a series of subsidiary gates to the fort's modern entrance, beside the original, Delhi Gate.

Brief history

Archeological evidence suggests the remote hilltop was fortified around the sixth century AD, when it was known as Mandapa-Durga, or "Durga's hall of worship" – later corrupted to "Mandu". Four hundred years later, the site gained in strategic importance when the powerful **Paramaras** moved their capital from Ujjain to Dhar, 35km north. Yet the plateau's natural defences proved unable to withstand persistent attacks by the Muslim invaders and the fort eventually fell to the sultans of Delhi in 1305.

While the Sultanate was busy fending off the Mongols on their northern borders a century or so later, Malwa's Afghan governor, Dilawar Khan Ghuri, seized the chance to establish his own independent kingdom. He died after just four years on the throne, however, leaving his ambitious young son at the helm. During **Hoshang Shah**'s illustrious 27-year reign, Mandu was promoted from pleasure resort to royal capital, and acquired some of the finest Islamic monuments in Asia.

Mandu's golden age continued under the **Khaljis**, who took over from the Ghuri dynasty in 1436. Another building boom and several protracted wars later, Mandu settled down to a lengthy period of peace and prosperity under **Ghiyath Shah** (1469–1500). He amassed a harem of 15,000 courtesans, and a bodyguard of 1000 women, whom he accommodated in the appropriately lavish Jahaz Mahal. The sybaritic sultan was poisoned by his son shortly after his eightieth birthday. His successor, Nasir Shah, died ten years later, and Mandu, dogged by feuds and the threat of rebellion, became an easy target for the militaristic sultan of Gujarat, who invaded in 1526. In the centuries that followed, control over the fort and its rapidly decaying monuments passed between a succession of independent rulers and the Mughals. By the time King James I's ambassador, **Sir Thomas Roe**, followed the mobile court of Emperor Jahangir here in 1617, most of the city lay in ruins, its mansions and tombs occupied by Bhil villagers whose descendants continue to scratch a living from the surrounding fields. Mandu today is a tranquil backwater that sees far fewer visitors than it deserves, save for the busloads of exuberant Indian day-trippers on weekends.

The Royal Enclave

Daily except Fri sunrise–sunset • ₹100 (₹5), video ₹25

Reached via the lane that leads west off the village square is the **Royal Enclave**. Just inside the entrance is a bookshop and a small **museum** (free) with a modest collection of stone carvings and pottery fragments. The Royal Enclave is dominated by Ghiyath Shah's majestic **Jahaz Mahal**, or "Ship Palace". The name derives from its unusual shape and elevated situation on a narrow strip of land between two large water tanks. A rooftop terrace, crowned with four domed pavilions, overlooks **Munja Talao** lake to the

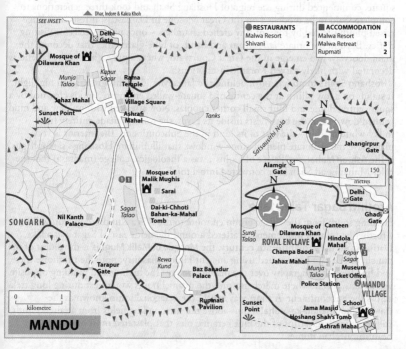

5

west, and the square, stone-lined **Kapur Sagar** to the east. From the northern balcony, you also get a good view of the geometric sandstone bathing pools.

The next building along the lane is the **Hindola Mahal**, or "Swing Palace" – so-called because its distinctive sloping walls supposedly look as though they are swaying from side to side. The design was, in fact, purely functional, intended to buttress the graceful but heavy stone arches that support the ceiling inside. At the far end of the T-shaped assembly hall, a long stepped ramp allowed the sultan to reach the upper storey on elephant-back.

Champa Baodi

Sprawling over the northern shores of Munja Talao are the dilapidated remains of a second royal pleasure palace. The **Champa Baodi** boasts an ingeniously complex ventilation and water-supply system, which kept its dozens of subterranean chambers cool during the long Malwan summers. Immediately to the north stands the venerable **Mosque of Dilawara Khan**, dating from 1405. The chunks of Hindu temple used to build its main doorway and colonnaded hall are still very evident.

The **Hathi Pol**, or "Elephant Gate", with its pair of colossal, half-decapitated elephant guardians, was the main entrance to the Royal Enclave but is now closed. To reach the edge of the plateau and the grand **Delhi Gate** you will have to return to the bazaar and follow the road out of Mandu. Built around the same time as Dilawara Khan's mosque, this great bastion, towering over the cobbled road in five sculpted arches, is the most imposing of the twelve that stud the battlements along the fort's 45km perimeter.

The village group

Daily sunrise–sunset • ₹100 (₹5), video ₹25

Some of the fort's best-preserved buildings are clustered **around the village**. Work on the magnificent pink-sandstone mosque, the **Jama Masjid** on the west side of the main square, commenced during the reign of Hoshang Shah and took three generations to complete. Said to be modelled on the Great Mosque in Damascus, it rests on a huge raised plinth pierced by rows of tiny arched chambers – once used as cells for visiting clerics. Beyond the ornate *jali* screens and bands of blue-glazed tiles that decorate the main doorway, you emerge in the Great Courtyard, where a prayer hall at the far end is decorated with finely carved Koranic inscriptions.

Hoshang Shah's tomb (c.1440), behind the Jama Masjid, is this group's real highlight. It stands on a low plinth at the centre of a square-walled enclosure, and is crowned by a squat central dome and four small corner cupolas. Now streaked with mildew and mud washed down from the bats' nests inside its eaves, the tomb is made entirely from milky-white marble – the first of its kind in the Subcontinent. The interior is very plain, save the elaborate pierced-stone windows that illuminate Hoshang's sarcophagus.

The **Ashrafi Mahal**, or "Palace of Coins", was a theological college (madrasa) that the ruler Muhammad Shah later converted into a tomb.

Around Sagar Talao lake

Heading south from the village group en route to the Rewa Kund group, you will find a further handful of monuments scattered around the fields east of Sagar Talao lake. Dating from the early fifteenth century, the **Mosque of Malik Mughis** is the oldest of the bunch, once again constructed using ancient Hindu masonry; note the turquoise tiles and fine Islamic calligraphy over the main doorway. The high-walled building opposite was a *caravanserai*, where merchants and their camel trains would rest during long treks across the Subcontinent. A short way south, the octagonal tomb known as the **Dai-ki-Chhoti Bahan-ka-Mahal** looms above the surrounding fields from a raised plinth, still retaining large strips of the blue ceramic tiles that plastered most of Mandu's beautiful Afghan domes.

The Rewa Kund ~~Group~~

Daily sunrise–sunset • ₹100 (₹5), video ₹25

The road to the **Rewa Kund Group** heads past herds of water buffalo grazing on the muddy foreshores of the lake, then winds its way gently through a couple of Bhil villages towards the far southern edge of the plateau; stately old baobabs line the roadside, like giant upturned root vegetables. The **Rewa Kund** itself, an old stone tank noted for its curative waters, lies 6km south of the main village. Water from it used to be pumped into the cistern in the nearby **Baz Bahadur Palace**. Bahadur, the last independent ruler of Malwa, retreated to Mandu to study music after being trounced in battle by Rani Durgavati. Legend has it that he fell in love with a Hindu singer named Rupmati, whom he enticed to his hilltop home with an exquisite palace. The couple eventually married, but did not live happily ever after. When Akbar heard of Rupmati's beauty, he dispatched an army to Mandu to capture her and the long-coveted fort. Bahadur managed to slip away, but his bride, left behind in the palace, poisoned herself rather than fall into the clutches of the attackers.

Rupmati Pavilion

The romantic **Rupmati Pavilion**, built by Bahadur for his bride-to-be, rests on a ridge high above the Rewa Kund; beneath its lofty terrace, the plateau plunges a sheer 300m to the Narmada Valley. The view is breathtaking, especially at sunset or on a clear day.

ARRIVAL AND DEPARTURE
MANDU

By bus Although there are a couple of direct buses to Mandu from Indore (2 daily; 3hr 30min–4hr), it's often quicker to travel to Dhar (every 30min–1hr; 2hr) and pick up one of the local services to Mandu (every 30min; 1hr 30min) from there.

By taxi A taxi to Mandu from Indore costs ₹2100–3000.

GETTING AROUND

By bike and auto-rickshaw If you don't have your own vehicle, the most pleasant way of getting around the fort and its widely dispersed monuments is by bicycle (₹100/ day from *Malwa Resort*, or half that from Ritik Bicycle Shop, near *Shivani* restaurant). Alternatively, rent an auto-rickshaw for a complete tour (around ₹250).

ACCOMMODATION

Malwa Resort 2km south of the square ✆ 07292 263235, ⓦ mptourism.com. This MP Tourism-run hotel is by some distance the most comfortable choice in town. It has a collection of air-cooled and a/c cottages, both with lake-facing verandas; the latter have separate seating and dressing areas and fridges. There's also a good restaurant and a bar. ₹2140

Malwa Retreat Just south of Hotel Rupmati ✆ 07292 263221, ⓦ mptourism.com. The rooms and (more comfortable) "Swiss" tents (₹2460) at this MP Tourism-run hotel are clean and compact, with partial views of the gorge; some of the rooms, however, also have water damage on the walls, so ask to see a few. ₹1385

Rupmati North end of the plateau near the Nagar Panchayat barrier ✆ 07292 263270. The overpriced, attached rooms here have red carpets, pink walls and brown bed covers – fortunately there's also a TV and a shared veranda with ravine views to take your mind of the decor, plus a decent restaurant. It's 1km from the bus stand, so ask the driver to be dropped off en route to the town centre. ₹1300

EATING

Avoid meat and *paneer*, as frequent power-cuts mean even places with refrigerators have problems keeping perishables fresh.

Malwa Resort 2km south of the square. One of the smarter restaurants in town, serving the usual MP Tourism menu: meat and veg Indian and Chinese dishes, with a few Continental options thrown in for good measure (mains ₹70–310). There's also an attached bar. Daily 8–10am, noon–3pm & 7–10.30pm.

Shivani Halfway between the square and the Nagar Panchayat barrier. This modest restaurant has a wider range of food than most of its competitors in Mandu, with dishes from the north and south of India, as well as a tasty Gujarati-style thali. Mains from ₹40. Daily 9am–9pm.

5

Ujjain

On the banks of the sacred Shirpa River, **UJJAIN**, 55km north of Indore, is one of India's seven holiest cities. Like Haridwar, Nasik and Prayag, it plays host every twelve years to the country's largest religious gathering, the **Kumbh Mela** (see box, p.264), which has in the past drawn an estimated 30 million pilgrims here to bathe. Outside festival times, Ujjain is great for people-watching, as pilgrims and locals alike go about their daily business. Around the main temples, you see modern Hinduism at its most kitsch, with all types of devotional paraphernalia, gaudy lighting and plastic flower garlands for sale. At the *ghats*, women flap wet saris dry, children splash in the water, and pujaris ply their trade beneath the rows of riverside shrines. A mini-Varanasi Ujjain is not, but the temples rising behind the *ghats* are majestic at dusk, and with the ringing of bells and incense drifting around, this atmospheric place can feel timeless.

The Western Railway cuts straight through the **centre** of Ujjain, forming a neat divide between the spacious and affluent residential suburbs to the south and the more interesting, densely packed streets northwest of the station. Unless you spend all day wandering through the **bazaar**, sightseeing in Ujjain usually means treading the **temple** trail, with a brief foray south of the *ghats* to visit the **Vedha Shala observatory**.

Brief history

Excavations north of Ujjain have yielded traces of settlement as far back as the eighth century BC. The ancient city was a major regional capital under the Mauryans (Ashok was once governor here), when it was known as **Avantika** and lay on the main trade route linking northern India with Mesopotamia and Egypt. According to Hindu mythology, Shiva later changed its name to **Ujjaiyini**, "He Who Conquers With Pride", to mark his victory over the demon king of Tripuri. Chandra Gupta II, renowned for his patronage of the arts, also ruled from here in the fourth and fifth centuries AD. Among the Nava Ratna, or "Nine Gems", of his court was the illustrious Sanskrit poet

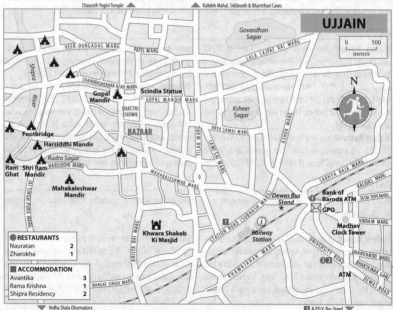

Map: **UJJAIN**

Chausath Yogini Temple — Kalideh Mahal, Siddavath & Bhartrihari Caves

Govardhan Sagar

VEER DURGADAS MARG — PATEL MARG — LALA LAJPAT RAI MARG

Shipra River

CHANDRASHEKHAR AZAD MARG

Gopal Mandir — **Scindia Statue**
GOPAL MANDIR MARG

CHATTRI CHOWK

Ksheer Sagar

ASHOK MARG

Footbridge

BAZAAR

Harsiddhi Mandir

Rudra Sagar

ARYA SAMAJ MARG

TILAK MARG

LAXMI PAN MARG

Ram Ghat — Shri Ram Mandir — HARSIDDHI MARG

Mahakaleshwar Mandir

MAHAKALESHWAR MARG

SAKHYA RAJA MARG

Dewas Bus Stand

Bank of Baroda ATM

KALIDAS MARG

TATIA TOPE MARG

GPO

JAI SINGH PURA MARG

AHILYA BAI MARG

Khwara Shakeb Ki Masjid

STATION ROAD (SUBHASH MARG)

Railway Station

Madhav Clock Tower

VIKRAM MARG

UNIVERSITY ROAD

DHANVANTRI MARG

BHARTWAR GANJ

KHAWATAHAN MARG

BHAGAT SINGH MARG

DEWAS ROAD

ATM

● **RESTAURANTS**
| Nauratan | 2 |
| Zharokha | 1 |

■ **ACCOMMODATION**
Avantika	3
Rama Krishna	1
Shipra Residency	2

▼ Vedha Shala Observatory

0 — 500 metres

N

▼ 3 & P.D.V. Bus Stand

Kalidasa, whose much-loved narrative poem *Meghduta* ("Cloud Messenger") includes a lyrical evocation of the city. (**E.M. Forster** visited Ujjain in 1914, determined to get an idea of what it looked like in Kalidasa's day. He soon admitted defeat, declaring: "Old buildings are buildings, ruins are ruins.")

Most of Ujjain's temples were razed in 1234 by Iltutmish, of the Delhi Slave Dynasty. Thereafter, the Malwan capital was governed by the sultans of Mandu, the Mughals, and **Raja Jai Singh** from Jaipur, who designed the Vedha Shala observatory (Ujjain straddles the Hindu first meridian of longitude). Ujjain's fortunes have declined since the early eighteenth century, except for a sixty-year renaissance between the arrival of the Scindias in 1750 and their departure to Gwalior. Today, nearby Indore dominates the region's industrial activity, leaving Ujjain to make its living by more traditional means.

Mahakaleshwar Mandir

Overlooking the river • No fixed opening times • Free

Ujjain's chief landmark, the **Mahakaleshwar Mandir**, crowning a rise above the river, is the logical place to start a tour of the town. Its gigantic saffron-painted sanctuary tower, a modern replacement built by the Scindias in the nineteenth century for one destroyed by Iltutmish in 1234, soars high above a complex of marble courtyards, water tanks and fountains, advertising the presence below of one of India's most powerful *shivalingams*. Housed in a claustrophobic subterranean chamber, the deity is one of India's twelve **jyotirlingam** – "lingam of light" – whose essential energy, or *shakti*, is "born of itself", rather than from the rituals performed around it, and is considered particularly potent, especially by Tantric followers, due to its unusual south-facing position.

Harsiddhi Mandir

West of the Mahakaleshwar Mandir • No fixed opening times • Free

From the Mahakaleshwar Mandir, head west down the hill past the Rudra Sagar tank to the auspicious **Harsiddhi Mandir**, which Hindu mythology identifies as the spot where Parvati's elbow fell to earth while Shiva was carrying her burning body from the *sati* pyre. Its main shrine, erected by the Marathas in the eighteenth century, houses (from left to right) images of Mahalakshmi (the goddess of wealth), Annapurna (goddess of food and sustenance), and Saraswati (goddess of wisdom).

Gopal Mandir

Northwest of Chattri Chowk, a chaotic market square in the heart of the bazaar • No fixed opening times • Free

Northwest of Chattri Chowk the picturesque **Gopal Mandir** was erected by one of the Scindia ranis in the early nineteenth century. With its blend of Mughal domes, Moorish arches and lofty Hindu sanctuary tower, the temple is a fine example of late Maratha architecture. Inside, it is worth noting the sanctum's silver-plated doors. These were fitted here by Mahaji Scindia, who rescued them from Lahore after they had been carried off by Muslim looters. The shrine room itself, lined with marble, silver and mother-of-pearl, contains icons of the presiding deity, Gopal (Krishna), and his parents, Shiva and Parvati.

The Vedha Shala observatory

1km southwest of the railway station • Daily dawn–dusk • ₹5; guides are free, though they may expect a tip

Ujjain was the birthplace of mathematical astronomy in India, research into the motion of the stars and planets having been carried out here since the time of

5

Ashoka. Later, Hindu astronomers fixed both the **first meridian** of longitude and the Tropic of Cancer here – the reason why Raja Jai Singh of Jaipur, governor of Malwa under the Mughal emperor Mohammad Shah, chose it as the site for another of his surreal open-air observatories. Built in 1725, the **Vedha Shala observatory** lies 1km southwest of the railway station, overlooking the Shirpa River. The complex is smaller than its more famous cousins in Delhi and Jaipur, the Jantar Mantars, but remains in excellent condition with very informative guides and labelling. Local astronomers still use its five instruments to formulate ephemeredes (charts predicting the positions of the planets), which you can buy at the site.

ARRIVAL AND DEPARTURE UJJAIN

By train The station, which sits on both branches of the Western Railway, is in the centre of town. There's an MP Tourism office in the railway station (Mon–Sat 10am–5pm; ☎ 0734 256 1544).

Destinations Bhopal (5–8 daily; 2hr 50min–4hr 45min); Gwalior (1–3 daily; 9hr 27min–13hr 55min); Indore (9–12 daily; 1hr 30min–2hr 25min); Jabalpur (1–2 daily; 11hr 5min–11hr 20min); Jaipur (2–3 daily; 8hr 40min–13hr 5min); Mumbai (1–2 daily; 12hr 30min–13hr 10min).

By bus Just northeast of the railway station is the Dewas Bus Stand, from where buses for Bhopal, Dhar (for connections to Mandu and Maheshwar) and Omkareshwar arrive and depart. The inconvenient PDV Bus Stand, next to MP Tourism's *Avantika*, 2km south of town, serves Indore.

By MP Bus MP Tourism sometimes runs buses to Indore and Omkareshwar; ask at the MP Tourism office for more information.

Destinations Bhopal (2–3 daily; 5–6hr); Dhar (4 daily; 4hr); Indore (every 30min; 1hr 30min–2hr); Omkareshwar (4–5 daily; 3hr 45min–4hr 30min).

GETTING AROUND

By auto-rickshaw or bicycle Ujjain is fairly spread out, so you'll need to get around by auto-rickshaw or by renting a bicycle (around R50/day) from the shop opposite the Dewas Bus Stand.

By taxi Taxis (around ₹1750–2500/day) can be arranged through the MP Tourism office.

ACCOMMODATION

Avantika Off Lal Bahadur Shastri Marg, 2km south of town ☎ 0734 251 1398, ⓦ mptourism.com. Also known as *Yatri Niwas*, this MP Tourism-run hotel has an institutional feel. The best bet for shoestring travellers is the partitioned dorm (₹200), which has comfortable beds and clean sheets; the private rooms are fine but overpriced. There's a decent restaurant too. **₹1060**

Rama Krishna Station Rd (Subhash Marg), opposite the railway station ☎ 0734 255 3017. A notch above the other flophouses in the station area; the large but tired rooms have attached bathrooms with fairly reliable hot water. While the rooms themselves are pretty clean, the bedding is not. Look out for the "RK" sign on the roof, as it's easy to miss the entrance. **₹400**

Shipra Residency University Rd ☎ 0734 255 1495, ⓦ mptourism.com. A tranquil, white-tiled courtyard is the centrepiece of this MP Tourism-run hotel (just about the best in town), around which are comfortable a/c rooms with fancy quilts. There's also a good restaurant and bar. **₹2460**

EATING

Ujjain suffers from a dearth of acceptable places to eat. There's a cluster of food stalls by the clock tower but, as with the inexpensive *dhabas* opposite the railway station, you should only frequent the most popular ones.

Nauratan Shipra Residency University Rd ☎ 0734 255 1495, ⓦ mptourism.com. Typical MP Tourism menu – veg Indian, tandoori and Chinese dishes, plus a few Western options like fish and chips – in relaxed surroundings, plus Ujjain's widest choice of alcoholic drinks. Mains from ₹70. Daily noon–3pm & 7–10.30pm.

Zharokha Grand Tower, Vikram Marg ☎ 0734 255 3699. A varied menu of north Indian standards, with particularly rich sauces, plus a few obligatory Chinese dishes thrown in for good measure. Daily 7.30am–3.30pm & 7–11pm.

DIRECTORY

Banks Indore is the nearest place to change money, but IDIBI Bank on University Rd and the State Bank of India, near the clock tower, have ATMs.

Maheshwar

Overlooking the north bank of the mighty Narmada River, 91km southwest of Indore, **MAHESHWAR** was the site of King Kartvirajun's ancient capital, **Mahishmati**, a city mentioned in both the Mahabharata and Ramayana. In the eighteenth century, Maharani **Ahilya Bai** built a palace and several temples here, giving the town a new lease of life. Today, it's a prominent port of call on the Narmada Hindu pilgrimage circuit, but well off the tourist trail.

The ghats

The waterfront **ghats** below an old sandstone palace make a quintessentially Indian spectacle. Parties of *yatris* take holy dips, while pujaris and groups of sadhus sit around murmuring prayers under raffia sunshades. For the best view of them, head for the overhanging balcony of the eighteenth-century **Ahilya Bai Mandir**, reached via steps under the facade of the palace behind.

The Rewa Society workshops

Palace and fort complex • Mon–Fri 10am–5pm • Free

The palace and fort complex houses the workshops of the **Rewa Society**, established by the maharani 250 years ago to promote the local handloom industry. Maheshwari **saris** are famous for their distinctive patterns and high quality; you can visit the weavers' workshops. Though descendants of the old ruling family still occupy parts of the building, a couple of rooms around the entrance courtyard have been given over to a small, eminently missable museum.

ARRIVAL AND DEPARTURE
MAHESHWAR

By bus All roads leading to Maheshwar are in a terrible state. If you're travelling from Indore, you'll need to change buses at the market town of Dhamnod.

Destinations Dhamnod (every 30min; 30min); Dhar (every 30min; 2hr); and Omkareshwar (every 30min–1hr; 3hr).
By taxi A taxi from Indore or Ujjain costs ₹1750–2500.

ACCOMMODATION AND EATING

★ **Ahilya Fort** On the banks of the river ☎ 011 4155 1575, ⊚ ahilyafort.com. This heritage hotel is run by the son of the last maharaja of Indore. The sixteenth-century fort houses gorgeously ornate rooms with stone walls and colonial-era furnishings. There's a pool and lovely gardens, and exquisite food is served in the restaurant (open to non-guests who reserve in advance). Two-night minimum stay. ₹26,640

Akash Deep Rest House Just to the right of fort car park ☎ 07283 273326. In the centre of town, the welcoming *Aakash Deep Rest House* has rather threadbare rooms with private bathrooms (some with partial views of the fort). It's acceptable for a night if you're on a tight budget. ₹300

Narmada Retreat 1km outside town ☎ 07283 273455, ⊚ mptourism.com. This MP Tourism-run hotel has cosy rooms in cottages and comfy a/c tents (₹2350), as well as an appealing restaurant. Make sure you bring mosquito repellent and a net. ₹2140

Omkareshwar

East of the main river crossing at Barwaha, the Narmada River dips southwards, sweeps north again to form a wide bend, and then forks around a 2km-long wedge-shaped outcrop of sandstone. Seen from above, the island, cut by several deep ravines, bears an uncanny resemblance to the "Om" symbol. This, coupled with the presence on its sheer south-facing side of a revered *shivalingam*, has made **OMKARESHWAR**, 77km south of Indore, one of central India's most sacred Hindu sites. Since ancient times, pilgrims have flocked here for *darshan* and a holy dip in the river, but in recent years, the town's

5

remoteness and loaded religious feel have made it a favourite with hard-core Western and Israeli dope-heads. Despite this, and the contentious Omkareshwar dam, the building of which led to the displacement of many thousands of people from nearby villages, the place manages to retain an authentic atmosphere among its temples, wayside shrines, bathing places and caves, which are strung together by an old paved pilgrims' trail.

The prominent white *shikhara* that soars above the **Shri Omkar Mandhata Mandir** is a relatively new addition to the dense cluster of buildings on the south side of the island. Below it, the ornate pillars in the assembly hall, or *mandapa*, are more representative of the shrine's great antiquity. Myths relating to the origins of the deity in the low-ceilinged sanctum date back to the second century BC. Another of India's 12 **jyotirlingams** ("lingams of light"), it is said by Hindus to have emerged spontaneously from the earth after a struggle between Brahma, Vishnu and Shiva.

The parikrama

Traditionally, the *parikrama* (circular tour) of Omkareshwar begins at the *ghats* below Shri Mandhata and proceeds clockwise **around the island**. The walk takes at least a couple of hours, so carry plenty of water.

The Triveni Sangam and the Gaudi Somnath Temple

The first section of the trail is a leisurely half-hour stroll from the footbridge to the pebble-strewn western tip of the island, where you'll find a small chai stall and a couple of insignificant shrines. The **Triveni Sangam**, or "Three-rivers Confluence", is an especially propitious bathing place where the Narmada River forks as it merges with the Kaveri River. From here, the path climbs above the fringe of fine white sand lining the northern shore until it reaches level ground. The ruins of the **Gaudi Somnath Temple** stand in the middle of the plateau, surrounded by a sizeable collection of sculpture mounted on concrete plinths. The sanctuary houses a colossal *shivalingam*, attended by an equally huge Nandi bull. At this point, drop down a steep flight of steps to the village, or continue east towards the old fortified town that crowned the top of the island before it was ransacked by Muslims in the medieval era. Numerous chunks of temple sculpture lying discarded among the rubble include a couple of finely carved gods and goddesses, used for shade by families of langur monkeys.

The Surajkund Gate and the Siddhesvara Temple

After scaling the sides of a gully, the trail leads under the large ornamental archway of the **Surajkund Gate**, flanked by 3m figures of Arjun and Bheema, two of the illustrious Pandava brothers. The tenth-century **Siddhesvara Temple** stands five minutes' walk away to the south, on a patch of flat ground overlooking the river. Raised on a large plinth decorated with rampaging elephants, it has some fine *apsara*s, or celestial dancers, carved over its southern doorway.

Back to the village

Of the two possible routes back to the village, one takes you along the top of the plateau before dropping sharply down, via another ruined temple and the **maharaja's palace**, to the Shri Mandhata temple. The other follows a flight of steps to the riverbank, and then heads past a group of sadhus' caves to the main *ghat*s.

ARRIVAL AND DEPARTURE   **OMKARESHWAR**

From the bus stand at the bottom of the village on the mainland, Omkareshwar's only street runs 400m uphill to a ramshackle **square**, where you'll find most of the *dharamshalas* and chai shops, and a handful of stalls hawking lurid puja

5

THE PILGRIMS' WAY

For those seeking the ascetic experience, the *dharamshalas* in the mainland village are inexpensive (around ₹50–100), and offer close-up experience of pilgrim culture. On the down side, rooms tend to be windowless cells, with washing facilities limited to a standpipe in the yard and communal toilets. One of the best is **Jat Samaj**, facing the river, to the right of the bridge on the main square – look for the rooftop figure on horseback. Alternatively head to **Ahilya Bai**, tucked away behind the Vishnu temple off the road to Mamaleshwar temple and the *ghats*, or its neighbour, **Tirole Kunbi Patel**.

paraphernalia (including the excellent stylized maps taken home by pilgrims as souvenirs). To **get to the island** itself, cross the high concrete footbridge or take one of the flat-bottomed ferries that shuttle between the *ghats* crouched at the foot of the river gorge.

By train Omkareshwar Road is the nearest railhead, but only slow passenger services stop here. Barwaha, on the north bank of the Narmada River, is the closest mainline railway station.

By bus Buses are generally more convenient than trains. In addition to the state services listed below, MP Tourism sometimes runs a/c buses to/from Indore and Ujjain; ask at the *Narmada Resort* for more information.

Destinations Dhamnod (every 30min; 3hr 30min); Indore (every 30min–1hr; 3–4hr); Maheshwar (every 30min–1hr; 3hr); Ujjain (4–5 daily; 3hr 45min–4hr 30min).

ACCOMMODATION AND EATING

Ganesh Guest House Near Tirole Kunbi Patel ☎ 07280 271370. This friendly place has a cool traveller vibe, good views and a "foreign tourists only" policy, though rooms are very spartan. Its restaurant, *Third Eye*, has a veg menu featuring so-so pizza and pasta, a sprinkling of Israeli and Indian dishes, tasty pancakes and some great Tibetan *momos* (steamed dumplings) and *thukpas* (soups). ₹300

Narmada Resort A couple of kilometres before the bus stand ☎ 07280 271455, ⓦ mptourism.com. This MP Tourism-run place is the smartest option in town. It has plain but clean rooms with private bathrooms and either a/c or air coolers, plus a reliable restaurant and bar. ₹1170

Himachal Pradesh

KI GOMPA, SPITI VALLEY

Himachal Pradesh

Ruffled by the lower ridges of the Shivalik Range in the far south, cut through by the Pir Panjal and Dhauladhar ranges in the northwest, and dominated by the great Himalayas in the north and east, Himachal Pradesh (HP) is India's most popular and easily accessible hill state. Sandwiched between the Punjab and Tibet, its lowland orchards, subtropical forests and maize fields peter out in the higher reaches where pines cling to the steep slopes of mountains whose inhospitable peaks soar in rocky crags and forbidding ice fields to heights of more than 6000m.

Together with deep gorges cut by rivers crashing down from the Himalayas, these mountains form natural boundaries between the state's separate districts. Each has its own architecture, from rock-cut shrines and *shikhara* temples to colonial mansions and Buddhist monasteries. Roads struggle against the vagaries of the climate to connect the larger settlements, which are way outnumbered by remote villages, many of which are home to seminomadic **Gaddi** and **Gujjar** shepherds.

An obvious way to approach the state is to head north from Delhi to the state capital, **Shimla**, beyond the lush and temperate valleys of **Sirmaur**. The former summer location of the British government, Shimla is a curious, appealing mix of grand homes, churches and chaotic bazaars, with breathtaking views. The main road **northeast** from Shimla tackles a pass just north of **Narkanda**, then follows the River Sutlej east towards **Sarahan**, with its spectacular wooden temple, before entering the eastern district of **Kinnaur**, much of which is accessible only to those holding **Inner Line permits** (see box, p.402). Kinnaur becomes more austere and barren as it stretches east to the Tibetan plateau, its beauty enhanced by delicate timber houses, temples and fluttering prayer flags.

Another road from Shimla climbs slowly northwest to **Mandi**, a major staging post for the state. To the north is Himachal's most popular tourist spot, the **Kullu Valley**, an undulating mass of terraced fields, orchards and forests overlooked by snowy peaks. Its epicentre is the continuously expanding tourist town of **Manali** – long a favourite hangout of Western hippies – set in idyllic mountain scenery and offering trekking, whitewater rafting and relaxing hot springs in nearby **Vashisht**. The sacred site of **Manikaran** in the Parvati Valley also has hot sulphur-free springs.

Beyond the Rohtang Pass in the far north of Kullu district, the high-altitude desert valleys of **Lahaul and Spiti** stretch beneath massive snow-capped peaks and remote settlements with Tibetan *gompas* dotting the landscape. **Permits** are needed for travel through to Kinnaur, but **Ki**, **Kaza** and **Tabo** have unrestricted access, as does the road through Lahaul to Leh in Ladakh.

THE TOY TRAIN TO SHIMLA

Highlights

❶ **The toy train** A rattly ride through stunning mountain scenery to the Raj-era hill station of Shimla. **See p.405**

❷ **Sarahan** A short detour en route to Kinnaur will be rewarded with fine views of the Sutlej Valley and a visit to the atmospheric Bhimakali temple. **See p.410**

❸ **Rewalsar** Buddhist pilgrimage site based around a sacred lake, with monasteries, temples, caves and hermitages. **See p.417**

❹ **Dharamsala** This relaxing hill station, home of the Dalai Lama, is an ever-popular place for rest, meditation retreats and trekking. **See p.418**

❺ **Dhauladhar trek** A fantastic five-day trek leading through Dhauladhar forest to the Indrahar Pass, visiting traditional villages. **See p.426**

❻ **Naggar** This quiet spot high up on the side of the Kullu Valley is a great place to relax and enjoy sweeping views. **See p.438**

❼ **Spiti Valley** Tiny Tibetan villages and beautiful white *gompas* dot Spiti's astonishing, weathered landscape. **See p.450**

❽ **Manali–Leh Highway** The second highest road in the world, passing through a vast wilderness between Himachal's honeymoon capital and Ladakh. **See p.455**

HIGHLIGHTS ARE MARKED ON THE MAP ON PP.400–401

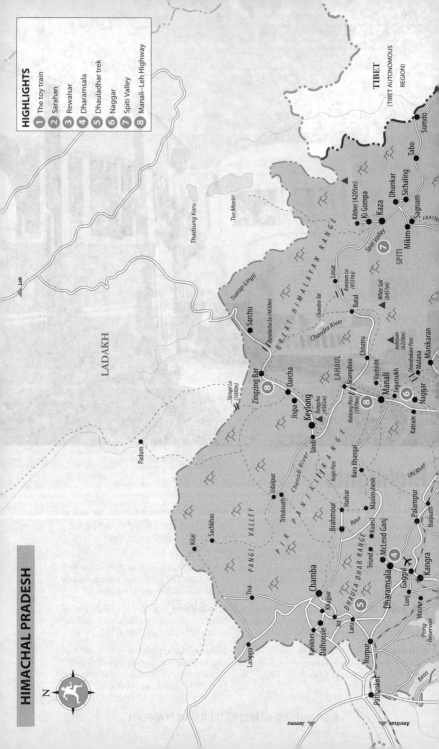

HIMACHAL PRADESH

N

TIBET

(TIBET AUTONOMOUS
REGION)

Sumdo

Tabo

Sichaling

Dhankar

Kibber (4205m)
Ki Gompa
Kaza
Sagnam

Mikim

Spiti River

SPITI

Spiti Valley 7

Leh

Thadsung Karu

Tso Moriri

Losar

Kunzum La
(4551m)

White Sail
(6451m)

LADAKH

Tsarap-Lingti

Sarchu

Baralacha La (4830m)

G R E A T   H I M A L A Y A N   R A N G E

Chandra-Tal

Batal

Chandra River

Chhatru

Chhatru

Indrasan
(6220m)

Chandrakani Pass

Malana

Manikaran

Vashisht
Manali
Jagatsukh

Katrain

Naggar 6

Zingzing Bar 8

Darcha

Jispa

Keylong

Shingo La
(5000m)

Padum

Rangcha
(4565m)

Tandi

LAHAUL

Gramphoo

Rohtang Pass
(3978m)

Manali 8

Kugti Pass

Chenab River

C H E N A B   R I V E R

P A N J A L   R A N G E

Udaipur

Triloknath

Bara Bhangal

Uhl River

Palampur

Baijnath

Sachkhas

Kilar

P I R   P A N J A L   V A L L E Y

Brahmour

Hadsar

Kuarsi
Manimahesh

Ravi

McLeod Ganj

Triund

4

Dharamsala

Kangra

Gaggal

Luni

Tisa

Chamba

Khajjiar

D H A U L A D H A R   R A N G E

5

Matur

Pong
Reservoir

Bairkhet

Dalhousie

Jot

Laru

Nurpur

Beas

Langera

Pathankot

Jammu

Amritsar

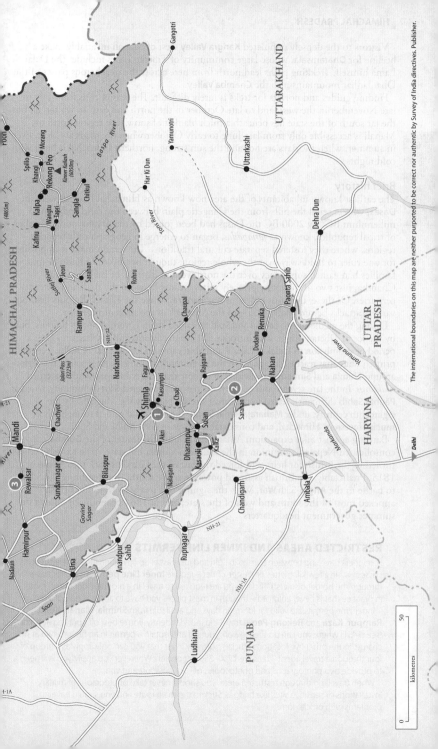

The international boundaries on this map are neither purported to be correct nor authentic by Survey of India directives. Publisher.

Visitors to the densely populated **Kangra Valley** west of Manali invariably make a beeline for **Dharamsala**, whose large community of Tibetan exiles includes the Dalai Lama himself. Trekking paths lead north from here across the treacherous passes of the Dhauladhar mountains into the **Chamba Valley**.

Finding guides and porters for **treks** is rarely difficult. The season runs from July to late November in the west, and to late October in the north and east. In **winter**, all but the far south of the state lies beneath a thick blanket of snow. The region north of Manali is accessible only from late June to early October when the roads are clear. Even in **summer**, when the days are hot and the sun strong, northern Himachal is beset with cold nights.

Brief history

The earliest known inhabitants of the area now known as Himachal Pradesh were the **Dasas**, who entered the hills from the Gangetic plain between the third and second millennium BC. By 2000 BC the Dasas had been joined by the **Aryans**, and a number of tribal republics, known as *janapadas*, began to emerge in geographically separate regions, where they fostered separate cultural traditions. The terrain made it impossible for one ruler to hold sway over the whole region, though by 550 AD Hindu Rajput families had gained supremacy over the northwestern districts of Brahmour and Chamba, just two of the many princely states created between the sixth and sixteenth centuries. Of these, the most powerful was **Kangra**, where the Katoch Rajputs held off various attacks before finally falling to the Mughals in the sixteenth century.

During the medieval era, **Lahaul and Spiti** remained aloof, governed not by Rajputs, but by the Jos of Tibetan origin, who introduced Tibetan customs and architecture. After a period of submission to Ladakh, Lahaul and Spiti came under the rajas of **Kullu**, a central princely state that reached its apogee in the seventeenth century. Further south, the region around **Shimla** and **Sirmaur** was divided into more than thirty independently governed *thakurais*. In the late seventeenth century, the newly empowered **Sikh** community, based at **Paonta Sahib** (Sirmaur), added to the threat already posed by the Mughals. By the eighteenth century, under **Maharaja Ranjit Singh**, the Sikhs had gained strongholds in much of western Himachal, and considerable power in both Kullu and Spiti.

Battling against Sikh expansion, Amar Singh Tapur, the leader of the **Gurkha** army, consolidated Nepalese dominion in the southern Shimla hill states. The *thakurai* chiefs turned to the **British** for help, and forced the last of the Gurkhas back into Nepal in 1815. Predictably, the British assumed power over the south, thus tempting the Sikhs to battle in the **Anglo-Sikh War**. With the signing of a treaty in 1846 the British annexed most of the south and west of the state, and in 1864 pronounced Shimla the summer government headquarters.

RESTRICTED AREAS AND INNER LINE PERMITS

Foreigners travelling between Sumdo in Spiti and just east of Spillo in Kinnaur – where the road passes within a few kilometres of Western Tibet – require **Inner Line permits**, valid for travel through the border districts. Officially you are required to travel in a group of four or more, but in practice that is never enforced – though in most places you have to apply as part of a group.

Inner Line permits are valid for fourteen days and available from **Shimla**, **Manali**, **Kullu**, **Rampur**, **Kaza** and **Rekong Peo**. If travelling independently, you're best off applying at **Kaza** (see p.451) where you can do the legwork yourself and obtain a permit in an hour or two at no charge. In the other five locations officials normally insist that you can only apply as a group of four through a travel agent – fees are ₹200–350 per person. Wherever you apply, you will need to provide two photographs and photocopies of your passport and visa.

When travelling through restricted areas, you should never take photographs of military installations or sensitive sites like bridges. Stick to the main route and you should have no problems with officialdom.

After Independence, the regions bordering present-day Punjab were integrated and named Himachal Pradesh ("Himalayan Provinces"). In 1956 HP was recognized as a Union Territory and ten years later the modern state was formed, with Shimla as its capital. Despite being a political unity, Himachal Pradesh is culturally very diverse. With more than ninety percent of the population living outside the main towns, and many areas remaining totally isolated during the long winter months, Himachal's separate districts maintain distinct customs, architecture, dress and agricultural methods. Though Hinduism dominates, there are substantial numbers of Sikhs, Muslims and Christians, and Lahaul, Spiti and Kinnaur have been home to Tibetan Buddhists since the tenth century. This may explain why the state has traditionally been a **stronghold** for the more inclusive Congress Party, although recent years have seen the BJP control the state government.

6

Shimla and around

SHIMLA, Himachal's capital, is India's largest and most famous hill station, where much of the action in Rudyard Kipling's colonial classic *Kim* took place. While the city is a favourite spot for Indian families and honeymooners, its size does little to win it popularity among Western tourists. It is however, a perfect halfway house between the plains and the Kullu Valley. It's also the starting post for forays into the remoter regions of Kinnaur and Spiti.

Whether you travel by road or rail from the south, the last stretch of the climb up to Shimla seems interminable. Deep in the foothills of the Himalayas, the hill station is approached via a sinuous route that winds from the plains at **Kalka** across nearly 100km of precipitous river valleys, pine forests, and mountainsides swathed in maize terraces and apple orchards. It's not hard to see why the British chose this inaccessible site as their summer capital. At an altitude of 2159m, the crescent-shaped ridge over which it spills is blessed with perennially cool air and superb **panoramas**.

Southeast of Shimla, **Kasauli** is a peaceful place to break your journey from Chandigarh in Punjab, while nearby **Nalagarh Fort** has been converted into the finest hotel in the state. The southernmost area of the state, **Sirmaur**, is Himachal's most fertile area, with the major Sikh shrine in **Paonta Sahib** as a noteworthy sight.

Northeast of Shimla, the apple-growing centre of **Narkanda** and **Sarahan**, site of the famous **Bhimakali temple**, set against a backdrop of the majestic Himalayas, can be visited in a two- or three-day roundtrip from Shimla, or en route to Kinnaur via the characterless transport hub of **Rampur**.

Brief history

Named after its patron goddess, Shamla Devi (a manifestation of Kali), the tiny village that stood on this spot was "discovered" by a team of British surveyors in 1817. Glowing reports of its beauty and climate gradually filtered to the imperial capital, Calcutta, and within two decades the settlement had become the Subcontinent's most fashionable summer resort. The annual migration was finally rubber-stamped in 1864,

---

WHEN TO VISIT SHIMLA

The **best time to visit** is during October and November, before the Himachali winter sets in, when the days are still warm and dry, and the morning skies are clear. From December to late February, heavy snow is common, and temperatures hover around, or below, zero. The spring brings with it unpredictability: warm blasts of air from the plains and flurries of freezing rain from the mountains. Accommodation can be scarce and expensive during the first high season (mid-April to the end of June), less so during the second high season of late September through early November. Expect larger crowds on weekends and holidays, notably Christmas and New Year. Whenever you come, bring warm clothes, as the nights can get surprisingly chilly.

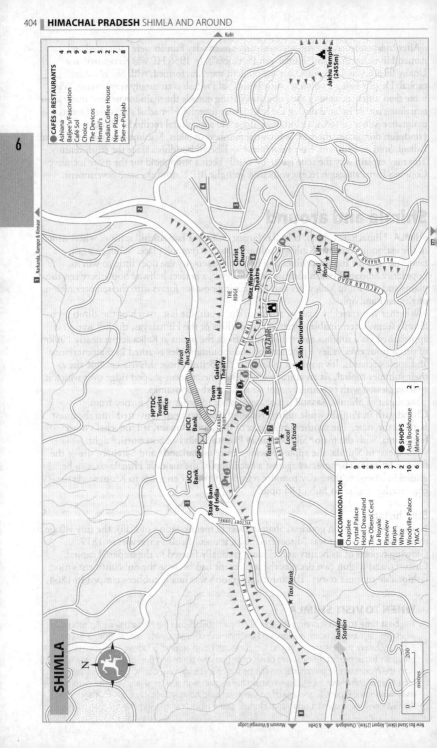

SHIMLA

N

▲ Kufri

Jakhu Temple (2455m)

Christ Church

THE RIDGE

Ritz Movie Theatre

Taxi Lift Rank

RAJ BHAVAN ROAD

CIRCULAR ROAD

LAKKAR BAZAAR

THE MALL

BAZAAR

Sikh Gurudwara

Gaiety Theatre

Rivoli Bus Stand

Town Hall

HPTDC Tourist Office

SCANDAL POINT

ICICI Bank

GPO

CART RD

Local Bus Stand

Taxis

UCO Bank

State Bank of India

VICTORY TUNNEL

THE MALL

Taxi Rank

Railway Station

◀ Nankanda, Rampur & Kinnaur

CAFÉS & RESTAURANTS

Ashiana	4
Bajee's/Fascination	3
Café Sol	9
Choice	6
The Devicos	1
Himani's	5
Indian Coffee House	2
New Plaza	7
Sher-e-Punjab	8

SHOPS

Asia Bookhouse	2
Minerva	1

ACCOMMODATION

Chapslee	1
Crystal Palace	9
Hotel Dreamland	4
The Oberoi Cecil	8
Le Royale	5
Pineview	3
Ranjan	7
White	2
Woodville Palace	10
YMCA	6

metres
0   200

▼ New Bus Stand (6km), Airport (21km), Chandigarh ▲ & Delhi   ▲ Museum & Viceregal Lodge

when Shimla – by now an elegant town of mansions, churches and cricket pitches – was declared the Government of India's official hot-season HQ. With the completion of the **Kalka–Shimla Railway** in 1903, Shimla lay only two days by train from Delhi. Its growth continued after Independence, especially after becoming state capital in 1966.

Today, Shimla is still a major holiday resort, popular mainly with nouveau riche Punjabis and Delhi-ites who flock here in their thousands during the May–June run-up to the monsoons, and then again in October, when many Bengalis also visit. Its faded colonial charm also appeals to foreigners looking for a taste of the Raj. The burra- and memsahibs may have moved on, but Shimla retains a decidedly **British feel**: pukka Indian gentlemen in tweeds stroll along The Mall smoking pipes, while neatly turned-out schoolchildren scuttle past mock-Tudor shop-fronts and houses with names like Braeside. At the same time, the pesky monkey troupes and chaotic mass of corrugated iron rooftops that make up Shimla's **bazaar** lend an unmistakeably Indian aspect to the town. The entire town was declared a no-smoking zone in October 2010.

6

The Ridge

Although Shimla and its satellite districts sprawl over the flanks of five or more hills, the centre is fairly compact, on and immediately beneath a shoulder of high ground known as "**the Ridge**". Shimla's busy social scene revolves around the broad and breezy piazza that straddles the Ridge, overlooking rippling foothills with the jagged white peaks of the Pir Panjal and Great Himalayan ranges on the horizon. It is said all water that drains off the north side of the Ridge ends up in the Arabian Sea, while from the south side it ends up in the Bay of Bengal. During high season it is a hive of activity, with entertainment provided by brass bands, pony rides and a giant screen showing sporting events. The Victorian Gothic spire of **Christ Church** is Shimla's most prominent landmark. The **stained-glass windows**, the finest in British India, depict (from left to right) Faith, Hope, Charity, Fortitude, Patience and Humility. There is still a service in English at 9am every Sunday. At the other end of the Ridge, **Scandal Point** is the focus of Shimla's famous mid-afternoon meet when crowds gather here to gossip.

The Mall

From the Ridge, a tangle of roads and lanes tumbles down in stages, each layer connected to the next by stone steps. **The Mall**, the main pedestrian thoroughfare, curves around the south slope of the hill. Flanked by a long row of unmistakeably British half-timbered buildings, Shimla's main shopping street was, until World War I, strictly out-of-bounds to

---

THE VICEROY'S TOY TRAIN

Until the construction of the **Kalka–Shimla Railway**, the only way to get to the Shimla hill station was on the so-called **Cart Road** – a slow, winding trail trodden by lines of long-suffering porters and horse-drawn tongas. By the time the 96km narrow-gauge line was completed in 1903, 103 tunnels, 24 bridges and 18 stations had been built between Shimla and the railhead at Kalka, 26km northeast of Chandigarh. These days, buses may be quicker, but a ride on the "toy train" is far more memorable – especially if you travel first-class, in one of the glass-windowed rail cars. Hauled along by a tiny diesel locomotive, they rattle at a leisurely pace through stunning scenery, taking between five and a half and seven hours to reach Shimla.

Along the route, you'll notice the guards exchanging little leather pouches with staff strategically positioned on the station platforms. The bags they receive in return contain small brass discs, which the drivers slot into special machines to alert the signals ahead of their approach. "Neal's Token System", in place since the line was first inaugurated, is a fail-safe means of ensuring that trains travelling in opposite directions never meet face to face on the single-track sections of the railway.

all "natives" except royalty and rickshaw-pullers. These days, rickshaws, man-powered or otherwise, are banned and non-Indian faces are in the minority. The quintessentially colonial **Gaiety Theatre** was renovated in 2008 and puts on regular performances.

The bazaar

Walk down any of the narrow lanes leading off The Mall, and you're plunged into a warren of twisting backstreets. Shimla's **bazaar** is the hill station at its most vibrant – a maze of dishevelled shacks, brightly lit stalls and minarets, cascading in a clutter of corrugated iron to the edge of Cart Road. Apart from being a good place to shop for authentic souvenirs, this is also one of the few areas of town that feels Himalayan: multicoloured Kullu caps (*topis*) bob about in the crowd, alongside the odd Lahauli, Kinnauri or Tibetan face.

The state museum

1.5km west of the centre via the Mall – take the right fork at the first intersection after the *Classic* hotel and left at the second, from where it is signposted • Tues–Sun 10am–1pm & 2–5pm, closed 2nd Sat of month • ₹50 (₹10), camera ₹50

The HP **state museum** is well worth the effort to get to. The ground floor of the elegant colonial mansion is given over largely to temple sculpture, and a gallery of magnificent **Pahari miniatures** – examples of the last great Hindu art form to flourish in northern India before the deadening impact of Western culture in the early nineteenth century. The Mughal-influenced Pahari or "Hill" school is renowned for subtle depictions of romantic love, inspired by scenes from Hindu epics. Among the museum's **paintings** are dozens of Mughal and Rajasthani miniatures and a couple of fine "Company" watercolours, produced for souvenir-hunting colonials by the descendants of the Mughal and Pahari masters. The *fakirs*, itinerant sadhus and mendicants they depict could have leapt straight from the pages of Kipling. One room is devoted to Mahatma Gandhi, packed with photos of his time in Shimla and amusing cartoons of his political relationship with the British.

The Viceregal Lodge

A 15min walk west of the state museum • Daily 9am–5pm; guided tours every 30min except 1–2pm • ₹50 (₹20)

Shimla's single most impressive colonial monument is the old **Viceregal Lodge**, summer seat of British government until the 1940s and today home to the **Institute of Advanced Studies**. The lodge is Shimla at its most British. The solid grey mansion, built in Elizabethan style with a lion and unicorn set above the entrance porch, surveys trimmed lawns fringed by pines and flowerbeds. Inside is just as ostentatious, though only sections of the ground floor are open to the public: a vast teak-panelled entrance

---

THE HIKE TO JAKHU TEMPLE

The early-morning hike up to **Jakhu**, or "Monkey", **Temple** is something of a tradition in Shimla. The top of the hill (2455m) on which it stands offers a superb panorama of the Himalayas – particularly breathtaking before the cloud gathers later in the day. The relentlessly steep climb takes thirty to forty-five minutes. The path starts just left of Christ Church; during the season, all you need do is follow the crowds.

After the hard walk up, the temple itself, a red-and-yellow-brick affair crammed with fairy lights and tinsel, comes as something of an anticlimax, although the new 30m-tall orange concrete statue of **Hanuman** is an impressive sight. The shrine inside houses what are believed to be the footprints of Hanuman himself. Legend has it that the monkey god, adored by Hindus for his strength and fidelity, rested on Jakhu after collecting healing Himalayan herbs for Rama's injured brother, Lakshmana. Watch out for the troupes of mangy monkeys around the temple. Pampered by generations of pilgrims and tourists, they have become real pests; hang on to your bag and don't flash food.

hall, an impressive library (formerly the ballroom) and the guest room. The **conference room**, hung with photos of Nehru, Jinnah and Gandhi, was the scene of crucial talks in the run-up to Independence. On the stone terrace to the rear of the building, a plaque profiles and names the peaks visible in the distance.

Prospect Hill

The short hike up to **Prospect Hill** (2176m), a popular picnic spot, ties in nicely with a visit to the Viceregal Lodge. By cutting through the woods to the west of the mansion, you can drop down to a busy intersection known as **Boileauganj**, from where a tarmac path climbs steeply up to the small shrine of Kamana Devi, which affords fine views.

6

ARRIVAL AND DEPARTURE SHIMLA

Wherever you arrive in Shimla, you'll be mobbed by **porters**. Most of the town is pedestrianized, and seriously steep, so you may be glad of the extra help to carry your gear, but it's better to politely refuse their offer to tout you a hotel.

By plane Shimla's airport lies 21km southwest of town on the Mandi road at Jubarhati. A taxi costs around ₹800 and there is no bus connection. There is one daily flight to Delhi (1hr 15min) but it is prone to cancellation due to bad weather. Also the only operator, Kingfisher (c/o Ambassador Travels, The Mall, ☎0177 265 8014), was on the verge of bankruptcy at the time of writing.

By train The train station is a 15min walk southwest of The Mall. The toy train connects Shimla with Kalka, where you can change onto the main broad-gauge line for Chandigarh and Delhi, the best services being *the Himalayan Queen* #4096 at 4.50pm or the faster *Shatabdi Express* #2012 at 5.45pm, both arriving in Delhi around 10pm. Toy train services depart from Shimla at 10.30am, 2.25pm, 4.25pm, 5.40pm and 6.15pm, while from Kalka they leave at 4am, 5.10am, 5.30am, 6am and 12.10pm; they should take around 5hr each, though it's often

longer. Reservations for onward journeys from Kalka can be made at Shimla Station (☎0177 265 2915, enquiries ☎131) or the booking booth next to the tourist office.

By bus Long-distance buses use the new multilevel bus stand 6km southwest of the centre, on the Chandigarh road. Frequen t minibuses link it to the Local Bus Stand on Cart Rd. Services include Chandigarh (every 15min; 4hr), Delhi (hourly; 10hr), Mandi (8 daily; 5hr), Kullu (8 daily 7–8hr), Dharamsala (4 daily; 10–11hr), Manali (8 daily; 8–9hr), Sarahan (3 daily; 7–8hr) and Rekong Peo (6 daily; 9–10hr). HPTDC run a deluxe bus to Manali (8.30am) and a/c Volvo bus to Delhi (8.30pm); both depart from more central Victory Tunnel and tickets should be booked at least a day in advance at the tourist office, while state bus tickets can be reserved at the adjacent ticket counter (Mon–Sat 10am–4.30pm) or at the bus stand.

GETTING AROUND AND INFORMATION

By taxi Taxis are the best way to get to the pricier hotels on the outskirts. The main Vishal Himachal Taxi Union rank (☎0177 265 7645) is 1km east of the Local Bus Stand, at the bottom of the lift (₹8 each way) that connects the east end of Cart Rd with The Mall. Another, more central, taxi rank can be found just above the Local Bus Stand on Cart Rd.

Tourist information The HPTDC main tourist office (daily: high season 9am–8pm; low season 9am–6pm;

☎0177 265 2561, ⓦhptdc.gov.in) is located on The Mall near Scandal Point. They organize whistle-stop sightseeing tours to destinations around Shimla, including Narkanda, and offer advice on local walks. To venture into the more remote and challenging regions such as Kinnaur and Spiti, check out our recommended mountaineering and trekking agencies on the Mall (see p.409).

ACCOMMODATION

Unsurprisingly for a state capital that is also a major holiday destination, **accommodation** is costlier than average. In May and June prices soar and it's essential to book in advance. At other times, most places are willing to bargain.

Chaplsee Between Lakkar Bazaar and Long Wood ☎0177 280 2542, ⓦchapslee.com. Exclusive, beautiful old manor house set in its own grounds on the edge of town and stuffed with antiques, plus a library, card room, tennis court and croquet lawn. Half-board, payment by credit card only. ₹**13,000**

Crystal Palace Circular Rd, near the lift ☎0177 265 7588, ⓦhotelcrystalpalace.com. Smart, functional and handily placed to take the lift up to The Mall, with modern, brightly coloured rooms and good facilities. ₹**1400**

★ **Dreamland** The Ridge, above Christ Church ☎0177 265 3005, ⓦhoteldreamlandshimla.com.

Welcoming and excellent value during the low season especially; all rooms are clean, with hot showers and cable TV. The pricier rooms boast fantastic views over to the Himalayas. Pleasant restaurant on the top floor, wi-fi and internet access. ₹900

The Oberoi Cecil The Mall ☎0177 280 4848, ⓦoberoihotels.com. Raj-era building, frequented by Rudyard Kipling among others. It is now an opulent chain hotel somewhat devoid of character, with little but the facade as a reminder of its past. Advance online discounts. ₹10,000

Pineview Mythe Estate, on the far side of the Victory tunnel ☎0177 265 8604, ⓦhotelpineview.in. A good location with an almost rural feel in an apple orchard facing north, with a wide choice of comfortable attached rooms and some deluxe suites. ₹700

Ranjan Just above the Local Bus Stand ☎0177 265 2818. Originally built in 1907, this large white building is showing its age. The attached rooms are large and basic, with some original fittings and common balconies supported by wooden columns. ₹550

Le Royale Jakhoo Rd ☎0177 265 1002, ⓔle_royale @hotmail.com. Modern and functional hotel offering great views from high above the Ridge and a variety of smart rooms of varying sizes, all with nice furnishings. ₹1500

White Lakkar Bazaar ☎0177 265 5276, ⓦhotelwhitesimla.com. Well-managed hotel with light rooms overlooking the Himalayas. Gleaming white marble and woodwork everywhere. The deluxe suite is excellent. Fixed prices all year. ₹1200

Woodville Palace Raj Bhavan Rd ☎0177 262 3919, ⓦwoodvillepalacehotel.com. A 20min walk south from Christ Church, this elegant 1930s mansion boasts huge rooms and suites, period furniture, lawns and a badminton court. ₹15,500

YMCA The Ridge, up the steps to the left of the Ritz movie theatre ☎0177 265 0021, ⓔymcashimla @yahoo.co.in. Large rooms, including seven attached. In-house dining hall (breakfast is included except Jan–March) and sun-terrace, along with cable TV, snooker tables, table tennis and internet café. ₹650/₹1500

EATING AND DRINKING

Few **restaurants** in Shimla retain any colonial ambience but standards have improved and a number of decent places complement the hotel restaurants, while the many **bakeries** and icecream parlours offer comfort for the sweet-toothed. For a really cheap and filling meal, try the fried potato patties (*tikki*) or chickpea curry and *puris* (*channa batura*) at one of the snack bars that line the steps opposite the Gaiety Theatre. Alternatively, the bazaar is good for cheap *dhabas*.

Ashiana The Ridge ☎0177 265 8464. HPTDC restaurant in a converted bandstand offering mainly non-veg Indian food, including tasty chicken *makhanwalla*, plus pizzas and a few Chinese dishes. Mains mostly ₹160–250. Daily 9am–10pm.

Baljee's The Mall ☎0177 281 4054. This hectic coffee house does a roaring trade in snacks, sweets and ice cream in the evenings especially. The *Fascination* restaurant upstairs offers a good selection of Indian and Chinese dishes for around ₹120–200, as well as sausage, egg and chips. Daily 11.30am–11pm.

★ **Café Sol** The Mall, on the roof of Combemere Hotel ☎0177 252 2242. Slick neon-lit cylindrical structure, good for reasonable Italian, Mexican and Thai dishes (₹180–500), as well as standard Indian food and tasty bakery items. Daily 11am–10.30pm.

★ **Choice** Middle Bazaar, down steps from Baljee's ☎0177 329 4626. Tiny Chinese and Tibetan restaurant with warm red walls and an exhaustive menu of delicious veg and non-veg dishes for ₹40–80. Daily noon–10.30pm.

The Devicos The Mall ☎0177 280 6335. The fairly plush restaurant downstairs does south Indian snacks for less than ₹100 and full-on Indian non-veg portions for

₹200–300. The ground floor is occupied by a *Coffee Day* franchise and there's a bar upstairs. Daily 10am–10.30pm.

Himani's The Mall ☎0177 265 2415. The ground floor is taken up by a flashy videogame arcade, a rather dowdy bar occupies the first floor and a family-style restaurant, pool den and sundeck are on the top floor. Menu includes tandoori chicken (full ₹240), south Indian cuisine and Continental dishes such as sizzlers (₹225). Daily 9am–9.30pm.

Indian Coffee House The Mall ☎0177 265 2982. Atmospheric, faded café with colonial ambience, offering the usual range of veg snacks such as masala dosa for ₹33, and attentive waiter service to the predominantly male clientele. Daily 8am–9pm.

New Plaza 60/1 Middle Bazaar, down the steps beside Himani's ☎0177 265 5438. Popular family restaurant. Good-value food including tasty meat sizzlers for around ₹200. Daily 10am–10.30pm.

Sher-e-Punjab The Mall ☎0177 280 3538. The best of the simple restaurants at the eastern end of the Mall. Hearty portions of spicy beans, chickpeas and dhal at ₹40–60, plus inexpensive meat and fish. Daily 7am–10.30pm.

DIRECTORY

Banks and exchange Various ATMs now line The Mall. Only the SBI will cash travellers' cheques, although cash can be exchanged at other banks and agents.

Bookshops Asia Bookhouse (☎0177 281 2217) and

Minerva (☎0177 280 3078), both on The Mall, stock a wide range paperbacks and reference titles.

Hospitals Indira Gandhi Medical College Hospital (☎0177 280 4251); Deen Dayal Hospital, near the ISBT (☎0177 265 4071).

Internet access There are a number of places dotted along and around The Mall. The *Dreamland hotel* has facilities too.

Permits Inner Line permits (see box, p.402) are issued at the Additional District Magistrate's office (Mon–Sat 10am–5pm, closed 2nd Sat of the month; ☎0177 265 7005) on the first floor of the modern courthouse, one street below The Mall.

Pharmacies Indu Medical, The Mall (9am–8pm).

Post The GPO (Mon–Sat 10am–6pm) is near Scandal Point on The Mall.

Travel agents Reliable operators on The Mall include City Travels, near Scandal Point (☎94180 20899, ✉citytravel shimla@gmail.com) and Great Himalayan Travels (☎0177 265 8934, ⌨ghtravels.com). The *YMCA* (see opposite) also organizes treks and safaris, as does Silver Dreams (☎0177 280 6897, ⌨blueskiestrekking.com) at the *Dreamland hotel*.

Kasauli

Though it sees few Western tourists, the small, slow-paced town of **KASAULI**, cradled by pine forests 77km southwest of Shimla, and with a touch of Raj architecture, makes a good stop-off on the way to or from Delhi. Crisscrossed by spindly cobbled streets, spreading along low ridges carpeted with forests and flower-filled meadows, Kasauli offers an abundance of gentle short strolls, such as the one to nearby Sanawar, or the scenic longer trek to Kalka, railhead for the toy train to Shimla.

ARRIVAL AND DEPARTURE KASAULI

By train The nearest railway station is 11km away at Dharampur on the Kalka–Shimla toy train line.

By bus There are frequent buses from Dharampur and direct hourly services from Shimla.

ACCOMMODATION AND EATING

Gian Post Office Rd ☎01792 272244. Stylish hotel, whose high-ceilinged rooms all have fireplaces, carpets and balconies, in true Raj style. The restaurant does good Indian, Chinese and Continental cuisine. ₹500

Ros-Common Lower Mall ☎01792 272005, ✉kasauli@hptdc.in. Overpriced state-run hotel with reasonable rooms of different prices and a standard restaurant. A more modern annexe is 500m away. ₹2200

Nalagarh

NALAGARH is an excellent place to break the journey between Delhi and Kullu, as it lies 60km from Chandigarh and just 12km off the main Chandigarh–Mandi road. Now an emerging industrial region, the town was capital of the medieval state of **Hindur**, founded by the Chandella Rajputs in 1100 AD. Its one outstanding feature is imposing **Nalagarh Fort**, now converted into the classiest hotel in Himachal Pradesh.

ARRIVAL AND DEPARTURE NALAGARH

By bus Nalagarh is most easily reached by bus from Chandigarh (every 1–2hr; 2hr).

ACCOMMODATION

★ **The Fort Resort** ☎01795 223179, ⌨nalagarh .in. Accommodation is in beautifully maintained suites, each with period furniture, and surprisingly good value. An atmospheric lounge bar overlooks terraced grounds with a tennis court, croquet lawn and swimming pool, and an Ayurvedic clinic offers massage. Breakfast included. ₹4500

Paonta Sahib

On the border with Uttarakhand, the town of **PAONTA SAHIB**, where pastel-yellow houses are packed tightly into the cobbled streets, holds an important shrine dedicated to **Guru Gobind Singh**, the tenth Sikh guru, who lived here in the late 1680s.

ARRIVAL AND DEPARTURE	PAONTA SAHIB

By bus Paonta Sahib provides good bus connections for travel between Shimla and points such as Mussoorie, Dehra Dun, Haridwar and Rishikesh.

ACCOMMODATION

The Yamuna 📞01704 222341, 📧paonta@hptdc.in. HPTDC hotel, on the banks of the River Yamuna, with pleasant rooms, a restaurant serving the predictable range of Indian and Chinese dishes and a bar. ₹700

Narkanda

A three-hour (65km) bus ride northeast of Shimla, the scruffy hill town of **NARKANDA** (2725m) makes a reasonable resting point on the bumpy, six-hour journey to Sarahan , and has a number of *dhabas* around the bazaar where you can grab a snack. This former staging post on the Hindustan–Tibet caravan route acts as the roadhead and main market town for the area's widely dispersed apple-and-potato-growers. There are some good rambles through the cedar forests that surround the town, and great **views** of the Himalayas. **Hatu Peak** (3143m), crowned by a lonely hilltop **Durga temple**, 7km east of town, looks out over the River Sutlej winding far below, and a string of white-tipped mountains to the north and east.

ARRIVAL AND DEPARTURE	NARKANDA

By bus Narkanda has good bus connections with Shimla (every 30min–1hr; 3hr).

ACCOMMODATION AND EATING

The Hatu On a hillside above town 📞01782 242430, 📧narkanda@hptdc.in. Fairly smart HPTDC hotel with large well-appointed rooms and great views from the manicured lawns. Also has ski equipment for hire, cable TV and a bar. ₹1300

Mahamaya Palace Above main road 📞01782 242448, 🌐hotelmahamayapalace.com. Spruced up Alpine-style hotel with lots of wood fittings, comfortable rooms, a huge deluxe suite and a decent restaurant. ₹650

Sarahan

Secluded **SARAHAN**, erstwhile summer capital of the Bhushar rajas, sits astride a 2000m ledge above the River Sutlej, near the Shimla–Kinnaur border. Set against a spectacular backdrop, the village harbours one of the northwestern Himalayas' most exotic spectacles – the **Bhimakali temple**. With its two multitiered sanctuary towers, elegantly sloping slate-tiled roofs and gleaming golden spires, it is the most majestic early timber temple in the Sutlej Valley – an area renowned for housing holy shrines on raised wooden platforms. Although most of the structure dates from the early twentieth century, parts are thought to be more than eight hundred years old.

A pair of elaborately decorated metal doors lead into a large courtyard flanked by rest rooms and a small carved-stone **Shiva shrine**. After ascending to a second, smaller yard, you pass another golden door, also richly embossed with mythical scenes, beyond which the innermost enclosure holds the two **sanctuary towers**. The one on the right houses musical instruments, flags, paladins and ceremonial weapons, some of which are on show in the small "museum" in the corner of the courtyard. Non-Hindus who want to climb to the top of the other, more modern tower (no photography) to view the highly polished gold-faced deity must don a saffron cap. Bhimakali herself is enshrined on the top floor, decked with garlands of flowers.

ARRIVAL AND DEPARTURE	SARAHAN

By bus There are several daily direct buses and many more local services from Jeori, 17km below Sarahan on the busy main road between Rampur and Kinnaur.

On foot Keen walkers might fancy ambling along the well-worn mule track to Sarahan from Jeori.

BLOOD SACRIFICE IN SARAHAN

The **Bhimakali** deity, a local manifestation of the Hindu goddess Kali/Durga, (see box, p.1174), has for centuries been associated with **human sacrifice**. Once every decade, until the disapproving British intervened in the 1800s, a man was killed here as an offering to the *devi*. Following a complex ceremony, his newly spilled blood was poured over the goddess's tongue for her to drink, after which his body was dumped in a deep well inside the temple compound. If no victim could be found, it is said that a voice would bellow from the depths of the pit, which is now sealed up.

The tradition of blood sacrifice continues in Sarahan to this day, albeit in less extreme form. During the annual **Astami** festival, two days before the culmination of **Dussehra**, a veritable menagerie of birds and beasts are put to the knife, including a water-buffalo calf, sheep, goat, fish, chicken, crab, and even a spider. The gory spectacle draws large crowds, and is a memorable alternative to the Dussehra procession in Kullu, which takes place at around the same time in mid-October.

6

ACCOMMODATION

Bushahr Guest House Behind the temple ☎01782 274238. This functional three-storey building has a range of clean, tidy and compact rooms arranged around maze-like corridors. Some rooms overlook the temple courtyard. ₹300

★ **Hotel Trehan's** Main road ☎01782 274205, ✉ hotel-trehan47@rediffmail.com. Welcoming hotel that looks out on the sheer mountainside and offers spacious attached rooms with attractive moulded ceilings and TV. Serves decent food too. ₹400

The Srikhand Opposite the temple ☎01782 274234, ✉ sarahan@hptdc.in. The building is an incongruous concrete monster but its rooms are reasonable and it has a delightful garden and a restaurant serving good veg meals on a relaxing terrace. Dorm ₹150, double ₹1500

Temple Guest House In the lower temple courtyard ☎01782 274248. The rooms are basic but pleasant and the dingy basement dorm offers some of the cheapest beds in the Himalaya. Dorm ₹75, double ₹200

Kinnaur

Before 1992, the remote backwater of **KINNAUR**, a rugged buffer zone between the Shimla foothills and the wild western extremity of Chinese-occupied Tibet, was strictly off-limits to tourists. Although visitors are now allowed to travel through the "**Inner Line**", and on to Spiti, Lahaul and the Kullu Valley, permits are still required (see p.402). Other areas of Kinnaur, notably the **Baspa Valley** and the sacred **Kinner-Kailash** massif visible from the mountain village of **Kalpa**, are completely open.

Straddling the mighty River Sutlej, which rises on the southern slopes of Mount Kailash, Kinnaur has for centuries been a major trans-Himalayan corridor. Merchants travelling between China and the Punjabi plains passed through on the **Hindustan–Tibet caravan route**, stretches of which are still used by villagers and trekkers. The bulk of the traffic that lumbers east towards the frontier, however, uses the newer NH-22, which veers north into Spiti just short of the ascent to Shipki La pass, on the Chinese border, which remains closed.

In the well-watered, mainly Hindu west of the region, the scenery ranges from subtropical to almost Alpine: wood-and-slate villages, surrounded by maize terraces and orchards, nestle beneath pine forests and vast blue-grey mountain peaks. Further east, largely beyond the reach of the monsoons, it grows more austere, and glaciers loom on all sides. **Buddhism** arrived in Kinnaur with the tenth-century kings of Guge, who ruled what is now southwestern Tibet. When **Rinchen Zangpo** (958–1055), the "Great Translator" credited with the "Second Spreading" of the faith in Guge, passed through, he left behind several monasteries and a devotion to a pure form of the Buddhist faith that has endured here for nearly one thousand years. In the sixteenth century, after Guge had fragmented into dozens of petty fiefdoms, the **Bhushar kings** took control of Kinnaur. They remained

6

TREKKING IN KINNAUR

Unfrequented mountain trails crisscross Kinnaur, offering **treks** ranging from gentle hikes to challenging climbs over high-altitude passes. The routes along the **Sutlej Valley**, punctuated with government resthouses and villages, are feasible without the aid of ponies, but away from the main road you need to be completely self-sufficient. **Porters** can usually be hired in Rampur, Rekong Peo and the Baspa Valley except in early autumn (Sept/Oct), when they're busy with the apple harvest.

THE KINNER-KAILASH CIRCUIT

The five- to seven-day *parikrama* (circumambulation) of the majestic Kinner-Kailash massif, a sacred pilgrimage trail, makes a spectacular trek for which you won't need an Inner Line permit. The circuit starts at the village of **MORANG**, on the left bank of the Sutlej, served by buses from Tapri or Rekong Peo. A track, passable by jeep, runs southeast from here to **Thangi**, the trailhead, and continues through Rahtak, over the **Charang La** pass (5266m) to **Chitkul** in the Baspa Valley. The trail then follows the river down to the beautiful village of **Sangla**, from where a couple of worthwhile day-hikes can be made – to **Kamru fort** behind the village, or the steep ascent to the **Shivaling La** pass, from where there are superb views of Raldang (5499m), the southernmost peak on the Kinner-Kailash massif. The final stage passes through the lower Baspa Valley, via Shang and Brua to **Karcham**, which overlooks the NH-22 highway. The best time for the Kinner-Kailash *parikrama* is between July and October; August is the most popular month with local pilgrims.

KAFNU TO KAZA, VIA THE PIN VALLEY

This challenging route across the Great Himalayan range, via the Kalang Setal glacier and the Shakarof La pass, is a dramatic approach to Spiti and the **Pin Valley**, and no restrictions apply. The trail, which is very steep, snow-covered, and hard to follow in places, should definitely not be attempted without ponies, porters, adequate gear and a reliable **guide**. It starts in earnest at Kafnu village, now connected to Wangtu on the main road by a paved surface, continuing via Mulling, Phustirang (3750m), and over the **Bhaba Pass** (4865m), a gruelling slog through snowfields, before dropping down into the beautiful and isolated **Pin Valley**. You can then trek onwards or get a vehicle to **Kaza** (see p.451). More of this route may become paved as the delayed Wangtu–Mudh road project painfully progresses.

CHITKUL TO HAR-KI-DUN

This ten-day trek to **Garhwal** (see p.295) passes along the edge of the Inner Line and is subject to restrictions. Starting from **Chitkul** and crossing the River Baspa to Doaria, the route then climbs up a side valley to follow a lateral moraine up to the Zupika Gad and then a steep ascent – the final section of which is up a crevassed glacier – to the **Borsu Pass** (5300m). The other side of the pass is down a steep snow-and boulder-field requiring some scrambling; you arrive a few days later in the beautiful valley of **Har-ki-Dun** in Garhwal. A guide is essential.

THE OLD HINDUSTAN–TIBET ROAD FROM KALPA TO THE RUPA VALLEY

Another route to consider is the relatively easy five-day trek starting at **Kalpa** and following the old Hindustan–Tibet road through the remote hamlets of upper Kinnaur (permits needed), past Shi Asu to the Rupa Valley. The views along the route are superb and the villagers are extremely hospitable. The road, now crumbling in places, is also ideal for mountain biking.

in power throughout the British Raj, when this was one of the battlegrounds of the espionage war played out between agents of the Chinese, Russian and British empires – the "Great Game" evocatively depicted in the novels of Rudyard Kipling.

Rekong Peo

East of Jeori, the road climbs high above the Sutlej into ever more remote territory, traversing sheer ravines on cable bridges, while tiny wooden villages, each with a pagoda-roofed temple, cling to the mountainsides. At **Wangtu** bridge, the trailhead for the Kinnaur–Pin Valley–Kaza trek (see box opposite), the highway switches to the north bank of the river beside the huge Karcham Dam hydro-electric project. Here a sturdy metal bridge bears right towards **Sangla** and the rest of the Baspa Valley, while the main highway continues to **REKONG PEO**, district headquarters of Kinnaur. Its batch of concrete houses and government buildings around a small maidan, 7km above the main road, gives it the air of an upstart frontier settlement. Apart from its moderately interesting **bazaar**, the only reason to stop is to buy trekking supplies, find a connection to Kalpa or obtain an Inner Line **permit** (see box, p.402).

6

ARRIVAL AND INFORMATION   REKONG PEO

By bus Buses drop off and pick up at the bend in the main bazaar before proceeding up the hill on the Kalpa road for 2km to the main bus stand, which can be reached on foot by the 500m path from the end of ITBP Rd. There are services almost hourly to Shimla (9–10hr), early morning departures direct to Mandi and Kaza (10–11hr), and direct buses to Chandigarh, Amritsar and Delhi. Several morning buses run to Sangla (2hr), some

continuing to Chitkul, and there are minibuses every 15–20min to Kalpa.

Tourist information The Tourist Info Centre (Mon–Sat 10am–5pm; ☎ 01786 222857) is in the open courtyard below the bazaar bus stop. This is also the official agent for Inner Line permits – they charge ₹350 but can take your photo and make copies of your passport as part of the service.

ACCOMMODATION AND EATING

There are a surprising number of **hotels** lining the upper side of the main bazaar, although most of these are rather overpriced. Those further up the hill and on side roads offer better value.

Fairyland On the road immediately above the main bazaar ☎ 98161 00037. Most easily accessed via the steps beside *Cafeteria Roof, Fairyland*'s modest but clean attached rooms have TV and great views of Kinner-Kailash. Generous portions in the restaurant. **₹350**
The Frontier In the middle of the main bazaar ☎ 88940 89191. This quiet family restaurant does a fair line in tandoori, Mughlai and Chinese dishes, which are also available in the typically male-dominated bar upstairs. Daily 8.30am–10pm.

Little Chef On the corner of the main bazaar ☎ 94180 92237. Brightly coloured mosaic table tops, intermittent wi-fi access and two computer terminals complement a wide-ranging menu of Indian, Chinese and Continental dishes in the ₹100–200 range. Daily 9am–9.30pm.
Mehfil ITBP Rd ☎ 01786 223600. Enjoying a central location but slightly removed from the bustling bazaar, this hotel has a range of attached rooms with TV and partial mountain views. **₹450**

Kalpa (Chini)

KALPA can be reached by the twisting 9km road from Rekong Peo or on foot along various steep tracks. Its narrow atmospheric lanes, crammed with rickety wooden shops, and dramatic location, high above the right bank of the Sutlej, make it by far the most attractive base in the immediate vicinity. The ancient Tibetan *gompa* here was founded by Rinchen Zangpo, and there is also a small Shiva temple. The village and its growing number of hotels are quite spread out up the hill and along the roads that radiate from the centre. Facing the village, the magnificent **Kinner-Kailash** massif sweeps 4500m up from the valley floor. The mountain in the middle, Jorkaden (6473m), is the highest, followed by the sacred summit of Kinner-Kailash (6050m) to the north, and the needle point of Raldang (5499m) in the south.

ARRIVAL AND DEPARTURE   KALPA (CHINI)

By bus Minibuses between Kalpa and Rekong Peo run every 15–20 min; there are three daily buses to Shimla

(6.30am, 11.30am & 2.30pm) and one to Sangla and Chitkul (8.30am).

ACCOMMODATION AND EATING

Apart from the hotel **restaurants**, there are just a few basic *dhabas* and tea houses. Hotel prices double in May, June and October.

★ Apple Pie Upper road ☎01786 226304, ⓦhotelapplepie.co.cc. Friendly place, painted sunshine yellow and containing three floors of nicely furnished, sizeable rooms with attractive artwork. Good restaurant too. ₹**700**

Blue Lotus Guest House In the village centre ☎01786 226001, ⓔbluelotus@gmail.com. This mundane concrete block offers the only real budget accommodation in Kalpa, with rooms priced according to their view. ₹**400**

Kinner Villa Upper road ☎01786 226006, ⓦkinnervilla .com. Expanded in 2012, this is the biggest resort around, with sleek, refurbished rooms, spotless bathrooms and a grassy lawn out front. ₹**2000**

Rakpa Regency Upper road ☎01786 245285, ⓦkinnaurhotels.com. Large hotel, popular with Bengalis, set in pleasant grounds. The front rooms have balconies with splendid views and there's a huge upstairs terrace. ₹**800**

The Baspa Valley

Hemmed in by the pinnacles of Kinner-Kailash to the north and the high peaks of the Garhwal range to the south, the 70km **River Baspa** rises in the mountain wilderness along the Indo–Tibetan border to flow through what was until recently one of Kinnaur's most beautiful and secluded areas. Much of the lower reaches of the valley below Sangla are now dominated by a massive and ugly hydro-electric plant but beyond Sangla the scenery remains unspoilt. Although the head of the valley is technically closed to tourists, there are still plenty of walking opportunities through side valleys. There are no official tourist offices nor any ATMs or banks that offer exchange in the Baspa Valley, although you may be able to pay in foreign currency or exchange small amounts at the pricier hotels.

Sangla

The valley's largest settlement, **SANGLA**, makes an excellent base to visit nearby **Kamru** village, 25 minutes' walk above Sangla, with its warren of lanes and slate-roofed stone houses, and its wood-and-stone gable-roofed **fort**. Tibetan prayer flags flutter in the breeze and the inhabitants retain Buddhist funerary rites, although they are now mostly Hindu and no longer read Tibetan. The inner sanctum of the **temple** below the fort is off-limits to visitors unless a goat is paid for and sacrificed.

ARRIVAL AND DEPARTURE   SANGLA

By bus Sangla is served by daily buses from Shimla, Rekong Peo and Kalpa. Two daily buses continue to Chitkul.

ACCOMMODATION

From late September through October Sangla fills up with Bengali holiday-makers so hotel options are increasing every year; the best **places to stay** are mostly dotted around the village outskirts.

Baspa Guest House Beside the bridge into town ☎98058 41254. This moderately attractive building with a flowery courtyard has a variety of attached doubles, the more expensive ones with cable TV. ₹**500**

Igloo Nature Camp 1km north of the village ☎88946 10946, ⓦigloonaturecamp.com. The most conveniently located of several luxury eco-camps in the Baspa Valley also organizes trekking tours. The spacious Swiss tents have attached bathrooms and there's a large mess tent. Breakfast included. ₹**3300**

Sangla Holiday Home At the far end of the bazaar ☎01786 242204, ⓦsanglaholidayhome.com. The upper storey of this friendly guesthouse boasts intricate wood carving and the attached rooms range from standard to deluxe. Expert trekking advice and guides available. ₹**600**

Sangla Resorts 300m south of the village ☎01786 242401, ⓔarunbhagat.negi@gmail.com. Perched on a hillock above apple orchards, this pleasant hotel has attached rooms of varying sizes and a dormitory. Dorm ₹**250**, double ₹**600**

EATING AND DRINKING

Ashiana Cafe In the middle of the bazaar ☎98058 41254. No-nonsense upstairs restaurant serving a standard range of Indian and Chinese main courses at a snip – non-veg items in the ₹60–80 range. Also open for breakfast. Daily 6am–10pm.

Tibetan Cafe In the middle of the bazaar ☎96252 91706. As the name suggests, this place specializes in extremely inexpensive momos, thukpa and chowmein for just ₹30–50. Two balcony tables overlook the bazaar. Daily 7.30am–8pm.

Chitkul

Twenty-five kilometres beyond Sangla, **CHITKUL** is as far up the valley as you can officially go, although the checkpoint at the far end of the village that marks the start of the guarded Inner Line is now unmanned and guides sometimes lead trekkers further up the valley. However, it's still better not to wander too far unaccompanied. Visible above the village, which is set on a rise with dramatic views of the opening valley, a trail winds steeply up to a huge saddle below the **Charang La pass** – the route of the Kinner-Kailash pilgrimage circuit (see box, p.412).

6

ARRIVAL AND DEPARTURE   CHITKUL

By bus There are several daily buses to Sangla (1hr), of which at least one or two go on to Rekong Peo and even Kalpa.

ACCOMMODATION AND EATING

★ **The Kinner Heights** Opposite the bus stand ☎ 98056 28801, ✉ kinnerheights@yahoo.com. Friendly Nepali-run place with fairly simple but clean attached rooms and an upstairs restaurant with floor cushions and a mostly basic menu. ₹400

Shahensha Resort Far end of village ☎ 98168 03505, ⓦ kinnaurhotels.com. One of the new breed of resorts,

painted blue and white, with smart rooms and balconies giving views along the river valley. ₹800

Thakur Guesthouse Near the bus stand ☎ 89882 09604. Old-fashioned wooden building with a mixture of pretty basic rooms, some of which are attached. The upper storey affords fine views. ₹500/₹300

Upper Kinnaur

Inner Line permits are required beyond the dull hamlet of **Spillo** for **upper Kinnaur**, the remote region east of Rekong Peo. Sparsely inhabited and increasingly bare, by the time the NH-22 has crossed the metal bridge beyond **Pooh** and starts to spiral up the greyish-brown slopes towards **Nako**, the terrain bears much more resemblance to Spiti or Ladakh than the greener Sutlej Valley.

Pooh and around

Several hours by road from Rekong Peo and within a day's hike of the frontier, the small town of **Pooh**, perched 4km above the main road, is the first main settlement you encounter. Evidence from inscriptions suggest that Pooh was, in the eleventh century, an important trading centre that fell under the influence of the Tibetan kingdom of Guge when the Great Translator, Rinchen Zangpo, travelled through the area. The temple here is devoted to Sakyamuni, with wooden columns supporting a high ceiling and a circumambulatory path around the altar.

Beyond Pooh, the road bends north, crossing the muddy Sutlej for the last time at **Khab**, where it meets the turquoise waters of River Spiti. To the northeast, Kinnaur's highest peak, **Leo Pargial II** (6770m), rises in a near-vertical 4000m wall which marks the border with Tibet and overlooks the old Indo–Tibet road at the **Shipki La pass** (5569m). The NH-22 continues north through the barren wastes of the Hanglang Valley, very similar to parts of Ladakh.

ARRIVAL AND DEPARTURE   POOH AND AROUND

By bus Very few buses go right up to Pooh, though you can get off anywhere along the main road below.

ACCOMMODATION

Om Guest House In the village centre ☎ 01785 232601. The best of the extremely limited choice here, the *Om* has decent rooms, two dorms and a good restaurant

serving all the usual Indian and Chinese favourites. Dorm ₹150, double ₹500

Nako

NAKO, the valley's largest village, nestling high above the River Spiti at 3640m around a small artificial **lake**, is now on the main Rekong Peo–Kaza road, which was redirected uphill to avoid the infamous **Malling Slide**. Unfortunately, the road still gets blocked during bad weather, as do many other points on the Kinnaur–Spiti circuit. In the northwest corner of the village, the eleventh-century complex of the **Nako Chokhor** (arrange entry through the Youth Club tent above the bus stand; ₹50) is attributed to Rinchen Zangpo; although it's in desperate need of restoration, its exquisite interior paintings are comparable to those in Alchi (see p.499). The finest building of all is the Serkhang or "Golden Hall", dedicated to the Tathagatas or Supreme Buddhas.

ARRIVAL AND DEPARTURE   NAKO

By bus One daily bus and numerous jeeps leave for Kaza via Tabo and for Rekong Peo.

ACCOMMODATION

Lake View Guest House Beside the lake ☎01785 236041. Enjoying by far the most scenic location, the attached rooms in this brightly painted place are fairly simple but clean and comfortable enough. **₹500**

Reo Purguil Near the bus stand ☎01785 236339. Best of the central trio of guesthouses, where all rooms have bathrooms and balconies. The restaurant is the best in town too. **₹400**

Northwest Himachal

From Shimla the main road winds west and north to the riverside market town of **Mandi**, an important crossroads linking the Kullu Valley and the hills to **the northwest**. The rolling foothills on this side of the state are warmer and more accessible than Himachal's eastern reaches, though less dramatic and considerably lower. The area sees little tourism outside **Dharamsala**, the British hill station turned Tibetan settlement, home to the Dalai Lama. Dharamsala is an excellent base for treks over the soaring Dhauladhar Range to the **Chamba Valley**, which harbours uniquely styled Hindu temples in **Brahmour** and **Chamba**. South of Chamba, the fading hill station of **Dalhousie** still has a certain ex-Raj charm, and is popular with Indian tourists who arrive in droves during the hot season.

The following section traces the River Beas and NH-21 as they weave from Mandi to Dharamsala, linking a string of quiet mountain towns and villages. While most visitors make the six-hour journey to Dharamsala in one go, those with more time can detour to sacred **Rewalsar**, just outside Mandi, or stop in the **Kangra Valley** to pick up the narrow-gauge train that trundles through patchwork fields and light forest to **Kangra**, just an hour away from Dharamsala and jumping off point for a couple of little-visited places of interest.

Mandi

The junction town of **MANDI**, 158km north of Shimla, straddles the River Beas, its riverside *ghats* dotted with stone temples where sadhus and pilgrims pray. Once a major trading post for Ladakhis heading south – *mandi* means market – the town still bustles with commercial activity, now centred on the attractive **Indira Market** and its sunken garden, in the centre of the town square. A collection of sixteenth-century Nagari-style temples sits above the town on **Tarna Hill**. On the summit is the main Kali temple, decorated with garish paintings of the fierce mother goddess draped in skulls and blood.

ARRIVAL AND DEPARTURE   MANDI

By bus The bus stand is 500m across the river on the east bank. There are departures every 30min or so for Rewalsar, Kullu, Manali and Pathankot, hourly for Baijnath and Dharamsala and several daily for Shimla, with more frequent connections in Bilaspur.

ACCOMMODATION AND EATING

Evening Plaza South side of main square 01905 225123, malhotralalji@hotmail.com. Typically functional business hotel, which has a range of slightly worn rooms of differing sizes, some with a/c. ₹440

Raj Mahal North of the town square 01905 222401, omeshwarsingh@yahoo.co.uk. This period-furnished palace, set in spacious shady gardens on an embankment, has spacious rooms, a good restaurant and an atmospheric gentlemen's bar. ₹1140

★ **Saffron** Regency Palms, northeast corner of main square 01905 222777. Cool a/c restaurant with subdued lighting, set in a stylish modern hotel, which serves ample portions of Indian, Chinese and some Continental cuisine for ₹100–200. Daily 7am–10pm.

Shiva South side of main square 01905 224211. The interior rooms are mostly windowless and not much cheaper than the far lighter ones facing the square. Food available by room service. ₹350

Rewalsar

If you've any interest in Buddhism it's worth taking a detour to **REWALSAR**, 24km southeast of Mandi, where three **Tibetan monasteries** (Nyingma, Drikung Kagyu and Drukpa Kagyu) mark an important place of pilgrimage. There are also Sikh and Hindu temples here, all of which draw a steady stream of pilgrims and tourists. The devout complete a *chora* around the small sacred lake and along narrow lanes full of shrines and stalls selling Tibetan curios, before lounging beneath the prayer flags on the lake's grassy fringes.

It's believed that Padmasambhava left many footprints and handprints in rocks and caves up in the hills around the lake, and steep paths lead up from the lake to **caves** that are used today as isolated meditation retreats. Of the three monasteries around the lake, **Tso-Pema Ogyen Heruka Gompa** is the most venerated and atmospheric; check out the tree planted in 1957 by the Dalai Lama, who visited India that year – two years before his exile from Tibet – to celebrate the 2500th anniversary of the Buddha's birth. Towering dramatically over the lake and visually dominating the Rewalsar setting is the large but much newer **Drukpa Kagyu Zigar Gompa**.

For **Hindus**, Rewalsar is regarded as the abode of the sage Lomas, for whose sake the lake was created with waters from the Ganga and Yamuna. Three small temples dedicated to Krishna, Lomas and Shiva, along with a Nandi bull statue and lakeside *ghats*, reflect Rewalsar's Hindu connections. On the west shore, the Sikh **gurudwara** attracts pilgrims retracing the steps of Guru Gobind Singh, who came here in 1702; this is one of the few associated with his life in Himachal. To the south a small **sanctuary** protects deer and Himalayan black bears.

ARRIVAL AND DEPARTURE   REWALSAR

By bus There are buses about every 30min from Mandi (1hr).

ACCOMMODATION AND EATING

There are several small but reasonable Tibetan restaurants near the lake, which serve *thukpa*, *momos* and noodles, and *dhabas* along the main road serving north Indian food.

Lotus Lake Just behind north lakeshore 01905 240239, lotuslake@yahoo.com. Standard hotel whose more expensive upper-storey rooms have lake views. The restaurant has a limited. ₹450

Nyingma Gompa Northwest lakeshore 01905 280226. Pretty basic cell-like rooms, many with lake views

and some with attached bathrooms, in the peaceful monastery buildings. ₹250/₹100

The Tourist Inn A short way back from the north shore 01905 240252, rewalsar@hptdc.in. Both blocks of this HPTDC hotel have fairly comfortable rooms with hot showers, although there are no views. ₹500

Baijnath

Although the nondescript village of **Joginder Nagar** is the eastern terminal of the Kangra Valley Railway, **BAIJNATH**, 21km further northwest, is perhaps a better spot to pick up the toy train, as more services originate here and it gives you a chance to visit the **Baidyanath Shiva temple**, parts of which are intricately carved and believed to date from 804 AD.

Kangra and around

Although most travellers bypass **KANGRA** on their way to Dharamsala, 18km further north, it's worth a brief detour. Kangra's crumbling, overgrown **fort** (daily sunrise–sunset; ₹100 (₹5)) was damaged by an earthquake in 1905 and is now inhabited by screeching green parrots that flit through a few simple temples still tended by priests. High gates, some British-built, span a cobbled path to the deserted ramparts. To get here, head 3km south on the road to Jawalamukhi, then turn up the 1km access road just before the bridge.

Masrur

Daily sunrise–sunset • ₹100 (₹5)

Thirty-five kilometres southwest of Kangra, the tiny village of **MASRUR** is the only place in the Himalayas with **rock-cut Hindu temples** similar to, though nowhere near as impressive as, those at Ellora in Maharashtra (see p.637). The fifteen temples, devoted to Ram, Lakshman and Sita, were hewn from natural rock in the ninth and tenth centuries.

Jawalamukhi

A simple whitewashed temple in the otherwise nondescript town of **JAWALAMUKHI**, 35km south of Kangra, protects one of north India's most important Hindu shrines. The sanctuary, crowned with a squat golden spire, contains a natural blue gas flame emitted from the earth, revered as a manifestation of the goddess of fire, Jawalamukhi.

ARRIVAL AND DEPARTURE   KANGRA AND AROUND

By bus Buses from all over the Kangra Valley and further afield pull into the bus stand 1km north of the town centre, where there are frequent connections to Dharamsala, as well as hourly services to both Masrur and Jawalamukhi.

By toy train Kangra can also be reached from Pathankot (see p.518) and Joginder Nagar by the narrow-gauge railway (see box, p.420).

ACCOMMODATION AND EATING

Jwalaji On the outskirts of Jawalamukhi ☎01970 222280, ✉jawalaji@hptdc.in. One of the better HPTDC hotels, with a range of spacious rooms, a dormitory, a full-service restaurant and a snack bar. Dorm ₹150, double ₹1300

Preet On the road to the bus stand, Kangra ☎01892 265260. The best rooms at this functional hotel are on the first floor, alongside a cosy little terrace. The restaurant is quite average. ₹400

Dharamsala and McLeod Ganj

Home to the Dalai Lama and Tibetan government in exile, and starting point for some exhilarating treks into the high Himalayas, **DHARAMSALA**, or more correctly, its upper town **McLEOD GANJ**, is one of Himachal's most irresistible destinations. Spread across wooded ridges beneath the stark rock faces of the Dhauladhar Range, the town is divided into two distinct and separate sections, separated by 10km of perilously twisting road and almost 1000m in altitude. Originally a British hill station, **McLeod Ganj** has been transformed by the influx of **Tibetan refugees** fleeing Chinese oppression in their homeland. Tibetan influence here is subsequently very strong, with temples, schools, monasteries, nunneries, meditation centres and the most extensive library of Tibetan history and religion. As well as playing host to hordes of foreign and domestic tourists, McLeod Ganj is a place of pilgrimage that attracts Buddhists and interested parties from

FROM TOP THE DALAI LAMA (P.423); THE MANALI–LEH HIGHWAY (P.455) >

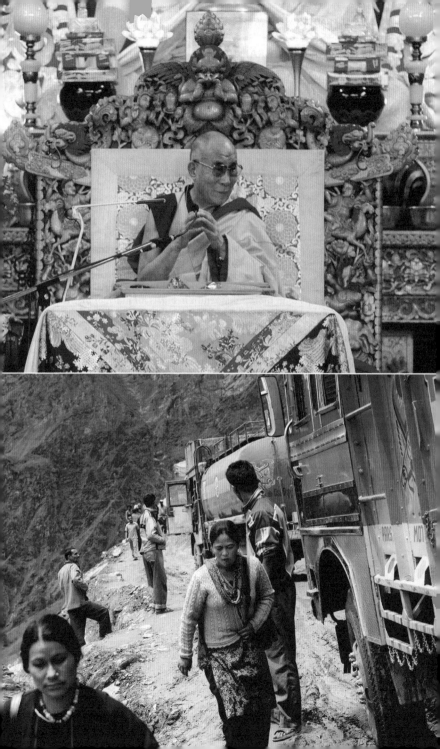

6

THE KANGRA VALLEY RAILWAY

India has five of the twenty or so vintage "toy trains" or narrow-gauge mountain railways in the world – three in the Himalayas and two of these in Himachal Pradesh. Most famous is the Kalka–Shimla line (see box, p.405), but the little-known 163km **Kangra Valley Railway** is also a magnificent engineering feat. Unlike the Kalka line, with its 103 tunnels and tortuous switchbacks, engineers of this route preferred bridges – 950 in all, many of which are still considered masterpieces – that give passengers uninterrupted views all the way from Pathankot to Joginder Nagar. Although it's slower than the equivalent road journey, the scenery along the way is far more impressive, particularly the stretch between Kangra and Mangwal.

There are six trains daily from Pathankot, departing between 2.30am and 4.30pm; four terminate at Baijnath (6hr 30min–7hr), while two go all the way to Joginder Nagar (10hr). In the opposite direction there are departures from Joginder Nagar at 7.30am and 12.20pm, and four more from Baijnath between 4.15am and 5.30pm. All services pass through Kangra.

all over the world, including Hollywood celebrities such as Richard Gere and Uma Thurman. Many people visit India specifically to come here, and its relaxed and friendly atmosphere can make it difficult to leave.

Despite heavy snows and low **temperatures** between December and March, McLeod Ganj receives visitors throughout the year. Summer brings torrential rains – this being the second wettest place in India – that return in bursts for much of the year. Daytime temperatures can be high, but you'll need warm clothes for the chilly nights.

Dharamsala

It's easy to see why most visitors bypass **Dharamsala** itself, a haphazard jumble of shops, offices and houses that spreads along several kilometres of gradually rising road. Apart from a couple of moderately lively bazaars, the only place of interest is the **Museum of Kangra Art** (Tues–Sun 10am–5pm; ₹50 (₹10)), which contains a small collection of Kangra miniatures and some modern art.

McLeod Ganj and aroud

The ever-expanding settlement of **McLeod Ganj** extends along a pine-covered ridge with valley views below and the near vertical walls of the Dhauladhar Range towering behind. Despite being named after David McLeod, the Lieutenant Governor of Punjab when the hill station was founded in 1848, little evidence of British occupation remains. The focal point of McLeod Ganj is its Buddhist **temple**, ringed with spinning red-and-gold prayer wheels. Today, Indian residents are outnumbered by Tibetans, who bedeck their ramshackle buildings with fluttering prayer flags: McLeod Ganj is not simply a political haven for them, but also home to their spiritual leader, the Dalai Lama, and to the Tibetan government in exile.

It's easy to **find your way around** McLeod Ganj. At its northern end, the road up from the lower town arrives at a small square that serves as the bus stand. Roads radiating from here head south to the Dalai Lama's Residence and the **Library of Tibetan Works and Archives**, northeast to the village of Dharamkot, the Tushita Retreat Meditation Centre and to the Tibetan Children's Village next to Dal Lake, and east to the hamlet of Bhagsu.

The Dalai Lama's Residence

Temple Rd

The Dalai Lama settled temporarily in McLeod Ganj in 1960; five decades later he's still here, and his **Residence** on the south edge of town has become his permanent home in exile. His own quarters are modest and most of the walled compound overhanging the valley is taken up by government offices. In front of the private enclosure, Dharamsala's main Buddhist temple, **Tsug Lakhang**, shelters images of Sakyamuni (the historical Buddha), Padmasambhava (who introduced Buddhism to Tibet) and Avalokitesvara (the *bodhisattva* of compassion) seated in meditation postures, surrounded by offerings from devotees. After paying homage to the Buddha inside, devotees complete a *kora*, a circumambulation of the temple complex (clockwise, starting at the trailhead below the monks' quarters), turning the numerous prayer wheels to send prayers out in all directions. Every afternoon monks from the nearby **Namgyal monastery** hold fierce but disciplined debates in the courtyard opposite the temple.

The Tibet Museum

Temple Rd • Tues–Sun 9am–5pm • ₹5

Next to the monastery, the **Tibet Museum** displays in graphic detail the plight of the Tibetan people since China invaded Tibet in 1949. Using photographs and video clips,

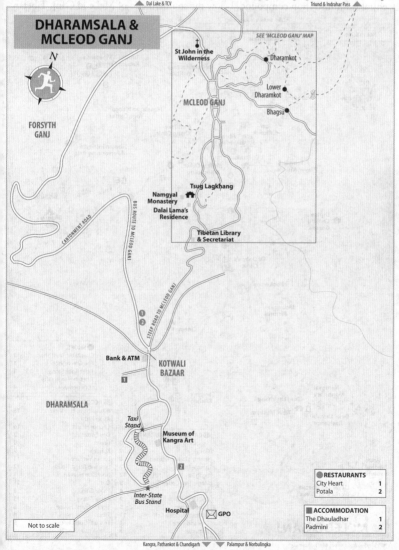

DHARAMSALA & MCLEOD GANJ

Dal Lake & TCV

Triund & Indrahar Pass

N

SEE 'MCLEOD GANJ' MAP

St John in the Wilderness

Dharamkot

MCLEOD GANJ

Lower Dharamkot

FORSYTH GANJ

Bhagsu

CANTONMENT ROAD

BUS ROUTE TO MCLEOD GANJ

Tsug Lagkhang

Namgyal Monastery

Dalai Lama's Residence

Tibetan Library & Secretariat

STEEP ROAD TO MCLEOD GANJ

Bank & ATM

KOTWALI BAZAAR

DHARAMSALA

Taxi Stand

Museum of Kangra Art

Inter-State Bus Stand

Hospital

GPO

RESTAURANTS
City Heart 1
Potala 2

ACCOMMODATION
The Dhauladhar 1
Padmini 2

Not to scale

Kangra, Pathankot & Chandigarh   Palampur & Norbulingka

the self-guided tour describes how Tibetan freedom fighters, backed by the CIA, waged an impossible guerrilla war against China that lasted into the 1970s. The upstairs hall features profiles of the museum curators – all refugees and ex-political prisoners – and a memorial to the 1.2 million Tibetans who have died in the conflict.

Library of Tibetan Works and Archives

Jogiwara Rd • Mon–Sat 9am–1pm & 2–5pm; closed 2nd & 4th Sat of month • Museum ₹10 • ☎ 01892 222467

The **Library of Tibetan Works and Archives** has one of the world's most extensive collections of original Tibetan manuscripts of sacred texts and prayers, books on all aspects of Tibet, information on Indian culture and architecture and a rich archive of historical photos. Decorated with bright Tibetan motifs, it is housed in the Tibetan Central Administration compound, below the southern end of McLeod Ganj. Tibetan

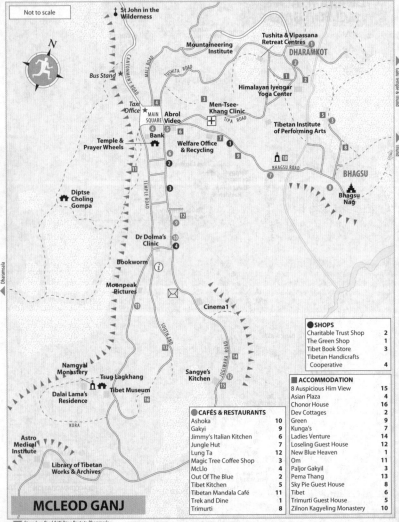

SHOPS

Charitable Trust Shop	2
The Green Shop	1
Tibet Book Store	3
Tibetan Handicrafts Cooperative	4

ACCOMMODATION

8 Auspicious Him View	15
Asian Plaza	4
Chonor House	16
Dev Cottages	2
Green	9
Kunga's	7
Ladies Venture	14
Loseling Guest House	12
New Blue Heaven	1
Om	11
Paljor Gakyil	3
Pema Thang	13
Sky Pie Guest House	8
Tibet	6
Trimurti Guest House	5
Zilnon Kagyeling Monastery	10

CAFÉS & RESTAURANTS

Ashoka	10
Gakyi	9
Jimmy's Italian Kitchen	6
Jungle Hut	7
Lung Ta	12
Magic Tree Coffee Shop	3
McLlo	4
Out Of The Blue	2
Tibet Kitchen	5
Tibetan Mandala Café	11
Trek and Dine	1
Trimurti	8

MCLEOD GANJ

Steep Jeep Road & Walking Route to Dharamsala

language and philosophy **courses** are held each weekday (see p.428), and a small **museum** on the first floor of the library displays Buddhist statues, finely moulded bronzes and mandalas (symmetrical images, used in meditation to symbolize spiritual journeys and the pattern of the universe).

Astro Medical Institute

Jogiwara Rd • Daily 9am–1pm & 2–5pm • Free

Just outside the library compound, the small **Astro Medical Institute** is staffed by monks who diagnose symptoms by examining the eyes, pulse and urine, and prescribe pills made of herbs, precious stones and sometimes animal products, mixed on particularly auspicious lunar dates. You can also have your horoscope prepared here.

Mountaineering Institute

Tushita Rd • Mon–Sat 10am–1.30pm & 2–5pm; closed 2nd Sat of month • ☎ 01892 221787

A minor road winds northeast from the McLeod Ganj Bus Stand to the **Mountaineering Institute**, which provides information on the region, including books and maps on the Dhauladhar Range, and organizes trekking expeditions.

Tushita Tibetan Buddhist Centre and Dhamma Sikhara

Tushita Rd

Continuing up the road from the Mountaineering institute you approach two Buddhist retreat centres, both beautifully situated in the midst of forests: the **Tushita Tibetan Buddhist Centre** was founded in 1972 by Lama Thubten Zopa Rinpoche, while just around the corner is **Dhamma Sikhara**, a Theravadan Vipassana centre. Meditation courses are held at both centres (see p.428).

Dharamkot and around

From the Dhamma Sikhara the road continues to Dharamkot, starting point for walks to **Triund** (2975m) and treks over the high passes to the Chamba Valley. Taking a path down through the wooded slopes north of Dharamkot brings you to the small, murky **Dal Lake**, the scene of an animal fair and Shaivite festival in September. It stands behind the **Tibetan Children's Village** (TCV), a huge complex providing education and training in traditional handicrafts for around two thousand students, many of whom are orphans or have been brought to safety by parents who have returned to Tibet. To the south, the creeping development has almost joined the village to the upper reaches of Bhagsu.

Bhagsu

Bhagsu Road heads east from McLeod Ganj's main square, skirting the hillside for 2km before reaching the village of **Bhagsu** with its ancient Shiva temple. The last few years have seen big changes here, with the construction of several hotels catering primarily for the domestic tourist market. However, it's still a pleasant enough place, with a few cafés near the temple complex. Beyond the temple a path meanders up the boulder-strewn

---

MEETING HIS HOLINESS THE DALAI LAMA

The **Dalai Lama** is in great demand. Tibetans fleeing their homeland come to him for blessing and reassurance; monks and nuns from all over India and Nepal look to him for spiritual guidance; and an ever-increasing number of Westerners arrive in Dharamsala hoping for a moment of his attention. As His Holiness no longer conducts public audiences, most visitors should count on attending one of his **public teachings**, which are advertised well in advance by the Office of His Holiness The Dalai Lama (Thekchen Choeling, McLeod Ganj; ☎ 01892 221343, ⓦ dalailama.com). **Private audiences** are granted to a select few and can only be arranged by writing at least four months in advance. The Dalai Lama's secretary receives hundreds of such letters each day and each case is reviewed on its merits.

slopes of a small stream up to a **waterfall**. If you're interested in studying tabla, contact Ashoka at the *Trimurti Guest House* (see p.427); he runs the **Trimurti International Music School** from his home. Note that in the past there have been occasional **attacks** on women walking between Bhagsu and McLeod Ganj, usually at night.

Tibetan Institute of Performing Arts

Mon–Sat 9am–noon & 1–5pm, closed 2nd & 4th Sat of month • ☎ 01892 221478, ⓦ tibetanarts.org

The **Tibetan Institute of Performing Arts** was founded in 1959 to preserve the Tibetan identity in exile. Around 150 people live on its campus, in the forests above McLeod Ganj overlooking Bhagsu, including artists, teachers, musicians and administrators. The TIPA troupe perform traditional *lhamo* operas, which derive from ancient masked dance dramas, and have played a morale-building role at Tibetan refugee camps throughout India, while also sharing Tibet's cultural heritage with international audiences. Visit its office for information on upcoming events and tours.

The Norbulingka Institute

8km from Dharamsala, near the village of Sidpur, Mon–Sat 8am–5pm • ☎ 01892 246402, ⓦ norbulingka.org

The **Norbulingka Institute**, is dedicated to preserving literary and artistic Tibetan culture. The complex of Tibetan-style buildings, built in 1985, is set amidst peaceful Japanese gardens, and centres on the two-storey **Deden Tsuglakhang temple**, which houses 1173 images of the Buddha and frescoes of the fourteen Dalai Lamas in the upper gallery. The

DHAULADHAR TREKS

0 (Approx.) 5
kilometres

TREKKING FROM DHARAMSALA

Dharamsala is one of the most popular starting points for **treks** over the rocky ridges of the Dhauladhar Range, which rise steeply from the Kangra Valley to 4600m. Trails pass through forests of deodar, pine, oak and rhododendron, cross streams and rivers and wind along vertiginous cliff tracks passing the occasional lake waterfall and glacier. Unless you are very experienced, you'll need a guide as the routes are steep and memorial stones testify to those who didn't make it. The **Mountaineering Institute** on Dharamkot Road (see p.423) can help arrange guides and porters, and stocks maps. Despite the availability of rough huts and caves, it's best to take a tent. The best **season** to trek here is from September to November, when the worst of the monsoon is over and before it gets too cold. Winter climbing should only be attempted by mountaineers experienced in using crampons and ice axes.

DHARAMSALA TO CHAMBA OVER INDRAHAR PASS

The most frequented route from Dharamsala to the Chamba Valley, over the **Indrahar Pass** (4350m), is arduous in places, but most trekkers manage it in around five days. The first section, from Dharamkot, winds through thick forest and steep rocky terrain for 9km to a grassy plateau at **Triund**. From here the path climbs to **Laqa Got**, and then on a seriously steep section up to the knife-edged Indrahar Pass where, weather permitting, you'll enjoy breathtaking views south to the plains and north to the snowy Pir Panjal peaks and Greater Himalayas. The descent is difficult in places and will take you via the Gaddi villages of **Kuarsi** and **Channauta** to the main road, from where you can pick up transport to Brahmour and Chamba by road.

OTHER ROUTES FROM DHARAMSALA TO CHAMBA

Several **other routes** cross the Dhauladhar Range, including the **Toral Pass** (4575m) which starts from **Tang Narwana** (1150m), 10km from Dharamsala. The most difficult route north is the five- or six-day trek across **Bhimghasutri Pass** (4580m), covering near-vertical rocky ascents, sharp cliffs and dangerous gorges. A much easier four- or five-day trek from Dharamsala crosses **Bleni Pass** (3710m) in the milder ranges to the northwest, weaving through alpine pastures and woods and crossing a few streams, before terminating at **Dunali**, on the Chamba road.

---

gilded copper statue of Sakyamuni in the hall downstairs is the largest of its kind outside Tibet. Elsewhere in the complex, the **Losel Doll Museum** shows colourful dioramas packed with traditionally clothed dolls.

ARRIVAL AND DEPARTURE MCLEOD GANJ AND DHARAMSALA

By plane Dharamsala's airport is 11km south at Gaggal. There is one daily flight to Delhi.

By bus State-run buses from Gaggal (every 30min; 30min), Shimla (3 daily; 10–11hr), Manali (3 daily; 10hr), Mandi (4 daily; 8–9hr), Pathankot (nearest railhead; every 30min; 3hr), Kangra (every 30min; 30min) and Delhi (6–8 daily; 15–16hr) pull into the bus stand on the south side of Dharamsala, though a very few private and deluxe buses from Delhi and Manali continue to McLeod Ganj.

GETTING AROUND AND INFORMATION

By taxi A shared taxi (₹20) between McLeod Ganj and Dharamsala takes just 15min. Taxi unions have fixed prices and a vehicle from McLeod Ganj to Dharamsala costs ₹200. Auto-rickshaws travel frequently from McLeod Ganj Bus Stand to Bhagsu (₹50) and the chai shop at Dharamkot (₹80).

By bus From 7.45am onwards numerous buses run between Dharamsala and McLeod Ganj (30min).

On foot To reach McLeod Ganj from Dharamsala, there is a steep 3km track that starts from behind the vegetable market, passing the Tibetan Library and Secretariat.

Tourist information McLeod Ganj's tourist office (Mon–Fri 10am–5pm, Sat 10am–2pm), on South End, provides basic accommodation and transport information. A good source of general info, news and local listings is ⓦmcllo .com or the free monthly news sheet *Contact*.

Tibetan Secretariat An information centre in Dharamsala's Tibetan Secretariat, beside the entrance to the compound, provides up-to-date news about the Tibetan community in Tibet and around the world.

ACCOMMODATION

Finding accommodation is only a problem during Losar, the Tibetan New Year (Feb/March). Almost all foreign visitors stay

6

in the upper town, **McLeod Ganj**, so there is little reason to stay in **Dharamsala** itself. Those planning long-term stays often head to the small settlements of **Bhagsu** or **Dharamkot**, where there is a mixture of rooms in family houses and a growing number of hotels, serving Indian tourists and hippie travellers, especially Israelis.

MCLEOD GANJ

8 Auspicious Him View Jogiwara Rd ☏ 01892 220567, ⊕ 8aushimview.com; map p.422. Fifteen spotless rooms, tastefully decorated with Tibetan art and wood panelling, in a spanking new block. Café and juice bar downstairs. ₹**1300**

Asian Plaza Main Chowk ☏ 01892 220855, ⊕ hotel asianplaza.com; map p.422. Snazzy new hotel with nicely decorated rooms and huge suites, right in the heart of town. Also has a rooftop restaurant that serves a standard range of Indian, Chinese and Continental. Free wi-fi. ₹**2200**

★ **Chonor House** South End ☏ 01892 221006, ⊕ norbulingka.org; map p.422. Part of the Norbulingka Institute for Tibetan Culture, with very well presented rooms decorated by artists, combining traditional Tibetan decor with modern comfort. There's also wi-fi and an excellent restaurant with garden seating. All proceeds go to Norbulingka. ₹**3500**

Green Bhagsu Rd ☏ 01892 221200, ⊕ greenhotel.biz; map p.422. Wide range of well-kept, comfortable rooms, with valley views, a good restaurant and adjacent internet café. Deservedly popular for being one of the better backpacker havens. ₹**800**

★ **Kunga's** Bhagsu Rd ☏ 01892 221180, ⊕ tenzin_dhonyo@yahoo.co.in; map p.422. Clean and centrally located with some non-attached rooms and a fantastic sun deck; larger rooms are spacious and light, with big balconies. Excellent new luxury block below. The fine Italian restaurant has wi-fi indoors. ₹**250**/₹**600**

Ladies Venture Jogiwara Rd ☏ 01892 221559, ⊕ shantiazad@yahoo.co.in; map p.422. Well-appointed rooms of varying size, some with shared bathrooms, in a welcoming hotel. Quiet location, with a garden and a small café. Fixed price year round. Dorm ₹**120**, double ₹**350**/₹**550**

Loseling Guest House Off Jogiwara Rd ☏ 01892 220085, ⊕ loselingmonastery.org; map p.422. Simple monastery-owned lodge, plain and well maintained with good views from an open roof terrace. Upstairs rooms are best and most in demand. Staff are sometimes extremely uncommunicative. Dorm ₹**100**, double ₹**260**

Om Near the bus stand ☏ 98163 29985, ⊕ omhotel @hotmail.com; map p.422. Simple, quiet and very friendly lodge on the western edge of town. A variety of rooms; the cheapest ones share squat toilet bathrooms and hot showers. The upper terrace and sociable restaurant are popular spots at sunset. ₹**250**/₹**450**

Paljor Gakyil TIPA Rd ☏ 01892 221443, ⊕ ngapal @yahoo.com; map p.422. Immaculate budget lodge with plain or carpeted rooms and great views over McLeod Ganj. Cheaper rooms only have cold water. To get

here, climb the steps between the *Seven Hills* and *Kalsang* guesthouses. ₹**200**

Pema Thang South End ☏ 01892 221871, ⊕ pema thang.net; map p.422. Friendly hotel, one of the best maintained on South End. Rooms all have heaters, hot showers and TV; you'll pay more for a good view. Popular with well-off Westerners interested in Buddhism. ₹**1650**

Tibet Bhagsu Rd ☏ 01892 221587, ⊕ hoteltibetdasa @yahoo.com; map p.422. Popular and central hotel with the superb *Snow Lion* restaurant; the downstairs valley-facing rooms offer the best value. Fixed prices all year. ₹**660**

Zilnon Kagyeling Monastery Bhagsu Rd ☏ 98827 45575, ⊕ ringtoptse@yahoo.co.in; map p.422. Basic and extremely cheap single and double rooms with shared facilities in an active *gompa*. Great quiet location and rooftop café. ₹**140**

BHAGSU

★ **Sky Pie Guest House** Off the left turning as you approach temple ☏ 01892 220497, ⊕ denisraaz8 @gmail.com; map p.422. Friendly and lively place with standard attached budget rooms in the old block and smarter ones with TV and balconies in the new block. ₹**300**

Trimurti Guest House Upper Bhagsu towards Dharamkot ☏ 01892 221364, ⊕ trimurtigarden.in; map p.422. A few rooms, all with shared bathrooms, in a quiet family place with a lawn and colourful shrine. The owner runs a small music school (see p.424). ₹**250**

DHARAMKOT

Dev Cottages Downhill from the main junction ☏ 01892 221558, ⊕ devcottage.com; map p.422. Smart and spacious new cottages, comfortably furnished and blessed with fine valley views and outdoor space. ₹**1500**

New Blue Heaven Downhill from the main junction ☏ 01892 221005, ⊕ sandeep74gill@yahoo.co.in; map p.422. Two-storey family house with a sociable terrace and garden. All rooms are simple but attached. ₹**800**

DHARAMSALA

The Dhauladhar Off Kotwali Bazaar ☏ 01892 224926, ⊕ dharamshala@hptdc.in; map p.421. Institutional-feeling HPTDC place with spacious attached rooms with constant hot water and balconies giving superb views over the plains to the south. Plus a good mid-priced restaurant, bar, garden terrace and lawns. ₹**1600**

Padmini Main Rd, near bus stand ☏ 01892 227378; map p.421. Striking brown-and-white striped building with reasonable rooms of different sizes, all attached with cable TV. ₹**500**

EATING AND DRINKING

While eating options in Dharamsala are fairly perfunctory, McLeod Ganj and its satellites are renowned for relaxed **restaurants** serving traveller staples and Tibetan dishes such as *thukpa* and *momos*, as well as fresh-baked Tibetan bread and cakes. There's not much nightlife but alcohol is available in a few places.

MCLEOD GANJ

Ashoka Jogiwara Rd ☎01892 221589; map p.422. Good spicy Indian food, as well as Chinese, Continental and Israeli dishes are served on two indoor levels and on a pleasant roof terrace for ₹100–200. Try the *karai* chicken. Daily 9am–10.30pm.

Gakyi Jogiwara Rd ☎98161 12763; map p.422. Humble and homely, with only five tables. Great Tibetan and Western veg dishes, plus the town's best fruit muesli and Tibetan bread. All items cost less than ₹100. Daily 7.30am–10pm.

Jimmy's Italian Kitchen Jogiwara Rd ☎01892 221883; map p.422. Hip Western-style upstairs café decorated with classic film posters. Good salads, baked potatoes, lattes and home-made desserts; dinners mainly ₹100–200. Daily 9am–10pm.

Jungle Hut Bhagsu Rd ☎98050 18235; map p.422. This bamboo structure perched on the top of the eponymous hotel offers the best views in the area. Food ranges from Western breakfasts through standard Indian and Chinese mains to ₹220 sizzlers. Daily 8am–9pm.

Lung Ta Jogiwara Rd ☎01892 220689; map p.422. Japanese vegetarian place with a constantly changing menu that usually includes miso soup, sushi, tempura vegetables and tofu steak; daily set menus ₹150. Profits go to assisting former Tibetan political prisoners. Mon–Sat noon–8.30pm.

McLlo Main Square ☎01892 221280; map p.422. Massive neon-lit monstrosity overlooking the square. Large selection of good Western food from ₹100, with trout around ₹300. The second-floor bar is the town's main drinking den. Daily 11am–midnight.

★ **Tibet Kitchen** Corner of Jogiwara Rd and main square ☎97362 54543; map p.422. Expertly run and stylishly decorated three-level restaurant-cum-café. The huge menu includes pan-Asian noodles, Italian and, most impressively, Bhutanese *datse* dishes in a spicy cheese sauce for ₹80–140. Daily 8am–9pm.

★ **Tibetan Mandala Café** Temple Rd ☎01892 220887; map p.422. Great hangout with a jolly proprietor, offering superb breakfasts, comfort food including cakes (₹40–60) and the best coffee in town. Wi-fi. Daily 6.30am–8pm.

BHAGSU

Magic Tree Coffee Shop Up the left turning as you approach temple ☎89881 56523; map p.422. Cosy little spot with a proper expresso machine, a modest selection of cakes and a mixture of rock and ethnic vibes. Daily 8am–11pm.

Trimurti Main Rd near temple ☎98168 68421; map p.422. This Punjabi restaurant on an open first-floor terrace is a firm favourite for its variety of veg dishes, including a filling ₹80 thali. Daily 7am–10pm.

DHARAMKOT

Out Of The Blue Down steps from the taxi stand ☎97367 41745; map p.422. There's a chillout zone with cushions upstairs and a grassy terrace outside. The pizza, Indian veg and Israeli meals cost ₹100–200. Daily 7am–midnight.

Trek And Dine Near the main junction ☎97363 65156; map p.422. Typically colourful spot with wall hangings and a cushioned corner, serving a range of inexpensive breakfasts, salads, pizza, pasta and Mexican dishes. Wi-fi available. Daily 7am–midnight.

DHARAMSALA

City Heart Near Kotwali Bazaar ☎01892 225290; map p.421. There's a basic ground-floor canteen and slightly more comfortable upstairs room. The food is mainly Bengali and tandoori, with some Chinese cuisine, all dishes around ₹80–150. Daily 9am–10.30pm.

Potala Near Kotwali Bazaar ☎86793 68859; map p.421. Very authentic Tibetan family restaurant tucked into a tiny upstairs room. Staples such as *thukpa* go for just ₹30–50. Daily 9am–9pm.

SHOPPING

Stalls and little shops along the main streets stock Tibetan trinkets, inexpensive warm clothing, incense, prayer bells, rugs and books.

Bookshops The Tibet Book Store is a good place to browse for books on Tibetan Buddhism, as is the Charitable Trust Shop, both on Jogiwara Rd in McLeod Ganj's main bazaar.

The Green Shop Bhagsu Rd. The Green Shop sells recycled painted cards, hand-painted T-shirts, books on the environment and filtered boiled water for ₹5.

Tibetan Handicrafts Cooperative Jogiwara Rd ☎01892 221415. This large handicrafts shop sells *thangkas* of all sizes, along with prayer flags and local garments.

6

DIRECTORY

Banks and exchange The Punjab National Bank (Mon–Fri 10am–2pm, Sat 10am–noon) in McLeod Ganj will change travellers' cheques and cash, as will the upper branch of State Bank of India in Dharamsala. There are a number of ATMs and several authorized exchange agencies in McLeod Ganj

Cinema Cinema1 and Abrol Video, both on Jogiwara Rd, show Hollywood flicks, often with a Tibetan or Indian theme.

Courses Numerous courses are available in McLeod Ganj, including dharma teachings, Tibetan language, Hindi, ancient Thai massage, yoga, tabla, karate, Xi Gung, Tai Chi, reiki, and Indian vegetarian and Tibetan cookery. Free classes on dharma are given in translation by Buddhist monks from 11am until noon most weekdays at the Library of Tibetan Works and Archives. Philosophy courses and three-month Tibetan language courses (beginning March, June & Sept) are also run from the library (contact the Secretary for Tibetan Studies, ☎01892 222467). Several places, such as *Sangye's Kitchen* (daily 10am–noon & 4–6pm; ₹250; ☎98161 64540) near the Post Office on Jogiwara Rd, offer Tibetan cooking lessons.

Hospitals The Tibetan Delek Hospital (☎01892 222053), above the Astro Medical Institute, is one of the best hospitals in the state and has Western doctors on call.

Internet access McLeod Ganj has a multitude of internet cafés, mostly charging ₹30/hr. Wi-fi networks are increasingly available.

Meditation Tibetan Buddhist meditation courses are held at the Tushita Meditation Centre in Dharamkot (office Mon–Sat 9.30–11.30am & 1–4.30pm; ☎01892 221866, ⒲tushita.info). Courses range from short retreats of eight to ten days to an intensive three-month summer purification retreat (Vajrasattva). The Vipassana Centre, next door, follows teachings more akin to Theravada Buddhism. They run ten-day silent retreats and daily sittings (register in person Mon–Sat 4–5pm or contact ☎01892 221309, ⒲sikhara.dhamma.org).

Teaching The Yong Ling School, Jogiwara Rd on the left past the post office, welcomes volunteer teachers. An excellent resource for jobs is Volunteer Tibet (⒲volunteertibet.org), whose office is opposite the school.

Tibetan settlement For enquiries about the Tibetan settlement, call in either at the Welfare Office on Bhagsu Rd in McLeod Ganj or directly at the Reception Centre below the post office, where donations of clothes, books, blankets and pens for new Tibetan arrivals are always gratefully accepted.

Travel agents General agents for all services include Himachal Travels (☎01892 221428), Tibet Tours & Travels (☎01892 221283), both on Jogiwara Rd, and Ways Tours & Travels, Temple Rd (☎01892 221910).

Yoga The Himalayan Iyengar Yoga Centre (⒲hiyogacentre .com) in Dharamkot runs five-day courses in Hatha yoga, starting every Thurs.

Dalhousie

The quiet, relaxed hill station of **DALHOUSIE** spreads over five low-level hills at the western edge of the Dhauladhar Range. While the town itself, mostly modern hotels interspersed with Raj-era buildings and low-roofed stalls, is unremarkable, the pine-covered slopes around it are intersected with paths and tracks ideal for short, undemanding walks.

Dalhousie owes its name to Lord Dalhousie, Governor General of Punjab (1849–56), who was attracted by the cool climate to establish a sanatorium here for the many British, who, like himself, suffered ill health. Early in the twentieth century, it was a popular alternative to crowded, expensive Shimla, but thereafter declined. Today Dalhousie is a favourite summer retreat for holidaying Punjabis, but receives only a handful of Western tourists, few of whom stay. A small population of Tibetans has lived here since the Chinese invasion of Tibet in 1959.

The town is spread over a series of hills with winding roads and steep paths connecting the two focal points, the chowks. **Gandhi Chowk**, with its restaurants and post office, is the busiest section. From here the Mall and Garam Sarak dip and curve 2km to **Subhash Chowk**, at the top end of the largely Muslim Sadar Bazaar. North of here, the bus stand and information office mark the main road out of town.

ARRIVAL AND INFORMATION

DALHOUSIE

By bus Dalhousie is usually approached by bus from Pathankot in the Punjab, 80km southwest, or through the Himalayan foothills from Dharamsala (2–3 daily; 6hr) and Shimla (1–2 daily; 13–14hr), both via Nurpur. Transport to Chamba (2hr 15min) usually goes via Banikhet, though four buses also travel via Khajjiar. Taxis to either chowk from the bus stand cost a rather steep ₹100.

Tourist information The tourist information office (Mon–Sat 10am–5pm; ☎01899 242136), 50m from the bus stand, provides transport information.

ACCOMMODATION AND EATING

Numerous **hotels** cater for Dalhousie's hot-season hordes and it is only between April and June that prices really shooot up. Most hotels have their own restaurants, numerous *dhabas* crowd the chowks, there are some independent **places to eat**.

★ **Crags** Garam Sarak Rd, 400m from Subhash Chowk ⓣ01899 242124, ⓔrnkagarwal@yahoo.in. A quiet and exceptionally friendly hotel with old-fashioned but comfortable rooms, a large terrace, tasty food (if pre-arranged) and great views down to the plains. ₹500

Momo's Corner In the Tibetan Market above the bus stand. Tiny hole-in-the-wall hut with just three tables but serving some of the tastiest *momos* (ten for ₹50) you will find, as well as chowmein. Daily 8am–8pm.

Moti Mahal Subhash Chowk ⓣ01899 242134. Fairly functional restaurant with indoor and courtyard seating, which does a decent selection of Indian and Chinese dishes for around ₹100–200, as well as cheaper snacks like masala dosa. Daily 9am–10pm.

Sher-e-Punjab Just below Subhash Chowk ⓣ94180 10413. The most established and reliable of three adjacent establishments with very similar names. Best for rich and tasty non-veg dishes for ₹170–240. Daily 9am–10pm.

Silverton Near the Circuit House above the Mall ⓣ01899 240674, ⓦheritagehotels.com/silverton. An old-world manor house with large rooms, all stylishly furnished with period furniture, and immaculate lawns set within private woodlands. ₹3000

Sky Ways Court Rd, 100m from Subhash Chowk ⓣ01899 242818. Rather characterless concrete building but the fairly large attached rooms with cable TV are good value and have uninterrupted views. ₹500

Youth Hostel A 5min walk behind the dhabas from the bus stand ⓣ01899 242189, ⓔyh_dalhousie@rediffmail.com. Well organised and extremely clean hostel, which has 15-bed dorms and attached doubles. Dorm ₹150, double ₹350

Around Dalhousie

From Dalhousie the road east zigzags through forests to **Khajjiar**, a popular local day out, before descending through terraced mountain slopes to **Chamba**, perched above the rushing River Ravi. It's a slow and relaxed place with some fascinating temples and a small art museum. **Brahmour**, three hours further east by bus and the final settlement on the road into the mountains, holds more Hindu temples – both towns make good bases for **treks** into the remote **Pangi Valley**.

Khajjiar

Heading east towards Chamba, the road descends through deodar forests to the meadow of **Khajjiar** where the small twelfth-century temple of **Khajjinag** looks down over a vast rolling green with a small lake cupped in the centre. Khajjiar is a popular day-trip from Dalhousie for Indian tourists who come to take pony rides. The road beyond Khajjiar dips across denuded and terraced hillsides down towards Chamba.

ARRIVAL AND DEPARTURE — KHAJJIAR

By bus Prince Travels at the bus stand in Dalhousie runs a tourist bus to Khajjiar and Chamba, departing at 10am and returning to Dalhousie at 6.30pm; in addition, four Chamba-bound state buses travel via Khajjiar every day.

ACCOMMODATION

Shining Star Resort On hill above town centre ⓣ01899 236336, ⓦshiningstarkhajjiar.com. Plush hotel with a range of comfortable rooms and luxurious suites, a decent restaurant and fine views from all but the cheapest rooms. ₹1000

Chamba

Shielded on all sides by high mountains, **CHAMBA** was ruled for an entire millennium by kings descended from Raja Sahil Verma, who founded it in 920 AD and named it after his daughter Champavati. Unlike Himachal states further south, it was never formally under Mughal rule and its distinct Hindu culture remained intact until the first roads were built to Dalhousie in 1870. When the state of Himachal Pradesh was formed in 1948, Chamba became the capital. Today, just a handful of visitors make it out here, passing through before or after trekking, or stopping off to see the unique **temples**.

6

6

CHAMBA FESTIVALS

Chamba's annual four-day **Suhi Mata Festival**, in early April, commemorates Rani Sunena, the wife of the tenth-century Raja Sahil Verma. A curious legend relates that when water from a nearby stream failed to flow through a channel supposed to divert it to the town, local brahmins advised Raja Verma that either his son or his wife would have to sacrifice themselves. The queen obliged; she was buried alive at the head of the channel, and the water flowed freely. Only women and children participate in the festival, dancing on the *chaugan* before processing with an image of Champavati (Rani Sunena's daughter who gave her name to the town) and banners of the clan's solar emblem to the Suhi Mata temple in the hills behind the town.

Minjar, a week of singing and dancing at the start of August to celebrate the growth of maize, is also peculiar to Chamba. Its climax comes on the last day, when a rowdy procession of locals, Gaddis and Gujjars, dressed in traditional costumes, leaves the palace and snakes down to the riverbank, where bunches of maize are thrown into the water. Before Independence, locals followed a custom whereby a male buffalo was pushed into the river; its drowning was an auspicious sign but if the beast managed to swim to the opposite bank bad fortune was expected for the coming year.

The *chaugan*, a large green used for sports, evening strolls and festive celebrations, marks the centre of town, overlooked by the imposing old **Rang Mahal** palace, now a government building.

Bhuri Singh museum

Tues–Sun 10am–5pm • Free

At the south end of the *chaugan*, the **Bhuri Singh museum** holds a reasonable display of local arts and crafts. Its eighteenth- and nineteenth-century **Kangra miniature paintings**, depicting court life, amorous meetings and men and women smoking elaborate hookahs, are much bolder than their Mughal-influenced Rajasthani equivalents. The museum's best feature is its small cache of **rumals**. Made by women since the tenth century, *rumals* are like embroidered paintings, depicting scenes from popular myth. Today just a few women continue this tradition, but a weaving centre in the old palace is attempting to revitalize the art.

The temples

The intimate complex of **Lakshmi Narayan temples**, behind Dogra Bazaar west of the *chaugan*, is of a style found only in Chamba and Brahmour. Three of its six earth-brown temples are dedicated to Vishnu and three to Shiva, all with profusely carved outer walls and curious curved *shikharas*, topped with overhanging wooden canopies and gold pinnacles added in 1678 in defiance of Aurangzeb's order to destroy all Hindu temples in the hill states. Niches in the walls contain images of deities, but many stand empty, some statues lost in the earthquake of 1905 and others looted more recently.

Entering the compound, you're confronted by the largest and oldest temple, built in the tenth century and enshrining a marble idol of Lakshmi Narayan. The buxom maidens flanking the entrance to the sanctuary, each holding a water vessel, represent the goddesses Ganga and Yamuna, while inside a frieze depicts scenes from the Mahabharata and Ramayana. Temples dedicated to Shiva fill the third courtyard. In the inner sanctuary, you'll see sturdy brass images of Shiva, Parvati and Nandi, inlaid with silver and copper brought from mines nearby. Outside the temple complex, **coppersmiths** manufacture curved ceremonial trumpets and brass hookahs.

Of Chamba's other temples, the most intriguing is the tenth-century **Chamunda Devi temple** high above the town in the north, a steep half-hour climb up steps that begin near the bus stand. Decorated with hundreds of heavy brass bells and protecting a fearsome image of the bloodthirsty goddess Chamunda, the temple is built entirely of wood, and commands an excellent view up the Ravi Gorge. Back in

TREKS AROUND CHAMBA AND BRAHMOUR

The most popular treks from Chamba lead south over the **Dhauladhar** via the Minkiani or Indrahar pass to Dharamsala. **Equipment** can be rented and porters and **guides** hired in Chamba and Brahmour. Mani Mahesh Travels in Chamba (☎ 01899 222507) organizes and equips treks.

TREKS IN THE PANGI VALLEY TO LAHAUL

Few trekkers make it to the spectacular, all but inaccessible **Pangi Valley**, between the soaring Greater Himalayan Range in the north and the Outer Himalayan Range in the south. Several peaks within it have never been climbed, and onward paths lead to Kashmir, Lahaul and Zanskar. The trek to Lahaul takes nine or ten days from **Traila** (90km north of Chamba) via Satraundhi (3500m) over the Sach Pass to Killar, Sach Khas, and finishing in Purthi from where you can take a bus via Tindi to **Udaipur**. Buses run from here to Keylong, capital of Lahaul, for connections northwards to Leh or south over the Rohtang Pass and down to Manali.

TREKS FROM BRAHMOUR

Trekking routes lead north from **Brahmour** (2130m) over the Pir Panjal Range across passes that are covered with snow for most of the year. The challenging six- to seven-day trek over **Kalichho Pass** (4990m), "the Abode of Kali", ends in the village of **Triloknath**, whose ancient temple to three-faced Shiva is sacred to both Hindus and Buddhists. Buses run from here to Udaipur, and on to Keylong and Manali.

Another demanding five- to six-day route crosses the **Kugti Pass** (5040m). From **Hadsar**, an hour by bus from Brahmour, the path follows the River Budhil for 12km to **Kugti**, then up to **Kuddi Got**, a vast flower-filled meadow (4000m). The next stage, over the pass, requires crampons and ice axes for an incredibly taxing six-hour climb. Having enjoyed views of the towering peaks of Lahaul and Zanskar from the summit, you plummet once again to the head of a glacier at **Khardu**, continuing down to Raape, 7km from **Shansha**, which is linked to Udaipur and Keylong by road.

Finally, a delightful three-day trek to the sacred lake of **Manimahesh** (4183m) starts from and returns to Hadsar. The awesome Manimahesh Kailash massif, with its permanent glaciers and ice fields, overlooks the lake.

town, south of the *chaugan* near the post office, the small, lavishly carved eleventh-century **Harirai temple** contains a smooth brass image of Vaikuntha, the triple-headed aspect of Vishnu.

ARRIVAL AND INFORMATION
CHAMBA

By bus Buses arrive at the cramped bus stand in the north of town. From Chamba, there is one bus a day for Dharamsala (9.30pm; 8–9hr), and two for Shimla (4am & 5pm; 15–16hr). There are buses every 30min to Banikhet and hourly to Pathankot, and a daily departure

to Amritsar (11pm; 8hr).
Tourist information The uninspiring tourist office (Mon–Sat 10am–5pm; ☎ 01899 224002) is part of the *Iravati* complex.

ACCOMMODATION AND EATING

Chamba has a fair number of mostly grubby budget **lodges** and cheap **restaurants**. Try the local speciality, *madhra*, a rich, oily and slightly bitter mix of beans and curd.

Chamunda View Below the bus stand ☎ 01899 224067. Just about the pick of the budget lodges, though still rather shabby. Still, the compact attached rooms are fine for a night. ₹**300**

City Heart Above the far end of the chaugan ☎ 01899 225930, ⊚ hotelcityheartchamba.com. The best hotel in town is a modern affair, with fairly smart attached rooms and probably the best restaurant too. ₹**1780**

The Iravati The nearest corner of the chaugan to the bus stand ☎ 01899 222671, ⊚ chamba@hptdc.in. HPTDC hotel offering comfortable, carpeted attached rooms with cable TV and a reliable, if unexciting, restaurant. ₹**1200**

Rishi Hotel Rishi, Dogra Bazaar ☎ 01899 224343. A popular hotel restaurant, with a good selection of both veg and non-veg meals for ₹70–180, mostly Indian with some Chinese. Daily 7am–10pm.

6

Brahmour

BRAHMOUR is a one-horse town of slate-roofed houses, apple trees and small maize fields, shadowed on all sides by high snowy peaks. The **temples**, whose curved *shikharas* dominate the large, neatly paved central square, are more dramatic and better preserved than their rivals at Chamba. The sanctuaries are unlocked only for puja in the mornings and evenings, permitting a glimpse of bold bronze images of Ganesh, Shiva and Parvati, unchanged since their installation in the seventh and eighth centuries when Brahmour was capital of the surrounding mountainous region. The efficient Mountaineering Institute has details of local **treks**, reliable guides and porters, and equipment for rent.

6

ARRIVAL AND DEPARTURE
BRAHMOUR

By bus There are several daily bus connections with Chamba (3hr), fewer with Dalhousie.

ACCOMMODATION AND EATING

Except during the September pilgrimage when everywhere is booked up, you can find **rooms** at the handful of guesthouses. **Food** is mainly confined to the stalls lining the main road between the bus stand and the square.

Divya Cottage In the centre of the village ☎ 01090 275033. Probably the best of the budget lodges, despite being drastically basic with barely furnished rooms and cramped attached bathrooms. ₹300

The Kullu Valley

The majestic **KULLU VALLEY** is cradled by the Pir Panjal to the north, the Parvati Range to the east, and the Barabhangal Range to the west. This is Himachal at its most idyllic, with roaring rivers, pretty mountain villages, orchards and terraced fields, thick pine forests and snow-flecked ridges. The valley extends 80km north from the mouth of the perilously steep and narrow **Larji Gorge**, near Mandi, to the foot of the **Rohtang Pass** – gateway to Lahaul and Ladakh.

In spite of the changes wrought by roads, immigration and, more recently, mass tourism, the Kullu Valley's way of life is maintained in countless timber and stone villages. Known as **paharis** ("hill people"), the locals – high-caste landowning Thakurs, and their (low-caste) sharecropping tenant farmers – still sport the distinctive Kullu cap, or *topi*. The women, meanwhile, wear colourful headscarves and *puttoos* fastened with silver pins and chains. Venture into the lush meadows above the tree line and you'll cross paths with nomadic **Gaddi** shepherds.

Most tourists make a beeline for **Manali** after a gruelling bus ride from Leh or Delhi. With its vast choice of hotels and restaurants, there is something here for everyone. Still an evergreen hippie hangout, it's India's number-one honeymoon spot, and is also popular with outdoors enthusiasts taking advantage of the fine **trekking**. Few travellers actually stay in **Kullu town** and the only real attraction is the annual **Dussehra festival** in October. Flights from Delhi to Bhuntur, just south of Kullu, offer a welcome but weather-dependent alternative to the long overnight bus journeys. To the north, **Naggar**'s castle, ancient temples and relaxed guesthouses make a pleasant change from the claustrophobic concrete of modern Manali, as do **Manikaran**'s sacred hot springs, up the spectacular **Parvati Valley**.

Brief history

Known in the ancient Hindu scriptures as **Kulanthapitha**, or "End of the Habitable World", the Kullu Valley for centuries formed one of the major trade corridors between Central Asia and the Gangetic plains, and local rulers, based first at **Jagatsukh** and later at Naggar and Sultanpur (now Kullu), were able to rake off handsome profits from the through traffic. This trade monopoly, however, also made it a prime target for invasion, and in the eighteenth and early nineteenth centuries the Kullu rajas were forced to

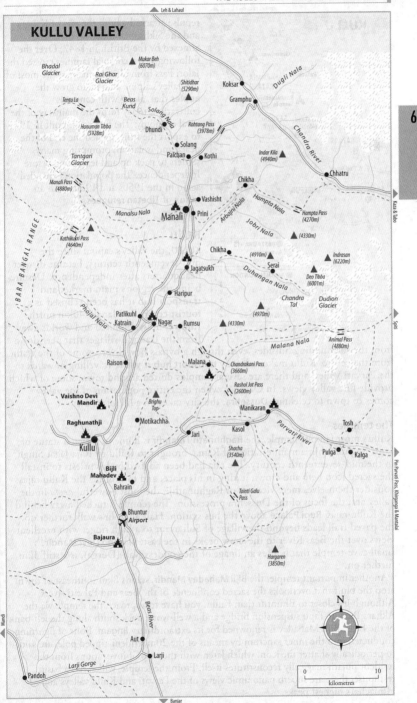

KULLU VALLEY

Leh & Lahaul

Bhadal
Glacier

Mukar Beh
(6070m)

Rai Ghar
Glacier

Shitidhar
(5290m)

Koksar

Dugli Nala

Tentu La

Beas
Kund

Gramphu

Chandra River

Hanuman Tibba
(5928m)

Solang Nala

Dhundi

Rohtang Pass
(3978m)

Indar Kila
(4940m)

Chhatru

Solang

Palchan

Kothi

Tantgari
Glacier

Chikha

Manali Pass
(4880m)

Vashisht

Manali

Prini

Arbojni Nala

Hampta Nala

Hampta Pass
(4270m)

Kaza & Tabo

Manalsu Nala

Jobri Nala

(4330m)

BARA BANGAL RANGE

Kathikukri Pass
(4640m)

Chikha

(4910m)

Indrasan
(6220m)

Jagatsukh

Serai

Duhangan Nala

Deo Tibba
(6001m)

Haripur

Chandra
Tal

Dudion
Glacier

Phojal Nala

Patlikuhl

Katrain

Nagar

Rumsu

(4970m)

(4330m)

Spiti

Malana Nala

Animal Pass
(4880m)

Raison

Malana

Chandrakani Pass
(3660m)

Rashol Jot Pass
(2600m)

Vaishno Devi
Mandir

Brighu
Top

Manikaran

Tosh

Raghunathji

Motikachha

Jari

Kasol

Parvati River

Kullu

Shacha
(3540m)

Pulga

Kalga

Pin Parvati Pass, Khirganga & Mantalai

Bijli
Mahadev

Bahrain

Tainti Galu
Pass

Bhuntur
Airport

Bajaura

Hargaren
(3850m)

Mandi

Beas River

N

Aut

Larji

Pandoh

Larji Gorge

0   10

kilometres

Banjar

6

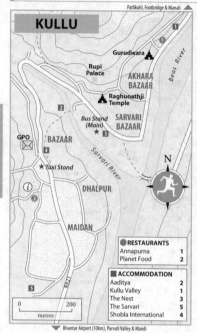

KULLU

Patlikuhl, Footbridge & Manali

Gurudwara

Rupi Palace

AKHARA BAZAAR

Raghunathji Temple

Bus Stand (Main)

SARVARI BAZAAR

GPO

BAZAAR

DHALPUR

Taxi Stand

MAIDAN

Beas River

Sarvari River

N

RESTAURANTS
Annapurna 1
Planet Food 2

ACCOMMODATION
Aaditya 2
Kullu Valley 1
The Nest 3
The Sarvari 5
Shobla International 4

0 200 metres

Bhuntur Airport (10km), Parvati Valley & Mandi

repulse attacks by both the raja of Kangra and the Sikhs, before seeing their lands annexed by the British in 1847. Over the following years, colonial families crossed the Jalori Pass from Shimla, making the most of the valley's alpine climate to grow the **apples** that, along with **cannabis** cultivation, today form the mainstay of the rural economy. The first road, built in 1927 to export the fruit, spelled the end of the peace and isolation, prompting many settlers to pack up and leave long before Independence. The population expanded again in the 1950s and 1960s with an influx of **Tibetan refugees**.

Kullu

KULLU, the valley's capital since the mid-seventeenth century, became district headquarters after Independence. Despite being the region's main market and transport hub it has been eclipsed as a tourist centre by Manali, 40km north. Kullu is noisy, polluted and worlds away from the tranquil villages that peer down from the surrounding hillsides, even though a bypass now diverts some of the traffic from the centre. Kullu makes a handy **transport hub** if you're travelling onwards to the Parvati Valley, and there are several **temples** dotted around town, some of which provide fine valley views. In October, when the entire population of the valley comes to town to celebrate **Dussehra**, the city takes on a life of its own.

The temples

Kullu's most famous temple, the **Raghunathji Mandir** is home to a sacred statue of Lord Raghunathji, a manifestation of Rama, brought to Kullu by Raja Jagat Singh in the mid-seventeenth century. The raja had been advised by his priests to install the sacred icon here and crown it king in his place, and to this day the Kullu rajas consider themselves mere viceroys of Raghunathji, the most powerful *devta* in the valley and the focus of the Dussehra procession. The temple is tucked away behind the Kullu rajas' **Rupi Palace** above the bus station. Half an hour's walk further up, the paved trail leads beyond the village of Sultanpur to a high ridge, with excellent views over the Beas River to the snow peaks in the east. **Vaishno Devi Mandir**, a small cave-temple that houses an image of the goddess Kali (Durga), is a stiff 3km further on.

Another important temple, the **Bijli Mahadev Mandir**, stands 8km southeast of town, atop the bluff that overlooks the sacred confluence of the Beas and Parvati rivers. Although it's closer to Bhuntur than Kullu, you have to approach the temple via the Akhara Bazaar–Tapu suspension bridge and a well-worn track south along the left bank of the Beas. Bijli Mahadev is renowned for its extraordinary **lingam**. Bolts of lightning, conducted into the inner sanctum by means of the 20m, trident-tipped pole, are said to periodically shatter the icon, which later, with the help of invocations from the resident pujari, magically reconstitutes itself. From the temple, which has a basic resthouse, there are superb panoramic views of the Parvati and Kullu valleys and Himachal's highest peaks.

DUSSEHRA IN THE VALLEY OF THE GODS

In the Kullu region, often dubbed the **"Valley of the Gods"**, the village deity reigns supreme. No one knows how many *devtas* and *devis* inhabit the hills south of the Rohtang Pass, but nearly every hamlet has one. The part each one plays in village life depends on his or her particular **powers**; some heal, others protect the "parish" borders from evil spirits, summon the rains, or ensure the success of the harvest. Nearly all, however, communicate with their devotees by means of **oracles**. When called upon to perform, the village shaman, or **gaur** – drawn from the lower castes – strips to the waist and enters a trance in which the *devta* uses his voice to speak to the congregation. The deity, carried out of the temple on a ceremonial palanquin, or *rath*, rocks back and forth on the shoulders of its bearers as the *gaur* speaks. His words are always heeded, and his decisions final; the *devta*-oracle decides the propitious dates for marriages, and for sowing crops, and arbitrates disputes.

DUSSEHRA

The single most important outing for any village deity is **Dussehra**, which takes place in the town of **Kullu** every October after the monsoons. Although the week-long festival ostensibly celebrates Rama's victory over the demon-king of Lanka, Ravana, it is also an opportunity for the *devtas* to reaffirm their position in the grand pecking order that prevails among them – a rigid hierarchy in which the Kullu raja's own tutelary deity Rama, alias **Raghunathji**, is king.

On the tenth day of the new, or "white" moon in October, between 150 and 200 *devtas* make their way to Kullu to pay homage to Raghunathji. As befits a region that holds its elderly women in high esteem, the procession proper cannot begin until **Hadimba**, the grandmother of the royal family's chief god, arrives from the Dunghri temple in Manali. Like her underlings, she is borne on an elaborately carved wooden *rath* swathed in glittering silk and garlands, and surmounted by a richly embroidered parasol, or *chhatri*. Raghunathji leads the great **procession** in his six-wheeled *rath*. Hauled from the Rupi palace by two hundred honoured devotees, the palanquin lurches to a halt in the middle of Kullu's maidan, to be circumambulated by the raja, his family, and retinue of priests. Thereafter, the festival's more secular aspect comes to the fore. **Folk dancers** perform for the vast crowds, and the maidan is taken over by market stalls, snake charmers, astrologers, sadhus and tawdry circus acts. The revelries finally draw to a close six days later on the full moon, when the customary **blood sacrifices** of a young buffalo, a goat, a cock, a fish and a crab are made to the god.

Kullu's Dussehra, now a major tourist attraction, has become increasingly staged and commercialized. Book accommodation well in advance, and be prepared for a crush if you want to get anywhere near the *devtas*.

ARRIVAL AND DEPARTURE

KULLU

By plane The single daily flight to Kullu from Delhi arrives in Bhuntur, 30min south of Kullu by bus.

By bus All long-distance buses pull in at the main bus stand in Sarvari Bazaar, on the north side of the Sarvari River. Local services heading north also drop and pick up passengers at the top of Dhalpur maidan. There are direct services to Manali (1hr 30min) every 15min and hourly via Naggar (2hr), a far more scenic route. Frequent southbound buses via Bhuntur pass right outside the airport.

By taxi Taxis to the airport are exorbitant (₹350) and should be booked in the union office (☎01902 222322) on the main road close to the tourist office.

INFORMATION

Permits The District Commissioner's office near Dhalpur maidan (Mon–Sat 10am–5pm, closed 2nd Sat of month; ☎01902 222727) is the place to apply for Inner Line permits (see box, p.402).

Tourist office HPTDC's tourist office (daily 10am–6pm, until 8pm April–June; ☎01902 222349), on the west side of Dhalpur *maidan*, can book tickets on HPTDC's deluxe buses to Delhi, Shimla and Chandigarh.

ACCOMMODATION AND EATING

Kullu has a reasonable choice of **accommodation**, although prices can double during high season and even quadruple for Dussehra. There are few **restaurants** outside the hotels but a predictable host of *dhabas* and chai stalls.

Aaditya Lower Dhalpur, 200m from the bus stand ☎01902 224263, ⊕hotelaaditya.com. Centrally located hotel, with decent attached rooms; the basic rooftop double is cheapest and has good views. ₹500

6

★ **Annapurna** Akhara Bazaar ☎ 01902 224162. Very simple restaurant serving superb vegetarian dishes, all under ₹100, from both ends of the country, including fine masala dosas. There's a baked goods and sweet counter outside. Daily 7.30am–10pm.

Kullu Valley Akhara Bazaar ☎ 01902 222223. Smart, brightly lit modern hotel, whose rooms are nicely furnished and spacious; most boast bathtubs. The cheaper ones without tubs are great value. ₹600

The Nest Next to the bus stand ☎ 01902 222685, ✉ hotelnest@rediffmail.com. The best hotel by the bus stand but suffers from noise. Clean, good-value attached doubles; two of the pricier second-floor rooms have tubs. ₹250

Planet Food North side of Dhalpur maidan ☎ 98179 72919. Fairly functional first-floor restaurant, which serves a mixture of snacks and Indian/Chinese main courses for ₹100–200. Fine if you can bear the cheesy Western music. Daily 10am–10pm.

The Sarvari South of the maidan and up a small lane ☎ 01902 222471. HPTDC chain hotel in a quiet location with a range of rooms in two blocks. Good valley views, Ayurvedic massage, a restaurant and bar. ₹1500

Shobla International Dhalpur ☎ 01902 222800, 🌐 shoblainternational.com. Kullu's top hotel, which has recently had a major revamp. Large, lavishly decorated and furnished rooms, a good mixed-cuisine restaurant and a relaxing lawn. ₹1650

The Parvati Valley

Hemmed in by giant-pinnacled mountain peaks, the **Parvati Valley**, which twists west from the glaciers and snowfields on the Spiti border to meet the Beas at Bhuntur, is the Kullu Valley's longest tributary. It's a picturesque place, with quiet hamlets perching precariously on its sides amid lush terraces and old pine forests. Though the landscape around **Jari** has been scarred by the ugly **Malana hydro project**, there is strong local pressure to at least camouflage the site. Visitors to the valley are an incongruous mix – a combination of Western hippies (especially Israelis) and van-loads of Sikh pilgrims bound for the *gurudwara* at **Manikaran**, 32km northeast of the Beas-Parvati confluence. Crouched at the foot of a gloomy ravine, this ancient religious site, sacred to Hindus as well as Sikhs, is famous for the **hot springs** that bubble out of its stony river banks.

To make the most of Parvati's stunning scenery you'll have to **hike**. Two popular trails thread their way up the valley: one heads north from the fascinating hill village of **Malana** (see box, pp.444–445), over the Chandrakhani Pass to Naggar; the other follows the River Parvati east to another sacred hot spring and sadhu hang-out, **Khirganga**. The trail continues from Khirganga to **Mantalai** with its Shiva shrine and over the awesome 5400m Pin-Parvati pass into **Spiti**. This serious snowfield is riddled with crevasses and takes several hours to cross. A guide is absolutely essential (see box opposite).

GETTING AROUND   THE PARVATI VALLEY

By bus Buses, some of them from Kullu, leave Bhuntur at least hourly for Manikaran (1hr 30min), passing through Jari and Kasol en route. The last bus back to Kullu, via Bhuntur, leaves around 6pm.

Jari and around

Spilling down the south side of the Parvati Valley, **JARI**, 15km from Bhuntur, looks across to the precipitous Malana *nala* in the north, and to the snow-flecked needles of the Baranagh Range on the eastern horizon. Like many of its lookalike cousins, the tatty settlement supports a small transient population of stoned Westerners, attracted by the top-quality *charas*. Those wanting a shortcut to **Malana** (see box, pp.444–445) can hire a vehicle up to the Malana hydro project roadhead, from where the village is a mere 4km trek.

Jari's unspoilt and far more attractive satellite village of **Mateura**, just ten minutes' walk up the hill from the main road, has spectacular views over the Parvati Range and is home to the small but important **Kali Anagha temple**.

ACCOMMODATION AND EATING   JARI AND AROUND

Om Shiva On the left-hand side as you enter Jari ☎ 01902 276202. The rooms are rather basic in this simple but welcoming guesthouse, but all have attached bathrooms. ₹300

Rooftop Restaurant & Guest House Upper side of Matheura ☎ 01902 275434. The rooms here are fairly

PARVATI DISAPPEARANCES

For more than a decade the Parvati Valley has seen the mysterious **disappearance** of at least twenty travellers. Most were travelling alone, although one incident in August 2000 involved three campers who were brutally attacked in their tent, thrown into the gorge and left for dead – one survived. Most of the vanished have never been found, including the Israeli who went missing in the most recently publicized case in July 2009. Several theories have been put forward to explain these disappearances, from drug-related accidents on the treacherous mountain trails, to attacks by bears or wolves or foul play by the numerous cannabis cultivators in the region; some even claim that the disappeared may have joined secret cults deep in the mountains. Most likely, however, they were victims of bandit attacks, motivated solely by money, with the wild waters of the River Parvati conveniently placed for disposing of bodies. Individual travellers should **take heed** and only use recognized guides on treks across the mountains. Don't attempt solo treks – even along the relatively simple trail over the Chandrakhani Pass between Naggar and Malana and the straightforward trek to the hot springs at Khirganga. There are many trekking agencies in Kullu and Manali who can put you in touch with a reputable guide.

small and basic but the real draw is the roof terrace overlooking the village, which serves the best food in the area. ₹**400**

Village Guest House Centre of Matheura village ☎01902 276070. A traditional wooden-balconied house, whose immaculate rooms have spotless bathrooms and satellite TV. Set in a wonderful garden, it's deservedly popular year-round. ₹**500**

Kasol

Beyond Jari, the road winds down towards the rushing grey-green Parvati, which it meets at **KASOL**, a pleasant village straddling a mountain stream and surrounded by forest. Kasol has grown in popularity, and now has a large resident population of *charas*-smoking travellers, most of whom are Israelis – earning it the nickname of "little Israel" from the locals. A trickle of trekkers also plod through on their way to or from the pass of Rashol Jot (2440m), a hard day's climb up the north side of the valley which provides an alternative approach to Malana and the Chandrakhani route to the Kullu Valley.

ACCOMMODATION AND EATING   KASOL

Accommodation ranges from basic rooms in village houses and simple lodges to more organized hotels, while Kasol's travellers' **cafés** are cheap and plentiful.

Alpine Guest House Off main road, by river bank ☎01902 273710, ⊛alpineguesthouse.net. Attractive two-storey building with spacious attached rooms, set in wooded grounds by the river. Warm and welcoming atmosphere too. ₹**600**

Deep Forest Up the hill just before the bridge ☎01902 273048. The nondescript and functional attached rooms here are nothing like as spectacular as the views which the hotel's slight elevation give it. ₹**500**

Moondance Restaurant and Bakery Just beyond the bridge ☎98161 53681. Choose between interior seating and a nicely terraced courtyard overlooking the river. All the travellers' favourites such as pancakes and shakes are available for ₹80–250, plus there are board games to play. Daily 8am–10.30pm.

Sandhya Palace Kasol 400m along the road to Manikaran ☎01902 273745, ⊛sandhyapalace.com. Pleasantly situated away from the centre, this upmarket hotel has comfortable deluxe rooms and wildly fluctuating rates that mean good deals off-season. ₹**2750**

Sasi Palace Just before the bridge ☎97363 68505. Blessed with a riverside location and gaily painted stone walls, and serving food from breakfast and snacks to filling Indian, Chinese and Western meals for ₹100–200. Daily 8am–11pm.

Taj Palace On the Jari side of the village ☎01902 273864. First-floor restaurant with pink walls and comfy seating, where you can enjoy a variety of Indian, Italian and other cuisines for less than ₹200. Daily 7am–midnight.

Manikaran

Just 4.5km along the pleasantly wooded main road beyond Kasol, clouds of steam billowing from the rocky riverbank herald the Parvati Valley's chief attraction. Hindu

6

mythology identifies **MANIKARAN** as the place where the serpent king Shesha stole Parvati's earrings, or *manikara*, while she and her husband Shiva were bathing in the river. When interrogated, the snake flew into a rage and snorted the earrings out of his nose. Ever since, boiling water has poured out of the ground. The site is also venerated by Sikhs, who have erected a massive concrete *gurudwara* over the springs.

Boxed in at the bottom of a vast, sheer-sided chasm, Manikaran is a damp, dark and claustrophobic place where you're unlikely to want to spend more than a night. Most of the action revolves around the springs themselves, reached via the lane that leads through the village from the footbridge. On the way, check out the finely carved pale-grey stone **Rama temple** just beyond the main square, and the pans of rice and dhal cooking in the steaming pools on the pavements. Down at the riverside **Shiva shrine**, semi-naked **sadhus** sit in the scalding waters smoking chillums. Sikh pilgrims, meanwhile, make their way to the atmospheric **gurudwara** nearby, where they take a purifying dip in the underground pool, sweat in the hot cave and then congregate upstairs to listen to musical recitations from the Sikhs' holy book, the Guru Granth Sahib. If you visit, keep your arms, legs and head covered; tobacco is prohibited inside the complex.

ACCOMMODATION AND EATING   MANIKARAN

Except during May and June, when Manikaran fills up with Punjabi visitors, **accommodation** is plentiful and inexpensive. Most hotels have a steaming indoor hot tub, which tends to leave them feeling rather damp. **Food**, which is strictly veg, is mostly found in local *dhabas*.

Fateh Guest House In an alley near the Rama temple ☎ 01902 209307. All the small and simple rooms have hot showers and TVs at this welcoming family guesthouse, the best value in town. ₹**200**

Holy Palace Between the Rama Temple and the gurudwara ☎ 98826 11193. This spacious, glorified *dhaba* has no clearly visible sign but offers a wide range of tasty Indian and Chinese dishes for less than ₹100, plus slightly pricier pizzas. Daily 8am–10pm.

Sharma Guest House At the gurudwara end of the bazaar ☎ 01902 273742. Simple lodge with basic rooms, the best of those near the *gurudwara*, but only has shared bathrooms. ₹**200**

Shivalik On the main road before the turn-off to the bus stand ☎ 01902 273817, ⊚ royalpalacehotels .com. Part of a small local chain, this solid brick hotel has large rooms with TVs and balconies with river views. ₹**500**

Naggar

Stacked up the lush, terraced lower slopes of the valley as they sweep towards the tree line from the left bank of the Beas, **NAGGAR** is the most scenic and accessible of the hill villages between Kullu and Manali, roughly 20km from each. Clustered around an old **castle**, this was the regional capital before the local rajas decamped to Kullu in the mid-1800s. A century or so later, European settlers began to move in. Seduced by the village's ancient **temples**, peaceful setting and unhurried pace, visitors often find themselves lingering in Naggar – a far less hippified village than those further north – longer than they intended. Numerous tracks wind up the mountain to more remote settlements, providing a choice of enjoyable **hikes**.

Naggar is a very pleasant place, often sadly overlooked by travellers making a beeline for Manali. The relaxed atmosphere, refreshing elevation, stunning views and a variety of interesting sites combine to make it an excellent spot to while away a few days.

The castle

Since it was erected by Raja Sidh Singh (c.1700), Naggar's central **castle**, astride a sheer-sided bluff, has served as palace, colonial mansion, courthouse and school. It is now a hotel, but nonresidents can wander in for ₹20 to admire the views from its balconies. Built in the traditional "earthquake-proof" *pahari* style (layers of stone bonded together with cedar logs), the castle has a central courtyard, a small shrine and a shop selling local handicrafts downstairs. The **Jagti Patt temple**'s amorphous deity, a triangular slab of rock strewn with rose petals and rupee notes, is said to have been borne here from its home on the summit of Deo Tibba by a swarm of wild honeybees – the valley's *devtas* in disguise.

The Nicholas Roerich Gallery

Tues–Sun: May–Aug 10am–1pm & 1.30–6pm; Sept–March 10am–1pm & 1.30–5pm • ₹50, camera ₹25, video ₹60; ticket includes admission to Urusvati-Himalayan Folk Art Museum • **Ⓦ** roerichtrust.org

Perched on the upper outskirts of the village, the **Nicholas Roerich Gallery** houses an exhibition of paintings and photographs dedicated to the memory of its former occupier, the Russian artist, writer, philosopher, archeologist, explorer and mystic. Around the turn of the beginning of the twentieth century, Roerich's atmospheric landscape paintings and esoteric philosophies – an arcane blend of Eastern mysticism and *fin de siècle* humanist-idealism – inspired a cult-like following in France and the United States. Financed by donations from devotees, Roerich was able to indulge his obsession with Himalayan travel, eventually retiring in Naggar in 1929 and dying here eighteen years later.

Urusvati-Himalayan Folk Art Museum

Tues–Sun: May–Aug 10am–1pm & 1.30–6pm; Sept–March 10am–1pm & 1.30–5pm • Admission included with Nicolas Roerich Gallery

A path winds further up from the Nicholas Roerich gallery above the road through the forest for around 100m to **Urusvati-Himalayan Folk Art Museum**. Founded by Roerich's wife in 1928, the museum has a collection of local folk art, costumes, more of Roerich's paintings, several paintings by his Russian followers, and a gallery of Russian folk art.

The temples

The largest and most distinctive of Naggar's ancient Hindu **temples** and shrines, the wooden pagoda-style **Tripuri Sundri** stands in a small enclosure at the top of the village, just below the road to the Roerich Gallery. Like the Dunghri temple in Manali, it is crowned with a three-tiered roof, whose top storey is circular. Its *devta* is the focus of an annual *mela* (mid-May) in which deities from villages are brought in procession to pay their respects.

Ten minutes' walk further up the hill – follow the stone steps that lead right from the road – brings you to a clearing where the old stone **Murlidhar** (Krishna) **Mandir** looks down on Naggar, with superb views up the valley to the snow peaks around Solan and the Rohtang Pass. Built on the ruins of the ancient town of Thawa, the shrine, set in a large courtyard, is strictly off-limits to non-Hindus.

Finally, on your way to or from the bus stand at the bottom of the village, look out for the finely carved stone *shikharas* of the **Gaurishankar Mandir**. Set in its own paved courtyard below the castle, this Shiva temple, among the oldest of its kind in the valley, houses a living lingam, so slip off your shoes before approaching it.

ARRIVAL AND INFORMATION   NAGGAR

Naggar village proper, its sights and accommodation lie some way above the small bazaar on the main road where the buses pull in. If you have your own vehicle, you can drive all the way up to the Roerich Gallery at the top of the village.

By bus Naggar is equidistant (21km) from Kullu and Manali and connected to both by hourly buses along the scenic east bank of the Beas. More frequent and faster services in either direction along the west bank can be joined at Patlikuhl, from where taxis and auto-rickshaws climb the 6km up to Naggar.

On foot You can walk from Patlikuhl on the old mule track – a hike of at least 1hr.

Trekking information If you are thinking of trekking around Naggar, you are advised to use guides, especially if crossing the Chandrakhani Pass to Malana (see pp.444–445). Himalayan Mountain Treks at *Poonam Mountain Lodge* (see p.441) have equipment, will arrange porters and guides, and can fix up jeep trips to Lahaul and Spiti. Local guides are also easy to find, though make sure they are reputable.

ACCOMMODATION

Alliance Guest House Halfway between the village and the Roerich Gallery **☎** 01902 248263, **✉** voyagealliance@yahoo.co.in. Popular guesthouse with simple, clean rooms, a self-catering flat (₹1500), a

6

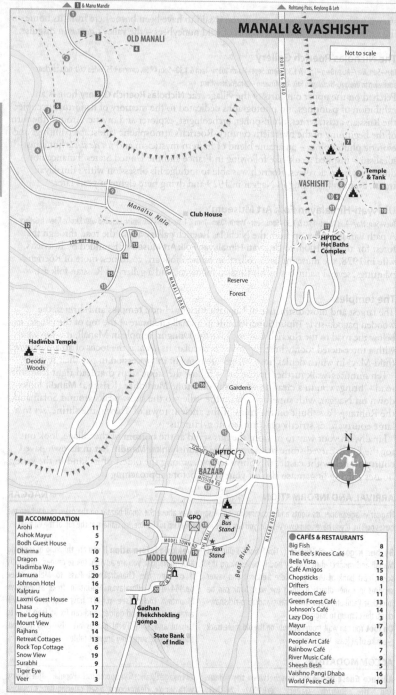

MANALI & VASHISHT

Not to scale

Old Manali

Vashisht

Temple & Tank

HPTDC Hot Baths Complex

Manalsu Nala

Club House

Reserve Forest

Hadimba Temple

Deodar Woods

Gardens

HPTDC ℹ

BAZAAR

GPO ✉

★ **Bus Stand**

MODEL TOWN

Taxi Stand

Beas River

Gadhan Thekchhokling gompa

State Bank of India

■ ACCOMMODATION	
Arohi	11
Ashok Mayur	5
Bodh Guest House	7
Dharma	10
Dragon	2
Hadimba Way	15
Jamuna	20
Johnson Hotel	16
Kalptaru	8
Laxmi Guest House	4
Lhasa	17
The Log Huts	12
Mount View	18
Rajhans	14
Retreat Cottages	13
Rock Top Cottage	6
Snow View	19
Surabhi	9
Tiger Eye	1
Veer	3

● CAFÉS & RESTAURANTS	
Big Fish	8
The Bee's Knees Café	2
Bella Vista	12
Café Amigos	15
Chopsticks	18
Drifters	1
Freedom Café	11
Green Forest Café	13
Johnson's Café	14
Lazy Dog	3
Mayur	17
Moondance	6
People Art Café	4
Rainbow Café	7
River Music Café	5
Sheesh Besh	
Vaishno Pangi Dhaba	16
World Peace Café	10

small lending library and a warm family atmosphere. ₹550
The Castle Upper end of village ☎01902 248316,
✉kullu@hptdc.in. Atmospheric castle, now one of
HPTDC's signature hotels, with well-furnished attached
doubles, some offering superb views from spacious
wooden balconies. The restaurant is also good. ₹1900
Negi's Family House Lower end of village ☎97360
42578. The four basic but clean rooms with shared
bathrooms in this welcoming family house are the cheapest
in the area. ₹200
★ **Poonam Mountain Lodge** Below the castle

☎94181 49827, ⚐poonammountain.in. Cosy doubles,
three with fireplaces for winter stays, wi-fi access, a lovely
outside seating area and good veg restaurant serving local
specialities, such as red rice, on request. Extremely
welcoming and knowledgeable owner, too. ₹500
Sheetal Hotel 50m from the castle ☎01902 248250,
⚐hotelsheetalnaggar.com. The wood-panelled rooms in
this ochre-coloured hotel are comfortable, with TV and
balconies. There's also a decent rooftop restaurant and
some nearby cottages are available. ₹770

6

EATING AND DRINKING

Ragini Hotel Rooftop Next to the Sheetal Hotel
☎01902 248185. The upstairs restaurant serves good food,
including grilled trout for around ₹300 and some Mexican
dishes. There is a pleasant café downstairs. Daily 7am–11pm.
★ **Under The Parachute** 150m from the castle
☎98173 15099. Friendly restaurant serving excellent
Italian cuisine and rainbow trout specials from ₹250 in a

downstairs room and more pleasant roof terrace, which is
indeed canopied by a real parachute. Daily 8am–10pm.
Zenith Café Just before the Roerich Gallery ☎97367
80119. Aptly named given its splendid views, this rooftop
joint does trout for a reasonable ₹260 and various Indian,
Chinese and Tibetan dishes for around half that. Daily
8am–10pm.

Manali

Himachal's main tourist resort, **MANALI**, stands at the head of the Kullu Valley, 108km
north of Mandi. Despite lying at the heart of the region's highest mountain range, it
remains easily accessible by road from the plains; after one hour on a plane and a short
hop by road, or sixteen hours on a bus from Delhi, you could be staring from your
hotel veranda across apple orchards and thick pine forests to the snowfields of Solang
Nala, which shine a tantalizing stone's throw away to the north. Manali has become
increasingly popular with domestic tourists (more than five million annually), and now
greets an eclectic mix of honeymooners, holiday-makers, hippies, trekkers and traders.

The Manali that lured travellers in the 1970s has certainly changed, although the
majestic mountain scenery, thermal springs and quality *charas* can still be enjoyed. **Old
Manali** retains some of its atmosphere, and the village of **Vashisht** across the valley, with
its increasing number of guesthouses and cafés, has become a popular place to chill out.
For those preferring to venture into the mountains, Manali makes an ideal **trekking**
base for short hikes and serious expeditions, and countless agencies can help put a
package together for you. The relaxing hotels in Manali's cleaner, greener outskirts, and
dozens of sociable cafés and restaurants ranged around a well-stocked **bazaar**, provide a
welcome relief from the rigours of the mountain trails. As well as treks around Manali
you can also explore the Kullu Valley (see box, pp.444–445).

The Mall

Manali's main street, **The Mall**, quite unlike its namesake in Shimla, is a noisy scene of
constant activity, fronted by the bus stand, several shopping markets, travel agents, and a
line of hotels and restaurants. It's a great place to watch the world go by – locals in
traditional caps, Tibetan women in immaculate rainbow-striped pinafores, Nepali porters,
Buddhist monks, the odd party of Zanskaris swathed in fusty woollen *gonchas*, souvenir-
hunting Indian tourists and a curious mix of Westerners. The grid of streets behind The
Mall is curiously known as **Model Town**, though it is scarcely a paradigm of town planning.

The bazaar

Manali's days as an authentic *pahari* bazaar ended when the mule trains were
superseded by Tata trucks, but it's still great for souvenir **shopping**. Woollen goods

6

ADVENTURE SPORTS AND TOURS AROUND MANALI

Considering the fierce whitewater that thrashes down the Kullu Valley during the spring melt, Manali's **rafting** scene is surprisingly low-key. Raft trips down the River Beas are offered between the end of May and early July, when water levels are highest, beginning at Piridi (above Bhuntur) around 15km downstream at Jhiri. The price (around ₹1500) should include meals, lifejackets, helmets and return travel; check exactly what you're paying for, as some unscrupulous operators expect you to make your own way back after the trip.

Skiing in the Solang Valley is popular from January to April – but the slope isn't much bigger than a cricket pitch and there is no proper ski centre. A new ski centre in conjunction with the Finnish government is still in the pipeline for the Rohtang Pass. The valley is also a popular spot for **paragliding**, **kitesurfing** (both ₹1500–2500) and **helicopter rides** (from ₹2500 per person). Rock climbing, canyoning and zorbing are gaining in popularity.

One of the best ways to explore Kullu is by **mountain biking**, which is possible from mid-June to mid-October; bike hire costs around ₹500/day for a European bike, plus ₹800 with a guide. Popular routes include the descent from Rohtang, the forest trail to the Bijli Mahadev Temple and the back road to Naggar.

Numerous agents offer jeep safaris and other guided tours to remote areas such as Lahaul, Spiti and Ladakh – prices vary wildly, as does what is included, so always shop around. Most of these operations also run treks on the most popular local routes (see box, pp.444–445) and further afield.

ADVENTURE SPORTS AND TOUR AGENCIES

Himalayan Adventurers Opposite the tourist office, Manali ☎01902 253050, ⓦhimalayan adventurersindia.com. Rup Negi and his experienced team offer the full range of activities from trekking, mountain biking and skiing to jeep and motorbike tours. There's even birdwatching.

Himalayan Extreme Centre Branches in Old Manali and Vaishisht ☎9816174164, ⓦhimalayan-extreme-center.com. The best all-round place for adrenalin-charged activities such as rafting, paragliding, rock climbing, canyoning and zorbing.

Himalayan Snowcats Old Manali ☎01902 252365, ⓦhelimanali.com. The principal agent for thrilling helicopter rides above the mountains.

Magic Mountain Jagatsukh, 6km south of Manali ☎98160 56934, ⓦmagicmountainadventures .com. Owner Raju Sharma specializes in mountain biking and leads tours himself. He can also arrange trekking, skiing and jeep safaris.

Tiger Eye Adventure Old Manali ☎01902 251092. Very efficient Dutch-run agency, which runs reliable trekking, bicycle, motorbike and jeep tours.

---

are the town's real forte, particularly the brilliantly patterned **shawls** for which the Kullu Valley is famous. Genuine pure-wool handloom shawls with embroidered borders start at around ₹600, but those made from finest pashmina cost several thousand rupees. Shop around and check out the fixed-price factory shops to get an idea of what's available: the government-sponsored Bhutico on The Mall opposite the tourist office, the Bodh Shawl factory shop just off The Mall south of the bus stand and The Great Hadimba Shop & Factory next to the Manu Temple in Old Manali are recommended; the NSC (New Shopping Centre) market near the bus stand also has a good selection.

Elsewhere around the bazaar, innumerable stalls are stacked with handwoven goods and pillbox Kullu **topis**. Those with gaudy multicoloured up-turned flaps and gold piping are indigenous to the valley, but you can also pick up the plain-green velvet-fronted variety favoured by Kinnauris. Manali's other specialities are **Tibetan curios** such as prayer wheels, amulets, *dorjees* (thunderbolts) and masks, musical instruments and *thangkas*. Few of the items hawked as antiques are genuine but it takes an expert eye to spot a fake. The same applies to silver **jewellery** inlaid with turquoise and coral, which can nonetheless be attractive and relatively inexpensive.

The Hadimba Temple

Resting on a wide stone platform fifteen minutes' walk northwest of the bazaar, the **Hadimba Temple** is Manali's oldest shrine and the seat of Hadimba (or "Hirma

Devi"), wife of Bhima. Considered to be an incarnation of Kali, Hadimba is worshipped in times of adversity, and also plays a key role in the Dussehra festival (see box, p.435). Hadimba is supposed to have given the kingdom of Kullu to the forefathers of the rajas of Kullu, and in veneration and affection the family to this day refer to her as "grandmother". The massive triple-tiered wooden pagoda, crowned by crimson pennants and a brass ball and trident (Shiva's *trishul*), dates from 1553, and is a replica of earlier ones that burned down in successive forest fires. The facade writhes with wonderful woodcarvings of elephants, crocodiles and folk deities. Entered by a door surmounted by wild ibex horns, the gloomy **shrine** is dominated by several large boulders, one of which shelters the stone on which goats and buffalo are sacrificed during important rituals. The hollow in its middle, believed to be Vishnu's footprint, channels the blood to Hadimba's mouth.

Soft-drinks stands, curio stalls and yak rides cater for visitors while the nearby **Kullu Cultural Museum** (₹10) displays detailed models of the valley's temples.

Old Manali

Old Manali, the village from which the modern town takes its name, lies 2km north of The Mall, on the far side of the Manalsu Nala. Built in the old *pahari* style, most of the houses of Old Manali have heavy stone roofs and wooden balconies hung with bushels of drying herbs and tobacco. Unlike its crowded, concrete offspring, the settlement retains an unhurried and traditional feel for most of the year, despite prolific tourist development. In summer, travellers on throaty Enfields roar through its lanes, guesthouses blare trance music and the cafés are thick with chillum smoke. In the wake of the tourists come the Kashmiris, Rajasthani tailors and other opportunists, eager to make good business before returning to Goa in the autumn.

To get here, head north up Old Manali Road, bear right at the fork in the road, and keep going until you reach the iron bridge across the river. A bit of leg work will bring you to the village proper, clustered on top of a steeply shelving ledge of level ground above the *nala*. It is also known as **Manaligarh** after its ancient citadel – now a ruined fort surrounded by a patchwork of maize terraces and deep-green orchards. At the centre of the village is an unusual, brash new temple dedicated to **Manu**, who laid the foundations of Hindu law that continues to today, as well as *varna* or "colour" – the basis of the caste system. Inscribed stones dating from the Middle Ages embedded into the concrete paving reveal the site's antiquity. Although Manali itself is considered safe, women should be wary of walking along the lane from town to Old Manali after dark; it has been the scene of several attempted **rapes** since the 1990s.

The gompas

Manali harbours the highest concentration of **Tibetan refugees** in the Kullu Valley, hence the prayer flags fluttering over the approach roads into town, and the presence, on its southern edge, of two **gompas**.

Capped with polished golden finials, the distinctive yellow corrugated-iron pagoda roof of the **Gadhan Thekchhokling Gompa** is an exotic splash of colour amid the ramshackle huts of the Tibetan quarter. Built in 1969, the monastery is maintained by donations from the local community and through the sale of **carpets** handwoven in the temple workshop. When they are not looking after the **shop**, the young lamas huddle in the courtyard to play *cholo* – a Tibetan dice game involving much shouting and slamming of wooden *tsampa* bowls on leather pads. Beside the main entrance, a roll of honour recounts the names of Tibetans killed during the violent political demonstrations that wracked China in the late 1980s.

The smaller and more modern of the two **gompas** stands nearer the bazaar, in a garden that in late summer blazes with sunflowers. Its main shrine, lit by dozens of bare electric bulbs and filled with fragrant Tibetan incense, houses a colossal gold-faced Buddha, best viewed from the small room on the first floor.

ARRIVAL AND DEPARTURE

By bus Most private buses pull into the bus stand 300m south of the State Bank of India at the bottom of town, while government buses use the main bus stand in the middle of The Mall. There is the usual mixture of ordinary and deluxe services to destinations such as Delhi (8–10 daily; 16–17hr), Dharamsala (3 daily; 10–11hr), Kaza (1 daily; 12–13hr), Keylong (6–8 daily; 5–6hr), Kullu (every 15min; 1hr 30min–2hr), Mandi (hourly; 4–5hr), Naggar (hourly; 1hr) and Shimla (6 daily; 9–10hr).

By motorbike Reliable well-serviced Enfields can be

rented for ₹800–1200/day from Hardev Motors on the road to Vashisht (☎ 98160 82825, ⦿ hardevmotors.com).

By taxi Manali's Taxi Operators' Union kiosk (☎ 01902 252450) lies just up from the tourist office; the taxis have fixed rates, which are sometimes negotiable off-season. You can book single seats in jeeps and Maruti Gypsy taxis to Leh (17–19hr; ₹800–2000) and Kaza (10–11hr; ₹700); numerous travel agents book the former, while the *Kiran Guest House* (near State Bank of India; ☎ 01902 253066) is the best sales and departure point for Kaza.

INFORMATION

Tourist information The functional but not over-helpful tourist office (Mon–Sat 10am–5pm, sometimes longer

hours April–June; ☎ 01902 252175) is at the north end of The Mall. You can make reservations for all state-run hotels

TREKS AROUND MANALI AND THE KULLU VALLEY

The Kullu Valley's spectacular alpine scenery makes it perfect for **trekking**. Trails are long and steep, but more than repay the effort with superb views, varied flora and the chance to visit remote hill stations. Within striking distance of several major trailheads, **Manali** is the most popular place to begin and end treks. While **package deals** (around ₹2000/person for three days with a group of four) offered by the town's many agencies can save time and energy, it is relatively easy to organize your own trip with maps and advice from the tourist office and the Mountaineering Institute at the bottom end of town. Porters and horsemen can be sought out in the square behind the main street. Always take a reliable **guide**, especially on less-frequented routes, as you cannot rely solely on **maps**. Some trekkers have reported difficulties when descending from the Bara Bangal Pass, as maps don't do the terrain justice.

The optimum trekking **season** is right after the monsoons (mid-Sept to late Oct), when skies are clear and pass-crossings easier. From June to August, you run the risk of sudden, potentially fatal snow, or view-obscuring cloud and rain. There are several good trekking agencies in Manali (see box, p.442).

MANALI TO BEAS KUND

The relatively easy trek to Beas Kund, a glacial lake at the head of Solang *nala*, is the region's most popular short hike. Encircled by 5000m-plus peaks, the well-used campground beside the lake, accessible in two days from Manali, makes a good base for side-trips up to the surrounding ridges and passes.

From **Palchan**, a village thirty minutes north of Manali by bus, follow the jeep track up the valley to **Solang**, site of a small ski station, resthouse and the Mountaineering Institute's log huts. The next two hours take you through pine forests and grassy meadows to the campground at **Dhundi** (2743m). A more strenuous walk of 5–6 hours the next day leads to **Beas Kund**. The hike up to the **Tentu La** Pass (4996m) and back from here can be done in a day, as can the descent to Manali via Solang.

MANALI TO LAHAUL, VIA THE HAMPTA PASS

The three-day trek from the Kullu Valley over the Hampta Pass to Lahaul, the old caravan route to Spiti, is a classic. Rising to 4330m, it is high by Kullu standards; do not undertake it without allowing good time to acclimatize. **Day one**, from the trailhead at **Jagatsukh** or Hampta (both villages near Manali) to the campground above **Sethen**, is an easy hike (4–5hr) up the verdant, forested sides of the valley. **Day two** (5hr) brings you to **Chikha**, a high Gaddi pasture below the pass; stay put for a day or so if you're feeling the effects of altitude. The ascent (700m) on **day three** to the **Hampta Pass** (4330m) is gruelling, but the views from the top – of Indrasan and Deo Tibba to the south, and the moonscape of Lahaul to the north – are sublime recompense. It takes six to seven hours of relentless rock-hopping and stream-crossing to reach **Chhatru**, on the floor of the Chandra Valley. From here, you can turn east

at the HPTDC office (☎ 01902 253531), two doors down.

Permits if you want to get an Inner Line Permit (see box, p.402) in Manali, you must do so through a registered travel agent (see box, p.442).

Railway booking There's an official Indian Railways reservation booth (Mon–Sat 8am–5pm, Sun 9am–2pm) next to the tourist office.

ACCOMMODATION

There are three main **accommodation** areas in Manali. Most longer-stay budget places are clustered in **Old Manali**, while many of Manali's classic hotels with gardens and character are dotted around the **northern and western outskirts**. In **central Manali**, numerous mid-range business and honeymoon hotels cluster on and behind The Mall. Tariffs rocket to at least double in most Manali hotels during **high season** (April–June), when you might want to check out availability at the Manali Hoteliers Association on The Mall (☎ 01902 253059, ⓦ manalistay.com). At most other times, competition keeps rates well down.

6

OLD MANALI

Ashok Mayur Main road through village ☎ 01902 252868, ✉ manurishi72@yahoo.com. Small, basic (verging on dingy) but friendly guesthouse where all rooms

towards Koksar and the **Rohtang Pass**, or west past the world's largest glacier, **Bara Shigri**, to **Batal**, the trailhead for the Chandratal–Baralacha trek (see box, p.452).

NAGGAR TO MALANA VIA THE CHANDRAKHANI PASS AND ONWARDS

The trek to Jari in the Parvati Valley from Naggar, 21km south of Manali, is quintessential Kullu Valley trekking, with superb scenery and fascinating villages. The roundtrip can be completed in three days, but you may be tempted to linger in **Malana** and explore the surrounding countryside. A **guide** is essential for several reasons: the first stage of the trek involves crossing a maze of grazing trails; Malana is culturally sensitive and requires some familiarity with local customs; and a number of people have **disappeared** in the Parvati Valley in recent years under suspicious circumstances (see box, p.437). The descent to the Parvati Valley is too steep for pack ponies, but porters are available in Naggar through the guesthouses, including Himalayan Mountain Treks at *Poonam Mountain Lodge* (see p.441).

The trail leads through the village of Rumsu and then winds through wonderful old-growth forests to a pasture just above the tree line, which makes ideal camping ground. From here, a climb of 4km takes you to the **Chandrakhani Pass** (3660m), with fine views west over the top of the Kullu Valley to the peaks surrounding Solang *nala* and north to the Ghalpo mountains of Lahaul. Some prefer to reach the base of the pass on the first day and then camp below the final ascent.

The inhabitants of **MALANA**, a steep 7km descent from the pass, are known for their frostiness and staunch traditions. Plans by regional developers to extend a paved road here are vehemently opposed by the insular locals. Although notions of **caste pollution** are not as strictly adhered to as they once were, you should observe a few basic "**rules**" in Malana: approach the village quietly and respectfully; stick to paths at all times; keep away from the temple; and above all, don't touch anybody or anything, especially children or houses. If you do commit a cultural blunder, you'll be expected to make amends: usually in the form of a ₹1000 payment for a sacrificial offering of a young sheep or goat to the village deity, **Jamlu**, one of the most powerful Kullu Valley gods. His **temple**, open to high-caste Hindus only, is decorated with lively folk carvings, among them images of soldiers – the villagers claim to be the area's sole remaining descendants of Alexander the Great's army. Popular **places to stay** include the *Renuka Guesthouse*, which has hot water, and the *Himalaya Guesthouse*, run by the former village headman. The owner of *Santu Ram's* is an authority on local trails. All the guesthouses offer simple meals and rooms cost ₹300 or less. The official camping ground lies 100m beyond the village spring.

The **final stage** of the trek takes you down the sheer limestone sides of Malana *nala* to the floor of the Parvati Valley – a precipitous 12km drop that is partially covered by a switchback road. From the hamlet of **Rashol**, you have a choice of three onward routes: either head east up the right bank of the river to **Manikaran** (see p.437); follow the trail southwest to the sacred **Bijli Mahadev Mandir**; or climb the remaining 3km up to the road at **Jari**, from where regular buses leave for Bhuntur, Kullu and Manali.

6

have shared bathrooms but many have small balconies warmed by the morning sun. Cheap singles. ₹200

Dragon Down lane from main road ☎ 01902 252790, ⓦ dragontreks.com. Newer hotel with brash exterior but comfortable, spacious attached rooms with hot water and balconies. The top floor of the new block has some great wooden-floored duplexes. Also fine restaurant, internet café and travel centre. ₹500

Laxmi Guest House On lane beyond Dragon ☎ 01902 253569. Small, friendly place with rickety wooden rooms, which stay cheap even in high season. The attached ones cost little more. Largely uninterrupted valley views and a small garden are the best features. ₹150/₹200

Rock Top Cottage Up stepped path just past Lazy Dog ☎ 98162 03901, ⓔ pappybaba@yahoo.com. Decent attached and non-attached rooms, with grubby walls but clean bathrooms and fine views. You can camp in the lovely garden. ₹250/₹300

★ **Tiger Eye** Signposted down lane towards top of village ☎ 01902 252718, ⓔ tigereyeindia@yahoo.com. Peaceful, newly built family guesthouse run by friendly Indian-Dutch couple. Immaculate rooms and balconies with great views, plus a TV and internet lounge. Well worth the little extra. ₹600

Veer On lane beyond Dragon ☎ 01902 252410, ⓔ veerguesthouse@hotmail.com. The functional rooms are in two blocks separated by a leafy garden and communal eating area. Some non-attached singles and some rooms with a/c and TV. ₹400

NORTHERN AND WESTERN OUTSKIRTS

Hadimba Way Log Huts area ☎ 01902 251552, ⓦ hotelhadimbaway.in. Best value of the several places in this quiet little enclave near the Hadimba Temple. Unusually, the upstairs rooms are cheaper than those on the ground floor. ₹600

The Log Huts Overlooking Manalsu Nala ☎ 01902

253225, ⓔ manali@hptdc.in. Luxurious but overpriced timber holiday cottages tucked away in the woods, with one or two double bedrooms, kitchens and most comforts including cable TV. ₹6000

Rajhans Between Old Manali Rd and Log Huts area ☎ 01902 252209, ⓦ hotelrajhansmanali.in. Stylish new four-storey brick building with valley views from the more luxurious higher rooms; all attached with TV. ₹700

Retreat Cottages Log Hut Rd ☎ 01902 252042, ⓦ retreatcottages.com. Immaculate, huge self-catering two- and three-bedroom suites with baths in a tastefully designed building. Recommended for groups of 6–8. Meals can also be ordered. ₹7500

CENTRAL MANALI

Jamuna Gompa Rd ☎ 01902 252506. Friendly old-style hotel. The attached rooms are clean and spacious enough and about as cheap as it gets in this quiet part of Manali. ₹350

★ **Johnson Hotel** Old Manali Rd ☎ 01902 253764, ⓦ johnsonhotel.in. Three-star comfort in an old colonial building. Spacious and neat wooden-floored rooms overlook the garden; the carpeted downstairs rooms are cheaper, with wood-burning heaters for winter. ₹3200

Lhasa Just off Model Town Rd ☎ 01902 252134. One of the friendlier and better-value places in the area, enhanced by the recent lick of blue and yellow paint. All rooms have bathrooms and TV. ₹300

Mount View Far end of Model Town Rd ☎ 01902 252465. Pleasant ivy-clad building in a quieter area with decent-sized and comfortably furnished doubles and a rooftop terrace with splendid views. ₹300

Snow View Model Town Rd ☎ 01902 253084, ⓦ hotelsnowviewmanali.com. Large, functional hotel with comfortable, decent-sized rooms, mainly aimed at business travellers. Facilities include cable TV, internet and 24hr room service. ₹1000

EATING AND DRINKING

Manali's wide range of **restaurants** reflects the town's melting-pot credentials: Tibetan *thukpa* joints stand cheek-by-jowl with south Indian coffee houses, Gujarati thali bars and Nepalese-run German pastry shops. Old Manali joints offer traveller-friendly **breakfasts** of eggs, porridge, pancakes, toast and jam, as well as a variety of cuisines.

CENTRAL AND NORTHWEST MANALI

Bella Vista Log Hut Rd, just across the bridge from Old Manali ☎ 01902 251985. This snazzy place is a self-billed Spanish café, with a range of tapas and main courses for ₹200–300. Daily 8am–10.30pm.

★ **Café Amigos** North end of The Mall ☎ 98161 18765. Wooden tables, colourful pottery, chilled-out music and a fantastic range of cakes and brownies, as well as main meals for around ₹200. Daily 8am–10pm.

Chopsticks The Mall ☎ 01902 252639. Very popular Tibetan-run restaurant with a pleasant atmosphere and

varied menu. Try the filter coffee and the great muesli, fruit and curd. Daily 9am–10pm.

Green Forest Café Off Log Hut Rd ☎ 01902 251042. Small local restaurant with some outdoor patio seating, serving the best *momos* and *thukpas* in Manali for well under ₹100. Daily 9am–8.30pm.

Johnson's Café Johnson Hotel, Old Manali Rd ☎ 01902 253023. A great café, with garden seating and an inviting menu including beer, fresh trout and crème caramel. Some items cost ₹300–400 but they're worth it. Daily 7.30am–10.30pm.

Mayur Mission Rd, just off The Mall ☎01902 252316. Exciting and extensive Indian menu featuring dishes from all over the Subcontinent for ₹150–200 – try the excellent *jalfrezi*. Candles, serviettes and classical Indian music create a pleasant vibe. Daily 8am–11pm.

Vaishno Pangi Dhaba School Rd, just off The Mall ☎94186 60693. One of the best cheap joints, serving dosas and other north and south Indian snacks such as masala dosa from only around ₹50. Daily 7am–11pm.

OLD MANALI

★ **The Bee's Knees Café** ☎97366 43833. Tented and canopied garden with gentle Indian music, where you can enjoy breakfast, snacks and Indian and Chinese food but the speciality is Mexican – a filling chicken burrito is only ₹120. Free wi-fi. Daily 8am–11pm.

Drifters Main Road ☎98050 33127. Hip new hotel restaurant with low tables and cushions downstairs, plus an outdoor terrace. Does grilled trout with the trimmings for around ₹300, somewhat less for other Indian, Chinese and Western dishes. Free wi-fi. Daily 9am–11pm.

Lazy Dog Main Rd ☎01902 254277. Popular restaurant overlooking the river, beautifully decorated

and fine for hanging out, if you like loud Western music. Specializes in Korean food – try the tasty *Kadimba* rice plate (₹200). Mon 4–11.30pm, Tues–Sun 10.30am–11.30pm.

Moon Dance Main Rd ☎98162 01046. Popular garden café and meeting place above the river with a varied menu that includes Mexican and Italian dishes for ₹100–150. Daily 9am–midnight.

People Art Café Main Rd ☎97367 87568. Small Russian-owned corner joint where you are given paper and crayons to draw with. Dishes like *sirniki* (curd fritters) and *draniki* (potato pancakes) make a change, plus they do fine Western breakfasts. Daily 8.30am–11pm.

River Music Café Next to bridge ☎01902 251140. Nice hang-out with outdoor tables or floor-cushion seating under shelter, plus a good sound system. Usual menu of Western, Indian and Chinese snacks and meals for ₹100–250. Daily 7am–11pm.

★ **Sheesh Besh** Main Rd ☎98829 37320. This self-proclaimed "fresh & funky" joint boasts colourful artwork and river views. Breakfast options include sausage and bacon, while the delicious non-veg mains only cost ₹120–140. Free wi-fi. Daily 8am–11pm.

6

Vashisht

Famous for its sweeping valley views and sulphurous hot-water springs, the ever-expanding village of **VASHISHT**, 3km northeast of Manali, is an amorphous jumble of traditional timber houses and modern concrete cubes, divided by paved courtyards and narrow muddy lanes. It is the epicentre of the local budget travellers' scene, with a good choice of guesthouses and cafés. The tranquil and traditional atmosphere is only interrupted by the occasional rave that takes place in the woods, or if the weather is poor, in one or two obliging hotels.

The only place for a **hot soak** is in the bathing pools of Vashisht's ancient temple (free), which is far more atmospheric anyway. Divided into separate sections for men and women, they attract a decidedly mixed crowd of Hindu pilgrims, Western hippies, semi-naked sadhus and groups of local kids.

Vashisht boasts two old stone **temples**, opposite each other above the main square and dedicated to the local patron saint Vashishta, guru of Raghunathji. The smaller of the two opens onto a partially covered courtyard and is adorned with elaborate woodcarvings. Those lining the interior of the shrine, blackened by years of oil-lamp and *dhoop* smoke, are worth checking out.

ARRIVAL AND DEPARTURE   VASHISHT

There are no buses to Vashisht, so most people arrive on foot or by auto-rickshaw from Manali.

ACCOMMODATION

Vashisht is packed with budget **guesthouses**, many of them old wooden buildings with broad verandas and uninterrupted vistas up the valley. A few larger **hotels** offer good-value, mid-range rooms. The only time you'll not be spoilt for choice is during high season (May–June).

Arohi Main On the main road into the village ☎01902 254421, ⓦarohiecoadventures.com; map p.440. Immaculate rooms with cable TV, intercom and balconies

overlooking the river. Rates are open to negotiation. Their agency can arrange various activities. ₹600

Bhrigu Hotel On the main road into the village

☏01902 253414, ⌨hotelbhrigu.com; map p.440.
Large hotel whose west-facing rooms all have attached
bathrooms and superb views from their spacious balconies.
Wi-fi and upstairs café with pool table. ₹**400**

Bodh Guest House In lane just beyond temple ☏01902
254165, ✉rajpeter2@rediffmail.com; map p.440. Sociable
bright blue and white guesthouse with smallish but cosy rooms,
all with common bathrooms. Wi-fi access ₹50/day. ₹**100**

★ **Dharma** A 5min walk up behind the temples
☏01902 252354, ⌨hoteldharmamanali.com; map
p.440. Complete with new wing. Most rooms have
fantastic views, as does the marble terrace with a swing

and loungers. There's even a tiny swimming pool, filled by
the hot springs. ₹**250**

Kalptaru Overlooking the temple tanks ☏01902
253443; map p.440. You can't get any closer to the baths
– with great-value rooms, all attached, with hot showers.
Small garden and veranda from which to watch the
bathers. ₹**200**

Surabhi Halfway up the main road ☏01902 252796,
⌨surabhihotel.com; map p.440. The airy, smart new
rooms upstairs are all nicely furnished and all views have of
the valley. The cheaper ground-floor rooms are colder and
darker. ₹**700**

EATING AND DRINKING

Big Fish On the main road, opposite the temples
☏88940 04509; map p.440. Upstairs restaurant serving
trout for around ₹200 and other travellers' favourites. Daily
7am–midnight.

Freedom Café On the main road into village
☏89883 15364; map p.440. Floor seating and a grassy
deck with good views; the Indian food is mostly in the
₹100–200 range, while trout goes for ₹300. Daily
7.30am–11pm.

Rainbow Café On the main road into village ☏98160
95744; map p.440. Sociable hangout offering traveller-
friendly staples such as pancakes, pasta and spring rolls, with
terrace views of the temple tanks. Daily 7am–11.30pm.

World Peace Café On the main road, above the
Surabhi hotel ☏98160 42796; map p.440. Standard
Indian/Western menu and prices but also Turkish coffee,
movies, board games and frequent live gigs. Has a roof
terrace too. Daily 7am–11pm.

Lahaul and Spiti

Few places on earth can mark so dramatic a change in landscape as the **Rohtang Pass**. To
one side, the lush green head of the Kullu Valley; to the other, an awesome vista of bare,
chocolate-coloured mountains, hanging glaciers and snowfields that shine in the dazzlingly
crisp light, with just flecks of flora deep in the valley to soften the stark image. The district
of **Lahaul and Spiti**, Himachal's largest, is named after its two subdivisions, which are, in
spite of their numerous geographical and cultural similarities, distinct and separate regions.

Lahaul

Lahaul, sometimes referred to as the Chandra-Bhaga Valley, is the region that divides the
Great Himalayas and Pir Panjal ranges. Its principal river, the Chandra, rises deep in the
barren wastes below the **Baralacha Pass**, and flows south, then west towards its confluence
with the River Bhaga near Tandi. Here, the two rivers become the Chenab, and crash
north out of Himachal to Kishtwar in Kashmir. Being closer to what rains the monsoon
brings across the Rohtang pass from the south, Lahaul's **climate** is less arid than in Ladakh
and Zanskar to the north and as a consequence, the key highway passes of Rhotang La and
Baralacha La are more prone to early snow than the higher examples further north. So it is
that between late October and late March, heavy snows close the passes and seal off the
region. The Rohtang Pass is usually closed on Tuesdays for maintenance and often gets
blocked by landslides following heavy rain. Despite such difficulties, Lahaulis, a mixture of
Buddhists and Hindus, enjoy one of the highest per capita incomes in the Subcontinent.
Using glacial water channelled through ancient irrigation ducts, Lahauli farmers manage to
coax a bumper crop of **seed potatoes** from their painstakingly fashioned terraces. The
region is also the sole supplier of **hops** to India's breweries, and harvests prodigious
quantities of wild herbs, used to make perfume and medicine. Much of the profit
generated by these cash crops is spent on lavish jewellery, especially seed-pearl necklaces

and coral-and turquoise-inlaid silver plaques, worn by the women over ankle-length burgundy or fawn woollen dresses. Lahaul's traditional costume and Buddhism are a legacy of the Tibetan influence that has permeated the region from the east.

Keylong

Lahaul's largest settlement and the district headquarters, **KEYLONG**, 114km north of Manali, is the last significant settlement on the long road journey to Ladakh. Although of little interest itself, the town lies amid superb scenery, within a day's climb of three Buddhist **gompas**. A couple of **stores** in the busy market sell trekking supplies – useful if you are heading off to Zanskar.

Lahauli Buddhists consider it auspicious to make a clockwise circumambulation – known as the **Rangcha Parikarma** – of the sacred **Rangcha Mountain** (4565m), which overlooks the confluence of the Bhaga and Chandra rivers. A well-worn trail that makes a long and arduous day-hike from Keylong, the route is highly scenic, and takes in the large **Khardung Gompa** along the way. A rough motorable road leads to Khardung (10km), but closer to Keylong and on the same side of the valley are two quiet and picturesque *gompas* high up the mountainside, **Shasher Gompa** (3km) and **Gungshal Gompa** (5km).

ARRIVAL AND INFORMATION   KEYLONG

By bus There are eight buses daily to Manali, the first one leaving at 5.30am and the last at 1.30pm. Note that onward transport to Leh can be difficult to arrange in high season (July & Aug), as most buses are full by the time they get to Manali.

Services There are no official foreign currency facilities here but the *Tashi Deleg* guesthouse will change money for a poor rate.

ACCOMMODATION AND EATING

Chanderbhaga On the main road, 1km towards Darcha ☎ 01900 222393. Comfortable but bland and typically overpriced HPTDC hotel. Half-board included with the more expensive rooms. HPTDC buses overnight at the tent camp. Dorm ₹200, double ₹1800.

Gyespa The Mall ☎ 01900 222207, ⊛ gyespahotels .webs.com. Neat three-storey hotel, which has compact but comfortable attached rooms with hot showers and a good multicuisine restaurant. Smarter new sister hotel above village. ₹300

Nordaling Paying Guest House On a path between the main road and the bus stand ☎ 01900 222294. Welcoming lodge that has bright, reasonably spacious rooms with bathrooms and cable TV, plus a decent restaurant. ₹500

Spiti

From its headwaters below the **Kunzum La** pass, the River Spiti runs 130km southeast to within the flick of a yak's tail of the border with Tibet, where it meets the Sutlej. The valley itself, surrounded by huge peaks with an average altitude of 4500m, is one of the highest and most remote inhabited places on earth – a desolate, barren tract scattered with tiny mud-and-timber hamlets and lonely lamaseries. Until 1992, Spiti in its entirety lay off-limits to foreign tourists. Now, only its far southeastern corner falls within the **Inner Line** – which leaves upper Spiti, including the district headquarters **Kaza**, freely accessible from the northwest via Lahaul. If you are really keen to complete the loop through the restricted area to or from Kinnaur (see p.411), you will need a **permit** (see box, p.402). The last main stop before reaching the restricted zone is the famed **Tabo** *gompa*, which harbours some of the oldest and most exquisite Buddhist art in the world.

Northwestern Spiti

From Grampoo, where the road along the Spiti Valley forks east from the Manali-Leh Highway, you have to bump along a wide but rough track for the first 80km. However, the gorge, waterfalls, snowy peaks and not least, the white-knuckle ascent over Kunzum La pass, make for a mind-boggling entry into the region. Near the pass it's possible with your own vehicle to detour 12km north to the small but picturesque **Chandertal Lake**

(4300m). Soon after crossing Kunzum La, the track reaches the sprawling village of **Losar**, (4113m), where you have to sign in at a police checkpoint. There are a couple of basic guesthouses and a few *dhabas* but little reason to stay here. From this point the track becomes a patchily surfaced road for the last section to Kaza.

Kaza and around

KAZA, 76km southeast of the Kunzum Pass, and 201km from Manali, is the subdivisional headquarters of **Spiti**. Overlooking the north bank of the River Spiti, it's the region's least picturesque town, but as the main market and roadhead it's a good base from which to head off on two- or three-day treks to monasteries and remote villages such as Kibber. Rates for porters and ponymen are comparable to those in Kullu. It is also possible to trek to Dhankar (32km) and on to Tabo (43km).

The town is divided into two parts by an almost dry creek that trickles into the River Spiti. On the west side, **New Kaza** is rather lacking in character but does boast a colourful modern monastery, just above the main road, which then loops round the head of the gorge towards the bus stand on the far side of **Old Kaza**. The old village is also accessible from New Kaza by a low footbridge, from the opposite side of which the bazaar winds down through a maze of alleys to the bus stand, passing most of the town's facilities on the way.

ARRIVAL AND DEPARTURE · KAZA AND AROUND

By bus There is one daily departure for Manali (5am; 12–13hr) and two for Tabo (2hr) at 7.30am and 2pm, the first of which goes all the way to Shimla (20–22hr) via Rekong Peo (11–12hr). The only bus to Mudh (2hr 30min) in the Pin Valley leaves daily at 3pm, returning the next morning. Likewise, there is a 4.15pm departure to Kibber that returns next day.

By taxi Jeeps are plentiful around the bus stand and cost roughly ₹2000 return for the Pin Valley or Tabo and ₹1200 for Kibber via Ki.

ACCOMMODATION

Amazingly, Kaza has about fifty mostly simple **places to stay**, spread roughly equally between New and Old Kaza, so bargaining down the rather inflated prices can produce good results.

Khangsar Hotel Main road, New Kaza ☎ 01906 222276. This pleasant hotel has large, comfortable attached rooms, most with TV, and a decent restaurant. Its nearby sister hotel *Deyzor* can take any overspill. ₹700

Parasol Retreat 200m below monastery, New Kaza ☎ 01902 200204. Modern building whose attractive rooms have soft furnishings and most have sweeping views. The attached agency runs tours and activities. ₹800

Sakya's Abode Main road near creek, New Kaza ☎ 01906 222254, ✉ sakya_abode@yahoo.com. This attractive place, built in traditional monastic style around a grassy lawn, offers smartish rooms and a cheap dorm. Dorm ₹200, double ₹660

Tashi Delek Off main bazaar, near bus stand ☎ 94596 66088. Conveniently placed for early morning departures, this ochre-coloured lodge has basic attached rooms. Those at the back have the best views. ₹500

Zangchuk Guest House Near the creek, Old Kaza ☎ 01906 222705. The attached rooms and facilities are very basic but there are excellent views from its peaceful terrace. New block under construction at the time of writing. ₹500

EATING AND DRINKING

Chandertal Cafe Main bazaar, Old Kaza ☎ 94189 72250. Simple Tibetan canteen serving great *thentuk*, *thukpa* and *momos*, all for well under ₹100. Check out the amusing and incongruous Rasta mural. Daily 6am–9pm.

Mahabudha Main bazaar, Old Kaza ☎ 94185 37545. Light upstairs restaurant with fine views from its large windows. It offers reasonable Indian and Chinese, including tasty pork dishes for ₹150–200. Daily 7am–9pm.

Sherab Food Corner Right below the monastery, New Kaza ☎ 94595 24121. Tiny and ultra-basic Tibetan joint, where you can get a superb non-veg *thukpa* for just ₹50, as well as *momos* and chowmein. Daily 6.30am–8pm.

★ **SÜI Café** Main bazaar, Old Kaza ☎ 94162 07750. Artistically decorated and run solely on solar power by Ecosphere (see p.452) upstairs, you can get a few savoury snacks such as *chaat* and *tsampa* nachos with cheese dip, plus great cakes, juices, coffee and even beer. Daily 8am–8pm.

6

TREKKING IN LAHAUL AND SPITI

Although parts of the old trade routes to Ladakh and Tibet are now sealed with tarmac, most of this remote and spectacular region is still only accessible on foot. Its trails, though well frequented in high season, are long, hard and high, so you must be self-sufficient and have a guide. Pack-horses and provisions are most readily available in **Manali**, or in **Keylong** and **Darcha** (Lahaul) and **Kaza** (Spiti) if you can afford to wait a few days. A good rope for river crossings will be useful, particularly in summer when the water levels are at their highest.

The **best time** to trek is July to early September, when brilliant blue skies make this an ideal alternative to the monsoon-prone Kullu Valley. By late September, the risk of snowfall deters many visitors from the longer expeditions. Whenever you leave, allow enough time to acclimatize to the **altitude** before attempting any big passes: AMS (Acute Mountain Sickness) claims victims here every season (see p.50).

LAHAUL: DARCHA TO PADUM VIA THE SHINGO LA PASS

The most popular trek is from **Darcha** over the **Shingo La** pass (5000m) to **Padum** in Zanskar. The trail passes through **Kargyak**, the highest village in Zanskar, and follows the Kargyak Valley down to its confluence with the Tsarap at **Purne**. There is a small café, shop, and camping ground here and it's a good base for the side trip to **Phuktal gompa**, one of the most spectacular sights in Zanskar. During the high season (July & Aug), a string of chai stall/tent camps spring up at intervals along the well-worn trail through the Tsarap Valley to Padum, meaning that you can manage without a guide or ponies from here on. Do not bank on finding food and shelter here at the start or end of the season.

LAHAUL: BATAL TO BARALACHA PASS

Lahaul's other popular trekking route follows the River Chandra north to its source at the **Baralacha Pass** (4920m) and makes a good extension to the Hampta Pass hike (see box, pp.444–445). Alternatively, catch a Kaza bus from Manali to the trailhead at **Batal** (3960m) below the **Kunzum La** (4551m). The beautiful milky-blue **Chandratal** ("Moon") **Lake** is a relentless ascent of 7hr from Batal, with stunning views south across the world's longest glacier, **Bara Shigri**, and the forbidding north face of the **White Sail** massif (6451m). The next campground is at **Tokping Yongma** torrent. **Tokpo Yongma**, several hours further up, is the second of the two big side-torrents and is much easier to ford early in the morning; from here it is a steady climb up to the **Baralacha Pass**. You can then continue to Zanskar via the Phirtse La, or pick up transport (prearranged if possible) down to Keylong and Manali or onwards to Leh.

SPITI: KAZA VIA THE PIN VALLEY TO MANIKARAN OR WANGTU

One of the best treks in **Spiti** is up the **Pin Valley**. The track alongside the River Pin, which passes a string of traditional settlements and monasteries, is now motorable as far as Mudh, around 40km south of Kaza. Over the next few years it is expected to be paved right through to Wangtu, but for now it forks beyond Mudh into two walking paths; the northern path over the Pin–Parvati Pass (5400m) to **Manikaran** in the Parvati Valley (see p.436), and the southern one to Wangtu in **Kinnaur** via the Bhaba Pass (4865m). The last section to Wangtu itself has also fallen to the roadbuilders, so you might decide just to hitch a ride.

DIRECTORY

Permits Anyone planning to continue on to Kinnaur can pick up a free Inner Line permit (see box, p.402) from the Additional Deputy Commissioner's office in New Kaza (Mon–Sat 9am–1pm & 2–5pm; closed second Sat).
Travel agents Spiti Holiday Adventure (☎01906 222711,

ⓦspitiholidayadventure.com) is the most reliable travel agent and also offers currency exchange, while Ecosphere (☎01906 222652, ⓦspitiecosphere.com) offers free water refills, a network of homestays and info about trekking and wildlife.

Ki Gompa

Set against a backdrop of snow-flecked mountains and clinging to the steep sides of a windswept conical hillock, **Ki Gompa** is a picture-book example of Tibetan architecture and one of Himachal's most exotic spectacles. Founded in the sixteenth century, Ki is the largest **monastery** in the Spiti Valley, supporting a thriving community of lamas whose Rinpoche, Lo Chien Tulkhu from Shalkar near Sumdo, is said to be the current incarnation of the "Great Translator" Rinchen Zangpo. His glass-fronted quarters crown the top of the complex, reached via stone steps that wind between the lamas' houses below. A labyrinth of dark passages and wooden staircases connects the prayer and assembly halls, home to collections of old *thangkas*, weapons, musical instruments, manuscripts and devotional images (no photography). Many of the rooms have seen extensive renovation since an earthquake struck in 1975; a new prayer hall, dedicated by the Dalai Lama, was also added in 2000. During the new moon towards late June or early July, Ki plays host to a large **festival** celebrating the "burning of the demon" when *chaam* dances are followed by a procession that winds its way down to the ritual ground below the monastery where a large butter sculpture is set on fire.

ARRIVAL AND DEPARTURE	KI GOMPA

By bus There is one bus daily from Kaza that arrives around 5pm and continues to Kibber. The return to Kaza passes through about 8am.

ACCOMODATION

Ki Gompa Guesthouse In the monastery ☏ 94186 26613. The monks rent out a few extremely basic, cell-like rooms in the monastery. Simple meals are included but there is only cold water. ₹300

Tashi Khangsar Guesthouse Located after the first bend in the road towards Kibber ☏ 01906 226277. Small, friendly and clean guesthouse with very simple rooms, most with shared bathrooms, fitting in well with the spartan surroundings. ₹150/₹250

Kibber

KIBBER (4205m) is among the highest settlements in the world with a driveable road and electricity. Jeep tracks, satellite dishes and the odd tin-roofed government building aside, its smattering of a hundred or so old Spitian houses is truly picturesque. Surrounded in summer by lush green barley fields, Kibber also stands at the head of a trail that picks its way north across the mountains, via the high glaciated **Parang La** pass (5600m) to Ladakh. Before the construction of roads into the Spiti Valley, locals used to lead ponies and yaks this way to trade in Leh bazaar. Some Manali-based trekking companies (see box, p.442) offer a seventeen-day trek from here to the lake of **Tso Moriri** in Ladakh (see p.492) and on to Leh.

ARRIVAL AND DEPARTURE	KIBBER

By bus Taking the 4.15pm bus from Kaza to Kibber (1hr) means you have to spend the night.

Other options Alternatively you could hire a jeep, hitch with a tour group, or forego transport altogether and walk the 16km of trails, although the outbound trip is nearly all uphill.

ACCOMMODATION

Norling Opposite the school at the start of the village ☏ 01906 200091. Typical of the handful of congenial lodges but slightly nicer than the adjoining *Rainbow* and with a better restaurant. All rooms have common hot bucket bathrooms. ₹200

Serkong In the centre of the village ☏ 01906 200156. Very quaint traditional rooms, all with common bathrooms, and a nice roof terrace for relaxing over a snack or tea in the sun. ₹250

Dhankar

Nearly a third of the way between Kaza and Tabo, near the meeting of the Pin and Spiti rivers, a rough road veers off to the east for 8.5km to Dhankar. The **Dhankar Gompa** (daily 8am–6pm; ₹25) on the uppermost peak behind the village of **DHANKAR** (3890m) is famed for its brilliant murals, probably painted in the seventeenth century, depicting the life of the Buddha. Although some of the work has been vandalized, the scenes depicting the Buddha's birth, rebirth and life in Kapilavastu and his rejection of worldly ways are spectacular. The *gompa*, much of which is in a sad state of repair and on the World Monument Fund's list of the hundred most endangered sites, also affords superb views down to the confluence of the main River Spiti and the Pin tributary.

ARRIVAL AND DEPARTURE   DHANKAR

Dhankar is not on a bus route so you will have to arrange your own transport (a taxi from Sichaling on the main road to Tabo is ₹200) or walk – the short cut starts from the storm shelter by the main road under the *gompa* 3km before Sichaling.

ACCOMMODATION

Dhankar Gompa guesthouse In the monastery. The much improved monastery guesthouse has simple attached and non-attached rooms, the latter with hot water, plus a dormitory and a terrace restaurant. Dorm ₹150, double ₹300/₹500

Tenzin Homestay Above the monastery near the Old Fort ⏺94592 70036. Welcoming family homestay with small, cosy rooms, all with shared baths, and splendid views across the valley. Food included. ₹500

Pin Valley

Thirty minutes east of Kaza a bridge at Attargu crosses the Spiti and begins a 156km run up the **PIN VALLEY** to **Gulling**, above which stands the important Nyingma *gompa* of Gungri, believed to date back to the eighth or ninth century. Across the river lies the slightly larger settlement of **Sagnam**. At the head of the valley, a rough road veers slightly southwest to **Mikim** and the **Pin Valley National Park** (unrestricted free access), which starts beyond the hamlet of **Phukchong** and is home to the ibex, red fox and snow leopard. Beyond Sagnam the road deteriorates rapidly, but vehicles can push ahead another 14km to **Mudh**, an enchanting hamlet with a tiny nunnery that peers over a breathtaking valley, the end of which is flanked by the pyramid-shaped Tordang Mountain.

ARRIVAL AND DEPARTURE   PIN VALLEY

By bus There is one bus from Kaza at 3pm, which returns the following morning.

ACCOMMODATION

The Hermitage On the edge of Phukchong ⏺94184 39294. By far the most comfortable place to stay in the valley, with neat attached rooms. It is primarily a meditation retreat. Half-board ₹1800

Himalayan Pin Parvati Guest House Mudh village centre ⏺94185 71167. Probably the best of the several simple guesthouses, with plain but clean rooms, all with common baths, and good healthy food. ₹350

Shambala Guesthouse Sagnam village centre ⏺01906 224221. The best of the small bunch at this delightful riverside location, with small but clean rooms and well-kept shared facilities. ₹250

Tara Guest House On the edge of Mudh ⏺94184 41453. Providing simple meals and a warm family welcome, the *Tara* is another good option. All rooms are basic, with shared baths. ₹300

Tabo

One of the main reasons to brave the rough roads of Spiti is to get to **Tabo Gompa**, 43km east of Kaza. The mud-and-timber boxes of the old *gompa* that nestle on the steep north bank of the Spiti may look drab but the multihued murals and stucco sculpture they contain are some of the world's richest and most important ancient Buddhist art treasures – the link between the cave paintings of Ajanta (see p.643) and the more exuberant Tantric art that flourished in Tibet five centuries or so later. According to an inscription in its main assembly hall, the monastery was established in 996 AD, when **Rinchen Zangpo** was disseminating dharma across the northwestern Himalayas. In addition to the 158 Sanskrit Buddhist texts he personally transcribed, the "Great Translator" brought with him a retinue of Kashmiri artisans to decorate the temples. The only surviving examples of their exceptional work are here at Tabo, at Alchi in Ladakh, and Toling and Tsaparang *gompas* in Chinese-occupied western Tibet.

The new *gompa*, inaugurated by the Dalai Lama in 1983, houses nearly fifty lamas and a handful of *chomos* (nuns), some of whom receive training in traditional painting techniques under a *geshe*, or teacher from eastern Tibet. Visitors are welcome to attend daily 6.30am puja. It's also worth exploring the caves across the main road, one of which houses more paintings, but you need to be let in by the *gompa* caretaker.

The Chogskhar

Daily 8am–5pm; unrestricted access to grounds • Donation

Enclosed within a mud-brick wall, Tabo's **Chogskhar**, or "sacred enclave", contains eight temples and 24 *chortens* (*stupas*). The largest and oldest structure in the group, the **Sug La-khang**, which includes the **Z'al** (House of Treasures), stands opposite the main entrance. Erected at the end of the tenth century, the "Hall of the Enlightened Gods" was conceived in the form of a three-dimensional mandala, whose structure and elaborately decorated interior functions as a mystical model of the universe complete with deities. There are three distinct bands of detail – the lower-level paintings depict episodes in the life of the Buddha and his previous incarnations; above are stucco gods and goddesses; and the top of the hall is covered with meditating Buddhas and *bodhisattvas*. Bring a torch to see the full detail of the murals.

The other temples date from the fifteenth and eighteenth centuries. Their contents illustrate the development of Buddhist iconography from its early Indian origins to the Chinese-influenced opulence of medieval Tibetan Tantricism that still, in a more lurid form, predominates in modern *gompas*.

ARRIVAL AND DEPARTURE   TABO

By bus Two buses per day travel to Kaza, the 3am departure going all the way to Manali. In the opposite direction, a bus passes through at around 9.30am on its way from Kaza to Rekong Peo in Kinnaur and on to Shimla.

ACCOMMODATION AND EATING

Café Kunzon Top In the village centre ☎ 94592 70055. Choose between the flowery courtyard and cushioned interior to enjoy tasty vegetarian food, including various types of Tibetan *tsampa*, curries and Western dishes such as rostis, all ₹40–80. Daily 7am–10pm.

Maitreya Guest House In the village centre ☎ 94189 81957. Friendly family guesthouse with comfortable attached rooms on two floors arranged around a leafy enclosure. The convivial restaurant does great *momos* and other food. ₹600

Millennium Monastic Guest House Outside the main monastery gates ☎ 01906 223333, ⊕ tabomonastery.org. The official monastery guesthouse is run by monks and has simple rooms, some attached, and a dorm. Also has a simple restaurant. Dorm ₹100, double ₹200/₹350

★ **Sidharth** On the road to the bus stand ☎ 94185 81203, ✉ dk22902@gmail.com. Bright new two-storey hotel with decent-sized attached rooms, all beautifully decorated and comfortably furnished. Small restaurant downstairs. ₹500

Tashi Khangsar Hotel Between the monastery and the river ☎ 01906 233346, ✉ vaneetrana23@gmail .com. Reasonably spacious and excellent-value attached rooms and a lovely large garden, with a parachute canopy for shade. ₹400

The Manali–Leh Highway

Since it opened to foreign tourists in 1989, the famous **Manali–Leh Highway** has replaced the old Srinagar–Kargil route as the most popular approach to Ladakh. In summer, a stream of vehicles set off from the Kullu Valley to travel along the second-highest road in the world, which reaches a dizzying altitude of 5328m at Tanglang La. Its surface varies wildly from fairly smooth asphalt through potholes of differing depths to dirt tracks sliced by glacial streams, traversing a starkly beautiful lunar wilderness. Depending on road conditions and type of vehicle, the 485km journey can take anything from seventeen to thirty hours' actual driving. Bus drivers invariably stop for a short and chilly night in one of the spartan **tent camps** along the route. These, however, are few and far between after September 15, when the highway officially closes; in practice, all this means

6

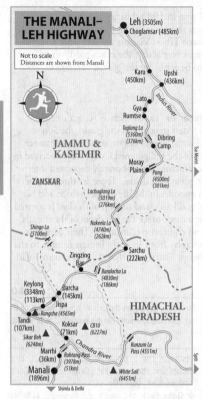

THE MANALI–
LEH HIGHWAY

Not to scale
Distances are shown from Manali

N

Leh (3505m)
Choglamsar (485km)

Karu
(450km) — Upshi
(436km)

Lato
Gya
Rumtse

Taglang La
(5360m)
(376km) — Dibring
Camp

Moray
Plains — Pang
(4500m)
(301km)

JAMMU &
KASHMIR

ZANSKAR

Lachuglang La
(5019m)
(276km)

Nakeela La
(4740m)
(262km) — Sarchu
(222km)

Shingo La
(5100m)

Zingzing
Bar

Baralacha La
(4830m)
(186km)

Keylong
(3348m)
(113km) — Darcha
(145km)

Jispa

Rangcha (4565m)

Tandi
(107km) — Koksar
(71km) — CB10
(6227m)

Sikar Beh
(6248m)

Marhi
(36km) — Rohtang Pass
(3978m)

Manali
(1896m) — White Sail
(6451m)

Chandra River

Kunzum La
Pass (4551m)

HIMACHAL
PRADESH

Indus River

Tsab Manté

Spiti

Shimla & Delhi

is that the Indian government won't airlift you out if you get trapped in snow. Yet some companies run regardless of this until the passes become blocked by snowfall in late October. Details on **transport** between Manali (see p.444) and Leh (see p.483) are covered in the respective town accounts.

Manali to Keylong

Once out of **Manali**, the road begins its long ascent of the **Rohtang Pass** (3978m) and, annoyingly, often gets clogged only an hour or so up, when trucks get bogged down in wet weather; it's not uncommon to have an unscheduled wait of up to four hours when this happens. Buses pull in for breakfast (or brunch) 17km before the pass at a row of makeshift *dhabas* at Marhi (3360m). Though not all that high by Himalayan standards, the pass itself is one of the most treacherous in the region and every year locals and tourists alike are caught unawares by sudden weather changes – hence Rohtang's name, which literally means "piles of dead bodies". The road descends from Rohtang to the floor of the **Chandra Valley**, finally reaching the river at **Koksar**, little more than a scruffy collection of chai stalls with a **checkpoint** where you have to enter passport details in a ledger – one of several such stops on the road to Leh. The next few hours are among the most memorable on the entire trip. Bus seats on the left are best, as the road runs across the northern slopes of the valley through the first Buddhist settlements, hemmed in by towering peaks and hanging glaciers towards **Keylong** (see p.450). The HPTDC super-deluxe and some other buses break the journey here, leaving the bulk of the journey to the second day (the opposite obviously applies when travelling to Manali from Leh).

Keylong to Sarchu

Beyond Keylong, the Bhaga Valley broadens, but its bare sides support very few villages. At **Darcha**, a lonely cluster of dry-stone huts and dingy tent camps, plus another checkpost, the landscape is still fairly green. All buses stop here for passengers to grab a hot bowl of Tibetan *thukpa* from a wayside *dhaba*. There's little else to do in Darcha, though the Shingo La trailhead – the main trekking route north to Zanskar (see p.504) – is on the outskirts. If you are not on one of the through Manali–Leh buses, you're better off stopping at **JISPA**, 7km south, a pleasant little village with ample camping along the river as well as the route's one proper hotel.

From Darcha, the surfaced road climbs steadily northeast to the **Baralacha La** pass (4950m). On the other side, some buses stop for the night at **SARCHU**, where the state-run tent camp is preferable to several more expensive camps dotted along the road. Note that Sarchu Serai is 2500m higher than Manali, and travellers coming straight from Manali might suffer from the higher altitude here.

CYCLING THE MANALI–LEH HIGHWAY

Touring cylists revere the Manali–Leh highway as one of the most challenging road rides in the world and each summer up to three hundred intrepid two-wheelers set off to attempt the nearly 500km route. While the **gradients** are rarely unrideable, the two-day ascents, rough tracks over the **passes** and, most crucially, the **altitude** demand respect and some preparation.

Hauling a fully laden bike up 50km climbs to well over 5000m may sound daunting, but the exhilaration can be rewarding – especially if you're set up to camp rather than relying on the noisy, dirty parachute camps. You'll need wind- and waterproof clothing, a warm fleece, sunglasses and headwear, plus a good supply of high-energy snacks like the blocks of peanut brittle found in the bazaars. A water filter increases your autonomy too as you'll drink at least three litres a day. Check your bike has a suitably low gearing for crawling up the passes (most MTBs will), and that you have near-new brake pads for the long descents that follow, as well as a secure baggage system. As for clothing, choose quick-drying items that will wick away sweat before it brings on exposure on a chilly pass.

Most riders set off from Manali (1900m) and take eight to ten days to get to Leh (3500m). However, starting in Leh gives you a chance to acclimatize before you set off, and involves less climbing (but no less drama). Whichever direction you take, don't fret too much about you or your bike packing up halfway, as you'll always be able to hitch a lift. If riding alone is not for you, choose between numerous **mountain-bike tour operators** in Manali (see box, p.442). For more information, see ⓦhimalayabybike.com.

Sarchu to Taglang La

Sarchu packs up for the season from September 15. Northbound buses that haven't overnighted in Keylong thereafter press on over **Lachuglang La** (5019m), the second highest pass on the highway, to the tent camp at **PANG** (4500m), which stays open longer. Unfortunately, this means that the drive through one of the most dramatic stretches of the route, through an incredible canyon, is in darkness. North of Pang, the road heads up to the fourth and final pass, the **Taglang La**, the highest point on the Manali–Leh Highway at a literally breathtaking 5328m. Drivers pull in for a quick spin of the prayer wheels and a brief photo session alongside the altitude sign and small shrine. If the weather's clear enough, you can gaze north beyond the multicoloured tangle of prayer flags across Ladakh to the Karakoram Range, just visible on the horizon.

Taglang La to Leh

Thirty kilometres beyond the pass is **Rumtse**, the first Ladakhi village. There are two basic guesthouse-cum-*dhabas* here, located opposite a store selling unperishable snacks. Just down the road the next village of **Gya** has a health clinic (with oxygen) and just back below the tree line, **Lato** has a particularly nice campsite in season, as well as a basic lodge. At **Upshi**, the road reaches the dramatic Indus Valley, tracing the **Indus River** past slender poplars, sprawling army camps and ancient monasteries. Traffic builds as you approach **Choglamsar**, then climb the final dusty kilometres to **Leh** (see p.479) – past the world's highest golf course – through the modern outskirts to the haberdashers, canny traders and wrinkled apricot-sellers of Leh's Main Bazaar.

ACCOMMODATION AND EATING   THE MANALI–LEH HIGHWAY

There are only very sparse accommodation options north of Keylong (see p.450), mostly at very basic **tent camps**, with the odd equally basic **guesthouse** thrown in. The one exception is the hotel listed below. Most of these places can rustle up simple **meals** and there are a few tented *dhabas* along the route too. If you are on a government bus, accommodation at the Chanderbhaga in Keylong (see p.450) is organized for you, whichever direction you are travelling in.

Hotel Ibex-Jispa Main Rd, Jispa ⓣ98160 36860, ⓦhotelibexjispa.com. Incongruously large four-storey building amid the mountain glory, housing 27 smart deluxe rooms and a twenty-bed dormitory. They can arrange adventure activities. Dorm ₹150, double ₹1800

Jammu and Kashmir

HOUSEBOAT, DAL LAKE

Jammu and Kashmir

India's northernmost and sixth-largest state, Jammu and Kashmir (usually shortened to J&K), is one of its most mountainous and staggeringly beautiful. It also encapsulates the cultural and religious diversity of the Subcontinent by falling into three distinct regions. The southwestern end of its thick bracket-shaped expanse is the Hindu-majority area around the winter capital of Jammu. Directly to the north across the first range of the Himalayas is the almost exclusively Muslim Kashmir, as infamous for its ongoing political woes (see box, pp.466–467) as it is renowned for its enchanting beauty. Finally, to the northeast, hugging the disputed borders with both Pakistan and China, the remote and rugged region of *Ladakh*, which occupies nearly seventy percent of the state according to its de facto borders, is populated mostly by adherents of Tibetan Buddhism.

Jammu is the state's largest city and the traditional stepping-stone into the region, worthy of a stopover in its own right for its imposing fort and admirable collection of temples. Most foreigners, however, head immediately for the summer capital of **Srinagar**, lynchpin of the famed Kashmir Valley, which also offers the green hills and meadows of **Gulmarg** and **Pahalgam**. Unless you fly direct to the enchanting capital of Ladakh, **Leh**, the decision of **when to visit Ladakh** is largely made for you: the passes into the region are only open between late June and late October, when the sun is at its strongest and the weather, at least during the day, pleasantly warm. From November onwards, temperatures drop fast, often plummeting to minus 40°C between December and February, when the only way in and out of Zanskar is along the frozen surface of the river. Leh is surrounded by numerous villages dominated by venerable monasteries such as **Tikse** and **Hemis** or, further west, **Lamayuru**. The latter provides a good stopover en route to **Kargil**, halfway along the Srinagar–Leh road and the jumping-off point for the isolated **Zanskar Valley**. Other sparsely populated but exquisite areas worth the bumpy detours involved in reaching them from Leh include the icy lakes of **Pangong Tso** and **Tso Moriri**, as well as the almost surreal **Nubra Valley**, with its sand dunes and wandering camels.

Brief history

The region that comprises the current state of J&K has been a cultural, religious and political crossroads for millennia. There is archeological evidence that the area around Jammu, whose name appears in the Mahabharata, was part of the **Harappan** civilization, based in the Indus Valley, one of the oldest in the world. Remains of other powerful kingdoms, such as those of the **Mauryas** and **Guptas**, have also been found near the city, although the foundation of Jammu itself is credited to the **Raja Jambu Lochan** in the late

TIKSE MONASTERY

Highlights

❶ Kashmir Valley This lush swathe of green is once more attracting visitors to trekking bases such as Pahalgam and Gulmarg. **See p.469**

❷ Dal Lake Lounging on a Kashmiri houseboat, surrounded by waterlilies, kingfishers and a stunning mountain range – unforgettable. See p.471

❸ Leh Medieval streets, a Tibetan-style palace, bazaars and looming snowy peaks. **See p.479**

❹ Tikse Along with Lamayuru and Hemis, the Indian Himalayas' most impressive monastery complex. **See p.489**

❺ Tso Moriri This exquisite high-altitude lake inhabited by nomadic herders features snow-fringed desert mountains and rare migratory birds. **See p.492**

❻ Nubra Valley Sand dunes, Bactrian camels and views of the mighty Karakorams await across the world's highest driveable road. **See p.494**

❼ Alchi Wonderful painted murals and stucco images are hidden behind the simple exterior of this ancient monastery. **See p.499**

❽ Zanskar Walled in by the Himalayas, during the winter this isolated valley can only be reached by following the frozen river route. See p.504

HIGHLIGHTS ARE MARKED ON THE MAP ON PP.462–463

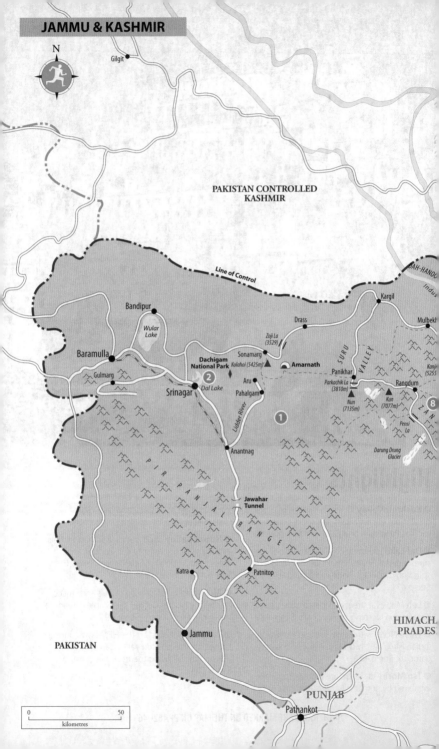

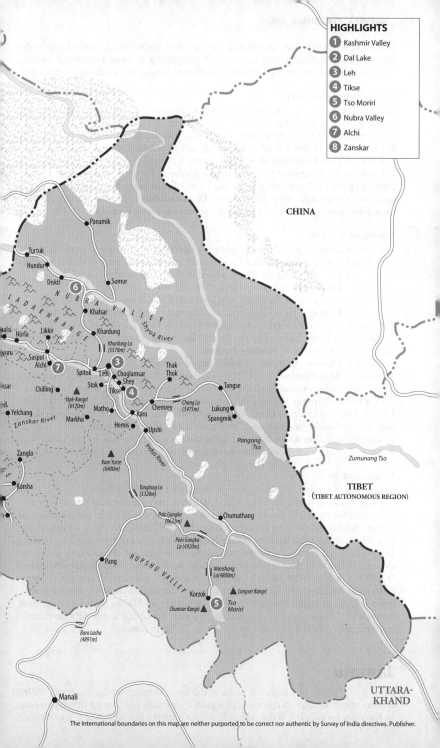

HIGHLIGHTS

1. Kashmir Valley
2. Dal Lake
3. Leh
4. Tikse
5. Tso Moriri
6. Nubra Valley
7. Alchi
8. Zanskar

CHINA

Panamik

Turtuk

Hundur

Diskit

Sumur

6 NUBRA VALLEY

LADAKH RANGE

alsi

Nurla

Likkir

Khalsar

yuru

Saspol

Khardung

Alchi **7**

Shyok River

Spitok

Khardung La (5578m)

3 Leh

Choglamsar

Thak Thok

ksar

Chilling

Stok

Shey

Tikse **4**

Tangse

Stok-Kangri (6120m)

Matho

Karu

Chemrey

Chang La (5475m)

Lukung

ed.

Yelchang

Zanskar River

Markha

Hemis

Upshi

Spangmik

Zangla

Kam Yurze (6400m)

Pangong Tso

Zumunang Tso

GE

Karsha

Indus River

Tanglang La (5328m)

TIBET
(TIBET AUTONOMOUS REGION)

Polo Gongka (6632m)

Chumathang

Rupshu Valley

Pang

Polo Gongka La (4920m)

Namshang La (4800m)

Bara Lacha (4891m)

Korzok

Chamser Kangri

5 Tso Moriri

Lungser Kangri

Manali

UTTARA-KHAND

fourteenth century. It later fell under the control of the **Sikhs** but after their defeat by the British in 1846, became part of the Hindu **Dogra dynasty** in the mid-nineteenth century. The majority of its people still identify themselves as Dogras and speak the Dogri dialect.

Developments in Kashmir

Kashmir, meanwhile, had become an important centre of Buddhism and, subsequently, Hinduism during the first half of the first millennium AD and these faiths co-existed side by side regardless of the region's rulers for the best part of a thousand years. In 1349, **Shah Mir** became the first Muslim ruler of Kashmir and it continued to be controlled by followers of Islam from **Mughals** to **Afghans** until it was taken over by the Sikhs and followed the same historical path as Jammu from the 1840s until Independence. Its problems since 1948 (see box, pp.466–467) have still not been resolved but under the guidance of its youngest ever chief minister, **Omar Abdullah**, (elected in January 2009), there is increased confidence of positive developments among Kashmiris.

The origins of Ladakh

The first inhabitants of Ladakh are thought to have been a mixture of nomadic herdsmen from the Tibetan plateau and a small contingent of early Buddhist refugees from northern India called the Mons, joined in the fourth or fifth century by the Indo-Aryan **Dards**, who introduced irrigation and settled agriculture. The first independent kingdom in the region was established in the ninth century by the maverick nobleman Nyima Gon, at around the same time as **Buddhism** was first disseminated by the wandering sage-apostles such as Padmasambhava (alias Guru Rinpoche). This was followed by the **Second Spreading**, among whose key proselytizers was the "Great Translator" **Rinchen Zangpo**.

Around the fourteenth century, Ladakh passed through a dark age before being reunified by **Tashi Namgyal** (ruled 1555–70), who established a new capital and palace at Leh. This power eventually succumbed to the mightier Mughals, when Aurangzeb demanded more tribute, ordered the construction of a mosque in Leh and forced the Ladakhi king to convert to Islam. Trade links with Tibet resumed in the eighteenth century, but Ladakh never regained its former status. Plagued by feuds and assassinations, the kingdom teetered into terminal decline, and was an easy target for the **Dogra** general Zorawar Singh, who annexed it for the maharaja of Kashmir in 1834.

Modern Ladakh

Ladakh became a part of J&K in independent India in 1948, following the first of the three Indo-Pak wars fought in the region. Tensions over the disputed line of control still flare up sporadically (see box, pp.466–467). When you consider the proximity of China, another old foe who annexed a large chunk of Ladakh in 1962, it's easy to see why this is India's most sensitive border zone. There is also a degree of internal friction. Long dissatisfied with the state government based in Srinagar, the Ladakhis finally saw the establishment of their region as the **Ladakh Autonomous Hill Development Council** (LAHDC) in September 1995, localizing – in theory – government control. A group of Ladakhi Buddhist and Muslim parties formed the unified **Ladakh Union Territory Front** in 2002 to push for separation from J&K and gain Union Territory recognition from Delhi. Despite local success in state elections, the Congress-led state government has repeatedly blocked moves to set up Union Territory status.

Jammu

Known as "the city of temples" because of the many shrines that dot the town, **JAMMU** is more attractive than its reputation suggests and worthy of at least a full day en route to Kashmir, for which it is the railhead (at least until the line to Srinagar is complete).

The main place of worship in town is the revered **Ragunath** temple, although it is surpassed in importance by **Vaishno Devi**, near Katra, some 60km north. The city also boasts the impressive **Bahu Fort**, which crowns a hill overlooking the River Tawi and the splendid **Baja-u-Bahu** gardens. The town's principal museum is the mildly absorbing **Amar Mahal**, which showcases period art.

Ragunath

Daily 6am–10pm

If you only have time to visit one of Jammu's many temples, it should be the buzzing **Ragunath**, about ten minutes' walk through the commercial lanes east of the bus stand. Once you've got through the tight security, you enter a large courtyard surrounded by multiple *shikharas* and two gardens. Within lies an inner courtyard, housing the main shrine of Lord Ragunath, an incarnation of Vishnu, and his two consorts, watched over by an orange-robed statue of Hanuman nearby.

Bahu Fort

Daily 9am–9pm • Free

The town's most imposing attraction is **Bahu Fort**, which stands proudly on a high bluff above the south bank of the River Tawi, around 3km southeast of the centre. The solid, squat battlements of the fort enclose some beautifully manicured lawns, although the principal draw for Hindus is the small **Mata Kali temple** within the complex.

Aquarium Awareness Centre

Daily 9am–9pm • ₹20

Next to Bahu Fort, the **Aquarium Awareness Centre** contains a mildly diverting assortment of more than four hundred varieties of fish and other marine creatures. Hilariously designed with a metallic casing in the shape of a fish, the museum is entered through its mouth and exited via the tail.

Baja-u-Bahu Gardens

Daily: summer 8am–10pm; winter 9am–9pm • ₹10

Descending in attractive tiers below the fort, the impressive **Baja-u-Bahu Gardens** contain a series of well-tended flower gardens and decorative pools, which act as swimming baths for the local monkeys. It's a favourite picnic spot for Indian tourists.

Amar Mahal Museum

Srinagar Rd • Daily 9am–12.50pm & 2–5.50pm, closes 4pm in winter • ₹45 (₹10)

A couple of kilometres northeast of the bus stand on the Srinagar Road, the **Amar Mahal Museum**, housed in a converted palace, is basically an art gallery with some regal memorabilia. The portraits and miniatures date mostly from the early twentieth century.

ARRIVAL AND DEPARTURE   **JAMMU**

By plane Jammu's airport (☎0191 243 7843) is 8km southwest of the city and has several daily flights to Delhi and Srinagar with Air India and Jet.

By train Trains from all over India pull into the station 4km south of the centre. There are at least seven daily trains from Delhi, of which the fastest is the *Uttar S Kranti* #12445 (dep. 8.50pm, arr. Jammu 6.35am). The most convenient

train to Delhi is the *Malwa Express* #12920 (dep. 9am, arr. Delhi 7pm).

By bus Numerous buses to Srinagar (11–12hr; ₹250–450) depart between 5am and 8am from the main bus stand, in the centre of town just north of the river. There are also frequent services to Pathankot, Amritsar, Delhi and other destinations. JKTDC buses depart from near the tourist

THE KASHMIR CONFLICT

The Himalayan state of **Kashmir** is the main reason why India and Pakistan have remained bitter enemies for most of the sixty-plus years since Independence. The region's troubles date from Partition, when the ruling Hindu maharaja Hari Singh opted to join India rather than Pakistan (see p.1163), and the geopolitical tug-of-war over the state has soured relations between the two countries ever since, at least until the last few years.

The conflict in Kashmir has taken two forms: firstly, a **military confrontation** between the Pakistani and Indian armies along the de facto border – on three occasions leading to fully fledged war (in 1947, 1965 and 1999); and, secondly, a violent **insurgency-cum-civil war** since 1989, during which both Kashmiri and foreign Muslim fighters have launched various attacks against Indian military and civilian targets inside Kashmir itself, leading to equally bloody reprisals by Indian security forces – a conflict which has now cost an estimated seventy thousand lives.

THE ROOTS OF THE PROBLEM

Following the cessation of hostilities in 1948, a UN resolution demanded a plebiscite should take place whereby the Kashmiri people would decide their own future. This India has resolutely refused to hold. The Ceasefire Line, or so-called **Line of Control**, became the effective border between India and Pakistan; the third of Kashmir held by Pakistan is referred to by those who support independence from India as **Azad (Free) Kashmir**. India lost a further slice of Kashmiri territory to the Chinese during the 1962 conflict (see p.1164) before a resumption of hostilities with Pakistan during the **Second Indo-Pakistan War** of 1965 (see p.1164). Again, Kashmir was the focus of attention, though at the end of the war both sides returned to their original positions. The **Simla Agreement** of 1972 committed both sides to renounce force in their dealings with one another, and to respect the Line of Control and the de facto border between their two states.

INSURGENCY AND CIVIL WAR

Simmering Kashmiri discontent with Indian rule and Delhi's political interference in the region, which had been due to gain virtual autonomy in return for joining India, began to transform into **armed resistance** around 1989 – the arrival of Mujahideen in the Kashmir Valley after the end of the war with Russia in Afghanistan is often blamed for the sudden surge of militancy. The key incident, however, was the unprovoked massacre, in 1990, of around one hundred unarmed protesters, by Indian security forces on **Gawakadal Bridge** in the capital, Srinagar. By the following year, violence and human-rights abuses had become endemic, both in the Kashmir Valley itself and further south around Jammu. **Curfews** became routine, and thousands of suspected militants were detained without trial amid innumerable accusations of torture, the systematic rape of Kashmiri women by Indian troops, disappearances of countless boys and men, and summary executions. The conflict continued to ebb and flow

office on Vir Marg, aka Residency Rd (see below) and sometimes from the railway station. City minibuses connect the railway station to the centre of the old town, via the main bus stand, every few minutes.

By jeep Between Jammu and Srinagar, many people choose to take a shared jeep (9–10hr; ₹560). You can organize this at one of the numerous travel agencies or where the jeeps gather below the flyover, west of the bus stand.

INFORMATION

Tourist office The helpful Tourist Reception Centre (Ⓣ0191 254 4527 Ⓦjktourism.org) is on Vir Marg, which starts around 10min walk north of the bus stand, opposite the Ragunath temple. It hands out quite a good map of the state and its two largest cities.

ACCOMMODATION

Finding a room is rarely a problem in Jammu, though there is little choice in the middle to upper end of the market. Most of the budget places are to be found on Gumat Bazaar or around the bus stand.

Diamond Gumat Bazaar Ⓣ0191 257 7792, Ⓔhotel diamondjmu@gmail.com. Plenty of adequate rooms of varying sizes, some with shared bathrooms and some a/c. Sees the most Western visitors, but not the best in

throughout the 1990s, with regular atrocities on both sides, while the region's once-thriving tourist industry was dealt a fatal blow when the extremist Al-Faran Muslim group kidnapped five tourists trekking near Pahalgam in 1995; one was beheaded, and the others were never found. At the end of the decade, the crisis brought India and Pakistan to the verge of yet another all-out war. With both countries now fully fledged **nuclear states**, Kashmir has become one of the world's most dangerous geopolitical flashpoints.

In May 1999, at least eight hundred Pakistani-backed Mujahideen crept across the Line of Control overlooking the Srinagar–Leh road near **Kargil** and began to occupy Indian territory. India moved thousands of troops and heavy artillery into the area, and swiftly followed up with an aerial bombardment. In the event the conflict was contained, and by July 1999 the Indian army had retaken all the ground previously lost to the militants. All-out war was only narrowly averted again in early 2003 after intense diplomatic pressure was brought to bear on both sides by US emissary **Colin Powell**. Within Kashmir, long-established organizations like the Jammu and Kashmir Liberation Front and the All Party Hurriyat Conference, which had traditionally adopted a secular and nationalist stance, were being increasingly eclipsed by militantly Islamic and pro-Pakistani groups such as Lashkar-e-Toiba and Jaish-e-Mohammad.

THE ROAD TO PEACE?

The first signs of genuine rapprochement came in May 2003, when Indian prime minister Vajpayee made a **declaration of peace**, announcing that hundreds of Pakistanis detained in Indian prisons since the Kargil war would be released. Pakistani prime minister Mir Zafarullah Khan Jamali responded by announcing that Pakistan would ease trade restrictions and improve travel and sporting links. In 2004 and 2005 the Indian and Pakistani governments also held their first-ever talks with Kashmiri separatists from the Hurriyat Conference, establishing a peaceful "Road Map" for progress in the region. A further round of Indo-Pak talks following the appointment of Manmohan Singh as India's new prime minister resulted in further small but encouraging signs of progress, symbolized by the inauguration, in April 2005, of a fortnightly **bus service** between Srinagar and Muzaffarabad in Pakistani-controlled Kashmir. Further détente was signalled in the aftermath of the devastating **earthquake** in Pakistani Kashmir in October 2005, which killed around 73,000 people in Pakistan and a further 1400 in Indian Kashmir, when the Line of Control was opened to speed up relief operations.

Various **long-term solutions** to the whole Kashmir issue are currently being mooted. These have ranged from India suggesting that the Line of Control (LoC) might be converted into a permanent border to Pakistan possibly even being prepared to give up all claims to Kashmir if India allowed it some form of self-government. Kashmir's future looks brighter now than it has for decades, although there is the perpetual risk that a single violent incident could trigger a new phase of conflict. Indeed, the shooting of a few Indian and Pakistani soldiers on each side of the border in January 2013 had raised tensions again at the time of writing.

terms of value. ₹550/₹750

Jammu Residency Vir Marg ☏ 0191 257 9554, ⌨ jktdc .co.in. Half a dozen fairly characterless government blocks, offering a range of rooms, some of them with a/c, and the odd luxury suite. ₹600

Nagima Gumat Bazaar ☏ 0191 256 6008. Very clean and welcoming Sikh-run establishment, containing just ten rooms, some of which are a/c and not much more expensive than the non-a/c ones. ₹500

Sri Math Vaishno Devi Right next to railway station entrance ☏ 0191 247 3275. Huge institutional behemoth with a rather off-putting security entrance and 10am checkout but clean spacious rooms (all a/c) and a cheap dorm. Dorm ₹60, double ₹650

Vivek Just south of bus stand ☏ 0191 254 7545, ✉ vish7337@yahoo.in. Centrally a/c hotel in a convenient location, with comfortable rooms and a snazzy lobby, though the restaurant's not great. ₹1740

EATING AND DRINKING

Though it's no gourmet's paradise, Jammu has plenty of cheap snack joints and vegetarian *vaishno dhabas*. Hotel restaurants are the best choice if you want meat and more comfortable surroundings.

Falak KC Residency, Vir Marg ☏ 0191 252 0770. This odd revolving restaurant on top of the smart business hotel has good Indian and international cuisine. Most main courses more than ₹300. Daily 12.30–11pm.

7

SECURITY CONCERNS AND SCAMS IN KASHMIR

Although the situation in Kashmir is calmer than it has been for twenty years, it is still essential to check the current state of affairs with reputable media sources before travelling – Ⓦkashmirtimes.com is a good local resource. No tourists have been directly targeted since 1995 (see box, pp.466–467) but if trouble is flaring up, then you will have to endure a very heavy **military presence** and may even run the risk of getting literally caught in the crossfire or an act of **terrorism**. You should not necessarily be put off by government advisories, however, as these tend to be extremely cautious and Kashmir has remained on the list of no-go areas even when at its most peaceful.

Once you are in Jammu and the Kashmir Valley, you will find that **security** is taken very seriously and the vast majority of tourist sites, such as temples, mosques, museums and forts, are heavily guarded. You are usually prohibited from taking bags or electronic items inside; tokens are given when you check them but if you are not comfortable about leaving possessions like cameras or mobile phones in the cloakroom, then it is better to lock them in your hotel. Both Jammu and Srinagar **airports** have extra-high security and passengers are often not allowed into the terminal until a certain time before departure – usually two hours but occasionally less. Sometimes no hand luggage is allowed on board, so it is best to check in advance.

The other potential pitfall to be aware of is the variety of **scams** perpetrated on unsuspecting tourists by unscrupulous Kashmiris, especially in Delhi's Paharganj area or Jammu. It is best to take with a pinch of salt any advice about safety in Kashmir (or the lack of it) from people who approach you. Some make out you will be in danger without a guide and then try to sell you a tour costing hundreds, if not thousands of dollars. These people should be avoided at all costs, as should agents trying to sell you rooms on houseboats (see p.471). At best you will be overcharged and in the worst case you will be seriously ripped off.

JKTDC Café Baja-u-Bahu Gardens. This simple café is a nice spot to enjoy a cup of tea or for a snack, such as a samosa or sandwich. Daily: summer 8am–10pm; winter 9am–9pm.

Mehfil Hotel Samrat, Gumat Bazaar ☎0191 254 7402. Reasonable veg and non-veg Indian and Chinese dishes such as American chop suey are available at this low-key hotel restaurant for around ₹100–150. Daily 7am–10pm.

Mughal Darbar Vir Marg ☎0191 257 0579. One of the best places to try Kashmiri cuisine, including its famous richly spiced mutton dishes (₹120–160). Beautifully decorated. Daily 8am–10.30pm.

Regal Opposite Ragunath temple entrance ☎99063 47288. Busy restaurant that feeds the hungry crowd of pilgrims with tasty veg food, ranging from north Indian curries to southern snacks. Most items cost less than ₹100. Daily 9am–10.30pm.

Around Jammu

Although most foreigners head straight towards the Kashmir Valley, there are a couple of places you might consider stopping near the road to Srinagar, which is predictably punctuated by army signs spouting militaristic slogans – "the power behind the punch" is a common one. Around 40km north of Jammu a road branches off to the small town of **Katra**, which is the base for the 12km hike to **Vaishno Devi** temple. One of the region's most important pilgrimage centres, the cave shrine is entered via an ankle-deep stream, whose chilly waters you must brave in order to get *darshan* of the image of the goddess, a triple incarnation of the female *shakti*.

A further 70km along, just as the pines start to take over from the deciduous forest, the main road passes by **Patnitop**, an alpine-style resort, popular with lowland Indians for its views, fresh air and relative accessibility.

ARRIVAL AND DEPARTURE

By bus/jeep Both Katra and Patnitop are connected by frequent buses and jeeps with Jammu. The latter is also

ACCOMMODATION

Saraswati Near Shalimar Garden, Katra ☎ 0191 254 9065, ⓦ jktdc.co.in. Nestled below the verdant mountains, this three-storey concrete government block contains a variety of rooms, some deluxe, others with common bathrooms. ₹600/₹800

AROUND JAMMU

only a short walk from the main Jammu–Srinagar road.

Tourist Establishment On hill above centre of resort, Patnitop ☎ 0191 257 9554, ⓦ jktdc.co.in. Set amid tall pines, this is the nicest of the three state-run hotels here. There is a choice between standard rooms and cute huts. Decent restaurant, too. ₹1500

Kashmir

Long before **KASHMIR** was immortalized in the eponymous Led Zeppelin song it had already achieved legendary status with Western travellers, from officers of the British Raj to the first hippie overlanders in the 1960s. No stint in the Subcontinent was complete without an idyllic sojourn on the famous houseboats of the capital **Srinagar** (see box, p.471), which is at the heart of the idyllic Kashmir Valley.

By the end of the 1980s, the **tourist business** was booming alongside agriculture, and had in fact overtaken it as the region's main source of income. This all came to an almost overnight halt with the onset of the conflict in 1989 (see box, pp.466–467). Only in recent years has the situation stabilized enough to see the number of visitors swell to more than a trickle, though it's still well below the 1980s zenith and domestic tourists continue to greatly outnumber foreigners. Most people content themselves with a visit to **Srinagar**, although the towns of **Gulmarg** and **Pahalgam**, both in prime trekking territory, are regarded as being safe these days, as is the lovely town of **Sonamarg** on the Kargil road. Nevertheless, before setting off for Kashmir, it is wise to check on the current security situation (see box opposite).

There could hardly be a greater contrast than that between the hot and dusty plains around Jammu and the cool green belt of the **Kashmir Valley**. Apart from the geographical divide, separated as they are by a rise in altitude of more than 1000m, there are huge cultural and religious differences. While the whole area around Jammu is predominantly Hindu, the Kashmir Valley and its capital, **Srinagar**, are distinctly Muslim, hence the notorious sectarian problems (see box, pp.466–467). The initial impression of the Vale of Kashmir, whether you approach it via the Jawahar Tunnel, which cuts through the mountains from Jammu in the south, or via the Zoji La pass from Kargil to the east, remains one of a lush rural paradise guarded by the grandeur of the surrounding peaks, the mighty **Pir Pinjal** range snow-capped except in the very height of summer. Vivid green fields of corn and wheat form a patchwork quilt with

KASHMIR'S CLIMATE

Although Kashmir's climate is not as harsh as in neighbouring Ladakh and the road up from Jammu is kept open by the army, the winter months see some seriously sub-zero temperatures and heaps of snow. If you do come between November and March, you will need to bring very warm clothing – locals wear a thick woollen cloak called a *pheran*. By contrast, as much of the Kashmir Valley, including Srinagar itself, is well under 2000m in altitude, high summer can be surprisingly hot, sometimes topping 35OC. Therefore, the late spring or early autumn is the best time to come, especially if you intend to do any trekking. The former sees the meadows carpeted in an abundance of flowers, while the latter offers warm golden days, chillier nights and the first signs of the foliage changing hue.

fruit orchards and groves of nut trees, principally walnut and almond. These are most often lined with towering poplars and willows, hence the preponderance, on the approach to the capital, of shops selling high-quality cricket bats. Heavy industry has yet to appear in the valley.

Srinagar

Steeped in tradition and set in one of the most dramatic locations in India, with majestic mountains pressing in on three sides, **SRINAGAR** is the summer administrative capital of J&K. All too often associated with strife in recent times, this city of almost a million inhabitants is most famous with tourists for the **houseboats** that line the fringes of **Dal Lake** and **Nageen Lake**, as well as the central section of the **Jhelum River**, a tributary of the Indus. The town has some other splendid attractions, which in recent years have once again been opened to visitors after long periods of being off-limits.

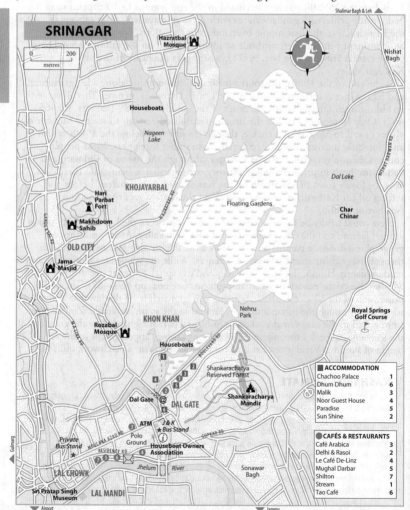

SRINAGAR

Shalimar Bagh & Leh

Hazratbal Mosque

Nishat Bagh

Houseboats

Nageen Lake

Dal Lake

KHOJAYARBAL

Hari Parbat Fort

Floating Gardens

Char Chinar

Makhdoom Sahib

OLD CITY

Jama Masjid

Nehru Park

KHON KHAN

Royal Springs Golf Course

Rozabal Mosque

Houseboats

Shankaracharya Reserved Forest

Shankaracharya Mandir

Dal Gate

DAL GATE

@

ATM

J&K Bus Stand

Private Bus Stand

Polo Ground

Houseboat Owners Association

LAL CHOWK

Jhelum River

Sonawar Bagh

Sri Pratap Singh Museum

LAL MANDI

Airport

Jammu

ACCOMMODATION	
Chachoo Palace	1
Dhum Dhum	6
Malik	3
Noor Guest House	4
Paradise	5
Sun Shine	2

CAFÉS & RESTAURANTS	
Café Arabica	3
Delhi & Rasoi	2
Le Café De-Linz	4
Mughal Darbar	5
Shilton	7
Stream	1
Tao Café	6

THE LULLABY OF LAPPING LAKES

Few experiences are as romantic as lounging on an exquisitely carved **houseboat**, watching kingfishers diving for their dinner between the floating lilies or gazing at the moon reflected on the darkened waters. These floating hotels of one to four rooms have existed for generations; many originated at the peak of the British Raj, when Victorian families would spend the entire hot season here. They originally chose to stay on boats to get around laws that forbade them from owning land.

Srinagar has no fewer than 1200 **houseboats** lining the shores of the **two main lakes**, Dal and Nageen, and the banks of the Jhelum River. And that's just the official ones. Consequently, it can seem like a bewildering business to know where to start looking. The golden rule is to ignore **touts** in town (or further afield) who try to get you to commit yourself with all sorts of promises. Some establishments are also infamous for poor service and rip-offs – most of those connected with the name Baktoo, in particular, should be given a wide berth.

One approach is to organize your stay through the **Houseboat Owners Association** (daily 8am–6pm; ☏0194 245 0326), whose office is opposite the Tourist Reception Centre on Residency Road. They produce a clear price list of the different categories of boat from Deluxe Class (₹5400 for a double with full board) down to D Class (₹1500 for the same). They will also help you negotiate moderate discounts on these prices at slack times such as late summer and off-season.

Undoubtedly the best way to find a houseboat, however, is to hole up in a town hotel for the first night and then hire a **shikara**, a colourful flat-bottomed water taxi that is steered with a heart-shaped paddle, to embark on a scouting mission. This way you can stop and look at a number of boats to compare prices, amenities and location. Once you've chosen your vessel, be sure to agree exactly what is included in the price, such as the number of meals, drinks or whether a daily *shikara* ride to the shore is part of the deal. It is also wise to make it clear if you do not want to be pestered by floating salesmen and that there should be no deterioration in houseboat service if you do turn them away. Note that some houseboats on the far side of Dal Lake and most on Nageen are accessible by road or footpath. Those on Nageen are generally a little cheaper. It is also worth noting that there has been a potential threat to the very existence of houseboats since a 2009 government mandate that they should install expensive sewage treatment units in order to prevent further water pollution. The allegedly corrupt Department of Lakes and Waterways has yet to enforce any regulations, though.

Chief among these are two of the most venerated mosques, **Jami Masjid**, deep in the heart of the atmospheric **Old City**, and the lakeside **Hazratbal**. Another important Islamic place of worship is the Sufi shrine of **Makhdoom Sahib**, halfway up to the inaccessible fort.

Srinagar, like the rest of Kashmir, is predominantly Muslim, even more so since the advent of serious trouble in 1990, when almost all the Hindu Pandits were driven out – though this region was known for centuries for its religious tolerance, where adherents of all the major eastern faiths lived side by side. The most important Hindu temple is the **Shankaracharya Mandir**, atop a hill overlooking Dal Lake.

The bustling centre of Srinagar, which revolves around the two main thoroughfares of Residency Road and MA Road, is not particularly appealing, although the bazaar area of **Lal Chowk** at the western end of these streets holds more interest. Of the city's secular sights, options include the engaging **Sri Pratap Singh Museum** and the Mughal pleasure gardens that surround the lake, such as **Shalimar Bagh** and **Nishat Bagh**.

Dal Lake

Srinagar would be a major draw on the strength of its Himalayan scenery alone, but it is the city's serene lakes and grand gardens that make it irresistible. There are actually several large bodies of water dividing the urban sprawl into its constituent neighbourhoods but by far the largest is **Dal Lake**, with a surface area of approximately 21 square kilometres. The lake is usually as flat as a mirror and incredibly photogenic, with the surrounding peaks reflected in the greenish-blue waters. Apart from the houseboats that cover its southern end, nearest the town centre, the lake is famous for its floating gardens, as well as the floating flower and vegetable market, best visited in the early morning.

Nehru Park, the lake's largest island, has pontoons for swimming (₹50/hr) and even waterskiing facilities (₹600 including lesson). The best way to tour the lake is on a *shikara* (see box, p.471). These officially cost ₹300 per hour to hire but, depending on your bargaining skills, you can get them for around ₹200. Some houseboats can arrange self-paddle *shikaras* for around ₹300 per day.

The Mughal gardens
Daily 6am–7pm • ₹10

The perimeter of Dal Lake is punctuated by lavishly ornamental gardens, a legacy of the seventeenth-century Mughal period. These collections of fountains, terraced lawns and flowerbeds reach their zenith in **Nishat Bagh**, halfway along the eastern shore, and **Shalimar Bagh**, set a little way back from the northeastern corner.

Hazratbal mosque

On the northwestern shore of Dal Lake stands **Hazratbal mosque**, whose huge white marble dome towers above its spacious courtyard. It is considered to be Kashmir's holiest shrine, as its plain but vast interior houses a single hair of the prophet Mohammed, purportedly brought from Medina centuries ago. The scene of heavy fighting during the worst of the insurgency, it is once more a tranquil spot that welcomes outsiders along with the constant stream of worshippers.

Nageen Lake

Tucked between the spit of land behind Hazratbal mosque and the Old City, **Nageen Lake** is much smaller than more famous Dal Lake. It does not have any particular sights but is more peaceful for that very reason and quite a popular choice for anymore wanting a more serene houseboat experience.

Jama Masjid

In the heart of the atmospheric **Old City**, crammed with wooden buildings displaying the typical Kashmiri architectural style of carved balustrades and ornate frames on windows and doors, stands **Jama Masjid**, Srinagar's largest mosque. Built of sturdy stone and brick with the distinctive pagoda-style wooden minarets unique to Kashmir, it was erected between 1398 and 1402 by Sikander But-Shikoh but has been destroyed by fire and rebuilt several times, most recently in 1961.

Rozabal

A couple of kilometres to the southeast of Jama Masjid, the small square mosque of **Rozabal**, with its simple octagonal dome, is purported to enshrine the tomb of Jesus by those who subscribe to the theory – the subject of Holger Kersten's *Jesus Lived In India*– that Christ actually lived to a ripe old age and died here in Kashmir. The mosque is kept locked but you may be able to peep inside through the gate. Note that this is the one place in Srinagar that foreigners sometimes encounter hostility from locals who do not appreciate this attention, so it is best to move on if asked.

Makhdoom Sahib

One of Kashmir's most vibrant places of worship, the Sufi shrine of **Makhdoom Sahib**, is located on the northern edge of the Old City, halfway up towards Hari Parbat Fort on the hill of the same name. The fort, occupied by the army, is not open to the public; the shrine is open to men only. Good views across Nageen Lake and further afield can be enjoyed by all from the nearby steps.

Sri Pratap Singh Museum

Tues–Sun 10am–4pm • ₹50 (₹10) • ⊕ spsmuseum.org

The outstanding **Sri Pratap Singh Museum** is in Lal Mandi, south across the Jhelum River from Lal Chowk. The former maharaja's palace houses a huge collection that includes archeological findings such as terracotta tiles and Buddhist tablets, decorative arts from enamelware to papier mâché, textiles, manuscripts and miniature paintings. At the time of writing most of the exhibits were in the process of being moved to the adjacent new building, though it was planned that the natural history and mineral sections should remain in the old palace.

Shankaracharya Mandir

Daily 7.30am–5pm

The city's main Hindu temple, **Shankaracharya Mandir**, occupies the crest of the eponymous hill south of the Boulevard. The temple itself is nothing special architecturally speaking and security is predictably tight, but the views across the city and lakes to the mountains beyond are quite breathtaking. The walk up is a gentle thirty-minute stroll, although security guards sometimes demand that you take an auto-rickshaw.

ARRIVAL AND DEPARTURE

SRINAGAR

By plane Srinagar's airport (☎0194 243 0334) lies 14km south of the city centre. Taxis into town cost a whopping ₹545; auto-rickshaws around half that. There are flights to Delhi (8–10 daily; 1hr 25min–2hr), Jammu (3–5 daily; 30min) and Leh (1 weekly on Weds; 1hr).

By bus Government buses and jeeps pull in on Residency Rd, a few minutes' walk south of Dal Gate, while the private bus stand is around 1km further west. Destinations

include Delhi (2 daily; 22–24hr), Jammu (10 daily; 11–12hr), Kargil (6–8 daily; 10–11hr) and Leh (4–6 daily; 2 days).

By jeep/minibus Jeeps run to Jammu (8–9hr), Kargil (6–7hr) and Leh (14–15hr), operating more flexible hours and costing at least half as much again than buses. Shared minibuses are the best way to travel within the Kashmir Valley.

INFORMATION

Tourist office The Tourist Reception Centre (☎0194 245 2691, ⊕ jktourism.org) is right beside the government bus stand on Residency Rd and claims to be open 24hr. It's not all that much help beyond selling a useful ₹10 map and handing out a few glossy brochures. Beware of the touts who hang around here and other arrival points to besiege tourists with offers of houseboats, guided tours and "cheap" carpets.

Services Nida Tours & Travel (on lakeside path north of Dal Gate, ☎0194 250 1684, ✉nidatours@yahoo.com) is principally a travel agent; they can book tickets and arrange treks (see p.477) or give useful advice on them, as can Kashmir Valley Travels (town side of Dal Gate, ☎0194 210 7527).

ACCOMMODATION

Although most foreign tourists stay on houseboats (see box, p.471), there are plenty of conventional hotels and lodges. During the domestic April–June high season the prices below are likely to double.

HOTELS

★ **Chachoo Palace** New Rd, Khon Khan, Dal Lake ☎99068 20423, ✉hotelchachoopalace@yahoo.com. This quaint wooden hotel with a lakeside lawn has the charm of a houseboat with easier access and cheaper prices. The comfortable attached rooms have TV and the friendly proprietors can also provide food. ₹**500**

Dhum Dhum Dal Gate ☎0194 245 0779. This backpackers' favourite is convenient for transport and the town but rather noisy. Rooms are passable, with bare-bones furniture and average bathrooms. ₹**400**

Malik Boulevard, Dal Lake ☎0194 247 3672,

⊕hotelmalik.in. A typically characterless square block beside the lake, with decent, well-furnished but somewhat overpriced rooms. The restaurant does standard Indian and Continental cuisine. ₹**1300**

Noor Guest House Abi-Buchara, Dal Lake ☎0194 245 0872, ✉noorguesthouse@gmail.com. Nice and colourful place with a great front lounge and delightful garden. Mixture of attached and non-attached rooms. Bicycles and motorbikes for rent. ₹**300**/₹**600**

Paradise Boulevard, Dal Lake ☎0194 250 0663, ⊕hotelparadisesgr.org. Several blocks of rather classy rooms that vary in size. Set just off the lakefront, and cheaper

7

than its mid-range competitors. Decent restaurant. ₹**1000**

Sun Shine Boulevard, Dal Lake ☎0194 247 2469, ⓦhotelsunshinesgr.com. Painted a suitably bright yellow, this modern hotel is among the best in this range. The smart rooms are more expensive with a lake view. There's a pleasant coffee shop on the roof. ₹**2000**

HOUSEBOATS

Prices are for a double room only unless otherwise indicated.

★ **Bendemeer** Khon Khan, Dal Lake ☎99067 46121, ⓔnewbendemeer@gmail.com. Accessible from the road, this beautifully carved deluxe- class boat provides expert service and excellent value. One of three adjacent vessels owned by the same people. Full board ₹**3000**

Dunhill Khon Khan Dal Lake ☎96229 46264. Also accessible from the road. You won't find a boat much cheaper than this simple two-room affair, run by a mother and daughter. Two meals cost an extra ₹500/day. ₹**600**

Kashmir View Dal Lake ☎99067 22897. The dining room, where meals are ordered à la carte, is particularly attractive. More rooms in the attached pontoon hotel. Free self-paddle *dunghy*, a wooden, canoe-type boat. Hotel ₹**600**, houseboat ₹**1000**

Lakeview East side of Nageen Lake ☎99065 32015.

Actually a group of eight jointly run houseboats with varying room sizes and standards of comfort – reception is in a nearby house. Well kept and good value. ₹**1000**

Mughal Sheraton Dal Lake ☎99068 64924, ⓔmughalsheraton@yahoo.co.in. This is the biggest of four sister boats, all with spacious and luxurious rooms. Three daily meals for two cost ₹1000 extra. ₹**2500**

New Bulbul Dal Lake ☎99064 76085. A small boat in a pleasantly open part of the lake and with a homely feel. Good value, especially if you take the full board option. Full board ₹**900**

Royal Pleasure Nageen Lake ☎0194 242 4675, ⓔroyaljeweller@rediffmail.com. A rarity in being a new construction but intricately carved in traditional style. Very friendly, and the owners also run treks. Half board ₹**1200**

Sea Palace Dal Lake ☎99067 22914. A small group of boats of varying sizes, with rooms of differing quality. One unusual feature is that some have baths. Two daily meals cost ₹600/couple. ₹**1000**

★ **Veena Palace** Dal Lake ☎97970 56134, ⓔfindous123@yahoo.co.in. Set in a water lily pond, this friendly place offers extremely good value. The rooms are not lavish but comfortable and attractively furnished. Meals for two cost ₹600 daily for veg, ₹800 for non-veg. ₹**500**

EATING AND DRINKING

The **local cuisine** of Kashmir is known as *wazwan* and is heavily meat-based, its signature dish being *rogan josh*, richly spiced mutton in a tomato sauce. Dishes often include **saffron**, as the costly spice is grown locally and therefore less expensive than elsewhere. Kashmiris are also famed for their green *kahwa* tea, drunk sweet and milkless but often spiced with cardamom or almond. Alcohol is still pretty hard to come by, though you may find it in a few flashy hotel bars.

CaféArabica Hotel Broadway, Moulana Azad Rd ☎0194 245 9001. The trendiest spot in town, serving coffee, snacks and main dishes, including trout fish for ₹300, at the back of the luxury hotel, which also has a bar. Daily 9am–11pm.

Le Café De-Linz Residency Rd ☎0194 247 2618. Housed in a unique but rather dingy round building, this restaurant offers a long Indian menu and some Chinese food, with most items around ₹100 or less. Daily noon–9pm.

Delhi & Rasoi Boulevard, Dal Lake ☎94197 78141. Simple pure veg restaurant with courtyard or interior seating, where you can enjoy south Indian snacks like *masala dosa* and *uttapam* for ₹60–70 or thalis for ₹150. Daily 8am–11pm.

Mughal Darbar Residency Rd ☎0194 248 2202. Mostly tandoori and particularly traditional *wazwan* dishes, with

some fish too. There is a bakery as well. Items cost ₹60–150. Daily 8am–10.30pm.

Shilton Residency Rd ☎99064 45609. As well as the standard Indian and Chinese menu, you can get reasonable steaks and local specialities in this popular establishment with a dark interior for around ₹120–400. Daily 9am–midnight.

Stream Boulevard, Dal Lake ☎0194 250 0244. Upmarket restaurant with an outdoor patio and interior with comfortable seating and sylish decor, offering lamb, chicken, veg, pizzas and the like for ₹200–400. Daily 11.30am–11pm.

★ **Tao Café** Residency Rd ☎0194 247 2230. One of Srinagar's most atmospheric restaurants, where you can dine in the lovely rose garden. There is a wide choice of favourites from India, China and Tibet for ₹100–200. Daily 10am–10pm.

Gulmarg

Some 56km west of Srinagar and at an elevation of around 2700m, **GULMARG**, whose name means "flower meadow", is a pleasant escape from the city but is rather more

geared towards domestic tourists and can get very crowded. It is also rather spread out, with no discernible centre. The meadow itself is 1km wide and more than 3km long, allowing ample room for picnics, pony rides and even one of the world's highest golf courses. The surrounding pine slopes can be ascended for a distant view of **Nanga Parbat** (8126m)to the north, in Pakistan-controlled Baltistan. Less active visitors can ascend one of these slopes on a gondola for the princely sum of ₹300 for the first stage and ₹500 for the second. In winter, the gondola is used to get to the top of Gulmarg's **skiing** slopes, which are underused but highly recommended for the quality of powdery snow. Government rates for skiing, displayed on boards around the resort, are ₹250 per hour, while equipment rental is ₹1000 per day. Two private operations that can arrange packages and lessons are Kashmir Alpine (☎0195 425 4638, ⊚kashmiralpine.com), which purports to be the world's smallest ski shop and also runs trekking expeditions during the warmer months, and the British-run Mountain Tracks (⊚ski-gulmarg .co.uk). Other activities include **pony riding** (₹300 for the first hour, then ₹200/hour) and **zorbing** (₹125/person for a 150m ride).

ARRIVAL AND DEPARTURE GULMARG

By bus/jeep Although there is an erratic bus service, the best way to get to Gulmarg from Srinagar is by shared jeep (₹80) or you can hire a vehicle for a day-trip for ₹1600.

ACCOMMODATION AND EATING

Accommodation is plentiful but uniformly overpriced, prices below doubling between April and June, Gulmarg's short season of popularity with domestic tourists. There are just a couple of restaurants outside the hotels, plus a smattering of *dhabas* in the centre of the bazaar.

Bakshi In the middle of the bazaar ☎0195 425 4566. Simple and popular canteen-style restaurant specializing in Jain pure veg dishes, including filling thalis for around ₹100. Daily 8am–9pm.

Gulmarg Sahara On road into town ☎0195 425 4505. Elongated first-floor hotel, all wood and corrugated iron, with reasonably comfortable rooms spread above its lounge and several adjacent shops. **₹1500**

New Zam Zam Far northern end of the bazaar ☎0195 425 4402, ⊜hotelzamzam@yahoo.in. Slightly faded but attractive wood-panelled hotel, with wicker chairs and old carpets adding a colonial feel. Good views from the balconies and a decent restaurant. **₹1200**

Welcome Hotel Towards the northern end of the bazaar ☎0195 425 4412, ⊚welcomehotelsgr.com. Large modern hotel with intricately carved wooden ceilings and functionally furnished rooms, plus a fairly decent restaurant. **₹2000**

Pahalgam and around

Kashmir's number-one trekking base (see box opposite), **PAHALGAM** enjoys a stunning location around 100km east of Srinagar in the deep-cut Lidder Valley, whose pine-crested ridges ascend sharply from each bank of the chilly, fast-flowing river. The town, whose altitude is 2139m, is mostly located on the slightly flatter east bank and the lower surrounding slopes. Main Market, the central thoroughfare of the modern town, runs parallel to the river and contains most of the facilities, while the more pleasant **old village** lies 1.5km north, beyond Pushwan Park with its fancy flowerbeds and topiary. The only sight of interest is the **Mamal temple**, across the bridge above the west bank of the river, but eager pony men tout rides at fixed government rates (₹300/hr) to various local beauty spots. Nearby **Aru** makes a quieter alternative base.

ARRIVAL AND INFORMATION PAHALGAM

By bus/jeep The bus service from Srinagar to Pahalgam is rather unreliable but it is easy to get a bus or shared jeep (₹70) to Anantnag (known locally as Islamabad) and another from there to Pahalgam (₹80).

Tourist information The Tourist Reception Centre on the main market (☎0193 624 3224) claims to be open 24/hr in season.

TREKKING IN KASHMIR

Despite being prime trekking territory, the security concerns of recent decades mean that relatively few foreigners take to the hills. The once booming industry is slowly picking up, however, and there have been no unpleasant incidents involving foreign tourists since 1995 (see box, pp.466–467). Given the tricky terrain and the delicate political situation, however, it is not recommended to set off without at least a **local guide**. Trekking agencies in Srinagar (see p.473) and some hotels mentioned in the text can provide fully organized treks with ponies, porters and all the requisite equipment.

Pahalgam is still the main base for treks, which vary in length and level of difficulty from the two-day round trips within the Lidder Valley to the week-long hike to Panikhar in Ladakh's Suru Valley (see p.503). You can also do some good walking from **Sonamarg**, the last main town in Kashmir before the Zoji La pass. Conditions for trekking are pretty hot and uncomfortable in high summer and the shoulder seasons of late spring and early autumn are the optimum time to trek; the best **map** is Sheet 1 in Leomann's India Himalaya series. For more general advice about trekking, see Basics (p.56).

AMARNATH TREK

Kashmir's most trodden route becomes crowded during the July/August full moon with thousands of pilgrims, who flock to see the natural ice lingam in the **Amarnath cave**, at an altitude of 3962m. The trek from Pahalgam usually takes four days and includes overnight stays at Chandanwari (2900m), Sheshnag (3720m) and Panchtarni (3933m). The final stage involves crossing the Mahagunas pass. After visiting the cave, you can either return the same way or make the more direct descent to Baltal, 8km east of Sonamarg on the Srinagar–Leh road.

KOLAHOI GLACIER TREK

The five-day trek from Pahalgam to the impressive but receding **Kolahoi glacier** (3400m) can be shortened by a day if you take a jeep to the first overnight stop at picturesque Aru (2414m). The next day the ascent is via alpine meadows and streams to Lidderwat (3049m), before a gentler stage to Satlanjan (3150m), which allows you to preserve energy for the steep climb to the glacier and back to Lidderwat on the following day. You can then walk back down to Aru or Pahalgam itself on the fifth day.

SONAMARG TO WANGAT TREK

This popular route takes you through a beautiful stretch of the mountains via a number of delightful **high altitude lakes**, where fishing is permitted with a permit (available through agents in Srinagar). The first staging post at Nichnai (3620m) affords views of the Thajiwas glacier before the second day's walking undulates to Kishanar (3819m). On the third day you cross over the 4191m Bazkal Gali pass and descend past Gadsar Lake to overnight at Dubta Pani (3280m). Next day's walking takes in the seven tiered lakes of Satsar en route to the region's largest body of water, Gangabal Lake (3507m) for a final night's camping before the descent to Wangat, where there are buses and jeeps to Srinagar.

ACCOMMODATION

★ **Beach Resort** Old village ☎94693 92930, ✉mehrajganai2001@gmail.com. Small guesthouse with comfortable rooms of varying sizes, the best of which overlook the lush lawn and river. The welcoming owners also run treks. ₹400

Pahalgam Hotel Main Market ☎01936 243252, ⓦpahalgamhotel.com. The town's premier hotel, occupying vast riverside grounds. The spacious rooms in its alpine-style blocks are lavishly furnished. This supposedly fixed price is negotiable off-season. Full board ₹7000

Paradise Main Marlet ☎01936 243368, ⓦparadisegroupofhotels.com. Functional if slightly dull hotel with wi-fi, adequate rooms and a decent restaurant on the ground floor. The same people own the fancier *Paradise Inn* beyond the old village. ₹1800

EATING

Dana Pani Main Market ☎01936 243234. Modern and clean place, great for filling Punjabi veg meals for ₹60–80. Also offers good south Indian cuisine. Daily 7.30am–10.30pm.

Prince Hotel Opposite the bus stand ☏01936 243130. This place has a slightly grubby appearance but is the best independent restaurant for Kashmiri *wazwan* cuisine, including lots of meat in rich spicy sauces. Daily 8am—10pm.

★**The Trout Beat** Pahalgam Hotel, Main Market ☏01936 243252. Expertly prepares the eponymous fish and other non-veg food.

Aru

The peaceful village of **Aru** is located is located a 12km jeep ride or gentle walk northwest of Pahalgam amid splendidly verdant mountain terrain. It has a growing reputation as a relaxed hangout and is particularly popular with chillum-toting Israelis. It also makes a good base for local hikes and longer treks, such as the three-day treks to the Thajiwas glacier (see below) or Amarnath cave (see box, p.477).

ACCOMMODATION AND EATING ARU

Rohella Centre of village ☏01936 211339, ✉rohellarafi@yahoo.co.in. Very friendly guesthouse with basic but clean rooms. The pick of the small bunch here, it also does decent food. ₹300

Sonamarg

The third rural location in Kashmir that has started to see a return of foreign travellers is **SONAMARG**, 84km northeast of Srinagar. Perched beside the River Sindh and surrounded by forests of pine, fir, beech and sycamore, with towering peaks all around, it is a scenic spot to break the journey to Kargil or Leh. This is also the place with the best display of spring and early summer flowers. A further attraction is that the **Thajiwas glacier** is just 4km away and so makes one of the easiest treks. The only downside is that its location on the vital Srinagar–Leh road means there is a fairly constant and noticeable military presence.

ARRIVAL AND INFORMATION SONAMARG

By bus Frequent buses ply the main route between Srinagar and Ladakh, although those heading east are liable to be full.
By jeep A seat in a shared jeep should cost around ₹200, while a whole vehicle will cost ₹1500 one way to Srinagar.
Trekking For local trekking with expert guidance and service, contact Shabir Ahmad Naik (☏94691 03995).

ACCOMMODATION AND EATING

Hill View Slightly north of main road ☏0194 2417351. Somewhat ugly block, containing spacious and modern but highly overpriced rooms. The restaurant does buffet lunch (₹250) and dinner (₹350). ₹3000
Narrinder Punjabi Middle of bazaar, main road ☏0194 2417205. Pretty basic place with a few no-frills attached rooms above a plain restaurant that serves tasty Punjabi food. ₹1000
Tourist Establishment West side of town ☏0194 245 7927, ⊛jktdc.co.in. Comfortable state government hotel set on a grassy meadow with large double rooms and some suites. They also manage the huts near Thajiwas glacier. ₹2000

Ladakh

LADAKH (La-Dags – "land of high mountain passes") is India's most remote and sparsely populated region, a high-altitude **desert** cradled by the Karakoram and Great Himalaya ranges and crisscrossed by myriad razor-sharp peaks and ridges. Variously described as "Little Tibet" or "the last Shangri-La", the culturally and administratively separate area is one of the last enclaves of Mahayana **Buddhism**, which has been the principal religion for nearly a thousand years. This is most evident in Ladakh's medieval **monasteries**: perched on rocky hilltops and clinging to sheer cliffs, these **gompas** are both repositories of ancient wisdom and living centres of worship.

The highest concentration of monasteries is in the **Indus Valley** near **Leh**, the region's

RESTRICTED AREAS AND PERMITS

Parts of Ladakh are still inaccessible to casual tourists, but with the easing of tensions along the border between India and China, much of this incredible land has been opened up. Three areas in particular are now firm favourites with travellers: the **Nubra Valley** bordering the Karakoram Range to the north of Leh; the area around **Pangong Tso**, the lake to the east of Leh; and the region of **Rupshu** with the lake of **Tso Moriri**, to the southeast of Leh. Indian and foreign visitors need **permits** to visit these areas. In theory, these are only issued to groups of at least four people accompanied by a guide, and only through a local tour operator. However, in practice travel agents are generally happy to issue permits to solo individuals travelling independently, though you'll have three imaginary friends (usually people applying at the same time) listed on the permit to bump up the numbers. As long as your name and passport number are on the permit, the checkpoints are quite relaxed about how many of you there are.

Permits are issued by the **District Magistrate's Office** in **Leh** but the office now only deals through Leh's many **tour operators** (see p.484), who charge a **fee** – usually around ₹100 per head. As some of the areas in question (such as Pangong Tso) are served by infrequent public transport, you may well find yourself using a tour operator anyway, in which case they will include your permit in the package. You will need two photocopies of the relevant pages of your passport and visa. Provided you apply in the morning, permits are usually issued on the same day. Once you have your permit, usually only valid for a maximum period of seven days, make at least five copies before setting off, as checkpoints sometimes like to keep a copy when you report in. They may also occasionally spot-check to see the original copy. If you go on an organized trip, however, the driver takes care of all this and you may never even handle your permit.

7

capital. Surrounded by sublime landscapes and crammed with hotels, guesthouses and restaurants, this atmospheric little town, a staging post on the old Silk Route, is most visitors' point of arrival and an ideal base for side trips. North of Leh, across the highest driveable pass in the world, **Khardung La**, lies the valley of **Nubra**, where sand dunes carpet the valley floor. It is also possible to visit the great wilderness around the lake of **Tso Moriri** in **Rupshu**, southeast of Leh, and to glimpse Tibet from the shores of **Pangong Tso** in the far east of Ladakh. For all these areas you will, however, need a permit (see above). West of Leh, beyond the windswept **Fatu La** and **Namika La** passes, Buddhist prayer flags peter out as you approach the predominantly Muslim district of **Kargil**. Ladakh's second largest town, at the mouth of the breathtakingly beautiful **Suru Valley**, is the jumping-off point for **Zanskar**, the vast wilderness in the far south of the state that forms the border with Lahaul in Himachal Pradesh.

Far beyond the reach of the monsoons, Ladakh receives little snow, especially in the valleys, and even less rain (just 100mm per year). Only the most frugal methods enable its inhabitants to **farm** the thin sandy soil, frozen solid for eight months of the year and scorched for the other four. In recent years, **climate change** has meant even drier winters with even less snow; the consequent loss of snow-melt has put pressure on traditional farming and irrigation, resulting in a real fear of drought.

GETTING AROUND   LADAKH

Two main "highways" connect Ladakh with the rest of India: the legendary Srinagar–Leh road and the route up from **Manali** (see p.441), almost 500km south. These two, plus the rough road from Kargil to Padum in Zanskar, also link the majority of Ladakh's larger settlements with the capital. **Bus services** along the main Indus Valley highway are frequent and reliable but grow less so the further away you get from Leh. To reach off-track side valleys and villages within a single day, it is much easier to splash out on a jeep **taxi** – either a Gypsy or a Tata Sumo – available in Kargil and Leh. The alternative, and more traditional way to get around the region, of course, is by **trekking**.

Leh

As you approach **LEH** for the first time, via the sloping sweep of dust and pebbles that divides it from the floor of the Indus Valley, you'll have little difficulty imagining how

FESTIVALS IN LADAKH

Most of Ladakh's Buddhist **festivals**, in which masked **chaam** dance dramas are performed by lamas in monastery courtyards, take place in January and February, when roads into the region are snowbound. This works out well for the locals, for whom the festivals relieve the tedium of the relentless winter, but it means that few outsiders get to experience some of the northern Himalayas' most vibrant and fascinating spectacles. Recently, however, a few of the larger *gompas* around Leh have followed the example of **Hemis**, and switched their annual festivals to the **summer** to attract tourists. The tourist office in Leh produces a listings booklet called *Ladakh*, giving dates for forthcoming years.

Gompas that hold their *chaams* (dance festivals) in winter or spring include **Matho** (mid-Feb to mid-March), **Spitok** (mid-Jan), **Tikse** (late Oct to mid-Nov) and **Diskit** (mid-Feb to early March) in Nubra. Other important festivals in Ladakh include **Losar** (the Tibetan/Ladakhi New Year), which falls any time between mid-December and early January.

SUMMER FESTIVALS

Hemis Tsechu: July 7–8, 2014; June 26–27, 2015. See p.490.
Karsha Gustor, Zanskar: July 24–25, 2014; July 14–15, 2015. See p.506.
Thak Thok Tsechu: Aug 6–7, 2014; July 25–26, 2015. See p.491.
Sani Nasjal, Zanskar: Aug 9–10, 2014; July 30–31, 2015.
Phyang Tsedup: July 24–25, 2014; July 14–15, 2015. See p.497.
Festival of Ladakh: Sept 1–15. This popular J&K Tourism-sponsored two-week event, held principally in Leh, is designed to extend the tourist season. It features archery contests, polo matches, Bactrian camels from Nubra and traditional Ladakhi dance along with some tedious speeches.

the old trans-Himalayan traders must have felt as they plodded in on the caravan routes from Yarkhand and Tibet: a mixture of relief at having crossed the mountains in one piece, and anticipation of a relaxing spell in one of central Asia's most scenic towns. Spilling out of a side valley that tapers north towards eroded snow-capped peaks and looks south towards the majestic **Stok-Kangri massif** (6120m), the Ladakhi capital sprawls from the foot of a ruined Tibetan-style palace – a maze of mud-brick and concrete flanked on one side by cream-coloured desert and on the other by a swathe of lush, irrigated farmland.

Despite being increasingly touristic, the abiding impression of Leh remains that of a lively yet laidback place to unwind after a long bus journey. Attractions in and around the town itself include the former **palace** and **Namgyal Tsemo gompa**, perched amid strings of prayer flags above the narrow dusty streets of the **old quarter**, whose layout has not changed since it was founded in the sixteenth century. A short walk north across the fields brings you to the small monastery at **Sankar**, which harbours accomplished modern Tantric murals and a thousand-headed Avalokitesvara deity. Leh is also a good base for longer **day-trips** out into the Indus Valley. Among the string of picturesque villages and *gompas* within reach by bus are **Shey**, site of a derelict seventeenth-century palace, and the spectacular **Tikse gompa**.

Brief history

Leh only became regional capital in the seventeenth century, when Sengge Namgyal shifted his court here from Shey, 15km southeast, to be closer to the head of the Khardung La–Karakoram corridor into China. The move paid off: within a generation the town had blossomed into one of the busiest markets on the Silk Road. Leh's prosperity, managed mainly by the Sunni **Muslim** merchants whose descendants live in its labyrinthine old quarter, came to an abrupt end with the closure of the Chinese border in the 1950s. Only after the Indo-Pak wars of 1965 and 1971, when India rediscovered the hitherto forgotten capital's strategic value, did its fortunes begin to look up. Today, khaki-clad *jawans* (soldiers) and their families from the nearby military and air force bases are the mainstay of the local economy in winter, when **foreign visitors**, to whom the region was opened up in 1974, are few and far between. Leh has more than doubled in size since the advent of tourism and is a far cry from the sleepy Himalayan town of the early 1970s.

The bazaar

After settling into a hotel or guesthouse, most visitors spend their first day in Leh soaking up the atmosphere of the **bazaar**. Eighty or so years ago, this bustling tree lined boulevard was the busiest market between Yarkhand and Kashmir. Merchants from Srinagar and the Punjab would gather to barter for pashmina wool brought down by nomadic herdsmen from western Tibet, or for raw silk hauled across the Karakorams on Bactrian camels. These days, though the street is awash with kitsch curio shops and handicraft emporiums, it retains a distinctly Central Asian feel. Even

7

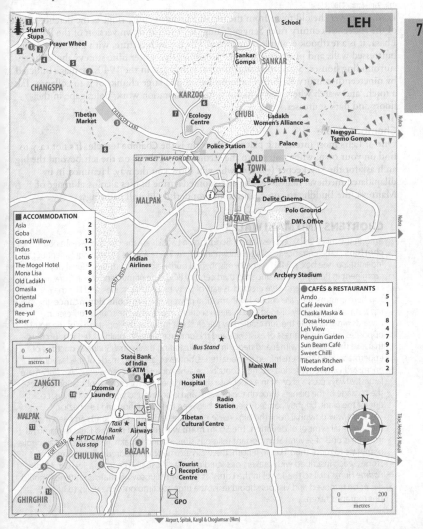

LEH

School

Shanti Stupa
Prayer Wheel

Sankar Gompa — SANKAR

CHANGSPA

KARZOO

Tibetan Market

CHANGSPA LANE

Ecology Centre

CHUBI

Ladakh Women's Alliance

Namgyal Tsemo Gompa

Police Station

Palace

SEE 'INSET' MAP FOR DETAIL

OLD TOWN

Chamba Temple

MALPAK

Delite Cinema

BAZAAR

Polo Ground

DM's Office

■ ACCOMMODATION	
Asia	2
Goba	3
Grand Willow	12
Indus	11
Lotus	6
The Mogol Hotel	5
Mona Lisa	8
Old Ladakh	9
Omasila	4
Oriental	1
Padma	13
Ree-yul	10
Saser	7

Indian Airlines

Archery Stadium

● CAFÉS & RESTAURANTS	
Amdo	5
Café Jeevan	1
Chaska Maska & Dosa House	8
Leh View	4
Penguin Garden	7
Sun Beam Café	9
Sweet Chilli	3
Tibetan Kitchen	6
Wonderland	2

Chorten

FORT ROAD

0   50
metres

ZANGSTI

State Bank of India & ATM

Dzomsa Laundry

MAIN BAZAAR

Bus Stand

SNM Hospital

Mani Wall

Radio Station

MALPAK

Taxi Rank

Jet Airways

Tibetan Cultural Centre

HPTDC Manali bus stop

CHULUNG

BAZAAR

N

GHIRGHIR

Tourist Reception Centre

GPO

0   200
metres

Airport, Spitok, Kargil & Choglamsar (9km)

Nubra

Nubra

Tikse, Hemis & Manali

ALTITUDE SICKNESS

As Leh is 3505m above sea level, some travellers, and especially those who arrive by plane from Delhi, experience mild **altitude sickness** (see p.50). The best way to avoid the symptoms – persistent headaches, dizziness, insomnia, nausea, loss of appetite or shortness of breath – is to rest for at least 48 hours on arrival. Drink 3–4 litres of water a day, avoid alcohol, and don't exert yourself.

if you're not shopping for trekking supplies, check out the surviving **provision stores** along the street, where bright pink, turquoise, and wine-red silk cummerbunds hang in the windows.

The palace

Daily 9am–5pm • ₹100 (₹5)

Lording it over the old town from the top of a craggy granite ridge is the derelict **palace** of the sixteenth-century ruler Sengge Namgyal. A scaled-down version of the Potala in Lhasa, it is a textbook example of medieval Tibetan architecture, with gigantic sloping buttressed walls and projecting wooden balconies that tower nine storeys above the surrounding houses. Since the Ladakhi royal family left in the 1940s, damage inflicted by nineteenth-century Kashmiri cannons has caused large chunks of it to collapse. Take a torch, and watch where you walk: in spite of restoration work, holes gape in the floors and dark staircases.

Chamba temple

One of Leh's most interesting places of worship is the **Chamba temple**. It's not easy to find on your own; when you get to the second row of shops on the left beyond the big arch ask for the key-keeper (*gonyer*), who will show you the way. Hemmed in by dilapidated medieval mansions, the one-roomed shrine houses a colossal image of Maitreya, the Buddha to come, and some wonderful old wall paintings.

CHORTENS AND MANI WALLS

Among the more visible expressions of Buddhism in Ladakh are the chess-pawn-shaped **chortens** at the entrance to villages and monasteries. These are the Tibetan equivalent of the Indian *stupa* (see box, p.346) – large hemispherical burial mounds-cum-devotional objects, prominent in Buddhist ritual since the third century BC. Made of mud and stone (now also concrete), many *chortens* were erected as acts of piety by Ladakhi nobles, and like their southern cousins, they are imbued with mystical powers and **symbolic significance**: the tall tapering spire, normally divided into thirteen sections, represents the soul's progression towards nirvana, while the sun cradled by the crescent moon at the top stands for the unity of opposites, and the oneness of existence and the universe. Some contain sacred manuscripts that, like the *chortens*, wither and decay in time, illustrating the central Buddhist doctrine of impermanence. Those enshrined in monasteries, however, generally made of solid silver and encrusted with semiprecious stones, contain the ashes or relics of revered *rinpoches* (incarnate lamas). Always pass a *chorten* in a clockwise direction: the ritual of circumambulation mimics the passage of the planets through the heavens and is believed to ward off evil spirits. Look out for the giant, brightly painted specimen between the bus station and Leh bazaar.

A short way downhill from the big *chorten*, near the radio station, stands an even more monumental symbol of devotion. The 500m **mani wall**, erected by King Deldan Namgyal in 1635, is one of several at important religious sites around Ladakh. Ranging from a couple of metres to more than 1km in length, the walls are made of hundreds of thousands of stones, each inscribed with prayers or sacred mantras – usually the invocation *Om Mani Padme Hum*: "Hail to the Jewel in the Lotus". It goes without saying that such stones should never be removed and visitors should resist the urge to climb onto the walls to have photographs taken.

Namgyal Tsemo Gompa

Daily 7–9am & 5–8pm

Once you are acclimatized to the altitude, the stiff early-morning hike up to **Namgyal Tsemo Gompa**, the monastery perched precariously on the shale-covered crag above Leh palace, is a great way to start the day. Two trails lead up to "the Peak of Victory", whose twin peaks are connected by giant strings of multicoloured prayer flags; the first and most popular path zigzags across its south side from the palace road, while a second scales the more gentle northern slope via the village of Chubi, the route followed by the lama from Sankar *gompa* (see below) who tends to the shrine each morning and evening. Alternatively, you could drive here along the dirt track that turns left off the main Khardung La highway, 2km north of the bus stand.

Approaching the *gompa* from the south, the first building you come to is the red-painted **Maitreya temple**. Thought to date from the fourteenth century, the shrine houses a giant Buddha statue flanked by *bodhisattvas*. However, its wall paintings are modern and of less interest than those in the **Gon-khang** (temple of protector deities) up the hill.

The Shanti Stupa

A relatively new addition to the rocky skyline around Leh is the toothpaste-white **Shanti Stupa** above Changspa village, nearly 3km west of the bazaar by road. Inaugurated in 1983 by the Dalai Lama, the "Peace Pagoda", whose sides are decorated with gilt panels depicting episodes from the life of the Buddha, is one of several such monuments erected around India by a "Peace Sect" of Japanese Buddhists. It can be reached by car, or on foot via a steep flight of more than 500 steps, which winds up from the end of Changspa Lane via the café just below the *stupa*. Its broad terrace makes an excellent spot to watch the sunrise, and is popular with early morning yogis.

Sankar Gompa

Daily 7am–6pm • ₹30

Nestled amid the shimmering poplar coppices and terraced fields of barley that extend up the valley behind Leh, **Sankar Gompa**, 2km north of the town centre, is among the most accessible monasteries in central Ladakh. You can get here either by car or on foot: turn left at the *Antelope Guesthouse* on the main road north out of Leh and then right onto the concrete path that runs alongside the stream. Sankar appears after about fifteen minutes' walk, surrounded by sun-bleached *chortens* and a high mud wall. You can also work your way through the fields behind the burgeoning tourist area of Karzoo.

The monastery, a small under-*gompa* of Spitok, is staffed by twenty monks, and is the official residence of the **Kushok Bakula**, Ladakh's head of the Gelug-pa sect. Above the **Du-khang** (main prayer hall) stands the *gompa*'s principal deity, Tara, in her triumphant, one-thousand-armed form as Dukkar, or "Lady of the White Parasol", presiding over a light, airy shrine room whose walls are adorned with a Tibetan calendar and tableaux depicting "dos and don'ts" for monks – some of which are very arcane indeed. Another flight of steps leads to the *gompa* **library** and, eventually, a roof terrace with fine views towards the north side of Namgyal Tsemo hill and the valley to the south.

ARRIVAL AND DEPARTURE — LEH

By plane There are flights from Leh airport to: Delhi (3–5 daily; 1hr 30min), Jammu (2 weekly; 1hr) and Srinagar (1 weekly; 45min). A taxi from the airport, 5km southwest of town on the main Srinagar highway, costs ₹200–250. Tickets can be booked and confirmed at the Air India/Tushita Travels office on Fort Rd (daily 10am–5pm; 01982 252076). The Jet office is located in the main bazaar (Mon–Sat 10am–5pm, Sun 10am–3pm; 01982 250999, jetairways.com), not far down from the mosque.

By bus Nearly all services (see relevant accounts for destinations around Leh) to Kargil (May–Oct 2–4 daily; 9–10hr), Manali (June–Sept 2–3 daily; 2 days; see p.448) and Srinagar (June–Oct 2–4 daily; 20–30hr) use the main bus stand, a 15min walk or a ₹60 taxi ride south of the bazaar, although deluxe HPTDC Manali buses terminate on Fort Road, near the *Hotel Dreamland*. Tickets for HPTDC's alternate-days "super-deluxe" bus to Manali (₹1800 including an overnight stop and meal in Keylong) can be booked at their upstairs office on Fort Rd (daily 10am–8pm; ☎9697 376404). Costing less than half the price are the ramshackle state transport corporation buses run by HPSRTC and J&KSRTC, bookable the day before departure at the town bus stand. Several agencies along Fort Rd sell tickets for private buses to Manali for around ₹1000–1200.

By jeep Jeeps are widely used for transportation around Ladakh and to destinations further afield, such as Manali (17–19hr; ₹1800–2000/person) and Srinagar (14–15hr; ₹1600–1800/person). They can be booked through travel agents or preferably direct from the Taxi Operators Co-operative (see below).

GETTING AROUND

By taxi The main rank of the Taxi Operators Co-operative (daily 6am–7pm; ☎01982 253039) is almost directly opposite the tourist information centre. Each driver carries a list of fixed fares to just about everywhere you might want to visit in Ladakh, taking into account waiting time and night halt charges. These rates apply to peak season; reductions of up to forty percent can be had at other times. Prices are high as the season is so short – expect to pay around ₹90 to Changspa,

₹750 return to Tikse, ₹1600 to Hemis and ₹7000 to Pangong Lake.

Bike rental Mountain bikes can be rented from Luna Ladakh Travel, Zangsti Rd (50m from Dzomsa Laundry), for ₹250/day.

Motorbikes Although several places now hire motorcycles, with the going rate starting around ₹700/day for an Enfield, you should check the bikes carefully. By far the most reliable agency is Enntrax Tours (☎01982 250603), just south of Fort Rd ; mopeds here are ₹500/24hr.

INFORMATION AND TOURS

Tourist office The main J&K tourist reception centre (Mon– Sat 10am–4pm; ☎01982 252094, ⊛jktourism .org), 3km from the bazaar on the airport road, is too far out of town and hardly worth visiting. The mini tourist information centre on Ibex Rd in the bazaar (June to mid-Sept; Mon–Sat 8am–6pm, Sun 10am–4pm, mid-Sep to May daily 10am–4pm; ☎01982 253462) is a bit more helpful.

Tour operators Reliable agents recommended for trekking and jeep safaris include: Yama Adventures,

Changspa Lane (☎01982 250833, ⊛yamatreks.com); Mountain Trails, 2 Hemis Complex, Zangsti Rd (☎01982 254855); Footprints, Fort Rd (☎01982 251799, ⊛footprintsindia.com); and Dreamland Trek & Tours, Fort Rd (☎01982 250784, ⊛dreamladakh.com). Alternatively, smaller agencies such as Oriental Travels, at the *Oriental Guest House* in Changspa (☎01982 253153), offer a more personalized service. Some agents also offer rafting on the River Indus (see box, p.496).

ACCOMMODATION

Leh is glutted with **accommodation**, much of it refreshingly neat and clean. Prices are subject to strict regulation but have crept up in recent years. Due to the short season, they do not fluctuate much but you can bargain in the shoulder months. Most of the town's cheap **guesthouses** are in the leafy areas of Changspa to the west and Karzoo to the north, where you may find a sunny en-suite "glass room" with a view all to yourself. Rooms in Leh's few **mid-range** and increasing number of **upmarket hotels** all come with attached bathrooms and piped hot water. **Homestays** can be arranged in villages on trekking routes around Leh, which offer a dinner, bed and breakfast for around ₹500–800/person (₹1000–1500/couple), with ten percent of the proceeds going towards village development programmes. Information and booking links can be found at ⊛himalayan-homestays.com.

Asia Changspa Lane ☎01982 253403, ⊛hotelasialadakh .com. Large riverside guesthouse consisting of three blocks, the oldest of which has shared bathrooms. Sociable roof terrace-cum-café, as well as yoga, meditation, reiki, Pranic healing and free wi-fi. ₹400/₹1000

Goba Down path off Changspa Lane ☎01982 253670, ⊛gobaguesthouse@gmail.com. Well-maintained traditional house with a pleasant garden and views of Shanti Stupa. Rooms are immaculate, and those in the new block have attached bathrooms. ₹200/₹800

Grand Willow Fort Rd ☎01982 251835, ⊛grandwillowladakh.com. Blessed with beautifully ornate wooden balconies and mountain views, the hotel's spacious rooms have cable TV and colourful soft furnishings. Good Ladakhi restaurant too. ₹2630

★ **Indus** Malpak, off Fort Rd ☎01982 252502, ⊜masters_adv@yahoo.co.in. Cheap singles and a wide range of doubles, all with attached bathrooms and solar-heated water. Central, pleasant, with a family atmosphere and open in winter. Fee for wi-fi. ₹400

Lotus Upper Karzoo ☎01982 250265, ⊛lotushotel .in. The laidback staff and leafy location make this a relaxing and welcoming option, although the rooms are better at other places. It's done in a traditional style and the more expensive rooms have mountain views. ₹3160

The Mogol Hotel Changspa Lane ☎01982 253439, ⊛hotelmogol.com. Smart new place with warm yellow external walls, welcoming staff and large, very comfortably furnished rooms, half of them with TV. ₹2900

Mona Lisa Down path off Changspa Lane ☏01982 252456, ✉riggs_pisces@yahoo.co.in. Run by a family who lovingly tend the vegetable garden. Simple attached rooms and a smarter new extension under construction. Breakfast available. ₹500

Old Ladakh Old town ☏01982 252951, ✉old_ladakh@rediff.com. Ladakh's first-ever guesthouse is homely and central, with a choice of rooms, some attached: the kitsch "deluxe" one (pink pillows and Tibetan rugs) is a real winner. New block with restaurant under construction. ₹300/₹600

★**Omasila** Changspa Lane ☏01982 252119, ⓦhotelomasila.com. Friendly, accommodating 35-room hotel, including five suites and six centrally heated rooms. The large terrace offers sweeping views and the dining room serves excellent dishes featuring home-grown vegetables. Open year round. ₹2800

★**Oriental** Below the Shanti Stupa, Changspa ☏01982 253153, ⓦoriental-ladakh.com. Genuinely welcoming guesthouse with spotless rooms (mostly attached), free filtered water, computers and wi-fi, superb views and nourishing home-cooked meals. Open all year; booking advisable in summer. ₹250/₹600

Padma Ghirghir, off Fort Rd ☏01982 252630, ⓦpadmaladakh.net. The traditional old building has immaculate rooms with shared baths and a kitchen; the modern annexe has centrally heated attached doubles and a rooftop restaurant. Both offer wi-fi, views and a garden. ₹660/₹2570

Ree-yul Zangsti, on lane off Fort Rd ☏01982 252911, ✉limbijal@rediffmail.com. Tucked in a quiet corner of the centre, boasting a lovely courtyard and exquisitely carved woodwork, this convivial place has clean rooms, all attached, some with TV. ₹700

Saser Karzoo, up the path from the Ecology Centre ☏01982 250162, ✉namy_z@yahoo.com. Modern hotel that successfully embraces elements of traditional architecture, with a pleasant garden courtyard and comfortable rooms with baths – a bargain during low season. ₹500

7

ENVIRONMENTAL ISSUES AND VOLUNTARY ORGANIZATIONS

Damage to the **environment** has become an issue of paramount importance in Ladakh. Although plastic bags are officially banned in Leh, as they clog up the vital river systems that the state so depends on, shopkeepers continue to use them. Plastic mineral-water bottles are a particular headache; you are advised to bring your own filtration system (see box, p.47) with you, or refill your plastic water bottles at guesthouses with filtered water or at Leh's **Dzomsa Laundry**, near the main bazaar. As well as providing safe water and delicious local juices, such as seabuckthorn, this establishment provides a vital service in ecologically sound washing, using biodegradable detergent and water at a safe distance from habitation. It also serves as a co-op for rural, semiliterate people.

With limited resources at their disposal, a handful of **voluntary organizations** battle to protect Ladakh's delicate environment and ancient culture. These include **LEDeG** (the Ladakh Ecological Development Group) – a local nongovernmental organization that aims to counter the negative impact of Western-style "development" by fostering economic independence and respect for traditional culture. Its headquarters are five minutes' walk north of the main bazaar at the **Ecology Centre** (Summer Mon–Fri 9.30am–5pm; winter Mon–Sat 10am–4pm; closed 2nd Sat of the month; ☏01982 253221, ⓦledeg.org), which has a small **library** and a **handicraft shop** selling locally made clothes, thangkas, T-shirts, books and postcards.

Helena Norberg-Hodge, the Swedish-born founder of LEDeG, is also behind the International Society for Ecology and Culture (**ISEC**) website (ⓦisec.org.uk), devoted to promoting sustainable ways of living in both "developing" and "developed" countries. ISEC employs **volunteers** in Ladakh on the **Farm Project** to help local farmers maintain traditional farming methods. Closely aligned to the Farm Project, the co-operative Women's Alliance of Ladakh (**WAL**), based in Chubi, north of central Leh (Mon–Sat 10am–5pm; ☏01982 250293, ⓦwomenallianceladakh.org), works to reinforce traditional Ladakhi culture. One of their more noticeable achievements was to ban plastic bags from Leh in 1998; the alliance now boasts more than five thousand members in one hundred villages. The best time to visit them is during one of their **festivals**, where you can sample local produce, pick up handicrafts and catch exhibitions of colourful traditional costume and folk dance performances.

Another group is **LEHO** (Ladakh Environment and Health Organization), which places its emphasis on the proper utilization of land and water resources and the management of livestock on a sustainable basis. Their office and showroom is on the first floor of the Himalaya Complex, beneath the Amdo restaurant on Main Bazaar (Mon–Sat 10am–5pm; ☏01982 253691, ✉sultanaleho@yahoo.com).

EATING AND DRINKING

As Leh's thriving restaurant and café scene has been cornered by the refugee community, **Tibetan food** has a high profile alongside tourist-oriented Chinese and European dishes. **Beer** is widely available in most of Leh's tourist restaurants, but while **chang**, a local barley brew, is harder to come by.

Amdo Main Bazaar ☎ 01982 253114. Popular Tibetan restaurant, offering freshly prepared food that is generally excellent but can take up to an hour to appear; main courses ₹50–80. Serves hearty *tsampa* porridge. Daily 10.30am–5.30pm.

Café Jeevan Changspa Lane ☎ 94191 29157. Very smart and clean pure-veg Sikh-run restaurant featuring a variety of cuisines in the ₹60–100 range. Lovely decor both downstairs and in the partially enclosed roof terrace. Daily 7am–11pm.

Chaska Maska & Dosa House South of Fort Rd ☎ 96229 68043. Cuisine from both ends of the Subcontinent plus a few western dishes. Best *masala dosas* in town, for ₹70. Daily 7am–11pm.

Leh View Main Bazaar ☎ 94697 73429. The best 360° view in town from the roof terrace is offset by painfully slow service and inflated prices, making this a better bet for a drink than a meal. Daily 8.30am–11pm.

Penguin Garden Old Rd, just off Fort Rd ☎ 96222 71777. A great place for a beer, *German Bakery* snacks or a multicuisine meal, such as ample sizzlers (around ₹150), in a leafy garden location, fairy lit at night. Daily 7am–10.30pm.

Sun Beam Café Fort Rd ☎ 99069 78621. Cute first-floor restaurant with wicker ceiling and colourful lanterns. Most Indian, Chinese, Continental and Tibetan mains cost ₹100–250. The best deal is *momos* with soup. Daily 7.30am–10.30pm.

Sweet Chilli Changspa Lane ☎ 01982 251855. Large garden restaurant surrounded by poplars, with firepits, a cushioned chill-out zone and Italian, Russian and Thai dishes as well as the usual food. Daily 10am–11pm.

★ **Tibetan Kitchen** Down alley off Fort Rd ☎ 96978 11510. Considered by many, locals and visitors alike, to offer the best Tibetan food in town. Great mutton *thukpas* for ₹90; *momos* a bit pricey at ₹120. Daily 11am–10.30pm.

★ **Wonderland** Changspa Lane ☎ 96229 72826. Excellent rooftop joint with a cushioned chill-out corner and unusually attentive service. Good selection of Indian, Chinese, Tibetan and Continental mains for ₹80–160. Daily 7am–10pm.

SHOPPING

Between June and September, Leh is swamped by almost as many transient Tibetan and Kashmiri **traders** as souvenir-hungry tourists. Most of the merchandise hawked in their temporary boutiques and stalls comes from outside the region: papier-mâché bowls, shawls and carpets from Srinagar, jewellery and miniature paintings from Jaipur, and "Himalayan" handicrafts, including *thangkas*, churned out in Nepal and by Tibetan refugees in Old Delhi. Prices tend to be high, so haggle hard, and don't be conned into shelling out for cleverly faked "antiques". Much of the "silver" on sale is in fact cheap white metal. There are quite a few **bookshops** dotted around the centre and along Changspa Lane; most have the usual selection of secondhand travellers' novels but one or two offer a wider selection.

TRADITIONAL ARTEFACTS AND CLOTHING

Tibetan and Ladakhi curios account for the bulk of the goods on sale in Leh's emporia, though most of these are run by Kashmiris. For authentic Ladakhi souvenirs, try the outfitters and provision stores dotted along the main bazaar. There are also some genuine Ladakhi/Tibetan markets in the bazaar and along Changspa Lane. Turquoise is sold by the *tolah* (there are eighty *tolahs* to a kilogram), and quality and age determine the price. You'll find vendors sitting on the main roads. The lanes running off the bazaar towards old town are home to hole-in-the-wall seamstress shops that can produce custom-fit local clothing, including dapper stovepipe hats (*tibi*), hand-dyed *gonchas*, raw silk cummerbunds, tie-dyed rope-soled shoes (*pabbu*) and Bhutanese cross-button shirts. Yak wool shawls go for around ₹800–1000. The handicraft shops at the environmental organizations (see box, p.485) are other sources of quality traditional clothing, including hand-knitted woollen jumpers, shawls, hats and socks. Most of the wool gathered in Ladakh lands up in the Kashmir Valley for milling and weaving, and few of the pashmina shawls on offer in the shops along Fort Rd are genuine. If money is no object, you could splash out on a *perak*, a long Ladakhi headdress, encrusted with turquoise, which costs upwards of ₹5000.

DIRECTORY

Banks and exchange The J&K Bank, 1st Floor, Himalaya Shopping Complex, Main Bazaar and the State Bank of India on the main market square have exchange facilities. Both these, plus the Punjab National Bank and a couple of other locations have ATMs. Private licensed operators include many hotels and travel agents around Fort Rd and along Changspa Lane.

Hospital Leh's overstretched, poorly equipped SNM

Hospital (☎ 01982 252014) is 1km south of the centre on the main road. For urgent medical treatment, contact a doctor through any upmarket hotel. PT Alamdar Chemist & Clinic (☎ 01982 252587), off the lower end of the bazaar, has a good English-speaking morning surgery from 9am.

Internet access Broadband internet cafés abound all over the main bazaar, Fort Rd and Changspa Lane. The standard charge is ₹1.50/min, wi-fi ₹1/min. Many hotels and some cafés now have free wi-fi.

Laundry Dzomsa Laundry (see box, p.485).

Libraries The Ecology Centre's excellent library (Mon–Sat 10am–4pm) keeps books on everything from agriculture to Zen Buddhism, as well as periodicals, magazines and files of articles on Ladakh and development issues. Students of Buddhism should check out the collection of books at the Chokhang Vihara Monastery, across from the State Bank of India, or the Tibetan Cultural Centre in the south of town.

Massage Indian Vedyashala on Changspa Lane (☎ 99069

99502) offers a range of Ayurvedic massages for around ₹500–1000.

Meditation, yoga and alternative therapy In high season small classes are run by the Mahabodhi Society in Changspa which specializes in Vipassana (☎ 01982 253689); their extensive complex in Devachan (☎ 01982 244155, ⓦ mahabodhi-ladakh.org) towards Choglamsar, 3km south of Leh, includes a meditation centre with courses ranging from three to seven days. The *Asia* guesthouse, Changspa Lane, houses a German-run Vajrayana Meditation and Healing Arts Centre.

Pharmacy Het Ram Vinay Kumar at the top of the main bazaar sells a range of allopathic pills and potions. For Tibetan medicine, two *amchis* at the LSTM Amchi Clinic, Changspa Lane (daily: July–Sept 8am–8pm; Oct–June 10am–4pm), speak English and charge ₹100 for a consultation using traditional diagnostic techniques.

Police ☎ 01982 252018, ☎ 100 for the operator.

Post The post office is in the main bazaar (Mon–Sat 10am–1pm & 2–5pm).

Southeast of Leh

Southeast of Leh, the Indus Valley broadens to form a fertile river basin. Among the spectacular Buddhist monuments lining the edges of the flat valley floor are **Shey**, site of a ruined palace and giant brass Buddha, and the stunning monastery of **Tikse**. Both overlook the main highway and are thus served by regular buses.

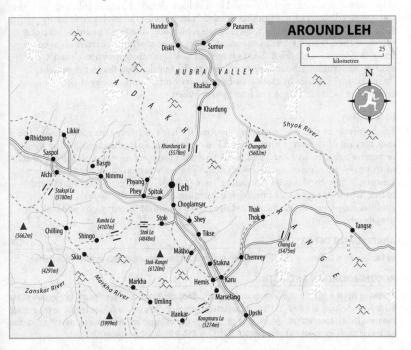

With the exception of **Stok Palace**, home of the Ladakhi queen, sights on the opposite (south) side of the Indus, linked to the main road by a relatively unfrequented and partly surfaced road, are harder to reach by public transport. South of Stok, **Matho** *gompa* is more famous for its winter oracle festivals than its art treasures, but is well worth a visit, if only for the superb views from its roof terrace. Further south still, continue to **Hemis**, Ladakh's wealthiest monastery and the venue for one of the region's few summer religious festivals. To side-step your fellow tourists without spending a night away from Leh, head up the austerely beautiful tributary valley back on the opposite side of the river from Hemis to the *gompas* of **Chemrey** and **Thak Thok**, the latter built around a fabled meditation cave.

East of Thak Thok, the road crosses the Chang La and then veers east to the high mountain lake of **Pangong Tso**, most of which lies in Tibet. Far more relaxing and inviting is the vast wilderness of **Rupshu**, with trekking possibilities around the shores of **Tso Moriri**, in the deep south. Permits are required for these three areas (see box, p.479).

Shey

SHEY, 15km southeast of Leh and once the capital of Ladakh, is now all but deserted, the royal family having been forced to abandon it by the Dogras midway through the nineteenth century. Only a semiderelict palace, a small *gompa* and a profusion of *chortens* remain, clustered around a bleached spur of rock that juts into the fertile floor of the Indus Valley. You can walk to Shey from Tikse monastery along a winding path that passes through one of Ladakh's biggest *chorten* fields with hundreds of whitewashed shrines of varying sizes scattered across the surreal desert landscape.

The palace

The **palace**, a smaller and more dilapidated version of the one in Leh, sits astride the ridge, below an ancient fort. Crowned by a golden *chorten* spire, its pride and joy is the colossal metal Shakyamuni Buddha housed in its ruined split-level temple (daily 6–9am; ₹30). Installed in 1633, the 12m icon allegedly contains a hoard of precious stones, mandalas and powerful charms. Entering from a painted antechamber, you come face to face with the Buddha's huge feet, soles pointing upwards. Upstairs, a balcony surrounding the statue's torso surveys the massive Buddha in better light. Preserved for centuries by thick soot from votary butter lamps, the gold-tinted murals coating the walls are among the finest in the valley.

Rock carving

Easily missed as you whizz past on the road is Shey's most ancient monument. The **rock carving** of the five Tathagata or "Thus gone" Buddhas, distinguished by their respective vehicles (*vahanas*) and hand positions (*mudras*), appears on a smooth slab of stone on the edge of the highway; it was probably carved soon after the eighth century, before the "Second Spreading" (see p.464). The large central figure with hands held in the gesture of preaching (turning the wheel of *dharma*), is the Buddha Resplendent, Vairocana, whose image is central in many of the Alchi murals (see p.499).

ARRIVAL AND DEPARTURE   SHEY

By bus Take any of the frequent Leh–Tikse minibuses to the main highway below the palace and walk up from there.

ACCOMMODATION AND EATING

Besthang Hotel A few minutes' walk down the lane behind the Shikhar ☏ 01982 252792. A converted traditional Ladakhi house with attached rooms, a pleasant garden and simple home cooking by arrangement. ₹**500**

Shilkhar On the main road. The only independent eating option in Shey, this no-frills restaurant serves a varied menu of Indian and Western food, most items costing ₹50–150. Daily 8am–8pm.

Tikse

Ladakh's most photographed and architecturally impressive *gompa* (₹30) is at **TIKSE**, 19km southeast of Leh. Founded in the fifteenth century, its whitewashed *chortens* and cubic monks' quarters rise in ranks up the sides of a craggy bluff, crowned by an imposing ochre- and red-painted temple complex whose gleaming golden finials are visible for kilometres in every direction. Tikse's reincarnation as a major tourist attraction has brought it mixed blessings: its constant stream of summer visitors spoils the peace and quiet necessary for meditation, but the income generated has enabled the monks to invest in major refurbishments, among them the **Maitreya temple** immediately above the main courtyard. Inaugurated in 1980 by the Dalai Lama, the shrine is built around a gigantic 14m gold-faced Buddha-to-come, seated not on a throne as is normally the case, but in the lotus position. The bright murals on the wall behind, painted by monks from Lingshet *gompa* in Zanskar, depict scenes from Maitreya's life. For most foreign visitors, however, the highlight of a trip to Tikse is the view from its lofty **roof terrace**. A patchwork of barley fields stretches across the floor of the valley, fringed by rippling snow-flecked desert mountains and a string of monasteries, palaces, and Ladakhi villages. To enjoy this impressive panorama accompanied by primeval groans from the *gompa*'s gargantuan Tibetan trumpets – played on the rooftop at the 7am puja – you'll have to stay overnight or arrange an early jeep from Leh.

7

ARRIVAL AND DEPARTURE   TIKSE

By bus Minibuses travel to Tikse (40min) via Shey (30min) from Leh every 30min. The last bus back to Leh leaves at 5pm.

ACCOMMODATION AND EATING

Chamba Hotel Down by the road ☎ 01982 267005. Offers reasonably comfortable attached rooms at rather inflated rates and a decent garden restaurant serving a varied menu from Tibetan food to pancakes, as well as a ₹300 buffet. April–Sept. **₹1500**

Monastery Guesthoue ☎ 01982 267005. The rooms behind the *gompa*'s simple but good restaurant are spacious and clean but only have shared facilities. This is one of Ladakh's most atmospheric places to stay, as you feel so much part of the monastic community. **₹400**

Stok

Just beyond the Tibetan refugee camp at **Choglamsar**, a road bears right across to the quieter west bank of the Indus. In the distance, at the head of a huge moraine, the elegant four-storey **Stok Palace** stands in the shadow of an intrusive TV mast, overlooking barley terraces studded with whitewashed farmhouses. Built early in the nineteenth century by the last ruler of independent Ladakh, it has been the official residence of the Ladakhi royal family since they were ousted from Leh and Shey two hundred years ago. The present gyalmo or "queen", Deskit Angmo, a former member of parliament, still lives here during the summer, and has converted one wing of her 77-room palace into a small **museum** (daily 8am–6pm; ₹30). The fascinating collection comprises some of the royal family's most precious heirlooms, including exquisite sixteenth-century **thangkas** illuminated with paint made from crushed rubies, emeralds and sapphires. The *pièces de résistance*, however, are the gyalmo's **peraks**. Still worn on important occasions, the ancient headdresses, thought to have originated in Tibet, are encrusted with slabs of flawless turquoise, polished coral, lapis lazuli and nuggets of pure gold. **Stok gompa** (dawn–dusk; ₹30), twenty minutes' walk up the valley, boasts a collection of dance-drama masks and some lurid modern murals painted by lamas from Lingshet *gompa* in Zanskar, the artists responsible for the Maitreya statue in Tikse (see above).

ARRIVAL AND DEPARTURE   STOK

By bus/taxi Buses leave Leh for Stok (40min) at 8am and 4.30pm. The last bus back to Leh leaves at 5.15pm. Alternatively, get off any more frequent bus along the east bank of the river at the junction in Choglamsar and take a taxi or even walk the last 4km.

ACCOMMODATION

Kalden Guest House At the foot of the palace 01982 242057. This friendly family guesthouse is extremely basic, with slightly tatty rooms and shared bathrooms, but fine for a night. ₹500

Skittsal 2km down the Choglamsar road 01982 242049, skittsal.com. Despite its panoramic valley views, this hotel seems unfeasibly large for such a remote location. The attached rooms are spacious but seriously overpriced. OK restaurant. May–Sep. ₹2800

Matho

MATHO, 27km south of Leh, straddles a spur at the mouth of an idyllic side-valley that runs deep into the heart of the Stok-Kangri massif. Though no less interesting or scenically situated than its neighbours, it sees comparatively few visitors. The *gompa* is the only representative in Ladakh of the **Sakyapa** sect, which held political power in thirteenth-century Tibet.

Despite its collection of 400-year-old *thangkas*, the monastery is best known for its **oracle festival**, Matho Nagran, held on the twenty-fifth and twenty-sixth day of the second Tibetan month (Feb/March). Two oracles, known as *rongzan*, are elected by lot every three years from among the sixty or so resident lamas. During the run-up to the big days, the pair fast and meditate in readiness for the moment when they are possessed by the spirit of the deity. Watched by crowds of rapt onlookers, they then perform all manner of death-defying stunts that include leaping blindfold around the *gompa*'s precipitous parapets while slurping kettle-fulls of *chang*, and slashing themselves with razor-sharp sabres without drawing blood. The events are rounded off with colourful *chaam* dances in the monastery courtyard, and a question-and-answer session in which the *rongzan*, still under the influence of the deity, make prophecies about the coming year.

You can admire the costumes and masks worn by the monks during the festivals in Matho's small **museum**, tucked away behind the Du-khang. Men are also permitted to visit the eerie **Gon-khang** on the roof, where the oracles' weapons and ritual garments are stored. The floor of the tiny temple lies under a deep layer of barley brought as harvest offerings by local villagers.

ARRIVAL AND DEPARTURE   MATHO

By bus Services leave Leh daily at 8am and 4.30pm, returning at 7.30am and 4pm.

Hemis

Daily 8am–6pm • ₹30

Thanks to its famous festival – one of the few held in summer, when the passes are open – **HEMIS**, 45km southeast of Leh, is visited in greater numbers than any other *gompa* in Ladakh. Every year in mid-July (see box, p.480), hundreds of foreigners join the huge crowds of locals, dressed in their finest traditional garb, which flock to watch the colourful two-day pageant. However, at other times, the rambling and atmospheric seventeenth-century **monastery** can be disappointingly quiet. Although it's one of the region's foremost religious institutions, only a skeleton staff of monks and novices are resident off-season. The main entrance opens onto the large rectangular courtyard where the festival **chaam dances** are performed. Accompanied by cymbal crashes, drum rolls and periodic blasts from the temple trumpets, the culmination of the event on the second day is a frenzied dismemberment of a dummy, symbolizing the destruction of the human ego, and thus the triumph of Buddhism over ignorance and evil. Once every twelve years, the Hemis festival also hosts the ritual unrolling of a giant *thangka*. The *gompa*'s prize possession, which covers the entire facade of the building, it was embroidered by women whose hands are now revered as holy relics. Decorated with pearls and precious stones, it will next be displayed in 2016. There is a **museum** (8am–6pm; ₹100 (₹50)) in the corner of the courtyard but the modest collection of *thangkas*, masks and musical instruments barely justifies the inflated fee.

ARRIVAL AND DEPARTURE

HEMIS

By bus Services are only frequent during the festival; at other times a single morning service leaves Leh at 9.30am and returns at noon, while another leaves at 4pm, staying the night at Hemis and returning at 7am. There are more frequent buses from Leh to Karu, a short taxi ride or long walk away.

ACCOMMODATION

Camping You can camp for free outside Chomoling village, 2km from Hemis.

Hemis Restaurant Below the monastery ☎01982 249072. There are a couple of tatty non-attached rooms, run by young *carrom*-playing monks, above the restaurant, which serves simple veggie food. You can camp for ₹100. ₹250

Hemis Spiritual Retreat Below the monastery ☎01982 249011. The rooms here also have shared bathrooms but are slightly better than those at *Hemis Restaurant*. Basic but tasty veg food is served in the garden. ₹300

Parachute Restaurant Chomoling, 2km from Hemis; no phone. Apart from local veg cuisine, this place also does western favourites such as a selection of pancakes and is a useful stop-off for trekkers heading for the Markha Valley. Daily 7am–8pm.

Chemrey

₹50, including museum

Clinging like a swallow's nest to the sides of a shaly conical hill, the magnificent *gompa* of **CHEMREY** sees very few visitors because of its location – tucked up the side valley that runs from Karu, below Hemis, to the Chang La pass into Pangong.

Founded in 1664 as a memorial to King Sengge Namgyal, the monastery is staffed by a dwindling community of around twenty Drugpa monks and their young novices. Its main **Du-khang**, off the courtyard on the lower level, boasts a fine silver *chorten* and a set of ancient Tibetan texts whose title pages are illuminated with gold-and-silver calligraphy. Upstairs in the revamped **Guru-La-khang** sits a giant brass statue of Padmasambhava. The new museum on the top floor houses statues, *thangkas*, scrolls and utensils.

ARRIVAL AND DEPARTURE

CHEMREY

By bus If you don't have your own vehicle, it takes around 50min to follow the dirt track down to the river and up to the monastery after the Leh–Thak Thok bus (see below) drops you off beside the main road.

Thak Thok

A few kilometres up the valley from Chemrey, above the village of **Sakti**, **THAK THOK** (pronounced *Tak-Tak* and meaning "rock roof") *gompa* shelters a cave in which the apostle Padmasambhava is said to have meditated during his epic eighth-century journey to Tibet. Blackened over the years by sticky butter-lamp and incense smoke, the mysterious grotto is now somewhat upstaged by the monastery's more modern wings nearby. As well as some spectacular twentieth-century wall paintings, the **Urgyan Photan Du-khang** harbours a collection of multicoloured yak-butter candle-sculptures made by the head lama. For a glimpse of state-of-the-art Buddhist iconography, head to the top of Thak Thok village, where a shiny new temple houses a row of huge gleaming Buddhas, decked out in silk robes and surrounded by garish modern murals.

Apart from during the annual **festival** (see box, p.480), Sakti is a tranquil place, blessed with serene views south over the snowy mountains behind Hemis.

ARRIVAL AND DEPARTURE

THAK THOK

By minibus Five minibuses a day leave Leh for Sakti (8am, 8.30am, noon, 2.30pm & 3.30pm); the last one back to Leh departs at 3.30pm.

ACCOMMODATION

There are plenty of ideal camping spots beside the river, although as ever you should seek permission before putting up a tent on someone's field.

7

Pangong Tso

Pangong Tso, 154km southeast of Leh, is one of the largest saltwater lakes in Asia, a long narrow strip of water stretching from Ladakh east into Tibet. Only a quarter of the 134km-long lake is in India, and the army, who experienced bitter losses along its shores in the war against China in 1962, jealously guard their side of the frontier. Until the mid-1990s, it was off-limits to visitors, and tourists still need a permit to come here (see box, p.479). The lake, at an altitude of 4267m, with the dramatic glacier-clad Pangong Range to its south and the Changchenmo Range reflected in its deep blue-green waters to the north, measures 8km across at its widest point and provides a tantalizing view of Tibet in the distance, although the bitter winds blowing over the brackish water make it one of the coldest places in Ladakh.

ARRIVAL AND DEPARTURE   PANGONG TSO

By bus The only public bus from Leh (Sun 6am) drops off visitors at the village of Spangmik before continuing to the restricted border area; it returns around 7am on Mon.

By jeep Most tourists come here on a two-day jeep safari from Leh (from ₹7000 for up to five people), organized by one of the many travel agents (see p.484).

ACCOMMODATION

There is basic accommodation and food at Spangmik but it is poor value, especially the hugely overpriced tent camp. Better deals can be had near other parts of the lake.

Padma Where the road first meets the lake ☏94198 19078, ✉tonybuddhist@yahoo.co.in. Meals are included with the rooms, which vary in size but all have shared bathrooms. They also rent tents with full board. ₹500

Tso Moriri

Famous for the large herds of *kiang*, or wild ass, which graze on its shores, the lake of **Tso Moriri**, 210km southeast of Leh, lies in the sparsely populated region of **Rupshu**. You need a permit to travel here (see box, p.479).

Nestling in a wide valley flanked by some of the highest peaks in Ladakh – **Lungser Kangri** (6666m) and **Chanmser Kangri** (6622m) – the 20km-long lake is home to flocks of migratory *nangpa* or bar-headed geese, as well as occasional herds of pashmina goats and camps of nomadic herders. Located on the shores of the lake at an altitude of 4595m, **Korzok** – the only large village in the area – is a friendly place with a small *gompa*. To help protect the fragile ecosystem against the influx of tourists, a new directive stipulates that no habitation can be built within 700m of the shoreline. Visitors should bring their own food supplies and make sure they take all their rubbish away.

The open spaces around Tso Moriri make for some pleasant **trekking**, including the relatively easy – if you are acclimatized – three-day, 40km circuit of the lake. Another route gaining popularity is the trail from Rumtse near Upshi via Tso Kar to Tso Moriri. Some trekking operators in Manali and Leh can arrange more ambitious routes such as the ancient trade route linking **Spiti** to Tso Moriri and Leh via Kibber. Treks start from around $50 per person per day in a group of four, which usually includes transport, food and tents.

ARRIVAL AND DEPARTURE   TSO MORIRI

By bus From Leh, three buses depart for Tso Moriri on the 10th, 20th and 30th of each month at 6am, returning the following day.

By jeep Most tourists visit on a jeep safari, which start at around ₹8500 for a two-day trip. These usually follow a circular itinerary through Upshi and Mahe Bridge, winding up at Korzok. From there they then continue on towards the Manali–Leh Highway, passing the lake of Tso Kar and Thukse village along the way.

FROM TOP TSO MORIRI; LEH (P.479) >

ACCOMMODATION

Accommodation is in local homestays dotted around the lake area and an overpriced tent colony or in Korzok, 1km back from the lake.

Lake View Guest House Just below Korzok bus stand ☎ 94193 45362. Fairly basic guesthouse with bright and breezy but rather tatty rooms and squat toilets in the shared bathrooms. ₹500

North of Leh: Nubra Valley

Until 1994, the lands north of Leh were off-limits to tourists and had been unexplored by outsiders since the nineteenth century. Now, the breathtaking **Nubra Valley**, unfolding beyond the world's highest stretch of driveable road as it crosses the **Khardung La** (5602m), can be visited with a seven-day **permit** (see p.479), which gives you enough time to explore the stark terrain and trek out to one or two *gompas*. The valley's mountain backbone looks east to the Nubra River and west to the Shyok River, which meet amid silver-grey sand dunes and boulder fields. To the north and east, the mighty Karakoram Range marks the Indian border with China and Pakistan. In the valley it's relatively mild, though **dust storms** are common, whipping up sand and light debris in choking clouds above the broad riverbeds.

Before the region passed into the administrative hands of Leh, Nubra's ancient kings ruled from a palace in **Charasa**, atop an isolated hillock opposite Sumur, home to the valley's principal monastery. Further up the Nubra River, the hot springs of **Panamik**, once welcomed by footsore traders, are blissfully refreshing after a day on a bumpy bus. By the neighbouring Shyok River, **Diskit**, surveyed by a hillside *gompa*, lies just 7km from **Hundur**, known for its peculiar high-altitude double-humped Bactrian camels.

The route north to Nubra, a steep and rough road that forces painful groans from buses and trucks, keeps Leh in sight for three hours before crossing the Khardung La, and ploughing down more gently towards the distant Karakoram Range. Due to its strategic importance as the military road to the battlefields of the Siachen Glacier, the road to Nubra is kept open all year round but conditions can be treacherous at any time.

ARRIVAL AND DEPARTURE NORTH OF LEH: NUBRA VALLEY

By bus Buses leave Leh for Panamik via Sumur (Tues & Thurs 6am; 7–8hr) and Hunder via Diskit (Tues & Sat 5.30am; 6–7hr). The buses return to Leh the next day and you should book your return journey on arrival.

By jeep Up to five people can rent a jeep from Leh taxi rank or any tour operator (see p.484). A complete three-day itinerary, including a visit to Diskit and Panamik, costs in the region of ₹8500 for the jeep plus driver.

GETTING AROUND

By bus There's one daily service between Diskit and Panamik, leaving Panamik at 7am and returning at 4pm.
By taxi There are few taxis in the valley but you can negotiate day-trips from Diskit or Sumur up either of the river branches for around ₹1200, or more like ₹2000 to go up both.

Sumur

Beyond the confluence of the Shyok and Nubra rivers, **SUMUR**, a sleepy oasis spread over a large area, is home to the valley's most influential monastery, **Samstem Ling gompa**, a pleasant forty-minute walk behind the village. Built in 1841, the *gompa* accommodates just under a hundred Gelug-pa monks of all ages. To catch the morning or evening pujas, you'll have to **stay** in Sumur.

ACCOMMODATION AND EATING SUMUR

AO Guesthouse 100m down lane from prayer wheel ☎ 01980 223506. Six of the basic doubles have attached baths, plus there's a relaxing garden, vegetarian café and camping for ₹100. ₹300/₹500

K-Sar Guest House 500m down lane from prayer wheel ☎ 01980 223574. All the spruce rooms are attached and you can camp for ₹300 in their spacious tents or for ₹100 in your own. ₹600

Silk Route Cottages At the top of the village ☎ 01982 253439, ⓦ hotelmogol.com. Nicely situated, spacious new bamboo cottages, all lavishly furnished. Managed by the *Hotel Mogol* in Leh. Four huge upmarket tents also available. ₹2800

Panamik

A one-hour bus journey (22km) up the valley from Sumur, **PANAMIK** (aka Pinchimik), a dusty hamlet overlooked by the pin-point summit of Charouk Dongchen, marks the most northerly point in India accessible to tourists. A kilometre past the underwhelming **hot springs**, beyond the stone walls that line the pitted road, is the village proper. Splitting into wide rivulets at this point, the sapphire Nubra seems shallow and tame, but it's not – heed local advice not to ford it, as there have been several reported accidents involving travellers.

A dot on the mountainside across the river, **Ensa gompa** is the main attraction. The walking route, three hours each way, passes through the village and crosses a bridge beyond the vast boulder field 3km upstream, then joins a wide jeep track above the river for several kilometres. Though the *gompa* is usually locked, the views from rows of crumbling *chortens* nearby make the climb worthwhile. If one of the few semiresident monks is there, however, you'll be shown inside to see the old wall paintings in the temples, and the footprint of Tsong-kha-pa, allegedly imprinted at this spot when he journeyed from Tibet to India in the fourteenth century.

ACCOMMODATION   PANAMIK

Bangka Guesthouse 600m beyond the hot springs ☎ 01980 247044. Typical of the handful of humble guesthouses in Panamik, this one is very basic with spartan rooms and shared bathrooms. ₹250

Hot Springs Guesthouse Just beyond the hot springs ☎ 01980 247043. Set in a pleasant flower-filled garden, the nearest place to the springs is also the only one with attached bathrooms, although the rooms lack character. ₹400

Diskit

DISKIT feels rather dull on first impressions, but it does possess an appealing old town, whose low, balconied houses lie below the main road before the diversion to the centre. Buses stop on Diskit's main road by the prayer wheel where the road descends through the old quarter to the bazaar, and then again on the new road to the bazaar, before continuing to Hundur. For the guesthouses, get off at the first bus stop. The main road climbs on past the newly constructed 30m statue of the seated Buddha up the hillside above the town to Diskit's picturesque **gompa**, built in 1420. If you're on foot, follow the long *mani* wall, which continues on the other side of the road, and trace the path that winds upwards from its end to the monastery – a steep walk of around thirty minutes. The *gompa*'s steps climb past the monks' quarters to the first of a group of temples (₹30). Local legend has it that a Mongol demon, a sworn enemy of Buddhism, was slain nearby, but his lifeless body kept returning to the *gompa*. What are reputed to be his wrinkled head and hand are now clasped by a pot-bellied protector deity in the spooky **Gon-khang**.

The diminutive **Lachung temple**, higher up, is the oldest here. Soot-soiled murals face a huge Tsong-kha-pa statue, topped with a Gelug-pa yellow hat. In the heart of the *gompa*, the **Du-khang**'s remarkable mural, filling a raised cupola above the hall, depicts Tibet's Tashilhunpo *gompa*, where the Panchen Lama is receiving a long stream of visitors approaching on camels, horses and carts. Finally, the **Kangyu Lang** (bookroom) and **Tsangyu Lang** temples act as storerooms for hundreds of Mongolian and Tibetan texts.

ACCOMMODATION AND EATING   DISKIT

Olthang Close to the main road prayer wheel ☎ 01980 220025. Offers a range of attached rooms and camping for ₹300. Home-grown vegetables from the picturesque garden are served for dinner in the dining hall, which doubles as a bar in the evenings. ₹400

★ **Sangam** Near the village centre ☎ 01980 220404. The newest and smartest place in the area, with a fine restaurant. Its spacious attached and non-attached rooms are great value. ₹250/₹700

Sangam View By the central village crossroads ☏ 94691 65249. Just about the only independent restaurant in the valley does a good range of Indian, Chinese and some Western

dishes for ₹60–150. May–Oct daily 7am–9pm.

Sunrise Diskit Along a mani wall to the right of the road down from the prayer wheel ☏ 01980 220011. This simple place offers cheap rustic rooms, shared bathrooms and a pleasant garden. ₹300

Hundur

Seven kilometres north of Diskit, **HUNDUR**, a tiny village in a wooded valley beyond some impressive sand dunes, was as far as foreigners could go along this part of the Nubra Valley until the Muslim village of **Turtuk**, towards the line of control, started opening up around the time of writing. Hundur's main monastery lies just below the main road, near the bridge and the end of the bus route. Further down and across the brook is a creaky, cobweb-filled old manor that once belonged to the local Zimskhang royal family, and is now occasionally unlocked by a key-keeper at the *Goba Guesthouse*. The village is renowned for its herd of Bactrian camels (a vestige of its days on the old trans-Karakoram trade route), which you will invariably encounter if you walk out onto the dunes. **Camel rides** start around ₹200 for a short lope across the sand.

ACCOMMODATION AND EATING   HUNDUR

Goba Gueshouse 400m down from the roadside gompa ☏ 01980 221083. This friendly hangout is a quaint, low-key affair with good food, a sunny yard and hundreds of flowers. The upstairs rooms are attached. ₹300/₹500

Semba On the road from Diskit ☏ 01980 221348. Small family guesthouse with just three rooms, all of which have

shared bathrooms. Doubles up as the village bar, though it never gets too rowdy. ₹200

Snow Leopard Signposted off the main road at the back of the village ☏ 01980 221097. Set in a beautiful vegetable garden, this secluded guesthouse has great views. All rooms are attached but the older ones have squat toilets. ₹250

West of Leh

Of the many *gompas* accessible by road **west of Leh**, only **Spitok**, piled on a hilltop at the end of the airport runway, and **Phyang**, which presides over one of Ladakh's most picturesque villages, can be comfortably visited on day-trips from the capital. The rest, including **Likkir** and the temple complex at **Alchi**, with its wonderfully preserved eleventh-century murals, are usually seen en route to or from **Kargil**. The 231km journey, which takes in a couple of high passes and some mind-blowing scenery, can be completed

RAFTING AND KAYAKING IN LADAKH

When water levels are high, between the end of June and late August, Leh's more entrepreneurial travel agents operate **rafting** trips on the River Indus and Zanskar River. The routes are tame in comparison with Nepal's, but floating downstream in a twelve-seater rubber inflatable is a hugely enjoyable way to experience the rugged and beautiful landscape. Two different stretches of the River Indus are most commonly used: from **Phey** near Spitok to the Indus-Zanskar confluence at **Nyemo** (3hr), and from Nyemo to below the ancient temple complex at **Alchi** (2hr 30min). Experienced rafters may also want to try the more challenging route between Alchi and Khalsi, which takes in the 1km-long series of rapids at **Nurla**. The annual multiday expedition down the River Zanskar to the Indus is by far the most rewarding as it also includes the spectacular road approach to Padum. A popular shorter route on the Zanskar is from Chiling to Nyemo (3hr).

Several adventure-tour operators in Leh offer whitewater rafting or kayaking on the Indus. **Tickets** should be booked at least a day in advance. One of the best operators is Splash Adventure Tours, Changspa Lane (☏ 01982 251042, ⊛ kayakindia.com); **prices** start from around ₹1300 for half-day trips. Make sure when you book that the price includes transport to and from the river, rental of life jackets and helmets, and meals, and that there is a waterproof strongbox for valuables.

in a single eight-hour haul, slightly less by jeep. To do this stretch of road justice, however, you should spend at least a few days making short forays up the side valleys of the Indus, where idyllic settlements and *gompas* nestle amid barley fields and mountains.

One of the great landmarks punctuating the former caravan route is the monastery of **Lamayuru**. Reached via a nail-biting sequence of hairpin bends as the highway climbs out of the Indus Valley to begin its meandering ascent of **Fotu La**, it lies within walking distance of some extraordinary lunar-like rock formations, at the start of the main trekking route south to Padum in Zanskar. Further west still, beyond the dramatic **Namika La** pass, **Mulbekh** is the last Buddhist village on the highway. From here on, *gompas* and *gonchas* give way to onion-domed mosques and flowing *salwar kameez*.

There is, on average, an accident a day on the narrow, high and twisting Leh–Kargil road. Tata trucks are the most prone to toppling off the tarmac, and it can take hours for the rescue vehicles from Leh and Kargil to arrive and then clear the road. In summer, **transport** along the highway is straightforward as ramshackle state and private buses ply the route; getting to more remote spots, however, can be hard and it is worth considering getting a group together to rent a **jeep** from tour operators in Leh (p.484).

Spitok

SPITOK gompa, rising incongruously from the end of the airport runway, makes a good half-day foray from Leh, 10km up the north side of the Indus Valley. The fifteenth-century **monastery**, which tumbles down the sides of a steep knoll to a tight cluster of farmhouses and well-watered fields, is altogether more picturesque. Approached by road from the north, or from the south along a footpath that winds through Spitok village, its spacious rooftops command superb views. The main complex is of less interest than the **Palden Lumo** chapel, perched on a ridge above. Although visiting soldiers from the nearby Indian army barracks consider the deity inside the temple to be Kali Mata, the key-keeper will assure visitors that what many consider to be the black-faced and bloodthirsty Hindu goddess of death and destruction is actually **Yidam Dorje Jigjet**. Coloured electric lights illuminate the cobwebbed chamber of veiled guardian deities whose ferocious faces are only revealed once a year. If you have a torch, check out the 600-year-old paintings on the back wall, partially hidden by eerie *chaam* masks used during the winter festival season.

ARRIVAL AND DEPARTURE   SPITOK

By bus/taxi Either take a taxi (around ₹120) from Leh or any of the buses heading west along the main Srinagar highway.

Phyang

A mere 17km west of Leh, **PHYANG gompa** looms large at the head of a secluded side valley that tapers north into the Ladakh Range from the Srinagar highway.

The *gompa* itself houses a fifty-strong community of lamas, but few antique murals of note, most of them having recently been painted over with brighter colours. Its only treasures are a small collection of fourteenth-century Kashmiri bronzes in the modern Guru-Padmasambhava temple and the light and airy **Du-khang**'s three silver *chortens*, one of which is decorated with a seven-eyed **dzi stone**. The gem, considered to be highly auspicious, was brought to Phyang from Tibet by the monastery's former head lama, whose ashes the *chorten* encases. Tucked away around the side, the shrine in the *gompa*'s gloomily atmospheric **Gon-khang** (₹30) houses a ferocious veiled protector deity and an amazing collection of weapons and armour plundered during the Mongol invasions of the fourteenth century. Also dangling from the cobweb-covered rafters are several sets of yak horns, believed to be 900-year-old relics of the Bon cult.

Phyang's annual **festival**, Phyang Tsedup, held between mid-July and early Aug (see box, p.480) to coincide with the tourist season, is the second largest in Ladakh after the one held in Hemis (see p.490). Celebrated with the usual masked *chaam* dances, the event is marked with a ritual exposition of a giant 10m brocaded silk *thangka*.

By bus Services from Leh all the way up to Phyang leave at 8am & 4pm, returning an hour later; however, the main highway, which has many more vehicles to and from Leh, is only a 30min walk away.

Likkir

Five kilometres to the north of the main Leh–Srinagar highway, shortly before the village of Saspol, the large and wealthy *gompa* of **LIKKIR**, home to around one hundred monks, is renowned for its new 23m-high yellow statue of the Buddha-to-come that towers serenely above the terraced fields. A pleasant break from the bustle of Leh, the village of Likkir offers a small but adequate choice of accommodation which, along with the sheer tranquillity of the surroundings, tempts many travellers to linger a few days.

The *gompa*, 3km up the valley from the village, was extensively renovated in the eighteenth century and today shows little sign of the antiquity related to the site. It overlooks the starting point for the popular two-day hike to Temisgang via Rhizong, which provides a comparatively gentle introduction to trekking in Ladakh.

TREKKING IN LADAKH AND ZANSKAR

The ancient footpaths that crisscross **Ladakh** and **Zanskar** provide some of the most inspiring **trekking** in the Himalayas. Threading together remote Buddhist villages and monasteries, cut off in winter behind high passes whose rocky tops bristle with prayer flags, nearly all are long, hard and high – but never dull. Whether you make all the necessary preparations yourself, or pay an agency to do it for you, **Leh** (see p.479) is the best place to plan a trek; the **best time** to trek is from June to September.

Trekking **independently** is straightforward if you have a copy of *Trekking in Ladakh* (see below), don't mind haggling and are happy to organize the logistics yourself. To find ponies and guides, head for the Tibetan refugee camp at Choglamsar, 3km south of Leh. Count on paying around ₹400 per horse and ₹300 per donkey each day – two people trekking through the Markha Valley, for example, would pay around $40 each for the entire week. By contrast, a **package trek** sold by a trekking agent in Leh will cost around $50 per day, and more if your group is less than four people.

You can **rent equipment**, including high-quality tents, sleeping bags, sleeping mats and duck-down jackets, either through your chosen agency or at somewhere like Spiritual Trek, Changspa Lane (☎01982 251701, ⊛spiritualtrekladakh.com). Expect to pay around ₹100–150 a day for a tent, ₹80–100 for a sleeping bag and ₹50–60 for a gas stove; if you're intending to climb Stok-Kangri you may need to dish out ₹50 for an ice axe. Independent trekkers might consider buying Indian equipment in the bazaar, and then later selling it on.

Minimize your impact in culturally and ecologically sensitive areas by being as **self-reliant** as possible, especially with food and fuel. Buying provisions along the way puts an unnecessary burden on the villages' subsistence-oriented economies, and encourages strings of unsightly "tea shops" (often run by outsiders) to sprout along the trails. Always burn kerosene, never wood – a scarce and valuable resource. Refuse should be packed up, not disposed of along the route, no matter how far from the nearest town you are, and plastics retained for recycling at the Ecology Centre (box, p.485) in Leh. Always bury your faeces and burn your toilet paper afterwards. Finally, do not defecate in the dry-stone huts along the trails; local shepherds use them for shelter during snow storms.

An excellent **book** covering everything you need to know to undertake an expedition in the region is Trailblazer's *Trekking in Ladakh* by Charlie Loram, on sale in bookshops in Leh. For information about trekking to **Zanskar** from the south, see "Trekking in Lahaul and Spiti" (box, p.452).

THE MARKHA VALLEY

The beautiful **Markha Valley** runs parallel with the Indus on the far southern side of the snowy Stok-Kangri massif, visible from Leh. Passing through cultivated valley floors, undulating

ARRIVAL AND DEPARTURE

By minibus The direct minibus from Leh (4pm; 3hr) goes past the village and makes the 3km haul up the valley to the *gompa*, returning to Leh at 7am the next morning. Otherwise, take any westbound vehicle, get dropped off at the turning from the main Leh–Kargil highway and walk the short but treeless 1km road to the village, where you can hire a taxi for the *gompa*.

ACCOMMODATION AND EATING

★ **Gaph-Chow** In the lower village ☎ 01982 252748. Friendly place with simple, comfortable rooms with attached baths, camping space in the lovely vegetable garden, internet, a garden café and traditional Ladakhi kitchen. Half-board ₹1200

Norboo Spon Just off the road to the monastery ☎ 01982 227145. Simple non-attached rooms. The owner offers woodcarving and *thangka*-painting lessons, as well as good trekking advice – aided by the scale model of the Likkir–Temisgang trek in his garden. Full board ₹800

Alchi

Driving past on the nearby Srinagar–Leh highway, you'd never guess that the spectacular sweep of wine-coloured scree 3km across the Indus from **Saspol** conceals one of the most significant historical sites in Asia. Yet the low pagoda-roofed

7

high-altitude grassland and snow-prone passes, the winding trail along it enables trekkers to experience life in a roadless region without having to hike for weeks into the wilderness – as a result, it has become the most frequented route in Ladakh. Do not attempt this trek without adequate wet- and cold-weather gear: snow flurries sweep across the higher reaches of the Markha Valley even in August.

The circuit takes six to eight days to complete, and is usually followed anticlockwise, starting from the village of **Spitok** (see p.497), 10km south of Leh. A more dramatic approach via **Stok** (see p.489) affords matchless views over the Indus Valley to the Ladakh and Karakoram ranges, but involves a sharp ascent of **Stok La** (4848m) on only the second day; don't try it unless you are already well acclimatized to the altitude.

LIKKIR TO TEMISGANG

A driveable road along the old caravan route through the hills between **Likkir** and **Temisgang** makes a leisurely two-day hike, which takes in three major monasteries (Likkir, Rhizong and Temisgang) and a string of idyllic villages. It's a great introduction to trekking in Ladakh, the perfect acclimatizer if you plan to attempt any longer and more demanding routes. Ponies and guides for the trip may be arranged on spec at either Likkir or Temisgang villages, both of which have small guesthouses and are connected by daily buses to Leh.

LAMAYURU TO ALCHI

Albeit short by Ladakhi standards, the five-day trek from **Lamayuru** to **Alchi** is one of the toughest in the region, winding across high passes and a tangle of isolated valleys past a couple of ancient *gompas*, and offering superb panoramic views of the wilderness south of the Indus Valley. It's very hard to follow in places, so don't attempt it without an experienced guide, ponies and enough provisions to tide you over if you lose your way.

PADUM TO LAMAYURU

The trek across the rugged Zanskar Range from **Padum** to **Lamayuru** on the Srinagar–Leh highway, usually completed in ten to twelve days, is a hugely popular but very demanding long-distance route, not to be attempted as a first-time trek nor without adequate preparation, ponies and a guide.

STOK-KANGRI

Visible from most of Leh, **Stok-Kangri** (6120m) is reputed to be the easiest peak above 6000m in the world. Several agents in Leh advertise five-day **climbing expeditions** via the village of Stok with a non-technical final climb for around $50 per head per day for a group of four. If you've got *Trekking in Ladakh* in your rucksack, it's straightforward to walk up it independently, though you'll need to carry enough food for three or four days.

Chos-khor (daily 8am–1pm & 2–6pm; ₹50), or "religious enclave", at **ALCHI**, 70km west of Leh, harbours an extraordinary wealth of ancient wall paintings and wood sculpture, miraculously preserved for more than nine centuries inside five tiny mud-walled temples. The site's earliest murals are regarded as the finest surviving examples of a style that flourished in Kashmir during the "Second Spreading". Barely a handful of the monasteries founded during this era escaped the Muslim depredations of the fourteenth century; Alchi is the most impressive of them all, the least remote and the only one you don't need a special permit to visit.

Legend tells that Rinchen Zangpo, the "Great Translator" (see p.464), stuck his walking stick in the ground here en route to Chilling and upon his return found it had become a poplar, an auspicious sign that made him build a temple on the spot. One tree near the entrance to the Chos-khor, denoted with a signboard, is symbolic of this event. The Chos-khor itself consists of five separate temples, various residential buildings and a scattering of large *chortens*, surrounded by a mud-and-stone wall. It is best to concentrate on the two oldest temples, the **Vairocana** and the **Sumtsek**, both in the middle of the enclosure, although the nearby **Manjushree** and **Lo-Tsawa** shrines also boast colourful murals and the former a huge, brightly painted statue of the Buddha of Wisdom.

The Vairocana

An inscription records that Alchi's oldest structure, the **Vairocana**, was erected late in the eleventh century. Its centrepiece is an image of Vairocana, the "Buddha Resplendent", flanked by the four main Buddha manifestations that appear all over Alchi's temple walls, always presented in their associated colours: Akshobya ("Unshakeable"; blue), Ratnasambhava ("Jewel Born"; yellow), Amitabha ("Boundless Radiance"; red) and Amoghasiddhi ("Unfailing Success"; green). The other walls are decorated with six elaborate mandalas, interspersed with intricate friezes.

The Sumtsek

Standing to the left of the Du-khang, the **Sumtsek** marks the highwater mark of early medieval Indian-Buddhist art. Its woodcarvings and paintings, dominated by rich reds and blues, are almost as fresh and vibrant today as they were nine hundred years ago when the squat triple-storey structure was built. The heart of the shrine is a colossal statue of **Maitreya**, the Buddha-to-come, his head shielded from sight high in the second storey. Accompanying him are two equally grand **bodhisattvas**, their heads peering serenely down through gaps in the ceiling. Each of these stucco statues wears a figure-hugging *dhoti*, adorned with different, meticulously detailed motifs. Avalokitesvara, the *bodhisattva* of compassion (to the left), has pilgrimage sites, court vignettes, palaces and pre-Muslim style *stupas* on his robe, while that of Maitreya is decorated with episodes from the life of Gautama Buddha. The robe of Manjushri, destroyer of falsehood, to the right, shows the 84 masters of Tantra, the *mahasiddhas*, adopting complex yogic poses in a maze of bold square patterns.

Among the exquisite **murals**, some repaired in the sixteenth century, is the famous six-armed green goddess Prajnaparamita, the "Perfection of Wisdom". Amazingly, this, and the multitude of other images that plaster the interior of the Sumtsek, resolve, when viewed from the centre of the shrine, into a harmonious whole.

| **ARRIVAL AND DEPARTURE** | **ALCHI** |

By bus Private buses leave Leh at 8am, taking 3hr to cover the 70km and returning at 3.45pm and 7am the next day. Otherwise you can board any Kargil-bound vehicle, get off at the metal truss bridge west of Saspol and walk across the river and up the remaining 6km.

ACCOMMODATION AND EATING

The number of places to stay has grown as Alchi's fame has spread but prices are generally quite high. Most serve food, so apart from a couple of *dhabas* in the village centre, there is just one independent restaurant.

Golden Oriole German Bakery Just above the Chos-kor ☎ 94692 79018. Sociable terrace restaurant with a sizeable menu of curries, Tibetan, Chinese and some Western favourites for ₹50–150. Daily 6am–10pm.

Heritage Home Right beside Chos-kor entrance ☎ 01982 227125. Pleasantly welcoming mid-range guesthouse with a shady courtyard. The attached rooms are quite large and decorated in traditional Ladakhi style. ₹1200

Lotsava About 50m below the main road into town ☎ 01982 227129. Very basic guesthouse with good views but layers of dust; with a little warning, the owner will serve filling breakfasts and evening meals in the small garden. ₹400/₹600

Samdupling 100m above the taxi stand ☎ 01982 221704, ✉ hotelsamdupling@gmail.com. Nicely located beside a small stream, this purpose-built modern hotel has spacious, comfortably furnished rooms and a reasonable restaurant with the standard choices of dishes. ₹2600

★ **Zimskhang** On both sides of the lane to the Chos-kor ☎ 01982 227086, ✇ zimskhang.com. On one side of the lane is a smart new hotel, while on the other there are cheaper non-attached rooms behind the pleasant garden restaurant. ₹400/₹2100

Lamayuru

If one sight could be said to sum up Ladakh, it would have to be **LAMAYURU gompa**, 130km west of Leh and 107km east of Kargil. Hemmed in by a moonscape of scree-covered mountains, the whitewashed medieval monastery towers above a scruffy cluster of tumbledown mud-brick houses from the top of a near-vertical, weirdly eroded cliff. A major landmark on the old silk route, the *gompa* numbers among the 108 (a spiritually significant number) founded by the Rinchen Zangpo in the tenth and eleventh centuries. However, its craggy seat, believed to have sheltered Milarepa during his religious odyssey across the Himalayas, was probably sacred long before the advent of Buddhism, when local people followed the shamanistic Bon cult. Just thirty lamas of the Brigungpa branch of the Kagyu school are now left, as opposed to the four hundred that lived here a century or so ago. Nor does Lamayuru harbour much in the way of art treasures. The main reason visitors make a stop on this section of the Srinagar–Leh road is to photograph the *gompa* from the valley floor, or to pick up the trail to the Prikiti La pass – gateway to Zanskar – that begins here.

The steep footpath from the highway above town brings you out near the main entrance to the monastery, where you should be able to find the lama responsible for issuing entrance tickets (₹50) and unlocking the door to the **Du-khang**. Lamayuru's newly renovated prayer-hall houses little of note other than a **cave** where Naropa, Milarepa's teacher, is said to have meditated, and a collection of colourful yak-butter sculptures. If you're lucky, you'll be shown through the tangle of narrow lanes below the *gompa* to a tiny **chapel**, whose badly damaged murals of mandalas and the Tathagata Buddhas date from the same period as those at Alchi (see p.499).

ARRIVAL AND INFORMATION LAMAYURU

By bus The daily Leh–Kargil and Kargil–Leh buses both depart around 5.30am from their respective towns of origin and pass through Lamayuru between 9am and 10am, stopping near the central chai stalls. Some private buses also pass through up to early afternoon.

Trekking Trekkers in search of reliable guides and ponies could ask at the *Dragon Guest House* (see below) or try arranging them in advance through their office in Leh (☎ 01982 253164).

ACCOMMODATION AND EATING

★ **Dragon Guest House** To left of footpath through village ☎ 01982 224510, ✉ dragon_skyabu@yahoo.com. The old hop-covered block has a range of non-attached rooms, including one covetable glass room, while the new block contains smarter en suites. The pleasant garden restaurant is the best place to eat in Lamayuru. ₹500/₹800

Moonland At first bend in road 400m west ☎ 01982 224576. Smartest place in area, modern but built in traditional Ladakhi style with a mixture of attached and non-attached rooms, plus a good restaurant. ₹600/₹1200

Niranjana Hotel Near the gompa entrance ☎ 01982 224555. This imposing four-storey building has twenty concrete rooms with good views of the surrounding valleys; the shared bathrooms have hot running water. ₹600

Zambala On main road opposite village ☎ 94695 35961. The best and friendliest of the roadside eateries offers simple rice and veg dishes for ₹90 and is a good place to wait for the bus. Daily 6am–10pm.

7

Mulbekh

West of Lamayuru, the main road crawls to the top of **Fotu La** (4091m), the highest pass between Leh and Srinagar, then ascends **Namika** ("Sky-Pillar") **La** (3760m), so called because of the jagged pinnacle of rock that looms above it to the south. Once across the windswept ridge, it drops through a dramatic landscape of disintegrating desert cliffs and pebbly ravines to the wayside village of **MULBEKH** – the last sizeable Buddhist settlement along the road before the Muslim Purki settlements around Kargil. The village is scattered around the banks of the River Wakha, lined with poplars and orchards of walnut and apricot trees and would be a sleepy hamlet were it not for the endless convoys of trucks and tourist buses that thunder through while the passes are open. Those visitors who stop at all tend only to stay long enough to grab a chai at a roadside *dhaba* and to have a quick look at the 7m-high **Maitreya** ("Chamba" in Tibetan) **statue** carved from the face of a gigantic boulder nearby. The precise origins of the shapely four-armed Buddha-to-be are not known, but an ancient inscription on its side records that it was carved between the seventh and eighth centuries, well before Buddhism was fully established in Tibet. The single-chambered *gompa* (₹10), in front of the statue and decorated with particularly beautiful murals, is dedicated to the thousand-armed Chenrazig (Avalokitesvara).

ACCOMMODATION AND EATING   MULBEKH

Maitreya Guest House 1km west along the main road ☎01985 270035. Comfortable and gaily decorated attached rooms can be found at this hospitable family guesthouse, which also serves healthy veg food. ₹300

Paradise On main road opposite the statue ☎01985 270010. A few shabby non-attached rooms nestle above a better canteen serving *thukpa*, dhal, rice, *momos* and butter tea during the day, booze by night. ₹300

Kargil

Though it is surrounded by awesome scenery, most travellers don't spend more than a few hours in **KARGIL**, capital of the area dubbed "Little Baltistan", which rises in a clutter of corrugated-iron rooftops from the confluence of the Suru and Drass rivers. As a halfway point between Leh and Srinagar, its grubby hotels fill up at night with weary bus passengers, who then get up at 4am and career off under cover of darkness. Although the town has expanded several kilometres along and above the riverside, the central area around the main bazaar, which loops round into a northerly orientation, is very compact and walkable. Woolly-hatted and bearded old men and slick youngsters stroll the streets past old-fashioned wholesalers with their sacks of grains, spices and tins of ghee, Tibetans selling Panasonic electricals and butchers displaying severed goats' heads on dusty bookshelves. The town feels more Pakistani than Indian, and the faces (nearly all male) and food derive from Kashmir and Central Asia. Western women should keep their arms and legs covered and may arouse mild curiosity.

The majority of Kargil's eighty thousand inhabitants, known as Purki, are strict **Muslims**. Unlike their Sunni cousins in Kashmir, however, the locals here are orthodox **Shias**, which not only explains the ubiquitous Ayatollah photographs, but also the conspicuous absence of women from the bazaar. You might even spot the odd black turban of an Agha, one of Kargil's spiritual leaders, who still go on pilgrimage to holy sites in Iran and have outlawed male-female social practices such as dancing. Descendants of settlers and Muslim merchants from Kashmir and Yarkhand, Purkis speak a dialect called **Purig** – a mixture of Ladakhi and Balti.

Brief history

Had it not been for the daring Indian reconquest of the region during the 1948 Indo-Pak War, Kargil would today be part of Baltistan, the region across the Ceasefire Line which it closely resembles. Indeed, Kargil is so close to the Ceasefire Line and Pakistani positions that it served as the logistics centre in the 1999 war (see box, pp.466–467) and was repeatedly targeted by Pakistani artillery. Aside from the odd building destroyed, however, much of the town escaped unscathed as the army bases and airport lie on the outskirts of town. Since further conflict in the summer of 2002 the dust has settled markedly and, as dialogue continues between India and Pakistan on Kashmir, tourist numbers have been steadily increasing.

ARRIVAL AND INFORMATION   KARGIL

By bus State buses arriving in Kargil from Leh and Srinagar pull in by the river, 150m below the middle of the bazaar, while private buses, minibuses and jeeps share a larger compound further south, just below the bazaar. Buses to Srinagar (9–10hr) leave mostly late night, to Leh (9–10hr) early morning, plus every 1–2hr until 2pm to Panikhar (3hr) and 3 afternoon departures to Mulbekh (1hr 30min).

Services to Padum (13–14hr) are notoriously unreliable.
By jeep Shared jeeps to Leh (7–8hr; ₹850), Padum (9–10hr; ₹1600) and Srinagar (6–7hr; ₹750) mostly leave early in the morning.
Tourist office The unreliable J&K tourism reception centre (Mon–Sat 10am–4pm; ☏ 01985 232721) is on the east side of town, on the river side of the taxi stand.

ACCOMMODATION

Since the closure of many hotels during the Kashmir crisis, budget options are very limited and room tariffs soar in July and August when most travellers pass through; the rates we quote reflect this, but discounts are usually available at other times.

Crown Near state bus stop ☏ 94191 77206, ✉ muntazir89@yahoo.com. Rambling old budget hotel that's seen better days but still attracts backpackers. Some rooms come with attached bathrooms and there's a cheap dorm. Dorm ₹**100**, double ₹**400**/₹**500**
Greenland Just off the lane heading towards the state bus stop ☏ 01985 232324, ✉ greenlandkargil@gmail .com. The old block has been renovated and painted, and while the new one is better both are overpriced. OK as a last resort. ₹**1500**

Siachen On a lane down to taxi stand ☏ 01985 233055, ✉ hotel_siachen_kargil@rediffmail.com. One of the best downtown hotels, large and comfortable with attached rooms, a few cheaper options on the first floor and a good restaurant. ₹**2450**
Tourist Marjina On the lane heading towards the state bus stop ☏ 94191 76212, ✉ saggedmargina@ yahoo.com. Reasonably large attached rooms, either in the rickety old wooden building or new block, under construction at the time of writing. ₹**800**

EATING

Eating options are rather limited and most restaurants are closed for breakfast but the street food can be delicious – chai, chapattis and omelettes, with hot Kashmiri bread slathered with butter. Spicy shish kebabs go for just ₹15 later in the day.

Karan Singh Punjabi Janata South end of Main Bazaar. One of the town's better *dhabas*: rich meat and veg dishes with spicy Indian sauces ladled onto platefuls of rice. You can eat well for less than ₹100. Daily 6am–7pm.
Las Vegas In the middle of the Main Bazaar ☏ 94191 76773. One of the more salubrious places, serving mainly non-veg Indian, Kashmiri and Chinese food, such as rogan josh and various chowmeins, for around ₹80–120. Daily noon–9pm.
Rubby South end of Main Bazaar ☏ 94197 19903. Popular restaurant serving local specialities including

yakhani (meat boiled in yogurt) and *gustaba* (meat balls), typical of Central Asian cuisine. Most items well under ₹100. Daily 10am–8pm.
Tibetan Food Restaurant Middle of Main Bazaar ☏ 94191 76095. All the favourites like *momos* and *thukpa*, dished up for around ₹50–80 in the simple upstairs dining room. Choice can be limited. Daily 10am–9pm.
Zojila Bakery Main Bazaar; no phone. A good place to stop for a morning tea, or to pick up bread and cookies. One of the few places for a sit-down brekkie. Daily 7am–7pm.

The Suru Valley

Dividing two of the world's most formidable mountain ranges, the **Suru Valley** winds south from Kargil to the desolate Pensi La – the main entry point for Zanskar. The first leg, usually undertaken in the pre-dawn darkness by bus, leads through the broad lower reaches of the Suru Valley, strewn with Muslim villages clustered around metal mosque domes. As you progress southwards, the pristine white ice-fields and twin pinnacles of **Nun-Kun** (7077m) nose over the horizon. Apart from a brief disappearance behind the steep sides of the valley at **Panikhar**, this awesome massif dominates the landscape all the way to Zanskar.

Shortly beyond Panikhar, the Suru veers east around the base of Nun-Kun, passing within a stone's throw of the magnificent **Parkachik Gangri** glacier. Having wound across a seemingly endless boulder field, closed in on both sides by sheer mountain walls, the road then emerges at a marshy open plain surrounded by snow peaks and mountainsides of near-vertical strata. **Juldo**, a tiny settlement whose fodder-stacked rooftops are strung with fluttering prayer flags, marks the beginning of Buddhist **Suru**.

The climb to the pass from **Rangdum gompa**, across the flat river basin from Juldo, is absolutely breathtaking. One glistening 6000m peak after another appears atop a series of side valleys, many lined with gigantic folds of rock and ice. The real high point, though, is reserved for the dizzying descent from **Pensi La** (4401m), as the road's switchbacks swing over the colossal S-shaped **Darung Drung Glacier**, whose milky-green meltwaters drain southeast into the Stod Valley, visible below.

Panikhar

Although by no means the largest settlement in the Suru Valley, **PANIKHAR**, three hours' bus ride south of Kargil, is a good place to break the long journey to Padum. Before the Kashmir troubles, it was a minor trekking centre, at the start of the Lonvilad Gali–Pahalgum trail. These days, despite the improving situation, it sees far fewer tourists, even in high season.

The main reason to stop is to hike to nearby **Parkachik La**, for panoramic views of the glacier-gouged north face of the mighty **Nun-Kun massif**. The **trail** up to the pass begins on the far side of the Suru, crossed via a suspension bridge thirty minutes south of the village. It may look straightforward from Panikhar, but the four-hour roundtrip climb to the ridge gets very tough indeed towards the top, especially if you're not used to the altitude. However, even seasoned trekkers gasp in awe at the sight that greets them when they finally arrive at the cairns. Capped with a plume of cloud and with snow streaming from its huge pyramidal peak, Nun sails 3500m above the valley floor, draped with heavily crevassed hanging glaciers and flanked by its sisters, multi-pinnacled Kun and saddle-topped Barmal.

ARRIVAL AND DEPARTURE   PANIKHAR

By bus There are buses every 1–2hr back to Kargil until around 5pm but no services on to Padum.

Hitching If you're looking for a lift to Padum, walk the 5km back down to the checkpost on the main road and try your luck there, the earlier the better.

ACCOMMODATION AND EATING

J&K Tourist Bungalow 100m from the bus stand ☎ 01985 259137. Large but rather dowdy attached rooms full of old furniture. The restaurant serves simple veg meals, the only food available in the village. ₹400

Kayoul Opposite the bus stand ☎ 94691 92810, ✉ saki_muna@yahoo.com. Extremely basic lodge, with a few small rooms, a tad grubby and all with common bathrooms. But it's the only alternative to the J&K place. ₹200

Zanskar

Walled in by the Great Himalayan Divide, **ZANSKAR**, literally "Land of White Copper", has for decades exerted the allure of Shangri-La on visitors to Ladakh. The region's staggering remoteness, extreme climate and distance from the major Himalayan trade routes has meant that the successive winds of change that have blown through the Indus Valley to the north had little impact here. The annual influx of trekkers and a driveable road have certainly quickened the pace of development, but away from the main settlement of **Padum**, the Zanskaris' way of life has altered little since the sage Padmasambhava passed through in the eighth century.

The nucleus of the region is a Y-shaped glacial valley system drained by three main rivers: the **Stot** (or Doda) and the **Tsarap** (or Lingit) join and flow north as the **Zanskar**. Lying to the leeward side of the Himalayan watershed, the valley sees a lot more snow than central Ladakh. Even the lowest passes remain blocked for seven or eight months of the year, while midwinter temperatures can drop to a bone-numbing minus 40oC. Fourteen thousand or so tenacious souls subsist in this bleak and treeless terrain – among the coldest inhabited places on the planet – muffled up for half the year inside their smoke-filled whitewashed crofts, with a winter's-worth of fodder piled on the roof.

Until the end of the 1970s, anything the resourceful Zanskaris could not produce for themselves (including timber for building) had to be transported into the region over 4000- to 5000-metre passes, or, in midwinter, carried along the frozen surface of the Zanskar from its confluence with the Indus at Nimmu – a ten- to twelve-day roundtrip that's still the quickest route to the Srinagar–Leh road from Padum. Finally, in 1980, a drivable dirt track was blasted down the Suru and over Pensi La into the Stot valley. Landslides and freak blizzards permitting (Pensi La can be snowbound even in August), the bumpy journey from Kargil to Padum can now be completed in as little as ten hours.

Padum

After a memorable trek or bus ride, **PADUM**, 240km to the south of Kargil, comes as a bit of an anticlimax. Instead of the picturesque Zanskari village you might expect, the region's administrative headquarters and principal roadhead turns out to be a desultory collection of typical concrete cubes, oily truck parks and tin-roofed government buildings. The settlement's only real appeal lies in its superb location. Nestled at the southernmost tip of a broad, fertile river basin, Padum presides over a flat patchwork of farmland enclosed on three sides by colossal walls of scree and snow-capped mountains.

Straddling a nexus of several long-distance trails, Padum is an important **trekking hub** and the only place in Zanskar where tourism has thus far made much of an impression. During the short summer season, you'll see almost as many weather-beaten Westerners wandering around its sandy lanes as locals – a mixture of indigenous Buddhists and Sunni Muslims. Even so, facilities are still limited to a

---

THE IMPACT OF TOURISM IN ZANSKAR

Just a handful of Zanskar's widely scattered **gompas** and settlements lie within striking distance of the road. The rest are hidden away in remote valleys, reached after days or weeks of walking. Improved communications may yet turn out to be a mixed blessing for Zanskar. While the road undoubtedly brought a degree of prosperity to Padum, it has also forced significant changes upon the rest of the valley – most noticeably a sharp increase in tourist traffic – whose **long-term impact** on the region's fragile ecology and traditional culture has yet to be fully realized. Increased tourism has, in fact, done little to benefit the locals financially, with agencies in Leh, Manali, Srinagar and even Delhi pocketing the money paid by trekking groups. Zanskaris, weary of seeing their region come second to Kargil, have been campaigning for years for a sub-hill council status with more control over development. Buddhist concerns have also been heightened in the face of state government mismanagement and occasional communal tensions with their Muslim neighbours. There has been some outside aid emerging – one excellent initiative is the Dutch-based **Stichting Zanskar Scholen** foundation (⊛zanskarscholen.com), which equips some of the impoverished state and monastery schools.

> ## ORGANIZING TREKS FROM PADUM
>
> Basic **trekking supplies** are sold at the hole-in-the-wall stores along the bazaar. Prices are much higher than elsewhere, so it pays to bring your own provisions with you from Kargil. Most trekkers arrange **ponies** through the tourist office or guesthouse owners, or you could try Zanskar Trek (☏01983 245053), who also supply guides (₹500–1000/day). Expect to pay around ₹300 per pony per day, depending on the time of year (ponies transport grain during the harvest, so they're more expensive in early September). If you have trouble finding a horse-wallah in Padum, ask at a neighbouring village, such as Pipiting, a thirty-minute walk north across the fields from Padum, where many of them live.

small tourist office and a small but growing number of shops, restaurants and guesthouses. Nor is there much to see while you're waiting for your blisters to heal. The only noteworthy sight within easy walking distance is a small **Tagrimo gompa** fifteen minutes' walk to the west.

7

ARRIVAL AND INFORMATION PADUM

By bus The private bus from Leh (2 days) via Kargil (11–12hr) is highly erratic, operating every 2–3 days during summer to no fixed timetable. The only services within the valley are from Padum to Zangla (Wed & Fri; 1hr 30min) and Karsha (1 daily; 1hr).

By taxi Due to the short season jeep taxis in Padum (through the Padum Taxi Union office on the main road are expensive: a trip to Karsha and back costs at least ₹1000.

Tourist office The J&K Tourist Office, as you enter the village on the main road (Mon–Sat 10am–4pm; ☏01983 245017) is good for general information and trekking advice.

Services There are no official exchange facilities in Padum. A couple of places have internet but connections are slow.

ACCOMMODATION

Chamling Kailash North end of main bazaar ☏94694 57379, ✉lobel@sancharnet.in. The best budget option, with comfortable attached rooms, decorated in Buddhist style and set around a pleasantly relaxing courtyard. ₹**500**

J&K Tourist Complex North end of main bazaar ☏01983 245017. Institutional but comfortable government lodge with well-maintained attached doubles, as well as dorm beds and tent sites (both ₹100). ₹**400**

★ **Marq Hotel** 200m west of main bazaar ☏01983 245021, ✆marqinnzanskar.com. The smartest place in town, with bright, spacious attached rooms, all of which have cable TV and splendid views. Relative luxury with a homely family feel and excellent food. ₹**2800**

Mont Blanc South end of main bazaar ☏01983 245183. Friendly French-run place with simple rooms, all with bathrooms and slight Gallic touches; also ₹100 tent pitches. ₹**600**

EATING AND DRINKING

Food supplies are plentiful in summer but start to dwindle as autumn approaches. Apart from the guesthouse restaurants, there are some good cheap *dhabas* and the odd noteworthy independent establishment.

Lhasa Middle of the main bazaar. The best of the Zanskari-cum-Tibetan joints, good for egg and local bread brekkies and well-prepared *momos* and *thukpas* later in the day. Daily 7am–9pm.

Shahi Darbar UP Restaurent (sic) Towards southern end of the main bazaar; no phone. Good cheap Indian *dhaba* that rustles up a tasty selection of veg and non-veg curries, with degrees of spiciness to suit all palates. Daily 10am–10pm.

Karsha

The hike across the fields from Padum to **KARSHA gompa**, Zanskar's largest Gelug-pa monastery, is the most rewarding and popular side trip. This cluster of whitewashed mud cubes clinging to the rocky lower slopes of the mountain north of Padum dates from the tenth to the fourteenth century. Of the prayer halls, the recently renovated Du-khang and Gon-khang at the top of the complex are the most impressive, while the small Chukshok-jal, set apart from the *gompa* below a ruined fort on the far side of a gully, contains Karsha's oldest wall paintings, contemporaneous with those at Alchi (see p.499). The tiny village is also a nicer place to stay than Padum.

En route to Karsha, you pass another large *gompa*, **Sani**, lauded as the oldest in Zanskar, and the only one built on the valley floor. Local legend attributes its foundation to the itinerant Padmasambhava (Guru Rinpoche) in the eighth century. Set apart from the temples a little to the north is a 2m-high Maitreya figure, carved out of local stone sometime between the eighth and tenth centuries.

ARRIVAL AND DEPARTURE   KARSHA

On foot The quickest way to get to Karsha on foot is to head north from Padum to the cable bridge across the Stot, immediately below the monastery. Set off early in the morning; the violent icy storms that often blow in from the south across the Great Himalayan Range around mid-afternoon make the 90min hike across the exposed river basin something of an endurance test.

By road Karsha can also be reached by road, via the bridge at Tungri, 8km northwest of Padum. There's a daily bus in summer that leaves Padum at 4pm, returning at 7am. Taxis cost around ₹800 one way.

ACCOMMODATION

Some villagers rent rooms to tourists – ask around or try the wonderful glass room belonging to Thuktan Thardot in Sharling Ward, just below the *gompa*.

Lobzang Guest House In the middle of the village. Pretty basic but atmospheric guesthouse with a handful of sparsely furnished rooms with shared facilities. Simple meals available. ₹**250**

Haryana and Punjab

GOLDEN TEMPLE, AMRITSAR

Haryana and Punjab

The prosperous states of Haryana and Punjab occupy the fertile river plain northwest of Delhi. Crossed by the five major tributaries of the Indus River, the former British-administered region of Punjab ("Five Rivers") was split down the middle at Independence. Indian Muslims fled west into Pakistan, Sikhs and Hindus east, in an exodus accompanied by horrific massacres. In 1966, Indira Gandhi, in response to Sikh pressure, made the Punjab Hills into Himachal Pradesh. The plains, meanwhile, were divided into the predominantly Sikh Punjab and the 96-percent Hindu Haryana, both governed from the specially built capital of Chandigarh.

There is little of tourist interest in the two states other than the **Golden Temple** in Amritsar and the wacky **Rock Garden of Chandigarh**, but the region, India's breadbasket, is very important to the nation's **economy**. Its farmers produce nearly a quarter of India's wheat and one third of its milk and dairy foods, while Ludhiana churns out ninety percent of the country's woollen goods. Helped by remittance cheques from millions of expatriates in the UK, US and Canada, the states' per capita income is almost double the national average.

Crossing Haryana and Punjab, you're bound to travel at some stage along part of the longest, oldest and most famous highway in India – the NH-1, alias the **Grand Trunk Road**, stretching 2000km from Peshawar, near the rugged Afghan–Pakistan frontier, to Kolkata on the River Hooghly. The first recorded mention of this trade corridor dates from the fourth century BC, when it was known as the Uttar Path (the "North Way").

Brief history

Punjab's first urban settlement, dating back to 3000 BC and now known as the **Harappan** civilization, was invaded by the Aryans around 1700 BC. Among the Sanskrit scriptures set down in the ensuing **Vedic** age was the **Mahabharata**, whose epic battles drew on real-life encounters between the ancient kings of Punjab at Karnal, 118km north of Delhi. Conquered by the Mauryans in the third century BC, it saw plenty more action as various invading Mughal armies passed through on their way from the Khyber Pass to Delhi – including Babur, who routed Ibrahim Lodi at Panipat in 1526.

Meanwhile, further north, **Sikhism** was beginning to establish itself under the tutelage of Guru Nanak (1469–1539). Based on the notion of a single formless God, the guru's vision of a casteless egalitarian society found favour with both Hindus and Muslims, in spite of Mughal emperor Aurangzeb's attempts to stamp it out. Suppression actually strengthened the Sikh faith in the long run, inspiring the militaristic and confrontational tenth guru **Gobind Singh** to introduce the Five Ks, part of a rigorous new orthodoxy called the **Khalsa**, or "Community of the Pure" (see p.1178).

Having survived repeated seventeenth-century Afghan invasions, the Sikh nation emerged to fill the power vacuum left by the collapse of the Mughals. Only in the 1840s, after two bloody wars with the British, was the Khalsa army finally defeated.

ROCK GARDEN, CHANDIGARH

Highlights

❶ Rock Garden, Chandigarh This bizarre and seemingly haphazard sculpture garden, assembled from rubbish by a local eccentric, and saved from demolition by public support, offers a curious contrast to the ordered city that surrounds it. **See p.515**

❷ The Golden Temple, Amritsar One of the great sights – and sounds – of India; *kirtan* (devotional songs) are performed throughout the day and into the night from the breathtaking golden Harmandir, which seems to float like a beautiful gilded boat upon the sacred pool surrounding it. **See p.520**

❸ Jallianwalla Bagh, Amritsar Site of the infamous Amritsar massacre, in which British troops gunned down unarmed demonstrators, as retold in a dramatic sound-and-light show. **See p.523**

❹ Border ceremony, Wagha Shorter and more colourful than a cricket match, the border ceremony is a highly charged event, especially on Sundays, when hundreds of people gather to swap honks, chants and cheers from the Indian and Pakistani sides. **See p.525**

HIGHLIGHTS ARE MARKED ON THE MAP ON P.512

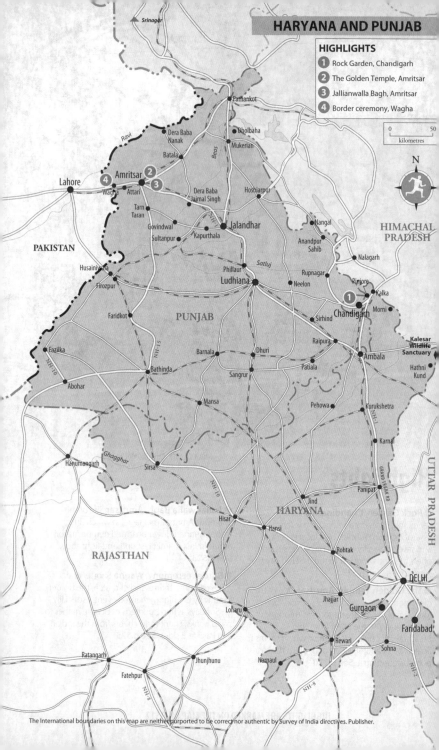

HARYANA AND PUNJAB

HIGHLIGHTS
1. Rock Garden, Chandigarh
2. The Golden Temple, Amritsar
3. Jallianwalla Bagh, Amritsar
4. Border ceremony, Wagha

0   50
kilometres

N

HIMACHAL
PRADESH

Srinagar

Pathankot

Dholbaha

Dera Baba
Nanak

Batala

Mukerian

Ravi

Beas

Lahore

Amritsar

Wagha

Attari

Dera Baba
Jaimal Singh

Hoshiarpur

Tarn
Taran

Govindwal

Kapurthala

Jalandhar

Nangal

PAKISTAN

Sultanpur

Anandpur
Sahib

Nalagarh

Husainiwala

Phillaur

Satluj

Rupnagar

Pinjore

Firozpur

Ludhiana

Neelon

Kalka

Morni

PUNJAB

Faridkot

Sirhind

Chandigarh

Kalesar
Wildlife
Sanctuary

Barnala

Dhuri

Raipura

Ambala

Fazilka

Bathinda

Sangrur

Patiala

Hathni
Kund

Abohar

Mansa

Pehowa

Kurukshetra

NH-10

Hanumangarh

Ghagghar

Sirsa

Karnal

NH-15

UTTAR
PRADESH

Panipat

GRAND TRUNK RD

RAJASTHAN

Jind

HARYANA

Hisar

Hansi

Rohtak

DELHI

Ratangarh

Jhunjhunu

Loharu

Jhajjar

Gurgaon

Faridabad

Fatehpur

Namaul

Rewari

Sohna

NH-8

NH-2

The International boundaries on this map are neither purported to be correct nor authentic by Survey of India directives. Publisher.

Thereafter, the Sikhs played a vital role in the Raj, helping to quash the Mutiny of 1857. The relationship only soured after the **Jallianwalla Bagh massacre** of 1919 (see box, p.523), which also ensured that the Punjab's puppet leaders (who hailed the general responsible as a hero) were discredited, leaving the way open for the rise of radicalism.

After Independence and Partition, things calmed down enough to allow the new state to grow wealthy on its prodigious agricultural output. As it did, militant Sikhs began to press for the creation of the separate Punjabi-speaking state they called Khalistan. A compromise of sorts was reached in 1966, when the Hindu district of Haryana and the Sikh-majority Punjab were nominally divided. However, the move did not silence the separatists, and in 1977 Indira Gandhi's Congress was trounced in state elections by a coalition that included the Sikh religious party, the **Akali Dal**.

A more sinister element entered the volatile equation with the emergence of an ultra-radical separatist movement led by **Sant Jarnail Singh Bhindranwale**. Covertly supported by the national government (who saw the group as a way to defeat the Akali Dal), Bhindranwale and his band waged a ruthless campaign of sectarian terror in the Punjab which came to a head in 1984, when they occupied Amritsar's Golden Temple; **Operation Blue Star**, Indira Gandhi's brutal response (see p.1165), plunged the Punjab into another ugly bout of communal violence. Four years later, history repeated itself when a less threatening occupation of the temple was crushed by **Operation Black Thunder**. Since then, the Punjab police have gone on to make considerable advances against the terrorists – helped, for the first time, by Punjabi peasant farmers, the **Jats**, who had grown tired of the inexorable slaughter. Most Akali Dal factions boycotted the 1992 elections, which saw Congress returned on a 22 percent turnout. Chief minister **Beant Singh** was killed by a car bomb in 1995, but this was the militants' last gasp. Public support had ebbed, and the police, using strong-arm tactics, were able to wipe out the paramilitary groups that had burgeoned during the 1980s. Subsequent state elections have seen a **return to normality**. An Akali Dal/BJP coalition – thrown out by Congress in 2002 – regained power in 2007, and held it in 2012, with voter turnout back to normal and no paramilitary violence.

Chandigarh

CHANDIGARH is the state capital of both Punjab and Haryana, but part of neither, being a Union Territory administered by India's federal government. Its history begins in 1947, when Partition placed the Punjab's main city of Lahore in Pakistan, leaving India's state of Punjab without a capital. Nehru saw this as an opportunity to realize his vision of a city "symbolic of the future of India, unfettered by the traditions of the past, (and) an expression of the nation's faith in the future". The job of designing it went to controversial Swiss-French architect Charles-Edouard Jeanneret, alias **Le Corbusier**.

Begun in 1952, Chandigarh was to be a groundbreaking experiment in town planning. Le Corbusier's blueprints were for an orderly grid of sweeping boulevards, divided into 29 neat blocks, or **Sectors**, each measuring 800m by 1200m, and interspersed with extensive stretches of green. The resulting city has been a source of controversy since its completion in the 1960s. Some applaud Le Corbusier's brainchild as one of the great architectural achievements of the twentieth century, but detractors complain that the design is self-indulgent and un-Indian. Le Corbusier created a city for fast-flowing traffic at a time when few people owned cars, while his cubic concrete buildings are like ovens during the summer – all but uninhabitable without expensive air-conditioning. The city has expanded from the first phase comprising sectors 1 to 30 (there is no Sector 13), through a second phase – sectors 31 to 47 – and is now into the third phase with (half-size) sectors 48 to 61. Satellite towns emulating Chandigarh's grid plan and sterile concrete architecture have also sprung up on either side, with Panchkula in Haryana and Mohali in Punjab easing the pressure on a city left with nowhere else to grow.

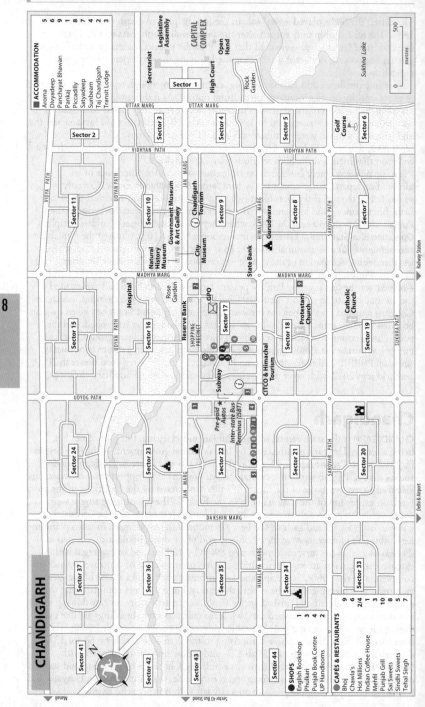

CHANDIGARH

ACCOMMODATION

Aroma	5
Divyadeep	6
Panchayat Bhawan	9
Pankaj	1
Piccadilly	8
Satyadeep	7
Sunbeam	4
Taj Chandigarh	2
Transit Lodge	3

SHOPS

English Bookshop	1
Phulkari	3
Punjab Book Centre	4
UP Handlooms	2

CAFÉS & RESTAURANTS

Bhoj	9
Chawla's	6
Hot Millions	2/4
Indian Coffee House	1
Mehfi	3
Punjab Grill	10
Sai Sweets	8
Sindhi Sweets	5
Tehal Singh	7

Sector 1

Legislative Assembly

Secretariat

CAPITAL COMPLEX

High Court

Open Hand

Rock Garden

Sukhna Lake

UTTAR MARG

Sector 2

Sector 3

Sector 4

Sector 5

Sector 6

Golf Course

VIDHYAN PATH

Sector 11

Sector 10

Government Museum & Art Gallery

Chandigarh Tourism

Sector 9

Sector 8

Sector 7

Natural History Museum

City Museum

State Bank

Gurudwara

MADHYA MARG

Hospital

Sector 15

Rose Garden

Reserve Bank

Sector 16

SHOPPING PRECINCT

GPO

Sector 17

Sector 18

Protestant Church

Sector 19

Catholic Church

Subway

CITCO & Himachal Tourism

UDYOG PATH

Sector 24

Sector 23

Pre-paid Autos

Inter-state Bus Terminus (ISBT)

Sector 22

Sector 21

Sector 20

DAKSHIN MARG

Sector 37

Sector 36

Sector 35

Sector 34

Sector 33

Sector 41

Sector 42

Sector 43

Sector 44

JAN MARG

HIMALAYA MARG

UDYAN PATH

SAROVAR PATH

SUKHNA PATH

VIDYA PATH

Railway Station

Delhi & Airport

Manali

Sector 43 Bus Stand

0 500 metres

8

Despite Chandigarh's shortcomings, its inhabitants are proud of their capital, which is cleaner, greener and more affluent than other Indian cities of comparable size, and boasts a rock garden said to be India's second most visited tourist site after the Taj Mahal.

Chandigarh's numbered **sectors** are further subdivided into lettered blocks, making route-finding relatively easy. Le Corbusier saw the city plan as a living organism, with the imposing **Capital Complex** to the north as a "head", the shopping precinct, **Sector 17**, a "heart", the green open spaces as "lungs", and the crosscutting network of roads, separated into eight different grades for use by various types of vehicles (in theory only), a "circulatory system".

The museums

Sector 10 • All Tues–Sun 10am–4.40pm • A ₹10 ticket covers the three museums, with a ₹5 camera charge for each

Situated in the green belt known as the Leisure Valley, Chandigarh's museums, located in Sector 10, form part of a cultural complex that includes the neighbouring Rose Garden. The **Government Museum & Art Gallery** houses a sizeable and informatively displayed collection of textiles, Harappan artefacts, miniature paintings and contemporary art, including five original Roerichs and a couple of A.N. Tagore's atmospheric watercolours. The ancient sculptures are the compelling exhibits, notably the Gandhara Buddhas with their delicately carved "wet-look" *lunghis* and distinctly Hellenic features – a legacy of Alexander the Great's conquests.

Next door, the small but appropriately modernist **City (Architecture) Museum** illustrates the planning and construction of Chandigarh, with models and photographs in a concrete pavilion based on one of Le Corbusier's designs. Beyond that, the **Natural History Museum** has a few stuffed animals, some bits of fossilized mammoths and diorama depictions of early humans.

8

The Capital Complex

Tight security following the 1995 assassination (in front of the Assembly building) of Punjab chief minister Beant Singh by Sikh nationalist hardliners means you'll need a **letter of permission** from the tourist office (see p.516) to visit the **Capital Complex** in Sector 1. The complex's most imposing edifice is the eleven-storey **Secretariat**, Chandigarh's highest building, which houses ministerial offices for both Haryana and Punjab, and has a roof garden with good views over the city. The resemblance of the **Legislative Assembly building**, or Vidhan Sabha (home to the legislatures of both states) to a power station is no coincidence: Le Corbusier was allegedly inspired by a stack of cooling towers he saw in Ahmedabad. Opposite the Secretariat is the most colourful building in the complex, the **High Court** (also serving both states), which is said to incorporate elements of the Buland Darwaza in Fatehpur Sikri, and is decorated inside with huge woollen tapestries. North of this is the black, 13m-high **Open Hand monument**, Chandigarh's adopted emblem. Weighing all of 45 tonnes, it revolves on ball bearings like a weather vane and stands for "post-colonial harmony and peace".

The Rock Garden

Uttar Marg, Sector 1 • Daily: April–Sept 9am–7pm; Oct–March 9am–6pm • ₹20 • ⓦ nekchand.com

Close to the Capital Complex, the **Rock Garden** is a surreal fantasyland fashioned from fragments of shattered plates, neon strip-lights, pots, pebbles, broken bangles and assorted urban-industrial junk. The open-air exhibition is a labour of love from of retired Public Works Department road inspector **Nek Chand**. Inspired by a recurrent childhood dream, he began construction in 1965. His intention was to create just a small garden, but by the time it was discovered in 1973 – to widespread astonishment – it covered 12 acres. Though it was completely illegal, the city council recognized it as a great artistic endeavour and, in a conspicuously enlightened decision, awarded Chand a salary to continue his work, and a workforce of fifty labourers to help. Opened to the public in 1976, the garden now covers 25 acres and contains several thousand sculptures.

Now over 85, Nek Chand continues to oversee work on the site, a labyrinth of more than a dozen different enclosures interconnected by narrow passages, arched walkways, streams, bridges, grottos, waterfalls, battlements and turrets. Stick to the path, or you could end up wandering the maze until the *chowkidar* finds you at closing time.

ARRIVAL AND DEPARTURE   CHANDIGARH

By plane Chandigarh's airport is 11km south of the city centre (₹100 by auto from the ISBT, ₹300 by taxi); destinations include Delhi, Mumbai and Srinagar. Airlines include Air India, 162–4, Sector 34-A ☎ 0172 262 4943 and Jet, airport, ☎ 0172 507 5674. Bajaj Travels, 96–7 Sector 17-C (☎ 0172 432 1000) are agents for several international and domestic airlines.

By train There's a rail reservation centre at the ISBT (Mon–Sat 8am–2pm & 2.15–8pm, Sun 8am–2pm). From the railway station 8km southeast of the centre there are direct trains to Delhi (7 daily; 3hr 32min–5hr 20min), Jodhpur (1 daily; 17hr 20min), Mumbai (1–2 daily; 27hr 25min) and Kolkata (1 daily; 30hr 45min). The superfast a/c *Shatabdi Express* runs to New Delhi

railway station (#12006 & #12012 dep. at 6.53am & 6.23pm). Second-class tickets cost ₹435, three times the bus price, but the journey is far more comfortable and almost twice as fast. Other useful daily trains include the #22926 *Paschim Express* (dep. 11.20am, arr. New Delhi 4.25pm).

By bus The main Inter-state Bus Terminal (ISBT) is on the south edge of the main commercial and shopping district, Sector 17, but daytime services to Punjab and Himachal Pradesh use the Sector 43 bus stand, connected to the ISBT by local bus. Tickets can be pre-booked at both terminals, or bought on the bus. There's a pre-paid auto-rickshaw counter across the road from the west side of the ISBT (next to the pedestrian underpass exit).

GETTING AROUND AND INFORMATION

By auto-rickshaw Chandigarh is too spread out to explore on foot, but cycle and auto-rickshaws cruise the streets. Cycle rickshaws are cheaper, but the drivers find the long haul up to the north end of town or to the railway station tough going, so allow plenty of time. A pre-paid auto from opposite the ISBT to the Rock Garden is around ₹50.

By taxi The main taxi stand (☎ 0172 270 4621; 24hr) is next to the ISBT's pre-paid auto-rickshaw booth, but there are others at, for example, the northeast and southeast corners of Sector 22.

Tourist information Chandigarh Tourism (ⓦ chandigarhtourism.gov.in) has information booths at the station (daily 6am–6pm) and in Plaza Market, Sector 17 (daily 10am–5pm). The second of these should be able to issue a permit to visit the Capital Complex (see p.515) – failing that, you may have to go their administrative office

next to the police HQ in Sector 9-D (☎ 0172 274 0420). Their tour and travel wing, CITCO (Chandigarh Industry and Tourism Development Corporation; daily 9am–5pm; ☎ 0172 270 3839, ⓦ citcochandigarh.com), is at the ISBT, and should be able to provide basic tourist information as well as selling tours). Himachal Pradesh's office (Mon–Sat 9am–6pm; ☎ 0172 270 7267), next door to CITCO at the ISBT, is useful for booking HP Tourist Development Corporation tours and buses to HP destinations such as Manali and Shimla. Punjab Tourism has an office at 3 Sector 38-A (☎ 0172 262 5951); Haryana Tourism's office is at 17–19 Sector 17-B (☎ 0172 270 2955; ⓦ haryanatourism. gov.in).

Tours CITCO at the ISBT can arrange half-day excursions in and around town (₹50) in an open-top tourist bus, visiting the museum and art gallery and the Rock Garden.

ACCOMMODATION

Chandigarh's sky-high property prices make its **accommodation** expensive, especially at the bottom end where choice is very limited.

GETTING TO SHIMLA

Chandigarh is an important transport hub for **Shimla**, most swiftly reached by bus from Sector 43 (every 10min; 4hr–4hr 30min). You can also get there on the slower but more congenial Viceroys' "Toy Train" (see box, p.405) from Kalka, 26km to the northeast and connected to Chandigarh by trains and frequent buses. The scenic 75km journey from Kalka to Shimla takes around 5hr (dep. 4am, 5.10am, 5.30am, 6am & 12.10pm).

Aroma Himalaya Marg, Sector 22-C ☏0172 270 0047 or 8, ⊛hotelaroma.com. A vintage Austin guards the doorway of this attractive-looking hotel, which has a range of bars and restaurants. The rooms are mock-classic, with laminated floors and slightly scuffed walls imitating an old-fashioned feel. All in all, it's a reasonable fall-back if the *Sunbeam*'s full. Breakfast included. ₹**3560**

Divyadeep Himalaya Marg, 1090–1 Sector 22-B ☏0172 270 1169. Pleasant budget hotel run by Sai Baba devotees. The rooms are decent enough, with a/c and hot running water, and there's a large rooftop area, though liquor is banned. If it's full, try the almost identically priced *Satyadeep*, a few doors away, above Sai Sweets at 1102–03 Sector 22-B (☏0172 270 3103), run by the same management. ₹**1200**

Panchayat Bhawan Madhya Marg, Sector 18 ☏0172 270 0791 or 2, ✉panchayatbhawan@yahoo.com. The cheapest place to stay in town, hostel-like but well kept, with dorms and large, clean rooms, some of them with a/c (₹936). Dorm ₹**100**, double ₹**624**

Pankaj Udyog Path, Sector 22-A ☏0172 270 9891. Squeaky-clean a/c rooms and fancy showers, but of the "regular" rooms only those on the top floor have exterior windows; bigger and better "deluxe" and "super deluxe" rooms (₹2217 and ₹2663) all have windows and a seating area. ₹**1437**

Piccadily Himalaya Marg, Sector 22-B ☏0172 270 7571 or 2, ⊛thepiccadily.com. Rather plush establishment with thickly carpeted corridors and rooms, central a/c, free wi-fi, classy restaurant, bar and coffee shop. Breakfast included. ₹**5404**

Sunbeam Udyog Path, Sector 22-B ☏0172 270 8100 to 07, ⊛hotelsunbeam.com. Upmarket hotel opposite the ISBT with swish marble lobby and comfortable rooms, though the decorative brickwork in front of the windows makes them a bit dark. ₹**3114**

★ **Taj Chandigarh** Block 9, Sector 17-A ☏0172 661 3000, ⊛tajhotels.com. Chandigarh's poshest option by a long chalk, in a well-designed building whose minimalist modern decor in cool, light colours makes it something like an elegant, beautiful version of one of Le Corbusier's concrete boxes. ₹**13,370**

Transit Lodge ISBT, Sector 17 ☏0172 464 4485. Cheap and cheerful, slap bang in the middle of the bus station, and institutional but clean with attached rooms and hot water; also has dorm accommodation. Rates include one meal. Dorm ₹**300**, double ₹**750**

EATING AND DRINKING

Bhoj Hotel Divyadeep, 1090–1 Sector 22-B ☏0172 270 5191. Classy pure-veg joint run by Sai Baba devotees, serving only thalis, at ₹140 (small) or ₹170 (large). Daily 11.30am–4pm & 7–10.30pm.

Chawla's Himalaya Marg, Sector 22-C ☏0172 270 5625, ⊛chawlachicken.com. The Punjab's most popular foodstuff is chicken, cooked in a variety of ways, and this small tandoori restaurant is renowned for its wonderful, rich cream chicken (₹375 for a whole one; but a ₹215 half portion will be more than enough). Daily 11.30am–11.30pm.

Hot Millions 76–79 Sector 17-D (upstairs) ☏0172 272 3222, ⊛hotmillions.biz. Part of a successful fast-food chain, selling everything from dosas to pizzas. This eat-in branch also has a good salad bar, and a menu of tandoori, Mughlai and Chinese cuisine (chicken sizzler ₹425), with a takeaway just downstairs (☏0172 270 4858). *Hot Millions 2* in Sector 17-C near *Mehfil* has a cool subterranean pub – *Down Under*. Restaurant Sun–Thurs 11am–10pm, Fri & Sat 11am–10.30pm; takeaways and Down Under Sun–Thurs 11.30am–11pm, Fri & Sat 11.30am–midnight.

Indian Coffee House 63–64 Sector 17-E ☏0172 270 4504. Budget co-op chain with a limited but cheap menu, including dosas, sandwiches and good coffee. All dishes are under ₹40 (masala dosa ₹36). Daily; winter 9am–9pm; summer 9am–10pm.

Mehfil 183–5 Sector 17-C ☏0172 270 3539. Preserve of Chandigarh's smart set, and *the* place to sample rich Mughlai and Punjabi cuisine in a/c comfort. Dishes include an excellent chicken tikka masala (₹310), or *rogan josh* (₹295). There's a ₹255 lunch combo on offer from noon to 4pm, and for dessert, they serve ice cream from the *Baskin Robbins* outlet directly opposite. Daily 11am–11pm.

Punjab Grill 120–22 Sector 17-C ☏0172 402 9444, ⊛punjabgrill.in. An elegant grill restaurant, where a perfect tandoori chicken will set you back ₹475, and tandoori pomfret costs ₹725. Daily 11.45am–4.30pm & 7–11pm.

Sai Sweets 1102–3 Sector 22-B (below the Satyadeep hotel) ☏0172 270 3103. One of the best sweetshops in town, where you can also sit down for a sticky *gulab jamun* (₹12), or for savoury snacks such as a really good *chana bhatura* (like *chana puri*, but bigger; ₹50). Daily 7.30am–8.30pm.

Sindhi Sweets 110 Sector 17-B ☏0172 507 5222. An excellent a/c sweets emporium, packed to the gunwales with silver-coloured confections of all sorts (takeaway only), and translucent *kesar* or *angoora petha* at ₹220/kg. Daily 9.30am–10.30pm.

Tehal Singh Himalaya Marg, 1116–7 Sector 22-B ☏0172 271 1189. Very popular chicken restaurant (with takeaway and delivery), doing the likes of tandoori chicken (₹220) or butter chicken (₹300), with decent-sized half portions available. *Singh's Chicken* right next door provides competition. Daily noon–1am.

8

SHOPPING

English Bookshop 30 Sector 17-E ☎0172 270 2542. A good general bookstore, centrally located in the middle of Sector 17's main shopping area. Mon–Sat 10am–8pm.

Phulkari 27 Sector 17-E ☎0172 270 6246. Several states run handicraft emporiums in the Sector 17 shopping complex, among them Punjab, whose Phulkari store stocks a good range of embroidered silk, woodwork and traditional pointed Punjabi shoes. Mon–Sat 10.30am–2pm & 3.30–8pm.

Punjab Book Centre 1126–7 Sector 22-B ☎0172 270 1952. A good mix of fiction and non-fiction – everything from Karl Marx to Jeffrey Archer – and in particular for books on Indian history and politics. Mon–Sat 10am–8pm.

UP Handlooms 139–41 Sector 17-C ☎0172 304 2248. For quality handloom products, this UP state emporium by Sector 17's Plaza Market is strong on block-printed calico garments, especially *salwar kameez*. Daily 10.30am–3pm & 3.30–7.30pm.

DIRECTORY

Banks and exchange Several banks around Bank Square in the northeast corner of Sector 17 change money, including UCO Bank, Punjab National Bank and State Bank of India. ATMs are common around town, including one at the station and two at the ISBT.

Hospitals Chandigarh's Government Multi Specialty Hospital is in Sector 16 (☎102 or ☎0172 276 8265), but is not as good as the PGI, Sector 12 (☎0172 274 6018).

Internet e-net, 63 Sector 17-E (upstairs from the *Indian Coffee House*; daily 10.30am–8pm; ₹40/hr).

Left luggage There is a cloakroom in the ISBT (₹5/day; 24hr except 12.30–1pm & 8.30–9pm).

Pharmacies Apollo Pharmacy, 16–17 Sector 34-A ☎0172 501 7225 (24hr).

Police ☎100.

8

Pathankot

The dusty town of **PATHANKOT**, 270km northwest of Chandigarh and 101km to the northeast of Amritsar, is an important cantonment and railway junction, close to the frontier with Pakistan and near the borders with Himachal Pradesh and Jammu. Pathankot itself is a friendly enough place, but there's nothing special to see here, and most travellers just pass through to pick up bus connections to Dharamsala, Dalhousie, Chamba and Kashmir, or to take the slow train east through the picturesque Kangra Valley.

ARRIVAL AND INFORMATION

By train The slow narrow-gauge passenger trains to Jogindernagar (daily 2.15am & 10pm; 9hr 10min–9hr 45min; plus four trains to Baijnath only) wind through the scenic Kangra Valley and make a pleasant alternative to the busy road to both Dharamsala (change at Kangra) and the Kullu Valley (bus from Joginder Nagar or Baijnath).

By bus Pathankot's bus station, on Railway Rd, 300m west of the railway station, has services to Amritsar (every

10min; 3hr), Chandigarh (35 daily; 6hr), Dharamsala (13 daily; 4hr), Jammu (every 15–30min; 3hr), Manali (5 daily; 12hr) and Shimla (2 daily; 12 hr).

Tourist information No local (Punjabi) tourist office, but Himachal Pradesh Tourism has a friendly branch at the railway station (in principle Mon–Sat 10am–5pm, but often open earlier, or closed briefly if the single member of staff needs a break; ☎0186 222 0316).

ACCOMMODATION

Railway Retiring Rooms At the station. If you've got a rail ticket, this is by far the best-value budget accommodation in town, all very ship-shape and correct, with attached bathrooms and hot water, plus a/c if you want it, but there's no phone and you can't book ahead, so you'll have to take your chances. Rooms can be rented for 12hr or 24hr. ₹200

Tourist Hotel Railway Rd (200m east of the railway station) ☎0186 222 0660. Reasonable attached rooms, of which, oddly, the cheaper ones have hot water, while the

bigger, pricier ones (₹800) don't. Not great value for money, but the best of the bunch along this stretch of Railway Road. ₹500

Venice 300m east of the station and then 400m south of Railway Rd on Dhangu Rd ☎0186 222 5061, ⓦvenicehotelindia.com. This is Pathankot's top business hotel, and its most comfortable address, with good rooms ranging from semi-deluxe to super-deluxe (the only real difference being the size). There's free wi-fi, a restaurant and a bar. ₹1720

Amritsar

The Sikhs' holy city of **AMRITSAR** is the largest city in Punjab: noisy and congested, but its old city in particular is as lively as any in India, and contains the fabled **Golden Temple**, whose domes soar above the teeming streets. Amritsar is also an important staging-post for those crossing the Indo–Pakistan frontier at Wagha, 29km west (see box, p.525).

Brief history

Amritsar was founded in 1577 by **Ram Das**, the fourth Sikh guru, beside a bathing pool famed for its healing powers. The land around the tank was granted in perpetuity by the Mughal emperor Akbar to the Sikhs. When merchants moved in to take advantage of the strategic location on the Silk Route, Amritsar expanded rapidly, gaining a grand new temple under Ram Das's son and heir, **Guru Arjan Dev**. Sacked by Afghans in 1761, the shrine was rebuilt by the Sikhs' greatest secular leader, **Maharaja Ranjit Singh**, who also donated the gold used in its construction.

Amritsar's **twentieth-century** history has been blighted by a series of appalling **massacres**. The first occurred in 1919, when thousands of unarmed civilian demonstrators were gunned down without warning by British troops in **Jallianwalla Bagh** (see box, p.523) – an atrocity that inspired Gandhi's Non-Cooperation Movement. Following the collapse of the Raj, Amritsar experienced some of the worst communal

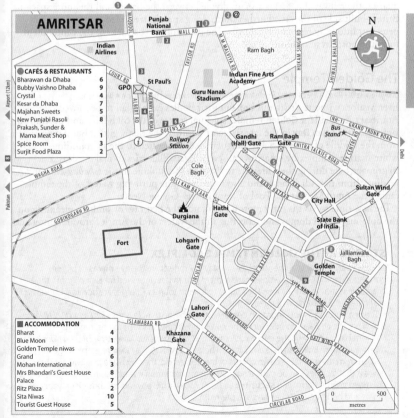

blood-letting ever seen on the Subcontinent. The Golden Temple, however, remained unaffected by the volatile politics of post-Independence Punjab until the 1980s, when as part of a protracted and bloody campaign for the setting up of a Sikh homeland, heavily armed fundamentalists under the preacher-warrior Sant Jarnail Singh **Bhindranwale** occupied the Akal Takht, a building in the Golden Temple complex that has traditionally been the seat of Sikh religious authority. The siege was brought to an end in early June 1984, when prime minister Indira Gandhi ordered an inept paramilitary attack on the temple, code-named **Operation Blue Star**. Bhindranwale was killed along with two hundred soldiers and two thousand others, including pilgrims trapped inside.

Widely regarded as an unmitigated disaster, Blue Star led directly to the assassination of Indira Gandhi by her Sikh bodyguards just four months later, and provoked the worst riots in the city since Partition. Nevertheless, the Congress government seemed to learn little from its mistakes. In 1987, Indira Gandhi's son, Rajiv Gandhi, reneged on an important accord with the Sikhs' main religious party, the Akali Dal, thereby strengthening the hand of the separatists, who retaliated by occupying the temple for a second time. This time, the army responded with greater restraint, leaving **Operation Black Thunder** to the Punjab police. Neither as well provisioned nor as well motivated as Bhindranwale's martyrs, the fundamentalists eventually surrendered.

The Golden Temple stands in the heart of the **old town**, itself a maze of narrow lanes and bazaars. Eighteen fortified **gateways** punctuate the aptly named **Circular Road**, of which only Lohgarh Gate (to the north) is original. Skirting the edge of the old quarter, the railway line forms a sharp divide between the bazaar and the more spacious British-built side of the city. Further north, long straight tree lined streets eventually peter out into leafy residential suburbs. The neat military barracks of the **cantonment** form the northwestern limits of the city.

The Golden Temple

Golden Temple Rd • There's a free bus to the Temple from the railway station forecourt (every 30min 4.30am–9pm)

Even visitors without a religious bone in their bodies cannot fail to be moved by Amritsar's resplendent **Golden Temple**, spiritual centre of the Sikh faith and open to all. Built by **Guru Arjan Dev** in the late sixteenth century, the richly gilded **Harmandir** rises from the middle of an artificial rectangular lake, connected to the surrounding white-marble complex by a narrow causeway. Every Sikh tries to make at least one pilgrimage here during their lifetime to listen to the sublime music (*shabad kirtan*), readings from the Adi Granth and also to bathe in the purifying waters of the temple tank – the **Amrit Sarovar** or "Pool of Immortality-Giving Nectar".

The best time to visit is early morning, to catch the first rays of sunlight gleaming on the bulbous golden domes and reflecting in the waters of the Amrit Sarovar. Sunset and

---

STAYING AT THE GOLDEN TEMPLE COMPLEX

Undoubtedly the most authentic places to stay in Amritsar are the five **niwas** or pilgrim hostels run by the Golden Temple management committee. Intended for Sikh pilgrims, these charitable institutions also open their doors to foreign tourists. Charges are nominal but stays are limited to a maximum of three nights.

The first building as you approach on the east side of the temple is the *Guru Arjan Dev Niwas*, which has the check-in counter for all the *niwas* and simple, spacious rooms. The most comfortable of the five is the new, excellent-value *Guru Hargobind Niwas*. The *Sri Guru Nanak Niwas* was where Bhindranwale and his men holed up prior to the Golden Temple siege in 1984.

Apart from the inevitable dawn chorus of throat-clearing, the downside of staying at these *niwas* is that facilities can be basic (*charpoy* beds and communal wash-basins in the central courtyard are the norm) and **security** can be a problem. It is advisable to book in advance as rooms and beds are almost always at a premium.

GOLDEN RULES

Visitors of all nationalities and religions are allowed into the Golden Temple provided they respect a few basic **rules**, enforced by patrolling guards. Firstly, tobacco, alcohol and drugs of any kind are forbidden. Before entering, you should also leave your shoes at the free cloakrooms, cover your head (cotton scarves are available outside the main entrance – or wear your Kullu hat) and wash your feet in the pool below the steps. **Photography** is permitted around the pool, but not inside any of the shrines.

evenings are an excellent time to tune in to the beautiful music performed in the Harmandir. The helpful information office (daily 7am–8pm) at the main entrance organizes **guided tours**, provides details on temple accommodation and has books and leaflets about the temple and Sikh faith.

The Parikrama

The principal north entrance to the temple, the **Darshini Deori**, leads under a Victorian **clocktower** to a flight of steps, from where you catch your first glimpse of the Harmandir, floating serenely above the glassy surface of the Amrit Sarovar. Dropping down as a reminder of the humility necessary to approach God, the steps end at the polished marble **Parikrama** that surrounds the tank, its smooth white stones set with the names of those who contributed to the temple's construction.

The shrines on the north edge of the enclosure are known as the **68 Holy Places**. Arjan Dev, the fifth guru, told his followers that a visit to these was equivalent to a pilgrimage around all 68 of India's most sacred Hindu sites. Several have been converted into a **Gallery of Martyrs**, in which paintings of glorious but gory episodes from Sikh history are displayed.

Four glass-fronted booths punctuate the Parikrama. Seated in each is a priest, or **granthi**, intoning verses from the Adi Granth (Sikh scriptures). The continuous readings are performed in shifts; passing pilgrims touch the steps in front of the booths with their heads and leave offerings of money.

At the east end of the Parikrama, the two truncated **Ramgarhia Minars** – brick watchtowers whose tops were blasted off during Operation Blue Star – overlook the Guru-ka-Langar (see below) and the main bathing **ghats**. Hang around here long enough and you'll see a fair cross-section of modern Sikh society parade past: families of Jat farmers, NRIs (Non-Resident Indians) on holiday from Britain and North America and the odd group of fierce-looking warriors carrying lances, sabres and long curved daggers. Distinguished by their deep-blue knee-length robes and saffron turbans, the ultra-orthodox **nihangs** (literally "crocodiles") are devotees of the militarist tenth guru, Gobind Singh.

The Guru-ka-Langar

For Sikhs, no pilgrimage to the Golden Temple is considered complete without a visit to the **Guru-ka-Langar**. The giant communal canteen, which overlooks the eastern entrance to the temple complex, provides **free food** to all comers. Sharing meals with strangers reinforces one of the central tenets of the Sikh faith, the **principle of equality**, instigated by the third guru, **Amar Das**, in the sixteenth century to break down caste barriers.

Some ten thousand chapatti and black dhal dinners are dished up here each day in an operation of typical Sikh efficiency, which you can witness for yourself by joining the queues that form outside the hall (open 24hr). The meal begins after grace has been sung by a volunteer, or *sevak*, and continues until everyone has eaten their fill. By the time the tin trays have been collected and the floors swept for the next sitting, another crowd of pilgrims has gathered at the gates, and the cycle starts again. Although the

8

meals are paid for out of the temple's coffers, most visitors leave a small donation in the boxes in the yard outside.

The Akal Takht

Directly opposite the ceremonial entrance to the Harmandir, the **Akal Takht** is the second most sacred shrine in the Golden Temple complex. A symbol of God's authority on earth, it was built by Guru Hargobind in the seventeenth century and came to house the Shiromani Gurudwara Parbandhak Committee, the religious and political governing body of the Sikh faith founded in 1925.

During the 1984 siege, **Bhindranwale** and his army used this golden-domed building as their headquarters, fortifying it with sandbags and machine-gun posts. When Indian paratroopers tried to storm the shrine, they were mown down in their hundreds while crossing the courtyard in front of it: the reason why the army ultimately resorted to much heavier-handed tactics to end the siege. Positioned at the opposite end of the Amrit Sarovar, tanks pumped a salvo of high-explosive squash-head shells into the delicate facade, reducing it to rubble within seconds. The destruction of the Akal Takht offended Sikh sensibilities more than any other aspect of the operation. The shrine has been largely rebuilt and now looks almost the same as it did before June 6, 1984. Decorated with elaborate inlay, its ground floor is where the Adi Granth is brought each evening from the Harmandir, borne in a gold-and-silver palanquin.

The Jubi Tree

The gnarled old **Jubi Tree** in the northwest corner of the compound was planted around 450 years ago by the Golden Temple's first high priest, or Babba Buddhaya, and is believed to have special powers. Women wanting a son hang strips of cloth from its branches, while marriage deals are traditionally struck in its shade for good luck – a practice the modern temple administration frowns upon.

The Harmandir

Likened by one guru to "a ship crossing the ocean of ignorance", the triple-storey **Harmandir**, or "Golden Temple of God" was built by Arjan Dev to house the Adi Granth, which he compiled from teachings of all the Sikh gurus; it is the focus of the Sikh faith. The temple has four doors indicating it is open to people of all faiths and all four caste divisions of Hindu society. The large dome and roof, covered with 100kg of gold leaf, is shaped like an inverted lotus, symbolizing the Sikhs' concern for temporal as well as spiritual matters.

The long causeway, or **Guru's Bridge**, which joins the Harmandir to the west side of the Amrit Sarovar, is approached via an ornate archway, the **Darshani Deorh.** As you approach the sanctum check out the amazing Mughal-style inlay work and floral gilt above the doors and windows.

The **interior** of the temple – decorated with yet more gold and silver, adorned with ivory mosaics and intricately carved wood panels – is dominated by the enormous **Adi Granth**, which rests on a sumptuous throne beneath a jewel-encrusted silk canopy. Before his death in 1708, Guru Gobind Singh, who revised the Adi Granth, declared that he was to be the last living guru, and that the tome would take over after him – hence its full title, the Guru Granth Sahib. *Granthi*s intone continuous readings from the text as the worshippers file past, accompanied by singers and musicians – all relayed by loudspeakers around the complex. Known as Shri Akhand Path, a single continuous reading of the Guru Granth Sahib is carried out in three-hour shifts and takes around 48 hours to complete.

ARRIVAL AND DEPARTURE   AMRITSAR

By plane The airport is 12km northwest of town (₹450 by taxi, R300 by auto-rickshaw). There are flights to Delhi with Air India (*MK International Hotel*, Ranjit Ave

📞 0183 250 8122 or 33), SpiceJet, Jet (airport 📞 0183 320 9847) and JetKonnect.

THE JALLIANWALLA BAGH MASSACRE

Just 100m northeast of the Golden Temple, a narrow lane leads between two tall buildings to **Jallianwalla Bagh** memorial park (daily: summer 6am–9pm; winter 7am–8pm), site of one of the bloodiest atrocities committed by the British Raj.

In 1919, a series of one-day strikes, or *hartals*, was staged in Amritsar in protest against the recent **Rowlatt Act**, which enabled the British to imprison without trial any Indian suspected of sedition. When the peaceful demonstrations escalated into sporadic looting, the lieutenant governor of Punjab declared martial law and called for reinforcements from Jalandhar. A platoon of infantry arrived soon after, led by **General R.E.H. Dyer**.

Despite a ban on public meetings, a mass demonstration was called by Mahatma Gandhi for April 13, the Sikh holiday of Baisakhi. The venue was a stretch of waste ground in the heart of the city, hemmed in by high brick walls and with only a couple of alleys for access. An estimated twenty thousand people gathered in Jallianwalla Bagh for the meeting. However, before any speakers could address the crowd, Dyer and his 150 troops, stationed on a patch of high ground in front of the main exit, opened fire without warning. By the time they had finished firing, ten to fifteen minutes later, hundreds of unarmed demonstrators lay dead and dying, many of them shot in the back while clambering over the walls. Others perished after diving for cover into the well that still stands in the middle of the *bagh*.

No one knows exactly how many people were killed. Official estimates put the death toll at 379, with 1200 injured, although the final figure may well have been several times higher; Indian sources quote a figure of two thousand dead. Hushed up for more than six months in Britain, the Jallianwalla Bagh massacre caused an international outcry when the story finally broke. It also proved seminal in the Independence struggle, prompting Gandhi to initiate the widespread civil disobedience campaign that played such a significant part in ridding India of its colonial overlords.

Moving first-hand accounts of the horrific events of April 13, 1919, and contemporary pictures and newspaper reports, are displayed in Jallianwalla Bagh's small **martyrs gallery**. The **well**, complete with chilling bullet holes, has been turned into a memorial to the victims.

There's a multilingual sound-and-light show every evening (7.30pm in summer, 6pm in winter), but it isn't really worth staying for.

By train The railway station is conveniently located in the centre of town, north of the old city. The best trains for Delhi are the daily superfast all-a/c chaircar *Amritsar–New Delhi Shatabdis* – the #12014 (dep. 5am, arr. 11.15am) and the #12030 (dep. 4.55pm, arr. 11.05pm). If you prefer to travel overnight, there's the #12904 *Golden Temple Mail* (dep. 9.25pm, arr. 7.05am), which continues to Mumbai (arr. 5.20am the following day). Other trains include the daily #13050 *Amritsar–Howrah Express* (dep. 6.10pm) via Varanasi (arr. 6.55pm next day) to Kolkata (arr. Howrah 3.45pm the day after that), and the twice-weekly #19782 *Amritsar–Jaipur Express* (Fri & Sun 5.50pm), which is faster than the #19772 (Tues & Thur 2.30pm) – both arrive in Jaipur at 7.30am.

By bus For Pathankot (every 10min; 3hr) and HP destinations, you are restricted to state transport buses from the large bus stand on Grand Trunk Rd (NH-1), north of the old city, where there are also services to Chandigarh (approximately every 30min; 4–6hr). Private buses, including a/c services, leave from around the railway station or outside on the street, just north of Gandhi (Hall) Gate. Agencies outside Gandhi (Hall) Gate and on Queens Rd operate deluxe and a/c buses to Chandigarh (3–5hr) and Delhi (10hr), but Delhi – 475km away – is a long and tiring road journey, and most people prefer to travel by train.

GETTING AROUND AND INFORMATION

By rickshaw You may find Amritsar too large and labyrinthine to negotiate on foot; if you're crossing town or are in a hurry, flag down an auto-rickshaw. Otherwise, stick to cycle rickshaws, which are the best way to get around the narrow, packed streets of the old quarter.

Tourist information PTDC's tourist office (Tues–Sun 9am–5pm; ☏ 0183 240 2452, ⊛ punjabtourism.gov.in), at the western exit from the railway station on Queens Rd, is friendly and helpful. They also run a Heritage Walk through the old city (₹75 (₹25) per person), starting at the City Hall daily at 8am and finishing at the Golden Temple.

GETTING TO PAKISTAN

For **Pakistan**, take one of the frequent buses to **Attari**, from where it's just 2km to the border at **Wagha** (see box opposite), or hire a taxi or auto from Amritsar. Rickshaws are available between Attari and Wagha. You'll have to cross into Pakistan by foot – it can take up to two hours to complete formalities. Tourists just wishing to watch the bizarre border spectacle can rent taxis (₹600) for the roundtrip, or take a shared taxi from outside the Golden Temple (₹100 per person) a couple of hours before the start. There is a **cross-border train** – the twice-weekly *Samjhauta Express* to Lahore in the Pakistani part of the Punjab – but whether it runs depends on the political situation, and at present it must be boarded at Delhi or Attari, not in Amritsar.

ACCOMMODATION

Amritsar's numerous **hotels** are spread out all over the city. While mid-range and upmarket accommodation is plentiful, budget options are limited; one solution is to stay in one of the Golden Temple's *niwas* (see box, p.520).

Bharat Off Railway Link Rd ☎0183 222 7536, ✉bharat_hotel@yahoo.com. Decent enough and handy for the station, offering a range of rooms of varying size, all with attached bathrooms and hot showers. Ignore any demands for spurious extra "taxes" when you check out. ₹650

Blue Moon Mall Rd ☎0183 222 0759, ✉hotelbluemoon@gmail.com. Friendly, helpful place, much better value than its more expensive competitors. The rooms are spacious and airy, and there's a decent restaurant (see opposite) open to non-residents. ₹1950

Grand Queens Rd, opposite the railway station ☎0183 256 2977, ⓦhotelgrand.in. Neat, clean, convenient and central with attached rooms around a pleasant garden courtyard, though windows all face inward. There's an adjacent bar decorated with Hollywood movie posters. A standard room (₹1426) is larger and more stylish than the cheapest (budget) rooms, but all have free wi-fi. They also offer day and night tours, the latter including the Wagha border ceremony. ₹700

Mohan International Albert Rd ☎0183 301 0100, ⓦmohaninternationalhotel.com. One of Amritsar's top hotels but overpriced, though it does have a/c, room service, a 24hr coffee shop and a pool. Popular in season (Nov–March) for Punjabi wedding receptions, which are colourful but noisy. Rates include breakfast. ₹3232

Mrs Bhandari's Guest House 10 Cantonment ☎0183 222 8509, ⓦbhandari_guesthouse.tripod.com. Wonderful old-fashioned rooms with wood fires and bathtubs in a colonial home with lawns, gardens and a small swimming pool. "British-style" three-course meals are available but pricey. You can camp in the grounds for ₹200/person. Popular with overland package tours, it's become an Amritsar institution. ₹2307

Palace Queens Rd, opposite the railway station ☎0183 256 5111. A facelift has massively improved things at this conveniently located and reasonably priced hotel where all the rooms have tiled floors and attached bathrooms, but wi-fi costs an extra ₹200/day. ₹600

Ritz Plaza 45 Mall Rd ☎0183 256 2836, ⓦritzhotel.in. Low-key but reasonably classy establishment, with central a/c, good-sized rooms and a relaxed atmosphere, surrounded by lawns; facilities include a pool, lounge bar, 24hr coffee shop and international restaurant, and it's wheelchair-accessible. Breakfast included. ₹5425

Sita Niwas 61 Sita Niwas Rd ☎0183 254 3092, ✉sitaniwas@yahoo.co.in. A good-value and popular budget option near *Guru Ram Das Niwas* and the Golden Temple, with a wide range of attached rooms. The very cheapest ones lack hot water, but it's only ₹100 more to get it. ₹500

Tourist Guest House Hide Market, near Bhandari Bridge, Grand Trunk Rd ☎0183 255 3830, ✉bubblesgoolry@yahoo.com. Popular with budget travellers since hippie trail days, offering a variety of rooms, of which the cheapest have shared bathrooms and hot water in buckets, but it doesn't cost much more for a very nice attached room with hot water. Wi-fi costs ₹100/day extra. Ignore commission-hungry rickshaw-wallahs telling you it's full. ₹300/₹500

EATING AND DRINKING

For inexpensive food, try the simple vegetarian **dhabas** around the Golden Temple and bus stand, which serve cheap and tasty *puris* and *chana* dhal. Local specialities include **Amritsari fish** (fillets of river fish fried in a spicy batter – river sole is the best, but *singara* is cheaper).

Bharawan da Dhaba Near the City Hall ☎0183 255 2275, ⓦbharawandadhaba.com. One of the best *dhabas* in Amritsar, founded in 1912 and now a full-sized restaurant, serving simple and inexpensive but good veg curries (₹100–140). Daily 8am–11pm.

Bubby Vaishno Dhaba 201 Gantagar Market (upstairs

in a mall opposite the Golden Temple main entrance) ☏ 98558 85007. A handy place for veg curries (such as *palak paneer* at ₹120), thalis (₹125–150) and breakfast options such as *parathas* or *puris*, plus a few south Indian dishes for good measure. Daily 24hr.

Crystal Crystal Chowk. One of the city's most popular restaurants, with Indian, Chinese and Western dishes served in comfortable surroundings, or from "fast-food" outlets on the street. A succulent *murgh makhani* (cream chicken) will set you back ₹300, as will a chicken tikka masala or a rogan josh. Daily 11am–11.30pm.

Kesar da Dhaba Passian Chowk, between Golden Temple and Durgiana Temple ☏ 0183 255 2103, ⓦ kesardadhaba.com. A limited menu of basic veg curries or thalis (₹106–140) in an establishment that's been going since 1916, but is well hidden away in the back streets (you'll need to ask for directions, or get a rickshaw to bring you). Daily 10.30am–6pm & 7–11pm.

Majahan Sweets Chowk Bijli (just off Hall Bazaar) ☏ 0183 254 1078. An excellent and long-established sweet shop (since 1947), and a very good place to try local sweet specialities such as lentil-based *dal pinni* (₹120/kg) and *matthi* (from ₹100/kg). Daily 8.30am–9.30pm.

New Punjabi Rasoli By Jallianwalla Bagh ☏ 0183 254 0140. Indian veg dishes, plus some Chinese and Continental, at reasonable prices (₹65–100). Most of the Indian dishes involve *paneer* (the *paneer* tomato is good, at ₹140), but there's also a delicious mushroom tikka masala (₹160). Daily 9am–11pm.

Prakash Meat Shop, **Sunder Meat Shop** and **Mama Meat Shop** Maqbool Rd, 500m north of Mall Rd. This trio of locally renowned *dhabas* are an Amritsar institution, frying up spicy mutton tikka or (for the brave) brain curry, on *tawas* (griddles) out front, at ₹100 a throw. Daily except Tues noon–midnight.

Spice Room Blue Moon Hotel, Mall Rd ☏ 0183 222 0759. An impressive choice of international dishes, including Indian, Western, Chinese and Tibetan, ranging from Middle Eastern mixed mezze (₹309) to *paneer* steak (₹379) and chicken pili-pili (₹399). Daily 12.30–3.30pm & 7.30–11.30pm.

Surjit Food Plaza GT 3–4 Nehru Plaza, Lawrence Rd ☏ 0183 222 2523. This bright restaurant (formerly a *dhaba* across the street) is an excellent place to try local specialities such as butter chicken (₹250) or Amritsari fish (₹300). Daily noon–3pm & 7–11pm.

DIRECTORY

Banks and exchange There are ATMs across town, including five in the railway station forecourt, one at the bus station and several around Jallianwalla Bagh. There's a clutch of forex bureaux opposite the train station on Railway Link Rd, many of which will change Pakistani rupees.

Hospitals The best in the city are Kakkar Hospital, Green Ave ☏ 0183 250 6015, and Munilal Chopra Hospital, 361 Mall Rd ☏ 0183 222 2072.

Internet A couple of places in Nehru Plaza, Lawrence Rd, including Cyber World at GF 55 (daily 9am–9pm; ₹30/hr).

Left luggage Baggage can be left for short periods at the Golden Temple's *gurudwaras*, or at the railway station or bus stand cloakroom.

Shopping Tablas (hand-drums), harmonia and other musical instruments are available at the shops outside the Golden Temple, where you can also buy cheap cassettes and CDs of the beautiful *kirtan* played in the shrine itself. Other possible souvenirs include a pair of traditional *Arabian Nights*-style Punjabi leather slippers (*jootis*), sold at stalls east of the temple's main entrance.

Swimming pools The *Mohan International* (₹500) and *Ritz Plaza* (₹500/hr) allow non-residents discretionary use of their pools.

8

BEDLAM AT THE BORDER

Every evening as sunset approaches, the **India-Pakistan border** closes for the night with a spectacular and somewhat Monty Pythonesque show. It takes place at a remote little place 27km west of Amritsar called **Wagha** (the nearest town, 2km away, is Attari), connected by frequent minibuses to Amritsar. Hundreds, if not thousands, of Indians make their way westwards to Wagha (and Pakistanis eastwards) to watch the popular tourist attraction from specially erected stands.

Indian guards sporting outrageous moustaches and outlandish hats perform synchronized speed marching along a 100m walkway to the border gate where they turn and stomp back. Raucous cheering, clapping and much blowing of horns accompanies the spectacle. Guards on the Pakistan side then emulate their neighbours' efforts to much the same sort of cacophony on the other side of the gate. The guards strut their military catwalk several times and then vanish into the guardhouse. Flags are simultaneously lowered, the gates slammed shut and the crowds on either side rush forward for a massive and congenial photo session. On both sides, more empathy than ever occurs on a cricket pitch permeates the air; photos are taken with the stone-faced guards and then everyone heads home – back to business as usual.

Gujarat

MEGHAWAL PEOPLE IN KUTCH

9

Gujarat

Heated in the north by the blistering deserts of Pakistan and Rajasthan, and cooled in the south by the gentle ocean breeze of the Arabian Sea, Gujarat forms India's westernmost bulkhead. The diversity of its topography – forested hilly tracts and fertile plains in the east, vast tidal marshland and desert plains in the Rann of Kutch in the west, with a rocky shoreline jutting into its heartland – can be compared to the multiplicity of its politics and culture. Home to significant populations of Hindus, Jains, Muslims and Christians, as well as tribal and nomadic groups, the state boasts a patchwork of religious shrines and areas steeped in Hindu lore. Gujarat is the homeland of Mahatma Gandhi, born in Porbandar and a long-time resident of Ahmedabad. In line with his credo of self-dependence, Gujaratis consistently rank at or near the top of the chart in terms of India's economic output, and have fanned around the world to settle abroad.

The region's prosperity dates as far back as the third millennium BC, when the Harappans started trading shell jewellery and textiles. The latter, Jain-dominated industry, remains an important source of income to the state. India's most industrialized state, Gujarat also boasts some of the Subcontinent's biggest oil refineries; thriving cement, chemicals and pharmaceutical manufacturing units; and a lucrative ship-breaking yard at Alang. Kandla is one of west India's largest ports, while much of the country's diamond-cutting and-polishing takes place in Surat, Ahmedabad and Bhavnagar. Rural poverty remains a serious problem, however, and health and education developments still lag behind economic growth.

Despite Gandhi's push for political change through non-violent means, his home state has often followed a different course, and Muslim-Hindu tensions have boiled more than to violence on a cyclical basis. Following the devastating January 2001 **earthquake**, centred in Kutch, the state suffered India's worst **communal rioting** since Partition, with more than a thousand people killed in 2002. Dozens more died in a 2008 string of bomb attacks in Ahmedabad. All these events added to the woes of a state already beleaguered by severe **water shortages** and **drought**.

Nevertheless, Gujarat has plenty to offer those who take time to detour from its more famous northerly neighbour Rajasthan, and it's free of the hassle tourists often encounter there. The lure of important **temple cities**, **forts** and **palaces** is balanced by the chance to search out unique **crafts** made in communities whose way of life remains scarcely affected by global trends. Gujarat's **architectural diversity** reflects the influences of its many different rulers – Buddhist Mauryans, Hindu rajas and Muslim emperors.

Ahmedabad, state capital until 1970 and the obvious place to begin a tour, harbours the first mosques built in the curious **Indo-Islamic** style, richly carved temples and

SUN TEMPLE AT MODHERA

Highlights

① Ahmedabad Superb Indo-Islamic architecture, bustling bazaars and Mahatma Gandhi's Sabarmati Ashram. **See p.534**

② Sun temple, Modhera This beautiful eleventh-century temple is the finest example of Solanki architecture in the country. **See p.544**

③ Kutch Distinct from the rest of Gujarat; traditional embroidery, costume and culture still thrive in this harsh and remote landscape. See p.545

④ Dwarka Krishna's ancient capital and India's westernmost holy town is always abuzz with pilgrims. **See p.558**

⑤ Gir National Park The last remaining habitat of the rare Asiatic lion. **See p.566**

⑥ Diu West India's most congenial beach venue, this relaxed island has a Portuguese flavour in its colonial architecture. **See p.568**

⑦ Palitana temples Hundreds of sumptuously carved Jain shrines and stunning views from the top of Shatrunjaya Hill. **See p.574**

⑧ Champaner and Pavagadh A Solanki fortress guarding a lost Muslim city and a sacred hill dotted with Hindu and Jain temples. **See p.578**

HIGHLIGHTS ARE MARKED ON THE MAP ON PP.530–531

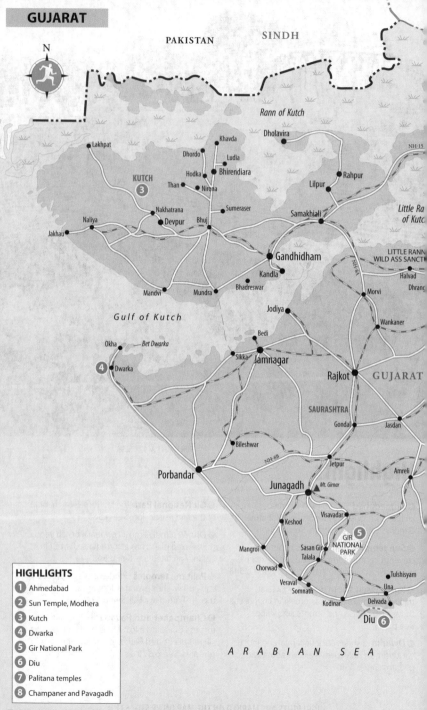

GUJARAT

PAKISTAN   SINDH

N

Rann of Kutch

Lakhpat

Dholavira

NH-15

Dhordo   Khavda

Ludia

KUTCH   Hodka Bhirendiara

3   Than   Nirona   Lilpur   Rahpur

Nakhatrana   Sumeraser   Samakhiali   Little Ra
Naliya   of Kutc
Jakhau   Devpur   Bhuj

LITTLE RANN
WILD ASS SANCT

Gandhidham   Halvad
Kandla   Dhranc
Mandvi   Mundra   Bhadreswar   Morvi

Gulf of Kutch   Jodiya   Wankaner

Bedi

Okha   Bet Dwarka   Sikka Jamnagar

4   Dwarka   Rajkot   GUJARAT

SAURASHTRA

Gondal   Jasdan

Bileshwar

NH-8B   Jetpur   Amreli

Porbandar   Junagadh   Mt. Girnar

Keshod   Visavadar

GIR   5
Mangroi   Sasan Gir NATIONAL
Talala   PARK
Chorwad   Tulshisyam
Veraval   Una
Somnath   Delvada
Kodinar
Diu 6

ARABIAN   SEA

HIGHLIGHTS

1 Ahmedabad
2 Sun Temple, Modhera
3 Kutch
4 Dwarka
5 Gir National Park
6 Diu
7 Palitana temples
8 Champaner and Pavagadh

The International boundaries on this map are neither purported to be correct nor authentic by Survey of India directives. Publisher.

9

step-wells dating from the eleventh century. Just north is the ancient capital of **Patan** and the Solanki sun temple at **Modhera**, while south is the Harappan site, **Lothal**. In the northwest, the largely barren region of **Kutch** was largely bypassed by Gujarat's foreign invaders, and consequently preserves a village culture where crafts long forgotten elsewhere are still practised.

The Kathiawar Peninsula, or **Saurashtra**, is Gujarat's heartland, scattered with temples, mosques and palaces bearing testimony to centuries of rule by Buddhists, Hindus and Muslims. Highlights include the superb Jain temples adorning the hills of **Shatrunjaya**, near Bhavnagar, and **Mount Girnar**, close to Junagadh. The temple at **Somnath** is said to have witnessed the dawn of time, and that at **Dwarka** is built on the site of Krishna's ancient capital. At **Junagadh**, ancient Ashokan inscriptions stand a stone's throw from flamboyant mausoleums and Victorian Gothic-style palaces. There's plenty of scope for spotting **wildlife**, too, including Asia's only lions, found in **Gir National Park**, blackbucks at **Velavadar National Park**, and the Indian wild ass in the **Little Rann Sanctuary**. Separated from the south coast by a thin sliver of the Arabian Sea, the island of **Diu**, a Union Territory and not officially part of the state, is fringed with beaches, palm groves and whitewashed Portuguese churches.

Brief history

The first known settlers in what is now Gujarat were the **Harappans**, who arrived from Sindh and Punjab around 2500 BC. Despite their craftsmanship and trade links with Africans, Arabs, Persians and Europeans, the civilization fell into decline in 1900 BC, largely due to severe flooding. From 1500 to 500 BC, little is known about the history of Gujarat but it is popularly believed the **Yadavas**, Krishna's clan, held sway over much of the state, with their capital at Dwarka. Gujarat's political history begins in earnest with the powerful **Mauryan** empire, established by Chandragupta with its capital at Junagadh and reaching its peak under Ashoka. After his death in 226 BC, Mauryan power dwindled; the last significant ruler was Samprati, Ashoka's grandson, a Jain who built fabulous temples at *tirthas* (pilgrimage sites) such as Girnar and Palitana. Rule then passed among a succession of warring dynasties and nomadic tribes throughout the first millenium AD, among them the native Gurjars (or Gujjar), from whom the modern state would derive its name.

A golden age

In the eleventh and twelfth centuries, Gujarat came under the sway of the **Solanki** (or **Chalukyan**) dynasty, originating from a Gurjar clan, which issued in a golden era in the state's architectural history. The Solankis built and rebuilt (following the devastating raid of Mahmud of Ghazni in 1027) splendid Hindu and Jain **temples** and **step-wells** throughout the state.

Foreign conquests

Muslim rule in Gujarat was established by the Khalji conquest in 1299. A century later, the **Sultanate of Gujarat** was founded when Muzaffar Shah declared independence from Delhi. Setting up a new capital at Ahmedabad, the Muzaffarid Dynasty ruled for two hundred years before the Mughal conquest of emperor Akbar in the sixteenth century. In the ensuing period, Muslim, Jain and Hindu styles were melded to produce remarkable **Indo-Islamic** mosques and tombs.

ALCOHOL IN GUJARAT

Gujarat is a **dry state**, but tourists can get free one-week alcohol permits from the bigger hotels. Avoid illicitly produced alcohol – the state has imposed the death penalty for its manufacture and sale, following a July 2009 incident in which 136 people died from drinking toxic alcohol. Alcohol is legally served in the Union Territory enclaves of Diu and Daman.

In the 1500s, the **Portuguese**, already settled in Goa, turned their attention to Gujarat. Having captured Daman in 1531, they took Diu four years later, building forts and typically European towns. The **British East India Company** set up its factory and headquarters in Surat in 1613, sowing the seeds of a prospering textile industry. British sovereignty over the state was established in 1818 when governor-generals signed treaties with about two hundred of Saurashtra's princely and petty states. The introduction of machinery upgraded textile manufacture, bringing substantial wealth to the region while putting many manual labourers out of business. Their cause was valiantly fought by Gujarat-born **Mahatma Gandhi** (see box, p.560), who led the momentous Salt March from Ahmedabad to Dandi. After Partition, Gujarat received an influx of Hindus from Sindh (Pakistan) and witnessed terrible sectarian fighting as Muslims fled to their new homeland.

The birth of modern Gujarat

In 1960, after the Marathi and Gujarati **language riots** (demonstrators sought the redrawing of state boundaries according to language, as had happened in the south), Bombay state was split and Gujarat created. The Portuguese enclaves were forcibly annexed by the Indian government in 1961. Post-Independence, Gujarat remained a staunch Congress stronghold until the fundamentalists of the BJP took control in 1991. The communal violence of 2002 pitted Muslim and Hindu neighbours against one another (see box below). More than a decade on, the religious and ethnic tension continues to cast a long shadow. Meanwhile, Gujarat remains one of India's most wealthy and prosperous states.

GODHRA AND GUJARAT'S COMMUNAL VIOLENCE

When the BJP shocked India with its landslide victory in the December 2002 election, analysts needed only to point to a single word as an answer for the victory – **Godhra**. The town was an anonymous railway depot until February 27, 2002, when a Muslim mob set fire to railway cars filled with Hindu pilgrims returning from the controversial temple at Ayodhya, killing 58.

The incident sparked huge **riots** across Gujarat. Muslim neighbourhoods burned while sword- and stick-wielding Hindus rampaged, looted and raped. In many cases, police forces allegedly stood by and watched. The official count death count reached almost one thousand, more than two thirds of them Muslim, while hundreds of thousands more were displaced.

Gujarat's BJP chief minister **Narendra Modi** earned the moniker "Muslim killer" for standing idly by as the violence continued. Just after the NGO Human Rights Watch reported Gujarat state officials "were directly involved" in the killings and that they were engaged in a "massive **cover-up** of the state's role in the violence", parliament attempted to censure the BJP government. Prime minister Atal Bihari Vajpayee apologized for not having "tried harder" to end the riots and announced a $31 million rehabilitation package.

Still, following a campaign filled with Hindutva rhetoric pledging to "to prevent" another Godhra, a blatant attempt to amass Hindu votes amid a climate of ethnic tension, Modi went on to secure a landslide win in the next election and has remianed in power ever since, becoming Gujarat's longest-serving chief minister and continuing to try to block prosecution of the rioters. In 2004, however, following protests against biased state authorities, the Supreme Court ordered more investigation into the riots, calling for a re-opening of more than two thousand dismissed cases. Just months before the 2007 state elections, respected magazine *Tehelka* published secretly filmed footage of senior Gujarati Hindu politicians, mainly from the BJP, describing their own active involvement in fanning the riots. The report alleged that Modi allowed the violence to continue unabated, ordered the police to side with Hindu rioters and sheltered the perpetrators from justice. Still, he was again resoundingly re-elected, and his name has subsequently been thrown about as a possible 2014 candidate for prime minister.

At last, in 2011, dozens of those guilty of the Godhra fire were convicted and sentenced, and in 2012, hundreds more of the rioters were convicted, including a former state minister, the first political implication in the post-Godhra riots.

For an in-depth account of the post-Godhra violence and the causes behind it, read Ward Berenschot's *Riot Politics: India's Communal Violence and the Everyday Mediation of the State* (2012).

9

Ahmedabad

A tangled mass of factories, mosques, temples and skyscrapers, Gujarat's commercial hub, **AHMEDABAD** (pronounced "Amdavad"), sprawls along the banks of the River Sabarmati, about 90km from its mouth in the Bay of Cambay. With a population of around seven million, it is the state's largest city and has long faced appalling pollution, dreadful congestion and repeated outbreaks of communal violence. However, the mix of medieval and modern makes it a compelling place to explore.

A wander through the bazaars and pols (residential areas) of the **old city** is rewarding. Ahmedabad is packed with diverse architectural styles, with more than fifty **mosques** and **tombs**, plus Hindu and Jain **temples** and grand **step-wells** (*vavs*). The **Calico Museum of Textiles** is one of the world's finest, while Gandhi's **Sabarmati Ashram** is an must-see for anyone with an interest in the Mahatma.

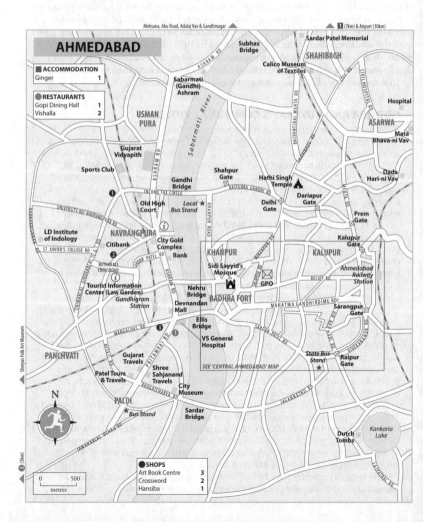

Particularly in the old city, it's advisable to cover your mouth and nose with a handkerchief to reduce inhalation of **carbon monoxide**. In 2002, a controversial **canal project** diverted water from the River Narmada into the Sabarmati, which previously had virtually dried up outside the monsoon. This has given the city a cooler feel, but Ahmedabad has a long way to go before it can breathe easily.

Brief history
When **Ahmed Shah** inherited the Sultanate of Gujarat in 1411, he moved his capital from Patan to Asawal, on the east bank of the Sabarmati, renaming it after himself. It quickly grew as artisans and traders were invited to settle, and its splendid mosques, intended to assert Muslim supremacy, heralded the new **Indo-Islamic** style of architecture. In 1572, Ahmedabad became part of the Mughal Empire and, on the back of a flourishing **textiles trade**, came to be regarded as India's most handsome city. However, two devastating famines, coupled with political instability, led the city into **decline**. It wasn't until 1817, when the newly arrived British lowered taxes, that the merchants returned. A new wave of prosperity came from the burgeoning opium trade, while the introduction of modern machinery re-established the Ahmedabad as a textile exporter. In the run-up to Independence, while **Mahatma Gandhi** was revitalizing small-scale textile production, the "Manchester of the East" became an important seat of political power and a hotbed for religious tension. While its reputation has been darkened by violent **communal rioting**, Ahmedabad remains today a booming hub for textiles as well as for IT, education, jewellery, chemicals and pharmaceuticals.

The old city
The historic heart of Ahmedabad is the **old city**, an area of about three square kilometres on the east bank of the river, dissected by the main thoroughfares of Relief Road and Mahatma Gandhi (MG) Road, and reaching its northern limits at **Delhi Gate**. It's best to start exploring in Lal Darwaja, taking in the squat buildings of the original citadel, **Bhadra**, the **mosques** and tombs of Ahmedabad's Muslim rulers, as well as vibrant bazaars and pols – labyrinths of high wooden havelis and narrow cul-de-sacs.

Bhadra Fort and around
Lal Darwaja

The solid fortified citadel, **Bhadra**, built of deep red stone in 1411 as Ahmedabad's first Muslim structure, is relatively plain in comparison to the city's later mosques. The palace is now occupied by offices and most of it is off-limits, but you can climb to the roof via a winding staircase just inside the main gateway. Across from the fort to the east is **Alif Shah's Mosque**, gaily painted in green and white. Further on, beyond the odoriferous meat market in **Khas Bazaar**, is **Teen Darwaja**, a triple gateway built during Ahmed Shah's reign that once led to the outer court of the royal citadel. A trio of pointed arches engraved with Islamic inscriptions and detailed carving spans the busy road below.

Sidi Saiyad's Mosque
Mirzapur Rd, Lal Darwaja • Daily 5am–11pm

Sidi Saiyad's Mosque, famed for the ten magnificent *jali* (lattice-work) screens lining its upper walls, sits in the centre of a busy roundabout. Built in 1573, the two semicircular screens on the western wall are its most spectacular, with floral designs exquisitely carved out of the yellow stone. Stonework within depicts heroes and animals from popular Hindu myths – one example of Hindu and Jain craftsmanship influencing an Islamic tradition that rarely allowed the depiction of living beings in its mosques. Women cannot enter this mosque, but the gardens around it afford good views of the screens.

9

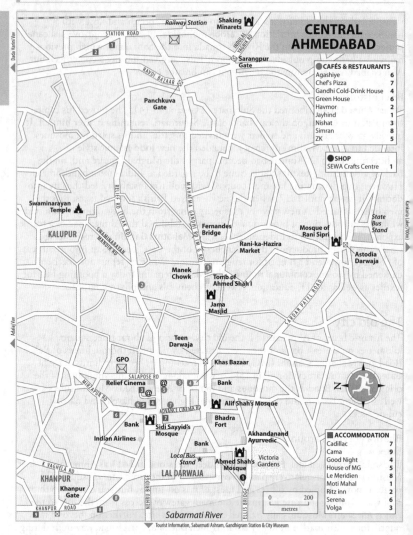

CENTRAL AHMEDABAD

CAFÉS & RESTAURANTS	
Agashiye	6
Chef's Pizza	7
Gandhi Cold-Drink House	4
Green House	6
Havmor	2
Jayhind	1
Nishat	3
Simran	8
ZK	5

SHOP	
SEWA Crafts Centre	1

ACCOMMODATION	
Cadillac	7
Cama	9
Good Night	4
House of MG	5
Le Meridien	8
Moti Mahal	1
Ritz inn	2
Serena	6
Volga	3

Tourist Information, Sabarmati Ashram, Gandhigram Station & City Museum

Ahmed Shah's Mosque

Jijabai Marg, west of Bhadra Fort, across from Victoria Gardens • Daily 5am–11pm

Ahmed Shah's small but artfully simple **mosque** was the private place of worship for the royal household. Sections of an old Hindu temple, perhaps dating back to 1250 AD, were used in its construction – hence the incongruous Sanskrit inscriptions on some of the pillars in the sanctuary. The zenana (women's chamber) is hidden behind pierced stone screens above the sanctuary in the northeast corner.

Jama Masjid

Mahatma Gandhi Rd • Daily 5am–11pm

The spectacular **Jama Masjid**, completed in 1424, stands today in its entirety except for two minarets destroyed by an earthquake in 1957. Always bustling, the mosque is busiest on Fridays, when thousands converge to worship. The 260 elegant pillars supporting the roof of the domed prayer hall (*qibla*) are covered with unmistakeably Hindu carvings, while close to the sanctuary's principal arch a large black slab is said to be the base of a Jain idol inverted and buried as a sign of Muslim supremacy.

Immediately outside the east entrance of the mosque, the square **Tomb of Ahmed Shah I**, who died in 1442, stands surrounded by pillared verandas. Women are not permitted to enter the central chamber, the site of his grave, or those of his son and grandson.

Manek Chowk
Manek Chowk Rd, east of Jama Masjid

The jewellery and textile market of **Manek Chowk** is filled with craftsmen working in narrow alleys amid newly dyed and tailored cloth. Further into the market, to the east, and surrounded by the dyers' colourful stalls, is the mausoleum of Ahmed Shah's queens, **Rani-ka-Hazira**. Its plan is identical to Shah's own tomb (see above), with pillared verandas clearly inspired by Hindu architectural tastes.

Mosque and tomb of Rani Sipri
Swami Vivekananda Rd, near Astodia Darwaja • Daily 5am–8pm

The small, elegant **mosque of Rani Sipri** was built in 1514 at the queen's orders. Her grave lies in front, sheltered by a pillared mausoleum. The stylish mosque shows more Hindu influence than any other in Ahmedabad: its pillared sanctuary has an open facade to the east and fine tracery work on the west wall.

Swaminarayan Temple
Swaminarayan Mandir Rd, Kalupur • Daily 6am–7pm

The brightly coloured **Swaminarayan Temple** presents a delicate contrast to the many hard-stone mosques in the city. Both the temple and the houses in the courtyard surrounding it are of finely carved wood, with elaborate and intricate patterns typical of the havelis of north and west Gujarat. The temple's main sanctuary is given over to Vishnu and his consort Lakshmi.

Shaking minarets
Indulal Yagnik Rd, near Sarangpur Darwaja • Daily 8am–6pm

Sidi Bashir's minarets are all that remain of this mosque built in 1452, which was named after one of Ahmed Shah's favourite slaves. More than 21m high, these are the best existing example of the "**shaking minarets**" – built on a foundation of flexible sandstone, probably to protect them from earthquake damage – once a common sight on Ahmedabad's skyline.

Dada Hari-ni Vav and Mata Bhava-ni Vav
Haripura, Asarwa, opposite railway yard, northeast Ahmedabad • Daily 8am–6pm • Free • Auto-rickshaw from Lal Darwaja ₹75

Northern Gujarat abounds with remarkable **step-wells** – deep, with elaborately carved walls and broad flights of covered steps leading to a shaft – but **Dada Hari-ni Vav**, just outside the city's old northeast boundaries, is among the finest. While it's a Muslim construction, built in 1500, the craftsmen were Hindu, and their influence is clear in the lavish and sensuous carvings on the walls and pillars. Visit around 11am when the sculpted floral patterns and shapely figurines inside are bathed in sunlight. **Bai Harir**'s lofty mosque and lattice-walled tomb stand just west of the well, while a couple of hundred metres north of the complex is the neglected **Mata Bhava-ni Vav**, probably constructed in the eleventh century, before Ahmedabad was founded. It's profoundly Hindu in character, and dedicated to Bhava-ni, an aspect of Shiva's consort Parvati.

9

> ## SEWA
>
> Almost ninety percent of women who work in India are self-employed. Outside the protection of labour laws and the minimum wage, they are subject to exploitation, often by unscrupulous banks and lenders. Ahmedabad, however, has maintained a tradition of self-help since the days of Gandhi, achieving global recognition as the base of the ground-breaking **Self-Employed Women's Association, SEWA** (☎ 079 25506444, ⓦ sewa.org). Founded in the early 1970s, SEWA provides legal advice, training, support and childcare, and runs its own co-operative bank.
>
> Following a major slump in the textile industry in 1984, SEWA set up training centres in weaving, sewing, dyeing and printing, providing efficient machinery. This helped to re-establish many women in the textile labour force, providing an outlet for their products. In 1987, a SEWA protest against *sati* (widow burning) and a campaign to have verbal divorce and polygamy banned in Gujarat resulted in a change in the law. SEWA also strongly opposes female foeticide, which is particularly widespread in Gujarat. With more than a million members nationwide, and more than 600,000 of them in Gujarat, the organization now tackles projects throughout India and overseas.
>
> SEWA's crafts are available from the organization's reception centre on the east side of Ellis Bridge (Mon–Sat 10am–6.30pm) and from its outlet, Hansiba, on CG Road at the Banascraft Chandan Complex (Mon–Sat 11am–9pm, Sun 11.30am–7.30pm).

Hathi Singh Temple

Shahibaug Rd, north of Delhi Gate • Daily 10am–noon & 4–7.30pm

The Jain **Hathi Singh Temple** is easily distinguished by its high carved column. Built entirely of white marble embossed with smooth carvings of dancers, musicians, animals and flowers, this serene temple is dedicated to Dharamnath, the fifteenth *tirthankara*, or "ford-maker", one of twenty-four great teachers sanctified by the Jains.

Calico Museum of Textiles

In the Sarabhai Foundation, opposite Shahibagh Underbridge • Tours (2hr) daily except Wed 10.30am & 2.45pm; arrive early as tours fill up quickly • Free • ☎ 079 27868172, ⓦ calicomuseum.com • Bus #101 or #105 from Lal Darwaja bus stand; an auto-rickshaw costs ₹60

The **Calico Museum of Textiles** is India's finest collection of textiles, clothes, furniture and crafts. Highlights of the **morning tour** include exquisite pieces made for the British and Portuguese, while from India's royal households there's an embroidered tent and Shah Jahan's robes. There are *patola* saris from Patan (see p.544) and extravagant *zari* work that gilds saris in heavy gold stitching, bringing their weight to nearly nine kilos. Other galleries are dedicated to embroideries, *bandhani* tie-and-dye, textiles made for overseas trade and woollen shawls from Kashmir and Chamba. The **afternoon tour** includes the galleries of *pichwais* and other temple paintings and decorations, including Jain statues housed in a replica haveli temple and centuries-old manuscripts and mandalas painted on palm leaves.

Sanskar Kendra (City Museum)

In the Sanskar Kendra complex, Bhagatcharya Rd • Tues–Sun 10am–6pm • Free, no photos• ☎ 079 26578369 • Bus #31 from Lal Darwaja bus stand; an auto-rickshaw costs ₹60

The **City Museum** is worth a visit, covering subjects such as the history of the city, urban growth, sociological development and the activities of Gandhi and the freedom movement. There is a **Kite Museum** (same hours) in the basement, showcasing the tradition of city's January Kite Festival, the world's largest.

Sabarmati (Gandhi) Ashram

Ashram Rd • Daily 8.30am–6.30pm • ☎ 079 27557277, ⓦ gandhiashram.org.in • Buses#13/1 and #13/2 connect the ashram to Lal Darwaja

The **Sabarmati Ashram** is where the Mahatma lived from 1917 until 1930, holding meetings with weavers and Harijans as he helped them find security and re-establish the manual textile industry in Ahmedabad. In keeping with the man's uncluttered lifestyle, the collection of his personal property is modest but poignant – wooden shoes, white seamless clothes and a pair of round spectacles. The ashram itself is no longer operating, but many people come here simply to sit and meditate.

ARRIVAL AND DEPARTURE AHMEDABAD

By plane The international airport (☎079 2869266) is 10km north of Ahmedabad and connected to the centre by pre-paid taxis (₹400–300), auto-rickshaws (around ₹100–200) and bus #105 (hourly 7am–10pm; ₹8), which terminates at Lal Darwaja, the local bus stand in the west of the old city. Free liquor permits can be obtained from the domestic terminal (☎079 22860631), from a counter across from the luggage belt (daily 8am–10pm). Indian Airlines have an office in town between Sidi Saiyad's Mosque and Nehru Bridge (☎079 26585622); Jet Airways are on Ashram Rd opposite Gujarat Vidyapith (☎079 27543304); and Kingfisher Airlines' office is at the airport (☎1800 2333131).

Destinations Bangalore (2 daily; 2hr); Delhi (14 daily; 1hr 30min); Jaipur (2 daily; 1hr); Kolkata (3 daily; 2hr 30min); Mumbai (21 daily; 1hr).

By train Ahmedabad's main railway station, locally known as Kalupur Station, is on Station Rd, a 2km walk (or ₹25 auto ride) from Lal Darwaja, while the less-used Gandhigram Station, used to connect destinations in Saurashtra, is on the west side of the river, just west of Ashram Rd. Ahmedabad is on the Delhi–Mumbai train line, and serves as the jumping-off point for most destinations within Gujarat, as well as for Mount Abu, Jodhpur, Ajmer and Udaipur in Rajasthan. There are reservation centres (Mon–Sat 8am–8pm, Sun 8am–2pm) at both stations.

By bus The ST bus stand is in the southeast of the old city, on Gita Mandir Rd by Astodia Gate. Reservation

centres are located on platforms 1 and 5 (daily 6.30am–2pm, 2.30–7.30pm & 8–9.45pm). From here, government buses link the entire state and beyond, while a/c "Volvo" buses, operated jointly by the Gujarat State Road Transport Corporation (GSRTC) and various private companies, link Rajkot, Surat, Vadodara and Bhuj. Additionally, numerous private bus agencies are set near the station as well as in Paldi, west of Sardar Bridge, offering a plenitude of bus services throughout the state and beyond. In the latter area are some of the most useful agencies, serving destinations statewide and beyond. Among them are Patel Tours & Travels (☎099 74378888, ⓦpateltoursandtravels.com), which has buses to Bhuj (8 daily; 8hr), Gujarat Travels (☎942 8521105, ⓦgujarattravels.co.in), which has buses to Mount Abu (3 nightly; 4–6hr), and Shree Sahjanand Travels (☎079 26575988, ⓦshreesahjanandtravels.com), which has a nightly bus to Diu (10.15pm; 9hr) and Mumbai (10.15pm; 10–11hr).

Destinations Bhavnagar (hourly; 4–5hr); Bhuj (about hourly; 7–8hr); Dholka (for Lothal; every 30min; 1hr 30min); Dhrangadhra (every 30min; 3hr); Dwarka (6 daily; 10–11hr); Gandhinagar (every 15min; 1hr); Jamnagar (about hourly; 6hr); Jodhpur (4 daily; 10–12hr); Mehsana (every 10min; 2hr); Mumbai (2 daily; 4hr); Palitana (12 daily; 5–6hr); Rajkot (every 30min; 4–5hr); Surat (every 15min; 6hr); Udaipur (12 daily; 6–7hr); Vadodara (every 15min; 2hr).

GETTING AROUND

By bus Ahmedabad AMTS (Ahmedabad Municipal Transport Service; ⓦamts.co.in) is useful for getting around the city, connecting all parts of town with Lal Darwaja's bus stand. In

addition, Ahmedabad's much-heralded BRTS (Bus Rapid Transit System; ⓦahmedabadbrts.com), also known as Janmarg, beats the traffic with exclusive lanes and median

RECOMMENDED DAILY TRAINS FROM AHMEDABAD

The services listed below are the most convenient and/or fastest trains from Ahmedabad. All run daily except the *Shatabdi Express* #2010 (daily except Sun).

Destination	Name	No.	Departs	Total time
Bhavnagar	*Bhavnagar Express*	#12971	5.45am	5hr 20min
Bhuj	*Nagari Express*	#19115	11.59pm	7hr 26min
Delhi	*Swarna J Raj Express*	#12957	5.45pm	13hr 45min
Dwarka	*Saurashtra Mail*	#19005	5.05am	9hr 41min
Jamnagar	*Saurashtra Mail*	#19005	5.05am	7hr 2min
Jodhpur	*Ranakpur Express*	#14708	12.10am	9hr 35min
Mumbai	*Shatabdi Express*	#12010	2.30pm	7hr 5min
	Gujarat Mail	#12902	10pm	8hr 25min
Porbandar	*Saurashtra Express*	#19215	8.05pm	9hr 45min
Udaipur	*Udaipur City Express*	#19944	11pm	10hr 20min

9

bus stations. Although the expanding network has proved an overall success, the line planned to pass near Lal Darwaja has yet to be completed, limiting the network's usefulness for travellers.

INFORMATION AND TOURS

Tourist office The helpful tourist office is in HK House, just off Ashram Rd, on the west side of the river (Mon–Sat 10.30am–1.30pm & 2–6pm, closed 2nd & 4th Sat of month; ☎079 26589172, ✆gujarattourism.com); the attached travel service can book airline tickets and arrange tours.

Tours The Ahmedabad Municipal Corporation (AMC) runs non-a/c city bus tours (daily 9am–1pm & 2–5pm; ₹60; ☎079 25507739) from platform D of the Lal Darwaja bus stand. Gujarat Tourism, partnered with Pinks Travels, runs a/c city bus tours (daily 7.45am–1.30pm & 1.45–8.15pm; ₹200; ☎1800 2337951) from the City Civic Centre, opposite the GLS School in the Law Garden, as well as full-day bus tours that take in more than a dozen Hindu and Jain temples (Sun 8am–8pm; ₹200) starting from Jalaram Temple. *House of MG* runs a heritage walk starting at the Swaminarayan Temple and ending at the Jama Masjid (daily 8–10.30am; ₹50 (₹30); ☎079 25391811 ext 509 or ☎98240 32866), as well as brilliant self-guided audio tours starting from *House of MG* itself (daily 8am–5pm; ₹100). Call to reserve any of these tours.

ACCOMMODATION

LAL DARWAJA

Cadillac Advance Cinema Rd ☎079 25507558; map p.536. Just about the best shoestring option, with welcoming staff but austere rooms with peeling paint, hard beds and squat toilets (some attached). Built in 1934, the hotel does have a spot of character, and there's a pleasant balcony overlooking the bustle of Lal Darwaja. ₹300/₹400

Good Night Opposite Sidi Saiyad's Mosque, Mirzapur Rd ☎079 25507181, ✆hotelgoodnight.co.in; map p.536. Neat and tidy rooms with private white-tiled bathrooms and TVs; some have a/c (starting at ₹1100). The a/c triples are good value at ₹1400. ₹600/₹1100

★ House of MG Opposite Sidi Saiyad's Mosque, Mirzapur Rd ☎079 25506946, ✆houseofmg.com; map p.536. This 1920s heritage hotel has spacious, individually decorated rooms fitted with flatscreen TVs and wi-fi, most with four-poster beds. The private courtyards have period furniture and old photos lining the walls, while playful touches like popcorn makers are found in each suite (₹14990). Two excellent restaurants and an indoor pool complete the package. ₹6490

Serena Mirzapur Rd ☎079 25510136; map p.536. Beyond the unprepossessing exterior are reasonable attached rooms with slightly grubby bathrooms and 24hr checkout; the more expensive have a/c (₹1080) and extra space. A decent fall-back if *Volga* and *Good Night* are full. ₹780

Volga Near Ankelsharia Hospital off Relief Rd ☎079 25509497, ✆hotelvolga.in; map p.536. Friendly service and spotless pastel-shaded attached rooms, each with TV, phone, wi-fi and 24hr checkout; some have a/c (₹1150), while the cheaper ones are a bit stuffy with only internal windows. As quiet as it gets in Lal Darwaja. ₹900

AROUND THE RAILWAY STATION

Moti Mahal Kalupur Rd ☎079 2121881; map p.536. Very well-kept, clean hotel offering identikit rooms, some with a/c (₹2000) and all with attached bathrooms and TVs. The hotel has three restaurants and a bar. ₹950

Ritz Inn Kalupur Rd ☎079 22123842, ✆hotelritzinn .com; map p.536. A recommended three-star with Art Deco flourishes and smart service. The charming rooms have black-and -white bathrooms, TVs, writing desks and wi-fi. ₹3300

KHANPUR DISTRICT

Cama Khanpur Rd ☎079 25601234, ✆camahotelsindia.com; map p.536. Large rooms featuring baths and carpets overlook the Sabarmati, although are somewhat let down by slightly dated decor. However, the manicured garden, pool, rooftop restaurant, liquor shop (noon–7pm) and 24hr coffee shop are ample compensation. 9am checkout. ₹5500

Le Meridien Khanpur Rd ☎079 25505505, ✆lemeridien.com/ahmedabad; map p.536. Service and standards are as high as you'd expect from this international chain, with an excellent restaurant, indoor pool, steam sauna, jacuzzi and gym. The rooms have wood-effect floors and leather furniture, as well as DVD players, wi-fi and views over the Sabarmati. ₹7500

NORTHERN AHMEDABAD

Ginger Drive-In Rd, behind Himalaya Mall, 7km north of the centre ☎079 66663333, ✆gingerhotels.com; map p.534. This slick branch of Tata's chain of stylized hotels is the most useful for the airport, with pared-down a/c attached rooms with coffee makers, fridges, wi-fi and "self check-in". ₹4000

EATING

Ahmedabad's most popular **restaurants** are clustered around Relief Rd, Salapose Rd and Badhra; great snack stalls line Khas Bazaar. If you are making only a brief stop in Gujarat, be sure to sample the state's delicious thali.

★ **Agashiye** House of MG, opposite Sidi Saiyad's Mosque, Mirzapur Rd ☎079 25506946; map p.536. One of the state's finest restaurants, with a roof terrace, cushions to sit on and an open kitchen: prices are steep (a regular thali is ₹500 for lunch and ₹450 for dinner), but the mouth-watering Gujarati thalis are as good as it gets. A series of recipe books is on sale, and cookery classes are in the pipeline. Daily noon–3.30pm & 7–10.45pm.

Chef's Pizza Opposite Cadillac, Advance Cinema Rd ☎079 73739900; map p.536. The deep-pan pizzas (₹80–200 for a regular) are surprisingly good at this tiny, clean and friendly fast-food joint that's popular among a younger crowd. Also on the menu are burgers, sandwiches and wraps. Daily 11am–11pm.

Gandhi Cold-Drink House Khas Bazaar; map p.536. Friendly, hole-in-the-wall place with plastic chairs out front and a range of refreshing milk and ice cream concoctions (around ₹15), including an Indonesian-style "Royal Faluda", unique to Ahmedabad, and a butterscotch lassi (both ₹30). Daily 10am–11pm.

Gopi Dining Hall Pritamrai Rd, west side of Ellis Bridge ☎079 26576388; map p.534. Named by *Newsweek* as one of the 101 Best Places to Eat Around the World in August 2012, Gopi is a welcoming all-veg place offering generous Gujarati and Kathiawadi thalis with unbeatable prices (₹120–180) and top service. It's very popular, so reserve ahead or wait in line. Daily 10.30am–3pm & 6.30–10.30pm.

Green House House of MG, Mirzapur Rd ☎079 25506946; map p.536. Cheaper than *Agashiye* (mains from ₹150), and almost as appealing: sit on wooden benches under an ivy-covered pavilion and tuck into snacks, light meals and sorbets, frozen yogurts, ice creams and lassis: try the saffron or rose flavours (₹125). Daily breakfast specials are also fantastic (₹250). Daily 7am–11pm.

Havmor Near Rupam Cinema, Relief Rd ☎079 25357373; map p.536. Set along one of Ahmedabad's most fume-choked streets, this tidy white-tiled branch of Gujarat's most famous ice cream company, founded here in 1944 and now spread as far as Punjab and Pune, serves south Indian dishes (masala dosa ₹99), fast food (pizza ₹50) and lots of ice cream (from ₹20). Daily 11.30am–10pm.

Jayhind Manek Chowk ☎079 22140714; map p.536. One of the best places to sample Ahmedabad's famous sweets, *Jayhind* has sold wonderful dry-fruit halwa, *ghari* and *mithai* by the kilo (₹400-700), as well as *kaju pista* roll (₹5–30) since 1948. Daily 9am–10.30pm.

Nishat Khas Bazaar ☎079 25507335; map p.536. With its huge flashing neon sign, this a/c restaurant is hard to miss. Its mutton *kadai* (₹105) and chicken tikka masala (₹130) are among the favourites. A cheaper, non-a/c restaurant with the same name is just up the street (chicken tikka masala ₹50) and just as popular with the locals. Daily 10am–11.15pm.

Simran FG Tower, Khanpur Rd ☎079 25511002; map p.536. Handy for the big hotels nearby, this a/c restaurant has cosy booths, an old fish tank, and curtains blocking out the bustle of Khanpur Rd; good choices include *tawa jhinga* (prawn curry; ₹155), mutton kebabs (₹150) and fish curry (₹145). Daily 11.30am–11pm.

★ **Vishalla** Narol Sarkhej Rd, 7km southwest of city centre ☎079 26602422. ⊛vishalla.com; map p.534. This fabulous open-air restaurant serves generous portions of pure-veg Gujarati cuisine in a charming village setting, complete with floor seating under thatched-roof huts and a variety of cultural performances. The set lunches (₹278) and dinners (₹548) are served on banana leaves. Don't miss the attached utensil museum (Tues–Sun 3–10pm; ₹50 (₹10); ⊛vechaar.com). It's well worth the trip to get here: from Lal Darwaja, take bus #31 or hire an auto-rickshaw (₹125 return). Tues–Sun 3–10pm.

ZK Relief Rd, opposite Relief Cinema ☎079 25506121; map p.536. A dimly lit restaurant with a pink-and-maroon colour scheme and an ancient fish tank. Trawling through the exhaustive menu – there's well over two hundred dishes – certainly builds up an appetite: the tandoori items (₹95–225) are particularly good. Daily 11am–4pm & 7–11pm.

DIRECTORY

Banks and exchange Foreign exchange is available at the Bank of India in Khas Bazaar, the Central Bank of India opposite Sidi Saiyad's Mosque and the State Bank of India opposite Lal Darwaja bus station (all Mon–Fri 11am–3pm, Sat 11am–1pm); Thomas Cook is at 208 Sakar III, off Ashram Rd near the old High Court; CITIBank has a branch on CG Rd at B/201 Fairdeal House, near Swastik Four Rd.

Bookshops Crossword (☎079 26468031), Shri Krishna Complex, near the Mithakali crossroad (see map, p.534); Art Book Centre (☎079 26582139), just off Mangaldas Rd, 350m east of Ellis Bridge (see map, p.534).

Cinemas City Gold Cinema (☎079 26587782), near the tourist office on Ashram Rd screens English and Hindi films (tickets ₹180).

Hospitals VS General, Ellis Bridge (☎079 26577621), is a large government hospital; for traditional treatments, try Akhandanand Ayurvedic, Akhandanand Rd (☎079 25507796).

Internet access Relief Cyber Café, opposite the Relief Cinema, and Planet Cyber Cafe, behind Relief Cinema (via alley next to Airtel office); both ₹20/hr.

Post office Salapose Rd (Mon–Sat 10am–7.30pm).

9

Around Ahmedabad

The most obvious day-trips from Ahmedabad are north to **Adalaj**, with its impressive step-well, and beyond to **Gandhinagar**, with its extraordinary Swaminarayan religious complex. South of town, the lake, pavilions and mausoleums of **Sarkhej** make a pleasant break from the crowded city, while further south is the ancient Harappan site at **Lothal**.

Adalaj Vav

19km north of Ahmedabad · Daily 8am–6pm · Free · Connected by frequent buses running between Ahmedabad and Gandhinagar; Adalaj village is 1km from the bus stop

One of Gujarat's most spectacular step-wells, **Adalaj Vav** stands in neat gardens. The monument, built in 1498 and now out of use, is best seen around noon, when sunlight penetrates to the bottom of the five-storey octagonal well shaft. Steps lead down to the cool depths through a series of platforms raised on pillars. Alive with exquisite sculptures, the walls, pillars, cornices and niches portray erotica, dancing maidens, musicians and animals.

Gandhinagar

The second state capital after Chandigarh to be built from scratch since Independence, uninspiring **GANDHINAGAR** is laid out in thirty residential sectors in an ordered style influenced by the architect **Le Corbusier**. There's little to warrant spending much time here, unless you wish to visit the headquarters of the Swaminarayan sect, **Akshardham**. This Hindu revivalist movement promotes Vedic ideals pronounced by Lord Swaminarayan (1781–1830).

Swaminarayan complex

J Rd, Sector 20, west side of Gandhinagar near the Sabarmati · Tues–Sun 9.30am–7.30pm · Free; audio animatronic shows ₹75 · ⓦ akshardham.com/gujarat

The Akshardham may advocate simplicity and poverty, but the colossal **Swaminarayan complex** is hugely extravagant. Built of six thousand tonnes of pink sandstone, it houses the gold-leafed statues of Swaminarayan and two other prominent gurus. The rest of the complex is a surreal **theme park**, with a Hall of Holy Relics containing possessions of Swaminarayan and state-of-the-art audiovisual shows. On September 24, 2002, 33 people were killed and 72 injured here by Pakistani suicide terrorists. Links were quickly made between the attack and the post-Godhra rioting (see box, p.533). Today, the only evidence of the **massacre** is the security presence at the entrance.

ARRIVAL AND DEPARTURE

GANDHINAGAR

By bus Regular buses connect Gandhinagar's ST bus stand (located in Sector 11 in the city's geographical centre) with Ahmedabad's ST bus stand (every 30min; 45min).
By train There are two daily trains to and from Ahmedabad

(departing from Ahmedabad at 8.55am and 10.05am; returning 3.32pm and 6.25pm; 1hr). The station is inconveniently located in Sector 14, about 2km east of the centre (auto-rickshaw ₹20).

ACCOMMODATION AND EATING

Cambay Spa and Golf Resort Sector 25 ☏079 23289000, ⓦthecambay.com. For some real pampering, try Cambay's beautiful, minimalist rooms complete with wi-fi, LCD screens, electronic safes and coffee makers. There's also a multicuisine restaurant, juice bar, spa and a nine-hole golf course. ₹9000

Toran Cafeteria Sector 9, near Gujarat Forensic Science University ☏972 7723948. A pleasant government-run place by the river bank, southeast of the centre, surrounded by gardens, and serving veg food only (fixed thali ₹85). Daily 8.30am–10pm.

Sarkhej

10km southwest of Ahmedabad • Daily 6am–10pm • Bus #31 from Lal Darwaja (45min)

9

Sarkhej holds a complex of beautiful monuments arranged around an artificial **lake**. On the southwest side of the lake, the square **tomb** of the revered saint Sheikh Ahmed Khattu, the spiritual mentor of Ahmed Shah, who died in 1445, is Gujarat's largest mausoleum. It was constructed by Ahmed Shah's successor, Mohammed Shah, in 1446. The later Sultan Mohammed Beghada (d. 1511) added palaces, a harem, a vast lake and, eventually, his own tomb as well. Sarkhej became a retreat of Gujarati sultans and today remains a charming escape from Ahmedabad.

Lothal

80km south of Ahmedabad, near the mouth of the River Sabarmati • **Site** Daily dawn to dusk • Free **Museum** Daily except Fri 10am–5pm • ₹50 (₹5) • Direct bus from Ahmedabad's ST bus stand (2 daily; 2hr); Ahmedabad's Gandhigram Station is connected by a metre-gauge railway to Lothal-Burkhi station (2 daily; 2–3hr), 4km from the site: either walk the rest of the way or hire an autorickshaw.

Near the mouth of the River Sabarmati, by the Gulf of Cambay, is **Lothal**, one of the largest excavated **Harappan** (or Indus Valley) sites (see box below). Foundations, platforms, crumbling walls and paved floors are all that remain of the prosperous sea-trading community that dwelled here between 2400 and 1900 BC, when a flood all but destroyed the settlement. A walk around the **central mound** reveals the old roads that ran past ministers' houses and through the acropolis. The lower town comprised a bazaar, workshops and residential quarters. Evidence has been found here of an even older culture, perhaps dating from the fourth millennium BC, known as the **Red Ware Culture**. You can see remains from this period and from the Indus Valley Civilization in the illuminating **museum** situated adjacent to the site.

Northern Gujarat

North of Gandhinagar, the district of Mahesana was the Solankis' seat of government between the eleventh and thirteenth centuries. Some remains of their old capital, **Anhilawada Patan**, still stand, including the extraordinary **Rani-ki-Vav** step-well, situated just outside the modern city of Patan, home to Gujarat's last remaining *patola* weavers. The big draw here is undoubtedly the ancient sun temple at **Modhera**, easily reached from the crowded city of **Mahesana** (Mehsana); it's also worth visiting the striking shrines at the Jain temple at **Taranga**.

THE INDUS VALLEY CIVILIZATION

Before the Mauryans took over in the fourth century BC, India's greatest empire was the **Indus Valley Civilization**. Sophisticated settlements dating back to 2500 BC were first discovered in 1924 on the banks of the Indus in present-day Sindh (Pakistan), at **Mohenjo Daro**. Further excavations in 1946 in Punjab revealed the city of **Harappa**, from the same era. In its prime, this great society spread from the present borders of Iran and Afghanistan to Kashmir, Delhi and southern Gujarat. It lasted until 1900 BC, when it was destroyed by heavy floods.

A prosperous and literate society, importing raw materials from regions as far west as Egypt and trading ornaments, jewellery and cotton, it also had a remarkable, centrally controlled political system. Each town was almost identical, with complex drainage systems. Lothal, close to the Gulf of Cambay in southern Gujarat, was a major port. Although much about this complex society remains unknown, similarities exist between the Indus Valley Civilization and present-day India. For example, like Hindus, the Indus Valley people had a strong custom of worshipping a mother goddess, and there is evidence of phallic worship, still popular among Shaivites.

9

Sun Temple at Modhera

Daily 8am–6pm • ₹200 (₹5) • Modhera is linked by road to Mahesana (45min by bus; return taxi fare around ₹450), Patan (every 30min; 1hr 15min), Zainabad (2 daily; 1hr 30min) and Ahmedabad (2–3hr)

If you visit only one town in northern Gujarat, make it **MODHERA**, where the eleventh-century **Sun Temple** is the state's best example of Solanki temple architecture. Almost a thousand years old, the temple has survived earthquakes and Muslim iconoclasm; apart from a missing *shikhara* and slightly worn carvings, it remains largely intact. The Solanki kings were probably influenced by Jain traditions; deities and their vehicles, animals, voluptuous maidens and complex friezes adorn the sandy brown walls and pillars. Within the *mandapa*, or pillared entrance hall, twelve *adityas* set into niches in the wall portray the transformations of the sun in each month of the year. Closely associated with the sun, *adityas* are the sons of Aditi, the goddess of infinity and eternity. Modhera's sun temple is positioned so that at the equinoxes the rising sun strikes the images in the sanctuary, which at other times languishes in a dim half-light. In front of the temple, 108 shrines adorn the rim of **Surya Kund**, a 100-square-metre rectangular pond.

Patan

The bustling modern town of **PATAN** was built on the ruins of the old city of **Anhilwara**, long-time capital of Gujarat. The old city served several Rajput dynasties between the eighth and the twelfth centuries before being annexed by the Mughals, then fell into decline when Ahmed Shah moved the capital to Ahmedabad in 1411. Little remains now except traces of fortifications scattered in the surrounding fields, as well as the stunning **Rani-ki-Vav**.

While modern Patan has few monuments, in the **Salvivad** area of town you can watch the complex weaving of silk *patola* saris, once the preferred garment of queens and aristocrats, and an important export of Gujarat, now made by just one extended family, the Salvis (Salvivado, Patolawala St; ☏02766 232274, ⊚patanpatola.com). The saris fetch anywhere from one to seven lakhs (₹100,000–700,000) and take around four to six months to produce. For smaller wallets, scarves are also available from ₹5000.

Rani-ki-Vav

2km northwest of Patan • Daily 8am–6pm • ₹100 (₹5)

Gujarat's greatest **step-well**, the **Rani-ki-Vav** was built for the Solanki queen Udaimati in 1050 and extensively restored during the 1980s, recreating as perfectly as possible the original extravagant carving. Near the well are the remains of the **Sahastralinga Talav**, the "thousand-lingam tank" built at the turn of the twelfth century, but razed during Mughal raids. This is part of the same **complex** that includes a modest open-air **museum**.

ARRIVAL AND DEPARTURE | **PATAN**

By bus Frequent buses from the ST bus stand in the centre of Patan connect with Mehsana (every 30min; 1hr 15min) and Ahmedabad (every 30min; 3hr).

ACCOMMODATION AND EATING

Navjivan 46 GIDC, southeast corner of Sidhpur Circle ☏02766 231035, ⊚hotelnavjivan.com. A no-frills hotel in business for more than three decades, offering simple and clean rooms (a/c ₹500) with attached bathrooms, and a pure-veg restaurant on site. ₹**250**

Neerav Near Kohinoor Cinema in the town centre ☏02766 222127. The decent rooms here have attached bathrooms and TVs, while some come with a/c (₹750). Gujarat and Punjabi thalis are offered in the attached restaurant. ₹**400**

The Jain temple at Taranga

60km northeast of Mehsana • Buses from Ahmedabad (3hr 30min) and Mehsana (1hr 30min) drop you off at Timba, from where shared jeeps (₹5) ply the remaining 8km to Taranga

Well off the tourist trail, the **hilltop temple complex** at **TARANGA** was built during the Solanki period. Its striking shrines are better preserved than the more famous sites of Mount Abu, Girnar and Shatrunjaya. The **Ajitanath Temple**, built of durable sandstone, is dedicated to the second of twenty-four *tirthankaras*, whose 5m statue stands just inside, his gaze remarkably calm and unmoving, even for a statue. There is little in the way of tourist facilities here, although you can get an inexpensive lunch at a *dharamshala*.

Kutch

Bounded on the north and east by marshy flats and on the south and west by the Gulf of Kutch and the Arabian Sea, the province of **KUTCH** (also Kuchchh or Kachchha) is a place apart. All but isolated from neighbouring Saurashtra and Sindh (Pakistan), the largely arid landscape is shot through with the colours of the heavily embroidered local dress. Kutchi legends can be traced in sculptural motifs, and its strong folk tradition is still represented in popular craft, clothing and jewellery designs. Few tourists make it here, but those who do are invariably enchanted. Launching from the central city of **Bhuj** – which was devastated by the 2001 earthquake – you can explore the region's craft villages, ancient fortresses, medieval ports and isolated monasteries. The treeless salt marshes to the north and east, the Great and Little **Ranns of Kutch**, breathtaking expanses of cracked white earth, can flood completely during a heavy monsoon, effectively turning much of the region into an inland sea from July to September. Home to the rare wild ass, the Ranns are also the only region in India where flamingos breed successfully. The southern district of **Aiyar Patti** supports crops of cotton,

---

KUTCHI PASTORAL GROUPS

Kutch has the most significant population of **pastoral communities** in Gujarat. Each tribe can be identified from its costume, and gains income from farming or crafts such as weaving, painting, woodcarving and dyeing.

The **Rabari,** the largest group, rear cattle, buffalo and camels, sell ghee, weave, and are known for their fine **embroidery**. Most of the men sport a white turban, white cotton trousers tight at the ankle and with baggy pleats above the knee, a white jacket (*khediyun*), and a blanket thrown over one shoulder. Rabari women dress in black pleated jackets or open-backed blouses, full black skirts and tie-dyed head cloths, and always wear heavy silver jewellery and ivory bangles around the upper arms. In **Bhujodi**, near Bhuj, the Rabari weave camel wool into blankets and shawls.

The **Bharvad** tribes infiltrated Gujarat from Vrindavan, close to Mathura in Uttar Pradesh. The men are distinguishable by the peacock, parrot and flower motifs sewn into their *khediyun*, and the women by their bright backless shirts, *kapadun*, rarely covered by veils. Mass marriages take place among the Bharvad every few years.

The wandering **Ahir** cattle-breeders, today prosperous entrepreneurs, came to Gujarat from Sindh, and settled as farmers. The men sport baggy trousers and the *khediyun*, together with a white loosely wound headcloth; the women dress like the Rabaris, with additional heavy silver nose-rings. The children's bright *topis*, or skull-caps, are like those common in Pakistan.

The **Charans**, long-established bards of Gujarat, encompass in their clans the Maldharis, who raise prize cattle, and the leather-workers known as Meghavals. They claim descent from a celestial union between Charan and a maiden created by Parvati. The women are often worshipped by other tribes, as their connection with Parvati links them closely to the mother goddess, Ashpura, highly popular in Kutch.

Said to have migrated from Pakistan, the **Jats** are an Islamic pastoral group. The men can be identified by their black dress, while young Jat girls have dainty plaits curving round the sides of their faces, and wear heavy nose-rings.

9

castor-oil plants, sunflowers, wheat and groundnuts. Northern Kutch, or **Banni**, by contrast, is semidesert with dry shifting sands and arid grasslands.

Brief history

Remains from the third millennium BC in eastern Kutch suggest migrating Indus Valley communities crossed the Ranns from Mohenjo Daro in modern Pakistan to Lothal in eastern Gujarat. Despite being so cut off, Kutch felt the effect of the Buddhist Mauryan empire, later coming under the control of Greek Bactrians, the Western Satraps and the powerful Guptas. The Arab invasion of Sindh in 720 AD pushed refugees into Kutch's western regions, and tribes from Rajputana and Gujarat crossed its eastern borders. Later in the eighth century, the region fell under the sway of the Gujarati capital Anhilawada (now Patan), and by the tenth century the Samma Rajputs, later known as the Jadejas, had infiltrated Kutch from the west and established themselves as rulers, making their capital at **Bhuj**. Jajeda rule was eventually interrupted by a brief period of British domination in the early nineteenth century, and soon afterwards Kutch was absorbed into the Indian Union in 1948. The region has largely retained its customs, laws and a thriving maritime tradition, built originally on trade with Malabar, Mocha, Muscat and the African coast.

Bhuj

In the heart of Kutch, the narrow streets and old bazaars of the walled town of **BHUJ** retain a medieval flavour unlike in any other Gujarati city. While much of it was reduced to rubble in the **earthquake** of January 2001 (which killed around twenty thousand people, destroyed 1.2 million homes in the region and severely damaged the famed Aina Mahal, known as the "Palace of Mirrors"), the $2 billion reconstruction has resulted in new infrastructure, new businesses and new jobs. Although the process was slow and not always smooth, reconstruction is now just about complete, and the city seems to have finally emerged from the tragedy.

Bhuj is overlooked from the east by the old, crumbling fort on Bhujia Hill, while the vast **Hamirsar Tank**, with a small park on an island in its centre, stands on its western edge. The remnants of the **old city** form an intricate maze of streets and alleyways leading to the **palace complex**, guarded by sturdy walls and high heavy gates, enclosing the Aina and Prag mahals.

Aina Mahal

Darbargadh • Daily except Thurs 9am–noon & 3–6pm • ₹10, camera ₹30, video camera ₹100

An eighteenth-century palace built during the reign of Maharao Lakho, and later turned into a museum showcasing the opulence of the royal dynasty, the **Aina Mahal** suffered much damage in the 2001 earthquake. Fortunately, despite its roof collapsing, the famed **Hall of Mirrors** remained largely intact; the interior has now been fully restored, but work is ongoing on the exterior. The chief architect of the palace, Ram Singh Malam, was an Indian seafarer who studied in Europe for seventeen years after being rescued from a shipwreck by Dutch sailors off the coast of Africa. His masterpiece was the tiled pleasure-chamber at the heart of the palace where the maharaja, soothed by an ingenious system of fountains, used to compose poetry and listen to music. Royal heirlooms on display include a couple of original Hogarths and a portrait of Catherine the Great.

Prag Mahal

Darbargadh • Mon–Sat 9am–noon & 3–6pm • ₹12; camera ₹30, video ₹100

The once-grand **Prag Mahal**, built in the 1860s and combining Mughal, British, Kutchi and Italian architectural styles, also suffered damage during the quake. Its main tower appears to be precariously held together by skewed stones. Visitors are currently only allowed inside the cavernous main hall. The palace was one of the locations used in the hit film *Lagaan* (2001).

Sharad Bagh Palace

Southwest corner of Hamirsar Tank • Daily 9am–noon & 3–6pm • ₹10, camera ₹20, video ₹100

The small but stately **Sharad Bagh Palace** was built in 1867 as the retreat of the last maharao. Its small porticoed buildings are delicately proportioned and include a plush drawing room, decked with hunting trophies, photographs and old clocks, and a dining room containing Maharao Madansinjhi's coffin. The palace's most appealing feature, however, is its well-tended garden.

Kutch Museum

Southeast of Hamirsar Tank • Daily except Wed & 2nd & 4th Sat of the month 10am–1pm & 2.30–5.30pm • ₹50 (₹5), camera ₹100

The worthwhile, two-storey **Kutch Museum** has topographical, historical and cultural exhibits on the region, with various Kutchi textiles and crafts showcased along with life-sized mannequins representing major Kutchi communities. There are also some interesting finds from the Indus Valley Civilization, found at Dholavira and tracing back four millennia.

Ramkund Tank

South of Hamirsar Tank, across from the Kutch Museum

From the southwest corner of the Hamirsar Tank, a path leads behind Ram Dhun Temple to the 250-year-old bone-dry **Ramkund Tank**. Made of hard grey stone and shaded with trees, it is decorated with skilfully crafted images of Kali, Vishnu, Nag and Ganesh, and bears small niches in the walls where oil lamps once glittered in the dusk as devotees prayed at the evening puja.

Folk Museum

Mandvi Rd, 100m west of Collector's Office • Tues–Sun 10.30am–1.15pm & 2–5pm • ₹50 (₹10), camera ₹50

Bhuj's private **Folk Museum**, also known as Bharatiya Sanskruti Darshan, contains fine examples of Kutchi pottery, embroidery, games, musical instruments, wall hangings and model reconstructions of typical Kutchi mud hut villages. Although less folk-related, at least as interesting is the museum's rare fossil of an extinct giant species of crocodile.

ARRIVAL AND DEPARTURE   **BHUJ**

By plane The airport is 5km north of the centre. Daily flights to Mumbai (1hr 30min) are run by Jet Airways (☏02832 253671, ⊛jetairways.com) and Kingfisher (☏1800 2093030, ⊛flyingfisher.com).

By train The railway station is set about 1.5km north of Aina Mahal (reservations office Mon–Sat 8am–8pm, Sun 8am–2pm). The best train services to Ahmedabad are the *Bhuj-Bandra Sayaji Express* #19116 (daily; dep. 10.15pm, arr. 5.05am), which continues to Mumbai's Bandra Terminus (arr. 2.05pm), and the *Ala Hazrat Express* #14312 (Tues, Thurs & Sun; dep. 12.25am, arr. 7.40pm), which continues to reach Jaipur and Delhi at 8.30am and 2.35pm respectively, the following day. There are several daily trains that travel to Gandhidham (1hr), but it's easier to take the bus.

By bus The bus stand is on ST Station Rd, about 500m east

of Harmirsar Lake. There are frequent state buses to Ahmedabad (every 30min; 8–9hr), Rajkot (hourly; 6–7hr) and Jamnagar (8 daily; 7–8hr), as well as to Mandvi (every 30min; 1hr 30min). Less frequent buses serve the villages of Khavda (5 daily; 2hr) and Dhordo (2 daily; 2hr 30min) in northern Kutch. Private bus operators are strung along Station Rd: Patel Tours and Travels (☏02832 657781, ⊛pateltoursandtravels.com), 100m west of the station, has buses to Ahmedabad (7 daily; 8hr), including a nightly a/c sleeper bus (10pm), and to Mumbai (via Ahmedabad; 20hr). Jay Somnath (☏02832 221919), opposite *Green Rock*, has buses to Rajkot (6 daily; 7hr).

By shared jeep A small shared jeep stand is about 200m east of the bus stand on the opposite side of ST Rd, with regular jeeps departing for Mandvi (45min).

INFORMATION

Tourist information Bhuj has no official tourist office; head instead to the tourist desk at Aina Mahal (daily except Sat 9am–noon & 3–6pm; ☏02832 291702 or ☏93742

35379, ⊜pkumar_94@yahoo.com), manned by the friendly and well-informed Pramod Jethi, who also organizes heritage walks (3hr; ₹500).

9

ACCOMMODATION

City Guest House Langa St, just off Shroff Bazar ☎02832 221067. If rupees are tight, head here for no frills but clean rooms – some with attached bathrooms – set around a small courtyard. 24hr checkout. ₹400

★ **Gangaram** Behind Aina Mahal ☎02832 222948, ✉hotelgangaram@yahoo.com. Run by the obliging Rajesh Jethi, a mine of information, this travellers' stalwart has clean rooms, some with a/c (₹1000) and all with private bathrooms. There's wi-fi in the lobby (₹30/hr), a roof terrace and a good restaurant (chicken curry ₹125). ₹600

Ilark Station Rd ☎02832 258999, ⊛hotelilark.com. A modern red-and-black-glass exterior shields one of the more chic hotels in town: all have laminate floors, large beds and big TVs. There are also two smart restaurants, a bookshop, flower shop, and – incongruously – a tree in the lobby. ₹2200

Kutch Safari Lodge 14km north of Bhuj, overlooking the Gorudra Reservoir ☎98250 13392, ⊛kutchsafaribhuj. com. This luxurious camp has white concrete huts resembling traditional *bhungas* (mud-brick and straw homes), a pool and a restaurant that often features live music; a good choice if you've got your own vehicle. ₹4350

Prince Station Rd ☎02832 256355, ⊛hotelprince online.com. After extensive renovations, this long-established mid-range choice has reopened with large and spotless attached a/c rooms, a foreign exchange counter, two restaurants and welcoming staff. ₹2450

Raj Mahel Near ST Station, behind Sur Mandir Cinema ☎02832 223000, ⊛hotelrajmahalkutch.com. This sparkling new, red-coated hotel in the centre of town gives Bhuj's older hotels a run for their money, with spotless rooms with attached bathrooms, some with a/c (₹999) and all with 24hr hot water and internet access. Dorm ₹200, double ₹650

EATING

Station Rd is the place to pick up the local **snack**, *dhabeli* (spiced lentils and peanuts in a bun). The *Prince* Hotel has a wine shop and can provide **alcohol permits**.

Anando Foods Near the Kutch Museum. Set underground, across from Alfred High School, is this hygienic fast-food joint serves inexpensive south Indian snacks, Chinese noodles, soups, fried rice, ice cream and pizzas ("Italian" ₹80). Daily 10am–10pm.

Gopi Gola Opposite Green Rock, ST Rd, 100m west of ST bus stand ☎099795 95293. With cosy blue booths and plenty of fans, this tiny creamery serves floats, faloodas, slushies and real thick milk shakes (₹50). A welcome retreat from the bustle of Bhuj's busy centre. Daily 10am–10.30pm.

Green Rock ST Rd, opposite Gopi Gola ☎02832 253644, ⊛greenrockrestaurant.com. Smart a/c restaurant with photos of Bollywood and cricket stars on the walls and an all-veg menu of north and south Indian, Chinese and Western dishes. Lunch thalis ₹150. Daily 11am–3pm & 7–10.30pm.

Jesal and Toral Hotel Prince, Station Rd. If you're feeling homesick you'll enjoy the fish fingers and beans on toast at *Jesal*. They also serve interesting north Indian fish dishes, plus veg and non-veg Indian and Chinese staples (mains ₹90–200). *Toral*, meanwhile, offers a lavish all-you-can-eat Gujarati thali (₹195). Daily: Jesal 7am–3pm, 7–11pm; Toral 11.30am–3pm & 7.30–11.30pm.

Nilam Opposite Prince Hotel, Station Rd ☎02832 224786. Courteous staff serve up excellent veg Indian and Chinese food – the sweetcorn and green pepper masala is recommended – plus inexpensive breakfasts and a vegetarian kebab special (₹105). Daily 11am–3pm & 7–11pm.

Park View ST Rd ☎02832 225655. Overlooking Bhuj's busiest street, this plush and popular a/c restaurant serves Punjabi, south Indian, Chinese and Mexican cuisine, to name just a few. The mouth-watering thalis may just be the best deal in Bhuj (₹225), while the Kaju curry (₹126) is also fantastic. Daily noon–3pm & 7–11pm.

DIRECTORY

Banks and exchange The State Bank of India on Hospital Rd changes cash and travellers' cheques, as does ICICI across the street. There are numerous ATMs.

Bike rental Santosh Cycle Centre, near the bus station, rents bicycles (₹35–60/day).

Internet Several internet cafés are scattered in Bhuj, including the a/c Burhani Cyber Cafe, near *Oasis Hotel*, and Western Cyber Café, near the new vegetable market (both ₹20/hr).

Around Bhuj

Bhuj is a useful base for visiting **outlying craft villages**. From Mandvi, Mundra and Kandla on the coast to Hodka, Dhordo and Khavda to the north, Kutch's ethnic diversity, including Rabari, Ahir, Jat, Muthwa, Harijan and Rajput communities, is reflected in its wide-ranging handicrafts. As well as the local villages, sights of interest include the ancient sights of **Dholavira**, the Khanpatha monastery at Than, and, of course, the vast and desolate **Great Rann of Kutch**.

GETTING AROUND

AROUND BHUJ

By public transport Villages are best reached by private transport; infrequent buses run from Bhuj to Dhordo (2 daily) and Khavda (3 daily).

Taxi and motorbike rental Exploring the area by taxi or motorcycle gives you the most freedom. Most hotels in Bhuj will organize motorbike hire, though many bikes are in a poor state of repair; a better bet is MK Auto (Mon–Sat 10am–8pm; ☎ 02832 222242; ₹500/day), a motorbike rental place a few metres west of *Green Rock* (see opposite).

Permits Permits are required for many of the outlying villages, and are available for free from the District Superintendent of Police's Office in Bhuj, a 5min walk

southeast of the Hamirsar Tank (Mon–Sat 11am–2pm & 3–6pm); the process takes about 15min; bring photocopies of your passport and visa well as the originals. Permits are sometimes granted at the Bhirendiara police post (Mon–Sat 9am–6pm), 50km north of Bhuj, marking the junction where the road turns northwest for Hodka and north for Khavda, but it's best to get it done in Bhuj.

Tours For advice on where to visit, talk to Pramod Jethi (see p.547), who runs tours to the craft villages (₹1300 by car; ₹100 by auto-rickshaw). Laxmi Tours & Travels (Shop 1 below *Hotel Sahara Palace*, opposite ST bus stand; Mon–Sat 9am–9pm; ☎ 02832 224258, ⓦ kutch-tourism.com) offers a range of regional tours.

Mandvi

The compact town of **MANDVI**, situated on the west bank of a wide tidal estuary, 60km southwest of Bhuj, faces the Arabian Sea to the south and supports a dwindling *dhow*-building industry. Merchants, seamen and later the British settled in this once-flourishing port; though few remained long, they left behind grand European-style mansions. Today, Mandvi has a leisurely feel, its cluttered shops and **markets** stocked with *bandhani* and silver. Shifting sands block the estuary along on its south side, forming a long, uncrowded **beach** that is good for swimming. By the

---

KUTCHI HANDICRAFTS

Kutch is renowned for its distinctive traditional crafts, particularly its **embroidery**, practised by pastoral groups like Hindu Rabaris and Ahirs, and Muslim Jats and Muthwas, as well as migrants from Sindh including the Sodha Rajputs and Meghwal Harijans. Traditionally, each community has its own stitches and patterns, though these distinctions are becoming less apparent with time.

The northern villages of Dhordo, Khavda and Hodko are home to the few remaining communities of **leather embroiderers**, who stitch flower, peacock and fish motifs onto bags, fans, horse belts, wallets, cushion covers and mirror frames. Dhordo is also known for its **woodcarving**, while Khavda is one of the last villages to continue the printing method known as **ajrakh**. Cloth is dyed with natural pigments in a lengthy process similar to batik, but instead of wax, a mixture of lime and gum is used to resist the dye in certain parts of the cloth when new colours are added. Women in Khavda also paint **terracotta pots**.

Rogan painting is practised by only a few artisans at Nirona in northern Kutch. A complex process turns hand-pounded castor oil into coloured dyes that are used to decorate cushion covers, bedspreads and curtains with simple geometric patterns. Craftsmen also make melodic **bells** (once used for communication among shepherds) coated in intricate designs of copper and brass. Silver jewellery is common, featuring in most traditional Kutchi costumes, but Kutchi **silver engraving**, traditionally practised in Bhuj, is a dwindling art form. The anklets, earrings, nose-rings, bangles and necklaces are similar to those seen in Rajasthan; many are made by the Ahir and Rabari communities living in both areas. The main centres for silver are Anjar, Bhuj, Mandvi and Mundra.

Kutchi clothes are distinctive not only for their fine embroidery and bold designs. The most common form of **cloth** printing is **bandhani** (tie-dye), a practice most concentrated in Mandvi and Anjar. Another unique craft is ilacha (*mashroo*-weaving), a combination of dyeing and weaving with silk yarn to create designs so detailed and complex as to appear embroidered.

9

estuary, you can see **dhows** being built by hand: around fifty men spend two years building each ship, the largest of which cost upwards of $500,000, and are bought by wealthy Gulf Arabs.

Vijay Vilas Palace

8km west of town (turn left after 4km) • Daily 9am–1pm & 3–6pm • ₹35, camera ₹50, video ₹200

Mandvi's little-visited **Vijay Vilas Palace** is a sandy-white domed building in almost 700 acres of land, built as a summer retreat by Kutch's maharao in the 1940s, and now often used as a film set. Inside, European furniture fills the high-ceilinged carpeted rooms, hunting trophies deck the walls and a grand stairway leads to the ladies' quarters on the first floor. The palace estate has a royal pavilion and a long private beach with a hotel (see below).

ARRIVAL AND DEPARTURE   MANDVI

By public transport Regular buses run from Bhuj's ST bus stand to Mandvi's ST bus stand (every 30min; 1hr 30min). Faster shared jeeps (45min–1hr; ₹45) also link the two towns.

ACCOMMODATION AND EATING

The Beach at Mandvi Palace Vijay Vilas Palace beach ☎ 02834 277597, ⓦ mandvibeach.com. Ten luxury a/c tents packed tightly together with private bathroom and veranda, as well as an excellent restaurant, *Dolphin* (daily 1–3pm & 7–9pm). Non-guests who stay for lunch (₹550/₹650 veg/non-veg) may also use the beach. ₹6000

★ **Rukmavati Guest House** On the waterfront near Bridge Gate ☎ 02834 223558, ⓦ rukmavatihotel.webs .com. Housed in a former hospital, this is Mandvi's best budget option: all rooms have private bathrooms with solar-heated water while some have a/c (₹1300) and nice balconies. There's a small library and friendly manager,

Vinod Bhatt, who has loads of local information. ₹650

Sea View On the waterfront near bus station ☎ 02834 224481, ⓦ hotelseaviewmandvi.com. Although they don't exactly have "sea views", those at the front look straight out onto the *dhow*-builders. Rooms are decent and brightly lit by large windows; most have a/c (₹1150). ₹650

Zorba the Buddha First Floor of Osho Hotel, KT Shah Rd, west of the bus stand. Set behind the old Bhid Gate downtown, this is the best bet for food other than *The Beach*, serving excellent veg thalis (₹70). Daily 11am–3pm & 7–10pm.

Southeast of Bhuj

The 50km journey **southeast** from Bhuj to **KANDLA**, one of the busiest ports on India's west coast, takes you past dry scrubland. In the small village of **Bhujodi**, about 9km out of Bhuj and 1km off NH-42 towards Ahmedabad, artisans weave thick shawls and blankets on pit looms dug into the floors of squat mud houses. You can buy their products from the small shop run by the Bhujodi Handweaving Co-op Society. Further along on this road are the villages of **Paddhar**, known for Rabari embroidery, and **Dhaneti**, a centre for Ahir embroidery. **Dhamadka** remains a centre for Ajrakh block-printing, although it has struggled to recover from the 2001 earthquake, after which many of its artisans were moved to the village of **Ajrakhpur**. Around 10km east of Bhuj, Ajrakhpur is home to the enterprise of Dr. Ismail Mohammed Khatri (☎ 02832 299786, ✉ dr.ismail2005@gmail.com), who can trace his Ajrakh block-printing heritage back at least nine generations.

The first main town beyond Bhuj, **ANJAR**, was the capital of Kutch until 1548. Badly affected by the earthquake, the town recovered much more slowly than Bhuj, with serious disruption to traditional craftsmaking – Ahir embroidery, *bandhani*, batik and nutcrackers. However, things have improved in recent years, and a crafts market is held here every Monday when Rabari people from more than 130 villages set up shop (8.30am–1pm).

North of Bhuj

North of Bhuj are some of the most interesting craft centres in Kutch, their colours accentuated by an increasingly desolate landscape. From the village of **BHIRENDIARA**, 50km north of Bhuj, known for its embroidery and patchwork as well as its beautiful mudwork (*liponkan*) interiors, the road forks. To the northwest is **HODKA**, followed by **DHORDO** at the end of the road, each of which features a cluster of grass-roofed mud huts decorated with traditional clay and whitewash patterns.

South of Bhirendiara and closer to Bhuj is **SUMERASER SHEIKH**, where NGO **Kala Raksha** (☎ 02808 277238, ⊛ kala-raksha.org) maintains an archive of antique textiles, a handicraft workshop, a museum and a fixed-price shop. Most of Kala Raksha's participants are women from marginalized communities, and this is a great place to learn about local embroidery, tie-dyeing, patchwork and inlay techniques. Call ahead to arrange a tour. Kala Raksha's work is vital, as the future of many of the craft centres is in doubt: the post-earthquake reconstruction created many largely unskilled labouring jobs, and these, with their higher wages, have lured many craft workers away from handicraft making.

Kalo Dungar

25km northeast of Khavda • Private transport is best; weekend buses depart in the evening from Khavda and return early morning

Kalo Dungar (Black Hills), Kutch's highest point, rises 462metres over the vast salt flats (or inland sea during monsoon season), offering unparalleled views of the Great Rann disappearing into the vast horizon, a truly edge-of-the-world vista. Pleasant pathways and viewing huts have been built along the slopes facing the Rann, and a 400-year-old temple nearby marks the spot where Dattreya, the three-headed incarnation of Lords Brahma, Vishnu and Shiva, once offered a band of starving jackals his own body as a meal (it regenerated itself as they ate). The priests here attract today's wild jackals with heaps of boiled rice offered as prasad, spilled onto a concrete platform at noon each day as visitors watch from a safe distance. For a donation, the neighbouring *dharamshala* also offers meals and lodgings to Kalo Dungar's trickle of visitors.

Banni Grasslands

50km north of Bhuj • Private transport is best; the Centre for Desert and Ocean offers pick up from Bhuj

Skirting the southern edge of the Great Rann are the semi-arid Banni Grasslands, home to a vast array of birds, including flamingos, pelicans, cranes, painted storks and hornbills. Ecologist Jugal Tiwari of the Centre for Desert and Ocean (☎ 02835 221284, ⊛ cedobirding.com) organizes informative birdwatching trips in the area; the centre is also somewhere you can buy local handicrafts.

Than and Dhinodar

60km northwest of Bhuj • Daily bus from Bhuj departs 5pm (2hr); return departs early morning

The monastery at **THAN** is home to a Tantric order of Hindu sadhus known as Kanphata ("split-ear") after the heavy agate rings they traditionally wear in their ears. This whitewashed complex at the foot of the hill encloses a handful of medieval temples, tombs and domed dwellings. Hardy travellers can spend the night in its *dharamshala* for a small donation. From Than, you can walk up a rocky ravine via an ancient pilgrims' trail to the mountaintop behind (3hr return), where **Dhinodar** is the site of a small painted temple, home to a Kanphata yogi, Hiranath Baba, and his acolytes; take ample water supplies.

ACCOMMODATION AND EATING   **NORTH OF BHUJ**

Devpur Homestay Darbargadh, Devpur village (40km northwest of Bhuj) ☎ 02835 283065, ⊛ sites.google .com/site/devpurhomestay. A sandstone fort built in 1905 in the Kutchi (or Roha) style and converted into a charming homestay with fancy a/c suites (₹3500) and simple bungalows, elegant courtyards, a tennis court and a vintage dining room serving set breakfasts (included), lunches and dinners. **₹1500**

Shaam-e-Sarhad Village Outside Hodka village, 50km north of Bhuj ☎ 02832 654124, ⊛ hodka.in.

This full-board resort is a sustainable tourism project run by the local Halepotra people. "Sunset at the Border", as the name means, offers accommodation in *bhungas* (circular mud huts) or luxury tents, all with attached Western-style toilets and some with a/c (₹3500). The resort offers craft workshops, birdwatching excursions and trips to local villages. A permit is required to visit, obtainable in Bhuj's District Superintendent of Police's Office. Oct–March only. **₹1500**

9

Dholavira

250km northeast of Bhuj • Daily 9am–dusk • No video

In the far north of Kutch, on an island surrounded by snow-white salt flats, the tiny village of **DHOLAVIRA** surrounds the remnants of a Harappan city that thrived six thousand or more years ago. Archeological digs started here in the 1970s after a local farmer ploughed up a small terracotta seal. Soon, the existence of a major planned city with monumental structures, a palace complex and an extraordinary water management system was revealed. Today, the archeological centre attracts barely a trickle of visitors.

ARRIVAL AND DEPARTURE   DHOLAVIRA

By bus There's a daily bus from Bhuj to Dholavira, departing at 2.30pm (7hr), returning at 5.30am. Due to the inconvenient bus schedule, it's best to visit with private transport.

ACCOMMODATION AND EATING

Toran Tourist Complex 1km south of Dholavira site 📞 02837 277395. The simple *bhunga*-style cottages at the state-run *Toran* hotel are Dholavira's only choice for accommodation, all with attached bathrooms and some with a/c (₹900). A basic cafeteria offers Gujarati thalis (₹80). **₹500**

Little Rann Wild Ass Sanctuary

Entrance to the sanctuary is near Bajana village, a 30min drive from Dasada • Oct–May daily 6am–6pm • ₹1050 (₹250) per vehicle seating up to six, SLR camera ₹500 (₹100)

Spanning 4850 square kilometres, the **Little Rann Wild Ass Sanctuary**, a vast salt-encrusted desert plain that becomes inundated during the rains (July–Sept), is home to an abundance of wildlife, including the endangered Indian **wild ass**. Usually seen in loosely knit herds, this handsome chestnut-brown-and-white member of the horse family is capable of running very fast. The sanctuary is also home to wolves, foxes, jackals, jungle and desert cats, nilgai and blackbuck antelopes and the chinkara gazelle. Large flocks of flamingo, pelicans and winter-visiting cranes can be seen at Bajana Lake; October to March is the time to see the migratory birds.

ARRIVAL AND GETTING AROUND   LITTLE RANN WILD ASS SANCTUARY

While the sanctuary headquarters is at **Dhrangadhra** near its southern edge, most tourist facilities are at **Dasada**, 70km to the northeast of Dhrangadhra. Although recommended, hiring a guide is not mandatory.

By train Dhrangadhra is served by several daily trains linking with Ahmedabad (3hr) and Bhuj (5hr). Dasada is 33km from Viramgam railway station, connected by regular buses and autos/taxis (₹400/₹600), which has frequent trains to Ahmedabad (1hr) and less frequent trains to Bhuj (6hr).
By bus Dhrangadhra is linked by frequent buses to Ahmedabad (every 30min; 3hr) and Bhuj (every 30min; 5hr), while buses from Dasada also connect with Ahmedabad (every 15min; 2hr 30min), Patan (2 daily; 2hr 30min; 5hr), Rajkot (6 daily; 4hr) and Bhuj (5 daily; 6hr).
By jeep You can rent a jeep for around ₹3000/day and a guide to take a tour of the sanctuary from Dasada, Dhrangadhra or any of the resorts (see below).

ACCOMMODATION

Desert Coursers 10km west of Dasada 📞 99983 05501 or 📞 94263 72113, 🌐 desertcoursers.net. Also called *Camp Zainabad*, this is a friendly eco-camp offering all-in stays that include comfortable thatched-roof *kooba* (traditional hut) accommodation, all meals and unlimited jeep safaris. Horse and camel safaris can be arranged (₹1000). The camp is also highly involved in numerous laudable social and cultural projects. Free pick up from Dasada bus station. **₹5400**
Eco Tour Camp Jogad village, 20km north of Halvad and about 45km northwest of Dhrangadhra (₹800 for pick-up from Dhrangadhra) 📞 02754 280560 or 📞 98255 48090, 🌐 littlerann.in. Among the best options for the Little Rann is wildlife photographer Devjibhai Dhamecha's excellent eco-camp close to Sumera Lake, on the very southern edge of the sanctuary. The camp offers full-board accommodation in traditional *koobas*, and it's also possible to stay at Devjibhai's welcoming family home in Dhrangadhra (₹1000). Safaris can arranged for ₹2000/₹3000 (6hr/8hr) per jeep. **₹2000**

Rann Riders 2km east of Dasada ☏ 99252 35014, ⓦ rannriders.com. This eco-resort has 28 a/c cottages with tiled or grass roofs, a restaurant, pool, gardens, several inviting hammocks and a friendly and helpful owner. Accommodation is on an a package that includes full board and the choice of a jeep, horse or camel safari. Free pick up from Dasada bus station. ₹**6000**

Saurashtra

SAURASHTRA, or the **Kathiawar Peninsula**, forms the bulk of Gujarat state, a large knob of land spreading south from the hills and marshes of the north out to the Arabian Sea, cut into by the Gulf of Cambay to the east and the Gulf of Kutch to the west. This is Gujarat at its most diverse, populated by cattle-rearing tribes and industrialists, with Hindu, Jain, Buddhist and Muslim architecture, modern urban centres and traditional bazaars.

Rajkot

RAJKOT, Gujarat's third largest city after Ahmedabad and Surat, is a typically sprawling, crowded and congested Indian city. Founded in the sixteenth century, Rajkot was ruled by the Jadeja Rajputs until merging with the Union of Saurashtra after Independence, and has since grown into a large industrial centre with a significant middle class. Best known for its association with **Mahatma Gandhi**, Rajkot has little to attract tourists save a museum and Gandhi's family residence in the **old city**, which is still home to a plenitude of typical Gujarati wooden-fronted houses with intricately carved shutters and stained-glass windows. Rajkot makes a good base for trips to nearby palaces.

Kaba Gandhi No Delo

Off Ghikantha Rd, 300m wast of Sanganwa Chowk • Mon–Sat 9am–noon & 3–5.30pm • Free

The Gandhis moved to **Kaba Gandhi No Delo** from Porbandar in 1881 when the Mahatma's father accepted an appointment as the diwan of Rajkot state. Tucked away in the narrow streets off the old city, the house has several rooms lined with artefacts and pictures stringing together the story of Gandhi's life.

Watson Museum

Jubilee Bagh • Mon–Sat, except 2nd & 4th Sat of month 9am–6pm • ₹50 (₹2)

Named after Colonel Watson, a British political agent from 1886 to 1893 largely responsible for documenting Saurashtran history, the **Watson Museum** features a somewhat dishevelled collection of artefacts and artworks. Gathered from some of the region's erstwhile royal families, the displays range from Mohenjo Daro relics to medieval statues and manuscripts and nineteenth century oil paintings.

ARRIVAL AND DEPARTURE   RAJKOT

By plane Jet Airways, Kasturba Rd (☏ 0281 2479623) and Air India (opposite GEB Office, Dhebar Rd; ☏ 0281 2234122) have daily flights to Mumbai. The airport is northwest of the centre (₹30 auto-rickshaw ride).

By train Rajkot's train station is about 2km north of the city centre (₹20 auto-rickshaw ride). Plenty of daily trains link Rajkot to Ahmedabad (4hr 30min), including the #19006 *Saurashtra Mail* (dep. 5.45pm, arr. 10.25pm), which continues to Mumbai Central (arr. 7.10am). Several daily trains also head to Junagadh (2hr) and Veraval (4hr).

By bus From the ST bus stand on Dhebar Rd there are regular state buses to Ahmedabad (every 30min; 4hr

30min), Jamnagar (every 30min; 2hr), Junagadh (hourly; 2hr–2hr 30min) and Bhuj (hourly; 7hr). Numerous private bus companies have offices clustered at Limda Chowk, each operating shuttles to private terminals on the outskirts of town: Eagle Travels (Ring Rd, opposite the Adani Hyper Market; ☏ 0281 554444) has comfortable daily a/c buses to Ahmedabad (4hr), Vadodara (6hr) and Mumbai (11hr); Mahasagar Travels (Moti Tanki Chowk; ☏ 0281 2466424) runs buses to Junagadh (hourly; 2hr); and Jay Somnath (Gondal Rd, 50m south of the Telegraph Office; ☏ 0281 2433315) has buses to Bhuj (daily; 5–6hr).

9

INFORMATION

Tourist office Rajkot's rather redundant tourist office (Mon–Sat 10.30am–1.30pm & 2–5.30pm, closed 2nd and 4th Sat of month; ☎028122 34507) is off Jawahar Rd, north of Sanganwa Chowk behind the State Bank of India.

Services The post office is on Sadar Rd, off Jawahar Rd, opposite Jubilee Gardens. Internet access is available at Try Matrix Cyber Café (City Plaza, Yagnik Rd) and Buzz Cyber Café (opposite *Lord's Banquet*, Kasturba Rd), both of which charge ₹20/hr.

ACCOMMODATION

Bhabha Panchnath Rd, off Jawahar Rd ☎0281 2220861, ⓦhotelbhabha.com. A good budget option just across from MKG High School, with small singles, doubles, triples and quads, all of which have TV and private bathroom. The more expensive rooms also come with tubs and a/c (₹955). The "deluxe coolers" are especially good deals if rupees are tight (₹575). **₹805**

Galaxy Jawahar Rd, 100m north of Sanganwa Chowk ☎0281 2222905, ⓦthegalaxyhotelrajkot .com. A refurbishment has brightened up this hotel and pushed prices up: the sizeable a/c rooms in creams and browns have TV and wi-fi, but the attached bathrooms could be better. It's on the third floor of a shopping complex, accessed via a creaking lift. **₹1990**

Imperial Palace Dr Yagnik Rd ☎0281 2480000, ⓦtheimperialpalace.biz. Rajkot's classiest hotel attracts visiting cricketers and Bollywood stars with sophisticated rooms, a pool and fitness suite and an excellent restaurant.

Rates include breakfast. Unusually for Gujarat, it's also wheelchair-accessible. **₹4900**

Jyoti Kanak Rd, 200m north of bus stand ☎0281 2225472, ⓔhoteljyoti@hotmail.com. The best of the scruffy and poky lodges in the area, *Jyoti is* bearable for a night, thanks largely to its welcoming manager. All rooms have attached bathrooms while some also have a/c (₹1250). **₹750**

Kavery Kanak Rd ☎0281 2239331, ⓦhotelkavery .com. This mid-range business hotel has spacious attached rooms with pale wood fittings and a superb in-house restaurant, *Bukhara*. Other perks include free airport pickup and wi-fi in the rooms. **₹1850**

Raviraj Palace Dhebar Rd, opposite Jivan Bank ☎0281 2227359, ⓔinfo@hotelravirajpalace.com. A brand new establishment with large windows and balconies (room 104's is especially spacious) in their fan-cooled and a/c (₹999) rooms. The four-person a/c rooms (₹1500) are a good deal. **₹800**

EATING

Look out for the Kathiawadi version of the Gujarati thali, spiced with ginger and garlic. Rajkot is also known for milk sweets like *thabdi halwas* and the saffron-flavoured *kesar pedas*.

Bukhara Hotel Kavery, Kanak Rd ☎0281 2239331. Smart a/c restaurant serving a Gujarati thali (₹150) at lunch and, for dinner, an exhaustive menu of top-notch north and south Indian, Chinese, Mexican and Italian dishes. Daily 11am–11pm.

Dhola Maru Hotel Grand Regency, Dhebar Rd ☎0281 2240100. Recommended hotel restaurant serving Indian, Chinese, Italian and Mexican dishes; its glass-walled kitchen is an attraction in itself and you can watch them prepare Indian breads like naan. Mains ₹150–275. Daily 11am–11pm.

★ **Lord's Banquet** Kasturba Rd. This efficient a/c place, serving superior north Indian food (₹80–150), is where locals go for a treat. You can specify the spiciness of your dish and even the crispiness of your roti. *Paneer* butter masala ₹127. Daily 12.30–3.30pm & 7.30–11.30pm

Temptations Kasturba Rd. Next to *Lord's Banquet* and run by the same management, this classy restaurant offers Chinese, Italian, Indian, American and Mexican dishes (chimichangas ₹188) as well as snacks and ice cream. Unique versions of the *The Last Supper* adorn the entrance. Daily 11am–midnight.

Sayla

In August or September, the quiet pastoral town of **SAYLA** bursts into life with one of Gujarat's most unique and colourful festivals, the Tarnetar Fair. To a flurry of Barwhadi tribal songs, dances and battles of poetry in a sport known as *duhas*, the local men strut in colourful turbans and embroidered jackets and sporting brightly decorated umbrellas. Tarnetar aims to celebrate youth, joy and artistry, while many of the bejewelled young women present have the primary aim of finding their future husbands. As the tradition goes, women have first choice.

ARRIVAL AND DEPARTURE
SAYLA

By bus Sayla's bus stand lies at the southern entrance to town, 600m north of the busy Rajkot–Ahmedabad highway, 87km from Rajkot (1hr 30min) and 135km from Ahmedabad (3hr). Several daily buses to both cities depart from here, but more frequent connections are available from the bus stand on the highway itself.

ACCOMMODATION

Bell Guest House Off Sayla Roundabout on NH-8A ☎ 97246 78145, ⓦ bellguesthouse.com. Built by Sayla's royal family for British colonial officers, this old bungalow has been converted into a comfortable homestay offering large a/c rooms with en-suite bathrooms and a fine restaurant. The shady grounds are home to a giant chessboard and an aged tennis court. ₹3000

Wankaner

The small city of **WANKANER** is named for its setting at the bend of the River Machchhu (wanka means "bend" and ner means "river"). The flamboyant **Ranjit Vilas Palace** (call ahead to visit; ☎ 02828 220000) stands on a hill overlooking the city. Home to the family that once ruled the state of the same name, it was built between 1899 and 1914, with an arched facade featuring a frenzy of architectural styles, combining Mughal domes with Doric columns, Victorian Gothic arches, stained-glass windows, chandeliers and Franco-Italian window panes that overlook the palace grounds, where stables are stocked with thoroughbred Kathiawadi stallions. The interior is at least as eccentric, with a stuffed animal collection that includes rhinos, Kodiak bears, several now-extinct Indian wildcats, and no less than seventeen tiger heads.

ARRIVAL AND DEPARTURE
WANKANER

By bus Wankaner's bus stand is in the southeast of town; regular buses run to Rajkot (every 30min; 1hr).

ACCOMMODATION

Motiwadi Royal Oasis 2km from Ranjit Vilas Palace ☎ 02828 22000. Splurge on the Art Deco splendour of the royal family's nearby summer home, built between 1875 and 1940, offering full-board with sumptuous rooms, two fine restaurants and a spacious indoor pool. ₹4600

Gondal

Once the capital city of a Jadeja Rajput clan, **GONDAL** houses a handful of extravagant royal residences. All contain memorabilia from the life of the widely admired scholar-maharaja Bhagwat Sinhji, responsible for making Gondal one of India's most prosperous states. The city is now a centre for beadwork embroidery, handloom weaving, silverware, brassware and Ayurvedic medicine. Good places for shopping include the market on Darbargadh Road and the Udyog Bharati emporium near the palace. The Naulakha Museum (daily 9am–noon & 3–6pm; ₹20) is housed in a crumbling riverside palace, displaying the various artefacts from Gondal's glory days, including the royal wardrobe and library and the weighing scale on which Bhagwat Sinhji measured himself against gold to be distributed as charity on his own golden jubilee.

ARRIVAL AND DEPARTURE
GONDAL

By bus The bus stand is near the city centre, about 500m south of *Orchard Palace*; regular buses link to Rajkot (every 30min; 1hr).

ACCOMMODATION

Orchard Palace Huzoor Palace ☎ 02825 24550, ⓦ gondalpalaces.com. Built as an annexe to the *Huzoor Palace*, the current royal residence, *Orchard Palace* was the official guesthouse of the maharajas from the late nineteenth century, deriving its name from a neighbouring grove of fruit trees. Although a bit pricey, all rooms have high ceilings, four-posters and period furniture, while the palace itself houses a royal car collection spanning a century. Price includes a guided tour of Gondal's palaces. ₹4800

9

Jamnagar

The busy hub of **JAMNAGAR** in northwest Saurashtra, founded in the sixteenth century, was one of the region's most important princely states. **K.S. Ranjitsinhji**, who played cricket for England alongside W.G. Grace, ruled Jamnagar at the start of the twentieth century, replacing run-down buildings with attractive constructions that still attest to his prosperous and efficient rule. In recent years, the city has become the world's undisputed refining hub, with the Reliance Industries' refinery just west of town stacking up well over a million barrels of oil each day. Visitors come to Jamnagar for its fabulous mix of architecture and renowned *bandhani* (tie-dye), sold in the markets near the Darbargadh; from October to May, a small number use the city as a base from which to explore the diverse intertidal sea life of the **Marine National Park** (60km west; ☎0288 2679355), which encompasses 42 islands strung along 120km of coastline.

The Old City

The most remarkable of Ranjitsinhji's constructions is **Willingdon Crescent**, the swooping arches of its curved facade overlooking the wide streets of Chelmsford Market and the old palace, the **Darbargadh**. In the heart of town, just off Ranjit Road, southwest of Bedi Gate, stands the late nineteenth-century **Ratan Bai Mosque**. This grand domed prayer-hall, its sandalwood doors inlaid with mother-of-pearl, is the unlikely neighbour to a magnificent pair of **Jain temples**, both decorated with extraordinary **murals**. The most spectacular of the two, **Shantinath Mandir**, is a maze of brightly coloured columns. The outer side of the large dome over **Adinath Mandir** is inlaid with gold and coloured mosaic and both temples have cupolas enriched with a design of mirrors above the entrance porch. The temples form the hub of **Chandni Bazaar**, an almost circular market area enlivened by carved wooden doors, mosaics and balconies.

Ranmal Lake and around

Some of Jamnagar's most interesting sites are set to the east of the man-made **Ranmal Lake**, at the centre of which stands the **Lakhota Palace**, an island fort built in the eighteenth century. It's only accessible from the north side, and upon entering you'll pass a guardroom containing muskets, swords and powder flasks, and the **museum** (daily except Wed and 2nd & 4th Sat of month 10am–1pm & 2–5.30pm; ₹50 (₹2)) on the upper floor, which holds a mediocre display of paintings, sculpture, folk art and coins. South of the lake stands the crumbling, circular **Bhujia Fort**, closed since becoming a casualty of the 2001 earthquake. To its northwest, on the edge of the old city, the **Bala Hanuman Temple** has been the scene of round-the-clock non-stop chanting ("Shree Ram, Jai Ram, Jai Jai Ram") since August 1 1964, a feat cited in the *Guinness Book of Records*.

ARRIVAL AND DEPARTURE	**JAMNAGAR**

By plane The airport is 6km west of town – an auto or taxi will cost around ₹60 or ₹180 respectively. Air India (Indra Mahal, Bhid Bhanjan Rd; ☎0288 2554768) operates flights to Mumbai (daily; 1hr).

By train The main railway station is 5km northwest of town. Regular trains connect with Ahmedabad (6–7hr), Rajkot (1hr 30min–2hr) and Dwarka (2–3hr). The #19005 *Saurashtra Mail* departs at 3.35pm and arrives in Rajkot at 5.15pm, Ahmedabad at 10.25pm, and Mumbai Central at 7.10am. In the other direction, the #19005 *Saurashtra Mail* departs Jamnagar at 12.09pm and arrives in Dwarka at 2.46pm.

By bus The bus station is 2km west of the town centre; an auto-rickshaw will cost around ₹30. When heading to Rajkot, buses can be hailed from outside *Hotel President*. Private buses leave from Pancheshwar Tower near Teen Batti: Patel Tours & Travels (☎0288 2552419, ⊕pateltoursandtravels.com) has buses to Ahmedabad (15 daily; 7hr) and Bhuj (3 daily; 7hr).

Destinations Ahmedabad (hourly; 7hr); Dwarka (hourly; 3–4hr); Junagadh (hourly; 4hr); Rajkot (every 30min; 2hr).

ADINATH TEMPLE, PALITANA >

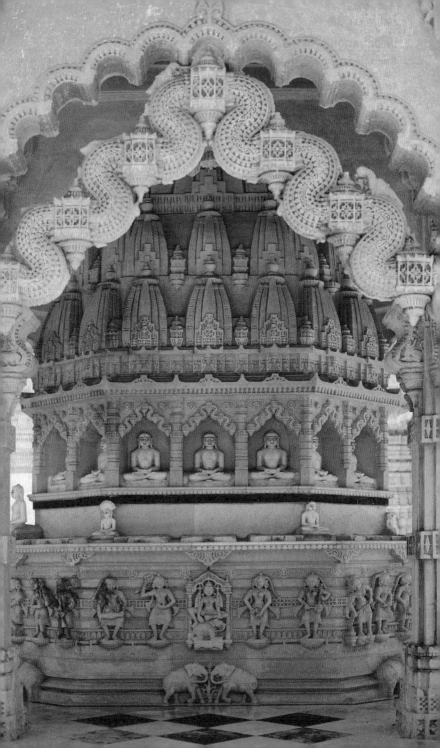

INFORMATION

Tourist office The information bureau (📞 0281 2234507) is at Jawahar House, behind the State Bank of Saurashtra.

Services Internet access is available at Venus, opposite the Post Office in Teen Batti, and Sify Iway (📞 0288 2661422), a 5min walk west of *Hotel President* (both ₹20/hr). Thomas Cook, opposite the town hall, and several banks on Ranjit Rd change money. Jamnagar's Ayurvedic University (📞 0288 2664866, 🌐 ayurveduniversity.com), 1km northwest of Teen Batti, runs a vast array of courses, and offers massage, yoga and mud-therapy sessions.

ACCOMMODATION

Aram Nand Niwas, Pandit Nehru Marg, Bedi Rd 📞 0288 2551701, 🌐 hotelaram.com. Palatial white building – once the home of a scion of the state's ruling family – with blue awnings, giving it something of the feel of a British seaside hotel. Its large a/c rooms, nostalgic for the days of the Raj and filled with European antiques, have a faded charm. Wi-fi and breakfast included. **₹1500**

Ashiana Third Floor, New Super Market, Bedi Gate Rd 📞 0288 2559110, 🌐 hotelashiana.com. Jamnagar's best budget option: spacious rooms with TV and bathroom, some with carpets and a/c (₹800), set right in the centre of town. There's wi-fi in the lobby, and the helpful staff can arrange onward bus, train or air tickets. **₹400**

President Teen Batti 📞 0288 2557491, 🌐 hotelpresident.in. A well-managed hotel, home to a/c rooms (₹1783) with wood-panelled walls and non-a/c rooms with somewhat grubby bathrooms. All have private balconies and TVs, while there's also a currency exchange, a good restaurant, wi-fi in the lobby and nautically themed decor throughout. Staff can organize birdwatching and sailing trips and visits to the nearby marine park. Free airport transfers. **₹780**

Punit Pandit Nehru Marg, just northwest of Teen Batti 📞 0288 2559275, 🌐 hotelpunit.com. A popular place with a small but pleasant roof terrace and airy turquoise rooms, which come with carpets and slightly dated decor. A/c rooms start at ₹700. **₹600**

EATING

⭐**7 Seas** Hotel President, Teen Batti 📞 0288 2557491. In line with the hotel's maritime theme, with a porthole-like door and paintings of the sea, *7 Seas* serves up some of Jamnagar's best non-veg food: the (mutton) sheek kebab curry (₹216) stands out, and the pineapple lassi (₹79) is not to be missed. 24hr.

Cafe Paradise Ranjit Rd. Look for the orange sign for this friendly, low-key restaurant, stacked with booths and offering a photo menu of Chinese and Punjabi meals, including chicken biriyani (₹130) and chicken lolipop (₹35 per piece). Daily 10am–11pm.

Kalpana Teen Batti 📞 0288 2554369. The decor may be ancient, but the tempting veg snacks – burgers, dosas, milk shakes and ice cream (₹25–120) – certainly hit the spot. Daily 9.30am–11pm.

Madras Old Station Rd, Teen Batti 📞 0288 3211543. A cramped dining room, with separate slightly more spacious a/c area, serving great Punjabi, south Indian (masala dosa ₹40), Jain and Chinese dishes, as well as fresh juices, ice cream and pizzas (₹75–85). Daily 10am–10.30pm.

Dwarka

Poised at the tip of the peninsula, at India's western edge, **DWARKA** is one of Hinduism's sacred Charm Dham, or "four abodes," thanks to its legendary role as Lord Krishna's capital following his flight from Mathura to the coast. In vivid contrast to the arid expanses further inland, Dwarka is surrounded with fertile wheat, groundnut and cotton fields, while the city itself is a labyrinth of narrow winding streets cluttered with crumbling temples. Today, these still resonate with the bustle of saffron-clad pilgrims and the clatter of celebratory drums. Dwarka really comes to life during the major Hindu **festivals**, especially Janmashtami (Aug/Sept), marking Krishna's birthday.

Dwarkadhish Temple

100m north of Gomti Ghat • Daily 7am–12.30pm & 5–9.30pm

Jagat Mandir, the elaborately carved tower of the sixteenth-century **Dwarkadhish Temple**, looms 78m over the town, comprising five storeys and 72 pillars while hoisting a giant flag made from more than fifty yards of cloth. It is believed that the original structure was built 2500 years ago by Vajranabha, Krishna's grandson, and that it has been destroyed by raging seas and rebuilt no less than six times. Non-Hindus may enter the shrine only after signing a form declaring respect for the religion.

ARRIVAL AND DEPARTURE

DWARKA

By train The train station is 2km northeast of town. Several daily trains connect Jamnagar (2–3hr) and Rajkot (4–5hr), while at least one daily train goes to Ahmedabad (9–10hr). The #19006 *Saurashtra Mail* departs daily at 12.48pm, travelling to Jamnagar (arr. 3.33pm), Rajkot (arr. 5.15pm), Ahmedabad (arr. 10.25pm) and Mumbai Central (arr. 7.10am).

By bus The bus stand is a 10min walk north of the old city centre on the Okha Rd. Services run from here to Jamnagar (3–4hr), Porbandar (3hr), Junagadh (5–6hr) and Veraval (6hr). More comfortable private bus companies have offices along Bhadrakali Rd, among them Shiv Shakti Travels (opposite *Hotel Guruprerna*; ☎02892 234601), which has buses to Jamnagar (hourly; 3hr 30min), Rajkot (hourly; 5hr 30min) and Bhuj (8.30pm daily; 9hr).

INFORMATION

Tours Dwarka Darshan (Vegetable Market; ☎02892 234093) runs tours (8am & 2pm; ₹50) to the underground *jyotirlingam* at the Nageshwar Temple, 16km from Dwarka.

Services Internet access is available at Shreeji Cybercafé (₹40/hr) opposite *Hotel Uttam*. There are several banks with ATMs along Bhadrakali Rd, including an HDFC.

ACCOMMODATION AND EATING

Guruprerna Opposite Bhadrakali Temple, Bhadrakali Rd ☎02892 234553, ✉hotelguruprerna@gmail.com. Institutional-style hotel with clean, comfortable rooms, all with attached bathrooms and some with a/c (₹1200). Its popular a/c restaurant, *Sharanam*, serves generous thalis (₹140). ₹850

Puroshotam Parotha House Opposite Guruprerna, Bhadrakali Rd ☎98988 10251. Small but extremely popular diner serving all-vegetarian Punjabi meals, including

excellent *paneer* tikka masala (₹90). Daily noon–10.30pm.

Shri Dwarkesh Bhojnalay Next to HDFC, Bhadrakali Rd. A hole-in-the-wall thali joint offering fantastic Gujarati food for pennies (thali ₹35). Daily 11am–2pm & 6–10pm.

Tulsi Opposite Dr. Ambadker Statue, Bhadrakali Rd ☎02892 235232. A bland business hotel with mostly clean and modern a/c (₹1200) and fan-cooled rooms with TVs, and hot water from 5–10am. ₹1000

Porbandar

Despite its links to legends of Krishna, **PORBANDAR**, once an international port and princely state capital, owes the bulk of its fame to Mahatma Gandhi, born here in 1869. Today, shrouded in a dim haze of excretions from the cement and chemical factories on its outskirts, the town is pretty grimy, despite the flow of remittances from its many emigrants overseas. Still, the Gandhi connection isn't Porbandar's only draw. Several lavish palaces are strung along the coast near the city's Chowpatty Seaface, including **Daria Rajmahal Palace**, now a college, and **Huzoor Palace**, occupied by the descendants of the former maharaja when they visit from London. An impressive old arched pavillion, **Grishmabhawan**, built for eighteenth-century poet Maharaja Sartanji, stands near the bus stand, while Porbandar's lake is a designated bird sanctuary (although you're more likely to spot **flamingos** – along with *dhow*-builders – at the creeks along the coast than here). Meanwhile, more than a thousand **whale sharks** visit the coast each year near Porbandar and Veraval: the Wildlife Trust of India (☎011 26326025, ⌨wti.org.in) can help organize dives or trips on research boats.

Gandhi's birthplace

Near Manek Chowk, Kasturba Rd • Daily 10am–noon & 3–6.30pm • Free but guides expect small donation

Porbandar's biggest attraction is **Gandhi's birthplace**, an old three-storey haveli. A swastika marks his exact birthplace. Faded traces of old paintings adorn some of the walls in the reading and prayer rooms on the upper floors, but little else remains. The neighbouring **Kirti Mandir**, completed in 1950, is a memorial to Gandhi and his wife, blending various religious architectural styles and displaying photographs and artefacts from the Mahatma's life.

ARRIVAL AND DEPARTURE

PORBANDAR

By plane Porbandar's airport is 7km east of town (₹50 auto-rickshaw ride). Jet Airways has daily flights to

Mumbai (dep. 3.50pm; 1hr 30min).

9

MAHATMA GANDHI – INDIA'S GREAT SOUL

Gujarat's most famous son, **Mohandas Karamchand Gandhi**, was born on October 2, 1869, in Porbandar. Although merchants by caste – Gandhi means grocer – both his grandfather and father rose to positions of political influence. Young Mohandas was shy and sickly, just an average scholar, but from early on he questioned the codes of power around him, even flouting accepted Hindu practice: he once ate meat for a year believing it would give him the physical edge the British appeared to possess. As a teenager, he began to develop an interest in spirituality, particularly the Jain principle of **ahimsa** (non-violence).

At 19, he moved to London to study law, outwardly adopting the appearance and manners of an Englishman while obeying his mother's wish that he resist meat, alcohol and women. Studying the Bible alongside the Bhagavad Gita, he came to view different religions as a collective source of truth from which all could draw spiritual inheritance.

After a brief spell back in India, Gandhi left again to practise law in South Africa. The plight of his fellow Indians there, coupled with his own indignation at being ejected from a first-class train carriage, fuelled his campaigns for racial equality. Gaining crucial victories for minorities against the practices of indentured labour, his public profile grew. At this time he opted to transcend material possessions, donning the peasant's handspun *dhoti* and shawl and taking a vow of celibacy. This turn to ascetic purity he characterized as *satyagraha*, derived from Sanskrit ideas of "truth" and "firmness"; it would become the touchstone of **passive resistance**.

Returning to India with his messianic reputation well established – the poet Tagore named him **"Mahatma"** (Great Soul) – Gandhi travelled the country campaigning for **swaraj** (home rule). He also worked tirelessly for the rights of women and untouchables, whom he called **Harijans** (children of God), and founded an ashram at Sabarmati outside Ahmedabad where these principles were upheld. Gandhi stepped up his activities in the wake of the brutal massacre of protesters at Amritsar, leading a series of self-sufficiency drives during the 1920s, which culminated in the great **salt march** from Ahmedabad to Dandi in 1930. This month-long 386km journey led a swelling band of followers to the coast, where salt was made in defiance of the British monopoly on production. It drew worldwide attention: although Gandhi was promptly imprisoned, British resolve was seen to have weakened. On his release, he was invited to a round-table meeting in London to discuss home rule. The struggle continued for several years and Gandhi served more time in jail, his wife Kasturba dying by his side in 1944.

As the nationalist movement gained strength, Gandhi grew more concerned about the state of Hindu-Muslim relations. He responded to outbreaks of communal violence by subjecting his own body to self-purification and suffering through fasting. After Independence, Partition left him with a deep sense of failure. In a bid to stem the ensuing violence, he again fasted in Calcutta as large numbers of Hindus and Muslims flowed between the new countries. Gandhi's commitment to the fair treatment of Muslim Indians and his intention to visit and endorse Pakistan as a neighbour enraged many Hindu fundamentalists. He survived an attempt on his life on January 20, 1948, only to be shot dead from close range by a lone Hindu gunman in Delhi ten days later. Prime minister Nehru announced the loss of a national radio: "Friends and comrades, the light has gone out of our lives and there is darkness everywhere."

By train The railway station is 1km northeast of the town centre; the daily #19216 *Saurashtra Express* departs at 9.05pm, reaching Ahmedabad at 6.10am and Mumbai at 7.15pm the following day.

By bus The ST bus stand is a short walk south of the town centre, with buses linking Dwarka (7 daily; 3hr), Jamnagar (3 daily; 4hr) and Junagadh (3.25pm daily; 3hr). Private bus offices are strung along MG Rd.

INFORMATION

Banks Banks along MG Rd change foreign currency, as does JK Forex, also on MG Rd, across from Natraj.
Internet access Skyline Cyber Cafe, beneath *Indraprasth* on ST Cross Rd (₹20/hr).

Travel agents Thankys Tours & Travel (MG Rd, near Dreamland Cinema; ☎0286 2244344) book taxis, trains and domestic flights. Eagle Travels (MG Rd, near Panchayat Office; ☎0281 2212089) has buses to Rajkot (5hr) and Ahmedabad (10hr).

ACCOMMODATION

Indraprasth Opposite Swaminarayan Temple, off ST Cross Rd ☎0286 2242681, ⊛hotelindraprasth .biz. One of the better value mid-range choices in Porbandar, offering straightforward fan-cooled and a/c (₹950) rooms in warm colours with TVs and private bathrooms. ₹500

Moon Palace MG Rd, 100m east of the main square ☎0286 2241172, ⊛porbandaronline.com /moonpalace. While the rooms – all with attached baths and TVs and some with a/c (₹700) – feel a bit sombre, they're clean, comfortable and good value. ₹400

★ **Natraj** MG Rd, close to Moon Palace ☎0286 2215658, ⊛hotelnatrajp.com. A notch above the competition: surprisingly cool, minimalist fan-cooled and a/c (₹800) rooms with attached bathrooms at bargain prices, plus a fine restaurant, wi-fi, currency exchange and a watersports centre offering boat trips. ₹350

Silver Palace Silver Complex, just off MG Rd ☎0286 2252591 or ☎94263 72953. Another good choice despite the somewhat grimy entrance, with spotless fan and a/c (₹999) rooms with TVs, fridges and various superfluous pieces of furniture, such as padded stools and mini tables. Ask to see a few, as some have lurid decor. ₹600

EATING

Moon Palace Moon Palace hotel, MG Rd. Popular restaurant serving Gujarati thalis (₹90), Punjabi dishes and Western snacks. It also opens early for breakfast. Daily 7.30am–11pm.

National MG Rd. This unassuming Muslim-run place serves delicious (but small) meat and veg meals (₹30–90) to a steady stream of contented customers. Daily 8am–10.30pm.

Natraj Natraj hotel, MG Rd ☎99798 77567. Run with the same style and quiet efficiency as the hotel, *Natraj* has an elegant, modern dining room and a varied menu of Indian and Chinese and even decent pizzas (veg ₹95) and pasta dishes – the latter a real rarity for Gujarat. Dining is limited to the fast-food menu until dinner begins (7pm). Daily 11am–11pm.

Swagat MG Rd, 250m east of the main square. A relaxed, softly lit place that offers good-quality, reasonably-priced Punjabi and south Indian veg dishes (₹30–85). It can get very busy at weekends. Daily 8.30am–3pm & 5.30–11pm.

Junagadh

The little-visited town of **JUNAGADH** (or Junagarh) is an intriguing small city with a striking skyline of domes and minarets. Its lively bazaars, Buddhist monuments, Hindu temples, mosques, Victorian Gothic-style archways and faded mansions – plus the magnificent Jain temples on **Mount Girnar** – make it well worth exploring.

From the fourth century BC to the death of Ashoka (*c*.232 BC), Junagadh was the Gujarat's capital under the Buddhist Mauryas. The brief reigns of the Kshatrapas and the Guptas came to an end when the town passed into the hands of the Hindu Chudasanas, who in turn lost out to Muslim invaders. Muslim sovereignty lasted until Independence when, although the nawab of Junagadh planned to unite with Pakistan, local pressure ensured that the city became part of the Indian Union. Because of the sanctity of Mount Girnar, 4km away, the **Shivratri Mela** (Feb/March) assumes particular importance in Junagadh, when thousands of saffron-clad sadhus set up camp here. Fireworks, processions, chanting, chillum-smoking and demonstrations of body-torturing ascetic practices run for at least five days and nights. Every November, up to a million people take part in the **Parikrama**, a three-day 36km walk around the base of Mount Girnar and the surrounding hills.

Chittakhana Chowk and around

Junagadh is fairly compact, focused on the busy market area around **Chittakhana Chowk**. To the north, near the railway station, quiet wide roads lead past the majestic **Maqbara monuments**, while in to the south, congested streets surround Circle Chowk, a fine semicircular terrace between towering Victorian Gothic-style gateways. Nearby is the extravagant **Durbar Hall** along with its modest museum, while MG Road continues south to bustling Kalwa Chowk.

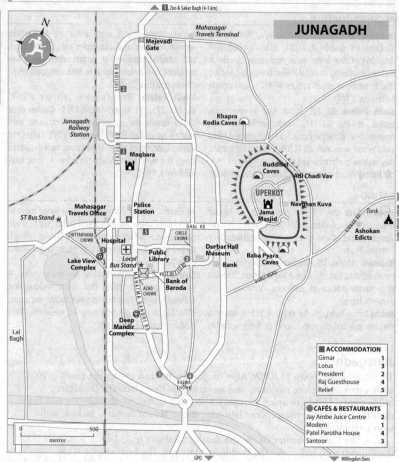

Maqbara

MG Rd, opposite the High Courts

Junagadh's chief Muslim monuments, the boldly decorated nineteenth-century **maqbara** (tombs), are unlike any other in Gujarat. These striking mausolea blend European, Indian and Islamic styles, crowned with multitude of bulbous domes. The most opulent tomb is the 1892 sepulchre of Mahabat Khan II, but more outstanding is that of Vizir Sahib Baka-ud-din Bhar, completed four years later and flanked on each corner by tall minarets hugged with spiral staircases.

Durbar Hall Museum

Post Office Rd, just west of the main entrance to Uparkot • Daily except Wed & 2nd & 4th Sat of each month 9am–12.15pm & 3–6pm • ₹50 (₹5), ₹2/photograph

The **Durbar Hall Museum** takes up part of the former palace of the babis of Junagadh, offering an intimate glimpse into their lavish lives. Silver chairs in the great hall stand in regal splendour around a large carpet, valuable silver clocks encase scruffy stuffed birds, huge coloured chandeliers hang from the ceiling and a royal gallery displays old portraits of the nawabs themselves.

Uparkot
Eastern end of Dhal Rd • Daily except 2nd & 4th Sat of month 7am–6.15pm • ₹50 (₹2)

The imposing fortified citadel of **Uparkot** is perched on a thickly walled mound to the east of the city and colonized by eagles, egrets and squirrels. Legend dates the fort's origins to the time of the Yadavas (Krishna's clan) who fled Mathura to settle in Dwarka, but historians believe it was built by Chandragupta Maurya in 319 BC. Rediscovered and repaired in 976 AD by Muslim conquerors, it regained its defensive importance, withstanding sixteen sieges over the next eight hundred years. A grand sequence of three high gateways cut into solid rock during the Muslim occupation stands at the entrance to the citadel, spanning a cobbled walkway that winds upwards to the summit of the raised fort, where the fort-like **Jama Masjid**, converted from a palace by a conquering Sultan in the fifteenth century, stands abandoned with its unique octagonal courtyard. The two fierce cannons opposite the mosque were brought here in 1538 after being used Diu fort against the Portuguese in 1530. About 200m northeast, more than 170 steps descend to the **Adi Chadi Vav** (well), believed to date from the fifteenth century. As impressive is the eleventh-century **Navghan Kuva** in the southeast of the citadel, consisting of a superb staircase winding around a well shaft to the dimly lit water level more than 52m below.

Buddhist caves
100m north of Jama Masjid • Daily 8am–6pm • ₹100 (₹5)

Near the Jama Masjid is a two-storey complex of monastic cells cut into the rock and arranged around courtyards. These **Buddhist caves** are the most recent of their kind in Junagadh, built in the third or fourth century AD. Worn traces of figurines and foliage can still be made out on the columns in the lower level.

Baba Pyara and Khapra Kodia caves
Baba Pyara caves 100m south of Uparkot walls • Daily 9am–6pm • ₹100 (₹5) • Khapra Kodia caves 300m north of Uparkot walls • Daily 9am–5pm • ₹100 (₹5)

Two clusters of Buddhist caves are found just beyond the walls of Uparkot. The **Baba Pyara caves**, hewn from the rock between 200 BC and 200 AD, consist of more than a dozen rooms opening to colonnades and a spacious courtyard, and were used by Buddhists until the time of Ashoka, then afterwards by Jains. Cut into a hill climbing towards Uparkot's southern walls, the caves are worth a wander. A little to the north of Uparkot are the slightly older, plainer **Khapra Kodia caves**, of which only the uppermost storey has survived.

Ashokan edicts
2km east of town on road to Girnar • Daily 8am–1pm & 2–6pm • ₹100 (₹5)

A rock engraved with the Buddhist **edicts of Ashoka**, Junagadh's most famous monarch, remains where it was placed in the third century BC, its impact somewhat marred by a modern shelter and concrete platform. Written in ancient brahmi script, the worn verses etched into the granite encourage the practice of dharma and equality, and beseech different religious sects to live in harmony and repent the evils of war. Situated on the pilgrim trail to Girnar, Ashoka's edicts had a lasting influence: as late as the seventh century AD there were about three thousand Buddhists in Junagadh, and more than fifty convents. Sanskrit inscriptions on the same rock were added during the reigns of King Rudraman (150 AD) and Skandagupta (455 AD), while both Gujarati and English translations accompany them today.

Mount Girnar
6km east of Junagadh • An auto-rickshaw costs ₹80

At more than 1116m, **Mount Girnar**, a steep-sided extinct volcano, is a major pilgrimage centre for Jains and Hindus, and has been considered sacred since before the

9

third century BC. It's best to start the roughly eight thousand-step ascent around 6am. The trail (6–7hr return), scattered with chai stalls, climbs through eucalyptus forests before zigzagging across the sheer rock face. On a plateau below the summit, the picturesque huddle of Jain temples has been renovated a little since its erection between 1128 and 1500. Neminath, the 22nd *tirthankara* who is said to have died on Mount Girnar after seven hundred years of meditation and asceticism, is depicted as a black figure in the lotus position holding a conch in the marble **Neminath temple**, the first on the left as you enter the "temple city".

The final two thousand steps to the summit of Mount Girnar are worth the effort, offering breathtaking views. At the top, a temple dedicated to the Hindu goddess **Amba Mata** attracts both Hindu and Jain pilgrims. Steps lead down from this temple and then up again along a narrow ridge towards **Gorakhnath Peak**, where a small shrine covers what are supposedly the footprints of the pilgrim Gorakhnath, and further to a third peak where the imprints of Neminath's feet are sheltered by a small canopy. At the most distant point of the ridge, a shrine dedicated to the fierce Hindu goddess **Kalika**, the eternal aspect of Durga, is a haunt for near-naked **Aghora ascetics** who express their absolute renunciation of the world by ritually enacting their own funerals.

ARRIVAL AND DEPARTURE

By train The station is just off Station Rd, to the northwest of the town centre. The *Jabalpur Express* #11463/#11465 departs at 11.35am to Rajkot (arr. 2pm) and Ahmedabad (6.25pm).

Destinations Ahmedabad (4 daily; 7hr); Delvada (for Diu; daily; 6hr); Rajkot (7 daily; 2hr); Sasan Gir (daily; 2–3hr); Veraval (8 daily; 2hr).

By bus The long-distance bus stand is 300m west of Chittakhana Chowk. Mahasagar Travels (bus terminal just east

of Majevadi Gate; offices on Dhal Rd near the railway station, ☎0285 2626085; and at Kalwa Chowk,☎0285 2621913) operates private buses to Ahmedabad (2 daily; 7hr); Rajkot (2 daily; 2hr 30min) and Mumbai (1 daily; 19–20hr); shuttle services are available from city offices to the main terminal.

Destinations Ahmedabad (hourly; 7–8hr); Diu (2 daily; 5hr); Jamnagar (hourly; 5hr); Porbandar (hourly; 3hr); Rajkot (hourly; 2hr 30min); Sasan Gir (hourly; 2hr); Veraval (hourly; 2hr); Una (for Diu; hourly; 4hr 30min).

INFORMATION

Tourist information The official tourist office is in *Hotel Girnar*, near the northern Majevadi Gate (☎0285 2621201), but staff at *Relief Hotel* provide the best information on the town's sites and Gir National Park.

Services XS Cyber Café (☎0285 2621468) in the Lake View Complex, behind the railroad tracks from *Modern Restaurant*, and Magic Net, 1st floor of the Deep Mandir

Complex about 200m south of Azad Chowk, both offer internet access for ₹15/hr. The main post office is 2km south of town; there's also a smaller branch next to the local bus stand on MG Rd. The State Bank of India opposite the Durbar Hall Museum changes dollars and sterling, and there are several ATMS scattered around town, including the Bank of Baroda near the bus stand.

ACCOMMODATION

If you're arriving in Junagadh during either Shivratri Mela or the Parikrama (see p.54), it's advisable to book rooms well in advance.

Girnar 2km north of town, near Majevadi Gate ☎0285 2621201. Run (without much enthusiasm) by Gujarat Tourism, *Girnar* has reasonable rooms with attached bathroom; some also have balconies and a/c (₹650) and there's a decent restaurant (thalis ₹50). Auto-rickshaws from the bus stand cost ₹20–30. **₹400**

Lotus Station Rd ☎0285 2658500, ⦿thelotushotel .com. A tranquil contrast to the dust and noise outside, *Lotus* is the town's smartest hotel. The swish rooms have marble floors and beige furniture, along with hot water, TV, refrigerator and wi-fi. **₹1450**

President Station Rd ☎0285 2625661. Handy if you have to catch an early train, this place has acceptable rooms, some with a/c (₹900) and all with private bathrooms. The larger, more expensive rooms face the noisy main road, so opt for one facing the courtyard. **₹600**

Raj Guesthouse Dhal Rd ☎0285 2623961. The space-challenged *Raj* is a good choice for backpackers looking to save a few rupees in one of its dirt-cheap rooms, cabins or dorm beds. Dorm **₹60**, double **₹200**

★ **Relief** Dhal Rd ☎ 0285 2620280, ⊛ reliefhotel .com. Welcoming and extremely knowledgeable staff, clean, bright and inexpensive rooms with attached bathrooms and a superior restaurant (in season) make *Relief* easily the best bet in town for backpackers. A/c rooms were in the works at the time of writing. ₹ **500**

EATING

Jay Ambe Juice Centre Post Office Rd, 50m south of Circle Chowk. The place to come for fresh fruit juices, milk shakes and ice cream: don't miss the drinks made from Junagadh's famous *kesar* (saffron) mangos (around ₹25). Daily 10am–11pm.

Modern Opposite the hospital ☎ 0285 2620928. An a/c dining hall serving bottomless spicy-sweet thalis (₹80). Tourists are unusual here, however, so you may have an audience while you eat. Daily 10am–10.30pm.

Patel Parotha House North of Kalwa Chowk ☎ 98989 96023. A clean and busy a/c restaurant with big windows overlooking Kalwa Chowk, serving generous Gujarati and Jain thalis (₹60). Daily 9am–11pm.

Santoor Northwest of Kalwa Chowk, MG Rd ☎ 0285 2625090. Delicious, reasonably priced Chinese, Punjabi and south Indian dishes (masala dosa ₹40), plus juices from locally grown fruit and milk shakes, served in cosy, dimly lit booths. Daily 11am–11pm.

Veraval

Midway between Porbandar and Diu sprawls the chaotic, congested fishing port of **VERAVAL**. While most visitors today use Veraval as a jumping-off point for the area's pilgrimage sites – such as **Somnath** – 6km to the east, such it was once a major port for *hajjis* en route to Mecca. The vicinity's various shrines to Vishnu and connection with Krishna – said to have lived here with the Yadavas – make it equally important for Vaishnavites today.

The city itself has little to hold visitors' interest, although its enormous **fishing harbour**, crammed with a dizzying number of colourful *dhows*, is worth a look. A kilometre along the road to Somnath is **Bhalka Tirtha**, a modest temple marking the spot where Shri Krishna was fatally mistaken for a deer, receiving an arrow wound while he slept on a deerskin. Beneath a tree planted in his memory is a marble statue of the reclining deity.

ARRIVAL AND DEPARTURE   VERAVAL

By train Veraval's train station (☎ 02876 220444) is just over 1km north of town. For longer journeys, it's often quicker to change at Rajkot. The *Pune Express* and *Jabalpur Express* depart at 7.50am and 9.55am respectively, connecting Junagadh (1hr 30min), Rajkot (4hr) and Ahmedabad (9hr), while there are two daily departures for Sasan Gir (9.45am & 1.55pm; 1hr 30min–2hr) and one for Delvada (4.20pm; 3hr), the nearest station to Diu.

By bus Veraval's bus stand (☎ 02876 221666) is on ST Rd near the centre of town, connecting major cities throughout Gujarat. Several private offices are set nearby, some of which offer overnight bus services.

Destinations Ahmedabad (5 daily; 9hr); Diu (4 daily; 3hr); Dwarka (4 daily; 6hr); Junagadh (hourly; 2hr); Porbandar (4 daily; 3hr); Rajkot (hourly; 4hr); Sasan Gir (every 2hr; 1hr 30min).

ACCOMMODATION AND EATING

Kaveri Akar Complex, ST Rd ☎ 02876 220842, ⊛ hotelkaveri.in. Just to the left when exiting the bus stand, this is the best option in town, with clean, bright and well-appointed a/c (₹850) and non-a/c rooms with TV, wi-fi and attached bathrooms. ₹ **500**

Sagar Riddhi Siddhi Complex, ST Rd ☎ 02876 223939. This a/c vegetarian restaurant near the clock tower offers a varied menu of south Indian, Chinese and Punjabi dishes (masala dosa 40; Punjabi thali ₹100). Daily 9am–3.30pm & 5–11pm.

Utsav Opposite the bus Stand, ST Rd ☎ 02876 222306. Just to the right when exiting the bus stand, this hotel has rooms that are much more habitable than the entrance to the grubby complex would suggest, with views high over the busy road. Some have a/c (₹650). ₹ **450**

Somnath

The town of **SOMNATH** consists of little more than a few streets between the bus stand and its giant temple, famed across India as the first of the twelve *jyotrilinga* of Shiva.

9

The temple is visible from all over town, towering over a reclaimed beach, much of which still resembles a construction zone.

Somnath Temple

Daily 6am–9.30pm • Aarti (prayer) times: 7am, noon, 7pm • Photography prohibited • **Sound and Light Show** 7.45–8.45pm • ₹20

Legend has it that the site of **Somnath Temple**, formerly known as **Prabhas Patan**, was dedicated to Soma, the juice of a plant used in rituals and greatly praised for its enlightening powers (and hallucinogenic effects) in the Rig Veda. The temple itself is believed to have appeared first in gold, at the behest of the sun god, next in silver, created by the moon god, a third time in wood at the command of Krishna and, finally, in stone, built by King Bhimdev, the strongest of the five Pandava brothers from the Mahabharata epic. The earliest definite record, however, dates the temple to the tenth century when it became rich from devotees' donations. Unfortunately, such wealth came to the attention of the brutal iconoclast Mahmud of Ghazni who destroyed the shrine and carried its treasure off to Afghanistan. The next seven centuries saw a cycle of rebuilding and sacking, though the temple lay in ruins for more than two hundred years after a final sacking by Aurangzeb before the most recent reconstruction began in 1950. Although very little of the original structure remains, the latest reconstruction follows the elegant style of the Solanki period, and merits a visit for its physical and spiritual grandeur.

Prabhas Patan Museum

A few hundred metres north of the temple • Daily except Wed and 2nd & 4th Sat of the month 8.30am–12.15pm & 2.30–6pm • ₹50 (₹2)

The **Prabhas Patan Museum** preserves the scant remains of previous constructions of the Somnath temple. In addition to the array of carved stone statues lined up in the open courtyard, the museum's collection includes lintels, vials of sacred water, sections of roof pillars, friezes, and *toranas* from the tenth to twelfth centuries.

Other temple sites

Tongas and rickshaws gather outside the bus station, ready to take pilgrims to the temple sites east of Somnath. Most important of these is **Triveni Ghat**, mentioned in the epics of the Ramayana and Mahabharata. Also called Triveni Sangam, this newly renovated bathing *ghat* lies at the confluence of the Hiran, Saraswati and Kapil rivers where they meet the Arabian Sea. A dip in the waters here is believed to be highly propitious. Before reaching the confluence, the road passes the ancient **Surya Mandir**, the Sun Temple, probably built during the Solanki period and now cramped by a newer temple and concrete houses built almost against its walls.

ARRIVAL AND DEPARTURE   SOMNATH

By bus and autorickshaw Somnath's bus stand is just a few hundred metres east of the Shiva temple. Buses run to Veraval's ST bus stand (every 15–30min; ₹12). Autos will charge around ₹50 for the trip.

ACCOMMODATION AND EATING

Aastha Khodiyar St, behind Central Bank ☏94281 89792. Just behind Central Bank and very close to the temple, with small but clean, tiled rooms, some with a/c (₹1000) and all with attached bathrooms and TVs. **₹400**

Bhabha Restaurant Khodiyar St. The original *Bhabha* sits just outside the *Aastha hotel*, while about 200m east is a new restaurant with the same name and owner. Both are popular, friendly joints offering good breakfasts and killer Punjabi thalis (₹120). Daily 8.30am–10.30pm.

Mayuram Triveni Rd, southeast of the bus stand ☏02876 231286. The sparkling, tiled rooms here, some with a/c (₹700), all have attached bathrooms and are among Somnath's best-value options, but be sure to book ahead. **₹400**

Gir National Park

15 Oct to 15 June daily 7–11am & 3–5.30pm; late monsoons can delay opening until early Nov • Six-person jeep ₹1600–1700 (arrange at Sasan Gir); permit per vehicle ₹3200–3400 (from park information centre); camera fee ₹250/person (₹50)

The **Asiatic lion**, which, thanks to hunting, forest-clearance and poaching, has been extinct in the rest of India since the 1880s, survives in the wild in just 1150 square kilometres of the gently undulating Gir Forest. **Gir National Park**, accessed via **Sasan Gir**, lies 60km southeast of Junagadh and 45km northeast of Veraval, and boasts more than four hundred lions in its 260 square kilometres. The park also shelters around three hundred leopards, as well as sambar (large deer), chousingha (four-horned antelope), chinkara (gazelle), jackal, striped hyena and wild boar. The wildlife shares the land with Maldhari cattle-breeders, many of whom have been relocated outside the sanctuary. Those who remain are paid compensation by the government for the inevitable loss of their livestock to marauding lions. In 2008, it emerged that some tourists had been paying to watch lions devour tethered cattle in cruel – and illegal – "*baitwalla* shows"; if anyone approaches you about one of these shows, inform the park's management team. Sightings of the lions aren't guaranteed, although summer is the best time to spot them.

Dewaliya

Daily except Wed 8–11am & 3–5pm • $20 (₹75) • Jeeps (₹200 return) leave regularly from Sasan Gir

For a guaranteed lion sighting, head for **Dewaliya**, a partially fenced-off area of the park known as the Gir Interpretation Zone, just 12km from Sasan Gir. You get a surprisingly good impression of the lions "in the wild" here – they still have to hunt for their food, even if the deer have limited space to escape.

ARRIVAL AND DEPARTURE   GIR NATIONAL PARK

By public transport Buses and trains connect Sasan Gir to Junagadh (2 daily; 2hr) and Veraval (2 daily; 1hr). From   Diu, head to Una and then catch a bus (2hr 15min).

INFORMATION

Park information centre The park's reception centre is in Sasan Gir village, next to *Sinh Sadan Guest House* (daily: mid-Oct to mid-Feb 6.30–10.30am & 3–5pm; mid-Feb to mid-June 6.30am–1pm & 4–5.30pm; ☎ 02877 285541).

ACCOMMODATION AND EATING

Amidhara Resort Off Railway Station Rd, Sasan Gir ☎ 02877 285950, ☎ amidhararesorts.com. These full-board lodgings are the plushest to be found near Gir, with   comfortable attached rooms and private cottages (₹8000). The attractive grounds include a pool, gym, billiards hall, badminton court and restaurant. **₹4500**

THE ASIATIC LION

The rare **Asiatic lion** (*panthera leo persica*) is paler and shaggier than its more common African cousin, with longer tail tassles, more prominent elbow tufts and a larger belly fold. Probably introduced to India from Persia, the lions were widespread in the Indo-Gangetic plains at the time of the Buddha. In 300 BC, Kautilya, the minister of Chandragupta Maurya, offered them protection by declaring certain areas *abharaya aranyas*, "forests free from fear." Later, in his rock-inscribed edicts, **Ashoka** admonished those who hunted the majestic animals.

The lion was favourite game for India's nineteenth-century rulers and by 1913, not long after it had been declared a protected species by the nawab of Junagadh, its population was reduced to twenty. Since then, Gir Forest has been recognized as a sanctuary (1969), and a national park (1975), while the number of lions has swelled to well over four hundred. However, they remain under serious threat from poachers, while illegal timber-felling in the forest is still common. Three major roads and a railway line bisect the park, which also has four temples that attract more than eighty thousand pilgrims each year; all this produces noise, pollution and littering. Moreover, when lions stray from the sanctuary – a common occurrence – there have been attacks on humans and livestock. Plans, meanwhile, to create another reserve outside Gujarat, possibly in Madhya Pradesh – to reduce the risk of the cats being wiped out by a particularly contagious disease or infection – continue to be resisted (for political rather than conservation reasons) by the state government. For more information, see ☎ asiatic-lion.org.

9

Gir Birding Lodge 2km west of Sasan Gir, opposite Bambhafod Naka ☎02877 296514, ☜girnationalpark.com. This full-board option has rooms in the main building and in cottages, complete with wood-fittings and four-posters; there's also a fine restaurant. The hotel's friendly naturalist-guide takes guests for birdwatching walks. ₹4000

Girl Jungle Resort 3km west of Sasan Gir, 500m east of Bhalchel Village ☎02877 285590, ☜girjungleresort.com.

With lovely gardens and pretty rooms that have checked floors and cane furniture, this is among Gir's best options. There's also a pool and an excellent restaurant overlooking the Hiran River. ₹3500

Umang Off Station Rd, Sasan Gir, 100m west of Sinh Sadan ☎02877 285728. One of the better cheap hotels, in a convenient location, offering bright but spartan rooms with attached bathrooms, some with a/c (₹1350), plus a dorm. Dorm ₹300, double ₹800

Diu

Set off the southern tip of Saurashtra is the tiny island of **DIU**, just 12km long and 3km wide. Under Portuguese control for more than four hundred years, until 1961, it is now governed as a Union Territory from Delhi along with its sister city of Daman (see p.579). The combination of relaxed atmosphere, historic charm, broad beaches and lack of alcohol restrictions makes Diu one of the most popular tourist destinations in the state. While its beaches are admittedly not as idyllic as Goa's, most visitors stay longer than intended.

Diu Town in the east is the island's main focus. A maze of alleys lined with distinctive Portuguese buildings form the hub of the **old town**, while the **fort** stands on the island's easternmost tip, staring defiantly out at the Gulf of Cambay. Along the northern coast, the island's main road runs past salt pans that give way to mud flats sheltering flocks of water birds, including flamingos that stop to feed in early spring. The route skirting the south coast passes rocky cliffs and beaches, the most popular of which is **Nagoa Beach**, before reaching the tiny fishing village of **Vanakbara** in the very west of the island.

Brief history

The earliest records of Diu date from 1298, when it was controlled by the Chudasana dynasty. Soon after, it fell into the hands of invading Muslims and by 1349 was ruled by Mohammed bin Tughluq who successfully boosted the shipbuilding industry. Diu prospered as a harbour and in 1510 came under the government of the Ottoman Malik Ayaz, who repelled besieging **Portuguese** forces in 1520 and 1521. Aware of Diu's strategic position for trade with Arabia and the Persian Gulf, and having already gained a toehold in Daman, the Portuguese did not relent. Under **Nuno da Cunha**, they once more tried, but

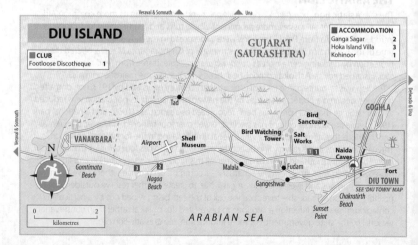

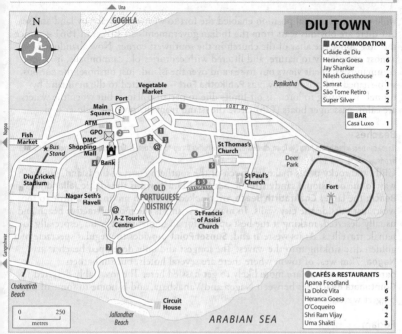

DIU TOWN

ACCOMMODATION
Cidade de Diu	3
Heranca Goesa	6
Jay Shankar	7
Nilesh Guesthouse	4
Samrat	1
São Tome Retiro	5
Super Silver	2

BAR
Casa Luxo	1

CAFÉS & RESTAURANTS
Apana Foodland	1
La Dolce Vita	6
Heranca Goesa	5
O'Coqueiro	4
Shri Ram Vijay	2
Uma Shakti	3

failed, to take the island in 1531. However, in 1535, Sultan Bahadur of Gujarat, facing pressure from both the Mughals and Portuguese, allowed da Cunha to build a fort in Diu. Three years later an Ottoman siege of Diu was repelled, cementing Portuguese control of Diu. The Portuguese held sway for more than four centuries, making Diu one of the world's longest-held colonial possessions. They were finally forced out in 1961 by Nehru's government, which, after a swift bombing campaign, declared Diu to be part of India.

Diu Town

Little **DIU TOWN** is protected by the fort in the east and a wall in the west. **Nagar Sheth Haveli**, one of the grandest of the town's distinctive Portuguese mansions, is on Makata Road, hidden in the web of narrow streets that wind through the residential Old Portuguese District. Fishermen make daily trips from the north coast in wooden boats; their catch is sold in the fish market opposite the bus stand (daily 9am–noon).

Diu's churches

Although the Christian population is dwindling along with the old language, a few old whitewashed **churches** in Diu's Farangiwada (Foreigner's Corner) are still used. Portuguese Mass is celebrated beneath the high ceilings and painted arches of **St Paul's**, widely considered to be India's most elaborate Portuguese church. To the northwest, the church of **St Thomas** now houses a sparsely stocked museum (daily 9am–9pm) and a guesthouse (see p.571), while to the south, the church of **St Francis of Assisi** is partly occupied by the local hospital.

The fort

East end of Fort Rd · Daily 8am–6pm · Free

Diu's serene **fort**, built by Nuno da Cunha in 1535, still stands robust, resisting the battering of the sea on three sides and sheltering birds, jackals and the town jail. Its

9

wide moat and coastal position enabled the fort to withstand attack by land and sea, but there are obvious scars from the Indian government's air strikes in 1961 – notice the hole above the altar of the church in the southwest corner. Now abandoned almost completely to nature, and littered with centuries-old cannonballs, it commands excellent views out to sea and over the island. Just offshore, the curious, ship-shaped old prison known as **Panikotha Fort** – connected to the mainland by tunnel, according to lore – is off-limits due to partial collapse, but when the waters are calm, passenger boats (₹25) circle the island from the port for a closer look.

Beaches

Nagoa can be reached by bus from Diu Town; check with the tourist office for up-to-date details; Gomtimata Beach can only be reached by private vehicle

Cliffs and rocky pools make up much of the southern coast of the island, giving way to the occasional sandy stretch. South of Diu Town is the idyllic **Jallandhar Beach**; the larger **Chakratirth Beach**, overlooked by a high mound, is a little to the west, just outside the city walls. In many ways this is the most attractive beach and usually deserted, making it the best option for an undisturbed swim, especially for female travellers. At its western end, **Sunset Point** provides the regular spectacle of a golden disc sinking into the waves. The longest and only developed beach is at **Nagoa**, 7km west of town, where there are several hotels, but sunbathers, particularly women, are more likely to get hassled here. The invariably deserted **Gomtimata Beach** lies between Nagoa and Vanakbara, and is home to some of Diu's biggest waves.

Fudam

3km west of Diu bus stand, 400m south of Airport Rd

FUDAM is an attractive village of pale yellow and sky grey Portuguese houses. The highlight is the old whitewashed church, known as Our Lady of Remedies, where a carved wooden altar with the Madonna and child remains inside.

Shell Museum

Just east of the airport on the Airport Rd • Daily 9am–6pm • ₹10

The **Shell Museum** is the vast personal collection – 42 years in the making – of Captain Devjibhai Vira Fulbaria, who spent a lifetime on the ocean picking up shells wherever he weighed anchor. With 2500 shells and detailed descriptions, this quirky, out-of-the-blue exhibit is certainly worth a look.

ARRIVAL AND DEPARTURE   DIU

Despite the generally shoddiness of roads connecting Diu to the rest of Saurashtra, buses remain the most comfortable and convenient means of transport here, and private buses are most often well worth the slight jump in price. Be warned that some buses may be inundated with drunken passengers on weekend nights, particularly Sundays.

By plane Diu's airport (☏ 02875 252365) is 6km west of town and served by Jet Airways (airport ☏ 02875 253542) flights to Mumbai (Sun–Fri; 2.35pm; 35min).

By train The nearest railway station to Diu is at Delvada, 8km up the Diu–Una road. From here, train #52952 (daily 2.25pm) departs for Sasan Gir (3hr 30min) and Junagadh (6hr), while the slow #52950 runs to Veraval (daily 8.05am; 3hr), where there are daily trains for Ahmedabad (9.50am & 7.40pm; 8–9hr).

By bus Buses arrive and depart from the bus stand by the bridge in Diu Town, just a few minutes' walk to the west of town. State bus services run to to Porbandar,

Rajkot, Junagadh and Veraval; for Palitana, take a bus to Bhavnagar and change at Talaja. Private tour operators operate more comfortable buses to Ahmedabad and Mumbai. Far better transport connections are found on the mainland, at Una bus stand, connected to Diu by auto-rickshaws and buses (6.30am–8pm; every 30min–1hr; 40min; ₹14).

Destinations Ahmedabad (2 daily; 8–9hr); Bhavnagar (9 daily; 6hr); Junagadh (8 daily; 5hr); Porbandar (2 daily; 7hr); Rajkot (5 daily; 7hr 30min); Veraval (10 daily; 2hr 30min).

GETTING AROUND

Auto-rickshaw Widely available across the island: ₹10–20 for trips within town and ₹50 to reach Nagoa Beach.
Bus DMC (Diu Municipal Council) buses depart from the main bus stand to Nagoa Beach at 7am, 11am and 4pm (returning 30min later), stopping at the airport along the way.
Bike and moped rental Numerous places near the main square rent out bikes (₹20–30/day), as well as mopeds and scooters (₹200–300/day).

INFORMATION

Tourist information The tourist office, next to Bandar Gate at the port (Mon–Sat 10am–1pm & 2–6pm; ☎ 02875 252653, ⊛ damandiutourism.com), opposite the main square, offers little beyond maps and brochures. A–Z Tourist Centre (daily 9am–11pm) on Vaniya St, near Pancharti Rd in the Old Portuguese District, offer basic information on the island and can arrange car, moped and scooter rental, as well as train, bus and flight tickets.

Services The main post office is on the western side of the main square (Mon–Sat 8am–noon & 2–5pm). The State Bank of India and A–Z Forex (☎ 02875 252210), both near the main square, exchange money; ICICI, Axis and State Bank all have ATMs near the main square. Several internet cafés are scattered around town, including Super Surfing (₹30/hr), below *Super Silver* Hotel, and A–Z Cyber Cafe in the A–Z Tourist Centre (₹30/hr).

ACCOMMODATION

Expect prices to rise during festival periods, particularly Diwali, Holi and New Year's, while in the off-season prices can come down by as much as seventy percent. Some people, especially women, may be put off at festival times by the rowdy atmosphere.

DIU TOWN

Cidade de Diu Off Collectorate Rd ☎ 02875 254595, ⊛ cidadedediu.com; map p.569. A wedding cake of a building, with clashing paint jobs illuminated by neon lights at night; the rooms are thankfully more tasteful. While the cheaper options are a bit worn, all are brightly painted and clean, while the more expensive rooms are spacious and come with a curvy balcony. A pool, bar and restaurant are attached. **₹2500**

Heranca Goesa Behind Diu Museum, Farangiwada ☎ 02875 253851, ⊜ heranca_goesa@yahoo.com; map p.569. A handful of non-a/c rooms in the very friendly Goan family home of Francisco and Alina: all are immaculate and have attached bathrooms, while those at the top of the house are the best. There's a large, breezy terrace for sunbathing with a view of all three of Diu's old churches. **₹400**

Jay Shankar Jallandhar Beach ☎ 02875 252424; map p.569. This old stalwart remains a popular travellers' haunt for its low prices and quiet setting. Rooms are quite worn, but there's a bar, restaurant, 24hr hot water, balconies and views of the sea from the rooftop terrace. Some rooms have a/c (₹700). **₹400**

Nilesh Guesthouse Next to Bank of India, 50m south of the mosque ☎ 02875 252319; map p.569. Just south of the mosque, this is one of Diu's best-value cheapies, with clean although somewhat characterless rooms with TVs and balconies, some with a/c (₹700). Staff are helpful and the bar and restaurant (Gujarati thali ₹60) are usually busy. **₹300**

Samrat Collectorate Rd ☎ 02875 252354, ⊜ samrat_diu@yahoo.com.in; map p.569. Samrat has the same owners (and similar clashing colour schemes) as *Cidade de Diu*, with which it shares a pool and bar. The pink and beige rooms here have TV and private bathrooms, while some also have a/c (₹1850) and balconies. **₹1240**

★**São Tome Retiro** St Thomas Church ☎ 02875 253137; map p.569. A classic place to soak up the chilled Diu vibe, with a handful of simple but colourful rooms set within one of Diu's most atmospheric old Portuguese churches. When it's full, as is often the case, you can sleep on the whitewashed roof (₹200) which offers unparalleled views of the island. The hosts, the D'Souza family, throw legendary all-you-can-eat BBQs (₹200) every other evening from September to April, open to non-guests. **₹400**

Super Silver Super Silver Complex ☎ 02875 252020, ⊜ supersilverdiu@yahoo.com; map p.569. A warm welcome and clean, excellent-value rooms with attached bathrooms and TVs, some with a/c (₹900), make *Super Silver* a popular choice with foreign travellers. There's pleasant seating in the shaded hallway and a lovely roof terrace overlooking the veggie market. On-site scooter rental (₹200–300/day) and internet cafe (₹40/hr). **₹400**

THE REST OF THE ISLAND

Ganga Sagar Nagoa Beach ☎ 02875 252249; map p.568. While it may be a bit of a dive, *Ganga Sagar* has economical tiled rooms, some a/c (₹1800), a pleasant common balcony, a lively bar (sometimes a tad too lively on weekends) and restaurant, and a great location right on the beach. **₹1500**

Hoka Island Villa Nagoa Beach ☎ 02875 253036, ⊛ resorthoka.com; map p.568. Pleasant hotel with enticing rooms, hammocks hanging in the communal areas, groves of palm trees, a small pool and a restaurant offering delicious fish dishes such as coconut prawn and tamarind fish curry (₹250). **₹2150**

9

Kohinoor Airport Rd, 1.5km west of Diu town ☎02875 252209, ⓦhotelkohinoordiu.com; map p.568. Diu's first three-star hotel, this resort has a vaguely Mediterranean feel, with comfortable attached rooms, pool, jacuzzi, restaurant, pastry shop, bar, gym and the *Footloose* disco. ₹**2650**

EATING

Apana Foodland Apana Hotel, Fort Rd ☎02875 253650, ⓦapanahoteldiu.com/apanas-foodland; map p.569. Large a/c restaurant with a garden terrace overlooking the sea, serving tasty north Indian cuisine and other specialities – the shark tikka (from ₹250) and grilled lobster (from ₹750) stand out. Daily 7am–5pm & 7–11pm.

La Dolce Vita Jallandar Beach ☎098242 03925; map p.569. This is one of Diu's most laid-back hangouts, complete with thatched roof, a small library, generous Continental breakfasts (₹80), special seafood meals at the regular BBQ parties (Mon & Fri; ₹200), and a helpful, English-speaking owner, Kishor. Daily 8am–10pm.

Heranca Goesa Behind Diu Museum ☎02875 253851; map p.569. An intimate place in a family home, and one of the only places to sample Portuguese and Goan food in Diu. The seafood's excellent and don't miss the delicious *bebinca* pudding, a rich, seven-layer cake made by the kilo (₹300) on request. Although special requests are taken for lunches and dinners, the restaurant is only open regularly for breakfasts. Daily 8am–10.30am.

O'Couqueiro Lane behind Cidade de Diu; map p.569. A family-run garden restaurant with hanging lanterns and palm trees, serving home-made muesli and yogurt, pasta dishes made with imported Italian olive oil and parmesan, and a handful of Portuguese options (mains ₹175–220). There's a slim selection of books and magazines to read, and international chillout music on the sound system. Daily 7.30am–10.30pm.

★ **Shri Ram Vijay** Just of Bunder Chowk (Main Square); map p.569. A wonderful slice of small-town Americana transported to Diu Town, this tiny parlour started up in 1933, still serves home-made ice cream (₹20–30/scoop), sundaes, banana splits, cream sodas and milkshakes. Daily 8.30am-1.30pm &3.30–9.30pm.

Uma Shakti Behind Veggie Market; map p.569. This hotel restaurant and bar serves good breakfasts of cornflakes, toast or pancakes, as well as more substantial Indian or Chinese meals. The breezy roof terrace, with views over Diu Town, is good for a sundowner. Mains ₹60–180. Daily 9am–10.30pm.

DRINKING

The availability of alcohol seems to be the greatest Portuguese legacy in Diu. You'll pay ₹50-60 for a Kingfisher.

Casa Luxo Bunder Chowk (Main Square); map p.569. Caught in a bit of a 1960s time-warp, this is one of Diu's more welcoming bars. Mon 9am–1pm, Tues–Sat 9am–1pm & 4-9pm.

Footloose Discotheque Kohinoor Hotel, Airport Rd, 1.5km west of Diu town; map p.568. In addition to the welcoming, modern *Rio Bar* (daily 11am–3pm & 7–11pm), *Kohinoor* Hotel houses Diu's only nightclub, *Footloose* Discotheque, air-conditioned with a spacious dance floor complete with flashy lighting effects. Sat & Sun 8–11pm.

Bhavnagar

The port of **BHAVNAGAR**, founded in 1723 by the Gohil Rajput Bhavsinghji, whose ancestors came to Gujarat from Marwar (Rajasthan) in the thirteenth century, is an important trading centre whose principal export is cotton. With few sights of its own, Bhavnagar does, however, boast a fascinating bazaar in the old city, and is an obvious place to stay for a night before heading southwest to the Jain temples of Palitana. For Gujarati industrialists, it serves as the jumping-off point for the massive, controversial and booming ship-breaking yard at **Alang**. The yard, where twenty thousand labourers work, has been off-limits to foreigners since Greenpeace red-flagged it for environmental damage, toxic spills and hazardous work. Bhavnagar has produced a string of artists and writers, notably poet **Jhaverchand Meghani**. Locals also claim to speak the most grammatically correct form of Gujarati.

The focus of interest is the **old city**, its vibrant markets overlooked by delicate wooden balconies and the pillared facades of former merchants' houses. The marble temple, **Ganga Devi Mandir**, by the Ganga Jalia Tank in the town centre, has a large dome and intricate latticework on its walls, while the **Takhteshwar Temple**, raised on a hill in the south of town, affords a good view over to the Gulf of Cambay in the east.

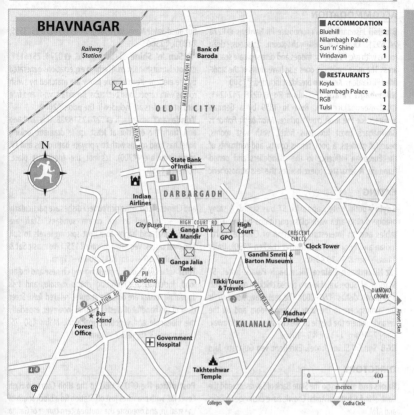

The Gandhi smriti museum and Barton museum

Off Crescent Circle • **Gandhi Smriti Museum** Mon–Sat 9am–1pm & 2–6pm, closed 2nd and 4th Sat of the month • Free **Barton Museum** • Mon–Sat 9am–1pm & 2–6pm, closed 2nd and 4th Sat of the month • ₹50 (₹2)

In the east of town by the clock tower, the **Gandhi Smriti Museum** exhibits old sepia photos of the Mahatma, who studied here at the Shamaldas Arts College & Sir PP Science Institute. Downstairs, the **Barton Museum** shows off a huge, haphazard collection of Buddhist, Jain and Hindu statues, medieval bronzes, Harappan terracotta as well as the odd skeleton.

ARRIVAL AND DEPARTURE   BHAVNAGAR

By plane The airport is 5km east of town on Airport Rd, a taxi or auto will cost ₹100 or R60 respectively. Jet Airways (ⓣ 0278 2433371) and Kingfisher both fly daily to Mumbai; tickets can also be bought from Tikki Tours and Travels (ⓣ 0278 2431477) in the Prithvi Complex in Kalanala.

By train Bhavnagar's train station is a few hundred metres north of the old city, at the top of Station Rd. An early morning train connects Ahmedabad (5hr 30min) on weekends, while the daily *Bhavnagar–Bandra Express* #12972 departs at 8.30pm, arriving in Ahmedabad at 1.55am, Vadodara at 3.55am and

Mumbai's Bandra Terminus at 10.20am.

By bus The ST bus stand is on ST Rd, a 10min walk from the centre of Bhavnagar. Private buses are operated by numerous firms along Waghawadi Rd, such as Tanna Travels (ⓣ 0278 2425218) at Crescent Circle, with services to Ahmedabad (4hr; hourly), Vadodara (7 daily; 4–5hr) and Mumbai (dep. 4pm; 13hr).

Destinations Ahmedabad (hourly; 5hr); Bhuj (6 daily; 11hr); Diu (4 daily; 7hr); Junagadh (4 daily; 6hr 30min); Palitana (every 30min; 1hr 15min); Rajkot (12 daily; 4hr); Vadodara (11 daily; 6hr); Velavadar (2 daily; 1hr).

9

ACCOMMODATION

Bluehill Jasunath Chowk, opposite Pil Gardens ☎ 0278 2426951, ✉ hotelbluehill@yahoo.com. Spacious, clean rooms with a/c, TVs, desks, fridges and cute separate seating areas. The more expensive ones also have views of the stork-filled Pil Gardens. American breakfast included. ₹**1500**

Nilambagh Palace ST Station Rd ☎ 0278 2424241, ✇ nilambagpalace.com. Built in 1859 by a German architect for the local crown prince, *Nilambagh Palace* is Bhavnagar's most luxurious hotel, with vast rooms, peaceful gardens, a pool, tennis courts, and remnants of the European influence in the chandeliers and period furniture. A separate annexe houses the less atmospheric

but good-value *Narayani Heritage Hotel* (☎ 0278 2513535; ₹1800). ₹**2500**

★ **Sun 'n' Shine** ST Station Rd ☎ 0278 2516131, ✇ hotelsunnshine.com. The high expectations generated by the elegant green marble lobby are matched by swish rooms with carpets and bathtubs. Breakfast, wi-fi and free airport transfers are included in the price. ₹**2000**

Vrindavan Darbargadh ☎ 0278 2518928. This rambling and, from the exterior at least, quite dramatic-looking hotel has tired rooms with tiny private bathrooms and TV, some with a/c (₹700). It's not the friendliest place, however. ₹**350**

EATING

Koyla Apollo Hotel, opposite ST bus stand. A shiny orange dining area with glass partitions between the tables and an interesting selection of Chinese, north Indian and Punjabi meals (butter chicken ₹190). Daily 11am–3pm & 7–10.45pm.

★ **Nilambagh Palace** Nilambagh Palace hotel, ST Station Rd. Superb and keenly priced chicken, mutton, fish and prawn dishes (₹60–200). The real draw, however, is the atmosphere in the stately dining room and on the veranda, where the bustle of the city seems a world away. Daily 7–10am, 1–3pm & 7–10pm.

RGB Sun 'n' Shine hotel. Excellent veg Gujarati, Jain

and Chinese food – the rich *paneer* dishes are particularly good – as well as ice cream sundaes. Staff are professional and happy to adjust spicing levels to suit personal tastes. Veg *tawa masala* ₹135. Live music Sat & Sun. Daily 7.30–10am & 11.30am–11pm.

Tulsi Kalanala Chowk. Appealing veg Chinese and Indian food, including a comforting *chana masala*, and less appealing muzak are on offer at quiet, relaxed *Tulsi*. Steer clear of the handful of Western dishes, however, especially the pineapple and vegetable macaroni. Mains ₹50–75. Daily noon–3.30pm & 7–11pm.

DIRECTORY

Banks and exchange The State Bank of Saurashtra and the Bank of India, both on Amba Chowk, have exchange facilities and ATM.

Internet access Cyber Café, near *Nimabagh Palace* (₹20/hr).

Post office The GPO is next to the High Court on High Court Rd, with branches just off Station Rd a block south of the station, and opposite the southeastern corner of Ganga Jalia Tank.

Blackbuck National Park

Velavadar, 65km north of Bhavnagar • Mid-Oct to mid-June daily 6am–6pm • ₹250 (₹20), plus ₹1000 (₹250) per vehicle, camera, ₹250 (₹5), mandatory guide ₹500 (₹100) • ☎ 0278 2880342 • No jeeps are available to hire on site; taxis available by Ganga Jalia Tank in Bhavnagar: day trips cost around ₹2000

Outside the tiny village of **Velavadar**, the 34-square-kilometre **Blackbuck National Park** is Gujarat's own slice of savannah. Bounding through the tall golden grass, however, are not impalas but blackbucks, spiral-horned Indian antelopes of which the park has the country's highest concentration. Prior to Independence their number stood at eight thousand, but habitat loss and hunting cut this figure down to two hundred by 1966. The park's blackbuck now number well over three thousand, making it a laudable success story. It is also home to endangered Indian wolves, striped hyenas, nilgai antelope, jackals, jungle cats and Indian foxes, as well as birds of prey like Stoliczka's bushchat and harrier hawks, at least 1500 of the latter arriving from Siberia each winter.

Palitana

For many visitors, the highlight of a trip to Saurashtra is a climb up the holy hill of **Shatrunjaya**, India's principal Jain pilgrimage site, just outside the dull town of **PALITANA**, 50km southwest of Bhavnagar.

Shatrunjaya

6km south of Palitana • Daily 7am–6pm • Free, camera ₹100 • Auto-rickshaws (about ₹40) and tongas run from near Palitana's bus stand to the foot of Shatrunjaya (10min)

More than nine hundred temples crown **Shatrunjaya**, said to be a chunk of the mighty Himalayas where the Jains' first *tirthankara*, Adinath, and his chief disciple gained enlightenment. While records show that the hill was a *tirtha* as far back as the fifth century, the existing temples date only from the sixteenth century, anything earlier having been lost in the Muslim raids of the 1500s and 1600s.

Climbing the wide steps up Shatrunjaya takes one to two hours, though, as with all hilltop pilgrimage centres, *dholis* (seats on poles held by four bearers; ₹1200–1500 return) are available for those who can't make it under their own steam. The views as you ascend are magnificent, and you should allow at least two more hours to see even a fraction of the temples.

The individual *tuks* (temple enclosures) are named after the merchants who funded them. Together they create a formidable city, laid over the two summits and fortified by thick walls. Each *tuk* comprises courtyards chequered in black-and-white marble and several temples whose walls are exquisitely and profusely carved with saints, birds, animals, buxom maidens, musicians and dancers. Many are two or even three storeys high, with balconies crowned by perfectly proportioned pavilions. The largest temple, dedicated to Adinath, in the Khartaravasi *tuk* on the northern ridge, is usually full of masked Svetambara nuns and monks, dressed in white and carrying white fly-whisks. The southern ridge and the spectacular Adishvara temple in its western corner are reached by taking the right-hand fork at the top of the path. On a clear day the view from the summit takes in the Gulf of Cambay to the south, Bhavnagar to the north and Mount Girnar to the west.

A path leads along the ridge and down into the valley of Adipur, 13km away; it's open for one day only, during the festival of **Suth Tera** (Feb/March), when up to fifty thousand pilgrims come to Shatrunjaya for this unique display of devotion.

Shri Vishal Jain Museum

400m from the start of the steps to Shatrunjaya • Daily 8am–12.30pm & 3–8.30pm • ₹10, no photos

The **Shri Vishal Jain Museum** displays a haphazard collection of artefacts, including centuries-old Jain idols, artwork, palm-leaf manuscripts, and a small temple set down the stairs towards the back. Despite being labelled only in Gujarati, the exhibits are worth the minuscule entry fee.

ARRIVAL AND INFORMATION | PALITANA

By train Palitana Station is 750m north of the bus stand, with three daily trains to Bhavnagar (1hr 15min).

By bus Buses arrive and depart from the bus stand in the north of town, 400m north of the bridge.

Departures Bhavnagar (hourly; 1hr–1hr 30min); Junagadh (2 daily; 6hr); Talaja for Diu (hourly in the morning; 1hr); Una for Diu (daily; 5hr).

Services The owner of the *Shravak* hotel is a good source for regional information. For internet, try Patel Computer, a 5min walk south of Shravak (₹20/hr).

ACCOMMODATION

Shravak Opposite the bus stand ☎02848 252428. Adequately clean rooms with attached bathrooms, cold-water showers and friendly staff, in a convenient location for moving on (although less so for falling asleep: the adjacent streets can remain noisy quite late). Hot water buckets are available 5–10am. ₹**300**

Takhatgadh Dharmsala Opposite Shri Vishal Jain Museum ☎02848 252167. A few hundred metres from the steps to Shatrunjaya, this three-storey dharamshala is one of Patitana's best deals, with a/c (₹500) and fan rooms, most sleeping three, facing onto a spacious, pink courtyard. ₹**200**

Vijay Vilas Palace Hotel Adpur, 4km from the bus station ☎02848 282371. A good option if you have your own vehicle (auto-rickshaw for around ₹60), the rooms in this converted 1906 European-style palace guesthouse have four-posters, old dressers and other early twentieth-century paraphernalia, some overlooking the western slopes of Shatrunjaya. An alternate path to the summit starts nearby. ₹**3500**

9

EATING

Bhojan Shala Parshwanath Jain Trust, beside Shri Vishal Jain Museum. This large dining hall on the ground floor of a four-storey yellow block, doubling as a *dharmashala* (₹200), serves generous and tasty Jain meals (₹30–50). Daily 7.30–9am, 11.30am–1.30pm & 4.30–6pm.

Jagruti Restaurant Opposite bus stand. The best place to eat other than in Palitana's hotels, this basic but friendly restaurant serves excellent Gujarati meals and snacks for pennies (thali ₹50). Daily 9am–10.30pm.

Southeastern Gujarat

Sandwiched between Maharashtra and the Arabian Sea, the seldom-visited **southeastern** corner of Gujarat harbours few attractions to entice you off the beaten path to or from Mumbai. **Vadodara** (Baroda), former capital of the Gaekwad rajas, is most appealing for its proximity to the old Muslim town of **Champaner** and the ruined forts and exotic Jain and Hindu temples crowning **Pavagadh Hill**. Further south, dairy pastures gradually give way to a swampy, malaria-infested coastal strip of banana plantations and shimmering saltpans cut by silty, sinuous rivers. The area's largest city is modern, industrial **Surat**, while in the far south of the state is the dreary former Portuguese territory of **Daman**.

Vadodara (Baroda)

VADODARA, also known as Baroda, is a congested industrial city with a youthful vibe owing to the presence of Gujarat's largest university, MSU. Although its old core retains some interest, with beautiful havelis, palaces and traditional bazaars, its main draw lies in its being the most convenient base for visiting the nearby sites of **Champaner** and **Pavagadh**. If you are here during the **Navratri** festival (late Sept/early Oct), you can join the throngs watching thousands of colourfully dressed women, men and children dancing into the small hours.

Sayaji Bagh

Entrance on Tilak Rd · **Baroda Museum & Picture Gallery** Reached from University Rd · Daily 10.30am–5pm · ₹200 (₹10)

Built and dedicated to the people of Vadodara by the beloved reformer Maharaja Sayajirao Gaekwad III, the large green park of **Sayaji Bagh** contains two museums and a planetarium, zoo and vintage toy train. The large Indo-Saracenic **Baroda Museum & Picture Gallery** holds art and textiles from all over the world, plus Gujarati archeological remains and Mughal miniatures.

Laxmi Vilas Palace

Nehru Rd **Laxmi Vilas Palace** Daily 10.30am–5.30pm · ₹100 (₹25) · **Maharaja Fateh Singh Museum** Tues–Sun 10.30am–4pm · ₹125 (₹25); photos · ☎ 0265 2426372

Laxmi Vilas Palace is the most extravagant of Vadodara's palaces, designed by Major Charles "Mad" Mant and commissioned at great expense by Maharaj Sayajirao Gaekwad III in 1890. Audio tours (1hr) are available of its Durbar Hall, armoury and palm-filled mosaic courtyards. The palace grounds are also home to the **Maharaja Fateh Singh Museum**, which holds a modest selection of European, Chinese, Japanese and Indian art, including many epic works of Raja Ravi Varma, personally commissioned by the maharaja of Baroda.

ARRIVAL AND DEPARTURE   VADODARA

By plane The airport is 6km northeast of the city (around ₹60 by auto-rickshaw). Jet Airways (opposite *WelcomHotel Vadodara*; ☎ 0265 2343441) and Indian Airlines (Fateh Gunj; ☎ 0265 2794747) have daily flights to Delhi; the former also flies daily to Mumbai.

By train Vadodara railway station is in Sayajigunj, within easy walking distance of most of the hotels. The crowded ticket reservation office is upstairs; you can bypass the hassle for a small fee if you buy your ticket from Yogi Krupa Travel Service on Station Rd (daily 8.30am–8.30pm;

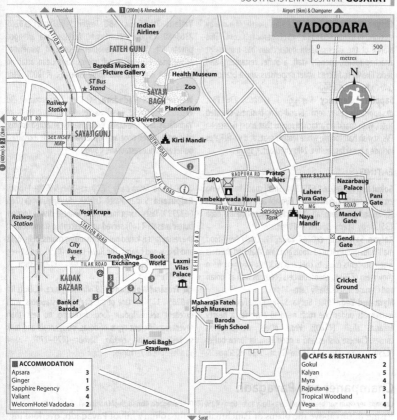

VADODARA

ACCOMMODATION

Apsara	3
Ginger	1
Sapphire Regency	5
Valiant	4
WelcomHotel Vadodara	2

CAFÉS & RESTAURANTS

Gokul	2
Kalyan	5
Myra	4
Rajputana	3
Tropical Woodland	1
Vega	4

☎0265 2794977). All trains travelling on the main Delhi–Mumbai line stop here. The *Shatabdi Express* #12009 runs to Ahmedabad (Mon–Sat; dep. 11.20am, arr. 1.10pm), while the *Shatabdi Express* #12010 is the quickest train to Mumbai (Mon–Sat; dep. 4.17pm, arr. Mumbai Central 9.35pm).

By bus The ST bus stand is in the west of town, 300m north of the train station. Few buses to Mumbai (frequent;

9–10hr) start at Vadodara, so they may be full when they arrive – the train is far better. Private bus companies with frequent services to Mumbai, Rajasthan and Madhya Pradesh line Station Rd.

Destinations Ahmedabad (frequent; 2hr 30min); Champaner (hourly; 1hr 30min–2hr); Diu (3 daily; 12hr); Rajkot (hourly; 8hr).

INFORMATION

Tourist information Gujarat Tourism, Narmada Bhavan, Jail Rd (Mon–Sat 10.30am–6pm, closed 2nd & 4th Sat of month; ☎0265 2427489).

Services Currency exchange is offered at the Trade Wings Exchange Bureau (opposite *Kalyan* restaurant, Sayajigunj),

and at the Bank of Baroda (Suraj Plaza, Sayajigunj), which has one of several ATMs in Sayajigunj. The GPO is off Raopura Rd in the centre of town; there's also a branch in Sayajigunj (just south of *Kalyan*). Internet access is available at New Speedy Cyber Café (₹15/hr), opposite the *Apsara* hotel.

ACCOMMODATION

Vadodara's numerous mid-range hotels are often full, so book ahead. The few budget options are in serious need of some loving care. Most hotels are in Sayajigunj, just a short walk southeast of the railway station.

Apsara Sayajigunj ☎0265 2225399. Probably the best of the shoestring options – hardly a ringing endorsement –

with ramshackle but (just about) habitable rooms with attached bathrooms and a friendly manager. **₹450**

9

Ginger Fatehgunj Camp Rd, 1km north of railway station ☎0265 6633333, ⓦgingerhotels.com. This branch of the über-modern hotel chain has minimalist attached rooms, friendly staff, a buffet restaurant, and perks like wi-fi, filtered water dispensers, and a branch of *Café Coffee Day*. ₹2500

Sapphire Regency Sayajigunj ☎0265 2361130, ⓦsapphireregency.com. Brand-new business-oriented hotel, with sparkling attached rooms that boast flatscreen TVs, stylish bathrooms, white leather seats and wi-fi. Rates include a breakfast buffet. 24hr checkout. ₹1900

Valiant 7th floor, BBC Tower Sayajigunj ☎0265 2363480, ⓦhotelvaliant.com. Accessed via an aged private lift, *Valiant* is another decent, if somewhat impersonal, business hotel; rooms have clean attached bathrooms and TVs, and some have a/c (₹1200). 24hr checkout. ₹950

WelcomHotel Vadodara RC Dutt (Racecourse) Rd ☎0265 2330033, ⓦitcwelcomgroup.in. One of Vadodara's few five-stars, with swanky attached rooms, plus an outdoor pool and gym. Rates include breakfast buffet at its fine restaurant. ₹9000

EATING

Gokul Koti Rd ☎0265 6552581. Small snack-bar serving excellent south Indian dishes, Punjabi and Gujarati thalis (₹90), and ice cream, all at low, low prices (masala dosa ₹35). Daily 11am–3pm & 7–10pm.

Kalyan Sayajigunj ☎0265 2362211. Lively "veg food mall" with multicoloured stools and thin, thatched shutters where students come to chat and tuck into anything from chowmein (₹70) to cheeseburgers (₹60), as well as Indian and Chinese snacks. Daily 7am–11pm.

Myra and Vega Hotel Surya, Sayajigunj. Two superior restaurants under one roof: head to *Myra* for a hearty Gujarati thali (₹180); *Vega* offers well-prepared curries, Chinese dishes and a good Punjabi lunch buffet (₹250). Vega daily 11.30am–2pm, 3.30–6.30pm &

7.30–11pm; Myra daily 11.30am–2pm & 7.30–11pm.

Rajputana Sadar Patel Chowk, Sayajigunj ☎0265 6622799. Tasty north Indian and Chinese dishes (*paneer butter masala* ₹140) served up in eccentric surroundings; the restaurant is kitted out with hanging chains, bells, dolls and fake wood beams. The Royal Lunch (₹150), an all-veg feast, runs from noon–3pm. Daily 11am–3pm & 6.30–11pm.

★ **Tropical Woodland** 139 Windsor Plaza, RC Dutt Rd ☎0265 2321495. One of the city's top restaurants, with excellent south Indian food, including no less than seventeen different types of dosas, main meals and milk shakes: try the *chikoo* flavour (₹70–270). Daily 11am–3pm & 7–10pm.

Champaner and Pavagadh

Champaner 48km northeast of Vadodara • Daily 8am–6pm • ₹250 (₹10) • **Pavagadh** 4km south of Champaner

Rising 820m above the plains of Panchmahal is the solitary hill of **Pavagadh**, overlooking the almost forgotten city – and World Heritage Site – of **CHAMPANER**. Although the city was fortified centuries earlier, in 1297 the Chauhan rajputs made Champaner their stronghold, fending off three Muslim attacks. It remained Gujarat's capital until 1536, when the courts moved to Ahmedabad and Champaner fell into decline. When the British arrived in 1803 it was almost completely overrun by the forest.

The massive city walls with inscribed gateways still stand, encompassing several houses, exquisite mosques and Muslim mausoleums, all imbued with a strange, time-warped atmosphere. The largest mosque is the exuberant **Jama Masjid**, east of the walls; two minarets stand either side of the main entrance, and the prayer halls are dissected by almost two hundred pillars supporting a splendid carved roof raised in a series of domes.

The **patha** (pilgrim's route) ascends 4km from Champaner to Pavagadh, passing the old battered gates of the fortress. Roughly midway up, the road ends along with a cluster of snack, souvenir and chai stalls, the cable-car station and Pavagadh's sole hotel. Continuing the ascent on foot, pilgrims pass numerous Jain temples and several sacred lakes along the trail to the summit, where the eleventh-century **Kalikamata Temple** stands, along with a shrine to the Muslim saint Sadan Shah on its roof.

ARRIVAL AND DEPARTURE   CHAMPANER AND PAVAGADH

CHAMPANER

From Champaner's bus stand, opposite the south gate, hourly buses link Halol, 7km west, where there are

services to Vadodara (every 15min; 1hr 30min) and Ahmedabad (5 daily; 3hr).

PAVAGADH
Regular shuttle buses depart from opposite Champaner's southern gate to the end of Pavagadh Hill Rd (halfway up the hill; 15min); otherwise it's a 1–2hr walk from the trailhead opposite Champaner's southern gate to the halfway point. From here, the trail to the summit is a 2hr walk or quick cable-car ride (7am–11pm; ₹98 return).

ACCOMMODATION

Hotel Champaner Halfway up Pavagadh Hill, near start of cable-car line ☎02676 245641. Halfway up Pavagadh, this somewhat bland government-run hotel is the only accommodation to be found on the hill. Fortunately, rooms are adequate, all with attached bathrooms and some with a/c (₹1200), boasting magnificent views over the plains of southern Gujarat. The attached restaurant serves decent veg thalis (₹70). ₹**600**

Surat

Sprawled around a tight bend in the Tapti River about 20km from the coast, **SURAT** is one of India's fastest growing industrial centres, and – since a 1994 wake-up call in the form of a plague outbreak – one of the country's cleanest cities. However, its appeal is mostly for history buffs, who come to see what few vestiges remain of the East India Company's first foothold on the Subcontinent.

ARRIVAL AND DEPARTURE   SURAT

Surat's ST bus station and main railway station are both about 3km east of the city centre.

By train There are frequent connections to regional hubs and beyond, including Vadodara (2hr), Ahmedabad (4hr), Mumbai (4–5hr), and Vapi (1hr), for Daman.
By bus Regular buses serve Mumbai (6hr), Ahmedabad (5–6hr) and all cities in between, as do dozens of private buses run by companies like Shubham Travels (☎98252 80517), near Delhi Gate.

ACCOMMODATION AND EATING

Finding a room can be hard on weekdays, so book ahead. Most of the big hotels have good restaurants.

Embassy Near Delhi Gate, Ring Rd ☎0261 2443170, ⓦembassyhotelsurat.com. A stylish mid-range hotel in a convenient location near both the train and bus stations. Its a/c rooms come with carpets, bathtubs, TV and complimentary breakfast. ₹**1800**

Omkar Eighth Floor, Omkar Chambers, Station Rd ☎0262 7419329. The best pick for backpackers, situated opposite the railway station, this is a busy, budget guesthouse with unfussy rooms that offer views over the city. ₹**400**

Daman

As a Union Territory, independent of the dry state that surrounds it, **DAMAN** is a weekend target for busloads of Gujarati men who come here to drink themselves senseless. The rest of the time it is quiet but generally disappointing, its pair of grubby beaches subject to massive tides. It does, however, offer fantastic **seafood** and some well-preserved **Portuguese churches**, **houses** and **forts**. To the north of the Damanganga River is **Nani** ("Little") **Daman**, home to most of the hotels, restaurants and bars, while on the south side is **Moti** ("Great") **Daman**, the old Portuguese quarter.

Brief history

Straddling the mouth of the **Damanganga River**, Daman made an obvious target for the Portuguese, who took it in 1531 from the Sultanate of Gujarat's Ethiopian governor, Siddu Bapita. The governor of Goa, Dom Constantino de Bragança, cajoled the sultan into ceding the territory 28 years later, after which it became the hub of the Portuguese trans-Arabian Sea trade with East Africa. The British occupation of Sindh in the 1830s strangled the town's opium business and lead to decline. Colonial rule, however, survived until 1961 when Nehru lost patience with the Portuguese and sent in the troops.

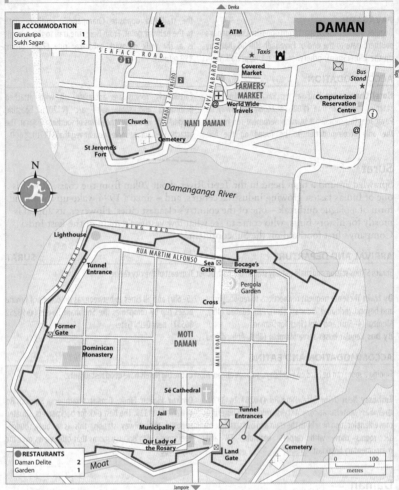

DAMAN

Devka

ATM

Taxis

Covered
Market

FARMERS'
MARKET

World Wide
Travels

Bus
Stand

Computerized
Reservation
Centre

SEAFACE ROAD

KAVI KHABARDAR ROAD

ESTRADA 2 FEVEREIRO

Church

NANI DAMAN

Cemetery

St Jerome's
Fort

N

Damanganga River

RING ROAD

Lighthouse

RUA MARTIM ALFONSO

Sea
Gate

Bocage's
Cottage

Tunnel
Entrance

Pergola
Garden

Cross

Former
Gate

MOTI
DAMAN

MAIN ROAD

Dominican
Monastery

Sé Cathedral

Jail

Tunnel
Entrances

Municipality

Our Lady of
the Rosary

Land
Gate

Cemetery

Moat

Jampore

0   100
metres

Nani Daman

Most of the action in **Nani Daman** centres on Seaface Road, which runs west from the market past rows of hotels, seedy bars and liquor stores to the **beach**, too polluted for a comfortable swim or sunbathe. To the south and directly behind the quay, the ramparts of **St Jerome's Fort**, erected between 1614 and 1672, offer views of the riverfront, dominated by fishing trawlers. The citadel encircles a Catholic church (now a school) and a walled Portuguese cemetery.

Moti Daman

The town's most impressive monuments lie in the colonial compound of **Moti Daman**. Inside its hefty walls, elegant mansions with verandas and colour-washed facades overlook leafy courtyards. Moti Daman's highlights are its **churches**, among the oldest and best-preserved Christian monuments in Asia. The grandest is the **cathedral** (Church of Bom Jesus) on the main square. Built in 1603, its gigantic gabled Baroque facade opens onto a lofty vaulted hall. Across the square, the

Church of Our Lady of the Rosary is crammed with ornate woodwork. **Main Road** links Moti Daman's two **gates**, installed in the 1580s following a Mughal invasion. A small cottage next to the northern Sea Gate was once home to the Portuguese poet Bocage, while atop the bastion facing the southern Land Gate is the cell where condemned prisoners spent their final days.

ARRIVAL AND DEPARTURE   DAMAN

By train The nearest station to Daman is at Vapi; train tickets can be reserved at the reservation centre (daily except Wed 9.30am–1.30pm & 4–9pm) opposite Daman's tourist office. The *Shatabdi Express* connects Ahmedabad (8.30am; 4hr 40min) and Mumbai (7.02pm; 2hr 30min).

By bus Daman's bus stand is east of Seaface Rd in Nani Daman; buses connect to Vapi, 12km east (every 30min; 25min), as do shared taxis (20min; ₹20), private taxis (₹120) and auto-rickshaws (₹80). From Vapi, there are many bus connections, including Mumbai (5 daily; 4–5hr) and Vadodara (10 daily; 6–7hr).

INFORMATION

Tourist information The tourist office (Mon–Fri 9.30am–1.30pm & 2–6pm; ☎0260 2255104, ⓦdamandiutourism.com) is on Zapabar Main Rd, just south of the bus stand.

Services There are two post offices: one in Nani Daman 100m west of the bus stand and one in Moti Daman opposite the Municipal Council Building. World Wide Travels (daily 9am–9pm; ☎0260 2255734) in *Hotel Maharaja* is the best place to change money, and there are several ATMs on Kavi Khabardar Rd. Further south on the same road, Speed Age offers internet access (₹20/hr).

ACCOMMODATION AND EATING

Daman Delite Gurukripa hotel, Seaface Rd. The place to come for a slap-up meal: choose from an extensive seafood menu (prawns ₹170) and finish with a nip of potent Goan *feni* (coconut spirit). Daily 7.30am–11pm.

Garden Seaface Rd. A terrace restaurant-bar serving reasonably priced tandoori pomfret (₹180) and lobster, as well as Goan meat and veg specialities. Daily 11am–11pm.

Gurukripa Seaface Rd ☎0260 2255046, ⓦhotelguru kripa.com. Though beginning to show its age, *Gurukripa* is well run, boasting large a/c attached rooms with wi-fi, plus a roof garden and a decent bar-restaurant. ₹**1550**

Sukh Sagar Estrada 2 Fevereiro ☎0260 2255089. This friendly little hotel, tucked away on a quiet street, has no-nonsense basic but clean a/c (₹1000) and fan-cooled rooms, as well as a budget restaurant. ₹**900**

Mumbai

CHHATRAPATI SHIVAJI TERMINUS (VICTORIA TERMINUS)

Mumbai

Ever since the opening of the Suez Canal in 1869, the principal gateway to the Indian Subcontinent has been Mumbai (Bombay), the city Aldous Huxley famously described as "the most appalling of either hemisphere". Travellers tend to regard time spent here as a rite of passage to be survived rather than savoured. But as the powerhouse of Indian business, industry and trade, and the source of its most seductive media images, the Maharashtran capital can be a compelling place to kill time. Whether or not you find the experience enjoyable, however, will depend largely on how well you handle the heat, humidity, traffic fumes and relentless crowds of India's most dynamic, Westernized city.

10

First impressions of Mumbai tend to be dominated by its chronic shortage of space. Crammed onto a narrow spit of land that curls from the swamp-ridden coast into the Arabian Sea, the city is technically an island, connected to the mainland by bridges and narrow causeways. In less than five hundred years, it has metamorphosed from an aboriginal fishing settlement into a megalopolis of more than sixteen million people – India's largest city and one of the biggest urban sprawls on the planet. Being swept along broad boulevards by endless streams of commuters, or jostled by coolies and hand-cart pullers in the teeming bazaars, you'll continually feel as if Mumbai is about to burst at the seams.

The roots of the population problem and attendant poverty lie, paradoxically, in the city's enduring ability to create wealth. Mumbai alone generates one third of India's tax income, its port handles half the country's foreign trade, and its movie industry is the most prolific in the world. Symbols of prosperity are everywhere: from the phalanx of office blocks clustered on Nariman Point, Maharashtra's Manhattan, to the expensively dressed teenagers posing in Colaba's trendiest nightspots.

The flip side to the success story is the city's much-chronicled poverty. Each day, an estimated five hundred economic refugees pour into Mumbai from the Maharashtran hinterland. Some find jobs and secure accommodation; many more end up living on the already overcrowded streets, or amid the squalor of some of Asia's largest slums, reduced to rag-picking and begging from cars at traffic lights.

However, while it would definitely be misleading to downplay its difficulties, Mumbai is far from the ordeal some travellers make it out to be. Once you've overcome the major hurdle of finding somewhere to stay, you may begin to enjoy its frenzied pace and crowded, cosmopolitan feel.

Nowhere reinforces your sense of having arrived in Mumbai quite as emphatically as the **Gateway of India**, the city's defining landmark. Only a five-minute walk north, the **Prince of Wales Museum** should be next on your list of sightseeing priorities, as much for its

CRICKET AT THE OVAL MAIDAN

Highlights

❶ The Gateway of India Mumbai's defining landmark, and a favourite spot for an evening stroll. **See p.590**

❷ Chhatrapati Shivaji Museum A fine collection of priceless Indian art, from ancient temple sculpture to Mughal armour. **See p.591**

❸ Maidans (parks) Where Mumbai's citizens escape the hustle and bustle to play cricket, eat lunch and hang out. **See p.592**

❹ CS (Victoria) Terminus A fantastically eccentric pile, and the greatest railway station ever built by the British. **See p.596**

❺ Haji Ali's Tomb Mingle with the crowds of Muslim worshippers who flock to the island tomb of Sufi mystic Haji Ali to listen to *qawwali* music on Thursday evenings. **See p.601**

❻ Elephanta Island Catch a boat across Mumbai harbour to see one of ancient India's most wonderful rock-cut Shiva temples. **See p.603**

❼ Bollywood blockbusters Check out the latest Hindi mega-movie in one of the city centre's gigantic Art Deco cinemas. **See p.618**

HIGHLIGHTS ARE MARKED ON THE MAP ON P.587

10

MUMBAI OR BOMBAY?

In 1996 Bombay was renamed **Mumbai**, as part of a wider policy instigated by the right-wing Maharashtrian nationalist Shiv Sena Municipality to replace names of any places, roads and features in the city that had connotations of the Raj. The Shiv Sena asserted that the British term "Bombay" derived from the Marathi title of a local deity, the mouthless "Maha-amba-aiee", Mumba Devi for short (see p.597). In fact, historians are unanimously agreed that the Portuguese, who dubbed the harbour "Bom Bahia" ("Good Bay") when they first came across it, were responsible for christening the site and that the later British moniker had nothing to do with the aboriginal Hindu earth goddess.

A couple of decades on, however, "Mumbai" seems to have definitively taken root with the dotcom generation and even outgrown the narrow agenda of its nationalist originators – just as "Bombay" outlived the Raj.

flamboyantly eclectic architecture as for the art treasures inside. The museum provides a foretaste of what lies in store just up the road, where the cream of Bartle Frere's Bombay – the **University** and **High Court** – line up with the open maidans on one side, and the boulevards of **Fort** on the other. But for the fullest sense of why the city's founding fathers

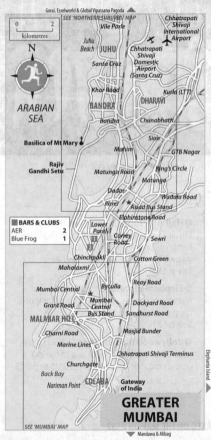

declared it Urbs Prima in Indis, you should press further north still to visit the **Chhatrapati Shivaji Terminus (CST)**, the high-water mark of India's Raj architecture.

Beyond CST lie the crowded bazaars and Muslim neighbourhoods of **central Mumbai**, at their liveliest and most colourful around **Crawford Market** and **Mohammed Ali Road**. Possibilities for an escape from the crowds include an evening stroll along **Marine Drive**, bounding the western edge of downtown, or a boat trip out to **Elephanta**, a rock-cut cave on an island in Mumbai harbour containing a wealth of ancient art.

Brief history

Mumbai originally consisted of seven **islands**, inhabited by small Koli fishing communities. In 1534, Sultan Bahadur of Ahmedabad ceded the land to the **Portuguese**, who subsequently handed it on to the English in 1661 as part of the Portuguese Infanta Catherine of Braganza's dowry during her marriage to Charles II. Bombay's safe harbour and strategic commercial position attracted the interest of the **East India Company**, based at Surat to the north, and in 1668 a deal was struck whereby they leased Bombay from Charles for a pittance.

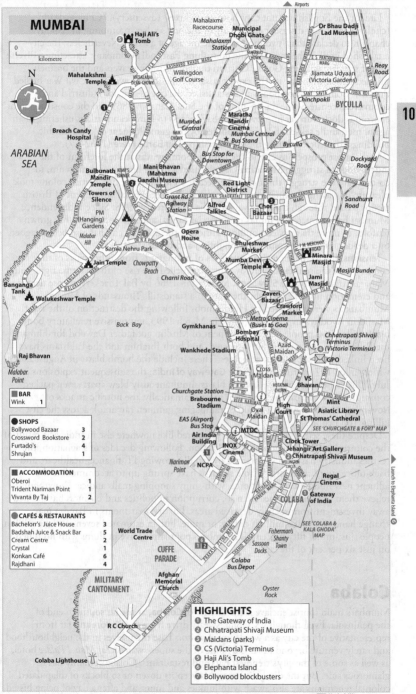

MUMBAI

0 ———— 1
kilometre

N

Airports

Mahalaxmi Racecourse

Municipal Dhobi Ghats

Mahalaxmi Station

Dr Bhau Dadji Lad Museum

Haji Ali's Tomb

Willingdon Golf Course

Jijamata Udyaan (Victoria Gardens)

Reay Road

BYCULLA

Chinchpokli

Mahalakshmi Temple

Breach Candy Hospital

Antilia

ARABIAN SEA

Mumbai Central

Maratha Mandir Cinema

Mumbai Central Bus Stand

Byculla

Dockyard Road

Bulbunath Mandir Temple

Mani Bhavan (Mahatma Gandhi Museum)

Red Light District

Sandhurst Road

Towers of Silence

Grant Rd Railway Station

Chor Bazaar

PM (Hanging) Gardens

Alfred Talkies

Bhuleshwar Market

Minara Masjid

Malabar Hill

Opera House

Mumba Devi Temple

Kamla Nehru Park

Jami Masjid

Masjid Bunder

Jain Temple

Chowpatty Beach

Zaveri Bazaar

Banganga Tank

Charni Road

Crawford Market

Walukeshwar Temple

Metro Cinema (Buses to Goa)

Back Bay

Gymkhanas

Bombay Hospital

Chhatrapati Shivaji Terminus (Victoria Terminus)

Raj Bhavan

Wankhede Stadium

Azad Maidan

GPO

Malabar Point

Cross Maidan

VS Bhavan

BAR
Wink   1

Churchgate Station

Brabourne Stadium

High Court

Mint

Asiatic Library

St Thomas' Cathedral

SEE 'CHURCHGATE & FORT' MAP

SHOPS
Bollywood Bazaar   3
Crossword Bookstore 2
Furtado's   4
Shrujan   1

EAS (Airport) Bus Stop

Oval Maidan

MTDC

Air India Building

INOX Cinema

Clock Tower

Jehangir Art Gallery

Chhatrapati Shivaji Museum

ACCOMMODATION
Oberoi   1
Trident Nariman Point 1
Vivanta By Taj   2

Nariman Point

NCPA

Regal Cinema

COLABA

Gateway of India

CAFÉS & RESTAURANTS
Bachelorr's Juice House   3
Badshah Juice & Snack Bar 5
Cream Centre   2
Crystal   1
Konkan Café   6
Rajdhani   4

World Trade Centre

CUFFE PARADE

SEE 'COLABA & KALA GHODA' MAP

Fisherman's Shanty Town

Sassoon Docks

Colaba Bus Depot

Oyster Rock

Launch to Elephanta Island

MILITARY CANTONMENT

Afghan Memorial Church

R C Church

HIGHLIGHTS
❶ The Gateway of India
❷ Chhatrapati Shivaji Museum
❸ Maidans (parks)
❹ CS (Victoria) Terminus
❺ Haji Ali's Tomb
❻ Elephanta Island
❼ Bollywood blockbusters

Colaba Lighthouse

Mandve & Alibag

10

Life for the English was not easy, however: "fluxes" (dysentery), "Chinese death" (cholera) and other diseases culled many of the first settlers, prompting the colony's chaplain to declare that "two monsoons are the age of a man". Nevertheless, the city established itself as the capital of the flourishing East India Company, attracting a diverse mix of settlers including Goans, Gujarati traders, Muslim weavers and the business-minded Zoroastrian Parsis. The export crisis in America following the Civil War fuelled the great Bombay **cotton boom** and established the city as a major industrial and commercial centre, while the opening of the Suez Canal in 1869 and the construction of enormous docks further improved Bombay's access to European markets ushering in an age of mercantile self-confidence embodied by the grandiloquent colonial-Gothic buildings constructed during the governership of **Sir Bartle Frere** (1862–67).

As the most prosperous city in the nation, Bombay was at the forefront of the **Independence** struggle; Mahatma Gandhi used a house here, now a museum, to co-ordinate the struggle through three decades. Fittingly, the first British colony took pleasure in waving the final goodbye to the Raj, when the last contingent of British troops passed through the Gateway of India in February 1948. Since Independence, Mumbai has prospered as India's commercial capital and the population has grown tenfold, to more than sixteen million, although the modern city has also been plagued by a deadly mixture of **communal infighting** and **terrorist attacks**.

Tensions due to the increasing numbers of immigrants from other parts of the country, and the resultant overcrowding, has fuelled the rise of the extreme right-wing Maharashtrian party, the **Shiv Sena**, founded in 1966 by Bal Thackery, whose death and cremation in 2012 brought the state to a standstill. Thousands of Muslim Mumbaikars were murdered by Hindu mobs following the destruction of the Babri Masjid in Ayodhya in 1992–93, while in March 1993, ten massive retaliatory **bomb blasts** killed 260 people. The involvement of Muslim godfather Dawood Ibrahim and the Pakistani secret service was suspected, and both Ibrahim and the Pakistanis have been linked with subsequent atrocities. These include the bomb blasts in August 2003, which killed 107 tourists next to the **Gateway of India**; the subsequent explosions in July 2006, when co-ordinated bomb blasts simultaneously blew apart seven packed commuter trains across the city; and, most dramatically, the horrific attacks of **November 26, 2008**, when a group of rampaging gunmen ran amok across the city, killing 166 people.

Despite these setbacks, Mumbai has prospered like nowhere else in India as a result of the country's ongoing **economic liberalization**. Following decades of stagnation, the textiles industry has been supplanted by rapidly growing IT, finance, healthcare and back-office support sectors. Whole suburbs have sprung up to accommodate the affluent new middle-class workforce, with shiny shopping malls and car showrooms to relieve them of their income. Even so, corruption in politics and business has drained away investment from socially deprived areas. Luxury apartments in Bandra may change hands for half a million dollars or more, but an estimated seven to eight million people (just under fifty percent of Mumbai's population) live in slums with no toilets, on just six percent of the land.

Colaba

Mumbai's main tourist enclave is the district of **Colaba**, at the far southern end of the peninsula. Even though it's a long, sweaty drive from the airport and far from representative of the city as a whole, most visitors base themselves in the neighbourhood and rarely venture beyond it. As the home of the super-swanky *Taj Mahal Palace* hotel, as well as some of the city's trendiest bars and restaurants, Colaba certainly has its glamorous side. But the dimly lit streets between its dozen or so blocks of dilapidated colonial tenements are also awash with junkies and touts, and after a day of being hissed

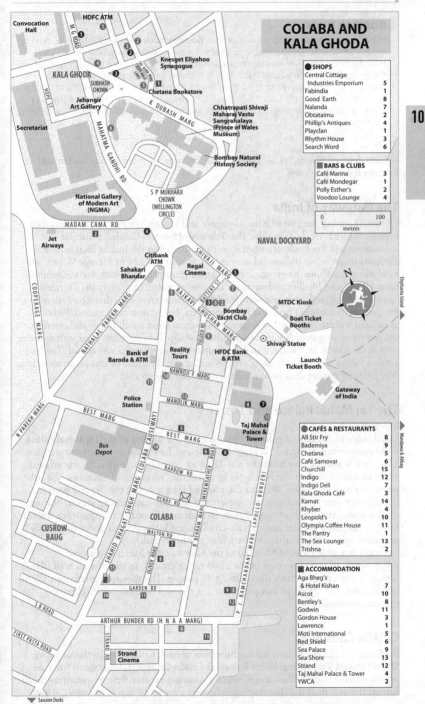

COLABA AND KALA GHODA

Convocation Hall

HDFC ATM

KALA GHODA

Knesget Eliyahoo Synagogue

SUBHASH CHOWK

Jehangir Art Gallery

Chetana Bookstore

Secretariat

K DUBASH MARG

Chhatrapati Shivaji Maharaj Vastu Sangrahalaya (Prince of Wales Museum)

Bombay Natural History Society

S P MUKHARJI CHOWK (WELLINGTON CIRCLE)

National Gallery of Modern Art (NGMA)

MADAM CAMA RD

Jet Airways

NAVAL DOCKYARD

Citibank ATM

Sahakari Bhandar

Regal Cinema

SHIVAJI MARG

MTDC Kiosk

Bombay Yacht Club

Boat Ticket Booths

Shivaji Statue

Bank of Baroda & ATM

Reality Tours

HFDC Bank & ATM

Launch Ticket Booth

NAWROJI F MARG

Police Station

MANDLIK MARG

Gateway of India

BEST MARG

BEST MARG

Taj Mahal Palace & Tower

Bus Depot

BARROW RD

HENRY RD

COLABA

CUSROW BAUG

WALTON RD

GARDEN RD

S B ROAD

ARTHUR BUNDER RD (H N A A MARG)

FIRST PASTA ROAD

Strand Cinema

Sassoon Docks

SHOPS

Central Cottage Industries Emporium	5
Fabindia	1
Good Earth	8
Nalanda	7
Obtataimu	2
Phillip's Antiques	4
Playclan	1
Rhythm House	3
Search Word	6

BARS & CLUBS

Café Marina	3
Café Mondegar	1
Polly Esther's	2
Voodoo Lounge	4

0   100
metres

CAFÉS & RESTAURANTS

All Stir Fry	8
Bademiya	9
Chetana	5
Café Samovar	6
Churchill	15
Indigo	12
Indigo Deli	7
Kala Ghoda Café	3
Kamat	14
Khyber	4
Leopold's	10
Olympia Coffee House	11
The Pantry	1
The Sea Lounge	13
Trishna	2

ACCOMMODATION

Aga Bheg's & Hotel Kishan	7
Ascot	10
Bentley's	8
Godwin	11
Gordon House	3
Lawrence	1
Moti International	5
Red Shield	6
Sea Palace	9
Sea Shore	13
Strand	12
Taj Mahal Palace & Tower	4
YWCA	2

10

Elephanta Island

Mandwa & Alibag

N

10

BOMBAY DUCK

Its name suggests some kind of fowl curry, but **Bombay duck** is actually a fish – to be precise, the marine lizard fish (*Harpalon nehereus*), known in the local dialect of Marathi as *bummalo*. How this long, ribbon-like sea creature acquired its English name no one is exactly sure, but the most plausible theory holds that the Raj-era culinary term no derives from the Hindustani for mail train, *dak*. The nasty odour of the dried fish is said to have reminded the British of the less salubrious carriages of the Calcutta–Bombay *dak* when it pulled into VT after three days and nights on the rails, its wooden carriages covered in the stinking mould that flourished in the monsoonal humidity.

---

at from doorways by sellers of "brown sugar" most people head for the bazaars and brighter lights of uptown.

The Gateway of India

Commemorating the visit of King George V and Queen Mary in 1911, India's own honey-coloured Arc de Triomphe, the **Gateway of India**, is Colaba's principal monument and the landmark most iconic of Mumbai in the Indian imagination. Featured in countless Bollywood movies, it was built in 1924 by George Wittet, whose brief was to combine the grandeur of a Roman triumphal arch with decorative motifs from Hindu and Muslim architecture. The resulting structure, every bit a symbol of "power and majesty", was originally intended to be a ceremonial disembarkation point for passengers alighting from the P&O steamers, but is, ironically, more closely associated with the moment in August 1947 when, amid much pomp and ceremony, the last remaining British soldiers on Indian soil slowly marched to their waiting troop ship as the Union Jack was lowered – to euphoric cheers from a vast crowd. The hour around sunset when thousands of visitors mill about the archway and plaza, munching *bhel puri* and having their photos taken, is the best tine to visit.

The Taj Mahal Palace and Tower

Apollo Bunder

Local pride in the face of colonial oppression is the subtext of the **Taj Mahal Palace and Tower** complex, directly behind the Gateway. Its patron, the Parsi industrialist J.N. Tata, is said to have built the old *Taj* as an act of revenge after he was refused entry to what was then the best hotel in town, the "whites only" *Watson's*. The ban proved to be its undoing. *Watson's* disappeared long ago, but the *Taj* still presides imperiously over the seafront, the preserve of Mumbai's air-kissing jet set, visiting cricket teams and heads of state. Lesser mortals are allowed in to experience the tea lounge, shopping arcades and vast air-conditioned lobby (there's also a fabulously luxurious loo off the corridor to the left of the main desk).

Almost as emblematic of Mumbai as the Gateway, the building featured prominently in news coverage of the 2008 terror attacks, in which a team of Islamist jihadis occupied it for three days, killing 31 people. The subsequent refit cost US 40 million and took a year to complete, but has restored the hotel to its glittering former splendour.

Colaba Causeway

Reclaimed in the late nineteenth century from the sea, Colaba's main thoroughfare, **Shahid Bhagat Singh Marg**, better known as **Colaba Causeway**, leads south from the tourist enclave towards the quieter military cantonment area. Few tourists stray much further down it than the claustrophobic hawker zone at the top of the street, whose shops are fronted by a line of covered incense and knick-knack stalls, but it's well worth doing so, if only to see the neighbourhood's earthy **fresh produce market** a couple of blocks south of the Strand cinema.

Sassoon Docks

Mumbai's wholesale seafood market, **Sassoon Docks**, lies a ten-minute walk beyond the southern end of Colaba Causeway. The greasy quaysides are at their liveliest immediately before and after sunrise, when coolies haul the night's catch in crates of crushed ice over gangplanks, while Koli women cluster around the auctioneers. The stench, as overpowering as the noise, comes mostly from bundles of one of the city's traditional exports, **Bombay duck** (see box opposite). Note that **photography** is strictly forbidden as the docks are adjacent to a sensitive naval area.

Afghan Memorial Church of St John the Baptist

Nanbhai Noos Marg • Buses #3, #11, #47, #103, #123 or #125 from SBS Marg (Colaba Causeway)

The **Afghan Memorial Church of St John the Baptist** was built in 1847–54 to commemorate British victims of the ill-fated First Afghan War, in which Elphinstone's expeditionary force was famously wiped out while trying to withdraw from Kabul down a tunnel of gorges to Jalalabad. Of the 16,500 troops and camp followers who set out on January 1, 1842, only forty survived the massacre, and only one British solider – William Brydon – arrived alive (a trickle of sepoys and one Greek civilian also made it back a couple of days later). The battle-scarred colours of the 44th Regiment of Foot, which provided the bulk of the British contingent, are among those displayed inside the church. Memorial plaques of coloured marble line the walls of the chancels, listing officers killed in action during the conflict.

Kala Ghoda and around

Immediately north of Colaba, **Kala Ghoda** ("Black Horse") district is named after the large equestrian statue of King Edward VII that formerly stood on the crescent-shaped intersection of MG Road and Subhash Chowk. Flanked by Mumbai's principal museum and art galleries, the neighbourhood has in recent years been re-branded as a "cultural enclave" – as much in an attempt to preserve its many historic buildings as to promote the contemporary visual arts that have thrived here since the 1950s. Fancy stainless-steel interpretative panels now punctuate the district's walkways, and on Sundays in December and January, the **Kala Ghoda Fair** sees portrait artists, potters and *mehendi* painters plying their trade in the car park fronting the Jehangir Art Gallery.

Chhatrapati Shivaji Museum

MG Rd • Daily except Tues 10.15am–6pm • ₹300 (₹25), camera ₹200, video ₹1000 – no tripods or flash • ⓦ themumbaimuseum.com

The **Prince of Wales Museum of Western India**, or **Chhatrapati Shivaji Maharaj Vastu Sangrahalaya** as it was renamed by the Shiv Sena, ranks among the city's most distinctive Raj-era constructions. It stands rather grandly in its own gardens off MG Road, crowned by a massive white Mughal-style dome, beneath which one of India's finest collections of paintings and sculpture is arrayed on three floors. The building was designed by George Wittet, of Gateway of India fame, and stands as the epitome of the hybrid **Indo-Saracenic** style – regarded in its day as an "educated" interpretation of fifteenth- and sixteenth-century Gujarati architecture, mixing Islamic touches with typically English municipal brickwork.

The foreigners' ticket price includes an **audio tour**, which you collect at the admissions kiosk inside, though you'll probably find it does little to enhance your visit. The heat and humidity inside the building can also be a trial. For a break, the institutional tea-coffee kiosk in the ground-floor garden is a much less congenial option than the *Café Samovar* outside (see p.612), but to exit the museum and re-enter (which you're entitled to do) you'll have to get your ticket stamped in the admissions lobby first.

Ground floor

The **Key Gallery** in the central hall of the **ground floor** provides a snapshot of the collection's treasures, including the fifth-century AD stucco Buddhist figures unearthed by archeologist Henry Cousens in 1909. The main **sculpture room** in the east wing displays other fourth- and fifth-century Buddhist artefacts, mostly from the former Greek colony of Gandhara. Important Hindu sculptures include a seventh-century Chalukyan bas-relief depicting Brahma seated on a lotus, and a sensuously carved torso of Mahisasuramardini, the goddess Durga, with tripod raised ready to skewer the demon buffalo.

Upper floors

The main attraction on the **first floor** has to be the museum's famous collection of **Indian painting**, which includes works from the Mughal emperors' private collections. More fine medieval miniatures are housed in the **Karl & Meherbai Khandalavala Gallery**, on the renovated east wing of this floor, along with priceless pieces of Ghandaran sculpture, Chola bronzes and some of the country's finest surviving examples of medieval Gujarati woodcarving. Indian **coins** are the subject of the **House of Laxmi Gallery**, also in the east wing, while the **second floor** showcases a vast array of Oriental ceramics and glassware. Finally, among the grisly **weapons** and pieces of armour stored in a small side gallery at the top of the building, look out for the cuirass, helmet and jade dagger which the museum only recently discovered belonged to no less than the Mughal emperor Akbar.

Jehangir Art Gallery

MG Rd • Daily 11am–7pm • Free

Technically in the same compound as the Prince of Wales Museum, though approached from further up MG Road, the **Jehangir Art Gallery** is Mumbai's longest-established venue for contemporary art, with five small halls specializing in twentieth-century arts and crafts from around the world. You never know what you're going to find – most exhibitions last only a week and exhibits are often for sale.

National Gallery of Modern Art

MG Rd, facing the museum and Mukharji Chowk • Tues–Sun 11am–6pm • ₹150 (₹10) • ⊕ ngmaindia.gov.in

Charting the development of modern Indian art from its beginnings in the 1950s to the present day, the **National Gallery of Modern Art (NGMA)** holds a mix of permanent and temporary exhibitions. The works are arrayed over five wonderfully light, semicircular galleries, interconnected by teak-and-chrome staircases. The installations, in particular, tend to be a lot more adventurous than those you'll find in the Jehangir across the road.

Around Oval Maidan

Northeast of Kala Ghoda stretches the yawning expanse of **Oval Maidan**, where impromptu cricket matches are held almost every day, against a backdrop of giant palms and even taller Raj-era buildings. Green during the monsoons and parched yellow for the rest of year, it is flanked on its eastern side by some of Mumbai's finest Victorian piles, dating from the high point of British power. The travel writer Robert Byron famously described them as forming an "architectural Sodom", claiming that "the nineteenth century devised nothing lower than the municipal buildings of British

India. Their ugliness is positively daemonic". Today, however, the massive erections of Empire appear not so much ugly as intriguing.

High Court
Karmaveer Bhaurao Patil Marg

Dominating the east side of Oval Maidan is the **Mumbai High Court**, originally the Old Secretariat, which the Raj historian G.W. Forrest described in 1903 "a massive pile whose main features have been brought from Venice, but all the beauty has vanished in trans-shipment". With its gigantic pitched roofs and balconies shaded by enormous rattan blinds, the building has changed little since. Take a peek inside, where lawyers in black gowns, striped trousers and white tabs bustle up and down the staircases, and office desks are piled high with dusty be-ribboned bundles of documents – a vision of Indian bureaucracy at its most Dickensian.

Mumbai University
MG Rd

Across AS D'Mello Road from the High Court stand the two major buildings comprising **Mumbai University** (established 1857), which were designed in England by Sir Gilbert Scott, architect of the Gothic extravaganza that is London's St Pancras railway station. Funded by the Parsi philanthropist Cowasjee "Readymoney" Jehangir, whose white marble statue appears in front of it, the **Convocation Hall** greatly resembles a church. Above the entrance, a huge circular stained-glass window features a wheel with spokes of Greek pilasters separating the signs of the zodiac. With all its polished teak and brass, the interior, currently closed to visitors for security reasons, could have been transported from a Victorian public school in the home counties of England.

Library and Rajabhai Clock Tower

It's a shame that at the time of going to print the University is closed to visitors, because one fantastic visit is to the **library**, just to see its splendid antique reading room, spanned by a vaulted wooden ceiling and illuminated by Gothic windows. Above it, Gilbert Scott's 79.2m-high **Rajabhai Clock Tower** is said to have been modelled on Giotto's campanile in Florence and formerly chimed tunes such as *Rule Britannia* and *Home Sweet Home*.

Fort

East of Oval Maidan stretches the spectacular **Fort** district, site of Mumbai's original British settlement and the first East India Company fort – hence the name. The sloping ramparts, moats and fortified gateways were pulled down in the mid-nineteenth century following the demise of the French threat to British supremacy in India, but this is still the commercial hub of the southern city and a great area for aimless wandering, with plenty of old-fashioned cafés, department stores and street stalls crammed in between the imposing Victorian buildings.

Horniman Circle

At the heart of the Fort district lies the spacious **Horniman Circle**, conceived in 1860 as the centrepiece of a newly planned Bombay by the then Municipal Commissioner, Charles Forjett, on the site of Bombay's "Green". Later, the space served as a cotton market and parade ground. The garden's wrought-iron gates and fences enclose a haven of vegetation where office workers bring their lunches and newspapers. Surrounding it are ranks of grand buildings whose paved arcades, crowned by grim-faced keystone heads, today provide accommodation for families of street sleepers.

10

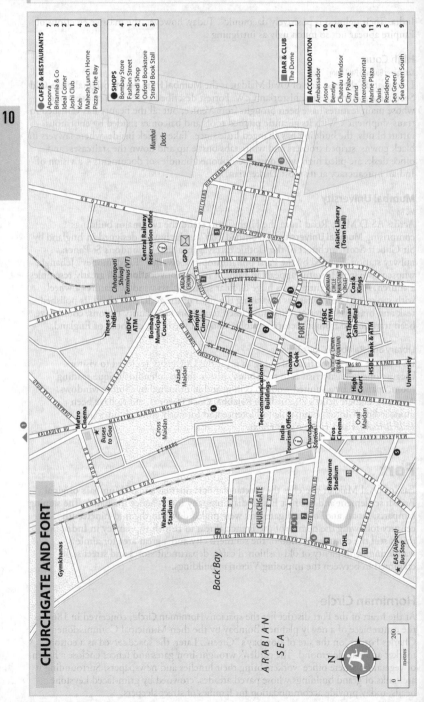

CHURCHGATE AND FORT

● **CAFÉS & RESTAURANTS**
Apoorva	7
Britannia & Co	3
Ideal Corner	2
Joshi Club	1
Koh	4
Mahesh Lunch Home	5
Pizza by the Bay	6

● **SHOPS**
Bombay Store	4
Fashion Street	1
Khadi Shop	2
Oxford Bookstore	5
Strand Book Stall	3

■ **BAR & CLUB**
The Dome	1

■ **ACCOMMODATION**
Ambassador	7
Astoria	10
Bentley	2
Chateau Windsor	8
City Palace	1
Grand	4
Intercontinental	6
Marine Plaza	3
Oasis	5
Residency	5
Sea Green/	
Sea Green South	9

Mumbai Docks

Central Railway Reservation Office

GPO

Asiatic Library (Town Hall)

Chhatrapati Shivaji Terminus (VT)

HORNIMAN CIRCLE

ELPHINSTONE CIRCLE

Cox & Kings

Times of India

HDFC ATM

Bombay Municipal Council

New Empire Cinema

Planet M

HSBC ATM

St Thomas' Cathedral

FORT

Thomas Cook

NUTAN CHOWK (FLORA FOUNTAIN)

HSBC Bank & ATM

Azad Maidan

High Court

University

Metro Cinema

Buses to Goa

Cross Maidan

Telecommunications Buildings

India Tourism Office

Churchgate Station

Eros Cinema

Oval Maidan

Wankhede Stadium

CHURCHGATE

Brabourne Stadium

DHL

EAS (Airport) Bus Stop

Gymkhanas

Back Bay

ARABIAN SEA

N

0 — 200 metres

DABAWALLAHS

Mumbai's size and inconvenient shape create all kind of hassles for its working population. One thing the daily tidal wave of commuters does not have to worry about, however, is where to find an inexpensive and wholesome home-cooked lunch. In a city with a wallah for everything, it will find them. The members of the **Nutan Mumbai Tiffin Box Suppliers Charity Trust (NMTSCT)**, known colloquially, and with no little affection, as "**dabawallahs**", see to that. Every day, around 5000 *dabawallahs* deliver freshly cooked meals to 200,000 suburban kitchens to offices in the downtown area. Each is prepared early in the morning by a wife or mother while her husband or son is enduring the crush on the train. She arranges the rice, dhal, *subzi*, curd and *parathas* into cylindrical aluminium trays, stacks them on top of one another and clips them together with a neat little handle.

This **tiffin box** is the linchpin of the whole operation. When the runner calls to collect it in the morning, he uses a special colour code on the lid to tell him where the lunch has to go. At the end of his round, all the boxes are carried to the nearest railway station and handed over to other *dabawallahs* for the trip into town. Between leaving the cook and reaching its final destination, the tiffin box will pass through at least half a dozen different pairs of hands, carried on heads, shoulder-poles, bicycle handlebars and in the brightly decorated handcarts that glide with such insouciance through the midday traffic.

WHERE TO FIND THEM

To catch them in action, head for **CST (VT)** or **Churchgate** stations around late morning, when the tiffin boxes arrive in the city centre to a chorus of "*lafka! lafka*" – "hurry! hurry!" – as the *dabawallahs* rush to make their lunch-hour deadlines. Nearly all come from the same small village near Pune and are related to one another. They collect around ₹2000–4000 per month in total.

One of the reasons the system survives in the face of competition from trendy fast-food outlets is that *dabba* lunches still work out a good deal cheaper, saving precious rupees for the middle-income workers who use the system. Competition has recently arisen from high-end takeaway joints in Mumbai, some of whom offer freshly prepared gourmet food delivered in tiffin tins. But the *dabawallahs* are not sitting on their heels in the face of the new competition, recently launching a website to facilitate booking online and by SMS.

Famous foreigners who have taken more than a passing interest in the *dabawallah* phenomenon include Sir Richard Branson (the Virgin tycoon spent a day accompanying a tiffin carrier on his round), Prince Charles (who invited some to his wedding with Camilla Parker-Bowles) and Bill Clinton, who took a tiffin lunch during a state visit.

The Asiatic Society Library

Shahid Bhagat Singh Marg • Mon–Sat 10am–7pm

The splendid Neoclassical building on the east side of Horniman Circle served as the city's former Town Hall, one of the few buildings in Mumbai that pleased Aldous Huxley: "(Among) so many architectural cads and pretentious bounders," he wrote in 1948, "it is almost the only gentleman." The Doric edifice, dating from 1833, was originally built to house the vast collection of the **Asiatic Society Library**, which is still open to the public. Save for the addition of electricity, little has changed here since the institution was founded. Reading rooms, lined with wrought-iron loggias and teak bookcases, are filled with scholars poring over mouldering tomes dating from the Raj. Among the ten thousand rare and valuable manuscripts stored here is a fourteenth-century first edition of Dante's *Divine Comedy*, said to be worth around US$3 million, which the Society famously refused to sell to Mussolini. Visitors are welcome but should sign in at the Head Librarian's desk on the ground floor.

St Thomas' Cathedral

VN Rd • Daily 7am–6pm

Just west off Horniman Circle stands the diminutive **St Thomas' Cathedral**, reckoned to be the oldest British building in Mumbai, blending Classical and Gothic styles. After the death of its founding father, Governor Aungier, the project was abandoned; the walls stood 5m high for forty-odd years until enthusiasm was rekindled in the second decade of the eighteenth century. It was finally opened on Christmas Day, 1718, complete with the essential "cannonball-proof roof". In those days, the seating was divided into useful sections for those who should know their place, including one for "Inferior Women". The whitewashed and polished brass-and-wood interior looks much the same at it did in the eighteenth century. Lining the walls are memorial tablets to British parishioners, many of whom died young, either from disease or in battle.

Chhatrapati Shivaji Terminus (Victoria Terminus)

Inspired by St Pancras Station in London, F.W. Stevens designed **Victoria Terminus**, the barmiest of Mumbai's buildings, as a paean to "progress". Built in 1887 as the largest British edifice in India, it's an extraordinary amalgam of domes, spires, Corinthian columns and minarets that was succinctly defined by the journalist James Cameron as "Victorian-Gothic-Saracenic-Italianate-Oriental-St Pancras-Baroque". In keeping with the current re-Indianization of the city's roads and buildings, this icon of British imperial architecture has been renamed **Chhatrapati Shivaji Terminus**, in honour of the famous Maratha warlord. The new name is a bit of a mouthful, however, and locals mostly still refer to it as **VT** (pronounced "vitee" or "wee-tee").

Few of the two million or so passengers who fill almost a thousand trains every day notice the mass of decorative detail. A "British" lion and Indian tiger stand guard at the entrance, and the exterior is festooned with sculptures executed at the Bombay Art School by the Indian students of John Lockwood Kipling, Rudyard's father. Among them are grotesque mythical beasts, monkeys, plants and medallions of important personages. To minimize the sun's impact, stained glass was employed, decorated with locomotives and elephant images. Above it all, "Progress" stands atop the massive central dome.

One regrettable addition to the station's fixtures is the polished black marble memorial next to its main entrance commemorating the 58 passengers and staff gunned down by terrorists during the 26/11 attack (see p.588).

Central Bazaar District

Sir JJ Rd, 1km north of CST (VT) station

Lining the anarchic jumble of streets beyond Lokmanya Tilak Road is Mumbai's bustling **central bazaar district** – a fascinating counterpoint to the wide and Westernized streets of downtown. In keeping with traditional divisions of guild, caste and religion, most streets specialize in one or two types of merchandise. If you lose your bearings, the best way out is to ask someone to wave you in the direction of **Mohammed Ali Road**, the busy road through the heart of the district (now surmounted by a gigantic flyover), from where you can hail a cab.

Crawford Market

Crawford (aka Mahatma Phule) **Market**, ten minutes' walk north of CST, is an old British-style covered market dealing in just about every kind of fresh food and domestic animal imaginable. Before venturing inside, stop to admire the **friezes** wrapped around its exterior – a Victorian vision of sturdy-limbed peasants toiling in the fields during his time, as designed by Rudyard Kipling's father, Lockwood, principal of the Bombay School of Art in 1865.

The **main hall** is still divided into different sections: pyramids of polished fruit and vegetables down one aisle, sacks of nuts or oil-tins full of herbs and spices down another. Around the back of the market, in the atmospheric wholesale wing, the pace of life is more hectic. Here, noisy crowds of coolies mill about with large reed-baskets held high in the air (if they are looking for work) or on their heads (if they've found some). Animal lovers should steer well clear of the market's eastern wing, where all kinds of unfortunate creatures are crammed into undersized cages. Beyond the pets section, the meat hall is not for the squeamish.

Jama Masjid and Zaveri Bazaar

Sheikh Memon St

The streets immediately **north of Crawford Market** and west of **Mohammed Ali Road** form one vast bazaar area, dominated by the domes and minarets of the chintzy white **Jama Masjid**, or "Friday Mosque" (*c*.1800). The nucleus of the building is an ancient water tank, which now serves as an ablution pool. Pillars rise directly from the murky green pond to support the main body of the mosque, whose halls are reached by stairways. Cutting north from the Jama Masjid is **Zaveri Bazaar**, the jewellery market where Mumbaikars come to shop for dowries and wedding attire. An estimated 65 percent of all India's gold, silver and precious gems trading is carried out in the brightly lit emporia lining the market's lanes.

Mumba Devi temple

Sheikh Memon St, Bhuleshwar

An important centre of Devi worship, the **Mumba Devi temple** rises from one of the most densely populated square miles on the planet – a maze of twisting lanes and alleyways, lined by five- or six-storey wooden-balconied tenement buildings. The present structure, with its tapering polychrome sanctuary tower, dates only from the nineteenth century, but the black-stone deity inside it, patron goddess of the city's Koli fisherfolk, is much older. Originally she occupied a shrine further south, just outside the walls of the East India Company's fort, but that site was commandeered to make way for VT station. Quite whether an English corruption of Mumba's name formed the root of "Bombay", as Maharashtran nationalists claim, is debatable, but there is no doubting the popularity of the modern temple, which throngs with worshippers from dawn until dusk. Colourful stalls selling floral offerings and other religious paraphernalia line the streets around it, where you'll encounter plenty of saffron-clad sadhus, their foreheads smeared with vibrant red vermilion powder.

Marine Drive

Netaji Subhash Chandra Marg, better known as **Marine Drive**, is Mumbai's seaside prom, an eight-lane highway with a wide pavement built in the 1920s on reclaimed land. The whole 3km stretch – still often referred to by Mumbaikars as the "Queen's Necklace" after the row of lights that illuminates its spectacular curve at night – is a favourite place for a stroll; the promenade next to the sea has uninterrupted views virtually the whole way along, while the peeling, mildewed Art Deco apartment blocks on the land side remain some of the most desirable addresses in the city.

Chowpatty Beach

Situated at the top of Marine Drive, **Chowpatty Beach** is a Mumbai institution. On evenings and weekends, Mumbaikars gather here in large numbers – not to swim (the sea is foul) but to wander, sit on the sand, munch kulfi and *bhel puri*, get their ears cleaned and gaze across the bay while the kids ride a pony or a rusty Ferris wheel. Once a year, in September, the **Ganesh Chathurthi** festival draws gigantic crowds as idols, both huge and small, of the elephant-headed god Ganesh are immersed in the sea against the iconic backdrop of skyscrapers. The beach is also the venue for the city's annual **Ram Lila** festival (mid-Oct) when the story of Rama's battle with the evil demon Ravana is performed over ten consecutive nights on a specially erected stage, culminating in the burning of a colossal Ravana effigy.

At the back of the beach, a bronze bust recalls the bravery of Tukaram Omble, the policeman who lost his life capturing terrorist Ajmal Kasab during the 2008 attacks. Omble held on to the gunman's AK47 long enough for his colleagues to overpower the attacker, but was shot several times in the process and later died of his injuries.

10

Mani Bhavan

19 Laburnum Rd • Daily 9.30am–6pm • Free, with optional donation

A ten-minute walk north from the middle of Chowpatty Beach along Pandita Ramabai Marg, **Mani Bhavan** was Gandhi's Bombay base between 1917 and 1934. Set in a leafy upper-middle-class road, the house has now been converted into a permanent memorial to the Mahatma. The lovingly maintained polished-wood interior is crammed with historic photos and artefacts – the most disarming of which is a friendly letter to Hitler suggesting world peace. Laburnum Road is a few streets along from the Bharatiya Vidya Bhavan music venue on KM Munshi Marg – if coming by taxi ask for the nearby Gamdevi Police Station.

Malabar Hill

Its shirt-tails swathed in greenery and brow bristling with gigantic skyscrapers, **Malabar Hill**, the promontory enfolding Chowpatty Beach at the north end of Back Bay, has been south Mumbai's most desirable neighbourhood almost since the city was founded. The British were quick to see the potential of its salubrious breezes and sweeping sea views, constructing bungalows at the tip of what was then a separate island – the grandest of them the Government House, originally erected in the 1820s and now the seat of the serving governor of Maharashtra, **Raj Bhavan**.

Although none of Malabar's landmarks can be classed as unmissable, its Hindu shrines and surviving colonial-era residences form an interesting counterpoint to the modernity towering on all sides. Bal Gangadhar Kher Marg (formerly Ridge Road) is the district's main artery. You can follow it from Mumbai's principal **Jain Temple** (see map, p.587), with its mirror-encrusted interior dedicated to Adinath, all the way to the tip of the headland, where the famous **Walkeshwar Temple** stands as the city's oldest Hindu shrine surviving *in situ*. According to the Ramayana, Rama fashioned a lingam out of sand to worship Shiva here, which over the centuries became one of the Konkan's most important pilgrimage centres. Today's temple, erected in 1715 after the original was destroyed by the Portuguese, is of less note than the **Banganga Tank** below it – a rectangular lake lined by stone *ghats* and numerous crumbling shrines.

THE TOWERS OF SILENCE

High on Malabar Hill, screened from prying eyes by a high wall and dense curtain of vegetation (and strictly closed to visitors), stand the seven **Towers of Silence**, where the city's dwindling Zoroastrian community (better known as Parsis) dispose of their dead. Pollution of the four sacred elements (air, water, earth and, holiest of all, fire) contradicts the most fundamental precepts of the 2500-year-old Parsi faith, first imported to India when Zoroastrians fled from Sassanid Persia to escape Arab persecution in the seventh century. So instead of being buried or cremated, the bodies are laid out on top of open-topped, cylindrical towers, called *dokhmas*, for their bones to be cleaned by **vultures** and the weather. The remains are then placed in an ossuary at the centre of the tower.

Central Mumbai: Mahalakshmi to Byculla

The centre of Mumbai, beyond Malabar Hill, is mostly made up of working-class neighbourhoods: a huge mosaic of dilapidated tenements, markets and industrial eyesores left over from the Victorian cotton boom. For relief from the urban cauldron, residents travel west to the seashore to worship at the **Mahalakshmi Temple** (if they're Hindus) or the island **tomb of Haji Ali** (if they're Muslims). Both make great excursions from south Mumbai, and can be combined with a foray across town to the recently revamped **Dr Bhau Dadji Lad Museum** in Byculla, calling en route at the **Mahalakshmi dhobi ghats** – one of the city's more offbeat sights.

10

Mahalakshmi Temple

Just off Bhulabhai Desai Rd • Buses #83, #124 or #132 will take you from Colaba to Haji Ali, within a stone's throw of the Mahalakshmi Temple

Mumbai's busy **Mahalakshmi Temple**, dedicated to the Hindu goddess of wealth and prosperity – the city's most sought-after attributes – stands on the shoreline off the frenetic Bhulabhai Desai intersection. The approach is via an alley lined with stalls selling spectacular floral offerings and devotional pictures. A heavy security cordon has to be crossed before entering the main shrine, where a statue of the *devi* glittering with

---

DHARAVI: THE £700 MILLION SLUM

Sprawling over 550 acres, **Dharavi**'s maze of dilapidated shacks and narrow, stinking alleyways is home to more than a million people. An average of 15,000 of them share a single toilet. Infectious diseases such as dysentery, malaria and hepatitis are rife; and there aren't any hospitals.

Despite the poverty, Dharavi has been described by the UK's *Observer* newspaper as "one of the most inspiring economic models in Asia": hidden amid the warren of ramshackle huts and squalid open sewers are an estimated fifteen thousand single-room factories, employing around a quarter of a million people and turning over a staggering £700 million (US$1 billion) annually. The majority of small businesses in Dharavi are based on **waste recycling** of one kind or another. Slum residents young and old scavenge materials from across the city and haul them back in huge bundles to be reprocessed. Aluminium cans are smelted down, soap scraps salvaged from schools and hotels are reduced in huge vats, leather reworked, disused oil drums restored and discarded plastic reshaped and remoulded. An estimated ten thousand workers are employed in the plastics sector alone. Ranging from ₹3000–15,000 per month, wages are well above the national average, and though Dharavi may not have any health centres, it does hold a couple of banks, and even ATMs.

As India's most iconic slum, Dharavi has also found an unlikely niche in the history of Indian and international **cinema**. The district provided many of the settings for Danny Boyle's multiple-Oscar-winning **Slumdog Millionaire**, as well as several of its leading child actors.

Despite its burgeoning international fame, Dharavi's future remains uncertain. The entire district is living in the shadow of a proposed US$40 billion **redevelopment project** which aims to bulldoze the entire slum. In return for agreeing to eviction, residents will be entitled to apartment space in new multistorey tower blocks. Schools, roads, hospitals and other amenities have also been promised. Opposition to the scheme among Dharavites has been all but unanimous, however, with slum dwellers insisting any future development should focus not on erecting a swanky new suburb but on improving existing conditions.

You can visit Dharavi yourself by joining one of the "**Slum Tours**" run by Reality Tours and Travels out of Colaba. Tickets for these engaging guided trips cost ₹650 (including transport), with a longer and more comfortable version with an a/c car for ₹1200. For more details, contact Krishna Pujari on ☎022 2283 3872 or ☎9820 822253, check out ⊕realitytoursandtravel.com, or just drop in to their booking office (Mon–Fri 10am–7pm, Sat 10am–4pm) off Colaba Causeway (SBS Marg), in Akber House on Nawroji Fardonji Marg, opposite the *Laxmi Vilas Hotel* (see map, p.589) – enter Akber House via the passageway through S. S. S. Corner next to the *New Apollo Restaurant*; the office is on the first floor, reached via a steep, narrow flight of steps and tiny corridor through the Unique Business Service Centre.

gold jewellery and bangles, and seated astride a tiger and demon, is propitiated by a constant stream of worshippers. Donations pile so high that the temple pujaris run a money-spinning sideline reselling them. While you're here, find out what your future holds by joining the huddle of devotees pressing rupees onto the rear wall of the shrine room. If your coin sticks, you'll be rich.

Haji Ali's Tomb

10

Occupying a small islet in the bay just north of the Mahalakshmi Temple is the mausoleum of the Muslim saint, Afghan mystic **Haji Ali Bukhari**. The site is a great place to head on Thursday and Friday evenings, when large crowds gather around the promontory to watch the sunset and listen to live **qawwali** music.

The tomb is connected to the mainland by a narrow concrete **causeway**, only passable at low tide. When not immersed in water, its entire length is lined with beggars supplicating passers-by and chanting verses from the Koran. Non-Muslims are welcome, but all visitors need to keep well covered (a headscarf should be worn by women).

Haji Ali Juice Centre

The traditional way to round off a trip to the mausoleum is to take a glass or two of fresh fruit juice at the legendary **Haji Ali Juice Centre**, just to the right of the entrance to the causeway. Customers either cram into the tiny dining hall or else order from their cars.

Mahalakshmi dhobi ghats

Bapurao Jagtap Marg • Buses #124 (from Colaba) and #153 (from Haji Ali) go to the *dhobi ghats*; trains run from Churchgate to Mahalakshmi station emerging from the station, turn left and follow the road over the rail tracks – the *ghats* will be below you on your left (the hawkers from the nearby slums who work the spot will show you the way).

On the face of it, the idea of going out of your way to ogle Mumbai's dirty washing sounds like a very perverse pastime. If you're passing, however, the **Mahalakshmi dhobi ghats**, near Mahalakshmi suburban railway station, are a sufficiently memorable spectacle to break a trip across town to see. Washing from all over the city is brought here each morning to be soaked in concrete vats and thumped by the resident *dhobis*. A trickle of curious foreign tourists gathers on Mahalakshmi road bridge for this uniquely Indian photo opportunity.

ANTILIA

If Mumbai is notorious for its poverty, then the city is no less famous for the glittering wealth of its richest inhabitants, and they don't come richer than **Mukesh Ambani**, chairman of the Reliance Industries petrochemical corporation. With a net worth of US$21 billion, Ambani is officially India's richest man, and his recently built home on Altamount Rd in the Cumballa Hill district of south-central Mumbai is said to be the world's most valuable piece of real estate. The futuristic, 27-storey skyscraper – known as **Antilia** – enjoys a majestic view over the Arabian Sea on one side, and Dharavi slum area on the other. Completed in 2010, it cost an estimated US$500–600 million to build, and is valued at somewhere between US$1–2 billion. Six floors are given over to a 168-car parking area. The building boasts nine elevators, three helipads, a glittering ballroom with solid silver balustrades and ceilings festooned with crystal chandeliers, hanging gardens of hydroponic plants and an ice room where the Ambanis can beat the summer heat in flurries of man-made snow.

Reaction to the appearance of this new behemoth on Mumbai's skyline has been mixed, to say the least. While most of the locals and sightseers regard it with wide-eyed wonder, members of India's intelligentsia – from industrialist J.R. Tata to novelist Arundhati Roy – have been less than complimentary, deploring the Ambanis' apparent lack of social conscience.

10

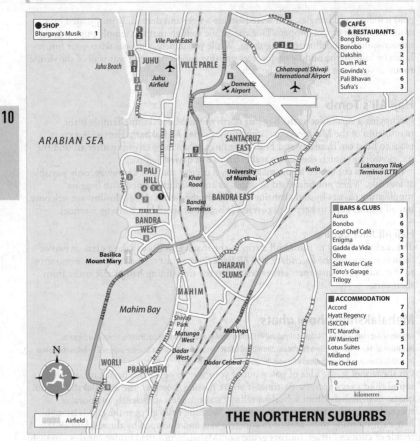

THE NORTHERN SUBURBS

Dr Bhau Dadji Lad Museum

DR Ambedkar Rd • Daily except Wed 10am–5.30pm • ₹100 (₹5) • ⏍ bdlmuseum.org

Way out in the post-industrial wasteland of Byculla, the **Dr Bhau Dadji Lad Museum** was originally opened in 1872 as the **Victoria and Albert Museum** – "one of the greatest boons the British have conferred on India", according to contemporary reports. The elegant, Palladian-style building, set amid classically planned botanical gardens (now home to a rather depressing zoo) has been restored to its former glory, and houses a collection of fascinating lithographs, prints, documents, uniforms and models relating to the development of Bombay. In the adjacent garden, the carved stone pachyderm after which the Portuguese are said to have named Elephanta Island presides over a collection of forlorn British statues, moved here during Independence beyond the reach of angry mobs.

Gorai

Just beyond the northern limits of Mumbai, **Gorai** is a low-lying, sparsely populated peninsula separated at its tip from the mainland by tidal creek. Among the city's residents, this isolated green belt, settled by Portuguese priests and Catholic converts in the sixteenth century, is famous for two starkly contrasting attractions: if you've a day to kill in Mumbai between flights, and can't face exploring the city, either the **Esselword** amusement park complex or adjacent **Global Vipassana Pagoda** might be worth considering – though be warned that getting to and from Gorai from downtown can take upwards of two hours at peak times.

Esselworld

Mon–Fri 10am–7pm, Sat & Sun 10am–8pm • ₹590/₹690 regular/peak for adults; ₹390/₹490 for children; combined Esselword & Water Kingdom ₹790/₹890 adult, ₹590/690 children • ⓦ esselworld.com

Mumbai's answer to Disneyland, **Esselword** is the first-choice destination for local families who can afford the trip – an island of American-style fun and frolics on the city's green fringe. It consists of two parts: the Esselworld amusement park, with its white-knuckle roller coasters, gentler kiddies' rides, ice rink and bowling alley; and the adjacent Water Kingdom, a vast complex of aqua slides featuring the world's largest wave pool, a huge play lagoon and some brilliant family-friendly rides. Crowds in both can be oppressive on weekends and holidays, but ease off during the week when admission charges drop.

Global Vipassana Pagoda

Daily dawn–dusk • ⓦ globalpagoda.org

Chugging across Gorai creek on the ferry, you could be forgiven for thinking yourself on a river somewhere in southeast Asia. From the far bank, the ethereal, gold-painted **Global Vipassana Pagoda** rises like something you'd expect to see shimmering over the waters of Burma's Ayeyarwady Delta. In fact the pagoda was built as a replica of the resplendent Shwedagon Paya in Yangon (Rangoon), Myanmar's most venerated Buddhist monument. Its gleaming golden pinnacle soars 99m – the height of a thirty-storey building – above the shoreline peaks and the adjacent amusement park, making it the world's largest freestanding dome, taller even than Bijapur's Golgumbaz.

An entrance way leads to a cavernous meditation hall measuring 280m in diameter and capable of accommodating eight thousand worshippers. Genuine relics of the Buddha, donated by the government of Sri Lanka and Mahabodhi Soceity of Bodh Gaya, are enshrined in the upper dome above the hall. Other structures in the landscaped complex include 21m-tall seated Buddha carved from a single piece of marble, a massive entrance gateway and towers containing a colossal Burmese-style bell and gong.

ARRIVAL AND DEPARTURE   GORAI

By train and launch Make for Borivali station on the suburban train line. Leave via the western exit, which brings you on to Chandavarkar Rd, where you can pick up a BEST bus #294 or #247 to Gorai Creek – or better still, jump in an autorickshaw for the 4km trip to the river. Once at the jetty, take the Esselworld launch (₹50), not the cheaper local Gorai ferry, as it the latter drops you a long way from the park.

By bus Modern Tours and Travels (☎ 022 2353 0888) run a private service (2hr 30min; ₹700 plus ferry) that also runs direct to Esselworld from Colaba each day, departing from outside the Regal Cinema at 8.30am. Book in advance.

By taxi Taxis charge around ₹500 for the 71km journey from Colaba, and can be in short supply for the return leg.

Elephanta

An hour's ride northeast across Mumbai harbour from Colaba, the island of **Elephanta** offers the best escape from the seething claustrophobia of the city – as long as you time your visit to avoid the weekend deluge of noisy day-trippers. Populated only by a small fishing community, it was originally known as **Gherapura**, the "city of Ghara priests", until the island was renamed in the sixteenth century by the Portuguese in honour of the carved elephant they found at the port – now on display outside the Dr Bhau Dadji Lad Museum in Byculla. Its chief attraction is its unique **cave temple**, whose massive **Trimurti** (three-faced) **Shiva sculpture** is as fine an example of Hindu architecture as you'll find anywhere.

By boat Boats set off every 30min from the Gateway of India (daily 9am–2.30pm; returning from Elephanta noon–5pm; book through the kiosks near the Gateway of India); note that boats may be cancelled due to adverse weather conditions during the monsoon. "Deluxe" boats (₹150 return) include a 30min tour with a government guide – ask for your guide at the cave's ticket office on arrival. Ordinary ferries (₹120 return) don't include the guided tour and are usually more packed. There's also a tourist tax of ₹10 payable on arrival, and a further admission charge of ₹10.

Information Cool drinks and souvenir stalls line the way up the hill, and, at the top, the MTDC *Chalukya* restaurant offers substandard food and warm beer, served on a terrace with good views out to sea. If you don't want to walk up the 120 steps to the caves there's a miniature train up from the jetty (₹10 return). Note that you cannot stay overnight on the island and that the caves are closed on Mondays.

The cave

Tues–Sun 9.30am–5pm • ₹500 (₹5)

Elephanta's impressive excavated eighth-century **cave**, covering an area of approximately 5000 square metres, is reached by climbing more than one hundred steps lined by souvenir and knick-knack stalls, to the top of the hill. Inside, the massive columns, carved from solid rock, give the deceptive impression of being structural. To the right as you enter, note the panel of **Nataraj**, Shiva as the cosmic dancer. Though spoiled by the Portuguese who, it is said, used it for target practice, the panel remains magnificent: Shiva's face is rapt, and with one of his left hands he removes the veil of ignorance. Opposite is a badly damaged panel of Lakulisha, Shiva with a club (*lakula*).

Each of the four entrances to the simple square main **shrine** – unusually, it has one on each side – is flanked by a pair of huge fanged *dvarpala* guardians (only those to the back have survived undamaged), while inside a large lingam is surrounded by coins and smouldering joss left by devotees. Facing the northern wall of the shrine, another panel shows Shiva impaling the demon Andhaka, who wandered around as though blind, symbolizing his spiritual blindness. The panel behind the shrine on the back wall portrays the marriage of Shiva and Parvati, but the cave's outstanding centrepiece is its powerful 6m bust of **Trimurti**, the three-faced Shiva, whose profile has become almost as familiar to Indians as that of the Taj Mahal.

Elephanta Hill

From Cave 1 you can follow a paved path around the north flank of the hillside past a string of other, unfinished excavations, which exemplify how the caves were originally dug out and carved. If you've the stamina, follow the dirt path that leads from the end of the paved trail beyond these to the summit of **Elephanta Hill**, a stiff hike of fifteen minutes. At the top you'll be rewarded by an encounter with a couple of rusting Portuguese cannons and a magnificent view back over Mumbai harbour to the distant city beyond.

Unless you're travelling by train to or from **Chhatrapati Shivaji Terminus** (formerly Victoria Terminus), be prepared for a long slog to or from the centre. The international and domestic **airports** are way north of the city, and ninety minutes or more by road from the main hotel areas, while from **Mumbai Central** railway or **bus station** you also face a laborious trip across town.

GETTING TO GOA

Easily the best-value way to travel the 500km from Mumbai to Goa is by **plane** – prices often compare favourably with the cost of the same journey on the Konkan Railway, which has two departures daily. Whatever your budget, think twice before attempting the hellish overnight **bus** journey.

BY PLANE

Around fifteen flights leave daily from Mumbai's domestic airport for Goa's **Dabolim airport** (code GOI). Flights are currently operated by Jet Airways, JetKonnect, IndiGo, SpiceJet, Go Air and Air India (see p.35). One-way fares start from around ₹2000; check ⓦ expedia.co.in and ⓦ cleartrip.com for the latest deals, or the websites of the airlines themselves (see p.35) for special offers and promotions.

Demand for seats can be fierce around Diwali and Christmas/New Year, when you're unlikely to get a ticket at short notice. At other times, one or other of the carriers should be able to offer a seat on the day you wish to travel – though perhaps not the lowest fares. If you didn't pre-book when you purchased your international ticket, check availability as soon as you arrive.

BY TRAIN

The **Konkan Railway** line runs daily express trains from Mumbai to Goa. However, these services are not always available at short notice from the booking halls at CST and Churchgate unless you've purchased an **Indrail Pass**. Don't, whatever you do, be tempted to travel "unreserved" class on any Konkan service, as the journey as far as Ratnagiri (roughly midway) is overwhelmingly crushed. There are a number of convenient overnight services (see box, p.607).

Fares range from a bargain-bucket ₹175 for basic second-class seated, to ₹320 for sleeper class, or ₹1300 for two-tier a/c. The priciest first-class tickets cost ₹2200 – roughly what you pay for a low-cost flight off peak.

BY BUS

The Mumbai–Goa bus journey ranks among the very **worst** in India. Depending on the type of bus you get and taking into account appalling road surfaces along the sinuous coastal route, fourteen to sixteen hours is a realistic estimate for the journey time.

Fares start at around ₹400 for a push-back seat on a beaten-up Kadamba (Goan government) or MSRTC coach. Tickets for these services are in great demand in season with domestic tourists, so **book in advance** at Mumbai Central. Quite a few **private overnight buses** (around a dozen daily) also run to Goa, costing from around ₹600 for no-frills buses up to ₹1000 for swisher a/c Volvo coaches with berths. Tickets are best booked at least a day in advance through the bus company, or online via ⓦ makemytrip.com. Apart from enabling you to compare services, the latter also allows you to check departure and pick-up points, which vary between operators. Few leave from south Mumbai. Among those that do is the largest operator for Goa, Paulo Travels (ⓦ paulotravels.com), whose recommended 8pm sleeper service from Dhobi Talao Junction on Fashion St (see map, p.594), is the fastest and most comfortable bus to catch, costing ₹950 single and taking just 10hr.

BY PLANE

INTERNATIONAL AIRPORT

Mumbai's busy international airport, Chhatrapati Shivaji (30km north of downtown; ⓦ csia.in), is divided into two terminals, 2B and 2C; the former hosts foreign carriers, while the latter handles exclusively Air India and Air India Express flights. All of the airlines have offices outside the main entrances.

Taxis While many of the more upmarket hotels send out courtesy coaches to pick up and drop off their guests, most people arriving in Mumbai use the pre-paid taxi desk in the arrivals hall. Fares are slightly higher than the normal meter rate, but at least you can be sure you'll be taken by the most direct route and it might save you having to haggle. It will cost ₹400 (or ₹500 a/c) to Colaba. Alternatively, if you want to book a car with driver, try Cool Cab (☎ 022 2216 4466, ⓦ citycoolcab.in) or Meru (☎ 022 4422 4422, ⓦ merucabs.com).

DOMESTIC AIRPORT

Internal flights land at Mumbai's domestic airport (26km to the north of downtown and 2km west of the international airport; ☎ 022 2626 4000; ⓦ csia.in). Terminal 1A handles Air India, while all other carriers use Terminals 1B and 1C.

Transfers If you're transferring directly from here to an

10

IN TRANSIT

If you're only passing through Mumbai between flights and need to sit out half the night, it's worth knowing that the *Leela Kempinski* and *Royal Meridien* five-stars are both a short, complimentary transfer bus ride from the international terminal at CST. Their a/c restaurants, coffee shops and bars make much more comfortable places to kill time than the departure lounge at the airport – and their toilets are in a different league.

international flight take the free "fly-bus" that shuttles every 30min between the two airports; look for the transfer counter in your transit lounge.

Information and taxis India Tourism and the MTDC both have 24hr information counters in the arrivals hall, and there's a foreign exchange counter and accommodation desk tucked away near the first-floor exit. The official "pre-paid" taxi counter on the arrivals concourse charges around ₹400 to Colaba (₹500 for a/c). For a car with driver, try Cool Cab (☎ 022 2216 4466, ⊛ citycoolcab.in) or Meru (☎ 022 4422 4422, ⊛ merucabs.com).

Domestic airlines Air India, Air India Building, Nariman Point (☎ 1800 227722); Air India Express, Air India Building, Nariman Point (☎ 022 2279 6330); GoAir (☎ 1800 222111); IndiGo Airlines, (☎ 099 1038 3838 or 1800 180 3838); Jet Airways/JetKonnect, B1, Amarchand Mansion, Ground Floor, Madam Cama Rd, Colaba (☎ 022 3989 3333); SpiceJet (☎ 1800 180 3333).

BY TRAIN

Three main rail networks service Mumbai: Western Railways, covering Gujarat, northern Madhya Pradesh and Rajasthan; Central Railways, covering Maharashtra and southern Madhya Pradesh; and the Konkan Railway, running south down the coast to Goa and beyond.

CHHATRAPATI SHIVAJI TERMINUS (CST)

Trains operating between Mumbai and most central, southern and eastern regions work out of Chhatrapati Shivaji Terminus or CST (formerly Victoria Terminus, or VT), the main railway station at the end of the Central Railway line. The station lies a 10- or 15min ride to/from Colaba; taxis wait at the busy rank outside the south exit, opposite the reservation hall.

MUMBAI CENTRAL

The terminus for Western Railway trains from northern India, Mumbai Central, is a 30min ride from Colaba; on arrival, take a taxi from the forecourt, or flag one down on the main road – it should cost around ₹250–300.

OTHER STATIONS

Some trains from south India run out of more obscure stations: Dadar is way up in the industrial suburbs; Kurla, arrival/departure point for a few trains to/from Bengaluru (Bangalore) and Kerala, is even further out, just south of

the domestic airport. From either, it's worth asking at the station when you arrive if there is another long-distance train going to Churchgate or CST (Victoria Terminus) shortly after – far better than trying to cram into either a suburban train or bus.

RESERVATIONS

The quickest and most convenient place for foreign nationals to make reservations on any of the networks is the efficient tourist counter (#14) on the first floor of the Western Railway's booking hall, next door to the Government of India tourist office in Churchgate (Mon–Fri 8am–8pm, Sat 8am–2pm; ☎ 022 2209 7577). Mumbai's other "Tourist Ticketing Facility" is on the first floor (counter #52) of the a/c Central Railway Reservation Office at CST (VT; Mon–Sat 8am–8pm, Sun 8am–2pm; ☎ 022 2262 2859). The office is on the right of the main station entrance (as you go in), just off the concourse where taxis pull up. In theory you may be required to produce a foreign currency encashment certificate or ATM slip to buy tickets here, though it's unlikely to be asked for. Tickets for seats on the Konkan Railway can be booked at either Churchgate or CST booking halls.

BY BUS

Although taxis, working from ranks immediately outside both airports and the train stations, are by far the most convenient form of onward transport, there are a number of bus services.

GOVERNMENT SERVICES

Nearly all interstate buses work from Mumbai Central Bus Stand, a stone's throw from the railway station of the same name. Government services use the main Maharashtra State Road Transport Corporation (MSRTC) stand itself. Suburban trains stop at Mumbai Central railway station opposite, but catching the suburban train out to Mumbai Central station and walking over the bridge across the main road to the bus stand is the kind of thing that only die-hards do these days.

BOOKING COUNTERS AND RESERVATIONS

States with bus company booking counters (daily 8am–8pm) here include Maharashtra, Karnataka and Goa. Few of their services compare favourably with train travel on the same routes. Reliable timetable information can be

RECOMMENDED TRAINS FROM MUMBAI

All the following trains run daily.

Destination	Name	No.	From	Departs	Duration
Aurangabad	*Tapovan Express*	#17617	CST	6.10am	7hr 5min
Bengaluru (Bangalore)	*Udyan Express*	#16529	CST	8.05am	24hr 45min
Bhuj	*Kutch Express*	#19131	Bandra	5.10pm	16hr 15min
Delhi	*Rajdhani Express*	#12951	MC	4.40pm	15hr 50min
Goa (Margao)	*Konkan– Kanya Express*	#10111	CST	11.05pm	11hr 40min
	Jan Shatabdi	#2051	Dadar	5.25am	8hr 45min
	Mangalore Express	#12133	CST	10.15pm	8hr 45min
Kochi (Cochin)	*Netravati Express* (Kurla)	#16345	LTT	11.40am	26hr 30min
Kolhapur	*Sahyadri Express*	#1023	CST	5.50pm	12hr 15min
Lonavala	*Udyan Express*	#16529	CST	8.05am	2hr 30min
Nasik	*Pushpak Express*	#12534	CST	8.20pm	3hr 30min
Neral (for Matheran)	*Deccan Express*	#11007	CST	7.10am	1hr 22min
Pune	*Udyan Express*	#16529	CST	Daily 8.05am	3hr 35min

10

difficult to obtain, reservations are not available on standard buses, and most long-haul journeys are gruelling overnighters. Among the exceptions are the deluxe buses run by MSRTC to Pune and Kolhapur; the small extra cost buys you more leg-room, fewer stops and the option of advance booking. The only problem is that most leave from the ASIAD bus stand in Dadar, or the new MSRTC stand in Thane, 30min and 60min respectively by road or rail north of Mumbai Central. Note that fares on services to popular tourist destinations such as Goa and Mahabaleshwar increase by as much as 75 percent during peak season.

PRIVATE BUSES

Private services operate from the roadside next to Mumbai Central railway station, a 2min walk west on the opposite side of busy Dr AN Marg (Lamington Rd). They cover most of the same routes as government buses and tend to be faster, more comfortable and easier to book in advance – though again, long-distance services invariably depart at night.

TIMETABLES

Timetable information is most easily researched online, via websites such as ⑩ makemytrip.com, which compare fares,

class of vehicles, journey durations, departure times and – crucially – departure points (services leave from different places and follow different routes out of the city).

Destinations The following refers only to MSRTC (government) services. For timetable information for private buses, check ⑩ makemytrip.com.

ASIAD Dadar to: Kolhapur (4 daily; 10hr); Nasik (hourly; 4–5hr); Pune (every 30min; 4hr).

Mumbai Central to: Aurangabad (2 daily; 10hr); Bengaluru (3 daily; 24hr); Bijapur (3 daily; 12hr); Goa (2 daily; 13–16hr); Mahabaleshwar (2 daily; 7hr 30min); Udaipur (1 daily; 15–16hr); Ujjain (1 daily; 16–17hr).

BY BOAT

Three companies – PNP, Maldar Catamarans and Ajanta – operate boat services from the Gateway of India to Mandawa jetty, on the far side of Mumbai harbour, from where buses shuttle to nearby Alibag, transport hub for the route southwards down the Konkan coast. Ranging from comfortable a/c catamarans (₹150) to bog-standard launches (₹100), the ferries leave roughly every hour; tickets should be purchased in advance from the PNP, Ajanta or Maldar company booths near the Gateway of India, on the north side of Shivaji Marg, next to the MTDC information counter.

GETTING AROUND

During peak hours in Mumbai **gridlock** is the norm, and you should brace yourself for long waits at junctions if you take to the roads by taxi, bus or auto. Local **trains** get there faster, but can be a real endurance test even outside rush hours.

10

BY TRAIN

Mumbai's local trains carry an estimated 6.1 million commuters each day between downtown and the sprawling suburbs in the north – half the entire passenger capacity of Indian Railways (see box, below). One line begins at CST (VT), running up the east side of the city; the other leaves Churchgate, travelling via Mumbai Central, Dadar to Santa Cruz and beyond. Services depart every few minutes from 5am until midnight, stopping at dozens of small stations. Carriages remain packed solid virtually the whole time, with passengers dangling precariously out of open doors to escape the crush, so start to make your way to the exit at least three stops before your destination. Peak hours (approximately 8.30–10am & 4–7pm) are the worst of all. Women are marginally better off in the "ladies carriages"; look for the crowd of colourful saris and *salwar kameezes* grouped at the end of the platform.

BUSES

BEST (☎022 2285 6262, ⊚bestundertaking.com) operates a bus network of labyrinthine complexity, covering every part of the city. You can check routes and bus numbers on their website; recognizing bus numbers in the street, however, can be more problematic, as numerals are written in Marathi (although in English on the sides). Avoid rush hours at all costs and aim, wherever possible, for the "Limited" ("Ltd") services, which stop less frequently. Tickets are bought from the conductor on the bus.

INFORMATION

Tourist information The best source of information in Mumbai is the excellent India Tourism (Mon–Fri 9am–6pm, Sat 9am–2pm; ☎022 2207 4333 or ☎022 2207 4334, ⊜indiatourism@mtnl.net.in) at 123 M Karve Rd, opposite Churchgate Station's east exit, with exceptionally helpful staff and lots of free maps and brochures. The Maharashtra State Tourism Development Corporation (MTDC) office is on Madam Cama Rd opposite the LIC Building at Nariman Point (Mon–Sat 9.30am–5.30pm; ☎022 2284 5678,

TAXIS AND CAR RENTAL

With rickshaws banished to the suburbs, Mumbai's ubiquitous black-and-yellow taxis are the quickest and most convenient way to nip around the city centre. In theory, all should have meters; in practice, particularly at night or early in the morning, many drivers refuse to use them. If this happens, either flag down another or haggle out a fare. As a rule of thumb, expect to be charged ₹20 for the first 1.5km and ₹12/km thereafter, plus a small sum for heavy luggage (₹5–10/article). A 25 percent supplement is levied for night journeys. The latest addition to Mumbai's hectic roads is the Cool Cab (☎022 2216 4466; ⊚citycoolcab.in), blue taxis with a/c and tinted windows; rates are around forty percent higher than in a normal cab.

CARS WITH DRIVERS

Cars can be rented per 8hr day (₹1500–1700 for a non-a/c, or 2200–2600 for a/c, depending on the car), plus ₹150/day driver allowance if the trip involves an overnight stay (the driver sleeps in the car). A maximum kilometre rate applies (usually 300km), after which there is a charge for every additional kilometre covered. A recommended travel agent who can arrange cars and drivers in Mumbai is Garha Tours & Travels (☎022 2635 0035 or ☎98670 28232, ⊜info@garhatours.com). Their office is out near the airport at 104 Atlantic Apartments, Swami Samarth Nagar, Lokhandwala Complex, Andheri (W).

⊚maharashtratourism.gov.in); staff here can reserve rooms in MTDC resorts, and also sell tickets for city sightseeing tours (see box opposite).

Listings For detailed listings, the most complete source is Mumbai's *Time Out* (⊚timeoutmumbai.net). Alternatively, check out the "Metro" page in the *Indian Express* or the "Bombay Times" section of the *Times of India*. All are available from street vendors around Colaba and downtown.

A "SUPER-DENSE" CRUSH

The suburban rail network in Mumbai is officially the busiest on the planet. No other line carries as many passengers, nor crams them into such confined spaces. At peak times, as many as 4700 people may be jammed into a nine-carriage train designed to carry 1700, resulting in what the rail company, in typically jaunty Mumbai style, refers to as "**Super-Dense Crush Load**" of 14–16 standing passengers per square metre. Not all of these actually occupy floor space, of course: ten percent will be dangling precariously out of the doors.

The busiest stretch, a 60km segment between Churchgate terminus and Virar in north Mumbai, transports nearly 900 million people each year, the highest of any rail network in the world. **Fatalities** are all too frequent: on average, six hundred die on the rail network annually (that's more than sixteen deaths per day), from falling out of the doors crossing the tracks or because they're hit by overhead cables while riding on the roof.

TOURS

A number of operators around the Gateway of India offer whistle-stop one-day city "darshan" tours by bus (around ₹175–200 non-a/c, not including admission charges) – an inexpensive but usually very rushed way to cram Mumbai's tourist highlights into a single day. These trips are pitched primarily at Indian visitors, so expect slow drives past the homes of Bollywood stars and the US$200-billion skyscraper of tycoon Mukesh Ambani (see box, p.601), as well as a crossing of the new Worli-Bandra Sea Link bridge. There are, however, some more foreigner-friendly alternatives.

The Bombay Heritage Walks ☎98218 or ☎87321, ⓦbombayheritagewalks.com. Focusing mainly on period buildings and colonial history, the excellent guided walks organized by architects Abha Bahl and Brinda Gaitonde last for 2hr and are offered mainly at weekends, though weekday evening outings can sometimes be arranged, depending on availability. Advance bookings essential.

MTDC Maharashtra Tourism's 1hr after-dark tours of downtown Mumbai's illuminated landmarks are on an open-top bus. Tickets bookable at the MTDC kiosk near the Gateway of India, which is also where they leave from. Weekends 7pm & 8.15pm; upper deck ₹150, lower deck ₹50.

Mumbai Magic ⓦmumbaimagic.com. A range of interesting walking and driving tours delving into various aspects of the city, from colonial architecture to Jewish heritage.

Reality Tours and Travels ⓦrealitytoursandtravel .com. Memorable trips out to the huge Dharavi shantytown (see box, p.600).

10

ACCOMMODATION

Finding **accommodation** at the right price when you arrive in Mumbai can be a real problem. Budget travellers, in particular, can expect a hard time finding decent but affordable accommodation. The best low-cost places tend to fill up days or weeks in advance, so you should book well ahead to avoid a stressful, sweaty room hunt. Tariffs in mid-range and upmarket places are also especially high for India. State-imposed **luxury tax** (currently ten percent), and **service charges** levied by the hotel itself further bump up bills; both these add-ons are included in the prices quoted in the following reviews. A short ride from the railway stations **Colaba** makes a handy base, and is where the majority of foreign visitors head first. The streets around the Gateway of India are chock-full of accommodation, and the area also offers more in the way of food and entertainment than neighbouring districts. At the western edge of the downtown area, swanky **Marine Drive** (officially Netaji Subhash Chandra Marg) is lined with four- and five-star hotels taking advantage of the panoramic views over Back Bay and the easy access to the city's commercial heart.

COLABA AND KALA GHODA

Aga Bheg's & Hotel Kishan Ground, 2nd & 3rd floor, Shirin Manzil, Walton Rd ☎022 2284 2227; map p.589. Muslim-run pair of budget guesthouses on different floors of the same building. Their differently priced rooms (₹1500–3000) are nice and clean, some very jazzily decorated. A/c costs ₹350 extra. **₹1500**

Ascot 38 Garden Rd ☎022 6638 5566, ⓦascothotel .com; map p.589. One of the oldest and most comfortable small hotels in Mumbai, updated with contemporary glass-and-marble designer interiors and spacious modern rooms. Their Deluxe rooms (₹8050) are twice the size of the Superiors. **₹7700**

Bentley's 17 Oliver Rd ☎022 2284 1474, ⓦbentleyshotel.com; map p.589. Dependable old Parsi-owned favourite in five different colonial tenements, all on leafy backstreets. Rooms (₹1500–3000, with optional a/c for ₹350 extra) are quiet, secure and spacious, if a little worn, though the overall shabbiness isn't compensated for by the rates, which are higher than you'd expect for the level of comfort. **₹1500**

Godwin Jasmine Building, 41 Garden Rd ☎022 2287 2050, ⓦmumbainet.com/hotels/godwin; map p.589. Smart three-star with large, international-standard rooms and great views from upper floors and rooftop garden (ask for #804, #805 or #806). Not quite in the same league as the nearby (and comparably priced) *Ascot* but a sound choice nonetheless. **₹7500**

Gordon House 5 Battery St ☎022 2289 4400, ⓦghhotel.com; map p.589. Chic designer boutique place behind the Regal cinema. Each floor has a differnt theme: "Scandinavian" (the easiest to live with), "Mediterranean" and "Country". Discounts at weekends. **₹10,000**

Lawrence 3rd floor, 33 Sri Sai Baba Marg (Rope Walk Lane), off K Dubash Marg, behind TGI's ☎022 2284 3618 or ☎6633 6107; map p.589. Close to the Jehangir Art Gallery, this is arguably south Mumbai's best rock-bottom choice, with five well-scrubbed doubles (plus two singles and two triples) with fans, and not-so-clean shared shower-toilets; breakfast included. Be warned though, it's a long slog up five floors of filthy wooden steps if the (decrepit) lift isn't working. Advance booking essential. **₹700**

10

Moti International 10 Best Marg ☎ 022 2202 1654, ✉ hotelmotiinternational@yahoo.co.in; map p.589. Quiet and friendly hotel in a characterful old colonial building. Rooms are cosy and clean; most (but not all) have windows. All come with a/c, fridge, TV and complimentary soap and towels. A/c costs ₹700 extra. Good value. ₹2500

Red Shield Red Shield House, 30 Boram Behram (Mereweather) Rd, near the Taj hotel ☎ 022 2284 1824, ✉ redshield@vsnl.net; map p.589. Ultra-basic bunk beds in cramped, stuffy dorms (lockers available), or larger good-value doubles. Rates include breakfast and lunch, served in a sociable canteen. Maximum one-week stay. Dorm ₹250, double ₹850

Sea Shore 4th floor, 1-49 Kamal Mansion, Arthur Bunder Rd ☎ 022 2287 4237; map p.589. Among the best budget deals in Colaba. The sea-facing rooms with windows are much nicer than the airless cells on the other side. Friendly management and free, safe baggage store. Non-attached bath only. ₹1000

Sea Palace Kerawalla Chambers, 26 PJ Ramchandani Marg (Apollo Bunder) ☎ 022 2284 1828, ⌨ seapalacehotel.net; map p.589. Best of the three mid-range hotels at the quiet end of the harbour front, although the rooms (₹6000–8500), come as a bit of a disappointment for the price, with old-fashioned decor and worn furnishings. All are a/c but sea views cost extra. Breakfast and light meals are served on a sunny terrace at the front. ₹6000

Strand PJ Kerawalla Chambers, Ramchandani Marg (Apollo Bunder) ☎ 022 2288 2222, ⌨ hotelstrand.com; map p.589. Popular mid-scale option on the seafront, with good harbour views from the pricier rooms. It's nicely situated and efficiently run, but very dowdy, with smudged walls, tired beige colour schemes, worn carpets and cheap mattresses. ₹5000

Taj Mahal Palace and Tower PJ Ramchandani Marg ☎ 022 6665 3366, ⌨ tajhotels.com; map p.589. Perhaps India's most famous hotel and the haunt of Mumbai's *beau monde*, with 546 luxury rooms, shopping arcades, a huge outdoor pool and a good spread of bars and restaurants. The hotel was at the centre of the terrorist attacks of November 2008 (see p.590), but reopened within a month, and has now been restored to its former glory after a US$40-million refit. Prices start from around US$400 in the Tower; considerably more in the Palace. ₹20,000

Vivanta By Taj 90 Cuffe Parade ☎ 022 6665 0808, ⌨ tajhotels.com; map p.587. Modern, business-oriented five-star occupying a seventeen-floor skyscraper just south of Colaba. A much more competitively priced option than its sister concern, the *Taj Mahal Palace and Tower*, though lacking old-world style and atmosphere. There is a large outdoor pool and an adjacent gym and steam room. ₹9000

★ **YWCA** 18 Madam Cama Rd ☎ 022 2202 5053, ✉ ywcaic@mtnl.net.in; map p.589. Relaxing, secure and quiet hostel (open to men as well as women) with spotless attached rooms. Rates include breakfast and a generous buffet dinner – a bargain for south Mumbai. Advance booking online is obligatory. ₹3150

MARINE DRIVE

Ambassador VN Rd ☎ 022 2204 1131, ⌨ ambassador india.com; map p.594. Landmark four-star with smart (albeit bland) modern rooms and a choice location close to sea and cafes. The revolving restaurant on the top floor (closed at the time of writing pending renovation) is another bonus. Double rooms offer the most competitively priced option in this bracket. ₹7000

Astoria Jamshedji Tata ☎ 022 6654 1234, ⌨ astoriamumbai.com; map p.594. Smart business hotel in refurbished 1930s Art Deco building near the Eros cinema. The rooms are nowhere near as ritzy as the lobby but offer good value this close to the centre. ₹7000

Bentley 3rd floor, Krishna Mahal, Marine Drive ☎ 022 2281 5244; map p.594. Not to be confused with *Bentley's* in Colaba (see p.609), this small, friendly guesthouse is across town on the corner of D Rd/Marine Drive, near the cricket stadium. The marble-lined a/c rooms are clean and comfortable for the price, though most share shower-toilets. Rates include breakfast. ₹2250

★ **Chateau Windsor** 5th floor, 86 Veer Nariman Rd ☎ 022 6622 4455, ⌨ chateauwindsor.com; map p.594. Impeccably neat and central, with unfailingly polite staff and a selection of attractively renovated rooms – many of them quaintly old-fashioned. Their "penthouse" option on the sixth floor is particularly nice, comprising an individual bungalow surrounded by pot plants. Very popular, so reserve well in advance. ₹5500

Intercontinental 135 Marine Drive ☎ 022 3987 9999, ⌨ mumbai.intercontinental.com; map p.594. Ultra-chic boutique hotel whose rooms have huge sea-facing windows and state-of-the-art gadgets (42-inch plasma screens and DVD players to name but two), while the rooftop pool, bars and restaurants, including the *Dome* (see p.616) rank among Mumbai's most fashionable. ₹12,000

Marine Plaza 29 Marine Drive ☎ 022 2285 1212, ⌨ hotelmarineplaza.com; map p.594. Ritzy but small luxury hotel on the seafront, with the usual five-star facilities and a (pseudo) Art Deco atrium lobby topped by a glass-bottomed rooftop pool. ₹10,000

Oberoi Nariman Point ☎ 022 2232 5757, ⌨ oberoihotels.com; map p.587. Enjoying a prime spot overlooking Back Bay, this hotel is traditionally the first choice of business travellers to the city – lacking the heritage character of the *Taj Mahal Palace and Tower*, but with fine views from its soaring tower and an atmosphere of glittering opulence throughout. It was severely damaged during the 2008 terror attacks, in which 32 staff and guests lost their lives, but has been fully renovated since. ₹34,000

Sea Green/Sea Green South 145 Marine Drive ☎ 022 6633 6525, ⓦ seagreenhotel.com & 145-A Marine Drive ☎ 022 6633 6535, ⓦ seagreensouth.com; map p.594. Jointly owned and enduringly popular pair of seafront hotels. Decor is old-fashioned going on shabby, and rates are quite high, although the sweeping bay views from front-facing rooms partly compensate. ₹4700

Trident Nariman Point (formerly the Hilton Towers) Nariman Point ☎ 022 6632 4343, ⓦ tridenthotels.com; map p.587. Sitting next to the *Oberoi* (see opposite) on Nariman Point, the *Trident* suffered slight damage during the 2008 attacks but reopened shortly afterwards. Currently the city's premier business hotel, with full five-star facilities and trimmings, including sea views from its pool. ₹9000

AROUND CHHATRAPATI SHIVAJI (VICTORIA) TERMINUS

City Palace 121 City Terrace ☎ 022 2261 5515, ⓦ hotelcitypalace.net; map p.594. Large and popular hotel bang opposite the station. Economy rooms are tiny and windowless (almost like in a capsule hotel), but have a/c and are perfectly clean. Deluxe rooms higher up the building are larger and have bird's-eye views. ₹3750

Grand 17 Shri SR Marg, Ballard Estate ☎ 022 6658 0506, ⓦ grandhotelbombay.com; map p.594. Characterful British-era three-star out near the old docks, nicely refurbished and with well-equipped rooms at competitive rates. ₹6500

Oasis 276 Shahid Bhagat Singh Marg ☎ 022 3022 7886, ⓦ hoteloasisindia.in; map p.594. Very well placed for CST station, and the best-value budget option in this area: rooms have good beds, clean linen and TVs. It's worth splashing out on a top-floor "deluxe" room as they offer better views. A/c costs ₹800 extra. ₹1400

★ **Residency** 26 Rustom Sidhwa Marg, off DN Rd ☎ 022 2262 5525, ⓦ residencyhotel.com; map p.594. Great little mid-range hotel, close to the best shopping areas. Its variously priced rooms (all with safe and wi-fi) offer unbeatable value, especially the no-frills "standard" options. Though some of the rooms are cramped and lacking external windows, they're well furnished and clean, and the staff are courteous. Book at least a fortnight in advance. ₹3500

JUHU AND AROUND THE AIRPORTS

★ **Accord** 32 Jawaharlal Nehru Rd, Near Canara Bank, Santa Cruz (East) ☎ 022 2611 0560, ⓦ hotelaccordindia.com; map p.602. If all you want is a simple, inexpensive, clean, secure, attached room for the night within easy reach of the airport, you won't do better than this place. Don't expect a palace: the decor is faded and the location, amid a tangle of busy roads and

overpasses, is dreadful; but they get the basics right. The windows are well soundproofed; staff are courteous; breakfast is included; and there's a 24hr complimentary transfer car to or from the airport, just 15min away. ₹3500

Hyatt Regency Airport Rd, Andheri (East) ☎ 022 6696 1234, ⓦ mumbai.regency.hyatt.com; map p.602. Ancient Hindu precepts on architecture and design were incorporated into this ultra-luxurious five-star, right next to the airport. The results are impressive, and a notch more stylish than the competition, with floor-to-ceiling windows, rain showers and dark marble floors. ₹12,000

ISKCON Guesthouse Juhu Church Rd, Juhu ☎ 022 2620 6860, ⓦ iskconmumbai.com (follow the "Guest House" link under "Temple" on the drop-down menu); map p.602. Idiosyncratic hotel run by the International Society for Krishna Consciousness. Rooms (some with a/c, ₹1500 extra) are very large and impeccably clean and comfortable for the price, though certain restrictions apply (no alcohol, meat or caffeine may be consumed on the premises). Forty days' advance booking is recommended. ₹3500

ITC Maratha Sahar Rd, Andheri (East) ☎ 022 28303030, ⓦ itchotels.in; map p.602. This palatial luxury hotel close to the airport has made an attempt to infuse some Maharashtra character into its decor, and holds a particularly pleasant pool in its central courtyard. The real selling point here, however, is a clutch of terrific Indian restaurants nearby. ₹8500

JW Marriott Juhu Tara Rd, Juhu ☎ 022 6693 3000, ⓦ marriott.com; map p.602. Palatial five-star complex with five opulent restaurants, three pools (one of them filled with treated salt water), a top-notch spa and blocks of luxury rooms looking through landscaped grounds to the beach. ₹10,000

Lotus Suites Andheri Kurla Rd, International Airport Zone, Andheri (East) ☎ 022 2827 0707, ⓦ lotussuites .com; map p.602. An "Eco-Four-Star at Three-Star prices" is how this environment-friendly hotel describes itself, designed using energy-saving materials and with "green" trimmings such as jute slippers and recycling bins in the rooms. A very comfortable option for the price. ₹6200

Midland Jawaharlal Nehru Rd, Santa Cruz (East) ☎ 022 2611 0414, ⓦ hotelmidland.com; map p.602. Dependable two-star with well-furnished twin-bedded rooms, just a short ride from the airport. It's right in front of the *Accord* (see above) but not as good value. Courtesy bus and breakfast Included in the price. ₹5200

The Orchid 70-C Nehru Rd, Vile Parle (East) ☎ 022 2616 4040, ⓦ orchidhotel.com; map p.602. Award-winning "Eco-Five-Star", built with organic and recycled materials and using low-toxin paints. Every effort is made to minimize waste of natural resources, with a water-recycling plant and "zero garbage" policy. ₹9000

10

EATING

Mumbai is crammed with interesting **places to eat**, from glamorous rooftop lounge bars to hole-in-the-wall kebab shops. The cafés, bars and restaurants of **Colaba** encompass just about the full gamut of possibilities, while a short walk or taxi ride north, **Kala Ghoda** and **Fort** are home to some of the best cafés and restaurants in the city, including its last traditional Parsi diners, whose menus (and sometimes decor as well) have changed little in generations. Watch out for the service charges levied on your bill by some of the more expensive places.

10

COLABA

All Stir Fry Gordon House Hotel; map p.589. Cool modern restaurant specializing in build-your-own meals using a selection of fresh veg, meat, fish, noodles and sauces, flash-cooked in a wok in front of you. The satay and dim sum are particularly good. ₹550 for unlimited servings. Daily 12.30–3pm & 7.30–11pm.

Bademiya Behind the Taj Mahal Palace & Tower on Tulloch Rd; map p.589. Legendary Colaba kebab-wallah serving delicious flame-grilled chicken, mutton and fish steaks (all at ₹120–150), as well as veg alternatives (₹90), wrapped in paper-thin, piping hot *rotis*, from benches on the sidewalk. Families from uptown drive here on weekends, eating on their car bonnets, but there are also little tables and chairs if you don't fancy a takeaway. Daily 6.30pm–late.

Busaba 4 Mandlik Marg ☎022 2204 3769, ⓦbusaba .net; map p.589. Sophisticated bar-restaurant specializing in Far Eastern cuisine (₹450–600). Thai, Korean, Vietnamese and Tibetan staples run alongside exotic salads. The big signature dish here, however, is Burmese *kaukswe*: a mound of noodles in a smooth, rich, coconut broth, topped with tender meat, fresh ginger, lime, fried onions and crispy wonton noodles. One of *the* places the city's high rollers like to pose (if they can't get a table at *Indigo* next door). Daily noon–3pm & 6.30pm–12.30am.

Café Samovar Jehangir Art Gallery, MG Rd ☎022 2284 8000; map p.589. Very pleasant and peaceful semi-alfresco café opening onto the museum gardens. Under swirling paddle fans and pieces of Indian folk art, you can chose from a wide array of à la carte options (prawn curry, *roti* kebabs and dhansak; most around ₹175–250) and great salads (₹125–150), with chilled guava juice or beer. Daily except Sun 11am–7.30pm.

Churchill 103 Colaba Causeway; map p.589. Tiny a/c Parsi diner, with a vast choice of filling, Continental comfort food, from pizza to pasta and burgers – ideal if you've had your fill of spicy food. For dessert or an afternoon treat, check the famous *Churchill* fridge for freshly baked treats such as gooey chocolate cake or blueberry cheesecake. No alcohol, no washrooms. Most mains ₹300–400. Daily 11am–11pm.

Indigo 4 Mandlik Marg ☎022 6636 8999, ⓦfoodindigo.com; map p.589. One of the city's most fashionable restaurants, for once deserving of the hype, and specializing in superb international and modern European cooking with a gourmet Indian twist (Kerala oysters with saffron ravioli, for example). Mains from around RS600–750; wine prices are astronomical. Count on US$50–60/head for three courses. Reservations essential. Daily noon–3pm & 7–11.45pm.

Indigo Deli Ground Floor, Pheroze Building, Chattrapati Shivaji Maharishi Marg ☎022 6655 1010; map p.589. This much loved gastro café-restaurant is a stalwart of the south Mumbai scene thanks to its menu of Continental comfort foods and NY deli-style staples – from burgers and hot dogs to thin-crust pizzas and perfect steak-frites – served in sleek designer comfort. Pick of the all-day breakfast selection is the chef's special "eggs-on-beach benedict'" where the eggs come on crab cakes instead of muffins. For dessert, try the organic lime pie, or croissant bread pudding with brandy sauce. Most mains ₹500–850. Daily 9am–12.30am.

Kamat Colaba Causeway; map p.589. Friendly little restaurant serving unquestionably the best south Indian breakfasts in the area, as well as the usual range of southern snacks (*iddli*, *vada*, *sambar*), delicious spring dosas and (limited) thalis for ₹85–160. Daily 8.30am–9.30pm.

STREET FOOD

Mumbai is renowned for distinctive street foods – especially **bhel puri**, a quintessentially Mumbai masala mixture of puffed rice, deep-fried vermicelli, potato, crunchy *puri* pieces, chilli paste, tamarind water, chopped onions and coriander. More hygienic, but no less ubiquitous, is **pao bhaji**, a round Portuguese-style bread roll served on a tin plate with griddle-fried, spicy vegetable stew, and **kanji vada**, savoury doughnuts soaked in fermented mustard and chilli sauce. And if all that doesn't appeal, a pit-stop at one of the city's hundreds of **juice bars** probably will. There's no better way to beat the sticky heat than with a glass of cool milk shaken with fresh pineapple, mango, banana, *chikoo* (small brown fruit that tastes like a sweet pear) or custard apple. Just make sure they hold on the ice – which may be made with untreated water.

★ **Konkan Café** Vivanta By Taj Hotel, Cuffe Parade ☏ 022 6665 0808; map p.587. Just the place to push the boat out: a sophisticated five-star hotel restaurant, done up in earthy terracotta red and banana-leaf green hues in homage to a Mangalorean home. They serve fine regional cuisine from coastal Maharashtra, Goa, Karnataka and Kerala. You can choose from their thali platters (₹1000–1500) or go à la carte: butter-pepper-garlic crab is to die for. Quite simply some of the most mouthwatering south Indian food you'll ever eat. Daily noon–3.30pm & 6.30–11.30pm.

Leopold's Colaba Causeway; map p.589. A Mumbai institution that played a starring role in Gregory David Roberts' *Shantaram*, *Leopold's* is the number-one hangout for India-weary Western travellers, who continue to cram onto its small tables for bland, overpriced Indian, Continental and Chinese tourist around food – despite (or perhaps because of) the fact that the café was one of the leading targets of the 2008 terror attacks (staff will show you the bullet holes in the walls, now discreetly hidden behind pictures). Expect to queue. Mains ₹250–400; beer ₹225. Daily 7am–12.30am.

Olympia Coffee House Colaba Causeway; map p.589. *Fin-de-siècle* Irani café with marble tabletops, wooden wall panels, fancy mirrors and a mezzanine floor for women. Waiters in Peshwari caps and *salwar kameezes* serve melt-in-the-mouth kebabs and delicious curd-based dips. It gets packed out at breakfast time for cholesterol-packed *masala kheema* (fried mutton mince), which regulars wash down with bright orange chai. A quintessential (and inexpensive) Bombay experience. Mains ₹75–100. Daily 8am–11pm.

The Sea Lounge Taj Mahal Palace and Tower; map p.589. Atmospheric 1930s-style lounge café on the first floor of the *Taj*, with fine Gateway and harbour views – good for High Tea (from around ₹750) or a decadent breakfast (₹1000). Daily 7am–midnight.

KALA GHODA

Chetana 34K Dubhash Marg, ☏ 022 2284 4968, ⓦ chetana.com; map p.587. Sumptuous pure-veg thalis (Maharashtran, Rajasthani or Gujarati, with a healthy low-calorie option at lunchtime; ₹350–440) served in a mellow, Indian-style interior (a/c) with booths and traditional art on the walls. You won't find better *desi* cooking at this price anywhere else in south Mumbai. Daily 12.30–3.30pm & 7.30–11.30pm.

Kala Godha Café 10 Rope Walk Lane ☏ 022 2263 3866, ⓦ kgcafe.in; map p.589. Tucked away up a narrow backline, this tiny café makes a hip little pit stop if you're visiting the nearby museums. High, whitewashed walls, long skylights and wood benches give a feeling of space even though it's pint-sized. The coffee and teas are first rate, and they do freshly baked light bites, sandwiches (₹100–200), salads (₹220–385), soups, waffles and fruit sundaes (₹100–200), as well as more filling main meals after 7.30pm. Free wi-fi (except between 12.30 and 3.30pm). Daily 8.30am–11.45pm.

★ **Khyber** 145 MG Rd, opposite Jehangir Art Gallery ☏ 022 2267 3227, ⓦ khyberrestaurant.com; map p.589. You enter this romantic Mughlai restaurant through a finely carved, cusp-arched sandstone facade, and the interior is no less enchanting. The cuisine is "Northwest Frontier" style: rich, creamy curries made with sublime blends of spices, and choice cuts of seafood, chicken or mutton kebabs flame-grilled or braised in traditional *tava* pans. Mains ₹350–450. Daily noon–3pm & 6.30–11pm.

The Pantry Yeshwant Chambers, Ground Floor, Military Square Lane ☏ 022 2267 8901; map p.589. A great option for a heat-beating light bite or gourmet brunch: with its cement floors, recycled Burmese hardwood table tops, white walls and dabs of pastel colour, the café has a fresh, airy feel and a menu featuring Continental crowd pleasers such as quiche (₹250), gorgonzola and apple sandwiches (₹200) and red-millet pancakes with strawberry compote (₹125). Also freshly baked pastries and flourless chocolate cake (70percent cocoa!). Daily 8.30am–11.30pm.

Trishna 7 Sai Baba Marg (Ropewalk Lane), Kala Ghoda ☏ 022 2261 4991, ⓦ trishna.co.in; map p.589. Visiting dignitaries and local celebs, from the President of Greece to Bollywood stars, have eaten in this dimly lit Mangalorean. There are wonderful fish dishes in every sauce going, including the signature butter-pepper-garlic crab (around ₹900–1250) and superb pomfret stuffed with green masala (₹650), plus cheaper north Indian standards. Very small, so book in advance. Mon–Sat noon–3.30pm & 6.30pm–midnight; Sun noon–3.30pm and 7.30pm–midnight.

CHURCHGATE AND FORT

Apoorva SA Brelvi Rd ☏ 022 2287 0335; map p.594. Popular Mangalorean, hidden up a side street off Horniman Circle (look for the tree trunk wrapped with fairy lights). The cooking is authentic and the seafood – simmered in spicy coconut-based gravies – comes fresh off the boat each day. Try their definitive Bombay duck, *surmai* (kingfish) in coconut gravy or delicious prawn *gassi*, served with perfect *sanna* and *appams*. Mains ₹250–650. Daily noon–3.30pm & 6.30pm–1.30am.

★ **Britannia & Co** Shri SR Marg, Ballard Estate; map p.594. Quirky little Parsi restaurant, famous as much for its quaint period atmosphere as for its wholesome Irani food. Most people come for the mouth-watering berry pulao (chicken, mutton or vegetable), made with deliciously tart dried berries imported from Tehran (₹300, but portions are gigantic). For afters, there's the house caramel custard. One of the city's unmissable eating experiences. Open Daily 11.30am–3.30pm.

10

10

Ideal Corner 12 F/G Hornby View, Gunbow St ☎022 2262 1930; map p.594. Another Parsi café with a cult following, dishing up delicious home-made specialities like *kchchidi* prawn, lamb or veg dhansak, chicken *farcha* and exceptional *lagan* custard – a Zoroastrian take on the classic British pud, flavoured with rose water and cardamom. Most mains ₹100–150. Mon–Sat 9am–4.30pm.

Koh Intercontinental Marine Drive, 135 Marine Drive ☎000 3987 9999, ⊛mumbai.interncontinental.com; map p.594. Magnificent Thai cuisine, devised by celeb chef Ian Kittichai, and served against a backdrop of chic contemporary designer decor. Lovers of sustainably sourced cooking should stay at home: most of the ingredients are flown in daily from far afield, from the Japanese white fish to Chilean sea bass. Count on ₹2000 for three courses. Reservations essential, even on weekdays. Daily 12.30pm–3pm & 7.30pm–midnight.

★ **Mahesh Lunch Home** 8-B Cawasji Patel St ☎022 2287 0938, ⊛maheshlunchhome.com; map p.594. Much like *Trishna* (see p.613) only a good bit cheaper and less touristy, this Mangalorean diner in the depths of Fort is famous across the city for its flavoursome seafood specialities, especially the Koliwada prawns, pomfret *gassi* (₹530) and fish curry (₹250), and the jumbo butter-garlic crab, which are sold by weight. Reservations recommended on weekends. Mon–Sat 11.30am–4pm & 6pm–midnight, Sun 7pm–midnight.

Pizza By the Bay Soona Mahal, 143 Marine Drive ☎022 2284 3646, ⊛pizzabythebay.in; map p.594. This bustling, high-end Italian on the corner of VN Rd and Marine Drive does a brisk trade in authentic Neapolitan pasta (₹400), pizza (₹350–500) and freshly baked treats, as well as European-style breakfasts. Reserve ahead for a table next to the window for breezy bay views. Long waits on weekends are the norm, even if you book. Count on spending upwards of ₹1000 for three courses. Daily 8.30am–11.30pm.

CHOWPATTY

Bachelorr's Juice House Chowpatty Sea Face, opposite Birla Krida Kendra, near Charni Rd station ☎022 2368 1408; map p.587. There's no better antidote to the brouhaha of the nearby beach than a "Strawberry Cream" at *Bachelorr's* – a tall milkshake crammed with whipped cream and pieces of fresh strawberry, which they do in any number of chocolate-based variations. No points for ambience. Daily 9am–midnight.

Cream Centre Fulchand Niwas 25/B, Chowpatty Sea Face ☎022 2367 9222; map p.587. This immaculately clean, pure-veg fast food joint facing Chowpatty Beach serves a huge range of Indian snacks, but the best, by far, is their famous *channa batura* (₹150) – a frisbee-sized pillow of deep-fried *puri*, which you poke with your finger to deflate

and use to mop up a bowl of creamy masala chickpeas, diced potatoes and onions. Daily noon–11.30pm.

Crystal 19 Chowpatty Sea Face, nr Wilson College; map p.587. Punjabis and lovers of north Indian home cooking travel here from across the city to eat *dhaba*-style dhal *makhani*, *alu jeera* and other spicy vegetarian dishes, served from a soot-blackened kitchen. For dessert, there's divine *kheer* (cardamon-flavoured rice pudding) and *amras* (mango pulp). A great little budget option if you're not phased by the grime, with most mains under ₹100. Daily noon–11pm.

CRAWFORD MARKET AND THE CENTRAL BAZAARS

Badshah Juice and Snack Bar Opposite Crawford Market, Lokmanya Tilak Rd; map p.587. Delicious kulfi, and dozens of freshly squeezed fruit juices, though most locals come for the *faloodas* – an incomparable, quintessentially Mumbai mix of vermicelli, basil seeds and tapioca pearls steeped in milk, ice cream and rose syrup. The ideal place to round off a trip to the market. Daily 9am–10pm.

★ **Joshi Club** 31-A Narottamwadi, Kalbadevi Rd ☎022 2205 8089; map p.594. Also known as *The Friends Union Joshi Club*, this eccentric thali canteen serves what many aficionados regard as the most genuine and tasty Gujarati-Marwari meals in the city, on unpromising Formica tables against a backdrop of grubby walls. ₹135 buys you unlimited portions of four vegetable dishes, dhal and up to four different kinds of bread, with all the trimmings (and banana custard). Daily 11am–3pm & 7–10pm.

Rajdhani Sheikh Memon St; map p.587. Approaching from Crawford Market, cross the road by the entrance and turn right past the Lokmanya Tilak Marg Police Booth Outstanding, eat-till-you-burst Gujarati thali joint. Very cramped and a notch pricier than average (₹300, or ₹349 for the "Special" Sun lunch), but the quality is high. It's on the road leading to the Jama Masjid. A dozen branches have opened across the city in recent years but this is the original and best. Mon–Sat noon–3pm & 6.30–11pm, Sun noon–3pm.

THE NORTHERN SUBURBS

Bong Bong 5 Silver Croft CHS, corner of 16th Rd and 33rd Rd, Bandra West ☎022 6555 5567; map p.602. The best of a select band of authentic Bengali restaurants in the suburbs, catering mainly for homesick movie-makers. Decorated with memorabilia, rickshaw murals and old photographs of Kolkata, it has cosy and sociable vibe and serves food packed with astounding flavours. Mains from ₹200–400. Daily 11.30am–12.30am.

★ **Dakshin Coastal** ITC Maratha, Sahar Rd, near the airport ☎022 2830 3030; map p.602. As far a cry from your regular *udipi* joint as it's possible to imagine, *Dakshin Coastal* showcases the sublime and varied cuisine of the south Indian shoreline. From the sun-dried chillis soaked in buttermilk appetizer to main-course delights such as Keralan-style prawns delicately cooked with raw mango and fresh coconut, everything is packed with intense flavours and exquisitely presented. Count on ₹1500–1700/head for the works. Mon–Sat 7–11.45pm; Sun 12.30–2.45pm.

★ **Dum Pukt** ITC Maratha, Sahar Rd, near the airport ITC Maratha, Sahar Rd ☎ 022 2830 3030; map p.602. One of few kitchens in India that faithfully recreates the cuisine of the Muslim Nawabs of Hyerabad and Awadh, where chefs developed a technique of slow cooking known as *dum*. If you've a monster appetite, go for the *raan-e-dum pukht* – a leg of marinated lamb stuffed with spices, baked in dough and finished with a shell of dried fruit, coconut and oven juices. The decor's as regal as the cooking. Count on ₹1700–2000/head for three courses. Daily 7–11.45pm.

Govinda's ISKCON Hare Krishna Mandir, Juhu Tara Rd, Juhu ☎ 022 2620 0337; map p.602. Sumptuous vegetarian thalis of sattvic cooking (no garlic or onions). Everything's been ritually offered to Krishna before being served, guaranteeing what the management describe as a "transcendental dining experience". At ₹230/head, it's certainly great value for Mumbai and there's often live *bhajan* singing. Daily noon–3pm & 6.30–9.30pm.

Pali Bhavan 10 Adarsh Nagar, Pali Naka, Near Costa Coffee, Bandra (West) ☎ 022 2651 9400; map p.602. An aura of Old India hangs over this quirkily styled restaurant up in Bandra, which delights as much for its decor of sepia photos and antique woodwork as its classy pan-Indian cuisine. The huge menu features dishes from across the country, given classy gourmet twists. Daily noon– 3.30pm & 7pm–1am.

Sufra's Carter Rd, Bandra (West) ☎ 022 2649 7259; map p.602. Handily situated opposite the Carter Rd promenade, *Sufra's* is a popular little Middle Eastern takeaway serving delicious *shawarmas* (₹150), stuffed with succulent chicken pieces oozing garlic sauce, in addition to so-so falafels and kebabs. You can eat on their little mezzanine, but most people head across the road to munch their wraps on the seafront. For dessert, they do scrumptious *ashtalieh* (₹90), a Lebanese sweet rice pudding with hints of rose water. Daily 11.30am–midnight.

DRINKING

Mumbaikars have an unusually easy-going attitude to alcohol; popping into a **bar** for a beer is very much accepted (for men at least), even at lunchtime. **Colaba Causeway** is the focus of the travellers' and local students' social scene but to sample the cutting edge of the city's nightlife, you'll have to venture to the **suburbs**, where the trendiest places have turned the city's draconian licensing laws to their advantage by serving gourmet food to complement the range of imported beers, wines and cocktails.

★ **AER** Four Seasons Hotel, 114 Dr E Moses Rd, Worli ☎ 022 2481 8000, ⬚ fourseasons.com; map p.586. With its all-white, Miami-vice-style jigsaw furniture and astounding panoramic views over the city, this alfresco bar on the 34th floor of a luxury skyscraper hotel has become the poster boy of Mumbai's lounge bars, even out-blinging the *Dome* on Marine Drive. Cocktails and champagne are half price between 5.30 and 8.30pm. Otherwise, it's Moet Chandon at ₹500/glass (or Kingfishers at a more reasonable ₹350). ₹1500 admission from 8pm Thurs–Sat. Daily 5.30pm–1.30am.

Aurus Nichani House, Juhu Tara Rd, Juhu ☎ 022 6710 6666, ⬚ dishhospitality.com; map p.602. Sexy beachside hangout, boasting a bar-restaurant inside and a relaxing terrace overlooking Juhu Beach, and a Goa-style soundtrack of techno/trance/house. Boasts its fair share of Bombabes and celebs, though the entry policy is less snooty than other places hereabouts. Sunday sunset time is their big night, when you'll be lucky to be let in unless you have contacts. Cover charge (redeemable against drinks or food) ₹2500. Daily 7.30pm–1.30am.

Bonobo 1 Kennilworth Phase II, 2nd Floor, off Linking Rd, Bandra ☎ 022 2605 5050; map p.602. Bonobo is the current high court of cool for the suburban art clique, hosting live gigs and DJ sets on Fridays and Saturdays in a (tiny) a/c

---

PERFORMING ARTS IN MUMBAI

Mumbai is a major centre for traditional **performing arts**, attracting the finest **Indian classical musicians** and **dancers** from all over the country. Frequent concerts and recitals are staged at venues such as Bharatiya Vidya Bhavan, KM Munshi Marg (☎ 022 2363 0224), the headquarters of the international cultural (Hindu) organization, and the National Centre for the Performing Arts, Nariman Point (NCPA; ⬚ ncpamumbai.com).

For **drama**, head out to the Prithvi Theatre (☎ 022 2614 9546, ⬚ prithvitheatre.org) on Juhu Church Road, a small but lively venue focusing mainly on Hindi-language theatre, along with some English productions.

10

performance space. A balmy rooftop bar soaks up the overspill, and doubles as a gastro diner where you can steel yourself for the night ahead with fabulous wild mushroom and truffle mascarpone risotto (₹550). Look out for much-acclaimed monthly "Wobble" night, mixing heavy drum 'n' bass and dubstep. Drinks ₹250–450. Daily 5.30pm–1.30am.

★ **Café Marina** Sea Palace Hotel Kerawalla Chambers, Apollo Bunder, Colaba; map p.589. If lounge-resto isn't your thing, and all you want is a reasonably priced cold beer, and something tasty to munch while savouring an expansive view, this place ticks all the boxes. Overlooking the harbour from a great rooftop vantage point, it offers local and imported bottled beers from ₹250–450. Daily 8.30am–11.30pm.

Café Mondegar Colaba Causeway; map p.589. Draught and bottled beer (₹150–350) and deliciously fruity cocktails are served in this small café-bar. The atmosphere is very relaxed, the music on the famous jukebox tends towards cheesy rock classics and the clientele is a mix of Westerners and local students; murals by a famous Goan cartoonist give the place a cheerful ambience. Daily 8.30am–1.30pm.

Cool Chef Café Thadani House, 329/A Worli Village, Worli Sea Face, off the Bandra–Worli Sea Link, near the Indian Coast Guard office ☎ 022 2430 1127, ⓦ coolchefcafe.com; map p.602. Located in a grubby, downbeat backstreet across the water from Bandra, this antique bungalow is the hub of Mumbai's nascent alternative scene. Dubstep DJs, crowd-funded indie bands, occasional karaoke, Grime Riot discos and street dance crews create a house party vibe, with a weird edge. Admission prices vary from ₹300–500 depending on the acts. Daily noon–1.30am.

The Dome Hotel InterContinental, 135 Marine Drive; map p.594. After **Aer** in Worli, this cool rooftop bar is easily south Mumbai's most alluring spot for a sundowner. Plush white sofas and candlelit tables surround the domed rotunda and a very sexy raised pool, while the views over Back Bay make even the sky-high drink prices (₹800 plus for a cocktail) feel worth it. Daily 5.30pm–1.30am.

Gadda da Vida Novotel Mumbai, Balraj Sahani Marg, Juhu Beach ☎ 022 6693 4444, ⓦ novotel.com; map p.602. Beach-front bars are like hens' teeth in Mumbai, but at *Gadda da Vida* (named after a hit from 1970s prog-rock band Iron Butterfly) you can sip your Caipiroska as the sun sets over Juhu's churning waves. House

DJs spin electro jazz early on, followed by dance anthems as the place fills up. ₹400 for a beer and ₹500–700 for cocktails. Daily 5.30pm–1.30am.

Indigo 4 Mandlik Rd, Colaba; map p.589. Attached to the fashionable *Indigo* restaurant (see p.612), this is the coolest hangout in Colaba, with edgy, stripped-bare decor and frequented by young media types and would-be wine buffs. Cover charge of ₹1000–2000 sometimes levied on Fri and Sat. Daily 5.30pm–1.30am.

Olive 4 Union Park Rd, Pali Hill (between Juhu and Bandra) ☎ 022 4340 8228, ⓦ olivebarandkitchen .com; map p.602. Nowhere pulls in Bollywood's A-list like *Olive*. If you want to rub shoulders with Hrithik, Katrina, Sushmita and Priyanka, Thursday evening (aka "see-and-be-seen night") is your best bet, though dress to kill – and come armed with a full wallet. Cover charges do not apply, but cocktails are in the region of ₹1000. Mon–Sat 7.30pm–1am, Sat & Sun noon–3.30pm & 7.30pm–1.30am.

Salt Water Café Rose Minar Annexe, 87 Chapel Rd, next to Mount Carmel Church. Bandra (West) ☎ 022 2643 4441, ⓦ saltwatercafe.in; map p.602. This smart all-day diner in swanky Bandra is renowned for its relaxed atmosphere, warm-toned designer decor, gastro food and drink-till-you-drop happy hours. During the day you can down unlimited quantities of sangria for ₹450, and on Weds–Sat between 11pm and 1am, ₹750 buys you unlimited vodka cocktails and Budweiser. Daily 9am–midnight.

Toto's Garage 30 Lourdes Heaven, Pali Junction, Bandra West ☎ 022 600 5494; map p.602. Neon-lit, garage-themed bar with a VW hanging from its ceiling. Hard rock, metal and grunge provide the soundtrack when the lads pile in for pitchers of draught beer after work. It's tiny and packed to the gills most of the time. Beer from ₹200/pint. Daily 6.30pm–12.30am.

Wink Vivanta by Taj (formerly Taj President), G.D. Somani Rd, 90 Cuffe Parade ☎ 022 6665 0808; map p.587. Seriously stylish lounge bar a short hop from Colaba. It's split into two areas, separated by a Japanese gauze screen: a sleek island bar, famous for its Winktini cocktails (₹700–1000); and a chillout area with angled bare-brick walls and comfy couches where you can chat and munch on wasabi peas until the DJ cranks up the volume around 11pm. It gets very busy on weekends with expats and the visiting business crowd. Daily 6pm–1am.

NIGHTCLUBS AND LIVE MUSIC

Despite a 1.30am curfew (only clubs within hotels are allowed to carry on later), Mumbai's **clubbing** scene remains the most full-on in India. Tiny, skin-tight outfits that show off razor-sharp abs and pumped-up pecs are very much the order of the day for boys, and spray-on mini-dresses and kitten heels are *de rigueur* for the girls. Dancefloors get as rammed as a suburban commuter train and the cover charges can be astronomical on weekends. Door policies and dress codes tend to be strict ("no ballcaps, no shorts, no sandals"), and, in theory, most clubs have a "couples-only" policy. In practice, if you're in a mixed group and don't appear sleazy you shouldn't have any problems.

★ **Blue Frog** D/2 Mathuradas Mills Compound, NM Joshi Marg, Lower Parel ☎ 022 6158 6158, ⊛ bluefrog .co.in; map p.586. Housed in an old warehouse in Mumbai's former mill district, *Blue Frog* is the city's hippest and most happening live music venue, showcasing leading Indian and international music acts and DJs – anything from rock to hip-hop and Indo-Jazz Fusion. Admission free before 9pm (except on Sun), otherwise ₹350 on Tues– Thurs & Sun, or ₹600 on Fri & Sat. Tues–Sat 6.30pm–1.30am, Sun 11.30am–5pm & 6.30pm–1.30am.

Enigma JW Marriott Hotel, Juhu Tara Rd; map p.602. Long considered the city's most exclusive nightclub, *Enigma* found itself upstaged by newcomers *Trilogy* and *Tryst* in 2010–2011 so it closed for a massive refit. With a pimped-up bar and new minimalist decor, it has been since early 2013 a "multi-purpose performance venue", hosting live bands, unplugged sessions and even stand-up comedy, alongside the usual club dance nights hosted by top-drawer DJs from India and abroad. Cover charge ₹2000–4000/couple, depending on the night. Fri & Sat 9pm–1.30am.

Polly Esther's Gordon House Hotel, Battery St, Colaba; map p.589. Uncool and unrepentant, this retro club, with its '70s decor, cheesy underlit dance floor and waiters wearing ludicrous fluoro-coloured Afro wigs, offers a refreshingly unpretentious alternative to the sleek lounge-restos of the suburbs. Live music, hip-hop, Bollywood and retro on different nights. Cover charge ₹1000–1200 includes ₹200 entry; the rest is redeemable at the bar. Sat & Sun 9.30pm–1.30am.

★ **Trilogy** Hotel Sea Princess, Juhu Tara Rd, Santacruz (W) ☎ 022 2646 9500, ⊛ trilogy.in; map p.602. Currently the party place of choice for the film industry's finest, *Trilogy* has it all: rude doormen, bartenders in fedoras, a glittering staircase, VVIP lounges, a huge dance floor (a rarity indeed in Mumbai) and sparkly LED chandeliers that festoon the ceiling and change colours in sync with the music. The DJs play mainstream dance (David Guetta, Skrillex and the like) for a mixture of teenyboppers from the 'burbs, Bollywood wannabes in spray-on clothes and thirty-somethings on occasional Big Nights Out. Drink prices are top whack (₹400 for beers, double that for shots and cocktails). Daily 10pm–3am.

Voodoo Lounge Arthur Bunder Rd, Colaba; map p.589. This cavernous, louche little dive off Colaba Causeway plays host to Mumbai's one and only gay club, from 9pm on Fri & Sat (it's dead and depressing the rest of the week). The atmosphere's welcoming for both gay and straight men and women, though most of the punters do come to cruise (avoid the loos if you're easily shocked) and the vibe can be seedy at times, with local prostitutes prominent in the mix. Admission ₹400/head. Daily 7pm–1.30am.

CINEMA

Not surprisingly for a city obsessed with the movies, Mumbai has hundreds of **cinema houses**, among them a handful of glorious ArtDeco halls dating from the twilight of the Raj. However, only a handful regularly screen **English-language** films. The rest feature the latest Bollywood blockbusters, which of course aren't shown with subtitles. For the latest **reviews and listings**, get hold of a copy of *Time Out Mumbai* magazine (₹50). Alternatively, look for the biggest, brightest hoarding, and join the queue. **Seats** in a comfortable a/c cinema cost ₹170–300, or less if you sit in the stalls (not advisable for women).

Regal Shahid Bhagat Singh Rd, Colaba ☎ 022 2202 1017. One of Mumbai's oldest and best-loved cinema halls, the Regal showed Laurel and Hardy's *The Devil's Brother* on its opening night in 1933. There's still only one screen, and the auditorium is filled with velvet seats. Shows both Hollywood and Bollywood, mainly to affluent middle-class professionals and students, so the vibe is generally civilized. The handiest cinema if you're based in south Mumbai.

Eros Cambata Building, 42 M. Karve Rd, opposite Churchgate Station ☎ 022 2282 2335, ⊛ erostheatre .com. Another of the Art Deco behemoths, the Eros can accommodate more than one thousand people. Screens mainly Hindi and Marathi movies, with occasional English-language offerings.

Metro Big M.G. Rd, Dhobi Talao Junction, Marine Lines ☎ 022 3984 4060, ⊛ bigcinemas.com. Opened by Metro-Goldwyn-Mayer in 1938, this is the granddaddy of the city's movie houses, with seating for nearly 1500 people until it was transformed into a six-screen multiplex in 2006. Facilities are top-notch. Screens mainly Hindi movies, but does show the odd Hollywood hit.

Inox Cross Road 2, 2nd Floor, Barrister Rajni Patel Marg, Nariman Point ☎ 022 6658 8888, ⊛ inoxmovies.com. Another big multiscreen venue, built only a few years ago in the retro Mumbai-Art Deco style.

SHOPPING

Mumbai is a great place to shop and prices compare well with other Indian cities. Locally produced **textiles** and export-surplus clothing are among the best buys, as are **handicrafts** from far-flung corners of the country. In the larger shops, rates are fixed and **credit cards** are often accepted; elsewhere, particularly when dealing with street vendors, it pays to haggle. Uptown, the **central bazaars** are better for spectating than serious shopping.

10

BOLLYWOOD REVOLUTION

Film is massive in India. The country produces around 1200 movies annually, half of them in the studios of north Mumbai. Known as "**Bollywood**", the home of the All-India cinema industry has experienced a sea change over the past decade, as its output has started to reach mass audiences of expat Indians in Europe and North America. The resulting global revenues have financed much higher production standards and a completely new approach to plot, acting styles and scripts – rendering redundant the old cinematic stereotypes of the so-called "masala format", which dominated Indian film for decades. Big song-and-dance numbers still very much have their place in the modern Bollywood blockbuster, as does melodrama. But the overall tone these days tends to be much more sophisticated, with glamorous foreign locations, more plausible story lines, cutting-edge camera work and even state-of-the-art CGI deployed to wow cinemagoers at home and abroad.

Whereas in the past, hit movies tended to incorporate a bit of everything – romance, laughs, fight scenes, chases, lurid baddies, a set of instantly recognizable stock characters and convoluted plots that emphasized traditional values – now the industry is making big bucks from more nuanced genre flicks. The four highest grossing movies of the past decade were a feel-good comedy (*3 Idiots*; 2009), a dark psychological thriller (*Ghajini*; 2008), an action movie (*Don 2*; 2011) and a sci-fi superhero blockbuster (*Ra I*; 2011) – all radical departures from the Bollywood mainstream.

Some elements, however, remain consistent. Not even the most serious Indian movie can do without at least two or three "item numbers" – the set-piece song-and-dance sequences that give all hit films their essential anthems. And the cult of the Bollywood star shows no sign of abating. A-listers in the industry enjoy almost god-like status (only the country's top cricketers come close to matching their exalted mass appeal). Images of the current heartthrobs appear everywhere, from newspapers to cheesy TV ads.

At the top of the heap stands the veteran, white-bearded eminence grise of Bollywood, **Amitabh Bachchan**, whose record-breaking career as a screen hero saw a startling revival in the 2000s after he came out of de facto retirement to host India's version of *Who Wants To Be A Millionaire*, called *KBC* (*Kaun Banega Crorepati*). Only a notch below him comes rival **Shah Rukh Khan**, the smouldering lead of countless romantic blockbusters and the man the *Los Angeles Times* dubbed "the world's biggest movie star" in 2011. In box office terms, however, neither the Big B nor SRK can these days claim the appeal of **Aamir Khan**, the actor-director-producer behind hits such as *Lagaan* and *3 Idiots* – the latter the highest grossing Indian movie of all time. Other leading men of the moment include **John Abraham**, **Hrithik Roshan** and Bollywood bad boy, **Salman Khan**.

Not surprisingly in such an image-obsessed industry, **female leads** tend to have a shorter shelf life than their male counterparts, although contemporary starlets such as **Priyanka Chopra**, **Katrina Kaif** and **Kareena Kapoor** are tackling increasingly demanding roles in an attempt to prove themselves as serious actresses.

Even so, their off-screen antics and romantic dalliances continue to capture more attention than their acting skills, as do any public appearance of India's biggest celebrity couple, star actor **Abhishek Bachchan** (son of Amitabh) and his wife **Aishwarya Rai**. A former Miss World whose extreme beauty and svelte figure are often credited as spearheading the crossover of Bollywood into Western cinemas, Aishwarya has maintained her great popularity despite having had her first child in 2011. The career trajectory of Bollywood actresses has tended to be downwards after marriage (the assumption being that Indian audiences aren't prepared to accept a married woman, or even worse, a mother, as a romantic heroine). But with two other Bollywood queens – **Madhuri Dixit Nene** and **Karisma Kapoor** –making comebacks after starting a family, the times may well be changing.

ANTIQUES

Bollywood Bazaar Mutton St; map p.587. The Chor Bazaar area, and Mutton Street in particular, is the centre of Mumbai's antiques trade. And one shop that's worth the trip alone for Indian film fans is the wonderful Bollywood Bazaar, which sells old posters and memorabilia. The priciest pieces are hand-painted specimens dating from the 1950s, or even earlier, but they also stock plenty of repro versions that make great souvenirs. Sat–Thurs 10am–7pm.

Phillip's Antiques ⓦ phillipsantiques.com, Colaba; map p.589. Although much more expensive than Chor Bazaar, this famous antique shop opposite the Regal cinema is well worth a browse – even if you're not buying. Brass, bronze and wood Hindu sculpture, silver jewellery, old prints and aquatints form the mainstay of its collection. Mon–Sat 10am–7pm.

CLOTHES AND TEXTILES

Mumbai produces the bulk of India's clothes, mostly the lightweight, light-coloured "shirtings and suitings" favoured by droves of uniformly attired office-wallahs. Better-quality cotton clothes (often stylish designer-label rip-offs) are available in shops along Colaba Causeway and Mandlik Marg (behind the *Taj Mahal Palace and Tower*).

Fabindia MG Road, Kala Ghoda; map p.589. It's worth checking out the local branch of the nationwide Fabindia chain, which has an excellent and very affordable selection of stylish modern Indian-style shirts, *kurtas*, *shalwar kameezes*, as well as beautifully made items for the home. Daily 11am–9.30pm.

"Fashion Street" MG Rd; map p.594. For cheap Western clothing, you can't beat this long row of stalls strung out along MG Rd between Cross and Azad Maidans west of CST, specializing in reject and export-surplus goods ditched by big manufacturers: mainly T-shirts, jeans, summer dresses and sweatshirts. Daily 10am–9pm.

Khadi shop (signed "Mumbai Khadi Gramodyog Sangh") 286 Dr D.N. Marg, near the Thomas Cook office; map p.594. For traditional Indian clothes, look no further than here. As Whiteaway & Laidlaw, this rambling Victorian department store used to kit out all the newly arrived burrasahibs with pith helmets, khaki shorts and quinine tablets. These days, its old wooden counters and shirt and sock drawers stock dozens of different hand-spun cottons and silks, sold by the metre or made up as vests, *kurtas* or block-printed *salwar kameezes*. Mon–Sat 10.30am–6.30pm.

Obtataimu 3 Ropewalk Lane, next to Kala Ghoda Café, Kala Ghoda ⓦ obataimu.com; map p.589. A canary-coloured Bajaj scooter advertises the presence of this cute little fashion boutique, which sells cloud-cotton T-shirts and pretty silk dresses, as well as fish-leather iPad cases, designer luggage and furniture. Daily 11am–10pm.

Shrujan Saagar Villa, 38 Bhulabahi Desai Rd, opposite Navroz Apartment ☎ 022 2352 1693, ⓦ shrujan.org; map p.587. A dazzling array of bags, belts, cushion covers, trousers, quilts, saris, shawls, skirts, tops and wall hangings, embroidered by tribal women from the Kutch region of Gujarat. All profits go to community development schemes. Mon–Sat 10.30am–6.30pm.

LIFESTYLE

Bombay Store Western India House, Sir PM Rd, Fort ☎ 022 4066 9999; map p.594. This department store in the Fort district is a great place to shop for souvenirs, with vibrant displays of traditional handicrafts, textiles, woodwork, silverware, repro vintage photos and funky fashion accessories and designer artefacts from the Elephant Company. Mon–Sat 10.30am–8pm, Sun 11am–6.30pm.

Good Earth 2 Reay House, next to Taj Mahal Palace and Tower Hotel ☎ 022 2202 1030; map p.589. Fine tableware, luxury bed linen, lanterns and exquisite clothes made from traditional Indian fabrics. Prices reflect its proximity to the *Taj*, but their stock is all original and beautifully displayed. Daily 11am–10pm.

Playclan Above FabIndia, 137 Jeroo Building, MG Rd, Kala Ghoda; map p.589. Colourful range of stationery, prints and mugs decorated with Indian icons such as Ambassador cars, Kathakali dancers, Bombay taxis and auto-rickshaws – perfect souvenirs. Daily 11am–9.30pm.

HANDICRAFTS

Regionally produced handicrafts are marketed in assorted state-run emporia at the World Trade Centre, down on Cuffe Parade, and along Sir PM Rd, Fort. The quality is consistently high – as are the prices, if you miss out on the periodic holiday discounts. Mereweather Rd (now officially B Behram Marg), directly behind the *Taj Mahal Palace and Tower*, is awash with Kashmiri handicraft stores stocking overpriced papier-mâché pots and bowls, silver jewellery, woollen shawls and rugs. Avoid them if you find it hard to shrug off aggressive sales pitches. Down at the south end of Colaba Causeway, around Arthur Bunder Rd, shops with mirrored walls and shelves are stacked with cut-glass carafes full of syrupy, fragrant essential oils. Incense is hawked in sticks, cones and slabs of sticky *dhoop* on the pavement nearby (check that the boxes haven't already been opened and their contents sold off piecemeal).

Central Cottage Industries Emporium 34 Shivaji Marg, near the Gateway of India in Colaba; map p.589. The size, central location and big range of inlaid furniture, wood- and metalwork, miniature paintings, jewellery, toys, clothing and textiles make this the single best all-round place to hunt for souvenirs. Also purveyors of a fine range of teas. Mon–Sat 10.30am–6.30pm.

BOOKSHOPS

Crossword Bookstore Mohammed Bhai Mansion, Huges Rd, Kemp's Corner, a 10min walk north of Chowpatty Beach ☎ 022 2384 2001; map p.587. Mumbai's largest retailer, in smart new a/c premises, complete with its own coffee bar. Mon–Fri 11am–8.30pm, Sat & Sun 11am–9pm.

10

Nalanda Ground floor, Taj Mahal Palace and Tower; map p.589. An exhaustive range of coffee-table tomes and paperback literature, though at top prices. Daily 11am–midnight.

Oxford Bookstore Apeejay House, 3 Dinsha Vacha Rd, Churchgate; map p.594. Not quite as large as Crossword, but almost, and much more easily accessible if you're staying downtown or in Colaba. It also has a very cool a/c café. Daily 8am–10pm.

Search Word Metro House, Shahid Bhagat Singh Marg (Colaba Causeway); map p.589. The best bookshop in Colaba, with shelves full of guides and a great range of Indian fiction – at discounts only rivalled by the Strand Book Stall in Fort. Daily 10am–10pm.

Strand Book Stall Next door to the Canara Bank, off PM Rd, Fort; map p.594. The best-value bookshop in the city centre, with a big selection of discounted Penguins and Indian literature. Daily 10.30am–10pm.

MUSIC AND MUSICAL INSTRUMENTS

Bhargava's Musik 4/5 Imperial Plaza, 30th Rd, Bandra ⓦbhargavasmusic.com; map p.602. The city's foremost music shop, up in the northern suburb of Bandra, stocks every conceivable kind of Indian instrument, from sitars and sarods to bamboo flutes and shruti boxes, as well as Western guitars, strings and drums. Mon–Sat 10.30am–8pm.

Furtado's Jer Mahal, Dhobitalao ☏022 6622 5454, ⓦfurtadosonline.com. Mostly Western-style woodwind, brass, keyboard and percussion, with a basic stock of Indian instruments. It's far more easily accessible than Bhargava's if you're based in south Mumbai. Mon–Sat 10.30am–8.30pm.

Rhythm House Subhash Chowk, opposite the Jehangir Art Gallery; map p.589. For cassettes and CDs, this is a good first stop; a veritable Aladdin's cave of classical, devotional and popular music from all over India, with a reasonable selection of Western rock, pop and jazz, as well as DVDs of classic and contemporary Hindi movies. Mon–Fri 10am–8.30pm, Sat & Sun 11am–8.30pm.

SPORTS

In common with most Indians, Mumbaikars are crazy about **cricket**. Few other spectator sports get much of a look-in, although the **horseracing** at Mahalakshmi draws large crowds on Derby days. Previews of all forthcoming events are posted on the back pages of the *Times of India*, and in *Time Out Mumbai*.

CRICKET

Cricket provides almost as much of a distraction as movies in the Maharashtrian capital, and you'll see games in progress everywhere, from impromptu sunset knockabouts on Chowpatty Beach to more formal club matches in full whites at the gymkhanas lined up along Marine Drive. The Indian season runs from October through February. Tickets for cup and test matches are almost as hard to come by as seats on commuter trains, but foreign visitors can sometimes gain preferential access to quotas through the Mumbai Cricket Association's offices on the first floor of Wankhede.

Brabourne Stadium Off Marine Drive. The world's most prolific batsman in both test and one-day cricket, Sachin Tendulkar, still lives in the city and plays regularly for its league-winning club side at the Brabourne Stadium.

Oval Maidan South Mumbai. This is the place to watch local talent in action, set against a wonderful backdrop of imperial-era buildings. Something of a pecking order applies here: the further from the path cutting across the centre of the park you go, the better the wickets and the classier the games become. Pitches

LAUGHTER YOGA

On the principle that laughter is the best medicine, Mumbai doctor Madan Kataria and his wife Madhuri – aka "the Giggling Gurus" – have created a new kind of therapy: *hasya* (laughter) yoga. There are now more than three hundred **Laughter Clubs** in India and many more worldwide; around 50,000 people join the Laughter Day celebrations in Mumbai on the first Sunday of May each year, with tens of thousands more participating in seventy countries worldwide.

Fifteen-minute sessions start with adherents doing yogic breathing whilst chanting "Ho ho ha ha", which develops into spontaneous "hearty laughter" (raising both hands in the air with the head tilting backwards), "milkshake laughter" (everyone laughs while making a gesture as if they are drinking milkshake), and "swinging laughter" (standing in a circle saying "aaee-oo-eee-uuu") before the rather fearsome "lion laughter" (extruding the tongue fully with eyes wide open and hands stretched out like claws, and laughing from the tummy). The session then winds up with holding hands and the chanting of slogans ("We are the laughter club member (sic)…Y…E…S!").

Laughter Clubs take place between 6am and 7am at various venues around the city, including Colaba Woods in Cuffe Parade and Juhu Beach. For the full story, go to ⓦlaughteryoga.org.

like these are where Sachin Tendulkar (see above), cut his cricketing teeth.

Wankhede Stadium Off Marine Drive. This 45,000-capacity stadium is where major test matches are hosted, amid an atmosphere as intense, raucous and intimidating for visiting teams as any in India.

HORSERACING AND HORSERIDING

Mahalakshmi Racecourse Near the Mahalakshmi Temple, just north of Malabar Hill ⓦarcmumbai .com. This is the home of the Royal Western India Turf Club – a throwback to British times that still serves as a prime stomping ground for the city's upper classes. Race meets are held twice weekly, on Wednesdays and Saturdays between November and March, and big days such as the 2000 Guineas and Derby attract crowds of 25,000. Entrance to the public ground is by ticket on the day. Seats for the colonial-era stand, with its posh lawns and exclusive *Gallops Restaurant* are, alas, allocated to members only. Race cards are posted in the sports section of the *Times of India* and at ⓦrwitc .com. On non-race days, the Mahalakshmi ground doubles as a riding track. Temporary membership of the Amateur Riding Club of Mumbai, another bastion of elite Mumbai, entitles you to use the club's thoroughbreds for classes. Full details on how to do this, along with previews of forthcoming club polo matches, are posted on the website.

DIRECTORY

Ambulance ☎101 for general emergencies; but you're nearly always better off taking a taxi.

Banks and exchange There are dozens of ATMs dotted around the city. All the major state banks downtown change foreign currency (Mon–Fri 10.30am–2.30pm, Sat 10.30am–12.30pm); some (eg the Bank of Baroda) also handle credit cards and cash advances. Thomas Cook's big Dr D.N. Marg branch (Mon–Sat 9.30am–7pm; ☎022 6160 3333), between the Khadi shop and Hutatma Chowk, can also arrange money transfers from overseas.

Consulates and high commissions Note that most of India's neighbours, including Bangladesh, Bhutan, Burma, Nepal and Pakistan, only have embassies in New Delhi and/or Kolkata (Calcutta). All of the following are open Mon–Fri only: Australia, Level 10, A Wing, Crescenzo Building, G Block, Plot C 38-39 Bandra Kurla (☎022 6757 4900, ⓦindia.highcommission.gov .au); Canada, Indiabulls Finance Centre, 21st Floor, Tower 2, Senapati Bapat Marg, Elphinstone Rd (West) (☎022 6749 4444, ⓦcanadainternational.gc.ca); Republic of Ireland, Kamanwalla Chambers, 2nd Floor, Sir PM Rd, Fort (☎022 6635 5635); South Africa, Gandhi Mansion, 20 Altamount Rd (☎022 2389 3725, ⓦdha .gov.za); United Kingdom, Naman Chambers, C/32 G Block, Bandra Kurla Complex, Bandra (East) (☎022 6650 2222, ⓦukinindia.fco.gov.uk); USA, C-49, G-Block, Bandra Kurla Complex, Bandra East (☎022 2672 4000, ⓦmumbai.usconsulate.gov).

Hospitals The best hospital in the centre is the private Bombay Hospital, New Marine Lines (☎022 2206 7676, ⓦbombayhospital.com), just north of the government tourist office on M Karve Rd. Breach Candy Hospital (☎022 2366 7949, ⓦbreachcandyhospital.org) on Bhulabhai Desai Rd, near the swimming pool, is also recommended by foreign embassies.

Internet access A couple of cramped 24hr places (₹40/hr) can be found in Colaba on Nawroji F Marg. If you have your own computer, wi-fi access is available at most of the city's mid- and high-end hotels, as well as at local branches of the *Barista* coffee shop chain (there's a branch next to the Regal Cinema in Colaba).

Libraries Asiatic Society (see p.595), Shahid Bhagat Singh Marg, Horniman Circle, Ballard Estate (Mon–Sat 10.30am–7pm); British Council (for British newspapers and magazines), A Wing, 1st floor, Mittal Tower, Nariman Point (Tues–Sat 10am–6pm); Bombay Natural History Society, Hornbill House, next to the Chhatrapati Shivaji Museum (ⓦbnhs.org; Mon–Fri 9.30am–5.30pm), has an international reputation for the study of wildlife in India. Visitors may obtain temporary membership, which allows them access to the library, natural history collection, occasional talks and the opportunity to join organized walks and field trips.

Pharmacies Saharkari Bandar Chemist at the top of SBS Marg, Colaba, is open until 8.30pm.

Police The main police station in Colaba (☎022 2285 6817) is on the west side of Colaba Causeway, near the crossroads with Best Marg.

Postal services The GPO (Mon–Sat 9am–8pm, Sun 9am–4pm) is around the corner from CST (VT) Station, off Nagar Chowk. The parcel office (10am–4.30pm) is behind the main building on the first floor. Packing-wallahs hang around on the pavement outside. DHL (☎1800 111 345) has eleven offices in Mumbai, the most convenient being the 24hr one under the *Sea Green Hotel* at the bottom of Marine Drive.

Travel agents The following travel agents are recommended for booking domestic and international flights, and cars with drivers: Cox and Kings India, 16 Bank St, Fort (☎1800 221235, ⓦcoxandkings.co.in); Sita World, 11th Floor, Bajaj Bhavan, Nariman Point; Thomas Cook, 324 Dr DN Rd, Fort (☎022 6160 3333, ⓦthomascook.co.in); Garha Tours & Travels, 104 Atlantic Apartments, Swami Samarth Nagar, Lokhandwala Complex, Andheri (W) (☎022 2635 0035 or 98670 28232, ✉info@garhatours.com).

10

Maharashtra

KAILASH TEMPLE, ELLORA

Maharashtra

Vast and rugged, the modern state of Maharashtra is the third largest in India and the second most visited by foreign tourists. As soon as you leave the seething endless concrete housing projects, petrochemical works and swamplands of its seething port capital, Mumbai, you enter a different world with a different history. Undoubtedly, Maharashtra's greatest treasures are its extraordinary cave temples and monasteries. The finest of all are found near Aurangabad, renamed after the Mughal emperor Aurangzeb and home to the Bibi-ka-Maqbara, dedicated to his wife. The busy commercial city is the obvious base for visits to the Buddhist caves at Ajanta, with their fabulous and still-vibrant murals, and the monolithic temples of Ellora, where the astonishing Hindu Kailash temple was carved in its entirety from one single rock.

Despite Maharashtra's early importance as a centre of Buddhism, the Hindu faith is very much at the core of the life in the state. Balancing modern industry alongside ancient associations with the Ramayana, the main pilgrimage centre has always been **Nasik**, a handy place to break journeys en route to Aurangabad. One of the four locations of the Kumbh Mela, the city is always a hive of devotional activity, and lies close to one of India's most sacred Shiva shrines, reached from the village of **Trimbak**. In the state's far northeastern corner, the city of **Nagpur** lies close to **Sevagram**, where Mahatma Gandhi set up his headquarters during the struggle for Independence.

Away from the cities, one of the most characteristic features of the landscape is a plenitude of **forts**. Rising abruptly a short distance inland from the sea, the Sahyadri Hills – part of the **Western Ghats** range – form a series of huge steps that march up from the narrow coastal strip to the edge of the **Deccan plateau**. These flat-topped hills could easily be converted into forts where small forces could withstand protracted sieges by large armies. Modern visitors can scale such windswept fortified heights at **Pratapgadh** and, most dramatically, **Daulatabad**.

During the nineteenth century, the mountains found another use. When the summer proved too much for the British in Bombay, they sought refuge in nearby **hill stations**, the most popular of which, **Mahabaleshwar**, now caters for droves of domestic tourists. **Matheran**, 800m higher, has a special attraction: a rickety miniature train. South of Matheran, a further series of magnificent rock-cut caves clustered around another resort town, **Lonavala**, provides the main incentive to break the journey to the modern, cosmopolitan city of **Pune**, famous for its **Osho** resort founded by the New Age guru Bhagwan Rajneesh, but most appealing for its atmospheric old town and burgeoning eating and drinking scene.

To the west, Maharashtra occupies 500km of the **Konkan coast** on the Arabian Sea, from Gujarat to Goa. The little-explored palm-fringed coast winds back and forth with

Highlights

❶ Nasik Pilgrimage centre and capital of India's nascent wine trade, this city is a fascinating combination of ancient and modern. **See p.627**

❷ Ellora caves A World Heritage Site that features breathtaking Hindu, Buddhist and Jain caves carved from solid volcanic rock, as well as the stunning Kailash temple. **See p.637**

❸ Ajanta caves Hidden in a remote horseshoe-shaped ravine, Ajanta's caves contain the finest surviving gallery of art from any of the world's ancient civilizations. **See p.643**

❹ Gandhi ashram, Sevagram Learn about the great man's life and beliefs at the last ashram he lived in. **See p.652**

❺ The Konkan coast This stretch of coastline remains relatively unspoilt with several appealing places to stay, including the small port of Murud-Janjira. **See p.653**

❻ Miniature train to Matheran Fantastic views across the Western Ghats are revealed during the switchback train journey up to this former British hill station. **See p.656**

❼ Pune Known as the "Oxford of the East", this sophisticated city is home to an absorbing old town, a riveting museum and some excellent places to eat and drink, plus the Osho ashram. **See p.660**

HIGHLIGHTS ARE MARKED ON THE MAP ON P.626

countless inlets, ridges and valleys; highlights include **Murud-Janjira**, whose extraordinary fortress was the only one never conquered by the Mughals, and **Ganpatipule**, the region's chief pilgrimage centre, where you can walk on kilometres of virtually deserted, palm-fringed beaches. By the time you reach **Kolhapur**, the main town in the far south of the state, famous for its temple and palace, Mumbai feels a world away.

Brief history

Maharashtra enters recorded history in the second century BC, with the construction of its first Buddhist caves. These lay, and still lie, in peaceful places of great natural beauty, but could never have been created without the wealth generated by the nearby caravan trade routes between north and south India.

The first Hindu rulers

The region's first Hindu rulers – based in Badami, Karnataka – appeared during the sixth century, and Buddhism was almost entirely supplanted by the twelfth century. Hinduism, in the form of the simple faith of Ramdas, the "Servant of Rama", provided the philosophical underpinning behind the campaigns of the Maharashtra's greatest warrior, **Shivaji** (1627–80), who remains a potent symbol for Maharashtrans, celebrated in prominently positioned equestrian statues across the state. The fiercely independent Maratha chieftain united local forces to place insurmountable obstacles in the way of

HIGHLIGHTS

1. Nasik
2. Ellora caves
3. Ajanta caves
4. Gandhi ashram, Sevagram
5. The Konkan coast
6. Miniature train to Matheran
7. Pune

MAHARASHTRA

MTDC HOTELS

The Maharashtra Tourism Development Corporation (**MTDC**) runs a number of hotels across the state, often occupying superb locations – though standards are variable – and can also organize stays in local B&Bs. The most useful of their resorts are listed in this chapter and can be booked either at MTDC offices or at ⓦ maharashtratourism.gov.in.

any prospective invader; so effective were their guerrilla tactics that he could even take on the mighty Mughals, who by 1633 had got as far as capturing Daulatabad. By the time he died, in 1680, he had managed to unite the Marathas into a stable and secure state, funded by the plunder gleaned through guerrilla raids as far afield as Andhra Pradesh. In response, Mughal Emperor **Aurangzeb** moved his court and capital south to the Deccan, first to Bijapur (1686) and then Golconda (1687), but still failed to subdue Shivaji's dynasty. Yet by the end of the eighteenth century the power of both had weakened and the British were able to take full control.

A nationalist consciousness

Maharashtra claims a crucial role in the development of a nationalist consciousness. An organization known as the Indian National Union, originally convened in Pune, held a conference in Bombay in 1885, which was thereafter known as the **Indian National Congress**. This loose congregation of key local figures from around the country was to change the face of Indian politics. At first, its aim was limited to establishing a national platform to raise the status of Indians, and it remained loyal to the British. In the long term, of course, it was instrumental in the achievement of Independence 62 years later, with many of the Congress's factional leaders over the years hailing from Maharashtra.

Post-Independence

With Independence, the Bombay Presidency, to which most of Maharashtra belonged, became known as Bombay State. Maharashtra as such was created in 1960 from the state's Marathi-speaking regions. Its manufacturing industries, centred on Mumbai and to a lesser extent cities such as Nagpur, Nasik, Aurangabad, Sholapur and Kolhapur, now account for around fifteen percent of the nation's output. Textiles have long been important – the Deccan soils supplied the world with cotton in the nineteenth century after its main source was interrupted by the American Civil War – but this is now also one of the premier high-tech industry regions, especially along the Mumbai–Pune corridor. Still, the majority of Maharashtra's population of more than 112 million are still engaged in agriculture.

Nasik

Lying at the head of the main pass through the Western Ghats, the fast-developing city of **NASIK** (or Nashik) makes an interesting stopover en route to or from Mumbai, 187km southwest. The city is one of the four sites of the world's largest religious gathering, the **Kumbh Mela** (see box, p.264), due to be hosted next in Nasik in 2015. Even outside festival times, the *ghat*-lined banks of the **River Godavari** are always animated.

According to the Ramayana, Nasik was where Rama (Vishnu in human form), his brother Lakshmana and wife Sita lived during their exile from Ayodhya, and the arch-demon Ravana carried off Sita from here in an aerial chariot to his kingdom, Lanka, in the far south. The scene of such episodes forms the core of the busy pilgrimage circuit – a lively enclave packed with religious specialists, beggars, sadhus and street vendors touting puja paraphernalia.

However, Nasik has a surprising dearth of historical buildings – even the famous temples beside the river only date from the **Maratha era** of the eighteenth century. Its only real monuments are the rock-cut caves at nearby **Pandav Lena**. Excavated at the peak of Buddhist achievement on the Deccan, these 2000-year-old cells hark back to the days when, as capital of the powerful **Satavahana** dynasty, Nasik dominated the all-important trade routes linking the Ganges plains with the ports to the west.

From Nasik, you can make an interesting day-trip to the highly auspicious village of **Trimbak**, from which a steep climb takes you to **Brahmagiri**, the source of the Godavari. Somewhat in contrast to its religious importance, Nasik is also the centre of Maharashtra's burgeoning **wine region** (see box opposite).

Ram Kund

Around 1km east of the bus stand

Always buzzing with a carnival atmosphere, the **Ram Kund** is the reason most people come to Nasik, although this sacred bathing tank can look more like an overcrowded municipal swimming pool than one of India's most ancient holy places. Among the Ram Kund's more arcane attributes is its capacity to dissolve bones – whence the epithet of **Astivilaya Tirth** or "Bone Immersion Tank".

Kala Ram Mandir

At the end of the narrow, uphill street opposite Ram Kund • No fixed opening times • Free

The square around the **Kala Ram Mandir**, or "Black Rama Temple", is the city's second most important sacred area. Among the well-known episodes from the Ramayana to occur here was the event that led to Sita's abduction, when Lakshmana sliced off the nose of Ravana's sister after she had tried to seduce Rama by taking the form of a voluptuous princess. Sita's cave, or **Gumpha**, a tiny grotto known in the Ramayana as Parnakuti ("Smallest Hut"), is just off the square.

The Kala Ram temple itself, at the bottom of the square, houses unusual jet-black deities of Rama, Sita and Lakshmana; these are very popular with visiting pilgrims, as access is free from all caste restrictions. The best time to visit is around sunset, after evening puja, when a crowd, mostly of women, gathers in the courtyard to listen to a traditional storyteller recount tales from the Ramayana and other epics.

Pandav Lena

8km southwest of Nasik • Daily sunrise– sunset • ₹100 (₹5) • An auto-rickshaw costs around ₹300 for a roundtrip, including waiting time.

A steep fifteen-minute climb up one of the precipitous conical hills that overlook the Mumbai–Agra Road, 8km southwest of Nasik, is **Pandav Lena**, a small group of 24 rock-cut caves famous for their well-preserved Pali inscriptions and fine ancient stone sculpture. Cave 18, the only *chaitya* hall, is one of the earliest, dating from the first century BC, and is notable for its striking facade, while Cave 3, the largest *vihara*, boasts some superb exterior stonework.

ARRIVAL AND DEPARTURE

NASIK AND AROUND

By plane Nasik's Gandhinagar airport is around 5km southeast of the city and has irregular flights to/from Mumbai; check the latest schedule at the tourist office (see opposite). A taxi to/from the airport costs around ₹200–300.

By bus There are three principal bus stands. Buses from Mumbai pull in at the Mahamarga Bus Stand, 10min by rickshaw from the city centre, while Aurangabad and Pune buses terminate at the central New City Bus Stand. The Old City Bus Stand is around 500m north along the Old Agra Rd

(also known as Swami Vivekanand Rd), and is primarily useful for buses to Trimbak; it's an easy walk from either stand to several inexpensive hotels and restaurants.

Destinations Aurangabad (every 1–2hr; 4hr–4hr 30min); Mumbai (hourly; 4hr); Pune (every 30min; 4–5hr); Trimbak (every 30min; 45min).

By train Nasik Rd railway station, the nearest railhead, lies 8km southeast of the centre; local buses regularly ply the route into town, and there is no shortage of shared taxis

INDIA'S WINE CAPITAL

With its temperate winters, rich soil and gently undulating landscape, Nasik's arid and dusty hinterland has over the past decade proved itself to be – incongruously enough – ideal for growing wine grapes, and the city has firmly established itself at the centre of India's fast-expanding wine industry.

TOURS AND TASTINGS

Sula Vineyards 14km west of Nasik ☎0253 223 0575, ⌨sulawines.com. The best-established producer, enthusiastically supported by Mumbai's urban sophisticates, Sula Vineyards is a slick and professional operation that wouldn't feel out of place in the Napa Valley. They run 45min tours of its winery (hourly 11.30am–5.30pm; ₹150 for four wine tastings, ₹250 for

six), concluding with a generous tasting session.
Vallée de Vin 32km southwest of Nasik ☎0253 220 4379, ⌨vallee-de-vin.com. Based in the Sanjegaon valley, Vallée de Vin is part of Grover Zampa Vineyards, India's second biggest wine producer (after Sula). Daily tours (11am–5pm; 45min; ₹125) are on offer; groups of six or more should book in advance.

11

and auto-rickshaws (about ₹200–300 for a trip to/from the city centre). There's a ticket booking office (Mon–Sat 8am–8pm, Sun 8am–2pm), near HDFC House, around 1km west of the city bus stands, though its easier to book online or via a travel agent.

Destinations Agra (1 daily; 17hr 30min); Delhi (3 daily; 20hr 18min–26hr 8min); Jalgaon (12–13 daily; 2hr 14min–3hr 54min); Mumbai (38 daily; 2hr 35min–5hr 30min); Nagpur (6–8 daily; 9hr 25min–20hr 15min).

INFORMATION

Tourist information The helpful MTDC tourist office (Mon–Sat 10am–5.30pm; ☎0253 257 0059) is at T1, Golf Club, Old Agra Rd, and easiest reached by cutting across the park opposite the New City Bus Stand.

Services The State Bank of India, between the two city bus stands on Old Agra Rd, has an ATM and changes money. Internet access is available at the Shree Sadguru Cyber Café, next door to the *Panchavati* hotel complex.

ACCOMMODATION

Most of Nasik's hotels, stretching along the Mumbai–Agra road en route to Pandav Lena, are pitched at business travellers, though there are a few more budget-friendly exceptions around the Old City Bus Stand chowk.

Beyond Sula Vineyards, 14km west of Nasik ☎0253 223 0141, ⌨sulawines.com. Each of the super-stylish en suites is named after a grape variety at this tranquil, wine-themed hotel in the grounds of Sula Vineyards. There's also an infinity pool, spa and gym, and you can go hiking or cycling. The rate listed here is for weekends; prices drop by almost 25 percent during the week. ₹**7650**

Gateway 7km southwest on Mumbai–Agra Rd ☎0253 660 4499, ⌨thegatewayhotels.com. Set behind beautifully landscaped grounds, with a gleaming marble lobby designed in mock-Maratha style, this outpost of the *Gateway* chain is one the most luxurious places to stay in the area, though rooms feels somewhat overpriced. ₹**7150**

Ginger Satpur MIDC ☎0253 661 6333, ⌨gingerhotels.com. Nasik outpost of this reliable chain of mid-range hotels offering efficient service, comfortable if bland rooms, wi-fi access, a small gym and an in-house branch of *Café Coffee Day*. The only downside is the location, on a busy road 4km northwest of the Mahamarga Bus Stand. It's much cheaper to book online in advance. ₹**3500**

Padma Sharanpur Rd ☎0253 257 6837. One of Nasik's better budget hotels, opposite the Old City Bus Stand, the *Padma* is a safe option. Its basic rooms all have private bathrooms (though there is only hot water between 6–9am) and TVs, and there's a restaurant and "permit room" (bar). ₹**700**

Panchavati 430 Chandak Vadi ☎0253 257 2291, ⌨panchavatihotels.com. Set mercifully off noisy MG Rd a 15min walk from the New City Bus Stand, this four-part complex has rooms to suit most pockets, all of them clean, attached and good value for money, though overall it's a little worn and institutional. At the bottom of the range is the budget *Panchavati Guest House*, followed by the mid-range *Panchavati Yatri*, the slightly swisher *Hotel Panchavati* and, at the top of the range, the *Panchavati Millionaire*. ₹**900**

Rajmahal Sharanpur Rd ☎0253 258 0501, ⌨hotelrajmahalnashik.com. A few doors down from the *Padma* hotel, the *Rajmahal* is a step up in quality, with bright, comfortable and fairly modern rooms (ask for one of the quieter ones away from the main road). Very good value. ₹**1225**

EATING AND DRINKING

Nasik's best-value meals are to be had in its traditional "keep it coming" thali restaurants, where for less than the price of a beer you can enjoy carefully prepared and tasty vegetable, pulse and lentil dishes, often including such regional specialities as *bajra* (wholemeal *rotis*) and *bakri* (hot oatmeal biscuits). The city's religious associations tend to mean that meat and alcohol are less easily available than elsewhere in Maharashtra, but most of the larger hotels have bars (known as "permit rooms" in Maharashtra) and several of the more expensive restaurants serve beers and spirits too.

Annapurna MG Rd. The service may be unsmiling, but the south Indian and Punjabi veg dishes at this keenly priced stalwart are as good as they come. Dosas (from around ₹50) are a speciality; try the perfectly spiced Mysore *paneer* masala dosa. Daily 11.30am–3pm & 6.30–10.30pm.

Khyber Panchavati hotel complex, 430 Chandak Vadi ☎0253 257 7871. Steer past the veg Indian and Chinese dishes, and go for of *Khyber's* top-notch non-veg Afghan-Mughlai kebabs, rich curries or tandoori fish dishes. The restaurant itself has a touch of style, with mosaic-patterned table tops, frosted glass partitions and fragrant incense. Mains ₹130–320. Daily 11.30am–3.30pm & 7–11.30pm.

Pangat Thali Panchavati hotel complex, 430 Chandak Vadi. Bustling Gujarati thali canteen where the industrious turbaned waiters will refill your tray with fresh, wholesome pure-veg morsels faster than you can chow them down. An unlimited thali costs ₹140. Daily 11.30am–3pm & 6.30–11pm.

Talk of the Town Suyojit Chambers, Trimbak Rd, near the New City Bus Stand ☎0253 257 1961. One of central Nasik's smarter restaurant-bars with a choice of dining halls, from the family-friendly to the smoky and masculine. The north Indian veg and non-veg dishes (mains ₹100–380) are generally pretty tasty, and there's a long list of alcoholic drinks. Daily 7am–midnight.

★ **Tasting Terrace** Sula Vineyards, 14km west of Nasik ☎0253 223 0575, ⊚sulawines.com. This breezy, first-floor bar looks out over acres of neat rows of vines towards the scenic Gangapur tank. The wine list focuses on Sula's range of whites, reds and rosés (the Merlot-Malbec is well worth sampling), as well as a small selection from other (mainly new world) producers. A glass of wine costs from around ₹150, and there's an ₹300 cover charge at weekends. There are two excellent restaurants – one serving Indian food, the other offering Italian cuisine – close by. Sun–Thurs 11am–10pm, Fri & Sat 11am–11pm.

Trimbak

Crouched in the shadow of the Western Ghats, 28km west of Nasik, the village of **TRIMBAK** – literally "Three-Eyed", another name for Lord Shiva, in Marathi – marks the spot where one of the four infamous drops of immortality-giving amrit nectar fell to earth from the kumbh vessel during the struggle between Vishnu's vehicle Garuda and the Demons – the mythological origin of the Kumbh Mela (see box, 264).

Trimbakeshwar Mandir temple

Numbering among India's most sacred centres for Shiva worship (it houses one of the twelve must sacred Shiva temples, known as *jyotirlingas*), the **Trimbakeshwar Mandir** temple, in the centre of the village, is unfortunately closed to non-Hindus. Its impressive eighteenth-century *shikhara* (tower), however, can be glimpsed from the backstreets nearby.

The source of the Godavari

Trimbak is also close to the source of one of India's longest and most sacred rivers, the **Godavari**; the spring can be reached via an ancient pilgrim trail that cuts through a cleft in an awesome, guano-splashed cliff face. The roundtrip to **Brahmagiri**, the source of the Godavari, takes between two and three hours. It's a strenuous walk, particularly in the heat, so make sure you take enough water.

From the trailhead at the edge of the village, the way is paved and stepped as far as the first level outcrop, where there are some welcome chai stalls and a small hamlet. Beyond that, either turn left after the last group of huts and follow the dirt trail through the woods to the foot of the **rock-cut steps** (20min), or continue straight on to the three **shrines** clinging to the base of the cliff above. The first is dedicated to the goddess Ganga, the second – a cave containing 108 lingams – to Shankar (Shiva), and the third to the sage Gautama Rishi, whose hermitage this once was.

The steps climb 550m above Trimbak to the remains of **Anjeri Fort** – a site that was, over the years, attacked by the armies of both Shah Jahan and Aurangzeb before it fell into the hands of Shaha-ji Raj, father of the legendary rebel-leader Shivaji. The **source** itself is another twenty minutes further on, across **Brahmagiri Hill**, in the otherwise unremarkable Gaumukh ("Mouth of the Cow") temple. From its rather unimpressive origins, this paltry trickle flows for nearly 1000km east across the entire Deccan to the Bay of Bengal.

ARRIVAL AND DEPARTURE · TRIMBAK

By bus/shared taxi Trimbak makes an easy day-trip from Nasik. Buses leave regularly from the Old City Bus Stand (every 30min; 45min). To return, you can catch a bus (which run until around 8pm) or one of the shared taxis that wait outside Trimbak Bus Stand.

Aurangabad and around

On first impressions, it's easy to see why many travellers regard **AURANGABAD** as little more than a convenient, though largely uninteresting, place in which to kill time on the way to **Ellora** and **Ajanta**. Yet given a little effort, this city of more than a million inhabitants can compensate for its architectural shortcomings. Scattered around its ragged fringes, the remains of fortifications, gateways, domes and minarets – including those of the most ambitious Mughal tomb garden in western India, the **Bibi-ka-Maqbara** – bear witness to an illustrious imperial past; the small but fascinating crop of **rock-cut Buddhist caves**, huddled along the flanks of the flat-topped, sandy yellow hills to the north, are remnants of even more ancient occupation.

Modern Aurangabad is one of India's fastest growing commercial and industrial centres, specializing in car, soft drink and beer production. It's a decidedly upbeat place, boasting plenty of restaurants, bars and interesting shops in the old city. Easy day-trips from Aurangabad include the dramatic fort of **Daulatabad**, and, just a little further along the Ellora road, the tomb of Emperor Aurangzeb at the Muslim village of **Khuldabad**.

Brief history

The city was founded in the early seventeenth century by **Malik Ambar**, an ex-Abyssinian slave and prime minister of the independent Muslim kingdom of the Nizam Shahis; many of the **mosques** and palaces he erected still endure, albeit in ruins. Aurangabad really rose to prominence, however, towards the end of the seventeenth century, when **Aurangzeb** decamped here from Delhi. At his behest, the impressive city walls and gates were raised in 1682 to withstand the persistent Maratha attacks that bedevilled his later years. Following his death in 1707, the city was renamed in his honour as it changed hands once again. The new rulers, the **Nizams of Hyderabad**, staved off the Marathas for the greater part of 250 years, until the city finally merged with Maharashtra in 1956.

The old city

The **old city**, laid out on a grid by Malik Amber in the early seventeenth century, still forms the core of Aurangabad's large **bazaar** area. It's best approached via **Gulmandi Square** to the south, along any of several streets lined with colourful

---

GOING DOOLALLY

In the days of the Raj, soldiers who cracked under the stresses and strains of military life in British India were packed off to recuperate at a psychiatric hospital in the small Maharashtran cantonment town of **Deolali**, near Nasik. Its name became synonymous with madness and nervous breakdown; hence the English phrase "to go doolally".

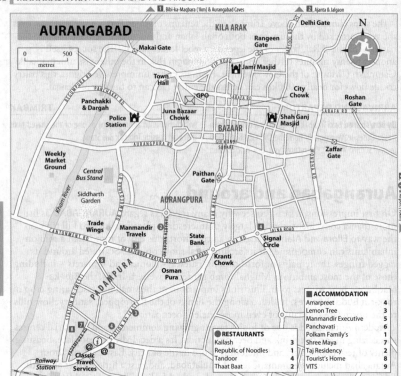

11

shops and stalls. Sections of Aurangzeb's city wall survive, though more impressive is the network of city **gates**, some of which have been restored to something approaching their former glory.

The Panchakki

Panchakki Rd, about 600m northwest of the Central Bus Stand • Daily 6.15am–9.15pm • ₹100 (₹5)

On the left bank of the Kham River is an unusual water-mill known as the **Panchakki**. Water pumped underground from a reservoir in the hills 6km away drives a small grindstone, once used to mill flour, and collects in an attractive fish-filled tank, shaded by a large banyan tree. The Panchakki forms part of the **Dargah** of Baba Shah Muzaffar, a religious compound built by Aurangzeb as a memorial to his spiritual mentor, a Chishti mystic. The complex makes a lively place to wander around in the early evening with lots of chai shops, *mehendi* (henna hand-painting) artists and souvenir shops.

The Bibi-ka-Maqbara

Around 2.5km north of the city centre • Daily sunrise–10pm • ₹100 (₹5) • The most practical way of getting here is by auto-rickshaw; a roundtrip encompassing the Bibi-ka-Maqbara and the caves (see opposite) costs around ₹300

Although it's the most impressive Islamic monument in the whole of Maharashtra, Aurangabad's Mughal tomb-garden, the **Bibi-ka-Maqbara**, has always suffered from comparison with the Taj Mahal, built forty years earlier, of which it's an obvious imitation. Completed in 1678, the mausoleum was dedicated by **Prince Azam Shah** to the memory of his mother **Begum Rabi'a Daurani**, Aurangzeb's wife. Lack of resources dogged the 25-year project, and the end result fell far short of expectations. Looking at the mausoleum from beyond the ornamental gardens and redundant fountains in front of it, the truncated minarets and ungainly entrance arch make the Bibi-ka-Maqbara appear ill-proportioned compared with the elegant height and symmetry of the Taj, an impression not enhanced by the abrupt discontinuation of marble after the first 2m – allegedly a cost-saving measure.

An enormous brass-inlaid **door** – decorated with Persian calligraphy naming the maker, the year of its installation and chief architect – gives access to the archetypal *charbagh* garden complex. Of the two entrances to the mausoleum itself, one leads to the inner balcony while the second drops through another beautiful door to the **vault** (visitors may no longer climb the minarets). Inside, an exquisite octagonal **lattice-screen** of white marble surrounds the raised plinth supporting Rabi'a Daurani's grave. Like her husband's in nearby Khuldabad, it is "open" as a sign of humility. The unmarked grave beside it is said to be that of the empress's nurse.

The caves

Around 3.5km north of the city centre • Daily sunrise–sunset • ₹100 (₹5) • The most practical way of getting to the caves is by auto-rickshaw; a roundtrip encompassing the Bibi-ka-Maqbara and caves costs around ₹300

Carved out of a steep-sided spur of the Sahyadri Range overlooking the Bibi-ka-Maqbara, Aurangabad's own **caves**, bear no comparison to those in nearby Ellora and Ajanta, but their fine **sculpture** makes a worthwhile introduction to rock-cut architecture. In addition, the infrequently visited site is peaceful and pleasant in itself, with commanding views over the city and surrounding countryside.

The caves, all Buddhist, consist of two groups, eastern and western (a third group is inaccessible), around 500m apart. The majority were excavated between the fourth and eighth centuries, under the patronage of two successive dynasties: the **Vakatkas**, who ruled the western Deccan from Nasik, and the **Chalukyas**, a powerful Mysore family who emerged during the sixth century. All except the much earlier Cave 4, which is a *chaitya* hall, are of the *vihara* (monastery) type, belonging to the Mahayana school of Buddhism. **Cave 3** is the most impressive of the western group, with vivid friezes adorning the pillars in the main chamber. In the eastern group, Cave 6 has some finely carved *bodhisattvas*, but it's the superb sculpture in **Cave 7** that provides the real highlight, including a couple of zaftig representations of Tara and, to the left of the Buddha in the sanctuary, a celebrated frieze showing a dancer in classic pose accompanied by six female musicians.

Daulatabad

Dominating the horizon 13km northwest of Aurangabad, the awesome hilltop citadel of **DAULATABAD** crowns a massive conical volcanic outcrop whose sides have been shaped into a sheer 60m wall of granite. Not least for the panoramic **views** from the top of the hill, Daulatabad makes a rewarding pause en route to or from the caves at Ellora, 17km northwest.

Brief history

It was the eleventh-century **Yadavas** who were responsible for scraping away the jagged lower slopes of the mount – originally known as **Deogiri**, "Hill of the Gods" – to form its vertical-cliff base, as well as the 15m-deep moat that encircles the upper portion of the citadel. Muslim occupation of Deogiri began in earnest with the arrival in 1327 of sultan Ghiyas-ud-Din **Tughluq**, who decreed that his entire court should decamp here from Delhi, an epic 1100km march that cost thousands of lives, and ultimately proved futile – within seventeen years, drought and famine had forced the beleaguered ruler to return to Delhi. Thereafter, the fortress fell to a succession of different regimes, including Shah Jahan's **Mughals** in 1633, before it was finally taken by the **Marathas** midway through the eighteenth century.

The fortress

Daily 6am–6pm • ₹100 (₹5)

Beyond the formidable sets of outer defences that enclose a series of high-walled courtyards at the foot of the hill, Daulatabad's labyrinthine **fortress** unfolds around the enormous **Chand Minar**, or "Victory Tower", erected in 1435. The Persian blue-and-turquoise tiles that once plastered it in complex geometric patterns have disappeared, but it remains an impressive spectacle, rising from the ruins of the city that once sprawled from its base. The **Jama Masjid**, back along the main path, is Daulatabad's oldest Islamic monument. Built in 1318, the well-preserved mosque comprises 106 pillars plundered from the Hindu and Jain temples which previously stood on the site. It now functions as a Bharatmata temple, much to the chagrin of local Muslims. Adjoining the mosque, the large stone-lined "Elephant" **tank** was once a central component in the fort's extensive water-supply system. Two giant terracotta pipes channelled water from the hills into Deogiri's legendary fruit and vegetable gardens.

From the Chand Minar, the main walkway continues through another set of bastions and fortified walls before emerging close to the **Chini Mahal**, or "Chinese Palace". The impressive **Mendha Tope** ("Ram-headed Cannon"), inscribed in Persian, rests on a squat stone tower just above. From here onwards, a sequence of macabre traps lay in wait for the unwary intruder. First, a moat infested with man-eating crocodiles (now spanned by an iron bridge) had to be crossed to reach the main citadel. Next the attackers would have had to clamber through a maze of claustrophobic, zigzagging passageways, the last of which was closed with an iron cover that could be heated to generate toxic gases.

From the final tunnel, it's a fairly steep ten-minute climb up a broad flight of steps to the **Baradari**, an attractive octagonal pavilion used by Shah Jahan during his visits to Daulatabad. The **views** from the flat roof of the building are superb, but an even more impressive panorama is to be had from the **look-out post** perched on the summit of the hill, marked with another grand cannon.

ARRIVAL AND INFORMATION
DAULATABAD

By bus/taxi Although Daulatabad features on the guided tours of Ellora from Aurangabad (see opposite), you'll have more time to enjoy it by travelling here on one of the buses (every 30min; 30min) that shuttle between Aurangabad and the caves. From Daulatabad, it is easy to catch another bus or shared taxi on to Khuldabad and Ellora; the stop is directly opposite the main entrance to the fort.

Visiting independently If you're not on a tour, try to arrive early as the place is often overrun with schoolchildren, and bring a torch as some of the passages in the fort are pitch-black and hopelessly confusing – one reason why you might also consider hiring a guide (around ₹600).

Khuldabad

22km north of Aurangabad • Tombs Sunrise–10pm • Free, but small tips and donations are expected. Buses run every 30min between Aurangabad and Ellora, stopping en route at Khuldabad's small bus stand (30min from Aurangabad, 10min from Ellora), a 10min walk from the tombs.

Nestled on a saddle of high ground, **KHULDABAD**, also known as **Rauza**, is an old walled town famous for a wonderful crop of onion-domed **tombs**. Among the Muslim notables deemed worthy of a patch of earth in this most hallowed of burial grounds ("Khuldabad" means "Heavenly Abode") were the emperor Aurangzeb himself, who raised the town's granite battlements and seven fortified gateways, a couple of nizams, and a fair few of the town's Chishti founding fathers.

The last of the great Mughals' tomb lies inside a whitewashed **dargah**, midway between the North and South gates. The grave itself is a humble affair decorated only by the fresh flower petals scattered by visitors, open to the elements instead of sealed in stone. The devout emperor insisted that it be paid for not out of the royal coffers, but with the money he raised in the last years of life by selling his own hand-quilted white skullcaps. Aurangzeb chose this as his final resting place primarily because of the presence, next door, of **Sayeed Zain-ud-Din**'s tomb, which occupies a quadrangle separating Aurangzeb's grave from those of his wife and second son, Azam Shah. Locked away behind a small door in the mausoleum is Khuldabad's most jealously guarded relic, the **Robe of the Prophet**, revealed to the public once a year on the twelfth day of the Islamic month of Rabi-ul-Awwal, when the tomb attracts worshippers from all over India. Directly opposite Zain-ud-Din's tomb is the **Dargah of Sayeed Burhan-ud-Din**, a Chishti missionary buried here in 1334. The shrine is said to contain hairs from the Prophet's beard, which magically increase in number when they are counted each year.

ARRIVAL AND DEPARTURE

BY PLANE
Chikal Thana airport Aurangabad's airport is 10km east of the city; a taxi to/from the city centre costs ₹200–300. Most of the smarter hotels offer a pick-up service. Jet Airways/JetKonnect and Air India both have daily flights to Mumbai (50min); the former also has weekly flights to Indore (50min), while the latter has a daily service to Delhi (1hr 50min).

BY TRAIN
Aurangabad railway station The train station stands on the southwest edge of the city centre, at the southern end of Station Rd West, within easy reach of most of the budget hotels. As Aurangabad is not on the main line, trains to and from the city are fairly limited (Jalgaon, 166km north, has the nearest mainline station, with services to a far greater range of destinations). The quickest train to Mumbai is the #12072 *Jan Shatabdi Express* (daily 6am; 6hr 30min); if you prefer to travel overnight, try the #17058 *Devagiri Express* (daily 11.25pm; 7hr 45min).
Destinations Delhi (1 daily; 22hr 30min); Hyderabad/Secunderabad (4 daily; 10hr 5min–12hr 35min); Mumbai

(4 daily; 6hr 45min–8hr 5min); Nasik (4 daily; 2hr 54min–3hr 53min).

BY BUS
State buses The hectic Central Bus Stand is 2.5km north of the railway station, off Dr Ambedkhar Rd. All the state transport corporation (MSRTC) buses arrive and depart from here.
Destinations Ellora (every 30min; 40min) via Daulatabad and Khuldabad; Jalgaon (every 30min; 3hr 30min–4hr) via Fardapur for Ajanta (2hr 30min–3hr); Mumbai (6–7 daily, including a nightly "luxury" bus; 8–10hr); Nagpur (around 6 daily; 12hr); Nasik (every 30min–1hr; 4hr 30min); Pune (every 30min–1hr; 5hr).
Private buses For a little more comfort, there are numerous private companies running a/c buses to most of the larger destinations; you can save yourself a lot of hassle by heading straight to the calm and efficient Manmandir Travels on Adalat Rd (☎ 0240 236 5748, ⌨ manmandir. co.in), which operates services to a wide range of destinations from its own private terminus – a far cry from the usual bedlam.

GETTING AROUND

By auto-rickshaw Aurangabad's sights lie too far apart to take in on foot. The city is, however, buzzing with auto-rickshaws; longer sightseeing trips work out much cheaper if you settle on a fare in advance (around ₹600–800/day).
By taxi Taxis can be hailed in the street or found at the

railway station and cars with drivers can be hired through travel agents such as the efficient Classic Travel Services (☎ 0240 233 7788, ⌨ aurangabadtravelservices .com), on the ground floor of the Tourist Reception Centre. Expect to pay from around ₹1200/day.

INFORMATION AND TOURS

Tourist information A counter at the airport (opens to meet incoming flights) provides basic information, while more detailed enquiries are fielded at the Tourist Reception Centre on Station Rd East, where helpful offices of both India Tourism (Mon–Fri 8.30am–6pm, Sat 8.30am–1.30pm ☎ 0240 233 1217) and MTDC (Mon–Fri plus the first and third Sat of the month

10am–1pm & 1.30–5.45pm; ☎ 0240 233 1513) are housed on the first floor; the manager Chandrashekar Jaiswal in particular is a mine of information.
Tour operators Various companies run daily guided tours of Aurangabad and the surrounding area, all operating to the same itineraries and departure times, and all generally rushed. Ellora and City tours usually include the

Bibi-ka-Maqbara, Panchakki, Daulatabad Fort, Aurangzeb's tomb at Khuldabad and the Ellora caves (though not the Aurangabad ones). Ajanta tours go to the caves only, but it's a long roundtrip to make in a day – if you want to spend more time at the site, stay at Fardapur (see p.649) or travel on to Jalgaon (see p.650). Classic Travel Services (see p.635) runs the best of the tours: Ellora and the city's sights (₹300 excluding entry fees); Ajanta (₹450 excluding entry fees); the Shirdi temple complex of guru Sai Baba (₹400), and the famous Paithani Weaving Centre (₹350).

ACCOMMODATION

Aurangabad's proximity to some of India's most important monuments, together with its "boom-city" status, ensures a profusion of **hotels**, though standards are variable. For local B&Bs, contact the MTDC.

Amarpreet Jalna Rd ☎0240 621 1133, ⓦamarpreethotel.com. This upper-mid-range hotel, on a main road just south of the old city, is a reliable choice, offering large, well-furnished rooms, a quality non-veg restaurant and a bar. Good value, especially if you book online. ₹3750

Lemon Tree 7/2 Chikalthana ☎0240 660 3030, ⓦlemontreehotels.com. Set around a large pool, this is the brightest, cheeriest – and certainly the most fragrant – of the upper-bracket business hotels lining the airport road. It has a couple of good restaurants (see below) and the appealing *Slounge* bar. The rate given here is for booking online in advance; rack rates are significantly higher. ₹5500

Manmandir Executive Adalat Rd ☎0240 236 5777, ⓦmanmandirmotels.com. Immaculately maintained budget business hotel above a private bus terminus (see p.635), with a range of sizeable, blandly comfortable rooms (the non-a/c options are particularly good value), plus a clean a/c dorm (₹300) for those on a really tight budget. ₹1450

Panchavati Off Station Rd West ☎0240 232 8755, ⓦhotelpanchavati.com. Decent, if unspectacular, hotel on the western edge of the city centre with economical rooms (all with private bathrooms; some with a/c), welcoming staff and a restaurant (whose menu even features a few Korean options). ₹950

Polkam Family's Nipat Niranjan Nagar, New Pahadsingpura ☎0240 240 0916. Aurangabad's nicest B&B: a couple of homely rooms in a charming and peaceful Muslim family home on the edge of town between the Bibi-ka-Maqbara and the caves. Book direct or via MTDC. ₹1200

Shree Maya Bharuka Complex, Padampura Rd, off Station Rd West ☎0240 233 3093. Friendly and very popular place with large, cleanish rooms (some a/c; all attached); standards vary, so ask to look at a few. There's also a chilled and sociable restaurant with good food, plus internet access (for a fee). ₹700

Taj Residency Ajanta Rd, 4km north of the centre ☎0240 661 3737, ⓦtajhotels.com. Aurangabad's most luxurious option is set in a domed, gleaming-white wedding cake confection. Rooms are tastefully finished in dark wood, and all come with bathtubs and a balcony. Facilities include a spa, large pool and croquet on the palm-fringed lawn. ₹9400

Tourist's Home Station Rd West ☎0240 233 7212 or ☎9326 262611. No-frills place set on a quiet, rambling campus, with rooms to suit most pockets. The smartest rooms (some with balconies and a/c) are in the renovated new wing, set back from the main road, while the high-ceilinged old wing has some of the city's cheapest doubles. ₹500

VITS Station Rd East ☎0240 235 0701, ⓦvitshotelaurangabad.com. This business hotel is the smartest central option, with an impressive atrium and plush rooms with a hint of style, plus a pool, small gym and spa, and a restaurant-bar. The rate given here is for booking online in advance; rack rates are a fair bit higher. ₹3500

EATING AND DRINKING

Aurangabad is chock-full of places to eat, with most restaurants serving either strictly vegetarian **Gujarati** food or meat-oriented north Indian dishes. As elsewhere in the state, non-veg places tend to be synonymous with dim lights, drawn curtains and a male clientele – with a few exceptions – while the veg restaurants attract families. **Drinking** is an exclusively male preserve, usually carried out in the many specially segregated bars (aka "permit rooms"), as well as the larger, more tourist-oriented hotels and restaurants.

Kailash Station Rd East ☎0240 233 8916. This recently revamped, pure veg restaurant serves inexpensive south Indian and Punjabi food, and is popular with local workers. Mains from around ₹70. Daily noon–3pm & 7–11pm.

Republic of Noodles Lemon Tree hotel ☎0240 660 3030. If you fancy something a little different, head to this award-winning Southeast Asian restaurant, which has an alfresco dining area by the pool. As well as some classic Thai and Vietnamese dishes, there are a few more unusual Burmese, Indonesian and Singaporean options. Expect to pay around ₹600-plus for dinner. Daily 7am–11pm.

Tandoor Shyam Chambers, Station Rd East ☎0240 232 8481. Dominated by an imposing bust of Egyptian pharaoh Tutankhamun, this welcoming traveller's favourite is one of the city's best-established non-veg restaurants. Tandoori chicken and mutton kebabs are the house specialities, while for monster appetites there's the full-on "sizzling tandoori platter" (big enough for two). Mains ₹130-450. Daily 11am–3pm & 6.30–11pm.

Thaat Baat Beneath Embassy Hotel, near Vivekanand College, Samarth Nagar Rd ☎ 0240 651 2666. There's a festive air at this fun, family-friendly thali place, where armies of waiters breezily ladle out dollops of tasty pure veg against a backdrop of Rajasthani puppets, paintings and handicrafts. A hearty feed and a drink will set you back around ₹150. Daily noon–3pm & 7–11pm.

DIRECTORY

Banks and exchange An efficient foreign exchange service is provided at Trade Wings (daily 9am–7pm) on Dr Ambedkhar Rd. ATMs are common throughout the city, including an ICICI Bank one opposite the Tourist Reception Centre.

Internet There are numerous internet cafés throughout town, including in the Classic Travel Services office (see p.635) and opposite the Tourist Reception Centre.

Shopping Aurangabad is famous for its Himroo and Paithani textiles, which are on sale (alongside cheaper imitations) throughout the city; Classic Travel Services runs a tour (see p.635) to the Paithani Weaving Centre.

Ellora

Palaces will decay, bridges will fall, and the noblest structures must give way to the corroding tooth of time; whilst the caverned temples of Ellora shall rear their indestructible and hoary heads in stern loneliness, the glory of past ages, and the admiration of ages yet to come.

Captain Seely, *The Wonders of Ellora*

Maharashtra's most visited ancient monument, the **ELLORA** caves, 29km northwest of Aurangabad, may not enjoy as grand a setting as their older cousins at Ajanta, but the amazing wealth of **sculpture** they contain more than compensates, and this is an unmissable stop if you're heading to or from Mumbai, 400km southwest. In all, 34 Buddhist, Hindu and Jain caves – some excavated simultaneously, in competition – line the foot of the 2km-long Chamadiri escarpment as it tumbles down to meet the open plains. The site's principal attraction, the colossal **Kailash temple**, rears from a huge, sheer-edged cavity cut from the hillside – a vast lump of solid basalt fashioned into a spectacular complex of colonnaded halls, galleries and shrines.

Brief history

The original reason why this apparently remote spot became the focus of so much religious and artistic activity was the busy **caravan route** that passed through here on its way between the prosperous cities to the north and the ports of the west coast. Profits from the lucrative trade fuelled a 500-year spate of excavation, beginning midway through the sixth century AD at around the same time that Ajanta, 100km northeast, was abandoned. This was the twilight of the **Buddhist** era in central India; by the end of the seventh century, **Hinduism** had begun to reassert itself. The Brahmanical resurgence gathered momentum over the next three hundred years under the patronage of the Chalukya and Rashtrakuta kings – the two powerful dynasties responsible for the bulk of the work carried out at Ellora, including the eighth-century Kailash temple. A third and final flourish of activity on the site took place towards the end of the first millennium AD, after the local rulers had switched allegiance from Shaivism to the **Jain** faith. A small cluster of more subdued caves to the north of the main group stand as reminders of this age.

Unlike the isolated site of Ajanta, Ellora did not escape the iconoclasm that accompanied the arrival of the **Muslims** in the thirteenth century. The worst excesses were committed during the reign of Aurangzeb who ordered the demolition of the site's "heathen idols". Although Ellora still bears the scars from this time, most of its best pieces of sculpture have remained remarkably well preserved, sheltered from centuries of monsoon downpours by the hard basalt hillside.

11

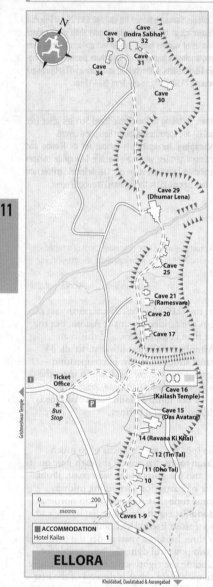

Cave 33
Cave (Indra Sabha) 32
Cave 31
Cave 34
Cave 30
Cave 29 (Dhumar Lena)
Cave 25
Cave 21 (Ramesvara)
Cave 20
Cave 17
Ticket Office
Cave 16 (Kailash Temple)
Cave 15 (Das Avatara)
Bus Stop
14 (Ravana Ki Khai)
12 (Tin Tal)
11 (Dho Tal)
10
Grishneshwar Temple
0   200
metres
Caves 1-9

ACCOMMODATION
Hotel Kailas   1

ELLORA

Khuldabad, Daulatabad & Aurangabad

The caves

Daily except Tues dawn–dusk • ₹250 (₹10) • If you've come in an auto-rickshaw or a taxi you will also need to buy an ₹10 parking ticket

All the **caves** are numbered, following a roughly chronological plan. Numbers 1 to 12, at the south end of the site, are the oldest, from the Vajrayana Buddhist era (500–750 AD). The Hindu caves, 13 to 29, overlap with the later Buddhist ones and date from between 600 and 870 AD. Further north, the Jain caves – 30 to 34 – were excavated from 800 AD until the late eleventh century. Because of the sloping hillside, most of the cave entrances are set back from the level ground behind open courtyards and large colonnaded verandas or porches.

To see the oldest caves first, turn right opposite Cave 16, the vast Kailash temple, and follow the main pathway down to Cave 1. From here, work your way gradually northwards again, avoiding the temptation to look around Cave 16, which is best saved until late afternoon when the bus parties have all left and the long shadows cast by the setting sun bring its extraordinary stonework to life.

A much-delayed modern **visitor centre** has been due to open for several years now.

The Buddhist group

The **Buddhist caves** line the sides of a gentle recess in the Chamadiri escarpment. All except Cave 10 are *viharas*, or monastery halls, which the monks would originally have used for study, solitary meditation and communal worship, as well as the mundane business of eating and sleeping. As you progress through them, the chambers grow steadily more impressive in scale and tone. Scholars attribute this to the rise of Hinduism and the need to compete for patronage with the more overtly awe-inspiring Shaivite cave-temples being excavated so close at hand.

Caves 1 to 9

Cave 2 is the first cave of interest, a large central chamber supported by twelve massive, square-based pillars while the aisles are lined with seated Buddhas. The doorway into the shrine room is flanked by two giant, bejewelled *dvarpalas*, or guardian figures: an unusually muscular Padmapani, the *bodhisattva* of compassion, on the left, and an opulent Maitreya, the "Buddha-to-come", on the right. Both are accompanied by their consorts. Inside the sanctum itself, a stately Buddha is seated on a lion throne, looking stronger and more determined than his serene forerunners in Ajanta.

Caves 3 and 4 lack the artifice of Cave 2, though the latter retains some fine capital work. **Cave 5** is the largest single-storey *vihara* in Ellora. Its enormous 36m-long rectangular assembly hall is thought to have been used by the monks as a refectory, and has two rows of benches carved from the stone floor.

Caves 6–9 were excavated at roughly the same time in the seventh century, and are reached via a single door and stairwell cut into the rock. On the walls of the antechamber at the far end of the central hall in **Cave 6** are two of Ellora's most famous and finely executed figures: Tara, the buxom female consort of the *bodhisattva* Avalokitesvara, stands to the left; on the opposite side, the Buddhist goddess of learning, Mahamayuri, is depicted with her emblem, the peacock, while a diligent student sets a good example at his desk below. From Cave 6, a short flight of steps leads up to diminutive **Cave 9**, with a fine frieze decorating the facade.

Caves 10, 11 and 12

Excavated in the early eighth century, **Cave 10** is one of the last and most magnificent of the Deccan's rock-cut *chaitya* halls. Steps lead from the left of its large veranda to an upper balcony, where a trefoil doorway flanked by flying threesomes, heavenly nymphs and a frieze of playful dwarfs leads to an interior balcony. Inside the long apsidal hall (which you may need to ask to be unlocked), the rib-vaulting effect on the ceiling imitates the beams that would have appeared in earlier freestanding wooden structures. A slender Buddha sits enthroned in front of a votive *stupa*, the hall's devotional centrepiece.

In spite of the rediscovery in 1876 of its hitherto hidden basement, **Cave 11** continues to be known as the **Dho Tal**, or "Two Floors" cave. Its top storey is a long columned assembly hall housing a Buddha shrine and, on its rear wall, images of Durga and Ganesh, the elephant-headed son of Shiva – evidence that the cave was converted into a Hindu temple after being abandoned by the Buddhists. **Cave 12** next door – the **Tin Tal**, or "three floors" – is another triple-storey *vihara*, approached via a large open courtyard. Again, the main highlights are on the uppermost level. The shrine room at the end of the hall, whose walls are lined with five large *bodhisattvas*, is flanked on both sides by seven Buddhas – one for each of the Master's previous incarnations.

The Hindu group

Ellora's seventeen **Hindu caves** are grouped around the middle of the escarpment, to either side of the majestic Kailash temple. Excavated at the start of the Brahmanical revival in the Deccan during a time of relative stability, the cave-temples throb with a vitality absent from their restrained Buddhist predecessors. In place of benign-faced Buddhas, huge **bas-reliefs** line the walls, writhing with dynamic scenes from the Hindu scriptures. Most are connected with **Shiva**, the god of destruction and regeneration (and the presiding deity in all of the Hindu caves on the site), although you'll also come across numerous images of Vishnu (the Preserver) and his various incarnations.

The same tableaux crop up time and again, a repetition that gave Ellora's craftsmen ample opportunity to refine their technique over the years leading up to their greatest achievement, the Kailash temple (Cave 16). Covered separately (see opposite), the temple is the highlight of any visit to Ellora, but you'll appreciate its beautiful sculpture all the more if you visit the earlier Hindu caves first. Numbers 14 and 15, immediately south, are the ones to go for if you're pushed for time.

Cave 14

Dating from the start of the seventh century AD, and among the last of the early excavations, **Cave 14** was a Buddhist *vihara* converted into a temple by the Hindus. The entrance to the bare sanctum is guarded by two impressive river goddesses, Ganga and Yamuna, while lining the ambulatory wall behind and to the right, seven heavy-breasted fertility goddesses, the **Sapta Matrikas**, dandle chubby babies on their laps.

Shiva's elephant-headed son, Ganesh, sits to their right beside two cadaverous apparitions, Kala and Kali, the goddesses of death. Superb **friezes** adorn the cave's long side-walls.

Cave 15

Like its neighbour, the two-storey **Cave 15**, reached via a long flight of steps, began life as a Buddhist *vihara* but was hijacked by the Hindus and became a Shiva shrine. Behind the Natya Mandapa ("Hall of Dance") in the centre of the courtyard, make for the upper level of the main structure to find some of Ellora's most magnificent sculpture. The cave's name, **Das Avatara**, is derived from the sequence of panels along the right wall, which show five of **Vishnu**'s ten incarnations (avatars).

A carved panel in a recess to the right of the antechamber shows Shiva emerging from a lingam. Brahma and Vishnu stand before the apparition in humility and supplication – symbolizing the supremacy of Shaivism in the region at the time the conversion work was carried out. Finally, halfway down the left wall of the chamber as you're facing the shrine, the cave's most elegant piece of sculpture shows Shiva as Nataraja, poised in a classical dance pose.

11

Caves 17 to 29

Only three of the Hindu caves strung along the hillside north of the Kailash temple are really worth exploring in depth. **Cave 21** – the **Ramesvara** – was excavated late in the sixth century. Thought to be the oldest Hindu cave at Ellora, it harbours some well-executed sculpture, including a fine pair of river goddesses on either side of the veranda, two wonderful door guardians and some sensuous loving couples, or *mithunas*, dotted around the walls of the balcony. **Cave 25**, further along, contains a striking image on the exterior ceiling of the main shrine of the sun god **Surya** speeding in his chariot towards the dawn.

From here, the path picks its way past two more excavations, then drops steeply across the face of a sheer cliff to the bottom of a small river gorge. Once under the seasonal **waterfall**, the trail climbs the other side of the gully to emerge beside **Cave 29**, the huge **Dhumar Lena**. Dating from the late sixth century, the cave boasts an unusual cross-shaped floor plan similar to the Elephanta cave in Mumbai harbour. Pairs of rampant lions guard its three staircases while, inside, the walls are covered with huge **friezes**. On the right-hand side of the (southern) entrance, a dice-playing scene shows Shiva teasing Parvati by holding her arm back as she prepares to throw. Left of the exit, Shiva skewers the Andhaka demon, while in the opposite wall panel he foils the many-armed Ravana's attempts to shake him and Parvati off the top of Mount Kailash; look for the cheeky dwarf baring his bum to taunt the evil demon.

The Kailash temple (Cave 16)

Cave 16, the colossal **Kailash temple**, is Ellora's masterpiece. Here, the term "cave" is not only a gross understatement but a complete misnomer. For although the temple was, like the other excavations, hewn from solid rock, it bears a striking resemblance to earlier freestanding structures in south India. The monolith is believed to have been the brainchild of the Rashtrakuta ruler **Krishna I** (756–773). One hundred years and four generations of kings, architects and craftsmen elapsed, however, before the project was completed. Climb up the track leading along the lip of the compound's north-facing cliff to the ledge overlooking the squat main tower, and you'll see why.

The sheer scale is staggering. Work began by digging three deep trenches into the top of the hill using pickaxes and lengths of wood which, soaked with water and stuffed into narrow cracks, expanded to crumble the basalt. Once a huge chunk of raw rock had been exposed in this way, the royal sculptors set to work. In all, around a quarter of a million tonnes of chippings and debris were cut from the hillside, with no room for improvisation or error. The temple was conceived as a giant replica of Shiva and Parvati's

Himalayan abode, the pyramidal **Mount Kailash**. Today, all but a few fragments of the thick coat of white-lime plaster that gave the temple the appearance of a snowy mountain have flaked off, to expose elaborately carved surfaces of grey-brown stone beneath. Around the rear of the tower, these have been bleached and blurred by centuries of erosion, as if the giant sculpture is slowly melting in the fierce Deccan heat.

The temple

The main **entrance** to the temple is through a tall stone screen, intended to mark the transition from the profane to the sacred realms. After passing between two guardian river goddesses, Ganga and Yamuna, you enter a narrow passage that opens onto the main forecourt, opposite a panel showing **Lakshmi**, the goddess of wealth, being lustrated by a pair of elephants. Custom requires pilgrims to circumambulate clockwise around Mount Kailash, so descend the steps to your left and head across the front of the courtyard towards the near corner.

From the top of the concrete steps in the corner, all three principal sections of the complex are visible: first, the shrine above the entrance housing Shiva's vehicle, **Nandi**, the bull; next, the intricate recessed walls of the main assembly hall, or **mandapa**, which still bear traces of the coloured plaster that originally coated the whole edifice; and finally, the sanctuary itself, surmounted by the stumpy, 29m, pyramidal tower, or **shikhara** (best viewed from above). These three components rest on an appropriately huge raised platform, borne by dozens of lotus-gathering elephants. As well as symbolizing Shiva's sacred mountain, the temple also represented a giant **chariot**. The transepts protruding from the side of the main hall are its wheels, the Nandi shrine its yoke, and the two life-sized, trunkless elephants in the front of the courtyard (disfigured by Muslim raiders) are the beasts of burden.

Most of the main highlights of the temple itself are confined to its side walls, which are plastered with vibrant **sculpture**. Lining the staircase that leads up to the north side of the *mandapa*, a long, lively narrative panel depicts scenes from the Mahabharata, and below this the life of **Krishna**. Continuing clockwise, the majority of the panels around the lower sections around the temple are devoted to **Shiva**. On the south side of the *mandapa*, in an alcove carved out of the most prominent projection, you'll find the finest piece of sculpture in the compound. It shows Shiva and Parvati being disturbed by the multiheaded **Ravana**, who has been incarcerated inside the sacred mountain and is now shaking the walls of his prison with his many arms. Shiva is about to assert his supremacy by calming the earthquake with a prod of his toe. Parvati, meanwhile, nonchalantly reclines on her elbow as one of her handmaidens flees in panic.

From here, head up the steps at the southwest corner of the courtyard to the **Hall of Sacrifices**, with its striking frieze of the seven mother goddesses, the Sapta Matrikas, and their ghoulish companions Kala and Kali (shown astride a heap of corpses). The sixteen-columned assembly hall is shrouded in a gloomy half-light designed to focus worshippers on the presence of the deity within. Using a portable arc light, the *chowkidar* will illuminate fragments of painting on the ceiling, where Shiva, as **Nataraja**, performs the dance of death.

The Jain group

Ellora's small cluster of four **Jain caves** is north of the main group, just a five-minute walk north along the path from Cave 29 or, alternatively, reachable from the Kailash temple via a curving asphalt road.

Excavated in the late ninth and tenth centuries, after the Hindu phase had petered out, the Jain caves are Ellora's swansong, featuring some fine decorative carving and a few exquisite paintings. Of principal interest is **Cave 32**, the **Indra Sabha** ("Indra's Assembly Hall"), a miniature version of the Kailash temple. The lower of its two levels is plain and incomplete, but the upper storey, guarded by huge *yaksha* and *yakshi* figures facing each other across the veranda, is crammed with elaborate stonework, notably the ornate pillars and the two *tirthankaras* guarding the entrance to the central shrine. The naked figure of Gomatesvara, on the right, is fulfilling a vow of silence in the forest. He is so deeply immersed in meditation that creepers have grown up his legs, and animals, snakes and scorpions crawl around his feet.

The Grishneshwar Mandir

Rising above the small village west of the caves, the cream-coloured *shikhara* of the eighteenth-century **Grishneshwar Mandir** pinpoints the location of one of India's oldest and most sacred deities. The lingam enshrined inside the temple's cavernous inner sanctum is one of the twelve "self-born" **jyotirlingas** ("linga of light"), thought to date back to the second century BC. Non-Hindus are allowed to join the queue for *darshan*, but men have to remove their shirts before entering the shrine itself.

ARRIVAL AND INFORMATION **ELLORA**

Most visitors use Aurangabad as a base for day-trips to the caves; if you prefer to take in the caves at a more leisurely pace and climb Daulatabad Hill, either spend the night at Ellora or leave Aurangabad early in the morning.

By bus There are regular MSRTC buses (every 30min; 40min) from Aurangabad to Ellora.

By tour Travel agencies in Aurangabad offer tours (see p.635), though these tend to be rather rushed.

By auto-rickshaw/taxi An auto-rickshaw for the roundtrip from Aurangabad costs around ₹700, including waiting time; a taxi costs about ₹1200.

Guides Official multilingual guides are on hand to take you on a tour of the most interesting caves (groups of up to five people around ₹750).

ACCOMMODATION AND EATING

Apart from the mediocre MTDC canteen inside the complex and the roadside *dhabas* opposite the bus stand, the only place to eat is at the restaurant inside *Hotel Kailas*.

Hotel Kailas Opposite the entrance to the caves ☎02437 244543, ⦿hotelkailas.com. This small, peaceful hotel has a mix of simple rooms close to the road and smarter cottages (₹3000) facing the caves themselves.

There's a decent restaurant, and a range of activities on offer, including trips to local markets, hikes, massages and even paragliding. **₹1500**

Ajanta

Hewn from the near-vertical sides of a horseshoe-shaped ravine, the caves at **AJANTA** occupy a site worthy of the spectacular ancient art they contain. Less than two centuries ago, this remote spot was known only to local tribespeople; the shadowy entrances to its abandoned stone chambers lay buried deep under a thick blanket of creepers and jungle.

The chance arrival in 1819 of a small detachment of East India Company troops, however, brought the caves' obscurity to an abrupt end. Led to the top of the precipitous bluff that overlooks the gorge by a young "half-wild" scout, the tiger-hunters spied what has now been identified as the facade of Cave 10 protruding through the foliage.

The British soldiers had made one of the most sensational archeological finds of all time. Further exploration revealed a total of 28 colonnaded caves chiselled out of the chocolate-brown and grey basalt cliffs lining the River Waghora. More remarkable still were the immaculately preserved **paintings** writhing over their interior surfaces. For, in addition to the rows of stone Buddhas and other **sculpture** enshrined within them, Ajanta's excavations are adorned with a swirling profusion of murals, depicting everything from battlefields to sailing ships, city streets and teeming animal-filled forests to snow-capped mountains. Even if you aren't wholly familiar with the narratives they portray, it's easy to see why these paintings are regarded as the finest surviving gallery of art from any of the world's ancient civilizations.

11

ROCK-CUT CAVES OF THE NORTHWESTERN DECCAN

The **rock-cut caves** scattered across the volcanic hills of the northwestern Deccan rank among the most extraordinary religious monuments in Asia. Ranging from tiny monastic cells to elaborately carved temples, they are remarkable for having been hewn by hand from solid rock. Their third-century BC origins seem to have been as temporary shelters for Buddhist monks when heavy monsoon rains brought their travels to a halt. Modelled on earlier wooden structures, most were sponsored by **merchants**, for whom the casteless new faith offered an attractive alternative to the old, discriminatory social order. Gradually, encouraged by the example of the Mauryan emperor Ashoka, the local ruling dynasties also began to embrace Buddhism. Under their patronage, during the second century BC, the first large-scale monastery caves were created at **Karla**, **Bhaja** and **Ajanta**.

THE HINAYANA SCHOOL

Around this time, the austere **Hinayana** ("Lesser Vehicle") school of Buddhism predominated in India. Caves cut in this era were mostly simple worship halls, or **chaityas** – long, rectangular apsed chambers with barrel-vaulted roofs and two narrow colonnaded aisles curving gently around the back of a monolithic **stupa**. Symbols of the Buddha's enlightenment, these hemispherical burial mounds provided the principal focus for worship and meditation, circumambulated by the monks during their communal rituals.

THE MAHAYANA SCHOOL

By the fourth century AD, the Hinayana school was losing ground to the more exuberant **Mahayana** ("Greater Vehicle") school. Its emphasis on an ever-enlarging pantheon of **bodhisattvas** (merciful saints who postponed their accession to nirvana to help mankind towards enlightenment) was accompanied by a transformation in architectural styles. *Chaityas* were superseded by lavish monastery halls, or **viharas**, in which the monks both lived and worshipped, and the once-prohibited image of the Buddha became far more prominent. Occupying the circumambulatory recess at the end of the hall, where the *stupa* formerly stood, the colossal **icon** acquired the 32 characteristics, or **lakshanas** (including long dangling ear-lobes, cranial protuberance, short curls, robe and halo) by which the Buddha was distinguished from lesser divinities. The peak of Mahayanan art came towards the end of the Buddhist age. Drawing on the rich catalogue of themes and images contained in ancient scriptures such as the **Jatakas** (legends relating to the Buddha's previous incarnations), Ajanta's exquisite wall **painting** may, in part, have been designed to rekindle enthusiasm for the faith, which was, by this point, already starting to wane in the region.

THE VAJRAYANA SECT

Attempts to compete with the resurgence of **Hinduism**, from the sixth century onwards, eventually led to the evolution of another, more esoteric religious movement. The **Vajrayana**, or "Thunderbolt" sect stressed the female creative principle, **shakti**, with arcane rituals combining spells and magic formulas.

BRAHMANISM

Ultimately, however, such modifications were to prove powerless against the growing allure of Brahmanism. The ensuing shift in royal and popular patronage is best exemplified by **Ellora** where, during the eighth century, many old *viharas* were converted into temples, their shrines housing polished *shivalinga* instead of *stupas* and Buddhas. Hindu cave architecture, with its dramatic mythological **sculpture**, culminated in the tenth century with the magnificent **Kailash temple**, a giant replica of the freestanding structures that had already begun to replace rock-cut caves. It was Hinduism that bore the brunt of the iconoclastic medieval descent of Islam on the Deccan, Buddhism having long since fled to the comparative safety of the Himalayas, where it still flourishes.

Brief history

Located close enough to the major trans-Deccan trade routes to ensure a steady supply of alms, yet far enough from civilization to preserve the peace and tranquility necessary for meditation and prayer, Ajanta was an ideal location for the region's itinerant

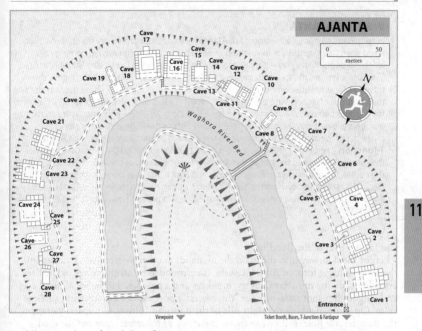

AJANTA

Viewpoint ▼   Ticket Booth, Buses, T-Junction & Fardapur ▼

Buddhist monks to found their first permanent monasteries. Donative inscriptions indicate that its earliest cave excavations took place in the second century BC.

In its heyday, Ajanta sheltered more than two hundred monks, as well as a sizeable community of painters, sculptors and labourers employed in excavating and decorating the cells and sanctuaries. Sometime in the seventh century, however, the site was abandoned – whether because of the growing popularity of nearby Ellora, or the threat posed by the resurgence of Hinduism, no one knows. By the eighth century, the complex lay deserted and forgotten, overlooked even by the Muslim iconoclasts who wrought such damage to the area's other sacred sites during the medieval era.

The caves

Tues–Sun 9am–5.30pm • ₹250 (₹10), "amenities fee" ₹10, video ₹25 • Entry tickets are sold at the booth at the main entrance, a 4km bus ride (a/c bus ₹20, non-a/c bus ₹10 one way) from the Ajanta T-junction

An obvious path leads up from the ticket booth to the grand **Mahayana** *viharas*; if you'd prefer to see the caves in chronological order, however, start with the smaller **Hinayana** group of *chaitya* halls at the bottom of the river bend (caves 12, 10 and 9), then work your way back up, via Cave 17. For help getting up the steps, sedan-chair bearers (around ₹500), or dhooli-wallahs, stand in front of the stalls below, while porters (around ₹150) are on hand to carry bags. Official **guides** make two-hour tours (around ₹700) which can be arranged through the ticket office; most deliver an interesting spiel but you may well feel like taking in the sights again afterwards at a more leisurely pace.

Cave 1

There's always a queue for **Cave 1**, which contains some of the finest and stylistically most evolved paintings on the site. By the time work on it began, late in the fifth century, *viharas* served not only to shelter and feed the monks, but also as places of worship in their own right. In common with most Mahayana *viharas*, the extraordinary murals lining the walls and ceilings depict episodes from the Jatakas, tales of the birth

VISITING AJANTA

In spite of its comparative remoteness, **Ajanta** receives an extraordinary number of visitors. If you want to enjoy the site in anything close to its original serenity, avoid coming on a weekend or public holiday – it takes a fertile imagination indeed to picture Buddhist monks filing softly around the rough stone steps when hundreds of riotous school children and throngs of tourists are clambering over them. Among measures to minimize the impact of the hundreds of visitors who daily trudge through is a ban on flash photography – though the introduction of low-impact lighting has aided close viewing – and strict limits on the numbers allowed into the most interesting caves at any given time. Another significant move to reduce the ecological impact on the area has been the creation of the **Ajanta T-junction** (see below). The best seasons to visit are either during the monsoon, when the river is swollen and the gorge reverberates with the sound of the waterfalls, or during the cooler winter months between October and March. At other times, the relentless Deccan sun beating down on the south-facing rock can make a trip around Ajanta a real endurance test. Whenever you go, take a hat, some sunglasses, a good torch and plenty of drinking water.

and former lives of the Buddha.

Left of the doorway into the main shrine stands another masterpiece. **Padmapani**, the lotus-holding form of Avalokitesvara, is surrounded by an entourage of smaller attendants, divine musicians, lovers, monkeys and a peacock. His heavy almond eyes and languid hip-shot *tribhanga* (or "three-bend") pose exudes a distant and sublime calm. Opposite, flanking the right side of the doorway, is his counterpart, **Vajrapani**, the thunderbolt holder. Between them, these two *bodhisattvas* represent the dual aspects of Mahayana Buddhism: compassion and knowledge.

The real focal point of Cave 1, however, is the large sculpted Buddha seated in the shrine room – the finest such figure in Ajanta. Using portable electric spotlights, guides love to demonstrate how the expression on the Buddha's exquisitely carved face changes according to where the light is held.

On the way out, you should be able to spot this cave's other famous trompe l'oeil, crowning one of the pillars (on the fourth pillar on the left as you face the exit): the figures of four apparently separate stags that, on closer inspection, all share the same head.

Cave 2

Cave 2 is another impressive Mahayana *vihara*, dating from the sixth century. Here, the ceiling is decorated with complex floral patterns, including lotus and medallion motifs. Sculpted friezes in the small subsidiary shrine to the right of the main chapel centre on a well-endowed fertility goddess, **Hariti**, the infamous child-eating ogress, and Kubera, the god of wealth. The side walls teem with lively **paintings** of the Jatakas and other mythological episodes. A mural on the left veranda shows the birth of the Buddha, emerging from under his mother's arm, and his conception when a white elephant appeared to her in a dream (bottom left).

Caves 3 to 9

Cave 3 is inaccessible but unfinished **Cave 4**, the largest *vihara* in the complex, is worth a quick look for its 28 pillars and huge Buddha. It's also worth popping into **Cave 6**, a two-storey *vihara* with a finely carved doorjamb and lintel around the entrance to its shrine room. Cave 8 is always closed; it contains the generator for the lights.

Cave 9, which dates from the first century BC, is the first *chaitya* you come to along the walkway. Resting in the half-light shed by a characteristic peepal-leaf-shaped window in the sculpted facade, the hemispherical **stupa**, with its inverted pyramidal reliquary, forms the devotional centrepiece of the 14m-long hall. The fragments of painting that remain, including the procession scene on the left wall, are mostly superimpositions over the top of earlier snake deities – *nagarajas*.

Cave 10

Although, like Cave 9, marred by the unsightly wire meshing used to keep out bats, the facade of **Cave 10**, a second-century BC *chaitya* hall – the oldest of its kind in the ravine – is still a grand sight. The cave's main highlights, however, are far smaller and more subdued. Along the left wall, you may be able to pick out the fading traces of painting (now encased in glass) that depict a scene in which a raja and his retinue approach a group of dancers and musicians surrounding a garlanded *bodhi* tree – a symbol of the Buddha (the Hinayanas preferred not to depict him figuratively); it's believed to be the earliest surviving Buddhist mural in India. Elsewhere on the walls is graffiti scrawled by the British soldiers who rediscovered the caves in 1819.

The apsidal-ended hall itself, divided by three rows of painted octagonal pillars, is dominated by a huge monolithic **stupa** at its far end. If there's no one else around, test out the *chaitya*'s amazing acoustics.

Caves 16 and 17

The next cave of interest, **Cave 16**, is another spectacular fifth-century *vihara*, with the famous painting known as the **Dying Princess** near the front of its left wall. The "princess" was actually a queen named **Sundari**, and she isn't dying, but fainting after hearing the news that her husband, King Nanda (Buddha's cousin), is about to renounce his throne to take up monastic orders. The opposite walls show events from Buddha's early life as **Siddhartha**.

Cave 17, dating from between the mid-fifth and early sixth centuries, boasts the best-preserved and most varied paintings in Ajanta. While you wait to enter, have a look at the frescoes on the **veranda**. Above the door, eight seated Buddhas, including Maitreya, the Buddha-to-come, look down. To the left, an amorous princely couple share a last glass of wine before giving their worldly wealth away to the poor. The wall that forms the far left side of the veranda features fragments of an elaborate "Wheel of Life". Inside the cave, the murals are, once more, dominated by the illustrations of the Jatakas, particularly those in which the Buddha takes the form of an animal to illustrate certain virtues. This is also where you'll find the exquisite and much-celebrated portrait

CAVE PAINTING TECHNIQUES

The basic **painting techniques** used by the artists of Ajanta to create the caves' lustrous kaleidoscopes of colour changed little over the eight centuries the site was in use, from 200 BC to 650 AD. First, the rough stone surfaces were primed with a thick coating of paste made from clay, cow-dung, animal hair and vegetable fibre. Next, a finer layer of smooth white lime was applied. Before this was dry, the artists quickly sketched the outlines of their pictures using red cinnabar, which they then filled in with an undercoat of *terre-verte*. The **pigments**, all derived from natural water-soluble substances (kaolin chalk for white, lamp soot for black, glauconite for green, ochre for yellow and imported lapis lazuli for blue), were thickened with glue and added only after the undercoat was completely dry. Thus the Ajanta paintings are not, strictly speaking, frescoes (always executed on damp surfaces), but **tempera**. Finally, once dry, the murals were painstakingly polished with a smooth stone to bring out their natural sheen. The artists' only sources of **light** were oil-lamps and sunshine reflected into the caves by metal mirrors and pools of water (the external courtyards were flooded expressly for this purpose), a constraint that makes their extraordinary mastery of line, perspective and shading – which endow Ajanta's paintings with their characteristic otherworldly light – all the more remarkable.

of a sultry, dark-skinned princess admiring herself in a mirror while her handmaidens and a female dwarf look on. The *chowkidars* will demonstrate how, when illuminated from the side, her iridescent eyes and jewellery glow like pearls against the brooding, dark background.

Cave 19

Excavated during the mid-fifth century, when the age of Mahayana Buddhism was in full swing, **Cave 19** is indisputably Ajanta's most magnificent *chaitya* hall, its **facade** teeming with elaborate sculpture. Inside, the faded frescoes are of less note than the sculpture around the tops of the pillars. The standing Buddha at the far end, another Mahayana innovation, is even more remarkable. Notice the development from the stumpier *stupas* enshrined within the early *chaityas* (caves 9 and 10) to this more elongated version. Its umbrellas, supported by angels and a vase of divine nectar, reach right up to the vaulted roof.

Caves 21 to 26

Caves 21 to 26 date from the seventh century, a couple of hundred years after the others, and form a separate group at the far end of the cliff. Apart from the unfinished **Cave 24**, whose roughly hacked trenches and pillars give an idea of how the original excavation was carried out here, the only one worth a close look is **Cave 26**. Envisaged on a similarly grand scale to Cave 19, this impressive **chaitya** hall was never completed. Nevertheless, the sculpture is among the most vivid and sensuous at Ajanta. On the left wall as you enter the cave, the colossal image of **Parinirvarna** (Siddhartha reclining on his deathbed) is the essence of tranquility. Note the weeping mourners below, and the flying angels and musicians above, preparing to greet the sage as he drifts into nirvana. Two panels down, and in dramatic contrast, the **Temptation of Mara** frieze depicts Buddha ensconced under a peepal tree as seven tantalizing sisters try to seduce him. Their father, the satanic Mara, watches from astride an elephant in the top left corner. The ruse to lead the Buddha astray fails, of course, eventually (bottom right) forcing the evil adversary and his daughters to retreat.

The viewpoint

The climb to the **viewpoint** from where the British hunting party first spotted the Ajanta caves is well worth the effort – the panorama over the Waghora gorge and its surrounding walls of bare, flat-topped mountains is spectacular. From the far side of the iron footbridge beneath Cave 8, steps lead up the opposite side of the ravine to a small tin-roofed shelter, where the full majesty of the sheer-sided gorge becomes clear. From here it's a stiff twenty-minute climb straight ahead to the clearly visible viewpoint at the ridge of the hill.

ARRIVAL AND DEPARTURE | AJANTA

By bus All MSRTC buses (every 30min) between Aurangabad (2hr 30min–3hr), 108km southwest, and the nearest railhead at Jalgaon (1hr), 58km north, stop on request at the Ajanta T-junction, which is 4km from the caves on the main road. Provided that you catch an early enough service up here, it's possible to see the caves, grab a bite to eat, and then head off again

in either direction (there are facilities for storing your luggage here).
By taxi A taxi for the roundtrip from Aurangabad, with waiting time, costs around ₹2700; from Jalgaon you can expect to pay about ₹1500.
By tour Travel agencies in Aurangabad offer rather rushed tours (see p.635) of Ajanta.

GETTING AROUND

The Ajanta T-junction All vehicles (including taxis and tour buses) must terminate at the Ajanta T-junction, where you'll find a tourist complex with snack joints,

toilets and hawker stalls; a much-delayed, state-of-the-art visitor centre has been due to open for several years, but was still idle at the time of research. After paying an

₹10 "amenities fee" to enter the complex, you catch one of the supposedly eco-friendly green buses regularly ply the route to and from the caves (non-a/c ₹10, a/c ₹20 one way).

ACCOMMODATION AND EATING

Since the first bus from the T-junction to the caves doesn't leave until 9am, there's little advantage in staying locally, though there are some reasonable accommodation options. For food, apart from the uninspiring MTDC dining halls just outside the entrance to the caves and at the *MTDC Holiday Resort*, you have a choice of Padmapani Park's pure veg restaurant and the nearby string of typical Maharashtran roadside *dhabas* that line the main highway.

MTDC Holiday Resort Fardapur ☎02438 244230. Located around 1.5km from the T-junction in the village of Fardapur, this hotel is pretty basic, with dowdy attached rooms and a low-cost dorm, as well as an unremarkable restaurant.Dorm ₹200, double ₹1760

MTDC T-Junction Guest House Close to the tourist complex ☎02438 244230. Set in attractive gardens a short wander from the tourist complex and the bus stop, this faded guesthouse has five spacious, split-level rooms,

all a/c, attached bathrooms and small private verandas. The main drawback is that, apart from the nearby snack stalls, there's nowhere to eat. ₹2820

Padmapani Park Fardapur ☎02438 244280, ⓦhotelpadmapaniparkajanta.com. At the edge of Fardapur, 1km walk from the *Holiday Resort*, is this simple, fairly clean hotel, popular with Indian tourists. The rooms are a bit shabby, but the restaurant is very good. ₹920

Lonar

Few visitors reach the crater at **LONAR** but those who do find this **meteorite-formed lake** an amazing and tranquil place. Referred to as "Taratirth" in a Hindu legend that correctly claimed it was created by a shooting star, the gigantic hole in the ground was formed about 50,000 years ago when a lump of space rock survived its fiery descent through the atmosphere to bury itself here. As the only such crater formed in basalt rock in the world, the site is not just a geological curiosity but also highly valuable to scientists – NASA has made extensive studies due to its apparent similarity to some lunar and Martian landscapes – though many of the lake's mysteries, such as the extreme alkalinity of its thick, sulphurous water, continue to baffle.

Numerous steep paths lead down to the lake from the rim, the principal one starting around 500m from the *MTDC Holiday Resort* and emerging in the basin near a twelfth-century temple dedicated to Shiva. A complete circuit of the lake, surrounded by forest and home to a rich array of birdlife, takes around three hours. En route you will discover numerous other seemingly lost Shaivite shrines. While huddling along a ravine etched into the crater's northeastern slope – an alternative path back up – is a fascinating cluster of temples, fed by a spring, or *dhar*, supposedly originating from the Ganges. Before leaving, it's well worth searching out the tenth-century Chalukyan **Daitya Sudana** temple in Lonar village, its walls inside and out crawling with a profusion of exquisite carvings of mythological scenes.

ARRIVAL AND INFORMATION

LONAR

By taxi The easiest way to get to Lonar is by taxi from Aurangabad, which costs ₹2500–3500 for a day-trip, depending on the car and your negotiating skills.

By bus There are two morning buses direct from Aurangabad (4hr), with the last bus back around 4pm;

services stop in the centre of Lonar village, around 2km from the lake.

Guides For more on the crater, it's worth hiring a local guide; Gajanan Kharat (☎07260 221428) is recommended.

ACCOMMODATION

MTDC Holiday Resort Opposite the crater ☎07260 22160. The only accommodation in Lonar is this rather ghostly hotel built for a tourist rush that never came. The

attached rooms are comfortable enough, though a little uninspiring, but the restaurant has a superbly sited terrace from which to survey the lake. ₹1000

Jalgaon

Straddling an important junction on the Central and Western Railway networks, as well as the main trans-Deccan trunk road, NH-6, **JALGAON** is a prosperous market town for the region's cotton and banana growers, and a key jumping-off point for travellers heading to or from the Ajanta caves, 58km south. Even though the town holds nothing of interest, you may find yourself obliged to hole up here to be well placed for a morning departure.

ARRIVAL AND INFORMATION

By train The railway station, on Station Rd, appropriately enough, is well served by mainline trains between Delhi, Kolkata and Mumbai, and convenient for most cities to the north on the Central Railway. Express services also pass through en route to join the Southeastern Railway.

Destinations Agra (7–8 daily; 14hr–17hr 58min); Bengaluru (1 daily; 24hr 10min); Bhopal (9–10 daily; 6hr 50min–9hr 15min); Chennai (1 daily; 23hr 5min); Delhi (7 daily; 17hr 50min–22hr); Gwalior (7–8 daily; 12hr 20min–16hr 7min); Mumbai (17–18 daily; 6hr 42min–8hr 40min); Nagpur (11–15 daily; 5hr 30min–9hr 5min); Pune (5 daily; 8hr 25min–11hr 12min); Wardha Junction (for Sevagram; 11–15 daily; 5hr 9min–6hr 45min); Varanasi (4–7 daily; 19hr 30min–28hr 25min).

By bus The busy MSRTC bus stand is 1.5km across town

from the railway station (around ₹30–40 in an auto-rickshaw). There are frequent buses to Aurangabad (every 30min; 3hr 30min–4hr), 160km away, all of which stop at the Ajanta T-junction (1hr). MSRTC also runs buses to Mumbai (1–2 daily; 9–11hr), Nagpur (1–2 daily; 9–10hr) and Pune (5–6 daily; 9–10hr), but preferable are the (generally overnight) buses run by the private companies such as Shree Durga Travels (☎0257 222 8124) and Uncle Travels (☎0257 224 1294); tickets can be booked at the travel agents that line up along Station Rd.

Services For internet try the Om Internet Café (₹20 /hr), on the first floor of the Golani Market shopping centre, just beyond the roundabout at the top of Station Rd. There's an ATM in the railway station, and numerous others around town.

ACCOMMODATION AND EATING

★ **Hotel Arya** Navi Peth, a 10min walk from the railway station ☎0257 222 6803. There's no better place to eat than this economical veg restaurant, which gets packed out at lunchtime. The menu's focus is north Indian and Punjabi (mains ₹30–90), though there are a few south Indian breakfast options too. To get here from the railway station, turn left at the top of Station Rd and then left again at the clock tower. The owners also run *Arya Niwas*, one of the town's best pure veg thali joints, which you pass en route from the station. Daily 7am–10.30pm.

★ **Plaza Hotel** Station Rd, 2min walk from the railway station ☎0257 222 7354, ✉hotelplaza_jal @yahoo.com. By far the best place to stay in Jalgaon – in fact one of the best budget hotels in India – is this

welcoming and very spruce hotel. Immaculately clean rooms come with attached bathrooms and feature a cool, white minimalist design; the huge a/c "deluxe" room (₹1300) is particularly good. The owner is very friendly and well-informed, and staff will provide tea in your room if you're leaving early in the morning. **₹550**

Royal Palace Mahabal Rd, 10–15min auto-rickshaw ride from the railway station ☎0257 223 3888, ✉hotelroyalpalace.in. The grand marble lobby, decorated with a glitzy chandelier, a reproduction of the Mona Lisa and fountain filled with fish, raise expectations that the mid-range rooms fail to match; still they are comfortable enough, and there's a good restaurant on site. Book online for a 10–20 percent discount. **₹2400**

Nagpur and around

Capital of the "land of oranges", **NAGPUR** is the focus of government attempts to develop industry in the remote northeastern corner of Maharashtra – most foreigners in the city are here for business rather than pleasure purposes. The trickle of visitors who do stop here tend to do so en route to Madhya Pradesh, or the Gandhian ashrams at **Sevagram** and **Paunar**, a two-hour journey southwest. The other worthwhile excursion is the ninety-minute bus ride northeast to the hilltop temple complex at **Ramtek**.

In the city itself, the most prominent landmark is the Sitabuldi Fort, standing on a saddle between two low hills above the railway station, though it's closed to the public.

North and west of the fort, the pleasantly green Civil Lines district holds some grand Raj-era buildings, dating from the time when this was the capital of the vast Central Provinces region.

ARRIVAL AND DEPARTURE

NAGPUR

Geographically at the virtual centre of India, Nagpur is handily placed for connections all across the country – though a long way from anywhere.

By plane The airport is around 8km southwest of the centre (around ₹200–250 by auto-rickshaw, a bit more by taxi).

Destinations Bhopal (6 weekly; 50min); Delhi (1 daily; 1hr 30min); Hyderabad (1 daily; 1hr 25min); Kolkata (1 daily; 1hr 30min); Mumbai (1–2 daily; 1hr 20min); Pune (2 daily; 1hr 15min); Raipur (1 daily; 40min).

By train Nagpur's busy central mainline railway station is a short auto-rickshaw (₹20–30) ride from the main hotel district along Central Ave. The quickest train to Mumbai is the #12290 *Nagpur CSTM Duront* (daily 8.50am; 11hr).

Destinations Bhopal (8–15 daily; 5hr 50min–8hr 40min); Chennai (4–10 daily; 16hr 45min–23hr 25min);

Delhi (7–14 daily; 14hr–21hr 40min); Hyderabad (2–5 daily; 8hr 25min–10hr 20min); Jabalpur (3–5 daily; 8hr 45min–19hr 30min); Jalgaon (11–15 daily; 5hr 30min–9hr 5min); Kolkata (4–7 daily; 17hr 25min–19hr 30min); Mumbai (7–9 daily; 11hr–23hr 40min); Nasik (6–8 daily; 9hr 25min–20hr 15min); Pune (2–3 daily; 15hr–17hr 40min); Wardha Junction (for Sevagram; 11–15 daily; 53min–1hr 22min).

By bus MSRTC buses pull in at the state bus stand, 2km southeast of the railway station.

Destinations Aurangabad (6 daily; 12hr); Jabalpur (3 daily; 7–8hr); Jalgaon (2 daily; 9hr); Pune (4 daily; 16hr); Ramtek (every 30min; 1hr 30min); Wardha (every 30min; 2–3hr).

INFORMATION

Tourist information The MTDC tourist office (Mon–Sat 10am–6pm; ☎ 0712 253 3325) is 2.5km west of the centre on West High Court Rd in Civil Lines, but is only useful for booking accommodation. If you're heading to Madhya Pradesh, you can get information from the helpful MP Tourism office on the fourth floor of

the Lokmat Building, Wardha Rd (Mon–Sat 10am–5pm except 2nd and 3rd Sat of the month; ☎ 0712 244 2378).

Services The State Bank of India on Kingsway, near the railway station, changes foreign currency. ATMs are common throughout the city.

ACCOMMODATION AND EATING

Grand Hotel Just off Central Ave, around 1km east of the bus stand ☎ 0712 661 7850. The *Grand* is one of the better budget hotels on Central Ave, though as standards are generally low, this isn't a ringing endorsement. The cleanish rooms here are a bit shabby, but OK for a night. ₹450

Naivedhyam Just off Jhowsi Rani Chowk in Sitabuldi ☎ 0712 256 3070. This swish, first-floor restaurant, right in the centre of town, is something of a Nagpur institution, serving up delicious veg Indian/Chinese food to a bizarre Hindi-Hawaiian music soundtrack. The "deluxe" thali (₹175) is a good bet. Daily noon–3.30pm & 7–10.30pm.

Pride Wardha Rd, opposite the airport ☎ 0712 229 1102,

ⓦ pridehotel.com. One of Nagpur's best top-end hotels, the *Pride* often plays host to visiting cricket teams. The en suites are spacious and fully equipped, though some have rather kitsch 1970s-era carpets and curtains. Facilities include a pool and gym, a clutch of fine cafés/restaurants and an appealing bar. Good online discounts available. ₹7520

Tuli International 1km northwest of the railway station ☎ 0712 665 3555, ⓦ tuligroup.com. Of Nagpur's numerous business-traveller-oriented hotels, this hotel in the quiet Sadar district probably has the most charm; its chandeliered lobby, carpeted corridors and chintzy decor give it an endearingly old-fashioned feel. Rooms are comfortable and there's a good restaurant and bar. ₹5250

Ramtek

The picturesque cluster of whitewashed hilltop temples and shrines at **RAMTEK**, 40km northeast of Nagpur on the main Jabalpur road (NH-7), is one of those alluring apparitions you spy from afar on long journeys through central India. According to the Ramayana, this craggy, scrub-strewn outcrop was the spot where Rama, Sita and Lakshmana paused on their way back from Lanka. Although few traces of these ancient times have survived, the site's old paved pilgrim trails, sacred lake, tumbledown shrines and fine views across the endless plains more than live up to its distant promise.

Ram Mandir and the Kalidas Smarak

Around 4.5km from the bus stand • **Kalidas Smarak** Daily 8.30am–8pm • ₹5

On the fringes of the town a flight of stone steps climbs steeply up the side of Ramtek hill to the **Ram Mandir**. Built in 1740, the temple stands on the site of an earlier fifth-century structure, of which only three small sandstone shrines remain. Just beneath the temple complex stands the circular **Kalidas Smarak**, a modern memorial to the great Sanskrit poet, Kalidasa. The pavilion's interior walls are decorated with painted panels depicting scenes from his life and works.

Ambala Lake

Just off the road that runs between the bus stand and the Ram Mandir

Another of Ramtek's sacred sites is Ambala Lake, a holy bathing tank that lies 1.5km along a pilgrims' trail at the bottom of the gully, enfolded by a spur of parched brown hills. Its main attractions are the temples and *ghats* clinging to its muddy banks. More energetic visitors may wish to combine a look with a *parikrama*, or circular tour of the tank, taking in the semiderelict cenotaphs and weed-choked shrines scattered along the more tranquil north and western shore.

ARRIVAL AND DEPARTURE   RAMTEK

By bus Frequent buses shuttle between Nagpur and Ramtek (every 30min; 1hr 30min). From the bus stand, an auto-rickshaw will take you the 4.5km to the Ram Mandir via Ambala Lake for around ₹100.

ACCOMMODATION

Rajkamal Resort Near the temple complex ☎07114 202761, ⍟rajkamalresorts.com. Most people visit Ramtek as a day-trip from Nagpur, but if you want to stay the night, try the *Rajkamal Resort*. It has acceptable, though overpriced rooms, as well as a picturesquely sited open-air restaurant serving so-so food. ₹**1500**

Sevagram

Main ashram compound Daily 6am–6pm • Free • **Visitors centre** Daily except Tues 10am–6pm • Free

SEVAGRAM, Gandhi's model "Village of Service", is set deep in the serene Maharashtran countryside, 9km from the railroad town of **WARDHA**. The Mahatma moved here from his former ashram in Gujarat during the monsoon of 1936, on the invitation of his friend Seth Jamnalal Bajaj. Right at the centre of the Subcontinent, within easy reach of the Central Railway, it made an ideal headquarters for the national, non-violent Satyagraha movement, combining seclusion with the easy access to other parts of the country Gandhi needed in order to carry out his political activities.

These days, the small settlement is a cross between a museum and living centre for the promulgation of Gandhian philosophies. Interested visitors are welcome to spend a couple of days here, helping in the fields, attending discussions and prayer meetings, and learning the dying art of hand-spinning. The older ashramites, or *saadhaks*, are veritable founts of wisdom when it comes to the words of their guru, Gandhiji.

Once past the absorbing visitors' centre, with its photos and documents recounting Gandhi's life, the real focal point of the ashram is the sublimely peaceful main compound entered a few hundred metres along the road. These modest rustic huts – among them the Mahatma's main residence – have been preserved exactly the way they were when the great man and his disciples lived here in the last years of the Independence struggle. A small *khadi* shop sells handloomed cloth and other products made on site.

ARRIVAL AND DEPARTURE SEVAGRAM

By train Wardha Junction railway station, 77km southwest of Nagpur and 9km west of Sevagram, is connected by regular services to Nagpur (11–15 daily; 53min–1hr 22min) and Jalgaon (11–15 daily; 5hr 9min–6hr 45min).

By bus Local buses (every 30min; around 20min) run

between Wardha and the crossroads outside the Kasturba Gandhi Hospital, from where it's a 1km walk to the ashram. Regular buses also connect Wardha and Nagpur (every 30min; 2–3hr).

By auto-rickshaw An auto-rickshaw from the bus stand to Sevagram and Paunar (see below) costs around ₹250.

ACCOMMODATION

Rustam Bhavan Guest House In the main ashram compound ☎07152 284753. If you want to spend some time at the ashram, you can stay in the basic but spotless *Rustam Bhavan Guest House*, though you will be expected to do a couple of hours' communal work a day. Simple, super-healthy veg meals are on offer. ₹100

Yatri Niwas Opposite the main compound ☎9822 797520 or ☎07152 284753. The *Yatri Niwas* provides accommodation in thatch-roofed brick huts, though it's a fair bit scruffier than the *Rustam Bhavan Guest House* nearby. ₹100

Paunar

Vinoba Bhave's ashram at **PAUNAR**, 3km from Sevagram has an altogether more dynamic feel than its more famous cousin at Sevagram. Bhave (1895–1982), a close friend and disciple of Gandhi, best remembered for his successful Bhoodan, or **land gift**, campaign to persuade wealthy landowners to hand over farmland to the poor, founded the ashram in 1938 to develop the concept of **swarajya**, or "self-sufficiency". Consequently, organic gardening, milk production, spinning and weaving have an even higher profile here than the regular meditation, prayer and yoga sessions. Another difference between this institution and the one up the road is that the *saadhaks* here are almost all female.

In the ashram's living quarters, Bhave's old **room** is kept as a shrine. Stone steps lead down from the upper level to a small terrace looking out over the **ghats**, where two small memorials mark the spots where a handful of Gandhi's, and later Bhave's, ashes were scattered onto the river. Every year, on January 30, the *ghats* are inundated with half a million people who come here to mark the anniversary of Gandhi's death.

ARRIVAL AND DEPARTURE PAUNAR

By bus Paunar can be reached by bus from Wardha (every 30min; 2–3hr); hop off at the old stone bridge, which is close to the ashram.

On foot Alternatively, you can walk the 3km from

Sevagram (see opposite). The path, a cart track that runs over the hill opposite the hospital crossroads, comes out in the roadside village 1km west of the Paunar ashram.

ACCOMMODATION AND EATING

Paunar Ashram 3km from Sevagram ☎07152 288388. As with Sevagram, it is possible to stay in one of the visitors' rooms at the ashram, though you should call

in advance to check there's space. Meals, made from organic, home-grown produce, are available on request. ₹100

The Konkan coast

Despite the recent appearance of a string of upscale resorts pitched at wealthy urbanites, the coast stretching south from Mumbai, known as the **Konkan**, remains relatively unspoilt. Empty beaches, backed by casuarina and areca trees and coconut plantations, regularly slip in and out of view, framed by the distant Ghats, while little fortified towns preserve a distinct coastal culture, with its own dialect of Marathi and fiery cuisine. The number of rivers and estuaries slicing the coast meant that for years this little-explored area was difficult to navigate, but the Konkan railway, which winds inland between Mumbai and Kerala via Goa, now renders it more easily accessible; proposals for a seaplane service from Mumbai was also announced in late 2012 – check the latest with the MPTDC.

There are numerous appealing **homestays** along the Konkan coast; ZaraHutke (☎98670 00918, ⓦzarahutke.in) has a good selection.

Murud-Janjira

The first interesting place to break the journey south is the small port of **MURUD-JANJIRA**, 165km south of Mumbai. A traditional trade centre that once belonged to a dynasty of former Abyssinian slaves known as the Siddis, it still features plenty of attractive wooden houses, some brightly painted and fronted by pillared verandas. The gently shelving beach is wide and safe for swimming, though you'll find the sea more inviting if you head further south or north.

In Murud, the 1661 Kasa Fort sits in the open sea 2km off the beach but cannot be visited, nor can the impressive nineteenth-century palace of the last nawab, which dominates the northern end of the bay. Fine views of the coast and surrounding countryside can be had, however, from the hilltop **Dattatreya Temple**, sporting an Islamic-style tower but dedicated to the triple-headed deity comprising Brahma, Vishnu and Shiva.

Janjira Fort

5km south of Murud • Daily 7am–5.30pm • Free • Local *hodka* boats (20min) sail to the fort from the Rajpuri jetty, a short auto-rickshaw ride away, though, since they seat 20 and only leave when full, at quiet times you may have to charter the boat yourself (around ₹500)

Just offshore some 5km south of Murud-Janjira stands the imposing sixteenth-century **Janjira Fort**, one of the few the Marathas failed to penetrate, and now a picture of majestic dereliction. The boat trip to the fort is a serene trip, and once there you're given an hour so to explore the formidable battlements, though the interior lies mostly in ruins.

ARRIVAL AND INFORMATION MURUD-JANJIRA

By bus and catamaran or ferry The nearest railhead to Murud is Roha, a 2hr bus ride away, which is why most travellers still reach the town by jumping on one of the roughly hourly hydrofoil catamarans or regular ferries (1hr) from the Gateway of India in Mumbai to Mandawa, on the southern side of Mumbai harbour (see p.607). Buses meet the boats and shuttle passengers straight to Alibag (45min), from where you can catch regular government buses to Murud (every 1–2hr; 2hr). Most direct bus services (every 1–2hr) from Mumbai Central take 6hr; there are also two faster buses (4hr 30min) which must be booked in advance. Buses stop along Murud's main street, Durbar Rd, parallel to the coast

Money Bring enough cash to cover your stay – at the time of writing there was no ATM in the village nor would the sole bank exchange foreign currency.

ACCOMMODATION AND EATING

The best of the accommodation is lined up along Durbar Rd. There is no shortage of regular, clean and inexpensive local eating options south of the chowk.

Dandekar Home Stay Just south of the chowk ☎9221 260260. Located on a narrow stretch of beach (look out for the "Rooms available here" sign), this friendly, family-run homestay has clean and simple rooms. Tasty meals can be provided on request. ₹750

Golden Swan Resort On the edge of town, 1km north of the chowk ☎02144 274078, ⓦgoldenswan.com. This resort is the most comfortable option In Murud, with a/c cottages (₹3760) sleeping up to six people and smart a/c rooms (some with views of the sea and the fort); prices drop by about a third during the week. There's also a restaurant and bike rental. ₹3405

Sea Shell Resort Darbar Rd, next to the police station ☎02144 274306, ⓦseashellmurud.com. This centrally located hotel has decent if rather plain rooms (with fans or a/c) overlooking the sea and a small pool shaded by palm trees, and a restaurant. Staff can arrange dolphin-spotting boat trips. ₹2500

Ganpatipule

Some 215km south of Murud-Janjira lies **GANPATIPULE**, a tiny village centred on a modern **Ganapati temple**. Approached via a long covered walkway, the temple is built around a Ganapati omnar, a naturally formed – though hardly accurate – image of the elephant god, which attracts thousands of Indian pilgrims each year. Much more impressive is Ganpatipule's spectacular white-sand **beach**, which extends for several kilometres either side of the village. The sea is generally safe for swimming, though you should exercise caution between June and October.

ARRIVAL AND DEPARTURE
GANPATIPULE

By train/bus To get to Ganpatipule, either make your way to Ratnagiri (on the Konkan railway and well connected by state and private buses to other cities in the state) and take a local bus (every 30min–1hr; 1hr 30min) the last 32km, or catch one of the direct MSRTC services from Mumbai (1–2 daily; 10hr) or Kolhapur (every 2–3hr; 4hr). Buses usually stop outside the *MTDC Resort*, though at festival times you may be dropped along the main road at the edge of the village, a 1.5km walk or rickshaw ride from the beach.

ACCOMMODATION AND EATING

★ **Atithi Parinay** 12km south of Ganpatipule ☎ 90499 81309, ✆ atithiparinay.com. Owned by an interior designer, this delightful homestay is a great place to unwind. Choose to stay in a comfortable "Swiss" tent (with an attached bathroom), cottage, bungalow or very atmospheric treehouse (₹3500). Home-cooked veg meals are on offer, as are a range of activities, including yoga, hiking, beach visits and trips to local palaces and temples. ₹**2700**

MTDC Resort In the centre of Ganpatipule ☎ 02357 235248. Set around neat lawns right at the heart of the village, this state-run resort has a range of reasonable rooms, some with breezy balconies, occupying a row of attractive two-storey villas a stone's throw from the sea; the "Konkani Huts", in a shaded beachside compound a 10min walk north, are poorly maintained and disappointing, however. There's a good restaurant-bar on site. ₹**2230**

Matheran

The quirky, Raj-era hill station of **MATHERAN**, 108km east of Mumbai, is set on a narrow north–south ridge at an altitude of 800m in the Sahyadri Range. From evocatively named viewpoints, at the edge of sheer cliffs that plunge into deep ravines, you can see way across the hazy plains – on a good day, so they say, as far as Mumbai. The town itself, shrouded in thick mist for much of the year, has, for the moment, one unique attribute: cars, buses, motorbikes and auto-rickshaws are prohibited. That, added to the journey up, on a **miniature train** that chugs its way through spectacular scenery to the crest of the hill, gives the town an agreeably quaint, time-warped feel.

Matheran (literally "mother forest") has been a popular retreat from the heat of Mumbai since the nineteenth century. These days, few foreign visitors venture up here, and those that do only hang around for a couple of days, to kill time before a flight or to sample the charms of Matheran's colonial-era hotels. The tourist season lasts from mid-September to mid-June (at other times it's raining or misty), and is at its most hectic around Diwali and Christmas, in April and May, and over virtually any weekend. There's really nothing up here to do but relax, explore the woods on foot or horseback and enjoy the fresh air and views.

As the crow flies, Matheran is only 6.5km from Neral on the plain below, but the train climbs up on 21km of track with no less than 281 curves, said to be among the sharpest on any railway in the world. Sadly, the steam engines that once handled the demanding haul puffed their last in 1980, to be replaced by cast-off diesels from Darjeeling, Shimla and Ooty. The train ride is a treat, especially if you get a window seat, but be prepared for a squash unless you travel to first class.

The points and forest walks

Matheran occupies a long, narrow, semicircular plateau, bounded for most of its extent by sheer cliffs. These taper at regular intervals into outcrops, or **points**, revealing through the tree canopy wonderful panoramas of distant hills and plains. Few visitors manage more than half a dozen in a single outing, but in midwinter when temperatures are pleasantly cool, it's possible to tick off the majority in a long day's trek.

For a quick taster, head south from the main bazaar past *Lord's Central* hotel on Matheran's eastern flank to Alexander Point, pressing on beyond it to Chowk Point – the most southerly of the mountain's spurs. This shouldn't take more than a couple of hours there and back. Another enjoyable route on an old cart track winds around the western rim, past a series of gorgeous British-era bungalows to Louisa, Coronation and Sunset (or Porcupine) points, the last – as its name

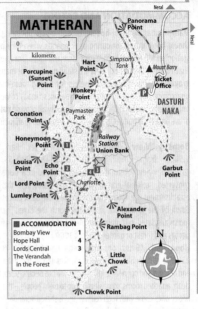

implies – regarded as the choicest place to see the sun go down.

Accurate topographical maps of the mountain and its many paths are all but impossible to come by, although there's a wonderful old British one proudly on display in the dining room of *Lord's Central* hotel, which walkers are welcome to consult

All the viewpoints are walkable, and horses and rickshaws are available (see below).

ARRIVAL AND INFORMATION
MATHERAN

By train To reach Matheran by rail you must first get to Neral Junction, served by frequent overground metro trains (around 19 daily) from Mumbai's CST and Dadar (1hr 45min–2hr 15min), terminating at Karjat, plus two daily fast services (1hr 22min). One or two daily fast trains (2hr 35min–3hr 9min) travel between Neral and Pune; there more frequent services between Pune and Karjat, from where you can backtrack to Neral on suburban services. From mid-October to mid-June, narrow-gauge trains chug up from Neral to Matheran (4 daily; 1hr 40min–2hr). During the monsoon services are dependent on the weather and best not relied on. All trains are timed to tie in with incoming mainline expresses, so don't worry about missing a connection if the one you're on is delayed – the toy train should wait

– but it's worth booking a day in advance at weekends in order to guarantee a seat. Matheran railway station is in the centre of the hill station on MG Rd, which runs roughly north–south.

By minibus or taxi A taxi from Mumbai (2hr 30min–3hr) to Matheran costs from around ₹1900, one to Pune costs from around ₹2000 (2hr 30min–3hr). Shared taxis (₹60/person, ₹300/car; 30min) and minibuses (₹60; 30min) shuttle regularly between Matheran and Neral. All motorized transport parks at the taxi stand next to the *MTDC Resort* at Dasturi Naka, 2km from Matheran.

Services Neither of Matheran's banks offers foreign exchange, though the ATM at the Union Bank, just south of the station, accepts foreign cards; nevertheless, it is worth bringing some cash with you just in case.

GETTING AROUND

By porter, horse and rickshaw From the taxi stand – after paying the entry toll (₹40 adults, ₹20 children) – you can walk with a porter (₹150–250), be led by a rather fragile-looking horse (₹150–300) or take a hand-pulled rickshaw (₹350–450) to your hotel; you are

expected to haggle. If you're happy to carry your own bags, follow the rail tracks, which cut straight to the middle of Matheran, rather than the more convoluted dirt road. Trips to the town's various viewpoints cost from ₹300 by horse and ₹450 by rickshaw.

ACCOMMODATION AND EATING

Matheran has plenty of **hotels**, though all are pricey – particularly at weekends, when rates almost double (and you should book ahead), or during peak periods when they become uniformly astronomical. Most are close to the railway station on MG Rd, with more expensive and more family-orientated places on the road behind it, Kasturba Bhavan. Note that 10am or 11am check-outs are standard, and that many places close down during the rainy off-season. **Single male travellers** should brace themselves for a long room-hunt as the town's hoteliers almost universally refuse beds to unaccompanied males ("stags"). The reason: so many come to the hill station from Mumbai to kill themselves. Most places only have hot water in the morning. Virtually all provide **full** or **half-board** at reasonable rates, but if you want to eat out, or are on a tight budget, try one of the numerous thali joints around the station.

Bombay View Southwest of Paymaster Park, 1.5km from the station ☎02148 230453, ⓦ bombayviewhotelmatheran.com. Housed in a huge converted colonial-era mansion and annexe, this establishment is a notch pricier than the more basic places down by the station, but just about worth the extra. The rooms are dated, but most have plenty of space, as well as sitouts and forest or garden views. ₹**3000**

Hope Hall MG Rd, opposite Lord's Central ☎02148 230253, ⓦ hopehallmatheran.com. Situated at the quiet end of town and open since 1875, *Hope Hall* has decent-sized, clean, attached rooms, some sleeping up to eight people – the better ones come with high ceilings and a shared veranda – scattered across a secluded yard. Badminton and table tennis facilities. Weekday discounts. 24hr check-out. ₹**2750**

Lords Central MG Rd ☎02148 230228, ⓦ matheran .com. Though worn at the edges – its wonky verandas, poinsettias, hard beds and tasty (and copious) set meals give it the feel of a 1930s boarding house – eccentric, Raj-era *Lords* is one of Matheran's best-loved institutions, thanks in no small part to its irreverent, anecdote-loving Parsi owners. It also boasts spectacular views from its poolside terrace garden. Rates include full board. ₹**4000**

★ **The Verandah in the Forest** 2km southwest of station ☎02148 230296, ⓦ neemranahotels.com. Set in woods a short way above Charlotte Lake, this sumptuously restored nineteenth-century bungalow is reason enough to come to Matheran. Apart from the evocative period decor and furnishings, its greatest asset is a huge west-facing veranda smothered in foliage – one of the most perfect spots in India for lunch (if pre-booked) or afternoon tea and biscuits (though beware the pilfering monkeys). Rates are reasonable and fairly constant throughout the year. ₹**4700**

Lonavala and around

Just thirty years ago, the town of **LONAVALA** (also spelt Lonavla), 110km southeast of Mumbai and 62km northwest of Pune, was a quiet retreat in the Sahyadri hills.

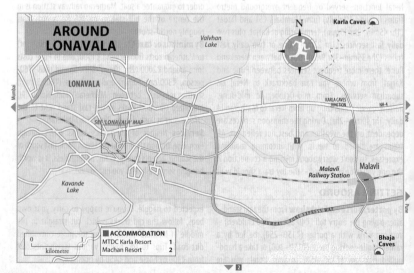

AROUND LONAVALA

■ ACCOMMODATION	
MTDC Karla Resort	1
Machan Resort	2

VISITING BHAJA AND KARLA

The two sites lie some 6km apart, to the east of Lonavala, and can be covered under your own steam by bus and/or train in a day, if you are prepared for a good walk (bring plenty of water), though it is easier to hire an **auto-rickshaw** (around ₹400–500) or taxi (about ₹800–1000) for the tour, both of which can usually be found at Lonavala railway station. It's a good idea to avoid weekends if you want to enjoy the caves in peace and quiet; Karla, in particular, gets swamped with noisy day-trippers to its Hindu shrine.

Since then, the place has mushroomed to cope with hordes of weekenders and second-home owners from the state capital, and is now only of interest as a base for the magnificent **Buddhist caves** of **Karla** and **Bhaja**, some of the finest rock-cut architecture in the northwest of the Deccan region. Though not on nearly such an impressive scale as Ajanta and Ellora, they harbour some beautifully preserved ancient sculpture, some of which dates from the Satavahana period (second century BC).

11

Bhaja

9km east of Lonavala • Daily 9am–5.30pm • ₹100 (₹5) • Passenger trains run roughly hourly from Lonavala (20–30min) to Malavli railway station, 2km from the caves; from here follow the road south of the station until it peters out (1.5km), from where it's a steep 10min climb up to the caves

The excavations at **caves** at **BHAJA** are among the oldest in India, dating from the late second to early first century BC, during the earliest, Hinayana, phase of Buddhism. You enter the complex opposite Bhaja's apsidal **chaitya** hall, which contains a *stupa* but no figures. Its 27 plain bevelled pillars lean inwards, mimicking the style of wooden buildings, and sockets in the stone of the exterior arch reveal that it once contained a wooden gate or facade. Most of the other caves consist of simple halls – *viharas* – with adjoining cells that contain plain shelf-like beds; many are fronted by rough verandas. Further south, beyond a mysterious dense cluster of fourteen **stupas**, the veranda of the **last cave**, a *vihara*, is decorated with superb carvings, which scholars have identified as the figures of the Hindu gods, Surya and Indra.

Karla

3km north of Karla Caves Junction on the Mumbai–Pune road and 11km from Lonavala • Daily 9am–5pm • ₹100 (₹5) • Three morning buses (generally 9am, 10am & 11.30am; 30min) head for the caves directly from Lonavala, with the last bus returning from Karla at 5pm

The rock-cut Buddhist *chaitya* hall at **KARLA** (also Karli), reached by steep steps that climb 110m, is the largest and best preserved in India, dating from the first century AD. Though partially obstructed by a modern Hindu temple housing a shrine to Ekviri, the enormous 14m-high facade of the hall, topped by a horseshoe-shaped window, is still an impressive sight. To the left of the entrance stands a *simhas stambha*, a tall column capped with four lions, while in the porch of the cave, dividing its three doorways, are panels of figures in six couples, presumed to have been the wealthy patrons of the hall. With their expressive faces and sensuous bodies, it's hard to believe these figures were carved around two thousand years ago.

Two rows of octagonal columns with pot-shaped bases divide the interior into three, forming a wide central aisle and, on the outside, a hall that allowed devotees to circumambulate the monolithic *stupa* at the back. Above each pillar's fluted capital kneel a pair of finely carved elephants, each mounted by two riders, one with arms draped over the other's shoulders. Amazingly, some of the timber rafters supporting the arched roof appear to date from the time when the hall was in use.

ARRIVAL AND INFORMATION

LONAVALA AND AROUND

By bus Lonavala's central bus stand is just off the old Mumbai–Pune road, but the train is an infinitely preferable way to travel.

By train The railway station is on the south side of town, a 10min walk from the bus stand area. Lonavala is on the

main railway line between Mumbai (every hour or so; 2hr–2hr 30min) and Pune (every hour or so; around 1hr), and most express trains stop here.

Services There's a small internet café, Balaji's, on the road running south from the railway station.

ACCOMMODATION AND EATING

With the odd exception, Lonavala's limited accommodation offers poor value, mainly because demand well outstrips supply for much of the year. **Rates** drop between October and March, and you can expect a 20–30 percent reduction on weekdays, but this isn't somewhere you're likely to want to unpack your bags. Lonavala holds a bewildering number of shops selling the local sweet speciality, **chikki** – a moreish amalgam of nuts, seeds or coconut set in rock-solid jaggery. Many of the town's hotels like to lay on **full board**, but you'll eat fresher food in places along the main street, which cater more for the brisk through-trade.

Citrus D Shahani Rd, a 5min auto-rickshaw ride from the bus or railway station ☎ 02114 279531, ⓦ citrushotels.com; map p.659. Slick Mumbai-style business hotel, somewhat incongruously tucked into a sleepy backstreet. The en suites have a minimalist, designer feel, and are arranged within lemon-fragranced blocks. There's a spa and a chic Astroturf-covered courtyard, and their excellent Italian/Mediterranean restaurant is the best of the hotel selection. Book via the website for the best deals. ₹7000

Machan Resort Jambulne, 17km south of Lonavala ☎ 95940 53113, ⓦ themachan.com; map p.658. Easily the best place to stay in the area (for those with deep

pockets), the *Machan* is an "off-grid" (all the electricity is generated by solar and wind power) eco-friendly resort in a rural location surrounding by 25 acres of grounds. Accommodation is provided in luxurious treehouses high above the canopy, making them a haven for birders. Rates include half-board. ₹12,000

MTDC Karla Resort 7km east of Lonavala, 1.5km west of Karla Junction ☎ 02114 282230; map p.658. Occupying a large, leafy compound a few hundred metres off the Mumbai–Pune road, this tranquil place has a range of good-value rooms and suites (₹2880) in chalets and cottages (₹2465), plus paddle boats for rent on the river behind. Check-out 9am. ₹1530

Pune

At an altitude of 598m, the prosperous city of **PUNE** (occasionally still anglicized as Poona), Maharashtra's second largest, lies close to the Western Ghat mountains (known here as the Sahyadri Hills), on the edge of the Deccan plains as they stretch away to the east. Capital of the Marathas' sovereign state in the sixteenth century until its rulers were deposed by the Brahmin Peshwa family, Pune was – thanks to its cool, dry climate – chosen by the British in 1820 as an alternative headquarters for the Bombay Presidency. Since colonial days, Pune has continued to develop as a major industrial city and now ranks along with Hyderabad, Bengaluru and Chennai as one of central/southern India's fastest growing business centres. Signs of the new prosperity abound, from huge hoardings advertising multistorey executive apartment blocks and gated estates, to coffee bars, a/c malls and hip clothing stores. Pune also has a couple of spiritual claims to fame: Koregaon Park is home to the famous Osho ashram (see p.662), while on the city's outskirts is *yogacharya* BKS Iyengar's illustrious yoga centre – a far more sober and serious institution.

Pune's centre is bordered to the north by the **River Mula** and to the west by the **River Mutha** – the two join in the northwest to form the Mutha-Mula, at Sangam

Bridge. The principal shopping area, and the greatest concentration of restaurants and hotels, is in the streets south of the railway station, particularly Connaught and, further south, **MG Road**. The old Peshwa part of town, by far the most interesting to explore, is towards the west between the fortified **Shaniwarwada Palace** and fascinating **Raja Dinkar Kelkar Museum**; old wooden *wadas* – palatial city homes – survive on these narrow, busy streets, and the Victorian, circular **Mahatma Phule Market** is always a hive of activity.

Raja Dinkar Kelkar Museum

1378 Shukrawar Peth • Daily 9.30am–5.30pm • ₹200 (₹50) • ☎ 020 2446 1556, ⓦ rajakelkarmuseum.com

Dinkar Gangadhar Kelkar (1896–1990), aside from being a celebrated Marathi poet published under the name Adnyatwasi, spent much of his life travelling and collecting arts and crafts from all over the country. In 1975, he donated his collection to the Maharashtran government for the creation of a museum dedicated to the memory of his son, Raja, who had died at the age of 12. Housed in a huge old-town mansion, the **Raja Dinkar Kelkar Museum** is a wonderful potpourri in which beauty and interest is

11

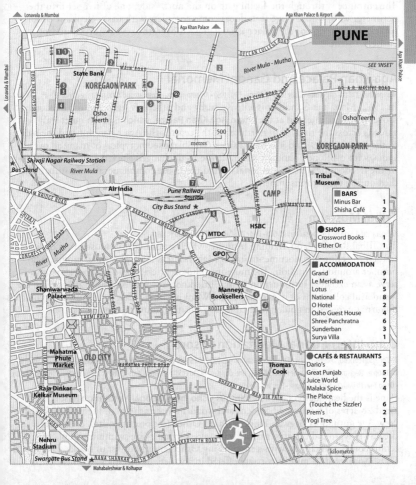

found in both artistic and everyday objects, though the sheer scale of the collection – 21,000 pieces strong – means that only a fraction can be shown at any one time. Paraphernalia associated with paan, the Indian passion, includes containers in every conceivable design: some mimic people, animals or fish, others are egg-shaped and in delicate filigree.

Also on show are musical instruments, superb Marathi and Gujarati textiles and costumes, domestic shrines, puppets, ivory games and a model of Shaniwarwada Palace, while curiosities include a suit of fish-scale armour, a collection of intricate noodle-makers and an entire cabinet full of "erotic nut cutters".

Shaniwarwada Palace

1km north of the Kelkar Museum • **Palace** Daily 8am–6pm • ₹100 (₹5) • **Sound-and-Light show** Daily except Tues 8pm • ₹25

In the centre of the oldest part of town only the imposing high walls of the **Shaniwarwada Palace** survived a huge conflagration in 1828. The chief residence of the Peshwas from 1732 until it was captured by the British in 1817, the building has little to excite interest today, though there's a **Sound-and-Light** show in English. The entrance is through the Delhi gate on the north side, one of five set into the perimeter wall, whose huge teak doors come complete with nasty elephant-proof spikes. The interior of the palace is now grassed over, the seven-storey building entirely absent.

Aga Khan Palace and Gandhi Memorial

5km northeast of the city centre • Daily 9am–5.30pm • ₹100 (₹5) • An auto-rickshaw costs around ₹100 from the city centre

In 1942, Mahatma Gandhi, his wife Kasturba and other key figures of the freedom movement were interned at the grand **Aga Khan Palace**, which is set in quiet leafy gardens across the river, 5km northeast of the centre. The Aga Khan donated the palace to the state in 1969, and it is now a small **Gandhi museum**, typical of many all over India, with captioned photos and simple rooms unchanged since they were occupied by the freedom fighters. A **memorial** behind the house commemorates Kasturba, who died during their imprisonment.

Tribal Museum

Koregaon Rd, 1.5km east of the railway station • Daily 10.30am–5.30pm • ₹200 (₹10)

The Tribal Research and Training Institute, which runs the **Tribal Museum**, is dedicated to the protection and documentation of Maharashtra's forty-plus tribal groups, who number around ten million. The museum's photos, artefacts and outdoor dioramas serve as an excellent introduction to this little-known world, but the highlights are the wonderful collections of dance masks and Worli paintings. Talk to the museum curator if you're interested in guided (but culturally sensitive) **tours** to tribal areas.

Osho International Meditation Resort

17 Koregaon Park Rd, 2km northeast of the railway station • ☎ 020 2401 9999, ⓦ osho.com • **Welcome Center** Daily 9am–12.30pm & 2–3.30pm • Registration for first-time visitors ₹1150, one-day pass ₹1130 (₹550), five-day pass ₹5080 (₹1016), spa/pool entry ₹200/day • **Osho Teerth** Daily 6–9am & 3–6pm • Free with day pass

Pune is the headquarters of the infamous **Osho International Meditation Resort**. Set amid 28 acres of landscaped gardens and woodland, the ashram of the now-deceased New Age guru, Shri Bagwan Rajneesh, aka "Osho" (see box opposite), comprises a dreamy playground of cafés, marble walkways, Olympic-size swimming pool, spas, tennis courts and clinics, with a shop selling Osho's enormous list of books, DVDs and CDs. Courses at its multiversity are offered in a variety of therapies and meditation techniques, alongside more offbeat **workshops** with titles such as "Disappear into the Painting", "Squeeze the Juice of Life" and "Doing Dying Differently".

This eco-friendly bubble follows a strict door policy, with security beefed up following the revelation of visits to Osho by Mumbai 26/11 conspirator **David Headley** – guided tours had at the time of writing been indefinitely cancelled, and in the wake of Pune's own attack in 2010 are unlikely to resume. If you're interested in taking a course, you must take your passport to the Welcome Center, where you'll have to take an on-the-spot HIV test in order to register. You'll need **two robes** (maroon for daywear, white for evenings), on sale at the ashram's "mini-mall". It is also possible to stay inside the resort at the pricey *Osho Guest House* (see p.665).

OSHO

It is well over forty years since followers began to congregate around **Bhagwan Rajneesh** (1931-90), the self-proclaimed New Age guru better known to his tens of thousands of acolytes worldwide as simply **Osho**. Underpinned by a philosophical mishmash of Buddhism, Sufism, sexual liberationism, Tantric practices, Zen, yoga, hypnosis, Tibetan pulsing, disco and unabashed materialism, the first Rajneesh ashram was founded in Pune in 1974. It rapidly attracted droves of Westerners, and some Indians, who adopted new Sanskrit names and a uniform of orange or maroon cottons and a bead necklace (*mala*) with an attached photo of the enlightened guru, in classic style, sporting long greying hair and beard.

FULFILMENT, UTOPIANISM AND TAX EVASION

Few early adherents denied that much of the attraction lay in Rajneesh's novel approach to fulfillment. His dismissal of Christianity ("Crosstianity") as a miserably oppressive obsession with guilt struck a chord with many, as did the espousal of liberation through sex. Rajneesh assured his devotees that material comfort was not to be shunned. Within a few years, satellite ashrams were popping up throughout Western Europe, and by 1980 an estimated 200,000 devotees had liberated themselves in 600 meditation centres across 80 countries.

To protect itself from pollution, nuclear war and the AIDS virus, the organization poured money into a utopian project, **Rajneeshpuram**, on 64,000 acres of agricultural land in Oregon, US. It was at this point that the tabloids and TV documentary teams really got interested in Rajneesh, now a multimillionaire. Infiltrators leaked stories of strange goings-on at Rajneeshpuram and before long its high-powered female executives became subject to police interest. Charges of tax evasion, drugs, fraud, arson and a conspiracy to poison several people in a neighbouring town to sway the vote in local elections provoked further sensation. Although he claimed to know nothing of this, Rajneesh pleaded guilty to breaches of US immigration laws and was deported in 1985. Following protracted attempts to resettle in 21 different countries, the Valium-addicted Rajneesh returned home to Pune, where he died in 1990, aged 59.

POST-RAJNEESH

The ashram went through a period of internal squabbles and financial trouble in the 1990s. At his death, Rajneesh appointed an inner circle to manage the group, though several departed and the Osho "brand" – which sells around four million books each year, supplemented by CDs, DVDs, paintings and photos – is now controlled from Zurich and New York. The Pune ashram wasn't seeing enough of this to meet its costs and consequently has had to relaunch and re-style itself, changing both its name (from Osho Commune International to **Osho International Meditation Resort**) and the pattern of life inside its walls; whereas in its heyday an average stay was three to six months, today people typically stay no more than two weeks and few followers live on site.

THE 2010 BOMBING

It was at least partly due to Osho's enduring popularity with foreigners that the nearby *German Bakery*, Koregaon Park's erstwhile hippie hangout, was targeted for a Mumbai-style terrorist attack in February 2010, which left seventeen dead and around sixty injured – a huge shock for this normally peaceful little enclave.

11

The beautiful gardens laid out to the east of the main Osho complex, known as **Osho Teerth**, are open to day-pass-holders. They make a serene place for a stroll, with babbling streams, stands of giant bamboo, mature trees and Zen sculpture artfully placed amid the greenery.

ARRIVAL AND DEPARTURE
PUNE

Pune's prominence as a business capital means that it's well connected to towns and cities in southern India. However, demand for seats on planes, trains and buses far exceeds supply, so book onward transport as soon as you can.

BY PLANE
Lohagaon airport Pune's airport, 10km northeast of the city centre, is a major hub, with regular direct flights to cities throughout India. It's a 15–30min journey to/from the city centre, depending on traffic; a taxi costs ₹250–500. Plans for a new international airport in Pune have been mooted.

BY TRAIN
Pune railway station The train station is in the centre of the city, south of the river; an auto-rickshaw to/from Koregaon Park costs around ₹50. It is one of the last stops for numerous long-distance trains to and from Mumbai, so rail services are excellent – despite many of them departing in the early morning; some terminate at Dadar (or worse still) Kurla, so always check first. Some services are much more convenient than others (see box opposite). Reservations for all trains should be made as far in advance as possible online, via a travel agency or at the reservation centre next to the station itself (Mon–Sat 8am–8pm, Sun 8am–2pm).
Destinations Bengaluru (2–4 daily; 19hr 40min–24hr 10min); Chennai (3 daily; 19hr 35min–24hr 40min); Delhi (3–5 daily; 20hr 5min–27hr 25min); Ernakulam (for Kochi; 1–2 daily; 24hr 35min–35hr 10min); Hyderabad/Secunderabad (3–5 daily; 10hr 45min–13hr 20min); Jalgaon (6–7 daily; 7hr 57min–9hr 43min); Kolhapur (5 daily; 7–8hr); Lonavala (roughly hourly; 48min–2hr 8min); Madgaon (for Goa; 1 daily; 13hr 5min); Mumbai (roughly hourly; 3hr–5hr 15min);

Nagpur (2–3 daily; 15hr 45min–18hr); Nasik (1 daily; 6hr 35min).

BY SHARED TAXI
For Mumbai, 24hr shared taxis leave from agencies at the taxi stand in front of Pune railway station – they're quicker than the buses, but only take you as far as Dadar.

BY BUS
Pune has three main bus stands. If you're unsure which station you require for your destination, ask at the enquiries hatch of the City Bus Stand or at the MTDC counter at the railway station. More comfortable private buses depart from offices throughout Pune; tickets can be bought from travel agencies in Koregaon Park.
City Bus Stand Next to the railway station, City Bus Stand is split into two sections, one serving Pune itself (with signs and timetables only in Marathi), the other for destinations south and west. Regular buses to Mumbai (via Lonavala) also leave from here.
Destinations Goa (3–4 daily; 11hr); Kolhapur (hourly; 5–6hr); Mahabaleshwar (hourly; 3hr 30min–4hr); Mumbai (every 15min; 3hr 15min).
Swargate and Shivaji Nagar stands The Swargate Bus Stand, about 5km south, close to Nehru Stadium, services Karnataka and some of the same destinations as City, while the stand next to Shivaji Nagar railway station, 3km west of the centre, runs buses every 30min to points north, such as Aurangabad (5hr) and Nasik (4–5hr).

INFORMATION

Tourist information The spectacularly unhelpful MTDC Tourist Office (Mon–Fri plus the first and third Sat of the month 10am–5.45pm; ☎020 2612 6867) is inside "I" block of Central Building (enter between

Ambedkar Chowk and Sadhu Vaswani Circle). They also have an information counter (officially the same times) opposite the railway station's first-class booking office.

ACCOMMODATION

Top-end hotels are springing up all over Pune, but there's a chronic shortage of budget and mid-range places, which explains why prices are high for what you get and vacancies like gold dust: advance booking is all but essential.

Grand MG Rd, near the Dr Ambedkar statue ☎020 2636 0728, ⓦgrandhotelpune.co.in. Set behind a dimly lit beer garden, the colonial-era *Grand* doesn't live up to its name, but is an acceptable budget choice for a night: the high-ceilinged doubles in the rear annexe are pretty clean, though scruffy; the bathroom-less, wood-partitioned

singles (₹400), however, are best avoided. ₹990
★ **Lotus** Plot No. 356, Lane No.5, Koregaon Park ☎020 2613 9701, ⓦhotelsuryavilla.com. Housed in an unassuming salmon-pink block in tranquil, leafy surroundings, the *Surya Villa's* renovated sister hotel is Koregaon's Park's best-value hideaway. Bright, spotless,

TRAINS TO AND FROM PUNE

Of the myriad rail services feeding in and out of Pune, the following are recommended as the fastest and/or most convenient:

Destination	Name	No.	Frequency	Departs	Journey time
Bengaluru	*Udyan Express*	#16529	Daily	11.45pm	21hr 5min
Chennai	*CSTM Chennai Express*	#11041	Daily	6.10pm	22hr 35min
Delhi	*Jhelum Express*	#11077	Daily	5.20pm	27hr 25min
Goa	*Goa Express*	#12780	Daily	4.35pm	13hr 5min
Hyderabad/ Konark	*Secunderabad Express*	#11019	Daily	7.05pm	12hr 45min
Kolhapur	*Sahyadri Express*	#11023	Daily	10.05pm	8hr
Mumbai CST	*Deccan Queen*	#12124	Daily	7.15am	3hr 10min

modern rooms are blessed with big windows, comfy beds and balconies; wi-fi access and a/c cost extra. A basic breakfast (included) is served to the rooms, and the location is handy for the area's best restaurants/bars. ₹**2230**

Le Meridien RBM Rd, just northwest of the railway station ☎020 6641 1111, ⊛starwoodhotels.com. Though no longer the biggest hotel in Pune, this vast cathedral of marble still feels like its most opulent and luxurious. Large, plush yet airy rooms come with thick honey-coloured carpets and huge beds; the rooftop bar (complete with two-tiered pool) is one of the city centre's most heavenly spaces for an evening drink and is open to non-guests. ₹**10,000**

National 14 Sassoon Rd, opposite the railway station ☎020 2612 5054. Huge, high-ceilinged, cleanish rooms in a rambling, sparse and dilapidated colonial mansion occupying a relatively peaceful plot set back from the main road. The smaller, quieter, cheaper rooms in the courtyard annexe have private sitouts. ₹**750**

★ **O Hotel** North Main Rd ☎020 4001 1000, ⊛ohotelsindia.com. Goa chic comes to Pune: outside, a forbidding sandstone-coloured tower block; inside, an exuberant designer playground of bold textures, shades and shapes. Rooms are suitably Zen-like, blending simple lines and stylish details with warm, muted tones and natural materials, and facilities include a gorgeous spa and spectacular rooftop infinity pool and bar, plus Indian and Japanese restaurants (worth a visit even if you're not staying). Book online in advance for the best deals. ₹**7050**

Osho Guest House Osho International Meditation Resort, 17 Koregaon Park Rd ☎020 6601 9900, ⊛osho .com. Within the grounds of the Osho ashram, and open only to attendees, this luxurious hotel offers stylish, minimalist, Zen rooms – though be warned that the accommodation is situated above the main auditorium, which, as the ashram likes to put it, "can make the 6am Dynamic Meditation hard to resist. ₹**9400**

Shree Panchratna 7 Tadiwala Rd ☎020 2605 9999, ⊛hotelshreepanchratna.in. Aimed at business travellers and located on a quiet side street close to the railway station, *Shree Panchratna* is well maintained and efficiently-run, if a little unexciting. The plain rooms all have a/c, private bathrooms, kettles, mini-fridges, wi-fi access and a fresh feel; some also have balconies. ₹**2950**

Sunderban 19 Koregaon Park ☎020 2612 4949, ⊛tghotels.com. Fine Art Deco mansion, set behind an immaculate expanse of lawn right next to the Osho ashram. The older rooms in the main house, furnished in swathes of leather and acres of teak and mahogany, are better value than those in the flashier modern garden block, though there are big discounts April–Sept and breakfast is included. There's a great Italian restaurant (see below) and a spa. ₹**3300**

Surya Villa 294/1 Koregaon Park ☎020 2612 4501, ⊛hotelsuryavilla.com. Sizeable if somewhat spartan rooms (with fans or a/c) spread over four floors in a suburban block close to Osho. It's hugely popular, mainly with long-staying foreign ashramites, so book well in advance. ₹**1760**

EATING AND DRINKING

Pune's affluent young things have money to burn these days, and new, innovative places to eat and drink open up every month to relieve them of their info-tech salaries, the largest concentration of them up at the eastern end of Koregaon Park. Booking is advisable at the smarter places at weekends.

CAFÉS AND RESTAURANTS

Dario's Hotel Sunderban ☎020 2605 3597, ⊛dario's .in. A tranquil, Italian veg restaurant with a lovely patio filled with plants and birdsong. The food – sandwiches, salads, risottos, pastas and pizzas, plus crêpes, waffles and

pastries for breakfast – is pretty authentic, and it is a great place for a glass of wine or a proper espresso or cappuccino. Mains ₹290–560. Daily 8am–11pm.

Great Punjab 5 Jewel Tower, Lane 5, Koregaon Park ☎020 2614 5060, ⊛thegreatpunjab.com. One of

Koregaon Park's most popular north Indians, offering generous kebabs, grills and tandoori dishes – and a long list of cocktails and spirits – in smart if subdued surroundings. Dedicated carnivores should sample the *karela kebab*, a mountain of succulent tandoori chicken stuffed with a robust mix of minced meat and herbs. Mains ₹250–700. Daily noon–3pm & 7–11pm.

Juice World 2436/B East Street Camp ☎020 2611 4318. Freshly squeezed fruit juices, milk shakes and *faloodas* (₹50–180) are the mainstay of this buzzing haunt just east of the top of MG Rd; lychee, *chikoo* and musk melon are some of the more unusual flavours on offer. It also serves piping-hot snacks such as *aloo paratha* and, throughout the afternoon and evening, tangy Bombay-style *pao bhaji*, which bubbles away on a huge counter griddle. Daily 8am–9/10pm.

Malaka Spice Lane 5, Koregaon Park ☎020 2615 1088, ⊛malakaspice.com. Longstanding Southeast Asian specialist, dishing up reasonably authentic stir-fries, curries and noodle dishes (mains ₹275–750) in arty surroundings. It's relaxed at lunchtime and intimate in the evening when the candlelit covered veranda and garden terrace twinkle with alluring fairy lights. It's also a good spot for a drink, especially if you catch the happy hour (Mon–Fri 4–7pm). Rather incongruously, a caricaturist is on hand, should you require his services. Daily 11am–11pm.

The Place (Touché the Sizzler) 7 Moledina Rd ☎020 2613 4632. Huge, succulent sizzlers (veg, fish, pork, mutton or beef; ₹310-440) and tender steaks are the house specialities of this popular Parsi-run old-timer in the city centre (somewhat bizarrely, the founder of the restaurant later opened a "sizzler restaurant" on the Isle of Man in the UK). Daily 11.30am–3.30pm & 7–10.45pm.

Prem's Main Rd, Koregaon Park ☎020 6601 2413. Tucked away from the main road, this cool, modern restaurant-bar is a hit for both its spot-on Indian and Chinese dishes (there are also a few decent Continental options) and its range of beers (including draught Hoegaarden) and spirits. Mains ₹180–380. Daily 8am–11.30pm.

Yogi Tree Hotel Surya Villa, 294/1 Koregaon Park ☎020 2612 1911. This is the favourite hangout of health-conscious Osho-ites, with a menu offering muesli, pancakes, sandwiches and filled croissants, hygienically prepared salads, decent pizza and pasta, and veg Indian and Chinese dishes. The desserts – including ice cream sundaes and banoffee pie – are great too. Mains ₹100–250. Daily 7am–11pm.

BARS

★ **Minus Bar** O Hotel ☎020 4001 1000. Soaring high over the cityscape, the *O*'s lantern-lit rooftop bar is Pune's dreamiest spot for a sundowner. Sink into a low-slung white-cushioned sofa, settle onto a Kutchi-patchwork beanbag or dabble your feet in the infinity pool as you muse over the enterprising list of cocktails (around ₹600–700; a Kingfisher will set you back ₹350 or so) and soak up the views. Daily noon–11.30pm.

★ **Shisha Café** ABC Farms, Koregaon Park ☎020 6520 0390, ⊛shishajazzcafe.in. One of the city's most congenial watering holes: a cavernous restaurant-bar awash with greenery and capped with a huge thatched roof hung with Persian carpets. Indo-Iranian food, notably kebabs (₹190–300) dominate the menu, and they serve a good range of beers (from ₹140), wines and spirits, plus hookahs and Turkish coffee. The walls are lined with posters of jazz greats, and live jazz and blues bands often play in the evenings (give them a call or check the website to see who's playing). Daily 10am–11.30pm.

SHOPPING

Crossword 1st floor of Sohrab Hall, Sassoon Rd ☎020 2605 9600. The best central bookshop, with an extensive range of English-language fiction and non-fiction. It also has an in-house branch of *Café Coffee Day*. Daily 10.30am–9pm.

Either Or 24 Sohrab Hall, Sassoon Rd ☎020 2605 7225, ⊛eithEror.in. This is an excellent place for souvenir shopping, with an extensive range of textiles, jewellery, household furnishings, crafts and music. It is located in the same complex as Crossword (see above). Daily 10.30am–8pm.

DIRECTORY

Banks and exchange For changing currency or travellers' cheques, Thomas Cook is at 13 Thacker House, just off General Thimmaya Rd (☎020 2634 6171, ⊛thomascook.in). There are countless ATMs throughout Pune.

Internet You can get online in many places, including at

the 24hr internet café on the first floor of the railway station and at Sonali Internet on Lane 7 in Koregaon Park. Almost all the hotels offer internet/wi-fi access.

Post office The very efficient GPO is on Sadhu Vasavani (Connaught) Rd.

Mahabaleshwar and around

The former capital of the Bombay Presidency, **MAHABALESHWAR**, 250km southeast of Mumbai and rivalling Matheran as the most visited hillresort in Maharashtra, is easily reached from Pune, 120km northeast. The highest point in the Western Ghats

(1372m), it is subject to extraordinarily extreme **weather** conditions. The start of June brings heavy mists and a dramatic drop in temperature, followed by a deluge of biblical proportions: up to 7m of rain can fall in the hundred days up to the end of September. As a result, tourists tend only to come here between October and early June; during April and May, at the height of summer, the place is packed.

For most foreign visitors, Mahabaleshwar's prime appeal is its location midway between Mumbai and Goa, but it holds enough good **hiking trails** to keep walkers here for a few days, with tracks through the woods to waterfalls and assorted vantage points overlooking the peaks and plains. One enjoyable route – along which you may well not see another soul – is the 3km forested walk along the **Tiger Path** bridleway to **Mumbai Point**, which starts around 1km southwest of the bus stand opposite the *Hotel Sathar*, just south of the Christian cemetery. The sunset panoramas from here can be breathtaking. If there's a group of you, you could rent a **boat** out on the **Venna Lake**, 2.5km north of town, though it's not as peaceful a pastime as you might think. Otherwise, the main activity in town is to amble up and down the animated pedestrianized **main bazaar** (Dr Sabne Road) – which with its chip shops, amusement arcades and popcorn stands bears a passing resemblance to a British seaside resort – and graze on the locally grown **strawberries** and other fruits for which the town is famous.

Pratapgadh

Around 24km west of Mahabaleshwar • Daily dawn–dusk • ₹5 • Taxis charge around ₹600 for the return trip to Pratapgadh, with waiting time; state buses (1hr) also do the journey each day, leaving the bus stand at 9am and returning at 11am

The seventeenth-century fort of **PRATAPGADH** stretches the full length of a high ridge affording superb views over the surrounding mountains. Reached by a flight of five hundred steps, it is famously associated with the Maratha chieftain, **Shivaji**, who lured the Mughal general Afzal Khan here from Bijapur to discuss a possible truce. Neither, it would seem, intended to keep to the condition that they should come unarmed. Khan attempted to knife Shivaji, who responded by killing him with the gruesome *wagnakh*, a set of metal claws worn on the hand. Modern visitors can see Afzal Khan's tomb, a memorial to Shivaji, and views of the surrounding hills.

ARRIVAL AND INFORMATION
MAHABALESHWAR AND AROUND

By bus The central State Bus Stand is at the northwest end of the bazaar. There are regular MSRTC buses to/from Mumbai (6–7 daily; around 7hr), Pune (every 30min–1hr; 3hr 30min) and Kolhapur (3–5 daily; 5hr 30min), and one each to Ratnagiri (6hr) and Panaji in Goa (12hr); for the latter, numerous agents in the bazaar sell tickets for more comfortable private buses entry.

Entry fees Note that there is a ₹20 entry fee for visitors, collected at toll booths at each end of town.

Services The bazaar is home to some unreliable internet cafés and plenty of ATMs.

GETTING AROUND

By taxi Auto-rickshaws are banned in Mahabaleshwar but taxis line up at the west end of the bazaar, charging around ₹50 for short hops in and around town.

By bike Bikes can be rented from a stall at the *Dreamland* hotel (see p.668).

ACCOMMODATION

As in many hill stations, despite an abundance of hotels, at busy times prices in Mahabaleshwar are well above average. Room rates are a moveable feast, particularly at the lower end of the scale, but fall roughly into three categories: peak months are April and especially May, when as at Diwali, Christmas and New Year, tariffs at the cheaper places double or even treble and the place is well worth avoiding. Prices quoted are for off-season, which broadly covers most of the rest of the year, bar long weekends ("mid-season"). The cheapest places to stay are on the Main Bazaar and the road parallel to it, Murray Peth. Two points to note: hoteliers in Mahabaleshwar refuse to take in single travellers, and many places close during the monsoon.

Deluxe Dr Sabne Rd ☏ 02168 260095. Decent budget hotels are thin on the ground in Mahabaleshwar, but the *Deluxe* is one of the better bets. Located above a fabrics shop, it has cramped but fairly clean and comfortable attached rooms with either a/c or fans. ₹**1200**

★ **Dina** 1km northeast of the bus stand ☏ 02168 260246, ⓦ dinahotel.com. Mahabaleshwar's most atmospheric heritage hotel, in a bungalow and annexe that date back to 1908, is set in beautifully tended flower gardens high above Venna Lake. Best are the spacious rooms in the main house, which feature four-poster beds and fine views from the partitioned veranda. Full-board. ₹**2750**

Dreamland Below the State Bus Stand ☏ 02168 260228, ⓦ hoteldreamland.com. Large, well-established resort hotel surrounded by extensive gardens. Rooms range from simple chalets or "cottages" to spacious a/c en suites (₹5000) with stupendous views. There's a pool, jacuzzi and sauna, a garden café, and a restaurant serving fine Indian and Chinese cuisine. ₹**4230**

MTDC Holiday Resort 2km southwest of the centre ☏ 02168 260318. Huge campus with a wide range of accommodation, all with sitouts, ranging from austere economy rooms through high-ceilinged standard rooms to spruce modern cottages accommodating four (₹3525), in a peaceful location; a 10min walk from Mumbai Point. ₹**1225**

EATING AND DRINKING

Grapevine Western end of Masjid Rd, which is parallel with the main bazaar ☏ 02168 261100. For something a bit different, make for the idiosyncratic *Grapevine*, where a decent list of wines, beers and spirits complements a delightfully eclectic (if expensive) menu ranging from Parsi home cooking to fish and chips and pasta with home-made pesto, all to a soundtrack of mid-1980s power ballad covers. Mains from ₹150. Daily noon–3pm & 7–10.30pm.

Kolhapur

KOLHAPUR, on the banks of the River Panchaganga 225km south of Pune, is thought to have been an important centre of the Tantric cult associated with Shakti worship since ancient times. The town probably grew around the sacred site of the present-day **Mahalakshmi temple**, still central to the life of the city, although there are said to be up to 250 other shrines in the area. With a population of almost 600,000, Kolhapur has become a major industrial centre, but has retained enough Maharashtran character to make it worthy of a stopover.

Mahalakshmi temple

In the centre of old Kolhapur, overlooking the town square • Daily dawn–10.30pm • Free

The **Mahalakshmi temple**, whose cream-painted sanctuary towers embellish the centre of Kolhapur's old town, is thought to have been founded in the seventh century, though what you see today dates from the early eighteenth century. The devout queue around the block from the complex's east gate for *darshan* at the image of the goddess Mahalakshmi, beneath the largest of five domed towers; you're welcome to join in.

Rajwada (Old Palace)

Near the Mahalakshmi Temple • No fixed opening times • Free

Presiding over the square just up the road from the Mahalakshmi temple, the **Rajwada**, or Old Palace, is still occupied by members of the former ruling Chhatrapati family, though its entrance hall is usually busy with worshippers to its Bhawani temple – you can access it by passing under the pillared porch that extends out into the town square.

Wrestling pit (Motibaug)

Close to the Rajwada • **Wrestlers training** June–Sept daily except Sat 6–9am & 4–6pm

Kolhapur is famous as a centre for traditional wrestling, or *kushti*. On leaving the Old Palace gates, turn right and head through the low doorway in front of you, from where a path picks its way past a couple of derelict buildings to the *motibaug*, or **wrestling pit**. At certain times of day, and in season, you come come and watch people training. Matches take place at the nearby **Khasbag Maidan** wrestling stadium.

New Palace

Shahaji Chhatrapati, 2km north of the town centre • Daily 9.30am–5.30pm • ₹30 (₹13)

The maharaja's **New Palace** was built in 1884, following a fire at the Rajwada. Designed by Major Mant, founding father of the Indo-Saracenic school of so much British colonial architecture, it fuses Jain and Hindu influences with local touches from the Rajwada while remaining indomitably Victorian, with a prominent clock tower. The present maharaja lives on the first floor, while the ground floor houses the **Shahaji Chhatrapati Museum**, a dozen or so rooms crammed with fascinating memorabilia that demonstrates above all else the Chhatrapati family's extraordinary history of bloodlust: among the maharaja's collection of portraits, costumes, embroidery, riding paraphernalia and old Raj-era photos is an astonishing array of swords, rifles and torture equipment, a gruesome display cabinet of a huntsman's homeware – fans fashioned from tails, an elephant's-foot occasional table – and, in the final room, a scandalous Who's Who of stuffed endangered species, including half the current tiger population of India. Rather less macabre is the spectacular church-like Durbar Hall, with its superb carvings and mosaic floor.

ARRIVAL AND INFORMATION

KOLHAPUR

By train The railway station is 400m west from the bus stand on Station Rd, near the centre of town.

Tourist information The MTDC tourist office (Mon–Fri plus 1st and 3rd Sat of the month 10am–5pm; ☎0231 269 2935)

is on Assembly Rd, a 15min walk north of the railway station (ask locally for the Collector's Office).

Services There are plenty of banks with ATMs lining Station and Assembly roads.

ACCOMMODATION AND EATING

There's no shortage of decent, good-value **accommodation** in Kolhapur, much of it within easy reach of the bus stand along Station Rd. Kolhapur is legendary across Maharashtra for its fiery **cuisine**. In addition to the hotels, restaurants – notably *Woodland* and *Padma Guest House* – there are several good, inexpensive places to eat around Station Square.

Hotel Tourist Station Rd ☎0231 265 0421, ⓦhoteltourist.co.in. The pick of a row of welcoming mid-range hotels a few minutes' walk east of the bus stand. Rooms (all are attached; a/c costs about ₹250 extra) are unfussy but large and well maintained; ask for one away from the road. It has veg and non-veg restaurants, and breakfast is included. 24hr check-out. **₹1225**

Padma Guest House Near Padma Talkies, Laxmipuri ☎0231 264 1387, ⓦpadmakolhapur.com. A reliable budget hotel with decent rooms (all with attached bathrooms, and TVs) and an excellent (and economical) restaurant specializing in fiery Kolhapuri cuisine – the tongue-tingling mutton curries are not to be missed. **₹755**

Shalini Palace On the outskirts of town, overlooking Rankala Lake ☎0231 263 0401, ⓔhotelshalinipalace

@rediffmail.com. The maharaja's former summer residence may have lost some of its grandeur but remains the most atmospheric place to stay. Furnishings are disappointingly modern throughout, though the enormous suites (₹7045) retain a few delightful period details. Even if you don't stay, it's worth considering a trip for a meal in the former Durbar Hall and a lakeside stroll in the extensive, verdant grounds. **₹2115**

★ **Woodland** 204 E Ward, Tarabai Park ☎0231 265 0941, ⓦhotelwoodland.net. Good-value and welcoming upper-bracket option in a peaceful suburb 2km north of the railway and bus stations. It has spacious, light and comfortable a/c rooms plus a terrific non-veg garden/veranda restaurant, *Sunderban*, and a "permit room" (bar). Rates include breakfast and wi-fi. 24hr check-out. **₹2935**

Goa

PALOLEM BEACH

Goa

The former Portuguese enclave of Goa, midway down India's southwest coast, has been a holiday destination since colonial times, when British troops and officials used to travel here from across the country for a spot of "R&R". Back then, the three Bs – bars, brothels and booze – were the big attractions. Now it's the golden, palm-fringed beaches spread along the state's 105km coastline that pull in the tourists – around two million of them each winter. Cheap air travel has spawned a dramatic rise in the number of domestic visitors in recent years, and planeloads of free-spending Russians have also started to pour in. Yet in spite of the increasing chaos of Goa's main resorts, it's still possible to find the odd quiet corner if you're prepared to explore and can avoid the busy Christmas–New Year period. If you know where to go, Goa can still be a wonderful place to recuperate from the travails of life on the road.

Serving as the linchpin for a vast trade network for more than 450 years, Goa was Portugal's first toe-hold in Asia. However, when the Portuguese empire began to flounder in the seventeenth century, so too did the fortunes of its capital. Cut off from the rest of India by a wall of mountains and hundreds of kilometres of un-navigable alluvial plain, it remained aloof from the wider Subcontinent until 1961, when the exasperated prime minister, Jawaharlal Nehru, finally gave up trying to negotiate with the Portuguese dictator Salazar and sent in the army.

It was shortly after the "Liberation" (or "Occupation" as some Goans still regard it), that the first **hippie travellers** came to the region on the old overland trail. They found a way of life little changed in centuries: back then Portuguese was still very much the lingua franca of the well-educated elite, and the coastal settlements were mere fishing and coconut cultivation villages. Relieved to have found somewhere culturally undemanding to party, the "freaks" got stoned, watched the mesmeric sunsets over the Arabian Sea and danced like lunatics on full-moon nights.

Since then, the state has been at pains to shake off its reputation as a druggy drop-out zone, and its beaches have grown in popularity year on year. Around two dozen stretches of soft white sand indent the region's coast, from spectacular 25km sweeps to secluded palm-backed coves. The level of development behind them varies a great deal; while some are lined by swanky Western-style resorts, the most sophisticated structures on others are palm-leaf shacks.

Which beach you opt for largely depends on what sort of holiday you have in mind. Developed resorts such as **Calangute** and **Baga** in the north, and **Colva** and **Benaulim** in the south, offer more accommodation than elsewhere. **Anjuna**, **Vagator** and **Chapora**, where places to stay are generally harder to come by, are the beaches to aim for if you've come to Goa to party. However, the bulk of budget travellers taking time out from tours of India end up in **Palolem**, in the far south beyond the reach of the charter transfer buses – though be warned that it too has become a major resort over the past decade, attracting literally thousands of long-stay visitors

12

NIGHT MARKET, ARPORA

Highlights

❶ Old Goa The belfries and Baroque church facades looming over the trees on the banks of the Mandovi are all that remains of this once splendid colonial city. **See p.682**

❷ Beach shacks Tuck into a fresh kingfish, lobster or tandoori pomfret, washed down with an ice-cold beer. **See p.690**

❸ Night market, Arpora Cooler and less frenetic than the flea market, with appealing goods on sale and a fun atmosphere. **See p.694**

❹ Flea market, Anjuna Goa's famous tourist bazaar is the place to pick up the latest party

gear, shop for souvenirs and watch the crowds go by. **See p.696**

❺ Aswem The hippiest spot on the north Goan coast to swim, fine dine and dance under the stars. **See p.703**

❻ Palacio do Deão An extravagant, painstakingly restored colonial-era mansion in south Goa, where you can eat lunch on a leafy garden terrace. **See p.714**

❼ Sunset stroll, Palolem Tropical sunsets don't come much more romantic than at this idyllic palm-fringed cove in the hilly deep south. **See p.720**

HIGHLIGHTS ARE MARKED ON THE MAP ON P.674

in peak season. For a quieter scene, you could head for **Patnem**, just over the headland from Palolem, or **Agonda**, further up the coast, where development is limited to a string of hut camps and family guesthouses. The only place where the **hippie scene** endures to any significant extent is **Arambol**, in the far north of the state, where you can dip in to any number of yoga styles and holistic therapies between spells on the beach.

GOA

HIGHLIGHTS

1 Old Goa
2 Beach shacks
3 Night Market, Arpora
4 Flea Market, Anjuna
5 Aswem
6 Palacio do Deão
7 Sunset stroll, Palolem

Some 10km from the state capital, **Panjim**, the ruins of the former Portuguese capital at **Old Goa** are foremost among the attractions away from the coast – a sprawl of Catholic cathedrals, convents and churches that draw crowds of Christian pilgrims from all over India. Another popular day excursion is to Anjuna's Wednesday **flea market**, a sociable place to shop for souvenirs and dance wear. In the south, the district of Salcete, and its main market town, **Margao**, is also littered with distinctively hybrid buildings in the form of Portuguese-era mansions, churches and seminaries. Finally, wildlife enthusiasts may be tempted into the interior to visit the nature reserves at **Cotigao** and **Netravali** in the far south.

The **best time to come** to Goa is during the dry, relatively cool winter months between late November and mid-March. At other times, either the sun is too hot for comfort, or the humidity, clouds and rain make life miserable. During peak season, from mid-December to the end of January, the weather is perfect, with temperatures rarely nudging above 32°C. Finding a room or a house to rent at that time, however – particularly over Christmas and New Year when tariffs double, or triple – can be a real hassle.

Brief history

Goa's sheer inaccessibility by land has always kept it out of the mainstream of Indian history; on the other hand, its control of the seas and the lucrative spice trade made it a much-coveted prize for rival colonial powers. Until a century before the arrival of the Portuguese, Goa had belonged for more than a thousand years to the kingdom of the **Kadamba** dynasty. They, in turn, were overthrown by the Karnatakan Vijayanagars, the Muslim Bahmanis, and Yusuf Adil Shah of Bijapur, but the capture of the fort at Panjim by **Afonso de Albuquerque** in 1510 signalled the start of a Portuguese occupation that was to last 451 years.

Goa Dourada ("Golden Goa")

As the colony expanded, its splendid capital (dubbed as "Goa Dourada", or "Golden Goa", due to its incredible prosperity) came to hold a larger population than Paris or London. Though Ismail Adil Shah laid siege for ten months in 1570, and the Marathas came very close to seizing the region, the greatest threat was from other European maritime nations, principally Holland and France. Meanwhile, conversions to **Christianity**, started by the Franciscans, gathered pace when St Francis Xavier founded the **Jesuit** mission in 1542. With the advent of the **Inquisition** soon afterwards, laws were introduced censoring literature and banning any faith other than Catholicism. Hindu temples were destroyed, and converted Hindus adopted Portuguese names, such as Da Silva, Correa and De Sousa, which remain common in the region. Thereafter, the colony, whose trade monopoly had been broken by its European rivals, went into gradual decline, hastened by the unhealthy, disease-ridden environment of its capital.

"Liberation"

Despite certain liberalization, such as the restoration of Hindus' right to worship and the final banishment of the dreaded Inquisition in 1820, the nineteenth century saw widespread civil unrest. During the British Raj many Goans moved to Bombay, and elsewhere in British India, to find work.

The success of the post-Independence Goan struggle for freedom owed as much to the efforts of the Indian government, which cut off diplomatic ties with Portugal, as to the work of freedom fighters such as **Menezes Braganza** and **Dr. Cunha**. After a "liberation march" in 1955 resulted in a number of deaths, the state was blockaded. Trade with Bombay ceased, and the railway was cut off, so Goa set out to forge international links, particularly with Pakistan and Sri Lanka: that led to the building of Dabolim airport, and a determination to improve local agricultural output. In 1961, prime minister Jawaharlal Nehru finally sent in the armed forces. Mounted in defiance of a United Nations resolution, "**Operation Vijay**" met only token resistance, and the Indian army overran Goa in two days. Thereafter, Goa (along with Portugal's other two enclaves, Daman and Diu) became part of India as a self-governing **Union Territory**, with minimum interference from Delhi.

Goa today

Since Independence, Goa has continued to prosper, bolstered by iron-ore exports and a booming tourist industry. Dominated by issues of statehood, the status of Konkani and the ever-rising levels of immigration, its political life has been dogged by chronic **instability**, with frequent changes of government and chief ministers, interrupted by occasional periods of **President's Rule**, when the state had to be governed directly from New Delhi.

At the start of the twenty-first century, renewed fears over the pace of change on the coastal strip started to dominate the news. A sudden influx of **Russian charter tourists** and high-rolling **property developers** from Delhi and Mumbai provoked a backlash from successive ruling coalitions, with a state-sponsored land grab of expatriate property. Hundreds of resident Europeans had their assets confiscated, and fled. A series of high-profile attacks on and by foreigners – notably the murder in 2008 of British teenager Scarlett Keeling – has done little to improve the state's image abroad. Meanwhile, as ever-improving infrastructural links with the rest of India render Goa's borders more porous, the survival of the region as a culturally distinct entity continues to hang in the balance.

12

ARRIVAL AND DEPARTURE GOA

TO AND FROM MUMBAI

By plane A couple of dozen flights shuttle between Mumbai and Goa's Dabolim airport daily, with fares from as low as ₹1000 (or even less) if you book well in advance with one of the no-frills airlines – or as much as ₹40,000 on New Year's Eve. Try SpiceJet, IndiGo, Go Air or JetKonnect (see p.35). Flying with Air India or Jet Airways will set you back around $100 each way.

By train Four to five services run daily on the Konkan Railway from Mumbai, the most convenient being the overnight *Mangalore Express* (#12133), which departs from CST at 10.15pm and arrives in Goa at 8.25am the following morning. Travelling in the other direction (ie *towards* Mumbai), the service to go for is the overnight *Konkan Kanya Express* (#10112), which departs from Margao (see p.710) at 4.45pm (or Karmali, near Old Goa, 11km west of Panjim, at 5.18pm), arriving at Mumbai CST at 5.50am the following day. The other fast train from Goa to CST is the *Mandovi Express* (#0104), departing Margao at 8.30am (or Karmali at 8.55am) and arriving at 9.45pm the same evening. Note that all KRC trains book up within days of the seats being released.

By bus A fleet of night buses covers the 500km between Goa and Mumbai – a terrible 14- to 18hr journey to be avoided at all costs. Paulo Travels is the top firm running the route, with a range of different services, from no-frills buses for ₹600 to swisher a/c Volvo coaches with berths costing ₹1600. For tickets, contact their office just outside the Kadamba Bus Stand, Panjim (☎0832 222 3736,

ⓦ paulotravels.com). In south Goa, the firm's main outlet is at the *Nanutel* hotel in Margao (☎0834 272 1516). Information on all departures and fares is available online.

TO AND FROM HAMPI

By train The most stress-free and economical way to travel between Hospet and Goa, the jumping-off place for Hampi, is the four-times-weekly train service. The *Vasco–Howrah Express* (#18048) departs every Tuesday, Thursday, Friday and Sunday at 7.50am, arriving 7hr 30min hours later. Fares range from ₹200 for a seat in an ultra-basic, crowded second-class compartment to ₹700 for second-class a/c – the most comfy option. Tickets can be bought on the day, but arrive at Margao by at least 6.30am, as the "queues" are invariably more like rugby scrums. There are also trains from Hospet to Goa (see p.1129).

By bus The bus journey covering the same route is no cheaper than the train (sleeper class) and is far more gruelling. Two or three clapped-out government services leave Panjim's Kadamba stand (platform #9) each morning for Hospet, the last one at 10.30am. Brace yourself for a long, hard slog; all being well, it should take nine or ten hours, but delays and breakdowns are frustratingly frequent.

TO AND FROM GOKARNA

By train The fastest and most convenient way to travel along the coast between Goa and Gokarna is on the Konkan Railway. At 2.45pm, the *Maru–Sagar Express*

(#12978) leaves Margao, passing through Chaudi at 3.25pm en route to Gokarna Rd, the town's railhead, where it arrives an hour later at 4.25pm. As this is classed as a passenger service, you don't have to buy tickets in advance; just turn up at the station 30min before the time of departure and pay at the regular ticket counter.

GETTING AROUND

By taxi Most foreign visitors travel around Goa in white or yellow-and-black Maruti van taxis. Fares are often posted at ranks, but they tend only to apply to peak season; at other times you should settle the sum in advance.

By bike A cheaper alternative is to rent either a bicycle (gearless, Indian-made cycles are on offer in all the resorts for around ₹150–200/day) or, for longer trips, a motorbike. Make sure the lights and brakes are in good shape, and be especially vigilant at night.

Central Goa

Known as the *Velhas Conquistas* ("Old Conquests"), the land wedged between the Mandovi and Zuari rivers in Central Goa was the first territory to be colonized by the Portuguese in the early sixteenth century, and still retains a more Christian feel than outlying districts. Gabled, whitewashed churches dominate most village squares, and you'll see plenty of old-style Portuguese dresses worn by Catholic women.

The Lusitanian atmosphere is most discernible of all in the older districts of the state capital, **Panjim**, and although the town attracts far fewer visitors than the coastal resorts, it certainly deserves a day or two's break from the beach, if only to visit the remains of **Old Goa**, a short bus ride away upriver. Further inland, the forested lower slopes of the Western Ghats, cut through by the main Panjim–Bengaluru (Bangalore) highway, shelter the impressive **Dudhsagar falls**, reachable only by 4WD jeep, and a small, but beautifully situated medieval Hindu temple at **Tambdi Surla**.

12

Panjim

Stacked around the sides of a lush terraced hillside at the mouth of the River Mandovi, **PANJIM** (also known by its Marathi name, **Panaji** – "land that does not flood") was for centuries little more than a minor landing stage and customs house, protected by a hilltop fort and surrounded by stagnant swampland. It only became state capital in 1843, after the port at Old Goa had silted up and its rulers and impoverished inhabitants had fled the plague.

EASY RIDING

Before you take to the road on a rented motorbike, there are a few things to consider. Officially, you need an international **driver's licence** to rent and ride anything, but in practice a standard licence will suffice if you're stopped and asked to produce your papers by the local police. All rented motorcycles should carry special yellow-and-black **licence plates**; make sure yours does, to avoid harassment by Goa's notoriously corrupt traffic cops. **Helmets** are also compulsory these days while riding on the highways, but not on backroads. Rates for motorbikes vary according to season, duration of rental and vehicle; most owners also insist on a **deposit** and/or passport as security. The cheapest bike, a scooter-style Honda Activa 100cc, which has automatic gears, costs ₹200–250 per day. Other options include the perennially stylish Enfield Bullet 350cc, although these are heavy, unwieldy and – at upwards of ₹500 per day – the most expensive bike to rent. **Fuel** is sold at service stations around the state (known locally as "petrol pumps"). In smaller settlements, including the resorts, it's sold in mineral-water bottles at general stores or through backstreet suppliers – but you should avoid these as some bulk out their petrol with low-grade kerosene or industrial solvent, which makes engines misfire and smoke badly.

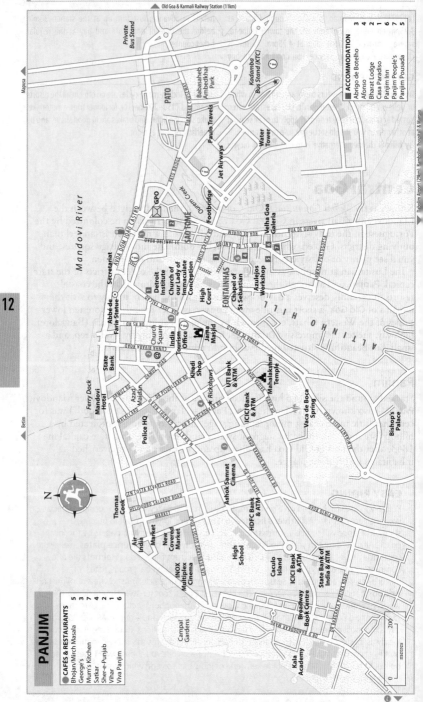

▲ Old Goa & Karmali Railway Station (11km)

PANJIM

CAFÉS & RESTAURANTS
Bhojan/Mirch Masala	5
George's	3
Mum's Kitchen	7
Satkar	4
Sher-e-Punjab	2
Vihar	1
Viva Panjim	6

ACCOMMODATION
Abrigo de Botelho	3
Afonso	4
Bharat Lodge	2
Casa Paradiso	1
Panjim Inn	6
Panjim People's	7
Panjim Pousada	5

Mandovi River

Dabolim Airport (29km); Bambolim (Ixori) & Margao

N

0   200   metres

Today, the town ranks among the least congested and hectic of any Indian capital. Conventional sights are thin on the ground, but the backstreets of the old quarter, **Fontainhas**, have retained a faded Portuguese atmosphere, with their colour-washed houses, *azulejo* tiled street names and Catholic churches.

Panjim's annual hour in the spotlight comes at the end of November each year when it hosts the **International Film Festival of India**, or IFFI (ⓦiffi.nic.in), for which a galaxy of Bollywood glitterati, and the odd foreign director, turn up to strut their stuff.

Fontainhas

The town's oldest and most interesting district, **Fontainhas**, comprises a dozen or so blocks of Neoclassical houses nestled at the foot of leafy Altinho Hill on the eastern edge of Panjim, across the creek from the bus stand. Many have retained their traditional coat of ochre, pale yellow, green or blue – a legacy of the Portuguese insistence that every Goan building (except churches, which had to be white) should be colour-washed after the monsoons. While some have been restored, the majority remain in a state of charismatic decay.

One of the district's oldest structures is the **Chapel of St Sebastian**, which stands at the centre of Fontainhas, at the head of a small square. The eerie crucifix inside, brought here in 1812, formerly hung in the Palace of the Inquisition in Old Goa. Unusually, Christ's eyes are open – allegedly to inspire fear in those being interrogated by the Inquisitors.

Just off the bottom of the square is a small workshop where you can watch traditional Goan *azulejos* being made. The main sales room, **Velha Goa Galeria**, is a couple of blocks away, next door to the *Panjim Inn*, which itself houses a small **art gallery** showcasing local talent (daily 10am–8pm).

Church Square

The leafy rectangular park opposite the India Government tourist office, known as **Church Square** or the **Municipal Gardens**, forms the heart of Panjim's commercial district. Presiding over its southeast side is the town's most distinctive landmark, the whitewashed Baroque facade of the **Church of Our Lady of the Immaculate Conception**. At the head of a crisscrossing laterite walkway, the church was built in 1541 for the benefit of sailors arriving here from Lisbon. The weary mariners would stagger up from the quay to give thanks for their safe passage before proceeding to the capital at Old Goa – the original home of the enormous bell that hangs from its central gable.

The Secretariat

Avda Dom Joao Castro

Running north from the church, Rua José Falcao brings you to the riverside, where Panjim's main street, Avenida Dom Joao Castro, holds the town's oldest surviving building. With its sloping tiled roofs, carved-stone coats of arms and wooden verandas, the stalwart **Secretariat** looks typically colonial. Yet it was originally the summer palace of Goa's sixteenth-century Muslim ruler, the Adil Shah. Later, the Portuguese converted it into a temporary resthouse for the territory's governors (who used to overnight here en route to and from Lisbon) and then a residence for the viceroy. Today, it houses municipal offices, though plans are afoot to transform it into a museum.

A hundred metres east, a peculiar statue of a man holding his hands over the body of an entranced reclining woman represents **Abbé de Faria** (1755–1819), a Goan priest who emigrated to France to become one of the world's first professional hypnotists.

ARRIVAL AND DEPARTURE | PANJIM

By plane European charter planes and domestic flights arrive at Dabolim airport (ⓣ0832 254 0788), 29km south of Panjim on the outskirts of Vasco da Gama, Goa's second city. Pre-paid taxis into town (45min; ₹700), booked at the office directly opposite the main exit, can be shared by up to four people.

Destinations Bengaluru (3–5 daily; 1hr); Delhi (6 daily; 2hr 30min); Hyderabad (2 daily; 1hr 30min); Kochi (5 weekly; 1hr 10min); Mangalore; (2 daily; 45min); Mumbai (12–17 daily).

By train There's no train station in town itself; the nearest one, on the Konkan Railway, is at Karmali (11km east of Panjim near Old Goa). State buses to central Panjim await arrivals. Bookings can be made at the KRC Reservations Office, on the first floor of the Kadamaba Bus Stand, Panjim (Mon–Sat 8am–8pm, Sun 8am–2pm). Make your bookings as far in advance as possible.

Destinations Gokarna Rd (1 daily; 2hr); Hospet for Hampi (4 weekly; 7hr); Mumbai (15 daily; 11–13hr 30min); Pune (1 daily; 12hr).

By bus Long-distance and local buses work out of Panjim's busy Kadamba Bus Stand, 1km east of the centre in the district of Pato. Tickets can be bought in advance at the Kadamba booking counters at the main bus stand (daily 9–11am & 2–5pm). Trips on private services may be purchased through the many travel agents immediately outside the station.

Destinations Arambol (12 daily; 1hr 45min); Calangute (every 30min; 45min); Gokarna (2 daily; 5hr 30min); Hampi (2 daily; 10hr); Mapusa (every 15min; 25min); Margao (every 15min; 55min); Mumbai (12 daily/nightly; 14–18hr); Pune (7 daily; 12hr).

GETTING AROUND

Rickshaws and pilots Auto-rickshaws are the most convenient way of getting around Panjim; flag one down at the roadside or head for one of the ranks around town. The trip from the bus stand to Fontainhas costs around

₹50. If you're not weighed down with luggage, motorcycle taxis – unique in India, and known throughout Goa as "pilots" – offer a cheaper and faster alternative.

INFORMATION

Tourist information GTDC's information counter, inside the concourse at the main Kadamba Bus Stand (daily 9.30am–1pm & 2–5pm; ☎0832 222 5620, ⓦgoa-tourism.com) is useful for checking train and bus

timings, but little else. The more reliable India Tourism office is across town on Church Square (Mon–Fri 9.30am–6pm, Sat 9.30am–1pm; ☎0832 222 3412, ⓦincredibleindia.org).

ACCOMMODATION

Finding a room can be a problem during **Dussehra** (Sept & Oct), Diwali (mid-Nov), the **IFFI film festival** in late November, and over Christmas and New Year. Note that **checkout times** vary.

Abrigo de Botelho Rua de Natal, Fontainhas ☎9822 100867, ⊜botelhoroty@gmail.com. The newest of the district's heritage boutique hotels, set on a quiet corner in one of the prettiest backstreets. Its rooms, which come in three categories (₹3000–5000), are all a/c, large and tastefully decorated, with beautiful wood and tiled floors. Complimentary breakfast is served in a secluded rear garden. ₹**3000**

★ **Afonso** St Sebastian Chapel Square, Fontainhas ☎0832 222 2359 or ☎9764 300165. This refurbished colonial-era house in a picturesque square is a safe bet if you can't quite afford the *Panjim Inn* down the road. Spotless attached rooms, friendly owners and rooftop terrace with views and cool ceramic mosaic floors – though someone's gone overboard with the textured wall paint. Single occupancy available. ₹**1500**

Bharat Lodge Sao Tome Rd, near the GPO ☎0832 222 4862. Good-value budget guesthouse, located at the heart of the old quarter in a terracotta-washed, 150-year-old building that has retained many of its original features despite extensive modernization. The rooms are large for the price, have quiet fans and good-sized bathrooms: ask for #106 or #102 if they're vacant. A/c costs ₹300 extra. ₹**1600**

Casa Paradiso Ghanekar Building, Rua Jose Falcao

☎0832 222 6291,ⓦcasaparadisogoa.com. This guesthouse is the only mid-range place outside Fontainhas worth considering. The location, on a busy thoroughfare close to the secretariat and Church Square, is none too inspiring, and there's no outside sitting space, but it is central and the rooms themselves are spotless, with a/c and shiny ceramic floors. ₹**1600**

★ **Panjim Inn/Panjim Pousada** E-212, Rua 31 de Janeiro, Fontainhas ☎0832 243 5628, ⓦpanjiminn.com. Grand 300-year-old townhouse, managed as a homely heritage hotel, with period furniture, antique photos, balconies and a veranda where meals and drinks are served. Their adjacent three-storey wing overlooking the river is in the same style, but with better views, while the *Pousada* annexe over the road has two lovely rearside rooms sharing a wooden balcony that overlooks a secret courtyard. Buffet breakfast included in the price. ₹**4000**

Panjim People's Rua 31 de Janeiro, Fontainhas ☎0832 222 1122, ⓦpanjiminn.com. Sister concern of the *Panjim Inn*, in a former high school opposite the original house (see above). It's more upmarket than their other two buildings, with newer a/c units and large flatscreen TVs in spacious rooms, all fitted with antique rosewood furniture, gilded pelmets and lace curtains. Rates include buffet breakfast. ₹**10,500**

EATING AND DRINKING

Catering for the droves of tourists who come here from other Indian states, as well as fussy, more price-conscious locals, Panjim is packed with good **places to eat**. Most are connected to a hotel, but there are also plenty of other independently run establishments offering quality food for far less than you pay in the coastal resorts. If you're unsure about which regional cooking style to go for, head for *The Fidalgo Food Enclave*, in the *Hotel Fidalgo* on 18th June Rd, which hosts six different outlets, from Goan to Gujarati.

Bhojan/Mirch Masala Hotel Fidalgo, 18th June Rd. Authentic, pure-veg Gujarati thali joint, in the a/c restaurant complex of a popular upscale hotel. You won't eat finer Indian vegetarian cuisine anywhere in Goa. ₹200 for the works. For equally superb non-veg, north Indian food (kebabs, curries, tandoori and the like) head next door to *Mirch Masala*. Daily noon–3pm & 5–11pm.

George's Emilio Gracia Rd. This is a great little Goan-Catholic café serving proper local food at local prices, on cramped tables near the Immaculate Conception church. Grab a seat under a fan and tuck into calamari chilli fry, prawn-curry-rice, millet-fried fish fillets or one of the good-value seafood thalis. Most mains around ₹150. Daily 10am–10pm.

★ **Mum's Kitchen** Dr D Bandodkar (DB) Marg (Panjim–Miramar Rd) ☎ 9011 095557, ⊛ mumskitchengoa.com. The owners of this great Goan restaurant in the suburb of Miramar, 10min by auto from the centre of Panjim, collected old family recipes from mothers, grandmas and aunties across the state in an attempt to revive disappearing culinary traditions. The results are as authentic and flavour-packed as any you'll encounter in Goa. Most mains ₹300–450. Daily 11am–11pm.

Satkar 18th June Rd. Popular south Indian snack and juice joint. There's a huge range of dishes, including Chinese and north Indian, but most people go for their fantastic masala dosas (₹60) and piping hot, crunchy samosas (₹15) – the best in town. Daily 8am–10pm.

Sher-e-Punjab Above Hindu Pharmacy, Cunha Rivara Rd, Municipal Gardens (Church Square) ☎ 0832 242 5657. This north Indian restaurant, an old Panjim favourite that recently had a major facelift, occupies a funky, glass-sided dining hall overlooking the square. Steer clear of the Goan and Chinese menu – Mughlai is the thing here: chicken, mutton and *paneer* prepared in the tandoor or steeped in rich, spicy and creamy sauces, which you scoop up with flaky naan breads. Mains ₹200–325. Daily 10.30am–11.30pm.

Vihar Around the corner from Venite, on Avda Dom Joao Castro. One of the best south Indian snack cafés in town, and more conveniently situated than its competitors if you're staying in Fontainhas. The only drawback is the traffic noise; best avoided during rush hours. Daily 7.30am–9.30pm.

★ **Viva Panjim** 178 Rua 31 de Janeiro, behind Mary Immaculate High School, Fontainhas. Traditional

12

GOAN FOOD AND DRINK

Not unnaturally, after 451 years of colonization, Goan **cooking** absorbed a strong Portuguese influence – palm vinegar (unknown elsewhere in India), copious amounts of coconut, tangy *kokum* and fierce local chillies also play their part. Goa is the home of the famous **vindaloo** (from the Portuguese *vinho d'alho*, literally "garlic wine"), originally an extra-hot and sour pork curry, but now made with a variety of meat and fish. Other **pork** specialities include spicy *chouriço* sausages, *sorpotel*, a hot curry made from pickled pig's liver and heart, *leitao*, suckling pig and *balchao*, pork in a rich brown sauce. Another traditional Goan Catholic dish is mutton *xacuti*, made with a sauce of lemon juice, peanuts, coconut, chillies and spices. The choice of **seafood**, often cooked in fragrant masalas, is excellent – clams, mussels, crab, lobster, giant prawns – while **fish**, depending on the type, is either cooked in wet curries, grilled, or baked in tandoori clay ovens. *Sanna*, like the south Indian *iddli*, is a steamed cake of fermented rice flour, but here sweetened with palm toddy. Sugar fiends will adore *bebinca*, a rich, delicious solid egg custard with coconut.

As for **drinks**, locally produced wine, spirits and beer are cheaper than anywhere in the country, thanks to lower rates of tax. The most famous and widespread **beer** is Kingfisher, which tastes less of glycerine preservative than it does elsewhere in India, but you'll also come across pricier Fosters, brewed in Mumbai and nothing like the original. Goan **port**, a sweeter, inferior version of its Portuguese namesake, is ubiquitous, served chilled in large wine glasses with a slice of lemon. Local **spirits** – whiskies, brandies, rums, gins and vodkas – come in a variety of brand names for less than ₹50–150 a shot, but, at half the price, local speciality **feni**, made from distilled cashew or from the sap of coconut palms, offers strong competition. Cashew *feni* is usually drunk after the first distillation, but you can also find it double-distilled and flavoured with ginger or cumin, producing a smooth liqueur.

Goan home cooking – *xacutis*, vindaloo, prawn *balchao*, *cafreal*, *amotik* and delicious freshly grilled fish – served by a charming local woman, Linda de Souza, in a pretty colonial-era backstreet. This place should be your first choice for dinner if you're staying in Fontainhas. Most mains ₹175–300. Mon–Sat 11.30am–3pm & 7–10.30pm, Sun 7–10.30pm.

DIRECTORY

Banks Nearly all the banks in town nowadays have ATMs, where you can make withdrawals using Visa or MasterCard; several are marked on our map (see p.678). The most efficient place to change currency and travellers' cheques is Thomas Cook, near the Air India/Indian Airlines office at 8 Alcon Chambers, Dr D Bandodkar (DB) Marg (Mon–Sat 9am–6pm; Oct–March also Sun 10am–5pm).

British Consular Assistant The British High Commission of Mumbai has a one-woman Consular Section in Panjim – a useful contact for British nationals who've lost passports, get into trouble with the law or need help dealing with a death. It's on the far western end of town, opposite the five-star *Marriott Hotel* at 303–304 Casa del Sol, Miramar (☎ 832 246 1110 or ☎ 832 246 1113; ✉ assistance@goaukconsular .org; Mon–Thurs 9.30am–3pm, Fri 9.30am–12.30pm; emergency out-of-hours number: ☎ 9111 2419 2100).

Cinema Panjim's swanky multiplex, the 1272-seater Inox, is in the northwest of town on the site of the old Goa Medical College, Dr D Bandodkar (DB) Marg (☎ 0832 242 0999, ⓦ inoxmovies.com). It screens all the latest Hindi blockbusters, and some English-language Hollywood movies; see the local press or their website for listings and booking details.

Hospital The state's main medical facility is the new Goa Medical College, aka GMC (☎ 0832 245 8700–07), 7km south on NH-17 at Bambolim, where there's also a 24hr pharmacy. Ambulances (☎ 102) are likely to get you there a lot less quickly than a standard taxi. Conditions are grim by Western standards. Less serious cases can receive attention at the Vintage Hospital, next to the fire brigade headquarters in Panjim's St Inez district (☎ 0832 564 4401–05). Better medical facilities are available in Margao, less than an hour away by road (see p.710).

Pharmacies Hindu Pharma, near the tourist office on Church Square (☎ 0832 222 3176), stocks a phenomenal range of Ayurvedic, homeopathic and allopathic medicines.

Old Goa

At one-time a byword for oriental splendour, Portugal's former capital in India, **OLD GOA**, was virtually abandoned following malaria and cholera epidemics from the seventeenth century onwards. Today, despite its UNESCO World Heritage Site status, you need considerable imagination to picture the once-great city at its zenith, when it boasted a population of several hundred thousand. The maze of twisting streets, piazzas and ochre-washed villas has vanished, and all that remains is a score of cream-painted churches and convents. Foremost among the surviving monuments is the tomb of **St Francis Xavier**, the legendary sixteenth-century missionary, whose desiccated remains

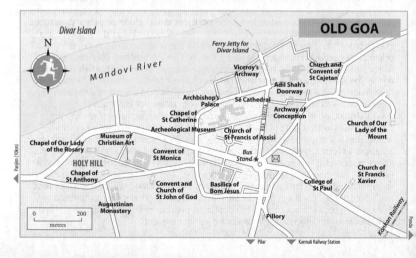

are enshrined in the **Basilica of Bom Jesus** – the object of veneration for Catholics from across Asia and beyond.

Viceroy's Archway

Old Goa's grandest mansions formerly lined the riverfront, and the best direction from which to approach the site is still from the north. Begin your tour at the **Viceroy's Archway** (1597), which would have been the first structure to greet new arrivals in the seventeenth century. Constructed to commemorate Vasco da Gama's first landfall in India, it features a Bible-toting figure resting his foot on the cringing figure of a "native" on one side, and a statue of Da Gama himself on the other.

Church of St Cajetan

A short way up the lane from the Archway, the spectacular domed **Church of St Cajetan** (1651) was modelled on St Peter's in Rome by monks from the Theatine Order. While it boasts a Corinthian exterior, non-European elements are also evident in the decoration, such as the cashew-nut designs in the carving of the pulpit.

The Sé (St Catherine's Cathedral)

The Portuguese viceroy Redondo (1561–64) commissioned the **Sé**, or **St Catherine's Cathedral**, southwest of St Cajetan's, to be "a grandiose church worthy of the wealth, power and fame of the Portuguese who dominated the seas from the Atlantic to the Pacific". Today it stands larger than any church in Portugal, although it was beset by problems, not least a lack of funds and the motherland's temporary loss of independence to Spain. It took eighty years to build and was not consecrated until 1640.

On the Tuscan-style exterior, the one surviving tower houses the **Golden Bell**, cast in Cuncolim (south Goa) in the seventeenth century. During the Inquisition its tolling announced the start of the gruesome autos-da-fé that were held in the square outside, when suspected heretics were subjected to public torture and burned at the stake. The scale and opulence of the Corinthian-style interior is overwhelming; no fewer than fifteen altars are arranged around the walls, among them one featuring a **Miraculous Cross**, said to heal the sick. The staggeringly ornate, gilded main **altar** is surrounded by panels depicting episodes from the life of St Catherine of Alexandria (died 307 AD).

Convent of St Francis of Assisi

Archeological Museum Daily except Fri 10am–6pm • ₹10

On the north side of Old Goa's central square stands the **Convent of St Francis of Assisi**, built by Franciscan monks in 1517. Today, the core of the **Archeological Museum** inside consists of a gallery of **portraits** of Portuguese viceroys, painted by local artists under Italian supervision. Other exhibits include coins, domestic Christian wooden sculpture, and downstairs in the cloister, pre-Portuguese Hindu sculpture. Next door, the **Church of St Francis** (1521) features fine decorative frescoes, *hidalgos'* tombstones in the floor paving, and paintings on wood showing the life of St Francis of Assisi.

Basilica of Bom Jesus

Site of the world-famous mausoleum of St Francis Xavier, the **Basilica of Bom Jesus**, on the south side of the main square, is India's most revered and architecturally accomplished church. Work on the building was started in 1589 and took sixteen years to complete. In 1964, it became the first church in South Asia to be promoted to a Minor Basilica, by order of Pope Pius XII, and today forms the main focus for Christian worship in the old colonial capital.

Is it believed that the design of the basilica is derived from the Gesù, the Jesuits' headquarters in Rome, and, with its idiosyncratic blend of Neoclassical restraint and Baroque extravagance, is typical of the late Renaissance. The sumptuous **facade**, the most ornate in Goa, is dominated by the IHS motif, standing for Iesus Hominum Salvator ("Jesus Saviour of Men") – a feature of all Jesuit churches.

Inside the church

The **interior** is positively plain by comparison, but no less impressive, dominated by a massive gilt altarpiece and a huge central statue of St Ignatius Loyola, founder of the Jesuit Order, accompanied by the Infant Jesus. Swathed in lush gold leaf, the gigantic **reredos** filling the far end of the nave remains the basilica's most arresting feature. Its undisputed treasure, however, is to be found in the south transept: the **mausoleum of St Francis** was installed in 1698, a century and a half after his death, gifted to the Jesuits by the last of the Medicis, Cosimo III (1670–1723), Grand Duke of Tuscany, in exchange for the pillow on which the saint's head was laid to rest. It took Florentine sculptor Giovanni Batista Saggini a decade to design and was made from precious marble and coloured jaspers shipped from Italy.

Holy Hill

If the heat hasn't got the better of you, head west up the lane leading from the bus stand to take in the cluster of monuments on **Holy Hill**, some of which date from the earliest phase of Christian building in Goa.

Convent of Santa Monica

The lane winds uphill, passing the weed-choked **Convent of Santa Monica** on the right. This was the only Goan convent at the time of its construction in 1627, and the largest one in Asia in its era. It housed around a hundred nuns and offered accommodation to women whose husbands were called away to other parts of the empire. As they had to remain away from the public gaze, the nuns attended mass in the choir loft of the adjacent **chapel**, where a Miraculous Cross rises above the figure of St Monica at the altar.

Museum of Christian Art

Museum Daily 9.30am–5pm • ₹10

Next door to the Convent of Santa Monica stands Goa's foremost **Museum of Christian Art**. Exhibits include processional crosses, ivory ornaments, damask silk clerical robes and some finely sculpted wooden icons dating from the sixteenth and seventeenth centuries, among them an unusual statue of John the Baptist wearing a tiger-skin wrap (in the style of the Hindu god Shiva).

Chapel of Our Lady of the Rosary

Crowning the very top of the Holy Hill, the **Chapel of Our Lady of the Rosary**, constructed in 1526 in the Manueline style (after the Portuguese king Manuel I, 1495–1521), features Ionic plasterwork with a double-storey portico, cylindrical turrets and a tower that commands fine views across the river from the terrace where Albuquerque surveyed the decisive battle of 1510. Its cruciform interior is unremarkable, except for the marble tomb of **Catarina a Piró**, believed to have been the first European woman to set foot in the colony. A commoner, she eloped here to escape the scandal surrounding her romance with Portuguese nobleman Garcia de Sá, who later rose to be governor of Goa. Under pressure from no less than Francis Xavier, Garcia eventually married her, but only *in articulo mortis* as she lay on her deathbed. Her finely carved tomb, set in the wall beside the high altar, incorporates a band of intricate Gujarati-style ornamentation, probably imported from the Portuguese trading post of Diu.

12

ST FRANCIS XAVIER

Francis Xavier, the "Apostle of the Indies", was born in 1506 in the old kingdom of Navarre, now part of Spain. When the Portuguese king, Dom Joao III (1521–57), received reports of corruption and dissolute behaviour among the Portuguese in Goa, it was Xavier whom the Jesuit Order selected to restore the moral climate of the colony.

Arriving after a year-long journey, the young priest embarked on a programme of missionary work throughout southern India, converting an estimated thirty thousand people – primarily by performing such miracles as raising the dead and curing the sick with a touch of his beads. Subsequent missions took him further afield to Sri Lanka, Malacca (Malaysia) and Japan, before his death from dysentery on the island of San Chuan (Sancian), off the Chinese coast in 1552.

Although credited with converting more people to Christianity than anyone other than St Paul, Francis Xavier owes his subsequent canonization principally to the legend surrounding the fate of his mortal remains, which, when exhumed in China a year after burial, were found to be in a perfect state of preservation. His body was later removed and taken to Old Goa, where it has remained ever since, enshrined in the **Basilica of Bom Jesus**.

PLUNDERED RELICS

St Francis's incorruptible corpse, however, has never rested entirely in peace. Chunks of it have been removed over the years by **relic hunters** and curious clerics: in 1614, the right arm was dispatched to the pope in Rome (where it allegedly wrote its name on paper), a hand was sent to Japan, and parts of the intestines to Southeast Asia. One Portuguese woman, Dona Isabel de Caron, even bit off the little toe of the cadaver; apparently, so much blood spurted into her mouth, it left a trail to her house and she was discovered.

Every ten years, the saint's body is carried in a three-hour ceremony from the Basilica of Bom Jesus to the Sé cathedral, where visitors file past, touch and photograph it. Around a quarter of a million pilgrims flock to view the corpse, these days a shrivelled and somewhat unsavoury spectacle. The next Exposition is scheduled for the winter of 2014–15.

ARRIVAL AND DEPARTURE

OLD GOA

By bus Just 25min by road from the state capital, Old Goa is served by buses every 15min from Panjim's Kadamba Bus Stand (₹10). Given how short the trip is, and the high charges levied by local taxis and auto-rickshaws, this is one excursion that's eminently do-able by public transport.

By auto-rickshaw The road to Old Goa is smooth enough to consider covering by auto-rickshaw. Count on ₹200 each way.

By taxi Taxis from Panjim charge around ₹400 to drop passengers in Old Goa.

Tambdi Surla

Six or seven hundred years ago, the Goan coast and its hinterland were littered with scores of richly carved stone temples. Only one, though, made it unscathed through the Muslim onslaught and the religious bigotry of the Portuguese era. Erected in the twelfth or thirteenth century, the tiny **Mahadeva temple** at **TAMBDI SURLA**, deep in the interior of Goa, owes its survival to its remote location in a tranquil clearing deep in the forest at the foot of the Western Ghats, which enfold the site in a wall of impenetrable vegetation.

The temple, dedicated to Shiva, was built from the finest weather-resistant grey-black basalt, carried across the mountains from the Deccan Plateau and richly carved in situ by the region's most accomplished craftsmen.

Despite its remoteness, Tambdi Surla sees large numbers of visitors, especially on weekends, when it becomes the target for numerous school trips – so if you want to enjoy the site's essential tranquillity come during the week.

ARRIVAL AND DEPARTURE

TAMBDI SURLA

By Taxi To get to Tambdi Surla you have to follow the course of NH4 east from the central Goan town of Ponda, which because it is used by streams of iron ore trucks is a nightmare on a scooter or motorbike. Go by taxi if you can afford it: drivers charge around ₹3000 for the roundtrip from the coast.

Dudhsagar waterfalls

Measuring a mighty 600m from head to foot, the famous **Dudhsagar waterfalls**, on the Goa–Karnataka border, are some of the highest in India, and a spectacular enough sight to entice a steady stream of visitors from the coast into the rugged Western Ghats. The Konkani name for the falls, which literally translated means "sea of milk", derives from clouds of foam kicked up at the bottom when the water levels are at their highest. Overlooking a steep, crescent-shaped head of a valley carpeted with pristine tropical forest, Dudhsagar is set amid impressive **scenery** that is only accessible on foot or by jeep.

The **best time to visit** is immediately after the monsoons, from October until mid-December, when water levels are highest, although the falls flow well into April.

ARRIVAL AND DEPARTURE DUDHSAGAR

By jeep The only practical way to get to Dudhsagar and back is by 4WD jeep from Colem (get to Colem by train from Vasco, Margao and Chandor, or by taxi from the north-coast resorts for around ₹3000). Look for the "Controller of Jeeps" in Colem, near the station. The cost of the onward 30- to 40min trip from Colem to the falls, across rough forest tracks and three river fords, is ₹2000–2500/person (travelling alone or in a pair you may have to wait for the vehicle to fill up); the drive ends with an enjoyable 10min hike.

North Goa

Development in North Goa is concentrated mainly behind the 7km, strip of white sand that stretches from the foot of **Fort Aguada**, crowning the peninsula east of Panjim, to Baga creek in the north. Encompassing the resorts of **Candolim**, **Calangute** and **Baga**, this is Goa's prime charter belt and an area most independent travellers steer well clear of.

Since the advent of mass tourism in the 1980s, the alternative "scene" has drifted progressively north away from the sunbed strip to **Anjuna** and **Vagator** – site of some of the region's loveliest beaches – and scruffier **Chapora**, still primarily a workaday fishing village. Further north still, **Arambol** has thus far escaped any large-scale development, despite the completion of the new road bridge across the Chapora River. **Aswem** and **Mandrem**, just south of Arambol, are this stretch of coast's hot tips: still reasonably off-track, though rapidly filling up.

ARRIVAL NORTH GOA

North Goa's market town, **Mapusa**, is the area's main jumping-off place if you're arriving overland from out of state. Travelling here by train via the **Konkan Railway**, get off at **Tivim** (Thivim), 12km east of Mapusa, from where you'll have to jump in a bus or taxi for the remaining leg.

Mapusa

MAPUSA (pronounced "Mapsa") is the district headquarters of Bardez *taluka*. A dusty collection of dilapidated, mostly modern buildings ranged around a busy central square, the town is of little more than passing interest, although it does host a lively daily fresh produce **market**. Anjuna's market may be a better place to shop for souvenirs, but Mapusa's is much more authentic. Local specialities include strings of spicy Goan sausages (*chouriço*), bottles of toddy (fermented palm sap) and large green plantains from nearby Moira.

Whatever you're looking for in the Mapusa market, it's a good idea to arrive as early in the morning as possible to beat the heat. After 11am temperatures can be extremely stifling.

ARRIVAL AND DEPARTURE

By train Tivim (Thivim), the nearest railway station to Mapusa, is 12km east in the neighbouring Bicholim district. Buses should be on hand to transport passengers into town. The Konkan Railway's *Konkan Kanya Express* #10111 arrives in Tivim at around 9.30am, leaving plenty of time to find accommodation in the coastal resorts west of Mapusa.

Destinations Chaudi (for Palolem; 1 daily; 1hr 30min); Gokarna Rd (1 daily; 2hr); Mumbai (8–12 daily; 9–12hr).

By bus You can pick up local services to Calangute, Baga, Anjuna, Vagator, Chapora and Arambol. These leave from the Kadamba Bus Stand, a 5min west of

the main square, where all state-run services from Panjim also pull in.

Destinations Anjuna (hourly; 30min); Arambol (12 daily; 1hr 45min); Baga (hourly; 30min); Calangute (every 30min; 30min); Chapora (every 30min; 30–40min); Mumbai (24 daily; 14–18hr); Panjim (every 15min; 25min); Pernem (6 daily; 1hr 45min); Vagator (every 30min; 25–35min).

By taxi Motorcycle taxis hang around the square to whisk lightly laden shoppers and travellers to the coast for around ₹75. Taxis charge considerably more (around ₹250), but you can split the fare with up to five people.

EATING

FR Xavier In the Municipal Market. For quick, authentic Goan food, you won't do better than the *FR Xavier*, which has been here since the Portuguese era. It serves scrumptious veg patties and beef "chops" (rissoles), as well as spicy meals of fish, prawn and chicken curry, and other local standards such as *cafreal*

and *xacuti*. Most mains cost less than ₹150. Daily 9am–9pm.

Ruchira Inside the Hotel Satyaheera on the north side of the main square. Best of the eating options on or around the main intersection, serving a standard multicuisine menu and cold beer. Daily 9am–9pm.

SHOPPING

Other India Bookstore Behind Mapusa Clinic ☎ 0832 226 3306, ⓦ otherindiabookstore.com. Hidden away behind the Mapusa Clinic, this bookstore is

a treasure trove of a vast range of titles relating to ecology, the environment and Goa in general; a full stock list is available online.

Candolim and around

CANDOLIM is prime package-tourist country, and not a resort that sees many backpackers, but, with a few pleasant places to stay tucked away down quiet back lanes, it can make a good first stop if you've just arrived in Goa. The busy strip running through the middle of town holds a string of banks and handy shops where you can stock up with essentials before moving further afield, and there are some great places to eat and drink, frequented mostly by boozy, middle-aged Brits and, increasingly, Russian charter tourists.

Fort Aguada

The one sight worth seeking out in the area is **Fort Aguada**, crowning the rocky flattened headland to the south, at the end of the beach. Built in 1612 to protect the northern shores of the Mandovi estuary from Dutch and Maratha raiders, the bastion encloses several natural springs, the first source of drinking water available to ships arriving in Goa after the long sea voyage from Lisbon. The ruins of the fort can be reached by following the main drag south from Candolim as it bears left, past the turning for the *Fort Aguada Beach Resort*; keep going for 1km until you see a right turn, which runs uphill to a small car park. Panoramic views extend from the top of the hill where a four-storey Portuguese **lighthouse**, erected in 1864 and the oldest of its kind in Asia, looks down over the vast expanse of sea, sand and palm trees.

Sinquerim Beach

From the base of Fort Aguada on the northern flank of the headland, a rampart of red-brown laterite juts into the bay at the bottom of what's left of **Sinquerim Beach**, which was virtually wiped out by a series of particularly heavy monsoon storms in 2009. This was among the first places in Goa to be singled out for upmarket tourism. The

Taj group's *Fort Aguada* resort, among the most expensive hotels in India, lords it over the sands from the slopes below the battlements.

ARRIVAL AND DEPARTURE CANDOLIM AND AROUND

By bus Buses to and from Panjim and Calangute stop every 10–15min or so at the stand opposite the *Casa Sea Shell*, in the middle of Candolim. A few head south here to the *Fort Aguada Beach Resort* terminus; you can also flag them down from anywhere along the main drag to Calangute.

Destinations Calangute (every 15min; 15min); Panjim (every 15min; 25min).

By taxi Maruti taxis are ubiquitous.

GETTING AROUND AND INFORMATION

Motorbike rental During the season there is often a dearth of motorcycles for rent, in which case search for one in Calangute – try *Gabriel's*. The nearest petrol pump lies 5km east on the main Panjim road, just beyond Nerul.

Services There are lots of ATMs dotted along the main drag and you can change money at any number of private exchange places in Candolim, although their rates are unlikely to be as competitive as those in Calangute.

ACCOMMODATION

Candolim is charter-holiday land, so **accommodation** tends to be expensive for most of the season. That said, if bookings are down you can find some great bargains here.

Casa Sea Shell Fort Aguada Rd, near Bom Successo ☎ 0832 247 9879, ⓦ seashellgoa.com. Long-established former charter hotel near the Nerul road junction where you've a choice between standard non-a/c rooms or larger, newer and better-furnished ones with flatscreen TVs and a/c. Facing each other across a palm-shaded garden, both blocks offer accommodation that's spacious for the price, impeccably clean, and well aired. Best of all, you get the run of a well-kept little pool. A/c costs ₹600 extra. ₹2250

⭐ **Dona Florina** Monteiro's Rd, Escrivao Waddo ☎ 0832 248 9051, ⓦ donaflorina.co.in. Large guesthouse in a superb location, overlooking the beach in the most secluded corner of the village. Its friendly owner, Jessie D'Souza, has added a breezy rooftop terrace with ceramic mosaic floors where guests can practise yoga. Well worth paying a little extra for if you want idyllic sea views. No car access. ₹1500

Marbella Sinquerim ☎ 0832 247 9551, ⓦ marbellagoa .com. Individually styled suites and spacious rooms in a beautiful house built to resemble a traditional Goan mansion. The decor, fittings and furniture are gorgeous, especially in the top-floor "Penthouse" (₹6000), and the whole place is screened by a giant mango tree. Unashamedly romantic and well worth splashing out on. ₹3000

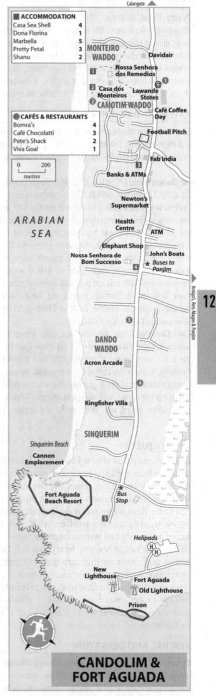

■ ACCOMMODATION	
Casa Sea Shell	4
Dona Florina	1
Marbella	5
Pretty Petal	3
Shanu	2

● CAFÉS & RESTAURANTS	
Bomra's	4
Café Chocolatti	3
Pete's Shack	2
Viva Goa!	1

CANDOLIM & FORT AGUADA

12

Arpojn, Reis Magos & Panjim

Pretty Petal Camotim Waddo ☎0832 248 9184, ⓦprettypetalsgoa.com. Not as twee as it sounds: very large, modern rooms, all with fridges, quality mattresses, balconies, and relaxing, marble-floored communal areas overlooking lawns. Their top-floor apartment, with windows on four sides and a huge balcony, is the best choice, though more expensive. Use of nearby swimming pool included. ₹**1700**

Shanu Escrivao Waddo ☎0832 248 9899. Eighteen good-sized, well-furnished rooms with narrow balconies right on the dunes, some of them with uninterrupted views of the sea. High season rates range from ₹700–2250. Ask the hospitable owners for #120 (or failing that #118, #111, #110 or #107). Breakfast is served in your room. ₹**700**

EATING AND DRINKING

Candolim's numerous beach **cafés** are a cut above your average seafood shacks, with pot plants, high-tech sound systems and prices to match. The further from the *Taj* complex you venture, the lower the prices become. Fancier places serving more ambitious cuisine line busy Fort Aguada Rd, alongside a string of enduringly popular local joints.

★ **Bomra's** Souza Waddo, 247 CHOGM (Fort Aguada) Rd ☎9822 149633 or ☎9822 106236, ⓦbomras.com. Understated, relaxed place, on a dimly-lit gravel terrace by the roadside. From the outside you'd never know this was one of Goa's gastronomic highlights, but the food – contemporary Burmese and Kachin cuisine – is superb. The menu's reassuringly short; try their spinach wraps in fragrant *tahini* sauce for starters, and the beef in peanut curry or snapper with lime and chilli, tofu and noodles for a main. They also do fantastic mojitos and, for dessert, delicious ginger crème brûlée. Count on ₹1000–1250 for three courses. Daily 6.30pm–late.

Café Chocolatti Near Acron Arcade. Goa's answer to Juliette Binoche's "Vianne Rocher" in the movie *Chocolat*, the British-raised owner of this delightful café in south Candolim, Nazneen, has conjured up a chocoholic heaven. Order a perfect cup of freshly ground coffee or a milk shake to drink in the garden, and indulge in gourmet Belgian-style truffles, tinged with chilli, mocha and orange, a succulent marmalade brownie, or crunchy almond-flavoured Italian biscuits. ₹150–200 for coffee and a treat. Daily 10am–9pm.

Pete's Shack Sequeira Waddo. One beach shack that deserves singling out because it's always professional and serves great healthy salads (₹125–250) with real olive oil, mozzarella and balsamic vinegar. All the veg is carefully washed in chlorinated water first, so the food is safe and fresh. The same applies to their seafood sizzler and tandoori main courses. For dessert, try the wonderful chocolate mousse, home-made carrot cake, brownies or cooling mint lassis. Daily 8.30am–late.

Viva Goa! CHOGM (Fort Aguada) Rd. Tasty, no-nonsense Goan food fresh from the market – musselfry, barramundi (*chonok*), lemonfish (*modso*) and sharkfish steaks fried *rechado* style in chilli paste or in millet (*rawa*) – served on a roadside terrace. Tourists are welcome, but it's essentially local food at local prices. Most mains around ₹150. Daily 11am–11pm.

Calangute

A 45-minute bus ride up the coast from Panjim, **CALANGUTE** was, in Portuguese times, where well-to-do Goans would come for their annual *mudança*, or change of air, in May and June, when the pre-monsoonal heat made life in the towns insufferable. It remains the state's busiest resort, but has changed beyond recognition since the days when straw-hatted musicians in the beachfront bandstand would regale smartly dressed strollers with Lisbon *fados* and Konkani *dulpods*. Mass package tourism, combined with a huge increase in the number of Indian visitors (for whom this is Goa's number-one beach resort), has placed an impossible burden on the town's rudimentary infrastructure. Hemmed in by four-storey buildings and swarming with traffic, the market area, in particular, has taken on the aspect of a typical makeshift Indian town of precisely the kind that most travellers used to come to Goa to get away from. In short, this is somewhere to avoid, although most people pass through here at some stage to eat: Calangute boasts some of the best **restaurants** in the state.

ARRIVAL AND DEPARTURE

By bus Buses from Mapusa (every 30min; 30min) and Panjim (every 15min; 45min) pull in at the small bus stand-cum-market square in the centre of Calangute. Some continue to Baga, stopping at the crossroads behind the beach en route. Destinations Mapusa (every 30min; 30min); Panjim (every 30min; 40min).

ACCOMMODATION

In spite of the encroaching mayhem, plenty of travellers get hooked on the village's mix of market town and beach resort, returning year after year to stay in little family guesthouses in the fishing *waddo*, where the life remains remarkably unchanged. Nowhere is far from the shore, but sea views are a rarity.

Camizala 5-33B Maddo Waddo ☎ 9689 156449. A lovely, breezy haven amid the brouhaha of Calangute, with four rooms, common verandas and sea views. About as close to the beach as you can get, and the *waddo* is very quiet. Cheap, considering the location. ₹800

CoCo Banana 1195 Umta Waddo ☎ 0832 227 6478 or ☎ 0832 227 9068, ⓦ cocobananagoa.com. Very comfortable, spacious chalets, all with bathrooms, fridges, fans, mosquito nets, kettles and extra-long mattresses. An additional ₹450 gets you a lot more space and verandas opening on to the garden. Down the lane beyond *Meena Lobo's* restaurant, it is run by a welcoming Swiss–Goan couple, Walter and Marina Lobo, who have been here for more than years. ₹750

Indian Kitchen Behind Our Lady of Piety Church ☎ 9822 149615, ⓦ indian-kitchen-goa.com. Highly decorated guesthouse with crazy mosaic tiling, brightly patterned walls and lanterns. The rooms, all attached, have fridges and music systems – and, amazingly for a budget hotel, there's a little pool to the rear. ₹1000

EATING AND DRINKING

Ever since *Souza Lobo* opened on the beachfront to cater for Goan day-trippers in the 1930s, Calangute has been somewhere people come as much to eat as for a stroll on the beach, and even if you stay in resorts elsewhere you'll doubtless be tempted down here for a meal.

A Reverie Near Goan Heritage Resort, Gauro Waddo ☎ 9823 174927 or ☎ 9326 114661. Over-the-top gourmet place on the south side of Calangute, centred on a grand, multilevel, terracotta-tiled canopy. Both the gastronomic menu and ambience are about as extravagant as Goa gets, but the prices aren't top whack (around ₹1500–2000/head, plus drinks). Signature dishes include beef *filet* with a scoop of mustard ice cream, and Himalayan trout with Thai herbs. Reservations recommended. Daily 7pm–late.

Florentine's 4km east of St Alex's Church at Saligao, next door to the Ayurvedic Natural Health Centre. It's well worth venturing inland to taste Florence D'Costa's legendary chicken *cafreal* (₹250) made to a jealously guarded family recipe that pulls in crowds of locals and tourists from across north Goa. The restaurant is a down-to-earth place, with prices to match, serving only chicken, some seafood and vegetarian snacks. Daily 6.30pm–late.

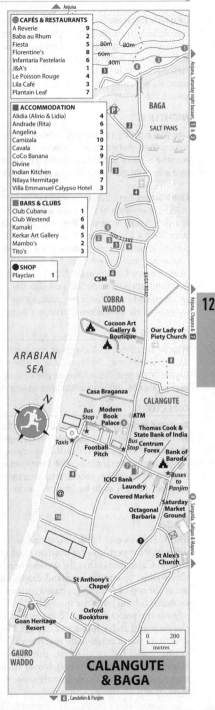

CAFÉS & RESTAURANTS
A Reverie	9
Baba au Rhum	2
Fiesta	5
Florentine's	8
Infantaria Pastelaria	6
J&A's	1
Le Poisson Rouge	4
Lila Café	3
Plantain Leaf	7

ACCOMMODATION
Alidia (Alirio & Lidia)	4
Andrade (Rita)	6
Angelina	5
Camizala	10
Cavala	2
CoCo Banana	9
Divine	1
Indian Kitchen	8
Nilaya Hermitage	7
Villa Emmanuel Calypso Hotel	3

BARS & CLUBS
Club Cubana	1
Club Westend	6
Kamaki	4
Kerkar Art Gallery	5
Mambo's	2
Tito's	3

SHOP
Playclan	1

CALANGUTE & BAGA

Infantaria Pastelaria Next to St John's Chapel, Baga road. Roadside terrace café run by *Souza Lobo* that gets packed out for its stodgy croissants, freshly baked apple pie and traditional Goan sweets (such as *dodol* and home-made *bebinca*). Top of the savoury list, though, are the prawn and veg patties (₹50), which locals buy by the boxload. Daily 8.30am–11pm.

Plantain Leaf Market area. The best *udipi* restaurant outside Panjim, if not all Goa, where waiters in matching shirts serve the usual range of delicious dosas and other spicy snacks in a clean, cool marble-lined canteen, with relentless background *filmi* music. Try their definitive *iddli-vada* breakfasts, delicious masala dosas (₹90) or the cheap and filling set thalis (₹135). Daily 7.30am–10.30pm.

NIGHTLIFE

Calangute's **nightlife** is surprisingly tame for a resort of its size, though it does boast the only old-school trance and dance venue with any credibility, tucked away in the jungle on the outskirts. Music of a more traditional Indian variety can be enjoyed at the Kerkar Art Gallery, amid suitably serene surroundings. Otherwise, take your pick from the string of shacks lined up along the beach, which stay open until the last punter staggers home.

Club Westend 4km inland at Sangolda ☎9188 8892 9079. Set on a hilltop in the Mollem Bhat Valley, this is the only place to party in the area. Weapon of choice: Goa trance. The look is a "unique jungle dance paradise", with two open-air dancefloors on separate levels, a rooftop pool, extravagantly neon ambient zones and exclusive VIP cabins. Admission fluctuates around ₹700–1500, and the clientele is mostly twenty-something, and Russian. Queues and crowds can be horrendous in peak season, but there's really nowhere else worth bothering with south of Vagator.

Fri & Sun 9pm–4.30am.

Kerkar Art Gallery Gauro Waddo at the south end of Calangute ☎0832 227 6017, ⓦsubodhkerkar.com. Weekly classical music and dance recitals, held in the candlelit back garden. The little concerts, performed by students and teachers from Panjim's Kala Academy, are kept comfortably short for the benefit of Western visitors, and are preceded by a short introductory talk. Tickets, available in advance or at the door, cost ₹400. Tues 6.45pm–8.30pm.

SHOPPING

Playclan Shop NoS-3, Ida Maria Resort, next to HDFC Bank ⓦplayclan.com. Delhi-based design collective Playclan have a great shop in Calangute offering quirky souvenirs and gifts. They create an alternative universe of instantly recognizable Indian symbols – gods, Kathakali dancers, rickshaws and "horn-ok-please" lorries – with which they decorate T-shirts, mugs, lighters and underwear. Daily 11am–8pm.

DIRECTORY

Banks and exchange Thomas Cook have a branch in the main market area (Mon–Sat 9.30am–6pm), where there's also an efficient ICICI Bank with 24hr ATM. Private currency changers on the same street include Wall Street Finances (Mon–Sat 9.30am–6pm), opposite the petrol pump and in the shopping complex on the beachfront, who exchange both cash and travellers' cheques at bank rates. At the Bank of Baroda (Mon–Fri 9.30am–2.15pm, Sat 9.30am–noon, Sun 9.30am–2pm), just north of the market on the Anjuna road, you can make encashments against Visa cards; commission is one percent of the amount changed, plus ₹150 for the authorization phone call.

Baga

BAGA, 10km west of Mapusa, is basically an extension of Calangute. The only difference between this far northern end of the beach and its more congested centre around Calangute is that the scenery here is marginally more varied and picturesque. Overlooked by a rocky headland draped in vegetation, a small tidal river flows into the sea at the top of the village, past a spur of soft white sand where ranks of brightly coloured fishing boats are moored.

Since the package boom, Baga has developed more rapidly than anywhere else in the state and today looks less like the Goan fishing village it was in the early 1990s and more like a small-scale resort on the Spanish costas, with a predominantly young, male, Indian clientele. But if you can steer clear of the lager louts, Baga boasts distinct advantages over its neighbours: a crop of excellent **restaurants** and a **nightlife** that's consistently more full-on than anywhere else in the state, if not all India.

ARRIVAL AND DEPARTURE

BAGA

By bus Regular buses from Mapusa via Calangute (hourly; 40 & 15mins respectively) terminate at the car park in the far north of Baga, next to *Britto's* restaurant.

ACCOMMODATION

Accommodation is harder to find in Baga than in Calangute, as even rooms in smaller guesthouses tend to be booked up well before the season gets under way. The majority of family-run places lie around the north end of the beach, where night have been a lot more peaceful since Goa's premier club, *Tito's*, acquired soundproofing.

★ **Alidia (Alirio & Lidia)** Baga Rd, Saunta Waddo ☎0832 227 6835, ⊛alidiabeachcottages.com. A compact resort hotel snuggled in the dunes, less than 1min walk from the beach, offering five types of accommodation – from standard non-a/c rooms (₹1800) and cottages (₹2000), to swankier a/c cottages and suites (₹2500/3500). It's efficiently run, stylishly designed (with wooden floors and traditional shell windows in the newer block), and swathed in creepers and foliage. A gorgeous little curvi-form pool, meanwhile, makes it great value in this bracket. ₹1800

Andrade (Rita) Just south of Tito's Lane, Saunta Waddo ☎0832 227 9087. Clean, simply furnished rooms, some of them sea-facing, in a pair of modern blocks attached to a family house. The slightly pricier ones to the rear are nicer, though you don't get the views. Friendly management, and close to the liveliest stretch of beach. A/c costs ₹300 extra. ₹1200

Angelina Saunta Waddo ☎0832 227 9145, ✉angelinabeachresort@rediffmail.com. Spacious, well-maintained rooms with large, gleaming tiled bathrooms and big balconies, in the thick of things off Tito's Lane. The best rooms are on the top storey of the newest of the three blocks. Unbeatable value for money in this enclave. A/c costs ₹500 extra. ₹1500

Cavala Baga Rd ☎0832 227 7587 or ☎0832 227 6090, ⊛cavala.com. Modern hotel in tastefully traditional laterite, with a pool in a plot across the road surrounded by banana groves. The twin-bedded rooms have separate balconies front and back; the rear-side ones look across open fields. Rooms range from simple non-a/c doubles (₹2500) to luxurious suites (₹4000–5000). ₹2500

Divine Near Nani's and Rani's north of the river ☎0832 227 9546 or ☎8879 312374, ⊛indivinehome.com. Run by a couple of hospitable animal-lovers, with rooms on the small side, if impeccably clean; some have attached shower-toilets, and there's a lovely upper terrace with sunbeds and shades, presided over by a menagerie of animal finials on the rooftops. ₹1000

Nilaya Hermitage Arpora Bhati ☎ 0832 227 6793, ⊛nilaya.com. Set on the crest of a hilltop 6km inland from the beach, with matchless views over the coastal plain, this ranks among India's most exclusive hotels, patronized by a very rich international jet set. The complex is a fantasy of rich Indian colours, fiddly ironwork and gilded pillars, opening onto a dreamy pool. Rooms from around $460 for two (or $700 over Christmas–New Year), including meals and airport transfers. ₹24,000

Villa Emmanuel Calypso Hotel Saunta Waddo ☎0832 227 5667 or ☎9923 653514. You can't stay any closer to the beach than this double-storey block, run by local family Manuel and Meena Fernandes. The beds are a bit basic, but most rooms have uninterrupted sea views. Rates increase the higher up the building the rooms are, peaking at ₹1300. The cheapest options are on the ground floor. ₹800

EATING

Nowhere else in the state offers such a good choice of quality **eating** as Baga. Restaurateurs – increasing numbers of them European expats or refugees from upper-class Mumbai – vie with each other to lay on the trendiest menus and most romantic, stylish gardens or terraces.

Baba au Rhum Arpora ☎98220 78759. This cool French patisserie-cum pizzeria hidden deep in the expat enclave of Arpora is a bit off the beaten track, but worth hunting out for its crumbly croissants, baguettes, pains au raisin, fruit salads, juices and perfect café au lait, served on heavy wood tables, with infectious World grooves playing in the background. To find it, turn left off the main Calangute–Anjuna road when you see their signboard. Mains ₹150–300; desserts and pastries ₹50–150. Thurs–Tues 8.30am–10pm.

Fiesta Tito's Lane ☎0832 227 9894, ⊛fiestagoa.com. Baga's most sumptuously decorated restaurant enjoys a perfect spot at the top of a long dune, with sea views from the veranda of a 1930s house. Giant paper lanterns and an old fishing boat filled with scatter cushions set the tone. The contemporary Mediterranean food is as delectable as the decor. Try their carpaccio of beef for starters, followed by lasagne, ravioli or the succulent wood-oven baked pizzas (₹325). Most starters and mains ₹400–650. Reservations recommended. Daily 7pm–midnight.

J&A's Baga Creek ☎0832 227 5274 or ☎9823 139488, ⊛italyingoa.com. Authentic Italian food (down to the imported Parmesan, sun-dried tomatoes

12

and olive oil) served in the gorgeous candlelit garden of a traditional fisherman's cottage. There's an innovative range of salads and antipasti, a choice of sumptuous pasta dishes, wood-fired pizzas and tender steaks (with rosemary potatoes) for mains, and their signature dish, seafood lasagne, is hard to beat. Count on ₹850/head for three courses; double that if you order wine. Daily 7–11pm.

Lila Café Baga Creek ☎0832 227 9843, ⓦlilacafegoa .com. Laid-back bakery-cum-snack-bar, run by a German couple who have been here for decades. Their healthy home-made breads and cakes are great, and there's an adventurous lunch menu featuring spinach à la crème,

aubergine pâté and smoked water-buffalo ham. Most mains under ₹250. Pastries and cakes ₹60–150. Open Daily 8.30am–8pm.

★ **Le Poisson Rouge** Baga Creek ☎0832 324 5800 or ☎9823 859276. The latest star addition to north Goa's gastronomic map, situated in an elegantly styled palm garden lit by pretty tea lights. Try the golden-fried Chapora calamari, served with basil hummus and a green coulis, followed by fragrant pomfret *filet* in anis-butter sauce, or asparagus risotto. Around ₹1200/head for three courses, plus wine. Reservations recommended. Daily 7–10.30pm.

NIGHTLIFE

Club Cubana Arpora ⓦclubcubana.com. *Cubana* occupies a hilltop just inland from the strip and is the most civilized nightspot in the area, especially for women. Only couples are admitted (₹1400 for two, includes drink and pizza); there's even a ladies-only dance floor. The music's so-so, but the vibe is much more chilled than male-dominated *Tito's*. Jeeps shuttle punters up the hill, and you can wallow in a curvi-form pool. On Weds girls get in for free (₹800 admission for guys). Daily 9.30pm–late.

Kamaki Tito's Lane, Saunta Waddo. Big-screen sports and a state-of-the-art karaoke machine account for the appeal of this a/c bar just up the lane from *Tito's*. ₹300 cover charge sometimes applies. Daily 8am–late.

Mambo's Tito's Lane, Saunta Waddo. Large, semi-open-air pub with wooden decor and a big circular bar that gets packed out most nights in season with a lively, mixed crowd. Karaoke and a mad rodeo bull are the big

draws, though drinks cost well above average (₹250 for a beer), and they slap on a ₹500 cover charge after 11pm, or when there's live entertainment. "Ladies Night" (Weds) means free entry and free drinks for women. Couples only. Nov & Dec daily 8pm–late; off-season 8–11pm.

Tito's Tito's Lane, Saunta Waddo ⓦtitosgoa.com. That Baga's nightlife has become legendary in India is largely attributable to this club. Every night hundreds of revellers, many of them men from other states, are lured in by TV images of skimpy dancewear and a thumping sound-and-light system. For Western women in particular, this can make for an uncomfortably loaded atmosphere. Biggest nights are Tues and Sat; music policy is lounge jazz till 11pm, then hip-hop, house, salsa and trance until late. Entry ₹850 including drinks; entry and drinks, are free for women. At Christmas, prices can soar above of ₹2000. Nov– Dec daily 8pm–late; off-season 8–11pm.

SATURDAY NIGHT BAZAARS

One of the few genuinely positive improvements to the north Goa resort strip over the past decade has been the **Saturday Night Bazaar**, held on a plot inland at **Arpora**, midway between Baga and Anjuna. Originally the brainchild of an expat German called Ingo, it's run with great efficiency and a sense of fun that's palpably lacking these days from the Anjuna Flea Market (see p.696). The balmy evening temperatures and pretty lights are also a lot more conducive to relaxed browsing than the broiling heat of mid-afternoon on Anjuna beach.

Although far more commercial than its predecessor in Anjuna, many old Goa hands regard this as far truer to the original spirit of the flea market. A significant proportion of the stalls are taken up by foreigners selling their own stuff, from reproduction Indian pop art to antique photos, the latest trance party wear, stunning antique and coconut-shell jewellery and techno DJ demos. There's also a mouth-watering array of ethnic food to choose from and a stage featuring live music from around 7pm until midnight, when the market winds up, as well as a couple of trendy bars with live DJs. Admission is free.

The original night market from which Ingo's splintered – Mackie's – lies nearby, close to the riverside In Baga. Spurned by the expatriate designers and stallholders, it is not quite as lively as its rival, though in recent years has made an effort to close the gap, with better live acts and more foreign stallholders.

Anjuna

ANJUNA, the next sizeable village up the coast from Baga, was, until a few years back, the last bastion of alternative chic in Goa – where the state's legendary full-moon parties were staged each season, and where the Beautiful Set would rent pretty red-tiled houses for six months at a time, make trance mixes and groovy dance clothes, paint the palm trees fluoro colours and spend months lazing on the beach. A small contingent of fashionably attired, middle-aged hippies still turn up, but thanks to a combination of the Y2K music ban (see box, p.699) and overwhelming growth in popularity of the flea market, Anjuna has seriously fallen out of fashion for the party set.

As a consequence, the scattered settlement of old Portuguese houses and whitewashed churches, nestled behind a long golden sandy beach, nowadays more closely resembles the place it was before the party scene snowballed than it has for a decade or more. There is, however, a downside to staying here: levels of substance abuse, both among

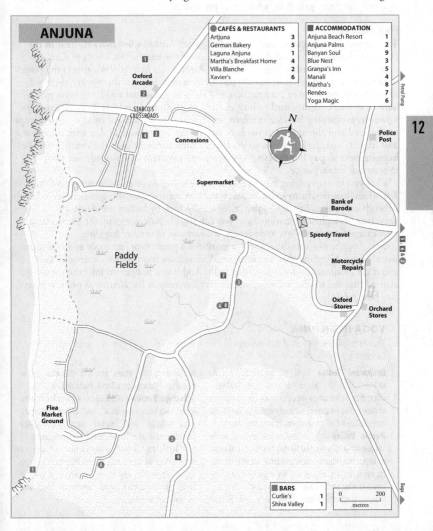

CAFÉS & RESTAURANTS	
Artjuna	3
German Bakery	5
Laguna Anjuna	1
Martha's Breakfast Home	4
Villa Blanche	2
Xavier's	6

ACCOMMODATION	
Anjuna Beach Resort	1
Anjuna Palms	2
Banyan Soul	9
Blue Nest	3
Granpa's Inn	5
Manali	4
Martha's	8
Renées	7
Yoga Magic	6

BARS	
Curlie's	1
Shiva Valley	1

12

visitors and locals, remain exceptionally high, and the village suffers more than its fair share of dodgy characters.

The beach

The north end of **Anjuna beach**, just below where the buses pull in, is no great shakes by Goan standards, with a dodgy undertow and lots of even dodgier Kashmiris selling hash, as well as parties of whisky-filled day-trippers in constant attendance. The vibe is much nicer at the far, southern end, where a pretty and more sheltered cove accommodates a mostly twenty-something tourist crowd. A constant trance soundtrack thumps from the shacks behind it, cranking up to become proper parties after dark, when *Curlie's* and neighbouring *Shiva Valley* take turns to max their sound systems, hosting international DJs through the season. Chai ladies and food stallholders sit in wait on the sands, just like for the raves of old, but the party grinds to a halt at 10pm sharp.

Flea market

The biggest crowds gather on Wednesdays, after Anjuna's **flea market**, held in the coconut plantation behind the southern end of the beach, just north of *Curlie's*. Along with the Saturday Night Market at Arpora (see box, p.694), this is the place to indulge in a spot of **souvenir shopping**. Two decades ago, the weekly event was the exclusive preserve of backpackers and the area's seasonal residents, who gathered here to smoke chillums and to buy and sell party clothes and jewellery. These days, however, everything is more mainstream. Pitches are rented out by the metre, drugs are banned and the approach roads to the village are choked all day with a/c buses and Maruti taxis ferrying in tourists from resorts further down the coast. Even the beggars have to pay **baksheesh** to be here. The mayhem is, however, fun to experience at least once.

What you end up paying for the exotic merchandise on offer – which ranges from Rajasthani handicrafts to south Indian stone carving and everything in between – largely depends on your ability to **haggle**. Prices are sky-high by Indian standards. Be persistent, though, and cautious, and you can usually pick things up for a reasonable rate, except from the Western designers, who are not so fond of haggling.

Even if you're not spending, the flea market is a great place just to sit and watch the world go by. Mingling with the suntanned masses are bands of strolling musicians, mendicant sadhus and fortune-telling bulls. And if you happen to miss the show, rest assured that the whole cast reassembles every Saturday at Baga/Arpora's night markets (see box, p.694).

YOGA IN ANJUNA

Thanks to the presence on its fringes of two world-class centres, Anjuna is a great place to develop your yoga skills.

Brahmani Centre Tito's White House, Anjuna ☎ 9545 620578, ⓦ brahmaniyoga.com. Brahmani offers drop-in Ashtanga yoga classes by expert teachers at their studio on the outskirts of the village just off the main Siolim Rd; all levels of ability are catered for.

Purple Valley Arpora ⓦ yogagoa.com. If you're looking for a fully fledged retreat or course, you won't do better than Purple Valley, which has accommodation for up to forty guests and what must be one of the loveliest yoga *shalas* (practice areas) in India. Their top-drawer teachers include Manju Jois and Sharath

Rangaswamy, the eldest son and grandson of the illustrious Ashtanga guru Shri K. Pattabhi Jois.

Satsanga Retreat Verla Cana, 4km inland from Anjuna ⓦ satsangaretreat.com. Offering retreats, yoga holidays and teacher training, Satsanga describes itself as a "home away from home" but with palm trees, tropical gardens and a swimming pool in a small village between Anjuna and Mapusa. The yoga space is beautiful and there are plenty of chillout areas and hammock spots. Ayurvedic food and massage are on offer too.

ARRIVAL AND DEPARTURE

By bus Buses from Mapusa (hourly; 30–40min) drop passengers at various points along the tarmac road across the top of the village, which turns north towards Chapora at the main Starco's crossroads. If you're looking for a room on spec, get off here as it's close to most of the guesthouses.

ACCOMMODATION

Anjuna Beach Resort De Mello Waddo ☎0832 227 4499 or ☎9822 176753 (Joseph), ⓦanjunabeachresort.com. This place offers 32 spacious, comfortable rooms with balconies, fridges, attached bathrooms and solar-heated water in two concrete blocks ranged around a pool. Those on the upper floors are best. There's also a block of apartments for long stayers; both are very good value, though the complex is showing signs of age. A/c costs ₹500 extra. Free wi-fi. ₹1500

Anjuna Palms De Mello Waddo ☎0832 227 3268 or ☎9822 686817 (Felix), ⓦanjunapalms.com. Cosy budget guesthouse, tucked away behind an old Portuguese-era house next door to the Oxford Arcade, with more character than most. It offers three types of rooms: larger, a/c ones with high ceilings (₹1200); more ramshackle options with shared bathrooms (₹550); and medium sized non-a/c with private bathrooms (₹950). All of them open on to a garden courtyard. Just a 5min walk from the beach. ₹550

Banyan Soul Peqqem Peddem, off Flea Market Rd ☎9820 707283, ⓦthebanyansoul.com. Leafy, designer-chic hotel on the quiet, southeastern fringes of the village, near the German Bakery. Shaded by an old banyan tree, the rooms are attractively decorated – though small for the price – and each has a private outdoor sitting area that's well screened from the neighbours. Some readers find this place a bit overpriced and boxed in; others love its tucked-away feel. ₹2500

Blue Nest Soronto Waddo ☎9763 063379. Jospah and Cecilia's little row of five old-fashioned rooms, with pitched-tiled roofs and wood rafters, is close to the main road through the village, but you wouldn't know it. Neatly painted, they're large for the price and have good thick mattresses, as well as nice little tiled verandas looking out over woodland. ₹500

Granpa's Inn Gaun Waddo ☎0832 227 3270, ⓦgranpasinn.com. Formerly known as Bougainvillea, Granpa's occupies a lovely 200-year-old house set in half an acre of lush gardens, with a kidney-shaped pool and shady breakfast terrace. They offer three categories of rooms: non-a/c standards (₹4000), a/c suites in the main house (₹4500)= and poolside suites (₹5500). Very popular despite the high tariffs, so book well ahead. ₹4000

Manali South of Starco's crossroads ☎0832 227 4421. Anjuna's most popular all-round budget guesthouse has simple rooms (with shared toilets) opening onto a yard, fans, safe deposit, money exchange, library, internet connection and a sociable terrace-restaurant. Good value; booking recommended. ₹400

Martha's 907 Montero Waddo ☎0832 227 3365, ⓔmpd8650@hotmail.com. Spotless attached rooms (₹800 for non-a/c, ₹1400 for a/c) run by a friendly family. Amenities include kitchen space, fans, free wi-fi and running, solar-heated water. Two pleasant houses and a villa also available – ideal for families (₹1000–1500/night). And their breakfasts are famous (see p.698). ₹800

Renées Montero Waddo ☎0832 227 3405 or ☎9850 462217. This is a little gem of a guesthouse. Swathed in greenery, welcoming and family run, it holds just half a dozen rooms, most of them surprisingly spacious, with garden-facing balconies. A few have simple kitchenettes and fridges. It's a tad pricier than the competition, but worth it. A/c costs ₹400 extra. ₹800

★ **Yoga Magic** ☎0832 652 3796 or ☎9370 565717, ⓦyogamagic.net. Innovative "Canvas Ecotel", offering low-impact luxury on the edge of Anjuna in Rajasthani hunting tents. The structures, ranging from standard lodges (₹6000 for minimum 3-night stay) to swankier suites (₹8400/₹10,500 for minimum 3-night stay) are all decorated with block-printed cotton and furnished with cushions, silk drapes and solar halogen lights. Loos are of the biodegradable, non-smelly compost kind. And there's a pool. ₹6000

EATING AND DRINKING

Responding to the tastes of its visitors, Anjuna boasts a good crop of quality cafés and restaurants, many of which serve healthy vegetarian dishes and juices. If you're hankering for a taste of home, call in at Orchard Stores on the southeastern side of the village, or the rival Oxford Arcade, on the opposite, north side, which both serve the expatriate and tourist community with a vast range of pricey imported delights and organic produce from around India.

Artjuna 972 Montero Waddo, on the flea market road, ⓦartjuna.com. Pretty little garden café serving up delicious salads, pesto omelettes, sandwiches of all varieties, a few sweet treats (all ₹120–200) and great coffee. There's a play area for kids, yoga and zumba for all ages and a beautiful shop. Sun–Fri 7am–10.30pm, Sat 7am–7pm.

★ **German Bakery** South Anjuna, on the road to Nirvana Hermitage ⓦgerman-bakery.in. The original and inimitable outlet of this much-copied wholefood café-restaurant, hidden away in a tree-shaded garden on the south side of the village, is Goa's ultimate travellers' hangout. Sitting beneath old trees strung with Tibetan prayer flags and Pipli lanterns, you can eat such rarities as buckwheat porridge (₹100), *kombucha* tea, wheat grass and lovely crunchy salads (₹170–250). There is a full menu of Italian, Indian, Tibetan and seafood, and of course the bakery's famous cakes and coffee. Daily 8am–11pm.

Laguna Anjuna De Mello Waddo, close to the flea market ⓦ lagunaanjuna.com. Pretty poolside resto in chic little boutique hotel which offers copious Goan fish thalis (₹250) and a full range of Indian delights. Daily 8am–11pm.

Martha's Breakfast Home Martha's guesthouse, 907 Montero Waddo. Secluded, very friendly breakfast garden serving fresh Indian coffee, crêpes, healthy juices, apple and cinnamon porridge, fruit salads with curd and – the house speciality – melt-in-the-mouth waffles with proper maple syrup (₹100). Daily 8–11am.

Villa Blanche Assagao ⓦ villablanche-goa.com. A short drive from Anjuna on the road to Mapusa, this great bistro-cum-bakery servers terrific light bites, including smoked salmon bagels with capers (₹250), heavier mains, such as German-style beef meatballs (₹200) and everything from healthy sprout salads to home-made ice creams. On Sundays it hosts a popular brunch (10am–3pm) which just keeps on giving for ₹600; booking is essential. Daily 9am–5.30pm.

Xavier's South Anjuna. Nestled in the palm forest just inland from the Flea Market ground, *Xavier's* has formed the hub of the south Anjuna alternative scene for decades, and is still going strong. Most people come for the seafood, kebabs, tikkas and tandoori dishes (₹200–300), but they also serve tasty Chinese and Italian, organic salads and delicious home-made pickles. Look for the sign on the left off the market lane. Daily 11am–3pm & 6.30–11pm.

NIGHTLIFE

Anjuna's far from the rave spot it used to be, but at least one big party is still held in the area around the Christmas–New Year full-moon period. The rest of the time, serious trance heads make the trek south to *Westend* or up to Vagator (see below) and Aswem (see p.703).

12

Curlie's/Shiva Valley South beach, Anjuna. A pair of adjacent shacks that together form the focus of a rather heavy, druggy scene, with large, mixed crowds of both Indian and Western tourists gathering from sunset until 10pm. Some kind of "arrangement" has clearly been made with the local police here: chillums and joints are smoked openly in and around the cafés, but arrests are commonplace along the paths and lanes behind. Be warned that rumours are rife of cops, or fake cops, extorting bribes and sexual favours from tourists caught in possession of illegal drugs. Drinks at regular shack prices. Admission free. Daily sunset–10pm.

SHOPPING

Artjuna House 972 Monteiro Vaddo ☎ 0832 227 4794, ⓦ artjuna.com. Chock full of everything from cute kids' clothes to antique furniture, *Artjuna's* delightful boutique offers an eclectic mix of jewellery by expat designers Moshe and Simona Bassi, as well as tribal adornments from Nagaland. They also do a fantastic collection of women's clothes and create unique leatherwork – all displayed in a lovely Portuguese villa. There's a nice little café too. Daily 10am–10pm.

DIRECTORY

Banks and exchange ATMs are clustered along the Mapusa Rd near the Bank of Baroda, which itself will make encashments against Visa cards, but doesn't offer foreign exchange.

Post office The village post office is on the Mapusa Rd near the bank.

Vagator

Barely a couple of kilometres of clifftops and parched grassland separate Anjuna from the southern fringes of **VAGATOR**. Spread around a tangle of winding back lanes, this is a more chilled, undeveloped resort that appeals, in the main, to southern European beach bums who come back year after year.

With the red ramparts of **Chapora fort** looming above it, Vagator's broad sandy beach – known as "Big Vagator" – is undeniably beautiful. However, a peaceful swim or lie on the sand is out of the question here as it's a prime stop for bus parties of domestic tourists. A much better option, though one that still sees more than its fair share of day-trippers, is the next beach south. Backed by a steep wall of crumbling palm-fringed

THE DARK SIDE OF THE MOON

Lots of visitors come to Goa expecting to be able to party on the beach every night, and are dismayed when the only places to dance turn out to be mainstream clubs they probably wouldn't look twice at back home. But the truth is that the full-on, elbows-in-the-air **beach party** of old, when tens of thousands of people would space out to huge techno sound systems under neon-painted palm trees, is well and truly a thing of the past in Goa – thanks largely to the stern attitude of the local government.

Goa's coastal villages saw their first big parties back in the 1960s with the influx of hippies to Calangute and Baga. Much to the amazement of the locals, the preferred pastime of these wannabe sadhus was to cavort naked on the sands together on full-moon nights, amid a haze of chillum smoke and loud rock music. The villagers took little notice of these bizarre gatherings at first, but with each season the scene became better established, and by the late 1970s the Christmas and New Year parties, in particular, had become huge events, attracting travellers from all over the country.

In the late 1980s, the local party scene received a dramatic shot in the arm with the coming of Acid House and techno. Ecstasy became the preferred dance drug as the rock and dub-reggae scene gave way to rave culture, with ever-greater numbers of young clubbers pouring in for the season on charter flights. Goa soon spawned its own distinctive brand of psychedelic music, known as Goa Trance, cultivated by artists such as Goa Gill, Juno Reactor and Hallucinogen.

The golden era for Goa's party scene, and Goa Trance, was in the early 1990s, when big raves were held two or three times a week in beautiful locations around Anjuna and Vagator. For a few years the authorities turned a blind eye to them. Then, quite suddenly, the plug was pulled: during the run up to the Y2K celebrations a ban on amplified-music was imposed between 10pm and 7am. More than a decade on, the curfew is still place but routinely flaunted: some places pay backhanders to stay open til the early hours, while during an election year it's early to bed for everyone again. As a consequence, the rave scene of former years has virtually disappeared, limited to a couple of established, above-board clubs – notably the *Nine Bar* and *Hilltop* in Vagator (see p.701), *Club Westend* in Sangolda (see p.692), and *Soma* Project at Aswem (see p.705).

12

laterite, **Ozran** (or "Little") **Vagator beach** is actually a string of three contiguous coves. To reach them you have to walk from where the buses park above Big Vagator, or drive to the end of the lane running off the main Chapora–Anjuna road (towards the *Nine Bar*), from where footpaths drop sharply down to a wide stretch of level white sand (look for the mopeds and bikes parked at the top of the cliff). Long dominated by Italian tourists, the southernmost – dubbed "Spaghetti Beach" – is the prettiest, with a string of well-established shacks, at the end of which a **face carved out of the rocks**, staring serenely skywards, is the most prominent landmark. Relentless racquetball, trance sound systems and a particularly sizeable herd of stray cows are the other defining features.

ARRIVAL AND INFORMATION   VAGATOR

By bus Hourly buses from Panjim and Mapusa, 9km east, pull in every 15min or so at the crossroads on the far northeastern edge of Vagator, near where the main road peels away towards Chapora. From here, it's a 1km walk over the hill and down the other side to the beach.

Information and money *Bethany Inn*, on the north side of the village, has a foreign exchange licence (for cash and travellers' cheques), and an efficient travel agency in the office on the ground floor. The nearest ATM is in Anjuna (see map, p.695).

ACCOMMODATION

Bethany Inn Just south of the main road ☎ 0832 227 3731 or ☎ 8221 30939 (Joseph), ⊛ bethanyinn.com. Eleven immaculate, self-contained rooms with mini-bar fridges, balconies and attached bathrooms (₹850–1200);

plus four additional a/c options in a new block, with big flatscreen TVs, larger balconies and more spacious tiled bathrooms (₹1800). ₹850

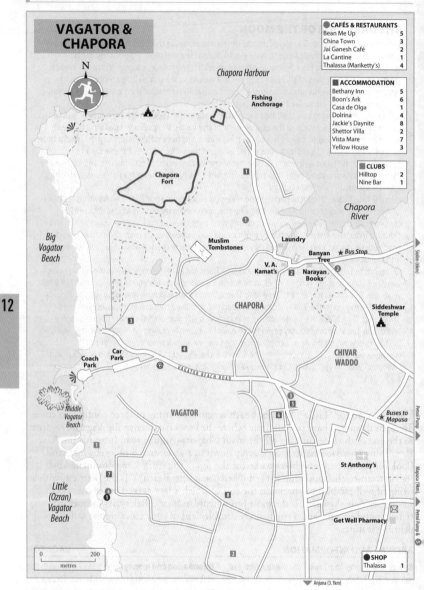

VAGATOR & CHAPORA

N

● CAFÉS & RESTAURANTS	
Bean Me Up	5
China Town	3
Jai Ganesh Café	2
La Cantine	1
Thalassa (Mariketty's)	4

■ ACCOMMODATION	
Bethany Inn	5
Boon's Ark	6
Casa de Olga	1
Dolrina	4
Jackie's Daynite	8
Shettor Villa	2
Vista Mare	7
Yellow House	3

■ CLUBS	
Hilltop	2
Nine Bar	1

● SHOP	
Thalassa	1

Chapora Harbour

Fishing Anchorage

Chapora Fort

Big Vagator Beach

Chapora River

Muslim Tombstones

Laundry

Banyan Tree   ★ Bus Stop

V. A. Kamat's

Narayan Books

CHAPORA

Siddeshwar Temple

CHIVAR WADDO

Coach Park

Car Park

@   VAGATOR BEACH ROAD

Middle Vagator Beach

VAGATOR

Buses to Mapusa

St Anthony's

Little (Ozran) Vagator Beach

Get Well Pharmacy

Siolim (6km)

Petrol Pump

Mapusa (9km)

Petrol Pump & @

Anjuna (3.1km)

0   200   metres

12

★ **Boon's Ark** Near Bethany Inn ☎ 0832 2274045 or ☎ 9822 175620, ⓦ boonsark.com. Honest, clean, family-run place offering modern rooms with excellent beds, stone shelves, fridges and pleasant little verandas opening on a well-tended courtyard garden. Owners Peter and Jessie Mungu also offer room service, money exchange and bikes to rent. A/c ₹300 extra. ₹**1500**

Dolrina Vagator Beach Rd ☎ 0832 227 3382. Nestled under a lush canopy of trees near the beach, Vagator's largest budget guesthouse features attached or shared bathrooms, a couple of larger family rooms, a sociable garden café, individual safe deposits and roof space. Single occupancy rates are available, and breakfast is served in their atmospheric rear garden. ₹**800**

★ **Jackie's Daynite** Beach Rd ☎ 0832 227 4330 or ☎ 9822 133789. The best all-round budget place in the village, perfectly placed within easy reach of both the *Nine Bar* and *Hilltop*. Jackie De Souza has been running a café and shop here for more than thirty years, and added rooms behind. They're clean and great value, though often booked up, so reserve in advance. A/c ₹400 extra. **₹800**

Vista Mare Ozran clifftop ☎ 9822 120980. Lovely big rooms behind a (quiet-ish) restaurant on the clifftop, boasting king-size beds, spacious attached bathrooms, marble-topped tables and huge verandas. A top location

and good value. A/c ₹500 extra. **₹1500**

Yellow House Big Vagator ☎ 9822 125869. Henriquita Moniz and son Jubert renovated this guesthouse behind Big Vagator beach, which now looks better than ever after more than twenty years in business. It's peaceful and secluded, despite the proximity of the surf, and the rooms are neat and pleasantly furnished, though not all have outside sitting space. A/c ₹400 extra. **₹1200**

EATING

Bean Me Up Near the petrol pump ☎ 0832 2273479. India's one and only tofu joint – the last word in Goan gourmet healthy eating. Design-your-own salads and fresh juices, or tuck into various tofu, tempeh and seitan combos steeped in creamy sauces, or pizzas from a real wood-fired oven. Mains (₹150–300) come with steamed spinach, fresh brown bread and hygienically washed greens. Daily 8am–11pm.

China Town Chapora crossroads, next to Bethany Inn. This small roadside restaurant, tucked away just south of the main drag, is perennially popular for its budget eats. The menu includes tasty seafood dishes

(₹200–250) in addition to a large Chinese selection and all the usual Goa-style travellers' grub. Daily 9am–11pm.

★ **Thalassa (Mariketty's)** Ozran clifftop ☎ 9850 033537. Stylish and hospitable, *Thalassa* serves honest, flavoursome and scrupulously authentic Greek cooking with excellent service, against a backdrop of swaying palms and the rippling ocean. Try and get there in time for the stunning sunset, and make sure to order a big glass of sangria. Mains around ₹250–600. Count on ₹1000 for three courses, plus drinks. Booking essential. Daily 9am–11.30pm.

NIGHTLIFE

Hilltop Ozran Vagator ☎ 9604 772788. *Hilltop's* big night is Sunday, when bumper crowds take to its pretty, circular dance floor, set in a coconut grove just back from the cliff top. The PA is heavy duty, the palm trunks painted regulation neon colours, chai mamas ring the arena with their flickering kerosene lamps and freshly baked nibbles, and foreign DJs do the honours on stage. They also host their own night market on Fridays. Admission ₹200. Fri & Sun 4–10pm.

Nine Bar Above Ozran beach ☎ 9623 102102, ⓦ club9bar.com. The spiritual home of Goa trance, where you can space out on a large open-air dance floor as the sun sets behind a curtain of palm trees and DJs spin beats from a chest-thumping rig. Drink prices are high (₹100 for beers) and there's a heavy security presence, with metal detector frisks at the entrance; photography is strictly prohibited. They play trance on Wed, but different dance genres through the week. The fun continues indoors after 10pm. Admission free. Daily 5pm–late.

SHOPPING

Thalassa Ozran clifftop. Attached to the popular Greek restaurant of the same name (see above), this boutique offers a range of stylish beach and evening wear, from beautiful floaty dresses in delicate fabrics to tribal

textiles and Rajasthani brocade umbrellas. There is also a selection from designer Miriam Strehlau, who favours bold prints and heavy embroidery – perfect attire for sipping sangria sundowners. Daily 11am–11pm.

Chapora

Huddled in the shadow of a Portuguese fort on the opposite, northern side of the headland from Vagator is **CHAPORA**, north Goa's main fishing port. The anchorage and boatyard below its brown-walled citadel forms the backbone of the village's economy, but there's always been a hard-drinking, heavy-smoking hippie tourist scene alongside it, revolving around the coffee shops and bars on the main street. For a brief period a few years back, Russian mafia types took over and squeezed the freaks out, but like migrating turtles they've returned to their old hangout in numbers undiminished by the recent changes in Goa. If this doesn't sound much like your bag, you'll probably be best off sticking to neighbouring Vagator.

The fort

Chapora's chief landmark is its venerable **old fort**, most easily reached from the Vagator side of the hill. At low tide, you can also walk around the bottom of the headland, via the anchorage and the secluded coves beyond it to Big Vagator, then head up the hill from there. The red-laterite bastion, crowning the rocky bluff, was built by the Portuguese in 1617 on the site of an earlier Muslim structure (thus the village's name – from Shahpura, "town of the Shah"). Deserted in the nineteenth century, it lies in ruins today, although the views up and down the coast from the weed-infested ramparts are still superb. Also worth a visit is the village's busy little fishing anchorage, where you can buy delicious calamari fresh off the boats most evenings.

ARRIVAL AND DEPARTURE   CHAPORA

By bus Buses run three times daily between Chapora and Panjim, and every 15min from Mapusa, with departures until 7pm. Most drop passengers at the old banyan tree at the far end of the main street, where the motorcycle pilots all hang out.

ACCOMMODATION

Casa de Olga ☎ 0832 227 4355 or ☎ 9822 157145. By far the most (in fact, the only) congenial place to stay in Chapora. It is an immaculate, red-and-white-painted little guesthouse near the fishing anchorage, run with great efficiency and enthusiasm by hosts Edmund and Elisa. Their nicest rooms are the five in a new block to the rear, which are all attached and have good-sized balconies (₹1000). There are cheaper non-attached alternatives at the front. ₹**500**

Shettor Villa Off the west side of the main street ☎ 0832 227 3766 or ☎ 9822 158154. Cheaper and more basic than *Casa de Olga*. Half a dozen of its rooms, ranged around a sheltered backyard, come with fans and attached bathrooms; the other eigteen share shower-toilets. ₹**450**

EATING

La Cantine Out on the road to the fishing anchorage. Justifiably the most popular place in Chapora to eat these days. Run by an expat chef called Max, it serves healthy, home-cooked food – chickpea and pumpkin soup, beetroot tartare (₹180), pasta al forno (₹300) and courgette quiche – in a basic roadside shack. Daily 9am–11pm.

Jai Ganesh Café Just up from the banyan tree. The focal point of the tourist scene, where Chapora's resident Westerners watch the world go by over fresh fruit juices and milk shakes (₹50–65). Daily 8am–sunset.

Morjim

Due to its relative isolation, the village of **MORJIM** was where Goa's first Russian tourists headed back in the early noughties. Nowadays dubbed "Morjimograd" by other foreign visitors, it's since become a resolutely Russian-only enclave, with hotels, guesthouses and rental villas controlled, if not owned outright, by Moscow mafiosi. A lot of sensational stories have appeared in the Indian media in recent years, reporting on the upscale prostitution and drug rackets run out of here. Although such reports do have a basis in truth, the majority of young sunseekers you see fizzing around Morjim on scooters are just regular, law-abiding holiday-makers. That said, the atmosphere in the guesthouses and restaurants can feel less than friendly, and most Western travellers find the experience of staying in Morjim a disconcerting one – not to mention eye-wateringly expensive – preferring to continue north to the more culturally mixed resorts of Aswem and Mandrem.

Morjim beach itself is dramatic and well worth at least a walk, especially in the early morning, when you'll see teams of fishermen hauling giant handnets from the surf. The spit at its southern end, opposite Chapora fort, is also a great birding hotspot.

ARRIVAL AND DEPARTURE   MORJIM

By bus Half a dozen buses per day skirt Morjim en route to Panjim, the first at 7am; heading the other way, you can pick up a direct bus from Panjim at 5pm, and there are frequent services from Mapusa via Siolim. They'll drop you on the main road, a 5min walk from the beachfront area at Vithaldas Waddo.

12

ACCOMMODATION

Because of the unwelcoming vibe, the hotels and guesthouses immediately behind the beach, in the dunes and along the beachfront road, are best avoided. One really nice option, however, stands on the riverfront, to the south of the village.

★ **Jardin d'Ulysse** Facing the riverbank on the village's south side ☎ 9822 581928, ✉ ulyssemorjim @gmail.com. Delightful GoanFrench-run place comprising five a/c "cottages" with tiled roofs, ochre-washed floors and kitchenettes. Down in the front garden, a small restaurant whips up an eclectic menu of steaks, scrumptious lasagne, Tibetan *momos* and salads for mostly French and British travellers. Owners Fleur and Gilbert are charming hosts, and always on hand to help arrange excursions, boat trips and scooters. **₹3000**

EATING

★ **Sublime** Morjim beach ☎ 9822 484051. Run by celebrity chef Chris Saleem Agha Bee, this funky little gastro beach shack in the heart of Morjim rustles up stylish, innovative cuisine deploying novel combos of fresh local ingredients: try the fish carpaccios (₹350) or ginger batter calamari (₹260) for starters, and Asiatic beef with wasabi mashed potatoes (₹400), or nut-crusted white fish with nori sesame stuffing (₹440) for mains. Ample veggie options include the popular mega organic salad (₹300). Booking essential. Daily 11am–11pm.

Aswem

Pretty **ASWEM**, the next settlement north of Morjim, could hardly be described as a proper resort. Officially inside the Coastal Protection Zone, its beachfront holds few permanent buildings and most of the accommodation is in temporary structures. And yet, over the past few seasons, the strip of soft white sand nestled beneath its *mand* of slender palms has become the place to see and be seen by India's seriously cool set. Mumbai millionaires, Bollywood A-listers and international celebs (including Paris Hilton) are regularly spotted in the swanky new resorts and clubs that recently opened in the dunes. A more down-to-earth scene holds sway around the headland to the south, which is family friendly, with lots of children playing on the beach. How long this stretch can hold out against the rising tide of bling, however, is anyone's guess.

12

ARRIVAL AND DEPARTURE ASWEM

By bus Sporadic buses from Panjim (3 daily; 1hr 30min) and Mapusa (4 daily; 40min) cover the quiet stretch of road running parallel to the beach inland, from where a 5min walk across paddy fields brings you to the shacks and hut camps attached to them.

ACCOMMODATION

With accommodation either ultra-basic or staggeringly expensive, most visitors ride up to Aswem for the day on scooters and decamp after sunset. A handful of places, however, offer reasonable value for money.

★ **Elsewhere** ☎ 022 2373 8757 or ☎ 9820 037387, ⊕ aseascape.com. A collection of dreamy nineteenth-century villas (or "beach houses") on the quietest patch of dunes, with cobalt-blue interiors and uninterrupted sea views from their pillared verandas. Absolutely the last word in Goan beachside chic, and very exclusive – though at Côte d'Azur prices and for weekly rental only. **₹58,000– 285,000/week.**

Leela Cottages Near La Plage ☎ 9823 400055, ⊕ leelacottage.com. Beautiful designer huts (all a/c) of various sizes and prices (₹6000–9500), grouped in a gated property under the palms just a stone's throw from the beach, but far enough away from the restaurants to remain peaceful and quiet (and free from cooking smells). The interiors are furnished with antiques collected from all over India. **₹6000**

Nifa Aswem Morjim Rd close to La Plage ☎ 0832 224 4400, ⊕ hotelnifa.com. A cheaper alternative set back on the roadside inland, *Nifa* has clean comfortable sea-facing rooms a short walk from the beach. There is a small pool on site. **₹1500**

Otter Creek ☎ 022 2373 8757 or ☎ 9820 037387, ⊕ aseascape.com. You have to cross a rickety footbridge to reach these luxury tents, nestled on the riverbank just behind the dunes, in the thick of a coconut plantation. Each is fitted with a bamboo four-poster, bathroom, veranda and jetty on the river. Plus you get access to the same empty bit of beach as *Elsewhere* (see above). **₹31,000– 90,000/week.**

THE TURTLE WIND

In early November, if a strong and steady on-shore breeze blows through the night at Morjim locals call it the locals call it a **turtle wind**. Such weather normally heralds the arrival of Goa's rarest migrant visitors, Olive Ridley marine turtles (*Lepidochelysolivacea*).

For as long as anyone can remember, the spoon-shaped spit of soft white sand at Temb, the southern end of Morjim beach, has been the nesting ground of these beautiful sea reptiles. Each winter, a succession of females emerge from the surf during the night and, using their distinctive flippers, crawl to the edge of the dunes to lay their annual clutch of 105–115 eggs. Just over two months later, the fresh hatchlings clamber out and crawl blinking over their siblings to begin the perilous trek back to the water, guided into the sea by moonlight.

Little more is known about how these enigmatic creatures spend the rest of their long lives (turtles frequently live for more than a century), but it is thought that the females return to the beaches where they were born to lay their own eggs. Some have been shown to travel as far as 4500km to do this.

THREATS FROM ALL SIDES

Once a thriving species, with huge populations spread across the Pacific, Atlantic and Indian oceans, the Olive Ridley is nowadays **endangered**. Aside from a wealth of traditional predators (such as crows, ospreys, gulls and buzzards, who pick off the hatchlings during their dash for the sea), the newborns and their parents are vulnerable to a host of threats from humans. In Morjim, as in most of Asia, the eggs are traditionally considered a delicacy and local villagers collect them to sell in Mapusa market. Many (perhaps as many as 35,000 worldwide) are killed accidentally by fishermen each year, caught up in fine shrimp nets or attracted by squid bait that is used to catch tuna. Floating litter, which the hapless turtles mistake for jellyfish, has also taken its toll over the past two decades, as have tar balls from oil spills, which coat the animals' digestive tracts and hamper the absorption of food. The growth of tourism poses an additional danger: electric lights behind the beaches throw the hatchlings off course as they scuttle towards the sea, and sand compressed by sunbathers' trampling feet damages nests, preventing the babies from digging their way out at the crucial time.

THE TROOPS RALLY

In a bid to revive numbers, locals are employed by the Goa Forest Department to watch out for the females' arrival in November and to guard the nests after the eggs have been laid until they hatch. You'll see them camped under palm-leaf shades on the beach, with the nests fenced in and marked by red and green signs.

So far, the government-led **conservation attempt** has not proved all that effective. After an initial leap in hatchling figures, recent results have been mixed, which the Forest Department ascribes to an increase in tourist activity.

Watching the nesting turtles is an unforgettable experience, although one requiring a certain amount of dedication, or luck. No one knows for sure when an Olive Ridley female will turn up, but with a strong turtle wind blowing at the right time, the chances are good. Much more predictable are the appearances of the hatchlings, who emerge exactly 54 days after their mothers laid the eggs. If you ask one of the wardens looking after the nests, they can tell you when this will be.

Simply Special Inn Aswem Morjim Rd near Papa Jolly ☎ 9823 400055, ⊛ simplyspecialinn.com. This is a really welcoming place with comfortable, pleasantly furnished rooms (some a/c with kitchenettes; ₹2000), an excellent rooftop restaurant and all-round friendly vibe. Hosts Mitushi and Asif run low-key cultural events throughout the season, including fair trade craft fairs and art exhibitions. **₹1500**

★ **Yab Yum** ☎ 0832 651 0392, ⊛ yabyumresorts.com. A campus of beautiful domed structures made from palm thatch, mango wood and laterite, with curvy moulded concrete floors and walls painted pale purple. Large and attractively furnished inside, the rooms have beds on platforms and comfy mattresses, glitter balls, paper lanterns and muslin drapes – though such alt-chic comes at a price (up to ₹7000 for suites). **₹5000**

Yoga Gypsys ☎ 0832 645 3077 or ☎ 9326 130115, ⊛ yogagypsys.com. This spot, in the coconut plantation under the Ajoba temple just north of La Plage, is arguably the finest nook on the coast hereabouts. The place holds five octagonal huts, made from dark mango wood. They're large, well spaced, have wraparound verandas, and are naturally cross-ventilated, with quality beds and simple, relaxing decor. There are also a couple of tipis (₹2500), yoga space and a great lounge area. **₹4500**

EATING

Gopal Just north of La Plage. Once the only shack on Aswem beach, now almost hidden by its more famous neighbour *La Plage*, *Gopal* still commands a loyal following of customers who want simple Indian food. It offers a typical Goan menu: a bit of everything from all over the world. Mains from ₹100–250. Daily 8am–11pm.

★ **La Plage** Aswem beach ☎ 9822 121712. Against a diaphanous backdrop of floaty white muslin and swaying palm trees, *La Plage* does a brisk trade in cool Gallic-Mediterranean snacks and drinks all served up by Nepali waiters in black *lunghis*. The menu changes a little each season but expect marinated kingfish carpaccio (₹280), their signature hamburger (₹350), seared rare tuna (the most ordered dish on the menu; ₹420) and, last but not least, a tempting chocolate thali offering five choco-rich desserts (₹520; it's not obligatory to share). Alcohol served between 4–7pm. Booking essential. Daily 8.30am–11pm.

Pink Orange Just north of La Plage. Great place to chill out, with low seating and comfy cushions. They serve up tasty breakfasts featuring pesto omelettes and a range of locally made cheeses (₹250), as well as a great choice of salads (₹180–250), a simple veg thali (₹150) and delicious home-made mushroom ravioli (₹220). Hosts Alex and Jai also run *Café Esperanto* on the roadside, which stays open during monsoon. As Jai doubles as a DJ, you can expect chilled beats and the odd daytime party here. Daily 9am–11pm.

Roma Near the Aswem inlet, before Yoga Gypsys. Pretty garden restaurant with delicious pizzas and an interesting selection of pastas (₹220–380). Definitely a cut above the usual Italian dishes. Wood-fired oven evenings only. Daily 11am–11pm.

NIGHTLIFE

Aswem has emerged as the new face of Goan nightlife, with a batch of chic beachfront clubs where you can jump off the dancefloor straight on to the sand.

Club Fresh Gawde Waddo, at the far south, Morjim side of the beach. The most ostentatious lounge bar/dance club on the north coast, incongruously set amid the dunes on the fringes of Morjim and Aswem. Going for that Ibiza/*Miami Vice* look, it's styled entirely in white and its mostly hip, rich, Russian clientele play along by dressing in white too. There's a 12m bar staffed by Ukrainians juggling bottles and cocktail shakers à la Tom Cruise, and a line-up of celebrity DJs (Paris Hilton did the honours on their opening night). Admission free, but drink prices are top whack (₹270–300 for beers; ₹400–500 for shots). Daily 11am–late.

Marbela Beach Aswem ⓦmarbelabeach.com. The name (sic) says it all. A fantasy ego-trip for metropolitan yuppies, this white-themed resort on the beachfront features a lounge bar blasting dance mixes into the night air from an outsize PA. After the 10pm wind down, punters either shuffle indoors to the soundproofed *Club M*, or over to the alfresco champagne bar. Admission free; drinks ₹250–300 for beers; ₹350–500 for shots and cocktails. Daily 5pm–late.

Soma Project In the grounds of La Cabana close to La Plage. Offering a welcome relief from wall-to-wall trance, *Soma's* changing roster of international DJs spin dubstep and world music, as well as the latest grooves from Copenhagen, Moscow and beyond. A refreshingly smiley, unpretentious vibe holds sway, and there are plenty of chillout areas as well as a swimming pool. Drinks ₹100–150; ₹250–350 for shots. Admission free. Daily sunset–late.

SHOPPING

Long gone are the Lamani sarong shacks. These days, Aswem is renowned for its rank of designer boutiques, including some from the likes of Jade Jagger.

Dust Aswem beach, close to La Plage. Beautifully chic beach creations – both clothes and accessories – made with raw silk and hand-block prints from tribal villages in north India. Thurs–Tues 10.30am–sunset.

Mandrem

From the far side of the creek bounding the edge of Aswem, a magnificent and largely empty beach stretches north towards Arambol – the last unspoilt stretch of the north

12

Goan coast. Whether or not **MANDREM** can continue to hold out against the developers remains to be seen, but for the time being, nature still has the upper hand here. Olive Ridley marine **turtles** nest on the quietest patches, and you're more than likely to catch a glimpse of one of the white-bellied **fish eagles** that live in the casuarina trees – their last stronghold in the north of Goa.

ARRIVAL AND INFORMATION — MANDREM

By bus Connected by regular buses from Mapsua (9 daily; 1hr 30min), the market area at Madlamaz is easy to reach by public transport, but getting to the beach area is trickier as auto-rickshaws are few and far between. Ask your guesthouse or hut camp for help.

Information A couple of small grocery stores, internet cafés and travel agents are on hand to provide essential services.

ACCOMMODATION

Most of the village's accommodation is tucked away inland at **Junasa Waddo**, where a growing number of small guesthouses, hotels and yoga retreats cater to a mixed, peace-and-quiet-loving crowd.

Ashiyana Junasa Waddo ⓦ ashiyana-yoga-goa.com. If you like your yoga retreats to be drop-dead gorgeous, look no further than here. Perched on the banks of the Mandrem River facing the sea from the middle of an old coconut *mand*, the centre offers world-class yoga, massage, meditation and satsang tuition with accommodation in Indonesian-style boutique treehouses and eco-lodges. All of them boast glorious sea views, and there's a wholefood-Ayurvedic-veg restaurant on site (guests only). Rates (₹6000–19,000/day, depending on the accommodation) include workshops. ₹**6000**

Mandala Just upriver from Ashiyana ☎ 9657 898021, ⓦ themandalagoa.com. Beautifully painted murals adorn the buildings at Mandala, a "back-to-nature

boutique resort". You can opt to stay in the main house with all mod cons (₹9000), in beautiful two-tier bamboo chalets based on the design of Keralan houseboats (₹6500) or overpriced tents with communal bathrooms in the coconut grove (₹3600). It's close to the beach, but there's no direct road access. ₹**3600**

Villa River Cat ☎ 0822 224 7928 or ☎ 9823 610001, ⓦ villarivercat.com. Quirky riverside hotel, screened from the beach by the dunes, with distinctive hippie-influenced decor and furniture. The sixteen rooms (₹4000–5000) are all individually designed: mosaics, shells, devotional sculpture and hammocks set the tone. Host Rinoo Seghal is an animal lover, so brace yourself for the menagerie of cats and dogs. ₹**4000**

EATING

★ **Café Nu** Junnaswada, small track before D'Souzas Residency ☎ 9850 658568. Lovely open-sided restaurant in pretty garden serving light gourmet bites from sublime chef Chris Saleem Agha Bee. There are plenty of fish dishes (₹250–350), the famous house hamburger (₹330) and, for the health-conscious, a copious organic salad (₹280). And the bon bon dessert (₹220) is legendary around these parts. Booking essential for dinner. Daily noon–3pm & 6–10pm.

O'Saiba Mandrem beach. Great views from this beach

shack, which serves up high-quality versions of the usual Indian and tandoori food. Expect delicious seafood including *hariyali* fish tikka with fresh mint sauce (₹250), a flavoursome *dal makhani* (₹120) and a fair number of Western favourites. Daily 8am–11pm.

The Well Garden Mandrem beach. Fantastic wood-baked pizzas (evening only), delicious pastas and tasty salads with feta and sprouts (₹150–300) – and be sure to leave room for the warm *chikoo* cake and chocolate sauce (₹180). Daily 11am–3pm & 6–10pm.

Arambol

ARAMBOL, 32km northwest of Mapusa, is easily the most populous village in the far north, and the area's main tourist hub. Traditionally a refuge for a hard-core hippie fringe, it nowadays attracts a lively and eclectic mix of travellers, the majority of whom stick around for the season, living in rented rooms, hut camps and small houses scattered behind the magnificent white-sand beach. As with most of north Goa, there's a strong showing of Russians here, but the well-heeled Muscovites still don't quite outnumber the spiritually inclined types from northern Europe who have long formed Arambol's mainstay. The two groups rub along harmoniously enough, and the overall vibe is inclusive and positive, with plenty of live music to enjoy in the evenings, lots of relaxed places to eat and drink, and more opportunities to learn new yoga poses and reshuffle your chakras than you could get through in several lifetimes, let alone a winter. Moreover, beach life is generally laidback too – except on weekends, when day-tripping drinkers descend en masse in SUVs from nearby Maharashtra.

The village and beaches

Arambol's main drag is a winding road lined cheek-by-jowl with clothes and bedspread stalls, travel agents, internet cafés and souvenir shops selling tourist knick-knacks. The lane bends downhill to the **main beach** – dotted with wooden outriggers and one of the most picturesque in south India. The best view of it is from the crucifix and small **Parasurama shrine** on the hilltop to the north, which is an especially serene spot at sunset. **After dark**, when the Hula-Hoopers, fire jugglers and *bhajan* singers have turned homewards, the candles and fairy lights of the shacks illuminate the beachfront to magical effect.

Bathing is possible here during the daytime, but less inspiring than around the headland at Paliem or "Lakeside" beach, reached by following the track through a series of rocky-bottomed coves. The path emerges at a broad strip of soft white sand hemmed in by cliffs. Behind here a small freshwater lake extends along the bottom of the valley into the jungle, lined with sulphurous mud, which, when smeared over the body, dries to form a surreal, butter-coloured shell.

■ ACCOMMODATION		● CAFÉS & RESTAURANTS	
Arun Huts	4	Cheeky Monkey	6
Atman	6	Double Dutch	7
Famafa	2	Dylan's (Toasted and Roasted)	9
Go-Ym	7	Eyes of Buddha	1
Ivon's	5	Fellini's	4
Om Ganesh Cottages	1	Lamuella	5
Silver Sands	3	Relax Inn	3
		Rice Bowl	2
		Sai Deep	8

Keep following the path around the back of the lake and you'll soon come to Paliem's famous **banyan tree**, a monster specimen with giant runners extending more than 60m – a popular chillum-smoking spot. Keen walkers can continue over the cliffs immediately north – Arambol's prime parascending venue – to reach the generally quiet **Kerim beach**.

ARRIVAL AND DEPARTURE
ARAMBOL

By bus Buses run between Panjim and Arambol, via Mapusa's main town stand, every 30min until noon, and every 90min thereafter, terminating at the small bus stop on the main road in Arambol. A faster private minibus service from Panjim arrives daily opposite the

chai stalls at the beach end of the village.
By taxi Taxis charge ₹1200 for the run from Dabolim airport to Arambol, and ₹350 for the 30min trip from the nearest railhead at Tivim (Thivim).

ACTIVITIES

Posters pinned to palm trees and café noticeboards around Arambol advertise an amazing array of activities, from kite surfing to reiki. Good places to get a fix on what's happening are the noticeboard at *Lamuella* and *Double Dutch's* "Bullshit Info" corner, which displays email addresses and meeting details for just about everyone who does anything – including their own popular dokra bronze casting workshops, held annually each January.

Dance The Temple of Dance Centre, Girkar Waddo, close to the **Kundalini Rooftop Garden**, offers sessions in great tribal fusion, contemporary, salsa, Bollywood and belly dance styles, and hosts a festival in January with more workshops and performances.

Paragliding Tandem rides rom the clifftops above Lakeside beach, run by a couple of German and British outfits who've been here for the best part of a decade, alternating between Goa and Manali. The cost of the flight includes all the equipment you'll need and full instruction. For more information, go to *Arambol Hammocks*, close to the *Rice Bowl* restaurant at the north end of the beach.

ACCOMMODATION

The cost of accommodation in Arambol has risen sharply over the past few seasons, reflecting the village's popularity with free-spending young Russians, but it's still nearly all pitched at budget travellers: no-frills, Goan-run guesthouses and expat-inspired hippie-chic predominate here rather than mainstream hotels.

Arun Huts Near Narayan Temple ☎ 9850 096468. Quirky little hut camp, run by local beautician, Mrs Mala Singh, in the thick of Arambol village. Just 60m from the sea, it comprises two rows of neatly painted wood huts, fitted with decent mattresses, attached shower toilets and fans. The whole earth-floored compound is smothered in banana trees, palms and flowers, and very atmospheric, especially in the evening. Good value. ₹850

Atman Girkar Waddo ☎ 8698 880135, ⓦ atmangoa. com. Lovely bamboo-and-wood tree huts on the south side of the beach, prettily thatched and decorated with coco mats, colourful sari drapes, original fractal-fluoro wall hangings, and bolsters on their spacious sit-out areas. Smiling Italian-Indian owners, Michaela and Sunil, also run a yoga space and small boutique, as well as a restaurant. ₹1500

Famafa Khalcha Waddo ☎ 0832 229 2516, ⓦ travelingoa .com/famafa. Large, anodyne concrete place just off the main drag; very close to the beach and great value for money. One of the few places that boast hot water showers. They don't take bookings and operate a 9am checkout, so get here early for a room. ₹600

Go-Ym Bag Waddo, close to Atman ☎ 9637 376335, ⓦ go-ym.com. Large mid-range resort with twelve tiled, vibrantly coloured cottages close to the beach. The tastefully decorated rooms come with comfortable beds. ₹2750

Ivon's Girkar Waddo ☎ 0832 224 2672 or ☎ 9822 127398. The pick of the budget bunch: immaculately clean, tiled rooms, all with attached bathroom and fronted by good-sized tiled balconies opening onto the dunes or a well-groomed family compound. ₹600

Om Ganesh Cottages In the cove between the village and Lakeside beach; book at the Om Ganesh stores on the main drag ☎ 0832 229 7614. Most desirable of the cottages stacked up the cliffside just south of Lakeside beach (₹600–1000). The sea views from their verandas are superb. Rates vary wildly according to demand, and advance booking (with a deposit) is all but essential by mid-season. They also have some new apartments near *Double Dutch* for monthly rental (₹15,000/month). ₹600

Silver Sands 4-S Tara Ankush ☎ 0832 224 2648 or ☎ 9923 667448. Huge, immaculately clean rooms with terracotta-tiled roofs and shining ceramic floors, overlooking the Narayan temple. The best ones are on the first storey of the newest block; cheaper budget options with shared bathrooms occupy the ground floor. Close to the beach and well maintained by resident owners, the Lavu family. ₹700

EATING

Thanks to its annually replenished pool of expatriate gastronomic talent, Arambol harbours a handful of unexpectedly good restaurants – not that you'd ever guess from their generally lacklustre exteriors. The village's alternative, Western European contingent cares more about flavours than fancy decor, and prices in the village reflect this. Russians with money to splurge, meanwhile, tend to gravitate towards the fancier seafood joints spread along the beachfront, where the day's catch is displayed on cold trays for selection, then grilled alfresco in front of you. Prices can be eye-popping, so get a quote before you order.

Cheeky Monkey Arambol beach. A cut above your average beach shack, offering a great variety of salads, home-made pastas and great stir-fried noodle dishes. Try the warm beetroot salad (₹180), pumpkin ravioli (₹220) and the one and only dessert on the menu, a knock-out hot chocolate pudding with cinnamon ice cream (₹220). Daily 9am–11pm.

★ **Double Dutch** Main St, halfway down on the right (look for the yellow signboard). Spread under a palm canopy in the heart of the village, this laidback café is the hub of alternative Arambol. Renowned for its melt-in-the-mouth apple pie, it also offers a tempting range of home-baked buttery biscuits, cakes, healthy salads and sumptuous main meals (from ₹175), including fresh buffalo steaks (₹340), the Indonesian veg thali (₹240) and perennially popular "mixed stuff" (stuffed mushrooms and capsicums with sesame pesto; ₹250). Daily 8am–11pm.

Dylan's (Toasted and Roasted) Behind Kinara restaurant and Golden Hands jewellers. Owner Raj insists that it's not just about the coffee and the cookies, but both are exceptional. He also hosts regular concerts and art shows. Mon–Sat 9am–11pm.

Eyes of Buddha North end of beach. Enduringly popular travellers' hangout, occupying a perfect spot overlooking the main beach. It's renowned above all for its mountainous fruit salad and curd breakfasts, and they serve up great north Indian food, tandoori fish and a few local Goan dishes: try the succulent *paneer* (₹170) and chicken kebabs (₹250) with hot naan bread. Daily 8am–11pm.

Fellini's Main St. Italian-run place serving delicious wood-fired pizzas (₹150–275), and authentic pasta or gnocchi with a choice of more than 20 sauces. It gets horrendously busy in season, so get here early if you want snappy service. Daily 11am–11pm.

⭐ **Lamuella** Main St. Lively little roadside café, serving healthy breakfasts, toasties, hummus plates and filling salads during the daytime, as well as energizing juice combos and herb teas. After sunset you can order from an eclectic dinner menu with amazing home-made mushroom ravioli and grilled fish (₹320) with chocolate fondant ice cream for dessert (₹200). Daily 8.30am–11pm.

Relax Inn North end of beach. Top-quality seafood straight off the boats, and authentic pasta (you get even more expat Italians in here than at *Fellini's*) – try the *vongole* (clam) sauce. Inexpensive (most mains around ₹200), but expect a wait as they cook to order. Daily 6–11pm.

Rice Bowl North end of beach. This place serves the best Chinese in Arambol, with a perfect view of the beach to match, and a pool table (₹100/hr). Any of their tasty noodle dishes are safe bets, as are the Japanese and Tibetan specialities. Most mains ₹200–250. Daily 8am–11pm.

Sai Deep At the bottom end of the village. This little *dhaba* is noted among those in this stretch and has a devoted following. They serve copious fruit salads as well as thalis, and a good travellers' breakfast menu of pancakes, eggs and curd at rock bottom prices. Daily sunrise–sunset.

NIGHTLIFE

Ash Girkar Waddo. With amazing art work, this open-air venue hosts everything from Russian shamanic singers to gypsy folk musicians and Sufi bands – the musicianship is of a consistently high standard, too. Naturally, most performances are accompanied by fire dancing – this is Arambol! Look out for posters to see what is coming up. Daily 6.30–11pm.

Loeki's Just up from the beachfront. Jam sessions and live bands are hosted by *Loeki's* on Sun and Thurs eves. Standards vary with whoever happens to blow in, but there have been some memorable impromptu gigs held here over the past few seasons. Sun & Thurs 7–11pm.

SHOPPING

Lamuella Opposite Shiv Krupa General Store, Arambol Main Road. In the heart of Arambol, *Lamuella* holds a great collection of clothes for women and children – with a few options for men – mostly from expat local designers. They also stock beautiful jewellery for every budget and homeware from fair trade collectives in India. There a café in the back garden to chill in afterwards. Daily 10am–10pm.

DIRECTORY

Banks and exchange There is an ATM close to the bus stand, and several places along the main village lane change money and do cash advances on debit and credit cards: try SS Travels opposite *Om Ganesh General Store*.

Post office On the east side of the village, beyond the big church.

YOGA IN ARAMBOL

Yogis and yoga classes are ubiquitous in Arambol, and of varying quality. Here are two of our favourites to help separate the wheat from the chaff.

Iyengar yoga teacher **Sharat** (ⓦhiyogacentre.com) holds five-day classes in his studio in Modlo Waddo. Prospective students should sign up at the centre from 1–3pm. To find it, head for the *Priya Guest House* and follow the "HIYC" signs from there.

Viriam Kaur's yoga classes, held amid the leafy retreat of a rooftop garden in Girkar Waddo, have attracted a strong following over the past few years – not least because it's among the few places in India where you can learn Kundalini yoga. Also trained in Western and Ayurvedic massage, Viriam and her partner Adam Divine offer individual sessions and training, as well as workshops and courses on chakra healing and other therapeutic techniques. Check out her website (ⓦorganickarma.co.uk) for dates, contact details and reviews.

Terekol

The tiny enclave of **TEREKOL** is the northernmost tip of Goa. Set against the backdrop of a filthy iron-ore complex, the old fort that dominates the estuary from the north – an ochre-painted building with turreted ramparts that wouldn't look out of place in coastal Portugal – was built by the Marathas at the start of the eighteenth century, but taken soon after by the Portuguese. These days, it serves as a low-key luxury heritage hotel, the *Fort Tiracol*.

ARRIVAL   TEREKOL

By ferry Terekol is reached on a clapped-out car ferry (every 30min; 5min) from the hamlet of Kerim (Querim), 42km from Panjim. If the tide is out and the water levels are too low for the ferry to run, you can either backtrack 5km, where there's another one, or arrange for the boatman at the jetty to run you across (for a negotiable fee).
By bus or taxi Sporadic buses cover the route, but you'll find the trip easier on a rented scooter or by taxi.

ACCOMMODATION

Fort Tiracol ☏ 8390 383917 or ☏ 02366 227631, ⓦ forttiracol.com. Seven luxurious rooms decorated in traditional ochre and white, with black-oxide floors, black-tiled drench showers and rustic wood and wrought-iron furniture; tariffs range from ₹9500 for a standard room to ₹12,500/night for the larger suites. Non-residents are welcome to visit the restaurant and stylish lounge bar, where you can eat authentic Goan cooking while enjoying what must rank among the finest seascapes in southern India. ₹9500

12 | South Goa

Backed by a lush band of coconut plantations and green hills, Goa's south coast is fringed by some of the region's finest **beaches**. An ideal first base if you've just arrived in the region is **Benaulim**, 6km west of the state's second city, **Margao**. The most traveller-friendly resort in the area, Benaulim stands slap in the middle of a spectacular 25km stretch of pure white sand. Although increasingly carved up by Mumbai time-share companies, low-cost accommodation here is plentiful and of a consistently high standard. Nearby **Colva**, by contrast, has degenerated over the past decade into an insalubrious sink resort. Frequented by huge numbers of day-trippers, and boasting few discernible charms, it's best avoided.

With the gradual spread of package tourism down the coast, **Palolem**, a ninety-minute drive south of Margao along the main highway, is Goa's most happening beach, attracting droves of sun seekers from November through March. Set against a backdrop of forest-cloaked hills, its bay is spectacular, though the crowds can feel overwhelming in high season. For a quieter scene, try **Agonda**, just up the coast, or **Patnem**, immediately south of Palolem. Among the possible day-trips inland, a crop of Portuguese-era mansions at **Chandor** and **Quepem** are your best options; and in the far south, the **Cotigao Wildlife Sanctuary** affords a rare glimpse of unspoilt forest and its fauna.

Margao

The capital of prosperous Salcete *taluka*, **MARGAO** – referred to in railway timetables and on some maps by its official government title, **Madgaon** – is Goa's second city, and if you're arriving in the state on the Konkan Railway, you'll almost certainly have to pause here to pick up onward transport by road. Surrounded by fertile rice paddy and plantain groves, the town has always been an important agricultural market, and was once a major religious centre, with dozens of wealthy temples and *dharamshala*s – however, most of these were destroyed when the Portuguese absorbed the area into their **Novas Conquistas** ("New Conquests") during the seventeenth century. Today, Catholic churches still outnumber Hindu shrines, but Margao has retained a cosmopolitan feel due to a huge influx of migrant labour from neighbouring Karnataka and Maharashtra.

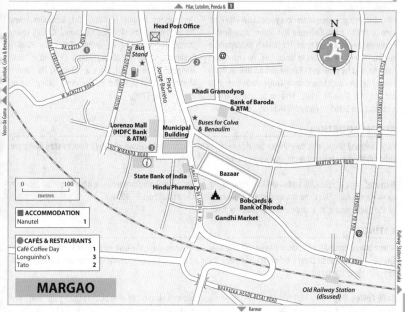

MARGAO

Largo de Igreja (Church Square) and around

A short auto-rickshaw ride north of the centre to **Largo de Igreja** square at the north end of town, **Church of the Holy Spirit** is the main landmark of the square, and indeed Margao's dishevelled colonial enclave. It was built by the Portuguese in 1675, and ranks among the finest examples of late Baroque architecture in Asia with an interior dominated by a huge gilt reredos dedicated to the Virgin. Just northeast of it, overlooking the main Ponda road, stands one of the state's grandest eighteenth-century palacios, **Sat Banzam Ghor** ("Seven Gables house"). Only three of its original seven high-pitched roof gables remain, but the mansion is still an impressive sight, its facade decorated with fancy scrollwork and huge oyster-shell windows.

Market area

Colonial-era vestiges aside, the main reason to come to Margoa is to shop at the town's **market**, the hub of which is a labyrinthine covered area. Just up the road, on the southeast side of the town's hectic main sqaure, stands the little government-run **Khadi Gramodyog** shop, which sells the usual range of hand-spun cottons and raw silk by the metre, as well as ready-made traditional Indian garments.

ARRIVAL AND DEPARTURE
MARGAO

By train Margao's huge railway station lies 3km south of the centre, its reservation office (Mon–Sat 8am–4.30pm, Sun 8am–2pm; ☎0832 271 2940) divided between the ground and first floors. Tickets for trains to Mumbai are in short supply, so make your reservation as far in advance as possible. If you're catching the train to Hospet (en route to Hampi; four weekly) get here early to avoid long queues. Several principal trains stop in Margao at unsociable times of night, but there's a 24hr information counter (☎0832 271 2790) and a round-the-clock pre-paid auto-rickshaw and taxi stand outside the exit.

Destinations Chaudi (1 daily; 45min); Gokarna (2 daily; 1hr 50min); Hospet (3 weekly; 8hr); Mangalore (5 daily; 4–6hr); Mumbai (4–5 daily; 9hr 30min–11hr 30min).

By bus Local private buses shuttling between Colva and Benaulim leave from in front of the *Kamat Hotel*, on the east side of Margao's main square. Arriving on

12

long-distance government services you can get off either here or at the main Kadamba Bus Stand, 3km further north, on the outskirts of town. The latter is the departure point for interstate services to Mangalore, via Chaudi and Gokarna, and for services to Panjim and north Goa. Paulo Travel's deluxe coach to and from Hampi works from a lot next to the *Nanutel* hotel, 1km or so south of the Kadamba Bus Stand on Padre Miranda Rd.

Destinations Agonda (4 daily; 2hr); Benaulim (every 30min; 15min); Chandor (hourly; 45min); Chaudi (every 30min; 1hr 40min); Colva (every 15min; 2hr 30min); Gokarna (2 daily; 4hr 30min); Hampi (1 nightly; 10hr); Mangalore (5 daily; 7hr); Mapusa (10 daily; 2hr 30min); Mumbai (2 daily; 16–18hr); Panjim (every 30min; 50min); Pune (1 daily; 12hr).

ACCOMMODATION

With Colva and Benaulim a mere 20min bus ride away, it's hard to think of a reason why you'd want to **stay** in Margao, although there is a reasonable option if you're stuck.

Nanutel Rua Padre Miranda ☎0832 270 0900, ⓦnanuindia.com. This three-star multistorey block north of the main square is a commendable place in town.

Pitched at visiting businessmen, it has 55 central a/c rooms and a small pool. ₹**2000**

EATING

After a browse around the bazaar, most visitors make a beeline for *Longuinho's*, the long-established hangout of Margao's English-speaking middle classes, before heading home. If you are on a tight budget, try one of the south Indian-style pure-veg cafés along Station Rd.

Café Coffee Day Shop 18/19 Vasanth Arcade, near Popular High School. Goa's answer to *Starbucks* has a super-cool a/c branch tucked away off the Municipal Gardens square, popular with local college kids. Aside from a perfect latte, it serves spicy savouries (such as mini-pizzas and salad wraps; ₹50–125) and, most memorably, a very sinful "sizzling brownie" (₹110), which will have chocoholics begging for loyalty cards. Daily 8.30am–10.30pm.
Longuinho's Luis Miranda Rd. Relaxing, old-fashioned café serving a selection of meat, fish and veg mains, freshly baked savoury snacks, cakes and drinks. The food isn't up to much these days, and the 1950s Goan atmosphere has been marred by the arrival of satellite TV,

but it's a pleasant enough place to catch your breath over a beer. Snacks ₹50–175; mains ₹200–300. Daily 8.30am–10pm.
Tato Tucked away up an alley off the east side of Praça Jorge Barreto. The town's brightest and best south Indian café serves the usual range of hot snacks (including especially good samosas at breakfast time, and masala dosas from noon). A bit cramped downstairs, but well worth the effort to find. For a proper meal, climb the stairs to their cool a/c floor, where you can order wonderful thalis (₹75) and a range of north Indian dishes, as well as all the *udipi* nibbles (₹50–100) that are dished up on the ground floor. Daily 8am–9.30pm.

DIRECTORY

Banks There are plenty of ATMs dotted around the town centre: try HDFC, in the Lorenzo Mall, on the west side of Praça Jorge Barreto just up from *Longuinho's*, or the Bank of Baroda on the opposite side of the square.
Cinema Margao boasts south Goa's principal cinema, the Osia Multiplex (☎0832 270 1717), out in the north of town near the Kadamba Bus Stand. It screens Hollywood

as well as Bollywood releases; tickets cost ₹100–150.
Hospitals Hospicio (☎0832 270 5664 or ☎0832 270 5754), Rua De Miranda, and the Apollo Victor Hospital, in the suburb of Malbhat (☎0832 272 8888 or ☎0832 272 6272, ⓦapollovictorhospital.com).
Post office The GPO is at the top of the central municipal gardens.

Around Margao

For a good dose of quirky colonial architecture, head **inland from Margao**, where villages such as **Loutolim** and **Chandor** are littered with decaying old Portuguese houses, most of them empty – the region's traditional inheritance laws ensure that old family homes tend to be owned by literally dozens of descendants, few of whom are willing or can afford to maintain them.

Braganza-Perreira/Menezes-Braganza house

Chandor • Daily except holidays, no set hours • just turn up between 10am and noon or 3 and 6pm, go through the main entrance, up the stairs and knock at either of the doors • Recommended donation ₹100/person • ☎ 0832 278 4227 & ☎ 9822 160009

Thirteen kilometres east of Margao across Salcete district's fertile rice fields lies sleepy **Chandor** village, a scattering of tumbledown villas and farmhouses ranged along shady tree lined lanes. The main reason to venture out here is to see the splendid **Braganza-Perreira/Menezes-Braganza house**, regarded as the grandest of Goa's colonial mansions. Dominating the dusty village square, the house, built in the 1500s by the wealthy Braganza family for their two sons, has a huge double-storey facade, with 28 windows flanking its entrance. Braganza de Perreira, the great-grandfather of the present owner, was the last knight of the king of Portugal; more recently, Menezes Braganza (1879–1938), a journalist and freedom fighter, was one of the few Goan aristocrats actively to oppose Portuguese rule. Forced to flee Chandor in 1950, the family returned in 1962 to find their house, amazingly, untouched. The airy tiled interiors of both wings contain a veritable feast of **antiques**.

Exploring the house

The house is divided into two separate wings, owned by different (and contrasting) branches of the old family. Both are open to the public, though there are no set hours as such. Furniture enthusiasts and lovers of rare Chinese porcelain, in particular, will find plenty to drool over in the Menezes-Braganza wing (to the right as you face the building). Next door, in the **Braganza-Perreira** portion, an ornate oratory enshrines St Francis Xavier's diamond-encrusted toenail, retrieved from a local bank vault. The house's most famous feature, however, is its ostentatiously grand ballroom, or **Great Salon**, where a pair of matching high-backed chairs, presented to the Braganza-Perreiras by King Dom Luís of Portugal, occupy pride of place.

Fernandes House

Chandor • A donation of around ₹100/person is expected • ☎ 0832 278 4245

An air of charismatic dilapidation hangs over the **Fernandes House**, on the south side of the village. One of the oldest surviving *palacios* in Goa, its core is of pre-conquest Hindu origin, overlaid by later accretions. Sara Fernandes, the present owner, receives visitors in the wonderful **salon** that extends the length of the building's first floor, abutting a bedchamber containing its original, ornately carved four-poster. Hidden in the bowels of the building below, a narrow passage fitted with disguised gun holes was where the family used to shelter when attacked by Hindu rebels and bandits such as the Ranes. **Visitors** are welcome to call any day of the week, but should telephone in advance.

Palacio do Deão

Quepem • Guided tours daily except Fri 10am–6pm • Free • ☎ 0832 266 4029, ⓦ palaciododeao.com

A superb colonial-era *palacio* stands at **Quepem**, a thirty-minute drive southeast of Margao on the fringes of the state's iron-ore belt. In 1787, a high-ranking member of the Portuguese clergy, **Father José Paulo de Almeida**, built a country house in the town. Known as the **Palacio do Deão**, it grew to become one of the most grandiloquent in the colony, and later served as a retreat for the colony's Viceroys. The *palacio* was recently restored to its former glory by a Goan couple who scoured libraries in Lisbon for original plans of the building, what you see today is a faithful approximation of how the house would have looked in José Paulo's day. The engaging guided **tour** lasts around half an hour, winding up on the lovely rear terrace overlooking the river where, by prior arrangement, you can enjoy a copious Indo-Portuguese lunch (₹500) – an experience not be missed.

12

Colva

A hot-season retreat for Margao's moneyed middle classes since long before Independence, **COLVA** is the oldest and largest – but least appealing – of south Goa's resorts. Its outlying *waddos* are pleasant enough, dotted with colonial-style villas and ramshackle fishing huts, but the beachfront is dismal: a lacklustre collection of concrete hotels, souvenir stalls and flyblown snack bars strewn around a bleak central roundabout. The atmosphere is not improved by the heaps of rubbish dumped in a rank-smelling ditch that runs behind the beach, nor by the stench of drying fish wafting from the nearby village. Benaulim, just a five-minute drive further south, has a far better choice of accommodation and range of facilities, and is altogether more salubrious.

Benaulim

The predominantly Catholic fishing village of **BENAULIM** lies in the dead centre of Colva beach, scattered around the coconut groves and paddy fields, 7km west of Margao. Two decades ago, the settlement had barely made it onto the backpackers'

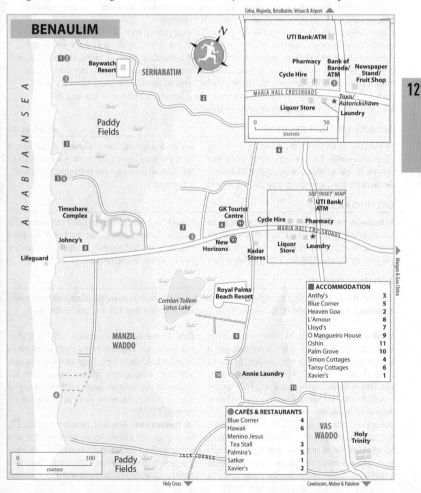

BENAULIM

Colva, Majorda, Betalbatim, Velsao & Airport

UTI Bank/ATM

Baywatch Resort

SERNABATIM

Pharmacy — Bank of Baroda/ATM — Newspaper Stand/Fruit Shop

Cycle Hire

MARIA HALL CROSSROADS

Taxis/Autorickshaws

Liquor Store — Laundry

0   50
metres

A R A B I A N   S E A

Paddy Fields

Timeshare Complex

Johncy's

Lifeguard

SEE INSET MAP

UTI Bank/ATM

GK Tourist Centre

Cycle Hire — Pharmacy

MARIA HALL CROSSROADS

New Horizons

Kadar Stores

Liquor Store — Laundry

Comlan Tollem Lotus Lake

Royal Palms Beach Resort

MANZIL WADDO

Annie Laundry

Margao & Goa Chitra

VAS WADDO

Holy Trinity

0   100
metres

Paddy Fields

JACK CORNER

Holy Cross   Cavelossim, Mobor & Palolem

■ **ACCOMMODATION**

Anthy's	3
Blue Corner	5
Heaven Goa	2
L'Amour	8
Lloyd's	7
O Mangueiro House	9
Oshin	11
Palm Grove	10
Simon Cottages	4
Tansy Cottages	6
Xavier's	1

● **CAFÉS & RESTAURANTS**

Blue Corner	4
Hawaii	6
Menino Jesus Tea Stall	3
Palmira's	5
Satkar	1
Xavier's	2

12

map. Nowadays, though, affluent holiday-makers from metropolitan India come here in droves, staying in the huge resort and time-share complexes mushrooming on the outskirts, while long-staying, heavy-drinking Brit pensioners and thirty-something European couples taking time out of trips around the Subcontinent make up the bulk of the foreign contingent.

Benaulim's rising popularity has certainly dented the village's old-world charm, but time your visit well (avoiding Diwali and the Christmas peak season), and it is still hard to beat as a place to unwind. The seafood is superb, accommodation and motorbikes cheaper than anywhere else in the state, and the beach is breathtaking, particularly around sunset, when its brilliant white sand and churning surf reflect the changing colours to magical effect. Shelving away almost to Cabo da Rama on the horizon, the beach is also lined with Goa's largest, and most colourfully decorated, fleet of **wooden outriggers**, and these provide welcome shade during the heat of the day.

Goa Chitra

Tues–Sun 9.15am–6pm, last tour 5.15pm • ₹300 • ☎ 0832 657 0877, ⓦ goachitra.com • To get to Goa Chitra by bike or motorcycle, head east from Maria Hall crossroads towards Margao, and take the first turning on your left at a fork after 1.5km; when you reach the T-junction ahead, turn sharply right – the museum lies another 500m on your right

Conventional sights are thin on the ground along this stretch of coast, though one exception stands out on the eastern fringes of Benaulim: a splendid new ethnographic museum, **Goa Chitra**. Set against a backdrop of a working organic farm, the exhibition comprises a vast array of antique agricultural tools and artefacts, ranging from giant cooking pots and ecclesiastical robes to tubas and sugarcane presses. The idea is to promote appreciation of the region's traditional agrarian lifestyle – a world of knowledge and skills fast disappearing today.

12

ARRIVAL AND INFORMATION	BENAULIM

By bus Buses connecting Margao and Benaulim run every 15min or so, working from the southeast side of the main square in Margao and Maria Hall crossroads in Benaulim.
Services Arranged around this busy junction are two well-stocked general stores, a couple of café-bars, a bank, pharmacy, laundry and the taxi and auto-rickshaw rank, from where you can pick up transport to the beach, 1.5km west.

GETTING AROUND

By motorbike and bicycle Signs offering motorbikes for rent are dotted along the lane leading to the sea: rates are standard, descending in proportion to the length of time you keep the vehicle (₹200/day is about average for a Honda Activa). Worth bearing in mind if you're planning to continue further south is that motorbikes are much cheaper to rent (and generally in better condition) here than in Palolem. Bicycles cost around ₹100/day to rent.

ACCOMMODATION

Aside from the unsightly time-share complexes and five-stars that loom in the fields around the village, most of Benaulim's **accommodation** consists of small budget guesthouses, scattered around the lanes 1km or so back from the beach.

L'Amour Beach Rd ☎ 0832 277 0404, ⓦ lamourbeachresortgoa.com. Benaulim's oldest hotel comprises a comfortable thirty-room cottage complex; its chalets (some a/c) are spacious and cool, with ceramic tiled floors and little verandas opening onto a central garden. Reasonable rates, but avoid the rooms on the first floor of the main block, which get horribly hot. ₹2000
Anthy's Sernabatim ☎ 0832 277 1680 or ☎ 9922 854566, ✉ anthysguesthouse@rediffmail.com. Nicely furnished rooms right on the sea, with high ceilings, tiny bathrooms and breezy verandas. A/c costs ₹400 extra. ₹1600

Blue Corner Sernabatim ☎ 9850 455770, ⓦ blue-corner-goa.com. Popular hut camp on the beach, run by an enthusiastic young crew. Large palm-leaf structures with fans, mosquito nets, attached shower-toilets and plywood sit-outs. Quiet and secure, and the bar-restaurant is one of the most happening places on the beach in the evenings. ₹2000
★ **Heaven Goa** 1 Ambeaxir, Sernabatim ☎ 0832 275 8442 or ☎ 9890 698202, ⓦ heavengoa.in. Run by a welcoming Swiss-Keralan couple, Karin & Sunil, this block of a dozen or so rooms occupies a plum spot, 10min back from the sea beside a lily pond alive with frogs, egrets and

water buffalo. The rooms are spacious and well set up (with wooden shelves, mosquito nets, shiny tiled floors and balconies overlooking the water). Expert Ayurvedic massages are offered; and they bake delicious fresh pizzas in a wood-fired oven, too. Unbelievable value in this bracket. ₹700

Lloyd's 1554 A Vas Waddo ☎0832 277 1492, ⓦlloydstouristrooms@gmail.com. With its garish yellow exterior, this place on the beach side of the village stands out in more ways than one. The rooms are really big for the price, with high ceilings, quality beds and fans, plus neat mozzie screens over the windows. And they offer of various sizes apartments upstairs for longer stays. ₹700

O Mangueiro House 1685/A, Vas Waddo (next to Carina Beach Resort) ☎0832 277 0408 & ☎9922 542217, ⓦmangogrovegoa.com. One of the oldest budget guesthouses in Benaulim, run by the affable Mr Caetano. Just 400m from the beach, the rooms are on the small side, but neat and clean, freshly painted each season, and with quality mattresses. Some have tiny balconies opening onto a sandy courtyard. Others face the road. There's also an equally good-value studio for longer stays (₹750) and a two-bedroom apartment (₹1400). ₹450

Oshin Mazil Waddo ☎0832 277 0069, ⓔinaciooshin @rediffmail.com. Large complex of old-style budget rooms set well back from the road. Opening onto leafy terraces, they're spacious and clean with attached bathrooms, balconies, fresh towels and complimentary soap; those on the top floor afford views over the treetops. A notch above most places in this area, and good value, but quite a walk from the beach. ₹600

Palm Grove Tamdi-Mati, 149 Vas Waddo ☎0832 277 0059, ⓦpalmgrovegoa.com. Secluded hotel surrounded by beautiful gardens, offering three classes of mostly a/c rooms (₹2000–3500), ranging from ropy to luxurious. A bike ride back from the beachfront, but very pleasant, and the management is welcoming. ₹2000

Simon Cottages Ambeaxir, Sernabatim ☎0832 277 0581. Perennially among the best budget deals in Benaulim, in a quiet spot at the unspoilt north side of the village and with huge rooms on three storeys, all with shower-toilets and verandas, opening onto a sandy courtyard. ₹450

Tansy Cottages Beach Rd ☎0832 277 0574, ⓔtansycottages@yahoo.in. Not the best of locations, and the shocking green-and-purple paintwork is hard to live with, but the rooms here are some of the nicest budget options in Benaulim: they're a generous size, with tiled floors and new attached bathrooms. A/c costs ₹300 extra. ₹500

★**Xavier's** Sernabatim ☎0832 277 1489, ⓔjovek @vsnl.in. Well-maintained, large rooms ranged around a lovely garden, virtually on the beach but within walking distance of the village centre. All rooms have private terraces, extra thick king-sized mattresses and low-slung cane chairs to lounge on, and the local owners, who have been here for decades, are genuinely hospitable. A peaceful, perfectly situated option – and great value. ₹1600

EATING AND DRINKING

Benaulim's proximity to Margao market, along with the presence of a large Christian fishing community, means its **restaurants** serve some of the tastiest, competitively priced seafood in Goa. The largest and busiest shacks flank the beachfront area, where *Johncy's* catches most of the passing custom. However, you'll find better food at lower prices at places further along the beach, which seem to change chefs annually; the only way to find out which ones offer the best value for money is to wander past and see who has the most customers.

Blue Corner Sernabatim. Great little beachside joint specializing in seafood and authentic Chinese. House favourites include "fish tomato eggdrop soup", scrumptious "dragon potatoes" and, best of all, their "Dave's steak" (₹350). Also featured on the eclectic menu are tasty Italian dishes, sizzlers and, for homesick veggies, a pretty good cauliflower cheese. Most mains ₹200–250. Daily 7am–late.

Hawaii South end of beach. Nadia and Vinod from Himachal Pradesh have run this welcoming little shack for more than a decade, and can claim one of the most loyal clienteles in the village, most of whom come for the Italian dishes, prepared with home-made pasta, fresh herbs, olive oil and proper cheese. The prawn lasagne and moussaka also get the thumbs up, and they do a zingy, fresh-mint mojito. During the day, a dedicated kids' play area is an additional attraction. Mains ₹150–200. Daily 8am–late.

Menino Jesus Tea Stall Sernabatim. If you've ever wondered what beach shacks were like thirty years ago, check this place out. It's where the local rickshaw drivers refuel on spicy fish-curry-rice plates, piping hot slices of millet-fried mackerel and *pao bhaji* for just ₹50. Rough and ready, but the food's delicious, and the sea view is perfect. Daily 11am–10pm.

Palmira's Beach Rd ☎0832 277 1309. Benaulim's best breakfasts: wonderfully creamy and fresh set curd, copious fruit salads with coconut, real espresso coffee, warm local bread (*bajri*) and the morning paper. For a light lunch, try their delicious prawn toast or tomato or ginger-carrot soups. Daily 7am–4pm.

Satkar Maria Hall Crossroads. No-frills locals' *udipi*

canteen that's the only place in the village where you can order regular Indian snacks – samosas (₹15), masala dosas (₹40), hot *pakoras* and spicy chickpea stew (*channa*) – and full thalis (₹60) – at regular Indian prices. And the *bhaji pau* breakfast here (₹25) is a must. Daily 8am–9.30pm.

★ **Xavier's** Sernabatim. Host Jovek's mum, Maria, does most of the masala preparation and cooking for this breezy

beachside restaurant, so the Goan dishes – prawn vindaloo, fish *caldin* and a knockout *chouriço* chilli-fry are highly recommended. Less spicy alternatives include a particularly tasty lemon rice; and of course, they do the usual range of market-fresh seafood. Facing one of the most tranquil stretches of the beach, the terrace is most atmospheric at night, with the waves crashing in only a few metres away. Most mains ₹150–250. Daily 8am–late.

DIRECTORY

Banks and exchange For changing money, the Bank of Baroda (Mon–Fri 9am–2pm, Sat 9–11.30am) on Maria Hall has a (temperamental) ATM; the UTI one around the corner on the main road is a bit more dependable. Currency and travellers' cheques may be changed at GK Tourist Centre, at the crossroads in the village centre, and New Horizons, diagonally opposite. It's worth comparing rates at the two.

Internet For internet access, GK Tourist Centre and New Horizons have broadband connections (₹40/hr).

Laundry Annie's, opposite Palm Grove, offers an inexpensive same-day laundry service. The Frank Bela laundry on the Maria Hall crossroads charges slightly more.

Agonda

AGONDA, 10km northwest of Chaudi, comes as a pleasant surprise after the chaos reigning elsewhere in Goa. Accommodation in this predominantly Catholic fishing village is in small-scale, family-run guesthouses and hut camps, the restaurant scene is relatively unsophisticated, and the clientele easy-going and health-conscious. Granted, you don't get a dreamy brake of palm trees as a backdrop, but since the Boxing Day tsunami of 2004 the beach has lost its menacing undertow and the sand is as clean as any in the state. Moreover, the surrounding hills and forest are exquisite.

The smart money says Agonda could all too soon go the way of Palolem (several large hut-camp owners there have recently purchased leases on land here in anticipation of a mass exodus) but for the time being the village deserves to be high on the from Palolem list for anyone seeking somewhere quiet and wholesome, with enough amenities for a relaxing holiday, but still plenty of local atmosphere.

12

AGONDA

Cabo Da Rama

■ ACCOMMODATION
Bioveda	4
Chris-Joana	7
Dersy's	11
H2O	10
Jardim A Mar	5
Kaama Kethna	8
Maria Paulo	6
Monsoon	2
Palm Beach Lifestyle Resort	9
Secret Garden	1
White Sand Beach Huts and Villas	3

● RESTAURANTS
Fatima Thali	5
Jardim A Mar	4
Madhu's	3
Monsoon	1
White Sand	2

0 — 200 metres

ARABIAN SEA

ATM

St. Anne's Church

Car Park **P**

Palolem

Palolem & B

ARRIVAL AND DEPARTURE   AGONDA

By bus Agonda is served by four daily buses from the nearest market town, Chaudi (dep. Chaudi 8.30am, 9.00am, 3.30pm & 4.30pm); two run to Margao (dep. Agonda 6.15am & 2.30pm). Most services stop at the junction on the main Palolem road, 1km east (you can usually find a rickshaw for the trip into the village), but a couple go as far as the church in the centre of Agonda.

ACCOMMODATION

Agonda gets seriously packed in peak season, and over Christmas and New Year you'll be lucky to find a bed anywhere on spec. Tariffs rocket by fifty percent or more at this time, but after Jan 15 settle back down again and remain on a par with those in Patnem and Palolem. Except for the upscale camps (which require payment in advance online) few places accept advance bookings so you'll probably have to plod around to find somewhere that suits, or else phone ahead from the comfort of a café table (though note that mobile coverage tends to be patchy hereabouts).

Bioveda Doval Kazan ☎9422 388982, ⊛bioveda.in. Comfortable huts with attached bathrooms opening onto the beach. A thirty-second skip from the surf and roofed with paddy thatch, they're attractively set up, cool and comfortable and equipped with quality beds, split-cane blinds and lots of other homely touches. The welcoming British-Keralan owners also run an excellent little Ayurveda centre on site where you can enjoy authentic massages by qualified staff. ₹1500

Chris-Joana Near the church ☎0832 264 7306 or ☎9421 155814, ✉belu_miranda5@yahoo.in. Smart modern house on the roadside just south of the Church. Its bargain-priced rooms are clean, light and airy, and have decent beds. Go for one on the rear side, overlooking the rooftops and creek to coconut plantations; the front ones get warm in the afternoons. ₹500

Dersy's South end of the beach, on the roadside ☎0832 264 7503. Spotlessly clean and cosy rooms, with tiled floors and good-sized bathrooms. Those on the first floor (front side) have a common sea-facing veranda that catches the breezes; you can lie in bed and hear the waves crashing just 100m away. They also run a couple of rows of competitively priced beach huts (₹1500) on the opposite side of the lane. ₹2000

H2O South of the church ☎9421 152150 or ☎9423 936994, ⊛h2oagonda.com. Currently the hippiest of the camps on the beach – and the most pricey, charging upwards of ₹7000/night in high season for a plywood chalet right on the sand. Painted black, the tiled huts are styled with cerise and turquoise drapes and quilts; each has a huge, semi-open-air bathroom and veranda with low sofas and bolsters. Garden rooms, set back from the beach-facing ones, are less priey alternatives. ₹5000

Jardim A Mar Doval Kazan ☎9420 820470, ⊛jardim-a-mar.com. Professionally run "palm-tree-garden resort", offering budget rooms (₹800–1500) and pricier beachside huts (₹2000–2600), nicely decorated with Rajasthani quilts and blockprint throws. Partly German-owned, it has a slicker feel than most of the competition. ₹1500

★ **Kaama Kethna** Gurawal, 2km southeast of Agonda off the Palolem road ⊛kaamakethna.net. This German-run eco-tourism and permaculture project just outside the village offers simply furnished treehouses (₹1000–2000), built high in the cashew canopy from palm leaf panels and wood, plus a few bamboo huts with spacious terraces at ground level. The site is wonderfully quiet and leafy, with colourful birds and monkeys flitting through the branches. Food grown on the farm is served in their little restaurant. Just a 15min cycle from the beach. ₹1000

Maria Paulo Just north of Dersy's towards the church ☎0832 264 7606, ⊛mariapauloagonda.com. This modern white building on the roadside is a bigger and slightly more anonymous guesthouse than the others in the village, which some might prefer. Six large, cool marble-floored rooms, all with quality beds and mozzie nets; the pricier ones (₹3000) have generous verandas and sea views. A/c costs double. Complimentary towels, soap and wifi. ₹2000

Monsoon North of St Anne's Church ☎9923 549360, ⊛monsoon-goa.com. Low-slung thatched huts in a secluded, peaceful setting behind the north end of the beach. Efficiently run by the resident German owner, it offers a pleasant parachute-shaded chillout terrace and dining area with a tiled roof. Family friendly (no bar). Huts from ₹1200–3500 depending on size and season; rooms up to ₹3500. Prices are especially high over Christmas. ₹800

Palm Beach Lifestyle Resort Behind Dersy's ☎0832 264 7783 or ☎9422 450380, ⊛palmbeachgoa.com. Simple but very pleasant, terracotta-coloured chalets, ranged over terraces under a coconut plantation. They all have attractive wood floors, comfy mattresses and sea views from raised decks. Far better value than comparable places on the beach. ₹1200

Secret Garden Doval Kazan ☎0832 264730 or ☎9421 152054. At the far north end of the beach, the *Secret Garden* is more ramshackle than most of the camps in Agonda, but has a special edge. The owners have lived here for four generations and have allowed a screen of vegetation to grow up between the plot and the sand, making it more secluded, quiet and private. There are only four simple huts (the topmost one with a has to die for), plus a couple of cottage-style rooms. Recommended for families. ₹2000

★ **White Sand Beach Huts and Villas** North of St Anne's Church ☎9823 548277, ⊛agondawhitesand.com. This campus of stylish huts has definitely raised the bar in Agonda. Made of local wood, thatch and bamboo, with stone tiled floors, the cottages are furnished like chic hotel rooms – though ranged around a busy bar-restaurant, and there's a minimum stay of three nights (₹3500). For greater seclusion, and unparalleled luxury

12

slap on the beach, treat yourself to a stay in one of their gorgeous villas (₹10,000) – huge, five-star boutique chalets in Balinese and Keralan styles, with decadent open-to-sky bathrooms and uninterrupted sea views from private terraces. **₹3500**

EATING AND DRINKING

Agonda's restaurants are as much hangouts as places to eat. Most are furnished with relaxing cane chairs, pretty Himalayan lanterns and lounge areas with bolsters, and are on or near the beach. Standards of cooking (and, alas, hygiene) vary wildly from year to year in many beachside places, mainly because the staff are predominantly untrained Nepalis and Assamese who work here for the season.

Fatima Thali Next to church. Tasty ₹60 veg thalis and spicy *bhaji pao* (₹25), served on cramped tables in a tiny roadside chai shop. Popular with locals and long-staying foreigners on tight budgets. Daily 8am–9pm.

Jardim A Mar Doval Kazan. A café-restaurant that ticks all the boxes: it's slap on the sand, well shaded (under palms and a Ladakhi parachute), with comfy cane chairs, hammocks and silk cushions scattered on lounge mats. And it's a great breakfast spot, churning out fresh fruit juices, proper coffee, grilled baguettes and, the house speciality, rice pudding, as well as a popular all-day menu. Most mains ₹200–300. Daily 8am–11pm.

Madhu's North side of beach. For years, the best tandoori outfit on the beach: great for fresh local fish and Indian dishes alike (₹150–200). It's inexpensive and always busy, so get here early. Daily noon–midnight.

Monsoon North side of the beach. One for the healthy eaters: great house muesli and copious fresh salads for breakfast (₹120–200); pasta, Tibetan *momos* (₹180), seared fish steaks and a focussed selection of curries the rest of the day. Served on a small sandy terrace on the beach. Daily 8am–10.30pm.

White Sand North of the church. One of the more sophisticated menus in Agonda, including eggs rösti for breakfast (₹140), steaks (₹250), seafood, tandoori chicken and cashew brown rice with beetroot *raita* (₹180) for lunch and dinner, as well as a good range of cocktails (₹180–250). Daily 8am–late.

DIRECTORY

Internet You'll find a string of places offering internet access along the tarmac lane leading north of the church.

Money exchange You will find ATMs at the junction opposite the church.

Palolem

Nowhere else in peninsular India conforms so obediently to the archetypal image of a paradise beach as **PALOLEM**, 35km south of Margao. Lined with a swaying curtain of coconut palms, the bay forms a perfect curve of golden sand, arcing north from a giant pile of boulders to a spur of the Sahyadri Hills, which tapers into the sea draped in thick forest. Palolem, however, has become something of a paradise lost over the past decade. It's now the most popular resort in Goa among independent foreign travellers, and is deluged from late-November. Visitor numbers become positively overwhelming in peak season, when literally thousands of people spill across a beach backed by an unbroken line of shacks and Thai-style huts camps.

Basically, Palolem in full swing is the kind of place you'll either love at first sight, or want to get away from as quickly as possible. If you're in the latter category, try smaller, less frequented **Patnem** beach, a short walk south around the headland, where the shack scene is more subdued and the sands marginally emptier.

ARRIVAL AND DEPARTURE · PALOLEM

By bus Regular buses run between Margao and Palolem, stopping at the end of the lane leading from the main street to the beachfront. Frequent services also run between Margao and Karwar (in Karnataka) via the nearby market town of Chaudi (every 30min; 2hr), 2km southeast across the rice fields. The last bus from Palolem to Chaudi/ Margao leaves at around 4.30pm; check with the locals for the precise times, as these change seasonally.

By train Chaudi is also the nearest railhead to Palolem; the station lies a short way north of the main bazaar. Rickshaws charge ₹100, taxis ₹200–250, for the ride to the beach.

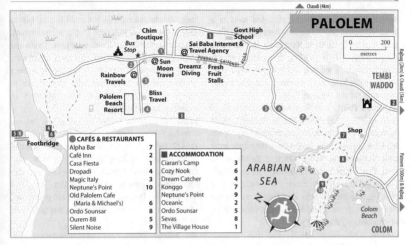

CAFÉS & RESTAURANTS

Alpha Bar	7
Café Inn	2
Casa Fiesta	1
Dropadi	4
Magic Italy	3
Neptune's Point	10
Old Palolem Cafe (Maria & Michael's)	6
Ordo Sounsar	8
Ourem 88	5
Silent Noise	9

ACCOMMODATION

Ciaran's Camp	3
Cozy Nook	6
Dream Catcher	4
Konggo	7
Neptune's Point	9
Oceanic	2
Ordo Sounsar	5
Sevas	8
The Village House	1

ACTIVITIES

Cycle rental A stall halfway along the main street charges the princely sum of ₹25/hr or ₹100/day.

Diving Dreamz Diving, in *Sea Shells Guest House*, Pundalik Gaitondi Rd (☎ 9326 113466, ⏻ dreamzdiving.com), offer guided dives to sites in much clearer waters than you get around Palolem.

Sailing Goa Sailing (☎ 9850 458865, ⏻ goasailing.com) has three 4.5m Prindle Catamarans for rent – by the hour (₹1250), half day (₹3000) or full day (₹4500) – ideal for exploring remote beaches in the area.

Surf canoes Available for rent at various places along the beach for ₹100/hr – great for paddles to the island at the top of the bay, or, weather permitting, around the headland to "Butterfly Beach".

Trekking Goa Jungle Adventure (☎ 9850 485641, ⏻ goajungle.com or ⏻ facebook.com/goajungleadventure) runs guided treks to natural swimming sites, as well as full-on canyoning and rafting trips from their base at Netravali, in the mountain area inland from Palolem. Rates, from ₹2000/half day for canyoning or ₹2000/full day for guided treks, include all equipment.

ACCOMMODATION

The local municipality's strict enforcement of a rule banning new concrete construction in Palolem (it went so far as to bulldoze without warning the entire resort a few years back) has ensured that most of the village's accommodation consists of simple palm-leaf huts or "treehouses".

Ciaran's Camp ☎ 0832 264 3477, ⏻ ciarans.com. "Camp" understates the sophistication of this compact resort in the centre of Palolem Beach, whose coir, coconut wood and terracotta-tiled chalets are ranged around a neatly manicured central lawn. You've a choice of sea-facing (₹4500) or super-plush a/c rooms (₹5000), which are like something from a four-star boutique hideaway. The whole place is exceptionally well run, with a popular double-decker bar-restaurant on site, safe lockers, wi-fi and pair of friendly Weimeraner hounds. ₹3500

Cozy Nook North end of the beach, near the island ☎ 0832 264 3550, ⏻ cozynookgoa.com. One of the most attractive set-ups in Goa, comprising bamboo huts in three styles. The nicest are the Robinson Crusoe-esque Deluxe options (₹3500), which have two storeys, with a chillout floor on top and bedroom below. The Sea Facing ones (₹3000) are ramshackle and jazzy, decked out in Rajasthani furniture; the

Semi Deluxe (₹2500) only have upper-floor rooms. Opening onto the lagoon on one side and the beach on the other, the site occupies a prime spot at the scenic north end of the bay. ₹2500

Dream Catcher North end of the beach behind Cozy Nook ☎ 0832 264 4873 or ☎ 9822 137446, ⏻ dreamcatcher.in. Individually styled, very glam Keralan-style huts in a neatly swept sandy compound, with more space, better mattresses, nicer textiles, bigger windows and sturdier foundations than most, in a plum position by the riverside. There's also a shaded yoga *shala* for classes, and a "chillout-ambient bar". Prices are on the high side, to say the least (₹3000–7000 depending on the category of hut), but so are the standards. ₹3000

Konggo Ourem ☎ 9422 059217 or ☎ 9764 267511. The most interesting huts currently on offer in Palolem,

12

ingeniously constructed around cliffs and rocks in a beautiful tropical garden alive with birds and butterflies, just behind the far south end of the beach. The larger ones (₹2000–3000) are huge, with long, deep decks, and plenty of room to do yoga and even cook your own meals while the bathrooms have proper plumbing. And they're good value given the great location. **₹2000**

Neptune's Point South Palolem ☎9822 584968 or ☎9764 686555, ✆neptunepoint.com. *Neptune's* occupies the sweet spot atop the boulder headland dividing Palolem and Patnem, and its huts, stacked up on the hillside under giant coconut palms, make the most of the stupendous views. They're basic by today's standards, but comfortable enough, and having the sea on three sides is a unique selling point. The only downside is the *Silent Noise* disco and movie evenings (see opposite), held on the premises twice weekly, which bring in big crowds. **₹1500**

Oceanic Tembi Waddo ☎0832 264 3059, ✆hotel-oceanic.com. A 10min walk inland from the beach (and also reachable via the backroad to Chaudi), *Oceanic* is owned and managed by a resident British couple. Its marble-floored rooms are stylishly designed, fresh, cool and relaxing, with large mosquito nets, blockprinted bedspreads and bedside lamps. There's also a pool on a forested patio behind, and a quality restaurant. **₹3250**

★ **Ordo Sounsar** Far northern end of Palolem beach, on the far side of the creek (look for the rickety footbridge to the right as you head for the island) ☎9822 488769 & ☎9422 639497, ✆ordosounsar.com. Run by a hospitable brother-and-sister team, Serafin and Shelly, this is Palolem's most idyllic hut camp, tucked away on the tranquil side of the river. The huts themselves are a generous size and comfortable, with great sit-outs to lounge on and funky thatched roofs; and there's an excellent restaurant. **₹1500**

Sevas Far southern end of the beach, on the hill dividing Palolem from Colom ☎0832 264 3977 or ☎9422 065437, ✆sevaspalolemgoa.com. Beautiful "ethnic" cabañas sporting traditional rice-straw roofs, mud-and-dung floors, hygienic squat-style loos and bucket baths. The huts come in two sizes: standard (₹1500) and deluxe (₹2500). They also offer massages and yoga classes, and there's a pleasant restaurant serving very good thalis for ₹200. **₹1500**

The Village House #196, near Government High School ☎0832 264 5767 or ☎9960 487627, ✆villageguesthousegoa.com. This British-run boutique guesthouse, on the fringes of Palolem a 10min walk from the beach, is the most comfortable and stylish place to stay in the area. Furnished with four-posters and vibrant silk bed covers, the a/c rooms are large – and the designer bathrooms palatial. A shady rear garden serves as a common breakfast area, and you can take your drinks out onto the veranda in the evenings. **₹3500**

EATING

Palolem's **restaurants** reflect the cosmopolitan make-up of its visitors. Each year, a fresh batch of innovative, ever more stylish places opens, many of them managed by expats.

Café Inn Pundalik Gaitondi Rd. The best coffee in Palolem, made with a proper Italian coffee machine by an Israeli duo. They get packed out for breakfast, and have a small but eclectic menu, including tasty shakshuka, smoked chicken pastrami sandwiches (₹150), tortilla wraps, BBQ prawn kebabs (₹250–350), cakes and pastries. The best reason to come here, though, is the legendary chocolate-espresso pie (₹100). Daily 10am–11pm.

Casa Fiesta Pundalik Gaitondi Rd. Popular place on the main drag, offering an appetizing menu of world cuisine: hummus, Greek salad, wood-oven baked pizzas, Mexican specialities and fish *pollichatu*; mains (mostly under ₹300) come with delicious roast potatoes. Daily 8.30am–11pm.

Dropadi Beachfront. This place enjoys both a top location and Palolem's best Indian chef, who specializes in rich, creamy Mughlai dishes and tandoori fish. Go for the superb *murg makhini*, crab masala with spinach, or tandoori jumbo prawns in basil sauce. Most main courses ₹200–350. Daily noon–11pm.

Magic Italy Beach Rd. On the busy approach to the seafront, this is south Goa's number-one Italian restaurant, serving home-made ravioli and tagliatelle, along with scrumptious wood-fired pizzas (₹150–300). Daily noon–11pm.

Old Palolem Café (Maria & Michael's) On lane running behind south side of beach. Great cheap eats in old Goan style, served at a no-frills roadside joint behind the beach huts. Pull up a plastic chair and tuck into a tin-plate thalis (veg and non-veg; ₹50/₹75), samosas (₹10) or patties (₹10). Daily 10am–8pm.

Ordo Sounsar Far northern end of Palolem beach. With most places using frozen fish instead of fresh these days, this laidback restaurant, on a terrace in a hut camp of the same name, is something special. Seasonal Goan seafood and vegetarian dishes are their specialities: pomfret stuffed with green chilli; papaya curry in coconut juice; green-pea *xacuti*; prawn *balchao*; shark *ambotik*; white cabbage in lime dressing – all made with the choicest and freshest ingredients. Count on ₹350–500 for two courses. Daily 8.30am–late.

★ **Ourem 88** On lane running behind south side of beach (behind Rococo Pelton Bar) ☎8698 827679. Tiny garden restaurant run by Brit expats Jodie and Brett, serving cleverly thought-out Euro gastro dishes made from fresh local ingredients. Try their superb steak with béarnaise sauce, melt-in-the-mouth chicken Kiev or oven-baked barramundi filet in a herb and parmesan crust,

leaving room for the divine pear and apple torte. Absolutely the finest dining in Palolem, prices are reasonable given the quality of the cuisine (around ₹750 for three courses, not including drinks). Tues–Sun 6pm–late.

DRINKING AND NIGHTLIFE

As with everywhere else in Goa, the ubiquitous 10pm amplified music ban is strictly observed in Palolem, although one crew has found a way of circumventing the rule.

Alpha Bar Behind the south side of the beach. An offshoot of *Silent Noise* which (silently) cranks up midweek with a similar mix of house, electro and hip-hop. Headphones cost ₹400. Thurs 9.30pm–late.

Neptune's Point South side of beach. A dreamy location for a sundowner, and on Weds they screen movies, which you can watch while enjoying a mojito from the bar. Admission free and drinks won't break the bank. Daily 11am–late.

Silent Noise Neptune's Point ⓦ silentnoise.in. On the rocky promontory at the far south end of the bay, the *Silent Noise* collective stages weekly headphone parties on Saturday nights (₹600), where the music is broadcast digitally to individual headsets instead of through PAs. You've a choice of house, electro and big beats mixes on three separate channels, synced with live AV screens, lights and lasers, and of course there's a dreamy view through the palm trees of India's most beautiful beach. Sat 9pm–4am.

DIRECTORY

Exchange Several agents in Palolem are licensed to change money; LKP Forex in the *Palolem Beach Resort* offers competitive rates. Sai Baba International, Sun Moon Travel and Rainbow Travels on the main street all do cash advances against Visa and MasterCard. The nearest ATM (for Visa and MasterCard withdrawals) is at the Corporation Bank in Chaudi (south end of the village on the main street).

Doctor Dr Sandheep, at the private Dhavalikar Hospital (ⓣ 0832 264 3147), 2km out of Palolem at Devabag on the road to Agonda.

Internet cafés Bliss Travel, on the left near the main entrance to the beach; ₹40/hr for the village's fastest broadband lines. Go armed with an extra layer – the a/c's fierce.

Pharmacy Palolem's main pharmacy is 1km out of the village on the Chaudi Rd, to your right just after the Agonda turning. It's closed on Sundays, but out of hours you can call at the pharmacist's house immediately behind the shop.

Telephones Bliss Travel (see above) is one of the few surviving IST/STD places in Palolem.

South of Palolem

If the bright lights of Palolem start to lose their allure, wander around the headland to the south, where the Hindu fishing hamlet of **Colom** offers a more sedate scene. The shacks and bar strip resurfaces in earnest once around the next promontory at **Patnem**, but even in peak season the beach here rarely gets packed. Finally, to the south of Patnem, **Rajbag** is a worthwhile destination for a fitness walk, but little more, thanks to the massive luxury resort behind it.

Colom

Once across the creek and boulder-covered spur bounding the south end of Palolem beach, you arrive at **COLOM**, a largely Hindu fishing village scattered around a series of rocky coves. Dozens of long-stay rooms, leaf huts and houses are tucked away under the palm groves and on the picturesque headland running seawards. This is the best place in the village to start an accommodation hunt – the lads at the *Boom Shankar* bar (see p.725) will know of any vacant places – but be warned that most of the rooms here are very basic indeed, with a few exceptions.

Patnem

A string of hut camps and shacks line the of colom beach south, **PATNEM**. The beach, curving for roughly 1km to a steep bluff, is broad, with little shade, and shelves quite steeply at certain phases of the tide, though the undertow rarely gets dangerously strong.

On the headland dividing Patnem from Colom, the **Harmonic Healing & Eco Retreat Centre** (☎8007 198029, ⓦharmonicingoa.com) is the place to come if you need to sort out your body and soul. Wrapped in greenery with panoramic views of the beach, the centre hosts daily yoga, reiki, pilates and Thai massage classes, as well as lessons in Bollywood dance and classical Indian singing (₹350 for drop-ins; ₹1400 for 60min treatment sessions).

Rajbag and beyond

At low tide, you can walk around the bottom of the steep-sided headland dividing Patnem from neighbouring **RAJBAG**, another kilometre-long sweep of white sand. Sadly, its remote feel has been entirely submerged by the massive five-star recently erected on the land behind it – much to the annoyance of the locals, who campaigned for four years to stop the project.

It's possible to press on even further **south from Rajbag** by crossing the Talpona River via a hand-paddled ferry, which usually has to be summoned from the far bank (fix a return price in advance). Once across, a short walk brings you to **Talpona Beach**, backed by low dunes and a line of straggly palms. From here, you can cross the headland at the end of the beach to reach **Galjibag**, a remote white-sand bay that's a protected nesting site for Olive Ridley marine **turtles**. A strong undertow means swimming isn't safe here.

ARRIVAL AND DEPARTURE   SOUTH OF PALOLEM

Patnem's is 1km or so closer to Chaudi than Palolem, and just a short hop from the **Konkan railway station**, and you can travel there directly by **auto-rickshaw** for around ₹75. The same road continues over a low, wooded rise to the turning for Colom. **Buses** also cover this route, starting at the Kadamaba stand at the north end of Chaudi bazaar and dropping passengers at the end of the short lane leading to Patnem beach – the best place to pick up transport back to Chaudi. Auto-rickshaws and taxis for the **return trip** to Chaudi hang around along the beachfront lane.

ACCOMMODATION

April 20 (aka Goyam Bungalows) Patnem ☎9822 685138 or ☎9890 877844, ⓦgoyam.net. Luxury, double-storeyed wooden bungalows painted pretty pastel colours, with tariffs ranging from ₹2500–5000, depending on size and time of year. Partly screened by casuarina trees, each is smartly furnished and fitted with bathrooms, mosquito nets and swings on sea-facing balconies; those at the front are the village's number-one des reses. **₹2500**

Boom Shankar Colom ☎0832 264 4035. Simply furnished, but clean attached rooms on the southern edge of the village, with lots of lounging space and fine views across the cove. They can also help you root out longer-term rentals in houses nearby. **₹1000**

Home Patnem ☎0832 264 3916, ⓦhomeispatnem.com. A chic little expat-run guesthouse, comprising an annexe of attached rooms under Mangalorean tiles, pleasantly decked out with textiles, coconut mats, lampshades and other touches to justify their hefty tariffs. **₹2500**

★ **Laguna Vista** ☎8554 949 8110, ⓔagunavista patnem@gmail.com. Basic but beautifully located thatched huts on their own quiet cove, with fans, loos, comfy mattresses, mozzie nets, fresh towels, safe lockers and perfect sunset views. There's a lovely yoga *shala* on site, a little boutique selling original clothes and jewellery, and a relaxing lounge-resto (see opposite). Run by a team of dynamic young expats, this is a very nicely put together camp and perfect for seclusion with a sociable hang-out on the doorstep. **₹1500**

Namaste Patnem ☎9850 477189. A standout choice among the string of budget traveller camps in Patnem is this dependable, lively budget option, run by the amiable Satay. Rates range from ₹1000–2500 depending on size and comfort of the hut, time of year and how far back you are from the sand; all have individual shower-toilets. **₹1000**

Papaya's Patnem ☎9923 079447, ⓦpapayasgoa.com. A delightfully green oasis, where water is recycled to keep the plants in their prime and power comes from solar panels. The eco-huts have four-posters, thick mattresses, breezy little sitouts and shaggy palm-frond fringes made from locally sourced materials. **₹2500**

EATING AND DRINKING

It's a safe bet you'll spend a few hours each day in one or other of the cafés in Colom or behind Patnem beach, and a couple of commendable places are tucked away just inland.

April 20 North end of Patnem beach ☏ 9673 501912. This swanky beachside restaurant, an offshoot of the popular *Dropadi* in Palolem, does superb seafood prepared in rich north Indian style: crab *makhini*, avocado prawns and tandoori sea bass (₹350–400) are their signature dishes. Daily noon–11pm.

Boom Shankar Colom. *Boom Shankar* does a great range of food – including its perennially popular fresh mozzarella and tomato salads (₹175) – and, with a rear terrace overlooking the bay and gorgeous views, is the perfect place for a sundowner. Daily 11am–late.

Capital Opposite Patnem Chai Shop. It's worth ambling up the lane from the beach for a meal at *Capital*. The roadside location isn't up to much, but they do fantastic salads (₹130–160) and a knockout spinach-mushroom cheeseburger (₹200), to name but two of the healthy, freshly prepared dishes on an extensive multicuisine menu. Daily 8.30am–11pm.

★ **Home** Middle of the beach, Patnem. Patnem's nicest beach café, serving mezzes, freshly baked bread, Swiss röstis, fresh salads (from around ₹175), proper Lavazza espresso and wonderful desserts (banoffee pie, warm apple tart with fresh cream and legendary brownies). It's a

particularly pleasant option for breakfast, with Chopin playing on the sound system and sparrows chirping in the palms. Daily 8am–10.30pm.

Laguna Vista Colom. Full-flavoured, healthy, organic meals made from local ingredients and served on a dreamy terrace with its toes in the waves by a young crew from four continents. The menu's eclectic and international – bruschetta, crunchy salads, chapatti wraps, falafels, Indian dishes and a BBQ (on Fri) – and prices restrained (count on ₹550 for two courses). They lay on live DJs for sunset, starting at 5.30pm, and show movies three nights a week from 7.30pm. Daily 8am–10pm.

Papaya Middle of Patnem beach. Succulent grilled seafood steaks and potato wedges (₹250) are the big hit at *Papaya*, but they also do a roaring trade in zingy Thai curries (₹190) and prawns with more-ish rösti potatoes and mushrooms (₹310). Daily 8am–late.

Patnem Chai Shop At the end of the lane leading from Patem beach, on the corner. The village chai shop is famous hereabouts for its crunchy samosas (₹6), *bhaji pao* (₹20) and delicious tea, attracting as many discerning expats as locals. Daily 8am–9pm.

12

Cotigao Wildlife Sanctuary

The **Cotigao Wildlife Sanctuary**, 10km southeast of Chaudi, was established in 1969 to protect a remote and vulnerable area of forest lining the Goa–Karnataka border. Best visited between October and March, Cotigao is a peaceful and scenic park that makes a pleasant day-trip from Palolem, 12km northwest. Encompassing 86 square kilometres of mixed deciduous woodland, the reserve is certain to inspire tree lovers, but less likely to yield many wildlife sightings: its tigers and leopards were hunted out long ago, while the gazelles, sloth bears, porcupines, panthers and hyenas that allegedly lurk in the woods rarely appear. You do, however, stand a good chance of spotting at least two species of monkey, a couple of wild boar and the odd gaur (the primeval-looking Indian bison), as well as plenty of birdlife.

A network of trails winds from the trailhead 3km beyond the centre to various named sites in the forest, but aren't way-marked and are very hard to follow. It is worth noting that most visitors complain about walking for hours without seeing anything of interest.

ARRIVAL AND DEPARTURE   COTIGAO WILDLIFE SANCTUARY

By bus Any of the buses running south on the NH-17 to Karwar via Chaudi will drop you within 2km of the gates.

However, to explore the inner reaches of the sanctuary, you really need your own transport.

INFORMATION

Interpretative Centre You have to pay your entry fees (₹25, plus ₹100 for a car, ₹25 for a motorbike; ₹50 for a camera permit) at the reserve's small interpretatice centre. The wardens here will show you how to get to a 25m-high treetop watchtower, overlooking a waterhole that attracts a handful of animals around dawn and dusk.

Accommodation You can also stay here at a rather unprepossessing little room (₹250/night), in the compound behind the main reserve gates.

Eating Food and drink may be available by prior arrangement, and there's a shop at the nearest village, 2km inside the park.

Kolkata and West Bengal

THE VICTORIA MEMORIAL AT SUNSET, KOLKATA

13

Kolkata and West Bengal

Unique among Indian states in stretching all the way from the Himalayas to the sea, West Bengal is nonetheless explored in depth by few travellers. That may have something to do with the exaggerated reputation of its capital, Kolkata (Calcutta), a sophisticated and friendly city that belies its popular image as poverty-stricken and chaotic. The rest of Bengal holds an extraordinary assortment of landscapes and cultures, ranging from the dramatic hill station of Darjeeling, within sight of the highest mountains in the world, to the vast mangrove swamps of the Sundarbans, prowled by man-eating Royal Bengal tigers. The narrow central band of the state is cut across by the huge River Ganges as it pours from Bihar into Bangladesh and here the Farrakha Barrage controls the movement of south-flowing channels such as the River Hooghly, the lifeline of Kolkata.

At the height of British rule, in the nineteenth and early twentieth centuries, Bengal flourished both culturally and materially, nurturing a uniquely creative blend of West and East. The **Bengali Renaissance** produced thinkers, writers and artists such as Bankim Chandra Chatterjee and **Rabindranath Tagore**, whose collective influence still permeates Bengali society more than a century later.

Not all of Bengal is Bengali; the current Nepalese-led separatist movement for the creation of an autonomous "Gurkhaland" in the Darjeeling area has focused on sharp differences in culture. Here, the Hindu Nepalese migration eastward from the nineteenth century onwards has largely displaced the indigenous tribal groups of the north, though Lamaist Tibetan Buddhism continues to flourish. In the southwest, on the other hand, tribal groups such as the Santhals and the Mundas still maintain a presence, and itinerant Baul **musicians** continue the region's traditions of song and dance, most often heard around Tagore's university at **Shantiniketan**; Tagore's own musical form, Rabindra Sangeet, is a popular amalgam of influences including folk and classical. Other historical specialities of Bengal include its ornate **terracotta temples**, as seen at Bishnupur, and its **silk** production, concentrated around **Murshidabad**, the state's last independent capital.

Bengal's own brand of Hinduism emphasizes the **mother goddess**, who appears in such guises as the fearsome Kali and Durga, the benign Saraswati, goddess of learning, and Lakshmi, the goddess of wealth. The most mysterious of all is Tara, an echo of medieval links with Buddhism; her temple at **Tarapith** is perhaps the greatest centre of Tantrism in the entire country.

LOCAL FERRY IN SUNDARBANS NATIONAL PARK

Highlights

❶ Victoria Memorial This monument to the British Empire in Kolkata is a dizzying blend of Mughal and Italian architecture. **See p.738**

❷ Eden Gardens Enjoy the chaos and spectacle of a match at Kolkata's famous cricket ground. **See p.740**

❸ Kumartuli Fascinating warren of lanes where artisans model lavish images of goddesses and demons out of straw, clay and pith. **See p.743**

❹ Sundarbans Float through the endless mangrove forests, home to a profusion of wildlife, including the majestic Bengal tiger. **See p.759**

❺ Shantiniketan This tranquil university town exudes the spirit of its founder, the poet and philosopher Rabindranath Tagore. **See p.762**

❻ Darjeeling A charming hill station with spectacular views and famously fine tea. **See p.769**

❼ Singalila Trek This Darjeeling trek features unforgettable mountain vistas, especially beautiful in April and May, when the rhododendrons are in bloom. **See p.777**

❽ Toy Train Take a leisurely journey on this Victorian railway, partly steam-driven, past the tea gardens that carpet the steep hillsides around Darjeeling. **See p.779**

❾ Kalimpong The horticultural capital of the northeast, with quiet walks, orchid nurseries and colourful markets. **See p.781**

HIGHLIGHTS ARE MARKED ON THE MAP ON P.730

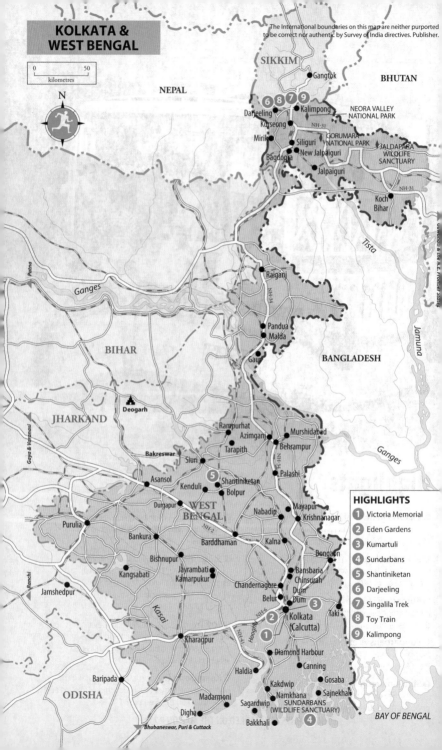

KOLKATA & WEST BENGAL

0   50
kilometres

N

The International boundaries on this map are neither purported to be correct nor authentic by Survey of India directives. Publisher.

SIKKIM
Gangtok
BHUTAN

NEPAL

⑥ ⑧ ⑦ ⑨
Darjeeling • Kalimpong
Kurseong   NEORA VALLEY
Mirik   NATIONAL PARK
Siliguri   GORUMARA
Bagdogra New Jalpaiguri NATIONAL PARK   JALDAPARA
                                         WILDLIFE
                          Jalpaiguri   SANCTUARY
                                    NH-31
                                         Koch
                                         Bihar
                                              Tista

Patna
Ganges
Raiganj
        NH-34
        Pandua
        Malda
Gaur   **BANGLADESH**

BIHAR

JHARKAND
Deogarh

Rampurhat
Azimganj Murshidabad
Tarapith   Behrampur
Bakreswar Siuri   Palashi
Asansol   Kenduli Shantiniketan ⑤
Durgapur   Bolpur
        WEST   Nabadip
Purulia **BENGAL**   Krishnanagar
Bankura   Mayapur
        NH-2
Bishnupur Barddhaman Kalna
                           Bongaon
Kangsabati Jayrambati   Bansbaria
Jamshedpur Kamarpukur Chinsurah
        Chandernagore Dum
Kasai   Belur   Dum ③
                Kolkata   Taki
        ② NH-6 (Calcutta)
Kharagpur   ①
        Hoogly
                Diamond Harbour
Baripada   Canning
Haldia
        Kakdwip Gosaba
ODISHA   Namkhana Sajnekhali
Madarmoni Sagardwip SUNDARBANS
Digha   (WILDLIFE SANCTUARY)
        Bakkhali   ④
Bhubaneswar, Puri & Cuttack   **BAY OF BENGAL**

Gaya & Varanasi
Ranchi
NH-31
Ganges
Jamuna
Darjeeling & the N.E. Frontier States

HIGHLIGHTS

① Victoria Memorial
② Eden Gardens
③ Kumartuli
④ Sundarbans
⑤ Shantiniketan
⑥ Darjeeling
⑦ Singalila Trek
⑧ Toy Train
⑨ Kalimpong

Brief history

Although Bengal was part of the Mauryan Empire during the third century BC, it first came to prominence in its own right under the Guptas in the fourth century AD. So dependent was it on trade with the Mediterranean that the fall of Rome caused a sharp decline, only reversed with the rise of the Pala dynasty in the eighth century.

After a short-lived period of rule by the highly cultured Senas, based at **Gaur**, Bengal was brought under Muslim rule at the end of the twelfth century by the first Sultan of Delhi, Qutb-ud-din-Aibak. Sher Shah Suri, who briefly usurped power from the Mughals in the mid-sixteenth century, developed the infrastructure and built the Grand Trunk Road, running all the way to the Northwest Province on the borders of his native Afghanistan. Akbar reconquered the territory in 1574, before the advent of the Europeans in the eighteenth century.

The Europeans

The Portuguese, who were the first to set up a trading community beside the Hooghly, were soon joined by the British, Dutch, French and many others. Rivalry between them eventually resulted in the ascendancy of the **British**, with the only serious indigenous resistance coming from the tutelary kingdom of **Murshidabad**, led by the young Siraj-ud-Daula. His attack on the fledgling British community of Calcutta in 1756 culminated in the infamous **Black Hole** incident (see box, p.740), when British prisoners suffocated to death. Vengeance, in the form of a British army from Madras under **Robert Clive**, arrived a year later. The defeat of Siraj-ud-Daula at the **Battle of Plassey** paved the way for British domination of the entire Subcontinent. Bengal became the linchpin of the British East India Company and its lucrative trading empire, until the company handed over control to the Crown in 1858.

Bengal today

Up to 1905, Bengal encompassed Orissa (Odisha) and Bihar; it was then split down the middle by Lord Curzon, leaving East Bengal and Assam on one side and Orissa, Bihar and West Bengal on the other. The move aroused bitter resentment, and the rift it created between Hindus and Muslims was a direct cause of the second Partition, in 1947, when East Bengal became East Pakistan. During the war with Pakistan in the early 1970s that resulted in the creation of an independent **Bangladesh**, up to ten million refugees fled into West Bengal. Shorn of its provinces, and with the capital moved from Calcutta to Delhi in 1911, the story of West Bengal in the twentieth century was largely a chronicle of decline.

The state's political life has been dominated by a protracted – and sometimes violent – struggle between the **Congress** and in recent years, the breakaway **Trinamool Congress**, against the major left-wing parties: the Marxist Communist Party of India, or **CPI(M)**, and the Marxist-Leninist **Naxalites** (Communist Party of India (ML)). In the 1960s and 1970s, the latter launched an abortive but bloody attempt at revolution. Bolstered by a strong rural base, the CPI(M) and allies emerged victorious in 1977 under the enigmatic Jyoti Basu (d.2010), weathering the collapse of world communism, and heralding the decades-long dominance by the **Left Front**. This long dominance by the CPI(M) came to a dramatic end in 2011, when the firebrand politician, **Mamata Banerjee**, who had honed her political skills supporting the oppressed poor in two notorious campaigns against industrialization, swept to power. While she inherited a state of political and industrial turmoil, **Didi**, or "Sister" as she is commonly known, has yet to redress the imbalance in the infrastructure and there are many who feel that she has been neither able to transend the grassroots struggle that brought her to prominence, nor to comprehend the complexities of what was once, and still is, a dynamic industrial powerhouse.

In Kolkata – booming with expatriate wealth and a surge in business confidence – political turmoil can seem a world away. Meanwhile in the north of the state, ethnic

13

political groups are calling for autonomy from Bengal. The fabric and future shape of the current state is by no means certain.

Kolkata (Calcutta)

One of the four great urban centres of India, **KOLKATA** is, to its proud citizens, the equal of any city in the country in charm, variety and interest. As the showpiece capital of the British Raj, it was the greatest colonial city of the Orient, and descendants of the fortune-seekers who flocked from across the globe to participate in its eighteenth- and nineteenth-century trading boom remain conspicuous in its cosmopolitan blend of communities. Despite this, there has been a recent rise in Bengali nationalism, which has resulted in the renaming of Calcutta as Kolkata (the Bengali pronunciation and official new name). This has yet to be universally embraced – leading English-language paper *The Telegraph* continues to use Calcutta.

Since Indian Independence, mass migrations of dispossessed refugees caused by twentieth-century upheavals within the Subcontinent have tested the city's infrastructure to the limit. The resultant suffering – and the work of Mother Teresa in drawing attention to its most helpless victims – has given Kolkata a reputation for poverty that its residents consider ill-founded. They argue that the city's problems – the continuing influx of refugees notwithstanding – are no longer as acute as those of Mumbai or other cities across the world. In fact, though Kolkata's mighty Victorian buildings stand peeling and decaying, and its central avenues are choked with traffic, the city exudes a warmth and buoyancy that leaves few visitors unmoved. Kolkata is expanding rapidly, with shopping malls, restaurants and satellite towns springing up all around the city. The downside of all this development, however, partly resulting from the huge increase in traffic, is some of the worst air pollution in the world, with some of the most chaotic road systems in the country.

In terms of the city's cultural life, Kolkata's Bengalis exude a pride in their artistic heritage and like to see themselves as the **intelligentsia** of India. The city is home to a multitude of **galleries** and huge Indian classical music festivals, with a thriving Bengali-language **theatre** scene and a cinematic tradition brought world renown by director Satyajit Ray.

Visitors still experience Kolkata first and foremost as a colonial city with the chief bastion of imperialism at its heart – the **Writers' Building**, the seat of state government – little changed over the decades. Grand edifices in a profusion of styles litter the old city and several venerable Raj institutions continue to survive, such as the racecourse, the reverence for cricket and several exclusive gentlemen's clubs. Kolkata's crumbling, weather-beaten buildings and anarchic streets can create an intimidating first impression. With time and patience, though, this huge metropolis unravels its secrets, providing a fascinating conglomerate of styles and influences. The **River Hooghly**, spanned by the remarkable cantilever Howrah Bridge, is not all that prominent in the life of the city. Instead its heart is the green expanse of the **Maidan**, which attracts locals from all walks of life for recreation, sports, exhibitions and political rallies. At its southern end stands the white marble **Victoria Memorial**, and close by rise the tall Gothic spires of **St Paul's Cathedral**. Next to the busy **New Market** area looms the eclectic **Indian Museum** housing one of the largest collections in Asia, ranging from natural history to art and archeology. Further north, the district centred on BBD Bagh is filled with reminders of the heyday of the East India Company, dominated by the bulk of the **Writers' Building**, built in 1780 to replace the original structure that housed the clerks or "writers" of the East India Company; nearby stand **St Andrew's Kirk** and the pillared immensity of the **GPO**. The city's old **Chinatown**, a short walk north of BBD Bagh, is a sad reminder of a once flourishing community, while on the edge of the frenetic, labyrinthine markets of **Barabazaar**, **synagogues** and the **Armenian church** are remnants of a once thriving cosmopolitan trade. The renowned temple of **Kalighat** is away to the south. Across the river, south of the marvellous **Howrah railway station**, lies the tranquillity of the **Botanical Gardens**.

Kolkata's **climate** is at its best during its short winter (Nov–Feb), when the daily maximum temperature hovers around 27°C, and the markets are filled with vegetables and flowers. Before the monsoons, the heat hangs unbearably heavily; the arrival of the rains in late June brings relief, but usually also floods that turn the streets into a quagmire. After a brief period of post-monsoon high temperatures, October and November are quite pleasant; this is the time of the city's biggest festival, **Durga Puja**.

THE FESTIVALS OF KOLKATA

Most of Kolkata's Hindu festivals are devoted to forms of the mother goddess, **Shakti**. **Kali**, the black goddess, a consort of Shiva, is most commonly depicted with four arms, standing on the prostrate Shiva after killing the demon Raktvirya, her tongue protruding in horror. A symbol of victory over evil, ten-armed **Durga** is shown sitting on a lion slaying the demon Mahisasura who assumed the shape of a buffalo. She has no temple but the two-week **Durga Puja** (Sept/Oct) is Kolkata's most lavish festival.

During the festivals images of the goddesses are placed in elaborate marquees called *pandals*. Supported by large donations and the local communities, *pandals* block off small streets for days. After the puja, the images are taken to the river for immersion, a colourful scene that's best viewed from one of the boat cruises offered by the West Bengal tourist office (see p.748). Following immersion, the images are fished out with cranes to avoid pollution caused by the materials and paints used in the statuary. *Pandals* worth visiting during Durga Puja, besides the popular one at Kumartuli, include those at Mohammed Ali Park near Chittaranjan Avenue, MG Marg crossing and nearby College Square. Baghbazar's *pandal* is the city's oldest and renowned for its simple elegance.

THE MAJOR FESTIVALS

Jaidev Mela (early Jan) Baul minstrels gather to commemorating Joydeb, the revered author of the *Gita Govinda*, held in the village of Kenduli, near Shantiniketan.

Ganga Sagar Mela (mid-Jan) During the winter solstice of Makar Sankranti, thousands of Hindu pilgrims and sadhus gather for a three-day festival at Sagardwip, 150km south where the Ganges meets the sea.

Dover Lane Music Festival (Jan/Feb) A week-long festival in south Kolkata, attracting many of the country's best musicians.

Saraswati Puja (Jan/Feb) Popular and important festival, dedicated to the goddess of learning and staged throughout Bengal.

Chinese New Year (Jan/Feb) Celebrated with a week-long festival of dragon dances, firecrackers and fine food, concentrated around Chinatown and the suburb of Tangra.

Muharram (dates determined by the lunar calendar; see ⓦwhen-is.com) Shi'ite Muslims mark the anniversary of the martyrdom of Hussein by severe penance, including processions during which they flagellate themselves.

Durga Puja (Sept/Oct) At the onset of winter, Durga Puja (known elsewhere as Dussehra) is the Bengali equivalent of Christmas. It climaxes on Mahadashami, the tenth day, when the images are immersed in the river.

Lakshmi Puja (Oct/Nov) Held five days after Mahadashami on the full moon, to honour the goddess of wealth.

Id ul Fitr (dates determined by the lunar calendar; see ⓦwhen-is.com) Celebrating the end of the fasting month of Ramadan and heralded by the new moon, this joyous festival features wonderful food at the restaurants and stalls around Park Circus.

Diwali and Kali Puja (Oct/Nov) Kali Puja is held on a moonless night when goats are sacrificed, and coincides with Diwali, the festival of light.

Christmas (Dec 25) Park Street and New Market are adorned with fairy lights and the odd Christmas tree. Plum pudding is sold, and Midnight Mass is well attended.

Poush Mela (late Dec) Held in Shantiniketan around Christmas, the *mela* brings in Bauls, the wandering minstrels who attract large audiences.

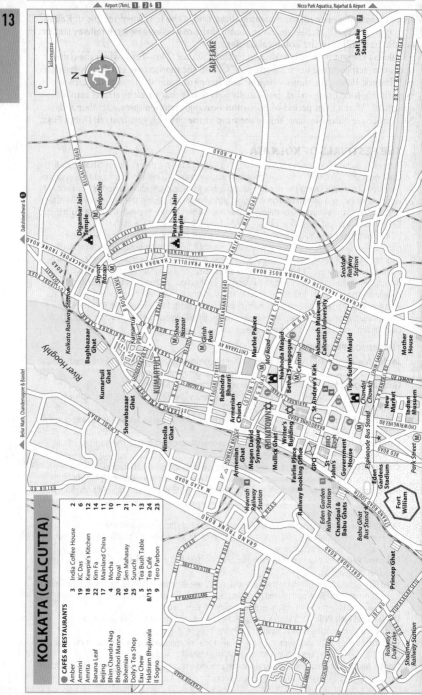

KOLKATA (CALCUTTA)

CAFÉS & RESTAURANTS

Amber	3	India Coffee House	2
Ammini	19	KC Das	6
Amrita	18	Kewpie's Kitchen	12
Banana Leaf	22	Kim Fa	14
Beijing	17	Mainland China	11
Bhim Chandra Nag	4	Mocha	10
Bhojohori Manna	20	Royal	1
Bohemian	16	Sen Mahasay	21
Dolly's Tea Shop	25	Suruchi	7
Eau Chew	5	Tea Bush Table	13
Haldiram Bhujiwala	8/15	Tea Café	24
Il Sogno	9	Tero Parbon	23

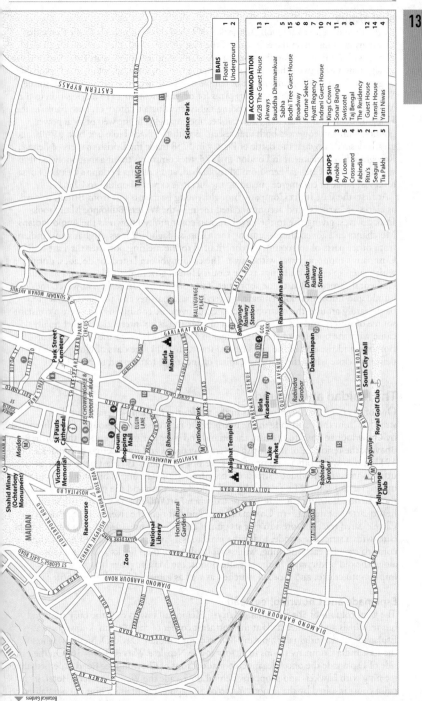

■ **BARS**

| Floatel | 1 |
| Underground | 2 |

■ **ACCOMMODATION**

66/2B The Guest House	13
Airways	1
Bauddha Dharmankuar Sabha	5
Bodhi Tree Guest House	15
Broadway	6
Fortune Select	7
Hyatt Regency	10
Indrani Guest House	2
Kings Crown	3
Sonar Bangla	11
Swissotel	3
Taj Bengal	9
The Residency	12
Transit House	14
Yatri Niwas	4

● **SHOPS**

Anokhi	3
By Loom	5
Crossword	4
Fabindia	5
Ritu's	2
Seagull	1
Tia Pakhi	5

13

Brief history

By the time the remarkable **Job Charnock** established the headquarters of the **East India Company** at **Sutanuti** on the east bank of the Hooghly in 1690, the riverside was already dotted with trading communities from European countries. A few years later, Sutanuti was amalgamated with two other villages to form the town of **Calcutta**, whose name probably originated from *kalikutir*, the house or temple of Kali (a reference to the **Kalighat** shrine). With trading success came ambitious plans for development; in 1715 a delegation to the Mughal court in Delhi negotiated trading rights, creating a territory on both banks of the Hooghly of around 15km long. Later, it became entangled in the web of local power politics, with consequences both unforeseen, as with the Black Hole (see box, p.740), and greatly desired, as when the Battle of Plassey in 1758 made the British masters of Bengal. Recognized by Parliament in London in 1773, the company's trading monopoly led it to shift the capital of Bengal here from Murshidabad, and Calcutta became a clearing house for a vast range of commerce, including the lucrative export of opium to China.

At first, the East India Company brought young bachelors out from Britain to work as clerks or "writers" and accommodated them in the **Writers' Building**. Many took Indian wives, giving rise to the new Eurasian community known as the **Anglo-Indians**. Merchants and adventurers – among them Parsis, Baghdadi Jews, Afghans and Indians from other parts of the country – contributed to the melting pot after the East India Company's monopoly was withdrawn. The ensuing boom lasted for decades, during which such splendid buildings as the Court House, government House and St Paul's Cathedral earned Calcutta the sobriquet "City of Palaces". In reality, however, the humid and uncomfortable climate, putrefying salt marshes and the hovels that grew haphazardly around the metropolis created unhygienic conditions that were a constant source of misery and disease. The death of Calcutta as an international port finally came with the opening of the Suez Canal in 1869, which led to the emergence of Bombay, and the end of the city's opium trade. In 1911, the days of glory drew to a definitive close when the imperial capital of India was transferred to New Delhi.

The Maidan and around

One of the largest city-centre parks in the world, the **Maidan** – literally "field" – stretches from the Esplanade in the north to the racecourse in the south, and is bordered by **Chowringhee Road** to the east, the Strand and river to the west and to the north, **Raj Bhavan**, the residence of the British governor-generals and the viceroys of India until 1911 and now the official home of the governor of Bengal. This vast open area stands in utter contrast to the chaotic streets of the surrounding city, and is big enough to swallow up several clubs, including the Calcutta Ladies Golf Club and the immaculate greens of the Calcutta Bowling Club. It was created when **Fort William**, now home to the military headquarters of the Eastern Command, was laid out near the river in 1758; Robert Clive cleared tracts of forest to give its guns a clear line of fire. Originally a haven for the elite, with a strict dress code, today the maidan is a favourite spot for ordinary citizens to come to exercise each morning, while shepherds graze their flocks and riders canter along the old bridleways. In the late afternoons, the Maidan plays host to scores of impromptu cricket and football matches, as well as games of kabadi (see p.56).

Esplanade and Chowringhee Road

The 46m column of **Shahid Minar** (Martyrs' Memorial) towers over the busy tram and bus terminals and market stalls at the northeast corner of the Maidan, known here as Esplanade. It was originally built in 1828 to commemorate David Ochterlony, who led the East India Company troops to victory in the Nepalese Wars of 1814–16. On the east side of Esplanade the once-elegant colonnaded front of **Chowringhee Road** is perpetually teeming with hawkers and shoppers. Behind the facade the Victorian **Grand Hotel**, its palm court inspired by the famous *Raffles* of Singapore, maintains a hint of colonialism.

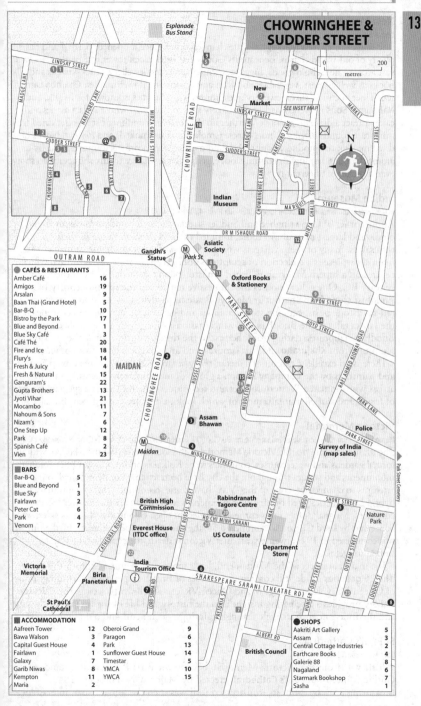

CHOWRINGHEE & SUDDER STREET

13

Esplanade Bus Stand

New Market

SEE INSET MAP

Indian Museum

Gandhi's Statue

Asiatic Society

Oxford Books & Stationery

Assam Bhawan

Maidan

Police

Survey of India (map sales)

Park Street Cemetery

British High Commission

Rabindranath Tagore Centre

Everest House (ITDC office)

US Consulate

Department Store

Nature Park

Victoria Memorial

Birla Planetarium

India Tourism Office

St Paul's Cathedral

British Council

● CAFÉS & RESTAURANTS	
Amber Café	16
Amigos	19
Arsalan	9
Baan Thai (Grand Hotel)	5
Bar-B-Q	10
Bistro by the Park	17
Blue and Beyond	1
Blue Sky Café	3
Café Thé	20
Fire and Ice	18
Flury's	14
Fresh & Juicy	4
Fresh & Natural	15
Ganguram's	22
Gupta Brothers	13
Jyoti Vihar	21
Mocambo	11
Nahoum & Sons	7
Nizam's	6
One Step Up	12
Park	8
Spanish Café	2
Vien	23

■ BARS	
Bar-B-Q	5
Blue and Beyond	1
Blue Sky	3
Fairlawn	2
Peter Cat	6
Park	4
Venom	7

■ ACCOMMODATION			
Aafreen Tower	12	Oberoi Grand	9
Bawa Walson	3	Paragon	6
Capital Guest House	4	Park	13
Fairlawn	1	Sunflower Guest House	14
Galaxy	7	Timestar	5
Garib Niwas	8	YMCA	10
Kempton	11	YWCA	15
Maria	2		

● SHOPS	
Aakriti Art Gallery	5
Assam	3
Central Cottage Industries	2
Earthcare Books	4
Galerie 88	8
Nagaland	6
Starmark Bookshop	7
Sasha	1

13

New Market
Lindsay St

The single-storey **New Market** has little changed inside since it opened in 1874 and has plenty of old-world charm. Beneath its Gothic red-brick clock tower, the market stocks a vast array of household goods, luggage, garments, textiles, jewellery, knick-knacks and books as well as meat, vegetables and fruit and a booming flower market. **Chamba Lama** sells Tibetan curios, silver jewellery and bronzes while **Sujata's** is known for its silk, and **Nahoum & Sons** is a renowned Jewish bakery and confectioner whose rolls, pastries and cakes attract a die-hard clientele. Further up the corridor, condiment stalls offer dried fruit, miniature rounds of salty Bandel cheese (smoked and unsmoked) and *amshat*, blocks of dried mango; the produce, poultry, fish and meat market nearby is unmistakeable by its aroma. Coolies, hoping for commission, eagerly offer assistance to any shopper who shows even a flicker of uncertainty.

Indian Museum
At the corner of Chowringhee and Sudder streets • Tues–Sun 10am–4.30pm • ₹150 (₹10)

At the corner of Chowringhee and Sudder streets, the stately **Indian Museum** is the oldest and largest museum in India, founded in 1814. Visitors come in their thousands, many of them villagers who call it the *jadu ghar* or "house of magic". The main showpiece is a collection of **sculptures** obtained from sites all over India, which centres on a superb Mauryan polished-sandstone **lion capital** dating from the third century BC. One gallery houses the impressive remains of the second-century BC Buddhist **stupa from Bharhut** in Madhya Pradesh, partly reassembled to display the red-sandstone posts, capping stones, railings and gateways. Carvings depict scenes from the Jataka tales of the Buddha's many incarnations. Along with a huge collection of Buddhist sculptures, dating from the first to the third centuries, you'll also see stone sculpture from **Khajuraho** and Pala bronzes, and archeological finds from other sites.

There is an excellent exhibit of Tibetan *thangkas* and Kalighat *pat* (see box, p.744) and paintings by the **Company School**, a group of mid-nineteenth-century Indian artists who emulated Western themes and techniques. Finally, there's a spectacular array of fossils and stuffed animals, most of which look in dire need of a decent burial.

Victoria Memorial
Memorial Tues–Sun 10am–5pm, closed 2nd Sat of the month • ₹150 (₹10) **Gardens** Daily 5.30am–7pm • ₹4 • ⓦ victoriamemorial-cal.org

The dramatic white marble **Victoria Memorial** at the southern end of the Maidan, with its formal gardens and watercourses, continues to be Kolkata's pride and joy. Other colonial monuments and statues throughout the city have been renamed or demolished, but attempts to change the name of the "VM" have come to nothing. This extraordinary hybrid building designed by Sir William Emerson, with Italianate statues over its entrances, Mughal domes in its corners, and elegant open colonnades along its sides, was conceived by Lord Curzon to commemorate the empire at its peak, though by the time it was completed in 1921, twenty years after Victoria's death, the capital of the Raj had shifted to Delhi.

The main entrance, at the Maidan end, leads into a tall chamber beneath the dome. The 25 **galleries** inside still contain mementoes of British imperialism including statues of Queen Mary, King George V and Queen Victoria. Well worth seeing, the **Calcutta Gallery** provides a fascinating insight into the history and life of the Indians of the city and the Independence struggle through paintings, documents and old photographs.

St Paul's Cathedral
Daily 9am–noon & 3–6pm

A little way from the Victoria Memorial, beyond the Birla Planetarium, stands the Gothic edifice of **St Paul's Cathedral**, erected by Major W.N. Forbes in 1847. Measuring 75m by 24m, its iron-trussed roof was then the longest span in existence.

13

For improved ventilation, the lancet windows inside extend to plinth level, and tall fans hang from the ceiling. The most outstanding of the many well-preserved memorials and plaques to long-perished imperialists is the stained glass of the west window, designed by Sir Edward Burne-Jones in 1880 to honour Lord Mayo, assassinated in the Andaman Islands. The original steeple was destroyed in the 1897 earthquake; after a second earthquake in 1934 it was remodelled on the Bell Harry Tower at Canterbury Cathedral.

The Academy of Fine Arts
Cathedral Rd • Daily 3–8pm • Free

South of the cathedral, the **Academy of Fine Arts** is a showcase for Bengali contemporary arts. As well as temporary exhibitions, it holds permanent displays of the work of artists such as Jamini Roy and Rabindranath Tagore (see box, p.763). A café and pleasant grounds enhance the ambience.

The Cultural Centre: Rabindra Sadan, Nandan and Sisir Mancha
1 AJC Rd • Daily 9am–8pm

Immediately south of the Academy of Fine Arts, the Cultural Centre features the large auditorium of **Rabindra Sadan** which, occasionally and especially in winter, features programmes of Indian classical music. Next door, **Nandan**, designed by Satyajit Ray, is a lively film centre (see p.755) and pays homage to the rich tradition of Bengal's filmmaking. Also within the complex, Bengali theatre is celebrated with its own auditorium, **Sisir Mancha**.

Park Street

Renamed by the CPI(M) as Mother Teresa Sarani – though few if any city folk use this name – **Park Street** is packed with restaurants, cafés and bars and has long been the hub of cosmopolitan and hedonistic Calcutta. Once famous for its live music, including a renowned jazz club now sadly gone, the western or Maidan end of the strip continues to support some of the liveliest nightlife in the city. The street also has been important in the history of the city, housing the Asiatic Society, the Survey of India and the iconic Raj-era monoliths of the Park Street Cemetery.

Asiatic Society
1 Park St • **Reading Room** Mon–Fri 10am–8pm, Sat 10am–5pm • Free

Close to Chowringhee Road, the **Asiatic Society**, established in 1784 by Orientalists including Sir William Jones, houses a huge collection of around 150,000 books and 60,000 manuscripts, some dating back to the seventh century. The society has a **reading room** open to the public as well as a **gallery** of art and antiquities that holds paintings by Rubens and Reynolds, a large coin collection and one of Ashoka's stone edicts.

Park Street Cemetery
Around 2km east along Park St from the Maidan • Mon–Fri 7.30am–4.30pm, Sat 7.30–11am • Donation or buy guide pamphlet ₹100

The disused **Park Street Cemetery** is one of the city's most haunting memorials to its imperial past. Inaugurated in 1767, it is the oldest in Kolkata, holding a wonderful concentration of pyramids, obelisks, pavilions, urns and headstones, beneath which many well-known figures from the Raj lie buried including Sir William Jones of the Asiatic Society. The epitaphs make poignant reading.

Central Kolkata

The commercial and administrative hub of both Kolkata and West Bengal is **BBD Bagh**, which die-hard Kolkatans still refer to as **Dalhousie Square**. The new official name, in a

13

THE BLACK HOLE OF CALCUTTA

Built in 1868 on the site of the original Fort William – destroyed by Siraj-ud-Daula in 1756 – the **GPO** on the west side of the square hides the supposed site of the **Black Hole of Calcutta**. On a hot June night in 1756, 146 English prisoners were forced by Siraj-ud-Daula's guards into a tiny chamber with only the smallest of windows for ventilation; most had suffocated to death by the next morning. By all accounts, the guards were unaware of the tragedy unfolding and, on hearing the news, Siraj-ud-Daula was deeply repentant. A memorial to the victims that formerly stood in front of the Writers' Building was moved in 1940 to the grounds of St John's Church, south of the GPO.

---

fine piece of irony, commemorates three revolutionaries hanged for trying to kill Lieutenant-Governor General Lord Dalhousie.

Beyond the headquarters of Eastern Railways on Netaji Subhash Road, you come to the heart of Kolkata's **commercial district**, clustered around the Calcutta Stock Exchange at the corner of Lyon's Range, which started out as a gathering of traders under a neem tree in the 1830s. The warren of buildings, houses all sorts of old colonial trading companies, including some still bearing Scottish names.

St John's Church

Daily 8am–5pm • ₹10

Of the eighteenth- and nineteenth-century British **churches** dotted around Central Kolkata, the most interesting is **St John's** just south of the GPO. Erected in 1787, it houses memorials to British residents, along with an impressive painting of *The Last Supper* by Johann Zoffany, in which prominent Calcuttans are depicted as apostles. In the grounds, Kolkata's oldest graveyard holds the tomb of **Job Charnock**, the city's founding father, who earned eternal notoriety for marrying a Hindu girl he saved from the funeral pyre of her first husband; he is one of the few colonialists still cherished amongst Bengalis.

Eden Gardens

Daily dawn–dusk • Free

Eden Gardens, the imposing site of the world-famous **cricket** ground (officially known as the **Ranji Stadium**), lies near the river close to Chandpal Ghat and has been described as the "Coliseum of Cricket". Watching a test match here is an unforgettable experience as the 100,000-seat stadium resounds to the roar of the crowd. Next to the stadium, towards the river, the pleasant palm-fringed **gardens** are a picture of tranquillity with a **Burmese pagoda** set against a little lake.

The Synagogues of BethEl and Magen David

Pollock St and Synagogue St (both off Brabourne Rd) • Sun–Thurs 10am–5pm • Gain permission from Nahoums Bakery in New Market who will arrange a guide to visit either of the synagogues

Now protected monuments, a short distance north of BBD Bagh and on the edge of Barabazaar (see opposite), the **synagogues** of **BethEl** and **Magen David** are reminders of the once flourishing community that played such an important role in the commercial life of the city. While the Jewish community has all but disappeared from Kolkata, the two synagogues remain lovingly preserved. Buried in the heart of a busy electrical goods market, BethEl's exterior, emblazoned with the Star of David, hides an immaculate, lofty hall with aisles awaiting a lost congregation. A short distance away, Magen David's church-like appearance is similar. Both feature striking stained glass, common throughout the synagogues of India.

North Kolkata

The amorphous area of **north Kolkata**, long part of the "native" town rather than the European sectors of the "white town", was where the city's prosperous nineteenth-century

KOLKATA GALLERIES

Bengal has a lively tradition of contemporary art, and with increased prosperity and speculation in fine art, galleries showing a high standard of work are burgeoning throughout the city. Exhibitions are listed in *The Telegraph*'s Sunday supplement *Graphiti* and *Explocity*, a free listings magazine available at the tourist office and some hotels. Besides the Academy of Fine Arts and the Ashutosh Museum, the following are worth checking out.

Aakriti Art Gallery 1st floor, Orbit Enclave, 12 3A, Picasso Bithi, Hungerford St ☎033 2289 3027, ⓦaakritiartgallery.com. A well-presented modern Indian art gallery with big-name exhibitions and a shop. Mon–Sat noon–7pm.

Birla Academy of Art and Culture 108 Southern Ave ☎033 2466 2843, ⓦbirlaart.com. Ancient and modern art with regular exhibitions of contemporary Indian artists. Tues–Sun 4–7pm.

Galerie 88 28-B Shakespeare Sarani ☎033 2290 2274, ⓦgalerie88.in. Private gallery showing contemporary Indian paintings plus specialist exhibitions and some big names. Also stocks art supplies. Mon–Sat 10am–7pm.

Rabindranath Tagore Centre ICCR, 9A Ho Chi Minh Sarani ☎033 2287 2680, ⓦtagorecentreiccr .org. Art and craft exhibitions in this government-run, cultural establishment with a number of galleries and auditoria. Mon–Sat 10am–7pm.

Bengali families created their little palaces, or *raj baris*, many of which are now in advanced and fascinating states of decay.

Barabazaar

North of BBD Bagh, the area known as **Barabazaar** has hosted a succession of trading communities; the Portuguese were here before Job Charnock landed at the fishing village that stood close by, and it later became home to Marwari and Gujarati merchants. The small hectic lanes south of MG Road are lined with shops and stalls selling everything from glass bangles to textiles.

At the northwest corner of Barabazaar, near Howrah Bridge, is Kolkata's oldest church, the **Armenian Church of Our Lady of Nazareth** (Sun 9am–11pm). Founded in 1724 by Cavond, an Armenian from Persia, it was built on the site of an Armenian cemetery in which the oldest tombstone dates to 1630. The Armenian community was already highly influential at the courts of Bengal by the time the British arrived, and played an important role in the early history of the East India Company. Later they helped start the lucrative jute industry and still have a small community in the city.

Nakhoda Masjid

East of Barabazaar on Rabindra Sarani (formerly Chitpore Rd)

The huge red **Nakhoda Masjid**, whose two lofty minarets rise to 46m, is the great Jama Masjid (Friday mosque) of the city. Completed in 1942, it was modelled on Akbar's Tomb at Sikandra near Agra; its four floors can hold ten thousand worshippers. The traditional Muslim market sells religious items along with clothes, dried fruit and sweets such as *firni*, made of rice.

Chinatown

Until relatively recently, the chaotic jumble of streets to the south along Rabindra Sarani housed a thriving **Chinatown**, restaurants, temples, markets, opium dens and all. A handful of Chinese families continue to live around the decaying environs of Chhatawala Gully, where a small early-morning street **market** (daily 6–7am) offers home-made pork sausages, noodles and jasmine tea. Today, the main focus of the city's Chinese community is at Tangra on the eastern edge of town, where dwindling numbers continue to nurture some of its customs and industries.

13

Marble Palace

North of MG Rd, on tiny Muktaram Babu St off Chittaranjan Ave • Tues, Wed & Fri–Sun 10am–4pm • Free; no photography

The ornate **Marble Palace** holds a lavish collection of statues, European antiques, Ming vases, and paintings by Rubens and Gainsborough. To join one of the free guided tours of this extraordinary pile, get a pass from the tourist offices at BBD Bagh or Shakespeare Sarani (see p.748). To the north of Marble Palace, **Sonagachi's** warren of lanes comprise Kolkata's largest red-light district.

Rabindra Bharati Museum

Dwarkanath Tagore Lane • Tues–Sun 10am–4.30pm • ₹50 (₹10)

A short walk northeast of the Marble Palace, the small campus of Rabindranath Tagore's liberal arts university, **Rabindra Bharati**, preserves the house where he was born and died as the **Rabindra Bharati Museum**, or Tagore House. A fine example of a nineteenth-century *raj bari*, the museum holds a large collection of Tagore's paintings.

College Street

The heart of Calcutta University and surrounded by its hallowed institutions, **College Street** is famed for its book vendors – forming one of the largest secondhand book markets in the world. While the emphasis is primarily on textbooks, browsing unearths far more. No trip is complete without a visit to the frenetic **India Coffee House**, which maintains its reputation as a meeting place for the intelligentsia.

Ashutosh Museum of Indian Art

Mon–Fri 11am–4.30pm • ₹10

In the Centenary Building just inside Calcutta University's College Street gateway, the **Ashutosh Museum of Indian Art** is dedicated to the arts of Bengal, with a superb collection from eighth-century Pala-dynasty sculpture to nineteenth-century painted scrolls and contemporary art. Few people come this way; you are more than likely to have the museum to yourself and a few officious staff.

The River Hooghly

Until silting rendered it impractical for large ships, the **River Hooghly**, a distributary of the Ganges, was responsible for making Calcutta a bustling port. The *ghats* lining the river's east bank serve as landings and places for ritual ablutions but hold, unlike in Varanasi, no mythological significance. Around 2km north of Howrah Bridge, beyond the cremation grounds of **Nimtolla Ghat**, lies **Kumartuli Ghat** and its community of artisans and sculptors. A short distance further north lies **Baghbazaar Ghat** where overladen barges of straw arrive for the artisans of Kumartuli. Baghbazaar, the Garden Market, stands on the original site of **Sutanuti**, its grand but decaying mansions epitomizing the long-vanished lifestyle of the Bengali gentry, the *bhadra log* (lampooned by Kipling in *The Jungle Book*, whose monkey troupe he called the "bandar log").

HOWRAH BRIDGE

One of Kolkata's most famous landmarks (officially called Rabindra Setu, though few people use this new name), **Howrah Bridge** (⊚ howrahbridgekolkata.gov.in) is 97m high and 705m long, spanning the river in a single leap to make it the world's third longest cantilever bridge. Erected with a maze of girders during World War II in 1943 to give Allied troops access to the Burmese front, it was the first bridge to be built using rivets. Joining the streams of pedestrians who walk across it each day is a memorable experience. **Vidyasagar Setu**, the second Hooghly bridge, built 3km south to relieve the strain, was 22 years in the making. It's a vast toll bridge with spaghetti-junction-style approaches high enough to let ships pass below.

The ghats

Boat trips around ₹250/hr

South of Howrah Bridge, in its shadow, set behind the busy flower market of **Mullick Ghat**, the **Armenian Ghat** is most animated at the first light of dawn, when traditional gymnasts and wrestlers, devotees of Hanuman the monkey god, come to practise. As the Strand – separated from the river by the Circular Railway line – heads south, it passes several warehouses, **Millennium Park** and Fairlie Place and comes to another cluster of *ghats*. Frequent ferries (7.30am–8pm) from **Chandpal Ghat** provide an easy alternative to Howrah Bridge and connect with several other useful *ghats* such as **Shibpur** (for the Botanical Gardens) and **Shobabazar** (for Kumartuli). **Babu Ghat**, near a messy bus terminus and identified by its crumbling colonnade, is used for early morning bathing, attended by pujaris (priests) and heavy-handed masseurs. Further south towards **Princep Ghat**, between Fort William and the river, the Strand comes into its own as a leafy promenade, pleasant during the early evenings with cafés, food stalls and boat rides from the small jetty near *Scoops* café.

Kumartuli

A short walk north of Shobabazar Ghat, lies the warren of **Kumartuli**, where a community of *kumars* or "potters" hand-craft lavish statues of voluptuous goddesses used for the city's religious festivals. In the days leading up to the great pujas, especially that of Durga, Kumartuli is a fascinating hive of activity. Statues take form from straw and river clay before being spray-painted and then clothed in all their finery. Although *pith* (banana tree marrow) is still used to decorate the statues, modern materials have made an impact. The community is also accessible from Shobabazar Metro Station – emerge from the west exit and walk west along a lane to Rabindra Sarani and an entrance to Kumartuli.

Botanical Gardens

10km south of Howrah Station • Daily 5.30am–5pm • ₹50 (₹10) • Buses #C6 (from Esplanade), #T9 (from Park St), #6 minibus (from Dharamtala via Howrah); taxis from the central Sudder St area cost around ₹250 one way; ferries ply to Shibpur Ghat from Chandpal Ghat (8am–8pm; ₹10 return)

The **Botanical Gardens** at Shibpur lie on the west bank of the Hooghly. Populated by countless bird species, the huge gardens are best seen in winter and spring, and early in the mornings before the heat of the day sets in. Their most famous feature is the world's largest **banyan tree**, 24.5m high and an astonishing 420m in circumference. The Orchid House, the Herbarium and the Fern Houses are also worth seeing, and there's an attractive riverside promenade.

South Kolkata

South of the Maidan and Park Street, Kolkata spreads towards **suburbs** such as **Alipore** and Ballygunge, both within easy distance of the centre. The thoroughfare that starts life as Chowringhee at Esplanade proceeds past **Kalighat** to **Tollygunge**, following the Metro line that terminates near the luxurious *Tollygunge Club* (see p.757) – the mansion of an indigo merchant now surrounded by immaculate golfing fairways and bridle-paths. Northeast of Tollygunge, beyond a white-tiled mosque built in 1835 by descendants of Tipu Sultan (see p.1165), lies the parkland of Rabindra Sarobar, known locally as the Lakes, a popular spot for early evening walks.

Alipore

Zoo Daily except Tues 9am–5pm • ₹20 National Library Mon–Fri 9am–8pm, Sat & Sun 9.30am–6pm • Free

Around 3km southwest of Park Street, elegant triple-arched gates just south of the popular **Zoo** and Aquarium lead to Belvedere, the former residence of the lieutenant-governor of Bengal, presented to Warren Hastings by Mir Jafar, and now serving as the

13

> ## KALIGHAT PAINTINGS
>
> Early in the nineteenth century, Kalighat was in its heyday, drawing pilgrims, merchants and artisans from all over the country. Among them were **scroll painters** from elsewhere in Bengal, who developed the distinctive style now known as **Kalighat pat**. Adapting Western techniques, using paper and water-based paints instead of tempera, they moved away from religious themes to depict contemporary subjects. By 1850, Kalighat *pat* had taken a dynamic new direction, satirizing the middle classes in much the same way as today's political cartoons. They serve as a witty record of the period, filled with images of everyday life, and can be found in galleries and museums around the world, and in the Indian Museum (see p.738) as well as the Birla Academy and Ashutosh Museum in Kolkata.

National Library. When the capital shifted to Delhi, this library was left behind; today it houses a huge collection of books, periodicals and reference material, as well as rare documents in an air-conditioned chamber. Day membership to the Reading Room is available with ID and two photographs

Kalighat
5km south of Park St off Ashutosh Mukherjee Rd (an extension of Chowringhee Rd)

Kolkata's most important temple, **Kalighat**, stands at the heart of a diverse and animated area, part residential, part bazaar. The destitute, hoping for charity from pilgrims, line the temple approaches and prostitutes linger on the thoroughfares and bridges offering their services in tragic, grimy circumstances. The typically Bengali temple itself, built in 1809 of brick and mortar but capturing the sweeping curves of a thatched roof, is dedicated to Kali, the black goddess, a form of Shakti. According to legend, Shiva went into a frenzy after the death of his wife Sati, dancing with her dead body and making the whole world tremble. In an attempt to stop him Vishnu took his solar discus and chopped the disintegrating corpse into 51 bits. The spot where each piece fell became a *pitha*, a sacred site for the female principal of divinity – Shakti. The shrine here marks the place where her little toe fell.

Open all hours, the temple is tended by avaricious priests who will try to whisk you downstairs to confront the dramatic monolithic image of the terrible goddess with her huge eyes and bloody tongue. The courtyard beyond the main congregational hall is used for sacrificing goats on special occasions. **Nirmal Hriday**, Mother Teresa's home for the destitute and dying, is on the northwest corner of the complex.

ARRIVAL AND DEPARTURE
KOLKATA (CALCUTTA)

BY PLANE
Netaji Subhash Bose International Airport Kolkata's airport (general ☎033 2511 8787, international ☎033 2511 9864, domestic ☎033 2511 9636), 20km north of the city centre, is served by international flights. Officially Netaji Subhash Bose International Airport, it is still universally known by its old name of Dum Dum. A sparkling new terminal 2 opened at the time of going to press; this will eventually combine international and domestic services and the adjacent domestic terminal will be phased out. Key amenities at the airport include money-exchange and a pre-paid taxi booth, an accommodation booking counter, a railway reservation desk, useful taxi counters and a city coach counter. The airport also has retiring rooms (₹1500 a/c, ₹600 dorm with flight and passport details) booked through the airport manager's office; there is a 24hr café outside the old domestic terminal.

Domestic airlines Air India, 39 Chittaranjan Ave (☎1800/180 1407 or ☎033 2211 2573 (24hr with a tourist counter); airport office enquiries ☎033 2511 9031, recorded flight enquiries: general ☎1400, arrivals ☎1402, departures ☎1403); Go Air (☎1800/222 111) Indigo (☎1800/180 3838); Jet Airways, 18-D Park St (☎033 3989 3333), airport enquiries (☎033 2511 9894}; Jet Konnect (☎1800/223020); Spicejet ☎(1800/180 3333).

Flight connections Kolkata has excellent domestic flights but its international connections are limited with direct flights to Bangkok, Singapore, Yangon (Burma (Myanmar)), Dhaka and Chittagong (Bangladesh), Kathmandu, Kunming (China), Kuala Lumpur, Hong Kong and Bhutan; Air India, Jet Airways, Emirates and Qatar fly, with changes, to Europe. Check *Graphiti, The Telegraph's* Sunday supplement, for current flight (and train) information.

MOTHER TERESA

Beatified by Pope John Paul II on October 19, 2003, **Mother Teresa**, Kolkata's most famous citizen (1910–97), was born Agnes Gonxha Bojaxhiu to Albanian parents, and grew up in Skopje in the former Yugoslavia. Joining the Sisters of Loreto, an Irish order, she was sent as a teacher to Darjeeling, where she took her vows in May 1931 and became Teresa. While working in Kolkata, she was moved by the terrible poverty around her; in 1948 she changed her nun's habit for the simple blue-bordered white sari that became the uniform of the **Missionaries of Charity**.

The best known of their many homes and clinics is **Nirmal Hriday** at 251 Kalighat Rd, a hospice for destitutes. Despite local resistance, Mother Teresa chose its site by Kalighat temple in the knowledge that many poor people come here to die next to a holy *tirtha* or crossing-place. Mother Teresa's piety and single-minded devotion to the poor won her international acclaim, and she was awarded the Nobel Peace Prize in 1979. Subsequently she also attracted a fair share of controversy with her fierce anti-abortion stance and was also accused of disregarding advances in medicine in favour of saving souls. Censure, however, seems iniquitous in the light of her immense contribution to humanity.

If you're interested in the work of the Missionaries of Charity, they can be contacted at **Mother House**, near Sealdah Station at 54-A AJC Bose Rd (☏033 2249 7115, closed Thurs; ⓦmotherteresa.org). Mother Teresa is buried here, and along with her tomb there is a small museum dedicated to her life. They run orientation workshops (a brief introduction to their work) on Mondays, Wednesdays and Fridays from 3pm to 5pm at nearby Shishu Bhavan, 78 AJC Bose Rd, which is an orphanage and a dispensary for children.

The appalling poverty highlighted by Mother Teresa has led to a number of NGO charities developing in the city. Established in 1979, **Calcutta Rescue** is a non-religious organization that runs clinics, schools and a crèche in Kolkata, as well as an outreach programme to help people in need further afield in West Bengal. For more information visit them online at ⓦcalcuttarescue.org or call ☏033 2217 5675.

An organization dedicated to the welfare and rehabilitation of street and slum children, **Hope** relies on volunteers and donors for its many projects throughout the city and further afield. For more information call ☏033 2472 2904 or visit ⓦhopefoundation.ie.

GETTING INTO TOWN

By taxi A pre-paid taxi from the airport to the central Sudder St area costs around ₹290. The private taxi booth run by Mega Cars charges around ₹500 for the same journey in an a/c car while Wenz Car Hire charge ₹690. The transport counters at the domestic terminal are clustered together near the exit.

By bus Express Volvo a/c coach services connect the airport with various points in the city, the most useful being the VS1, which travels to Dharamtala, handy for the Sudder St area (₹40). Luggage allowance is one bag plus hand luggage per person, as these are essentially commuter coaches.

By Metro and circular railway An alternative is to take a taxi (around ₹100) or the shuttle bus to the Dum Dum Metro station (5km), and then the Metro (see p.747) into town; Sudder St is a short walk from Park Street station. Bear in mind that you can't take large items (bikes, sports equipment etc) onto the Metro system. Dum Dum is also a terminus for the Circular Railway to Eden Gardens (Chandpal Ghat) (7.50am–6.45pm; ₹5) from where Sudder St is a short taxi ride away.

BY TRAIN

Kolkata has three main railway stations: Howrah, Sealdah and Kolkata, with two others, Santragachi and Shalimar, as subsidiary hubs. Unfortunately, none of the stations are currently linked to the Metro system but the east–west line, under construction at the time of writing, will have stations at Howrah and Sealdah.

Howrah Howrah – the point of arrival for most major trains from the south and west – stands on the far bank of the Hooghly, 2km west of the centre. To reach the central downtown area, traffic has to negotiate Howrah Bridge – the definitive introduction to the chaos of the city. Avoid the touts and taxis outside the station building, and head straight for the pre-paid taxi booth, from where the fare to central Sudder St and the Park St areas is around ₹100. Minibuses and buses also operate from Howrah to destinations all over the city, but tend to be very crowded. A good alternative is to follow the signs from the station gate and take a ferry (₹5) across the Hooghly to Babu Ghat or the adjacent Chandpal Ghat, close to BBD Bagh, and pick up a metered taxi or bus from there.

Kolkata Kolkata Station (or Terminus, also known as Chitpur Station) lies 1km from Shyambazar Metro station, from where it is a convenient seven stops south to Park St (for Sudder St hotels). There isn't a pre-paid booth but auto-rickshaws to Shyambazar are available and there is a taxi rank. The Circular Railway connects the station with Eden Gardens (handy for the Sudder St area).

RECOMMENDED TRAINS FROM KOLKATA

Destination	Name	No.	From	Departs	Total time
Allahabad	Kalka Mail	#12311	Howrah	7.40pm	13hr 20min
Bhubaneswar	Falaknuma Express	#12703	Howrah	7.25pm	6hr 20min
Bolpur	Shantiniketan Express	#12337	Howrah	10.10am	2hr 15min
	Kanchenjunga Express	#15657	Sealdah	6.35am	2hr 45min
Chennai	Coromandel Express	#12841	Howrah	2.50pm	26hr 25min
Delhi	Rajdhani Express*	#12301/05	Howrah	4.55pm	17hr
	Rajdhani Express*	#12313	Sealdah	4.50pm	17hr 30min
Gaya	Mumbai Mail	#12321	Howrah	10pm	7hr 22min
Guwahati	Saraighat Express	#12345	Howrah	13.50pm	17hr 40min
Mumbai	Howrah Mumbai Duronto Express*	#12262	Howrah	8.20pm	26hr 10min
	Gitanjali Express	#12860	Howrah	1.50pm	31hr 30min
New Jalpaiguri**	Darjeeling Mail	#12343	Sealdah	10.05pm	9hr 55min
	Kanchenjunga Express	#15657	Sealdah	6.35am	11hr 40min
Patna	Danapur Express	#12351	Howrah	8.35pm	9hr 30min
Puri	Puri Express	#12837	Howrah	10.35pm	8hr 55min
	Falaknuma Express	#12703	Howrah	7.25pm	7hr
Raxaul (for Birganj in Nepal)	Mithila Express	#13021	Howrah	3.45pm	16hr 45min
Varanasi	Amritsar Mail	#13005	Howrah	7.10pm	14hr 5min

*A/c only
**Connect here for taxis to Siliguri, Darjeeling, Kalimpong, Sikkim and Gangtok.

Santragachi Several major trains now stop here in transit but the station, 7km to the west of Howrah, is also the terminus for a few long distance trains on the Southeastern Railways network. Taxis and buses are available and there is an a/c Volvo bus (V2) all the way to the airport via Park Circus.

Shalimar Shalimar, the city's newest station, lies 5km to the south of Howrah and across Vidyasagar Setu Bridge from Kolkata, with a handful of trains along the Southern Railways network. A taxi costs around ₹110 to Sudder St and there is an occasional and irregular ferry service to Garden Reach and Babu Ghat.

Sealdah Sealdah Station, with its own pre-paid taxi booth in the car park, is on the eastern edge of the centre close to the Sudder St area. Once the main terminus for trains from the north, Sealdah now shares this role with Kolkata Station.

BOOKING TICKETS

Centralized information on train connections is available on ☎033 2230 3545 or ☎033 2230 3535. For general reservation enquiries call ☎033 2230 3496. You can also book online (see p.34) or through agents around Sudder St.

Railway Reservation Offices Of the numerous computerized booking offices throughout the city the convenient ones are: Fairlie Place (BBD Bagh), Howrah and Sealdah stations, Bentinck St (Esplanade) and Alexandra Court, 61 Chowringhee Rd, Rabindra Sadan (Mon–Sat 8am–8pm, Sun & hols 9am–2pm).

Foreign Tourist Office The tourist office on the first floor of the Eastern Railways office, in the northwest corner of BBD Bagh at 6 Fairlie Place, books tourist quota train tickets (Mon–Sat 10am–5pm, Sun & hols 10am–2pm; ☎033 2222 4206). You'll need to bring proof of encashment (an exchange or ATM receipt) to reserve a berth if paying in rupees.

BY BUS

While the main highways and expressways to the west and northwest of the city are relatively quick, having undergone modernization in recent years, much of the state's roads are in appalling condition. Buses are generally cheaper but can be a painful experience, especially on the northern route to Siliguri (Darjeeling).

Esplanade bus stand The largest, the most chaotic and the most convenient of Kolkata's bus terminals less than 500m north of the tourist hub of Sudder St, Esplanade is not a single terminal but rather a collection of bus services to numerous points throughout the state. These include the Rocket Bus travelling the 560km route to Siliguri (7pm; 13hr; ₹400 & ₹500, Santanu Booking Counter ☎9331062749); which offers reclining seats as well as a sleeper coupe (singles will be required to share). Among the most efficient and luxurious services from the terminus is Royal Cruiser (☎033 2252 1415), who have their office within the Esplanade Metro station (entrance opposite Grand Hotel), with climate-controlled Volvo buses to Siliguri (7pm) and Puri (9pm) among other key destinations. Several buses from here head to Basanti and the Sundarbans (especially early morning) and for points south to Diamond Harbour and beyond.

Babu Ghat bus stand Some long-distance buses from the south, including Puri and Ranchi, terminate at Babu Ghat bus stand, not far from Fort William on the east

bank. State transport companies (Orissa Roadways ☎ 943 314 34280; West Bengal State Transport (☎ 033 241 6388) have their booths here. Among the private companies, the Dolphin (☎ 943 323 6077) service to Puri departs at 9pm and arrives in Puri at 7am; the bus is a basic "sleeper" but some sleeper coaches offer coupes – do check first; others have reclining seats.

GETTING AROUND

The **Metro**, India's first and Kolkata's pride and joy, provides a fast, clean and efficient way to get around. The river is also used for transport, with the *ghats* near Eden Gardens at the hub of a **ferry** system. You can beat the traffic by jumping on one of the frequent ferries from Chandpal Ghat to Howrah Station, though they're crowded at rush hour. Metered **taxis** remain the most convenient mode of transport and radio cabs (private taxis) provide more comfort at a price. There is a bewildering plethora of **buses** plying through the city and the few trams left are a reminder of bygone days. While using public transport, be wary of **pickpockets**, especially on crowded buses.

By Metro Kolkata's Russian-designed Metro, inaugurated in 1984, is still every bit as good as its inhabitants proudly claim, with trains operating punctually every few minutes. Services run from 7am to 9.45pm Monday to Saturday and 3pm to 9.45pm on Sundays. Tickets are cheap, starting at ₹4, and you can travel the entire length of the north–south line from Dum Dum near the airport to Kavi Nazrul Islam (Garia) in the south for just ₹12. Single tickets work on a token system and are valid for 90min from purchase – touch the token on the turnstyle to enter and drop into the slot to exit. Smart Cards allow multiday travel and cost ₹100 (refundable) plus charges from ₹100. Recharge

machines are available at certain stations including Park Street.

By bus Kolkata supports a vast and complicated bus network (for route information, check ⓦ calcuttaweb.com), in operation each day roughly between 5am and 11pm, and subject to overcrowding and the occasional pickpocket. Most buses stop far from the kerb, making getting on and off a hazard. Useful routes include: #S8 from Howrah via Esplanade to Gariahat; #S17 from Chetla near Kalighat via Esplanade to Dakshineshwar; and #5 and #6, which both travel via Howrah and the Esplanade-Chowringhee area, and stop at the Indian Museum at the head of Sudder St. Buses with an "S" prefix denote special express buses, which

ONWARD TRAVEL

TO BANGLADESH

Kolkata is the main gateway to Bangladesh from India. The Bangladesh Consulate is at 9 Circus Ave (Mon–Fri 9am–5pm; ☎ 033 2247 5208, ext 207 for visa section). Visas must be obtained in advance and will be issued on the same day if you submit your passport before 10am. You can reach Bangladesh by train or road or a combination of both, and there are several flights daily from Kolkata to Dhaka. Departing Kolkata Station, the *Maitri Express* (#13108/9) (Tues & Sat 7.10am) – buy tickets from the Foreign Tourist Bureau, Fairlie Place (see opposite) – is the only direct train to Dhaka and you need a visa to book. An alternative is to take an early train from Sealdah to Bangaon and cross the border to take another train from Benapole. Numerous travel agents around Sudder and Marquis streets sell tickets for private buses to Dhaka, which depart from the Esplanade stand, but some involve a change at the border. Private buses such as Shyamoli Paribahan, 10 Marquis Street (☎ 033 2252 0693), to Dhaka depart from Esplanade while government-run WBSTC and BRTC buses operate from Esplanade and Salt Lake International Karunamoyee terminal (☎ 033 2359 8448), a ₹180 taxi ride from the centre, to Dhaka (Tues, Thurs & Sat from 5.30am; 12hrs); you will need to show your visa to book.

TO THE ANDAMAN ISLANDS

Flights with Air India, Jet Air and Jet Konnect leave daily for Port Blair. To go by ship (there are three to four sailings a month), you'll need to book through the Shipping Corporation of India, 13 Strand Road (☎ 033 2248 2354; from ₹4080, dorms and bunks from ₹1790); the journey takes three to five days, so bring plenty to read and food to supplement the dull meals. Free thirty-day permits are granted on arrival.

13

charge marginally more. The a/c Volvo buses run on several useful routes including the VS1 from Esplanade to the airport and the V1 between Tollygunge (via Gariahat) and the airport. These are commuter buses, so getting on with luggage mid-route can be a problem when the buses are full. In addition, there are private brown-and-yellow minibuses which travel at inordinate speeds. Their destinations are painted boldly in Bengali and English on their sides and route numbers are occasionally visible; #128 connects Howrah with Esplanade.

By tram Kolkata's cumbersome trams (ⓦcalcuttatramways.com), barely changed save for a lick of paint since they started operating in 1873, have been phased out, but certain routes linger on and a "new" model has been introduced with high glass windows. Female travellers may well be glad of the rush-hour women-only coaches. Routes include, among others, #1, Esplanade to College St.

Taxis Painted either yellow or black and yellow, taxis in Kolkata are extremely good value, especially on long journeys such as to and from the airport (around ₹300 for a 20km ride), but a few drivers can be unwilling to take you on short journeys or to areas they don't like the sound of. There's a 25 percent night-time surcharge (10pm–6am). Up to two pieces of luggage are free, but there's an additional charge for further pieces and for placing bags in the boot. Most cabs have working meters and tend to use them in conjunction with the conversion charts they are obliged to carry. Pre-paid taxis are available at some railway stations and the airport.

Private taxis Several private taxi companies, also referred to as radio cabs, with vehicles at the airport and railway stations as well as the major hotels, provide more safety and luxury with a/c and printed receipts. Firms include Kolkata Cabs (☎4433 3222), Mega Cab (☎4141 4141) and Blue Arrow (☎13658 or ☎9239 244416). Charges start from ₹80/hr plus ₹8.50/km. Some levy a minimum charge.

Rickshaws Despite efforts to ban them, Kolkata still has human-drawn rickshaws, though they're only available in the central areas of the city, especially around New Market where some pullers supplement their meagre income by acting as touts and pimps. Most of the rickshaw-pullers are Bihari pavement-dwellers, who live short and very hard lives. Haggle for a realistic price but feel free to give a handful of baksheesh too.

Car rental Autoriders, 10-A Ho Chi Min Sarani (☎033 2282 3561); Avis, *Oberoi Grand* hotel, 15 Chowringhee Rd (☎033 3399 0099), ⓦavis.co.in; Wentz 3 (☎09330018001 or ☎033 3958 7217); they have a counter at the airport or you can book online ⓦwenzcars.com.

Ferries The ferry system provides a pleasant alternative to the city's manic roads. The most useful ferry terminal is Chandpal Ghat near Eden Gardens and a short taxi ride from Sudder St, from where, along with Howrah Station, you can get ferries downriver to Shibpur for the Botanical Gardens and upriver to Shobabazar, useful for visiting Kumartuli. Ferry prices start at a mere ₹5.

INFORMATION

English-language newspapers Newspapers such as the *The Telegraph*, *Hindusthan Standard* and *Statesman* remain the primary source for information on what's on but the best is *The Telegraph*'s Sunday supplement *Graphiti*. *Explocity Kolkata* is a free listings magazine available at the tourist office and some hotels.

India Tourism office 4 Shakespeare Sarani (Mon–Fri 9am–6pm, Sat 9am–1pm; ☎033 2282 5813), off Chowringhee Rd. Provides general information on Kolkata, West Bengal and destinations further afield, and can assist with itineraries. Get your Marble Palace (see p.742) pass here.

West Bengal Tourist Bureau (WBTDC) 3/2 BBD Bagh

East (Mon–Sat 10.30am–4.30pm; ☎033 2248 5168, ⓦwestbengaltourism.gov.in). Arranges tours of Kolkata and package trips throughout West Bengal. They also issue permits and book tours and accommodation in the Sundarbans (Mon–Fri only).

State tourist offices The most useful of the many offices representing other states in Kolkata are those that cover the northeastern states and assist in securing permits for these areas (see box, p.839) and the Andaman and Nicobar islands. Andaman and Nicobar, 2nd Floor, DP-7, Sector 5 (☎033 2357 4897); Arunachal Pradesh, Block CE, 109 Sector 1, Salt Lake (☎033 2321 3627); Assam, 8 Russel St (☎033 2229 5094);

WHAT'S IN A NAME?

Though most of the old British **street names** in Kolkata were officially changed years ago, habits die hard and some of the original names continue to be widely used in tandem with the new. The most important of these is Chowringhee or Jawaharlal Nehru Road (still called Chowringhee). Other name changes to note are BBD Bagh (still often referred to by its old name of Dalhousie Square or simply "Dalhousie"), Mirza Ghalib Street (Free School St), Dr Mohammed Ishaque Road (Kyd St), Muzaffar Ahmed Street (Ripon St), Ho Chi Minh Sarani (Harrington St), AJC Bose Road (Lower Circular Rd), Shakespeare Sarani (Theatre Rd), Rabindranath Tagore Street (Camac St), Lenin Sarani (Dharamtala) and Rabindra Sarani (Chitpore Rd).

Manipur, 26 Rowland Rd (☏ 033 2475 8075); Meghalaya, 120 Shantipally, EM Bypass (☏ 033 2441 2159); Mizoram, 24 Old Ballygunge Rd ☏ (033 2461 5887); Nagaland, 11 Shakespeare Sarani (☏ 033 2282 5247); Orissa (Odisha), 41 & 55 Lenin Sarani (☏ 033 2249 3653); Sikkim, 4 1 Middleton St (☏ 033 2281 5328); Tripura, 1 Pretoria St (☏ 033 2282 5703).

TOURS

WALKING TOURS

If you want to devise your own walking itineraries, the essential companion is A Jaywalker's Guide to Calcutta by Soumitra Das, and the AtoZ of the city, Eicher Kolkata City Map, makes an excellent companion – both are available at bookshops such as Oxford (see p.756).

Calcutta Walks 9A Khairu Place, Chandni Chowk ☏ 98301 84030, ⓦ calcuttawalks.com. Very well organized and well-informed upmarket agency that concentrates on walks and tours of the city; from ₹1500.

Help Tourism ☏ 033 2455 0917 (see below). Help's walking tours provide a great insight into the historic heart of the city. Tours are between 4–5hr long and start at ₹1000.

Kali Travel Home ☏ 94321 45532 (see below). A welcoming agency run by two Australian aficionados of the old city. Tours give you an in-depth view, warts and all 3 start at ₹700.

Walks of Kolkata F25, 1st floor Kamalalaya Centre, 156A Lenin Sarani ☏ 98317 61003, ⓦ walksofkolkata .com. Themed walks and tailor-made itineraries run by Swati with lots of flexibility including tours for individuals. From ₹2500.

Assam Bengal Navigation Company 3B Dirang Arcade, GNB Rd, Guwahati ☏ 0361 266 7871, ⓦ assambengalnavigation.com. Luxurious operators with an international network who charge in US dollars and provide multiday cruises along the Hooghly as well as in Assam and elsewhere on converted river steamers.

Vivada Cruises 14 Southern Ave ☏ 033 2463 1990 or ☏ 98839 33033, ⓦ vivadacruises.com. Along with timed cruises along the Hooghly, Vivada also provide a multiday cruise to Varanasi and wildlife cruises on the Sunderbans; they also charter boats.

TOUR OPERATORS

Help Tourism 67A Kali Temple Rd, Kalighat ☏ 033 2455 0917, ⓦ helptourism.com. Ethically minded, this pioneering agency has helped establish several wildlife projects and offers a wide range of tours including to the Sundarbans and wildlife-viewing in north Bengal.

Himalayan Footprints 77 Netaji Subhas Rd ☏ 98300 33896. Informative and flexible wildlife tours, nature treks and trips to the Sundarbans, Sikkim and Darjeeling.

Kali Travel Home 5A Ishwar Chakraborty Lane, Burtola ☏ 94321 45532, ⓦ traveleastindia.com. This knowledgeable Australian agency is keen to share their enthusiasm for the city and for Bengal with tailor-made guided tours, cooking classes and farm stays.

WBTDC 3/2 BBD Bagh East ☏ 033 2248 5168. Government-run tours are especially useful during the pujas; the office also offers city tours and statewide tours by coach, from ₹430.

TRAVEL AGENTS

Thomas Cook Chitrakoot Building, 2nd Floor, 230 AJC Bose Rd ☏ 033 2247 5378. Deals with inbound tours and international flights and foreign exchange. For domestic and international flights, there are numerous agents around Sudder St.

ACCOMMODATION

As soon as you arrive in Kolkata, taxi drivers are likely to assume that you'll be heading for Sudder St, near New Market, where you'll find a heady mix of travellers, businessmen and Bangladeshis in transit. As the main travellers' hub in Kolkata and close to all amenities, the area is a sociable place to stay, with numerous budget or mid-range hotels; the latter tend to be overpriced and poor value for money, and if you're after a modicum of luxury, you may have to look further afield.

SUDDER STREET, NEW MARKET, ESPLANADE AND AROUND

Aafreen Tower 9A Kyd St ☏ 033 2229 3280; map p.737. An efficient budget business hotel with a quirky exterior glass lift. The rooms are clean and exceptional value, especially those with a/c. There isn't a restaurant but staff will supply meals from surrounding cafés. ₹700

Bawa Walson 5A Sudder St ☏ 033 2252 1512, ⓦ walson .bawahotels.com; map p.737. A new addition to the strip, this chain hotel offers smart, modern and tastefully decorated rooms but at an extraordinary price unless you are able to score one of their great web offers. The Courtyard restaurant serves platter meals including tandoori. ₹7200

Broadway 27A Ganesh Chandra Ave ☏ 033 2236 3930; map pp.734–735. Established in 1937, this old hotel, near Chandni Chowk Metro station, offers basic non-a/c rooms on the edge of the commercial district; cheaper rooms come with shared baths. The Art Deco restaurant and bar downstairs, with its high ceilings and lazy fans, exudes a faded atmosphere. 24hr check-out. ₹715

Capital Guest House 11-B Chowringhee Lane ☏ 033 2252 0598; map p.737. Set in a large courtyard away from the bustle of Sudder St, rooms in this purpose-built block

13

are plain but functional with hot water by the bucket; some have a/c. ₹**590**

Fairlawn 13-A Sudder St ☎033 2252 1510, ⊛fairlawnhotel.com; map p.737. Chock-full of memorabilia, this famous and old-fashioned family-run hotel exudes a charmingly faded and eccentric Raj atmosphere, though the absence of modernization doesn't suit all tastes. Non-residents can drink in the lush garden bar, popular in the evenings. ₹**3700**

Galaxy 3 Stuart Lane ☎033 2252 4565; map p.737. This small hotel, with just four rooms, is clean and good value despite the lack of light and position, with hot water with an a/c option too. ₹**650**

Kempton 3 Marquis St ☎033 4017 7888, ⊛hotelkempton. in; map p.737. Just around the corner from Sudder St, this business hotel, with its smart modern design and decor, represents great value especially for its cheaper rooms. There is a multicuisine restaurant and a café. ₹**3850**

Maria 5/1 Sudder St ☎033 2252 0860; map p.737. The sizeable budget rooms – some with attached baths – in this old high-ceilinged, faded building are often booked up; there is also a dorm (₹100), a reliable internet café and a pleasant terrace upstairs. The place is peeling, however ,and you'll need plenty of insect repellent. ₹**600**

Modern Lodge 1 Stuart Lane ☎033 2242 5960; map p.737. Cramped place, with a relaxing roof terrace; despite the surly – sometimes downright rude – service, it's been popular with budget travellers since the 1960s, and has a lot of history; there are better rooms upstairs and some with attached baths. ₹**150**

Oberoi Grand 15 Chowringhee Rd ☎033 2249 2323, ⊛oberoihotels.com; map p.737. The white Victorian facade of this luxurious hotel, established in 1938, is very much part of the fabric of the city. Service is attentive, and the interior has been completely revamped in a modern-meets-traditional style; facilities include a swimming pool and Thai and Indian restaurants; security is very tight. ₹**24,100**

Paragon 2 Stuart Lane ☎033 2252 2445; map p.737. This has long been a popular traveller haunt, offering dark and dingy rooms downstairs, and better ones, though small, around the popular rooftop courtyard; some rooms come with attached baths and there are also two Dorm ₹**110**, double ₹**270**

Timestar 2 Tottee Lane ☎033 2252 8028; map p.737. The fair-sized rooms in this peeling old villa, quietly located down a small drive, come with fans but hot water by the bucket; some have TV too and there is an a/c option. ₹**500**

YMCA 25 Chowringhee Rd ☎033 2249 2192; map p.737. Near the Indian Museum, with a grand but dilapidated wood-lined entrance, offering spacious, high-ceilinged rooms upstairs with morning tea and breakfast included; those with a/c are better value. Temporary membership

(₹50/week) also allows access to a well-kept snooker table and table tennis. Breakfast is included. ₹**1200**

PARK STREET, CHOWRINGHEE AND AROUND

Fortune Select 21B Loudon St ☎033 3988 4422; map pp.734–735. New business hotel in a leafy residential road just off Park St with smart, contemporary design. Its prime location makes it worth considering, along with good amenities including restaurant, bar and coffee shop, a gym and a swimming pool. ₹**9200**

Park 17 Park St ☎033 2249 9000, ⊛theparkhotels .com; map p.737. Modern five-star boutique hotel in a good location on a cosmopolitan street; amenities include swimming pool, health club, late check-out and good food at the three restaurants, plus a popular nightclub and a bar with live music. Comfortable and stylish. ₹**12,500**

Sunflower Guest House 7 Royd St ☎033 2229 9401, ⊛sunflowerguesthouse.com; map p.737. A sizeable and well-maintained old building managed by one of the city's old *rajbari* families and serviced by a quaint lift; most of its spotless guestrooms – all with attached baths – are on the top three floors, with the penthouse rooms providing good views; there's a spacious lobby and a small roof garden with food to order. ₹**750**

YWCA 1 Middleton Row ☎033 2229 7033, ✉ywcacal @bsnl.in; map p.737. Safe for women and especially good for longer stays, this clean, central hostel with plain but adequate rooms, some a/c off Park St, is built around a pleasant courtyard with a tennis court. Book in advance. Rates include breakfast. ₹**760**

SOUTH KOLKATA

66/2B The Guest House 66/2B Purna Das Rd ☎033 2464 6422, ⊛662btheguesthouse.com; map pp.734–735. Situated in pleasant part of town, handy for the lakes and Gariahat, and in an area becoming increasingly lively with good restaurants and trendy shopping, this guesthouse has spacious rooms in classic Calcutta style; there is a coffee shop downstairs and their *Tero Parbon* restaurant, specializing in Bengali cuisine, lies around the corner. ₹**2100**

★ **Bodhi Tree Guest House** 48/44 Swiss Park ☎033 2424 3871, ⊛bodhitreekolkata.com; map pp.734–735. A stunning little boutique guesthouse colourfully and artistically presented, across the tracks from the lakes and close to the Rabindra Saravar Metro station; rooms are themed and are priced according to length of stay. ₹**2200**

Indrani Guest House 3-B Lovelock St ☎033 2486 6712 or ☎09830 269511; map pp.734–735. A comfortable family house offering B&B and optional home-cooking in a residential part of the city off Ballygunge Circular Rd. There's a limited number of homely rooms, so book ahead; discounts available for longer stays. ₹**1540**

13

The Residency Guest House 50/1C Purna Das Rd ☎ 033 2466 9382; map pp.734–735. Spotless a/c rooms with tiled floors in a residential area just off Gol Park and within walking distance of the lakes and Gariahat. The custom-built guesthouse is welcoming and the complimentary breakfast is served in their swish sister establishment, the *Restaurant on the First Floor*, next door. ₹3300

Transit House 11-A Raja Basanta Roy Rd ☎ 033 2466 2700, ✉ transit1@vsnl.net; map pp.734–735. Excellent, safe and comfortable guesthouse with sizeable rooms; away from the centre but in an interesting location close to markets and the lakes, and not far from the Metro and Kalighat. Handy for anyone going to the Sunderbans Tiger Camp (see p.759). ₹900

ELSEWHERE IN THE CITY

Airways No. 2 Airport Gate, Jessore Rd, Kolkata airport ☎ 033 2512 7280; map pp.734–735. An inexpensive but welcoming place in the vicinity of the airport, with basic but clean rooms and a rooftop restaurant. Handy for early departures and late arrivals. ₹700

Bauddha Dharmankuar Sabha Nalanda Square, 1 Buddhist Temple St, behind Bowbazar police station and Bow Barracks ☎ 033 2211 7138, ⊛ bengalbuddhist.com; map pp.734–735. A Buddhist *vihara* with very cheap, basic rooms and a haven within the heart of the commercial district. Don't expect leafy tranquillity but rather a safe, institutional place. You will need to share bathrooms and gates close early; it is popular so book at least a week ahead. ₹200

Hyatt Regency JA-1 Sector 3, Salt Lake City ☎ 033 2335 1234 or ☎ 1600 228001, ⊛ kolkata.regency.hyatt .com; map pp.734–735. Plush hotel with luxurious rooms on the Eastern Bypass, en route to the airport and handy for the city too. It's built to impress, with capacious lobbies, restaurants,

a palm-fringed swimming pool and all facilities. ₹13800

Kings Crown Nazrul Islam Ave (VIP Rd), near the airport ☎ 033 2573 1712; map pp.734–735. On the Ultadunga road a convenient 2km from the airport, two blocks offer a good range of accommodation from plain singles to comfortable a/c rooms, along with a decent restaurant and bar; convenient for early or late flights. ₹1500

Sonar Bangla Eastern Bypass ☎ 033 2345 4545, ⊛ itcwelcomgroup.in; map pp.734–735. Busy hotel whose popularity rests on its convenient location between city and airport and its excellent range of restaurants, bars and nightclubs. All the comforts and services you'd expect from a five-star, and a relaxed welcome. ₹9250

Swissotel City Centre, New Town ☎ 033 6626 6666, ⊛ swissotel.com/kolkata; map pp.734–735. Luxurious new hotel with all amenities and very well placed for the airport. There are a number of good restaurants, cafés and bars, a health centre and a rooftop swimming pool from where you can watch the planes fly by. The upmarket shopping mall next door offers alternative dining and designer brands. ₹9500

Taj Bengal 24-B Belvedere Rd, Alipore ☎ 033 2223 3939, ⊛ tajhotels.com; map pp.734–735. Opulent showpiece hotel and still the prime address in the city, attempting to amalgamate Bengali features with the usual *Taj* grandeur. Excellent range of restaurants, including Chinese and Indian, and a pool and nightclub. Peak season rates can be astronomical but at other times there are good deals to be had on the web. ₹16,575

Yatri Niwas Howrah South Station ☎ 033 2660 1742; map pp.734–735. Convenient for late arrivals or early starts but you will have to show a relevant long-distance reservation. It offers basic dormitory, standard and a/c rooms (₹550); there are great foodhalls at both the main and the South Station. Dorm ₹100, double ₹350

EATING

Although locals love to **dine out**, traditional Bengali cooking was, until recently, restricted to the home; however, some excellent restaurants now offer the chance to taste this wonderful fish-based cuisine. The most popular cuisine when dining out is Chinese, spiced and cooked to local tastes: the city has a rich tradition including its own Chinatown at **Tangra** (closes early around 10pm) on the road to the airport. You'll also find several good south Indian restaurants, as well as rich Muslim cooking and the *kathi* roll, which is now part and parcel of Kolkata's cuisine. Coffee culture is growing with the usual chain cafés throughout the city and there is a handful of purveyors of fine tea. Numerous patisseries and confectioneries work hard to keep up with demand. Restaurants and cafés around **Sudder St** cater for Western travellers while roadside chai shops and street food stalls around BBD Bagh are extremely popular for lunch.

NEW MARKET AND SUDDER STREET

Arsalan 119-A Ripon St ☎ 033 6569 9579; map p.737. Large restaurant that serves a selection of Chinese and other food; you're best off sticking to its Mughlai cuisine – such as the kebabs and excellent biriyanis (try the rich mutton Lucknow biryani, ₹190) – for which it is famous. There are other branches off Park St and on AJC Bose Rd. Daily 10am–10pm.

Baan Thai *Oberoi Grand* hotel, 15 Chowringhee Rd ☎ 033 2249 2323; map p.737. Although expensive – upwards of

₹2000/person – this in-hotel restaurant offers by far the best Thai cooking in town, with dishes like *Kai yang* (barbecue chicken with lemongrass) as well as standards such as red curry. Daily noon–3pm & 7–11pm.

Blue and Beyond 9th floor, *Hotel Lindsay*, 8-A Lindsay St; map p.737. This rooftop bar and restaurant provides an excellent vantage point over New Market and the surrounding city, especially at dusk for a (pricey) beer. Good Indian and reasonable Chinese dishes – such as sliced fish

13

in chilli wine sauce (₹250) – plus good-value breakfasts and buffets on offer. Daily noon–11pm.

Blue Sky Café Sudder St; map p.737. Budget travellers' haunt halfway down the strip on a corner, providing all the old favourites, including good breakfasts. Clean and well run, with a/c, it's a popular meeting place. Mains from ₹40. Daily 8am–11pm.

Fresh & Juicy 2 7 Sudder St; map p.737. Despite its fruity theme, this small café has a good and varied travellers' menu from breakfasts and "snakes" (snacks) to Chinese *haka*. Around ₹120 for a meal. Daily 8am–11pm.

Nahoum & Sons F-20, New Market; map p.737. Legendary Jewish bakery and confectioner selling delicious fruitcake, cashew macaroons, cheese straws and chicken patties. Selections start at around ₹40. Mon–Sat 8am–8pm.

Nizam's 22–25 Hogg Market; map p.737. The original restaurant here gave birth to the legendary *kathi* roll – a tasty sheesh kebab, rolled into a *paratha* of white flour. It's still worth a visit for a snacky meal, or try their egg roll or biryani. Expect to pay around ₹100. Daily 11am–11pm.

★ **Spanish Café** 7 Sudder St; map p.737. Tucked away in the far right corner of the courtyard, this is the most traveller-friendly place on the strip, with the usual breakfast menu and great coffee; there is a good selection of Spanish and Italian dishes including gazpacho and *espinacas salteadas* (spinach and seafood, ₹100). Daily 8am–11pm.

AROUND PARK STREET

Amber Café 2A Middleton Row; map p.737. Bright, new and popular family restaurant run by the owners of celebrated *Amber*; no alcohol and disappointing coffee, but the food is great, with sandwiches, platter meals (from ₹250) and specialities such as chicken tikka masala wrap (₹225). Daily noon–11pm.

Amigos 11/1 Ho Chi Minh Sarani, Jubilee Court ✆033 4060 2507; map p.737. New restaurant, with a Tex-Mex based menu, which at the time of going to press was awaiting its liquor licence. Well received by critics, it also offers the usual pizza selection. Try the Mango Tequila Pescado (fish with chillies and mangoes) and expect to pay around ₹700 for a meal. Daily noon–11pm.

Bar-B-Q 43 Park St; map p.737. An old and reliable favourite, offering Chinese and much-lauded tandoori cuisine in pleasant a/c surroundings with a bar downstairs; the special lunch menu includes Persian delicacies such as *chelo* kebabs on rice. Mains around ₹450. Daily noon–11pm.

Bistro by the Park 2A Middleton Row; map p.737. Tasteful and fresh decor in this popular modern bistro with a varied menu including pan-fried fish (₹375); great for lunch. Daily noon–11pm.

Café Thé 9A Ho Chi Minh Sarani; map p.737. This modern bistro in an exhibition centre, with an extensive tea list including iced tea, is proving to be a popular and arty meeting place. The menu offers surprises including smoked haddock coated in Welsh rarebit, shepherds pie, sandwiches and lasagne, along with Indian and Chinese. Best at lunch or early evenings; expect to pay around ₹400. Daily 10am–8pm.

Fire and Ice Kanak Building, 41 Chowringhee Rd ✆033 2288 4073; map p.737. A trendy bistro and bar (with free wi-fi) serving authentic Italian cuisine including pizzas and *al fiumé* (fresh river prawns in olive oil, ₹560); full meals around ₹800. Can get packed in the evenings. Daily noon–11pm.

Flury's 18 Park St, on the corner of Middleton Row; map p.737. A Kolkata landmark, this once-legendary Swiss teashop and patisserie, founded in 1927, has been completely revamped Little of the old atmosphere remains, but it's still a popular place and worth visiting for all-day English breakfasts (₹370) or cakes (from ₹45), patties, home-made chocolates and pastries – try the rum balls. Other branches at Alipur, South City Mall and Salt Lake, Sector 3. Daily 8am–9pm.

Gupta Brothers 42-A Park Mansions, Mirza Ghalib St; map p.737. Excellent, clean and cheap vegetarian snack bar and sweet counter with a good Rajasthani restaurant upstairs. Try the tandoori *bharwan aloo*, for around ₹45. Daily noon–10pm.

Jyoti Vihar 3A/1 Ho Chi Minh Sarani; map p.737. The most popular south Indian café in town can get packed, especially at lunchtime. It is an eat-and-run place, cramped on two floors, but its reputation is justified with excellent dosas starting from ₹55. Daily noon–8pm.

Mocambo 25-B Park St, around the corner on Mirza Ghalib St; map p.737. A firm favourite for its good cooking and hugely varied menu running from their renowned chicken Kiev to pizza – lobster thermador is occasionally available. Smart, yet relaxed. Expect to pay from ₹600. Daily noon–11pm.

One Step Up 18-A Park St; map p.737. Bright bistro offering a range of options, from sandwiches and light meals to tandoori and pastries. Especially popular at lunch, but also good for an early evening drink. From ₹120. Daily noon–11pm.

Park 17 Park St ✆033 2249 3121; map p.737. This upmarket hotel has developed a reputation for some of the finest dining in town. *Zen*, a Terence Conran restaurant, serves dishes from Thailand, China, Japan and Indonesia; *Saffron* specializes in Indian cuisine; the 24hr *Atrium* coffee bar also provides a good food menu. Expect to pay from ₹800 for a night out. Daily noon–11pm.

CHANDNI CHOWK AND AROUND

Amber 11 Waterloo St ✆033 2248 6520; map pp.734–735. A Kolkata landmark that refuses to fade away, serving celebrated Mughlai and tandoori cuisine with mains from

₹250. Plush and dimly lit, it covers three floors, with a bar downstairs. Daily noon–11pm.

Eau Chew P32 Mission Row Extension, Ganesh Chandra Ave ☎ 033 2237 8260; map pp.734–735. A legendary family-run restaurant and a remnant from the heyday of Chinatown, this unassuming place above a petrol station produces authentic Chinese food. The chimney stew, cooked slowly around a metal coal-burning container, is especially good; alternatives include the roast duck or the roast pork. From ₹250 for a meal. Daily noon–11pm.

India Coffee House 15 Bankim Chatterjee St, just off College St; map pp.734–735. Atmospheric, historic landmark café in the heart of the university area where students and intellectuals continue to meet. It's good for a light meal (from ₹60) and a break from trawling the bookshops of College St. Daily 8am–8pm.

AJC BOSE ROAD AND AROUND

★ **Kewpie's Kitchen** 2 Elgin Lane ☎ 033 2486 9880; map pp.734–735. Private home with a restaurant annexe, offering traditional Bengali food fit for a *jamai babu* (son-in-law) first entering his wife's home – try their *luci* (puris) and the fish and prawn preparations including *malai chingri* (prawns in cream) and *dab-er-chingri* (prawns in green coconut). Their set *thalas* (thali) start from ₹265 but expect to pay more. Tues–Sun 12.30–3pm & 7–10.30pm.

Mocha 209 Karnani Estate, AJC Bose Rd ☎ 033 3020 7406; map pp.734–735. Down the side of the old multistorey building, this popular chain restaurant and coffee bar comes dressed in loud clashing colours with reds, blues yellows and greens combined with edge-glow pink Perspex, swings and a shisha bar thankfully shut upstairs on the mezzanine. The broad menu appeals to teenagers and grown-ups alike and the coffees are great. Meals around ₹500. Daily 11am–11pm

Suruchi 89 Elliot Rd ⊚ abwu.org; map pp.734–735. Run by the All Bengal Women's Union, a charity for rehabilitated prostitutes and their children, and a good place to taste Bengali home-cooking – try the *mocha chingri* (prawns with banana flower). Unpretentious atmosphere and reasonable prices (from ₹100); recommended for lunch despite its poor location. Mon–Fri 12.30–3pm.

SOUTH KOLKATA

★ **Ammini** 21C Monohar Pukur Rd ☎ 033 3221 6769; map pp.734–735. Smart, modern bistro in a residential part of town, serving excellent and great-value Keralan cooking. Try the *kari meen* (fish curry) with *appam* (rice hoppers). Expect to pay around ₹400.

Banana Leaf 73 Rashbehari Ave, Lake Market; map pp.734–735. Plain decor and a fast turnaround for this extremely popular restaurant that cooks up some of the best south Indian food in town. Try their dosas or lemon

rice. An entire "meal" including cashewnut *uttapam* costs just ₹112. Daily noon–9pm.

Bhojohori Manna 18/1A Hindustan Rd ☎ 033 2466 3941; map pp.734–735. Popular chain serving Bengali food, with a huge menu – the main feature should be a fish or *chingri* (prawn) dish, or try the *kosha mangsho* (mutton curry). Expect to queue. There's a small branch on nearby Ekdalia Rd and a tiny branch at 11A Esplanade next to KC Das. Daily noon–9pm.

Bohemian 32 4 Old Ballygunge 1st Lane, Bondel Rd ☎ 033 6460 1001; map pp.734–735. The current talk of the town, serving Kolkata nouvelle cuisine in a simple but chic environment. There is a bewildering variety on offer, from Strogonoff to traditional Bengali prawn *gondhoraj* and almost everything else in between, including the ubiquitous pizza and pasta menu. Expect to pay around ₹700. Daily noon–3pm & 7–11pm.

Dolly's Tea Shop Dakshinapan Shopping Centre, Dhakuria; map pp.734–735. A small but iconic tea shop that lights up this cheerless concrete complex, with rattan furniture, a peaceful ambience and a great selection of teas and snacks including sandwiches and cakes. Mon–Sat 10am–6pm.

Tea Bush Table 5B Ashton Rd, near Hotel Samilton, off Sarat Bose Rd ☎ 033 4001 3937; map pp.734–735. A new and trendy café with chic design and an inventive menu including an extensive list of teas from the traditional to oriental exotic varieties, such as Pu-erh from China. They serve all-day breakfasts as well as sandwiches, salads and pasta. Expect to pay from ₹85 for tea and around ₹400 for a meal. Mon–Fri 11am–11pm, Sat & Sun 9am–11pm.

Tea Cafe P557 Lake Road Extension, opposite Vivekananda Park ☎ 033 4006 5500 or ☎ 84200 50213; map pp.734–735. This small bistro near the lakes, with smart but simple decor, is part of a Goa-based chain with additional influences from Kerala. This mixed heritage is reflected in the contemporary menu, which ranges from salads, sandwiches and pasta to Keralan *kachiya moru* (fish curry with buttermilk) and *Peixe-a-Portuguesa* (Portuguese/ Goan fish stew). Book ahead and expect to pay ₹500 for a meal. Mon–Fri 11am–10pm, Sat & Sun 11am–10.30pm.

ELSEWHERE IN THE CITY

Beijing 77/1 Christopher Rd, Tangra; map pp.734–735. Owned by a celebrated restaurateur, this restaurant has an extensive menu featuring favourites such as Peking chicken and steamed fish and Meifoon noodles. The bar is well stocked. Expect to pay around ₹700 for a meal with a drink. Daily noon–3pm & 7–10pm.

Haldiram Bhujiwala 58 Chowringhee Rd; map pp.734–735. A snack bar, sweetshop and café all rolled into one, this self-service vegetarian chain offers good if predictable food, with everything from samosas, thalis (from ₹110) and dosas to ice cream. Other branches on

13

SWEETSHOPS

Milk-based sweets such as the small and dry *sandesh* are a Bengali speciality. Though the white *rosogulla*, the brown (deep-fried) *pantua* and the distinctive black *kalojam*, all in syrup, are found elsewhere in north India, the best examples are made in Kolkata. Others worth trying are *lal doi* – a delicious red steamed yogurt made with jaggery – or white *mishti doi*, yogurt made with sugar. Sweetshops serve savoury snacks in the afternoons such as deep-fried pastry strips called *nimki* (literally "salty"); *shingara*, a delicate Bengali samosa; and *dalpuri*, *paratha*-like bread made with lentils.

Amrita 16-A Sarat Bose Rd; map pp.734–735. Excellent *mishti doi*.

Bhim Chandra Nag Surya Sen St, off College St; map pp.734–735. Best of several good sweetshops in the area.

Ganguram's 46-C Chowringhee Rd; map pp.737. Once-legendary sweetshop near Victoria Memorial, with branches all over the city; try *mishti doi* and *sandesh*.

KC Das 11 Esplanade East and 57-A Ripon St; map pp.734–735. The city's most famous sweetshop and a key location with a café and an a/c mezzanine; try their *rosogolla*. Other branches include Block B, Laketown.

Sen Mahasay 171-H Rashbehari Ave; map pp.734–735. Next to Gariahat Market, renowned for its *sandesh*; there are several other branches throughout the city including Shyambazaar.

Vien 34-B Shakespeare Sarani; map pp.737. Small, popular sweetshop, with excellent *sandesh* amongst other offerings.

Middleton Row and on Gariahat Rd in Ballygunge in a multi-floored supermarket. Mon–Sat 11am–8pm.

Kim Fa 47 South Tangra Rd ☎033 2329 2895; map pp.734–735. This small Chinese restaurant is still one of Tangra's best, serving excellent Hakka cuisine and popular with the local community. Try the Thai soup, garlic prawns and chilli king prawns, which can be quite potent. From ₹300. Daily noon–3pm & 7–10pm.

Mainland China 3-A Gurusaday Rd ☎033 2287 2206; map pp.734–735. Chic Chinese restaurant with elegant service and excellent seafood; widely considered the city's finest, but perhaps a bit overdone and, for some, overcooked. Expect to pay around ₹1000 for a night out. Daily noon–3pm & 7–11pm.

Royal Near Nakhoda Masjid, Rabindra Sarani; map pp.734–735. No trip to this area is complete without a visit to this legendary Muslim restaurant for a biriyani or a chicken or mutton *champ* (chop) cooked in aromatic spices and accompanied by *rumali* roti (thin "handkerchief" bread). It's basic, but there is an a/c room which charges more. Expect to pay around ₹200. Daily 11am–11pm.

Il Sogno Horizon Building, 57 Chowringhee Rd (AJC Bose Rd) ☎090070 67459; map pp.734–735. Smart new restaurant serving excellent and authentic Italian food presented by celebrated chef Davide Lucio Cananzi, but the service is chaotic and, at the time of going to press, they were still awaiting a liquor licence. Try the sea bass or the torched linguini bolognaise. Expect to pay around ₹800 a head. Daily noon–3pm & 7–11pm.

DRINKING AND NIGHTLIFE

The formerly tense, all-male atmosphere of Kolkata's **bars** is becoming a thing of the past, with designer-style places attracting a young, professional clientele. Shisha bars are popular, but you will need to put up with the smoke. As well as the places below, the big hotels are a good option for a quiet drink; some of them also have discos. At the time of going to press, due to a late-night rape in 2012, bars and discos along Park St have had to shut by 11pm. Most discos do not allow single males and entry is from ₹500.

Bar-B-Q 43 Park St; map p.737. On the ground floor of this popular restaurant, this is one of the more stylish bars on the strip and the food is good with tandoori and kebabs. Daily noon–11pm.

Blue and Beyond 9th floor, Hotel Lindsay, 8-A Lindsay St; map p.737. The terrace up here is probably the best spot for a relaxing drink and a nibble at dusk, with the bustle of New Market below yet out of earshot. Daily noon–11pm.

Fairlawn 13-A Sudder St; map pp.734–735. The small but popular beer garden and café with lush vegetation and parasols, makes a pleasing setting for a late afternoon or evening drink accompanied by a snacky meal. Daily 11am–11pm.

Floatel 9/10 Kolkata Jetty, Strand Rd; map pp.734–735. The *Anchor Bar* at water level is a fine place to languish in a/c splendour and watch crowded ferries passing by. The bar-restaurant upstairs with its expansive deck catches the river breeze, but is sometimes booked for events. Daily noon–11pm.

Park Hotel 17 Park St; map p.737. This hotel is brimming with bars and discos. *Tantra* is still the liveliest nightclub in town, starting at 7pm most days and 4pm on weekends, and attracting a well-heeled crowd with celebrities and fashion shows and live music on Sundays (from ₹500). Dimly lit yet lively, and essentially a pub, *Someplace Else* (no cover) features live bands playing Indian hits and Western rock; the poolside *Aqua* serves food and DJs pump out lounge music in the evenings; and the cocktail bar *Roxy*, designed with a stunning mix of aluminium and brick, offers an ample wine list (from ₹350) to a smart crowd. Daily noon–11pm.

Peter Cat 18-A Park St; map p.737. Plush and pleasant, this long-term favourite with diners and drinkers alike

maintains a good reputation as a bar, offering drinks from cocktails to beer, as for well as its food, including the much-lauded *chelo* kebab. Daily noon–11pm.

Underground Hotel Hindustan, 235/1 AJC Bose Rd; map pp.734–735. A long-standing popular nightclub with a young well-heeled crowd, offering a big dance floor where regular and guest DJs mix everything from hip-hop to Goan trance. From ₹500. Daily 7–11pm.

Venom Fort Knox, 6 Camac St; map p.737. All the rage in the evenings with a trendy, young clientele. There's a lounge bar as well as a dancefloor where the DJ pumps out a variety of music from bhangra to rock and roll. Daily 7–11pm.

ENTERTAINMENT

Scratch the surface and you can find some surprisingly eclectic traditions, from rock and roll in the bars of Park St to occasional snatches of jazz from a fading scene (best portrayed in the recent documentary *Finding Carlton*).

Cinema Cinemas showing English-language films several times each day can be found along Chowringhee near Esplanade and New Market. All are a/c; some, like Metro, 5 Jawaharlal Nehru Rd, Esplanade, and Elite, SN Banerjee Rd, are fine examples of Art Deco. Names to look for include Inox, a modern multiplex at the Forum on Elgin Rd (other branches at City Centre Salt Lake, City Centre II Rajarhat and South City). Nandan (☏ 033 2223 1210), behind Rabindra Sadan on AJC Bose Rd, is the city's leading art house cinema with a library, archives and three auditoria; Nandan also hosts the Kolkata Film Festival in mid-November (🌐 kff.in) with films shown at venues throughout the city.

CLASSICAL MUSIC

Kolkata has an unassailable reputation as the most discerning centre of classical Indian music in the country.

The main concert season runs from winter to spring, with the huge week-long Dover Lane Music Festival, held in south Kolkata around the end of January and early February, attracting many of India's best musicians. Other popular venues for single- and multiday festivals include Rabindra Sadan. Of the many non-religious festivals each year, the Ganga Utsav, held over a few weeks around the end of January at Diamond Harbour, involves music, dance and theatrical events.

Music classes One of the country's leading north Indian classical music research institutes, Sangeet Research Academy in Tollygunge (☏ 033 2377 3395, 🌐 itcsra.org) offers long-term courses in various music forms and a three-month short-term residential course ($500/month). They also host free Wednesday evening concerts as well as occasional concerts on Saturdays.

SHOPPING

Compared to Delhi, Kolkata has limited tourist shopping. However, there are many characterful **markets**, including the wide-ranging **New Market** (see p.738), as well as local institutions such as **Barabazaar** to the north (see p.741) and **Gariahat Market**, with its produce market best in the early mornings, in south Kolkata. Modern **shopping malls** – good for books, clothes, designer labels, leather and jewellery and restaurants – include Forum, 10/3 Elgin Rd; Emami Shoppers City at Lord Sinha Rd; South City Mall on Prince Anwar Shah Rd, South Kolkata; City Centre II at Rajarhat near the airport. Typical **Bengali handicrafts** to look out for include **metal** *dokra* items from the Shantiniketan region northwest of the city: animal and bird objects are roughly cast by a lost-wax process to give them a wiry look. Long-necked, pointy-eared terracotta horses from Bankura, in all sizes, have become something of a cliché. *Kantha* **fabrics** display delicate line stitching in decorative patterns. Bengal boasts several good centres of cotton and **silk** weaving, producing legendary **saris** such as the Baluchari style from Murshidabad.

BOOKS

The month-long Kolkata Book Fair, held at the Milan Mela ground off the EM Bypass in January and February, is now among the biggest of its kind in the country and provides a good opportunity to pick up books at a discount. The shops and the roadside stalls of College St are well worth a browse, with an occasional rare gem turning up amid stacks of science and computer studies books.

Crossword 8 Elgin Rd; map pp.734–735. Large modern bookshop on two floors, with a good selection including novels, illustrated books and travel, plus a music section and a café. Other branches can be found in South City Mall and City Centre, Salt Lake. Mon–Sat 10am–8pm.

Earthcare Books 10 Middleton St; map p.737. At the back of a yard, this small and modest but focused bookshop

13

specializes in books on green issues, and publishes several titles too. Mon–Sat 10am–7pm.

Seagull 31-A SP Mukherjee Rd ⓣ033 2476 5869, ⓦseagullindia.com. Pleasant little bookshop owned by interesting and creative publishers; their resource centre, a block away, has a library and holds special exhibitions and events. Mon–Sat 10am–6pm.

Starmark Emami Shoppers City, 3 Lord Sinha Rd. Extensive bookshop with an adequate range from fiction and travel to magazines as well as music and DVDs in a popular shopping complex. Other branches include South City Mall and City Centre, Salt Lake. Mon–Sat 10am–8pm.

Oxford Books & Stationery 17 Park S. An upmarket a/c bookshop with a small music section and the *Cha Bar* café upstairs. Nice atmosphere, but the collection is fairly limited. Mon–Sat 10am–8pm.

EMPORIA

Good selections of most handicrafts, including textiles and saris, can be found in various state emporia, many of which, such as Gujari (Gujarat), are located in the large Dakhsinapan shopping complex south of Dhakuria Bridge near Gol Park and the lakes. Offering fixed (if slightly high) prices, these are the simplest places to start shopping.

Assam 8 Russel St. Part of Assam House, selling handicrafts and textiles from Assam including fabrics in *pat* and *moga*, two techniques of silk manufacturing. Mon–Sat 10am–5pm.

Central Cottage Industries 7 Chowringhee Rd, Esplanade. Part of the national chain, with handicrafts, jewellery, silver, and fabrics from all over India, though service is apathetic and the stock is a bit faded. Mon–Sat 9.30am–6pm.

Nagaland 13 Shakespeare Sarani. A fine assortment of Naga shawls, with red bands and white and blue stripes on black backgrounds. As with Scots tartan, certain patterns denote particular tribes. Mon–Sat 10am–5pm.

Sasha 27 Mirza Ghalib St. This women's self-help group has a good collection of handicrafts and textiles including *kantha*. Mon–Sat 9.30am–5pm.

FABRICS, CLOTHING AND BOUTIQUES

Along with several designer boutiques, a wide range of fabric is available to buy and outlets can direct you toward good (and very cheap) tailors; there are several around Mirza Ghalib St and New Market. You can still get shoes made to order at one of the few remaining Chinese shoe shops around Bentinck St.

Anokhi 2nd Floor, Forum, 10/3 Elgin Rd. This is one branch of the national chain renowned for its chic Rajasthani hand-printed cottons with a wide range from clothing to furnishing. Mon–Sat 10am–8pm.

By Loom 58B Hindusthan Park. A small but stunning selection of handicrafts, textiles and saris fusing traditional handlooms and contemporary design to great effect. Mon–Sat 10am–7pm.

Fabindia 234 3-A AJC Bose Rd and 16 Hindusthan Park near Gariahat. Good selection of hand-printed *kurtas* and *salwar kameez* as well as shirts, fabrics and furnishings from this trendy chain boutique; they use natural dyes which run, so use a cool wash and separate colours. Other branches at City Centre, City Centre II and South City malls. Mon–Sat 10am–7pm.

Ritu's 4 Woodburn Court, Lala Lajpat Rai Sarani. Chic boutique for *salwar kameez* from a designer who started out here in Kolkata before rising to international fame dressing the likes of Jemima Khan and Princess Diana. Another branch is at South City Mall, Anwar Shah Rd. Mon–Sat 10am–7pm.

Tia Pakhi 49/13 Hindustan Park. Small but delightful selection of gifts and home furnishings featuring traditional craft with contemporary design, in the increasingly chic part of town. Mon–Sat 10am–7pm.

MUSICAL INSTRUMENTS

Kolkata is renowned for its sitar and sarod makers – expect to pay upwards of ₹12500 for a decent instrument, much more for a premium one. Manoj Kumar Sardar & Bros, 8A Lalbazaar St, opposite Lalbazaar Police Station (ⓣ033 2237 5835, ⓦmonojkrsardar.com) makes good sitars and sarods to order; they also have a small selection of off-the-shelf instruments. Radha Krishna Sharma, 58 Vivekananda Rd, north of College St (ⓣ09831116953), is similar. The legendary Hemen & Co, Triangular Park, Rashbehari Ave (ⓣ033 2466 2607), has made sarods for some famous musicians and makes pricey instruments to order; it's now run by the son of the original owner. Shops around Sudder St are strongest on Western instruments, but their traditional instruments are invariably of inferior quality and may be beyond tuning; Rabindra Sarani (Chitpore Rd) has a concentration of shops of varying quality, many catering to the wedding-band trade. Kolkata must produce more tabla players than any other city; tabla makers can be found next to Kalighat Bridge and at Keshab Sen St off College St.

SPORTS

Sport is enthusiastically followed in Kolkata, with **football** matches – especially those between the two leading clubs, Mohan Bagan and East Bengal – and **cricket** test matches drawing huge crowds. There are two major stadium complexes, **Ranji** at Eden Gardens and **Salt Lake** on the eastern edge of the city. The **Maidan**, home to the Calcutta Bowling Club and the Ladies Golf Club, is a favourite venue for impromptu cricket and football matches, and the scene of regular race

13

meets in winter and spring run by the Calcutta Turf Club which also has **polo** on the grounds at the centre of the racecourse. The curious sport of **kabadi**, a fierce form of tag played by two teams on a pitch the size of a badminton court, can also be seen around the Maidan. The *Hindusthan International Hotel*, 235-1 AJC Bose Rd (☎ 033 2247 2394), allows non-residents to use their **swimming pool** on a daily basis (₹500). Across the road from the superbly equipped Tollygunge Club, where (with the right connections) you might get to use the pool and tennis courts, the elite Royal Calcutta Golf Club is the world's second oldest **golf club**, after St Andrews in Scotland.

DIRECTORY

Ambulance Call ☎ 102, or the Red Cross ☎ 033 2248 3636; St John's Ambulance Brigade ☎ 033 2476 1935; or Bellevue Clinic ☎ 033 2287 2321.

Banks and currency exchange Kolkata airport has a 24hr branch of the State Bank of India (SBI), as well as Thomas Cook at the international terminal. There are numerous private foreign exchange bureaux around Sudder St, New Market and in the vicinity of Park St, some offering very competitive rates. Banks that offer foreign exchange around the centre include SBI, 38B Chowringhee Rd and 1 Strand Rd; Standard Chartered Bank, 41 Chowringhee Rd and Citibank, 43 Chowringhee Rd. Other currency exchange bureaux include Thomas Cook, 19B Shakespeare Sarani (☎ 033 6652 6625) (other offices at Salt Lake and Lake Gardens), and American Express, 21 Old Court House St, near the West Bengal Tourist Office (☎ 033 2248 9491). The ATM machines at banks such as SBI, Axis and HSBC, among others, take MasterCard, Visa, Cirrus and Maestro.

Consulates Bangladesh, 9 Circus Ave (Sheikh Mujib Sarani) (☎ 033 4012 7500); Bhutan, 48 Tivoli Court, 1A Ballygunge Circular Rd (☎ 033 4012 3999); Canada, Duncan House, 31 Netaji Subhash Rd (☎ 033 2242 6820); China, EC-72 Sector 1, Salt Lake (☎ 033 4004 8169); Germany, 1 Hastings Park Rd, Alipur (☎ 033 2479 1141); Burma (Myanmar), 57K Ballygunge Circular Rd (☎ 033 2485 1658); Nepal, 1 National Library Ave, Alipore (☎ 033 2456 1224); Singapore, 8 AJC Bose Rd (☎ 033 2247 4990); South Africa, 225-D AJC Bose Rd (☎ 033 2247 4107); Sri Lanka, Nicco House, 2 Hare St (☎ 033 2248 5102); Thailand,18-B Mandeville Gardens (☎ 033 2440 7836); UK, 1A Ho Chi Minh Sarani (☎ 033 2288 5172); USA, 5/1 Ho Chi Minh Sarani (☎ 033 3984 2400).

Hospitals Cheap, government-run hospitals are notoriously mismanaged, and private medical care, if expensive by comparison, is infinitely superior. In case of serious illness, you are best advised to contact your consulate. Good private clinics include Belle Vue, 9 Loudon St (☎ 033 2287 2321), Ruby General, EM Bypass, Kasba (☎ 033 2442 0291); and Woodlands Nursing Home, 8/5 Alipore Rd (☎ 033 2456 7075).

Internet Net access (from ₹15 an hour) is easily available throughout the city – look for Sify iWays. Of the places around Sudder St, by far the most pleasant is Gomukh, 7 Sudder St, at the back of the courtyard, with a gift shop and an excellent café next door – remove your shoes.

Permits and visas The Foreigners' Registration Office is at 237-A AJC Bose Rd (☎ 033 2247 0549).

Pharmacies Deys Medical Stores, 6 Lindsay St and 20-A Nelly Sengupta Sarani; Angel, 151 Park St (24hr); Dhanwantary Clinic, 65 Diamond Harbour Rd (24hr); Welmed, 4–1 Sambhunath Pandit St (24hr Mon & Tues).

Police ☎ 100. The central police station is on Lal Bazaar St, BBD Bagh (☎ 033 2241 3230). Others include Park St (☎ 033 2226 8321).

Postal services The GPO, on the west side of BBD Bagh, houses the poste restante and a philatelic department. If you're staying in the Sudder St area, the New Market Post Office, Mirza Ghalib St, is much more convenient. Sending parcels is easiest from the large and friendly post office on Park St, where enterprising individuals will handle the entire process for you for a negotiable fee. For a quicker service, DHL has several offices including one at 6 Kedia Villa, Marquis St (☎ 033 2217 1675).

Around Kolkata

The Hindu temples of **Dakshineshwar** and **Belur Math**, and even the great Vaishnavite centres of **Nabadip** and **Mayapur** further north, can be taken in as day-trips on local trains from Kolkata's Sealdah and Howrah stations.

Dakshineshwar

Oct–March 6am–12.30pm & 3–8.30pm, April–Sept 6am–12.30pm & 3.30–9pm • Free • Local trains run from Sealdah to Dakshineshwar

At the edge of Kolkata, 20km north of Esplanade on the east bank of the river, the popular temple of **Dakshineshwar** stands in the shadow of Bally Bridge. Built in

13

1855, it was a product of the Bengali Renaissance, consecrated at a time when growing numbers of middle-class Hindus were questioning their faith. Typical Bengali motifs – a curved roof reminiscent of local village huts, nine chhatris and beehive cupolas – dominate the design. The mystic and influential religious philosopher **Ramakrishna** once officiated here, and his room, beside the main gate, now houses a collection of his personal effects. His life is beautifully portrayed in Romain Rolland's biography, *The Life of Ramakrishna*. Not far from the main temple, **Yogoday Satsanga Math** is the headquarters of the Self-Realization Fellowship, founded in California in 1925 by the author of *Autobiography of a Yogi*, **Paramahansa Yogananda**.

Belur Math

April–Sept 6–11.30am & 4–7pm; Oct–March 6.30am–noon & 3.30–6pm • Free • ⓦ belurmath.org • The Math is best visited along with a trip to Dakshineshwar; Local trains run from Howrah to Belur Math (5 daily, 25min)

Across the bridge from Dakshineshwar, 3km south along the west bank of the Hooghly, is the serene forty-acre riverfront campus of **Belur Math**. Founded by a disciple of Ramakrishna, **Swami Vivekananda**, and completed (after his death) in 1938, the monastery houses temples and museums dedicated to the Mission. It incorporates elements from several world religions; the gate is inspired by early Buddhist sculpture, the windows by Islamic architecture, and the ground plan is based on the Christian cross. After the *math* closes in the evenings, you may stay for **arati** (evening worship), held at the Sri Ramakrishna Temple, followed by meditation till around 8pm.

Nabadip and Mayapur

An important centre for Vaishnava pilgrimage, the little town of **Nabadip** (or Nawadip) lies on the west bank of the Hooghly, around 100km north of Kolkata. Once the eleventh-century capital of Bengal under the Sen dynasty, Nabadip was also the home of Hindu sage **Sri Chaitanya** (1486–1533) and its temples are alive with his devotees singing *kirtan* (devotional song). A 50km *padakrama*, or foot pilgrimage, links the various Vaishnava sites spread across nine islands. Nabadip may be a Vaishnava town, but its most atmospheric temple is the **Kali Bari** at Poramatolla, tucked into the folds of one of the most impressive banyan trees you are ever likely to see.

Across the river from Boral Ghat (ferry ₹5), the jetty at Nabadip, the Vaishnava centre of **Mayapur**, run by the Hare Krishna sect of ISKCON, draws huge crowds at weekends, visitors thronging to the labyrinthine temple complex where a gigantic basilica is under construction. One way of exploring the area is on the afternoon boat ride (₹30) that takes in some of the holy islands, but this is part pilgrimage and is accompanied with lectures.

ARRIVAL AND INFORMATION   NABADIP & MAYAPUR

By train Several trains from Howrah run to Nabadip, 2.5km from the main Boral Ghat (₹30 by cycle rickshaw). An alternative is to take a train from Sealdah to Krishnagar, then a bus or auto rickshaw to Mayapur Ghat and then a ferry.

Tourist Information ISKCON's Mayapur Tourism Centre, Opposite Gada Bhavan (ⓦ visitmayapur.com) also organizes transport from Kolkata and you can book online.

ACCOMMODATION

ISKCON's Shri Mayapur Dham ☏ 03472 245620, ⓦ mayapurguesthouse.com. The well-run Mayapur complex has a huge variety of accommodation from simple pilgrim rooms to a/c splendour in one of several guesthouses. You can book online. Besides the two dining halls with set meal times, there is a restaurant open till 9pm; the entire site is vegetarian and alcohol is forbidden. **₹400**

The Sundarbans and the Gangetic Delta

13

South of Kolkata down to the coast, the Hooghly fringes one of the world's largest estuarine deltas, the **Sundarbans**, a 10,000-square-kilometre expanse of mangrove swamp and forested islets formed by silt swept down from the Himalayas and home to the world's largest population of **tigers**. Closer to the city, the former colonial port of **Diamond Harbour** is a popular weekend break and lies en route to **Sagardwip**, a sacred island where the Ganges reaches the sea. The expansive **beaches** of the delta provide quiet respite and are within easy reach of Kolkata.

Sundarbans Tiger Reserve

The cluster of mangrove-covered islands known as the **Sundarbans** or "beautiful forest", lie in the Ganges Delta, stretching east from the mouth of the Hooghly to Bangladesh. They are home to the legendary **Royal Bengal tiger**, which has adapted remarkably well to this watery environment, swimming from island to island and covering distances of as much as 40km in one day. The region has been designated a UNESCO World Heritage Site and its abundant wildlife also includes saltwater crocodiles, Gangetic dolphins, otters and monitor lizards. All the half-million or so people sharing this delicate ecosystem, regardless of religion, worship Banbibi, the goddess of the forest, and her Muslim consort Dakshin Rai, supreme ruler of the Sundarbans.

Along with a crocodile and turtle hatchery, the Project Tiger compound at **Sajnekhali** also houses a shrine to Banbibi. There is a **watchtower** here, but others like Dobanki, where an aerial walkway skirts the top of the mangroves, and Netidhopani, which sits near the ruins of a four-hundred-year-old temple, are far more attractive. As getting to the Sundarbans on your own is a laborious process, you might want to opt for an all-inclusive package tour. Be aware, though, that tiger sightings are rare.

ARRIVAL AND INFORMATION

SUNDARBANS TIGER RESERVE

Season The Sundarbans are open from September to March.

Travel to Sajnkhali Travelling independently, and not through a pre-arranged tour package, is an adventure in itself – take a train to Canning from Sealdah, a shared taxi from Canning to Godhkali, a ferry to Gosaba Bazaar, a rickshaw or cycle van to Pakhirala Tigar Mor (6km), and finally a ferry to Sajnekhali. Alternatively, take an early bus from Kolkata's Babu Ghat to Basanti (6 daily; 3hr; from 6.45am), an auto to Godhkali (Gosaba Ghat), a ferry to Gosaba Bazaar, and then as above. Scheduled ferries cross the estuarine channel from Pakhirala to Sanjnekhali (7am & 6pm) or you could negotiate a country boat; boats are also available at Godhkali or Dayapur near Gosaba.

Permits Foreigners require a permit (free) in advance from the WB Tourist Centre in Kolkata (see p.748) to visit the Sundarbans; tour companies will arrange them for you.

Entry fee Visitors need to pay entry fees (₹40)to the national park at Sajnekhali.

Transport within the reserve All transport is by boat, which can be rented from the Boatman Association with the help of the lodge staff (from ₹1000 depending on your itinerary). You have to take along a Project Tiger guide (₹600 (₹300)) and pay an entry fee of ₹340 (video camera ₹200). The loud diesel motors scare wildlife away, but when they cut their engines the silence is awesome.

ACCOMMODATION

The only accommodation within the reserve is at the *Tourist Lodge* at Sajnekhali. All other accommodation is on the fringes but some of these are well managed with attractive tours (see box, p.749) arranged from Kolkata.

Sajnekhali Tourist Lodge Sajnekhali ☎03218 214960; reservations: WBTDC, 3/2 BBD Bagh, Kolkata ☎033 4401 2659. This ramshackle wooden lodge on stilts is devoid of all charm except for its unique access to the core forest; there is a dorm and rates include basic meals. The caged approach and the institutional atmosphere add to a certain feeling of incarceration and you are best advised to remain upstairs after dark. The boat ride option is thoroughly recommended. The compound also houses the Project Tiger office as well as a shrine to Banbibi, and monitor lizards roam free. Dorm ₹**500**, double ₹**1200**

Sunderban Tiger Camp Opposite Sajnekhali ☎033 3293 5749, ⊛sunderbantigercamp.com. Well-organized and popular package including pick up from

PLANNING YOUR VISIT TO THE SUNDERBANS

WBTDC organize two- and three-day packages with the option of staying either on the boat, at the *Sunderban Tiger Camp* or at the *Sajnekhali Tourist Lodge* (from ₹2800). The cruises can get crowded and noisy. In season, Vivada Cruises (☎033 2463 1990, ⊕vivadacruises.com) offers luxury cruises to the Sundarbans. Alternatively you can arrange your own boat at Gosaba Ghat in Godhkali (see p.759).. Tailor-made tours by private operators (from ₹18,000 for a three-day itinerary) are more peaceful and leisurely: try Kali Travel Home (see p.749), or Neil Law of Himalayan Footprints (see p.749) who runs his own camp and boats. Help Tourism (see p.749) also have a deservedly good reputation.

south Kolkata and boat excursions. Accommodation is in tents, huts and cottages, including some with a/c, near Gosaba; also popular as a WBTC tour. **₹6310**

Sunderbans Jungle Camp & Sundergaon Earth Villa Bali Island. ☎033 2455 0917, ⊕kolkata @helptourism.com. Run by Help Tourism partly in conjunction with conservationist Belinda Wright, the camp on the edge of the reserve is a tasteful mix of rustic tradition and contemporary comfort. They have their own boat and employ local villagers. Their all-inclusive package includes engagement with the community along with wildlife tours, and pick up from Kolkata. **₹32,000**

Along the Hooghly to the sea

South of Kolkata the Hooghly merges with the delta, gaining girth rapidly as it approaches Sagardwip and the islands at the river's mouth. The river scenery is particularly popular with city folk at the weekends, who come to enjoy the breeze of **Diamond Harbour**, 50km south of Kolkata. At the far southern end of the Delta, the casuarina-lined beaches provide a welcome retreat from the grime of Kolkata.

Hindus revere **Sagardwip**, also known as Sagar Island, as the point where the Ganges meets the sea. At the mouth of the Hooghly, it is accessible by ferry from Harwood Point near Diamond Harbour and from Namkhana further south. The confluence is venerated at the **Kapil Muni Temple**, on an island that bears the brunt of the savage Bay of Bengal cyclones and is gradually being submerged. On Makar Sankranti (mid-Jan), during the **Sagar Mela**, hundreds of thousands of pilgrims from all over India descend on the island, cramming into the water to bathe. Facilities are limited at the best of times but alternatives include Diamond Harbour and the island beaches such as **Bakkhali** at the western reaches of the Sunderbans.

ARRIVAL AND DEPARTURE

To Diamond Harbour The trip down to Diamond Harbour from the city, by bus or train from Sealdah Station, is a popular day's excursion for Kolkatans who come to enjoy the river cruises.

To Sagardwip Direct buses from Esplanade travel to Harwood Point during the *mela*; the island can also be reached from Namkhana (3hr) on the suburban railway network from Kolkata's Sealdah Station, from where the quiet casuarina-lined beach at Bakkhali is easily accessible.

ALONG THE HOOGHLY TO THE SEA

Once on Sagardwip, the temple is a further 32km from the ferry, and can be accessed by bus or taxi.

To Sagar Mela WBTDC (see p.748) organize a coach trip as well as a cruise (from ₹5000/person) to visit the mela. The advantage of the cruise is that you can stay on the boat and avoid the crush.

To Bakkhali Trains from Sealdah travel to Namkhana where a rickshaw takes you to a ferry and a bus to Bakkhali.

ACCOMMODATION

DIAMOND HARBOUR

Diamond Harbour Tourist Lodge ☎03174 255246. Run by the WBTDC, this is large institutional block with plain a/c and fan-ventilated rooms, some of them tiny and cramped; the service is poor and the food basic but it does have grand views of the river–though that might not be enough to warrant a stay. **₹550**

Ganga Kutir Raichak ☎03174 275632 or ☎033 4040 4040, ⊕gangakutir.com. Luxurious new resort by one of Bengal's leading Marwari developers, with a spa and gourmet restaurant, and a swimming pool that blends into the river scenery. The sister concern, *Ffort*, is older, with a more traditional ambience. **₹15,800**

SAGARDWIP AND AROUND

Sagardwip has limited accommodation, especially during the *mela*, with a handful of lodges, ashrams and *dharamshalas* offering basic accommodation; you'll find much greater choice at Bakkhali. Bring mosquito repellent, and if staying at Sagardwip, bring your own sleeping bag.

Bharat Seva Ashram Near Kapil Muni Temple, Sagardwip. Basic dharamshala near the temple, geared towards pilgrims and almost impossible to book during the mela; there are simple rice restaurants nearby for food. You are expected to give a donation, as suggested here, to the caretaker. ₹**200**

Tourist Lodge Bakkhali ✆03210 225260 or ✆033 2248 8271. Extensive government-run lodge with elaborate garden and kitsch sculptures of a flock of flamingos. The a/c rooms are generously sized and it is the only accommodation here with direct access to the expansive beach beyond the casuarinas. They have their own restaurant, and there are other places to eat in the vicinity. ₹**1650**

Youth Hostel Near Kapil Muni Temple, Sagardwip ✆033 2248 0626. With plain and cheap rooms and no restaurant but basic cafes nearby, this extensive hostel is one of the few places to stay on the island. ₹**150**

Central Bengal

A low-lying rural region where the pace of life is in stark contrast to that of Kolkata, **central Bengal** has a few sights to tempt tourists off the Kolkata–Darjeeling route. **Shantiniketan**, built on the site of Rabindranath Tagore's father's ashram, is a haven of peace, and a must for anyone interested in Bengali music, art and culture. The other highlights of the region include a cluster of exquisite terracotta temples in **Bishnupur**, the ruins of **Gaur**, the region's seventh-century capital, and the palaces of **Murshidabad**, capital of Bengal's last independent dynasty. With the Maoist insurgency along the borders of Jharkhand and Odisha, the southwestern districts of Bengal have become too dangerous to visit.

Bishnupur

A sleepy backwater town 150km northwest of Kolkata, **Bishnupur** is a famous centre of Bengali learning, renowned above all for its exquisite **terracotta temples**. It was the capital of the Malla rajas, under whose patronage one of India's greatest schools of **music** developed. The roots of Bishnupur's long tradition of temple building are in the basic form of the domestic hut translated into temple architecture. Built of brick and faced with finely carved terracotta decoration, the temples combine striking simplicity of form with vibrant texture.

Several temples (daily 9am–5pm; pass for all sites ₹100 (₹5)) lie scattered in a wide area around Bishnupur. **Raas Mancha**, built in 1587 by Bir Hambir in a unique pyramidal style, is used to display the images of Krishna and Radha during the annual Raas festival. Nearby, the well-preserved **Shyamarai**, built in 1643, is a particularly fine example of terracotta art, while the smaller **Jorbangla** has fine detail. The unassuming tenth-century **Mrinmoyee temple** encloses the auspicious *nababriksha*, nine trees growing as one. To the north of town and dating from 1694, the **Madan Mohan**, with its domed central tower and scenes from the life of Krishna, is one of the largest.

ARRIVAL AND DEPARTURE   BISHNUPUR

By train Of the express trains that connect Kolkata to Bishnupur, the basic *Rupashi Bangla Express* (#12883 #12884) is the most convenient for a day-trip, departing Howrah Station at 6am.

ACCOMMODATION

Basudah ✆09432 145532, ⊛traveleastindia.com. A rural idyll in an adobe farmhouse 16km from Bishnupur, devoted to organic farming, conservation and research. This is the best way to see Bengali village life in all its simplicity. Kali Travel Home arrange the recommended three-day package from Kolkata, which includes transport. ₹**18,200**

Tourist Lodge ✆033 2210 3199, reserve via the WBTDC (see p.748). Close to Raas Mancha, this extensive government-run complex, with a range of fair-sized plain rooms from basic doubles to a/c deluxe, is the most convenient for visiting the sites. The restaurant serves Bengali rice-based meals. Book well ahead during the festival season. ₹**600**

13

Shantiniketan

Despite rapid growth and encroachment into the tribal Santhal habitat, the peaceful haven of **Shantiniketan**, 136km northwest of Kolkata, remains a world away from the clamour and grime of the city. Founded by Nobel Laureate **Rabindranath Tagore** in 1921 on the site of his father's ashram, both the settlement and its liberal arts university **Vishwa Bharati** were designed to promote the best of Bengali culture. Towards the end of the Bengali Renaissance, Tagore's vision and immense talent inspired a whole way of life and art; the university and school still operate under this momentum.

Centred around the **Uttarayan** complex of buildings, designed by Tagore, the university is very much in harmony with its surroundings, despite its recent growth as Kolkatans have settled or built holiday homes nearby. Well-known graduates include Indira Gandhi and Satyajit Ray, and departments such as **Kala Bhavan** (art) and **Sangeet Bhavan** (music) still attract students from all over the world.

The renowned **Bauls**, Bengal's wandering minstrels, who play a unique style of folk music, gather during the afternoon at the informal **shanibarer haat** (Saturday market) held under the trees by Shriniketan's canal, where Shantal tribals also gather to sell their crafts. The large fair of **Poush Mela**, between December 22 and 25, attracts numerous Bauls each year.

Kala Bhavan Archive

Daily except Tues 10am–5pm • Free, with special permission from the head of department

The **Kala Bhavan Archive** houses twentieth-century Bengali sculpture and painting, including works by eminent artists such as Abanendranath and Gaganendranath Tagore, Nandalal Bose and Rabindranath Tagore himself, as well as a collection of Chinese and Japanese art.

The Vichitra Museum

Uttarayan • Thurs–Mon 10.30am–1pm & 2–4.30pm, Tues 10.30am–1pm • ₹5

Also known as the Rabindra Bhavan Museum, the **Vichitra Museum** captures the spirit of Tagore's life and work with a collection of his paintings, manuscripts and personal effects.

ARRIVAL AND DEPARTURE   SHANTINIKETAN

By train Bolpur, 3km south of Shantiniketan, is the nearest railway station, on the main line between Kolkata and Darjeeling, served by several trains via Burddhaman (or Burdwan). The best train for Bolpur from Kolkata is the *Shantiniketan Express* #12337, which leaves Howrah at 10.10am and terminates at Bolpur at 12.25pm, departing for Howrah 30min later. Baul singers occasionally busk in second-class carriages. If you're heading on from Shantiniketan to Darjeeling, the best of the daily express trains is the *Darjeeling Mail* #12343, which stops late at night (12.34am) in Bolpur but arrives in New Jalpaiguri (NJP) at 8am the next morning. The best daytime train is the *Kanchenjunga Express* #15657, which departs at

9.40am and arrives at NJP at 6.20pm. Reservations are available from the Shantiniketan reservations counter (Mon–Sat 10am–3pm) near the post office, though this has limited quotas; the computerized reservations counter at Bolpur Station offers more choice.

By bus The main bus stand is at Jamboni, 2km west towards Surul with connections to Kenduli and Rampurhat (Tarapith) among other destinations.

By cycle rickshaws or bike Cycle rickshaws are the chief means of transport in the area and generally very reliable, but the best way to experience Shantiniketan is to cycle – ask at your hotel or at one of the bicycle shops along the main road.

ACCOMMODATION

The Shantiniketan area holds a reasonable amount of accommodation, with several options along the noisy main Shantiniketan–Bolpur Rd, and more appealing places around the fringes of the campus and especially Shyambati where there is a small choice. Expect to pay a lot more during Poush Mela when you are advised to book well ahead.

Babli Farm Illambazar Rd ☎ 03463 271285, ⊛ babli .org. An agricultural and forestry project that works with the local community to develop a balanced ecosystem. The

farm features beautiful, traditional cottages and a healthy menu in their restaurant – this is open to non-residents but it's advisable to book ahead. **₹800**

13

RABINDRANATH TAGORE

The Bengali poet and literary giant **Rabindranath Tagore** (1861–1941) has inspired generations of artists, poets and musicians. He developed an early interest in theatre, and set his poems to music – this was to become, as Rabindra Sangeet, one of the most popular musical traditions in Bengal. Introduced to England and the West by the painter William Rothenstein and the poet W.B. Yeats, Tagore had his collection of poems, *Gitanjali*, first published in translation in 1912, and the following year was awarded the Nobel Prize for Literature. Though he preferred to write in Bengali, and encouraged authors in other Indian languages, he was also a master of English prose. Not until he was in his 70s did his talent as an artist and painter emerge, developed from scribblings on the borders of his manuscripts. Tagore was an enormous inspiration to many, including his students, the illustrious painter Nandalal Bose, and later the filmmaker Satyajit Ray, who based several of his films on the works of the master.

Bolpur Lodge Bolpur ☎03463 252662 or ☎09800 119894. Large, long-established and welcoming lodge, set away from the bustle of the main road with a pleasant courtyard. Rooms are large, plain and good value, either fan-cooled or with a/c. There's also a reasonable restaurant. ₹**350**

Bonpulak Shyambati ☎03463 261193. Three pleasant, airy rooms in a friendly family home with a small, colourful garden on the edge of the campus; meals on request. ₹**500**

★ **Chhuti** 241 Charu Palli, Jamboni ☎03463 252692, ⓦchhutiresort.com. Comfortable and well-laid out cottages with an ethnic touch, some with a/c, and a restaurant. Still the most pleasant option around Shantiniketan; credit cards accepted with a 2 percent charge. ₹**1540**

Malancha Shyambati Bazaar ☎094343 48742. In the middle of the market, with small, plain rooms and convenient cafés nearby. Handy for the university. ₹**500**

Hotel Shantiniketan Bhubandanga ☎03463 254434. Bright pink hotel with a pleasant garden and a quiet location down a lane; the cheaper rooms are good value but hot water comes by the bucket. ₹**750**

Shantiniketan Tourist Lodge Bolpur Tourist Lodge Rd ☎03463 252699, reservations ☎033 2210 3199. Large government-run place midway between Bolpur and Shantiniketan, with some a/c rooms, good-value cottages, a pleasant garden and a restaurant. The a/c rooms are a bit overpriced. ₹**700**

EATING

Alcha Ratanpalli ⓦalchastore.com. A delightful little garden café that combines a bookshop, a library (refundable deposit), a gallery and a small but excellent boutique selling clothes and furnishings; it's also good for breakfasts, grilled sandwiches, snacks and cake. Daily 8–10.30am & 4–8pm.

Ghare Baire Gitanjali Complex, Siuri Rd. This is as smart

as it gets in Shantiniketan, with a pleasant upmarket ambience and an eclectic menu including mocktails (from ₹50), Chinese dishes for when you need to get away from dhal bhaat and south Indian food. But the Bengali cuisine is best – try the special thali with fish or mutton (₹225); the vegetarian classic thali is great value (₹80). Daily noon–8pm.

Tarapith

One of the most important centres of Tantric Hinduism, **Tarapith** is easily visited on a day-trip and features in William Dalrymple's recent book *Nine Lives*. The temple and the cremation ground, in a grove beside the river littered with shrines 50km north of Shantiniketan, are popular with Tantric sadhus, and it's not uncommon to witness rituals involving skulls and cremation ashes. The temple, in a perpetually busy courtyard, is dedicated to the mysterious and feared goddess Tara, who appears here with a silver face and large eyes. The lanes leading to the temple are a hive of activity where pilgrims procure offerings and liaise with temple priests (*panda*) to officiate in deeply personal ceremonies.

ARRIVAL AND DEPARTURE
TARAPITH

By train The *Ganadevta Express* #13017 departs Howrah at 6.05am, passing through Bolpur near Shantiniketan (8.52am) and arriving at Rampurhat railway station, 8km north of Tarapith, at 10.20am; the

4.45pm *Rampurhat Express* #12348 returns via Shantiniketan. Buy tickets in advance – as the time of departure approaches, the station and the footbridges become uncomfortably chaotic.

13

By auto-rickshaw Shared *tempos* (auto-rickshaws); (₹30), the main mode of public transport, regularly ply the path between Tarapith and Rampurhat station. To reserve an auto-rickshaw, negotiate at the stands.

ACCOMMODATION AND EATING

Amantran Rampurhat Rd, 3km from the temple ⊕ 03461 253133 or ⊕ 09836 066999. This welcoming place offers a wide selection of sleeping options: airy rooms; a selection of small cottages, some a/c (the non-a/c rooms are expensive); and a good restaurant and bar. The landscaped garden, popular during the wedding season, has a small lake and a non-chlorinated swimming pool in the hot season. ₹**1800**

Bengal Lodge Near the river ⊕ 09775 164636. Just 50m from the temple gates, this popular, good-value lodge offers a choice of plain or a/c rooms close to the temple and next to the cremation grounds and the small ceremonial ghat. There is a popular dhal *bhaat* restaurant downstairs. ₹**350**

Sonar Bangla Rampurhat Rd ⊕ 03461 253827, ⊕ hotelsonarbangla.com/tarapith/. This is the most luxurious hotel in the centre of town with an incongruous resort-like atmosphere, large grounds and a block at the back that looks down onto a central, well-designed landscape garden and pool. The non-a/c rooms are overpriced; the best, and most expensive, rooms are those clustered around the swimming pool. The restaurant has an extensive menu but service can be slow. ₹**1125**

Kendubilwa

The town of **Kendubilwa**, also known as **Kenduli**, 42km west of Shantiniketan on the bank of a wide shallow river, is the birthplace of **Jaidev**, the author of Gita Govinda, and the spiritual home of the Bauls. Its small terracotta temple is engulfed each year in mid-January when the **Jaidev Mela** attracts streams of pilgrims, as well as a collection of yogis and sadhus who gather among the banyan trees to hear the **Bauls** perform through the night. Over the years the *mela* has grown to include a wide range of stalls and a funfair. During the *mela*, special buses leave regularly from Bolpur (2hr).

Murshidabad

Set in the brilliant green landscape of rural Bengal and close to the commercial town of **Behrampur**, **Murshidabad**, 219km north of Kolkata, represents the grand and final expression of independent Bengal before the arrival of the British. Several eighteenth-century monuments along the banks of the Hooghly stand as melancholic reminders of its days as the last independent capital of Bengal.

Established early in the eighteenth century by the **Nawab Murshid Quli Khan**, Mzurshidabad was soon eclipsed when the forces of Siraj-ud-Daula were defeated by Robert Clive at the Battle of Plassey in 1757, as a result of which the British came to dominate Bengal from the new city of Calcutta. Clive described Murshidabad as equal to London, with several palaces and seven hundred mosques; today most of its past glory lies in ruins, though it is still renowned for cottage industries, especially silk weaving.

Murshidabad's intriguing mixture of cultures is reflected in its architectural styles, which range from the columned **Hazarduari** to the **Katra Mosque**, built by Murshid Quli Khan in the style of the mosque at Mecca. A large oxbow lake, the **Moti Jheel** or **Pearl Lake**, guards the desolate ruins of Begum Ghaseti's palace, where Siraj-ud-Daula reigned before his defeat, and which was subsequently occupied for a while by Clive. To the south and across the river, **Khushbagh**, the **Garden of Delight**, holds the tombs of many of the nawabs, including Alivardi Khan and Siraj-ud-Daula.

Hazarduari

Lalbagh • Sat–Thurs 10am–4.30pm • ₹100 (₹15) • ⊕ murshidabad.net

Hazarduari, the nawab's Italianate palace, designed by General Duncan Macleod of the Bengal Engineers, with its mirrored banqueting hall, circular durbar room, armoury and library of fine manuscripts, is now a museum; some of the paintings are in dire need of restoration, but the portrait collection is excellent.

The main transport hub for Murshidabad is Behrampur, 11km to the south. Auto-rickshaws (₹30), cycle rickshaws and ferries provide access to the sites of Murshidabad.

By train A few trains run to Behrampur from Kolkata (4–6hr), including the *Hazarduari Express* #13113 (6.50am from Chitpur) which also stops at Murshidabad (5hr 20min); there is more choice from Azimganj, 20km and a ₹800 taxi-ride away with trains like *Kamrup Express* #15959 (from Howrah, arriving to 2.40pm) travelling on to NJP and Assam.

By bus Most long-distance buses arrive and depart from Behrampur Station with connections to Kolkata's Esplanade (5–6hr), as well as Malda (3hr 30min).

By ferry A regular short ferry service (8am–5pm; ₹3) from near Hazarduari in Lalbagh is the only direct means of access to places across the river, including Khushbagh.

ACCOMMODATION

Manjusha Near Hazarduari ☎ 03482 70321. This is a welcoming place, beautifully situated, overlooking the timeless river. However, the rooms are disappointingly dingy. The catering is poor but a short walk along the river leads to restaurants. The early morning boat ride, arranged here, to Khushbagh is thoroughly recommended. ₹400

Sunshine Panchanantala, Behrampur ☎ 03482 277322. With a handy location close to the main highway and away from the chaos of central Behrampur, yet not far from Murshidabad if you have transport, this hotel offers a range from plain basic rooms to good-value a/c, and a multicuisine restaurant. ₹800

Malda and around

Famous for its mangoes, the large, unattractive commercial town of **Malda**, 340km north of Kolkata, makes a good base to explore the historic sites of **Gaur** and **Pandua**, both earlier capitals of Bengal.

Gaur

Spread across a landscape of lush paddy fields, **Gaur**, 16km south of Malda, was the seventh-century capital of King Sasanka, and then successively belonged to the Buddhist Palas and the Senas. The latter, the last Hindu kings of Bengal, were violently displaced by the Muslims at the start of the thirteenth century. The city was sacked in 1537 by Sher Shah Suri, and its remaining inhabitants wiped out by plague in 1575.

Gaur lay buried in silt for centuries, but excavations have revealed the extensive remains of a city that once boasted more than a million inhabitants. Recent finds include a vast brick **palace** complete with waterways and a mint. A *ghat* with chains for anchoring barges suggests that the River Ganges may have once flowed past the palace. Elsewhere, Gaur's sites include various large tanks, such as the 1.5km long **Sagar Dighi** from 1126, and the extensive embankments. **Dakhil Darwaza**, an impressive red-brick gateway built in 1425 during the Muslim period, leads into the **Fort**, in the southeast corner of which a colossal wall encloses the ruins of the old palace. The **Qadam Rasul Mosque** nearby was built in 1531 to contain the Prophet's footprint in stone.

Pandua

The splendid **Adina Masjid** at **Pandua**, 18km north of Malda, was built around 1370 and was the largest mosque in the Subcontinent in its day. It now lies in ruins, but these still betray the origin of much of the building materials – carved basalt masonry from earlier Hindu temples was used to support 88 brick-built arches and 378 identical small domes, the design following that of the eighth-century mosque of Damascus. Other monuments include the **Eklakhi mausoleum** – one of the first square brick tombs in Bengal, with a carved Ganesh on the doorway, and **Qutb Shahi Masjid**, or the Golden Mosque.

ARRIVAL AND GETTING AROUND **MALDA AND AROUND**

By train Malda Town station, near the centre, is on the main line between Kolkata and north Bengal, served by several good trains such as the *Kanchenjunga Express*

#15657/#15658 (daily; 7hr).

By taxi Taxis to both Gaur and Pandua charge around ₹2500 for the day.

13

Golden Park NH-34 ☎03512 262251, ⓦhotelgoldenpark.com. Malda's most luxurious address, 8km to the north of town but convenient for a visit to Pandua, offers clean, comfortable rooms, a/c and a decent restaurant and a bar; facilities include a travel desk. The hotel is popular for events including weddings, but at other times can feel soulless. ₹2150

Purbanchal NH-34 ☎03512 266183. One of a clutch of budget business hotels around the centre, with a range of rooms including some a/c, choose a room away from the highway to avoid noise. The hotel has one of the better restaurants in town and a dimly lit bar. ₹500

Darjeeling and North Bengal

North Bengal, where the Himalayas soar from the flat alluvial plains towards Nepal, Sikkim and Bhutan, holds some magnificent mountain panoramas, and also some of India's most attractive **hill stations**. Most visitors pass as quickly as possible through **Siliguri** en route to **Darjeeling**, **Kalimpong** and the small, mountainous state of Sikkim. If you've time on your hands, it's worth making a detour east of Siliguri to explore the sub-Himalayan **Dooars**, with its patchwork of tea gardens and forests that encompasses the **Jaldapara Wildlife Sanctuary**, home to the one-horned rhino, bison and wild boar.

The region has its fair share of political turmoil. The Gurkhaland movement, centred around Darjeeling, and the Kamtapuri Liberation Front, which purports to represent most of north Bengal south to Malda, have called for a complete break from the state of West Bengal. Occasional strikes called by the Gurkha movement can paralyse the Darjeeling hills and affect traffic. Tourist traffic is usually allowed to exit the district, but you may have to pay an exorbitant fee to the taxi driver. You should check the press and with your hotel before travelling to the region.

Siliguri and New Jalpaiguri

A major commercial hub and Bengal's second city, ever-expanding **Siliguri** has a thriving tea-auction centre and serves as the gateway to Darjeeling, Kalimpong, Sikkim and Bhutan. Together with its main railway station, **New Jalpaiguri** – commonly referred to as NJP – and the airport at **Bagdogra**, it forms an unavoidable link between the rail and air connections to Kolkata and Delhi, and the roads up into the mountains. The border with Nepal at **Kakarbitta** nearby is open to tourists, though the bus journey from here to Kathmandu is an arduous one.

Most tourists pass straight through Siliguri, but travel connections may mean that you have to stop overnight. Besides teeming bazaars such as Bidhan Market, there's little of interest to see save the impressive **Tashi Gomang Stupa** (daily 5am–noon & 1–5pm) in the small Tibetan enclave 2km or so from the centre on Sevoke Road. The **Darjeeling Himalayan Railway**'s (see box, p.779) route to Darjeeling has been disrupted due to track conditions but a short Jungle Safari departing Siliguri Junction (10am) provides an experience of this unique railway.

ARRIVAL AND DEPARTURE   **SILIGURI AND NEW JALPAIGURI**

BY PLANE

Bagdogra airport, 12km west of Siliguri, is served by flights from Delhi, Kolkata, Guwahati, Bhutan and Bangkok; there's also a helicopter service from here to Gangtok in Sikkim (see p.811).

Taxis Taxis booked through the pre-paid counter at the airport run directly to Siliguri (₹390), Darjeeling (₹2500), Kalimpong (₹2000) and Gangtok (₹2800), though you can

negotiate cheaper fares from the stand outside the gates with returning taxis.

Flights Air India, Jet Airways, Spicejet and Go Air fly from Bagdogra airport to Kolkata, Delhi and Guwahati; Druk Air flies to Bangkok (Tues & Sat; ⓦdrukair.com.bt) and also connects with Paro in Bhutan (Wed & Sun). For tickets, try Heat Flexi Holidays, 34 Bidyasagar Rd, Khalpara (☎0353 250 4631) or Cox & Kings,

Ganeshayan Building, Sevoke Rd (☏9851 000802). Spicejet (☏0353 255 0950) and Jet Airways (☏0353 243 5876) have offices at *Hotel Vinayak,* Hill Cart Rd (☏0353 243 1495).

By helicopter Flights to Gangtok (daily 11am & 2.30pm; ₹2200) leave from Bagdogra, weather permitting, only with a full load of five passengers and with a maximum baggage allowance of 10kg. For reservations book in advance through Sikkim Tourism Development Corporation (☏03592 203960, ⓦsikkimstdc.com). The sole Siliguri agent is the Tourist Service Agency (TSA) in Pradhan Nagar, the lane opposite the bus terminal (☏0353 251 0872 or ☏09434 467236).

BY TRAIN

New Jalpaiguri (NJP) Station Siliguri does have its own railway station, once used by the Toy Train (though this service is currently suspended due to track conditions), but the New Jalpaiguri (NJP) Station, 4km east, is the main rail junction in the region, with trains to and from Kolkata, Delhi and Assam. Reservations can be made at NJP railway station or the Central Railway Booking Office (daily 8am–4pm), Bidhan Rd, near Kanchenjunga Stadium in Siliguri. The best train to Kolkata is the *Darjeeling Mail* #12344 (10hr), which terminates at Sealdah, while the most convenient for Delhi is the efficient *Rajdhani Express* #12423 (25hr 30min), which also passes through Patna with connections for Gaya and Bodhgaya. The *Rajdhani* #12435 (Mon & Fri; 20hr) stops at Varanasi (13hr 50min); on other days take the *Rajdhani* #12423 and change at Mughal Sarai.

Auto-rickshaws and taxis Cycle and auto-rickshaws (₹45 and ₹120) ply the route between NJP and Siliguri, battling through the often-gridlocked market, while shared Vikrams (auto-taxis) charge ₹30 a seat; taxis charge up to ₹500. Use the pre-paid booth outside the main station for local and long-distance journeys in auto-rickshaws as well as taxis.

BY BUS OR SHARED JEEP

Tenzing Norgay Bus Terminal Most buses arriving at Siliguri terminate at the Tenzing Norgay Bus Terminal on Hill Cart Rd at Pradhan Nagar, close to most hotels and taxis to Darjeeling. Overnight Volvo "luxury" buses to Kolkata (12hr) are an alternative to the train (₹1200 for

a/c), and have the advantage of depositing you in Esplanade, near the central Sudder St area. However, the roads are dire, so be prepared for a severe rattling. Gupta Tour & Travels (☏94340 46540), opposite *Hotel Heritage,* Pradhan Nagar, are the most comfortable but usually need prior booking; cheaper alternatives include the Rocket Bus, booked at TNBT (☏0353 251 8879). Standard buses run from Siliguri to Kolkata, Patna and Guwahati, although the train is far more comfortable. Frequent buses also travel to Chalsa and Madarihat, convenient for the wildlife sanctuaries.

To Darjeeling and Kalimpong The easiest way to get to Darjeeling is by shared jeep. These depart from in front of NJP Station, and Sevoke More and Tenzing Norgay Bus Terminal in Siliguri, where jeep transport syndicates have their own ticket booths and the prices are fixed. Shared taxis to Darjeeling depart when full (3–5hr; ₹150). For a bit more comfort, take two seats up in front or a whole taxi (negotiate with returning taxis for reduced rates). Shared taxis to Kalimpong (₹110) depart from Panitanki More across the bridge while buses to Kalimpong depart from around the bus terminal.

To Sikkim Regular buses and shared jeeps run to Gangtok from around the bus terminus in Pradhan Nagar. Sikkim Nationalized Transport, opposite the bus terminus (daily 6am–4pm; ☏0353 251 1496), runs bus services to Gangtok (departures 7.30am–1.30pm; ₹90), and other points in Sikkim. Get a Sikkim permit (see box, p.810) from Sikkim Tourism next door; shared jeeps (₹200) are also obtainable here and on the main road outside the gates; a reserved jeep costs ₹2000. There are also helicopter flights from Bagdogra (see opposite).

To Kathmandu To reach Kathmandu in Nepal, travel to Panitanki, the crossing (24hr) on the Indian side of the border, and use a cycle rickshaw (₹40) to get to the Nepalese side at Kakarbitta (7am–7pm). Shared taxis (₹90), regular buses from the terminal or outside it (from ₹20) and taxis (₹1000) travel to Panitanki, where you can pick up a Nepalese visa for $30 in cash. Kakarbitta offers a greater choice of onward buses to Kathmandu (17hr). For a lot more luxury, take a flight from Bhadrapur (25km and a 45min taxi ride from Kakarbitta) to Kathmandu with Buddha Air or Yeti Airlines. Flights can be booked through Siliguri agencies or at Kakarbitta itself.

INFORMATION

Tourist office West Bengal's Tourist Office (WBTDC; Mon–Fri 10.30am–4pm; ☏0353 251 7561), opposite the bus station at Pradhan Nagar, books rooms in tourist lodges in places such as Jaldapara Wildlife Sanctuary and offers wildlife package tours; at the next desk, the Forest Department officer books forest lodges such as at Lava near

Neora Valley. There are information-only tourist counters at NJP station and Bagdogra airport.

Sikkim Tourism Opposite the bus stand in the same compound as Sikkim Nationalized Transport, the Sikkim Tourist Office (Mon–Sat 10am–4pm; ☏0353 251 2646), provides information and Sikkim permits (see box, p.810).

13

Tour operators Siliguri's best private tour operator, Help Tourism, First Floor, Malati Bhavan, 143 Hill Cart Rd (☎ 0353 253 5896, ⊚ helptourism.com), organizes wildlife tours, village homestays, and treks and tours off the beaten track.

ACCOMMODATION

It is worth noting that some of the cheap hotels around the bus terminal – the *Delhi* and the *Shere-e-Punjab* in particular – have dubious reputations, especially in their treatment of women guests.

Apsara 18 Patel Rd, Pradhan Nagar ☎ 0353 251 4252. Down a lane parallel to the main road and opposite Tenzing Norgay Bus Terminal, this is a friendly budget hotel, handy for transport links and amenities and with basic, clean rooms, all with attached baths; hot water is by the bucket (₹10). **₹400**

Holydon NJP Station Rd ☎ 0353 269 1335. Friendly and inexpensive hotel, the closest decent place to the railway station, with some a/c rooms, a restaurant and a bar that can get busy in the evenings. **₹400**

Manila Pradhan Nagar ☎ 0353 251 9342. Spotless and modern and one of a choice of decent hotels close to the taxi and bus stand, with attentive service, comfortable rooms, money exchange (with an ATM next door) and a good restaurant. **₹880**

Marinas Naxalbari Rd, Bagdogra ☎ 0353 255 1371, ⊚ marinasmotel.com. A very pleasant garden hotel, handy both for the airport (with free transfers) and the Nepal border at Kakarbitta. The reasonably priced rooms all have attached baths, and there's a restaurant, a bar and

Glenary's coffee shop. **₹2500**

Nirvana 18 Patel Rd, Pradhan Nagar ☎ 9832 014001. Right behind *Khana Khazana* restaurant, this conveniently located multistorey block offers a bit more comfort than *Apsara* next door. The small, carpeted rooms come with attached baths. **₹600**

Sinclairs Pradhan Nagar ☎ 0353 251 7674, ⊚ sinclairshotels.com. Upmarket old hotel that remains popular for its convenient location near the crossroad to Darjeeling and handy for all points including the airport. Comfortable, if a bit expensive with large refurbished rooms and complimentary breakfast, a good restaurant, a garden and a (summer only) swimming pool. **₹5460**

Vinayak Hill Cart Rd ☎ 0353 243 3131. A reliable mid-range hotel conveniently located in the centre of town yet close to the taxi stands, with a choice of small but adequate rooms including some with a/c. The restaurant downstairs serves good Indian food. **₹900**

EATING

City Centre Uttorayan Complex NH31. This modern shopping mall, handy for the airport, has the usual mix of shops including a Crossword bookshop and a cinema, along with several places to eat including the snacky *Tea Junction* and the multicuisine *Zizzi*. There is also a food court. Daily noon–9pm.

Kalpataru Pice Hotel Rani Tanki More, Sevoke Rd. This no-frills rice-based restaurant is renowned throughout the hills for its traditional Bengali fish dishes – try the *chital* or the *rohu*. Daily noon–10pm.

Khana Khazana Pradhan Nagar, opposite the bus

terminal. A very pleasant restaurant, and a good stop for travellers as it is handy for bus and taxi connections. Serving everything from dosas to pizzas, this is still one of the best options in town. Daily 9am–10pm.

Punjabi Kadhai Siddhi Arcade, near Anandloke Nursing Home, Sevoke Rd. This smart, new restaurant with pleasant decor makes a good night out; it is around 1km from the centre and popular for its great Punjabi cooking including tandoori. Expect to pay around ₹350/person for a meal. Daily noon–10pm.

DIRECTORY

ATMs There are several ATM including one opposite the *Manila Hotel* on Hill Cart Rd and around Sevoke More; Axis is generally the easiest to use.

Changing money The bureau at the *Delhi Hotel* across from the bus terminal on Hill Cart Rd; State Bank of India, Mangaldeep Building, Hill Cart Rd, or Cox & Kings, Ganeshayan Building, Sevoke Rd (☎ 985 100 0802)

Hospitals Neotia Getwel, Uttarayan (☎ 0353 305 3000, ⊚ neotiahealthcare.com). With state-of-the-art facilities, this is by far the best hospital in the region, servicing the hills and Sikkim as well.

Post office The main post office is on Kacheri Rd, with branches near the Central Railway Booking Office and the bus terminal.

Jaldapara Wildlife Sanctuary and around

Apart from the Darjeeling hills, most of North Bengal is well off the beaten track, and few travellers make detours from the Darjeeling–Sikkim–Nepal route.

13

Probably the best reason to do so is to visit one of a string of **wildlife sanctuaries** that, along with tea gardens, carpet the **Dooars** along the southern approaches to the Himalayas.

The largest of these, **Jaldapara Wildlife Sanctuary**, 124km from Siliguri, was established in 1943 to protect wildlife from the encroachment of tea cultivation. Set against a backdrop of forested foothills on the banks of the River Torsa, Jaldapara's 216 square kilometres hold large tracts of tall elephant grass, best explored by a dawn elephant ride. Fifty highly endangered one-horned rhinoceros, as well as wild elephants, *sambar* and hog deer reside in the sanctuary.

More accessible but not as extensive, the twin parks of **Gorumara National Park** and **Chapramari Wildlife Sanctuary** (Oct–May), 80km east of Siliguri, shelter similar fauna and there is an elephant camp at adjacent **Dhupjhora**.

ARRIVAL AND INFORMATION   JALDAPARA WILDLIFE SANCTUARY AND AROUND

By train The closest train station is at Madarihat, 7km from the reserve and 1km from the sanctuary gates, with a limited service from both Siliguri and NJP. From here taxis run to Hollong in the heart of the forest for around ₹150. Alternatively, more trains travel via New Mal Junction to Hasimara 18km from the reserve including *Kanchan Kanya* (#13149), which departs Siliguri Junction at 8.05am. The nearest railway station to Lataguri, the entry point to Gorumara is New Mal Junction (30km) with a choice of transport including buses and taxis.
By bus A handful of buses and trains run from Siliguri

and NJP to Madarihat and in season there is a handy tourist bus departing NJP at 8.30am via Siliguri, Gorumara and Lataguri (see p.867) to arrive around 2.20pm at *Jaldapara Tourist Lodge* (₹100). Enquire at the tourist office at Siliguri.
Fees and rides A ₹200 (₹50) fee is payable at the entrance to the park (camera fees extra). Elephant safaris (5–8am; ₹600 (₹300)) start at *Hollong* and Hollong guests get first preference. Jeep safaris are also available from ₹600/person. Access to Gorumara is via Lataguri (₹200(₹80)) by jeep.

ACCOMMODATION AND EATING

Book either of the Tourist Lodges through either Kolkata (see p.748) or Siliguri (see p.767) WBTDC offices. The WBTDC packages from Siliguri (from ₹8225) are all inclusive, including transport, accommodation, meals and elephant rides.

Gachbari Dhupjhora Elephant Camp ☎03561 266340. Though it's hardly luxurious, this most atmospheric of the forest lodges, in the form of a basic treehouse, provides a good chance of seeing wildlife from the veranda. Don't expect room service or a hot water, and book well in advance – the number quoted is for the Forest Officer, who manages reservations. Cheaper rooms are available in six basic cottages and there is a garden restaurant. ₹3000
Hollong Forest Lodge ☎03563 262228. Extremely popular due to its situation; it's the only lodge within the

sanctuary itself. Simple rooms but a great location. ₹2858
Jaldapara Jungle Camp Birpara, Madarihat ☎09733 267517, ⊚jaldaparacamp.com. A welcoming place around 3km from the sanctuary, with comfortable wood-built jungle cabins, a well-ordered campus and their *Aranya Restaurant* serving good Bengali cooking. They will arrange safaris and transport. ₹1100
Jaldapara Tourist Lodge ☎03563 262230. Extensive complex where the new concrete block is more comfortable than the more atmospheric old wing. Book your ride here. ₹2500

Darjeeling

Part Victorian holiday resort, part major tea-growing centre, **Darjeeling** (from *Dorje Ling*, "the place of the thunderbolt") straddles a ridge 2200m up in the Himalayas, almost 600km north of Kolkata. Over fifty years since the British departed, the town remains as popular as ever with holiday-makers from the plains, and promenades such as the Mall and the Chowrasta still burst with life. The greatest appeal for visitors has to be its stupendous mountain vistas – with Kanchenjunga (the third highest mountain in the world) and a vast cohort of ice-capped peaks dominating the northern horizon. However, the infrastructure created under the Raj has been unable to cope with the ever-expanding population leading to acute shortages of water and electricity, and chaos on the hopelessly inadequate roads.

13

Still, Darjeeling remains a colourful and lively, cosmopolitan place, with good shopping and dining, plenty of walks in the surrounding hills and attractions such as the **Toy Train** and colourful Buddhist monasteries. The best seasons to visit – and to attempt the magnificent trek to Sandakphu to see Everest – are after the monsoons and before winter (late September to late November), and spring (mid-February to May).

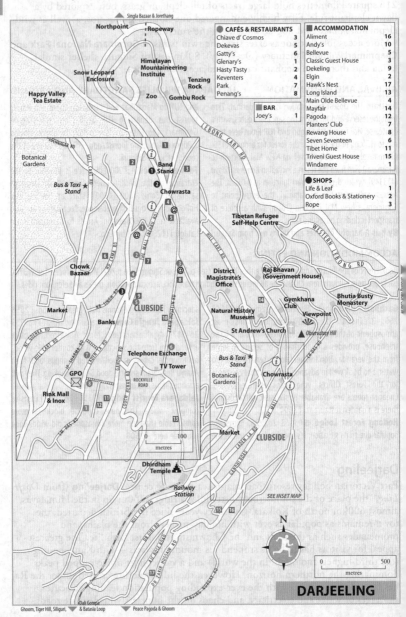

CAFÉS & RESTAURANTS
Chiave d' Cosmos	3
Dekevas	5
Gatty's	6
Glenary's	1
Hasty Tasty	2
Keventers	4
Park	7
Penang's	8

BAR
Joey's	1

ACCOMMODATION
Aliment	16
Andy's	10
Bellevue	5
Classic Guest House	3
Dekeling	9
Elgin	2
Hawk's Nest	17
Long Island	13
Main Olde Bellevue	4
Mayfair	14
Pagoda	12
Planters' Club	7
Rewang House	8
Seven Seventeen	6
Tibet Home	11
Triveni Guest House	15
Windamere	1

SHOPS
Life & Leaf	1
Oxford Books & Stationery	2
Rope	3

DARJEELING

Brief history

Until the nineteenth century, Darjeeling belonged to **Sikkim**. However in 1817, after a disastrous war with Nepal, Sikkim was forced to concede the right to use the site as a health sanatorium to the **British**, who had helped to broker a peace settlement. Darjeeling soon became the most popular of all hill resorts, especially after the Hill Cart Road was built in 1839 to link it with Siliguri. **Tea** arrived a few years later, and with it an influx of Nepalese labourers and the disappearance of the forests that previously carpeted the hillsides. The town's growing economic significance led Britain to force a treaty on the Sikkimese in 1861, thereby annexing Darjeeling and Kalimpong. In the early 1900s, Darjeeling's reputation grew as one of the most glamorous and far-flung outposts of the British Empire. Subsequently it became a centre for mountaineering and played a key role in the conquest of the greater Himalayas.

After Independence, the region joined West Bengal, administered from Calcutta, but calls for autonomy grew, taking shape in the **Gurkhaland** movement of the 1980s, led by the **Gurkha National Liberation Front (GNLF)**. The subsequent violent campaign ended a decade later and, once in power, GNLF politicians grew complacent, fuelling discontent and leading to their overthrow by the **Gorkha Jana Mukti Morcha (GJMM)** in 2007. The GJMM victory reinvigorated the push for an autonomous Gurkhaland, employing wildcat strikes designed to cripple West Bengal's hold on the region. Despite unhappiness with the West Bengal government, support for the GJMM, who adminster through Gurkhaland Territorial Administration (GTA), is far from unanimous – local opposition, however, is vigorously and sometimes violently put down.

The Chowrasta and Clubside

The heart of Victorian Darjeeling is the **Chowrasta**, an expansive traffic-free promenade resplendent with a bandstand, high above the busy bazaar on Hill Cart Road. One of the four main roads leading off it is the **Nehru Road** (also called the **Mall**), it descends from Chowrasta to **Clubside**, the area below the prestigious **Planters' Club,** otherwise known as the **Darjeeling Club**. Established in 1868, this venerable institution was the centre of Darjeeling high society. Today, visitors are welcome to stay and sample the faded ambience and facilities such as the bar and snooker room, as long as they buy temporary membership.

Observatory Hill and around

Taking the right fork from the northern end of the Chowrasta, near the bandstand, brings you to the **viewpoint** from where you can survey the Kanchenjunga massif and almost the entire state of Sikkim. From near the *Windamere Hotel* steps, ascend the pine-covered hillside to the top of **Observatory Hill**, the original site of the Bhutia Busti monastery. Streaming with prayer flags, the shrine at the summit, dedicated to the wrathful Buddhist deity Mahakala, whom Hindus worship as Shiva, reflects a garish hybrid of styles. Another faded Raj-era institution, the **Gymkhana Club** (day membership ₹50, week ₹250; ☎0354 225 4342, ⍟darjeelinggymkhanaclub.com), stands near Observatory. Temporary membership allows visitors to play billiards, roller skate or take advantage of the small library and bar. A few streets below, the small and little-visited **Natural History Museum** (daily except Thurs 10am–4.30pm; ₹10) holds a large collection of moths and butterflies, stuffed animals and birds, and a natural-habitat display complete with sound effects.

A steep but pleasant walk down from near Government House, or a circuitous taxi ride, leads to the **Tibetan Refugee Self-Help Centre** (closed Sun). Founded in 1959 after the Chinese invasion of Tibet, it houses around seven hundred refugees, most of whom make carpets or Tibetan handicrafts. The community also has a hospital and a school. Tourists are welcome to watch the activities; the shop sells handicrafts and carpets, which they will ship for you. Around the same altitude, and a short distance away, is the small, picture-postcard **Bhutia Busti Monastery** (daily 8am–6pm) re-established here from its original site on Observatory Hill. An alternative approach is the pleasant 1km

13

DARJEELING TEA

Although the original appeal of Darjeeling for the British was as a hill resort with easy access from the plains, inspired by their success in Assam they soon realized its potential for growing **tea**. Today, the Darjeeling tea industry continues to flourish, producing China Jat, China Hybrid and Hybrid Assam. A combination of factors, including altitude and sporadic rainfall, have resulted in a relatively small yield – only three percent of India's total – but the delicate black tea produced here is considered to be one of the finest in the world. It is also some of the most expensive with varieties fetching more than ₹18,000 a kilo at auction.

Grades such as Flowery Orange Pekoe (FOP) or Broken Orange Pekoe (BOP) are determined by quality and length of leaf as it is withered, crushed, fermented and dried.

Happy Valley Tea Estate off Lebong Cart Rd. To watch the process for yourself, call in at the Happy Valley Tea Estate; it's a 30min walk from town. Just follow the signs from the Hill Cart Rd near the District Magistrate's office. Tues–Sat 8am–noon & 1–4.30pm, Sun 8am–noon.

BUYING TEA

As for **buying**, try the Chowrasta Tea Store, Chowrasta; The House of Tea on the Mall and Tea Cosy at the Rink Mall offer try-before-you-buy, with the latter's menu set clearly by the seasons (otherwise known as "flushes"). However, for the best price and an enthusiastic explanation of tea, explore the labyrinth of Chowk Bazaar to find Radhika & Son near the Laxmi Bhandar. Such vendors usually trade in unblended tea bought directly from tea gardens. The typical cost of a kilo of good middle-grade tea is ₹600–800. You can taste life on a tea plantation either through the luxurious *Glenburn TE* or at *Makaibari* (see p.779).

walk downhill along the steep CR Das Road from the Chowrasta. Linked to Phodong in Sikkim, the *dukhang* (prayer hall) houses a venerated copy of the Tibetan Book of the Dead – the Bardo Thodol.

Darjeeling Zoo (Padmaja Naidu Zoological Park)

Birch Hill • Daily except Thurs 8.30am–4pm • ₹100 (₹30), including HMI ticket (see below)

The promenade north from the Chowrasta leads to Darjeeling's well-maintained **Zoo**. The zoo's snow leopard breeding centre (closed to the public), established in 1986, is the only place in the world to have successfully bred this endangered species, while Project Panda has produced several Red Pandas.

Himalayan Mountaineering Institute

Museum Daily except Thurs 9am–4.30pm • Included in zoo ticket price (see above)

The **Himalayan Mountaineering Institute** (HMI) (see box, p.774), reached via the zoo and covered by the same ticket, is one of India's most important training centres for mountaineers. Its first director was **Sherpa Tenzing Norgay**, Sir Edmund Hillary's climbing partner on the first successful ascent of Everest, who lived and died in Darjeeling, and is buried in the Institute's grounds. In the heart of the leafy complex, the **HMI Museum** is dedicated to the history of mountaineering, with equipment old and new, a relief map of the Himalayas, and a collection of costumes of hill people.

The **Everest Museum** in the annexe recounts the history of ascents on the world's highest peak, from Mallory and Irvine's ill-fated 1924 expedition to Tenzing and Hillary's triumph in 1953 and the record-breaking 20hr 24min climb by Kaji Sherpa in 1998.

Northpoint and the Ropeway

Daily in season 10am–4pm • ₹200

Below the HMI at Northpoint, where the views of Sikkim open out, and near the Gothic ramparts of **St Joseph's College**, the cable car or **Ropeway** has restarted its

13

DARJEELING TOUR AND ADVENTURE OPERATORS

Darjeeling is brimming with tour and trek operators, and some of the budget hotels such as *Long Island* and *Triveni Guest House* provide cost-effective, reliable trekking services for the Singalila Ridge.

Adventures Unlimited 142 Dr Zakir Hussein Rd ☎ 9933 070013, ⊛ adventuresunlimited.in. Gautam runs an excellent operation including both motorbike and mountain-bike tours, as well as rental (motorbikes from ₹1200, mountain bikes from ₹450/day) with a deposit; he also organizes kayaking on the Teesta and, of course, trekking.

Himalayan Mountaineering Institute ☎ 0354 225 4087, ⊛ himalayanmountaineeringinstitute .com (see p.772). Basic and advanced mountaineering courses, including a women-only expedition. Trips, centred around their Chaurikhang Base Camp at the foot of Rathong Glacier in Sikkim, are run with military precision and last 28 days ($650 (₹4000)). However, this is an economical and unique introduction to Himalayan mountaineering. The more rewarding advanced course requires previous mountaineering experience; to join either course, you must be aged between 17 and 40 and should be fit. Apply at least three months in advance.

Himalayan Travels 18 Gandhi Rd ☎ 0354 225 6956 or ☎ 9434 209847. An efficient organization run by the affable K.K. Gurung, one of the first and most experienced operators in town, offering tours and treks throughout Darjeeling, Sikkim and Bhutan.

Red Panda Triveni Guest House, 85/1 Dr Zakir Hussein Rd ☎ 9932 673511. Efficient budget trek operator who specializes in the Singalila trek.

Trek-Mate Singalila Arcade, Nehru Rd ☎ 0354 225 6611 or ☎ 9832 083241, ✉ chagpori @satyam.net.in. Tsewang Trogawa runs this very helpful agency, arranging treks to Sandakphu and West Sikkim. They provide guides and porters and rents out sleeping bags, down jackets and day packs, and organize day-treks as well as village homestays near Tukdah.

---

operation after a terrible accident in 2003. A popular day-trip destination, the cable car travels down past tea gardens to Tukvar Tea Estate towards Singla and the Sikkim border.

Lloyd Botanical Gardens

Chowk Bazaar • Mon–Sat 6am–5pm • Free

Lochnagar Road winds down from the bus stand in the bazaar to enter the **Lloyd Botanical Gardens**, resplendent with pines, willows and maples that cover the hillside. A quiet spot with tended flowerbeds and meandering walkways, the gardens were established in 1878 and feature a central glasshouse filled with ferns and orchids and other flowers.

Nipponjan Myohoji Buddhist Temple

Daily 4.30am–7pm • Prayers 4.30am & 4.30pm

Heading out of town on AJC Bose Road, just past Lal Kothi, you come to the discreetly hidden **Nipponjan Myohoji Buddhist Temple**, usually referred to as the Peace Pagoda, a peaceful spot for meditation, yoga or taichi, with great views over the valley to Kanchenjunga. The temple itself has a small museum upstairs.

Around Darjeeling

One really unmissable part of the Darjeeling experience is the early-morning mass exodus to **Tiger Hill** to watch the sunrise. This can easily be combined with a visit to the old monastery of **Ghoom**, and the huge monastery at **Sonada** on Hill Cart Road towards Siliguri.

Tiger Hill

Viewing tower from ₹20 • Jeeps from ₹100/seat or ₹1200 reserved from Clubside (see opposite)

In good weather and in season, more than two hundred jeeps and taxis, packed with tourists leave from Clubside in Darjeeling around 4am each morning, careering 12km through Ghoom to catch the dramatic sunrise at **Tiger Hill**. This incredible viewpoint (2585m) on the eastern extremity of the Singalila Range provides a 360-degree Himalayan panorama, with the steamy plains bordering Bangladesh to the south, the Singalila ridge with Everest beyond to the west, Kanchenjunga and Sikkim to the north, and the Bhutan and Assam Himalayas trailing into the distance to the northeast. From left to right, the **peaks** include: Lhotse (which actually looks larger than Everest); Everest itself; Makalu; then, after a long gap, the rocky summit of Kang on the Sikkim–Nepal divide; the prow of Jannu in Nepal; Rathong; tent-like Kabru south and north; Talung; Kanchenjunga main, central and south; Pandim; Simvo; horned Narsing; and the fluted pyramid of Siniolchu. If you're feeling energetic you could opt to walk back from Tiger Hill visiting the *gompas* of Ghoom on the way.

Senchal Wildlife Sanctuary

Senchal • ₹50 • ☎ 0354 54308

Tiger Hill also gives access to the small **Senchal Wildlife Sanctuary**, which, at just 38 square kilometres is home to a variety of fauna including barking deer, jackals, wild boar, the occasional black bear and a leopard. It is best to explore on foot or by mountain bike – Adventures Unlimited (see box opposite) rent out bikes and can give advice or arrange a trip to the sanctuary.

Ghoom and other monasteries

Often obscured in cloud, **Ghoom** (2438m), with its charming little railway station and tiny bazaar on the edge of Jorebangla, holds several interesting monasteries. The most venerated of these is **Yiga Choling**, or the Old Ghoom Monastery (signposted from the bazaar), tucked off the main thoroughfare above a brash resort. Built in 1850 by Sharap Gyatso, a renowned astrologer, the monastery consists of a single chambered temple and a few residential buildings. Inside the prayer hall is a huge figure of Maitreya, the Buddha of the future – a statue of an exceptionally high standard of workmanship, with fine detail above and around the bronze face.

Back on the main road, the **Shakya Choling** *gompa* has expanded in recent years, while **Samten Choling**, a small but colourful *gompa* on a bend in the main road to Darjeeling, is sometimes included on the jeep tours to Tiger Hill.

Thupten Sanga Choling

Halfway between Ghoom and Darjeeling on the main road stands the imposing **Thupten Sanga Choling**, otherwise known as the **Dali Gompa**, inaugurated by the Dalai Lama in 1993. This is a very active **Drukpa Kagyu** *gompa* with two hundred monks. The huge meditation hall is richly decorated with exquisite murals and ceiling mandalas.

Sonada Monastery

☎ 0354 246 6716, ☜ paldenshangpa.org

South of Ghoom, down the Hill Cart Road towards Kurseong, the influential **Sonada Monastery** or **Samdrub Darjay Choling**, founded in the 1960s, was the seat of **Kabje Kalu Rinpoche** who developed a large American and French following. Today the monastery continues under the tutelage of his incarnate Yangsi Kalu Rinpoche. Rooms are occasionally available for retreat.

ARRIVAL AND DEPARTURE   **DARJEELING**

Virtually all travellers arriving in Darjeeling from the plains come via Siliguri, whether by the Toy Train or by road Jeeps and buses stop at the **bus stand** in the lower half of the town, from where it's a bit of an uphill trek to the main hotel area. Most taxis and some jeeps drop you off at **Clubside** near the **Mall** (officially Nehru Rd), at the upper end of town. Porters are available (from ₹100) at the bus stand and bazaar, but be aware that some act as touts. Darjeeling is best explored on foot – in fact much of it that is closed to all vehicles.

13

By plane The nearest airport to Darjeeling is Bagdogra, 100km to the south (see p.766); allow plenty of time to get there by taxi. Tickets for Jet Airways and other airlines are available through Clubside Tours and Travels, JP Sharma Rd (☎0354 225 4646), and Pineridge Travels, Nehru Rd, Chowrasta (☎0354 225 3912), which also handles Druk Air's flights to Bangkok and flights from Bhadrapur in Nepal to Kathmandu. Air India has its office on the Chowrasta (☎0354 225 4230).

By train If and when the Toy Train (see box, p.779) to Siliguri is operational, it leaves at 9.15am, weather and landslides permitting, and takes a leisurely seven to eight hours. Railway reservations (daily 8am–2pm) for selected main line trains out of NJP can be made at Darjeeling's station a couple of days before departure. They have tourist quotas, but if stuck, try Gupta Tours & Travel, near the station at 5 Chachan

Mansion (☎0354 225 4616), who can get tickets when quotas are "full" for a fee.

By bus Due to poor road conditions, it is best to avoid the handful of buses and minibuses that run to Siliguri from the bus stand near Chowk Bazaar. For overland bus travel to Kathmandu, head to the border town of Kakarbitta in Nepal to get a choice of coaches (see p.767).

By jeep Shared taxis and jeeps charge ₹150 (Siliguri) and ₹175 (NJP). In the mornings, jeeps run regularly to Gangtok, Siliguri, Mirik, Kalimpong and Jorethang (for West Sikkim; foreigners need permits), and are by far the most efficient way to travel, especially if you pay for two front seats for yourself. Book in advance if you can at the jeep stand (next to the bus stand); each route has its own syndicate, and some have two or three

Destinations Gangtok services (4hr 30min; ₹180) run frequently between 7am and 2pm.

INFORMATION

Permits Foreigners planning to head on to Sikkim need a permit (free). Acquiring one is painless formality at the Sikkim Tourism's office at Main Old Bellevue, Nehru Rd (Mon–Sat 10am–4pm). You will need to bring a photocopy of your passport and visa plus a passport photograph. Initial 30-day permits are extendable to a maximum of three months once you're in Gangtok (see p.811). Permits are free and single-entry only, you cannot re-enter within three months. Travelling to

Gangtok, you can get a permit at the Rangpo border checkpoint (but not at the Naya Bazaar crossing for West Sikkim). Getting a permit in Darjeeling allows you the option of travelling directly to West Sikkim on a hair-raising 27km road descending through tea plantations to Jorethang via Naya Bazaar.

GTA Tourism 4 Silver Fir, Bhanu Sarani, 100m to the north of Chowrasta (daily: in season 9am–1pm & 2–5pm; off-season 10am–4.30pm; ☎0354 225 4879) provides

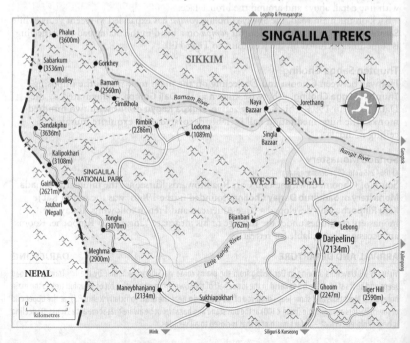

SINGALILA TREKS: THE MANEYBHANJANG–PHALUT TRAIL

13

The single ridge of the **Singalila Range** rises near Darjeeling and extends all the way to the summit of Kanchenjunga. Unfortunately, although some longer trails have been opened in Sikkim (see p.804), there is no provision yet to link them to the initial lower sections of the ridge to **Sandakphu** (3636m) and **Phalut** (3600m) in Darjeeling District.

Easily accessible from Darjeeling, the later stages of the Maneybhanjang–Phalut trail provide magnificent views of the higher ranges; lightweight expeditions are possible as there are trekking huts (from ₹150) and lodges (₹300–1000) and simple food stalls along the way. The walking is demanding and you should bring your own sleeping bag and warm clothes as the weather can be unpredictable.

Maneybhanjang, a small town and roadhead 27km from Darjeeling, is the usual starting point for the route, with the finest views found along the **Sandakphu–Phalut** section of the trail while trekking north. You will need to get an **entry fee** from the Forestry Department (₹300 (₹100), camera ₹150 (₹100)) to enter the **Singalila National Park**, and regulation states that you has to take a **guide** (₹800/day) – available through the Highlander Guides and Porters Welfare Association (☏97340 56944, ⊕highlanderguidesandporters.com). Take an early shared jeep to Maneybhangjang from Chowk Bazaar in Darjeeling to start the trek the same day.

Several organizations arrange porters, from ₹400/day as well as **guides**, from ₹650 (around ₹700 for an English-speaking guide), as part of all-inclusive packages (from ₹1800/day); among others, Trek-Mate in Darjeeling (see box, p.774) will **rent out equipment** (sleeping bags ₹30 a day, plus ₹1500 deposit). The **best time** to trek is after the monsoon (Oct & Nov), and during spring (Feb–May). It gets hot at the end of April and into May, but this is an especially beautiful season, with the rhododendrons in bloom. Several permutations are possible, including a trek to the Sikkim border at Jorethang; an alternative is to use the idyllic *Karmi Farm* (see p.779) as a base.

THE CLASSIC ROUTE

DAY 1 Start from Maneybhanjang with a sharp climb to **Meghma**; the trail eases to the hut at **Tonglu** (3070m). One variation bypasses Tonglu to Tumling where there are lodges, including the *Shikar Lodge*, but most strong walkers should be able to press on to Gairibas, or to Kalipokhari where there are a couple of lodges including *Sherpa*.

DAY 2 From Tonglu head on to **Kalipokhari** and **Bikhebhanjang**. The trail then rises steeply to **Sandakphu** (3636m), which has a trekkers' hut and lodges such as the friendly *Sherpa Chalet*.

DAY 3 The panorama opens out as you leave Sandakphu en-route to **Sabarkum**. There's no shelter or food here, but if you drop down to the right for thirty minutes to **Molley**, you'll find a trekkers' hut.

DAY 4 Retrace your steps to Sabarkum and continue along the ridge to **Phalut** (3600m), where there is a trekkers' hut. The panorama from here is particularly impressive.

DAY 5 Either retrace your steps to Sandakphu or follow the trail from Phalut via **Gorkhey**, where there is plenty of choice of accommodation including *Pasang* or *Shanti Lodge*. You could walk on to **Ramam** (2560m), home of the welcoming *Sherpa Hotel*, among others, or descend from Sabarkum to the pleasant riverside village of Sirikhola where accommodation is available at *Goparma Lodge*. A road is being constructed to Sirikhola which when open will allow access back to Darjeeling.

DAY 6 The final day leads to **Rimbik** (2286m); check with locals before setting off as the route is confusing. In Rimbik there's the warm and cosy *Sherpa*, where they'll help arrange bus tickets to Darjeeling; alternatives include the *Sherpa Tenzing*. Rimbik is a roadhead served by buses and jeeps (6–7am, noon–1pm) heading to Darjeeling; you could also set off by taxi or on foot to *Karmi Farm* near Bijanbari.

---

information on treks and tours, transport and whitewater rafting on the River Teesta (from ₹450). Their booths at Clubside and the railway station are of limited use.

WB Tourist Bureau Pineridge Building, The Mall (Mon–Fri 10am–4.30pm; ☏0354 225 5351) is useful for information on North Bengal and especially the wildlife parks and tourist bungalows, and for West Bengal in general.

Sikkim Tourism (Mon–Sat 10am–4pm), *Olde Bellevue Hotel*, opposite *Glenary's*, Nehru Rd. The office's primary, and extremely useful function is to issue Sikkim permits for foreign tourists (see box, p.810); they also provide general information for potential visitors to the state.

13

ACCOMMODATION

Darjeeling has more than three hundred hotels, placing considerable strain upon the infrastructure. The main thing to establish before you check in anywhere is the **water** situation; many cheaper places only provide water in buckets, and charge extra if you like it hot. Off-season (late June to Sept & late Nov to April) **discounts** can be up to fifty percent.

CENTRAL DARJEELING

Aliment 40 Dr Zakir Hussein Rd ☎ 0354 225 5068. Popular travellers' hangout with friendly management and internet access, but plain rooms, the more expensive of which have TV. The restaurant upstairs is the best in this part of town with an eclectic mix from pancakes to Tibetan food and Nepalese thalis (from ₹100). ₹600

Andy's 102 Dr Zakir Hussein Rd ☎ 0354 225 3125. Run by a retired couple, this is the best of the ridgetop guesthouses: safe, with large, immaculate rooms and great views towards Kalimpong and Bhutan, but no restaurant. Hot water is time managed and doors close early. This is essentially a comfortable family home. ₹600

Bellevue The Chowrasta ☎ 0354 225 4075. Dominating the Chowrasta, this once grand hotel, linked to Tibetan nobility, offers large, wood-panelled rooms with fireplaces. Service is low-key and meals need to be pre-arranged, but there are plenty of restaurants nearby and its location makes it well worth considering. ₹1600

Classic Guest House CR Das Rd ☎ 0354 225 7025. This excellent spot, just a couple of minutes below Chowrasta, offers five clean, large and comfortable wood-lined rooms with verandas and dramatic views. Despite its proximity to the centre and good restaurants, it is peaceful and quiet. Wi-fi costs ₹100. ₹2200

★ **Dekeling** 51 Gandhi Rd, above Dekevas restaurant ☎ 0354 225 4159, ⓦ dekeling.in. In a great central location, approached up steep steps, with the luxury of running hot water and a large range of rooms – some come with great views and the timbered ones upstairs are charming. The new wing at the back is the most comfortable and a bit quieter in the early mornings. The Tibetan owners are especially helpful and there is a welcoming log fire in winter; good off-season discounts too. Their *Hawk's Nest Villa*, a 10min walk away, has four luxurious suites with fireplaces, good home cooking and a garden. ₹850

★ **Elgin** 32 HD Lama Rd ☎ 0354 225 7226, ⓦ elginhotels.com. Premier heritage hotel, opulent and well maintained, with good facilities and an old-fashioned, formal atmosphere that captures the spirit of Darjeeling. Rates include all meals, and the tea service is the best in town. ₹9400

Long Island 11/A/2 Dr Zakir Hussein Rd ☎ 0354 225 2043. Tucked away on the other side of the ridge beyond the telecom tower, this is a friendly place with some of the best budget rooms on the ridgetop, most with shared baths and hot water by the bucket; there are more comfortable rooms at a price. The family-run café has a small but varied menu and there is an excellent trekking service. ₹300

Main Olde Bellevue Above Bellevue, 1 Nehru Rd, Chowrasta ☎ 0354 225 4178, ⓦ darjeelinghotel.com. A large property with rooms overlooking Nehru Rd in two new blocks and an old rambling chalet with plenty of atmosphere, wooden rooms and creaky floors. It's on the top of the hill, with great views, and close to all amenities. ₹1500

Mayfair Below Government House, The Mall ☎ 0354 225 6376, ⓦ mayfairhotels.com. Once a maharaja's summer retreat, the rooms and garden cottages here offer ostentatious luxury. Facilities include restaurants, a bar and health spa; the gardens are immaculate, and the garden restaurant offers great views. The price includes breakfast and dinner. ₹13,800

Pagoda 1 Upper Beechwood Rd ☎ 0354 225 3498. Keenly priced budget rooms, a fire in the lounge, free hot water by the bucket and a quiet, central location close to Laden La Rd and the post office with all amenities within easy reach. ₹600

Planters' Club The Mall ☎ 0354 225 4348 or ☎ 94340 48572. A local landmark (also known as the *Darjeeling Club*) with old-fashioned rooms, coal fires (₹200), a billiard room, bar, restaurant and library. Residential guests must take temporary membership (₹50); non-guests can use the facilities for ₹225. ₹2800

Rewang House Dr Zakir Hussein Rd ☎ 9474 030016. Plain student rooms in a convivial family home with running hot water and breakfast and dinner included in the price. The owner runs an educational charity and welcomes volunteers. ₹800

Seven Seventeen HD Lama Rd ☎ 0354 225 5099, ⓦ hotel717.com. Extensive, well-run hotel with airy rooms. It's just above the bazaar, so no mountain views. Credit cards are accepted for undiscounted rooms; there is a cheaper annexe up the road. Exchange facilities. ₹2360

Tibet Home Manjushree Centre, 12 Gandhi Rd ☎ 0354 225 2977. This non-profit cultural centre offers eight large, comfortable and well-appointed rooms with attached baths and hot water. Students of the centre get discounts. ₹1760

Triveni Guest House 85/1 Dr Zakir Hussein Rd ☎ 9932 673511. Plain, roomier and a bit cheaper than the *Aliment* opposite, but not as popular, with hot water by the bucket (₹10). Friendly, with a decent restaurant where breakfasts start at ₹70 and a reliable and economical trekking service. ₹350

Windamere Observatory Hill ☎ 0354 225 4041, ⓦ windamerehotel.com. The most iconic and celebrated of Darjeeling's hotels has accommodated a pantheon of rich and

13

famous guests in its old-world cottages decked out with Raj memorabilia; it also has a modern wing with comfortable suites but less character. Expensive, but well worth a visit for tea on the lawn or the occasional concert. ₹**10,900**

AROUND DARJEELING

Glenburn Tea Estate Off Kalimpong Rd ☎ 033 2288 5630, ⓦ glenburnteaestate.com. You can get a taste of the opulence of a tea-manager's lifestyle but at a price, with this collection all-inclusive package including from the airport and all meals. The extensive estate, en route to Kalimpong, stretches down the hillside to the Rangeet River, and offers of riverside camping and fishing. ₹**24100**

★ **Karmi Farm** Near Bijanbari ⓦ karmifarm.com, ⓔ karmifarm@yahoo.co.uk. Overlooking the Ramam River valley with vistas of West Sikkim, the idyllic farm, with comfortable rooms and good views, occasionally organizes yoga camps and makes an excellent base should you wish to trek the Singalila ridge. ₹**2000**

Makaibari Tea Estate Pankhabari Rd, Kurseong ☎ 9733 004577, ⓦ makaibari.com. The pioneering owner of this organic tea estate has encouraged homestays around the plantation in the workers' houses. Rustic but comfortable rooms and meals. ₹**1200**

THE DARJEELING HIMALAYAN RAILWAY: THE TOY TRAIN

Completed in 1881, the small-gauge (2ft or 610mm) **Darjeeling Himalayan Railway** was designed as an extension of the North Bengal State Railway, climbing from **New Jalpaiguri**, via **Siliguri**, for a tortuous 88km up to **Darjeeling**. Given World Heritage status by UNESCO in 1999, the **Toy Train** follows the Hill Cart Road, crossing it at regular intervals and even sharing it with traffic. The Toy Train is no longer an essential mode of transport but is certainly a tourist attraction, and currently runs from Kurseong to Darjeeling. Work is continuing on repairing the landslide damaged sections and the line should reopen to Siliguri by the end of 2013. A handful of steam engines are still in use but diesel engines are now de rigueur on the long route.

Weather permitting, first-class coaches with large viewing windows provide magnificent views as the journey progresses and the scenery gradually unfolds; second class can be fun but crowded. At its highest point at Jorebungalow near Ghoom (2438m), 7km short of Darjeeling, the dramatic panorama of the Kanchenjunga Range is suddenly revealed. Just beyond Ghoom, the train does a complete circle at the Batasia Loop – the most dramatic of the three loops encountered along the way. Another method used to gain rapid height are the **reversing stations** where the track follows a "Z" shape.

Some travellers may find the entire route from Siliguri painfully slow. The diesel-driven section from Kurseong is well worth the time, however or alternatively you could take the short ride from Darjeeling to Ghoom.

THE TOY TRAIN TO GHOOM

In season, four steam-driven **Joy Ride** tourist trains (₹260 return) leave Darjeeling at 10.40am, and travel up to Ghoom, where they stop for just fifteen minutes (not enough time to view the monasteries), before returning to Darjeeling with another brief stop at Batasia Loop for views of the Himalayas. Although sold as a package, you could the service is return on the regular diesel service. Alternative transport back to Darjeeling includes buses or shared jeeps, or you can take the top road for a quiet walk back, enjoying stupendous views along the way and a visit to the **Peace Pagoda** in the woods above the Dali Gompa.

INFORMATION

Train times The regular Toy Train currently departs Kurseong at 3pm, stops at Ghoom at 5.05pm and arrives at Darjeeling at 5.50pm, traffic permitting. The train to Kurseong departs from Darjeeling at 10.15am. A second service has been recently introduced leaving Kurseong at 7am and returning from Darjeeling at 4pm.

Booking tickets For more information on the Toy Train, contact the Darjeeling Himalayan Railway Society (ⓦ dhrs.org), or, in India, the Director at Elysia Building, near Himali School, Kurseong 734203 (☎ 0354 200 5734, ⓦ dhr.in). Book ahead as there are rarely more than three coaches on a train.

ACCOMMODATION

Cochrane Place Kurseong, 1km below the bazaar ☎ 099320 35660, ⓦ imperialchai.com. *Cochrane Place* is a rambling old villa with grand views, plenty of memorabilia, atmospheric if creaky rooms, a dorm and good food. Dorm ₹**736**, double ₹**2786**

13

EATING AND DRINKING

Chiave d' Cosmos 44 1H TN Rd. This tiny little café serves a good range of sandwiches, grills and pizzas and a small selection of good Italian dishes and decent coffee. The roof is a great place in the late afternoon. Daily 10am–9pm.

Dekevas 51 Gandhi Rd. Popular with travellers and locals alike, this no-smoking restaurant with pleasant Tibetan decor offers the usual mixed menu, including a wide range of Tibetan dishes and a very good-value breakfast. Daily 8am–9pm.

Gatty's Below Omni Guest House, nr TV Tower, Dr Zakir Hussain Rd. The closest one gets to a nightclub in Darjeeling with a lively motorbike theme (Gautam runs motorbike tours), this bistro also has a small but eclectic menu including lasagne and chicken pakoras (from ₹180). There is free wi-fi and a large screen in the adjacent room to catch the latest football. A great place for a beer in the evenings, the bar is liveliest after 9pm. Daily 6–11.30pm.

Glenary's The Mall. Darjeeling's most reputable eating place, renowned for its patisserie and tearooms, has a restaurant upstairs serving tasty sizzlers and great tandoori. The coffee shop downstairs, accompanied by an internet café, is a popular place to meet and spend time, in the basement, the American-styled bar serves burgers and pizzas. Daily 8am–9pm.

Hasty Tasty The Mall. Offering Indian fast food, and very popular with Indian holidaymakers, this self-service place serves tasty cheese dosas and superb veg thalis. However, the service is hardly hasty. Daily 11am–8pm.

Joey's Opposite Rink Plaza. A small and intimate pub, where Punam makes everyone welcome – a popular rendezvous for visitors and locals alike. Not renowned for its food but rather its beer, ambience and chat. Currently undergoing a major facelift. Daily 5–10pm.

Keventers Clubside. A landmark café serving toasted sandwiches and fried breakfasts that include bacon and ham. The terrace above the crossroads is excellent for people-watching, even if the service is poor. A delicatessen downstairs sells cheese, ham and sausages. Daily 8am–6pm.

Park 41 Laden La Rd. Widely considered to offer Darjeeling's finest north Indian and tandoori cuisine, served in plush surroundings with a bar. Reasonable Thai cooking as well; in season, the papaya salad is especially good. Daily noon–3pm & 6–11pm.

Penang's Opposite the GPO, above Laden La Rd. As much a bar as a café, this cheap, grubby yet popular local haunt serves excellent *momos* and *thukpa* and their chilli chicken is legendary. Daily noon–9.30pm.

SHOPPING

Life & Leaf Chowrasta ⊕lifeandleaf.org. This fair trade shop sells village handicrafts and produce including tea. Daily 11am–5pm.

Oxford Books & Stationery Chowrasta. A pleasant place to browse with a selection of novels, maps, non-fiction and coffee-table books. They will ship. Daily

10am–5pm.

Rope NB Singh Rd (below Clubside). Rope has a good selection of trekking gear, but is expensive. Shops in the Singalila Market, The Mall also offer equipment, including jackets and sleeping bags – mainly imitation gear from Nepal but at a good price. Daily 9am–4pm.

DIRECTORY

Banks and exchange There are several ATMs on Laden La Rd. The State Bank of India here also changes money and travellers' cheques; a short distance down the road, HDFC at Rink Mall offers foreign exchange. Licensed private foreign-exchange vendors offer an alternative but charge a bit more than the bank rate. Among these, the *Hotel Mohit* and *Hotel Seven Seventeen* are both on HD Lama Rd. Poddar's, 8 Laden La Rd near the GPO, is also good for cash advances on credit/debit cards.

Cinema Inox, Rink Mall (⊕0354 225 7183). A modern new multiplex with three auditoria and the latest from Bollywood and Hollywood; it can be loud so, depending on the film, take some cotton wool.

Hospital Try Planters' Hospital, Planter's Club, The Mall (⊕0354 225 4327); Mariam Nursing Home, The Mall (⊕0354 225 4327). The Tibetan Medical & Astro Institute, *Hotel Seven Seventeen*, 26 HD Lama Rd (⊕0354 225

4735), is part of the Dalai Lama's medical organization, Men-Tsee-Khang, and has a clinic and a well-stocked dispensary. There is also a Women's Clinic (Mon–Sat 1.30–5pm, Sun 10am–1pm) under *Hotel Springburn*, 70 Gandhi Rd.

Post office The main post office (Mon–Fri 9am–5pm, Sat 9am–noon) is on Laden La Rd.

Tibetan studies The Manjushree Centre of Tibetan Culture, 12 Gandhi Rd (⊕0354 225 6714, ⊕manjushree-culture.org), founded in 1988 to preserve and promote Tibetan culture, offers part-time Tibetan language classes (Mon–Sat 4–6pm) and more intensive three-, six- and nine-month courses and holds seminars, talks, video shows and exhibitions. The Chagpori Medical Institute at Takdah (en route to Teesta) runs excellent long courses in Tibetan medicine; ask at the Manjushree Centre.

Kalimpong

Though it may seem grubby at first, the quiet hill station of **Kalimpong**, 50km east of Darjeeling, has much to offer, including a colourful market, an extraordinary profusion of orchids and other flowers, great views of Kanchenjunga, several monasteries and lots of potential for walks in the surrounding hills, which are still home to the original **Lepcha** community. Like Darjeeling, Kalimpong once belonged to Sikkim, and later to Bhutan. Unlike Darjeeling, however, this was never a tea town or resort but a trading centre on the vital route to Tibet. Despite a large military presence, Kalimpong's recent history has been one of neglect, decaying infrastructure and water shortage. A deep-rooted dissatisfaction has simmered for several years, spearheaded by the Gurkhaland movement (see p.771), but political uncertainties and wildcat strikes have not detracted from Kalimpong's charm. The **earthquake** in September 2011 (see box, p.809) devasted parts of the town, but today its quiet leafy avenues offer a breath of fresh air after the razzmatazz of Darjeeling.

Tenth Mile

Kalimpong spreads along a curving ridge to either side of its main market area, known as **Tenth Mile**. Though there are few of the curio and tourist emporia so abundant in Darjeeling, there are plenty of places selling Buddhist handicrafts and religious paraphernalia, which attract wholesale buyers from all over India. Silk brocade, Tibetan incense, made-to-order monks' attire and silver bowls predominate. Of the tourist shops, both Kaziratna Shakya and Himalayan Handicrafts on Rishi Road have good selections and workshops; the wholesale shops are centred around RC Mintri Road.

KALIMPONG

■ ACCOMMODATION
Cloud 9	6
Deki Lodge	2
Gompus	3
Himalayan	7
Holumba Haven	8
Orchid Retreat	1
Sherpa Lodge	4
Silver Oaks	5
Windsongs	9

● CAFÉS & RESTAURANTS
3C's	5
Cakes-r-us & Pizza	2
Cloud 9	7
Gompus	3
Kalash	4
King Thai	6
Lees	1

Rinkingpong Hill

Rinkingpong Hill, also known as **Durpin Dara**, looms above Kalimpong 4km to the southwest and is best visited at dawn. At its highest point, **Zong Dog Palri Phodrang Gompa**, also known as Durpin ("telescope") Monastery, built in 1957 to house three copper statues brought from Tibet in the 1940s, was modelled on Guru Rinpoche's mythical "pure realm" palace and consecrated by the Dalai Lama. Despite the communication masts and the army campus next door, the *gompa*'s roof is a great place to take in the sunrise accompanied by the chanting of the monks below; you are welcome to sit in for the prayers.

The wooded roads leading up Rinkingpong Hill hide several interesting old manor houses. **Morgan House** was built for a British jute merchant but now serves as a tourist lodge, where tea on the lawn captures the atmosphere of the period; the views are stunning.

St Teresa's Church

Some 2km above town up the hill, **St Teresa's Church** was built in 1929 by a Swiss missionary and borrows heavily from vernacular Buddhist monastic architecture, mimicking a Bhutanese *gompa*. There's beautiful carving inside and out: note the doors, adorned with the eight sacred Buddhist symbols.

Thirpai Choling Gompa and Thongsa Gompa

Above Tenth Mile, to the east of town, a short walk up Deolo Hill brings you to the **Thirpai Choling Gompa**, a breakaway Gelugpa monastery founded in 1892 and recently renovated, which once venerated the controversial image of Dorje Shugden, a deity proscribed by the Dalai Lama.

Also near Tenth Mile and below the main road, the meditation halls of **Thongsa Gompa**, a small Bhutanese monastery founded in 1692, completely renovated recently, are covered with beautiful murals. Some of these are sexually explicit, depicting *yabyum*, the coupling of divine opposites.

Deolo Hill

Daily 9am–6pm • ₹5

The summit of **Deolo Hill** (1704m) is a popular picnic spot, with a DGHC tourist lodge and restaurant, and a superb vista that ranges from the steamy Teesta Valley far below to the summit of Kanchenjunga, with the frontier ridge and the passes of Nathula and Jelepla into Tibet clearly visible.

ARRIVAL AND DEPARTURE	KALIMPONG

Kalimpong, only accessible by road, is served by regular buses, taxis and jeeps from Darjeeling, Siliguri and Gangtok. Most buses and jeeps run from the Motor Stand in the central market area. In case you need assistance, ask at the Help Desk at nearby *Sherpa Lodge*.

By jeep A shared jeep (1pm, ₹110) to the NJP railway station, booked in advance through the Railway Agency on Rishi Rd (☎ 03552 259954), is especially useful for evening train departures such as the *Darjeeling Mail* to Kolkata. Each route has its own syndicate and ticket office. Bear in mind that the last reliable transport links are mid-afternoon.

Destinations Darjeeling (2hr 30min–4hr; ₹100), Siliguri (2hr 30min; ₹100, reserved ₹1400), Gangtok (3hr; ₹120). Other destinations include NJP, Lava, Kakarbitta (Nepal border), Pelling and Ghezing.

By taxi Himalayan Travellers (☎ 94341 66498) is good for

reserved taxis and the Motor Transport Syndicate (☎ 99327 66064) runs services to Darjeeling (7am–3pm).

By bus Although slower than jeeps, buses to Siliguri (₹60) are generally more comfortable; similarly, the bus to Gangtok is worth considering compared to a shared jeep (7am; ₹60).

Train and air tickets Dynamic Solutions, Jopa Complex on Main Rd (☎ 03552 257874), is good for all air tickets; for train tickets, head to the Railway Agency on Rishi Rd (daily 10am–4pm), although their quota for NJP is low.

HORTICULTURE

Kalimpong is renowned for its **horticulture**, especially its orchids, cacti, amaryllis, palms and ferns. There are round fifty nurseries, such as **Sri Ganesh Mani Pradhan** at Twelfth Mile and **Pineview** (₹10) on Atisha Road, which specializes in exotic cacti. Although Kalimpong blossoms all year long, the **best time** to see orchids in bloom is between mid-April and mid-May, when the **flower festival** is usually held.

INFORMATION

Tourist information GTA tourist office, Damber Chowkh (daily 9.30am–5pm; ☎ 03552 257992), provides general information and arranges whitewater rafting on the Teesta (from ₹350). A better bet for local information is the extremely helpful Travel Help Desk at *Sherpa Lodge* near the Motor Stand (☎ 89720 29913).

Tour operators Gurudongma Tours and Treks (☎ 03552 255204, ◍ gurudongma.com) specializes in ornithological, culinary and trekking trips and has its own farmhouse (see box, p.784). 2 Travel Help Desk organizes village tours, local walks and tailor-made

itineraries including trips to the Neora Valley; they will also arrange mountain bike tours. Mondo Challenge, an educational charity that welcomes volunteers, also runs one- and two-day village treks (☎ 03552 260026, ◍ kalimpongvillagetour.wordpress.com). Not for the faint-hearted, the Swedish-run Himalayan Eagle offers tandem paragliding flights (Sept–June ☎ 9635 156911) from near Deolo; you will need to sign a disclaimer as they are not fully insured. Its sister operation, (◍ himalayanbiketours.se) organizes motorbike tours of the region and accepts payment in euros.

ACTIVITIES

Markets On Wednesdays and Saturdays, Tenth Mile gets very lively as villagers flock in from the surrounding areas for the principal weekly markets.

Traditional paper workshops The Gangjong Paper

Factory (Mon–Sat 9am–4.30pm) welcomes visitors to their handmade paper workshop down steps off Printam Rd; access to Himalayan Handmade Paper, on KD Pradhan Rd near Thirpai, is easier and they also have a shop.

ACCOMMODATION

Cloud 9 Ringkingpong Rd ☎ 98320 39634. Five spacious, airy and well-kept rooms with grand views across the distant town. It's above a restaurant and bar that's especially lively when the owner Binodh is around – expect guitar jams and Beatles covers. **₹1650**

Deki Lodge Tirpai Rd ☎ 03552 255095. A 10min walk from the Motor Stand, this clean and very welcoming Tibetan-run hotel offers a wide choice, from budget rooms with hot water by the bucket to comfortable doubles with running hot water in the new wing at the rear; internet is available. **₹730**

Gompus Damber Chowk ☎ 03552 2558181, ◍ gompuskalimpong.com. This legendary place bang in the centre of town has been completely revamped into a smart, mid-range business hotel with large rooms all with TV and modern plumbing, on three floors above a popular restaurant and bar. **₹1760**

Himalayan Upper Cart Rd ☎ 03552 255248, ◍ himalayanhotel.com. Historic hotel, in the process of changing hands, full of Tibetan memorabilia, set amid exquisite, leafy gardens in an unspoilt spot above town; the modern cottages are luxurious but lack the ambience of the old house with its large wood-panelled rooms. **₹5600**

★ **Holumba Haven** 8.5 Mile, near the Fire Station ☎ 03552 256936, ◍ holumba.com. Beautifully presented cottages set in a plant nursery resplendent with tree ferns and complete with a menagerie of birds. Some cottages come with their own kitchens, or you can have home-cooked meals with the informative and

extremely welcoming owners. This is essentially a homestay and so doesn't provide all the amenities of a hotel. **₹950**

Orchid Retreat 12 Mile ☎ 03552 274489, ◍ theorchid retreat.com. A family-run plant nursery that has been partly converted into a comfortable homestay; beyond the initial modern buildings the grounds drop steeply away into a lush garden decorated with tree ferns and exotic flora, where a handful of wooden chalets built in vernacular style provide a quiet haven. **₹2950**

Sherpa Lodge Ongden Rd ☎ 89720 29913. Convenient central location with eight good budget rooms, four with attached bathrooms, and a lovely terrace for breakfast overlooking the playground. Hot water is by the bucket. The owner is very helpful and runs an information and travel desk on the ground floor. **₹500**

Silver Oaks Ringkingpong Rd ☎ 03552 255296, ◍ elginhotels.com. One of the grandest addresses in town, with a central location, spacious, plush rooms with conservative decor, and a good restaurant; the garden is a pleasant setting for tea or drinks in the evenings. **₹8200**

★ **Windsongs** 8 Mile ☎ 03552 256556, ◍ windsongs kalimpong.com. A palm nursery and family home with a handful of rooms, some in the plush new block. However the single cottage in the manicured garden, where the bathroom window opens out to the most impressive view in the hills – from the Teesta to the top of Kanchenjunga (a distance around 8000m), makes this the best spot in town. **₹3200**

EATING AND DRINKING

3C's Main Rd. A popular bistro with a snack bar, coffee shop and a patisserie counter; good for breakfast and for lunch. Try

their *rumali* roti and *paneer* tikka. Daily 10am–6pm.

Cakes-r-us & Pizza SBG Rd, near GTA tourist office. A

13

VILLAGE TOURISM AND HOMESTAYS

Offering the chance to explore the rural landscape and experience local culture, organized **village tourism** is becoming increasingly popular. The main operators include Gurudongma and Holumba (see p.783) in Kalimpong, Help Tourism (see p.768) in Siliguri and Himalayan Footprints in Gangtok (see box, p.814).

Farm House ☎ 9002 692611, ⊛ awakeandshine .org. This homestay run by Gurudongma is a tranquil and rustic yet luxurious development on the beautiful Samthar Plateau, an 80km drive from Kalimpong. The rate shown here includes dinner; they will arrange cheaper alternatives. ₹13,500

Gurung Guest House Tinchuley Village House ☎ 9733 326309, ⊛ tinchuley.com. Situated 28km from Kalimpong near Takdah, this well-run guesthouse,

with some delightful wood-lined rooms plus a modern block, provides a comfortable retreat with a small tea and cardamom plantation and nature trails nearby. ₹1000

Turuk Kothi ☎ 9434 109881, ⊛ turukkothi heritagehome.com. Across the border into Sikkim, 35km from Kalimpong, this is a grand manor house set in an idyllic plantation that dates back to the late nineteenth century. ₹3000

pleasant patisserie with *Pizza* across the hall offering pizza and Indian food to eat in or take away. Daily 10am–6pm.

Cloud 9 Ringkingpong Rd ☎ 98320 39634. A welcoming bar and a restaurant with occasional live music and a varied menu. With some notice, they can produce a special Bhutanese meal including spicy chese curry, red rice and pork and *pakshya pa* (boiled pork). Expect to pay around ₹400 with drinks and dinner. Daily noon–1pm.

Gompus Damber Chowk. A famous and popular bar and restaurant in the centre of town with a wide menu but best known for *momos* and *thukpa*; expect to pay around ₹200 for a meal. Great place for a long, cold beer. Daily 8am–9pm.

Kalash Main Rd. An excellent vegetarian restaurant that

has had a recent makeover, and offers good wholesome cooking with thalis for just ₹130. Daily noon–6pm.

King Thai Ma Supermarket, near the police station. A popular local bar and restaurant serving Indian and Chinese, rather than Thai food expect to pay around ₹300 for a meal. Local bands play here occasionally but sadly evenings often disintegrate into fights at around 9pm. Daily noon–10pm.

Lees Above Maya Liang, SBG Rd. Authentic Chinese restaurant it's owned by and named after the chef. Try the steamed golden chicken or spare ribs; it's best to come for lunch as he closes early in the evenings. Expect to pay around ₹300. Daily noon–6pm.

DIRECTORY

ATMs Of the handful of ATMs, the most useful are next to the State Bank of India on Main Rd, ICICI next door and Axis on DS Gurung Rd above the Motor Stand, accepting credit and debit cards.

Changing money On all of which accept Main Rd near DGHC office, Soni Emporium and neighbouring Kaziratna

Shakya change cash and travellers' cheques.

Hospital Adarsha Nursing Home, SD Giri Rd (☎ 89679 68474), is one of the best hospitals in town for emergencies.

Post office The main post office is near the town centre, above the bazaar area just behind the police station.

Around Kalimpong

Although the **Lepchas**, the original inhabitants of the area, have lost their traditional way of life in most parts of Darjeeling and Sikkim, their lifestyle has remained relatively untouched in the unspoilt forest-covered hills and deep river valleys to the south of Kalimpong.

Lava and Neora Valley National Park

Lying on an old trade route to Bhutan, the small town of **Lava** (2184m) with a colourful Tuesday market, 35km from Kalimpong and accessible by shared jeep, makes an ideal base for exploring the nature trails of **Neora Valley National Park**. A 880-hectare reserve stretching along a narrow river valley, with a huge variation in wildlife and abundant orchids and birds, the park has been designated a tiger reserve but sightings are extremely rare. As well as black bear and red panda Neora Valley is home to packs of wild dogs.

Lava is also convenient for approaching the **Rachela Pass** (3152m) on the Sikkim–Bhutan border, which provides excellent views of the Chola Range including Chomalhari (7314m), the sacred mountain of Bhutan.

Walking around Lava

Pleasant **trails** lead west from Lava towards **Budhabare**, a market town in the Git River Valley, which has a sprinkling of Lepcha, Gurkha and Bhutia villages. The track continues through forest to **Kafer Lolegaon** where the sunrise is legendary and there is a Heritage Forest walk along a canopy trail. You can get here via a rough road from Kalimpong, but if you're fit, you could walk the trail that crosses the Relli River near the village of the same name and climbs directly to Kalimpong. Alternatively, you could **cycle** through the area – ask at the Travel Help Desk in Kalimpong (see p.783) for routes.

ARRIVAL AND INFORMATION LAVA AND NEORA VALLEY NATIONAL PARK

By jeep or bus The crossroads at the centre of Lava serves as a shared taxi stand with regular connections to Kalimpong and also to Siliguri; buses make the same journey. The turn-off to Kafir Lolegaon is 5km away on the Kalimpong road. There is less transport on this route and so it is best to travel early.

Permits The Travel Help Desk in Kalimpong (see p.783) can arrange the necessary guides and permits (₹200 (30)) as well as transport for a multiday trek through the sanctuary staying at remote forest resthouses; they can also advise on treks around Lava. The Forest Department (☎03561 24907), 1km above Lava on the Kalimpong road, opposite the small Wildlife Museum (free), also manages permits.

Park entry Jeeps from Lava to the gate of Neora Valley NP (15km) charge the earth (₹3000). The road is too rutted to take ordinary vehicles. Leave the vehicle by the park gates where there is a café and the checkpost to register your permit. Access into the park is on foot.

ACCOMMODATION AND EATING

Lava has limited accommodation within the town but the surrounding area offers a choice from forest bungalows to places with a bit more luxury. Further afield, Lolegaon has a handful of hotels to choose from. There are a few basic restaurants around the taxi stand in the centre.

Forest Rest House Lava ☎03552 255780, ⓦwbfdc.com. On the edge of town and a short drive off the main Kalimpong road, this is a pleasant and quiet place to stay, though booking it through the Forest Department is a pain. If passing through Siliguri, book through the Tourist Office (see p.767) or try their office off Rinkingpong Rd in Kalimpong. **₹600**

Neora Valley Jungle Camp Kolakham, Lava ☎0353 253 5896, ⓦhelptourism.com. The most luxurious accommodation in the vicinity of the national park and run by experienced wildlife experts, this is hardly a camp but rather a collection of tasteful stone and wood cottages with expansive views of Sikkim. Transport there from Lava is extra. **₹5000**

Paradise Lava Bazaar, Lava ☎9932 889565, ⓦparadisehotelsgroup.com. One of Lava's better hotels, with partially wood-lined rooms with TV and attached baths with hot water when electricity allows; there is also a decent restaurant catering mainly for Bengali visitors. They also have a branch at Rishyap, a pleasant 4km walk away through the woods. **₹700**

Tree Fern Lolegaon ☎9932 371313, ⓦresorttreefern.com. With nine picturesque wooden cottages on a steep sloping garden this is probably the best place to stay at Lolegaon, with hot water and attached baths and a restaurant. **₹1650**

Bihar and
Jharkhand

YOUNG MONKS, MAHABODHI TEMPLE

Bihar and Jharkhand

Bihar occupies the flat eastern Ganges basin, south of Nepal, between Uttar Pradesh and West Bengal. To its south, Jharkhand, occupying the hilly Chotanagpur plateau north of Orissa, was hewn out of Bihar in 2000, following agitation by its tribal majority. Both states are beset by poverty, lack of infrastructure, inter-caste violence, corruption and general lawlessness.

14

Although visitors are usually unaffected by the banditry and guerrilla war, Buddhist pilgrims and tourists have on occasion been robbed and few travellers spend much time here, which is a shame, because the region offers a fascinating mix of **religious history**. Check the **safety situation** with your government's foreign ministry and the local press (Ⓦpatnadaily.com and Ⓦbihartimes.in are good sources of information) before travel; local state and tourist authorities tend to downplay safety concerns. The region is generally best avoided during local elections, when tensions run high, and riots and violent crime are not uncommon.

Patna

PATNA, Bihar's capital, dates back to the sixth century BC, but shows few signs today of its former glory as the centre of the Magadhan and Mauryan empires. A sprawling metropolis hugging the south bank of the Ganges, Patna stretches for around 15km in a shape that has changed little since Ajatasatru (491–459 BC) shifted the Magadhan capital here from Rajgir.

The first Mauryan emperor, **Chandragupta**, established himself in what was then **Pataliputra** in 321 BC, and pushed the limits of his empire as far as the Indus; his grandson **Ashoka** (274–237 BC), one of India's greatest rulers, held sway over even greater domains. To facilitate Indo-Hellenic trade, the Mauryans built a Royal Highway from Pataliputra to Taxila, Pakistan, which later became the Grand Trunk Road. The city experienced two revivals, first when the first Gupta emperor, **Chandra Gupta**, made it his capital early in the fourth century AD, and then again when it was rebuilt in the sixteenth century by Afghan ruler Sher Shah Suri.

Every March the city celebrates its illustrious history with several days of music, dancing and public events during the **Pataliputra Mahotsava** festival.

Note that Patna has a higher crime rate than other Indian cities, and it's not a good idea to walk around on your own at night.

Golghar

Patna's most notable monument is the **Golghar**, also called "the round house", a huge colonial-era grain store built in 1786 to avoid a repetition of 1770's terrible famine; thankfully, it never needed to be used. Overlooking the river and Gandhi Maidan, its two sets of stairs spiralling up to the summit were designed so coolies could carry grain up one side, deliver their load through a hole at the top, and descend down the other. Sightseers now clamber up for views of the mighty river and the city.

| **Lalu and the caste wars: politics in Bihar** p.793 | **Madhubani paintings** p.796 **Meditation courses in Bodhgaya** p.799 |

NALANDA

Highlights

❶ **Sonepur Mela** This month-long festival and cattle fair is a spectacular gathering of pilgrims, sadhus and animals. **See p.794**

❷ **The Mahabodhi Temple** A cutting from the tree under which the Buddha attained enlightenment is the focal point of Bodhgaya's renowned temple, which really does have an air of calm, meditative holiness about it. **See p.797**

❸ **Mahakala Caves** Climb a path lined with hopeful beggars to see the caves where Buddha underwent years of bodily mortification before realizing that this was not the true path to enlightenment. **See p.801**

❹ **Rajgir** A dusty Buddhist pilgrimage town filled with shrines, as well as therapeutic hot springs, and a chairlift to take you up to a Peace Pagoda on a hill. **See p.801**

❺ **Nalanda** The site of a fifteen-hundred-year-old university, from the days when Buddhism dominated India, strewn with the remains of ancient *stupas* and monasteries. **See p.802**

HIGHLIGHTS ARE MARKED ON THE MAP ON P.790

Gandhi Museum

Ashok Rajpath, just northwest of Gandhi Maidan • Daily except Sat 10am–6pm • Free • Ⓦ gandhisangrahalaypatna.org

Patna's **Gandhi Museum** is really more like a book in museum format, consisting largely of text and photos illustrating, in one room, the Mahatma's life, and in another, the history of the independence movement in Bihar. One or two of Gandhi's personal effects are also on display, but are labelled in Hindi only.

BIHAR & JHARKHAND

HIGHLIGHTS

1. Sonepur Mela
2. The Mahabodhi Temple
3. Mahakala Caves
4. Rajgir
5. Nalanda

The International boundaries on this map are neither purported to be correct nor authentic by Survey of India directives. Publisher.

Patna Museum

Buddha Marg • Tues–Sun 10.30am–4.30pm • ₹500 (₹100), camera ₹100, video ₹500

The **Patna Museum**, although faded and run-down, has an excellent collection of sculptures. Among its most famous exhibits is a polished sandstone female attendant, or *yakshi*, holding a fly-whisk, dating back to the third century BC. There are also Jain images from the Kushana period, a group of Buddhist *bodhisattvas* from Gandhara (in northwest Pakistan), some freakishly deformed stuffed animals and a gigantic fossilized tree thought to be 200 million years old. Don't bother paying the ₹500 (₹100) extra to see the Buddha relic.

14

Harimandir Sahib

In the most interesting area of Patna – the older part of town, 10km east of Gandhi Maidan – filthy congested lanes lead to **Harimandir Sahib**, the second holiest of the four great Sikh shrines known as *takhts* (thrones). Set in an expansive courtyard off the main road, the dazzling white onion-domed marble temple is dedicated to Guru Gobind Singh, born in Patna in 1660. Visitors can explore the courtyard and even venture inside where devotional music is often playing. Remove your shoes and cover your head before entering. Shared auto-rickshaws cost ₹10 from Gandhi Maidan Bus Stand.

Qila House

Jalan Ave • Visits by appointment • ☎ 0612 264 2354

A short way northeast of Harimandir Sahib, the private **Qila House** (or Jalan Museum) holds a fine collection of art, including Chinese paintings and Mughal filigree work in jade and silver. Among the antiques are porcelain items that once belonged to Marie Antoinette, and Napoleon's four-poster bed. To the west, the East India Company's **Old Opium Warehouse** at **Gulzarbagh** is now home to a government printing press.

Saif Khan's Mosque

Midway between Harimandir Sahib and Gandhi Maidan stands **Saif Khan's Mosque**, also called "the mosque of stone". That is indeed what it is made from, but the stone is hidden behind layers of whitewash, with pretty green highlights. The mosque was commissioned in 1621 by the son of the Mughal emperor Jahangir, Parwez Shah, who was governor of Bihar at the time (although it doesn't actually look very Mughal), and it attracts visitors from all over India to this day.

ARRIVAL AND DEPARTURE
PATNA

By plane Patna's airport is 5km west of town (around ₹200 by taxi, ₹100 by auto). Flights serve Delhi (6 daily with Air India, Jet, IndiGo and Go Air), Kolkara (2–3 daily with Jet, JetKonnect and IndiGo) and Ranchi (1 daily with Go Air). Air India are at South Gandhi Maidan (☎ 0612 222 2554); Jet's office is at the airport (☎ 0612 222 3045).

By train All mainline train services arrive at Patna Junction station, in the west of the city. Patna Junction is the most important railway station in the region, and has a foreigners' reservation window (No. 7) on the upper floor of the booking office. The best train to Kolkata (Howrah) is the *Janshatabdi Express* #2024 (Mon–Sat; dep. 5.45am, arr. 1.25pm); overnight services include the *Vibhuti Express* #12334 (daily; dep. 10.35pm, arr. 7.30am). For destinations beyond Kolkata, the *Northeast Express* #12506 leaves Patna

at 10.20pm daily, reaching New Jalpaiguri (for Darjeeling) at 8.20am and Guwahati at 4.45pm. In the other direction, to Varanasi, the *Shramjeevi Express* #12391 (daily; dep. 10.50am, arr. just after 3pm) is a good option. The *Rajdhani Express* #12309 at 7.25pm (arr. 7.35am next day) and the *Sampark Kranti Express* #12393 at 6pm (arr. 8.35am next day) are the pick of several daily trains to New Delhi. For Mumbai, the *Rajendra Nagar* #12142 leaves daily at 11.10am, arriving at 3.30pm the next day. Seven daily trains cover the 2–3hr journey to Gaya, of which the fastest is the 6.15am *Janshatabdi* #12365 (arr. 8.10am), which continues on to Ranchi (arr. 1.55pm). Only one inconvenient weekly train links Patna directly with Puri, and no trains arrive in Gaya at a convenient time for the daily *Purshottam Express* #12802 (which leaves Gaya at 1.35pm, arriving in

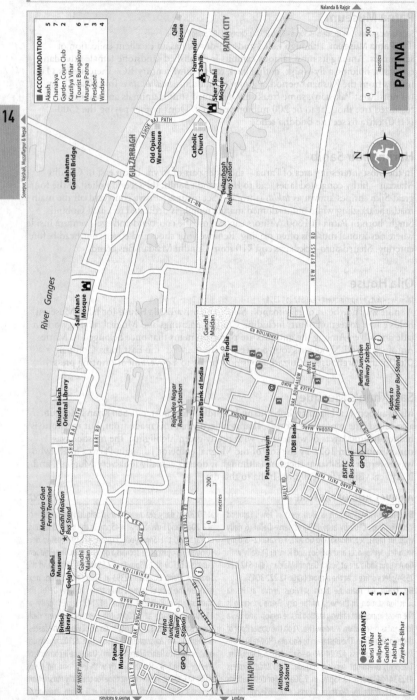

14

Sonepur, Vaishali, Muzaffarpur & Nepal

PATNA

ACCOMMODATION	
Akash	5
Chanakya	7
Garden Court Club	2
Kautilya Vihar	6
Tourist Bungalow	1
Maurya Patna	3
President	3
Windsor	4

Qila House

PATNA CITY

Harimandir Sahib

Sher Shahi Mosque

Old Opium Warehouse

Catholic Church

Gulzarbagh Railway Station

GULZARBAGH

ASHOK RAJ PATH

NH-19

Mahatma Gandhi Bridge

River Ganges

Saif Khan's Mosque

NEW BYPASS RD

Khuda Baksh Oriental Library

Rajendra Nagar Railway Station

BARI RD

ASHOK RAJ PATH

Mahendra Ghat Ferry Terminal

Gandhi Maidan Bus Stand

Gandhi Museum

Golghar

British Library

Patna Museum

BAILEY RD

SEE 'INSET' MAP

GPO

Gandhi Maidan

EXHIBITION RD

DAK BUNGALOW ROAD

FRASER ROAD

Patna Junction Railway Station

MITHAPUR

Mithapur Bus Stand

Muner & Varanasi

Airport

Gandhi Maidan

Air India

EXHIBITION RD

State Bank of India

BUDDHA MARG

DAK BUNGALOW ROAD

FRASER ROAD

HOTEL LANE

Patna Junction Railway Station

Autos to Mithapur Bus Stand

Patna Museum

IDBI Bank

BUDDHA MARG

BAILEY RD

BIR CHAND PATEL PATH

BSRTC Bus Stand

GPO

● RESTAURANTS	
Bansi Vihar	4
Bellpepper	3
Gandhi's	1
Takshila	5
Zayeka-e-Bihar	2

N

0 500 metres

0 200 metres

LALU AND THE CASTE WARS: POLITICS IN BIHAR

For years, Bihar languished at the bottom of almost every measure of development: from literacy rates to GDP. Author William Dalrymple described it as "the most ungovernable and anarchic state in India", even though it is blessed with ample coal and iron deposits and large tracts of arable land. The problem was caused by a disastrous combination of virulent inter-caste conflict and criminal misgovernance.

After Indian Independence, Bihar was ruled by a mafia of high-caste landowners, with the lower castes – who together with untouchables and tribal people make up more than seventy percent of the state's population – marginalized to the point of persecution. All that seemed set to change in 1991 when a rabble-rouser from a lowly caste of buffalo milkers, **Lalu Prasad Yadav**, united the "backward castes", the Muslims and the untouchables under a banner of social justice, winning that year's state election by a landslide. In power, Lalu delighted with his common touch; he spontaneously unclogged traffic congestion in Patna by walking the streets with a megaphone and filled the grounds of his official residence with buffalo.

Unfortunately Lalu proved little better than his predecessors. His cabinet of caste brethren included men wanted for murder and kidnapping, and violence remained the main tool of political persuasion – as one election candidate said: "Without one hundred men with guns you cannot contest an election in Bihar." Much of the state degenerated into virtual civil war as the upper castes, lower castes, Maoist (Naxalite) guerrillas, police and private armies clashed violently.

Lalu's career appeared to be over in 1997, when he was imprisoned for a short spell for embezzling billions of rupees. He responded by getting his illiterate wife **Rabri Devi** proclaimed chief minister. Even though his RJD party was toppled in the 2005 state elections, Lalu went on to serve as minister for railways from 2004 to 2009, and remains a member of Parliament.

Meanwhile, at state level, things have changed for the better. In 2005 a Janata Dal (U)–BJP coalition under Lalu's chief opponent Nitish Kumar took power, and the situation began to improve. With less obvious domination by organized crime, investors are returning, bringing new employment opportunities. Now, the Biharis who faced so much prejudice as emigrant workers in states like Maharashtra are beginning to find jobs at home, and in 2011 (Kumar's coalition having retained power in the 2010 elections) one study even concluded that Bihar was the least corrupt state in India. Poor it may still be, but at long last things in Bihar have started to turn around.

Puri at 5.30am), so take a morning bus to Gaya for that.

By bus For all destinations it's wise to stick to daytime services. State-run buses to Sonepur, Muner and Hajipur (for Vaishali) use the Gandhi Maidan Bus Stand. Private buses leave from the chaotic Mithapur Bus Stand, 2km south of the railway station (shared autos connect the two), where there is no enquiry office or departure board, and you'll have to depend on touts to guide you to a bus. For Nalanda and Rajgir, you may have to change at Bihar Sharif. Private

companies offer bus tickets to Kathmandu with a voucher for the bus across the border, but it's just as easy – and generally wiser – to make your own way to Raxaul (see p.796), cross the border, and find a bus on the Nepali side. The best services to Raxaul and Ranchi are the a/c buses run by Bihar State Roadways (BSRTC) from their stand in Bir Chand Patel Path (☎0612 250 6099, ⊛gauravluxury.com). BSRTC hope to serve more destinations in the near future; details should appear on their website.

INFORMATION

Tourist information The Bihar State Tourism Development Corporation is at *Kautilya Vihar Tourist Bungalow* (Mon–Sat 10.30am–5.30pm; ☎0612 222 5411, ⊛bstdc.bih.nic.in), with a booth at Patna Junction (daily 8am–8pm, but often closed; ☎0612 220 5755). Bihar

Tourism can arrange tours and car rental, but many drivers won't go to isolated areas for fear of dacoits. India Tourism are in the Institution of Engineers Building, near R-Block roundabout, Hardinge Rd (☎0612 657 0640, ⊛itopat @gmail.com).

ACCOMMODATION

Akash Hotel Alley (just off Fraser Rd) ☎0612 223 9599. One of Patna's better shoestring hotels, *Akash* has a motley collection of fairly clean, compact rooms; it's often full, but is located in an alley full of cheap hotels,

although not all of them are authorized to accept foreigners guests. ₹500

Chanakya Bir Chand Patel Path ☎0612 222 0590, ⊛hotelchanakyapatna.com. This looming hotel has

14

tastefully furnished beige- and apricot-coloured attached rooms. There's also a classy bar, a currency exchange and two top restaurants serving Indian and Chinese, or Mughal and Afghan dishes. ₹6458

Garden Court Club Patna Super Market, Fraser Rd ☎0612 320 2279, ⒲gardencourtclub.com. Accessed via an ancient lift, this small hotel in a shopping complex has a handful of neat and tidy rooms with TVs, and is the best -value cheapie in town. It also has a rooftop restaurant (see below). ₹700

Kautilya Vihar Tourist Bungalow Bir Chand Patel Path ☎0612 222 5411, ⒲bstdc.bih.nic.in. The Bihar State Tourism Development Corporation's rambling hotel has cavernous, brightly coloured but rather overpriced doubles, a reasonable dorm, free wi-fi in the lobby, and a relaxed rooftop restaurant. Dorm ₹200, double ₹1174

Maurya Patna Fraser Rd, South Gandhi Maidan ☎0612 220 3040, ⒲maurya.com. Service can be impersonal, even surly, at this five-star, but the luxurious rooms – decorated in a range of styles, from colonial to oriental – swimming pool and fine restaurants tend to make up for it. ₹13,658

President Off Fraser Rd ☎0612 220 9203, ⒲hotelpresidentpatna.com. Its decor may not have been updated since the 1970s, but *President* remains a good option. Although the rooms are a little stuffy, they're clean and boast multicoloured bedspreads. The management is also a good source of transport information. ₹1761

Windsor Exhibition Rd ☎0612 220 3250, ⒲hotelwindsorpatna.com. A reassuringly well-run mid-range hotel, good value, with nicely furnished modern attached rooms, an internet café and an excellent restaurant (see below). ₹1996

EATING AND DRINKING

There are several decent **restaurants** strung along Fraser Rd, although some double as bars in the evening when the custom is all male. Keep an eye out for *littis* – baked balls of spiced chickpea dough – a Bihari speciality sold by street vendors.

Bansi Vihar Fraser Rd ☎0612 222 4804. A narrow, dimly lit dining hall packed with locals, who come to sample tasty south Indian snacks, primarily dosas, of which there are 22 varieties (₹52–95), as well as *uttapams* and the odd Chinese dish. Daily 8am– 10.30pm.

★ **Bellpepper** Hotel Windsor, Exhibition Rd ☎0612 220 3250. A cosy and intimate little place serving excellent tandoori dishes such as chicken *malai tikka* (₹230) and kebabs such as chicken *seekh* kebab (₹240). Daily 12.30– 3.30pm & 7.30–10.30pm.

Gandhi's Fraser Rd ☎0612 392 5468. A polished and super-hygienic pure-veg basement restaurant that serves a rich *paneer* butter masala (₹140) and seasonal hot *gulab jamun* (₹35). Daily 10am–10pm.

Takshila Hotel Chanakya, Bir Chand Patel Path ☎0612 222 0590. A top-notch restaurant specializing in Mughlai and Afghan meat dishes, with kebabs, Peshwari-style tandoori chicken (₹399 for half a bird), and in the evenings, set menus at ₹499 veg, or ₹599 non-veg. Daily 12.30–3.30pm & 7.30–11pm.

Zayeka-e-Bihar Garden Court Club, Fraser Rd ☎0612 320 2279. The food is good here, served on a delightful rooftop terrace, and the menu offers tempting dishes such as *Zayeka-e-Bihar bhujia* (spicy fried vegetables; ₹120) and *Bihari machh* (fish in mustard gravy; ₹130), but the service is pretty shoddy, and often many of the things on the menu aren't available. Worth a punt none the less. Daily 10am–10pm.

DIRECTORY

Banks The SBI, West Gandhi Maidan, handles foreign exchange; ATMs are dotted around town.
Internet Cyber City, G-9, ground floor, Hem PLaza, Frazer Rd (daily 9am–7pm; ₹15/hr); Windsornet at the *Windsor*

hotel (daily 6.30am–8.30pm; ₹30/hr).
Travel agents Ashok Travel in the *Hotel Pataliputra Ashok* (☎0612 250 4238); Thomas Cook at the *Maurya Patna* (☎0612 645 5266).

Around Patna

Patna is a good base for exploring Nalanda, Rajgir and **Vaishali**, but there are also places of interest closer at hand, notably the fabulous hilltop *dargah* at **Muner**, 27km west. If you're in Bihar between early November and early December, don't miss the **Sonepur Mela**, staged 25km north of Patna across the huge Gandhi Bridge – Asia's longest river bridge – at the confluence of the Gandak and the Ganges. Cattle, elephants, camels, parakeets and other animals are brought for sale, pilgrims combine business with a dip in the Ganges, sadhus congregate, and festivities abound. The event is memorably described by Mark Shand in his quixotic *Travels on My Elephant* (see p.1188). The Bihar State Tourism Development Corporation in Patna (see p.793) organizes tours and maintains a tourist village at Sonepur during the *mela*.

Muner

Muner is served by buses (approximately hourly) from Gandhi Maidan Bus Stand in Patna

The imposing but sadly neglected red-sandstone shrine of Sufi saint Yahia Muneri, 1km west of **Muner**, was built in 1605. Every year, around February, a three-day *urs*, or festival, in the saint's honour attracts pilgrims from far and wide, with *qawwals* by Sufi musicians from Delhi and Ajmer. Muner is also known for its **sweets**, particularly lentil *ladoos*.

Vaishali

Set amid paddy fields 55km north of Patna, the quiet village of **VAISHALI** was the site of the Buddha's last sermon. Named after King Visala, who is mentioned in the Ramayana, Vaishali is also believed by some historians to have been the first city-state in the world to practise a democratic, republican form of government. After leaving his family and renouncing the world, Prince Gautama studied here, but eventually rejected his master's teachings and found his own path to enlightenment. He returned to Vaishali three times and on his last visit announced his final liberation – *Mahaparinirvana* – and departure from the world, in around 483 BC. A hundred years later, the second Buddhist Council was held in Vaishali and two *stupas* erected.

A small but well-presented **archeological museum** (daily except Fri 10am–5pm; ₹10) provides a glimpse into the ancient Buddhist world. A short path next to the Coronation Tank (Abhishekh Pushkarni) leads off to the remains of the **stupa** where the ashes of the Buddha were reputedly found in a silver urn.

Two kilometres north among the ruins of **Kolhua** (daily except Fri 10am–5pm; ₹100 (₹5)), the remarkably well-preserved **Ashokan Pillar** was erected by the Mauryan emperor (273–232 BC) to commemorate the site of Buddha's last sermon. Known locally as Bhimsen-ki-lathi (Bhimsen's Staff), the 18.3m-high pillar, made of polished red sandstone, is crowned by a lion sitting on an inverted lotus, which faces north towards Kushinagar, where Buddha died. Jains of the Svetambara sect, who believe that the last *tirthankara*, **Mahavira**, was born in Vaishali in 599 BC, have erected a **shrine** in the fields 1km east of Kolhua.

ARRIVAL AND DEPARTURE   VAISHALI

Most people take in Vaishali as a **day-trip** from Patna, and the best way to do that is to hire a taxi (Bihar Tourism can sort you one for around ₹1500). You could take a bus from Gandhi Maidan Bus Stand to Hajipur, then one to Lalganj and one from there to Vaishali, but that would take too long to do the roundtrip in one day. There is no accommodation in Vaishali as such, but Hajipur has a handful of very simple hotels.

The road to Nepal

Some 55km north of Vaishali, **KESARIYA** (Kessaputta) has an impressive five-terraced eighth-century *stupa* said to have been built on top of another erected by the Buddha's Licchavi disciples after he announced he was about to attain nirvana and gave them his begging bowl as a souvenir. To get to Kesariya, take a bus (3hr) from Vaishali to **Chakia**, 20km away, then a taxi or rickshaw to the site.

In 1917, **MOTIHARI**, a poor and lawless town 298km north of Patna, was the site of one of Gandhi's first acts of civil disobedience – he refused bail after being

14

MADHUBANI PAINTINGS

Jitwarpur, a village on the outskirts of the small town of **Madhubani**, in northern Bihar, is home to a vibrant tradition of folk art. Madhubani **paintings** by local women were originally decorations for the outside of village huts. Illustrating mythological themes – including images of local deities as well as Hindu gods and goddesses – the paintings were eventually transferred onto handmade paper, often using bright primary colours to fill the strong black line drawings. **Fabrics** printed with Madhubani designs have become very chic; these days they tend to be professionally made elsewhere, and are sold in the expensive boutiques of India's major cities, although you can still pick them up cheaply in Madhubani itself.

Buses connect Patna to Madhubani (5hr 30min), where there are some basic hotels; rickshaws can take you on to Jitwarpur.

arrested for protesting the plight of local farmers, who were being forced to grow indigo for the British textile industry. There's a small **museum** with photos and items such as Gandhi's walking stick and slippers. Motihari was also the birthplace of **George Orwell**, whose father worked here as a government opium agent. There are *dharamshalas* if you want to stay.

The border crossing for **Nepal** is at **RAXAUL**, a grubby, mosquito-infested town with limited amenities – you're much better off staying over the border in Birganj.

ARRIVAL AND INFORMATION   THE NEPALESE BORDER

By train There's a daily train to Raxaul from Howrah.

By bus Raxaul is served by a couple of a/c buses a day from the BSRTC bus stand in Patna (see p.793).

Crossing the border The border between Raxaul and the Nepalese town of Birganj, 5km away (₹50 by auto-rickshaw), is open 24hr, but in practice you may not be able to cross at night if the border officials have gone to bed. In particular, if you need to buy a Nepalese visa

(US$30), you should try to arrive by 6pm. From Birganj bus park (1km east of town) there are frequent buses to Kathmandu (9hr), and less frequently to Pokhara (11hr).

Services The foreign exchange bureaux in Raxaul will only change Indian to Nepalese rupees or vice-versa, but Birganj has facilities for travellers' cheques and US dollars.

ACCOMMODATION

Kaveri Main Rd, Raxaul ☎06255 221148. If you do have to spend the night, this functional hotel is about the best Raxaul has to offer. **₹300**

Gaya

GAYA, 100km south of Patna, is a transit point for visitors to **Bodhgaya**, 13km away. Gaya has no real tourist attractions but many Hindus come here to honour their parents a year after death by offering *pinda* – funeral cakes – at the massive **Vishnupad temple** (no entry to non-Hindus). Pilgrims also bathe at the riverside *ghats*. **Brahmajuni Hill**, 1km southeast of the Vishnupad temple, is said to be where Buddha preached his fire sermon.

ARRIVAL AND INFORMATION   GAYA

By train Most people arrive by train. Auto-rickshaws will take you to Bodhgaya from the station (₹150, though you may find one shared), or you can take a cycle rickshaw to Kacheri Bus Stand and continue to Bodhgaya by shared auto (₹20). If you arrive after dark, stay overnight in Gaya as the route between the two can be unsafe.

Information There is a rather useless tourist office in the railway station (Mon–Sat 8am–8pm but often closed; ☎0631 242 0155).

Internet I-Way (Mon–Sat 9am–9pm, Sun 9am–4pm; ₹30/hr) and Vishal Cyber World (daily 8am–9pm; ₹30/hr), both on a narrow alley off Station Rd.

ACCOMMODATION

Ajatsatru Station Rd (opposite the station)
📞 0631 243 4584, ✉ hotel.ajatsatru@gmail.com. The standard rooms are quite basic, although they have attached bathrooms with water heaters, and there are cleaner and more cheerful (but still overpriced) a/c rooms (₹1260). The downstairs restaurant has decent Indian and Chinese food (daily 7am–11pm; veg biriyani ₹60, chicken biriyani ₹100). ₹630

Akash Close by on Laxman Sahay Rd 📞 0631 222 2205. Simple rooms with attached bathrooms, but hot water comes in a bucket (free on request). They also have their own generator, so there's electricity even during Gaya's frequent power cuts. ₹400

Railway Retiring Rooms At the station. If you have a train ticket, these are your best bet for a one-night stay: functional but large and clean with attached bathrooms and hot running water. There are some a/c rooms (₹600) and a dorm (₹200). To get a place, however, you have to join the scrum at the enquiries office just outside the station entrance. ₹300

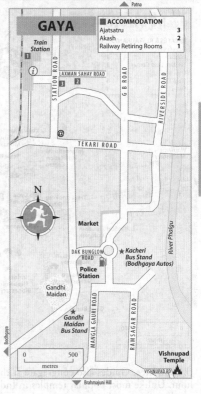

GAYA

ACCOMMODATION	
Ajatsatru	3
Akash	2
Railway Retiring Rooms	1

Bodhgaya and around

The world's most important Buddhist pilgrimage site, **BODHGAYA**, 13km south of Gaya, is wonderfully relaxed, with an array of monasteries, temples and retreats. Its focal point is the **Mahabodhi Temple**, where Buddha attained enlightenment.

The temple dates from the seventh century AD and flourished up to the sixteenth century, when it fell into the hands of Hindu priests, who professed to be baffled by its origins. In the early nineteenth century, British archeologists rediscovered its significance, and Bodhgaya has since been rejuvenated by overseas Buddhists, who have built monasteries, temples and shrines on the site. From November to February, Bodhgaya is home to an animated community of exiled **Tibetans**, often including the Dalai Lama, as well as a stream of international Tibetophiles. Meditation courses (see box, p.799) attract others, while large monasteries from places like Darjeeling bring their followers to attend ceremonies and lectures. From mid-March to mid-October, the region becomes oppressively hot and Bodhgaya returns to its quiet ways.

The Mahabodhi Temple is also sacred to Hindus, who regard Buddha as an incarnation of Vishnu, and dominate the management, despite protests from the Buddhist world. The dispute is exacerbated by the contrasting forms of worship: Buddhists have a solitary inward approach; Hindus prefer spectacle and noisy ceremony.

Mahabodhi Temple

Daily 4am–9pm • Camera ₹20, video ₹500

The elegant single spire of the **Mahabodhi Temple** rises to a lofty height of 55m, and is visible throughout the surrounding countryside. Within the temple complex, which is liberally sprinkled with small *stupas* and shrines, the main brick temple stands in a hollow encircled by a stone railing dating from the second century BC. Shoes are tolerated within the grounds but not inside the temple: they can be left at

14

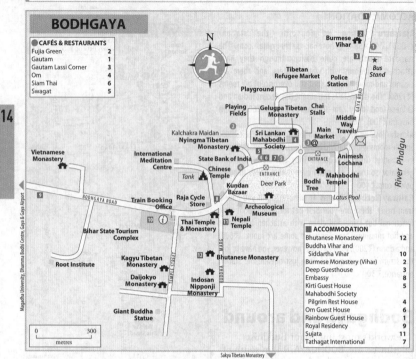

BODHGAYA

CAFÉS & RESTAURANTS
Fujia Green	2
Gautam	1
Gautam Lassi Corner	3
Om	4
Siam Thai	6
Swagat	5

ACCOMMODATION
Bhutanese Monastery	12
Buddha Vihar and Siddhartha Vihar	10
Burmese Monastery (Vihar)	2
Deep Guesthouse	3
Embassy	8
Kirti Guest House	5
Mahabodhi Society Pilgrim Rest House	4
Om Guest House	6
Rainbow Guest House	1
Royal Residency	9
Sujata	11
Tathagat International	7

the entrance. Guides also congregate at the entrance and charge around ₹100 per hour. Unlike most popular temples in India, this UNESCO World Heritage Site exudes an atmosphere of peace and tranquillity. Extensively renovated during the nineteenth century, it is supposed to be a replica of a seventh-century structure that in turn stood on the site of Ashoka's original third-century BC shrine. Inside the temple, a single chamber holds a large gilded image of the Buddha, while upstairs is a balcony and a small, plain meditation chamber.

The Bodhi Tree

At the rear of the temple to the west, the large **Bodhi Tree** grows out of an expansive base, attracting scholars and meditators, but it's only an off-shoot of the one under which the Buddha attained enlightenment. Many legends surround the destruction of the original, but it is generally thought that Ashoka, when he sent his daughter Sangamitra to Sri Lanka as an emissary of Buddhism, had sent a cutting with her. This was planted at Anuradhapuram, and a cutting from that was later brought back to Bodhgaya and replanted. Pilgrims tie coloured thread to its branches and Tibetans accompany their rituals with long lines of butter lamps. A sandstone slab with carved sides next to the tree is believed to be the **Vajrasana**, or "thunder-seat", upon which Buddha sat facing east.

Animesh Lochana Temple

The small white **Animesh Lochana Temple** to the right of the compound entrance marks the spot where Buddha stood and gazed upon the Bodhi Tree in gratitude. Numerous ornate *stupas* from the Pala period (seventh to twelfth centuries) are littered around the grounds and next to the temple compound to the south is a rectangular lotus pool where Buddha is believed to have bathed.

Temples and monasteries

Modern monasteries and temples around the Mahabodhi Temple open from around 7am until noon and between 2pm and 6pm. Some are very simple, while others, like the **Thai Temple**, with its unmistakeable roof, are elaborate confections. The **Gelugpa Tibetan Monastery**, or *gompa*, is within the Tibetan quarter northwest of the main shrine. The complex includes a central prayer hall, large prayer wheel and residential buildings. The bigger of the two other Tibetan monasteries further west belongs to the **Kagyu** sect; its spacious main prayer hall is decorated with beautiful modern murals, Buddha images and a large Dharma Chakra, or "Wheel of Law". The other two major Tibetan schools also have monastic representation here – there's a **Nyingma** *gompa* next to the Chinese temple and a small **Sakya** *gompa* south of the Bhutanese Monastery and Indosan Nipponji Temple.

Next to the Kagyu Tibetan Monastery, the **Daijokyo Monastery** captures in concrete some elements of a traditional Japanese temple and belongs to the Nichiren sect. Opposite, the **Indosan Nipponji Temple** has an elegant and simple hut-like roof and a beautiful image of the Buddha inside its main hall. Next door, the exquisite **Bhutanese Monastery** features finely painted murals and ceiling mandalas. In a decorative garden at the end of the road, the imposing 25m Japanese-style **Giant Buddha Statue** was consecrated by the Dalai Lama in 1989.

Archaeological Museum

Daily except Fri 8am–5pm • ₹10

Bodhgaya's **Archaeological Museum**, west of the Mahabodhi Temple complex, has a collection of locally discovered sculptures. Its prize exhibit is the stone balustrade that once surrounded the Bodhi Tree in the Mahabodhi Temple. The pink sandstone parts date from the first or second century BC, but the granite ones are newer, dating from the sixth or seventh century AD.

MEDITATION COURSES IN BODHGAYA

Especially during the winter high season, **meditation courses** are available in either of the two distinct traditions of Buddhism: Mahayana (the Great Vehicle), epitomized by the various forms of Tibetan Buddhism which spread across China and Japan; and Hinayana (or Theravada), as practised in Sri Lanka, Thailand and other parts of southeast Asia. Check noticeboards in the various cafés, and ask at the *Root Institute* or the *Burmese Vihar*.

Root Institute for Wisdom Culture ☎ 0631 220 0714, ⊕ rootinstitute.com. The Root Institute for Wisdom Culture is a real haven, a semi-monastic dharma centre 2km west of the main temple with pleasant gardens, a shrine room, library and accommodation. It organizes residential courses, focusing on the Mahayana tradition. There are drop-in meditation classes, one-day workshops and longer courses on Buddhism, yoga and meditation between October and March. A ten-day course, including fee, food and accommodation, typically costs around ₹10,000, depending on what is included; it's best to book well in advance. The institute is always looking for volunteers (minimum three months) for general tasks and to help in its charitable school and polio, TB and mobile clinics.

Dhamma Bodhi International Meditation Centre ☎ 0631 220 0437, ⊕ bodhi.dhamma.org. The Dhamma Bodhi International Meditation Centre, a Vipassana centre, is a few kilometres out of town near Magadha University on Dobi Rd, and holds regular courses throughout the year.

International Meditation Centre ☎ 0631 220 0707. The International Meditation Centre, a couple of hundred metres behind the Chinese temple, runs Vipassana courses for beginners and advanced students; donations are accepted as there are no fixed fees.

Burmese Vihar ☎ 0631 220 0721. Although not currently running meditation courses, the Burmese Vihar has useful information on meditation courses and is involved in voluntary social-work projects.

14

ARRIVAL AND INFORMATION

By plane Gaya's international airport (☎0631 221 0129) is around 12km west of Bodhgaya, and is connected by Air India to Varanasi (1 daily; 35min) and Kolkata (2 weekly; 1hr 5min), as well as having flights (for the benefit of pilgrims) to Burma, Bhutan, Nepal and Thailand.

By bus From Bodhgaya, you'll need to travel back to Gaya for most onward services, although, especially in season, there are private buses from Kalchakra Maidan to destinations such as Ranchi, Raxaul, Varanasi, Siliguri and even Thimpu.

By auto There are auto-rickshaws to Bodhgaya from outside Gaya railway station (₹150; less if you can find a shared one), and shared autos from Kacheri Bus Stand, a couple of kilometres south (₹20). An auto from the airport is around ₹100.

Tourist information The main tourist office in the Bihar State Tourism Corporation complex (Mon–Sat 10am–5pm; ☎0631 220 0672) is distinctly unenlightening but has a computerized train reservation booth next door (Mon–Sat 8am–noon). Middle Way Travels (☎0631 220 0648, ✉middleway_2006@yahoo.com), near the entrance to the temple, can arrange local tours and car rental, and book train, bus and flight tickets. The Sri Lankan Mahabodhi Society (☎0631 220 0742, ✉mbsi_1891@yahoo.com), responsible for reviving Bodhgaya in the nineteenth century, maintains a small centre northwest of the Mahabodhi Temple and can offer advice on accommodation and courses.

ACCOMMODATION

Outside the pilgrimage season (Nov–Feb) discounts of up to fifty percent are available in most hotels. Many **monastery guesthouses** welcome tourists, subject to the same rules as the pilgrims – in particular no smoking, alcohol or sex.

MONASTERIES

Bhutanese Monastery Buddha Marg ☎0631 220 0710. An old guesthouse, next to the monastery and full of character, with single and family rooms, some with private bathroom and hot water. ₹500/₹700

Burmese Monastery (Vihar) Gaya Rd ☎0631 220 0721. Set in a pleasant garden, the rooms at this guesthouse are inexpensive, but boxy and with shared bathroom facilities. The absence of fans and the prevalence of biting insects will test your Buddhist indifference to personal comfort. ₹150

Mahabodhi Society Pilgrim Rest House (Sri Lankan Guest House) Bodhgaya Rd ☎0631 220 0742, ✉mbsi_1891@yahoo.com. Very popular with pilgrims and often full, with a dorm, a handful of private rooms and a modest veg canteen. No fixed price: payment by donation.

HOTELS

Buddha Vihar and **Siddartha Vihar** Bihar State Tourism Corporation complex ☎0631 220 0445, ✉bodhgaya.bstdc@gmail.com. Of these two adjoining state-run hotels, the first has three- to ten-bed dorms, while the second has extremely good-value bright, spacious, attached doubles, and prices don't rise in high season. Dorm ₹75–150, double ₹578

★ **Deep Guesthouse** Gaya Rd, near the Burmese Vihar ☎0631 220 0463. One of Bodhgaya's best budget lodges, offering a warm welcome and sociable atmosphere. Rooms are smallish but super-clean with attached bathrooms and 24hr hot water. ₹700

Embassy Bodhgaya Rd ☎0631 220 0711, ⊕hotelembassybodhgaya.com. No-frills marble-floored rooms with gleaming bathrooms at this reliable mid-range hotel in the centre of town. ₹1320

Kirti Guest House Close to Kalchakra Maidan ☎0631 220 0744, ✉kirtihouse744@yahoo.com. The Dalai Lama beams benevolently over the reception at this serene guesthouse run by the Tibetan Monastery and accessed over a short bridge. The rooms are fresh and bright, with discounts off season, and for ₹500 more you get a wood-panelled suite. ₹2500

Om Guest House Bodhgaya Rd ☎99340 57498. Not for the claustrophobic, rather overpriced, and without the communal vibe of some other traveller places, *Om* nevertheless delivers spick-and-span rooms with attached bathrooms and primrose yellow walls in a central location. ₹800

Rainbow Guest House Gaya Rd, near the Burmese Vihar ☎0631 220 0308. Not very central, but good value, with attached rooms, (reasonably) hot water and friendly staff, at monastery guesthouse prices but without the religious strictures. ₹400

★ **Royal Residency** Domuhan Rd (Bodhgaya Rd) ☎0631 220 1156, ⊕theroyalresidency.net. An immaculate but pricey option favoured by well-heeled Japanese visitors. The rooms boast sleek wooden floors and fittings, cream-coloured walls and minimalist decor. There's also excellent dining and, for a minimum of fifteen takers, they'll heat up a Japanese-style communal bath. ₹7632

Sujata Buddha Marg ☎0631 220 0481, ⊕sujatahotel .com. The a/c attached rooms are a little plain but come with balconies, gold-flecked bedspreads and sparkling bathrooms with tubs. ₹6458

Tathagat International Bodhgaya Rd ☎0631 220 0106, ⊕hoteltathagatbodhgaya.net. Slightly cramped but comfortable rooms with mini-sofas, checked curtains and private balconies in a prominent whitewashed building opposite the deer park. Staff can book train and flight tickets. ₹4110

EATING

Bodhgaya has Bihar's widest range of places to eat, catering for visitors from all around the world. During November and February, **Tibetan tent restaurants** spring up throughout town – follow the crowds to find the best ones.

Fujia Green Kalchakra Maidan ☎ 99340 58923. An ever-popular Tibetan restaurant housed in a cross between a hut and a tent, with Christmas-style decorations and a vast array of *momos* (stuffed dumplings; ₹35–65) and hearty *thukpa* (noodle soup; ₹25–40). Daily 7am–9.30pm.

Gautam Gaya Rd, opposite the Burmese Vihar. A restaurant in a shack serving traveller-oriented menus with big breakfasts, banana pancakes (₹50) and cinnamon rolls (₹30). Daily 5am–9pm.

Gautam Lassi Corner Opposite the Mahabodhi Temple entrance. A bustling low-key refreshment kiosk that does a brisk trade in refreshing lassis (flavoured with syrups such as rose and pineapple; ₹30), and freshly squeezed juices (₹25). Daily 6.30am–9pm.

Om Bodhgaya Rd. Backpacker stalwart, serving dosas, chocolate chip cookies and apple pie as well as excellent-value thalis (₹40) and set breakfasts (₹70), with big portions and small prices. Daily 7am–9pm.

★ **Siam Thai** Bodhgaya Rd ☎ 0631 220 0429. Appealing restaurant with reasonable Thai food. Try the *tom yum* soup (₹140–160) and the red chicken curry (₹180). Thai food can be very hot, so ask them to go easy on the chilli if you prefer it mild. Daily 8am–10pm.

Swagat Hotel Tathagat International, Bodhgaya Rd ☎ 0631 220 0106. The menu at this hotel restaurant has a tempting selection of veg and chicken burgers, north Indian dishes like *rogan josh* (₹280) and decent stabs at Continental mainstays such as chicken Kiev (₹225). Daily 6am–10pm.

DIRECTORY

Banks The State Bank of India (Mon–Fri 10.30am–4.30pm, Sat 10.30am–1.30pm) has foreign exchange and an ATM (there are others to its west along Bodhgaya Rd). Middle Way Travels (see opposite) also changes cash and travellers' cheques. It's worth comparing rates and commissions before choosing where to change.

Bicycle rental The Raja Cycle Store, next door to the *Embassy* hotel (☎ 99317 11505), is a good place to rent bicycles.

Internet Galaxy (daily 9am–8pm; ₹30/hr) is one of a cluster of very similar internet places opposite the Mahabodhi Temple entrance.

Mahakala Caves

No buses; access by auto-rickshaw from Bodhgaya

In remote, almost desert-like surroundings on the far side of the Falgu River, 12km northeast of Bodhgaya, sit the **Mahakala** (or Dungeshwari) **Caves**, where Buddha did the severe penance that resulted in the familiar image of him as a skeletal, emaciated figure. After years of extreme self-denial at Mahakala, he realized its futility and walked down to Bodhgaya, where he achieved nirvana. A short climb from the base of the impressive cliff leads to a Tibetan monastery and the small caves. A Buddhist shrine inside the main cave is run by Tibetans, although a Hindu priest has set up in competition.

Rajgir

Eighty kilometres northeast of Bodhgaya, the small market town of **RAJGIR** nestles in rocky hills that witnessed the meditations and teachings of both the Buddha and Mahavira, the founder of Jainism. The capital of the Magadha kingdom before Pataliputra (Patna), Rajgir was also where King Bimbisara converted to Buddhism. Rajgir is also regarded as a health resort because of its **hot springs**, which can get unpleasantly crowded.

A Japanese shrine at **Venuvana Vihara** marks the spot where a monastery was built for Buddha to live in, while at **Griddhakuta** (Vulture's Peak), on Ratnagiri Hill, 3km from the town centre, Buddha set in motion his second "Wheel of Law". The massive modern **Peace Pagoda**, built by the Japanese, dominates Ratnagiri Hill and can be reached by a rickety chairlift (daily 8.15am–1pm & 2–5pm, last ticket 4.30pm; ₹60). Griddhakuta is actually halfway down the hill, so you may prefer to wander down from here rather than climb back up to take the chair lift. Look out for the 26 Jain shrines

14

on top of these hills, reached by a challenging trek attempted almost solely by Jain devotees. On an adjacent hill, in the **Saptaparni cave**, the first Buddhist council met to record the teachings of the Buddha after his death.

ARRIVAL AND DEPARTURE
RAJGIR

By train There are three daily trains from Patna, one of which actually starts in Delhi.

By bus Rajgir is connected by bus to Gaya, Nalanda and

sometimes Patna (for the latter you often have to change at Bihar Sharif, 25km away).

ACCOMMODATION AND EATING

Gautam Vihar 300m from the bus stand on the road to Nalanda ☏ 06112 255273. Run by the state tourist authority, this place has spacious rooms with pleasant verandas, a decent dorm and a hit-and-miss garden restaurant. Dorm ₹125, double ₹700

Green Hotel Opposite the Japanese temple complex (2km south of the bus stand) ☏ 98358 58246. A small restaurant ("hotel" does not imply accommodation) with a relaxed atmosphere, serving reasonably priced food including a choice of thalis (₹80–280 veg, ₹120–350 non-veg). Daily 8am–10pm.

★ **Indo Hokke** 4km west of the bus stand ☏ 06112

255245, ⊕ theroyalresidency.net. A unique hotel, which fuses Japanese and Indian architectural influences. It has Japanese- and Western-style rooms, a communal Japanese bath (if there's sufficient demand), and the outstanding *Lotus* restaurant, which serves Indian, Chinese and Japanese dishes. ₹5500

Siddharth In Kund Market (1km south of the bus stand) ☏ 06112 255616, ✉ siddarthrajgir@gmail.com. Handy for the nearby hot spring, but otherwise not great for hot water, which is limited to the hours of 6–10am and 7–8pm. It's decent enough, but a little pricey for what you get. ₹1200

Nalanda and around

Daily 9am–5.30pm or sunset if earlier • ₹100 (₹5)

Founded in the fifth century AD by the Guptas, the great monastic **Buddhist university** of **NALANDA** attracted thousands of international students and teachers until it was sacked by the Afghan invader Bhaktiar Khilji in the twelfth century. Courses included philosophy, logic, theology, grammar, astronomy, mathematics and medicine. Education was provided free, supported by the revenue from surrounding villages and benefactors such as the eighth-century king of Sumatra.

Excavations have revealed nine levels of occupation on the site, dating back to the time of the Buddha and Mahavira in the sixth century BC. Most of it is now in ruins, but the orderliness and scale of what remains is staggering evidence of the strength of Buddhist civilization in its prime. The **site** is strewn with the remains of *stupas*, temples and eleven monasteries, their thick walls impressively intact. Nalanda is now part of the modern Buddhist pilgrimage circuit, but even casual tourists will appreciate taking the time to walk through the extensive site, or climb its massive 31m **stupa** for commanding views. Informative booklets available at the ticket booth render the numerous guides unnecessary.

Nalanda Museum (daily except Fri 9am–5pm; ₹5) houses antiquities found here and at Rajgir, including Buddhist and Hindu bronzes and a number of undamaged statues of the Buddha. **Nava Nalanda Mahavihara**, the Pali postgraduate research institute, houses many rare Buddhist manuscripts, and is devoted to study and research in Pali literature and Buddhism.

ARRIVAL AND DEPARTURE
NALANDA AND AROUND

By train The railway station, 2km east of the bus stop, is served by three daily trains each way between Rajgir and Patna.

By bus Buses every 30min or so between Rajgir and

Bihar Sharif (35km northeast, change here for Patna) stop at the turning to Nalanda, from where rickshaws are available for the remaining 2km to the gates of the site.

EATING

Tourist Cafeteria By the site entrance ☏ 99736 19507. Veg and non-veg food, both Indian and foreign, including chicken biriyani (₹150), or American chop suey (₹160). Nothing special, but decent enough. Daily 7am–10pm.

Pawapuri

Buses to Pawapuri run from Bihar Sharif

Eighteen kilometres east of Nalanda, at **PAWAPURI**, Mahavira, the founder of Jainism, is said to have attained enlightenment. He died and was cremated here around 500 BC, and the site is now a major draw for pilgrims, who come to visit the **Jalamandir**, a white marble temple in the centre of a lotus pond.

Bihar School of Yoga

☏ 06344 222430, ⊕ biharyoga.net • Trains from Kolkata, Patna, Delhi and Mumbai serve Jamalpur (6km distant), or buses from Bihar Sharif

Eighty kilometres east of Pawapuri, at **MUNGER**, is the **Bihar School of Yoga** Founded by Swami Niranjananda Saraswati, the ashram is the world's first accredited yoga university and runs popular four-month yoga courses (in English) from October to January, although short stays are also possible. It has a sister school at Rikhia in Jharkhand.

Jharkhand

Carved out of Bihar in 2000, after years of agitation by its largely *adivasi* population, **JHARKHAND** yields almost forty percent of India's minerals, but suffers from extreme poverty, lawlessness and Naxalite (Maoist guerrilla) activity, and is rarely visited by tourists. Its main attraction is the beautiful *sal* forests of **Palamau (Betla) National Park**, with its beautiful Sal forests, but sadly these have been damaged by years of drought and although the park is part of Project Tiger (see box, p.1182), tiger sightings are now rare; more problematically, police conducting an anti-Naxalite campaign in the state have requisitioned all the park's tourist accommodation, and although this is supposed to be on a temporary basis, it is not clear when the park's lodges and state-run tourist bungalow will again be open to tourists. Other forest reserves and parks pepper the state, including **Hazaribagh National Park** in the north, but bandits and Naxalites are active in these areas, and around **Parasnath temple**, so it's vital to check the **security situation** before venturing out, and you should avoid travelling at night anywhere in the state.

TOURS

JHARKHAND

Palamau National Park If the situation is safe and you want to visit Palamau National Park, consider going on an excursion from Ranchi, the state capital, with Ashok Travels at the *Hotel Ranchi Ashok* (☏ 0651 248 1856) or Suhana Travels (☏ 94311 71394) on Station Rd.

ACCOMMODATION

⭐ **BNR Hotel** ☏ 0651 246 1241, ⊕ chanakyabnrranchi .com. The best accommodation in Ranchi is at this atmospheric Raj-style old railway hotel, now completely refurbished and super-elegant. ₹4760

Sikkim

THE PEMAYANGTSE GOMPA

Sikkim

The tiny and beautiful state of Sikkim lies to the south of Tibet, sandwiched between Nepal to the west and Bhutan to the east. Measuring just 65km by 115km, its landscape ranges from sweltering deep valleys just 300m above sea level to lofty snow peaks such as Kanchenjunga (Kanchendzonga to the locals) which, at 8586m, is the third highest mountain in the world. A small but growing network of tortuous roads penetrates this rugged and beautiful Himalayan wilderness.

15

For centuries Sikkim was an isolated, independent Buddhist kingdom, until war with China in the early 1960s led the Indian government to realize the area's strategic importance as a crucial corridor between Tibet and Bangladesh. As a result of its annexation by India in 1975, Sikkim has experienced dramatic changes. Now a fully fledged Indian state, it is predominantly Hindu, with a population made up of 75 percent **Nepalese Gurungs**, and less than twenty percent **Lepchas**, its former rulers. Smaller proportions survive of **Bhutias**, of Tibetan stock, and **Limbus**, also possibly of Tibetan origin, who gave the state its name – *sukh-im*, "happy homeland". Nepali is now the lingua franca and the Nepalese are socially and politically the most dominant people in the state. However, the people of Sikkim continue to jealously guard their freedom and affluence and remain untouched by the Nepalese Gurkhas' autonomy movement in neighbouring Darjeeling. Although only Sikkimese can hold major shares in property and businesses, partnerships with Indian (non-Sikkimese) entrepreneurs and subsidies to indigenous Sikkimese industry have led to prosperity – fuelled by its special status within the union.

Historically, culturally and spiritually, Sikkim's strongest links are with Tibet. The main draws for visitors are the state's off-the-beaten-track **trekking** and its many **monasteries**, more than two hundred in all, mostly belonging to the ancient **Nyingmapa** sect. **Pemayangtse** in West Sikkim is the most historically significant, and houses an extraordinary wooden mandala depicting Guru Rinpoche's Heavenly Palace. **Tashiding**, a Nyingmapa monastery built in 1717, surrounded by prayer flags and *chortens* and looking across to snowcapped peaks, is considered Sikkim's holiest. **Rumtek** is the seat of the **Gyalwa Karmapa** – head of the **Karma Kagyu** lineage – and probably the wealthiest monastery in Sikkim. Besides monasteries and the staggering beauty of the land, many come to Sikkim to trek. The capital, **Gangtok**, a colourful, bustling cosmopolitan town, is home to a bewildering array of trekking agents only too happy to take your money in dollars and to arrange the necessary permits.

Sikkim's gigantic mountain walls and steep wooded hillsides, drained by torrential rivers such as the **Teesta** and the **Rangit**, are a botanist's dream. The lower slopes abound in **orchids**, sprays of cardamom carpet the forest floor, and the land is rich with apple orchards, orange groves and terraced paddy fields (to the Tibetans, this was

RED PANDA, VARSHEY RHODODENDRON SANCTUARY

Highlights

❶ Chaam Experience this mysterious and colourful lama dance, held in most monasteries around the harvest festival of Losung (early December). **See p.811**

❷ Rumtek One of Sikkim's most venerated monasteries, Rumtek is home to the Black Hat sect, and hosts a spectacular festival in February. **See p.817**

❸ Pemayangtse A wonderful, highly venerated seventeenth-century monastery perched on a commanding ridge with glorious views. **See p.825**

❹ Varshey Rhododendron Sanctuary Magnificent views and gentle trails through a botanical paradise. **See p.825**

❺ Monastery Trail: West Sikkim You won't need porters or special permits to walk the rewarding circuit from Pelling to Kecheopalri, Yuksom and Tashiding, staying at village homestays enroute. **See p.828**

❻ Dzongri and Singalila Trails High-altitude treks through rhododendron forests, across high meadows and past remote lakes with breathtaking views of mighty Kanchenjunga. **See p.829**

❼ Tashiding An especially sacred monastic complex on a conical hill with marvellous views. **See p.830**

❽ Yumthang Walk through this spectacular rhododendron-filled valley with icy pinnacles towering overhead. **See p.833**

HIGHLIGHTS ARE MARKED ON THE MAP ON P.808

Denzong, "the land of rice"). At higher altitudes, monsoon mists cling to huge tracts of lichen-covered forests, where countless varieties of rhododendron carpet the hillsides and giant magnolia trees punctuate the deep verdant cover. Higher still, approaching the Tibetan plateau, larch and dwarf rhododendron give way to meadows abundant with gentians and potentilla. Sikkim's forests and wilderness areas are inhabited by a wealth of fauna, including extremely elusive snow leopards, tahr (wild goat on the Tibet plateau), *bharal* or blue sheep, black bear, flying squirrels and the symbol of Sikkim – the endangered **red panda**.

HIGHLIGHTS

1. Chaam
2. Rumtek
3. Pemayangtse
4. Varshey Rhododendron Sanctuary
5. Monastery Trail: West Sikkim
6. Dzongri and Singalila Trails
7. Tashiding
8. Yumthang

SIKKIM

0   20
kilometres

CHINA

N

Kangchengyaa (6889m)

Pauhunri (7125m)

Gurudogmar

Fluted Peak (6084m)

Chopta Valley

Thangu

Chombu (6362m)

Yume Samdong (Zero Point)

Nepal Peak (6910m)

G R E A T   H I M A L A Y A

8 Yumthang (3645m)

Green Lake (4850)

Tangchung Khang (6010m)

Lama Wangden (5868m)

Kanchenjunga (8586m)

Zemu Glacier

Siniolchu (6887m)

Lachen (2977m)

Kyeshong La (3790m)

Lachung (2734m)

Lachung

NEPAL

Simvo (6812m)

KANCHENDZONGA NATIONAL PARK

DZONGU

Teesta

CHINA (TIBET AUTONOMOUS REPUBLIC)

Talung Glacier

Pandim (6691m)

Tolung

Chungthang (1579m)

Kabru (7338m)

Kokthang (6147m)

Goecha La (4940m)

Jopuno (5935m)

Narsing (5825m)

Singhik

Chaurikhang

Zemanthang (4453m)

Samiti Lake

Mangan

Tosar Lake

Kangla (5200m)

Dzongri La (4400m)

Thansing (3930m)

SIKKIM

Lampokhari Lake

Dzongri (4030m) Tsokha

Bakhim

Labrang

Rangit

Nathu La (4328m)

Danfeybhir Yar (4400m)

Khecheopalri Lake

Yoksum (1780m)

Phodong

Lingdum

Phensang

Serathang

Dzongri Trail

5

Ralang

Rumtek

Tsomago Lake (3767m)

Chewabhanjang (3170m)

Pelling

3 7 Tashiding

2

Gangtok

Maenam (3235m)

Ranipool

4

Gyalshing

Pemayangtse

Uttarey (1695m)

Hee

Legship

Kewzing

Ravangla

1

NH-31A

Assam Lingzey

Varshe (3030m)

Dentam

Rinchenpong

Tendong (2757m)

Singtam

Hilley

Phalut

Soreng

Naya Bazaar

Samdruptse

Namchi

Rangpo

Aritar

BHUTAN

Sombare

Daramdin

Jorethang

Melli

Teesta

WEST BENGAL

WEST BENGAL

Darjeeling

Teesta Bazaar

Kalimpong

The international boundaries on this map are neither purported to be correct nor authentic by Survey of India directives. Publisher.

EARTHQUAKES, LANDSLIDES AND DAMS

Although a common occurrence throughout the Himalayas, the earthquake of September 2011, with its epicentre at Mangan 42km northwest of Gangtok, was particularly destructive, leaving around sixty people dead and a trail of destruction as far away as Gangtok. The effects of the magnitude 6.9 quake were felt throughout the region, in Nepal and as far away as Kolkata. Much of the destruction took place around **hydro-electric** projects disrupting roads and infrastructure. To compound the state's communication nightmare, unseasonal rains in 2012 resulted in deadly **landslides** and loss of life and in North Sikkim being virtually cut off from the rest of the state for several weeks.

Industrialization and the construction of dams and numerous hydro-electric projects on Sikkim's rivers, such as the **Teesta**, has brought pressure on the state's diminishing indigenous population especially in Dzongu, the heartland of the Lepchas, threatening their lifestyle and heritage. Although the voice of their **protest** is now all but lost, the destruction of habitat and the extraordinary strain on the state's fragile road system is self-evident. For more information, visit ⓦ weepingsikkim.blogspot.com.

15

Brief history

No one knows quite when or how the **Lepchas** – or the Rong, as they call themselves – came to Sikkim, but their roots can be traced back to the animist Nagas of the Indo-Burmese border. **Buddhism**, which arrived from Tibet in the thirteenth century, took its distinctive Sikkimese form four centuries later, when three Tibetan monks of the old Nyingmapa order, disenchanted with the rise of the reformist Gelugpas, migrated south and gathered at Yoksum in western Sikkim. Having consulted the oracle, they sent to Gangtok for a certain Phuntsog Namgyal, whom they crowned as the first **chogyal** or "righteous king" of Denzong in 1642. Both the secular and religious head of Sikkim, he was soon recognized by Tibet, and set about sweeping reforms. His domain was far larger than today's Sikkim, taking in Kalimpong and parts of western Bhutan.

Over the centuries, territory was lost to the Bhutanese, the Nepalese and the **British**. Sikkim originally ceded Darjeeling to the East India Company as a spa in 1817, but was forced to give up all claim to it in 1861 when the kingdom was declared a protectorate of the British. **Tibet**, which perceived Sikkim as a vassalage, objected and invaded in 1886, but a small British force sent in 1888 to Lhasa helped the British consolidate their hold. By importing workers from Nepal to work in the tea plantations of Sikkim, Darjeeling and Kalimpong, the British sought to diminish the strong Tibetan influence and helped alter the ethnic make-up of the region, with the new migrants soon outnumbering the indigenous population.

After Indian Independence, the reforming and intensely spiritual eleventh chogyal, **Tashi Namgyal**, strove hard until his death in 1962 to prevent the dissolution of his kingdom. Officially Sikkim was a protectorate of India, and the role of India became increasingly crucial, with the Chinese military build-up along the northern borders that culminated in an actual invasion early in the 1960s. His son **Palden Thondup**, the last chogyal, married as his second wife an American, Hope Cook, whose reforms as gyalmo (queen) did not prove popular and also came to irritate the Indian government. The embattled chogyal eventually succumbed to the demands of the Nepalese majority, and Sikkim was **annexed** by India in 1975 after a referendum with an overwhelming 97 percent majority. The chogyal remained as a figurehead until his death in 1981.

The state continues to be treated with care by the Indian government, partly through a lingering sense of unease amongst the disaffected Sikkimese minority and an increasingly complex ethnic patchwork but, more importantly, because Sikkim remains a bone of contention between India and China. Today, the **Sikkim Democratic Front** forms the government of Sikkim; generous government subsidies and loans have helped to ensure that people remain generally contented, while extensive road-building is bringing benefits to remote communities despite the many landslides in recent years.

PERMITS AND TREKKING IN SIKKIM

Though foreigners need to obtain an **Inner Line Permit** (ILP) to visit Sikkim, getting one is a mere, if irritating, formality. Permits can be obtained in advance along with your Indian visa, but agencies abroad charge exorbitant fees so are best avoided. In India Sikkim permits are **free** and can be arranged through the agencies below. Permits are date-specific and initially valid for thirty days from entry; **extensions** are normally available up to a maximum of sixty days. Note that when you do leave Sikkim, you will not be allowed to re-enter within three months.

Airport immigration At the four main entry points: Delhi, Mumbai, Kolkata, Chennai.

Foreigners' Regional Registration Offices In Delhi, Mumbai, Kolkata and Chennai.

Sikkim House 12–14 Panchsheel Marg, Chanakyapuri, New Delhi (☎011 2611 5346.

Sikkim Tourism *Hotel Olde Bellevue*, Nehru Rd, opposite *Glenary's Restaurant*, Darjeeling.

Sikkim Tourist Centre SNTC Bus Stand, Hill Cart Rd, Siliguri (☎0354 251 2646).

Sikkim Tourist Information Centre Sikkim House, 4 1 Middleton St, Kolkata (☎033 2281 7905).

TREKKING AND MOUNTAINEERING PERMITS

Although the potential is huge, **high-altitude trekking** in Sikkim remains a restricted and expensive business. Firstly, foreigners have to acquire **trekking permits** (aka **Protected Area Permits**) for high-altitude treks, which also act as entry permits for these areas. These are available only from the Sikkim Tourism offices in Gangtok and Delhi. Foreigners have to pay for the services of Gangtok-based tour operators (see box, p.814) in US dollars, to provide essential accompanying guides.

Check papers before you set off, and itineraries too as you don't want to be rushed, especially at altitude. Trekking parties consist of a minimum of two people; tour operators charge an official daily rate that ranges from $70 to $150 per head per day depending on group size and route.

While most major peaks require special permits for **mountaineering** and permission from the Indian Mountaineering Foundation in Delhi (see p.116) with at least three months' notice, the Sikkim government, through the appropriate **Gangtok trekking operator**, hands out permits for Frey's Peak (5830m) near Chaurikhang on the Singalila Ridge; Thingchenkang (6010m) near Dzongri and Jopuno (5935m) in West Sikkim; and Lama Wangden (5868m) and Brumkhangse (5635m) in North Sikkim. Recommended Gangtok agents include Namgyal (see box, p.814).

The high-altitude treks most commonly offered by the operators are the Dzongri–Goecha La route. plus its variation starting from Uttarey (see box, p.825) and the Singalila Ridge (see box, p.829). The exhilarating trek from Lachen to Green Lake is possible, but permission must be obtained from Delhi (most easily arranged through a Gangtok agent) at least three months in advance. At the moment, Dzongri still bears the brunt of the trekking industry in the state, and the pressure is beginning to tell severely on the environment.

Low-altitude hikes often come without the restriction of permits, and makes Sikkim an alluring destination for quiet walks off the beaten track. The **rhododendron trails** around Varshey, West Sikkim, for example, are particularly pleasant. A word of warning: avoid trekking unaccompanied in forest areas due the risk of surprising **black bears**.

Some areas, such as Nathu La on the border with Tibet in East Sikkim, and Gurudongma Lake in North Sikkim remain completely off-limits to foreigners.

OBTAINING PERMITS

Permits can be instantly acquired at the **Sikkim border** at Rangpo; go to the tourist office for an application form and then cross the road to have it registered by the police. In case you are arriving via Darjeeling, obtain your permit there (see p.776). In order to apply, you'll need two passport photographs, and photocopies of your passport and visa details.

As well as Gangtok and its surroundings in East Sikkim, the general Sikkim permit (ILP) covers all of South Sikkim and most areas in the east and west of the state, apart from most high-altitude treks. Sensitive border areas, like Tsomgo Lake (also known as Changu or Tsangu) in East Sikkim, most of North Sikkim except for Mangan and its immediate vicinity, and all high-altitude treks including the Singalila Ridge and Dzongri, require the additional **Protected Area Permit** or PAP (see above); foreigners can only enter these areas in groups of at least two accompanied by representatives of approved travel agents who arrange the permits.

Gangtok

Capital of Sikkim, the overgrown and colourful hill-town of **GANGTOK** (1870m) occupies a rising ridge in the southeast of the state, on what used to be a busy trade route into Tibet. Today, rapid development means an ugly assortment of concrete multistorey buildings is growing virtually unchecked, and the urban sprawl retains only a few traditional Sikkimese architectural elements. However, a short amble soon leads you away from the congested centre to bring you occasional glimpses of the snow-capped Himalayas, and on a good day you can see Kanchenjunga, the horned peak of Narsing (5825m) and the fluted pyramid of Siniolchu (6887m) poking above the surrounding hills.

While modern Gangtok epitomizes the recent changes in Sikkimese culture and politics, its Buddhist past is the root of its appeal for visitors, evident in the collection at the **Institute of Tibetology** and the charming **Enchey Monastery**, as well as the impressive **Rumtek Monastery**, 24km west of town. However, the **palace** on the tree lined promenade, the **Ridge** above town, used by the chogyals between 1894 and 1975, is now out of bounds, part-occupied by the government and a closed chapter in Sikkim's heritage. Sikkim's pride and joy, the **orchid**, is nurtured at several sites in and around Gangtok, and celebrated at the Flower Show Complex also on the Ridge.

Most of the town itself looks west; one explanation for the lack of development east of the ridge is that tradition dictates that houses face northwest, towards Kanchenjunga, Sikkim's guardian.

15

Enchey Monastery

Right at the top of town just below a colossal telecom tower, 3km from the centre and reached by several roads (the most picturesque follow the west side of the ridge), **Enchey Monastery** is a small two-storey Nyingmapa *gompa*. Visitors are welcome; the **best time** to go is between 7am and 8am, when the monastery is busy and the light is good.

The monastery was built in the mid-nineteenth century on a site blessed by the Tantric master Druptob Karpo, who was fabled for his ability to fly. Surrounded by tall pines, and housing more than a hundred monks, it is a gem of a place but suffered some damage in the 2011 earthquake. Built by the Chogyal on traditional Tibetan lines, the prayer hall's beautifully painted porch is filled with murals of protective deities and the wheel of law, while the conch shells that grace the doors are auspicious Buddhist symbols. Enchey holds an annual *chaam*, or **masked lama dance**, during the Losung festival, determined by the lunar calendar but usually held in early December.

Ganesh Tok and Around

A spectacular viewpoint festooned with prayer flags, a short, and steep 1km climb past the TV tower from Enchey, **Ganesh Tok** provides a sweeping view of the city sprawling below. A further 5km up the road to Tsomgo Lake, **Hanuman Tok** (2300m) is another viewpoint with vistas of eastern Sikkim, and is the cremation ground of the Royal Family, with *chortens* containing relics of the deceased; the Hanuman temple after which the spot is named is more recent.

Himalayan Zoological Park

Daily 9am–4pm • ₹10, car ₹50

The entrance to the 506-acre **Himalayan Zoological Park** is opposite Ganesh Tok, and is a good walk in itself if you don't have a car. Visitors come in the hope of catching a glimpse of the red pandas, snow leopards, bears and Tibetan wolves that roam the extensive open-air enclosures.

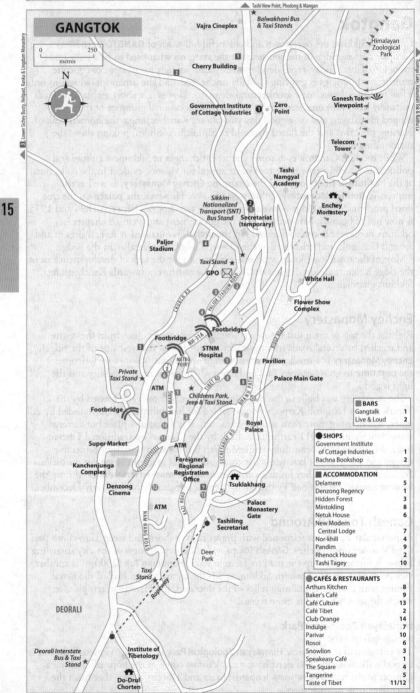

GANGTOK

0 — 250
metres

N

Lower Sichey Busty, Helipad, Ranka & Lingdum Monastery

Tsomgo Lake, Hanuman Tok & Nathu La

Tashi View Point, Phodong & Mangan

Vajra Cineplex

Balwakhani Bus & Taxi Stands

Himalayan Zoological Park

Cherry Building

Government Institute of Cottage Industries

Zero Point

Ganesh Tok Viewpoint

Telecom Tower

Tashi Namgyal Academy

Sikkim Nationalized Transport (SNT) Bus Stand

Secretariat (temporary)

Enchey Monastery

Paljor Stadium

Taxi Stand

GPO

White Hall

Flower Show Complex

CHURCH RD

PALJOR STADIUM ROAD

RIDGE ROAD

Footbridge

Footbridges

NH-31A

STNM Hospital

Pavilion

Palace Main Gate

Private Taxi Stand

METRO POINT

TIBET RD

Footbridge

M G MARG

ATM

Childrens Park, Jeep & Taxi Stand

BHANU PATH

Royal Palace

SECRETARIAT RD

Super Market

ATM

Kanchenjunga Complex

Foreigner's Regional Registration Office

Denzong Cinema

Tsuklakhang

Palace Monastery Gate

ATM

KAZI ROAD

NAM NANG ROAD

Tashiling Secretariat

Deer Park

Taxi Stand

Ropeway

Institute of Tibetology

DEORALI

Deorali Interstate Bus & Taxi Stand

Do-Drul Chorten

10 , 14 , Rumtek, Darjeeling & Siliguri

BARS
Gangtalk	1
Live & Loud	2

SHOPS
Government Institute of Cottage Industries	1
Rachna Bookshop	2

ACCOMMODATION
Delamere	5
Denzong Regency	1
Hidden Forest	3
Mintokling	8
Netuk House	6
New Modern Central Lodge	7
Nor-khill	4
Pandim	9
Rhenock House	2
Tashi Tagey	10

CAFÉS & RESTAURANTS
Arthurs Kitchen	8
Baker's Café	9
Café Culture	13
Café Tibet	2
Club Orange	14
Indulge	7
Parivar	10
Rosoi	3
Snowlion	6
Speakeasy Café	1
The Square	4
Tangerine	5
Taste of Tibet	11/12

The Ridge

Midway between MG Marg and Enchey, the quiet leafy promenade of the **Ridge** is a popular spot, with the Flower Show Complex and a small park at the northern end, and at the southern end, the **Royal Palace**. South of the compound, the Secretariat was devastated by the 2011 earthquake and is being rebuilt.

The Royal Palace and Tsuklakhang

Visitors (without cameras) are usually granted access to **Tsuklakhang**, the royal chapel at the far end of the Royal Palace compound, best accessed through the rear gates of the compound (which are normally left unmanned). The monastic complex has several resident monks and the chapel has impressive murals, Buddhist images and a vast collection of manuscripts. Here too there's a lama dance, known as *kagyat*, at the end of December, during which the main gates are open to the public; some years the *kagyat* takes place in Pemayangtse (see p.825). Across the lawns, ponies graze where flowers once bloomed in manicured beds, and the **Royal Palace** lies forlorn and abandoned, a prisoner of circumstance.

Institute of Tibetology

Mon–Sat 10am–4pm, closed 2nd Sat of each month • ₹10

South of Gangtok at Deorali, 3km from the centre, set in wooded grounds, is the museum-cum-library of the **Institute of Tibetology** with its impressive and invaluable collection of books and rare manuscripts, as well as religious and art objects such as exquisite *thangkas* (scrolls) and a photography archive. You can also get here from the upper town via the ropeway cable car (see p.815).

Do-Drul Chorten

A couple of hundred metres east of the Institute of Tibetology on the brow of the hill, an imposing whitewashed *chorten*, known as the **Do-Drul Chorten** – one of the most important in Sikkim – dominates a large, lively monastic seminary. The *chorten* is capped by a gilded tower, whose rising steps signify the thirteen steps to nirvana; the sun and moon symbol at the top stands for the union of opposites and the elements of ether and air, surrounded by 108 prayer wheels. Behind the monastic complex, a prayer hall houses a large image of **Guru Rinpoche** (Padmasambhava) who brought Buddhism to Tibet at the request of King Trisong Detsen in the eighth century AD. He later travelled through Sikkim hiding precious manuscripts (*termas*) in caves, for discovery at a future date by *tertons*. Curiously, part of the head of the image projects into the ceiling protected by a raised section of roof; belief has it that the image is slowly growing.

ARRIVAL AND DEPARTURE	GANGTOK

BY ROAD

With the deterioration in Sikkim's roads, shared jeeps and taxis are the most popular and efficient mode of transport, the busiest route being between Gangtok and Siliguri, the main transport hub in West Bengal, with the nearest airport (Bagdogra, 124km) and railway station (NJP, 117km). Due to the Gurkha agitation in neighbouring Darjeeling district this route sees occasional closures, though the authorities endeavour to keep it open especially for emergency and tourist traffic.

By jeep Most travellers arrive by jeep from Siliguri (see p.766) in west Bengal (4hr 30min), the current

transport centre for the railhead at New Jalpaiguri (NJP) and for Bagdogra airport. Shared jeeps also run from Darjeeling and Kalimpong. Jeeps to North Sikkim depart from Balwakhani/Vajra; book in advance at the Interstate Taxi Stand at Deorali, off NH31-A near the Police Headquarters.

Destinations From the Interstate Taxi Stand: Darjeeling (5–6hr; ₹180); Kalimpong (3–4hr; ₹120), New Jalpaiguri (NJP; ₹250); Siliguri (5–6hr; ₹200). From the South West/ Ranka Stand Gyalshing (4–5hr; ₹180); Jorethang (3–4hr; ₹130); Pelling (5–6hr; ₹200); Rumtek (1hr; ₹50).

TREKKING, TOUR AND ADVENTURE OPERATORS

All high-altitude treks in Sikkim have to be conducted in groups and arranged through the following **travel agents** or **tour operators**, all based in Gangtok, who will also secure the necessary permits.

Blue Sky Tours & Travels Tourism Building, MG Marg ☏ 98323 70680. Very helpful agency specializing in jeep safaris, particularly in north Sikkim. Avoid their ski packages, however.

Fly Sikkim Adventure Khal Goan, Ranka ☏ 97350 17094, ⊚ facebook.com/flysikkimadventure. Offering regular flights (from ₹2000/15min) around Ranka near Lingdum and Tashi View Point – be sure to check your insurance covers it.

Himalayan Footprints Pineli Cottage, Upper Syari ☏ 99326 51962, ⊚ abouthimalayas.com. One of the few agencies run by a woman, excelling in nature tours and treks off the beaten track and village homestays. They run an extensive network throughout northeast India including Arunachal Pradesh and Assam, and also offer mountain bike safaris.

Hub Outdoors Bojoghari, Near Tashi Viewpoint ☏ 94342 03848, ⊚ facebook.com/HUBOUTDOOR. Great adventure operator that specializes in trekking and mountain biking adventures. They also rent mountain bikes for ₹900/day, less for multiday excursions. They have a shop and another branch on Tibet Rd.

Khangri Tours & Treks Tibet Rd ☏ 03592 206050, ⊚ khangri.com. Owner Tsering Dorjee is an experienced trekking guide and a keen amateur

botanist who can arrange cultural and monastic tours and treks throughout Sikkim, and who pioneered routes like the soft trek to Tosar Lake.

Namgyal Treks & Tours Tibet Rd ☏ 03592 203701 or ☏ 94340 33122, ⊚ namgyaltreks.net. Namgyal Sherpa is a highly capable and experienced high-altitude trek and expedition operator, recognized by both the Sikkim and Central Government tourist offices.

Sikkim Adventure 6th Mile, Tadong ☏ 03592 251250, ⊚ sikkim-adventure.com. Sailesh Pradhan runs a plant nursery and is an extremely knowledgeable and enthusiastic botanist, and a specialist guide for trips focused around Sikkim's rich flora. Those interested in botany and horticulture should pay his nursery a visit.

Sikkim Tours & Travels Church Rd ☏ 03592 202188, ⊚ sikkimtours.com. Owner Lukendra is tremendously helpful and experienced, and specializes in nature tours and photography, birdwatching, homestays and treks; he also offers treks off the beaten path and mountain bike tours.

Tashila Tours and Travels Below TNSS School Hall ☏ 03592 229842, ⊚ tashila.com. Experienced operator offering trekking, mountainbiking, kayaking and river-rafting expeditions, angling and monastery tours.

BY BUS AND TRAIN

If you're determined to suffer the buses you can choose between SNT (Sikkim Nationalized Transport) or a number of private operators; services run to Siliguri and Bagdogra Airport in West Bengal and Jorethang in south Sikkim. All buses run by Sikkim Nationalized Transport (SNT), the state carrier, use the SNT Bus Stand on Paljor Stadium Rd, but passengers may prefer to be dropped off earlier at Metro Point, MG Marg, which is more convenient for the tourist office and most hotels. Non-SNT buses stop at the Interstate Stand, Deorali, 2km south of the centre. SNT has a train reservations counter (Mon–Sat 8am–2pm, Sun 8am–noon; ☏ 03592 222016), but the reservations quota for Gangtok is highly inadequate so you are advised to book in Siliguri or online.

BY AIR

By plane An airport is being constructed at Pakyong (32km) southeast of Gangtok, to take small passenger aircraft, and should be operational by 2014. Until then, flights from Bagdogra can be booked either through Josse & Josse, MG Marg (☏ 03592 224682), agents for Jet Airways, or through Silk Route Tours and Travels, first floor, *Green Hotel*, MG Marg (☏ 03592 223354), who also sell tickets for the various airlines flying from Biratnagar (2hr from Siliguri) in eastern Nepal to Kathmandu.

By helicopter Sikkim Tourism Development Corporation, next to the tourist office (☏ 03592 203960 or ☏ 94750 11220) sells tickets for the helicopter flight (subject to weather conditions; daily 11am; ₹2200) to Bagdogra to connect with Indian Airlines and Jet flights; note that the flights only operate with a full load of five passengers and baggage allowance is a mere 10kg.

GETTING AROUND

By taxi Shared local taxis are the most common way of travelling the main highway (Gangtok to Deorali around ₹10). After 9pm, taxis become scarce but reserved taxis are available from stands near the SNT Bus Stand, the Private

Bus Stand at Deorali, the Lall Bazaar supermarket, Children's Park between MG Marg and Tibet Rd, and the Main Line (Bansi Lal). All taxis carry a rate chart and are generally honest.

By the ropeway With terminals at the Secretariat, Nam Nang and Deorali, the ropeway (daily 9am–5pm) provides a spectacular view of the southern city but is an expensive way to get around by local standards (₹60 return, no one-way fare) and is not particularly useful for most accommodation. While it's scheduled to run every 12min, in practice it waits to fill up before moving on.

INFORMATION AND TOURS

Helicopter bookings and tours STDC (☎03592 203960 or ☎94750 11220), next to the tourist office on MG Marg, sell tickets for their spectacular helicopter flights that operate on demand (from ₹7590/15min flight; entire aircraft charter ₹1500/min) to West Sikkim, Yumthang, Gangtok and, the most breathtaking of them all, a 90min Kanchenjunga trip up the Zemu Glacier. Cameras aren't allowed on some routes.

ACCOMMODATION

Gangtok's **hotels** are expensive in high season (has broadly speaking April–June and Sept–Nov), but offer discounted rates at other times. Rooms with views are invariably more expensive. As the town spreads so has the choice of accommodation, with some excellent hotels and guesthouses springing up along the highway at Deorali and Tadong and as far south as Ranipul, and a growing number of alternatives within striking distance of town.

15

CENTRAL GANGTOK

Delamere Church Rd ☎03592 227646 or ☎92335 00158, ⊕hoteldelamere.com. This smart little hotel has undergone a major makeover and offers spotless, well-appointed rooms with tiled floors and good facilities but no good views. Also features a multicuisine restaurant; it's a short walk to the Metro Point. ₹2310

Denzong Regency Cherry Banks ☎03592 201565, ⊕denzongregency.com. In a very pleasant location with quiet grounds; away from the bustle of the bazaar but yet within easy walking distance, this luxurious hotel exudes a sense of Sikkimese history and offers large suite-like rooms and a high level of service. ₹9500

★Mintokling Bhanu Path (Tashiling Rd) ☎03592 208553, ⊕mintokling.com. Run by an old Sikkimese family, with a lovely garden and a quiet location near the palace, high above the market yet in pleasant walking distance. Its twelve airy rooms have good views over the valley to the mountains. ₹2030

★Netuk House Tibet Rd ☎03592 206778, ⊕netukhouse@gmail.com. A family home near the centre extended into a boutique hotel offering warm, atmospheric and beautifully presented rooms with Sikkimese decor, and boasting a pleasant roof terrace. The rate quoted here includes full board; B&B also available. ₹4500

New Modern Central Lodge Tibet Rd ☎03592 201361. Long-popular budget hotel close to the centre and geared towards backpackers, with a traveller-friendly restaurant and some rooms with attached baths and running hot water. Dorms ₹150/₹600

Nor-khill Paljor Stadium Rd ☎03592 205637, ⊕elginhotels.com. Luxurious former royal guesthouse of the Chogyal, this landmark hotel is one of the finest addresses in town. Plush rooms in grand Sikkimese style, a good restaurant and cosy bar, but the location, overlooking the sports stadium, is poor and you will need transport. Prices include all meals. ₹9500

★Pandim Secretariat Rd ☎03592 207540 or ☎98320 80172. Welcoming and pleasant family-run hotel with recently refurbished smart rooms with modern bathrooms, and a superb location high above town – the rooftop restaurant has dramatic views and the Sikkimese cuisine, made to order, is excellent. ₹950

AROUND GANGTOK

★Hidden Forest Lower Sichey Busty ☎03592 205197, ⊕hiddenforestretreat.org. A 2km taxi ride from the SNT bus terminus and Paljor Stadium brings you to this peaceful idyll, with organic food, a pleasant terrace garden and sublimely comfortable cottages in a family-run nursery that specializes in orchids and azaleas. Extremely good value. ₹2200

Rhenock House Jeewan Theeng Marg, Development Area ☎03592 201146 or ☎98320 96281, ⊕renakvilla .com. 1.5km north of Metro Point, this is a contemporary villa set in a manicured garden with restful, wood-floored rooms, a lounge with plenty of reading, a restaurant and cosy bar and views across to Gangtok from the garden. Wi-fi as well as use of a PC. ₹3850

★Tashi Tagey NH-31A, near State Bank of India, Tadong ☎03592 231631, ⊕tashitagey.com. A welcoming and extremely helpful Tibetan family run this hotel 4km from central Gangtok. Clean and homely, with a good restaurant, great for Tibetan home-cooking and Indian food; rooms continue in the annexe and are much quieter in the spacious new block at the back. From here it's a steep 15min walk up to Do-Drul *chorten*, and an easy ₹12 taxi ride to Gangtok. ₹1160

15

EATING, DRINKING AND NIGHTLIFE

Arthurs Kitchen Tibet Rd. A good little café with a traveller-friendly, multicuisine menu and an enticing selection of Sikkimese traditional meals including Lepcha, Nepali and Bhotiya (₹280) with prior notice. Daily 9am–9.30pm.

Baker's Café MG Marg. A modern patisserie a short walk from the tourist office, with a tempting selection of cakes and pizzas, as well as good filter coffee and fruit drinks. There's another outlet on the national highway near the Private Bus Stand. Daily 9am–9pm.

Café Culture Bhanu Path. This tiny, popular daytime restaurant below the *Pandim* hotel prides itself on good wholesome food with a broad menu featuring an eclectic range from sandwiches and *momos* to Bhutanese food. With prior notice they will create a traditional Sikkimese six-course meal. Daily noon–3pm.

Café Tibet NH-31A, past the hospital. Run by the *Hotel Tibet*, this lively café is popular with students, serving pizzas and burgers, croissants, cakes and ice cream. Daily 10am–8pm.

Gangtalk MG Marg. A lively and popular place with a rock/pop feel and if you can find space, a great veranda for people-watching on the busy strip below. It is good for beer or for a light meal with a menu that ranges from burgers to *momos*. Daily noon–10pm.

Live & Loud Tibet Rd. A hip bar/restaurant with large sofas and live music, particularly at weekends when it gets packed for bands brought in from far and wide. Daily 6–11pm.

Parivar MG Marg. The most popular of the vegetarian restaurants, with a menu that is strongest on south Indian cuisine and thalis. In season it gets packed with visiting Indian

families looking for a taste of home. Daily noon–10pm.

Rosoi MG Marg, next to the tourist office. An old favourite in the heart of town, now reinvented as a good-value, multicuisine vegetarian restaurant best for Indian food; there's no bar, however. Daily noon–10pm.

Snowlion Hotel Tibet, Paljor Stadium Rd ☎03592 222523 or ☎03592 223468. Still the best restaurant in Gangtok. The superb Tibetan and Indian food, with a selection of Sikkimese and Japanese dishes, is expensive by local standards (from around ₹800 a meal) but highly recommended. Daily noon–10pm.

Speakeasy Café Rachna Bookshop, Development Area. This café of the celebrated bookshop and cultural hub offers snacks and coffee but also puts on occasional live music. There are regular talks, exhibitions, performances and symposiums upstairs. Daily 11am–2pm & 5–9pm.

The Square Paljor Stadium Rd, next to Mount Jopuno. Bright little café-bistro offering a small but varied menu including good Thai, Continental and Nepalese cuisine. There's a bar, and you get great views. Daily noon–11pm.

Taste of Tibet Hotel Bayul, MG Marg. A café popular with locals for its good wholesome local cuisine, serving *momos*, *thukpa* and the ubiquitous chowmein all at reasonable prices. There is another branch a short distance south along MG Marg; around ₹250/head. Daily noon–11pm.

Tangerine Chumbi Residency hotel, Tibet Rd. Plush, elegant yet affordable restaurant serving Indian, Chinese and Sikkimese specialities, including the intriguing *churpi ningro* (cheese and fern). The adjacent lounge bar is good for a relaxing drink. Expect to pay ₹600 for a meal. Daily noon–11pm.

SHOPPING

The town's best shopping areas are the **Main Market**, stretching for 1km along the pedestrianized MG Marg, and the local produce bazaar in the concrete **Kanchenjunga Shopping Complex**. Stalls sell dried fish, dri (female yak) cheese (*churpi*), and yeast for making the local beer, *tomba*. This is also a good place to buy everyday supplies. Curio shops on MG Marg and on Paljor Stadium Rd sell turquoise and coral jewellery, plus religious objects such as silver ritual bowls and beads.

Government Institute of Cottage Industries NH-31A, north of the centre. Workshops and a retail outlet for traditional Sikkimese handicraft including carpets, hand-loomed fabrics, *thangka* paintings and wooden objects; prices are fixed and you can visit the workshops. Mon–Sat 10am–4pm.

Rachna Bookshop Development Area, 1km north of

Metro Point ☎03592 204336, ⊕rachnabooks.com. This is far more than just a great bookshop – there are poetry and other readings, seminars, art exhibitions and even concerts hosted. The owner, Raman, is a keen jazz aficionado and music is central to the theme with a good café downstairs. Mon–Sat 10am–8pm.

FLAVOURS OF SIKKIM

Sikkimese food is a melange of Nepalese, Tibetan and Indian influences; rice is a staple and dhal is readily available, while **gyakho** is a traditional chimney stew served on special occasions. Sikkimese delicacies include **ningro** (fern rings), **shisnu** (nettle soup), **phing** (glass noodles), and **churpi** (dri cheese) cooked with chillies.

SOMETHING TO KEEP OFF THE CHILL

Most restaurants serve **alcohol** and "foreign" liquor, such as brandy and beer, is cheap enough. Look out for **tomba**, a traditional drink usually served in winter, consisting largely of fermented millet, with a few grains of rice for flavour, served in a wooden or bamboo mug and sipped through a bamboo straw. The mug is occasionally topped up with hot water; once it's been allowed to sit for a few minutes, you're left with a pleasant warm, milky beer that's best on a cold evening.

You will usually find *tomba* in the less salubrious places, where the mixture might be doctored to make it stronger; for a better-quality brew, try the more expensive hotels. Note that the Sikkimese have **alcohol-free** days during full moon.

DIRECTORY

Banks and exchange Axis Bank has a choice of several ATMs accepting Visa, MasterCard and Maestro along MG Marg and elsewhere, including one next to Sikkim Tourism. State Bank of India (SBI), near the tourist office and Metro Point, changes most currencies and travellers' cheques; some tour operators also offer competitive rates. If you're travelling into the interior, note exchange facilities and ATMs are few and far between beyond here.

Cinema Of Gangtok's cinemas, X'Cape, at Vajra Cineplex, Balwakhani, is state of the art while Denzong in Lall Market has been around for years – both show a mix of Indian and Hollywood films.

Hospital The STN Memorial Hospital, on the junction of NH-31A and Paljor Stadium Rd, has a 24hr emergency wing and an ambulance service (☏ 03592 228765); Central Referral Hospital, 5th Mile, Tadong (☏ 03592 231138) has more facilities.

Internet Besides hotel access, Gangtok has several internet cafés (around ₹30/hr) including the Web Centre, NH-31A near *Café Tibet,* and New Light on Tibet Rd.

Police ☏ 100.

Post office The main branch is on Paljor Stadium Rd.

Around Gangtok

The most obvious destinations for day-trips from Gangtok are the great Buddhist monasteries of **Rumtek** to the southwest, and **Phodong** to the north. Indian tourists flock to **Tsomgo Lake** and beyond, to the Tibetan border at **Nathu La**.

Tsomgo Lake and around

Tsomgo Lake (pronounced "Changu"), 35km northeast of Gangtok and just 20km from the Tibetan border at **Nathu La**, is a scenic spot at an altitude of 3750m. It is popular with Indian and foreign visitors alike, all of whom need permits arranged through travel agents (see box, p.814). Indian visitors flock here to sample the high-mountain environment and, hopefully, experience their first thrill of snow in the colder months. It's possible to visit the **Kyongnosla Alpine Sanctuary** (3350m) en route, where a profusion of wild flowers bloom between May and August and migratory birds stop over in winter on their annual journey from Siberia to India. Only Indians are allowed up to the trade post at **Serathang** and **Nathu La** (4130m), where, at a motley collection of border buildings, they hope to catch a glimpse of Chinese soldiers.

Rumtek

Visible from Gangtok, and a popular 24km day-trip southwest of the capital, **RUMTEK** is one of Sikkim's largest and most impressive *gompas* and the main seat of the **Karma Kagyu** lineage – also known as the **Black Hat** sect – founded during the twelfth century by the first Gyalwa Karmapa, Dusun Khyenpa (1110–93).

Foreigners need to register passport details at the **checkpoint** off the bazaar; even Indians and locals are sometimes asked for ID.

15

THE KARMA KAGYU AND RUMTEK

Dusun Khyenpa established the Tsurphu monastery in central Tibet near Lhasa, which became the headquarters of the **Karma Kagyu** for eight centuries until the Chinese invasion of Tibet in 1959. The sixteenth **Karmapa**, Rangjung Rigpe Dorje, fled Tibet for Sikkim, where he was invited to stay at the old Rumtek *gompa*. Within a couple of years, the Karmapa had begun the work of building a new monastery at **Rumtek** to become his new seat on land donated by the Sikkimese King Chogyal Tashi Namgyal. One of the great Tibetan figures of the twentieth century, the sixteenth Karmapa was very influential in the spread of Tibetan Buddhism to the West, setting up over two hundred Karma Kagyu centres and raising funds for the rebuilding of Tsurphu. When he died in 1981, he left behind a wealthy monastery and a huge and lucrative international network, but one bitterly divided by an ugly squabble over his rightful successor. Two reincarnate Karmapas have now emerged as the main contenders to the throne – one blessed by the Dalai Lama and ensconced in Dharamsala, the other in nearby Kalimpong. A heavily armed security presence is to keep the peace but is a sad intrusion into the otherwise impressive monastery.

The main temple

Daily 6am–5pm • ₹10; no photography allowed

The **main temple**, with its ornate facade covered in intricate, brightly painted wooden latticework, overlooks the expansive **courtyard**. Large red columns support the high roof of the **prayer hall**, where the walls are decorated with murals and *thangkas*. Visitors may attend daily rituals here, when lines of monks sit chanting.

Karma Shri Nalanda Institute of Buddhist Studies

The **Karma Shri Nalanda Institute of Buddhist Studies**, behind the main temple, built in 1984 in traditional Tibetan style, is the most ornate of all the buildings of Rumtek. Monks spend a minimum of nine years studying here, followed by an optional three-year period of isolated meditation. The ashes of the sixteenth Karmapa are contained in a gilded 4m-high *chorten* or *stupa*, studded with turquoise and coral, which sits in the **Golden Stupa** hall opposite the Institute.

Old Rumtek gompa

Two kilometres beyond the new monastery and Rumtek village, a flower-and-prayer-flag-lined path leads to the simple **Old Rumtek Gompa**, the original monastery, founded in 1740 and recently renovated. The quiet setting, surrounded by empty outbuildings in traditional Sikkimese alpine style, with latticed wooden windows, is a world away from the charged atmosphere of the main complex.

Lingdum

The most rewarding route to Rumtek is via the impressive **Zum Gharwang** *gompa* of **Lingdum**, completed in 1998 and an easy 14km taxi ride (₹30) from the centre of Gangtok. A haven of peace surrounded by deep woodland, Lingdum is a grand example of modern monastic architecture, with an expansive terrace and courtyard. Inside, delicate and detailed murals, with a predominance of pastel colours, depict the life of the Buddha.

ARRIVAL AND DEPARTURE   **RUMTEK**

By jeep If you don't arrange your own transport, the best way to get to Rumtek is in one of the shared jeeps that leave Gangtok from the Private Taxi Stand near Zero Point when full (₹50). Few shared taxis travel after 2pm, but those that do will charge a lot more after dark. You can arrange a return to Gangtok.

ACCOMMODATION AND EATING

Rumtek has a limited choice of budget **accommodation**, but an increasing number of more upscale resorts offering a quiet alternative to crowded Gangtok. In Rumtek itself, noodles and chai are available at the **teashops** clustered near the monastery gate and at the **bazaar**.

SIKKIM HOMESTAYS

If you're interested in getting a taste of rural Sikkimese life, you might want to try a **homestay**, which provides an interesting insight into local communities and their customs. Home-stays are especially useful on forest treks such as the Pelling round via Kecheopalri. While several homestays remain word-of-mouth, those networks listed through the Ecotourism and Conservation Society of Sikkim (☎9733088003, ⒲sikkimhome-stay.com or ⒲rpgecoss@gmail.com) include **Yuksam** (contact Mr Pema Bhutia; ☎9832 452527), **Pastenga** in eastern Sikkim (contact Mr Huna Rai; ☎9832 033679), **Dzongu** (contact Dr N.T. Lepcha; ☎9434 179160) and **Kewzing**.

Bamboo Resort Sajong, 1km before the monastery gates ☎03592 252516 or ☎98320 61986, ⒲bamboo resort.com. A boutique hotel where Swiss chic meets formal Sikkimese style, set against a backdrop of forest with views towards Gangtok and Nathu La in the far distance. There's a herb garden, library and a meditation room and mountain bikes are available to explore the countryside. Each bedroom has a unique colour scheme and breakfast and dinner are included in the price. ₹4200

Sun-Gay ☎03592 252221. A welcoming guesthouse between the checkpost and monastery gates, this is by far the best of the budget options, boasting large clean rooms, good home cooking, an expansive terrace and a garden; the cheaper rooms share bathrooms. ₹400

Teen Taley Eco Garden Resort Lower Sajong ☎03592 252256, ⒲sikkimresort.com. Around 2km from Rumtek and spread over six acres, this place is geared towards families, with a small farm and guided walks, mountain bikes for hire, pony riding and a pick-your-own vegetable garden. The mix of cottages, deluxe rooms and suites uses a blend of vernacular and modern architecture. ₹2500

Zurmang Tara Hotel Lingdum ☎99330 08818. Run by Lingdum Monastery, with comfortable if plain rooms above a decent restaurant serving local and Indian food, this is a wonderful spot for a quiet retreat and to get a close look at the workings of the great monastery. ₹700

Phodong and Labrang

The road to **Phodong**, another living but far less ostentatious monastery 38km north of Gangtok on the Mangan road, passes Kabi Lunchok, a pleasant wooded spot marking a historic treaty between the Lepchas and the Bhutias, and some spectacular waterfalls.

On a high spur of 3km above the small Phodong Bazaar, Phodong commands superb views, with a simple square main temple and several outhouses. Built in the early eighteenth century, this was Sikkim's pre-eminent Kagyu monastery until the growth of Rumtek in the 1960s. It too hosts colourful lama dances, similar to the *chaam* of Rumtek, each December.

A rough road leads a further 4km up from Phodong to another renovated old monastery – the unusual octagonal **Labrang**. A cluster of *chortens* between these two monasteries marks the ruins of **Tumlong**, Sikkim's capital city for most of the nineteenth century.

South Sikkim

Ignored by most travellers en route to higher trekking trails and the great *gompas* of west Sikkim, **southern Sikkim** nevertheless offers quiet charm, its lichen-covered forests draped with a stunning array of orchids and inhabited by rare and endangered animals. The region is dominated by the great, forested peak of **Maenam** – towering high above the town of **Ravangla** – a challenging day-trek and famous for its plants and flowers and for the tremendous view from its summit. Easier options such as the delightful jungle walk to the lesser heights of **Tendong** are just as rewarding, while high above the district capital **Namchi**, the gigantic statuary of **Samdruptse** and **Solophok** are clearly visible from as far away as Darjeeling. Sikkim's sole tea garden, the organic **Temi Tea Estate**, welcomes visitors and provides a good base from which to explore the area.

Jorethang

The busy market town and crucial transport hub of **JORETHANG** lies in the very south of the state, just across the River Rangit from Singla Bazaar in West Bengal and a mere 30km north of Darjeeling, which is just visible high above the tea plantations. It is a useful supply stop, with a few decent budget **hotels** that are useful should you miss your connection and need to stay the night.

ARRIVAL AND DEPARTURE   JORETHANG

All regular transport terminates at the main transport hub, the **Plaza**, a multistorey building right in the middle of town. All the respective companies have ticket counters here and will help you find the right connection.

By jeep Few jeeps leave Jorethang after 1pm and the rule of thumb is to travel early.
Destinations Darjeeling (2hr; ₹110); Gangtok (4–5hr; ₹130); Legship (1hr; change here for Pelling, Ravangla, Yoksum and Tashiding); Namchi (1hr; ₹40); Siliguri (4–5hr; ₹130). There are less frequent services to Gyalshing and Varsh.

By bus Jorethang is well connected by bus with the rest of Sikkim.
Destinations Gangtok (7.30am); Namchi (8.30am); Pelling (3pm); Siliguri (8am).

ACCOMMODATION AND EATING

Aanie Heem Circular Road, Jorethang Bazaar ☎ 96098 59956. A popular hotel in the middle of town with small rooms, some with attached baths, and a good restaurant serving the usual Indian and Chinese mix; handy for the Plaza for early connections. ₹500

Club Mahendra Baiguney Sisney ☎ 03595 276575 or ☎ 96799 98482. This luxurious development in the river valley feels a bit out of place, with swimming pool, spa and manicured lawns and great service. Although a timeshare, it can be booked with prior notice and represents the highest level of comfort in this part of Sikkim; useful for recuperating after long drives. ₹3950

The Namgyal ☎ 03595 276852 or ☎ 96478 75723. Next to the bridge on the edge of town, this tried and tested hotel has good-value doubles with running hot water above a decent restaurant and bar. ₹526

Namchi and around

Some 79km southeast of Gangtok, 24km northwest of Jorethang and pleasantly situated on a saddle at 1676m above sea level, busy **NAMCHI** is the administrative centre for south Sikkim. Although the area is a magnet for domestic tourists due to the extraordinary statuary that is springing up around it, the town itself has little to offer save a handful of monasteries including the impressive Nyingmapa **Doling Gompa**.

Samdruptse

Daily 7am–5pm • ₹20 • To get here, it's a steep, gruelling climb past Ngadak Monastery, or an easier jeep ride (₹200) to the ornamental Rock Garden, from where you'll need to make a 3km climb up steps to the statue; taxis from Namchi's Central Park to the car park near the statue cost ₹500

High above town, 8km to the north of Namchi along the undfolding ridge, the gigantic 41m statue of Guru Rinpoche (Padma Sambhava) known as **Samdruptse** sits on a ridge gazing south towards Darjeeling. Inaugurated by the Dalai Lama in 2004, the statue cost ₹67,600,000 (around US$16 million) to build, and is large enough to contain a meeting hall.

Damthang and Tendong Hill

Faint forest trails lead north from Samdruptse through the forest to **Tendong Hill** (2623m) where a small monastery sanctifies the sacred spot revered by the Lepchas, who believe that the hill saved them from the great flood that once submerged the earth. An easier and more direct route to Tendong starts from the hamlet of **Damthang**, 14km north of Namchi on the Ravangla road and accessible by shared taxi, from where it's a 6km trek along a pleasant brick-paved trail through dense, protected forest. On a

PUJA CEREMONY AT THE RUMTEK GOMPA (P.817) >

clear day, the views from the summit stretch from the plains of Bengal to the high Himalayas, and in good weather it's worth camping at the top to catch the sunrise. Beware of **black bears** – don't go alone.

ARRIVAL AND DEPARTURE
NAMCHI AND AROUND

By jeep Namchi is well connected to all points in Sikkim as well as Siliguri, Kalimpong and Darjeeling, and jeeps are frequent between 6am and 2pm. The main transport hub is the multistorey Car Parking Plaza below Central

Square where all jeeps, taxis and buses converge; use the pre-paid booths.
Destinations Gangtok (₹120); Gyalshing (₹100); Jorethang (₹40); Ravangla (₹60).

INFORMATION AND SERVICES

Information The Sikkim Tourism office on Stadium Rd, near Dak Bungalow, above the District Hospital (Mon–Sat 9am–5pm, Sun 10am–1pm; ☎03595 248536) is useful for information on the area.

Services There's an internet café below *Kesang*, and several ATMs in the vicinity of the square, including State Bank of India and Axis; both take credit and debit cards (Visa and MasterCard).

ACCOMMODATION AND EATING

Namchi offers an increasing choice of accommodation. Most places are clustered around the pedestrianized main square, Central Park, resplendent with two magnificent trees including a pipal with an aquarium built around it. As most of the interest is beyond the town itself, consider one of several alternative options.

Cherry Resort Temi Tea Estate ☎03592 261570 & ☎97335 45592, ⊛cherryresort.com. Equidistant between Namchi and Ravangla, this hotel at Temi Tea Estate makes a convenient base to discover central Sikkim. Despite the rather institutional look of the commanding block, it provides a good degree of comfort with large rooms, a good restaurant and bar and high level of service. Tours can be arranged. ₹**3450**

Dungmali Solophok Rd ☎9434126992 & ☎8902232559. Although 4km above town, this welcoming family-run guesthouse with its organic kitchen garden and adjacent woodland is well worth the trek. Most rooms benefit from the great views, and the home cooking

is wholesome. It is within walking distance of both town and Solophuk. ₹**1000**

Samdruptse Jorethang Rd ☎03595 264263. A popular and convenient stop offering a large range of rooms, from grubby cubbyholes with shared facilities to more luxurious ones upstairs with attached baths; the bar and restaurant is one of the most popular in town, serving local, Indian and Chinese food, though the canteen-like atmosphere can be a bit frenetic. ₹**600**

Zimkhang Central Square ☎03595 264263 or ☎96098 56114. Near the fountain, this conveniently located budget hotel, close to all amenities, has decent clean rooms above a popular local bar and restaurant. ₹**700**

Ravangla and around

Spread across a high saddle, 65km west of Gangtok and 52km east of Pelling, the sleepy market town of **RAVANGLA** (also known as Ravang and Rabang) makes for a convenient stopover, especially for anyone interested in trekking through one of the last remaining **rhododendron forests** in south-central Sikkim. The fabulous **Maenam Sanctuary** remains a botanist's dream, covering the flanks of the gigantic forested peak which looms over the town.

Ravangla itself has a sizeable Tibetan settlement, with a handicrafts centre and shop at the **Kheunpheling Carpet Centre** in the refugee camp to the south. Steps north of the bazaar lead to a completely renovated **Nyingmapa monastery** and behind it, the lavish formal park of the **Shakyamuni Project** dominated by a giant statue of the Buddha.

Mane Chorkeling Monastery and the Tathagatha Centre

A short, steep walk from the north end of Ravangla Bazaar leads to the lavishly renovated Nyingmapa **Mane Chorkeling** *gompa* with a landscaped garden, which, along with the old chapel within the grounds, is dedicated to Shakyamuni and Guru Rimpoche, accompanied by a host of stucco images of the wrathful protectors. This is the site of the annual three-day **Pang Lhabsol festival** in late August, which celebrates the worship of Kanchenjunga and draws thousands of Sikkimese to enjoy the traditional sports and **Pangtoed Chaam**, a festival of masked dances unique in that it is performed here, not by monks, but by *zigtempas* or lay people.

Maenem

The summit of **Maenam** (3235m), 10km from Ravangla bazaar, is home to a small chapel to Guru Rinpoche (Padma Sambhava) and boasts superlative views especially of the horned summit of Narsing (5825m). Feasible as a day-trek, the stiff 1000m **ascent** of Maenam (2hr 30min–4hr) starts with steps rising from the bazaar up to the *gompa* before trailing off through the sanctuary where you may even be lucky enough to glimpse wildlife, including the elusive red panda, black bear and a variety of birds. The route through the forest is confusing and you may want to take a local guide (₹500), arranged through hotels in town or at the forest gate 1km above town where you pay an entry fee to the sanctuary (₹50). To catch the sunrise from the dilapidated shelter, bring a good sleeping bag, food and water.

Ralang

Monasteries in the vicinity of Ravangla include the old and the new *gompas* at **Ralang**, 13km to the north, with shared jeeps (₹40) travelling the route on demand. The old *gompa*, **Karma Rabtenling**, is linked to the ninth Karmapa and was founded in 1730. The new Ralang monastery, **Palchen Choeling**, built in 1995 in much the same style as Rumtek, is one of the largest temple buildings in Sikkim with numerous resident monks.

ARRIVAL AND DEPARTURE   RAVANGLA AND AROUND

Be advised that you can't be assured of regular transport much after noon.

By jeep Jeeps leave from the stand at the crossroads towards the southern end of the market, heading to Gangtok (₹100) and Namchi (₹60) via Damthang (₹30), as well as Legship and Gyalshing. To get to Pelling (₹100) you may need to change at Gyalshing.

By bus Buses travel to Gyalshing at around 11am and to Gangtok at around 9am and there are two to Namchi (9am & 1pm) with connections to Siliguri. The shortest route to Darjeeling is via Namchi, where you may have to change for a jeep or bus to Jorethang, and again there for Darjeeling.

ACCOMMODATION

There's a reasonable choice of accommodation on offer in and around Ravangla, most centred around the small bazaar, but with more choice along the Kewzing-Legship Rd. Alternatively you can stay at the Temi Tea Estate, 11km away (see opposite).

Annexe at Mount Narsing Village Resort 3km along the Kewzing road ☏ 8145 294900, ⓦ rabong-borong .com. A quiet idyll in a stunning location, a steep 20min walk (or precarious jeep drive) up from the main resort.

Comfortable chalets, built partly of local materials, are ringed around the main lodge, with a restaurant boasting an open fire; the service is suitably low-key. Their tour operation Yuksom Tours & Travels specializes in this region. **₹2750**

> ## NARSING & RANGIT TRAILS
>
> Numerous trails and permutations explore this corner of Sikkim, forming the watershed dominated by the elegant peak of Narsing (5825m) – climbing not permitted – and offering the promise of a **high-altitude trek** without the restriction of a special permit. The region abounds with high mountain **lakes** as well as **hot springs** along the river Rangit, best accessed via Ralang and Borong or from Tashiding (see p.830). However, the region is most famous for its **holy caves** including **Lhar Rinchen Nying Phug** (3785m), one of the four in Sikkim associated with Guru Rinpoche, which lies en-route to the mountain lakes of Panchpokhari (3–4 days). The little-visited trek starts at **Labdang** connected to **Tashiding** (13km) by jeep. Local **guides** are available at Labdang (from ₹200/day) and through *Sanu's* homestay in Tashiding, while complete itineraries are available through hotels *Zumthang* and *Narsing* in Ravangla.

15

Bon Farm House Kewzing Busti ☎973590 0165, ⓦsikkimbonfarmhouse.com. An idyllic spot surrounded by terraced fields just outside the sleepy market town of Kewzing, itself 8km east of Ravangla, Chewang Rinchen Bonpo's farmhouse has well-furnished wood-lined rooms, marrying rustic vernacular style with modern amenities including attached bathrooms. The Bon community offers nature walks and monastic tours. Full board is available. ₹2600

Queen Hill Ralang Road ☎9733244089. This recently built and local-run hotel with simple rooms but hot water and attached bathrooms is well located at the quiet end of the bazaar near the footpath to the monastery; the restaurant serves a mix of local, Chinese and Indian food. ₹600

Wildflower Retreat Borong ☎9433119535 & ⓦthewildflowerretreat.com. 5km down the road from Ralang, with rustic cottages in a picturesque garden; catering is limited. This is a good spot to unwind, enjoy the wonderful views of Narsing or walk to the hot springs (6km) by the Rangit river. ₹1650

Zumthang Kewzing Rd ☎9733061311, ⓦhotel zumthang.webs.com, ✉zumthang@yahoo.com. On the outskirts of Ravangla, the delightful family offer a warm welcome and large, clean rooms, some with balconies; Karma can organize Buddhist retreats, voluntary work and home-stays. Very informative about the area and along with nature treks, can arrange tours of Ralang Monastery. ₹800

15

West Sikkim

This beautiful land, characterized by great tracts of virgin forest and deep river valleys, is home to ancient monasteries such as **Pemayangtse** and **Tashiding** and the rapidly developing tourist hub and hill-station of **Pelling**. The old capital, **Yoksum**, lies at the start of the trail towards Dzongri and Kanchenjunga. In the far west, along the border with Nepal, the watershed of the Singalila Range rises along a single ridge, with giants such as Rathong and Kabru culminating in Kanchenjunga itself. Only two high-altitude trails are currently easily accessible but require **permits** (see box, p.810), and are expensive; however, several low-altitude treks with numerous variations provide ample opportunities to enjoy the wonderful profusion of orchids, rhododendron forests, waterfalls and terraced hillsides with a backdrop of majestic vistas. If you're coming directly from **Darjeeling** via Jorethang for a high-altitude trek, arrange permits and itineraries in advance.

Gyalshing & Legship

The bustling market town of **GYALSHING** (pronounced and also known as **Geyzing**), 110km west of Gangtok, is the administrative centre and transport hub of western Sikkim, and a good place to stock up on provisions and extend **permits**, which you can do through the Superintendent of Police (Mon–Sat 10am–4pm) at **Tikjuk**, midway between Gyalshing and Pelling. There are a handful of **hotels** around the main square in the centre of Gyalshing should you miss connections. At the bottom of the climb up to Gyalshing, **LEGSHIP** (14km) is an important regional road junction and the gateway to western Sikkim. Nestling deep in the shadows of the Rangit Valley, Legship is dull with little to see save a temple across the river and grubby hot springs down the road, but you may find yourself here waiting for onward transport.

ARRIVAL AND DEPARTURE

GYALSHING

All jeeps and buses from Gyalshing to Gangtok, Ravangla, Yoksum (via Tashiding), Namchi, Jorethang and Siliguri pass through Legship; frequent jeeps connect Legship to Gyalshing and Jorethang but not much after 4pm.

By jeep Taxis and jeeps depart from the main square for Pelling and other local destinations; most have left by midday, with the exception of those to Pelling which continue regularly until dark. If reserving a taxi, Omnis tend to be cheaper as they can travel up the steep short-cut to Pelling, which is closed to jeeps.

Destinations Gangtok (4–5hr; ₹180); Pelling (30min; ₹30); Jorethang (2–3hr; 6–7 daily; change here for Darjeeling); Siliguri (5–7hr; ₹180).

By bus An SNT bus to Gangtok leaves at 8am and to Siliguri at 8am via Jorethang where there are better connections and jeeps to Darjeeling.

ACCOMMODATION AND EATING

Attri Gyalshing ☎ 03595 250602. A few yards up from the market on the Tikjuk Rd, yet a quiet spot, this lodge has plain but functional rooms with attached baths, and is one of the best options in the centre of town. There is no restaurant but there are cafés around the corner including

Denkhang near the crossroads. ₹600

Trishna Legship ☎ 03595 250887. Dominating the crossroads at Legship, this basic hotel has small rooms with attached baths but hot water by the bucket. The hotel restaurant is the best place in town to eat. ₹400

Pemayangtse

Daily 7am–5pm · ₹20 (₹10)

Perched at the end of a ridge with a grand panorama of the entire Parekh Chu watershed including the Kanchenjunga massif, the hallowed monastery of **Pemayangtse**, 118km

---

WEST SIKKIM WALKS

The rhododendron forests, wooded hills and river valleys at the heart of the Singalila forests, crisscrossed by numerous trails, allow independent walkers to explore the region, generally without the headache of red-tape (permits) and the expense of tour operators and expedition costs. Apart from the occasional forest lodge or guesthouse, a growing network of **home-stays** allows the intrepid trekker to wander off the beaten track especially along the **Monastery Trail** (see box, p.828) from Pelling. On the western boundaries of the state, the rhododendron forests are best seen around Varshey.

RHODODENDRON WALKS

The Singalila range's rhododendron forests, lauded by the famous botanist Sir JD Hooker who travelled here in 1848, are best visited between mid-April and mid-May when the flowers are in full bloom. Of these forests, the **Varshey Rhododendron Sanctuary** (aka Barsey or Varsey) covers 104 square kilometres, ranges in altitude from 2840m to 4250m and is home to black bear, red panda and pheasant. Entry to the forest is via **Hilley**, **Soreng** or **Dentam** and entry permits (₹50 (₹25), tents and camera extra) for the sanctuary are available from forestry departments at **Hilley**, **Soreng**, **Uttarey** and **Gangtok**. The most popular route is the 8km roundtrip from Hilley to **Varshey** (3030m), which offers majestic views. You can extend the walk to Uttarey (3–4 days with tented accommodation), from where you can either take transport out or continue on foot to the small town of Dentam.

From Dentam, a river-valley trail leads to the quiet village of **Rinchenpong** (4–5hr), a good base for West Sikkim village walks; another trail from Dentam leads east up the ridge to **Pelling** (4–5hr). There are numerous permutations and possibilities for trekking in this region including an extension (with prior arrangement with tour operators and the appropriate permits) into the long high-altitude **Singalila Ridge trek** to Dzongri and beyond (see box, p.829).

ACCOMMODATION

Choice of accommodation by the sanctuary is limited and it is best to look a bit further afield such as at Soreng, Rinchenpong bazaar and Kaluk, where there is increasing choice.

Dhungay Home-stay Hee Bermiok ☎ 97332 69413, ⓦ dhungayhome-stay.com. An extensive traditional farm with an organic garden, provides comfortable rooms and local cuisine, and arranges tours and treks; handy for the Singalila rhododendron forests. ₹1800

Gurash Kunj Lodge Varshey ☎ 95938 34627. Very handy for the sanctuary, this well situated but disappointing "trekkers" lodge offers just one double room and a dorm (₹300), and is very basic indeed. ₹600

Nagbeli Uttarey ☎ 89725 54514, ⓦ nagbeliresort. com. Above the small Uttarey Bazaar and handy for the

rhododendron treks, the hotel, popular with Bengali travellers, has comfortable if small rooms some in a concrete block and others in a wooden chalet set in a colourful garden; treks can be organized. ₹1130

★ **Yangsum Farm** Rinchenpong ☎ 94341 79029, ⓦ yangsumfarm.com. The sylvan environs of this working hill-farm 3km below the bazaar, provides a quiet retreat with large, comfortable rooms furnished in local style but with modern amenities and good home-cooking. Thendup can arrange decent village and forest walks and all-inclusive treks including guides for the Singalila trails. Rates include meals. ₹5500

15

from Gangtok and a mere 2km from Pelling, is poised high above the River Rangit. It's a 9km journey along the main road from Gyalshing; or you can take a steep, 4km short-cut through the woods past a line of *chortens* and the otherwise uninteresting remains of Sikkim's second capital, **Rabdantse**, now made into a pleasant park.

Pemayangtse, the "Perfect Sublime Lotus", founded in the seventeenth century by Lhatsun Chempo, one of the three lamas of Yoksum, and extended in 1705 by his reincarnation, is one of the most important *gompas* in Sikkim and belongs to the Nyingmapa sect. The views and the surrounding woods create an atmosphere of meditative solitude. Surrounded by outhouses featuring intricate woodwork on the beams, lattice windows and doors, the main *gompa* itself is plain in comparison. Built on three floors, it centres around a large hall which contains images of Guru Rinpoche and Lhatsun Chenpo (the latter was an enigmatic Tibetan lama who is the patron saint of Sikkim), and an exquisite display of *thangkas* and murals. On the top floor, a magnificent wooden sculpture carved and painted by Dungzin Rinpoche, a former abbot of Pemayangtse, depicts Sang Thok Palri, the celestial abode of Guru Rinpoche, rising above the realms of hell. The extraordinary detail includes demons, animals, birds, Buddhas and *bodhisattvas*, *chortens* and flying dragons, and took him just five years to complete.

Pelling and around

The quiet, relatively new yet rapidly swelling town of **PELLING**, situated 2085m above sea level only 2km beyond Pemayangtse, is most notable for its expansive views north towards the glaciers and peaks of Kanchenjunga. High above forest-covered hills, in an amphitheatre of cloud, snow and rock, the entire route from Yoksum over Dzongri La to the Rathong Glacier can be seen. Frenetic building activity hasn't detracted from Pelling's quiet charm, with numerous hotel terraces that allow you to gaze in awe at the world's third-highest peak, as well as easy access to attractive walks in the hinterland. One noticeable element missing is a bazaar, though a few shops are now beginning to appear.

ARRIVAL AND DEPARTURE   PELLING AND AROUND

By jeep From the crossroads of Upper Pelling also called Zero Point, shared jeeps travel regularly (6am–3pm) between Pelling and Gyalshing (₹30); there are also twice-daily services to Gangtok via Ravangla (7.30am & noon; ₹200), and one jeep daily for Siliguri (7am; ₹250). Special shared taxis to Kecheopalri (₹70) are booked through *Hotel Kabur* who also arrange an early afternoon service to Yuksom (₹80); the regular route to Yuksom via Tashiding entails a change at Gyalshing but leave as early as possible to make the connections. Father Travels (see below) runs a direct jeep service to Gangtok leaving at 7.30am and direct jeeps to Darjeeling are also available in season.

By bus A single bus (7am, ₹165) leaves for Siliguri (5hr 30min) via Jorethang from Lower Pelling. Book in advance at SNT, *Hotel Pelling*, Lower Pelling (☎03595 250707).

INFORMATION AND TOURS

Information The Tourist Information Centre near the helipad (daily 10am–4pm) is good for general and travel information, as is the excellent local website, ⓦ gopelling.net. Avoid the pretend tourist information centre above the crossroads. For the best in local, trekking and transport information, consult *Hotel Garuda* who also keep an interesting travellers' log, or ask at *Hotel Kabur*.

Tours If you have less time on your hands, tour operators such as Let's Go Tour & Treks (☎9733018237) in Upper Pelling and Father Jeep Service (☎03595 258219) can arrange day-trips by jeep (from ₹1800 for half-day and around ₹3000 for 6–8 people or ₹225/person for a full day). Both hotels *Garuda* and *Kabur* provide reliable travel services and can arrange local treks, village tours and logistics for the Monastery Trail (see box, p.828).

ACCOMMODATION

Most of Pelling's **hotels**, whose rates rise steeply in the high seasons (March–May & Sept–Nov) are spread along a 2km stretch of road between Upper, Middle and Lower Pelling, with Lower Pelling gearing itself more towards the domestic market and Upper Pelling offering the finest views. Here you'll find several attractive options and new luxury developments away from the concrete jungle.

Dubdi Near the helipad, Upper Pelling ☎03595 258349 & ☎9733098921. This small hotel, located in a quiet corner above town and tucked beside the gates to the Norbu Ghang, is a lot less expensive than its neighbour, *Norbu Ghang*, with very comfortable, spacious and spotless rooms, some with great views. ₹1000

The Elgin Mount Pandim Just below Pemayangtse monastery ☎03595 250756, ⌨elginhotels.com. Darjeeling-style elegance has turned this old government hotel into the most luxurious address in western Sikkim. Every room has a view of the snowy peaks, the multi-cuisine restaurant is excellent and the quiet, unspoilt location makes this the ideal base from which to explore the area. ₹8850

★ **Garuda** The crossroads, Upper Pelling ☎03595 258 319 & ☎97330 76484. A long-popular travellers' haunt with internet access and travel desk, this well-run family hotel offers a wide range from basic doubles to deluxe balconied suites and dorms, with a 40 percent off-season discount; their useful comment books are useful for trekking information. The restaurant boasts good food including a Sikkimese set meal, beer and *tomba* (see below) in winter. Dorms ₹200, double ₹500

★ **Kabur** Pemayangtse Road, Upper Pelling ☎03595 258 504 & ☎97759 72112. A welcoming place, 200m from the crossroads, with internet access and a very helpful local trek-and-tour operation. The doubles are carpeted, with hot water and heaters in winter and there's an expansive rooftop terrace complete with sun loungers and great views. The restaurant that opens on to it offers a healthy range of meals, including Sikkimese cuisine and is a great place to catch the sunset over a beer. Very good value. ₹200

Ladakh Upper Pelling ☎97331 63551. A rapidly dying breed in Pelling – a traditional, rustic Sikkimese house with six rooms and a dorm popular with drivers; you will need to share the common bathrooms with squat toilets, but all is about to change in this humble but welcoming place; a proud new block comprising modern bathrooms was about to open at the time of writing. Dorms ₹150, double ₹350

Pachhu Village Resort Chumbong ☎94341 03512, ⌨pellingresort.com. Great location about 2km from town (₹200 by taxi) and part of a community dedicated to organic farming, with a kitchen garden and a cheese dairy nearby. All their 7 immaculate suites, wood-lined and designed in modern-Sikkimese style, have panoramic views and rates include half-board with trek and tours on offer. ₹3450

Phamrong Upper Pelling ☎03595 258218 & ☎97330 76484, ✉mailphamrong@yahoo.com. Conveniently located at the crossroads, an old favourite in need of a makeover, with a wide range of comfortable rooms, hot running water and breakfast included. The restaurant serves Sikkimese, Indian and Chinese food, and there are good views from some of the more expensive rooms. Internet available. ₹2600

15

EATING AND DRINKING

Most of the best **restaurants** are to be found in hotels, but traditional Sikkimese food is rather rarer than *dhal bhat* due to the strong Bengali presence. Upper Pelling has several cafés, and for fine dining try the conservative menu at *Mount Pandim*. Pelling is a good place to sample a *tomba* (warm millet beer) usually made and served in cooler months; it's best in Sikkimese-run hotels like *Garuda* and *Kabur*.

Garuda The Crossroads, Upper Pelling. A popular restaurant and bar on the ground floor of the hotel, with a good mix of Indian and Chinese plus local cuisine – traditional Sikkimese food made with prior notice. Daily 9am–10pm.

Kabur Pemayangtse Road. Welcoming place with a rooftop restaurant and bar and great terrace and a place for a long drink at dusk. The menu is varied with Chinese, Indian and local and Sikkimese delicacies with notice. Daily 9am–10pm.

Melting Point Middle Pelling. One of the few exceptions from hotel restaurants, this great independent multi-cuisine restaurant is tastefully decorated and boasts a pleasant veranda and views, though its popularity means you may not get a seat outside. The choice is ample, including some local specialities such as the Fingsha Rice with chicken (₹150); it is also good for a late afternoon beer. Daily 11.30am–9pm.

DIRECTORY

Banks and ATM Nearby the post office, there's a State Bank of India ATM, but no official facilities for changing money.
Internet There is an internet café at the post office during office hours (₹30/hr).
Post office The post office is in Upper Pelling just above the crossroads.

Sanga Choling

A new road blasted up the steep ridge from near the helipad just above Pelling makes a good 4km walk to reach the small but highly venerated Nyingmapa monastery of **Sanga Choling**, one of the oldest *gompas* in Sikkim and another of Lhatsun Chenpo's creations. Gutted by fire, it was rebuilt in 1948 and houses some of the original clay statues including a stunning Samantha Bhadra.

15

THE MONASTERY TRAIL

You won't need a guide for this most rewarding circuit which has come to be known as the **Monastery Trail**, taking in the highlights of western Sikkim including several holy places and monasteries; do ask advice from either hotels *Kabur* or *Garuda* in **Pelling**, where you can pick up a rough map of the trail. Each section takes between 4–7 hours and the growing network of **home-stays** allows the intrepid trekker to explore off the beaten track. Most walkers start the popular 3–4 day trail from Pelling via **Darap** to **Kecheopalri**, then continue to **Yuksom** (with a steep descent and a knee-grinding ascent to the small town) where there are some decent hotels and home-stays. Continuing from Yuksom takes in monasteries such as Dubdi (above Yuksom), Hongri and Sinon before descending to **Tashiding**. To return to Pelling, walk down to Sakyung from where there is an unrelenting ascent to Pelling. Along with several extensions, alternative routes from Tashiding include walking to Borong, Ralang and **Ravangla** (see p.822) with a dip in a hot spring along the Rangit River; the advantage of this variation is that it would help you get on to the road for Gangtok. For trail information in Tashiding ask at *Sanu's* home-stay (see p.831).

Khecheopalri Lake

Surrounded by forests and hidden in a mountain bowl (2000m) 33km northwest of Pelling, **Khecheopalri Lake** (₹10), known as the "Wishing Lake", is sacred to the Lepchas. A footpath from the tiny bazaar and road head, past the picturesque *anni gompa* (nunnery) leads to the lake, which attracts pilgrims of all faiths. Legend has it that if a leaf drops onto the lake's surface, a guardian bird swoops down and picks it up, thereby maintaining the purity of the water. A path up from beyond the police station in the bazaar, leads to the small Khecheopalri *gompa* (1km) that serves a scattered farming community occupying the plateau above the lake, with great views of Mount Pandim (6691m). The village **home-stays** and natural serenity make this place to linger for a day or more and walks include those to sacred caves such as **Dufuk**.

INFORMATION   KHECHEOPALRI

Transport There are irregular jeep services to Pelling and Yuksom.

Accommodation Although there is some basic accommodation around Kecheopalri's tiny bazaar, the best places are the homestays on the plateau above.

Eating The bazaar has a couple of basic restaurants serving local cuisine.

Guides Guides are available for exploring the area and charge around ₹500/day.

ACCOMMODATION

Family Guest House (Trekkers Hut) Kecheopalri Bazaar ☎97330 76496. Basic yet pleasant and friendly hostel 300m before the bazaar with shared bathrooms and vegetarian meals (₹100) on order. They provide information on the area and arrange guides. **₹300**

★ **Lake View Nest Home-stay** Kecheopalri Gompa ☎95939 76635. For reservations contact Deepen Pradhan at Hotel Kabur, Pelling ☎97359 45589. Welcoming home-stay on the plateau, with comfortable rooms and a modern shared bathroom downstairs. Wholesome food and great views and a glimpse of pastoral life

abound. Chumden, the owner, will organize guides and give advice on walks in the region. To get there turn right once in the hamlet and walk a slightly descending trail for 200m; price includes meals. **₹650**

Pala Home-stay Kecheopalri Gompa (contact through Lake View Nest home-stay). Near the gompa, the lama owner, Chumden's father, offers traditional wooden chalet rooms and shared bathrooms; he also organizes meditation courses. One of several home-stays around the hamlet; price includes meals. **₹500**

Yoksum

The sleepy, spread-out hamlet of **YOKSUM** at the end of the road and at the entrance to the Rathong Chu gorge, 40km north of Pemayangtse, holds a special place in Sikkimese history. This was the spot where three lamas converged from different directions across the Himalayas to enthrone the first religious king of Sikkim, Chogyal Phuntsog Namgyal, in

WEST SIKKIM HIGH-ALTITUDE TREKS

Two **high-altitude treks** are currently allowed in Sikkim. The first, from **Yoksum** to **Dzongri**, in the shadow of Kanchenjunga, passes through huge tracts of forest and provides incredible mountain vistas; all-inclusive rates from a decent agency are from around $50 per head per day including **permits**. The second, the **Singalila Ridge**, explores the remote high pastures of the Singalila frontier range with breathtaking views of the massif. Trekkers for either of the two must have special permits (see box, p.810) and travel in groups of at least two organized by authorized agencies (see box, p.814). For general advice on trekking equipment and health issues, see Basics, p.56.

THE DZONGRI TRAIL

Although Dzongri is the junction of several trails, the prescribed route onwards leads to **Goecha La** via Zemanthang and Samiti Lake. Well-marked and dotted with basic accommodation, the trail, also used by yak herders, is at its best in May when the rhododendrons bloom.

DAY 1 It takes approximately 6hr to climb the 16km from **Yoksum** (1780m) to **Tsokha** (3048m). The forested trail begins gently before arriving at the Parekh Chu above its confluence with the Rathong. The next 4.5km involve a knee-grinding ascent, entering the lichen zone and cloud forests, past the *Forest Rest House* at **Bakhim** (2684m) to the Tibetan yak herders' settlement of Tsokha where there are a couple of trekkers huts.

DAY 2 This day can be spent acclimatizing yourself to the altitude at Tsokha, perhaps with a 5km trek towards Dzongri, to a watchtower for superb views of Kanchenjunga and Pandim.

DAY 3 The 11km section from **Tsokha** to **Dzongri** (4030m) takes at least 5hrs, rising through beautiful pine and rhododendron forests to **Phedang Meadows** (3450m), before continuing to the hut at Dzongri.

DAY 4 Once again, it's worth staying around Dzongri for further acclimatization. This gives you the opportunity to climb Dzongri Hill above the hut for views of Kanchenjunga's craggy south summit and the black rocky tooth of Kabur, a holy mountain towering above Dzongri La (4400m), a pass that leads to the HMI base camp 12km away at Chaurikhang and the Rathong Glacier (a recommended variation).

DAY 5 The 8km trek from **Dzongri** to **Thangsing** (3841m) takes around 4hrs, descending against an incredible backdrop of peaks to a rhododendron forest, crossing a bridge and continuing through woods to the *Trekkers Hut* at **Thangsing** at the end of a glacial valley.

DAY 6 The 10km short, sharp shock up to **Samiti Lake** (4303m) takes around 3hrs through alpine meadows traversing glacial moraine before arriving at the emerald-green **Samiti Lake** (local name Sungmoteng Tso). If you are still going strong, you could continue to **Zemanthang** (4453m) where there's a trekkers hut.

DAY 7 The climax of the trek, and also its most difficult section by far simply due to its high altitude. From **Samiti Lake**, the 14km roundtrip climb takes around 4hrs up to **Goecha La** and 2–3hrs back down again. The trail follows glacial moraine to Zemanthang, before a final grinding rise following cairns and the occasional prayer flag to the narrow defile at Goeche La (5000m), where Kanchenjunga South is clearly visible on a clear day.

DAY 8 Most of the long 24km hike from **Samiti Lake** back to **Tsokha** is downhill and takes around 8hrs, involving a short cut after the bridge to avoid Dzongri. There are several variations to this finish.

THE SINGALILA RIDGE

Itineraries for **Singalila Ridge** treks range between ten and nineteen days and though more expensive due to the area's remoteness, they prove exceptionally rewarding, with views from Everest to the huge Kanchenjunga massif ahead. It's best done from south to north facing the views as the trail rises towards the snows through remote alpine pastures and past hidden lakes. The most common variations starts from the road head at **Uttarey** (1965m), 28km to the west of Pelling and ascends to **Chewabhanjang** (3170m) on the Sikkim–Nepal frontier. Thereafter, the trail rarely descends below 3500m, high above the tree line and past several lakes; the highest point of the trail is the **Danfeybhir Tar**, a pass at 4400m. The route descends to **Gomathang** (3725m), a yak-herders' shelter on the banks of the Boktochu, then passes through a delightful forests of silver fir and rhododendron before arriving at the welcome sight of the bungalow at **Dzongri** connecting with the main trekking trails.

15

1642. Named the "Great Religious King", he established Tibetan Buddhism in Sikkim. Lhatsun Chenpo is supposed to have buried offerings in Yoksum's **Norbugang Chorten**, a vast white stupa built with stones and earth from different parts of Sikkim, to be found in **Norbugang Park** (1km), which also houses the **Coronation Throne**, a simple stone throne of the first chogyal. In front of the throne, a large footprint embedded in a rock belongs to one of the lamas. Disappointing today, **Kathok Lake**, a small scummy pond nearby at the top end of town, was also part of the original ceremony.

The village's main role these days is as the start of the high-altitude **Dzongri Trail**, but unless you have a trekking permit, you're not supposed to venture any further and the authorities are quite vigilant. So long as you're not carrying a backpack they may allow a day-trip along the main trail to the Parekh Chu and its confluence with the Rathong Chu – a 28km roundtrip.

Dubdi Monastary

High above Yoksum, prayer flags announce the site of the **Dubdi Monastery**, built in 1701 and one of the oldest monasteries in Sikkim. To get here, walk past the bazaar to the hospital at the top of the village. The road ends here and a path threads past water-wheels and a small river and rises through the forest to arrive at the *gompa* on an expansive shelf. It's best to enquire in the bazaar or the KCC office (see box opposite) before you set out as it's often shut.

By jeep There are no buses to or from Yoksum itself, but the regular jeep services (book the night before at the bazaar) start early (6.30–7.30am) to Gyalshing (₹100) via Tashiding (₹50), Pelling (₹100), Jorethang (₹120) and to Gangtok (₹220) via Ravangla; you're unlikely to get any shared transport after 1pm.

Information Kangchendzonga Conservation Committee (KCC), Gompa Rd (see box opposite) (daily 10am–4pm) provide information and will assist with home-stays and other travel-related enquiries.

Internet Available at the Community Information Centre (₹50/hr) above the bazaar.

Trekking Of the few operators Raj Gurung, Red Panda in the bazaar (☎97331 96470) is a knowledgeable, enthusiastic and experienced operator who rose through the ranks and knows the area well. He can arrange Dzongri Trail permits with two days notice and is reasonably priced at $40/head for two. He can also arrange local guides (₹250). Also enquire at KCC.

ACCOMMODATION AND EATING

Most options are around the small market area. The KCC (see box opposite) at the Visitors Information Centre, at the head of town (☎9832 452527) organizes several **home-stays** (from ₹600 including food) around the village. Besides hotel restaurants, the only other **places to eat** are cafés – such as the popular *Guptas* and the friendly *Yak* – along the main drag, which serve snacks and basic meals.

Pemathang ☎90020 90180. Approaching Yoksum's tiny market, this guesthouse offers a range of clean, airy rooms most with attached bathrooms, and a small but picturesque garden; there is a trekking agency next door. **₹400**

Tashi Gang ☎99330 07720. Just above the bazaar, the oldest and still the best of Yoksum's mid-range hotels is now being thoroughly and tastefully revamped amalgamating traditional Sikkimese style with modern amenities; it also has a decent restaurant. **₹1980**

Wild Orchid ☎03595 241212. A rustic traditional house, centrally located, that offers basic budget rooms with shared bathrooms. **₹300**

Yuksam Residency ☎99331 33330. This central and plush hotel in the bazaar has a bit too much marble for a mountain village and can feel cold. It has a strong Buddhist theme and offers a high level of comfort with the more expensive rooms offering more warmth, clad in wood. **₹3200**

Tashiding

Considered the holiest in Sikkim, the beautiful *gompa* of **Tashiding** occupies the point of a conical hill 19km southeast of Yoksum, high above the confluence of the Rangit and the Rathong. "The Devoted Central Glory" was built in 1717, after a rainbow was

CONSERVATION AND THE KANCHENJUNGA NATIONAL PARK

Established in 1996 with the help of the Sikkim Biodiversity and Ecotourism Project, the **Khangchendzonga Conservation Committee** (KCC) aims to promote ecological awareness to locals and visitors alike. The KCC's main concern is the impact of tourism on the fabric of the **Kanchenjunga National Park**, and their methods include planting trees, involving local participation in the planning and organizing clean-up campaigns. Conservation has also been embraced by the Sikkim government, which has put in place a code of conduct, banning the use of wood for fuel in preference to kerosene; however, wood fires continue to be part and parcel of the Sikkim landscape. KCC initiatives include keeping trails clean, promoting eco-awareness, training local workers as porters and guides, and organizing self-help initiatives. For more information on the KCC, contact their coordinator Pema Chewang Bhutia at Visitors Information & Bioliverity Centre, Gompa Road, Yoksum (☎03595 241 211, ☎9832 452527 & ☎9733 158268, ✉kcc_sikkim@hotmail.com); they also arrange low-altitude trail **guides** for ₹500 a day.

seen to connect the site to Kanchenjunga. While a new road has eaten its way through the forest to the monastery, the climb is still recommended – the well-marked path leaves the main road near an impressive *mani* wall (inscribed with the mantra *Om mani padme hum*: "Hail the jewel in the lotus" in silver paint) and leads steeply past rustic houses and fields and along a final flag-lined approach. On the fifteenth day of the first month of the Tibetan New Year, devotees from all over Sikkim gather in Tashiding for the **Nyingmapa Bhumchu festival**, when they are blessed with the holy water from an ancient bowl said by legend never to dry up. Oracles consult the water's level to determine the future.

On the increasingly popular **monastery trail**, Tashiding provides a good base from which to explore the **treks** along watershed of Mt Narsing and the Rangit River, with several holy lakes and caves a few days walk away (see box, p.823).

ARRIVAL AND DEPARTURE

TASHIDING

By jeep Leaving from the bottom of the main street of Tashiding's tiny Senik Bazaar, 2km below the monastery, one or two timetabled jeeps (7–9am) and a handful of unscheduled jeeps connect Tashiding to Yoksum (₹40), Legship (₹40), Gyalshing (₹90) and one at noon to Gangtok (₹180). The last regular shared jeeps depart at 9am.

On foot Several trails through the forests and along

stretches of roads, make trekking an alternative option to public transport; the route to Yuksom climbs up to Sinon Gompa before traversing high ground while the route to Pelling descends to Sakyung before a final relentless climb; you can also walk to Ravangla via Borong and Ralang. For more detail and numerous other trekking possibilities including guides, consult Sanu at her home-stay.

ACCOMMODATION AND EATING

Accommodation around Tashiding's Senik Bazaar is generally disappointing, though there are some fabulous home-stays on the footpath up to the monastery and some in the monastery compound itself. The bazaar has a handful of local cafés.

Mount Siniolchu Guesthouse ☎97333 42511. At the top end of the bazaar, this simple guesthouse with wood rooms, plain beds and shared baths downstairs, is a welcoming place and close to cafés and a short walk from the taxi stand at the crossroads. ₹200

★ **Sanu Homestay** ☎96350 60062, ✉sanubhutia @rocketmail.com. Just 300m uphill through the entrance gates, this brilliant village home-stay in the monastery community, offers a warm welcome and good home-cooking from an organic garden. There are just three wonderful rooms with a shared bath outside that features hot showers but squat toilets. Sanu is a font of knowledge for the area and can help arrange treks, guides or just

directions for those wanting to go it alone. Her sister Sonam next door runs a similar home-stay and there are more uphill. ₹400

Tashiding Lodge ☎03595 243249. Handy for both the taxi stand and the walk up to the monastery, between the market and the gates, this budget lodge has some rooms with good views but shared bathrooms, and there are cafés in the vicinity. ₹300

Yatri Niwas Tourist Lodge ☎98326 23654. A good location near the gates, this government lodge offers a degree of comfort, with large all with attached baths and hot water and food to order. There is a pleasant garden though there is a distinct lack of atmosphere. ₹400

North Sikkim

A fragile road etches its way up the Teesta valley and splits at Chungthang with one branch bearing northwest to Lachung and beyond, the other due north to Lachung, to the beautiful valley of Yumthang and eventually Zero Point on the high plateau.

The huge **earthquake** of 2011, with its epicentre near the capital Mangan, severed the roads to north Sikkim leaving over sixty people dead. To make matters worse, unexpected late-season rains a year later in 2012 caused deadly **landslides** that once again isolated the region for several weeks.

INFORMATION

Monsoons Every year throughout the monsoon, landslides take out stretches of road, making travel even more tedious – at the height of the tourist season around five hundred jeeps battle their way up and down the tortuous and inadequate roads to and from Gangtok.

Permits Access much of spectacular North Sikkim is restricted: visitors are allowed in only with the necessary permits, and some areas along the borders remain completely out of bounds. Groups armed with Protected Area Permits (see box, p.810) can go as far north as Thangu

past Lachung, at the edge of the plateau; only Indians – similarly armed – can travel further on to the spectacular lake of Gurudongma, near the source of the Teesta on the Tibetan plateau. North of Mangan, foreigners are only allowed up in groups of two or more, and the jeep safaris are sold inclusive of transport and accommodation, with the choices in the hands of tour operators. In general, permits for North Sikkim (extendable through the Superintendent of Police in Mangan) are only good for five days and a further seven for trekking.

Mangan

Travelling north past Phodong, the highway reaches the town of **MANGAN**, 67km north of Gangtok, the district capital of North Sikkim perched high above the Teesta valley. Recovering after the devastating earthquake of 2011 which all but demolished the bazaar and destroyed **Rinzing Gompa**, Mangan is nevertheless a convenient stop on an arduous route to the north. The town itself has little interest other than its busy bazaar, a handful of hotels and the District Headquarters, 2km above town, a relatively easy place to get a **permit** if you haven't already picked one up in Gangtok.

INFORMATION   MANGAN

Tours and permits Contact Khangri Treks & Tours of Gangtok (☎ 03592 226050) to arrange trekking guides,

permits and information on the area.

ACCOMMODATION AND EATING

Tamarind ☎ 03592 234297 & ⓦ tamarindhotels.in. Mid-market splendour bang in the centre of town with marble lobbies, a good vegetarian restaurant, internet access and large spotless rooms with modern plumbing. It

also accepts credit cards. ₹**2700**

Tshana Residency ☎ 94344 45079. On the highway, this welcoming family home with traditional wood-lined rooms offers modern facilities and the rates include meals. ₹**2200**

Dzongu

Few visit the magnificent, untouched valley and pristine heart of Sikkim – the Lepcha homeland of **Dzongu**, that branches northwest from Mangan towards Kanchenjunga. At the heart of the valley, the ancient *gompa* of **Tholung**, devastated by the 2011 earthquake, has been re-housed in a new *gompa* and is home to ancient treasures of the Chogyals; these are displayed every three years to the public with the next exhibition, known as Kamsel, due in January 2015. Few roads penetrate Dzongu and the only way to get to Tholung is on foot from the road-head (20km, 5hr). A few good **home-stays** allow visitors to explore the pastoral life of the region abundant with forest walks, challenging **treks** and **mountain bike** trails. A five-day trek starts at Lingza and passes through Tholung, Thizon and across **Kyeshong La** (3790m) taking in the best of Dzongu.

Homestays themselves are able to provide all logistics from Mangan including transport and there is an official price list and rates covering the entire itinerary.

Dzongu Lee Lingdong ☎96098 64255, ✉reepjong @gmail.com, ⊛dzongulee.com. A comfortable Lepcha family home in traditional style with modern amenities offering five guest rooms, wholesome food, and a variety of village and forest walks and activities including mountain biking arranged.; there are hot springs nearby. Price is all-inclusive. ₹3000

Mayal Lang Passingdan ☎94344 46088, ⊛mayal lyang.com. A traditional mountain home with all-inclusive simple colourful rooms, shared bathroom and with a lush garden; treks and walks arranged. ₹3000

Sohar Dho Tingvong ☎98002 54465, ✉dupdenl @yahoo.com. Nestling amongst the terraced fields with a backdrop of forests and mountain views, this welcoming family home offers comfortable rooms, good food and trekking services, and full-board is included. ₹3000

Lachung and around

Forty kilometres north of Mangan lies **CHUNGTHANG**, set in a deep valley that sees little sunlight, a grubby town with a destructive hydro-electric project at the confluence of the Teesta and Lachung rivers. The road forks here with the one to the right climbing rapidly to the group of small settlements of **LACHUNG**, the "big pass", a mere fifteen kilometres west of Tibet. Across the river from the main cluster of settlement, **Lachung Monastery** is a two-storey Tibetan-style *gompa* belonging to the Nyingmapa sect worth visiting especially for its wonderful murals. The Bhotia people of Lachung and Lachen practise a unique social system known as *Dzumsa* – a sort of gathering of elders that controls everything from grazing rights to law and order.

As the road north ascends past yak pastures, it enters the **Shingba -Rhododendron Sanctuary** announcing the start of **Yumthang** (3645m), 25km north of Lachung, with spectacular rock and ice pinnacles towering to 6000m on either side. This beautiful tree lined valley does not have accommodation but boasts somewhat neglected hot sulphur springs. A pleasant purpose-made **walking trail** leads 10km along the valley floor, back to the sanctuary gates – due to the high altitude and problems with acclimatization, descent rather than ascent is recommended. Past Yumthang, the road continues up the valley and emerges on the high plateau land at **Yumesamdong** or **Zero Point** (the end of the road), at an altitude of 4770m with a backdrop, weather permitting, of the snowy sentinels along the Tibet border.

Lachen and around

The other road from Chungthang leads 26km to **LACHEN** and a further 36km to **THANGU**, tantalizingly close to the Tibetan plateau and as far as foreign tourists are allowed to go. This is the route to the sacred **Gurudongma Lake**, considered blessed by Guru Rinpoche and the source of the River Teesta, set against a spectacular backdrop of icy peaks. A short day-hike (5km each way) from Thangu (no special trekking permit needed) leads to the picturesque **Chopta Valley** (4400m).

Several interesting **high-altitude treks** are now open to group tours in this isolated region, including the challenging **Lachen to Green Lake** (4850m) trek, which takes nine days there and back, and offers great views of Mount Siniolchu (6887m) across the Zemu glacier and the gigantic east face of Kanchenjunga. You'll need to make your plans well in advance however, with red tape invariably proving a dampener.

15

The Northeast

KAZIRANGA NATIONAL PARK

The Northeast

The least explored, most mysterious and arguably the most beautiful region of India, the Northeast, known as the "Seven Sisters", is connected to the rest of the country by a narrow stretch of land between Bhutan and Bangladesh, and was all but sealed off from the outside world until relatively recently. Arunachal Pradesh shares an extremely sensitive frontier with Chinese-occupied Tibet and, together with Nagaland, Manipur and Mizoram, a 1600km-long border with Myanmar.

Many insurgencies, caused by a vast ethnic diversity, have fractured the region since Independence, with tribal groups pushing for autonomy as well as fighting each other. A huge influx of Bangladeshis in the last decade and the displacement of many indigenous people has created further tension. Though there has been improvement in security in some areas, others remain disturbed with occasional clashes and armed conflict on the fringes. Permits (see p.839) are required for travel in certain regions, notably Arunachal Pradesh, while some other areas, such as the Manipur hills and Nagaland's eastern fringes, remain highly volatile. Tourists, however, are not a target of violence and the extraordinary diversity of peoples and spectacular landscapes make a visit to the region well worth the effort. One of the world's wettest monsoon belts, the area also boasts an astounding array of flora and fauna, estimated to represent fifty percent of India's entire biodiversity.

Until the 1960s the region comprised just two states, the North East Frontier Agency, now Arunachal Pradesh, and Assam, but separatist pressures further divided it into the seven states, now officially joined by an eighth – Sikkim. **Assam** consists of the flat, low-lying Brahmaputra valley. Its capital, **Guwahati**, boasts two of India's most important ancient temples and is the gateway to the region, while an encounter with a one-horned rhino in the magnificent **Kaziranga National Park** is a highlight of any trip to the Northeast.

The other six states occupy the surrounding hills, and are quite distinct from the rest of India in landscape, climate and peoples. **Meghalaya** has beautiful lakes and includes the wettest places on earth, Cherrapunjee and Mawsynram. Its capital, **Shillong**, retains some of the colonial atmosphere from its days as east India's summer capital. Majestic **Arunachal Pradesh**, one of India's most remote states, is inhabited by a fascinating range of peoples, many of Tibetan origin. In the state's northwestern corner, close to Bhutan, lies the Buddhist monastery of **Tawang**, in sight of the mountainous border with Tibet, while in the far northeast is the remote wilderness of **Namdapha National Park**. To the south, the lush mountains of **Nagaland** are home to fourteen distinctive tribal groups. **Mizoram**, in the Lushai hills, is predominantly Christian and has one of the highest literacy rates in India.

Manipur is perhaps the most fractured of all the Northeast states and unsafe for travel off the beaten track (see p.841), wracked by numerous insurgencies and inter-factional disputes. **Tripura**, on the other hand, with its long history of insurgency, is far more settled today, with plans a for major rail link and an improved road system; you are still

Highlights

❶ **Tea tourism, Assam** Stay at one of the grand bungalows to get a taste of the lifestyle of a plantation owner. **See p.845**

❷ **Kaziranga National Park, Assam** Spot the rare one-horned rhino on a dawn elephant ride or take a jeep safari deep into the jungle where, with luck, you can see wild elephant or indeed, the elusive tiger. **See p.846**

❸ **Majuli Island, Assam** Fascinating Hindu monasteries, nurturing a unique way of life and artistic traditions, on one of the world's largest river islands. **See p.847**

❹ **Tawang Monastery, Arunachal Pradesh** In a remote corner that was once Tibet, the largest Buddhist monastery in India maintains an ancient, unbroken tradition. The quiet chapel commemorating the sixth Dalai Lama lies close by. **See p.857**

❺ **Namdapha National Park, Arunachal Pradesh** A beautiful and remote wildlife park in the far northeastern corner of the state, bordering Burma, with habitat ranging from the steamy foothills to the snow line, home to a huge variety of wildlife including the Hoolock gibbon and elusive big cats. **See p.859**

❻ **Hornbill Festival, Nagaland** An unmissable occasion and the highlight of the Northeast calendar, bringing together all the Naga tribes in their finery with music, dance and martial art displays. **See p.860**

HIGHLIGHTS ARE MARKED ON THE MAP ON P.838

THE NORTHEAST

HIGHLIGHTS

1 Tea tourism, Assam

2 Kaziranga National park, Assam

3 Majuli Island, Assam

4 Tawang monastery, Arunachal Pradesh

5 Namdapha National park, Arunachal Pradesh

6 Hornbill Festival, Nagaland

N

CHINA
(TIBET
AUTONOMOUS
REPUBLIC)

Siang River

West Siang River

Siang River

Dihong River

Lohit River

DANAKOSHA

Tuting

Roing

Parasuram-kund

Bhismaknagar

Tezu

NAMDAPHA
NATIONAL
PARK

5

Namsai

Miao

Pasighat

Along

Oiramghat

Murkong Selek

DIBRU SAIKHOWA
NATIONAL PARK

Digboi

NH 37

ARUNACHAL
PRADESH

Daporijo

Tinsukia

Margherita

Ledo

Dibrugarh

Ziro

Sibsagar

Mon

MYANMAR
(BURMA)

6

North
Lakhimpur

Harmuti

Itanagar

Naharlagun

Majuli

3

Nimatighat

Jorhat

NAGALAND

Dirang

Munna

Sela Pass

Bangachang

Tawang

4

Bomdila

Rupa

Tipi

Kalaktang

Bhalukpong

Sangrua

Bokakhat

Mokokchung

Tuensang

Mt Saramati

Wokha

NAMERI
NATIONAL
PARK

Tezpur

Nagaon

KAZIRANGA
NATIONAL PARK

2

Dimapur

Tuophena

Kohima

Khonoma

Kisama

Ukhrul

BHUTAN

Brahmputra

Nalbari

Madan
Kamdev

Lumding

ASSAM

1

Maibong

MANIPUR

MANAS
NATIONAL
PARK

Hajo

Sualkuchi

Guwahati

Nartiang

Cachar
Hills

Imphal

Loktak
Lake

Barpeta

NH 31

Lake
Baraponi

Jowai

Jaintia
Hills

Haflong

Moirang

KEIBUL LAMJAO
NATIONAL PARK

Shillong

Mawphlang

NH-44

Mawlynnong

Khasi
Hills

Dawki

Silchar

Mawsynram

Cherrapunjee

Tamabil

MEGHALAYA

GARO
HILLS

Williamnagar

Siju

Baghmara

Sylhet

Lalaghat

Dharmanagar

Kailashahar

Kolasib

Tura

Kumarghat

Aizawl

Champhai

Unakoti

TRIPURA

MIZORAM

NH 54

BANGLADESH

Akhaura

Agartala

Udaipur

SEPAHIJALA
NATURE RESERVE

Neermahal

Dhaka

Comilla

CHITTAGONG
HILL TRACTS

Noakhali

Chittagong

0   100
kilometres

The International boundaries on this map are neither purported to
be correct nor authentic by Survey of India Publisher.

advised to exercise caution if travelling in the eastern hills. The people of Manipur are closely related to the neighbouring Burmese population, while Tripura, bordered by Bangladesh on three sides having been cut off from the Bangladeshi plains during the 1947 Partition, is distinctly Bengali to the west with the hill tribes to the east.

The best **time to visit** the Northeast is from November to April, although the high mountain areas are extremely cold by December and anywhere in the hills can get cold; winter fog can disrupt journeys in Upper Assam. It rains heavily from May to the end of September. In two weeks you could travel from West Bengal to Guwahati, Shillong and Kaziranga, while three weeks would be enough to cover the main sights of Assam and Meghalaya. A month would enable you to enjoy the two most beautiful and

---

ACCESS, PERMITS AND TOUR OPERATORS

Although the region is gradually opening up for tourism, **regulations** can change according to the current state of security, so check the latest information with the Indian Embassy, Consulate, Tourist Office or visa agency before travelling. However, it is best to get any permit while in India through a tour operator (see below) or through an agent in Guwahati – allow two days to arrange all necessary paper work and travel arrangements.

PERMITS

Currently **Arunachal Pradesh** is the only one of the seven states that requires both Indian and foreign visitors to obtain **Restricted** or **Protected Area Permits** ($50 for a maximum of thirty days) prior to entry. Parties should theoretically consist of a minimum of two accompanied by a travel agent though, in practice, the other person may have been "delayed"; allow up to three working days to obtain the permit. **Nagaland**, **Mizoram** and **Manipur** currently only require registration on arrival at the entry point at the border and again with the Superintendent of Police within 24 hours of arrival. Indian nationals do require Inner Line Permits for Nagaland (₹50), Mizoram (₹120) and Arunachal Pradesh (₹25) prior to entry; those Indians travelling to Mizoram by road will also need an ILP but for those arriving by air, permits are issued on arrival.

Make several **photocopies** of your passport and permits while travelling through the region. To obtain **Inner Line Permits**, Indian citizens should apply with two passport photographs to representatives of the state governments concerned. Applications should only take a day to process, and can be extended for up to six months in the relevant state capital. Passes are valid for the full period they are allocated for, no matter how many times you enter and exit a state, but in practice, especially for Arunachal, you may find yourself negotiating with border guards.

RECOMMENDED TOUR OPERATORS

The following operators are able to provide detailed itineraries along with any necessary permits.

Explore Nagaland Greenwood Villa, Kigwema, Nagaland ☎09856 343037, ⊛explorenagaland.com. Well-organized and informative tour operator whose services range from arranging local guides to entire itineraries.

Gurudongma Tours & Treks *Gurudongma Lodge*, Kalimpong, West Bengal ☎03552 255204, ⊛gurudongma.com. Highly professional team arranging tours, trekking, mountain-biking, tribal and wildlife holidays with particular expertise in birdwatching trips (⊛allindiabirding.com).

Himalayan Footprints (About Himalayas) Kolkata ☎09830 033896, ✉info@abouthimalayas.com. Specializing in wildlife and adventure tours, they have an excellent network throughout the

Northeast including Sikkim, working closely with local partners.

Himalayan Holidays Bomdila ☎03782 222017 or ☎09436 045063, ⊛himalayan-holidays.net. They specialize in western Arunachal and Tawang but have a good network throughout the northeast.

Jungle Travels India GNB Rd, Silpukhuri, Guwahati, Assam ☎0361 266 0890, ⊛jungletravelsindia.com. Guwahati-based agent organizing excellent group and tailor-made tours, including luxury cruises.

Purvi Discovery Jalannagar, Dibrugarh, Assam ☎0373 230 1120, ⊛purviweb.com. Upmarket and efficient operator that specializes in tea tours as well as wildlife, fishing, golf, riding and tribal culture.

16

remote states, Arunachal Pradesh and Nagaland. To take in all the states together, including Mizoram, you'll need considerably longer.

Assam

Assam is dominated by the mighty **River Brahmaputra**, and its vast, lush valley sandwiched between the Himalayan foothills to the north and the Meghalayan hills and plateau to the south. An attractive state carpeted by plantations, forests and paddy fields, Assam is one of India's few **oil** regions, and produces around sixty percent of the nation's **tea**. However, the industry is not as profitable as it once was, and for the marginalized *baganiyas* (tea workers), mainly *adivasis* – tribal people brought in from central India by the British to work as indentured labourers on the plantations – depressingly little has changed since colonial times.

Social divisions and ethnic strife have lead to long-term **instability** in the state. The separatist group United Liberation Front of Asom (**ULFA**) began an armed struggle for independence in 1985, and in the early 1990s Assamese nationalism sparked opposition from Bodos, Cachars and other ethnic minorities. Bangladeshi migration into Assam has been a bone of contention for indigenous Assamese, resulting in the deadly clashes of 2012 between migrant Bangladeshis and Bodos that left several dead in the western districts of the state. Despite the seemingly unsurmountable ethnic tensions, occasional violence reported in the press, *bandh*s and political in-fighting, the situation has vastly improved along with the infrastructure. More and more visitors are enjoying the delights of **wildlife** and **tea tourism** as tourists are rarely embroiled in the strife that underlies the social fabric of Assam.

Guwahati

The state capital, **GUWAHATI** (or Gauhati), lies on the banks of the mighty **Brahmaputra**. Although some of the old town still retains its character, Guwahati is a rapidly expanding city of shopping malls and heaving bazaars and as it is the main gateway to the region you will probably need to stay here for a night or two. Guwahati's main attractions are the **Kamakhya**, **Navagraha** and **Umananda** temples, while northwest of the city are the silk village of **Sualkuchi**, the pilgrimage site of **Hajo** and **Manas National Park**.

As the main hub for the region's lucrative tea industry, Guwahati's **Assam Tea Auction Centre** at Dispur is the largest trade centre in the world for the CTC (crush, tear and curl) tea so characteristic of Assam; visits require prior permission from the Senior Manager (☏0361 233 1845). Elsewhere, the bustling markets of **Paltan Bazaar**, **Pan Bazaar** and **Fancy Bazaar**, Guwahati's main shopping areas, are bunched in the centre on either side of the railway, with the older residential areas north of the tracks spread along the riverside. Assamese **silk**, wooden rhinos and other crafts are sold at several shops on GNB Road, including at the **State Emporium**.

The temples of Kamakhya, Navagraha and Umananda

On the commanding Nilachal Hill, overlooking the river 8km west of the centre, the important Kali temple of **Kamakhya**, with its beehive-shaped *shikhara*, is a good example of the distinctive Assamese style of architecture. As one of the *shakti pithas*, it marks the place where Sati's yoni (vulva) landed when her body fell to earth in 51 pieces. As at many of the *shakti* temples of Assam, Kamakhya maintains a strong tradition of *bali* (animal sacrifice) usually around noon. You can get here from Kacheri by bus or in a Trekker (shared taxi; ₹15).

East of the centre, on a wooded hill popular with monkeys, the single-domed **Navagraha** temple – the "temple of the nine planets", an ancient seat of astrology and

16

WARNINGS AND TRAVEL ADVICE

If travelling to Manipur, you are advised to the services of a local travel agent who can ensure smooth travel as well as make any security arrangements necessary (see box, p.866). Nagaland has had a long-term insurgency issue, which only rarely affects the main areas but is still rife along the eastern border with Burma. Sporadic violence does plague Assam as well, where the western districts around Kokrajhar have been devastated by ethnic clashes between Bangladeshi migrants and Bodos in 2012. The entire region is prone to wildcat strikes known as *bandhs* (lockouts) when shops, restaurants and public transport shut down – do check before and while travelling. Avoid driving any distance at night, even through Assam, due to the threat of banditry often in the guise of insurgency.

GENERAL ADVICE

Although the **roads** in the Assam valley are being gradually modernized along the southern shores of the Brahmaputra, elsewhere and especially in the hills and mountains of the Northeast, the roads are generally in a terrible state and journeys can prove tedious and painfully slow. **Trains** along the valley from Guwahati to Upper Assam and Dimapur are reasonable, and there are a handful of fast trains. **Flights** are the most convenient mode of travel, with major airports at Guwahati, Agartala (Tripura), Aizawl (Mizoram), Dibrugarh, Silchar, Dimapur and Imphal. At the time of going to press, the useful but ageing **helicopter** service run by Pawan Hans was grounded following a spate of accidents. If and when the helicopter service passes its airworthiness certificate, it will provide the most convenient method of travelling to the interior, especially around Arunachal Pradesh which has some of the worst roads in the country. Larger groups could consider chartering flights through Northeast Shuttles (☎033 2567 6284, ⓦnortheastshuttles.com) for some airports. Some of the **ferries** along the Brahmaputra are useful, especially those connecting Majuli Island with the north and south shores of the Brahmaputra, while upmarket cruises provide a languid and leisurely way of discovering the river and surrounding areas.

Arranging **car rental** makes sense but for the mountains of Arunachal ensure you rent a large vehicle such as a Sumo or Bolero. **Money changing** facilities are few and far between outside Guwahati; larger destinations such as state capitals do have **ATM**s but you should travel with enough cash just in case.

16

astronomy – wonderful acoustics, especially in the mornings when priests chant prayers for clients in search of solace. Housed in a single red dome, the central lingam is encircled by a further eight representing the planets. Outside the temple, fortune-tellers (*jyotish*) will read your future.

The Shiva temple of **Umananda** stands on Peacock Island in the middle of the Brahmaputra. Its location atop a steep flight of steps is more dramatic than the temple itself, but you may get to see some rare golden langur monkeys. Ferries leave regularly from Kachari and Umananda Ghat (₹30 return).

ARRIVAL AND DEPARTURE   GUWAHATI

BY PLANE

Airport Guwahati's Lok-Priya Gopinath Bordoloi Airport, 18km southwest of the city centre, has regular flights to Agartala, Aizawl, Bagdogra, Delhi, Dibrugarh, Dimapur, Imphal, Jorhat, Kolkata, Lilabari, Mumbai and Silchar.

Transport A taxi to the airport costs around ₹500 (45min) – book through the pre-paid booth in the arrivals hall. ASTC's a/c airport bus connects with flights and runs to Paltan Bazaar (₹130) and Volvo Point, Ulubari (9–10 daily); alternatively, shared minibuses (₹150) leave when full from outside *Hotel Mahalaxmi*, next to *Hotel Nandan* on GS Rd.

Helicopter flights For helicopter flights to Naharlagun (near Itanagar), Shillong, Tawang and elsewhere, check with Pawan Hans (☎0361 241 6720) which was grounded at the time of going to press and undergoing stringent airworthiness tests.

BY TRAIN

The main railway station is in the town centre. Several trains link Guwahati to Delhi; the *Rajdhani Express* #12423 (Mon, Wed, Thurs, Fri & Sun 7.05am; 27hr 5min) is the fastest. For Jorhat, the *Shatabdi Express* #12067 (Mon–Sat) 6.30am; 6hr 50min) is the quickest train; it also calls at Lumding (2hr 52min) and Dimapur (4hr 15min). The *Kamrup Express*

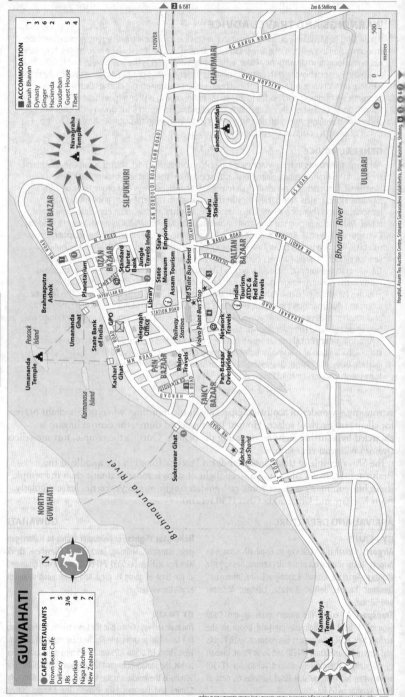

16

GUWAHATI

CAFÉS & RESTAURANTS
Brown Bean Cafe	1
Delicacy	5
JBs	3/6
Khorikaa	4
Naga Kitchen	7
New Zealand	2

■ ACCOMMODATION
Baruah Bhavan	1
Dynasty	3
Ginger	6
Hacienda	2
Suudarban	5
Guest House	4
Tibet	4

NORTH GUWAHATI

N

Brahmaputra River

Peacock Island

Umananda Temple

Karmanasa Island

Umananda Ghat

Kachari Ghat

Sukreswar Ghat

Machkowa Bus Stand

Kamakhya Temple

Navagraha Temple

UZAN BAZAR

SILPUKHURI

Brahmaputra Ashok

Planetarium

State Bank of India

GPO

Telegraph Office

Library

Railway Station

PAN BAZAR

FANCY BAZAR

Rhino Travels

Standard Charter Bank

Jungle Travels India

State Museum

Assam Tourism

State Emporium

Old State Bus Stand

Volvo Point–Bus Stop

India Tourism, ATDC & Red River Travels

Network Travels

Pan Bazaar Overbridge

Nehru Stadium

Gandhi Mandap

CHANDMARI

ULUBARI

PALTAN BAZAR

Bharalu River

RG BARUA ROAD

GN BORDOLOI ROAD (GNB ROAD)

MG ROAD

MC ROAD

LAMB ROAD

STATION ROAD

HB ROAD

GS ROAD

SOLPARA ROAD

B BARUA ROAD

BK KAKOTI ROAD

REHABARI ROAD

0   500   metres

Zoo & Shilong

Hospital, Assam Tea Auction Centre, Srimanta Sankaradeva Kalakshetra, Dispur, Basistha, Shilong

Hajo, Airport (18km), Saraighat Bridge, Sualkuchi, Manas National Park, Manas National Park & Tezpur

#15959 (daily 4.05pm; 13hr 20min) travels to Dibrugarh. For Kolkata (Howrah), the *Kamrup Express* #15960 (daily 7.50am; 22hr 20min) is a convenient option. Other important railway stations include Kamakhya Junction, where most of the main trains to the west also stop.

BY BUS

The new Inter-state Bus Terminus (ISBT) is inconveniently located on NH-37, 9km to the east. Public buses leave from here to destinations throughout the region, including Kaziranga (hourly; 5hr), Siliguri (5–7 daily; 12hr) and Tezpur (1–2 hourly; 4–5hr). Most of the private bus companies are based in hectic and chaotic Paltan Bazaar to the south of the station and at the Volvo Point, off GS Rd at Ulubari.

BY TAXI

Shared taxis and Sumos to Shillong (3hr 30min) and other destinations depart when full from the old bus stand, opposite *Hotel Tibet* in Paltan Bazaar.

INFORMATION AND TOURS

Cruises For those with time (and money), the Assam Bengal Navigation Company runs cruises on the Brahmaputra; book direct (☎0361 260 2223, �☷assambengalnavigation.com), or through Jungle Travels India (see box, p.839).

Tourist office Assam Tourism is on Station Rd next to the Tourist Lodge (daily except Sun and 2nd & 4th Sat of month: March–Oct 10am–5pm; Nov–Feb 10am–4.15pm; ☎0361 254 7102, ⓦassamtourism.org). The state's commercial wing ATDC, 4th floor, Asom Paryatan Bhavan, AK Rd, Paltan Bazaar (☎0361 263 3654) along with their Red River travel services downstairs, offers a full service including city tours, car rental, flight bookings, cruises, tours and excursions to Kaziranga and Manas; next door the India Tourism office (Mon–Fri 9.30am–5pm; ☎0361 234 1603) provides information on the Northeast and general tourism.

Tours and travel Nature Hunt, 1st floor, 96 Barthakur Mill Rd, Ulubari (☎0361 245 0330 or ☎99575 77417, ⓦnaturehunttours.com) is a young team that arranges wildlife and adventure tours. Rhino Travels, MN Rd, Pan Bazaar (☎0361 254 0666), offers a range of tours including safaris at Manas. Network Travels, Paltan Bazaar (☎0361 260 5335, ⓦnetworktravelsindia.net), arranges tours, permits and air tickets; it's also one of the region's largest private bus operators.

ACCOMMODATION

★ **Baruah Bhavan** 40 MC Rd, Uzanbazar ☎0361 254 1182, ⓦheritagehomeassam.com. A comfortable family home converted into a luxurious guesthouse with five twin rooms and one double; each room has its own theme. The roof terrace is very pleasant in the evenings and there is a garden and good home cooking. The bazaar in which it is located is close to the river and handy for an early morning stroll to the fish market. ₹2000

Dynasty SS Rd, Fancy Bazaar ☎0361 251 6021, ⓦdynastyhotel.in. Expectations are raised by the imposing palm-shaded entrance, water feature and opulent lobby, though not quite met by the smart but overpriced attached rooms. Of the four restaurants and bars, the *Tandoor* restaurant is one of the best in town and the *Roof Top* barbecue is a good spot in the evenings; there is a gym and a spa. It is bang in the middle of the bazaar, so be prepared for some noise seeping through the sealed windows. ₹6500

Ginger IHM Campus, VIP Rd, behind the Tennis Association of Assam, Borbari ☎08876 723500, ⓦgingerhotels.com. Cool branch of the swish *Tata Group* chain, with great-value, minimalist attached rooms, w-ifi, gym and modish touches like "self check-in". The location is inconvenient for the centre but handy for the route to Shillong and elsewhere. There is a restaurant and a *Café Coffee Day*. You should be able get 60 percent off of the published rate if you book online. ₹4500

★ **Hacienda** Geetanagar ☎0361 241 5555 or ☎033 2245 7389, ⓔheritagetourismindia.com. Set in immaculate grounds on a hill, this luxurious and exclusive villa belongs to one of Assam's leading industrialists and the property, full of fine art and antiques (including Chippendale furniture and bone china), represents the finest levels of hospitality. They are also able to arrange your entire Northeast itinerary with notice, and specialize in tea and wildlife tours. ₹10,000

★ **Suudarban Guest House** Just off Buddha Hall, ME Rd, Paltan Bazaar ☎0361 273 0722, ⓔsuudarbanguesthouse@yahoo.com. At the end of a lane off a strip full of small hotels, this popular and friendly place, by a canal, is the pick of the budget lodges with good-value – generally pink – attached rooms with TVs. The corridors are brightened up with houseplants, framed photos and religious posters. ₹700

Tibet AT Rd, Paltan Bazaar ☎0361 251 9815, ⓔhoteltibet@redimail.com. The best of the budget lodges clustered around the old bus station right in the centre of the bazaar, with cleanish, boxy rooms on a busy strip. It can be noisy, however, so bring earplugs. The restaurant downstairs serves good Indian, Chinese and Tibetan food. ₹299

16

EATING AND NIGHTLIFE

Most of Guwahati's mid-range and upmarket hotels have good restaurants and there are several chain restaurants and fast-food joints, mostly along the sprawling GS Rd. Make sure to try Assamese cuisine which as such as fish *tainga*, far less spice and oil than north Indian cooking. Guwahati has a fledgling music and club scene (check out *Eclectic Vibes* magazine ⓦ facebook.com/eclecticvibes).

★ **Brown Bean Cafe** HC Rd, Uzanbazaar ⓦ brownbeancafe.com. Excellent coffee shop close to the river and handy for Umananda Ghat and local markets, with plenty of reading material and a range of coffee and teas all carefully explained in the menu. The accompanying restaurant serves Chinese and European food (chilli chicken ₹210). Daily 10am–10pm.

Delicacy GS Rd, 2km south of Bharalu River. Ignore the unprepossessing location beneath an overpass, *Delicacy* is the place to come for authentic northeastern cuisine. Huge portions of duck, pigeon, pork, chicken and freshwater fish are served with unusual accompaniments like banana flowers, sesame seeds and bamboo shoots (mains from ₹120). Daily noon–3pm & 7–10pm.

JBs MG Rd, near the main ferry point. Overlooking the Brahmaputra, the trendy and popular *JBs* has a pleasant first-floor a/c restaurant with an eclectic mixed menu that ranges from traditional Indian dishes to Italian and Chinese: the rich *paneer makhani* and *paneer do-pyaza* are particularly good. Downstairs is a snack bar and bakery.

There's another branch at Christian Busti, GS Rd, just over 1km south of Bharalu River. Daily 11am–10pm.

★ **Khorikaa** Opp. Bora Service Petrol Pump, GS Rd. Legendary Assamese thali restaurant run by celebrated chef Atul Lahkar. Located upstairs, with a canteen-like atmosphere it gets packed at lunch and is a must for anyone keen to sample authentic local cuisine; try the duck with bamboo shoots (₹140). Daily noon–3pm & 7–10pm.

Naga Kitchen Opp. Pantaloons, GS Rd and opp. Doordarshan, RG Baruah Rd. Pleasant relaxed and trendy restaurant with two branches in the city, serving Chinese, seafood and, of course, Naga cuisine. Try their Naga speciality of fish, banana flowers and fern or chicken and bamboo shoots; expect to pay around ₹400/head. Daily noon–10pm.

New Zealand GNB Rd, opp. State Museum. Pleasant little café and ice cream parlour serving sundaes smoothies and frozen yogurt. You can also get sandwiches here plus puff pastries, cakes and coffees. Daily 10am–9pm.

DIRECTORY

Banks and exchange Standard Chartered Bank, GNB Rd, and the State Bank of India, MG Rd, change travellers' cheques and foreign currencies. Thomas Cook (ⓣ0361 222 9932) is on GS Rd, 3km south of Bharalu River. There are ATMs all over town, including next to Standard Chartered Bank.

Hospital Down Town Hospital (ⓣ0361 233 6906); Guwahati Medical College Hospital (ⓣ0361 252 8417).

Internet access There are numerous internet cafés (₹20–30/hr) throughout the city including I-Way on Lamb Rd and Pace Travels in Paltan Bazaar.

Police Emergencies ⓣ 100; HB Rd (ⓣ0361 254 0138).

Post office ARB Rd, just a round the corner from the State Bank of India.

Hajo and Sualkuchi

HAJO, 38km northeast of Guwahati, is a pilgrimage site for Hindus, Buddhists and Muslims, worth seeing for its mix of religious temples, including the Hindu **Hayagriba-Madhava Mandir**. Muslims believe visiting the **Poa Mecca Mosque** here four times is equivalent to a pilgrimage to Mecca. Nearby **Sualkuchi** is renowned for its golden *muga* silk, named after the rich amber colour of the *muga* cocoon, exclusive to Assam.

Manas National Park

Oct–March • ₹250 (₹50), vehicle ₹300, camera ₹500 (₹50)

MANAS NATIONAL PARK, 80km west of Guwahati on the border with Bhutan, has been on UNESCO's list of endangered World Heritage Sites since 1992. Troubled by insurgency and poachers, and plagued by development, the park's population of large mammals had sadly declined and sightings of tigers and elephants are now relatively rare. However, several rhinos have been relocated successfully from Kaziranga and a recent photographic audit between India and Bhutan counted fourteen tigers. Consisting of two ranges, Bansbari and Koklabari, Manas is well worth visiting for its varied natural beauty, with buffalo and rhino grazing on expansive stretches of sand and grass, and *sal* forests flanking the Manas River.

INFORMATION | MANAS NATIONAL PARK

Manas has a handful of **lodges** including at Mathanguri and some in the main town, **Barpeta Road**, which has good train and road links to Guwahati and transport hire for the park.

Bansbari Lodge ☎0361 260 2223, ⌨assambengal navigation.com. Close to the park gates and the most comfortable of Manas's places to stay, with full packages including food, elephant and jeep safaris and optional travel from Guwahati. Foreign visitors pay a premium (price shown here) while Indians pay around a third. ₹**7500**

Tezpur

TEZPUR, 174km northeast of Guwahati, is a busy administrative and commercial hub on the north bank of the Brahmaputra. It is a convenient and sometimes essential stop en route to Arunachal Pradesh and provides good road links to Kaziranga National Park (83km) on the south bank across the 3km long Kolia Bhomora Bridge. It is also a good place to find out about visiting Nameri National Park.

ARRIVAL AND DEPARTURE | TEZPUR

By bus Tezpur's ASTC bus stand, on Jenkins Rd, state buses to Guwahati (1–2 hourly; 4–5hr), Jorhat (hourly; 4hr), Kaziranga (hourly; 2hr) and Itanagar (1–2 daily; 5hr). An alternative transport hub for those passing through is **Mission Charali** 4km to the north. Most transport to Bhalukpong and West Himachal, Guwahati and sees points east and south across the bridge, stops here.
By Sumo/taxi Jenkins Rd is lined with Sumo stands, with daily services to Bomdila (7hr), Dirang (9hr) and Tawang (14–18hr) (a break at Bomdila or Dhirang is recommended) in west Arunachal; shared taxis also travel to Itanagar. Travel early.

INFORMATION

Post office The GPO is on Head Post Office Rd, parallel to the main road.
ATMs No banks change foreign currency, but there are plenty of ATMs.
Internet Dhungana Cyber Café in the Anjana Complex, NB Rd, 100m north of *Chinese Villa* Baliram complex, offers internet access (₹30/hr).
Tourist office The tourist office (daily except Sun and 2nd & 4th Sat of month 10am–5pm; ☎03712 221 016), is in the Prashanti *Tourist Lodge* on KP Agarwalla Rd.

ACCOMMODATION AND EATING

Baliram Complex Cnr NB and NC roads. This glass-clad complex in the bazaar has restaurants on every floor and is literally the food centre of town (a vertical food hall) with something for everyone from Indian food to ice cream. It is extremely popular in the evenings. A good place to start is *Chinese Villa* on the second floor, resplendent with red hanging lamps, where there's a separate Indian menu. Opt for the Chinese dishes (₹90–180), such as barbecued lamb. Daily 11am–10.30pm.
Basant Main Rd ☎03712 230831. A comfortable budget hotel in the centre of town that's popular with visiting businessmen. It offres decent-sized doubles but you pay a lot more for a/c. There is also a good Indian restaurant – *Usha*. ₹**450**
★ **KF Mission** Charali, 4km north of the bus station ☎03712 237825, ✉fkfood@gmail.com. Next to the busy and convenient crossroads, *KF* is a welcome surprise: immaculate, contemporary rooms with slick attached bathrooms, modern art, flatscreen TVs and tea/coffee-making facilities make this "boutique" hotel one of Assam's most stylish. There is a bright patisserie and an ice-cream parlour on the ground floor, while the smart a/c multicuisine restaurant upstairs serves Indian and Chinese food as well as pizzas and coffee – try their chicken korma and expect to pay around ₹450 for a meal. Next door, the dimly-lit and equally smart bar is a good place for a long drink after a tiring journey. ₹**2350**
Prashanti Tourist Lodge KP Agarwalla Rd ☎03712 221016. Although it has seen better days, the pleasantly located government-run lodge is still an acceptable choice, with quiet and pretty cleansimple rooms. ₹**800**
★ **Wild Mahseer** Sonitpur, 30km north of Tezpur ☎03714 234354 or ☎091670 38491, ⌨wildmahseer .com. These four luxurious colonial-era bungalows are based on the Addabari Tea Estate and are handy for the journey to Tawang. Prices include full board and activities: aside from enjoying the peace and quiet, guests can fish, cycle or hike. Good value out of season (May–Oct) Card payments are not currently accepted. ₹**5600**

16

Kaziranga National Park

A World Heritage Site covering 430 square kilometres on the southern bank of the Brahmaputra, **KAZIRANGA NATIONAL PARK**, 217km east of Guwahati, occupies a vast valley floor against a backdrop of the Karbi Anglong Hills. Its rivulets, shallow lakes and semi-evergreen forested highlands blend into marshes and flood plains covered with tall elephant grass teeming with deer and wild buffalos. However, the big draw, is the park's famous yet highly endangered one-horned **rhinos**, best observed from the back of an elephant first thing on a winter's morning. **Tiger** sightings are relatively rare, despite the park's official claim to have the highest density of tigers of any park in the world.

Jeeps take you deeper into the forest than elephants, but cannot get nearly as close to the rhinos and buffalo. The abundant birdlife includes egrets, herons, storks, fish eagles, kingfishers and a grey pelican colony.

Kaziranga is open from November to early April. Avoid visiting on Sundays, when it gets busy with noisy groups. During the monsoons (June–Sept), the Brahmaputra bursts its banks, **flooding** the low-lying grasslands and causing animals to move to higher ground within the park. In 2012, monsoon floods ravaged Kaziranga, leading to a huge death toll among the animals including several rhinos. Traditional animal migration routes have been choked by overdevelopment around Kaziranga. To compound the extreme pressures on the park, population growth has lead to **land encroachment** and **poaching** which is now endemic. In the first quarter of 2013 alone, poachers killed around sixteen rhinos for their precious horns prompting surveillance drones to be introduced. So far, the authorities have proved incapable of protecting the park.

ARRIVAL AND INFORMATION   KAZIRANGA NATIONAL PARK

Kaziranga consists of four directional ranges, with the administrative centre at Kohora. Major towns nearby include Jorhat (100km), with access to the railway network and Majuli, and Tezpur (54km) useful if you're travelling to west Arunachal.

By bus There are hourly buses to Kaziranga from Tezpur (2hr), Jorhat (1hr 30min) and Guwahati (5hr), as well as less frequent services to Dibrugarh (5–7 daily; 6hr). State and private buses all stop at Kohora, the main gate, on the NH-37 (AT Rd), with Network Travels serving as the pick-up and drop-off point.

By plane Jorhat is the nearest airport (90km; 1hr 30min) with flight connections to Guwahati and Kolkata. Taxis charge ₹2200.

Tourist information For information, visit the tourist office (☎ 03776 262423) in *Bonani*, in the *Tourist Complex*, Kohora. This is where you book park entry and rides; they will also book transport. The current tourist officer has been very pro-active in developing trekking and eco-tourism in the nearby Karbi hills.

Park entry and safaris Entrance fee ₹500 (₹50), vehicle ₹400, camera ₹500 (₹50), video ₹1000 (₹500). Elephant rides (5.30–7.30am & 3–4pm; ₹1525 (₹525)) in all four ranges of the park give priority to foreign tourists who are

made to pay a lot more and get first preference. The result is that, at the height of the season, Indians are often left out. Jeep safaris (7–9.30am & 1.30–3.30pm, ₹1300–₹2500) can be a bit cramped but go deeper into the park. Book at least the day before at the *Tourist Complex* at Kohora or ask your hotel to arrange them.

Travel and tours Horlank Namsing (☎ 78963 94105 or ☎ 98548 72861) provides guides for walks in Karbi Anglong hills and has a restaurant on a picturesque hillock overlooking a river, a short distance from the *Tourist Complex* (Danny Gam at the tourist office can give you more information). He can also arrange village homestays. Hoon of Himalayan Footprints (☎ 9954 262530 or ☎ 9830 033896) arranges tours and transport throughout the Northeast and can also arrange Arunachal Permits (see box, p.839) and transport to Bomdila and Tawang. Jungle Travels (☎ 92070 42330; ✉ info@jungletravels.in) provide exclusive, upmarket holidays around Kaziranga with multiday cruises on the Brahmaputra.

ACCOMMODATION AND EATING

Kaziranga has a large selection of places to stay with numerous "resorts" cropping up south of the main highway. Accommodation is now reaching saturation point; an alternative is to seek out one of several **homestays** around Bogorijuri. There is a selection of **restaurants** along the highway but most of the lodges and resorts have their own catering. If possible, try local **Karbi cuisine**, consisting of simple, oil-free meals cooked in bamboo containers.

16

Diphlu River Lodge Kuthuri ☎0361 266 7871, ⊛diphluriverlodge.com. Beautifully designed – rustic look, luxurious feel – cottages on stilts with a high level of service and well organized tours, safaris and boat rides; booked through the luxury brand of Assam Bengal Navigation which also offers cruises down the Brahmaputra but all for an extraordinary price; rates are almost half for Indians (shown here as per person price for foreigners) and off-season discounts are highly attractive. ₹**14000**

IORA The Retreat Kohora ☎03776 262437, ⊛kazirangasafari.com. Huge, well-organized resort with a whole range of tours including elephant and jeep rides within the park in season, and visits to tea gardens; there are restaurants, a shop, cycle hire and a spa and swimming pool. However, its 20-acre spread feels more like an upper class ghetto rather than a retreat. ₹**5100**

Nature-Hunt Eco Camp Kohara ☎09435 515011, ⊛naturehunttours.com. A young and enthusiastic team run this small resort tucked into a corner of a tea garden nursery, with rustic cottages and luxury tents with adjacent bathrooms. There is a central lounge with bonfires in the evenings, a restaurant serving local cuisine and a range of

elephant and jeep safaris on offer. Ronnie is able to provide tours throughout the Northeast and will also arrange tours to Majuli. ₹**1800**

Tourist Complex ☎03776 262429. There are four state-run lodges are in the complex, *Aranya* (₹1676) is the most comfortable, with a range of clean but characterless attached rooms with balconies or verandas, a decent restaurant and bar; *Bonani* (₹1000) has a vaguely colonial feel, large, worn rooms (some with a/c) and – unsettlingly – several animal skulls dotted around; *Bonoshree* (₹600) has tatty but acceptable doubles; *Kunjaban* is the most basic, with several dorms (₹150, plus ₹100 for bed linen) ask for one of the three-bed rooms. ₹**600**

Wildgrass ☎03776 266 2085, ⊛oldassam.com. Kaziranga's original "resort" has mellowed with age and is well worth considering with its extensive grounds containing over 200 types of plants, atmospheric lounge and cottages plus more contemporary housing; there is a restaurant and bar and a pleasant veranda. They offer well-planned tours of the park; the owner is a mine of information on the area. Rates include breakfast. ₹**2400**

16

Upper Assam

Around 310km northeast upriver from Guwahati, **Jorhat** has an airport and road connections to Kaziranga, Nagaland, Guwahati, Kolkata and northern Arunachal Pradesh. You will almost certainly have to wade through the city at some point on your trip, but for now it is noteworthy as a transport hub alone.

The unique Vaishnavite culture of **Majuli**, reputedly the world's largest river island, and **Sibsagar**, former capital of the Ahoms, are also close by. Further north, **Dibrugarh** is opening up as a gateway to northern Nagaland and eastern Arunachal Pradesh, and is full of **tea plantations** to explore. There is good birdwatching at **Dibru-Saikhowa National Park**, while **Digboi** has an interesting oil museum and war memorial.

Majuli

Within striking distance of Jorhat, **MAJULI** is often described as one of the largest inhabited river islands in the world, but **erosion** in recent years is threatening its claim and, indeed in the long run, its future. Regardless of its precise status, Majuli is a fascinating place and a true gem of the Northeast, largely because of its unique Vaishnavite *sattras* (Hindu monasteries), though it is also a haven for birdwatchers.

There are 22 *sattras* – institutions that contain elements of a temple, monastery, school and centre for the arts – on Majuli: each consists of a prayer hall (*namghar*) surrounded by living quarters for devotees, and *ghats* for bathing. Music, song and dance are essential elements of the devotional life of the *sattras* and you may be lucky enough to catch one of the performances are sometimes arranged for large that parties of visitors.

ARRIVAL AND INFORMATION   MAJULI

By ferry Ferries for Majuli's Kamalabari Ghat leave from Nimatighat (8.30am, 10.30am, 2pm, 3pm & 4pm; 2hr 30min; ₹20, vehicle ₹700), accessible by bus or taxi and shared taxi (₹30; 1hr) from Jorhat. As the ferry timings only

give you an hour or so on the island, it is inadvisable to visit as a day-trip. You'll get more out of the experience if you stay overnight, with return ferries to Nimatighat running at 7.15am, 7.30am, 8.30am, 1.30pm & 3pm. A word of warning: the ferries can get uncomfortably crowded, with people sitting on the corrugated roof and vehicles loaded on the back, and the single cabin can feel low in the water. It is also possible to travel north from Majuli, with two morning ferries from Luhitghat, 3km north of Garamur; they arrive at Khabalughat on the north bank, from where there are buses to north Lakhimpur, and from there, buses on to Itanagar or Tezpur, and a train to Guwahati.

Tour guides Tirtha Bhuyan Borgayan, Sri Sri Uttar Kamalabari Sattra (☎09401 834909, ✉tirthabhuya @gmail.com) is a *bhakat* (monk) and provides a unique insight into life in *sattras*. Jyoti Narayan Sarma, NLK Rd, Garamur (☎09435 657282, ✉majulitourism@gmail. com) is the most organized and commercial of Majuli's tour operators and can co-ordinate tours beyond the island.

Tinsukia

The gateway to the remote reaches of Upper Assam and eastern Arunachal, **TINSUKIA**, 47km east of Dibrugarh, is the commercial hub of the region, the centre for several key industries including tea. During World War II, the remarkable construction of the 1736km-long Stillwell Road, also known as the **Ledo Road**, provided a vital link with the Chinese Nationalists helping the Allies in their campaign against the Japanese. With the amenities of a modern city, shopping malls and all, Tinsukia is a good base from which to explore the island reserve of the **Dibru-Saikhowa National Park** (10km) renowned for its birds and herds of wild horses that initially arrived in the area as pack animals from the war.

ARRIVAL AND INFORMATION   TINSUKIA

By train Tinsukia is on the main railway network (New Tinsukia Station) with trains such as the *Kamrup Express* #15960 (daily) and the *Jan Shatabdi Express* #12068 (daily except Sun) to Guwahati via Dimapur. run to New Tinsukia Station, 10km from the park's southern entry point at Guijan.

Information Information for Dibru-Saikhowa National Park is available from the Range Officer at the entry point at Guijan (☎0374 233 7569).

Tours Purvi Discovery (see box, p.839) offer wildlife tours to Dibru-Saikhowa as well as upmarket tea tourism with stays in tea estates.

ACCOMMODATION AND EATING

Inspection Bungalow Guijan, Tinsukia ☎0374 233 7569. This picturesque simple and basic forest bungalow built on stilts is booked through the Forest Officer. Local food is available on request. ₹600

KF ATC Mall, GNB Rd, Tinsukia ☎03742 330128,

✉kftinsukia@gmail.com. A branch of this small chain of boutique hotels with comfortable and modern a/c rooms and a great multicuisine restaurant with a patisserie and a bar. ₹2400

Meghalaya

Meghalaya, one of India's smallest states, occupies the plateau and rolling hills between Assam and Bangladesh. Its people are predominantly Christian, belonging to three main ethnic groups, the Garos, Jaintias and the matriarchal Khasis – throughout these hills, women do most of the work and the household management. The state has a high literacy rate and teaching is in English. Much of Meghalaya ("the land of the rainclouds") is covered with lush forests, rich in orchids; these "blue hills" bear the brunt of the Bay of Bengal's monsoon-laden winds and are among the wettest places on earth. Stupendous waterfalls are a standard feature of the state, many to be seen on the outskirts of the capital, **Shillong**; however, the most dramatic of these plummet from the plateau to the south, around **Cherrapunjee**.

Meghalaya's hills rise to almost 2000m, making for a pleasantly cool year-round climate. The **Jaintia Hills** offer good walking and caving, and the state is laced with historical sights such as **Nartiang** near **Jowai**, which has an impressive collection of monoliths. Elsewhere, the **sacred forests**, crucibles of biodiversity to be found throughout the Khasi Hills, remain jealously protected. To the south of Shillong, walks through pristine forests and across one of the most intriguing features of the region, the **living root bridges** around the village of **Mawlynnong**, make the **East Khasi Hills** one of the highlights of the Northeast. Although the state has seen its share of political turmoil since its inception in 1972, all in all Meghalaya remains a charming land of misty forests and hospitable people.

Shillong

With its rolling hills of conifers and pineapple shrubs, **SHILLONG** was known to the British as "the Scotland of the East" – an impression first brought to mind by **Barapani** (or **Umiam**), the picturesque loch-like reservoir 23km from town on the Guwahati highway, and the sight of the local Khasi women wearing gingham and tartan shawls. At an altitude of around 1500m, Shillong became a popular hill station for the British,

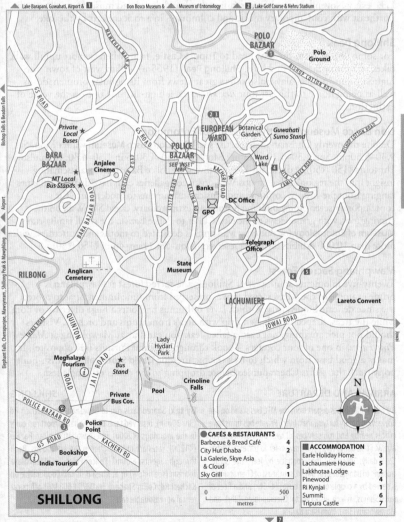

SHILLONG

CAFÉS & RESTAURANTS
Barbecue & Bread Café	4
City Hut Dhaba	2
La Galerie, Skye Asia & Cloud	3
Sky Grill	1

ACCOMMODATION
Earle Holiday Home	3
Lachaumiere House	5
Lakkhotaa Lodge	2
Pinewood	4
Ri Kynjai	1
Summit	6
Tripura Castle	7

0 — 500 metres

who built it on the site of a thousand-year-old Khasi settlement and made it Assam's capital in 1874.

Sadly, with uncontrolled growth, choking traffic jams and water shortages – despite the rain – the city today has lost much of its charm. Some of the original Victorian town around the centre, known as the European Ward, however, is still preserved, with garden villas and the sylvan environs of **Ward Lake**. North of the polo ground is one of Asia's oldest golf courses, founded in 1898 by a group of British civil servants.

A local sport and popular gambling tradition, **siat khnam** involves teams of Khasi men firing arrows at a target while punters throughout the city bet on the final two digits of the total. Daily games start around 3.30pm opposite Nehru Stadium. Of the town's markets, including the busy **Police Bazaar** in the centre, the **Iewduh** (Mon–Sat) or Bara Bazaar, is Meghalaya's oldest and most traditional market, run mainly by women. The **Shillong Autumn Festival** (⊛shillongautumnfestival.com), held at Umiam Lake every November, combines traditional cultural dance and music from all over the northeast with contemporary music and culminates in a rock concert by the lake.

Shillong Peak

For some respite from the city, head to **Tripura Castle**, from where a short uphill walk takes you into pine-forested hills. **Shillong Peak** (1965m), 10km west of town, the highest point in Meghalaya, also offers great views from its popular promenade, as well as being home to the last four *ilex khasiana*, a high-altitude tree on the verge of extinction.

Don Bosco Museum and the Museum of Entomology

Despite the overtly Christian message, the sparkling **Don Bosco Museum** winter Mon–Sat 9.30–5.30pm, Sun 1.30–5.30; summer Mon–Sat 9.30–4.30, Sun 1.30–4.30; compulsory 1hr tours ₹150 (₹50); ⊛dbcic.org 3km northwest of Police Bazaar, offers a fascinating insight into the region's tribal groups Well-organized galleries each have dedicated themes ranging from pre-history, costumes and musical instruments to modern art. The contemporary seven-storey building features an extraordinary, caged Sky Walk on the curving roof, with grand views of the city. Closer to Police Bazaar, the small family-run **Museum of Entomology** (or Butterfly Museum) is dedicated to moths and butterflies, with more than 10,000 exhibits lovingly preserved (Mon–Sat 11am–4pm; ₹150 (₹50).

Mawphlang Sacred Forest

Twenty-five kilometres southwest of Shillong, the **sacred forest** at **Mawphlang** is a prime example of the Khasi sacred grove, preserved from time immemorial to protect the since delicate biodiversity. A thick layer of humus harbours a huge diversity of flora while the trees, draped with lichen drip with area's from arums and orchids. Visitors should not pick anything, not even a fallen leaf. You can stay at Mawphlang at *Maple Pine Farm*, in one of four cottages – book through Cultural Pursuits (see opposite). It makes a good base from which to trek the picturesque **David Scott Trail**, a British-built pony track that skirts Cherrapunjee before dropping to the plains of Bangladesh.

ARRIVAL AND DEPARTURE	SHILLONG

By bus Public buses depart from the MTC bus stand on Jail Rd, leaving hourly for Guwahati (4hr). Private bus firms have offices nearby and run services all over the Northeast. For Aizawl (1–2 daily; 18hr) you may prefer to travel to Silchar (2–3 daily; 10hr) and then continue by jeep. The border crossing to Bangladesh at Dawki, southeast of Cherrapunjee, is served by a couple of private buses (4–5hr) and a fleet of taxis/Sumos, which also run to Cheerapunjee (2hr) and Mawsynram (3hr), from Bara Bazaar.

By taxi Shared taxis run to Guwahati from Kacheri Rd (3hr 30min); reserved taxis to Guwahati airport run early in the mornings (₹2000) and Guwahati's Paltan Bazaar (₹1200); rates are much higher in the afternoons. Book through agents around Police Point, at Meghalaya Tourism (see below) or at Khasi Hills Taxi Cooperative on Kacheri Rd; Collin Shaborg (☎08794 608346) offers car rental at reasonable rates.

INFORMATION AND TOURS

Tourist offices Meghalaya Tourism, Jail Rd, opposite the bus station (daily 9am–6pm; ☎0364 222 6220, ⓦ meghalayatourism.org) provides information and organizes tours; they also arrange cars. The India Tourism office is upstairs on GS Rd (Mon–Fri 9.30am–5.30pm, Sat 9.30am–2pm; ☎0364 222 5632).

Tours The highly recommended Cultural Pursuits at *Hotel Alpine Continental*, (☎98560 41205, ⓦ culturalpursuits.com) arranges good-value

tailor-made tours throughout the region, including homestays in Khasi villages. Their treks and tours include Garo Wangala and the David Scott Trail to Cherrapunjee. Meghalaya Tourism runs a good-value day-trip to Cherrapunjee (8am–4.30pm; from ₹260) and a city tour (8.30am–2.30pm; from ₹200). Meghalaya Adventurers Association, Mission Compound near the Synod Complex (☎0364 254 5621) offer trips to explore the spectacular caves of the region.

ACCOMMODATION

Shillong has a wide range of **accommodation**, although staying on GS Rd can be noisy. For a quiet and central location look around the European Ward area. Further afield, Umiam Lake offers scenic tranquillity while the village of Mawphlang offers homestay accommodation and an insight into Khasi life.

Earle Holiday Home Oakland Rd ☎0364 222 8614. Central and popular, with a range of clean but twee rooms (think lino floors and garish bed covers) in a traditional Meghalayan house or a more modern annexe; there's a good restaurant and a distinct holiday camp feel. ₹550

Lachaumiere House Upper Lachaumiere ☎0364 250 1239 or ☎98560 08720, ⓦ lachaumierehouse.com. A family-run, grand manorhouse with pleasant lawns and home comforts and an adjacent cottage in the grounds; set in a residential area yet close to all amenities. ₹3100

Lakkhotaa Lodge Near the golf course ☎0364 259 0523, ⓦ lakkhotaalodge.com. A boutique hotel with a wild mix of colours and styles from American to Chinese to Indian. There are just nine rooms, each named after a different Native American tribe: "Cherokee", with a four-poster bed and a jacuzzi, stands out. It also has an excellent restaurant, open to non-guests who book ahead. ₹6500

Pinewood European Ward, Rita Rd ☎0364 222 3116, ☎pinewoodhotel@dataone.in. Government-run hotel that dates back to the late 1800s and consists of a main blockhouse and several wood-lined cottages, some in need of a facelift while others have a lot of character, scattered around extensive grounds above Ward Lake. The restaurant

is reasonable and there is a comfortable bar, which is pleasant earlier on and later gets animated with locals discussing politics. ₹2800

★ **Ri Kynjai** 20km north of Shillong ☎9862 420300, ⓦ rikynjai.com. Set in 45 acres of forest in a spectacular location beside Umiam Lake, the region's best hotel has luxury rooms and stunning cottages; the latter are raised on stilts, have traditional "upturned boat" roofs and come with fireplaces and jacuzzis. The restaurant specializes in Northeastern cuisine, and there's a spa. ₹8000

Summit 23 Upper Lachaumiere ☎0364 222 6216. A family home at the top of the town yet close to the centre, with a well-planned guesthouse in the garden offering comfort and a secure and pleasant environment with meals to order. ₹1500

★ **Tripura Castle** (also known as *Royal Heritage*) Tripura Castle Rd ☎0364 250 1111, ⓦ tripuracastle .com. Beautiful hotel in an inspiring hilltop location 3km south of town, next to the Maharaja of Tripura's former summer home. The charming rooms have wooden floors and brass fireplaces, while the maharaja Suite has a mahogany bed once slept in by Tagore. The recently developed annexe next door is equally comfortable and there is a good restaurant and bar. ₹5200

EATING AND DRINKING

The flourishing local music scene has earned Shillong the nickname "**rock city**". For performances look out for posters; bands to look out for include Soulmate and Lou Majaw.

★ **Barbecue & Bread Café** GS Rd. Down a short flight of steps and beyond the fish tank is an authentic and very popular Chinese restaurant decked out with paper lamps and oriental trinkets. There are excellent chicken, pork and seafood dishes including chicken wonton soup; expect to pay ₹250. Upstairs, the *Bread Café* delivers good coffee, cakes and sandwiches. Daily 10am–10pm.

City Hut Dhaba Earle Holiday Home. A cabin-like dining room with an extravagant water feature, *City Hut Dhaba*

has a menu of more than 300 items, including interesting dishes like spicy duck *chatpata*. Wrap up warm, as it can be decidedly chilly in the evenings. Expect to pay around ₹250 for a meal. Daily 10am–10pm.

La Galerie, Skye Asia & Cloud 9 Hotel Centre Point, Police Bazaar. This landmark hotel has been the centre of Shillong dining and nightlife for several years. *La Galerie* is its multicuisine restaurant and good for a quick bite (₹60–200); the fifth floor, with its grand views over the town centre, has the far more atmospheric and refined *Skye Asia* with rattan chairs and soft sofas and a good pan-Asian menu (mains ₹180–300) featuring well-executed Thai soups and *satays*, Korean barbecued chicken and Japanese *teppanyaki*. It is adjoined to the chic bar *Cloud 9*, one of the happening bars in town, with the occasional DJ and a ladies night on Friday. Daily 10am–10pm.

Sky Grill Hotel Polo Towers, near Polo Ground. This upmarket hotel has a selection of restaurants and bars, when the weather permits, the best of these is the *Sky Grill* on the terrace, offering a barbecue deal in the evenings including a beer or soft drink for ₹745. Daily 10am–10pm.

DIRECTORY

Banks and ATMs SBI, Kacheri Rd, changes money and travellers' cheques; there is an ATM outside and several throughout Shillong.

Internet Internet joints are thin on the ground (from ₹20/ hr)– try malls around Police Bazaar, Kacheri and Keating roads.

Post office The GPO is on Kacheri Rd, as is the State Bank of India, which has foreign exchange facilities.

Cherrapunjee and around

CHERRAPUNJEE, 56km south of Shillong in the Khasi Hills, is a spread out settlement with the town of of **Sohra** at its centre. It has achieved fame as the wettest place on earth: the highest daily rainfall ever recorded fell here in 1876 – 104cm in 24 hours. The area's numerous waterfalls are most impressive during the steamy monsoon season when awesome torrents plunge down to the Bangladeshi plains often obscured by rain clouds.

Every eight days a market is held here, with tribal jewellery, honey and local produce on offer. Of the various points of interest, the **Noh Kalikai waterfall**, **Bangladesh viewpoint**, **Mawsmai village** and **cave** and **Mawjinbuin cave** near **Mawsynram**, which is even wetter than Cherra itself, are all within a few kilometres. An easy way of seeing them all is to join Meghalaya Tourism's **day-trip** (see p.851) which leaves Shillong at 8am. Alternatively, a taxi for the day costs around ₹2000.

The double-decker **living root bridges** below Cherrapunjee around **Nongriat**, accessed by a knee-grinding descent, are well worth a visit. One of the marvels of Meghalaya, these bridges, made from the ficus elastica tree, some of which hundreds of years, are carefully entwined and grown to span rivers and ravines.

ACCOMMODATION   CHERRAPUNJEE

★ **Cherrapunjee Holiday Resort Village** Laitkynsew ☎9436 115925, ⚲cherrapunjee.com. Around 12km from Sohra, this friendly and welcoming place sits on a ledge looking down to villages, hills and the Bangladesh plains in the distance and makes an ideal base for exploring the area. The main building has six large comfortable rooms with attached bathrooms around a central hall and restaurant, there is also a new annexe next door for more comfort, and a dorm (₹450). The restaurant offers a range from local cuisine to *dhal bhaat* and a lot more. They offer itineraries and have useful information on walks and treks including the walk down to Nongriat and the David Scott Trail (see p.850). ₹2125

Polo Orchid Mawsmai ☎8794 701636, ⚲hotelpolotowers.com. Part of the upmarket Shillong chain, this hotel, perched on a cliff 7km (₹100 by taxi) from Sohra, is handy for waterfalls and cliff walks. However with its expanse of stone floors and comfortable, urban-style rooms, It feels out of place and is overpriced. The *Rain Café* upstairs provides a good panorama and a decent menu designed for day-trippers from Shillong. ₹5000

Mawlynnong and Dawki

Reputedly the cleanest village (anywhere), **MAWLYNNONG**, 86km southease of Shillong in the **East Khasi Hills** is a marvel of community ecological awareness where everything is beautifully cared for and all rubbish careful recycled and processed. This is also a good place to see a living root bridge. Alas, the tree guesthouse at Mawlynnong had been damaged (check the latest situation with Cultural Pursuits). A challenging bamboo walkway, the Sky View, climbs to the forest canopy providing distant views.

Nearby **DAWKI**, 96km from Shillong, is the most important of the

Meghalaya–Bangladesh border crossings to **Tamabil**, two and a half hours from Sylhet. There's no Bangladesh visa office in Meghalaya, so you will need to acquire a visa beforehand; Kolkata has a consulate. From Dawki to Shillong the last buses and Sumos leave around 11am; alternatively, a taxi costs ₹3000 to and from Shillong. There are no official currency exchange facilities at the crossing.

Arunachal Pradesh

Arunachal Pradesh, "the land of the dawn-lit mountains", is one of India's last unspoilt wilderness. A wealth of fascinating cultures, peoples and **tribes** – plus a staggering five hundred species of orchid – are found in its glacial terrain, alpine meadows and subtropical rainforests.

The capital, **Itanagar**, is north of the Brahmaputra across from Jorhat. In the far west of the state, the road from **Bhalukpong** on the Assamese border to the monastery of **Tawang** climbs steadily through rugged hills, streams and primeval forests, crossing the dramatic **Sela Pass** (4300m) midway. Along the route lie the Buddhist towns of **Bomdila** and **Dirang**. In the far northeast, **Namdapha National Park** is home to clouded and snow leopards. Arunachal's remote and unspoilt central highlands, home to a myriad tribes, hides some of the best the Himalayas have to offer including, the mysterious Buddhist land of **Pemako**.

Despite its beauty, tourism has been discouraged because of the extremely sensitive border with Chinese-occupied Tibet in the north and Myanmar in the east. In 1962, the Chinese invaded Arunachal Pradesh, reaching the outskirts of Tezpur in Assam, a 300km incursion that India has never forgotten. Since then, a strong military presence has been adopted in the area with China laying claim to much of the state. All visitors require a **permit** (see box, p.839) to enter the state.

Itanagar

Just under 400km northeast of Guwahati, **ITANAGAR**, the state's quiet capital, is of little interest but an important transport hub for anyone travelling to the central plateau. You may find you need to spend a night or two here organizing permits and logistics. Surrounded by low, wooded hills, the town spreads along a 4km stretch of road running between Zero Point, where the better hotels are located, and Ganga Market, the animated main bazaar, which has cheaper accommodation and the bus station. The **Government Sales Emporium** above Zero Point sells interesting handicrafts. Six kilometres west of town, **Gyakar Sinyi** (Ganga Lake), cupped in a jungle hollow, is a popular picnic spot.

ARRIVAL AND INFORMATION ITANAGAR

By bus and Sumo State and private buses connect Itanagar with Guwahati (10–11hr) and destinations throughout the state, but be aware that most roads are in terrible condition. Sumos and shared jeeps are quicker but

you will need a day of rest after a journey; destinations include Along (12hr), Bomdila (10–12hr), Hapoli (8hr) and Pasighat (6–7hr).

Tourist office There's an intermittently open tourist office

ARUNACHAL PRADESH'S TRIBAL GROUPS

Arunachal Pradesh is stunningly diverse, with 26 major tribal groups, each with its own culture, dialect, dress, social structure and traditions. Polygamy remains common among many of them, as does the religious blend of Hindu, Buddhist and animist beliefs. The main ethnic groups include Monpas, Sherdukpens, Apatani, Wanchos, Noctes, Tangsas, Singphos, Khamptis, Mishmis, Mijis, Galos, Padams, Miwongs, Tagins and Puroiks. However, within all the groups, tradition is slowly giving way to modern influences, particularly among the younger generation, who increasingly wear Western clothes, watch Bollywood flicks and eat Chinese food.

16

(☎0360 221 4745, ⊛arunachaltourism.com) behind the Akash Deep complex in Ganga Market.
Tour Operators Abor Country Travels & Expeditions, B Sector, below Raj Bhavan (☎0986 355 3243,

⊜aborcountry@gmail.com) organizes treks, whitewater expeditions and tours of Arunachal and elsewhere in the Northeast.

ACCOMMODATION AND EATING

Moomsie Kogey Complex, below Zero Point ☎0360 229 0971. A smart mid-range hotel mixing modern facilities with vernacular style and offering a large choice from cheap, poky doubles to decent a/c rooms; the restaurant is one of the best in town a wide menu from local fish dishes to Chinese and tandoori and also a bakery. ₹500

Arun Subansiri Below Zero Point ☎ 0360 221 2806. Established and extensive landmark hotel below the museum and monastery, with a range of rooms all with

attached baths and hot water and a good restaurant that also has a decent patisserie. ₹1600

Todo B Sector, Near Mithun Gate, NH-52A ☎0360 229 0347, ⊛hoteltodo.in. One of Itanagar's fanciest addresses with plenty of marble, some garish decor, honeymoon-like suites and decent doubles on the southern edge of town; there is a good restaurant, *Ajir*, with a mixed menu including Thai red curry but best on Indian food. The *Kame* bar also has occasional discos. ₹2200

West Arunachal

Bordered by Bhutan and Tibet, the isolated hills and valleys of **western Arunachal** climb to some of the remotest glaciers and peaks in the Himalayas. Most of the 6000m-plus mountains – except **Gori Chen** (6488m) and **Nyegi Kangsang** (7047m) – remain completely unknown. The main road, in a perpetual state of disrepair, runs from **Bhalukpong** on the Assamese border to near the Tibet frontier at **Tawang**, ending high in the mountains at one of Asia's largest monasteries. On this bone-shaking, sometimes terrifying yet spectacular journey along some of the worst stretches of road you are ever likely to encounter, you rise from the steamy foothills to the high market town of **Bomdila** with its Buddhist monasteries and occasional yak; further on lies **Dirang**, an ancient fortress town, before the endless climb up through the **Sela Pass** to Tawang.

Bomdila

Set on a spur of the Thagla Ridge at 2530m, the dividing line between rainforests to the south and subalpine valleys to the north, **BOMDILA** is a quiet, pleasant, spread-out settlement with a handy bazaar in the lower town and quiet walks above. There is a handful of **Tibetan Buddhist monasteries** here – the largest, a Gelugpa *gompa*, known as the **Bomdila Monastery** – Gentse Gaden Rabhyel Ling – high above town, was inaugurated by the Dalai Lama in 1997. The gompa holds a spectacular *chaam* (festival of lama masked dance) around mid-November which attracts plenty of local people including **Monpa** women in distinctive pink knitted gowns and yak-hair hats. The older *gompa*, at the end of the bazaar in the lower town, houses a large blue Medicine Buddha statue. A few kilometres beyond Bomdila, the snow-covered peaks of Gori Chen (6488m) and Kangto (7042m) come into view, weather permitting.

ARRIVAL AND INFORMATION   BOMDILA

All transport arrives at the new **Parking Complex** in the middle of town, where there are some convenient hotels. Local transport is available here and the lower bazaar is a short walk away. You will need a taxi for the main Bomdila monastery (₹150). There are travel offices in the Parking Complex and an internet café, though electricity and bandwidth is a problem; most mobile services do not work in West Kameng except for VSNL.

By bus There are just two routes out of Bomdila: onward and upward towards Tawang, and back down to

Bhalukpong. State buses, for those who are willing to take a severe rattling, run from the new bus station in the lower

16

part of town to Tezpur (1 daily; 9–11hr).

By shared taxi/jeep The most common form of transport to and from Bomdila; you should pre-book at the taxi stand and be prepared for early departures for all long-distance journeys including Bhalukpung (₹300) and Tezpur (₹350). There are regular taxis to Dirang and a handful of early-morning taxis to Tawang (185km; 7hr; ₹470). For Itanagar, it is best to stay overnight at Bhalukpung or

Tezpur before continuing on.

Tourist office Tourist information (☎03782 222049) is at the *Tourist Lodge*, but the desk is not always manned.

Tours The professional and excellent Himalayan Holidays (☎03782 222017 or ☎09436 045063), ABC Building, Main Market & Parking Complex, arranges sightseeing trips and treks and complete itineraries and provides internet access (₹40/hr). They can also arrange transport (Tawang ₹6500).

ACCOMMODATION AND EATING

★ **Doe-Gu-Khil** Gentse Gaden Rabgyel Ling Monastery ☎03782 223232 or ☎09402 292774, ✉yipe_bg@yahoo.com. A wonderful, quiet spot within the monastery compound and just below the main complex, with spotless and well-presented rooms with attached baths around a courtyard; the vegetarian food is cooked to order. You will need to book early for the *chaam*. ₹**700**

Highlanders' Inn Near DC Bungalow, Upper Gompa Rd ☎03782 223795. Friendly and welcoming hotel close to the *gompa* and a fall-back if *Doe-Gu-Khil* is full. The large, plain rooms, all with attached baths, suffer from the sound of vehicles warming up in the early mornings so opt for a room at the back; the restaurant's menu is limited, catering

for Indian budget travellers. ₹**800**

Tourist Lodge Near Police Station ☎03782 222049. 1km uphill from the Parking Complex, this government establishment has a pleasant setting and large tatty rooms set around a central pond; there are no geysers but hot water is provided by the bucket and the heaters are well worth the extra ₹100. Meals are basic. ₹**150**

Tsepal Yangjom Main Bazaar ☎03782 222286. At the heart of the lower market, this established hotel has comfortable wood-lined rooms with attached baths and the best restaurant in town serving local, Chinese and Indian cuisine – try the boiled chicken and bamboo shoots (₹180). ₹**2440**

Old Dirang and New Dirang

Ninety minutes beyond Bomdila, the ancient fortress town of **OLD DIRANG** (1690m), also known as **Dirang Dzong**, or "**fort**", commands the lower river valley. Take the steps up just before the bridge to the walled medieval settlement (signed) where within the warren of stone houses and lanes shared by human and livestock alike, and besides the odd TV dish, time seems to have stood still. The *dzong* stands more or less abandoned in the centre of the settlement and is often locked. The rest of Old Dirang with quite a few medieval buildings and a 500-year-old *gompa* above town, is worth a walk through with the odd tethered yak and notice a strong aroma of local brew.

NEW DIRANG, 5km further up the valley, is the main market and transport hub, with fruit orchards on the outskirts and a yak-breeding farm. Of the several **monasteries** in the area, there is the **Kalachakra** *gompa* dedicated to the Wheel of Life and the old **Liung** *gompa*, belonging to one of the oldest sects of Tibetan Buddhism. Further up the road towards Tawang, a footpath leads down to **hot springs**, a popular bathing spot for local villagers. About 8km away, the **Sangti Valley** is the winter home of the black-necked crane and a popular place for birdwatching.

ACCOMMODATION   DIRANG

The best places to stay are located along the main highway around 1km before the bazaar of new Dirang.

★ **Pemaling** ☎03780242 615 or ☎094027 83255, ✉pemalingdirang@yahoo.co.in. On the approach to the new town from Old Dirang, this well-run hotel provides a good alternative to staying at Bomdila, with comfortable in attached rooms with floral decor, and a restaurant with good cooking and wonderful vistas. ₹**2450**

Samdup Khang ☎03780 200 315 or ☎094028 69201. A newish hote,l close to the centre of New Dirang on the

main road, offering a range of rooms from small doubles to more upstairs luxurious options, all with attached baths; the modern restaurant serves a range of Indian and Chinese food. ₹**1000**

Tourist Lodge ☎03780 242157. Tucked beside *Pemaling*, with grand wood-lined rooms in front and some smaller ones at the back. All have attached baths and hot water when electricity allows; the management is low-key and the catering basic but the place has potential. ₹**1100**

16

The Sela Pass and around

The gruelling yet spectacular road from Dirang to **Tawang** (a 10–12hr drive), an improbable highway perpetually under construction, rises steadily from the river valley through alpine scenery past waterfalls and grazing yaks. The endless switchbacks climb up to the dramatic 4300m **Sela Pass**, where you can take tea and have cheese *momos* in front of a *bakari* (wood-fired oven) at the café by the gate. The pass is snowed in for around six months a year, though ill-equipped jeeps still brave the journey. Of the many memorials to those who lost their lives during the 1962 Chinese invasion the most impressive is the **Jaswant Singh Memorial**, 13km beyond the pass that commemorates a battle when a tiny Indian contingent held off the Chinese army for several days before finally being overrun.

Tawang

Some 180km beyond Bomdila, the great Buddhist monastery of **TAWANG**, the largest in India, dominates the land of the Monpas. Perched at around 3500m and looking out onto a semicircle of peaks, snow-capped for much of the year, Tawang, on the edge of Tibet and peering down to Bhutan, feels like the end of the road, with long cold nights and plenty of snow in winter.

A bone of contention between India and China, Tawang has always been of special significance to Tibetans and the Dalai Lama who fled Tibet in 1959 and travelled surreptitiously through here on his way into exile. His pre-incarnation, the **Sixth Dalai Lama** was born on the outskirts of the town.

The three-day **Torgya festival** in January, shortly before Losar (Tibetan New Year), celebrates the life of the first king of Mon and is accompanied by a *chaam* (lama dance) to ward off evil spirits. Recently established, the **Tawang Festival**, held towards the end of October, celebrates the community with cultural shows.

Tawang Monastery

Daily dawn–dusk • Camera ₹20, video ₹100 **Museum** ₹20

Established by Merak Lama Lodre Gyatso in 1680 under the auspices of the Fifth Dalai Lama, when this area was part of Greater Tibet, the highly influential **Tawang Monastery** is a huge fortress-like complex with a warren of buildings, a couple of kilometres beyond the town. It houses around five hundred monks and is renowned for its collection of priceless manuscripts and *thangkas*. There is a small **museum** filled with Buddhist ornaments and relics, and a vast library. Rebuilt in the 1990s, the main *dukhang* (temple hall) dominated by an 8m-high statue of Shakyamuni along with spectacular murals, was consecrated by the present **Dalai Lama** whose 2009 visit brought much displeasure to the Chinese government. The abbot, Gyalshey Rimpoche, has declared the entire region to be free from the slaughter of animals – one reason why so many yaks freely in these parts.

Urgyelling

As you descend south from Tawang, a bifurcation in the road (5km), adorned by ceremonial gates, leads to the small chapel of **Urgyelling**. Set in a peaceful grounds, the chapel commemorates the birth here of the **Sixth Dalai Lama**, Tsanyang Gyatso in 1683. The monastery was sacked when Tsanyang Gyatso was deposed but he prophesised he would return and that when one of the three grand trees he planted died, catastrophe would befall Tibet. In 1959 one of the trees died in a storm and that very year the 14th Dalai Lama (the present), fleeing Tibet, sought refuge at this very spot.

ARRIVAL AND INFORMATION

TAWANG

By bus and jeep Daily jeeps run from Tawang to Bomdila, Dirang and Tezpur – book in advance from ticket agents

near the bus stand; transport leaves early.
By taxi A one-way taxi trip to the monastery costs around

16

₹150 but it's worth asking the driver to wait as it can be difficult to find one for the return journey; it is also a pleasant walk. A taxi to Bomdila costs ₹5000.

Tourist office The *Tourist Lodge* has a small tourist office, but Himalayan Holidays (☎03794 223151), opposite *Hotel Gorichen*, Main Bazaar, is a better source of information.

ACCOMMODATION AND EATING

★ **Dolma Khangsar** Near Monastery gates ☎03794 223271 or ☎94360 51011. Four excellent wood-lined, suite-like rooms with attached baths and hot water, in a welcoming family home with good vegetarian cooking and a great location next to the monastery. A brisk 3km walk up from the bazaar (or a taxi ride). **₹1240**

Gakyi Khang Zhang Near DC Office ☎03794 224647 & ☎09402 605115, ⓦgkztawang.com. Off Monastery Rd, 1km above the bazaar, this is the fanciest address around, with comfortable rooms all with hot water and a restaurant as well as a lounge bar that features the occasional DJ (when there's a cover charge; ₹150). **₹1240**

Siddhartha Main Rd, Nehru Market ☎03794 222515 or ☎94366 35998. One of the better hotels around the

bottom end of the main market, with a small range from semi- to super-deluxe and not much perceptible variation; all have attached bathrooms and hot water. The internet fee is ₹65 and there is a good restaurant. **₹850**

Snow Yak 1st floor, Main Bazaar. With modern decor and a relaxed ambience, this pleasant lunchtime restaurant offers a mixed menu, best to go local with *thenduk* (noodle soup) from ₹70 or the specials, such as *churpa* (cheese) dishes from ₹120.

Tawang Opposite SBI ☎03794 223271 or ☎94360 51011. Franchise hotel run by the welcoming Sonam, with the most comfortable and spacious rooms in the centre of town, just 200m above the crossroads. There is hot water and a small restaurant or room service with a limited menu that's best for Indian food. **₹1000**

16

Central and Eastern Arunachal

Pristine forests mark the watersheds of the Siang, Dibang and Lohit rivers an unspoilt wilderness gradually opening up to visitors in search of exploration and adventure. The town of **Hapoli** (**Ziro**) makes a good base for exploring this land of rain clouds, forests, swirling paddy terraces and the fascinating **Apatani villages** where animist beliefs and the worship of **Donyi-Polo** (sun and moon) are still very much alive. The Apatanis are just one of the many **tribes** that inhabit these remote forests and hills of Central Arunachal. Beyond Hapoli, the fragile highway etches through forested hills to the settlement of **Along**; further south the River Siang, battling through the jungles, merges into the mighty Brahmaputra at **Pasighat**, close to the urban centres of Upper Assam. Further east, the remote valleys of the **Dibang** and **Lohit** rivers, inhabited by the Mishmi, Singpho and Khampti tribes, descend from snow-covered passes through subtropical forests where in the far east corner of the state, the pristine **Namdapha National Park** harbours a huge variety of fauna and flora.

Hapoli (Ziro)

The quiet, yet slowly expanding town of **HAPOLI** (still known widely by its former name **Ziro**), 150km north of Itanagar, is surrounded by the terraced fields and rolling pine-clad hills of the Apatani plateau, 1780m above sea level. Besides the colourful market, where you will come across local delicacies such as dried rat and other unusual meat, Ziro provides a base for exploring the surroundings. Hills and village communities. There aresome great forest walks around the plateau where you can still see Apatani men with impressive facial tattoos and women with bamboo nose-plugs. **Old Ziro** is a scenic 7km walk away, and the **Talley Valley Wildlife Sanctuary**, renowned for its clouded leopard, makes a good two-day trek.

ARRIVAL AND INFORMATION

HAPOLI

By bus and taxi The roads to and from Hapoli in any direction may be a gruelling challenge but they're currently the only way to access the region, pending the possible resumption of the helicopter service. Sumo services run to Along, Daporijo, Itanagar and Pasighat – allow 9hrs for

Itanagar; during the monsoons the roads get almost impassable.

Tours and information With tourism in its infancy, NGOs such as NgunuZiro (☎09436 224834, ⓔ NgunuZiro@gmail. com, ⓦfacebook.com/NgunuZiro) provide vital information and assistance for exploring the area. Peak Tour and Travels (☎03788 225221) can organize local tours, other established tour operators in the region include Abor County Travels &

Expeditions, Itanagar (☎09863 553243, ✉aborcountry @gmail.com).

ACCOMMODATION AND EATING

Blue Pine Pai Gate ☎03788 224812 or ☎03788 225223. On the outskirts of town, 2km from the centre, the hotel offers plain and simple rooms with shared or attached bathrooms, and a good restaurant. ₹600

Ziro Valley Resort Biirii ☎03788 224 278 or ☎09856 910173. Midway between the old and new

towns, in a pleasant location surrounded by fields, this extensive lodge offers a range of rooms featuring the local panelled building style and pastel colours. Modern amenities include attached baths and hot water, electricity permitting. ₹1000

Along and Pasighat

East of Hapoli, the River Siang, having started life as the Tsangpo on the Tibet plateau, tumbles through the lush rainforests around the small towns of **ALONG** and **PASIGHAT**, to eventually form the Brahmaputra. Few visitors travel this tortuous road through the land of the Adis and the Mishmis, but there are numerous opportunities for **trekking** and river adventures including some of the most challenging **whitewater** in the Himalayas.

ARRIVAL AND DEPARTURE

ALONG AND PASIGHAT

By bus and taxi The towns can be reached from Itanagar (7hr to Along; 10hr to Pasighat); the easiest routes are via North Lakhimpur along the Brahmaputra valley on the NH-52 rather than the hill roads through Hapoli. Shared Jeeps run from Itanagar and Hapoli, but

having your own vehicle makes the journey a lot easier, quicker and more comfortable. A 30min drive from Pasighat is Oiramghat, from where a daily ferry runs to Dibrugarh (see p.847).

ACCOMMODATION

Aagaam Yubo Complex, Nehru Chowk, Along ☎03783 223640 or ☎0943 664055. Plain, a/c rooms with Western-style bathrooms and hot water make this one of the best options in Along, it also has a decent restaurant. ₹800

Oman Main Bazaar, Pasighat ☎03862 224464. Friendly and central, offering clean but basic rooms with attached bathrooms and buckets of hot water. ₹500

Namdapha National Park

Oct–April • ₹50 (₹10), jeep ₹100, ordinary camera ₹75, camera with a zoom lens ₹400, video ₹750

The beautifully remote **NAMDAPHA NATIONAL PARK**, covering an area of 1985 square kilometres, is unique for its massive range of altitudes (200–4500m) and its huge biodiversity Close to the Burmese border, Namdapha is home to tigers, leopards (clouded and snow), elephants, red pandas, deer and the endangered Hoolock gibbon, although you are unlikely to spot any big wildlife on a short visit.

THE BEYUL OF PEMAKO

An arduous multiday expedition, the trek to the **Beyul of Pemako** (the hidden paradise in the shape of a lotus) is probably the most rewarding adventure of the eastern Himalayas. Inhabited by the Mishmis and Adis, this remote and mysterious land of forest, cloud, lakes and high mountain crags, overlooked by the distant snows of Namche Barwa in Tibet, is especially sacred to Buddhists. They believe that Guru Rimpoche (Padmasambhava) blessed the region with hidden spiritual treasures that can only be accessed through the challenge of pilgrimage. The journey, which starts at Pasighat or Along, passes through Tuting and climaxes with the circumambulation of the five lakes of Danakosha high in the district of Dibang. For more information contact The Greener Pastures, Dibrugarh (☎09435 747471, ⊕thegreenerpastures.com) or Abor Country Travels & Expeditions, Itanagar (☎09863 553243, ✉aborcountry@gmail.com).

16

ARRIVAL AND INFORMATION

By bus Buses to and from Miao pass through Margherita, 64km southwest, and the convenient Tinsukia, 40km further southwest in Assam, where rail services run to Guwahati. Dibrugarh is a further 47km beyond Tinsukia, with connections to central Arunachal.

NAMDAPHA NATIONAL PARK

Information The park headquarters are at Miao (Field Director: ☎03807 222249) where you can book forest resthouses as well as elephant safaris. The best source of information is ⓦnamdapha.in, run by the Nature Conservation Foundation.

ACCOMMODATION

In addition to the basic forest resthouses at Deban, within the park, there is limited choice at Miao.

Eco-Tourist Guest House Miao ☎9436 228763. Run by a local NGO, the guesthouse has just four comfortable rooms

and a caretaker who will provide simple meals. Book in advance and they will look after your entire itinerary. ₹600

Nagaland

On the Burma border, south of Arunachal Pradesh and east of Assam, **Nagaland** is physically and conceptually at the very edge of the Subcontinent. Home to the fiercely independent Nagas, its hills and valleys were only opened up to tourism in 2000. One of India's most beautiful states, it was once renowned for its head-hunters but is now ninety percent Christian.

A visit to a Naga village provides a fascinating insight into a rapidly disappearing way of life. Most tour operators will arrange trips here and it is a good idea and far more informative to use a guide, as some Nagas are tired of having their homes on show. If you do visit, bring a gift and offer money for the village to the chief (or *angh*).

Traditional Angami villages surround the capital of **Kohima**, including **Khonoma**. From **Mon** you can see various Konyak villages such as **Shangnyu**. The Ao tribe inhabits **Mokokchung**, while **Tuensang** is home to six different tribes. The state's terrain is also ideal for trekking and mountain biking. A good time to visit is during the **Hornbill**

THE NAGAS

Naga warriors have long been feared and respected, and have practised head-hunting within living memory. They are also skilful farmers, growing twenty different species of rice. They differentiate between the soul and the spirit, believing the soul resides in the nape of the neck, while the spirit, in the head, holds great power and brings good fortune. Heads of enemies and fallen comrades were once collected to add to those of the community's own ancestors. Some tribes tattooed their faces with swirling horns to mark success in **head-hunting**. The heads themselves were kept in the men's meeting house (*morung*) in each village, which was decorated with fantastic carvings of animals, elephant heads and tusks – you can still see examples in many villages. After decades of Christianity, dominated by the Baptists, age-old traditions were fading away and festivals such as the Hornbill (see above) have recently been introduced in an attempt to reinstate traditional Naga culture. Today, music is an important feature of modern Naga youth culture with numerous bands, a music school and even the occasional jazz festival.

Politically, Nagaland has seen a series of violent insurgencies and a powerful independence movement. The Naga were bought within the Indian union when, following a series of Naga raids on Assamese villages, the British sought to push them back into the hills. Despite two victories over the British The Angami Naga were made to sign a truce in 1879 and went on to be loyal to the British; during World War II the Nagas fought valiantly against the Japanese. At the time of Independence, the Nagas found their land divided, with the larger area falling to Burma; India's promise of self-determination never materialized and today sections of Naga society still yearn for autonomy while politicians wrangle. Though a ceasefire is officially in place, violence occasionally flares up and the politics of independence have disintegrated into a quagmire of inter-political rivalries that pays little heed to the wellbeing of the Naga people.

16

Festival (⊕hornbillfestival.com), held in the first week in December, which showcases Naga art, dance, music and sport. Check to see if you'll need a **permit** to enter Nagaland (see box, p.839).

Kohima and around

KOHIMA, Nagaland's capital, was established below the large Angami **Kohima Village** by the British in the nineteenth century and has been developing and spreading rapidly over the last few years. Traditional Naga villages – including **Khonoma**, 20km beyond Kohima, **Jakhema** and **Kigwema** – are just a short drive away while Kohima itself is an incresingly cosmopolitan place, with traditional markets being replaced by modern shopping centres. Elsewhere the strength of Christianity is nowhere better epitomized than in the soaring gabled rooflines, inspired by the *morung* of the new Catholic Cathedral to the south of the city.

World War II Cemetery

Spread loosely over the saddle of two large hills, Kohima forms a pass that played a strategic role during World War II. The Imphal–Dimapur highway – the route along which the Japanese hoped to reach the plains of India – crosses the saddle at the foot of the **World War II Cemetery** at the heart of Kohima. Designed by Edwin Lutyens on the site of the battle that climaxed over the District Commissioner's tennis court, the cemetery stands as a tribute to the Allies who died during the three-month Battle of Kohima, which ended in June 1944 with a death toll of more than ten thousand soldiers. A plaque towards the bottom of the cemetery bears the poignant message "When you go home tell them of us and say, for your tomorrow, we gave our today".

Kohima village

The large Angami settlement of **Kohima Village** is set on a high hill overlooking modern Kohima and approached through ceremonial gates a short way from the centre of town. A few of the buildings still sport the traditional pitched roofs and crossed "house-horns" on the gables, a mark of seniority, and its tightly knit labyrinth of lanes maintains a definite Naga feel. Carved heads to signify family status, grain baskets in front of the houses, and troughs used to make rice beer are among the distinctive features.

Kisama and around

Daily: May–Sept 8am–6pm; Oct–April 8am–4.30pm • ₹10

The **Naga Heritage Village** at **Kisama**, a showcase of Naga arts and crafts 10km south of Kohima, is well worth the visit to see the collection of *morung* from most of the tribes of Nagaland. It is a beautiful spot, right under the wooded **Japfu Peak** (3048m), which makes a rewarding day **trek** (Oct–May) from near Kisama and provides grand views of Kohima and beyond, especially at sunset or sunrise. The nearby Angami village of **Kigwema**, 3km further on, feels untouched and is well worth a walk through with a guide. Nino Zhasa (☏09856 343037) arranges guided tours of Kigwema and guides for trekking to Japfu; she also arranges **homestays** in and around Kigwema.

Khonoma

Khonoma, 20km northwest of Kohima and a rewarding day out, is where the Angami warriors made their final stand against the British in 1879. It's a rare animist village that celebrates the festival of Sekrenyi (Purification of the Soul) in late February. Renowned as a "green village" where tradition is carefully preserved, Khonoma is surrounded by magnificent swirls of rice terraces irrigated by a complex system of bamboo water pipes. Behind the village lies the scenic **Dzükou valley**, part of the Khonoma Nature Conservation and Tragopan Sanctuary, graced with waterfalls and

16

wonderful viewpoints. Several houses around Khonoma offer homestay facilities – contact Vikedono, Baby's Homestay (☎94366 19378).

ARRIVAL AND INFORMATION KOHIMA AND AROUND

By bus Most private buses from Imphal are through services to Dimapur and don't go into the town centre, so ask the driver to drop you off at the *Japfu* hotel. State buses drop you at the stand in the town centre. There are state and private buses in all directions; tickets for private buses can be bought from agents in the centre or on Phool Bari. State buses to Dimapur run every 30min, and daily to Mokokchung and Imphal.

By Sumo Frequent Sumos to Dimapur depart from the taxi stand 200m up from the bus station.

By car From Kohima, roads lead west to the railhead and airport at Dimapur, north to Mokokchung and south to

Imphal. From Mokokchung, the road continues to Jorhat in Assam.

Tourist office The tourist office (Mon–Fri 10am–4pm; ☎0370 224 3124, ⍟tourismnagaland.com) is below the *Japfu*.

Tour operators Nagaland is blessed with several good tour operators including Nino Zhasa of Explore Nagaland (☎09856 343037, ⍟explorenagaland.com) based around Kohima and Kigwema, who can assist with your entire itinerary including good homestays. For wildlife tours contact Gurudongma and for adventure treks contact Abor Country (see p.854).

ACCOMMODATION

Kohima has a good choice of mid-range **hotels** except during the Hornbill Festival you should book around eight months in advance. There are several **homestays** around the city, and during the festival quite a few extra homes welcome guests.

Aradura Inn near Little Flower School and the Cathedral ☎09862 469939, ⍟aradurainn.com. A hotel with pleasant grounds and good views of the southern end of town. It offers a selection of mid-range rooms with beautiful wood floors and attached baths; the sitting room is homely and there is a popular restaurant/café (see below); expect genuine local hospitality. ₹**1705**

★ **Green Wood Villa** Kipfüzha Sector, Kigwema ☎09856 343037. A contemporary house close to the Heritage Village at Kisama, with all the comforts of home and great views from the roof garden; Nino organizes tours across Nagaland as well as treks up to Japfu peak (see p.861). She can also arrange homestays around the village and in Kohima. This is the best place to stay for the Hornbill Festival but you will need to book well in advance. Off-season discounts are extremely good value (from ₹500). ₹**1600**

The Heritage Officers Hill, near DC Bungalow ☎094360 00044, ⍟info@theheritage.in. A handful of beautiful wood rooms with fireplaces in this grand manor

that was once the District Commissioner's house, set within extensive grounds on a hill just south of the cemetery; meals are on order and there are occasional concerts in the grounds. Run by the affable Thejal, a successful musician who also runs the *Dream Café* in town. ₹**1500**

★ **Razhü Pru** Mission Compound ☎0370 229 0291, ⍟razhupru@yahoo.co.in. A lovely old manorhouse, conveniently located, with large rambling rooms, well decorated throughout with Naga art, and a great atmosphere, 200m uphill past the Kohima Village gates. The restaurant serves good multicuisine meals including Naga dishes. ₹**2000**

The Orchid Chandmari Rd, Midland, near cemetery ☎90894 34838, ⍟orchidluxuryhotel@gmail.com. Slightly off the main road and a bit quieter than the others, this extensive hotel has modern amenities, offering large comfortable rooms with spotless stone floors and kettles for tea or coffee. The restaurant, finished in marble and chrome, offers Indian and Chinese food plus Naga specialities to order. ₹**2600**

EATING

Kohima has an increasing choice of **restaurants** outside the hotels. While international mixed menus are popular, you can also find some good Naga cooking based around rice with boiled vegetables, bamboo shoots and meat, and the infamous Naga chilli. The city also has a choice of popular cafés for light meals and snacks, but bear in mind that everything, besides hotels, shuts down early (by 7pm) and there is a state-wide ban on alcohol. Much of town is closed on Sunday.

Aradura Spur Cafe Aradura Inn. A relaxed and elegant restaurant and café with soft sofas, dining areas and an open kitchen, serving a multicuisine menu along with Naga dishes. This is a popular place, especially in the early evenings, and can get a bit smoky. Daily 10am–7pm.

Café Caffeine Jasokie Place, Main Town. Near the overhead bridge, this spotless fourth floor restaurant is bright and breezy with some inventive graphics and decor. The extensive menu stretches from sandwiches to spaghetti bolognaise (₹150) and lasagne (₹200) as well as offering snacks and coffee. Mon–Sat 10am–6pm.

★ **Chingtsüong** Razhü Point, Main Town ☎09436 001855. If you are looking for an authentic Naga meal, this is the place to come, as the owner is dedicated to promoting Naga cuisine. Despite the plastic chairs, this small upstairs restaurant with its smoky bamboo walls has plenty of atmosphere, and with advance notice, you may even be able to sample *zhütho*, the traditional Naga rice beer (despite the ban on alcohol). Also with advance notice (3–4hr) you can get an à la carte meal but otherwise the daily set menus (recommended) offer tasty meals such

pork or fish with bamboo shoots. The owner will keep the restaurant open in the evenings, with prior booking, for larger groups. Mon–Sat noon–7pm.

Dream Café Jasokie Place, Main Town. At the back of the UCO building, off the crossroads near the bottom of the cemetery, this small café and patisserie, owned by a renowned local musician, is the trendiest place in town. It's a great meeting place, with free wi-fi, pizzas (from ₹120), cakes and coffee, though sometimes you will need to wait for a space. Occasional live music on Friday and Saturday. Mon–Sat 10am–6pm.

Dimapur

For most, bustling **DIMAPUR**, 74km northwest of Kohima, the main gateway to the state, comes as a disappointing introduction, feeling much like any other Assam town. Don't let this put you off as, though Nagaland has a lot more to offer. Almost unavoidable, the town provides all the vital air, road and train connections linking Nagaland to the other states of the Northeast and especially Assam and Manipur. On the riverside edge of town are the **Kachari ruins**, fertility symbols dating back to the thirteenth-century Kachari kingdom.

ARRIVAL AND DEPARTURE   DIMAPUR

The main modes of transport in Dimapur are auto-rickshaws and shared taxis. The Nagaland checkpost is around 2km from the centre of town.

By plane Dimapur's airport is 4km out of town off the Kohima road. JetKonnect, Jet Airways and Air India fly to Kolkata, there are currently no direct connections to any other Northeast destinations.

By train Nagaland's sole railhead, Dimapur has trains to Dibrugarh, Simaluguri (for Sibsagar) and Tinsukia in Assam. The best service for Guwahati is the *Jan Shatabdi*

Express #12068 (daily except Sun 4.30pm; 4hr 30min); in the other direction (#12067) it travels to Jorhat (10.45am; 2hr 35min).

By taxi and bus The main transport hub is the railway station, from where shared taxis, marked yellow, ply regularly to Kohima (₹150; 3hr) services slow down after mid-afternoon. State and private buses run to Kohima (3hr) from the Nagaland State Transport stand adjacent to the station. Private buses to Guwahati, Jorhat, Imphal and Itanagar leave from near Super Market Junction.

ACCOMMODATION AND EATING

Dimapur has a limited choice of accommodation with a handful of budget and business hotels. There are couple of good restaurants and a surprisingly lively music scene.

★ **Jumping Bean** 1st Floor, Ana-Ki, near Tata Parking, Circular Rd ☎03862 284619, ✉jumpingbeancafe @gmail.com. With a very varied menu, from oriental and Korean through to great sandwiches, pasta and coffee, the popular bistro is a hub for the town's lively contemporary music scene. Bands play every second Friday of the month, when it stays open late. Daily 10am–7pm.

Niathu Resort 7th Mile, Chumukedima ☎03862 241489, ⊛niathugroup.com. The most luxurious of Dimapur's hotels, the resort consists of cottages with an

oblique reference to Naga traditional style coupled with large areas of marble flooring, modern amenities and a multi-cuisine restaurant. There is a spa and swimming pool and pleasant gardens. It's handy for the airport, but the cheaper rooms are disappointing. ₹3900

Tragopan Circular Rd ☎03862 230291, ✉hoteltragopan@indya.com. Busy and popular business hotel across the tracks and close to the *Jumping Bean* café, with comfortable rooms, attached baths and a decent restaurant. ₹800

Mon and around

In the far northeast of Nagaland, 70km southeast of Sibsagar in Assam, **MON** is the regional capital of the **Konyak** tribe, mainly attractive as a base for visits to the surrounding villages. Look out for older Konyaks with elaborate and iconic facial tattoos and goat-horn earrings.

16

In early April, the Konyaks celebrate the colourful six-day spring **Aoling festival**, turning out in all their finery to mark the beginning of the new year. A bumpy 23km drive northeast from Mon, **Shangnyu** is a typical Naga village where the welcoming *angh*'s home is packed with horns and animal skulls; the village also has a small but interesting museum.

ARRIVAL AND DEPARTURE
MON AND AROUND

By bus and jeep Buses and jeeps to Mon run from Dibrugarh (at least 7hr) via Sibsagar in Assam, bypassing the need to go through Dimapur and Kohima – but be prepared for dreadful roads and check current permit regulations before you set off.

ACCOMMODATION

Helsa Cottage Mon ☏0386 922 1246 or ☏8974 63314. A welcoming place that looks a bit like a tourist lodge, with large rooms, attached bathrooms, little electricity and beds with mosquito nets; the food is reasonable and they can arrange guides. ₹1200

Mokokchung and around

A vibrant hill town southwest of Mon and 160km (5hr by jeep) north of Kohima, **Mokokchung** is Nagaland's third largest urban centre, yet remains a quiet backwater in terms of tourism. Just 104km from Jorhat and more easily reachable from Assam than Kohima or Dimapur, Mokokchung makes a good base for exploring the surrounding Ao villages, including **Longkhum**, 17km away, which has a small museum and a guesthouse.

Tuensang

Tuensang, 115km east of Mokokchung, lies at the centre of a region inhabited by six different tribes – the Phom, Khiamniungan, Chang, Yimchunger and Sangtam. From here it's a two-day drive to **Thanamir**, and the start of a stunning two-day trek between tribal villages to **Mount Saramati**, Nagaland's highest peak (3826m), near the Burmese border. En route, there are basic places to stay at **Kiphere**. Check the security situation with your tour operator before setting off.

Mizoram

Heading south from Assam into **Mizoram**, "land of the highlanders", a winding mountain road takes you into forests and bamboo-covered hills. Mizoram is a gentle pastoral land, and the **Mizos** are a welcoming people who see very little tourism. Whitewashed churches dot the landscape, giving it more of the feel of a Central American country than a state squashed between Burma and Bangladesh.

The Mizos, who migrated from the Chin Hills of Burma, were regularly raiding tea plantations in the Assam Valley right into the late nineteenth century; only in 1924 did the British finally manage to bring about some semblance of control. They opened up what were then the **Lushai Hills** to missionaries who converted much of the state to Christianity. **Aizawl**, the capital, is a large sprawling city built on impossibly steep slopes. In the heart of the state, traditional Mizo communities occupy the crests of a series of ridges, each village dominated by its chief's house and *zawlbuk*, or bachelors' dormitory. An egalitarian people, without gender or class distinctions, the Mizos remain proud of their age-old custom of *Tlawmgaihna*, a code of ethics that governs hospitality. They enjoy a 95 percent literacy rate and are culturally more influenced by the Christian West than by mainstream India; music is an important part of Mizo life and an integral part of the Mizo Christian service. You may need a **permit** to enter (see box, p.839).

Aizawl

One of India's remotest state capitals, **AIZAWL** (1250m), with the Tropic of Cancer passing straight through it, perches precariously on the steep slopes of a sharp ridge. Although the views are of hills rather than snowy mountains, it has something of the feel of a Himalayan hill station. There are few monuments or temples, but the markets are interesting and there are some extraordinary churches, including the imposing **Solomon's Temple**, looking a bit like a cardboard cut-out, at Chawlhhmun. Everything closes on Sunday, when many people go to church dressed in their best.

Zarkawt is the main downtown area, with **Bara Bazaar** (daily except Sun 6am–3pm) the city's main attraction: everything from Mizo music to bespoke shoes can be bought here.

The **Durtlang Hills** immediately north of Aizawl, and **Luangmual**, 7km west, provide pleasant **walking** country – both are easy day-trips. Buses leave for Luangmual from outside the Salvation Army Temple.

ARRIVAL AND INFORMATION — AIZAWL

The easiest way of travelling to Mizoram is by air as the overland routes are long and tedious. To the north, the busy commercial hub of **Silchar**, 180km away in Assam, provides the most convenient train station, has an airport, and is connected to other areas by Assam's improving highways.

By plane Aizawl's Lengpui Airport, 35km west, has flights to Guwahati, Imphal and Kolkata. A taxi to the airport costs around ₹800; shared taxis (₹200), with pre-paid tickets sold at the arrivals hall, leave for Aizawl when full so you may have to wait for an hour or so.

By bus and Sumo The only recommended road out of Mizoram leads to Silchar, with Sumos (4–6hr; ₹350) the best way to travel, and there are several agents in Zarkawt. Private bus companies in Zarkawt also run services to Silchar. Sumos and state buses both travel to Shillong and Guwahati (both 14–18hr) via Silchar.

Tourist office There's a tourist office at Bungkawn (Mon–Fri 9am–5pm; T 0389 231 3475).

Travel and tours *David's Clover* are extremely good at arranging transport and tours around Mizoram for guests. Faith Travel & Tours, B27, 1st floor, Ramklun Venglai, opposite Lalbiakliana Petrol Station (T 08575 142075) provides tour packages and vehicles with optional guides, and can arrange air tickets too.

Services The State Bank of India, near First AR Ground, has an ATM and a foreign exchange counter.

ACCOMMODATION

★ **David's Clover** Zarkawt T 0389 230 5736, E hotelclover@hotmail.com. This ageing, central, family-run, mid-range hotel is run on a B&B basis. It offers comfortable attached rooms and some quirky wiring; each room boast a TV, fridge and wi-fi access. The owners, and especially Dolly, are extremely helpful and will arrange transport and suggest itineraries; the multicuisine restaurant is great. ₹1500

Regency B49 Zarkawt Main St T 0389 234 9334 or W regencyaizawl.com. The fanciest address in town, with a mock international lobby; lavish marble provides a promising introduction but the rooms themselves are uninspiring. There is a good travel service and the restaurant is trendy and bright. ₹1050

★ **RH Inn** Zarkawt A54 Main St T 0389 234 1987 or T 09856 560892. Down steps opposite the *Regency*, this central and charming guest house has immaculate, great-value, large, suite-like homely doubles and a restaurant and

BAMBOO, RATS AND REVOLUTION

Mizoram's two main species of bamboo flower every 48–50 years, attracting hordes of rats that devour crops, leading to famine. The first time this happened, in 1959, the government was seriously unprepared, which led **Laldenga** to found the **Mizo Famine Front** (MFF) to combat famine. It transformed into the **Mizo National Front** (MNF), a guerrilla group fighting for secession. The government's heavy-handed response in 1967 boosted support for the MNF who relied on essential Pakistani assistance that came to an end with Bangladeshi independence. The MNF eventually came to the negotiating table and statehood was granted in 1986 in return for an end to the insurgency. Mizoram is now the most peaceful of the "seven sisters." However, in 2007 the bamboo began to flower again, the rat population grew and crops were devastated but the famine, this time was thankfully not as devastating.

terrace with good views, a rarity in central Aizawl. ₹1050

Ritz Near Machhunga Point, Bara Bazaar ☎ 0389 231 0409, ⊛ ritzaizawl.com. A good option, popular with business travellers; staff are friendly, and there's a range of rooms, most with attached bathrooms and TVs, as well the excellent *Blue Berry* multicuisine restaurant. ₹1500

EATING

The best restaurants are in hotels and there a couple of good cafés around. For local cuisine, mild by Indian standards, try the modest restaurants around Bara Bazaar. The state is dry and most places close around 7pm.

★ **The Coffee Place** 1st Floor, Mamre Shopping Complex, next to Regency, Zarkawt. Welcoming café with great coffee and cakes and a good place to spend time catching up with writing and reading; this is a popular student hang-out and a good place to find out what is happening in Aizawl. Daily 10am–7pm.

David's Kitchen Zarkawt. Part of the *David's Clover* hotel and an old favourite serving Indian and Chinese food and Mizo cuisine. They also have a local café next door. Expect to pay around ₹500/head. Daily noon–9pm.

Jojo's 1st Floor, Mamre Shopping Complex, next to Regency, Zarkawt. Popular little kitchen restaurant next to *The Coffee Place*, serving Chinese and local food and light meals. Daily noon–7pm.

Magnolia 1st floor, Regency Hotel, Zarkawt. This is the smartest restaurant in town, all bright yellow walls and white leather chic. The wide-ranging menu offers a variety from pasta to tandoori. Try the sesame oven-roasted fish (₹180) and expect to pay around ₹600. Daily noon–9pm.

Manipur

16

Manipur, stretching along the border with Burma, centres on a vast lowland area watered by the lake system south of its capital **Imphal**. This far corner is home to the **Meithei**, who despite their own fascinating version of Vaishnava Hinduism, remain resolutely independent in their thinking. With its myriad **tribes**, including Naga, Manipur feels closer to Southeast Asia than mainstream India and many locals speak neither English nor Hindi. Manipur's **matriarchal society** means that women do most of the work and also champion political causes, with well-publicized protests against the violation of women and the people of Manipur, by paramilitary groups stationed in the state. The strength of Manipuri women is no better exemplified than by the universal popularity and success of the inspiring boxer and five-times World Champion and Olympic medallist, Mary Kom.

Although the vale of Imphal is now all but devoid of trees, the outlying hills are still forested and shelter exotic birds and animals like the spotted linshang, Blyth's tragopan and even the clouded leopard, as well as numerous varieties of orchid. The unique natural habitat of **Loktak Lake** is home to the sangai deer – the dancing deer of the reed beds and a symbol of Manipur.

Manipur's **history** can be traced back to the founding of Imphal in the first century AD. After long periods of independent and stable government, the state was

---

SAFETY IN MANIPUR

Over decades, Manipur has been wreaked by waves of violence through insurgency, drug- and arms-trafficking across the Burmese border, and brutal inter-factional **conflict**, making it one of the most volatile states in the union. Daily reports of violence appear in the local papers and any visitor to the state cannot help but notice the heightened security, with well-armed paramilitary and commandos visible almost everywhere. While the vale of Imphal is more or less safe, the hills and border regions demand extreme caution. Make adequate travel arrangements and travel into Imphal by air if possible – the road to Dimapur is prone to closures and the road to Silchar is not recommended. Some governments, including that of the UK, advise against all but essential travel to the state. That said, visitors who take care are unlikely to be affected, but do check the security situation and permit requirements (see boxes p.839 & P.841) beforehand.

incorporated into India at the end of the Indo-Burmese war in 1826, before coming under British rule in 1891. During World War II, much of Manipur was occupied by the Japanese, with 250,000 British and Indian troops trapped under siege in Imphal for three months. Thanks to a massive RAF air-lift from Agartala, they held out, and when Japanese troops received the order to end the Imphal campaign, it was in effect the end of the campaign to conquer India. Manipur became a fully fledged Indian state in 1972.

Imphal and around

Encircled by distant hills, Manipur's capital, **IMPHAL** (785m), lies at the northern end of the lake district and sprawls around the extensive grounds of what was once the medieval fortress of **Kangla**. The **Polo Ground** adjacent to Kangla plays an important role in Manipuri tradition; according to popular legend, the Manipuri game of *Sagol Kangjei* is the inspiration for modern polo, and every November the Sangai Festival features a polo tournament with teams drawn from as far afield as Europe.

Close to the main gates of Kangla, the **Shaheed Minar** memorial commemorates the failed Meithei revolt against British occupation in 1891, while a short distance south is the **State Museum** (Tues–Sun 10am–4.15pm; ₹20(₹3)), a showcase for Manipuri culture with tribal art and costumes and a historical collection along with stuffed animals. At the heart of Imphal, along Kangchup Road, the fascinating **Khwairamband** bazaar (daily), also known as *ima keithel* (mother's market), now re-housed in a new complex in three sections, is run by more than three thousand Meithei women, making it the largest of its kind in Asia. Upstairs, above the produce hall, where there is a pleasant cafeteria, you can look down on the bustling scene below. Southeast of Kangla,the Vaishnavite temple of **Shri Shri Govindjee**, where priests perform rituals addressing the deities according to the times of day, is well worth a visit, especially in the afternoon when you may be lucky to catch a glimpse of a **Manipuri dance** rehearsal in the hall opposite. Nearby lies the old **Royal Palace**, closed to the public.

The Commonwealth War Graves Commission immaculately maintains the **British War Cemetery**, 500m north of the *Tourist Lodge* on Imphal Road while south of the city near Bishnupur, a Japanese memorial stands as a poignant reminder of the war. Closed to the public for years due to it being a paramilitary camp, the large park behind the boulevard of Kanglawat holds some remains of the old palace of **Kangla**, taken by the British following the war of 1891.

ARRIVAL AND DEPARTURE
IMPHAL

By plane Imphal Airport, 6km to the south, is well connected to Guwahati and Kolkata and sees a handful of flights to Aizawl. Airlines servicing Imphal include Air India, Jet Airways, JetKonnect and Indigo. There are no airport bus connections to the city centre; taxis charge ₹300; shared taxis ₹10 and reserved taxis ₹150. Foreigners currently do not need permits but need to enter passport details at the desk just inside the arrivals hall.

By bus and taxi The new Inter-state Bus Terminal is being built on Stadium Rd but for the time being AOC (Assam oil Corporation), corner on Dimapur Rd acts as the main hub with buses to Nagaland and beyond (6.30am &

10.30am) including Guwahati (579km; ₹700) via Kohima (6hr; ₹300) and Dimapur (215km; 7hr; ₹400), the closest railhead. Winger shared taxis travel the same route (6am & 10.30am; ₹600) and are a bit faster; for bookings try DI Sumo and Winger Service (☏ 9862 071071). Some private buses depart from their offices while the Silchar buses (200km; 14hr; ₹400) leave from Silchar Parking near Khwairamband – note, however, that this service, due to occasional strikes and unpredictable security and road conditions, is not recommended. Several private bus companies operate from MG Ave near the State Bank of India, and also have stands on DM Rd outside *Hotel Tampha*.

INFORMATION

Tourist office The state tourist office (April–Sept Mon–Sat 9.30am–5pm; Oct–March closes 4.30pm; closed 2nd Sat of month; ☏ 0385 222 0802, ⓦ tourismmanipur.nic.in) is at the Directorate of Tourism building behind the *Hotel Imphal*, off

the main Dimapur road. The India Tourism office is on Jail Rd (Mon–Sat 9.30am–5.30pm; ☏ 0385 222 1131).

Banks & ATMs The State Bank of India on MG Ave has a foreign exchange service. There is an ATM there and others

16

throughout the centre.

Tours Classic Traveller at *The Classic* hotel (☎ 9862 805292, ✉ rajib@theclassichotel.in) is well organized, offering day-tours of the entire Imphal valley (from ₹3000). Seven

Sisters, MG Ave (☎ 9862 188454 or ☎ 0385 244 3977) offer tours and book transport and also air tickets. Travel World, at the airport (☎ 9856 805960) book cars at the tours and air tickets.

ACCOMMODATION AND EATING

Imphal has a few decent hotels, where you will find the best restaurants, but there are no bars – Manipur is a dry state and everything, outside the hotels, shuts down around 7pm.

Anand Continental Khoyathong Rd ☎ 0385 222 3422. One of the better city-centre hotels, offering smallish but comfortable rooms with attached baths and one of the best restaurants in town, *Host*. ₹850

★ **The Classic** North AOC, Dimapur Rd ☎ 0385 244 3967, ⒲ theclassichotel.in. Opposite the Kangla grounds, this is the most opulent of Imphal's hotels, with a swish lobby, a good restaurant and great breakfasts. The comfortable rooms have modern amenities but recive a bit of traffic noise, despite the sealed windows; service is friendly but slow. There is a good café, which

has occasional live music, and an excellent travel desk. ₹2300

Imphal North AOC, Dimapur Rd ☎ 0385 242 3344. The large rambling tourist lodge on the northern edge of town offers sizeable rooms with attached baths, some of them a/c, plus a restaurant and very helpful staff should you need to arrange transport or require information. ₹500

Nirmala MG Ave ☎ 0385 222 9014. This business hotel, in the centre of town, has a large range of rooms from poky simple doubles through to a/c suites. The a/c restaurant has a good multicuisine menu. ₹820

Loktak Lake

South of Imphal, Lotak Lake is home to a unique community of fishermen who live on circular floating atolls of matted vegetation. Much of the lake is taken up by the **Keibul Lamjao National Park** (daily 9am–5pm; ₹200 (₹30)). home to the unique and endangered sangai deer that live on the reed beds. Avoid the hill at **Sendra**, which is now a paramilitary camp surrounded by litter. You can get a boat out to Sendra Island where there is a tourist bungalow and cafeteria. To get to the national park gates, drive on for 5km past Sendra; the viewing tower on a hill with views down to the reed beds is a good 1.5km walk or drive past the gate. You will need binoculars and lots of patience to catch sight of any wildlife. On the way to Loktak, the small town of **MOIRANG**, 45km south of Imphal, is the traditional centre of Meithei culture, with a temple devoted to the pre-Hindu deity **Thangjing**. In April 1944, the Indian National Army under Netaji Subhas Chandra Bose planted its flag at Moirang, having fought alongside the Japanese against the British Indian Army for the cause of Independence. A **memorial** and small **museum** (daily; ₹20 (₹2)) commemorate the event.

Tripura

Surrounded by Bangladesh on three sides, the lush mountains, hills and valleys of **TRIPURA** became part of India in 1949 when the princely state joined the union. Its fate and culture has been closely entwined with Bengal, while indigenous ethnic groups form around thirty percent of the population, mostly around the northern and eastern districts bordering Assam. Partition and the subsequent creation of East Pakistan (now Bangladesh) in 1948, followed by war, famine and military regimes forced millions of Bangladeshis to flee into Tripura, where they now outnumber the indigenous people – such as the Tripuri, a Tibeto-Burman ethnic group – which has caused resentment and **conflict** over the decades. In 2013, elections returned the CPI(M) government, making Tripura one of the last communist-held states in India. Today, **Agartala**, the capital, is a relaxed city with a palace and a few temples, with **Udaipur**, a town of lakes and temples, and the fairy-tale palace at **Neermahal** easily accessible. Of particular note is **Tripura Sundari**, one of the Northeast's most important temples. It is located just outside Udaipur, and well worth a visit. A handful of sanctuaries, such as **Gumti**, **Rowa**, **Trishna** and **Sepahijala**, protect the state's few remaining forests while to the northeast the medieval Shaivite rock carvings of **Unakoti** are now accessible after years of strife.

Agartala

Agartala, Tripura's capital, is a laid-back administrative centre. Its main attraction is the gleaming white **Ujjayanta Palace**, completed in 1901. Set amid formal gardens and artificial lakes, this huge building, now home to the State Legislative Assembly, covers around eight hundred acres. Across the road, one of many temples nearby and open to the public, the **Jagannath Temple** with its orange tower rises from an octagonal plinth.

    Kamala Sagar lake, 27km south of Agartala, is overlooked by a small Kali temple with a twelfth-century sandstone image of Mahishasuramardini, a form of Durga, while on the road south to Udaipur the **Sepahijala** (25km) nature reserve and botanical gardens is actually a vast zoo dedicated to the preservation of animals such as the Hoolock gibbon.

ARRIVAL AND INFORMATION   AGARTALA

By plane The airport, 12km north, has good daily flights to Guwahati, Kolkata and Imphal, serviced by Air India, Jet Airways, JetKonnect, Spice Jet and Indigo. Pre-paid counters for autos (₹130) and taxis (₹260) link the airport with the centre of Agartala. At the time of going to press, the Pawan Hans Helicopter service was suspended.

By train Agartala has limited connections to Lumding and Silchar in Assam, linking into the national rail network. A major extension should be complete by the end of 2014, bringing high-speed services including the *Rajdhani* to the state.

By bus or Sumo Arriving by bus, you'll probably be dropped off at one of the private company offices on LN Bari Rd, or at the state bus stand at Krishna Nagar. State buses leave from Inter-state Bus Terminal (3km) for the gruelling stop-start convoy to Silchar (12hr), Shillong (20hr) and Guwahati. Private buses depart from LN Bari Rd, 100m east of the palace. Buses heading north from Agartala have to travel in three-daily army-escorted convoys from Teliamura to Kumarghat (the nearest railhead), leaving at 6am, 8am and 11.30am. Buses and Sumos to Udaipur (every 30min; 2hr) leave from the South Bus Station near Shankar Chowmohoni.

To and from Bangladesh Agartala is 2km from the border with Bangladesh but there is no official currency exchange. Rickshaws on the Bangladeshi side can take you to Akhaura Junction, 4km away, from where there are trains to Comilla, Sylhet and Dhaka (2hr 30min). The Bangladeshi Embassy (Mon–Thurs 8.30am–1pm & 2–4.30pm, Fri 8.30am–noon; ☏0381 222 4807), next to the *Brideway* hotel, issues visas.

Tourist information The tourist office (TTDC) is temporarily housed at Kunjaban, opposite the Governor's House (Mon–Sat 10am–5.30pm, Sun 3–5pm; ☏0381 232 5930, ⓦtripuratourism.nic.in) while its premises at the Palace Compound are being renovated. The office provides information and organizes good-value tour packages around Tripura. It also books accommodation in all the tourist lodges.

ACCOMMODATION AND EATING

Abhishek Durga Bari Rd. Centrally located and popular, this multicuisine restaurant, strong on Indian food, has a small a/c dining room and a pleasant courtyard which is popular for alfresco eating in the evenings, weather permitting. There is a dining hall popular for events and weddings, which might explain the tacky plastic seating that lets down the ambience; expect to pay around ₹300. Daily noon–3 & 6–10pm.

★ **Executive Inn** 9 Mantri Bari, Chowmuhani ☏0381 232 5047, ✉hotelexecutiveinn@yahoo.com. Set in its own courtyard behind the ICICI ATM, this centrally located efficient little hotel offers excellent value with well-presented and huge double rooms, dark downstairs and best on the top floor. The rooms range from plain doubles to a/c suites and there is an excellent restaurant next door – *Blossom*. ₹880

Ginger Khejurbagan, Airport Rd ☏0381 241 1333, ⓦgingerhotels.com. Efficient *Tata* group chain hotel with spotless, if soulless, rooms reminiscent of a hospital and modelled on a *Travelodge*, but with welcoming staff and an attractive meal plan including great breakfasts; there is a *Coffee Café Day* downstairs at the back of the hotel. You can pick up good discounts online and even, occasionally, at their airport counter. ₹4300

16

Odisha

CARVINGS AT KONARK TEMPLE

17

Odisha

Despite being one of India's poorest states, Odisha – formerly known as Orissa (many road signs and web addresses still carry the old name), boasts a rich and distinctive cultural heritage. The state's coastal plains have the highest concentration of historical and religious monuments – Odisha's principal tourist attractions. Puri, site of the famous Jagannath temple and one of the world's most spectacular devotional processions, the Rath Yatra, combines the heady intensity of a Hindu pilgrimage centre with the hedonistic pleasures of the beach. Just a short hop off the main Kolkata–Chennai road and railway, the town is a popular destination for backpackers. Konark, a short way up the coast, has the ruins of Odisha's most ambitious medieval temple, whose surfaces writhe with exquisitely preserved sculpture, including some eyebrow-raising erotica. The ancient rock-cut caves and ornate temples of Bhubaneswar, the state capital, hark back to the era when it ruled a kingdom stretching from the Ganges delta to the mouth of the River Godavari.

Away from the central "golden triangle" of sights, foreign travellers are few and far between, though you'll see plenty of Bengali tourists travelling throughout coastal Odisha. In the winter, the small islands dotted around **Chilika Lake**, a huge saltwater lagoon south of Bhubaneswar, is good for birdwatchers. Further north, in the **Bhitarkanika Sanctuary**, a remote stretch of beach is the nesting site for rare Olive Ridley **turtles**.

From the number of temples in Odisha, you'd be forgiven for thinking Brahmanical Hinduism was its sole religion. In fact, almost a quarter of the population are **adivasi**, or "tribal" (literally "first") people, thought to have descended from the area's pre-Aryan aboriginal inhabitants. In the more inaccessible corners of the state many of these groups have retained unique cultural traditions and languages, though dam builders, missionaries, "advancement programmes" initiated by the state government, and the activities of Maoist rebels continue to threaten their way of life. Tourism poses another danger (see box, p.902).

Brief history

Other than scattered fragmentary remains of prehistoric settlement, Odisha's earliest archeological find dates from the fourth century BC. The fortified city of **Sisupalgarh**, near modern Bhubaneswar, was the capital of the **Kalinga** dynasty, about which little is known. In the third century BC, the ambitious Mauryan emperor **Ashoka** routed the Kalingan kingdom in a battle so bloody that the carnage was supposed to have inspired his legendary conversion to **Buddhism**. Rock edicts erected around the empire extol the virtues of the new faith, dharma, as well as the principles that Ashoka hoped to instil in his vanquished subjects. With the demise of the Mauryans, Kalinga enjoyed something of a resurgence. Under the imperialistic **Chedi** Jain dynasty, vast sums were spent expanding the capital and on carving elaborate monastery caves into the nearby hills of

Highlights

❶ Bhubaneswar Hidden in the suburbs of the state capital are around five hundred temples with unique architecture and elaborate sculptures. Check out the majestic Lingaraj Mandir. **See p.875**

❷ Udaigiri and Khandagiri Among Odisha's premier historical sites, these 2000-year-old sandstone caves, once occupied by Jain monks, feature some fascinating carvings and friezes. **See p.883**

❸ Olive Ridley turtles Endangered Olive Ridley turtles journey to Gahirmatha beach for one night in February or March to lay their eggs – an unforgettable scene. **See p.886**

❹ Puri With one of India's holiest temples and a laidback traveller scene, Puri is an essential stop-off for pilgrims and backpackers alike. **See p.887**

❺ Rath Yatra Pilgrims flock to Puri to celebrate Lord Jagannath during the frenetic midsummer "Car Festival". **See p.891**

❻ Konark Dating back to the thirteenth century, this elegant Hindu temple sits astride a huge stone chariot and is decorated by some extraordinary erotic carvings. **See p.896**

HIGHLIGHTS ARE MARKED ON THE MAP ON P.874

17

Khandagiri and **Udaigiri**. During the second century BC, however, the kingdom gradually splintered into warring factions and entered a kind of Dark Age. The influence of Buddhism waned, Jainism all but vanished, and **Brahmanism**, disseminated by the teachings of the Shaivite zealot Lakulisha, started to resurface as the dominant religion.

A golden age

Odisha's golden age, during which the region's prosperous Hindu rulers created some of South Asia's most sophisticated art and architecture, peaked in the twelfth century under the **Eastern Gangas**. Fuelled by the gains from a thriving trade network (which extended as far east as Indonesia), the Ganga kings erected magnificent **temples** where Shiva worship and arcane tantric practices adopted by earlier Odishan rulers were replaced by new forms of devotion to Vishnu. The shrine of the most popular royal deity of all, Lord Jagannath, at Puri, was by now one of the four most hallowed religious centres in India.

In the fifteenth century, the **Afghans of Bengal** swept south to annex the region, with Man Singh's **Mughal** army hot on their heels in 1592. That even a few medieval Hindu monuments escaped the excesses of the ensuing iconoclasm is miraculous, and **non-Hindus** have never since been allowed to enter the most holy temples in Puri and Bhubaneswar. In 1751 the **Marathas** from western India ousted the Mughals as the dominant regional power. The East India Company, meanwhile, was also making inroads along the coast, and 28 years after Clive's victory at Plassey in 1765, Odisha finally came under **British rule**.

Post Independence

Following **Independence**, the state has sustained rapid **development**. Discoveries of coal, bauxite, iron ore and other minerals stimulated considerable industrial growth and improvements to infrastructure. Despite such urban progress, however, Odisha

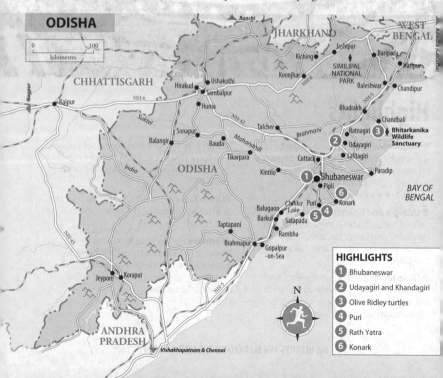

ODISHA

0 — 100
kilometres

JHARKHAND

WEST BENGAL

Kolkata (Calcutta)

Ranchi

Jashipur
Baripada
Kiching
Haripur
Keonjhar
SIMILIPAL NATIONAL PARK
Baleshwar
Chandipur

CHHATTISGARH
Ushakothi
Hirakud
Sambalpur
Huma
Bhadrakh
Chandbali
Bhitarkanika Wildlife Sanctuary
Raipur
Nagpur
Suktel
Sonapur
Talcher
Brahmani
Ratnagiri
Balangir
Bauda
Mahanadi
Udayagiri
Lalitagiri
Indra
ODISHA
Tikarpara
Cuttack
Kintilo
Bhubaneswar
Paradip
Pipli
Konark
Balugaon
Chilika Lake
Puri
Taptapani
Barkul
Satapada
Rambha
Brahmapur
Gopalpur-on-Sea

BAY OF BENGAL

Jeypore
Koraput

ANDHRA PRADESH

Vishakhapatnam & Chennai

N

HIGHLIGHTS
1 Bhubaneswar
2 Udayagiri and Khandagiri
3 Olive Ridley turtles
4 Puri
5 Rath Yatra
6 Konark

remains a poor rural state (around 55 percent of children are malnourished, for example), heavily dependent on agriculture to provide for the basic needs of its forty million or so inhabitants.

Events of recent years have damaged the state's reputation. Violent **Maoist** (Naxalite) activity in rural areas has increased, drawing an often equally violent response from government forces. In March 2012, two Italian travellers visiting tribal areas in the Kandhamal area were kidnapped by Naxalites and held for almost a month, before being released unharmed. There have also been attacks against the state's **Christian minority** by Hindu fundamentalists, who, in 2008, killed at least seventy people and forced tens of thousands from their homes.

An ongoing campaign by environmental and human rights groups, meanwhile, has been vociferous in its opposition to the multinational corporation **Vedanta**, which is pushing ahead with plans to develop a bauxite mine on Niyamgiri mountain in eastern Odisha, considered sacred by the local *adivasi* community.

GETTING AROUND   ODISHA

Travelling around Odisha presents few practical problems if you stick to the more populated coastal areas. **NH-5** and the **Southeast Railway**, which cut in tandem down the coastal plain via Bhubaneswar, are the main arteries of the region. A branch line also runs as far as Puri, connecting it by frequent, direct express **trains** to Delhi, Kolkata and Chennai. Elsewhere, **buses** are the best way to travel.

Bhubaneswar

With its featureless 1950s architecture, **BHUBANESWAR** may initially strike you as surprisingly dull for a city with a population of around three-quarters of a million and a history of settlement stretching back more than two thousand years. However, the southern suburbs harbour the remnants of some of India's finest medieval **temples,**

ODISHAN FESTIVALS

The chances of coinciding with a **festival** while in Odisha are good, since the state celebrates many of its own as well as all the usual Hindu festivals.

Makar Mela (mid-Jan). Pilgrims descend on a tiny island in Chilika Lake to leave votive offerings in a cave for the goddess Kali.

Adivasis Mela (Jan 26–Feb 1). Bhubaneswar's "tribal" fair is a disappointing cross between New York's Coney Island and an agricultural show, though it does feature good live music and dance.

Magha Saptami (Jan & Feb). During the full-moon phase of Magha, a small pool at Chandrabhaga beach, near Konark, is swamped by thousands of worshippers in honour of Surya, the sun god and curer of skin ailments.

Panashankranti (early April). In various regions, on the first day of Vaisakha, saffron-clad penitents carrying peacock feathers enter trances and walk on hot coals.

Chaitra Parba (mid-April). Santals (the largest of Odisha's many *adivasi* groups) perform *Chhou* dances at Baripada in Mayurbhunj district, northern Odisha.

Ashokastami (April & May). Bhubaneswar's own Car Festival (a procession of temple chariots), when the Lingaraj deity takes a dip in the Bindu Sagar tank.

Sitalasasthi (May & June). Commemorates the marriage of Shiva and Parvati, celebrated in Sambalpur and Bhubaneswar.

Rath Yatra (June & July). The biggest and grandest of Odisha's festivals. Giant images of Lord Jagannath, his brother Balabhadra and his sister Subhadra make the sacred journey from the Jagannath temple to Gundicha Mandir in Puri.

Bali Yatra (Nov & Dec). Commemorates the voyages made by Odishan traders to Indonesia. Held at full moon on the banks of the River Mahanadi in Cuttack.

Konark Festival (early Dec). A festival of classical dance featuring Odishan and other regional dance forms in the Sun Temple at Konark.

17

which are made all the more atmospheric by the animated religious life that continues to revolve around them, particularly at festival times.

Brief history

Bhubaneswar first appears in history during the fourth century BC, as the capital of ancient **Kalinga**. It was here that Ashoka erected one of the Subcontinent's best-preserved rock edicts – still in place 5km south of **Dhauli**. Under the **Chedis**, ancient Kalinga gained control over the thriving mercantile trade in the region and became the northeast seaboard's most formidable power.

Bhubaneswar then declined, re-emerging as a regional force only in the fifth century AD, when it became an important Shaivite centre. Coupled with the formidable wealth of the **Sailodbhavas** two centuries later, the growing religious fervour fuelled an extraordinary spate of temple construction. Between the seventh and twelfth centuries some seven thousand shrines are believed to have been erected around the **Bindu Sagar** tank. Most

ODISHAN TEMPLES

Odishan temples constitute one of the most distinctive regional styles of religious architecture in South Asia. They were built according to strict templates set down one thousand years or more ago in a body of canonical texts called the *Shilpa Shastras*. These specify not only every aspect of temple design, but also the overall symbolic significance of the building. Unlike Christian churches or Islamic mosques, Hindu shrines are not simply places of worship but objects of worship in themselves – recreations of the "Divine Cosmic Creator-Being" or the particular deity enshrined within them. For a Hindu, to move through a temple is akin to entering the very body of the god glimpsed at the moment of *darshan*, or ritual viewing, in the shrine room. In Odisha, this concept also finds expression in the technical terms used in the *Shastras* to designate the different parts of the structure: the foot (*pabhaga*), shin (*jangha*), torso (*gandi*), neck (*kantha*), head (*mastaka*) and so forth.

THE DEUL

Most temples are made up of two main sections. The first and most impressive of these is the **deul**, or sanctuary tower. A soaring, curvilinear spire with a square base and rounded top, the *deul* symbolizes Meru, the sacred mountain at the centre of the universe. Its intricately ribbed sides, which in later buildings were divided into rectangular projections known as *raths*, usually house images of the accessory deities, while its top supports a lotus-shaped, spherical *amla* (a motif derived from an auspicious fruit used in Ayurvedic medicine as a purifying agent). Above that, the vessel of immortality, the *kalasha*, is crowned by the presiding deity's sacred weapon, a wheel (Vishnu's *chakra*) or trident (Shiva's *trishul*). The actual deity occupies a chamber inside the *deul*. Known in Oriya as the **garbha griha**, or inner sanctum, the shrine is shrouded in womb-like darkness, intended to focus the mind of the worshipper on the image of God.

THE JAGAMOHANA

The **jagamohana** ("world delighter"), which adjoins the sanctuary tower, is a porch with a pyramidal roof where the congregation gathers for readings of religious texts and other important ceremonies. Larger temples, such as the Lingaraj in Bhubaneswar and the Jagannath in Puri, also have structures that were tacked on to the main porch when music and dance were more commonly performed as part of temple rituals. Like the *jagamohana*, the roofs of the **nata mandir** (the dancing hall) and **bhoga-mandapa** (the hall of offerings) are pyramidal. The whole structure, along with any smaller subsidiary shrines (often earlier temples erected on the same site), is usually enclosed with in a walled courtyard.

AN EVOLVING STYLE

Over the centuries, Odishan temples became progressively grander and more elaborate. It's fascinating to chart this transformation as you move from the earlier buildings in Bhubaneswar to the acme of the region's architectural achievement, the stunning Sun Temple at **Konark** (see p.896). Towers grow taller, roofs gain extra layers, and the **sculpture**, for which the temples are famous all over the world, attains a level of complexity and refinement unrivalled before or since.

were razed in the Muslim incursions of the medieval era, but enough survived for it to be possible in even a short visit to trace the evolution of Odishan architecture from its small, modest beginnings to the gigantic, self-confident proportions of the **Lingaraj** – the seat of Trimbhubaneshwara, or "Lord of Three Worlds", from which the modern city takes its name. A relative backwater until after Independence, Bhubaneswar was only declared the new state capital after nearby Cuttack reached bursting point in the 1950s.

The temples

Of the five hundred or so **temples** that remain in Bhubaneswar only a handful are of interest to anyone but the most ardent temple-phile. They are quite spread out in the south of the city, but it's possible to see the highlights in a day by auto-rickshaw (see p.880). The majority are active places of worship, so dress appropriately, remove your shoes (and any leather items) at the entrance and seek permission before taking photographs, particularly inside the buildings. The resident priest will expect a donation if he's shown you around, but don't believe the astronomical amounts recorded in the ledgers you'll be shown. Entry is free to all temples except the Rajarani.

The central group
Just west of Lewis Rd, around 2.5km south of the railway station

The compact **central group** includes some of Bhubaneswar's most celebrated temples, most notably the well-preserved **Parasurameswara Mandir** and the exquisite, tenth-century **Muktesvara Mandir**.

Parasurameswara Mandir

The best-preserved and most beautiful early example in the central group, the lavishly decorated **Parasurameswara Mandir**, stands in the shade of a large banyan tree. Dating from around 650 AD, the shrine's plain, rectangular assembly hall (*jagamohana*), simple stepped roof and squat beehive-shaped tower (*deul*) typify the style of the late seventh century. Besides the sheer quality of the building's exterior sculpture, Parasurameswara is significant in marking the then-recent transition from Buddhism to Hinduism. Look out for panels depicting Lakulisha, the proselytizing Shaivite saint whose sect was largely responsible for the conversion of Odisha to Hinduism in the fifth century. More graphic assertions of Hindu supremacy mark corners of the *deul*, where rampant lions crouch or stand above elephants, symbols of the beleaguered Buddhist faith.

Muktesvara Mandir

Erected in the mid-tenth century, the **Muktesvara Mandir** is often described as the gem of Odishan architecture for its compact size and exquisite sculptural detail. It stands in a separate walled courtyard, beside the small **Marichi Kund** tank (whose waters are believed to cure infertility). The temple was constructed two hundred years after the Parasurameswara, and represents the new, more elaborate style that had evolved in Bhubaneswar. Its *jagamohana* sports the more distinctively Odishan pyramidal roof, while the *deul*, though similar in shape to earlier sanctuary towers, places more emphasis on vertical rather than horizontal lines. Directly facing the main entrance, the ornamental **torana** (gateway), topped by two reclining female figures, is Muktesvara's masterpiece.

On the edge of Muktesvara's terrace, the unfinished **Siddhesvara** was erected at around the same time as the Lingaraj, but is far less imposing.

The eastern group
Just east of Lewis Rd, around 2.5km south of the railway station

The two key temples in the **eastern group** are the **Rajarani Mandir**, widely considered to be one of the most beautiful temples in Bhubaneswar, and the **Brahmesvara Mandir**, which continues to host a living deity.

17

Rajarani Mandir

Daily sunrise–sunset • ₹100 (₹5), video ₹25

Although it was never completed, the twelfth-century **Rajarani Mandir** ranks among the very finest of Bhubaneswar's later temples. From the far end of the well-watered gardens in which it stands, the profile of the *deul* dominates first impressions. The best of the sculpted figures for which Rajarani is famous surround the sides of the tower, roughly 3m above the ground, where the **dikpalas** ("guardians of the eight directions"), separated from one another by exquisite female *nayikas*, protect the main shrine.

Brahmesvara Mandir

Unlike most of its neighbours, the eleventh-century shrine within **Brahmesvara Mandir** still houses a living deity, as indicated by the saffron pennant flying from the top of the sanctuary. Here, as at Rajarani, *dikpalas* preside over the corners, with a fierce Chamunda on the western facade (shown astride a corpse and holding a trident and severed head), while curvaceous maidens admire themselves in mirrors or dally with their male consorts. An inscription, now lost, records that one Queen Kovalavati once made a donation of "many beautiful women" to this temple, recalling that **devadasis**, the dancers-cum-prostitutes who were to become a prominent feature of Odishan temple life in later years (see box, 899), made an early appearance here. Non-Hindus are barred from the central shrine, whose majestic Nandi bull has testicles well polished by years of propitious rubbing from worshippers.

The Bindu Sagar group

West of the central group around the Bindu Sagar

The largest group of temples is clustered around the **Bindu Sagar** ("ocean drop tank"). This small artificial lake, mentioned in the Puranas, is said to contain nectar, wine and water drawn from the world's most sacred rivers. It's the main bathing place both for pilgrims visiting the city and for the Lingaraj deity, who is taken to the pavilion in the middle once every year during Bhubaneswar's annual **Car Festival** (Ashokastami) for his ritual purificatory dip. The hours around sunrise and sunset are the most evocative time for a stroll here, when the residents of the nearby *dharamshalas* file through the smoky lanes to pray at the *ghats*.

Lingaraj Mandir

Immediately south of the Bindu Sagar stands Odisha's most stylistically evolved temple. Built early in the eleventh century by the Ganga kings, one hundred years before the Jagannath temple at Puri, the mighty **Lingaraj Mandir** has remained a living shrine. For this reason, foreign visitors are not permitted inside, but there is a **viewing platform** overlooking the north wall of the complex, from where all four of the principal sections of the building are visible. The two nearest the entrance, the *bhoga-mandapa* (hall of offering) and the *nata mandir* (hall of dances), associated with the rise of the *devadasi* system (see box, p.899) are both later additions. Beautiful **sculpture** depicting the music and dance rituals that would once have taken place inside the temple adorns its walls.

The immense 45m *deul* is the literal and aesthetic high-point of the Lingaraj. The rampant lion projecting from the curved sides of the tower, and the downtrodden elephant beneath him, one more symbolize the triumph of Hinduism over Buddhism. On the top, the typical Odishan motif of the flattened, ribbed sphere (*amla*) supported by gryphons, is crowned with Shiva's trident. As in the Brahmesvara temple, the long saffron pennant announces the living presence of the deity below.

The **shrine** inside is unusual. The powerful 2.5m-thick Svayambhu ("self-born") lingam that it contains, one of the twelve *jyotrilingas* in India, is known as "Hari-Hara" as it is considered half Shiva, half Vishnu – an extraordinary amalgam thought to have resulted from the ascendancy of Vaishnavism over Shaivism in the twelfth and thirteenth centuries. Unlike other lingams, which are bathed every day in a concoction prepared from hemlock, Svayambhu is offered a libation of rice, milk and bhang by the brahmins.

Vaital Deul Mandir

The **Vaital Deul** temple, one of the group's oldest buildings, is a real feast of Tantric art. The building was erected around 800 AD in a markedly different style from most of its contemporaries in Bhubaneswar, drawing heavily on earlier Buddhist influences. Among the panels of Hindu deities encrusting its outer walls, you can make out examples of some of India's earliest erotic sculpture.

Once you have proceeded past the four-faced lingam post at the main entrance (used for tethering sacrificial offerings), your eyes soon adjust to the darkness of the **interior**, whose grotesque images convey the macabre nature of the esoteric rites once performed here. Durga, in her most terrifying aspect as **Chamunda**, peers out of the half-light from behind the grille at the far end of the hall – her withered body, garlanded with skulls and flanked by an owl and a jackal, stands upon a rotting corpse. In front of her a man picks himself up from the floor, having filled his skull-cup with blood from the decapitated body nearby.

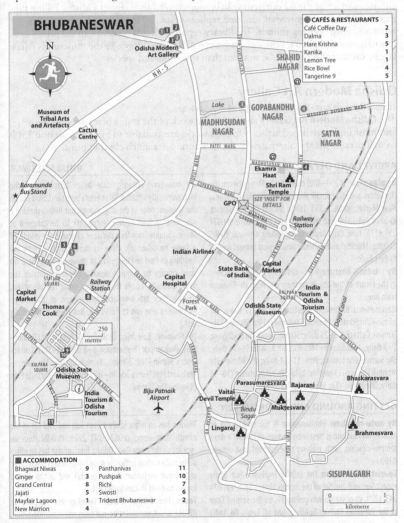

BHUBANESWAR

N

NH-5

Odisha Modern
Art Gallery

**SHAHID
NAGAR**

Museum of
Tribal Arts
and Artefacts

Cactus
Centre

Lake

**MADHUSUDAN
NAGAR**

**GOPABANDHU
NAGAR**

MAHARSHI DAYANAND MARG

**SATYA
NAGAR**

PATEL MARG

Baramunda
Bus Stand

GOPABANDHU MARG

MADHUSUDAN MARG

Ekamra
Haat

Shri Ram
Temple

GPO

SEE 'INSET' FOR
DETAILS

MAHATMA
GANDHI MARG

Railway
Station

JAN PATH

Indian Airlines

RAJPATH

Capital
Market

CUTTACK ROAD

Capital
Hospital

State Bank
of India

KALPANA
SQUARE

**India
Tourism &
Odisha
Tourism**

EKAMRA MARG

UDYAN MARG

Forest
Park

Odisha State
Museum

Dava Canal

RN NAGAR

STATION
SQUARE

Railway
Station

Capital
Market

Thomas
Cook

JAN PATH

RAJPATH

CUTTACK ROAD

0   250
metres

KALPANA
SQUARE

Odisha State
Museum

India
Tourism &
Odisha
Tourism

Biju Patnaik
Airport

EKAMRA MARG

Parasumaresvara

Rajarani

Bhaskaresvara

Vaital
Devil Temple

Bindu
Sagar

Muktesvara

Lingaraj

Brahmesvara

SISUPALGARH

0   1
kilometre

● CAFÉS & RESTAURANTS	
Café Coffee Day	2
Dalma	3
Hare Krishna	5
Kanika	1
Lemon Tree	1
Rice Bowl	4
Tangerine 9	5

■ ACCOMMODATION			
Bhagwat Niwas	9	Panthanivas	11
Ginger	3	Pushpak	10
Grand Central	8	Richi	7
Jajati	5	Swosti	6
Mayfair Lagoon	1	Trident Bhubaneswar	2
New Marrion	4		

17

Odisha State Museum

At the top of Lewis Rd • Tues–Sun 10am–5pm • ₹50 (₹5) • ☏ 0674 243 1597

The **Odisha State Museum** has a collection of "tribal" artefacts, manuscripts and archeological finds, including pre-twelfth-century Buddhist statues and reproductions of **chitra muriya**, the folk murals seen in village houses around Puri. The museum's real highlight, however, is its collection of antique **painting** and illuminated **palm-leaf manuscripts** (see box, p.896). Only New Delhi's National Museum holds finer examples of this traditional Odishan art form.

Museum of Tribal Arts and Artefacts

NH-5, close to the Baramunda bus stand • Mon–Sat 10am–5pm • Free

The anthropological **Museum of Tribal Arts and Artefacts** exhibits the distinctive cultures and art of the 62 different tribal groups spread throughout Odisha. Filling the gardens outside are somewhat idealized replicas of *adivasi* dwellings, decorated with more authentic-looking murals. The **library** reputedly holds copies of all the books and journals ever compiled on the *adivasi* groups of Odisha. Opposite the museum is Asia's largest **cactus collection**, home to more than one thousand species.

Odisha Modern Art Gallery

132 Forest Walk, Surya Nagar • Mon–Sat 11am–1.30pm & 4–8pm, Sun 4–8pm

The **Odisha Modern Art Gallery** showcases the work of the state's best contemporary and most underprivileged artists. Original works are available to buy from around ₹500 to well over ₹15,000 – alternatively you can settle for a much cheaper print.

ARRIVAL AND DEPARTURE

BHUBANESWAR

By plane Taxis (₹200–300) cover the 2–3km between the city centre and Biju Patnaik airport. Air India (Raj Path, near New Market; ☏ 0674 253 0380), IndiGo (at the airport; ☏ 0124 661 3838) and Jet Airways (at the airport; ☏ 0674 259 6176) have daily flights to Bengaluru, Chennai, Delhi, Kolkata, Mumbai and Vishakapatnam, plus several weekly to Port Blair.

By train Bhubaneswar railway station, located in the centre of the city, is on the main Howrah–Chennai train line.

Destinations Brahmapur (Berhampur; 12–17 daily; 2hr 25min–2hr 50min); Chennai (2–4 daily; 19hr 50min–21hr 30min); Cuttack (15–25 daily; 30min); Gaya (for Bodhgaya; 1–3 daily; 13hr 55min–14hr 40min); Kolkata (8–14 daily; 6hr 50min–8hr 30min); Puri (11–14 daily; 1hr 40min–2hr 40min); Varanasi (3 weekly; 19hr); Vishakapatnam (10–16 daily; 6hr 30min–7hr 55min).

By bus Long-distance state buses terminate at the inconveniently situated Baramunda bus stand, 5km out on the western edge of the city, though not before making a whistle-stop tour of the centre. Ask to be dropped at Station Square (look for a statue of a horse in the middle of a large roundabout), close to most hotels. If you are heading to Puri or Pipli, you can shave up to an hour off your journey by flagging down a bus from outside the State Museum, rather than getting on at the bus stand, though they are invariably jam-packed at this stage. (Minibuses also run to Puri/Pipli, but travel dangerously fast.)

Destinations Baleshwar (Balasore; 6–8 daily; 3hr 30min–5hr); Brahampur (Berhampur; 6–8 daily; 4–5hr); Cuttack (every 30min–1hr; 30min); Konark (hourly; 1hr 30min–2hr); and Puri (every 30min–1hr; 1hr 15min–2hr), via Pipli (45min–1hr 15min).

GETTING AROUND AND INFORMATION

By auto-rickshaw Bhubaneswar is too spread out to explore on foot and is best seen by auto-rickshaw; a day's temple-viewing, with waiting time, should cost around ₹300.

Tourist information The Odisha Tourism office (daily except Sun and 2nd Sat of the month 10am–5pm; ☏ 0674 243 1299, ⓦ orissatourism.gov.in;) is on the second floor of the Paryatan Bhavan building, just off Lewis Rd. India

Tourism has an office (daily except Sun and 2nd Sat of the month 9am–6pm; ☏ 0674 243 2203, ⓦ odishatourism .gov.in) on the same floor. Odisha Tourism also has an office at the train station (officially daily 24hr, though this is more of a vague aspiration than a reality) and at the airport (opens to meet incoming flights).

Tours The Odisha Tourism Development Corporation (OTDC), which handles state-run tours and accommodation, has an office at the *Panthanivas* hotel (☎0674 243 0764, ⓦpanthanivas.com). It offers city tours and guided half- and full-day trips (from ₹275, excluding entry fees) to various destinations throughout the state.

ACCOMMODATION

While the better-class hotels are spread out all over the city, the budget places – which are generally fairly poor – are mainly grouped around the **railway station** or near the busy **Kalpana Square** junction at the bottom of Cuttack Rd, a 5min auto-rickshaw ride away.

Bhagwat Niwas 9 Buddha Nagar ☎0674 231 3708. Managed by an Aurobindo devotee, this shoestring hotel is nothing to write home about, but has simple, relatively clean rooms that are just about acceptable for a night or two. Some of the more expensive options come with a/c, and there's an inexpensive restaurant. 24hr checkout. **₹400**

Ginger Jaidev Vihar, 4km from the railway station ☎1860 266 3333, ⓦgingerhotels.com. The city's best mid-range hotel offers unfussy service and modern if characterless en suites with flatscreen TVs. There's an on-site restaurant, a *Café Coffee Day* branch, a small gym and an ATM. Book online in advance to knock around 50 percent off the rack rates. **₹4300**

Grand Central Old Station Rd ☎0674 231 3411, ⓦhotelgrandcentral.com. In a convenient if unprepossessing location, *Grand Central* has dated but comfortable a/c rooms with TVs; the more expensive ones come with tubs and mini-bars. The superb restaurant serves fine dosas. Book online for a 20 percent discount. **₹2600**

Jajati MG Marg, top end of Station Square ☎0674 250 0352, ⓔsahuramesh2003@hotmail.com. A popular hotel with a lime-green exterior located within striking distance of the railway station. Although a little frayed around the edges, the rooms (with either a/c or fans) are decent enough and pretty good value. **₹600**

Mayfair Lagoon 8-B Jaydev Vihar, 4km from the railway station ☎0674 236 0101, ⓦmayfairhotels.com. This luxury hotel is something of an oddity: sumptuous cottages with dark-wood fittings and super-expensive villas (₹19,500) with four-poster beds and Jacuzzis surround an ornamental lake; the attractive grounds, meanwhile, are filled with kitsch life-sized models of crocodiles, deer and sundry other beasts. Two excellent restaurants and a fine bar are added perks. **₹10,800**

New Marrion 6 Jan Path ☎0674 238 0850, ⓦhotelnewmarrion.com. Smart, upper-mid-range hotel with good-value attached rooms, a curvy pool, forex facilities and a travel agency, as well as several good restaurants and a bar (open to non-guests). Online prices can be up to 50 percent lower than the rack rates. **₹6450**

Panthanivas Lewis Rd ☎0674 243 2314, ⓦpanthanivas.com. An institutional OTDC-run hotel close to the museum and temples with dated but large and comfortable a/c rooms. There are a couple of good restaurants, and the 8am checkout is negotiable when they're not too busy. **₹2350**

Pushpak 68 Buddha Nagar ☎0674 231 0185. Despite the rather dusty exterior, the friendly *Pushpak* is the pick of the Kalpana Square hotels. The attached rooms are large and clean, and have either fans or a/c; there are three decent restaurants and a bar. 24hr check-out. **₹1750**

Richi Station Square ☎0674 253 4619, ⓔhotelrichi @sify.com. An ugly concrete monolith right next to the railway station (so not the quietest), *Richi* remains a popular choice for those with early-departing or late-arriving trains. The rooms are OK if you don't look too closely. **₹750**

Swosti 103 Jan Path ☎0674 253 4678, ⓦswosti.com. The older and cheaper of the city's two *Swostis* shows its age, but remains a reliable option. The slightly overpriced a/c attached rooms have tubs, mini-bars and thoughtful touches like hairdryers and kettles. There's also a good travel agency, a couple of restaurants and a bar. **₹4300**

Trident Bhubaneswar Nayapalli, 4km from the railway station ☎0674 230 1010, ⓦtridenthotels .com. The city's top hotel is exquisitely furnished with antique textiles, stone and metalwork. Facilities include an excellent restaurant, an efficient travel centre, exchange facilities, a pool and even a running track. **₹12,000**

EATING

The few restaurants that specialize in traditional **Odishan cuisine**, or include some Odishan dishes on their menus, are well worth seeking out. Look out for *chenna poda* (cheesecake stuffed with almonds), *raswadi* (thickened milk with balls of curd) and *gajar ka halwa* (a rich sweet made from grated carrots).

Café Coffee Day Ginger hotel ☎98802 63333, ⓦcafecoffeeday.com. This Indian chain serves the best coffee (₹50–115) in Bhubaneswar, as well as teas, smoothies and milk-shakes, and a selection of (pricey) sandwiches, pastries, snacks, cakes and cookies. There are several other branches in the city too. Daily 24hr.

Dalma 157 Madhusudan Nagar ⓦdalmahotels.com. Named after the state's signature dish (potato, *brinjal* and

17

other vegetables cooked in dhal), this modest restaurant is the place to go for traditional regional cuisine. The fish curry is excellent, and there are some fine crab and prawn dishes. There are a couple of other branches away from the centre. Mains from ₹70. Daily noon–3pm & 7–10.30pm.

Hare Krishna Jan Path, just north of the junction with MG Marg ☎0674 253 4188. Waiters in dinner jackets rather than *dhotis* serve strictly ISKCON-style food (the Hare Krishna movement's cuisine, without garlic or onions): vegetarian and delicious. Mains around ₹50–150. Daily 11am–3pm & 7–10.30pm.

Kanika Mayfair Lagoon ☎0674 666 0101. Specializing in traditional Odishan food, this is one of the city's best restaurants and one of two in the *Mayfair Lagoon* worth visiting (see p.881). If you fancy a post-dinner drink and dance, head to the *Mayfair's* British-style pub and club. Mains ₹150–500. Daily noon–3pm & 7.30–11pm.

Lemon Grass Mayfair Lagoon ☎0674 666 0101. The second of two excellent restaurants in this hotel. This one serves top quality Thai, Chinese, Japanese and Indonesian cuisine amid decor that steers just the right side of Far Eastern pastiche. Mains ₹150–500. Daily noon–3pm & 7.30–11pm.

Rice Bowl Shahid Nagar, 1.5km north of the railway station ☎0674 254 7862. This first-floor, a/c restaurant, which gets packed out with local families on the weekends, produces above-average Chinese food, as well as some good fish and prawn curries. Mains ₹70–200. Daily 12.30–10pm.

Tangerine 9 Jan Path, just north of the junction with MG Marg ☎0674 253 3009. With well over 250 Indian and Chinese dishes (₹70–289) on offer, the menu here can be a little overwhelming: if you're having trouble deciding, opt for one of the tasty kebabs or the tandoori pomfret. Daily noon–3pm & 7–10.30pm.

SHOPPING

Ekamra Haat Madhusan Marg, north of the railway station ⊛ekamrahaat.in. This is a permanent craft market with stalls selling all manner of goods from across Odisha and beyond. Daily 10am–10pm.

Modern Book Depot At the top of Station Square. Houses a small collection of English-language fiction. Opening times are erratic. Daily 10am–6pm.

DIRECTORY

Banks and exchange The State Bank of India (Mon–Fri 10am–4pm, Sat 10am–2pm, closed 2nd Sat of month) on Raj Path changes foreign currencies, as does Thomas Cook (Mon–Fri 9am–5pm, Sat 10am–2pm, closed 2nd Sat of month; ☎0674 253 5222), at 130 Ashok Nagar, Jan Path. ATMs are numerous, notably around Kalpana Square and on Jan Path.

Dance Dance lessons can be arranged through the Odisha Dance Academy, 64 Kharwal Nagar, Unit 3 (☎0674 240 8494), while the Utkal Sangeet Mahavidyalaya, Odisha's premier college of performing arts, on Sachivalaya Marg (☎0674 241 0234), hosts regular music, dance and drama events.

Hospitals and pharmacies The Capital Hospital is near the airport on Sachivajaya Marg; for casualty, call ☎0674

240 0688. There's a well-stocked pharmacy onsite. The Red Cross (☎0674 240 2005 or ☎0674 239 2005) provides a 24hr ambulance service.

Internet There are plenty of internet cafés around Station Square, Cuttack Rd and Jan Path. Iway, next to the *Swosti* hotel, and beside the exhibition ground near the Shri Ram Temple, has a reasonably quick connection.

Police station Raj Path, near the State Bank of India (☎0674 253 3732).

Post office On the corner of MG Marg and Sachivalaya Marg (Mon–Sat 9am–7pm).

Travel agents Discover Tours (463 Lewis Rd, ☎0674 243 0477), is the most reliable operator for cultural and wildlife tours. The *New Marrion*, *Swosti* and *Trident* hotels all have good in-house agencies.

Around Bhubaneswar

A number of places around Bhubaneswar can be easily visited on a day-trip from the city. Fifteen minutes by auto-rickshaw out of the centre, the second-century BC caves at **Khandagiri** and **Udaigiri** offer a glimpse of the region's history prior to the rise of Hinduism. **Dhauli**, just off the main road to Puri, boasts an even older monument: a rock edict dating from the Mauryan era, commemorating the battle of c.260 BC that gave emperor Ashoka control of the eastern seaports, and thus enabled his missionaries to export the state religion across Asia. **Pipli**, 20km south, is famous for its appliqué work and colourful lampshades.

Nandankanan Zoological Park

20km north of Bhubaneswar • Daily: April–Sept 7.30am–5.30pm, Oct–March 8am–5pm • ₹100 (₹20) • ☎ 0674 246 6077, ⊛ nandankanan.org • Buses run from Kalpana Square in Bhubaneswar (every 30min–1hr; 1hr) or you can rent a taxi for the day

The **Nandankanan Zoological Park**, one of India's better zoos, is a good place for families to spend a few hours. Its animal collection includes rhinos, giraffes, Asiatic lions and some white tigers, and there's a toy train, paddle boats and a cable car.

Udaigiri and Khandagiri caves

6km west of Bhubaneswar • Daily 8am–5pm • ₹100 (₹5), video ₹25 • The OTDC in Bhubaneswar (see p.880) runs day-trips to the caves that also take in Dhauli or you can take a bus (every 30min–1hr; 30–45min) from Bhubaneswar's old city bus stand near Capital Market

More than two thousand years ago, caves chiselled out of the malleable yellow sandstone of a pair of low hills 6km west of Bhubaneswar were home to a community of **Jain monks**. Nowadays, they're clambered over by langur monkeys and occasional parties of tourists. Though by no means in the same league as the caves of the Deccan, **Udaigiri** and **Khandagiri** rank among Odisha's foremost historical monuments.

Inscriptions show that the **Chedi** dynasty, which ruled ancient Kalinga from the first century BC, was responsible for the bulk of the work. There are simple monk's cells, as well as royal chambers where the hallways, verandas and facades are encrusted with **sculpture** depicting court scenes, lavish processions, hunting expeditions, battles and dances. The later additions (from medieval times, when Jainism no longer enjoyed royal patronage in the region) are more austere, showing the 24 heroic Jain prophet-teachers, or *tirthankaras*.

From Bhubaneswar, the caves are approached via a road that follows the route of an ancient **pilgrimage path**. As you face the hills with the highway behind you, Khandagiri ("Broken Hill") is on your left and Udaigiri ("Sunrise Hill") is on your right.

Udaigiri

The **Udaigiri** caves occupy a fairly compact area around the south slope of the hill. **Cave 1** (Rani Gumpha or "Queen's Cave"), off the main pathway to the right, is the largest and most impressive of the group. A long frieze across the back wall shows rampaging elephants, panicking monkeys, sword fights and the abduction of a woman, perhaps illustrating episodes from the life of Kalinga's King Kharavela. **Caves 3** and **4** contain sculptures of a lion holding its prey and elephants with snakes wrapped around them, and pillars topped by pairs of peculiar winged animals. **Cave 9**, up the hill and around to the right, houses a damaged relief of figures worshipping a long-vanished Jain symbol. The crowned figure is thought to be the Chedi king, Vakradeva, whose donative inscription can still be made out near the roof. Inside the sleeping cells of all the caves, deep grooves in the stone wall at the back and in the floor were designed to carry rainwater down from the roof as an early air-conditioning system.

To reach **Cave 10**, return to the main steps and climb towards the top of the hill. Its popular name, "Ganesh Gumpha", is derived from the elephant-headed Ganesh carved on the rear wall of the cell on the right. From here, follow the path up to the ledge at the very top of Udaigiri hill for good views and the ruins of an old **chaitya hall**, probably the main place of worship for the Jain monks who lived below.

Below the ruins are **Cave 12**, shaped like the head of a tiger, and **Cave 14**, the Hathi Gumpha, known for the long **inscription** in ancient Magadhi carved onto its overhang. This relates in glowing terms the life history of King Kharavela, whose exploits brought in the fortune needed to finance the cave excavation.

17

Khandagiri

The caves on the hill opposite udaigiri , **Khandagiri**, can be reached either by the long flight of steps leading from the road, or by cutting directly across from Hathi Gumpha via the steps that drop down from Cave 17. The latter route brings you out at **Caves 1** and **2**, known as Tatowa Gumpha ("Parrot Caves") for the carvings of birds on their doorway-arches. Cave 2, excavated in the first century BC, is the larger and more interesting. On the back wall of one of its cells, a few faint lines in red Brahmi script are thought to have been scrawled two thousand years ago by a monk practising his handwriting. The reliefs in **Cave 3**, the Ananta Gumpha ("Snake Cave"), contain the best of the sculpture on Khandagiri hill, albeit badly vandalized in places. **Caves 7** and **8**, left of the main steps, were former sleeping quarters, remodelled in the eleventh century as sanctuaries. Both house reliefs of *tirthankaras* on their walls as well as Hindu deities which had become part of the Jain pantheon by the time conversion work was done. From the nineteenth-century **Jain temple** at the top of the hill there are clear views across the sprawl of Bhubaneswar to the white dome of Dhauli.

Dhauli

Around 8km south of Bhubaneswar • No fixed opening times • Free • Unless you're on a tour, getting to Dhauli involves a 2km walk – get off the bus from Bhubaneswar's old city bus stand (every 30min–1hr; 30–45min) at Dhauli Chowk, and make your way along the avenue of trees to the rock edict, from where the road begins its short climb up the hill

The gleaming white **Vishwa Shanti Stupa** on **Dhauli Hill**, 8km south of Bhubaneswar on the Pipli road, overlooks the spot where the Mauryan emperor **Ashoka** defeated the Kalingas in the decisive battle of 260 BC. Apart from bringing the prosperous Odishan kingdom to its knees, the victory also led the emperor, allegedly overcome by remorse at having slain 150,000 people, to renounce the path of violent conquest in favour of the spiritual path preached by Gautama Buddha. Built in 1972, the modern *stupa*, which eclipses its older predecessor nearby, is a memorial to this legendary change of heart, and the massive religious sea-change it precipitated.

After his conversion, Ashoka set about promulgating the maxims of his newly found faith in **rock edicts** installed at key sites around the empire. One such inscription, in ancient **Brahmi**, the ancestor of all non-Islamic Indian scripts, still stands on the roadside at the foot of Dhauli hill, etched in a rock featuring a beautifully carved figure of an elephant (symbolizing Buddhism). The Dhauli edict includes a mixture of rambling philosophical asides, discourses on animal rights and tips on how to treat your slaves. Particularly of note are the lines claiming the Buddhist doctrine of non-violence was being recognized by "the kings of Egypt, Ptolemy and Antigonus and Magas", which proved for the first time the existence of a connection between the ancient civilizations of India and the West. The inscription diplomatically omits the account that crops up elsewhere describing how many Kalingas Ashoka put to the sword before he finally "saw the light".

Pipli

A 15min drive beyond Dhauli on the road to Puri • Buses between Bhubaneswar and Puri pass through Pipli (every 30min–1hr; 1hr–1hr 30min to/from Bhubaneswar, 30min–1hr to/from Puri)

Splashes of bright colour in the shop-fronts along the main street announce your arrival in **PIPLI**, Odisha's **appliqué** capital (see box, p.896). Much of what the artisans now produce is shoddy kitsch compared with the painstaking work traditionally undertaken for the Jagannath temple. Express enough interest and you'll be shown some of the better-quality pieces for which Pipli is justly famed. Bedspreads, wall-hangings and small *chhatris* (awnings normally hung above household and temple shrines) are the most authentic goods on offer. The shops do not open early; the best time to wander around is in the evening, when gas lamps and devotional music make the experience much more atmospheric.

Ratnagiri, Udayagiri and Lalitgiri

95km northeast of Bhubaneswar • Daily 8am–5pm • ₹100 (₹5), video ₹25 • The three sites are relatively inaccessible by public transport, so it is better to rent a car for a day (around ₹1200) or take an organized tour (the OTDC offers one for ₹685)

Nestled among picturesque verdant hills 95km northeast of Bhubaneswar are the remains of three Buddhist universities, **Ratnagiri**, **Udayagiri** and **Lalitgiri**. The sites lie around 10km apart and are best reached in a day-trip or by hiring a car for the day.

Ratnagiri

Museum daily except Fri 10am–5pm • ₹2

RATNAGIRI, the most impressive of the sites, lies 20km from the main road on top of a hill overlooking the River Keluo. When Chinese chronicler Hiuen T'sang visited the university in 639 AD, it had already been a major Buddhist centre for at least two hundred years. In those days the sea reached much further inland, and would have been visible from this point – which may in part account for the choice of location. **Missionaries** were trained in such places before being sent away to China and Southeast Asia.

Two **monasteries** lie below the enormous *stupa* at the top of the hill. The larger and better-preserved one, dating from the seventh century, has a paved courtyard surrounded by cells and a beautifully carved doorway made from local blue-green chlorite stone. The shrine inside houses a majestic Buddha. A **museum** houses the antiquities and architectural remains collected from the excavations at all three sites.

Udayagiri

Ten kilometres back towards the main road from Ratangiri, **UDAYAGIRI** is the largest Buddhist complex in Odisha. Its main structure is a large *stupa*, better preserved than its counterpart at Ratnagiri. Of the two monasteries here, which flourished between the seventh and twelfth centuries, only one has been excavated. It features a large seated Buddha in its central shrine and an intricately carved entrance, along with an inscribed step-well. More rock-cut sculptures adorn the crest of the hill behind the monastery.

Lalitgiri

The turning for **LALITGIRI** is about 10km further along the main road towards Paradip. Most of the ruins of the four monasteries here are thought to date from around the ninth century, although inscriptions on an apsidal temple suggest that the site may have been occupied as early as the first century AD. Excavations in 1982 of the large *stupa* at the top of the hill revealed a gold casket containing a fragment of bone, believed to be a relic of the Buddha. The hilltop also provides grand panoramic views.

Northern Odisha

Cuttack, Odisha's second city in the north of the state, straddles the Mahanadi River. Devoid of attractions, it detains few travellers on the long journey to or from Kolkata. Once clear of Cuttack's polluted outskirts, however, you soon find yourself amid the flat paddy fields, palm groves and mud-walled villages of the **Mahanadi Delta**. Twisting through it is one of India's busiest transport arteries; the main railway line and NH-5 follow the path of the famous pilgrim trail, the **Jagannath Sadak**, which once led from Kolkata to Puri.

The area's biggest attraction is **Bhitarkanika Wildlife Sanctuary**, 130km northeast of Bhubaneswar, which has outstanding natural scenery, an abundance of fauna and flora and is visited by the endangered Olive Ridley turtles. **Similipal National Park**, close to the state border with West Bengal, is also impressive.

17 Bhitarkanika Wildlife Sanctuary

Covering 672 square kilometres overlying the Brahmani-Baitarani delta, the mangrove forests and wetlands of the **BHITARKANIKA WILDLIFE SANCTUARY** constitute one of the richest ecosystems of its type in India. As well as more than two hundred species of birds, it's a refuge for saltwater crocodiles, monitor lizards, rhesus monkeys and a host of other reptiles and mammals, and incorporates the Olive Ridley turtle nesting beaches at Gahirmatha, Rushikulya and Devi. The best time to visit is between November and March, when most of the migratory birds that flock to the sanctuary are in situ, although the nesting season for the herons usually ends around the middle of November. If you're hoping to witness the arrival of Olive Ridley turtles, check first at the tourist office in Bhubaneswar (see p.880) to find out exactly when – or indeed if – they are expected. Other highlights include the crocodile conservation programme at Dangmar Island and the heronry at Bagagahana.

ARRIVAL AND INFORMATION   BHITARKANIKA WILDLIFE SANCTUARY

To minimize costs if you're visiting the sanctuary independently, it is possible to use the small port of Chandbali as a base for day-trips. The hassle of reaching one of Bhitarkanika's entry points and obtaining permits, boat transportation and accommodation, means it's much easier to take an organized trip.

By bus or train Chandbali is linked by bus to Bhubaneswar, 190km away (6–8 daily; around 4–5hr). Alternatively, head to Bhadrak, the nearest railhead, 60km away (11–20 trains daily between Bhadrak and Bhubaneswar; 2hr 12min–3hr 8min); regular buses (around 6 daily; 1hr 30min–2hr) connect Bhadrak and Chanbali.

By boat There are several agents based around the jetty in Chandbali who can arrange park entry permits and boats (around ₹2500/day; be prepared to haggle). If you want to obtain the permit yourself you'll need to contact the elusive Assistant Conservator of Forests, also based at the jetty (☎06786 220372).

Tours Discover Tours in Bhubaneswar (see p.882), Heritage Tours in Puri (see p.894) and Nature Camp (see opposite) all arrange tours to the sanctuary.

Opening times and entry fees Bhitarkanika Wildlife Sanctuary is open daily between August and mid-May. Entry permits cost ₹1000 (₹20).

OLIVE RIDLEY TURTLES

Every year around February or March, a strip of beach at the end of Odisha's central river delta witnesses one of the world's most extraordinary natural spectacles. Having swum right across the Pacific and Indian oceans, an average of around 200,000 female **Olive Ridley marine turtles** crawl onto the sand to nest. Almost as soon as the egg laying is complete, they're off again into the surf to begin the journey back to their mating grounds on the other side of the world.

No one knows quite why they travel such distances, but for local villagers the arrival of the giant turtles has traditionally been something of a boon. Turtle soup for breakfast, lunch and dinner, and extra cash from market sales. Over the years the annual slaughter began to turn into a green gold rush, and turtle numbers plummeted drastically until the Bhitarkanika Sanctuary on **Gahirmatha beach**, 130km northeast of Bhubaneswar, was set up in 1975 at the personal behest of Indira Gandhi. Weeks before the big three- or four-day invasion, coastguards monitor the shoreline and armed rangers aim to keep poachers at bay. For wildlife enthusiasts it's a field day.

In recent years, however, **environmental threats** have impacted on the turtles' habitat. Several hundred local families have begun to cultivate land within the sanctuary, water quality has been jeopardized by the growth of illegal prawn farms, and trawlers have been caught illegally fishing in the area without "turtle excluder devices". The turtles are further menaced by industrial pollution and the construction of a large seaport at Dhamra, 15km from Gahirmatha. Several conservation organizations, including Greenpeace and the WWF, are monitoring the area. In January 2010, the bodies of around one thousand dead turtles (according to official estimates) were found on the beach; although this is horrifyingly high, it was less than half of the figure for the previous year.

ACCOMMODATION

It is possible to stay at one of the inexpensive forest lodges at Dangmal, Ekakula, Gupti or Habalikathi, though these are very basic options suitable only for very hardy travellers. You have to bring your own food and water, which the *chowkidar* will cook for you, and unless you use an agent, the only way to book this accommodation is in advance through the Divisional Forest Officer in the less than accessible outpost of Rajnagar (☎ 06729 272460).

Ayanyanivas Chandbali ☎06786 220397, ⓦpanth anivas.com. Located near the jetty in Chandbali, the OTDC-run *Ayanyanivas* is fine for a night or two. It has scruffy but acceptable rooms (with either fans or a/c), as well as a low-cost Dorm ₹280, double and a reasonable restaurant. ₹700
Nature Camp Bankuala Village ☎0674 653 3812, ⓦbhitarkanikatour.com. Also known as *Bhitarkanika*

Village Retreat, Nature Camp is the best place to stay in the area: accommodation is provided in comfortable "Swiss" tents with attached bathrooms, and there is a good restaurant. Rates are for two people for a two-night, three-day package including accommodation, meals, transfers to/from Bhubaneswar, and trips to the sanctuary. ₹22,000

Similipal National Park

Originally a royal hunting ground, **SIMILIPAL NATIONAL PARK** was one of the first Project Tiger reserves (see box, p.1182) and remains – despite suffering serious problems – one of the last true wildernesses left in eastern India, home to tigers, leopards, wild elephants and 231 species of birds.

In March 2009, Maoist rebels launched an attack in the park: several buildings were blown up, forestry department vehicles were set on fire and a group of tourists was robbed. The state authorities responded by closing the park until 2011, when it was re-opened for day visitors. This closure resulted in most of the forestry department officials fleeing their posts, and there were reports of increased illegal tree-felling, hunting and poaching. Despite a government crackdown, rebel groups remain active in the region and the security situation is prone to change, so check the latest updates with the Odisha Tourism office in Bhubaneswar (see p.880) before setting off.

ARRIVAL AND INFORMATION   SIMILIPAL NATIONAL PARK

By train Independent travellers should head to the town of Baripada, around 25km east of the Pithabata entrance to the park; there are some basic places to stay there, and you can organize onward transport to the park. The *BBS BPO Express* #12892 (daily except Sat; dep. 5.10pm; 4hr 50min) runs from Bhubaneswar to Baripada; the *BGY BBS Express* #12891 (daily except Sun; departs 5.09am; 4hr 50min) does the return journey.

Tours The easiest way to visit the park is on an organized tour – try Discover Tours in Bhubaneswar (see p.882) or Heritage Tours in Puri (see p.894).
Opening times and entry fees Similipal National Park is open daily from mid-November to mid-June. The entry fee (₹1000 (₹40), plus ₹100/camera) is payable at either of the park's two entrances, Tulsibani and Pithabata.

Puri

As the home of Lord Jagannath and his siblings, **PURI** ranks among Hindu India's most important sacred sites, visited by a vast number of pilgrims each year. The crowds peak during the monsoons for **Rath Yatra**, the famous "Car Festival", when millions pour in to watch three giant, multicoloured chariots being drawn up the main thoroughfare. At the centre of the maelstrom, the **Jagannath temple** soars above the town's medieval heart and colonial suburbs like some kind of misplaced space rocket. Non-Hindus aren't allowed inside its bustling precincts, but don't let this deter you; Puri's streets and beach remain the focus of intense devotional activity year round, while its bazaars are crammed with collectable religious souvenirs associated with Lord Jagannath.

Three distinct types of visitor come to Puri: middle-class Bengalis lured by the combined pleasures of puja and promenade; young Western and Japanese backpackers enjoying the low-key traveller scene; and thousands of pilgrims, mainly from rural eastern India, who flock in to pay their respects to Lord Jagannath. Over the years the

17

three have staked out their respective ends of town and stuck to them. It all makes for a rather bizarre and intoxicating atmosphere, where you can be transported from the intensity of Hindu India to the sea and back to the relative calm of your hotel veranda at the turn of a bicycle wheel.

Brief history

Until the seventh and eighth centuries, Puri was little more than a provincial outpost along the coastal trade route linking eastern India with the south. Then, thanks to its association with the Hindu reformer **Shankaracharya** (Shankara), the town began to feature on the religious map. Shankara made Puri one of his four *mathas*, or centres for the practice of a radically new, and more ascetic form of Hinduism. Holy men from across the whole Subcontinent came here to debate the new philosophies – a tradition carried on in the town's temple courtyards to this day. With the arrival of the **Gangas** at the beginning of the twelfth century, this religious and political importance was further consolidated. In 1135, Anantavarman Chodaganga founded the great temple in Puri, and dedicated it to **Purushottama**, one of the thousand names of Vishnu – an ambitious attempt to integrate the many feudal kingdoms recently conquered by the Gangas. Under the Gajapati dynasty in the fifteenth century Purushottama's name changed to **Jagannath** ("Lord of the Universe"). Henceforth **Vaishnavism** and the devotional worship of Krishna, an incarnation of Vishnu, was to hold sway as the predominant religious influence in the temple. Puri is nowadays one of the four most auspicious pilgrimage centres, or *dhams*, in India.

Western-style leisure **tourism**, centred on the town's long sandy beach, is a comparatively new phenomenon. The British were the first to spot Puri's potential as a resort. When they left, the Bengalis took over their bungalows, only to find themselves sharing the beach with an annual migration of young, chillum-smoking Westerners attracted to the town by its abundant hashish. Today, few vestiges of this era remain. Thanks to a concerted campaign by the municipality to clean up Puri's image, the "scene" has dwindled to little more than a handful of cafés, and is a far cry from the swinging hippie paradise some still arrive here hoping to find.

The Jagannath temple

Northwest of the town centre, off Grand Rd · **Raghunandan Library** Mon–Sat 10am–noon & 4–6pm · Donation expected (around ₹10–20 is fine); when the library is closed, touts hang around outside the temple offering views from the rooftops of nearby buildings – try not to pay more than ₹50

The mighty **Jagannath temple** in Puri is one of the four holy *dhams*, or "abodes of the divine", drawing pilgrims, or *yatris*, here to spend three auspicious days and nights near Lord Jagannath, the presiding deity. The present temple structure, modelled on the older Lingaraj temple in Bhubaneswar, was erected at the start of the twelfth century by the Ganga ruler Anantavarman Chodaganga.

Viewing the temple

Despite the temple's long-standing "caste no bar" rule, non-Hindu visitors are obliged to view proceedings from the flat roof of the **Raghunandan Library**, directly opposite the main gate. One of the librarians will show you up the stairs to the vantage point overlooking the East Gate. You should make a donation for this service – but don't believe the big sums written in the ledger.

From the rooftop a fine view encompasses the immense **deul**, at 65m by far the loftiest building in the entire region. Archeologists have removed the white plaster from the tower to expose elaborate **carving** similar to that on the Lingaraj. Crowning the very top, a long scarlet pennant and the eight-spoked wheel (*chakra*) of Vishnu announce the presence of Lord Jagannath within.

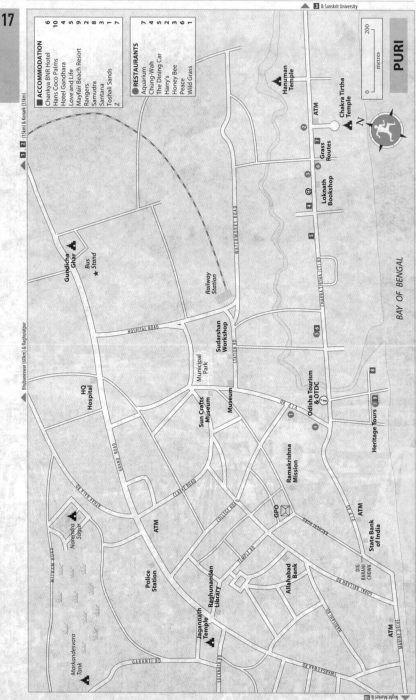

PURI

0 _____ 200
metres

BAY OF BENGAL

■ ACCOMMODATION
Chankya BNR Hotel   6
Hans Coco Palms   10
Hotel Gandhara   4
Love and Life   5
Mayfair Beach Resort   9
Rangers   2
Samudra   8
Santana   3
Toshali Sands   1
Z   7

● RESTAURANTS
Aquarium   7
Chung-Wah   4
The Dining Car   5
Harry's   2
Honey Bee   3
Peace   6
Wild Grass   1

Hanuman Temple

Chakra Tirtha Temple

ATM

Grass Routes

Loknath Bookshop

Gundicha Ghar

Bus Stand

Railway Station

Sudarshan Workshop

Municipal Park

Museum

Odisha Tourism & OTDC

Heritage Tours

HQ Hospital

HOSPITAL ROAD

WATERWORKS ROAD

CHAKRA TIRTHA ROAD

STATION RD

UR PITA BLVD

Sun Crafts Museum

Ramakrishna Mission

GPO

State Bank of India

ATM

ATM

Narendra Sagar

Markandesvara Tank

Jagannath Temple

Raghunandan Library

Police Station

Allahabad Bank

DIG BARANI CHOWK

GRAND ROAD

CLARKE ROAD

COLLEGE ROAD

TEMPLE RD

GOSAL RAILWAY RD

DR NAYAK RD

GANDHI ROAD

KACHERI ROAD

UR PITA BLVD

MIRZAN ROAD

GARANTI RD

LOCKRATI RD

MARINE DRIVE

SWARGADWAR RD

The pyramidal roofs of the temples' adjoining halls, or *mandapas*, rise in steps towards the tower. The one nearest the sanctuary, the *jagamohana* (Assembly Hall), is part of the original building, but the other two, the smaller *nata mandir* (Dance Hall) and the *bhoga-mandapa* (Hall of Offerings) nearest the entrance, were added in the fifteenth and sixteenth centuries. These halls still see a lot of action during the day as worshippers file through for *darshan*, while late every night they become the venue for devotional music. Female and transvestite dancers (*maharis* and *gotipuas*) once performed episodes from Jayadev's Gita Govinda, the much-loved story of the life of Krishna, for the amusement of Lord Jagannath and his siblings. Nowadays, piped songs have replaced the traditional theatre.

THE JAGANNATH DEITIES AND RATH YATRA

Stand on any street corner in Odisha and you'll probably be able to spot at least one image of the black-faced **Jagannath deity**, with his brother **Balabhadra** and sister **Subhadra**; each figure is legless, with undersized arms and prominent eyes. The origins of this peculiar symbol are shrouded in **legend**. One version relates that the image of Lord Jagannath looks the way it does because it was never actually finished. King Indramena, a ruler of ancient Odisha, once found the god Vishnu in the form of a tree stump washed up on Puri beach. He carried the lump of wood to the temple and, following instructions from Brahma, called the court carpenter Visvakarma to carve out the image. Visvakarma agreed – on condition that no one set eyes on the deity until it was completed. The king, however, unable to contain his excitement, peeped into the workshop; Visvakarma, spotting him, downed tools and cast a spell on the deity so that no one else could finish it.

RATH YATRA

The Jagannath deities are also the chief focus of Puri's annual "Car Festival", the **Rath Yatra** – just one episode in a long cycle of rituals that begins in the full moon phase of the Oriya month of Djesto (June & July). In the first of these, the **Chandan Yatra**, special replicas of the three temple deities, are taken to the **Narendra Sagar** where for 21 consecutive days they are smeared with *chandan* (sandalwood paste) and rowed around in a ceremonial, swan-shaped boat. At the end of this period, in a ceremony known as **Snana Yatra**, the three go for a dip in the tank, after which they head off for fifteen days of secluded preparation for Rath Yatra.

The Car Festival proper takes place during the full moon of the following month, Asadho (July & Aug). Lord Jagannath and his brother and sister are placed in their chariots and dragged by 4200 honoured devotees through the assembled multitudes to their summer home, the **Gundicha Ghar** ("Garden House"), 1.5km away. If you can find a secure vantage point and escape the crush, it's an amazing sight. The immense chariots are draped with brightly coloured cloth and accompanied down Grand Road by elephants, the local raja (who sweeps the chariots as a gesture of humility and equality with all castes) and a cacophony of music and percussion. Each chariot has a different name and a different-coloured cover, and is built anew every year to rigid specifications laid down in the temple's ancient manuals. Balabhadra's *rath*, the green one, leads; Subhadra is next, in black; and lastly, in the 13m-tall chariot with eighteen wheels and a vivid red and yellow drape, sits Lord Jagannath himself. It takes eight hours or more to haul the *raths* to their resting place. After a nine-day holiday, the sequence is performed in reverse, and the three deities return to the temple to resume their normal lives.

Conventional wisdom has it that the procession commemorates Krishna's journey from Gokhul to Mathura; historians cite the similarity between the *raths* and temple towers to claim it's a hangover from the time when temples were made of wood. Whatever the reason for the Car Festival, its devotees take it very seriously indeed. Early travellers spoke of fanatics throwing themselves under the gigantic wheels as a short cut to eternal bliss (whence the English word "**Juggernaut**", meaning an "irresistible, destructive force"). Contemporary enthusiasts are marginally more restrained, but like most mass gatherings in India, the whole event teeters at times on the brink of complete mayhem.

17

The kitchens

Outside the main building, at the left end of the walled compound surrounding the temple, are the **kitchens**. The food prepared here, known as *mahaprasad*, and blessed by Lord Jagannath, is said to be so pure that even a morsel taken from the mouth of a dog and fed to a brahmin by a Harijan (an "untouchable") will cleanse the body of sin. Devotees mill around carrying pieces of broken pots full of dhal and rice; they can only offer food to the deity from an imperfect pot as Lord Jagannath is the only perfection in this world.

The temple employees

Among the ten thousand or so daily recipients of the *mahaprasad* are the six thousand employees of the temple itself. These **servants** are divided into 96 hereditary and hierarchical orders known as *chhatisha niyoga*, and include the priests who minister to the needs of the deities (teeth cleaning, dressing, feeding, getting them ready for afternoon siesta, and so forth), as well as the teams of craftspeople who produce all the materials required for the daily round of rituals.

The bazaar

Grand Rd, close to the Jagannath temple

The crowded streets around the Jagannath temple buzz with activity – commercial as much as religious. **Grand Road**, Puri's broad main thoroughfare, is lined with a lively **bazaar**, many of its stalls specializing in *rudraksha malas* (Shaivite "rosaries" made of 108 beads), Ayurvedic cures and the ubiquitous images of Lord Jagannath. Look out too for the wonderful "religious maps" of Puri.

Swargadwar

Around 2.5km west of the town centre

The **Swargadwar** cremation ground, one of India's most auspicious mortuary sites, is situated well beyond the south corner of the beach. Although anyone can watch the ceremonies from a respectful distance, over-inquisitive tourists are definitely not welcome.

The Markandesvara tank

North of the Jagannath temple • To get here, follow the temple's north wall up to a little road junction in the far corner, then turn right and stick to the same narrow twisting backstreet for about 1km; the journey is best attempted by bike

The **Markandesvara tank**, a large, steep-sided bathing place, is said to have been the spot where Vishnu once resided in the form of a neem tree while his temple was buried deep under a sand dune. There's no sign of the tree, but the temples on the south side are worth a look, particularly the smaller of the group, which contains images of the Jagannath trio.

Narendra Sagar

East of the Markandesvara tank • To get here, retrace your route from Markandesvara tank down the lane as far as the first road junction, then bear left and continue for another 1km or so

The **Narendra Sagar** is Puri's most holy tank. A small temple stands in the middle, joined to the *ghats* by a narrow footbridge. During the annual **Chandan Yatra**, a replica deity of Lord Jagannath, Madan Mohan, is brought here every day for his dip. The temple itself is plastered with vivid **murals** that you can photograph on payment of the set fee listed nearby. The list also advertises the range of services offered by the temple *pujaris*, including the unlikely sounding "throw of bone" and "throw of hair" – references to the tank's role as another of Puri's famous mortuary ritual sites.

Sun Crafts Museum

VIP Rd • Daily 6am–10pm • Free

The **Sun Crafts Museum** showcases the more commercial side of the Lord Jagannath phenomenon. Run by a Hare Krishna devotee, it houses an extensive collection of images of the deity and his siblings, in various forms. There is also a workshop where little wooden replicas are carved and painted, before being dispatched to ISKCON centres around the world. A more controversial image of Lord Jagannath depicts him mounted on the centre of a Christian crucifix – some regard it as a symbolic demand for religious tolerance in light of the hostility between Hindus and Christians in Odisha. You may have to ask discreetly to be shown it.

Sudarshan workshop

Station Rd • No fixed opening hours

The **Sudarshan workshop** is one of the few traditional stone-carvers' yards left in Puri. The sculptors and their apprentices are more interested in pursuing their art than selling it to tourists, but gladly direct potential customers to the factory **shop** next door. Most of the pieces here are large religious icons carved out of khondalite – the multicoloured stone used in the Sun Temple at Konark.

The beach

South of town centre

If a peaceful swim and a spot of sunbathing are your top priorities, you may be disappointed with **Puri beach**; the stretch in front of the fishing village is a 3km-long open-air toilet and rubbish dump. For a more salubrious dip, press on beyond the Sanskrit University, 3km further east.

In the west end of town, along **Marine Parade**, the atmosphere is more akin to a British Victorian holiday resort. This stretch is very much the domain of the domestic tourist industry and the beach is much cleaner here. It's a pleasant place to stroll and becomes highly animated after sunset when the nightly souvenir market gets going.

Local fishermen patrol the beach as **lifeguards**; recognizable by their triangular straw hats and *dhotis*, they wade with their punters into the surf and literally hold their hands to keep them on their feet – the **undertow** claims victims every year, so weak swimmers should be careful. When not saving lives, the fishermen are busy at the CT Road end of the beach, engaged in the more traditional industries of mending nets and boats.

Note that there have been reports of attacks and **muggings** on quieter stretches of the beach, so take care.

ARRIVAL AND DEPARTURE   PURI

By train Trains arriving at Puri's end-of-line station, in the north of town, are greeted by fired-up rickshaw-wallahs sprinting alongside in the race to catch a foreigner. (You'll encounter similar "rickshaw rage" at the bus stand and the Jagannath temple, caused by competition for the commission offered by the hotels.) Puri is joined to the main Kolkata–Chennai routes by a branch line of the busy South East train network, but there is a far greater range of services from both Bhubaneswar and Khurda Rd, 44km away.

Destinations Bhubaneswar (11–14 daily; 1hr 40min–2hr 40min); Gaya (for Bodhgaya; 1–2 daily; 15hr 10min–16hr

10min); Kolkata (4–6 daily; 7hr 30min–9hr 40min); Varanasi (3 weekly; 20hr 33min).

By bus The bus stand is in the north of the city, a 10min rickshaw ride from the centre through the bumpy back-streets. Minibuses and jeeps also run to Bhubaneswar and Konark, though often travel dangerously fast.

Destinations Bhubaneswar (hourly; 1hr 30min–2hr 30min); Konark (hourly; around 1hr); Satapada on Chilika Lake (every 30min–1hr; 1hr 30min–2hr).

By car The tourist office and the town's travel agencies (see p.894) can organize cars and drivers; expect to pay from ₹1200 for a roundtrip to Konark and ₹1400 to Satapada.

GETTING AROUND

By bike Puri is fairly spread out but flat, so bicycles (around ₹50/day) are ideal for getting around and exploring the maze of streets around the Jagannath temple. There are several places to rent them on Chakra Tirtha (CT) Rd, in the travellers' enclave between the *Gandhara* and *Love and Life*.

By moped/motorbike Mopeds and motorbikes (from

₹300/day) are rented out by a couple of travel agents and shops along CT Rd for full or half-days and are useful for trips up the coast to Konark; standards vary, however.

By rickshaw and auto-rickshaw Auto-rickshaws are relatively thin on the ground, though one or two are always hanging around the railway and bus stations and the smarter hotels. Cyclerickshaws are more common.

17

INFORMATION AND TOURS

Tourist information The main Odisha Tourism office is on CT Rd (daily except Sun & 2nd Sat of the month 10am–5pm; ☎06752 222664); there's also a (fairly unhelpful) counter at the railway station (officially daily 24hr).

Tours The OTDC, which has a booking counter close to the main Odisha Tourism office, offers a range of tours, including one taking in the main sights of Puri and Konark (₹200) and another that visits Chilika Lake (₹290). Gandhara Travel, at the *Hotel Gandhara* (see below) also offers tours, including to Konark during the dance festival, as well as flight and train bookings. Heritage Tours (☎06752 223656, ⊛heritagetoursorissa .com), based at the *Mayfair Beach Resort*, is well-established and reliable, offering a wide range of tours throughout the state and beyond. Grass Routes on CT Rd (☎06752 220560, ⊛grassroutesjourneys.com) arranges excellent themed-tours of the Puri and the surrounding area, including to Chilika Lake, plus cookery classes.

ACCOMMODATION

Virtually all of Puri's **hotels** are on or near the beach, where a strict distinction is observed: those aimed at domestic tourists are lined up behind Marine Drive, the promenade on the west end of the beach, while budget-conscious Westerners are sandwiched further east around CT Rd between the high-rise resort hotels and the fishing village; this backpackers' enclave is sometimes referred to as **Pentakunta**. The less expensive hotels are quiet during the summer months, but the pricier accommodation tends to be booked solid well in advance of Rath Yatra. Checkout is 8am for most hotels, although off-season this rule is less rigidly enforced.

Chankya BNR Hotel CT Rd ☎06752 223006, ⊛therailhotel.com. A must for Rajophiles, this renovated hotel – formerly the *South Eastern Railway Hotel* – retains much of the old-world charm that once made it the premier bolthole for Calcutta's burra- and memsahibs. The rooms are comfortable, and there's an atmospheric restaurant (see opposite). Check out the old train engine in the neatly manicured gardens out front. ₹2800

Hans Coco Palms Marine Drive ☎06752 230038, ⊛hanshotels.com. A modern complex in a superb setting some 2km west of the town centre; all the rooms are a/c and overlook the sea. There's a pool, bar and restaurant, and the beach here is pleasant. Booking in advance via the website can save you a fair bit. ₹8500

★ **Hotel Gandhara** CT Rd ☎06752 224623, ⊛hotelgandhara.com. Easily the best mid-range hotel in town and consequently very popular, so advance bookings are a must year-round. All the spick-and-span rooms are en suite, some have a/c and a few have sea views. There's a swimming pool, restaurant serving good Indian, Japanese and Western dishes, internet café, money exchange, and an efficient travel agency. ₹1160

Love and Life CT Rd ☎06752 224433, ✉loveandlife @hotmail.com. Although its claims of being a "luxury resort" are well wide of the mark, *Love and Life* is a decent choice. Popular with Puri's many young Japanese visitors, it has an easy-going atmosphere, a good restaurant and clean attached rooms either in the main block or in cottages in the garden. ₹900

Mayfair Beach Resort Off CT Rd ☎06752 227800, ⊛mayfairhotels.com. The smartest hotel in Puri has tastefully decorated rooms and cottages surrounded by palm trees, a pool and an appealing stretch of beach to the front. Facilities include a gym, massage centre, bar and a fine restaurant (see opposite). ₹10,800

Rangers Midway between Puri and Konark ☎06752 211057, ⊛rangersatv.webs.com. As close to a secluded beach paradise as you're likely to find around here, though not actually that convenient for visiting either Puri or Konark. There's a mix of accommodation including colourful rooms and three types of tents (camping ₹300), which vary in comfort. In addition, there's a restaurant and numerous activities are on offer, including quad biking, surfing, parasailing and trekking. ₹600

Samudra Off CT Rd ☎06752 222705, ⊛samudrapuri. com. This well-run hotel is one of the better lower-mid-range options in Puri with a range of rooms, the better and more expensive of which are on the second floor and have sea-facing balconies. The restaurant isn't bad, either. ₹1100

Santana At the end of CT Rd ☎06752 251491, ⊛indiasantana.com. A small, pleasant hotel with a good set-up for travellers (it's particularly popular with Japanese visitors). The economy rooms are narrow and sparsely-furnished, but the more expensive ones are larger and have a/c. All have bright mauve, green or purple walls and wonderfully clashing orange curtains. ₹500

Toshali Sands Konark Rd, 9km north of town ☎06752 250571, ⊛toshalisands.com. A self-styled "ethnic village" consisting of a/c rooms and attractive cottages

(₹7750) grouped around a garden and a pool. Popular with tour groups, *Toshali Sands* also has a good restaurant, a gym and a sauna. Rates include free pick up from the railway station. ₹6445

Z CT Rd ☎06752 222554, ⊛zhotelindia.com. A Puri institution, the *Z* (pronounced "jed") is based in a mansion once owned by the raja of Serampore.

There is a range of rooms – the cheaper ones share facilities, the more expensive options are attached (₹1500) – with sea views and plenty of communal areas, including a TV lounge, a kitchen and a large garden. It was under renovation at the time of research, so prices are likely to rise a bit in the future. ₹500

EATING AND DRINKING

Most of the **restaurants** along CT Rd offer inexpensive thalis, and there's good **fresh fish** to be had, though better food can be found at the smarter hotels. An interesting alternative is the sacred food, or *mahaprasad*, the creation of four hundred cooks in the Jagannath temple kitchens and available from stalls in the nearby Anand Bazaar.

Aquarium Mayfair Beach Resort ☎06752 227800. This sea-life-themed restaurant with an open-air veranda is Puri's best option for a sophisticated evening out. The menu is a delicious and adventurous mix of Chinese, Indian and Western dishes, plus a few local specialities, with the focus firmly on seafood. Mains ₹175–450. Daily noon–3pm & 7.30–11pm.

Chung-Wah Hotel Lee Garden, VIP Rd. Run by a Chinese family from Kolkata, *Chung-Wah* offers authentic food (including a range of tempting fish and prawn dishes), big portions and a quick turnover. Mains ₹80–230. Daily 11.30am–3pm & 6.30–10.30pm.

The Dining Car Chanakya BNR hotel ☎06752 223006. A stately, a/c restaurant with high ceilings and evocative black-and-white photos of the South Eastern Railway in years gone by. The menu features the usual Indian and Chinese staples, as well as few attempts at Western dishes, such as fish and chips. Mains ₹65–225. Daily 1–3pm & 8–11pm.

Harry's Hotel Lotus, CT Rd. This pure-veg restaurant serves tasty Indian food (from around ₹50) made

without onions or garlic in the Hare-Krishna ISKCON tradition, as well as fresh fruit juices. Daily noon–3pm & 7–10.30pm.

★**Honey Bee** CT Rd. This peaceful, a/c bakery-pizzeria is ideal for homesick travellers. The thin-crust pizzas (₹165–425) are surprisingly good, there's an inventive range of sandwiches and soups (including gazpacho), and even bacon is on offer. In addition, there's a proper coffee machine and tempting home-made cakes, pastries and breads. Daily 8.30am–2pm & 6–10pm.

Peace CT Rd. This traveller stalwart is a friendly place, with tables in a shady garden. The menu has good breakfast options, juices, tasty Indian and Chinese food, fresh fish and seafood, and various attempts at western dishes. Mains ₹35–200. Daily 8/9am–10/11pm.

Wild Grass Corner of VIP Rd and College Rd, 2km from CT Rd. Popular with locals, *Wild Grass* is hit and miss – if you catch it on a good day, you'll find well-prepared tandoori, seafood, vegetarian and Odishan dishes at reasonable prices (₹50–150). Noon–3pm & 7–10pm.

SHOPPING

Bookshops Loknath Bookshop on CT Rd (see map, p.890) has a selection of secondhand books.

Crafts and markets Several shops on Temple Rd stock

a good range of local crafts at fixed prices, and there's a lively evening market on the beach off Marine Drive, south of *Puri Hotel*.

DIRECTORY

Banks and exchange The State Bank of India beyond the *Nilachal Ashok Hotel*, on VIP Rd, changes travellers' cheques and dollars, sterling and euros. It has an ATM here and another on CT Rd, close to *Z* hotel, two of several in the town. You can also change money at Allahabad Bank on Temple Rd, 200m up from the GPO towards the temple, and at *Hotel Gandhara*.

Hospitals Puri's main "HQ" hospital (☎06752 223742) is outside the town centre on Grand Rd. Hotels such as the

Mayfair can help find doctors in an emergency.

Internet access There are numerous cyber cafés along CT and VIP Rds; *Hotel Gandhara* has a particularly fast connection (₹40/hr).

Police The main police station is on Grand Rd, near the Jagannath temple. There is another branch at the Kacheri Rd, VIP Rd junction (☎06752 222025).

Post office The GPO, which has poste restante, is on Kacheri Rd.

17

ODISHAN ART AND ARTISTS

Few regions of India retain as rich a diversity of **traditional art forms** as Odisha. While a browse through the bazaars and emporia in Puri and Bhubaneswar provides a good idea of local styles and techniques, a trip out to the **villages** where the work is actually produced is a much more memorable way to shop. Different villages specialize in different crafts – a division that harks back to the origins of the caste system in Odisha. Patronage from the nobility and wealthy temples during medieval times allowed local artisans, or *shilpins*, to refine their skills over generations. As the market for arts and crafts expanded, notably with the rise of **Puri** as a pilgrimage centre, **guilds** were formed to control the handing down of specialist knowledge and separate communities established to carry out the work. Today, the demand for **souvenirs** has given many old art forms a new lease of life.

STONE SCULPTURE

With modern temples increasingly being built out of reinforced concrete, life forOdisha's stone sculptors is getting tougher. To see them at work, head for Pathuria Sahi ("Stonecarvers' Lane") and the famous Sudarshan workshop on Station Road in **Puri** (see p.893), where mastercraftsmen and apprentices still fashion Hindu deities and other votive objects according to specifications laid down in ancient manuals.

PAINTING

Patta chitra, classical Odishan painting, is closely connected with the Jagannath cult. Traditionally, artists were employed to decorate the inside of the temples in Puri and to paint the deities and chariots used in the Rath Yatra. Later, the same vibrant colour-schemes and motifs were transferred to lacquered cloth or palm leaves and sold as sacred souvenirs to visiting pilgrims. In the village of **Raghurajpur** near Puri, where the majority of the remaining artists, or *chitrakaras*, now live, men use paint made from the local mineral stones. Specialities include sets of *ganjiffa* – small round cards used to play a trick-taking game based on the struggle between Rama and the demon Ravana, as told in the Ramayana.

PALM-LEAF MANUSCRIPTS

Palm leaves, or *chitra pothi*, have been used as writing materials in Odisha for centuries. Using a sharp stylus called a *lohankantaka*, the artist first scratches the text or design onto the surface

Konark and around

Time runs like a horse with seven reins,
Thousand-eyed, unageing, possessing much seed. Him the poets mount; His wheels are all beings.

The Artharva Veda

If you see only one temple in Odisha, it should be **KONARK**, 35km north of Puri and one of India's most visited ancient monuments. Standing imperiously in its compound of lawns and casuarina trees, this majestic pile of oxidizing sandstone is considered to be the apogee of Odishan architecture and one of the finest religious buildings anywhere in the world.

The temple is all the more remarkable for having languished under a huge mound of sand since it fell into neglect around three hundred years ago. Not until the dune and heaps of collapsed masonry were cleared away from the sides, early in the twentieth century, did the full extent of its ambitious design become apparent. In 1924, the Earl of Ronaldshay described the newly revealed temple as "one of the most stupendous buildings in India which rears itself aloft, a pile of overwhelming grandeur even in its decay". A team of seven galloping horses and 24 exquisitely carved wheels found lining the flanks of a raised platform showed that the temple had been conceived in the form of a colossal chariot for the sun god **Surya**, its presiding deity.

Equally sensational was the rediscovery among the ruins of some extraordinary **erotic sculpture**. Konark, like Khajuraho (see p.365), is plastered with loving couples locked in ingenious amatory postures drawn from the *Kama Sutra* – a feature that

of palm leaves, then applies a paste of turmeric, dried leaves, oil and charcoal that, when rubbed off, emphasizes the etching. Palm-leaf flaps are often tied onto the structure so an innocent etching of an animal or deity can be lifted to reveal *Kama Sutra* action. The best places to see genuine antique palm-leaf books are the National Museum in **New Delhi** or the State Museum in Bhubaneswar.

TEXTILES

Distinctive textiles woven on handlooms are produced throughout Odisha. Silk saris from **Brahmapur** and **Sambalpur** are the most famous, though **ikat**, which originally came to Odisha via the ancient trade links with Southeast Asia, is also typical. It is created using a tie-dye-like technique known as *bandha*, also employed by weavers from the village of **Nuapatna**, 70km from Bhubaneswar, who produce silk *ikats* covered in verses from the scriptures for use in the Jagannath temple.

APPLIQUÉ

The village of **Pipli** (see p.884) has the monopoly on appliqué, another craft rooted in the Jagannath cult. Geometric motifs and stylized birds, animals and flowers are cut from brightly-coloured cloth and sewn onto black backgrounds. Pipli artists are responsible for the chariot covers used in the Rath Yatra as well as for the small canopies, or *chhatris*, suspended above the presiding deity in Odishan temples.

METALWORK

Tarakashi (literally "woven wire"), or silver filigree, is Odisha's best-known metalwork technique. Using lengths of wire made by drawing strips of silver alloy through small holes, the smiths create distinctive ornaments, jewellery and utensils for use in rituals and celebrations. The designs are thought to have come to India from Persia with the Mughals, though the existence of an identical art form in Indonesia, with whom the ancient Odishan kingdoms used to trade, suggests that the technique itself may be even older. *Tarakashi* is now only produced in any quantity in **Cuttack** and is a dying as an art form.

may well explain the comment made by one of Akbar's emissaries, Abul Fazl, in the sixteenth century: "Even those who are difficult to please," he enthused, "stand astonished at its sight."

Apart from the temple, a small **museum** and a fishing **beach**, Konark **village** has little going for it. Sundays and public holidays are particularly busy here: aim to stay until sunset after most of the tour groups have left, when the rich evening light works wonders on the natural colours in the khondalite sandstone.

Brief history

Inscription plates attribute the founding of the temple to the thirteenth-century Ganga monarch **Narasimhadeva**, who may have built it to commemorate his military successes against the Muslim invaders. Local legend attributes its aura of power to the two very powerful magnets said to have been built into the tower, with the poles placed in such a way that the idol was suspended in mid-air.

The temple's 70m tower became a landmark for European mariners sailing off the shallow Odishan coast, who knew it as the "**Black Pagoda**", and the frequent incidence of shipping disasters along the coast was blamed on the effect of the aforesaid magnets on the tidal pattern. The tower also proved to be an obvious target for raids on the region. In the fifteenth century, Konark was sacked by the Yavana army, causing sufficient damage to allow the elements to get a foothold. As the sea receded, sand slowly engulfed the building and salty breezes set to work on the spongy khondalite, eroding the exposed surfaces and weakening the superstructure. By the end of the

17

nineteenth century, the tower had disintegrated completely, and the porch lay buried up to its waist, prompting one art historian of the day to describe it as "an enormous mass of stones studded with a few peepal trees here and there".

Restoration only really began in earnest in 1901, when British archeologists set about unearthing the immaculately preserved hidden sections of the building and salvaging what they could from the rest of the rubble. Finally, trees were planted to shelter the compound from the corrosive winds, and a museum opened to house what sculpture was not shipped off to Delhi, Kolkata and London.

The temple
Daily dawn–8pm • ₹250 (₹10)

The main entrance to the **temple** complex on its eastern, sea-facing side brings you out directly in front of the **bhoga-mandapa**, or "hall of offerings". Ornate carvings of amorous couples, musicians and dancers decorating the sides of its platform and stocky pillars suggest that the now roofless pavilion, a later addition to the temple, must originally have been used for ritual dance performances.

To get a sense of the overall scale and design, stroll along the low wall that bounds the south side of the enclosure before you tackle the ruins proper. As a giant model of Surya's war chariot, the temple was intended both as an offering to the Vedic sun god and as a symbol for the passage of time itself – believed to lie in his control. The seven **horses** straining to haul the sun eastwards in the direction of the dawn (only one is still intact) represent the days of the week. The **wheels** ranged along the base stand for the twelve months, each with eight spokes detailed with pictures of the eight ideal stages of a woman's day.

The sanctuary tower

With the once-lofty **sanctuary tower** now reduced to little more than a clutter of sandstone slabs tumbling from the western wing, the **porch**, or *jagamohana*, has become Konark's real centrepiece. Its impressive pyramidal roof, rising to a height of 38m, is divided into three tiers by rows of lifelike statues – mostly musicians and dancers serenading the sun god on his passage through the heavens. Though now blocked up, the huge cubic **interior** of the porch was a marvel of medieval architecture. The original builders ran into problems installing its heavy ornamental ceiling, and had to forge 10m iron beams as support – a considerable engineering feat for the time.

Sculpture and erotica

Marvellously elaborate **sculpture** embellishes the temple's exterior with a profusion of deities, animals, floral patterns, bejewelled couples, voluptuous maidens, mythical beasts and aquatic monsters. Some of Konark's most beautiful **erotica** is to be found in the niches halfway up the walls of the porch; look for the telltale pointed beards of sadhus, clearly making the most of a lapse in their vows of chastity. Many theories have been advanced over the years to explain the lascivious scenes here and elsewhere on the temple. The most convincing explanation is that the erotic art was meant as a kind of metaphor for the ecstatic bliss experienced by the soul when it fuses with the divine cosmos – a notion central to **Tantra** and the related worship of the female principle, **shakti**, which were prevalent throughout medieval Odisha.

Carved wheels and friezes

Moving clockwise around the temple from the south side of the main staircase, you pass the intricately carved **wheels** and extraordinary **friezes** that run in narrow bands above and below them. These depict military processions (inspired by King Narasimhadeva's tussles with the Muslims) and hunting scenes, featuring literally thousands of rampaging elephants. In the top frieze along the south side of the platform, the appearance of a giraffe proves that trade with Africa took place during the thirteenth century.

The Surya statue

Beyond the porch, a double staircase leads to a shrine containing a **statue of Surya**. Carved out of green chlorite stone, this serene image – one of three around the base of the ruined sanctuary tower – is considered to be one of Konark's masterpieces. The other two statues in the series are also worth a look, if only to compare their facial expressions which, following the progress of the sun around the temple, change from wakefulness in the morning (south) to heavy-eyed weariness at the end of the day (north). At the foot of the western wall there's an altar-like platform covered with carvings: the kneeling figure in its central panel is thought to be King Narasimhadeva.

Konark dance festival

In early December, the temple hosts one of India's premier **dance festivals**, drawing an impressive cast of both classical and folk dance groups from all over the country. For the exact dates and advance bookings, contact the Odisha Tourism offices in Bhubaneswar or Puri.

The archeological museum

Near the *Yatrinivas* hotel, a 10min walk from the temple compound • Daily except Fri 10am–5pm • ₹10

The **archeological museum** has lost most of its best pieces to Delhi, but still has fragments of sculpture, much of it erotic. Outside, a small shed in the northeast corner

---

ODISSI DANCE

Even visitors who don't normally enjoy classical dance cannot fail to be seduced by the elegance and poise of Odisha's own regional style, **Odissi**. Friezes in the Rani Gumpha at Udaigiri (see p.883) attest to the popularity of dance in the Odishan courts as far back as the second century BC. By the time the region's Hindu "golden age" was in full swing, it had become an integral part of religious ritual, with purpose-built dance halls, or *nata mandapas*, being added to existing temples and corps of dancing girls employed to perform in them.

DEVADASIS

Devadasis, literally "wives of the god", were handed over by their parents at an early age and symbolically "married" to the deity. They were trained to read, sing and dance and, as one disapproving early nineteenth-century chronicler put it, to "make public traffic of their charms" with male visitors to the temple. Gradually, ritual intercourse (a legacy of the Tantric influence on medieval Hinduism) degenerated into pure prostitution, and dance, formerly an act of worship, grew to become little more than a form of commercial entertainment. By the colonial era, Odissi was all but lost.

RESURGENCE

Its resurgence followed the rediscovery in the 1950s of the **Abhinaya Chandrika**, a fifteenth-century manual on classical Odishan dance. Like Bharatanatyam, India's most popular dance style, Odissi has its own highly complex language of poses and steps. Based on the *tribhanga* "hip-shot" stance, movements of the body, hands and eyes convey specific emotions and enact episodes from well-known religious texts – most commonly the **Gita Govinda** (the Krishna story). Using the *Abhinaya* and temple sculpture, dancers and choreographers were able to reconstruct this grammar into a coherent form and within a decade Odissi was a thriving performance art once again. Today, ironically, dance lessons with a reputed guru have become *de rigueur* for the young daughters of Odisha's middle classes.

LIVE PERFORMANCES

Unfortunately, catching a **live performance** is a matter of being in the right place at the right time. The only regular recitals take place in the Jagannath temple. If, however, you're not a Hindu, the annual **festival of dance** at Konark, in the first week of December, is your best chance of seeing Odisha's top performers. If you're keen to learn, check out the several dance academies in Bhubaneswar that run **courses** for beginners (see p.882).

17

of the enclosure houses a stone architrave bearing images of **nine planet deities**, the Navagrahas. This originally sat above one of the temple's ornamental doorways and is now kept as a living shrine.

Chandrabhaga beach

3km south of the temple compound

Chandrabhaga beach is a quiet and clean alternative to Puri's dirty sands. Although far from ideal for swimming or sunbathing, it's nonetheless a pleasant place to wander in the late afternoon and watch the fishermen and their catch.

ARRIVAL AND INFORMATION

KONARK

By bus, jeep and minibus Regular buses (hourly; around 1hr) travel the 33km between Puri and Konark; the last one back to Puri leaves around 6.30pm. Jeeps and minibuses also shuttle along this route, though they often driven recklessly. From Bhubaneswar, there are hourly buses (2–3hr) to Konark; some involve a change at Pipli.

By auto-rickshaw From Puri, an auto-rickshaw will do the return journey to Konark, with waiting time, for about ₹500–600.

By car A car (and driver) for the Puri-Konark roundtrip, including waiting time, costs from ₹1200.

On a tour The OTDC offices in Puri and Bhubaneswar offer several different tours that visit Konark; prices start at ₹200.

Information The Odisha Tourism office is in the *Yatrinivas* hotel (daily except Sun & 2nd Sat of the month 10am–5pm; ☎ 06758 236821).

ACCOMMODATION AND EATING

Few people stay in Konark, but the **accommodation** here is convenient if you want to enjoy the temple in peace after the day-trippers have left. For **food** you have a choice between the row of thali and tea stalls opposite the temple or a more substantial meal in one of the hotel restaurants.

Labanya Lodge Just outside the village on the beach road ☎ 06758 236824. The *Labanya Lodge* is the most backpacker-friendly place in Konark, with a small garden, internet access and bikes for rent. The rooms vary though, so make sure you look at a few. ₹400

Lotus Eco Village Ramchandi beach, about 7km southwest of Konark ☎ 06758 236161, ⓦ lotusresort konark.com. Easily the most stylish place to stay in the area, this peaceful complex is designed to look like a traditional village and sits right on the beach. Accommodation is in wood-panelled cottages or more spacious villas (₹9200), and there's a restaurant and small spa; at the time of research, a swimming pool and bar were in the pipeline. ₹7000

Panthanivas Opposite the entrance to the temple compound ☎ 06758 236831, ⓦ panthanivas.com. The location could not be more convenient for visiting the temple, but this OTDC-run hotel is pretty gloomy, with scruffy, cleanish attached rooms. It also has a so-so restaurant. ₹750

Yatrinivas A 10min walk from the temple compound ☎ 06758 236820, ⓦ panthanivas.com. Another OTDC-run hotel, the *Yatrinivas* is a better option than the *Panthanivas*, with pleasant gardens and a decent restaurant that is often packed out with tour parties at lunchtime. The fan-cooled or (more expensive) a/c rooms are fine for a night. ₹750

Southern Odisha

Along the stretch of coast between Puri and Andhra Pradesh there are a couple of scenic detours that may tempt you to break the long journey south. Three hours south of the capital, at the foot of a barren, sea-facing spur of the Eastern Ghats, is India's largest saltwater lake. **Chilika**'s main attractions are the one million or so migratory birds that nest here in winter. Seventy kilometres further on, **Gopalpur-on-Sea** is a decidedly low-key beach town. **Brahmapur** (formerly Berhampur), 16km inland, is southern Odisha's biggest market town, and the main transport hub for the sinuous route west through the hills to the spa station of **Taptapani** and "tribal districts" beyond.

Chilika Lake

Were it not for its glass-like surface, **CHILIKA LAKE**, Asia's largest lagoon, could easily be mistaken for the sea; from its mud-fringed foreshore you can barely make out the narrow strip of marshy islands and sand-flats that separate the 1100-square-kilometre expanse of brackish water from the Bay of Bengal. Come here between December and February, and you'll see a variety of **birds**, from flamingos, pelicans and painted storks to fish eagles, ospreys and kites, many of them migrants from Siberia, Iran and the Himalayas. Chilika is also one of the few places in India where the **Irrawaddy dolphin** can be spotted.

The best way to see the lake and the birdlife is on a boat trip. Unfortunately, tourists are currently banned from visiting Nalabana Island, a designated bird sanctuary, which has dramatically reduced the chances of seeing the migratory birds at close quarters. The state authorities claim this is to protect the birds from the disruption caused by visitors, but the move has been criticized by local travel agencies and boat operators, who are hopeful the policy will be overturned. In the meantime, it's still possible to see the migratory birds by taking a boat cruise or by visiting some of Chilika's other islands, which offer decent birdwatching opportunities, though not as good as those on Nalabana.

By and large, the fishing villages and fabled island "kingdom" of **Parikud** on the eastern side of the lake are passed up in favour of the boat ride to the *devi* shrine on **Kalijai** island. Legend has it that a local girl once drowned here on the way to her wedding across the lake, and that her voice was subsequently heard calling from under the water. Believing the bride-to-be had become a goddess, local villagers inaugurated a shrine to her that over the years became associated with **Kali** (Shiva's consort Durga in her terrifying aspect). Each year at Makar Sankranti, after the harvest, pilgrims flock to the tiny island from all over Odisha and West Bengal to leave votive offerings in the sacred cave where the deity was enshrined.

Satapada, on the coastal side 45km from Puri, is the best place to stay on the lake; the surrounding waters offer the best chance of seeing dolphins. The scenery surrounding **Barkul** is less impressive than at Satapada, and you're further from most of the islands, but it does have the best accommodation around the lake. **Rambha**, 135km from Bhubaneswar, is well placed for walks around the more scenic southern corner of the lake and for boat rides to Parikud.

ARRIVAL AND DEPARTURE   CHILIKA LAKE

By bus Satapada is linked to Puri by daily buses (every 30min–1hr; 1hr 30min–2hr). To get to Barkul, take a bus from Puri or Bhubaneswar towards Brahmapur (6–8 daily; around 3hr 30min–4hr) and get off at Balugaon, where you can get an auto-rickshaw for the remaining 7km to Barkul.

INFORMATION AND TOURS

Tourist information Satapada is home to an informative visitor centre (daily 10am–5pm; ₹10), while the *Yatrinivas* (see below) houses the tourist office (daily except Sun & 2nd Sat of month 10am–5pm; ☎ 0675 262077).

Tours Travellers can take trips on OTDC motor launches (₹130) or cheaper rowing boats from Barkul and Satapada;

it costs around ₹500–1000hr to rent a motorboat for yourself. The manager at the Barkul *Panthanivas* can help with arrangements. Alternatively, numerous travel agencies, including the *Gandhara's* in-house travel agency (see p.894) in Puri and the OTDC offices in Bhubaneswar and Puri run day-trips to Chilika.

ACCOMMODATION AND EATING

Panthanivas Barkul ☎ 06756 222 0488, ☗ pantha nivas.com. The OTDC-run *Panthanivas* offers spacious, though dated, rooms and a fine restaurant; especially recommended is the *chinguri charchari* (shrimp with fried vegetables). If you plan to visit between September and March, it's best to book ahead at the Bhubaneswar or Puri OTDC offices. ₹**1000**

Yatrinivas Satapada ☎ 06752 262077, ☗ panthanivas .com. Run by the OTDC, *Yatrinivas* provides the best accommodation in Satapada, though this isn't necessarily a ringing endorsement; some rooms have private balconies overlooking the well-tended gardens that run down to the lake, and the restaurant serves delicious thalis and fresh fish. ₹**650**

17

"TRIBAL" TOURISM

Most of Odisha's **adivasi** groups live in the remote southwest of the state. Once you have ventured over the pass above the hot springs of Taptapani (see opposite), the appearance of pots attached to sago palms and windowless mud huts with low thatched roofs indicates that you have arrived in the traditional land of the **Saoras**. Further west around the Koraput and Jeypore area live the **Dongria Kondh**, the **Koya** and the **Bondas**.

"Tribal tourism" was very popular in Odisha, but in 2012 it was effectively banned by the state authorities (although some unscrupulous tour operators do attempt to circumvent the rules). The reason behind the move was a series of newspaper articles that highlighted a number of exploitative, unethical and degrading "human safaris" in both Odisha (particularly involving the Bondas) and the Andaman Islands. The situation was then exacerbated by the kidnapping of two Italian travellers (see p.875).

Adivasi villages saw little or no share of the spoils of the tours, a situation they were – and continue to be – justifiably angry about. Whichever way you look at it, turning up in an isolated and **culturally sensitive** place with a camera is a pretty unsound way of "meeting" the locals, and a glance from a car is hardly likely to enlighten you on traditions that have existed for centuries.

Restrictions may well be loosened in the future, so it is worth checking the latest situation with Odisha Tourism in Bhubaneswar (see p.880) or one of the more responsible travel agencies such as Grass Routes in Puri (see p.894) or Discover Tours in Bhubaneswar (see p.882).

Gopalpur-on-Sea

More than two thousand years ago, when the Kalingas were accruing wealth from the pearl and silk trade with Southeast Asia, **GOPALPUR-ON-SEA**, formerly the ancient port of Paloura, must have been a swinging place. Today, the only time you're likely to encounter much action is during festivals and holidays, when the village is temporarily inundated with Bengali holiday-makers. For the rest of the year, its desultory collection of seafront hotels stands idle, left to the odd backpacker and armies of industrious fishermen (*katias*) hauling in hand nets on Gopalpur's endless empty shoreline. Paradise it certainly isn't, but if you're looking for a spot along the coast to unwind and enjoy the warm sea breezes, this is as appealing a place as any. **Sunbathing** on the beach will quickly make you the centre of attention, but its uncrowded sands, punctuated by coconut groves, sleepy lagoons and tiny creeks, make a good setting for a rejuvenating walk.

ARRIVAL AND DEPARTURE   GOPALPUR-ON-SEA

By train or bus Getting to Gopalpur-on-Sea is easiest via the town of Brahmapur (Berhampur), which is connected to Bhubaneswar by numerous trains (12–17 daily; 2hr 25min–2hr 50min) and buses (6–8 daily; 4–5hr).

By auto-rickshaw, jeep and minibus Minibuses and jeeps depart when full from Brahmapur's centrally located bus stand for the 16km trip (around 30min) to Gopalpur. You'll be dumped at the top of Gopalpur's main street, a 10min walk from the seafront and most of the hotels. Alternatively an auto-rickshaw straight to your hotel from Brahmapur costs around ₹200–250.

ACCOMMODATION AND EATING

Standards are fairly low at Gopalpur's **hotels**, which are also comparatively expensive: it's worth haggling – only during holiday and festival times are they likely to be full. As for **eating**, there's a surprising dearth of seafood, though some restaurateurs can be cajoled into cooking the odd pomfret or prawn curry, given sufficient warning.

Mayfair Palm Beach Resort Overlooking the beach ☎ 0680 666 0101, ⊛ mayfairhotels.com. The smartest hotel in town, which opened in December 2012, is housed in a building that dates back to 1914. The en suites, however, are decidedly modern, and many boast sea views. There's also a pool and an excellent restaurant and bar. At the time of research, there were plans afoot for a spa. ₹**10,800**

Mermaid On the north side of the beach ☎ 0680 224 2050. A friendly place, popular with holidaying Kolkatans, with plain, somewhat scruffy rooms and private sea-facing balconies. With advance notice, non-residents can enjoy delicious Bengali thalis. ₹**700**

Sea Side Breeze On the beach ☏ 0680 224 2075. The only hotel actually on the beach, *Sea Side Breeze* has large, cleanish rooms, many with sea views. There's also a good-value restaurant serving tasty seafood. The welcoming manager can arrange trips on a fisherman's boat in the backwaters of nearby "Blue Bay". ₹**600**

Swosti Palm Resort Near the Lighthouse ☏ 0680 224 2453, ⓦ swosti.com. One of Gopalpur's more comfortable hotels, if rather overpriced. Its a/c rooms are pleasant, but nothing special, and most lack a view of the sea. The restaurant, however, is strong on seafood: the *chengudi malai* (prawns in coconut cream) and *macha tarkari* (fish curry) are both worth a try. Booking online can save you around 25 percent. ₹**4600**

Taptapani

One possible foray from the coast, if you're tempted by the lure of the nearby hills, is the trip to the spa village of **TAPTAPANI**, nestled in the *ghats* 51km west of Brahmapur. Little more than a line of dingy snack stalls and mildewed bungalows deep in the forest, it's the kind of place to which government servants pray not to be posted. Pilgrims, however, come here in large numbers for the legendary **hot springs**, which are believed to cure infertility. The boiling sulphurous water bubbles out of a cleft in the mountainside and is piped into a small pool, where little rocks smeared with vermilion and hibiscus petals mark the presence of the living deities believed to reside in the water (it is prohibited to dip any part of the body in the pool).

ARRIVAL AND DEPARTURE   TAPTAPANI

By bus Regular buses (hourly; 1hr 15min–2hr) travel   between Brahmapur and Taptapani.

ACCOMMODATION AND EATING

Panthanivas Just down the hill from the springs ☏ 06816 255031, ⓦ panthanivas.com. You can enjoy the hot springs in privacy at the atmospheric OTDC-run *Panthanivas* as the water is pumped straight into capacious sunken bathtubs in some of the more expensive rooms.

Despite the fine views, the place is rarely full, which is just as well, as there's nowhere else to stay in the vicinity (book in advance just to be on the safe side). There's also a decent restaurant. ₹**1150**

Andhra Pradesh

CHARMINAR, HYDERABAD

Andhra Pradesh

18

Although Andhra Pradesh occupies a great swathe of eastern India, stretching more than 1200km along the coast from Orissa to Tamil Nadu and reaching far inland from the fertile deltas of the Godavari and Krishna rivers to the semi-arid Deccan Plateau, most foreign travellers simply pass through en route to its more attractive neighbours. This is understandable, as places of interest are few and far between, but the sights Andhra Pradesh does have are absorbing enough to warrant at least a brief stop-off.

Now a major hi-tech hub, the capital, **Hyderabad**, is an atmospheric city with lively bazaars, the eclectic Salar Jung Museum and the mighty **Golconda Fort**. **Warangal**, 150km northeast, has Muslim and Hindu remains from the twelfth and thirteenth centuries, while the region's Buddhist legacy is preserved in museums at sites such as **Nagarjunakonda** and **Amaravati**. In the east, the city of **Vijayawada** has little to recommend it, though it is a convenient access-point for Amaravati. Similarly, in the northeast, the fast-growing city of **Visakhapatnam** is little more than a handy place to break up a long trip. By contrast, the temple town of **Tirupati** in the far southeast is a fascinating, impossibly crowded pilgrimage site. In the southwest, **Puttaparthy** attracts a more international pilgrim crowd, who still flock to the ashram of the late spiritual leader Sai Baba.

Although modern industries have grown up around the capital, and shipbuilding, iron and steel are important on the coast, most people in Andhra Pradesh remain poor. Away from the Godavari and Krishna deltas, where the soil is rich enough to grow rice and sugar cane, the land is in places impossible to cultivate, which has contributed to the desperate plight of many farmers (see p.908).

Brief history

The earliest accounts of the region, from the third century BC, refer to a people known as the Andhras. The **Satavahana dynasty** (second century BC to second century AD), also known as the Andhras, came to control much of central and southern India from their second capital at Amaravati on the Krishna. They enjoyed extensive international trade and were great patrons of Buddhism. Subsequently, the Pallavas, the Chalukyas and the Cholas all held sway. By the thirteenth century, the Kakatiyas of Warangal were under constant threat from Muslim incursions, while later on, after the fall of their city at Hampi, the Hindu Vijayanagars transferred operations to Chandragiri near Tirupati.

The next significant development was in the mid-sixteenth century, with the rise of the Muslim **Qutb Shahi dynasty**. In 1687, the son of the Mughal emperor Aurangzeb seized Golconda. Five years after Aurangzeb died in 1707, Hyderabad's viceroy declared independence and established the Asaf Jahi dynasty of **nizams**. In return for allying with the British against Tipu Sultan of Mysore, the nizam dynasty was allowed to retain a certain degree of autonomy even after the British had come to dominate India.

During the Independence struggle, harmony between Hindus and Muslims in Andhra Pradesh disintegrated. **Partition** brought matters to a climax, as the nizam wanted to join other Muslims in the soon-to-be-created state of **Pakistan**. In 1949 the capital erupted in riots, the army was brought in and Hyderabad state was admitted to

The Oneness university and temple p.921   Shri Satya Sai Baba p.922

PILGRIMS AT TIRUMALA HILL

Highlights

❶ Hyderabad A predominately Islamic city, as well as a focal point of twenty-first century hi-tech India, with a compelling combination of monuments, museums and bazaars. **See p.909**

❷ Golconda Fort Set in a lush landscape just west of Hyderabad, the Qutb Shahi dynasty's capital boasts a dramatic and well-preserved fort with amazing acoustics. **See p.912**

❸ Warangal This sleepy town features two important Hindu monuments: a rambling medieval fort and an exquisitely carved thousand-pillared Shiva temple. **See p.916**

❹ Nagarjunakonda Now surrounded by a vast artificial lake, this peaceful place boasts various Buddhist monuments, including a huge statue, and a fine museum. **See p.917**

❺ Amaravati At this village on the banks of the Krishna river, fine carvings surround the foundation mound of a great Buddhist stupa. **See p.919**

❻ Tirumala Hill The world's most visited pilgrimage centre, crowned by the crowded, vibrant and colourful Venkateshvara Vishnu temple. **See p.920**

HIGHLIGHTS ARE MARKED ON THE MAP ON P.908

the Indian Union. Andhra Pradesh state was created in 1956 from Telugu-speaking regions (although Urdu is widely spoken in Hyderabad) that had previously formed part of the Madras Presidency on the east coast and the princely state of Hyderabad to the west. Today almost ninety percent of the population is Hindu, with Muslims largely concentrated in the capital.

In 1999, the pro-business Telugu Desam party eventually wrestled the power long held by Congress, and over the following five years there was huge development around Hyderabad, most famously, **HITEC City**. However, rural areas – where drought and economic crisis led to thousands of farmer suicides – were neglected. In 2004 Congress regained control of the state government, although they were also criticized for not doing enough to help farmers, and suicides have continued with alarming frequency, though the numbers fell in 2012.

In December 2009, following a high-profile hunger strike, the Indian government surprisingly bowed to pressure from the Telangana Rashtra Samithi (TRS) party and announced plans to carve a new state, **Telangana**, out of northwestern Andhra Pradesh. Although welcomed by TRS supporters who claimed their region had long been neglected, the decision sparked widespread protests, strikes and political resignations. The Indian government subsequently set up a commission to examine the practicalities of the issue and a formal decision had still not been announced in early 2013, where there was a further wave of violent clashes in Hyderabad.

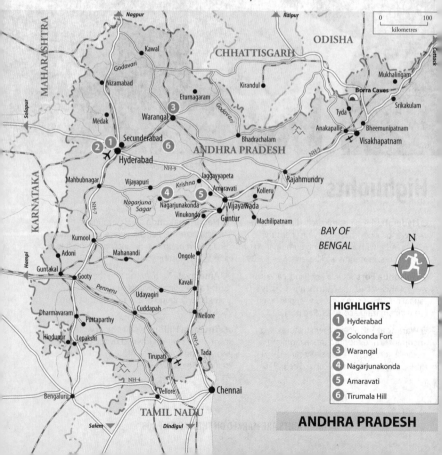

HIGHLIGHTS

1. Hyderabad
2. Golconda Fort
3. Warangal
4. Nagarjunakonda
5. Amaravati
6. Tirumala Hill

ANDHRA PRADESH

Hyderabad/Secunderabad

A melting pot of Muslim and Hindu cultures, the capital of Andhra Pradesh comprises the twin cities of **HYDERABAD** and **SECUNDERABAD**, with a combined population of around eight million. Secunderabad, of little interest, is the modern administrative city founded by the British, whereas Hyderabad, the old city, has teeming **bazaars**, **Muslim monuments** and the absorbing **Salar Jung Museum**. Hyderabad declined after Independence, with tensions often close to the surface due to lack of funding. Nowadays, although the overcrowded old city still suffers from substandard amenities, the conurbation as a whole is booming. In recent years Hyderabad has overtaken Bengaluru to become India's foremost computer and **IT centre**.

The Hyderabad metropolitan area has three distinct sectors: **Hyderabad**, divided between the old city and newer areas towards HITEC City; **Secunderabad**, the modern city; and **Golconda**, the old fort. The two cities are basically one big sprawl, separated by a lake, **Hussain Sagar**. The most interesting area, south of the River Musi, holds the **bazaars**, the **Charminar** and the **Salar Jung Museum**. North of the river, the main shopping malls are found around **Abids Circle** and **Sultan Bazaar**. Four kilometres west of Hyderabad railway station lies the posh **Banjara Hills** district. Beyond here is the exclusive residential area of **Jubilee Hills**, while a further 6km brings you to **HITEC City**.

Brief history

Hyderabad was founded in 1591 by **Mohammed Quli Shah** (1562–1612), 8km east of Golconda, the fortress capital of the Golconda empire. Unusually, the new city was laid out on a grid system, with huge arches and stone buildings that included Hyderabad's most famous monument, the **Charminar**. At first it was a city without walls; these were only added in 1740 as defence against the Marathas. Legend has it that a secret tunnel linked the city with the spectacular **Golconda Fort**, 11km away.

For the three hundred years of Muslim reign, there was harmony between the predominantly Hindu population and the minority Muslims. Hyderabad was the most important focus of Muslim power in south India at this time; the princes' fabulous wealth derived primarily from the fine gems, particularly diamonds, mined in the Kistna Valley at Golconda. The famous **Koh-i-Noor** diamond was found here – the only time it was ever captured was by Mughal emperor Aurangzeb, when his son seized the Golconda Fort in 1687. It ended up, cut, in the British royal crown.

Since 2009, Hyderabad's future status has been thrown into question by the drawn-out **Telangana** decision (see opposite). If the state is divided, it is unclear if the city would be part of the new state, remain part of Andhra Pradesh or serve as a joint capital for both states.

Salar Jung Museum

Daily except Fri 10am–5pm • ₹150 (₹10) • No photography • ⊕ salarjungmuseum.in

The unmissable **Salar Jung Museum**, on the south bank of the River Musi, houses part of the huge collection of Salar Jung, one of the nizam's prime ministers, and his ancestors. A well-travelled man of wealth, he bought whatever took his fancy from both East and West, from the sublime to, in some cases, the ridiculous. His extraordinary hoard includes Indian jade, miniatures, furniture, lacquer-work, Mughal opaque glassware, fabrics, bronzes, Buddhist and Hindu sculpture, manuscripts and weapons. The museum gets very crowded on weekends.

Charminar

Daily 9am–5.30pm • ₹150 (₹10)

A maze of bazaars teeming with people, the old city has at its heart the **Charminar** or Four Towers, a triumphal arch built at the centre of Mohammed Quli Shah's city in

18

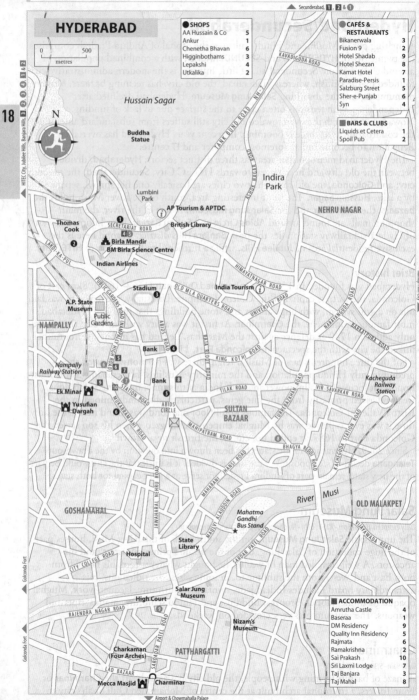

Secunderabad, ▲ 1, 2 & 3

HYDERABAD

0 ————— 500
metres

● SHOPS

AA Hussain & Co	5
Ankur	1
Chenetha Bhavan	6
Higginbothams	3
Lepakshi	4
Utkalika	2

● CAFÉS & RESTAURANTS

Bikanerwala	3
Fusion 9	2
Hotel Shadab	9
Hotel Shezan	8
Kamat Hotel	7
Paradise-Persis	1
Salzburg Street	5
Sher-e-Punjab	6
Syn	4

■ BARS & CLUBS

Liquids et Cetera	1
Spoil Pub	2

■ ACCOMMODATION

Amrutha Castle	4
Baseraa	1
DM Residency	9
Quality Inn Residency	5
Rajmata	6
Ramakrishna	2
Sai Prakash	10
Sri Laxmi Lodge	7
Taj Banjara	3
Taj Mahal	8

Hussain Sagar

Buddha Statue

Lumbini Park

Indira Park

NEHRU NAGAR

Thomas Cook

AP Tourism & APTDC
British Library

SECRETARIAT ROAD

Birla Mandir
BM Birla Science Centre

Indian Airlines

HIMAYATNAGAR ROAD

Stadium

India Tourism

OLD MLA QUARTERS ROAD

UNIVERSITY ROAD

A.P. State Museum

NAMPALLY

Public Gardens

PUBLIC GARDENS ROAD

NAMPALLY HIGH ROAD

ABIDS ROAD

RAJA REDDY ROAD

KING KOTHI ROAD

Bank

Nampally Railway Station

STATION ROAD

MUKARAMJAHI ROAD

Bank

TILAK ROAD

Ek Minar

Yusufian Dargah

ABIDS CIRCLE

SULTAN BAZAAR

Kacheguda Railway Station

VIR SAVARKAR ROAD

MAHIPATRAM ROAD

BHAGYA REDDY ROAD

GOSHAMAHAL

JAWAHARLAL NEHRU ROAD

MALNI ALIUDDIN ROAD

MAHARANI JHANSI ROAD

River Musi

OLD MALAKPET

VIJAYAWADA ROAD

Mahatma Gandhi Bus Stand

State Library

Hospital

SARDAR PATEL ROAD

CITY COLLEGE ROAD

RAJENDRA NAGAR ROAD

High Court

Salar Jung Museum

Nizam's Museum

PATTHARGATTI

Charkaman (Four Arches)

LAD BAZAAR

SARDAR PATEL ROAD

Mecca Masjid

Charminar

Airport & Chowmahalla Palace

KAVADIGUDA ROAD

NH-7

TANK BUND ROAD

LAKDI KA PUL

NARAYANGUDA ROAD

BARKATPURA ROAD

TIRUMALA NAGAR ROAD

KACHEGUDA STATION ROAD

Ramoji Film City

1591 to commemorate an epidemic of the plague. It features four graceful 56m-high minarets, housing spiral staircases to the upper storeys. The (now defunct) mosque on the roof is the oldest in Hyderabad. The yellowish colour of the building is due to a special stucco made of marble powder, gram and egg yolk. The **Charkaman**, or Four Arches, north of the Charminar, were built in 1594; the western arch, **Daulat-Khan-e-Ali**, was at one time adorned with rich gold tapestries.

Lad Bazaar

The Charminar marks the beginning of the fascinating **Lad Bazaar**, which leads to Mahboob Chowk, a market square featuring a mosque and Victorian clock tower. Lad Bazaar specializes in everything you could possibly need for a Hyderabadi marriage, including bangles, rosewater, herbs, spices and cloth. You'll also find silver filigree jewellery, antiques, *bidri*-ware, hookah paraphernalia and, in the markets near the Charminar, **pearls** – so beloved of the nizams that they ground them into powder to eat. Hyderabad is still the centre of India's pearl trade.

Mecca Masjid

Daily 8am–noon & 3–8pm

Southwest, behind the Charminar, the **Mecca Masjid** was constructed in 1598 and can hold three thousand devotees, with room for up to ten thousand more in the courtyard. On the left of the courtyard are the tombs of the nizams. In May 2007, the mosque was rocked by a powerful bomb; the incident killed fourteen people. The perpetrators were never caught and since this and subsequent bombings, security has been very tight throughout the city.

Chowmahalla Palace

Khilwat 20-4-236, Motigalli • Daily except Fri 10am–5pm • ₹150 (₹40), camera ₹50 • ⓦ chowmahalla.com

The 150-year-old **Chowmahalla Palace**, southwest of the Mecca Masjid, was used by the nizams to entertain royal visitors and official guests. Inspired by the Shah's palace in Tehran, it is actually a (partially restored) complex of four palaces, a grand Durbar Hall, elegant courtyards and fountain-filled gardens.

North of the river

Just south of the railway station, the **Yusufian Dargah**, with its striking bulbous yellow dome, is the shrine of a seventeenth-century Sufi saint of the venerable Chishti order. About 1km north of the station, set in tranquil public gardens, the **State Museum** (daily except Fri & 2nd Sat of each month 10.30am–5pm; ₹10) displays a modest collection of bronzes, prehistoric tools and weapons.

The **Birla Venkateshwara Mandir** (daily 7am–noon & 3–9pm; no photography) on Kalapahad ("black mountain") Hill, north of the public gardens, is open to all. Constructed in 1976, the temple itself is not of great interest, but affords fine views. Nearby is the mildly diverting **BM Birla Science Centre** (daily 10.30am–8pm, closes 3pm on Fri; ₹20; ⓦbirlasciencecentre.org), which has a lot of satellite hardware and photos, sensory perception machines and a small dinosaur display, plus a **planetarium** (English shows at 11.30am, 4pm & 6pm; ₹25).

Hussain Sagar

Hussain Sagar, the large expanse of water separating Hyderabad from Secunderabad, lends a welcome air of tranquillity to the busy conurbation and the area is a popular place for a stroll, especially at sunset. In its centre stands a large stone statue of the **Buddha Purnima** ("Full Moon Buddha"), erected in 1992. Regular **boats** (₹45 return) chug out to the statue from Lumbini Park, just off Secretariat Road. The park was the site of one of two bombs that exploded in August 2007, claiming 44 lives, so security is predictably tight.

Golconda Fort

Daily 9am–5pm • ₹100 (₹5) • Sound-and-light show: English: March–Oct 7pm, Nov–Feb 6.30pm; 1hr; ₹50 • Bus #66G from Charminar via Nampally

Golconda, 122m above the plain and 11km west of old Hyderabad, was the capital of the seven Qutb Shahi kings from 1518 until the end of the sixteenth century, when the court moved to Hyderabad itself. Well preserved and set in thick green scrubland, it is one of India's most impressive forts, boasting 87 semicircular bastions and eight mighty gates, complete with gruesome elephant-proof spikes. Set aside a day to explore the fort, which covers an area of around four square kilometres.

Entering the **fort** by the Balahisar Gate, you come into the Grand Portico, where guards clap their hands to show off the fort's acoustics. To the right is the **mortuary bath**, where the bodies of deceased nobles were ritually bathed prior to burial. If you follow the arrowed anticlockwise route, you pass the two-storey residence of ministers Akkana and Madanna before starting the stairway ascent to the Durbar Hall. Halfway along the steps, you arrive at a small, dark cell named after the court cashier **Ramdas**, who while incarcerated here produced the clumsy carvings and paintings that litter the gloomy room.

Nearing the top, you come across the small, pretty mosque of Ibrahim Qutb Shah; beyond here is an even tinier temple to Durga. The steps are crowned by the three-storey **Durbar Hall** of the Qutb Shahis, on platforms outside which the monarchs would sit and survey their domains.

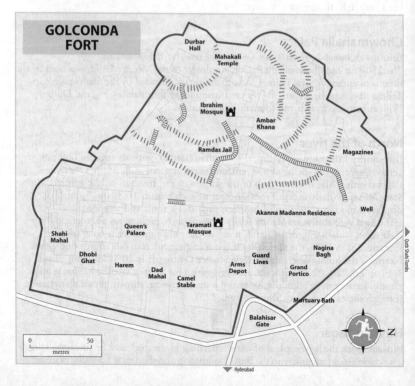

GOLCONDA FORT

18

The ruins of the **queen's palace**, once elaborately decorated with multiple domes, stand in a courtyard centred on an original copper fountain that used to be filled with rosewater. You can still see traces of a "necklace" design on one of the arches, at the top of which a lotus bud sits below an opening flower with a cavity at its centre that once contained a diamond. At the entrance to the **palace** itself, four chambers provided protection from intruders. Passing through two rooms, the second of which is overgrown, you come to the **Shahi Mahal**, the royal bedroom. Originally it had a domed roof and niches on the walls that once sheltered candles or oil lamps. Golconda has a nightly **sound-and-light** show.

Tombs of the Qutb Shahi kings

Daily except Fri 9.30am–4.30pm • ₹20 • Bus #123 or #142S from Charminar

There are 82 **tombs** about 1km north of Golconda Fort's outer wall. Set in peaceful gardens, they commemorate commanders, relatives of the kings, dancers, singers and royal doctors, as well as all but two of the Qutb Shahi kings. Faded today, they were once brightly coloured in turquoise and green.

The western suburbs

Most of Hyderabad's new-found wealth is concentrated in the city's western suburbs. The nearest of these is **Banjara Hills**, around 4km from Nampally, which comprises spacious residences in quiet streets surrounding Road No.1, a glitzy strip of trendy shops, restaurants and bars. The Western appearance and dress, particularly of the young women here, is a sharp contrast to the niqabs and saris ubiquitous in the old city. Several kilometres further west you enter the even leafier and more upmarket district of **Jubilee Hills**, which is largely residential.

The upturn in Hyderabad's fortunes was driven by its becoming a hi-tech hub in the late 1990s, earning it the nickname "Cyberabad", although it is also home to other industries including car manufacture. **HITEC City** itself is several square kilometres of modern blocks and complexes about 10km from the city centre. Although strict security prevents casual visits by those with no business within the complexes, you can get a flavour by touring the area, which is bordered on the south and west by a large lake and beautiful rock formations, reminiscent of Hampi.

Ramoji Film City

Daily 9am–6pm • ₹600 • ⓦ ramojifilmcity.com

Ramoji Film City (RFC), 25km east of central Hyderabad, is the world's largest film studio complex. Covering nearly two thousand acres, with around five hundred set locations, it can produce up to sixty movies simultaneously. Although you cannot see films actually being made, you can tour the facades, enjoy rides such as the Ramoji Tower simulated earthquake and watch a dance and stunt show. The easiest way to get here is on a tour from Hyderabad (see p.914).

ARRIVAL AND DEPARTURE   HYDERABAD/SECUNDERABAD

BY PLANE

Modern and efficient Rajiv Gandhi International Airport is around 20km south of central Hyderabad. Until the metro connection is complete, the airport is only linked to the city by taxis (about ₹900) and Pushpak Airport Liner buses (every 10–15min; ₹100–200); heading to the airport, you can catch these from the Secretariat.

Airlines Go Air, Babukhan Estate, Basheerbagh (☎ 040 2326 0037) Indian Airlines, opposite Assembly, Hill Fort Rd,

Saifabad (☎ 040 2343 0334); IndiGo, 2nd floor, 5-9-86/1 Chapel Rd (☎ 1800 180 3838); Jet Airways, Hill Fort Rd, ☎ 040 3989 3333; Kingfisher Airlines (☎ 1800 425 7008); SpiceJet (☎ 1800 180 3333).

Destinations There are frequent international flights and excellent domestic connections to Bengaluru (10–12 daily; 1hr–1hr 30min); Chennai (12–15 daily; 1hr–1hr 30min); Delhi (13–16 daily; 2–4hr); Goa (2–3 daily; 1hr 45min); Kochi (4 daily; 1hr 45min); Kolkata (5 daily; 2–3hr);

18

Mumbai (14–16 daily; 1hr 15min–3hr 30min) and many other cities.

BY TRAIN

Many long-distance trains terminate at Secunderabad; your ticket is valid for any connecting train to Hyderabad (Nampally) railway station. The two stations are also linked to each other – and other points in the city, such as Banjara Hills and HITEC City – by the overground Hyderabad Metro (or MMTS). The railways reservations office at Hyderabad (daily 8am–8pm) is to the left as you enter the station: counter 211 is for tourists. The Secunderabad reservation complex is more than 400m to the right as you exit the station: counter 34 is for foreigners.

Destinations Daily train services from Hyderabad (Nampally) station include: the *Charminar Express* #12760 to Chennai (6.30pm; 13hr 45min); the *Sabari Express* #17230 to Trivandrum via Ernakulam (noon; 30hr 55min); the *Mumbai Express* #17032 to Mumbai (8.40pm; 16hr 25min); the *East Coast Express* #18646 to Kolkata (10am; 30hr 10min) via

Vijayawada, Visakhapatnam and Bhubaneswar; and the *Rayasaleema Express* #17429 to Tirupati (3.35pm; 15hr 5min). Most northeast-bound services call at Warangal and Vijayawada. From Secunderabad, the *Konark Express* #11020 travels to Mumbai (11.45am; 16hr 10min). The *Bangalore Express* #12785 (7.05pm; 11hr 20min) departs from Kacheguda station, around 3km east of Nampally.

BY BUS

The long-distance Mahatma Gandhi Bus Stand occupies an island in the River Musi, 3km southeast of Nampally railway station.

Destinations From the long-distance bus stand, regular bus services run to destinations throughout the state and beyond, including Bidar (hourly; 4hr), Tirupati (10 daily; 12hr), Vijayapuri for Nagarjunakonda (6 daily; 4hr), Vijayawada (every 15min; 6hr) and Warangal (every 15min; 3hr). Various "deluxe" private buses depart for Bengaluru, Chennai, Mumbai and other major cities from outside Hyderabad (Nampally) railway station.

GETTING AROUND AND INFORMATION

Car rental Air Travels in Banjara Hills (📞 040 2332 8561, ✉ airtravels@yahoo.com) and Classic Travels in Secunderabad (📞 040 2775 5645).

Tourist information AP Tourism office (daily except Sun 10am–5pm; 📞 040 2345 3110, 🌐 aptourism.in) is on Secretariat Rd, near the huge flyover. The APTDC office next door (daily 7am–8pm; 📞 040 2345 3036, 🌐 aptdc.in) and the other APTDC office, on Sardar Patel Rd, Secunderabad (📞 040 2789 3100), exist principally to book their tours. The Incredible India office is in the new tourist plaza at Begumpet (Mon–Fri 9am–5pm; 📞 040 2326 1360), along with the offices of many other states. A good source of information is the monthly magazine, *Channel 6* (₹30;

🌐 channel6.in), available from most bookstalls.

Guided tours APTDC operates a number of good-value guided tours. The times quoted below are when tours set off from the Secunderabad office; the pick-up time in Hyderabad is 15–20min later. There's a city tour (daily 7.45am–6.30pm; ₹300); a Golconda Fort sound-and-light show tour (daily 2–9pm; ₹230 including entry); and a Ramoji Film City tour (daily 7.45am–6.30pm; ₹800 including entry). For the latter, tours run by private agents in Nampally may be more convenient. The Nagarjuna Sagar tour (Sat & Sun 7.30am–10pm; ₹500 excluding entry) is a rushed but convenient way to reach this fascinating area (see p.917).

ACCOMMODATION

The area to the east of **Hyderabad (Nampally) railway station** has the cheapest accommodation, but you're unlikely to find anything acceptable for less than ₹500: avoid the grim little collection of five lodges with "Royal" in their name. A little over 1km north of Secunderabad railway station, several decent places can be found on **Sarojini Devi Rd**.

HYDERABAD

Amrutha Castle 5-9-16 Saifabad, opposite the Secretariat 📞 040 4443 3880, 🌐 bestwestern amruthacastle.com. This extraordinarily kitsch hotel, which looks like a fairy castle, won't be to everyone's taste, but is undoubtedly a fun place to stay. The turreted attached rooms have faux wooden beams, fortified doors and paintings of famous royals. Although there's no moat, you can take a dip in the rooftop pool. ₹4800

★ **DM Residency** 5-8-196/B Nampally 📞 040 6644 7734, ✉ hoteldmresidency@gmail.com. Set back from the Nampally hubbub, this new hotel is kept scrupulously clean by the overtly helpful staff. The rooms are

comfortable, with flatscreen TVs and there's wi-fi in the lobby. Good single and a/c rates. ₹1100

Quality Inn Residency Nampally High Rd 📞 040 3061 6161, 🌐 theresidency-hyd.com. A business traveller-oriented hotel with central a/c and comfy attached rooms set around a looming atrium. While the standard rooms are fine, the "classic" ones are pretty slick, particularly their plate glass desks. ₹3900

Rajmata Nampally High Rd, opposite railway station 📞 040 6666 5555, ✉ royalrajmata@gmail.com. Set back from the road, the popular *Rajmata* has a slightly overpriced collection of cleanish attached rooms: all have TVs and some also boast a/c. ₹900

Sai Prakash Station Rd ☎040 2461 1726, ⓦhotelsaiprakash.com. The vast marble lobby gives way to keenly-priced all a/c rooms with flatscreen TVs and contemporary blue-and-brown flower motifs on the walls: the bathrooms, however, are decidedly cramped. It also offers wi-fi access and two decent restaurants. ₹1800

Sri Laxmi Lodge Gadwal Compound, Station Rd ☎040 6663 4200. Down a small lane opposite the *Sai Prakash*, *Sri Laxmi* is one of the city's better shoestring options. The rooms – if not always the sheets – are clean and have attached showers and squat toilets. A TV costs ₹50 extra. ₹400

★ **Taj Banjara** Road No.1, Banjara Hills, 4km from the centre ☎040 6666 9999, ⓦtajhotels.com. In a pleasant lakeside location, with all the usual top-notch facilities including a pool, three classy restaurants and a 24hr coffee shop. Online specials are invariably lower than the official rates. ₹6300

Taj Mahal 4-1-999 Abids Rd ☎040 6651 1122, ⓦhoteltajmahalindia.com. This peeling white-and-pale-green 1920s building has a patio garden, spiral staircase and plenty of character. The rooms themselves are plainer, but feature high ceilings, a/c, flatscreen TVs and fridges; those on the upper floor are better, though more expensive. ₹1750

SECUNDERABAD

Baseraa Sarojini Devi Rd ☎040 2770 3200, ⓦbaseraa .com. The smartest hotel within walking distance (around 15min) of the station, *Baseraa* boasts modern attached rooms with a/c, TV, minibar and wi-fi access. ₹2900

Ramakrishna St John's Rd ☎040 2783 4567, ☎2782 0933. With some a/c rooms, this comfy upper-budget-range hotel, in a large concrete block opposite the railway reservation complex, is the best option in the immediate station area. ₹900

EATING AND DRINKING

Plenty of places specialize in **Hyderabadi cuisine**, such as authentic biriyanis, and the famously chilli-hot Andhra cuisine. Hyderabadi cooking is derived from Mughlai court cuisine, featuring sumptuous meat dishes with northern ingredients such as cinnamon, cardamom, cloves and garlic, and traditional southern vegetarian dishes with an array of flavourings like cassia buds, peanuts, coconut, tamarind leaves, mustard seeds and red chillies. There are numerous **bars**, particularly along Road No.1 in Banjara Hills and the burgeoning Jubilee Hills area further west.

HYDERABAD

Bikanerwala 6-3-190/Z Road No.1, Banjara Hills ☎040 6666 1111. At this bustling fast-food joint the focus is firmly on north Indian cuisine, with authentic *bhel puri*, *channa bhatura* and *aloo tikki* (₹30–100) all on offer, as well as sweets. Daily 8.30am–11.30pm.

Fusion 9 6-3-249/A Road No.1, Banjara Hills ☎040 6557 7722. Expensive (mains ₹350–475) but quality cuisine from regions as diverse as Mexico, Europe, the Middle East and Southeast Asia, served in a smart modern lounge. The same owners run the similarly good *F9 Diner* in Priyanka Plaza, Kondapur, near HITEC City. Daily 11am–11pm.

Hotel Shadab Saroadar Patel Rd, Patthargatti ☎040 2456 1648. While there are some fine meat and fish tandoori items on the menu, the main reason to visit *Hotel Shadab* is for its excellent mutton and chicken biriyanis (₹125–180), some of the best in the city. You may have to queue for a table, but it's worth the wait. Daily 5am–11pm.

★ **Hotel Shezan** MJ Rd, Nampally ☎040 2461 7867. People flock for the excellent and filling biriyanis, a snip at ₹130. Some Western and Chinese dishes are also served in the tiered open-air dining hall. Daily noon–11pm.

Kamat Hotel Station Rd, opposite Sai Prakash hotel ☎040 2320 3351. At this conveniently located branch of the hygienic veggie chain, waiters in white shirts with red lapels serve up inexpensive veg dosas, *iddlis*, *vadas*, thalis and mains (₹40–100). Daily 7am–10pm.

Liquids et Cetera Road No.1, Banjara Hills ☎040 6625 9907. Very trendy nightclub that hosts theme nights such as

Barbie Fridays and Bollywood Bling. Attracts celebrities from the Mumbai entertainment scene. Daily 8pm–2am.

Salzburg Street Amrutha Castle hotel, 5-9-16 Saifabad ☎040 4443 3880. Overlooking the lobby's water feature, this restaurant has unusual, but well-executed, options like prawns cooked in a "Northwest Frontier" style and the Korean-Indian fusion *kimchi paneer*, as well as some more traditional Indian and Chinese dishes. Mains ₹150–300. Daily 11am–10.30pm.

Sher-e-Punjab Corner of Nampally High Rd and station slip road ☎040 2320 4448. In a convenient, if not particularly appealing location, this popular basement restaurant offers tasty north Indian veg and non-veg food at low prices: many under ₹100 and full tandoori chicken ₹230. Daily 10am–10.30pm.

Spoil Pub Road No.1, Jubilee Hills ☎040 6451 3333. Popular pub that offers a range of entertainment from Ladies Nite to House of Noise. ₹79 snacks and drinks until 8.30pm. Daily 5–11pm.

★ **Syn** Taj Deccan hotel, Road No.1, Banjara Hills 6666 3939. This hip restaurant is the place to come for authentic Thai, Vietnamese and Japanese cuisine (mains from ₹250). It features a teppanyaki counter, and a slick bar that, alongside the usual range of alcoholic drinks, also serves "detox cocktails". Daily noon–11pm.

SECUNDERABAD

Paradise-Persis Sarojini Devi Rd ☎040 6631 3721. This very popular modern multirestaurant complex bashes

18

out fine Hyderabadi cuisine, as well as Chinese. The biriyanis are recommended, but don't miss out on the succulent mutton kebabs. Mains ₹80–250. Daily 8am–11pm.

SHOPPING

All the shops listed below are in central Hyderabad and operate core hours of Mon–Sat 10am–8pm, sometimes later. Lad Bazaar (see p.911) in the old city remains the most absorbing place to browse for anything from saris to spices.

AA Hussain & Co Arastu Trust Building, 5-8-551 Abids Rd ☎040 2320 3724. This old-fashioned bookshop, which has not changed much in the seventy years or more that it has existed, offers a vast selection of titles on most subjects.

Ankur 6-1-84 Secretariat Rd ☎040 2323 4901. A huge range of beautiful silks and saris of varying quality and extent can be found at this well-stocked shop.

Chenetha Bhavan A little south of the railway station, Nampally ☎040 2460 2845. This modern shopping complex is stuffed with handloom shops, specializing in both clothes and carpets.

Higginbothams 9 Lal Bahadur Stadium ☎040 2323 7918. The main Hyderabad branch of the venerable national chain has a diverse collection of novels, reference and academic books.

Lepakshi Gunfoundry, MG Rd ☎040 2323 5028. The flagship branch of the AP government emporium stocks a wide range of handicrafts from all over the state.

Utkalika Opposite DGP Office, Saifabad ☎040 2324 0510. This government of Odisha handicrafts emporium has a modest selection of silver filigree jewellery, handloom cloth, *ikat* tie-dye, Jagannath papier-mâché figures and buffalo bone carvings.

DIRECTORY

Banks and exchange State Bank of Hyderabad, MG Rd, and Federal Bank, 1st floor, Orient Estate, MG Rd exchange foreign currency; both open Mon–Fri 10.30am–2.30pm, the latter also Sat 10.30am–12.30pm. Alternatively try Thomas Cook (☎040 2329 6521) at Nasir Arcade, Secretariat Rd, or LKP forex (☎040 2321 0094) on Public Gardens Rd, 10min walk north of Nampally Station; both open Mon–Sat 9.30am–6pm. ATMs are ubiquitous.

Hospitals The government-run Gandhi Hospital is in Secunderabad (☎040 2770 2222); the private CDR Hospital is in Himayatnagar (☎040 2322 1221); and there's a Tropical Diseases Hospital in Nallakunta (☎040 2766 7843).

Internet access Some of the quickest connections are at Reliance Web World (₹20/hr), which has numerous branches, including on the second floor of a shopping mall near Abids Circle.

Library You must be a member or a British citizen to use the British Library, Secretariat Rd (Tues–Sat 11am–7pm; ☎040 2323 0774).

Pharmacies Apollo Pharmacy (☎040 6060 2424) has branches throughout the city, some open 24hr.

Police ☎040 2323 0191. In an emergency call ☎100.

Travel agents Travel Club forex (☎040 2321 0417), Nasir Arcade, Saifabad, close to Thomas Cook; and Kamat Travels in the *Hotel Sai Prakash* complex (☎040 2460 6617).

Around Hyderabad

As you head north from Hyderabad, the landscape becomes greener and hillier, sporadically punctuated by photogenic black-granite rock formations. There is little to detain visitors here except **Warangal**, which has a medieval fort and a Shiva temple. South of the capital, swathes of flat farmland stretch into the centre of the state, where the Nagarjuna Sagar Dam has created a major lake with the important Buddhist site of **Nagarjunakonda**, now an island, in its waters.

Warangal

WARANGAL – "one stone" – 150km northeast of Hyderabad and just about possible to visit as a day-trip, was the Hindu capital of the Kakatiyan empire in the twelfth and thirteenth centuries. Like other Deccan cities, it changed hands many times between the Hindus and the Muslims – something reflected in the remains you see today.

Warangal's **fort** (daily 9am–5pm; ₹100 (₹5)), 4km south of the city, is famous for its two circles of fortifications: the outer made of earth with a moat, and the inner of stone. Four roads into the centre meet at the ruined Shiva temple of **Swayambhu**

(1162). At its southern gateway, another Shiva temple, from the fourteenth century, is in much better shape; inside, the remains of an enormous lingam came originally from the Swayambhu shrine. Also inside the citadel is the **Shirab Khan**, or **Audience Hall**, an early eleventh-century building very similar to Mandu's Hindola Mahal (see p.388).

Some 6km north of town just off the main road beside the slopes of Hanamkonda Hill, the largely basalt Chalukyan-style "**thousand-pillared**" Shiva temple (daily 6am–6pm) was constructed in 1163. A low-roofed building on several stepped stages, it features superb carvings and shrines to Vishnu, Shiva and Surya, the sun god. They lead off the *mandapa*, whose numerous finely carved columns give the temple its name. In front, a polished Nandi bull was carved out of a single stone. A Bhadrakali temple stands at the top of the hill.

18

ARRIVAL AND INFORMATION
WARANGAL

By train There are at least 20 services daily between Hyderabad and Warangal, taking 2–3hr.

By bus There are buses every 15–30min between Warangal and Hyderabad, taking around 3hr.

Getting around The easiest way to cover the site is to rent a bike from one of the stalls on Station Rd (₹5–10/hr). An auto-rickshaw to either the fort or the temple costs

around ₹100, if you negotiate hard.

Tourist information There's an AP Tourism office (☎ 0870 244 6606; daily except Sun 10am–5pm) opposite the Royal Engineering College.

Internet Internet facilities are available at Durga Xerox on Station Rd, almost opposite the *Vijaya Lodge*.

ACCOMMODATION AND EATING

Ashoka Main Rd, Hanamkonda ☎0870 257 8491, ⓦhotelashoka.in. Near the thousand-pillared temple, this place has carpeted a/c rooms with TV and fridge but dodgy service. The restaurant provides Indian and Chinese standards; there's also an attached bar. **₹1100**

Bharati Mess Station Rd. The best of the vegetarian restaurants in the station area, offering huge and wholesome unlimited refill meals for around ₹70, all made

with fresh ingredients. Daily 7am–10pm.

Surya Station Rd ☎0870 244 1834. A decent budget option very close to the station, with clean attached rooms and a good restaurant serving a range of inexpensive food. **₹700**

Vijaya Lodge Station Rd ☎0870 225 1222. The pick of the extremely basic lodges near the station, with grubby but not unhygienic rooms, some with shared bathrooms. **₹250/₹400**

Nagarjunakonda

NAGARJUNAKONDA, or "Nagarjuna's Hill", 166km south of Hyderabad and 175km west of Vijayawada, is all that remains of the vast area, rich in archeological sites, that was submerged when the huge Nagarjuna Sagar Dam was built across the River Krishna in 1960. Many nearby villages had to be relocated to higher ground when the valley was flooded. Ancient settlements in the valley were first discovered in 1926, and extensive excavations carried out between 1954 and 1960 uncovered more than one hundred sites dating from the early Stone Age to late medieval times. Nagarjunakonda was once the summit of a hill, where a fort towered 200m above the valley floor; now it is just a small oblong island near the middle of Nagarjuna Sagar lake. Several Buddhist monuments have been reconstructed, in an operation reminiscent of that at Abu Simbel in Egypt, and a **museum** exhibits the more remarkable ruins of the valley. **VIJAYAPURI**, the village on the shore of the lake, overlooks the colossal dam itself, which produces electricity for the whole region.

Boats arrive on the northeastern edge of **Nagarjunakonda island** (daily 9am–5pm) at what remains of one of the gates of the fort, built in the fourteenth century and renovated by the Vijayanagar kings in the mid-sixteenth century. Low, damaged, stone walls skirting the island mark the edge of the fort, and you can see ground-level remains of the Hindu temples that served its inhabitants. Well-kept gardens lie between the jetty and the museum, beyond which nine Buddhist monuments from various sites in the valley have been rebuilt. West of the jetty, there's a reconstructed third-century AD bathing *ghat*.

18

The stupas

The **maha-chaitya**, or *stupa*, constructed at the command of King Chamtula's sister in the third century AD, is the area's earliest Buddhist structure. It was raised over relics of the Buddha – said to include a tooth – and has been reassembled in the southwest of the island. Nearby, a towering **Buddha statue** stands beside a ground plan of a monastery that enshrines a smaller *stupa*. Close by are other **stupas**; the brick walls of the *svastika chaitya* have been arranged in the shape of swastikas, common emblems in early Buddhist iconography.

The museum

Daily except Fri 10.30am–5pm • ₹100 (₹5)

The **museum** houses stone friezes decorated with scenes from the Buddha's life, and statues of the Buddha in various postures. Earlier artefacts include metal axe-heads and knives (dating from the first millennium BC). Later exhibits include inscribed pillars from Ikshvaku times. Medieval sculptures include a thirteenth-century *tirthankara* (Jain saint) and a seventeenth-century Ganesh.

ARRIVAL AND INFORMATION NAGARJUNAKONDA

By bus Nagarjunakonda can easily be reached from Hyderabad (4hr; all the regular Macherla services stop at Vijayapuri) or Vijayawada (6hr; a direct service runs daily at 11am and frequent services leave from Guntur).

Getting around Tickets for boats to the island (daily 9am & 1.30pm; 45min; ₹90) go on sale 25min before

departure. Each boat leaves the island 90min after it arrives, so if you want to see the ruins and museum in detail, take the morning boat and return in the afternoon.

Tourist information The AP Tourism office (daily except Sun 10am–5pm; ☎08680 277364) is near the bus stand.

ACCOMMODATION

Accommodation at Vijayapuri is limited and there are two distinct settlements 6km apart on either side of the dam. For easy access to the sites it's better to stay near the jetty on the right bank of the dam; ask the bus driver to leave you at the launch station.

Nagarjuna Motel Complex 500m beyond the boat jetty ☎08642 278188. This functional but drab-looking concrete complex has adequate rooms, some with a/c, and a basic restaurant. **₹500**

Vijay Vihar On the near side of the dam as you approach the lake from Hyderabad ☎08680 277362, ⓦaptdc.in. APTDC runs the comfortable all-a/c *Vijay Vihar*. The better rooms are more expensive at weekends. **₹1300**

Eastern and northern Andhra Pradesh

One of India's least visited areas, **eastern Andhra Pradesh** is sandwiched between the Bay of Bengal in the east and the red soil and high peaks of the Eastern Ghats in the north. Its one architectural attraction is the ancient Buddhist site of **Amaravati**, near the city of **Vijayawada**, whose sprinkling of historic temples is far overshadowed by impersonal, modern buildings. For anyone with a strong desire to explore, however, pockets of natural beauty along the coast and in the hills of eastern Andhra Pradesh can offer rich rewards. At the northern tip of the state, the nondescript city of **Visakhapatnam** is a useful place to break up a journey to northern India.

Vijayawada

Almost 450km north of Chennai, a third of the way to Kolkata, **VIJAYAWADA** is a bustling commercial centre on the banks of the Krishna delta, 90km from the coast. This mundane city, alleviated by a mountain backdrop of bare granite outcrops and some urban greenery, is seldom visited by tourists, but is an obvious stop-off point for visits to nearby **Amaravati**. The **Kanaka Durga** (also known as Vijaya) **temple** on

Indrakila Hill in the east, dedicated to the city's patron goddess of riches, power and benevolence, is the most interesting of Vijayawada's handful of temples. Across the river, roughly 3km out of town, is an ancient, unmodified cave temple at **Undavalli**, a tiny rural village reachable on any Guntur-bound bus, or the local #13 service.

ARRIVAL AND INFORMATION VIJAYWADA

By train Vijayawada's railway station, on the main Chennai–Kolkata line, is in the centre of town: the daily *Janmabhoomi Express* #12805 (11.50am; 6hr 35min) is a convenient service to Hyderabad (Secunderabad).

By bus Regular buses to Amaravati (hourly; 1hr 30min–2hr), Hyderabad (every 15min; 6hr) and Visakhapatnam (hourly; 6–9hr) depart from the Pandit Nehru bus stand.

1.5km west of the station, on the other side of the Ryes Canal.

Tourist information There's a tourist office (Mon–Sat 10am–5pm; 0866 252 3966) at the railway station, and APTDC has an office in the town centre at the *Hotel Ilapuram* complex, Gandhi Nagar (same times; 0866 257 0255).

ACCOMMODATION AND EATING

Monika Lodge Just off Elluru Rd about 300m northeast of the bus stand 0866 257 1334. One of the cheapest lodges in town but a bit dingy, with cramped and very basic attached rooms. ₹350

Narayana Swamy Achutaramaiah St 0866 257 1221. Good-value lodge, with spotless rooms, some with a/c and TV. If full, try the *Sri Ram* opposite; it's very similar. ₹500

Raj Towers Elluru Rd 0866 257 1311. At the top end of the budget range, this tall modern block offers pleasantly

furnished a/c rooms with cable TV and has a decent restaurant. ₹1000

Swarna Palace Corner of Atchutaramaiah St and Elluru Rd 0866 257 7222, swarnapalace @rediffmail.com. Reliable upper-mid-range place, with spacious and comfortable, though rather overpriced, a/c rooms. Its fourth-floor *Palace Heights* restaurant serves hearty portions of Indian, Chinese and Continental food, and there's a bar. ₹3000

Amaravati

Site Daily except Fri 10am–5pm • ₹100 (₹5) Museum Same hours • ₹2

Little more than a village on the banks of the Krishna, 33km from Vijayawada, **AMARAVATI** is the site of a Buddhist settlement formerly known as Chintapalli, where a *stupa* larger than those at Sanchi (see p.345) was erected over relics of the Buddha in the third century BC, during the reign of Ashoka. The *stupa* no longer stands, but its size is evident from the mound that formed its base. There was a gateway at each of the cardinal points, one of which has been reconstructed, and the meticulously carved details show themes from the Buddha's life. A Kalachakra initiation programme was conducted by the Dalai Lama here in January 2006 to commemorate 2550 years since the Buddha's birth.

Exhibits at the small but fascinating **museum** date from the third century BC to the twelfth century AD and include Buddha statues with lotus symbols on the feet, tightly curled hair and long ear lobes – all traditional indications of an enlightened teacher.

ARRIVAL AND DEPARTURE AMARAVATI

By bus Buses run hourly from Vijayawada to Amaravati (1hr 30min–2hr) and more frequently from Guntur (every 15min;

45min–1hr), a dull market town in between. The excavated site and museum are less than 1km from the bus stand.

ACCOMMODATION AND EATING

RKS Rest House Temple St 08645 255516. Typical of the basic lodges dotted around the temple, this place offers

no creature comforts but is OK for a night. ₹350

Visakhapatnam

Andhra Pradesh's second largest city, 650km east of Hyderabad and 350km north of Vijayawada, **VISAKHAPATNAM** (commonly known as Vizag) is a busy port and home to major shipbuilding, oil refining and steel industries. Apart from a few decent beaches

18

and some interesting temples, the main point of interest is the **Submarine Museum** (Tues–Sun 2–8.30pm, Sun also 10am–12.30pm; ₹25) on Beach Road, which is the decommissioned Russian-built *INS Kurusara*. Most of all, the city is a useful place to break up a long journey along the east coast.

ARRIVAL AND DEPARTURE
VISAKHAPATNAM

By train Visakhapatnam's railway station, on the main Chennai–Kolkata line, is close to the port. The best service in both directions is the superfast *Coromandel Express* #12842 (10.10pm) to Bhubaneshwar (6hr 25min) and Kolkata (13hr 40min); #12841 to Chennai (4.45am; 12hr 50min).

By bus Regular buses for Vijayawada (every 30min; 6–8hr) and Hyderabad (hourly; 11–13hr) leave from the bus stand, south of the city centre.

ACCOMMODATION AND EATING

Gateway Beach Rd ☎ 0891 662 3670, ⓦ thegateway hotels.com. The top-end *Taj Hotels*-run *Gateway* has recently renovated sea-facing attached rooms and an excellent Chinese restaurant. ₹5800

Haritha Hotel Beach Rd ☎ 0891 256 2333, ⓦ aptdc .in. This mid-range APTDC hotel offers comfortable, if slightly institutional, standard and a/c rooms. Breakfast included. ₹1100

Karanths Hotel 33-1-55 Patel Marg ☎ 0891 256 0347. By far the best place if you're just overnighting between trains

and want to stay by the station. Very clean attached rooms with cable TV and polite service. ₹500

Sandy Lane Beach Rd ☎ 0891 273 6997. Housed in an attractive Raj-era mansion and with seating at the back of the beach, this bar-restaurant offers chilled beer and fresh seafood for ₹100–200. Daily 11am–11pm.

YMCA Beach Rd ☎ 0891 275 5826. The reliable and predictably popular *YMCA*, which boasts a splendid seaside location, has a few economical attached rooms and a dorm. Dorm ₹150, double ₹600

Southern Andhra Pradesh

The further south you travel from the fertile lands watered by the great Krishna and Godavari rivers, the less hospitable the terrain becomes, especially in the rocky southwest of the state. For Hindus, the main attraction in southern Andhra Pradesh is the **Venkateshvara temple**, outside **Tirupati**, India's most popular Vishnu shrine, where several thousand pilgrims come each day to receive *darshan*. **Puttaparthy**, the community founded by the deceased spiritual leader Sai Baba, and the **Oneness University** (see box opposite) are the only other places in the region to attract significant numbers of visitors. All three places are closer to Chennai in Tamil Nadu and Bengaluru in Karnataka than to other points in Andhra Pradesh.

Tirumala Hill and Tirupati

Set in a stunning position, surrounded by wooded hills capped by a ring of vertical red rocks, the **Sri Venkateshvara temple** at Tirumala, 170km northwest of Chennai, is said to be one of the richest places of pilgrimage in the world, and is certainly the most popular, drawing more devotees than Rome or Mecca. With its many shrines and *dharamshalas*, the whole area around Tirumala Hill, an enervating drive 700m up in the Venkata hills, provides a fascinating insight into contemporary Hinduism practised on a large scale.

The road trip up Tirumala Hill is a lot less terrifying now that there's a separate route down; the most devout, of course, climb the hill by foot. The steep **trail** starts at Alipuri, 4km from the centre of Tirupati; all the pilgrim buses pass through – look out for a large Garuda statue and the soaring *gopura* of the first temple. There are drinks stalls all along the route, which is covered for most of the way. The walk takes at least four hours, and an early start is recommended. When you get to the top, you will see barbers giving pilgrims tonsures as part of their devotions.

At the bottom of the hill, the **Sri Kapileswaraswami** temple at Kapilateertham is the only Tirumala temple devoted to Shiva.

The Venkateshvara temple

General entry free; sudarshan ₹50; special entry and e-darshan ₹300 • ⓦ ttdsevaonline.com

The **Venkateshvara temple** (aka Sri Vari) dedicated to **Vishnu** and started in the tenth century, has been renovated to provide facilities for the thousands of pilgrims who visit daily; weekends, public holidays and festivals are even busier. Unless your visit is intended to be particularly rigorous, you should buy one of the **special darshan** tickets, as this can reduce the time it takes to get inside by quite a few hours, perhaps even more than a day. All types of tickets can be purchased from booths near the temple entrance and even in advance online. Before entering the temple non-Hindus have to sign a declaration of faith in Lord Venkateshvara and provide photocopies of the picture and visa pages from their passports, along with the originals. Note that **no electronic devices** are allowed inside the temple.

At the entrance is a colonnade, lined with life-sized copper or stone statues of royal patrons. The *gopura* gateway leading to the inner courtyard is decorated with sheets of embossed silver; a gold *stambha* (flagstaff) stands outside the inner shrine next to a gold upturned lotus on a plinth. Outside, opposite the temple, is a small museum, the **Hall of Antiquities** (daily 8am–8pm). Your *darshan* tickets entitle you to enter the museum via shorter queues opposite the exit.

Tirupati

The hill is 11km as the crow flies from its service town of **TIRUPATI**, but double that by road. The town is almost entirely modern and pretty unappealing, as well as being predictably crowded with the constant flow of pilgrims. A five-minute walk from the railway station, the one temple in Tirupati itself that's definitely worth a look is **Govindarajaswamy**, whose modern grey *gopura* is clearly visible from many points in town. The inner sanctum is open to non-Hindus and contains a splendid large black reclining Vishnu. In its own compound by the side entrance stands the fine little Venkateshvara Museum of Temple Arts (daily 8am–8pm; ₹5). The temple's impressive bathing tank lies 200m to the east.

THE ONENESS UNIVERSITY AND TEMPLE

A few kilometres from the small town of Tada, around 70km east of Tirupati, lies the startling complex of the **Golden City**, home to the **Oneness University**. The focal point of this community is the stunning and gigantic three-storey **Oneness Temple**, built in brilliant white marble and visible for miles around. The largest pillarless hall in Asia, it is capable of housing up to five thousand people. The huge edifice has an impressive meditation hall on the upper storey and beneath it areas for communal worship and events, most notably *darshan* with the founders of the Oneness Movement, **Sri Bhagavan** (born March 15, 1949 in Natham, Tamil Nadu) and his partner **Amma** (born August 15, 1954 in Sangam, Andhra Pradesh). Often referred to as Kalki Bhagavan, as many followers have declared him to be the tenth incarnation of Vishnu, the guru has always disavowed this title, concentrating instead on promoting his core message of seeking union with the divine.

After the couple married in 1976, they founded the Jeevashram school in 1984, originally located at Satyaloka, a remote location in the Eastern Ghats near the Andhra and Karnataka borders. Here they developed the philosophy of Oneness, wherein every individual feels connected to all that is and gradually awakens to a state of higher consciousness. This is achieved by the process of **deeksha blessing**, whereby divine energy is transferred directly to the recipient by a gentle touching of the head around the crown chakra. In the early 1990s, the school relocated to **Nemam**, in Tamil Nadu north of Chennai, before finding its new home at the Golden City at the turn of the millennium.

The temple is not open to casual visitors but those genuinely interested can arrange a visit in advance and be given a tour. You can find out more about the movement and get details on the four-week-long **deepening process** at the university by logging onto ⓦ onenessuniversity.org. If you do arrange to go independently, it is better to hire a taxi from Tirupati or Chennai as the complex is very difficult to reach by public transport.

Tiruchanur Padmavati temple

Between Tirupati and Tirumala Hill, the **Tiruchanur Padmavati temple** is another popular pilgrimage halt. A gold *vimana* tower with lions at each corner surmounts the sanctuary, which contains a black stone image of goddess Lakshmi with one silver eye. A ₹50 ticket allows you to jump the queue to enter the sanctuary.

Chandragiri Fort

Daily except Fri 10am–5pm • ₹100 (₹5) • **Sound-and-light-show** English: Nov–Feb 7.30pm; March–Oct 8pm; 45min; ₹30

In the sixteenth century, **Chandragiri**, 11km southwest of Tirupati, became the third capital of the Vijayanagars. It was here that the British negotiated the acquisition of the land to establish Fort St George, the earliest settlement at what is now Chennai. The original fort, thought to date from around 1000 AD, was taken over by Haider Ali in 1782, followed by the British in 1792. A small **museum** is housed in the main building, the Indo-Saracenic Raja Mahal. Another building, the **Rani Mahal**, stands close by, while behind that is a hill with two freestanding boulders that was used as a place of public execution during Vijayanagar times. There's a nightly **sound-and-light** show.

ARRIVAL AND DEPARTURE
TIRUMALA HILL AND TIRUPATI

By plane There are flights to Hyderabad (3 daily; 1hr) and Mumbai (1 daily; 1hr 45min) from the airport, 14km outside Tirupati.

By train The railway station is right in the centre of Tirupati. The best way of getting to Tirupati is by train from Chennai (6–8 daily; 2hr 30min–4hr); the trip can just about be done in a day if you get the *Saptagiri Express* #16057 (6.25am; 3hr 5min). There are several connections to Hyderabad (4–6 daily; 12–15hr).

By bus The bus stand is 500m east of the train station. From Hyderabad it's a long haul (8–10 daily; 13–16hr). Frequent express bus services run to Chennai (every 15–30min; 3hr 30min–4hr). There are hourly buses to both Kanchipuram (5hr), three of which continue to Mahabalipuram (7hr), and Bengaluru (7hr).

GETTING AROUND AND INFORMATION

By bus A special section at the back of Tirupati bus stand has services every few minutes to Tirumala Hill; you can also access the hill via a local bus stop outside the railway station.

Tourist information The AP Tourism office (daily 7am–9pm; ☏ 0877 225 5385) is on the second floor of the Sri Devi Complex, Tilak Rd.

SHRI SATYA SAI BABA

Born on November 23, 1926, in Puttaparthy, **Satyanarayana Raju** allegedly displayed prodigious talents from an early age. His apparently supernatural abilities initially caused some concern to his family, who took him to Vedic doctors and eventually to be exorcised. Having been declared possessed by the divine rather than the diabolical, at the age of 14 he calmly announced he was the new incarnation of **Sai Baba**, a saint from Shirdi in Maharashtra who died eight years before Satya was born.

Gradually his fame spread and a large following developed. In 1950 the **ashram** was inaugurated and a decade later Sai Baba was attracting international attention; he still has millions of devotees worldwide, more than two years after his death on April 27, 2011. Just 5ft tall, with a startling Hendrix-style Afro, his smiling, saffron-clad figure can be seen on posters, photos and murals all over south India. Though his **miraculous powers** reportedly included the ability to materialize *vibhuti*, sacred ash, with curative properties, Sai Baba always claimed this to be unimportant, emphasizing instead his message of **universal love**. During his last years a number of ex-followers made serious accusations about coercion and even sexual abuse on the part of the guru himself, which have been vehemently denied.

Predictably, following the passing of the guru, there have been further rumours of corruption by the trustees of his organization, casting its future into some doubt. Whatever your feelings about the divinity of Sai Baba, the atmosphere around the ashram remains undeniably peaceful. You can find out more about the Sai organization at ⓦ saibaba.ws.

ACCOMMODATION AND EATING

Unless you're a pilgrim seeking accommodation in the *dharmshalas* near the temple, all the decent places to stay are in Tirupati. Eating is almost exclusively vegetarian, and there are many cheap "meals" places in town and on Tirumala Hill.

Annapurna 349 G Car St, opposite the railway station ☏ 0877 225 0666. On a busy corner, this modern hotel has spacious, sparsely furnished attached rooms with tiled floors, TVs and either fans or a/c. The a/c restaurant serves south Indian snacks, thalis, Chinese and north Indian dishes. ₹1100

Bhimas Deluxe 34–38 G Car St, near the railway station ☏ 0877 222 5521, ✉ bhimasdeluxehotels @rediffmail.com. Despite an unappealing grey colour-scheme, the attached a/c rooms with TV here are a decent choice; 12hr "transit rooms" are available for two thirds of the regular rate. ₹1650

Mayura 209 TP Area ☏ 0877 222 5925, ✉ mayurahotels@yahoo.co.in. The best of the mid-range hotels opposite the bus station, offering average rooms with clean bathrooms and TV. ₹1500

★ **The Orchid** Fortune Kences hotel, opposite the bus stand ☏ 0877 225 5855. The excellent ₹799 evening buffet is one of the few places to enjoy non-veg food, with superb chicken and lamb dishes, followed by a great range of desserts. À la carte available too. Daily 7–11pm.

Sindhuri Park Opposite the bathing tank ☏ 0877 225 6430, ⊛ hotelsindhuri.com. One of the smartest places in the town centre, this all-a/c hotel has comfortable – if unremarkable – attached rooms with good views of the tank and temple. The restaurant offers a good range of Indian *paneer* and veg dishes, as well as banana split for dessert. ₹2340

Sri Vignesh Residency 191 Railway Station Rd ☏ 0877 645 2547. The bright yellow exterior rather masks the dingy interior. Still, the cell-like attached rooms are among the best budget deals in town. ₹400

Puttaparthy

Deep in the southwest of the state, amid the arid rocky hills bordering Karnataka, a thriving community has grown up around the once insignificant village of **PUTTAPARTHY**, birthplace of spiritual leader **Sai Baba**. Centring on **Prasanthi Nilayam** (Abode of Peace), the ashram where Sai Baba used to reside most of the year, the town has schools, a university, hospital and sports centre that offer up-to-date and free services to all. The ashram itself is a huge complex, with canteens, shops, a museum and library, and a vast assembly hall. The museum (daily 10am–noon) contains detailed displays on the world's major faiths and presents a positive unitarian message.

ARRIVAL AND DEPARTURE   PUTTAPARTHY

By plane The small airport, 6km from the ashram, is currently closed and its future uncertain.

By train The railway station, named Sri Satya Sai Prasanti Nilayam, is 8km from town on the main north–south route, from which you should be able to get a shared auto-rickshaw to the ashram for around ₹15: the daily *Kacheguda Express* #17604 (7pm; 10hr) travels to

Hyderabad. There are more services to and from Dharmavaram, 42km away, connected to Puttaparthy by regular buses.

By bus Buses from Bengaluru (every 30min–1hr; 4hr), Hyderabad (4–6 daily; 12–13hr), Tirupati (hourly; 6–7hr) and Chennai (8–10 daily; 8–9hr) stop at the stand outside the ashram entrance.

ACCOMMODATION AND EATING

Many visitors stay in the ashram accommodation, which is strictly segregated by sex, except for families. Costs are minimal, and although you can't book in advance, you can enquire about availability at the secretary's office (☏ 08555 287583). Outside the ashram, many of the hotels are overpriced. The ashram also has a canteen open to non-residents.

Bamboo Nest Chitravathi Rd ☏ 99064 34576. Delicious Tibetan *momos* (dumplings) and *thukpas* (thick noodle soups) are available at this popular and sociable haunt. Most items under ₹100. Daily 9.30am–2pm & 4.30–9pm.

Sai Ganesh Guest House Gopuram Rd ☏ 08555 287460. This small and cosy lodge near the police station is one of the best budget options. ₹500

Sai Towers Near the ashram entrance ☏ 0855 287270,

⊛ saitowers.com/hotel. Charges a lot for its smallish fan and a/c rooms, except for some much cheaper singles, but has a good veg restaurant downstairs. ₹1900

Sri Sai Sadan Gopuram Rd ☏ 08555 287507, ✉ srisaisadan@yahoo.com. Decent-value hotel, whose rooms all have a fridge, TV, phone and balcony with views of the countryside or the ashram, plus there's a meditation room and rooftop restaurant. ₹900

18

The Andaman Islands

RAJAN ON THE BEACH, HAVELOCK

19

The Andaman Islands

India's most remote state, the Andaman Islands are situated more than 1000km off the east coast in the middle of the Bay of Bengal, connected to the mainland by flights and ferries from Kolkata, Chennai and Vishakapatnam. Thickly covered by deep green tropical forest, the archipelago supports a profusion of wildlife, including some extremely rare species of bird, but the principal attraction for tourists lies in the beaches and the pristine reefs that ring most of the islands. Filled with colourful fish and kaleidoscopic corals, the crystal-clear waters of the Andaman Sea feature some of the world's richest and least spoilt marine reserves – perfect for snorkelling and scuba diving. Although parts of the archipelago still see few visitors, the Andamans are now firmly on the tourist circuit.

For administrative purposes, the Andamans are grouped with the **Nicobar Islands**, 200km further south, but these remain strictly off-limits to foreigners, as well as Indians with no direct business there. Approximately two hundred islands make up the Andaman group and nineteen the Nicobar. They are of varying size, the summits of a submarine mountain range stretching 755km from the Arakan Yoma chain in Burma to the fringes of Sumatra in the south. All but the most remote are populated in parts by **indigenous tribes** whose numbers have been slashed dramatically as a result of nineteenth-century European settlement and, more recently, rampant **deforestation**, now banned at least in theory.

With the timber-extraction cash cow now largely tethered, the hope is that **tourism** will replace tree-felling as the main source of revenue on the Andamans. However, the extra visitor numbers envisaged are certain to overtax an already inadequate infrastructure, aggravating seasonal water shortages and sewage disposal problems. Given India's track record with tourism development, it's hard to be optimistic about how these issues will be managed. Consequently, it's no small mercy that plans to allow flights from Southeast Asia and even further afield to enter India at Port Blair seem to be on permanent hold, as the impact on this culturally and ecologically fragile region could be catastrophic.

The point of arrival for boats and planes is the small but busy capital, **Port Blair** in **South Andaman**, which holds almost half the total population. The only island to have fully developed a tourist infrastructure is **Havelock**, although its smaller neighbour **Neil** is heading in the same direction. The other places where foreigners can spend the night are on the large islands of **Middle** and **North Andaman**, connected to South Andaman by the Andaman Trunk Road (ATR), diminutive **Long Island** and remote **Little Andaman**, a long voyage to the south.

The outlying islands are richest in natural beauty, with the beaches of **Smith** and the coral around **Cinque** of particular note. Such spots are not always easy to reach, as connections and transport can be erratic, frequently uncomfortable and severely limited.

Native people of the Andaman and Nicobar islands p.930
Andaman Trunk Road closure p.934

Scuba diving in the Andaman Islands p.938

SCUBA DIVING

Highlights

❶ Wandoor The white sandy beach and islets of the Mahatma Gandhi National Marine Park are the most popular day-trip destination from capital Port Blair, and a good appetizer for more remote parts. **See p.937**

❸ Scuba diving The Andamans' beautiful coral reefs teem with vivid underwater life. w**See p.938**

❷ Havelock Island For the best diving and partying, head for Havelock, still laidback and friendly despite being the most developed of the Andamans. **See p.939**

❹ Long Island This is the place to head to get an idea of what Havelock was like two decades ago and a chance to unwind in a friendly, laidback village. **See p.942**

❺ North Andaman The long haul by bus or boat from Port Blair is worthwhile for the backdrop of thick rainforest and the dazzling tropical beaches when you arrive. **See p.944**

❻ Little Andaman As very few travellers make it to the archipelago's southernmost island, you may well have the stunning forest-fringed beaches to yourself. **See p.945**

HIGHLIGHTS ARE MARKED ON THE MAP ON P.928

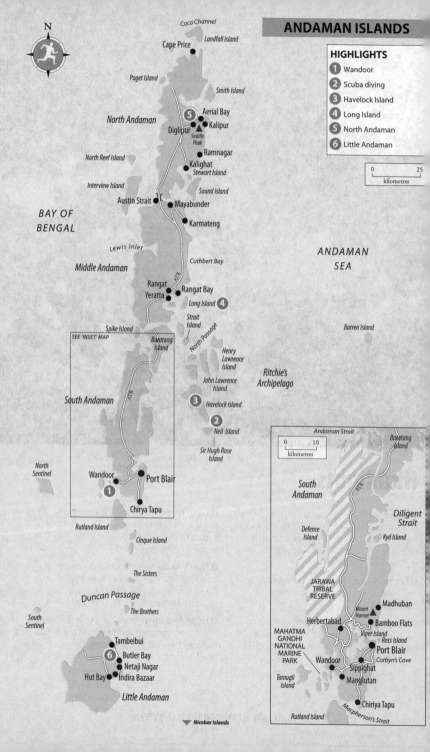

ANDAMAN ISLANDS

HIGHLIGHTS

1. Wandoor
2. Scuba diving
3. Havelock Island
4. Long Island
5. North Andaman
6. Little Andaman

0   25
kilometres

Coco Channel

Landfall Island

Cape Price

Paget Island

Smith Island

North Andaman

⑤ Aerial Bay

Diglipur   ● Kalipur

Saddle Peak

● Ramnagar

North Reef Island

Kalighat

Stewart Island

Interview Island

Sound Island

Austin Strait   ● Mayabunder

BAY OF BENGAL

● Karmateng

Lewis Inlet

ANDAMAN SEA

Middle Andaman

Cuthbert Bay

Rangat   ● Rangat Bay

Yeratta

Long Island ④

Strait Island

Barren Island

North Passage

Spike Island

SEE 'INSET' MAP

Baratang Island

Henry Lawrence Island

Ritchie's Archipelago

John Lawrence Island

South Andaman

③ Havelock Island

②

Neil Island

Sir Hugh Rose Island

North Sentinel

Wandoor   ● Port Blair

①

Chirya Tapu

Rutland Island

Cinque Island

The Sisters

Duncan Passage

The Brothers

South Sentinel

Tambeibui

● Butler Bay

⑥   ● Netaji Nagar

Hut Bay   ● Indira Bazaar

Little Andaman

▽ Nicobar Islands

Inset map

Andaman Strait

0   10
kilometres

Baratang Island

South Andaman

Diligent Strait

Kyd Island

Defence Island

JARAWA TRIBAL RESERVE

Mount Harriet   ● Madhuban

Herbertabad   ● Bamboo Flats

MAHATMA GANDHI NATIONAL MARINE PARK

Viper Island   Ross Island

Wandoor   **Port Blair**

Sippighat   Corbyn's Cove

Tamugli Island

Manglutan

Chiriya Tapu

Rutland Island

Macpherson's Strait

Brief history

The earliest mention of the Andaman and Nicobar islands is found in **Ptolemy**'s geographical treatises of the second century AD. Other records from the Chinese Buddhist monk I'Tsing some five hundred years later and Arabian travellers who passed by in the ninth century depict the inhabitants as fierce and cannibalistic. It is unlikely, however, that the Andamanese were cannibals, as the most vivid reports of their ferocity were propagated by Malay pirates who held sway over the surrounding seas, and needed to keep looters well away from trade ships that passed between India, China and the Far East.

During the eighteenth and nineteenth centuries, **European missionaries** and trading companies turned their attention to the islands with a view to colonization. A string of unsuccessful attempts to convert the Nicobaris to Christianity was made by the French, Dutch and Danish, all of whom were forced to abandon their plans in the face of hideous diseases and a severe lack of food and water. Though the missionaries themselves seldom met with any hostility, several fleets of trading ships that tried to dock on the islands were captured, and their crews murdered, by Nicobari people.

In 1777, the British Lieutenant Archibald Blair chose the South Andaman harbour now known as **Port Blair** as the site for a **penal colony**, although it was not successfully established until 1858, when political activists who had fuelled the Mutiny in 1857 were made to clear land and build their own prison. Out of 773 prisoners, 292 died, escaped or were hanged in the first two months. Many also lost their lives in attacks by Andamanese tribes who objected to forest clearance, but by 1864 the number of convicts had grown to three thousand. The prison continued to confine political prisoners until 1945 and still stands as Port Blair's prime "tourist attraction" (see p.931).

During World War II the islands were occupied by the **Japanese**, who tortured and murdered hundreds of indigenous islanders suspected of collaborating with the British, and bombed the homes of the Jarawa tribe. British forces moved back in 1945, and at last abolished the penal settlement. After **Partition**, refugees – mostly low-caste Hindus from Bengal – were given land in Port Blair and North Andaman, where the forest was clear-felled to make room for rice paddy, cocoa plantations and new industries. Since 1951, the population has increased more than tenfold, further swollen by repatriated Tamils from Sri Lanka, ex-servicemen given land grants, economic migrants from poorer Indian states including thousands of Bihari labourers, and the legions of government employees packed off here on two-year "punishment postings". This replanted population greatly outnumbers the Andamans' indigenous people (see box, p.930), who currently comprise around 0.5 percent of the total.

INFORMATION   **THE ANDAMAN ISLANDS**

Climate The climate remains tropical throughout the year, with temperatures ranging from 24°C to 35°C and humidity levels never below seventy percent. By far the best time to visit is between January and April. From mid-May to October, heavy rains flush the islands, often bringing violent cyclones that leave west-coast beaches strewn with fallen trees, while in November and December less severe rains arrive with the northeast monsoon.

Health It's worth pointing out that a minority of travellers fall sick in the Andamans. The dense tree cover, marshy swamps and high rainfall combine to provide the perfect breeding ground for mosquitoes, and malaria is endemic in even the most remote settlements. Sandflies are also ferocious in certain places and tropical ulcer infections from scratching the bites is a frequent hazard.

Permits Foreign tourists are only permitted to visit certain parts of the Andaman group and some of those only as day-trips. Free thirty-day permits are granted on arrival by both sea and air and can be extended at Port Blair, Havelock and Neil for fifteen days on production of an outbound ticket.

Time Despite being so far east, the islands run on Indian time, so the sun rises as early as 4.30am in summer and darkness falls soon after 5pm.

South Andaman

South Andaman is the most heavily populated of the Andaman Islands – particularly around the capital, **Port Blair** – thanks in part to the drastic thinning of tree cover to make way for settlement. Foreign tourists can only visit its southern and east-central reaches – including the beaches at **Corbyn's Cove** and **Chiriya Tapu**, the fine reefs on the western shores at **Wandoor**, 35km southwest of Port Blair, and the environs of **Madhuban** and **Mount Harriet**, on the east coast across the bay from the capital. With your own transport it's easy to find your way along the narrow bumpy roads that connect small villages, weaving through forests and coconut fields, and skirting the swamps and rocky outcrops that form the coastline.

19

Port Blair

An odd combination of refreshingly scenic hills and characterless tin-roofed buildings tumbling towards the sea in the north, east and west, and petering out into fields and forests in the south, **PORT BLAIR** merits only a short stay. There's little to see here – just

---

NATIVE PEOPLE OF THE ANDAMAN AND NICOBAR ISLANDS

Quite where the **indigenous population** of the Andaman and Nicobar islands originally came from is a puzzle that has preoccupied anthropologists since Alfred Radcliffe-Brown conducted his famous field work among the Andamanese at the beginning of the twentieth century. Asian-looking groups such as the Shompen may have migrated here from the east and north when the islands were connected to Burma, or the sea was sufficiently shallow to allow transport by canoe, but this doesn't explain the origins of the black populations, whose appearance suggests African roots.

The survival of the islands' first inhabitants has long been threatened by traders and colonizers, who introduced disease and destroyed their territories through widespread tree-felling. Thousands also died from addiction to the alcohol and opium that the Chinese, Japanese and British exchanged for valuable shells. Many have had their populations decimated, while others like the Nicobarese have assimilated to modern culture, often adopting Christianity. The indigenous inhabitants of the Andamans, divided into *eramtaga* (those living in the jungle) and *ar-yuato* (those living on the coast), traditionally subsisted as hunter-gatherers, living on fish, turtles, turtle eggs, pigs, fruit, honey and roots. For more information on the islands' original inhabitants, visit Survival International's website, Ⓦ survival-international.org.

THE GREAT ANDAMANESE

Although they comprised the largest group when the islands were first colonized, only around fifty **Great Andamanese** now survive. In the 1860s, the Rev Henry Corbyn set up a "home" for the tribe to learn English on Ross Island, insisting that they wear clothes and attend reading and writing classes. Five children and three adults from Corbyn's school were taken to Calcutta in 1864, where they were shown around the sights but treated more as curiosities themselves. Within three years, almost the entire population had died, victims of either introduced diseases or addiction. In recent years the surviving Great Andamanese were forcibly settled on Strait Island, north of South Andaman, as a "breeding centre", where they were forced to rely on the Indian authorities for food and shelter. Sadly, the last speaker of Bo, one of the oldest Andamanese languages, died in January 2010.

THE JARAWAS

The **Jarawas**, who were shifted from their original homes when land was cleared to build Port Blair, currently number between 250 and 400 and live on the remote western coasts of Middle and South Andaman. They are hemmed in by the Andaman Trunk Road (ATR), which since the 1970s has cut them off from hunting grounds and freshwater supplies. During the 1980s and 1990s, encroachments on their land by loggers, road builders and settlers met with fierce resistance, and dozens, possibly hundreds, of people died in **skirmishes**, mostly on or near the

the **Cellular Jail** and a few small **museums** – but as it's the point of arrival for the islands and the place with the most facilities, you may well find yourself staying longer than you'd ideally want to. The hub of the town's activities and facilities is the cluster of streets known as Aberdeen Bazaar. Generally, street names are in short supply all over town, and are rarely used.

Cellular Jail

GB Pant Rd · **Jail and museum** Tues–Sun 9am–noon & 2–5pm · ₹10, camera ₹20 **Sound-and-light show** Mon, Wed & Fri 6.45pm · ₹20

Port Blair's only firm reminder of its gloomy past, the sturdy brick **Cellular Jail**, overlooks the sea from a small rise in the northeast of town. Built between 1896 and 1905, its tiny solitary cells were quite different and far worse than the dormitories in other prison blocks erected earlier. Only three of the seven wings that originally radiated from the central tower now remain. Visitors can peer into the 3m by 3.5m cells and imagine the grim conditions in which the prisoners lived. Cells were dirty and poorly ventilated, drinking water was limited to two glasses per day, and the convicts were expected to wash in the rain as they worked clearing forests and building prison quarters. Food, brought

ATR. Some more amicable **contact** between settlers and tribals was subsequently made through gift exchanges at each full moon, although the initiative was later cancelled. These meetings nevertheless led to some Jarawas becoming curious about what "civilization" had to offer, and they started to hold their hands out to passing vehicles and even visiting Indian settlements near their territory. Despite the authorities trying to minimize contact, it is still common for Jarawas to approach buses, and some private vehicles ignore the rules and stop for photo shoots. The government has increased Jarawa land by 180 square kilometres, but lodged an ongoing appeal over a 2002 Indian Supreme Court order to close the ATR – a ruling made following protests by international pressure groups such as Survival International. A disturbing legal reversal made early in 2013 has also once again allowed "human safaris" to take place.

THE ONGE

Relations with the **Onge**, who call themselves the **Gaubolambe**, have been relatively peaceful. Distinguished by their white-clay and ochre body paint, they continue to live in communal shelters and construct temporary thatched huts on Little Andaman. The remaining population of around one hundred retain their traditional way of life on two small reserves. Contact with outsiders is limited to an occasional trip into town to purchase liquor, and visits from rare parties of anthropologists. The reserves are strictly off-limits to foreigners, but you can learn about the Onge's traditional hunting practices, beliefs and rituals in Vishvajit Pandya's wonderful ethnographic study, *Above the Forest*.

THE NICOBAR PEOPLE

On the Nicobars, the most assimilated and numerous tribe, the **Nicobarese**, are of Mongoloid descent and number over twenty thousand. They live in villages, ruled by a headman, and have largely cordial relations with the Indian settlers. By contrast, only very limited contact is ever had with the isolated **Shompen** tribe of Great Nicobar, whose population of around three thousand manage to lead a traditional hunting-and-gathering existence. The most elusive tribe of all, the **Sentinelese**, live on North Sentinel Island west of South Andaman. Following the first encounter with Indian settlers in 1967, some contact was made with them in 1990, after a team put together by the local administration left gifts on the beaches every month for two years, but subsequent visits have invariably ended in a hail of arrows and two Indian fishermen who ventured too close to the island were killed in 2006. Since the early 1990s, the authorities have effectively given up trying to contact the Sentinelese, who are estimated to number anywhere between fifty and two hundred. Flying in or out of Port Blair, you pass above their island, ringed by a spectacular coral reef. It's reassuring to think that the people sitting at the bottom of the plumes of smoke drifting up from the forest canopy still manage to resist contact with the outside world.

19

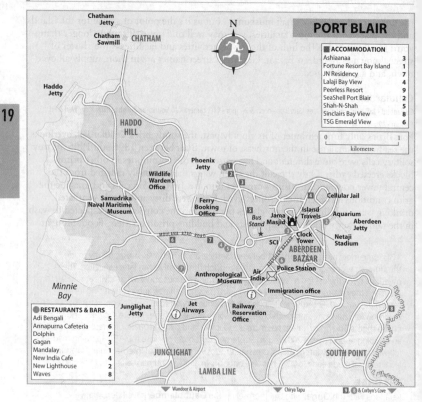

from the mainland, was stored in vats where the rice and pulses became infested with worms; more than half the prison population died long before their twenty years' detention was up. Protests against conditions led to several hunger strikes, and frequent executions took place at the gallows that still stand in squat wooden shelters in the courtyards, in full view of the cells. The **sound-and-light show** outlines the history of the prison, and a small **museum** by the entrance gate exhibits lists of convicts, photographs and grim torture devices.

Anthropological Museum

MG Rd • Daily except Thurs 9am–1pm & 1.30–4.30pm • ₹10, camera ₹20

On the south side of the centre, close to the Directorate of Tourism, the **Anthropological Museum** has exhibits on the Andaman and Nicobar tribes, including weapons, tools and rare photographs of the region's indigenous people taken in the 1960s. Among the most striking of these is a sequence featuring the Sentinelese, taken on April 26, 1967, when a party of Indian officials made the first contact with the tribe. After scaring the aborigines, the visitors marched into one of their hunting camps and made off with the bows, arrows and other artefacts now displayed in the museum.

Samudrika Naval Maritime Museum

Haddo Rd, Delanipur • Tues–Sun 9am–5.30pm • ₹10

To the northwest of town in the area known as Delanipur, the **Samudrika Naval Maritime Museum** is an excellent primer if you're heading off to more remote islands, with a superlative shell collection and informative displays on various aspects of local marine biology. One of the exhibits features a cross-section of the different corals you can expect to see on the Andamans' reefs, followed by a rundown of the various threats these fragile organisms face, from mangrove depletion and parasitic starfish to clumsy snorkellers.

ARRIVAL AND DEPARTURE   PORT BLAIR

Port Blair is the departure point for all flights and ferry crossings to the **Indian mainland**; it is also the hub of the Andamans' inter-island bus and ferry network. **Booking tickets** (especially back to Chennai, Kolkata or Vishakapatnam) can be time-consuming, and many travellers are obliged to come back here well before their permit expires to make reservations before heading off to more pleasant parts of the islands again. Port Blair has an efficient computerized Southern Railways reservation office near the Secretariat (Mon–Sat 8.30am–1pm & 2–4pm) – useful for travellers intending to catch onward **trains** from their port of arrival on the mainland.

19

BY PLANE

Veer Savarkar airport The smart airport terminal is less than 4km south of town at Lamba Line. Taxis and auto-rickshaws are on hand for short trips into town (₹50), while mid- or upper-range hotels usually have shuttle buses to collect guests. Local buses also frequently ply the route to town from outside the shop on the far side of the main road, barely 100m from the terminal building.

To and from the mainland Port Blair is currently served by four flights daily from Chennai and Kolkata (both 2hr), operated by Air India, Jet Airways, Spicejet and Go Air; Air India also have a daily flight from Bhubaneshwar (2hr). Flights at peak times like Diwali, Christmas and New Year through to February can be heavily subscribed, so book early. These periods also see prices soar as high as ₹20,000 one way; at other times they can be as low as ₹5000. The Air India office (☎03192 233108) is diagonally opposite the tourist office, while Jet Airways (☎03192 236922) is on the first floor at 189 Main Rd, Junglighat, next to the Incredible India office. Spicejet and Go Air can only be booked online or through travel agents such as the efficient Island Travels (Mon–Sat 9am–6pm; ☎03192 233034), between the clock tower and marina.

Inter-island services In 2012 a new private seaplane service (☎03192 244312, ✉andamanseaplane@gmail .com) started to Havelock (Mon–Sat 2 daily; 20min) and Diglipur (Mon–Sat 1 daily; 50min); tickets are costly at ₹4100 and ₹10,500 respectively.

BY BOAT

Jetties Port Blair has two main jetties: boats from the mainland moor at Haddo Jetty, nearly 2km northwest of Phoenix Jetty, arrival point for inter-island ferries. The Director of Shipping Services (DSS; ☎03192 245555) at Phoenix Jetty has the latest information on boats and ferries, but you can also check details of forthcoming departures in the shipping news column of the local newspaper, the *Daily Telegrams*. Boats can get cramped and uncomfortable, sometimes lacking shade outside and space inside; take adequate supplies of food and water, as minimal sustenance is sold on board.

To and from the mainland Services to and from Chennai (see p.958) can be relied upon to leave in each direction once every week to ten days, while those to and from Kolkata (see box, p.747) sail roughly every two weeks; boats to and from Vishakapatnam are altogether more erratic, averaging once a month in each direction – call the Shipping Office there on ☎0891 256 5597 for more information. Although much cheaper than flying (from ₹1500), sea crossings are long (3–5 days), uncomfortable and often delayed by bad conditions. Tickets for all three mainland ports (Chennai, Kolkata and Vishakapatnam) are now handled by the DSS and go on sale a week in advance of departure at the allotted booths within the Computerized Reservation Centre (Mon–Fri 9am–1pm & 2–4pm, Sat 9am–noon) at Phoenix Jetty. When they do go on sale, it's wise to be there to join the fray ahead of time. Make sure you get a ticket before your permit expires, as you will need to show it to get the fifteen-day extension (see p.929).

Inter-island services Most of the islands open to foreign tourists are accessible by government-run boats from Phoenix Jetty. Details of sailings to and from Port Blair for the following two to three days are posted in the *Daily Telegrams* newspaper. More details of boat services between destinations outside the capital appear in the relevant accounts of this guide. The only way to guarantee a passage is to book tickets in advance at the Inter-Island booths in the Computerized Reservation Centre at Phoenix Jetty, though any unsold tickets are issued prior to departure on the quay. You can avoid these scrums by paying an agent such as Island Travels to get a ticket for you. Fares are very reasonable, even allowing for the two-tier pricing system for islanders and non-islanders: Havelock, for example, costs ₹200–350, Little Andaman a mere ₹60. Havelock also has a smart private catamaran service, the *Makruzz* (1–2 daily; 2hr; from ₹775; ☎makruzz.com).

Destinations Aerial Bay on North Andaman (3 weekly; 7–9hr); Havelock (2–4 daily; 2hr–3hr 30min); Hut Bay on Little Andaman (4–6 weekly; 6–9hr); Long Island (4 weekly; 5–6hr); Neil (1–3 daily; 2hr); Rangat on Middle Andaman (4 weekly; 6–7hr).

ANDAMAN TRUNK ROAD CLOSURE

Because of the sensitivities surrounding the Jarawa tribal reserve and concerns over undesirable contact with tourists, the Andaman Trunk Road (**ATR**) was closed to foreigners between Port Blair and Rangat at the time of writing. The situation is constantly under review, so check with a local travel agent or the tourist office in advance of your visit.

19

BY BUS

Buses connect Port Blair with most of the major settlements on Middle and North Andaman via the Andaman Trunk Road (see box above). From the mildly chaotic bus stand in the centre of town, there are government services to Rangat (5.45am & 11.45am; 6hr), Mayabunder (5am & 9.45am; 9hr) and Diglipur (4am & 4.30am; 11hr). Several private companies, including Ananda (☎03192 233252), who have an office near the bus stand, run deluxe or video coach services to the same destinations; these leave from outside the bus stand between 5am and 10am. Tickets for both categories of service are cheap at ₹120–300.

GETTING AROUND

By taxi and auto-rickshaw Taxis gather opposite the bus stand in central Port Blair. They all have meters and there's a pre-paid booth, but negotiating the price before leaving is the usual practice. Expect to pay at least ₹100 for a trip from the centre of town to Corbyn's Cove; auto-rickshaws try to charge just as much as taxis but a ride within town shouldn't cost more than ₹30–40.

By bus Local buses run from the bus stand frequently to Wandoor (hourly) and less so to Chiriya Tapu (every 2hr), so they can be used for day-trips Note that the Andaman Trunk Road (ATR) was closed to foreigners at the time of writing; check with the tourist office for updates.

By motorbike It's pleasant to rent a motorbike or scooter but there are few outlets – try Green Island Tours & Travels (☎03192 230226), near the clock tower in Aberdeen Bazaar. The only petrol pumps are on the crossroads west of the bus stand and on the airport road.

INFORMATION AND TOURS

Tourist information The counter at the airport (☎03192 232414) hands out a useful general brochure, but trying to get more than basic tour and hotel information from the main A&N Directorate of Tourism office (Mon–Fri 9am–5pm, Sat 9am–1pm; ☎03192 232747, ⓦand.nic.in), situated in a modern building diagonally opposite Air India, can be frustrating. Further southwest on Junglighat Main Rd, the Incredible India office (Mon–Fri 8.30am–5pm; ☎03192 233006, ⓦincredibleindia.org) is not much better.

Permits The Immigration Office (Mon–Fri 8.30am–1pm & 2–5.30pm, Sat 8.30am–1pm; ☎03192 239247) in Aberdeen Bazaar, is the place to go for the free fifteen-day permit extension (see p.929). If you intend to visit Interview Island (see p.943), you must first obtain a free permit from the Chief Wildlife Warden, whose office (☎03192 233270) is next to the zoo in Haddo.

Services It's wise to stock up on rupees in Port Blair as the banks and agencies here are the only places on the islands officially allowed to exchange cash and travellers' cheques. There are several ATMs dotted around town (and now a couple on Havelock too).

Tours The A&N Directorate of Tourism town tours are a waste of time, but their harbour cruises (daily 3–5pm; ₹100) are more worthwhile, departing from Phoenix Jetty for fleeting visits to the floating docks and Viper Island (see p.936); there are also excursions to Ross Island (see p.936), as well as day-trips to Mount Harriet (8am; from ₹275; see p.937) and Wandoor/Mahatma Gandhi National Marine Park (see p.937); the bus tour to Wandoor (Tues–Sun 8am; ₹150) connects with the 9.30am boat to the marine park.

ACCOMMODATION

Port Blair boasts numerous places to stay, though not much in the mid-range. The abundance of options means availability is only an issue around Christmas and New Year, when prices are also hiked; they drop during the monsoon season.

Ashiaanaa Marine Hill ☎94742 17008, ⓔshads _maria@hotmail.com. An attractive ochre-coloured building, very conveniently located for Phoenix Jetty. This friendly place offers a selection of decent-sized, mostly attached rooms, some with balconies. ₹300/₹550
Fortune Resort Bay Island Marine Hill ☎03192 234101, ⓦfortunehotels.in. Port Blair's swishest hotel is elegant and airy with polished dark wood. All rooms have carpets and balconies overlooking Phoenix Jetty. There's a good restaurant, gardens and an open-air seawater swimming pool. Check for online deals. ₹7000
JN Residency Moulana Azad Rd ☎03192 232148, ⓔjnresidency@gmail.com. Completely transformed from the old Jaganath, this comfortable lodge now has TV and optional a/c in all the rooms, which have shared balconies. ₹900

Lalaji Bay View RP Rd. ☎03192 230551, ✉lalajibayviewbookings@gmail.com. Popular budget guesthouse in an elevated position up above Aberdeen Bazaar, which offers good-value attached rooms. It also has a good sociable rooftop restaurant that serves beer, but service is slow. ₹600

Peerless Resort Corbyn's Cove ☎03192 229263, ⓦpeerlesshotels.com. The setting is lovely, with a white-sand beach opposite, and gardens of palms, jasmine and bougainvillea, but the balconied a/c rooms and cottages are a bit tatty for the prices they charge. There's a bar and mid-priced restaurant with an average evening buffet. ₹6500

★ **SeaShell Port Blair** Marine Hill ☎03192 242773, ⓦseashellportblair.com. Excellent modern hotel suited for business travellers and tourists alike. Spacious, beautifully furnished and decorated rooms with great

showers and flatscreen TVs. The more expensive rooms have balconies overlooking the sea. ₹5000

Shah-N-Shah Mohanpura ☎03192 233696, ✉apsaratours786@yahoo.com. Conveniently located between the bus stand and Phoenix Jetty, this is basic but friendly and comfortable, with mostly attached rooms and a travel agent. Cheap single occupancy. ₹300/₹500

Sinclairs Bay View On the coast road to Corbyn's Cove ☎03192 227824, ⓦsinclairshotels.com. Clifftop hotel offering spotless carpeted rooms with balconies, large bathrooms and dramatic views, as well as a much-improved restaurant. ₹7500

★ **TSG Emerald View** 25 Moulana Azad Rd ☎03192 246488, ⓦandamantsghotels.com. Smart mid-range place with a sparkling new lobby and spacious, colourfully furnished a/c rooms, boasting all mod cons. Also has a decent restaurant. ₹2300

19

EATING AND DRINKING

★ **Adi Bengali** Moulana Azad Rd ☎99332 50583. Simple but sparkling clean place serving tasty Bengali dishes such as *parsha* fish curry, a snip at ₹50. Also offers chicken and a range of veg dishes. Daily 7am–10pm.

Annapurna Cafeteria Aberdeen Bazaar, towards the post office ☎03192 234199. Port Blair's best south Indian joint, serving a range of huge crispy dosas, plus north Indian and Chinese meals, delicious coffee and wonderful *pongal* at breakfast. The lunchtime thalis are also good. Mains ₹60–125. Mon–Sat 6.30–10.30am & 3.30–10.30pm.

Dolphin Marthoma Church Complex, Golgha ☎03192 243933. Pleasantly decorated with cane chairs and blinds, serving carefully prepared Indian and Chinese dishes, as well as some Continental options and a few house specialities involving chicken and seafood (around ₹80–100). Daily noon–10pm.

Gagan Aberdeen Bazaar, opposite the clock tower ☎03192 212140. Simple canteen with a decent range of north and south Indian veg and non-veg dishes for around ₹60–150, including tasty fried fish. Daily 7am–10pm.

Mandalay Fortune Resort, Marine Hill ☎03192 234101. À la carte main courses (₹200–350) or, when demand allows, a reasonable dinner buffet for around ₹500, can be enjoyed in the airy open restaurant with great bay views. Service can be a bit lax for its class. The adjacent *Nico Bar* is a decent bet for a drink. Daily noon–10.30pm.

New India Café Moulana Azad Rd ☎96795 09398. Below the *Jaimathi* lodge this cheap restaurant wins no prizes for decor but bashes out a log menu of veg and meat dishes (₹50–100). Expect to wait if you order anything that's not already prepared. Daily 7am–3pm & 6–10pm.

New Lighthouse Near Aberdeen Jetty ☎03192 237356. Popular place with outdoor seating, where you can catch the sea breeze while feasting on some of the cheapest lobster and other seafood (₹150–250) in India. Daily 11am–10.30pm.

Waves Peerless Resort, Corbyn's Cove ☎03192 229263. Slightly pricey but very congenial alfresco hotel restaurant under a shady palm grove, and one of the few places in town you can order a beer with your meal. Most dishes ₹200–300. Daily 11am–11pm.

Around Port Blair

At some point, you're almost certain to find yourself killing time in Port Blair, waiting for boats to show up or tickets to go on sale. Rather than wasting days in town, it's worth exploring the **coast** of South Andaman which, although far more densely populated than other islands in the archipelago, holds a handful of easily accessible beauty spots and historic sites. Among the latter, the ruined colonial monuments on **Viper** and **Ross islands** can be reached on daily harbour cruises or regular ferries from the capital (see opposite). For **beaches**, head to nearby **Corbyn's Cove**, or cross South Andaman to reach the more pleasingly secluded **Chiriya Tapu**, which is easily accessible on a day-trip if you rent a motorbike or scooter, and is the jumping-off point for *Cinque*. By far the most rewarding way to spend a day out of town, however, is to catch the tourist boat from **Wandoor** to **Jolly Buoy** or **Red Skin islands** in the **Mahatma Gandhi**

National Marine Park opposite, which boasts some of the Andamans' best snorkelling. The other area worth visiting is **Mount Harriet** and **Madhuban** on the central part of South Andaman, north across the bay from Port Blair.

Viper Island

First stop on the A&N Tourism harbour cruise from Port Blair is generally **Viper Island**, named not after the many snakes that doubtless inhabit its tangled tropical undergrowth, but a nineteenth-century merchant vessel that ran aground on it during the early years of the colony. Lying a short way off Haddo Jetty, it served as an isolation zone for the main prison, where escapees and other convicts were sent to be punished. Whipping posts and crumbling walls, reached from the jetty via a winding brick path, remain as relics of a torture area, while occupying the site's most prominent position are the original gallows.

Ross Island

₹20 • Several daily boats from Phoenix Jetty

Eerie decaying colonial remains are to be found on **Ross Island**, at the entrance to Port Blair harbour, where the British sited their first penal settlement in the Andamans. Originally cleared by convicts wearing iron fetters, Ross witnessed some of the most brutal excesses of British colonial history, and was the source of the prison's infamy as **Kalapani**, or Black Water. Of the many convicts transported here, distinguished by their branded foreheads, the majority perished from disease or torture before the clearance of the island was completed in 1860. Thereafter, it served briefly as the site of Rev Henry Corbyn's **Andaman Home** – a prison camp created with the intention of "civilizing" the local tribespeople – and then the headquarters of the revamped penal colony before the British were forced to evacuate by the Japanese entry into World War II. Little more than the hilltop **Anglican church**, with its weed-infested graveyard, has survived the onslaught of tropical creepers and vines.

Corbyn's Cove

The best beach within easy reach of the capital lies 6km southeast, at **Corbyn's Cove**, a small arc of smooth white sand backed by a swaying curtain of palms. There's a large hotel here, *Peerless Resort* (see 935), but the water isn't particularly clear, and bear in mind that lying around scantily clothed may bring you considerable attention from crowds of local workers.

Chiriya Tapu

For a little isolation, take a bus 30km south of Port Blair to **Chiriya Tapu** ("Bird Island"), at the tip of South Andaman. The walkable track running beyond this small fishing village leads through thick jungle overhung with twisting creepers to a large bay, where swamps give way to shell-strewn beaches. Other than at lunchtime, when it often receives a deluge of bus parties, the beach offers plenty of peace and quiet, forest walks on the woodcutters' trails winding inland and easy access to an inshore reef. However, the water here is nowhere near as clear as at outlying spots in the archipelago.

Cinque Island

Cinque, two hours south of Chiriya Tapu, actually comprises two islets, joined by a spectacular sand isthmus with shallow water either side that covers it completely at high tide. The main incentive to come here is the superb diving and snorkelling around the reefs. However, heaps of dead coral on the beach attest to damage wreaked by the Indian navy during the construction of the swish "cottages" overlooking the beach. Rumour has it that these were built for the visit of a Thai VIP in 1996, but local government officials now use them as bolt holes from Port Blair.

Although there are no **ferries** to Cinque, it is possible to charter a dinghy and boatman for around ₹2000/day from Chiriya Tapu. Foreigners are not allowed to stay the night.

Wandoor

Much the most popular excursion from Port Blair is to **WANDOOR**, 30km southwest. The long white **beach** here is littered with the dry, twisted trunks of trees torn up and flung down by annual cyclones. It's fringed not with palms but with dense forest teeming with birdlife. You should only snorkel here at high tide, as the coral is easily damaged when the waters are shallow.

ACCOMMODATION   **WANDOOR**

Sea Princess Beach Resort 500m back from the car park ☎03192 280002, ⓦseaprincessandaman.com. This smart resort, set in nicely landscaped grounds, offers luxury cottages, rooms and suites. The restaurant is also very pleasant. ₹**5400**

Wandoor Paradise Resort On the beach ☎94342 72135. The only budget option in Wandoor are the two ramshackle huts here, though the seaside location is made less idyllic because the restaurant is mainly a drinking den. ₹**500**

The Mahatma Gandhi National Marine Park

Park entry ₹500 (₹50) • Boats from Wandoor Tues–Sun 10am; ₹450

Most people take a cruise around the fifteen islets comprising the **Mahatma Gandhi National Marine Park**, which boasts one of the richest coral reefs in the region. From the jetty at Wandoor, the boats chug through broad creeks lined with dense mangrove swamps and pristine forest to either **Red Skin Island** or, more commonly, **Jolly Buoy**. The latter, an idyllic deserted island, boasts an immaculate shell-sand beach ringed by a bank of superb coral. The catch is that the boat only stops for around an hour, which isn't nearly enough time to explore the shore and reef. While snorkelling off the edges of the reef, beware of **strong currents**.

Mount Harriet and Madhuban

Park entry ₹250 (₹25) • Passenger ferries from Chatham Jetty every 30min, vehicle ferries from Phoenix Jetty 8 daily

The richly forested slopes of **Mount Harriet** make for some decent exercise and can easily be visited on a day-trip from Port Blair. From the ferry landing at **Bamboo Flats**, it's a pleasant 7km stroll east along the coast and north up a path through trees hung with thick vines and creepers to the 365m summit, which affords fine views back across the bay. An intermittent bus service runs between Bamboo Flats and Hope Town, where the uphill path starts, and saves you the 3km coastal stretch. Alternatively, jeeps and taxis are available to take you all the way to the top, but they charge at least ₹500. The Mount Harriet National Park checkpost is on the road so you probably won't be asked if you take the path. It's 2.5km from the checkpost up to the resthouse and viewing tower at the summit. If you have strong legs, you can reach the small settlement of **Madhuban** on the coast northeast of the mountain by the 16km round route via Kala Patthar (Black Rock) and back via the coast. There is a decent beach at Madhuban but not much else.

Neil

Tiny, triangular-shaped **Neil** is the most southerly inhabited island of **Ritchie's Archipelago**, barely two hours northeast of Port Blair on a fast ferry. The source of much of the capital's fresh fruit and vegetables, its fertile centre, ringed by a curtain of stately tropical trees, comprises vivid patches of green paddy dotted with small farmsteads and banana plantations. The beaches are mediocre by the Andamans' standards but worth a day or two en route to or from Havelock and, as it is far less developed with less than ten accommodation options, some visitors prefer it to its busier neighbour for more extended stays.

Neil boasts five **beaches**, all of them within easy cycling distance of the small bazaar just up the lane from the jetty. The best place to swim is **Neil Kendra**, a gently curving bay of white sand on the north coast which straddles the jetty and is scattered with picturesque

19

wooden fishing boats. This blends into **Bharatpur** to the east and **Lakshmangar**, which continues for nearly 3km west: to get to Lakshmangar by road, head right when the road from the jetty meets the bazaar and follow the road for around twenty minutes until it dwindles into a surfaced track, then take a right. Wrapped around the headland, the beach is a broad spur of white-shell sand, with shallow water offering good snorkelling, although footing is difficult when entering the water at any time other than high tide.

Exposed to the open sea and thus prone to higher tides, **Sitapur** beach, 6km southeast of Neil Kendra, is also appealing and has the advantage of a sandy bottom extending

SCUBA DIVING IN THE ANDAMAN ISLANDS

The seas around the Andaman Islands are some of the world's most unspoiled. Marine life is abundant, with an estimated 750 species of fish existing on one reef alone, and parrot, trigger and angel fish living alongside manta rays, reef sharks and loggerhead turtles. Many species of fish and coral are unique to the area, and fascinating ecosystems exist in ash beds and cooled lava based around the volcanic Barren Island. For a quick taste of marine life, you could start by **snorkelling**; most hotels can supply masks and snorkels, though some equipment is in dire need of replacement. The only way to get really close, and venture out into deeper waters, is to **scuba dive**. The undisputed home of **diving** is Havelock, with eight centres up and running at the last count, and there are also operators on Neil, Long and South Andaman.

PRICES AND COURSES

Prices are very similar at all the centres, with certified divers paying around ₹2500 for one tank, ₹4000 for two; more economical packages, often including accommodation and food, are available for multiple dives, while Discover Scuba introductory days go for ₹4500–5000. **Courses** cost about ₹14,000 for a basic four-day PADI open-water qualification, ₹15,000 for advanced or ₹50,000 to go all the way up to Divemaster, including all the tanks.

DIVING ADVICE

Underwater, it's not uncommon to come across schools of reef shark, which rarely turn hostile, but one thing to watch out for and avoid is the **black-and-white sea snake**. Though these seldom attack – and, since their fangs are at the back of their mouths, would find it difficult to get a grip on any human – their bite is twenty times deadlier than that of the cobra.

Increased tourism inevitably puts pressure on the delicate marine ecosystem, and poorly funded wildlife organizations can do little to prevent damage from insensitive visitors. Ensure your presence in the sea around the reefs does not harm the coral by observing the following **Green Coral Code** while diving or snorkelling:

• Never touch or walk on living coral, or it will die.
• Try to keep your feet away from reefs while wearing fins; the sudden sweep of water caused by a flipper kick can be enough to destroy coral.
• Always control the speed of your descent while diving; enormous damage can be caused by divers landing hard on a coral bed.
• Never break off pieces of coral from a reef, and remember that it is illegal to export dead coral from the islands, even fragments you may have found on a beach.

DIVE CENTRES

Andaman Bubbles Beach #5, Havelock ☎ 03192 282140, ⓦ andamanbubbles.com. Top-quality centre with excellent equipment and nitrox diving.

Barefoot Scuba Beach #3, Havelock ☎ 03192 282181, ⓦ diveandamans.com. A PADI 5-star rated operator with expert divemasters. Offers occasional dives with Rajan the elephant.

Dive India Beach #5, Havelock ☎ 03192 214247, ⓦ diveindia.com. One of the more established operations on Havelock. It has another branch on Neils, too.

India Scuba Explorers Neil Kendra, Neil ☎ 94742 38646, ⓦ indiascubaexplorers.com. Small but professional German-run dive centre.

Infinity Scuba Andamans Chiriya Tapu, South Andaman ☎ 94760 71098, ⓦ infinityscubandamans .com. An ex-Indian Navy commander leads groups to Cinque and other sites around South Andaman.

Lacadives Wandoor, South Andaman ☎ 98209 28271, ⓦ lacadives.com. After nearly twenty years of experience in the Lakshadweeps, Lacadives now explore the reefs around South Andaman.

into the sea. The ride there across Neil's central paddy land is pleasant, but there are no facilities beyond the two new guesthouses on intermediate **Ram Nagar** beach.

ARRIVAL AND DEPARTURE — NEIL

By boat Neil is well connected with Havelock (1–2 daily; 1hr 30min) and Port Blair (1–3 daily; 2hr), plus there are four weekly ferries to Long Island (4hr 30min) and Rangat (5hr 30min–6hr).

GETTING AROUND

By bus An hourly bus runs between the bazaar and Sitapur. You can also rent bicycles (₹60/day) or mopeds (₹300/day) at guesthouses or stalls in the market.

ACCOMMODATION

A-N-D Beach Resort 250m east of the jetty, Neil Kendra ⊕ 01392 214722. Tucked along the path behind the beach, this welcoming place has some very cheap huts with common bathrooms and a few attached ones, as well as a decent restaurant. ₹200/₹500

Breakwater Ram Nagar ⊕ 95318 52332. This group of ten or so attached huts near the beach is well constructed around a patch of open land. The restaurant does good food and is a sociable gathering place. ₹500

Kalapani Ram Nagar ⊕ 94–742 74991. Though not quite as appealing as those at nearby *Breakwater*, the huts here are perfectly habitable and some of them have shared facilities. ₹300/₹500

SeaShell Lakshmangar ⊕ 03192 242773, ⊕ seashellneil.com. The latest venture from the *SeaShell* group is by far Neil's most upmarket resort, with superbly furnished thatched cottages set in lush landscaped gardens. ₹5000

★ **Tango Beach Resort** Lakshmangar ⊕ 03192 282634, ⊕ tangobeachandaman.com. This friendly place right on the beach offers a range of accommodation from small bamboo huts to larger ones with verandas and the pricey Lagoon suites. It also has one of the best resort restaurants. ₹500

EATING

Blue Sea Ram Nagar beach ⊕ 94760 13330. This newly opened joint just back from the beach offers good seafood, pasta and Indian dishes, as well as filling sizzlers for around ₹200. Daily 8.30am–11pm.

★ **Gyan Garden** 500m west of the bazaar ⊕ 94742 39576. Far and away the best place to eat, this delightful and welcoming garden restaurant cooks fresh fish (₹150–200) and home-grown veg dishes are also a speciality. Daily 8am–10pm.

Hotel Chand In the bazaar ⊕ 94742 22395. Small *dhaba*-style establishment, which serves up tasty, albeit somewhat oily, food. It's mostly Indian, with fish thali for ₹110, but there are some Western dishes too. Daily 6am–10.30pm.

Havelock

Havelock is the largest island in Ritchie's Archipelago, and the most intensively cultivated, settled – like many in the region – by Bengali refugees after Partition. Thanks to its regular ferry connections with the capital, it is also visited in greater numbers than anywhere else in the Andamans. In recent peak seasons, approaching a thousand tourists can be holed up here at one time, including an increasing number of well-heeled Indians, which has led to an explosion in accommodation and tourist shops, many (as in the rest of the country) owned by Kashmiris.

The east coast

Havelock's hub of activity is not the **jetty village**, which just has a few stalls, a couple of dowdy lodges, the odd restaurant and the police station, but the **Main Bazaar**, which you come to if you follow the road straight ahead from the jetty for 2km, passing Beach #2 on the way. Here you'll find a greater variety of shops and places to eat, the only bank and the island's main junction.

If you take the left turn through the busier strip of Main Bazaar, the road leads on past **beaches #3 and #5**, where most of the beach huts and resorts are located. As on

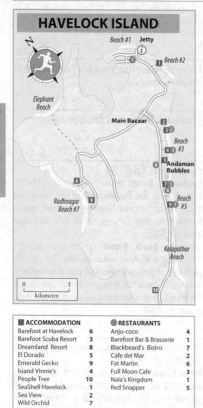

HAVELOCK ISLAND

Beach #1   Jetty

Beach #2

Elephant Beach

Main Bazaar

Beach #3

Andaman Bubbles

Radhnagar Beach #7

Beach #5

Kalapathar Beach

0   1
kilometre

■ ACCOMMODATION		● RESTAURANTS	
Barefoot at Havelock	6	Anju-coco	4
Barefoot Scuba Resort	3	Barefoot Bar & Brasserie	1
Dreamland Resort	8	Blackbeard's Bistro	7
El Dorado	5	Cafe del Mar	2
Emerald Gecko	9	Fat Martin	6
Isiand Vinnie's	4	Full Moon Cafe	3
People Tree	10	Nala's Kingdom	1
SeaShell Havelock	1	Red Snapper	5
Sea View	2		
Wild Orchid	7		

Neil's north coast, these east-facing beaches, though exquisitely scenic, have fairly thin strips of golden-white sand, and when the sea recedes across the lumps of broken coral and rock lying offshore, swimming becomes all but impossible. After Beach #5 the road continues south for several kilometres before turning slightly inland and eventually petering out at **Kalapathar** beach. The entire southern half of Havelock consists of impenetrable forest.

The west coast

The right turn from the island's main junction leads 9km through paddy fields and other crops before dropping through some spectacular woodland to **Radhnagar** (Beach #7), a 2km arc of perfect white sand, backed by stands of giant *mowhar* trees and often touted as the most beautiful in India. The water is a sublime turquoise colour and, although the coral is sparse, marine life here is diverse and plentiful, especially among the rocks around the corner from the main beach (accessible at low tide). The main drawback, which can make sunbathing uncomfortable, is a preponderance of pesky sandflies.

As the nesting site for a colony of Olive Ridley **turtles** (see box, p.886), Radhnagar is strictly protected by the Forest Department, whose wardens ensure tourists don't light fires or sleep on the beach. There's not much accommodation here but a clutch of *dhabas* provides ample sustenance for day-trippers.

A couple of kilometres before the road descends to Radhnagar, a path on the right leads over a hill and down through some scattered settlements to far wilder **Elephant Beach**, although the only trunks you are likely to spot are those of huge fallen trees. Snorkelling here is good, and coral reefs are accessible from the shore, but it can be tough to find the way unless somebody takes you; look out for the start of the path at a sharp bend in the road with a Forest Department noticeboard in a small clearing, and then keep asking the way whenever you see a local.

ARRIVAL AND INFORMATION   HAVELOCK

By boat Havelock's main jetty is on the north side of the island, at the village known as Beach #1. After registering with the police as you disembark, it's best to make your own way to where you plan to stay, though if you've booked in advance, most places arrange pick up.

Destinations Ferries: Long Island (4 weekly; 4hr–4hr 30min); Neil (1–2 daily; 1hr 30min); Port Blair (2–4 daily; 2hr–3hr 30min); Rangat (4 weekly; 5hr–5hr 30min). There are also 1–2 daily *Makruzz* catamaran sailings for Port Blair.

By plane There is a new seaplane service to Port Blair

(Mon–Sat 2 daily; 20min).

Tourist information When staffed, the small tourist office just outside the jetty gates is moderately helpful (daily 8am–5pm; ☎ 94742 22245).

Services The only place to change money is the State Co-operative Bank (Mon–Fri 9am–1pm, Sat 9–11am), at the Main Bazaar, 2km inland of the main jetty, although there are now two ATMs en route. Numerous places now offer satellite broadband internet connections, but charge an exorbitant ₹300/hr.

GETTING AROUND

By bus From the jetty buses run hourly from 6.30am to Radhnagar (aka Beach #7), the last returning at 6pm. Another service runs several times daily to Kalapathar, passing down the east coast, where the bulk of the accommodation is located.

By bike You can rent a scooter, motorbike (around ₹350/day) or cycle (₹60/day) at the guesthouses.

ACCOMMODATION

With the only fully developed tourist scene in the Andamans, Havelock now has around seventy accommodation establishments to choose from, offering everything from the most basic huts to luxuriously furnished cottages. Prices can rise by fifty percent from mid-December to mid-January, and drop considerably between May and October.

Barefoot at Havelock Radhnagar ☎03192 220191, ⓦbarefoot-andaman.com. Havelock's most luxurious resort, with fan-cooled duplexes, "Nicobari" cottages, a/c "Andaman" villas and new top-quality Rajasthani tents. The fine restaurant and bar area are also attractive timber-and-thatch structures. ₹4900

★ **Barefoot Scuba Resort** Beach #3 ☎03192 282343, ⓦdiveandamans.com. The home of Barefoot's dive centre offers luxury Rajasthani tents and smart bamboo duplexes with attached bathrooms, as well as humble huts for people on dive packages. ₹2500

Dreamland Resort Radhnagar ☎03192 282120. Just 200m back along the main road from where it meets the beach, offering ten basic blue raffia huts with shared bathrooms. The only cheapie at Havelock's best beach. ₹500

El Dorado Beach #5 ☎03192 282451, ⓦeldoradoathavelock.com. This mixture of huts (with or without bathrooms) and small cottages is separated from the sea by a grassy palm grove. ₹500/₹900

Emerald Gecko Beach #5 ☎03192 206084, ⓦemerald-gecko.com. The nicest mid-range resort, with ten modest huts (with or without private bathroom) and half a dozen superbly designed two-tier cottages. Breakfast included. ₹1200

Island Vinnie's Beach #3 ☎03192 282187, ⓦislandvinnie.com. Spacious and beautifully constructed Swiss-style tented cabañas, all with attached bathrooms, as well as more humble huts, some with shared facilities. ₹500/₹900

People Tree Kalapathar ☎94760 71979, ⓦpeople-tree .in. The most remote place to stay on the island, with five spacious duplexes and four huge bungalows, plus a café on the opposite side of the road. They can arrange for you to be picked up when you arrive on Havelock. ₹3000

SeaShell Havelock Beach #2 ☎03192 211830, ⓦseashellhavelock.com. Arranged around a manicured lawn barely 1km from the jetty, the two dozen or so sturdy and spacious a/c chalets offer all mod cons including flatscreen TVs. ₹5500

Sea View Beach #3 ☎03192 282442. Very simple but spacious eco-friendly bamboo huts, all with attached bathrooms and mosquito nets. The restaurant does decent, mostly Indian food. ₹600

★ **Wild Orchid** Beach #5 ☎03192 282472, ⓦwildorchidandaman.com. Easily the best value higher-end resort, for its classy cottages (some with a/c), splendidly constructed timber restaurant and lounge, and all-round laidback atmosphere. Breakfast included. ₹5000

EATING AND DRINKING

Anju-coco Beach #5 ☎94760 76405. The best of the small crop of independent roadside restaurants, occupying expanded new premises. Serves filling ₹50 breakfasts, cheap fish and chips, Tibetan *momos* and some more adventurous dishes for ₹250–350. Daily 8am–10.30pm.

Barefoot Bar & Brasserie Main jetty ☎94742 24212. Smart upper-storey wooden deck with film posters and expensive food such as bruschetta and canapés. Most mains around ₹300 and seafood sizzlers up to ₹800. Inexpensive lunchtime thalis served downstairs. Daily 11am–4.30pm & 6–10pm.

★ **Blackbeard's Bistro** Emerald Gecko, Beach #5 ☎03192 206084. The lovely open dining area has a bar and furniture created from recycled timber, and often offers rare dishes such as ceviche as well as fresh fish cooked in delicious and imaginative sauces for ₹300–350. Daily 7–10.30am, noon–2pm and 6–9.30pm.

Café del Mar Barefoot Scuba Resort, Beach #3 ☎03192 282343. Convivial joint serving Indian, Chinese and Western dishes. Excellent meat and seafood specials for ₹200–250. Daily 6.30am–9pm.

Fat Martin Around the corner from Wild Orchid Beach #5 ☎94760 71965. Tiny place with just three tables serving superb masala dosas for ₹60, as well as soups, other vegetarian snacks and lassi. Daily 7am–8pm.

★ **Full Moon Café** Island Vinnie's, Beach #3 ☎98319 00166. Wide menu, including some genuinely spicy Indian cuisine, as well as Western favourites and fresh seafood, mostly ₹200–300. Try the succulent fish tikka. Daily 7am–11pm.

Nala's Kingdom Main jetty ☎01392 282233. The most salubrious place in the jetty area, serving Bengali, south Indian, Chinese and various fish dishes for under ₹200. Great thalis too. Daily 7am–4pm & 7–9.30pm.

Red Snapper Wild Orchid, Beach #5 ☎ 03192 282472. Excellent upmarket seafood, meat and veg menu, served in classy surroundings. Most dinners are in the ₹350–500 range. Occasional recitals of traditional Bengali music. Daily 7–10.30am, noon–2.30pm & 6.30–9pm.

Long Island

19

Just off the southeast coast of Middle Andaman, **Long Island** is attracting a growing number of travellers, with a couple of excellent beaches in **Marg Bay** and **Lalaji Bay**. Both of these are most easily approached by chartering a fisherman's dinghy from the jetty (around ₹500 each way), although Lalaji can be reached on foot by following the red arrows across the island and then turning left along the coast. You should not attempt this at high tide, and even when the sea is out it's quite an obstacle course of rocks and fallen trees.

The main settlement by the jetty has the island's only facilities, which amount to a handful of shops, a couple of basic *dhabas*, and the only two places to stay.

ARRIVAL AND DEPARTURE   LONG ISLAND

By boat Long Island has four weekly ferries to and from Havelock (4hr–4hr 30 min), Neil (5hr–5hr 30min), Port Blair (6–7hr) and Rangat (1hr), as well as a small local ferry connection with Yeratta (2 daily; 1hr 15min), 9km from Rangat.

ACCOMMODATION AND EATING

Blue Planet Signposted with blue arrows from the jetty ☎ 03192 215923, ⓦ blueplanetandamans.com. Around a dozen adjoining rooms of varying sizes, some attached, arranged compactly around the courtyard restaurant whose centrepiece is a giant *mowhar* tree. Also a couple of large cottages and campsite nearby. ₹350/₹1000
Forest Office Guesthouse Near the jetty ☎ 03192 278532. Some people see if there is any availability at the Forest Office's guesthouse, which has a couple of spartan attached rooms usually occupied by officials. ₹500
Hotel GKR Opposite the village football pitch ☎ 94742 08368. A very basic restaurant that serves south Indian snacks, fish fry and fairly skimpy thalis for ₹100. Daily 6am–9pm.

Middle Andaman

For most travellers, **Middle Andaman** is a gruelling rite of passage to be endured en route to or from the north. The sinuous Andaman Trunk Road, hemmed in by walls of towering forest, winds through kilometres of jungle, and crosses the strait that separates the island from its neighbour, **Baratang**, by means of a rusting flat-bottomed ferry. The island's frontier feeling is heightened by the knowledge that the impenetrable forests west of the ATR comprise the **Jarawa Tribal Reserve** (see box, p.930). Of its two main settlements, the more northerly **Mayabunder**, the port for alluring **Interview Island** (see opposite), is slightly more appealing than characterless inland **Rangat** because of its pleasant setting by the sea, but neither town gives any reason to dally. Baratang, meanwhile, has some interesting mud volcanoes and limestone caves, which can be accessed on the boat trips that run daily except Sunday according to demand (₹300).

Rangat

At the southeast corner of Middle Andaman, **RANGAT** consists of a ramshackle sprawl around two rows of chai shops and general stores divided by the ATR. However, as a major staging-post on the journey north, it's impossible to avoid – just don't get stranded here if you can help it.

ARRIVAL AND DEPARTURE   RANGAT

By boat The four weekly ferries from Port Blair via Havelock, Long Island and Neil dock at Rangat Bay, 8km east, from where you can take a bus or auto-rickshaw into town; there are also small daily ferries to Long Island from nearby Yeratta.

By bus Rangat is served by two daily government buses to Port Blair (6–7hr) as well as some private services, which pass through in the morning from further north.

There are several daily buses to Mayabunder (2hr 30min–3hr) and Diglipur (4hr 30min–5hr).

ACCOMMODATION AND EATING

APWD Rest House 📞03192 274237. The Andaman Public Works Department (APWD)'s *Rest House*, pleasantly situated up a winding hill from the bazaar with views across the valley, is the best place to stay and eat, providing good, filling fish thalis (₹100). ₹**600**

Aroma Restaurant Main Rd 📞94742 73527. Other than a couple of *dhabas*, this first-floor place, offering north and south Indian and Chinese staples, is the only place to eat in town. Daily 11am–10pm.

Hawksbill Nest 15km north at Cuthbert Bay (aka RRO) 📞03192 279159. The rooms (some a/c) are characterless but comfortable at this A&N Tourism hotel, which is

invariably empty. Buses between Rangat and Mayabunder stop here on request and there is a fine beach nearby. Dorm ₹**150**, double ₹**600**

RK Lodge 📞03192 274237. The newish *RK Lodge*, just off the main road, is the best of the handful of private establishments, with compact attached rooms. ₹**400**

Sea Shore Lodge 📞03192 274464. If you have an early ferry out of Rangat Bay, it's better to stay down near the jetty at the friendly *Sea Shore Lodge*. Basic meals can be had from the motley conglomeration of stalls between the lodge and the jetty. ₹**500**

Mayabunder

Only 70km north of Rangat by road, **MAYABUNDER** is perched on a long promontory right at the top of the island and surrounded by mangrove swamps. Unfortunately, the bus journey from Rangat can exceed three hours due to continual stops on the surprisingly populated route. Home to a large minority of former Burmese **Karen** tribal people who were originally brought here as cheap logging labour by the British, the village is more spread out and more appealing than Rangat. At the brow of the hill, before it descends to the jetty, a small hexagonal wooden structure houses the **Forest Museum** (Mon–Sat 8am–noon & 1–4pm; free), which holds a motley collection of turtle shells, snakes in formaldehyde, dead coral and a crocodile skull.

ARRIVAL AND DEPARTURE   MAYABUNDER

By bus Some of the buses from Port Blair (9–10hr) and Rangat (2hr 30min–3hr) now continue over the new

bridge to Diglipur on North Andaman (2hr from Mayabunder).

ACCOMMODATION AND EATING

Anmol Lodge Middle of the bazaar in the village centre 📞03192 262695. This once humble lodge has been fully renovated so all rooms are now attached, with cable TV and some a/c. Food must be pre-ordered. ₹**500**

APWD Rest House Next door to the Forest Museum 📞03192 273211. The rooms (some a/c) are large and very comfortable, plus there's a pleasant garden and gazebo

overlooking the sea, and a dining room serving good set meals (around ₹100). Often booked up by officials. ₹**600**

Sea'N'Sand 1km south of the centre 📞03192 273454, ✉thanzin_the_great@yahoo.co.in. Nicely located by the sea, this very welcoming Karen-run lodge has a range of simple rooms, mostly attached, and a reasonable restaurant. ₹**300**/₹**600**

Interview Island

Mayabunder is the jumping-off place for **Interview Island**, a windswept nature sanctuary off the remote northwest coast of Middle Andaman – if you've come to the Andamans to watch **wildlife**, it should be top of your list. Large and mainly flat, it is completely uninhabited save for a handful of unfortunate forest wardens, coastguards and policemen, posted here to ward off poachers. Foreigners aren't permitted to spend the night on the island, and to do a day-trip you must first obtain a ₹500 **permit** from the Forest Museum in Mayabunder (see above). The only way to reach Interview is to charter a private fishing dinghy from Mayabunder jetty for around ₹4000. Arrange one

19

the day before and leave at first light. Ask your boatman to moor by the **beach** at the southern tip of the island, which has a perennial freshwater pool inside a low cave; legend has it that the well, a nesting site for white-bellied **swifts**, has no bottom. At the forest post, where you have to sign an entry ledger, ask the wardens about the movements of Interview's feral **elephants**, descendants of trained elephants deserted here by a Kolkata-based logging company after its timber operation failed in the 1950s. **Saltwater crocodiles** are found on the island's eastern coastline.

19

North Andaman

Shrouded in dense jungle, **North Andaman** is the least populated of the region's large islands, crossed by a single road linking its scattered Bengali settlements. Although parts have been seriously logged, the total absence of driveable roads into northern and western areas has ensured blanket protection for a vast stretch of convoluted coastline, running from Austin Strait in the southwest to the northern tip, Cape Price; it's reassuring to know at least one extensive wilderness survives in the Andamans.

Despite the completion of the ATR's final section and the bridge from Middle Andaman, the main settlement of **DIGLIPUR** continues to exist in relative seclusion. Known in the British era as Port Cornwallis, North Andaman's largest settlement is another disappointing market town where you're only likely to pause long enough to pick up a local bus further north to the coast. Unless you are catching a boat (to Smith or Ross islands or back to Port Blair) straightaway from the port of **Aerial Bay**, 9km northeast, it's better to continue another 9km to **Kalipur**, where there's an excellent deserted beach, backed by lush forest and covered in photogenic driftwood. Swimming is best at high tide because the water recedes across rocky mud pools. Offshore snorkelling is also excellent, especially along the reef that runs towards the islet barely 500m away.

It's possible to walk from Kalipur to **Saddle Peak**, the highest mountain in the Andamans at 737m, which rises dramatically to the south, swathed in lush jungle. Permission to make the three- to four-hour climb must be obtained from the Range Officer at the forest checkpost near the start of the ascent, but don't attempt it without a guide and plenty of drinking water. Another enjoyable day-trip is to the **limestone caverns**, 12km south near Ramnagar beach, best accessed by dinghy from Kalipur. You can arrange a dinghy, or guide for the Saddle Peak climb, at *Pristine Beach Resort* (see opposite).

Smith and Ross islands

Many tourists find their way up here in order to explore the various **islands** dotted around the gulf north of Aerial Bay, particularly **Smith** and **Ross** (not to be confused with its namesake near Port Blair), whose white sandbars, coral reefs and flora are splendid. At low tide it is possible to walk between the two islands. Mercifully, plans to build a luxury resort on Smith have floundered. You can organize the requisite ₹500 permit from the Wildlife Information booth at Aerial Bay and rent a boat (₹2000) for the return trip yourself, or through one of the area guesthouses – try *Pristine Beach Resort* (see opposite).

ARRIVAL AND DEPARTURE

NORTH ANDAMAN

By boat There are three boats a week in each direction from Aerial Bay to Port Blair (7–9hr).

By bus Several buses a day leave in the early morning for Port Blair (11–12hr) via Mayabunder (2hr) and Rangat (4hr

30min–5hr). There are 10–12 daily buses from Diglipur to Aerial Bay (20min) and Kalipur (45min).

By plane There is a new seaplane service to Port Blair (Mon–Sat 1 daily; 50min).

ACCOMMODATION AND EATING

DIGLIPUR

APWD Rest House ☏ 03192 272203. On the hill above

the main road, the *APWD Rest House* offers the village's nicest accommodation. ₹600

Maa Yashoda On the main road ☎ 99332 55086. This selection of ultra-basic rooms above a shop have bathrooms but not a lot else. ₹300

KALIPUR

★ **Pristine Beach Resort** ☎ 03192 271793. Easily the most congenial place to stay on North Andaman, with a huge range of options from small non-attached huts

through sturdy duplexes to luxury cottages, all set in lovely grounds near the beach. Very good restaurant too (most dishes ₹150–200). ₹300/₹600

Turtle Resort ☎ 03192 272553. Typically institutional A&N Tourism hotel, which enjoys a prime location on a hilltop above the bay. The rooms are plain but large. Dorm ₹150, double ₹600

Little Andaman

Little Andaman is the furthest point south in the archipelago that foreigners can travel to on their tourist permit. Most of the island has been set aside as a tribal reserve for the **Onge** and is thus off-limits. It was also the only island open to foreigners to sustain extensive damage in the 2004 **tsunami**, but although a number of buildings were destroyed, and 64 people died, Little Andaman has recovered well. Relatively few visitors make it down here, although a slight improvement in tourist infrastructure renders it increasingly worthwhile for those who do, and it seems the word is out.

The main settlement, **INDIRA BAZAAR**, is 2km north of the jetty at **Hut Bay**, which curves gradually round in a majestic 8km sweep, the quality of the sand and beauty of the adjacent jungle increasing the further north you go. The top stretch is named **Netaji Nagar** after the village on the island's only road, which runs behind it. En route, you can detour 1km inland at the huge signpost about 2.5km north of Indira Bazaar to see the **White Surf Waterfalls** (daily dawn–dusk; ₹20). Made up of three 10- to 15m-high cascades, it's a relaxing spot; you can clamber into the right-hand fall for a soothing shower – yet crocodiles are said to inhabit the surrounding streams. Over the headland at the top of Hut Bay, 12km or so from the jetty, lies the smaller but equally picturesque crescent of **Butler Bay**. There's not much to do here but swim, sunbathe or look around the slightly eerie remains of the government beach resort, which was swept away by the tsunami – that is unless you've brought your surfboard with you: Little Andaman has a cult reputation among surfers for having some of the best conditions anywhere in South Asia.

ARRIVAL AND DEPARTURE   LITTLE ANDAMAN

By boat Daily ferries from Port Blair arrive at Hut Bay, the   faster ones making the voyage in less than 6hr.

GETTING AROUND

Bike rental Bicycles (₹50/day) and mopeds (₹250/day) can be rented through the guesthouses, but are in very   short supply.

ACCOMMODATION AND EATING

Blue View Netaji Nagar ☎ 97344 80842. A motley mixture of huts and rooms, all with shared facilities, spaced around open ground, plus a good seafood restaurant (dishes ₹150–200). ₹200

★ **Jina Resort** Netaji Nagar ☎ 94760 38057. Pleasant and welcoming place with a sociable eating area and great banana leaf fish (₹200) on the menu. There are huts and rooms of varying sizes but all are non-attached. ₹200

Palm Grove Indira Bazaar ☎ 94342 99212. Decent government-run restaurant which offers a limited menu of fish, chicken and veg dishes, mostly Indian. Filling thalis go for ₹110. Daily 7am–9pm.

Sealand Tourist Home Indira Bazaar ☎ 03192 284306. The best place to stay in the main settlement is this two-storey lodge, whose splendid bay-front location is only marred by the architect's inexplicable decision to have all windows facing the interior. Some rooms a/c, all attached. ₹400

Vvet Guest House Indira Bazaar ☎ 03192 284155. Functional government-run guesthouse whose staff can take some persuading to let you stay, but the small, pleasant garden makes the wrangling just about worthwhile. ₹300

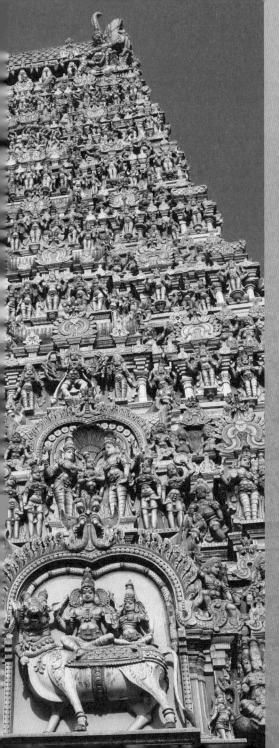

Tamil Nadu

MEENAKSHI TEMPLE, MADURAI

Tamil Nadu

When Indians refer to "the South", it's usually Tamil Nadu they're talking about. While Karnataka and Andhra Pradesh are essentially cultural transition zones buffering the Hindi-speaking north, and Kerala and Goa maintain their own distinctively idiosyncratic identities, the peninsula's massive Tamil-speaking state is India's Dravidian Hindu heartland. Traditionally protected by distance and the military might of the southern Deccan kingdoms, the region has, over the centuries, been less exposed to northern influences than its neighbours. As a result, the three powerful dynasties dominating the south – the Cholas, the Pallavas and the Pandyans – were able, over a period of more than a thousand years, to develop their own unique religious and political institutions, largely unmolested by marauding Muslims.

The most visible legacy of this protracted cultural flowering is a crop of astounding **temples**, whose gigantic gateway towers, or *gopuras*, still soar above just about every town. It is the image of these colossal wedge-shaped pyramids, high above the canopy of dense palm forests, or against patchworks of vibrant green paddy fields, which Edward Lear described as "stupendous and beyond belief". Indeed, the garishly painted deities and mythological creatures sculpted onto the towers linger long in the memory of most travellers.

The great Tamil temples, however, are merely the largest landmarks in a vast network of **sacred sites** – shrines, bathing places, holy trees, rocks and rivers – interconnected by a web of ancient pilgrims' routes. Tamil Nadu harbours 274 of India's holiest Shiva temples, and 108 are dedicated to Vishnu. In addition, five shrines devoted to the five Vedic elements (Earth, Wind, Fire, Water and Ether) are to be found here, along with eight to the planets, as well as other places revered by Christians and Muslims. Scattered from the pale orange crags and forests of the Western Ghats, across the fertile deltas of the **Vaigai** and **Kaveri** rivers to the Coromandel coast on the Bay of Bengal, these sites were celebrated in the hymns of the Tamil saints, composed between one and two thousand years ago. Today, so little has changed that the same devotional songs are still widely sung and understood in the region and it remains one of the last places in the world where a classical culture has survived well into the present.

The Tamils' living connection with their ancient Dravidian past has given rise to a strong **nationalist movement**. With a few fleeting lapses, one or other of the pro-Dravidian parties has been in power here since the 1950s, spreading their anti-brahmin, anti-Hindi proletarian message to the masses principally through the medium of movies. Indeed, since Independence, the majority of Tamil Nadu's political leaders have been drawn from the state's prolific **cinema** industry.

With its seafront fort, grand mansions and excellence as a centre for the performing arts, the state capital **Chennai** is nonetheless a hot, chaotic, noisy Indian metropolis that

20

KODAIKANAL, THE GHATS

Highlights

❶ Mamallapuram Stone-carvers' workshops, a long sandy beach and wonderful Pallava monuments have made this a top tourist attraction. **See p.963**

❷ Puducherry Former French colony that has retained the ambience of a Gallic seaside town: croissants, a promenade and gendarmes wearing képis. **See p.975**

❸ Thanjavur Home to some of the world's finest Chola bronzes, this town is dominated by the colossal tower of the Brihadishwara Temple. **See p.988**

❹ Madurai The love nest of Shiva and his consort Meenakshi, this busy city's major

temple hosts a constant round of festivals. **See p.997**

❺ Kanyakumari At the southern tip of the Subcontinent, Kanyakumari marks the sacred meeting point of the Bay of Bengal, Indian Ocean and Arabian Sea. **See p.1006**

❻ The Ghats The spine of southern India, excellent for trekking through lush mountains and tea plantations from its refreshingly cool hill stations. **See p.1008**

❼ Mudumalai Wildlife Sanctuary This densely forested park is becoming increasingly popular for its wild elephants and excellent accommodation. **See p.1019**

HIGHLIGHTS ARE MARKED ON THE MAP ON P.950

still carries faint echoes of the Raj. However, it is a good base for visiting **Kanchipuram**, a major pilgrimage and sari-weaving centre, filled with reminders of an illustrious past.

Much the best place to start a temple tour is in nearby **Mamallapuram**, a seaside village that – quite apart from some exquisite Pallava rock-cut architecture – boasts a long and lovely beach. Further down the coast lies the one-time French colony of **Puducherry**, now home to the famous Sri Aurobindo ashram; nearby, **Auroville** has

TAMIL NADU

0   50
kilometres

N

ANDHRA PRADESH

KARNATAKA

Mysore

Bengaluru

NH-4

Krishnagiri

NH-7

NH-46

Pulicat

Tiruttani

Arakkonam

Chennai

Ranippettai

Vellore

Dakshina Chitra

Kanchipuram

Madhuranthakam

Chengalpattu

Mamallapuram ❶

VEDANTHANGAL BIRD SANCTUARY

Palar

NH-45

TAMILNADU

Tiruvannamalai

Gingee

Tindivanam

Villupuram

Auroville

Puducherry ❷

Ponnaiyar

MUDUMALAI WILDLIFE SANCTUARY ❼

Theppakkadu

Masinagudi

Dodabetta

Udhagamandalam (Ooty)

Gudalur

Kotagiri

Coonoor

Mettupalayam

Mysore

Stanley

Yercaud

Salem

Vriddhachalam

Cuddalore

Chidambaram

BAY OF BENGAL

Kaveri

Erode

Namakkal

Gangaikondacholapuram

Tiruppur

NH-47

Coimbatore ❻

Nilgiri Blue Mountain Railway

Pollachi

Karur

Kaveri

Kulittalai

Srirangam

Tiruchirapalli

Mayiladuturai

Swamimalai

Darasuram

Kumbakonam

Thiruvaiyaru

Thanjavur ❸

Thiruvarur

Tharamgambadi

Karaikal

Nagur

Nagappattinam

Velankanni

INDIRA GANDHI WILDLIFE SANCTUARY

Kochi

Palani

Lake Vyapuri

Kollidam

Pudukottai

Tiruthuraipondi

Vedaranyam

Kodaikanal

Dindigul

KERALA

Vaigai

Tiruparankundram

Algarkovil

Madurai ❹

Karaikkuai

Alappuzha

Manamadurai

NH-49

Jaffna

Shrivilliputhur

Rajapalaiyam

NH-7

Ramanathapuram

Mandapam

Rameshwaram

Palk Strait

Talaimannar

Mannar

SRI LANKA

Gulf of Mannar

Adam's Bridge

Kollam

NH-47

Kuttalam

Tenkasi

Tirunelveli

Tuticorin

Thiruvananthapuram

NH-7A

Palayankottai

Kovalam

Mundanthurai

Nanguneri

Tambraparni

Tiruchendur

LAKSHADWEEP SEA

Maruntha Malai

Padmanabhapuram

Suchindram

Nagercoil

Kanyakumari ❺

HIGHLIGHTS

❶ Mamallapuram
❷ Puducherry
❸ Thanjavur
❹ Madurai
❺ Kanyakumari
❻ The Ghats
❼ Mudumalai Wildlife Sanctuary

carved out a role for itself as a popular New Age centre. The road south from Puducherry puts you back on the temple trail, leading to the tenth-century Chola kingdom and the extraordinary architecture of **Chidambaram**, **Gangaikondacholapuram**, **Kumbakonam** and **Darasuram**. For the best Chola bronzes, however, and a glimpse of the magnificent paintings that flourished under Maratha rajas in the eighteenth century, travellers should head for **Thanjavur**. Chola capital for four centuries, the city boasts almost a hundred temples and was the birthplace of Bharatanatyam dance, famous throughout Tamil Nadu.

In the very centre of Tamil Nadu, **Tiruchirapalli**, a commercial town just northwest of Thanjavur, held some interest for the Cholas, but reached its heyday under later dynasties, when the temple complex in neighbouring **Srirangam** became one of south India's largest. Among its patrons were the Nayaks of **Madurai**, whose erstwhile capital further south, bustling with pilgrims, priests, peddlers, tailors and tourists, is an unforgettable destination. **Rameshwaram**, on the long spit of land reaching towards Sri Lanka, and **Kanyakumari** at India's southern tip are both important pilgrimage centres, and have the added attraction of welcome cool breezes and vistas over the sea.

While Tamil Nadu's temples are undeniably its major attraction, the hill stations of **Kodaikanal** and **Udhagamandalam (Ooty)** in the west of the state are popular destinations on the well-beaten tourist trail between Kerala and Tamil Nadu. The verdant, cool hills offer mountain views and gentle trails through the forests and tea and coffee plantations. You can also spot wildlife in the teak forests of **Mudumalai Wildlife Sanctuary** and bamboo groves of **Indira Gandhi Wildlife Sanctuary**, situated in the Palani Hills.

20

Brief history

Since the fourth century BC, Tamil Nadu has been shaped by its majority **Dravidian** population, a people of uncertain origins and physically quite different from north Indians. The influence of the powerful *janapada*s, established in the north by the fourth and third centuries BC, extended as far south as the Deccan, but they made few incursions into **Dravidadesa** (Tamil country). Incorporating what is now Kerala and Tamil Nadu, Dravidadesa was ruled by three dynasties: the **Cheras**, who held sway over much of the Malabar coast (Kerala), the **Pandyas** in the far south and the **Cholas**, whose realm stretched along the eastern Coromandel coast.

In the fourth century, the **Pallava** dynasty established a powerful kingdom centred in **Kanchipuram**. By the seventh century, the successors of the first Pallava king, Simhavishnu, were engaged in battles with the southern Pandyas and the forces of the Chalukyas, based further west in Karnataka. This was also an era of social development. **Brahmins** became the dominant community. The emergence of *bhakti*, devotional worship, placed temples firmly at the centre of religious life, and the inspirational *sangam* literature of saint-poets fostered a tradition of dance and music that has become Tamil Nadu's cultural hallmark.

In the tenth and eleventh centuries, the Cholas experienced a profound revival, ploughing their new wealth into the construction of splendid and imposing temples. Subsequently, the **Vijayanagars**, based in Hampi (Karnataka), resisted Muslim incursions from the north and spread to cover most of south India by the sixteenth century. This prompted a new phase of architectural development, including the introduction of colossal *gopura*s. In Madurai, the Vijayanagar governors, **Nayaks**, set up an independent kingdom whose impact spread as far as Tiruchirapalli.

Simultaneously, the south experienced its first significant wave of **European settlement**. First came the Portuguese, followed by the British, Dutch and French. The Western powers soon found themselves engaged in territorial disputes, most markedly between the French, based in **Pondicherry**, and the British, whose stronghold since 1640 had been Fort St George in **Madras**. It was the British who prevailed, confining the French to Pondicherry.

As well as occasional rebellions against colonial rule, Tamil Nadu also saw anti-brahmin protests, in particular in the 1920s and 1930s. **Independence** in 1947 signalled the need for state boundaries, and by 1956 the borders had been demarcated on a linguistic basis. Thus in 1965 Madras Presidency became **Tamil Nadu**.

Since Independence, Tamil Nadu's industrial sector has mushroomed. The state was a Congress stronghold until 1967, when the **DMK** (Dravida Munnetra Kazhagam), championing the lower castes and reasserting Tamil identity, won a landslide victory on a wave of anti-Hindi and anti-central government sentiment. Power has ping-ponged back and forth between the DMK and the breakaway party AIADMK ever since (see box, p.954).

INFORMATION   TAMIL NADU

Climate Temperatures in Tamil Nadu, which usually hover around 30°C, peak in May and June, when they often soar above 40°C away from the coast. The state is barely affected by the southwest monsoon that pounds much of India from June to September: it receives most of its rain between October and December, when the odd cyclone may well make an appearance. The cooler, rainy days, however, bring their own problems: large-scale flooding can disrupt road and rail links and imbue everything with an all-pervasive dampness.

Accommodation and eating Accommodation throughout the state is good and plentiful. Most hotels have their own dining halls that, together with local restaurants, usually serve sumptuous and unlimited thalis (known here simply as "meals"), tinged with tamarind and presented on banana leaves. Indigenous dishes are almost exclusively vegetarian.

20 Chennai

In the northeastern corner of Tamil Nadu on the Bay of Bengal, **CHENNAI** (still commonly referred to by its former British name, **Madras**) is India's fourth largest city, with a population nudging seven and a half million. Hot, congested and noisy, it's the major transport hub of the south and most travellers stay just long enough to book a ticket for somewhere else. The attractions of the city itself are sparse, though it does boast fine specimens of **Raj architecture**, pilgrimage sites connected with the apostle **Doubting Thomas**, superb **Chola bronzes** at its state museum, and plenty of classical music and dance performances.

Geographically Chennai divides into three main sectors. North of the River Cooum stands **Fort St George**, site of the first British outpost in India and **George Town**, the commercial centre, which developed during British occupation. George Town's principal landmark is **Parry's Corner** located at the southern end of Rajaji Salai. Sandwiched between the Cooum and Adyar rivers is **Central Chennai**, the modern, commercial heart of the metropolis, crossed and served by the city's main thoroughfare, **Anna Salai**. East of Anna Salai is the atmospheric old Muslim quarter of **Triplicane** and beyond is the long straight **Marina** with its massive beach, fishing boats and hordes of domestic tourists, saris and trousers hitched up, enjoying a paddle. Further south along the coast is the district of **Mylapore**, inhabited by the Portuguese in the 1500s, with its two important places of pilgrimage and tourist attractions, **Kapalishvara Temple** and **San Thomé Cathedral**.

Brief history

As capital of Tamil Nadu, Chennai is a comparatively modern creation, like Mumbai and Kolkata. It was founded as a fortified trading post by the **British East India Company** in 1639, north of the ancient Tamil port of **Mylapore** and the Portuguese settlement of San Thomé. It was completed on St George's Day in 1640 and thus named **Fort St George**. Over the course of the following century and a half, as capital of the **Madras Presidency**, which covered most of south India, the city expanded to include many surrounding villages. It was briefly lost to the French but three years later, in 1746, the British re-established control under **Robert Clive** (Clive of India) and continued to use it as their southern base, although it was surpassed in national importance by Calcutta.

The city's renaissance began after Independence, when it became the centre of the Tamil **movie industry**, and a hotbed of **Dravidian nationalism**. Renamed Chennai in 1997, the metropolis has boomed since the Indian economy opened up to foreign investment in the early 1990s. The flip side of this rapid economic growth is that

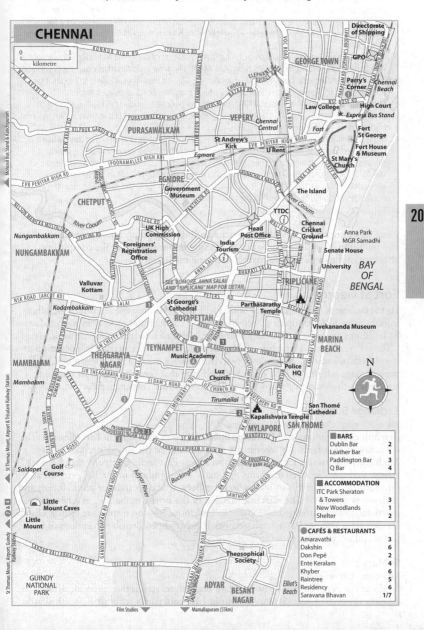

20

OF MOVIE STARS AND MINISTERS

One notable difference between the Chennai-based Tamil movie industry and the mainstream Bollywood movies from Mumbai is the influence of **politics** on Tamil films. Traditional folk ballads about low-caste heroes vanquishing high-caste villains were perfect propaganda vehicles for the nascent Tamil nationalist movement, the Dravida Munnetra Kazhagam (**DMK**). It is no coincidence that the party's founding father, **C.N. Annadurai**, was a top screenplay and script writer. He and his colleagues used the popular film genres of the time to convey their political ideas to the masses and this politicization of the big screen created the **fan clubs**, or *rasigar manram*s, that play a key role in mobilizing support for the nationalist parties in elections.

Perhaps the most influential fan club of all time was that of superstar Marudur Gopalamenon Ramachandran, known to millions simply as "**MGR**". He generated fanatical grass-roots support in the state and rose to become chief minister in 1977. His eleven-year rule is still regarded by liberals as a dark age of chronic corruption, police brutality, political purges and rising organized crime. When he died in 1987, two million people attended his funeral and even today, MGR's statue, sporting trademark sunglasses and lamb's-wool hat, is revered across Tamil Nadu at roadside shrines.

MGR's political protégée, and eventual successor, was teenage screen starlet **Jayalalitha**, a convent-educated brahmin's daughter whom he recruited to be both his leading lady and mistress. After 25 hit films together, Jayalalitha followed him into politics, becoming leader of the AIADMK, the party MGR set up after being expelled from the DMK in 1972. Despite allegations of fraud and corruption Jayalalitha enjoyed two spells as chief minister in the early noughties and assumed power for her third stint in 2011.

Chennai's infrastructure has been stretched to breaking point: poverty, oppressive heat and pollution are more likely to be your lasting impressions than the conspicuous affluence of the city's modern marble shopping malls.

Fort St George

Fort St George is quite unlike any other fort in India. Facing the sea amid state offices, it looks more like a complex of well-maintained colonial mansions than a fort. Many of its buildings are today used as offices and are a hive of activity during the week.

The fort was the first structure of Madras town and the first territorial possession of the British in India. Construction began in 1640 but most of the original buildings were damaged during French sieges replaced later that century. The most imposing structure is the slate-grey-and-white eighteenth-century colonnaded **Fort House**.

Exchange Building
York St • Daily except Fri 9am–5pm • ₹100 (₹5), no photography

The modestly proportioned **Exchange Building** houses the excellent **Fort Museum**. The collection within faithfully records the central events of the British occupation of Madras with portraits, regimental flags, weapons, East India Company coins, medals, stamps and thick woollen uniforms that make you wonder how the Raj survived as long as it did. The first floor is now an **art gallery**, where portraits of prim officials and their wives sit side by side with fine sketches of the British embarking at Chennai in aristocratic finery, attended by Indians in loincloths. Also on display are etchings by the famous artist **Thomas Daniell**, whose work largely defined British perceptions of India at the end of the eighteenth century.

St Mary's
Fort St George • Daily 9am–5pm

South of the Fort Museum, past the State Legislature, stands the oldest surviving Anglican church in Asia, **St Mary's**, built in 1678 and partly renovated after the battle of 1759. It's distinctly English in style, crammed with plaques and statues in memory of British soldiers, politicians and their wives. The grandest plaque, made of pure silver, was presented by Elihu Yale, former governor of Fort St George (1687–96) and founder of Yale University. A collection of photographs of visiting dignitaries, including Queen Elizabeth II, is on display in the entrance porch.

George Town

Bus #18 from Anna Salai

North of Fort St George, the former British trading centre of **George Town** remains the focal area for banks, offices, shipping companies and street stalls. This network of streets harbours a fascinating medley of architecture: eighteenth- and nineteenth-century churches, Hindu and Jain temples and a scattering of mosques, interspersed with grand

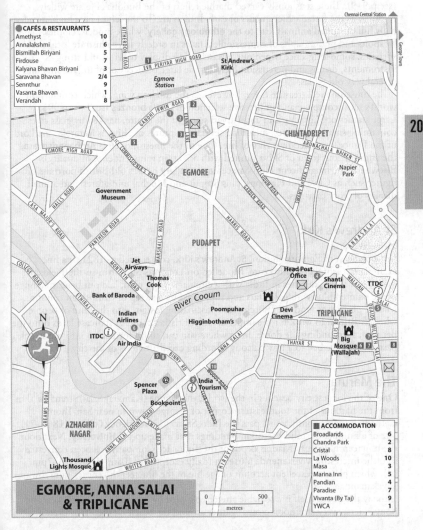

● CAFÉS & RESTAURANTS	
Amethyst	10
Annalakshmi	6
Bismillah Biriyani	5
Firdouse	7
Kalyana Bhavan Biriyani	3
Saravana Bhavan	2/4
Sennthur	9
Vasanta Bhavan	1
Verandah	8

■ ACCOMMODATION	
Broadlands	6
Chandra Park	2
Cristal	8
La Woods	10
Masa	3
Marina Inn	5
Pandian	4
Paradise	7
Vivanta (By Taj)	9
YWCA	1

EGMORE, ANNA SALAI & TRIPLICANE

0 500 metres

20

mansions. In the east, on Rajaji Salai, the **General Post Office** occupies a robust earth-red Indo-Saracenic building constructed in 1884. George Town's southern extent is marked by the bulbous white domes and sandstone towers of the **High Court** and the even more opulent towers of the **Law College**, both showing strong Islamic influence.

Government Museum

Pantheon Rd • Daily except Fri 9.30am–5pm • ₹250 (₹15), camera ₹200, video camera ₹500 • Bus #23C from Anna Salai for Pantheon Rd, south of Egmore railway station

The Chennai **Government Museum** contains some remarkable archeological finds from south India and the Deccan. Inside the deep-red, circular **main building**, built in 1851, the first gallery is devoted to archeology and geology; the highlights are the dismantled panels, railings and statues from the second-century AD *stupa* complex at **Amaravati** (see p.919). These sensuously carved marble reliefs of the Buddha's life are widely regarded as the finest achievements of early Indian art. To the left of here high, arcaded halls full of stuffed animals lead to the **ethnology gallery**, where models, clothes, weapons and photographs of expressionless faces in orderly lines illustrate local tribal societies, some long since wiped out. A fascinating display of wind and string **instruments**, drums and percussion includes the large predecessor of today's sitar and several very old tablas.

The museum's real treasure trove, however, is the modern wing, which contains the world's most complete and impressive selection of **Chola bronzes** (see box, p.991). Large statues of Shiva, Vishnu and Parvati stand in the centre, flanked by glass cases containing smaller figurines, including several sculptures of Shiva as **Nataraja**, the Lord of the Dance, encircled by a ring of fire. One of the finest models is **Ardhanarishvara**, the androgynous form of Shiva (united with Shakti in transcendence of duality). Elsewhere, the magnificent Indo-Saracenic **art gallery** houses old British portraits of figures such as Clive and Hastings, plus Rajput and Mughal miniatures, and a small display of ivory carvings.

St Andrew's Kirk

Off Periyar EVR High Rd

Just northeast of Egmore Station, **St Andrew's Kirk**, consecrated in 1821, is a fine example of Georgian architecture. Modelled on London's St Martin's-in-the-Fields, it's one of just three churches in India with a circular seating plan, laid out beneath a huge dome painted blue with gold stars and supported by a sweep of Corinthian columns. Marble plaques around the church give a fascinating insight into the kind of people who left Britain to work for the imperial and Christian cause. A staircase leads onto the flat roof, surrounding the dome, from where you can climb further up into the steeple past the massive bell to a tiny balcony affording excellent views of the city.

The Marina

One of the longest city beaches in the world, the **Marina** (Kamaraj Salai) stretches 5km from the harbour at the southeastern corner of George Town to near San Thome Cathedral. Going south, you'll pass the Indo-Saracenic **Presidency College** (1865–71), one of a number of stolid Victorian buildings that make up the **University**. Next door, the nineteenth-century Madras depot of the Tudor Ice Company has been converted into the interesting **Vivekananda Museum** (daily except Wed10am–noon & 3–7pm; ₹2), which gives an excellent account of the life of the nineteenth-century saint, Swami Vivekananda.

Today the **beach** itself is a sociable stretch, peopled by idle paddlers, picnickers and pony-riders; every afternoon crowds gather around the beach market. However, its location, just a little downstream from the port, which belches out waste and smelly fumes, combined with its function as the toilet for the fishing community, detract somewhat from its natural beauty.

Mylapore

Buses #4, #5 or #21 from the LIC building on Anna Salai

Long before Madras came into existence, **Mylapore**, south of the Marina, was a major settlement; the Greek geographer Ptolemy mentioned it in the second century AD as a thriving port. During the Pallava period (fifth to ninth centuries) it was second only to Mamallapuram.

An important stop on the St Thomas pilgrimage trail, **San Thomé Cathedral** (daily 6am–8pm) marks the eastern boundary of Mylapore, lying close to the sea at the southern end of the Marina on San Thomé High Road. Although the present neo-Gothic structure dates from 1896, it stands on the site of two earlier churches built over the tomb of St Thomas; his relics are kept inside, accessed by an underground passage from the museum at the rear of the courtyard.

The large **Kapalishvara temple** sits just under 1km west of the San Thomé cathedral off RK Mutt Road. Seventh-century Tamil poet-saints sang its praises, but the present structure, dedicated to Shiva, probably dates from the sixteenth century. The huge (40m) *gopura* towering above the main east entrance, plastered in stucco figures, was added in 1906. Surrounding an assortment of busy shrines, where priests offer blessings for devotees and non-Hindus alike, the courtyard features an old tree where a small shrine to Shiva's consort, Parvati, shows her in the form of a peahen (*mayil*) worshipping a lingam.

Little Mount Caves

Little Mount, off Mount Rd • Bus #18A, #18B, or #52C from Anna Salai

St Thomas is said to have sought refuge from persecution in the **Little Mount Caves**, 8km south of the city centre. Entrance to the caves is beside steps leading to a statue of Our Lady of Good Health. Inside, next to a small natural window in the rock, are impressions of what are believed to be St Thomas' handprints, created when he made his escape through this tiny opening. Behind the new circular church of Our Lady of Good Health is a natural **spring**. Tradition has it that this was created when Thomas struck the rock, so the crowds that came to hear him preach could quench their thirst; samples of its holy water are on sale.

St Thomas Mount

Mount Rd • Take a suburban train to Guindy railway station and walk from there

It's said that St Thomas was speared to death while praying before a stone cross on **St Thomas Mount**, 11km south of the city centre. **Our Lady of Expectation Church** (1523), at the summit of the Mount, can be reached by 134 granite steps marked with the fourteen stations of the Cross, or by a road which curls its way to the top, where a huge old banyan tree provides shade.

Theosophical Society headquarters

Adyar Bridge Rd, Besant Nagar (south of Mylapore) • **Grounds** Mon–Sat 8.30–10am & 2–4pm **Bookshop** Mon–Sat 9am–noon & 3–6pm **Library** Tues–Sun 9am–5pm • @intl. hq@ts-adyar.org • Buses #5, #5C or #23C from George Town/Anna Salai

The **Theosophical Society** was established in New York in 1875 by American Civil War veteran Colonel Henry S. Olcott and the eccentric Russian aristocrat Madame Helena Petrovna Blavatsky, who claimed to have occult powers. Based on a fundamental belief in the equality and truth of all religions, the society in fact

20

propagated a modern form of Hinduism, praising all things Indian and shunning Christian missionaries. Needless to say, its two founders were greeted enthusiastically when they transferred their operations to Madras in 1882, establishing their headquarters near Elliot's Beach in Adyar.

The society's buildings still stand today, sheltering several shrines and an excellent **library** of books on religion and philosophy. The collection includes 800-year-old scroll pictures of the Buddha; rare Tibetan xylographs; exquisitely illuminated Korans; a giant copy of Martin Luther's *Biblia* printed in Nuremberg three hundred years ago; and a thumbnail-sized Bible in seven languages. Anybody is welcome to look around, but to gain full use of the library you have to register as a member.

The 270 acres of woodland and gardens surrounding the society's headquarters make a serene place to sit and restore the spirits. In the middle, a vast 400-year-old **banyan tree**, said to be the second largest in the world, can provide shade for up to three thousand people at a time.

ARRIVAL AND DEPARTURE CHENNAI

BY PLANE

Chennai airport The airport, in Trisulam, 16km southwest of the city centre on NH-45, is comprehensively served by international and domestic flights. Jet Airways (43/44 Montieth Rd; Mon–Sat 9.30am–1.30pm & 2–5.30pm; ☎044 3989 3333)) and Air India (Marshalls Rd; Mon–Sat 9.30am–1pm & 1.45–5.30pm) have frequent daily flights to Delhi, Mumbai, Bengaluru and Hyderabad as well as to Port Blair. The international and domestic terminals are a short walk from each other. The main concourse has a 24hr post office, currency exchange facilities and a couple of snack bars. The Tamil Nadu Tourist Information

Centre at the arrivals exit can book accommodation, and there's a computerized ticket reservation counter (Mon–Sat 8am–2pm & 2.15–8pm, Sun 8am–2pm) immediately outside the domestic terminal exit.

Getting in to town The quickest and cheapest way to get into town is by suburban train (see opposite) from Trisulam Station, 500m from the airport on the far side of the road, to Park, Egmore and North Beach stations (30–40min). There are pre-paid taxi counters at both terminals for the ever-increasingly congested ride to the main hotels or railway stations; from the main road, rickshaws charge ₹300. Taxis straight down the coast to Mamallapuram cost

RECOMMENDED TRAINS FROM CHENNAI

Destination	Name	No.	From	Departs	Duration
Bengaluru	*Shatabdi Express*	#12007	Central	6am*	4hr 50min
	Bangalore Express	#12609	Central	1.35pm	6hr 30min
Coimbatore	*Kovai Express*	#12675	Central	6.15am	7hr 30min
	Cheran Express	#12673	Central	10.10pm	7hr 55min
Hyderabad	*Charminar Express*	#12759	Central	6.10pm	13hr 50min
Kanyakumari	*Kanyakumari Express*	#12633	Egmore	5.30pm	13hr 20min
Kochi/Ernakulam	*Alleppey Express*	#16041	Central	8.45pm	11hr 48min
	Trivandrum Mail	#12623	Central	7.45pm	10hr 35min
Kodaikanal Road	*Pandian Express*	#12637	Egmore	9.20pm	7hr 47min
Madurai	*Vaigai Express*	#12635	Egmore	1.20pm	8hr 5min
Mettupalayam (for Ooty)	*Nilgiri Express*	#12671	Central	9.15pm	9hr
Mumbai	*Mumbai Express*	#11042	Central	11.55am	26hr
	Dadar Express	#12164	Egmore	6.50am	23hr 10min
Mysore	*Shatabdi Express*	#12007	Central	6am*	7hr
	Mysore Express	#16222	Central	9.30pm	10hr 30min
Rameshwaram	*R'waram Express*	#16713	Egmore	5pm	11hr 45min
Thanjavur	*Trichy Express*	#16853	Egmore	8.15am	6hr 38min
Tiruchirapalli	*Guruvayur Express*	#16127	Egmore	7.40am	5hr 30min
	Vaigai Express	#12635	Egmore	1.20pm	5hr 5min
Thiruvananthapuram	*Trivandrum Mail*	#12623	Central	7.45pm	15hr 35min
Tirupati	*Saptagiri Express*	#16057	Central	6.25am	3hr 5min

*Except Wed; a/c only

around ₹1100. Buses #70 and #70a go to Mofussil Bus Stand (see below) in Koyambedu suburb, from where you can connect to other destinations.

BY TRAIN

Stations Chennai has two main long-distance railway stations – Egmore and Central, both in the northern sector of the city and just 1.5km apart. Egmore Station is the arrival point for most trains from Tamil Nadu and Kerala. The booking office at Egmore, up the stairs left of the main entrance handles bookings for both Egmore and Central stations. There is also an efficient tourist reservation counter (Mon–Sat 8am–8pm, Sun 8am–2pm) on the first floor of the Moore Market Complex (next to the main Central station building), which sells tickets for trains from both stations. Both stations have left-luggage offices. The occasional service for southern Tamil Nadu leaves from the suburban Tambaram Station.

BY BUS

Mofussil Bus Stand Buses from all long-distance destinations use the huge Mofussil Bus Stand, inconveniently situated in the suburb of Koyambedu, more than 10km west of the centre. Mofussil is linked to other parts of Chennai by a host of city buses, which depart from the well-organized platforms outside the main terminal: buses #27, #15B, #15F and #17E go to the Egmore/Central area and Parry's Corner; bus #27B also goes on to Triplicane; while buses #70 and #70A link the bus stand with the airport. Note that most buses from Mamallapuram, Puducherry and other towns to the south of Chennai stop at Guindy suburban railway station; taking a train in from there saves time.

Destinations The six platforms at Mofussil are each divided into thirty-odd bays, with frequent services to destinations throughout Tamil Nadu and neighbouring states, including Bengaluru (every 15–30min; 8–11hr); Chengalpattu (every 5–10min; 1hr 30min–2hr); Chidambaram (20 daily; 5–7hr); Coimbatore (every 30min; 11–13hr); Kanchipuram (every 20min; 1hr 30min–2hr); Kanyakumari (10 daily; 16–18hr); Kodaikanal (1 daily; 14–15hr); Kumbakonam (every 30min; 7–8hr); Madurai (every 20–30min; 10hr); Mamallapuram (every 15–30min; 2hr); Puducherry (every 15–30min; 4–5hr); Rameshwaram (3 daily; 14hr); Thanjavur (20 daily; 8hr 30min); Thiruvananthapuram (6 daily; 20hr); Tiruchirapalli (every 15–30min; 8–9hr); Tirupati (every 30min–1hr; 4–5hr); Tiruvannamalai (every 20–30min; 4–5hr); Udhagamandalam (Ooty) (2 daily; 15hr).

BY BOAT

Boats leave Chennai every week/ten days for Port Blair, capital of the Andaman Islands. The first thing you'll need to do is contact the Directorate of Shipping at 17 Rajaji Salai, Jawahar Building, George Town (☎044 2522 6873, ⊛ and .nic.in) to find out when the next sailing is and when tickets go on sale, usually during the week prior to departure. There are no ticket sales on the day of sailing. Permits for up to a month are given on arrival in Port Blair. The Andaman Information Centre Mon–Fri 10am–5.30pm, Sat 10am–1pm; (☎044 2536 0952) is in the Tamil Nadu Tourism Complex, 2 Wallajah Rd, Triplicane. For more details, in the Andaman Islands chapter (see p.933).

GETTING AROUND

Chennai's sights and facilities are spread over such a wide area that it's impossible to get around without using some form of **public transport**. Most visitors jump in auto-rickshaws, but outside rush hours you can travel around comfortably by **bus** or on the suburban **train** (Mass Rapid Transport System). Line 2 of the Chennai metro, which connects with the MRST and runs 22km from Chennai central station to St Thomas Mount, is due to open in 2013. The 32.1km line 1, which will connect Washermanpet in the north of the city to the airport in the south, is scheduled to open in 2014.

By train If you want to travel south from central Chennai to Guindy (Deer Park) or the airport, the easiest way to go is by suburban train (aka the MRST). Services run every 15min (on average) between 4.30am and 11pm, prices are minimal, and they only get overcrowded during rush hours (around 7–9am & 4–6pm). Buy a ticket before boarding. City trains travel between Beach (opposite the GPO), Fort, Park (for Central), Egmore, Nungambakkam,

CHENNAI TOURS

One good way to get around the sights of Chennai is on a TTDC **bus tour**; bookings are taken at their office (see p.960). They're good value, albeit rushed, and the guides can be very helpful. The TTDC **half-day tour** (daily 8am–1pm or 1.30–6.30pm; ₹215 non-a/c, ₹230 a/c) takes in Fort St George, the Government Museum (Birla Planetarium on Fri), the Snake Park, Kapalishvara Temple, and Marina Beach. TTDC also offer good-value **day-trips**, including visits to Mamallapuram, Kanchipuram (daily 6.30am – 7pm; ₹680 non-a/c, ₹750, a/c), and Puducherry (Sat & Sun 6.30am–7pm; ₹680 non-a/c, ₹800 a/c), with meals included in the tariff; check at their office for other itineraries and further details.

Kodambakkam, Mambalam (for T Nagar and silk shops), Saidapet (for Little Mount Church), Guindy, St Thomas Mount and Trisulam (for the airport).

By bus Local bus routes radiate out from the amalgamated Express and Broadway bus stands, between Central train station and George Town. On Anna Salai and other major thoroughfares buses have dedicated stops, but on smaller streets you have to flag them down, or wait with the obvious crowd. Numbers of services to specific places of interest in the city are listed in the relevant accounts, while those to and from the Mofussil Bus Stand are listed in "Arrival and departure" (see p.959).

By rickshaw Auto-rickshaw drivers in Chennai are notorious for demanding high fares from locals and tourists alike. The diversions and one-way systems in place due to the construction of the metro are having a considerable effect on

journey times and hence rickshaw prices. It's worth asking two or three drivers to compare prices and then haggle. If you need to get to the airport or station early in the morning, expect to pay around ₹350. Arrange in advance.

By taxi Chennai's yellow-top Ambassador taxis have meters but drivers often refuse to use them, so prepare yourself for some hard bargaining. At around ₹150 from Central Station to Triplicane, they're practically pricing themselves out of business. For this reason, more reliable and economical radio taxis such as Bharati Call Taxi (☎044 2814 2233) are popular.

By car Private cars (with driver) can be booked at any of the city's upmarket hotels, through TTDC or with one of the numerous private tour agents such as Welcome Tours & Travels, 150 Anna Salai (☎044 2846 0908, ☎allindiatours .com).

INFORMATION

Tourist information The Tamil Nadu Tourism Development Office (Mon–Fri 10am–1.30pm & 2–5.45pm; ☎044 2538 3333, ☎tamilnadutourism.org), 2 Wallajah Rd, Triplicane, houses several other state tourist offices including the office of the Andamans. You can pick up Chennai and Tamil Nadu maps here. There is another branch opposite the Central railway station at 4 EVR Salai (Mon–Fri 10am–1.30pm &

2pm–5.45pm; ☎044 2538 4356). The India Tourism Office 154 Anna Salai (Mon–Fri 9am–6pm; ☎044 2846 0285, ☎incredibleindia.org) provides information, maps and brochures for the whole of India.

Services A useful and centrally located travel agent and exchange facility is Thomas Cook, 45 Montieth Rd, Mon–Sat 10.30am–6pm ☎044 6677 4600.

ACCOMMODATION

Finding an inexpensive **place to stay** in Chennai can sometimes be a problem. With the 24hr check-out system it's difficult to predict availability and some of the cheaper places don't take advance bookings. The good news is that standards in the cheapies are better than in other cities. Most of the mid-range and inexpensive hotels are around the railway station in **Egmore** and further east in **Triplicane**. The bulk of the top hotels are in the south of the city and several offer courtesy buses to and from the airport.

EGMORE

★ **Chandra Park** 9 Gandhi Irwin Rd, opposite the station ☎044 2819 1177, ☎hotelchandrapark.com; map p.955. Clean-cut business hotel with central a/c, foreign exchange, 24hr coffee shop, bar and rooftop restaurant. The spacious, light and well-furnished standard rooms are a very good deal. **₹1500**

Masa 15/1 Kennet Lane ☎044 2819 3344, ☎2819 1261; map p.955. Cleanish, modern building close to the station with good-value rooms (deluxe ₹660; a/c ₹1200), all with attached bathrooms and TV. No advance booking. **₹520**

Marina Inn 55/31 Gandhi Irwin Rd ☎044 2819 2919, ☎marinainn.in; map p.955. Very smart business-style hotel with central a/c a couple of hundred metres to the right as you exit Egmore station. The double rooms, though not big, are tastefully decorated and very clean, with 32" LCD TVs; there's also a multicuisine restaurant and bar. **₹2520**

Pandian 15 Kennet Lane ☎044 2819 1010, ☎hotelpandian.com; map p.955. Very smart two-star hotel with spotless rooms, breakfast included and free wi-fi

for an hour. There are some singles (from ₹850) while doubles with a/c cost ₹1900. **₹1400**

★ **YWCA** 1086 Periyar EVR High Rd ☎044 2532 4234, ☎igh@ywcamadras.org; map p.955. Attractive hotel in quiet gardens behind Egmore Station, with spotless, spacious rooms (a/c ₹1685), safe-deposit and a good restaurant. A highly recommended, safe and friendly place; book in advance. Rates include a buffet breakfast. **₹1225**

ANNA SALAI AND TRIPLICANE

Broadlands 18 Vallaba Agraharam St, Triplicane ☎044 2854 5573, ☎broadlandshotel@yahoo.com; map p.955. Reception is in an old whitewashed house, from which stretches a maze of corridors, outbuildings and courtyards. This is a budget travellers' enclave with character. There's a wide range of rooms and prices, with singles starting from ₹250 and a/c doubles for up to ₹1000, some with private balconies. **₹380**

Cristal 34 CNK Rd, Triplicane ☎044 2851 3011; map p.955. Down a lane off Quaide Milleth Salai (opposite *Hotel Firdouse*) and thus a little quieter, this is as cheap as it gets in Chennai. Rooms are tiled and all have attached showers. The a/c rooms range from ₹650–1000 depending on size and facilities. **₹300**

La Woods 1 Woods Rd ☎ 044 2846 0677, ✉ admin @lawoodshotel.com; map p.955. Good-value mid-range hotel with central a/c. The comfortable and nicely decorated rooms have modern plumbing, lighting and media hub, while Italian marble flooring throughout gives a bright and airy feel. **₹3600**

★ **Paradise** 17/1 Vallaba Agraharam St, Triplicane ☎ 044 2859 4252, ✉ paradisegh@hotmail.com; map p.955. A friendly and dependable hotel, offering inexpensive rooms with attached bathrooms, TVs and a choice of Western or Indian loos. There are two blocks, old and new, right next to each other; rooms (a/c ₹700) in the new block are slightly bigger and cleaner. There's also a large roof terrace, travel facilities and exchange. Good value. **₹400**

Vivanta (By Taj) Binny Rd ☎ 044 6600 0000, ✉ vivantabytaj.com; map p.955. Dating from the Raj era, this whitewashed Art Deco five-star near Anna Salai is a Chennai institution. The large heritage rooms feature Victorian decor, dressing rooms and verandas overlooking the pool; there is also a range of suites from ₹21,600. Plus a

health club, 24hr coffee shop, two excellent restaurants (see p.962) and a bar. **₹13,200**

OUTSIDE THE CENTRE

ITC Park Sheraton & Towers 132 TTK Rd ☎ 044 2499 4101, ✉ itcwelcomgroup.in; map p.953. The last word in American-style executive luxury. There are three excellent restaurants, a 24hr coffee shop, gym and spa. The spacious rooms with plush furnishings make it an excellent choice for business travellers. **₹12500**

New Woodlands 72–75 Dr Radhakrishnan Salai ☎ 044 2811 3111, ✉ newwoodlands.com; map p.953. Sprawling complex of spacious, self-contained apartments called cottages (non-a/c ₹4000; a/c ₹5485) and clean, reasonably sized rooms (deluxe ₹3300) in the main block. There are also two good restaurants, wi-fi and a swimming pool. **₹2300**

Shelter 19–21 Venkatesa Agraharam St, Mylapore ☎ 044 4924 1919, ✉ hotelshelter.com; map p.953. A stone's throw from the Kapalishvara Temple, this sparklingly clean luxury three-star hotel with good restaurants and a bar is better value than most upmarket places. **₹5100**

20

EATING

Amaravathi Corner of Cathedral and TTK roads ☎ 044 2811 7000; map p.953. One of four dependable options in this complex of regional speciality restaurants, south of the downtown area. This one does excellent Andhran food, including particularly tasty biriyanis (from ₹225). Daily noon–4pm & 7–11pm.

Amethyst Next to Corporation Bank, White's Rd ☎ 044 4599 1633; map p.955. Delightful garden café with tables set among ferns and palms along a veranda and in an a/c hall. There are toasted sandwiches (₹200), a range of coffees (₹140), fresh veg and fruit juices (from ₹135) and a three-course à la carte menu (₹800). Expensive, but the greenest place in town. Daily 10am–10pm.

Annalakshmi 1st floor, Sigapi Achi Building (behind Air India office), 18/3 Rukmani Lakshmipathy Rd ☎ 044 2852 5109; map p.955. This beautifully decorated restaurant is a charitable venture run voluntarily by Sivananda devotees, whose profits go to the community. You can choose between set menus with different Ayurvedic properties (₹575/₹1200) or order à la carte (around ₹200/dish). Tues–Sun 11am–3pm & 7–9pm.

Bismillah Biriyani 1 Triplicane High Rd, next door to Taj Sports & Dresses near the junction with Wallajah Rd; map p.955. A tiny *dhaba*, the best of many such places on this road, with just six tables. They serve up tasty chicken in tandoori, kebab and biriyani form. Daily 7–11pm.

★ **Dakshin/Khyber/Residency** ITC Park Sheraton & Towers, 132 TTK Rd ☎ 044 2499 4101; map p.953. The *Dakshin* is one of the country's top south Indian restaurants,

serving a range of unusual dishes, including seafood in marinated spices, Karnataka mutton biriyani and *appam*. Live Carnatic music in the evenings. Book in advance and expect to pay around ₹800 for a meal with starter and drink. The *Khyber* offers meaty poolside barbecues; the *Residency* serves multicuisine. Daily 12.15–3pm & 7.15–11pm.

Don Pepé 1st floor, above Hot Breads, 73 Cathedral Rd ☎ 044 2811 0343; map p.953. Swish a/c Tex-Mex joint, serving a predictable menu of fajitas, enchiladas, tortillas and burritos, plus a selection of average pasta dishes (dubbed "Euro-Mex"). Meat dishes cost in the region of ₹300. Daily 11am–10pm.

Ente Keralam 1 Kasturi Estate, First St Poes Garden, a 10min walk from the Chola Sheraton Hotel ☎ 044 4232 8585; map p.953. Food is served in seven separate rooms at this top-notch Keralan restaurant, giving it a homely feel. Try a backwater speciality, Karimeen fish (₹365–585 depending on size), one of their veggie coconut curries (₹185) or the meat dishes (around ₹330). The lunchtime menu offers sixteen dishes for ₹225. Daily noon–3pm & 7–11pm.

Firdouse 307 Quaide Milleth Salai ☎ 044 4215 7174; map p.955. One of the best local restaurants on this street, with an extensive menu of north and south Indian food: *aloo parathas*, a range of chicken dishes, vegetarian options and biriyanis. It's clean, service is good and there's a separate a/c dining area. Daily 11am–midnight.

Kalyana Bhavan Biriyani 424 Pantheon Rd, Egmore ☏ 044 2819 3111; map p.955. As the name suggests, this is a specialist biriyani place, serving tasty plain (₹65), chicken (₹110) and mutton versions (₹120) on banana leaves, accompanied by aubergine sauce and a semolina sweet. Daily 11am–4pm & 6–9pm.

Raintree 636 Anna Salai ☏ 044 4393 9999; map p.953. The rooftop restaurant, *Up North*, with great city views, a pool and bar, serves traditional Punjabi cuisine and kebabs (veg dishes ₹425, meat dishes ₹525). On the ground floor, the spacious and immaculate *Kitchen* serves superb all-you-can-eat buffets (breakfast, lunch and dinner ₹597/₹956/₹1136). Up North daily 7.30–11pm; Kitchen daily 6.30–9.30am, 12.30–3pm & 7–11pm.

★ **Saravana Bhavan** Thanigai Murugan Rathinavel Hall, 77 Usman Rd, T Nagar ☏ 044 2819 2055; map p.953. This famous south Indian fast-food chain is an institution among the Chennai middle class, with other branches opposite the bus stand in George Town, in Egmore and in the forecourt of the Shanti cinema (at the top of Anna Salai). Try one of their many thalis (from ₹80) and finish with freshly made *ladoo* or *barfi* from their sweets counter. Mains ₹50. Daily 6am–10pm.

Sennthur 154 Anna Salai, opposite Spencer Plaza ☏ 044 6546 8316; map p.955. Large, centrally located "banana-leaf" restaurant very popular with locals. There are two main eating areas, non-a/c at the front and a slightly more expensive a/c hall at the back. "Meals" are served from 11.30am–3.30pm (standard meals ₹60; specials with extra dishes and dessert ₹100); north Indian dishes are ₹70. Daily 7am–11pm.

Vasanta Bhavan 20 Gandhi Irwin Rd ☏ 044 2819 2354; map p.955. Easily the best "meals" joint among many around Egmore Station, with ranks of attentive waiters and delicious pure-veg food – ₹70 for a limited thali and ₹120 unlimited. It's busy, spotlessly clean, and their coffee and sweets are delicious. Daily 6am–10.30pm.

Verandah Vivanta by Taj, Binny Rd ☏ 044 6600 0000; map p.955. Perfect venue for a posh Sun morning breakfast buffet, with fresh coffee served in silver pots. The blow-out lunchtime buffets (Mon–Sat 12.30–3pm; ₹650) are also excellent. Reserve in advance.

DRINKING AND ENTERTAINMENT

While there is plenty of **entertainment** on offer in Chennai, many travellers tend head to down the coast to nearby Mamallapuram or to the Tamil temple towns as soon as possible. Triplicane, one of the main tourist accommodation areas, is almost dry and most of the top night spots are located in the top-end hotels. The annual Carnatic music festival runs from mid-December to mid-January, with the main concerts taking place at the music academy on TTK Rd. You can find details of other classical music and dance performances in the local *What's On* guide.

Dublin Sheraton Park Hotel, 132 TTK Rd, Alwarpet, Chennai ☏ 90251 59067; map p.953. Guest DJs keep the music varied at this loud and popular, three-floor club and there's a good selection of wines, beers and cocktails on offer.

Leather Bar Park Hotel Plot 601, Anna Salai ☏ 90251 78535; map p.953. A favourite of Chennai's young moneyed crowd – especially at weekends – this smart bar gains its name from the black leather furniture throughout. Their wide range of drinks include plenty of cocktails, which you sip al-fresco on the spill-out terrace area.

Paddington Sports Bar 132 Chamiers Rd, Nandanam ☏ 90251 48252; map p.953. Large sports bar complete with billiards room, smart restaurant area and a goalpost shaped bar. They also serve Indian and Chinese food.

QBar Hilton Chennai, 10th Floor, 124/1 Jawaharlal Nehru Salai, Guindy ☏ 90251 83174; map p.953. Poolside rooftop club with a chillout soundtrack provided by the resident DJ. They serve a good selection of beers and wines, cocktails and mocktails.

The northeast

Fazed by the heat and air pollution of Chennai, most visitors escape as fast as they can, heading down the Coromandel coast to India's stone-carving capital, **Mamallapuram**. En route, it's worth stopping at **Dakshina Chitra**, a folk museum 30km south of Chennai, where traditional buildings from across south India have been beautifully reconstructed. Further inland, **Kanchipuram** is an important pilgrimage and silk-sari-weaving town from where you can loop southwest to the atmospheric temple town of **Tiruvannamalai**, situated at the base of the sacred mountain, Arunachala. Along the coast, you can breakfast on croissants and espresso coffee in the former French colony of **Puducherry**. A short way north, **Auroville**, the Utopian settlement founded by followers of the Sri Aurobindo Ghose's spiritual successor, The Mother, provides a New Age haven for soul-searching Westerners and an economy for the local population.

Mamallapuram and around

Scattered around the base of a colossal mound of boulders 58km south of Chennai is the small seaside town and UNESCO World Heritage Site of **MAMALLAPURAM** (formerly Mahabalipuram). From dawn till dusk, the rhythms of chisels chipping granite resound down its sandy lanes – evidence of a stone-carving tradition that has endured since this was a major port of the Pallava dynasty, between the fifth and ninth centuries. It is only possible to speculate about the purpose of much of the boulder sculpture, but it appears that the friezes and shrines were not made for worship at all, but rather as showcases for the talents of local artists. Due in no small part to the maritime activities of the Pallavas, their style of art and architecture had wide-ranging influence, spreading from south India as far north as Ellora, as well as to Southeast Asia.

Mamallapuram's monuments divide into four categories: open-air **bas-reliefs**, structured **temples**, man-made **caves** and **rathas** ("chariots" carved in situ from single

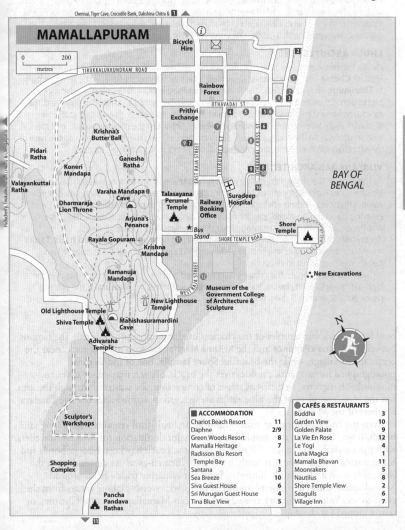

MAMALLAPURAM

Chennai, Tiger Cave, Crocodile Bank, Dakshina Chitra & **1**

0 — 200 metres

TIRUKKALUKKUNDRAM ROAD

Bicycle Hire

Rainbow Forex

OTHAVADAI ST

Prithvi Exchange

Krishna's Butter Ball

Pidari Ratha

Koneri Mandapa

Ganesha Ratha

Valayankuttai Ratha

Varaha Mandapa II Cave

Dharmaraja Lion Throne

Arjuna's Penance

Rayala Gopuram

Ramanuja Mandapa

Krishna Mandapa

Talasayana Perumal Temple

Railway Booking Office

Suradeep Hospital

Bus Stand

SHORE TEMPLE ROAD

Shore Temple

BAY OF BENGAL

New Excavations

Museum of the Government College of Architecture & Sculpture

New Lighthouse Temple

Old Lighthouse Temple

Shiva Temple

Mahishasuramardini Cave

Adivaraha Temple

Sculptor's Workshops

Shopping Complex

Pancha Pandava Rathas

EAST RAJA STREET

WEST RAJA STREET

THIRUKULA ST

OTHAVADAI CROSS ST

20

■ ACCOMMODATION	
Chariot Beach Resort	11
Daphne	2/9
Green Woods Resort	8
Mamalla Heritage	7
Radisson Blu Resort Temple Bay	1
Santana	3
Sea Breeze	10
Siva Guest House	6
Sri Murugan Guest House	4
Tina Blue View	5

● CAFÉS & RESTAURANTS	
Buddha	3
Garden View	10
Golden Palate	9
La Vie En Rose	12
Le Yogi	4
Luna Magica	1
Mamalla Bhavan	11
Moonrakers	5
Nautilus	8
Shore Temple View	2
Seagulls	6
Village Inn	7

THE TEMPLES OF TAMIL NADU

No Indian state is more dominated by its **temples** than Tamil Nadu, where temple architecture catalogues the tastes of successive dynasties and testifies to the centrality of religion in everyday life. Most temples are built in honour of Shiva, Vishnu and their consorts; all are characterized not only by their design and sculptures, but also by constant activity: devotion, dancing, singing, pujas, festivals and feasts. Each is tended by brahmin priests, recognizable by their *dhotis* (loincloths), a sacred thread draped over the right shoulder, and marks on the forehead. One to three horizontal (usually white) lines distinguish Shaivites; vertical lines (yellow or red), often converging into a near-V shape, are common among Vaishnavites.

DRAVIDA ARCHITECTURE

Dravida, the temple architecture of Tamil Nadu, first took form in the Pallava port of **Mamallapuram**. A step-up from the cave retreats of Hindu and Jain ascetics, the earliest Pallava monuments were **mandapas**, shrines cut into rock faces and fronted by columns. This sculptural skill was transferred to freestanding temples, **rathas**, carved out of single rocks and incorporating the essential elements of Hindu temples: the dim inner sanctuary, the *garbhagriha*, capped with a modest tapering spire featuring repetitive architectural motifs.

CHOLA ARCHITECTURE

Pallava themes were developed in Karnataka by the Chalukyas and Rashtrakutas, but it was the Shaivite **Cholas** who spearheaded Tamil Nadu's next architectural phase, in the tenth century. In **Thanjavur**, Rajaraja I created the Brihadeshvara Temple principally as a status symbol; its proportions far exceed any attempted by the Pallavas. Set within a vast walled courtyard, the sanctuary, fronted by a small *mandapa*, stands beneath a sculpted *vimana* that soars more than 60m high. Most sculptures once again feature Shiva, but the *gopuras* each side of the eastern gateway to the courtyard were an innovation, as were the lions carved into the base of the sanctuary walls, and the pavilion erected over Nandi in front of the sanctuary.

VIJAYANAGAR ARCHITECTURE

By the time of the thirteenth-century **Vijayanagar** kings, the temple was central to city life, the focus for civic meetings, education, dance and theatre. The Vijayanagars extended earlier structures, adding enclosing walls around a series of **prakaras**, or courtyards, and erecting freestanding *mandapas* for use as meeting halls, elephant stables, stages for music and dance, and ceremonial marriage halls (*kalyan mandapas*). Raised on superbly decorated columns, these *mandapas* became known as **thousand-pillared halls**. **Tanks** were added, doubling as water stores and washing areas, and used for festivals when deities were set afloat in boats.

Under the Vijayanagars, the *gopuras* were enlarged and set at the cardinal points over the high gateways to each *prakara*, to become the dominant feature. **Madurai** is the place to check out Vijayanagar architecture.

boulders to resemble temples or the chariots used in temple processions). The famous bas-reliefs, **Arjuna's Penance** and the **Krishna Mandapa**, adorn massive rocks near the centre of the village, while the beautiful **Shore Temple**, one of India's most photographed monuments, presides over the beach. Sixteen man-made caves and monolithic structures, in different stages of completion, are scattered through the area, but the most complete of the nine *rathas* are in a group, named after the five Pandava brothers of the Mahabharata.

Given the co-existence of so many stunning archeological remains with a long sandy **beach**, it was inevitable this would become a major destination for Western travellers, with the inevitable presence of Kashmiri emporia, beach hawkers, budget hotels and fish restaurants – and more recently hordes of Chennai-escapees descending at the weekends as well. The sandy hinterland and flat estuarine paddy fields around Mamallapuram also harbour a handful of sights well worth making forays from the coast to see. You can take any coastal bus between Mamallapuram and Chennai, or rent a moped for the day.

The Shore Temple

Daily 6am–6pm (ticket office closes 5.30pm) • ₹250 (₹10), includes Pancha Pandava *rathas* if visited on the same day

With its unforgettable silhouette, visible for kilometres along the beach, Mamallapuram's **Shore Temple** dates from the early eighth century and is considered to be the earliest stone-built temple in south India. Today, due to the combined forces of wind, salt and sand, much of the detailed carving has eroded, giving the whole temple a soft, rounded appearance.

The taller of the towers is raised above a cell that faces out to sea – don't be surprised to see mischievous monkeys crouching inside. Approached from the west through two low-walled enclosures lined with small Nandi (bull) figures, the temple comprises two lingam shrines (one facing east, the other west), and a third shrine between them housing an image of the reclining Vishnu. Recent excavations, revealing a tank containing a structured stone column thought to have been a lantern, and a large Varaha (boar incarnation of Vishnu) aligned with the Vishnu shrine, suggest that the area was sacred long before the Pallavas chose it as a temple site.

The Krishna Mandapa

A little to the west of the village centre, off Shore Temple Road, the enormous bas-relief known as the **Krishna Mandapa** shows Krishna raising Mount Govardhana aloft in one hand. The sculptor's original intention must have been for the rock above Krishna to represent the mountain, but the seventeenth-century Vijayanagar addition of a columned *mandapa*, or entrance hall, prevents a clear view of the carving. Krishna is also depicted seated milking a cow, and standing playing the flute. Other figures are *gopas* and *gopis*, the cowboys and girls of his pastoral youth.

Arjuna's Penance

Another bas-relief, **Arjuna's Penance** (also referred to as the "Descent of the Ganges") is a few metres north, opposite the modern Talasayana Perumal Temple. The surface of this rock erupts with detailed carving, most notably endearing and naturalistic renditions of animals. On the left-hand side, Arjuna, one of the Pandava brothers and a consummate archer, is shown standing on one leg. He is looking at the midday sun through a prism formed by his hands, meditating on Shiva, who is represented by a nearby statue fashioned by Arjuna himself. The Shiva Purana tells that Arjuna made the journey to a forest on the banks of the Ganges to do penance, in the hope that Shiva would part with his favourite weapon, the *pashupatashastra*, a magic staff or arrow. Shiva eventually materialized in the guise of Kirata, a wild forest-dweller, and picked a fight with Arjuna over a boar they both claimed to have shot. Arjuna only realized he was dealing with the deity after his attempts to drub the wild man proved futile; narrowly escaping death at the playful hand of Shiva, he was finally rewarded with the weapon. To the right of Arjuna, a natural cleft represents the **Ganges**, complete with *nagas* – water spirits in the form of cobras. You may well see sudden movements among the carved animals: lazing goats often join the permanent features.

Ganesha Ratha

Just north of Arjuna's Penance a path leads west to a single monolith, the **Ganesha Ratha**. Its image of Ganesh dates from this century; some say it was installed at the instigation of England's King George V. The sculpture at one end, of a protecting demon with a tricorn headdress, is reminiscent of the Indus Valley Civilization's 4000-year-old horned figure known as the "proto-Shiva".

Varaha cave

Behind Arjuna's Penance, southwest of the Ganesha *ratha*, is the **Varaha Mandapa II Cave**, whose entrance hall has two pillars with horned lion-bases and a cell flanked by two *dvarpalas*, or guardians. One of four **panels** shows the boar-incarnation of Vishnu, who

20

stands with one foot resting on the *naga* snake-king as he lifts a diminutive Prithvi – the earth – from the primordial ocean. Another is of Gajalakshmi, the goddess Lakshmi seated on a lotus being bathed by a pair of elephants. Trivikrama, the dwarf brahmin who becomes huge and bestrides the world in three steps to defeat the demon king Bali, is shown in another panel, and finally a four-armed Durga is depicted in another.

Krishna's Butter Ball

A little way north of Arjuna's Penance, precipitously balanced on the top of a ridge, is a massive, natural, almost spherical boulder called **Krishna's Butter Ball**. Picnickers and goats often rest in its perilous-looking shade.

The lighthouses

South of Arjuna's Penance at the highest point in an area of steep paths, unfinished temples, ruins, scampering monkeys and massive rocks, the **New Lighthouse** affords fine views east to the Shore Temple, and west across paddy fields and flat lands littered with rocks. Next to it, the **Olakanesvara** ("flame-eyed" Shiva), or **Old Lighthouse Temple**, used as a lighthouse until the early twentieth century, dates from the Rajasimha period (674–800 AD).

Mahishasuramardini Cave

Nestling between the two lighthouses is the **Mahishasuramardini Cave**, whose central image portrays Shiva and Parvati with the child Murugan seated on Parvati's lap. Shiva's right foot rests on the back of the bull Nandi, and Parvati sits casually, leaning on her left hand. On the left wall, beyond an empty cell, a panel depicts Vishnu reclining on the serpent, his attitude of repose contrasted with the weapon-brandishing demons, Madhu and Kaithaba. Other figures seek Vishnu's permission to chase them. Opposite, an intricately carved panel shows the eight-armed goddess Durga as Mahishasuramardini, the "crusher" of the buffalo demon Mahishasura. The panel shows Durga riding a lion, in the midst of the struggle. Accompanied by dwarf *ganas*, she wields a bow and other weapons; Mahishasura, equipped with a club, can be seen to the right, in flight with fellow demons.

Government Museum of Architecture and Sculpture

West Raja St • Mon–Sat 9am–1pm & 2–5pm • ₹10

The tiny **Government Museum of Architecture and Sculpture** near the lighthouse, has a rather motley collection of unlabelled Pallava sculpture found in and around Mamallapuram.

Pancha Pandava Rathas (Five Rathas)

Daily 6am–6pm (ticket office closes 5.30pm) • ₹250 (₹10) including the Shore Temple on the same day

In a sandy compound 1.5km south of the village centre stands the stunning group of monoliths known as the **Pancha Pandava Rathas**, the five chariots of the Pandavas. Dating from the period of Narasimhavarman I (c.630–670 AD), they consist of five separate freestanding sculptures that imitate structured temples plus some beautifully carved life-sized animals.

The "architecture" of the *rathas* reflects a variety of styles and stands almost as a model for much subsequent development in the southern style. Carving was always executed from top to bottom, enabling the artists to work on the upper parts with no fear of damaging anything below. Intriguingly, it's thought that the *rathas* were never used for worship.

The southernmost and tallest of the *rathas*, named after the eldest of the Pandavas, is the pyramidal **Dharmaraja**. Set on a square base, the upper part comprises a series of diminishing storeys, each with a row of pavilions. Four corner blocks, each with two panels and standing figures, are broken up by two pillars and pilasters supported by squatting lions. Figures on the panels include Ardhanarishvara (Shiva and female consort in one figure), Brahma, the king Narasimhavarman I and Harihara (Shiva and Vishnu combined). The central tier includes sculptures of Shiva Gangadhara and one of the earliest representations in Tamil Nadu of the dancing Shiva, Nataraja, who became all-important in the region. Alongside, the **Bhima** *ratha*, the largest of the group, is the least complete. Devoid of carved figures, the upper storeys, like in the Dharmaraja, feature false windows and repeated pavilion-shaped ornamentation.

The Arjuna and Draupadi *rathas* share a base. Behind the **Arjuna**, the most complete of the entire group and very similar to the Dharmaraja, stands a superb unfinished sculpture of Shiva's bull Nandi. **Draupadi** is unique in terms of rock-cut architecture, with a roof that appears to be based on a straw-thatched hut. There's an image of Durga inside, but the figure of her lion vehicle outside is aligned side-on and not facing the image, suggesting this was not a real temple. To the west, close to a life-sized carving of an elephant, stands the *ratha* named after the twin brothers **Nakula and Sahadeva**.

Tiger Cave

Main highway, 4km north of Mamallapuram • Daily sunrise–sunset • Free

Set amid trees close to the sea, the extraordinary **Tiger Cave** contains a shrine to Durga, approached by a flight of steps that passes two subsidiary cells. Following the line of an irregularly shaped rock, the cave is remarkable for its elaborate exterior, which features multiple lion-heads surrounding the entrance to the main cell. If you sit for long enough, the section on the left with seated figures in niches above two elephants begins to resemble an enormous owl.

Crocodile Bank

14km north of town on the road to Chennai • Tues–Sun 8am–6pm • ₹35, camera ₹20, video camera ₹100 • ⓦ madrascrocodilebank.org

The **Crocodile Bank** at Vadanemmeli was set up in 1976 by the American zoologist Romulus Whittaker to protect and breed indigenous crocodiles. The Bank has been so successful (from fifteen crocs to five thousand in the first fifteen years) that its remit now extends to saving endangered species, such as turtles and lizards, from around the world.

Low-walled enclosures in its garden compound house hundreds of inscrutable crocodiles, soaking in ponds or sunning themselves on the banks. Breeds include the fish-eating, knobbly-nosed gharial, and the world's largest species, the saltwater *Crocodylus porosus*, which can grow to 8m in length. You can watch feeding time at about 4.30pm on Monday or Thursday or have your own brief feeding session any time for a fee of ₹20. The temptation to take photos is tempered by the sight of those hungry saurians clambering over each other to snap up the chopped flesh, within centimetres of the top of the wall.

Another important field of work is conducted with the collaboration of local Irula people, whose traditional expertise is with snakes. Cobras are brought to the bank for **venom collection**, to be used in the treatment of snakebites. Elsewhere, snakes are repeatedly "milked" until they die, but here only a limited amount is taken from each snake, enabling them to return to the wild. To visit this section costs an extra ₹5.

Dakshina Chitra

Main Coast Rd • Daily except Tues 10am–6pm • ₹200 (₹75) • ⓦ dakshinachitra.net

Occupying a patch of sand dunes midway between Chennai and Mamallapuram, **Dakshina Chitra**, literally "Vision of the South", is one of India's best-conceived folk museums, devoted to the rich architectural and artistic heritage of Kerala, Karnataka, Andhra Pradesh and Tamil Nadu. Set up by the Chennai Craft Foundation, the museum exposes visitors to many disappearing traditions of the region, which you might otherwise not be aware of, from tribal fertility cults and Ayyannar field deities to pottery and leather shadow puppets.

20

A selection of traditional buildings from across peninsular India has been painstakingly reconstructed using original materials. Exhibitions attached to them convey the environmental and cultural diversity of the south, most graphically expressed in a wonderful textile collection featuring antique silk and cotton saris from various castes and regions. Snacks are available on site.

ARRIVAL AND DEPARTURE

By train The nearest railway station is in Chengalpattu, 29km to the northeast for mainline trains to Chennai, Tiruchirapalli and beyond. There are frequent bus connections from Chengalpattu to Mamallapuram (see below).

By bus The bus stand is in the centre of the village next to Perumal Temple. Two main routes connect Chennai and Mamallapuram – the East Coast Rd and the Old Mamallapuram Rd – with 32 buses daily starting from 4.15am. There are 32 services daily from Mamallapuram to Chennai (4.15am–9pm), 12 daily to Kanchipuram and

MAMALLAPURAM AND AROUND

regular services to Chengalpattu (change for Tiruvannamalai). Puducherry buses (from Chennai) run every 20min but don't come in to Mamallapuram – you need to either walk the 1.5km westwards to the East Coast Rd (or take an auto-rickshaw; ₹50), and flag down a bus at the bus stop.

By taxi Taxis to and from the centre of Chennai cost around ₹1300 or ₹1100 to and from the airport. Puducherry is a ₹1600 ride. Mamallapuram suffers badly from aggressive touting by a small number of hotels; ignore the touts and walk to your chosen destination – it's a small place.

GETTING AROUND AND INFORMATION

Bike and motorbike rental By far the best way to get to the important sites is by bicycle. You can rent bikes from shops on East Raja St for ₹10/hr or ₹50/day. Scooters and Enfield motorcycles can also be rented for around ₹300/day, from Poornima Travels, next to *Moonrakers* restaurant. You can also

check at your guesthouse.

Tourist information The Government of Tamil Nadu Tourist Office (Mon–Fri 10am–1pm & 2–5.45pm; ☎044 2744 2232) is one of the first buildings you see in the village, on your left as you arrive from Chennai.

ACCOMMODATION

Chariot Beach Resort 69 Five Rathas Rd ☎044 2498 6364, ⬢chariotbeachresorts.com. A luxurious resort at the southern end of town with massive garden area, unobstructed sea views and a 57m swimming pool. All rooms are spacious and beautifully furnished, and there's also the option of luxurious cottages (₹17,400) and sea-facing suites (₹19,200). ₹**12,600**

Daphne Fishermens Colony (reception at Daphne's Hotel Othavadai, Cross St); no phone bookings. The very last guesthouse on the beach strip with just nine rooms on three floors, a roof terrace and sea views. ₹**800**

★ **Green Woods Resort** 12 Othavadai Cross St ☎044 2744 3318, ⬢greenwoods_resort@yahoo.com. Very friendly and extremely good-value family-run place, set round a beautifully kept courtyard garden. There's a wide range of very clean rooms (the best a/c rooms cost just ₹1400), some with swing chairs, private balconies, terraces and TVs, plus excellent Ayurvedic massage on site and a nice restaurant (see opposite). ₹**350**

Mamalla Heritage 104 East Raja St ☎044 2744 2060, ⬢hotelmamallaheritage.com. Efficient and modern hotel on the main road through the village with comfortable and spotless a/c rooms overlooking a courtyard. There's a choice of standard and slightly bigger deluxe (₹3120) rooms, all with fridge and TV, and there are two very good restaurants on site (see opposite). ₹**2880**

Radisson Blu Resort Temple Bay 1km north of town, 57 Kovalam Rd ☎044 2744 3636, ⬢radissonblu .com. A luxurious resort with a swimming pool and excellent restaurant, which backs right on to the beach. There are eight different categories of room, from standard doubles to sea-view villas with jacuzzis and sit-out areas (₹23,490). ₹**13,800**

Santana 178 Othavadai St ☎94442 90832. Six sizeable and spotless first-floor rooms (a/c ₹1300); the seafront one is a gem, sandwiched in between their popular ground-floor beachside restaurant and roof terrace. They also offer a travel service. ₹**800**

★ **Sea Breeze** Othavadai Cross St ☎044 2744 3035, ⬢seabreezehotel.com. The only bona fide beach resort within the village, featuring a range of rooms and prices according to size and view – the large sea view rooms with private balcony and king size beds are the best. The swimming pool is open to non-residents (₹400/day) and there's an Ayurveda centre. ₹**1440**

Siva Guest House 2 Othavadai Cross St ☎044 2744 3534, ⬢sivaguesthouse.com. A small but clean and tidy lodge with just fifteen rooms, which are spread over three floors. Mandala-patterned bedsheets add flavour and there is a choice of non-a/c and a/c rooms (₹1300). Good value. ₹**600**

Sri Murugan Guest House 42 Othavadai St ☎044 2744 2662, ⬢srimuruganguesthouse.com. Bigger than many of the surrounding hotels, with 25 rooms (including some singles for ₹450 and a/c rooms for ₹1300), but retaining a peaceful vibe. Service is courteous and there's a breezy rooftop restaurant. ₹900

Tina Blue View 48 Othavadai St ☎044 2744 2319. Established family guesthouse with simple turquoise and whitewashed rooms, some in the main block and others in an annexe in their pleasant garden. All rooms have attached bathrooms and mosquito nets. There are also some single rooms (₹300) and the popular *Seagulls* rooftop restaurant (see below). ₹500

EATING AND DRINKING

Mamallapuram is crammed with small restaurants specializing in **seafood** – tiger prawns, pomfret, tuna, shark and lobster – usually served marinated and grilled with chips and salad; always establish in advance exactly how much it will cost. As this is a travellers' hangout, there are also numerous places offering the usual array of pasta, pancakes and bland Indian dishes. **Beer** is widely available, but it's pricey (₹150–200). If you want to enjoy real Indian food, head to the *dhabas* by the bus stand and the banana-leaf places on East Raja St.

Buddha 46 Othavadai St ☎97890 70754. Yellow walls adorned with Buddhas and the leafy outlook create a pleasant ambience. The usual travellers' breakfasts are available (omelette, toast and muesli), plus noodles and sizzlers during the day and seafood in the evening. There's also an unexpected range of cocktails at ₹180. Daily 7am–11pm.

Garden View Green Woods Resort, 12 Othavadai Cross St ☎044 2744 3318. Friendly first-floor terrace restaurant, which serves superb vegetable biriyanis, seafood (₹130–190), curries spiced as requested (around ₹80) and the usual pancakes and the like. There's a choice of views – the relaxed garden or busier street. Daily 8am–10pm.

★ **Golden Palate** Mamalla Heritage Hotel, 104 East Raja St ☎044 2744 2060. Blissfully cool café with a/c and tinted windows, serving the best veg food in the village: ₹130 "meals" at lunchtime (noon–3pm), north Indian tandoori in the courtyard in the evenings and wonderful ice cream sundaes. The equally popular rooftop *Waves* restaurant serves chicken (₹240) and grilled fish (₹320). Golden Palate daily 7am–10.30pm; Waves daily noon–4pm & 7–11pm.

Luna Magica Bajanai Kovil St, Fisherman Colony ☎98401 00519. Beach restaurant serving top-notch seafood, kept alive in a tank and sold by weight. They specialize in tiger prawns and lobster in a choice of tasty sauces such as tomato or garlic butter and also offer fish curry, grilled fish and tuna steak. Red wine and cold beer are available but expensive. Daily 7.30am–10pm.

Mamalla Bhavan Shore Temple Rd, opposite the bus stand. A very popular pure-veg and "meals" joint that's invariably packed. At ₹60, their unlimited lunchtime "meals" (11.30am–3.30pm) are a bargain, and they also serve good south Indian breakfasts including *pongal*, masala dosas and coffee. Daily 6.30am–9.30pm.

Moonrakers 34 Othavadai St ☎044 2744 2115. Cool jazz and blues sounds, great fresh seafood and slick service ensure this place, with its three floors, is often packed with travellers. The owners are constantly touting passers-by for custom. Good seafood platter (fish, prawns, calamari) for ₹450. Daily 11.30am–11.30pm.

Nautilus Othavadai Cross St. Popular café/restaurant run by a French chef. The menu features soups, a wide range of French salads (₹80–110), ratatouille (₹130), seafood, beef and the usual travellers' favourites at reasonable prices. Daily 6am–11pm.

Shore Temple View Santana, 178 Othavadai St ☎94442 90832. Two restaurants (ground floor and rooftop) in the same beachfront building serving lobster per kilo, fish dishes (₹200) and seafood platters with rice and salad (₹500). The rooftop has a pleasant breeze. Daily 6.30am–11pm.

Seagulls Tina Blue Hotel, 48 Othavadai St ☎044 2744 2319. A large and pleasant rooftop restaurant serving a decent, extensive seafood menu including tuna steak with chips and salad, seafood platters (around ₹400), fish and prawn curries (₹190–230), veggie dishes (₹110) and chicken (from ₹160). Proceeds go to a local orphanage. Daily 7am–11pm.

La Vie En Rose West Raja St ☎94448 77544. Peaceful garden restaurant with pleasant views across the local temple tank. Offers a Western-oriented menu including a few salads, soups, chicken, prawn and fish dishes for around ₹150 and some veggie dishes (₹90). Daily 11am–11pm.

Village Inn Thirukulam St, off Othavadai St ☎94441 16406. A small, pleasant restaurant with cane furniture and classical Indian music, serving up grilled seafood, good fish curry (₹150) and veggie dishes (₹80). One of the cheaper places for beer. Daily 9am–10.30pm.

Le Yogi 19 Othavadai St ☎98407 60340. Run by a French/Indian couple, this relaxed place is a good spot to chill. They serve French crêpes (₹70–95), a range of salads with brown sesame bread (₹120–140), pasta dishes (₹140) and good coffee and lassis. Daily 8am–11pm.

DIRECTORY

Banks and exchange There are many places to change money, two of the best are Prithvi Exchange 12/23 East Raja St (daily 9.30am–7pm; ☎044 2744 3265), and The Rainbow Forex, 14 Othavadai St (daily 9.30am–9pm; ☎044 2744 2442).

Bookshops There are a few secondhand bookshops in town

20

including Apollo Books, 150/1 Fisherman Colony (daily 9am–10pm; ☎ 044 2744 2992), which has a good selection of new and secondhand books in several languages.

Hospital If you need medical treatment, Suradeep Hospital 15, Thirukulam St (☎ 044 2744 2335) is highly recommended.

Internet There are many internet places, including Lakshmi Cottage, 5 Othavadai Cross St (☎ 044 2744 2463;

₹40/hr and the Hi Tech Net Centre) 21 Othavadai St (☎ 044 2744 2494; ₹30/hr). If you want to Skype, check prices beforehand.

Travel agents Delhi-based Hi! Tours at 125 East Raja St (☎ 044 2744 3260, ⊕ hi-tours.com) offer car rental, ticketing and other services; Travels Partners (☎ 98403 77033, ✉ travelspartners@gmail.com) on Othavadai St provide friendly service.

Kanchipuram

KANCHIPURAM is situated on the Vegavathi River 70km southwest of Chennai. Ask any Tamil what Kanchipuram (aka "Kanchi") is famous for, and they'll probably say silk saris, shrines and saints – in that order. A dynastic capital throughout the medieval era, it remains one of the country's seven holiest cities, sacred to both Shaivites and Vaishnavites, and among the few surviving centres of goddess worship in the south. Year round, pilgrims pour through for a quick puja stop on the Tirupati tour circuit and, if they can afford it, a spot of shopping in the sari emporia. For non-Hindu visitors, however, Kanchipuram holds less appeal. Although the temples are undeniably impressive, the town itself is unremittingly hot, with only basic accommodation and amenities. Some people prefer to visit Kanchipuram as a **day-trip** from Chennai or Mamallapuram, both of which are a two-hour bus ride away.

Established by the **Pallava** kings in the fourth century AD, Kanchipuram served as their **capital** for five hundred years, and continued to flourish throughout the Chola,

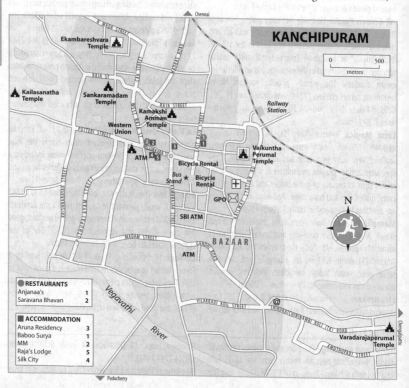

KANCHIPURAM

0   500
metres

Chennai

Ekambareshvara Temple

Kailasanatha Temple

Sankaramadam Temple

RAJA ST

RAJA STREET

Kamakshi Amman Temple

Western Union

PUTTERI STREET

Railway Station

Vaikuntha Perumal Temple

ATM

Bicycle Rental

Bus Stand   Bicycle Rental

GPO

SBI ATM

MADAM STREET

BAZAAR

ATM

N

Vegavathi River

VILAKKADI KOIL STREET

THIRUKATCHININAMBI KOIL (TK) ROAD

Varadarajaperumal Temple

AMUTHUPADI STREET

Chengalpattu

● RESTAURANTS
Anjanaa's	1
Saravana Bhavan	2

■ ACCOMMODATION
Aruna Residency	3
Baboo Surya	1
MM	2
Raja's Lodge	5
Silk City	4

Puducherry

20

Pandya and Vijayanagar eras. Under the Pallavas, it was an important scholastic forum, and a meeting point for Jain, Buddhist and Hindu cultures. Its **temples** dramatically reflect this enduring political prominence, spanning the years from the peak of Pallava construction to the seventeenth century, when the ornamentation of the *gopuras* and pillared halls was at its most elaborate. You might need to be a little firm to resist the attentions of pushy puja-wallahs, who try to con foreigners into overpriced ceremonies. If you've come for silk, head for the shops that line Gandhi and Thirukatchininambi roads.

Ekambareshvara Temple

North Mada St • Daily; closed noon–4pm • Camera ₹20, video ₹100

On the north side of town, Kanchipuram's largest temple and most important Shiva shrine, the **Ekambareshvara Temple** – also known as Ekambaranatha – is easily identified by its colossal whitewashed *gopuras*, which rise to almost 60m. The main temple contains some Pallava work, but was mostly constructed in the sixteenth and seventeenth centuries, and stands within a vast walled enclosure beside some smaller shrines and a large fish-filled water tank.

The entrance is through a high-arched passageway beneath an elaborate *gopura* in the south wall which leads to an open courtyard and a majestic "thousand-pillared hall", or *kalyan mandapa*. This faces the tank in the north and the sanctuary in the west that protects the emblem of Shiva (here in his form as **Kameshvara**, Lord of Desire), Prithvi lingam (one of five lingams in Tamil Nadu that represent the elements, in this case *Prithvi*, the earth). Behind the sanctum, accessible from the covered hallway around it, an eerie bare hall lies beneath a profusely carved *gopura*, and in the courtyard a venerable **mango tree** represents the tree under which Shiva and Kamakshi were married. This union is celebrated during a festival each April, when many couples are married in the *kalyan mandapa*.

Sankaramadam

Raja St • Daily; closed noon–4pm

Kanchipuram is the seat of a line of holy men bearing the title **acharya**, whose line dates back perhaps as far as 1300 BC to the saint Adi Sankaracharya. The 68th acharya, the highly revered Sri Chandrasekharendra Sarasvati Swami, died in January 1994 at the age of 101. Buried in the sitting position, as is the custom for great Hindu sages, his mortal remains are enshrined in a *samadhi* at the **Sankaramadam**, a *math* (monastery for Hindu renouncers) down the road from the Ekambareshvara Temple. Lined with old photographs from the life of the former swami, with young brahmin students chanting Sanskrit verses in the background, it's a typically Tamil blend of simple sanctity and garish modern glitz. The *math*'s two huge elephants are available to bestow blessings upon visiting pilgrims for a small fee.

Kailasanatha Temple

Western outskirts • Daily; closed noon–4pm

The **Kailasanatha Temple**, the oldest structure in Kanchipuram and the finest example of Pallava architecture in south India, is situated among several low-roofed houses just over 1km west of the town centre. Built by the Pallava king Rajasimha early in the eighth century, its intimate size and simple carving distinguish it from the town's later temples. Usually quieter than its neighbours, the shrine becomes the focus of vigorous celebrations during the **Mahashivratri festival** each March. Like its contemporary, the Shore Temple at Mamallapuram, it is built of soft sandstone, but its sheltered position has spared it from wind and sand erosion, and it remains remarkably intact, despite some rather clumsy renovation work.

Kamakshi Amman Temple

Raja St • Daily; closed noon–4pm

Built during Pallava supremacy and modified in the fourteenth and seventeenth centuries, the **Kamakshi Amman Temple**, north of the bus stand, combines several styles, with an ancient central shrine, gates from the Vijayanagar period, and high, heavily sculpted, creamy *gopuras* set above the gateways.

This is one of India's three holiest shrines to Shakti, Shiva's cosmic energy depicted in female form, usually as his consort. The goddess Kamakshi, a local form of Parvati, shown with a sugar-cane bow and arrows of flowers, is honoured for having lured Shiva to Kanchipuram, where they were married, and thus having forged the connection between the local community and the god. In February or March, deities are wheeled to the temple in huge wooden "cars", decked with robed statues and swaying plantain leaves.

ARRIVAL AND DEPARTURE

KANCHIPURAM

By train The railway station in the northeast of town sees twelve daily passenger services from Chengalpattu (originating in Chennai, Arakkonam, Tirupathi and Puducherry) and two express trains (the weekly *Mumbai–Madurai Express* and bi-weekly *Mumbai–Nagercoil Express*).

By bus Buses from Chennai, Mamallapuram and

Chengalpattu stop at the stand in the town centre just off Kosa St.

Destinations Chennai (every 10min; 1hr 30min–2hr); Madurai (3 daily; 8hr); Puducherry (10 daily; 3–4hr); Salem (11 daily; 8hr), change for Coimbatore; Tiruchirapalli (12 daily; 8hr); Tiruvannamalai (9 daily; 3–4hr).

GETTING AROUND AND INFORMATION

By bike The best way to get around Kanchi is by bicycle. Most of the main roads are fairly wide and traffic just about manageable. Bikes are available (₹7/hr) from stalls at both the west and northeast entrances to the bus stand.

Services There are many ATMs along Kamarajar St and

Nellukara St, including the SBI ATM just along from Silk City, but the nearest official foreign exchange places are in Chennai and Mamallapuram. There is a Western Union on West Raja St, and several internet places along Kamarajar St.

ACCOMMODATION AND EATING

Anjanaa's Baboo Soorya, 85 East Raja St ☎044 2722 2555. An excellent Chettinad restaurant on the ground floor of the hotel, serving a range of veggie/prawn biriyanis (₹100–160), a few veggie dishes (₹120) and fiery chicken, mutton and fish cooked Chettinad style for ₹160. Across the reception is their large and busy a/c bar serving cold beers for ₹200. Daily 10.30am–3.30pm & 6.30–10.30pm.

Aruna Residency 15 Ulakalanthar Maada St, tucked away 50m down from the main junction ☎044 2722 4274. A large, quiet mid-range place that offers very good deals on single occupancy rooms. The double rooms (a/c ₹1350), complete with TV, are a good size, light and airy. ₹1100

Baboo Soorya 85 East Raja St ☎044 2722 2555, ⓦhotelbaboosoorya.com. The smartest place in town and set back from the noise of the main road in its own grounds. The 38 rooms (a/c ₹1800) are well kept and represent good value. There's also a restaurant and a/c bar. It's a good idea to book in advance. ₹1500

MM 65/66 Nellukkara St ☎044 2722 7250, ⓦmmhotels.com. Large, clean, medium-priced hotel, situated right in the heart of the town. The wood-panelled

a/c rooms (₹1800) have armchairs but are a little on the small side; the non-a/c rooms are plainer but slightly bigger. ₹1260

Raja's Lodge 20-B Nellukkara St ☎044 2722 2603. One of the best budget options in town with friendly staff, but the rooms are a little on the small side and somewhat dingy. The same rooms can be a/c activated for an extra ₹300. ₹550

Saravana Bhavan MM Residency, 65/66 Nellukkara St ☎044 2722 7250. An offshoot of the famous Chennai pure-veg restaurants, this is the most popular place in town. Limited "meals" (10.30am–4pm & 7–10pm) cost ₹80, specials ₹95 and Punjabi dishes ₹225. South Indian snacks are available all day. The ground-floor a/c room (8am–10pm) has the same menu but higher tariffs. Daily 6.30am–10.30pm.

Silk City 1st Floor, 77 Nellukara St ☎044 2722 7573, ⓔhotelsilkcity@gmail.com. Brand new hotel in a central location with immaculate spacious a/c rooms. A kettle, TV and towels are provided in all rooms, and the large attached bathrooms are spotless. Excellent value. No alcohol. ₹1439

20

VEDANTHANGAL BIRD SANCTUARY

One of India's most spectacular bird sanctuaries lies roughly 1km east of the village of **Vedanthangal**, 30km from the east coast and 86km southwest of Chennai. The **sanctuary** is busiest with birdlife between December and February, when it's totally flooded. The rains of the northeast monsoon, sweeping through in October or November, bring local and migratory water birds including some that nest and settle here until the dry season (usually April), when they leave for wetter areas. Abundant trees on mounds above water level provide perfect nesting spots, alive by January with fledglings. Visitors can watch the avian action from a path at the water's edge, or from a watchtower (fitted out with strong binoculars). Try to come at sunset, when the birds return from feeding. Common Indian **species** to look out for are openbill storks, spoonbills, pelicans, black cormorants, and herons of several types. You may also see ibises, grey pelicans, migrant cuckoos, sandpipers, egrets (which paddle in the rice fields), and darting bee-eaters.

ARRIVAL AND DEPARTURE

By bus Getting to Vedanthangal can present a few problems. The nearest town is Maduranthakam, 8km east, on NH-45 between Chengalpattu and Tindivanam, from where there are hourly buses to the sanctuary. Alternatively, direct services run every hour or two from Chengalpattu.

By taxi Taxis make the journey from Maduranthakam for ₹500 but cannot be booked from Vedanthangal.

INFORMATION

Opening hours Daily 5.30am–6pm. The best months to visit are Nov–Feb, although weekends and holidays can be crowded and noisy.

Entry fees Entry to the sanctuary is ₹5 (camera ₹50, video recorders ₹125).

Accommodation To arrange accommodation, call the Forest Ranger (☎ 94442 66213) or Wildlife Warden in Chennai (☎ 044 2235 1471)

Tiruvannamalai

Synonymous with the fifth Hindu element of fire, **TIRUVANNAMALAI**, 100km southwest of Kanchipuram, ranks, along with Madurai, Kanchipuram, Chidambaram and Trichy, as one of the five holiest towns in Tamil Nadu. Its name, meaning "Red Mountain", derives from the spectacular extinct volcano, **Arunachala**, which rises behind it, and which glows an unearthly crimson in the dawn light. This awesome natural backdrop, combined with the colossal **Arunachaleshvara Temple** in the centre of town, make Tiruvannamalai one of the region's most memorable destinations. Well off the tourist trail, it's a perfect place to get to grips with life in small-town Tamil Nadu, especially for anyone with an interest in Hinduism.

Mythology identifies Arunachala as the place where Shiva asserted his power over Brahma and Vishnu by manifesting himself as a lingam of fire, or **agni-lingam**. The event is commemorated each year at the rising of the full moon in November/December, when a vast vat of two thousand litres of ghee and a 30m-wide wick is lit by priests on the summit of Arunachala. This symbolizes the fulfilment of Shiva's promise to reappear each year to vanquish the forces of darkness and ignorance with firelight.

The sacred Red Mountain is also associated with the famous twentieth-century saint, **Sri Ramana Maharishi**, who chose it as the site for his twenty-three-year meditation retreat. A crop of small ashrams has sprung up on the edge of town below Sri Ramana's Cave, some of them more authentic than others, and the ranks of white-cotton-clad foreigners floating between them have become a defining feature of Tiruvannamalai.

Arunachaleshvara Temple

Known to Hindus as the "Temple of the Eternal Sunrise", the enormous **Arunachaleshvara Temple**, built over a period of almost a thousand years, consists of three concentric courtyards whose gateways are topped by tapering *gopuras*, the largest of which cover the east and north gates. The best spot from which to view the precinct, a breathtaking spectacle against the sprawling plains and lumpy, granite Shevaroy Hills, is the path up to Sri Ramana Maharishi's meditation cave, Virupaksha (see below), on the lower slopes of Arunachala. To enter the temple, however, head for the huge eastern gateway, which leads through the thick outer wall carved with images of deities, local saints and teachers. In the basement of a raised hall to the right before entering the next courtyard is the Parthala lingam, where Sri Ramana Maharishi is said to have sat in a state of Supreme Awareness while ants feasted on his flesh.

The caves

Opposite the western entrance of the temple complex, a path leads up a holy hill (15min) to the **Virupaksha Cave**, where the Maharishi stayed between 1899 and 1916. He personally built the bench outside and the hill-shaped lingam and platform inside, where all are welcome to meditate in peace. When this cave became too crowded, Ramana shifted to another, hidden away a few minutes further up the hill. He named this one, and the small house built onto it, **Skandasramam**, and lived there between 1916 and 1922. The inner cave here is also set aside for meditation, and the front patio affords splendid views across the temple, town and surrounding plains.

Sri Ramana ashram

Main Rd · ⦿ sriramanamaharshi.org

The caves can also be reached via the pilgrims' path winding uphill from the **Sri Ramana ashram**, 2km south of the temple along the main road. This simple complex is where the sage lived after returning from his retreat on Arunachala, and where his body is today enshrined. The *samadhi* has become a popular place for Sri Ramana's devotees on pilgrimage, but interested visitors are welcome to stay in the dorms here. There's also an excellent bookshop (8am–11am & 2–6pm) stocking a huge range of titles on the life and teachings of the guru, as well as quality postcards, calendars, devotional music and DVDs.

ARRIVAL AND INFORMATION

TIRUVANNAMALAI

By train The railway station, 500m east of the temple, is on the line main Tirupati–Madurai line, with a daily service in each direction.

By bus Buses arrive at the town bus stand on Chinnakadai St, 1km north of the temple. Coming from the coast, it's easiest to make your way on one of the numerous buses from Tindivanam, which pass through Gingee. There are excellent bus connections to Chennai (every 10min), Chengalpattu (every 10min, change for

Mamallapuram), Puducherry (every 30min), Trichy (hourly) and Kanchipuram (every 2hr).

Services There is intermittent internet access at the Image Computer Centre, 52 Car St, and Sri Sai, 14-A Kadambarayam St. There are a few ATMs and a couple of Western Union offices but the best place to change money and travellers' cheques is the India Boutique/Forex, 138 Raj Chettiyar Complex on Chengam Rd, near the Ashram (⦿04175 238248).

ACCOMMODATION

Arunachala 5 Vada Sannathi St ⦿04175 228300. Large, clean and comfortable hotel situated right outside the main temple entrance. There is a choice of non-a/c and a/c rooms (₹1125), all of which are a good size and have

TVs. Not the quietest place to stay, but certainly atmospheric. ₹825

Park 26 Kosmadam St ⦿04175 222471. Reliable budget option a 5min walk from the junction of North and

---

THE PRADAKSHANA

During the annual Kartiggai festival, Hindu pilgrims are supposed to perform an auspicious circumambulation of Arunachala, known as the **Pradakshana** (*pra* signifies the removal of all sins, *da* the fulfilment of desires, *kshi* freedom from the cycle of rebirth, and *na* spiritual liberation). Along the way, offerings are made at a string of shrines, tanks, temples, lingams, pillared meditation halls, sacred rocks, springs, trees, and caves related to the Tiruvannamalai legends. Although hectic during the festival, the paved path linking them all together is quiet for most of the year, and makes a wonderful day-hike, affording fine views of the town and its environs.

East Car St. The rooms (some small singles for ₹200; a/c ₹650) are fairly basic but clean, with TVs and buckets but no showers. There's a vegetarian canteen on the ground floor. ₹**400**

Ramakrishna 34-F Polur Rd, 5min from the bus station on the main Gingee road (turn right out of the bus station and veer left at the fork) ☎04175 250005, ✉hotelramakrishna@hotmail.com. One of the best places in town, with sizeable, clean rooms with TV and attached bathrooms and a choice of Indian or Western loos (different prices). There are also larger deluxe rooms from ₹700 and a/c rooms from ₹900. Excellent a/c restaurant next door to the reception (see below). ₹**400**

SASA Lodge Chinnakadai St, almost opposite the bus stand ☎04175 252293. One of the cheapest lodges in town, painted a bright blue and white. Rooms (some with a/c, ₹750) are basic and clean enough, but most of them are windowless. The front-facing rooms have light but are rather noisy. ₹**450**

Trishul 6 Kanagarayar St ☎04175 222219, ⊕hoteltrishul.com. Tucked away down a lane off Kosmadam St near the *Park* in a quiet location away from the hustle, this hotel has a rooftop terrace with views of the temple, a good restaurant and a bafflingly dark a/c bar. Choice of decent-sized non-a/c and a/c rooms (₹2080). ₹**1687**

EATING

Nala Residency 21 Anna Salai ☎04175 222322. A couple of hundred metres beyond the *Park*, this hotel restaurant has an extensive menu (veg and non-veg) and serves quality food. Veggie dishes cost around ₹70 and chicken dishes ₹100. Try the delicious butter *paneer* masala. Daily 7.30am–midnight.

★ **Ramakrishna** 34-F Polur Rd ☎04175 250005. Excellent food served quickly and efficiently in a/c cooled comfort. Good breakfasts, excellent eleven-dish "meals" (11am–3pm; ₹85) and a range of north and south Indian food available in the evenings. Daily 6.30am–10.30pm.

Udipi Brindhavan Car St ☎04175 222693. Located down a small lane opposite the temple's east entrance, this long and narrow *dhaba* is a typical *udipi* restaurant, serving very cheap lunchtime "meals" (11am–4pm; ₹45) and excellent parottas. Daily 6am–11pm.

Vickys Trishul Hotel 6 Kanagarayar St ☎04175 222219. Posh a/c ground-floor restaurant with a vaguely oriental vibe and decor, and a wall-length aquarium. Veggie dishes around ₹70, chicken dishes ₹100, the usual "meals" option (noon–3pm; veg ₹80; non-veg ₹120) and tandoori in the evenings. Daily 7.30am–10.30pm.

20

Puducherry

First impressions of **PUDUCHERRY** (**Pondicherry**, also often referred to simply as Pondy), the former capital of French India, can be unpromising. Instead of the leafy boulevards and *pétanque* pitches you might expect, its messy outer suburbs and bus stand are as cluttered and chaotic as any typical Tamil town. Closer to the seafront, however, the atmosphere grows tangibly more Gallic, as the bazaars give way to rows of houses whose shuttered windows and colourwashed facades wouldn't look out of place in Montpellier. For anyone familiar with the British colonial imprint, the town can induce culture shock with it's richly ornamented Catholic churches, French road names and policemen in De Gaulle-style *képis*, and *boules* played in the dusty squares. Many of the seafront buildings were damaged by the 2004 tsunami, but Puducherry's tourist infrastructure remained intact.

Brief history

Known to Greek and Roman geographers as "Poduke", Puducherry was an important staging post on the second-century maritime trade route between Rome and the Far East. When the Roman Empire declined, the Pallavas and Cholas took control and were followed by a succession of colonial powers, from the Portuguese in the sixteenth century to the French, Danes and British, who exchanged the enclave several times after the various battles and treaties of the Carnatic Wars in the early eighteenth century. Puducherry's heyday, however, dates from the arrival of the French governor Joseph **Dupleix**, who accepted the governorship in 1742 and immediately set about rebuilding a town decimated by its former British occupants. It was he who instituted the street plan of a central grid encircled by a broad oblong boulevard, bisected north to south by a canal dividing the "Ville Blanche", to the east, from the "Ville Noire", to the west.

Although relinquished by the French in 1954 – when the town became the headquarters of the **Union Territory of Pondicherry**, administering the three other former colonial enclaves scattered across south India – Puducherry's split personality still prevails. The seaside promenade, **Goubert Salai** (formerly Beach Road), has the forlorn look of an out-of-season French resort, complete with its own white Hôtel de Ville. Many visitors are grave Europeans in white Indian costume, busy about their

PUDUCHERRY

Auroville & Chennai

Sri Aurobindo Paper Factory

Aurodhan Art Gallery

CAFÉS & RESTAURANTS	
Adiyar Anandha Bhavan	1
Bombay Ananda Bhavan	2
Café Lune	5
Hot Breads	3
La Terrasse	11
Le Club	8
Le Rendezvous	7
Madame Shanthe's	6
Poudou Poudou	9
Qualithé	4
Satsanga	10

THIYAGA RAJA STREET
C KOIL STREET
MA KOIL STREET
TD KOIL STREET
KA COVIL STREET
SRI AUROBINDO STREET
SUPRAYA CHETTIAR STREET
C KOIL STREET
A MADAM STREET
RUE NEHRU

SARDAR VALLABHAI PATEL SALAI (NORTH BLVD)
HOLLANDAL STREET
DERICHEMONT STREET
DUPUY STREET
RUE DE LA MARINE

Sri Aurobindo Ashram

Market

RANGA PILLAI STREET
VELLAJA STREET
NIDARAJAPAVER ST
SAINT THERESA STREET
SINNA PAPPARA STREET
LAPPORTH STREET
MONTHORSIER STREET
C MUDHALIAR STREET
LAL BAHADUR SASTREETRI STREET
BUSSY STREET
RUE DE BAZAR SAINT LAURENT

Puducherry Government Museum

Raj Nivas

GPO

GOVERNMENT PLACE

Gandhi Memorial

UCO Bank

RUE MARE DE LABOURDONNAIS

Hôtel de Ville

SURCOUF STREET

State Bank of India

PDTC

New Bus Stand, Villupuram, Cuddalore & Mass Hotel

ANNA SALAI (WESTREET) BLVD
MAHATMA GANDHI ROAD
MISSION STREET
CAP ANDRE STREET
GINGEE SALAI
RUE ST LOUIS STREET
RUE SUFFREN STREET
AMBOUR SALAI
RUE ROMAIN ROLLAND
RUE DUMAS
GOUBERT SALAI (BEACH RD)
RUE ELLAIMANE COLI
RUE BUSSY
RUE DE BOURBON

Botanical Gardens

Sacred Heart of Jesus

Water Tower

Railway Station

BAY OF BENGAL

ACCOMMODATION	
Amala Lodge	4
Aruna	1
French Guest House	3
Hotel de l'Orient	7
International Guest House	5
Park Guest House	8
Soorya International	6
Surya Swastika	2

SUBRAIYAH SALAI (SOUTH BLVD)

DR AMBEDKHAR SALAI

Sports Complex

New Pier

N

0   200
metres

20

spiritual quest. It was here that **Sri Aurobindo Ghose** (1872–1950), a leading figure in the freedom struggle in Bengal, was given shelter after it became unwise for him to live close to the British in Calcutta. His ashram attracts thousands of devotees from all around the world, most particularly from Bengal.

Goubert Salai

Puducherry's beachside promenade, **Goubert Salai**, is a favourite place for a stroll, though there's little to do other than watch the world go by. The Hôtel de Ville, today housing the Municipal Offices building, is still an impressive spectacle, and a 4m-tall Gandhi memorial, surrounded by ancient columns, dominates the northern end. Nearby, a French memorial commemorates French Indians who lost their lives in World War I.

Just north of the Hôtel de Ville, a couple of streets back from the promenade, is the leafy old French-provincial-style square now named **Government Place**. On the north side, the impressive, gleaming white **Raj Nivas**, official home to the present lieutenant-governor of Puducherry Territory, was built late in the eighteenth century for Joseph Francis Dupleix.

Pondicherry Government Museum

Ranga Pillai St • Tues–Sun 10am–1pm & 2–5pm • ₹50 (₹2)

The **Pondicherry Government Museum** is opposite Government Place. The archeological collection includes Neolithic and two-thousand-year-old remains from Arikamedu, a few Pallava (sixth- to eighth-century) and Buddhist (tenth-century) stone sculptures, bronzes, weapons and paintings. Alongside are a bizarre assembly of French salon furniture and bric-à-brac from local houses, including a velvet S-shaped "conversation seat".

Sri Aurobindo Ashram

Rue de la Marine • Daily 8am–noon & 2–6pm • Free, no children under three, Photography with permission • ⓦ sriaurobindosociety.org.in

The **Sri Aurobindo Ashram** is one of the best-known and wealthiest ashrams in India. Founded in 1926 by the Bengali philosopher-guru, Aurobindo Ghosh, and his chief disciple, personal manager and mouthpiece "The Mother", it serves as the headquarters of the Sri Aurobindo Society, or SAS. Today the SAS owns most of the valuable property and real estate in Puducherry, and wields what many consider to be a disproportionate influence over the town. The **samadhi**, or mausoleum, of Sri Aurobindo and "The Mother" is covered daily with flowers and usually surrounded by supplicating devotees with their hands and heads placed on the tomb. Inside the main building, an incongruous and very bourgeois-looking Western-style room, complete with three-piece suite and Persian carpet, is where "The Mother" and Sri Aurobindo chilled out. The adjacent bookshop sells a range of literature and tracts, while the building opposite hosts frequent cultural programmes.

Botanical Gardens

Subbaiyah Salai • Daily 8am–noon & 2–6pm • Free; aquarium ₹5

Established in 1826, the **Botanical Gardens** offer many quiet paths to wander. The French planted nine hunderd species here, experimenting to see how they would do in Indian conditions; one mahogany tree, the *Khaya senegalensis*, has grown to a height of 25m. You can also see an extraordinary fossilized tree, found about 25km away in Tiravakarai. The aquarium inside the gardens is uninspiring.

ARRIVAL AND DEPARTURE	PUDUCHERRY

By train Puducherry's railway station is in the south, a 5min walk from the sea off Subbaiyah Salai. There are daily express and passenger trains to Chennai and Tirupati and weekly fast express trains to Bhubaneshwar (Wed), Mangalore (Tues), New Delhi (Wed) and Howrah, Kolkata (Wed).

20

By bus All buses pull into New Bus Stand, which lies on the western edge of town. From here, auto-rickshaws charge at least ₹50 into the old town, taxis double that, but you can jump in a *tempo* to central Ambour Salai for ₹5–10.

Destinations Bengaluru (4 daily; 10–12hr); Chennai (every 10–20min; 2hr 30min–3hr); Chidambaram (every 20min; 2hr); Coimbatore (10 daily; 9hr); Kanchipuram (10 daily; 3–4hr); Kanyakumari (hourly; 12–13hr); Madurai (hourly; 9–10hr); Mamallapuram (every 10–20min; 1hr 30min–2hr); Thanjavur (hourly; 5hr); Tiruchirapalli (every 30min; 5–6hr); Tiruvannamalai (every 20min; 2hr).

GETTING AROUND AND INFORMATION

By auto-rickshaw Puducherry is well served by auto-rickshaws, which can negotiate the narrow and chaotic streets efficiently.

By bicycle Many tourists like to rent a bicycle from one of the many stalls dotted about town, such as Sri Durga Pharameshwari Cycle Stores, 106-B Mission St (☏ 98941 21133) and Ganesh Cycle Store, 39 Mission St (☏ 0413 222 2801).

By scooter For trips further afield such as Auroville, it is possible to rent mopeds and scooters from agencies around town. A passport or driving licence is required. Check at the helpful Tourist Office or wander along Mission St to compare prices and models.

Tourist information The Puducherry Tourism Development Corporation (PTDC) office is at 40 Goubert Salai (daily 8am–8pm; ☏ 0413 233 9497, ✉ tourismpondy@sify.com). The staff are extremely helpful, providing leaflets and a city map, and information about Auroville; they can also book you onto their city tours (half-day 1.30–5pm, non-a/c ₹150, a/c ₹200; full-day 9.45am–5pm, non-a/c ₹250, a/c ₹300) and help arrange car rental.

Services There are plenty of ATMs around the town. Muthu Forex, 161 Mission St (☏ 0413 222 4239) changes travellers' cheques and has a Western Union transfer facility. Thomas Cook is at 2A Rue Labourdonnais (☏ 0413 222 4008). Other places to change money include the State Bank of India, 15 Suffren St, and UCO Bank on Rue Mahe de Labourdonnais. The GPO is on Ranga Pillai St (Mon–Sat 8am–5pm). Internet access is available throughout central Puducherry; try iWay at 36 Nidarajapayar St.

ACCOMMODATION

Puducherry's **basic lodges** are concentrated around the main market area, Ranga Pillai St and Rue Nehru. Guesthouses belonging to the **Sri Aurobindo Ashram** offer good value for money, but come with a lot of regulations, curfews and overpowering "philosophy of life" notices and are not overtly welcoming.

Amala Lodge 92 Ranga Pillai St ☏ 0413 233 8910. This centrally located hotel is one of the best of the budget options. The rooms are clean enough but a little bit on the small side. There is also a three-bed room available with a/c for ₹800. **₹300**

Aruna 3 Zamindar Garden, SV Patel Rd ☏ 0413 233 7756, ✉ hotelarunapondy@gmail.com. Located on a quiet side street, up in the northern sector of town. It has pleasant double rooms (some a/c, ₹95) with TV and balcony, some of which catch the morning sun. **₹700**

French Guest House 38 Ambour Salai ☏ 0413 420 0853. Clean, reasonably sized rooms, including some family suites, in a welcoming centrally located hotel. The a/c rooms are slightly cleaner and brighter but twice the price. **₹300**

★ **Hotel de l'Orient** 17 Rue Romain Rolland ☏ 0413 234 3067, ✉ neemranahotels.com. A beautiful, UNESCO heritage-accorded French house boasting sixteen individually decorated rooms with French antiques, tiled balconies and long shuttered windows overlooking the leafy courtyard restaurant. Four categories of room with the most expensive, featuring an ante room and four-poster bed, costing ₹7500. **₹3500**

International Guest House 47 NSC Bose Salai ☏ 0413 233 6699, ✉ ingh@aurosociety.org. The largest Aurobindo establishment in town, with dozens of very large, clean rooms, some of which are a/c (₹1050). It's a good budget option but typically institutional, with a 10.30pm curfew. Often full, so best book in advance. Rooms in the new wing are slightly more expensive. **₹500**

Park Guest House Goubert Salai ☏ 0413 223 3644, ✉ parkgh@sriaurobindoashram.org.in. Another Sri Aurobindo Society place with the same strict rules (no alcohol and a 10.30pm curfew) for ashram visitors only. Spotless and very comfortable rooms (a/c ₹800) with mosquito nets and sitouts, overlooking garden and sea. Bike rental, laundry and restaurant but no TV. **₹600**

Soorya International 55 Ranga Pillai St ☏ 0413 222 7486, ✉ hotelsooryainternationalin.com. Decent, centrally a/c hotel, located in the centre of town. Good-sized-comfortable standard rooms and bigger deluxe rooms complete with sofa and balcony. It also has a multicuisine restaurant. **₹1575**

Surya Swastika 11 Eswaran Koil St ☏ 0413 234 3092, ✉ suryaswastika@sify.com. A traditional Tamil guesthouse in a quiet corner of town, with nine basic rooms dotted around a covered central courtyard. Quintessential budget traveller's place – incredibly cheap, friendly and clean enough. **₹180/₹220**

20

EATING AND DRINKING

If you've been on the road for a while and are hankering for healthy salads, fresh coffee, crusty bread, cakes and real pastry, you'll be spoilt for choice in Puducherry. **Beer** is available just about everywhere (except the SAS-owned establishments) and is half the regular Tamil Nadu price at around ₹60 a bottle.

Adiyar Anandha Bhavan Rue Nehru ☏0413 222 3333. Very popular pure veg restaurant with three counters under one roof. Samosas, *chaat* and snacks on the left, a sweet counter in the centre and veggie dishes to the right. Pay first and show receipt. Daily 7am–11pm.

Bombay Ananda Bhavan 199 Mission St ☏0413 222 8293. Clean and very popular south Indian pure veg joint, serving good south Indian breakfasts (*pongal* and *vada* ₹40), excellent masala dosas for ₹35 and the usual lunchtime "meals" for ₹60. Daily 7am–10pm.

Café Lune Rue Suffren, near the State Bank of India. This tiny café, which opened in 1961, is popular with the locals, who gather to drink coffee, prepared with great pomp and style. The ultra-cheap lunchtime plate of lemon rice and *vada* is very good. Mon–Fri 7am–1pm & 4–7pm; Sat 4–7pm.

Hot Breads 42 Ambour Salai ☏0413 222 7886. Squeaky-clean *boulangerie*-café popular with the French expats. Classic crusty croissants, fresh baguettes and delicious savoury pastry snacks are available, their tempting smells wafting out onto the street. Also serves pizza, burgers and hotdogs. Daily 7.30am–9.30pm.

★ **La Terrasse** 5 Subbiah Salai ☏0413 222 0809. Popular French restaurant, especially for European backpackers, who hang out here to devour croissants and al fresco cappuccino. The prawn dishes and pizzas (₹90–200) are excellent, and there's a range of Indian, Chinese and French food. Daily except Wed 8.30am–9pm.

Le Club 38 Rue Dumas ☏0413 233 9745. One of the best-known restaurants in town. The menu is predominantly French and features their famous *coq au vin* (₹420), *steak au poivre* (₹400), seafood dishes (around ₹400), a full wine list and cocktails (₹350). Daily 8am–10.30pm.

Le Rendezvous 30 Rue Suffren ☏0413 222 7677. Seafood sizzlers (around ₹350), pizza and tandoori brochettes are some of the specialities of this popular expat-oriented restaurant. Fresh croissants and espresso are served for breakfast, while seafood later on dishes range from ₹290–800. You can dine indoors or on the terrace. Daily except Tues 11am–3.30pm & 6–10pm.

★ **Madame Shanthé's** 40A Rue Romain Rolland ☏0413 222 2022. Very friendly rooftop restaurant, with lovely ambience and evening illuminations, that serves tasty French, Indian and Chinese dishes. Their speciality is seafood: pasta *marinara* (₹200) and a superb, excellent-value seafood platter (fish, calamari and prawns; ₹220). Daily 11am–11pm.

Poudou Poudou 31 Rue Labourdonnais. One of the only Indian restaurants in the old part of town, this place also serves some seafood (fish curry ₹100) and continental cuisine. There is a small a/c dining area and two rooftop terraces. Most dishes cost less than ₹130. Daily 10am–11.30pm.

Qualithé 3 Rue Mahe de Labourdonnais, opposite Government Place. A dim and somewhat seedy ground-floor bar-restaurant, serving a small range of dishes, including fried rice and a few mains that are chalked up each day outside. Its popularity is due to its range of whisky and strong beers. Daily 6–10.30pm.

Satsanga 54 Rue Labourdonnais ☏0413 222 5867. The menu here is prepared by the French *patron*: organic salads with fresh herbs, tzatziki, garlic bread, sauté potatoes and *tagliatelle alla carbonara*. The plat du jour includes fresh fish and there's a range of French beef dishes for ₹285. Two dining areas – a courtyard or rooftop. Tues–Sun 12–3pm & 6–11pm.

Auroville

The most New Age place anywhere in India must surely be **AUROVILLE**, the planned "City of Dawn", 10km north of Pudicherry, straddling the border of the Union Territory and Tamil Nadu. Founded in 1968, Auroville was inspired by "The Mother", the spiritual successor of Sri Aurobindo. Around 1700 people live in communes (two thirds of them non-Indians), with such names as Fertile, Certitude, Sincerity, Revelation and Transformation, in what it is hoped will eventually be an ideal city for a population of fifty thousand. Architecturally experimental buildings, combining modern Western and traditional Indian elements, are set in a rural landscape of narrow lanes, deep red earth and lush greenery. Income is derived from agriculture, handicrafts, alternative technology, educational and development projects and Aurolec, a computer software company.

Considering how little there is to see here, Auroville attracts a disproportionately large number of day-trippers – much to the chagrin of its inhabitants, who rightly point out that you can only get a sense of what the settlement is all about if you stay a while. Interested visitors are welcomed as paying guests in most of the communes (see below), where you can work alongside permanent residents.

The Visitor Centre

Daily 9am–5.30pm • ☎ 0413 262 2239, ⓦ auroville.org

The Visitor Centre is the focal point of any tourist visit to Auroville. You need to get tickets here for an exterior viewing of Matri Mandir, but before they are issued, you're shown a short video presentation about the village. The adjacent bookshop has plenty of literature on Auroville and it's worth checking the notice board, which has details of **activities** in which visitors may participate (including yoga, reiki and Vipassana meditation, costing around ₹200/session). The nearby **Bharat Niwas** houses a permanent exhibition on the history and philosophy of the settlement. There are also three quality handicraft outlets and several pleasant vegetarian cafés serving snacks, meals and cold drinks.

Matri Mandir

Mon–Sat 10am–noon & 2–4pm, Sun 10am–noon • Free • tickets available from the Visitor Centre • To obtain "concentration entry" for the Matri Mandir to meditate on the crystal, you must book two days ahead

Begun in 1970, the space-age **Matri Mandir** – a gigantic, almost spherical hi-tech meditation centre at the heart of the site – was conceived as "a symbol of the Divine's answer to man's inspiration for perfection". Earth from 124 countries was symbolically placed in an urn, and is kept in a concrete cone in the amphitheatre adjacent to Matri Mandir, from where a speaker can address an audience of three thousand without amplification. The focal point of the interior of the Matri Mandir is a 70cm crystal ball symbolizing the neutral but divine qualities of light and space.

ARRIVAL AND INFORMATION   **AUROVILLE**

Auroville lies 15km north of Puducherry, off the main Chennai road; you can also get here via the coastal highway, turning off at the village of Chinna Mudaliarchavadi.

By bus Buses from Puducherry run every 20–30min but as Auroville is spread over some fifty square kilometres it's best to come with your own transport.
By auto-rickshaw or taxi From Puducherry to Auroville costs around ₹250 for the 30min journey in an auto-rickshaw or around ₹350 in a taxi.
On a tour Alternatively, there's the PTDC half-day tour from Puducherry (see p.978).

ACCOMMODATION AND EATING

The information desk at the visitor centre is a good place to enquire about **paying guest accommodation** in Auroville's guesthouses. Tariffs are high – from ₹860 to ₹4500 including all meals. Alternatively you can check availability in the many smaller guesthouses via the new booking system being launched on ⓦ aurovilleguesthouses.org. Officially there's no lower limit on the time you have to stay, but visitors are encouraged to stick around for at least a week and to help out on communal projects. There are many excellent privately run restaurants dotted around the ashram and a café at the visitor centre.

Central Tamil Nadu: the Chola heartland

To be on the banks of the Cauvery listening to the strains of Carnatic music is to have a taste of eternal bliss

Tamil proverb

Continuing south of Puducherry along the Coromandel coast, you enter the flat landscape of the **Kaveri** (aka Cauvery) **Delta**, a watery world of canals, dams, dykes and rivulets that has been intensively farmed since ancient times. Just 160km in diameter, it forms the verdant rice-bowl core of Tamil Nadu, crossed by more than thirty major rivers and countless streams. The largest of them, the River Kaveri, known in Tamil as Ponni, "The Lady of Gold" (a form of the Mother Goddess), is revered as a conduit of liquid *shakti*, the primordial female energy that nurtures the millions of farmers who live on her banks and tributaries. The landscape here is one endless swathe of green paddy fields, dotted with palm trees and little villages of thatched roofs and market stalls; it comes as a rude shock to land up in the hot and chaotic towns.

This mighty delta formed the very heartland of the **Chola** empire, which reached its apogee between the ninth and thirteenth centuries, an era often compared to classical Greece and Renaissance Italy both for its cultural richness and the sheer scale and profusion of its architectural creations. Much as the Cholas originally intended, every visitor is immediately in awe of their huge temples, not only at cities such as **Chidambaram**, **Kumbakonam** and **Thanjavur**, but also out in the countryside at places like **Gangaikondacholapuram**, where the magnificent temple is all that remains of a once-great city. Exploring the area for a few days will bring you into contact with the more delicate side of Chola artistic expression, such as the magnificent **bronzes** of Thanjavur.

Chidambaram

CHIDAMBARAM, 58km south of Puducherry, is so steeped in myth that its history is hard to unravel. As the site of the *tandav*, the cosmic dance of Shiva as **Nataraja**, King of the Dance, it's one of the holiest sites in south India, and a visit to its **Sabhanayaka Temple** affords a fascinating glimpse into ancient Tamil religious practice and belief. The legendary king **Hiranyavarman** is said to have made a pilgrimage here from Kashmir, seeking to rid himself of leprosy by bathing in the temple's Shivaganga tank. In thanks for a successful cure, he enlarged the temple. He also brought three thousand brahmins, of the Dikshitar caste, whose descendants, distinguishable by top-knots of hair at the front of their heads, are the ritual specialists of the temple to this day.

Few of the fifty *maths* (monasteries) that once stood here remain, but the temple itself is still a hive of activity and hosts numerous **festivals**. The two most important are ten-day affairs, building up to spectacular finales: on the ninth day of each, temple chariots process through the four Car streets in the **car festival**, while on the tenth there is an **abhishekham**, when the principal deities in the Raja Sabha (thousand-pillared hall) are anointed. For exact dates (one is in May/June, the other in Dec/Jan), contact any TTDC tourist office and plan well ahead, as they are very popular. Other local festivals include fire-walking and *kavadi* folk dance (dancing with decorated wooden frames on the head) at the Thillaiamman Kali (April/May) and Keelatheru Mariamman (July/Aug) temples.

Chidambaram revolves around the Sabhanayaka Temple and the busy market area that surrounds it, along North, East, South and West Car streets. The town also has a large student population, based at Annamalai University to the east, a centre of Tamil studies.

Sabhanayaka Nataraja Temple
Daily 4am–noon & 4–10pm

For south India's Shaivites, the **Sabhanayaka Nataraja Temple**, where Shiva is enthroned as Lord of the Cosmic Dance (Nataraja), is the holiest of holies. Its huge *gopuras*, whose lights are used as landmarks by sailors far out to sea in the Bay of Bengal, soar above a 55-acre complex, divided by four concentric walls. The oldest parts now standing were built under the Cholas, who adopted Nataraja as their chosen deity and crowned several kings here. If you have the time the best way to tackle the complex is to work slowly inwards from the third enclosure in clockwise circles.

Frequent **ceremonies** take place at the innermost sanctum, the most popular being at noon and 6pm, when a fire is lit, great gongs are struck and devotees rush forward to catch a last glimpse of the lingam before the doors are shut. On Friday nights before the temple closes, during a particularly elaborate puja, Nataraja is carried on a palanquin accompanied by music and attendants carrying flaming torches and tridents. At other times, you'll hear ancient devotional hymns from the Tevaram.

20

The gopuras

The west *gopura* is the most popular entrance, as well as being the most elaborately carved and probably the earliest (c.1150 AD). Turning north (left) from here, you come to the colonnaded **Shivaganga tank**, the site of seven natural springs. From the broken pillar at the tank's edge, all four *gopuras* are visible. In the northeast corner, the largest building in the complex, the **Raja Sabha** (fourteenth- to fifteenth-century) is also known as "the thousand-pillared hall"; tradition holds that there are only 999 actual pillars, the thousandth being Shiva's leg. During festivals the deities Nataraja and Shivakamasundari are brought here and mounted on a dais for the anointing ceremony, *abhishekha*.

The importance of **dance** at Chidambaram is underlined by the reliefs of dancing figures inside the east *gopura*, demonstrating 108 *karana*s (a similar set is to be found in the west *gopura*). A *karana* is a specific point in a phase of movement prescribed by the extraordinarily comprehensive Sanskrit treatise on the performing arts, the *Natya Shastra* (c.200 BC–200 AD) – the basis of all classical dance, music and theatre in India.

The second enclosure

To get into the square **second enclosure** head for its western entrance (just north/of the west *gopura* in the third wall), which leads into a circumambulatory passageway. Once beyond this second wall you may become disorientated as the roofed inner enclosure sees little light and is supported by a maze of colonnades.

Govindaraja shrine

The innermost **Govindaraja shrine** is dedicated to Vishnu – no surprise, as most Shiva temples have a Vishnu shrine inside them, though no Vaishnavite temple has a shrine for Shiva. The deity is attended by non-Dikshitar brahmins who, it is said, don't always get along with the Dikshitars. From outside the shrine, non-Hindus can see through to the most sacred part of the temple, the **Kanaka Sabha** and the **Chit Sabha**, adjoining raised structures, roofed with copper and gold plate and linked by a hallway. The latter houses bronze images of Nataraja and his consort Shivakamasundari; behind and to the left of Nataraja, a curtain, sacred to Shiva and strung with rows of leaves from the bilva tree, demarcates the most potent area of all. Within it lies the **Akashalingam**, known as the *rahasya*, or "secret", of Chidambaram: made of the most subtle of the elements, Ether (*akasha*) – from which Air, Fire, Water and Earth are born – the lingam is invisible – signifying the invisible presence of God in the human heart.

A crystal lingam, said to have emanated from the light of the crescent moon on Shiva's brow, and a small ruby Nataraja are worshipped in the Kanaka Sabha. They are ritually bathed in the flames of the priests' camphor fire or oil lamps six times a day. This inner area is where you're most likely to hear **oduvars**, hereditary singers from the middle, non-brahmin castes, intoning verses of ancient Tamil poetry. The songs with which they regale the deities at puja time, drawn from compilations such as the Tevaram or earlier Sangam, are believed to be more than a thousand years old.

ARRIVAL AND INFORMATION   CHIDAMBARAM

By train The railway station is just over 1km southeast of the centre. There are daily trains to Chennai Egmore (5hr 38min) and Tiruchirapalli (3hr 30min).

By bus Buses from Chennai, Thanjavur, Mamallapuram and Madurai pull in at the bus stand, about 500m from the temple. Destinations Buses run to: Chengalpattu (every 20–30min; 4hr 30min–5hr); Chennai (every 20–30min; 5–6hr); Coimbatore (6 daily; 7hr); Kanchipuram (hourly; 7–8hr);

Kanyakumari (3 daily; 10hr); Kumbakonam (every 10min; 2hr 30min); Madurai (6 daily; 8hr); Puducherry (every 15–20min; 2hr); Thanjavur (every 15–20min; 4hr); Tiruchirapalli (every 30min; 5hr); Tiruvannamalai (hourly; 3hr 30min).

Tourist information The TTDC tourist office (Mon–Fri 9.45am–5.45pm; ☎ 04144 238739) is next to *Vandayar Gateway Inn* hotel on Railway Feeder Rd. Friendly, helpful staff but not a lot of leaflets.

FROM TOP MAMALLAPURAM (P.963); BRIHADISHWARA TEMPLE, THANJAVUR (P.990); MUDUMALAI WILDLIFE SANCTUARY (P.1019) >

Services None of the banks in Chidambaram change money, although the *Saradharam* hotel, near the bus stand, will change cash and there is an ICICI Bank ATM in the forecourt, as well as a couple more on South Car St. Internet access is widely available: try the *Saradharam* or *I-Castle* by the east entrance to the temple.

ACCOMMODATION

Akshaya 17/18 East Car St ☎ 04144 220192, ⊛ hotel-akshaya.com. Pleasant, clean, mid-range hotel, with a garden backing right onto the temple wall. There's a choice of non-a/c and a/c rooms (₹2250), though the non-a/c are much better value, and a couple of restaurants. ₹1100

★ **Mansoor Lodge** 91 East Car St ☎ 04144 221072. A cheap, friendly and good-value hotel, right opposite the temple. The rooms (some singles at ₹250) have tiled floors and clean bathrooms and there is a TV in each one. ₹400

Raja Rajan 162 West Car St ☎ 04144 222690. Close to the west gate of the temple, this is another budget option with clean rooms and tiled bathrooms. There are some cheap singles (₹250) and good-value a/c rooms (₹730). ₹350

Ritz 2 VGP St, near the bus stand ☎ 04144 646675, ✉ alritzhotel@gmail.com. One of the better places in town, this comfortable hotel is conveniently located and has good-sized clean rooms (a/c ₹1200), all with TV, and a good restaurant. ₹1000

Sabanayagam 7 East Sannathi St, off East Car St ☎ 04144 220896. Despite its flashy exterior, this is a run-of-the-mill budget place located 10m down the main temple entrance lane. Rooms (some windowless; a/c ₹990) are clean, but off dim corridors with a choice of Western or Indian toilets. ₹525

Saradharam 19 Venugopal Pillai St, opposite the bus stand ☎ 04144 221336, ⊛ hotelsaradharam.co.in. Large, clean, well-kept rooms, some with balconies, in a modern building; a/c rooms (₹2159) include breakfast. The hotel also has three decent restaurants (including the multicuisine *Anupallavi*), a garden, bar, laundry service and foreign exchange. ₹1089

EATING

New Moorthy Café 4 Bolenarayanan Street (on corner with VGP street). A street level restaurant which is very popular with the locals. There's a wide range of chicken dishes for ₹80 and a few veggie dishes for around ₹50. Their superb *paneer* butter masala (₹60) has a serious kick. Daily 11am–11pm.

RK Residency 30 VGP St ☎ 04144 226713. There are two restaurants in this hotel – a vegetarian one on the fourth floor and non-veg one opposite the reception – both serving reasonably priced Indian and Chinese dishes. Daily 8am–10pm.

Sri Krishna Vilas 93 East Car St ☎ 94432 12328. Simple but very good south Indian food served in a clean environment with deities adorning the walls and early morning pujas. Small range of breakfast dishes including tasty *pongal*. No menu as such – just ask for what you want. Daily 7.15am–2pm & 4–10pm.

Thillai Ganesa Bhavan 137/4 SP Kovil St, opposite the hospital ☎ 98652 82004. Around the corner from the bus station, this small place, adorned with Lakshmi pictures on the walls, is a popular choice. they serve tasty south Indian breakfasts, good coffee and lunchtime "meals" (₹50) from 11am–3.30pm. Daily 6.30am–10pm.

Gangaikondacholapuram

Devised as the centrepiece of a city built by the Chola king Rajendra I (1014–42) to celebrate his conquests, the magnificent **Brihadishwara Temple** (a replica of the Tanjore temple) stands in the tiny village of **GANGAIKONDACHOLAPURAM** in Ariyalur District, 35km north of Kumbakonam. The tongue-twisting name means "the town of the Chola who took the Ganges". Under Rajendra I, the Chola empire did indeed stretch as far as the great river of the north, an unprecedented achievement for a southern dynasty. Aside from the temple and the rubble of Rajendra's palace, 2km east at Tamalikaimedu, nothing of the city remains. Nonetheless, this is among the most extraordinary archeological sites in south India, outshone only by Thanjavur, and the fact that it's devoid of visitors most of the time gives it a memorably forlorn feel.

Brihadishwara Temple

Daily 6am–noon & 4–8pm • Free

Dominating the village landscape, the **Brihadishwara Temple** sits in a well-maintained grassy courtyard, flanked by a closed *mandapa* hallway. Over the sanctuary, to the right, a massive pyramidal tower (*vimana*) rises 55m in nine diminishing storeys.

Turning right (north) inside the courtyard, before you reach a small shrine to the goddess **Durga**, containing an image of Mahishasuramardini (the slaying of the buffalo demon), you come across a small well, guarded by a lion statue, known as Simhakinaru and made from plastered brickwork. King Rajendra is said to have had Ganges water placed in the well to be used for the ritual anointing of the lingam in the main temple. The lion, representing Chola kingly power, bows to the huge Nandi respectfully seated before the eastern entrance of the temple, in line with the *shivalingam* contained within.

Directly in front of the eastern entrance to the temple stands a small altar for offerings. Two parallel flights of stairs ascend to the *mukhamandapa* or porch, which leads to the long pillared *mahamandapa* hallway, the entrance of which is flanked by a pair of large guardian deities. Immediately inside the temple a guide can show you the way to the tower, up steep steps. On either side of the temple doorway, sculptures of Shiva in his various benevolent (*anugraha*) manifestations include him blessing Vishnu, Devi, Ravana and the saint Chandesha. In the northeast corner, an unusual square stone block features carvings of the nine planets (*navagraha*). A number of **Chola bronzes** (see box, p.991) stand on the platform; the figure of Karttikeya, the war god, carrying a club and a shield, is thought to have had particular significance

The base of the main temple sanctuary is decorated with lions and scrollwork. Above this decoration, running from the southern to the northern entrance of the *ardhamandapa*, a series of sculpted figures in plastered niches portray different images of Shiva. The most famous is at the northern entrance, showing Shiva and Parvati garlanding the saint Chandesha, who here is sometimes identified as Rajendra I.

Archeological Museum
Daily except Fri 10am–1pm & 2–5.45pm • Free

Two minutes' walk northeast along the main road (turn right from the car park), the tiny **Archeological Museum** contains Chola odds and ends discovered locally. The finds include terracotta lamps, coins, weapons, tiles, bronze, bangle pieces, palm-leaf manuscripts and an old Chinese pot.

ARRIVAL AND INFORMATION   **GANGAIKONDACHOLAPURAM**

By bus Although it is marginally closer to Chidambaram, bus connections are better to and from Kumbakonam, running every 15min or so. Some Trichy to Chidambaram services also stop here.

Information Be sure not to get stuck here between noon and 4pm when the temple is closed. Facilities are minimal, with little more than a few cool-drinks stands. Parts of the interior are extremely dark, and a torch is useful.

Kumbakonam and around

Sandwiched between the Kaveri (Cauvery) and Arasalar rivers, 74km southwest of Chidambaram and 38km northeast of Thanjavur, is **KUMBAKONAM**. Hindus believe this to be the place where a water pot (*kumba*) of *amrita* – the ambrosial beverage of immortality – was washed up by a great deluge from atop sacred Mount Meru in the Himalayas. Shiva, who just happened to be passing through in the guise of a wild forest-dwelling hunter, for some reason fired an arrow at the pot, causing it to break. From the shards, he made the lingam that is now enshrined in **Kumbeswara Temple**, whose *gopuras* today tower over the town, along with those of some seventeen other major shrines. A former capital of the Cholas, who are said to have kept a high-security treasury here, Kumbakonam is the chief commercial centre for the Thanjavur region. The main bazaar, **TSR Big Street**, is especially renowned for its quality costume jewellery.

The main reason to stop in Kumbakonam is to admire the exquisite sculpture of the **Nageshwara Swami Shiva Temple**, which contains the most refined Chola stone carving still in situ. The town also lies within easy reach of the magnificent Darasuram and Gangaikondacholapuram temples, both spectacular ancient monuments that see very few visitors. The village of Swamimalai, just a bike ride away, is the state's principal centre for traditional **bronze casting**.

Kumbeswara Temple

Nageshwaram Rd • Daily 6am–noon & 4–8pm • Free

Surmounted by a multicoloured *gopura*, the east entrance of Kumbakonam's seventeenth-century **Kumbeswara Temple**, home of the famous lingam from which the town derived its name, is approached via a covered market selling a huge assortment of cooking pots, a local speciality, as well as the usual glass bangles and trinkets. At the gateway, you may meet the temple elephant, with a painted forehead and necklace of bells. Beyond the flagstaff, a *mandapa* houses a fine collection of silver *vahanas*, vehicles of the deities, used in festivals, and *pancha loham* (compound of five metals) figures of the 63 Nayanmar poet-saints.

Sarangapani Temple

Off ISR Big St • Daily 6am–noon & 4–8pm • Free

The principal and largest of the Vishnu temples in Kumbakonam is the thirteenth-century **Sarangapani Temple**, entered through a ten-storey pyramidal *gopura* gate, more than 45m high. The **central shrine** dates from the late Chola period, with many later accretions. Its entrance, within the innermost court, is guarded by huge *dvarpalas*, identical to Vishnu whom they protect. Between them are carved stone *jali* screens, each different, and in front of them stands the sacred, square *homam* fireplace. During the day, rays of light from tiny ceiling windows penetrate the darkness around the sanctum, designed to resemble a chariot with reliefs of horses, elephants and wheels. A painted cupboard contains a mirror for Vishnu to see himself when he leaves the sanctum sanctorum.

Nageshwara Swami Shiva Temple

The small **Nageshwara Swami Shiva Temple**, in the centre of town, is Kumbakonam's oldest, founded in 886 and completed a few years into the reign of Parantaka I

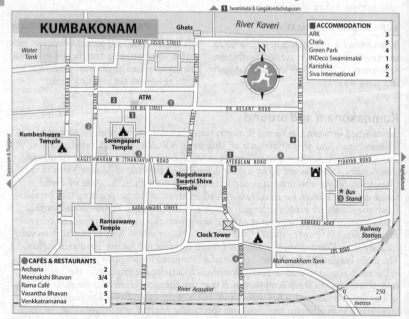

(907–c.940). First impressions are unpromising, as much of the original building has been hemmed in by later Disney-coloured additions, but beyond the main courtyard, occupied by a large columned *mandapa*, a small *gopura*-topped gateway leads to an inner enclosure where the earliest Chola shrine stands. Framed in the main niches around its sanctum wall are a series of exquisite stone figures, regarded as the finest surviving pieces of **ancient sculpture** in south India. With their languid stance and mesmeric, half-smiling facial expressions, these modest-sized masterpieces far outshine the more monumental art of Thanjavur and Gangaikondacholapuram.

Mahamakham

Indira Gandhi Rd • Daily 6am–noon & 4–8pm • Free

The most famous and revered of many sacred **water tanks** in Kumbakonam, the **Mahamakham** in the southeast of town is said to have filled with ambrosia (*amrit*) collected from the pot broken by Shiva. Every twelve years, when Jupiter passes the constellation of Leo, it is believed that water from the Ganges and eight other holy rivers flows into the tank, thus according it the status of *tirtha*, or sacred river crossing. At this auspicious time, as many as four million pilgrims come here for an absolving bathe; the last occasion was in early 2004.

Darasuram

From Kumbakonam it is a ₹6 bus journey, ₹20 by auto-rickshaw or an easy 5km bike ride (on the Thanjavur route) southwest; the route is flat enough, but keep your wits about you on the main Thanjavur highway

The **Airavateshwara Temple**, built by King Rajaraja II (c.1146–73), stands in the village of **DARASURAM**. This superb, if little-visited, Chola monument ranks alongside those at Thanjavur and Gangaikondacholapuram; but while the others are grandiose, emphasizing heroism and conquest, this is far smaller, exquisite in proportion and detail and said to have been decorated with *nitya-vinoda*, "perpetual entertainment", in mind. At this temple, Shiva is called Airavateshwara because he was worshipped here by Airavata, the white elephant belonging to Indra, king of the gods.

Darasuram's finest pieces of sculpture are the Chola black-basalt images adorning wall niches in the *mandapa* and inner shrine. These include images of Nagaraja, the snake-king, with a hood of cobras, and Dakshinamurti, the "south-facing" Shiva as teacher, expounding under a banyan tree.

Swamimalai

To reach Swamimalai from Darasuram, return to the main road from the temple and ask directions in the bazaar; Swamimalai is only 3km north, but cycling between the two involves several turnings, so expect to have to ask directions again. From Kumbakonam, the route is more straightforward; cross the Kaveri at the top of Town Hall St (north of the centre), turn left and follow the main road west through a ribbon of villages

SWAMIMALAI, 8km west of Kumbakonam, is revered as one of the six sacred abodes of Lord Murugan, Shiva's son, whom Hindu mythology records became his father's religious teacher (*swami*) on a hill (*malai*) here. The site of this epic role-reversal now hosts one of the Tamils' holiest shrines, the **Swaminatha Temple**, crowning the hilltop of the centre of the village, but of more interest to non-Hindus are the **bronze-casters'** workshops dotted around the bazaar and the outlying hamlets.

Known as **sthapathis**, Swamimalai's casters still employ the "lost wax" process perfected by the Cholas to make the most sought-after temple idols in south India. Their finished products are displayed in numerous showrooms along the main street, from where they are exported worldwide, but it is more memorable to watch the *sthapathis* in action, fashioning the original figures from beeswax and breaking open the moulds to expose the mystical finished metalwork inside.

ARRIVAL AND INFORMATION

KUMBAKONAM

By train Kumbakonam's small railway station, in the southeast of town 2km from the main bazaar, is well served by trains both north and south, and has a left-luggage office (24hr) and decent (non-a/c and a/c) retiring rooms (₹500/₹700).

By bus The hectic bus stand is in the southeast of town, just northwest of the railway station. All the timetables are in Tamil, but there's an enquiry office with English-speaking staff. Buses leave for Gangaikondacholapuram

(every 30min), Puducherry (hourly) and Thanjavur (every 5–10min) many going via Darasuram. Frequent services run to Chennai (every 30min), Trichy (every 5–10min) and there's a daily service to Bengaluru at 6pm.

Services There are a few small internet places on TSR Big St, where there is also an ICICI ATM machine, 100m from the *Siva International* hotel.

ACCOMMODATION

ARK 21 TSR Big St ✆ 0435 242 1942, ✉ info@hotelark .com. Centrally located hotel with five floors and fifty spacious and very clean rooms, all with TV and decent-sized bathrooms. The non-a/c rooms are very good value, while a/c rooms cost ₹1325. There's also an a/c bar serving overpriced beer. **₹900**

Chela 9 Ayekulam Rd ✆ 0435 243 0336, ✇ hotelchela .com. Large mid-range place located between the bus stand and the centre, with a pale green mock-classical front. The good-sized clean rooms (a/c ₹990) have soap, fresh towels and TV and there's a multicuisine restaurant and bar. **₹770**

Green Park 10 Lakshmi Vilai St ✆ 0435 240 3912, ✇ hotelgreenpark.co.in. Excellent-value business-oriented hotel with a choice of non-a/c and a/c rooms (₹1300) – all comfortable, clean and with TV. There's also a coffee shop and the *Suvai* vegetarian restaurant. **₹900**

INDeco Swamimalai In the hamlet of Thimmakkudy,

6km west of Kumbakonam ✆ 0435 248 0044, ✇ indecohotels.com. Set in its own grounds, this heritage resort is in a beautifully restored nineteenth-century brahmin's mansion, modern facilities in teak-and rosewood-furnished rooms. Suites ₹8820. Small swimming pool and massage. **₹5280**

Kanishka 18/450 Ayekulam Rd opposite the Chela ✆ 0435 2425231, ✇ hotelkanishka.in. A pleasant, friendly, business hotel with a range of comfortable, good-sized rooms, ranging up to ₹1238 for a/c executive rooms with king-size beds. The non-a/c doubles are very good value. **₹770**

Siva International 104/5 TSR Big St ✆ 0435 242 4013. This huge hotel complex is one of the tallest buildings in town. The rooms (a/c ₹770) are a good size and it's clean enough, but there are some grungy corridors. Great views from the rooftop. **₹472**

EATING

Archana Big Bazaar St. Right in the thick of the market, serving good-value south Indian "meals" (₹50) and great *uttapams*, this place is popular with the locals. Foreigners aren't often seen here, though will be made very welcome. Beware: it can get hot and stuffy inside. Daily 6am–10.30pm.

Meenakshi Bhavan Ayekulam Rd ✆ 0435 6454251. Excellent, clean south Indian veg joint, which serves some rarer snacks like *adai*, a form of spicy rice cake, and very good dosas for ₹30–45. "Meals" are ₹60 or ₹110 in the a/c room. Daily 7am–11pm.

Rama Café 17 Indira Gandhi Rd. This tiny café right by the Mahamakham tank is a great place to sit, chill and take in the

view. It serves simple veg "meals" (₹45), a range of snacks and south Indian coffee. Daily except Tues 7am–10pm.

Vasantha Bhavan Bus stand ✆ 0435 6533996. South Indian veg restaurant serving full range of south Indian breakfasts to fuel any onward journey. "Meals" are served from 11am (₹60) and there's also chai and coffee on offer. Daily 6am–midnight.

Venkkatramanaa 40 Gandhi Park North ✆ 0435 2400736. Huge and very popular restaurant, adorned with pictures of Sri Ramana. There's no English menu, but the staff are friendly and helpful. A small range of dishes including "meals" (₹55) and south Indian specials (₹75). Daily 5am–9.45pm.

Thanjavur

One of the busiest commercial towns of the Kaveri Delta, **THANJAVUR** (aka Tanjore), 55km east of Tiruchirapalli and 35km southwest of Kumbakonam, is nevertheless well worth a visit. Its history and treasures – among them the breathtaking **Brihadishwara Temple**, Tamil Nadu's most awesome Chola monument – give it a crucial significance to south Indian culture. The home of the world's finest Chola bronze collection, it holds enough of interest to keep you enthralled for at least a couple of days plus it's a good base for short trips to nearby Gangaikondacholapuram, Darasuram and Swamimalai.

Thanjavur divides into two sections, separated by the east–west **Grand Anicut Canal**. The **old town**, north of the canal and once entirely enclosed by a fortified wall, was chosen, between the ninth and the end of the thirteenth century, as the capital of their extensive empire by all the Chola kings save one. None of their secular buildings survive, but you can still see as many as ninety temples, of which the Brihadishwara most eloquently epitomizes the power and patronage of Rajaraja I (985–1014), whose military campaigns spread Hinduism to the Maldives, Sri Lanka and Java. Under the Cholas, as well as the later Nayaks and Marathas, literature, painting, sculpture, Carnatic classical music and Bharatanatyam dance all thrived here. Quite apart from its own intrinsic interest, the Nayak **royal palace compound** houses an important library and museums including a famous collection of bronzes.

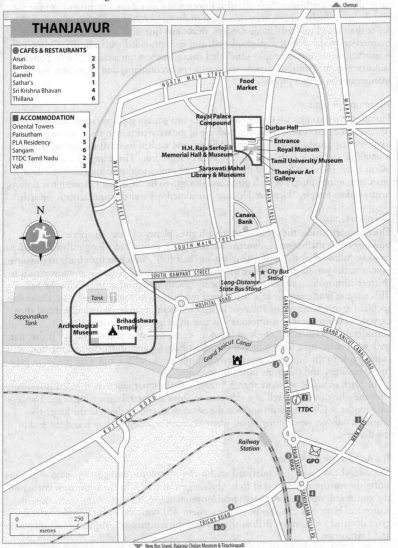

THANJAVUR

● **CAFÉS & RESTAURANTS**

Arun	2
Bamboo	5
Ganesh	3
Sathar's	1
Sri Krishna Bhavan	4
Thillana	6

■ **ACCOMMODATION**

Oriental Towers	4
Parisutham	1
PLA Residency	5
Sangam	6
TTDC Tamil Nadu	2
Valli	3

20

New Bus Stand, Rajaraja Cholan Museum & Tiruchirapalli

Of major local **festivals**, the most lavish celebrations at the Brihadishwara Temple are associated with the birthday of King Rajaraja, in October. An eight-day celebration of **Carnatic classical music** is held each January at the Panchanateshwara Temple at **Thiruvaiyaru**, 13km away, to honour the great Carnatic composer-saint, Thyagaraja.

Brihadishwara Temple
Temple Daily 6am–8pm • ☎ 04362 274476 **Museum** Daily 9am–6pm • Free

Thanjavur's skyline is dominated by the huge tower of the **Brihadishwara Temple**, which for all its size and UNESCO World Heritage status lacks the grandiose excesses of later periods. The temple was constructed as much to reflect the power of its patron, King Rajaraja I, as to facilitate the worship of Shiva. Profuse **inscriptions** on the base of the main shrine provide incredibly detailed information about the organization of the temple, showing it to have been rich, both in financial terms and in ritual activity. No fewer than four hundred female dancers, **devadasis** (literally "slaves to the gods", married off to the deity), were employed, and each provided with a house. Other staff – another two hundred people – included dance teachers, musicians, tailors, potters, laundrymen, goldsmiths, carpenters, astrologers, accountants and attendants for all manner of rituals and processions.

The temple entrance
Entrance to the complex is on the east, through two **gopura** gateways some way apart. Although the outer one is the larger, both are of the same pattern: massive rectangular bases topped by pyramidal towers with carved figures and vaulted roofs. At the core of each is a monolithic sandstone lintel, said to have been brought from Tiruchirapalli, more than 50km away. The outer facade of the inner *gopura* features mighty, fanged *dvarpala* door guardians, mirror images of each other, and thought to be the largest monolithic sculptures in any Indian temple. "Elephant blessings' are sometimes available just through the arch.

The main temple
Once you are inside, the gigantic **courtyard** gives plenty of space to appreciate the buildings. The **main temple**, constructed of granite, consists of a long pillared *mandapa* hallway, followed by the *ardhamandapa*, or "half-hall", which in turn leads to the inner sanctum, the *garbha griha*. Above the shrine, the pyramidal 61m *vimana* tower rises in thirteen diminishing storeys, the apex being exactly one third of the size of the base. This *vimana* is an example of a "structured monolith", a stage removed from the earlier rock-cut architecture of the Pallavas, in which blocks of stone are assembled and then carved. As the stone that surmounts it is said to weigh eighty tonnes, there is considerable speculation as to how it got up there; the most popular theory is that the rock was hauled up a 6km-long ramp. Others have suggested the use of a method comparable to the Sumer Ziggurat style of building, in which logs were placed in gaps in the masonry and the stone raised by leverage.

The black *shivalingam*, more than 3.5m high, in the **inner sanctum**, is called Adavallan, "the one who can dance well" – a reference to Shiva as Nataraja, the King of the Dance, who resides at Chidambaram and was the *ishtadevata*, chosen deity, of the king. The lingam is only on view during pujas, when a curtain is pulled back to reveal the god to the devotees.

The Archeological Museum
Outside, the walls of the courtyard are lined with **colonnaded passageways** – the one along the northern wall is said to be the longest in India. In the southwest corner of the courtyard, the small **Archeological Museum** houses an interesting collection of sculpture. Here you can also buy the excellent ASI booklet, *Chola Temples*, which gives detailed accounts of Brihadishwara and the temples at Gangaikondacholapuram and Darasuram.

Royal Palace Compound

East Main St (a continuation of Gandhiji Rd)• **Palace Compound** Daily 9am–6pm • Free **Durbar Hall** Daily 10am–5pm • ₹50 (₹10), camera ₹30, video ₹100

Members of the erstwhile royal family still reside in the **Royal Palace Compound**, 2km northeast of Brihadishwara Temple. Work on the palace began in the mid-sixteenth century under Sevappa Nayak, the founder of the Nayak kingdom of Thanjavur; additions were made by the Marathas from the end of the seventeenth century onwards. Dotted around the compound are several reminders of Thanjavur's past under these two dynasties, including an exhibition of oriental manuscripts and a superlative museum of **Chola bronzes**. Unfortunately, many of the palace buildings remain in a sorry state, despite various promises of funds for renovation.

Remodelled by Shaji II in 1684, the **Durbar Hall**, or hall of audience, houses a throne canopy decorated with the mirrored glass distinctive of Thanjavur. Although damaged, the ceiling and walls are elaborately painted. Five domes are striped red, green and yellow, and on the walls, friezes of leaf and pineapple designs and trumpeting angels in a night sky show European influence. The **courtyard** outside the Durbar Hall was the setting for one of the more poignant moments in Thanjavur's turbulent history when, in 1683, the last of the Nayak kings gave himself up to the king of Madurai. Its most imposing structure, the Sarja Madi or "seven-storey" bell tower, built by Serfoji II in 1800, is closed to the public due to its unsafe condition.

Saraswati Mahal Library Museum

Daily 10am–1pm & 1.30–5pm • Free

The **Saraswati Mahal Library** holds one of the most important oriental manuscript collections in India, used by scholars from all over the world. The library is closed to the general public, but a small **museum** displays a bizarre array of books and pictures from the collection. Among the palm-leaf manuscripts is a calligrapher's *tour de force* in the form of a visual mantra, where each letter in the inscription "Shiva" comprises the god's name repeated in microscopically small handwriting. Most of the Maratha manuscripts, produced from the end of the seventeenth century, are on paper; they

20

CHOLA BRONZES

Originally sacred temple objects, **Chola bronzes** are the only art form from Tamil Nadu to have penetrated the world art market. The most memorable bronze icons are the **Natarajas**, or dancing Shivas. The image of Shiva, standing on one leg, encircled by flames, with wild locks caught in mid-motion, has become almost as recognizably Indian as the Taj Mahal.

The principal icons of a temple are usually stationary and made of stone. Frequently, however, ceremonies require an image of the god to be led in procession outside the inner sanctum, and even through the streets. According to the canonical texts known as *Agamas*, these moving images should be made of metal. Indian bronzes are made by the **cire-perdue** ("**lost wax**") process, known as *madhuchchishtavidhana* in Sanskrit. Three layers of clay mixed with burned grain husks, salt and ground cotton are applied to a figure crafted in beeswax, with a stem left protruding at each end. When that is heated, the wax melts and flows out, creating a hollow mould into which molten metal – a rich five-metal alloy (*panchaloha*) of copper, silver, gold, brass and lead – can be poured through the stems. After the metal has cooled, the clay shell is destroyed, and the stems filed off, leaving a unique completed figure, which the caster-artist, or *sthapathi*, remodels to remove blemishes and add delicate detail.

Those bronzes produced by the few artists practising today invariably follow the Chola model; the chief centre is now **Swamimalai** (see p.987). Original Chola bronzes are kept in many Tamil temples, but as the interiors are often dark it's not always possible to see them properly. Important **public collections** include the Royal Palace Compound at Thanjavur (see above), the Government Museum at Chennai (see p.956) and the National Museum, New Delhi (see p.87).

include a superbly illustrated edition of the Mahabharata. Sadists will be delighted to see the library managed to hang on to their copy of the explicitly illustrated **Punishments in China**, published in 1804. Next to it, full rein is given to the imagination of French artist **Charles Le Brun** (1619–90), in a series of pictures on the subject of physiognomy. Animals such as the horse, bullock, wolf, bear, rabbit and camel are drawn in painstaking care above a series of human faces which bear an uncanny, if unlikely, resemblance to them. You can buy postcards of this scientific study and exhibits from the other palace museums in the **shop** next door.

Thanjavur Art Gallery

East Main St • Daily 9am–1 & 3pm–6pm • ₹60 (₹7), camera or video ₹100 (₹30)

A magnificent collection of **Chola bronzes** – the finest of them from the Tiruvengadu hoard, unearthed in the 1950s – fills the **Thanjavur Art Gallery**, a high-ceilinged audience hall with massive pillars, dating from 1600. The elegance of the figures and delicacy of detail are unsurpassed. A tenth-century statue of Kannappa Nayannar (#174), a hunter-devotee, shows minutiae right down to his embroidered clothing, fingernails and the fine lines on his fingers. The oldest bronze, four cases left of the main doorway (#58), shows Vinadhra Dakshinamurti ("south-facing Shiva") who, with a deer on one left hand, would have originally been playing the *vina* – the musical instrument has long since gone. However, the undisputed masterpiece of the collection shows Shiva as Lord of the Animals (#86), sensuously depicted in a skimpy loin-cloth, with a turban made of snakes. Next to him stands an equally stunning Parvati, his consort (#87), but the cream of the female figures, a seated, half-reclining Parvati (#97), is displayed on the opposite side of the hall.

20

ARRIVAL AND INFORMATION

By train Thanjavur's only railway station is located south of the old town, canal and Bridhadshwara temple complex. The tourist information office, GPO and hotels are all within easy walking distance. They are daily trains to Chenai Egmore (7hr 30min), Trichy (40min), Kumbakonam (42min) and Rameshwaram (8hr 5min).

By bus Most buses, including those from Madurai, Tiruchirapalli, and Kumbakonam, terminate at the New Bus Stand, 4km southwest of the centre. Rickshaws into town from here cost ₹100, or you can jump on one of the #74 or #75 buses that shuttle to and from the centre every few minutes. Some buses from Chennai and Puducherry still pull in at the old long-distance State

Bus Stand, opposite the City Bus Stand, at the southern end of the old town.

Destinations Kumbakonam (every 5min; 1hr 30min), Madurai (every 15min 6hr); Trichy (every 5min, 1hr 30min).

Tourist information The TTDC tourist office (Mon–Fri 10am–5.45pm; ☎04362 230984) is located in the compound of *TTDC Tamil Nadu* hotel on Gandhiji Rd.

Services The GPO is along a side road opposite the train station. You can change money at Canara Bank on South Main St and there are a few ATMs dotted around the town, including one at the railway station. One good internet access point is Gemini Soft, on the first floor of the *Oriental Towers* hotel, Srinivasam Pillai Rd.

ACCOMMODATION

Oriental Towers 2889 Srinivasam Pillai Rd ☎04362 230450, ⓦ hotelorientaltowers.com. Huge hotel-cum-shopping complex, with small swimming pool, internet access, a multicuisine restaurant and luxurious central a/c rooms. Four rooms on each floor have good temple views, while deluxe rooms are larger and cost an extra ₹500. Good value. **₹3120**

Parisutham 55 Grand Anicut Canal Rd ☎04362 231801, ⓦ hotelparisutham.com. Luxurious hotel with spacious, centrally a/c rooms, a large palm-fringed pool, Ayurvedic treatments, multicuisine restaurant, craft shop, foreign exchange and travel agent. It's a tad overpriced and popular with tour groups, so book ahead. **₹10900**

PLA Residency 2886 Srinivasam Pillai Rd ☎04362 270204, ⓦ plaresidency.com. Small but immaculate rooms with large flatscreen TVs and fab attached bathrooms with modern plumbing and serious shower-heads. It's worth paying an extra ₹200 for the bigger exec double. **₹1680**

Sangam Trichy Rd ☎04362 239451, ⓦ hotelsangam .com. Luxury four-star hotel on the edge of town with comfortable a/c rooms, an excellent restaurant (see opposite), pool (₹200 for non-residents) and beautiful Tanjore paintings – the one in the lobby is worth a trip here in itself. **₹6700**

TTDC Tamil Nadu Gandhiji Rd ☎04362 231325, ⓦ ttdconline.com. A 10min walk from the railway station, this state-run hotel, once the raja's guesthouse, manages to maintain lots of character. Large, comfortable and very clean rooms (a/c ₹1350 and deluxe ₹1912) have a sofa and armchairs, all of them are set around a pleasant enclosed garden. ₹880

★ **Valli** 2948 MKM Rd ☎04362 231580,

✉arasu_tnj@rediffmail.com. At the end of an industrial lane, this friendly hotel has clean rooms (a/c ₹1463), with a choice of Indian or Western loos (₹715), a rooftop terrace and convenient but rather average restaurant. The best budget option in town. ₹605

EATING AND DRINKING

Arun Court Rd ☎04362 277310. Conveniently located on the corner of Gandhiji and Court Roads, this small pure-veg south Indian restaurant has an extensive menu featuring 96 dishes, most of which cost around ₹50. Try the masala dosas (₹40). Daily 6.30am–10pm.

Bamboo PLA Residency, 2886 Srinivasam Pillai Rd ☎04362 270204. Light and airy rooftop restaurant with a welcome cool breeze serving pure veg "meals" at lunchtime for ₹50 and a range of north Indian dishes and breads in the evening. Daily 11.30am–3pm & 6.30–10.30pm.

Ganesh 2905 Srinivasam Pillai Rd ☎04362 277032. Large, clean south Indian *dhaba* situated on the first floor. Serves a wide range of veg dishes, a selection of noodle dishes (₹40–80), masala dosas (₹32) and tandoori food after 4pm. Daily 7am–10.30pm.

Sathar's 167 Gandhiji Rd ☎04362 277032. The most popular non-veg restaurant in town, serving a variety of

chicken dishes, all costing around ₹120, and a few veggie dishes for ₹100. There are three separate sections, including an a/c hall upstairs. Daily 12.30–4.30pm & 6.30–11.30pm.

★ **Sri Krishna Bhavan** 68a VAC Nagar Trichy Rd ☎04362 233344. Very clean and popular pure-veg restaurant, which serves delicious, unlimited thalis for just ₹50 and a good range of curries (₹65–70) and breads. Their a/c hall is open from 10am–10pm. Daily 7am–10pm.

★ **Thillana** Sangam, Trichy Rd ☎04362 239451. Swish multicuisine restaurant renowned for its superb lunchtime south Indian thalis (₹250). In the evening, the extensive à la carte menu, featuring superb *chettinad* specialities (₹190), is served up with live Carnatic music from 7–11pm (count on ₹600/head). Daily noon–3pm & 7–11pm.

20

Tiruchirapalli (Trichy) and around

TIRUCHIRAPALLI – more commonly referred to as **Trichy** – stands in the plains between the Shevaroy and Palani hills, just under 100km north of Madurai. Dominated by the dramatic Rock Fort, it's a sprawling commercial centre with a modern feel. Most of its business is in the southern **Trichy Junction** district, where the **bazaars**, immediately north of the Junction, heave with locally made cigars, textiles and fake diamonds, made into inexpensive jewellery and sewn into dance costumes. Head north along Big Bazaar Road and you're confronted by the dramatic profile of the **Rock Fort**, topped by the seventeenth-century Vinayaka (Ganesh) Temple. There are several British churches dotted around the town, the most notable of which is **Our Lady of Lourdes**, west of the Rock Fort, which is modelled on the basilica of Lourdes.

North of the fort, the River Kaveri marks a wide boundary between the crowded business districts and the somewhat more serene temples a beyond the river. The spectacular **Ranganathaswamy Temple** in **Srirangam**, 6km north of central Trichy, is so large it holds much of the village within its courtyards. Also north of the Kaveri is the elaborate **Sri Jambukeshwara Temple**.

Brief history

The precise date of Trichy's foundation is uncertain, but though little early architecture remains, it is clear that between 200 and 1000 AD control of the city passed between the Pallavas and Pandyas. The Chola kings who gained supremacy in the eleventh century embarked upon ambitious building projects, reaching a zenith with the Ranganathaswamy Temple. In the twelfth century, the Cholas were ousted by the Vijayanagar kings of Hampi, who then stood up against Muslim invasions until 1565, when they succumbed to the might of the sultans of the Deccan. Less than fifty years later the Nayaks of Madurai came to power, constructing the fort and firmly establishing Trichy as a trading city. After almost a century of struggle against the

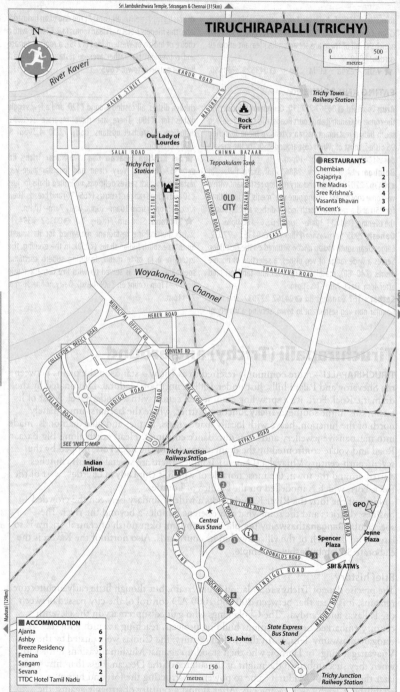

Sri Jambukeshwara Temple, Srirangam & Chennai (315km)

TIRUCHIRAPALLI (TRICHY)

River Kaveri

KARUR ROAD

MADURA RD

Trichy Town
Railway Station

Rock
Fort

NAVAB STREET

Our Lady of
Lourdes

SALAI ROAD   CHINNA BAZAAR

Trichy Fort
Station

Teppakulam Tank

● RESTAURANTS
Chembian	1
Gajapriya	2
The Madras	5
Sree Krishna's	4
Vasanta Bhavan	3
Vincent's	6

SHASTRI RD

MADRAS TRUNK RD

WEST BOULEVARD ROAD

BIG BAZAAR ROAD

BOULEVARD ROAD

EAST

OLD
CITY

Woyakondan Channel

THANJAVUR ROAD

Thanjavur

MUNICIPAL OFFICE RD

HEBER ROAD

COLLECTOR'S OFFICE ROAD

CONVENT RD

RACE COURSE ROAD

CLEVELAND ROAD

DINDIGUL ROAD

MADURAI ROAD

SEE 'INSET' MAP

BYPASS ROAD

Indian
Airlines

Trichy Junction
Railway Station

Madurai (129km)

1

2
2

WILLIAMS ROAD

3

GPO

ROYAL ROAD

Central
Bus Stand

MACQUEL COURT LANE

i

4   3   6

5

McDONALDS ROAD

Spencer
Plaza

9 5

6

Jenne
Plaza

BIRDS ROAD

SBI & ATM's

ROCKINS ROAD

6

7

DINDIGUL ROAD

MADURAI ROAD

State Express
Bus Stand

St. Johns

■ ACCOMMODATION
Ajanta	6
Ashby	7
Breeze Residency	5
Femina	3
Sangam	1
Sevana	2
TTDC Hotel Tamil Nadu	4

0   150
metres

Trichy Junction
Railway Station

Airport (6km)

20

French and British, who both sought lands in southeast Tamil Nadu, the town came under British control until it was declared part of Tamil Nadu state in 1947.

The Rock Fort

Daily 6am–8pm • ₹3, camera ₹20, video camera ₹100 • ☎ 0431 270 4621, ⓦ rockforttemple.com • Bus #1 from outside the railway station or Dindigul Rd

The massive sand-coloured rock on which Trichy's **Rock Fort** rests towers to a height of more than 80m, its irregular sides smoothed by wind and rain. The Pallavas were the first to cut into it, but it was the Nayaks who grasped the site's potential as a fort, adding only a few walls and bastions as fortifications. From the entrance, off China Bazaar, a long flight of red-and-white painted steps cuts steeply uphill, past a series of Pallava and Pandya rock-cut temples (closed to non-Hindus), to the **Ganesh Temple** crowning the hilltop. The views from its terrace are spectacular, taking in the Ranganathaswamy and Jambukeshwara temples to the north, their *gopuras* rising from a sea of palm trees, and the cubic concrete sprawl of central Trichy to the south.

Sri Ranganathaswamy Temple

Srirangam • Daily 5.30am–9pm • ₹10; camera ₹50, video ₹100; official guides ₹300/2hr • Frequent buses from Trichy pull in and leave from the southern gate

The **Sri Ranganathaswamy Temple** at **Srirangam**, 6km north of Trichy Junction, is among the most revered shrines to Vishnu in south India, and also one of the largest and liveliest. Enclosed by seven rectangular walled courtyards and covering more than sixty hectares, it stands on an island defined by a tributary of the River Kaveri. This location symbolizes the transcendence of Vishnu, housed in the sanctuary reclining on the coils of the snake Adisesha, who in legend formed an island for the god, resting on the primordial Ocean of Chaos.

The temple complex

A gateway topped with an immense and heavily carved *gopura*, completed in the late 1980s, leads to the outermost courtyard, the latest of seven built between the fifth and seventeenth centuries. Most of the present structure dates from the late fourteenth century, when the temple was renovated and enlarged after a disastrous sacking in 1313.

The first **three courtyards** form the hub of the temple community, housing ascetics, priests, musicians and souvenir shops. On reaching the fourth wall, the entrance to the temple proper, visitors remove footwear and can purchase camera and video camera tickets before passing through a high gateway, topped by a magnificent *gopura* and lined with small shrines to teachers, hymn-singers and sages. In earlier days, this **fourth** *prakara* would have formed the outermost limit of the temple, and was the closest members of the lowest castes could get to the sanctuary. It contains some of the finest and oldest buildings of the complex, including a temple to the goddess **Ranganayaki** in the northwest corner where devotees worship before approaching Vishnu's shrine. On the eastern side of the *prakara*, the heavily carved "thousand pillared" *kalyan mandapa*, or hall, was constructed in the late Chola period. The pillars of the outstanding **Sheshagiriraya Mandapa**, south of the *kalyan mandapa*, are decorated with rearing steeds and hunters, representing the triumph of good over evil.

To the right of the gateway into the fourth courtyard, a small **museum** houses a modest collection of stone and bronze sculptures and some delicate ivory plaques. For ₹10, you can climb to the roof of the fourth wall from beside the museum and take in the view over the temple rooftops and *gopuras*, which increase in size from the centre outwards.

20

Inside the gate to the **fifth courtyard** – the final section of the temple open to non-Hindus – is a pillared hall, the **Garuda Mandapa**, carved throughout in typical Nayak style. Maidens, courtly donors and Nayak rulers feature on the pillars that surround the central shrine to Garuda, the man-eagle vehicle of Vishnu.

ARRIVAL AND DEPARTURE
TIRUCHIRAPALLI (TRICHY) AND AROUND

By plane Trichy's airport (enquiries and bookings ☎ 0431 248 0233) is 8km south of the centre and has daily flights to and from Chennai, several weekly to Thiruvananthapuram and Kozhikode, and frequent services to Sri Lanka and the Gulf states. The journey into town, by taxi (around ₹250) or bus (#7, #28, #59, #63 or #K1) takes less than 30min.

By train The main railway station, Trichy Junction, which has given its name to the southern district of town, is within easy reach of most hotels and restaurants.

Destinations Bengaluru (1 daily; 8hr 55min); Chengalpattu (6–7 daily; 4hr–5hr 20min); Chennai (7–9 daily; 5hr 20min–7hr); Coimbatore (2 daily; 4hr 55min–5hr 10min); Kanyakumari (3 daily; 7hr 30min–9hr); Kochi (1 daily; 9hr 30min); Kodaikanal Rd (2–4 daily; 1hr 50min–2hr 15min); Madurai (8–9 daily; 2hr 45min–3hr 30min); Thanjavur (2 daily; 1hr 10min–1hr 25min).

By bus There are two main bus stands in Trichy, State Express and Central. The State Express stand is almost opposite the railway station and is used by more of the Tamil Nadu state buses, while the Central Stand, at the other end of Rockins Rd, serves more private buses. The efficient local city service (#1) that leaves from the platform on Rockins Rd, opposite the *Shree Krishna* restaurant, is the most convenient way of getting to the Rock Fort, the temples and Srirangam. Auto-rickshaws are also widely available.

Destinations Chengalpattu (every 20–30min; 7–8hr); Chennai (every 20–30min; 8hr 30min–9hr 30min); Coimbatore (every 30min; 5hr); Kanchipuram (3 daily; 7hr); Kanyakumari (every 30min; 10–12hr); Kodaikanal (8–10 daily; 5hr); Madurai (every 30min; 4–5hr); Puducherry (every 30min; 5–6hr); Thanjavur (every 10min; 1hr–1hr 30min); Tiruvannamalai (5 daily; 6hr).

INFORMATION

Tourist information The tourist office (Mon–Fri 10am–5.30pm; ☎ 0431 246 0136), which offers travel information but no maps, is just outside the *Tamil Nadu* hotel, opposite the Central Bus Stand.

Services There are many plces to change money. The Karur Vysya Bank ATM on the ground floor just outside Jenne Plaza is good, and in the Plaza is the Highway Forex office (Mon–Sat 10am–6pm). The State Bank of India on

Dindigul Rd exchanges American Express and Thomas Cook travellers' cheques; there are several ATMs clustered together here, including SBI's own. There are more ATMs in the vicinity of the bus stands. Many hotels have wi-fi and there are plenty of internet points, including Netpark in Jenne Plaza and the two branches of iWay near the Central Bus Stand.

ACCOMMODATION

Ajanta 6A, Rockins Rd ☎ 0431 241 5501. A huge, 85-room complex centred on its own Vijayanagar shrine, and with an opulent Tirupati deity in reception, which is popular with middle-class pilgrims. The clean, plain rooms (a/c ₹1485; good-value singles ₹490) come with towels provided. **₹825**

Ashby 17-A Rockins Rd ☎ 0431 246 0652, ⊛ ashbyhotel .com. This atmospheric Raj-era place is first choice for most foreign tourists, though it's seen better days. The rooms (a/c ₹1575) are large and clean, with cable TV and mosquito coils, and there's a decent little courtyard restaurant. **₹660**

★ **Breeze Residency** 3/14 McDonald's Rd ☎ 0431 404 5333, ⊛ breezeresidency.com. This large, centrally located a/c hotel boasts good-sized, comfortably furnished rooms, a nicely decorated foyer, swimming pool and a very good restaurant, *The Madras* (see opposite). **₹4930**

Femina 109 Williams Rd, near the Central Bus Stand ☎ 0431 241 4501, ⊛ feminahotles.in. Well-maintained,

sprawling block of a/c rooms (deluxe ₹3600), some with balconies offering views of the Rock Fort. The hotel also houses two plush restaurants, travel services, shops, a pool, fitness centre and 24hr coffee bar. **₹2040**

Sangam Collector's Office Rd ☎ 0431 241 4700, ⊛ hotelsangam.com. Trichy's top hotel, with all the facilities expected of a four-star: a very nice swimming pool (₹200 for non-residents) and an excellent restaurant, *The Chembian* (see opposite), with live music at weekends. Deluxe rooms ₹6600. **₹4080**

Sevana 5 Royal Rd (next to the Gajapriya) ☎ 0431 241 5201. Set in its own grounds 100m back from the main road, this hotel lacks character but offers clean, spacious doubles with king-size beds and towels provided. There's a good-value 33 percent discount for single occupancy and the a/c tariff (₹1265) includes breakfast. **₹660**

TTDC Tamil Nadu McDonald's Rd ☎ 0431 241 4346, ⊛ ttdconline.com. One of TTDC's better hotels, and just far

20

enough from the bus stand to escape the din. There are two categories of a/c rooms (standard ₹1045; larger deluxe ₹1560), all with cable TV, but the non-a/c rooms are better value. ₹715

EATING

Chembian Sangam hotel, Collector's Office Rd ☏ 0431 424 4555. This excellent restaurant offers a range of delicious Indian dishes as well as unusually good Western and Chinese cuisine, in an atmospheric, beautifully decorated dining hall. Non-veg mains around ₹250. Live Carnatic music at weekends. Daily noon–3pm & 7–11pm.

Gajapriya Royal Rd ground floor of the Gajapriya hotel. Non-veg north Indian and noodle dishes are specialities of this small but blissfully cool and clean a/c restaurant. Meat dishes cost around ₹100. Daily 6.30–11pm

The Madras Breeze Residency, 3/14 McDonald's Rd ☏ 0431 404 5333. Worth a visit for their excellent-value lunchtime (₹250) and dinner buffets (₹324), which feature a wide range of Indian and Chinese dishes and a few random Mexican treats thrown into the mix. Daily 12.30–3.30pm & 7.30–11pm.

Shree Krishna 1 Rockins Rd, opposite the Central Bus Stand ☏ 0431 241 4737. Delicious and very filling American or south Indian set breakfasts (₹100), unlimited banana-leaf thalis at lunchtime (₹65) and a range of veggie curries (₹50–60) in the evenings – all served with a smile. Daily 6am–11pm.

Vasanta Bhavan Abhirami Hotel Complex, 10 Rockins Rd, opposite Central Bus Stand ☏ 0431 241 5001. Trichy's best-known south Indian restaurant, serving up unbeatable value lunchtime "meals" (₹70) and the standard range of snacks the rest of the day. The fast-food counter serves dosas and *uttapams* all day. Daily 6am–11pm.

Vincent's 6 Madurai Rd, next to Spencer Plaza and Vincent's bakery ☏ 90039 25210. Set back from the road in its own terrace garden, with mock pagodas, concrete bamboo and a multicuisine menu that includes tasty chicken tikka and fish dishes. The bakery (9am–10pm) sells great cakes and coffee. No alcohol. Daily noon–3pm & 6.30–10pm

20

Madurai

One of the oldest cities in South Asia, **MADURAI**, on the banks of the River Vaigai, has been an important centre of worship and commerce for as long as there has been civilization in south India. It was often described as "the Athens of the East" and indeed, when the Greek ambassador Megasthenes visited in 302 BC, he wrote of its splendour and described its queen, Pandai, as "a daughter of Herakles". The Roman geographer Strabo also wrote of Madurai, complaining that the city's silk, pearls and spices were draining the imperial coffers of Rome. It was this lucrative trade that enabled the **Pandyan** dynasty to erect the mighty **Meenakshi-Sundareshwarar temple**. Although now surrounded by a sea of modern concrete cubes, the massive *gopuras* of this vast complex, writhing with multicoloured mythological figures and crowned by golden finials, remain the greatest man-made spectacle of the south. No fewer than 15,000 people pass through its gates every day and on Fridays (sacred to the goddess Meenakshi) numbers swell to more than 25,000, while the temple's ritual life spills out into the streets in an almost ceaseless round of festivals and processions.

Although considerably enlarged and extended through the ages, the overall layout of Madurai's **old city**, south of the River Vaigai, has remained largely unchanged since the first centuries AD, comprising a series of concentric squares centred on the massive **Meenakshi Temple**. Aligned with the cardinal points, the street plan forms a giant mandala, whose sacred properties are activated during the regular mass clockwise circumambulations of the central temple. **North of the river**, Madurai becomes markedly more mundane and irregular. You're only likely to cross the Vaigai to reach the city's more expensive hotels or the Gandhi Museum.

Brief history

Although invariably interwoven with myth, the traceable history and fame of Madurai stretches back well over 2000 years. Numerous natural **caves** in local hills,

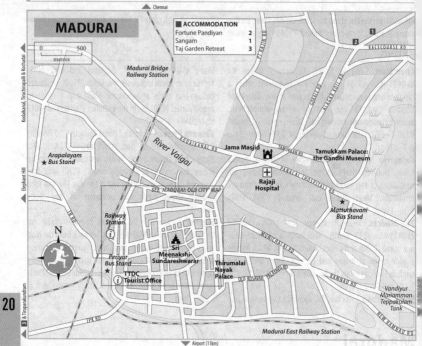

and boulders often modified by the addition of simple rock-cut beds, were used both in prehistoric times and by ascetics such as the Ajivikas and Jains, who practised withdrawal and penance.

Madurai appears to have been capital of the Pandyan empire without interruption for at least a thousand years. It became a major commercial city, trading with Greece, Rome and China, and *yavanas* (a generic term for foreigners) were frequent visitors to Pandyan seaports. The Tamil epics describe them walking around town with their eyes and mouths wide open with amazement. Under the Pandya dynasty, Madurai also became an established seat of Tamil culture, credited with being the site of three **sangams**, "literary academies", said to date back ten thousand years and which supported some eight thousand poets.

The Pandyas' capital fell in the tenth century, when the **Chola** king Parantaka took the city. In the thirteenth century, the Pandyas briefly regained power until the early 1300s, when the notorious **Malik Kafur**, the Delhi Sultanate's "favourite slave", made an unprovoked attack during a plunder-and-desecration tour of the south, and destroyed much of the city. Forewarned of the raid, the Pandya king, Sundara, fled with his immediate family and treasure, leaving his uncle and rival, Vikrama Pandya, to repel Kafur. Nevertheless, the latter returned to Delhi with booty said to consist of "six hundred and twelve elephants, ninety-six thousand *mans* of gold, several boxes of jewels and pearls and twenty thousand horses".

Shortly after this raid Madurai became an independent Sultanate. In 1364, it joined the Hindu **Vijayanagar** empire, ruled from Hampi and administered by governors, the **Nayaks**. In 1565, the Nayaks asserted their own independence. Under their supervision and patronage, Madurai enjoyed a renaissance, being rebuilt on the pattern of a lotus centring on the Meenakshi Temple. Part of the palace of the most illustrious of the Nayaks, **Thirumalai** (1623–55), survives today. The city remained under Nayak control until the mid-eighteenth century when it was gradually taken over by the British. A hundred years later the British de-fortified Madurai, filling its moat to create the four Veli streets that today mark the boundary of the old city.

Sri Meenakshi-Sundareshwarar Temple

Daily 4am–12.30pm & 4–10pm • Camera ₹50, video camera ₹250

Enclosed by a roughly rectangular 6m-high wall, in the manner of a fortified palace, the **Sri Meenakshi-Sundareshwarar Temple** is one of the largest temple complexes in India. Much of it was constructed during the Nayak period between the sixteenth and eighteenth centuries, but certain parts are very much older.

For the first-time visitor, confronted with a confusing maze of shrines, sculptures and colonnades, and unaware of the logic employed in their arrangement, it's very easy to get disorientated. Quite apart from the estimated 33,000 sculptures to arrest your attention, the life of the temple is absolutely absorbing, with the endless round of puja ceremonies, loud *nagaswaram* and *tavil* music, weddings, brahmin boys under religious instruction in the Vedas, the prostrations of countless devotees and the glittering market stalls inside the east entrance. Even if you're not lucky enough to see a festival procession, something is always going on to make this one of the most compelling places in Tamil Nadu.

Approximately fifty priests live and work here, recognizable by the white *dhotis* tied between their legs and silk cloth worn around their waists.

The entrance

Madurai takes the **gopura**, prominent in all southern temples, to its ultimate extreme. The entire complex has no fewer than twelve such towers. Built into the outer walls, the four largest reach a height of around 46m and are covered with a profusion of gaily painted stucco gods and demons.

20

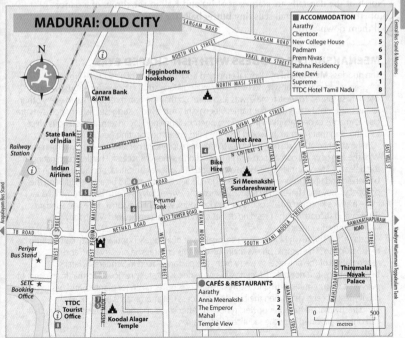

MADURAI: OLD CITY

N

Higginbothams bookshop

Canara Bank & ATM

State Bank of India

Railway Station

Indian Airlines

Market Area

Bike Hire

Sri Meenakshi-Sundareshwarar

Perumal Tank

TB ROAD

Periyar Bus Stand

SETC Booking Office

TTDC Tourist Office

Koodal Alagar Temple

Thirumalai Nayak Palace

Arapalayam Bus Stand

Central Bus Stand & Museums

Vandiyur Mariamman Teppakkulam Tank

■ ACCOMMODATION	
Aarathy	7
Chentoor	2
New College House	5
Padmam	6
Prem Nivas	3
Rathna Residency	1
Sree Devi	4
Supreme	1
TTDC Hotel Tamil Nadu	8

● CAFÉS & RESTAURANTS	
Aarathy	5
Anna Meenakshi	3
The Emperor	2
Mahal	4
Temple View	1

0 ————— 500
metres

▼ Airport (11km)

The most popular **entrance**, on the east side, leads directly to the Shiva shrine. Another entrance nearby, through a towerless gate, leads to the adjacent Meenakshi shrine deep inside. In the **Ashta Shakti Mandapa** ("Eight Goddesses Hallway"), a market sells puja offerings and souvenirs. Sculpted pillars illustrate different aspects of the goddess Shakti, and Shiva's 64 miracles at Madurai.

Golden Lotus Tank

Continuing straight on from the Ashta Shakti Mandapa, you cross East Ati Street and having passed through the seven-storey **Chitrai gopura** you then enter a passageway which leads to the eastern end of the **Pottamarai Kulam** ("Golden Lotus Tank"), where Indra bathed before worshipping the *shivalingam*. From the west side of the tank you can see the glistening gold of the Meenakshi and Sundareshwar *vimana* towers. Facing Meenakshi, just beyond the first entrance and in front of the sanctum sanctorum, stands Shiva's bull-vehicle, Nandi. At around 9pm, the moveable images of the god and goddess are carried to the **bed chamber**. Here the final puja ceremony of the day, the **lalipuja**, is performed, when for thirty minutes or so the priests sing lullabies (*lali*), before closing the temple for the night.

Every Friday (6–7pm) Sundareshwar and Meenakshi are brought to the sixteenth-century **Oonjal Mandapa**, where they are placed on a swing (*oonjal*) and serenaded by members of a special caste, the Oduvars.

Sundareshwarar Shrine

Walking back north, past the Meenakshi shrine and through a towered entrance, you arrive at the Sundareshwarar shrine. Inside is the huge monolithic Ganesh, **Mukkuruni Vinayaka**, thought to have been unearthed during excavation of the Mariamman Teppakulam tank. Chubby Ganesh is wellknown for his love of sweets and during the annual **Vinayaka Chaturthi festival** (Sept), a special prasad (food offering) is concocted using 300 kilos of rice, 10 kilos of sugar and 110 coconuts.

North of the flagstaffs are statues of Shiva and Kali in the throes of a dance competition; a nearby stall sells tiny **butter balls** for visitors to throw at the deities "to cool them down".

MEENAKSHI: THE GODDESS WITH FISH-SHAPED EYES

The goddess **Meenakshi** of Madurai emerged from the flames of a sacrificial fire as a three-year-old child, in answer to the Pandyan king Malayadvaja's prayer for a son. The king, not only surprised to see a female, was also horrified that she had three breasts. In every other respect, she was beautiful, as her name, Meenakshi ("fish-eyed"), suggests; fish-shaped eyes are classic images of desirability in Indian love poetry. Dispelling his concern, a mysterious voice told the king that Meenakshi would lose the third breast on meeting her future husband.

In the absence of a male heir, the adult Meenakshi succeeded her father as Pandyan monarch. With the aim of world domination, she embarked on a series of successful battles, culminating in the defeat of Shiva's armies in his Himalayan abode, Mount Kailash. Shiva then appeared on the battlefield and upon seeing him, Meenakshi immediately lost her third breast thus fulfilling the prophecy. They then travelled to Madurai, where they were duly married. They assumed a dual role – firstly as king and queen of the Pandya kingdom, with Shiva assuming the title Sundara Pandya, and secondly as the presiding deities of the Madurai temple, into which they subsequently disappeared.

Today, their shrines in Madurai are the focal point of a hugely popular fertility cult centred on their "coupling". The temple priests maintain that this ensures the preservation and regeneration of the universe, so every night the pair are placed in Sundareshwar's bedchamber – but not before Meenakshi's nose ring is carefully removed so that in the heat of passion it won't cut her husband. However, fidelity is never taken for granted, and has to be ritually tested each year when the beautiful goddess Cellattamman is brought to Sundareshwar "to have her powers renewed". After she is spurned, she flies into a fury that can only be placated with the sacrifice of a buffalo.

20

The Thousand Pillar Hall

Art Museum Daily (daily 6.30am–12.30pm & 4–9pm; ₹5 extra if you have a temple ticket; temple camera ticket valid here)

Leaving through the east gateway of the Sundareshwaar shrine you come to the fifteenth-century **Ayirakkal Mandapa**, (thousand-pillared hall) in the northeast corner, which now houses the temple **Art Museum**. Throughout the hall, large sculptures of strange mythical creatures and cosmic deities rear out at you from the broad stone pillars, some of which have startlingly metallic-like musical tones when tapped.

Vandiyur Mariamman Teppakulam

Ramnad Rd • Bus #4 or #4A

At one time, the huge **Vandiyur Mariamman Teppakulam** tank in the southeast of town, with its constant supply of water, flowing via underground channels from the Vaigai, was always full. Nowadays it is only filled during the spectacular Teppam **floating festival** (Jan/Feb), when pilgrims take boats out to the goddess shrine in the centre. Before their marriage ceremony, Shiva and Meenakshi are brought in procession to the tank, where they float on a beautifully illuminated raft pulled by devotees, that encircles the shire. The boat trip is the overture to a seduction that reaches its passionate conclusion later that night in the temple. This traditionally makes the Teppam the most auspicious time of year for young couples to get married.

Thirumalai Nayak Palace

Mahlyadampokki St • **Palace** Daily 9am–5pm • ₹50 (₹10), camera ₹30, video camera ₹100, includes Palace Museum **Sound-and-Light Show** English 6.45–7.35pm; ₹50 • Tamil 8–8.50pm; ₹25; tickets issued 15min before the show • ☎ 0452 233 2945

Today only a quarter of the seventeenth-century **Thirumalai Nayak Palace**, located 1.5km southeast of the Meenakshi Temple, survives. Much of it was dismantled by Thirumalai's grandson, Chockkanatha Nayak, and used to build a new palace at Tiruchirapalli. The remains were renovated in 1858 by Lord Napier, then governor of Madras, and once again in 1971 for the Tamil World Conference. The palace originally consisted of two residential sections, a theatre, private temple, harem, royal bandstand, armoury and gardens. The **Palace Museum** in an adjacent hall includes unlabelled Pandyan, Jain and Buddhist sculptures, terracottas and an eighteenth-century print of the palace in a dilapidated state. A nightly **Sound-and-Light Show** (in both English and Tamil) recalls the story of the Tamil epic, Shilipaddikaram, and the history of the Nayaks.

Tamukkam Palace: the Gandhi Memorial Museum

Tamukkan Rd **Museum** Sat–Thurs • 10am–1pm & 2–5.45pm • Free **Library** Daily except Fri 10am–1pm & 2–5.45pm • Free • Bus #1, #2, #11, #13 #14 #17 #24 (from Periyar bus stand 20min)

Across the Vaigai, 5km northeast of the centre near the Central Telegraph Office, stands **Tamukkam**, the seventeenth-century multipillared and arched palace of Queen Rani Mangammal. Built to accommodate such regal entertainment as elephant fights, Tamukkam was taken over by the British, used as a courthouse and collector's office, and in 1955 became home to the Gandhi and Government museums. The **Gandhi Memorial Museum** charts the history of India since the landing of the first Europeans, viewed in terms of the freedom struggle. The perspective is national, but where appropriate, reference is made to the role played by Tamils. Wholeheartedly critical of the British, it states its case clearly and simply, quoting the condemnation by Englishman John Sullivan of his fellow countrymen's insulting treatment of Indians. One chilling artefact, kept in a room painted black, is the bloodstained *dhoti* the Mahatma was wearing when he was assassinated. Next door to the museum, the **Gandhi Memorial Museum Library** houses a reference collection, open to all, of fifteen thousand books, periodicals, letters and microfilms.

ARRIVAL AND DEPARTURE

By plane Madurai's small domestic airport (☎0452 269 0433), 12km south of the centre, is served by daily flights to and from Chennai, Mumbai, Delhi, Bengaluru, Hyderabad and three flights a week to Kochi. Jet Airways (offices at the airport) have two daily flights to Chennai and Air India (7-A West Veli St near the post office; ☎0452 269 0433) five weekly. SpiceJet operate the Hyderabad and Bengaluru routes. To get to the airport, catch a taxi (around ₹250) or take city bus #10A from the Periyar Bus Stand.

By train The reservations office is to the left of the main hall. There's a small veg canteen on Platform 1, and a pre-paid auto-rickshaw and taxi booth outside the main entrance. Madurai is well connected with most major towns and cities in south India. For further timetable details, ask the Tourism Department Information Centre, to the right of the ticket counters. It's possible to reach the railhead for Kodaikanal by train, but the journey is much faster by express bus.

By bus The Central Bus Stand is the arrival point for all services except those from Kerala and west Tamil Nadu, which arrive at Arapalayam Bus Stand. The Central Bus stand is 7km from the centre, east of the river, and is connected to the centre by city buses #700 and #75, while Arapalayam Bus Stand is in the northwest, about 2km from the railway station. Periyar bus stand, on West Veli St, is for local city buses. Next to Periyar is the Tamil Nadu State Express reservation office (8am–2pm & 4pm–8pm) for a/c buses to Chennai and other destinations including several Keralan towns and Bengaluru.

Destinations (from the Central Bus Stand unless otherwise stated): Chengalpattu (every 20–30min; 9hr); Chennai (every 20–30min; 11hr); Chidambaram (6 daily; 8hr); Coimbatore (Arapalayam stand, every 30min; 5–6hr); Kanchipuram (4 daily; 10–12hr); Kanyakumari (every 30min; 6hr); Kochi/Ernakulam via Kottayam (Arapalayam stand, 9 daily; 10hr); Kodaikanal (Arapalayam stand, hourly; 4hr); Kumbakonam (8 daily; 6hr–6hr 30min); Kumily, for Periyar Wildlife Sanctuary (Arapalayam stand, hourly; 5hr); Mysore (5 daily; 10hr); Puducherry (hourly; 9–10hr); Rameshwaram (every 30min–1hr; 4hr); Thanjavur (every 30min; 4–5hr); Thiruvananthapuram, Kerala (hourly; 7hr); Tiruchirapalli (every 30min; 4–5hr); Tirupati (4 daily; 15hr). There are no direct services from Madurai to Ooty – you need to change in Coimbatore.

GETTING AROUND AND INFORMATION

Bike rental Cheap bike rental is available at SV, West Tower St, near the west entrance to the temple, or the stall on West Veli St, opposite the *Tamil Nadu* hotel.

Tourist information The TTDC tourist office, on West Veli St (Mon–Fri 10am–5.45pm, plus Sat 10am–1pm during festivals; ☎0452 233 4757), is useful for general information and maps, and can provide information on car rental and approved guides. If you want a taxi to see the outlying sights, head to the rank at the main railway station, which abides by government set rates; a 5hr city tour will cost ₹1000. In the main hall of the railway station itself you'll find a very helpful branch of the Tourism Department information centre (daily 6.30am–8.30pm).

Services The State Bank of India is at 6 West Veli St and there are many 24hr ATMs in town, including those at the Canara Bank on West Perumal Maistry St and the UTI Bank on Station Rd. Madurai's GPO is at the corner of West Veli and North Veli streets (Mon–Sat 8am–7.30pm, Sun & hols 9am–4.30pm; Speedpost 10am–7pm). Internet access is widely available: try Net Tower, next to the *Hotel International*, Friends, just round the corner at 13/8 Kaka Thoppu St, or the two branches of iWay on West Perumal Maistry St.

ACCOMMODATION

Aarathy 9 Perumal Koil, West Mada St ☎0452 233 1571, ☎0452 233 6343; map p.999. Popular hotel in a great location overlooking the Koodal Alagar Temple; it's often booked up. All rooms (a/c from ₹1089) have TV and some have balconies, but there's quite a range so it's worth checking a few. Good a/c restaurant and alfresco eating in the courtyard. ₹770

Chentoor 106 West Perumal Maistry St ☎0452 307 7777 ☜hotelchentoor.in; map p.999. Good-value, tower block hotel with very nice, clean a/c rooms (slightly bigger

RECOMMENDED TRAINS FROM MADURAI

Destinaton	Name	No.	Departs	Duration
Bengaluru	*Tuticorin–Mysore Express*	#16731	7.50pm	10hr 50min
Chennai	*Vaigai Express*	#12636	6.45am	7hr 55min
	Pandian Express	#12638	8.35pm	9hr
Coimbatore	*Nagercoili–Coimbatore Express*	#16611	1.05am	6hr 5min
Nagercoil	*Chennai–Guruvayur Express*	#16127	4.35pm	5hr
Trichy	*Vaigai Express*	#12636	6.45am	2hr 5min

20

"royal" rooms ₹2280) with TV and king-size beds. Also has a good rooftop restaurant. **₹1800**

Fortune Pandyan Racecourse Rd, north of the river ☎0452 4356789, ⓦfortunehotels.in; map p.998. Smart, centrally a/c hotel with a range of large, comfortable rooms all with TV and lavishly decorated with period-style furnishings. Quiet and relaxed, but some way from the centre. Good restaurant, a bar, exchange facilities and travel agency. **₹5520**

New College House 2 Town Hall Rd ☎0452 234 2971, ⓔcollegehouse_mdu@yahoo.co.in; map p.999. This huge, maze-like place has more than 200 rooms, and one of the town's best "meals" canteens. The very cheapest rooms are grubby, but there are some cleaner deluxe rooms for an extra ₹345. Likely to be vacancies here when everywhere else is full. **₹550**

Padmam 1 Perumal Tank West St ☎0452 234 0702, ⓔhotel_padmam@hotmail.com; map p.999. Clean, comfortable modern hotel in central location with a rooftop restaurant. All rooms have TV, some have small balconies and a few are a/c (₹2160). The front rooms, which overlook the ruined Perumal tank and have views of the temple *gopuras*, are more expensive. **₹1440**

Prem Nivas 102 West Perumal Maistry St ☎0452 234 2532, ⓦhotelpremnivas.com; map p.999. The swanky exterior belies a slightly grubby interior, although bed linen is clean and the rooms (a/c ₹1440; good-value singles ₹475) are a reasonable size, with flatscreen TV. **₹750**

Rathna Residency 109 West Perumal Maistry St ☎0452 437 4444, ⓦhotelrathnaresidency.com; map p.999. This is a standard mid-range hotel with central a/c and clean, decent-sized rooms (deluxe rooms cost an extra ₹479), all with wi-fi. There's also a money exchange facility and a good restaurant, *The Sangam*. **₹1800**

Sangam Alagar Koil Rd ☎0452 424 4555

ⓦhotelsangam.com; map p.998. Situated in its own grounds, this plush, centrally a/c hotel has very comfortable rooms (deluxe ₹7195 with bath and sofa) a bar and currency exchange. There is a decent swimming pool (₹200 for non-residents), nice gardens and an excellent restaurant. **₹5096**

★ **Sree Devi** 20 West Avani Moola St ☎0452 234 7431; map p.999. This small hotel, right next to the temple, has spotless non-a/c doubles and is a popular choice with travellers. The "deluxe" a/c rooftop room (₹1200) has a great view of the western *gopura*. No restaurant, but they will order in food and beer on request. **₹550**

Supreme 110 West Perumal Maistry St ☎0452 234 3151, ⓦhotelsupreme.in; map p.999. A large, central hotel in a seven-storey block with comfortable rooms (a/c ₹3300), some of which have temple views. There are good facilities, including free wi-fi, foreign exchange, a travel counter, an a/c ground floor restaurant and an overpriced rooftop restaurant with fab views. Lukewarm reception. **₹2580**

★ **Taj Garden Retreat** 40 TPK Rd, Pasumalai Hills ☎0452 663 3000, ⓦthegatewayhotels.com; map p.998. Madurai's most exclusive hotel, a beautifully refurbished colonial house in 25 acres of manicured gardens in the hills, overlooking the city from 6km away. Superior rooms (₹8400) in the old colonial building are the most atmospheric, but the executive rooms (₹9600) have the best views. There is a gourmet restaurant, swimming pool, tennis court and bar. **₹7200**

TTDC Hotel Tamil Nadu Unit I West Veli St ☎0452 233 7471, ⓦttdconline.com; map p.999. Situated a little out of the way from the atmosphere of the temples and the bazaar, this hotel offers spacious rooms overlooking a leafy courtyard. The non-a/c rooms are very good value; the a/c rooms (from ₹1500) are larger and very comfortable. **₹880**

EATING

When the afternoon heat gets too much, head for one of the **juice bars** dotted around the centre, where you can order freshly squeezed pomegranate, pineapple, carrot or orange juice for around ₹25/glass. Madurai is hardly a drinking town, but most of the pricier hotels have a bar, perhaps the most eccentric being the *Apollo 96*, a sci-fi-themed extravaganza at the *Supreme* hotel (see above).

Aarathy Aarathy Hotel, 9 Perumal Koil, West Mada St ☎0452 233 1571; map p.999. This place serves south Indian breakfasts (7–10.30am), very good lunchtime thalis (11.30am–3.30pm; ₹90) and a good range of veg and non-veg dishes (4.30–10.30pm). There's an a/c dining room and tables in a courtyard, where the temple elephant is led twice a day. Daily 6am–10.30pm.

★ **Anna Meenakshi** West Perumal Maistry St; map p.999. One of the best-value places to eat in the centre, this upmarket branch of *New College House's* more traditional canteen serves good pure-veg food. Delicious coconut and lemon rice "meals" (₹60), banana leaf "meals" (₹90) and

north Indian dishes (₹110). Daily 6am–11pm.

★ **The Emperor** Chentoor hotel, 106 West Perumal Maistry St ☎0452 307 7777; map p.999. With a lovely breeze and great city and temple views, this mulicuisine rooftop restaurant is a great place to eat. They serve good Indian food, including biriyanis, chicken dishes (₹110) and sizzlers, and Chinese dishes. Daily 6am–11pm.

Mahal 21 Town Hall Rd ☎0452 234 2700; map p.999. Well-established and nicely decorated street-level restaurant serving small but tasty portions of fish and chips (₹150), plus tandoori items (₹120) and south Indian veg snacks (around ₹65). Daily noon–10.30pm.

20

Temple View Supreme Hotel, 110 West Perumal Maistry St ☎ 0452 234 3151; map p.999. This is one of Madurai's most popular rooftop restaurants, with great views of the city and temple. The pure-veg food is average and the service a little lax, but it's still worth checking out. Main courses ₹95–125. Daily 4pm–midnight.

SHOPPING

Old Madurai is crowded with **textile and tailors' shops**, particularly in West Veli, Avani Moola and Chitrai streets, and Town Hall Rd. At the tailors' shops near the temple, locally produced textiles are generally good value, and tailors pride themselves on turning out faithful copies of favourite clothes in a matter of hours. Unfortunately, most of the **souvenir shops** in the vicinity of the temple employ touts who invite tourists to "come and enjoy temple view free of charge only looking". It's worth doing once as the views from the shops are impressive, but getting back down to street level without making a purchase at hugely inflated prices is quite a challenge. South Avani Moola Street is packed with **jewellery**, particularly gold shops, while stores on West Veli Street sell crafts, oil lamps, Meenakshi sculptures and *khadi* cloth and shirts.

Rameshwaram

The sacred island of **RAMESHWARAM**, 163km southeast of Madurai and less than 20km from Sri Lanka across the Gulf of Mannar, is, along with Madurai, south India's most important pilgrimage site. Rameshwaram is mentioned in the Ramayana as the place where the god Rama, as an incarnation of Vishnu, worshipped Shiva, and consequently attracts followers of both Vishnu and Shiva. The **Ramalingeshwara Temple** complex, with its magnificent pillared walkways, is the most famous on the island, but there are several other small temples of interest, such as the **Gandhamadana Parvatam**, sheltering Rama's footprints, and the **Nambunayagi Amman Kali Temple**, frequented for its curative properties. **Danushkodi** (Rama's Bow) at the eastern end is where Rama is said to have bathed. The boulders peppering the sea between here and Sri Lanka, making "Rama's bridge" (*Rama Sethu*), were strategically placed by Hanuman's monkey army so they could cross to Lanka in their search for Rama's wife Sita, after her abduction by the demon king Ravana. The town offers uncommercialized **beaches** (not India's most stunning) where you can unwind, bathe and do ablutions.

Rameshwaram, whose streets radiate out from the vast block enclosing the Ramalingeshwara, is always crowded with day-trippers and ragged mendicants who camp outside the Ramalingeshwara and the **Ujainimahamariamman**, the small goddess shore temple. An important part of their pilgrimage is to bathe in the main temple's sacred tanks and in the sea; the narrow strip of beach is shared by groups of bathers, relaxing cows and mantra-reciting *swamis* sitting next to sand lingams. As well as fishing – prawns and lobsters for packaging and export to Japan – shells are a big source of income in the coastal villages.

Ramalingeshwara Temple

The core of the **Ramalingeshwara** (or Ramanathaswamy) **Temple** was built by the Cholas in the twelfth century to house two much-venerated **shivalingams** associated with the Ramayana. After rescuing his wife Sita from the clutches of Ravana, Rama was advised to atone for the killing of the demon king – a brahmin – by worshipping Shiva. Rama's monkey lieutenant, Hanuman, was despatched to the Himalayas to fetch a *shivalingam*, but when he failed to return by the appointed day, Sita fashioned a lingam from sand (the *Ramanathalingam*) so the ceremony could proceed. Hanuman eventually made it back bearing a lingam and in order to assuage the monkey's guilt Rama decreed that in future, of the two, Hanuman's should be worshipped first. The lingams are now housed in the inner section of the Ramalingeshwara, but can only by viewed by Hindus. Much of what can be visited dates from the 1600s, when the temple received generous endowments from the Sethupathi rajas of Ramanathapuram.

The temple is enclosed by high walls, which form a rectangle with huge pyramidal *gopura* entrances on each side. Each gateway leads to a spacious closed ambulatory, flanked on either side by continuous platforms with massive pillars set on their edges. These **corridors** are the most famous attribute of the temple, their extreme length – 205m, with 1212 pillars on the north and south sides – giving a remarkable impression of receding perspective. Before entering the inner sections of the temple, pilgrims are expected to bathe at each of the 22 temple **tirthas** (tanks) in the temple – hence the groups of dripping-wet pilgrims, most of them fully clothed, making their way from tank to tank, to be soaked by bucket-wielding temple attendants. Monday is Rama's auspicious day, when the Padilingam puja takes place. **Festivals** of particular importance at the temple include **Mahashivaratri** (ten days during Feb/March), **Brahmotsavam** (ten days during March/April) and **Thirukalyanam** (July/Aug), celebrating the marriage of Shiva to Parvati.

ARRIVAL AND INFORMATION   RAMESHWARAM

By train The railway station is 1km southwest of the centre; trains from Chennai and further afield all terminate here. There are daily services to Chennai Egmore (13hr 30min) via Trichy (5hr 30min) and Thanjavore (6hr 25min).

By bus The NH-49 links Madurai to Mandapam on the coast and the impressive 2km-long Indira Gandhi Bridge links the mainland to the island of Rameshwaram. Buses from Madurai, Trichy and beyond arrive at the bus stand 2km west of the centre Bus #1 (every 10min) connects the bus stand and temple.

Destinations Ultra-deluxe buses daily to Chennai (4.30pm; ₹450) and Bengaluru (4.30pm; ₹550); frequent services to Trichy and Madurai.

Tourist information The main TTDC tourist office, a dilapidated two-storey peach-coloured building next to the bus stand (daily 10am–5.45pm; ☎04573 221371) gives out information about guides, accommodation and boat trips but opens rather erratically.

Services The post office is on Pamban Rd. There are a couple of internet places near the west entrance to the temple offering intermittent access between the power cuts. Bicycles are available to rent from stalls in the four Car streets around the temple.

ACCOMMODATION

Until recently **accommodation** in Rameshwaram was restricted to the fairly basic lodges and modest hotels on the four streets around the temple. However, a rash of modern star hotels has sprung up along the road into town offering decent alternatives. The temple authorities also provide pilgrim rooms; ask at the Devasthanam Office, East Car St (☎04573 221223). During holidays and festivals, rooms are like gold dust and just as priey.

Chola Lodge 25 North Car St ☎04573 221307. A large white building halfway along North Car St, the quietest of the Car streets. The rooms are fairly basic but clean and come with a TV and a choice of Indian or Western loos. ₹400

Daiwik NH-49 near the bus stand ☎04573 223222, ⊛daiwikhotels.com. This is one of several new hotels on the main highway into town. Immaculate, spacious and comfortable rooms with king-size beds and flatscreen TV 's. Deluxe rooms ₹1000 more. On site massage and restaurant. ₹3500

Maharaja's 7 Middle St ☎04573 221271, ✉hotelmaharajas@gmail.com. Located near the west gate of the temple, this hotel has clean and comfortable rooms with attached bathrooms and TV. Some rooms have temple views from the balcony. The a/c rooms are twice the price. ₹524

Shriram Hotel Island Star 41-A South Car St ☎04573 221472. This is a fair-sized hotel with clean and pleasantly appointed rooms, most of which have sea views. The non-a/c rooms are quite good value; a/c doubles are twice the price. ₹400

★ **TTDC Hotel Tamil Nadu** Near the beach, 500m from the corner of North Car and East Car streets ☎04573 221277, ⊛ttdconline.com. The best option in the temple area of Rameshwaram, situated in its own grounds with restaurant and bar. There are some sea-facing rooms and cheaper ones (a/c from ₹1560) in the new block with outdoor seats. ₹880

Venkatesh West Car St ☎04573 221296. This is a no-frills three-storey hotel, with clean, decent-sized rooms all of which have TV and an attached bathroom. The a/c rooms cost fifty percent more. ₹650

Vinayaga 5 Railway Feeder Rd ☎04573 222361 ⊛vinayagahotel.com. A pleasant hotel in a three-storey block just 100m from the railway station precinct. Clean and well kept, with 45 light, spacious and airy a/c rooms (deluxe rooms cost an extra ₹400), it's a couple of kilometres from the temple area but quieter for it. ₹1992

20

EATING

Abhirami Shore Rd, near the east entrance to the main temple ☏ 04573 221178. Reasonably clean south Indian veg joint en the way to the seashore, with street views from the tables. Lunchtime "meals" are served from 11.30am–3pm at the pilgrim price of ₹40. Daily 6.30am–11.30pm.

Anandha Bhavan 1/4 West Car St ☏ 97873 44774. Clean and spacious south Indian-style restaurant serving good south Indian breakfasts. "Meals" available from 11.30am–3.30pm (₹50) plus pure veg dishes costing ₹40–70. Daily 7am–11pm.

Ashoka Bhavan West Car St. South Indian vegetarian place serving the usual range of cheap south Indian breakfasts and a limited range of regional "meals" including north Indian (₹60) and south Indian (₹40). Daily 7am–10pm.

Chola Hotel West Bazaar St. This small "hotel" is a food-only place and not to be confused with the lodge of same name; a good choice for carnivores, with biriyanis and other dishes, including chicken, mutton, liver and "head curry" all from ₹50. Daily noon–11pm.

Ganesh Mess Middle St, off Car St West. A small restaurant with just eight tables and pleasant and friendly service. Their lunchtime "meals" cost ₹50 and they also serve masala dosas (₹35) and other south Indian snacks throughout the day. Daily 7.15am–10.30pm.

TTDC Hotel Tamil Nadu Near the beach. Gigantic, noisy, high-ceilinged glass building serving all-you-can-eat pure veg breakfast, lunch and dinner buffets (₹77/₹102/₹102). There is also an a/c bar in the grounds opposite reception. Daily 7.30am–10am; 12.30pm–2.30pm & 7.30–9.30pm.

Kanyakumari

At the southernmost extremity of India, **KANYAKUMARI** is almost as compelling for Hindus as Rameshwaram. It's significant not only for its association with a virgin goddess, Devi Kanyakumari, but also as the meeting point of the Bay of Bengal, Indian Ocean and Arabian Sea. Watching the sun rise and set from here is the big attraction, especially on full-moon day in April, when it's possible to see both the setting sun and rising moon on the same horizon. Although Kanyakumari is in the state of Tamil Nadu, most foreign visitors arrive on day-trips from Kerala. While the place is of enduring appeal to pilgrims and those who just want to see India's tip, some may find it bereft of atmosphere, its magic obliterated by ugly concrete buildings and hawkers. Kanyakumari was devastated by the 2004 tsunami. Although the seafront and jetty have since been rebuilt, parts of the fishing village are still in ruins.

Kumari Amman Temple

Sannathi St • Daily 4.30am–12.15pm & 4–8.15pm

The shoreline **Kumari Amman Temple** is dedicated to the virgin goddess **Devi Kanyakumari**, who may have originally been the local guardian deity of the shoreline but was later absorbed into the figure of Devi, or Parvati, consort of Shiva. The image of Devi Kanyakumari inside the temple wears a diamond nose stud of such brilliance that it's said to be visible from the sea. Male visitors must be shirtless and wear a *dhoti* before entering the temple; non-Hindus are not allowed in the inner sanctum. It is especially auspicious for pilgrims to wash at the bathing *ghat* here.

Gandhi Mandapam

Daily 7am–7pm

Resembling a prewar British cinema, the **Gandhi Mandapam**, 300m northwest of the Kumari Amman Temple, was actually conceived as a modern imitation of an Orissan temple. It was so designed that at noon on October 2, Mahatma Gandhi's birthday, the sun strikes the auspicious spot where his ashes were laid prior to immersion in the sea.

The rocks

Ferry every 20min; daily 7.45am–4pm • ₹30, 150 people/boat

Possibly the original sacred focus of Kanyakumari were the two **rocks**, about 60m apart, jutting out of the sea 500m off the coast. They can be reached by the Poompuhar ferry service leaving from the jetty on the east side of town. Known as the Pitru and Matru *tirthas*, they attracted the attention of the Hindu reformer Vivekananda (1862–1902), who swam out to the rocks in 1892 to meditate on the syncretistic teachings of his recently dead guru, Ramakrishna Paramahamsa. Incorporating elements of architecture from around the country, the 1970 **Vivekananda Memorial** (daily 8am–4pm; ₹50) houses a statue of the saint. The footprints of Devi Kanyakumari can also be seen here, at the spot where she performed her penance. The other rock features an imposing 40m-high statue of the ancient Tamil saint **Thiruvalluvar**.

Wandering Monk Museum (Vivekananda Puram)

Beach Rd, just round the corner from Rock St • Daily 8am–noon & 4–8pm • ₹10

The small Wandering is dedicated to the life and teachings of Vivekananda. A sequence of 41 panels in English, Tamil and Hindi provide a meticulously detailed account of the *swami*'s odyssey around the Subcontinent at the end of the nineteenth century.

ARRIVAL AND INFORMATION	KANYAKUMARI

By train Trains from all over the Subcontinent (even Jammu – at 86hr the longest rail journey in India) stop at the railway station in the north of town, 2km from the seafront.

Destinations from Kanyakumari and nearby Nagercoil: Bengaluru (1 daily; 19hr 30min); Chennai (2–3 daily; 13hr 15min–15hr 25min); Coimbatore (2 daily; 11hr 55min); Kochi (2 daily; 6hr 15min–6hr 30min); Madurai (6 daily; 4hr 20min–5hr 15min); Mumbai (2 daily; 47hr 20min); Thiruvananthapuram (4 daily; 1hr 35min–2hr); Tiruchirapalli (5 daily; 7hr 15min–8hr 15min).

By bus The Express Bus Stand, near the lighthouse on the west side of town, is served by regular buses from Thiruvananthapuram, Madurai, Rameshwaram and Chennai.

Destinations Chennai (7 daily; 16–18hr); Kovalam (10–12 daily; 2hr); Madurai (every 30min; 6hr); Puducherry (1 daily; 12–13hr); Rameshwaram (3 daily; 10hr); Thiruvananthapuram (every 30min–1hr; 2hr 30min–3hr); Tiruchirapalli (every 30min; 10–12hr).

Tourist information The main Tamil Nadu tourist office on Beach Rd (Mon–Fri 10am–1pm & 2–5.30pm; ☎04652 246276) has maps and brochures.

ACCOMMODATION

★ **Lakshmi Tourist Home** East Car St ☎04652 246333, ☎04652 246627. This smart hotel is a popular choice with comfortable rooms, some of which are sea-facing. Choice of non-a/c and a/c rooms (₹1800). There's also an excellent non-veg restaurant. ₹990

Maadhini East Car St ☎04652 246787, ⌨hotelmaadhini.com. Large hotel right on the seafront above the fishing village. Comfortably furnished rooms, (a/c rooms 33 percent more expensive) some with fine sea views. It has one of the best restaurants in town (see below), an a/c bar and a rooftop terrace. ₹1500

Manickam Tourist Home North Car St ☎04652 246787. Large hotel block and sister hotel to the *Maadhini* (same owners). It has spacious, clean rooms (a/c ₹3500, some with balconies and sea views. Avoid the basement

rooms. Also has a rooftop terrace. ₹1500

Samudra Sannathi St ☎04652 246162, ☎hotelsamudra@yahoo.com. Smart hotel towards the bottom of Sannathi Str near the temple entrance. It has forty well-furnished deluxe rooms (a/c ₹1800) all facing the sea. All rooms have cable TV and the hotel also has its own generator. ₹1250

TTDC Hotel Tamil Nadu Near the lighthouse on Seafront ☎04652 246257, ⌨ttdconline.com. Up the hill and a little further from the temple and main drag. Choice of accommodation in a range of rooms in the main block or cottages (₹2500). The a/c doubles are ₹1500. The more expensive rooms have sea views. The on-site restaurant (7.30–10pm) serves veg and non-veg. ₹750

EATING

Archana Maadhini Hotel East Car St ☎04652 246787. A comfortable a/c basement dining hall option that has an extensive veg and non-veg multicuisine menu. In the

evening (7–10.30pm) you can also eat in their al fresco courtyard and they boast the town's widest selection of ice creams. Daily 7am–10.30pm.

Saravana Bhavan Sannathi St ☎04652 246357. Opposite the *Samudra*, to which it belongs, this very large dining hall is arguably the best of Kanyakumari's many "meals" restaurants, although service can be slow. Serves the usual snacks in the morning and evening and ₹70 "meals" at lunchtime. Daily 6.30am–10pm.

Sebaa 2/19 South Car Street ☎04652 246396. On the corner of South and East Car streets, this pleasant restaurant serves up a range of prawn and fish dishes, including biriyanis (₹180), a range of seafood curries and some chicken dishes for ₹120. Daily 11am–10.30pm.

Sree Devi Tiffin Stall Top of Rock St at junction with Beach Rd. Small but very popular local *dhaba*, serving *parathas*, omelettes and various snacks, along with a small selection of chicken curries (₹40). It's also a great place to sit, enjoy a chai and watch the world go by. Daily 6am–11pm.

The Ghats

Around sixty million years ago, what is today called peninsular India was a separate land-mass drifting northwest across the ocean towards central Asia. Geologists believe this mass originally broke off from the African continent along a fault line. This line is still discernible today as the north–south ridge of volcanic mountains, known as the **Western Ghats**, which stretch 1400km down the west coast of India. Rising to a height of around 2500m, it is India's second highest mountain chain after the Himalayas.

Forming a natural barrier between the Tamil plains and coastal Kerala and Karnataka, the Ghats (literally "steps") soak up the bulk of the southwest monsoon, which drains east to the Bay of Bengal via the mighty Kaveri and Krishna river systems. The massive amount of rain that falls here between June and October (around 2.5m) allows for an incredible **biodiversity**. Nearly one third of all of India's flowering plants can be found in the dense evergreen and mixed deciduous forests cloaking the Ghats, while the woodland undergrowth supports the Subcontinent's richest array of wildlife.

It was this abundance of game, and the cooler temperatures of the range's high valleys and grasslands, that attracted the British away from the withering summer heat on the southern plains. They also realized the economic potential of the local climate, fertile soil and plentiful rainfall. As the forests were felled to make way for tea plantations, and the region's many tribal groups – among them the Todas – were forced deeper into the mountains, permanent **hill stations** were established. Today, as in the days of the Raj, these continue to provide welcome escapes from the incessant heat, as well as romantic getaways for the emergent Indian middle classes and nostalgia for foreign tourists.

The best known of the hill resorts is **Udhagamandalam** (formerly Ootacamund, and known just as "Ooty") nestling in the **Nilgiris** (from *nila-giri*, "blue mountains"). The ride up to Ooty on the **miniature railway** via Coonoor is fun, and the views breathtaking, but the town centre suffers from heavy traffic pollution and actually has little to offer. Further south and reached by a scenic switchback road, the other main hill station is **Kodaikanal**. The lovely walks around town provide views and fresh air in abundance, while the bustle of Indian tourists around the lake makes a pleasant change from life in the city.

The forest areas lining the state border harbour Tamil Nadu's principal **wildlife sanctuaries**, **Indira Gandhi** and **Mudumalai**, which comprise part of the vast **Nilgiri Biosphere Reserve**, the country's most extensive tract of protected forest. Road building, illegal felling, hydro-electric projects and overgrazing have whittled away large parts of this huge wilderness area over the past two decades, but what's left is still home to an array of wildlife. The main route between Mysore and the cities of the Tamil plains wriggles through the Nilgiris, and you may well find yourself pausing for a night or two along the way. Whichever direction you're travelling in, a stopover in the dull textile city of **Coimbatore** is hard to avoid.

Kodaikanal

Perched on top of the Palani range, around 120km northwest of Madurai, **KODAIKANAL**, also known as **Kodai**, owes its perennial popularity to its hilltop position which, at an altitude of 2133m, affords breathtaking views over the blue-green reaches of the Vaigai plain. Raj-era bungalows and flower-filled gardens add atmosphere, while short walks out of the centre lead to rocky outcrops, waterfalls and dense *shola* forest. With the more northerly wildlife sanctuaries and forest areas of the Ghats closed to visitors, Kodai's outstandingly scenic hinterland also offers south India's best **trekking** terrain.

After a while in the south Indian plains, a retreat to Kodai's cool heights is more than welcome. However, in the height of summer (April–July) when temperatures compete with those in the lowlands, it's not worth the trip – nor is it a good idea to come during the monsoon (Oct–Dec), when the town is shrouded in mist and drenched by heavy downpours. From January to early March the nights are chilly so the **peak tourist season** runs from April to June, when prices soar.

The lake

Kodai's focal point is its **lake**, sprawling like a giant amoeba over 60 acres just west of the town centre. This is a popular place for strolls or bike rides along the 5km path that fringes the water's edge; a leisurely circumambulation is a very pleasant way to wile away an hour or two and also makes a good excuse for an evening indulging in Kodai's locally made chocolate. Pedal boats (₹50) and rowing boats (RS65–190) can be rented on the eastern shore while romantics might select a shikara ride (with boatman) for ₹250. Horseriding is also an option here – ₹100 to be led along the lakeside for 1km and ₹400

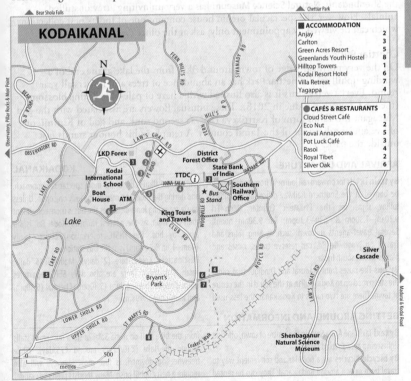

KODAIKANAL

▲ Bear Shola Falls

▲ Chettiar Park

N

■ ACCOMMODATION

Anjay	2
Carlton	3
Green Acres Resort	5
Greenlands Youth Hostel	8
Hilltop Towers	1
Kodai Resort Hotel	6
Villa Retreat	7
Yagappa	4

● CAFÉS & RESTAURANTS

Cloud Street Café	1
Eco Nut	2
Kovai Annapoorna	5
Pot Luck Café	3
Rasoi	4
Royal Tibet	2
Silver Oak	6

FERN HILLS RD
SIVANAD RD
FERN RD
HILL'S RD
LAW'S GHAT RD

Observatory, Pillar Rocks & Moir Point

BEAR SHOLA RD
OBSERVATORY RD
LKD Forex
District Forest Office
Kodai International School
TTDC ⓘ
State Bank of India
PT ROAD
ANNA SALAI
Boat House
ATM
Southern Railway Office
★ **Bus Stand**
WOODVILLE RD
IDAIYAR RD
King Tours and Travels
CLUB RD
LAKE RD
Lake
NOYCE RD
LAW'S GHAT RD

Silver Cascade

Bryant's Park

LOWER SHOLA RD
UPPER SHOLA RD
ST. MARY'S RD
Coaker's Walk

Shenbaganur Natural Science Museum

Madurai & Kodai Road

0   500
metres

for an hour's ride. Shops, restaurants and hotels are concentrated in a rather congested area east of and downhill from the lake. The only monuments to Kodai's colonial past are the neat **British bungalows** that overlook the lake, and Law's Ghat Road on the eastern edge of town. The British first moved here in 1845, to be joined later by members of the American Mission, who set up schools for European children.

Bryant's Park

Park Daily 9am–6.30pm, last entry 6pm • ₹15, camera ₹30, video camera ₹75 Coakers Walk Daily 7.30am–6.30pm • ₹5 camera ₹10

Southeast of the lake is **Bryant's Park**, with tiered flowerbeds, rhododendrons, pine, eucalyptus and wattle. A flower show is held here in May. A path, known as **Coaker's Walk**, skirts the hill, winding from the *Villa Retreat* to *Greenlands Youth Hostel* (10min), offering remarkable views that stretch as far as Madurai on a clear day.

Pillar Rocks and Bear Shola Falls

One of Kodai's most popular natural attractions is the **Pillar Rocks**, 7km south of town, where a series of granite cliffs rise more than 100m above the hillside. To get here, follow the westbound Observatory Road from the northernmost point of the lake (a steep climb) until you come to a crossroads; the southbound road passes the gentle **Fairy Falls** on the way to Pillar Rocks. Some 2km west of the lake, the signposted **Bear Shola Falls** is now barely a trickle of water but remains a popular picnic and photo-stop for local tourists.

Shenbaganur Natural Science Museum

Wed–Mon 10am–5pm • ₹10, camera ₹10

Southeast of the town centre, about 3km down Law's Ghat Road (towards the plains), the **Shenbaganur Natural Science Museum** has a very uninviting array of stuffed animals. However, the spectacular orchid house contains one of India's best collections, which can be viewed by appointment only; ask at the office (see opposite).

Chettiar Park

On the very northeast edge of town, around 3km from the lake at the end of a winding uphill road, **Chettiar Park** has an abundance of trees and flowers all year round. Every twelve years it is also flushed with a haze of pale-blue **Kurinji blossoms** (the next flowering is due in 2018). These unusual flowers are associated with the god Murugan, the Tamil form of Karttikeya (Shiva's second son), and god of Kurinji, one of five ancient divisions of the Tamil country. A temple in his honour stands just outside the park.

ARRIVAL AND DEPARTURE KODAIKANAL

By train Tickets for onward rail journeys from Kodai Rd can be booked at the Southern Railway office, at the GPO - follow signs for the Philatelic Counter (Mon–Fri 9.30am–1.30pm & 2.30–3.30pm; Sat 9.30am–noon). Several travel agents in town, such as King Tours and Travels on Woodville Rd, can reserve trains, buses and planes within south India.

By bus The buses from Madurai and Dindigul that climb the steep road up to Kodai pull in at the stand in the centre of town. There are two roads to Kodaikanal: the less-used

route from Palani is by far the more spectacular approach, and during the monsoon may be the only one open. Unless you're travelling long-distances the bus is more convenient than the train, as the nearest railhead, Kodai Rd, is 3hr away by bus. The TNSTC reservation counter (daily 10am–1pm & 2–4pm) is at the bus station.

Destinations Coimbatore (2 daily); Madurai 15 daily; Palani (10 daily). There are also daily SETC departures (ultra-deluxe) to Bengaluru (5.30pm), Chennai (6.30pm) and Kanyakumari (9am).

GETTING AROUND AND INFORMATION

By taxi Taxis line Anna Salai in the centre of town, offering sightseeing at high fixed rates.

By bicycle Bicycles are a popular and convenient way to travel both in and around Kodaikanal. They can be rented

from the bike stall on Anna Salai or from numerous stalls around the lake (₹10/hr or around ₹75/day). While freewheeling downhill is fun, most journeys will also require a hefty uphill push. Many tourists prefer to wander around at their own pace on foot.

Tourist information The tourist office (Mon–Fri 10am–5.45pm; ☎04542 241675) on Anna Salai (Bazaar Rd) and *Greenlands Youth Hostel* (☎04542 241099) can arrange treks of varying lengths and The 5hr trek around Kodaikanal is popular diffculty as is the three-day trek across the mountains to Munnar in Kerala. Rates depend on group numbers. Check food and accommodation details.

Services There are many internet access points in town but with varying degrees of speed and connection. Quick .Net on PT Rd is one of the better ones but also a little more expensive. There are several foreign exchange places; the State Bank of India and Canara Bank are both on Anna Salai, and there is an SBI ATM near the *Carlton* hotel.

ACCOMMODATION

Kodaikanal's inexpensive **lodges** are grouped at the lower end of Anna Salai. It is worth asking whether blankets and hot water are provided (the latter should be free, but you may be charged in budget places).

Anjay Anna Salai ☎04542 241089, ⓦhotelanjay.com. Simple, clean and pleasant hotel centrally located near the bus stand. Rooms are smarter than you'd expect from the outside, all with balconies and TV; the deluxe rooms (from ₹100 more) have the best views. **₹660**

Carlton Off Lake Rd ☎04542 240056, ⓦkrahejahospitality.com. The most luxurious hotel in Kodaikanal, a spacious, tastefully renovated and well-maintained colonial house overlooking the lake. All rooms have a lake view and exude Raj-era charm. There are also cottages (₹14500) within the grounds, a restaurant, bar and comfortable lounge. All rates include meals. **₹10000**

Green Acres Resort 11/213 Lake Rd ☎04542 242384, ⓦgreenacresresort.biz. Pleasant resort set in its own extensive grounds on a quiet corner of the lake with lovely gardens and swings. There is a wide range of different rooms priced, according to size and hot water availability, up to ₹5058 for the exec deluxe. **₹2117**

Greenlands Youth Hostel Coaker's Walk, off St Mary's Rd ☎04542 241099, ⓦgreenlandskodaikanal. com. An attractive old stone house with unrivalled views and sunsets from its deep verandas. There's a variety of rooms (up to ₹1320) with wooden beds, open fireplaces (wood costs ₹50) and attached bathrooms, and also a dorm. Very popular with groups, so book ahead. Dorm **₹250**, double **₹660**

Hilltop Towers Club Rd ☎04542 240413, ⓦhilltopgroup.in. Decent hotel, 5min from the lake, with modern, comfortable rooms featuring arched doors, large beds and TV. There's also a cosy and romantic honeymoon suite (₹3960) with a circular bed, plus three good restaurants and a bakery. **₹3180**

Kodai Resort Hotel Noyce Rd, near Coaker's Walk ☎04542 241301, ⓦkodairesorthotel.com. Large complex of fifty incongruous-looking but very pleasant cottages housing comfortable bedrooms with king-sized beds, TVs and huge individual roof terraces with good views. Also a health club, restaurant and resident emu. **₹4200**

Villa Retreat Coaker's Walk, off Club Rd ☎04542 240940, ⓦvillaretreat.com. Comfortable old stone house, with more character than most, situated in lovely gardens that afford superb views. Though a touch overpriced, rooms (priced according to views) have 24hr hot water; some also have real fires. **₹2878**

★**Yagappa** Noyce Rd ☎04542 241235, ✉yagappa resort@yahoo.com, ⓦyagappaheritageresort.com Good mid-range budget option with very clean rooms in three buildings, set around a lawn-cum-courtyard with views to the rear. There's a choice of standard and deluxe rooms (with balcony ₹1920) and a small dining area for guests only. **₹1680**

EATING

Cloud Street Café PT Rd. Large pleasant, upstairs café with traveller's vibe and secondhand book swap. Veggie breakfasts (₹125) with mushrooms, tomatoes and beans are served until 11.30am after which there are wood-oven pizzas (from ₹175), cakes and chocolate brownies. Daily 8.45am–8.30pm.

Eco Nut J's Heritage Complex, PT Rd. One of south India's few bona fide Western-style wholefood shops, and a great place to stock up on trekking supplies: muesli, home-made jams, breads, pickles and muffins, high-calorie "nutri-balls" and delicious cheeses from Auroville. Daily 9am–5.30pm.

Kovai Annapoorna Goldan Sands Hotel, Anna Salai 7 Road junction ☎04542 246181. Large, second-floor dining area with huge glass front and accompanying views.

They serve good south Indian breakfasts including pongal (8am–10.30am), "meals" (12.30–4pm; ₹80) and specials (₹120) including chapatti and curd. Daily 8am–8.30pm.

Pot Luck Café PT Rd. Tiny café with just a few tables squeezed onto a narrow veranda serving travellers' favourites including waffles, pancakes, club sandwiches, spaghetti (₹100) and tempting drinks such as Mayan hot chocolate (₹55). Wed–Mon 11am–7pm.

Rasoi Anna Salai, above the Cocoa Bean. Tiny first-floor *dhaba* with just eight tables, serving delicious Punjabi and Gujarati food: excellent *aloo parathas* (₹45), a range of north Indian vegetarian dishes (around ₹75), limited Punjabi thalis (₹100) and unlimited Gujarati thalis (₹150). Daily 10am–10pm.

20

★ **Royal Tibet** J's Heritage Complex, PT Rd ☎04542 243804. Small, friendly Tibetan joint, with dishes ranging from thick home-made bread to particularly tasty *momos*, soups and noodles. There's a range of chicken, mutton, beef and vegetarian dishes all for under ₹110. Daily 12–9pm.

Silver Oak Carlton Hotel, off Lake Rd ☎04542 240056. Splash out at Kodai's top hotel on their evening buffet spread (veg and non-veg; ₹675), rounded off with a *chhota* peg of Scotch in the bar. Lunchtime buffet also available (₹600) and a barbecue lunch every Sun (₹725). Daily 1–3pm & 7.30–10.30pm.

Indira Gandhi (Anamalai) Wildlife Sanctuary

Indira Gandhi (Anamalai) Wildlife Sanctuary is a 958-square-kilometre tract of forest on the southern reaches of the Cardamom Hills, 37km southwest of the busy junction town of **Pollachi**. Vegetation ranges from *shola*-grassland to dry deciduous to tropical evergreen, and the sanctuary is home to lion-tailed macaques (black-maned monkeys), gaur, *sambar*, spotted and barking deer, sloth bear, as well as leopards and tigers. Birds such as hornbills and frogmouths are also seen here. It s possible to **trek** through the giant creaking stands of bamboo with a guide and the Forestry Department also runs **safari tours** by minibus and **elephant safaris**. For reservations, contact the park reception office (see below).

ARRIVAL AND DEPARTURE   INDIRA GANDHI (ANAMALAI) WILDLIFE SANCTUARY

By bus There are good bus connections between Pollachi and both Coimbatore and Palani. From Pollachi there are three buses a day (6.15am, 11.15am & 3.15pm) up to the park's reception centre (☎04253 238360) at Top Slip. Rented cars/taxis, available at Pollachi, run to

the official entrance at the Sethumadai checkpost from 6.30am–6pm daily. Private vehicles can drive into the park with prior permission from the Field Director, Wildlife Warden Office, 178 Meenkarai Rd, Pollachi (☎04253 225356).

ACCOMMODATION AND EATING

The Forestry Department runs six **resthouses**, ranging from the basic *Hornbill* to the luxurious *Pillar Top*. Most are within easy walking distance of the reception centre and should be booked in advance through the Field Director in Pollachi. The canteen next to the reception centre serves basic **meals** and drinks and the local shop has equally basic provisions.

Coimbatore

Visitors tend only to use the busy industrial city of **COIMBATORE** as a stopover on the way to Ooty, 90km northwest. Once you've climbed up to your hotel rooftop to admire the blue, cloud-capped haze of the Nilgiris in the west, there's little to do here other than kill time wandering through the nuts-and-bolts bazaars, lined with lookalike textile showrooms, "General Traders" and shops selling motor parts.

ARRIVAL AND DEPARTURE   COIMBATORE

By train For Ooty, catch the daily #2671 *Nilgiri Express* at 5.15am, which gets into Mettupalayam in time to connect with the Toy Train (see box, p.1017) for Ooty.
Destinations Bengaluru (2–3 daily; 6hr 45min–9hr); Chennai (5–6 daily; 7hr 50min–8hr 55min); Ernakulam, for Kochi (7–8 daily; 4hr 20min–5hr 30min); Hyderabad (1 daily; 21hr 20min); Kanyakumari (2 daily; 11hr 45min); Madurai (1–2 daily; 6hr 15min–6hr 35min); Mettupalayam, for Ooty (1 daily; 1hr); Mumbai (2 daily; 31hr 15min–32hr 40min); Thiruvananthapuram (4–5 daily; 9hr 5min–10hr 25min); Tiruchirapalli (2 daily; 5hr 15min–5hr 45min).
By bus Coimbatore has five main bus stands, three of which are fairly near each other in the northern part of

town, a couple of kilometres north of the railway station. The Thiruvalluvar Bus Stand is the main state and interstate station; buses to and from Ooty, Coonoor and Mettupalayam use the Mettupalayam New Bus Stand 4km out of town. The busy central Bus Stand, 200m from *TTDC Tamil Nadu* guest house serves local city buses. The south of town holds a fourth bus stand, Ukkadam (which serves Palani, Pollachi, Madurai, Trichy and towns in northern Kerala). Local buses ply the routes between bus and train stations.
Destinations Bengaluru (hourly; 8–9hr); Chennai (every 30min–1hr); Kodaikanal (4 daily; 6hr); Madurai (every 30min; 5–6hr); Mysore (3 daily; 6hr); Udhagamandalam (Ooty) (every 30min; 3hr 30min–4hr); Palakaad (hourly;

20

2hr); Palani (hourly; 2hr 30min–3hr); Pollachi (every 30min; 1hr); Puducherry (10 daily; 9hr); Rameshwaram (2

daily; 14hr); Thrissur (hourly; 5hr); Tiruchirapalli (every 30min; 5hr).

ACCOMMODATION

Most of Coimbatore's **accommodation** is concentrated around the bus stands and railway station. The cheapest options line Nehru St and Shastri Rd, but avoid the rock-bottom places facing the bus stand itself, which are plagued with traffic noise from around 4am onwards.

Blue Star 369-A Nehru St ☎0422 223 0635, ⓦhotelbluestar.in. Impeccably clean rooms (a/c ₹1920), some with balconies, quiet fans and bathrooms, in a modern multistorey building a 5min walk from the bus stands. One of the best mid-range hotels in this area. ₹990.

City Tower 56 Sivasamy Rd ☎0422 223 0681, ⓦhotelcitytower.com. A smart, centrally air-conditioned hotel, five minutes walk south of the Central Bus Stand, with decent rooms featuring leatherette and vinyl. The "executive" rooms (₹4080) are more spacious and have a mini-bar and balcony. ₹3480

KK Residency 7 Shastri Rd ☎0422 430 0222, ⓔhotelkkresidency@gmail.com. Large, business-style hotel in a tower block behind the Central Bus Stand, with

very clean rooms (a/c ₹1560; good deals for single occupancy) and a couple of good restaurants. ₹735

New Vijaya Lodge 8/81 Geetha Hall Rd ☎0422 230 1570, ⓔnewvijayalodgemka@yahoo.com. Close to the railway station and one of the best (of many) budget options on this street. Rooms (a/c ₹1200) are clean, simple and compact, with TV, hot water in the mornings and towels provided. ₹600

TTDC Tamil Nadu 2 Dr Nanjappa Rd ☎0422 230 2176, ⓦttdconline.com. Conveniently located opposite the Central Bus Stand, with clean, pleasant rooms (a/c ₹1350). There's a tourist information service and its own very good restaurant next door. Often fully booked, so phone ahead. ₹880

EATING

Cloud 9 City Tower, 56 Sivasamy Rd ☎0422 223 0681. This covered rooftop restaurant with city views is one of the best in town. It has a comprehensive multicuisine menu with fish dishes for ₹250, chicken ₹180 and veggie dishes for ₹120. Daily noon–3pm & 7–11.30pm.

The Malabar KK Residency ☎94866 54402. First-floor restaurant in the *KK Residency* block, popular for its non-veg Keralan specialities. It also serves a range of chicken dishes (₹100) and a few vegetarian dishes including biriyani (₹70). Daily 11am–11pm.

★ **Naalukettu** Nehru St opposite the Blue Star

☎0422 223 1402. Stylish, clean and reasonably priced restaurant with nice courtyard garden and interior. They serve a range of veg and non-veg food including plain biriyani (₹80), prawn biriyani (₹150) and chicken dishes (₹88). Daily 12noon–10.30pm.

Nachiyappar Chettinad 2 Dr Nanjappa Rd ☎0422 230 2176. Large restaurant (part of the *TTDC* hotel) serving delicious, fiery Chettinad dishes (around ₹125), the usual south Indian breakfasts and unlimited lunchtime "meals'" (noon–4pm; ₹65) alongside a good range of other veg and non-veg dishes. Daily 7.30am–11pm.

20

Coonoor

At an altitude of 1858m, **COONOOR**, a scruffy bazaar and tea-planters' town on the Nilgiri Blue Mountain Railway (see box, p.1017) lies at the head of the Hulikal ravine, on the southeastern side of the Dodabetta mountains, 27km north of Mettupalayam and 19km south of Ooty. Thanks to its proximity to its more famous neighbour, Coonoor has avoided Ooty's overcommercialization, and can make a pleasant place for a short stop.

Coonoor consists of two "levels", **Lower Coonoor**, with its small but atmospheric hill market, which specializes in leaf tea and fragrant essential oils and **Upper Coonoor**, with its old Raj-era bungalows and narrow lanes with flower-filled hedgerows. At the top lies **Sim's Park**, a lush botanical garden on the slopes of a ravine with hundreds of rose varieties (daily 8am–6.30pm; ₹15, camera ₹35, video ₹75).

Around the town, rolling hills and valleys carpeted with spongy green tea bushes and stands of eucalyptus and silver oak offer some of the most beautiful scenery in the Nilgiris, immortalized in many a Hindi-movie dance sequence. Cinema fans from across the south flock here to visit key locations from their favourite blockbusters, among them **Lamb's Nose** (5km) and **Dolphin's Nose** (9km), former British picnicking

---

COONOOR'S TEA ESTATES

Visible from far away as tiny orange or red dots amid the green vegetation, **tea-pickers** work the slopes around Coonoor, carrying wicker baskets of fresh leaves and bamboo rods that they use like rulers to ensure that each plant is evenly plucked. Once the leaves reach the factory, they're processed within a day, producing seven grades of tea. **Orange pekoe** is the best and most expensive; the seventh lowest grade, a dry dust of stalks and leaf swept up at the end of the process, will be sold on to make instant tea. To visit a tea or coffee plantation, contact UPASI (United Planters' Association of Southern India) at Glenview House, Coonoor, (☎0423 223 0270, ⓦupasi.org), just along from *Vivek Tourist Home*.

---

spots with paved pathways and dramatic views of the Mettupalayam plains. If you take an early morning bus to Dolphin's Nose, it's possible to walk the 9km back into town via Lamb's Nose – a very pleasant scenic amble that takes you through tea estates and dense forest.

ARRIVAL AND INFORMATION

COONOOR

By train The railway station is in Lower Coonoor across the bazaar from the bus station. There are four trains daily to Ooty (7.45am, 10.40am, 12.35pm & 4.40pm) and one daily service to Mettupalayam at 3.15pm, which arrives at 5.30pm. Tickets to Ooty cost ₹3 ordinary class and ₹85 first class and it's ₹4/₹110 to Mettupalayam. The ticket office is open daily 7.30am–5.30pm.

By bus Buses from Mettupalayam, Coimbatore and Ooty arrive at the bus stand, a large blue building at the entrance to Lower Coonoor. Local buses run to Dolphin's Nose every two hours, starting at 7am.

Services There are a few ATMs in Coonoor – including the SBI ATM near the *gateway* and ICICI Circle's ATM between Bedford and Sim's Park. Ooty offers a much wider range. There is an internet place, I-Net, next door to the Dragon restaurant at Bedford Circle.

ACCOMMODATION

There are a few decent places to stay in Coonoor but it's spread over a wide area, so it's best to arrive early to look for a room; you'll need an auto-rickshaw to find most of the hotels. Expect to pay around ₹50 from the bus stand to Bedford Circle.

Gateway (By Taj Group) Church Rd, Upper Coonoor ☎0423 222 5400, ⓦtajhotels.com. Luxurious but overpriced colonial-era hotel with spectacular views from the gardens. Ayurvedic treatments, excellent lunchtime buffets (₹805) and a range of sports and activities. The largest "superior" rooms cost ₹10,200 but all prices are a third cheaper during off-peak periods. **₹9600**

Sree Venkateshwara Lodge Cash Bazaar ☎0423 220 6309. Large building 100m down from the railway station, and the best option in Lower Coonoor, offering clean, average-sized attached rooms, all with TV. **₹660**

Velan (aka Ritz) Ritz Rd, Bedford Circle ☎0423 223 0784, ⓦvelanhotels.com. Mid-range hotel with character, set in a great location on the outskirts of town. It has deep balconies, fine views and spacious rooms – the standard rooms have tiled floors, while the deluxe rooms

(₹3000) have wooden floors. **₹2400**

Vivek Tourist Home 42 Figure of Eight Rd, near Bedford Circle ☎0423 223 0658, ⓦhotelvivek.com. Clean rooms in a slightly institutional atmosphere; some have tiny balconies overlooking the lawn and tea terraces. Standard rooms have hot water by bucket only in the morning; deluxe rooms (₹1800) have 24hr hot showers. **₹990**

★**YWCA Guest House** Wyoming, near Nankem hospital, 500m down from Bedford Circle ☎0423 223 4426, ⓦywcaagooty.com. There are only fourteen rooms – five doubles, five singles (₹345) and dorms – in this Victorian-era house, full of character on a bluff overlooking town. Superb home-cooked meals are available at very reasonable rates, and there's a flower garden with fine views of the tea terraces. No alcohol. Dorm **₹135**, double **₹810**

EATING

Dragon Bedford Circle ☎0423 223 2158. Chinese restaurant serving up authentic Chinese dishes including spring rolls (₹90–130), a range of chop suey (₹120–150), chowmein (₹120–150) and a few Indian dishes. Daily 10am–4pm & 6.30–11pm.

Mirchi Bedford Circle ☎90035 57477. Clean restaurant with pleasant decor serving a range of veg (₹100) and non-veg (₹150) Indian food including a selection of spicy Chettinad dishes. They also serve soups (₹60) and lunchtime "meals". Daily 10am–11pm.

Tamizhamgam Pronounced "Tamirangum" Mount Rd near the bus stand. This is Coonoor's most popular vegetarian "meals" joint, serving the usual south Indian breakfasts, lunchtime "meals" and snacks throughout the day. Daily 7am–10pm.

Venky's Cash Bazaar, Lower Coonoor, next to Sree Venkateshwara Lodge ☎ 0423 2236740. Large pure-veg place serving traditional south Indian breakfasts, a choice of lunchtime "meals" (11.30am–4pm), including south Indian (₹45) and north Indian (₹110) thalis, and a few noodle dishes. Daily 7.30am–10pm.

Udhagamandalam (Ooty)

In the early nineteenth century, when the British burra sahib John Sullivan first ventured into this region of the Nilgiris through the Hulikal ravine and "discovered" **UDHAGAMANDALAM** (anglicized to **Ootacamund**, abbreviated to Ooty), the territory was the traditional homeland of the pastoralist **Toda** hill tribe. Until this moment, the Todas had lived in almost total isolation from the cities of the surrounding plains and Deccan plateau lands. Sullivan quickly realized the agricultural potential of the area, acquired tracts of land for ₹1 per acre from the Todas, and set about planting flax, barley and hemp, as well as potatoes, soft fruit and, most significantly, **tea**, all of which flourished in the mild climate. Within twenty years, the former East India Company clerk had made a fortune. Needless to say, he was soon joined by other fortune-seekers, and a town was built, complete with artificial lake, churches and stone houses that wouldn't have looked out of place in Surrey or the Scottish Highlands. **Ooty** was the "Queen of Hill Stations" and the most popular hill retreat in India outside the Himalayas.

By a stroke of delicious irony, the Todas outlived the colonists whose cash crops originally displaced them – but only just. Having retreated with their buffalo into the surrounding hills and wooded valleys, they continue to preserve a more-or-less traditional way of life, albeit in greatly diminished numbers. Until the mid-1970s "Snooty Ooty" continued to be "home" to the notoriously snobbish British inhabitants who chose to "stay on" after Independence. Since then, visitors have continued to be attracted by Ooty's cool climate and peaceful green hills, forest and grassland. However, indiscriminate **development** and a deluge of domestic holiday-makers, means that the quaint vestiges of the Raj have been somewhat diluted and are now few and far between.

Situated 2286m above sea level, the town sprawls over a large area with plenty of winding roads and steep climbs. The focal point is **Charing Cross**, a busy junction at the end of **Commercial Road**, the main shopping street running south to the big bazaar and municipal vegetable market.

Botanical Gardens

Woodhouse Rd • Daily 7am–6.30pm • ₹15, camera ₹30, video ₹75 • ☎ 0423 244 2545

A little way north of Charing Cross, the **Botanical Gardens**, laid out in 1847 by gardeners from London's Kew Gardens, consist of fifty acres of immaculate lawns, lily ponds and beds, with more than a thousand varieties of shrubs, flowers and trees. There's a refreshment stand in the park, and shops in the small Tibetan market sell ice creams and snacks. The **Rose Garden** (daily 7am–6.30pm; ₹20, camera ₹30, video ₹75), south of Charing Cross along a lane off Etienne's Road, has 2800 varieties of rose and is the largest collection in the whole of India. It's worth a visit for any budding botanists and gardeners, particularly in season, when the flowers proudly flaunt their petals and perfumes.

St Stephen's Church

Mysore–Ooty road

Northwest of Charing Cross, the small Gothic-style **St Stephen's Church** was one of Ooty's first colonial structures, built in the 1820s on the site of a Toda temple; timber

20

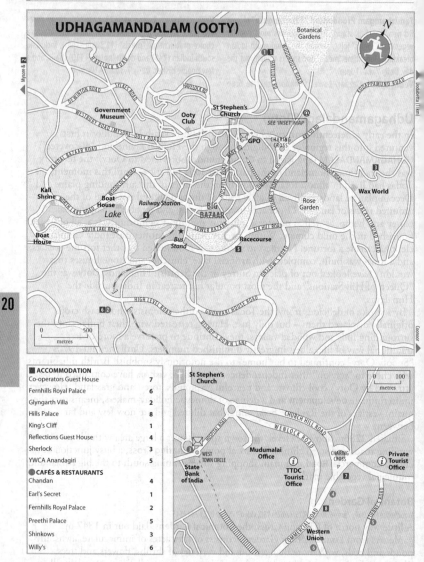

ACCOMMODATION

Co-operators Guest House	7
Fernhills Royal Palace	6
Glyngarth Villa	2
Hills Palace	8
King's Cliff	1
Reflections Guest House	4
Sherlock	3
YWCA Anandagiri	5

CAFÉS & RESTAURANTS

Chandan	4
Earl's Secret	1
Fernhills Royal Palace	2
Preethi Palace	5
Shinkows	3
Willy's	6

for its bowed teak roof was taken from Tipu Sultan's palace at Srirangapatnam and hauled up here by elephant. The area around the church gives some idea of what the hill-station must have looked like in the days of the Raj. To the right is the rambling and rather dilapidated **Spencer's store**, which opened in 1909 and sold everything a British home in the colonies could ever need; it's now a computer college.

Government Museum

Mysore-Ooty Rd • Daily except Fri & 2nd Sat of month 9.30am–5.30pm • ₹100 ₹(5)

Also in the northwest of town, a couple of kilometres further along the Mysore Road, the modest **Government Museum** houses a few tribal objects, sculptures and crafts.

THE NILGIRI BLUE MOUNTAIN RAILWAY

The famous narrow-gauge **Nilgiri Blue Mountain Railway** climbs up from Mettupalayam on the plains, via Hillgrove (17km) and Coonoor (27km) to Udhagamandalam, a journey of 46km that passes through sixteen tiny tunnels, eleven stations and nineteen bridges. It's a slow haul of four and a half hours or more – sometimes the train moves little faster than walking pace, and always takes at least twice as long as the bus – but the **views** are absolutely magnificent, especially along the steepest sections in the Hulikal ravine.

The line was built between 1890 and 1908, paid for by the tea-planters and other British inhabitants of the Nilgiris. It differs from India's two comparable narrow-gauge lines, to Darjeeling and Shimla, for its use of the so-called **Swiss rack system**, by means of which the tiny locomotives are able to climb gradients of up to 1 in 12.5. Special bars were set between the track rails to form a ladder, which cogs of teeth, connected to the train's driving wheels, engage like a zip mechanism. Because of this novel design, only the original locomotives can still run the steepest stretches of line, which is why the section between Mettupalayam and Coonoor has remained one of South Asia's last functioning **steam routes**. The chuffing and whistle screeches of the tiny train, echoing across the valleys as it pushes its blue-and-cream carriages up to Coonoor (where a diesel locomotive takes over) rank among the most romantic sounds of south India, conjuring up the determined gentility of the Raj era. Even if you don't count yourself as a trainspotter, a boneshaking ride on the Blue Mountain Railway should be a priority.

The lake

Boathouse daily 9am–6pm • ₹5, camera ₹10, video ₹100

Situated in the southwest corner of Ooty, the long and narrow **lake**, constructed in the early 1800s, is still one of Ooty's main tourist attractions, despite being somewhat polluted by sewage. Renting one of a range of lake-worthy vessels is a quintessential part of the domestic holiday scene, with a small percentage of foreigners also choosing to brave the waters. Once inside the boathouse, various boats can be rented (paddle boats ₹60–100, rowing boats ₹80–110, charter motor boats seating 8–15 people ₹250–450). Back outside, you can rent a horse and ride around the lake for ₹350 per hour. The circumference of the lake is about 4.5km and makes for a very pleasant walk, conveniently peppered with juice and chai stalls.

Wax World

Coonoor Rd • Daily 9.30am–8pm • ₹25, camera ₹10 • ☎ 97903 43296, ✉ info@waxworld.in

A couple of kilometres from Charing Cross, **Wax World** is a rather lifeless exhibition of twenty famous and infamous social and political figures, mostly from the twentieth century. Interesting in its own way, and with helpful guides to commentate, you may pick up the odd historical nugget. Watch out for the "disturbing scene". There are no Bollywood divas or sports heroes as yet.

ARRIVAL AND DEPARTURE

UDHAGAMANDALAM (OOTY)

By train Ooty's station for the miniature Nilgiri Blue Mountain Railway (see box above) from Coonoor and Mettupalayam is near Big Bazaar and close to the bus station. The station has a booking office (6.30am–7pm), where you can buy tickets for the Nilgiri Blue Mountain Railway, and a reservation counter (daily 8am–12.30pm & 2.30–4.30pm) for booking onward services to most other destinations in the south. Four trains daily (9.15am, 12.15pm, 2pm & 6pm) pootle down the narrow-gauge track to Coonoor but only the 2pm train continues down to Mettupalayam, on the main broad-gauge network, arriving at 6.30pm. If you are Chennai-bound you can connect with the daily #2672 *Nilgiri Express*, which departs at 7.45pm.

By bus Buses from Mysore and Coimbatore arrive at the bus stand, in the southwest of Ooty, near the Racecourse and Big Bazaar. Auto-rickshaws and taxis are available just outside the bus stand. There is an enquiry office (7am–8pm) on the left side of the station (as you enter) on the first floor. Both Tamil Nadu and Karnataka State Transport run regular and super-deluxe state buses out of Ooty.

20

Destinations Bengaluru (9 daily), Masingudi (4 daily), Mettupalayam (every 10 min), Mysore (every 30min) and other destinations in Tamil Nadu and Kerala. Private buses to Mysore, Bengaluru and Kodaikanal can be booked at the bigger hotels and agents dotted around the town.

INFORMATION

Tourist information The TTDC tourist office (Mon–Sat 10am–5.45pm; ☎ 0423 244 3977) is at the TTDC *Hotel Tamil Nadu* just above Wenlock Rd. You can book tours here, including a mammoth day-trip (daily 9am–8pm; ₹250/head or ₹1800/car) that includes Kamarajasagar Dam, Mudumalai and a jungle ride. There's also a day trip around Ooty and Coonoor (daily 9am–6pm; ₹200/head, ₹1200/car), which goes to Ooty Lake, Doddabetta Peak, the Botanical Gardens, Sim's Park, Lamb's Nose Dolphin's Nose and a tea garden. There's a private tourist information centre (Mon–Sat 10am–1pm & 2–6pm) in the clocktower building at Charing Cross that gives out leaflets and hotel information. The Mudumalai Forestry Department and ranger's office (10am–1pm & 2–5.45pm ☎ 0423 244 4098, ✉ fdmtr@tn.nic. in) is just up behind the TTDC office.

Services Ooty's post office is northwest of Charing Cross at West Town Circle, near St Stephen's Church. There are numerous internet outlets across town, especially around Charing Cross. The State Bank of India on West Town Circle changes travellers' cheques and currency as does the Western Union Office on Commercial R d. There are also several ATMs dotted around town.

ACCOMMODATION

Ooty's accommodation in Ooty is a lot more expensive than in many places in India and during the peak season (April and May), prices can rise by thirty to a hundred percent. It also gets very crowded, so you may have to hunt around.

Co-operators Guest House Commercial Rd, just along from Charing Cross ☎ 0423 244 4046. This centrally located hotel is a good budget option. Set slightly back from the main road, the Raj-era building has clean rooms and yellow-and-turquoise balconies overlooking a courtyard. **₹825**

Fernhills Royal Palace Fernhill Post, High Level Rd ☎ 0423 2443911, ⊕ fernhillspalace.co.in. Luxury heritage hotel in the maharaja of Mysore's former palace. The original exterior remains but the interior has been tastefully renovated into a range of suites of varying size and opulence. **₹10800**

Glyngarth Villa Golf Club Rd, 4.5km from town centre on the Mysore Rd ☎ 0423 244 5754, ⊕ glyngarthvilla .com. A 160-year-old colonial villa set in four acres of greenery. The five comfortable double rooms, with wooden panelling, exude colonial atmosphere. There are also four stylish attic suites (₹5062) in a new wooden cottage, each with a loft bedroom, sitting area with leather sofa and armchairs and modern bathrooms. **₹3600**

Hills Palace Commercial Rd ☎ 0423 244 6483, ⊕ eghplanet.com. Centrally located place set back from the main road and insulated from the traffic noise. Friendly, with spotlessly clean rooms (bigger rooms cost an extra ₹450), all with 24hr hot water and TV. Great value in low season. **₹1575**

King's Cliff Havelock Rd ☎ 0423 245 2888, ⊕ littlearth .in. Imposing ancestral mansion with nine lavishly furnished rooms, standard and deluxe (₹5969), each with a Shakespeareian theme. The place is full of character and has a stylish lounge and dining room. **₹3689**

Reflections Guest House North Lake Rd ☎ 0423 244 3834, ✉ reflectionsin@yahoo.co.in. Homely, relaxing guesthouse by the lake, just 5min walk from the railway station. Rooms open onto a small terrace and most of them have lake views. Easily the best budget option in Ooty, but it's small and fills up quickly, so book in advance. **₹600**

★ **Sherlock** Tiger Hill Rd, 3km east of Charing Cross ☎ 0423 244 1641, ⊕ littlearth.in/sherlock. Beautifully landscaped Victorian mansion with a Conan Doyle theme and stunning views from the grassy terrace. All nine rooms, standard or deluxe (₹3469), are tastefully furnished and have sitouts. Friendly service and good food, too. **₹3469**

YWCA Anandagiri Etienne's Rd ☎ 0423 244 4262, ⊕ ywcaagooty.com. Charming 1920s building set in spacious grounds near the racecourse. There are seven different types of room (tariffs vary according to size and hot water availability), chalets (₹1299) and a dorm. Excellent value and popular, so best book ahead. Dorm **₹110**, double **₹345**

EATING

Chandan Nahar Hotel, Commercial Rd, near Charing Cross. Carefully prepared north Indian specialities, a selection of tandoori vegetarian dishes and a range of lassis and milk shakes, served inside a posh restaurant or on a small lawnside terrace. Main courses ₹110. Daily 12.30–3.30pm & 7.30–10.30pm.

Earl's Secret King's Cliff, Havelock Rd ☎ 0423 245 2888. Extensive menu of more than two hundred quality dishes, including quail, chicken, seafood and veggie as well as delicious home-baked desserts, served in atmospheric surroundings. Expect to pay ₹300–450 for a main course. The hotel's resident singer/guitarist serenades diners from

8.45pm. Daily noon–3pm & 7–11pm.

Fernhills Royal Palace High Level Rd ☎0423 244 3911. Lavish buffets served in delightful dining room (formerly a ballroom) – breakfast (₹277), lunch (₹745) and dinner (₹745) – which are well worth the cost for a one-off treat. There's also a smaller à la carte restaurant with lawn views next door, serving meat (₹350) and veggie dishes (₹275). Daily 7.30am–10.30am, 12.30–3.30pm & 7.30–10.30pm.

★ **Preethi Palace** Etienne's Rd near Charing Cross ☎0423 244 2789. Excellent and very popular restaurant serving great lunchtime "meals" (north Indian ₹60; south Indian ₹85; Gujarati ₹130) and a range of delicious pure-veg food throughout the day including tandoori breads. Daily 7am–10pm.

Shinkows 42 Commissioners Rd ☎0423 244 2811. Good-value, authentic Chinese restaurant serving decent-sized portions on the spicy and pricey side – main meat and fish courses are around ₹190; veggie dishes ₹50–160. Daily noon–4pm & 6.30–10pm.

Willy's KRC Arcade, Walsham Rd. Second floor café, with a pleasant, laidback ambience and featuring a 70s-style dolphin mural. It's a good place to chill out over a coffee, cake or toasted sandwich and browse the impressive lending library. A range of Indian savoury snacks is also available. Daily 10am–10pm.

Mudumalai Wildlife Sanctuary

Elephant Camp Daily 8.30am–9am & 5.30–6pm • ₹15 **Vehicle safari tour** Daily 7–9am & 4–6pm; 40min • ₹135/person, camera ₹25, video camera ₹150 • ☎0423 252 6235

Set 1140m up in the Nilgiri Hills, the **MUDUMALAI WILDLIFE SANCTUARY** covers 322 square kilometres of deciduous forest, split by the main road from Ooty (64km to the southeast) to Mysore (97km to the northwest). Occupying the thickly wooded lower northern reaches of the hills, it boasts one of the largest populations of elephants in India, along with wild dogs, gaur (Indian bison), common and Nilgiri langurs and bonnet macaques (monkeys), jackals, hyenas, sloth bears and even a few tigers and leopards. The abundant local flora includes the dazzling red flowers of the flame of the forest.

The main focus of interest by the park entrance at **Theppakkadu** is the **Elephant Camp** show, where you can watch the sanctuary's tame pachyderms being fed and bathed. This is also the starting point for the government **safari tour**, which is the only way of accessing the official park limits. However, you may well see more creatures if you take a private **jeep tour** or **guided trek** into some of the parts of Mudumalai that are outside the state-controlled area. These can be arranged through your guesthouse or direct at Nature Safari in Masinagudi (☎0423 252 6340, ✉saveelephasmaximus@yahoo.co.in).

ARRIVAL AND DEPARTURE   MUDUMALAI WILDLIFE SANCTUARY

By bus The main route to Mudumalai from Ooty plied by buses to Mysore and Bengaluru takes 2hr 30min to reach Theppakkadu. The alternative route, a tortuous journey of very steep gradients and hairpin bends, can only be attempted by taxis, 4WD and minibuses. These take around 1hr and end up in Masinagudi, which is closer to most of the area's accommodation.

ACCOMMODATION

Jungle Retreat Bokkapuram, 6km southwest of Masinagudi ☎0423 252 6469, ⊛jungleretreat.com. The biggest and most luxurious sanctuary resort, with eco-friendly swimming pool and a range of accommodation including dorm beds, luxury treehouses (₹4706) and exec rooms (₹5883). The meals tariff (₹1470/day) covers three sumptuous buffet meals and unlimited tea and coffee. They can also arrange treks and plantation visits. Dorm ₹525, double ₹2941

Secret Ivory Masinagudi ☎0423 252 6844 ⊛secretivory.com. Luxury guesthouse with just eight rooms (deluxe ₹2175) and a treehouse (₹4069). They serve delicious farm-fresh veg, grown on their own land and also organize treks and safaris. ₹1980

TTDC Hotel Tamil Nadu Theppakkadu ☎0423 252 6580, ⊛ttdconline.com. The somewhat dowdy TTDC hotel is one of the park's budget options. There is a choice of doubles, four-bed family rooms (₹1400) and very cheap dorm accommodation. Dorm ₹125, double ₹600

Wild Haven Chadapatti, 6km south of Masinagudi ☎0423 252 6490, ⊛wildhaven.in. This lodge is in open land with great mountain views. There is a choice of simple, spacious double rooms in the stone block or accommdation in their cottages (₹2906). ₹3487

20

Kerala

PAPANASAM BEACH, VERKALA

21

Kerala

The state of Kerala stretches for 550km along India's southwest coast, divided between the densely forested mountains of the Western Ghats inland and a lush, humid coastal plain of rice paddy, lagoons, rivers and canals. Its intensely tropical landscape, fed by the highest rainfall in peninsular India, has intoxicated visitors since the ancient Sumerians and Greeks sailed in search of spices to the shore known as the Malabar Coast. Equally, Kerala's arcane rituals and spectacular festivals – many of them little changed since the earliest era of Brahmanical Hinduism – have dazzled outsiders for thousands of years.

Travellers weary of India's daunting metropolises will find Kerala's cities smaller and more relaxed. The most popular is undoubtedly the great port of **Kochi** (Cochin), where the state's long history of peaceful foreign contact is evocatively evident in the atmospheric old quarters of Mattancherry and Fort Cochin. In Kerala's far south, the capital, **Thiruvananthapuram** (Trivandrum), is gateway to the nearby palm-fringed beaches of **Kovalam** and **Varkala**, and provides visitors with varied opportunities to sample Kerala's rich cultural and artistic life.

One of the best aspects of exploring Kerala, though, is the actual travelling – especially by **boat**, in the spellbinding Kuttanad region, around historic **Kollam** (Quilon) and **Alappuzha** (Alleppey). Cruisers and beautiful wooden barges known as *kettu vallam* ("tied boats") ply the **backwaters**, offering tourists a window on village life in India's most densely populated state. Furthermore, it's easy to escape the heat of the lowlands by heading for the **hills**, which rise to 2695m. Roads pass through landscapes dotted with churches and temples, tea, coffee, spice and rubber plantations, and natural forests, en route to wildlife reserves such as **Periyar**, where herds of mud-caked elephants roam freely in vast tracts of jungle.

Kerala is short on the historic monuments prevalent elsewhere in India, and most of its ancient temples are closed to non-Hindus. Following an unwritten law, few buildings in the region, whether houses or temples, are higher than the surrounding trees, which in urban areas often creates the illusion that you're surrounded by forest. Typical features of both domestic and temple architecture include long, sloping tiled and gabled roofs that minimize the excesses of rain and sunshine, and pillared verandas; the definitive examples are Thiruvananthapuram's **Puttan Malika Palace**, and **Padmanabhapuram Palace**, in neighbouring Tamil Nadu, but easily reached from the capital.

Huge amounts of money are lavished upon many, varied, and often all-night **festivals** associated with Kerala's temples. Fireworks rend the air, while processions of

ELEPHANTS PLAY THEIR PART IN THE PURAM FESTIVAL

Highlights

❶ **Ritual theatre** Elaborately costumed, arcane dance dramas, such as kathakali and theyyem, are an essential part of the Kerala experience. **See p.1026**

❷ **Varkala** Chill out in a cliff-top café, sunbathe on the beach or soak up the atmosphere around the town's busy temple tank. **See p.1037**

❸ **The backwaters** Explore the beautiful waterways of Kerala's densely populated coastal strip on a rice barge or punted canoe, following the narrow, overgrown canals right into the heart of the villages. **See p.1046**

❹ **The High Range** The tea plantations, pepper groves and grassy mountains around Munnar and Periyar are the perfect antidote to the heat and humidity of the coast. **See pp.1050–1059**

❺ **Fort Cochin** Dutch, Portuguese, British and traditional Keralan townhouses line the backstreets of Malabar's old peninsular port. See the grandest of them from the inside by staying in a heritage hotel. **See p.1061**

❻ **Temple festivals** Parades of extravagantly decorated elephants, backed by drummers and firework displays, form the focal point of Kerala's Hindu festivals. **See p.1074**

HIGHLIGHTS ARE MARKED ON THE MAP ON P.1024

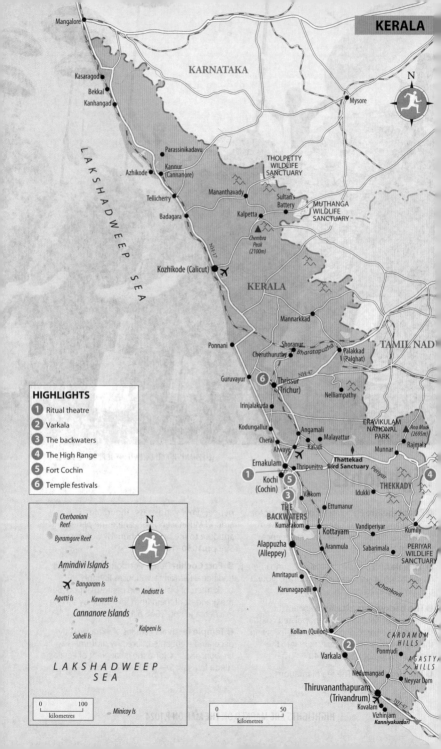

caparisoned elephants are accompanied by some of the loudest (and deftest) drum orchestras in the world. Thrissur's famous **Puram** festival (April/May) is the most astonishing, but smaller events take place throughout the state – often outdoors, with all welcome to attend. **Theatre** and **dance** also abound; not only the region's own female classical dance form, **mohiniyattam** ("dance of the enchantress"), but also the martial-art-influenced **kathakali** dance drama, which has for four centuries brought gods and demons from the Mahabharata and Ramayana to Keralan villages. Its two thousand-year-old predecessor, the Sanskrit drama **kudiyattam**, is still performed by a handful of artists, while localized rituals known as **theyyem**, where dancers wearing decorative masks and hats become "possessed" by temple deities, remain a potent ingredient of village life in the north. Few visitors witness these extraordinary all-night performances, but from December through March it is possible to spend weeks hopping between village festivals in northern Kerala, experiencing rituals little altered in centuries.

A word of warning, however, for budget travellers. Kerala ranks among the most **expensive** regions of India. **Accommodation** is particularly pricey – and tends to be of a correspondingly high standard. Cheap places to stay are thin on the ground everywhere, but especially in the coastal resorts, hill stations and backwater areas, where it's not uncommon to pay upwards of ₹2000 for a room in a modest guesthouse in season.

Brief history

Ancient Kerala is mentioned as the land of the **Cheras** in a third-century BC Ashokan edict, and in several even older Sanskrit texts, including the Mahabharata. Pliny and Ptolemy also testify to thriving trade between the ancient port of Muziris (now known as Kodungallur) and the Roman Empire. Little is known about the region's early rulers, whose dominion covered a large area, but whose capital, Vanji, has not so far been identified. At the start of the ninth century, King Kulashekhara Alvar – a poet-saint of the Vaishnavite *bhakti* movement known as the *alvars* – established his own dynasty. His son and successor, Rajashekharavarman, is thought to have been a saint of the parallel Shaivite movement, the *nayannars*. The great Keralan philosopher **Shankaracharya**, whose *advaitya* ("non-dualist") philosophy influenced the whole of Hindu India, was alive at this time.

Eventually, the prosperity acquired by the Cheras through trade with China and the Arab world proved too much of an attraction for the neighbouring **Chola** empire, who embarked upon a hundred years of sporadic warfare with the Cheras at the end of the tenth century. Around 1100, the Cheras lost their capital at Mahodayapuram in the north, and shifted south to establish a new capital at Kollam (Quilon).

Direct trade with Europe commenced in 1498 with the arrival in the capital, Calicut, of a small Portuguese fleet under **Vasco da Gama** – the first expedition to reach the coast of India via the Cape of Good Hope and Arabian Sea. After an initial show of cordiality, relations between him and the local ruler, or Zamorin, quickly degenerated, and da Gama's second voyage four years later was characterized by appalling massacres, kidnapping, mutilation and barefaced piracy. Nevertheless, a fortified trading post was soon established at Cochin from which the Portuguese, exploiting old enmities between the region's rulers, were able to dominate trade with the Middle East. This was gradually eroded away over the ensuing century by rival powers France and Holland. An independent territory was subsequently carved out of the Malabar Coast by Tipu Sultan of Mysore, but his defeat in 1792 left the British in control right up until Independence.

Kerala can claim some of the most startling **radical** credentials in India. In 1957 it was the first state in the world to democratically elect a communist government, and still regularly returns communist parties in elections. Due to reforms made

21

KERALAN RITUAL THEATRE

Among the most magical experiences a visitor to Kerala can have is to witness one of the innumerable ancient drama rituals that play such an important role in the cultural life of the region. **Kathakali** is the best known; other less publicized forms, which clearly influenced its development, include the classical Sanskrit **kudiyattam**.

Many Keralan forms share broad characteristics. A prime aim of each performer is to transform the mundane to the world of gods and demons; his preparation is highly ritualized, involving otherworldly costume and mask-like make-up. In *kathakali* and *kudiyattam*, this preparation is a rigorously codified part of the classical tradition. One-off **performances** of various ritual types take place throughout the state, building up to fever pitch during April and May before pausing for the monsoon (June–Aug). Finding out about such events requires a little perseverance, but it's well worth the effort; enquire at tourist offices, or buy a Malayalam daily paper such as the *Malayalam Manorama* and ask someone to check the listings for temple festivals, where most of the action invariably takes place. Tourist *kathakali* is staged daily in **Kochi** (see p.1059) but to find authentic performances, contact **performing arts schools** such as Thiruvananthapuram's Margi (see p.1030) and Cheruthuruthy's Kerala Kalamandalam (see p.1077); *kudiyattam* artists work at both, as well as at Natana Kairali at Irinjalakuda, which is accessible from Thrissur (see p.1974).

KATHAKALI

Here is the tradition of the trance dancers, here is the absolute demand of the subjugation of body to spirit, here is the realization of the cosmic transformation of human into divine.

Mrinalini Sarabhai, classical dancer

The image of a *kathakali* actor in a magnificent costume with extraordinary make-up and a huge gold crown has become Kerala's trademark. Traditional performances, of which there are still many, usually take place on open ground outside a temple, beginning at 10pm and lasting until dawn, illuminated by the flickers of a large brass oil lamp centre-stage. Virtually nothing about *kathakali* is naturalistic, because it depicts the world of gods and demons; men play both the male and female roles.

Standing at the back of the stage, two musicians play driving rhythms, one on a bronze gong, the other on heavy bell-metal cymbals; they also sing the dialogue. Actors appear and disappear from behind a hand-held curtain and never utter a sound, save the odd strange cry. Learning the elaborate hand gestures, facial expressions and choreographed movements, as articulate and precise as any sign language, requires rigorous training which can begin at the age of 8 and last ten years. At least two more **drummers** stand left of the stage; one plays the upright *chenda* with slender curved sticks, the other plays the *maddalam*, a horizontal barrel-shaped hand drum. When a female character is "speaking", the *chenda* is replaced by the hourglass-shaped *ettaka*, a "talking drum" on which melodies can be played. The drummers keep their eyes on the actors, whose every gesture is reinforced by their sound, from the gentlest embrace to the gory disembowelling of an enemy.

during the 1960s and 1970s, Kerala currently has the most equitable land distribution of any Indian state. Poverty appears far less acute than in other parts of the country, with life expectancy and per capita income well above the national averages. Kerala is also justly proud of its reputation for healthcare and education, with **literacy** rates that stand, officially at least, at 91 percent for men and 88 percent for women. Industrial development is negligible, however: potential investors from outside tend to fight shy of dealing with such a politicized workforce.

Thiruvananthapuram

Kerala's capital, **THIRUVANANTHAPURAM** (still widely known as **Trivandrum**), is set on seven low hills just a couple of kilometres inland from the Arabian Sea. Despite its

Although it bears the unmistakeable influences of *kudiyattam* and indigenous folk rituals, *kathakali*, literally "story-play", is thought to have crystallized into a distinct theatre form during the seventeenth century. The plays are based on three major sources: the **Hindu epics** the Mahabharata, Ramayana and the Bhagavata Purana. While the stories are ostensibly about god-heroes such as Rama and Krishna, the most popular characters are those that give the most scope to the actors – the villainous, fanged, red-and-black-faced *katti* ("knife") anti-heroes; these types, such as the kings Ravana and Duryodhana, are dominated by lust, greed, envy and violence. David Bolland's *Guide to Kathakali*, widely available in Kerala, gives invaluable scene-by-scene summaries of the most popular plays and explains in simple language a lot more besides.

When **attending a performance**, arrive early to get your bearings before it gets dark, even though the first play will not begin much before 10pm. (Quiet) members of the audience are welcome to visit the dressing room before and during the performance. The colour and design of the mask-like make-up, which specialist artists take several hours to apply, reveal the character's personality. The word *pacha* means both "green" and "pure"; a green-faced *pacha* character is thus a noble human or god. Red signifies *rajas*, passion and aggression, black denotes *tamas*, darkness and negativity, while white is *sattvik*, light and intellect. Once the make-up is completed, elaborate wide skirts are tied to the waist, and ornaments of silver and gold are added. Silver talons are fitted to the left hand. The transformation is complete with a final prayer and the donning of waist-length wig and crown. Visitors new to *kathakali* will almost undoubtedly get bored during such long programmes, parts of which are very slow indeed. If you're at a village performance, you may not always find accommodation, so you can't leave during the night. Be prepared to sit on the ground for hours, and bring some warm clothes. Half the fun is staying up all night to witness, just as the dawn light appears, the gruesome disembowelling of a villain or a demon *asura*.

KUDIYATTAM

Three families of the Chakyar caste and a few outsiders perform the Sanskrit drama **kudiyattam**, the oldest continually performed theatre-form in the world. Until recently it was only performed inside temples and then only in front of the uppermost castes. Visually it is very similar to its offspring, *kathakali*, but its atmosphere is infinitely more archaic. The actors, eloquent in sign language and symbolic movement, speak in the compelling intonation of the local brahmins' Vedic chant, unchanged since 1500 BC.

A single act of a *kudiyattam* play can require ten full nights; the entire play takes forty. A great actor, in full command of the subtleties of expression through gestures, can take half an hour to do such a simple thing as murder a demon, berate the audience, or simply describe a leaf fall to the ground. Unlike *kathakali*, *kudiyattam* includes comic characters and plays. The ubiquitous Vidushaka, narrator and clown, is something of a court jester, and traditionally has held the right to criticize openly the highest in the land without fear of retribution.

administrative importance – demonstrated by wide roads, multistorey office blocks and gleaming white colonial buildings – it's an easy-going state capital by Indian standards, with enclaves of traditional red-tiled gabled houses breaking up the bustle of its modern concrete core, and a swathe of parkland spreading north of the centre. Although its principal sight, the **Sri Padmanabhaswamy temple**, is closed to non-Hindus the city holds enough of interest to fill a day. Foremost among its sights is the splendid **Puttan Malika Palace**, one of the state's best museums, and a typically Keralan market, **Chalai bazaar**.

Both the palace and bazaar are in the oldest and most interesting part of the city, the **Fort** area in the south. At the opposite, northern side of the centre, the **Sri Chitra Art Gallery** and **Napier Museum** showcase painting, crafts and sculpture in a leafy park. In addition, schools specializing in the martial art *kalarippayat* and the dance/theatre forms of *kathakali* and *kudiyattam* offer an insight into the Keralan obsession with physical training and skill.

21

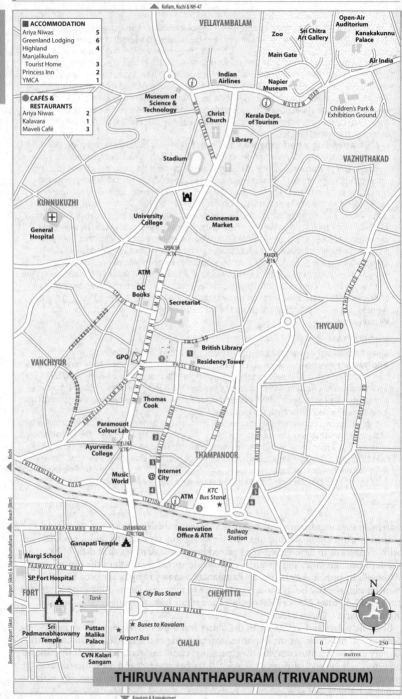

Kollam, Kochi & NH-47

ACCOMMODATION

Ariya Niwas	5
Greenland Lodging	6
Highland	4
Manjalikulam Tourist Home	3
Princess Inn	2
YMCA	1

CAFÉS & RESTAURANTS

Ariya Niwas	2
Kalavara	1
Maveli Café	3

VELLAYAMBALAM

Open-Air Auditorium

Zoo

Sri Chitra Art Gallery

Kanakakunnu Palace

Main Gate

Air India

Indian Airlines

Napier Museum

Museum of Science & Technology

Christ Church

Kerala Dept. of Tourism

Children's Park & Exhibition Ground

MUSEUM ROAD

Library

VAZHUTHAKAD

Stadium

KUNNUKUZHI

Connemara Market

University College

General Hospital

SPENCER JCTN

BAKERY JCTN

VAZHUTHACAD ROAD

MG RD

ATM

DC Books

Secretariat

THYCAUD

STATUE RD

CHITRAKKULAM ROAD

YMCA RD

British Library

Residency Tower

GPO

PRESS ROAD

VANCHIYUR

AMBUJAVILASAM ROAD

MAHATMA GANDHI ROAD

Thomas Cook

Paramount Colour Lab

MANJALIKULAM ROAD

Ayurveda College

COLLEGE JCTN

LAIKKAL HOSPITAL RD

AMRITO ROAD

S COIL RD

THAMPANOOR

Music World

Internet @ City

KTC Bus Stand

ATM

STATION ROAD

CHETTIKULANGARA ROAD

Kochi

Beach (8km)

OVERBRIDGE JUNCTION

Reservation Office & ATM

Railway Station

THAKARAPARAMBU ROAD

Ganapati Temple

Margi School

POWER HOUSE ROAD

PADMAVILASAM ROAD

SP Fort Hospital

Airport (6km) & Shankumukham

Beemapalli Airport (4km)

FORT

Tank

City Bus Stand

CHENTITTA

Sri Padmanabhaswamy Temple

Puttan Malika Palace

CHALAI BAZAAR

Buses to Kovalam

Airport Bus

CHALAI

CVN Kalari Sangam

N

0   250
metres

THIRUVANANTHAPURAM (TRIVANDRUM)

Kovalam & Kanyakumari

Sri Padmanabhaswamy temple

21

Padmanabha, the god Vishnu reclined on a coiled serpent with a lotus flower sprouting from his belly button, is the presiding deity of the **Sri Padmanabhaswamy temple**, a vast complex of interlocking walled courtyards, shrines and ceremonial walkways in the south of the city. The iconic image of the temple's seven-tiered, Tamil-style *gopura* gateway, reflected in the waters of the adjacent bathing tank, graced the front pages of many newspapers across the world in June 2011 when it was discovered that a vast horde of **treasure** had been discovered in vaults below its inner sanctum. Sealed inside the secret chambers were sacks of diamonds, a thousand kilograms of gold, thousands of pieces of gem-encrusted jewellery and, the pièce de résistance, an exquisite 1m-tall gold **image of Vishnu** shimmering with precious stones. Experts are still debating the value of the items, with estimates ranging from US$40–200 billion. Either way, the find makes this by far the richest place of worship in the world.

Non-Hindus are unfortunately not permitted inside, but the main approach road to Sri Padmanabhaswamy, with its stalls full of religious souvenirs and offerings, makes an atmospheric place for a stroll, particularly in the early morning when worshippers take ritual baths in the tank.

Puttan Malika Palace

Tues–Sun 8.30am–12.30pm & 3–5.30pm • ₹20, camera ₹15

The **Puttan Malika Palace** immediately southeast of the Sri Padmanabhaswamy temple became the seat of the Travancore rajas after they left Padmanabhapuram at the end of the nineteenth century. The cool chambers, with highly polished plaster floors and delicately carved wooden screens, house a crop of dusty royal heirlooms, including a solid crystal throne gifted by the Dutch. The real highlight, however, is the elegant Keralan architecture itself. Beneath sloping red-tiled roofs, hundreds of wooden pillars, carved into the forms of rampant horses (*puttan malika* translates as "horse palace"), prop up the eaves, and airy verandas project onto the surrounding lawns.

The royal family have always been keen patrons of the arts, and the open-air **Swathi Sangeetotsavam festival**, held in the grounds during the festival of Navaratri (Oct/Nov), continues the tradition. Performers sit on the palace's raised porch, flanked by the main facade, with the spectators seated on the lawn. For details, ask at the KTDC tourist office.

CVN Kalari Sangam

S St, East Fort • ☎ 0471 2474182, ⊛ cvnkalari.in

Around 500m southeast of the temple in East Fort, the red-brick **CVN Kalari Sangam** ranks among Kerala's top **kalarippayat** gymnasiums. It was founded in 1956 by C.V. Narayanan Nair, one of the legendary figures credited for the martial art's revival, and attracts students from across the world. From 6.30am to 8am (Mon–Sat) you can watch fighting exercises in the sunken *kalari* pit that forms the heart of the complex. Foreigners may join courses, arranged through the head teacher, or *gurukkal*, although prior experience of martial arts and/or dance is a prerequisite.

Chalai Bazaar

Thiruvananthapuram's main source of fresh produce and everyday items is the kilometre-long **Chalai Bazaar**, which runs east from MG Road in East Fort, from opposite the main approach to the temple. Lined with little shops selling flowers, incense, spices, bell metal lamps and fireworks, it's a great area for aimless browsing. On your left (north side) as you enter the street, look out for United Umbrella Mart,

21

which sells brightly coloured temple parasols used in elephant processions. Further down on the opposite side of the road, the delightfully old-fashioned Ambal Coffee Works in another source of authentically Keralan souvenirs.

The Margi Theatre School

West Fort • ☎ 0471 247 8806, ⓦ margitheatre.org

Thiruvananthapuram has for centuries been a crucible for Keralan classical arts, and the **Margi Theatre School**, at the western corner of the Fort area, is one of the foremost colleges for **kathakali** dance drama and the more rarely performed **kudiyattam** theatre form (see box, p.1026). Most visitors venture out here to watch one of the authentic *kathakali* or *kudiyattam* performances staged once each month in its small **theatre**, details of which are posted on the school's website.

To reach Margi, head to the SP Fort hospital on the western edge of Fort and then continue 200m north; the school is set back from the west side of the main road in a large red-tiled and tin-roofed building, behind the High School (the sign is in Malayalam).

The Napier Museum

LMS Vallayambalam Rd • Tues–Sun 10am–5pm • ₹5

A minute's walk east from the north end of MG Road, opposite Kerala Tourism's information office, brings you to the entrance to Thiruvananthapuram's **public gardens**. As well as serving as a welcome refuge from the noise of the city, the park holds the city's best museums. Give the dusty and uninformative Natural History Museum a miss and head instead for the more engaging **Napier Museum**. Built at the end of the nineteenth century, it was an early experiment in what became known as the "Indo-Saracenic" style, with tiled, gabled roofs, garish red-, black- and salmon-patterned brickwork, and a spectacular interior of stained-glass windows and loud turquoise, pink, red and yellow stripes. Highlights of the collection include fifteenth-century Keralan woodcarvings, minutely detailed ivory work, a carved temple chariot (*rath*), plus Chola and Vijayanagar bronzes.

Sri Chitra Art Gallery

Next to Zoological Gardens • Tues–Sun 10am–5pm • ₹50

You pass through the main ticket booth for the city's depressing, faded zoo to reach the **Sri Chitra Art Gallery**, which shows paintings from the Rajput, Mughal and Tanjore schools, along with pieces from China, Tibet and Japan. The meat of the collection, though, is made up of works by the celebrated artist **Raja Ravi Varma** (1848–1906), a local aristocrat who achieved fame and fortune as a producer of Hindu mythological prints – forerunners of India's quirky calendar art. Varma's style was much criticized by later generations for its sentimentality and strong Western influence, but in his time he was regarded as the nation's greatest living artist.

Also on view at the Sri Chitra, in rooms to the rear of the main building, are a couple of minor **Tagores**, and some striking, strongly coloured Himalayan landscapes by the Russian artist-philosopher and mystic, **Nicholas Roerich**, who resided in the Kullu Valley for two decades until his death in 1947 (see p.439).

ARRIVAL AND DEPARTURE   **THIRUVANANTHAPURAM**

BY PLANE

Beemapalli airport Connected to most major Indian cities, as well as Sri Lanka, the Maldives and the Middle East, Beemapalli airport lies 6km southwest of town.

You'll find a Kerala Tourism information booth (in theory 24hr), ATM and Thomas Cook foreign exchange facility just before the exit of the arrivals concourse.

21

GETTING INTO TOWN

By shuttle The best way to get to and from the airport is on the state-of-the-art, a/c airport bus (₹20), which runs between the arrivals concourse and the City bus stand in East Fort. It completes a second leg between here and Kovalam (much to the chagrin of local taxi drivers).

By auto-rickshaw and taxi Auto-rickshaws can get you into the centre for around ₹150 and there's also a handy pre-paid taxi service (pay before departure; ₹240 for the railway station, ₹450 for Kovalam's Lighthouse Beach).

BY BUS

Inter-state buses The long-distance KSRTC Thampanoor bus stand is opposite the train station in the southeast of the city, within walking distance of most of the city's budget accommodation. This is the place to catch services to Varkala – look out for the 90min "super-fast" highway buses; there is an inter-village service too, which takes 2hr 30min. Heading north up the coast (to Kollam, Alleppey, Ernakulam or Thrissur), aim for the 6am or 5.30pm "super-deluxe a/c" specials – you can buy tickets for all long-distance routes in advance at the reservations hatch, main bus stand concourse (daily 6am–10pm). The Tamil Nadu bus company, TNSRTC, has its own counter on the same concourse. Numerous private bus companies also run inter-state services; many of the agents are on Aristo Rd near the *Greenland Lodging*.

INFORMATION AND TOURS

Tourist information In addition to at the airport (see opposite), Kerala Tourism has an information counter at the KSRTC Thampanoor bus stand (Mon–Sat 10am–5pm; ☎0471 232 7224); while KTDC hosts a visitor reception centre next to the *KTDC Chaithram* hotel on Station Rd (daily 7am–9pm; ☎0471 233 0031), where you can book accommodation in their hotel chain and tickets for various

Local services Local buses (including those for Kovalam) depart from City bus stand, in East Fort, a 10min walk south from the KSRTC Thampanoor and railway stations. Services to Kovalam leave from the stand on the roadside – be prepared for a crush if you attempt this journey in the late-afternoon rush hour.

Destinations Alappuzha/Alleppey (every 15–20min; 3hr 30min); Ernakulam/Kochi (every 30min; 5hr); Kanyakumari (5 daily; 2hr 15min); Kollam (every 15–20min; 1hr 40min); Kovalam (every 20–30min); Kumily/Periyar (3 daily; 7hr 45min); Madurai (8 daily; 7hr); Neyyar Dam (hourly; 1hr 30min); Varkala (4 daily; 90min).

BY TRAIN

Kerala's capital is well connected by train with other towns and cities in the country, although getting seats at short notice on long-haul journeys can be a problem. Make reservations as far in advance as possible from the efficient computerized booking office at the station on the south side of the city centre (Mon–Sat 8am–2pm & 2.15–8pm, Sun 8am–2pm). There's a handy pre-paid auto-rickshaw counter on the arrivals concourse.

Destinations Alappuzha/Alleppey (10 daily; 3hr 15min–5hr); Chennai/Madras (6 daily; 16hr 25min–17hr 30min); Ernakulam/Kochi (25 daily; 3hr 50min–5hr); Kanyakumari (3 daily; 2hr 40min); Kollam/Quilon (24 daily; 55min–1hr 20min); Madurai (3 daily; 6hr 45min–9hr).

guided tours.

Tours Most of the KTDC tours, including the city tours (daily 7.30am––7pm; ₹300), are too rushed, but if you're really pushed for time and want to reach the tip of India, try the Kanyakumari tour (daily 8am–9pm; ₹700), which takes in Padmanabhapuram Palace (except Mon), Suchindram temple, and Kanyakumari in Tamil Nadu.

ACCOMMODATION

Accommodation is a lot easier on the pocket in Thiruvananthapuram than at nearby Kovalam Beach. That said, this is one city where budget travellers, in particular, should consider spending a couple of hundred rupees more than they might usually.

RECOMMENDED TRAINS FROM THIRUVANANTHAPURAM

The following trains are recommended as the fastest and/or most convenient from Thiruvananthapuram.

Destination	Name	No.	Departs	Duration
Alappuzha	*Netravati Express**	#16346	daily 9.50am	2hr 55min
Chennai	*Chennai Mail**	#12624	daily 2.30pm	16hr 25min
Ernakulam/Kochi	*Jan Shatabdi*	#12082	daily 2.20pm	3hr 50min
Kanyakumari	*Kanyakumari Express*	#16381	daily 9.35am	2hr 40min
Kollam	*Kerala Express*	#12625	daily 11.15am	1hr
Madurai	*Anantapuri Express*	#16124	daily 4.10pm	6hr 45min

*via Kollam, Varkala, Kottayam and Ernakulam

21

Ariya Niwas Aristo Rd, Thampanoor ☎ 0471 233 0789. Large, spotless and airy rooms with comfy beds and great city views from its upper floors. Good value and just 2min walk from the railway station, with an excellent "meals" restaurant on the ground floor (see below). A/c ₹1000 extra. ₹1000

Greenland Lodging Aristo Rd, Thampanoor ☎ 0471 232 8114. An efficient lodge with immaculate en-suite rooms (some a/c). The best low-cost option in the vicinity of the bus stand and railway station – though you'll have to book ahead. ₹680

Highland Manjalikulam Rd, Thampanoor ☎ 0471 233 3200, ⊛ highland-hotels.com. The rooms in this lower mid-range option fail to live up to the promise of the six-storey concrete- and tinted-glass facade, but it's well managed, just a short walk from the stations, and easy to find. ₹1100

Manjalikulam Tourist Home Manjalikulam Rd, Thampanoor ☎ 0471 233 0776, ⊛ mthkerala.com.

Don't be fooled by the shining glass- and marble- ground floor – above lurks a basic budget place offering variously priced rooms, but all of them clean and with good, comfy mattresses. No single occupancy. A/c ₹500 extra. ₹700

Princess Inn Manjalikulam Rd, Thampanoor ☎ 0471 233 9150, ✉ princess_inn@yahoo.com. Well-scrubbed, respectable cheapie close to the stations. One of the more welcoming and better-value small hotels in this busy enclave, though it's a bit more of a plod up the lane from Station Rd than some. A/c ₹400 extra. ₹750

★ **YMCA** YMCA Rd, near the Secretariat ☎ 0471 233 0059, ⊛ ymcatvm.org. Neat, smartly furnished rooms at bargain rates for the levels of comfort. The "luxury" options (₹700) are enormous and have high ceilings, quiet fans (some with a/c), TVs and spacious bathrooms. Amazing value, though you'll probably need to book at least two weeks in advance. ₹350

EATING

Freshly cooked dosas, *iddli-vada-sambar*, biriyanis and other traditional snacks are available at streetside cafés across town, including the perennially popular *Indian Coffee House* chain, which runs several branches in the city centre – most famously the circular *Maveli Café* next to the KSRTC bus stand in Thampanoor.

★ **Ariya Niwas** Ariya Niwas hotel, Aristo Rd, Thampanoor. Top-class south Indian vegetarian thalis (₹75) dished up on banana leaves in a scrupulously clean non-a/c dining room on the hotel's ground floor, or in the pricier a/c dining hall on the first storey. Hugely popular with everyone from office workers to company directors and their families, and deservedly so: there's really nowhere better to eat in the city. Daily 7.30am–9.30pm.

Kalavara Press Rd. One of the city's most popular multicuisine restaurants, down a side street off MG Rd. Their dining room is a bit dowdy, but in the evening they open their more attractive rooftop terrace with a pitched-tile shelter. The furniture's plastic, but the food (mostly

non-veg) is tasty and inexpensive: fish, beef, mutton and pork dominate the menu, and they do fish curry "meals" from 12.30pm to 2pm. Most mains under ₹175. Daily noon–3pm & 6.30–10pm.

Maveli Café Next to the bus station on Station Rd, Thampanoor. Part of the *Indian Coffee House* chain, this bizarre red-brick, spiral-shaped café (designed by the renowned expatriate British architect, Laurie Baker) is a Thiruvananthapuram institution. Inside, waiters in the trademark *ICH pugris* serve dosas (₹35), *vada*s, greasy omelettes, mountainous biriyanis (₹60) and china cups of the usual (weak and sugary) filter coffee. An obligatory pit-stop, though a grubby one. Daily 7am–10pm.

DIRECTORY

Banks and exchange A string of big banks along MG Rd have ATMs and change travellers' cheques and currency; there are additional ATMs next to the KTDC Tourist Reception Centre opposite the railway station, and immediately outside the station exit, next to the reservations hall. Thomas Cook has a foreign exchange counter at the airport and at its travel agency on the ground floor of the Soundarya Building (near the big Raymond's tailoring store), MG Rd (Mon–Sat 9.30am–6pm).

Dentist Kamala Dental Speciality Hospital, Sri Mulam

Club Junction, Vazhuthacaud (☎ 0471 233 8420, ⊛ kamaladental.com).

Hospitals SP Fort Hospital (☎ 0471 245 0540), just down the road from the Margi School in West Fort, has a 24hr casualty and specialist orthopaedic unit; the private Cosmopolitan Hospital, in Pattom (☎ 0471 244 8182) is also recommended.

Internet access Internet City on Manhalikulam Rd charges ₹20/hr and is convenient if you're staying in Thampanoor.

Kovalam and around

You have to envy the travellers who first discovered **KOVALAM** back in the 1970s. Before the appearance of the crowds and sunbeds that nowadays spill over the resort's quartet of beaches, not to mention the warren of hotels, shops and restaurants crammed into the palm groves behind them, this must have been a heavenly location. Four decades of unplanned development, however, have wrought havoc on the famous headland and its golden sand bays. Virtually every conceivable patch of dry ground behind the most spectacular of them, **Lighthouse Beach**, has been buried under concrete, along with most of the area's Keralan character.

Since the suspension in 2009 of direct charter flights from Europe, Russian package tourists have colonized Kovalam in a big way. Signs in Cyrillic script pop up along the beachfront from mid-December onwards, and the local lobsters are steamed in vodka rather than white wine.

The beaches

Kovalam consists of four distinct coves, each with markedly different characters. It takes around 45 minutes to an hour to walk from one end of them the other, but there's no shortage of potential pit-stops along the way to restore your energies.

Lighthouse Beach

Lighthouse Daily 3–5pm • ₹25 (₹10), camera ₹20

The largest and most developed cove at Kovalam, known for obvious reasons as **Lighthouse Beach**, is where most foreign tourists congregate. Lined by a paved esplanade, its seafront of shops and hotels extend along the full length of the bay, overlooked by the eponymous **lighthouse** at the southern end. You can scale the 142 spiral steps and twelve ladder rungs to the observation platform for a fine view.

Hawah Beach

A small rocky headland divides Lighthouse Beach from **Hawah Beach** (or **Eve's Beach**) – almost a mirror image of its busier neighbour, although backed for most of its length by empty palm groves. In the morning, before the sun-worshippers arrive, it functions as a base for local fishermen, who hand-haul their massive nets through the shallows, singing and chanting as they coil the endless piles of rope.

Kovalam Beach

Kovalam Beach, the third of the coves, is dominated from on high by the angular chalets of the five-star *Leela Kempinski*. Coachloads of excited Keralan day-trippers descend here on weekends, but at other it times offers a peaceful alternative to the beaches further south. To get there, follow the road downhill past the bus terminus.

Samudra Beach

The most northerly of Kovalam's quartet, **Samudra Beach** was until recently a European package tourist stronghold, though the large hotels clustered just beyond

---

> **WARNING: SWIMMING SAFETY**
>
> Due to unpredictable rip currents and a strong undertow, especially during the monsoons, **swimming** from Kovalam's beaches is not always safe. The introduction of blue-shirted lifeguards has reduced the annual death toll, but at least a couple of tourists still drown here each year, and many more get into difficulties. Follow the warnings of the safety flags at all times and keep a close eye on children. There's a first-aid post midway along Lighthouse Beach.

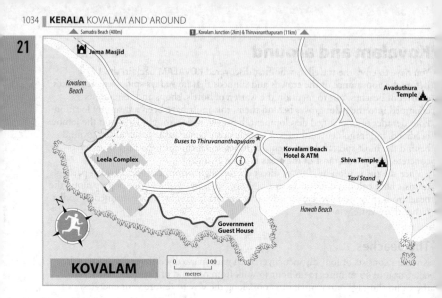

Jama Masjid

Kovalam
Beach

Avaduthura
Temple

Buses to Thiruvananthapuram

Kovalam Beach
Hotel & ATM

Leela Complex

Shiva Temple

Taxi Stand

Hawah Beach

Government
Guest House

KOVALAM

0   100
metres

it, on the far side of a low, rocky headland, nowadays host mainly metropolitan Indian and Russian holiday-makers.

ARRIVAL AND DEPARTURE   KOVALAM

By bus Buses from Thiruvananthapuram loop through the top of the village before coming to a halt outside the gates of the *Leela Kempinski*, on the promontory dividing Hawah and Kovalam beaches. If you don't intend to stay at this northern end of the resort, get down just past *Hotel Blue Sea* where the road bends – a lane branching to the left drops steeply downhill towards the top of Hawah Beach. The bus journey generally takes 30–45

min. Heading in the other direction (into the city) pick up the bus from outside the gates of the *Leela*. Long-distance services heading down the coast towards Kanyakumari stop at Kovalam Junction on the main highway.

By auto-rickshaw or taxi You can cover the 14km from Thiruvananthapuram more quickly by auto-rickshaw (₹150–200) or taxi (₹500–600).

INFORMATION

Tourist information The friendly tourist office (daily 10am–5pm, closed Sun in low season; ☎0471 248 0085, ⓦkeralatourism.org), just inside the *Leela Kempinski* gates,

close to where the buses pull in, stocks the usual range of glossy leaflets and can offer up-to-date advice about cultural events in the area.

ACCOMMODATION

Kovalam is chock-full of **accommodation** in all categories. Little of it could be considered great value by Keralan standards, but you may be able to pick up some last-minute discount if business is slack. Expect to be plagued by commission touts as you arrive; to avoid them, approach via the back paths.

★ **Amruthamgamaya (Amrutam)** Panagodu, near Venganoor, 6km northeast ☎0471 248 4600 or ☎9048 813159, ⓦamruthamgamaya.com. A great option if you want to base yourself away from the busy coastal strip, but within striking distance of the beaches. It's essentially an Ayurveda centre, but with comfortable accommodation in beautiful, large rooms overlooking a terraced garden. Veg meals are served on a high rooftop overlooking a sea of palm trees, and there's a gorgeous pool. Great value, but tricky to find: phone ahead for directions. Rates include half

board, with superb Keralan food. **₹3500**

Beach Hotel II Above Fusion restaurant, Lighthouse Beach ☎0471 248 6575, ⓦthebeachhotel-kovalam .com. Stylish, German-run hotel at the quiet end of Lighthouse Beach. Its ten rooms (some a/c) all have big, sea-facing balconies, and are light, spacious and airy, with terracotta-tiled floors and block-printed cotton bedspreads. Not to be confused with its sister concern, *Beach Hotel I*, below *Waves* restaurant, which isn't nearly as nice. A/c costs ₹1000 extra. **₹3500**

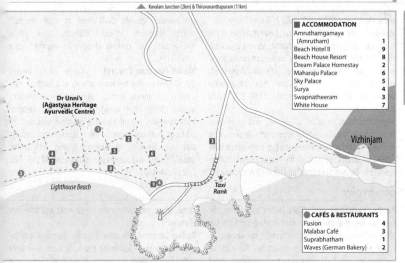

Kovalam Junction (2km) & Thiruvananthapuram (11km)

ACCOMMODATION

Amruthamgamaya (Amrutham)	1
Beach Hotel II	9
Beach House Resort	8
Dream Palace Homestay	2
Maharaju Palace	6
Sky Palace	5
Surya	4
Swapnatheeram	3
White House	7

Dr Unni's
(Agastyaa Heritage
Ayurvedic Centre)

Vizhinjam

Lighthouse Beach

Taxi Rank

CAFÉS & RESTAURANTS

Fusion	4
Malabar Café	3
Suprabhatham	1
Waves (German Bakery)	2

Beach House Resort Lighthouse Beach ☎ 8129 413850 (Naza). Tiny, garish yellow place on the seafront offering unusually large rooms with kitchenettes. Best, though, is the romantic wood-panelled Kerala-style penthouse on the roof (₹2500), which boasts superb sea views – well worth a splurge. **₹1500**

Dream Palace Homestay Lighthouse Beach ☎ 9447 694165 (John). Half a dozen pleasant rooms in a modern block set a 3min walk back from the beachfront, with marble floors, dark varnished furniture, sprung mattresses, kitchenettes, fancy headboards and tiny balconies. Excellent value. **₹1000**

Maharaju Palace 30m behind Lighthouse Beach ☎ 0471 248 5320, ⓦ maharajupalace.com. This Dutch-owned guesthouse, a block in from the beach, offers boutique style at affordable rates. Occupying a modern house in a well-kept tropical garden, its marble-lined rooms are impeccably clean and decorated with Indian handicrafts and comfy cane chairs on the verandas. Breakfast included. **₹2500**

Sky Palace Lighthouse Beach ☎ 9745 841222. Basic but comfortable option two blocks back from the waterfront, just a thirty-second walk from the beach. The very clean en-suite rooms, opening onto a sociable common veranda, are a good size, with gleaming floors and crisp white sheets. **₹700**

Surya Lighthouse Beach ☎ 0471 248 1012, ⓔ kovsurya@yahoo.co.in. Professionally run budget travellers' guesthouse down a narrow lane from the seafront. It's secure and quiet, with pleasant rooms for the price. A/c ₹900 extra. If it's full, try the *White House* next door (see below). **₹900**

Swapnatheeram (formerly Sri Krishna Palace) Lighthouse Beach ☎ 0471 248 4685, ⓦ swapnatheeram.com. Great-value mid-range place run by an exceptionally friendly local family, a 1min walk from the beach. Their spotless rooms are spacious and immaculately clean, with quality mattresses and complimentary towels and soap – some have sea views. Breakfast included. A/c ₹600 extra. **₹1300**

White House Lighthouse Beach ☎ 0808 879 1292, ⓔ whitehousekovalam@gmail.com. Basic guesthouse fronting a leafy plot. Quiet, clean and set back from the beach. Rooms 203 & 204 are pick of the crop. **₹1000**

EATING, DRINKING AND NIGHTLIFE

Lighthouse Beach is lined with identikit cafés and restaurants specializing in **seafood**: pick from displays of fresh fish, lobster, tiger prawns, crab and mussels that are then weighed, grilled over a charcoal fire or cooked in a *tandoor* (traditional clay oven), and served with rice, salad or chips. Meals are **pricey** by Indian standards and service is often painfully slow, but the food is generally very good and the ambience convivial. **Nightlife** in Kovalam is sedate, revolving around the beachfront cafés. Beer and spirits are served in most places, albeit in discreet china teapots from under the table due to tight liquor restrictions.

⭐ **Fusion** Lighthouse Beach. Along with *Waves*, this is the liveliest place on the main beach, with three innovative menus (Eastern, Western and fusion), served on a first-floor terrace overlooking the bay. Try the fish creole in orange vinaigrette with cumin potatoes, one of the Keralan seafood specialities, or home-made tagliatelle and chilli

21

pesto. Most mains ₹150–400. Daily 7.30am–10pm.

Malabar Café Lighthouse Beach;. Deservedly one of the most popular spots on the beachfront, serving a jack-of-all-trades menu of pizzas, burgers, superb tandoori seafood and pick-your-own lobsters, as well as Keralan staples such as fish *pollichathu* (₹350) and fish curry with tapioca (₹350). Most other mains ₹120–350. Daily 7.30am–late.

Suprabhatham Near the Silverstar, next to a small Shiva temple. Simple, popular vegetarian café-restaurant in a well-shaded garden, where you can order inexpensive Indian breakfasts, as well as an extensive multicuisine menu: the "Bengali aubergine" and "chunky avocado salad"

are popular specials. Staff tend to start on stiff whisky slammers around 10.30pm, after which the service and cooking degenerate rapidly. Daily 8am–11pm.

Waves (German Bakery) Lighthouse Beach. By day this shaded rooftop terrace functions as a laidback café serving light meals, German cakes and delicious freshly ground coffee. After sunset, its atmospheric designer lighting makes a great backdrop for more sophisticated cooking: seafood curries, fish steaks with sesame and coriander crust, or steamed prawns with lemon and chilli sauce. Two courses plus drinks around ₹550–700. Daily 7.30–10pm.

DIRECTORY

Banks, exchange and ATMs There's an ATM in the *Kovalam Beach Hotel*, on the road leading up from the southern end of Hawah Beach; otherwise, the nearest are up at Kovalam Junction, 2km inland on the national highway (roughly ₹100 return in an auto-rickshaw), where both ICICI and Canara Bank have sub-branches. Pheroze Framroze, near the entrance to the *Leela Kempinski* and bus

stand, offers competitive rates for currency and travellers' cheques.

Tailors Dozens of little tailor shops are crammed in to the alleyways behind Lighthouse Beach. You can have light cotton clothes made to measure, or get them to copy your favourite garment from home, using a wide choice of coloured calico.

South of Kovalam: Vizhinjam and beyond

A tightly packed cluster of tiled fishermens' huts, **VIZHINJAM** (pronounced "Virinyam"), on the opposite (south) side of the headland from Lighthouse Beach, was once the capital of the Ay kings, the earliest dynasty in south Kerala. A number of simple small shrines survive from those times, and can be made the focus of a pleasant afternoon's stroll through coconut groves, best approached from the centre of the village rather than the coast road – brace yourself for the sharp contrast between hedonistic tourist resort and workaday fishing village. Note too another stark divide:

AYURVEDA IN KERALA

"Health tourism" is very much a buzz phrase in Kerala these days, and resorts such as Kovalam and Varkala are packed with places to de-stress and detox – the majority of them based on principles of **Ayurveda medicine**. The Keralan approach to India's ancient holistic system of medicine has two distinct elements: first, the body is cleansed of toxins generated by imbalances in lifestyle and diet; secondly, its equilibrium is restored using herbal medicines, mainly in the form of plant oils applied using a range of different **massage** techniques. A practitioner's first prescription will often be a course of **panchakarma** treatment – a five-phase therapy during which harmful impurities are purged through induced vomiting, enemas and the application of medicinal oils poured through the nasal cavity. Other less onerous components, tailored for the individual patient, may include: *dhara*, where the oils are blended with ghee or milk and poured on to the forehead; *pizhichi*, in which four masseurs apply different oils simultaneously; and, the weirdest looking of all, *sirovashti*, where the oils are poured into a tall, topless leather cap placed on the head. Alongside these, patients are prescribed special balancing foods, and given vigorous full-body massages each day.

Standards of both treatment and hygiene vary greatly between establishments, as do the prices. Female travellers also sometimes complain of sexual harassment at the hands of opportunistic male masseurs; cross-gender massage is forbidden in Ayurveda. The application of dodgy oils that can cause skin problems is another risk you might be exposed to at a backstreet clinic. Your best bet is to follow tips from fellow travellers and, if you're unsure, check the state of any treatment rooms in advance.

between the Christian quarter to the south, with its towering Catholic church, and Muslim quarter to the north, spreading below a gigantic mosque.

Golden-sand beaches fringe the shore stretching **southwards from Vizhinjam**, interrupted only by the occasional rock outcrop and tidal estuary. This dramatic coastline, with its backdrop of thick coconut plantations, can appear peaceful compared with Kovalam, but it's actually one of the most densely populated corners of the state. Over the past decade, virtually every metre of land backing the prettiest stretches of coast has been bought up and built on. Even so, it's worth renting a scooter to explore the back lanes and more secluded beaches, where poor Christian fishing villages stand in surreal juxtaposition with luxury beach resorts and Ayurveda spas.

Padmanabhapuram Palace
Tues–Sun 9am–4.30pm • ₹50 (₹20), camera ₹20 • Frequent buses run there along the main highway from Thiruvananthapuram and Kovalam; hop on any service heading to Nagercoil or Kanyakumari and get off at Thakkaly (sometimes written Thuckalai)

Although now officially in Tamil Nadu, **PADMANABHAPURAM**, 63km southeast of Thiruvananthapuram, was the capital of Travancore between 1550 and 1750, and maintains its historic links with Kerala, from where it is still administered. With its exquisite wooden interiors, coconut-shell floors and antique furniture and murals, the **palace** represents the apogee of regional building, and fully merits a visit. Just **avoid weekends**, when the complex gets overrun with bus parties.

Varkala

Devout Hindus have for hundreds, and possibly thousands, of years travelled to **VARKALA**, 54km north up the coast from Thiruvananthapuram, to immerse ashes of recently deceased relatives in the surf. Against a backdrop of superb, burnt-clay coloured cliffs, the ancient rituals are still performed daily on **Papanasam beach**, despite the presence just a stone's throw away of a fully fledged tourist resort, focused around the northern end of the bay.

The dramatic location, coupled with comparatively low-key development, makes Varkala a more appealing place to spend a beach holiday than Kovalam. Tightly crammed along the rim of crumbling North Cliff, its row of restaurants and small hotels stare out across a vast sweep of ocean – a view that can seem almost

21

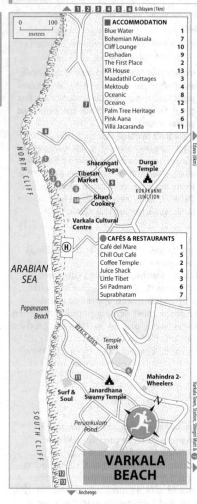

ACCOMMODATION
Blue Water	1
Bohemian Masala	7
Cliff Lounge	10
Deshadan	9
The First Place	2
KR House	13
Maadathil Cottages	3
Mektoub	4
Oceanic	8
Oceano	12
Palm Tree Heritage	5
Pink Aana	6
Villa Jacaranda	11

CAFÉS & RESTAURANTS
Café del Mare	1
Chill Out Café	5
Coffee Temple	2
Juice Shack	4
Little Tibet	3
Sri Padmam	6
Suprabhatam	7

transcendental after sunset, when a myriad tiny fishing boats light up their lanterns.

The beach

Known in Malayalam as Papa Nashini ("sin destroyer"), Varkala's beautiful white-sand **beach** has long been associated with ancestor worship. Devotees come here after praying at the ancient Janardhana Swamy Temple on the hill to the south, then perform mortuary rituals on the beach, directed by specialist pujaris (priests). The best time to watch the rites is in the **early morning**, just after sunrise. And note that it's best to keep your camera in your bag.

Janardhana Swamy Temple

Varkala's ancient **Janardhana Swamy Temple** is reached by following the stepped path up the hill from the crossroads in the village centre, or by heading up the lane that climbs steeply south from the beachfront area. **Non-Hindus** are not permitted to enter the inner sanctum of the shrine, but you can peep over the perimeter walls from the encircling path – a pleasant stroll in the morning, when the temple elephant is led around the lanes on her exercise walk.

Enshrining a form of Vishnu, the temple is adorned with brightly painted images of Hanuman, Rama's monkey general. Among its treasures is a bell salvaged from a Dutch ship that was wrecked on the beach in the eighteenth century – the ship's captain donated it in a gesture of thanksgiving after his entire crew escaped with their lives.

Papanasam Beach

Backed by sheer red laterite cliffs, Varkala's coastline is imposingly scenic and the **beach** relatively relaxing – although its religious associations do ensure that attitudes to public nudity (especially female) are less liberal than other coastal resorts in India. Western sun-worshippers are supposed to keep to the northern end (away from the main puja area reserved for the funerary rites) where they are serviced by a nonstop parade of local "hallo-pineapple-coconut?" vendors.

Whistle-happy lifeguards ensure the safety of **swimmers** by enforcing the no-swim zones beyond the flags: the undercurrent is often strong, claiming lives every year. **Dolphins** are often seen swimming quite close to the coast, and, if you're lucky, you may be able to swim with them by arranging a ride with a fishing boat. Sea otters can also occasionally be spotted playing on the cliffs by the sea.

North Cliff

Few of Varkala's Hindu pilgrims make it as far as the **North Cliff** area, the focus of a well-established tourist scene that's becoming increasingly dominated by Russian charter tourists. Bamboo and palm-thatch cafés, restaurants and souvenir shops jostle for space close to the edge of the mighty escarpments, which plunge vertically to the beach below in a dramatic arc. Several steep flights of steps cut into the rock provide shortcuts from the sand, and you can also get here via the gentler path that starts from the beachfront, or along the metalled road winding its way up from the village.

South Cliff

Lined with mid-range hotels and guesthouses, the cliff-top area running south of the main beachfront – known locally as **South Cliff** – is a much quieter neighbourhood of leafy lanes and large residential houses – a legacy of the lingering presence of numerous clean-living Brahmin families. The beach below the cliff, reached via rock-cut steps from several of the hotels, largely disappears at low tide, but offers a blissfully secluded spot to swim when the water recedes, though you should watch out for the sharp laterite boulders lurking in the surf.

Odayam

North of Varkala the shoreline grows a lot less densely populated, though the large, gaudily painted houses dotted around its hinterland of leafy lanes bear witness to the considerable affluence flooding in with remittance cheques from the Gulf states. You can comfortably walk the kilometre or so from the north end of Varkala cliff to **ODAYAM**, a mixed Hindu and Muslim village where a cluster of modest guesthouses has sprung up to service the small black-sand beach. Room rates are on the high side, but it can be well worth paying for the extra seclusion when Varaka's cliff-top area is firing on all cylinders.

ARRIVAL AND DEPARTURE	VARKALA

Varkala beach lies 4km west of Varkala town, which is grouped around a busy market roundabout. Auto-rickshaws are numerous; the trip between the beach and town shouldn't cost more than ₹50–60, and frequent local buses also cover the route (₹5).

By train The town's railway station – Varkala-Sivagiri – is 500m north of the central junction, and is served by express and passenger trains from Thiruvananthapuram, Kollam and most other Keralan towns on the mainline.
Destinations Alleppey (3 daily; 2hr); Kochi (hourly; 3hr 30min–4hr 30min); Kollam (every 30min; 25min); Thiruvananthapuram (every 30min; 1hr).
By bus While some buses from Thiruvananthapuram's Thampanoor stand, and from Kollam to the north, continue on to within walking distance of the beach and

cliff-top area, most terminate in Varkala village. If you can't get a direct bus to Varkala, take any "superfast" or "limited stop" bus running along the main NH-47 highway to Kallamballam, 15km east, from where slower local minibus services (₹25), auto-rickshaws (₹130–150) and taxis (₹200–250) can take you to the beach.
Destinations From Varkala Junction to: Alleppey (1 daily; 3hr 30min); Kollam (3 daily; 1hr); Thiruvananthapuram (every 30min; 1hr 30min–2hr). There are more frequent departures to and from Kallamballam.

GETTING AROUND

By motorcycle Scooters may be rented from Mahindra2Wheelers (Mon–Sat 9.30am–5pm; ☏ 9846 701975), near Temple Junction, and Wheels of South India, a business of no fixed abode that works up in North Cliff (☏ 9847 080412 or ☏ 9387 974698). The

nearest petrol pump is in Varkala town – 300m north of the main circle, on the left side of Station Rd as you head towards the railway station.
By taxi Recommended for airport drops and local sightseeing day-trips is Unni (☏ 9846 690300).

ACCOMMODATION

Varkala offers a wide choice of **accommodation**. The hotels up on **North Cliff** are most people's first choice, with more inspiring views than those lining the road to the beach, but there are some even better options on quieter **South Cliff** if you don't mind being away from the thick of things. For greater seclusion and a vivid taste of the area's lush palm forest and paddy fields, try **Odayam**, 1km north along the coastal path. All areas are accessible by road.

NORTH CLIFF

Bohemian Masala Thiruvambadi, North Varkala ☎ 9287 215567 or ☎ 9567 441286, ⓦ thebohemianmasala.com. A chic hippie haven of ethnic thatched huts in a gorgeous garden. They come in three styles: Primitive (₹1800); Cosmic (₹5200); and Universe, with king-sized bed (₹7600). The interiors are a bit gloomy, but cool and nicely fitted out using Indian handicrafts. Groovy earth-floored restaurant and in-house Ayurveda massages. **₹5200**

Cliff Lounge North Cliff ☎ 9895 633896, ⓦ clifflounge .com. The nicest mid-range place on North Cliff, set back behind the strip but with uninterrupted sea views from its spacious double rooms. All have breezy balconies and are pleasantly decorated with arty touches by your Keralan-German hosts, Sajeer and Elizabeth. ₹1000 extra for a/c. **₹3500**

Deshadan North Cliff ☎ 9846 031005, ⓦ deshadan .com. The smartest and most efficiently run of Varkala's small-scale resort complexes. Centred on a great little swimming pool, its twelve individually themed rooms are tastefully styled, with hand-painted furniture and ethnic colour schemes. A pair of two-bedroomed cottages in the garden suit families well. Quality Ayurveda centre on site. **₹4250**

Oceanic North Cliff ☎ 0470 302 1330 & ☎ 9846 096912, ⓔ oceanicresidence@yahoo.co.in. Very pleasant rooms, with flowering climbers trailing from its balconies, close to the cliff-top. Among the better-run, better-value budget options close to the strip. **₹1500**

SOUTH CLIFF

KR House South Cliff ☎ 0470 260 6400 or ☎ 9349 741998. A gem of a budget place – in a plum spot on South Cliff. Comfy mattresses, spotless bathrooms and balconies overlooking a narrow garden running to the cliff edge, from where a flight of steps drops steeply down to the beach. Away from the bustle of North Cliff, it's quiet, and run with great efficiency by the kindly Mr Ramchandran. **₹1000**

★ **Oceano** South Cliff ☎ 9349 392022 or ☎ 4703 251546, ⓦ oceanocliff.com. Set on the highest stretch of secluded South Cliff, rooms in this Dutch-owned guesthouse are light, cool, stylish and good value, with spectacular views from the pricier sea-facing suites (₹5500). You eat meals in little thatched gazebos on the cliff edge, from where steps lead to the beach via a plunge pool and spectacularly sited yoga platform. **₹2500**

Villa Jacaranda Temple Rd West, South Cliff ☎ 0470 261 0296, ⓦ villa-jacaranda.biz. Bijou boutique guesthouse nestled amid the leafy lanes of quiet South Cliff, near the temple. Run by a refugee from London, it is small (just four rooms) but perfectly formed, with cool wooden furniture, crisp white sheets, fresh jasmine flowers in your room and a fragrant garden. Room 4 has expansive sea views from its private terrace. **₹5000**

ODAYAM

Blue Water Near Parambil temple, Odayam ☎ 9446 848534, ⓦ bluewaterstay.com. A nicely set up, welcoming option, comprising nine varnished palm-wood chalets with tiled roofs – not all that spacious, but comfortably furnished, with floating flowers in terracotta pots, cane blinds and silk throws on the beds. All have sea views. The open-sided restaurant, overlooking the waves at the bottom of a terraced plot, is also the best place to eat and drink hereabouts. **₹6000**

The First Place Odayam ☎ 0470 299 2090 or ☎ 9746 983783, ⓦ thefirstplace-odayam.com. Eco-friendly Swedish-run guesthouse on the bluff overlooking the beach, with its own shady garden. The rooms aren't large, but they're nicely done – freshly painted with little wooden shelves, glossy red-oxide floors and mozzie nets. One of them serves as a classroom for Swedish kids, making this a particularly commendable option for young families. **₹1500**

Maadathil Cottages Manthara Temple Rd ☎ 9746 113495 (Muhajir), ⓦ maadathilcottages.com. Row of locally owned and - run holiday cottages in traditional Keralan style (gabled, red-tiled roofs, wood railings and split-cane blinds) at a sweet spot under the coconut trees behind Odayam beach. There's a pricier, larger cottage with a lovely rear veranda looking on to a lotus pond filled with egrets and butterflies. **₹4500**

Mektoub Odayam ☎ 9447 971239, ⓦ mektoubkerala .com. A perfect place to soak up the unspoilt vibe that still holds sway in Odayam. In an idyllic setting between coconut groves and paddy fields, it comprises a campus of red laterite buildings with spacious rooms and sea-facing verandas. Bargain rates considering the level of comfort, and owner Rafik is a great cook. It's hard to find; worth phoning ahead to be met. **₹3000**

★ **Palm Tree Heritage** Odayam ☎ 9946 055036, ⓦ palmtreeheritage.com. Stylish, Swedish-owned boutique place right behind the beach, set in well watered gardens. The architecture is delightful and the interiors cool and comfortable, blending traditional, hand-made Keralan woodwork and modern comforts, including

luxurious bathrooms. The food's terrific and staff unfailingly courteous. ₹7000
Pink Aana Odayam ☎9895 056543, ⓦpinkaana.at. Directly behind the beach with uninterrupted ocean views

from just four large, varnished bamboo huts. They're cool, well spaced and nicely furnished (with thick mattresses and sizeable bathrooms), and a stone's throw from the sand. Kids' beds available on request. ₹4000

EATING, DRINKING AND NIGHTLIFE

Varkala's cliff-top **café-restaurants** specialize in locally caught seafood (you'll also find plenty of Italian, Thai and Mexican items on offer – but they won't taste much like the real thing). Prices are high, even by Keralan standards, and service painfully slow, but the superb location more than compensates. Although alcohol is available in just about all the cliff-top places, due to Varkala's religious importance **beer** tends to be served in discreet teapots. Once the restaurants finish serving, **nightlife** is generally low-key.

★ **Café del Mare** North Cliff. The most professionally run place to eat on North Cliff, with an Italian coffee machine and polite, uniformed service. It offers the usual jack-of-all-trades menu, but they can actually cook everything on it. Made with imported cheeses, the Italian dishes are especially good (try the baked aubergine lasagne) and there are plenty of light bites and healthy salads. Most mains ₹250–400. Daily 8am–late.

Coffee Temple North Cliff. Hot contender (along with *Café del Mar*) for the crown of "Best Coffee in Varkala" and with a loyal following. The premises are poky, the Brit ex-pat service a bit random, and the cakes uninspiring *German Bakery* fare, but the mugs of brown stuff they make here are truly scrumptious. Espresso from ₹65. Daily 8am–11pm.

Juice Shack North Cliff. Fresh juices churned out by the larger-than-life, resplendently bearded Umesh and his team. They also do a range of healthy snacks (wraps and crunchy salads; ₹90) and host popular buffets (₹300) on Wed and Sat (buy your ticket in advance). Daily 8am–10pm.

Little Tibet North Cliff. Decorated with cheerful prayer flags and Buddhist *thangkas*, this large, bamboo-and-palm-thatch place catches the breezes at a prime cliff-edge location. Mexican and Italian specialities, but most people come for the tasty Tibetan *momo* dumplings (₹120–190) and *thukpa* soup (₹130). Very friendly, professional service. Daily 8am–late.

Sri Padmam Temple Junction. This dingy-looking café on the temple crossroads serves freshly made, cheap and tasty south Indian veg food (including ₹45 "meals" at lunchtime). You can walk through the front dining room to a large rear terrace affording prime views of the tank – particularly atmospheric at breakfast time. Daily 8am–9pm.

Suprabhatam Varkala village, 4km east of the beach. The cheapest and best pure veg joint in Varkala, just off the main circle in a dining hall lined with coir mats. Their dosas and other fried snacks aren't great, but the lunchtime "unlimited" rice-plate "meals" (noon–3pm; ₹45), featuring the usual *thoran*, *avial*, dhal, *rasam*, buttermilk, curd, *papad* and red or white rice, pull in streams of locals and foreigners alike. Daily 8am–9pm.

DIRECTORY

Banks and ATMs There's an ATM on Temple Junction, and several banks up in Varkala village, just off the main crossroads.
Cookery classes Learn how to make delicious north Indian and Keralan dishes with local chef, Sajeer, at Khan's Cookery Classes, held daily in a spruce little kitchen behind the *Chill Out Café* on North Cliff. Rates are ₹600/₹800 for veg/non-veg; book ahead on ☎9895 633896.
Internet Centres in Varkala charge ₹40/hr for broadband, but the connection is usually slow.

Post office Just north of temple junction (Mon–Sat 10am–2pm), near the *Suprabhatam* restaurant.
Yoga and meditation Sharangati, on the Thiruvambadi Rd behind North Cliff, offers expert tuition in both yoga and meditation, as well as weekly detox juice fasts and sitar recitals. Most students sign up for an all-inclusive package (₹3000/day, plus ₹800 for anyone sharing the same room), covering two daily yoga and two daily meditation sessions, all meals and comfortable accommodation. Full details at ☎9048 694762, ⓦsharangi-yogahaus.com.

Kollam (Quilon)

Sandwiched between the sea and Ashtamudi ("eight inlets") Lake, **KOLLAM** (pronounced "Koillam", and previously known as Quilon), was for centuries the focal point of the Malabar's spice trade. Phoenicians, Arabs, Greeks, Romans and Chinese all

21

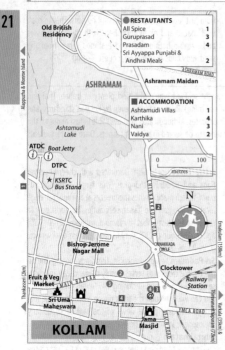

Old British Residency

RESTAUTANTS
All Spice 1
Guruprasad 3
Prasadam 4
Sri Ayyappa Punjabi & Andhra Meals 2

ASHRAMAM ROAD

ASHRAMAM — Ashramam Maidan

ACCOMMODATION
Ashtamudi Villas 1
Karthika 4
Nani 3
Vaidya 2

Ashtamudi Lake

ATDC Boat Jetty

DTPC

★ KSRTC Bus Stand

0 — 100
metres

N

Bishop Jerome Nagar Mall

Fruit & Veg Market

Sri Uma-Maheswara

CHINNAKKADA CIRCLE

Clocktower

Railway Station

MAIN BAZAAR

PAIKKADA ROAD

YMCA ROAD

Jama Masjid

BEACH ROAD

KOLLAM

Alappucha & Monroe Island

Thankaserri (2km)

Ernakulam (158km)

Thiruvananthapuram (72km)

Varkala (59km) &

dispatched ships to the city, before the rise of Calicut and Cochin eclipsed the port. These days, it's a workaday market town and busy transport hub for the southern backwater region, with surprisingly few vestiges of its former prominence. Many travellers stay overnight here, however, en route to or from Alleppey on the excursion boats that leave each morning from its lakeside ferry jetty. To kill time in the evening, take a stroll through the town's traditional **bazaar**, with its old wooden houses and narrow backstreets lined by coir warehouses, rice stores and cashew traders. A short auto-rickshaw ride south, Kollam's **beach** provides a welcome escape if the traffic of the centre get too much.

Government Guest House (old British Residency)

Residency Rd, Ashtamudi Lake

Of the few surviving colonial vestiges, the only one worth a detour is the former **British Residency**, a magnificent 250-year-old mansion on the shores of the lake, now used as a **Government Guesthouse**. Among the last monuments surviving in India from the earliest days of the Raj, it perfectly epitomizes the openness to indigenous influences that characterized the era, with typically Keralan gable roofs surmounting British pillared verandas. There are no set visiting hours – just turn up and ask the manager if you can have a look around.

ARRIVAL AND DEPARTURE

KOLLAM (QUILON)

By train Kollam's busy mainline railway station lies east of the clocktower that marks the centre of town, easily reached by auto-rickshaw. Note that most Thiruvananthapuram-bound trains do not stop in Varkala.
Destinations Alappuzha/Alleppey (9 daily; 1hr 15min–2hr); Ernakulam/Kochi (every 30min; 3–4hr); Thiruvananthapuram (hourly; 1hr 15min–2hr 30min); Varkala (hourly; 20–30min).

By bus The KSRTC bus stand is on the west side of town, near the boat jetty on Ashtamudi Lake. You can book express buses in advance but not local or "limited stop" services.
Destinations Alappuzha/Alleppey (hourly; 2hr); Ernakulam/Kochi (every 45min–1hr; 3–3hr 20min); Thiruvananthapuram (every 30min; 1hr 45min).

By boat There are some backwater ferry services from Kollam (see box opposite).

INFORMATION

Tourist office The District Tourism Promotion Council (DTPC) has a tourist office (daily 9am–6pm; ☎0474 274 5625, ⊕dtpckollam.com) at the boat jetty on Ashtamudi Lake, where you can book tickets for the daily tourist

backwater cruises (see box opposite). The local Alappuzha Tourism Development Council office (ATDC; daily 7am–9pm; ☎0474 276 7440, ⊕atdcalleppey.com), across the road, offers comparable services.

ACCOMMODATION

Ashtamudi Villas 2km north of Kollam, on the far side of Thevally Bridge ☎9847 132449, ⊕ashtamudivillas .com. Buried deep in the backwaters on the outskirts of town, this place is situated right on the water's edge, with

hammocks strung between the palm trees. The rooms, in a row of eco-friendly brick-built chalets, are spacious, bright and cool (get the detached one if it's available). You can phone ahead to arrange a pick up. ₹**1500**

BACKWATER CRUISES FROM KOLLAM

DTPC and ATDC run popular **cruises from Kollam to Alappuzha** (10.30am; 8hr; ₹400) on alternate days, with stops for lunch and tea. Tickets for both can be bought on the day from the tourist offices at the boat jetty on Ashtamudi Lake, and at some of the hotels. The same companies also offer exclusive overnight *kettu vallam* cruises, and DTPC runs half-day canal trips to nearby **Monroe Island** (daily 9am–1pm & 2–6.30pm; ₹500), as well as guided village tours taking in Ayurveda factories, coir-makers, boat-builders and bird-nesting sites. You may find that you get a far better impression of backwater life by hopping between villages on the very cheap **local ferries**. DTPC and ATDC have timetables and route information; tickets are sold on the boats themselves.

Karthika Off Main Rd, near the Jama Masjid mosque ☎ 0474 275 1831. Large, popular, central budget hotel offering a range of acceptably clean, plain rooms (some a/c) ranged around a courtyard that centres, rather unexpectedly, on three huge nude figures. ₹500

★ **Nani** Opposite the clocktower ☎ 0474 275 1141, ⓦ hotelnani.com. Kollam's most stylish hotel, in a quirky, Keralan-gabled redbrick tower block near the railway station. The comfortably furnished standard rooms are the real bargain, though couples might appreciate the extra space of the "executive" deluxe options (₹2500–3000). ₹1800

Vaidya Residency Rd, Chinnakkada ☎ 0474 274 8432, ⓦ thevaidyahotel.com. Fine if you just want somewhere comfortable to crash for a night and aren't fussy about the view. On the north side of town, the business-orientated, characterless rooms have no balconies and zero outlook, but are clean, and huge for the price. The standard ones (referred to as "deluxe") are the best value. ₹2250

EATING

All Spice Off Chinnakkada Circle, above Supreme Bakers. Determinedly Western, brightly lit fast-food joint, frequented by the town's middle-class families, and foreign tourists escaping Indian food. The a/c certainly hits the spot but the burgers, pizzas and fried chicken (₹70–s150) are less appealing than the north Indian and Chinese dishes (₹100–150). Daily noon–10pm.

Guruprasad Main bazaar. Cramped and sweaty, but wonderfully old-school "meals" (₹50) on the market's main street: blue-and-cream walls, framed ancestral photos and Hindu devotional art provide the typical backdrop for great pure-veg rice plates and *udipi*-style snacks. Daily 7.30am–10pm.

★ **Prasadam** Nani Hotel, opposite the clocktower ☎ 0474 275 1141, ⓦ hotelnani.com. Kollam's best food, served in plush a/c comfort. Traditional south Indian thalis are the most popular lunchtime options from an exhaustive menu. This is also a great place for fresh local seafood and backwater cuisine, like the *karimeen pollichathu* (white fish steamed in banana leaf; ₹225) and a blow-out seafood platter. Daily 7.30–10am, noon–3pm & 7–10.30pm.

Sri Ayyappa Punjabi and Andhra Meals Main Road, near *Dhanya Super Market*. Situated down a tiny alleyway off Kollam's main bazaar, this place is a real hidden gem. Look for the signboard just east of the Indian Bank, on the north side of the road. Superb Punjabi cuisine (a rarity in these parts) includes a delicious *paneer* butter masala (₹45) and dhal fry (₹35), hot naan breads and heavenly lassis. Mon–Sat noon–9.30pm.

DIRECTORY

ATM ATMs can be found in the smart Bishop Jerome Nagar shopping mall, just south of the main road between the jetty and the clocktower. The efficient ICICI bank also has a dependable ATM, next to the *Vaidya* hotel.

Internet Cyber.com, just south of the clock-tower on the first floor of Yeskay Towers, charges just ₹35/hr.

Alappuzha (Alleppey)

From the mid-nineteenth century, **Alappuzha** (or "**Alleppey**" as it was known in British times) served as the main port for the backwater region. Spices, coffee, tea, cashews, coir and other produce were shipped out from the inland waterways to the sea via its grid of canals and rail lines. Tourist literature loves to dub the town as "the Venice of the East", but in truth the comparison does few favours to Venice. Apart from a handful of colonial-era warehouses and mansions, and a derelict pier jutting into the

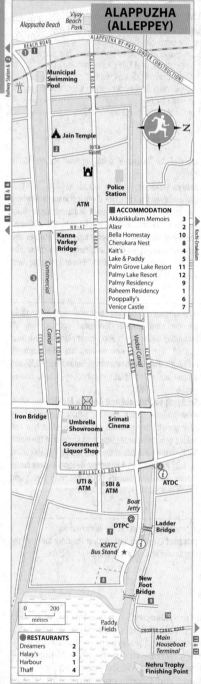

ALAPPUZHA (ALLEPPEY)

Alappuzha Beach | Vijay Beach Park

BEACH ROAD

ALAPPUZHA BY-PASS (UNDER CONSTRUCTION)

CULLEN ROAD

Municipal Swimming Pool

Jain Temple

DUTCH SQUARE

Police Station

ATM

NH-47

Kanna Varkey Bridge

Commercial

CCSB ROAD

Canal

Vadai Canal

VCSB ROAD

YMCA ROAD

Iron Bridge

Umbrella Showrooms

Srimati Cinema

Government Liquor Shop

MULLAKKAL ROAD

UTI & ATM

SBI & ATM

ATDC

Boat Jetty

DTPC

Ladder Bridge

KSRTC Bus Stand

New Foot Bridge

Paddy Fields

SHOMUR CANAL ROAD

Main Houseboat Terminal

Nehru Trophy Finishing Point

Railway Station & 2

Kochi Ernakulam

0   200
metres

ACCOMMODATION
Akkarikkulam Memoirs	3
Alasr	2
Bella Homestay	10
Cherukara Nest	8
Kait's	4
Lake & Paddy	5
Palm Grove Lake Resort	11
Palmy Lake Resort	12
Palmy Residency	9
Raheem Residency	1
Pooppally's	6
Venice Castle	7

RESTAURANTS
Dreamers	2
Halay's	3
Harbour	1
Thaff	4

sea from a sun-blasted **beach**, few monuments survive, while the old canals enclose a typically ramshackle Keralan market of bazaars and noisy traffic.

That said, Alappuzha makes a congenial place to while away an evening en route to or from the backwaters. Streams of visitors do just that during the winter season, for the town has become Kerala's pre-eminent **rice boat cruising** hub, with an estimated four hundred *kettu vallam* moored on the fringes of nearby Vembanad and Punnamada lakes. To cash in on the seasonal influx, the local tourist offices lay on excursion boats for day-trips, while in mid-December the sands lining the west end of town host a popular **beach festival**, during which cultural events and a procession of fifty caparisoned elephants are staged with the dilapidated British-built pier as a backdrop.

Alappuzha's really big day, however, is the second Saturday of August, in the middle of the monsoon, when it serves as the venue for one of Kerala's major spectacles – the **Nehru Trophy snake boat race**. This event, first held in 1952, is based on the traditional Keralan enthusiasm for racing magnificently decorated longboats, their raised rears designed to resemble the hood of a cobra. Each boat carries 25 singers, and 100 to 130 enthusiastic oarsmen power the craft along, all rowing to the rhythmic *vanchipattu* ("song of the boatman"). There are a number of prize categories, including one for the women's race; sixteen boats compete for each prize in knockout rounds. Similar races can be seen at Aranmula and at Champakulam, 16 kilometres by ferry from Alappuzha. The ATDC office will be able to tell you the dates of these other events, which change every year.

ARRIVAL AND DEPARTURE   ALAPPUZHA

By bus The filthy KSRTC bus stand is at the northeast edge of town, 1min from the boat jetty. For Fort Cochin, catch any of the fast Ernakulam services along the main highway and get down at Thoppumpady (7km south), from where local buses run the rest of the way.

Destinations Ernakulam/Kochi (every 30min; 1hr 30min); Kollam (9 daily; 1hr 15min–2hr); Kottayam (every 20min; 1hr 20min); Thiruvananthapuram (every 30min; 3hr 30min); Varkala (1 daily; 3hr 30min).

By boat The main boat jetty is on Vadai Canal, close to the KSRTC bus stand, from where the daily tourist ferries to and from Kollam run, as well as cheaper local (and less direct) ferries to and from Kottayam (dep. 7.30am, 9.35am, 11.30am, 2.30pm & 5.15pm). Regular services also connect Alappuzha with Champakulam, where you pick up less frequent boats to Neerettupuram and Kidangara, and back to Alappuzha. This round route ranks among Kuttanad's classic trips; the tourist offices can help you make sense of the timetables (also found at ⓦswtd.gov.in).

By train The station, on the main Thiruvananthapuram–Ernakulam line, lies 3km southwest across town, on the far side of Alappuzha's main waterway, Commercial Canal. As the backwaters prevent trains from continuing directly south beyond Alappuzha, only a few major daily services and a handful of passenger trains depart from here. For points further north along the coast, take the *Jan Shatabdi Express* (#12076) and change at Ernakulam, as the afternoon *Alleppey–Cannanore Express* (#16307), which runs as far as Kozhikode and Kannur, arrives at those destinations rather late at night. It is, however, a good bet if you want to get to Thrissur.

Destinations Ernakulam/Kochi (12 daily; 1hr–1hr 30min); Thiruvananthapuram (10 daily; 3hr–3hr 40min); Varkala (6 daily; 2hr–2hr 40min).

INFORMATION

Tourist information The town has several rival tourist departments, all of them eager to offer advice and book you onto their respective houseboat tours. The most conveniently situated – at the jetty itself on VCSB (Vadai Canal South Bank) Rd – are the DTPC tourist reception centre (daily 9am–5pm; ☎0477 225 1796) and adjacent Kerala Tourism office (Mon–Sat 10am–5pm; ☎0477 226 0722, ⓦkeralatourism.org). DTPC sell tickets for their ferries, backwater cruises and charter boats, and can help you fathom the intricacies of local ferry timetables. Though many of the houseboat booking agencies dotted around town call themselves "tourist information offices" – they're nothing of the kind; their sole purpose is to sell their cruises.

ACCOMMODATION

There are some great **homestay** possibilities if you're willing to travel to the outskirts and pay a little more, along with some good options, a taxi-ride away, in the surrounding **backwaters** and further up the coast. Nearly everywhere, whatever its bracket, has some kind of tie-in with a houseboat operator: good-natured encouragement tends to be the order of the day rather than hard-sell tactics, but you may be able to negotiate a reduction on your tariff if you do end up booking a backwater trip. Whenever you come, and wherever you choose to stay, brace yourself for clouds of **mosquitoes**.

ALLEPPEY TOWN

Alasr Commercial Canal, North Bank Rd, West of Kochukada Bridge ☎9947 820002 or ☎9605 066611, ⓦalasrholidays.com. Bona fide heritage hotels offering rooms for less than ₹1000 are as rare as hen's teeth in Kerala, but *Alasr* is just that – a splendid 200-year-old merchant's mansion overlooking one of Alleppey's main canals, offering a range of huge, affordable rooms of various sizes. There's none of the style and retro-chic of a boutique place, but the location can't be topped. ₹**700**

★ **Bella Homestay** Nr Nehru Trophy Finishing Point ☎0906 179196 or ☎0477 223 0201, ⓦbellakerala.com. Tucked away in a leafy, quiet backstreet, this homestay in a modern house within walking distance of the Punnamada

---

DAY CRUISES AND CANOE TRIPS AROUND ALLEPPEY

The obvious destination for a day-trip out of Alleppey is to the lakes on the town's north and eastern fringes: Punnamada and Vembanad. Reaching them from town is most straightforward by water. For short cruises, it's possible to charter diesel-powered motorboats (₹300/hr) or more sedate, twin-decked country boats (₹350/hr) from ATDC/DTPC, though their safety record hasn't been great of late. A better option would be to dispense with engines altogether and opt for a guided village tour in a hand-paddled canoe. Aside from being more "green", these allow you to penetrate narrow waterways beyond the range of the other tourist boats. DTPC offer their own punted tours, carrying two people for ₹200/hr.

A recommended private operator who's been ferrying tourists around Alappuzha's off-track backwaters for years is Mr K.D. Prasenan (☎9388 844712), based at the *Palm Grove Lake Resort* on the Punnamada Kayal, 3.5km north of the boat jetty (see above). In a slender 10m boat, he offers 5hr- and 9hr trips (₹1250/₹2500 respectively), for two people, including lunch.

A less expensive alternative, charging ₹750/1000 for one/two people per 5hr trip is Mr Joseph on ☎9446 584905, ✉josephshibin@yahoo.com.

21

jetty is a great mid-range option. Rooms are spacious, pleasantly furnished and impeccably clean, and the hospitality from Keralan-Polish hosts Biju and Natasha is warm. Superb value given the quality of the accommodation, and they do fine breakfasts. ₹1550

Cherukara Nest 9 774 Cherukara Building ☎0477 225 1509 or ☎9947 059628. 1940s "heritage" home, on a quiet canal road just a short walk around the corner from the KSRTC bus stand. Breakfast is served in an old courtyard under a huge mango tree. Eco-friendly houseboat cruises are a sideline. A/c costs double. ₹750

Palm Grove Lake Resort Punnamada Kayal, 3.5km north of boat jetty ☎0477 223 5004 or ☎9446 430434, ⊛palmgrovelakeresort.com. Near where the canal meets Punnamada Lake, this relaxed resort overlooks the

water – a perfect, tranquil spot from which to watch the snake boat races. Shaded by areca and coconut palms, its pretty cottages have gabled tile roofs, private outdoor showers and sitouts opening onto the garden. A/c ₹1000 extra. ₹2000

Palmy Lake Resort Thathampally, 2km north of boat jetty ☎0477 223 5938 & ☎9447 667888, ⊛palmyresort .com. Spacious, neatly painted red-tiled "cottages" (a/c and non-a/c), grouped behind a modern family home on the northeastern limits of town. It isn't actually on the lake, but offers exceptional value for money; all rooms have private pillared verandas opening onto a restful garden. Phone ahead for free pick up. ₹850

★ **Palmy Residency** Off VCNB Rd, near main houseboat terminal ☎0477 223 5938 or ☎9447 667888,

KUTTANAD: THE BACKWATERS OF KERALA

One of the most memorable experiences for travellers in India is the opportunity to take a boat journey on the **backwaters of Kerala**. The area known as **Kuttanad** stretches for 75km from Kollam in the south to Kochi in the north, sandwiched between the sea and the hills. This bewildering labyrinth of shimmering waterways, composed of lakes, canals, rivers and rivulets, is lined with dense tropical greenery and preserves rural Keralan lifestyles that are completely hidden from the road.

The region's bucolic way of life has long fascinated visitors. And the ever entrepreneurial Keralans were quick to spot its potential as a visitor destination – particularly after it was discovered that foreigners and wealthy tourists from India's cities were prepared to pay vast sums in local terms to explore the area aboard converted **rice barges**, or *kettu vallam*. Since its inception two decades ago, the houseboat tour industry has grown exponentially in both size and sophistication, and has brought with it major environmental drawbacks as well as increased prosperity. You can, however, explore this extraordinary region in lower-impact ways, too.

TOURIST CRUISES

The most popular excursion in the Kuttanad region is the full-day journey between **Kollam** and **Alappuzha**. All sorts of private hustlers offer their services, but the principal boats are run on alternate days by the ATDC and the DTPC (see p.1045). The double-decker boats leave from both Kollam and Alappuzha daily, departing at 10.30am (10am check-in); tickets (₹400) can be bought in advance or on the day at the ATDC/DTPC counters, other agents and some hotels. Both companies make three stops during the 8hr journey, including one for lunch, and another at the **Mata Amritanandamayi Math** at Amritapuri around 3hr north of Kollam (see p.1041). Although this is by far the main backwater route, many tourists find it too long, with crowded decks and intense sun. There's also something faintly embarrassing about being cooped up with a crowd of fellow tourists, madly photographing any signs of life on the water or canal banks, while gangs of kids scamper alongside the boat screaming "one pen, one pen".

VILLAGE TOURS AND CANOES

Quite apart from their significant environmental impact, most boats are too wide to squeeze into the narrower inlets connecting small villages. To reach these more idyllic, remote areas, therefore, you'll need to charter a punted **canoe**. The slower pace means you cover less distance in an hour, but the experience of being so close to the water, and those who live on it, tends to be correspondingly more rewarding. You'll also find more formal "**village tours**" advertised across the Kuttanad area, tying together trips to watch coir makers, rice farmers and boat builders in action with the opportunity to dine in a traditional Keralan village setting.

KETTU VALLAM (HOUSEBOATS)

Whoever dreamed up the idea of showing tourists around the backwaters in old rice barges, or

ⓦpalmyresort.com. Up a side street a 10min walk from Main Canal/bus stand, this well-run, peaceful guesthouse (an offshoot of the *Palmy Lake Resort*) has six rooms – the cheaper ones are great no-frills options, with mozzie nets and attached bathrooms. Unbeatable value in the budget bracket. ₹750

Raheem Residency Beach Rd ⓣ0477 223 9767, ⓦraheemresidency.com. The glossiest of Alappuzha's heritage hotels occupies a grand 140-year-old mansion on the beachfront. Sumptuously restored by its Irish owner (TV celeb Bibi Baskin), the building encloses six richly furnished a/c rooms, equipped with huge carved four-posters and original wood- and glass- window shutters. Gorgeous swimming pool, hammocks on the roof terrace and a breezy open-sided restaurant. ₹6500

Venice Castle Behind Canara Bank, close to KSRTC bus stand ⓣ477 223 777 & ⓣ99470 84414, ⓦvenicecastle .com. Substantial modern Keralan home a stone's throw from the bus stand and town centre, but sheltered behind a screen of lush greenery. Huge rooms for the price, and well aired, with comfy beds, decent bathrooms and views over mango and palm trees. The only catch is its proximity to the noisiest mosque in town (less than perfect at 4.30am). ₹1000

ALLEPPEY BACKWATERS

Akkarikkulam Memoirs Chennamkary ⓣ0477 276 2345, ⓦakkarakalammemoirs.com. One of the few proper heritage hotels in the backwaters (as opposed to homestays), in a recently converted Syrian-Christian mansion overlooking

kettu vallam, could never have imagined that, two decades on, six hundred or more of them would be chugging around Kuttanad waterways. These **houseboats**, made of dark, oiled jackwood with canopies of plaited palm thatch and coir, are big business, and almost every accommodation seems to have one. The flashiest are fitted with a/c rooms, jacuzzis and widescreen plasma TVs on their teak sun decks and have bottles of imported wine in their fridges. At the opposite end of the scale are rough-and-ready transport barges with gut-thumping diesel engines, cramped bedrooms and minimal washing facilities.

Rates vary hugely depending on the quality, more than double over Christmas and New Year, and halve off-season during the monsoons. In practice, ₹7500–18,000 is the usual bracket for a trip on a two-bedroom, a/c boat with a proper bathroom, including three meals, in early December or mid-January. The cruise should last a minimum of 22 hours, though don't expect to spend all of that on the move: running times are carefully calculated to spare gas. From sunset onwards you'll be moored at a riverbank.

You'll save quite a lot of cash, and be doing the fragile ecosystem a big favour, by opting for a more environmentally friendly **punted** *kettu vallam*. Rice barges were traditionally propelled by punt, and though it means you travel at a more leisurely pace, the experience is silent (great for wildlife-spotting) and altogether more relaxing.

Houseboat operators work out of **Kollam** and **Kumbakonam**, but most are in **Alappuzha**, where you'll find the lowest prices – but also the worst congestion on more scenic routes. Spend a day shopping around for a deal (your guesthouse or hotel-owner will be a good first port of call) and always check the boat over beforehand. It's also a good idea to get the deal fixed on paper before setting off, and to withhold a final payment until the end of the cruise in case you're not satisfied.

Dependable operators include: **Lakes and Lagoons** (ⓣ0477 223 6181, ⓦlakeslagoons .com); **Angel Queen** (ⓣ9895 189095 or ⓣ9847 504216, ⓦangelqueencruise.com); **Ben's Holidays** (ⓣ9847 505578& ⓣ9447 174999, ⓦbens-holidays.com); and **Yeskay Tours** (ⓣ9895 019242 or ⓣ9895 860674, ⓦyeskaytours.com).

LOCAL FERRIES

Kettu vallam may offer the most comfortable way of cruising the backwaters, but you'll get a much more vivid experience of what life is actually like in the region by jumping on one of the local ferries that serve its towns and villages. Particularly recommended is the trip from **Alappuzha to Kottayam** (dep 7.30am, 9.35am, 11.30am, 2.30 & 5.15pm; 2hr 30min; ₹10), which winds across open lagoons and narrow canals, through coconut groves and islands. Arrive early to get a good place with uninterrupted views.

Good places to aim for from Alappuzha include Neerettupuram, Kidangara and Chambakulam; all are served by regular daily ferries, but you may have to change boats once or twice along the way, killing time in local cafés and toddy shops (all of which adds to the fun, of course).

21

the Pamba River. Great value, and the rates include a sunset cruise, use of a rowing boat, bicycles, night fishing tours and guided walks around the area. ₹5500

Kait's Champakulam, 15km southeast of Alappuzha ☎0477 273 6223 or ☎9447 249184, ⊕kaitshome.com. Lovely little mid-priced homestay right on the river bank, with just four rooms divided between two blocks, both facing the river in a garden patrolled by pet ducks. ₹2500

Lake & Paddy Pamba riverside, 2.5km east of town centre at Chungam. Tiny and colourful budget guesthouse, run by hospitable brothers, situated right on the Pamba river with rice fields to the rear. Two lovely tile-floored cottages make the most of the green views (₹800);

two other cheapie rooms in the main house are bamboo lined. A fantastic location for watching village and river life roll by, and easily reached by government ferry from Alleppey or auto-rickshaw. ₹500

Pooppally's Ponga, Pooppally, on the Pamba River ☎0477 276 2034 or ☎9343 575080, ⊕pooppallys.com. This old ancestral mansion is a typically Syrian-Christian home with double-gabled roof and guest rooms in twin wings opening on to a central courtyard garden next to the river. They're not overly large, but have delightful wood-pillared verandas. If it's free, splash out on the romantic, 200-year-old *nalukettu* (₹4500), which sits on stilts above a pond in the back garden. *Pooppally's* is accessible by ferry or road. ₹3500

EATING

Aside from the **restaurants** listed below, most of Alappuzha's homestays and guesthouses provide meals for guests, usually delicious, home-cooked Keralan cooking that's tailored for sensitive Western palates.

★ **Dreamers** Alleppey beach. With its sea view and rustic decor, this Italian-run place is like a cross between a treehouse and dune shack. The menu lists Italian specialities – fresh pasta and pizza with real olive oil (₹200–250) – plus a handful of Eastern dishes, fresh salads and local seafood (the roast crab is a winner). Springsteen, Clapton and Rihanna dominate a rather random soundtrack. Daily 11am–11pm.

Halay's CCSB Rd. Proper Keralan-Muslim restaurant that's been an Alleppey institution for generations. Much of its old-world character disappeared in a recent facelift, but the food's as delicious as ever. Nearly everyone comes for their blow-out chicken biriyanis (₹130), to be enjoyed with the legendary house date pickle. Daily noon–3pm & 5–10pm.

Harbour Beach Rd. All the food served in this gleaming little seafront restaurant is prepared in the kitchens of the swanky *Raheem Residency* next door, so quality and freshness are assured. Grilled prawns, Alappuzha-style chicken curry and Kuttanadi fish all on offer. It's also one of the few places in town serving ice-cold beers. ₹100–200. Daily noon–3pm & 7–11pm.

Thaff YMCA Junction. It looks a bit down on its luck from the outside, but this is the best place in town for inexpensive non-veg Indian food, from local fish to chicken and mutton specialities, and all the standard veggie dishes. Intense Keralan flavours and rock-bottom prices are guaranteed, with filling thalis for ₹60. Daily 8–10am, 11am–3pm & 4–10pm.

DIRECTORY

Banks You can change money at the efficient UTI bank on Mullackal Rd (Mon–Sat 9.30am–4.30pm). Both it and the State Bank of India opposite have reliable ATMs.

Internet Widely available for ₹30–40/hr, with several outlets along the road facing the boat jetty; Mailbox, on VCSB Rd, a 5min walk west of Mullackal Rd, boasts the town's fastest connection.

THREATS TO THE BACKWATER ECOSYSTEM

The **African moss** that often carpets the surface of the narrower waterways may look attractive, but it is a symptom of the many serious **ecological problems** currently affecting the region, whose population density ranges from between two and four times that of other coastal areas in southwest India. This has put growing pressure on land, hence a greater reliance on fertilizers, which eventually work their way into the water and cause the build-up of moss. Illegal land reclamation poses the single greatest threat to this fragile ecosystem. In little more than a century, the total area of water in Kuttanad has been reduced by two-thirds, while mangrove swamps and fish stocks have been decimated by pollution and the spread of towns and villages around the edges of the backwater region. Tourism adds to the problem, as the film of oil from motorized ferries and houseboats spreads through the waters, killing yet more fish, which has in turn led to a reduction of more than fifty percent in the number of bird species found in the region.

Kottayam and around

21

Some 76km southeast of Kochi and 37km northeast of Alappuzha, **KOTTAYAM** is a compact, busy Keralan town strategically located between the backwaters and the mountains of the Periyar Wildlife Sanctuary. For Keralans, it's synonymous with **money**, both old and new. The many **rubber plantations** around it, introduced by British missionaries in the 1820s, have for more than a century formed the bedrock of a booming local economy, most of it controlled by landed **Syrian Christians**.

The churches

The presence of two thirteenth-century **churches** on a hill 5km northwest of the centre (accessible by auto-rickshaw) attests to the area's deeply rooted Christian heritage. Two eighth-century Nestorian stone crosses with Palavi and Syriac inscriptions, on either side of the elaborately decorated altar of the **Valliapalli** ("big") church, are among the earliest solid traces of Christianity in India. The visitors' book contains entries from as far back as the 1890s, including one each from the Ethiopian king, Haile Selassie and a British viceroy. The apse of the nearby **Cheriapalli** ("small") church is covered with lively paintings, thought to have been executed by a Portuguese artist in the sixteenth century. If the doors are locked, ask for the key at the church office (9am–1pm & 2–5pm).

Kumarakom Bird Sanctuary

Daily dawn – dusk • ₹45

A twenty-minute bus ride west of Kottayam brings you to the shores of **Vembanad Lake**, where the **Kumarakom Bird Sanctuary**, spread over a cluster of islands in the lagoon, forms the focus of a line of ultra-luxurious resorts on the water's edge. Between November and March, the wealthy metropolitan Indian tourists who holiday here are joined by flocks of migratory birds, though not in large enough numbers to entice non-specialists.

Bay Island Driftwood Museum

Mon–Sat 10am–5pm, Sun 11.30am–5.30pm • ₹50 • ⓦ bayislandmuseum.com

Birds, or representations of them, feature prominently in the area's most bizarre visitor attraction, the **Bay Island Driftwood Museum**, just off the main road on the outskirts of Kumarakom village, in which lumps of driftwood collected by a former schoolteacher are exhibited in an idiosyncratic gallery.

Ettumanur

Another possible day-trip from Kottayam is the magnificent Mahadeva (Shiva) temple at **ETTUMANUR**, 12km north on the road to Ernakulam, whose entrance porch holds some of Kerala's most celebrated medieval **wall paintings**. The most spectacular depicts Nataraja (Shiva) executing a cosmic *tandava* dance, trampling evil in the form of a demon underfoot. Foreigners can enter the temple for free, but you'll need to buy a camera ticket (₹20; video ₹50) from the counter on the left of the main gateway.

ARRIVAL AND INFORMATION   **KOTTAYAM AND AROUND**

By train The railway station, 2km north of the centre, sees a constant flow of traffic between Thiruvananthapuram (3hr 30min) and points north, including Ernakulam/Kochi (1hr 30min).

By bus Kottayam's KSRTC bus stand, 500m south of the centre on TB Rd (not to be confused with the private stand for local buses on MC Rd), is an important stop on routes to and from major towns in south India.

21

Destinations Ernakulam (every 30min; 2hr); Kollam (5 daily; 2hr 30min); Kumily/Periyar (every 30min; 3–4hr); Madurai (4 daily; 7hr); Thiruvananthapuram (every 15–30min; 4hr).

Tourist information and services DTPC maintain a tiny

tourist office at the jetty (daily 9am–5pm; ☎0481 256 0479). The best place to change money is the Canara Bank on KK Rd, which also has one of several ATMs around the main square. Internet facilities are available at Intimacy (₹30/hr), also on KK Rd, just north of the KSRTC bus stand.

ACCOMMODATION

Akkara Mariathuruthu ☎0481 251 6951, ⊕akkara.in. Just a 15min drive out of town, this welcoming homestay occupies an ancestral Syrian-Christian homestead sitting proudly on the riverbank – an idyllic, typically Keralan building, with traditional gabled architecture and interiors that can't have changed much in forty years. Access is by road or dugout canoe. A/c ₹500 extra. **₹3500**

Arcadia TB Rd ☎0481 256 9999, ⊕arcadiahotels.net. The town's top hotel, occupying its tallest building – a towering, white, angular monster block just south of the centre. Its rooms look much nicer from the inside, however, and are very good value (especially the "standard doubles"); there's also a fantastic rooftop pool on the fourteenth floor, as well as a restaurant (*Déja Vu*) and bar (*Fahrenheit*). **₹2200**

★ **GK's Riverview** Thekkakarayil, Kottaparambil, near Pulikkuttssery, 4km by water from Kumarakom ☎0481 259 7527 or ☎9447 197527, ⊕gkhomestay-kumarakom.com. Award-winning homestay, buried deep in the watery wilds between Kottayam and Kumarakom. The accommodation comprises four comfortable guest rooms in a separate block behind a family home, overlooking paddy fields. Owners George and Dai are charming hosts and mines of information about the area; they'll pick you up from Kottayam if you phone ahead. **₹3500**

Homestead KK Rd ☎0481 256 0467. The best mid-price option: "your key to a soft pillow" goes their slogan, though the beds in the economy rooms are rock hard and it's well worth shelling out an additional ₹150 for a "deluxe" with more space, better furniture and thicker mattresses. **₹650**

EATING

Anand KK Rd. For a delicious, pureveg thali or *udipi* snack, you won't do better than the *Anand* on the ground floor of the *Anand Lodge*, just off the northeast side of the main square. The a/c family hall is the more relaxing of the two wings and meals only cost ₹10 more. Offers a range of different rice meals for under ₹100, and scrumptious

masala dosas for ₹50. Daily 8am–9pm.

Meenachil Homestead Hotel KK Rd. Quality non-veg Keralan food, such as Kuttanadi chicken curry (₹135), plus Punjabi-style tandoori (₹100–150), Chinese duck dishes and set Keralan "meals" (₹60 veg, ₹70 non-veg). Daily 8am–9.30pm.

Periyar and around

One of the largest national parks in India, the **Periyar Wildlife Sanctuary** occupies 777 square kilometres of the Cardamom Hills region of the Western Ghats. The majority of its visitors come in the hope of seeing **wild elephants** – or even a rare glimpse of a **tiger** – grazing the shores of the reservoir at the heart of the reserve. Daily safari boats ferry hundreds of day-trippers around this sprawling, labyrinthine lake, where sightings are most likely at the height of the dry season in April. However, for the rest of the year, wildlife is less abundant than you might expect given Periyar's overwhelming popularity.

Just a few hours by road from the Keralan coastal cities, and Madurai in Tamil Nadu, it ranks among India's busiest reserves, attracting thousands of visitors over holiday periods. The park's ageing infrastructure, however, has struggled to cope with the recent upsurge in numbers. Just how overburdened facilities had become was horribly revealed in September 2009 when an excursion boat capsized on the lake, killing 45 tourists. Since the so-called **Thekkady disaster**, strict restrictions have been imposed, but the lake safari experience hasn't improved; most foreign visitors leave disappointed, not merely with the park, but also its heavily commercialized surroundings and apparent paucity of wildlife.

That said, if you're prepared to **trek** into the forest, Periyar can still be worth a stay. Elephant, *sambar*, Malabar giant squirrel, gaur, stripe-necked mongoose and wild

21

boar are still commonly spotted in areas deeper into the park, where birdlife is also prolific. Another selling point is Periyar's much vaunted **eco-tourism** initiative. Instead of earning their livelihoods through poaching and illegal sandalwood extraction, local Manna people are these days employed by the Forest Department to protect vulnerable parts of the sanctuary. Schemes such as "Border Hiking", "Tiger Trail" and "Jungle Patrol" tours, in which visitors accompany tribal wardens on their duties, serve to promote community welfare and generate income for conservation work.

In addition, the area around Periyar holds plenty of engaging day-trip destinations, such as **spice plantations** and an **elephant camp**, as well as lots of scope for **trekking** in the surrounding hills and forest. It's also a lot cooler up here than down on the more humid coast, and many foreign visitors are glad of the break from the heat.

Kumily

As beds inside the sanctuary are in short supply, most visitors stay in nearby **KUMILY**, a typical High Range town, centred on a hectic roadside market, 1km or so north of the main park entrance (known as **Thekkady**). Hotels and Kashmiri handicrafts emporia have spread south from the bazaar to within a stone's throw of the park, and tourism now rivals the spice trade as the area's main source of income. That said, you'll still see plenty of little shops selling local herbs, essential oils and cooking spices, while in the

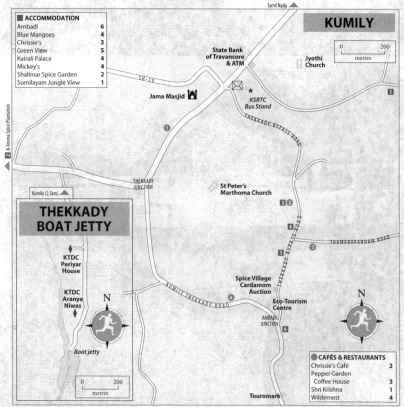

Tamil Nadu

KUMILY

ACCOMMODATION
Ambadi	6
Blue Mangoes	4
Chrissie's	3
Green View	5
Kairali Palace	4
Mickey's	4
Shalimar Spice Garden	2
Sumilayam Jungle View	1

0   200
metres

State Bank of Travancore & ATM

Jyothi Church

SH-19

Jama Masjid

KSRTC Bus Stand

THEKKADY BYPASS ROAD

& Aroma Spice Plantation

THEKKADY JUNCTION

St Peter's Marthoma Church

Kumily (2.5km)

THEKKADY BOAT JETTY

KTDC Periyar House

KTDC Aranya Niwas

N

THAMARAKANDAM ROAD

KUMILY THEKKADY ROAD

Spice Village Cardamom Auction

Eco-Tourism Centre

AMBADI JUNCTION

N

Boat jetty

0   200
metres

CAFÉS & RESTAURANTS
Chrissie's Café	2
Pepper Garden Coffee House	3
Shri Krishna	1
Wildernest	4

Touromark

Forest check post (400m) & Park entrance, Periyar Lake, KTDC Hotels & Thekkady Boat Jetty (see inset)

busy **cardamom sorting yard** behind the *Spice Village* resort, rows of Manna women sift through heaps of fragrant green pods using heart-shaped baskets.

The Periyar Wildlife Sanctuary

Daily 6am–6pm • ₹300 (₹25) • ⓦ periyartigerreserve.org

Centred on a vast artificial **lake** created by the British in 1895 to supply water to the drier parts of neighbouring Tamil Nadu, the **Periyar Wildlife Sanctuary** lies at altitudes of between 900m and 1800m, and is correspondingly cool: temperatures range from 15°C to 30°C. The royal family of Travancore, anxious to preserve favourite hunting grounds from the encroachment of tea plantations, declared it a forest reserve, and built the Edapalayam Lake Palace to accommodate their guests in 1899.

Seventy percent of the protected area, which is divided into core, buffer and tourist zones, is covered with evergreen and semi-evergreen forest. The **tourist zone** – logically enough, the part accessible to casual visitors – surrounds the lake, and consists mostly of semi-evergreen and deciduous woodland interspersed with grassland, both on hilltops and in the valleys. Although excursions on the lake (either by diesel-powered launch or paddle-powered bamboo raft) are the standard ways to experience the park, you can get much more out of a visit by **walking** with a local guide in a small group away from the crowd. However, avoid the period immediately after the monsoons, when **leeches** make hiking virtually impossible. The **best time to visit** is from December until April, when the dry weather draws animals from the forest to drink at the lakeside.

Wildlife viewing and tours

By far the best option for wildlife viewing from the lake is to sign up for one of the Forest Department's excellent **bamboo rafting trips**, which start with a short hike from the boat jetty at 8am and return at 5pm, with a minimum of three hours spent on the water. The rafts carry four or five people and, because they're paddled rather than motor-driven, can approach the lakeshore in silence, allowing you to get closer to the grazing animals and birds. Tickets cost ₹1500 per person and may be booked in advance from the eco-tourism centre on Ambadi Junction (see p.1054). Note that during busy periods places sell out quickly, so reserve as far ahead as possible.

As for the **boat tours**, though these are considerably less expensive it's quite a hassle to book yourself on one, and the trips themselves can come as a disappointment. It's unusual to see many animals – engine noise and the presence of dozens of other people make sure of that. To maximize your chances of sighting elephants, wild boar or *sambar* grazing by the water's edge, take the 7.30am service (for which you'll need to wear warm clothing in winter).

The best trips are run by the **Forest Department** (7.30am, 11.30am, 1pm & 4pm; ₹150). Their boats are smaller and shabbier than the KTDC vessels, but can get closer to the banks (and thus the wildlife) – more importantly, they are the only ones with upper decks (seats on the lower decks are a waste of time). Since the 2009 disaster, however, when 45 tourists died after one of these launches tipped over, only twenty people are permitted to travel on the upper decks and tickets sell out very fast; you'll need to be at the lakeside at least two hours before the scheduled departure time (or 90 min for the 7.30am boat). Sales counters are just above the main **visitor centre** (daily 6am–6pm; ☎04869 224571), next to the boat jetty; the Forest Department will issue two seats per person. You'll need to fill in an indemnity form, and wear a life-jacket at all times.

Walks and treks

Although you can – leeches permitting – trek freely around the fringes of Periyar, access to the sanctuary itself on foot is strictly controlled by the Forest Department. Their community-based eco-tourism programme offers a variety of structured

21

THE AYAPPA CULT

During December and January, Kerala is packed with huge crowds of men wearing black *dhotis*; you'll see them milling about train stations, driving in overcrowded and gaily decorated jeeps and cooking a quick meal on the roadside by their tour bus. They are pilgrims on their way to the Sri Ayappa forest temple (also known as Hariharaputra or Shasta) at **Sabarimala**, in the Western Ghats, around 200km from both Thiruvananthapuram and Kochi. The **Ayappa devotees** can seem disconcertingly ebullient, chanting "*Swamiyee Sharanam Ayappan*" ("Give us protection, god Ayappa") in a lusty call-and-response style reminiscent of English football fans.

Ayappa – the offspring of a union between Shiva and Mohini, Vishnu's beautiful female form – is primarily a Keralan deity, but his appeal has spread phenomenally in the last thirty years across South India, to the extent that this is said to be **the largest pilgrimage in the world**, with as many as 40–50 million devotees each year. Pilgrims are required to remain celibate, abstain from intoxicants, and keep to a strict vegetarian diet for 41 days before setting out on the four-day walk through the forest from the village of **Erumeli** (61km, as the crow flies, northwest) to the shrine at Sabarimala. Less-keen devotees take the bus to the village of Pampa, and join the 5km queue. When they arrive at the modern temple complex, pilgrims who have performed the necessary penances may ascend the famous eighteen **gold steps** to the inner shrine. There they worship the deity, throwing donations down a chute that opens onto a subterranean conveyor belt, where the money is counted and bagged.

The pilgrimage reaches a climax during the festival of **Makara Sankranti**, when massive crowds congregate at Sabarimala. On January 14, 1999, 51 devotees were buried alive when part of a hill crumbled under the crush of a stampede. The pilgrims had gathered at dusk to catch a glimpse of the final sunset of **makara jyoti** ("celestial light") on the distant hill of Ponnambalamedu.

Although males of any age and even of any religion can take part in the pilgrimage, **females** between the ages of 9 and 50 are barred.

walking tours, ranging from short rambles to three-day expeditions, all guided by local Manna tribal wardens. Tickets should be booked in advance from the eco-tourism centre on Ambadi Junction (see below), where you can also pick up brochures and leaflets on the trips.

ARRIVAL AND DEPARTURE

By bus Buses from Kottayam (every 30min; 4hr), Ernakulam (10 daily; 5hr) and Madurai in Tamil Nadu (at least hourly; 5hr 30min) pull in to the scruffy bus stand east of the main bazaar. Auto-rickshaws will run you

PERIYAR AND AROUND

from here to the visitor centre inside the park for around ₹60–70, stopping at the park entrance at Thekkady for you to pay the fee.

INFORMATION

Tourist information To book any of the Periyar Tiger Reserve's popular eco-tourism tours (see p.1053), you'll have to walk down the Thekkady Rd to the eco-tourism centre on Ambadi Junction (daily 9am–8pm, last tickets sold at 7.30pm; ☎04869 224571) – or better still, book in advance.

Services Both the State Bank of Travancore (which has an ATM), near the bus stand, and the Thekkady Bankers in the main bazaar can change currency and travellers' cheques. Internet facilities are available around Thekkady Junction for about ₹40/hr.

TOURS AND TREKS

Tours As well as the attraction of the wildlife sanctuary, tours to tea factories and spice plantation are offered by almost every hotel and tourist agency in Kumily. Unfortunately, many places have become heavily commercialized, so it's worth shopping around; often the best way to organize a tour is to ask at your hotel. The only certified organic spice garden in the area, and a particularly enjoyable one to visit, is the Aroma at

Chelimada, a short walk west of Kumily on the Kottayam Rd; contact the owner, Mr Sebastian ("Baby"), on his cell phone (☎9495 367837). Most of the plantations charge around ₹250/person for a 90min tour with guide and vehicle. The Forest Department runs village tours (6am–2.30pm; ₹1000) from the eco-tourism centre to a remote tribal settlement on the Tamil Nadu side of the mountains bordering Periyar. You're transported 10km by taxi to the start of the route, which is covered by bullock cart and coracle through a variety of different habitats and farmland. Profits go to the development of the local community.

Treks The windy, grassy ridgetops and forests around Periyar afford many fine treks, with superb views over the High Range guaranteed. One especially rewarding half-day trip is the hike up Kurusamalai (3hr), the peak towering to the northwest of Kumily, whose summit is crowned with a Holy Cross. As the summit falls within the national park boundaries, you're only permitted to hike to it under the auspices of the eco-tourism centre (see opposite), who market it as their "Cloud Walk" (₹300). Although hilly, this area is also good cycling territory; you can rent bikes from stalls in the market, and Touromark (T 04869 224332, W touromark.com), midway between Kumily and Thekkady, have imported 21-speed mountain bikes for rent. They also offer guided trips, ranging from 4hr/15km hacks through local spice gardens, coffee plantations and woodlands to a three-night/four-day ride across the Cardamom Hills to Munnar.

ACCOMMODATION

Kumily has **accommodation** to suit all pockets, with a number of small homestay guesthouses on the fringes of the village offering particularly good value. The three government-run places actually inside the park are either ludicrously expensive or shabby, or both, and thus not listed here.

Ambadi Ambadi Junction, Thekkady Rd T 04869 222193, W hotelambadi.com. Wood and red bricks dominate the architecture of this hotel, packed higgledy-piggledy onto the side of the road to the park. It offers three categories of rooms, all excellent value and with lots of Keralan character. Best are the "duplexes" (₹2500), which have beds on mezzanine floors and balconies sporting old-style pillars overlooking woodland. ₹2000

Blue Mangoes Bypass Rd T 04869 224603 or T 9744 995253. Simple en-suite rooms (with sitouts and balconies) in an impeccably clean modern block, plus a larger family "cottage". Rock-bottom rates, but good bedding and a quiet location. Owner Bobby speaks excellent English. ₹450

Chrissie's Bypass Rd T 04869 224155 or T 9447 601304, W chrissies.in. Smart 4-storey hotel below the bazaar, run by expats Chrissie (from the UK) and Adel (from Egypt). It's pricier than most homestays in the area, but you get more privacy and better views, and relaxing, homely interiors. There's also a great yoga *shala* on the rooftop, and popular little café-restaurant on the ground floor (see p.1056). ₹2000

Green View Bypass Rd T 04869 211015 & T 9447 432008, W sureshgreenview.com. One of Kumily's most popular homestays, in a newish house just off the Thekkady Rd. The 17 rooms range from basic options with bucket hot water to large en-suite ones with solar-heated showers and balconies looking across the valley to Kurusamalai Mountain (₹2000). A lovely rear garden attracts lots of wild birds. If it's full, try the identically priced *Rose Garden* next door (T 04869 223146). ₹650

Kairali Palace Bypass Rd T 04869 224604 or T 9895 187789. Outstandingly attractive homestay in a fusion building that blends traditional and modern styles, with gabled roofs, and wooden railings wrapped around the airy first-floor terrace. Its en-suite rooms are well furnished for the price. ₹800

Mickey's Bypass Rd T 04869 222196 or T 9447 284160. One of the oldest guesthouses in Kumily, whose smiling owner, Sujata, offers a range of rooms and cottages (₹1000), all with balconies or sitouts littered with comfortable cane furniture. ₹650

Shalimar Spice Garden Murikaddy, 6km from Kumily T 04869 222132, W shalimarkerala.net. Teak huts in traditional Keralan style with elephant-grass roofs, whitewashed walls, chic interiors and verandas looking straight onto forest, on the edge of an old cardamom and pepper estate. Facilities include a beautiful Ayurveda centre, outdoor pool set amid the trees and an open-sided restaurant where you can fine dine at rough-hewn granite tables. ₹12,500

★ **Sumilayam Jungle View** On the eastern edge of town T 04869 223582 or T 9446 136407, E jungleview8@yahoo.com. The best-value budget homestay in Kumily, a 10min plod (or short auto-rickshaw ride) from the bus stand – literally on the Tamil Nadu–Kerala border. The clean, bright, attached bedrooms are all comfortably furnished; those on the upper storey open onto a marble-floored veranda just metres from jungle. Nocturnal wildlife-spotting walks into the adjacent forest are offered for free by your welcoming host, Mr Ramachandran. ₹850

EATING

You're more likely to take **meals** at your guesthouse or hotel than eat out in Kumily, but for a change of scene the following places are the best options within walking distance of the bazaar.

Chrissie's Café Bypass Rd. This relaxing expat-run café, on the ground floor of *Chrissie's* hotel, pulls in a steady stream of foreigners throughout the day and evening for its delicious pizzas (₹175–250), made with Kodai mozzarella;

21

check out the specials board. They also do healthy breakfasts, homemade cakes and proper coffee. Count on ₹400–500/head. Daily 8am–9pm.

Pepper Garden Coffee House Thamarkandam Rd. In a garden filled with cardamom bushes behind a prettily painted blue-and-green house, a former park guide and his wife whip up tempting travellers' breakfasts (date and raisin pancakes, porridge with jungle honey, fresh coffee and Nilgiri tea), in addition to home-cooked lunches of veg fried rice, curry and dhal, using mostly local organic produce. Mains ₹65–150. Daily 8.30am–9.30pm.

Shri Krishna Bypass Rd. Run by a Bihari family, this pure-veg restaurant serves authentic north Indian dishes, including cheap and filling Gujarati and Marwari thalis (₹70–110), served on the usual tin trays or leaves. Daily 8am–9pm.

Wildernest Thekkady Rd. Filling Continental buffet breakfasts (fruit, juices, cereals, eggs, toast, peanut butter, home-made jams and freshly ground coffee; ₹225) served in the ground-floor café of a stylish small hotel. They also serve afternoon tea and cakes (including a delicious, very British warm plum cake). Daily 8am–7pm.

Munnar

MUNNAR, 130km east of Kochi and 110km north (4hr 30min by bus) of the Periyar Wildlife Sanctuary, is the centre of Kerala's principal tea-growing region. A scruffy agglomeration of corrugated-iron-roofed cottages and tea factories, its centre on the valley floor fails to live up to its tourist-office billing as "hill station", but there's plenty to enthuse about in the surrounding mountains, whose lower slopes are carpeted with lush tea gardens and dotted with quaint old colonial bungalows. Above them, the grassy ridges and crags of the High Range – including peninsular India's highest peak, **Ana Mudi** (2695m) – offer superlative trekking routes, many of which can be tackled in day-trips from the town.

It's easy to see why the pioneering Scottish planters who developed this hidden valley in the 1870s and 1880s felt so at home here. At an altitude of around 1600m, Munnar enjoys a refreshing **climate**, with crisp mornings and sunny blue skies in the winter – though as with all of Kerala, torrential rains descend during the monsoons. Munnar's greenery and cool air draw streams of well-heeled honeymooners and weekenders from south India's cities. However, increasing numbers of foreign visitors are stopping for a few days too, enticed by the superbly scenic bus ride from Periyar, which takes you across the high ridges and lush tropical forests of the Cardamom Hills, or for the equally spectacular climb across the Ghats from Madurai.

Clustered around the confluence of three mountain streams, Munnar town is a typical hill bazaar of haphazard buildings and congested market streets, which you'll probably want to escape at the first opportunity.

Kanan Devan Hills Tea Museum

Nallathany Rd • Tues–Sun 10am–4pm • ₹50 • ⓦ kdhptea.com/TeaMuseum.html

Although it doesn't physically demonstrate how tea is made, the **Kanan Devan Hills Tea Museum**, 2km northwest of the centre, is worth a visit for its collection of antique machinery and exhibition of photos of the area's tea industry, ranging from 1880s pioneers to the modern Tata tea conglomerate. The highlight of the visit is a short audiovisual presentation outlining how tea was introduced to the region and how it is processed today, rounded off with a tasting session; and there's a shop selling various KDH products.

The High Range Club

The social hub of the colonial period, and an important cultural icon in Munnar, the famous **High Range Club** is perched on a balcony overlooking the river on the southeastern edge of town. Indians were only officially permitted to enter the premises as recently as 1948, but these days non-members of any race are welcome to visit the typically Raj-era building for a round of golf, or to enjoy a G&T served on the lawns

TREKKING IN MUNNAR

Given the stupendous scenery rearing on all sides of Munnar, the **hiking scene** is surprisingly undeveloped. For anything more ambitious than a ramble through the tea gardens, it makes sense to use the services of a guide. The owner of the *Green View* guesthouse (see p.1055) and his enthusiastic young team (ⓦmunnartrekking.com) lead groups of two or more on interesting routes; rates range from ₹400–500 per person for soft treks to ₹550–800 for longer, more challenging outings; transport to and from the trailheads is included.

by liveried retainers. In the men-only bar, the walls are hung with rows of hunting trophies and topees. Stiff-upper-lip dress codes apply throughout: no T-shirts or sandals, and formal evening wear after 7pm on Saturdays.

Around Munnar

Although south India's highest peak, Ana Mudi, is off-limits due to the Nilgiri tahr conservation programme, several of the other summits towering above Munnar can be reached on day-treks through the tea gardens. Buses also wind their way up to the aptly named **Top Station**, a hamlet famed for its views and meadows of **Neelakurunji plants**, and to the more distant nature sanctuaries of Eravikulam and Chinnar, where you can spot Nilgiri tahr, elephant and many other wild animals. To reach the most remote attractions, however, you might want to hire a taxi for the day.

Top Station

One of the most popular **excursions** from Munnar is the 34km climb through some of the Subcontinent's highest tea estates to **TOP STATION**, a tiny hamlet on the Kerala–Tamil Nadu border which, at 1600m, is the highest point on the inter-state road. The settlement takes its name from the old aerial **ropeway** that used to connect it with the valley floor, the ruins of which can still be seen in places.

Eravikulam National Park

Daily 7am–6pm • ₹200 (₹40) • ⓦeravikulam.org

Encompassing 100 square kilometres of moist evergreen forest and grassy hilltops in the Western Ghats, the **Eravikulam National Park**, 13km northeast of Munnar, is the last stronghold of one of the world's rarest mountain goats, the **Nilgiri tahr**. Its innate friendliness made the tahr pathetically easy prey during the hunting frenzy of the colonial era. Today, however, numbers are healthy, and the animals have regained their tameness, largely thanks to the efforts of the American biologist Clifford Rice, who studied them here in the early 1980s. Unable to get close enough to observe the creatures properly, Rice followed the advice of locals and attracted them using salt, and soon entire herds were congregating around his camp. The tahrs' salt addiction also explains why so many hang around the park gates at **Vaguvarai**, where visitors – despite advice from rangers – slip them salty snacks.

You're almost guaranteed sightings of tahr from the minute you enter the park gates, reached by shuttle bus (₹20). From there, you can walk a further 1500m up a winding

THE NEELAKURUNJI PLANT

Apart from the marvellous views over the Tamil plains, Top Station is renowned for the very rare **Neelakurunji plant** (*Strobilatanthes*), which grows on the mountainsides. The plant only flowers once every twelve years, when huge crowds climb up to admire the cascades of violet blossom spilling down the slopes (the next flowering is due in Oct/Nov 2018). You can get here by **bus** from Munnar (10 daily from 5.30am; 1hr 30min), and jeep taxis do the return trip for ₹1200. Views are best before the mist builds at 9am.

21

single-track road before the rangers turn you around, but expect to do so in the company of hundreds of other tourists on weekends – a rather hollow experience.

Chinnar Wildlife Sanctuary

Daily 6am–7pm • ₹100 (₹10) • ⓦ chinnar.org

Although it borders Eravikulam, the **Chinnar Wildlife Sanctuary** is far less visited, not least because its entrance lies a two-hour drive from Munnar along 58km of winding mountain roads. The reserve, in the rain shadow of the High Range and thus much drier than its neighbour, is one of the best spots in the state for birdwatching, with 225 species recorded to date. But the real star attractions are the resident **grizzled giant squirrels**, who scamper in healthy numbers around the thorny scrub here, and the near-mythical "**white bison of Manjampatti**", thought to be an albino Indian gaur.

ARRIVAL AND DEPARTURE   MUNNAR

By bus State-run and private buses pull into the town bus stand in the modern main bazaar, near the river confluence and Tata headquarters; state buses continue through town, terminating nearly 3km south. For most hotels you should ask to be dropped off at Old Munnar, 2km south of the centre, near the ineffectual DTPC tourist office (daily 8.30am–7pm; ☎ 04865 231516).

Destinations Ernakulam/Kochi (hourly; 5hr 30min); Kottayam (5 daily; 5hr).

ACTIVITIES

To arrange **treks and camping trips** in the Chinnar Wildlife Sanctuary, you have to call at the **Forest Information Centre** – aka Wildlife Warden's Office – near Mount Carmel Church in the centre of Munnar town (☎ 04865 231587). There is a range of different eco-tourism adventures on offer including **day-walks** that can be arranged on spec at a counter next to the Chinnar Forest Check Post. The most popular route is a three- to four-hour itinerary taking in a number of prehistoric rock art and dolmen sites. **Longer routes** involve stays in a very basic log hut with no running water (₹1500/person, plus ₹300 for each additional person) or poorly maintained tree house (₹1000/person plus ₹250 for each additional person); the **prices** include dinner and breakfast, and the services of a (non-English-speaking) guide.

ACCOMMODATION

Munnar's **accommodation** costs significantly more than elsewhere in the High Range region, reflecting the high demand for beds from middle-class tourists from the big cities. Rooms at the low end of the scale are in particularly short supply; the few that exist are blighted by racket from the bus stand and bazaar. There are some options outside town that would suit travellers with their own transport.

Anaerangal Camp at Suryanelli 25km east of Munnar on the Periyar road ☎ 0484 209 2280 or ☎ 0484 401 2700, ⓦ munnarcamps.com. Half a dozen spacious luxury tents, fitted with quality beds and bathrooms, facing a magnificent panorama of mountain peaks, lake and forest. Delicious Keralan food, prepared at kitchens on site, is included in the rate, along with lakeside trekking, cycle rides, plantation visits and an evening camp fire. An inspiring location and friendly service. ₹4500

British County ET City Rd, Anachal, 12km from Munnar ☎ 0484 2371761 or ☎ 98470 4468, ⓦ touristdesk.in /britishcounty.htm. On a ridge enjoying a vast valley view, this property, run by the Tourist Desk in Kochi (see p.1065), has just four simply furnished rooms. They're clean and comfortable enough, but the real attraction here is the terrace, disturbed by nothing but birdcalls and the wind in the trees. Cook Ranjit rustles up tasty Indian food; rates cover full board. ₹4000

Casa del Fauno Peak Gardens Chinnakanal, 25km east of Munnar on the Periyar road ☎ 0484 304 8769 or ☎ 9895 766444, ⓦ casadelfauno.in. This glossily restored former tea bungalow boasts spectacular views and light, varnished wood interiors, with designer furniture and top-class service. French windows open on to well-kept lawns, where you can dine on the finest locally sourced food. ₹5500

Green View Sri Parvati Amman Kovil St, near the KSRTC bus stand ☎ 04865 230189 or ☎ 9447 825447 (Deepak). Clean and friendly budget guesthouse on the valley floor, down a side road just off the main drag, with rooms of various sizes – the best of them, #402, is a tiny double with big windows and hill views. Pitched squarely at foreign back-packers, it's run by an enthusiastic, competent young crew who do a sideline in guided day-treks (see box, p.1057). ₹600

★ **High Range Club** Kanan Devan Hills Rd ☎ 04865 230253, ⓦ highrangeclubmunnar.com. This old Raj-era club, founded by British planters in 1909, must have been a nightmare of suffocating imperialism in its heyday. Now the faded colonial ambience, with lounges filled with 1940s furniture and moth-eaten hunting trophies, feels undeniably quaint. The club's guest wing holds three kinds of rooms and cottages (₹3000–4000), varying in size and comfort. Rates include full board. ₹**2500**

JJ Cottage Sri Parvati Amman Kovil St, near the KSRTC bus stand ☎ 04865 230104. Next door to *Green View*, and very much in the same mould, though it's been open longer, charges higher rates and tends to get booked up earlier. Like its neighbour, the nicest of its clean, variously sized rooms is the one at the top (frontside), which has wood-panelled walls and fine views. A warm family welcome is guaranteed. ₹**650**

Royal Retreat Kanan Devan Hills Rd ☎ 04865 230440, ⓦ royalretreat.co.in. Pleasant, efficiently run roadside motel at the south end of town. Go for a "super-deluxe" room if possible: they're south-facing, have brick fireplaces and cane furniture, and are fronted by a cheerful little flower garden. ₹**2750**

Zina Cottages Kad ☎ 04865 230349 or ☎ 9447 190954. British-era stone bungalow, nestled amid tea gardens high on the hillside above Munnar. The basic rooms lack outlook and can be chilly, but the flower-filled front terrace has magnificent views across the town to Ana Mudi, and the young host will fill you in on local walks over flasks of hot tea in his sitting room. Come here less for creature comforts than for atmosphere, of which it has plenty. ₹**750**

EATING

The **thattukada** (hot food stall market) just south of the main bazaar, opposite the taxi stand, gets into its stride around 7.30pm and runs through the night, serving delicious, piping-hot Keralan food – dosas, *parottas*, *iddiappam*, green-bean curry, egg masala – ladled onto tin plates and eaten on rough wood tables in the street.

Food Count Main bazaar. The most hygienic non-veg option in the main bazaar is *Food Count*, on the ground floor of the *Munnar Inn*, serving samosas, veg cutlets, sandwiches and light meals (₹50–200). Daily 8am–9.30pm.

Saravan Bhavan Munnar Market. The best pure-veg south Indian restaurant in town, serving the standard

range of tasty *udipi* dosas (₹30–50) and thali meals (₹70) – in addition to popular mini-iddli plates and delicious buttermilk. Tucked away down a narrow side street, but there's a large sign on the roadside in the main bazaar, directly behind the Gandhi statue. Daily 8am–9pm.

DIRECTORY

Banks and ATMs There are numerous ATMs around town, and you can change money at the State Bank of Travancore and the State Bank of India.

Internet Internet access is available from a couple of places including Alpha Computer Centre (₹50/hr), next to the Tamil Nadu bus stand.

Kochi (Cochin)

Spreading across islands and promontories between the Arabian Sea and the backwaters, **KOCHI** (long known as Cochin) is Kerala's prime tourist destination. Its main sections – modern **Ernakulam** and the old peninsular districts of **Mattancherry** and **Fort Cochin** to the west – are linked by bridges and a complex system of ferries. Although some visitors opt to stay in the more convenient Ernakulam, the overwhelming majority base themselves in Fort Cochin, where the city's complex history is reflected in an assortment of architectural styles. Spice markets, Chinese fishing nets, a synagogue, a Portuguese palace, India's first European church and seventeenth-century Dutch homes can all be found within an easy walk.

Brief history

Kochi sprang into being in 1341, when a flood created a safe natural port that swiftly replaced Muziris (now Kodungallur, 50km north) as the chief harbour on the Malabar Coast. The royal family moved here in 1405, after which the city grew rapidly, attracting Christian, Arab and Jewish settlers from the Middle East. The history of **European** involvement from the early 1500s onwards is dominated by the aggression of the Portuguese, Dutch and British, who successively competed to control the port and its lucrative spice trade. From 1812 until Independence in 1947 it was administered by

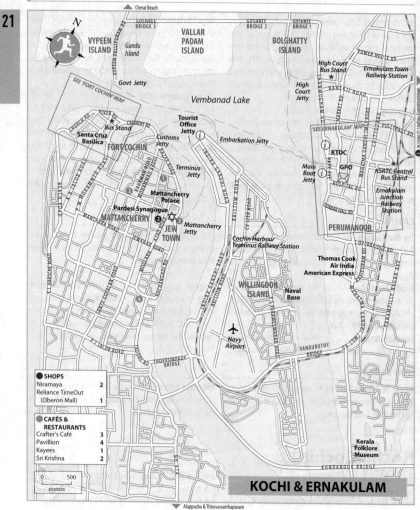

Cherai Beach

VYPEEN ISLAND

Gundu Island

GOSHREE BRIDGE 3

VALLAR PADAM ISLAND

GOSHREE BRIDGE 2

GOSHREE BRIDGE 1

BOLGHATTY ISLAND

POWER HOUSE RD.

High Court Bus Stand

Ernakulam Town Railway Station

Govt Jetty

Vembanad Lake

High Court Jetty

Tourist Office Jetty

Embarkation Jetty

KTDC

Santa Cruz Basilica

FORT COCHIN

Customs Jetty

Main Boat Jetty

GPO

KSRTC Central Bus Stand

Bus Stand

Terminus Jetty

Ernakulam Junction Railway Station

Mattancherry Palace

Pardesi Synagogue

MATTANCHERRY

JEW TOWN

Mattancherry Jetty

Cochin Harbour Terminus Railway Station

PERUMANOOR

Thomas Cook Air India American Express

WILLINGDON ISLAND

Naval Base

Navy Airport

VANDURUTHY BRIDGE

THOPPUMPADY BRIDGE

Kerala Folklore Museum

KUNDANOOR BRIDGE

KOCHI & ERNAKULAM

● SHOPS
Niramaya 2
Reliance TimeOut (Oberon Mall) 1

● CAFÉS & RESTAURANTS
Crafter's Café 3
Pavillion 4
Kayees 1
Sri Krishna 2

0   500
metres

Alappuzha & Thiruvananthapuram

a succession of *diwans*, or finance ministers. In the 1920s, the British expanded the port to accommodate modern ocean-going ships, and Willingdon Island, between Ernakulam and Fort Cochin, was created by extensive dredging.

Old Kochi: Fort Cochin and Mattancherry

Old Kochi, the thumb-shaped peninsula whose northern tip presides over the entrance to the city's harbour, formed the focus of European trading activities from the sixteenth century onwards. With high-rise development restricted to Ernakulam across the water, its twin districts of **Fort Cochin**, in the west, and **Mattancherry**, on the headland's eastern side, have preserved an extraordinary wealth of early colonial architecture, spanning the Portuguese, Dutch and British eras – a crop unparalleled in India. As you approach by ferry, the waterfront, with its sloping red-tiled roofs and ranks of peeling, pastel-coloured *godowns* (warehouses), offers a view that can have changed little in centuries.

Closer up, however, Old Kochi's historic patina has started to show some ugly cracks. The spice trade that fuelled the town's original rise is still very much in evidence. But over the past decade, an extraordinary rise in visitor numbers has had a major impact. Thousands of tourists pour through daily during the winter, and with no planning or preservation authority to take control, the resulting rash of new building threatens to destroy the very atmosphere people come here to experience. That said, tourism has also brought some benefits, inspiring renovation work to buildings that would otherwise have been left to rot.

Fort Cochin

Fort Cochin, the grid of old streets at the northwest tip of the peninsula, is where the Portuguese erected their first walled citadel, Fort Immanuel, which the Dutch East Indian Company later consolidated with a circle of well fortified ramparts. Only a few fragments of the former battlements remain (the outline of the old walls is traced by the district's giant rain trees, some of which are more than two centuries old), but dozens of other evocative European-era monuments survive.

A good way to get to grips with Fort Cochin's many-layered history is to pick up the free **walking-tour maps** produced by Kerala Tourism and the privately run Tourist Desk (see p.1065). They lead you around some of the district's more significant landmarks, including the early eighteenth-century Dutch Cemetery, Vasco da Gama's supposed house and several traders' residences.

Walking around the old quarter you'll come across several small exhibition spaces and galleries – evidence of Fort Cochin's newfound status as one of India's contemporary art hubs. The scene takes centre stage in mid-December when the annual **Kochi-Muziris Biennale** (ⓦkochimuzirisbiennale.org) draws artists and collectors from across the country with its mix of film, installation, sculpture, painting, performance art and new media hosted by half a dozen different venues.

Chinese fishing nets

The huge, elegant **Chinese fishing nets** lining the northern shore of Fort Cochin add grace to the waterfront view, and are probably the single most familiar photographic image of Kerala. Traders from the court of Kublai Khan are said to have introduced them to the Malabar region. Known in Malayalam as *cheena vala*, they can also be seen throughout the backwaters further south. The nets, which are suspended from poles and operated by levers and weights, require at least four men to control them.

St Francis church and around

Parade Ground • Daily 8.30am–6.30pm

South of the Chinese fishing nets on Church Road (the continuation of River Road) is the large, typically English **Parade Ground**. Overlooking it, the **Church of St Francis** was the first built by Europeans in India. Its exact age is not known, though the stone structure is thought to date back to the early sixteenth century. The facade, meanwhile, became the model for most Christian churches in India. Vasco da Gama was buried here in 1524, but his body was later removed to Portugal. Under the Dutch, the church was renovated and became Protestant in 1663, then Anglican with the advent of the British in 1795. Inside, the earliest of various tombstone inscriptions placed in the walls dates from 1562.

Mattancherry

Mattancherry, the old district of red-tiled riverfront wharves and houses occupying the northeastern tip of the headland, was once the colonial capital's main market area – the epicentre of the Malabar's spice trade, and home to its wealthiest Jewish and Jain

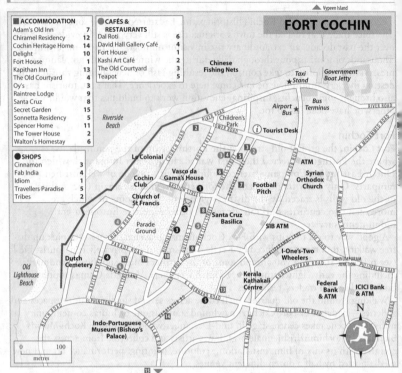

Vypeen Island

FORT COCHIN

◼ ACCOMMODATION	
Adam's Old Inn	7
Chiramel Residency	12
Cochin Heritage Home	14
Delight	10
Fort House	1
Kapithan Inn	13
The Old Courtyard	4
Oy's	3
Raintree Lodge	9
Santa Cruz	8
Secret Garden	15
Sonnetta Residency	5
Spencer Home	11
The Tower House	2
Walton's Homestay	6

● CAFÉS & RESTAURANTS	
Dal Roti	6
David Hall Gallery Café	4
Fort House	1
Kashi Art Café	2
The Old Courtyard	3
Teapot	5

● SHOPS	
Cinnamon	3
Fab India	4
Idiom	1
Travellers Paradise	5
Tribes	2

merchants. Like Fort Cochin, its once grand buildings have lapsed into advanced states of disrepair, with most of their original owners working overseas. When Mattancherry's Jews emigrated en masse to Israel in the 1940s, their furniture and other un-portable heirlooms ended up in the **antique shops** for which the area is now renowned – though these days genuine pieces are few and far between.

Mattancherry Palace

Jew Town Rd • Daily except Fri 10am–5pm • ₹2

The sight at the top of most itineraries is **Mattancherry Palace**, on the roadside a short walk from the Mattancherry Jetty, 1km or so southeast of Fort Cochin. Known locally as the Dutch Palace, the two-storey building was actually erected by the Portuguese, as a gift to the raja of Cochin, Vira Keralavarma (1537–61) – though the Dutch did add to the complex. While its squat exterior is not particularly striking, the interior is captivating, with some of the finest examples of Kerala's underrated school of **mural** painting, along with Dutch maps of old Cochin, coronation robes belonging to past maharajas, royal palanquins, weapons and furniture.

Jew Town and Pardesi Synagogue

Synagogue Lane • Daily except Sat 10am–noon & 3–5pm • ₹2

The neighbourhood immediately behind and to the south of Matancherry Palace is known as **Jew Town**, home of a vestigial Jewish community whose place of worship is the **Pardesi (White Jew) Synagogue**. Founded in 1568 and rebuilt in 1664, the building is best known for its interior, an incongruous hotchpotch paved with hand-painted eighteenth-century blue-and-white tiles from Canton. An elaborately carved Ark houses four scrolls of the Torah, on which sit gold crowns presented by the maharajas of Travancore and Cochin, testifying to good relations with the Jewish community. The synagogue's oldest artefact is a fourth-century copperplate inscription from the raja of Cochin.

Ernakulam

With its fast-paced traffic, broad streets and glittering gold emporia, **ERNAKULAM** has more of a big-city feel than Thiruvananthapuram – despite the fact it's marginally smaller. Other than the contemporary art on display at the small **Durbar Hall Art Gallery** on Durbar Hall Road (daily 11am–7pm; free), and the remarkable **folklore museum** (see below) on the southern outskirts, there's little in the way of sights – if you spend any time here, it'll probably be to eat at one of the area's famous Keralan **restaurants**.

Running parallel to the seafront, roughly 500m inland, **Mahatma Gandhi (MG) Road** is its main thoroughfare, where you'll find some of the largest textile stores, jewellery shops and hotels.

Kerala Folklore Museum

Theyvara, nr Kundulur Bridge • Daily 9.30am–7pm • ₹200 • ☎ 0484 266 5452, ⓦ folkloremuseum.org

Ernakulam's one outstanding visitor attraction is the **Kerala Folklore Museum**, on the distant southeast fringes of the city. Housed in a multistorey laterite building encrusted with traditional wood- and tile-work, the collection of antiques includes dance-drama masks and costumes, ritual paraphernalia, musical instruments, pieces of temple architecture, Thanjavur paintings, cooking utensils, portraits and ancestral photographs – to name but a few of the categories amassed by founder and avid antiques collector, George Thaliyath.

Its crowning glory is an exquisitely decorated **theatre** on the top floor, where evening performances of *kathakali* and *theyyem* are given against a backdrop of swirling Keralan temple murals and dark wooden pillars (see box, p.1069). Auto-rickshaws charge around ₹75–100 for the trip out to the museum from the Main Boat Jetty in Ernakulam – ask for Theyvara (aka "Shantinagar") Junction, or Kundulur Bridge.

ARRIVAL AND DEPARTURE

KOCHI (COCHIN)

By plane Kochi's international airport (ⓦ cochinairport.com) – one of India's most modern and efficient – is at Nedumbassery, near Alwaye (aka Alua), 29km north of Ernakulam. A pre-paid taxi into town costs around ₹550 and takes 45min or so, traffic permitting. If you'd prefer to be met from your flight with an a/c car, call Mr Haris of Ashik Taxis on ☎ 9288 157145 or ☎ 9656 798481. Modern, comfortable a/c airbuses also cover the route more or less hourly, running to Fort Cochin (9 daily; 45min–1hr 30min; ₹70).

By train There are two main railway stations, Ernakulam Junction, near the centre, and Ernakulam Town, 2km

further north. The Cochin Harbour Terminus, on Willingdon Island, serves the island's luxury hotels. Ernakulam Town lies on Kerala's main broad-gauge line and sees frequent services to and from Thiruvananthapuram via Kottayam, Kollam and Varkala. In the opposite direction, trains connect Ernakulam and Thrissur, and Chennai across the Ghats in Tamil Nadu. Since the opening of the Konkan Railway, a few express trains travel along the coast all the way to Goa and Mumbai. Although most long-distance express and mail trains depart from Ernakulam Junction, a couple of key services leave from Ernakulam Town. To

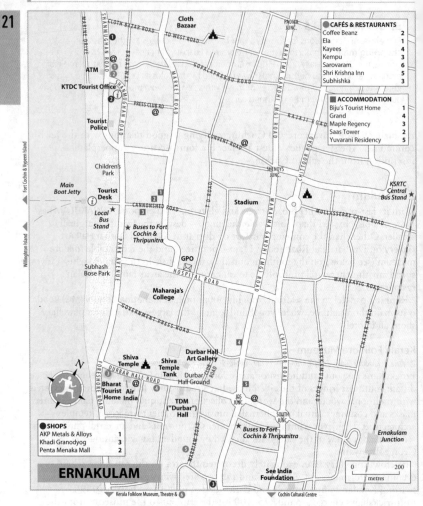

▼ Kerala Folklore Museum, Theatre & ⑥   ▼ Cochin Cultural Centre

confuse matters further, a few also start at Cochin Harbour station, so be sure to check the departure point when you book your ticket. The main reservation office, good for trains leaving all the stations, is at Ernakulam Junction.

Destinations Alleppey (16 daily; 1hr–1hr 30min); Bengaluru (5 daily; 11hr 20min–13hr); Chennai (7 daily; 12–15hr); Goa (4 daily; 12hr 25min–15hr); Kozhikode (15 daily; 3hr 50min–4hr 40min); Mumbai (6 daily; 20hr 45min–27hr); Varkala (hourly; 3–4hr).

By bus The KSRTC Central bus stand (☎0484 237 2033), beside the railway line east of MG Rd and north of Ernakulam Junction, is for state-run long-distance services. Reservations for services originating here can be made up to twenty days in advance. There are also

two stands for pricier private services: the Kaloor Stand (rural destinations to the south and east) is across the bridge from Ernakulam Town railway station on the Alwaye Rd, while the High Court Stand (buses to Kumily, for Periyar Wildlife Reserve, and north to Thrissur, Guruvayur and Kodungallur) is opposite the High Court ferry jetty. The Fort Cochin bus terminus serves tourist buses, local services to Ernakulam and the airport bus.

Destinations Alleppey (every 15–30min; 1hr 30min); Coimbatore (8–11 daily; 4–5hr); Kottayam (hourly; 2hr); Kozhikode/Calicut (every 1–2 hr; 5hr–5hr 30min); Kumily (9–10 daily; 5hr 30min–6hr); Munnar (every 30–45min; 5hr); Thiruvananthapuram (every 30min; 5hr); Thrissur (every 15min; 1hr 45min).

RECOMMENDED TRAINS FROM KOCHI/ERNAKULAM

The trains listed below are recommended as the fastest and/or most convenient services from Kochi. If you're heading to **Alappuzha** for the backwater trip to Kollam, take the bus, as the only trains that can get you there in time invariably arrive late.

Destination	Name	No.	Station	Departs	Duration
Bengaluru (**Bangalore**)	*Kanyakumari–Bangalore Express*	#16525	ET	daily 5.55pm	12hr
Kozhikode (**Calicut**)	*Netravati Express*	#16346	EJ	daily 2.05pm	5hr
Madgaon	*Rajdhani*	#12431	EJ	Tues & Thurs	11hr 40min
Mumbai	*Netravati Express*	#16346	EJ	daily 2.05pm	26hr 35min
Thiruvananthapuram	*Netravati Express*	#16345	ET	daily 2.20pm	4hr 20min
Varkala	*Malabar Express*	#16330	ET	daily 3.40pm	4hr

EJ = Ernakulam Junction
ET = Ernakulam Town
* = a/c only, meals included

GETTING AROUND

By ferry Kochi's dilapidated ferries provide a cheap and relaxing way to reach the various parts of the city. The most popular route for visitors is the one connecting Ernakulam's Main Boat Jetty and Fort Cochin/Matancherry's Customs Jetty (5.50am–9.30pm; every 20–30min). Also leaving from Ernakulam are ferries to Bolghatty Island (6.30am–9pm; every 30min), and Vypeen Island (7am–9.30pm; every 20–30min). The latter has two routes – one direct, and another slower service via Willingdon Island. From Fort Cochin's Government Jetty (10min walk west of Customs Jetty), you can also hop on a flat-bottomed vehicle ferry across the harbour mouth to Vypeen Island (6.30am–9pm; every 15min). Tickets should be purchased prior to embarkation from the hatch (separate queues for ladies and gents). All these routes are traced on our main Kochi map (see p.1060).

By bus KSRTC is in the process of upgrading its ageing fleet with new, state-of-the-art, low-floored Volvo buses, coloured bright green or orange. The new vehicles – used on prime routes such as the run between Fort Cochin and the airport – are cleaner and more comfortable, but there remain plenty of the old rust buckets in circulation and they're invariably crammed to bursting point. Frequent services run throughout the day between Ernakulam and Fort Cochin, though the ferry is a lot more enjoyable. If you miss the last boat back at 9.30pm, don't wait around for a bus (departures are sporadic and horrendously packed at that time of night); jump in an auto-rickshaw instead (₹250–300).

By bike Bicycles can be rented from many hotels and guesthouses in Fort Cochin.

By motorbike I-One's-Two Wheelers, at 1 946-A Njaliparambu (the lane opposite the entrance to the Kerala Kathakali Centre, near the Basilica in Fort Cochin) has Enfields for rent, as well as a few automatic Honda Activas. You'll need to leave your passport as security. Contact Ivan Joseph (☏ 9847 155306, ⓦ rentabikecochin.com).

INFORMATION

Tourist information India Tourism's main office (Mon–Fri 9am–5.30pm, Sat 9am–noon; ☏0484 266 8352, ⓦ incredibleindia.org), providing reliable information and qualified guides for visitors, is inconveniently situated on Willingdon Island, between the *Vivanta by Taj Malabar Hotel* and Tourist Office Jetty; they also have a desk at the airport. KTDC's reception centre, on Shanmugham Rd, Ernakulam (daily 8am–7pm; ☏0484 235 3234, ⓦ ktdc.com), books rooms in their hotel chain and organizes sightseeing and backwater tours. For general advice the two most convenient sources are the Kerala Department of Tourism's office next to the Government Jetty in Fort Cochin (Mon–Sat 10.15am–5pm; no phone, ⓦ keralatourism.com), and the tiny, independently run Tourist Desk (daily 8am–6.30pm; ☏0484 237 1761, ⓦ touristdesk.in) near the entrance to the Main Boat Jetty in Ernakulam (follow the path branching to the right – north – as you approach the jetty terminal, or to the left if arriving from Fort Cochin). The Tourist Desk also runs a subsidiary office on Tower Rd in Fort Cochin (same hours; ☏0484 221 6129). Both hand out maps of the town and backwaters – and walking-tour maps and guides to Fort Cochin – but the latter is more helpful when it comes to checking ferry and bus times, and for finding temple festivals in the area and further afield.

21

TOURS AND BACKWATER TRIPS

Backwater trips KTDC offers day-trips into the backwaters south of Kochi (daily 8.15am–5.30pm; ₹650), but they're not as good as those run by the Tourist Desk (daily 8.30am–6.30pm; ₹650; book at their counters in Fort Cochin and Ernakulam; ⓦtouristdesk.in /watervalleytour.htm). The cost includes hotel pick-up, transfer to the departure point near Vaikom, 30km south, a morning cruise (in a motorized boat) on the open backwaters, a village tour, a Keralan lunch buffet on board the *kettu vallam* and an afternoon trip through narrow waterways in a much smaller punted canoe. In a similar vein are the community-based tours run by the villagers of Kumbalanghi on Kallancherry Island (ⓣ0484 224 0329 or ⓣ9388 975508, ⓦkumbalanghivillagetours.com), profits from which go to the farmers, coir producers and fishermen who show you around (see p.1071).

Cruises If you are pushed for time, KTDC's half-day Kochi boat cruise (daily 9.30am–1pm & 2.30–6pm; ₹200) is a good way to orient yourself, but it doesn't stop long in either Mattancherry or Fort Cochin. Book at the reception Centre on Shanmugham Rd (see p.1065).

Elephants The Tourist Desk at the Main Jetty in Ernakulam (ⓣ0484 237 1761) and Tower Rd in Fort Cochin runs elephant-spotting tours to Wayanad, and beach and backwater stays in its own guesthouses around Kannur.

ACCOMMODATION

Most foreign visitors opt to stay in **Fort Cochin**, with its uncongested backstreets and charming colonial-era architecture. There are, however, drawbacks: room rates are grossly inflated (especially over Christmas and New Year), with few options at the budget end of the scale. **Ernakulam** may suffer a dearth of historic ambience, but it's far more convenient for travel connections and offers lots of choice and better value in all categories. Wherever you choose to stay, book well in advance.

ERNAKULAM

★ **Biju's Tourist Home** Corner of Cannonshed and Market roads ⓣ0484 238 1881, ⓦbijustouristhome .com; map p.1064. The pick of the budget bunch: a friendly, efficiently run hotel just a 5min walk from the boat jetty, with thirty spotless, well-aired and sizeable rooms. It has its own clean water supply and offers a cheap same-day laundry service. Phone reservations accepted. A/c ₹1000 extra. **₹750**

Grand MG Rd ⓣ0484 238 2061, ⓦgrandhotelkerala .com; map p.1064. This is the most classically glamorous place to stay in central Ernakulam. Spread over three floors of a 1960s building, its relaxing a/c rooms are done in retro-colonial style, with varnished wood floors and split-cane blinds. Surprisingly low rates given the level of comfort and location. **₹3600**

Maple Regency XL/1511 Cannonshed Rd ⓣ0484 235 5156 or ⓣ0484 237 1711, ⓔmapleregency @airtelmail.in; map p.1064. The best of the few rock-bottom options in the streets immediately east of the Main Boat Jetty, with thirty cheap, clean, non-a/c rooms. To the rear, a couple of old ancestral bungalows (₹800, ₹1400 a/c), dating from 1891, have been converted into pleasant chalet-style "cottages", with red-tiled floors, long pillared verandas and a lot more charm than anything else in this price bracket. **₹540**

Saas Tower Cannonshed Rd ⓣ0484 236 5319, ⓦsaastower.com; map p.1064. Since its refit, this tower-block hotel, with 72 well-furnished rooms, has become the best-value mid-range option in the city. It's completely lacking character, but very smart, central and well placed for the Fort Cochin ferry. **₹2200**

Yuvarani Residency Jos Junction, MG Rd ⓣ0484 237 7040, ⓦyuvaraniresidency.com; map p.1064. Comfortable, central and well-managed three-star with a choice of carpeted or tiled rooms (₹2000–3500) – and especially good showers. The popular Keralan seafood restaurant hosts live music recitals daily (except Tues), and there's a bar and a coffee shop. **₹2000**

FORT COCHIN

Adam's Old Inn 1/430 Burgher St ⓣ0484 221 7595, ⓦadamsoldinn.com; map, p.1062. The best budget option in the Fort district, with well-scrubbed little en-suite rooms opening onto a central corridor – only the "deluxe" one to the rear has a terrace. There's a helpful travel agent on the ground floor. **₹1000**

Chiramel Residency 1 296 Lilly St ⓣ0484 221 7310, ⓦchiramelhomestay.com; map p.1062. A great seventeenth-century heritage homestay, with welcoming owners and five lofty and carefully restored non-a/c rooms set around a fancily furnished communal sitting room. All have big wooden beds, teak floors and modern bathrooms. **₹2500**

★ **Cochin Heritage Home** Vadatazha Rd, nr Bishop's Palace ⓣ0484 221 6123 or ⓣ9447 432636, ⓦcochinheritage.com; map p.1062. The property with the most traditional Keralan character in Fort Cochin. With their high beamed ceilings, oxide tiled floors and antique wooden doors, the rooms are simply but attractively furnished, and open onto a polished-pillar veranda where breakfast is served in the mornings in the shade of split-cane blinds. There are only four rooms, so book ahead. Rates include breakfast. **₹3000**

Delight Ridsdale Rd, opposite the parade ground ☎0484 221 7658 or ☎9846 121421, ⓦdelightfulhomestay.com; map p.1062. Occupying an annexe tacked onto a splendid 300-year-old Portuguese mansion, David and Flowery's homestay holds seven spacious, comfortable and well-aired rooms, all equipped with new bathrooms and quiet ceiling fans. Some open onto a lovely courtyard garden; another has a long veranda overlooking the parade ground. Breakfast included. ₹2000

Fort House 6A Calvathy Rd ☎0484 221 7103, ⓦhotelforthouse.com; map p.1062. Stylishly simple rooms flank a sandy courtyard littered with pot plants and votive terracotta statues. Those in the better block (rooms #1–6) have comfy king-sized beds and good showers in their chic wet-room bathrooms – though the a/c units can be noisy. Avoid the older budget block on the west side. Rates include breakfast. ₹6000

Kapithan Inn 931 KL Bernard Rd ☎0484 221 6560, ⓦkapithaninn.com; map p.1062. Scrupulously clean, very nicely furnished rooms in a friendly homestay behind Santa Cruz Basilica, with four smarter, larger a/c cottages (₹1500) to the rear (large enough for families). Bargain rates for the level of comfort. ₹1000

The Old Courtyard 1/371–2 Princess St ☎0484 221 6302, ⓦoldcourtyard.com; map p.1062. Another delightful heritage hotel, with eight rooms around a seventeeth-century courtyard, framed by elegant Portuguese arches and bands of original *azulejo* tiles. For once the decor and antique furnishings (including romantic four-posters) are in keeping with the building – though perhaps a bit dark and lacking mod cons. Upper-storey rooms are less disturbed by noise from the courtyard restaurant (see p.1069). ₹3500

Oy's Burgher St ☎9947 594903, ⓦoys.co.in; map p.1062. Pleasant, clean and friendly backpackers' hideaway, with just three cosy rooms, down the lane from *Kashi Arts Café*. Barred windows look onto a little raised terrace and there's a pleasant little travellers' café on the ground floor. ₹800

Raintree Lodge Peter Celli St ☎0484 325 1489 & ☎9847 029000, ⓦfortcochin.com; map p.1062. Five outstandingly smart rooms furnished in modern style (two of them with tiny balconies) in a cosy guesthouse that's within easy walking distance of the sights, but still tucked away. The really nice thing about this place is its plant-filled roof terrace, which has panoramic views. ₹2500

Santa Cruz Peter Celli St ☎0484 221 6250 or ☎9847 518598; map p.1062. Half of the rooms in this small guesthouse behind St Francis' Church have windows opening onto an enclosed corridor, but the others are well ventilated – and they're all impeccably clean, neatly tiled and freshly painted, with new beds. Those on the upper floor are nicest. A/c costs an extra ₹600 – well

worth it as the rooms can get stuffy at night. You'll also need a mozzie net. ₹900

Secret Garden 745 Bishop Garden Lane, near Pattalam Market ☎9895 581489, ⓦsecretgarden.in; map p.1062. Buried in a maze of narrow back lanes, this is a hidden gem, run by Icelandic architect, Thóra Guðmundsdóttir. The white-walled rooms, which have high wooden ceilings, hand-carved beds and traditional terracotta tiled floors, all open onto balconies fronting an exotic garden with a good-size pool. Rates include (optional) morning yoga, and use of the house computer, books and bicycles. ₹7000

Sonnetta Residency 387 Princess St ☎0484 221 5744 or ☎9895 543555, ⓦsonnettaresidency.com; map p.1062. This small guesthouse has to be one of the cleanest places to stay in Kerala: the surfaces are gleaming, bed linen boil-washed and bathrooms polished. It lacks character, and has no outside sitting space, but is efficiently run and provides a secure, convenient base, with some of the cheapest a/c rooms (₹550 extra) in the district. ₹1100

Spencer Home 298 Parade Rd ☎0484 221 5049, ⓦspencerhome-fortkochi.blogspot.co.uk; map p.1062. Warm-toned wood pillars and gleaming ceramic tiled floors line the verandas fronting this Portuguese-era house's eleven immaculate rooms, which open onto a painstakingly kept garden. Peaceful and good value for the area. A/c ₹500 extra. ₹1500

The Tower House 320–321 Tower St ☎0484 221 6960, ⓦneemranahotels.com; map p.1062. The graceful period house opposite the Chinese fishing nets, is perfectly situated. Airy interiors are scrupulously in period, and there's a secluded pool. Don't expect the slick service of other places in this bracket, nor Fort Cochin's usual exorbitant rates. ₹5000

★ **Walton's Homestay** 39 Princess St ☎0484 221 5309 & ☎9249 721935, ⓦwaltonshomestay.com; map p.1062. Among Cochin's most characterful homestays, run by philosopher and local historian Mr Christopher Edward Walton in a centuries-old Dutch house. The rooms, many of which open onto a delightful rear garden, have been beautifully renovated, with modern bathrooms, ceiling fans, solar-powered hot water and comfy beds (a/c ₹400 extra). Book-swap library and yoga classes available; breakfast on the terrace is included. ₹1600

KUMBALANGHI VILLAGE

Gramam Neduveli House North Kumbalangi ☎0484 2240278 or ☎9447 177312, ⓦkeralagramam .com. Welcoming homestay offering accommodation in a beautifully converted coconut warehouse, slap on the banks of a lagoon. Chill in a hammock under the palms, go for cycle and canoe rides around the village, watch

21

local fishermen and toddy tappers at work and generally soak up the peaceful rural atmosphere. Host Byju and Lyma's home cooking is also great. Rates are for full board. ₹**4250**

★ **Kallancherry Retreat** Kumbalanghi village, 24km south of Ernakulam ☎0484 224 0564 or ☎9847

446683. Charming little family homestay, a world away from the crowded streets of Fort Cochin, set under palm trees on the banks of a huge lagoon just a 30min ride out of town. The en-suite rooms are squeaky clean and have balconies. ₹**2000**

EATING

Until the authorities shut them down a few years back, the quintessential Kochi dining experience was to buy a fish straight from the **Chinese fishing nets** in the Fort, then have it grilled at one of the stalls nearby. Instead, foreign tourists these days tend to congregate at the pavement joints along the nearby **Tower Rd**, drinking warm beer disguised in teapots. The food served in these cafés, however, is notoriously unhygienic. Your rupees will stretch further in **Ernakulam**, where you'll find some of the best traditional food in all south India.

ERNAKULAM

Coffee Beanz Shanmugham Rd; map p.1064. Trendy a/c cappuccino bar, patronized in the main by well-heeled students from the local management college shrieking into their mobiles over a full-on MTV soundtrack. The din notwithstanding, it's a good spot to beat the heat and grab a good coffee or quick meal (burgers, grilled sandwiches, dosas and fish curries, mostly under ₹200). Daily 11am–11pm.

Ela Shanmugham Rd; map p.1064. Great-value, a/c Keralan speciality place where nothing costs more than ₹200. The vibe is upbeat and trendy, but the non-veg food's very trad: *meen pollichathu*, deliciously rich Syrian-Christian vegetable stew, lamb-coconut curry and light, spongy *appam*s to soak it all up. Lots of old-style desserts, too, including *payasam* and more-ish banana fritters. Mon–Sat 11am–11pm, Sun 8am–10pm.

Kayees Durbar Hall Rd; map p.1064. This salubrious branch of the city's most famous Muslim restaurant is a modern dining hall in the heart of the downtown area, with an a/c section on the first floor. The menu is comprehensive, but everyone comes for the Malabari biriyanis (veg, chicken or mutton; ₹85–105), served with *Kayees'* mellow palm-date pickle and Arabian tea. Packed at lunchtime, and on Sundays. Pay for your meal token in advance. Daily 11.30am–2pm & 5.30–9pm.

Kempu Ground floor, Bharat Tourist Home, Durbar Hall Rd ☎0484 235 3501; map p.1064. A great place to regroup during a shopping trip on nearby MG Rd. The decor – terracotta murals, thick stone floors and dark Keralan wood – is soothing, and the south Indian bites dependably good. Try their *bonda* – spicy vegetable and peanut balls (₹35), served with coconut-chilli *chatni* that's so thick you have to spread it with a knife. This place was up for sale at the time of writing, so check it's still open before your visit. Daily 3.30pm–2am.

★ **Sarovaram** Bypass Rd, Kudunnur; map p.1064. People travel from all across the city for *Sarovaram's* famous lunchtime *sadyas* (₹100), served on banana leaves in a

typical Laurie Baker building, with exposed bricks and stone floors. The pure veg food is unrivalled in the city and the atmosphere is much more Keralan, though it's a long trek across town – but happily combined with a trip to the nearby Folklore Museum (see p.1063). Lunchtimes only. Daily noon–3pm.

Shri Krishna Inn Warriam Rd; map p.1064. The sumptuous south Indian thalis served in this smart a/c vegetarian restaurant are on a par with nearby *Subhishka's*, but the decor is more appealingly traditional, with lathe-turned wooden pillars and earthy-toned Keralan murals setting the tone. As well as unlimited thalis (₹100–130), they do a huge range of ice creams. Daily noon–2.30pm & 7–9pm.

Subhishka Bharat Tourist Home, Durbar Hall Rd ☎0484 235 3501; map p.1064. The same banana leaf *sadyas* as at *Sarovaram* (₹100 unlimited), only served in more contemporary surroundings, with incongruous music. It's a great place for crowd-watching, especially on Sundays when everyone appears in their best saris and shirts for the big family meal. At the time of writing the hotel was up for sale; phone ahead. Daily 7am–3.30pm & 7–11pm.

FORT COCHIN

★ **Dal Roti** 1 293 Lilly St; map p.1062. The first choice among Fort Cochin's hungry travellers, despite the generally grubby state of its walls, erratic service and shortage of tables. You'll know why as soon as you taste their signature *kati* rolls – deliciously flaky wraps filled with egg, chicken or vegetables – or good-value thalis (a refreshingly honest ₹200 for the works). The food is authentic north Indian and full of smoky, spicy flavours you don't get to enjoy that often in Kerala. Wed–Mon noon–3.30pm & 6.30–10.30pm.

David Hall Gallery Café Parade Ground; map p.1062. Delicious pizzas (₹200–250), made in a proper pizza oven and served alfresco in a lovely green oasis behind the David Hall art space. They also serve crêpes, freshly ground coffee, quality teas and juices. Don't miss the amazing seventeenth-century Dutch timbers on your way through the exhibition space. Daily noon–9pm.

Fort House 2 6A Calvathy Rd; map p.1062. Carefully prepared Keralan specialities – including delicious *karimeen pollichathu* or grilled fish steak – served on a romantic, candlelit jetty. The food is consistently good, and not too pricey (most mains ₹300–400), and the location's perfect for watching the ships chugging in and out of the docks. Daily noon–3pm & 6–11pm.

Kashi Art Café Burgher St; map p.1062. Chichi gallery café, with floors made from pebbles and railway sleepers, patronized mainly by well-heeled metropolitan Indian tourists. Freshly ground espresso (₹70) is the big draw, along with their famous house cakes (the old-fashioned chocolate gateau is legendary; ₹100), but they also do light meals and savoury snacks – check the specials board, and expect perfunctory service. Daily 8.30am–7.30pm.

The Old Courtyard 371–2 Princess St; map p.1062. Few places capture the feel of old-world Cochin as vividly as this courtyard restaurant, with candlelit tables arranged beneath Portuguese vaulted arches. The food (most mains ₹325–350) is as fine as the location – try the baked seafood spaghetti, or fish grilled with coriander butter – and the *patronne*-chef is a dessert wizard. Frequent live Carnatic music 7.30–9pm, and it's also a nice spot for breakfast. Daily 8–10am, noon–3pm & 6.30–11pm.

Teapot Peter Celli St; map p.1062. With its massive collection of teapots from around the world, shabby-chic colour-washed wood floors and walls, tea-chest tables and funky little mezzanine floor, this backstreet tearoom has been giving *Kashi* some much-needed competition. Quality teas (₹70) and coffees (₹40) are the mainstay, but they also do light meals (₹200–250) and delicious homemade cakes. Daily 8.30am–7.30pm.

KATHAKALI IN KOCHI

Kochi is the only city in Kerala where you are guaranteed the chance to see live **kathakali**, the state's unique form of ritualized theatre (see box, p.1026). Whether in its authentic setting, in temple festivals held in winter, or at the shorter tourist-oriented shows that take place year-round, these mesmerizing dance dramas – depicting the struggles of gods and demons – are an unmissable feature of Kochi's cultural life.

Four venues in the city currently hold daily shows, each preceded by an **introductory talk** at around 6.30pm. You can watch the dancers being made up if you arrive an hour or so beforehand; keen photographers should turn up well before the start to ensure a front-row seat. **Tickets** (usually around ₹250) can be bought at the door. Most visitors only attend one performance, but you'll gain a much better sense of what *kathakali* is all about if you take in at least a couple. The next step is an **all-night recital** at a temple festival, or one of the performances given by the top-notch Ernakulam Kathakali Club, which stages night-long plays by Kerala's leading actors once a month, either at the TDM Hall in Ernakulam or at the Ernakulathappan Hall in the city's main Shiva temple. For details phone ☎0484 236 9357, or drop in at the Tourist Desk at the Main Boat Jetty, Ernakulam (see p.1065).

Dr Devan's Kathakali See India Foundation, Kalathiparambil Cross Rd, near Ernakulam Junction railway station ☎0484 236 6471. The oldest tourist show in the city, introduced by the inimitable Dr Devan, who gets the ball rolling with a discourse on Indian philosophy and mythology. 6.45–8pm (make-up 6pm; ₹250).

Folklore Museum Bypass Rd, southeastern edge of Ernakulam ☎0484 2665452, ⓦfolkloremuseum .org. The most atmospheric venue – an a/c theatre decorated with wonderful Keralan murals and traditional wooden architecture – though it's quite pricey (₹400), and a long trek across town if you're staying in Fort Cochin. Try to combine a performance with a tour of the museum downstairs (see p.1063), and maybe a meal at nearby *Sarovaram* (see opposite). Taxis charge ₹100–150 from central Ernakulam.

Kerala Kathakali Centre Bernard Master Lane,

near Santa Cruz Basilica, just off KB Jacob Rd, Fort Cochin ☎0484 221 7552. Popular performances in a dedicated a/c theatre by a company of graduates of the renowned Kalamandalam academy. You usually get to see three characters, and the music is live. Shows (₹250) 6–7.30pm (make-up 5pm), plus *kalarippayat* (4–5pm), and live Carnatic music (8.30pm).

Rhythms Theatre (Greenix) Opposite Fort House, Fort Cochin ☎0484 221 7000, ⓦgreenix.in. You've a choice between a short kathakali recital (₹250) or longer culture show (₹450) combining excerpts from *kathakali* plays with displays of *mohiniyattam* dance, *kalarippayat* martial art and, on Sundays, *theyyem*, set against a combination of live and pre-recorded music. Performances aren't of the highest standard, but the evening is more likely to appeal to kids, as costumes and acts change in quick succession. Note that cameras cost ₹50 extra.

21

MATANCHERRY

Crafters Café Next to Heritage Arts shop on Jew Town Rd; map p.1060. Handy pit-stop if you're visiting the nearby synagogue. Tables on their wonderful little blue-pillared balcony are great for people watching as you enjoy a plate of delicious butterfly prawns (₹250), *appam* with coconut-veg stew (₹120) or a freshly cut sandwich (₹100–150). They also do proper espresso and cakes. Daily 9.30am–6.30pm.

★ **Kayees** Rahmathulla Hotel, New Rd, Matancherry; map p.1060. This Muslim joint in the backstreets of Matancherry is legendary across the state for its fragrant biriyanis, prepared fresh each morning according to a traditional, closely guarded Malabari recipe. There are frequently queues out the door, so get here before 1pm (or ideally earlier than that) to avoid disappointment. You've a choice of chicken (₹85) or mutton (₹95) biriyanis,

accompanied by the wonderful house date pickle. Noon–1.30pm & 5.30–7pm.

Pavillion Abad Hotel, Moulana Azad Rd, Chullikkal ☎0484 222 8211; map p.1060. The upscale option if you want a quality, good-value meal without having to travel up to Fort Cochin. The modern a/c dining hall is devoid of character, but spotlessly clean and both the food and service are first-rate, particularly the local seafood (the hotel's owners are fish exporters), served with piping hot *appam*. ₹300–450/head. Daily noon–3pm & 7–11pm.

Sri Krishna Café Matancherry Palace/Cheralai Rd; map p.1060. Typical south Indian, pure veg restaurants are thin on the ground on this side of the water, so it's worth jumping in a rickshaw from Fort Cochin to eat at this famous old *udipi* café in the temple district of Matancherry, where traditional Keralan "meals" cost under ₹40. Daily 11am–4pm.

SHOPPING

While serious shopping in **Ernakulam** tends to be focused on the **mega malls** to the north of the city (see box, p.1063), over in the tourist enclave of Fort Cochin, a combination of lookalike Kashmiri emporia (best avoided) and more individual boutiques, handicraft and curios shops cater for the passing foreign trade. **Jew Town** is the hub of an established **antiques** scene, with some of the largest and most spectacular showrooms in India – a legacy of the post-1960s exodus of the district's Jewish population to Israel, when a large amount of family furniture was left behind. Some approach the scale of small museums, with chunks of temple masonry, carved wood pillars, religious sculpture, doors, windows and even, in one instance, a huge Keralan snake boat for sale – though don't expect to find any bargains. **Original art** by local painters also features prominently in the galleries of Jew Town.

AKP Metals and Alloys Broadway, Ernakulam ⓦakpmetallodrome.com; map p.1064. The city's largest metalware emporium, showcasing a vast selection of traditional Keralan items in brass, copper, silver and bell metal. Mon–Sat 10.30am–8pm.

Cinnamon Trinity Hotel, 658 Ridsdale Rd, Parade Ground, Fort Cochin; map p.1062. The Fort Cochin branch of the hip Bengaluru lifestyle chain sells clothes, shoes and items for the home from a range of top Indian designers in a light and airy boutique. Womens' garments are particularly striking: unusual pieces in gorgeous natural colours. Mon–Sat 10am–7pm.

Fab India 279(I), Napier St, near Parade Ground, Fort Cochin ⓦfabindia.com; map p.1062. Specializing in garments made from traditional Indian textiles, the nationwide chain boasts five branches in the city, the most convenient of them in Fort Cochin. Browse a huge range of vibrant *kurtas*, tops, skirts, bedspreads and cushion covers – all at reasonable (fixed) rates. Mon–Sat 10.30am–8.30pm.

Idiom Opposite the Dutch Palace, Jew Town, Mattancherry; and on Bastion St near Princess St, Fort Cochin; map p.1062. The two branches of Idiom are the best places to browse for books on travel, Indian and Keralan culture, flora and fauna, religion and art; they also have an excellent range of fiction. Mon–Sat 10am–8.30pm.

Khadi Gramodyog Bhavan Pallimuku, MG Rd; map p.1064. The usual assortment of climate-friendly, hand-spun cotton and silk, sold by length or as ready-made garments, as well as items for the home, incense, honey, sandalwood and other village handicrafts at fixed prices. Mon–Sat 10.30am–8pm.

Niramaya 622 Quiros St, nr Jewish Synagogue, Mattancherry ⓦayurvastraonline.com; map p.1060. This innovative little boutique in Jew Town sells clothes made from organic cotton infused with healing Ayurvedic herbs. Dyed in subtle colours, they're perfect for the sticky Keralan heat. Also bed linen and yoga mats from natural materials. Mon–Sat 10am–6pm, Sun 10am–1pm.

Penta Menaka Mall Marine Drive; map p.1064. The best place in the city for electronic goods, computer/video games and movies – at a fraction of the price you'd pay back home (they're mostly pirated). Daily 10.30am–9.30pm.

Reliance TimeOut Level 02, Oberon Mall, north Ernakulam; map p.1060. The widest range of branded CDs and DVDs in the city – both regional and international – along with a huge section of books, toys and writing and art materials. Mon–Fri 10.30am–9.30pm, Sat & Sun 10.30am–10pm.

Travellers' Paradise KL Bernard Master Rd, Fort Cochin ⓦbloominthenaturalway.com; map p.1062. French designer Sophie Debiève set up this collective to market original pieces made by local Keralan women – mostly silk and cotton in beautiful Indian colours, and incorporating floral French print motifs. The range includes original household linen, bags and cards. Mon–Sat 10am–6pm.

Tribes Next to Head Post Office, Fort Cochin Ⓦtribesindia.com; map p.1062. Jewellery, textiles, paintings, terracotta and stone work, metal crafts and organic food products produced by tribal communities across the country. Stand-out pieces range from bead necklaces by the Wancho of Arunachal Pradesh, to coral bracelets from the Konyak Nagas and vibrant Pithora ritual art by the Bhils of Madhya Pradesh. Profits go toward development projects in the artists' communities. Mon–Sat 10am–6pm.

DIRECTORY

Banks All the major south Indian banks have branches on MG Rd in Ernakulam. To exchange travellers' cheques, the best place is Thomas Cook (Mon–Sat 9.30am–6pm), near the Air India Building at Palal Towers, also on MG Rd. ATMs can be found all over the centre of Ernakulam. In Fort Cochin, the Canara Bank has an ATM on Kanumpuram Junction.

Cinemas The eight-screen multiplex at LuLu Mall (Ⓦlulushoppingmall.com), 7km north of the centre (see box, p.1063), hosts regular screenings of English-language movies as well as Malluwood and Bollywood releases.

Dentist The Emmanuel Dental Centre, Noble Square, Kadavanthara (Ⓣ0484 220 7544, Ⓦcosmeticdentalcentre .com) is an international-standard practice that does routine dental procedures as well as more advanced cosmetic work.

Hospitals The 600-bed Medical Trust Hospital on MG Rd (Ⓣ0484 235 8001, Ⓦmedicaltrusthospital.com) is one of the state's most advanced private hospitals and has a 24hr casualty unit and ambulance service.

Laundry The municipal laundry in Fort Cochin is the Dhobi Khanna, on the south side of the district, a 3km/₹40 rickshaw ride from the tourist enclave. ₹10–15 for shirts; ₹25 for trousers. Allow 24hrs.

Taxis Ashik Taxis (Ⓣ9288 157145 or Ⓣ9656 798481) cover the entire state, and offer day-trips at fair prices.

Around Kochi

While the majority of visitors use the city as a base for day-trips into the surrounding backwaters and satellite villages, there's nothing to stop you doing the opposite, basing yourself in quiet backwater locations out of town – such as **Vypeen Island** to the north, or **Kumbalanghi** to the south – and travelling in to see the sights by bus, taxi or auto-rickshaw. There is some outstanding accommodation in Kumbalanghi village, in the form of homestays (see p.1067).

Backwater trips

Coir-production, rope-making, toddy-tapping, fishing and crab-farming are the main sources of income in the backwater villages south of Kochi. Easily reachable via the national highway, they're scattered over an expanse of huge lagoons and canals, flowing west behind a near continuous beach.

You can dip into the region for a day on one of the popular trips run out of Fort Cochin by KTDC and the Tourist Desk (see p.1065), or with a community-based tourism initiative based at Kumbalanghi village (see p.1066) – an award-winning project where proceeds are shared among the locals. The cost of the latter tour is ₹1400 (or ₹800 without lunch). You also have to budget for transport to and from the village. The trip is most easily done by auto-rickshaw (₹300–350 each way); if travelling by bus, head for Perumamapadappu, aka "Perumbadapu" on Google maps, and catch an auto from there for the remaining couple of kilometres.

Thripunitra

Some 12km southeast of Ernakulam and a short bus or auto-rickshaw ride from the bus stand just south of Jos Junction on MG Road, the small suburban town of **THRIPUNITRA** is worth a visit for its dilapidated colonial-style **Hill Palace**, now an eclectic museum, as well as its fabulous temple festival, held in mid November each year.

21

The Hill Palace
Tues–Sun 9am–5pm • ₹10

The royal family of Cochin at one time had around forty palaces – the **Hill Palace** was confiscated by the state government after Independence, and has slipped into dusty decline over the past decades. One of the museum's finest exhibits is an early seventeenth-century wooden *mandapa* (hall) featuring carvings of episodes from the Ramayana. Of interest too are the silver filigree jewel boxes, gold and silver ornaments, and ritual objects associated with grand ceremonies. Artefacts in the **bronze gallery** include a *kingini katti* knife, whose decorative bells belie the fact that it was used for beheading, and a body-shaped cage in which condemned prisoners would be hung while birds pecked them to death.

Sri Purnathrayisa Temple
Performances of theatre, classical music and dance, including all-night **kathakali** performances, are held over a period of eight days during the annual **Vrishikolsavam** festival (Oct/Nov) at the **Sri Purnathrayisa Temple** on the way to the palace. Inside the temple compound, both in the morning and at night, massed drum orchestras perform *chenda melam* in procession with fifteen caparisoned elephants.

Cherai Beach
The closest beach to Kochi worth the effort of getting to is **Cherai**, 25km north on **Vypeen Island**. A 3km strip of golden sand and thumping surf, it's sandwiched on a narrow strip of land between the sea and a very pretty backwater area of glassy lagoons. Chunky granite sea defences prevent the waves from engulfing the ribbon of fishing villages that subsist along this strip. Nowhere, however, is the sand more than a few metres wide at high tide, and the undertow can get quite strong. Even so, Cherai is gaining in popularity each year, and a row of small resorts and guesthouses has sprung up to accommodate the trickle of mainly foreign travellers who find there way up here from Fort Cochin.

ARRIVAL AND DEPARTURE
CHERAI BEACH

By ferry and bus To get to Cherai, you can jump on the car ferry (*jangar*) across to Vypeen Island from the jetty next to Brunton Boatyard in Fort Cochin, then transfer onto the hourly bus waiting on the other side, or catch one of the more frequent buses from opposite the High Court Jetty in Ernakulam.

By scooter Alternatively, you can, hire a scooter (see p.1065) and ride up – in which case, a preferable route to the main road is the more picturesque coastal lane hugging the sea wall; you can pick this up by turning west (left) down a bumpy backroad at Nayarambalam, 1km north of Narakkal, or via any of the lanes peeling left further on.

ACCOMMODATION

Brighton Beach House 783 Palli Fort, 2km north of Cherai ☎0484 310 7661, ⓦbrightonbeachhouse.org. Fairly basic en-suite rooms (some a/c) opening on to a yard right next to the sea wall, a 5min drive north of the main beachfront. Meals and sundowners are served in a small gazebo-cum-sun terrace overlooking the sand, which is particularly narrow here. ₹2500

La Dame Rouge Kizhakke Veedu, Manapilly ☎0484 2481 062 or ☎9249 410523, ⓦladamerouge.com. This small, French-owned boutique guesthouse is a true labour of love – beautifully designed and run by host Marco, a former consular official who's been here for decades. The rooms and duplex suites are exquisitely decorated, with colour-washed walls, four-posters and Indian antiques

– and the location, near a huge backwater, is superb. Canoe trips to the local market, Ayurvedic massages and fragrant Indo-Gallic fusion cooking are all on offer. Rates include breakfast and dinner. ₹5500

Kuzhupilly Beach House Kuzhupilly, 4.5km south of Cherai ☎484 2531456 or ☎9447 107028, ⓦkuzhupillybeachhouse.com. Little budget guesthouse just 30min by taxi from the Vypeen–Fort Cochin ferry dock, but overlooking a deserted stretch of beach and backwaters. The best rooms (₹2500) are on the upper floor and have fine sea views. Delicious, authentic Keralan home cooking is also on offer, along with bicycles and canoe tours. You can get most of the way there by bus (much cheaper); phone ahead for instructions. ₹2000

THEYYEM RITUAL, KANNUR (P.1084)>

21

Ocean Breath Cherai ☏ 9847 635206, ⓦ beachandbackwater.com. The best-value budget option in Cherai, and the one with most Keralan atmosphere. No sea views (it's set back across the road from the sea wall) but the rooms are pleasant, with high, traditional Keralan ceilings and carved gables, shiny ceramic floors and small sitouts. ₹**1200**

Thrissur

THRISSUR (Trichur), a bustling market hub and temple town roughly midway between Kochi (74km south) and Palakkad (79km northeast) on the NH-47, is a convenient base for exploring the cultural riches of central Kerala. Close to the Palghat (Palakkad) Gap – an opening in the natural border made by the Western Ghat mountains – it presided over the main trade route into the region from Tamil Nadu and Karnataka. For years Thrissur was the capital of Cochin state, controlled at various times by both the Zamorin of Kozhikode and Tipu Sultan of Mysore.

Today, Thrissur derives most of its income from remittance cheques sent by expatriates in the Gulf – hence the predominance of ostentatious modern houses in the surrounding villages. As the home of several influential art institutions, the town also prides itself on being the cultural capital of Kerala. One of the state's principal Hindu temples, **Vadukkunnathan**, is here too, at the centre of a huge circular maidan that hosts all kinds of public gatherings, not least Kerala's most extravagant, noisy and sumptuous festival, **Puram**.

THRISSUR PURAM

Thrissur is best known to outsiders as the venue for Kerala's biggest annual festival, **Puram**, which takes place on one day in the Hindu month of Medam (April–May; ask at a tourist office or check online for the exact date). Inaugurated by Shaktan Tampuran, the raja of Cochin, between 1789 and 1803, the event is the culmination of eight days of festivities spread over nine different temples to mark obeisance to Lord Shiva, at the peak of the summer's heat. Like temple festivals across Kerala, it involves the stock ingredients of caparisoned elephants, massed drum orchestras and firework displays, but on a scale, and performed with an intensity, unmatched by any other.

Puram's grand stage is the long, wide path leading to the southern entrance of **Vadukkunnathan Temple** on the Round. Shortly after dawn, a sea of onlookers gathers here to watch the first phase of the 36-hour marathon – the **kudammattom**, or "Divine Durbar" – in which two majestic **elephant processions**, representing Thrissur's Tiruvambadi and Paramekkavu temples, advance towards each other down the walkway, like armies on a medieval battlefield, preceded by ranks of drummers and musicians. Both sides present thirteen tuskers sumptuously decorated with gold caparisons (*nettipattom*), each ridden by three young Brahmins clutching objects symbolizing royalty: silver-handled whisks of yak hair, circular peacock-feather fans and colourful silk umbrellas fringed with silver pendants. At the centre of the opposing lines, the principal elephant carries an image of the temple's presiding deity. Swaying gently, the elephants stand still much of the time, ears flapping, seemingly oblivious to the crowds and huge orchestra that plays in front of them, competing to create the most noise and greatest spectacle. When the music reaches its peak around sunset, the two groups set off towards different districts of town. This signals the start of a spectacular **firework display** that begins with a series of deafening explosions and lasts through the night, with the teams once again trying to outdo each other to put on the most impressive show.

If you venture to Thrissur for Puram, be prepared for packed buses and trains, and book **accommodation** well in advance. As is usual for temple festivals, many men use the event as an excuse to get hopelessly drunk. Women are thus advised to dress conservatively and only to go to the morning session, or to watch with a group of Indian women – and at all times avoid the area immediately in front of the drummers, where the "rhythm madmen" congregate.

Vadakka Madham Brahmaswam

21

Thakkemadham Rd • Daily 7.30am–2.30pm • Free

The mighty Vadukkunnathan Temple, in the centre of the Round, may be closed to non-Hindus, but you can gain a sense of how ancient its roots are at the nearby **Vadakka Madham Brahmaswam**, five minutes' walk west of the temple on Thakkemadam Road, where young Namboodiri Brahmin boys attend **chanting** classes at a traditional *madham*, or college. Wearing traditional white *mundu*, sacred threads and ash marks on their skin, the students sit cross-legged in traditional Keralan halls while they repeat verses from 3000-year-old texts modelled for them by their gurus. If you'd like to visit, telephone (☏0487 244 0877) to ensure classes will be in progress; donations towards the *madham*'s activities are welcome.

Basilica of Our Lady of Dolours

Church Rd • Tues–Fri 10am–1pm & 2–6pm, Sat & Sun 10am–1pm & 2–7.30pm • ₹15

Not to be outdone by the scale of the Hindu temple across town, the vast Indo-Gothic **Basilica of Our Lady of Dolours** (Puthan Pally in Malayalam) dominates the skyline southeast of the Round, thanks to its gigantic 79m bellfry – allegedly the largest church tower in Asia. You can scale the mighty edifice, either via a lift or 350-step staircase, from the top of which superb views extend across the palm forest surrounding Thrissur.

Archeological Museum

Karunkaram Nambiar Rd • Tues–Sun 9.30am–1pm & 2–4.30pm • ₹10

Of the town's **museums**, grouped to the north of the Round, the only one worth visiting – not least for the splendid Keralan architecture of the former palace it's housed in – is the **Archeological Museum**, opposite the Priya Darshini bus stand, a five-minute walk north of the Round on Karunkaram Nambiar Road. Former residence of the Cochin royal family, the 200-year-old **Shaktan Thampuran Palace** is beautifully decorated with intricate wood- and tile-work. Exhibits include fifteenth- and eighteenth-century hero stones, a fearsome selection of beheading axes and a massive iron-studded treasury box.

ARRIVAL AND DEPARTURE
THRISSUR

The principal point of orientation in Thrissur is the Round, a road (subdivided into North, South, East and West) which circles the Vadukkunnathan Temple complex and maidan in the town centre.

By train On the main line to Chennai and other points in neighbouring Tamil Nadu, and with good connections to Kochi and Thiruvananthapuram, the railway station is 1km southwest.

By bus The KSRTC long-distance bus stand is opposite the station. The Shakthan Thampuran bus stand, on TB Rd, around 1km from Round South, serves local destinations south such as Irinjalakuda, Kodungallur and Guruvayur.

INFORMATION

Tourist information The primary purpose of the volunteer-run DTPC tourist office (Mon–Sat 10am–5pm; ☏0487 232 0800), on Palace Rd opposite the Town Hall (5min walk off Round East), is to promote the Puram festival, but they also hand out maps of Thrissur.

ACCOMMODATION

Thrissur has plenty of competitively priced mid-range hotels but only a couple of decent budget ones. If you're planning to be here during **Puram**, book well in advance and bear in mind that room rates soar – some of the more upmarket hotels, and those overlooking the Round, charge up to ten times their usual prices.

Ashoka Inn TB Rd ☏0487 244 4333, ⌂ashokainn .co.in. Best value among the business-oriented three-stars in the Shakthan Thampuran bus stand district, in a gleaming, glass-sided tower block with spacious, impeccably clean rooms. ₹4000

21

Elite International Chembottil Lane, off Round South ☎ 0487 242 1033, ⓦ hoteleliteinternational.com. Pronounced "Ee-light", this massive gunmetal-grey tower block in the centre of town has some rooms with balconies overlooking the green. They're huge for the price, but dowdy. Rates include breakfast. **₹700**

Gurukripa Lodge Chembottil Lane ☎ 0487 242 1895, ⓦ gurukripalodge.com. Run with great efficiency by the venerable Mr Venugopal, the *Gurukripa*, just off Round South, offers a variety of simple en-suite rooms, (including several great-value singles) ranged around a long inner courtyard. **₹300**

★ **Kuruppath** Mannadiara Lane, off Kuruppam Rd ☎ 9495 260000 or ☎ 9846 045696, ⓦ kuruppathheritage.com. An impeccably restored heritage bungalow, cowering amid the high-rise tower blocks in the heart of town, just a stone's throw from Round South. Filled with dark wood and antique tiles, the interiors are light, cool and astonishingly peaceful considering the location. Rates include meals. **₹5000**

EATING AND DRINKING

There are plenty of dependable places to eat in Thrissur, with many hotels and busy "meals" joints lining the Round. From 8.30pm, you can also join the auto-rickshaw-wallahs, hospital visitors, itinerant mendicants, Ayappa devotees and students who congregate at the popular **thattukada** hot food market on the corner of Round South and Round East, opposite the Medical College Hospital. The rustic Keralan cooking – omelettes, dosas, *parottas*, *iddiappam*, bean curries and egg masala – is freshly prepared, delicious and unbelievably cheap.

Akshaya Luciya Palace, Marar Rd, just off the southwest corner of the Round. Hotel restaurant where waiters in bow ties serve quality Keralan meals at lunchtime (₹110) in a blissfully cold a/c dining hall. From 7.30pm you can order from an exhaustive multicuisine menu, sitting outside in a pleasant garden illuminated by fairy lights. Beer is permitted with meals. Daily noon–3pm & 6–10.30pm.

★ **Bharath Hotel** Chembottil Lane, 50m down the road from the Elite Hotel. Thrissur's top pure-veg place, packed from 7.30am onwards. The food is unfailingly fresh and delicious, and the queues stretch out the door on weekends. Be sure to leave room for the *ada*, a mix of sugar cane, coconut and rice steamed in a banana leaf (which tastes disconcertingly like old-fashioned British treacle pudding). Daily 7.30am–9.30pm.

DIRECTORY

Banks There are ATMs all over the centre of town. The best place to change money and travellers' cheques is the UTI Bank in the City Centre Shopping building (Mon–Fri 9.30am–3.30pm, Sat 9.30am–1.30pm) on Round West. The UAE Exchange & Financial Services (Mon–Sat 9.30am–6pm, Sun 9.30am–1.30pm) in the basement of the *Casino Hotel*

building also changes currency and travellers' cheques.

Internet Available for ₹30/hr at Hugues Net on the top floor of the City Centre Shopping building and at SS Consultants next to the *Luciya Palace* hotel.

Post office The main post office is on the southern edge of town, just off Round South.

Around Thrissur

If Thrissur is the crucible of central Kerala's cultural and political life, then its hinterland serves as its main storehouse, dotted with towns, villages and pilgrimage sites where both contemporary party politics and ancient art traditions are pursued with great enthusiasm, despite the disruptive impact on local life of mass out-migration.

Guruvayur

GURUVAYUR, 19km west of Thrissur, is the site of south India's most revered Krishna temple, with hundreds of thousands of Hindu pilgrims pouring in all year to worship at the shrine. As usual, non-Hindus are barred from entering, but it's still worth coming on a day-trip to visit the **Punnathur Kotta Elephant Camp**, 4km north of town, where the temple's elephants reside (daily 8am–6pm; ₹5, camera ₹25). Some 67 pachyderms, aged from 10 to 98, live in the park, munching for most of the day on specially imported piles of fodder. They're cared for by their personal *mahouts*, who wash and scrub them several times a week in the sanctuary pond. As with domestic elephants everywhere, only approach an animal if the wardens allow you, as they can be unpredictable and dangerous.

Cheruthuruthy

CHERUTHURUTHY, on the banks of the Bharatpuzha (aka "Nila") River 32km north of Thrissur, is internationally famous as the home of **Kerala Kalamandalam** (Ⓦkalamandalam. org), the state's flagship training school for *kathakali* and other indigenous Keralan performing arts. The academy was founded in 1927 by the revered Keralan poet Vallathol (1878–1957), and has since been instrumental in the large-scale revival of interest in unique Keralan art forms. Non-Hindus are welcome to attend performances of *kathakali*, *kudiyattam* and *mohiniyattam* performed in the school's wonderful **theatre**, which replicates the style of the wooden, sloping-roofed traditional *kuttambalam* auditoria found in Keralan temples. You can also sit in on classes, watch demonstrations of mural painting, and visit exhibitions of costumes by signing up for the fascinating "**a day with the masters**" cultural programme (Mon–Sat 9.30am–1pm; ₹1000, including lunch).

ARRIVAL AND DEPARTURE   CHERUTHURUTHY

By train Served by express trains to and from Mangalore, Chennai and Kochi, the nearest mainline railway station is Shoranur Junction, 3km south.

By bus Buses heading to Shoranur from Thrissur's Priya Darshini (aka "Wadakkancheri") stand pass through Cheruthuruthy.

ACCOMMODATION

River Retreat Heritage Ayurvedic Resort 2km from Kalamandalam ☎04884 262244, Ⓦriverretreat.in. Accommodation in Cheruthuruthy is limited to the luxurious *River Retreat Heritage Ayurvedic Resort*, former palace of the raja of Cochin. The three-star hotel and Ayurveda spa occupies an idyllic position on the banks of the Nila, where you can swim in a crystalline pool, partly shaded by coconut palms. **₹330**

Kozhikode (Calicut)

Formerly one of Asia's most prosperous trading capitals, the busy coastal city of **KOZHIKODE** (Calicut), 225km north of Kochi, occupies an extremely important place in Keralan legend and history. It's also significant in the chronicles of European involvement on the Subcontinent, as Vasco da Gama landed at nearby Kappad beach in 1498. After centuries of decline following the Portuguese destruction of the city, Kozhikode is once again prospering thanks to the flow of remittance cheques from the Gulf – a legacy of its powerful, Moppila-Muslim merchant community, who ran the local ruler's (Zamorin's) navy and trade. The recent building boom has swept aside most monuments dating from the golden age, but a few survive, notably a handful of splendid Moppila **mosques**, distinguished by their typically Keralan, multitiered roofs.

The Moppila Mosques

The three most impressive mosques lie off a backroad running through the **Muslim** quarter of **Thekkepuram**, 2km southwest of the maidan (the auto-rickshaw-wallahs will know how to find them). Start at the 1100-year-old **Macchandipalli Masjid**, between Francis Road and the Kuttichira Tank, whose ceilings are covered in beautiful polychrome stucco and intricate Koranic script. A couple of hundred metres further north, the eleventh-century **Jama Masjid**'s main prayer hall, large enough for a congregation of twelve hundred worshippers, holds another elaborately carved ceiling. The most magnificent of the trio of mosques, however, is the **Mithqalpalli** (aka **Jama'atpalli**) **Masjid**, hidden down a lane behind Kuttichira tank.

21

Resting on 24 wooden pillars, its four-tier roof and turquoise walls were built more than seven hundred years ago.

ARRIVAL AND DEPARTURE

By plane Kozhikode's international airport (@calicutairport.com), at Karippur, 23km south of the city, is primarily a gateway for emigrant workers flying to and from the Gulf, but also has direct flights to many other Indian cities, including Mumbai, Delhi, Kochi, Chennai and Hyderabad. A taxi from the airport into town costs around ₹550.

Destinations Chennai (1–2 daily; 1hr 20min); Cochin (1 daily; 45min); Coimbatore (1 daily; 35min); Hyderabad (1 daily; 1hr 50min); Mumbai (34 daily; 1hr 40min–2hr).

By train The railway station (@ 0495 270 1234), near the centre of town, is served by coastal expresses, slower passenger trains, and superfast express trains to and from Goa, Mumbai, Kochi and Thiruvananthapuram.

Destinations Bangalore (1 daily; 12hr); Chennai (4 daily; 12–18hr); Goa (22 daily; 8–11hr 30min); Kannur (every 30–60min; 1hr 20min–1hr 45min); Kochi/Ernakulam (every 30min; 4–5hr); Mumbai (20 daily; 19–22hr); Thiruvananthapuram (hourly; 7hr 15min–10hr).

By bus There are three bus stands. Government-run services pull in at the KSRTC bus stand, on Mavoor Rd (aka Indira Gandhi Rd). Private long-distance – mainly overnight – buses stop at the New Moffussil private stand, 500m away on the other side of Mavoor Rd. The Palayam bus stand, off MM Ali Rd, just serves the city.

Destinations Bengaluru/Bangalore (8–10 daily; 10–11hr); Kannur (hourly; 1hr 30min–3hr); Kalpetta/Wayanad (every 30min; 1hr 45min); Kottayam (8–12 daily; 7–8hr); Ooty (3–4 daily; 5hr 30min–6hr); Thrissur (hourly; 3hr 30min).

INFORMATION

Tourist office KTDC's tourist information booth (officially daily 9am–7.30pm; @ 0495 270 0097), at the railway station, has information on travel connections and sights, but opening hours are erratic. The main KTDC tourist office (@ 0495 272 2391), in the *Malabar Mansion* hotel at the corner of SM St, can supply only limited information about the town and area.

ACCOMMODATION

Hotels in Kozhikode are plentiful, except at the bottom end of the range, where decent places are few and far between. This is one city where travellers on tighter budgets might be tempted to upgrade. Most establishments operate 24hr check-outs; because of the amount of traffic to and from the airport, the better-value ones rarely have vacancies at short notice so **reserve well ahead**.

Alakapuri Guest House Chinthavalappu Junction, MM Ali Rd, near the Palayam bus stand @ 0495 272 3451. Opening on to a large central garden, the rooms in this popular place range from old-fashioned, spartan, non-a/c doubles to more spacious "cottages" with polished wood chairs, pillared sitouts and sofas (₹1600). All of them are neatly painted and clean; a/c costs an additional ₹500. In the evening, you can eat on the lawn or in their cavernous dining hall under the watchful gaze of a giant plaster elephant. ₹1000

Beach Heritage Beach Rd, 2km west of the centre @ 0495 276 2056, @ beachheritage.com. Dating from 1890, the premises of the colonial-era Malabar English Club, with its closely cropped lawns and high-pitched tiled roofs, now house a heritage hotel retaining plenty of period feel. The six rooms come with balconies or private patios, split-cane blinds, paddle fans and a/c. Those on the upper floor are larger and have the best sea views. Good value. ₹3500

Calicut Tower Markaz Complex, off Mavoor IG Rd @ 0495 272 3202, @ calicuttower@yahoo.com. This ninety-room tower block, tucked away down a quiet side-street off the main drag and popular mainly with visiting Gulf Arab medical tourists, offers by far the best value in Kozhikode's lower-mid-range bracket. Impeccably clean, with shiny tiled floors and well-scrubbed bathrooms, its "standard a/c" rooms (just ₹350 pricier than the stuffier non-a/c options) are huge for the price. Strictly no alcohol. ₹1800

★ **Harivihar** 4km north of the centre in the residential suburb of Bilathikulam @ 0495 276 5865, @ harivihar .com. Ancestral home of the Kadathanadu royal family, converted into a particularly desirable heritage homestay. Set among lawns, herb beds, lotus ponds and an original laterite-lined bathing tank (which guests are welcome to use), the mansion is a model of traditional Keralan refinement. Distractions include short courses in yoga, astrology, cookery and Indian mythology, and treatments at their top-grade Ayurvedic centre. ₹9000

Sea Queen Beach Rd @ 0495 236 6604, @ seaqueenhotel.com. Bright yellow-and-blue brick building next to a lorry park on the seafront. It's a good option if your budget can stretch to one of the pleasant, spacious a/c rooms, the best of which is the sea-facing "a/c-deluxe" (#213; ₹2200). The non-a/c rooms are fusty and not nearly as nice. Breakfast, served alfresco on the rooftop, is included in the price. ₹1500

EATING

21

Kozhikode is famous for its **Moppila cuisine**, which has its roots in the culinary traditions of the city's former Arab traders. Fragrant chicken biriyanis and seafood curries with distinctive Malabari blends of spices crop up on most non-veg restaurant menus. **Mussels** are also big news here; deep-fried in their shells in crunchy, spicy millet coatings, they're served everywhere during the season (Oct–Dec; at any other time, they'll have been imported and won't be as fresh). Finally, no Kozhikode feast is complete without a serving of the city's legendary **halwa**: a sticky Malabari sweet made from rice flour, coconut, jaggery (unrefined sugar) and ghee. It comes in a dazzling variety of colours and flavours.

★ **Paragon** Off the Kannur Rd, ⦿ paragonrestaurant .net. *Paragon* has been a city institution since it opened in 1939. Don't be put off by the gloomy setting beneath a flyover: the Malabari cooking here is as good as you'll find anywhere. Seafood dishes are the house speciality – especially fish tamarind, fish-mango curry, *pollichathu*, *mollee* – but there are dozens of alternatives. Whatever you order, make sure it's accompanied by their famously light *appam* and *parotta* combo. Most mains ₹150–225. Daily 6am–10.45pm.

Sagar Mavoor/IG Rd. Another old favourite of Calicut's middle classes, now with two branches. Both are housed in distinctive laterite buildings, with non-a/c on the ground floor, and brighter a/c "family" dining halls on the floors above. Ignore the generic north Indian-Chinese-multicuisine menu. Everyone comes for the Malabari dishes such as egg curry, fish korma and, best of all, the flavour-packed chicken

pollichathu. Most mains under ₹175. Daily 6am–midnight.

Sanjeevanam MN's Ave, near 4th Railway Gate, off PT Usha Rd. The perfect, pure veg antidote to all those rich Malabari meals across town, *Sanjeevanam* specializes in healthy, additive-free, sattvic cooking. Their sumptuous lunchtime thali, "rajakeeam" (noon–3pm; ₹150), is out of this world, featuring twenty or more items. Noon–3pm & 6.30–9.30pm.

Zain's Hotel Convent Cross Rd ⦿ 0495 236 6331. An unassuming, red-painted family house down a dingy lane in the west end of town is hardly what you'd expect the Holy Grail of Moppila cuisine to look like, but people travel from across the city to eat here. You'll find a choice of biriyanis (fish, chicken or mutton; ₹100–150), various fiery seafood curries, and a range of different *pathiris* – the definitive Malabari rice-flour bread. Most mains ₹125–175. Daily noon–3pm & 6–11pm.

DIRECTORY

Bank and exchange The UAE Exchange on Bank Rd, next to *Hyson Heritage* (Mon–Sat 9.30am–1.30pm & 2–6pm, Sun 9.30am–1.30pm) changes cash and travellers' cheques, while the Union Bank of India and the State Bank of India, opposite each other on MM Ali Rd, are two of many

large branches with ATMs.

Internet Available at the Hub, on the first floor of the block to the right of *Nandhinee Sweets*, MM Ali Rd, and at Internet Zone, near KTDC *Malabar Mansion* (both ₹30/hr).

Wayanad

The seven mountains encircling the hill district of **Wayanad**, 70km inland from Kozhikode, enfold some of the most dramatic scenery in all of south India. With landscapes varying from semitropical savanna to misty tea and coffee plantations, and steep slopes that rise through dense forest to distinctive, angular summits of exposed grassland, the region ranges over altitudes of between 750m and 2100m. Even at the base of the plateau, scattered with typically ramshackle Indian hill bazaars, it's noticeably cooler than down on the plains.

The main Mysore–Kozhikode highway, NH-17, slices through Wayanad. Since the late 1990s, it has been the source of new income in the form of over-stressed dot-com executives and their families from Bangalore and Delhi, with numerous high-end resorts, eco-hideaways and plantation stays springing up to service the screen-weary. Even if you can't afford to stay in one of these bijou retreats, however, there are plenty of reasons to venture up here. Abutting the Tamil Nadu and Karnatakan borders, the twin reserves of **Muthanga** in the southeast, and **Tholpetty** in the north, collectively comprise the **Wayanad Wildlife Sanctuary** – part of the world-famous Nilgiri Biosphere and one of the best places in India to spot wild **elephant**.

21

Kalpetta and southern Wayanad

If you're travelling on all but the most flexible of budgets, you'll probably have to stay in the district's capital, **KALPETTA**. A hectic market hub straddling the main road, the town has little to commend it as a place to hang out, but does have the only budget accommodation in the area, as well as good transport connections to points east, notably the **Muthanga Wildlife Sanctuary**, the southern portion of the Wayanad reserve.

Muthanga Wildlife Sanctuary

Daily 7–10am & 3–6pm • ₹110, camera ₹25

Some 40km east of Kalpetta, the sanctuary is noted primarily for its elephants, but also shelters Indian bison (gaur), deer, wild boar, bear and a handful of tigers. **Trekking** in the sanctuary is only allowed during the morning slot; guides for the three-hour route charge ₹175. If you opt for the two-hour, 22km jeep trip, you'll also have to pay for a guide (₹150), the vehicle's rental (₹400) and entry fee (₹50) on arrival at the park gates.

ACCOMMODATION

KALPETTA AND SOUTHERN WAYANAD

★ **Aranyakam** Valathur–Rippon, Meppadi ☎04936 280261 or ☎9447 781203, ⍇aranyakam.com. Rooms and suites in a handsome Keralan-style bungalow, with wood floors and verandas on both sides, the rear ones just a few metres from the coffee bushes. Best options, if you can stretch to them, are their two huts (₹6000/7500), which look across a spectacular wilderness of pristine forest and mountain. ₹3500

Chandragiri Main Rd, Kalpetta ☎04936 203049. The best cheapie in town, in a modern block in the centre, and the only place with beds under ₹750 that you'd want to sleep in. It has three kinds of room, varying in size from tiny to small, but they're well scrubbed and well aired. ₹700

Green Gates TB Rd, Kalpetta North ☎04936 202001, ⍇greengateshotel.com. Modern three-star hotel, tucked away in its own lush grounds 300m north of the tourist office, offering a variety of rooms in the main multistorey block (₹3000), or more private cottages to its rear (₹5250). There's a pool, plenty of chillout space in the gardens, and an Ayurveda centre. The most comfortable option in Kalpetta, but not a great location. ₹3000

Tranquil Kappamudi Estate, Kolaggappara ☎04936 220244 or ☎9947 588507, ⍇tranquilresort.com. The crème de la crème of Wyanad's homestays, set amid 400 acres of rambling coffee, cardamom and vanilla plantations. The planter's bungalow itself holds eight comfy rooms (from $335), all opening on to a glorious veranda wrapped in manicured gardens, and there are two palatial treehouses ($435–470) as well as a large pool. The cooking's terrific, and the Dey family are perfect hosts. Minimum two nights. ₹17,800

Woodlands Main Rd Kalpetta ☎04936 202547, ⍇thewoodlandshotel.com. Dependable place on the main drag at the north end of town. Its rooms are a little worn, but comfortable enough for a night, and the staff are unfailingly courteous; there's secure parking, and separate veg and non-veg restaurants on the ground floor. A/c ₹500–1000 extra. ₹1200

North Wayanad

The teak forest takes over completely as you climb towards the northern limits of Wayanad, tracked by the savanna grass summits of the Brahmagiri massif. Some travellers use the pot-holed trunk road cutting north towards Mysore to reach the Nagarhole National Park or the Kodagu (Coorg) district in neighbouring Karnataka. But the majority of people who venture up here do so for a glimpse of wild elephants at the **Tholpetty Wildlife Sanctuary**, on the state border.

Tholpetty Wildlife Sanctuary

Jeep safaris Daily 7–9am & 3–5pm; 90min • ₹300–350; *Pachyderm Palace* will make the arrangements for you if you're staying there •
Guided treks Daily 8am–1pm • ₹1000 for up to four people

Forming the northern sector of the Wayanad reserve, **Tholpetty Wildlife Sanctuary**, 25km northeast of Mananthavady, is one of the best parks in south India for sighting elephants, as well as bison, boar, *sambar*, spotted deer, macaques and

Nilgiri langurs. Tigers also inhabit the reserve and their pug marks are commonly encountered along the muddy margins of forest trails, although you'd be lucky indeed to see any big cats in the flesh these days; decades of poaching have reduced the population to vestigial numbers.

The Forest Department runs 24km **jeep safaris** from the park's main gates along a network of rutted tracks, passing through stands of old teak and bamboo groves, interspersed with boggy waterholes where watchtowers and observation huts have been erected. You can also join **guided treks**, though the pace can be brisk, and stops few and far between.

Taxis charge ₹600 for the trip from Mananthavady to Tholpetty, and the frequent KSRTC buses to Kutta will drop you off at the sanctuary entrance. Buses back to Mananthavady run until 8.45pm.

Sree Thirunelli

One of Wayanad's most celebrated temples, **Sree Thirunelli**, lies in a remote part of the district 30km northwest of Mananthavady, reached via a bumpy backroad winding west off the Kogadu road. Set amid an awesome amphitheatre of mountains draped in vegetation, the temple is an unusual mix of Keralan tiled roofs and north Indian-style pillared halls.

A dozen **buses** daily connect Mananthavady to Thirunelli; jeeps will run you out there for around ₹300.

ACCOMMODATION   **NORTH WAYANAD**

★ **Agraharam Cottages** Near Sree Thirunelli temple, 30km north of Mananthavady ☎9605 005020 or ☎9605 005024, ⓦagraharamcottages.com. It is surprising to find this campus of tidy little chalets with red-tiled roofs and verandas, set amid neatly cropped lawns, in such a remote spot. It's a welcoming place that makes a tranquil base for visiting the adajcent temple, and for forays on foot into the surrounding woods and hills. The appam breakfasts and fish curry suppers are superb. ₹**5000**

Pachyderm Palace Near the Tholpetty Forest Check Post; book through the Tourist Desk in Kochi on ☎0484 237 1761, ⓦtouristdesk.in. Traditional Keralan bungalow with five simple rooms and garden hut on stilts.

Many guests are initially surprised by how basic rooms are for the price, but are invariably won over by the authentic Keralan cuisine (rates are all-inclusive) and friendly welcome. Jeeps for wildlife drives can be arranged here, along with guides for treks into the nearby Brahmagiri range. ₹**2500**

Wildlife Resort 500m from the Tholpetty Forest Check Post ☎9656 566977 or ☎9744 770500, ⓦwildliferesorts.in. The most comfortable option within easy walking distance of the Tholpetty park gate. Its recently built laterite, red-tiled "cottages", set in steeply sloping gardens just off the main road, are bland, and a tad overpriced, but well furnished (with good mattresses) and private sitouts. ₹**4000**

The far north

The beautiful coast **north of Kozhikode** is a seemingly endless stretch of coconut palms, wooded hills and virtually deserted beaches. The small fishing towns ranged along it hold little of interest for visitors, most of whom bypass the area completely – missing out on some exquisite, quiet coves, and the chance to see **theyyem**, the extraordinary masked trance dances that take place in villages throughout the region between November and May.

Kannur (Cannanore)

KANNUR (Cannanore), a large, predominantly Moppila Muslim fishing and market town 92km north of Kozhikode, was for many centuries the capital of the Kolathiri rajas, who prospered from the maritime spice-trade through its port. India's first Portuguese Viceroy, Francisco de Almeida, took the stronghold in 1505, leaving in his

21

wake an imposing triangular bastion, **St Angelo's Fort**. This was taken in the seventeenth century by the Dutch, who sold it a hundred or so years later to the Arakkal rajas, Kerala's only ruling Muslim dynasty.

These days, the town is the largest in the northern Malabar region – a typically Keralan market and transport hub jammed with giant gold emporia and silk shops, and seething with traffic. Land prices are booming ahead of the proposed construction of an international airport, which will doubtless see more skyscrapers rise on the outskirts. Kannur's few sights can be slotted into a morning, but increasing numbers of travellers are using the beaches to the south as bases from which to venture into the hinterland in search of **theyyem** rituals.

St Agnelo's Fort

Daily 8am–6pm • Free

Accessed through a gateway on its northern side, **St Agnelo's Fort** remains in good condition and is worth visiting to scale the massive laterite ramparts, littered with British cannons, for views over the town's massive Norwegian-funded fishing anchorage.

Arakkal Heritage Museum

Mon–Sat 10am–6pm • ₹25

The splendid whitewashed building facing the beachfront below the fort – once the raja and bibi of Arrakal's palace – now houses the government-run **Arakkal Heritage Museum**. Here documents, weapons, various pieces of 400-year-old rosewood furniture and other heirlooms relating to the family's history are displayed – though they're somewhat upstaged by the old building itself, with its high-beamed ceilings and original floorboards.

Folklore Museum

Chirakkal Mon–Sat 10.30am–12.30pm & 2.30–4.30pm • ₹10 • ☎ 0497 277 8090 • Rickshaws charge ₹150–200 for the trip, and buses run every 30min from the Padanna Paalam bus stand on the north edge of Kannur town

Extravagant costumes worn in *theyyem* and other less-known local art and ritual forms, including the Muslim dance style *oppana*, dominate the collection of the **Folklore Museum**, 5km north of Kannur town in the village of **Chirakkal**, just off NH-17. Housed in the 130-year-old palace, the engaging collection also features masks and weapons used in Patayani rituals performed in local Bhadrakali temples, and displays of *todikkalam* murals.

Kanhirode Co-operative

13km east of Kannur • Mon–Sat 9am–3.30pm • ☎ 0497 285 7865, ⓦ weaveco.com

Local guesthouse owners can point you toward **handloom weaving workshops** dotted around nearby villages – a legacy of the old calico cotton trade. One that's used to receiving visitors is the **Kanhirode Co-operative**, 13km northeast of Kannur on the main road to Mattanur, which employs around four hundred workers to make upholstery and curtain fabrics, plus material for luxury shirts and saris.

ARRIVAL AND DEPARTURE
KANNUR (CANNANORE)

Straddling the main coastal transport artery between Mangalore and Kochi/Thiruvananthapuram, Kannur is well connected by bus and train to most major towns and cities in Kerala, as well as Mangalore in Karnataka.

By train The busy town railway station, right in the centre of town, is Kannur's principal landmark, and the best place to pick up auto-rickshaws and taxis for trips further afield. Kerala Tourism have an info counter on the main concourse (Mon–Sat 7 9am–4pm; ☎ 0497 270 3121) where you can find out about homestays and forthcoming *theyyem* rituals.

Destinations Goa (22 daily; 6hr 40min–9hr); Kochi/ Ernakulam (hourly; 5hr 30min–6hr 30min); Kozhikode (every 30–60min; 1hr 20min–1hr 45min); Mangalore (hourly; 2–3hr); Mumbai (20 daily; 16–21hr).
By bus Most local services, including those from other towns in Malabar, work out of the New Bus Stand, a 5min walk

southeast of the railway station; the hub for long-distance Kerala state services is the KSRTC stand, a shot hop by auto-rickshaw north. Fleets of private buses – the most garishly painted coaches in India – also cover the same routes.

Destinations The following refers only to Kerala and Karnataka State Transport Corporation services: Kalpetta, Wayanad (2 daily; 4hr); Kochi/Ernakulam (4–6 daily; 8hr); Kozhikode/Calicut (hourly; 1hr 30min–3hr); Madurai (1 nightly; 11hr 30min–13hr); Mangalore (3 daily; 4–5hr); Mysore (5 daily; 8hr).

ACCOMMODATION

Kannur's noisy and congested centre is jammed with **hotels**, but you'll find better options further east in the cantonment district behind **Baby Beach**, and further north at **Palliyamoola Beach** (a ₹75 ride away), where a number of small resorts and homestays stand close to the sea. Southeast of town down the coast, a string of four spectacular beaches hold even more desirable places to stay.

Blue Mermaid Thottada Beach ☎ 9497 300234, ⓦ bluemermaid.in. Tiny homestay resort comprising a modern block of spacious, well-furnished a/c rooms, a detached cottage on the headland (₹3800), and romantic bamboo honeymoon lodge (₹4000) – all in a heavenly setting overlooking one of the area's loveliest beaches. Keralan meals, yoga lessons and Ayurveda on site. **₹3200**

Chera Rocks 14km south at Chera Kalle, Tayeechery ☎ 0490 234 3211 or ☎ 9446 610131, ⓦ cherarocks .com. If you're dreaming of a room where you can watch the moonlight on the waves and fall asleep to the sound of surf crashing through the coconut trees, look no further. Here is a pretty three-bedroom cottage (₹5300) huddled in a palm grove behind an idyllic beach, and less pricey "deluxe" rooms occupying a white house set back just behind it. Rates include full board and station pick-up. **₹2800**

★ **Costa Malabari** 10km south near Thottada village; book through the Tourist Desk, Main Jetty, Kochi ☎ 0484 237 1761, ⓦ costamalabari.com. Three traditional Keralan bungalows, surrounded by cashew and coconut groves on the bluff above pretty Thottada Beach. *Costa Malabari II* is the pick of the crop, perched on a cliff-top where a flight of rickety wooden steps descend to a golden sand cove. The food, served on a picturesque veranda, gets rave reviews. Pick-up from Kannur by arrangement. **₹2500**

Ezhara Beach House House 347, near Ezhara Moppila School, Ezhara Kadappuram, Kuttikkagam ☎ 0497 283 5022 or ☎ 9846 819941, ⓦ ezharabeachhouse.com. Tucked under the palms on the edge of a traditional Moppila quarter, this old, blue-painted bungalow is a great place to experience village life at close quarters. It's a stone's throw from the sand and within easy walking distance of long, empty beaches. Hyacinth and Georgio are great hosts. Rates include breakfast and dinner. **₹3000**

★ **Kannur Beach House** Thottada ☎ 9847 186330 or ☎ 9847 184535, ⓦ kannurbeachhouse.com. Sandwiched on a sliver of land between a river and the beach, this friendly little guesthouse has a sublime location and the rooms, with their antique wooden doors and windows, luminous interiors and lovely verandas, are perfect havens. Rates include meals. **₹3000**

Palmgrove Heritage Mill Rd, near Government Guesthouse, Kannur town ☎ 0497 270 3182, ⓦ palmgroveheritageretreat.com. Dating from the 1930s, this former palace once belonged to the last raja of Arikkal but now accommodates an offbeat little heritage hotel, with a choice of bargain rooms or threadbare suites in the old portion (₹1700), and large, modern, good-value doubles (₹600–800) in the two adjacent, multistorey blocks. **₹600**

Pranav Beach Rd, Palliyamoola ☎ 0497 274 1148 or ☎ 9387 478285, ⓦ pranavbeachresort.in. A well-run little resort, in a palm grove a stone's throw from the beach to the north of town, which offers a wide range of accommodation, from attractive a/c laterite cottages with pillared sitouts to smaller cabins made of palm wood. Fabulous Malabari meals are included in the price. **₹1500**

EATING

Komala Vilas Tucked down a side street opposite the railway station exit. Packed with commuters and travellers in transit, this diminutive place is the best traditional *udipi* restaurant in town, serving the usual range of south Indian *iddli-vada*, dosas and rice meals for next to nothing. Meals ₹35. Daily 7am–9pm.

DIRECTORY

Banks and exchange The State Bank of India has an ATM opposite the main exit to the railway station, and another on Fort Rd, where you'll also find a branch of Thomas Cook that changes money. Wall Street Forex, at the top of Fort Rd, are the local Western Union agents and also exchange currency and travellers' cheques.

Internet access and books Padinharakandy, 150m south of the pink City Centre Mall on Fort Rd. Inside the mall itself, DC Books is the best place in town to stock up on reading material.

THEYYEM

Theyyem (or *theyyam*) – the dramatic spirit-possession ceremonies held at village shrines throughout the northern Malabar region in the winter – rank among Kerala's most extraordinary spectacles. More than four hundred different manifestations of this arcane ritual exist in the area around Kannur alone, each with its own distinctive costumes, elaborate jewellery, body paints, face make-up and, above all, gigantic headdresses (*mudi*).

Unlike in *kathakali* and *kudiyattam*, where actors impersonate goddesses or gods, here the performers actually become the deity being invoked, acquiring their magical powers. These allow them to perform superhuman feats, such as rolling in hot ashes or dancing with a crown that rises to the height of a coconut tree. By watching the *theyyem*, members of the audience believe they can partake of the deity's powers – to cure illness, conceive a child or get lucky in a business venture.

Traditionally staged in small clearings (*kaavus*) attached to village shrines, *theyyem* rituals are always performed by members of the lowest castes; Namboodiri and other high-caste people may attend, but they do so to venerate the deity – a unique inversion of the normal social hierarchy. Performances generally have three distinct phases: the *thottam*, where the dancer, wearing a small red headdress, recites a simple devotional song accompanied by the temple musicians; the *vellattam*, in which he runs through a series of more complicated rituals and slower, elegant poses; and the *mukhathezhuttu*, the main event, when he appears in full costume in front of the shrine. From this point on until the end of the performance, which may last all night, the *theyyem* is manifest and empowered, dancing around the arena in graceful, rhythmic steps that grow quicker and more energetic as the night progresses, culminating in a frenzied outburst just before dawn, when it isn't uncommon for the dancer to be struck by a kind of spasm.

Increasing numbers of visitors are making the journey up to Kannur to experience *theyyem*, but **finding rituals** requires time, patience and stamina. The best sources of advice are local guesthouse owners, who can check the Malayalai newspapers for notices; **websites** such as ⓦtheyyemcalendar.com can also point you in the right direction. Anyone pushed for time might consider a trip out to **Parassinikadavu** (see below), where a form of *theyyem* is staged daily.

North from Kannur

The only village in Kannur district where you can be guaranteed a glimpse of *theyyem* is **Parassinikadavu**, a thirty-minute drive north of Kannur, where temple priests don elaborate costumes, dance and make offerings to the god Muthappan each morning and evening. With an early enough start, it's possible to catch the morning session and still have time to continue north to explore the little-visited **Valiyaparamba backwater** region. Local ferries crisscross this fascinating necklace of lagoons, and there's even a company running houseboat trips – though foreign tourists are few and far between.

Pressing on further north into Kasaragod district, it's worth splashing out on a night in one of the boutique retreats that have sprung up recently – the loveliest of them near the roadside town of **Nileshwaram**, at the head of the Valiyaparamba backwaters. Larger hotel complexes, pitched at wealthy holidaymakers from Bangalore, are beginning to appear further north still around **Bekal Fort**, where you can walk along some impressive ramparts overlooking kilometres of empty coast.

Parassinikadavu

The **Parassini Madammpura** temple in the village of **PARASSINIKADAVU**, 20km north of Kannur beside the River Valapatanam, is visited in large numbers by Hindu pilgrims for its *theyyem* rituals (daily 6.30–8.30am & 5.45–8.30pm). Elaborately dressed and accompanied by a traditional drum group, the resident priest, or *madayan*, becomes possessed by the temple's presiding deity – Lord Muthappan,

Shiva, in the form of a *kiratha*, or hunter – and performs a series of complex offerings. The two-hour ceremony culminates when the priest/deity dances forward to bless individual members of the congregation – an extraordinary spectacle, even by Keralan standards.

ARRIVAL AND DEPARTURE

By bus and taxi Regular local buses leave Kannur for Parassinikadavu from around 7am, dropping passengers at the top of the village. If you want to get here in time for the earliest *theyyem*, however, you'll have to fork out for one of the Ambassador taxis that line up outside Kannur bus stand (around ₹400 return). Cabbies sleep in their cars, so you can arrange the trip on the spot by waking one up; taxis may also be arranged through most hotels. Either way, you'll have to leave around 4.30am – or else spend the night nearer the temple.

ACCOMMODATION

Thai Resort 80m from the temple ☎ 0497 278 4242. Shaded by coconut trees, seven circular stone cottages are dotted around a well-kept garden with cool, comfortable rooms. They're a bit gloomy, but well aired, and the location's perfect. ₹2200

Thapasya Heritage Temple Rd ☎ 0497 2782944 or ☎ 9447065108, ⓦ thapasyaheritage.com. Situated on the hillside just south of the village, this is by far the best-value budget option within walking distance of the temple, and is very popular because of it. The building's modern, the beds have crisp linen and comfy mattresses, and the bathrooms are clean. A/c from ₹1000–1300. ₹650

Karnataka

THE PALACE OF MYSORE, BENGALURU

Karnataka

22

Created in 1956 from the princely state of Mysore, Karnataka – a derivation of the name of the local language, Kannada, spoken by virtually all of its 53 million inhabitants, known as Kannadigas – marks a transition zone between central India and the Dravidian deep south. Along its border with Maharashtra and Andhra Pradesh, a string of medieval walled towns studded with domed mausoleums and minarets recall the era when this part of the Deccan was a Muslim stronghold. The coastal and hill districts that dovetail with Kerala are quintessential Hindu south India, lush with tropical vegetation and soaring temple *gopuras*. In between are scattered several extraordinary sites, notably the ruined Vijayanagar city at Hampi, whose lost temples and derelict palaces stand amid an arid, rocky landscape of surreal beauty.

Coastal Karnataka is one of the wettest regions in India, its **climate** dominated by the seasonal monsoon, which sweeps in from the southwest in June, dumping an average of 4m of rain on the coast before it peters out in late September. Running in an unbroken line along the state's palm-fringed coast, the **Western Ghats**, draped in dense deciduous forests, impede the path of the rain clouds east. As a result, the landscape of the interior – comprising the southern apex of the triangular Deccan trap, known here as the **Mysore plateau**, is considerably drier, with dark volcanic soils in the north, and poor quartzite-granite country to the south. Two of India's most sacred rivers, the Tungabhadra and Krishna, flow across this sun-baked terrain, draining east to the Bay of Bengal.

Karnataka's principal attractions are concentrated at opposite ends of the state, with a handful of less-visited places dotted along the coast between Goa and Kerala. Road and rail routes dictate that most itineraries take in the brash state capital, **Bengaluru**, a go-ahead, modern city that epitomizes the aspirations of the country's new middle classes, with glittering malls, fast-food outlets and a nightlife unrivalled outside Mumbai. The state's second city, **Mysore**, appeals more for its Raj-era ambience, nineteenth-century palaces and vibrant produce and incense markets. It also lies within easy reach of several important historical monuments.

A clutch of unmissable sights lie further northwest, dotted around the dull railway town of **Hassan**. Around nine centuries ago, the Hoysala kings sited their grand dynastic capitals here, at the now middle-of-nowhere villages of **Belur** and **Halebid**, where several superbly crafted temples survive intact. More impressive still, and one of India's most extraordinary sacred sites, is the 18m Jain colossus at **Sravanabelagola**, which stares serenely over idyllic Deccan countryside.

West of Mysore, the Ghats rise in a wall of thick jungle cut by deep ravines and isolated valleys. Within, the coffee- and spice-growing region of **Kodagu (Coorg)** offers an entrancing, unique culture and lush, misty vistas. Most Coorgi agricultural produce is shipped out of **Mangalore**, a useful if uninspiring place to pause on the journey along

KUDLEE BEACH, GOKARNA

Highlights

❶ Bengaluru Booming silicon city offers the best shopping, nightlife and dining this side of Mumbai, not to mention a few great parks, plus the odd palace and temple. **See p.1092**

❷ Mysore The sandalwood city oozes relaxed, old-world charm and has lots to see, including the opulent Maharaja's Palace and a photogenic market. **See p.1102**

❸ Halebid and Belur Two wonderfully ornate and architecturally unique Hoysala temples set deep in the slow-paced Karnataka countryside. **See p.1112 & p.1113**

❹ Gokarna This vibrant Hindu holy town is blessed with atmospheric temples and exquisite crescent beaches and is ideal for serious unwinding. **See p.1125**

❺ Hampi The crumbling remains of the Vijayanagar kingdom, scattered among a stunning boulder-strewn landscape bisected by the Tungabhadra River. **See p.1131**

❻ Bijapur Known as the "Agra of the South" for its splendid Islamic architecture, most famously the vast dome of the Golgumbaz. **See p.1142**

❼ Bidar Rarely visited Muslim outpost in the remote northeast of the state, famed for *bidri* metalwork and magnificent medieval monuments. **See p.1147**

HIGHLIGHTS ARE MARKED ON THE MAP ON P.1091

Karnataka's beautiful **Karavali coast**. Interrupted by countless mangrove-lined estuaries, the state's 320km-long, reddish-coloured coastline contains plenty of fine beaches, mostly devoid of facilities. Few Western tourists visit the famous Krishna temple at **Udupi**, an important Vaishnavite pilgrimage centre, and fewer still venture into the mountains to see India's highest waterfall at **Jog Falls**, set amid some of the region's most spectacular scenery. However, the atmospheric Hindu pilgrimage town of **Gokarna**, further north up the coast, is a well-established hideaway for budget travellers, owing to its string of exquisite beaches.

Winding inland from the mountainous Goan border, NH-4A and the rail line comprise sparsely populated **northern Karnataka**'s main transport artery and lean towards this region's undisputed highlight, the ghost city of Vijayanagar, better known as **Hampi**. Scattered around boulder hills on the south banks of the Tungabhadra River, the ruins of this once splendid capital occupy a magical site and make a great spot to hole up in. The jumping-off place for Hampi is **Hospet**, from where buses leave for the bumpy journey north across the rolling Deccani plains to **Badami**, **Aihole** and UNESCO World Heritage Site **Pattadakal**. Now lost in countryside, these tiny villages – once capitals of the **Chalukya** dynasty – are still littered with ancient rock-cut caves and finely carved stone temples.

Further north still, in one of Karnataka's most remote and poorest districts, craggy hilltop citadels and crumbling wayside tombs herald the formerly troubled buffer zone between the Muslim-dominated northern Deccan and the Dravidian-Hindu south. **Bijapur**, capital of the Bahmanis, harbours south India's finest collection of Islamic architecture, including the world's second largest freestanding dome, the Golgumbaz. The first Bahmani capital, **Gulbarga**, site of a famous Muslim shrine and theological college, has retained little of its former splendour but the more isolated **Bidar**, where the Bahmanis moved in the sixteenth century, deserves a detour en route to or from Hyderabad. Perched on a rocky escarpment, its crumbling red ramparts include Persian-style mosaic-fronted mosques, mausoleums and a sprawling fort complex evocative of Samarkand on the Silk Route.

Brief history

Like much of southern India, Karnataka has been ruled by successive Buddhist, Hindu and Muslim dynasties. The influence of Jainism has also been marked; India's very first emperor, **Chandragupta Maurya**, is believed to have converted to Jainism in the fourth century BC, renounced his throne and fasted to death at Sravanabelagola, now one of the most visited Jain pilgrimage centres in the country.

During the first millennium AD, this whole region was dominated by power struggles between the various kingdoms controlling the western Deccan. From the sixth to the eighth centuries, the **Chalukya** kingdom included Maharashtra, the Konkan coast on the west and the whole of Karnataka. The **Cholas** were powerful in the east of the region from about 870 until the thirteenth century, when the Deccan kingdoms were overwhelmed by General Malik Kafur, a convert to Islam.

By the medieval era Muslim incursions from the north had forced the hitherto warring and fractured Hindu states of the south into close alliance, with the mighty **Vijayanagars** emerging as overlords. Their lavish capital, Vijayanagar, ruled an empire stretching from the Bay of Bengal to the Arabian Sea and south to Cape Comorin. Yet the Muslims' superior military strength triumphed in 1565 at the Battle of Talikota, when the **Bahmanis** laid siege to Vijayanagar, reducing it to rubble and plundering its opulent palaces and temples.

Thereafter, a succession of Muslim sultans held sway over the north, while in the south of the state, the independent **Wadiyar rajas** of Mysore, whose territory was comparatively small, successfully fought off the Marathas. In 1761, the brilliant Muslim campaigner Haider Ali, with French support, seized the throne. His son, Tipu Sultan, turned Mysore into a major force in the south before he was killed by the

British at the **battle of Srirangapatnam** in 1799. After Tipu's defeat, the British restored the Wadiyar family to the throne. Apart from a further half century of colonial rule in the mid-nineteenth century, they kept it until Karnataka was created by the merging of the states of Mysore and the Madras Presidencies in 1956.

Following Independence, the political scene was dominated by the **Congress** party, with the exception of some Janata Dal administrations in the 1980s, until, following an unstable period of president's rule, the **BJP** took control in May 2008. However, ructions within the party and the resignation of the chief minister in 2011 guaranteed a testing time at the autumn 2013 elections.

22

Bengaluru (Bangalore) and around

The political hub of the region, **BENGALURU** is a world apart from the rest of the state and in many ways India's most Westernized urban centre. From a charming, verdant "Garden City" of just over 600,0000 people at Independence, Bengaluru has been completely transformed by the technology boom into both a trendy, high-speed business hub and a bustling, smog-choked megalopolis of more than eight million. These days, signs of the West are thick on the ground: *Starbucks*-like *Café Coffee Day*s on nearly every corner, a flash new airport and ultra-modern metro (still far from completion) and legions of hard-working, free-spending twenty- and thirty-somethings in designer T-shirts and mini-skirts.

Bengaluru's few attractions are no match for those elsewhere in the state, and the city's comparative local advantages are ten-a-penny in the West. That said, it's an efficient transport hub, well served by plane and bus, and at nearly 1000m climate. Paired with first-rate shopping, dining and nightlife, this vibrant city can still deliver a few days' respite from south India's more taxing inconveniences.

The centre of modern Bengaluru lies about 4km east of Kempe Gowda Circle (and the bus and railway stations), near **MG Road**, where you'll find most of the mid-range accommodation, restaurants, shops, tourist information and banks. Leafy **Cubbon Park**, and its less than exciting museums, lie on its eastern edge, while the oldest, most "Indian" part of the city extends south from the railway station, a warren of winding streets at their most dynamic in the hubbub of the **City** and **Gandhi markets**.

Bengaluru's tourist attractions are spread out: monuments such as **Tipu's Summer Palace** and the **Bull Temple** are some way south of the centre. Most, if not all, can be seen on a

---

BENGALURU BACKLASH?

In recent decades Bengaluru has experienced a **seismic societal shift**, predominantly due to the endless job opportunities presented by computer software and back-office services. The population grew by nearly forty percent to 5.7 million in the decade ending in 2001, and is now approaching eight and a half million. By late 2007 every fifth city resident hailed from a different state and Bengaluru's **software industry** had become a US$8 billion behemoth.

Many locals blame IT professionals for skyrocketing living costs, choking **pollution** and the rise of a liberal, West-leaning bar and disco culture, not to mention **traffic jams**, regular power failures and crippling seasonal **water shortages**. In addition, due to higher salaries and bright futures, IT professionals are favoured in the competitive marriage market, creating further tension.

Yet hope springs eternal. After more than two decades of hand-wringing and debate, the first section of a much-needed subway system – known locally as the metrorail – has opened and started to alleviate the city's infamous traffic jams. The **international airport**, opened in 2008, facilitates the smooth passage of tourists and business visitors alike. Longtime residents may never regain their urban idyll, but with compromise and elbow grease Bengaluru may yet inspire civic pride.

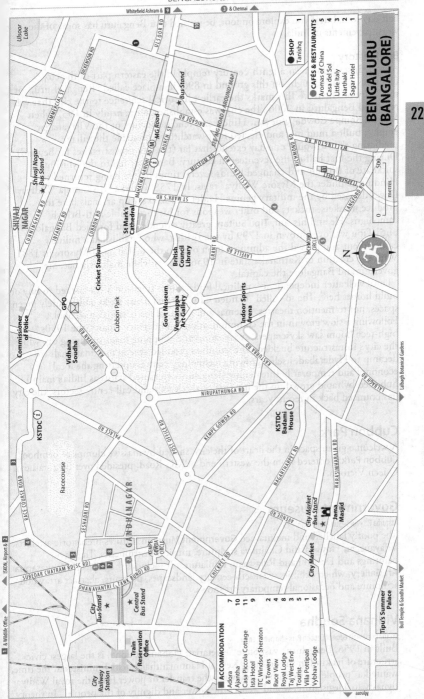

BENGALURU (BANGALORE)

22

0 | 500
metres

● SHOP

Tanishq	1

● CAFÉS & RESTAURANTS

Aromas of China	5
Casa del Sol	4
Little Italy	3
Narthaki	2
Sagar Hotel	1

■ ACCOMMODATION

Adora	7
Ajantha	10
Casa Piccola Cottage	11
Ista Hotel	9
ITC Windsor Sheraton & Towers	2
Race View	4
Royal Lodge	8
Taj West End	3
Tourist	1
Villa Pottipati	5
Vybhav Lodge	6

half-day tour, but if you explore on foot, be warned that Bengaluru has some of the worst pavements in India.

Brief history

A stone inscription near a tenth-century temple in the eastern part of the city describes a battle fought on this ground in 890, in a place called "Bengaval-uru," or the "City of Guards." This marks the earliest historical reference to the city that was **renamed** Bengaluru in 2006. The city was established more firmly in 1537 when Magadi **Kempe Gowda**, a devout Hindu and feudatory chief of the Vijayanagar empire, built a mud fort and erected four watchtowers outside the village, predicting that it would one day extend that far (the city now stretches far beyond). During the first half of the seventeenth century, Bangalore fell to the Muslim sultanate of Bijapur and changed hands several times before being returned to Hindu rule under the Mysore Wadiyar rajas. In 1758, Chikka Krishnaraja Wadiyar II was deposed by the military genius Haider Ali, who set up arsenals here to produce muskets, rockets and other weapons for his formidable anti-British campaigns. He and his son, **Tipu Sultan**, greatly extended and fortified Bangalore until Tipu was overthrown in 1799 by the British, who established a military cantonment and passed the administration over to the maharaja of Mysore in 1881. With the creation of Karnataka state in 1956, the erstwhile maharaja became governor and Bangalore the capital.

Until well after Independence, political leaders, film stars and VIPs flocked to buy or build homes here. The so-called "Garden City" offered many parks and leisurely green spaces, not to mention theatres, cinemas and a lack of restrictions on alcohol. Following a slow growth in the communications and defence sectors, the 1990s high-tech boom saw skyscrapers, swish stores and shopping malls springing up, while the city's infrastructure buckled. The stumbles prodded several multinationals to decamp to Hyderabad, itself a growing technology centre, upsetting the local economy and temporarily threatening Bengaluru's treasured status as India's main IT hub. Led by rapid growth in the international telecom and call-centre sectors, the city has bounced back in recent years.

Cubbon Park

A welcome green space in the heart of the city, shaded by massive clumps of bamboo, **Cubbon Park** is entered from the western end of MG Road, presided over by a statue of Queen Victoria.

Government Museum

Kasturba Rd • Tues–Sun 10am–5pm • ₹5

The poorly labelled and maintained **Government Museum** features prehistoric artefacts, Vijayanagar, Hoysala and Chalukya sculpture, musical instruments, Thanjavur paintings and Deccani and Rajasthani miniatures. It includes the adjacent **Venkatappa Art Gallery**, which exhibits twentieth-century landscapes, portraits, abstract art, wood sculpture and occasional temporary art shows.

Vidhana Soudha

On the northwest edge of Cubbon Park • No public entry

Built in 1956, Bengaluru's vast State Secretariat, **Vidhana Soudha**, is the largest civic structure of its kind in the country. Kengal Hanumanthaiah, chief minister at the time, wanted a "people's palace" that, following the transfer of power from the royal Wadiyar dynasty to a legislature, would "reflect the power and dignity of the people". In theory

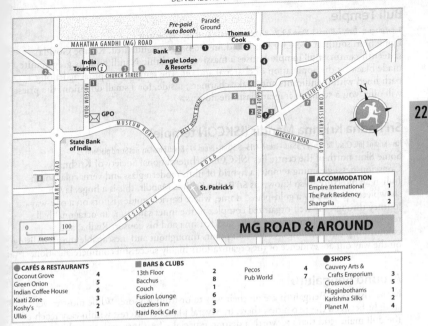

MG ROAD & AROUND

■ ACCOMMODATION
Empire International	1
The Park Residency	3
Shangrila	2

● CAFÉS & RESTAURANTS			■ BARS & CLUBS					● SHOPS	
Coconut Grove	4		13th Floor	2	Pecos	4		Cauvery Arts &	
Green Onion	5		Bacchus	8	Pub World	7		Crafts Emporium	3
Indian Coffee House	6		Couch	1				Crossword	5
Kaati Zone	3		Fusion Lounge	6				Higginbothams	1
Koshy's	2		Guzzlers Inn	5				Karishma Silks	2
Ullas	1		Hard Rock Cafe	3				Planet M	4

its design is entirely Indian, but its overall effect is not unlike the bombastic colonial architecture built in the so-called Indo-Saracenic style.

Lalbagh Botanical Gardens

Daily 6am–7pm • ₹10 • Buses #298M, #348E & #348F from City Bus Stand

Inspired by the splendid gardens of the Mughals and the French botanical gardens at Puducherry in Tamil Nadu (see p.977), Sultan Haider Ali set to work in 1760 laying out the **Lalbagh Botanical Gardens**, 4km south of the centre. Originally covering forty acres, just beyond his fort – where one of Kempe Gowda's original watchtowers can still be seen – the gardens were expanded under Ali's son Tipu, who introduced numerous exotic species of plants, and today they house an extensive horticultural seedling centre. The British brought in gardeners from Kew in 1856 and built a military bandstand and a glasshouse, based on London's Crystal Palace, which hosts wonderful flower shows. Now spreading over 240 acres, the gardens are pleasant to visit during the day, but tend to attract unsavoury characters after around 6pm. Great sunsets and city views can be had from the central hill, which is topped by a small shrine.

Tipu's Summer Palace and around

(daily 9am–5pm; ₹100 (₹5))

Just southeast of the City Market near the fairytale-like **Jama Masjid** – whitewashed and rambling and still in regular use – lies **Tipu's Summer Palace**, a two-storey, mostly wooden structure built in 1791. Similar in style to the Daria Daulat Palace at Srirangapatnam (see p.1108), the palace is in a far worse state, with most of its painted decoration destroyed. Next door, the **Venkataramanaswamy Temple**, dating from the early eighteenth century, was built by the Wadiyar rajas. The *gopura* entranceway was erected in 1978.

Bull Temple

Basavanagudi • Daily 7.30am–1.30pm & 2.30–8.30pm • Buses #34 & #37 from City Bus Stand

Lying 6km south of the City Bus Stand, in the Basavanagudi area, Kempe Gowda's sixteenth-century **Bull Temple** houses a massive monolithic Nandi bull, its grey granite made black by the application of charcoal and oil. The temple is approached along a path lined with mendicants and snake charmers; inside, for a small donation, the priest will offer you a string of fragrant jasmine flowers.

22

Sri Radha Krishna Mandir (ISKCON temple)

Hare Krishna Hill, Chord Rd • Daily 7.15am–1pm & 4.15–8.30pm • Buses #78 & #80 from City Bus Stand platform 23

Some 8km north of the centre lies ISKCON's (International Society of Krishna Consciousness) gleaming temple, a hybrid of ultra-modern glass and vernacular south Indian architecture. Also known as **Sri Radha Krishna Mandir**, this is a huge, lavish showpiece crowned by a gold-plated dome, where barriers guide visitors on a one-way journey through the well-organized complex to the inner sanctum, an octagonal hall resplendent with golden images of the god Krishna and his consort Radha, and colourfully painted ceilings. Collection points throughout and inescapable merchandising on the way out are evidence of the organization's highly successful commercialization.

Around Bengaluru

Many visitors to Bengaluru are on their way to or from Mysore. While most travel straight between the two cities, there are several places of interest within easy reach of the dull main road that are worth a detour, especially for those with special interest in folk culture, dance or spiritual renewal.

Janapada Loka Folk Arts Museum

On the Mysore road • Daily 9am–5.30pm • Museum ₹100 (₹20); video show ₹10; boating ₹20 • ⓦ janapadaloka.org • Any Bengaluru–Mysore bus, except nonstop express services, can drop you here

The **Janapada Loka Folk Arts Museum**, 53km southwest of Bengaluru, gives a fascinating insight into the region's culture. The collection is impressive: there's an amazing array of Karnatakan hunting implements, weapons, ingenious household gadgets, masks, dolls and shadow puppets, plus carved wooden *bhuta* (spirit) sculptures and larger-than-life temple procession figures, manuscripts, musical instruments and *yakshagana* theatre costumes. A small **restaurant** serves simple food.

Nrityagram Dance Village

Hasaragatta • Tues–Sat 10am–2pm • Village entrance fee ₹20; guided tours with lunch and demonstration ₹1250/person (minimum ten) • ☏ 080 2846 6313, ⓦ nrityagram.org

Anyone wishing to see or study classical dance in a rural environment should check out **Nrityagram Dance Village**, a delightful, purpose-built model village 30km west of Bengaluru, designed by the award-winning architect Gerard de Cunha and founded by the late Protima Gauri. Gauri had a colourful career in media and film, and eventually came to be renowned as an exponent of Odissi dance (see p.899). The school continues without her and attracts pupils from all over the world. It hosts regular performances and lectures on Indian mythology and art, and also offers courses in different forms of Indian dance.

ARRIVAL AND DEPARTURE	BENGALURU (BANGALORE)
BY PLANE	much-discussed express rail is up and running, you can get
Airport The new Bengaluru International Airport (ⓦ bengaluruairport.com) is 35km northeast of the city in Devanahalli. It's the busiest in south India and the most spacious in the country, with top-notch facilities. Until the	into the city by the dedicated Airport Taxi (₹650–700; ☏ 080 4422 4422) or an efficient a/c Vayu Vajra bus; the most useful routes to visitors are the round-the-clock #9 from Central Bus Stand (every 20–50min; 45min–1hr 15min; ₹180) and #7A

from MG Rd (11 daily; 50min–1hr 20min; ₹180).

Airlines Air India (☎080 2227 7747); Go Air (☎1 800 222111); Indigo (☎080 6678 5450); Jet Airways (☎080 3989 3333); Kingfisher (☎080 4197 9797); SpiceJet (☎1 800 180 3333).

Destinations Chennai (18–19 daily; 50min); Delhi (23–26 daily; 2hr 30min–3hr 30min); Goa (2–4 daily; 1hr); Hyderabad (10–12 daily; 1hr–1hr 30min); Kochi (5–6 daily; 1hr–1hr 20min); Mumbai (16–20 daily; 1hr 30min–1hr 45min); Thiruvananthapuram (6 daily; 1hr 45min).

BY TRAIN

Stations Bengaluru is well connected by train to all parts of India. Bangalore City railway station is west of the centre, near Kempe Gowda Circle, opposite the main bus stands; for the north of the city, it's better to board or disembark at Bangalore Cantonment Station north of the centre. Trains to Goa and a handful of trains to other destinations leave from Yeshwanthpur railway station (☎080 2337 7161) in the north of the city. Bangalore City has pre-paid auto-rickshaw and taxi booths in the forecourt and the computerized reservation office (Mon–Sat 8am–2pm & 2.15–8pm, Sun 8am–2pm; ☎132) is in a separate building, to the left as you approach the station; counter 14 is for foreigners.

Destinations The most useful services from Bangalore City include: *Shatabdi Express* #12008 (daily except Wed 4.15pm; 5hr 10min) to Chennai; *Karnataka Express* #12627 (daily 7.20pm; 39hr 20min) to Delhi; *Hampi Express* #16592 (daily 10pm; 9hr 45min) to Hospet; *Udyan Express* #16530 (daily 8.10pm; 23hr 40min) to Mumbai; *Shatabdi Express*

#12007 (daily except Wed 11am; 2hr) or *Tippu Express* #12614 (daily 3pm; 2hr 30min) to Mysore; *Kacheguda Express* #12786 (daily 6.20pm; 11hr 20min) to Hyderabad (Kacheguda station) and *Kanniyakumari Express* #12429 (daily 9.40pm) to Thiruvananthapuram (18hr) via Ernakulam (for Kochi; 12hr 20min).

BY BUS

Long-distance government buses, including those from other states, arrive at the busy Central (KSRTC) Bus Stand, opposite the railway station. There is a comprehensive timetable in English in the centre of the concourse. Most services can be booked in advance at the computerized counters near Bay 13 (daily 7.30am–7.30pm). For general enquiries, call ☎080 2287 3377. Tickets for the numerous private bus companies can be bought from the agencies on Tank Bund Rd, on the opposite side of the bus stand from the train station; operators include Sharma (☎080 2670 2447) and National (☎080 2660 3112), which advertise a multitude of destinations, including sleeper coaches to Goa and Mumbai. The most reliable of the private bus companies is Vijayanand Travels (☎080 2297 1257), whose distinctive yellow-and-black luxury coaches depart from their depot nearby.

Destinations Chennai (hourly; 8hr); Hassan (every 15–30min; 4hr); Hospet (2 daily; 10hr); Hyderabad (6 daily; 15–16hr); Madikeri (hourly; 6hr); Mangalore (every 30min–1hr; 9–10hr); Mumbai (2–4 daily; 23–24hr); Mysore (every 10–15min; 3hr); Ootacamund (6 daily; 7hr 30min–8hr); Puttaparthy (every 30min–1hr; 4hr); Tirupati (hourly; 7hr).

22

GETTING AROUND

By bus Bengaluru's extensive bus system radiates from the City Bus Stand (☎080 222 2542), near the railway station. Most buses from platform 17 travel past MG Rd. Along with regular buses, BMTC also operates a deluxe express service, Pushpak, on a number of set routes (#P109 terminates at Whitefield ashram) as well as a handful of night buses. Other important city bus stands include the City Market Bus Stand (☎080 670 2177) to the south of the railway station and Shivaji Nagar (☎080 286 5332) to the northeast of Cubbon Park.

By metro Bengaluru's long-awaited Namma Metro (ⓦbmrc.co.in) finally opened to much fanfare in 2012, although only the six stations on the raised section of the Purple Line from MG Rd eastwards to Byappanahalli were in operation at the time of writing. Trains run every 15min from 6–8am until 8–10pm and tickets cost ₹10–15.

By auto-rickshaw The easiest way of getting around is

by metered auto-rickshaw; fares start at ₹20 for the first kilometre and ₹8/km thereafter. Most meters do work and drivers are usually willing to use them, although you will occasionally be asked for a flat fare, especially during rush hour. Expect to pay ₹60–70 from the City Bus Stand to MG Rd.

By car and taxi You can book chauffeur-driven cars and taxis through several agencies including the Cab Service, Sabari Complex, 24 Residency Rd (☎080 2558 6121), and the 24hr Dial-a-Car service (☎080 2526 1737, ⓔdialacar @hotmail.com).

Car rental Avis, the *Oberoi* hotel, 37–39 MG Rd (☎080 2558 5858), ⓦavis.com; and Hertz, Unit 12 Raheja Plaza, 17 Commissariat Rd (☎080 2559 9408, ⓦhertz.com) both have airport outlets. For long-distance car rental and tailor-made itineraries, try one of the travel agents listed in the Directory (see p.1100) or any KSTDC office (see p.1098).

INFORMATION

Tourist information For information on Bengaluru, Karnataka and neighbouring states, go to the excellent India Tourism Office (Mon–Fri 9.30am–6pm, Sat 9am–1pm;

☎080 2558 5417, ⓦincredibleindia.org), in Triumph Tower, 48 Church St, where you can pick up free maps for both city and state. Apart from booths at the City railway station (daily

7am–8pm; ☎ 080 2287 0068) and at the airport, Karnataka State Tourist Development Corporation also has two city offices: there's one at Badami House, NR Square (daily 6.30am–10pm; ☎ 080 2227 5883, ✆ karnatakatourism.org), where you can book tours; another, the head office, is on the second floor of Khanija Bhavan, Race Course Rd (Mon–Sat 10am–5.30pm, closed second Sat of month; ☎ 080 2235 2901, ✆ karnatakatourism.org).

For information about what's on, pick up the twice-monthly listings magazine *Travel & Shop* (✆ travelandshop.in), available at most hotels and tourist offices, or the online guide *Time Out Bengaluru* (✆ timeoutbengaluru.net).

National parks information For information on any of Karnataka's national parks, call at the Wildlife Office, Forest Department, Aranya Bhavan, Malleswaram (☎ 080 2334 1993), or try Jungle Lodges & Resorts, Floor 2, Shrungar Shopping Centre, off MG Rd (☎ 080 2559 7021, ✆ junglelodges.com). The latter, a quasi-government body, promotes eco-tourism through a number of upmarket forest lodges, including the much-lauded *Kabini River Lodge* (see p.1110) near Nagarhole.

ACCOMMODATION

Due to the great number of business visitors it receives, Bengaluru offers a wealth of upmarket lodgings, as well as serviced apartments. Decent **budget accommodation** is also available, mostly concentrated around the Central Bus Stand and railway station.

AROUND THE RAILWAY STATION AND CENTRAL BUS STAND

Adora 47 SC Rd ☎ 080 2287 2280; map, p.1093. Above a quality south Indian veg restaurant, this is a top budget place and a popular backpacker choice. Though bland, the rooms are clean and sizeable, and some have a/c. ₹750

Royal Lodge 252 SC Rd ☎ 080 2226 6951, ✆ royallodge .in; map, p.1093. A large, functional budget hotel, which has been upgraded in recent years without much of a price hike. All rooms are attached, except a few poky singles, and each has a TV. ₹650

Tourist Ananda Rao Circle ☎ 080 2226 2381; map, p.1093. One of Bengaluru's best all-round budget lodges, with four floors wrapped round a courtyard and a veg restaurant. Small rooms, long verandas, friendly family management and no reservations, so it fills up fast. ₹350

Vybhav Lodge 60 SC Rd ☎ 080 2287 3997; map, p.1093. A tad grubby and frayed at the edges but not a bad fall-back. All the rooms are extremely compact and the cell-like attached singles with TV are very inexpensive. ₹400

AROUND THE RACECOURSE AND CUBBON PARK

ITC Windsor Sheraton & Towers 25 Golf Course Rd ☎ 080 2226 9898, ✆ sheraton.com; map, p.1093. Ersatz palace, now a luxurious five-star, mainly for overseas businesspeople with rates to match. Facilities include broadband, gym, pool, jacuzzi, a fine restaurant and popular Irish pub. ₹8500

Race View 25 Race Course Rd ☎ 080 4069 6111; map, p.1093. Large business hotel with sizeable wood-panelled rooms. Those at the front do overlook the racecourse but also the busy road. The a/c rooms cost just a little more. ₹850

Taj West End Race Course Rd ☎ 080 2225 5055, ✆ tajhotels.com; map, p.1093. Begun as a British-run boarding house in 1887, these lodgings were upgraded with fabulous gardens and long colonnaded walkways. The old wing is bursting with character, with broad verandas overlooking acres of grounds. Good online deals. ₹12,500

Villa Pottipati 142 4th Main, 8th Cross, Malleswaram ☎ 080 2336 0777, ✆ neemranahotels.com; map, p.1093. A heritage hotel in the northwestern suburbs, wrapped in a garden of jacaranda trees and flowering shrubs. Its rooms ooze old-world style, with pillared verandas, deep bathtubs and direct access to an outdoor swimming pool. Gourmet meals, prepared by a French chef, are also served. ₹3000

MG ROAD AND AROUND

⭐ **Ajantha** 22-A MG Rd ☎ 080 2558 4321, ✆ hotelajantha.in; map, p.1093. Best value in this area, with basic but larger than average attached rooms and some spacious, three-room cottages, located at the end of a quiet lane but near all the action. Veg restaurant, internet, bakery, travel agent and grocery all on site. ₹1350

⭐ **Casa Piccola Cottage** 2 Clapham St ☎ 080 2227 0754, ✆ casacottage.com; map, p.1093. Tranquillity awaits at these cottages, set in well-maintained grounds just over 1km south of MG Rd. The cottages and apartments are enormous, comfortable and well appointed, and the free breakfasts are excellent; wi-fi is also available. ₹3500

Empire International 36 Church St ☎ 080 2559 3743, ✆ hotelempire.in; map, p.1095. Smart new hotel with popular restaurant and very comfortable rooms boasting modern decor and good facilities. The slightly cheaper sister concern *Hotel Empire*, similar but without the finer touches, is a few blocks north of MG Rd, and charges ₹1050 for a double. ₹1850

Ista Hotel 1/1 Sami Vivekananda Rd ☎ 080 2555 8888, ✆ istahotels.com; map, p.1093. This gorgeous new ultra-luxurious hotel, with breezy, safari-themed bar, infinity pool, jacuzzi and gym, is a secluded sanctuary. Some of the spacious rooms have marble baths and views of Ulsoor Lake; suites have large garden balconies. Online deals available. ₹7000

22

Park Residency Pinto Towers, 36 Residency Rd ☎080 2558 2151, ⓦparkresidency.net; map, p.1095. This concrete behemoth offers good value, considering the central location, with clean, sizeable rooms, all with fridge, TV and some a/c. Filling Indian or Continental breakfast included. ₹2000

Shangrila 182 Brigade Rd ☎080 4112 1622, ⓔshangrila_htl@yahoo.co.in; map, p.1095. A welcoming Tibetan-run lodge that's right in the thick of things; the comfy standard rooms are decent value and the a/c ones are a great deal. Good Tibetan/Chinese restaurant, too. ₹900

EATING

With unmissable sights thin on the ground but tempting cafés and restaurants on every corner, you could easily spend most of your time in Bengaluru **eating**. Nowhere else in south India will you find such gastronomic variety. Around **MG Rd**, pizzerias, burger chains, ritzy ice cream parlours and gourmet French restaurants stand cheek by jowl with regional cuisine from Andhra Pradesh and Kerala, Mumbai *chaat* cafés and snack bars.

Aromas of China G3–4 Shiva Shankar Plaza, 19 Lalbagh Rd, Richmond Circle ☎080 4111 3355; map, p.1093. Among the city's top Chinese restaurants, delicacies offering such as dim sum and duck, as well as above-average versions of all the favourites. Mains ₹200–400. Daily noon–3.30pm & 7–11.30pm.

★ **Casa del Sol** 3rd floor, Devatha Plaza, 131 Residency Rd ☎080 4151 0101; map, p.1093. The ₹250 lunch buffet is worth every paise and the Sunday brunches are festive, all-you-can-drink affairs. An evening cocktail on the cool, comfortable terrace is a real treat. Daily 11am–11pm.

Coconut Grove Church St ☎080 2559 6262; map, p.1095. Mouth-watering and moderately priced gourmet Keralan, Chettinad and Coorg cuisine. Veg, fish and meat preparations are served in traditional copper thalis on a leafy terrace, and there's a wide range of seafood dishes. Main dishes ₹300–450. Its *Coco Grove* cocktail bar is a good spot for a drink. Daily 12.30–3.30pm & 7–11.30pm.

Green Onion Residency Rd Cross ☎080 2532 7146; map, p.1095. No-nonsense first-floor Chinese canteen serving all the usual favourites, a few Thai dishes and Tibetan veg *momos*. Mains ₹80–135. Daily noon–10.30pm.

Indian Coffee House Church St ☎080 2558 7088; map, p.1095. Now occupying incongruous modern premises but still old-fashioned at heart, with turbaned waiters serving tasty finger foods (₹30–80) and fine filtered coffee. The perfectly fluffy scrambled eggs are superb. Daily 8.30am–8.30pm.

Kaati Zone Church St ☎080 6566 0000; map, p.1095. Fast, clean and cheap, with *kaati* rolls (₹40–60) almost as

good as those you get in Kolkata (Calcutta). Try the Turkish kebab Varieties. Daily 11am–11pm.

★ **Koshy's** St Mark's Rd ☎080 2221 3793; map, p.1095. Spacious colonial-style café with cane blinds, pewter teapots and cotton-clad waiters. It serves tasty Indian specialities and international favourites like fish and chips for ₹100–200. Its adjacent sister establishment, *Jewel Box*, is much more upmarket. Daily 9am–11pm.

★ **Little Italy** 1135 100 Feet Rd, Indiranagar ☎080 2520 7171; map, p.1093. Whether dining on the bamboo-bordered terrace or in the elegant dining room, you'll get fantastic Italian food here, particularly the risottos and tomato-based pasta dishes for ₹300–400. There's also an extensive wine list. Daily noon–3pm & 7–11pm.

Narthaki Just off SC Rd ☎080 2287 3636; map, p.1093. The best restaurant in the railway station and bus stand area. Filling veg meals are served on the first floor, while on the second there is a restaurant-bar with a full menu of Indian and Chinese dishes. The chicken chilli is a belter. Mains ₹120–180. Daily 11.30am–11.30pm.

Sagar Hotel 48 SC Rd ☎080 2291 4197; map, p.1093. First-floor Andhra-style family restaurant serving filling biriyanis for little more than ₹100, as well as dishes from other parts of India. There's an a/c bar upstairs. Daily 11.30am–4pm & 6.30–11pm.

Ullas Above cinema, MG Rd ☎080 2558 7486; map, p.1095. Superb pure-veg restaurant, with a terrace and indoor section. Excellent lunchtime thalis (₹50–100) and a good choice of curries, plus Bombay *chaat*. Daily 9am–10pm.

DRINKING AND NIGHTLIFE

Bengaluru's hordes of bright young things have money to burn and a thriving **nightlife** in which to do it. A night on the town generally kicks off with a bar crawl along **Brigade Rd**, **Residency Rd** or **Church St**, where there are scores of swish **pubs**. Drinking alcohol does not have the seedy connotations it does elsewhere in India; you'll even see young Indian women enjoying a beer with their mates. Note that most clubs operate a couples-only policy. For a quiet, more elegant tipple head for the bars of the five-star **hotels**.

★ **13th Floor** 13th Floor, Ivory Tower, 84 MG Rd ☎080 4178 3355; map, p.1095. Lean over the outward facing bar, cool cocktail in hand, and enjoy the hubbub of

the city from a bird's-eye view. Classy and cosmopolitan, with stunning city and sunset views and cool postmodern decor, *13th Floor* is an absolute must, but come early because it fills up fast. Daily 7–11.30pm.

Bacchus 8 Papanna St, off St Mark's Rd ☎ 080 4033 3888; map, p.1095. The bar in this startlingly designed establishment features four distinct spaces with cantilevered platforms, and hosts theme nights including gigs, comedy, drinking games and wine tastings. ₹750 entry on Wed, Fri & Sat. Daily noon–11pm.

★ **Couch** 1st Floor, SAI Complex, MG Rd, near corner of Museum Rd ☎ 080 4151 2838; map, p.1095. Cool and cavernous two-level lounge with stone floors and stylishly mismatched retro furnishings. Grab a booth near the front windows and enjoy a well-made cocktail or two as life zooms by below. Also offers a full international menu. Daily 11am–11pm.

Fusion Lounge 185 Deena Complex, Brigade Rd ☎ 080 4114 2912; map, p.1095. Dazzling hi-tech lounge-cum-nightclub with different spaces for pricey but excellent food, DJ nights, karaoke and live performances. Daily 7–11.30pm.

Guzzlers Inn 48 Rest House Rd, off Brigade Rd ☎ 080 4112 2513; map, p.1095. A decent Indian stab at an English pub offering MTV, Star Sport, snooker, pool and good draught beer. Half-price afternoon happy hour. Daily 11am–11.30pm.

★ **Hard Rock Café** 40 St Mark's Rd, at Church ☎ 080 4124 2222; map, p.1095. This gorgeous, multiroom space inside an old stone library is well established as the buzzing nexus of Bengaluru nightlife, not to mention the finest bar and grill in town. With high, vaulted ceilings, grey stone walls and subtle accents, it feels both lived in and new. Daily noon–11pm.

Pecos 34 Rest House Rd, off Brigade Rd ☎ 080 2558 6047; map, p.1095. Three dank levels of rock posters and ageing wood make up the definitive Bengaluru dive. The tunes are hard-driving, the beer's cheap and the Indian grub ain't half bad. Daily 10.30am–11pm.

Pub World 65 Laxmi Plaza, Residency Rd ☎ 080 2558 5206; map, p.1095. The city's second oldest pub, this stylish place has lots of TVs and semi-private booths with crimson couches, popular with trendy young professionals. Daily 11am–11pm.

SHOPPING

The bustling area around **MG Rd** is the hub of Bengaluru shopping, with lots of new malls along its main section selling designer goods a little cheaper than in the West, as well as quality Indian clothing and accessories. **Dickenson Rd** //'to the is particularly strong on good jewellery, and there are many fine individual stores around, too, but you won't find the array of travellers' garb and trinkets so evident in places like Hampi or Gokarna. The free *Travel & Shop* magazine has a huge list of establishments.

Cauvery Arts & Crafts Emporium 49 MG Rd ☎ 080 2558 1118; map, p.1095. This state government-run outlet sells all manner of wooden toys and gadgets, sandalwood sculptures, inlaid rosewood coffee tables, metalwork, carpets, rugs and hundreds of other gift items. Daily 10am–8pm.

Crossword 32 Residency Rd ☎ 080 2558 2411; map, p.1095. A bookshop that stocks all the latest titles along with music, movies a great magazine selection. There's a *Café Coffee Day* inside. Daily 10.30am–9pm.

Higginbothams 74 MG Rd ☎ 080 2558 7359; map, p.1095. The main Bengaluru branch of the venerable national chain has a diverse collection of fiction, plus academic and reference books. Daily 9.30am–8.30pm.

Karishma Silks 45 MG Rd ☎ 080 2558 1606; map, p.1095. Vast, colourful range of pure silks, embroidered sari, cottons and *salwar kameez*, with something to suit most budgets. Daily 10.15am–8.45pm.

Planet M 9 Curzon Complex, Brigade Rd ☎ 080 4068 2888; map, p.1095. The largest music shop in the MG Rd area, with a huge choice of modern and classical Indian music, alongside a selection of international sounds, DVDs and magazines. Daily 11am–10pm.

Tanishq 121 Dickenson Rd ☎ 080 2555 0907; map, p.1093. If you have the money to splash out on some really special jewellery, head for this place a treasure trove of diamonds, gold and silver. Daily 10am–8pm.

DIRECTORY

Banks and exchange Thomas Cook, 55 MG Rd (☎ 080 2558 1338); TT Forex, 180 Cunningham Rd (☎ 080 2225 1201); Weizmann Forex Ltd, 56 Residency Rd (☎ 080 6628 4463) are all open Mon–Sat 9.30am–6pm). Banks have better rates; the State Bank of Mysore on MG Rd is the most convenient. There are many ATMs dotted around the city, especially in the MG Rd area.

Hospitals Victoria Hospital, near City Market (☎ 080 2670 1150). Dr Suresh Nao (☎ 98450 21614), a family practice

physician based in central Bengaluru, can recommend treatments and/or the closest hospital.

Internet Internet cafés are widely available across the city, generally charge ₹20–30/hr and are open until 9pm at least.

Libraries The British Council (English-language) library, 23 Kasturba Rd Cross (Mon–Sat 10.30am–6.30pm; ☎ 080 2221 3485), has newspapers and magazines that visitors are welcome to peruse in a/c comfort.

22

22

ART OF LIVING INTERNATIONAL CENTRE

Ved Vignam Maha Vidya Peeth (☎080 6726 2626, ⊕artofliving.org), the main centre of the **Art of Living** organization founded in 1982 by **Sri Sri Ravi Shankar** (not to be confused with the great sitar maestro), occupies 24 acres of lush green hilly land 21km south of Bengaluru on Kanakapura Road in Udayapura. Its centrepiece is the splendid, lotus-like **Vishalakshmi Mantap** temple, which is surrounded by more shrines, an amphitheatre and an ashram boasting lodgings, restaurants and a host of other facilities including a "Wellness Centre", bookshop, Ayurvedic spa and even a wedding hall. The organization – now with centres worldwide and NGO status – was founded by the guru after he discovered **Sudarshankriya**, a powerful stress-reducing breathing technique that is the focal point of his teachings. If you are interested in courses or volunteering, you can register through the website, or simply drop in to attend regular events like music, meditation and *darshan* led by the guru on most Wednesdays and Saturdays from 4.30pm. Get here by taking bus #211F from City Bus Stand.

Pharmacies Al-Siddique Pharma Centre, opposite Jama Masjid near City Market, and Janata Bazaar, in the Victoria Hospital, near City Market, are open all night.
Police ☎100.
Post office On the corner of Raj Bhavan Rd and Cubbon Rd, at the northern tip of Cubbon Park (Mon–Sat 10am–7pm, Sun 10.30am–1.30pm).
Travel agents For flight booking and reconfirmation, and other travel necessities, try Sahara Global at Unit G2, 35 Church St (☎080 6535 0001) or Gullivers Tours & Travels at South Black 201–202 Manipal Centre, Dickenson Rd, just north of MG Rd (☎080 2558 8001).

Mysore

A centre of sandalwood-carving, silk and incense production, **MYSORE** is one of south India's more appealing cities. Nearly 160km southwest of Bengaluru, the city is Karnataka's most popular tourist destination by a long shot, attracting about 2.5 million visitors each year. Nevertheless, it remains a charming, old-fashioned and undaunting town, changed by neither an IT boom nor its new-found status as a top international yoga destination. That said, the erstwhile capital of the Wadiyar rajas can be a little disappointing at first blush: upon stumbling off a bus or train you're not so much embraced by the scent of jasmine blossoms or gentle wafts of sandalwood as smacked by a cacophony of tooting, careering buses, bullock carts, motorbikes and tongas. Still, give it a few days and Mysore will cast a spell on you.

In addition to its official tourist attractions, chief among them the **Maharaja's Palace**, Mysore is a great city simply to stroll around. The evocative, if dilapidated, pre-Independence buildings lining market areas such as **Ashok Road** and **Sayaji Rao Road** lend an air of faded grandeur to a busy centre that teems with vibrant street life. Souvenir stores spill over with the famous **sandalwood**; the best place to get a sense of what's on offer is the government-run **Cauvery Arts and Crafts Emporium** on Sayaji Rao Road (closed Thurs), which stocks a wide range of local crafts that can be shipped overseas. The city's famous **Devaraja Market** on Sayaji Rao Road is one of south India's most atmospheric produce markets: a giant complex of covered stalls groaning with bananas (the delicious *nanjangod* variety), luscious mangoes, blocks of sticky *jaggery* and conical heaps of lurid *kumkum* powder.

Brief history

In the tenth century Mysore was known as Mahishur – "the town where the demon buffalo was slain" (by the goddess Durga). Presiding over a district of many villages, the city was ruled from about 1400 until Independence by the Hindu **Wadiyars**. Their rule was only broken from 1761, when the Muslim Haider Ali and his son Tipu Sultan

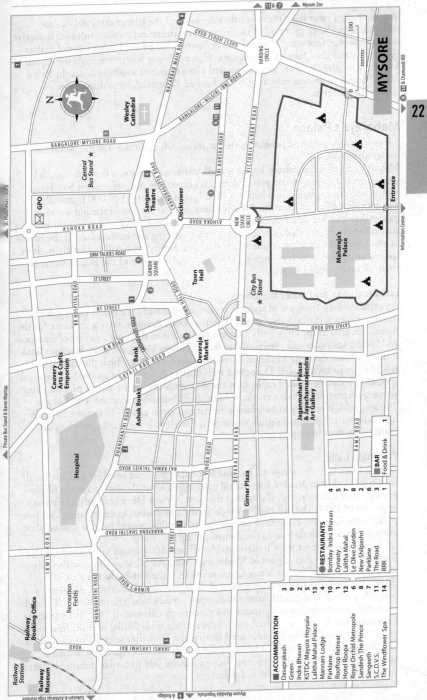

MYSORE

22

0 metres 100

■ ACCOMMODATION

Dasaprakash	3
Green	9
Indra Bhavan	2
KSTDC Mayura Hoysala	5
Lalitha Mahal Palace	13
Mannars Lodge	4
Parklane	10
Rooftop Retreat	1
Hotel Roopa	12
Royal Orchid Metropole	6
Sandesh The Prince	8
Sangeeth	7
S.C.D.V.S.	11
The Windflower Spa	14

● RESTAURANTS

Bombay Indra Bhavan	4
Dynasty	5
Lalitha Mahal	7
Le Olive Garden	8
New Shilpashri	2
Parklane	6
The Road	3
RRR	1

■ BAR

Food & Drink	1

took over. Two years later, the new rulers demolished the labyrinthine old city to replace it with the elegant grid of sweeping, leafy streets and public gardens that survive today. However, following Tipu Sultan's defeat in 1799 by the British colonel Arthur Wellesley (later the Duke of Wellington), Wadiyar power was restored. As the capital of Mysore state, the city thereafter dominated a major part of southern India. In 1956, when Bangalore became capital of newly formed Karnataka, its maharaja was appointed governor.

Maharaja's Palace

There are six gates in the perimeter wall but entrance is on the south side only • Daily 10am–5.30pm • ₹200 (₹20); shoes and cameras must be left in the cloakroom

Mysore's centre is dominated by the walled **Maharaja's Palace**, a fairytale spectacle topped with a shining brass-plated dome. It's especially magnificent on Sunday nights and during festivals, when it is illuminated by nearly 100,000 lightbulbs. It was completed in 1912 for the 24th Wadiyar raja, on the site of the old wooden palace that had been destroyed by fire in 1897. In 1998, after a lengthy judicial tussle, the courts decided in favour of formally placing the main palace in the hands of the Karnataka state government but the royal family, who still hold a claim, have lodged an appeal, which is ongoing. Twelve temples surround the palace, some of them of much earlier origin.

Entrance area and outer buildings

An extraordinary amalgam of styles from India and around the world crowds the lavish interior. Entry is through the Gombe Thotti or **Dolls' Pavilion**, once a showcase for the figures featured in the city's lively Dussehra celebrations and now a gallery of European and Indian sculpture and ceremonial objects. Halfway along, the brass **Elephant Gate** forms the main entrance to the centre of the palace, through which the maharaja would drive to his car park. Decorated with floriate designs, it bears the Mysore royal symbol of a double-headed eagle, now the state emblem. To the north, past the gate, stands a ceremonial wooden elephant *howdah*. Elaborately decorated with 84kg of 24-carat gold, it appears to be inlaid with red and green gems – in fact the twinkling lights are battery-powered signals that would have let the *mahout* know when the maharaja wished to stop or go.

The main halls

Walls leading into the octagonal **Kalyana Mandapa**, the royal wedding hall, are lined with a meticulously detailed frieze of oil paintings, executed over a period of fifteen years by four Indian artists, illustrating the great Mysore Dussehra festival (see box opposite) of 1930. The hall itself is magnificent, a cavernous space featuring cast-iron pillars from Glasgow, Bohemian chandeliers and multicoloured Belgian stained glass arranged in peacock designs in the domed ceiling.

Climbing a staircase with Italian marble balustrades, past an unnervingly realistic life-size plaster-of-Paris figure of Krishnaraja Wadiyar IV, lounging comfortably with his bejewelled feet on a stool, you come into the **Public Durbar Hall**, an orientalist fantasy like something from *A Thousand and One Nights*. A vision of brightly painted and gilded colonnades, open on one side, the massive hall affords views out across the parade ground and gardens to Chamundi Hill. The maharaja gave audience from here, seated on a throne made from 280kg of solid Karnatakan gold. These days, the hall is only used during the Dussehra festival, when it hosts classical concerts. The smaller **Private Durbar Hall** features especially beautiful stained glass and gold-leaf painting. Before leaving you pass two embossed silver doors – all that remains of the old palace.

MYSORE DUSSEHRA FESTIVAL

Following the tradition set by the Vijayanagar kings, the ten-day festival of **Dussehra** (Sept/Oct), to commemorate the goddess Durga's slaying of the demon buffalo, Mahishasura, is celebrated in grand style at Mysore. Scores of cultural events include concerts of south Indian classical (Carnatic) music and dance performances in the great Durbar Hall of the **Maharaja's Palace**. On Vijayadasmi, the tenth and last day of the festival, a magnificent procession of mounted guardsmen on horseback and caparisoned elephants – one carrying the palace deity, Chaamundeshwari, on a gold *howdah* – marches 5km from the palace to Banni Mantap, site of a sacred banyan tree. There's also a floating festival in the temple tank at the foot of **Chamundi Hill**, and a procession of chariots around the temple at the top. A torchlit parade takes place in the evening, followed by a massive firework display and much jubilation on the streets.

Jaganmohan Palace: Jayachamarajendra Art Gallery

300m west of the Maharaja's Palace • Daily 8am–5pm • ₹100 (₹20); no cameras

Built in 1861, the **Jaganmohan Palace** was used as a royal residence until 1915, when it was turned into a picture gallery and museum by Maharaja Krishnaraja Wadiyar IV. Most of the "contemporary" art on show dates from the 1930s, when a revival of Indian painting was spearheaded by E.B. Havell and the Tagore brothers, Rabindranath and Gaganendranath, in Bengal.

Nineteenth- and twentieth-century **paintings** dominate the first floor; among them the work of the pioneering oil painter Raja Ravi Varma who, although not everyone's cup of tea, has been credited for introducing modern techniques to Indian art. Games on the upper floor include circular *ganjifa* playing cards illustrated with portraits of royalty or deities, and board games delicately inlaid with ivory. There's also a cluster of musical instruments, among them a brass *jaltarang* set and glass xylophone. Another gallery, centring on a large wooden Ganesh seated on a tortoise, is lined with paintings, including Krishnaraja Wadiyar sporting with the "inmates" of his zenana during Holi.

Mysore Zoo

1km east of the Maharaja's Palace • Daily except Tues 8.30am–5.30pm • ₹40, camera ₹20

Officially named **Sri Chamarajendra Zoological Gardens**, **Mysore Zoo** is one of the oldest and best in India. Established as far back as 1882, it was opened to the public in 1902 and has grown to encompass 245 beautifully landscaped acres, with admirably spacious compounds for most of the animals that live here. As well as all the usual big **mammals**, including some fine leopards and tigers, the zoo boasts South Asia's only **gorilla** and a pair of tapirs. There are also many species of birds and reptiles to be admired, though some of their cages do not make viewing the animals easy. The zoo even has a very cheap canteen and an admirable policy of charging a deposit on water bottles, which can be claimed back at the exit.

Chamundi Hill

3km southeast of the city **Temple** Daily 7am–2pm, 3.30–6pm & 7–9pm • Free but special entrance ₹10 • Bus #201 from the City stand

Chamundi Hill, 3km southeast of the city, is topped with a temple to the chosen deity of the Mysore rajas – the goddess Chamundi, or Durga, who slew the demon buffalo Mahishasura. It's a pleasant, easy bus trip to the top; the walk down, past a huge Nandi, Shiva's bull, takes about thirty minutes. Take drinking water to sustain you, especially in the middle of the day – the walk isn't very demanding, but by the end of it, after more than a thousand steps, your legs are likely to be a bit wobbly.

Inside the twelfth-century **temple**, which is open to non-Hindus, is a solid gold Chamundi figure. Outside, in the courtyard, stands a fearsome, if gaily coloured, statue

YOGA IN MYSORE

Despite the passing in 2009 of its founder, Sri Pattahbi Jois, the world-renowned **Ashtanga Yoga Insitute** (Ⓦkpjayi.org), 2.5km northwest of town, is still a revered pilgrimage destination for devotees. The surrounding neighbourhood has in recent years turned into a bustling expat haven, filled with cafés, guesthouses, restaurants and internet cafés. The institute doesn't offer drop-in classes; students must register for a minimum of one month (around ₹30,000), and book at least two months in advance.

In contrast, **Mysore Mandala Yogashala**, at 581 Dewans Rd, Laxmipuram (closed Sat & Mon; ☎0821 425 6277, Ⓦmandala.ashtanga.org), is a self-contained retreat, offering excellent instruction, an organic café, well-tended garden, cultural events and, uniquely in Mysore, drop-in classes. Two-hour Ashtanga classes (₹500) run at 6am and 4.30pm, with the slightly less strenuous ninety minute Hatha classes (₹400) at 6.30am and 5pm.

of the demon Mahishasura. Overlooking the path down the hill, the magnificent 5m **Nandi**, carved from a single piece of black granite in 1659, is an object of worship himself, adorned with bells and garlands and tended by his own priest. Minor shrines, dedicated to Chamundi and the monkey god Hanuman, among others, line the side of the path; at the bottom, a little shrine to Ganesh lies near a chai shop. From here it's usually possible to pick up an auto-rickshaw or bus back into the city, but at weekends the latter are often full. If you walk on towards the city, passing a temple on the left with a big water tank (the site of the floating festival during Dussehra), you come after ten minutes to the main road between the *Lalitha Mahal Palace* and the city; there's a bus stop, and often auto-rickshaws, at the junction.

ARRIVAL AND DEPARTURE

By train The railway station is 1.5km northwest of the centre. For long hauls, the best way to travel is by train, usually with a change at Bengaluru (6–7 daily; 2–3hr); the fastest service is the a/c *Shatabdi Express* #2008 (daily except Wed 2.15pm; 2hr), which continues to Chennai (7hr 10min). There are ten services daily to Hassan, of which the *Talguppa Intercity Express* #16206 (6am; 1hr 50min) is the fastest.

By bus Mysore has three bus stands: major long-distance KSRTC and other state services pull in to Central, near the heart of the city, where there are advance booking counters. The Private stand is about 1km northwest of here and a host of agents there can make bookings for

private buses to many destinations. Local buses, including services for Chamundi Hill and Srirangapatnam, stop at the City stand, next to the northwestern corner of the Maharaja's Palace.

Destinations State-run services from Central Bus Stand: Channarayapatna (for Sravanabelagola; hourly; 2hr 30min); Hassan (every 15–30min; 3hr); Hubli (4–6 daily; 9hr); Kochi (6 daily; 11–12hr); Madikeri (every 30min–1hr; 3hr); Mangalore (every 30min–1hr; 7hr); Ootacamund (via Bandipur National Park; 8 daily; 5hr). Overnight services to Goa leave from the Private stand at 4pm and 5pm, getting to Panjim at 9am and 10am respectively.

INFORMATION AND TOURS

Tourist information The helpful Karnataka Tourism office (Mon–Sat 9.30am–5.30pm; ☎0821 242 2096) is located in Exhibition Buildings on Purandasa Rd, opposite the entrance to the Maharaja's Palace.

Tours The KSTDC office (daily 6.30am–8.30pm; ☎0821 242 3652) at the KSTDC hotel *Mayura Hoysala*, 2 Jhansi

Laxmi Bai Rd, is of little use except to book one of its marathon city tours (8.30am–8.30pm; ₹210), which only leaves with a minimum of ten passengers. You might also consider the Belur, Halebid and Sravanabelagola tour (Tues & Thurs 7.30am–9pm; ₹550) – it's great value but often rushed.

ACCOMMODATION

Finding a room is only a problem during Dussehra (see box, p.1105) and the Christmas/New Year period, when the popular places are booked up weeks in advance and prices predictably soar. Check-out is generally noon.

Dasaprakash Gandhi Square ☎0821 244 2444, Ⓦmysoredasaprakashgroup.com. Large, crumbling yet charming hotel complex arranged around a spacious paved

courtyard. It's busy, clean and efficient, with some rather overpriced a/c rooms, cheap singles and an excellent veg restaurant. **₹675**

★ **Green** Chittaranjan Palace, 2270 Vinoba Rd, Jayalakshmipuram ☎0821 251 2536, ⓦ greenhotelindia.com. This former royal palace on the western outskirts has been refurbished as an elegant, eco-conscious two-star hotel among landscaped gardens. The rooms are a decent size, and facilities include lounges, verandas, a croquet lawn and well-stocked library. All profits go to charities and environmental projects. Book in advance and arrange a pickup. ₹3750

Hotel Roopa 2724-C Bangalore–Nilgiri Rd ☎0821 244 0044, ⓦ hotelroopa.com. Bright modern hotel block with compact but comfy rooms at surprisingly reasonable prices. Very handy for the palace and a good buffet breakfast is included. ₹1075

Indra Bhavan Dhanavantri Rd ☎0821 242 3933, ⓔ hotelindrabhavan@rediffmail.com. A dilapidated old lodge full of character, with attached singles and doubles. The "ordinary" rooms are a little grubby, but the good-value "deluxe" ones have clean tiled floors and open onto a wide common veranda. Two good veg restaurants. ₹300

KSTDC Mayura Hoysala 2 Jhansi Lakshmi Bai Rd ☎0821 242 5349, ⓦ karnatakaholidays.net. Reasonably priced rooms and suites in a colonial-era mansion. There's a terrace restaurant and beer garden, which is good value, but the food is uninspiring. The budget *Yatri Niwas* in the same compound offers rooms for ₹750. ₹1050

Lalitha Mahal Palace T Narasipur Rd ☎0821 252 6100, ⓦ lalithamahalpalace.in. On a slope overlooking the city in the distance, this white, Neoclassical palace was built in 1931 to accommodate the maharaja's foreign guests. Now it's a Raj-style fantasy, decked with stunning period furniture and popular with tour groups. Rooms range from the cute turret rooms to the "Viceroy Suite" (₹50,000). The tea lounge, restaurant (see p.1108) and pool are open to non-residents (₹225). ₹40000

Mannars Lodge Chandragupta Rd ☎0821 244 8060. Budget hotel near the Central Bus Stand and Gandhi Square. Spruced up of late but overall still very plain, though the "deluxe" rooms do have TV. Deservedly popular with backpackers but no advance booking. ₹650

★ **Parklane** 2720 Sri Harsha Rd ☎0821 243 0400, ⓦ parklanemysore.com. A complete overhaul has transformed the *Parklane* into a swish yet affordable

boutique hotel. Appealingly misshapen rooms, all with a/c, contemporary furnishings and most with balconies, encircle a skylit atrium; wi-fi available. ₹1800

★ **Rooftop Retreat** 2.5km from bus stand in Gayathripuram ☎0821 245 0483. This delightful apartment homestay in a tranquil neighbourhood offers an Indian twist on the B&B experience, with a warm welcome and superb food. Bright blues and cosy creams dominate the mostly wood furnishings, and you can enjoy delightful mornings and evenings on the rooftop patio. Must reserve in advance. ₹1200

Royal Orchid Metropole 5 Jhansi Lakshmi Bai Rd ☎0821 425 5566, ⓦ royalorchidhotels.com. Luxurious heritage hotel built in 1920 by the maharaja of Mysore amid pleasant gardens. Rooms have high ceilings and a sense of grandeur. There's also a small outdoor pool and gym. The fine *Tiger Trail* multicuisine restaurant serves buffet breakfast and lunch in the central courtyard. ₹7000

Sandesh The Prince 3 Nazarbad Main Rd ☎0821 243 6777, ⓦ sandeshtheprince.com. Smart, stylish four-star with comfortable, well-furnished rooms and an impressive, skylit foyer. Facilities include travel desk, foreign exchange, outdoor pool (₹300/day to non-residents) with barbecue, and an excellent Ayurvedic centre and beauty parlour. ₹5000

Sangeeth 1966 Narayana Shastri Rd, near the Udipi Krishna temple ☎0821 242 4693. One of Mysore's best all-round budget deals: bland and a bit boxed in, but friendly and very good value, with a new rooftop restaurant. ₹400

S.C.D.V.S. Sri Harsha Rd ☎0821 242 1379, ⓔ hotelscvds@yahoo.com. Friendly modern lodge with some a/c rooms and cable TV in most. Some of the upper-storey rooms have balconies overlooking the palace. ₹750

The Windflower Spa Maharanapratap Rd, 3km southeast of town ☎0821 252 2500, ⓦ thewindflower.com. Whitewashed Balinese-style cottages surround a small lagoon on these gorgeous, sprawling grounds at the base of Chamundi Hill. Amenities include spa and massage, billiards and table football, an elegant bar, lagoon restaurant (see p.1108) and an outdoor pool with waterfall. ₹6400

EATING AND DRINKING

Mysore has scores of **places to eat**, from numerous south Indian "meals" joints dotted around the market to the opulent *Lalitha Mahal Palace*. To sample the renowned Mysore *pak*, a sweet, rich crumbly mixture made of ghee and maize flour, queue at Guru Sweet Mart, a small stall at KR Circle that's considered to be the best sweetshop in the city. Another speciality from this part of the world is *malligi iddli*, a delicate jasmine-flavoured *iddli* usually served in the mornings and at lunch.

Bombay Indra Bhavan Sayaji Rao Rd ☎0821 542 0521. Comfortable and popular veg restaurant that serves both south and north Indian cuisine and sweets. You can get a top-class masala dosa for ₹30. Daily 7.30am–8.30pm.

Dynasty Palace Plaza hotel, Sri Harsha Rd ☎0821 241 7592. Classy ground-floor dining room complemented in evenings by a breezy covered rooftop restaurant with a broad international menu (mains

22

22

₹120–200), full bar, and pleasant decor. Daily 7am–11pm.

Food & Drink Maharaja Shopping Complex, Bangalore–Mysore Rd ☎92415 57015. Advertising itself as a music bar, this joint is still more of a drinking den, with a wide selection of drinks and a jarring mixture of Western and Indian sounds. Daily noon–11pm.

Lalitha Mahal Palace T Narasipur Rd ☎0821 252 6100, ⍉lalithamahalpalace.in. Sample the charms of this palatial five-star hotel with a hot drink in the atmospheric tea lounge, or an à la carte lunch in the grand dining hall, accompanied by live sitar music. Buffet dinners for around ₹1000 on special occasions. The old-style bar also boasts a full-size billiards table. Daily 11am–2pm & 7–10.30pm.

★ **New Shilpashri** Gandhi Square ☎0821 244 8558. Encircled by leafy potted plants, this rooftop terrace is one of the best spots in the city to enjoy a sun-dipped egg and toast breakfast or a cool evening cocktail. Quality north Indian food like tasty tandoori and foreign dishes such as chicken stroganoff go for ₹100–150. Plenty of good veg options too. Daily 8am–11pm.

★ **Le Olive Garden** Windflower Spa ☎0821 252 2500. Excellent, reasonably priced Indian, Chinese and Western dishes served to the sound of falling water and croaking frogs at this quasi-jungle hideaway. Daily noon–11pm.

Parklane Sri Harsha Rd ☎0821 243 0400. Congenial courtyard restaurant-cum-beer balcony, with moderately priced veg and non-veg (meat sizzlers are a speciality), fake trees and live Indian classical music every evening. The hotel rooftop space is a real stunner, with full bar, pool and fantastic views. Popular with travellers and locals alike. Daily 8am–11pm.

The Road Sandesh The Prince, 3 Nazarbad Main Rd ☎0821 243 6777. Lined with plush booths – several of which are inside faux classic cars – this upmarket, American road trip-themed restaurant/club serves a good lunch menu before the tables are cleared at 7pm and patrons take to the circular wooden dancefloor, usually to guest DJs (₹300–400 cover at weekends). Daily noon–11.30pm.

RRR Gandhi Square ☎0821 244 1979. Superb Andhra canteen with a small but plush a/c room at the back. Gets packed at lunchtimes and at weekends, but it's well worth the wait for its excellent chicken biriyani, fried fish and set menus served on banana leaves. Daily 11.30am–4.30pm & 7–10pm.

Around Mysore

Mysore is a jumping-off point for some of Karnataka's most popular destinations. At **Srirangapatnam**, the fort, palace and mausoleum date from the era of Tipu Sultan, the "Tiger of Mysore", while the superb Hoysala temple of **Somnathpur** is an architectural masterpiece. If you're heading south towards Ootacamund, Bandipur National Park pales in comparison to Mudumalai across the Tamil Nadu border, although **Nagarhole National Park**, three hours southwest of Mysore towards the Kerala border, can be more rewarding.

Srirangapatnam

The island of **Srirangapatnam**, in the River Kaveri, 14km northeast of Mysore, measures 5km by 1km. Long a site of Hindu pilgrimage, it is named after its tenth-century Sriranganathaswamy Vishnu temple. The Vijayanagars built a fort here in 1454, and in 1616 it became the capital of the Mysore Wadiyar rajas. However, Srirangapatnam is more famously associated with **Haider Ali**, who deposed the Wadiyars in 1761, and even more so with his son **Tipu Sultan**. During his seventeen-year reign – which ended with his death in 1799, when the future Duke of Wellington took the fort at the bloody battle of "Seringapatnam" – Tipu posed a greater threat than any other Indian ruler to British plans to dominate India. Born in 1750, of a Hindu mother, he inherited his father Haider Ali's considerable military skills, but was also an educated, cultured man, whose lifelong desire to rid India of the hated British invaders naturally brought him an ally in the French. He obsessively embraced his popular name of the **Tiger of Mysore**, surrounding himself with symbols and images of tigers; much of his memorabilia is decorated with the animal or its stripes, and, like the Romans, he is said to have kept tigers for the punishment of criminals.

Sriranganathaswamy temple

300m east of station • Daily 8am–1pm & 4–8pm

At the heart of the fortress, the great temple of **Sriranganathaswamy** still stands proud and virtually untouched by the turbulent history that has flowed around it, and remains, for many devotees, the island's prime draw. Developed by succeeding dynasties, the temple consists of three distinctive sanctuaries and is entered via an impressive five-storeyed gateway and a hall that was built by Haider Ali. The innermost sanctum, the oldest part of the temple, contains an image of the reclining Vishnu.

22

Daria Daulat Bagh

2km east of the station • Daily 9am–5pm Fri • ₹100 (₹5)

The former summer palace, the **Daria Daulat Bagh**, literally "wealth of the sea", was used to entertain Tipu's guests. At first sight, this low, wooden colonnaded building set in an attractive formal garden fails to impress. But the superbly preserved interior is remarkable, with its ornamental arches, tiger-striped columns and floral decoration on every centimetre of the teak walls and ceiling. A much-repainted mural on the west wall relishes every detail of Haider Ali's victory over the British at Pollilore in 1780.

Gumbaz mausoleum

3km east of Daria Daulat Bagh • Daily except Fri 9am–5pm • Free

An avenue of cypresses leads from an intricately carved gateway to the **Gumbaz mausoleum**. Built by Tipu Sultan in 1784 to commemorate Haider Ali, and later also to serve as his own resting place, the lower half of the grey-granite edifice is crowned by a dome of whitewashed brick and plaster, spectacular against the blue sky. Ivory-inlaid rosewood doors lead to the tombs of Haider Ali and Tipu, each covered by a pall (tiger stripes for Tipu), and an Urdu tablet records Tipu's martyrdom.

ARRIVAL AND DEPARTURE   SRIRANGAPATNAM

Srirangapatnam is a small island, but places of interest are quite spread out; tongas, auto-rickshaws and bicycles are available on the main road near the bus stand.

By train All the Mysore–Bengaluru trains pull in to the station near the temple and fort.

By bus Frequent buses (including #313 and #316) take 30min from Mysore City Bus Stand.

ACCOMMODATION

Fort View Resorts ☏08236 252777, ⓦfortviewresorts.com. This smart and elegant place set in its own grounds not far from the fort entrance is the area's best-value hotel, with spacious rooms, some a/c, and manicured grounds. ₹1200

Mayura River View 3km east from the bus stand ☏08236 252114, ⓦkarnatakaholidays.net. The KSTDC hotel-cum-restaurant is rather institutional in feel but occupies a pleasant spot beside the River Kaveri. Its rooms and cottages (all a/c) are overpriced, however. ₹2500

Somnathpur: Keshava Vishnu temple

Daily 9am–5pm • ₹100 (₹5)

Built in 1268, the exquisite **Keshava Vishnu temple**, in the sleepy hamlet of **SOMNATHPUR**, was the last important temple to be constructed by the Hoysalas; it is also the most complete and, in many respects, the finest example of this singular style (see box, p.1113). Somnathpur itself, just ninety minutes from Mysore by road, is little more than a few neat tracks and some attractive simple houses with pillared verandas.

Like other Hoysala temples, the Keshava was built on a star-shaped plan. ASI staff can show you around and also grant permission to clamber on the enclosure walls, so you can get a marvellous bird's-eye view of the modestly proportioned structure. It's best to do this as early as possible, as the black stone gets very hot to walk on in bare feet later in the day. The temple is a *trikutachala*, "three-peaked hills" type, with a tower on each shrine. Its high plinth (*jagati*) provides an upper ambulatory, which on its outer edge allows visitors to approach the upper registers of the profusely decorated walls. Among the many superb images here are an unusually high proportion of Shaivite figures for a Vishnu temple. As at Halebid, a lively frieze details countless episodes from the Ramayana, Bhagavata Purana and Mahabharata. Intended to accompany circumambulation, the panels are "read" (there is no text) in a clockwise direction. Unusually, the temple is autographed; all its sculpture was the work of one man, named Malitamba. Outside the temple stands a *dvajastambha* column, which may originally have been surmounted by a figure of Vishnu's bird vehicle Garuda.

ARRIVAL AND DEPARTURE
SOMNATHPUR

By bus There are no direct buses from Mysore to Somnathpur. Private buses run from Mysore to Tirumakudal Narasipur (1hr), from where there are regular buses to Somnathpur (20min).

ACCOMMODATION AND EATING

There is nowhere to stay near the temple and the only food available is biscuits or maybe a samosa or fruit from a street-seller.

Talakadu Jaladhama 25km southeast of Somnathpur ☎08227 271196, ✉jaladhana @hotmail.com. Tucked in the backwaters of a dammed section of the Cauvery river, this exquisite resort offers secluded cottages, some with rooftop hot tubs and herb gardens. Boating and sports activities are available and the resort can be reached by direct private bus from Mysore. ₹**7000**

Nagarhole National Park

₹200 (₹75), camera ₹20 payable at check post

NAGARHOLE ("Snake River") **NATIONAL PARK**, together with Bandipur and Tamil Nadu's Mudumalai, forms the **Nilgiri Biosphere Reserve**, one of India's most extensive tracts of protected forest. The park extends 640 square kilometres north from the River Kabini, which has been dammed to form a picturesque artificial lake. During the dry season (Feb–June), this perennial water source attracts large numbers of animals, making it a potentially prime spot for viewing wildlife. The forest here is of the moist deciduous type – thick jungle with a 30m-high canopy – and more impressive than Bandipur's drier scrub.

However, disaster struck Nagarhole in 1992, when friction between local pastoralist "tribals" and the park wardens over grazing rights and poaching erupted into a spate of arson attacks. Thousands of acres of forest were burned to the ground. The trees are steadily growing back, but it will be years before animal numbers completely recover. An added threat to the fragile jungle tracts of the region is a notorious female gang of wood smugglers from Kerala, who have developed a fearsome and almost mythical reputation. Consequently, Nagarhole is most worth visiting at the height of the dry season, when its muddy riverbanks and grassy swamps, or *hadlus*, offer decent chances of sighting gaur (Indian bison), elephant, *dhole* (wild dog), deer, boar, and even the odd tiger or leopard. The park is best avoided altogether during the monsoon season.

ARRIVAL AND INFORMATION
NAGARHOLE NATIONAL PARK

By bus Two daily buses from Mysore's Central stand go to Hunsur (3hr), 10km from the park's north gate, where you can find transport, mostly in the form of jeeps, to the Forest Department's two resthouses.

Information The Nagarhole visitor centre organizes elephant rides (₹75) and schedules bus tours a round the sanctuary (6–9am & 3.30–6pm; ₹100).

ACCOMMODATION

Forest Department resthouses Inside the park; book through the Forest Department offices in Mysore ☎0821 248 0901 or Bengaluru ☎080 2334 1993. These simple rustic cabins are scantily furnished and you must arrive (either by jeep or rented vehicle) at the park gates well before dusk – the road through the reserve to the lodges closes at 6pm, and is prone to "elephant blocks". ₹500

Jungle Inn Veerana Hosahalli ☎08222 246022, ⓦjungleinn.in. An upmarket option, this inn is close to the park entrance and arranges wildlife safaris. It has a mixture of different sized rooms and huge Swiss tented cottages, and staff can arrange pick ups from Hunsur. ₹2500

Kabini River Lodge Approached via the village of Karapura, 3km from the park's south entrance; book through Jungle Lodges & Resorts ☎080 2559 7021, ⓦjunglelodges.com. Set in its own leafy compound on the lakeside, this former maharaja's hunting lodge offers all-in deals that include meals and transport around the park with expert guides. It's impossible to reach by public transport, so you'll need to rent a car to get here. Online specials at slack times. ₹7000

Hassan and around

The unprepossessing town of **HASSAN**, 118km northwest of Mysore, is visited in large numbers because of its proximity to the Hoysala temples at **Belur** and **Halebid**, both northwest of the town, and the Jain pilgrimage site of **Sravanabelagola** to the southeast. Some travellers end up staying a couple of nights but with a little forward planning you shouldn't have to linger for long, as the town is a busy and fairly unappealing sprawl of concrete. Set deep in the serene Karnatakan countryside, Belur, Halebid and Sravanabelagola offer considerably more appealing surroundings.

ARRIVAL AND INFORMATION

HASSAN

By train The railway station, served by regular trains from Mysore (10 daily; 2–3hr), is 2km east of the town centre on BM Rd. There are also several daily trains to Mangalore (5–6hr), one of them overnight.

By bus Hassan's KSRTC Bus Stand is in the centre of town, at the northern end of Bus Stand Rd, and served by frequent buses from Mysore (every 15–30min; 3hr). In order to see the surrounding sights by bus, you'll need at least two days. Belur and Halebid can be comfortably covered in one day; it's best to take one of the earliest hourly buses to Halebid (1hr) and move on to Belur (30min), from where services back to Hassan are more frequent (6.30am–6.15pm; 1hr 10min). Sravanabelagola, however, is in the opposite direction, and not served by direct buses; you have to head to Channarayapatna (every 30min from 6.30am; 1hr), aka "CR Patna", on the main Bengaluru highway and pick up one of the regular buses (30min) or any number of minibuses from there.

By car Apart from taking a tour, the only way to see Sravanabelagola, Belur and Halebid in one day is by car, which some visitors share; most of the hotels can fix this up for around ₹2500/day.

Tourist information AVK College Rd (Mon–Sat 10am–5.30pm; ☎08172 268862).

ACCOMMODATION

DR Karigowda Residency BM Rd, under 1km west from railway station ☎08172 264506. Immaculate budget hotel: friendly, comfortable and amazing value. Single occupancy possible; a/c good value. ₹550

Hoysala Village Resort Belur Rd, 6km northwest of the centre ☎08172 256065. Government-run luxury cottages and suites in a quiet rural setting. Multicuisine restaurant and a pool, which is open to non-residents (₹100/hr). ₹8100

Southern Star BM Rd, 500m from the train station ☎08172 251816, ⓦhotelsouthernstar.com. New hotel with a variety of rooms and all mod cons. It's better value than most and the *Karwar* restaurant is excellent. ₹3300

Vaishnavi Lodging Harsha Mahal Rd ☎08172 263885. Hassan's best budget lodge, with big clean rooms (all with phone and TV) and a veg restaurant. Reservations recommended; for a bit of quiet, ask for a room in the back. ₹400

EATING AND DRINKING

Cocktails BM Rd ☎81456 05143. Three-level restaurant and bar with breezy rooftop. Skip the grub and enjoy an evening drink in the open air. Daily 11am–11pm.

Harsha Mahal Below Harsha Mahal Lodge, Harsha Mahal Rd ☎08172 268533. Excellent veg canteen that serves freshly cooked *iddli* and stunningly good dosas, as well as some north Indian dishes. Daily 7.30am–10pm.

Swarna Gate In the Suvarna Regency, PB 97, BM Rd ☎08172 264006. This plush non-veg restaurant and bar with a few tables overlooking the garden is one of Hassan's finest. The varied menu is not cheap, with most curries going for at least ₹200. Daily 7am–10.30pm.

Upper Deck Harsha Mahal Rd ☎96023 56743. Small, modern terrace café offering coffees, ice creams and tasty *chaats* on a first-floor balcony. Popular with students. Daily 7am–9pm.

22

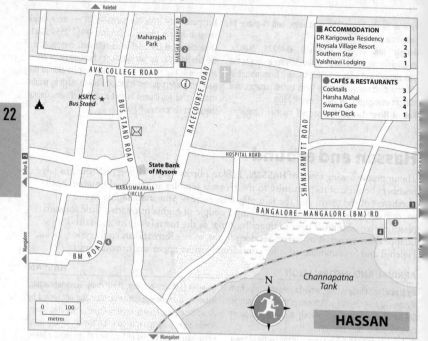

Belur & 2

Mangalore

ACCOMMODATION
DR Karigowda Residency	4
Hoysala Village Resort	2
Southern Star	3
Vaishnavi Lodging	1

CAFÉS & RESTAURANTS
Cocktails	3
Harsha Mahal	2
Swarna Gate	4
Upper Deck	1

HASSAN

Halebid

Now little more than a scruffy village of brick houses and chai stalls, **HALEBID**, 32km northwest of Hassan, was once the capital of the powerful Hoysala dynasty, who held sway over south Karnataka from the eleventh until the early fourteenth centuries. Once known as **Dora Samudra**, the city was renamed *Hale-bidu*, or "Dead City", in 1311 when Delhi sultanate forces under the command of Ala-ud-Din-Khalji swept through and reduced it to rubble. Despite the sacking, several large Hoysala temples (see box opposite) survive, two of which, the **Hoysaleshvara** and **Kedareshvara**, are superb, covered in exquisite carvings. Note that Belur (see opposite) has superior facilities to those found in Halebid, making it a far better base for exploration of the Hoysala region.

The Hoysaleshvara temple

In the centre of the village • **Temple** Daily sunrise–sunset • Free **Archeological museum** Daily except Fri 10am–5pm • ₹5

The **Hoysaleshvara** temple was started in 1141, and after some forty years of work it was still unfinished; this possibly accounts for the absence here of the type of towers that feature at Somnathpur, for example. It is no longer known which deities were originally worshipped, though the double shrine is thought to have been devoted at one time to Shiva and his consort. In any event, both shrines contain *shivalinga* and are adjoined by two linked, partly enclosed *mandapa* hallways in which Nandi bulls stand.

Hoysaleshvara also features many Vaishnavite images. The **sculptures**, which have a fluid quality lacking in the earlier work at Belur (see opposite), include Brahma aboard his goose vehicle Hamsa, Krishna holding up Mount Govardhana, another where he plays the flute and Vishnu (Trivikrama) bestriding the world in three steps. One of the most remarkable images is of the demon king **Ravana** shaking Shiva's mountain abode, Mount Kailash, populated by numerous animals and figures with Shiva and Parvati seated atop. Secular characters, among them dancers and musicians, occupy the same

22

HOYSALA TEMPLES

The **Hoysala** dynasty, who ruled southwestern Karnataka between the eleventh and thirteenth centuries, built a series of distinctive temples centred primarily at three sites: **Belur** and **Halebid**, close to modern Hassan, and **Somnathpur**, near Mysore. At first sight, and from a distance, the buildings, all based on a star-shaped plan, appear to be modest structures, compact and even squat. Yet on closer inspection, their profusion of fabulously detailed and sensuous sculpture, covering every centimetre of the exterior, is astonishing. Detractors often class Hoysala art as decadent and overly fussy, but anyone with an eye for craftsmanship will be sure to marvel.

The intricacy of the carvings was made possible by the material used in construction: a soft **soapstone** that on oxidization hardens to a glassy, highly polished surface. The level of detail, similar to that seen in sandalwood and ivory-work, became increasingly free and more fluid as the style developed, and reached its highest point at Somnathpur. Beautiful bracket figures, often delicate portrayals of voluptuous female subjects, were placed under the eaves, fixed by pegs top and bottom. A later addition (except possibly in the Somnathpur temple), these serve no structural function.

Another technique more usually associated with wood is the unusual treatment of the massive stone **pillars**: lathe-turned, they resemble those of the wooden temples of Kerala. They were probably turned on a horizontal plane, pinned at each end, and rotated with the use of a rope. It may be no coincidence that, to this day, wood turning is still a local speciality.

---

register as the gods, and you'll come across the odd erotic tableau featuring voluptuous, heavily bejewelled maidens. A narrative frieze, on the sixth register from the bottom, follows the length of the Nandi *mandapa*s and illustrates scenes from the Hindu epics.

A small **archeological museum** next to the temple houses a collection of Hoysala art and other finds from the area.

The Jain bastis
600m south of the Hoysaleshvara temple

The Jain *basti*s (temples) stand virtually unadorned; their only sculptural decoration consists of ceiling friezes inside the *mandapa*s and elephants at the entrance steps, where there's an impressive donatory plaque. The thirteenth-century temple of **Adi Parshwanatha** is dedicated to the 23rd *tirthankara*, Parshvanath, while the newer **Vijayanatha** built in the sixteenth century is dedicated to the sixteenth *tirthankara*, Shantinath. The *chowkidar* at the Parshwanatha temple will demonstrate various tricks made possible by the carved pillars' highly polished surfaces; some are so finely turned they sound metallic when struck.

ARRIVAL AND DEPARTURE   HALEBID

By bus Buses run to Hassan (every 30min–1hr until   8.30pm; 1hr) and to Belur (hourly until 8pm; 30min).

ACCOMMODATION

Shantala Opposite Hoysaleshvara temple ☏ 08177 273224. KSTDC hotel set in a small garden offering three comfortable, if overpriced, doubles with verandas, plus a four-bed room – all should be booked in advance. This is also the only place to eat, apart from a handful of daytime chai stalls. ₹**1000**

Belur

BELUR, 37km northwest of Hassan, on the banks of the Yagachi River, was the Hoysala capital prior to Halebid, during the eleventh and twelfth centuries. Still active, the **Chennakeshava temple** is a fine and early example of the singular Hoysala style, built by King Vishnuvardhana in 1117 to celebrate his conversion from Jainism, victory over Chola forces at Talakad and his independence from the Chalukyas. Today, its grey-stone *gopura*, or gateway tower, soars above a small, bustling market town – a popular pilgrimage site from October to December, when busloads of Ayappan devotees stream through en route to Sabarimala (see box, p.1054). The **Car festival** held around March or April takes place over twelve days and has a pastoral feel, attracting farmers from the surrounding countryside who conduct a bullock cart procession through the streets to the temple.

Chennakeshava temple

West of the bus stand • Daily 7.30am–8.30pm; main shrine opens for worship 8.30–10am, 11am–1pm, 2.30–5pm & 6.30–8.30pm

Chennakeshava temple stands in a huge walled courtyard, surrounded by smaller shrines and columned *mandapa* hallways. Lacking any form of superstructure, it appears to have a flat roof. If it ever had a tower, it would have disappeared by the Vijayanagar (sixteenth-century) period. Both the sanctuary and *mandapa* are raised on the usual plinth (*jagati*), creating the jagged star shape. Double flights of steps, flanked by minor towered shrines, afford entry to the *mandapa* on three sides; this hallway was originally open but, in the 1200s, pierced stone screens carved with geometric designs and scenes from the Puranas were inserted between the lathe-turned pillars. The quantity of **sculptural decoration**, if less mature than in later Hoysala temples, is staggering.

Within the same enclosure, the **Kappe Channigaraya temple** has some finely carved niche images and a depiction of Narasimha (Vishnu as man-lion) killing the demon Hiranyakashipu. A few metres west, fine sculptures in the smaller **Viranarayana** shrine include a scene from the Mahabharata of Bhima killing the demon Bhaga.

ARRIVAL AND INFORMATION

BELUR

By bus Buses from Hassan and Halebid arrive at the small bus stand in the middle of town, a 10 min walk west along the main street from the temple.

Bike rental There are auto-rickshaws available, but a good way to explore the area, including Halebid, is to rent a bicycle (₹5/hr) from one of the stalls around the bus stand.

Tourist information The tourist office (Mon–Sat 10am–5pm) is located within the KSTDC *Mayuri Velapuri* compound on Temple Rd.

ACCOMMODATION AND EATING

Kalpavriksha Just off Temple Rd ☎ 98276 30455. Just about the only place to eat meat in Belur, this small restaurant offers a standard range of Indian and Chinese main courses for around ₹100–150, as well as south Indian snacks. Daily 7am–10pm.

Mayuri Velapuri Temple Rd ☎ 08177 222209. This KSTDC hotel is the most comfortable place to stay, with five clean non-a/c and ten a/c rooms; breakfast is included. The two dorms are rarely occupied, other than during the March–May pilgrim season. Dorm ₹150, double ₹1000

Sumukha Residency ☎ 08177 222039. A third of the way to the temple heading west from the bus stand is this fairly modern and comfortable place. ₹500

Vishnu Lodge Near the bus stand ☎ 08177 222263. Above a great veg restaurant and sweet shop, this is the best-value place, with sizeable rooms (some with TV) but tiny attached bathrooms where hot water is only available in the mornings. ₹400

Sravanabelagola

The sacred Jain site of **SRAVANABELAGOLA**, 49km southeast of Hassan and 93km north of Mysore, consists of two hills and a large tank. On one of the hills, Indragiri (also known as Vindhyagiri), stands an extraordinary 18m-high monolithic statue of a naked male figure, **Gomateshvara**. Said to be the largest freestanding sculpture in India, this tenth-century colossus, visible from kilometres away, makes Sravanabelagola a key pilgrimage centre, though surprisingly few Western travellers find their way out here. Spend a night or two in the village, however, and you can climb Indragiri Hill before dawn to enjoy the serene spectacle of the sun rising over the sugar cane fields and outcrops of lumpy granite that litter the surrounding plains – an unforgettable sight.

Sravanabelagola is linked in tradition with the Mauryan emperor Chandragupta, who is said to have starved himself to death on the second hill in around 300 BC, in

accordance with a Jain practice. The hill was renamed Chandragiri, marking the arrival of Jainism in southern India. At the same time, a controversy regarding the doctrines of Mahavira, the last of the 24 Jain **tirthankaras** (literally "crossing-makers", who assist the aspirant to cross the "ocean of rebirth"), split Jainism into two separate branches – *svetambara*, "white-clad" Jains, are more common in north India, while *digambara*, "sky-clad", are usually associated with the south. Truly ascetic *digambara* devotees go naked, though few do so away from sacred sites.

The monuments at Sravanabelagola probably date from no earlier than the tenth century, when a General Chamundaraya is said to have visited Chandragiri in search of a Mauryan statue of Gomateshvara. Failing to find it, he decided to have one made. From the top of Chandragiri he fired an arrow across to Indragiri Hill; where the arrow landed he had a new Gomateshvara sculpted from a single rock.

Indragiri Hill

South of main road

Gomateshvara is approached from the tank between the two hills by 620 steps, cut into the granite of **Indragiri Hill**, which pass numerous rock inscriptions on the way up to a walled enclosure. Shoes must be deposited at the stall to the left of the steps, and you can leave bags at the site office nearby. Take plenty of water if it's hot, as there is none available on the hill. Entered through a small wagon-vaulted *gopura*, the **temple** is entirely dominated by the towering figure of Gomateshvara. With elongated arms and exaggeratedly wide shoulders, his proportions are decidedly non-naturalistic. The sensuously smooth surface of the white granite is finely carved: particularly the hands, hair and serene face. As in legend, ant-hills and snakes sit at his feet and creepers appear to grow on his limbs.

Chandragiri Hill

North of main road

Leaving your shoes with the keeper at the bottom, take the rock-cut steps to the top of the smaller **Chandragiri Hill**. Fine views stretch south to Indragiri and, from the north on the far side, across to a river, paddy and sugar cane fields, palms and the village of Jinanathapura, where there's another ornate Hoysala temple, the Shantishvara *basti*.

Rather than a single large shrine, as at Indragiri, Chandragiri holds a group of *basti*s in late Chalukya Dravida style, within a walled enclosure. Caretakers will take you around and open up the closed shrines. Save for pilasters and elaborate parapets, all the temples have plain exteriors. Named after its patron, the tenth-century **Chamundaraya** is the largest of the group, dedicated to Parshvanath. Inside the twelfth-century **Chandragupta**, superb carved panels in a small shrine tell the story of Chandragupta and his teacher Bhadrabahu. Traces of painted geometric designs survive and the pillars feature detailed carving. Elsewhere in the enclosure stands a 24m-high *manastambha*, "pillar of fame", decorated with images of spirits, *yakshis* and a *yaksha*. No fewer than 576 inscriptions dating from the sixth to the nineteenth centuries are dotted around the site, on pillars and on the rock itself.

Bhandari Basti and monastery (math)

The road east from the foot of the steps at Chandragiri leads to two interesting Jain buildings in town. To the right as you face the hill, the **Bhandari Basti** (1159), housing a shrine with images of the 24 *tirthankaras*, was built by Hullamaya, treasurer of the Hoysala raja Narasimha. Two *mandapa* hallways, where naked *digambara* Jains may sometimes be seen discoursing with devotees clad in white, lead to the shrine at the back.

At the end of the street, the *math* (monastery) was the residence of Sravanabelagola's senior *acharya*, or guru. Thirty male and female monks are attached to the *math*; normally a member of staff will be happy to show visitors around. Among the rare palm-leaf manuscripts in the library, some more of which are than a millennium old, are works on mathematics and geography, and the Mahapurana, hagiographies of the *tirthankara*s. Next door, a covered walled courtyard is edged by a high platform on three sides, on which a chair is placed for the *acharya*. A collection of tenth-century bronze *tirthankara* images is housed here, and vibrant murals detail the various lives of Parshvanath. The hills where the *tirthankara*s stood to gain *moksha* are represented in a model, somewhat resembling a jelly mould, with tacked-on footprints.

ARRIVAL AND INFORMATION   SRAVANABELAGOLA

By bus You can reach Sravanabelagola from Hassan with one change of bus (see p.1111), although many people choose the easier option of a tour from Mysore or Bengaluru.
Bike rental Crisscrossed by winding back roads, the idyllic

countryside around Sravanabelagola is mostly flat and thus perfect cycling terrain. Bicycles are available for rent at Saleem Cycle Mart, on Masjid Rd, opposite the northeast corner of the tank.

ACCOMMODATION AND EATING

There are plenty of *dharamshalas* to choose from if you want to stay, managed by the temple authorities and offering simple, scrupulously clean rooms, many with their own bathrooms and sitouts, ranged around gardens and courtyards, and most costing under ₹300 per night. The 24hr accommodation office (☎ 08176 657258), located inside the *SP Guest House*, next to the bus stand clock tower, will allocate you a room.

Hotel Raghu Opposite the main tank ☎ 08176 257238. Very simple attached rooms but clean enough and the only

private option around. It also has the best of the many small local restaurants – try the excellent thali. **₹600**

Kodagu (Coorg)

The hill region of **Kodagu**, formerly known as **Coorg**, lies 100km west of Mysore in the Western Ghats, its eastern fringes merging with the Mysore plateau. Rugged mountain terrain is interspersed with cardamom jungle, coffee plantations and fields of lush rice paddy, making it one of south India's most beautiful areas. Not much has changed since Dervla Murphy spent a few months here with her daughter in the 1970s (the subject of her classic travelogue, *On a Shoestring to Coorg*) and was entranced by the landscape and people, whose customs, language and appearance set them apart from their neighbours (see box, p.1119).

If you plan to cross the Ghats between Mysore and the coast, the route through Kodagu is definitely worth considering. Some **coffee plantation** owners open their doors to visitors. A good time to visit is during the festival season in early December, or during the **Blossom Showers** around March and April when the coffee plants bloom with white flowers, but be aware that some people find the strong scent overpowering.

Kodagu is relatively undeveloped apart from a new crop of homestays, and "sights" are hard to come by, but the countryside is idyllic and the climate refreshingly cool even in summer. Many visitors **trek** through the unspoilt forest tracts and ridges that fringe the district. On the eastern borders of Kodagu around Kushalnagar, large **Tibetan settlements** have transformed a once barren countryside into fertile farmland dotted with busy monasteries, some of which house thousands of monks.

Brief history

The first records of a kingdom here date from the eighth century, when it prospered from the salt trade passing between the coast and the cities on the Deccan. Under the Hindu **Haleri rajas**, the state repulsed invasions by its more powerful neighbours, including Haider Ali and his son Tipu Sultan (see p.1161). A combination of hilly terrain, absence of roads (a deliberate policy on the part of defence-conscious Kodagu kings) and the tenacity of its highly trained army ensured Kodagu was the only Indian kingdom never to be conquered.

22

In 1834, after ministers appealed to the British to help depose their despotic king, Vira Rajah, Kodagu became a princely state with nominal independence, which it retained until the creation of Karnataka in 1956. **Coffee** was introduced during the Raj and, despite plummeting prices on the international market, this continues to be the linchpin of the local economy, along with pepper and cardamom. Although Kodagu is Karnataka's wealthiest region, and provides the highest tax revenue, it does not reap the rewards – some villages are still without electricity – and this, coupled with the distinct identity and fiercely independent nature of the Kodavas (see box opposite), has given rise to an autonomy movement known as **Kodagu Rajya Mukti Morcha**. Methods used by the KRMM include cultural programmes and occasional strikes; violence is very rare.

Madikeri and around

Nestling beside a curved stretch of craggy hills, **MADIKERI**, capital of Kodagu, undulates around 1300m up in the Western Ghats, roughly midway between Mysore and the coastal city of Mangalore. The gradually increasing number of foreigners who travel up here find it a pleasant enough town, with red-tiled buildings and undulating roads that converge on a bustling bazaar, but most move on to home and plantation stays in the verdant Coorg countryside within a couple of days.

Omkareshwara Shiva

1km northwest of bus stand • **Temple** Daily **Museum** Tues–Sun 9am–5pm, except 2nd Sat

The **Omkareshwara Shiva** temple, built in 1820, features an unusual combination of red-tiled roofs, Keralan Hindu architecture, Gothic elements and Islamic-influenced domes. The fort and palace, worked over by Tipu Sultan in 1781 and rebuilt in the nineteenth century, now serve as offices and a prison. Within the complex, **St Mark's Church** holds a small **museum** of British memorabilia, Jain, Hindu and village deity figures and weapons. Also worth a look are the huge square **tombs of the rajas** which, with their Islamic-style gilded domes and minarets, dominate the town's skyline.

Raja's Seat

On the western edge of town near the Valley View hotel • Daily 6am–8pm • ₹5

The early eighteenth-century Kodagu king was no dummy – he chose one of the best sunset vantage points in south India for **Raja's Seat**, a popular grassy park and garden that fills up just before dusk. At 7pm a water-and-light show set to Bollywood tunes dazzles the locals.

Abbi Falls

8km southeast of the town • Auto-rickshaws charge ₹300 for the return journey including waiting time

Madikeri is the centre of the lucrative coffee trade, and a walk to **Abbi Falls** is a good introduction to coffee-growing country. The pleasant road, devoid of buses, winds through the hill country past plantations and makes for a good day's outing. At the litter-strewn car park at the end of the road, a gate leads through a private coffee plantation, sprinkled with cardamom sprays and pepper vines, to the bottom of the large stepped falls (fenced off so no swimming is possible) that are most impressive during and straight after the monsoons.

ARRIVAL AND INFORMATION   **MADIKERI AND AROUND**

By bus Madikeri has regular bus connections with Bengaluru (hourly; 6hr), Hassan (6 daily; 4hr), Mangalore (every 30min–1hr; 4hr) and Mysore (every 30min–1hr; 3hr). The KSRTC state bus stand is at the lowest part of town, towards its eastern side, below the main bazaar;

private buses from villages around the region pull into a car park 100m west.

Tourist information Travel Coorg (daily 10am–6pm; ☎08272 321009, ⍟travelcoorg.in), located at the back of the bus stand, offers useful information on the area,

THE KODAVAS

Theories abound as to the origins of the **Kodavas**, or **Coorgis**, who today comprise less than one sixth of the hill region's population. Fair-skinned and with their own language and customs, they are thought to have migrated to southern India from Kurdistan, Kashmir or even Greece, though no one knows exactly why or when. One popular belief holds that this staunchly martial people, who since Independence have produced some of India's leading military brains, are descended from Roman mercenaries who fled here following the collapse of the Pandyan dynasty in the eighth century; some even claim connections with Alexander the Great's invading army. Whatever their origins, the Kodavas have managed to retain a distinct identity apart from the freed plantation slaves, Moplah Muslim traders and other immigrants who have settled here. More akin to Tamil than Kannada, their language is Dravidian, yet their religious practices, based on ancestor veneration and worship of nature spirits and the river, differ markedly from those of mainstream Hinduism. Land tenure in Kodagu is also quite distinctive: women have a right to inheritance and ownership and are also allowed to remarry.

Spiritual and social life for traditional Kodavas revolves around the **ain mane**, or ancestral homestead. Built on raised platforms to overlook the family land, these large, detached houses, with their beautiful carved wood doors and beaten-earth floors, generally have four wings and courtyards to accommodate various branches of the extended family, as well as shrine rooms, or **Karona Kalas**, dedicated to the clan's most important forebears. Key religious rituals and rites of passage are always conducted in the *ain mane*, rather than the local temple. However, you could easily travel through Kodagu without ever seeing one, as they are invariably away from roads, shrouded in thick forest.

including treks and homestays. Coorg Travels (☎08272 225817) also arranges treks, tours and homestays. For information on Kodagu's forests and forest bungalows contact the Conservator of Forests, Deputy Commissioner's Office (☎08272 225708) at the fort, which is uphill en route to Raja's Seat. To arrange coffee plantation visits, contact the Codagu Planters Association on Mysore Rd (☎08272 226273).

ACCOMMODATION

★ **Caveri** School Rd ☎08272 225492. Below the private bus stand, this large hotel has been upgraded but remains good value, with large, nicely furnished double rooms. There's a ground-floor restaurant and their adjacent *Capitol* bar serves the spicy local delicacy *pondhi* (pork) curry. ₹850

Chitra School Rd ☎08272 225372, ⓦhotelchitra .co.in. Good-value hotel, with neat, well-kept rooms (the slightly pricier ones have cable TV) and a dorm. Excellent non-veg restaurant-cum-bar downstairs. Dorm ₹200, double ₹700

Coorg International Convent Rd ☎08272 228071, ⓦcoorginternational.com. A 10min rickshaw ride west of the centre, this is one of the few upmarket options in town. A large but slightly characterless hotel with comfortable Western-style rooms, it also has a multicuisine restaurant, exchange facilities, and shops. ₹5000

Daisy Bank Heritage Inn General Thimaya Rd (aka Mysore Rd), northwest side of town ☎08272 321172. The high-ceilinged rooms are subtly decorated and all named after flowers, lending a pastoral air to this converted mansion. All rooms have spotless bathrooms and flatscreen TVs. ₹1250

★ **Rainforest Retreat at Mojo Plantation** 13km north of Madikeri, near Galibeedu village ☎08272 265636, ⓦrainforestours.com. Informed hosts Sujata and Annu Goel have carved a thrumming idyll out of their little wedge of Kodagu plantation, with excellent organic meals (included) and warmly furnished cottages and tents set amid lush rainforest. All profits go to their NGO, which fosters environmental awareness and sustainable agriculture in the region. ₹2000

★ **The School Estate** 30km southeast from Madikeri ☎08274 258358, ⓦschoolestate.in. Set amid beautifully landscaped grounds surrounded by coffee, cardamom and vanilla plantations, *The School Estate* is an absolute charmer. Owner Rani Aiyapa is an excellent chef, and leads weekly cooking classes. The rooms are enormous, with rosewood beds and a number of homely touches that lend a refined English bed-and-breakfast feel, and the grounds are gorgeous. ₹3500

Valley View Raja Rd ☎08272 228387, ⓦkarnatakaholidays.net. A stiff walk up past Raja's Seat, this KSTDC hotel offers enormous old-fashioned rooms, many with excellent views. The restaurant serves booze and has an open terrace with epic views. ₹1800

EATING

Athithi Opposite the Town Hall ☏ 99010 40200. Tucked just off the main road, this place has an outdoor terrace, as well as indoor seating, where you can enjoy south Indian and tandoori pure veg cuisine for ₹60–150. Daily 7am–10pm.

★ **Choice** School Rd ☏ 08272 225585. Head for the spacious upstairs roof "garden" of this three-storey restaurant and tuck into huge portions of Indian and Chinese food. The American chop suey is a winner at ₹120. Daily 8.30am–10.30pm.

Karavali Fish Land Down the lane opposite the Fort ☏ 98457 89989. Sparkling clean family restaurant that specializes in fish, including a great-value ₹60 thali, although there are plenty of veg and meat options too. Daily 8am–10.30pm.

Mangalore

Many visitors only come to **MANGALORE** on their way somewhere else. As well as being fairly close to the Kodagu (Coorg) hill region, it's also a stopping-off point between Goa and Kerala, and is the nearest coastal town to the Hoysala and Jain monuments near Hassan, 172km east.

Mangalore was one of the most famous ports of south India. It was already well known overseas in the sixth century as a major source of pepper; the fourteenth-century Muslim writer Ibn Battuta noted its trade in pepper and ginger and the presence of merchants from Persia and Yemen. In the mid-1400s, the Persian ambassador Abdu'r-Razzaq saw Mangalore as the "frontier town" of the Vijayanagar empire (see p.1132), which was why the Portuguese captured it in 1529. Nowadays, the modern port, 10km north of the city proper, is principally known for the processing and export of coffee and cocoa (mostly from Kodagu), and cashew nuts (from Kerala). It is also a centre for the production of *beedi* cigarettes.

Mangalore's strong Christian influence can be traced back to the arrival further south of St Thomas (see p.1179). Some 1400 years later, in 1526, the Portuguese founded one of the earliest churches on the coast, although today's **Rosario Cathedral**, with a dome based on St Peter's in Rome, dates only from 1910. Closer to the centre, on Lighthouse Road, fine restored fresco, tempera and oil murals by the Italian Antonio Moscheni adorn the Romanesque-style **St Aloysius College Chapel**, built in 1885.

Manjunatha temple

At the foot of Kadri Hill, 3km north of the centre

Mangalore's tenth-century **Manjunatha temple** is an important centre of the Shaivite and tantric **Natha-Pantha cult**. Thought to be an outgrowth of Vajrayana Buddhism, the cult is a divergent species of Hinduism, similar to certain cults in Nepal. Enshrined in the sanctuary are a number of superb **bronzes,** including a 1.5m-high seated Lokeshvara (Matsyendranatha), made in 958 AD and considered to be the finest southern bronze outside Tamil Nadu. To see it close up, visit at *darshan* times (6am–1pm & 4–8pm), although the bronzes can be glimpsed through the wooden slats on the side of the sanctuary. If possible, time your visit to coincide with *mahapooja* (8am, noon & 8pm) when the priests give a fire blessing to the accompaniment of raucous music. Opposite the east entrance, steps lead via a reddish-coloured path to a curious group of minor shrines. Beyond this complex stands the **Shri Yogishwar Math**, a hermitage of Tantric sadhus set round two courtyards.

Ullal

10km south of Mangalore • Local bus #44A runs to Ullal from the junction at the south end of KS Rao Rd (centre of town)

If you're looking to escape the city for a few hours, then head out to the village of **ULLAL**, where a long sandy **beach** stretches for kilometres, backed by wispy fir trees. It's a deservedly popular place for a stroll, particularly in the evening when Mangaloreans come out to watch

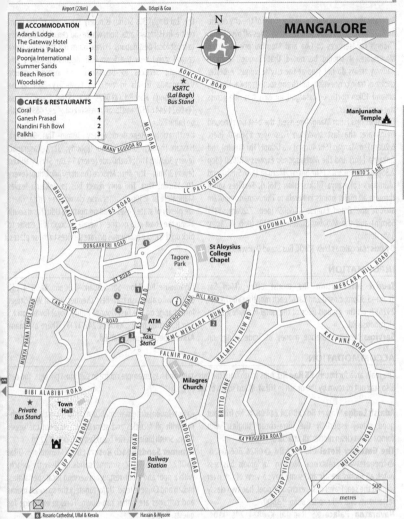

the sunset, but a strong undertow makes swimming difficult, and at times unsafe. You might be better off using the pool at the *Summer Sands Beach Resort* (see p.1122), immediately behind the beach. Towards the centre of Ullal, and around 700m from the main bus stand, is the *dargah* of **Seyyid Mohammad Shareeful Madani**, a sixteenth-century saint who is said to have come from Medina in Arabia, floating across the sea on a handkerchief. The extraordinary nineteenth-century building with garish onion domes houses the saint's tomb, which is one of the most important Sufi shrines in southern India. Visitors are advised to follow custom and cover their heads and limbs and wash their feet before entering.

ARRIVAL AND INFORMATION

MANGALORE

By plane Bajpe airport, 22km north of the city (bus #22 or #47A or taxis for ₹400–500), has regular services to Bengaluru (3–5 daily; 50min–1hr 10min), Goa (1 daily; 55min), Hyderabad (1 daily; 1hr 35min), Kochi (1 daily; 45min) and Mumbai (5–6 daily; 1hr 30min). There are also daily connections with the Gulf states.

22

By train The railway station, to the south of the city centre on Station Rd, sees daily services from cities all over India. Though rail services to Goa and Mumbai operate from Mangalore, it should be noted that through Konkan Railway trains do not stop at the city terminus. A better choice of train connections north and south is at Kankanadi, around 10km north, or Kasargod, an easy bus ride across the Kerala border.

Destinations From Mangalore itself, the best northbound trains are: the fast *Madgaon Passenger* #56640 (dep. 6.20am) to Margao (6hr 40min) via Udupi (1hr 40min) and Gokarna (4hr) and the *Matsyaganda Express* #12620 (dep 2.35pm) to Gokarna (4hr 5min), Margao (6hr 5min) and Mumbai's Lokmanya Tilak station (16hr). Services south through all major points in Kerala to Thiruvananthapuram include the *Ernad Express* #16605 (dep. 7.20am; 13hr 55min) and the *Malabar Express* #16630; (dep. 6.25pm; 14hr 40min).

By bus Mangalore's busy KSRTC Bus Stand (known locally as the "Lal Bagh" Bus Stand) is nearly 3km north of the town centre, in Hampankatta, from where you can catch city buses to most local destinations. Private buses use the much more central stand near the Town Hall. Agents for luxury and overnight services to Bengaluru and beyond include Vijayananda Travels in the PVS Centenary Building on Kudmulranga Rao Rd (☎ 0824 249 3536), Anand Travels (☎ 0824 244 6737) and Ideal Travels (☎ 0824 242 4899), both on Falnir Rd.

Destinations Bengaluru (every 30min–1hr; 9–10hr); Hassan (hourly; 6hr); Kannur (hourly; 3hr); Kasaragod (every 30min; 1hr); Kozhikode (every 1–2hr; 5hr); Madikeri (every 30min–1hr; 4hr); Mysore (hourly; 7hr); Udupi (every 10–15min; 1hr). The only direct bus to Gokarna leaves Mangalore at 1.30pm; otherwise, change at Kumta. There are plenty of state buses heading north to Udupi and south along the coast into northern Kerala, though it is easier to pick up the more numerous private services to those places.

INFORMATION

Tourist information The tourist office (Mon–Sat 10am–5.30pm, closed 2nd Sat of each month; ☎ 0824 244 2926) is on the ground floor of the *Hotel Indraprashta* on Lighthouse Rd.

Services You can change money at Trade Wings on Lighthouse Rd (Mon–Sat 9.30am–5.30pm; ☎ 0824 242 6225), who also cash travellers' cheques, and at Wall Street Interchange on the first floor of Utility Royal Towers on KS Rao Rd (same hours; ☎ 0824 242 1717). There are many ATMs, especially on KS Rao Rd.

ACCOMMODATION

The main area for hotels, **KS Rao Rd**, runs south from the bus stand and has an ample choice to suit most pockets. You can also stay out of town by the beach in **Ullal**, 10km south of the city.

Adarsh Lodge Market Rd ☎ 0824 244 0878. No frills but good value, especially the ultra-cheap singles, with compact but clean rooms, all attached. ₹400

The Gateway Hotel Old Port Rd ☎ 0824 666 0420, ⓦ thegatewayhotels.com. Modern *Taj* group business hotel; all rooms are a/c and some have a view of the river joining the sea. Travel desk, exchange, pool, bar, two classy restaurants and 24hr coffee shop. ₹3800

Navaratna Palace KS Rao Rd ☎ 0824 244 1104, ⓦ navaratnapalace.com. Preferable to its adjacent older sister, *Navaratna*, with better rooms (some a/c) for little extra cost. Also two good a/c restaurants: the non-veg *Heera Panna* and *Palimar* (pure veg). ₹700

Poonja International KS Rao Rd ☎ 0824 244 0171, ⓦ hotelpoonjainternational.com. Smart, mostly a/c, high-rise with all facilities and stunning views from the upper floors. South Indian buffet breakfast included. ₹1200

Summer Sands Beach Resort Chota Mangalore, Ullal ☎ 0824 246 7690, ⓦ summersands.in. Near the beach, with a pool and a bar-restaurant serving local specialities, Indian and Chinese food. Unfortunately the spacious rooms and cottages are rather run-down. Foreign exchange for guests. ₹2500

Woodside KMC Mercara Trunk Rd ☎ 0824 244 0296, ⓦ hotelwoodsidemangalore.com. Now occupying a sparkling new building nearly 1km from its former location, the hotel offers some of the best-value rooms (some a/c) and a good veg restaurant, *Xanadu*. ₹990

EATING

Coral Ocean At the Ocean Pearl hotel, Navabharat Circle ☎ 0824 241 3800. As the name suggests, there's an excellent seafood selection here, plus rich Mughlai dishes. Despite the luxury hotel setting, many items are around the very reasonable ₹300 mark. Daily 11am–11pm.

Ganesh Prasad Down a lane running off KS Rao Rd ☎ 0824 425 5932. Classic pure veg canteen, churning out all the south Indian favourites, from crispy dosas to gut-busting lunchtime "meals" (₹60). Daily 7am–9.30pm.

Nandini Fish Bowl Down a lane running off KS Rao Rd ☎ 78469 60022. The *Nandini Fish Bowl* rustles up tasty fish and chicken for around ₹100, with prawn dishes at ₹200. Daily 11am–3.30pm & 7–11pm.

Palkhi Balmatta New Rd ☏ 0824 244 4929. This airy family rooftop restaurant offers a wide menu of north Indian, Chinese, Continental and Mangalorean cuisine, with main courses in the ₹200–250 range. Daily 10.30am–11pm.

North of Mangalore: coastal Karnataka

Whether you travel the **Karnatakan (Karavali) coast** on the Konkan Railway or along the busy NH-17, southern India's smoothest highway, the route between Goa and Mangalore ranks among the most scenic anywhere in the country. Crossing countless palm- and mangrove-fringed estuaries, the railway line stays fairly flat, while the recently upgraded road, dubbed by the local tourist board as "The Sapphire Route", scales several spurs of the Western Ghats, which here creep to within a stone's throw of the sea, with spellbinding views over long, empty beaches and deep blue bays. Highlights are the pilgrim town of **Udupi**, site of a famous Krishna temple, and **Gokarna**, another important Hindu centre that provides access to exquisite unexploited beaches. A decent inland road winds through the mountains to **Jog Falls**, India's biggest waterfall, which can also be approached from the east.

Udupi

UDUPI (also spelt Udipi), on the west coast, 60km north of Mangalore, is one of south India's holiest Vaishnavite centres. The Hindu saint **Madhva** (1238–1317) was born here, and the **Krishna temple** and *maths* (monasteries) he founded are visited by hundreds of thousands of pilgrims each year. The largest numbers congregate during the late winter, when the town hosts a series of spectacular **car festivals** and gigantic, bulbous-domed chariots are hauled through the streets around the temple. Even if your visit doesn't coincide with a festival, Udupi is a good place to break the journey along the Karavali coast. Thronging with pujaris and pilgrims, its small sacred enclave is wonderfully atmospheric.

The Krishna temple and maths

Udupi's **Krishna temple** lies five minutes' walk east of the main street, surrounded by the eight **maths** founded by Madhva in the thirteenth century. Legend has it that the

---

KAMBLA

If you're anywhere between Mangalore and Bhatkal from October to April and come across a crowd gathering around a waterlogged paddy field, pull over and spend a day at the races – Karnatakan style. Few Westerners ever experience it, but the spectacular rural sport of **Kambla**, or **bull racing**, played in the southernmost district of coastal Karnataka (known as Dakshina Kannada), is well worth seeking out.

Two contestants, usually local rice farmers, take part in each race, riding on a wooden plough-board tethered to a pair of prize bullocks. The object is to reach the opposite end of the field first, but points are also awarded for style, and riders gain extra marks – and roars of approval from the crowd – if the muddy spray kicked up from the plough-board splashes the special white banners, or *thoranam*, strung across the course at a height of 6 to 8m.

Generally, race days are organized by wealthy landowners on fields specially set aside for the purpose. Villagers flock in from all over the region, as much for the fair, or *shendi*, as the races themselves: men huddle in groups to watch cockfights (*korikatta*), women haggle with bangle sellers and kids roam around sucking sticky *kathambdi goolay*, the local bonbons. It is considered highly prestigious to be able to throw such a party, especially if your bulls win any events or, better still, come away as champions. Known as *yeru* in Kannada, racing bulls are thoroughbreds who are rarely, if ever, put to work. Pampered by their doting owners, they are massaged, oiled and blessed by priests before big events, during which large sums of money are often won and lost.

idol enshrined within was discovered by the saint himself after he prevented a shipwreck. The grateful captain of the vessel offered Madhva his precious cargo as a reward, but the holy man asked instead for a block of ballast, which he broke open to expose a perfectly formed image of Krishna. Believed to contain the essence (*sannidhya*) of the god, this deity draws a steady stream of pilgrims, and is the focus of almost constant ritual activity. It is cared for by *acharyas*, or pontiffs, from one or other of the *maths*. They perform pujas (5.30am–8.45pm) that are open to non-Hindus; men are only allowed into the main shrine bare-chested.

22

ARRIVAL AND INFORMATION
UDIPI

By train Udupi's railway station is at Indrali on Manipal Rd, 3km west from the centre, and there are at least five trains in each direction daily.

By bus Udupi's three bus stands are dotted around the amorphous square in the centre of town: the KSRTC and private stands form a practically indistinguishable gathering spot for the numerous services to Mangalore and more long-distance buses to Mysore and Bengaluru and between northern Kerala and Goa. There are hardly any direct buses to

Gokarna or Jog Falls, so you usually have to change at Kumta or Honavar for both. The City stand is down some steps to the north and handles private services to local villages.

Tourist information The tourist office is near the temple in the Krishna Building, on Car St (Mon–Sat 10am–5.30pm; ☏ 0820 252 9718). The pamphlet *Udupi: an Introduction*, on sale in the stalls around the sacred enclave, is another rich source of background detail on the temple and its complex rituals.

ACCOMMODATION AND EATING

As a busy pilgrimage town, Udipi offres ample inexpensive **accommodation**, which is only likely to approach capacity during a major festival. For non-veg food or alcohol, you'll have to try a posh hotel restaurant, as the vast majority are pure veg.

Adarsha Below the Janardhana hotel. As you might expect of the masala dosa's birthplace, there are many fine, simple south Indian restaurants here where you can sample these and other veg favourites; and this is one of the best. Daily 2am–9.20pm.

Durga International Just west of City Bus Stand ☏ 0820 253 6971, ✉ durga-hotel@yahoo.com. Airy and efficient lodge with a variety of attached rooms, all with TV and some a/c, on the upper storeys of a modern block. ₹850

Janardhana South of the KSRTC Bus Stand ☏ 0820 252 3880, ✉ janardhanahotel@gmail.com. Clean but fairly mundane hotel with simple attached rooms of different sizes, most with cable TV and some a/c. ₹700

Sriram Residency Opposite the GPO ☏ 0820 253 0761, ✉ hotelsriramresidency@yahoo.co.in. Plushest place in the centre, though costing no more than most, with a smart lobby and comfortable a/c rooms. One of the two restaurants is a fine non-veg, and there's a bar too. ₹700

Sri Vidyasamudra Choultry Opposite Krishna temple ☏ 0820 252 0820. Foreigners are welcome in this ultra-basic lodge for pilgrims. The front rooms overlooking the temple are incredibly atmospheric. ₹150

Vyavahar Lodge Kankads Rd ☏ 0820 252 2568. Basic but friendly and clean lodge between the bus stands and temple. The singles are especially good value. ₹400

Jog Falls

Vehicle entry fee applies

Hidden in a remote, thickly forested corner of the Western Ghats 240km northeast of Mangalore, **Jog Falls** are the highest waterfalls in India. Today, however they are rarely as spectacular as they were before the construction of a large dam upriver, which impedes the flow of the River Sharavati over the sheer red-brown sandstone cliffs. Still, the surrounding scenery is gorgeous, with dense scrub and jungle carpeting sparsely populated, mountainous terrain. The views of the falls from the opposite side of the gorge is also impressive, unless, that is, you come during the monsoons, when mist and rain clouds envelop the cascades. Another reason not to come here during the wet season is that the extra water, and abundance of leeches at this time, make the excellent **hike** to the floor valley a trial; if you can, head up here between October and January. The trail starts just below the bus park and winds steeply down to the water, where you can enjoy a refreshing dip. The whole patch opposite the falls has been landscaped for appealing viewing, with its own impressive entrance gate and attractively designed reception centre.

ARRIVAL AND INFORMATION

By bus Jog Falls is connected by the well-paved NH-206 that crosses the Ghats from the coast south of Kumta (6 buses daily to the falls from Kumta; 3hr), which is connected by frequent buses to Gokarna. Coming from the south, it is slightly quicker to connect at Honavar (4–6 daily; 2hr 30min). On the inland side, there are hourly services to Shimoga, from where you can change onto buses for Hospet and Hampi. Change at Sagar instead for buses to Udupi, Mysore, Hassan and Bengaluru.

Tourist information The tourist office (Mon–Sat 10am–1.30pm & 2.30–5.30pm), upstairs at the new reception centre, opens rather erratically but can supply information on transport and vehicle rental.

ACCOMMODATION AND EATING

Accommodation is limited and was largely a KSTDC monopoly until a couple of homestays opened up in recent years. Apart from the standard government canteen at the *Gerusoppa Tunga Block*, the only other food options are at the enclave of small chai stalls and shops that cluster within the reception centre.

Gerusoppa Sharavathi Block 200m west of reception centre ☏ 08186 244732, ⓦ karnatakholidays.net. Ugly concrete KSTDC hotel whose vast, old-fashioned rooms are comfortable enough, with good views, but are grossly overpriced. ₹1800

Gerusoppa Tunga Block Next to the reception centre ☏ 08186 244732, ⓦ karnatakholidays.net. Humbler than the *Mayura Sharavathi*, whose reception it shares, with basic attached doubles and a shabby ten-bed dorm.

Dorm ₹180, double ₹800

JMJ Homestay More than 1km southeast of the reception centre, beyond the canal ☏ 94822 08755. Friendly homestay with four comfortable, rustic rooms. No food served. ₹500

PWD Inspection Bungalow 400m west of the reception centre ☏ 08186 244333. The a/c attached rooms are spacious and nicely situated on a hillock above the main road. ₹1500

Gokarna

Among India's most scenically situated sacred sites, **GOKARNA** lies between a broad white-sand beach and the verdant foothills of the Western Ghats, 230km north of Mangalore. Yet this compact little coastal town – a Shaivite centre for more than two

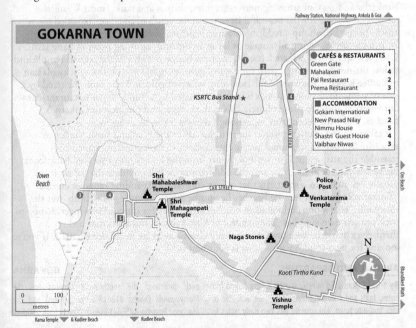

GOKARNA TOWN

Railway Station, National Highway, Ankola & Goa

KSRTC Bus Stand ★

● CAFÉS & RESTAURANTS
Green Gate 1
Mahalaxmi 4
Pai Restaurant 2
Prema Restaurant 3

■ ACCOMMODATION
Gokarn International 1
New Prasad Nilay 2
Nimmu House 5
Shastri Guest House 4
Vaibhav Niwas 3

Town Beach

Shri Mahabaleshwar Temple

CAR STREET

Shri Mahaganpati Temple

Naga Stones

Kooti Tirtha Kund

Police Post

Venkatarama Temple

MAIN ROAD

Om Beach

Bhandiker Math

Vishnu Temple

N

0   100
metres

Rama Temple ▼ & Kudlee Beach   ▼ Kudlee Beach

22

millennia – remained largely "undiscovered" by Western tourists until the early 1990s, when it began to attract dreadlocked and didgeridoo-toting neo-hippies fleeing the commercialization of Goa, just over 60km away. Now it's firmly on the tourist map, although the town retains a charming local character, as the Hindu pilgrims pouring through still far outnumber the foreigners who flock here in winter.

A hotchpotch of wood-fronted houses and red terracotta roofs, Gokarna is clustered around a long L-shaped bazaar. Its broad main road – known as **Car Street** – runs west to the town beach, which is a sacred site in its own right. Hindu mythology identifies it as the place where Rudra (another name for Shiva) was reborn after a period of penance through the ear of a cow from the underworld.

Gokarna is also the home of one of India's most powerful *shivalinga* – the **pranalingam**, which came to rest here after being carried off by Ravana, the evil king of Lanka, from Shiva's home on Mount Kailash in the Himalayas.

The temples

The *pranalingam* is enshrined in the medieval **Shri Mahabaleshwar temple**, at the far west end of the bazaar. It is regarded as so auspicious that a mere glimpse of it will absolve a hundred sins, even the murder of a brahmin. Pilgrims shave their heads, fast and take a ritual dip in the sea before *darshan*. For this reason, the tour of Gokarna traditionally begins at the beach, followed by a puja at the **Shri Mahaganpati temple**, a stone's throw east of Shri Mahabaleshwar, to propitiate the elephant-headed god Ganesh. Sadly, owing to some ugly incidents involving insensitive behaviour by a minority of foreigners, tourists are not allowed into the inner sancta of the main two temples but the parts you can visit are still extremely atmospheric. One interesting holy place you can get right into is **Bhandikeri Math**, a short way east of the bathing tank. This three-hundred-year-old temple and learning centre has shrines to the deities Bhavani Shankar, Uma Maheshwar and Maruthi.

The beaches

Notwithstanding Gokarna's numerous temples, shrines and tanks, most Western tourists come here for the beautiful **beaches** to the south of the more crowded town beach, beyond the lumpy, reddish-coloured headland that overlooks the town. Many lounge for weeks, taking advantage of lax attitudes and imbibing potent bhang lassis.

To pick up the trail, take a left off Car Street beside the Shri Mahaganpati temple and follow the newly cemented path for twenty minutes uphill and across a rocky plateau to **Kudlee Beach**. This wonderful 1km-long sweep of golden-white sand sheltered by a pair of steep-sided promontories is now punctuated by around fifteen restaurant-cum-hut ventures and one proper hotel. This is the longest and broadest of Gokarna's beaches, and with decent surf too, though the water can be dangerous.

It takes around twenty minutes more to hike over the headland from Kudlee to exquisite **Om Beach**, so named because its distinctive twin crescent-shaped bays resemble the auspicious Om symbol. Apart from the luxury resort set well back from the beach, largely flimsy huts and the odd hammock still populate the palm groves, usually belonging to restaurants that offer a constantly expanding range of cuisine.

Gokarna's two most remote beaches lie another thirty-minute walk/climb over the rocky hills. **Half Moon** and **Paradise** beaches are mainly for intrepid sun-lovers happy to pack in their own supplies. The handful of illegal shacks and stalls that had set themselves up there were unceremoniously cleared away by the police in 2012. If you're looking for near-total isolation, this is your best bet.

ARRIVAL AND DEPARTURE

GOKARNA

By train Gokarna Rd railway station is 9km inland but buses, taxis and auto-rickshaws (₹200) are available to take you into town. Gokarna Rd has two daily trains in each direction: the southbound services are the *Matsyaganda Express* #12619 (dep. 3.08am) and the *Madgaon Passenger* #56641 (dep. 3.28pm), both to Udupi

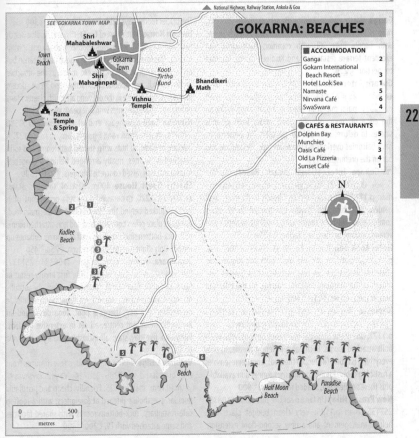

National Highway, Railway Station, Ankola & Goa

GOKARNA: BEACHES

SEE 'GOKARNA TOWN' MAP

Shri Mahabaleshwar

Town Beach

Gokarna Town

Shri Mahaganpati

Kooti Tirtha Kund

Bhandikeri Math

Vishnu Temple

Rama Temple & Spring

Kudlee Beach

Om Beach

Half Moon Beach

Paradise Beach

N

■ ACCOMMODATION	
Ganga	2
Gokarn International Beach Resort	3
Hotel Look Sea	1
Namaste	5
Nirvana Café	6
SwaSwara	4

● CAFÉS & RESTAURANTS	
Dolphin Bay	5
Munchies	2
Oasis Café	3
Old La Pizzeria	4
Sunset Café	1

22

0   500
metres

and Mangalore; the trains north are the *Matsyaganda Express* #12620 (dep. 3.08am) to Margao and Mumbai and the *Madgaon Passenger* #56640 (dep. 10.23am) to Margao. A couple of other weekly expresses also call here, but more regular express connections can be found in either Kumta or Ankola.

By bus The KSRTC Bus Stand, 300m north of Car St, is within easy walking distance of Gokarna's limited accommodation. The town is well connected by direct daily bus to Goa (5hr) and several towns in Karnataka, including Bengaluru (13–14hr), Hospet/Hampi (10hr) and Mysore (13hr), via Mangalore (6hr) and Udupi (5hr). You can change at Ankola on the main highway for more services north into Goa. For more buses to Hospet and Hampi and the best connections to Jog Falls, change at Kumta.

GETTING AROUND

By bike Bicycles are available for rent from a stall next to the *Pai Restaurant*, for ₹5/hr or ₹50/day.

By Auto-Rikshaw and taxi Auto-rickshaws and taxis cost ₹150–200 to Om Beach and auto-rickshaws just ₹80 along the paved path that goes three quarters of the way to Kudlee.

ACCOMMODATION

There is a better range of **guesthouses** than of bona fide **hotels** in Gokarna. As a last resort, you can nearly always find a bed in one of the spartan pilgrims' hostels, or **dharamshalas**, dotted around town. There is an increasing number of options at the **beaches**, from basic huts to a couple of new resorts. Prices can double over the Christmas/New Year period.

22

Ganga North end of Kudlee Beach ☎08386 257195, map p.1127. One of the more established beach joints, with simple huts (all with common bathrooms), an excellent terrace restaurant and Kudlee's fastest internet connection. ₹250

Gokarn International On the main road into town ☎08386 256622, ✉hotelgokarn@yahoo.com, map p.1125. Popular mid-scale place in a four-storey block on the edge of town, offering good value, from no-frills singles to deluxe, carpeted a/c doubles. The better ones have balconies overlooking the palm tops. Restaurant and bar on the premises. ₹450

★ **Gokarn International Beach Resort** Kudlee Beach ☎08386 257843, ✉hotelgokarn@yahoo.com, map p.1127. Set back from the beach in its own small garden, this compact, newly constructed hotel offers comfortable mid-price rooms with small kitchenettes and verandas, some of them sea-facing. ₹1200

Hotel Look Sea Kudlee Beach ☎93411 56506, map p.1127. All but four of these basic huts and rooms have shared facilities but many enjoy excellent beach views. Fine muesli in the morning; football matches on the telly and beer in the evening. ₹150/₹400

Namaste Northwest end of Om Beach ☎08386 257141, �🌐namastecafeombeach@gmail.com, map p.1127. One of the more popular beach options, with well-built attached rooms. Each has a different theme: in one, everything is round (including the bed); another resembles a rustic log cabin. Phone and internet connection available, plus there's a pleasant, shaded restaurant. ₹900

New Prasad Nilay On lane near the bus stand ☎08386 257135, map p.1125. Very clean budget place with helpful management and a new second-floor extension.

The pricier rooms have cable TV and balconies. ₹300

Nimmu House Southwest of Car St, towards Kudlee Beach ☎08386 256730, ✉nimmuhouse@yahoo.com, map p.1125. This foreigners' favourite is in a great leafy location but prices spike in peak season. Double rooms in the attractive modern block are spacious, attractive and have decent mattresses, while those in the old wing are much plainer. Many upper rooms have balconies with fine beach views. ₹500

Nirvana Café Southeast end of Om Beach ☎08386 329851, ✉suresh.nirvana@gmail.com, map p.1127. A mixture of bamboo huts with shared bathrooms and solid attached brick ones, neatly arranged behind a congenial restaurant with raised concrete loungers. ₹250/₹500

Shastri Guest House 100m east of the bus stand ☎08386 256220, ✉narasimha.shastri@gmail.com, map p.1125. Tucked behind the Shastri Clinic on the main road, this quiet place offers both attached and non-attached rooms with rock-bottom single rates, as well as roomier cottages up the hill. Only slightly more in high season. ₹250/₹450

SwaSwara Above Om Beach ☎08386 257132, 🌐swaswara.com, map p.1127. The first luxury resort in Gokarna, this *CGH Earth* property offers beautifully designed wood villas spread over terraces on a hillside overlooking the bay. There's a pool, yoga dome and an Ayurvedic treatment centre, all set in extensive gardens. Minimum five-day stay; all-inclusive packages per villa US$2275.

Vaibhav Lodge Off the main road, a few minutes from the bus stand ☎08386 256714, ✉vaibhavnivas97 @gmail.com, map p.1125. Friendly, cheap and justifiably popular guesthouse pitched at foreigners, with a rooftop café-restaurant; rock-bottom rooms with shared facilities and some attached with TV. ₹200/₹400

EATING AND DRINKING

Gokarna town offers a good choice of **places to eat**, with a string of busy "meals" joints along Car Street and the main road. The beaches now have a plethora of places offering travellers' favourites. Look out for the local sweet speciality *gadbad*, several layers of different ice creams mixed with chopped nuts and chewy dried fruit.

Dolphin Bay Southeastern Om Beach ☎98452 65608, map p.1127. Typically laidback place at the back of the beach, offering Western and Indian food, plus a fine range of lassis. Fish costs ₹100–150. Daily 8am–10pm.

Green Gate At Om Hotel, near the new bus stand ☎08386 256244, map p.1125. The more pleasant of this hotel's two restaurants offers a range of Mexican, Italian and Israeli dishes, as well as fish and sizzlers for around ₹200. The bar downstairs has a small garden area. Daily 8am–11pm.

Mahalaxmi At the beach end of Car St ☎94825 56667, map p.1125. Service can be rather slow, but you won't feel much need to hurry, waiting on this sea-view rooftop perch for tasty veg curries or veg with a creamy cheese sauce (all under ₹100). Daily 8am–10pm.

Munchies South-central Kudlee Beach ☎96482 37456, map p.1125. One of the newer and most relaxing spots on Kudlee, with pleasant shady seating and tasty grilled seafood and curries in the ₹100–200 range. Daily 8am–11pm.

Oasis Café South-central Kudlee Beach ☎99010 94690, map p.1127. You can dig your feet in the soft sand at this friendly hangout, nicely decorated with colourful lanterns and wall hangings. A range of offerings from lamb to momos and Thai dishes only cost around ₹100. Daily 8am–11pm.

★ **Old La Pizzeria** South-central Kudlee Beach ☎78297 28872, map p.1127. A few tables on the sand and a cosy atmosphere within make this one of the prime beach dining spots, with some of the best pizzas (₹100–170) in south India, plus fish, burgers and Mexican. Daily 9am–11pm.

Pai Restaurant Main Rd ☎ 08386 256755, map p.1125. An excellent spot for fresh and tasty veg thalis for ₹50, masala dosas and crisp *vadas*, plus teas and coffees at any time of day. Daily 7am–9.30pm.

★ **Prema Restaurant** At the beach end of Car St ☎ 94810 52117, map p.1125. Welcoming veg canteen with delicious dosas, superb toasted English muffin sandwiches, lots of other veg dishes and the best *gadbad* in town. Daily 8am–9pm.

Sunset Café Central Kudlee Beach ☎ 98868 97597, map p.1127. This very popular restaurant offers a range of veg, chicken and seafood dishes such as calamari sizzler for ₹160, and guarantees prime sunset views accompanied by Arabian Sea breezes. Daily 8am–10.30pm.

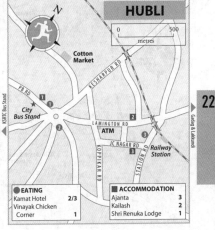

● EATING		■ ACCOMMODATION	
Kamat Hotel	2/3	Ajanta	3
Vinayak Chicken		Kailash	2
Corner	1	Shri Renuka Lodge	1

Hubli

Karnataka's second most industrialized city, **HUBLI**, just east of the Ghats and 418km northwest of Bengaluru, has little to offer tourists except for its transport connections to Mumbai, Goa, the coast of Uttar Kannada (Northern Karnataka), Hampi and other points in the interior.

ARRIVAL AND DEPARTURE   HUBLI

By train Hubli's railway station is right in the town centre and is well connected to Bengaluru, Mumbai, Pune, Hassan and Hospet.

By bus Hubli's efficient KSRTC Bus Stand is 2km south of the centre, and can be reached by bus from the railway station or the chaotic City Bus Stand, about 1km west of the station. There are connections to most towns in Karnataka, most usefully to Ankola (every 30min–1hr; 3hr 30min–4hr) for Gokarna; handy if you do not happen to coincide with one of the four daily direct buses.

ACCOMMODATION AND EATING

Ajanta JC Nagar Rd ☎ 0836 236 2216. This no-nonsense lodge near the station has a range of rooms, including very cheap singles with shared bathroom, and various attached double. ₹400

Kailash Lamington Rd ☎ 0836 235 2235. Conveniently located between the railway station and the bus stand, this efficient business hotel offers good-value a/c rooms and a decent restaurant. ₹600

Kamat Hotel ☎ 0836 222 9254. There are two branches of the famous south Indian food chain that bashes out excellent vegetarian meals and snacks. One is by the traffic island at the bus stand end of Lamington Rd, the other opposite the railway station. Both daily 7am–10pm.

Shri Renuka Lodge Opposite the City Bus Stand ☎ 0836 225 3615. This large and well-organized lodge offers a good range of reasonable rooms, some with a/c, and has its own veg restaurant. ₹500

Vinayak Chicken Corner Opposite the City Bus Stand ☎ 0836 426 1468. A good spot for inexpensive non-veg food, especially delicately spiced fried chicken, and beer. Daily 11am–11pm.

Hospet

Charmless **HOSPET**, about ten hours from both Bengaluru and Goa, is of little interest except as the jumping-off place for the extraordinary ruined city of **Hampi** (Vijayanagar), 13km northeast. If you arrive really late, or want a more upmarket hotel, it makes sense to stay here and catch a bus or auto-rickshaw out to the ruins the following morning.

ARRIVAL AND DEPARTURE   HOSPET

By train Hospet's railway station is 1.5km north of the centre. Note that the Hospet-based auto-rickshaws that gather on the forecourt charge at least ₹200 to Hampi but if you walk a short way along the road, you can usually bargain a returning

22

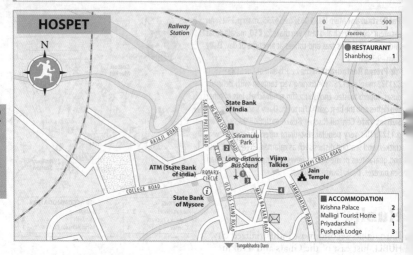

HOSPET

N

Railway Station

0 — 500 metres

● RESTAURANT
Shanbhog 1

RAJAJI ROAD

MG ROAD (STATION) ROAD
SARDAR PATEL ROAD

State Bank of India

Sriramulu Park

ATM (State Bank of India)

ROTARY CIRCLE

COLLEGE ROAD

OLD BUS STAND ROAD

MAIN BAZAAR ROAD

Long-distance Bus Stand

Vijaya Talkies

HAMPI CROSS ROAD

Jain Temple

JAMBUNATHA ROAD

State Bank of Mysore

■ ACCOMMODATION
Krishna Palace   2
Malligi Tourist Home   4
Priyadarshini   1
Pushpak Lodge   3

▼ Tungabhadra Dam

Hampi auto down to under ₹100. Hospet has one direct train daily to Bengaluru, the overnight *Hampi Express* #16591 (dep. 8.45pm; 9hr 25min); change at Guntakal Junction (3hr) for numerous southbound and northbound expresses. For connections to the coast and Goa, head west to Hubli (4 daily; 3–4hr). For connections to Badami and Bijapur, change at Gadag (4 daily; 1hr 20min–2hr).

By bus The bus stand is in the centre, just off MG (Station) Rd, which runs south from the railway station. Bookings for long-distance routes can be made at the ticket office on the bus stand concourse (daily 8am–noon & 3–6pm), where there's also a left-luggage facility. Regular buses run the 30min route to Hampi, some via Kamalapuram, until

around 7.30pm. There are KSRTC buses to destinations throughout the state, but journeys are slow so the only ones worth taking are to Gadag (every 30min; 2hr), Hubli (every 30min; 3hr) or Guntakal (hourly; 2hr 30min–3hr), for the better rail and road connections in those towns. Many tourists opt for the apparently easy option of a private sleeper coach to Goa or Gokarna which depart between 7 and 8pm (9–10hr; ₹800), operated by Paulo Travels (☎08394 225867) from beside the hotel *Priyadarshini*. Unfortunately, these are usually overbooked, overcrowded and, if you are travelling to Gokarna, you will be offloaded for a transfer at Ankola in the wee hours, whatever you are told to the contrary.

INFORMATION

Tourist information The tourist office at the Rotary Circle (Mon–Sat: June–March 10am–5.30pm; April & May 8am–1.30pm; ☎08394 228537) offers limited information and sells tickets for KSTDC tours of Hampi.

Services Full exchange facilities are available at the *Malligi* hotel. Enfield motorbikes are available for rent (or sale) from Bharat Motors (☎08394 224704) near Vijaya Talkies cinema.

ACCOMMODATION AND EATING

Krishna Palace MG Rd ☎08394 294300, ⓦ krishnapalacehotel.com. Snazzy newish a/c hotel, with smartly furnished rooms and an ostentatious lobby. Popular with eastern Europeans. ₹4000

Malligi Tourist Home 6/143 Jambunatha Rd, a 2min walk southeast of the bus stand ☎08394 228101, ⓦ malligihotels.com. Several blocks of luxurious a/c rooms and suites separated by manicured lawns. There is also a large outdoor swimming pool (₹100/hr for non-residents), a smart restaurant, billiards and massage facilities, in addition to a small bookshop, internet access, and an efficient travel service. ₹2200

Priyadarshini MG Rd ☎08394 228838. Large and

bland, but spotless and decent value, especially the a/c rooms (some with balconies). Two good restaurants: the veg *Naivedyam* and, in the garden, the excellent non-veg *Manasa*, which has a bar. ₹1200

Pushpak Lodge MG Rd ☎08394 421380. With basic but clean attached rooms, this is the best low-priced lodge in town and is conveniently, if noisily, located right by the bus stand. ₹400

Shanbhog Next to the bus station. An excellent little Udupi restaurant that's a perfect pit stop before heading to Hampi, particularly since it opens early for breakfast. Daily 6.30am–9.30pm.

Hampi (Vijayanagar)

Among a surreal landscape of golden-brown boulders and leafy banana fields, the ruined "City of Victory," **Vijayanagar**, better known as **HAMPI** (the name of the main local village), spills from the south bank of the River Tungabhadra.

This once dazzling Hindu capital was devastated by a six-month Muslim siege in the second half of the sixteenth century. Only stone, brick and stucco structures survived the ensuing sack – monolithic deities, crumbling houses and abandoned temples dominated by towering *gopuras* – as well as the sophisticated irrigation system that channelled water to huge tanks and temples.

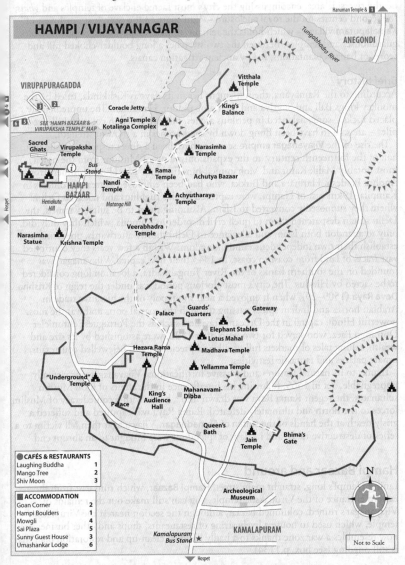

HAMPI / VIJAYANAGAR

Hanuman Temple & **1**

Tungabhadra River

ANEGONDI

VIRUPAPURAGADDA

Vitthala Temple

3 **2**

Coracle Jetty

King's Balance

6 **5**

SEE 'HAMPI BAZAAR & VIRUPAKSHA TEMPLE' MAP

Agni Temple & Kotalinga Complex

Sacred Ghats

Virupaksha Temple

Narasimha Temple

Bus Stand

3

Rama Temple

Achutya Bazaar

Nandi Temple

HAMPI BAZAAR

Hemakuta Hill

Matanga Hill

Achyutharaya Temple

Hospet

Narasimha Statue

Krishna Temple

Veerabhadra Temple

Palace

Guards' Quarters

Gateway

Elephant Stables

Hazara Rama Temple

Lotus Mahal

Madhava Temple

Yellamma Temple

"Underground" Temple

King's Audience Hall

Mahanavami-Dibba

Palace

Queen's Bath

Jain Temple

Bhima's Gate

● **CAFÉS & RESTAURANTS**

Laughing Buddha	1
Mango Tree	2
Shiv Moon	3

■ **ACCOMMODATION**

Goan Corner	2
Hampi Boulders	1
Mowgli	4
Sai Plaza	5
Sunny Guest House	3
Umashankar Lodge	6

N

Archeological Museum

KAMALAPURAM

Kamalapuram Bus Stand ★

Not to Scale

Hospet

Thus, most of Hampi's monuments are in disappointingly poor shape, appearing a lot older than their four or five hundred years. Sadly, a misguided government plan to turn the whole area into a sterile heritage enclosure (see box, p.1134) has started to devastate the core area of **Hampi Bazaar** as well. Yet, at least for the time being, the serene riverside setting and air of magic that still lingers over the site, sacred for centuries before a city was founded here, make it one of India's most extraordinary locations. Many find it difficult to leave and spend weeks chilling out in cafés, wandering to whitewashed hilltop temples and gazing at the spectacular sunsets.

Although spread over 26 square kilometres, the **ruins** of Vijayanagar are mostly concentrated in two distinct groups: the first lies in and around Hampi Bazaar and the nearby riverside area, encompassing the city's most sacred enclave of temples and *ghats*; the second centres on the **royal enclosure** – 3km south of the river, just northwest of **Kamalapuram** village – which holds the remains of palaces, pavilions, elephant stables, guardhouses and temples. Between the two stretches a long boulder-choked hill and scores of banana plantations, fed by ancient irrigation canals.

Brief history

According to the Ramayana, the settlement began its days as Kishkinda, ruled by the monkey kings Bali and Sugriva and their ambassador, Hanuman. The unpredictably placed rocks – some balanced in perilous arches, others heaped in colossal, hill-sized piles – are said to have been flung down by their armies in a show of strength.

The rise of the **Vijayanagar empire** seems to have been a direct response, in the first half of the fourteenth century, to the expansionist aims of Muslims from the north, most notably Malik Kafur and Mohammed-bin-Tughluq. Two Hindu brothers from Andhra Pradesh, Harihara and Bukka, who had been employed as treasury officers in Kampila, 19km east of Hampi, were captured by the Tughluqs and taken to Delhi, where they supposedly converted to Islam. Assuming them to be suitably tamed, the Delhi sultan despatched them to quell civil disorder in Kampila, which they duly did, only to abandon both Islam and allegiance to Delhi shortly afterwards, preferring to establish their own independent Hindu kingdom. Within a few years they controlled vast tracts of land from coast to coast. In 1343 their new capital, Vijayanagar, was founded on the southern banks of the River Tungabhadra, a location long considered to be sacred by Hindus. The city's most glorious period was under the reign of **Krishna Deva Raya** (1509–29), when it enjoyed a near monopoly of the lucrative trade in Arabian horses and Indian spices passing through the coastal ports and was the most powerful Hindu capital in the Deccan. Travellers such as the Portuguese chronicler Domingo Paez, who stayed for two years after 1520, were astonished by its size and wealth, telling tales of markets full of silk and precious gems, bejewelled courtesans, ornate palaces and fantastic festivities.

Thanks to its natural features and massive fortifications, Vijayanagar was virtually impregnable. Yet in 1565, following his interference in the affairs of local Muslim sultanates, the regent Rama Raya was drawn into a battle with a confederacy of Muslim forces to the north and ultimately defeated. Rama Raya was captured and suffered a grisly death at the hands of the **sultan of Ahmadnagar**. Vijayanagar then fell victim to a series of destructive raids, and its days of splendour were brought to an abrupt end.

Hampi Bazaar and around

Lining Hampi's long, straight main street, **Hampi Bazaar**, which runs east from the eastern entrance of the Virupaksha temple, you can still make out the remains of Vijayanagar's ruined, columned bazaar, although the section nearest the Virupaksha temple, which used to house a lively string of restaurants, shops and other businesses, now resembles a war zone thanks to a badly handled clean-up and restoration plan that is still ongoing (see box, p.1134).

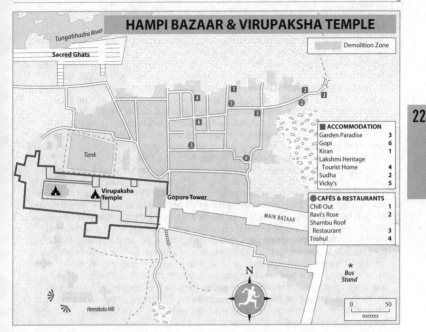

HAMPI BAZAAR & VIRUPAKSHA TEMPLE

Tungabhadra River

Sacred Ghats

Demolition Zone

Tank

Virupaksha Temple

Gopura Tower

MAIN BAZAAR

Hemakuta Hill

N

Bus Stand

0   50
metres

■ ACCOMMODATION
Garden Paradise	3
Gopi	6
Kiran	1
Lakshmi Heritage Tourist Home	4
Sudha	2
Vicky's	5

● CAFÉS & RESTAURANTS
Chill Out	1
Ravi's Rose	2
Shambu Roof Restaurant	3
Trishul	4

22

The Virupaksha temple

Daily 6.30am–12.30pm & 2–8.30pm • ₹2 but free during arati (daily 6.30–8am & 6.30–8.30pm)

Dedicated to a local form of Shiva known as Virupaksha or Pampapati, the functioning **Virupaksha temple** dominates the village, drawing a steady flow of pilgrims from all over southern India. Also known as **Sri Virupaksha Swami**, the temple is at its liveliest and most atmospheric during *arati*. The complex consists of two courts, each entered through a towered *gopura*.

A colonnade surrounds the inner court, usually filled with pilgrims dozing and singing religious songs. If the temple elephant, Lakshmi, is around when you enter, you can get her to bless you by placing a rupee in her trunk. In the middle, the principal temple is approached through a *mandapa* hallway whose carved columns feature rearing animals. Rare Vijayanagar-era paintings on the *mandapa* ceiling include aspects of Shiva, a procession with the sage Vidyaranya, the ten incarnations of Vishnu and scenes from the Mahabharata.

The riverside

The sacred **ford** in the river is reached from the Virupaksha's north *gopura*; you can also get there by following the lane around the impressive temple **tank**. A *mandapa* overlooks the steps that originally led to the river, now some distance away. A small **motor boat** plies from this part of the bank, ferrying villagers to the fields and tourists to the increasingly popular enclave of **Virupapuragadda**. This is replaced by the traditional old coracle after dark. The road left from the sacred ford through the village eventually loops back towards the hilltop Hanuman temple, about 5km east, and on to Anegondi – a recommended round walk.

Matanga Hill

The place to head for sunrise is the boulder hill immediately east of Hampi Bazaar. From

22

SACRILEGE IN A SACRED SETTING

Until the summer of 2011, the local people of Hampi Bazaar had lived a peaceful and largely idyllic existence amid the Vijayanagar ruins for several centuries. Indeed, in recent decades many of them had been making a decent living from the increasing number of travellers who came to marvel at the sites and hang out in the cafés and guesthouses. All that changed very abruptly when a long-awaited **government scheme** to fence off the whole 26-square-kilometre area in order to protect its UNESCO World Heritage status finally got out of legal gridlock and began to be implemented. All residents were removed from the bazaar and, despite vocal protests, the **bulldozers** moved in with grim purpose. As of early 2013, a whole swathe of the modern buildings around 30–40m on either side of the main bazaar and along the main lane from the temple to the river had been destroyed. By a supreme stroke of irony, considering that the aim of all this was to enhance the visitor experience, even the tourist office was flattened.

The project is being conducted in phases and, as they have been so slow in clearing the rubble from this initial phase, it could take anything from five to ten years to complete. In the meantime, the locals who have not already been deprived of their income – and thankfully that includes most of the guesthouses near the river and all of those across it – feel they are living on borrowed time because nobody knows when the next stage of demolition will begin. Ultimately even all the businesses on the opposite bank of the river will also be removed. Predictably, the **compensation packages** offered to those displaced are risible: just ₹125,000 per enterprise is barely enough to dig foundations for a new property in today's economic climate. Even if the guesthouse and restaurant proprietors did find the money to relocate to the land that has been made available 4km away, outside the projected fence, it is hardly guaranteed that travellers would choose to stay there. For the foreigners who have been enchanted by Hampi over the years it is heartbreaking that the magic of staying amid a former kingdom seems certain to disappear. For the locals whose homes and livelihoods are being swept away it is nothing short of a tragedy.

the end of the main street, an ancient paved pathway winds up a rise, at the top of which the magnificent Achyutharaya temple (see below) is revealed. The views improve as you progress up **Matanga Hill**, and a small stone temple (named Veerabhadra) at its summit provides an extraordinary vantage point. The problem of muggings early in the morning along this path seems to have waned but it's probably still a good idea to be vigilant if there are only one or two of you.

The riverside path

To reach the Vitthala temple (see below), walk east from the Virupaksha, the length of Hampi Bazaar, where a huge monolithic **Nandi** statue gazes across at the main temple from its shrine. Just before you reach these, a path on the left, staffed at regular intervals by conch-blowing sadhus and an assortment of other ragged mendicants, follows the river past a couple of cafés and numerous shrines, including a Rama temple – home to hordes of fearless monkeys. Beyond at least four Vishnu shrines, a paved and colonnaded **bazaar** leads due south to the **Achyutharaya temple** (aka Tiruvengalanatha), whose beautiful stone carvings – among them some of Hampi's famed erotica – are being restored by the ASI. Back on the main path again, make a short detour across the rocks leading to the river to see the little-visited waterside **Agni temple**; next to it, the Kotalinga complex consists of 108 (an auspicious number) tiny *lingas*, carved on a flat rock. As you approach the Vitthala temple, to the south is an archway known as the **King's Balance**, where the rajas were weighed against gold, silver and jewels to be distributed to the city's priests.

Vitthala temple

Daily 6am–6pm • ₹250 (₹10); ticket also valid for the Lotus Mahal (see p.1137) on the same day

Although the area of the **Vitthala temple** does not show the same evidence of early cult worship as Virupaksha, the ruined bridge to the west probably dates from before Vijayanagar times. The bathing *ghat* may be from the Chalukya or Ganga period, but as the temple has fallen into disuse it seems that the river crossing (*tirtha*) here has not had the same sacred significance as the Virupaksha site. Now part of the UNESCO World Heritage Site, the Vitthala temple was built for Vishnu, who according to legend was too embarrassed by its ostentation to live here.

The open *mandapa* features slender monolithic granite musical **pillars** which were constructed so as to sound the notes of the scale when struck. Today, due to vandalism and erosion from being repeatedly beaten, heavy security makes sure that no one is allowed to touch them. Guides, however, will happily demonstrate the musical resonance of other pillars on an adjacent structure. Outer columns sport characteristic Vijayanagar rearing horses, while friezes of lions, elephants and horses on the moulded basement display sculptural trickery – you can transform one beast into another simply by masking one portion of the image.

In front of the temple, to the east, a stone representation of a wooden processional **rath**, or chariot, houses an image of Garuda, Vishnu's bird vehicle. Now cemented, at one time the chariot's wheels revolved.

Anegondi and beyond

With more time, and a sense of adventure, you can head across the River Tungabhadra to **ANEGONDI**, a fortress town predating Vijayanagar, and its fourteenth-century headquarters. The most pleasant way to get here is to take a coracle from the ford 1.5km east of the Vitthala temple; these circular rush baskets, which are today reinforced with plastic sheets, also carry bicycles, which are a good way to visit Hampi's many monuments. A bridge was constructed at this point but it collapsed and there are no plans to rebuild.

Forgotten temples and fortifications litter Anegondi village and its quiet surroundings. The ruined **Huchchappa-matha temple**, near the river gateway, is worth a look for its lathe-turned black stone pillars and fine panels of dancers. **Aramani**, a ruined palace in the centre, stands opposite the home of the descendants of the royal family; also in the centre, the **Ranganatha temple** is still active. A huge wooden temple chariot stands in the village square. The only **accommodation** here is in village houses and you can get basic snacks at the local stalls.

Pampla Sarovar

To complete a five-kilometre loop back to Hampi from Anegondi (the simplest route if you have wheels), head left (west) along the turning just north of the village, which winds through sugar cane fields and eventually comes out near Virupapuragadda. En route you can visit the sacred **Pampla Sarovar**, signposted down a dirt lane to the left. The small temple above this square bathing tank, tended by a *swami* who will proudly show you photos of his pilgrimage to Mount Kailash, is dedicated to the goddess Lakshmi and holds a cave containing a footprint of Vishnu. If you are staying around Anegondi, this quiet and atmospheric spot is best visited early in the evening during *arati* (worship).

Hanuman temple

A worthwhile detour off the road north of the river leading west from Anegondi is the hike up to the tiny whitewashed **Hanuman temple**, perched on a rocky hilltop, from where you gain superb views over Hampi, especially at sunrise and sunset. The steep climb up to it takes around thirty minutes. An alternative walking route back involves following the path a further 2km back towards the river until you reach an impressive old **stone bridge** dating from Vijayanagar times. The bridge no longer spans the river but just beyond it, to the west, another small motor boat (₹10) returns you to a point about halfway between the Vitthala temple and Hampi Bazaar.

Hemakuta Hill and around

Directly above Hampi Bazaar, **Hemakuta Hill** is dotted with pre-Vijayanagar temples that probably date from between the ninth and eleventh centuries. Aside from the architecture, the main reason to clamber up here is to admire the **views** of the ruins and surrounding countryside. With views across the boulder-covered terrain and banana plantations, the sheer western edge of the hill is Hampi's number-one sunset spot, attracting a crowd of blissed-out tourists most evenings, along with a couple of entrepreneurial chai-wallahs and little boys posing for photos in Hanuman costumes.

A couple of interesting monuments lie on the road leading south towards the main, southern group of ruins. The first of these, a walled **Krishna temple complex** to the west of the road, dates from 1513. Although dilapidated in parts, it features some fine carving and shrines.

Hampi's most-photographed monument stands just south of the Krishna temple in its own enclosure. Depicting Vishnu in his incarnation as the Man-Lion, the monolithic **Narasimha** statue, with its bulging eyes and crossed legs strapped into yogic pose, is one of Vijayanagar's greatest treasures.

The southern and royal monuments

The most impressive remains of Vijayanagar, the city's **royal monuments**, lie some 3km south of Hampi Bazaar, spread over a large expanse of open ground. Before tackling the ruins proper, it's a good idea to get your bearings with a visit to the small **Archeological Museum** (daily except Fri 10am–5pm; free) at Kamalapuram, which can be reached by bus from Hospet or Hampi. Among the sculpture, weapons, palm-leaf manuscripts and paintings from Vijayanagar and Anegondi, the highlight is a superb scale model of the city, giving an excellent bird's-eye view of the entire site.

Bhima's Gate

The route to the monuments is well signposted. After 200m or so you reach the partly ruined massive **inner city wall**, made from granite slabs, which runs 32km around the city, in places as high as 10m. Just beyond the wall, the **citadel area** was once enclosed by another wall and gates, of which only traces remain. To the east, the small *ganigitti* ("oil-woman's") fourteenth-century **Jain temple** features a simple stepped pyramidal tower of undecorated horizontal slabs. Beyond it is **Bhima's Gate**, once one of the principal entrances to the city, named after the Titan-like Pandava prince and hero of the Mahabharata. Like many of the gates, it is "bent", a form of defence that meant anyone trying to get in had to make two 90° turns. Bas-reliefs depict such episodes as Bhima avenging the honour of his wife, Draupadi, by killing the general Dushasana. Draupadi vowed she would not dress her hair until Dushasana was dead; one panel shows her tying up her locks, the vow fulfilled.

Queen's Bath

To the west of the Jain temple, the plain facade of the 15m-square **Queen's Bath** belies its glorious interior, open to the sky and surrounded by corridors with 24 different domes. Eight projecting balconies overlook where once was water; traces of Islamic-influenced stucco decoration survive. Women from the royal household would bathe here and umbrellas were placed in shafts in the tank floor to protect them from the sun. The water supply channel can be seen outside.

Mahanavami-Dibba

Northwest of the Queen's Bath is **Mahanavami-Dibba** or "House of Victory", built to commemorate a successful campaign in Orissa. A 12m pyramidal structure with a square base, it is said to have been where the king gave and received honours and gifts. From here he watched the magnificent parades, music and dance performances, martial arts displays, elephant fights and animal sacrifices that made celebration of the ten-day Dussehra festival famed throughout the land. Carved reliefs decorate the sides of the platform.

King's Audience Hall

To the west of the Mahanavami-Dibba, another platform – the largest at Vijayanagar – is thought to be the basement of the **King's Audience Hall**. Stone bases of a hundred pillars remain, in an arrangement that has caused speculation as to how the building could have been used; there are no passageways or open areas.

Lotus Mahal

Daily 6am–6pm • ₹250 (₹10); ticket also valid for the Vitthala temple on the same day

The two-storey **Lotus Mahal**, in the north of the compound and part of the **zenana enclosure**, or women's quarters, was designed for the pleasure of Krishna Deva Raya's queen: a place where she could relax, particularly in summer. Displaying a strong Indo-Islamic influence, the pavilion is open on the ground floor, whereas the inaccessible upper level contains windows and balcony seats. A moat surrounding the building is thought to have provided water-cooled air via tubes.

Elephant Stables

Just northeast of the Lotus Mahal, the **Elephant Stables**, a series of high-ceilinged, domed chambers, entered through arches, are the most substantial surviving secular buildings at Vijayanagar – a reflection of the high status accorded to elephants, both ceremonial and in battle.

Hazra Rama temple

To the west of the compound lies Hemakuta Hill, site of the rectangular enclosure wall of the small **Hazara Rama** ("One thousand Ramas") temple. Thought to have been the private palace shrine, it features a series of medallion figures and bands of detailed friezes showing scenes from the Ramayana.

ARRIVAL AND INFORMATION   **HAMPI (VIJAYNAGAR)**

By bus Buses from Hospet terminate close to where the road joins the main street in Hampi Bazaar, halfway along its dusty length.

Tourist information A sign in the inner courtyard of the Virupaksha temple claims there to be a tourist office, after the official one was demolished, but it never seems to be open. The numerous private agencies can help with most travel-related enquiries.

Services Stalls such as Raju, just up the lane from *Vicky's* guesthouse, has motorbikes and scooters for rent (around ₹150–200/day). Most guesthouses rent bicycles (₹80/day) but the bumpy terrain does make cycling hard work. There are no ATMs or banks but agents can offer exchange; rates are rather poor, so it's better to stock up on cash in Hospet.

ACCOMMODATION

Hampi Bazaar remains the best place to stay for access to the sites, choice of restaurants and other facilities. There are no fancy hotels but around forty guesthouses of varying size and calibre. Some travellers prefer to stay across the river in **Virupapuragadda**, which is now well developed and has caught up in price. Prices are pretty low most of the year apart from the Christmas to mid-January peak, when they at least double.

HAMPI BAZAAR

Garden Paradise Far northeast end of the village ☎08394 241954, ✉elango14in@yahoo.com; map p.1133. Five attached and seven non-attached huts with mosquito nets, set in an excellent riverside location. Also a chilled-out multicuisine restaurant area. **₹500**

Gopi Centre of the village ☎08394 241695, ✉kirangopi2002@yahoo.com; map p.1133. One of the more established places with small, simple rooms in the old building and smart but expensive a/c options in another block round the corner. **₹600**

Kiran Beside the river ☎08394 204159,

22

@ gowdakiran96@yahoo.co.in; map p.1133. The basic rooms here are compact but clean enough and among the cheapest left in the area. The rooftop restaurant has fine views of the river and the temple. ₹300

★ **Lakshmi Heritage Tourist Home** Down the lane towards the river ☎ 08394 241456; map p.1133. Smart and spacious a/c rooms with new furniture and colourful decoration, plus hot running water all the time. Good discounts at slack times. ₹1500

★ **Sudha** Northeast end of the village ☎ 94810 42336; map p.1133. One of the nicest, friendliest places to stay. The rooms vary in size but are generally larger and decorated more nicely on the slightly pricier upper storey. Rooftop Nepali restaurant. ₹400

Vicky's Just east of the village centre ☎ 94805 61010, @ vikkyhampi@yahoo.co.in; map p.1133. Small, clean rooms, now all attached, in one of the village's oldest lodges. Friendly and deservedly popular for its rooftop restaurant. ₹800

ACROSS THE RIVER

Goan Corner 500m inland and east of boat crossing, Virupapuragadda ☎ 94487 18951, @ sharmila .thakur@gmail.com; map p.1131. Large complex between lush paddy fields and attractive boulders with a range of rooms and huts, some with attached bathrooms. Lively restaurant. ₹250/₹350

Hampi Boulders Narayanpet, Bandi Harlur ☎ 92426 41551, @ hampisboulders.com; map p.1131. Overlooking a bend in the River Tungabhadra, this small, quirky

resort hotel is the best upscale option, a 30min car ride from Hampi Bazaar. There are two grades of cottages, moulded around giant boulder outcrops, with palms, mango trees and brakes of bamboo for shade. Meals are so-so Indian buffets and they have a natural rock-cut swimming pool. ₹7000

★ **Mowgli** Far west end of main road, Virupapuragadda ☎ 08394 329844, @ mowglihampi .com; map p.1131. The smartest option right across the river, offering a range of rooms and cottages, including two with a/c, with comfy sitouts and private balconies, some with fantastic views, as well as a welcoming restaurant, set against a gorgeous paddy and river backdrop. ₹1200

Sai Plaza Main road, Virupapuragadda ☎ 08533 287017, @ saiplazahampi.com; map p.1131. These fifteen bungalows enclosing an attractive courtyard garden are relaxed and welcoming. The restaurant has delicious lassis and sandwiches and excellent views across the river. ₹400

★ **Sunny Guesthouse** 500m inland of boat crossing, Virupapuragadda ☎ 08533 287005, @ sunnyguesthouse@yahoo.com; map p.1131. Nicely landscaped gardens with brightly painted bungalows and two sets of compact rooms, some with piped hot water. Their *Sheesh Besh* restaurant is a popular hangout. ₹400

Umashankar Lodge Main road, Virupapuragadda t08533 287067; map p.1131. Cosy, popular spot with small but clean attached rooms (the upstairs ones rather overpriced) set round a leafy courtyard. ₹300

EATING

Hampi has a plethora of traveller-oriented **restaurants**, with many of the most popular attached to guesthouses in the bazaar, or among the growing row of joints in Virupapuragadda. As a holy site, the main village is strictly alcohol-free and almost entirely vegetarian. There are no such restrictions on the other side of the river.

Chill Out Centre of village ☎ 94820 48655; map p.1133. One of the newer places, and it out-chills some of the older ones, with cushioned seating and bright decoration. Veg sizzlers go for ₹160. Wi-fi available. Daily 8am–10.30pm.

Laughing Buddha Main road, Virupapuragadda ☎ 94827 67374; map p.1131. Good for set breakfasts and meat dishes such as schnitzel for around ₹150, with a generally relaxed atmosphere and film screenings every evening. Daily 8am–10pm.

★ **Mango Tree** 300m west of Sacred Ford ☎ 94487 65213; map p.1131. Wonderfully relaxed riverside hangout on tiered stone terraces, serving good veg food, especially the pasta dishes for around ₹100. Flies are a problem during the day. Daily 7.30am–9.30pm.

Ravi's Rose East end of village ☎ 08533 241957; map p.1133. This small rooftop joint is one of the best places for authentic Indian food (₹80–160): there are even some

genuinely spicy dishes on request, and great lassis too. Good sound system, playing mostly western sounds. Daily 7am–10pm.

Shambu Roof Restaurant Centre of village ☎ 94487 95096; map p.1133. Set breakfasts, snacks, a variety of dosas and a special thali for ₹100 are among the items available. The rooftop setting guarantees fine views of the temple, particularly at dawn and sunset. Daily 8am–10.30pm.

Shiv Moon Riverside path, 500m east of the village ☎ 94807 26462; map p.1131. A good place to break the journey to or from the Vitthala temple, serving pastas and standard curries, all in the ₹100–150 range. Daily 6am–10pm.

★ **Trishul** Southeast side of village ☎ 94805 03605; map p.1133. Featuring chicken, tuna, lasagne, pizza and apple crumble, plus Mexican and Israeli cuisine, this is one of Hampi's widest menus, promising the rare treat of non-veg dishes. Daily 7am–11pm.

Badami, Aihole and Pattadakal: Monuments of the Chalukyas

Now quiet villages, **Badami**, **Aihole** and **Pattadakal**, the last a UNESCO World Heritage Site, were once the capital cities of the **Chalukyas**, who ruled much of the Deccan between the fourth and eighth centuries. The astonishing profusion of **temples** in the area beggars belief. Badami's and Aihole's cave temples, stylistically related to those at Ellora (see p.637), are some of the most important of their type. Among the many freestanding temples are some of the earliest in India, and uniquely, it is possible to see both northern (*nagari*) and southern (Dravida) architectural styles side by side.

Badami

Surrounded by a yawning expanse of flat farmland, **BADAMI**, capital of the Chalukyas from 543 AD to 757 AD, extends east into a gorge between two red sandstone hills, each topped by an ancient fort complex. The southern hill is riddled with cave temples, while the northern one is studded with early structural temples. Beyond the village, to the east, is an artificial lake, **Agastya**, said to date from the fifth century. Badami's small selection of hotels and restaurants makes it an ideal base from which to explore the Chalukyan remains at Aihole and Pattadakal, as they do not possess such facilities. Be aware that the whole Badami area is home to numerous troupes of monkeys, especially around the monuments, and they will crawl all over you if you produce food.

Southern Fort cave temples

Daily sunrise–sunset • ₹100 (₹5)

Badami's earliest monuments are a group of sixth-century **caves** cut into the hill's red sandstone, each connected by steps leading up the hillside.

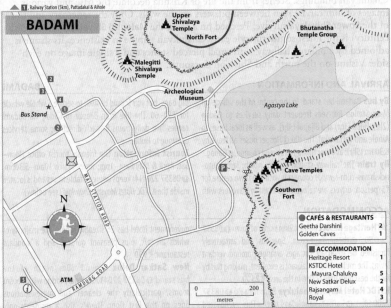

▲ 1 Railway Station (5km), Pattadakal & Aihole

BADAMI

Upper Shivalaya Temple
North Fort
Bhutanatha Temple Group
Malegitti Shivalaya Temple
Archeological Museum
Agastya Lake
Bus Stand
P
Cave Temples
Southern Fort
N

● CAFÉS & RESTAURANTS
Geetha Darshini	2
Golden Caves	1

■ ACCOMMODATION
Heritage Resort	1
KSTDC Hotel	
Mayura Chalukya	5
New Satkar Delux	2
Rajsangam	4
Royal	3

MAIN STATION ROAD

ATM

RAMDURG ROAD

0   200
metres

▼ Banashankeri

22

About 15m up the face of the rock, **Cave 1**, a Shiva temple, is probably the earliest. Entrance is through a triple opening into a long porch raised on a plinth decorated with images of Shiva's dwarf attendants, the *ganas*. Outside, to the left of the porch, a *dvarpala* door guardian stands beneath a Nandi bull. On the right is a striking 1.5m-high image of a sixteen-armed dancing Shiva. He carries a stick-zither-type *vina*, which may or may not be a *yal*, a now-extinct musical instrument, on which the earliest Indian classical music theory is thought to have been developed.

A little higher, the similar **Cave 2** is a Vishnu shrine that holds some impressive sculpture and painting. Climbing again, steps and slopes lead upwards past a natural cave containing a smashed image of the Buddhist *bodhisattva*, Padmapani (he who holds the lotus), before steps on the right lead up to the fort.

Cave 3 (578 AD) stands beneath a 30m-high perpendicular bluff. The largest of the group, with a facade measuring 21m from north to south, it is also considered to be the finest, for the quality of its sculptural decoration. Treatment of the pillars is extremely elaborate, featuring male and female bracket figures, lotus motifs and medallions portraying amorous couples.

To the east of the others, **Cave 4** is a Jain temple that overlooks Agastya Lake and the town. It's a much simpler shrine, dating from the sixth century. Lining the walls are figures of the 24 *tirthankaras*, both seated and standing and mostly without their identifying emblems. Here, the rock is striped.

After seeing the caves it is possible to climb up to the fort and walk east where, hidden in the rocks, a carved panel shows Vishnu reclining on the serpent Adisesha, attended by a profusion of gods and sages. Continuing, you can skirt the gorge and descend on the east to the Bhutanatha temples at the lakeside.

North Fort

North of Agastya Lake, a number of structural temples can be reached by steps. The small **Archeological Museum** (daily except Fri 10am–5pm; ₹2) contains sculpture from the region. Although now dilapidated, the **Upper Shivalaya temple** is one of the earliest Chalukyan buildings. Scenes from the life of Krishna decorate the base and various images of him can be seen between pilasters on the walls. Only the sanctuary and tower of the **Lower Shivalaya** survive. Perched on a rock, the **Malegitti Shivalaya** (late seventh century) is the finest southern-style early Chalukya temple in existence. Its shrine is adjoined by a pillared hallway with small pierced stones and a single image on each side: Vishnu on the north and Shiva on the south.

ARRIVAL AND INFORMATION

BADAMI

By bus Badami bus stand, in the centre of the village on Main Station Rd, sees frequent daily services to Gadag (2hr), Hubli (3hr) and Bijapur (4hr), as well as local buses to Aihole and Pattadakal. The direct Hospet buses all leave by 8.30am (5hr); at other times you should change in Gadag.
By train The railway station is 5km north; large auto-rickshaws-cum-*tempos* connect it with the town centre for ₹5/person; drivers are reluctant to cram in travellers with big bags, but you should be able to secure a whole vehicle for ₹50–60. The line from Bijapur to Gadag via Badami carries five daily trains in each direction; some services continue to Hubli.
Tourist information The friendly tourist office (Mon–Sat: April & May 8am–1pm; June–March 10am–5.30pm; ☎08357 220414) keeps unpredictable hours and is located inside the *KSTDC Hotel Mayura Chalukya* (see below).

ACCOMMODATION

★ **Heritage Resort** Almost 2km north of town ☎08357 220250, ⊕theheritage.co.in. Spacious and attractively furnished detached a/c cottages arranged around verdant lawns. The multicuisine restaurant is excellent, making this by far the best upmarket option in the area. ₹2500
KSTDC Hotel Mayura Chalukya Ramdurg Rd ☎08357 220046, ⊕karnatakaholidays.net. This renovated government hotel has 26 sizeable rooms, the majority of which are a/c, plus pleasant gardens and a standard restaurant. ₹990
New Satkar Delux Around 80m north of the bus stand ☎08357 220417. Friendly lodge with decent rooms, particularly the cleaner and more spacious ones on the first floor. There's also a residents-only

restaurant in the back garden, which serves excellent food. ₹**600**

Rajsangam Opposite the bus stand ☎08357 221991, ⓦhotelrajsangaminternational.com. The priciest in-town option offers spacious singles, deluxe doubles, and suites with balconies. It also has two good restaurants: the

Banashree serves pure veg food and the *Shubashree* is non-veg and has a bar. ₹**1400**

Royal 50m north of the bus stand ☎81231 43258. Good-value new lodge, built of brightly painted concrete and marble, with simply furnished but clean attached rooms, all with flatscreen TVs. ₹**700**

EATING

Geetha Darshini 100m south of the bus stand ☎90363 56378. This is a small but top-notch south Indian joint whose *iddlis*, *vadas* and dosas are out of this world. Daily 6am–9pm.

Golden Caves Just south of the bus stand ☎94487 29812. Serves good inexpensive non-veg Indian and Chinese food, indoors or in the airy courtyard. Full tandoori chicken ₹300 and cheap fish. Daily 7.30am–11pm.

Aihole

No fewer than 125 temples, dating from the Chalukyan and the later Rashtrakuta periods (sixth to twelfth centuries), are found in the tiny village of **AIHOLE** (Aivalli), near the banks of the River Malaprabha. Lying in clusters within the village, in surrounding fields and on rocky outcrops, many of the temples are remarkably well preserved, despite being used as dwellings and cattle sheds. Reflecting both its geographical position and spirit of architectural experimentation, Aihole boasts northern (*nagari*) and southern (Dravida) temples, as well as variants that failed to survive subsequent stylistic developments.

Two of the temples are **rock-cut caves** dating from the sixth century. The Hindu **Ravanaphadigudi**, northeast of the centre, a Shiva shrine with a triple entrance, contains fine sculptures of Mahishasuramardini, a ten-armed Nateshan (the precursor of Shiva Nataraja) dancing with Parvati, Ganesh and the Sapta Matrikas ("seven mothers"). A two-storey cave, plain save for decoration at the entrances and a panel image of Buddha in its upper veranda, can be found partway up the hill to the southeast, overlooking the village. At the top of that hill, the Jain **Meguti** temple, which may never have been completed, bears an inscription on an outer wall dating it to 634 AD. You can climb up to the first floor for fine views of Aihole and the surrounding country.

Durga temple

In the Archeological Survey compound near the centre of the village • Daily 6am–6pm • ₹100 (₹5)

The late seventh- to early eighth-century **Durga temple**, one of the most unusual, elaborate and large in Aihole, stands close to others on open ground. It derives its name not from the goddess Durga but from the Kannada *durgadagudi*, meaning "temple near the fort". A series of pillars – many featuring amorous couples – forming an open ambulatory continue from the porch around the whole building. Other sculptural highlights include the decoration on the entrance to the *mandapa* hallway and niche images on the outer walls of the now-empty semicircular sanctum.

Archeological Museum

Just outside the entrance to the Durga temple • Daily except Fri 10am–5pm • Free

The small **Archeological Museum** displays a modest collection of early Chalukyan sculpture and sells the booklet *Glorious Aihole*, which includes a site map and accounts of the monuments.

Ladh Khan

A short way south of the Durga temple, beyond several other shrines

The **Ladh Khan** temple (named after the Muslim who made it his home) is perhaps the best known of all at Aihole. Now thought to have been constructed at some point between the end of the sixth century and the eighth, it was originally seen as one of the country's temple prototypes. Inside stands a Nandi bull and a small sanctuary containing a *shivalingam* is next to the back wall. Both may have been later additions, with the original inner sanctum located at the centre.

By bus Six daily buses run to Aihole from Badami (1hr 30min) via Pattadakal (45min) from 5.30am to 9pm; the   last bus returns around 6pm.

Pattadakal

On a bend in the River Malaprabha 22km northeast of Badami, the village of **PATTADAKAL** served as the site of Chalukyan coronations between the seventh and eighth centuries; in fact, it may have been used solely for such ceremonies. Like Badami and Aihole, the area boasts fine Chalukyan architecture, with particularly large mature examples; as at Aihole, both northern and southern styles can be seen.

Temple compound

Daily 6am–6pm • ₹250 (₹10) Pattadakal is connected by regular state buses and hourly private buses to Badami (45min) and Aihole (45min).

Pattadakal's main group of monuments stand together in a well-maintained **temple compound**, next to the village, and have been designated a UNESCO World Heritage Site. The site is used for a major annual **dance festival** at the end of January or early February.

Earliest among the temples, the **Sangameshvara**, also known as **Shri Vijayeshvara** (a reference to its builder, Vijayaditya Satyashraya; 696–733), shows typical southern features. To the south, both the **Mallikarjuna** and the enormous **Virupaksha**, side by side, are in the southern style, built by two sisters who were successively the queens of Vikramaditya II (733–46). Along with the Kanchipuram temple in Tamil Nadu, the Virupaksha was probably one of the largest and most elaborate in India at the time. Interior pillars are carved with scenes from the Ramayana and Mahabharata, while in the Mallikarjuna the stories are from the life of Krishna.

The largest northern-style temple, the **Papanatha**, further south, was probably built after the Virupaksha in the eighth century. Outside walls feature reliefs (some of which, unusually, bear the sculptors' autographs) from the Ramayana, including, on the south wall, Hanuman's monkey army.

Bijapur and the north

The dry and dusty far northern region of Karnataka is as distinct culturally as it is in terms of landscape. Predominantly Muslim, at least in the larger settlements, it boasts some wonderful Islamic architecture and shrines in the venerable city of **Bijapur**, bustling **Gulbarga** and flyblown **Bidar**.

Bijapur

Boasting some of the Deccan's finest Muslim monuments, **BIJAPUR** is often billed as "the Agra of the South". The comparison is partly justified: for more than three hundred years, this was the capital of a succession of powerful rulers, whose domed mausoleums, mosques, colossal civic buildings and fortifications recall a lost golden age of unrivalled prosperity and artistic refinement. Yet there the similarities between the two cities end. A provincial market town of just 210,000 inhabitants, modern Bijapur is a world away from the urban frenzy of Agra. With the exception of the mighty **Golgumbaz**, which attracts busloads of day-trippers, its historic sites see only a slow trickle of tourists, while the ramshackle town centre is surprisingly laidback, dotted with peaceful green spaces and colonnaded mosque courtyards. In the first week of February the town hosts an annual **music festival**, which attracts several renowned musicians from both the Carnatic (south Indian) and the Hindustani (north Indian) classical music traditions.

Unlike most medieval Muslim strongholds, Bijapur lacked natural rock defences and had to be strengthened by the Adil Shahis with huge **fortified walls**. Extending some 10km around the town, these ramparts, studded with cannon emplacements (*burjes*) and watchtowers, are breached in five points by *darwazas*, or strong gateways, and several smaller postern gates (*didis*). In the middle of the town, a further hoop of crenellated battlements encircled Bijapur's **citadel**, site of the sultans' apartments and durbar hall, of which only fragments remain. The Adil Shahis' **tombs** are scattered around the outskirts, while most of the important **mosques** lie southeast of the citadel.

Brief history

Bijapur began life in the tenth century as **Vijayapura**, the Chalukyas' "City of Victory". Taken by the Vijayanagars, it passed into Muslim hands for the first time in the thirteenth century with the arrival of the sultans of Delhi. The Bahmanis administered the area for a time, but it was only after the local rulers, the **Adil Shahis**, won independence from Bidar by expelling the Bahmani garrison and declaring this their capital that Bijapur's rise to prominence began.

Burying their differences for a brief period in the late sixteenth century, the five Muslim dynasties that issued from the breakdown of Bahmani rule – based at Golconda, Ahmednagar, Bidar and Gulbarga – formed a military alliance to defeat the Vijayanagars. The spoils of this campaign, which saw the total destruction of Vijayanagar (Hampi), funded a two-hundred-year building boom in Bijapur during which the city's most impressive monuments were built. However, old enmities between rival Muslim sultanates on the Deccan soon resurfaced, and the Adil Shahis' royal coffers were gradually squandered on fruitless and protracted wars. By the time the British arrived on the scene in the eighteenth century, the Adil Shahis were a spent force, locked into a decline from which they and their capital never recovered.

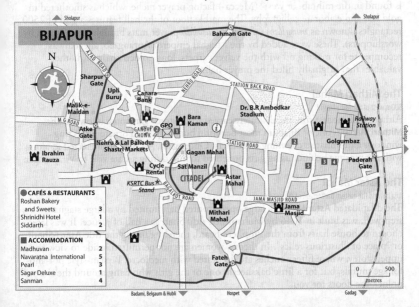

BIJAPUR

N

Sholapur — Bahman Gate — Sholapur

Sharpur Gate
Upli Buruj
Canara Bank
AZAD ROAD
NEHRU ROAD
STATION BACK ROAD
Dr. B.R Ambedkar Stadium
Malik-e-Maidan
M G ROAD
Atke Gate
GANDHI CHOWK
GPO
Bara Kaman
Railway Station
Nehru & Lal Bahadur Shastri Markets
STATION ROAD
Golgumbaz
Ibrahim Rauza
Gagan Mahal
Paderah Gate
Cycle Rental
Sat Manzil
Astar Mahal
KSRTC Bus Stand
CITADEL
BIJAI ROAD
JAMA MASJID ROAD
Mithari Mahal
Jama Masjid
Fateh Gate
Gulbarga
Gadag

CAFÉS & RESTAURANTS
Roshan Bakery and Sweets	3
Shrinidhi Hotel	1
Siddarth	2

ACCOMMODATION
Madhuvan	2
Navaratna International	5
Pearl	3
Sagar Deluxe	1
Sanman	4

0   500
metres

Badami, Belgaum & Hubli ▼   Hospet ▼   Gadag ▼

22

The Golgumbaz

Daily 6am–6pm • ₹100 (₹5)

The vast **Golgumbaz** mausoleum, Bijapur's most famous building, soars above the town's east walls, visible for kilometres in every direction. Built towards the end of the Adil Shahis' reign, the building is a fitting monument to a dynasty on its last legs – pompous, decadent and ill-proportioned, but conceived on an irresistibly awesome scale.

The cubic tomb, enclosing a 170-square-metre hall, is crowned with a single hemispherical **dome**, the largest in the world after St Peter's in Rome (which is only 5m wider). Spiral staircases wind up the four seven-storey octagonal towers that buttress the building to the famous **Whispering Gallery**, a 3m-wide passage encircling the interior base of the dome from where, looking carefully down, you can get a real feel of the sheer size of the building. Arrive here just after opening time to avoid the bus tours and to experiment with the extraordinary acoustics. The **view** from the mausoleum's ramparts, which overlook the town and its monuments to the dark-soiled Deccan countryside beyond, is superb.

Set on a plinth in the centre of the hall below are the gravestones of the ruler who built the Golgumbaz, **Mohammed Adil Shah**, along with those of his wife, daughter, grandson and favourite courtesan, Rambha. At one corner of the grounds stands the simple gleaming white shrine to a Sufi saint of the Adil Shahi period, **Hashim Pir**, which attracts *qawwals* (singers of devotional *qawwali* music) each February to the annual three-day *urs*.

The Jama Masjid

A little under 1km southwest of the Golgumbaz • No shorts or skirts

The **Jama Masjid** presides over the quarter that formed the centre of the city during Bijapur's nineteenth-century nadir under the nizam of Hyderabad. It was commissioned by Ali Adil Shah, the ruler credited with constructing the city walls and complex water supply system, as a monument to his victory over the Vijayanagars at the battle of Talikota in 1565, and is widely regarded as one of the finest mosques in India. As it is a living place of worship, you should not enter improperly dressed.

Simplicity and restraint are the essence of the colonnaded prayer hall below, divided by gently curving arches and rows of thick plaster-covered pillars. Aside from the odd geometric design and trace of yellow, blue and green tile-work, the only ornamentation is found in the mihrab, or west- (Mecca-) facing prayer niche, which is smothered in gold leaf and elaborate calligraphy. The marble floor of the hall features a grid of 2500 rectangles, known as *musallahs* (after the *musallah* prayer mats brought to mosques by worshippers). These were added by the Mughal emperor Aurangzeb, allegedly as recompense for making off with the velvet carpets, long golden chain and other valuables that originally filled the prayer hall.

The Mithari Mahal

800m west of the Jama Masjid

Although of modest size, the delicately carved three-storey gatehouse known as the **Mithari Mahal** is one of Bijapur's most beautiful buildings, with ornate projecting windows and minarets crowning its corners. Once again, Ali Adil Shah erected it, along with the mosque behind, using gifts presented to him during a state visit to Vijayanagar.

The Astar Mahal

Just beyond the eastern battlement of the citadel

The dilapidated **Astar Mahal**, a large open-fronted hall fronted by a large stagnant step-well, was built in 1646 by Mohammed Adil Shah as a hall of justice. It was later chosen to house hairs from the Prophet's beard, thereby earning the title **Asar-i-Sharif**, or "place of illustrious relics". In theory, women are not permitted inside to view the upper storey, where fifteen niches are decorated with mediocre, Persian-style pot-and-foliage murals, but for a little baksheesh, one of the girls who hang around the site will unlock the doors for you.

The citadel

Bijapur's **citadel** stands in the middle of town, hemmed in on all but its north side by battlements. Most of the buildings inside have collapsed, or have been converted into government offices, but enough remain to give a sense of how imposing this royal enclave must once have been.

The best-preserved monuments lie along, or near, the citadel's main north–south artery, Anand Mahal Road, reached by skirting the southeast wall from the Astar Mahal. The latter route brings you first to the **Gagan Mahal**. Originally Ali Adil Shah's "Heavenly Palace", this now-ruined hulk later served as a durbar hall for the sultans, who would sit in state on the platform at the open-fronted north side, watched by crowds gathered in the grounds opposite. West off Anand Mahal Road, the five-storey **Sat Manzil** was the pleasure palace of the courtesan Rambha, entombed with Mohammed Adil Shah and his family in the Golgumbaz. In front stands an ornately carved water pavilion, the **Jal Mandir**, now left high and dry in an empty tank.

22

Malik-e-Maidan and Upli Buruj

Guarding the principal western entrance to the city is one of several bastions that punctuate Bijapur's battlements. This one, the Burj-i-Sherza ("Lion Gate") sports a colossal cannon, known as the **Malik-e-Maidan**, literally "Lord of the Plains". It was brought here as war booty in the sixteenth century, and needed four hundred bullocks, ten elephants and an entire battalion to haul it up the steps to the emplacement. Inscriptions record that the cannon, whose muzzle features a relief of a monster swallowing an elephant, was cast in Ahmednagar in 1551.

A couple more discarded cannons lie atop the watchtower visible a short walk northeast of the Malik-e-Maidan. Steps wind around the outside of the oval-shaped **Upli Buruj**, or "Upper Bastion", to a gun emplacement that affords unimpeded views over the city and plains.

The Ibrahim Rauza

Under 1km west of the ramparts • Daily 6am–6pm • ₹100 (₹5)

Set in its own walled compound, the **Ibrahim Rauza** represents the apogee of Bijapuri architecture. Whereas the Golgumbaz impresses primarily by its scale, the appeal of this tomb complex lies in its grace and simplicity. Beyond the reach of most bus parties, it's also a haven of peace, with cool, colonnaded verandas and flocks of iridescent parakeets careening between the mildewed domes, minarets and gleaming golden finials.

Opinions differ over whether the tomb was commissioned by Ibrahim Adil Shah (1580–1626), or his favourite wife, Taj Sultana, but the former was the first to be interred here, in a gloomy chamber whose only light enters via a series of exquisite pierced-stone windows. Made up of elaborate Koranic inscriptions, these are the finest examples of their kind in India. More amazing stonework decorates the exterior of the mausoleum, and the equally beautiful **mosque** opposite, the cornice of whose facade features a stone chain carved from a single block. The two buildings, bristling with minarets and cupolas, face each other from opposite sides of a rectangular raised plinth, divided by a small reservoir and fountains. Viewed from on top of the walls that enclose the complex, you can see why its architect, Malik Sandal, added a self-congratulatory inscription in his native Persian over the tomb's south doorway, describing his masterpiece as "A beauty of which Paradise stood amazed".

ARRIVAL AND INFORMATION   **BIJAPUR**

By train The railway station is just east of the Golgumbaz, outside the old city walls, and 3km northeast of the bus stand. Destinations Badami (2hr 20min–2hr 35min); Gadag (4hr 10min–4hr 50min); Hubli (5hr 45min–6hr 30min); Yesvantpur (2–3 daily; 15hr 30min–17hr 50 min);

By bus State and inter-state buses from as far afield as Mumbai and Aurangabad pull into the KSRTC Bus Stand on the southwest edge of the town centre. KSRTC run deluxe buses to Bengaluru, Hubli, Mumbai and Hyderabad. Heading to Badami, it is often quicker to take the first bus to Bagalkot and change there. VRL runs private services to Bengaluru (3 buses from 7pm) and operates other overnight buses to Mangalore (via Udupi) and Mumbai. These can be booked through Vijayanand Travel, terrace floor, Shastri Market, Gandhi Chowk (☎ 08352 251000) or its other branch just south of the bus stand.

Destinations Aurangabad (12hr); Badami (4hr); Bagalkot (2hr); Bengaluru (13hr); Gulbarga (4hr); Hubli (6hr); Hyderabad (10hr); Mangalore (15hr); Mumbai (12hr).

Tourist information The tourist office (Mon–Sat 10am–5.30pm; ☎ 08352 250359) behind the *Hotel Adil Shahi* annexe on Station Rd, can help with arranging itineraries and guides.

GETTING AROUND

By bus Frequent local buses, largely uncrowded, connect the bus stand with the Golgumbaz and the train station.

By auto-rickshaw Auto-rickshaws don't have meters and charge a minimum of ₹20; although most of Bijapur is covered by a fare of ₹40, they are a much more expensive way of getting around the monuments, when they charge at least ₹300 for a 4hr tour.

By tonga or tempo Tongas are available from near the bus stand, while *tempos* ply the main road between the bus stand, the Golgumbaz and the train station.

By bike Bijapur is flat, relatively uncongested, and generally easy to negotiate by bicycle; rickety Heros are available for rent from several stalls outside the bus stand for ₹5/hr.

ACCOMMODATION

Madhuvan Station Rd ☎ 08352 255571. With a bright yellow exterior and a variety of rooms, from overpriced ordinary doubles to more comfortable a/c options, this is a safe bet. The restaurant serves good-value thalis at lunchtime. Currency exchange available for guests. **₹950**

Navaratna International Just off Station Rd ☎ 08352 222771. The huge, shiny-tiled rooms at this quiet hotel are great value for this price. Good service, veg and non-veg restaurants and a popular palm-shaded dining (and drinking) area. **₹600**

★ **Pearl** Station Rd ☎ 08352 256002. Bright modern hotel with clean, sizeable rooms. The front ones have

balconies and those at the top afford views of the Golgumbaz. The smart attached annexe at the back has quality a/c rooms. **₹900**

Sagar Deluxe Near Bara Kaman ☎ 08352 259234. A fine budget option that is close to the action yet tucked away on a quiet side street. Simple but adequate attached rooms, including cheap singles and great value a/c. **₹380**

Sanman Station Rd ☎ 08352 251866. Best value among the budget places, if a tad grubby, and right opposite the Golgumbaz. The more expensive rooms have TV and the rooftop restaurant/bar offers excellent evening views of the mausoleum. **₹200**

EATING

Roshan Bakery and Sweets MG Rd. Among other goodies, this popular place whips up the perfect budget takeaway brunch: flaky, rich and delicious croissants filled with boiled egg and veg. All items cost less than ₹20. Daily 7am–9pm.

Shrinidhi Hotel Gandhi Chowk ☎ 93720 44576. Probably the best choice for good south Indian veg food,

from *vada* and *dosa* snacks to full-on thalis for around just ₹60. Daily 7am–10pm.

★ **Siddarth** ☎ 08352 220338. Above the main market, this sprawling rooftop bar-restaurant offers tasty non-veg Indian cuisine such as tandoori chicken for ₹200, plus a good selection of booze. Daily 10am–10pm.

Gulbarga

GULBARGA, 165km northeast of Bijapur, was the founding capital of the Bahmani dynasty and the region's principal city before the court moved to Bidar in 1424. Later captured by the Adil Shahis and Mughals, it has remained a staunchly Muslim town, and bulbous onion domes and mosque minarets still soar prominently above its ramshackle concrete-box skyline. The town is also famous as the birthplace of the *chishti*, or saint, Hazrat Gesu Daraz (1320–1422), whose tomb, situated next to one of India's foremost Islamic theological colleges, is a major shrine.

In spite of Gulbarga's religious and historical significance, its **monuments** pale in comparison with those at Bijapur, or even Bidar. Unless you're particularly interested in medieval Muslim architecture, few are worth breaking a journey to see.

The Dargah

The one monument that warrants a look is the **Dargah**, a tomb complex on the edge of town around 2km northeast of the train station. Approached via a broad bazaar, this marble-lined enclosure centres on the tomb of Hazrat Gesu Daraz, affectionately known to his devotees as **Bandah Nawaz**, or "the long-haired one who brings comfort to others". The saint was spiritual mentor to the Bahmani rulers, and it was they who erected his beautiful double-storeyed mausoleum, now visited by hundreds of thousands of Muslim pilgrims each year. Women are not allowed inside, and men must wear long trousers. The same applies to the neighbouring tomb, whose interior has retained its exquisite Persian paintings. The Dargah's other important building, open to both sexes, is the **madrasa**, founded by Bandah Nawaz and enlarged during the two centuries after his death.

22

The fort

Encircled by 16m-thick crenellated walls, fifteen watchtowers and an evil-smelling stagnant moat, Gulbarga's deserted **fort** lies 1km north of the train station. The great citadel now lies in ruins behind the town's large artificial lake, with its sole surviving building the beautiful fourteenth-century **Jama Masjid**. Thought to have been modelled by a Moorish architect on the great Spanish mosque of Cordoba, it is unique in India for having an entirely domed prayer hall.

ARRIVAL AND DEPARTURE

GULBARGA

By train Gulbarga's mainline railway station lies 1.5km east of the bus stand, along Mill Rd. Station Rd, the town's other main artery, runs due north of here past the lake to the busy Chowk crossroads, at the heart of the bazaar.
Destinations Bengaluru (4 daily; 11hr 40min–14hr); Chennai (3 daily, 13hr 35min–16hr 45min); Hyderabad (4–8 daily; 4hr 10min–8hr 5min); Mumbai (9–11 daily; 9hr

45min–12hr); Pune (9–11 daily; 6hr 30min–7hr 40min); .
By bus Daily KSRTC buses from Bijapur, Bidar and beyond pull in to the State Bus Stand on the southwest edge of town. Frequent local buses such as #206 run from the bus stand via the crossroads near the station to the Dargah.
Destinations Hourly to Bijapur (4hr) and Bidar (3hr); less frequently further afield.

ACCOMMODATION AND EATING

Central Park Station Rd, nearly 1km north of station ☎08472 273231, ⍟centralparkgulbarga.com. Clean, modern business hotel whose simple but smart rooms all have TV and wi-fi connections, and some come with a/c. Good non-veg restaurant. ₹600

Kamat The venerable chain restaurant has several branches in Gulbarga including a pleasant one at Station Chowk, specializing in veg "meals" (all under ₹100) as well as *iddlis* and dosas; try *joleata roti*, a local bread cooked either hard and crisp or soft like a chapatti. Daily 7am–10pm.

Prashant First lane on the right after leaving the station ☎08472 221456, ✉muralidharbai2002 @gmail.com. Decent rooms of varying sized and

amenities, and surprisingly quiet for its location. ₹620
Prince Mill Rd ☎08472 251088. Opposite the bus stand and a little to the left, this well-maintained hotel has decent-sized rooms, all attached with TV. ₹450
Rajdhani Mill Rd ☎97417 37143. Most of the mains such as chicken and mutton cost well under ₹200 at this simple basement restaurant on the way towards the station from the bus stand. Daily 11am–11pm.
Southern Star Near the Fort, Super Market ☎08472 224093. The pricier rooms have fort views, but even if you don't stay the vast side-courtyard offers relaxing alfresco dining and is a great spot to watch the sun set behind the fort. ₹800

Bidar

Lost in the far northeast of Karnataka, **BIDAR**, 284km northeast of Bijapur, is nowadays a provincial backwater, better known for its fighter-pilot training base than the gently decaying monuments nearby. Yet the town, half of whose 140,000 population is still Muslim, has a gritty charm, with narrow red-dirt streets ending at arched gates and open vistas across the plains. Littered with tile-fronted tombs, rambling fortifications and old mosques, it merits a visit if you're travelling between Hyderabad (150km east) and Bijapur, although you should expect little in the way of Western comforts, and lot's of curious approaches from locals.

In 1424, following the break-up of the Bahmani dynasty into five rival factions, **Ahmad Shah I** shifted his court from Gulbarga to a less constricted site at Bidar. Revamping the town with a new fort, splendid palaces, mosques and ornamental gardens, the Bahmanis ruled from here until 1487, when the Barid Shahis took control. They were succeeded by the Adil Shahis from Bijapur, and later the Mughals under Aurangzeb, who annexed the region in 1656, before the nizam of Hyderabad acquired the territory in the early eighteenth century.

The heart of Bidar is its medieval **old town**, encircled by crenellated ramparts and eight imposing gateways (*darwazas*). This predominantly Muslim quarter holds many Bahmani-era mosques, havelis and *khanqahs* – "monasteries" set up by the local rulers for Muslim cleric-mystics and their disciples.

Mahmud Gawan's madrasa

The highlight of the old town is the impressive ruined **Mahmud Gawan's madrasa**, whose single minaret soars high above the city centre. The distinctively Persian-style building, originally surmounted by large bulbous domes, once housed a world-famous library. However, this burnt down after being struck by lightning in 1696, and several of the walls and domes were blown away when gunpowder stored here by Aurangzeb's occupying army caught fire and exploded. Today, the madrasa is little more than a shell, although its elegant arched facade has retained large patches of the vibrant Persian glazed tile-work that once covered most of the exterior surfaces.

The Fort
At the far north end of the street running past the madrasa

A rambling, crumbling monument valley to the fifteenth-century Bahmani Empire, the Bidar **Fort** retains a serene, austere beauty. Though locals have incorporated the vast rolling spaces into their lives – young boys play cricket in the grassy turf, terraces are planted with rice and scooters and small trucks ply its roads – its appeal remains undiminished.

The fort was founded by the Hindu Chalukyas and strengthened by the Bahmanis in the early fifteenth century. Despite repeated sieges, it remains largely intact, encircled by 10km of ramparts that drop away in the north and west to 300m cliffs. The main southern entrance is protected by equally imposing man-made defences: gigantic fortified gates and a triple moat formerly crossed by a series of drawbridges. You can complete the round of **the ramparts** in ninety minutes, taking time out to enjoy the views over the red cliffs and across the plains.

Rangin Mahal

The first building of note inside the fort is the exquisite **Rangin Mahal**, on the left after the third and final entrance gateway. Mahmud Shah built this "Coloured Palace" after

---

BIDRI

Bidar is renowned as the home of a unique damascene metalwork technique known as **bidri**, developed by the Persian silversmiths who came to the area with the Bahmani court in the fifteenth century. These highly skilled artisans engraved and inlaid their traditional Iranian designs onto a metal alloy composed of lead, copper, zinc and tin, which they blackened and polished. The resulting effect – swirling silver floral motifs framed by geometric patterns and set against black backgrounds – has since become the hallmark of Muslim metalwork in India.

Bidri objets d'art are displayed in museums and galleries all over the country. But if you want to see pukka *bidri*-wallahs at work, take a walk down Bidar's **Siddiq Talim Road**, which cuts across the south side of the old town, where skull-capped artisans tap and burnish vases, goblets, plates, spice boxes, betel-nut tins and ornamental hookah pipes, as well as less traditional objects – coasters, ashtrays and bangles – that crop up (at vastly inflated prices) in silver emporiums as far away as Delhi and Kolkata.

an unsuccessful uprising of Abyssinian slaves in 1487 forced him to relocate to a safer site inside the citadel. The palace's relatively modest proportions reflect the Bahmanis' declining fortunes, but its interior comprises some of the finest surviving Islamic art in the Deccan, with superb woodcarving above the door arches and Persian-style mother-of-pearl inlay on polished black granite surfaces. If the doors to the palace are locked, ask for the keys at the nearby **ASI museum** (daily 8am–1pm & 2–5pm; free), which is not otherwise worth a visit.

Solah Khamb
Opposite the ASI Museum

An expanse of gravel is all that remains of the royal gardens, overlooked by the austere **Solah Khamb** mosque (1327), Bidar's oldest Muslim monument, whose most outstanding feature is the intricate pierced-stone calligraphy around its central dome. From here, continue west through the ruins of the former royal enclosure – a rambling complex of half-collapsed palaces, baths, zenanas and assembly halls – to the fort's west walls.

Ashtur: the Bahmani tombs

As you look from the fort's east walls, a cluster of eight bulbous white domes floats alluringly above the trees in the distance. Sited nearly 5km east of Bidar (leave the old town via Dulhan Darwaza gate) and dating from the fifteenth century, the mausoleums at **Ashtur** are the final resting-places of the Bahmani sultans and their families, including the son of the ruler who first decamped from Gulbarga, Ala-ud-Din Shah I. His remains by far the most impressive tomb, with patches of coloured glazed tiles on its arched facade, and a large dome whose interior surfaces writhe with sumptuous Persian paintings. Reflecting sunlight onto the ceiling with a small pocket mirror, the *chowkidar* picks out the highlights, among them a diamond, barely visible among the bat droppings.

The tomb of Ala-ud-Din's father, the ninth and most illustrious Bahmani sultan, Ahmad Shah I, stands beside that of his son, decorated with Persian inscriptions. Beyond this are two more minor mausoleums, followed by the partially collapsed tomb of Humayun the Cruel (1458–61), cracked open by a bolt of lightning. Continuing along the line, you can chart the gradual decline of the Bahmanis as the mausoleums diminish in size, ending with a sad handful erected in the early sixteenth century, when the sultans were no more than puppet rulers of the Badrid Shahis.

ARRIVAL AND DEPARTURE   **BIDAR**

By train Bidar lies on a branch line of the main Mumbai–Secunderabad–Chennai rail route and can only be reached by slow passenger train.

By bus Most visitors arrive by bus at the KSRTC Bus Stand on the far northwestern edge of town, around 2km from the centre. The best connections are with Gulbarga (every 15min; 3hr) and Hyderabad (every 30min; 4hr).

ACCOMMODATION AND EATING

Extremely grubby lodges predominate in Bidar but the good news is that none of the handful of better **hotels** listed below cost very much. These are the best **places to eat** too, along with the odd basic veg restaurant.

Ashoka 1.5km west from the bus stand near Dr Ambedkar Circle ☏ 08482 227621. Standard business hotel with reasonably comfortable, good-value deluxe rooms, some of them a/c. The restaurant is fairly good, too. ₹450

Mayura Opposite the bus stand ☏ 08482 228142. Ugly concrete block but with large rooms that have optional a/c. The serves restaurant food, quite tasty but it doubles as a slightly unsavoury bar. ₹500

Sapna International 300m north of the bus stand ☏ 08482 220991. Bidar's nicest lodgings, with big, clean rooms and a good non-veg restaurant. ₹500

Udupi Krishna On Dr Ambedkar Circle ☏ 92065 77811. A very humble place but undoubtedly one of the best independent restaurants in town, serving up unlimited pure veg thalis for lunch and south Indian breakfasts. Daily 6.30am–9.30pm.

22

MURALS, KERALA

Contexts

History

India's history is as complex and as multifaceted as you would expect from such a huge, populous and culturally varied country – a place that was home to one of the world's earliest civilizations and the birthplace of four major global religions, as well as having spawned more dynasties, monarchs and kingdoms than even the most determined historian can keep track of. Broadly speaking, the history of India divides into two parts: the history of the Aryan north, heavily influenced by successive waves of invaders from the uplands of Central Asia, and the much more self-contained history of the Dravidian south.

The Indus Valley Civilization

The earliest human presence in the Indian subcontinent can be traced back to the Early, Middle and Late **Stone Ages** (400,000–200,000 BC), when the country was first settled by seminomadic hunters and gatherers. Village settlements gradually developed over the next four thousand years across the Indus Valley as their inhabitants began to use copper and bronze, domesticate animals, make pottery and trade with their neighbours.

By around 2500 BC, the village settlements of the Indus Valley had begun to develop into one of the world's earliest civilizations – roughly contemporaneous with those of Sumer and ancient Egypt. Known variously as the **Indus Valley Civilization** or the **Harappan Civilization**, this first great Subcontinental culture spread across a sizeable proportion of what is now southern Pakistan and the periphery of western India. Much of what is known about it comes from the remains of two great cities on the Indus, **Harappa** in the north and **Mohenjo Daro** in the south (both in present-day Pakistan). Laid out on a grid, both cities boasted large houses made from uniformly sized baked bricks, an elaborate system of covered drains (the world's first urban sanitation system) and large granaries. The absence of royal palaces and the large numbers of religious figurines found at both sites suggest that the Indus Valley Civilization was a theocratic state of priests, merchants and farmers.

The Indus Valley Civilization displayed remarkable longevity, surviving for a thousand years until its sudden demise around 1700 BC, probably caused by a catastrophic series of floods.

The Vedic Age (1500–600 BC)

The written history of India begins with the invasions of the charioteering **Indo-European** or **Aryan** tribes, which dealt the final death blow to the enfeebled Indus Civilization. The arrival of the Aryans marks the beginning of the so-called **Vedic Age**, named after the earliest Indian literature, the Vedas (see p.1172). The Aryans were one

10,000–3000 BC	2400 BC	1700 BC	1500–1000 BC
Spectacular Mesolithic rock art is created in Bhimbetka, central India.	Harappan people construct India's oldest known port city, at Lothal in Gujarat	Natural disasters and climate change precipitate the demise of the Harappan Civilization.	The world's oldest surviving sacred texts, the Vedas, are composed in northern India.

of the various nomadic tribes who emerged out of the vast steppes of Central Asia, marauding and eventually colonizing Europe, the Middle East and the Indian Subcontinent.

Aryan culture was diametrically opposed to that of the Indus Civilization. Seminomadic hunters and pastoralists when they first reached the Subcontinent, the Aryans gradually adopted the farming techniques learned from the peoples they conquered as they spread eastwards into India.

The Aryans' hymns, written down in the Vedas, describe the inter-tribal conflicts characteristic of the period, but also express an underlying sense of solidarity against the indigenous peoples, whom the Aryans referred to as **Dasas**. Originally a general term for "enemies", it came to denote "subjects" as they were colonized within the expanding land of the Aryans. The Aryans began to emphasize purity of blood as they settled among the darker aboriginals, and their original class divisions of nobility and ordinary tribesmen were hardened to exclude the Dasas. At the same time, the priests, the sole custodians of the increasingly complex religion and sacrificial rituals, began to claim high privileges for their skill and training. By 1000 BC, Aryan society had become divided into four classes, or **varnas** (literally "colour"): priests (brahmins), warriors (*kshatriya*), peasants (*vaishya*) and serfs (*shudra*), a division that still survives today. The first three classes covered the main divisions within the Aryan tribes; the Dasas and other non-Aryan subjects became the *shudras*, who served the three higher classes. Many of India's most important religious texts and epics also date from this period, including the Sama, Yajur and Atharva Vedas, Brahmanas and the Upanishads (see p.1172), while the **Mahabharata** and the **Ramayana** (see box, p.1173) also claim to relate to this era.

By the fifth century BC the scattered states of north India had been consolidated into five great kingdoms: Magadha, Kashi, Koshala, Vatsa and the republic of the Vrijjis. Eventually, **Magadha** emerged supreme, under Bimbisara (543–491 BC), who was also, according to legend, a personal friend and great patron of the **Buddha**, his almost exact contemporary. Bimbisara's son and successor Ajatashatru (491–461 BC) moved the capital of Magadha to **Pataliputra** (the forerunner of modern Patna) and either annihilated the other kingdoms in the Ganges valley or reduced them to the status of vassals. In the middle of the fourth century BC, the **Nanda** dynasty usurped the Magadhan throne; Mahapadma Nanda conquered Kalinga (Odisha and the northern coastal strip of Andhra Pradesh) and gained control of parts of the Deccan. The disputed succession after his death coincided with significant events in the northwest; out of this confusion the first of India's empires was born.

The Mauryan Empire (320–184 BC)

North India's burgeoning prosperity was by now beginning to attract the attention of ambitious rulers in Central Asia – something that was to become a recurrent theme in Indian history over the next thousand years. **Darius I**, the third Achaemenid emperor of Persia, had already conquered the kingdom of Gandhara (in what is now northern Pakistan and eastern Afghanistan) around 520 BC. Far more significant, however, was the later invasion by **Alexander the Great**, who defeated Darius III, the last Achaemenid, crossed the Indus in 326 BC, and then overran the Punjab. Alexander

C. 1000 BC	C. 563–483BC	326 BC	265–232 BC
Rise of the caste system.	Lifetime of Gautama Buddha, founder of the Buddhist faith.	Alexander the Great crosses the Indus and remains in India with his Macedonian army for two years.	Reign of the Mauryan emperor Ashoka.

was in India for just two years, and although he left garrisons and appointed satraps to govern the conquered territories, their position following his death in 323 BC became increasingly untenable.

The disruption caused by Alexander's brief incursion was seized upon by **Chandragupta Maurya**, the ruler of Magadha, who had overthrown the last of the Nanda dynasty in around 320 BC. Chandragupta is said to have met Alexander the Great and was probably inspired by his exploits; his 500,000-strong army drove out the Greek garrisons in the northwest and annexed all the lands east of the Indus.

From about 297 BC onwards, Chandragupta's son Bindusara extended the empire as far south as Mysore, before being succeeded in around 269 BC by his son, **Ashoka**, the most famous of India's early rulers. Ashoka ruthlessly consolidated his power for the first eight years of his reign, but then – allegedly sickened by the terrible carnage caused by his conquests – abruptly converted to Buddhism and renounced the use of violence in favour of the law of moral righteousness, or dharma. His adoption of Buddhism, however, did not interfere with his imperial pragmatism, and he continued to govern the newly acquired territory with a firm military hand. By the end of his reign, Ashoka's empire stretched from Assam to Afghanistan and from Kashmir to Mysore; only the three Dravidian kingdoms of the Cholas, Cheras and Pandyas in the southernmost tip of the Subcontinent remained independent. After Ashoka's death in 232 BC, the empire began to fall apart, and in 184 BC the last of the Mauryans, Brihadratha, was assassinated by one of his generals, bringing to an end nearly 140 years of Mauryan rule.

The age of invasions (184 BC–320 AD)

The five hundred years following the collapse of the Mauryan Empire are the most complex and confusing in Subcontinental history, marked by political fragmentation and a new and seemingly endless series of **invasions** from the northwest. The period is sometimes referred to as India's "Dark Age", although despite the lack of any unified central power it was also one of economic dynamism and considerable cultural achievement.

The first invaders were the **Bactrian Greeks** of Gandhara, who occupied the Punjab and extended their power as far as Mathura in Uttar Pradesh.

Yet the arrival of newcomers from Central Asia soon threatened the Greek position in Bactria. Large-scale movements of central Asian Yueh-Chi nomads had precipitated the migration of the **Shakas** (Scythians), from the Aral Sea area, who displaced the **Parthians** (Pahlavas) from Iran, who in turn wrested control of Bactria from the Greeks (who henceforth administered their Indian territories from a new capital in Kabul). The finer details of these various population movements remain unclear, and they were probably more in the nature of migrations than invasions. Whatever the details, both the Yueh-Chi and Shakas continued to drift slowly in the direction of India, finally arriving during the first century AD. The Shakas were the first to arrive, establishing themselves in northwestern India until the coming of the **Kushan** branch of the Yueh-Chi, who drove the Shakas off into Gujarat and Malwa (the area around Ujjain).

Despite the disintegration of the Mauryan Empire and the proliferation of rival kingdoms, the period from 200 BC to 300 AD was also one of unprecedented

261 BC	Mid-2nd century BC	1st and 2nd century AD
Terrible loss of life at the Battle of Kalinga (in modern day Odisha) prompts Ashoka's conversion to Buddhism.	First rock-cut cave monasteries excavated in the Deccan region.	Andhra Dynasty erect magnificent *stupas* around India, the greatest at Sanchi.

economic wealth and cultural development. Urban centres began to develop all over India, while external trade, both overland and maritime, opened up lines of communication with the outside world stretching as far as Arabia and southeast Asia by sea, and China and the Mediterranean by land via the **Silk Route**.

The rise of the south

Meanwhile, the first great kingdom of southern India was flexing its muscles. Between the second century BC and the second century AD the **Andhra** or **Satavahana** dynasty, which originated in the region between the Godavari and Krishna rivers (modern-day Andhra Pradesh and Maharashtra), began to make inroads into much of south and central India. The dynasty survived until the middle of the third century, when its territories were carved up by rival dynasties including the Pallavas (see below), who took control of their territories in Andhra Pradesh.

Further south, the three kingdoms of the **Cheras** on the Malabar Coast in the west, the **Pandyas** in the central southern tip of the peninsula, and the **Cholas** on the east coast of Coromandel – together comprising much of present-day Tamil Nadu and Kerala – had been developing almost completely independently of north India. Society was divided into groups based on the geographical domains of hills, plains, forest, coast and desert rather than class or *varna*, though brahmins did command high status. Although agriculture, pastoralism and fishing were the main occupations, trade in spices, gold and jewels with Rome and southeast Asia underpinned the region's prosperity.

From the middle of the first century BC, however, conflicts between the three states intensified. This enervating warfare rendered them vulnerable; early in the fourth century AD, the **Pallavas** overran the Chola capital of Kanchipuram, and by 325 AD had taken control of Tamil Nadu. The Pallavas remained a dominant power in the south until the ninth century AD, and thus became one of the longest ruling dynasties in Indian history.

The Guptas (320–650)

During the fourth century AD, a second great Indian empire began to emerge in the north: the **Guptas**. The parallels with the earlier Mauryan Empire are striking. Both were founded in the year 320 (BC and AD respectively) by a king named Chandragupta (though the later king is usually written as two words, Chandra Gupta), and both emerged from within the famous old kingdom of Magadha. **Chandra Gupta** (reigned c.320–335) appears to have been the ruler of a minor statelet within the old Magadhan kingdom, who acquired considerable new territory through intermarriage with the famous Licchavi clan, one of the Mauryas' principal enemies six hundred years previously. Chandra Gupta thus found himself master of a powerful kingdom in the Gangetic plain, which controlled the vital east–west trade route. His son and heir, **Samudra Gupta** (c.335–376 AD), expanded the frontiers of his realm from Punjab to Assam, while the empire reached its apogee under his successor, **Chandra Gupta II** (376–415 AD), who subjugated the Shakas in Gujarat and reunified the whole of northern India, with the exception of the northwest.

375–415 AD	460–477 AD	543 AD	700–728 AD
The Golden Age of Classical India during the reign of Chandra Gupta II.	Ajanta's finest cave paintings are commissioned by Emperor Harishena.	Chalukya Dynasty found their capital at Badami, erecting India's first freestanding stone temples.	Pallava Dynasty build the famous Shore Temple at Mamallapuram.

The era of these three imperial Guptas, along with the subsequent reign of Harsha Vardhana (606–647 AD) of Kanauj, is generally seen as the **Classical Age** of Indian history, one of cultural and artistic brilliance, religious ferment and political stability. Secular **Sanskrit literature** reached its perfection in the works of Kalidasa, the greatest Indian poet and dramatist, who was a member of Chandra Gupta II's court. The cave paintings of **Ajanta** and **Ellora** inspired Buddhist artists throughout Asia, and Yashodhara's detailed analysis of painting in the fifth century prescribed the classical conventions for the new art form. In **sculpture**, the images of the Buddha produced in Sarnath and Mathura embodied the simple and serene quality of classicism. In **architecture**, the Gupta era saw the birth of a new style of **Hindu temple** which would became India's classic architectural form. The era of the Guptas produced great thinkers as well: six systems of **philosophy** evolved, which refuted Buddhism and Jainism. One of them, **Vedanta**, has continued as the basis of all philosophical studies in India to this day.

The Guptas performed Vedic sacrifices to legitimize their rule, and patronized popular forms of Hinduism, such as devotional religion (*bhakti*) and the worship in temples of images of Vishnu, Shiva and the goddess Shakti, deities who were attracting increasing numbers of devotees during this era. Buddhism continued to thrive, however, with thousands of monks dwelling at Mathura as well as hundreds in Pataliputra itself.

The Gupta Empire remained relatively peaceful during the long reign of Kumara Gupta (c.415–455), who succeeded Chandra Gupta II, but by the time Skanda Gupta (c.455–467) came to the throne, western India was again threatened by invasions from Central Asia, this time by the **White Huns**, nomads from Central Asia who had already established themselves in Bactria. Skanda managed to repel White Hun raids, but after his death their disruption of central Asian trade seriously destabilized the empire. By the end of the fifth century, the Huns had wrested the Punjab from Gupta control, and further incursions early in the sixth century dealt a death blow to the Gupta Empire, which had completely disintegrated by 550 AD.

Kingdoms of central and south India (500–1250)

Meanwhile, significant events were taking place in central and south India. The history of the period was dominated by three major kingdoms: the **Pallavas**, who had supplanted the Satavahanas in the Andhra region and made Kanchipuram their capital back in the fourth century; the **Pandyas** of Madurai, who had established their own regional kingdom by the sixth century; and the **Chalukyas** of Vatapi (Badami in Karnataka), who had expanded into the Deccan in the middle of the sixth century. All three kingdoms intermittently fought one another, but their military strength was so evenly matched that none was able to gain ascendancy.

The Chalukyas were eventually overthrown in 753 by Dantidurga, the founder of the **Rashtrakuta** kingdom (whose rulers also tried their luck in the north, briefly gaining possession of Kanauj). The Pallavas survived their arch-enemies by about a hundred years, then succumbed to a combined attack of the Pandyas and the **Cholas**. The Cholas were a major new force in Tamil Nadu, conquering the Thanjavur region in the ninth century and taking Madurai from the Pandyas in 907, before being defeated by the Rashtrakutas in the middle of the tenth century, who were themselves replaced by the revived Chalukyas in 973 AD.

757–790 AD	**788–820 AD**	**Early 11th century**
Excavation of Kailash temple at Ellora in Maharashtra.	The philosopher Adi Shankara spreads the doctrine of Vedanta, the most widely followed tradition in Hinduism today.	The Cholas establish an empire stretching from the far south of India to Sumatra.

Ultimately, the chief beneficiaries of these dynastic toings-and-froings were the Cholas, who were able to regain lost territories and expand further during the eleventh and twelfth centuries. The great Chola kings **Rajaraja I** (985–1014) and **Rajendra I** (1014–1044) launched a series of campaigns against the Cheras, Pandyas and Chalukyas, and by the end of the eleventh century the Cholas were supreme in the south, although incessant campaigning had exhausted their resources. Ironically, their destruction of the Chalukyas sowed the seeds of their own downfall. Former Chalukya feudatories, such as the **Yadavas** of Devagiri in the northern Deccan and the **Hoysalas**, around modern Mysore, set up their own kingdoms; the latter attacked the Cholas from the west while the Pandyas directed a new offensive from the south. By the thirteenth century, the **Pandyas** had superseded the Cholas as south India's major power, while the Yadavas and Hoysalas controlled the Deccan until the advent of the Delhi sultans in the fourteenth century.

Despite constant political and military conflicts, this period was very much the classical age of the south. The ascendancy of the Cholas was complemented by the crystallization of Tamil culture; the religious, artistic, and institutional patterns of this period dominated the culture of the south and influenced developments elsewhere in the Subcontinent. In the sphere of religion, for instance, the great philosophers Shankara and Ramanuja, as well as the Tamil and Maharashtrian saints, had a significant impact on Hinduism in north India.

Kingdoms in north India (650–1250)

In north India, Harsha Vardhana's death was followed by a century of confusion, with assorted kingdoms competing to control the Gangetic valley. In time, the **Pratihara-Gurjaras**, from western India, and the **Palas**, of Bihar and Bengal, emerged as the main rivals, although both were weakened by repeated incursions from the Deccan by the **Rashtrakutas**, who briefly occupied Kanauj in 916. The Pratiharas regained their capital, but the tripartite struggle sapped their strength and they were unable to repel the invasion of Kanauj by Mahmud of Ghazni (see opposite) in 1018. The struggle for possession of Kanauj depleted the resources of all three competing powers and resulted in their almost simultaneous decline, while various smaller feudatory kingdoms began to assert their independence. Kingdoms emerged in Nepal, Kamarupa (Assam), Kashmir and Odisha, all with their own cultural identities, customs, literatures and histories. The Eastern Gangas of **Kalinga** (roughly equivalent to modern Odisha) also achieved political independence and unity in the twelfth century.

Meanwhile, in the west, the celebrated **Rajputs** began to emerge as a new element within Indian society. Their origins remain the subject of considerable speculation, although they probably descended from the various invaders who arrived in India between the third and sixth centuries, including the Pratihara-Gurjaras, Huns and Shakas and perhaps others. Whatever their origins, they acquired respectable Hindu genealogies and were given *kshatriya* status. By the tenth century, the most important Rajput clans, like the Chauhans of Ajmer, the Guhilas of Chittaurgarh, the Chandellas of Bundelkhand, and the Tomaras of Haryana (who founded modern Delhi in 1060), had all established small regional kingdoms spread across modern-day Rajasthan, Gujarat, Madhya Pradesh and other parts of the north.

1000–27	**1192**	**1198**
The Muslim warlord Mahmud of Ghazni mounts seventeen bloody incursions into Hindu India from Afghanistan.	Muhammad of Ghor defeats Prithviraj III at the Battle of Tarain, laying the foundations of the Delhi Sultanate.	Qutbu'd-Din Aibak erects the Qutub Minar victory tower in Delhi, marking the start of Muslim rule in India.

The Rajputs fought among each other incessantly, however, and failed to grasp the significance of a new factor, which entered the politics of north India at the start of the eleventh century. **Mahmud of Ghazni** (971–1030), a Turkish chieftain who had established the powerful Ghaznavid kingdom at Ghazni in Afghanistan, made seventeen plundering raids into India between 1000 and 1027, looting Mathura, Kanauj and Somnath, among other places. The powerful Rajput clans of northern India were still busy fighting one another almost two centuries later when **Muhammad of Ghor** (1162–1206) seized Ghaznavid possessions in the Punjab at the end of the twelfth century, and then turned his attention towards the wealthy lands further east. **Prithviraj III**, the legendary hero of the Chauhans of Ajmer, patched together an alliance to defeat the Turkish warlord at Tarain (north of Delhi) in 1191; but Muhammad returned the next year with a superior force and defeated the Rajputs. He had Prithviraj executed before returning home, leaving his generals to complete his conquest.

The Delhi Sultanate (1206–1526)

Muhammad of Ghor was assassinated in 1206 and his empire immediately disintegrated, leaving his Turkish general **Qutbu'd**, a former slave, as the autonomous ruler of Muhammad's former Indian territories. Aiback thus became the founder of the so-called "Slave Dynasty", the first part of which would eventually come to be known as the **Delhi Sultanate**, which would remain the major political force in the north until the early sixteenth century. The sultanate marked an important turning-point in Indian history. Islam rather than Hinduism suddenly became the religion of the country's rulers, while Delhi, rather than Kanauj or Pataliputra, became the most important city in the north.

Aiback's son-in-law **Iltutmish** (1211–36) extended the sultanate's territories from the Sind to Bengal by the time he died, but a period of confusion followed, with five different rulers in just six years. Not until **Ghiyas-ud-Din Balban** took effective control in 1246 did the sultanate attain any degree of stability, despite repeated threats from yet another set of foreign interlopers, the **Mongols**, who had been launching raids into western India from around 1220 and continued to attack the edges of the sultanate.

Ghiyas-ud-Din's death in 1287 was followed by the inevitable period of dynastic mayhem that only ended in 1290, when Aiback's Slave Dynasty came to an end, replaced by the **Khalji** dynasty. The Khalji family had entered India with Muhammad of Ghor, and subsequently carved out their own Muslim fiefdom in Bengal and Bihar. The first Khalji sultan, the elderly Feroz Shah I, was soon done away with by the implacable **Ala-ud-Din Khalji** (1296–1315), one of the most fearsome of all Indian rulers. A hard man for hard times, Ala-ud-Din was faced immediately by a series of further Mongol attacks. Delhi was besieged twice and its hinterlands plundered before the invaders suffered a resounding defeat at the hands of the new sultan in 1300, after which they left him alone. Having seen off the Mongols, Ala-ud-Din set out to conquer Gujarat and Rajasthan in a series of expeditions between 1299 and 1311, before turning his attention to the Deccan and the south. Even so, his military campaigns were more a question of exacting tribute and raising funds than of building a stable empire.

1325–51	1498	1510
Mohammed bin Tughluq forces the entire population of Delhi to march 1200km south to a new capital at Daulatabad.	Vasco da Gama completes the sea route across the Arabian Sea to land in Calicut on the Malabar Coast (Kerala).	The Portuguese admiral, Alfonso Albuquerque, takes the strategically vital port of Goa.

A fresh imperial impetus came from the **Tughluq** dynasty, which succeeded the Khaljis in 1320. Under **Mohammed bin Tughluq** (1325–51), the sultanate reached its largest extent, comparable in size to Ashoka's empire, although the onerous taxes required to finance Mohammed's military campaigns provoked a series of revolts, while the new Hindu kingdom of **Vijayanagar** took advantage of the decline of the sultanate's authority to extend its influence from its capital near **Hampi. Firoz Shah Tughluq** (1351–88) reversed the fortunes of the sultanate to some extent, thanks to the comparative mildness of his rule, but arguments over the succession after his death in 1388 further weakened the sultanate, as did an attack by the ruthless **Timur**, the Central Asian despot known to the West as Tamerlane, who sacked Delhi in 1398. By the end of the fourteenth century, the Delhi Sultanate had been reduced to just one of several competing Muslim states in northern India.

The greatly weakened sultanate was next taken over by the Afghan-descended Khizr Khan (1414–21), whose **Sayyid** dynasty ruled until 1444, to be succeeded by the **Lodis**, under whom the sultanate experienced a modest revival. **Sikander Lodi** (1489–1517) was particularly energetic and successful, annexing Jaunpur and Bihar, but his successor, Ibrahim, was unable to quell dissension among his Afghan feudatories, one of whom enlisted the support of Babur, the ruler of Kabul, who defeated Ibrahim at Panipat in 1526.

The early Mughal Empire (1526–1605)

For Babur – the founder of India's most famous dynasty, the **Mughals** – India appears to have been something of an afterthought. A direct descendant of Timur (and also distantly related to Genghis Khan), Babur was born in Uzbekistan and spent most of his life in Afghanistan, where he seized control of Kabul. It was only relatively late in life, hearing of the military weakness of the Lodis, that he decided to attack India.

His battle-hardened forces easily routed the very last Delhi sultan, Ibrahim Lodi, at the Battle of Panipat in 1526, which gave him tenuous control of Delhi and Agra, although his position remained unsafe until his troops had first defeated a far stronger Rajput force led by Rana Sanga of Mewar, at the Battle of Kanwaha in 1527, and then the allied forces of assorted Afghan chiefs. Shortly afterwards, his failing health forced him to retire to Agra, where he died in 1530.

Humayun, his son and successor, was a volatile character, alternating between bursts of energetic activity and indolence. He subdued Malwa and Gujarat, only to lose both while he "took his pleasure" in Agra. The Afghan-descended **Sher Shah Suri** (also known as Sher Khan or Sher Khan Sur) of south Bihar soon assumed the leadership of the Afghan opposition and, after two resounding defeats, Humayun was forced to seek refuge in Persia in 1539. He returned fifteen years later, however, to annihilate the forces of Sher Shah Suri's successor, Sikander Sur. Humayun died the following year after a fall in the Purana Qila in Delhi, leaving his 13-year-old son **Akbar** to succeed to the throne.

Fortunately for the young emperor, Humayun's experienced general **Bairam Khan** was on hand to serve as guardian and regent to help him through the difficult early years of his reign. Bairam first overcame the challenge of the Hindu general Hemu at the second Battle of Panipat in 1556, recovered Gwalior and Jaunpur, and handed over a

1526	1556	1569	1600
Babur defeats Ibrahim Lodi's forces at the Battle of Panipat to found the Mughal Dynasty.	Humayun, Babur's son, dies after falling down a flight of steps in Delhi.	Humayun's successor, Akbar, builds Fatehpur Sikri.	The British East India Company is formed.

consolidated kingdom of north India to Akbar in 1560. Akbar's own first military campaigns were against the **Rajputs**; and within a decade he had subdued all the Rajput domains except Mewar (Udaipur) by a clever combination of diplomacy and force. By the end of his reign in 1605 he controlled a broad sweep of territory stretching from the Bay of Bengal to Kandahar in Afghanistan.

In 1565, Akbar had the small fort built by Sikander Lodi in **Agra** demolished and replaced by the magnificent new Agra Fort, the centrepiece of a newly revitalized city that would henceforth rival Delhi as the major centre of Mughal power. Not content with this, in the late 1560s, he embarked on the creation of an entire new city, the remarkable but short-lived **Fatehpur Sikri**, which served for a brief period as the capital of the empire.

Akbar was as clever a politician and administrator as he was a successful general. In addition to involving Hindu landowners and nobles in political life, Akbar adopted a conscious policy of religious toleration aimed at widening his power base, abolishing the despised poll tax on non-Muslims (*jizya*) and tolls on Hindu pilgrimages.

The later Mughals (1605–1761)

The reign of **Jahangir** (1605–27) was a time of brisk economic and expansionist activity conjoined with artistic and architectural brilliance. Jahangir himself was a contradictory character: an alcoholic and a sadist, but also a notable connoisseur of art as well as an able and determined military commander who succeeded in extending the bounds of the already very considerable domains bequeathed to him by Akbar.

Jahangir's son **Shah Jahan** came to power in 1628, having already proved himself an outstanding commander during his father's reign. Despite his considerable military abilities, however, it is as perhaps the greatest patron of architecture the world has ever known that Shah Jahan is best remembered. In 1648 he officially moved the Mughal capital from Agra back to Delhi, celebrating the translocation with the construction of the new city of **Shahjahanabad** (now better known as Old Delhi), though it was in Agra that he left his greatest mark, with his myriad embellishments to the city's fort and, pre-eminently, in the creation of the **Taj Mahal**.

Shah Jahan's reign witnessed the entry of a new force into Indian history: the **Marathas**, a potent military power in central India. A group of militant Hindus from Maharashtra in central India, the Marathas had carved out a kingdom of their own under their inspirational chief, **Shivaji**, and soon began to turn their attentions northwards. Shah Jahan had responded to the Maratha threat by sending his third son, the ambitious young **Aurangzeb**, to the Deccan to take charge of Mughal interests in the region, although his military successes were repeatedly undermined by Shah Jahan's oldest son and preferred heir **Dara Shikoh**, who was anxious to destabilize Aurangzeb's military exploits lest they create a threat to his own prestige. The anticipated struggle between the two brothers erupted in 1658 when Shah Jahan fell suddenly and seriously ill. Shah Jahan recovered, but not before Aurangzeb had seen off Dara Shikoh, wiping out his army in a series of encounters that culminated in a rout at Ajmer. The thirty-year reign of the ailing emperor ended ignominiously. Aurangzeb had him incarcerated in Agra Fort, where he remained until his death in 1666.

Though lacking the charisma of Akbar or Babur, Aurangzeb evoked an awe of his own and proved to be a firm and capable administrator, who retained his grip on the

1615	**1658**	**1659**
Sir Thomas Roe, British ambassador to the Mughal court, negotiates trade rights with Jahangir.	Aurangzeb, last, most devout and austere of the great Mughal emperors, ascends to the throne after murdering his brothers.	The Maratha warlord, Shivaji, defeats the sultan of Bijapur to become the most powerful chief in peninsular India.

increasingly unsettled empire until his death at the age of 88. In contrast to the extravagance of the other Mughals, Aurangzeb's lifestyle was pious and disciplined. However, his religious dogmatism ultimately alienated the Hindu community whose leaders had been so carefully cultivated by Akbar. Hindu places of worship were again the object of iconoclasm and the *jizya* tax on non-Muslims was reintroduced.

The chief threat to Mughal rule in this period came from the Maratha chief, Shivaji, who established a compact and well-organized kingdom in western India, while the nearby Muslim kingdoms of Bijapur and Golconda allied themselves with him. Meanwhile, Guru Tegh Bahadur, the leader of the important new **Sikh** religion, was executed in 1675 for refusing to embrace Islam; his son, Guru Gobind, transformed the religious community into a military sect that became increasingly powerful in the Punjab. Aurangzeb's confrontation with the Rajputs over the Jodhpur succession in 1678 resulted in another war, and the alienation of most of his Rajput partners in the empire.

Aurangzeb's attention, however, was turning steadily south. In 1681 he transferred his base to the Deccan, where he spent the rest of his extremely long life overseeing the subjugation of the Bijapur and Golconda kingdoms and trying to contain the increasingly belligerent Marathas. In 1689, he succeeded in capturing and executing Shivaji's son, and by 1698 the Mughals had overrun almost the whole of the peninsula.

Aurangzeb's son, Bahadur Shah, succeeded in 1707 but reigned for just five years. His death in 1712 marked the beginning of the end for the Mughals, as their empire disintegrated. By the 1720s the rulers of Hyderabad, Avadh (Lucknow) and Bengal were effectively independent; the Marathas overwhelmed the rich province of Malwa in 1738; Hindu landholders everywhere were in revolt; and **Nadir Shah** of Persia dealt a serious blow to the empire's prestige when he invaded India, defeated the Mughal army and sacked Delhi in 1739.

The East India Company (1600–1857)

India's trading potential had attracted European interest ever since 1498, when Vasco da Gama landed on the Malabar (Keralan) Coast. During the ensuing century Portuguese, Dutch, English, French and Danish companies had all set up coastal trading centres, exporting textiles, sugar and indigo. British interests in India were formalized by the creation of the **East India Company**, granted a royal charter by Elizabeth I in 1600, whose representatives arrived at Surat in Gujarat in 1608, quickly establishing 27 trading posts around the country, including Fort George and Fort William (out of which the cities of Madras and Calcutta would subsequently develop), as well as at the fledgling settlement of Bombay.

It was in the south that European trading initiatives first took on a political significance, after the onset of the War of the Austrian Succession in 1740. Armed conflict between French and English trading companies along the south Indian coast soon developed into a minor war over the succession of the nizam of Hyderabad. Sporadic fighting continued until the end of the Seven Years' War in Europe and the Treaty of Paris in 1763 put an effective end to French ambitions in India. Meanwhile, **Robert Clive**'s defeat of the rebellious young nawab of Bengal at Plassey in 1757 had decisively augmented British power; by 1765 the enervated Mughal emperor legally recognized the Company by granting it the revenue management of Bengal, Bihar and Orissa.

1666	**1739**	**1757**
Shivaji and his son, Sambhaji, escape from Aurangzeb's court by hiding in a box of sweets.	With the Mughul dynasty in decline, the Persian King Nadir Shah sacks Delhi, slaughtering tens of thousands.	Robert Clive's victory over the nawab of Bengal at Plassey lays the foundation for two centuries of British rule in India.

For the next thirty years, the British in India contented themselves with developing trade and repulsing Indian offensives against their three major settlements in Calcutta, Bombay and Madras, though by the end of the century the defeat of **Tipu Sultan** of Mysore, the Company's best-organized and most resolute enemy, and the subjugation of the nizam of Hyderabad, resulted in the annexation of considerable territories, and by 1805 nearly all the other rulers in India recognized British suzerainty. A long-drawn-out series of conflicts between the British and Marathas (the so-called three "Maratha Wars" of 1774–1818) finally extinguished the Marathas as an effective military threat.

Following the subjugation of the Marathas, the British established a series of treaties with the rulers of Rajasthan and with most of India's other surviving independent kingdoms, collectively known as the so-called **princely states**, stretching from Hyderabad in the south to Kashmir in the north. Under these treaties, the various kingdoms retained their autonomy more or less intact and received a guarantee of military protection in exchange for pledging their loyalty to the British Crown and agreeing to certain political, mercantile and financial concessions. The much-abused city of Delhi, the traditional capital of north India, fared less well, as the British established their capital at the burgeoning new city of **Calcutta**. Not until 1911 would Delhi recapture its mantle as the north's imperial city.

The 1857 uprising

The new British **colony**, however, was in a state of social and economic collapse as a result of the almost incessant conflicts of the previous hundred years. The controversial "Doctrine of Lapse", whereby autonomous states were gradually annexed, was widely resented. In addition, the Company's policy, after 1835, of promoting European literature and science (with English replacing Persian as the official state language), the suppression of local customs such as *sati* and child marriage, and the deployment of Indian troops overseas (resulting in loss of caste) were increasingly perceived as part of a covert British attack on traditional Hindu and Muslim religious and cultural practices.

The final spark which ignited a full-blown uprising by the Indian army was supplied when troops were issued with cartridges for a new Enfield rifle rumoured to have been smeared in cows' and pigs' grease (polluting to both Hindus and Muslims). The resultant **1857 uprising** (traditionally referred to by the British as the "Indian Mutiny" or "Sepoy Rebellion", and by Indian historians as the "First War of Independence") began with a rebellion of Indian troops (sepoys) at Meerut on May 10, 1857, and Delhi was seized the next day. The rebellion quickly spread across most of central northern India, where mutineers seized Lucknow and Kanpur. The British authorities were caught by surprise, though control was gradually reasserted. Delhi and Kanpur were both retaken in September, and the final recapture of Lucknow in March 1858 effectively signalled the end of the uprising. Bloody reprisals ensued.

The Raj and Indian nationalism (1857–1947)

The uprising had important consequences for subsequent British rule in the Subcontinent. The governing powers of the East India Company were abolished and

1799	1857	1858	1911
Tipu Sultan is killed at the Battle of Srirangapatnam, securing British control of the far south.	Sepoys mount a rebellion against British rule.	The so-called "Mutiny" is brutally repressed. Large areas of Delhi are razed and hundreds of suspected rebels summarily executed.	Delhi succeeds Calcutta as the British capital.

the British Crown assumed the direct administration of India in the same year. Henceforth, British India was no longer merely a massive trade operation, but a fullyfledged independent kingdom, or **Raj**, as the period of British rule in the Subcontinent subsequently became known.

As a British colony, India assumed a new position in the world economy. Its trade benefited from the railways developed by the British, and Indian businessmen began to invest in a range of manufacturing industries. However, India subsidized the British economy as a source of cheap raw materials and as a market for manufactured goods, and its own economy and agriculture remained underdeveloped. British civil servants dominated the higher echelons of the administration, often introducing policies contrary to Indian interests and cultural traditions. Public demonstrations eventually forced the British to sanction the creation of the **Indian National Congress** party (usually known simply as "Congress") in 1885, and by 1905 Congress had adopted self-government as a political aim. In 1906, concerns about the predominantly Hindu Congress led to the foundation of the **All-India Muslim League** to represent the country's Muslims.

The Morley-Minto Reforms of 1909 paved the way for Indian participation in provincial executive councils and made allowance for separate Muslim representation. At the **Great Durbar** of 1911, held in honour of the new king, George V, the capital was moved back to **Delhi**, with the construction of yet another imperial city, so-called "New" Delhi, to celebrate the relocation (though it wasn't finished until 1931). A few years later, the Royal Proclamation of 1917 promised a gradual development of dominion-style self-government; and two years later the Montagu-Chelmsford Reforms attempted to implement the declaration.

At this point an England-educated lawyer, **Mohandas Karamchand Gandhi** (see see box, p.560) – better known as the Mahatma, or "Great Soul" – took up the initiative, espousing a political philosophy based on non-violence and the championing of the untouchables, whom he renamed the Children of God (Harijan). Gandhi began by organizing India-wide one-day strikes and protests, though these were mercilessly crushed by the government – as in the infamous incident (see box, p.523) in 1919 when troops under General Dyer dispersed a meeting at Jallianwalla Bagh in Amritsar by firing on the unarmed crowd, killing 379 and wounding 1200.

By 1928 Congress was demanding complete independence. The government offered talks, but the more radical elements in Congress, now led by the young **Jawaharlal Nehru**, were in a confrontational mood. Gandhi, in turn, led a well-publicized 386km "salt march" from his ashram in Sabarmati to make salt illegally at Dandi in Gujarat in defiance of a particularly unpopular British tax. This demonstration of non-violent civil disobedience (*satyagraha*) fired the popular imagination, leading to more processions, strikes, and mass imprisonments over the next few years, which in turn led to the formulation of the new **Government of India Act** in 1935, although this still fell short of offering the country complete independence. Congress remained suspicious of British intentions, and despite Gandhi's overtures refused to accommodate Muslim demands for representation. **Mohammed Ali Jinnah**, who assumed the leadership of the Muslim League in 1935, initially promoted Muslim-Hindu cooperation, but he soon despaired of influencing Congress and by 1940 the League passed a resolution demanding an independent Pakistan.

1915	**1919**	**1930**	**1931**
Gandhi returns to India from South Africa.	British troops open fire on unarmed civilians during a demonstration in Amritsar, killing 379 people.	Gandhi leads "Salt Satyagraha" to protest against British rule. Sixty thousand are imprisoned in its wake.	The Gandhi-Irwin Pact secures the release of all political prisoners.

Confrontations between the government, Congress and the Muslim League continued throughout World War II, despite the promise, in 1942, by a Britain increasingly reliant on Indian troops, of postwar Independence. Gandhi introduced the **Quit India** slogan and proposed another campaign of civil disobedience; Jinnah, meanwhile, preached his "two nations" theory and inspired mass Muslim support with his rhetoric against "Hinduization". A spate of terrorist activities across the country left one thousand dead and sixty thousand imprisoned. By the end of the war, the British government accepted that complete independence for India could no longer be postponed.

Unfortunately, British attempts to find a solution that would preserve a united India while allaying Muslim fears disintegrated in the face of continued intransigence from both sides, and they gradually realized that the division – or so-called **Partition** – of the existing country of India into separate Muslim and Hindu states was inevitable. **Lord Mountbatten** was appointed viceroy to supervise the handover of power. The Subcontinent was **partitioned** on August 15, 1947, and Pakistan came into existence. The new boundaries cut through both Bengal and the Punjab; Sikhs, Muslims and Hindus who had been neighbours became enemies overnight. Five million Hindus and Sikhs from Pakistan, and a similar number of Muslims from India, were involved in the ensuing two-way exodus, and the atrocities cost half a million lives. Mahatma Gandhi, who had devoted himself to ending the communal violence after Partition, was **assassinated** in January 1948 by a Hindu extremist antagonized by his defence of Muslims.

India under Nehru (1947–64)

Jawaharlal Nehru, India's first and longest-serving prime minister, proved to be a dynamic and extremely popular leader during his seventeen years in office, building the foundations of a democratic secular nation, and guiding the first stages of its agricultural and industrial development. The franchise was made universal for all adults and, with 173 million eligible to vote, in 1951 India became the **world's largest democracy**.

Despite Independence, there was still the problem of the 562 **princely states** within India, covering no less than two fifths of the country's total area, and which remained technically autonomous under the terms of ongoing British treaties. At Independence rulers of several of these states had yet to decide whether they were going to join India or Pakistan. Nehru's able deputy prime minister, Sardar Vallabhai Patel, was made responsible for encouraging the rulers of the recalcitrant statelets to join the new India, including sending a detachment of Indian troops into the territory of the Muslim nizam of **Hyderabad**, who had resisted joining the union even though the majority of his state's population was Hindu. Some parts of the Subcontinent retained their independence for even longer. The **French** enclaves at Pondicherry and Chandernagor were not incorporated until the 1950s, while the Portuguese refused to accept the new situation, until in 1961 Nehru finally sent in the army to annex **Goa**.

The most serious legacy of Partition concerned the Himalayan state of **Kashmir**. At Independence, Kashmir's Hindu maharaja Hari Singh remained undecided as to which of the two new countries he wished to join. Jinnah naturally assumed Kashmir would join Pakistan, given that three-quarters of its inhabitants were Muslims; Nehru was

Aug 15, 1947	**Jan 30, 1948**	**1948**
India is partitioned as Nehru is sworn in as the country's first prime minister– millions are displaced.	Mahatma Gandhi is shot at point-blank range by a Hindu fanatic while attending a prayer meeting in Delhi.	Indian troops and Pakistani insurgents clash for the first time in Kashmir, leading to the fateful partition of the region.

equally determined to keep it for India. Meanwhile, the maharaja continued to prevaricate. Events reached a head in October 1947, when Islamic partisans from Pakistan's tribal areas suddenly arrived in the Kashmir valley to encourage the maharaja to join with Pakistan. Hari Singh, fearing he was about to be overthrown, immediately determined to join India instead. Shortly afterwards Indian troops were airlifted into the valley, and began to battle with the Islamic insurgents. Although war was never officially declared, and no regular Pakistani military units were involved, the fighting is usually described as the **First Indo-Pakistan War**. By the time the UN brokered a ceasefire in 1948, Pakistani insurgents had secured a sizeable slice of Kashmiri territory, which Pakistan retains to this day.

Elsewhere in the region, Nehru attempted to promote Asian unity by following a policy of peaceful **non-alignment**, although this was repeatedly threatened by **Chinese aggression**. The Chinese invasion of Tibet in 1950 brought the Chinese right up to India's border (and a flood of refugees into India itself, including the Dalai Lama, who arrived in 1959), while in 1962 Chinese troops brushed aside Indian border patrols and began to move down into Assam. This "invasion" (although it was really more a show of force) ended soon afterwards, and while the humiliating inability of the Indian army to repel the interlopers did not officially spell the end of India's policy of non-alignment (it continues to this day), Nehru immediately signed a defence treaty with the US, and the Chinese retained small areas of Indian territory in Kashmir and Assam which they still hold.

Indira Gandhi (1966–84)

In 1946, the whole nation mourned Nehru's death which prevented him from witnessing the restoration of India's military prestige in the **Second Indo-Pakistan War** of 1965. Pakistani leader General Ayub Khan, perhaps wishing to test the resolve of new Indian premier **Lal Bahadur Shastri**, launched a series of skirmishes into disputed areas of Gujarat, and followed this up with attempts to infiltrate Kashmir and provoke a pro-Pakistani uprising. Full-scale fighting broke out in Kashmir and to the south, and the Indian army responded by driving Pakistani forces back to within 5km of a virtually defenceless Lahore before a ceasefire was agreed, with both sides returning to their previous borders. Despite this triumph, Lal Bahadur Shastri died shortly afterwards, in January 1966, leaving Nehru's daughter **Indira Gandhi** to establish herself as the new leader of Congress.

The 49-year-old Indira – or "Mrs Gandhi", as she is often called (though no relation to the Mahatma; she acquired her surname through marriage to a Parsi named Feroze Gandhi, who had died in 1960) – was initially chosen as a popular but easily manipulated figurehead by Congress chiefs. Gandhi herself had different plans. She moved rapidly to shore up her own power, and then – after consolidating her mandate in fresh elections in 1971 – launched Congress along a populist socialist path, nationalizing the banks, abolishing the former maharajas' privy purses, and introducing new legislation on corporate profits and land holdings. By this time, India was experiencing massive industrial growth and had also made a spectacular agricultural breakthrough with its **Green Revolution**, becoming self-sufficient in food by the early 1970s thanks to the introduction of high-yield grains.

1959	1961	1966
Tibet's spiritual leader, the Dalai Lama, flees to India, taking up residence with his cabinet in Dharamsala.	451 years of Portuguese rule in Goa come to an end as Nehru orders in the Indian army.	Nehru's niece, Indira Gandhi, becomes leader of the Congress Party and India's third prime minister.

Gandhi also had to deal with the increasingly chaotic situation in **East Pakistan** (present-day Bangladesh), which had declared independence from (West) Pakistan in 1971. Pakistani troops had been sent in to bring the East Pakistanis back into line, causing a mass exodus of refugees into India. Gandhi astutely waited until she had the moral support of the international community before launching simultaneous attacks in West and East Pakistan on December 4. By December 15, Pakistani forces in Bangladesh had capitulated.

Back at home, Gandhi was proving less successful. After widespread agrarian and industrial unrest against the rate of inflation and corruption within the Congress Party, she declared a **State of Emergency** on June 26, 1975, suspending all civil rights, censoring the press and imprisoning some twenty thousand of her opponents, real or imagined. The "Emergency" lasted eighteen months, characterized by the enforced sterilization of men and brutal slum-clearances in Delhi and elsewhere. When she finally released her opponents and called off the Emergency in January 1977, the bitterness she had engendered resulted in her ignominious defeat in the March elections. The ensuing **Janata** coalition under Morarji Desai fell apart within two years, and his premiership was terminated by a vote of no confidence in 1979. Gandhi, now apparently forgiven, swept back into office in January 1980.

Four years afterwards, Gandhi made the second, fatal, mistake of her career. A group of rebels demanding a separate Sikh nation – Khalistan – took control of the **Golden Temple** in Amritsar early in 1984, from where they organized a campaign of violence, killing hundreds of Hindus and moderate Sikhs. Gandhi sent in the tanks in June 1984, but two days of raging combat desecrated the Sikhs' holiest shrine as well as giving Khalistan its first martyrs. In October that year, Gandhi's Sikh bodyguards took revenge by assassinating her at her house in Delhi. The city was then engulfed in massive communal **rioting**, during which Hindu mobs went about Delhi systematically murdering Sikhs – according to some reports locating their victims with the help of electoral rolls supplied by Congress politicians.

Communal conflict (1984–95)

Following Gandhi's death, it was left to her sole surviving son, **Rajiv Gandhi** (a former pilot) to take up leadership of Congress. He came to power in December 1984 on a wave of sympathy boosted by his reputation as "Mr Clean", an image given added meaning by the **Bhopal** gas tragedy (see box, p.341) just two weeks before the elections. The opposition subsequently rallied under the leadership of **V.P. Singh**. Elections in 1989 did not give Singh's Janata Party a majority, but he managed to form a coalition government with the support of the "Hindu first" Bharatiya Janata Party, or **BJP**, led by **L.K. Advani**.

Singh was immediately confronted by problems in the Punjab and Kashmir, but it was an even more emotive issue that brought down his government in less than a year. Advani's populist BJP were demanding that the Babri Masjid mosque in **Ayodhya**, built by Babur on the supposed site of the birthplace of Rama, god-hero of the Ramayana, should be replaced by a Hindu temple. Advani set off towards Ayodhya in October 1990, accompanied by thousands of supporters, with the avowed intention of destroying the mosque. Singh ordered Advani's arrest, and the inevitable withdrawal of the BJP from his coalition government resulted in a vote of no confidence.

June 26, 1975–March 21, 1977	1984	Oct 31, 1984
In response to widespread civil unrest, Indira Gandhi declares a "State of Emergency", suspending elections and civil liberties.	Militant Sikhs occupy the Golden Temple in Amritsar. Indira Gandhi orders in the troops. A massacre ensues.	Indira Gandhi's Sikh bodyguards take revenge by shooting the prime minister in her garden, unleashing a communal bloodbath.

New elections were called. Shortly afterwards, while campaigning in Tamil Nadu in May 1991, Rajiv Gandhi was assassinated by Tamil Tigers seeking revenge for India's military opposition to their "freedom fight" in Sri Lanka. It was left to **P.V. Narasimha Rao** to steer Congress through the elections and form a new coalition government, which immediately embarked on a far-reaching programme of **economic liberalization**, dismantling trade barriers and allowing multinationals such as Coca-Cola, Pepsi and KFC to enter the Indian market for the first time.

At the same time, the BJP increased its seats in the Lok Sabha (the Lower House of Parliament) from 80 to 120 and Advani became leader of the opposition, amid growing popular support for the rebuilding of Rama's temple in Ayodhya. The situation finally came to a head in December 1992, as Hindu extremists incited crowds of fanatical devotees to tear down the Babri Masjid at Ayodhya in a blaze of publicity. The demolition was followed by terrible **riots** in many parts of the country, especially Bombay and Gujarat, where Muslim families and businesses were targeted. A few months later, a massive series of bomb blasts ripped through **Bombay**, killing 260 people and destroying some of the city's most important commercial buildings. No one claimed responsibility, though the attacks were thought to have been orchestrated by Islamic groups in retaliation for Hindu violence against their fellow Muslims.

Against this backdrop of uncertainty, the rise of right-wing Hindu-fundamentalist parties gathered pace. The BJP took advantage of the power struggle in the Congress Party to rekindle regional support. Their new rallying cry was **Swadeshi** – a campaign against the Congress-led programme of economic liberalization and, in particular, the activities of newly arrived companies such as Coca-Cola, Pepsi and KFC (one of whose branches was forced to close by the BJP-controlled Delhi municipality).

The rise of the BJP (1996–99)

The BJP emerged from the **general election** of May 1996 as the single largest party but were unable to muster a majority and were ousted a couple of weeks later by the hastily formed **Unified Front** (UF) coalition. The UF soldiered on until March 1998, after which the **BJP** finally struggled to power as the head of a new conservative coalition government under **Atal Bihari Vajpayee**.

This time, the party managed to stay in office for thirteen months, as opposed to the thirteen days of its previous spell in government. The BJP had promised change and the restoration of national pride, and one of its early acts in government was to conduct five underground **nuclear tests** in May 1998, provoking Pakistan to respond in kind. There was a chorus of world criticism, and US-led financial **sanctions** were imposed on both nations.

Ongoing tensions in **Kashmir** did little to calm local and international fears. In May 1999, at least eight hundred Pakistani-backed Mujahideen crept across the so-called Line of Control (the de facto border) overlooking the Srinagar–Leh road near **Kargil** and began to occupy Indian territory. India moved thousands of troops into the area, and within days the two countries were poised on the brink of all-out war. In the event the conflict was contained, and by July 1999 the Indian army had retaken all the ground previously lost to the militants.

1984	Dec 3, 1984	1990
Rajiv Gandhi, Indira's eldest son, succeeds his mother and initiates a period of sweeping economic reforms.	2200 die after toxic gas escapes from an American-owned fertilizer plant in Bhopal, Madhya Pradesh.	More than one hundred innocent civilians are gunned down by Indian security forces on the Gawakadal Bridge in Srinagar.

Shortly afterwards, the Congress Party, reinvigorated under the leadership of **Sonia Gandhi**, the Italian-born widow of the former prime minister Rajiv, collaborated with the Jayalalitha's AIADMK (see box, p.954) to bring about the downfall of the BJP government. At the start of the campaign, Congress hopes were high that, with a Gandhi once again as party leader, it could revive the popular support lost after years of infighting and corruption scandals. Unfortunately for them, the wave of **patriotism** that swept India after the Kargil victory in Kashmir was a godsend for Vajpayee (cynics argued it may well have been the hidden policy behind the army's uncompromising response to the crisis). Riding high on the feel-good factor, his party inflicted the biggest defeat Congress had sustained since 1947.

The new millennium

India's political problems were temporarily eclipsed by a succession of catastrophic **natural disasters**. In 2000, **record rainfalls** wreaked havoc. An estimated twelve million people were left marooned or homeless as river levels rose by as much as 4m in places. An even worse tragedy lay in store for millions of Gujaratis when, on the morning of January 26, 2001 – Indian Republic Day – a massive **earthquake** measuring 7.9 on the Richter scale levelled a vast area in the northwest of the state, killing around 19,000 and rendering hundreds of thousands of people homeless.

Meanwhile in Delhi, Vajpayee's party also came in for flak when the prime minister announced the **creation of three new states**: Jharkhand, Chhattisgarh and Uttaranchal (later changing its name to Uttarakhand), made up of remote parts of Bihar, Madhya Pradesh and Uttar Pradesh respectively.

Around this time, the wider world started to become aware, for the first time, of south India's burgeoning **hi-tech revolution**, centred on the cities of Bangalore and Hyderabad. **Bangalore** had led the way in the early 1980s, and by the mid-1990s had become a major player in the international software market. Yet by the turn of the millennium its pre-eminence was being challenged by the even more spectacular emergence of **Hyderabad** (quickly nicknamed "Cyberabad"), which thanks to massive state subsidies had begun to attract leading global players including Microsoft and Dell – although the rural poor of southern India saw very little of this newly generated wealth, further exacerbating the gap between rich and poor, which commentators quickly christened the "digital divide".

To the brink of war

During late 2001, **Indo-Pak relations** and the **Kashmir** question returned to the fore as India entered one of the most volatile periods in its modern history. In October, the **State Assembly building in Srinagar** was destroyed by Islamist suicide car-bombers, while in December, three Muslim gunmen stormed the **Parliament Building** in New Delhi, killing several police guards, before they were picked off by army marksmen. Pakistani involvement was inevitably suspected. Then, in early 2002, a Muslim mob in **Godhra**, Gujarat, attacked a trainload of Hindu pilgrims returning from Ayodhya: 38 died and 74 were injured, although this paled in comparison with the reprisal killings that followed, in which around two thousand people (mostly Muslims) were slaughtered.

May 21, 1991	1992	Dec 1992–Jan 1993
Rajiv Gandhi assassinated by Tamil Tiger suicide bomber while campaigning near Chennai.	A mob of Hindu extremists destroy the Babri Masjid mosque in Ayodhya, sparking riots and killings across India.	Scores die in a spate of communal disturbances in Bombay. Terrible reprisal bombings take place two months later.

Anti-Muslim sentiment in India was further fuelled only a month after Godhra when an Islamist suicide squad commandeered a tourist bus and used it to attack the **Kaluchak** army cantonment near Jammu. Coming only four months after the attack on the Indian parliament, and hot on the heels of yet another promise by Pakistan to clamp down on cross-border militancy, the atrocity provoked outrage in Delhi. Vajpayee, bowing to the hawks on the right of his own party, called for a "decisive battle", initiating a massive build-up of troops on the border. An estimated million men at arms were involved in the ensuing standoff as India and Pakistan edged to the brink of all-out **war**. Once again, however, US diplomacy diffused the crisis and the armies stood down.

In 2003, the Archaeological Survey of India released its long-awaited **report on Ayodhya**. To no one's surprise, the ASI panel of "experts", appointed by the right-wing BJP government, declared they'd found evidence to show there had been a temple, in effect condoning the tearing down of the mosque. Rubbing salt in old wounds, the ruling did little to quell post-Godhra tensions; and when, on August 25, 2003 (the day after the Ayodhya report was published), two **bombs** ripped through the centre of downtown Mumbai, commentators were quick to identify the Babri Masjid dispute as the provocation.

The return of Congress

Despite continuing sectarian troubles, with India booming as never before, Vajpayee and his BJP-led coalition decided to cash in on the perceived feel-good factor and call a snap **election** in **May 2004**, although far from increasing his majority as he'd expected, Vajpayee and his government were thrown out in the most dramatic political turnaround of recent times. Congress gained the largest share of the vote and **Sonia Gandhi** was duly invited to form a government. However, she stunned supporters by "humbly declining" the invitation and stepped down. Eventually, former finance minister, 71-year-old **Manmohan Singh**, stepped into the breach and was named as prime minister, the first Sikh ever to lead the country.

As the architect of the important liberalizing economic reforms enacted during the early 1990s, Singh seemed like the perfect candidate to oversee India's continuing economic and technological growth (as Singh himself once put it, "India happens to be a rich country inhabited by very poor people"). In April 2007 the country launched its first commercial space rocket, and the following month saw the government announce the strongest economic growth figures (an impressive 9.4 percent) for twenty years.

Despsite a rapid shrink in growth figures to between 6 and 7 percent over the past few years, India's technological and economic transformation continues apace. The country is now the world's second largest exporter of computer software after the US, generating sales of around a billion dollars a year, focused on the southern cities of Bengaluru and Hyderabad, which have also become home to innumerable international call centres thanks to the cities' educated, English-speaking workforce.

Yet such spectacular developments have had little effect on the lives of India's rural poor. In an attempt to address the ever-widening divide between the nation's increasingly affluent middle classes and the rest of the country, Singh's coalition

May 1996	May 11, 1998	1999	Jan 26, 2001
A far-right Hindu nationalist party, BJP, wins the general election.	India detonates its first atomic bomb. Pakistan follows suit soon after.	India and Pakistan on the brink of war after insurgents occupy Kargil, in Ladakh.	20,000 die and 167,000 are injured after a massive earthquake devastates northwest Gujarat on India's Independence Day.

government launched the nation's largest-ever rural jobs scheme in February 2006 with the aim of freeing around sixty million families from poverty, although this promised "New Deal" has yet to bear fruit. Progress has also been made on the looming **nuclear threat** hanging over the Subcontinent, with agreements now in place with the US and Pakistan.

Terrorist violence continues to plague the country, even so, including many attacks by Pakistan-based Islamic militants designed to derail the ongoing peace process in Kashmir, or to avenge attacks by Hindu mobs against Muslims in India. Bomb attacks in October 2005 and September 2008 killed almost a hundred people in Delhi, while in February 2007, 68 passengers (ironically, most of them Pakistani) were killed by bomb blasts on a train travelling from New Delhi to Lahore. Even the normally peaceful city of Jaipur became a target in May 2008, when seven bombs exploded in various busy streets around the Pink City, killing 63 people. It is **Mumbai**, however, which has suffered the worst from terrorist atrocities. In July 2006 a series of bombs blasts exploded almost simultaneously on seven commuter trains, leaving more than two hundred dead, while the horrific wave of co-ordinated attacks by Pakistani gunmen in **November 2008** brought the city to its knees, temporarily at least. Images of the burning *Taj Palace* hotel and the blood-spattered concourse of CST station were beamed live around the world, producing a sense of global compassion and outrage, while also raising alarming questions about India's security and economic prospects.

Challenges and potential

Despite these various setbacks, **elections in 2009** saw an unexpected landslide victory for the Congress-led coalition, with Manmohan Singh becoming the first Indian leader since Nehru in 1952 to be returned directly to power after a five-year term. Singh's low-key and scandal-free leadership, concentrating on economic fundamentals, the alleviation of poverty and improving relationships with Pakistan, has proved popular in a country that has enjoyed more than its fair share of big-talking but ineffective politicos.

In many ways Singh's business-oriented but socially conscious leadership provides the perfect template for how India will hope to develop in the coming decades. Many of India's citizens are enjoying increasing levels of affluence, while the country's **economy** (which has grown at an average rate of over seven percent for the past decade) continues to grow thanks to its increasingly skilled and educated workforce, as well as rocketing levels of foreign investment. All of which raises the genuine possibility that India will shortly become one of the global economic superpowers of the 21st century; according to estimates by Goldman Sachs, the country is on course to overtake France, Germany and former colonial masters Britain by around 2015, and to become the world's third largest economy (after the USA and China) by 2035.

Still, huge **challenges** remain. The most obvious is the simple fact that, for all India's spectacular economic progress, millions of its inhabitants continue to live in abject poverty, while rampant development is placing increasing strains on the country's outdated infrastructure. The always volatile relationship with Pakistan is another source of uncertainty, while the spectre of home-grown Hindu fundamentalism – as well as

Dec 2001	2006	April 20, 2007
Islamist gunmen attack the Indian parliament building in protest at the government's Kashmir policy.	Bangalore-based IT giant, Infosys, celebrates its 25th anniversary by announcing profits of US$2 billion.	Former Miss World and Indian screen goddess, Ashwariya Rai, weds Abhishek Bachchan in India's "Wedding of the Century".

threats from Islamic militants from abroad – is still very much alive and well. Meanwhile, a string of violent regional movements continue to sporadically challenge the authority of central and state governments; these range from Islamic jihadis in Kashmir and tribal insurgents in the northeastern hill states to the neo-Marxist Naxalite revolutionaries who continue to disrupt life in the impoverished eastern states of Chhattisgarh, Odisha, Bihar and Jharkhand.

In 2011–12, there arose yet another challenge to the stability of India's national government, in the form of a mass movement against the phenomenon many ordinary Indians regard as the root cause of the country's most pressing problems: **corruption**. Demonstrations voicing outrage at abysmal standards in public life – at local, state and national levels – coalesced around the unlikely figure of a former flower-seller and social activist from Maharashtra named Anna Hazare, who staged a series of high-profile, Gandhian-style hunger strikes to lobby for a strengthening of anti-corruption legislation. The movement was fuelled by widespread outrage at a string of well-publicized corruption cases, notably those surrounding India's hosting of the 2010 Commonwealth Games – an event marred by the failure of the Indian government to complete the facilities on schedule after US$4bn/£2.71bn of public funds earmarked for the event went missing.

A damning World Health Organization report on poverty in the same year further exposed the extent to which government money in India routinely ends up in the wrong pockets. Among the most disturbing of the WHO's statistics was that an estimated 40 percent of Indian children are malnourished – a fact prime minister Singh admitted was "a national shame".

Anna Hazare's hunger strikes started to lose their potency in 2012, but the corruption issue and plight of India's poor remained centre stage as more than are hundred thousand peasants marched from all over the country to Delhi to lobby for greater land rights. The conciliatory tone with which their demands were met by Congress ministers (who face a national election in 2014) diffused the crisis before the marchers arrived in the capital. But the outpouring of support they received all over India hinted at the scale of rising discontent, especially in rural areas, where the fruits of the recent economic boom are yet to make an impact.

Fears over India's **faltering economy** dominated the news in late 2012, as growth rates remained stubbornly sluggish at just over 6 percent. Those who identified corruption and government inefficiency as the culprits felt vindicated after a massive electricity blackout in July paralyzed the country, leaving 700 million people without power.

Earlier in the year, a new set of figures had emerged indicating how little impact on **gender inequalities** the increased prosperity had made. One report showed how sex-selective abortions, the cause of India's notoriously imbalanced gender ratio, were more prevalent in developed, affluent states, such as Haryana. Among the country's urban middle classes, the status and profile of women, both at home and in the workplace, has improved greatly since Independence. But the same is not true of rural areas, where the lot of women has improved little, and where domestic violence and rape more often than not go unpunished by the police.

The yawning gulf between middle-class-urban and rural-peasant India was underlined by events following the so-called **Delhi rape case** of December 2012, when a young physiotherapy student died after being brutally gang raped on a moving bus in the

2008	Nov 2008	2009
Tata launch the US$2500 "Nano", the world's cheapest car.	Terrorists launch a bloody attack on Mumbai; 164 die.	*3 Idiots*, starring Aamir Khan and Kareena Kapoor, becomes the highest-grossing Bollywood movie of all time.

capital. Galvanized by the atrocity, the educated classes poured on to the streets protesting at perceived police indifference to sexual violence and poor treatment generally of women in India. Demonstrations were held at cities across the country, garnering worldwide media attention. Yet when, just weeks later in February 2013, the bodies of three young girls were discovered in a Maharashtran village well, a veil of silence seemed to fall over the Indian media. Only after local mothers blocked the national highway did the local police mount an investigation, in the course of which tests proved the girls had been raped before being murdered.

The outrage expressed in the wake of these high-profile crimes exposed deep cultural fault lines in India – a country whose recent boom, far from alleviating the plight of the poorest, seems only to have increased disparities in wealth. Whether or not India can continue to evolve at its present pace and achieve its longed-for position on the global stage will be determined not merely by the power of its economy, but also by the extent to which it is able to balance the needs of rich and poor, and curb the corruption endemic in public life.

2010	2012	Dec 2012–Feb 2013
Growth rates exceed ten percent as the Indian economy goes into overdrive despite recession elsewhere in the world.	A government report claims that three million girls were unborn in 2011 as a result of female foeticide.	Crowds take to the streets across the country to express outrage at the rape and murder of a young student on a moving bus in Delhi.

Religion

Four out of five Indians are Hindus, and Hinduism permeates every aspect of life in the country, from the commonplace details of daily life up to national politics. After Hindus, Muslims are the largest religious group, and have been an integral part of Indian society since the twelfth century. The more recently established Sikh faith was founded in reaction to the caste laws and ritual observances of Hinduism and now boasts millions of adherents. The far older Jain religion also still commands a sizeable following, and there are also small communities of Buddhists, Christians and Iranian-descended Zoroastrians, or Parsis.

Hinduism

Hinduism is the product of several thousand years of evolution and assimilation. It has no founder or prophet, no single creed, and no single prescribed practice or doctrine; it takes in hundreds of gods, goddesses, beliefs and practices, and widely variant cults and philosophies. Some are recognized by only two or three villages, others are popular right across the Subcontinent. Hindus call their beliefs and practices **dharma**, which defines a way of living in harmony with natural and moral law while fulfilling personal goals and meeting the requirements of society.

The Vedic age

The origins of Hinduism date back to the arrival of the **Aryans** (see p.1151). The Aryans believed in a number of gods associated with the elements, including **Agni**, the god of fire, **Surya**, the sun god, and **Indra**, the chief god. Most of these deities faded in importance in later times, but Indra is still regarded as the father of the gods, and Surya was widely worshipped until the medieval period.

Aryan religious beliefs were first set down in a series of four books, the **Vedas** (from the Sanskrit word *veda*, meaning "knowledge"). Transmitted orally for centuries, the Vedas were finally written down, in Sanskrit, between 1000 BC and 500 AD. The earliest and most important of the four Vedas, the **Rig Veda**, contains more than a thousand hymns to various deities, while the other three (the Yajur Veda, Sama Veda and Atharva Veda) contain further prayers, chants and instructions for performing the complex sacrificial rituals associated with this early Vedic religion.

The Vedas were followed by further religious texts, including the **Brahmanas**, a series of commentaries on the Vedas for the use of priests (brahmins) and, more importantly, the **Upanishads**, which describe in beautiful and emotive verse the mystic experience of unity of the soul (*atman*) with Brahma, the absolute creator of the universe, ideally attained through asceticism, renunciation of worldly values and meditation. In the Upanishads the concepts of **samsara**, a cyclic round of death and rebirth characterized by suffering and perpetuated by desire, and **moksha**, liberation from *samsara*, became firmly rooted. As fundamental aspects of the Hindu world view, both are accepted by all but a handful of Hindus today, along with the belief in **karma**, the certainty that one's present position in society is determined by the effect of one's previous actions in this and past lives.

Hindu society

The stratification of Hindu society is rooted in the **Dharma Sutras**, a further collection of scriptures written at roughly the same time as the later Vedas. These defined four hierarchical classes, or **varnas** (from *varna*, meaning "colour", perhaps a reference to

THE MAHABHARATA AND THE RAMAYANA

Eight times as long as the *Iliad* and *Odyssey* combined, the **Mahabharata** was written around 400 AD and tells of a feuding *kshatriya* family in northern India during the fourth millennium BC. The chief character is **Arjuna**, who, with his four brothers, represents the **Pandava** clan, supreme fighters and upholders of righteousness. The Pandava clan are resented by their cousins, the evil **Kauravas**, led by Duryodhana, the eldest son of Dhrtarashtra, ruler of the Kuru kingdom.

When Dhrtarashtra hands his kingdom over to the Pandavas, the Kauravas are understandably less than overjoyed. The subsequent battle between the Pandavas and Kauravas is described in the sixth book, the famous **Bhagavad Gita**. Krishna steps into battle as Arjuna's charioteer. Arjuna is in a dilemma, unable to justify the killing of his own kin in pursuit of a rightful kingdom. Krishna consoles him, reminding him that his principal duty is as a warrior, and convincing him that by fulfilling his dharma he not only upholds law and order by saving the kingdom from the grasp of unrighteous rulers, he also serves the gods in the spirit of devotion and thus guarantees himself eternal union with the divine in the blissful state of *moksha*.

The Pandavas finally win the battle and Yudhishtra, one of the five Pandava brothers, is crowned king. Eventually Arjuna's grandson, Pariksit, inherits the throne, and the Pandavas trek to Mount Meru, the mythical centre of the universe and the abode of the gods, where Arjuna finds Krishna's promised *moksha*.

THE RAMAYANA

The Ramayana tells the story of **Rama**, the seventh of Vishnu's eight incarnations. Rama is the oldest of four sons born to Dasaratha, the king of Ayodhya, and heir to the throne. When the time comes for Rama's coronation, Dasaratha's scheming third wife Kaikeyi has her own son Bharata crowned instead, and has Rama banished to the forest for fourteen years. In an exemplary show of filial piety, Rama accepts the loss of his throne and leaves the city with his wife Sita and brother Laksmana.

One day, Suparnakhi, the sister of the demon **Ravana**, spots Rama in the woods and instantly falls in love with him. Being a virtuous husband, Rama rebuffs her advances, while Laksmana cuts off her nose and ears in retaliation. In revenge, Ravana kidnaps Sita, who is borne away to one of Ravana's palaces on the island of **Lanka**.

Determined to find Sita, Rama enlists the help of the monkey god **Hanuman**, and the two of them gather an army and prepare to attack. After much fighting, Sita is rescued and reunited with her husband. On the long journey back to Ayodhya, Sita's honour is brought into question. To prove her innocence, she asks Laksmana to build a funeral pyre and steps into the flames, praying to Agni, the fire god. Agni walks her through the fire into the arms of a delighted Rama. They march into Ayodhya guided by a trail of lights laid out by the local people. Today, this illuminated homecoming is commemorated by Hindus all over the world during **Diwali**, the festival of lights. At the end of the epic, Rama's younger brother gladly steps down, allowing Rama to be crowned as the rightful king.

difference in appearance between the lighter-skinned Aryans and the darker indigenous Dravidian population). Each *varna* was assigned specific religious and social duties, with Aryans established as the highest social class. In descending order the *varnas* are: **brahmins** (priests and teachers), **kshatriyas** (rulers and warriors), **vaishyas** (merchants and cultivators) and **shudras** (menials). The first three classes, known as "twice-born", are distinguished by a sacred thread worn from the time of initiation, and are granted full access to religious texts and rituals. Below all four categories, groups whose jobs involve contact with dirt or death (such as undertakers, leather-workers and cleaners) were classified as **untouchables**. Though discrimination against untouchables is now a criminal offence, in part thanks to the campaigns of Mahatma Gandhi, the lowest stratum of society has by no means disappeared.

Within the four *varna*s, social status is further defined by **jati**, classifying each individual in terms of their family and job (for example, a *vaishya* may be a jewellery seller, cloth merchant, cowherd or farmer). A person's *jati* determines his **caste**, and lays restrictions on all aspects of life from what sort of food he can eat, religious obligations and contact with other castes, to the choice of marriage partners. There are almost three thousand *jatis*; the divisions and restrictions they have enforced have repeatedly been the target of reform movements and critics.

A Hindu has three **aims in life**: to fulfil his social and religious duties (dharma); to follow the correct path in his work and actions (*karma*); and to gain material wealth (*artha*). These goals are linked with the four traditional stages in life. The first is as a child and student, devoted to learning from parents and guru. Next comes the stage of householder, expected to provide for a family and raise children. That accomplished, he may then take up a life of celibacy and retreat into the forest to meditate alone, and finally renounce all possessions to become a homeless ascetic, hoping to achieve the ultimate goal of *moksha*. The small number of Hindus who follow this ideal life assume the final stage as saffron-clad **sadhus** who wander throughout India, begging for food and retreating to isolated caves, forests and hills to meditate. They're a common feature in most Indian towns and many stay for long periods in particular temples. Not all have raised families: some assume the life of a sadhu at an early age as *chellas*, pupils of an older sadhu.

The main deities

Alongside the Vedas and Upanishads, the most important Hindu religious texts are the **Puranas** – long mythological stories about the Vedic gods – and the two great epics, the **Mahabharata** and **Ramayana** (see box, p.1173), thought to have been completed by the first century AD, though subsequently retold, modified and

---

HINDU GODS AND GODDESSES

VISHNU

With four arms holding a conch, discus, lotus and mace, **Vishnu** is blue-skinned, and often shaded by a serpent, or resting on its coils, afloat on an ocean. He is usually seen alongside his half-man-half-eagle vehicle, Garuda. **Vaishnavites**, often distinguishable by two vertical lines of paste on their foreheads, recognize Vishnu as supreme lord, and hold that he has manifested himself on earth nine times. The most important avatars are Rama (see box, p.1173) and **Krishna**, the hero of the Bhagavad Gita. The cult of Krishna evolved into the popular *bhakti* movement – the attempt to achieve *moksha* through devotion to god, and without the intercession of officiating Brahmin priests, finding expression in emotional songs concerning the quest for union with the divine. Krishna is represented in various ways: most popularly he is shown as the playful cowherd who seduces and dances with cowgirls (*gopis*), giving each the illusion that she is his only lover. He is also pictured as a small, chubby, mischievous baby, known for his butter-stealing exploits. Like Vishnu, Krishna is blue, and often shown dancing and playing the flute.

SHIVA

Shaivism, the cult of **Shiva**, was also inspired by *bhakti*, requiring selfless love from devotees in a quest for divine communion, but Shiva has never been incarnate on earth. He is presented in many different aspects, such as **Nataraja**, Lord of the Dance, **Mahadev**, Great God, and **Maheshvar**, Divine Lord, source of all knowledge. Though he does have several terrible forms, his role extends beyond that of destroyer, and he is revered as the source of the whole universe.

Shiva is often depicted with four or more faces, holding a trident, draped with serpents, and bearing a third eye in his forehead. In temples, he is identified with the lingam, or phallic symbol, resting in the yoni, a representation of female sexuality. Whether as statue or lingam, Shiva is accompanied by his bull-mount, Nandi, and often by a consort, who also assumes various forms, and is looked upon as the vital energy, **shakti**, that empowers him.

While Shiva is the object of popular devotion all over India, as the terrible **Bhairav** he is also the god of the Shaivite **ascetics**, who renounce family and caste ties and perform extreme meditative and yogic practices.

embellished on numerous occasions and in various different regional languages. The Puranas and the two great epics helped crystallize the basic framework of Hindu religious belief, which survives to this day, based on a supreme triumvirate of deities. **Brahma**, the original Aryan godhead, or "creator", was joined by two gods who had begun to achieve increasing significance in the evolving Hindu world-view. The first, **Vishnu**, "the preserver", was seen as the force responsible for maintaining the balance of the cosmos whenever it was threatened by disruptive forces, incarnating himself on earth nine times in various animal and human forms, or avatars, to fight the forces of evil and chaos, most famously as Rama (the god-hero whose exploits are described in the Ramayana) and as Krishna (who appears at the most significant juncture of the Mahabharata). The second, **Shiva**, "the destroyer" (a development of the Aryan god Rudra, who had played a minor role in the Vedas), was charged with destroying and renewing the universe at periodic intervals, though his powers are not merely destructive, and he is worshipped in myriad forms with various attributes (see box below). The three supreme gods are often depicted in a trinity, or *trimurti*, though in time Brahma's importance declined, and Shiva and Vishnu became the most popular deities – the famous Brahma temple at Pushkar is now one of the few in India dedicated to this venerable but rather esoteric god.

Depicted in human or semihuman form and accompanied by an animal "vehicle", other gods and goddesses who came alive in the mythology of the Puranas are still venerated across India. River goddesses, ancestors, guardians of particular places and protectors against disease and natural disaster are as central to village life as the major deities.

OTHER GODS AND GODDESSES

Chubby and smiling, elephant-headed **Ganesh**, the first son of Shiva and Parvati, is invoked before every undertaking (except funerals). Seated on a throne or lotus, his image is often placed above temple gateways, in shops and houses; in his four arms he holds a conch, discus, bowl of sweets (or club) and a water lily, and he's always attended by his vehicle, a rat. Ganesh is regarded by many as the god of learning, the lord of success, prosperity and peace.

Durga, the fiercest of the female deities, is an aspect of Shiva's more conservative consort, Parvati (also known as Uma), who is remarkable only for her beauty and fidelity. Among Durga's many aspects, each a terrifying goddess eager to slay demons, are Chamunda, Kali and Muktakeshi, but in all her forms she is Mahadevi (Great Goddess). Statues show her with ten arms, holding the head of a demon, a spear and other weapons; she tramples demons underfoot, or dances upon Shiva's body.

The comely goddess **Lakshmi**, Vishnu's consort, is usually shown sitting or standing on a lotus flower, and sometimes called Padma (lotus). Lakshmi is the embodiment of loveliness and grace, and the goddess of prosperity and wealth. She appears in different aspects alongside each of Vishnu's avatars, including Sita, wife of Rama, and Radha, Krishna's favourite *gopi*. In many temples she is shown as one with Vishnu, in the form of Lakshmi Narayan.

India's great monkey god, **Hanuman**, features in the Ramayana as Rama's chief aide in the fight against the demon-king of Lanka. Depicted as a giant monkey clasping a mace, Hanuman is seen as Rama and Sita's greatest devotee – as his representatives, monkeys find sanctuary in temples all over India.

The most beautiful Hindu goddess, **Saraswati**, the wife of Brahma, with her flawless milk-white complexion, sits or stands on a water lily or peacock, playing a lute, sitar or *vina*. She is revered as the goddess of music, creativity and learning.

Closely linked with the planet Saturn, **Shani** is feared for his destructive powers. His image, a black statue with protruding blood-red tongue, is often found on street corners; strings of green chillies and lemon are hung in shops and houses each Saturday (*Saniwar*) to ward off his evil influences.

Practice and pilgrimage

In most Hindu homes, a chosen deity is worshipped daily in a shrine room. Outside the home, worship takes place in temples and consists of **puja** – sometimes a simple act of prayer, but more commonly a complex process when the god's image is circumambulated, offered flowers, rice, sugar and incense, and anointed with water, milk or sandalwood paste (which is usually done on behalf of the devotee by the temple priest). The aim in puja is to take **darshan** – glimpse the god – and thus receive his or her blessing. Worshippers leave the temple with prasad, an offering of food or flowers taken from the holy sanctuary. **Temple ceremonies** are conducted by priests who tend the image in daily rituals in which the god is symbolically woken, bathed, fed, dressed and, at the end of each day, put back to bed. In many villages, shrines to *devatas*, village deities who function as protectors, are more important than temples.

Strict rules address **purity and pollution**, the most obvious of them requiring high-caste Hindus to limit their contact with potentially polluting lower castes. Above all else, **water** is the agent of purification, used in ablutions before prayer and revered in all rivers, especially Ganga (the Ganges). *Ghats*, steps leading to the water's edge, are common in all river- or lakeside towns, used for bathing, washing clothes and performing religious rituals.

India also has a wealth of **pilgrimage** sites visited by devotees eager to receive *darshan* and attain merit.

Islam

Muslims – some thirteen percent of the population – form a significant presence in almost every town, city and village. The belief in only one god, Allah, the condemnation of idol worship and the observance of their own strict dietary laws and specific festivals all set Muslims apart from their Hindu neighbours, with whom they have co-existed, not always peacefully, for centuries.

The first Muslims to settle in India were traders who arrived on the southwest coast in the seventh century. Much more significant was the invasion of north India under **Mahmud of Ghazni** (see p.1157), while more raids from Central Asia followed in the twelfth century, resulting in the partial colonization of India, while the invading Muslims set themselves up in Delhi as sultans.

Many Muslims who settled in India intermarried with Hindus, Buddhists and Jains, and the community spread. A further factor in its growth was missionary activity by **Sufis**, who stressed the attainment of inner knowledge of God through meditation and mystical experience. Their use of music, particularly *qawwali* singing, and dance, shunned by orthodox Muslims, appealed to Hindus, for whom singing played an important role in religious practice. Muslims are enjoined to pray five times daily. They may do this at home or in a **mosque** – always full at noon on Friday, for communal prayer (the only exception being the Druze of Mumbai, who hold communal prayers on Thursday).

The position of **women** in Islam is a subject of great debate. It's customary for women to be veiled – though in larger cities many women don't cover their heads – and in strictly orthodox communities most wear a *burqa*, usually black, that covers them from head to toe. Like other Indian women, Muslim women take second place to men in public, but in the home they wield great influence. Contrary to popular belief, polygamy is not widespread; while it does occur (Mohammed himself had several wives), many Muslims prefer monogamy and several sects actually stress it as a duty. In marriage, women receive a dowry as financial security.

Buddhism

Buddhism was born on the Indian Subcontinent, developing as an offshoot of – and a reaction to – Hinduism, with which it shares many assumptions about the nature of existence. For a time it became the dominant religion in the country, though from around the fourth century AD onwards it was gradually eclipsed by a resurgent Hinduism (which cleverly reappropriated the Buddha, claiming him to be an incarnation of Vishnu), and the subsequent arrival of Islam more or less finished it off. Today Buddhists make up only a tiny fraction of the population – outside north India's numerous Tibetan refugee camps, only Ladakh and Sikkim now preserve a significant Buddhist presence.

The founder of Buddhism, **Siddhartha Gautama**, known as the **Buddha** ("awakened one"), was born into a wealthy *kshatriya* family in Lumbini, north of the Gangetic plain in present-day Nepal, around 566 BC. Brought up in luxury as a prince, he married at an early age, but renounced family life when he was 30. Unsatisfied with the explanations of worldly suffering proposed by religious gurus, and convinced that asceticism did not lead to spiritual realization, Siddhartha spent years wandering the countryside and meditating. His enlightenment is said to have taken place under a *bodhi* tree in **Bodhgaya** (Bihar). Soon afterwards he gave his first sermon in **Sarnath**, near Varanasi. For the rest of his life he taught, expounding **dharma**, the true nature of the world, human life and spiritual attainment. Before his death (c.486 BC) in Kushinagara (UP), he had established the **Sangha**, a community of monks and nuns who continued his teachings.

The Buddha's world-view incorporated the Hindu concept of *samsara*, and *karma* and *moksha*, which Buddhists call **nirvana** (literally "no wind"). The most important concept outlined by the Buddha was that all things are subject to the inevitability of **impermanence**. There is no independent inherent self due to the inter-connectedness of all things, and our egos are the biggest obstacles on the road to enlightenment.

Tibetan Buddhism

Buddhism was introduced to **Tibet** in the seventh century AD, and integrated to a certain extent with the indigenous **Bon** cult. Practised largely in Ladakh, along with parts of Himachal Pradesh and Sikkim, Tibetan Buddhism recognizes the historical Buddha alongside a host of other Buddhas past and to come, and incorporates elaborate rituals into its worship. There is also a heavy emphasis on teachers, known as lamas, and reincarnated teachers, known as *tulkus*. The **Dalai Lama**, the head of Tibetan Buddhism, is the fourteenth in a succession of incarnate *bodhisattvas*, the representative of Avalokitesvara (the *bodhisattva* of compassion), and the leader of the exiled Tibetan community based in Dharamsala. With more than 100,000 Tibetan **refugees** now living in India, including the Dalai Lama and the Tibetan government in exile, Tibetan Buddhism is probably the most accessible and flourishing form of Buddhism in India, and there are numerous opportunities for study (see p.60). Tibetan Buddhist devotees hang prayer flags, turn prayer wheels, and set stones carved with mantras (religious verses) in rivers, thus sending the word of the Buddha with wind and water to all corners of the earth.

Jainism

The number of **Jains** in India is small – accounting for less than one percent of the population – but has been tremendously influential for at least 2500 years. A large proportion of Jains live in Gujarat, and all over India they are commonly found working as merchants and traders. Similarities to Hinduism, and a shared respect for nature and non-violence, have contributed to the decline of the Jain community through conversion to Hinduism, but there is no antagonism between the two religions.

Focused on the practice of **ahimsa** (non-violence), Jains follow a rigorous discipline to avoid harm to all **jivas**, or "souls", which exist in humans, animals, plants, water, fire, earth and air. They assert that every *jiva* is pure and capable of achieving liberation from existence in this universe. However, *jivas* are obscured by **karma**, a form of subtle matter that clings to the soul, which is born of action and binds the *jiva* to physical existence. For the most orthodox Jain, the only way to dissociate *karma* from the *jiva* is to follow the path of asceticism and meditation, rejecting passion, attachment and impure action.

The Jain doctrine is based upon the teachings of **Mahavira**, or "Great Hero", the last in a succession of 24 **tirthankaras** ("crossing-makers") said to appear on earth every 300 million years. Mahavira (c.599–527 BC) was born as Vardhamana Jnatrputra into a *kshatriya* family near modern Patna. Like his near-contemporary the Buddha, Mahavira rejected family life at the age of 30 and spent years wandering as an ascetic in an attempt to conquer attachment to worldly values.

His teachings were written down in the first millennium BC and Jainism prospered throughout India. Not long after, there was a schism. On the one hand the **Digambaras** ("sky-clad") believed that nudity was an essential part of world renunciation, and that women are incapable of achieving liberation from worldly existence. The **Svetambaras** ("white-clad"), however, disregarded the extremes of nudity, incorporated nuns into monastic communities and even acknowledged a female *tirthankara*. Today the two sects worship at different temples, but the number of naked Digambaras is minimal. Many Svetambara monks and nuns wear white masks to avoid breathing in insects, and carry a "fly-whisk", sometimes used to brush their path; none will use public transport and they often spend days or weeks walking barefoot to a pilgrimage site.

Sikhism

Sikhism, India's youngest religion, remains dominant in the Punjab, while its adherents have spread throughout northern India. The movement was founded by **Guru Nanak** (1469–1539), who was born into an orthodox Hindu *kshatriya* family near Lahore. Nanak was among many sixteenth-century poet-philosophers, sometimes referred to as *sants*, who formed emotional cults, drawing elements from both Hinduism and Islam. Nanak declared that "God is neither Hindu nor Muslim and the path which I follow is God's"; he regarded God as **Sat**, or truth, who makes himself known through gurus. Though he condemned the rituals of Brahmins, Nanak did not attack Islam or Hinduism – he simply regarded the many deities as names for one supreme God, and encouraged his followers to shift religious emphasis from ritual to meditation. In common with Hindus, Nanak believed in a cyclic process of death and rebirth (*samsara*), but asserted that liberation (*moksha*) was attainable in this life by all women and men regardless of caste, and that religious practice could and should be integrated into everyday practical living.

Guru Nanak was succeeded by **Guru Angad**, who continued to lead the community of Sikhs (literally, "disciples"), the so-called **Sikh Panth**, and wrote his own and Nanak's hymns in a new script, **Gurumukhi**, which is today used as the script of written Punjabi. Eight further gurus successively led the Sikh Panth after Guru Angad's death in 1552, gradually developing Sikhism into a powerful independent religious movement. **Guru Ram Das** (1552–74) founded the sacred city of **Amritsar**; his successor, **Guru Arjan Dev**, compiled the gurus' hymns in a book called the **Adi Granth**, built the Golden Temple to house it and also became Sikhism's first martyr when Jahangir executed him. Throughout their history, the Sikhs have had to battle to protect their faith and their people, especially against the Mughals; Aurangzeb had **Guru Teg Bahadur** beheaded in 1675, an event that heralded the era of his son and successor, **Guru Gobind Singh**, who was to revolutionize the entire movement.

Gobind Singh, the last leader, was largely responsible for moulding the community as it exists today. In 1699, he founded the brotherhood of the **Khalsa**. The aims of the Khalsa are to assist the poor and fight oppression; to have faith in one god and to abandon superstition and dogma; to worship god; and to protect the faith with steel. The Khalsa requires members to renounce tobacco, halal meat and sexual relations with

Muslims, and to adopt the **five Ks**: *kangha* (comb), *kirpan* (sword), *kara* (steel bracelet), *kachcha* (short trousers) and *kesh* (unshorn hair) – the last requirement means that Sikh men are usually instantly recognizable thanks to their luxuriant beards and distinctive turbans. Less visibly, Guru Gobind Singh replaced traditional caste names with Singh for men (meaning "lion" – although this name is not unique to Sikhs, being a common Hindu surname as well) and Kaur ("princess") for women. Finally, Guru Gobind Singh also compiled a standardized version of the Adi Granth, which contains the hymns of the first nine gurus as well as poems written by Hindus and Muslims, and installed it as his successor, naming it **Guru Granth Sahib**. This became the Sikh's spiritual guide, while political authority rested with the Khalsa.

Demands for a separate Sikh state – **Khalistan** – and fighting in the eighteenth century, and later after Independence, have burdened Sikhs with a reputation as military activists, and their bravery and martial traditions mean that they continue to make up an important part of the Indian army. Despite this, Sikhs regard their religion as one devoted to egalitarianism, democracy and social awareness. Though to die fighting for the cause of religious freedom is considered to lead to liberation, the use of force is officially sanctioned only when other methods have failed.

Christianity

The **Apostle Thomas** is said to have arrived in Kerala in 54 AD, and according to popular tradition the Church of San Thome is the oldest Christian denomination in the world, with many tales of miracles by "Mar Thoma", as Thomas is known in Malayalam. According to tradition, Thomas was martyred in 72 AD at Mylapore in **Madras**. The tomb has since become a major place of pilgrimage, while the Portuguese added the Gothic **San Thome Cathedral** to the site in the late nineteenth century.

From the sixteenth century onwards, the history of the Church in India is linked to the spread of foreign Christians across the Subcontinent. In 1552, St Francis Xavier arrived in the Portuguese trading colony of **Goa** to establish missions to reach out to the Hindu "untouchables". In 1559, at the behest of the Portuguese king, the Inquisition arrived in Goa. Jesuit missionaries carried out a bloody and brutal campaign to "cleanse" the small colony of Hindu and Muslim religious practice. Early British incomers took the attitude that the Subcontinent was a heathen and polytheistic civilization waiting to be proselytized and made significant numbers of converts – as Christianity is intended to be free of caste stigmas, it can be attractive to those seeking social advancement, and of the two million Christians in present-day India, most are *adivasi* (tribal) and *dalit* (untouchable) people.

The position of Christians in Indian society remains uncertain. In early 1999, Christian communities in some areas, notably in Gujarat and Orissa, were subject to forced "reconversions" and attacks. These were allegedly carried out by Hindu extremists incensed by proselytizing evangelists targeting low-caste Hindus. Following an international outcry, some states passed laws banning "forced conversions", but in December 2002, a riot was only narrowly averted after police acted to prevent 1500 *dalit* people from attending a mass-conversion in Chennai (Madras).

The **Hindu influence** on Christianity remains marked, in any case, and in many churches you can see devotees offering the Hindu *arati* (a plate of coconut, sweets and rice), and women wearing *tilak* dots on their foreheads. In the same way that Hindus and Muslims consider pilgrimage to be an integral part of life's journey, Indian Christians have numerous devotional sites, including St Jude's Shrine in **Jhansi** and the Temple of Mother Mary in **Mathura**. This sharing of traditions works both ways. At Christmas, for instance, you can't fail to notice the brightly coloured paper stars and small Nativity scenes glowing and flashing outside schools, houses, shops and churches throughout India.

Zoroastrianism

Of all India's religious communities, Western visitors are least likely to come across – or recognize – **Zoroastrians**, who have no distinctive dress and few houses of worship. Most live in Mumbai, where they are known as **Parsis** (Persians) and are active in business, education and politics. Zoroastrian numbers – roughly ninety thousand – are rapidly dwindling due to a falling birth rate and absorption into wider communities.

The religion's founder, **Zarathustra** (Zoroaster), lived in Iran around the sixth or seventh century BC, and was the first religious prophet to expound a dualistic philosophy, based on the opposing powers of good and evil. For him, the absolute, wholly good and wise God, **Ahura Mazda**, together with his holy spirit and six emanations present in earth, water, the sky, animals, plants and fire, is constantly at odds with an evil power, **Angra Mainyu**, who is aided by **daevas**, or evil spirits. Five daily prayers, usually hymns, uttered by Zarathustra and standardized in the **Avesta**, the main Zoroastrian text, are said in the home or in a temple, before a fire, which symbolizes truth, righteousness and order. For this reason, Zoroastrians are often, incorrectly, called "fire-worshippers".

Wildlife

India's vast range of habitats support a staggering range of wildlife, with around 65,000 species of fauna including 1200 birds and 340 mammals (India is the only country in the world where you can see both wild lions and tigers) plus a staggering 13,000 varieties of flowering plant. The lush deodar and rhododendron forests of the lower Himalayas are home to bears and blackbucks, while the fabled snow leopard and yak inhabit the higher mountains. Down on the Gangetic plain, the warm climate, forests and numerous lakes and rivers support a rich array of birdlife, while the Sunderbans mangrove swamps in the east are famous for their population of unusual swimming tigers. Camels, both wild and domesticated, can be found in the deserts of Rajasthan, while elsewhere in the west the dry climate supports spotted deer, leopards and the famous Asiatic lion. Further south, the dry Deccan plateau is thick with sandalwood forests, the home of wild elephants, while at the very southern tip of India you'll find elephants, butterflies and jewel-like birds under the canopy of the teak and rosewood rainforest.

Mammals

The Indian **elephant**, distinguished from its African cousin by its long front legs and smaller ears and body, is still widely used as a beast of burden in many parts of the country. Elephants have worked and been tamed in India for three thousand years, and there is still a sizeable population of wild elephants across the country. Another pachyderm, the lumbering **one-horned rhinoceros**, retains a tenuous foothold in the northeast of the country, with around eleven hundred living in the protected Manas and Kaziranga wildlife sanctuaries in Assam.

Indian **tigers** are fast becoming extinct in the wild (see box, p.1182), but you still stand a reasonable chance of coming across one in a national park – for the next few years at least. The other **big cats** have fared even worse than the tiger. The **Asiatic lion** (see box, p.567) now clings on in just one tiny patch of Gujarat, while the ghostly grey- and black-spotted **snow leopard** of the Himalayas is so rare as to be almost legendary. Only the plains-dwelling **leopard** (also known as the panther) can still be commonly found, especially in forested places near human settlement where domestic animals make easy prey. Other indigenous felines include the rare multicoloured marbled cat, the miniature leopard cat, the jungle cat, the fishing cat, and a kind of lynx called the caracal.

Deer and antelope, the larger cats' prey, are much more abundant. The often solitary *sambar* is the largest of the **deer**. Smaller and more gregarious are *chital* (spotted deer), while other deer include the elusive mountain-loving muntjac (barking deer) and the para (hog deer). The smallest deer in India is the nocturnal chevrotain, known because of its size (just 30cm high), as the mouse deer. **Antelopes** include the nilgai ("blue cow"), the endangered blackbuck and the unique forest-dwelling four-horned chowsingha (swamp deer). The desert-loving gazelle is known as the *chinkara* ("the one who sneezes") due to the sneeze-like alarm call it makes.

The most common **monkeys** are the feisty red-bottomed rhesus macaque and the black-faced "Hanuman" langurs, often found around temples. Wild monkeys include the Assamese macaque and pig-tailed macaque in the northern hills, and the bonnet macaque in the steamy tropical jungles of the south.

The shaggy **sloth bear** is hard to spot in the wild, although you may see captive bears being forced to dance near tourist sites; other bears include the black and brown varieties. Of the **canines**, the scavenging striped hyena and the small pest-eating Indian fox are fairly common, though the desert-dwelling Indian wolf is under threat of extinction.

The wild **buffalo** has a close genetic relationship with the domesticated water buffalo. More exotic members of the cow family are the hill-loving **gaur**, an Indian bison which stands 2m across at the shoulders, and the nimble, mountain-dwelling **yak**.

Reptiles

The 238 species of **snake** in India (of which fifty are poisonous) extend from the 10cm-long worm snake to nest-building king cobras and massive pythons. Poisonous snakes include the majestically hooded cobra, the yellow-brown Russell's viper, the small krait and the saw-scaled viper. **Lizards** are also common, with every hotel room

THE INDIAN TIGER: SURVIVAL OR EXTINCTION?

Few animals command such universal fascination as the **tiger**, and India is one of the very few places where this rare and enigmatic big cat can still be glimpsed in the wild, stalking through the teak forests and terai grass – a solitary predator, with no natural enemies save one.

As recently as the beginning of the twentieth century, up to 100,000 tigers still roamed the Subcontinent, even though tiger hunting had long been the "sport of kings". It was the trigger-happy British who brought tiger hunting to its most gratuitous excesses, however. Photographs of pith-helmeted, bare-kneed burra sahibs posing behind mountains of striped carcasses became a hackneyed image of the Raj.

In the years following Independence, **demographic pressures** nudged the Indian tiger perilously close to extinction. As the human population increased in rural districts, more and more forest was cleared for farming, depriving large carnivores of their main source of game and of the cover they needed to hunt. Forced to turn on farm cattle as an alternative, tigers were drawn into direct conflict with humans; some animals, out of sheer desperation, even turned man-eater and attacked human settlements. **Poaching** has taken an even greater toll. The black market has always paid high prices for dead animals – a tiger pelt alone can fetch US$12,500 in China – and for the various body parts believed to hold magical or medicinal properties.

Numbers had plummeted to below two thousand by 1973, the year in which India's ambitious **Project Tiger** was inaugurated. Nine areas of pristine forest were set aside for the remaining tigers. Demand for tiger parts did not end with Project Tiger, however, and the poachers remained in business, aided by organized smuggling rings. India's worst-case conservation scenario was finally played out in 2005, when it was discovered that the entire population of big cats at Sariska Tiger Reserve had mysteriously vanished at the hands of poachers.

Well-organized guerrilla groups operate with virtual impunity out of remote national parks, where inadequate numbers of poorly armed and poorly paid wardens offer little more than token resistance. Project Tiger officials are understandably reluctant to jeopardise lucrative tourist traffic by admitting that sightings are getting rarer, but the prognosis looks very gloomy indeed.

Today, though there are 23 Project Tiger sites, numbers continue to fall. Official figures optimistically claim a **population** of 3000 to 3500, but independent evidence is more pessimistic – a survey in 2012 suggested that numbers had fallen to just 1700, down from 3642 at the last major count a decade earlier. Estimates claim that one tiger is being poached every day in India, and the most pessimistic experts believe that India's most exotic animal could face extinction in the wild within less than a decade.

seeming to have a resident gecko to keep the place free of insects. The colourful garden lizard and Sita's lizard are both found throughout India. Olive Ridley marine turtles (see p.704 & p.886) nest at remote beaches along the east and southwest coasts. **Crocodiles** are common throughout the Subcontinent.

Birds

You don't have to be an aficionado to enjoy India's abundant **birdlife**. The country has a spectacular array of resident avifauna, while its geographical location also attracts many migratory species from colder countries to the north during the winter months.

Three common species of **kingfisher** frequently crop up amid the paddy fields and wetlands of the coastal plains. Other common and brightly coloured species include the grass-green, blue and yellow **bee-eaters**, the stunning **golden oriole** and the brilliant-blue **Indian roller**. **Hoopoes**, recognizable by their elegant black-and-white tipped crests, also flit around fields and villages, as do several kinds of **bulbuls**, **babblers** and **drongos**. Paddy fields and ponds often teem with water birds. The most ubiquitous of these is the snowy-white **cattle egret**, which can often be seen riding on the backs of cows and buffalo. Look out, too, for the mud-brown **paddy bird**, India's most common heron, distinguished by its pale green legs, speckled breast and hunched posture.

Common birds of prey such as the **brahminy kite** and the **pariah kite** are widespread around towns and fishing villages, where they vie with raucous gangs of house **crows** and **white-eyed jackdaws** for scraps. Pink-headed **king vultures** and the **white-backed vulture**, which has a white ruff around its bare neck and head, also show up whenever there are carcasses to pick clean. A bird whose call is a regular feature of the Western Ghat forests is the wild ancestor of the domestic chicken – the **jungle fowl**. Finally, among India's abundant **forest birds**, one species every enthusiast hopes to glimpse is the magnificent **hornbill**, with its huge yellow beak sporting a long curved casque on top.

Music

India is home to a staggering variety of different musical traditions, both ancient and modern, ranging from archaic styles of Hindu devotional chanting to the eclectic sounds of contemporary film scores. For many outsiders, the country's aural signature is provided by north Indian classical music, one of the world's most instantly recognizable sounds, with its twanging tanpuras and complex tabla beats. There's also Bollywood's huge treasury of film songs, or filmi, to explore, as well as a rich folk music tradition.

Indian classical music: ragas and talas

Underlying all Indian classical music is the concept of the **raga** (or *raag*, from the Sanskrit word meaning "colour"). Put simplistically, a raga is simply a musical scale or mode (loosely equivalent to the "key" of a piece of Western music), determining which notes can and can't be played during a particular piece. The raga defines the basic musical material and expressive content of each particular piece, meaning that while Indian classical musicians are renowned for their **improvisation**, this only takes place within strictly defined limits – the mark of a good performer is his or her ability to improvise extensively without stepping outside the boundaries of the chosen raga.

Just as the raga organizes melody, so the rhythm of a piece is organized using metric cycles known as **talas**. A *tala* is made up of a number of beats, with each beat being defined by a combination of rhythm pattern and timbre. There are literally hundreds of *talas*, the most common being the sixteen-beat *teen tala* (four times four beats).

The performance of a raga follows a set pattern. First comes the **alap**, a slow, meditative introduction in free rhythm which explores the chosen raga, carefully introducing its constituent notes one by one. In the next two sections, the **jor** and the **jhala**, the instrumentalist introduces a rhythmic element, developing the raga through a series of increasingly complex variations. Only in these and the final section, the **gat**, does the percussion instrument – usually the tabla or (in south India) the *mridangam* – enter. The soloist introduces a short, fixed phrase (known as "the composition") to which he returns between flights of improvisation. The *gat* itself is subdivided into three sections: a slow tempo passage known as *vilambit*, increasing to a medium tempo section called *madhya*, and leading finally to the fast concluding *drut*.

Musical instruments

The best-known Indian instrument is the **sitar**. This has six or seven main strings, plucked with a plectrum, along with between eleven and nineteen sympathetic strings. The curved neck allows the player to alter the pitch by pulling strings sideways across the fret to provide the pitch-bends so characteristic of Indian music. The **surbahar**, effectively a bass sitar, is played in the same way. Smaller than a sitar, the **sarod** has two resonating chambers connected by a metal fingerboard, and ten metal strings, plucked with a fragment of coconut shell (plus a further fifteen sympathetic strings underneath).

The **sarangi** is a fretless bowed instrument with a very broad fingerboard and three or four main strings of gut, plus anything up to forty sympathetic metal strings. Some claim it is the most difficult musical instrument to play in the world. The *sarangi* is capable of a wide range of timbres and its sound is likened to that of the human voice, meaning that it is often used to accompany vocal recitals. The word **bansuri** refers to a wide variety of

INDIAN CLASSICAL MASTERS ON CD

There's a huge variety of Indian – especially north Indian – classical music available on CD, including recordings by many of the country's leading virtuosos of the past fifty years. Perhaps the best-known and most recorded Indian classical artist is sitar player **Ravi Shankar** (1920–2012), who made numerous solo recordings, as well as duetting with artists ranging from Ali Akbar Khan (see below) to Yehudi Menuhin. Other legendary sitar players include **Nikhil Banerjee** (1931–86) and **Vilayat Khan** (1928–2004), while it's also worth searching out recordings by **Imrat Khan** (b.1935, and younger brother of Vilayat), the acknowledged master of the soulful *surbahar* (bass sitar).

Rivalling Ravi Shankar for recorded legacy is the internationally revered *sarod* virtuoso **Ali Akbar Khan** (1922–2009), while the hauntingly atmospheric music of **Hariprasad Chaurasia** (b.1938), India's leading master of the *bansuri* (bamboo flute), is also essential listening for anyone with even a passing interest in Subcontinental music. Less well-known, but equally rewarding, are the recorded performances of **Sultan Khan** (b.1940) and **Ram Narayan** (b.1927), two of modern India's greatest masters of the *sarangi*, while recordings by leading *shehnai* virtuoso **Bismillah Khan** (1916–2006) are also worth looking out for – albeit that the instrument is something of an acquired taste. Many notable recordings also feature **Alla Rakha** (1919–2000), perhaps the finest tabla virtuoso of recent years. For **Carnatic** music, try some of the many recordings by violin wizard L. Subramanian, saxophone supremo Kadri Gopalnath, or the much rarer recordings by **Sundaram Balachander** (1927–90), one of the twentieth century's leading exponents of the soulful *veena*.

bamboo (*banse*) flutes, either end-blown or side-blown. The **shehnai**, traditionally used for wedding music, is a double-reed, oboe-type instrument with up to nine finger holes.

The **tabla** is a set of two small drums, tuned to the tonic, dominant or subdominant notes of the raga and played with the palms and fingertips to produce an incredible variety of sounds and timbres. Predating the tabla, the **pakhavaj** is nearly 1m long and was traditionally made of clay, although wood is now more popular. It has two parchment heads, each tuned to a different pitch.

The instruments of **Carnatic music** (see p.1186) include the **vina**, which resembles the sitar but has no sympathetic strings; the **mridangam** double-headed drum; and the enormous **nadaswaram** (or *nagaswaram*), a kind of metre-long oboe, commonly used during temple ceremonies. The **violin** (slightly modified to suit Indian musical requirements) is also widely used.

Finally, perhaps the most ubiquitous but self-effacing of all Indian musical instruments is the **tanpura** (or *tambura*), a type of fretless lute with (usually) four or five wire strings. It's the tanpura that supplies the instantly recognizable, buzzing drone that underpins all Indian classical music. The tanpura is traditionally played by an advanced student of the lead performer – considered a rare and special honour for the pupil concerned.

Classical vocal music

Dhrupad is the oldest and most austere form of north Indian classical music. *Dhrupads* typically consist of two sections: a long and entirely wordless introductory *alap* during which the singer(s) vocalize a sequence of syllables deriving from the mantra "Hari Om Narayana Taan Tarana Tum", followed by a much shorter and faster section sung to the accompaniment of a *pakhavaj* drum. During the eighteenth century the rather severe *dhrupad* was largely displaced by the much more flamboyant **khayal** – described as the "bel canto of Indian music" – a form that allows for far greater displays of virtuosity. *Khayal* is typically accompanied by tabla and harmonium, along with a bowed instrument such as a *sarangi* or violin, which mirrors the vocal line.

Thumri are essentially love songs, written from a female perspective and sung in a language known as Braj Bhasha, a literary dialect of Hindi particularly associated with

Lucknow. The singer is always accompanied by the tabla, as well perhaps as the tanpura, the *sarangi* or the *surmandal*, and sometimes the violin or harmonium. Still more song-like than the *thumri* is the **ghazal**. In some ways the Urdu counterpart of *thumri*, the *ghazal* was introduced to India by Persian Muslims and is a poetic rather than a musical form – many favourite *ghazals* are drawn from the works of great Urdu poets.

Carnatic music

Southern India's classical music – known as **Carnatic** (or "Karnatak") music – is essentially similar to Hindustani classical music in its overall concept but differs in many details, usually ascribed to the far greater Islamic influence in the north. To the Western ear, Carnatic music is emotionally direct and impassioned, without the restraint that characterizes much of the north's music.

Song is at the root of south Indian music, and forms based on song are paramount, even when the performance is purely instrumental. The vast majority of the texts are religious, and the temple is frequently the venue for performance. The most important form is the *kriti*, a devotional song, hundreds of which were written by the most influential figure in the development of Carnatic music, the singer **Thyagaraja** (1767–1847).

Folk music

There are many kinds of **Indian folk music** (*Lok Sangeet*), but the main regional strands are those of Rajasthan, the Punjab (spread across both India and Pakistan), and Bengal. In **Rajasthan**, music is always played for weddings and theatre performances, and often at local markets or gatherings. There is a whole cast of professional musicians who perform this function, and a wonderful assortment of earthy-sounding stringed instruments like the *kamayacha* and *ravanhata* that accompany their songs.

Bengal is best known for the music of the **Bauls**, an order of wandering mystics and musicians who subscribe to a syncretic mix of Sufi and *bhakti* Hindu mystical beliefs expressed primarily through song, typically accompanied by the *ektara*, a one-stringed drone instrument.

The **Punjab** is most closely associated with **bhangra**. This was originally a kind of folk dance, performed as part of harvest festival celebrations and accompanied by music on the *dhol* and *dholki* drums, *ektara* and *tumbi* (a kind of single-string guitar); but since the 1980s has become a global pop phenomenon both in its traditional form and in contemporary dance, house and hip-hop fusions, created mainly by Asian musicians in the UK.

Filmi

Indian **popular music** is intimately bound up with the country's massive film industry. Music plays a crucial role in Bollywood movies and up until the 1990s virtually all Indian popular music consisted of songs, known as **filmi**, taken from the soundtracks to these movies. The most striking feature of these Bollywood *filmi* is their incredibly eclectic style, offering a fascinating snapshot of changing musical fashions over the past five decades, all seen from a uniquely Indian point of view.

Early film scores tended to be rooted in Indian folk and classical music, but from the 1960s onwards Bollywood film composers such as the famous **R.D. Burman** began to soak up an incredible range of musical influences in their work, from big band rock'n'roll to the techno and electronic creations of the innovative **A.R. Rahman**. Bollywood *filmi* are performed by so-called **playback singers**, the invisible artists who record the songs that the film's actors and actresses then mime along to. Many of these singers have achieved massive fame in their own right, including the legendary Asha Bhosle and her sister Lata Mangeshkar, along with male singers such as Kishore Kumar and Mohammed Rafi.

Books

India is one of the most written-about places on earth, and there are a bewildering number of titles available covering virtually every aspect of the country, ranging from scholarly historical dissertations to racy travelogues. Books marked ★ are particularly recommended.

HISTORY, SOCIETY AND REPORTAGE

Charles Allen *Plain Tales from the Raj*. First-hand accounts from erstwhile sahibs and memsahibs of everyday British India, organized thematically.

A.L. Basham *The Wonder That Was India*. This veritable encyclopedia by one of India's foremost historical authorities positively bristles with erudition.

Oliver Blach *India Rising: Tales From a Changing Nation*. Part reportage, part travel writing, India Rising is a personalized account of the modern nation state drawn from a broad cast of everyday lives, ranging from millionaire entrepreneurs to slum dwellers. A vivid account of the contradictions and challenges at the heart of India's rise, and its extraordinary potential.

Katherine Boo *Behind the Beautiful Forevers*. Award-winning investigative journalist Katherine Boo spent three years exploring the Annawadi slum near Mumbai airport, and her account, tracing the impact of a violent crime on the community, races along with an almost cinematic intensity.

Elizabeth Bumiller *May You Be the Mother of a Hundred Sons*. Lucid exploration of the Indian woman's lot, drawn from dozens of first-hand encounters in the 1990s – since when surprisingly little has changed.

David Burton *The Raj at Table*. Vividly evokes the quirky world of British India – commendable both for its extraordinary recipes and as a marvellous piece of social history.

Liz Collingham *Curry*. Original and entertaining account of Indian history seen through its food, from Mughlai biriyanis to Mulligatawny soup.

Larry Collins and Dominique Lapierre *Freedom at Midnight*. Readable, if shallow, account of Independence, highly sympathetic to the British and, particularly, to Mountbatten, who was the authors' main source of information.

Anne de Courcy *The Fishing Fleet*. The hitherto untold story of the many British women who, in response to a dearth of eligible bachelors at home, travelled to India in the late nineteenth century in search of husbands. Drawing on mainly unpublished memoirs, diaries and letters, the narrative yields a vivid picture of the Raj at its height from the memsahib's female perspective.

Siddartha Deb *The Beautiful and the Damned: Life in the New India*. Another brilliant portrait of the country, this time focusing on a handful individuals whose tragi-comic lives epitomize some of the tensions underlying India's modern metamorphosis.

★ **William Dalrymple** *The Last Mughal*. Masterful account of Delhi's part in the 1857 uprising. Using Urdu as well as English sources, Dalrymple tells us what it was like for the insurgents, the British, the Mughal court and – most importantly – the ordinary people of Delhi.

★ **William Dalrymple** *Nine Lives: In Search of the Sacred in Modern India*. The stories of nine different people who follow contrasting religious paths through the vortex of rapid social and cultural change. Each of Dalrymple's subjects are beautifully defined, revealing a wealth of insight into both India's past and present.

William Dalrymple *Return of a King*. The definitive account of the East India Company's ill-fated 1839 invasion of Afghanistan, in which 20,000 Indian and British soldiers perished – a true parable for our times.

★ **William Dalrymple** *White Mughals*. Compelling account of the previously forgotten story of British political officer James Achilles Kirkpatrick's marriage to the great-niece of the nizam of Hyderabad's prime minister.

Louis Fischer *The Life of Mahatma Gandhi*. Veteran American journalist Louis Fischer knew his subject personally, and his book provides an engaging account of Gandhi as a man, politician and propagandist.

Patrick French *Liberty or Death*. The definitive account (and a damning indictment) of the last years of the British Raj.

Patrick French *India*. French brings his earlier history up to date with a snapshot of the modern nation divided into themes (politics, economy and religion). Drawing on encounters with Indians from contrasting backgrounds, it manages to be scholarly yet wide-ranging at the same time – and a highly enjoyable read.

M.K. Gandhi *The Story of My Experiments with Truth*. Gandhi's fascinating record of his life, including his spiritual and moral quests and gradual emergence to the fore of national politics.

Bamber Gascoigne *The Great Mughals*. Concise, entertaining and eminently readable account of the lives of the first six great Mughals.

Anand Giridharadas *India Calling*. An intimate portrait of the country written from the perspective of a young American born of Indian parents who emigrated to the US in the 1970s. It's particularly revealing of the impact of new technology and economic change on families.

Christopher Hibbert *The Great Mutiny*. Account of the 1857 uprising, told entirely from the British point of view, in easy prose and with some compelling first-hand material from the British side.

John Keay *The Honourable Company: A History of the English East India Company*. Readable and balanced account of the East India Company and its strange role in Subcontinental history.

★ **John Keay** *India: A History*. The best single-volume history currently in print. Keay manages to coax clear, impartial and highly readable narrative from five thousand years of fragmented events, enlivened with plenty of quirky asides.

John Keay *Into India*. As an all-round introduction to India, this book – originally written in 1973 but reissued in 1999 – is the one most often recommended by old hands, presenting a wide spread of history and cultural background, interspersed with lucid personal observations.

Dominique Lapierre and Javier Moro *Five Past Midnight in Bhopal*. The definitive account of the world's worst industrial disaster, weaving the portraits of its victims together into an outstanding piece of investigative journalism.

Edward Luce *In Spite of the Gods*. The most authoritative account of the state of the nation currently in print, packed full of sobering statistics and myth-busting facts that challenge common misconceptions about the country.

★ **Suketu Mehta** *Maximum City: Bombay Lost and Found*. Acclaimed portrait of India's largest city, mixing memoir and travelogue, along with penetrating insights into the history, society and people of Mumbai.

Geoffrey Moorhouse *India Britannica*. A balanced, lively survey of the rise and fall of the British Raj.

Palagummi Sainath *Everybody Loves a Good Drought*. A classic report on India's poorest districts, telling the stories of individual villages that are usually lost in a maze of development statistics.

Amartya Sen *The Argumentative Indian*. A provocative and sharply written collection of essays on identity, religion, history, philosophy and – above all – what it means to be Indian.

Mala Sen *Death By Fire*. Later made into a controversial movie, this book uses the infamous Roop Kanwar case as a springboard to explore some of the wider issues affecting women in contemporary Indian society.

Mark Tully *India: the Road Ahead*. Few commentators understand India as well as Mark Tully, the veteran BBC correspondent, who has written a string of books since the early 1990s cataloguing the country's rapid change. This is his latest, but they're all worth hunting out, from *No Full Stops* (1992) to *India In Slow Motion* (2003) and *India's Unending Journey* (2008).

TRAVEL

James Cameron *An Indian Summer*. Affectionate and humorous description of the veteran British journalist's visit to India in 1972, and his marriage to an Indian woman.

★ **William Dalrymple** *City of Djinns*. Dalrymple's account of a year in Delhi sifts through successive layers of the city's past using a blend of inspired historical sleuth-work and interviews with a cast of characters ranging from Urdu calligraphers to local pigeon fanciers. The *Age of Kali* (published in India as In the *Court of the Fish-Eyed Goddess*) is a collection of essays drawn from ten years' travel in India.

Alexander Frater *Chasing the Monsoon*. Frater's wet-season jaunt up the west coast and across to Shillong took him through an India of muddy puddles and grey skies: an evocative account of the country as few visitors see it, now something of a classic.

Tim Mackintosh-Smith *The Hall of a Thousand Columns*. Quirky, learned and entertaining travelogue following the footsteps of Ibn Battuta through the Delhi of the Tughluq sultan Muhammad Shah and thence south to Kerala, with lashings of offbeat Subcontinental Islamic history en route.

V.S. Naipaul *An Area of Darkness*. One of the finest (and bleakest) books ever written about India: a darkly comic portrait of the country based on a year of travel around the Subcontinent in the early 1960s – dated, but still essential reading. Naipaul followed this up with *India: A Wounded Civilisation*, a damning analysis of Indian society written during the Emergency of 1975–77, and the altogether sunnier *India: A Million Mutinies Now*, published in 1990.

Tahir Shah *Sorcerer's Apprentice*. A journey through the weird underworld of occult India. Travelling as an apprentice to a master conjurer and illusionist, Shah encounters hangmen, baby renters, skeleton dealers, sadhus and charlatans.

Mark Shand *Travels on My Elephant*. Award-winning account of a 965km ride on an elephant from Konarak in Odisha to Bihar, and full of incident, humour and pathos. For the sequel, *Queen of the Elephants*, Shand teams up with an Assamese princess who's the country's leading elephant-handler.

Eric Shipton and H.W. Tilman *Nanda Devi: Exploration and Ascent*. Two classics of Himalayan mountaineering literature published in a single volume, recounting the famous expeditions of 1934 and 1936. Shipton's work, in particular, is a masterpiece of the genre: beautifully written and enthralling from start to finish.

FICTION

Aravind Adiga *The White Tiger*. Brilliantly dark satire on the "New" India, set largely in Delhi and featuring the relationship between a wealthy employer and his impecunious but murderously ambitious servant.

Mulk Raj Anand *Untouchable* and *Coolie*. First published in 1935, *Untouchable* gives a memorable worm's-eye view of the brutal life of an untouchable sweeper, while the subsequent *Coolie* (1936) describes the death of a 15-year-old child labourer.

⭐ **Vikram Chandra** *Sacred Games*. More than a decade elapsed between the publication of Chandra's award-winning debut novel, *Red Earth and Pouring Rain*, inspired by the life of Anglo-Indian soldier James Skinner, and this, his second offering – an epic, page-turning tale of friendship and betrayals, love and violence set in modern Mumbai.

Anita Desai *Fasting, Feasting*. One of India's leading female authors' eloquent portrayal of the frustration of a sensitive young woman stuck in the stifling atmosphere of home while her spoilt brother is packed off to study in America.

Kiran Desai *The Inheritance of Loss*. Warm, wise and beautifully told family tale straddling India and the US, set in the 1980s, with most of the action unfolding near Kalimpong against a backdrop of Nepalese insurgency.

E.M. Forster *A Passage to India*. Set in the 1920s, this withering critique of colonialism is memorable as much for its sympathetic portrayal of middle-class Indian life as for its insights into cultural misunderstandings.

Rudyard Kipling *Kim*. Cringingly colonialist at times, of course, but the atmosphere of India and Kipling's love of it shine through in this subtle story of an orphaned white boy. Kipling's other key works on India are two books of short stories: *Soldiers Three* and *In Black and White*.

Rohinton Mistry *A Fine Balance*. Compelling novel focusing on two friends who leave their lower-caste rural lives for the urban opportunities of the big smoke (in this case a fictionalized Mumbai). Mistry's *Such a Long Journey* is an acclaimed account of a Mumbai Parsi's struggle to maintain personal integrity in the face of betrayals and disappointment.

R.K. Narayan *Gods, Demons and Others*. Classic Indian folk tales and popular myths told through the voice of a village storyteller. Many of Narayan's beautifully crafted books, full of touching characters and subtle humour, are set in the fictional south Indian territory of Malgudi.

Gregory David Roberts *Shantaram*. Entertaining, albeit rather over-long, semi-autobiographical account of an escaped Australian convict taking refuge in India (mainly Mumbai), with memorable, if occasionally clichéd, depictions of the country and its people.

⭐ **Arundhati Roy** *The God of Small Things*. Haunting Booker Prize-winner about a well-to-do south Indian family caught between the snobberies of high-caste tradition, a colonial past and the diverse personal histories of its members.

⭐ **Salman Rushdie** *Midnight's Children*. This story of a man born at the very moment of Independence, whose life mirrors that of modern India itself, won Rushdie the Booker Prize and the enmity of Indira Gandhi, who had it banned in India. Set in Kerala and Mumbai, *The Moor's Last Sigh* was the subject of a defamation case brought by Shiv Sena leader Bal Thackeray.

⭐ **Vikram Seth** *A Suitable Boy*. Vast, all-embracing tome set in UP shortly after Independence; wonderful characterization and an impeccable sense of place and time make this an essential read for long train journeys.

William Sutcliffe *Are You Experienced?* Hilarious novel sending up the backpacker scene in India. Wickedly perceptive and very readable.

Tarun J. Tejpal *The Alchemy of Desire*. Set mainly in the Himalayas, this sensuous contemporary tale focuses on two lovers, mixing its exploration of human relationships with wider reflections on India in the twentieth century.

ART, ARCHITECTURE AND RELIGION

Roy Craven *Indian Art*. Concise general introduction to Indian art, from Harappan seals to Mughal miniatures.

⭐ **Diana L. Eck** *Banaras – City of Light*. Thorough disquisition on the religious significance of Varanasi, and a good introduction to the practice of Hindu cosmology.

Dorf Hartsuiker *Sadhus: Holy Men of India*. The weird world of India's itinerant ascetics exposed in glossy colour photographs and erudite but accessible text.

Stephen P. Huyler *Meeting God*. Unrivalled overview of the beliefs and practices of contemporary Hinduism, accompanied by fine photographs.

George Michell *The Hindu Temple*. A reasonable primer, introducing Hindu temples, their significance and architectural development.

Wendy O'Flaherty (transl) *Hindu Myths*. Translations of key myths from the original Sanskrit texts, providing an insight into the foundations of Hinduism.

Paramahansa Yogananda *Autobiography of a Yogi*. Uplifting account of religious awakening and spiritual development by one of the most internationally influential Hindu masters.

Language

No fewer than **22 major languages** are officially recognized by the Indian constitution, while numerous minor ones and more than a thousand dialects are also spoken across the country. When independent India was organized, the present-day states were largely created along linguistic lines, which helps the traveller make some sense of the complex situation. Considering the continuing prevalence of **English**, there is rarely any necessity to speak a local language, but some theoretical knowledge of the background and learning at least a few words of one or two can only enhance your visit.

The main languages of northern India, including the country's eastern and western extremities, are all **Indo-Aryan**, the easternmost subgroup of the Indo-European family that is thought to have originated somewhere between Europe and Central Asia several millennia BC, before tribal movements spread its progeny in all directions. The oldest extant Subcontinental language is Sanskrit, one of the three "big sisters" (along with Latin and Greek) upon which philologists have created the model of proto-Indo-European language. It's known to have been spoken early in the second millennium BC, although it was not written down until much later, and is the vehicle for all the sacred texts of Hinduism. Sanskrit remained the language of the educated until around 1000 AD and gradually developed into the modern tongues of northern India: Hindi, Urdu, Bengali, Gujarati, Marathi, Kashmiri, Punjabi and Oriya.

North India

Hindi is the pre-eminent language in the north, and the main language in the states of Uttar Pradesh, Madhya Pradesh, Rajasthan, Haryana, Bihar and Himachal Pradesh, as well as being widely used as a second language in other states. Hindi is very closely related to **Urdu**, the main language of Pakistan. Both Hindi and Urdu developed in tandem around the markets and army camps of Delhi (the term Urdu derives from the Turkish word for "camp") during the establishment of Muslim rule around the start of the second millennium AD. Whereas Hindi later returned to the Sanskrit roots of its Hindu speakers, however, and adopted the classical **Devanagari** script, Urdu became culturally more closely linked with Islam and is written in **Perso-Arabic** script. The vocabulary of each also reflects these cultural and religious ties. The scripts of Punjabi, Bengali and Gujarati are among those that have developed out of Devanagari and still bear some resemblance to it.

Other important languages spoken in north India include **Bengali** (West Bengal and Tripura), **Nepali** (West Bengal and Sikkim), **Gujarati** (Gujarat), **Punjabi** (Punjab, Delhi), **Kashmiri** and **Dogri** (Kashmir), **Assamese** and **Bodo** (Assam), **Oriya** (Odisha) and **Maithili** (Bihar).

South India

The four most widely spoken south Indian languages, **Tamil** (Tamil Nadu), **Telugu** (Andhra Pradesh), **Kannada** (Karnataka) and **Malayalam** (Kerala) all belong to the Dravidian family, the world's fourth largest group of languages. These and related minor languages grew up quite separately among the non-Aryan peoples of southern India over thousands of years, and the earliest written records of Tamil date back to the third century AD. The exact origins of the Dravidian group have not been established, but it is possible that proto-Dravidian was spoken further north in prehistoric times before the people were driven south by the Aryan invaders.

INDIAN ENGLISH

During the British Raj, **Indian English** developed its own characteristics, many of which have survived to the present day. It was during this period that Indian words also entered the vocabulary of everyday English, among them veranda, bungalow, sandal, pyjamas, shampoo, jungle, turban, caste, chariot, chilli, cardamom, pundit and yoga. The traveller to India soon becomes familiar with other terms in common usage that have not spread so widely outside the Subcontinent: *dacoit, dhoti, panchayat, lakh* and *crore* are but a few. A full list of Anglo-Indianisms can be found in the famous Hobson-Jobson Anglo-Indian dictionary.

Perhaps the most endearing aspect of Indian English is the way it has preserved forms now regarded as highly old-fashioned in Britain. Addresses such as "Good sir" and questions like "May I know your good name?" are commonplace, as are terms like "tiffin" and "cantonment". This type of usage reaches its apogee in the more flowery expressions of the media, which regularly feature in the vast array of daily newspapers published in English. Thus headlines often appear such as "37 perish in mishap", referring to a train crash, or passages like this splendid report of a bank robbery: "The miscreants absconded with the loot in great haste. They repaired immediately to their hideaway, whereupon they divided the iniquitous spoils before vanishing into thin air."

Language in India since Independence

With **Independence** it was decided by the government in Delhi that Hindi should become the **official language** of the newly created country. A drive to teach Hindi in all schools followed and more than half the country's population are now reckoned to have a decent working knowledge of the language. However, there has always been strong **resistance** to the imposition of Hindi in certain areas, especially the **Tamil-led** Dravidian south, and the vast majority of people living below the Deccan plateau have little or no knowledge of it.

This is where **English**, the language of the ex-colonists, becomes an important means of communication. Not surprisingly, given India's rich linguistic diversity, **English** remains a **lingua franca** for many people. It is still the preferred language of law, higher education, much of commerce and the media, and to some degree political dialogue; and for many educated Indians, not just those living abroad, it is actually their first language. All this explains why Anglophone visitors can often soon feel surprisingly at home despite the huge cultural differences. It is not unusual to overhear everyday contact between Indians from different parts of the country being conducted in English, and stimulating conversations can often be had, not only with students or businesspeople, but also with chai-wallahs and shoeshine boys.

USEFUL HINDI WORDS AND PHRASES

GREETINGS

Hello (slightly formal; not used for Muslims)	Namaste/Namaskar
Hello (formal; to a Muslim)	As salaam alaykum (in reply) Alaykum as salaam
Goodbye	Namaste
Goodbye (to a Muslim)	Khudaa haafiz
See you later	Phir mileynge
How are you? (formal)	Aap kaise hai?
How are you? (familiar)	Kya hal hai?
brother (informal; not to be used to older men)	bhaaii
sister (informal; not to be used to older women)	diidi
sir	sahib
sir (Muslims only)	hazur

BASIC WORDS

yes (informal /more formal)	haa/ji haa
no (informal/ more formal)	nahi/ji nahi
OK	acha/tiik hai
I/me	mai
you (formal)	aap
you (familiar; and to children)	tum
and/more	aur
how?	kaise?
how much?	kitna?
thank you	dhanyavad/shukriya

(formal; Indians don't usually say thank you during everyday transactions. There's no direct Hindi equivalent to the English word "please")

good	acha
very good	bahut acha
bad	buraa
big	barra
small	chhota
hot	garam
hot (spicy)	mirchi
cold	thanda
clean	saaf
dirty	gandaa
open	khulaa
expensive	mehngaa
please come	aiiye
go	jao
run (also "take a run" or "scram")	bhaago
enough	bas

BASIC PHRASES

My name is...	Mera naam...hai
What is your name? (formal)	Aapka naam kya hai?
What is your name? (familiar, and to children)	Tumhara naam kya hai?
I'm from...	Mai...se hu
We're from...	Hum...se hai
Where do you come from?	Aap kaha se aate hai?
I understand	Samaj gayaa
I don't understand	Samaj nahin aayaa
I don't know	Maluum nahi
I don't speak Hindi	Mai Hindi nahi bol sakta hu
Please speak slowly	Dhiire boliye
Sorry	Ma'af kiijiye
It is OK?	Tiik hai?
How much is this?	Yeh kitne ka hai?
I don't need it (literally "not needed"); useful response to persistent touts	Nahi chai'iya
Do you have...?	...hai?
I/we like it	Acha lugta hai
I'm fine	Tiik hai
What work do you do?	Kya kam karte hai?
Do you have any brothers or sisters?	Bhaai behan hai?
Oh dear!	Arey!

GETTING AROUND

Where is the...?	...kaha hai?
I want to go to...	Mai...jaana chaata hu
Where is it?	Kaha hai?
How far?	Kitna duur?
Which is the bus for Agra?	Agra ki bas kaha hai?
What time does the train leave?	Gaarii kab jayegi?
Stop!	Ruko!
Wait!	Thehero!

ACCOMMODATION

I need a room	Mujhe kamra chai'eeye
How much is the room?	Kamra kitne ka hai?
I am staying for one night	Mai ek raat ke liiye theheroonga

HEALTH

I have a headache	Sir me dard hai
I have a pain in my stomach	Mere pate me dard hai
The pain is here	Dard yaha hai
Where is the doctor's clinic?	Daktar ka clinic kaha hai
Where is the hospital?	Haspital kaha hai?
Where is the pharmacy?	Dawaaii khana kaha hai?
medicine	dawaaii
ill	bimar
pain	dard
stomach	pate
eye	aankh
nose	naak
ear	kaan
back	piith
foot	paao

NUMBERS AND TIME

zero	shunya
one	ek
two	do
three	tiin
four	char
five	paanch
six	che
seven	saat
eight	aath
nine	nau
ten	das
eleven	gyaarah
twelve	baarah
thirteen	terah
fourteen	chaudah
fifteen	pandrah
sixteen	solah
seventeen	satrah
eighteen	ataarah

nineteen	unniis	tomorrow/yesterday	kal
twenty	biis	day	din
thirty	tiis	afternoon	dopahar
forty	chaaliis	evening	shaam
fifty	pachaas	night	raat
sixty	saath	week	haftaah
seventy	sattar	month	mahiinaa
eighty	assii	year	saal
ninety	nabbe	Monday	somvaar
one hundred	ek sau	Tuesday	mangalvaar
one thousand	ek hazaar	Wednesday	budhvaar
one hundred thousand	ek lakh	Thursday	viirvaar
		Friday	shukravaar
ten million	ek crore	Saturday	shanivaar
today	aaj	Sunday	ravivaar

FOOD AND DRINK GLOSSARY

BASICS

khaana	food
chawaal	rice
chamach	spoon
chhoori	knife
kanta	fork
plate	plate
chini	sugar
chini nahi	no sugar (eg in tea)
kali mirch	black pepper
gur	jaggery (unrefined sugar)
namak	salt
mirch	pepper
mirchi	chilli hot
mirchi kam	less hot
garam	hot
thanda	cold
dahi	yogurt
dhal	curried lentils, sometimes reduced to a kind of broth; traditionally served as an accompaniment to all Indian meals
garam masala	spice mix (literally "hot spices") added to dishes as hot seasoning
ghee	clarified butter; often used instead of cooking oil, or to flavour food
gravy	any kind of curry sauce; nothing to do with British gravy
jeera	cumin
lal mirch	red pepper
masala	generic term indicating either a spice mixture or somethin spicy

methi	fenugreek
paan	digestif (see box, p.44)
paneer	unfermented cheese
sabji	any vegetable

DRINKS

bhang lassi	lassi flavoured with bhang (cannabis)
botal vaala paani	mineral water
chai	tea
doodh	milk
falooda	traditional Mughlai dessert, usually made with milk, ice cream, nuts and sweets
kaapi or kaafi	coffee
lassi	yogurt drink, served either plain or flavoured with salt or fruit
pani	water
peenay ka pani	drinking water (not mineral water)

MEAT AND FISH

chingri	prawns
gosht	meat, usually mutton
keema	minced meat
macchi	fish
murg	chicken

VEGETABLES AND FRUIT

aam	mango
alu	potatoes
baingan or brinjal	eggplant (aubergine)
bhindi	okra (ladies' fingers)

chana	chickpeas	dum	steamed in a casserole; the most common dish is *dum aloo*, with potatoes
gaajar	carrot		
gobi	cauliflower		
kaddoo	pumpkin		
kela	banana	jalfrezi	dish cooked with tomatoes and green chilli; medium-hot to hot
palak	spinach		
piaz	onions		
sabji	vegetables (literally, "greens")		
		karahi	cast-iron wok that has given its name to a method of cooking with dry spices to create dishes of medium strength
santaraa	orange		
seb	apple		
sag	spinach		
tamatar	tomato		

DISHES AND COOKING TERMS

		karhi	dhal-like dish made from dahi and gram flour
alu baingan	potato and aubergine; usually mild to medium		
		kofta	balls of minced vegetables or meat in a curried sauce
alu gobi	potato and cauliflower; usually mild		
alu methi	potato with fenugreek leaves, usually medium-hot	korma	mild sauce made with curd (and perhaps cream)
		malai kofta	vegetable balls in a rich cream sauce; usually medium-mild
alu mutter	potato and pea curry; usually mild		
baingan bharta	baked and mashed aubergine mixed with onion	momo	Tibetan dumplings
		mughlai masala	Mughal-style mild, creamy sauce
bhindi bhaji	gently spiced, fried okra	mulligatawny	classic Anglo-Indian-style vegetable soup; moderately spicy
bhuna	roasted and then thickened-down medium-hot curry sauce		
		murg makhani	butter chicken
		mutter paneer	paneer and peas curry
biriyani	rice baked with saffron or turmeric, whole spices and meat (sometimes vegetables), and often hard-boiled egg; rich	palak paneer	paneer and spinach
		pathia	thickened curry with lemon juice; hot
		pomfret	a flatfish popular in Mumbai and Kolkata
		pongal	spicy rice and dhal
chana masala	spicy chickpeas; usually medium-hot	pulau	rice, gently spiced and pre-fried
cutlet	fried cutlet of minced meat or chopped vegetables	raita	chilled yogurt flavoured with mild spices, sometimes with the addition of small pieces of cucumber and tomato; usually eaten as an accompaniment to a main course
dhal gosht	meat cooked in lentils; usually hot		
dhal makhani	lentils cooked with cream		
dhansak	curry sauce made from reduced lentils; usually medium-hot	rasam	south Indian-style spicy soup
		rogan josh	deep-red lamb curry, a classic Mughlai dish; medium-hot
dopiaza	onion-based sauce; medium-mild		

sambar	soupy lentil and vegetable curry with asafoetida and tamarind
shahi paneer	"royal" paneer; slightly more elaborate version of standard paneer curry, sometimes including fruit and nuts
seekh kebab	minced lamb grilled on a skewer
shami kebab	small minced lamb cutlets
tarka dhal	lentils with a masala of fried garlic, onions and spices
thali	combination of vegetarian dishes, chutneys, pickles, rice and bread served as an all-in-one meal
vindaloo	Goan vinegared meat (sometimes fish) curry, originally pork; very hot

BREADS AND PANCAKES

appam*	south Indian-style rice pan cake speckled with holes, soft in the middle
bhatura	soft bread made of white flour and traditionally accompanying *chana*; common in Delhi
chapatti	unleavened bread made of wholewheat flour
dosa*	crispy south Indian rice pancake; can be served in various forms, the best known of which is the masala dosa, when the dosa is wrapped around a filling of spicy potato curry
iddli*	south Indian steamed rice cake, usually served with *sambar*
kaathi	filled wraps
kachori	small thick cakes of salty deep-fried bread
loochi	delicate puri often mixed with white flour; cooked in Bengal

Mughlai paratha	*paratha* with egg
naan	white leavened bread kneaded with yogurt and baked in a *tandoor*
papad or poppadum*	crisp, thin, chickpea-flour cracker
paratha or parantha	wholewheat bread made with butter, rolled thin and griddle-fried; a little bit like a chewy pancake, sometimes stuffed with meat or vegetables
puri	crispy, puffed-up, deep-fried wholewheat bread
roti	loosely used term; often just another name for chapatti, though it should be thicker, chewier, and baked in a *tandoor*
uttapam*	thick, south Indian-style rice pancake often cooked with onions

SNACKS (CHAAT), SWEETS AND DESSERTS

barfi or burfi	traditional sweet made with milk; a bit like fudge
bhaji or bhajia	pieces of vegetable deep-fried in chickpea batter, served as a main course or a street snack
bhel puri	mix of puffed rice, potato and crunchy puri with tamarind sauce; a Mumbai speciality, though now popular nationwide
gulab jamun	classic Indian sweet made from deep-fried dough balls served in syrup
halwa	traditional sweet made from lentils, nuts and fruit, baked in a large tray and cut into small squares
jalebi	flour batter, which is deep fried and soaked in sugar syrup

south Indian terminology; all other terms are either in Hindi or refer to north Indian cuisine.

raj kachori a crisp *puri* usually filled with chickpeas and doused in curd and sauce

kheer delicate, Mughal-style rice pudding

kulfi Indian-style ice cream, often flavoured with pistachio

ladoo or **ladu** sweets made from small balls of gram flour and semolina

pakora pieces of vegetable deep-fried in chickpea batter; a popular street snack

rasgulla curd cheese balls flavoured with rosewater; a popular dessert

samosa parcels of vegetable and potato (and sometimes meat) wrapped up in triangles of pastry and deep-fried

vada* doughnut-shaped, deep-fried lentil cake (also spelt *vadai*, *vade*, *wadi*, etc)

vada pao* a *vada* served in a bun with chutney

Glossary

aarti evening temple puja of lights

adivasi official term for tribal person

ahimsa non-violence

amrita nectar of immortality

anda literally "egg": the spherical part of a *stupa*

angrez general term for Westerners

apsara heavenly nymph

arak or **araq** liquor distilled from rice or coconut

asana yogic seating posture; small mat used in prayer and meditation

ashram centre for spiritual learning and religious practice

asura demon

atman soul

avatar reincarnation of Vishnu on earth, in human or animal form

ayah nursemaid

Ayurveda ancient system of medicine employing herbs, minerals and massage

baba respectful term for a sadhu or an old man

bagh garden, park

baithak reception area in private house

baksheesh tip, donation or alms

bandh general strike

bandhani tie-dye

baniya another word for shopkeeper/trader/merchant

baniyan a cotton vest

banyan vast fig tree, used traditionally as a meeting place, or shade for teaching and meditating

baoli or **baori** step-well

bastee or **bustee** slum area

beedi Indian-style cigarette, with tobacco rolled in a leaf

begum a Muslim woman of high status

betel leaf chewed in paan, with the nut of the areca tree; also loosely applies to the nut

bhajan song in praise of god

bhakti religious devotion expressed in a personalized or emotional relationship with the deity

bhang pounded marijuana leaf, often mixed in lassi

Bharat Hindi name for India

Bharat Mata literally "Mother India"; a representation of India personified as a maternal goddess

bhawan or **bhavan** building, house, palace or residence

Bhotia Himalayan people of Tibetan origin

bhumi earth

bindu seed, or the red dot (also bindi) worn by women on their foreheads as decoration

bodhi enlightenment

bodhi tree or **bo tree** peepal tree (*ficus religiosa*), associated with the Buddha's enlightenment

bodhisattva in Buddhism an enlightened being

brahmin priest; a member of the highest caste group

burj tower or bastion

burqa a loose robe worn by orthodox Muslim women that covers the entire body

burra sahib colonial official, boss, or a man of great importance

cantonment area of town occupied by military quarters

caste social status acquired at birth

cella chamber, often housing the image of a deity

cenotaph ornate tomb

chaat snack

chaddar literally a sheet, can also mean a shawl

chaitya Buddhist temple or *stupa*

chajja sloping dripstone eave

chakra discus; focus of power; energy point in the body; wheel, often representing the cycle of death and rebirth

chandan sandalwood paste

chandra moon

chang Ladakhi beer made from fermented millet, wheat or rice

chappal sandals or flip-flops (thongs)

charas hashish

charbagh Persian-style garden divided into quadrants

charpoy traditional Indian bed; wooden-framed, with rope stretched across it

chhatri domed stone pavilion, often erected over a tomb

chillum cylindrical clay or wood pipe for smoking charas or ganja

Chisthti a follower of the Sufi saint Khwaja Muin-ud-Din Chishti of Ajmer

choli short, tight-fitting blouse worn with a sari

chor robber

chorten monument, often containing prayers, texts or relics, erected as a sign of faith by Tibetan Buddhists

choultry quarters for pilgrims adjoined to south Indian temples

chowk crossroads or courtyard

chowki police post

chowkidar watchman/caretaker

coolie porter/labourer

crore ten million

cupola small dome

dabba box; lunch box

dacoit bandit

dalit "oppressed", "out-caste". The term is preferred by so-called "untouchables" as a description of their social position

dargah tomb of a Muslim saint

darshan vision of a deity or saint; receiving religious teachings

darwaza gateway; door

dawan servant

deg cauldron for food offerings, often found in *dargahs*

deul Odishan temple or sanctuary

deva god

devadasi temple dancer

devi goddess

devta deity

dhaba food hall selling local dishes

dham important religious site, or a theological college

dharamshala resthouse for pilgrims

dharma sense of religious and social duty (Hindu); the law of nature, teachings, truth (Buddhist)

dhobi laundryman

dholak double-ended drum

dhoop thick pliable block of strong incense

dhoti white ankle-length cloth worn by males, tied around the waist, and hitched up through the legs

dhurrie woollen rug

digambara literally "sky-clad": a Jain sect, known for the habit of nudity among monks, though this is no longer commonplace

diwan or dewan chief minister

diwan-i-am public audience hall

diwan-i-khas hall of private audience

Dravidian of the south, but usually related to the family of languages used by aboriginal races of India who were pushed south

du-khang main temple in a *gompa*

dukka tank and fountain in courtyard of mosque

dupatta veil worn by Hindu and Muslim women with *salwar kameez*

durbar royal audience or council of state

dvarpala guardian image placed at sanctuary door

dzo domesticated half-cow half-yak

Eve-teasing sexual harassment of women, either physical or verbal

fakir ascetic Muslim mendicant

feni Goan spirit, distilled from coconut or cashew fruits

finial capping motif on temple pinnacle

gandharvas Indra's heavenly musicians

ganj area or neigbourhood

ganja marijuana buds

garbhagriha temple sanctuary, literally "womb-chamber"

garh fort

gari vehicle or car

ghat mountain, landing platform, or steps leading to water

ghazal melancholy Urdu song

godown warehouse

go-khang temple in a *gompa* devoted to protector (gon) deities

gompa Tibetan, or Ladakhi, Buddhist monastery

goonda ruffian

gopi young cattle-tending maidens who feature as Krishna's playmates and lovers in popular mythology

gopura towered temple gateway, common in south India

guru teacher of religion, music, dance, astrology etc

gurudwara Sikh place of worship

haj Muslim pilgrimage to Mecca

hajji Muslim engaged upon, or who has performed, the haj

hammam sunken Persian-style bath

Harijan title – "Children of God" – given to "untouchables" by Gandhi

hartal strike

haveli elaborately decorated mansion

hijra eunuch or transvestite

Hinayana literally "lesser vehicle": the name given to the original school of Buddhism by later sects

hookah water pipe for smoking strong tobacco or marijuana

howdah bulky elephant-saddle, sometimes made of pure silver, and often shaded by a canopy

hypostyle a building or room in which the roof is supported by columns (usually numerous) rather than walls, arches or vaulting

idgah area laid aside in the west of town for prayers during the Muslim festival Id-ul-Zuha

imam Muslim leader or teacher

imambara tomb of a Shi'ite saint

Indo-Saracenic overblown Raj-era architecture that combines Muslim, Hindu, Jain and Western elements

ishwara god

iwan the main (often central) arch in a mosque

jagirdar landowner

jali latticework in stone, or a pierced screen

jama or jami Friday, as in Jama Masjid, or "Friday mosque"

janapadas small republics and monarchies; literally "territory of the clan"

jangha the body of a temple

jarokha small canopied balcony, often containing a window seat

Jat major north Indian ethnic group; particularly numerous in eastern Rajasthan around Bharatpur

Jataka popular tales about the Buddha's life and teachings

jati caste, determined by family and occupation

jawab a building constructed to mirror another building opposite it, thus creating symmetry

jawan soldier

jhuta soiled by lips: food or drink polluted by touch

-ji suffix added to names as a term of respect

jihad striving by Muslims, through battle, to spread their faith

johar old practice of self-immolation by women in times of war

jyotrilinga twelve sacred sites associated with Shiva's unbounded lingam of light

Kailasa or **Kailash** mountain in western Tibet: Shiva's abode and the traditional source of the Ganges and Brahmaputra; the earthly manifestation of the "world pillar", Mount Meru

kalasha pot-like capping stone characteristic of south Indian temples

kama satisfaction

karma weight of good and bad actions that determine status of rebirth

katcha raw, crude, unsound, weak

kavad small decorated box that unfolds to serve as a travelling temple

khadi home-spun cotton; Gandhi's symbol of Indian self-sufficiency

khan honorific Muslim title

khana dwelling or house

khejri small tree found throughout the desert regions of Rajasthan

kirtan hymn-singing

kot fort

kothi residence

kotla citadel

kotwali police station

kovil term for a Tamil Nadu temple

kshatriya the warrior and ruling caste

kumkum red mark on a Hindu woman's forehead (widows are not supposed to wear it)

kund tank, lake, reservoir

kurta long men's shirt worn over baggy pyjamas

lakh one hundred thousand

lama Tibetan Buddhist monk and teacher

lathi heavy stick that can be used for support or as a weapon

lingam phallic symbol in places of worship, representing the god Shiva

liwan prayer hall or covered area of a mosque

loka realm or world, eg *devaloka*, world of the gods

lunghi male garment; long wraparound cloth worn tucked in around the waist flowing down to the ankles

madrasa Islamic school

maha- great or large

mahadeva literally "great god", and a common epithet for Shiva

mahal palace; mansion

mahant in Hinduism, a high-ranking pandit; in Sikhism, the manger of a *gurudwara*

maharaja (maharana, maharawal) prince, especially one who rules

maharani the wife of a maharaja, or the woman holding the rank of maharaja

mahatma great soul

Mahayana "Great Vehicle": a Buddhist school that has spread throughout Southeast Asia

mahout elephant driver or keeper

maidan large open space or field

makara crocodile-like animal featuring on temple doorways and symbolizing the river Ganges. Also the vehicle of Varuna, the Vedic god of the sea

mala necklace, garland or rosary

mandala religious diagram

mandapa hall, often with many pillars, used for various purposes such as weddings or dances

mandi market

mandir temple

mantra sacred verse, often repeated as an aid to meditation

mardana area for use of men in a haveli or palace

marg road

masjid mosque

mataji means "mother", it is also used as a polite form of address to an older woman or a female sadhu

math or **mutt** Hindu or Jain monastery

mayur peacock

medhi terrace

mehendi henna

mela festival

memsahib respectful address to European women

mihrab niche in the wall of a mosque indicating the direction of Mecca

minaret high slender tower, characteristic of mosques

minbar pulpit in a mosque from which the Friday sermon is read

mithuna amorous couples in Hindu and Buddhist figurative art

mohalla neighbourhood

moksha blissful state of freedom from rebirth aspired to by Hindus, Sikhs and Jains

mudra symbolic hand gestures used in meditation and dance that also feature in Hindu, Buddhist and Jain art

muezzin man behind the voice calling Muslims to prayer from a mosque

mullah Muslim teacher and scholar

muqarna a style of Islamic moulded vaulting

nadi river

naga mythical serpent; alternatively, a person from Nagaland

nala gorge cut by a seasonal stream

natak drama

natya dance

nautch dance

nawab Muslim landowner or prince

nilgai blue bull

nirvana (or, in Pali, *nibbana*) Buddhist equivalent of *moksha*

nizam title of Hyderabad rulers

NRI non-resident Indian: someone entitled to Indian nationality but resident abroad

nullah stream gorge in the mountains

om or **aum** symbol denoting the origin of all things, and ultimate divine essence, used in meditation by Hindus and Buddhists

paan betel nut, lime, calcium and aniseed wrapped in a leaf and chewed as a digestif. Mildly addictive

pada foot, or base, also a poetic meter

padma lotus; another name for the goddess Lakshmi

pagoda multistoreyed Buddhist monument

paisa There are a hundred paisa in a rupee

pali original language of early Buddhist texts

panchayat village council

parikrama ritual circumambulation around a temple, shrine or mountain

Parsi Zoroastrian

pietra dura inlay work, traditionally consisting of semiprecious stones set in marble; particularly associated with Agra

pir Muslim holy man

pol fortified gate

pradakshina patha processional path circling a monument or sanctuary

prakara enclosure or courtyard in a south Indian temple

pranayama breath control, used in meditation

prasad food blessed in temple sanctuaries and shared among devotees

prayag auspicious confluence of two or more rivers

puja worship

pujari priest

pukka ripe, mature, firm and stable; also correct and acceptable, in the very English sense of "proper"

punkah type of manually operated ceiling fan, widely used during the Raj era, hand-pulled by a so-called "punkah-wallah"

punya religious merit

purdah literally "curtain": the enforced segregation and isolation of women within a haveli or palace or, more figuratively, within society in general. General term for wearing a veil

purnima full moon

pyjama men's baggy trousers

qawwali devotional singing popular among Sufis

qibla wall in a mosque indicating the direction of Mecca

qila fort

raag or **raga** series of notes forming the basis of a melody

Raj rule; monarchy; in particular the period of British imperial rule 1857–1947

raja a ruler or landlord

Rajput princely rulers who once dominated much of north and west India

rakshasa demon

rangoli geometrical pattern of rice powder laid before houses and temples

rani a queen or princess of a raja

rath chariot

rawal chieftain or ruler of a minor principality

rekha deul Odishan towered sanctuary

rinpoche literally "precious one", a highly revered Tibetan Buddhist lama, considered to be a reincarnation of a previous teacher

rishi "seer"; philosophical sage or poet

rudraksha beads used to make Shiva rosaries

rumal handkerchief, particularly finely embroidered in Chamba state (HP)

sadar "main"; eg Sadar Bazaar

saadhak a person who is engaged in an all-encompassing course in spirituality to achieve realization of the self and God

sadhu Hindu holy man with no caste or family ties

sagar lake

sahib respectful title for gentlemen; general term of address for European men

salwar kameez long shirt and baggy ankle-hugging trousers worn by Indian women

samadhi final enlightenment; a site of death or burial of a saint

sambar species of Asian deer

samsara cyclic process of death and rebirth

sangam sacred confluence of two or more rivers, or an academy

sangeet music

sannyasi homeless, possessionless ascetic (Hindu)

sarai resting place for caravans and travellers who once followed the trade routes through Asia

sari dress for Indian women: a length of cloth wound around the waist and draped over one shoulder

sati one who sacrifices her life on her husband's funeral pyre in emulation of Shiva's wife. No longer a common practice, and officially illegal

satyagraha Gandhi's campaign of non-violent protest, literally "grasping truth"

scheduled castes official name for "untouchables"

sepoy infantry private, an Indian soldier in the British army during the colonial period

seva voluntary service in a temple or community

shaikh Muslim holy man or saint

Shaivite Hindu recognizing Shiva as the supreme god

shankha conch, symbol of Vishnu

shastra treatise

sheesh mahal "glass palace"; usually a small room or apartment decorated with mirrorwork mosaics

shikar hunting

shikhara temple tower or spire common in northern Indian architecture

shloka verse from a Sanskrit text

shri or sri respectful prefix; another name for Lakshmi

shudra the lowest of the four *varnas*; servant

singh or singha lion

sitout veranda

soma medicinal herb with hallucinogenic properties used in early Vedic and Zoroastrian rituals

stambha pillar, or flagstaff

sthala site sacred for its association with legendary events

stupa large hemispherical mound, representing the Buddha's presence, and often protecting relics of the Buddha or a Buddhist saint

suchalaya toilet

sulabh convenient toilet

surma black eyeliner, also known as kohl

Surya the sun, or sun god

sutra or sutta verse in Sanskrit and Pali texts (literally "thread")

svetambara "white-clad" sect of Jainism that accepts nuns and shuns nudity

swami master; title for a holy man

swaraj "self-rule"; synonym for independence, coined by Gandhi

tala rhythmic cycle in classical music; in sculpture a *tala* signifies one face-length

tandoor clay oven

tank square or rectangular water pool in a temple complex, for ritual bathing

tanpura the instrument producing the drone that accompanies all Indian classical music

tempo three-wheeled taxi

terma precious manuscript (Tibetan Buddhist term)

thakur usually Rajput landowner

thangka Tibetan religious scroll painting

Theravada "Doctrine of the Elders": the original name for early Buddhism, which persists today in Sri Lanka and Thailand

thug member of a north Indian cult of professional robbers and murderers

tiffin light meal

tiffin carrier stainless-steel set of tins used for carrying meals

tilak red dot smeared on the forehead during worship, and often used cosmetically

tirtha river crossing considered sacred by Hindus, or the transition from the mundane world to heaven; a place of pilgrimage for Jains

tirthankara "ford-maker" or "crossing-maker": an enlightened Jain teacher who is deified – 24 appear every 300 million years

tola the weight of a silver rupee: 180 grains, or approximately 11.6g

tonga two-wheeled horse-drawn cart

topi cap

torana arch, or freestanding gateway of two pillars linked by an elaborate arch

trimurti the Hindu trinity

trishula Shiva's trident

tuk fortified enclosure of Jain shrines or temples

tulku reincarnated teacher of Tibetan Buddhism

untouchables members of the lowest strata of society, considered polluting to all higher castes

urs Muslim saint's-day festival

vahana the "vehicle" of a deity: the bull Nandi is Shiva's *vahana*

vaishya member of the merchant and trading caste group

varna literally "colour"; one of four hierarchical social categories: brahmins, *kshatriyas*, *vaishyas* and *shudras*

vav step-well, common in Gujarat

Vedas sacred texts of early Hinduism

vedika railing around a *stupa*

vihara Jain or Buddhist monastery

vimana tower over temple sanctuary

waddo south Indian term meaning ward or subdivision of a district

-wallah suffix implying occupation, eg rickshaw-wallah

wazir chief minister to the king

yagna Vedic sacrificial ritual

yaksha pre-Vedic folklore figure connected with fertility and incorporated into later Hindu iconography

yakshi female *yaksha*

yali mythical lion

yantra cosmological pictogram, or instrument used in an observatory

yatra pilgrimage

yatri pilgrim

yogi sadhu or priestly figure possessing occult powers gained through the practice of yoga (female: yogini)

yoni symbol of the female sexual organ, set around the base of the lingam in temple shrines

yuga aeon: the present age is the last in a cycle of four *yugas*, *kali-yuga*, a "black age" of degeneration and spiritual decline

zamindar landowner

zenana women's quarters; segregated area for women in a mosque, haveli or palace

Small print and index

A ROUGH GUIDE TO ROUGH GUIDES

Published in 1982, the first Rough Guide – to Greece – was a student scheme that became a publishing phenomenon. Mark Ellingham, a recent graduate in English from Bristol University, had been travelling in Greece the previous summer and couldn't find the right guidebook. With a small group of friends he wrote his own guide, combining a highly contemporary, journalistic style with a thoroughly practical approach to travellers' needs.

The immediate success of the book spawned a series that rapidly covered dozens of destinations. And, in addition to impecunious backpackers, Rough Guides soon acquired a much broader readership that relished the guides' wit and inquisitiveness as much as their enthusiastic, critical approach and value-for-money ethos.

These days, Rough Guides include recommendations from budget to luxury and cover more than 200 destinations around the globe, as well as producing an ever-growing range of eBooks and apps.

Visit **roughguides.com** to see our latest publications.

Rough Guide credits

Editors: Eleanor Aldridge, Emma Gibbs, Charlie Melville and Neil McQuillian
Layout: Ankur Guha
Cartography: Swati Handoo
Picture editor: Natascha Sturny
Proofreader: Sam Cook
Managing editor: Keith Drew
Assistant editor: Prema Dutta
Production: Charlotte Cade
Cover design: Nicole Newman, Ankur Guha

Editorial assistant: Olivia Rawes
Senior pre-press designer: Dan May
Design director: Jason Mitchell
Travel publisher: Joanna Kirby
Digital travel publisher: Peter Buckley
Operations coordinator: Helen Blount
Publishing director (Travel): Clare Currie
Commercial manager: Gino Magnotta
Managing director: John Duhigg

Publishing information

This ninth edition published October 2013 by
Rough Guides Ltd,
80 Strand, London WC2R 0RL
11, Community Centre, Panchsheel Park,
New Delhi 110017, India
Distributed by the Penguin Group
Penguin Books Ltd,
80 Strand, London WC2R 0RL
Penguin Group (USA)
345 Hudson Street, NY 10014, USA
Penguin Group (Australia)
250 Camberwell Road, Camberwell,
Victoria 3124, Australia
Penguin Group (NZ)
67 Apollo Drive, Mairangi Bay, Auckland 1310,
New Zealand
Penguin Group (South Africa)
Block D, Rosebank Office Park, 181 Jan Smuts Avenue,
Parktown North, Gauteng, South Africa 2193
Rough Guides is represented in Canada by Tourmaline
Editions Inc. 662 King Street West, Suite 304, Toronto,
Ontario M5V 1M7
Printed in Singapore by Toppan Security Printing Pte. Ltd.

1216pp includes index
A catalogue record for this book is available from the
British Library
ISBN: 978-1-40936-670-6

MIX
Paper from
responsible sources
FSC® C018179

Help us update

We've gone to a lot of effort to ensure that the ninth
edition of **The Rough Guide to India** is accurate and up-
to-date. However, things change – places get "discovered",
opening hours are notoriously fickle, restaurants and
rooms raise prices or lower standards. If you feel we've got
it wrong or left something out, we'd like to know, and if
you can remember the address, the price, the hours, the
phone number, so much the better.

Please send your comments with the subject line
"**Rough Guide India Update**" to ✉ mail@uk.roughguides
.com. We'll credit all contributions and send a copy of the
next edition (or any other Rough Guide if you prefer)
for the very best emails.

Find more travel information, connect with fellow
travellers and plan your trip on ⓦ roughguides.com

Acknowledgements

David Abram: Thanks to Sinna of Aadi Kerala in Kochi/
Ernakulam for once again sharing his expertise on all
matters Keralan, and being my much needed "Mr Fixit"
in the deep south. Sarah and Ajit, and the delightful staff
at Amruthamgayam in Kovalam provided the softest
of landings, for which I was most grateful. Thank you to
Elisabeth Hauss for her insider's tips on Varkala. In Goa,
thanks to Christhe and Ermina in Benaulim for the home
from home, and to Victoria McCulloch in Arambol, for
bashing out a huge amount of juicy info in such a short
time. Finally, to the kindly staff of the Hotel Panchavati in
Nasik, who picked me up and dusted me down after my
misadventures in the far north of Maharashtra, I can only
apologize for my dishevelled state and thank them for their
kind hospitality.
Daniel Jacobs: Ramesh Wadhwa, Anil, Rajesh and also
Gajinder, Cheeta Ram, Sabir and everybody at the Tourist
Rest House in Agra, the Goverdhan Hotel in Fatehpur

Sikri, Khim and Gopal at Khim's, Hotel Jhansi in Jhansi,
Chandigarh Tourism and Himachal Pradesh Tourism in
Chandigarh, Himachal Pradesh Tourism in Pathankot,
Punjab Tourism in Amritsar, UP Tourism in Agra and Jhansi,
India Tourism in Varanasi, and BSTDC in Delhi and Patna.
Emma Boyle: Many thanks to; Gavin for his invaluable
insider advice; Camilla for her unfailing humour and
support; Abhinav and Abhineet, and equally Satinder, for
their company and invaluable pearls of Jaipur wisdom;
Krishna for his support in Udaipur; Ramesh and Rajesh for
their insider info on Nawalgarh and map; Jaggi for providing
a refuge in Jodhpur; Indar, Raj and Dev for their assistance
in Jaisalmer; Jitu in Bikaner; Sudhir for the wonderful
Chittorgarh town and fort motorbike tour; Anoop for his
hospitality in Pushkar; and last but not least, Abhay and
Raul for their many updates on Ranthambhore National
Park. As always, thanks to B and my family for their patience
and support.

ABOUT THE AUTHORS

David Abram A regular visitor to India for over thirty years, David wrote the original edition of this book back in the early 1990s, and has worked on every one since. Annual research trips to the subcontinent have taken him from Zanskar to Kanniyakumari over the years, and most points in between. He's currently writing a guide to Myanmar.

Nick Edwards Since studying in Oxford, has spent much of his life in Greece, India, America and elswhere. Recently returned to his native South London with spouse Maria, he avidly follows Spurs, psychedelic sounds and the peace movement.

Mike Ford Mike Ford first visited India back in 1985 and has travelled extensively in every state except Goa and the Andamans. He is a keen photographer and has led treks through Ladakh, Zanskar, Spiti, Sikkim and Arunachal Pradesh. In his free time he plays tabla in and around Bristol for classical musicians and kirtan wallahs. Chai, samosas and Bollywood films keep him tuned in between his India trips.

Shafik Meghji A travel writer, journalist and editor based in south London, Shafik Meghji has travelled extensively throughout India since his first visit in 2003. He also co-authors the Rough Guides to Argentina, Bolivia, Chile and Nepal, and contributes to the Rough Guides to Australia, Egypt, Central America on a Budget, and South America on a Budget, among others. He blogs at ⓦunmappedroutes.com, and you can follow him on Twitter @ShafikMeghji.

Devdan Sen Born and bred in India, travelled extensively in his own country and studied Indian classical music for several years before enrolling in SOAS, University of London. Based in Surrey, he works in publishing and travels to India frequently.

Gavin Thomas first visited Inida in 1991 and has been returning regularly ever since. He is also the author of the Rough Guides to Sri Lanka and Dubai, and co-author of the *Rough Guide to Rajasthan, Delhi and Agra*

Mike Ford: A big thank you to Mr D. Karunanidhi in Chennai. Thanks to Mira in Tiruvannamalai for uplifting chai and chat on the Girivalam. Thanks and *om shanti* to all the India co-authors. In the UK, thanks to the team of editors and cartographers who've also done a great job and to friends and family. It's been a mind-expanding, photogenic, pot-holed and brilliant journey.

Nick Edwards: Nick would like to thank the following fine locals for help along the way: Manzoor Chachoo and family in Srinagar; Mehraj Ganai and family in Pahalgam; Ravi of Poonam Mountain Lodge in Naggar; Vinayak Jishtu in Shimla; Benny & Lynda and all at Wild Orchid/ Emerald Gecko on Havelock; the Barefoot Scuba folk for the unforgettable dive with Rajan; Alex at Pristine Resort in Kalipur; Balaji and family in Mamallapuram; all at Sudha Lodge in Hampi and Nimmu House in Gokarna. Blessings to Tejasa for facilitating the Oneness Temple visit. Many thanks to Ellie for holding it all together editorially at RG HQ in London. Cheers to the following new friends for company and info along the way: David & Jessica in HP, Doug in Karnataka and Trent of LP in the Andamans. Finally, a special mention for the old friends who shared another magical Indian experience with me ~ John, Laura,

Phil, Murray and, of course, my beloved Maria. Oh, and no thanks to the Hyderabad rickshaw wallah for briefly abducting Maria!

Shafik Meghji: Many thanks to all the locals and travellers who helped out along the way with their recommendations, directions and – very occasionally – horror stories. A special *dhanyavad* must go to: my fellow authors for all their help and advice; Charlie Melville for her sterling editing work; Katie and Jehan Bhujwala and everyone at Shergarh Tented Camp for their hospitality and insight into all things tiger-related; David Symes and Ryan Newson at On The Go Tours; Keef Llewellyn-Burke and Gemma Williams for their good company in Khajuraho and Orchha; Darryl Andrade for good times in Pune and Matheran; Jean, Nizar and Nina Meghji; and Sioned Jones, for all her love and support.

In London, thanks to the numerous people who have worked so tirelessly to manage this huge book over twelve months of research, writing and editing, and squeeze it into the new design: Kathryn, Keith, Emma, Charlie and Ellie in editorial; Katie and Swati in cartography; Natascha for the pictures; and Sam for an excellent proofread.

Readers' updates

Thanks to all the readers who have taken the time to write in with comments and suggestions (and apologies if we've inadvertently omitted or misspelt anyone's name):

Eshan Amin, Darren Battle, Elias Baumgarten, Lyn Bell, Lara Bianciardi, Ewa Bikowska, Tom and Lara Bold, Maegan ChadwickDobson, Jane and Ian Christie, Philip Clendenning, Gemma Cribbin, Courtney Crook, Jan Draper, Jonathan Duff, Elinor, Jamal Essayah, Tom Evans, Jed Farlow, Elise Fischbach, Mathilde Fixl, Kurt en Greet, Sandy Grimwade, Oliver Harris, Doug Henning, Nicole Heyman, Susan Hinds, Rhiannon Horrell, Rowena Hou, Richard Hunt, Gill Hunter, Benjamin Jonas, Hassel Johns, Wes Kitura, Andreas Klaar, Tim Laslavic, Ollie Legge, Brett Lewis, Maria, Jennie Miller, Mini, George Mitton, Lynea Newcomer, Charlotte Norton, Vikas Pathak, James Perryman, Justin Petty, Sarah Porter, Irina Radonici, Philip Shanahan, Pat Sheafor, Shenshan, Iwona Sliz, Hela Shamash, John Smith, Hannah Thomas, Valerie Thompson, Arthur Ward and Carrick Whitney.

Photo credits

Index

Maps are marked in grey

STATE AND UNION TERRITORY (UT) ABBREVIATIONS

AN	Andaman and Nicobar (UT)	LD	Lakshadweep (UT)
AP	Andhra Pradesh	MH	Maharashtra
AR	Arunachal Pradesh	ML	Meghalaya
AS	Assam	MN	Manipur
BR	Bihar	MP	Madhya Pradesh
CH	Chandigarh (UT)	MZ	Mizoram
CT	Chattisgarh	NL	Nagaland
DD	Daman and Diu (UT)	OR	Odisha
DL	Delhi (Capital Territory)	PB	Punjab
DN	Dadra and Nagar Haveli (UT)	PY	Puducherry (UT)
GA	Goa	RJ	Rajasthan
GJ	Gujarat	SK	Sikkim
HP	Himachal Pradesh	TN	Tamil Nadu
HR	Haryana	TR	Tripura
JH	Jharkhand	UP	Uttar Pradesh
JK	Jammu and Kashmir	UA	Uttarakhand
KA	Karnataka	WB	West Bengal
KE	Kerala		

Map symbols

The symbols below are used on maps throughout the book

- ✈ Airport
- ✈ Domestic airport
- ★ Bus stop
- P Parking
- ✉ Post office
- (i) Information office
- @ Internet access
- ⛽ Fuel station
- ✚ Hospital
- ⚑ Golf course
- ⊙ Statue
- Ⓜ Metro station
- Ⓗ Helipad

- ♦ Point of interest
- 🌿 Viewpoint
- ♈ Lighthouse
- 🌺 Country park
- ⌂ Mountain lodge
- ♜ Fortress
- 🏛 Palace
- 🏚 Haveli
-)(Bridge
- ⊟ Ghat
- ⊠ Entrance gate
- 🚣 Boat
- 🌴 Palm tree

- ⛰ Mountain range
- ▲ Mountain peak
- ⌒ Cave
- Reef
- ♨ Hot spring pool
- ∥ Pass
- ▲▲▲ Escarpment
- Cliff
- Waterfall
- Swamp
- Park
- Beach
- Glacier

- Building
- Church (town)
- ♱ Church (regional)
- Market
- Stadium
- ⊞ Cemetery
- Muslim Cemetery
- ✦ Hindu/Jain temple
- ⚑ Muslim monument
- 🛕 Buddhist temple
- Chinese temple
- 🎋 Shrine
- Monastery

Listings key

- ■ Accommodation
- ● Café/restaurant
- ■ Bar/club
- ● Shop